LAROUSSE

POCKET
DICTIONARY

GERMAN
ENGLISH

ENGLISH
GERMAN

TASCHEN-
WÖRTERBUCH

DEUTSCH
ENGLISCH

ENGLISCH
DEUTSCH

LAROUSSE

21, rue du Montparnasse 75283 Paris Cedex 06

Editor-in-Chief/*Gesamtleitung*
Patrick White

Project Manager/*Koordinierung*
Helen Bleck

Editorial Team/*Redaktion*
Joaquín Blasco, Stuart Fortey, Helen Galloway, Elaine O'Donoghue,
Christina Reinicke, Stefan Rosenland, Veronika Schilling, Anna Stevenson

with/*mit*
Alexander Behrens, Anna Canning, Lynda Carey, Steffen Krug, Elisabeth
Lauer, Dörthe and Günter Lügenbuhl, Friedemann Lux, Úna ní Chiosáin,
Ruth Noble, Ingrid Schumacher, Alan Seaton, Liliane Seifert, Katerina Stein

Data Management/*Datenverwaltung*
Abdul Aziz Ndao

Artistic Director/*Graphische Gestaltung*
Sophie Compagne

with/*mit*
Ruth Noble, Cédric Pignon

Series Editor/*Verantwortlich für die Wörterbuchreihe*
Ralf Brockmeier

with/*mit*
Marc Chabrier

© Larousse/VUEF, 2002

ISBN 2-03-540019-8

Sales/*Vertrieb*: Houghton Mifflin Company, Boston.
Library of Congress Catalog Card Number
has been applied for.

Typeset by Ingénierie Graphisme Services, France

Contents
Inhaltsverzeichnis

Achevé d'imprimer par l'Imprimerie
Maury-Eurolivres à Manchecourt
Nº de projet 10090384 - 7 - OTB 50º
Nº de projet 10090719 - 3 - OTB 52º
Dépôt légal : janvier 2001 - Nº d'imprimeur : 91427

Imprimé en France - (Printed in France)

Preface

This new dictionary has been designed as a reliable and user-friendly tool for use in all language situations. It provides accurate and up-to-date information on written and spoken German and English as they are used today.

Its 55,000 words and phrases and 80,000 translations give you access to German texts of all types. The dictionary aims to be as comprehensive as possible in a book of this size, and includes many proper names and abbreviations, as well as a selection of the most common terms from computing, business and current affairs.

The new German spelling system has been used throughout, with both old and new forms shown on the German-English side of the dictionary.

Carefully constructed entries and a clear page design help you to find the translation that you are looking for fast. Examples (from basic constructions and common phrases to idioms) have been included to help put a word in context and give a clear picture of how it is used.

The dictionary provides extra help for students of German with the inclusion of boxes on German life and culture, the education system, false friends and common phrases that appear within the dictionary text itself.

Vorbemerkung

Dieses neue Wörterbuch wurde als zuverlässiger und benutzerfreundlicher Begleiter für Schule, Beruf und Freizeit entwickelt. Es gibt schnell und präzise Auskunft über den aktuellen Wortschatz des Englischen und des Deutschen in seiner geschriebenen und gesprochenen Form.

55 000 Wörter und Ausdrücke mit ihren 80 000 Übersetzungen eröffnen den Zugang zu englischen Texten aller Art. Um dieses Nachschlagewerk innerhalb des vorgegebenen Umfangs so umfassend wie möglich zu gestalten, wurden zudem viele Eigennamen und Abkürzungen sowie eine Auswahl der gebräuchlichsten Begriffe aus den Bereichen EDV/Internet, Wirtschaft und Tagespolitik aufgenommen.

Die Schreibung des Deutschen folgt konsequent den neuen amtlichen Rechtschreibregeln, im deutsch-englischen Teil werden zur besseren Auffindbarkeit alte und neue Formen nebeneinander angegeben.

Mit großer Sorgfalt gestaltete Einträge und eine übersichtliche Seitengestaltung helfen dem Benutzer, die gesuchte Übersetzung schnell zu finden. Zusätzlich veranschaulichen zahlreiche Beispiele (von grammatischen Basiskonstruktionen und gebräuchlichen Kollokationen bis zu idiomatischen Wendungen) die Benutzung des betreffenden Wortes im Kontext.

Als Hilfestellung für den deutschsprachigen Benutzer enthält dieses Wörterbuch zahlreiche in den Text integrierte Kästchen mit landeskundlichen Erläuterungen und vielfältigen Hinweisen zum Sprachgebrauch.

V

Boxes

 False friends

actual	gift	rent
to become	gymnasium	sender
to blame	handy	sensible
brave	local	serious
chef	marmalade	to spend
eventual	ordinary	sympathetic
famous	overhear	tablet
fantasy	photograph	taste
to fasten	prospect	temperamental
fraction	receipt	warehouse

 Common phrases

comparison	goodbye	regret
making comparisons	saying goodbye	regretting
confirmation	indifference	relief
requesting confirmation	luck wishing good luck	suggest
console	opinion	suggesting
consoling	giving opinions	supposition
conversation	permission	making suppositions
starting a conversation	asking permission	surprise
delight	promise	uncertainty
desire	promising	
desiring	reassure	
disappointment	reassuring	

 School and culture

A Level	fish and chips	Ivy League
BBC	foot	national curriculum
comprehensive school	feet and inches	Ofsted
Congress	gap year	private schools
cricket	GCSE	SATs
dates	general election	school dinners
Declaration of	head	tabloids
Independence	head of year	tea
detention	Hogmanay	Thanksgiving

Zusatzinformationen

 falsche Freunde

aktuell	Fraktion	Sender
bekommen	Gift	sensibel
blamieren	Gymnasium	seriös
brav	Handy	spenden
Chef	Lokal	sympathisch
eventuell	Marmelade	Tablett
famos	ordinär	Taste
Fantasie	Prospekt	temperamentvoll
fasten	Rente	überhören
Fotograf	Rezept	Warenhaus

 Wortschatz für den Alltag

bedanken
  sich bedanken
bitten
egal egal sein
einladen
Erlaubnis
  um Erlaubnis bitten
Glückwünsche
Mitgefühl
  Mitgefühl zeigen

Thema
  das Thema wechseln
verabreden
  sich verabreden
verabschieden
  sich verabschieden
verbieten
Vorliebe
  Vorlieben haben

Vorschlag
  Vorschläge machen
weigern
  sich weigern
widersprechen
wünschen
zusammenfassen
zustimmen

 Schulsystem und Landeskunde

Abiturfeier
Autobahn
Berliner Mauer
bitte
Brief
  blauer Brief
Datum
FKK (Freikörperkultur)
Gesamtschule
Grundgesetz

Grundkurs
Hauptschule
Kaffee
  Kaffee und Kuchen
Karneval
Leistungskurs
Note
Nummernschild
Orientierungsstufe
Projektwoche

Realschule
Reichstag
Schülervertretung
Schulferien
Schultüte
Sekundarstufe
Vertrauenslehrer

Abkürzungen

Abbreviations

Akkusativ	*A*	accusative
Abkürzung	*abk/abbr*	abbreviation
abwertend	*abw*	pejorative
bezeichnet die subjektive negative Wertung des Sprechers, z. B. **Banause**		implies disapproval, e.g. **Banause**
Adjektiv	*adj*	adjective
Verwaltung	ADMIN	administration
Adverb	*adv*	adverb
Flugwesen, Luftfahrt	AERON	aeronautics, aviation
Landwirtschaft	AGRIC	agriculture
amerikanisches Englisch	*Am*	American English
amtssprachlich, formell	*amt*	official language
Anatomie	ANAT	anatomy
Archäologie	ARCHAEOL	archaeology
Architektur	ARCHIT	architecture
Astrologie	ASTROL	astrology
Astronomie	ASTRON	astronomy
australisches Englisch	*Austr*	Australian English
Kfz-Technik	AUT(O)	automobile, cars
Hilfsverb	*aux*	auxiliary
Biologie	BIOL	biology
Botanik	BOT	botany
britisches Englisch	*Br*	British English
kanadisches Englisch	*Can*	Canadian English
Chemie	CHEM	chemistry
Handel	COMM	business
ein zusammengesetztes Substantiv bildend	*comp*	compound-forming element a noun used to modify
ein Substantiv, das zur näheren Bestimmung eines anderen dient, z. B. gardening in **gardening book** oder airforce in **airforce base**		another noun, e.g. gardening in **gardening book** or airforce in **airforce base**
Komparativ	*compar*	comparative
Datenverarbeitung	COMPUT	computers, computer science
Konjunktion	*conj*	conjunction
Bauwesen	CONSTR	construction, building trade
Verlaufsform	*cont*	continuous
Kochkunst	CULIN	culinary, cooking
Dativ	*D*	dative
demonstrativ, hinweisend	*dem*	demonstrative
Determinant	*det*	determiner
bezeichnet Artikelwörter und andere artikelähnliche Substantivbegleiter		indicates articles and similar
Wirtschaft	ECON	economics
Datenverarbeitung	EDV	computers, computer science
eigentliche Bedeutung	*eigtl*	literal
Elektrotechnik	ELEKTR/ELEC	electricity, electronics
etwas	*etw*	something
Femininum	*f*	feminine noun
umgangssprachlich	*fam*	informal
übertragene Bedeutung	*fig*	figurative
Finanzen	FIN	finance, financial

Abkürzungen

Abbreviations

Flugwesen, Luftfahrt	FLUG	aeronautics, aviation
gehoben	*fml*	formal
Fotografie	FOTO	photography
Femininum im Plural	*fpl*	plural feminine noun
Fußball	FTBL	football
nicht trennbar	*fus*	inseparable
Genitiv	G	genitive
gehoben	*geh*	formal
generell, allgemein	*gen*	generally
Geografie	GEOGR	geography, geographical
Geologie	GEOL	geology, geological
Geometrie	GEOM	geometry
Grammatik	GRAM(M)	grammar
Geschichte	HIST	history
humorvoll	*hum*	humorous
Industrie	IND	industry
unbestimmt	*indef*	indefinite
umgangssprachlich	*inf*	informal
Interjektion	*interj*	interjection
unveränderlich	*inv*	invariable
kennzeichnet bei Substantiven die Übereinstimmung der Plural- und Singularform, wie z. B. bei sheep *pl inv*: **four sheep**		applied to a noun to indicate that plural form same as singular, e.g. **sheep** *pl inv*: **four sheep**
ironisch	*iron*	ironic
jemand	*jd*	someone (nominative)
jemandem	*jm*	someone (dative)
jemanden	*jn*	someone (accusative)
jemandes	*js*	someone (genitive)
Komparativ	*kompar*	comparative
Konjunktion	*konj*	conjunction
Kochkunst	KÜCHE	culinary, cooking
Rechtswesen	LAW	legal
Linguistik	LING	linguistics
eigentliche Bedeutung	*lit*	literal
		in conjunction with *fig*, shows that both a literal and fiigurative sense is being covered by the same translation
Maskulinum	*m*	masculine noun
Mathematik	MATH	mathematics
Medizin	MED	medicine
Meteorologie	METEOR	weather, meteorology
Maskulinum und Femininum	*mf*	feminine and masculine noun
Militärwesen	MIL	military
Maskulinum im Plural	*mpl*	plural masculine noun
Musik	MUS	music
Mythologie	MYTH	mythology
Schifffahrt	NAUT	navigation
Norddeutsch	*Norddt*	northern German

Abkürzungen

Abbreviations

Neutrum bei Städte- und Ländernamen	*nt*	neuter noun (used with placenames)
Städte und Ländernamen gehören zu den Neutra. Sie werden in den meisten Fällen ohne Artikel benutzt: **ich fahre nach Deutschland/nach Berlin.** Es gibt jedoch Ausnahmen: **das Deutschland/das Berlin der 90er Jahre**		The names of countries and cities are generally neutral, and used without an article: **ich fahre nach Deutschland/ nach Berlin.** There are some exceptions, however: **das Deutschland/das Berlin der 90er Jahre**
Zahlwort	*num*	numeral
ohne Plural	*ohne pl*	uncountable noun
sich	*o.s.*	oneself
ostdeutsch	*Ostdt*	East German
österreichisch	*Österr*	Austrian
abwertend	*pej*	pejorative
bezeichnet die subjektive negative Wertung des Sprechers, z. B. **bimbo, catty**		implies disapproval, e.g. **bimbo, catty**
Perfekt	*perf*	perfect
persönlich	*pers*	personal
Fotografie	PHOT	photography
Redewendung(en)	*phr*	phrase(s)
Physik	PHYS	physics
Plural	*pl*	plural
Politik	POL	politics
besitzanzeigend	*poss*	possessive
Partizip Perfekt	*pp*	past participle
Präposition	*präp*	preposition
Präsens	*präs*	present
Präteritum	*prät*	preterite
Vorsilbe	*pref*	prefix
Präposition	*prep*	preposition
Pronomen	*pron*	pronoun
Psychologie	PSYCH	psychology, psychiatry
Eisenbahn	RAIL	railways
Rechtswesen	RECHT	law
reflexives Verb	*ref*	reflexive verb
regelmäßig	*reg*	regular
Religion	REL(IG)	religion
Redewendung(en)	*RW*	phrase(s)
salopp	*salopp*	very informal
jemand	*sb*	someone
Schifffahrt	SCHIFF	navigation
Schule	SCH(ULE)	school
Schweizerdeutsch	*Schweiz*	Swiss German
schottisches Englisch	*Scot*	Scottish English
trennbar	*sep*	separable
singular	*sg*	singular
Slang	*sl*	slang
Sport	SPORT	sport

Abkürzungen

Abbreviations

Börse	ST EX	stock exchange
etwas	*sthg*	something
Subjekt	*Subj/subj*	subject
süddeutsch	*Süddt*	southern German
Superlativ	*superl*	superlative
Technik, Technologie	TECH	technology, technical
Telekommunikation, Fernmeldewesen	TELEKOM/TELEC	telecommunications
Fernsehen	TV	television
Druckwesen	TYPO	printing
Plural	U	uncountable noun
Universität	UNI(V)	university
unregelmäßig	*unreg*	irregular
unveränderlich	*unver*	invariable
Verb	*vb*	verb
intransitives verb	*vi*	intransitive verb
unpersönliches Verb	*v impers*	impersonal verb
salopp	*vinf*	very informal
vor dem Substantiv zeigt an, dass die Übersetzung grundsätzlich attributiv verwendet wird, d. h. unmittelbar vor dem Substantiv steht, welches es näher bezeichnet	*vor Subst*	before noun indicates that the translation is always used attributively, i.e. directly before the noun which it modifiies
transitives Verb	*vt*	transitive verb
vulgär	*vulg*	vulgar
Wirtschaft	WIRTSCH	economics
Zoologie	ZOOL	zoology
kulturelle Entsprechung	≃	cultural equivalent
a) Im Verb: Trennbarkeit des deutschen Verbs b) Im zusammengesetzten Substantiv: Angaben zum Plural unter dem Wort nach dem Balken (z. B. steht der Plural von Ablbild unter dem Stichwort Bild)	I	a) In a German verb: indicates that verb is separable b) In a compound noun: shows the root of the word, where the plural will be found (e.g. the plural of Ablbild is under the headword Bild)

Lautschrift

Deutsche Vokale

[a]	**Aff**e, Ban**a**ne
[aː]	**A**rzt, **A**ntrag
[ɐ]	Galli**er**
[ɐ̯]	D**e**ssert
[e]	B**e**ton
[eː]	**e**del
[ɛ]	**e**cht, H**ä**ndler
[ɛː]	R**ä**tsel, Dess**e**rt
[ə]	Akti**e**
[iː]	v**ie**r
[i]	R**a**dio
[i̯]	Kalz**i**um
[ɪ]	W**i**nter
[o]	Mel**o**die
[oː]	apr**o**p**o**s
[o̯]	l**o**yal
[ɔ]	s**o**llen
[ø]	**ö**kologisch
[øː]	**Ö**l
[œ]	K**ö**chin, P**u**mps
[u]	K**u**vert, akt**u**ell
[uː]	K**u**h
[u̯]	Silh**ou**ette
[ʊ]	K**u**nst
[y]	B**ü**chse, S**y**stem
[yː]	T**ü**r
[y̯]	N**u**ance

Deutsche Diphthonge

[ai̯]	D**ei**chsel
[au̯]	**Au**ge
[ɔy̯]	**Eu**roCity

Deutsche Nasale

[ã]	Ch**an**son
[ãː]	Abonnem**ent**
[ɛ̃ː]	P**oin**te
[õ]	Chans**on**

Halbvokale

Jubil**ä**um	
Hard**w**are	

Konsonanten

Ba**b**y	
ich	
A**chs**e, Ka**v**iar	
Duett, Me**d**ien	

Phonetics

English vowels

[ɑː]	b**ar**n, c**ar**, l**augh**
[æ]	p**a**t, b**a**g, m**a**d
[ɒ]	p**o**t, l**o**g
[e]	p**e**t, t**e**nd
[ɜː]	b**ur**n, l**ear**n, b**ir**d
[ə]	m**o**ther, supp**o**se
[iː]	b**ea**n, w**ee**d
[ɪ]	p**i**t, b**i**g, r**i**d
[ɔː]	b**or**n, l**aw**n
[uː]	l**oo**p, l**oo**se
[ʌ]	r**u**n, c**u**t
[ʊ]	p**u**t, f**u**ll

English diphthongs

[aɪ]	b**uy**, l**igh**t, **ai**sle
[au]	n**ow**, sh**ou**t, t**ow**n
[eɪ]	b**ay**, l**a**te, gr**ea**t
[əu]	n**o**, r**oa**d, bl**ow**
[ɪə]	p**eer**, f**ier**ce, **i**dea
[eə]	p**air**, b**ear**, sh**are**
[ʊə]	p**oor**, s**ure**, t**our**
[ɔɪ]	b**oy**, f**oi**l

Semi-vowels

[j]	**y**ou, spanie**l**
[w]	**w**et, **wh**y, t**w**in

Consonants

[b]	**b**ottle, bi**b**
[ç]	
[k]	**c**ome, **k**itchen
[d]	**d**og, di**d**

Lautschrift

Gin	[dʒ]	jet, fri**dg**e
Fantasie, **v**ier	[f]	**f**ib, **ph**ysical
Al**g**erien, **g**ut	[g]	**g**ag, **g**reat
Hobby	[h]	**h**ow, per**h**aps
alphabetisch, **L**aser	[l]	**l**ittle, he**l**p
Samme**l**surium	[l̩]	
Material, Alar**m**	[m]	**m**etal, co**mb**
große**m**	[m̩]	
November, A**n**gabe	[n]	**n**ight, di**nn**er
liebe**n**	[n̩]	
si**ng**en	[ŋ]	su**ng**, parki**ng**
Pony, Pa**pp**e	[p]	**p**op, **p**eople
A**pf**el	[pf]	
Revue, **r**ot	[r]	**r**ight, ca**rr**y
Slalom, e**ss**en	[s]	**s**eal, pea**c**e
Stadion, **Sch**ule	[ʃ]	**sh**eep, ma**ch**ine
Toas**t**, Vol**t**	[t]	**t**rain, **t**ip
Konversa**t**ion	[ts]	
Chili	[tʃ]	**ch**ain, wre**tch**ed
	[θ]	**th**ink, fif**th**
	[ð]	**th**is, wi**th**
Vase, **W**agen	[v]	**v**ine, li**v**id
Ma**ch**t, la**ch**en	[x]	lo**ch**
Sau**c**e, **S**onne	[z]	**z**ip, hi**s**
E**t**age	[ʒ]	u**s**ual, mea**s**ure

Phonetics

Die Betonung der deutschen Stich-wörter wird mit einem Punkt für einen kurzen betonten Vokal (z. B. **Berg**) und mit einem Strich für einen langen betonten Vokal (z. B. **Magen**) angegeben.

German headwords have the stress marked either by a dot for a short stressed vowel (e.g. **Berg**) or by an underscore for a long stressed vowel (e.g. **Magen**). A phonetic transcription is only given when the pronunciation is problematic.

Der Hauptton eines englischen Wortes ist durch ein vorangestelltes [ˈ] markiert, der Nebenton durch ein vor-angestelltes [ˌ].

The symbol [ˈ] indicates that the follo-wing syllable carries primary stress and the symbol [ˌ] that the following syl-lable carries secondary stress.

Das Zeichen [ʳ] zeigt in der engli-schen Phonetik an, dass der End-konsonant „r" ausgesprochen wird, wenn das folgende Wort mit einem Vokal beginnt. Im amerikanischen Englisch wird dieses „r" so gut wie immer mitgesprochen.

The symbol [ʳ] in English phonetics indicates that the final "r" is pro-nounced only when followed by a word beginning with a vowel. Note that it is nearly always pronounced in American English.

Warenzeichen

Als Warenzeichen geschützte Wörter sind in diesem Wörterbuch durch das Zeichen ® gekennzeichnet. Die Markie-rung mit diesem Symbol oder sein Fehlen hat keinen Einfluss auf die Rechtskräftigkeit eines Warenzeichens.

Trademarks

Words considered to be trademarks have been designated in this dictionary by the symbol ®. However, neither the presence nor the absence of such designation should be regarded as affecting the legal status of any trademark.

How to use the dictionary

How to find the word or expression you are looking for:

First ask yourself some basic questions:
Is it a single word, a hyphenated word or an abbreviation?
Is it a compound noun?
Is it a German separable verb?
Is it a German feminine form?
Is it a phrase?
Is it a reflexive verb?
Is it a German irregular verb form?

Single words, hyphenated words and abbreviations

As a rule, you can find the word you are looking for in its alphabetical order. If you want to translate an English word into German, you should look on the English–German side of the dictionary, and if you want to know what a German term means, you should look on the German–English side. The word in **bold** at the start of each entry is called the 'headword'.

Entries beginning with a capital appear after those spelled the same way but with a small letter.

> **kosten** vi [probieren] to have a taste …
> **Kosten** pl costs …

Words with a hyphen, a full stop or an apostrophe come after those spelled the same way but without any of these punctuation marks.

> **so** adv [auf diese Art] like this; [auf jene Art] like that.
> **s. o.** (abk für siehe oben) see above.

In some cases, the entry is followed by a number in superscript. This means that just before or just after there is another entry, also followed by a number, which is written the same way but which has a completely different meaning or pronunciation. You must take care not to choose the wrong entry.

> **modern**[1] (perf hat/ist gemodert) vi to moulder.
> **modern**[2] <> adj modern; [modisch] fashionable <> adv - **1.** [zeitgemäß] in a modern way; ~ **denken** to have modern ideas - **2.** [zeitgenössisch] in a modern style.

You will sometimes see words preceded by a grey lozenge, called subentries. English phrasal verbs fall into this category.

> **afternoon** [ɑːftə'nuːn] n Nachmittag der; **in the** ~ am Nachmittag; **good** ~ guten Tag. ◆ **afternoons** adv esp Am nachmittags.
> **amount** [ə'maʊnt] … ◆ **amount to** vt fus - **1.** [total] sich belaufen auf (+ A) - **2.** [be equivalent to] hinausllaufen auf (+ A).

If you are looking up a noun which has a form with an initial capital which has a different meaning from the form without a capital, you should look at the form without a capital.

> **advent** ['ædvənt] *n* [of invention] Aufkommen *das;* [of period] Beginn *der.* ◆ **Advent** *n* RELIG Advent *der.*

If you are looking up a noun which, in the plural, has a different meaning from the noun in its singular form (like **glass/glasses** in English), you will find it under the singular form; the plural form will be there as a sub-entry, indicated by the symbol ◆.

> **glass** [glɑːs] ◇ *n* - 1. [gen] Glas *das;* **a ~ of wine** ein Glas Wein - 2. *(U)* [glassware] Glaswaren *pl* ◇ *comp* Glas-. ◆ **glasses** *npl* [spectacles] Brille *die;* [binoculars] Fernglas *das;* **a pair of ~es** eine Brille.

Some plural nouns appear as headwords in their own right when they are never or rarely used in the singular (e.g. **Teigwaren** in German, **scissors** in English).

Compound nouns

A compound is a word or expression which has a single meaning but is made up of more than one word, e.g. **point of order, kiss of life, virtual reality, International Monetary Fund**. It is a feature of this dictionary that English compounds appear in the A–Z list in strict alphabetical order. The compound **blood group** will therefore come before **bloodhound** which itself precedes **blood poisoning**.

> **blood group** *n* Blutgruppe *die.*
> **bloodhound** ['blʌdhaʊnd] *n* Bluthund *der.*
> **blood poisoning** *n* Blutvergiftung *die.*

Most compounds in German have their two elements joined together to form a single word. A vertical line is used to separate the constituent elements of a compound.

> **Schul|jahr** *das* - 1. [Jahr] school year - 2. [Klasse] year.

In order to check the plural of this noun, you should refer to the entry **Jahr**.

> **Jahr** (*pl* -e) *das* year; **im ~(e) 1992** in 1992; **die 90er ~e** the nineties; **seit ~en** for years …

Other German compound nouns made up of two separate words are entered in the same way as English compounds, e.g. **Schwarze Markt** *der*, **Rote Kreuz** *das*.

German separable verbs

Verbs of the type **an sein** which used to be written in one word (**anlsein**) are now written in two words following the German spelling reform but are still entered in the same place alphabetically.

> **anlsehnlich** *adj* - **1.** [groß] considerable - **2.** [schön] attractive.
>
> **an sein** (*perf* ist an gewesen) *vi* (*unreg*) to be on.
>
> **anlsetzen** *vt* [in Stellung bringen - Werkzeug] to place in position ...

German feminine forms

The feminine form of a German noun is entered alongside the masculine form when the two forms are identical or alphabetically adjacent. **Lehrerin** is thus entered at **Lehrer**.

> **Lehrer, in** (*mpl* -; *fpl* -nen) *der, die* [in Schule] teacher; [in Sportverein] instructor.

Otherwise the feminine appears as a separate headword.

> **Ärztin** ['ɛːɐ̯t͡stɪn] (*pl* -nen) *die* doctor.

Phrases

If looking for a phrase, you should look first under the noun that is used in the phrase. If there is no noun, then you should look under the adjective, and if there is no adjective, under the verb. Phrases appear in entries in bold, the symbol ~ standing for the headword.

> **Zeit** (*pl* -en) *die* [gen] time; **in letzter ~** lately; **im Laufe der ~** in the course of time; **von ~ zu ~** from time to time; **die ~ stoppen** to stop the clock; **~ raubend** time-consuming; **~ sparend** time-saving; **sich** (*D*) **für jn/etw ~ nehmen** to spend time on sb/sthg; **sich** (*D*) **die ~ (mit Kartenspielen) vertreiben** to pass the time (playing cards); **sich** (*D*) **~ lassen** to take one's time ...

Some very fixed phrases like **in spite of** in English or **auf jeden Fall** in German are entered under the first important element and preceded by ➡.

> **spite** [spaɪt] ◇ *n* (*U*) Bosheit *die* ◇ *vt* ärgern. ➡ **in spite of** *prep* trotz (+ G).
>
> **Fall** (*pl* Fälle) *der* [gen] case ... ➡ **auf alle Fälle** *adv* - **1.** [unbedingt] definitely - **2.** [vorsichtshalber] in any case. ➡ **auf jeden Fall** *adv* in any case ...

Reflexive verbs

German reflexive verbs are entered under the main form, after the symbol ➡.

> **anlschnallen** *vt* [Skier, Rollschuhe] to put on; [Sicherheitsgurt] to fasten. ➡ **sich anschnallen** *ref* to fasten one's seat belt.

German irregular verb forms

If you are unsure what the infinitive of a certain verb form is, and so where to look for it, then it may be an irregular form. These irregular forms are entered in the A–Z list.

> **aß** *prät* ⊏▷ essen.

How to find the right translation

Once you have found the word or phrase that you are looking for, there may be several different translations given from which to choose. However, all the necessary information to help you find the right translation is given.

Step 1 Imagine that you want to translate 'he accepted the blame' into German.

Go first to the entry **accept** on the English-German side of the dictionary. At sense 3 you will find the verb used in this context: **ein|gestehen**.

> **accept** [ək'sept] *vt* - **1.** [gift, advice, apology, invitation, offer] an|nehmen - **2.** [change, situation] akzeptieren, hin|nehmen - **3.** [defeat, blame] ein|gestehen; [responsibility] übernehmen - **4.** [subj: shop, bank] akzeptieren; [subj: machine] nehmen ...

Step 2 Go now to the entry for the second word that needs to be translated, **blame**.

NB It is important first to find the correct grammatical category (each category is introduced by ◇). **Blame** is a noun in this example and so you should look under the noun category (labelled *n*).

> **blame** [bleɪm] ◇ *n* Schuld *die;* **to take the ~ for sthg** die Schuld für etw auf sich *(A)* nehmen ◇ *vt* beschuldigen; **to ~ sthg on sb/sthg** jm/etw die Schuld an etw *(D)* geben ...

Step 3 On examining the noun category, you will find that the translation used is **Schuld**.

Step 4 The words selected can now be put together in the phrase to be translated, to give: **er hat die Schuld eingestanden**.

Extra information given in this dictionary

Labelling the gender of German nouns

The gender of German nouns is indicated on both sides of the dictionary by the definite article placed after the noun (*der* for masculine, *die* for feminine and *das* for neuter).

The label *pl* was chosen to mark plural forms in order to avoid the confusion with *die*.

> **Baum** (*pl* Bäume) *der* tree.
>
> **Hand** (*pl* Hände) *die* [Körperteil] hand ...
>
> **Kind** (*pl* -er) *das* child ...
>
> **Kosten** *pl* costs ...

When a German noun accompanied by an adjective is given as a translation on the English–German side, the adjective ending (-**er**, -**e** or -**es**) tells you what gender the noun is and no *der, die* or *das* label is given. At the entry **Arabic numeral**, for example, the gender of **Ziffer** is indicated by the -**e** ending of the adjective **arabische**.

> **Arabic numeral** *n* arabische Ziffer.

German adjectives only used attributively

With German adjectives of this type, the feminine form is shown first, followed by the masculine and neuter endings.

> **letztere, r, s** <> *adj* the latter; **in ~m Fall** in the latter case <> *pron* the latter.

German adjectives used as nouns

Nominalized German adjectives are, like all other nouns, labelled with the definite article. When used with an indefinite article, the ending of this type of noun changes according to the gender. Hence **Blinde** *der, die* becomes **ein Blinder** and **eine Blinde**.

> **Blinde** (*pl* -n) *der, die* blind man (*f* blind woman).

Labelling case information

Some German prepositions can take either the accusative or dative case and these are always labelled accordingly, e.g. at the entry ***adept: to be ~ (at sthg)*** (in etw *(D)*) geschickt sein.

Case is also indicated when it is not predictable, e.g. ***to be able to afford sthg*** sich *(D)* etw leisten können. Here the reflexive pronoun is dative, rather than the usual accusative.

Indicating the auxiliary

We indicate when a verb can be conjugated with both the auxiliary verb **haben** and the auxiliary verb **sein**, as at the entry **fahren**.

> **fahren** (*präs* fährt; *prät* fuhr; *perf* hat/ist gefahren) *vi*

Separability of German verbs

A vertical line is used in the dictionary after the prefix of a verb to indicate that it is separable.

> **ab|fahren** (*perf* hat/ist abgefahren) (*unreg*)
> ◇ *vi (ist)* [losfahren] to leave; [Zug] to depart, to leave; **auf jn/etw ~** *fam fig* to be into sb/sthg ◇ *vt (hat)* [Ladung] to take away ...

German prefixes as translations for English adjectives

Some English adjectives are translated by a noun prefix that is joined to the noun to form a compound noun.

Thus, when translating **aggregate amount** into German, the prefix **Gesamt-** should be joined to **Summe** to give **Gesamtsumme**.

> **aggregate** ['ægrɪgət] ◇ *adj* Gesamt-;
> **~ earnings** Gesamtverdienst *der* ◇ *n* [total] Gesamtsumme *die*; **on ~** ingesamt.

Alphabetical order and new German spelling

The German spelling reform sometimes means changes in alphabetical order on the German–English side of the dictionary. In order to help the reader to find what they are looking for, we have decided to show both the old and the new spellings in cases like these.

When the new spelling of a word means that its alphabetical order must be changed, the old spelling is always given but with a cross-reference to the new spelling where the full entry appears.

> **Stängel** (*pl* -) *der* stalk.
> **Stengel** *der* = Stängel.

In many cases, however, the new spelling is alphabetically very close to the old one. In these cases, a cross-reference is not necessary.

> **Potenzial, Potential** [potɛn'tsjaːl] (*pl* -e)
> *das* potential.

Sometimes cross-references are used when both the old spelling and new spelling are allowed. In these cases, the entry appears at the new spelling.

> **selbständig** = selbstständig.
>
> **selbstständig** *adj* - 1. [unabhängig] independent - 2. [im Beruf] self-employed ...

Compound words which used to be written in one word but which are now written in two have been left in their 'usual' place.

Kennen lernen thus appears where **kennenlernen** did before.

> **kennen** (*prät* kannte; *perf* hat gekannt) *vt* to know …
> **kennen lernen** *vt* [Person] to get to know, to meet …
> **Kenntnis** (*pl* -nisse) *die* knowledge …

In some cases, however, we have left the old spelling and given a cross-reference to the new spelling.

> **rad|fahren** *vi* (*unreg*) ▷ Rad.
> **Rad** (*pl* Räder) *das* - **1.** [von Fahrzeug] wheel - **2.** [Fahrrad] bike; ~ **fahren** to cycle - **3.** [von Maschine] cog.

On the English–German side, only the new spelling is used without any labelling.

> **river** ['rɪvəʳ] *n* Fluss *der* …

When both the old and new spellings are allowable, just the new spelling is shown in translations.

> **photography** [fə'tɒgrəfɪ] *n* (U) Fotografie *die*.

Boxes

False friends

To help you avoid translation errors, boxed notes have been inserted into the text that point out and explain the most common false friends, i.e. German and English words that look alike but have different meanings. You will find notes relating to German terms on the German–English side of the dictionary. Examples with their translations are given to help you put the words in context, as at **sensibel**.

> **sensibel**
>
> The German word sensibel is a false friend which has to do with feelings rather than the mind, and so it corresponds to the adjective "sensitive", not "sensible". Sie ist immer ein <u>sensibles</u> Kind gewesen therefore translates as "She was always a <u>sensitive</u> child".
> The English word "sensible" is most commonly translated by vernünftig. So if you want to tell someone in German: "Be <u>sensible</u>!" you could say Sei doch <u>vernünftig</u>!

Information on cultural items and the education system

Information on the education system in Germany has been added to this book in order to help English-speakers to understand the German system, which differs considerably from that in Britain and the US. The notes contain precise definitions of the terms used, or general information on common practices, as at **blauer Brief**.

> **blauer Brief**
>
> In German schools pupils receive marks ranging from 1 (excellent) to 6 (unsatisfactory). If a pupil's level of achievement slips (e.g. from 4 to 5 or from 5 to 6), the school will send home an official letter three months before the end of the school year to warn parents that the pupil may have to sit the year again. Pupils refer to such a letter as ein blauer Brief.

In addition, boxes have been included on cultural phenomena in German-speaking countries that English-speakers might find odd or of interest. These cover topics ranging from usage information, such as how to express the date and the use of the word **bitte**, to important historical items such as **Berliner Mauer**.

Common phrases grouped by subject

These boxes bring together the different ways in German that a certain idea can be expressed. A variety of common German phrases are presented, together with their translations, that can be used in the same context. For example, when wanting to suggest something, the English user will have several options in the box at the English entry **suggest**.

📖 Datum

In written German, the date is given as a number followed by a full stop (10. Mai 2000). However, when reading the date aloud, or if writing the date out in full, ordinal numbers are used (zehnter Mai 2000 or zehnter fünfter 2000). In abbreviated form, the day, month and year are separated by full stops (10.05.00). When referring to something happening on a particular date, the ordinal number is always preceded by am and has the dative ending -en (am zehnten Mai).

---

suggesting

Kann ich Ihnen helfen? Can I help you?
Was kann ich für Sie tun? How can I be of help?
Wenn Sie möchten, unternehme ich das für Sie. I'll do that for you if you like.
Ich schlage vor, wir gehen alle zusammen ins Kino. Why don't we all go to the movies?
Ich hätte da eine Idee. I've got an idea.

Infinitive Infinitiv	Present Präsens	Past Tense Präteritum	Past Participle Perfekt
beginnen	beginnt	begann	hat begonnen
beißen	beißt	biss	hat gebissen
biegen	biegt	bog	hat gebogen
bitten	bittet	bat	hat gebeten
bleiben	bleibt	blieb	ist geblieben
brechen	bricht	brach	hat/ist gebrochen
bringen	bringt	brachte	hat gebracht
denken	denkt	dachte	hat gedacht
dürfen	darf	durfte	hat gedurft/dürfen
essen	isst	aß	hat gegessen
fahren	fährt	fuhr	hat/ist gefahren
finden	findet	fand	hat gefunden
fliegen	fliegt	flog	hat/ist geflogen
fließen	fließt	floss	ist geflossen
fressen	frisst	fraß	hat gefressen
geben	gibt	gab	hat gegeben
gehen	geht	ging	ist gegangen
gelten	gilt	galt	hat gegolten
geschehen	geschieht	geschah	ist geschehen
gießen	gießt	goss	hat gegossen
greifen	greift	griff	hat gegriffen
haben	hat	hatte	hat gehabt
halten	hält	hielt	hat gehalten
hängen	hängt	hing/hängte	hat gehangen/gehängt
heben	hebt	hob	hat gehoben
heißen	heißt	hieß	hat geheißen
helfen	hilft	half	hat geholfen
kennen	kennt	kannte	hat gekannt
kneifen	kneift	kniff	hat gekniffen
kommen	kommt	kam	ist gekommen
können	kann	konnte	hat können/gekonnt
lassen	lässt	ließ	hat gelassen/lassen
laufen	läuft	lief	hat/ist gelaufen
leiden	leidet	litt	hat gelitten
leihen	leiht	lieh	hat geliehen
lesen	liest	las	hat gelesen
liegen	liegt	lag	hat gelegen
lügen	lügt	log	hat gelogen
messen	misst	maß	hat gemessen
mögen	mag	mochte	hat gemocht/mögen
müssen	muss	musste	hat gemusst/müssen
nehmen	nimmt	nahm	hat genommen
nennen	nennt	nannte	hat genannt
quellen	quillt	quoll	ist gequollen

Infinitive *Infinitiv*	Present *Präsens*	Past Tense *Präteritum*	Past Participle *Perfekt*
raten	rät	riet	hat geraten
reißen	reißt	riss	hat/ist gerissen
rennen	rennt	rannte	ist gerannt
riechen	riecht	roch	hat gerochen
rufen	ruft	rief	hat gerufen
saufen	säuft	soff	hat gesoffen
schieben	schiebt	schob	hat geschoben
schießen	schießt	schoss	hat/ist geschossen
schlafen	schläft	schlief	hat geschlafen
schlagen	schlägt	schlug	hat/ist geschlagen
schließen	schließt	schloss	hat geschlossen
schmeißen	schmeißt	schmiss	hat geschmissen
schneiden	schneidet	schnitt	hat geschnitten
schreiben	schreibt	schrieb	hat geschrieben
schreien	schreit	schrie	hat geschrie(e)n
schwimmen	schwimmt	schwamm	hat/ist geschwommen
sehen	sieht	sah	hat gesehen
sein	ist	war	ist gewesen
senden	sendet	sandte	hat gesendet/gesandt
singen	singt	sang	hat gesungen
sitzen	sitzt	saß	hat gesessen
sprechen	spricht	sprach	hat gesprochen
springen	springt	sprang	hat/ist gesprungen
stehen	steht	stand	hat gestanden
stehlen	stiehlt	stahl	hat gestohlen
sterben	stirbt	starb	ist gestorben
stoßen	stößt	stieß	hat/ist gestoßen
streiten	streitet	stritt	hat gestritten
tragen	trägt	trug	hat getragen
treffen	trifft	traf	hat getroffen
treiben	treibt	trieb	hat/ist getrieben
treten	tritt	trat	hat getreten
trinken	trinkt	trank	hat getrunken
tun	tut	tat	hat getan
verlieren	verliert	verlor	hat verloren
waschen	wäscht	wusch	hat gewaschen
wenden	wendet	wendete/wandte	hat gewendet/gewandt
werden	wird	wurde	ist geworden/worden
werfen	wirft	warf	hat geworfen
wissen	weiß	wusste	hat gewusst
wollen	will	wollte	hat gewollt/wollen

Infinitive *Infinitiv*	Past Tense *Präteritum*	Past Participle *Perfekt*
arise	arose	arisen
awake	awoke	awoken
be	was, were	been
bear	bore	born(e)
beat	beat	beaten
become	became	become
begin	began	begun
bend	bent	bent
beseech	besought	besought
bet	bet (also betted)	bet (also betted)
bid	bid (also bade)	bid (also bidden)
bind	bound	bound
bite	bit	bitten
bleed	bled	bled
blow	blew	blown
break	broke	broken
breed	bred	bred
bring	brought	brought
build	built	built
burn	burnt (also burned)	burnt (also burned)
burst	burst	burst
buy	bought	bought
can	could	-
cast	cast	cast
catch	caught	caught
choose	chose	chosen
cling	clung	clung
come	came	come
cost	cost	cost
creep	crept	crept
cut	cut	cut
deal	dealt	dealt
dig	dug	dug
do	did	done
draw	drew	drawn
dream	dreamed (also dreamt)	dreamed (also dreamt)
drink	drank	drunk
drive	drove	driven
dwell	dwelt	dwelt
eat	ate	eaten
fall	fell	fallen
feed	fed	fed
feel	felt	felt

Irregular English verbs

Infinitive *Infinitiv*	Past Tense *Präteritum*	Past Participle *Perfekt Perfekt*
fight	fought	fought
find	found	found
flee	fled	fled
fling	flung	flung
fly	flew	flown
forbid	forbade	forbidden
forget	forgot	forgotten
forsake	forsook	forsaken
freeze	froze	frozen
get	got	got (*Am* gotten)
give	gave	given
go	went	gone
grind	ground	ground
grow	grew	grown
hang	hung (also hanged)	hung (also hanged)
have	had	had
hear	heard	heard
hide	hid	hidden
hit	hit	hit
hold	held	held
hurt	hurt	hurt
keep	kept	kept
kneel	knelt (also kneeled)	knelt (also kneeled)
know	knew	known
lay	laid	laid
lead	led	led
lean	leant (also leaned)	leant (also leaned)
leap	leapt (also leaped)	leapt (also leaped)
learn	learnt (also learned)	learnt (also learned)
leave	left	left
lend	lent	lent
let	let	let
lie	lay	lain
light	lit (also lighted)	lit (also lighted)
lose	lost	lost
make	made	made
may	might	-
mean	meant	meant
meet	met	met
mistake	mistook	mistaken
mow	mowed	mown (also mowed)
pay	paid	paid
put	put	put

Infinitive *Infinitiv*	Past Tense *Präteritum*	Past Participle *Perfekt Perfekt*
quit	quit (also quitted)	quit (also quitted)
read	read	read
rend	rent	rent
rid	rid	rid
ride	rode	ridden
ring	rang	rung
rise	rose	risen
run	ran	run
saw	sawed	sawn
say	said	said
see	saw	seen
seek	sought	sought
sell	sold	sold
send	sent	sent
set	set	set
shake	shook	shaken
shall	should	-
shear	sheared	shorn (also sheared)
shed	shed	shed
shine	shone	shone
shoot	shot	shot
show	showed	shown
shrink	shrank	shrunk
shut	shut	shut
sing	sang	sung
sink	sank	sunk
sit	sat	sat
slay	slew	slain
sleep	slept	slept
slide	slid	slid
sling	slung	slung
slit	slit	slit
smell	smelt (also smelled)	smelt (also smelled)
sow	sowed	sown (also sowed)
speak	spoke	spoken
speed	sped (also speeded)	sped (also speeded)
spell	spelt (also spelled)	spelt (also spelled)
spend	spent	spent
spill	spilt (also spilled)	spilt (also spilled)
spin	spun	spun
spit	spat	spat
split	split	split
spoil	spoiled (also spoilt)	spoiled (also spoilt)

Irregular English verbs

Infinitive *Infinitiv*	Past Tense *Präteritum*	Past Participle *Perfekt*
spread	spread	spread
spring	sprang	sprung
stand	stood	stood
steal	stole	stolen
stick	stuck	stuck
sting	stung	stung
stink	stank	stunk
stride	strode	stridden
strike	struck	struck (also stricken)
strive	strove	striven
swear	swore	sworn
sweep	swept	swept
swell	swelled	swollen (also swelled)
swim	swam	swum
swing	swung	swung
take	took	taken
teach	taught	taught
tear	tore	torn
tell	told	told
think	thought	thought
throw	threw	thrown
thrust	thrust	thrust
tread	trod	trodden
wake	woke (also waked)	woken (also waked)
wear	wore	worn
weave	wove (also weaved)	woven (also weaved)
wed	wedded	wedded
weep	wept	wept
win	won	won
wind	wound	wound
wring	wrung	wrung
write	wrote	written

A

a, A [a:] (pl - ODER -s) *das* - **1.** [Buchstabe] a, A - **2.** MUS A.

Aal (pl -e) *der* eel.

aalglatt *adj abw* slippery.

a.a.O. (*abk für* am angegebenen Ort) loc. cit.

Aas (pl -e ODER Äser) *das* - **1.** (pl Aase) [Kadaver] carrion (U) - **2.** (pl Äser) salopp abw [Luder] devil; **kein ~** salopp not a damned single person.

ab ◇ *präp* (+ D) - **1.** [zeitlich] from; **~ 8 Uhr** from 8 o'clock; **~ 18 (Jahren)** over (the age of) 18 - **2.** [räumlich] from; **~ Werk** ex works; **9.30 ~ Köln** leaving Cologne at 9.30 - **3.** [bei einer Reihenfolge] over; **Einkünfte ~ 15 000 Euro** incomes over 15,000 euros ◇ *adv* - **1.** [räumlich] off; **weit ~ gelegen** situated a long way away - **2.** [auffordernd]: **~ ins Bett!** get to bed! - **3.** [elliptisch] off; *fig* **Hut ~!** hats off!; *siehe auch* ab sein. ➡ **ab und zu, ab und an** *adv* now and then.

ab|arbeiten *vt* to work off.

Ab|art *die* variety.

abartig *adj* deviant.

Abb. (*abk für* Abbildung) fig.

Abbau *der* (*ohne pl*) - **1.** [Demontage - von Bühne, Gerüst] taking down; [- von Maschine] dismantling - **2.** [Reduzierung] reduction - **3.** [beim Bergbau] mining - **4.** CHEM & BIOL breaking down.

ab|bauen ◇ *vt* - **1.** [abbrechen - Kulissen, Bühne, Zelt] to take down; [- Maschine] to dismantle - **2.** [reduzieren] to reduce - **3.** CHEM & BIOL to break down - **4.** [im Bergbau] to mine ◇ *vi* to go downhill.

ab|bekommen *vt* (unreg) - **1.** [Anteil, Partner, Prügel] to get; **Schaden ~** to get damaged; **hast du etwas ~?** [Verletzung] did you get hurt? - **2.** *fam* [Fleck] to get off.

ab|bestellen *vt* to cancel.

ab|bezahlen *vt* to pay off.

ab|biegen (*perf* hat/ist abgebogen) (unreg) ◇ *vi* (ist) to turn off; **nach links/rechts ~** to turn left/right ◇ *vt* (hat) [verhindern - Vorhaben] to avert; [- Thema] to change.

Ab|bild *das* picture.

ab|bilden *vt* to depict.

Ab|bildung *die* - **1.** [Bild] illustration - **2.** [Wiedergabe] depiction.

ab|binden *vt* (unreg) - **1.** [ausziehen] to undo - **2.** MED to ligature.

ab|blasen *vt* (unreg) *fam* to call off.

ab|blättern (*perf* ist abgeblättert) *vi* to flake off.

ab|blenden ◇ *vt* - **1.** [Lampe] to screen - **2.** [Scheinwerfer] to dip *Br*, to dim *Am* ◇ *vi* - **1.** FOTO to stop down - **2.** AUTO to dip *Br* ODER dim *Am* one's headlights.

Abblend|licht *das* dipped *Br* ODER dimmed *Am* headlights (pl).

ab|blitzen (*perf* ist abgeblitzt) *vi fam*: **bei jm ~** to get short shrift from sb.

ab|blocken *vt* to block.

ab|brechen (*perf* hat/ist abgebrochen) (unreg) ◇ *vt* (hat) - **1.** [Stück, Ast] to break off; [Bleistift] to break - **2.** [Vorhaben, Beziehungen, Reise, Studium] to break off; [Streik] to call off ◇ *vi* - **1.** (hat) [im Gespräch] to break off - **2.** (ist) [Geräusch] to stop.

ab|brennen (*perf* hat/ist abgebrannt) (unreg) ◇ *vt* (hat) - **1.** [Haus] to burn down - **2.** [Feuerwerk] to let off ◇ *vi* (ist) to burn down.

ab|bringen *vt* (unreg): **jn von seiner Meinung ~** to make sb change his/her mind; **jn davon ~, aus dem Fenster zu springen** to stop sb from jumping out of the window; **das bringt uns vom Thema ab** we're getting off the subject.

ab|bröckeln (*perf* ist abgebröckelt) *vi* to flake off.

Ab|bruch *der* - **1.** [Ende] breaking off; **einer Sache** (D) **keinen ~ tun** *fig* not to harm sthg - **2.** [Zerstörung] demolition.

abbruchreif *adj* fit only for demolition.

ab|buchen *vt* WIRTSCH: **~ (von)** to debit (to).

Abc [a(:)be(:)'tse:] *das* ABC.

ab|danken *vi* to abdicate.

ab|decken *vt* - **1.** [gen] to cover - **2.** [abräumen - Tisch] to clear; [- Dach] to take off.

Abdeckung (*pl* -en) *die* - **1.** [zum Schutz] cover - **2.** WIRTSCH covering.

ab|dichten *vt* [gegen kalte Luft] to insulate; [gegen Wasser] to waterproof; [Gefäß] to make airtight; [Fenster] to draughtproof.

Ab|dichtung *die* [gegen kalte Luft] insulation; [gegen Wasser] waterproofing; [von Fenster] draughtproofing; [von Gefäß] making airtight.

ab|drehen (*perf* hat/ist abgedreht) ⋄ *vt* (*hat*) - **1.** [Wasser, Gas] to turn off - **2.** [Knopf, Schraube] to twist off - **3.** [Film, Szene] to shoot ⋄ *vi* (*hat, ist*) [den Kurs ändern] to turn away.

Abdruck (*pl* -drücke) *der* - **1.** [Spur] imprint - **2.** [Druck] printing.

ab|drucken *vt* to print.

ab|drücken ⋄ *vt* [abquetschen] to constrict; **jm die Luft ~** to squeeze the breath out of sb ⋄ *vi* [schießen] to pull the trigger.

➥ **sich abdrücken** *ref* to leave an impression.

Abend (*pl* -e) *der* evening; **am ~** in the evening; **gestern/heute/morgen ~** yesterday/this/tomorrow evening; **guten ~!** good evening!; **zu ~ essen** to have one's dinner ODER evening meal; **bunter ~** social evening.

Abend|brot *das* cold supper.

Abend|essen *das* dinner, evening meal.

Abend|kasse *die* box office (*where tickets may only be bought immediately before performance*).

Abend|kurs *der* evening class.

abendlich *adj* evening (*vor Subst*).

Abend|mahl *das* REL (Holy) Communion.

Abend|programm *das* evening programme (*pl*) ODER viewing (*U*).

abends *adv* in the evening; **spät ~** late in the evening.

Abenteuer (*pl* -) *das* - **1.** [Erlebnis] adventure - **2.** [Wagnis] venture - **3.** [Liebesverhältnis] affair.

abenteuerlich *adj* - **1.** [waghalsig] adventurous - **2.** [fantastisch] fantastic.

Abenteurer, in (*mpl* -; *fpl* -nen) *der, die* adventurer.

aber ⋄ *konj* but ⋄ *adv*: **das ist ~ nett!** how nice!; **~ gerne!** of course!; **~ immer!** *fam* sure!; **jetzt ist ~ Schluss!** that's enough now!; **du kommst ~ spät!** you're a bit late, aren't you?

Aber|glaube, -n *der* superstition.

abergläubisch *adj* superstitious.

ab|fahren (*perf* hat/ist abgefahren) (*unreg*) ⋄ *vi* (*ist*) [losfahren] to leave; [Zug] to depart, to leave; **auf jn/etw ~** *fam* fig to be into sb/sthg ⋄ *vt* (*hat*) - **1.** [Ladung] to take away - **2.** [Strecke] to go over - **3.** [Reifen] to wear down - **4.** [Fahrkarte] to get full use out of.

Ab|fahrt *die* - **1.** [Start] departure; **Vorsicht bei der ~ des Zuges!** stand clear of the doors, the train is about to depart! - **2.** [Autobahnabfahrt] exit - **3.** [Skiabfahrt] descent.

Abfahrts|zeit *die* departure time.

Ab|fall *der* - **1.** [Hausmüll] refuse; [industriell] waste - **2.** (*ohne pl*) [Rückgang] drop, fall.

Abfall|beseitigung *die* waste disposal.

ab|fallen (*perf* ist abgefallen) *vi* (*unreg*) - **1.** [herunterfallen] to fall off - **2.** [übrig bleiben] to be left over; **was fällt für mich ab?** what do I get out of it? - **3.** [schlechter sein]: **gegen jn/etw ~** to suffer by comparison with sb/sthg - **4.** [sich neigen] to slope (down) - **5.** [sich verringern] to drop, to fall.

abfällig ⋄ *adj* disparaging ⋄ *adv* disparagingly.

ab|fangen *vt* (*unreg*) - **1.** [Brief, Anruf, Transport] to intercept - **2.** [Person] to catch - **3.** [Schlag] to ward off - **4.** [Flugzeug] to regain control of.

ab|färben *vi* to run.

ab|fassen *vt* to write.

ab|fertigen *vt* - **1.** [Waren] to prepare for dispatch; [Gepäck] to check in; [Schiff, Flugzeug] to prepare for departure - **2.** [Passagier, Antragsteller] to attend to.

Ab|fertigung *die* - **1.** [von Gepäck] check-in; [von Waren] preparation for dispatch; [von Schiff, Flugzeug] preparation for departure - **2.** [von Passagier, Antragsteller] attending to.

ab|feuern *vt* [Gewehr, Schuss] to fire; [Rakete] to launch.

ab|finden *vt* (*unreg*) [entschädigen]: **jn mit etw ~** to give sb sthg in compensation.

➥ **sich abfinden** *ref*: **sich mit etw ~** to come to terms with sthg.

Abfindung (*pl* -en) *die* [für einen Verlust] compensation; [für die vorzeitige Entlassung] severance pay.

ab|fliegen (*perf* ist abgeflogen) *vi* (*unreg*) to take off.

ab|fließen (*perf* ist abgeflossen) *vi* (*unreg*) [Spülwasser] to drain away; [Regenwasser] to run away.

Ab|flug *der* - **1.** [von Flugzeug] take-off - **2.** [Flughafenbereich] departures (*U*).

Ab|fluss *der* - **1.** [Öffnung - von Waschbecken, Dusche] plughole - **2.** [von Kapital] flight - **3.** [von Spülwasser] draining away; [von Regenwasser] running away.

ab|fragen *vt* to call up; **jn (etw) ~** to test sb (on sthg).

Abfuhr (*pl* -en) *die*: **jm eine ~ erteilen** to rebuff sb.

ab|führen ⋄ *vt* - **1.** [festnehmen] to take away - **2.** [vom Thema] to lead away ⋄ *vi* MED to act as a laxative.

Abführ|mittel *das* laxative.

ab|füllen *vt* - **1.** [Flüssigkeit]: **Wein in Fla-**

schen ~ to bottle wine - **2.** [Flaschen, Säcke] to fill - **3.** *fam* [betrunken machen]: **jn** ~ to get **sb** plastered.

Abgabe (*pl* -n) *die* - **1.** [Übergabe - von Gutachten] handing over; [- von Arbeit] handing in - **2.** [von Stimmen] casting - **3.** [Verkauf] sale - **4.** [von Ball] passing - **5.** [von Wärme, Sauerstoff] giving off. ◆ **Abgaben** *pl* [Steuern] taxes.

abgabenfrei *adj* exempt from tax.

abgabenpflichtig *adj* taxable.

Abgangszeugnis *das* leaving certificate.

Abgase *pl* exhaust fumes.

ab|geben *vt* (*unreg*) - **1.** [abliefern - Brief, Geschenk] to hand over; [- Arbeit] to hand in; [- an der Garderobe] to leave - **2.** [verkaufen] to sell - **3.** [teilen]: **jm etw** ~ to give **sb** sthg - **4.** [äußern - Erklärung] to make; [- Meinung] to give; [- Stimme] to cast - **5.** [abtreten] to give up - **6.** [darstellen - Figur] to cut; **einen guten Vater** ~ to make a good father - **7.** SPORT [werfen] to pass - **8.** [ausströmen] to give off - **9.** [abfeuern] to fire. ◆ **sich abgeben** *ref*: **sich mit etw (nicht)** ~ (not) to concern o.s. with sthg; **sie gibt sich mit ganz obskuren Typen ab** she mixes with some really dubious types.

abgebrüht *adj fam* hard-boiled, tough.

abgedroschen *adj* well-worn, hackneyed.

ab|gehen (*perf* ist abgegangen) (*unreg*) ◇ *vi* - **1.** [sich lösen] to come off - **2.** [verlassen]: **von etw** ~ to leave sthg - **3.** [abfahren] to leave, to depart - **4.** [abgeschickt werden] to go off - **5.** [abgerechnet werden] to be taken off ODER deducted - **6.** [abzweigen] to branch off - **7.** [abweichen]: **von seiner Meinung** ~ to change one's mind; **von seinen Forderungen** ~ to drop one's demands - **8.** [verlaufen] to go; **es ist gut abgegangen** it went well; **es geht ab** *salopp* things are really buzzing - **9.** [fehlen]: **ihm geht jedes Feingefühl ab** he lacks any sensitivity ◇ *vt* [Strecke, Straße] to walk along; [Grundstück] to walk over.

abgekämpft *adj* worn-out.

abgekartet *adj*: **ein ~es Spiel** a put-up job.

abgelegen *adj* remote.

abgemacht *adj* settled; **abgemacht!** it's a deal!

abgemagert *adj* emaciated.

abgeneigt *adj*: **einer Sache** (*D*) **(nicht)** ~ **sein** (not) to be opposed to sthg.

abgenutzt *adj* [Türgriff, Fußboden] worn; [Gerät] worn-out.

Abgeordnete (*pl* -n) *der, die* [im Bundestag] member of parliament; [im Landtag] representative.

Abgesandte *der, die* envoy.

abgeschieden *adj* remote.

Abgeschiedenheit *die* remoteness.

abgesehen *adv*: ~ **von jm/etw** apart from sb/sthg. ◆ **abgesehen davon, dass ...** *konj* apart from the fact that ...

abgespannt *adj* exhausted.

abgestanden *adj* [Bier] flat; [Luft] stale; [Wasser] stagnant.

abgestorben ◇ *pp* ▷ absterben ◇ *adj* - **1.** [Baum, Ast] dead - **2.** [Fuß, Bein] numb.

abgestumpft *adj* - **1.** [gefühllos] hardened - **2.** [apathisch] apathetic.

abgetragen *adj* worn-out.

ab|gewinnen *vt* (*unreg*): **jm etw** ~ to win sthg from sb; **einer Sache** (*D*) **Geschmack** ~ to acquire a taste for sthg.

ab|gewöhnen *vt*: **jm etw** ~ to get sb to give sthg up; **sich** (*D*) **etw** ~ to give sthg up.

ab|grenzen *vt* - **1.** [abtrennen - mit Zaun] to fence off; [- mit Mauer] to wall off - **2.** [unterscheiden] to differentiate. ◆ **sich abgrenzen** *ref*: **sich von jm/etw** ~ to distance o.s. from sb/sthg.

Abgrenzung (*pl* -en) *die* - **1.** [Grenze] boundary - **2.** [Begrenzung] definition.

Ab|grund *der* abyss; **vor dem** ~ **stehen** *fig* to be on the edge of the abyss.

abgrundtief ◇ *adj* profound, deep ◇ *adv* profoundly, deeply.

ab|gucken *vt fam* to copy; **etw von** ODER **bei jm** ~ to copy sthg from sb.

ab|hacken *vt* to chop off.

ab|haken *vt* to check off.

ab|halten *vt* (*unreg*) - **1.** [veranstalten] to hold - **2.** [fern halten]: **jn von etw** ~ to keep sb from sthg.

abhanden *adv*: **mir ist meine Brille** ~ **gekommen** my glasses have gone missing.

Abhandlung *die* treatise.

Abhang *der* slope.

ab|hängen ◇ *vt* (*reg*) - **1.** [Bild] to take down - **2.** [Anhänger, Wagon] to uncouple - **3.** [Konkurrenten, Verfolger] to shake off ◇ *vi* (*unreg*): **von jm/etw** ~ to depend on sb/sthg.

abhängig *adj*: **von etw** ~ **sein** [von Wetter, Geschmack, Zufall] to depend on sthg; [von Hilfe, Vormund] to be dependent on sthg; [von Drogen] to be addicted to sthg.

Abhängigkeit (*pl* -en) *die* - **1.** [gen] dependence; ~ **von etw** dependence on sthg - **2.** [von Drogen] addiction.

ab|härten ◇ *vt* to toughen up ◇ *vi*: **dieses Wetter härtet ab** this weather toughens you up. ◆ **sich abhärten** *ref* to toughen (o.s.) up.

ab|hauen (*perf* ist abgehauen) *vi fam* [verschwinden] to clear off.

ab|heben (*unreg*) ◇ *vt* - **1.** [vom Konto] to withdraw - **2.** [am Telefon] to pick up - **3.** [beim Kartenspiel] to cut ◇ *vi* [abfliegen] to take off. ➡ **sich abheben** *ref:* **sich von jm/etw** ODER **gegen jn/etw** ~ to stand out against sb/sthg.

ab|heften *vt* to file away.

ab|hetzen *vt* to drive hard. ➡ **sich abhetzen** *ref* to rush one's socks off.

Abhilfe *die:* ~ **schaffen** to take remedial action.

ab|holen *vt* [Paket, Ware] to collect; [Person] to pick up.

ab|holzen *vt* [Wald, Allee] to clear; [Bäume] to cut down.

ab|hören *vt* - **1.** [heimlich anhören - Gespräch] to listen in on; [- Telefon] to tap - **2.** [abfragen] to test; **jm etw** ~ to test sb on sthg - **3.** [abhorchen] to sound.

Abi (*pl* -s) *das abk für* Abitur.

Abitur (*pl* -e) *das* ≃ A levels (*pl*) *Br,* ≃ SATs (*pl*) *Am, final examination at a German 'Gymnasium', qualifying pupils for university entrance.*

Abitur|feier *die party at end of school studies.*

Abiturfeier

The Abiturfeier is a party for students who have reached the end of their school studies. This normally takes place once the exams are over but before the results have been published. Final year students, parents and teachers are all invited to attend, and during the course of the evening the overall grades are announced. The party often takes the form of a dance or a show.

Abiturient, in [abituri'ɛnt, ɪn] (*mpl* -en; *fpl* -nen) *der, die pupil who is taking/has taken the 'Abitur'.*

Abitur|zeugnis *das certificate awarded to a pupil who has passed the 'Abitur'.*

ab|kapseln ➡ **sich abkapseln** *ref* to cut o.s. off.

ab|kaufen *vt* - **1.** [kaufen]: **jm etw** ~ to buy sthg from sb - **2.** *fam* [glauben]: **diese Geschichte kaufe ich dir nicht ab!** I'm not buying that story (of yours)!

ab|klappern *vt fam:* **etw (nach etw)** ~ to scour sthg (for sthg).

ab|klingen (*perf* ist abgeklungen) *vi* (*unreg*) [Fieber] to die down.

ab|knöpfen *vt:* **jm etw** ~ to get sthg out of sb.

ab|kochen *vt* to sterilize (*by boiling*).

ab|kommen (*perf* ist abgekommen) *vi* (*unreg*): **von etw** ~ [Kurs, Weg] to deviate from sthg; [Thema] to get off sthg; [Gewohnheit, Vorhaben] to give sthg up, to abandon sthg.

Abkommen (*pl* -) *das* agreement.

abkömmlich *adj* available.

ab|können *vt* (*unreg*) *salopp:* **ich kann ihn/es nicht ab** I can't stand ODER stick *Br* him/it.

ab|kriegen *vt fam* - **1.** [gen] to get; **das Auto hat was abgekriegt** the car got damaged; **einen/eine** ~ to get a man/woman - **2.** [Deckel, Schraube, Fleck] to get off.

ab|kühlen (*perf* hat/ist abgekühlt) *vi* - **1.** [Temperatur] to cool down - **2.** [Stimmung, Engagement] to cool. ➡ **sich abkühlen** *ref* [Person] to cool down ODER off; [Verhältnis] to cool; **es hat sich abgekühlt** it has got cooler.

Abkühlung *die* cooling.

ab|kürzen *vt* - **1.** [Weg]: **den Weg** ~ to take a short cut - **2.** [Wort] to abbreviate - **3.** [Besuch, Reise] to cut short; [Verfahren] to shorten.

Abkürzung *die* - **1.** [von Weg] short cut - **2.** [von Wörtern] abbreviation.

ab|laden *vt* (*unreg*) - **1.** [abräumen] to unload - **2.** [erzählen]: **seinen Kummer bei jm** ~ to unburden o.s. to sb.

Ablage *die* - **1.** [für Papiere, Akten] filing cabinet - **2.** [Abheften] filing.

Ablagerung *die* [Sediment] deposit.

ab|lassen (*unreg*) ◇ *vt* - **1.** [Luft] to let out - **2.** [Wasser] to drain off ◇ *vi:* **von jm** ~ [in Ruhe lassen] to leave sb alone; **von etw** ~ [aufgeben] to give sthg up.

Ablauf *der* - **1.** [Verlauf] course; **um den friedlichen** ~ **der Veranstaltung zu gewährleisten ...** to ensure that the event passes off peacefully ... - **2.** [Abfluss] drain; [Rinne] outlet - **3.** [Ende] expiry.

ab|legen ◇ *vt* - **1.** [Mantel] to take off - **2.** [sich abgewöhnen] to get rid of - **3.** [Eid, Prüfung] to take - **4.** [Akten] to file ◇ *vi* - **1.** [Garderobe] to take one's coat/hat/etc off - **2.** [Schiff] to cast off.

Ableger (*pl* -) *der* - **1.** [von Pflanzen] cutting - **2.** [Filiale] subsidiary.

ab|lehnen *vt* - **1.** [Angebot, Vorschlag] to reject; [Einladung] to refuse, to turn down - **2.** [Rauschgift, Schusswaffen] to disapprove of.

Ablehnung (*pl* -en) *die* - **1.** [von Angebot] rejection; [von Einladung] refusal; **auf** ~ **stoßen** to be rejected - **2.** [Missbilligung] disapproval.

ab|leisten *vt:* **den Wehrdienst** ~ to do one's military service.

ab|leiten *vt* - **1.** [Rauch, Gas] to draw off - **2.** [folgern, zurückführen]: **etw von** ODER **aus etw** ~ [Wort, Recht] to derive sthg from sthg - **3.** [Gleichung] to differentiate.

Ableitung *die* - **1.** [von Rauch, Gas] drawing off - **2.** [von Wort, Formel] derivation.

ab|lenken *vt* - **1.** [zerstreuen] to distract; **jn von der Arbeit** ~ to put sb off their work - **2.** [Aufmerksamkeit, Verdacht] to divert

- 3. [weglenken - Angriff] to ward off; [- Bewegung] to deflect.

Ablenkung (pl -en) die **- 1.** [Zerstreuung] distraction **- 2.** [Richtungsänderung] deflection.

ab|lesen vt (unreg) **- 1.** [lesen] to read out **- 2.** [den Stand feststellen] to read **- 3.** [erraten]: **er liest ihr jeden Wunsch von den Augen ab** he can always tell what she wants from the look in her eyes.

ab|liefern vt to deliver.

ab|lösen vt **- 1.** [ersetzen] to take over from **- 2.** [abmachen] to take off. ◆ **sich ablösen** ref **- 1.** [sich abwechseln] to take turns **- 2.** [abgehen] to come off.

Ablösung die **- 1.** [Zahlung] paying off **- 2.** [Ersatzperson] relief.

ab|luchsen ['apluksn] vt: **jm etw ~** to get sthg out of sb.

ABM [a:'be:'ɛm] (pl -) (abk für Arbeitsbeschaffungsmaßnahme) die job creation scheme.

ab|machen vt **- 1.** [entfernen] to take off **- 2.** [verabreden] to agree on; **einen Termin ~** to make an appointment.

Abmachung (pl -en) die agreement.

ab|magern (perf ist abgemagert) vi to get thinner.

Abmarsch der departure.

ab|marschieren (perf ist abmarschiert) vi [bei Wandern] to set off; MIL to march off.

ab|melden vt **- 1.** [Personen]: **ein Kind von der Schule ~** to give notice of a child's removal from school; **sie ist bei mir abgemeldet** fam fig I've had it ODER I'm through with her **- 2.** [Gegenstände - Telefon] to have disconnected; [- Auto] to take off the road. ◆ **sich abmelden** ref: **sich polizeilich ~** to notify the police that one is moving away; **sich bei einem Verein ~** to cancel one's membership of a club.

Abmeldung die **- 1.** [beim Einwohnermeldeamt] notification that one is moving away **- 2.** [von der Schule] notification of a child's removal from school.

ab|messen vt (unreg) to measure.

ABM-Stelle die job created as part of a job creation scheme.

ab|mühen ◆ **sich abmühen** ref to struggle.

ab|nehmen (unreg) ◇ vt **- 1.** [herunternehmen - Vorhänge, Wäsche] to take down; [- Hut, Deckel] to take off; [- Hörer] to pick up **- 2.** [wegnehmen]: **jm etw ~** to take sthg (away) from sb **- 3.** [entlasten]: **jm etw ~** to relieve sb of sthg **- 4.** [kontrollieren] to inspect **- 5.** [kaufen]: **jm etw ~** to buy sthg from sb **- 6.** [glauben]: **das nimmt dir keiner ab!** nobody will buy that! **- 7.** [entgegennehmen - Prüfung] to conduct; **jm ein Versprechen ~** to make sb give a promise

- 8. [amputieren]: **jm einen Finger ~** to take sb's finger off **- 9.** [entnehmen]: **jm Blut ~** to take sb's blood **- 10.** [verlieren - Gewicht] to lose ◇ vi **- 1.** [leichter werden] to lose weight **- 2.** [sich verringern - Temperatur, Luftdruck, Ressourcen] to decrease; [- Mond] to wane.

Abnehmer, in (mpl -; fpl -nen) der, die buyer.

Abneigung die aversion.

ab|nutzen, ab|nützen vt to wear out. ◆ **sich abnutzen, sich abnützen** ref to wear out.

Abo (pl -s) das fam abk für Abonnement.

Abonnement [abɔnə'mã:] (pl -s) das **- 1.** [einer Zeitung] subscription **- 2.** [im Theater] season ticket.

abonnieren vt to subscribe to.

ab|packen vt to pre-pack.

ab|passen vt **- 1.** [Person] to catch **- 2.** [Moment] to wait for.

ab|pflücken vt to pick.

ab|prallen (perf ist abgeprallt) vi **- 1.** [zurückspringen - Ball] to bounce back, to rebound; [- Kugel] to ricochet **- 2.** [Vorwurf, Worte]: **an jm** ODER **von jm ~** to make no impression on sb.

ab|putzen vt to wipe.

ab|quälen ◆ **sich abquälen** ref [sich plagen]: **sich mit etw ~** to struggle with sthg.

ab|raten vi (unreg): **(jm) von etw ~** to advise (sb) against sthg.

ab|räumen vt [Geschirr] to clear away; [Tisch] to clear.

ab|reagieren vt: **etw an jm ~** to take sthg out on sb. ◆ **sich abreagieren** ref: **sich an jm ~** to take it out on sb.

ab|rechnen ◇ vi [Kassiererin] to cash up; **mit jm ~** [zahlen] to settle up with sb; [sich rächen] to get even with sb ◇ vt [abziehen] to deduct.

Abrechnung die **- 1.** [Bilanz, Rechnung] accounts (pl) **- 2.** [Rache] reckoning.

ab|reiben vt (unreg) **- 1.** [Schmutz] to rub off **- 2.** [Hände] to wipe **- 3.** [Kind, Hund] to rub down.

Abreibung (pl -en) die thrashing.

Abreise die departure.

ab|reisen (perf ist abgereist) vi to depart.

ab|reißen (perf hat/ist abgerissen) (unreg) ◇ vt (hat) **- 1.** [Papier] to tear off **- 2.** [Haus] to pull down ◇ vi (ist) **- 1.** [Teil, Knopf, Etikett] to come off; [Faden] to break off **- 2.** [Kontakt] to break off.

ab|richten vt to train.

ab|riegeln vt **- 1.** [verschließen] to bolt **- 2.** [Gelände] to cordon off.

Abriss der **- 1.** [Zerstörung] demolition **- 2.** [Darstellung] outline.

ab|rollen (perf hat/ist abgerollt) ◇ vt (hat)

[abspulen] to unwind ⬦ *vi (ist)* - **1.** [von einer Rolle] to unwind - **2.** [ablaufen] to go - **3.** SPORT to go into a roll.

ab|rücken (*perf* hat/ist abgerückt) ⬦ *vt* (hat) to move away ⬦ *vi (ist)* [wegrücken]: **von jm/etw ~** [sich entfernen] to move away from sb/sthg; [sich distanzieren] to distance o.s. from sb/sthg.

Ab|ruf *der* EDV retrieval. ⬥ **auf Abruf** *adv*: **auf ~ bereit stehen** to be standing by.

ab|rufen *vt* (*unreg*) EDV to retrieve.

ab|runden *vt* - **1.** [Zahl, Summe] to round down - **2.** [Ecke, Küche, Programm] to round off.

abrupt ⬦ *adj* abrupt ⬦ *adv* abruptly.

ab|rüsten ⬦ *vi* to disarm ⬦ *vt* to get rid of.

Abrüstung *die* disarmament.

ab|rutschen (*perf* ist abgerutscht) *vi* - **1.** [wegrutschen] to slip - **2.** [Schüler]: **er ist in Mathematik abgerutscht** his marks in mathematics have gone down.

ab|sacken (*perf* ist abgesackt) *vi* - **1.** [sinken - Flugzeug, Druck] to drop; [- Gebäude] to subside - **2.** [Leistung]: **sie ist in Chemie abgesackt** her marks in chemistry have got worse.

Ab|sage *die* - **1.** [von Termin, Veranstaltung] cancellation - **2.** [Zurückweisung]: **jm/einer Sache eine ~ erteilen** to reject sb/sthg.

ab|sagen ⬦ *vt* to cancel ⬦ *vi* to cancel.

ab|sägen *vt* - **1.** [sägen - Baum] to saw down; [- Brett] to saw off - **2.** *fam* [entlassen] to axe.

ab|sahnen *fam* ⬦ *vt* to cream off ⬦ *vi* to make a killing.

Ab|satz *der* - **1.** [von Schuhen] heel - **2.** [Verkauf] sales (*pl*) - **3.** [im Text] paragraph.

ab|saufen (*perf* ist abgesoffen) *vi* (*unreg*) - **1.** *salopp* [im Wasser - Schiff] to go to the bottom; [- Person] to go to a watery grave - **2.** *fam* [Motor] to flood.

ab|schaffen *vt* - **1.** [Regelung] to abolish - **2.** [aufheben] to do away with - **3.** [weggeben] to get rid of.

ab|schalten *vi & vt* [ausschalten] to switch off.

ab|schätzen *vt* - **1.** [Menge, Zahl] to estimate - **2.** [Menschen] to weigh up.

Abscheu *die* ODER *der* disgust, revulsion.

abscheulich ⬦ *adj* disgusting ⬦ *adv* disgustingly.

ab|schicken *vt* to post *Br,* to mail *Am.*

ab|schieben (*perf* hat/ist abgeschoben) (*unreg*) ⬦ *vt* (hat) - **1.** [außer Landes] to deport - **2.** *fam abw* [versetzen] to shunt off ⬦ *vi (ist)* *salopp abw* [fortgehen] to push off.

Abschied (*pl* -e) *der* - **1.** [Trennung, Weggehen] parting; **von jm/etw ~ nehmen** to say

goodbye to sb/sthg - **2.** [Entlassung] resignation; **seinen ~ nehmen** to resign.

ab|schießen *vt* (*unreg*) - **1.** [Flugzeug] to shoot down - **2.** [Kugel, Gewehr] to fire; [Pfeil] to shoot; [Rakete] to launch - **3.** [töten] to shoot - **4.** [Körperteil]: **ihm ist ein Bein abgeschossen worden** his leg has been shot off - **5.** *fam* [entlassen]: **jn ~** to give sb the boot, to kick sb out.

ab|schirmen *vt* to shield.

ab|schlachten *vt fam* to slaughter.

ab|schlagen *vt* (*unreg*) - **1.** [verweigern]: **jm etw ~** to refuse sb sthg - **2.** [abtrennen - durch Schneiden] to chop off; [- durch Schlagen] to knock off.

abschlägig ⬦ *adj* unfavourable ⬦ *adv*: **etw ~ bescheiden** to refuse sthg.

Abschlepp|dienst *der* (vehicle) recovery service.

ab|schleppen *vt* - **1.** [Auto, Schiff] to tow away - **2.** *fam* [Person] to pick up.

Abschlepp|seil *das* towrope.

ab|schließen (*unreg*) ⬦ *vt* - **1.** [Tür] to lock - **2.** [Tätigkeit] to finish - **3.** [Geschäft] to conclude; [Vertrag] to sign; [Versicherung] to take out - **4.** WIRTSCH to balance ⬦ *vi* [mit etw enden]: **mit etw ~** to finish with sthg; **mit der Vergangenheit ~** to draw a line under the past; **mit Verlust ~** to show a loss.

abschließend ⬦ *adj* concluding ⬦ *adv* in conclusion.

Ab|schluss *der* - **1.** [Ende] end; **zum ~ der Tagung spricht Professor Schulz** Professor Schulz will bring the conference to a close - **2.** [von Geschäft] conclusion; [von Vertrag] signing; [von Versicherung] taking out - **3.** [Abschlusszeugnis von Hochschule] degree.

Abschluss|zeugnis *das* school-leaving certificate.

ab|schmecken *vt* - **1.** [würzen] to season - **2.** [kosten] to taste.

ab|schmieren ⬦ *vt* - **1.** [Motor] to lubricate; [Fahrradkette] to grease - **2.** *fam* [abschreiben] to crib ⬦ *vi fam* [Flugzeug] to nosedive; [Computer, Programm] to crash.

ab|schminken *vt*: **jn ~** to remove sb's make-up. ⬥ **sich abschminken** *ref*: **sich ~** to remove one's make-up.

ab|schnallen (*perf* hat/ist abgeschnallt) *vt* (hat) to unfasten. ⬥ **sich abschnallen** *ref* to unfasten one's seatbelt.

ab|schneiden (*unreg*) ⬦ *vt* - **1.** [Stück] to cut off - **2.** [Weg]: **jm den Weg ~** to block sb's way - **3.** [Wort]: **jm das Wort ~** to cut sb off ⬦ *vi*: **gut/schlecht ~** to do well/badly.

Ab|schnitt *der* - **1.** [im Text, von Strecke] section - **2.** [von Formular, Karte] detachable portion; [von Scheck] counterfoil; [von Eintrittskarte] stub - **3.** [Zeitraum] period - **4.** MATH segment.

ab|schrauben vt to unscrew.

ab|schrecken vt - **1.** [abhalten] to deter - **2.** [mit kaltem Wasser - Eier] to put into cold water.

Abschreckung (pl -en) die deterrent.

ab|schreiben vt (unreg) - **1.** [kopieren] to copy - **2.** WIRTSCH [aufgeben] to write off.

Ab|schrift die copy.

Ab|schuss der - **1.** [von Flugzeug] shooting down - **2.** [von Gewehr] firing; [von Rakete] launching - **3.** [von Wild] shooting.

abschüssig adj sloping.

ab|schütteln vt eigtl & fig to shake off.

ab|schwächen vt to lessen. ➤ **sich abschwächen** ref to grow weaker.

ab|schweifen (perf ist abgeschweift) vi [Gedanken, Blick] to wander; **vom Thema ~** to digress.

ab|schwellen (perf ist abgeschwollen) vi (unreg) - **1.** [Schwellung] to go down - **2.** [Geräusch] to fade (away).

absehbar adj foreseeable; **in ~er Zeit** in the foreseeable future.

ab|sehen (unreg) ⬦ vt [Folgen] to foresee; **das Ergebnis ist abzusehen** it's possible to tell what the result will be ⬦ vi - **1.** [verzichten]: **von etw ~** to refrain from sthg - **2.** [ausnehmen]: **sieht man davon ab, dass er taub ist, ist er kerngesund** if you ignore the fact that he's deaf, he's perfectly healthy - **3.** [wollen]: **es auf etw (A) abgesehen haben** to be after sthg; **es darauf abgesehen haben, alle zu verärgern** to be intent on annoying everyone - **4.** [ärgern]: **es auf jn abgesehen haben** to have it in for sb.

ab|seifen vt [Kind] to soap down.

ab|seilen vt to lower down on a rope. ➤ **sich abseilen** ref - **1.** [mit einem Seil] to abseil - **2.** fam [verschwinden] to leg it.

ab sein (perf ist ab gewesen) vi (unreg) - **1.** [entfernt]: **dieses Dorf ist weit von allem ab** this village is far away from everything - **2.** [abgetrennt] to have come off.

abseits ⬦ präp: **~ eines Ortes** ODER **von einem Ort** away from a place ⬦ adv out of the way; **sich ~ halten** to keep oneself to oneself.

Abseits das - **1.** SPORT offside - **2.** [Isolation]: **ins ~ geraten** to be left out in the cold.

ab|senden vt to send off.

Ab|sender der - **1.** [Person] sender - **2.** [Adresse] sender's name and address.

Absenderin (pl -nen) die sender.

ab|setzen vt - **1.** [herunternehmen - Hut, Brille] to take off - **2.** [hinstellen, hinlegen] to put down - **3.** [aussteigen lassen] to drop off - **4.** [Betrag]: **etw von der Steuer ~ (können)** to (be able to) deduct sthg from one's tax

- **5.** [Ware] to sell - **6.** [entmachten - König] to depose - **7.** [Aufführung] to drop, to take off - **8.** [Medikament] to come off - **9.** [Kleidung] to trim. ➤ **sich absetzen** ref - **1.** [fliehen] to take off - **2.** [sich ablagern] to be deposited - **3.** [sich entfernen]: **sich von etw ~** to pull away from sthg - **4.** [sich abheben]: **sich gegen etw ~** to stand out against sthg.

ab|sichern vt to make safe. ➤ **sich absichern** ref to cover o.s.; **sich gegen etw ~** to protect o.s. against sthg.

Ab|sicht die intention; **es war nicht meine ~, dir zu schaden** I didn't mean to harm you.

absichtlich ⬦ adj deliberate, intentional ⬦ adv deliberately, intentionally.

absolut ⬦ adj absolute ⬦ adv absolutely; **das gefällt mir ~ nicht** I don't like that at all.

absolvieren [apzɔlˈviːrən] vt [Kurs] to complete; [Prüfung] to pass.

ab|sondern vt - **1.** [Sekret] to secrete - **2.** [isolieren] to isolate. ➤ **sich absondern** ref to isolate o.s.

ab|spalten vt CHEM to separate. ➤ **sich abspalten** ref: **sich (von etw) ~** to break away (from sthg).

ab|speisen vt: **jn mit etw ~** to fob sb off with sthg.

ab|sperren vt - **1.** [abriegeln] to seal off - **2.** [verschließen] to lock.

Ab|sperrung die - **1.** [Schranke, Sperre] barrier - **2.** [Absperren] sealing off.

ab|spielen vt to play. ➤ **sich abspielen** ref to take place.

Ab|sprache die arrangement; **nach vorheriger ~** after prior consultation.

ab|sprechen vt (unreg) - **1.** [vereinbaren] to agree on - **2.** [verweigern, aberkennen]: **jm etw ~** [Recht] to deny sb sthg; [Fähigkeit] to deny that sb has sthg. ➤ **sich absprechen**: **wir hatten keine Zeit, uns abzusprechen** we had no time to agree on what to say/do.

ab|springen (perf ist abgesprungen) vi (unreg) - **1.** SPORT to jump - **2.** [sich lösen] to come off - **3.** fam [zurücktreten]: **von etw ~** to back out of sthg.

ab|spülen ⬦ vt - **1.** [Geschirr] to wash - **2.** [Schmutz] to wash off ⬦ vi to wash up Br, to wash the dishes Am.

ab|stammen vi: **von jm/etw ~** to be descended from sb/sthg.

Abstammung die descent.

Ab|stand der [räumlich] distance; [zeitlich] interval; **50 Meter ~** a distance of 50 metres; **von jm/etw ~ halten** to keep one's distance from sb/sthg.

ab|statten vt: **jm einen Besuch ~** to pay sb a visit.

ab|stauben vt - 1. [putzen] to dust - 2. fam [mitnehmen]: **etw bei jm ~** to get sthg off sb.

Abstecher (pl -) der detour.

ab|stehen (perf hat/ist abgestanden) vi (unreg): **von etw ~** to stick out from sthg.

abstehend adj: **er hat ~e Ohren** his ears stick out.

ab|steigen (perf ist abgestiegen) vi (unreg) - 1. [hinunterklettern] to get off - 2. SPORT to be relegated - 3. [übernachten] to stay.

ab|stellen vt - 1. [Gerät, Strom, Wasser] to turn off - 2. [Last] to put down; [Möbel] to store, to put; [Auto, Fahrrad] to park - 3. [Missstand] to put an end to - 4. [freistellen]: **jn zu etw ~** to assign sb to sthg.

Abstell|raum der storage room.

ab|stempeln vt - 1. [stempeln - Dokument] to stamp; [- Briefmarke] to postmark - 2. abw [anprangern]: **jn zu** ODER **als etw ~** to label sb sthg.

ab|sterben (perf ist abgestorben) vi (unreg) to die off.

Abstieg (pl -e) der - 1. [vom Berg] descent - 2. [sozial, finanziell] decline - 3. SPORT relegation.

ab|stimmen ⟨⟩ vi [wählen] to vote ⟨⟩ vt - 1. [einstellen]: **etw auf jn/etw ~** to adapt sthg to sb/sthg; [Farben] to match sthg to sb/sthg - 2. [absprechen]: **etw mit jm ~** to agree on sthg with sb. ⟵ **sich abstimmen** ref: **sich mit jm (über etw (A)) ~** to agree (on sthg) with sb.

Ab|stimmung die - 1. [Wahl] vote - 2. [Koordinierung] coordination - 3. [Absprache] agreement.

ab|stoßen vt (unreg) - 1. [wegdrücken] to push off - 2. [verkaufen] to sell off - 3. [anekeln] to repel - 4. [abnützen - Farbe] to knock off.

abstoßend ⟨⟩ adj repulsive ⟨⟩ adv repulsively.

abstrakt ⟨⟩ adj abstract ⟨⟩ adv in the abstract.

ab|streiten vt (unreg) to deny.

Ab|strich der - 1. [Einschränkungen] reservation; **~e machen** to make concessions - 2. MED swab; [vom Gebärmutter] smear.

ab|stufen vt - 1. [Löhne, Preise, Farben] to grade - 2. [Haare] to layer.

ab|stumpfen (perf hat/ist abgestumpft) ⟨⟩ vt (hat) - 1. [Subj: Lärm, Monotonie] to dull the senses of - 2. [Subj: Leid, Schmerz] to harden ⟨⟩ vi (ist): **gegen etw ~** to become inured to sthg.

Ab|sturz der crash.

ab|stürzen (perf ist abgestürzt) vi [Flugzeug & EDV] to crash; [Bergsteiger] to fall.

ab|suchen vt: **etw (nach jm/etw) ~** to search sthg (for sb/sthg).

absurd adj absurd.

Abt (pl Äbte) der abbot.

ab|tasten vt to feel.

ab|tauen (perf hat/ist abgetaut) ⟨⟩ vt (hat) to defrost ⟨⟩ vi (ist) [Eis] to thaw; [Kühlschrank] to defrost.

Abtei (pl -en) die abbey.

Ab|teil das compartment.

ab|teilen vt to divide off.

Ab|teilung[1] die - 1. [einer Firma, im Kaufhaus] department - 2. MIL unit.

Ab|teilung[2] die [Trennung] dividing off.

Äbtissin (pl -nen) die abbess.

ab|tragen vt (unreg) - 1. [Erde, Steine - Subj: Wind, Wasser] to erode; [Subj: Person] to remove (layer by layer) - 2. [Kleidung] to wear out - 3. [Schulden] to pay off.

ab|treiben (perf hat/ist abgetrieben) (unreg) ⟨⟩ vt (hat) [Kind] **sie will das Kind ~** she wants to have an abortion ⟨⟩ vi - 1. (hat) MED [Abort vornehmen] to carry out an abortion; [Abort vornehmen lassen] to have an abortion - 2. (ist) [Boot] to be driven off course.

Abtreibung (pl -en) die abortion.

ab|trennen vt - 1. [abschneiden - Coupon, Blatt] to detach; [- Ärmel, Saum] to cut off - 2. [abteilen] to divide off.

ab|treten (perf hat/ist abgetreten) (unreg) ⟨⟩ vt (hat) - 1. [Absätze] to wear down - 2. [Rechte] to relinquish; **etw an jn ~, jm etw ~** to let sb have sthg ⟨⟩ vi (ist) [fortgehen] to make one's exit.

ab|trocknen vt to dry; **sich die Hände ~** to dry one's hands. ⟵ **sich abtrocknen** ref to dry o.s.

ab|verlangen vt: **jm etw ~** to demand sthg from sb.

ab|wägen vt to weigh up; **zwei Dinge gegeneinander ~** to weigh up two things against each other.

ab|wählen vt - 1. [Politiker] to vote out (of office) - 2. [Schulfach] to drop.

ab|wälzen vt: **etw auf jn ~** to shift sthg onto sb.

ab|wandeln vt to vary.

ab|wandern (perf ist abgewandert) vi - 1. [fortgehen] to migrate - 2. [Kapital] to be removed.

Ab|wandlung die adaptation.

ab|warten ⟨⟩ vt to wait for; **ich kann es kaum ~, in Urlaub zu fahren** I can hardly wait to go on holiday ⟨⟩ vi to wait and see.

abwärts adv downwards; **alle, vom Assistenten ~** everyone from the assistant down.

Abwasch der (ohne pl) washing-up Br, dishes Am (pl).

ab|waschen (unreg) ⟨⟩ vt - 1. [Geschirr] to wash - 2. [Schmutz] to wash off ⟨⟩ vi to wash up Br, to wash the dishes Am.

Ab|wasser *das* [von Haushalt] sewage *(U)*; [von Industrie] effluent *(U)*.

ab|wechseln ['apvɛksln] ◆ **sich abwechseln** *ref* to alternate; **sich mit jm ~** to take turns with sb.

abwechselnd ['apvɛkslnt] *adv* alternately.

Abwechselung ['apvɛkslʊŋ], **Abwechslung** (*pl* -en) *die* change.

abwegig *adj* bizarre.

Abwehr *die* - **1.** [Widerstand] resistance - **2.** SPORT & MIL defence.

ab|wehren ◇ *vt* - **1.** [Schlag, Angriff] to ward off - **2.** [Störung] to deter ◇ *vi* to refuse.

ab|weichen (*perf* ist abgewichen) *vi* (*unreg*): **von etw ~** to deviate from sthg; **seine Ansichten weichen von meinen ab** his opinions differ from mine.

abweichend *adj* different.

ab|weisen *vt* (*unreg*) - **1.** [ablehnen] to reject - **2.** [Person] to turn away.

abweisend ◇ *adj* unfriendly ◇ *adv* dismissively.

ab|wenden *vt* (*unreg*) - **1.** [wegdrehen]: **den Kopf ~** to turn away; **den Blick ~** to look away - **2.** [Unglück] to avert. ◆ **sich abwenden** *ref* to turn away; **sich von jm/etw ~** to turn one's back on sb/sthg.

ab|werfen *vt* (*unreg*) - **1.** [von Flugzeug] to drop - **2.** [Geld]: **Gewinn ~** to yield a profit.

ab|werten *vt* to devalue.

ab|wertend *adj* pejorative.

abwesend ◇ *adj* - **1.** [nicht anwesend] absent - **2.** [unkonzentriert] absent, absentminded ◇ *adv* absently.

Abwesenheit *die* absence; **in js ~** in sb's absence; **durch ~ glänzen** *iron* to be conspicuous by one's absence.

ab|wickeln *vt* - **1.** [Schnur] to unwind - **2.** [Geschäft] to complete - **3.** [Institution] to wind up, to close down.

Abwicklung (*pl* -en) *die* - **1.** [Abschluss] completion - **2.** [Auflösung] closing down.

ab|wiegen *vt* (*unreg*) to weigh out.

ab|wimmeln *vt fam* to get rid of.

ab|wischen *vt* - **1.** [Fläche] to wipe - **2.** [Dreck] to wipe off.

ab|würgen *vt fam* - **1.** [Motor] to stall - **2.** [beenden, unterdrücken] to stifle.

ab|zahlen *vt* to pay off.

ab|zählen ◇ *vt* to count ◇ *vi* to use a counting-out rhyme.

Ab|zeichen *das* badge.

ab|zeichnen *vt* to draw. ◆ **sich abzeichnen** *ref* - **1.** [sich ankündigen] to emerge - **2.** [sich zeigen] to stand out.

ab|ziehen (*perf* ist/hat abgezogen) (*unreg*) ◇ *vt* (*hat*) - **1.** [Schürze, Mütze] to take off; [Schlüssel] to take out - **2.** [subtrahieren - Nummer] to subtract; [- Betrag] to de

duct - **3.** [Bett] to strip - **4.** [Soldaten] to withdraw - **5.** [veranstalten]: **eine Schau** ODER **Show ~** *salopp* to make a fuss - **6.** [Haut]: **einem Kaninchen die Haut ~** to skin a rabbit ◇ *vi* (*ist*) - **1.** [Gas] to clear - **2.** *fam* [Person] to clear off.

Ab|zug *der* - **1.** [von Kamin] flue; [Belüftung] vent - **2.** [Foto] print; [Druck] proof - **3.** [Subtraktion] deduction; **nach ~ der Unkosten** after costs - **4.** [Fortgehen] withdrawal - **5.** [am Gewehr] trigger.

abzüglich *präp*: **~ einer Sache** *(G)* less sthg.

ab|zweigen (*perf* hat/ist abgezweigt) ◇ *vi* (*ist*) to branch off ◇ *vt* (*hat*) to put aside.

Abzweigung (*pl* -en) *die* turning.

Achse ['aksə] (*pl* -n) *die* - **1.** [Linie & MATH] axis; **auf ~ sein** *fig* to be on the move - **2.** [von Auto] axle.

Achsel ['aksl] (*pl* -n) *die* shoulder; **mit den ~n zucken** to shrug one's shoulders.

achselzuckend *adv* with a shrug.

acht *num* eight; *siehe auch* sechs.

Acht[1] ◆ **außer Acht** *adv*: **etw außer ~ lassen** to disregard sthg. ◆ **in Acht** *adv*: **sich in ~ nehmen** to be careful; **sich vor etw** *(D)* **in ~ nehmen** to watch out for sthg. ◆ **Acht geben** *vi* (*unreg*) to take care; **auf jn/etw ~ geben** to look after sb/sthg.

Acht[2] (*pl* -en) *die* eight; *siehe auch* Sechs.

Achte (*pl* -n) *der, die, das* eighth; *siehe auch* Sechste.

achte, r, s *adj* eighth; *siehe auch* sechste.

Achteck (*pl* -e) *das* octagon.

achtel *adj* (*unver*) eighth; *siehe auch* sechstel.

Achtel (*pl* -) *das* [der achte Teil] eighth.

achten ◇ *vt* to respect ◇ *vi*: **auf etw ~** to pay attention to sthg; **auf jn ~** to look after sb.

Achter|bahn *die* roller coaster.

achtfach ◇ *adj* eightfold ◇ *adv* eight times.

Acht geben *vi* ▷ Acht[1].

achthundert *num* eight hundred.

achtlos ◇ *adj* careless ◇ *adv* carelessly.

achtmal *adv* eight times.

achttausend *num* eight thousand.

Achtung *die* - **1.** [Respekt] respect - **2.** [Vorsicht]: **Achtung!** look out!; [formell] attention, please!; **~, Stufe!** mind the step!; **~, fertig, los!** SPORT on your marks, get set, go!

achtzehn *num* eighteen; *siehe auch* sechs.

Achtzehn (*pl* -en) *die* eighteen; *siehe auch* Sechs.

achtzig *num* eighty; **auf ~ sein** *fam* to be livid; *siehe auch* sechs.

Achtzig *die* eighty; *siehe auch* Sechs.

Achtziger|jahre, achtziger Jahre *pl*: **die ~** the eighties.

ächzen *vi* to groan.

Acker (*pl* Äcker) *der* field.

Ackerbau *der* agriculture; ~ **treiben** to farm.

ADAC [a:de:'a:'tse:] (*abk für* Allgemeiner Deutscher Automobil-Club) *der* ≃ AA *Br*, ≃ AAA *Am*.

addieren *vt* MATH to add up.

Adel *der* nobility.

adelig = adlig.

Ader (*pl* -n) *die* vein.

Adjektiv (*pl* -e) *das* adjective.

adjektivisch ['at jektɪ:vɪʃ] GRAM <> *adj* adjectival <> *adv* adjectivally.

Adler (*pl* -) *der* eagle.

adlig, adelig *adj* noble.

Admiral (*pl* -e ODER Admiräle) *der* MIL admiral.

adoptieren *vt* to adopt.

Adoption (*pl* -en) *die* adoption.

Adoptiveltern *pl* adoptive parents.

Adoptivkind *das* adopted child.

Adressbuch *das* - **1.** [privat] address book - **2.** [von Stadt, Gemeinde] directory.

Adresse (*pl* -n) *die* address.

adressieren *vt* to address; **etw an jn** ~ to address sthg to sb.

Adria *die*: **die** ~ the Adriatic.

Advent [at'vɛnt] *der* Advent; **erster/ zweiter** ~ first/second Sunday in Advent.

Adventskranz *der* Advent wreath.

Adverb [at'vɛrp] (*pl* -ien) *das* adverb.

adverbial [atvɛr'bja:l] GRAM <> *adj* adverbial <> *adv* adverbially.

Affäre (*pl* -n) *die* - **1.** [Skandal, Liebschaft] affair; **sich aus der** ~ **ziehen** to get out of it - **2.** [Angelegenheit] matter.

Affe (*pl* -n) *der* - **1.** [Tier - klein] monkey; [- groß] ape - **2.** *salopp abw* [blöder Kerl] jerk, twit *Br*.

affektiert *abw* <> *adj* affected <> *adv* affectedly.

affig *fam abw* <> *adj* stuck-up <> *adv* in a stuck-up way.

Afrika *nt* Africa.

Afrikaner, in (*mpl* -; *fpl* -nen) *der*, *die* African.

afrikanisch *adj* African.

After (*pl* -) *der* anus.

AG [a:'ge:] (*pl* -s) (*abk für* Aktiengesellschaft) *die* ≃ plc *Br*, ≃ corp. *Am*.

Ägäis *die*: **die** ~ the Aegean.

Agent, in (*mpl* -en; *fpl* -nen) *der*, *die* - **1.** [Spion] secret agent - **2.** [Vermittler] agent.

Agentur (*pl* -en) *die* agency.

Aggression (*pl* -en) *die* aggression.

aggressiv <> *adj* aggressive <> *adv* aggressively.

Agrarpolitik *die* agricultural policy.

Ägypten [ɛ'gyptn] *nt* Egypt.

Ägypter, in (*mpl* -; *fpl* -nen) *der*, *die* Egyptian.

ägyptisch *adj* Egyptian.

ah *interj*: ah! [Ausdruck der Verwunderung] oh!; [Ausdruck plötzlichen Verstehens] ah!

aha *interj* aha!

Aha-Erlebnis *das* revelation.

ähneln *vi*: **jm/einer Sache** ~ to resemble sb/ sthg.

ahnen *vt* - **1.** [im Voraus fühlen] to have a premonition of - **2.** [vermuten] to suspect.

ähnlich <> *adj* similar; **jm/etw** ~ **sein** to be similar to ODER like sb/sthg <> *adv* similarly; **jm/etw** ~ **sehen** to look like sb/sthg; **das sieht dir/ihm** ~! that's just like you/him!

Ähnlichkeit (*pl* -en) *die* similarity.

Ahnung (*pl* -en) *die* - **1.** [Vorgefühl] premonition; **ich habe so eine** ~, **als ob ...** I have the feeling that ... - **2.** [Vorstellung, Vermutung] idea; **keine** ~! I've no idea!; **keine/nicht die geringste** ~ **haben** to have no/not the faintest idea.

ahnungslos <> *adj* unsuspecting <> *adv* unsuspectingly.

Ahnungslosigkeit *die* lack of suspicion.

ahoi *interj* SCHIFF ahoy!

Ahorn (*pl* -e) *der* maple.

Ähre (*pl* -n) *die* ear (*of corn*).

Aids ['eidz] (*abk für* Acquired Immune Deficiency Syndrome) *nt* Aids.

Aidskranke *der*, *die* Aids sufferer.

Akademie (*pl* -n) *die* academy.

Akademiker, in (*mpl* -; *fpl* -nen) *der*, *die* university graduate.

akademisch *adj* academic.

Akazie (*pl* -n) *die* acacia.

Akkord (*pl* -e) *der* chord. ← **im Akkord** *adv* WIRTSCH: **im** ~ **arbeiten** to do piecework.

Akkordeon (*pl* -s) *das* accordion.

Akku (*pl* -s) *der* storage battery; [für Radio, Walkman] rechargeable battery.

Akkumulator (*pl* -en) *der* - **1.** ELEKTR storage battery - **2.** EDV accumulator.

Akkusativ (*pl* -e) *der* accusative.

Akne *die* acne.

Akrobat, in (*mpl* -en; *fpl* -nen) *der*, *die* acrobat.

akrobatisch <> *adj* acrobatic <> *adv* acrobatically.

Akt (*pl* -e) *der* - **1.** [Handlung, Aufzug] act - **2.** [Bildnis] nude - **3.** [Zeremonie] ceremony.

Akte (*pl* -n) *die* file; **etw zu den** ~**n legen** to shelve sthg.

aktenkundig *adj*: **ein** ~**er Vorgang** an occurrence which is on record.

Aktentasche *die* briefcase.

Aktie ['aktsiə] (*pl* -n) *die* share; **die** ~**n steigen/fallen** share prices are rising/falling.

Aktiengesellschaft *die* ≃ public limited company *Br,* ≃ corporation *Am.*

Aktienkurs *der* share price.

Aktion (*pl* -en) *die* - **1.** [Tätigkeit] action; **in ~ sein/treten** to be in/go into action - **2.** [Verkauf] sale; [Werbung] promotion.

Aktionär, in [aktsioˈnɛːɐ̯, rɪn] (*mpl* -e; *fpl* -nen) *der, die* shareholder.

aktiv ◇ *adj* active ◇ *adv* actively.

Aktiv *das* GRAM active.

aktivieren [aktiˈviːrən] *vt* - **1.** [System, Alarm] to activate - **2.** [Person] to mobilize.

Aktivität [aktiviˈtɛːt] (*pl* -en) *die* activity.

Aktualität *die* relevance; **an ~ gewinnen** to become topical.

aktuell *adj* - **1.** [Theaterstück, Buch] topical; [Thema, Problem] current - **2.** [modisch] fashionable.

aktuell

The German term **aktuell** corresponds to the English "current" rather than "actual". So the phrase **Ein Thema von aktuellem Interesse** means "a topic of current interest".
"Actual" in the sense of "real" or "true", and its adverbial form "actually", are usually translated by **wirklich**, in **Wirklichkeit** or **eigentlich**. So the question "What did he actually say?" might be rendered in German as **Was hat er eigentlich gesagt?**

Akupunktur (*pl* -en) *die* acupuncture.

Akustik (*ohne pl*) *die* - **1.** PHYS acoustics (*U*) - **2.** [Schallverhältnisse] acoustics *pl.*

akut ◇ *adj* - **1.** [vordringlich] urgent - **2.** MED acute ◇ *adv* - **1.** [vordringlich] urgently - **2.** MED acutely.

AKW [aːkaːˈveː] (*pl* -s) (*abk für* Atomkraftwerk) *das* nuclear power station.

Akzent (*pl* -e) *der* - **1.** GRAM [Betonung] stress - **2.** [Tonfall] accent - **3.** RW: **~e setzen** to set a new trend.

akzeptieren *vt* to accept.

Alarm (*pl* -e) *der* alarm; **~ schlagen** to raise the alarm; **es war blinder ~** it was a false alarm.

Alarmanlage *die* [von Gebäude] burglar alarm; [von Auto] car alarm.

alarmieren *vt* - **1.** [aufschrecken] to alarm - **2.** [rufen] to alert.

Albaner, in (*mpl* -; *fpl* -nen) *der, die* Albanian.

Albanien *nt* Albania.

albanisch *adj* Albanian.

albern ◇ *adj* silly ◇ *adv* in a silly way ◇ *vi* to fool around.

Albino (*pl* -s) *der* albino.

Albtraum *der* nightmare.

Album (*pl* Alben) *das* album.

Alge (*pl* -n) *die* - **1.** [Seetang] piece of seaweed; **~n** seaweed (*U*) - **2.** [Algenpest verursachend]: **~n** algae.

Algebra *die* algebra.

Algerien *nt* Algeria.

Algerier, in [alˈgeːrɪ̯e, rɪn] (*mpl* -; *fpl* -nen) *der, die* Algerian.

algerisch *adj* Algerian.

alias *adv* alias.

Alibi (*pl* -s) *das* - **1.** RECHT alibi - **2.** [Ausrede] excuse.

Alimente *pl* maintenance (*U*) *Br,* child support (*U*) *Am.*

alkalisch *adj* alkaline.

Alkohol (*pl* -e ODER Alkoholika) *der* - **1.** (*pl* Alkohole) CHEM alcohol - **2.** (*pl* Alkoholika) [Getränk] alcohol; **unter ~ stehen** *amt* to be under the influence (of alcohol).

alkoholabhängig *adj*: **~ sein** to be an alcoholic.

alkoholfrei *adj* alcohol-free.

Alkoholgehalt (*pl* -e) *der* alcohol content.

Alkoholiker, in (*mpl* -; *fpl* -nen) *der, die* alcoholic.

alkoholisch ◇ *adj* alcoholic ◇ *adv* alcoholically.

Alkoholismus *der* alcoholism.

all *det* all (of); **~ das Warten** all this waiting.

All *das*: **das ~** space.

alle (*nt* -s) ◇ *det* - **1.** [sämtliche] all; **~ Kleider** all the clothes; **~ beide** both (of them); **~ fünf überlebten** all five survived; **wir ~** all of us - **2.** [verstärkend]: **in ~r Ruhe** in peace and quiet; **in ~r Öffentlichkeit** quite openly; **~ Welt** everyone - **3.** [allerlei]: **~r Art** all kinds of drinks; **~s Mögliche** all kinds of things - **4.** [im Abstand von] every; **~ 50 Meter/zwei Wochen** every 50 metres/two weeks ◇ *pron* - **1.** [auf Personen bezogen] all, everyone; **~ sind gekommen** everyone came, they all came; **~ einsteigen!** all aboard! - **2.** [auf Sachen bezogen] all, everything; **das ist ~s** that's all ODER everything ◇ *adj fam*: **die Milch ist ~** we've run out of milk. ◆ **trotz allem** *adv* in spite of everything. ◆ **vor allem** *adv* above all.

Allee (*pl* -n) *die* [Straße] avenue.

allein ◇ *adj* - **1.** [für sich] alone; **heute Abend war ich ~ zuhause** I was on my own at home this evening - **2.** [einsam] lonely ◇ *adv* - **1.** [für sich] alone - **2.** [selbstständig] on one's own, by oneself - **3.** [einsam] alone; **~ zurückbleiben** to stay behind by oneself; **~ herumstehen** to stand around on one's own; **~ dastehen** to be all alone in the world - **4.** [nur] only; **~ das Handgepäck wiegt 50 kg** the hand luggage alone weighs 50 kg ◇ *konj geh* however. ◆ **ganz allein**

◇ *adj* - **1.** [für sich] all alone - **2.** [einsam] all on one's own, all by oneself ◇ *adv* - **1.** [für sich, einsam] all alone - **2.** [selbstständig] all on one's own, all by oneself. ▸ **von allein** *adv* by oneself/itself.

allein erziehend *adj:* **~e Mutter** single mother.

Allein|gang *der* single-handed effort. ▸ **im Alleingang** *adv* single-handedly.

alleinig *adj* sole.

allein stehend *adj* - **1.** [ledig] single - **2.** [allein wohnend]: **eine ~e Person** a person who lives alone.

Alleinstehende (*pl* -n) *der, die* - **1.** [ledig] single person - **2.** [allein wohnend] person who lives alone.

allemal *adv fam*: **dich schlage ich ~** I could beat you no sweat ▷ **Mal**.

allenfalls *adv* at most.

allerbeste, r, s *adj* very best.

allerdings *adv* - **1.** [als Antwort] certainly - **2.** [einschränkend] though.

allererste, r, s *adj* very first.

Allergie (*pl* -n) *die* allergy.

allergisch ◇ *adj* allergic; **gegen etw ~ sein** MED to be allergic to sthg; [etw nicht ausstehen können] not to be able to stand sthg ◇ *adv* - **1.** MED allergically; **auf etw ~ reagieren** to have an allergic reaction to sthg - **2.** [ablehnend]: **auf Lügen reagiere ich wirklich ~** I really can't stand people lying.

allerhand ◇ *adj* (*unver*) all sorts of; **das ist ja ~!** [erbost] that really is the limit!; [anerkennend] that's not bad at all! ◇ *pron* all sorts of things.

Allerheiligen *nt* All Saints' Day.

allerhöchstens ['ale'høːkstn̩s] *adv* at the very most.

allerlei *det* all sorts of.

allerletzte, r, s *adj* - **1.** [letzte] very last - **2.** [schlecht] most awful.

Allerletzte *das*: **das ist ja das ~!** that's the absolute limit!

Allerseelen (*ohne Artikel*) All Souls' Day.

allerseits *adv*: **guten Tag/Abend ~** good afternoon/evening everyone.

alles ▷ **alle**.

allesamt *adv* all together.

Alles|kleber *der* all-purpose glue.

Allgäu *das*: **das ~** the Allgäu.

allgemein ◇ *adj* - **1.** [gen] general - **2.** [Interesse, Sprachgebrauch] common; [Wehrpflicht, Wahlrecht] universal ◇ *adv* generally. ▸ **im Allgemeinen** *adv* in general.

Allgemeinbildung *die* general education.

allgemein gültig ◇ *adj* universal ◇ *adv* universally.

Allgemeinheit (*pl* -en) *die* - **1.** [Öffentlichkeit] general public - **2.** [Undifferenziertheit]

generality. ▸ **Allgemeinheiten** *pl* [Floskel] generalities.

Allheil|mittel *das* cure-all, panacea.

Alligator (*pl* -gatoren) *der* alligator.

alliiert *adj* allied.

Alliierte *pl* allies; **die ~n** HIST the Allies.

alljährlich ◇ *adj* annual ◇ *adv* every year.

allmächtig *adj* almighty.

allmählich ◇ *adj* gradual ◇ *adv* gradually.

allseits *adv* everywhere.

Alltag *der* everyday life.

alltäglich ◇ *adj* - **1.** [täglich] daily - **2.** [üblich] everyday ◇ *adv* every day.

Alltagstrott *der* daily grind.

allwissend *adj* all-knowing, omniscient.

allzu *adv* far too. ▸ **allzu sehr** *adv* far too much. ▸ **allzu viel** *adv* far too much.

Alm (*pl* -en) *die* mountain pasture.

Almosen (*pl* -) *das* alms (*pl*).

Aloe ['aːloe] (*pl* -n) *die* aloe.

Alpen *pl*: **die ~** the Alps.

Alpen|veilchen *das* cyclamen.

Alpen|verein *der organization which promotes study of the Alps and organizes mountain hikes etc*.

Alpen|vorland *das* (*ohne pl*) foothills (*pl*) of the Alps.

Alpha (*pl* -s) *das* alpha.

Alphabet [alfa'beːt] (*pl* -e) *das* alphabet.

alphabetisch ◇ *adj* alphabetical ◇ *adv* alphabetically.

alpin *adj* alpine.

Alptraum *der* = Albtraum.

als *konj* - **1.** [zur Kennzeichnung eines Zeitpunkts] when; **~ es dunkel wurde** when it got dark; **erst ~** only when - **2.** [zur Kennzeichnung einer Zeitspanne] as - **3.** [bei Vergleich]: **sie ist besser ~ ihr Bruder** she is better than her brother; **der Wein ist besser, ~ ich dachte** the wine is better than I thought it would be; **mehr ~** more than - **4.** [bei Vergleich vor Konjunktiv] as if, as though; **es sieht so aus, ~ würde es bald regnen** it looks like it's going to rain soon; **~ ob** as if, as though - **5.** [zur Kennzeichnung einer Eigenschaft] as; **ich verstehe es ~ Kompliment** I take it as a compliment; **~ Kind** as a child.

also ◇ *interj* well; **~ doch!** so I was right (after all)!; **~ gut** ODER **schön!** oh, all right then!; **na ~!** what did I tell you!, there you are!; **~ dann!** *fam* right then!; **~ bitte!** [Unmut ausdrückend] for heaven's sake! ◇ *adv* - **1.** [das heißt] that is - **2.** [demnach] so; **da lag ~ der Fehler!** so that's where the mistake was - **3.** [endlich] so; **die Sache ist ~ erledigt** so the matter is settled.

alt (*kompar* älter; *superl* älteste) *adj* - **1.** [gen]

old; **12 Jahre ~** 12 years old; **wie ~ bist du?** how old are you?; **zwei Jahre älter** two years older; **dieser ~e Schmarotzer!** *abw* the old sponger! **- 2.** [antik] antique **- 3.** [historisch] ancient; **~e Sprachen** classics, classical languages; **das ~e Rom** ancient Rome **- 4.** *RW:* **~ aussehen** *salopp* to be up shit creek.

Alt (*pl* **-e** ODER **-**) *<>* *der* (*pl* **Alte**) MUS alto *<>* *das* (*pl* **Alt**) [Bier] *type of dark German beer.*

Altar (*pl* Altäre) *der* altar.

Altbau (*pl* -ten) *der* old building.

altbekannt *adj* [Methode] well-known.

altbewährt *adj* proven.

Altbier *das type of dark German beer.*

Alte (*pl* -n) *<>* *der, die* **- 1.** [alter Mensch] old man (*f* old woman) **- 2.** *salopp abw* [Elternteil, Gatte] old man (*f* old girl) **- 3.** *salopp abw* [Vorgesetzter] boss, guvnor *Br* **- 4.** [Gleiche]: **ganz der/die ~** exactly the same *<>* *das* (*ohne pl*): **alles beim ~n lassen** to leave everything just as it is.

alteingesessen *adj* long-established.

Altenheim = Altersheim.

Altentagesstätte *die* old people's day centre.

Alter (*pl* -) *das* **- 1.** [Lebensalter] age; **im ~ von 12 Jahren** at the age of 12; **eine Frau mittleren ~s** a middle-aged woman; **bis ins hohe ~ war er gesund** he remained healthy until a ripe old age **- 2.** [Altsein] old age.

älter *adj* **- 1.** *⟾* **alt - 2.** [ziemlich alt] elderly.

Ältere (*pl* -n) *der:* **der ~** the Elder.

altern (*perf* hat/ist gealtert) *vi* **- 1.** [Person] to age **- 2.** [Cognac, Käse] to mature.

alternativ *<>* *adj* alternative *<>* *adv* **- 1.** [wahlweise] alternatively **- 2.** [unkonventionell]: **~ leben** to have an alternative lifestyle.

Alternative [alterna'tiːvə] (*pl* -n) *die* alternative.

altersbedingt *adj* age-related.

Altersgenosse *der* contemporary.

Altersgenossin *die* contemporary.

Altersgrenze *die* **- 1.** [Höchstalter, Mindestalter] age limit **- 2.** [Rentenalter] retirement age.

Altersgruppe *die* age group.

Altersheim, Altenheim *das* old people's home.

altersschwach *adj* **- 1.** [Person] old and infirm **- 2.** [Gegenstände] decrepit.

Altersversorgung *die* [privat] provision for one's old age; [vom Staat] provision for the elderly.

Altertum (*pl* -tümer) *das* [Antike] antiquity.

⬥ Altertümer *pl* [antike Objekte] antiquities.

Älteste (*pl* -n) *der, die* **- 1.** [ältestes Kind] eldest **- 2.** [älteste Person] eldest person.

althergebracht *adj* traditional.

altklug *<>* *adj* precocious *<>* *adv* precociously.

altmodisch *<>* *adj* old-fashioned *<>* *adv* in an old-fashioned way.

Altpapier *das* paper for recycling; **aus ~** made from recycled paper.

Altpapiercontainer *der* paper recycling bin.

altsprachlich *adj* *⟾* Gymnasium.

Altstadt *die* old town.

Alu *das fam* aluminium *Br,* aluminum *Am.*

Alufolie *die* tinfoil *UK.*

Aluminium *das* aluminium *Br,* aluminum *Am.*

am *präp* **- 1.** (*an* + *dem*) at the; **~ Flughafen** at the airport; **das Schönste ~ Urlaub ist es, lange schlafen zu können** the nicest thing about holidays is being able to sleep in; **ich möchte ~ Ausflug teilnehmen** I would like to take part in the trip **- 2.** (*nicht auflösbar*) [in geografischen Angaben]: **~ Meer** by the sea **- 3.** (*nicht auflösbar*) [im Datum] on the; **~ Abend** in the evening; **~ Montag** on Monday; **~ 4. Oktober** on 4. October; **~ Anfang des Jahres** at the start of the year **- 4.** (*nicht auflösbar*) [in Superlativen]: **~ schönsten** the most beautiful **- 5.** (*nicht auflösbar*) *fam* [vor substantivierten Infinitiven]: **ich bin ~ Arbeiten** I am working; *siehe auch* an.

amateurhaft *abw* *<>* *adj* amateurish *<>* *adv* amateurishly.

Amboss (*pl* -e) *der* **- 1.** [Schmiedegerät] anvil **- 2.** MED incus.

ambulant MED *<>* *adj* outpatient *<>* *adv* [behandeln] as an outpatient.

Ambulanz (*pl* -en) *die* MED outpatients' department.

Ameise (*pl* -n) *die* ant.

Ameisenhaufen *der* anthill.

amen *interj* amen!

Amen *das* [Zustimmung] blessing, approval.

Amerika *nt* America.

Amerikaner, in (*mpl* -; *fpl* -nen) *der, die* American.

amerikanisch *adj* American.

Ami (*pl* -s) *der fam* Yank.

Aminosäure *die* amino acid.

Ammoniak *das* ammonia.

Amnestie (*pl* -n) *die* amnesty.

Amöbe (*pl* -n) *die* amoeba.

Amok *der:* **~ laufen** to run amok.

Ampel (*pl* -n) *die* traffic lights (*pl*); **rote ~** red light.

Ampere [amˈpɛːɐ̯] (*pl* -) *das* amp, ampere.

Amphitheater *das* amphitheatre.

amputieren *vt* to amputate.

Amsel (*pl* -n) *die* blackbird.

Amt (*pl* Ämter) *das* - **1.** [Behörde] department; [Gebäude] office; **von ~s wegen** on official orders - **2.** [Stellung] position; [wichtige politische oder kirchliche Stellung] office - **3.** [Pflicht] duty; [Aufgabe] task.

amtierend *adj*: **der ~e Bundeskanzler** the German chancellor in office.

amtlich <> *adj* official <> *adv* officially.

Amtsgeheimnis *das* official secret.

Amtsgericht *das* ≃ county court *Br*, ≃ district court *Am*.

Amtssitz *der* seat of office.

Amtssprache *die* official language.

Amtszeit *die* term of office.

Amulett (*pl* -e) *das* amulet.

amüsieren *vt* to amuse. ◆ **sich amüsieren** *ref* to have fun; **sich über jn/etw ~** [auslachen] to make fun of sb/sthg; [lustig finden] to find sb/sthg funny.

an <> *präp* - **1.** (+ D) [räumlich] at; **an einem Tisch sitzen** to be sitting at a table; **~ der Wand** on the wall; **~ der Hauptstraße** on the main road; **~ einem Gymnasium Lehrer** teacher at a grammar school - **2.** (+ A) [räumlich] to; **sich ~ den Tisch setzen** to sit down at the table; **etw ~ die Wand lehnen** to lean sthg against the wall - **3.** (+ D) [zeitlich] on; **~ diesem Tag** on that day; **~ Fulda 15.09** arriving at Fulda at 15.09 - **4.** (+ D) [stellt Bezug her]: **~ Krebs leiden** to have cancer; **~ etw zweifeln** to doubt sthg - **5.** (+ D) [aus dieser Menge]: **genug ~ Beweisen haben** to have enough proof - **6.** (+ D) [mithilfe von] with; **am Stock gehen** to walk with a stick; **jn ~ der Stimme erkennen** to recognize sb by their voice - **7.** (+ A) *fam* [ungefähr]: **~ die 30 Grad** about 30 degrees - **8.** (+ A) [stellte Bezug her]: **~ jn denken** to think about sb; **sich ~ jn/etw erinnern** to remember sb/sthg - **9.** *RW*: **~ und für sich** generally; **~ sich** in itself <> *adv* - **1.** [elliptisch]: **Licht ~!** turn the light on! - **2.** [zeitlich]: **von jetzt ~** from now on.

Analogie (*pl* -n) *die* analogy.

Analphabet, in (*mpl* -en; *fpl* -nen) *der, die* illiterate (person).

Analyse (*pl* -n) *die* analysis; [von Blut] test.

analysieren *vt* to analyse; [Blut] to test.

Ananas (*pl* - ODER -se) *die* pineapple.

Anarchie (*pl* -n) *die* anarchy.

Anarchist, in (*mpl* -en; *fpl* -nen) *der, die* anarchist.

Anästhesie (*pl* -n) *die* anaesthesia.

Anatomie (*pl* -n) *die* anatomy.

anbahnen *vt* [Geschäft, Treffen] to prepare; [Gespräch] to start. ◆ **sich anbahnen** *ref* to be on the way.

anbändeln *vi* *fam*: **mit jm ~** to start going out with sb.

Anbau *der* - **1.** [Gebäudeteil] extension - **2.** [Bauen] building (*of extension*) - **3.** [von Pflanzen] growing.

anbauen *vt* - **1.** [Gebäude] to add (*as an extension*) - **2.** [Pflanze] to grow.

anbehalten *vt* (*unreg*) to keep on.

anbei *adv* *amt* enclosed.

anbeißen (*unreg*) <> *vt* to take a bite of <> *vi* - **1.** [Fisch] to bite - **2.** *fig* [Käufer] to take the bait.

anbelangen *vt*: **was jn/etw anbelangt** as far as sb/sthg is concerned.

anbeten *vt* to worship.

anbiedern ◆ **sich anbiedern** *ref* *abw*: **sich bei jm ~** to curry favour with sb.

anbieten *vt* (*unreg*) to offer. ◆ **sich anbieten** *ref* - **1.** [Mensch] to offer one's services; **sie bot sich an, uns die Stadt zu zeigen** she offered to show us round the city - **2.** [Sache]: **der Montag bietet sich als Termin für das Treffen an** Monday would be the best day for the meeting - **3.** [geeignet erscheinen]: **folgende Möglichkeiten bieten sich an** we have the following possibilities.

Anbieter, in (*mpl* -; *fpl* -nen) *der, die* supplier.

anbinden *vt* (*unreg*) to tie (up).

Anblick *der* sight.

anblicken *vt* to look at.

anbraten *vt* (*unreg*) to brown.

anbrechen (*perf* hat/ist angebrochen) (*unreg*) <> *vt* (*hat*) - **1.** [Verpackung] to open - **2.** [Knochen] to crack - **3.** [Geldschein] to break into <> *vi* (*ist*) *geh* [Tag] to dawn; [Morgen] to break; [Nacht] to fall.

anbrennen (*perf* hat/ist angebrannt) (*unreg*) <> *vt* (*hat*) [mit Feuer] to set fire to <> *vi* (*ist*) [Essen] to burn; **nichts ~ lassen** *fam* *fig* never to let a single chance go by.

anbringen *vt* (*unreg*) - **1.** [befestigen] to put up - **2.** [Kritik] to make - **3.** *fam* *abw* [mitbringen] to bring back.

Anbruch *der* [von Epoche] dawning; **bei ~ der Dunkelheit** when darkness falls/fell.

anbrüllen *vt* *fam* to bawl out; **gegen etw ~** to shout above sthg.

andächtig <> *adj* reverent <> *adv* reverently.

andauern *vi* to continue.

andauernd <> *adj* continual <> *adv* continually.

Andenken (*pl* -) *das* - **1.** [Erinnerung] memory; **zum ~ an jn/etw** in memory of sb/sthg - **2.** [Gegenstand, Souvenir] souvenir.

andere, r, s <> *adj* - **1.** [unterschiedlich] different - **2.** [übrig, weitere] other <> *pron*: **der/die/das ~** the other (one); **ein ~r/eine ~** [bei Dingen] a different one; [bei Personen] someone else; **ich habe noch zwei ~** I've got two others; **unter ~m** among other things.

anderenfalls = andernfalls.

andererseits, andrerseits *adv* on the other hand.

andermal ➡ **ein andermal** *adv* another time, some other time.

ändern *vt* to change; [Kleid] to alter; **das lässt sich nicht ~** there's nothing to be done about it. ➡ **sich ändern** *ref* to change.

andernfalls, anderenfalls *adv* otherwise.

anders ◇ *adv* - **1.** [andersartig, verschieden] differently; **sie sieht ganz ~ aus als ihre Schwester** she doesn't look at all like her sister; **~ ausgedrückt** put another way; **so und nicht ~!** this way only! - **2.** [sonst] else; **jemand/irgendwo ~** somebody/somewhere else; **niemand ~ als du kann uns jetzt noch helfen** only you can help us now ◇ *adj* different; **das muss ~ werden** this has got to change; **mir wird ganz ~** I feel weird.

andersherum *adv* the other way round.

anderswo *adv* elsewhere, somewhere else.

anderthalb *num* one and a half.

Änderung (*pl* -en) *die* [gen] change; [an Kleid] alteration.

anderweitig ◇ *adj* other ◇ *adv* - **1.** [anderswo] elsewhere - **2.** [auf andere Weise] otherwise.

andeuten *vt* - **1.** [ansprechen] to hint at; **~, dass** to hint that ... - **2.** [umreißen, skizzieren] to outline.

Andeutung *die* hint; **eine ~ machen** to drop a hint.

Andrang *der* crush; **es herrscht großer ~** there is a great crush.

andrehen *vt fam* [verkaufen] **jm etw ~** to flog sb sthg.

andrerseits = andererseits.

androhen *vt*: **jm etw ~** to threaten sb with sthg.

Androhung *die*: **unter ~ von etw** under threat of sthg.

anlecken (*perf* ist angeeckt) *vi* - **1.** [stoßen]: **an etw ~** to bang against sthg - **2.** [sich unbeliebt machen]: **bei jm/überall ~** to rub sb/everybody up the wrong way.

aneignen *vt*: **sich** (*D*) **etw ~** [lernen] to pick sthg up; *abw* [nehmen] to take sthg (for o.s.).

aneinander *adv* [drücken, befestigen] together; [reiben] against one another; [denken] about one another; **sich ~ gewöhnen** to get used to one another.

aneinander fügen *vt* to put together. ➡ **sich aneinander fügen** *ref* to fit together.

aneinander geraten (*perf* ist aneinander geraten) *vi* (*unreg*) to clash.

aneinander grenzen *vi* [Länder] to border

on one another; [Gärten, Wohnungen] to be adjacent.

aneinander hängen *vi* (*unreg*) [einander lieben] to be attached to one another.

aneinander legen *vt* to lay down next to each other.

Anekdote (*pl* -n) *die* anecdote.

anlekeln *vt* to make sick.

anerkannt *adj* recognized.

anlerkennen *vt* (*unreg*) - **1.** [Leistung, Begabung] to acknowledge - **2.** [Meinung, Person] to accept - **3.** [Autorität, Staat, Vaterschaft] to recognize.

Anerkennung (*pl* -en) *die* - **1.** [von Leistung, Begabung] acknowledgement - **2.** [von Meinung, Person] acceptance - **3.** [von Autorität, Staat, Vaterschaft] recognition.

anlfachen *vt* to fan.

anlfahren (*perf* hat/ist angefahren) (*unreg*) ◇ *vt* (*hat*) - **1.** [bei Unfall] to run into - **2.** [Ziel] to approach - **3.** [Last] to deliver - **4.** [tadeln] to scold ◇ *vi* (*ist*) [losfahren] to start.

Anlfall *der* fit.

anlfallen (*perf* hat/ist angefallen) (*unreg*) ◇ *vi* (*ist*) [Kosten] to be incurred ◇ *vt* (*hat*) [angreifen] to attack.

anfällig *adj*: **für etw ~ sein** to be prone ODER susceptible to sthg.

Anlfang *der* beginning, start; **~ April** at the beginning of April; **von ~ an** from the beginning ODER start; **von ~ bis Ende** from start to finish.

anlfangen (*unreg*) ◇ *vi* - **1.** [gen] to begin, to start; **mit etw ~** to start sthg, to begin sthg; **wer fängt an?** who's first?; **er fängt schon wieder an!** there he goes again! - **2.** [machen]: **er weiß nichts mit sich anzufangen** he doesn't know what to do with himself; **mit etw nichts ~ können** [verstehen] not to be able to get anywhere with sthg; [gebrauchen] not to be able to use sthg ◇ *vt* [beginnen] to begin, to start.

Anfänger, in (*mpl* -; *fpl* -nen) *der, die* beginner; **ein blutiger ~** a total beginner.

anfänglich ◇ *adj* initial ◇ *adv* initially.

anfangs *adv* at first.

Anfangsbuchstabe *der* [von Wort] first letter; [von Name] initial.

Anfangsstadium *das* initial stages (*pl*).

anlfassen ◇ *vt* - **1.** [berühren] to touch - **2.** [behandeln] to treat - **3.** [angehen] to handle ◇ *vi* [helfen] to lend a hand; **mit ~** to lend a hand.

anlfechten *vt* (*unreg*) [anzweifeln - Testament] to contest; [- Urteil] to appeal against.

anlfertigen *vt* [Anzug, Schrank] to make; [Bericht] to write; [Protokoll] to take down; **ein Porträt ~ lassen** to have a portrait done.

Anfertigung *die* (*ohne pl*) [von Anzug, Möbeln] making; [von Bericht] writing; [von Protokoll] taking down.

an|feuchten vt [Lippen, Briefmarke] to moisten; [Haut] to moisturize; [Lappen] to wet.

an|feuern vt to spur on.

an|flehen vt to beg.

an|fliegen (perf hat/ist angeflogen) (unreg) ⟨⟩ vt (hat) [Subj: Flugzeug] to approach; [Subj: Fluggesellschaft] to serve, to fly to ⟨⟩ vi (ist): **angeflogen kommen** to come flying up.

An|flug der - 1. [von Flugzeug, Hubschrauber]: **im ~ (auf etw** (A)) **sein** to be approaching (sthg) - 2. [Spur] hint.

an|fordern vt to ask for; [per Post] to send off for.

An|forderung die - 1. [Bestellung] request - 2. [Anspruch] demand; **einer ~ genügen** to meet a requirement; **den ~en einer Sache gewachsen sein** to be up to the demands of sthg.

An|frage die amt enquiry.

an|freunden ⟐ **sich anfreunden** ref to make friends; **sich mit jm ~** to make friends with sb; **ich freunde mich langsam mit der Idee an** the idea is growing on me.

an|fühlen vt to feel. ⟐ **sich anfühlen** ref to feel.

an|führen vt - 1. [nennen] to quote - 2. [täuschen] to take in - 3. [führen] to lead.

An|führer, in der, die leader.

Anführungs|zeichen pl quotation marks, inverted commas.

An|gabe die - 1. [Hinweis] detail - 2. [Aufschneiderei] showing off.

an|geben (unreg) ⟨⟩ vt - 1. [nennen, zitieren - Personalien, Grund] to give; [- Zeuge] to name - 2. [bestimmen - Richtung, Kurs] to set - 3. [behaupten] to claim, to allege ⟨⟩ vi [aufschneiden] to show off; **mit etw ~** to show off about sthg.

Angeber (pl -) der show-off.

Angeberin (pl -nen) die show-off.

angeblich ⟨⟩ adj alleged ⟨⟩ adv allegedly.

angeboren adj [Krankheit] congenital; [Talent, Abneigung] innate.

An|gebot das - 1. [Anbieten] offer; **~ und Nachfrage** supply and demand - 2. [Sortiment] range; **etw im ~ haben** to offer sthg.

angebracht ⟨⟩ pp ⟐ anbringen ⟨⟩ adj appropriate.

angebunden ⟨⟩ pp ⟐ anbinden ⟨⟩ adj: **kurz ~ sein** to be brusque.

angegriffen ⟨⟩ pp ⟐ angreifen ⟨⟩ adj [Gesundheit, Position] weakened.

angeheitert adj merry.

an|gehen (perf hat/ist angegangen) (unreg) ⟨⟩ vi (ist) - 1. [Licht] to go on; [Feuer] to catch

- 2. [akzeptabel sein]: **es geht nicht an, etw zu tun** it's not on to do sthg - 3. [vorgehen]: **gegen jn/etw ~** to fight sb/sthg ⟨⟩ vt (hat) [betreffen] to concern; **jn etwas ~** to concern sb; **das geht dich nichts an** it's none of your business.

angehend adj future.

an|gehören vi: **einer Sache** (D) **~** to belong to sthg.

Angehörige (pl -n) der, die - 1. [Verwandte] relative - 2. [Mitglied] member.

Angeklagte (pl -n) der, die defendant.

Angel (pl -n) die - 1. [zum Fischen] fishing rod - 2. [Scharnier] hinge.

angelaufen ⟨⟩ pp ⟐ anlaufen ⟨⟩ adj [Silber, Messing] tarnished.

An|gelegenheit die matter; **kümmere dich um deine eigenen ~en!** mind your own business!

angeln ⟨⟩ vi - 1. [fischen] to fish - 2. [suchen]: **nach etw ~** [suchen] to fish around for sthg ⟨⟩ vt - 1. [fischen] to fish for; [fangen] to catch - 2. [erobern]: **sich** (D) **jn ~** to land o.s. sb.

angemessen ⟨⟩ adj: **(einer Sache** (D)) **~** appropriate (to sthg) ⟨⟩ adv appropriately.

angenehm ⟨⟩ adj pleasant ⟨⟩ adv pleasantly.

angenommen ⟨⟩ pp ⟐ annehmen ⟨⟩ adj [Kind] adopted; [Name] assumed. ⟐ **angenommen, dass** adv assuming (that).

angeregt ⟨⟩ adj lively ⟨⟩ adv: **sich ~ unterhalten** to have a lively conversation.

angeschlagen adj - 1. [kaputt] chipped - 2. [krank] groggy; **gesundheitlich ~ sein** to be in poor health.

angesehen ⟨⟩ pp ⟐ ansehen ⟨⟩ adj respected.

Angesicht das: **im ~ einer Sache** (G) in the face of sthg; **von ~ zu ~** face to face.

angesichts präp: **~ einer Sache** (G) in view of sthg.

angespannt ⟨⟩ adj tense ⟨⟩ adv closely.

Angestellte (pl -n) der, die employee; [im Büro] white-collar worker.

angestrengt ⟨⟩ adj [Miene] strained; [Versuch] concerted ⟨⟩ adv [arbeiten, rudern, zuhören] hard.

angetan ⟨⟩ pp ⟐ antun ⟨⟩ adj: **von jm/ etw ~ sein** to be keen on sb/sthg.

angewiesen ⟨⟩ pp ⟐ anweisen ⟨⟩ adj: **auf jn/etw ~ sein** to be dependent on sb/ sthg.

an|gewöhnen vt: **sich** (D) **~, etw zu tun** to get into the habit of doing sthg; **jm etw ~** to get sb used to sthg.

An|gewohnheit die habit.

angewurzelt adv: **wie ~ stehen bleiben** to stand rooted to the spot.

Angler, in (*mpl* -; *fpl* -nen) *der, die* angler.

Anglistik *die (ohne pl)* English language and literature.

an|greifen (*unreg*) ◇ *vt* - **1.** [gen] to attack - **2.** [Gesundheit] to affect - **3.** [Projekt] to tackle - **4.** [Vorrat] to draw on - **5.** *Süddt* [anfassen] to touch ◇ *vi* to attack.

Angreifer, in (*mpl* -; *fpl* -nen) *der, die* attacker.

An|griff *der* attack; **etw in ~ nehmen** *fig* to set about sthg.

angriffslustig ◇ *adj* aggressive ◇ *adv* aggressively.

angst *adj:* **mir wird ~ und bange** I'm scared stiff.

Angst (*pl* Ängste) *die* - **1.** [Furcht] fear; **vor jm/etw ~ haben** to be afraid of sb/sthg; **es mit der ~ zu tun bekommen** to get scared; **jm ~ machen** to frighten sb - **2.** [Sorge]: **~ um jn/etw haben** to be anxious about sb/sthg.

Angst|hase *der fam abw* chicken.

ängstigen *vt* to frighten. ◆ **sich ängstigen** *ref:* **sich vor jm/etw ~** to be frightened of sb/sthg; **sich um jn/etw ~** to be anxious about sb/sthg.

ängstlich ◇ *adj* nervous ◇ *adv* - **1.** [furchtsam] nervously - **2.** [genau] very carefully.

an|gucken *vt fam* to look at; [Fernsehsendung] to watch; **sich** (*D*) **etw ~** to look at sthg; [Fernsehsendung] to watch sthg.

an|haben *vt* (*unreg*) - **1.** [Kleidung] to have on, to be wearing - **2.** [Schaden]: **jm/einer Sache nichts ~ können** to be unable to harm sb/sthg.

an|halten (*unreg*) ◇ *vi* - **1.** [Fahrzeug] to stop - **2.** [Zustand] to last ◇ *vt* [Bewegung] to stop; [Taxi] to hail; **den Atem ~** to hold one's breath.

anhaltend *adj* lasting.

Anhalter (*pl* -) *der* [Mitfahrer] hitchhiker; **per ~ fahren** to hitchhike.

Anhalterin (*pl* -nen) *die* [Mitfahrerin] hitchhiker.

Anhalts|punkt *der* clue.

anhand, an Hand *präp:* **~ einer Sache** (*G*) with the aid of sthg.

Anhang *der (ohne pl)* - **1.** [Nachwort] appendix - **2.** *fam* [Familie] relatives (*pl*); **mit ~ auf einem Fest erscheinen** to go to a party with someone.

an|hängen ◇ *vt* (*reg*) - **1.** [Wagen]: **etw an etw** (*A*) **~** [Waggon] to couple sthg to sthg; [Anhänger] to hitch sthg to sthg - **2.** [Zeit]: **etw an etw** (*A*) **~** to tag sthg onto sthg - **3.** [angebliche Schuld]: **jm etw ~** to pin sthg on sb ◇ *vi* (*unreg*): **einer Sache** (*D*) **~** to be an adherent of sthg.

Anhänger (*pl* -) *der* - **1.** [von Fahrzeugen] trailer; [von Straßenbahn] carriage (*other than front carriage*) - **2.** [Person - von Kandidat, Mannschaft] supporter; [- von Sekte] member - **3.** [Schmuck] pendant.

Anhängerin (*pl* -nen) *die* [von Kandidat, Mannschaft] supporter; [von Sekte] member.

anhänglich *adj* [Hund, Partner] devoted.

Anhäufung (*pl* -en) *die* accumulation.

an|heben *vt* (*unreg*) - **1.** [heben] to lift - **2.** [vergrößern] to raise.

an|heuern ◇ *vt* - **1.** [Matrosen] to sign on - **2.** [Arbeitskräfte] to take on ◇ *vi* [auf einem Schiff] to sign on.

Anhieb ◆ **auf Anhieb** *adv* straight off.

An|höhe *die* rise.

an|hören *vt* - **1.** [hören]: **sich** (*D*) **etw ~** to listen to sthg; **etw mit ~** to overhear sthg; **ich kann das nicht mehr mit ~** I can't bear to listen to it any longer - **2.** [erraten]: **jm seine Freude/Wut ~** to hear the joy/anger in sb's voice - **3.** *amt* [Zeugen] to give a hearing to. ◆ **sich anhören** *ref* to sound.

Anis *der* aniseed.

an|kämpfen *vi:* **gegen jn/etw ~** to fight against sth/sthg.

An|kauf *der* purchase.

Anker (*pl* -) *der* anchor; **vor ~ gehen/liegen** to drop/be at anchor.

ankern *vi* to anchor; [Anker werfen] to drop anchor; [vor Anker liegen] to be at anchor.

an|ketten *vt* to chain.

An|klage *die* - **1.** [vor Gericht] charge; **gegen jn ~ erheben** to bring a charge against sb - **2.** [öffentlich] accusation - **3.** [Kläger] prosecution.

an|klagen *vt* - **1.** [vor Gericht]: **jn (wegen etw) ~** to charge sb (with sthg) - **2.** [öffentlich] to accuse.

An|klang *der:* **(bei jm) ~ finden** to meet with (sb's) approval.

an|kleben *vt* to stick.

an|klopfen *vi* to knock.

an|knüpfen ◇ *vt* - **1.** [Seil]: **etw an etw** (*A*) **~** to tie sthg to sthg - **2.** [Gespräch] to strike up ◇ *vi* [Worte, Vorlesung]: **an etw** (*A*) **~** to take sthg up.

an|kommen (*perf ist angekommen*) *vi* (*unreg*) - **1.** [am Ziel] to arrive; **sie kommt mit dem Auto an** she's coming by car - **2.** [näher kommen] to approach - **3.** [mit Idee, Vorschlag]: **mit etw ~** to come up with sthg - **4.**: **bei jm gut/schlecht** ODER **nicht ~** to go down well/badly with sb/sthg; [sich durchsetzen]: **gegen jn/etw nicht ~** to be no match for sb/sthg - **5.** [wichtig sein]: **es kommt auf jn/etw an** it depends on sb/sthg; **es kommt darauf an** it depends; **es kommt mir vor allem auf die Qualität an** what matters to me is quality - **6.** [riskieren]: **es auf etw** (*A*) **~ lassen** to run the risk of sthg.

an|kreiden vt: **jm etw ~** to hold sthg against sb.

an|kreuzen vt to mark with a cross.

an|kündigen vt to announce. ◆ **sich ankündigen** ref: **der Herbst kündigt sich an** autumn is on its way.

Ankunft die arrival.

an|kurbeln vt to boost.

an|lächeln vt to smile at.

an|lachen vt - **1.** [lachen] to look smilingly at - **2.** [erobern]: **sich** (D) **jn ~** to land o.s. sb.

An|lage die - **1.** [Park - städtisch] park; [- von Schloss, Gebäude] grounds (pl) - **2.** [Gelände - militärisch] installation; [- für Sport] facilities (pl) - **3.** [Geldanlage] investment - **4.** [Bau] construction.

Anlass (pl Anlässe) der - **1.** [Grund] cause; **dazu gibt es keinen ~** there's no call for that - **2.** [Ereignis] occasion.

an|lassen vt (unreg) - **1.** [eingeschaltet lassen] to leave on - **2.** [starten] to start (up) - **3.** [anbehalten] to keep on.

Anlasser (pl -) der AUTO starter.

anlässlich präp: **~ einer Sache** (G) on the occasion of sthg.

an|lasten vt: **jm etw ~** [verantwortlich machen für] to blame sb for sthg; [Verbrechen, Charakterfehler] to accuse sb of sthg.

An|lauf der - **1.** [Schwung] run-up; **~ nehmen** to take a run-up - **2.** [Versuch] attempt.

an|laufen (perf hat/ist angelaufen) (unreg) ⟨⟩ vi (ist) - **1.** [beginnen] to begin, to start; [Motor, Maschine] to start; [Film] to open - **2.** [Körperteil]: **rot/blau ~** to go red/blue - **3.** [Metall] to tarnish; [Fensterscheibe, Brille] to steam up - **4.** [sich nähern]: **angelaufen kommen** to come running up ⟨⟩ vt (hat) [Hafen] to call at.

an|legen ⟨⟩ vt - **1.** [Garten, Park, Beet] to lay out; [Straße] to plan - **2.** [Kartei, Sammlung] to start - **3.** [Vorrat] to lay in - **4.** [beabsichtigen]: **es darauf ~, etw zu tun** to be determined to do sthg - **5.** [Geld] to invest - **6.** [anlehnen]: **etw (an etw** (A)**) ~** to lay sthg (on sthg) - **7.** [umbinden] to put on - **8.** [Subj: Tier] to lay back; **die Ohren ~** to lay back its ears - **9.** [Waffe] to raise to one's shoulder - **10.** geh [anziehen - Geschmeide] to put on ⟨⟩ vi - **1.** [Schiff] to dock - **2.** [mit Gewehr]: **auf jn/ etw ~** to aim at sb/sthg. ◆ **sich anlegen** ref: **sich mit jm ~** to pick a fight with sb.

Anlege|stelle die mooring.

an|lehnen vt - **1.** [Tür, Fenster] to leave ajar - **2.** [an die Wand] to lean; **etw an etw** (A) **~** to lean sthg against sthg. ◆ **sich anlehnen** ref: **sich an etw** (A) **~** to lean against sthg; fig to draw upon sthg.

Anlehnung (pl -en) die: **in ~ an einen Roman entstanden** based on a novel.

An|leitung die - **1.** [Hinweis] instruction;

unter js ~ under sb's guidance - **2.** [Text] instructions (pl).

an|lernen vt to train.

an|liegen vi (unreg) - **1.** [sitzen]: **eng ~** to be tight - **2.** fam [zu erledigen sein]: **was liegt heute an?** what do we have to do today?

Anlieger (pl -) der resident.

an|locken vt [Kunden] to attract; [mit Köder] to lure.

an|lügen vt (unreg) to lie to.

Anm. abk für Anmerkung.

an|machen vt - **1.** [Gerät] to turn on, to switch on - **2.** [Salat] to dress - **3.** salopp [ansprechen] to chat up Br, to hit on Am.

an|malen vt [bemalen] to paint.

an|maßen vt: **sich** (D) **~, etw zu tun** to presume to do sthg.

anmaßend adj presumptuous.

Anmelde|formular das application form.

an|melden vt - **1.** [beim Amt - Auto, Wohnsitz, Gewerbe] to register; [- Fernseher] to get a licence for; [- Patent] to apply for - **2.** [in Schule, Kurs] to enrol - **3.** [zu Termin] to make an appointment for; **sind Sie für heute angemeldet?** do you have an appointment for today? - **4.** [Besuch] to announce. ◆ **sich anmelden** ref - **1.** [für Kurs] to enrol - **2.** [zu Termin] to make an appointment.

Anmeldung die - **1.** [beim Amt] registration; [eines Patents] application - **2.** [in Schule, Kurs] enrolment - **3.** [zu Termin] making an appointment - **4.** [Rezeption] reception.

an|merken vt - **1.** [spüren]: **jm etw ~** to notice sthg in sb; **sich** (D) **nichts ~ lassen** not to show one's feelings - **2.** [sagen] to comment.

Anmerkung (pl -en) die - **1.** [im Text] note - **2.** [gesprochen] comment.

an|nähern vt to bring closer. ◆ **sich annähern** ref: **sich einander ~** to approach one another.

annähernd adv nearly.

Annäherung (pl -en) die approach; **die ~ von Wallonien an Flandern** the rapprochement between the Walloons and the Flemish.

Annahme (pl -n) die - **1.** [Meinung] assumption; **in der ~, dass ...** on the assumption that ... - **2.** [von Paket, Brief] receipt; [von Geschenk] acceptance.

annehmbar ⟨⟩ adj acceptable ⟨⟩ adv reasonably (well).

an|nehmen vt (unreg) - **1.** [empfangen, zustimmen, akzeptieren, zulassen] to accept; [Anruf] to take - **2.** [vermuten] to assume - **3.** [Staatsangehörigkeit, Namen, Kind] to adopt; [Dialekt, Gewohnheit] to pick up - **4.** [Gestalt] to take on.

Annehmlichkeit (pl -en) die: **-en** [Vorteile] advantages; [Bequemlichkeiten] comforts.

Annonce [a'nɔŋsə] (*pl* -n) *die* advertisement.

annoncieren [anɔŋ'siːrən] ◇ *vi* to place an advertisement ◇ *vt* to advertise.

annullieren *vt* [Ehe] to annul; [Vertrag] to cancel.

anöden *vt fam* to bore to tears.

anonym ◇ *adj* anonymous ◇ *adv* anonymously.

Anorak (*pl* -s) *der* anorak.

anordnen *vt* - **1.** [befehlen] to order - **2.** [Gegenstände] to arrange.

Anordnung *die* - **1.** [Aufstellung] layout - **2.** [Befehl] order; **auf js ~** (*A*) on sb's orders; **~en treffen** to make arrangements.

anpacken ◇ *vt* - **1.** [mit Händen] to grab - **2.** [behandeln]: **jn hart ~** to treat sb harshly - **3.** [lösen] to tackle ◇ *vi* [helfen]: **mit ~** to lend a hand.

anpassen *vt*: **etw einer Sache** (*D*) **~** to adapt sthg to sthg. **sich anpassen** *ref* to adapt.

Anpassung (*pl* -en) *die* adaptation.

Anpfiff *der* - **1.** [im Fußball] kick-off - **2.** *fam* [Tadel] ticking-off.

anpflanzen *vt* to plant.

anpöbeln *vt* to shout abuse at.

anprangern *vt* to denounce.

anpreisen *vt* (*unreg*) [Waren] to tout.

Anprobe *die* fitting.

anprobieren *vt* to try on.

anrechnen *vt* - **1.** [einbeziehen] to take into account; **jm etw hoch ~** to think highly of sb for sthg - **2.** [berechnen] to charge for.

Anrecht *das* - **1.** [Recht]: **ein ~ auf etw** (*A*) **haben** ODER **besitzen** to have the right to sthg - **2.** [Abonnement] subscription.

Anrede *die* form of address.

anreden *vt* - **1.** [ansprechen] to speak to - **2.** [mit Titel]: **den Chef mit „Herr Professor" ~** to address the boss as 'Professor'; **jn mit seinem Vornamen ~** to call sb by their first name.

anregen *vt* - **1.** [beleben] to stimulate - **2.** [empfehlen] to propose - **3.** [ermutigen]: **jn ~, etw zu tun** to encourage sb to do sthg.

Anregung *die* - **1.** [Belebung] stimulation - **2.** [Anreiz] incentive.

Anreise *die* journey (there).

anreisen (*perf* ist angereist) *vi* to travel (there).

Anreiz *der* incentive.

anrempeln *vt* to barge into.

anrichten *vt* - **1.** [Abendessen] to prepare - **2.** [Schaden] to cause; **da hast du was Schönes angerichtet!** you've really gone and done it now!

anrücken (*perf* ist angerückt) *vi* - **1.** [Truppen] to move in - **2.** *fam* [auftauchen] to show up.

Anruf *der* call.

Anrufbeantworter (*pl* -) *der* answering machine.

anrufen (*unreg*) ◇ *vt* [telefonieren] to call, to phone ◇ *vi* to call, to phone; **bei jm ~** to call ODER phone sb.

anrühren *vt* - **1.** [berühren - Person, Gegenstand] to touch; [- Thema] to touch on - **2.** [rühren] to mix.

ans *präp* (*an + das*): **~ Fenster klopfen** to knock on the window; *siehe auch* an.

Ansage *die* announcement.

ansagen *vt* to announce; **jm/etw den Kampf ~** to declare war on sb/sthg.

ansammeln *vt* to collect. **sich ansammeln** *ref* - **1.** [anhäufen, anstauen] to pile up - **2.** [versammeln] to gather.

Ansammlung *die* - **1.** [Anhäufung] accumulation - **2.** [Versammlung] gathering.

Ansatz *der* - **1.** [Anfang, Anzeichen] first sign; **im ~ stecken bleiben** to fall at the first hurdle; **gute Ansätze zeigen** to show promising signs - **2.** [von Körperteil] base - **3.** MATH formulation.

ansaugen *vt* to suck in.

anschaffen *vt*: **sich** (*D*) **etw ~** to get o.s. sthg.

Anschaffung (*pl* -en) *die* acquisition, purchase.

anschalten *vt* to turn on.

anschauen *vt* to look at; **sich** (*D*) **etw ~** to have a look at sthg.

anschaulich ◇ *adj* clear ◇ *adv* clearly.

Anschein *der* appearance; **dem** ODER **allem ~ nach** apparently; **es hat den ~, als ob it** looks like, it appears that.

anscheinend *adv* apparently.

anschieben *vt* (*unreg*) to push-start.

Anschlag *der* - **1.** [Attentat - auf Person] assassination attempt; [- auf Botschaft] attack; **einen ~ auf jn verüben** to make an attempt on sb's life; **einen ~ auf etw** (*A*) **verüben** to attack sthg, - **2.** [Zettel, Plakat] notice - **3.** [auf der Schreibmaschine] keystroke; **50 Anschläge pro Zeile** 50 characters per line - **4.** [am Klavier] touch.

anschlagen (*perf* hat/ist angeschlagen) (*unreg*) ◇ *vt* - **1.** [Plakat] to put up - **2.** [Geschirr] to chip - **3.** [wählen] to adopt - **4.** [Taste] to strike - **5.** [beim Stricken] to cast on - **6.** [verletzen]: **sich** (*D*) **den Kopf an etw** (*D*) **~** to knock one's head against sthg ◇ *vi* - **1.** [wirken] to work - **2.** [bellen] to start barking.

anschließen *vt* (*unreg*) - **1.** [verbinden - Telefon, Wasserhahn] to connect; [- Elektrogerät] to plug in - **2.** [folgen lassen] to add - **3.** [festschließen]: **etw an etw** (*A*) **~** to lock sthg to sthg. **sich anschließen** *ref* [mitmachen]: **sich jm/einer Sache ~** to join sb/

sthg; **sich einer Meinung ~** to endorse an opinion.

anschließend <> *adv* afterwards <> *adj* ensuing.

Anschluss *der* - **1.** [an Zug, Telefon] connection; **den ~ verpasst haben** *fig* to be left behind; **kein ~ unter dieser Nummer** the number you have dialled has not been recognized - **2.** [Telefonapparat] extension - **3.** [zu Freunden]: **~ finden** to meet people - **4.** [Folge]: **im ~ an etw** *(A)* following sthg - **5.** POL Anschluss.

anschmiegen ◆ **sich anschmiegen** *ref*: **sich an jn/etw ~** to snuggle up to sb/sthg.

anschnallen *vt* [Skier, Rollschuhe] to put on; [Sicherheitsgurt] to fasten. ◆ **sich anschnallen** *ref* to fasten one's seat belt.

anschneiden *vt (unreg)* - **1.** [schneiden] to cut into - **2.** *fig* [ansprechen] to broach.

anschreiben *(unreg)* <> *vt* - **1.** [Schulden]: **sie ließ ihre Einkäufe ~** she asked to pay for her purchases later - **2.** [per Brief] to write to <> *vi*: **~ lassen** to pay later.

anschreien *vt (unreg)* to shout at.

Anschrift *die* address.

Anschuldigung *(pl -en) die* accusation.

anschwellen *(perf ist angeschwollen) vi (unreg)* - **1.** [Körperteil] to swell - **2.** [Gewässer] to rise - **3.** [Geräusch] to grow louder.

anschwemmen *vt* to wash up.

ansehen *(unreg)* <> *vt* - **1.** [anblicken] to look at; **sich** *(D)* **etw ~** [zur Unterhaltung] to go and see sthg; **sich** *(D)* **jn/etw ~** [zur Prüfung] to look at sb/sthg - **2.** [erkennen]: **man sieht ihm sein Alter nicht an** he doesn't look his age; **man sieht ihr ihre Müdigkeit nicht an** her tiredness doesn't show - **3.** [erachten]: **jn/etw als etw ~** to regard sb/sthg as sthg - **4.** [ertragen]: **etw nicht (mit) ~ können** not to be able to stand sthg <> *vi*: **sieh mal an!** fancy that!

Ansehen *das* [Ruf] reputation.

ansehnlich *adj* - **1.** [groß] considerable - **2.** [schön] attractive.

an sein *(perf ist an gewesen) vi (unreg)* to be on.

ansetzen <> *vt* - **1.** [in Stellung bringen - Werkzeug] to place in position; [- Trinkgefäss, Blasinstrument] to raise to one's lips - **2.** [Termin] to arrange; [Preis] to fix - **3.** [Stück]: **etw an etw** *(A)* **~** to attach sthg to sthg - **4.** [Person]: **jn auf etw** *(A)* **~** to put sb on sthg - **5.** [zubereiten] to prepare - **6.** [anlagern]: **Rost ~** to get rusty <> *vi* [anfangen] to begin; **zum Sprung ~** to get ready to jump; **das Flugzeug setzte zur Landung an** the plane was commencing its descent. ◆ **sich ansetzen** *ref* [sich ablagern - Rost, Schimmel] to form; [- Kalk] to accumulate, to build up.

Ansicht *(pl -en) die* - **1.** [Meinung] opinion,

view; **der gleichen/anderer ~ sein** to be of the same/a different opinion; **meiner ~ nach** in my view ODER opinion - **2.** [Betrachtung]: **zur ~** [zur Probe] on trial ODER approval - **3.** [Abbildung] view. ◆ **Ansichten** *pl* opinions, views.

Ansichtskarte *die* postcard.

ansonsten *adv* otherwise.

anspannen *vt* - **1.** [Muskel] to tense; [Seil] to tauten - **2.** [anstrengen] to put under strain - **3.** [Pferd] to harness.

Anspannung *die* strain; **nervöse ~** nervous tension.

anspielen <> *vi*: **auf jn/etw ~** to allude to sb/sthg <> *vt* SPORT to play the ball to.

Anspielung *(pl -en) die* allusion.

anspornen ['anʃpɔrnən] *vt* to spur on; **jn zu etw ~** to spur sb on to sthg.

Ansprache *(pl -n) die* speech.

ansprechbar *adj*: **nicht ~ sein** [wegen Krankheit, Ohnmacht, Trunkenheit] to be in no fit state to talk to anybody.

anspringen *(perf hat/ist angesprungen) (unreg)* <> *vt (hat)* [angreifen] to pounce on <> *vi (ist)* - **1.** [Auto, Motor] to start - **2.** *fam* [reagieren]: **auf etw** *(A)* **~** to jump at sthg.

Anspruch *der* - **1.** [Recht] claim; **auf etw ~ haben** to be entitled to sthg - **2.** [Forderung] demand; **hohe Ansprüche an jn stellen** to demand a lot of sb; **jn/etw in ~ nehmen** to make demands on sb/sthg; **viel Zeit in ~ nehmen** to take a lot of time; **ich nahm seine Hilfe gern in ~** I was happy to accept his help.

anspruchslos ['anʃpruxsloːs] *adj* - **1.** [bescheiden] unpretentious; [Leben] simple - **2.** [Publikum, Person, Lektüre] undemanding - **3.** [Pflanze] easy to look after.

anspruchsvoll ['anʃpruxsfɔl] *adj* demanding; [Zeitung] quality *(vor Subst)*.

anstacheln ['anʃtaxln] *vt* [Ehrgeiz] to fire; **jn zu etw ~** to goad sb into sthg.

Anstalt *(pl -en) die* - **1.** [Institution] institution - **2.** [Irrenanstalt] mental hospital, institution.

Anstand *der* [gutes Benehmen] decency.

anständig <> *adj* decent; **eine ~e Tracht Prügel** *fam* a real hiding <> *adv* - **1.** [ordentlich, integer] decently - **2.** *fam* [kräftig]: **~ bezahlen** to pay well; **~ reinhauen** to stuff one's face.

anstandslos *adv* without hesitation.

anstarren *vt* to stare at.

anstatt *präp*: **~ js/einer Sache** instead of sb/sthg. ◆ **anstatt dass** *konj*: **~ dass wir reden ...** instead of talking ... ◆ **anstatt zu** *konj* instead of.

anstecken <> *vt* - **1.** [infizieren, mitreißen] to infect; **jn mit etw ~** to infect sb with sthg, to give sthg to sb; **er hat uns alle mit seinem**

Lachen angesteckt his laughter was infectious - **2.** [Zigarette, Kerze] to light; [Haus] to set fire to - **3.** [Orden, Brosche] to pin on; [einen Ring] to put on ◇ *vi* to be infectious.
➨ **sich anstecken** *ref:* **sich (bei jm) mit etw ~** to catch sthg (from sb).

ansteckend *adj* infectious.

Ansteckung (*pl* -en) *die* infection.

an|stehen *vi* (*unreg*) - **1.** [in Schlange] to queue *Br*, to stand in line *Am*, to stand in line for sthg *Am* - **2.** [Problem] to be on the agenda; [Termin] to be fixed.

an|steigen (*perf* ist angestiegen) *vi* (*unreg*) to rise.

anstelle *präp:* **~ js/einer Sache, ~ von jm/etw** instead of sb/sthg.

an|stellen *vt* - **1.** [Gerät] to turn on - **2.** [Angestellte] to employ, to take on; **in einem Großbetrieb angestellt sein** to work in a big factory - **3.** [zustande bringen - Beobachtung, Vergleich] to make; [- Unfug] to get up to; [- Blödsinn] to talk; **sie hat alles Mögliche angestellt** she tried everything; **wie soll ich das ~?** how am I supposed to do that?
➨ **sich anstellen** *ref* - **1.** [Schlange stehen] to queue *Br*, to stand in line *Am* - **2.** [sich benehmen] to act; **sie stellte sich sehr geschickt an** she got the hang of it very quickly.

An|stellung *die* position.

Anstieg (*pl* -e) *der* - **1.** [Zunahme] rise - **2.** [Aufstieg] ascent.

an|stiften *vt:* **jn zu etw ~** to incite sb to sthg.

Anstoß *der* - **1.** [Anlass] impetus (*U*); **den ~ zu etw geben** to provide the impetus for sthg - **2.** [Ärger]: **an etw** (*D*) **~ nehmen** to take offence at sthg - **3.** [im Fußball] kick-off.

an|stoßen (*perf* hat/ist angestoßen) (*unreg*) ◇ *vt* (hat) [mit dem Fuß] to kick; [mit dem Ellenbogen - mit Gewalt] to elbow; [- heimlich] to nudge; **sich das Knie am Tisch ~** to bang one's knee on the table ◇ *vi* - **1.** (*ist*) [anecken]: **mit der Schulter am Schrank ~** to bang one's shoulder on the cupboard - **2.** (hat) [angrenzen]: **an etw** (*A*) **~** to adjoin sthg - **3.** (hat) [mit Gläsern]: **(mit jm) auf jn/etw ~** to drink to sb/sthg (with sb).

an|strahlen *vt* - **1.** [beleuchten - Bauwerk] to floodlight; [- Schauspieler] to spotlight - **2.** [anlächeln] to beam at.

an|streichen *vt* (*unreg*) - **1.** [streichen] to paint - **2.** [kennzeichnen] to mark.

an|strengen ['anʃtrɛŋən] *vt* - **1.** [ermüden] to strain - **2.** [Kräfte, Fantasie, Kopf] to use - **3.** [Prozess] to start. ➨ **sich anstrengen** *ref* [sich bemühen] to make an effort, to try.

Anstrengung (*pl* -en) *die* effort.

Anstrich *der* - **1.** [Farbe] coat of paint - **2.** [Schein] air; **einer Sache** (*D*) **einen seriösen ~ geben** to lend authority to sthg.

Ansturm *der* - **1.** [Angriff] assault - **2.** [Andrang] rush.

an|stürmen (*perf* ist angestürmt) *vi:* **gegen etw ~** [Festung] to storm sthg.

Antarktis *die* Antarctic.

Anteil (*pl* -e) *der* - **1.** [Teil] share - **2.** [Teilnahme]: **an etw** (*D*) **~ haben** to participate in sthg; **an etw** (*D*) **~ nehmen** [bemitleiden] to share in sthg; [sich beteiligen] to participate in sthg.

Anteilnahme *die* - **1.** [Mitleid] sympathy - **2.** [Interesse] interest.

Antenne (*pl* -n) *die* - **1.** TECH aerial - **2.** [Gefühl]: **eine/keine ~ für etw haben** to have a/no feel for sthg.

Anthrax (*pl* -) *das* anthrax.

Antialkoholiker, in [antiˈalkoˈhoːlike, rɪn] (*mpl* -; *fpl* -nen) *der, die* teetotaller.

antiautoritär [antiˈautoriˈtɛːɐ] ◇ *adj* permissive ◇ *adv* permissively.

Antibiotikum [antiˈbjoːtikum] (*pl* -ka) *das* antibiotic.

antifaschistisch *adj* antifascist.

antik [anˈtiːk] *adj* - **1.** [klassisch] classical - **2.** [alt] antique.

Antike [anˈtiːkə] *die:* **die ~** (classical) antiquity.

Antikörper *der* antibody.

an|tippen *vt* - **1.** [Gegenstand] to tap - **2.** [Thema] to touch on.

antiquarisch *adj* second-hand.

Antiquität [antikviˈtɛːt] (*pl* -en) *die* antique.

Antrag ['antraːk] (*pl* Anträge) *der* - **1.** [Bitte] application; **einen ~ auf etw** (*A*) **stellen** to apply for sthg - **2.** [im Parlament] motion - **3.** [Formular] application form.

Antragsformular *das* application form.

an|treffen *vt* (*unreg*) to find.

an|treiben *vt* (*unreg*) - **1.** [Wagen] to drive; [Motor, Gerät] to power - **2.** [Person] to urge on; **jn zur Eile ~** to urge sb to hurry - **3.** [anschwemmen] to wash up.

an|treten (*perf* hat/ist angetreten) (*unreg*) ◇ *vt* (hat) - **1.** [beginnen] to start - **2.** [Erbschaft] to come into ◇ *vi* (*ist*) - **1.** [sich aufstellen] to line up - **2.** [kämpfen]: **gegen jn ~** [in Fußball, Tennis] to play sb; [im Boxen] to fight sb; [in Wahl] to stand against sb.

Antrieb *der* - **1.** [Kraft] drive; **mit elektrischem ~** electrically-powered - **2.** [Motivation] impetus; **etw aus eigenem ~ tun** to do sthg on one's own initiative..

an|trinken *vt* (*unreg*): **sich** (*D*) **Mut ~** to fill o.s. with Dutch courage.

Antritt *der* (ohne *pl*) - **1.** [Beginn] start - **2.** SPORT: **er hat einen schnellen ~** he has a good turn of pace.

an|tun *vt* (*unreg*) - **1.** [Unrecht] to do; **wie konntest du mir das ~?** how could you do that to me?; **sich** (D) **etwas ~** to take one's own life - **2.** [Gutes]: **jm zu viel Ehre ~** to do sb too much justice - **3.** [lieben]: **das Bild hat es mir angetan** I really like the picture.

Antwort ['antvɔrt] (pl -en) die - **1.** [Erwiderung] answer; [auf Brief] reply; **die ~ auf etw** (A) the answer to sthg; **~/keine ~ geben** to reply/not to reply - **2.** [Reaktion] response; **als ~ auf** (+ A) in response to.

antworten <> vi - **1.** [erwidern] to answer; **auf etw** (A) **~** to answer sthg, to reply to sthg - **2.** [reagieren] to respond <> vt [auf Fragen] to answer, to reply.

an|vertrauen vt: **jm etw ~** to entrust sb with sthg. ◆ **sich anvertrauen** ref: **sich jm ~** to confide in sb.

an|wachsen ['anvaksn] (perf ist angewachsen) vi (unreg) - **1.** [festwachsen] to take root - **2.** [wachsen] to increase.

Anwalt ['anvalt] (pl Anwälte) der - **1.** [Rechtsanwalt] lawyer - **2.** fig [Fürsprecher] advocate.

Anwältin ['anvɛltɪn] (pl -nen) die - **1.** [Rechtsanwältin] lawyer - **2.** fig [Fürsprecherin] advocate.

Anwalts|büro das [Firma] firm of lawyers.

Anwärter, in (mpl -; fpl -nen) der, die: **ein ~ (auf etw** (A)) a candidate for sthg.

an|weisen vt (unreg) - **1.** [zeigen] to show; **jm etw ~** to show sthg to sb - **2.** [beauftragen]: **jn ~, etw zu tun** to instruct sb to do sthg.

An|weisung die - **1.** [Befehl] instruction; **~ haben, etw zu tun** to have instructions to do sthg - **2.** [Zahlung - per Bank] payment; [- per Post] postal order.

anwendbar adj: **(auf jn/etw) ~ sein** to be applicable (to sb/sthg).

an|wenden vt - **1.** [Hilfsmittel, Gewalt, List] to use - **2.** [Methode, Regel]: **etw auf jn/etw ~** to apply sthg to sb/sthg.

An|wendung die - **1.** [Verwendung, Einsatz] use - **2.** [von Methode, Regel] application.

an|werben vt (unreg) to recruit.

anwesend adj present; **bei etw ~ sein** to be present at sthg.

Anwesenheit die presence; **in js ~** (D), **in ~ von jm** in sb's presence.

an|widern ['anvi:dɐn] vt to fill with repulsion.

Anwohner, in (mpl -; fpl -nen) der, die resident.

Anzahl die number.

an|zahlen vt to pay a deposit on; **100 Euro ~** to pay a deposit of 100 euros.

An|zahlung die deposit, down payment.

An|zeichen das sign.

Anzeige ['antsaigə] (pl -n) die - **1.** [in Zeitung] advertisement; [Brief] announcement - **2.** [Instrument] display - **3.** [Strafanzeige]

charge; **gegen jn ~ erstatten** to bring a charge against sb.

an|zeigen vt - **1.** [melden] to report - **2.** [zeigen] to show.

Anzeigen|teil der advertisements section.

an|zetteln ['antsɛtln] vt to instigate.

an|ziehen (unreg) <> vt - **1.** [Kleidung] to put on; **sich** (D) **etw ~** to put sthg on - **2.** [Person]: **jn ~** to dress sb - **3.** PHYS [anlocken] to attract - **4.** [Schraube, Tau] to tighten; [Bremse] to apply - **5.** [Körperteil] to draw up <> vi - **1.** [steigen] to rise - **2.** [beschleunigen] to accelerate. ◆ **sich anziehen** ref [Person] to get dressed; **sich warm ~** to dress warmly.

anziehend adj attractive.

Anziehungs|kraft die - **1.** PHYS (gravitational) attraction - **2.** [Reiz] attractiveness, appeal.

An|zug der - **1.** [Kleidungsstück] suit - **2.** [Nähern]: **im ~ sein** to be approaching.

anzüglich ['antsy:klɪç] <> adj lewd <> adv lewdly.

an|zünden vt [Streichholz, Kerze] to light; [Haus] to set fire to.

Apartment = Appartement.

Aperitif [aperi'ti:f] (pl -s) der aperitif.

Apfel ['apfl] (pl Äpfel) der apple.

Apfel|baum der apple tree.

Apfel|kuchen der apple cake.

Apfel|mus das apple sauce (usually eaten as dessert).

Apfel|saft der apple juice.

Apfelsine [apfl'zi:nə] (pl -n) die orange.

Apfel|wein der cider.

Apostel [a'pɔstl] (pl -) der apostle.

Apostroph [apo'stro:f] (pl -e) der apostrophe.

Apotheke [apo'te:kə] (pl -n) die pharmacy, chemist's Br, drugstore Am.

Apotheker, in (mpl -; fpl -nen) der, die pharmacist, chemist Br, druggist Am.

Apparat [apa'ra:t] (pl -e) der - **1.** [Gerät] device - **2.** [Telefon]: **am ~!** speaking! - **3.** [von Partei, Staat] apparatus - **4.** salopp [Riesending] whopper.

Appartement [apartə'mã:], **Apartment** [a'partmənt] (pl -s) das [Wohnung] flat Br, apartment Am.

Appell [a'pɛl] (pl -e) der - **1.** [Aufruf] appeal - **2.** MIL roll call.

appellieren vi: **an jn/etw ~** to appeal to sb/sthg.

Appetit [ape'ti:t] der appetite; **~/keinen ~ auf etw** (A) **haben** to feel/not to feel like sthg; **guten ~!** enjoy your meal!

appetitlich adj appetizing.

applaudieren [aplau'di:rən] vi to applaud.

Applaus [a'plaʊs] *der (ohne pl)* applause; **jm ~ spenden** to applaud sb.

Aprikose [apri'koːzə] *(pl -n) die* apricot.

April *der (ohne pl)* April; **~, ~!** April fool!; *siehe auch* September.

April|scherz *der* April fool's trick.

apropos [apro'poː] *adv* by the way; **~ Pizza, hast du Hunger?** talking of pizza, are you hungry?

Aquarell [akva'rɛl] *(pl -e) das -* **1.** [Bild] watercolour - **2.** [Farbe]: **in ~ malen** to paint in watercolours.

Aquarium [a'kvaːrjʊm] *(pl Aquarien) das* aquarium.

Äquator [ɛ'kvaːtɔr] *der (ohne pl)* equator.

Ära [ˈɛːra] *(pl Ären) die* era.

Araber, in [ˈarabɐ, rɪn] *(mpl -; fpl -nen) der, die* Arab.

Arabien *nt* Arabia.

arabisch *adj* [Kultur, Volk, Politik] Arab; [Sprache, Literatur] Arabic; [Halbinsel, Landschaft] Arabian.

Arabisch(e) *das (ohne pl)* Arabic; *siehe auch* Englisch(e).

Arbeit ['arbaɪt] *(pl -en) die -* **1.** [gen] work; **die ~en am Tunnel** the work on the tunnel; **bei der ~ sein** to be working; **ihr Wagen ist in ~** your car is being worked on; **zur ~ gehen** to go to work - **2.** [Arbeitsstelle] job; **keine ~ haben** to be out of work; **~ suchen** to be looking for work ODER a job - **3.** [Leistung, Werk] work - **4.** [Klassenarbeit] test - **5.** [wissenschaftlich] paper.

arbeiten *vi -* **1.** [Person] to work; **bei der Post ~** to work for the Post Office; **zu Hause ~** to work from home; **an etw** *(D)* **~** to work on sthg; **an sich** *(D)* **~** to work hard - **2.** [funktionieren - Maschine] to operate; [- Herz] to function ⇔ *vt* to make; **sich** *(D)* **die Finger** ODER **Hände wund ~** to work one's fingers to the bone. ➤ **sich arbeiten** *ref:* **sich nach oben ~** to work one's way up.

Arbeiter *(pl -) der* worker.

Arbeiterin *(pl -nen) die* worker.

Arbeitgeber, in *(mpl -; fpl -nen) der, die* employer.

Arbeitnehmer, in *(mpl -; fpl -nen) der, die* employee.

Arbeits|amt *das* job centre *Br*, employment agency *Am*.

Arbeits|aufwand *der:* **der ~ ist zu hoch** it would take too much effort.

arbeitsfrei *adj:* **zwei ~e Nachmittage in der Woche** two afternoons off a week.

Arbeits|kraft *die:* **sich** *(D)* **seine ~ erhalten** to keep o.s. fit for work. ➤ **Arbeitskräfte** *pl* workers.

Arbeits|kreis *der* [Lerngruppe] study group; [Ausschuss] working party.

arbeitslos *adj* unemployed.

Arbeitslose *(pl -n) der, die* unemployed person; **die ~n** the unemployed.

Arbeitslosigkeit *die (ohne pl)* unemployment.

Arbeits|markt *der* labour market.

Arbeits|platz *der -* **1.** [Stellung, Job] job - **2.** [Ort] workplace; **dort am Fenster ist mein ~** I work over there by the window.

arbeitsscheu *adj* workshy.

Arbeits|speicher *der* EDV RAM.

Arbeits|stelle *die -* **1.** [Stellung] job - **2.** [Ort, Abteilung] department.

Arbeits|suche *die:* **auf ~ sein** to be looking for work ODER a job.

Arbeits|tag *der* working day.

Arbeits|teilung *die* division of labour.

Arbeits|unfall *der* industrial accident.

Arbeits|vermittlung *die* [private Agentur] employment agency.

Arbeits|weise *die* [von Person] way of working; [von Maschine] mode of operation.

Arbeits|zeit *die* working hours *(pl)*.

Arbeits|zimmer *das* study.

Archäologe [arçɛo'loːgə] *(pl -n) der* archaeologist.

Archäologin [arçɛo'loːgɪn] *(pl -nen) die* archaeologist.

Arche ['arçə] *(pl -n) die:* **die ~ Noah** Noah's Ark.

Architekt, in [arçi'tɛkt, ɪn] *(mpl -en; fpl -nen) der, die* architect.

Architektur [arçitɛk'tuːɐ] *die (ohne pl)* architecture.

Archiv [ar'çiːf] *(pl -e) das* archive.

archivieren [arçi'viːrən] *vt* to (store in an) archive.

ARD [aːɛr'deː] *(abk für Arbeitsgemeinschaft der öffentlich-rechtlichen Rundfunkanstalten der Bundesrepublik Deutschland) die German public broadcasting network, responsible for the Erstes Programm TV channel.*

Arena [a'reːna] *(pl Arenen) die* arena.

arg [ark] *(kompar ärger; superl ärgste)* ⇔ *adj* [schlimm] bad; [sehr schlimm] terrible; **js ärgster Feind** sb's arch enemy ⇔ *adv* [schlimm] badly; [sehr schlimm] terribly.

Argentinien *nt* Argentina.

Ärger ['ɛrgɐ] *der (ohne pl) -* **1.** [Verärgerung] annoyance; [Zorn] anger - **2.** [Problem] trouble; **(jm) ~ machen** to cause (sb) trouble.

ärgerlich ⇔ *adj -* **1.** [verärgert] annoyed; [zornig] angry; **auf jn/über etw** *(A)* **~ sein** [verärgert] to be annoyed with sb/at sthg; [zornig] to be angry with sb/at sthg - **2.** [unangenehm] annoying ⇔ *adv* [verärgert] angrily.

ärgern *vt* to annoy. ➤ **sich ärgern** *ref* to get annoyed; **sich über jn/etw ~** to get annoyed with sb/at sthg.

Ärgernis (*pl* -se) *das* - 1. [Ärgerliches] nuisance - 2. RECHT: **Erregung öffentlichen ~ses** offence against public decency.

Argument (*pl* -e) *das* argument.

argumentieren *vi* to argue.

Argwohn *der* (*ohne pl*) suspicion.

argwöhnisch ◇ *adj* suspicious ◇ *adv* suspiciously.

Arie ['aːriə] (*pl* -n) *die* aria.

aristokratisch *adj* aristocratic.

Arithmetik *die* (*ohne pl*) arithmetic.

Arkaden *pl* ARCHIT arcade (*sg*).

Arktis *die* Arctic.

arm (*kompar* ärmer; *superl* ärmste) ◇ *adj* poor; **um etw ärmer sein** to have lost sthg; **er ist nun um 50 Euro ärmer** he's now 50 euros worse off ODER the poorer; **~ dran sein** *fam* to be in a bad way ◇ *adv* poorly; **jn ~ essen** to eat sb out of house and home.

Arm (*pl* -e) *der* - 1. [gen] arm; **jn/etw im ~ haiten** to hold sb/sthg in one's arms - 2. *RW:* **jn auf den ~ nehmen** to pull sb's leg, to thwart sb; **jn mit offenen ~en aufnehmen** to welcome sb with open arms. ◆ **Arm in Arm** *adv* arm in arm.

Armatur (*pl* -en) *die* [von Maschine, Auto] instrument. ◆ **Armaturen** *pl* [im Badezimmer] fittings.

Armatur|brett *das* AUTO dashboard.

Arm|band (*pl* -bänder) *das* [Schmuck] bracelet; [von Uhr] strap.

Armband|uhr *die* wristwatch, watch.

Arm|binde *die* armband.

Arme (*pl* -n) *der, die* - 1. [Bedauernswerte] poor thing; **du ~r!** you poor thing! - 2. [Mittellose] poor man/woman; **die ~n** the poor.

Armee [ar'meː] (*pl* -n) *die* army.

Ärmel (*pl* -) *der* sleeve; **die ~ hochkrempeln** *eigtl & fig* to roll up one's sleeves.

Ärmelkanal *der:* **der ~** the (English) Channel.

Arm|lehne *die* arm, armrest.

ärmlich ◇ *adj* [Wohnung, Kleidung] shabby; [Verhältnisse] miserable ◇ *adv* shabbily.

armselig *adj* - 1. [ärmlich] shabby - 2. [gering] meagre.

Armut *die* (*ohne pl*) poverty.

Aroma (*pl* -s ODER Aromen) *das* - 1. [Geruch] aroma - 2. [Würze] flavouring.

arrangieren [arãˈʒiːrən] *vt* [Treffen, Feier, Musik] to arrange. ◆ **sich arrangieren** *ref:* **sich mit jm ~** [sich verständigen] to come to an understanding with sb.

arrogant ◇ *adj* arrogant ◇ *adv* arrogantly.

Arroganz *die* (*ohne pl*) arrogance.

Arsch (*pl* Ärsche) *der salopp* - 1. [Gesäß] arse *Br*, ass *Am* - 2. [Blödmann] arsehole *Br*, ass-

hole *Am* - 3. *RW:* **jm in den ~ kriechen** *vulg* to lick sb's arse *Br* ODER ass *Am*.

Arsen *das* (*ohne pl*) arsenic.

Art (*pl* -en) *die* - 1. [Weise] way; **eine einfache ~, etw zuzubereiten** a simple way of preparing ODER to prepare sthg; **etw auf eine andere ~ tun** to do sthg another way; **auf gesunde ~** healthily; **auf diese ~ wird er nie gewinnen** he'll never win like this ODER this way; **die ~ und Weise(, wie)** the way (that); **Bratkartoffeln nach ~ des Hauses** the chef's special fried potatoes - 2. (*ohne pl*) [Wesen] nature; [Verhalten] behaviour; **das entspricht nicht ihrer ~, sich zu beschweren** it's not like her to complain - 3. [Sorte] sort, kind; **eine ~ Grippe** a sort ODER kind of flu; **in dieser ~** in this form; **das Schloss ist in seiner ~ einmalig** the castle is the only one of its kind - 4. BIOL species.

Artensterben *das* (*ohne pl*) dying out of species.

Arterie (*pl* -n) *die* artery.

Arterio|sklerose *die* arteriosclerosis (*U*).

Arthritis *die* arthritis.

artig ◇ *adj* good ◇ *adv:* **sie hat den Teller Spinat ~ aufgegessen** she ate up all her spinach like a good girl.

Artikel (*pl* -) *der* - 1. [in der Zeitung, im Gesetz] article; [im Wörterbuch] entry - 2. [Ware] item, article - 3. GRAM: **der bestimmte/unbestimmte ~** the definite/indefinite article.

artikulieren *vt* to articulate.

Artillerie (*pl* -n) *die* MIL artillery.

Artischocke (*pl* -n) *die* artichoke.

Artist, in (*mpl* -en; *fpl* -nen) *der, die* [im Zirkus] (circus) performer.

artistisch *adj* acrobatic.

Arznei (*pl* -en) *die* medicine.

Arzt [aːʁtst] (*pl* Ärzte) *der* doctor, GP.

Arzt|helfer, in *der, die* [im Wörterbuch] receptionist.

Ärztin ['ɛːʁtstɪn] (*pl* -nen) *die* doctor.

ärztlich *adj* medical.

Arzt|praxis *die* doctor's practice.

as, As (*pl* as, As) *das* MUS A flat.

As (*pl* -se) *das* = **Ass**.

Asbest (*pl* -e) *das* asbestos.

Asche (*pl* -n) *die* [von Feuer] ashes (*pl*); [von Zigarre, Vulkan] ash.

Aschen|becher *der* ashtray.

Aschen|puttel (*pl* -) *das* Cinderella.

Ascher|mittwoch *der* Ash Wednesday.

Asiat, in (*mpl* -en; *fpl* -nen) *der, die* Asian.

asiatisch *adj* Asian.

Asien *nt* Asia.

asozial ◇ *adj* antisocial ◇ *adv* antisocially.

Aspekt (*pl* -e) *der* aspect.

Asphalt [as'falt] (*pl* -e) *der* asphalt.

asphaltieren *vt* to asphalt.

aß *prät* [➤ essen.

Ass (*pl* -e) *das* [Spielkarte, Person] ace.

Assistent, in (*mpl* -en; *fpl* -nen) *der, die* assistant.

assistieren *vi* to assist; **jm bei etw ~** to assist sb with sthg.

Ast (*pl* Äste) *der* branch; **sich** *(D)* **einen ~ lachen** *fam fig* to laugh o.s. silly.

AStA ['asta] (*pl* ASten) (*abk für* Allgemeiner Studentenausschuss) *der* students' union.

Aster (*pl* -n) *die* aster.

Astgabel *die* fork in a branch.

Ästhetik [ɛs'te:tɪk] (*pl* -en) *die* - 1. (*ohne pl*) [das Schöne] aesthetic - 2. [Wissenschaft] aesthetics *(U)*.

Asthma *das* asthma.

Astrologie *die* (*ohne pl*) astrology.

astrologisch *adj* astrological.

Astronaut, in (*mpl* -en; *fpl* -nen) *der, die* astronaut.

Astronomie *die* (*ohne pl*) astronomy.

Asyl (*pl* -e) *das* - 1. (*ohne pl*) [Zuflucht] asylum - 2. [Obdachlosenasyl] hostel.

Asylant (*pl* -en) *der* asylum seeker.

Asylantin (*pl* -nen) *die* asylum seeker.

Asylbewerber, in *der, die* asylum seeker.

Asylrecht *das* (*ohne pl*) right of asylum.

asymmetrisch *adj* asymmetrical.

Atem *der* (*ohne pl*) - 1. [die Atmung] breathing - 2. [die Atemluft] breath; **außer ~ sein** to be out of breath; **~ holen** [einatmen] to breathe in; [sich ausruhen] to catch one's breath - 3. *RW:* **jn in ~ halten** [in Spannung versetzen] to keep sb on tenterhooks.

atemberaubend ⬦ *adj* breathtaking ⬦ *adv* breathtakingly.

atemlos ⬦ *adj* breathless ⬦ *adv* breathlessly.

Atemnot *die* (*ohne pl*) difficulty in breathing.

Atempause *die:* **eine ~ einlegen** ODER **machen** to take a breather.

Atemzug *der* breath.

Atheist, in (*mpl* -en; *fpl* -nen) *der, die* atheist.

Äther *der* (*ohne pl*) ether.

Äthiopien *nt* Ethiopia.

Athlet, in (*mpl* -en; *fpl* -nen) *der, die* athlete.

athletisch ⬦ *adj* athletic ⬦ *adv* athletically.

Atlantik *der:* **der ~** the Atlantic (Ocean).

Atlas (*pl* -se ODER Atlanten) *der* - 1. [Buch] atlas - 2. (*pl* Atlasse) [Satin] satin.

atmen *vt & vi* to breathe.

Atmosphäre (*pl* -n) *die eigtl & fig* atmosphere.

Atmung *die* (*ohne pl*) breathing.

Atoll (*pl* -e) *das* atoll.

Atom (*pl* -e) *das* atom.

atomar *adj* - 1. [von Atomen] atomic - 2. [mit Atomkraft] nuclear.

Atombombe *die* atom ODER atomic bomb.

Atomkraft *die* (*ohne pl*) nuclear power.

Atomkraftwerk *das* nuclear power station.

Atomkrieg *der* nuclear war.

Atommacht *die* nuclear power (*country*).

Atommüll *der* (*ohne pl*) nuclear waste.

Atomsprengkopf *der* nuclear warhead.

Atomwaffe *die* nuclear weapon.

Attentat (*pl* -e) *das* [erfolglos] assassination attempt; [erfolgreich] assassination.

Attentäter, in (*mpl* -; *fpl* -nen) *der, die* [erfolglos] would-be assassin; [erfolgreich] assassin.

Attest (*pl* -e) *das* doctor's certificate.

Attraktion (*pl* -en) *die* attraction.

attraktiv *adj* attractive.

Attrappe (*pl* -n) *die* dummy.

Attribut (*pl* -e) *das geh* [Merkmal & GRAM] attribute.

au *interj* [Ausdruck von Schmerz] ouch!, ow!

Aubergine [ober'ʒi:nə] (*pl* -n) *die* aubergine *Br*, eggplant *Am*.

auch *adv* - 1. [ebenfalls] also, too; **ich ~ me too**; **ich ~ nicht** me neither; **~ das noch!** that's the last thing I need! - 2. [sogar] even - 3. [wirklich]: **sie war unkonzentriert, aber es war ja ~ schon spät** she couldn't concentrate, but it WAS late - 4. [verstärkend]: **dass du ~ immer kleckern musst!** do you HAVE to make such a mess!; **hast du die Tür ~ wirklich zugemacht?** are you sure you closed the door? - 5. [egal]: **wo ~ (immer)** wherever; **was ~ (immer)** whatever; **wer ~ (immer)** whoever; **wie dem ~ sei** be that as it may.

Audienz (*pl* -en) *die* audience.

audiovisuell [audjovi'zuɛl] *adj* audiovisual.

auf ⬦ *präp* - 1. (+ *D, A*) [räumlich] on; **~ dem/den Tisch** on the table; **~ dem Land** in the country; **~s Land** to the country; **~ einen Berg steigen** to climb a mountain; **~ der Post** at the post office; **~ eine Feier gehen** to go to a party; **~ die Uni gehen** to go to university - 2. (+ *D*) [zeitlich – während]: **~ der Reise** on the journey; **~ der Hochzeit/Feier** at the wedding/party - 3. (+ *A*) [zur Angabe der Art und Weise]: **~ diese Art** in this way; **~ Deutsch** in German; **~ jeden Fall** in any case - 4. [feste Verbindungen]: **~ Reisen gehen** to go on a tour; **von heute ~ morgen** overnight - 5. (+ *A*) [zur Angabe eines Wunsches]: **~ ihr Wohl!** your good health! - 6. [zur Angabe eines Verhältnisses]: **~ ein Kilo Obst kommt ein Pfund Zucker** add a pound of sugar for every kilo of fruit ⬦ *adv* - 1. [offen]

open; **Tür ~!** open the door! **- 2.** [aufgestanden] up; **ich bin seit zehn Uhr ~** I've been up since ten o'clock **- 3.** [feste Verbindungen]: **~ einmal knallte es** suddenly there was a bang; **er aß alle Süßigkeiten ~ einmal** he ate all the sweets in one go <> *interj* [los, weg]: **~ in die Kneipe!** (let's) go to the pub! ◆ **auf und ab** *adv* **- 1.** [herauf und herunter] up and down **- 2.** [hin und her] back and forth.

auflatmen *vi* to breathe a sigh of relief.

Aufbau (*pl* -ten) *der* **- 1.** (*ohne pl*) [Bauen - von Zelt, Gerüst] putting up; [- von Ruinen] rebuilding **- 2.** (*ohne pl*) [Gründung] building up **- 3.** (*ohne pl*) [Struktur] structure **- 4.** [Anbau] superstructure.

auflbauen *vt* **- 1.** [bauen - Zelt, Gerüst] to put up; [- Ruinen] to rebuild **- 2.** [gründen, schaffen] to build up **- 3.** [zusammensetzen - Kulissen, Modelleisenbahn] to build; **aus etw aufgebaut sein** to be made up ODER composed of sth **- 4.** TELEC [Verbindung] to establish **- 5.** [ordnen] to structure **- 6.** [fördern]: **jn zu** ODER **als etw ~** to make ODER turn sb into sthg **- 7.** [trösten]: **jn ~** to give sb strength **- 8.** [begründen]: **etw auf etw** (D) ~ to base sthg on sthg. ◆ **sich aufbauen** *ref fam* [sich hinstellen] to plant o.s.

auflbäumen ◆ **sich aufbäumen** *ref* **- 1.** [Pferd] to rear (up) **- 2.** [Person]: **sich gegen jn/etw ~** to rebel against sb/sthg.

auflbauschen *vt* [übertreiben] to blow up.

auflbekommen *vt* (*unreg*) **- 1.** [öffnen] to get open **- 2.** *fam* [aufessen] to manage (to eat) **- 3.** [Schulaufgabe] to get for homework.

auflbereiten *vt* to process; [Trinkwasser] to purify.

auflbessern *vt* **- 1.** [verbessern] to improve **- 2.** [erhöhen] to increase.

auflbewahren *vt* [in Tresor] to keep; **etw (für jn) ~** to look after sthg (for sb); **die Milch kühl ~** to store the milk in a cool place.

Aufbewahrung *die* storage.

auflbieten *vt* (*unreg*) **- 1.** [Kraft] to summon up; [Einfluss] to use **- 2.** [Polizei, Militär] to call out.

auflblasen *vt* (*unreg*) [Ballon, Luftmatratze] to blow up, to inflate; [Backen] to puff out.

auflbleiben (*perf* ist aufgeblieben) *vi* (*unreg*) **- 1.** [wach bleiben] to stay up **- 2.** [offen bleiben] to stay open.

auflblenden <> *vt* to turn on full beam *Br* ODER high beam *Am* <> *vi* to put one's headlights on full beam *Br* ODER high beam *Am*.

auflblicken *vi* **- 1.** [hochsehen] to look up **- 2.** [bewundern]: **zu jm ~** to look up to sb.

auflblitzen (*perf* aufgeblitzt) *vi* [Licht] to flash.

auflblühen (*perf* ist aufgeblüht) *vi* **- 1.** [blühen] to blossom **- 2.** [aufleben] to blossom (out) **- 3.** [wachsen] to flourish.

auflbrauchen *vt* to use up.

auflbrausen (*perf* ist aufgebraust) *vi* **- 1.** [erklingen] to break out **- 2.** [hochfahren] to flare up.

auflbrechen (*perf* hat/ist aufgebrochen) (*unreg*) <> *vt* (*hat*) [mit Gewalt öffnen - Tür] to force open; [- Schloss] to force; [- Deckel] to force off; [- Wohnung, Auto, Tresor] to break into <> *vi* (*ist*) **- 1.** [abreisen] to set off (for) **- 2.** [aufreißen] to open.

auflbringen *vt* (*unreg*) **- 1.** [beschaffen] to raise **- 2.** [einsetzen] to summon up **- 3.** [einführen - Gerücht] to start **- 4.** [wütend machen] to make angry **- 5.** [öffnen können] to get open.

Aufbruch *der* (*ohne pl*) departure.

auflbrummen *vt fam*: **jm etw ~** [Strafe] to slap sthg on sb.

auflbürden *vt*: **jm/sich etw ~** [Verantwortung] to burden sb/o.s. with sthg.

aufldecken *vt* **- 1.** [aufschlagen] to turn back **- 2.** [entdecken] to uncover **- 3.** [Spielkarten]: **seine Karten** ODER **sein Spiel ~** to show one's hand **- 4.** [im Bett]: **jn ~** to pull the covers off sb.

auidrängen *vt*: **jm etw ~** to force sthg onto sb. ◆ **sich aufdrängen** *ref* **- 1.** [Person] to impose; **er hat sich uns vor der Reise aufgedrängt** he imposed himself on us before we set off **- 2.** [Idee]: **dieser Gedanke/ Verdacht drängte sich mir auf** I couldn't help thinking/suspecting that; **diese Idee drängt sich einem ja sofort auf, wenn man seinen Bericht hört** this idea comes immediately to mind on hearing his report.

aufldrehen <> *vt* **- 1.** [Wasserhahn, Gas] to turn on; [Deckel] to unscrew; [Flasche, Dose] to open **- 2.** *fam* [laut stellen] to turn up <> *vi fam* **- 1.** [schnell fahren] to put one's foot down **- 2.** [in Stimmung kommen] to get going.

aufdringlich <> *adj* [Person] pushy; [Farbe] loud; [Parfüm] overpowering <> *adv* insistently.

aufeinander *adv* **- 1.** [einer auf dem anderen] one on top of the other; **sie liegen ~** they are lying on top of each other **- 2.** [gegenseitig] one another; **sie passen ~ auf** they look out for each other.

aufeinander folgen (*perf* sind aufeinander gefolgt) *vi* to come one after the other.

aufeinander prallen (*perf* sind aufeinander geprallt) *vi* **- 1.** [zusammenstoßen] to crash into one another **- 2.** [sich widersprechen] to clash.

aufeinander stoßen (*perf* sind aufeinander gestoßen) *vi* (*unreg*) **- 1.** [Köpfe, Waggons] to bump into each other **- 2.** [Meinungen] to clash.

Aufenthalt (*pl* -e) *der* **- 1.** [Anwesenheit]

stay; **der ~ im Bereich des Krans ist gefährlich** keep well clear of the crane - **2.** [Unter-
brechung] stop; **in Köln haben wir eine Stunde ~** we'll have an hour to wait in Cologne.

Aufenthalts|genehmigung *die* resi-
dence permit.

Aufenthalts|ort *der* place of residence.

Auferstehung *die (ohne pl)* resurrection.

auf|essen *vt (unreg)* to eat up.

auf|fädeln *vt* to string.

auf|fahren *(perf ist aufgefahren) (unreg)*
<> *vi* - **1.** [im Auto]: **dicht auf den Vorder-
mann ~** to sit right on the tail of the car in
front; **auf jn/etw ~** to run into sb/sthg
- **2.** [erschrecken] to start; **aus dem Schlaf ~** to
awake with a start <> *vt* - **1.** [heranfahren] to
bring up - **2.** *fam* [anbieten] to lay on - **3.** [auf-
schütten] to put down.

Auffahrt *(pl -en) die* - **1.** [zur Autobahn] slip
road *Br*, on-ramp *Am* - **2.** [zu einem Gebäude]
drive - **3.** [Aufstieg] climb - **4.** *Schweiz* [Him-
melfahrt] Ascension Day.

Auffahr|unfall *der* rear-end collision.

auf|fallen *(perf ist aufgefallen) vi (unreg)* to
stand out; **mir ist nichts Besonderes an ihm
aufgefallen** nothing in particular struck me
about him; **das ist mir aufgefallen** I've noticed that.

auffallend <> *adj* striking <> *adv* stri-
kingly.

auffällig <> *adj* [Kleidung, Auto] ostentatious; [Farbe] loud; [Verhalten] odd, unusual
<> *adv* [geschminkt] ostentatiously; [häufig]
surprisingly.

auf|fangen *vt (unreg)* - **1.** [Ball] to catch
- **2.** [Worte, Spruch, Signal] to pick up
- **3.** [Stoß, Schlag] to cushion; [Inflation, Preis-
steigerung] to offset - **4.** [sammeln] to collect.

Auffang|lager *das* transit camp.

auf|fassen *vt* to understand; **etw als etw ~**
to take sthg as sthg.

Auffassung *die* opinion; **zu der ~ kommen, dass ...** to come to the conclusion that
...; **nach js ~** in sb's opinion.

Auffassungs|gabe *die (ohne pl)* intelli-
gence; **eine schnelle ~ haben** to be quick on
the uptake.

auf|flackern *(perf ist aufgeflackert) vi*
[leuchten] to flicker into life.

auf|fliegen *(perf ist aufgeflogen) vi (unreg)*
- **1.** [fliegen] to fly up - **2.** [sich öffnen] to fly
open - **3.** *fam* [entdeckt werden - Vorhaben] to
be uncovered; [- Bande] to be broken up.

auf|fordern *vt* - **1.** [bitten]: **jn zum Platz-
nehmen ~** to ask sb/on invite sb to be seated
- **2.** [befehlen]: **jn dazu ~, etw zu tun** to require sb to do sthg - **3.** [zum Tanz] to ask to
dance.

Aufforderung *die* - **1.** [Bitte] request, invitation - **2.** [Befehl] demand.

auf|frischen <> *vt* - **1.** [erneuern - Bezug] to
freshen up; [- Farbe] to brighten up; [- Mö-
bel] to renovate - **2.** [erweitern - Kenntnisse]
to brush up on; [- Erinnerung] to refresh
<> *vi* [Wind] to freshen.

auf|führen *vt* - **1.** [auf der Bühne] to per-
form - **2.** [nennen, auflisten] to give, to list.
<> **sich aufführen** *ref abw* [sich benehmen]
to behave.

Aufführung *die* [Vorstellung] performance.

auf|füllen *vt* - **1.** [nachfüllen] to top up
- **2.** [füllen] to fill up - **3.** [ergänzen] to replenish.

Aufgabe *die* - **1.** [Pflicht] task; **das ist nicht
meine ~** that's not my responsibility - **2.** [Ka-
pitulation] surrender - **3.** *(ohne pl)* [von Ge-
schäften]: **die Einzelhändler wurden zur
~ genötigt** the retailers were forced to give
up their businesses - **4.** [eines Pakets] posting
Br, mailing *Am*; [einer Anzeige] placing
- **5.** [SCHULE - in Prüfung] question; [- in Ma-
thematik] problem; [- Übung] exercise;
[- Schulaufgabe] homework (U).

Aufgaben|bereich *der* area of responsi-
bility.

Aufgang *(pl Aufgänge) der* - **1.** [Treppe]
stairs *(pl)* - **2.** [Leuchten] rising.

auf|geben *(unreg)* <> *vt* - **1.** [Gewohnheit,
Stelle, Geschäft] to give up; **das Rauchen ~** to
give up smoking - **2.** [Person] to give up on;
[Plan, Idee, Hoffnung] to give up; [Wett-
kampf, Spiel] to pull out of; **ich gebe es auf!** I
give up! - **3.** [auftragen] to set; **jm etw ~** to set
sb sthg - **4.** [Bestellung] to place; **eine Anzeige ~** to place an advert in the paper - **5.** [ver-
schicken] to send <> *vi* [aufhören, kapitulie-
ren] to give up.

aufgebläht *adj* [Ballon, Verwaltungsappa-
rat] inflated; [Bauch] swollen; [Backen]
puffed-out.

Aufgebot *das* - **1.** [an Personen] contin-
gent; [an Maschinen, Waren] array - **2.** [für
Hochzeit] banns *(pl)*; **das ~ bestellen** to publish the banns.

aufgebracht <> *pp* |> **aufbringen**
<> *adj* [wütend] angry.

aufgedunsen *adj* bloated.

auf|gehen *(perf ist aufgegangen) vi (unreg)*
- **1.** [Sonne, Mond] to rise - **2.** [Knoten, Knopf]
to come undone - **3.** [sich öffnen] to open
- **4.** [Rechnung] to work out - **5.** [verschwin-
den]: **in etw (D) ~** to disappear into sthg; **in
Flammen ~** to go up in flames - **6.** [sich einset-
zen]: **in etw (D) ~** to be wrapped up in sthg
- **7.** [deutlich werden]: **jm ~** to dawn on sb
- **8.** [Teig, Kuchen] to rise.

aufgehoben <> *pp* |> **aufheben** <> *adj*:
(bei jm) gut/schlecht ~ sein to be/not to be in
good hands (with sb).

aufgeklärt *adj* enlightened.

aufgelegt adj: **gut/schlecht ~ sein** to be in a good/bad mood.

aufgeregt <> adj excited <> adv excitedly.

aufgeschlossen <> pp ▷ aufschließen <> adj open-minded; **etw gegenüber** ODER **für etw ~ sein** to be open to sthg.

aufgeweckt adj bright.

aufgreifen vt (unreg) - **1.** [fangen] to pick up - **2.** [übernehmen] to take up.

aufgrund präp: **~ einer Sache** (G) because of sthg.

auflhaben (unreg) <> vt - **1.** [Hausaufgaben] to have for homework - **2.** [tragen] to have on, to be wearing - **3.** [offen lassen - Mantel, Tür] to have open; [- Knopf] to have undone <> vi [geöffnet sein] to be open.

auflhalten vt (unreg) - **1.** [offen halten - Tür, Tasche] to hold open; **die Hand ~** to hold out one's hand; **die Augen ~** to keep one's eyes open; **jm etw ~** to hold sthg open for sb - **2.** [anhalten - Entwicklung, Inflation] to put a check on - **3.** [stören] to hold up; **ich möchte Sie nicht ~** I don't want to keep you. ◆ **sich aufhalten** ref [sich befinden] to stay.

auflhängen <> vt - **1.** [hinhängen - Mantel, Plakat] to hang up; [- Bild] to hang; [- Wäsche] to hang out - **2.** [erhängen] to hang - **3.** [mit etw begründen]: **etw an etw** (D) **~** to base sthg on sthg <> vi [am Telefon] to hang up. ◆ **sich aufhängen** ref fam [sich erhängen] to hang o.s.

Aufhänger (pl -) der - **1.** [Halterung] loop - **2.** fig [Grund, Anstoß] pretext.

auflhäufen vt to pile up. ◆ **sich aufhäufen** ref to pile up.

auflheben vt (unreg) - **1.** [nehmen] to pick up - **2.** [aufbewahren] to keep; **etw gut ~** to keep sthg safe - **3.** [Gesetz, Verordnung] to repeal; [Verbot, Embargo] to lift; [Visapflicht] to end - **4.** [ausgleichen]: **etw/einander ~** to cancel sthg/each other out. ◆ **sich aufheben** ref to cancel each other out.

auflheitern vt [Person] to cheer up. ◆ **sich aufheitern** ref - **1.** [fröhlich werden] to cheer up - **2.** [sonnig werden] to clear up.

auflhellen vt [heller machen] to lighten. ◆ **sich aufhellen** ref - **1.** [Gesicht, Miene] to light up - **2.** [Wetter, Himmel] to clear up.

auflhetzen vt to stir up; **jn gegen jn/etw ~** to stir sb up against sb/sthg.

auflholen <> vt [Verspätung] to make up <> vi [Sportler, Wirtschaft] to catch up.

auflhorchen vi - **1.** [horchen] to prick up one's ears - **2.** [aufmerksam werden] to sit up and take notice.

auflhören vi - **1.** [nicht weitermachen] to stop; **~, etw zu tun** to stop doing sthg; **mit etw ~** to stop sthg; **mit dem Rauchen ~** to stop smoking - **2.** [kündigen] to finish - **3.** [zu

Ende sein - Film, Straße, Weg] to end; [- Lärm, Regen] to stop; [- Nebel] to lift; **da hört sich doch alles auf!** fig that's the limit!

auflklappen vt to open.

auflklären vt - **1.** [Missverständnis] to clear up; [Mord] to solve - **2.** [informieren]: **jn über etw** (A) **~** to tell sb about sthg - **3.** [über Sexualität informieren] to explain the facts of life to. ◆ **sich aufklären** ref - **1.** [sich auflösen] to be cleared up - **2.** [sonnig werden] to clear up.

Auflklärung die - **1.** [von Irrtum] clearing up; [von Verbrechen] solving - **2.** [Information] informing - **3.** [Information über Sexualität] sex education - **4.** HIST Enlightenment.

Auflkleber der sticker.

auflknöpfen vt to unbutton.

auflkommen (perf ist aufgekommen) vi (unreg) - **1.** [entstehen] to arise; [Sturm] to get up; **keine Zweifel ~ lassen** to leave no room for doubt - **2.** [übernehmen, zahlen]: **für jn/ etw ~** to pay for sb/sthg - **3.** [aufstehen können] to get up - **4.** [landen] to land.

auflkriegen vt fam - **1.** [öffnen können - Tür, Paket] to get open; [- Knoten] to get undone - **2.** [aufessen]: **etw nicht ~** not to eat sthg up.

auflladen vt (unreg) - **1.** [Lasten]: **etw auf etw** (A) **~** to load sthg onto sthg - **2.** [aufbürden]: **jm/sich etw ~** to burden sb/o.s. with sthg - **3.** [Batterie] to charge.

Auflage die - **1.** [von Büchern] edition; [von Zeitung] circulation - **2.** [Bedingung] condition; **jm zur ~ machen, dass ...** to make it a condition for sb that ....

aufllassen vt (unreg) - **1.** [Tür, Jacke] to leave open; [Knopf] to leave undone - **2.** [Hut, Mütze] to keep on.

aufllauern vi: **jm ~** to lie in wait for sb.

Auflauf der - **1.** [Speise] bake - **2.** [Menschenansammlung] crowd.

auflaufen (perf ist aufgelaufen) vi (unreg) - **1.** [sich festfahren]: **auf etw** (A) **~** to run aground on sthg - **2.** [abblocken]: **jn ~ lassen** SPORT to bodycheck sb - **3.** [steigen]: **auf etw** (A) **~** to mount up to sthg.

auflleben (perf ist aufgelebt) vi - **1.** [Person] to liven up - **2.** [Gespräch, Erinnerung] to revive.

aufllegen <> vt - **1.** [Tischtuch, Schallplatte, Schminke, Kohle] to put on; [Besteck] to put out - **2.** [Produkt, Buch] to bring out - **3.** [am Telefon] to hang up <> vi [am Telefon] to hang up.

aufllehnen ◆ **sich auflehnen** ref: **sich gegen jn/etw ~** to rebel against sb/sthg.

auflleuchten (perf hat/ist aufgeleuchtet) vi to light up.

auflisten vt to list.

aufllockern vt - **1.** [Erde, Boden] to break up; [Muskeln] to loosen up - **2.** [Stimmung,

Rede] to liven up. ◆ **sich auflockern** ref - 1. [Sportler] to limber up - 2. [Bewölkung] to break up; [Knoten] to loosen.

auf|lösen vt - 1. [in Flüssigkeit, in Bestandteile] to dissolve; **etw in etw** (D) **~** to dissolve sthg in sthg - 2. [Staatenverbund, Demonstration, Versammlung] to break up; [Vertrag] to cancel; [Verlobung] to break off; [Parlament] to dissolve - 3. [Betrieb, Haushalt] to break up. ◆ **sich auflösen** ref - 1. [Tablette, Kristalle] to dissolve; [Nebel] to lift; [Bewölkung] to break up; **sich in etw** (D) **~** to dissolve in sthg; **er hat sich in Luft aufgelöst** he vanished into thin air - 2. [Menge, Versammlung] to disperse.

Auf|lösung die - 1. [in Flüssigkeit, in Bestandteile] dissolving; **ein Bildschirm mit hoher ~** a high-resolution screen - 2. [von Koalition, Demonstration, Versammlung] breaking up; [von Vertrag] cancellation; [von Verlobung] breaking off; [von Parlament] dissolving - 3. [von Betrieb, Haushalt] breaking up.

auf|machen ◇ vt - 1. [gen] to open; [Schnur, Knopf, Jacke] to undo - 2. [gestalten] to make ◇ vi - 1. [öffnen] to open the door; **jm ~** to let sb in - 2. [Geschäft] to open. ◆ **sich aufmachen** ref [abreisen]: **sich ~ (nach)** to set off (for).

Aufmachung (pl -en) die - 1. [Gestaltung] layout - 2. [Kleidung] appearance.

aufmerksam ◇ adj - 1. [konzentriert] attentive; **jn auf jn/etw ~ machen** to draw sb's attention to sb/sthg - 2. [höflich] thoughtful ◇ adv attentively.

Aufmerksamkeit (pl -en) die - 1. [Konzentration] attentiveness - 2. [Mitbringsel] gift.

auf|muntern vt [aufheitern] to cheer up; [ermutigen] to encourage.

Aufnahme (pl -n) die - 1. [Empfang] reception; **~ in etw** (A) [Verein, Intensivstation] admission into sthg - 2. [Beginn - von Kontakt] establishment; [- von Arbeit, Gespräch, Verhandlungen] start - 3. [Aufzeichnung] recording; [von Diktat] taking down - 4. [Fotografie] photograph.

aufnahmefähig adj receptive.

Aufnahme|prüfung die entrance examination.

auf|nehmen vt (unreg) - 1. [aufheben, ergreifen] to pick up - 2. [empfangen - in Klub] to admit; [- Gast] to receive; [- Asylant] to take in; **Namen auf einer Liste ~** to include names on a list; **ein Wort im Wörterbuch ~** to include a word in the dictionary; **jn bei sich** (D) **~** to take sb in - 3. [essen]: **Nahrung ~** to eat - 4. [Informationen] to take in; [Vorschlag] to take up - 5. [reagieren auf]: **etw mit Begeisterung ~** to receive sthg enthusiastically - 6. [beginnen - Gespräch, Arbeit, Verhandlungen] to start; [- Thema, Tätigkeit] to take up; **mit jm Kontakt ~** to contact sb - 7. [konkur-

rieren]: **es mit jm/etw ~ können** to be a match for sb/sthg - 8. [sich leihen - Kredit, Hypothek] to get, to obtain; [- Geld, Summe] to borrow - 9. [Foto] to take - 10. [auf Tonband] to record.

auf|opfern ◆ **sich aufopfern** ref: **sich für jn/etw ~** to sacrifice o.s. for sb/sthg.

auf|päppeln vt [nach Krankheit] to nurse back to health.

auf|passen vi to pay attention; **auf jn/etw ~** [Kind, Tasche] to keep an eye on sb/sthg; **auf Fehler ~** to watch out for mistakes; **pass bloß auf, wenn ich dich erwische!** just you wait until I catch you!

auf|platzen (perf ist aufgeplatzt) vi to burst (open).

Aufprall (pl -e) der impact.

auf|prallen (perf ist aufgeprallt) vi: **auf etw** (A) **~** to hit sthg.

Auf|preis der extra charge.

auf|pumpen vt to pump up.

Aufputsch|mittel das stimulant.

auf|quellen (perf ist aufgequollen) vi (unreg) to swell up.

auf|raffen ◆ **sich aufraffen** ref [sich entschließen]: **sich dazu ~, etw zu tun** to face up to doing sthg.

auf|ragen vi to rise up.

auf|räumen ◇ vt - 1. [ordnen] to tidy up - 2. [forträumen] to tidy away ◇ vi - 1. [ordnen] to tidy up - 2. [etw beenden]: **mit etw ~** to put an end to sthg.

auf|rechnen vt: **etw gegen etw ~** to compare sthg with sthg.

aufrecht ◇ adj - 1. [gerade] upright - 2. [Demokrat, Haltung] upstanding ◇ adv [gerade] upright.

aufrecht|erhalten vt (unreg) to maintain.

auf|regen vt [ärgern] to annoy; [beunruhigen] to upset. ◆ **sich aufregen** ref to get worked up; **sich über jn/etw ~** to get worked up about sb/sthg.

aufregend adj exciting.

Aufregung die excitement; **das schlechte Wahlergebnis versetzte die Partei in ~** the bad election result caused a great stir in the party.

aufreibend adj [anstrengend] exhausting.

auf|reißen (perf hat/ist aufgerissen) (unreg) ◇ vt (hat) - 1. [öffnen - Brief, Verpackung] to tear open; [- Tür, Fenster] to fling open; [- Mund, Augen] to open wide - 2. salopp [kennen lernen] to pick up ◇ vi (ist) [Naht] to split; [Wolkendecke] to break up.

aufreizend ◇ adj provocative ◇ adv provocatively.

auf|richten vt - 1. [hochziehen - Kranken] to sit up; [- Rücken] to straighten (up) - 2. [aufstellen] to erect - 3. [trösten] to lift. ◆ **sich aufrichten** ref [sich hochziehen] to sit up.

aufrichtig ⬦ *adj* sincere ⬦ *adv* sincerely.

Aufrichtigkeit *die (ohne pl)* sincerity.

auflrücken *(perf ist aufgerückt) vi* to move up; **zum Direktor ~** to be promoted to headmaster.

Auflruf *der* appeal.

auflrufen *vt (unreg)* - 1. [nennen, rufen] to call - 2. [auffordern]: **jn zu etw ~** to appeal to sb for sthg.

Aufruhr *(pl -e) der* - 1. [Aufstand] uprising - 2. [Unruhe] turmoil.

auflrunden *vt*: **~ (auf (+ A))** to round up (to).

auflrüsten *vi* to rearm; **wieder ~** to rearm.

Auflrüstung *die* rearmament.

aufs *präp* = auf + das.

auflsagen *vt* [Text] to recite.

auflsammeln *vt* to pick up.

aufsässig *adj* rebellious.

Auflsatz *der* - 1. [Schularbeit] essay *Br*, paper *Am* - 2. [Abhandlung] paper - 3. [Aufbau] upper section.

auflsaugen *vt* to soak up.

auflschauen *vi* - 1. [mit Bewunderung]: **zu jm ~** to look up to sb - 2. *Süddt* [aufblicken] to look up.

auflscheuchen *vt* - 1. [verscheuchen] to startle - 2. *fig* [stören] to disturb.

auflschieben *vt (unreg)* - 1. [verschieben] to put off - 2. [öffnen - Tür, Fenster] to slide open; [- Riegel] to slide back.

Auflschlag *der* - 1. [Aufprall] impact - 2. [auf den Preis] extra charge - 3. [am Hosenbein] turn-up *Br*, cuff *Am*; [am Ärmel] cuff - 4. SPORT serve; **er hat ~** it's his serve.

auflschlagen *(perf hat/ist aufgeschlagen) (unreg)* ⬦ *vt (hat)* - 1. [öffnen - Buch, Zeitung, Augen] to open - 2. [Ei, Schale] to crack (open); [Eis] to break - 3. [verletzen]: **sich das Knie ~** to cut one's knee - 4. [aufbauen - Bett, Zelt] to put up; [- Lager] to pitch - 5. [dazurechnen]: **etw auf etw** *(A)* **~** to add sthg onto sthg ⬦ *vi* - 1. *(ist)* [aufprallen]: **auf etw** *(A)* **~** to hit sthg - 2. *(hat)* SPORT to serve.

auflschließen *(unreg)* ⬦ *vt* to unlock ⬦ *vi* - 1. [öffnen]: **jm ~** to unlock the door for sb - 2. [nachrücken] to move up.

Auflschluss *der (ohne pl)*: **über etw** *(A)* **~ geben** to provide information about sthg.

aufschlussreich *adj* informative.

auflschneiden *(unreg)* ⬦ *vt* to cut open ⬦ *vi* [angeben] to boast.

Auflschnitt *der* sliced cold meat and/or cheese.

auflschrauben *vt* [Deckel] to unscrew; [Glas] to screw the lid off.

auflschrecken *(perf hat/ist aufgeschreckt)* ⬦ *vt (hat)* to startle ⬦ *vi (ist)* to start.

Auflschrei *der eigtl & fig* cry; **ein ~ ging durchs Volk** there was a public outcry.

auflschreiben *vt (unreg)* - 1. [notieren] to write down - 2. [Strafzettel geben] to book.

Auflschrift *die* inscription.

Auflschub *der* period of grace.

auflschütten *vt* - 1. [nachfüllen] to pour on - 2. [anhäufen - Damm, Wall] to build up.

Auflschwung *der* - 1. [Auftrieb] upturn; **sein Optimismus gab uns ~** his optimism gave us a lift - 2. SPORT swing-up.

auflsehen *vi (unreg)* [hochschauen] to look up; **zu jm ~** [bewundern] to look up to sb.

Aufsehen *das*: **~ erregen** to cause a stir; **~ erregend** sensational.

Aufseher, in *(mpl -; fpl -nen) der, die* [im Gefängnis] warder.

auf sein *(perf ist auf gewesen) vi (unreg) fam* - 1. [offen sein] to be open - 2. [wach sein] to be up.

auflsetzen ⬦ *vt* - 1. [gen] to put on - 2. [schreiben] to draft ⬦ *vi* [landen] to touch down. ➡ **sich aufsetzen** *ref* [sich aufrichten] to sit up.

Auflsicht *die (ohne pl)* - 1. [Kontrolle] supervision; **die ~ über jn/etw haben** to supervise sb/sthg - 2. [Person] supervisor.

auflsitzen *(perf hat/ist aufgesessen) vi (unreg)* - 1. *(ist)* [aufsteigen - auf Motorrad] to get on; [- Pferd] to mount - 2. *(ist)* [sich täuschen lassen]: **jm ~** to be taken in by sb - 3. *(hat)* [wach bleiben] to sit up.

auflspannen *vt* to put up.

auflsparen *vt*: **sich** *(D)* **etw ~** to save sthg.

auflsperren *vt* - 1. [aufschließen] to unlock - 2. [offen halten] to open wide.

auflspielen ➡ **sich aufspielen** *ref* [angeben] to give o.s. airs; **sich als Chef/Genie ~** to play the boss/genius.

auflspringen *(perf ist aufgesprungen) vi (unreg)* - 1. [aufstehen]: **~ (vor** *(+ D)*) to jump up (with) - 2. [sich öffnen - Blüte, Tür] to burst open; [- Haut, Hände] to chap - 3. [springen]: **auf etw** *(A)* **~** to jump onto sthg.

auflstacheln *vt*: **jn (zu etw) ~** to spur sb on (to sthg).

auflstampfen *vi*: **mit dem Fuß ~** to stamp one's foot.

Auflstand *der* uprising, rebellion.

aufständisch *adj* rebellious.

auflstauen *vt* to dam. ➡ **sich aufstauen** *ref* [Wasser] to collect; [Gefühle, Wut] to get bottled up.

auflstecken *vt* - 1. [hochstecken] to pin up - 2. *fam* [aufgeben, abbrechen] to give up.

auflstehen *(perf hat/ist aufgestanden) vi (unreg)* - 1. *(ist)* [sich erheben] to get up - 2. *(hat)* [offen stehen] to stand open.

auflsteigen *(perf ist aufgestiegen) vi (unreg)* - 1. [auf Motorrad, Fahrrad, Pferd] to get on; **auf etw** *(A)* **~** [Fahrrad, Pferd] to get on sthg - 2. [Bergsteiger, Hubschrauber, Ballon] to climb; [Vogel] to soar; **auf einen Berg ~** to climb a mountain - 3. [Rauch] to rise; [Nebel] to lift - 4. [Erfolg haben] to be promoted.

auf|stellen vt - 1. [hinstellen - Schachfiguren, Kegel, Lampe] to set up; [- Schild] to put up - 2. [aufbauen - Gerüst, Gitter] to put up - 3. [Liste, Plan] to draw up - 4. [Theorie, Behauptung] to put forward - 5. [auswählen] to select - 6. [Ohren] to prick up; [Stacheln] to raise. ◆ **sich aufstellen** ref - 1. [sich hinstellen] to take up one's position - 2. [sich aufrichten - Haare] to stand on end.

Auf|stellung die - 1. [Hinstellen - von Schachfiguren, Kegeln, Lampe] setting up; [- von Schild] putting up - 2. [Aufbau - von Gerüst, Gitter] putting up - 3. [von Liste, Plan] drawing up - 4. [von Theorie, Behauptung] putting forward - 5. [Wahl] selection.

Auf|stieg (pl -e) der - 1. [Aufsteigen] ascent - 2. [Erfolg] promotion.

auf|stocken vt - 1. [höher bauen] to raise the height of - 2. [vergrößern] to increase.

auf|stoßen (perf hat/ist aufgestoßen) (unreg) ⟨⟩ vt (hat) [öffnen] to push open ⟨⟩ vi - 1. (ist) [stoßen]: **mit etw auf etw** (D) ~ to hit sthg with sthg - 2. (hat) [rülpsen] to belch - 3. (ist) fam [unangenehm auffallen]: **sein Verhalten ist mir sauer** ODER **übel aufgestoßen** his behaviour left a nasty taste in my mouth.

aufstrebend adj up-and-coming.

auf|stützen vt to prop up. ◆ **sich aufstützen** ref to support o.s.

auf|suchen vt to go to.

Auf|takt der - 1. [Anfang] start - 2. MUS upbeat.

auf|tanken vt [Auto] to fill up; [Flugzeug] to refuel; **Benzin ~** to fill up with petrol Br ODER gas Am.

auf|tauchen (perf ist aufgetaucht) vi - 1. [aus dem Wasser] to surface - 2. [sichtbar werden] to appear - 3. [aufkommen] to arise - 4. [gefunden werden, ankommen] to turn up.

auf|tauen (perf hat/ist aufgetaut) vt (hat) vi (ist) [Lebensmittel] to defrost; [Boden, Eis] to thaw.

auf|teilen vt - 1. [verteilen] to share out - 2. [einteilen] to divide up; **etw in etw** (A) ~ to divide sthg up into sthg.

Auf|teilung die - 1. [Verteilung]: **~ (unter** (+D)) sharing out (amongst) - 2. [Einteilung]: **~ (in** (+A)) division (into).

auf|tischen vt - 1. [servieren] to serve up - 2. fam fig [erzählen] to come out with.

Auftrag (pl Aufträge) der - 1. [Befehl, Aufgabe] task; **jm einen ~ geben** ODER **erteilen** to give sb a task - 2. [Bestellung] order; **etw in ~ geben** [Untersuchung, Reparatur] to order sthg; [Studie, Gemälde] to commission sthg.

auf|tragen (unreg) ⟨⟩ vt - 1. [aufstreichen] to apply - 2. [bestellen]: **jm ~, etw zu tun** to tell sb to do sthg; **sie hat mir Grüße an dich aufgetragen** she asked me to pass on her regards to you - 3. [abtragen] to wear out ⟨⟩ vi: **dick ~** fam [übertreiben] to go over the top.

Auftraggeber, in (mpl -; fpl -nen) der, die [Kunde] client.

auf|treffen (perf ist aufgetroffen) vi (unreg) to land.

auf|treiben (perf hat aufgetrieben) vt (unreg) (hat) [finden] to find.

auf|treten (perf ist aufgetreten) vi (unreg) - 1. [treten] to tread - 2. [sich benehmen] to behave - 3. [erscheinen - Person] to appear; [- Problem, Gefahr, Frage] to arise.

Auftreten das - 1. [Benehmen] behaviour - 2. [Erscheinen] occurrence.

Auf|trieb der buoyancy; **jm/einer Sache ~ geben** fig to give sb/sthg a lift.

auf|tun (unreg) fam [finden] to come across. ◆ **sich auftun** ref eigtl & fig to open up.

auf|türmen vt to pile up. ◆ **sich auftürmen** ref [Masse, Probleme] to pile up; [Berge] to tower.

auf|wachen (perf ist aufgewacht) vi to wake up.

auf|wachsen ['aufvaksn] (perf ist aufgewachsen) vi (unreg) to grow up.

Aufwand der - 1. [Einsatz - von Geld] expenditure; **es ist mit viel ~ verbunden** it takes a lot of time/effort/etc - 2. [Luxus] extravagance.

aufwändig ⟨⟩ adj extravagant ⟨⟩ adv extravagantly.

auf|wärmen vt - 1. [warm machen] to warm up - 2. fam fig [wieder erwähnen] to bring up again. ◆ **sich aufwärmen** ref to warm o.s up.

aufwärts adv upwards; **von 50 cm³ ~** from 50 cm³ ODER upwards.

aufwärts gehen (perf ist aufwärts gegangen) vi (unreg): **mit den Verkaufszahlen geht es aufwärts** the sales figures are looking up.

auf|wecken vt to wake up.

auf|weisen vt (unreg) [zeigen] to show; **der Plan weist Mängel auf** the plan contains flaws.

auf|wenden vt [Geld, Zeit] to spend; [Energie, Kraft] to use (up).

aufwendig adj & adv = aufwändig.

auf|werfen vt (unreg) - 1. [anhäufen - Erde, Kies] to pile up - 2. [ansprechen] to raise.

auf|werten vt [Währung] to revalue; [Ansehen, Status] to enhance.

auf|wickeln vt to wind up.

auf|wiegeln vt abw to incite; **jn gegen jn ~** to stir sb up against sb.

Auf|wind der upcurrent; ~ **bekommen** fig to get a boost; ~ **haben** to be going strong.

auf|wirbeln vt & vi to swirl up.

auf|wischen vt to mop up.

auf|wühlen vt - **1.** [zerwühlen] to churn up - **2.** [erregen] to stir up.

auf|zählen vt to list.

Auf|zählung die list.

auf|zeichnen vt - **1.** [zeichnen] to draw - **2.** [aufnehmen] to record.

Aufzeichnung die [Aufnahme] recording. ➡ **Aufzeichnungen** pl [Notizen] notes; **sich** (D) ~**en machen** to take notes.

auf|ziehen (perf hat/ist aufgezogen) (unreg) ⬦ vt (hat) - **1.** [Uhr, Spielzeugauto] to wind up - **2.** [erziehen - Kind] to bring up; [- Tier] to raise - **3.** [öffnen] to open - **4.** [necken] to tease; **jn mit etw** ~ to tease sb about sthg - **5.** fam [organisieren - Geschäft, Arbeitsgruppe] to set up; [- Fest, Kampagne] to organize ⬦ vi (ist) [Gewitter] to brew; [Wolken] to mass.

Auf|zucht die rearing.

Auf|zug der - **1.** [Lift] lift Br, elevator Am - **2.** abw [Aufmachung] get-up - **3.** [Akt] act.

auf|zwingen vt (unreg): **jm etw** ~ to force sthg onto sb. ➡ **sich aufzwingen** ref: **der Gedanke zwingt sich regelrecht auf** the thought is unavoidable.

Auge (pl -n) das - **1.** [Sehorgan] eye; **ein blaues** ~ a black eye; **mit bloßem** ~ with the naked eye; **mit eigenen** ~**n gesehen haben** to have seen sthg with one's own eyes; **ihm wurde schwarz vor** ~**n** everything went black - **2.** [Würfelpunkt] dot - **3.** RW: **(große)** ~**n machen** to stare wide-eyed; **seinen** ~**n nicht trauen** not to believe one's eyes; **jn aus den** ~**n verlieren** to lose touch with sb; **ein** ~ **zudrücken** to turn a blind eye; **jn/etw im** ~ **behalten** to keep an eye on sb/sthg; **in meinen/seinen**/etc ~**n** as I see/he sees/etc it; **jn/etw mit anderen** ODER **neuen** ~**n sehen** to see sb/etw differently; **jn/etw nicht aus den** ~**n lassen** not to take one's eyes off sb/sthg; **unter vier** ~**n** in private; **etw vor** ~**n haben** to have sthg in mind.

Augen|arzt, ärztin der, die eye specialist, ophthalmologist.

Augen|blick der moment; **im** ~ at the moment; **jeden** ~ at any moment, any time.

augenblicklich ⬦ adj - **1.** [sofortig] immediate - **2.** [jetzig] current ⬦ adv - **1.** [umgehend] immediately - **2.** [jetzig] currently.

Augen|braue die eyebrow.

Augen|farbe die: **welche** ~ **hat sie?** what colour are her eyes?

Augen|höhe die: **in** ~ at eye level.

Augen|winkel der: **jn/etw aus den** ~**n beobachten** to watch sb/sthg out of the corner of one's eye.

Augen|zeuge, zeugin der, die eyewitness.

augenzwinkernd adv with an air of complicity.

August der August; siehe auch September.

Auktion [aʊk'tsioːn] (pl -en) die auction.

Aula (pl -s) die hall.

Aupair|mädchen, Au-pair-Mädchen [oˈpɛːrmɛːtçən] das au pair.

aus ⬦ präp (+ D) - **1.** [heraus] out of; ~ **dem Haus gehen** to go out of the house, to leave the house; **Rauch kam** ~ **dem Fenster** smoke was coming out of the window - **2.** [zur Angabe der Herkunft] from; ~ **Amerika** from America; **ein Lied** ~ **den 70er Jahren** a song from the seventies - **3.** [zur Angabe des Materials]: ~ **Plastik** made of plastic; **Möbel** ~ **Eschenholz** ash furniture - **4.** [zur Angabe der Zugehörigkeit]: **einer** ~ **der Gruppe** a member of the group - **5.** [zur Angabe der Entfernung] from; ~ **50 m Entfernung** from 50 m away - **6.** [zur Angabe des Grundes]: ~ **welchem Grund?** for what reason?, why?; ~ **Spaß** for fun; ~ **Habgier** from greed, out of greed ⬦ adv - **1.** [elliptisch]: **Licht** ~! lights out! - **2.** [zu Ende] over; ~ **und vorbei** all over.

Aus das end; **ins** ~ **gehen** SPORT to go out (of play).

aus|arbeiten vt [Plan, Liste, Vertrag] to draw up; [Methode, Vorschlag] to work out.

Ausarbeitung (pl -en) die [von Plan, Liste, Vertrag] drawing up; [von Methode, Vorschlag] working out.

aus|arten (perf ist ausgeartet) vi to degenerate; **in** (+ A) ODER **zu etw** ~ to degenerate into sthg.

aus|atmen vt & vi to breathe out.

aus|baden vt: **etw** ~ **müssen** to pay (the price) for sthg.

Aus|bau der - **1.** [Beseitigung] removal - **2.** [Erweiterung - von Netz, Haus] extension; [- von Dachboden] conversion; [- von Kenntnissen] expansion.

aus|bauen vt - **1.** [beseitigen] to remove - **2.** [erweitern - Netz, Haus] to extend; [- Dachboden] to convert; [- Kenntnisse] to expand; [- Kontakte] to intensify, to strengthen.

aus|bessern vt [Schaden, Zaun] to repair; [Kleidungsstück] to mend.

aus|beulen vt - **1.** [glätten] to beat out - **2.** [verformen] to make baggy.

Aus|beute die gain.

aus|beuten vt to exploit.

aus|bilden vt - **1.** [schulen] to train; **sich zu etw** ~ **lassen** to train to be sthg - **2.** [hervorbringen] to develop.

Ausbilder, in (mpl -; fpl -nen) der, die instructor (f instructress).

Aus|bildung die [beruflich, fachlich] training; [schulisch] education; **in der ~ sein** [beruflich, fachlich] to be a trainee; [schulisch] to be in education.

Ausbildungs|zeit *die* period of training, traineeship.

aus|bleiben (*perf* ist ausgeblieben) *vi* (*unreg*) - **1.** [Besserung, Katastrophe] to fail to materialize; [Gäste, Touristen] to fail to turn up; **das bleibt nicht aus** that's inevitable - **2.** [nicht nach Hause kommen] to stay out.

Aus|blick *der* view; **ein ~ auf etw** (A) *fig* a look ahead to sthg.

ausbooten *vt* to oust.

aus|brechen (*perf* hat/ist ausgebrochen) (*unreg*) <> *vi* (ist) - **1.** [Gefangene, Krieg, Panik, Epidemie] to break out; **aus etw ~** to break out of sthg - **2.** [verfallen]: **in Gelächter ~** to burst out laughing; **in Tränen ~** to burst into tears - **3.** [Auto] to spin out of control - **4.** [Vulkan] to erupt <> *vt* (hat) [herausbrechen] to break off.

aus|breiten *vt* to spread out; **etw über jm/etw ~** to spread sthg out over sb/sthg. → **sich ausbreiten** *ref* - **1.** [sich verbreiten] to spread - **2.** *fam* [sich breit machen] to spread o.s. out.

Aus|bruch *der* - **1.** [Flucht] break-out - **2.** [Beginn] outbreak; **nach einer Woche kam die Krankheit vollends zum ~** after a week the disease broke out fully - **3.** [von Vulkan] eruption - **4.** [Gefühlsäußerung] outburst.

aus|brüten *vt* eigtl & *fig* to hatch.

Aus|dauer *die* [Beharrungsvermögen] perseverance; SPORT stamina.

ausdauernd <> *adj* persevering; **ein ~er Läufer** a runner with a lot of stamina <> *adv* untiringly.

aus|dehnen *vt* - **1.** [Einzugsgebiet, Einfluss] to expand; [Gummiband] to extend; [Kleidungsstück] to lengthen - **2.** [zeitlich] to extend. → **sich ausdehnen** *ref* [Metall, Handel] to expand; [Feuer] to spread; [Weite] to stretch out; **sich auf etw** (A) **~** [Brand, Hysterie, Aktivitäten] to spread to sthg.

aus|denken *vt* (*unreg*): **sich** (D) **etw ~** [Geschichte, Plan] to think sthg up; [Geschenk] to think of sthg; **da musst du dir schon etwas anderes ~!** *fam* you'll have to do better than that!

Aus|druck (*pl* -drücke ODER -e) *der* - **1.** (*pl* Ausdrücke) [Formulierung] expression - **2.** (*ohne pl*) [Zeichen] expression; **einer Sache** (D) **~ geben** ODER **verleihen** *geh* to express sthg - **3.** (*pl* Ausdrucke) EDV printout.

aus|drucken *vt* EDV to print (out).

aus|drücken *vt* - **1.** [Orange, Schwamm, Saft] to squeeze - **2.** [Zigarette] to stub out - **3.** [aussprechen] to express; **etw mit einfachen Worten ~** to put sthg simply - **4.** [zeigen - Gefühle, Dank] to express, to show.

→ **sich ausdrücken** *ref* - **1.** [Person] to express o.s. - **2.** [Freude, Gier, Intoleranz] to reveal itself.

ausdrücklich <> *adj* explicit <> *adv* explicitly.

Ausdrucks|weise *die* way of expressing o.s.

auseinander *adv* apart; **auseinander! break it up!; die Schwestern sind sechs Jahre ~** there's six years between the two sisters.

auseinander fallen (*perf* ist auseinander gefallen) *vi* (*unreg*) to fall apart.

auseinander gehen (*perf* ist auseinander gegangen) *vi* (*unreg*) - **1.** [sich trennen - Gruppe] to break up; [- Wege] to diverge; [- Personen] to part - **2.** [Vorhang] to open - **3.** [Meinungen] to differ - **4.** [Ehe] to break up.

auseinander halten *vt* (*unreg*) to distinguish.

auseinander laufen (*perf* ist auseinander gelaufen) *vi* (*unreg*) - **1.** [Gruppe] to disperse - **2.** [Eis, Käse] to melt; [Farbe] to run.

auseinander leben → **sich auseinander leben** *ref* to drift apart.

auseinander nehmen *vt* (*unreg*) to dismantle.

auseinander setzen *vt*: **jm etw ~** to explain sthg to sb. → **sich auseinander setzen** *ref* - **1.** [sich beschäftigen]: **sich mit etw ~** to examine sthg - **2.** [sich streiten]: **sich mit jm ~** to argue with sb.

Auseinandersetzung (*pl* -en) *die* - **1.** [mit Thema]: **~ (mit)** examination (of) - **2.** [Streit] argument; [Debatte] debate.

aus|fahren (*perf* hat/ist ausgefahren) (*unreg*) <> *vt* (hat) - **1.** [spazieren fahren - im Rollstuhl, Kinderwagen] to take out for a walk - **2.** [ausklappen - Antenne] to extend; [- Fahrwerk] to lower - **3.** [liefern] to deliver - **4.** [sehr schnell fahren] to drive flat out <> *vi* (ist) - **1.** [spazieren fahren - im Rollstuhl, Kinderwagen] to go for a walk - **2.** [hinausfahren - Zug] to depart.

Aus|fahrt *die* - **1.** [Stelle] exit; **'~ freihalten!'** 'keep clear!' - **2.** [Auslaufen] departure.

aus|fallen (*perf* ist ausgefallen) *vi* (*unreg*) - **1.** [Haare, Zahn] to fall out - **2.** [nicht stattfinden] to be cancelled; [Fußballspiel] to be postponed - **3.** [Verdienst, Einnahme] to be lost - **4.** [Maschine] to break down; [Bremse, Signal] to fail - **5.** [Mitarbeiter] to be absent; [Athlet] to pull out - **6.** [sich erweisen]: **der Sieg fiel deutlich aus** it was a clear victory; **gut/schlecht ~** to turn out well/badly.

ausfallend *adj* abusive; **~ werden** to become abusive.

Ausfall|straße *die* arterial road.

aus|fegen <> *vt* to sweep out <> *vi* to sweep up.

aus|fertigen vt amt [Vertrag, Testament] to draw up; [Pass, Zeugnis, Rechnung] to issue.

ausfindig adv: **jn/etw ~ machen** to find sb/ sthg.

aus|fließen (perf ist ausgeflossen) vi (unreg) to leak.

Ausflucht (pl Ausflüchte) die excuse; **Ausflüchte machen** to make excuses.

Aus|flug der die; **einen ~ machen** ODER **unternehmen** to go on a trip.

Ausflugs|lokal das cafe or pub in the countryside to which you can drive or walk out.

Aus|fluss der - **1.** [im Waschbecken] plughole - **2.** [Ausfließen] leaking - **3.** MED discharge.

aus|fragen vt to interrogate.

aus|fressen vt (unreg): **er hat mal wieder etwas ausgefressen** fam he's been up to his tricks again.

Ausfuhr (pl -en) die - **1.** [Ware] export - **2.** [Tätigkeit] exporting.

aus|führen vt - **1.** [spazieren führen - Familie, Hund] to take for a walk - **2.** [exportieren] to export - **3.** [realisieren - Reparatur, Befehl, Plan] to carry out; [- Freistoß, Schritte] to take - **4.** [erklären] to explain.

ausführlich <> adj detailed <> adv in detail.

aus|füllen vt - **1.** [Formular, Antrag] to fill in ODER out; [Kreuzworträtsel] to do; [Scheck] to make out - **2.** [füllen] to fill (up) - **3.** [verbringen]: **seine Zeit mit etw ~** to spend one's time doing sthg - **4.** [zufrieden stellen] to fulfil.

Aus|gabe die - **1.** [Ausgeben] distribution; [von Befehl, Banknoten] issuing; [von Essen] serving - **2.** [von Geld] expenditure; **~n** expenditure (U) - **3.** [Edition] edition.

Aus|gang der - **1.** [von Gebäude] exit; [von Wald] edge; [von Ort] end - **2.** (ohne pl) [Ausgeherlaubnis] time off; [von Soldaten] pass - **3.** [Ende] outcome.

Ausgangs|lage die starting position.

Ausgangs|punkt der starting point.

Ausgangs|sperre die curfew.

aus|geben vt (unreg) - **1.** [verteilen] [Lebensmittel, Decken] to hand out; [Befehl, Banknoten] to issue; [Essen] to serve - **2.** [Geld] to spend - **3.** fam [zu Drink einladen]: **jm einen ~ to buy sb a drink - 4.** [bezeichnen]: **sich als jd/etw ~** to pretend to be sb/sthg; **jn/etw als** ODER **für jn/etw ~** to pass sb/sthg off as sb/ sthg.

ausgebucht adj fully booked.

ausgedient adj: **dieser Sessel hat nun ~ I/ we/**etc no longer have any use for this armchair.

ausgedörrt adj [Kehle, Erde] parched; [Pflanze] withered.

ausgefallen <> adj unusual <> adv unusually.

ausgeflippt adj fam weird, freaky.

ausgeglichen adj [Mensch, Persönlichkeit] balanced; [Spiel] even; [Klima] stable; [Leistung] steady.

aus|gehen (perf ist ausgegangen) vi (unreg) - **1.** [ins Kino, in die Disko] to go out - **2.** [verlöschen - Kerze, Lampe] to go out; [- Motor] to stop; [- Heizung, Computer] to go off - **3.** [enden] to end - **4.** [hervorgebracht werden]: **von jm ~** to come from sb - **5.** [zugrunde legen]: **von etw ~** to assume sthg; **davon ~, dass ... to** assume (that) ... - **6.** [ausfallen] to fall out - **7.** [zu Ende gehen] to run out; **mir gehen die Ideen aus** my ideas are running out ODER drying up.

ausgehungert adj starved.

ausgelassen <> adj exuberant <> adv exuberantly.

ausgelaugt adj worn-out.

ausgemergelt adj [Körper, Mensch] emaciated.

ausgenommen konj - **1.** [es sei denn] unless - **2.** [außer] except.

ausgeprägt <> adj pronounced <> adv particularly.

ausgerechnet adv: **~ heute** today of all days; **~ mir muss das passieren** it had to happen to me of all people.

ausgereift adj perfected.

ausgeschlossen adj out of the question.

ausgesprochen <> adj [Ähnlichkeit, Begabung] definite; [Abneigung, Vorliebe] marked; [Glück, Zufall] real <> adv extremely, really.

ausgestorben adj: **wie ~** dead, deserted.

ausgewachsen ['ausgevaksn] adj [erwachsen] fully-grown.

ausgewogen adj balanced.

ausgezeichnet <> adj excellent <> adv excellently.

ausgiebig <> adj [Beratungen, Untersuchungen] extensive; [Frühstück] large; [Spaziergang] long <> adv extensively; **~ frühstücken** to eat a large breakfast.

aus|gießen vt (unreg) to pour out.

Ausgleich (pl -e) der - **1.** [Gleichgewicht] balance; **er schafft sich einen ~ zu seiner Arbeit, indem er sich sportlich betätigt** he balances out his work by doing sport - **2.** [Wiedergutmachung] compensation; **zum** ODER **als ~ in return - 3.** SPORT equalizer.

aus|gleichen (unreg) <> vt [Unterschiede, Unregelmäßigkeiten] to even out; [Mängel, Ungerechtigkeit] to make up for; [Gegensätze] to reconcile; [Konflikt] to settle; [Konto] to balance <> vi SPORT to equalize. ◆ **sich ausgleichen** ref [Unterschiede] to even out; [Konto] to balance.

aus|graben vt (unreg) to dig up.

Aus|grabung die excavation, dig.

Ausguck (*pl* -e) *der* lookout (post).

Aus|guss *der* drain.

aus|haken *vt* to unhook.

aus|halten (*unreg*) ⋄ *vt* - **1.** [ertragen] to stand; **den Vergleich mit etw ~** to bear comparison with sthg; **mit ihr ist es nicht auszuhalten** she's unbearable - **2.** *abw* [bezahlen] to keep; **sich von jm ~ lassen** to be kept by sb ⋄ *vi* [durchhalten] to hold out.

aus|handeln *vt* to negotiate.

aus|händigen *vt* to hand over.

Aus|hang *der* notice.

aus|hängen ⋄ *vi* (*unreg*) [angeschlagen sein] to be up; **die Liste hängt am schwarzen Brett aus** the list is up on the noticeboard ⋄ *vt* (*reg*) - **1.** [anschlagen] to put up - **2.** [Tür] to take off its hinges.

Aushängeschild (*pl* -er) *das fig* advertisement.

aus|heben *vt* (*unreg*) - **1.** [ausschaufeln] to dig out - **2.** [aushängen] to take off its hinges - **3.** [Verbrechernest] to raid.

aus|hecken *vt* to think up.

aus|helfen *vi* (*unreg*) to help out.

Aus|hilfe *die* - **1.** [Aushelfen] assistance; **zur ~ arbeiten** to help out - **2.** [Aushilfskraft] temporary worker; [im Büro] temp.

Aushilfs|kraft *die* temporary worker; [im Büro] temp.

aushilfsweise *adv* on a temporary basis.

aus|höhlen *vt* [Stamm] to hollow out.

aus|holen *vi* - **1.** [mit dem Arm] to move one's arm back - **2.** [beim Erzählen]: **weit ~** to go back a long way.

aus|horchen *vt* to sound out.

aus|kennen ➡ **sich auskennen** *ref* to know one's way around; **sich in einer Stadt ~** to know one's way around a town; **sich mit Computers ~** to know a lot about computers.

aus|kippen *vt* to tip out.

aus|klammern *vt* [Thema] to leave aside.

aus|klappen *vt* to open out.

aus|klingen (*perf* hat/ist ausgeklungen) *vi* (*unreg*) (hat, ist) [Musik, Tag, Fest] to come to an end.

aus|klinken (*perf* hat/ist ausgeklinkt) ⋄ *vt* (hat) to release ⋄ *vi* (ist) to come free. ➡ **sich ausklinken** *ref* to come free.

aus|klopfen *vt* [Teppich] to beat; [Pfeife] to knock out; [Kleidungsstück] to dust down.

aus|knipsen *vt fam* to switch off.

aus|knobeln *vt* - **1.** *fam* [auslosen - mit Würfeln] to throw dice to decide - **2.** [ausklügeln] to work out.

aus|kommen (*perf* ist ausgekommen) *vi* (*unreg*) - **1.** [genug haben] to get by, to manage; **mit etw ~** [Proviant] to make sthg last; [Gehalt] to get by on sthg; [Hilfe] to manage with sthg, to get by with sthg - **2.** [sich vertragen] to get on; **mit jm gut/schlecht ~** to get on well/badly with sb; **mit jm nicht ~** not to get on with sb.

aus|kosten *vt geh* to enjoy to the full.

aus|kratzen *vt* [Schüssel] to scrape out.

aus|kundschaften *vt* to spy out.

Auskunft (*pl* Auskünfte) *die* - **1.** [Information] information (U); **eine ~ bekommen** to get some information - **2.** (*ohne pl*) [Auskunftsschalter] information desk; [Fernsprechauskunft] directory enquiries.

Auskunfts|schalter *der* information desk.

aus|kurieren *vt* to cure.

aus|lachen *vt* to laugh at.

aus|laden *vt* (*unreg*) - **1.** [entladen] to unload - **2.** [nach einer Einladung]: **jn ~** to tell sb not to come.

ausladend *adj* overhanging; [Hinterteil] protruding; [Bewegung] sweeping.

Aus|lage *die* display. ➡ **Auslagen** *pl* expenses.

Ausland *das* (*ohne pl*): **im ~** abroad; **ins ~** abroad.

Ausländer (*pl* -) *der* foreigner.

ausländerfeindlich ⋄ *adj* xenophobic ⋄ *adv*: **~ eingestellt sein** to be xenophobic.

Ausländerfeindlichkeit *die* (*ohne pl*) hostility to foreigners, xenophobia.

Ausländerin (*pl* -nen) *die* foreigner.

ausländisch *adj* foreign.

Auslands|gespräch *das* international call.

Auslands|korrespondent, in *der*, *die* foreign correspondent.

Auslands|reise *die* trip abroad.

aus|lassen *vt* (*unreg*) - **1.** [Absatz, Einzelheit] to leave out, to miss out; [Chance, Gelegenheit] to miss - **2.** [abreagieren]: **etw an jm ~** to take sthg out on sb. ➡ **sich auslassen** *ref fam* [sich äußern]: **sich über jn/etw ~** *abw* to bitch about sb/sthg.

aus|lasten *vt* - **1.** [Betrieb, Maschine] to run at full capacity - **2.** [beanspruchen] to keep fully occupied; **mit etw ausgelastet sein** to be kept fully occupied by sthg.

Auslauf *der* (*ohne pl*) room (to run about).

aus|laufen (*perf* ist ausgelaufen) *vi* (*unreg*) - **1.** [Tank, Fass] to leak - **2.** [Flüssigkeit] to leak out - **3.** [Schiff] to set sail - **4.** [Modell, Serie] to be discontinued - **5.** [Vertrag, Amtszeit] to expire.

aus|laugen *vt* - **1.** [Bestandteile entziehen]: **der Boden wurde völlig ausgelaugt** the soil was completely stripped of its nutrients - **2.** [erschöpfen] to wear out.

aus|lecken *vt* to lick out.

aus|leeren *vt* to empty; [Glas, Tasse, Flasche] to drain, to empty.

aus|legen *vt* - **1.** [Waren] to display; [Köder, Gift] to put down - **2.** [auskleiden]: **ein Zim-**

mer mit Teppich ~ to carpet a room; **einen Schrank (mit Papier)** ~ to line a cupboard (with paper) - **3.** [vorstrecken]: **jm etw** ~ to lend sb sthg - **4.** [interpretieren] to interpret; **sein Zögern wurde ihm als Ängstlichkeit ausgelegt** his hesitation was interpreted as fear.

aus|leiern (*perf* hat/ist ausgeleiert) *vt* (*hat*) *vi* (*ist*) [Kleidungsstück] to stretch.

Ausleihe (*pl* -n) *die* - **1.** (*ohne pl*) [Ausleihen] lending - **2.** [Ausleihstelle] issue desk.

aus|leihen *vt* (*unreg*): **jm etw** ~ to lend sb sthg; **sich** (*D*) **etw** ~ to borrow sthg.

Auslese *die* (*ohne pl*) - **1.** [Selektion] selection - **2.** [Wein] *quality wine made from specially selected grapes.*

aus|liefern *vt* - **1.** [Verbrecher]: **jn jm** ~ to hand sb over to sb - **2.** [liefern] to deliver.

aus|liegen *vi* (*unreg*) to be on display; [Gift, Köder] to be down.

aus|löschen *vt* - **1.** [löschen] to extinguish, to put out - **2.** [vernichten] to erase; [Spuren] to cover; [Bevölkerung] to annihilate.

aus|losen *vt* to draw lots for.

aus|lösen *vt* - **1.** [Alarm, Mechanismus] to set off, to trigger - **2.** [Krieg, Panik, Freude] to cause.

Auslöser (*pl* -) *der* - **1.** FOTO (shutter release) button - **2.** [Ursache] trigger.

aus|machen *vt* - **1.** [Radio, Licht, Motor] to turn off; [Zigarette] to put out - **2.** [vereinbaren - Treffen] to arrange; [- Termin] to make; **wir haben ausgemacht, nichts zu verraten** we agreed not to say anything; **ich habe mit ihr ausgemacht, dass wir ins Kino gehen** I arranged to go to the cinema with her - **3.** [stören]: **macht es Ihnen etwas aus, wenn ich rauche?** do you mind if I smoke?; **das macht ihm nichts aus** it doesn't matter to him - **4.** [betragen] to come to; **der Umweg hat eine Stunde ausgemacht** the diversion took an hour - **5.** [bedeuten]: **viel** ~ to make a big difference; **wenig** ~ not to make much difference - **6.** *geh* [erkennen] to make out - **7.** [bilden - Reiz] to be, to constitute.

aus|malen *vt* - **1.** [ausfüllen] to colour in - **2.** [schildern] to describe vividly - **3.** [sich vorstellen]: **sich** (*D*) **etw** ~ to imagine sthg.

Ausmaß *das* extent.

aus|merzen *vt* to eradicate; [Erinnerungen] to obliterate.

aus|messen *vt* (*unreg*) to measure.

aus|mustern *vt* - **1.** MIL: **wegen seines Herzfehlers wurde er ausgemustert** the army rejected him because of his bad heart - **2.** [aussondern] to take out of service; [abgetragene Kleidung] to sort out.

Ausnahme (*pl* -n) *die* exception; **mit ~ von** with the exception of; **eine ~ machen** to make an exception.

Ausnahmezustand *der*: **den ~ verhängen** to declare a state of emergency.

ausnahmslos *adv* without exception.

ausnahmsweise *adv*: ~ **dürfen die Kinder aufbleiben** the children can stay up just this once.

aus|nutzen, aus|nützen *vt* - **1.** [nutzen] to use, to make use of; [Gelegenheit, Vorteil] to use, to make the most of - **2.** [missbrauchen] to take advantage of, to exploit.

aus|packen <> *vt* to unpack; [Paket, Geschenk] to unwrap <> *vi fam* to spill the beans.

aus|plaudern *vt* to give away.

aus|pressen *vt* - **1.** [Frucht] to squeeze - **2.** [ausbeuten] to squeeze dry.

aus|probieren *vt* to try out.

Auspuff (*pl* -e) *der* exhaust.

aus|pumpen *vt* to pump out; **jm den Magen** ~ to pump sb's stomach out.

aus|quetschen *vt* - **1.** [auspressen] to squeeze - **2.** *fam* [ausfragen] to grill; **jn über etw** (*A*) ~ to grill sb about sthg.

aus|radieren *vt* - **1.** [durch Radieren] to rub out, to erase - **2.** *fig* [zerstören] to wipe out.

aus|rangieren *vt fam* [Kleidung, Möbel] to throw out; [Fahrzeug] to scrap.

aus|rauben *vt* [Person] to rob; [Geschäft] to loot.

aus|räumen *vt* - **1.** [entfernen, leeren] to clear out - **2.** *fam* [ausrauben] to clean out - **3.** [Missverständnis] to clear up; [Zweifel] to dispel.

aus|rechnen *vt* to calculate, to work out; **sich** (*D*) **etw** ~ to work sthg out for o.s.; **sie hatte sich gute Chancen ausgerechnet** she had fancied her chances.

Ausrede *die* excuse; **faule ~** *fam* feeble excuse.

aus|reden <> *vi* to finish speaking <> *vt*: **jm etw** ~ to talk sb out of sthg.

aus|reichen *vi* to be enough; **es muß bis März** ~ it has to last until March.

ausreichend <> *adj* - **1.** [genügend] sufficient; **eine ~e Anzahl von Teilnehmern** enough participants - **2.** SCHULE *mark 4 on a scale of 1 to 6, indicating a pass, but only just* <> *adv* sufficiently; **wir haben ~ für die Party eingekauft** we bought enough for the party.

Ausreise *die*: **bei der ~** on leaving the country.

Ausreisegenehmigung *die* exit visa.

aus|reisen (*perf* ist ausgereist) *vi*: **nach Deutschland** ~ to leave for Germany; **aus einem Land** ~ to leave a country.

aus|reißen (*perf* hat/ist ausgerissen) (*unreg*) <> *vi* (*ist*) *fam* to run away <> *vt* (*hat*) [Unkraut] to pull up.

aus|renken *vt:* **jm/sich** *(D)* **den Arm ~** to dislocate sb's/one's arm.

aus|richten *vt* - **1.** [übermitteln]: **jm etw ~** to tell sb sthg; **ich soll Ihnen Grüße von meiner Tante ~** my aunt sends her regards; **kann ich etwas ~?** can I take a message? - **2.** [erreichen] to achieve; **ich habe bei der Behörde nichts ~ können** I didn't get anywhere with the authorities - **3.** [Text] to align - **4.** [anpassen]: **etw auf jn/etw ~, etw nach jm/etw ~** to gear sthg towards sb/sthg.

aus|rotten *vt* [Rasse, Ungeziefer] to exterminate; [Aberglauben] to eradicate.

aus|rücken *(perf* ist ausgerückt*)* *vi* - **1.** MIL to move out - **2.** *fam* [weglaufen] to run away.

aus|rufen *vt (unreg)* - **1.** [rufen] to cry, to exclaim - **2.** [öffentlich] to announce; **jn ~ lassen** to page sb - **3.** [verkünden]: **einen Streik ~** to call a strike.

Ausrufe|zeichen, Ausrufungszeichen *das* exclamation mark.

aus|ruhen ⟨⟩ *vi* to rest ⟨⟩ *vt* to rest; **die Beine/die Arme ~** to rest one's legs/arms. ➡ **sich ausruhen** *ref* to rest, to have a rest.

aus|rüsten *vt* [Truppe] to equip; [Schiff] to fit out; **ein Auto mit einem Katalysator ~** to fit a car with a catalytic converter. ➡ **sich ausrüsten** *ref* to equip o.s.

Aus|rüstung *die* - **1.** [das Ausstatten - von Truppe] equipping; [- von Schiff] fitting out - **2.** [Ausstattung] equipment *(U).*

aus|rutschen *(perf* ist ausgerutscht*)* *vi* to slip; **das Messer ist ihr ausgerutscht** the knife slipped out of her hand.

Ausrutscher *(pl -) der* slip.

Aus|sage *die* - **1.** [Äußerung - vor Gericht] statement; **nach ~ eines Fachmanns** according to an expert - **2.** [Inhalt] message.

Aussagekraft *die* expressiveness.

aus|sagen ⟨⟩ *vt* - **1.** [ausdrücken]: **etw über jn/etw ~** to say sthg about sb/sthg, to reveal sthg about sb/sthg - **2.** [vor Gericht] to state ⟨⟩ *vi* to testify, to give evidence.

aus|schalten *vt* - **1.** [abstellen] to switch off, to turn off - **2.** [ausschließen] to eliminate.

Ausschau *die (ohne pl):* **nach jm/etw ~ halten** to look out for sb/sthg.

aus|schauen *vi* - **1.** [ausblicken]: **nach jm/etw ~** to look out for sb/sthg, to be on the lookout for sb/sthg - **2.** *Süddt & Österr* [aussehen] to look; **er schaut gut aus** he looks well; **es schaut mit jm/etw gut/schlecht aus** things are looking good/bad for sb/sthg.

aus|scheiden *(perf* hat/ist ausgeschieden*)* *(unreg)* ⟨⟩ *vi (ist)* - **1.** [aus Gruppe]: **aus etw ~** to leave sthg - **2.** [SPORT - verlieren] to get knocked out; [- wegen Verletzung] to pull out - **3.** [wegfallen] to be ruled out ⟨⟩ *vt (hat)* [Giftstoff] to reject; [Eiter] to secrete.

aus|schenken *vt* to serve.

aus|schildern *vt* to signpost.

aus|schlafen *vi (unreg)* to have a lie-in.

Aus|schlag *der* - **1.** [auf Haut] rash - **2.** [das Entscheidende]: **den ~ geben** to be the decisive factor.

aus|schlagen *(perf* hat/ist ausgeschlagen*)* *(unreg)* ⟨⟩ *vt (hat)* - **1.** [entfernen]: **er hat ihm einen Zahn ausgeschlagen** he knocked out one of his teeth - **2.** [ablehnen] to turn down ⟨⟩ *vi* - **1.** *(hat)* [treten] to kick out - **2.** *(hat, ist)* [Zeiger, Pendel] to swing - **3.** *(hat, ist)* [Pflanze, Baum] to produce leaves.

ausschlaggebend *adj* decisive.

aus|schließen *vt (unreg)* - **1.** [Grund, Erklärung, Möglichkeit] to rule out; [Irrtum] to prevent; [Zweifel, Unsicherheit] to remove - **2.** [ausstoßen]: **jn von etw ~** to expel sb from sthg - **3.** [aussperren] to lock out. ➡ **sich ausschließen** *ref* - **1.** [sich aussperren] to lock o.s. out - **2.** [sich fernhalten - Person] to rule o.s. out; **diese beiden Möglichkeiten schließen sich gegenseitig aus** these two possibilities rule each other out.

ausschließlich ⟨⟩ *adj* exclusive ⟨⟩ *adv* exclusively ⟨⟩ *präp (+ G)* excluding.

Aus|schluss *der* [von expulsion; **unter ~ der Öffentlichkeit** RECHT in camera.

aus|schmücken *vt* - **1.** [Raum] to decorate - **2.** [Geschichte] to embellish.

aus|schneiden *vt (unreg)* to cut out.

Aus|schnitt *der* - **1.** [Zeitungsausschnitt] cutting *Br,* clipping *Am* - **2.** [Halsausschnitt] neckline; **ein Kleid mit tiefem ~** a low-cut dress - **3.** [Auszug] excerpt; [eines Romans] excerpt, extract; [eines Films] clip, excerpt; [eines Bilds] detail.

aus|schöpfen *vt* - **1.** [Schüssel] to scoop out - **2.** *fig* [ausnutzen] to exhaust.

Aus|schreibung *die* [von Stelle, Wettbewerb] advertisement; [von Projekt] call for tenders.

Ausschreitungen *pl* violent clashes.

Aus|schuss *der* - **1.** [Gremium] committee - **2.** *(ohne pl)* [Ausschussware] rejects *(pl).*

aus|schütteln *vt* to shake out.

aus|schütten *vt* - **1.** [Gefäß] to empty; [Flüssigkeit] to pour out - **2.** [auszahlen] to pay out, to distribute.

ausschweifend *adj* [Fantasie] wild; [Leben] debauched.

aus|sehen *vi (unreg)* to look; **sie sieht gut aus** she looks good; **es sieht nach Regen aus** it looks like rain; **es sieht danach aus, als würden wir gewinnen** it looks like we will win, it looks as if we will win; **mit dem Zuschuss sieht es gut aus** things are looking good as far as the grant is concerned; **wie siehts aus?** *fam* how's things?; **sehe ich danach aus, als würde ich stehlen?** do I look as if I would steal?; **so siehst du aus!** *fam fig* you can think again!, nothing doing!

aus sein (*perf* ist aus gewesen) *vi* (*unreg*) - **1.** [zu Ende sein] to be over; **mit dem Trinken ist es aus** no more drinking for me; **es ist aus mit ihm** he's had it; **es ist aus zwischen ihnen** it is over between them - **2.** [nicht an sein] to be out - **3.** SPORT to be out - **4.** [erpicht sein]: **auf etw** (*A*) ~ *fam* to be after sthg; **sie ist darauf aus, mir etw zu verkaufen** she is out to sell me sthg.

außen *adv* outside; **von ~** from (the) outside; **nach ~** outwards.

Außen|handel *der* (*ohne pl*) foreign trade.

Außen|minister, in *der, die* foreign minister.

Außen|politik *die* (*ohne pl*) foreign policy.

Außen|seite *die* outside.

Außenseiter, in (*mpl* -; *fpl* -nen) *der, die* outsider.

Außenstehende (*pl* -n) *der, die* outsider.

Außen|welt *die* (*ohne pl*) outside world.

außer ◇ *präp* (+ *D*) - **1.** [außerhalb] out of; **~ Haus sein** to be away from home; **~ Atem sein** to be out of breath; **~ Betrieb** out of order; **~ sich sein (vor)** to be beside o.s. (with) - **2.** [abgesehen von] except (for), apart from; **alle ~ ihm** everyone except (for) him; **nichts ~ ...** nothing but ... - **3.** [zusätzlich] in addition to, as well as ◇ *konj* except; **ich komme, ~ es regnet** I'll come, unless it rains.

außerdem *adv* also; **es ist viel zu spät, ~ regnet es** it's far too late and it's raining too.

äußere *adj* - **1.** [Wand, Umstände] external; [Ähnlichkeit, Schein] outward - **2.** [auswärtig] foreign.

Äußere *das* (*ohne pl*) (outward) appearance.

außergewöhnlich ◇ *adj* - **1.** [ungewöhnlich] unusual - **2.** [sehr gut] exceptional ◇ *adv* exceptionally, remarkably.

außerhalb ◇ *präp* (+ *G*) outside; **~ der Stadt** outside town; **~ der Öffnungszeiten** outside opening hours ◇ *adv* [nicht im Stadtgebiet] out of town.

außerirdisch *adj* extraterrestrial.

äußerlich ◇ *adj* - **1.** [an der Außenseite] external - **2.** [nach außen hin] outward; [oberflächlich] superficial ◇ *adv*: **~ war sie ruhig** she was outwardly calm; **die Salbe ist ~ anzuwenden** the ointment is for external application; **~ betrachtet** on the face of it.

Äußerlichkeiten *pl* - **1.** [Umgangsform und Aussehen] appearances - **2.** [Unwesentliches] trivialities.

äußern *vt* to express. ◆ **sich äußern** *ref* - **1.** [seine Meinung sagen]: **sich über jn/etw ~** to give one's opinion on ODER about sb/sthg; **sich zu etw ~** to comment on sthg - **2.** [sich

zeigen]: **sich in etw** (*D*) ~ to reveal itself in sthg.

außerordentlich ◇ *adj* extraordinary ◇ *adv* extremely, extraordinarily; **der Film hat mir ~ gut gefallen** I thought the film was extremely good.

äußerst *adv* extremely.

außerstande, außer Stande *adj*: **zu etw ~ sein** to be incapable of sthg.

äußerste *adj* - **1.** [Ende] furthest; [Rand] outermost - **2.** [größte] extreme; **von ~r Dringlichkeit** of the utmost urgency, extremely urgent - **3.** [Termin] latest possible; [Preis, Angebot] final - **4.** [schlimmste] extreme.

Äußerung (*pl* -en) *die* [offizielle Aussage] statement; [Bemerkung] remark.

aus|setzen ◇ *vt* - **1.** [verlassen] to abandon - **2.** [versprechen] to offer - **3.** [ausliefern] to expose - **4.** [beanstanden]: **dieser Kunde fand an allem etwas auszusetzen** this customer found fault with everything ◇ *vi* [Herz] to stop; [Motor] to cut out; **sein Atem setzte kurzzeitig aus** he stopped breathing momentarily; **beim Spiel ~** to miss a go. ◆ **sich aussetzen** *ref*: **sich einer Sache** (*D*) ~ to expose o.s. to sthg.

Aussicht (*pl* -en) *die* - **1.** [Sicht] view - **2.** [Zukunftsperspektive] prospect; **sie hat eine Beförderung in ~** she's in line for promotion; **jm etw in ~ stellen** to promise sb sthg.

aussichtslos *adj* hopeless.

aussichtsreich *adj* [Vorhaben] promising; **ein ~er Kandidat** a candidate who stands a good chance of succeeding.

Aussichts|turm *der* lookout tower.

aus|söhnen *vt* to reconcile. ◆ **sich aussöhnen** *ref*: **sich mit sb/etw ~** to become reconciled with sb/to sthg.

aus|sortieren *vt* to sort out.

aus|spannen ◇ *vt* - **1.** [ausbreiten] to spread - **2.** *fam* [wegnehmen]: **jm die Freundin/den Freund ~** to pinch sb's girlfriend/boyfriend ◇ *vi* to relax.

aus|sperren *vt* to lock out.

aus|spielen *vt* - **1.** [einsetzen] to bring to bear - **2.** [im Sport] to outplay - **3.** [manipulieren]: **jn gegen jn ~** to play sb off against sb.

aus|spionieren *vt* - **1.** [Geheimnis, Versteck] to uncover - **2.** [Person] to spy on.

Aus|sprache *die* - **1.** [Artikulation] pronunciation; **eine gute/schlechte ~ haben** to have a good/bad accent - **2.** [Gespräch] discussion (*to resolve a dispute*).

aus|sprechen *vt* (*unreg*) - **1.** [artikulieren] to pronounce - **2.** [ausdrücken] to express; [Urteil, Strafe] to deliver. ◆ **sich aussprechen** *ref* - **1.** [sich äußern]: **sich über etw ausführlich ~** to say what's on one's mind about sthg - **2.** [Stellung nehmen]: **sich gegen/für**

jn/etw ~ to come out against/in favour of sb/sthg - **3.** [offen sprechen]: **sich mit jm ~ to** talk things through with sb.

aus|spucken <> *vi* to spit <> *vt* - **1.** [spucken] to spit out - **2.** *fam* [ausgeben, bezahlen] to cough up - **3.** *fam* [erbrechen] to puke up.

aus|spülen *vt* to rinse out.

aus|statten *vt* [mit Geräten] to equip; [mit Lebensmitteln, Kleidung, Geld] to provide.

Ausstattung (*pl* -en) *die* - **1.** [mit Möbeln] furnishing; [mit Geräten] equipping; [mit Lebensmitteln, Kleidung, Geld] provision - **2.** [Ausrüstung] equipment; [von Küche, Auto] fittings (*pl*) - **3.** [Einrichtung] furnishings (*pl*).

aus|stehen (*unreg*) <> *vt* to endure; **jn/etw nicht ~ können** *fam* not to be able to stand sb/sthg <> *vi* [Zahlung] to be outstanding; **die Antwort steht noch aus** we're still waiting for an answer.

aus|steigen (*perf* ist ausgestiegen) *vi* (*unreg*) - **1.** [herausateigen] to get out; **aus einem Bus/Zug** to get off a bus/train - **2.** *fam* [ausscheiden]: **aus einem Geschäft ~** to pull out of a deal - **3.** [aus Gesellschaft] to drop out (from society).

Aussteiger, in (*mpl* -; *fpl* -nen) *der, die* drop-out.

aus|stellen *vt* - **1.** [zeigen - Waren] to display; [- Kunstwerke] to exhibit - **2.** [ausfertigen - Scheck, Rezept] to make out; [- Visum] to issue; **einen Scheck auf jn ~** to make out a cheque to sb - **3.** [ausschalten] to turn off.

Aus|stellung *die* exhibition.

aus|sterben (*perf* ist ausgestorben) *vi* (*unreg*) [Tierart] to become extinct; [Tradition] to die out.

Aus|steuer *die* dowry.

Ausstieg (*pl* -e) *der* - **1.** [Öffnung] exit - **2.** (*ohne pl*) [Rückzug]: **sie haben den ~ aus der Kernenergie beschlossen** they have decided to abandon nuclear energy.

aus|stoßen *vt* (*unreg*) - **1.** [ausschließen] to expel - **2.** [hervorstoßen - Schrei] to give; [- Seufzer] to heave; [- Fluch] to utter - **3.** [produzieren] to emit.

aus|strahlen <> *vt* - **1.** [verbreiten] to radiate - **2.** [senden] to broadcast <> *vi* [strahlen - Licht] to shine.

Aus|strahlung *die* - **1.** [Wirkung] charisma - **2.** [Senden] broadcasting.

aus|strecken *vt* [Zunge] to stick out; [Fühler] to put out; **die Beine/Arme ~** to stretch one's legs/arms. <> **sich ausstrecken** *ref* to stretch out.

aus|suchen *vt* to choose; **sich** (*D*) **etw ~ to** choose sthg.

Austausch *der* exchange; [von Spielern] substitution.

austauschbar *adj* interchangeable.

aus|tauschen *vt* - **1.** [mitteilen] to exchange - **2.** [auswechseln] to replace; **einen Spieler (gegen einen anderen) ~** to substitute a player (with another).

aus|teilen *vt* [Prospekte] to hand out; [Karten] to deal (out); [Essen] to dish out.

Auster (*pl* -n) *die* oyster.

aus|toben *vt*: **seine Wut an jm ~** to vent one's fury on sb. <> **sich austoben** *ref* to let off steam.

aus|tragen *vt* (*unreg*) - **1.** [Zeitung, Post] to deliver - **2.** [ausfechten]: **einen Streit mit jm ~** to have it out with sb - **3.** [Wettkampf] to hold - **4.** [im Mutterleib] to carry to term. <> **sich austragen** *ref* to sign out.

Australien *nt* Australia.

Australier, in [aus'tra:lie, rin] (*mpl* -; *fpl* -nen) *der, die* Australian.

australisch *adj* Australian.

aus|treiben *vt* (*unreg*) - **1.** [verbannen] to exorcize - **2.** [abgewöhnen]: **jm etw ~** to cure sb of sthg.

aus|treten (*perf* hat/ist ausgetreten) (*unreg*) <> *vt* (*hat*) - **1.** [ersticken - Funken] to stamp out; [- Zigarette] to tread out - **2.** [abnutzen] to wear down - **3.** [weiten] to break in <> *vi* (*ist*) - **1.** [ausscheiden]: **aus etw ~** to leave sthg - **2.** [zur Toilette gehen] to answer the call of nature.

aus|trinken (*unreg*) <> *vt* [Kaffee, Bier] to drink up, to finish; [Glas] to drain, to finish <> *vi* to drink up.

Austritt *der* [aus Partei] resignation; **die Kirche hat zahlreiche ~e zu verzeichnen** a lot of people have left the Church.

aus|trocknen (*perf* hat/ist ausgetrocknet) *vt* (*hat*) & *vi* (*ist*) [Haut, Brot, Boden] to dry out; [See] to dry up.

aus|tüfteln *vt* to work out.

aus|üben *vt* [Beruf] to practise; [Amt] to hold; [Einfluss, Druck] to exert; [Macht] to exercise, to wield.

aus|ufern (*perf* ist ausgeufert) *vi* to get out of hand.

Aus|verkauf *der* sale.

ausverkauft *adj* sold out.

Aus|wahl *die* - **1.** (*ohne pl*) [Wahl] choice - **2.** [Auslese] selection - **3.** [Sortiment] range.

aus|wählen *vt* to choose, to select.

aus|walzen *vt* - **1.** [walzen] to roll out - **2.** *abw* [breittreten] to drag out.

aus|wandern (*perf* ist ausgewandert) *vi* to emigrate.

Auswanderung *die* (*ohne pl*) emigration.

auswärtig *adj* - **1.** [extern] external - **2.** [aus einem anderen Ort] from another town; [Mannschaft] away (*vor Subst*) - **3.** [außenpolitisch] foreign.

Auswärtige Amt *das* foreign ministry.

auswärts *adv* [spielen, übernachten] away from home; ~ **essen** to eat out.

aus|waschen *vt (unreg)* [Fleck] to wash out; [Kleidungsstück] to wash; [Pinsel] to rinse.

aus|wechseln ['ausvɛksln] *vt* [Reifen, Batterien] to replace; [Spieler] to substitute; **wie ausgewechselt sein** to be a different person.

Aus|weg *der* way out.

ausweglos *adj* hopeless.

aus|weichen *(perf* ist ausgewichen) *vi (unreg)* **- 1.** (+ D) [Fußgänger, Hindernis] to avoid; [Schlag] to dodge; [Auto] to get out of the way of **- 2.** (+ D) [Frage, Entscheidung, Blick] to avoid **- 3.** [zurückgreifen]: **auf etw** (A) ~ to switch to sthg.

ausweichend *adj* evasive.

aus|weinen   **sich ausweinen** *ref:* **sich bei jm** ~ to cry on sb's shoulder.

Ausweis *(pl -e) der* [Personalausweis] identity card; [von Mitglied] membership card; [Zugangsberechtigung] pass.

aus|weisen *vt (unreg)* **- 1.** [verbannen] to deport, to expel **- 2.** [erkennen lassen]: **jn als etw** ~ to identify sb as sthg.   **sich ausweisen** *ref* to show one's identification.

Ausweis|kontrolle *die* identity card check.

Ausweispapiere *pl* papers, identification *(U).*

Ausweitung *(pl -en) die* **- 1.** [Vergrößerung] expansion **- 2.** [eines Streiks] spreading.

auswendig *adv* by heart; **etw** ~ **wissen** ODER **können** to know sthg by heart.

Aus|wertung *die* evaluation.

Aus|wirkung *die* effect, impact; **die** ~ **auf jn/etw** the effect ODER impact on sb/sthg.

aus|wringen *(prät* wrang aus; *perf* ausgewrungen) *vt (unreg)* to wring out.

Auswuchs ['ausvuːks] *der*   **Auswüchse** *pl* excesses.

aus|zahlen *vt* **- 1.** [Gehalt, Lohn] to pay **- 2.** [Teilhaber] to buy out; [Arbeiter] to pay off.   **sich auszahlen** *ref* to pay off.

aus|zählen *vt* to count up.

aus|zeichnen *vt* **- 1.** [mit Preisschild] to price **- 2.** [ehren]: **jm mit einem Preis** ~ to award a prize to sb **- 3.** [charakterisieren]: **große Biegsamkeit zeichnet diesen Werkstoff aus** this material is characterized by its great flexibility.   **sich auszeichnen** *ref* [Person] to distinguish o.s.; [Produkt] to stand out.

aus|ziehen *(perf* hat/ist ausgezogen) *(unreg)* *vt (hat)* **- 1.** [ablegen] to take off; **die Jacke** ~ to take off one's jacket **- 2.** [entkleiden] to undress **- 3.** [vergrößern - Tisch, Antenne] to pull out **- 4.** [herausziehen] to pull out *vi (ist)* [umziehen] to move out.   **sich ausziehen** *ref* to undress; **sich die Schuhe** ~ to take one's shoes off.

Auszubildende *(pl -n) der, die* trainee.

Aus|zug *der* **- 1.** [Ausschnitt] excerpt **- 2.** [Kontoauszug] statement **- 3.** [Umzug] move.

auszugsweise *adv:* **ein Roman** ~ **abdrucken** to publish a novel in instalments.

Auto *(pl -s) das* car; **mit dem** ~ **fahren** to go by car, to drive.

Auto|atlas *der* road atlas.

Auto|bahn *die* motorway *Br,* freeway *Am.*

Autobahn

At over 11,000 km, the German motorway network, construction of which began in the prewar era, is the second longest in the world after the United States. There is no speed limit on German motorways, although there is a recommended limit of 130 km/h. No toll is charged for using the motorway.

Autobahn|gebühr *die* toll.

Autobahn|kreuz *das* interchange.

Autobahn|meisterei *(pl -en) die* motorway *Br* ODER freeway *Am* maintenance department.

Auto|bus *der* bus.

Auto|fahrer, in *der, die* (car) driver.

autogene Training *das* autogenics *(U), relaxation technique based on self-hypnosis, developed by German neurologist J.H. Schultz.*

Auto|gramm *das* autograph.

Automat *(pl -en) der* [für Getränke, Zigaretten] vending machine.

Automatik *(pl -en) die* automatic mechanism.

Automatik|getriebe *das* automatic transmission.

automatisch *adj* automatic *adv* automatically.

automatisieren *vt* to automate.

Autonomie *(pl -n) die* autonomy.

Autor *(pl -toren) der* author.

Auto|radio *das* car radio.

Auto|rennen *das* **- 1.** [Sportart] motor racing **- 2.** [Wettkampf] motor race.

Autorin *(pl -nen) die* author.

autoritär *adj* authoritarian.

Autorität *(pl -en) die* authority.

Auto|unfall *der* car accident.

Auto|verkehr *der* car traffic.

avantgardistisch [avɑ̃ˈgardɪstɪʃ] *adj* avant-garde.

Avocado [avoˈkaːdo] *(pl -s) die* avocado.

Axt *(pl* Äxte) *die* axe.

Azalee *(pl -n) die* azalea.

Azubi *(pl -s) der, die fam* trainee.

B

b, B [be:] (*pl* - ODER -s) *das* - **1.** [Buchstabe] b, B - **2.** [MUS - Note] B flat; [- Vorzeichen] flat.
➤ **B** (*abk für* Bundesstraße) *die* ≃ A road *Br,* ≃ state highway *Am.*

Baby ['be:bi] (*pl* -s) *das* baby.

Baby|sitter, in ['be:bisitɐ, rɪn] (*mpl* -; *fpl* -nen) *der, die* babysitter.

Bach (*pl* Bäche) *der* stream; **den ~ runterge-hen** *fam* to go down the tubes.

Backbord *das* (*ohne pl*) SCHIFF port.

Backe (*pl* -n) *die* [Wange, von Po] cheek.

backen (*präs* bäckt ODER backt; *prät* backte ODER buk; *perf* hat gebacken) <> *vt* - **1.** [im Ofen] to bake - **2.** [braten] to fry <> *vi* to bake.

Backen|zahn *der* molar.

Bäcker (*pl* -) *der* baker.

Bäckerei (*pl* -en) *die* bakery.

Bäckerin (*pl* -nen) *die* baker.

Back|form *die* baking tin.

Back|ofen *der* oven.

Back|pulver *das* baking powder.

Back|stein *der* brick; **ein Gebäude aus ~** a brick building.

bäckt *präs* ➤ backen.

Bad (*pl* Bäder) *das* - **1.** [Badezimmer] bathroom - **2.** [Baden - im Meer] bathing (*U*); [- in der Wanne] bath; **ein ~ in der Menge neh-men** *fig* to press the flesh - **3.** [Schwimmbad] (swimming) pool - **4.** [Kurort] spa town.

Bade|anzug *der* swimming costume, swimsuit.

Bade|hose *die* swimming trunks (*pl*).

Bade|kappe *die* swimming cap.

Bade|mantel *der* bathrobe.

Bade|meister, in *der, die* [im Schwimm-bad] pool attendant; [am Strand] lifeguard.

baden <> *vt* [Kind] to bath *Br,* to bathe *Am;* [Wunde] to bathe <> *vi* - **1.** [in der Wanne] to have a bath - **2.** [schwimmen] to swim; **~ ge-hen** to go for a swim; **wenn das passiert, werde ich bei** ODER **mit meinen Plänen ~ ge-hen** *fam* if that happens, I can kiss my plans goodbye. ➤ **sich baden** *ref* to have a bath.

Bade|wanne *die* bath (tub).

Bade|zimmer *das* bathroom.

baff *adj:* **(ganz) ~ sein** *fam* to be gob-smacked.

Bafög ['ba:fœk] (*abk für* Bundesausbil-dungsförderungsgesetz) *das* [Stipendium] maintenance which is half grant and half loan awarded to students and trainees by the State; **~ bekommen** to get a grant.

Bagger (*pl* -) *der* mechanical digger.

baggern <> *vt* [Graben] to dig; [Fahrrinne] to dredge <> *vi fam* [Mädchen anmachen]: **er baggert schon wieder** he's on the pull again.

Bahn (*pl* -en) *die* - **1.** [Eisenbahn] train; **mit der ~ fahren** to travel by train ODER rail - **2.** [Institution] railway *Br,* railroad *Am;* **die ~** [Deutsche Bahn] German rail company; **bei der ~ arbeiten** to work for the railways - **3.** [Weg] path; **wir haben freie ~** AUTO the road is clear, *fig* the way is clear - **4.** [von Rakete, Planet] path - **5.** SPORT [in Schwimmbad, Stadion] lane; **40 ~en schwimmen** to swim 40 lengths - **6.** [Straßenbahn] tram *Br,* street-car *Am* - **7.** [Streifen - von Stoff] length; [- von Tapete] strip - **8.** RW: **auf die schiefe ~ gera-ten** to fall into bad ways; **jn aus der ~ werfen** to shatter sb.

bahnbrechend *adj* pioneering.

BahnCard® ['ba:nka:d] (*pl* -s) *die* card offering 50% discount on German rail fares.

Bahn|damm *der* railway embankment.

bahnen *vt:* **jm/sich einen Weg ~** to clear a path for sb/o.s.

Bahn|hof *der* (railway) station.

Bahn|steig (*pl* -e) *der* platform.

Bahnsteig|kante *die* platform edge.

Bahn|über|gang *der* level crossing *Br,* grade crossing *Am.*

Bahre (*pl* -n) *die* - **1.** [für Kranke] stretcher - **2.** [für Tote] bier.

Baiser [bɛˈze:] (*pl* -s) *das* meringue.

Bakterien *pl* bacteria, germs.

Balance [baˈlãsə] *die* balance.

balancieren [balãˈsi:rən] (*perf* hat/ist ba-lanciert) *vt* (*hat*) & *vi* (*ist*) to balance.

bald *adv* - **1.** [in Kürze, schnell] soon - **2.** *fam* [fast] almost, nearly - **3.** *fam* [endlich]: **hältst du jetzt ~ den Mund?** just shut up, will you? ➤ **bis bald** *interj* see you soon ODER later!

Baldrian (*pl* -e) *der* valerian.

balgen *vi* to tussle. ➤ **sich balgen** *ref:* **sich (mit jm um etw) ~** to tussle (with sb over sth).

Balkan *der:* **der ~ the** Balkans.

Balken (*pl* -) *der* beam.

Balkon [balˈkɔŋ, balˈko:n] (*pl* -s ODER -e) *der* balcony.

Ball (*pl* Bälle) *der* ball; **am ~ bleiben** [nicht aufhören] to stick at it; [auf dem Laufenden bleiben] to keep up to date.

Ballade (*pl* -n) *die* ballad.

Ballast *der* ballast.

Ballaststoffe *pl* roughage (*U*).

ballen *vt:* **die Faust ~** to clench one's fist. ➤ **sich ballen** *ref* [Schnee, Lehm]: **sich zu etw ~** to form into sth.

Ballen (pl -) der - **1.** [Packen] bale - **2.** [von Hand] ball of the hand; [von Fuß] ball of the foot.

ballern fam ◇ vi - **1.** [schießen] to spray bullets - **2.** [schlagen]: **gegen an etw** (A) ~ **to hammer on sthg** ◇ vt - **1.** [ohrfeigen]: **jm eine/ein paar** ~ to sock sb one - **2.** [werfen]: **etw gegen etw** ~ to smash sthg against sthg.

Ballett (pl -e) das ballet; **ins** ~ **gehen** to go to the ballet.

Ballon [ba'lɔŋ] (pl -s) der balloon.

Ball|spiel das ball game.

Ballungs|gebiet das, **-raum** der conurbation.

Balsam der eigtl & fig balm.

Balte (pl -n) der native/inhabitant of the Baltic.

Baltikum das: **das** ~ the Baltic.

Baltin (pl -nen) die native/inhabitant of the Baltic.

baltisch adj Baltic.

balzen vi to perform a courtship display.

Bambus (pl -se) der bamboo.

banal ◇ adj banal ◇ adv banally.

Banane (pl -n) die banana.

Bananen|republik die abw banana republic.

Banause (pl -n) der abw philistine.

Banausin (pl -nen) die abw philistine.

Band¹ [bant] (pl Bänder ODER Bände) ◇ das (pl Bänder) - **1.** [aus Stoff] band; [als Zierde] ribbon - **2.** [Tonband] tape; **etw auf** ~ **aufnehmen** to tape sthg - **3.** [Fließband] conveyor belt; **am laufenden** ~ fig continuously - **4.** [aus Bindegewebe] ligament ◇ der (pl Bände) [Buch] volume; **das spricht Bände** fig that speaks volumes.

Band² [bɛnt] (pl -s) die band.

Bandage [ban'da:ʒə] (pl -n) die [Verband] bandage.

bandagieren [banda'ʒi:rən] vt to bandage.

Band|breite die - **1.** ELEKTR bandwidth - **2.** fig [Vielzahl] range.

Bande (pl -n) die - **1.** [von Verbrechern, Kindern] gang - **2.** [SPORT - von Bahn, Spielfeld] barrier; [- von Billardtisch] cushion.

bändigen vt [Tier] to tame; [Kind] to control.

Bandit (pl -en) der bandit.

Band|maß das tape measure.

Band|nudeln pl tagliatelle (U).

Band|scheibe die ANAT disc.

Band|wurm der - **1.** [Wurm] tapeworm - **2.** fig [Gebilde]: **dieser Satz ist ein** ~ this sentence is never-ending.

bange adj anxious; **mir ist/wird** ~ I am/I'm getting worried.

Bange die: **keine** ~! don't worry!

Bank (pl Bänke ODER -en) die - **1.** (pl Bänke) [in Park, Schule] bench; [in Kirche] pew; **etw auf**

die lange ~ **schieben** fig to put sthg off - **2.** (pl Banken) [Geldinstitut] bank.

Bank|anweisung die banker's order.

Bankett (pl -e) das banquet.

Bank|geheimnis das banking confidentiality.

Bankier [baŋ'kje:] (pl -s) der banker.

Bank|konto das bank account.

Bank|leit|zahl die bank sort code.

Bank|note die banknote.

Bank|raub der bank robbery; **einen** ~ **verüben** to rob a bank.

Bank|räuber, in der, die bank robber.

bankrott adj bankrupt.

Bankrott (pl -e) der bankruptcy; ~ **gehen** to go bankrupt.

Bank|überfall der bank raid.

Bank|verbindung die account details (pl).

bannen vt - **1.** [fesseln] to hold spellbound - **2.** [Gefahr] to ward off; [bösen Geist] to exorcize.

Banner (pl -) das banner.

Baptist, in (mpl -en; fpl -nen) der, die Baptist.

bar ◇ adj - **1.** [mit Bargeld] cash; ~**es Geld** cash - **2.** [pur - Zufall] pure; [- Unsinn] sheer ◇ adv [in Bargeld] (in) cash. ➡ **gegen bar** adv [verkaufen] for cash. ➡ **in bar** adv in cash.

Bar (pl -s) die - **1.** [Nachtlokal] bar (often also a brothel) - **2.** [Theke] bar.

Bär (pl -en) der the bear; **jm einen** ~**en aufbinden** fig to pull sb's leg.

Baracke (pl -n) die hut.

Barbar, in (mpl -en; fpl -nen) der, die barbarian.

barbarisch ◇ adj barbaric ◇ adv barbarically.

barfuß adv barefoot.

barg prät ▷ bergen.

Bar|geld das cash.

bargeldlos ◇ adj cashless ◇ adv: ~ **zahlen** to use a cashless payment method.

Bariton (pl -s) der baritone.

Barkeeper ['ba:ɐ̯ki:pɐ] (pl -) der barman.

barock adj baroque.

Barock der ODER das (ohne pl) baroque period.

Barometer das barometer.

Baron [ba'ro:n] (pl -e) der baron.

Baronesse [baro'nes(ə)] (pl -n) die daughter of a baron.

Baronin [ba'ro:nɪn] (pl -nen) die baroness.

Barrel ['bɛral] (pl -s ODER -) das barrel.

Barren (pl -) der - **1.** [Block] bar - **2.** [Turngerät] parallel bars (pl).

Barriere [ba'rje:rə] (pl -n) die barrier.

Barrikade (pl -n) die barricade; **sie ging auf die** ~**n** fig she was up in arms.

barsch (superl barsch(e)ste) ◇ adj curt ◇ adv curtly.

Barsch *(pl -e) der* [Fisch] perch.

Bar|scheck *der* uncrossed cheque.

Bart *(pl* Bärte*) der* - **1.** [Gesichtshaar] beard - **2.** [Schlüsselbart] bit - **3.** *RW:* **jm um den ~ gehen** ODER **streichen** to butter sb up.

bärtig *adj* bearded.

Bar|zahlung *die* payment in cash.

Basar, Bazar *(pl -e) der* bazaar.

Basel *nt* Basel, Basle.

basieren *vi:* **auf etw** *(D)* **~** to be based on sthg.

Basilikum *das* basil.

Basis *(pl* Basen*) die* - **1.** [Grundlage] basis - **2.** MIL base - **3.** POL grass roots *(pl);* **an der ~ arbeiten** to work at grass-roots level.

Baske *(pl -n) der* Basque.

Baskenland *das:* **das ~** the Basque Country.

Basket|ball ['ba:skətbal] *der* basketball.

Baskin *(pl -nen) die* Basque.

baskisch *adj* Basque.

Bass *(pl* Bässe*) der* - **1.** [Stimme, Sänger] bass - **2.** [Kontrabass] double bass; [Bassgitarre] bass (guitar).

Bassist, in *(mpl -en; fpl -nen) der, die* - **1.** [im Orchester] double bass player; [in Rockgruppe] bass player, bass guitarist - **2.** [Sänger] bass.

Bass|schlüssel *der* MUS bass clef.

Bast *der* raffia.

Bastelei *(pl -en) die* - **1.** [Basteln] handicrafts *(pl)* - **2.** [Reparaturversuche]: **er hat genug von der ewigen ~** he's had enough of tinkering around all the time.

basteln ⟨⟩ *vt* to make; **Weihnachtsgeschenke ~** to make one's own Christmas presents ⟨⟩ *vi* to do handicrafts; **sie bastelt gerne** she likes making things herself; **an etw** *(D)* **~** to tinker with sthg.

Bastler, in *(mpl -; fpl -nen) der, die* handicrafts enthusiast.

BAT [be:'a:'te:] *(abk für Bundesangestelltentarif) der statutory salary scale for public employees.*

Batterie *(pl -n) die* - **1.** [Stromspeicher] battery - **2.** [große Menge] array.

batteriebetrieben *adj* battery-powered.

Batzen *(pl -) der fam:* **das hat mich einen ~ Geld gekostet** that cost me a packet.

Bau *(pl -ten* ODER *-e) der* - **1.** [das Bauen] construction; **in** ODER **im ~ sein** to be under construction - **2.** *(ohne plural)* [Baustelle] building site - **3.** *(pl* Bauten*)* [Gebäude] building - **4.** *(pl Baue)* [von Kaninchen] burrow; [von Fuchs] den; [von Dachs] set.

Bau|arbeiten *pl* construction work *(U).*

Bau|arbeiter, in *der, die* construction worker.

Bauch *(pl* Bäuche*) der* stomach; **sich** *(D)* **den ~ voll schlagen** *fam* to stuff o.s. ODER one's

face; **mit etw auf den ~ fallen** *fig* to make a botch ODER mess of sthg.

bauchig *adj* bulbous.

Bauch|nabel *der* navel.

Bauch|schmerzen ['bauxʃmɛrtsn] *pl* stomachache *(U).*

Bau|denkmal *das* listed building.

bauen ⟨⟩ *vt* - **1.** [anlegen, errichten] to build - **2.** [herstellen] to make; [Auto, Flugzeug] to build, to make - **3.** *fam* [verursachen - Unfall] to cause; **Mist ~** to mess up ⟨⟩ *vi* - **1.** [arbeiten, bauen lassen] to build; **an etw** *(D)* **~** to be building sthg - **2.** [vertrauen]: **auf jn/etw ~** to rely on sb/sthg.

Bauer *(pl -n* ODER *-) ⟨⟩ der (pl Bauern)* - **1.** [Landwirt] farmer; HIST peasant - **2.** [Schachfigur] pawn - **3.** [Spielkarte] jack ⟨⟩ *das* ODER *der (pl Bauer)* [Vogelkäfig] (bird) cage.

Bäuerin *(pl -nen) die* [Frau des Bauern] farmer's wife; [Landwirtin] farmer.

bäuerlich ⟨⟩ *adj* rural ⟨⟩ *adv:* **sich ~ kleiden** to wear rustic clothes.

Bauern|frühstück *das fried potatoes with scrambled egg and pieces of bacon.*

Bauern|hof *der* farm.

baufällig *adj* dilapidated.

Bau|firma *die* construction firm, building contractor.

Bau|genehmigung *die* planning permission *(U).*

Bau|land *das (ohne pl)* development site.

Baum *(pl* Bäume*) der* tree.

baumeln *vi* to dangle; **die Beine ~ lassen** to dangle one's legs.

Baum|schule *die* (tree) nursery.

Baum|stamm *der* tree trunk.

Baum|sterben *das* forest dieback.

Baum|stumpf *der* tree stump.

Baum|wolle *die* cotton.

Bau|satz *der* kit.

Bausch *(pl -e* ODER *Bäusche) der* ball.

bauschen *vt* [Kleidungsstück] to puff out; [Segel] to fill. ◆ **sich bauschen** *ref* [Vorhänge, Segel] to billow; [Ärmel] to puff out.

Bau|sparkasse *die* building society *Br,* savings and loan association *Am.*

Bau|stein *der* - **1.** [zum Bauen] brick - **2.** [zum Spielen] building block - **3.** [Bestandteil] constituent part, component.

Bau|stelle *die* building site; [auf einer Straße] roadworks *(pl).*

Bauten *pl* ⟹ Bau.

Bau|unternehmer, in *der, die* building contractor.

Bau|werk *das* building.

Bayer, in *(mpl -n; fpl -nen) der, die* Bavarian.

bayerisch = bayrisch.

Bayerisch = Bayrisch.

Bayerische = Bayrische.

Bayern *nt* Bavaria.

bayrisch, bayerisch ⬦ *adj* Bavarian ⬦ *adv* like a Bavarian.

Bayrisch(e), Bayerisch(e) *das* Bavarian (dialect).

Bazille *(pl -n) die* = Bazillus.

Bazillus *(pl -en) der* microbe.

Bd. *(abk für Band)* vol.

beabsichtigen *vt* to intend.

beachten *vt* - **1.** [befolgen - Vorschriften, Verbot] to observe; [- Ratschläge, Anweisungen] to follow - **2.** [berücksichtigen - Umstände, Gefahr] to take into consideration; **jn nicht ~** to take no notice of sb.

beachtlich ⬦ *adj* [Leistung, Verbesserung, Erfolg] considerable; [Position] important ⬦ *adv* considerably.

Beachtung *die* - **1.** [Befolgung - von Regeln] observing - **2.** [Berücksichtigung] consideration; **unter ~ aller Umstände** taking everything into consideration; **einer Sache** *(D)* **~ schenken** to take sthg into consideration; **jm keine ~ schenken** to take no notice of sb; **~ finden** to be taken into consideration.

Beamte *(pl -n) der* State employee *(e.g. teacher, policeman, civil servant).*

Beamtenschaft *die (ohne pl)* State employees *(pl).*

Beamtin *(pl -nen) die* State employee *(e.g. teacher, policewoman, civil servant).*

beängstigend ⬦ *adj* frightening ⬦ *adv* frighteningly.

beanspruchen *vt* - **1.** [fordern] to claim - **2.** [Material, Bremsen] to wear out - **3.** [strapazieren - Geduld, Person] to tax; **wir möchten Ihre Gastfreundschaft nicht länger ~** we don't want to impose on you any longer - **4.** [Raum, Zeit, Energie] to take up.

Beanspruchung *(pl -en) die* - **1.** [von Material, Nerven] strain - **2.** [im Beruf] demands *(pl).*

beanstanden *vt* to complain about.

Beanstandung *(pl -en) die* complaint.

beantragen *vt* - **1.** [verlangen] to apply for - **2.** [vorschlagen] to propose.

beantworten *vt* to answer.

Beantwortung *(pl -en) die:* **die ~ der Frage** the answer to the question.

bearbeiten *vt* - **1.** [mit Werkzeug] to work - **2.** [Text] to edit; [Musikstück] to arrange; **ein Buch für den Film ~** to adapt a book for the screen - **3.** [betreuen] to deal with - **4.** *fam* [misshandeln - Schlagzeug] to bang away at; **jn mit den Fäusten ~** to do sb over - **5.** *fam* [beeinflussen] to work on.

Bearbeitung *(pl -en) die* - **1.** [von Werkstück, Metall] working - **2.** [von Text] editing; [von Musikstück] arranging; [für Film, Fernsehen] adaptation - **3.** [von Antrag] processing.

beatmen *vt:* **jn künstlich ~** to give sb artificial respiration.

Beatmung *(pl -en) die:* **künstliche ~** artificial respiration.

beaufsichtigen *vt* to supervise.

beauftragen *vt:* **jn ~, etw zu tun** [bitten] to tell sb to do sthg; [Auftrag erteilen] to commission sb to do sthg; **beauftragt sein, etw zu tun** to be charged with doing sthg.

Beauftragte *(pl -n) der, die* representative.

bebauen *vt* [mit Gebäuden] to build on, to develop; **ein Gelände mit Häusern ~** to build houses on a site.

beben *vi* - **1.** [durch Explosion] to shake - **2.** [Hände, Person, Stimme] to tremble.

Beben *(pl -) das* - **1.** [von Händen, Person, Stimme] trembling - **2.** [Erdbeben] earthquake.

Becher *(pl -) der* - **1.** [Kaffeebecher - ohne Henkel, aus Pappe, Styropor] cup; [- ohne Henkel, aus hartem Kunststoff] beaker; [- mit Henkel, aus Porzellan] mug - **2.** [Pokal] goblet - **3.** [für Joghurt] pot; [für Eis] tub.

Becken *(pl -) das* - **1.** [Waschbecken] basin; [Spülbecken] sink; [Schwimmbecken] pool - **2.** [Körperteil] pelvis - **3.** [Instrument] cymbal.

bedacht ⬦ *pp* ▷ **bedenken** ⬦ *adj* - **1.** [vorsichtig] careful - **2.** [bemüht]: **auf etw** *(A)* **~ sein** to be concerned about sthg ⬦ *adv* [vorsichtig] carefully.

bedächtig ⬦ *adj* - **1.** [langsam] deliberate - **2.** [nachdenklich - Person, Miene] thoughtful; [- Worte] well-considered ⬦ *adv* - **1.** [langsam] deliberately - **2.** [überlegt - sprechen] with well-considered words.

bedanken ➡ **sich bedanken** *ref* to say thank you; **ich möchte mich herzlich ~** thank you very much; **sich bei jm für etw ~** to thank sb for sthg.

 sich bedanken

> Thanks! Danke!
> Many thanks/Thanks a lot! Vielen Dank!/ Danke sehr!
> Thank you for your help. Vielen Dank für deine Hilfe.
> I'm very grateful for your support. Ich bin für Ihre Unterstützung sehr dankbar.
> I really appreciate this. Ich bin dafür wirklich dankbar.

Bedarf *der* need; **~ an etw** *(D)* **haben** to be in need of sthg. ➡ **bei Bedarf** *adv* should the need arise.

bedauerlich *adj* regrettable.

bedauern *vt* - **1.** [Irrtum, Unüberlegtheit] to regret - **2.** [Person] to feel sorry for; **bedaure!** I'm sorry!

Bedauern *das* - **1.** [Mitleid] sympathy - **2.** [Reue] regret.

bedauernswert adj - **1.** [Irrtum] regrettable - **2.** [Person] pitiable.

bedecken vt to cover. ◆ **sich bedecken** ref [Himmel] to cloud over.

bedeckt ◇ pp ▷ **bedecken** ◇ adj [Himmel] overcast.

bedenken (prät bedachte; perf hat bedacht) vt - **1.** [überlegen] to consider - **2.** geh [beschenken - im Testament] to remember.

Bedenken (pl -) das - **1.** [Nachdenken] consideration - **2.** [Zweifel] doubt.

bedenklich adj - **1.** [prekär] serious - **2.** [besorgt] anxious - **3.** [fragwürdig] dubious.

Bedenkzeit die: jm ~ **geben** to give sb some time to think it over.

bedeuten vt - **1.** [gen] to mean; **viel/nichts ~** to mean a lot/nothing; **jm viel/wenig/nichts ~** to mean a lot/not to mean much/to mean nothing to sb; **das hat nichts zu ~** that doesn't matter - **2.** geh [zu verstehen geben]: **jm etw ~** to indicate sthg to sb.

bedeutend ◇ adj - **1.** [wichtig] important - **2.** [groß] considerable ◇ adv [sehr] considerably.

Bedeutung (pl -en) die - **1.** [Sinn] meaning - **2.** [Wichtigkeit] importance; **einer Sache** (D) **große/keine ~ beimessen** to attach great/no importance to sthg.

bedienen ◇ vt - **1.** [Person] to serve; **mit diesem Produkt sind Sie gut bedient** this product is a good deal - **2.** [Maschine] to operate ◇ vi to serve. ◆ **sich bedienen** ref to help o.s.; **~ Sie sich!** help yourself!

Bedienung (pl -en) die - **1.** [Versorgung] service - **2.** [Steuerung, Anwendung] operation - **3.** [Kellner] waiter; [Kellnerin] waitress.

Bedienungsanleitung die operating instructions (pl).

bedingen vt [verursachen] to bring about.

Bedingung (pl -en) die [Voraussetzung] condition; **eine ~ stellen** to stipulate a condition; **unter einer ~** on one condition. ◆ **Bedingungen** pl [Umstände] conditions.

bedingungslos ◇ adj unconditional ◇ adv unconditionally.

bedrängen vt [unter Druck setzen] to pressurize; [mit Truppen] to advance on; **jn mit Fragen ~** to badger sb with questions.

bedrohen vt to threaten.

bedrohlich ◇ adj [Situation, Aussehen] threatening; [Nähe, Intensität] dangerous ◇ adv [ansehen] threateningly; [nah, schnell] dangerously.

Bedrohung (pl -en) die threat.

bedrücken vt to depress.

bedrückt adj - **1.** [Person] depressed - **2.** [Schweigen, Stimmung] oppressive.

Bedürfnis (pl -se) das need.

bedürftig adj needy.

beeilen [bəˈaɪlən] ◆ **sich beeilen** ref to hurry; **beeile dich!** hurry up!

beeindrucken [bəˈaɪndrʊkn̩] ◇ vt to impress ◇ vi to make an impression.

beeinflussen [bəˈaɪnflʊsn̩] vt to influence.

beeinträchtigen [bəˈaɪntrɛçtɪɡn̩] vt [Bewegungsfähigkeit, Sicht] to impair; [Produktion, Stimmung] to affect adversely; [Wert, Qualität] to reduce; [Gesundheit] to damage; [Konzentration] to hamper.

Beeinträchtigung [bəˈaɪntrɛçtɪɡʊŋ] (pl -en) die [von Bewegungsfähigkeit, Sicht] impairment; [von Produktion, Stimmung] adverse effect; [von Wert, Qualität] reduction; [von Gesundheit] damaging; [von Konzentration] hampering.

beenden [bəˈɛndn̩] vt to end.

beengt [bəˈɛŋt] adv: ~ **wohnen** to live in cramped conditions.

beerben [bəˈɛrbn̩] vt: **jn ~** to inherit sb's estate.

beerdigen [bəˈeːɐ̯dɪɡn̩] vt to bury.

Beerdigung [bəˈeːɐ̯dɪɡʊŋ] (pl -en) die funeral.

Beerdigungsinstitut das funeral directors (pl).

Beere (pl -n) die berry.

Beet (pl -e) das [mit Blumen] flowerbed; [mit Gemüse] vegetable patch.

Beete ◆ **rote Beete** beetroot.

befahl prät ▷ **befehlen**.

befahrbar adj [Straße, Weg] passable; [Fluss] navigable.

befahren (präs befährt; prät befuhr; perf hat befahren) ◇ vt to use ◇ adj: **eine stark ~e Straße** a busy street.

befangen ◇ adj - **1.** [schüchtern] shy - **2.** RECHT partial - **3.** geh [gefangen]: **in dem Glauben ~ sein, dass ...** to labour under the misconception that ... ◇ adv shyly.

Befangenheit die - **1.** [Schüchternheit] shyness - **2.** RECHT partiality.

befassen (präs befasst; prät befasste; perf hat befasst) vt: **jn mit etw ~** geh to assign sthg to sb. ◆ **sich befassen** ref: **sich mit einer Frage ~** to look into a question; **sich intensiv mit einem Thema ~** to study ODER look at a matter in great detail.

Befehl (pl -e) der - **1.** [Aufforderung] order - **2.** EDV command.

befehlen (präs befiehlt; prät befahl; perf hat befohlen) ◇ vt to order; **jm ~, etw zu tun** to order sb to do sthg; **du hast mir gar nichts zu ~** I don't take orders from you ◇ vi: **über jn/etw ~** to command sb/sthg.

Befehlsform die GRAM imperative.

befestigen vt - **1.** [anbringen]: **etw an etw** (D) **~** to attach sthg to sthg; **etw mit Schrauben an der Wand ~** to screw sthg to the wall - **2.** [verstärken - Stadt] to fortify; [- Ufer, Damm] to reinforce; [- Straße] to make up.

Befestigung (pl -en) die - **1.** [das Anbringen]

attaching - **2.** [die Verstärkung - von Stadt] fortification; [- von Ufer, Damm] reinforcement; [- von Straße] making up.

befiehlt *präs* ▷ befehlen.

befinden (*prät* befand; *perf* hat befunden) *vt:* etw für gut/richtig ~ *geh* to deem sthg good/right. ◆ **sich befinden** *ref* to be; **sein Büro befindet sich im ersten Stock** his office is on the first floor.

Befinden *das* (state of) health.

beflecken *vt* to stain.

befohlen *pp* ▷ befehlen.

befolgen *vt* [Rat] to follow; [Befehl, Vorschrift] to obey.

befördern *vt* - **1.** [transportieren] to transport - **2.** [im Beruf] to promote.

Beförderung *die* - **1.** [Transport] transportation - **2.** [im Beruf] promotion.

Beförderungslmittel *das* means of transport.

befragen *vt* - **1.** [Person, Zeugen] to question - **2.** [Karten, Wahrsagerin] to consult.

Befragung (*pl* -en) *die* questioning.

befreien *vt* [Gefangenen] to free; [Land, Volk] to liberate; [Tier] to set free; **jn von etw ~** [von Diktatur, Schmerzen] to free sb from sthg; [vom Unterricht] to excuse sb from sthg.

Befreiung *die* [von Gefangenen, Tier] freeing; [von Land, Volk] liberation; [der Frau] emancipation; **eine ~ vom Unterricht kommt nicht in Frage** there's no question of you being excused from classes.

befreundet *adj* [Länder] friendly; **mit jm ~ sein** to be friends with sb.

befriedigen *vt* to satisfy.

befriedigend *adj* - **1.** [zufrieden stellend] satisfactory - **2.** SCHULE ≃ C, *mark equivalent to 3 on scale of 1 to 6.*

Befriedigung *die* - **1.** [Zufriedenheit] satisfaction - **2.** [Zufriedenstellung] satisfying.

befristen *vt* to put a time limit on; **ihre Tätigkeit ist auf ein Jahr befristet** her contract only runs for one year.

befristet *adj* [Vertrag] fixed-term, temporary.

befruchten *vt* to fertilize.

Befruchtung (*pl* -en) *die* fertilization; **künstliche ~** artificial insemination.

befugt *adj:* **zur Unterschrift ~ sein** to be authorized to sign.

Belfund *der* [ärztlich] results (*pl*); [von Fachmann] findings (*pl*); **'ohne ~'** MED 'negative'.

befürchten *vt* to fear.

Befürchtung (*pl* -en) *die* fear.

befürworten *vt* to support.

Befürworter, in (*mpl* -; *fpl* -nen) *der, die* supporter.

begabt *adj* talented.

Begabung (*pl* -en) *die* talent.

begann *prät* ▷ beginnen.

Begebenheit (*pl* -en) *die* occurrence; **eine wahre ~** something that really happened.

begegnen *vi* [entgegenkommen, treffen]: **jm ~** to meet sb; **etw** (*D*) **~** [Gefahr] to face sthg; **einer Person mit Freundlichkeit ~** to treat sb in a friendly manner. ◆ **sich begegnen** *ref* [treffen] to meet.

Begegnung (*pl* -en) *die* meeting.

begehen (*prät* beging; *perf* hat begangen) *vt* - **1.** [verüben - Mord, Verbrechen] to commit; [- Fehler] to make; **eine Dummheit ~** to do something stupid - **2.** *geh* [feiern] to celebrate - **3.** [benützen] to use.

begehren *vt* to desire; **sehr begehrt sein** to be much sought after.

begeistern *vt:* **sie begeisterte das Publikum** she delighted the audience; **man kann ihn für nichts ~** you can't make him enthusiastic about anything. ◆ **sich begeistern** *ref:* **sich für etw ~** [Idee] to be enthusiastic about sthg; [Film, Hobby] really to like sthg.

begeistert ◇ *adj* [Reiter, Schwimmer] enthusiastic, keen; [Publikum] delighted; **von dieser Idee bin ich gar nicht ~** I'm not very enthusiastic about ODER keen on that idea ◇ *adv* enthusiastically.

Begeisterung *die* [über Idee, Beschluss, für Hobby] enthusiasm; [über Leistung] delight.

begierig *adj* [Blicke] longing; [Lippen, Hände] eager; **nach etw** ODER **auf etw** (*A*) **~ sein** to be eager for sthg; **darauf ~ sein, etw zu tun** to be eager to do sthg ◇ *adv* eagerly.

begießen (*prät* begoss; *perf* hat begossen) *vt* - **1.** [mit Wasser] to water - **2.** [feiern] to celebrate with a drink.

Beginn *der* beginning, start. ◆ **zu Beginn** *adv* at the beginning ODER start.

beginnen (*prät* begann; *perf* hat begonnen) ◇ *vt* to begin, to start ◇ *vi* to begin, to start; **mit etw ~** to begin sthg, to start sthg.

beglaubigen *vt* to certify.

Beglaubigung (*pl* -en) *die* [Bescheinigung] certificate.

begleiten *vt* to accompany.

Begleiter, in (*mpl* -; *fpl* -nen) *der, die* companion; [beim Musizieren] accompanist.

Begleitlerscheinung *die* side effect.

Begleitung (*pl* -en) *die* - **1.** [Begleiten]: **sie kam in ~** she came with someone; **in ~ einer Freundin** accompanied by a friend - **2.** MUS accompaniment - **3.** [Begleitperson] escort; [Freund] companion.

beglückwünschen *vt:* **jn zu etw ~** to congratulate sb on sthg.

begnadigen *vt* to pardon.

Begnadigung (*pl* -en) *die* pardon.

begnügen ◆ **sich begnügen** *ref:* **sich mit etw ~** to make do with sthg.

begonnen *pp* ▷ beginnen.

begraben (*präs* begräbt; *prät* begrub; *perf* hat begraben) *vt* - **1.** [beerdigen] to bury - **2.** [beenden, vergessen - Streit] to bury; [- Hoffnung, Vorhaben] to abandon.

Begräbnis (*pl* -se) *das* funeral.

begreifen (*prät* begriff; *perf* hat begriffen) *vt & vi* to understand.

begrenzen *vt* - **1.** [Zeit, Geschwindigkeit] to limit, to restrict - **2.** [Fläche, Raum]: **der Park wird vom Fluss begrenzt** the river forms the park's boundary.

Begrenzung (*pl* -en) *die* - **1.** [von Zeit, Geschwindigkeit] restriction, limit - **2.** [von Fläche, Raum] boundary.

Begriff *der* - **1.** [Wort] term - **2.** [Vorstellung] idea, concept; **im ~ sein** ODER **stehen, etw zu tun** to be about to do sthg; **jm ein ~ sein** to mean something to sb; **sich** (*D*) **einen ~ von etw machen** to get an idea of sthg.

begriffsstutzig *adj abw* slow.

begründen *vt* - **1.** [erklären] to justify; **sie begründete ihr Verhalten mit persönlichen Problemen** she gave personal problems as the reason for her behaviour - **2.** [gründen - Firma, Stadt, Religion] to found; [- Theorie] to originate.

Begründer, in (*mpl* -; *fpl* -nen) *der, die* [von Religion, Stadt, Firma] founder; [von Theorie] originator.

Begründung *die* - **1.** [Angabe von Gründen] reason - **2.** [Gründung - von Firma, Stadt, Religion] founding; [- von Stil] establishment.

begrüßen *vt* - **1.** [grüßen] to greet - **2.** [gut finden] to welcome.

Begrüßung (*pl* -en) *die* greeting; [von Gästen] welcome.

begünstigen *vt* to favour.

begutachten *vt* - **1.** [Subj: Fachmann] to examine and report on - **2.** [betrachten] to have a look at.

begütert *adj* well-to-do.

behaart *adj* hairy.

behäbig *adj* [Mensch] portly; [Ausdrucksweise, Schritte] ponderous.

behaglich ◇ *adj* [Sessel] comfortable; [Wärme] cosy ◇ *adv* comfortably.

behalten (*präs* behält; *prät* behielt; *perf* hat behalten) *vt* - **1.** [nicht abgeben] to keep - **2.** [sich merken] to remember.

Behälter (*pl* -) *der* container.

behandeln *vt* - **1.** [gen] to treat; **jn gut/schlecht ~** to treat sb well/badly - **2.** [Problem, Thema] to deal with.

Behandlung *die* treatment.

beharren *vi* to insist; **auf etw** (*D*) **~** to insist on sthg.

beharrlich ◇ *adj* persistent ◇ *adv* persistently.

behaupten *vt* - **1.** [versichern] to claim - **2.** [verteidigen - Vorteil, Position] to maintain. ◆ **sich behaupten** *ref* - **1.** [sich durchsetzen] to assert o.s. - **2.** [gewinnen]: **sich gegen jn ~** to overcome sb.

Behauptung (*pl* -en) *die* - **1.** [Aussage] claim - **2.** [Verteidigung] maintenance.

beheben (*prät* behob; *perf* hat behoben) *vt* to rectify.

beheimatet *adj*: **~ in** (+ *D*) [Pflanze, Tierart] native to; [Person] from.

beheizen *vt* to heat.

behelfen (*präs* behilft; *prät* behalf; *perf* hat beholfen) *vi*: **sich** (*D*) **mit/ohne etw ~** to make do with/without sthg.

behelfsmäßig *adj* [Unterkunft, Konstruktion] makeshift; [Ersatz] temporary.

beherbergen *vt* to put up.

beherrschen *vt* - **1.** [Land, Stadt] to rule - **2.** [Leidenschaft, Markt] to control - **3.** [dominieren] to dominate - **4.** [meistern - Pferd, Wagen] to have control of; [- Arbeit, Sport, Instrument] to have mastered; [- Sprache] to have a command of. ◆ **sich beherrschen** *ref* to control o.s.

beherrscht ◇ *adj* self-controlled ◇ *adv* with self-control.

Beherrschung *die* - **1.** [von Leidenschaft] control; **die ~ verlieren** to lose control - **2.** [von Pferd, Wagen] control; [von Instrument] mastery; [von Sprache] command.

beherzigen *vt* to take to heart.

behilflich *adj*: **jm bei etw ~ sein** to help sb with sthg.

behindern *vt* - **1.** [Verkehr, Sicht] to obstruct - **2.** [Person]: **jn bei etw ~** to hinder sb in sthg.

behindert *adj* handicapped.

Behinderte (*pl* -n) *der, die* handicapped person; **die ~n** the handicapped.

Behinderung (*pl* -en) *die* - **1.** [Behindern] obstruction - **2.** [Handicap] handicap.

Behörde (*pl* -n) *die* authority. ◆ **Behörden** *pl* authorities.

behutsam ◇ *adj* careful ◇ *adv* carefully.

bei *präp* (+ *D*) - **1.** [räumlich - nahe] near; [- innen] at; **das Hotel ist gleich ~m Bahnhof** the hotel is right next to the station; **Bernau ~ Berlin** Bernau near Berlin; **~m Arzt** at the doctor's; **sie arbeitet ~ einem Verlag** she works for a publishing company; **~ meiner Tante** at my aunt's; **~ mir** at my house; **die Schuld liegt allein ~ mir** *fig* I alone am to blame; **ein Kind ~ der Hand nehmen** to take a child's hand, to take a child by the hand - **2.** [zusammen mit einer Person] with; **ich bleibe ~ dir** I'm staying with you - **3.** [zeitlich] at; **~ Beginn** at the beginning; **~ der Arbeit** at work; **~ seiner Beerdigung** at his funeral; **Vorsicht ~m Ein- und Aussteigen be**

careful when getting on and off; **~m Sport brach er sich den Arm** he broke his arm (while) playing sports - **4.** [als Teil einer Menge] among; **einige dieser Stilelemente finden sich auch ~ Picasso** some of these stylistic touches are also found in Picasso's work - **5.** [zur Angabe von Umständen]: **~ Tag/ Nacht** by day/night; **~ Gelegenheit** some time - **6.** [zur Angabe der Ursache]: **~ Regen fällt der Ausflug aus** if it rains the trip will be cancelled; **~ deinem Talent solltest du Maler werden** with your talent you should be an artist. ➤ **bei sich** adv: **hast du Geld ~ dir?** have you got any money on you?; **~ sich** (D) **sein** (fig to be (feeling) o.s.

bei|behalten vt (unreg) [Methode] to keep to; [Gegenstände] to keep.

bei|bringen vt (unreg) - **1.** [lehren]: **jm etw ~** to teach sb sthg - **2.** [mitteilen]: **jm etw (schonend) ~** to break sthg (gently) to sb - **3.** [zufügen]: **jm etw ~** to inflict sthg on sb - **4.** amt [bringen] to produce.

Beichte (pl -n) die confession.

beichten <> vt to confess; **jm etw ~** to confess sthg to sb <> vi to confess.

beide <> pron [zwei] both; **die ~n** both of them; **diese ~n** these two; **ihr ~n** you two <> adj - **1.** [zwei]: **die ~n Pferde** both (of) the horses, these two horses; **diese ~n Exemplare** both (of) these copies, these two copies - **2.** [alle zwei] both. ➤ **beides** pron both.

beiderlei det both.

beiderseitig adj mutual.

beiderseits präp (+ G) on both sides of.

beidseitig <> adj mutual <> adv on both sides.

beieinander adv together.

Beifahrer, in (mpl -; fpl -nen) der, die front-seat passenger.

Beifahrer|sitz der passenger seat.

Beifall der applause; **~ spenden** ODER **klatschen** to applaud.

beifällig <> adj approving <> adv approvingly.

bei|fügen vt: **einer Sache** (D) **etw ~** to enclose sthg with sthg.

beige [be:ʃ] adj beige.

Beigeschmack der - **1.** [von Esswaren]: **das Bier hat einen bitteren ~** the beer tastes slightly bitter - **2.** [von Begriff] connotation; **die ganze Affäre hatte einen bitteren ~** the whole affair left a bitter taste in the mouth.

Beihilfe die - **1.** [finanziell] financial aid - **2.** [kriminell] aiding and abetting; **jm ~ leisten** to aid and abet sb.

bei|kommen (perf ist beigekommen) vi (unreg): **jm ~** [fertig werden mit] to get the better of sb.

Beil (pl -e) das axe.

Beilage die - **1.** [Speise] side dish; **mit Reis**

als ~ served with rice - **2.** [zu Zeitung] supplement - **3.** amt [Belegen] enclosure.

beiläufig <> adj casual <> adv casually, in passing.

bei|legen vt - **1.** [beifügen]: **einer Sache** (D) **etw ~** to enclose sthg with sthg - **2.** [schlichten] to resolve.

Beileid das (ohne pl) condolences (pl); **herzliches** ODER **aufrichtiges ~!** my sincere condolences!

beiliegend adj amt enclosed; **~ übersenden wir Ihnen ...** please find enclosed ...

beim präp (bei + dem): **ich bin ~ Essen** I'm eating at the moment; **~ letzten Test** in the last test; **sie war ~ Arzt** she was at the doctor's; **sie traf ihn ~ Einkaufen** she met him while she was shopping; **~ Rasenmähen helfen** to help with mowing the lawn; siehe auch bei.

bei|messen vt (unreg): **einer Sache** (D) **große/keine Bedeutung ~** to attach great/no importance to sthg.

Bein (pl -e) das leg.

beinah, beinahe adv almost, nearly.

Beiname der epithet.

beinhalten [bəˈɪnhaltn̩] vt to contain.

Beipack|zettel der instruction leaflet.

bei|pflichten vi: **jm/einer Sache ~** to agree with sb/sthg.

beisammen adv together.

Beisammensein das get-together.

Beisein das: **im ~ von jm, in js ~** in the presence of sb, in sb's presence.

beiseite adv aside, to one side; **~ lassen** to leave aside ODER to one side; **~ legen** to put aside.

Beisetzung (pl -en) die funeral.

Bei|spiel das example; **sich** (D) **an jm ein ~ nehmen** to follow sb's example; **sich** (D) **ein ~ an etw** (D) **nehmen** to take sthg as one's example. ➤ **zum Beispiel** adv for example.

beispielhaft <> adj exemplary <> adv in exemplary fashion.

beispiellos <> adj unprecedented; [Unverschämtheit] unbelievable <> adv unprecedentedly.

beispielsweise adv for example.

beißen (prät biss; perf hat gebissen) <> vt to bite <> vi - **1.** [mit den Zähnen] to bite; **in etw** (A) **~** to bite into sthg - **2.** [brennen] to sting; **Qualm beißt in den Augen** smoke makes your eyes sting. ➤ **sich beißen** ref - **1.** [mit den Zähnen] to bite each other - **2.** [Farben] to clash.

bei|stehen vi (unreg): **jm ~** to stand by sb.

bei|steuern vt: **etw (zu etw) ~** to contribute sthg (to sthg).

Beitrag (pl Beiträge) der - **1.** [Geld, Mitarbeit] contribution; [als Vereinsmitglied] subscription - 2. [Artikel] article.

bei|tragen *(unreg)* ◇ *vt* to contribute ◇ *vi*: **zu etw ~** to contribute to sthg.

bei|treten *(perf ist beigetreten)* *vi (unreg)*: **etw** *(D)* **~** to join sthg.

Bei|tritt *der* [zur EU] entry; [zu Verein] joining.

beizeiten *adv* in good time.

bejahen *vt* [Frage] to say yes to; [Standpunkt] to approve of.

bekämpfen *vt* [Feind, Kriminalität] to fight; [Schädlinge] to control.

Bekämpfung *die*: **die ~ von etw** the fight against sthg; [von Schädlingen] the control of sthg.

bekannt *adj* well-known.

Bekannte *(pl -n) der, die* acquaintance.

Bekannten|kreis *der* circle of acquaintances.

Bekannt|gabe *die* announcement.

bekannt geben *vt (unreg)* to announce.

bekanntlich *adv* as is well known.

bekannt machen *vt* [Beschluss, Plan] to announce; [Fremde, Gäste] to introduce; **jn mit jm ~** to introduce sb to sb; **jn/sich mit etw ~** to familiarize sb/o.s. with sthg.

Bekanntschaft *(pl -en) die* - **1.** [Kennen, Bekannte] acquaintance; **mit jm ~ schließen** to make sb's acquaintance - **2.** [Bekanntenkreis] acquaintances *(pl)*.

bekehren *vt* to convert. ◆ **sich bekehren** *ref*: **sich (zu etw) ~** to convert (to sthg).

bekennen *(prät bekannte; perf hat bekannt) vt* [Sünde] to confess; [Fehler] to admit. ◆ **sich bekennen** *ref*: **sich zu etw ~** [Glauben] to profess sthg; [Überzeugung] to declare one's support for sthg; [Attentat] to claim responsibility for sthg.

beklagen *vt* to mourn. ◆ **sich beklagen** *ref*: **sich (bei jm über jn/etw) ~** to complain (about sb/sthg to sb).

bekleckern *vt*: **etw mit etw ~** to spill sthg on sthg. ◆ **sich bekleckern** *ref*: **sich mit etw ~** to spill sthg on o.s.

bekleidet *adj*: **mit etw ~ sein** to be wearing sthg.

Bekleidung *die (ohne pl)* - **1.** [Kleidung] clothes *(pl)* - **2.** *geh* [von Posten, Amt] tenure.

beklemmend ◇ *adj* oppressive ◇ *adv* oppressively.

Beklemmung *(pl -en) die* anxiety.

beklommen ◇ *adj* anxious ◇ *adv* anxiously.

bekommen *(prät bekam; perf hat/ist bekommen)* ◇ *vt (hat)* to get; [Zug, Bus, Krankheit] to catch; **ich bekomme noch 100 Euro von dir** you owe me 100 euros; **was ~ Sie?** what would you like?; **was ~ Sie dafür?** how much is it?; **es sind keine Karten mehr zu ~**

there are no more tickets available ODER to be had; **Prügel/eine Strafe ~** to be beaten/punished; **sie bekommt ein Kind** she's expecting (a baby); **Besuch ~** to have visitors; **etw geschenkt/geliehen ~** to be given/lent sthg; **Angst/Hunger ~** to get frightened/hungry; **seine Stimme bekam einen zärtlichen Ton** his voice took on a gentle tone ◇ *vi (ist)*: **jm gut ~** [Essen] to agree with sb; **der Wein ist mir nicht ~** the wine disagreed with me.

📖 **bekommen**

The German verb bekommen meaning "to get" is a false friend easily confused with the English "to become". So the phrase Was hast du zum Geburtstag geschenkt <u>bekommen</u>? means "What did you <u>get</u> for your birthday?"
The English "to become" or "to get" in the sense of "to change state" is translated by werden. Es ist plötzlich dunkel ge<u>worden</u> could be translated as "It's <u>become</u> dark all of a sudden."

---

bekräftigen *vt* [Meinung, Kritik] to confirm, to reinforce; **jn in etw** *(D)* **~** to confirm sb in sthg.

bekreuzigen ◆ **sich bekreuzigen** *ref* to cross o.s.

bekritzeln *vt* to scribble on.

bekümmert ◇ *adj* worried ◇ *adv* worriedly.

belächeln *vt abw* to laugh at.

beladen *(präs belädt; prät belud; perf hat beladen) vt*: **etw (mit etw) ~** to load sthg (with sthg).

Belag *(pl Beläge) der* - **1.** [von Bremsen] lining; [von Straße] surface; [von Fußboden] covering - **2.** [auf Brot] topping - **3.** [auf der Zunge] fur; [auf den Zähnen] film.

belagern *vt* to besiege.

Belagerung *(pl -en) die* siege.

Belang *(pl -e) der* [Bedeutung]: **von/ohne ~ sein (für jn)** to be important/of no importance (to sb). ◆ **Belange** *pl* [Interessen] interests.

belangen *vt* RECHT: **jn (für etw) ~** to prosecute sb (for sthg).

belasten *vt* - **1.** [mit Gewicht] to put a load on; **etw mit etw ~** to weight sthg down with sthg - **2.** [Umwelt] to pollute; [Leber] to put a strain on - **3.** [beanspruchen] to weigh heavily on; **jn mit etw ~** to burden sb with sthg - **4.** [besorgen]: **jn ~** to weigh on sb's mind - **5.** RECHT to incriminate - **6.** [finanziell - Konto] to debit; **ein Haus mit einer Hypothek ~** to mortgage a house.

belästigen *vt* to bother; [sexuell] to harass.

Belästigung (*pl* -en) *die* annoyance; [sexu-ell] harassment.

Belastung (*pl* -en) *die* - **1.** [mit Gewicht] load - **2.** [von Umwelt] pollution - **3.** [psychisch] strain - **4.** [von Konto] debiting.

belauern *vt* [Person] to spy on; [Verhalten] to observe secretly.

belaufen (*präs* beläuft; *prät* belief; *perf* hat belaufen) ◆ **sich belaufen** *ref*: **sich auf etw** (A) ~ to amount to sthg.

belauschen *vt* to eavesdrop on.

belebt *adj* busy.

Beleg (*pl* -e) *der* - **1.** [Quittung] receipt - **2.** [Nachweis] proof.

belegen *vt* - **1.** [mit Belag]: **etw mit etw** ~ [Brot] to top sthg with sthg; [Boden] to cover sthg with sthg - **2.** [besuchen] to enrol for - **3.** [okkupieren] to occupy - **4.** [einnehmen]: **den ersten/zweiten Platz** ~ to come first/second - **5.** [nachweisen - Zahlung] to provide proof of; [- Behauptung, Argument] to back up; [- Zitat] to reference.

Belegschaft (*pl* -en) *die* workforce.

belegt *adj* - **1.** [mit Aufschnitt]: **~es Brot/Brötchen** open sandwich/roll; **ein ~es Brot mit Käse** a slice of bread with cheese on it - **2.** [Zunge] furred - **3.** [besetzt - Zimmer] occupied; [- Hotel, Kurs] full - **4.** [Stimme] hoarse.

belehren *vt* to instruct; **jn über etw** (A) ~ to instruct sb about sthg; [Rechte] to inform sb of sthg; **jn eines Besseren/anderen** ~ to teach sb better/otherwise.

beleibt *adj* corpulent.

beleidigen *vt* [Person] to insult; [Empfinden] to offend.

Beleidigung (*pl* -en) *die* insult; **~ des guten Geschmacks** offence against good taste.

beleuchten *vt* - **1.** [Denkmal, Brunnen] to illuminate; [Straße, Raum] to light - **2.** [Thema] to examine.

Beleuchtung (*pl* -en) *die* - **1.** [mit Licht] lighting - **2.** [Lampen, Scheinwerfer] lights (*pl*) - **3.** (*ohne pl*) [von Thema, Theorie] examination.

Belgien *nt* Belgium.

Belgier, in ['bɛlgiɐ, rɪn] (*mpl* -; *fpl* -nen) *der, die* Belgian.

belgisch *adj* Belgian.

belichten *vt* to expose.

Belichtung *die* FOTO exposure.

Belieben *das*: **nach** ~ as you like; **das steht** ODER **liegt in deinem** ~ that is up to you.

beliebig ◇ *adj* any; **eine ~e Summe** any amount ◇ *adv*: **viel/viele** as much/many as you like; **~ lange** as long as you like.

beliebt *adj* popular; **beim jm** ~ **sein** to be popular with sb; **sich bei jm** ~ **machen** to make o.s. popular with sb.

Beliebtheit *die* popularity.

beliefern *vt*: **jn (mit etw)** ~ to supply sb (with sthg).

bellen *vi* to bark.

belohnen *vt* to reward.

Belohnung (*pl* -en) *die* - **1.** [Belohnen] rewarding - **2.** [Lohn, Entgelt] reward.

Belüftung *die* ventilation.

belügen (*prät* belog; *perf* hat belogen) *vt* to lie to.

bemalen *vt* [anmalen] to paint.

bemängeln *vt* to criticize.

bemerkbar *adj* noticeable; **sich ~ machen** [Person] to attract attention; [Sache] to become apparent.

bemerken *vt* - **1.** [wahrnehmen] to notice - **2.** [sagen] to remark.

bemerkenswert ◇ *adj* remarkable ◇ *adv* remarkably.

Bemerkung (*pl* -en) *die* remark.

bemitleiden *vt* to feel sorry for.

bemühen *vt geh* [Anwalt, Gutachter] to call on. ◆ **sich bemühen** *ref* - **1.** [sich anstrengen] to try; **sich ~, etw zu tun** to try to do sthg - **2.** [suchen]: **sich um jn/etw** ~ to look for sb/sthg, to try to find sb/sthg - **3.** [sich kümmern]: **sich um jn** ~ to take care of sb.

Bemühung (*pl* -en) *die*: **~en** efforts.

benachbart *adj* [Personen, Dörfer] neighbouring; [Disziplinen] related.

benachrichtigen *vt* to inform.

benachteiligen *vt* to disadvantage; [Minderheiten] to discriminate against.

benehmen (*präs* benimmt; *prät* benahm; *perf* hat benommen) ◆ **sich benehmen** *ref* to behave; **sich gut/schlecht** ~ to behave well/badly.

Benehmen *das* behaviour.

beneiden *vt*: **jn (um etw)** ~ to envy sb (sthg).

beneidenswert ◇ *adj* enviable ◇ *adv* enviably.

Benelux-Länder *pl* Benelux countries.

benennen (*prät* benannte; *perf* hat benannt) *vt* to name; RECHT to call.

Bengel (*pl* -) *der* little rascal.

benommen ◇ *adj* groggy ◇ *adv* groggily.

benoten *vt* to mark.

benötigen *vt* to need.

benutzen, benützen *vt* to use.

Benutzer, in (*mpl* -; *fpl* -nen) *der, die* user.

Benutzung *die* use.

Benzin (*pl* -e) *das* petrol Br, gas Am; **bleifreies/verbleites** ~ unleaded/leaded petrol Br ODER gas Am; **~ tanken** to fill up with petrol Br ODER gas Am.

Benzinkanister *der* petrol can Br, gas can Am.

beobachten *vt* - **1.** [observieren] to observe

- 2. [überwachen] to watch **- 3.** [bemerken] to notice.

Beobachter, in *(mpl -; fpl -nen) der, die* observer.

Beobachtung *(pl -en) die* observation.

bepackt *adj* loaded up.

bequem ⋄ *adj* **- 1.** [gemütlich] comfortable; **es sich** *(D)* ~ **machen** to make o.s. comfortable **- 2.** [faul] lazy **- 3.** [Lösung, Weg] easy ⋄ *adv* **- 1.** [liegen, sitzen] comfortably **- 2.** [leicht] easily.

Bequemlichkeit *(pl -en) die* **- 1.** [Gemütlichkeit] comfort **- 2.** [Faulheit] laziness.

beraten *(präs* berät; *prät* beriet; *perf* hat beraten) ⋄ *vt* **- 1.** [Rat geben] to advise; **jn bei etw** ~ to advise sb on sthg **- 2.** [besprechen] to discuss ⋄ *vi*: **über etw** *(A)* ~ to discuss sthg. ◆ **sich beraten** *ref*: **sich mit jm über etw** *(A)* ~ to discuss sthg with sb.

Berater, in *(mpl -; fpl -nen) der, die* adviser.

beratschlagen *vi* to discuss; **über etw** *(A)* ~ to discuss sthg.

Beratung *(pl -en) die* **- 1.** [Ratgeben] advice **- 2.** [Besprechung] discussion.

Beratungsstelle *die* advice centre.

berauben *vt*: **jn einer Sache** *(G)* ~ to rob sb of sthg.

berauschend ⋄ *adj* intoxicating ⋄ *adv*: ~ **wirken** to have an intoxicating effect.

berechenbar ⋄ *adj* **- 1.** [Summe, Größe] calculable **- 2.** [Person, Reaktion] predictable ⋄ *adv* predictably.

berechnen *vt* **- 1.** [ausrechnen] to calculate **- 2.** [anrechnen] to charge.

berechnend ⋄ *adj* calculating ⋄ *adv* calculatingly.

Berechnung *die* calculation; **aus** ~ **handeln** to act in a calculating manner.

berechtigen *vt*: **jn zu etw** ~ to entitle sb to sthg.

berechtigt *adj* justified.

Berechtigung *(pl -en) die* **- 1.** [Genehmigung] right **- 2.** [Korrektheit] legitimacy.

bereden *vt* [besprechen]: **etw (mit jm)** ~ to discuss sthg (with sb).

Bereich *(pl -e) der* **- 1.** [Gebiet] area **- 2.** [Aufgabe, Thema] field.

bereichern *vt* to enrich. ◆ **sich bereichern** *ref*: **sich (an jm/etw)** ~ to make money (at sb's expense/from sthg).

Bereicherung *(pl -en) die* enrichment.

bereisen *vt* to travel around.

bereit *adj* **- 1.** [fertig]: ~ **sein** to be ready **- 2.** [gewillt]: ~ **sein, etw zu tun** to be willing to do sthg; **sich** ~ **erklären, etw zu tun** to agree to do sthg.

bereithaben *vt* to have ready.

bereithalten *vt (unreg)* to have ready. ◆ **sich bereithalten** *ref*: **sich zu** ODER **für etw** ~ to be ready for sthg.

bereitmachen *vt* to get ready. ◆ **sich bereitmachen** *ref* to get ready.

bereits *adv* already; ~ **um sechs Uhr** as early as six o'clock.

Bereitschaft *die* **- 1.** [Wille] willingness **- 2.** [Bereitschaftsdienst] emergency service; ~ **haben** [Polizei, Feuerwehr] to be on standby; [Arzt] to be on call.

bereitstehen *vi (unreg)* [Fahrzeug, Koffer] to be ready; [Sanitäter, Polizei] to be on standby.

Bereitstellung *die* provision.

bereitwillig ⋄ *adj* willing ⋄ *adv* willingly.

bereuen *vt* [Fehler, Worte, Verhalten] to regret; [Sünde] to repent of.

Berg *(pl -e) der* [Erhöhung, große Menge] mountain; [kleiner] hill. ◆ **Berge** *pl* mountains; **in die** ~**e fahren** to go to the mountains.

bergab *adv* downhill; **mit jm/etw geht es** ~ sb/sthg is going downhill.

bergan = bergauf.

bergauf, bergan *adv* uphill; **mit jm/etw geht es** ~ things are looking up for sb/sthg.

Bergbau *der* mining.

bergen *(präs* birgt; *prät* barg; *perf* hat geborgen) *vt* **- 1.** [Verunglückte] to rescue; [Leiche, Unfallwagen] to recover; [Boot] to salvage **- 2.** *geh* [enthalten]: **etw in sich** *(D)* ~ to involve sthg.

Bergführer, in *der, die* mountain guide.

Berghütte *die* mountain hut.

bergig *adj* mountainous.

Bergmann *(pl -leute) der* miner.

Bergsteigen *das* (mountain) climbing.

Bergsteiger, in *der, die* (mountain) climber; [professionell] mountaineer.

Bergung *(pl -en) die* [von Verletzten] rescue; [von Leiche, Unfallwagen] recovery; [von Boot] salvage.

Bergwacht *die (ohne pl)* mountain rescue service.

Bergwandern *das* hill walking.

Bergwerk *das* mine.

Bericht *(pl -e) der* report; **über etw** *(A)* ~ **erstatten** to report on sthg.

berichten ⋄ *vt* to report ⋄ *vi* to report; **von jm/etw** ODER **über jn/etw** ~ to report on sb/sthg.

Berichterstattung *die* reporting.

berichtigen *vt* to correct.

Berichtigung *(pl -en) die* correction.

Berlin *nt* Berlin.

Berliner *(pl -)* ⋄ *der* **- 1.** [Person] Berliner **- 2.** [Gebäck] doughnut *(filled with jam)* ⋄ *adj (unver)* Berlin *(vor Subst)*.

Berlinerin *(pl -nen) die* Berliner.

berlinerisch *adj* Berlin *(vor Subst)*.

Berliner Mauer *die* Berlin Wall.

Berliner Mauer

Built in 1961 to halt the exodus of citizens fleeing to the West, the Berlin Wall split the city of Berlin in two, isolating West Berlin in the middle of the GDR. A powerful symbol of the partition of Germany up until 1989, and of the predicament of the German people, it was a grim reminder of the Cold War, of state repression and of the death that lay in store for any East German who tried to escape across it.

Berliner Philharmoniker *pl* Berlin Philharmonic *(sg)*.

Bern *nt* Bern, Berne.

Bernstein *der* amber.

bersten (*präs* birst; *prät* barst; *perf* ist geborsten) *vi* [Schiff, Gebäude] to break up; [Glas, Eis] to shatter.

berüchtigt *adj* notorious; **für** ODER **wegen etw ~ sein** to be notorious for sthg.

berücksichtigen *vt* - 1. [Vorschlag, Wunsch] to take into consideration; **wenn man berücksichtigt, dass ...** considering (that) ... - 2. [Bewerber, Antrag] to consider.

Beruf (*pl* -e) *der* profession; **was sind Sie von ~?** what do you do (for a living)?

berufen[1] *adj* - 1. [fähig] competent - 2. [bestimmt]: **zu etw ~ sein** to have a vocation as sthg.

berufen[2] (*prät* berief; *perf* hat berufen) *vt* to appoint; **jn ins Ausland ~** to post sb abroad. ◆ **sich berufen** *ref*: **sich auf jn/etw ~** to quote sb/sthg as one's authority.

beruflich ◇ *adj* professional ◇ *adv* [reisen] on business.

Berufsausbildung *die* vocational training.

Berufsberatung *die* career guidance.

Berufsleben *das* working life.

Berufsschule *die* vocational school *(attended part-time by apprentices)*.

Berufssoldat *der* professional soldier.

berufstätig *adj*: **~ sein** to have a job, to work; **sie ist nicht ~** she doesn't work.

Berufstätige (*pl* -n) *der*, *die* working person; **die ~n** the working population.

Berufsverkehr *der* rush-hour traffic.

Berufung (*pl* -en) *die* - 1. [Ruf] appointment; [ins Ausland] posting - 2. RECHT appeal; **~ einlegen** to appeal - 3. [Begabung] vocation - 4. [Bezug] reference; **unter ~ auf jn/etw** with reference to sb/sthg.

beruhen *vi*: **auf etw** (*D*) **~** to be based on sthg; **etw auf sich** (*D*) **~ lassen** to let sthg rest.

beruhigen *vt* to calm (down). ◆ **sich be-**

ruhigen *ref* [Person] to calm down; [Lage] to settle down; [Meer] to become calm.

Beruhigung (*pl* -en) *die* [von Person, Meer] calming; [von Lage] settling down.

Beruhigungsmittel *das* sedative.

berühmt *adj* famous; **wegen** ODER **für etw ~ sein** to be famous for sthg.

Berühmtheit (*pl* -en) *die* - 1. [Berühmtsein] fame - 2. [Person] celebrity.

berühren *vt* - 1. [anfassen] to touch - 2. [beeindrucken] to move.

Berührung (*pl* -en) *die* - 1. [Anfassen] touch - 2. [Kontakt]: **mit jm/etw in ~ kommen** to come into contact with sb/sthg.

besänftigen *vt* to soothe.

Besatzung *die* - 1. [Personal] crew - 2. MIL occupying forces *(pl)*.

beschädigen *vt* to damage.

Beschädigung *die* - 1. [Beschädigen] damaging - 2. [Schaden] damage *(U)*.

beschaffen ◇ *vt* to obtain; **jm etw ~ to** get sb sthg; **sich** (*D*) **etw ~** to get sthg ◇ *adj*: **das Material ist so ~, dass es große Belastungen aushält** the nature of the material means that it can withstand heavy loads.

Beschaffenheit *die* - 1. [Art] nature - 2. [Zustand] condition.

beschäftigen *vt* - 1. [anstellen] to employ; **er ist bei Siemens beschäftigt** he works for Siemens - 2. [ablenken] to keep busy - 3. [beanspruchen - Frage] to preoccupy; **sie ist im Moment sehr beschäftigt** she is very busy at present. ◆ **sich beschäftigen** *ref*: **sie beschäftigt sich intensiv mit Religion** she's heavily involved in religion; **wir ~ uns gegenwärtig mit der Frage, wie ...** we are currently considering ODER looking at the issue of how to ...

Beschäftigte (*pl* -n) *der, die* employee.

Beschäftigung (*pl* -en) *die* - 1. [Tätigkeit - Arbeit] occupation; [- Hobby] activity - 2. [Arbeitsstelle] job; **eine ~ suchen** to be looking for work; **ohne ~ sein** to be out of work - 3. [Anstellen] employment - 4. [Auseinandersetzung]: **~ mit etw** [Thema, Problem] consideration of sthg.

Bescheid (*pl* -e) *der* [Entscheidung] decision; **den ~ vom Finanzamt erwarten** to be waiting for an answer from the tax office; **~ wissen** to know; **jm ~ sagen** ODER **geben** [benachrichtigen] to let sb know; *fam* [jm die Meinung sagen] to give sb a piece of one's mind.

bescheiden ◇ *adj* - 1. [anspruchslos, einfach] modest; [Benehmen] unassuming - 2. [Essen] frugal; [Ergebnis, Leistung] mediocre ◇ *adv* [sich kleiden, leben] simply.

bescheinigen *vt* [mit Zeugnis] to certify; **den Empfang von etw ~** to sign for sthg; **sich etw ~ lassen** to get sthg confirmed in writing.

Bescheinigung (pl -en) die - **1.** [bescheinigen] certification - **2.** [Schein] certificate.

bescheißen (prät beschiss; perf hat beschissen) vt salopp: **jn (um etw)** ~ to con sb (out of sthg).

Bescherung (pl -en) die giving of Christmas presents.

beschießen (prät beschoss; perf hat beschossen) vt to fire on.

beschimpfen vt to insult; [mit groben Worten] to swear at.

Beschimpfung (pl -en) die insult; ~**en** abuse (U).

beschissen vulg <> pp ▷ bescheißen <> adj shitty <> adv [sich benehmen] shittily; **es geht mir** ~ things are going like shit for me.

beschlagen (präs beschlägt; prät beschlug; perf hat/ist beschlagen) <> vt (hat) [Pferd] to shoe; [Schuhsohlen] to stud <> vi (ist) to mist ODER steam up <> adj well-informed; **in etw** (D) ~ **sein** to be well up on sthg.

beschlagnahmen vt to confiscate.

beschleunigen <> vt [Tempo, Schritte] to quicken; [Abreise] to hasten; [Arbeitsprozess] to speed up <> vi to accelerate.

Beschleunigung (pl -en) die [von Verfahren, Entwicklung] speeding up; [von Auto] acceleration.

beschließen (prät beschloss; perf hat beschlossen) <> vt - **1.** [entscheiden] to decide on; ~, **etw zu tun** to decide to do sthg; [Gesetz] to pass; [Vorhaben] to approve - **2.** geh [beenden] to end <> vi [beraten]: **über etw** (A) ~ to decide on sthg.

Beschluss der decision; **einen** ~ **fassen** to take a decision.

beschmutzen vt [Teppich, Kleidung] to soil; [Wand] to stain; **jm/sich das Kleid** ~ to get sb's/one's dress dirty.

beschränken vt to limit, to restrict. ➭ **sich beschränken** ref: **sich auf etw** (A) ~ [Sache] to be confined to sthg; [Person] to confine o.s. to sthg.

beschränkt adj - **1.** abw [engstirnig] narrow-minded - **2.** [dürftig] limited; **in ~en Verhältnissen leben** to live in straitened circumstances - **3.** abw [dumm] slow, dim.

beschreiben (prät beschrieb; perf hat beschrieben) vt - **1.** [darstellen, formen] to describe; [Weg] to tell - **2.** [voll schreiben] to write on.

Beschreibung die description.

beschriften vt to label; [Brief] to address; [Etikett] to write on.

beschuldigen vt to accuse; **jn einer Sache** (G) ~ to accuse sb of sthg.

Beschuldigung (pl -en) die accusation.

beschützen vt to protect; **jn vor etw** (D) ~ to protect sb from sthg.

Beschützer, in (mpl -; fpl -nen) der protector.

Beschwerde (pl -n) die [Klage] complaint. ➭ **Beschwerden** pl [Schmerzen] trouble (U); ~**n im Kreuz haben** to have back problems ODER trouble with one's back.

beschweren vt [belasten] to weight down. ➭ **sich beschweren** ref: **sich (über jn/etw)** ~ to complain (about sb/sthg).

beschwichtigen vt [Person] to placate; [Zorn] to calm.

beschwindeln vt to dupe.

beschwingt adj [Stimmung] lively; [Melodie] lilting.

beschwipst adj tipsy.

beschwören (prät beschwor; perf hat beschworen) vt - **1.** [beeiden] to swear to - **2.** [erscheinen lassen - Geister] to invoke; [- Bilder] to conjure up; [- Erinnerungen] to evoke - **3.** [bitten] to entreat, to implore.

beseitigen vt - **1.** [entfernen - Fleck] to remove; [- Abfall] to get rid of, to dispose of; [- Schwierigkeiten, Missbrauch] to eliminate; [- Schnee] to clear away - **2.** [ermorden] to eliminate.

Beseitigung (pl -en) die - **1.** [Entfernung - von Fleck] removal; [- von Abfall] disposal; [- von Schwierigkeiten, Missbrauch] elimination - **2.** [Ermordung] elimination.

Besen (pl -) der broom.

besessen adj - **1.** [verrückt]: **wie** ~ like someone possessed - **2.** [begeistert]: **von etw** ~ **sein** to be obsessed with sthg.

besetzen vt - **1.** [Stelle, Rolle] to fill - **2.** [Sitzplatz, Haus, Gebiet, Land] to occupy - **3.** [verzieren]: **etw mit etw** ~ to trim sthg with sthg.

besetzt adj occupied; [Telefon] engaged; [Sitz] taken; **nicht** ~ [Büro] closed.

Besetzung (pl -en) die - **1.** [von Posten] filling - **2.** [Team - von Schauspielern] cast; [- von Sportlern] team - **3.** [von Land, Gebiet, Haus] occupation.

besichtigen vt [Museum] to visit; [Wohnung] to view; [Stadt] to go sightseeing in.

Besichtigung (pl -en) die [von Museum] visit; [von einer Wohnung] viewing; [von einer Stadt] sightseeing; [Führung] tour.

besiegen vt - **1.** [Feind] to defeat; [Mannschaft] to beat - **2.** [Zweifel, Neugier] to overcome.

Besiegte (pl -n) der, die loser.

Besinnung die: **die** ~ **verlieren** to lose consciousness.

Besitz der - **1.** [Eigentum] property - **2.** [Besitzen] possession - **3.** [Landgut] estate.

besitzen (prät besaß; perf hat besessen) vt to possess, to own; [Recht, Qualität] to have.

Besitzer, in (mpl -; fpl -nen) der, die owner.

besondere, r, s adj [speziell] special; [außergewöhnlich] particular; ~ **Kennzeichen**

distinguishing features; **im Besonderen** *(adv)* in particular, especially.

Besonderheit *(pl -en)* die special feature, peculiarity.

besonders <> *adv* - 1. [vor allem, sehr] especially, particularly - 2. [gut]: **nicht ~** not very well <> *adj*: **nicht ~ sein** to be not very good; **der Film ist nicht ~** the film isn't up to much.

besorgen *vt* - 1. [beschaffen] to get (hold of); **jm/sich etw ~** to get sb/o.s. sthg - 2. [sich um etw kümmern] to see to.

besorgt <> *adj* worried; **um jn ~ sein** to be worried about sb; **rührend um jn ~ sein** to be concerned for sb's wellbeing <> *adv* anxiously; **~ aussehen** to look worried.

Besorgung *(pl -en)* die [Einkäufe] purchase; **~en** shopping *(U)*.

bespielen *vt* to record on.

bespitzeln *vt* to spy on.

besprechen *(präs bespricht; prät besprach; perf hat besprochen)* *vt* - 1. [erörtern]: **etw (mit jm) ~** to discuss sthg (with sb) - 2. [rezensieren] to review - 3. [aufnehmen] to record (one's voice) on. ◆ **sich besprechen** *ref*: **sich (mit jm über etw) ~** to confer (with sb about sthg).

Besprechung *(pl -en)* die - 1. [Beratung] discussion; **in einer ~ sein** to be in a meeting - 2. [Rezension] review.

bespritzen *vt* - 1. [nass machen] to splash - 2. [beschmutzen] to spatter.

besser <> *adj & kompar* - 1. [als Komparativ von gut] better; [ziemlich gut] good; **das hier ist schon ein ~es Gerät** this is a pretty good machine; **das Hotel ist eine ~e Absteige** the hotel is just a glorified dosshouse; **~ ist ~** better safe than sorry - 2. [gesellschaftlich gehoben] superior <> *adv* better.

Bessere *(pl -n)* der, die, das better; **~s zu tun haben** to have better things to do.

bessern *vt* to improve; [Verbrecher] to reform. ◆ **sich bessern** *ref* [Wetter, Zustand] to improve; [Mensch] to mend one's ways.

Besserung die improvement. ◆ **gute Besserung** *interj* get well soon!

Bestand der - 1. [Bestehen] continued existence; **~ haben** to last - 2. [Vorrat] stock.

bestanden *pp* ▷ bestehen.

beständig <> *adj* - 1. [dauernd] constant - 2. [gleich bleibend - Wetter] settled; [- Freund] faithful; [- Mitarbeiter] reliable - 3. [widerstandsfähig]: **gegen etw ~ sein** to be resistant to sthg <> *adv* - 1. [dauernd] constantly - 2. [zuverlässig] steadily, reliably.

Bestandsaufnahme die stocktaking.

Bestandteil der component.

bestätigen *vt* to confirm; [Urteil] to uphold. ◆ **sich bestätigen** *ref* to be confirmed, to prove true.

Bestätigung *(pl -en)* die confirmation; [von Urteil] upholding.

beste, r, s <> *adj* best; **sich ~r Gesundheit erfreuen** to enjoy the best of health <> *adv*: **am ~n gehe ich jetzt** I'd better go now.

Beste *(pl -n)* der, die, das best (one); **das ~ aus etw** *(D)* **machen** *fig* to make the best of sthg; **es steht nicht zum ~n mit jm/etw** things are not looking good for sb/sthg; **eine Anekdote zum ~n geben** to tell a story; **jn zum ~n halten** *fig* to pull sb's leg.

bestechen *(präs besticht; prät bestach; perf hat bestochen)* <> *vt* to bribe <> *vi*: **sie besticht durch ihre Schlagfertigkeit** she makes an impression with her quick-wittedness.

bestechlich *adj* open to bribery.

Besteck *(pl -e)* das [Essbesteck] cutlery *(U)*; **ein ~** a place setting.

bestehen *(prät bestand; perf hat bestanden)* <> *vi* - 1. [existieren] to exist; **es steht ... there is ...** - 2. [sich zusammensetzen]: **das Buch besteht aus zehn Kapiteln** the book consists of ten chapters; **der Rahmen besteht aus Kunststoff** the frame is made of plastic - 3. [beinhalten]: **ihre Aufgabe besteht in der Planung des Projekts** her job consists of ODER involves planning the project; **das Problem besteht darin, dass ...** the problem is that ... - 4. [beharren]: **auf etw** *(D)* **~** to insist on sthg - 5. [standhalten]: **vor jm/etw ~** to stand up to sb/sthg <> *vt* to pass.

◆ **bestehen bleiben** *(perf ist bestehen geblieben)* *vi (unreg)* - 1. [übrig bleiben] to remain - 2. [Vorschrift] to be upheld.

bestellen <> *vt* - 1. [anfordern] to order; **sich** *(D)* **etw ~** to order sthg (for o.s.) - 2. [reservieren] to book, to reserve - 3. [kommen lassen] to summon - 4. [ausrichten]: **jm Grüße ~** to give ODER send one's regards to sb; **kann ich ihm etwas (von dir) ~?** can I give him a message (from you)? - 5. [bearbeiten] to cultivate; **es ist um jn/etw schlecht bestellt** sb/sthg is in a bad way <> *vi* to order.

Bestellung *(pl -en)* die - 1. [Anforderung, Waren] order - 2. [Reservierung] booking, reservation - 3. [Bearbeitung] cultivation. ◆ **auf Bestellung** *adv* to order; **wie auf ~** as if by command.

bestenfalls *adv* at best.

bestens *adv* very well.

bestialisch <> *adj abw* [Mord, Tat] brutal <> *adv* - 1. *abw* [grausam] brutally - 2. *fam* [unerträglich] dreadfully.

Bestie *(pl -n)* die - 1. [Raubtier] beast - 2. *abw* [Unmensch] brute.

bestimmen <> *vt* - 1. [Preis, Termin] to fix; **jn zum Nachfolger ~** to designate sb as one's successor - 2. [vorsehen]: **für jn/etw bestimmt sein** to be intended for sb/sthg - 3. [ermitteln] to determine; [Pflanze] to classify; [Bedeutung] to define - 4. [Charakter] to determine; [Stadtbild, Atmosphäre] to characterize <> *vi* - **1.** [entscheiden] to decide; **sie bestimmt in dieser Firma** she makes the decisions in this firm - **2.** [verfügen]: **über etw (frei) ~ können** to be able to do what one likes with sthg.

bestimmt <> *adj* - **1.** [gewiss] certain; [genau] particular - **2.** [festgelegt] fixed - **3.** GRAM definite; **der ~e Artikel** the definite article - **4.** [entschieden] definite, firm <> *adv* - **1.** [entschieden] firmly, decisively - **2.** [sehr wahrscheinlich] no doubt; [sicher] certainly; **das ist ~ kein Problem** I'm sure that won't be a problem; **etw ~ wissen** to know sthg for sure ODER certain; **ganz ~** definitely.

Bestimmtheit *die* firmness, decisiveness; **mit ~** [entschlossen] decisively.

Bestimmung *die* - **1.** *(ohne pl)* [von Preis, Frist] fixing - **2.** [Vorschrift] regulation; **eine gesetzliche ~** a legal provision - **3.** [Zweck] (intended) purpose; **ein Schiff seiner ~ übergeben** to launch a ship - **4.** [Ermitteln] determining; [von Pflanze] classification; [von Begriff, Bedeutung] definition - **5.** GRAM modifier.

Bestleistung *die* SPORT best performance; **ihre persönliche ~** her personal best.

Best.Nr. *(abk für Bestellnummer)* order no.

bestrafen *vt*: **jn (für etw) ~** to punish sb (for sthg); **jn mit Gefängnis ~** to sentence sb to imprisonment.

Bestrafung *(pl -en) die* punishment; [gerichtlich] sentence.

bestreiten *(prät bestritt; perf hat bestritten) vt* - **1.** [leugnen - Meinung, Aussage] to contest; [- Beschuldigung] to deny; **sich nicht ~** it is indispensable - **2.** [finanzieren] to pay for - **3.** [gestalten] to carry.

bestürmen *vt* - **1.** MIL to storm - **2.** [bedrängen]: **jn mit Fragen ~** to bombard sb with questions.

bestürzt <> *adj*: **über etw (A) ~ sein** to be dismayed about sthg <> *adv* in dismay.

Bestzeit *die* SPORT fastest time.

Besuch *(pl -e) der* - **1.** [Besuchen] visit; [von Schule, Kirche] attendance; **bei jm zu ~ sein** to be staying ODER visiting sb - **2.** *(ohne pl)* [Gast] visitor, guest; [Gäste] visitors *(pl)*, guests *(pl)*; **wir haben ~** we have a visitor/visitors.

besuchen *vt* to visit; [Kirche, Schule, Vorlesung] to attend.

Besucher, in *(mpl -; fpl -nen) der, die* visitor.

besucht *adj*: **gut/schlecht ~** well/poorly attended.

betätigen *vt* [Hebel] to operate; [Bremse] to apply. **~ sich betätigen** *ref*: **sich politisch/sportlich ~** to engage in politics/sport.

betäuben *vt* - **1.** MED to anaesthetize - **2.** [Trauer, Schmerz] to deaden, to dull.

beteiligen *vt*: **jn an etw (D) ~** to give sb a share in sthg. **~ sich beteiligen** *ref*: **sich an etw (D) ~** to participate in sthg; [Kosten] to contribute to sthg.

Beteiligung *(pl -en) die* - **1.** [Mitwirkung]: **~ (an etw (D))** participation (in sthg); [an Verbrechen] involvement (in sthg) - **2.** [an Gewinn] share.

beten <> *vi* to pray; **um** ODER **für etw ~** der to pray for sthg; **für jn ~** to pray for sb <> *vt* to say.

beteuern *vt* to declare.

Beton [be'tɔŋ] *(pl -s) der* concrete.

betonen *vt* - **1.** [aussprechen] to stress - **2.** [hervorheben] to emphasize, to stress.

Betonung *(pl -en) die* - **1.** [Betonen] stress - **2.** [Hervorhebung] emphasis.

Betracht *(ohne Artikel)* **~ in Betracht** *adv*: **jn/etw in ~ ziehen** [erwägen] to consider sb/sthg; [berücksichtigen] to take sb/sthg into account; **(nicht) in ~ kommen** (not) to be worth considering. **~ außer Betracht** *adv*: **etw außer ~ lassen** to disregard sthg.

betrachten *vt* - **1.** [ansehen] to look at; **(D) etw (näher) ~** to have a (closer) look at sthg - **2.** [beurteilen] to regard - **3.** [überprüfen] to examine, to consider. **~ sich betrachten** *ref* to look at o.s.

Betrachter, in *(mpl -; fpl -nen) der, die* observer.

beträchtlich <> *adj* considerable <> *adv* considerably.

Betrachtung *(pl -en) die* - **1.** [Betrachten] contemplation - **2.** [Überlegung] reflection.

Betrag *(pl Beträge) der* amount *(of money)*.

betragen *(präs beträgt; prät betrug; perf hat betragen) vt* [Preis, Rechnung] to amount ODER come to; **die Entfernung von A zu B beträgt 10 Kilometer** A is 10 kilometres away from B. **~ sich betragen** *ref*: **sich gut/schlecht ~** to behave well/badly.

betreffen *(präs betrifft; prät betraf; perf hat betroffen) vt* [angehen] to concern; [Auswirkungen haben auf] to affect; **was mich/diese Angelegenheit betrifft** as far as I am/this matter is concerned.

Betreffende *(pl -n) der, die* person concerned.

betreiben *(prät betrieb; perf hat betrieben) vt* - **1.** [vorantreiben] to pursue - **2.** [führen - Gewerbe] to carry on; [- Laden] to run - **3.** [antreiben]: **mit etw betrieben werden** to be driven by sthg; **diese Anlage wird mit Solarenergie betrieben** this system is solar-powered.

betreten¹ <> *adj* embarrassed <> *adv* sheepishly.

betreten² *(präs betritt; prät betrat; perf hat betreten) vt* to enter; [Rasen] to walk on; [Bühne] to walk onto.

betreuen vt to look after, to take care of; [Sportler] to coach.

Betreuer, in (mpl -; fpl -nen) der, die [von Kindern] child-minder; [von Sportlern] coach; [von Touristen] guide; [von Alten] care worker.

Betreuung die care; [von Sportler] coaching.

Betrieb (pl -e) der - 1. [Unternehmen] company, firm; [Produktionsstätte] plant; **heute ist er nicht im ~** he is not at work today - 2. [Tätigkeit] operation - 3. [Treiben, Verkehr]: **es ist** ODER **herrscht viel ~** it is very busy. **◆ in Betrieb** adv in operation; **etw in ~ setzen** [Maschine] to start (up) sthg; [Fabrik] to commission sthg. **◆ außer Betrieb** adv out of order; **etw außer ~ setzen** [Maschine] to stop sthg, to shut down sthg; [Fabrik] to decommission sthg.

betriebsam adj busy.

Betriebs|rat der - 1. [Gremium] works council - 2. [Mensch] works council member.

Betriebs|system das EDV operating system.

Betriebs|wirtschaft die business administration.

betrinken (prät betrank; perf hat betrunken) **◆ sich betrinken** ref to get drunk.

betroffen ◇ pp ☞ betreffen ◇ adj - 1. [bestürzt] shaken, upset; [Schweigen] stunned - 2. [nicht verschont]: **von etw ~ sein** to be affected by sthg ◇ adv: **jn ~ ansehen** to look at sb in consternation.

betrübt adj [Gesicht] sad; [Stimmung] gloomy; **über etw** (A) **~ sein** to be sad about sthg.

Betrug der fraud; **das ist ja ~!** this is daylight robbery!

betrügen (prät betrog; perf hat betrogen) ◇ vt to cheat; [Ehepartner] to cheat on; **jn um etw ~** to cheat sb out of sthg ◇ vi to cheat.

Betrüger (pl -) der conman, con artist.

Betrügerei (pl -en) die swindling.

Betrügerin (pl -nen) die con artist.

betrunken ◇ pp ☞ betrinken ◇ adj drunk.

Bett (pl -en) das - 1. [gen] bed; **ins** ODER **zu ~ gehen** to go to bed; **das ~ machen** to make the bed - 2. [Federbett] duvet, quilt.

Bett|decke die [aus Wolle] blanket; [gesteppt] quilt, duvet.

betteln vi to beg; **um etw ~** to beg for sthg.

betten vt: **jn auf etw** (A) **~** to lay sb (down) on sthg.

Bettler, in (mpl -; fpl -nen) der, die beggar.

Betttuch (pl -tücher) das sheet.

Bett|wäsche die bed linen.

Bett|zeug das (ohne pl) bedding, bedclothes (pl).

beugen vt - 1. [Körper, Finger, Gesetz] to bend - 2. [Substantiv, Adjectiv] to inflect; [Verb] to conjugate. **◆ sich beugen** ref - 1. [sich lehnen] to lean - 2. [sich unterwerfen]: **sich einer Sache** (D) **~** to submit ODER bow to sthg.

Beule (pl -n) die [am Kopf] lump; [am Auto] dent.

beunruhigen [bəˈʊnruːɪgn̩] vt to worry; **über etw** (A) **beunruhigt sein** to be worried about sthg.

beurlauben [bəˈuːɐ̯laʊbn̩] vt [suspendieren] to suspend.

beurteilen [bəˈuːɐ̯taɪln̩] vt to judge; [Größe, Qualität] to assess; **jn falsch ~** to misjudge sb.

Beurteilung [bəˈuːɐ̯taɪlʊŋ] (pl -en) die judgement; [von Größe, Qualität] assessment.

Beute die - 1. [von Einbrecher] loot - 2. [von Raubtier] prey.

Beutel (pl -) der [Sack] bag.

bevölkern vt - 1. [bewohnen] to inhabit - 2. [füllen] to fill.

Bevölkerung (pl -en) die population.

bevollmächtigen vt to authorize.

bevor konj before.

bevor|stehen vi (unreg) to be imminent.

bevorzugen vt - 1. [vorziehen] to prefer - 2. [protegieren] to give preferential treatment to.

bewachen vt to guard.

Bewacher, in (mpl -; fpl -nen) der, die guard.

bewaffnen vt to arm. **◆ sich bewaffnen** ref to arm o.s.

Bewaffnung (pl -en) die - 1. [Ausrüstung] armament, arming - 2. [Waffen] arms (pl).

bewahren vt - 1. [Person]: **jn vor etw** (D) **~** to protect sb from sthg - 2. [Nerven, Ruhe] to keep.

bewähren ◆ sich bewähren ref to prove one's/its worth.

bewahrheiten ◆ sich bewahrheiten ref to prove (to be) true.

Bewährung die - 1. [Profilierung] test, trial - 2. RECHT probation; **auf** ODER **mit ~** on probation.

bewaldet adj wooded.

bewältigen vt [Arbeit, Problem] to cope with; [js Tod, die Vergangenheit] to come to terms with; [Papierberge] to get through.

bewässern vt to irrigate.

bewegen[1] (prät bewegte; perf hat bewegt) vt (reg) - 1. [gen] to move - 2. [beschäftigen] to concern, to preoccupy. **◆ sich bewegen** ref - 1. [körperlich] to move; [im Freien] to take ODER get some exercise - 2. [sich verhalten] to act.

bewegen² (*prät* bewog; *perf* hat bewogen) *vt* (*unreg*) *geh* : **jn zu etw ~** [veranlassen] to induce sb to do sthg; [überreden] to prevail upon sb to do sthg.

beweglich *adj* agile; [Hebel] movable.

bewegt *adj* - **1.** [unruhig - Leben] eventful; [- See, Meer] choppy - **2.** [Stimme, Worte] emotional.

Bewegung (*pl* -en) *die* - **1.** [körperlich, politisch] movement; **etw in ~ setzen** to set sthg in motion; **sich in ~ setzen** [Person] *fam* to get moving; [Zug] to start to move - **2.** [körperlich] exercise.

Bewegungsfreiheit *die* freedom of movement; [Handlungsspielraum] room for manoeuvre.

bewegungslos <> *adj* motionless <> *adv*: **~ dastehen** to stand there motionless.

Beweis (*pl* -e) *der*: **ein ~** a piece of evidence; **~e** evidence, proof.

beweisen (*prät* bewies; *perf* hat bewiesen) *vt* - **1.** [gen] to prove; [Unschuld] to establish - **2.** [Mut] to show.

bewerben (*präs* bewirbt; *prät* bewarb; *perf* hat beworben) ◆ **sich bewerben** *ref* to apply; **sich bei einer Firma ~** to apply for a job with a firm; **sich um etw ~** to apply for sthg.

Bewerber, in (*mpl* -; *fpl* -nen) *der, die* applicant.

Bewerbung *die* application.

bewerfen (*präs* bewirft; *prät* bewarf; *perf* hat beworfen) *vt*: **jn/etw mit etw ~** to pelt sb/sthg with sthg.

bewerten *vt* to assess, to evaluate; [Klassenarbeit] to mark; **etw zu hoch/niedrig ~** to overrate/underrate sthg.

bewilligen *vt* [Antrag] to approve; [Hilfe, Kredit] to grant.

bewirken *vt* to cause; **es bewirkte das Gegenteil** it had the opposite effect; **wir haben bewirkt, dass jetzt Nachtbusse eingesetzt werden** we have managed to get them to lay on a night bus service.

bewohnen *vt* to inhabit.

Bewohner, in (*mpl* -; *fpl* -nen) *der, die* inhabitant.

bewölkt *adj* cloudy, overcast.

Bewölkung *die* (*ohne pl*) - **1.** clouding over - **2.** [Wolken] clouds (*pl*).

bewundern *vt* to admire.

Bewunderung *die* admiration.

bewusst <> *adj* - **1.** [absichtlich] deliberate - **2.** [bedacht] conscious; **ihre Absichten sind mir ~** I am aware of her motives; **ihre Absichten wurden mir ~** I realized what her motives were; **einer Sache** (*G*) **~ sein** to be aware of sthg <> *adv* - **1.** [absichtlich] deliberately - **2.** [bedacht] consciously.

bewusstlos *adj* unconscious.

Bewusstlosigkeit *die* (state of) unconsciousness.

Bewusstsein *das* - **1.** [Wissen] awareness - **2.** [geistige Klarheit] consciousness; **bei ~ sein** to be conscious; **das ~ verlieren** to lose consciousness.

bezahlen <> *vt* [Ware, Leistung] to pay for; [Person, Miete, Rechnung] to pay <> *vi* to pay; **wir möchten bitte ~!** may we have the bill please?

bezahlt *adj* paid.

Bezahlung *die* - **1.** [von Ware, Rechnung] payment - **2.** [Entgelt] pay.

bezeichnen *vt* - **1.** [nennen] to call; **jn/etw als etw ~** to describe sb/sthg as sthg - **2.** [markieren] to mark, to indicate.

bezeichnend *adj* characteristic; **~ für etw sein** to be characteristic of sthg.

Bezeichnung *die* - **1.** [Benennung] name; [Beschreibung] description - **2.** [Markierung] marking.

beziehen (*prät* bezog; *perf* hat bezogen) *vt* - **1.** [Kissen, Sofa] to cover; **das Bett frisch ~** to change the bedclothes - **2.** [Haus, Wohnung] to move into - **3.** [Ware, Zeitung, Einkünfte] to get; [Arbeitslosenhilfe] to receive - **4.** [anwenden]: **etw auf sich** (*A*) /**jn ~** to understand sthg to refer to o.s./to sb; **eine Aussage auf sich** (*A*) **~** to take a remark personally. ◆ **sich beziehen** *ref* - **1.** [angewendet werden]: **sich auf jn/etw ~** to refer to sb/sthg; **meine Kritik bezog sich nicht auf Sie** my criticism wasn't aimed at you - **2.** [sich berufen]: **sich auf etw** (*A*) **~** to refer to sthg - **3.** [sich bewölken]: **der Himmel bezieht sich** the sky is clouding over.

Beziehung *die* - **1.** [Kontakt - zu Person] relationship; **~en** [politisch] relations; **gute/ schlechte ~en zu jm haben** to be on good/ bad terms with sb; **er verfügt über gute ~en** he has lots of contacts - **2.** [Verhältnis] connection - **3.** [Hinsicht] respect.

beziehungsweise *konj* - **1.** [genauer gesagt] or rather, that is - **2.** [oder] or; **die Kinder sind ins Kino, ~ ins Schwimmbad gegangen** the children have either gone to the cinema or gone swimming - **3.** [jeweils] and ... respectively; **die Uhren kosten 300 ~ 400 DM** the watches cost 300 DM and 400 DM respectively.

Bezirk (*pl* -e) *der* district; [von Kirche] diocese.

Bezug (*pl* Bezüge) *der* - **1.** [Überzug] cover - **2.** [Beziehung]: **auf etw** (*A*) **~ nehmen** *amt* to refer to sthg; **in Bezug auf etw** (*A*) with regard to sthg. ◆ **Bezüge** *pl* income (*U*).

Bezugsperson *die* person to whom one looks for guidance, support etc.

bezwecken *vt*: **etw mit etw ~** to aim to achieve sthg by sthg.

bezweifeln *vt* to doubt.

BGB [be:ge:'be:] (*abk für* Bürgerliches Gesetzbuch) *das* German civil code.

BH [be:'ha:] (*pl* -s) (*abk für* Büstenhalter) *der* bra.

Bhf. *abk für* Bahnhof.

Bibel (*pl* -n) *die* bible.

Biber (*pl* -) *der* [Tier] beaver.

Bibliothek (*pl* -en) *die* library.

biegen (*prät* bog; *perf* hat/ist gebogen) ⟨⟩ *vt* (*hat*) to bend ⟨⟩ *vi* (*ist*) [Auto, Fahrer]: **um die Ecke ~** to go round the corner. ⟼ **sich biegen** *ref* to bend.

Biegung (*pl* -en) *die* bend.

Biene (*pl* -n) *die* bee.

Bier (*pl* -e) *das* beer; **ein großes/kleines ~** a half-litre/30 cl glass of beer.

Bier|dose *die* beer can.

Bier|garten *der* beer garden.

Bier|glas *das* beer glass.

bieten (*prät* bot; *perf* hat geboten) *vt* - **1.** [anbieten] to offer; [Schutz, Chance] to provide; **jm etw ~** to offer sb sthg; [Gelegenheit, Schutz] to provide sb with sthg - **2.** [zeigen] to present; **einen schrecklichen Anblick ~** to look terrible - **3.** [gefallen]: **sich** (*D*) **etw nicht ~ lassen** not to stand for sthg. ⟼ **sich bieten** *ref*: **es bot sich eine Gelegenheit an** opportunity came up.

Bikini (*pl* -s) *der* bikini.

Bilanz (*pl* -en) *die* - **1.** WIRTSCH balance; [schriftlich] balance sheet - **2.** [Ergebnis] outcome.

Bild (*pl* -er) *das* - **1.** [gen & TV] picture; [Gemälde] painting; [Zeichnung] drawing; [Foto] photograph - **2.** [Anblick] sight - **3.** [Vorstellung] idea, impression; **sich** (*D*) **ein ~ von jm/etw machen** to get an idea of sb/sthg - **4.** [Metapher] image - **5.** RW: **über etw** (*A*) **im ~e sein** to be in the picture (about sthg).

bilden ⟨⟩ *vt* [gen] to form ⟨⟩ *vi*: **lesen bildet** reading improves your mind. ⟼ **sich bilden** *ref* - **1.** [sich formen] to form - **2.** [sich informieren] to educate o.s.

Bilder|buch *das* picture book.

Bild|hauer, in *die* (*mpl* -; *fpl* -nen) *der*, *die* sculptor (*f* sculptress).

bildlich ⟨⟩ *adj* - **1.** [Darstellung] pictorial - **2.** [Wendung, Ausdruck] figurative ⟨⟩ *adv* - **1.** [darstellen] pictorially - **2.** [gesprochen] figuratively.

Bild|schirm *der* screen.

Bildschirmschoner (*pl* -) *der* EDV screen saver.

Bildung (*pl* -en) *die* - **1.** [Ausbildung] education; **eine umfassende ~ besitzen** to be well-educated ODER cultured - **2.** [Formung] formation.

Bildungs|politik *die* education policy.

Bildungs|weg *der*: **der zweite ~** *second chance for people outside the education system to obtain educational qualifications.*

Billard ['bɪljart] *das* billiards (*U*).

billig ⟨⟩ *adj* - **1.** [preiswert] cheap - **2.** *abw*

[schlecht - Anzug, Papier, Scherz, Trick] cheap; [- Ausrede] feeble ⟨⟩ *adv* cheaply; **die Vase habe ich ~ gekauft** I got the vase cheap.

Billig|angebot *das* special offer.

Billig|lohn|land *das*: **Arbeiter aus Billiglohnländer wie Indonesien** cheap labour from countries like Indonesia.

bimmeln *vi* to ring.

bin *präs* ⟹ sein.

Binde (*pl* -n) *die* - **1.** [Verband] bandage - **2.** [über den Augen] blindfold; [um den Arm] armband - **3.** [Damenbinde] sanitary towel.

Binde|mittel *das* binding agent.

binden (*prät* band; *perf* hat gebunden) ⟨⟩ *vt* - **1.** [zusammenbinden] to tie together - **2.** [festbinden]: **etw an etw** (*A*) **~** to tie sthg to sthg - **3.** [Krawatte] to knot; [Schleife, Knoten] to tie - **4.** [Soße, Buch, durch Vertrag] to bind ⟨⟩ *vi* to bind. ⟼ **sich binden** *ref* [heiraten] to get married.

Binde|strich *der* hyphen.

Bind|faden *der* string.

Bindung (*pl* -en) *die* - **1.** [Verbundenheit] bond; [Verpflichtung] commitment - **2.** [Ski-bindung] binding.

Binnen|markt *der* internal market; [von EU] single market; **der europäische ~** the European single market.

Biochemie *die* biochemistry.

Biokost *die* health food.

Biologe (*pl* -n) *der* biologist.

Biologie *die* biology.

Biologin (*pl* -nen) *die* biologist.

biologisch *adj* - **1.** [der Biologie] biological - **2.** [natürlich - Farben] natural; [- Brot] organic.

birgt *präs* ⟹ bergen.

Birke (*pl* -n) *die* birch.

Birn|baum *der* pear tree.

Birne (*pl* -n) *die* - **1.** [Frucht] pear - **2.** [Glühbirne] light bulb - **3.** *fam* [Kopf] nut.

birst *präs* ⟹ bersten.

bis ⟨⟩ *präp* (+ *A*) - **1.** [zeitlich] until; **wir bleiben ~ morgen** we're staying until tomorrow; **von Montag ~ Freitag** from Monday to Friday, Monday through Friday *Am*; **~ auf weiteres** until further notice; **~ bald!** see you soon!; **~ dann!** see you then!; **~ morgen!/später!** see you tomorrow/later! - **2.** [spätestens] by; **das muss ~ Mittwoch fertig sein** it must be ready by Wednesday - **3.** [räumlich] to; **es sind noch 200 km ~ Berlin** there are still 200 km to Berlin; **~ auf die Haut durchnässt** soaked to the skin ⟨⟩ *konj* until; **warte, ~ ich komme** wait until I'm there. ⟼ **bis auf** *präp* (+ *A*) except for, apart from. ⟼ **bis zu** *präp* up to; **~ zu 20 Personen** up to 20 people.

Bischof (*pl* Bischöfe) *der* bishop.

bischöflich *adj* episcopal.

bisher *adv:* ~ hat sie nicht angerufen she hasn't called so far; **wir haben das ~ immer so gemacht** until now we've always done it this way.

bisherig *adj* [ehemalig] former; **sein ~es Verhalten** his behaviour up to now.

bislang *adv:* ~ hat sie nicht angerufen she hasn't called so far; **wir haben das ~ immer so gemacht** until now we've always done it this way.

Bison (*pl* -s) *der* bison.

biss *prät* ⊳ **beißen**.

Biss (*pl* -e) *der eigtl & fig* bite.

bisschen *adj* [wenig]: **das ~ Regen macht doch nichts** that little bit of rain won't do any harm. ◆ **das bisschen** *pron:* **das ~ kannst du jetzt auch noch essen** you can eat that little bit up. ◆ **ein bisschen** ⊳ *adj* [etwas] a bit of, a little; **ein ~ Kaffee** a drop of coffee ⊳ *adv* [ein wenig] a bit; **ein ~ bleiben** to stay a while. ◆ **kein bisschen** ⊳ *adj:* **wir haben kein ~ Brot** we have no bread at all ⊳ *adv* [nicht] not at all. ◆ **ach du liebes bisschen** *interj* oh, dear!

Bissen (*pl* -) *der* [Stück] bite.

bissig *adj eigtl & fig* vicious; '**Vorsicht, ~er Hund**' 'beware of the dog'.

bist *präs* ⊳ **sein**.

Bistum (*pl* -tümer) *das* diocese.

bitte ⊳ *adv* please ⊳ *interj* - **1.** [als Bitte, Aufforderung] please; **bedient euch, ~!** please help yourselves!; **~! Hier ist Ihr Kaffee!** here's your coffee for you; **~ sehr! Kommen Sie herein!** (do) come in!; **~ schön! was möchten Sie kaufen?** yes Sir/Madam, how can I help you? - **2.** [als Antwort]: **danke! - ~!** thanks! - don't mention it!; **Entschuldigung! - ~!** sorry! - that's all right!; **kann ich nur einen Apfel nehmen? - ~!** may I have an apple? - of course!; **~ sehr** ODER **schön!** [Antwort auf einen Dank] don't mention it!, you're welcome! - **3.** [als Nachfrage] pardon?, sorry?; **wie ~?** pardon?, sorry? - **4.** [am Telefon]: **ja ~?** hello? - **5.** [zur Selbstbestätigung]: **na ~!** there you are, you see!

bitte

In Germany, bitte is used when making a request ("please") or in response to danke (in the sense of "don't mention it" or "you're welcome"). The following dialogue illustrates both uses: Kann ich bitte telefonieren? "May I use your phone? Aber natürlich! "Of course!" Danke. "Thank you." Bitte sehr. "Don't mention it".

Bitte (*pl* -n) *die* [Anliegen] request; **eine ~ um etw** a request for sthg.

bitten (*prät* bat; *perf* hat gebeten) ⊳ *vt*

- **1.** [höflich auffordern]: **jn ~, etw zu tun** to ask sb to do sthg; **ich bitte Sie, etwas leiser zu sein!** please be a little quieter!; **jn um etw ~** to ask sb for sthg; **ich bitte Sie um Aufmerksamkeit!** may I have your attention, please! - **2.** [einladen]: **jn zu sich ~** to ask sb to come to one ⊳ *vi* [Bitte aussprechen]: **um etw ~** to ask for sthg; **ich bitte um Ruhe!** silence, please!

bitten

Could you give me a hand with these bags? Könntest du mir mit diesen Taschen helfen?
Can you tell him I'll phone back? Können Sie ihm ausrichten, ich rufe zurück?
Would you pass the salt, please? Könnte ich bitte das Salz haben?
I was wondering whether you could lend me £10? Könntest du mir vielleicht 10 Pfund leihen?
Would you mind getting me some stamps while you're out? Kannst du mir auf dem Weg ein paar Briefmarken mitbringen?

bitter ⊳ *adj* - **1.** [gen] bitter - **2.** [Ironie] biting - **3.** [Not] desperate; [Armut] abject ⊳ *adv* - **1.** [gen] bitterly; **~ schmecken** to taste bitter - **2.** [benötigen] desperately.

Bitterkeit *die eigtl & fig* bitterness.

Bizeps (*pl* -e) *der* biceps (*sg*).

BKA [be:ka:'a:] (*abk für* Bundeskriminalamt) *das Federal Office for criminal investigation*.

Blähungen *pl* wind (*U*).

Blamage [bla'ma:ʒə] (*pl* -n) *die* disgrace.

blamieren *vt* [kompromittieren] to disgrace. ◆ **sich blamieren** *ref* [sich bloßstellen] to disgrace o.s.

blamieren

The German verb blamieren means "to disgrace" or, in its reflexive form, "to disgrace oneself" – it does not mean "to blame". So the phrase Er hat sich vor allen Leuten blamiert might be rendered in English as "He disgraced himself in front of everybody".
To translate the English verb "to blame", you should use a construction such as jm die Schuld an etw geben. The phrase "You can't blame him for that" can therefore be translated into German as Dafür kann man ihm nicht die Schuld geben.

blank *adj* - **1.** [glänzend] shiny - **2.** [pur] sheer, pure - **3.** [unbedeckt] bare; **~ sein** *fam* to be broke.

Blase (*pl* -n) *die* - **1.** [auf der Haut] blister

- 2. [Luftblase] **bubble - 3.** [Harnblase] **bladder.**

Blasebalg (*pl* -bälge) *der* bellows (*pl*).

blasen (*präs* bläst; *prät* blies; *perf* hat geblasen) ⬦ *vt* **- 1.** [gen] to blow **- 2.** [Trompete, Horn] to play ⬦ *vt* **- 1.** [gen] to blow **- 2.** *vulg* : **jm einen ~** to give sb a blow job ⬦ *vi* **- 1.** [gen] to blow **- 2.** [auf Trompete, Horn] to play.

Blasinstrument *das* wind instrument.

Blaskapelle *die* brass band.

blass (*kompar* blasser ODER blässer; *superl* blasseste ODER blässeste) *adj* **- 1.** [Haut] pale **- 2.** [Erinnerung, Ähnung] **vague;** [Hoffnung] faint.

Blässe *die* paleness.

bläst *präs* ⬦ blasen.

Blatt (*pl* Blätter) *das* **- 1.** [von Pflanzen] leaf **- 2.** [Papier] sheet **- 3.** [Seite] page **- 4.** [Zeitung] paper **- 5.** *RW:* **ein unbeschriebenes ~ sein** [unbekannt] to be an unknown quantity; [unerfahren] to be inexperienced; **kein ~ vor den Mund nehmen** not to mince one's words; **das ~ hat sich gewendet** the tide has turned.

blättern (*perf* hat/ist geblättert) ⬦ *vi* **- 1.** (*hat*) [umschlagen]: **in etw** (D) ~ to leaf through sthg **- 2.** (*ist*) [abblättern] to flake (off) ⬦ *vt* (*hat*) [Geldscheine] to count out.

Blätterteig *der* puff pastry.

blau (*kompar* blauer; *superl* blau(e)ste) *adj* **- 1.** [Farbe] blue **- 2.** [geprellt]: **ein ~es Auge** a black eye; **ein ~er Fleck** a bruise **- 3.** [betrunken]: ~ **sein** *fam* to be sloshed **- 4.** [geschwänzt] *fam:* **einen ~en Montag machen** to skip ODER skive off *Br* work on Monday.

Blau *das* [Farbe] blue.

blauäugig *adj* **- 1.** [Augen] blue-eyed **- 2.** [naiv] naïve.

Blaubeere *die* bilberry, blueberry.

Blaue (*pl* -n) ⬦ *das* **- 1.** [Farbe] blue **- 2.** [Unbekannte]: **ins ~** [fahren] with no particular place to go; [reden] aimlessly ⬦ *der fam* [Hundertmarkschein] *a one-hundred-mark note.*

Blauhelm *der* blue beret.

bläulich *adj* bluish.

Blaulicht *das* [Signal] flashing blue light (*on ambulance etc.*).

blaumachen *vi fam* [schwänzen] to stay away from school/work.

Blazer ['blɛːzɐ] (*pl* -) *der* blazer.

Blech (*pl* -e) *das* **- 1.** [Metall] sheet metal **- 2.** [Backblech] baking sheet *Br,* cookie sheet *Am* **- 3.** *fam* [Unsinn] rubbish.

blechen *fam vt & vi* to fork out.

Blechinstrument *das* brass instrument.

Blechschaden *der* bodywork damage (*U*).

Blei *das* [Metall] lead.

Bleibe (*pl* -n) *die* place to stay.

bleiben (*prät* blieb; *perf* ist geblieben) *vi* **- 1.** [an einem Ort] to stay; **wo bleibst du**

denn so lange? [bei Eintreffen] what kept you? **- 2.** [in einem Zustand] to remain; **sie ist ganz die Alte geblieben** she hasn't changed a bit; **wir ~ in Kontakt** we keep in touch; **bei etw ~** to stick to sthg; **es bleibt also dabei, morgen um zehn Uhr** ten o'clock tomorrow morning, like we said, then?; **das bleibt unter uns** it's strictly between ourselves **- 3.** [als Übriges] to be left; **uns ~ nur noch wenige Tage** we only have a few days left.

bleibend *adj* lasting.

bleiben lassen *vt* (*unreg*) **- 1.** [unterlassen] to leave be **- 2.** [aufgeben] to give up.

bleich *adj* pale.

bleifrei *adj* unleaded.

Bleistift *der* pencil.

Bleistiftspitzer (*pl* -) *der* pencil sharpener.

Blende (*pl* -n) *die* **- 1.** [vor Fenster] blind, screen; AUTO visor **-** [FOTO - Objektivöffnung] diaphragm; [- Blendenzahl] aperture.

blenden ⬦ *vt eigtl & fig* to dazzle ⬦ *vi* [Licht] to be dazzling.

blendend ⬦ *adj* dazzling ⬦ *adv* marvellously; **du siehst ~ aus!** you look dazzling!

Blick (*pl* -e) *der* **- 1.** [der Augen] look; [kurz] glance; **den ~ heben/senken** to raise/lower one's eyes; **einen ~ auf etw** (A) **werfen** to glance at sthg; **sie würdigte mich/es keines ~es** she did not deign to look at me/it **- 2.** [Ausblick] view **- 3.** [Urteil] eye **- 4.** *RW:* **keinen ~ für etw haben** not to appreciate sthg.

blicken *vi* to look; **sich (nicht) ~ lassen** (not) to show one's face; **das lässt tief ~** that explains a lot.

Blickpunkt *der:* **im ~ der Öffentlichkeit** in the public eye.

blieb *prät* ⬦ bleiben.

blies *prät* ⬦ blasen.

blind ⬦ *adj* **- 1.** [gen] blind; ~ **für etw sein** to be blind to sthg **- 2.** [versteckt] **-** Passagier **- 3.** [falsch] **-** Alarm ⬦ *adv* blindly.

Blinddarmentzündung *die* appendicitis (*U*).

Blinde (*pl* -n) *der, die* blind man (*f* blind woman).

Blindenschrift *die* braille.

Blindheit *die eigtl & fig* blindness.

blinken *vi* **- 1.** [funkeln - Metall] to gleam; [- Sterne] to twinkle; [- Wasser, Edelstein] to sparkle **- 2.** [signalisieren - Verkehr] to indicate; [Signal geben] to signal.

Blinker (*pl* -) *der* indicator *Br,* turn signal *Am.*

Blinklicht *das* flashing light.

blinzeln *vi* [mit einem Auge, als Zeichen] to wink; [mit beiden Augen] to blink.

Blitz (*pl* -e) *der* **- 1.** [am Himmel] lightning (*U*); **ein ~ a** flash of lightning; **wie der ~** like lightning **- 2.** [Blitzlicht] flash.

Blitzableiter (*pl* -) *der* lightning conductor.

blitzblank *adj* [Geschirr] sparkling clean; [Wohnung] spotless.

blitzen ⬦ *vi* - 1. [am Himmel]: **es blitzt** there is lightning - 2. [funkeln - Schmuck, Wohnung] to sparkle; [- Metall] to gleam ⬦ *vt fam* [fotografieren] to take a flash photo of; **geblitzt werden** to be caught by a speed camera.

Blitzlicht *das* flash.

Blitzschlag *der* flash of lightning; **vom ~ getroffen werden** to be struck by lightning.

blitzschnell ⬦ *adj* lightning ⬦ *adv* like lightning.

Block (*pl* Blöcke ODER -s) *der* - 1. (*pl* Blöcke) [Stück] block - 2. (*pl* Blöcke) [aus Papier] pad - 3. (*pl* Blöcke, Blocks) [Häuserblock] block - 4. (*pl* Blocks) [Gruppe - von Staaten] bloc; [Fraktion] faction.

Blockade (*pl* -n) *die* blockade.

Blockflöte *die* recorder.

Blockhaus *das* log cabin.

blockieren ⬦ *vt* - 1. EDV [versperren] to block - 2. [zum Stillstand bringen] to obstruct ⬦ *vi* [Motor] to jam; [Räder] to lock.

Blockschrift *die* block capitals (*pl*).

blöd, blöde *fam* ⬦ *adj* stupid ⬦ *adv* stupidly.

Blödsinn *der fam* rubbish.

blond *adj* blond (*f* blonde).

Blondine (*pl* -n) *die* blonde.

bloß ⬦ *adv* - 1. *fam* [lediglich] only, just; **jetzt ~ noch etwas drehen** now just turn it some more - 2. [zum Ausdruck von Ratlosigkeit]: **was sollen wir ~ machen?** what on earth shall we do? - 3. [zum Ausdruck von Ärger]: **warum musstest du ~ den Schlüssel stecken lassen?** why did you have to go and leave the key in the lock? - 4. [zum Ausdruck einer Drohung]: **hau ~ ab!** just push off, all right?; **unterschreib das ~ nicht!** don't you dare sign that! - 5. [zum Ausdruck einer Aufforderung]: **~ keine Panik!** just don't panic! - 6. [zum Ausdruck eines Wunsches]: **hätte ich ~ nichts gesagt!** if only I hadn't said anything! ⬦ *adj* - 1. [nackt] bare; **mit ~en Füßen** barefoot; **mit ~em Auge** with the naked eye - 2. [rein] sheer.

bloßstellen *vt* to show up; [Betrüger] to unmask.

bluffen [blœfn] *abw vt & vi* to bluff.

blühen *vi* - 1. [Pflanze] to bloom, to flower; [Baum] to blossom - 2. [florieren] to flourish - 3. *fam* [drohen]: **das kann dir auch noch ~!** you could still be in for it!

blühend *adj* - 1. [Pflanze] blooming, flowering; [tree] blossoming - 2. [frisch] radiant - 3. [ausufernd]: **eine ~e Fantasie** a vivid imagination.

Blume (*pl* -n) *die* [Pflanze] flower.

Blumenkohl *der* cauliflower.

Blumenstrauß *der* bunch of flowers.

Blumentopf *der* flowerpot.

Bluse (*pl* -n) *die* blouse.

Blut *das* blood; **~ spenden** to give blood; **~ stillend** styptic.

Blutabnahme *die* blood test.

Blutbad *das* bloodbath.

Blutdruck *der* blood pressure.

Blüte (*pl* -n) *die* - 1. [Pflanzenteil] flower, bloom; [von Baum] blossom - 2. [das Blühen] flowering, blooming; [von Baum] blossoming; **in voller ~** in full flower; [Baum] in full blossom - 3. [Aufschwung] flowering.

Blutegel (*pl* -) *der* leech.

bluten *vi* to bleed; **aus der Nase ~** to have a nosebleed.

Bluter, in (*mpl* -/ *fpl* -nen) *der, die* haemophiliac.

Bluterguss *der* MED haematoma; [blauer Fleck] bruise.

Blütezeit *die* - 1. [von Pflanze] flowering period - 2. [von Kultur, Reich] heyday.

Blutgefäß *das* blood vessel.

Blutgruppe *die* blood group.

blutig ⬦ *adj* bloody ⬦ *adv* - 1. [befleckt]: **jn ~ schlagen** to beat sb to a pulp - 2. [niederschlagen] bloodily.

Blutkonserve *die* unit of stored blood (*for transfusions etc.*).

Blutkörperchen (*pl* -) *das* corpuscle; **weiße/rote ~** white/red blood cells.

Blutkreislauf *der* blood circulation.

Blutprobe *die* - 1. [Untersuchung] blood test - 2. [entnommenes Blut] blood sample.

Blutspender, in *der, die* blood donor.

Blutübertragung *die* blood transfusion.

Blutung (*pl* -en) *die* bleeding; MED haemorrhage; [Monatsblutung] period.

blutunterlaufen *adj* bloodshot.

Blutwurst *die* black pudding *Br*, blood sausage *Am*.

BLZ *abk für* Bankleitzahl.

Bö = Böe.

Bock (*pl* Böcke) *der* - 1. [Kaninchen, Reh] buck; [Ziege] billy-goat; [Schaf] ram; **stur wie ein ~** as stubborn as a mule; **ein geiler ~** *salopp* a randy old goat - 2. SPORT (vaulting) horse - 3. [Gerüst] trestle - 4. *RW*: **darauf hab ich keinen ~** I can't be fagged.

Bockbier *das* bock, *strong dark beer*.

bockig *adj* [trotzig] contrary.

Bockspringen *das* - 1. SPORT vaulting - 2. [Spiel] leapfrog.

Bockwurst *die type of pork sausage, usually boiled and eaten in a bread roll with mustard.*

Boden (*pl* -) *der* - 1. [Grund] ground; [Erdreich] soil; **auf deutschem ~** on German soil; **er hat den ~ unter den Füßen verloren** [beim

Klettern] he lost his footing; [im Leben] his world has fallen apart - **2.** [Fußboden] floor; **zu ~ gehen** [im Boxsport] to go down - **3.** [von Gefäß, Koffer, Meer] bottom - **4.** [Speicher] loft - **5.** RW: **am ~ zerstört** absolutely shattered; **an ~ gewinnen/verlieren** to gain/lose ground.

bodenlos adj - **1.** [tief] bottomless - **2.** [unglaublich] incredible.

Bodenpersonal das ground staff.

Bodenschätze pl mineral resources.

Bodenturnen das floor exercises (pl).

Böe (pl -n), **Bö** (pl -en) die gust.

bog prät ▷ biegen.

Bogen (pl - ODER Bögen) der - **1.** [Biegung] curve; **dort macht die Straße einen ~ nach links** the road curves to the left there; **einen ~ um jn/etw machen** to steer clear of sb/sthg; **in hohem ~** [Wasser] in a great arc; **in hohem ~ hinausgeworfen werden** ODER **hinausfliegen** to be thrown out on one's ear - **2.** [Bauwerk] arch - **3.** [Schusswaffe & MUS] bow - **4.** [Blatt] sheet.

Bogenschießen das archery.

Bohle (pl -n) die thick plank.

Böhmen nt Bohemia.

Böhmerwald der Bohemian Forest.

Bohne (pl -n) die bean; **dicke/grüne ~n** broad/green beans; **das interessiert mich nicht die ~** fam I'm not in the slightest bit interested in that.

bohnern vt to polish.

bohren ▷ vt - **1.** [Loch] to drill; [Brunnen, Schacht] to sink - **2.** [hineinstoßen] to stick, to thrust ▷ vi - **1.** [mit einem Bohrer] to drill; **nach Öl/Wasser ~** to drill for oil/water; **in** ODER **an einem Zahn ~** to drill a tooth; **in der Nase ~** to pick one's nose - **2.** fam [drängen] to keep on. ➡ **sich bohren** ref [eindringen]: **sich in etw** (A) **~** to bore one's way into sthg.

bohrend adj [Blick] piercing; [Schmerz] gnawing; [Fragen] probing.

Bohrer (pl -) der [Gerät] drill.

Bohrlmaschine die drill.

Bohrung (pl -en) die drilling.

böig adj gusty.

Boiler [bɔylɐ] (pl -) der boiler.

Boje (pl -n) die buoy.

Bolzen (pl -) der bolt.

bombardieren vt to bombard; **jn mit etw ~** eigtl & fig to bombard sb with sthg.

Bombe (pl -n) die bomb.

Bombenlanschlag der bomb attack.

Bombenlerfolg der fam smash hit.

Bombenlstimmung die fam wild atmosphere.

Bon [bɔŋ] (pl -s) der - **1.** [Beleg] receipt - **2.** [für Speisen und Getränke] voucher.

Bonbon [bɔŋ'bɔŋ] (pl -s) der ODER das sweet.

Bonn nt Bonn.

Bonze (pl -n) der abw bigwig.

Boom [buːm] (pl -s) der boom.

Boot (pl -e) das boat; **mit** ODER **in einem ~ fahren** to go by boat; **~ fahren** to go boating; **wir sitzen alle in einem** ODER **im selben ~** fig we are all in the same boat.

Bord (pl -e) ▷ das [Brett] shelf ▷ der SCHIFF & FLUG side; **von ~ gehen** to disembark; **alle Vorsicht über ~ werfen** to throw caution to the winds. ➡ **an Bord** ▷ adv on board; **alle Mann an ~!** all aboard! ▷ präp (+ G) on board.

Bordell (pl -e) das brothel.

Bordlkarte die boarding card.

Bordsteinlkante die kerb.

borgen vt - **1.** [entleihen] to borrow; **etw von** ODER **bei jm ~** to borrow sthg from sb; **sich** (D) **etw ~** to borrow sthg - **2.** [verleihen]: **jm etw ~** to lend sb sthg.

Borke (pl -n) die bark.

Börse (pl -n) die - **1.** [Geldbeutel] purse - **2.** WIRTSCH stock market; [Gebäude] stock exchange; **das Unternehmen geht an die ~** the company is being floated (on the stock market).

bösartig adj - **1.** [Verhalten, Mensch, Bemerkung] malicious; [Hund] vicious - **2.** [Krankheit] malignant.

Böschung (pl -en) die bank.

böse ▷ adj - **1.** [schlecht] bad; [verwerflich] wicked, evil - **2.** [wütend]: **(über etw** (A)**) ~ sein/werden** to be/get angry (about sthg); **auf jn ~ sein, jm ~ sein** to be angry with sb - **3.** fam [schlimm] bad; [Entzündung] nasty - **4.** [frech, ungezogen] naughty ▷ adv - **1.** [schlimm] badly; **sich ~ erkälten** to catch a nasty cold - **2.** [bösartig]: **es war nicht ~ gemeint** I didn't mean it nastily - **3.** [wütend] angrily.

Böse (pl -n) ▷ der, die villain ▷ das: **nichts ~s tun/vorhaben** not to do/mean any harm; **etw ~s sagen** to say sthg nasty; **nichts ~s ahnen** to be unsuspecting.

Bösewicht (pl -er ODER -e) der - **1.** [Schuft] villain - **2.** [Schlingel] rascal.

boshaft ▷ adj - **1.** [böse] wicked, evil - **2.** [höhnisch] malicious ▷ adv [höhnisch] maliciously.

Bosheit (pl -en) die - **1.** [Gesinnung] malice - **2.** [Handlung] malicious thing.

Bosnien-Herzegowina nt Bosnia-Herzegovina.

bosnisch adj Bosnian.

Boss (pl -) der boss; [von Bande] leader.

böswillig ▷ adj malicious ▷ adv [handeln] maliciously.

bot prät ▷ bieten.

Botanik die botany.

botanisch adj botanical ▷ Garten.

Bote (*pl* -n) *der* - **1.** [gen] messenger; [von Kurierdienst] courier - **2.** [Vorbote] herald.

Botin (*pl* -nen) *die* - **1.** [gen] messenger; [von Kurierdienst] courier - **2.** [Vorbotin] herald.

Botschaft (*pl* -en) *die* - **1.** [Mitteilung] message - **2.** [diplomatische Vertretung] embassy.

Botschafter, in (*mpl* -; *fpl* -nen) *der, die* ambassador.

Bouillon [bul'jɔŋ] (*pl* -s) *die* bouillon.

Boulette = Bulette.

Boulevard [bul(ə)'vaːɐ̯] (*pl* -s) *der* boulevard.

Boulevardpresse *die* tabloid press, sensationalist press.

Boulevardtheater *das* light theatre.

Boutique, Butike [bu'tiːk] (*pl* -n) *die* boutique.

Bowle ['boːlə] (*pl* -n) *die* punch.

Bowling ['boːlɪŋ] (*pl* -s) *das* bowling.

Box (*pl* -en) *die* - **1.** [Lautsprecherbox] speaker - **2.** [Kasten] box - **3.** [an Rennstrecke] pit; [in Pferdestall] box; [in Garage] space.

boxen ◇ *vi* to love ◇ *vt* - **1.** SPORT to fight - **2.** [schlagen] to punch. ◆ **sich boxen** *ref* [kämpfen] to fight.

Boxer (*pl* -) *der* [Hund & SPORT] boxer.

Boxkampf *der* boxing match.

boykottieren [bɔykɔ'tiːrən] *vt* to boycott.

brach *prät* ⊳ brechen.

brachte *prät* ⊳ bringen.

Branche ['brãːʃə] (*pl* -n) *die* (branch of) industry; [Gewerbe] trade.

Brand (*pl* Brände) *der* - **1.** [Feuer] fire - **2.** [Brennen]: **vor dem ~ des Lagers** before the camp caught fire; **etw in ~ setzen** ODER **stecken** to set fire to sthg; **in ~ geraten** to catch fire - **3.** *fam* [Durst] raging thirst.

Brandenburg *nt* Brandenburg.

Brandenburger Tor *das* Brandenburg Gate.

brandneu *adj* brand-new.

Brandstifter, in *der, die* arsonist.

Brandstiftung *die* arson.

Brandung (*pl* -en) *die* surf.

Brandwunde *die* burn.

brannte *prät* ⊳ brennen.

Branntwein *der* spirits (*pl*); **Whisky ist ein ~** whisky is a type of spirit.

Brasilianer, in (*mpl* -; *fpl* -nen) *der, die* Brazilian.

brasilianisch *adj* Brazilian.

Brasilien *nt* Brazil.

brät *präs* ⊳ braten.

braten (*präs* brät; *prät* briet; *perf* hat gebraten) *vt & vi* [in der Pfanne] to fry; [im Ofen mit Fett] to roast; [im Ofen ohne Fett] to bake.

Braten (*pl* -) *der* roast.

Brathähnchen *das* roast chicken.

Bratkartoffeln *pl* fried potatoes.

Bratpfanne *die* frying pan.

Bratsche (*pl* -n) *die* MUS viola.

Bratwurst *die* (fried) sausage.

Brauch (*pl* Bräuche) *der* custom.

brauchbar ◇ *adj* [Vorschlag] useful; [Material, Kleidung] usable ◇ *adv* usefully; **~ arbeiten** to do acceptable work.

brauchen ◇ *vt* - **1.** [benötigen] to need; **jn/etw für** ODER **zu etw ~** to need sb/sthg for sthg - **2.** [verbrauchen] to use (up) - **3.** [verwenden]: **jn/etw (nicht) ~ können** (not) to be able to use sb/sthg ◇ *aux* [müssen] to need; **ihr braucht nicht zu grinsen** there's no need for you to grin.

Braue (*pl* -n) *die* brow, eyebrow.

brauen *vt* [Bier, Tee] to brew; [Trank] to make.

Brauerei (*pl* -en) *die* brewery.

braun ◇ *adj* - **1.** [Farbe] brown; **~e Butter** *butter melted in frying pan until brown* - **2.** [nationalsozialistisch] Nazi ◇ *adv* [farbig] brown; [braten] until brown; *siehe auch* braun gebrannt.

Braun *das* brown.

Bräune *die* suntan.

bräunen (*perf* hat/ist gebräunt) ◇ *vt* (hat) - **1.** [Körper, Gesicht] to tan - **2.** [Zwiebeln] to brown; [Zucker] to caramelize ◇ *vi* - **1.** (hat) [durch Sonne] to tan - **2.** (ist) [Braten] to turn brown. ◆ **sich bräunen** *ref* [durch Sonne - Person] to get a tan; [- Haut] to go brown; [sonnenbaden] to sunbathe.

braun gebrannt *adj* tanned.

Braunkohle *die* brown coal, lignite.

Brause (*pl* -n) *die* - **1.** [Getränk, Pulver] sherbet - **2.** [Dusche] shower.

brausen (*perf* hat/ist gebraust) *vi* - **1.** (hat) [Meer, Wind] to roar; [Beifall] to thunder - **2.** (ist) [sich fortbewegen] to race.

Braut (*pl* Bräute) *die* - **1.** [am Hochzeitstag] bride - **2.** [Verlobte] fiancée - **3.** *salopp* [Mädchen] bird *Br*, chick *Am*.

Bräutigam (*pl* -e) *der* - **1.** [am Hochzeitstag] bridegroom - **2.** [Verlobter] fiancé.

Brautpaar *das* bride and groom (*pl*).

brav *adj* - **1.** [artig] good - **2.** [bieder] plain.

---

brav

The German **brav** is a false friend which does not mean "brave" but "good" in the sense of "well-behaved". So the phrase **Wenn du brav bist, bekommst du ein Eis** can be translated as "If you're good, you'll get an ice-cream".
The English word "brave" in the sense of "courageous" corresponds to the German **tapfer**, so "**brave** soldiers" would be **tapfere Soldaten**.

bravo ['braːvo] *interj* bravo!

BRD [beːɛrˈdeː] (*abk für* Bundesrepublik Deutschland) *die* FRG.

brechen (*präs* bricht; *prät* brach; *perf* hat/ist gebrochen) ◇ *vt* **- 1.** (*hat*) [gen] to break; [Ast] to break off; [Rose, Blume] to pluck; [Trotz, Hartnäckigkeit] to overcome; [Ehe] to break up; **jm/sich den Arm ~** to break sb's/one's arm **- 2.** (*hat*) [erbrechen] to vomit (up) ◇ *vi* **- 1.** (*ist*) [durchbrechen] to break **- 2.** (*hat*) [erbrechen] to vomit, to be sick **- 3.** (*hat*) [Kontakt abbrechen]: **mit jm ~** to break off contact with sb **- 4.** (*hat*) [Brauch aufgeben]: **mit einer Tradition ~** to break with a tradition **- 5.** (*ist*) [durchkommen] to burst out. ◆ **sich brechen** *ref* [Schall] to echo; [Licht] to be refracted; [Wellen] to break.

brechend *adv*: **~ voll** full to bursting.

Brechreiz *der* nausea (U).

Brei (*pl* -e) *der* purée; [aus Haferflocken] porridge; [aus Kartoffeln] mashed potatoes (*pl*); [aus Gries] semolina.

breit ◇ *adj* **- 1.** [gen] wide; [Schultern, Gesicht, Hüften, Aussprache] broad; **ein ~es Lachen** a guffaw **- 2.** [allgemein] general ◇ *adv* **- 1.** [seitlich ausgedehnt]: **~ gebaut** sturdily built **- 2.** [ausgedehnt - darstellen] in great detail; [- lächeln] broadly; **~ lachen** to guffaw.

breitbeinig *adv* [dastehen] with one's legs apart; **~ gehen** to walk with a rolling gait.

Breite (*pl* -n) *die* **- 1.** [Ausdehnung] width **- 2.** [geografische Lage] latitude.

Breitengrad *der* (degree of) latitude.

breit machen *vt*: **die Beine ~** *fam* to spread one's legs. ◆ **sich breit machen** *ref fam* **- 1.** [Raum beanspruchen] to take up a lot of room **- 2.** [sich einquartieren] to make o.s. at home **- 3.** [sich verbreiten] to spread.

breitschlagen *vt* (*unreg*) *fam* [überreden] to talk round; **sich zu etw ~ lassen** to let o.s. be talked into sthg.

breitschultrig, breitschulterig *adj* broad-shouldered.

Bremsbelag *der* brake lining.

Bremse (*pl* -n) *die* **- 1.** [Bremsvorrichtung] brake **- 2.** [Insekt] horsefly.

bremsen ◇ *vi* [halten] to brake ◇ *vt* **- 1.** [Fahrzeug] to brake **- 2.** [Entwicklung, Person] to slow down.

Bremslicht *das* brake light.

Bremspedal *das* brake pedal.

Bremsweg *der* braking distance.

brennbar *adj* flammable.

brennen (*prät* brannte; *perf* hat gebrannt) ◇ *vi* **- 1.** [gen] to burn; [Haus, Wald, Gardine] to be on fire, to burn; **es brennt!** fire! **- 2.** [Lampe, Birne] to be on **- 3.** [Wunde, Augen] to smart; [Füße] to be sore **- 4.** [erregt sein]: **auf etw** (*A*) **~** to be dying for sthg ◇ *vt*

- 1. [Loch] to burn **- 2.** [Ziegel, Ton] to fire; [Schnaps] to distil; [Mandeln] to roast **- 3.** *fam* [CD-Rom] to burn.

Brenner *der*: **der ~** the Brenner Pass.

Brennholz *das* firewood.

Brennnessel, Brenn-Nessel *die* stinging nettle.

brenzlig *adj* **- 1.** [Geschmack] burnt; **ein ~er Geruch** a smell of burning **- 2.** *fam* [heikel] dicey.

Brett (*pl* -er) *das* **- 1.** [aus Holz] plank; **schwarzes ~** noticeboard **- 2.** [zum Spielen] board.

Brettspiel *das* board game.

Brezel (*pl* -n) *die* pretzel.

bricht *präs* ▷ brechen.

Brief (*pl* -e) *der* letter.

blauer Brief

In German schools pupils receive marks ranging from 1 (excellent) to 6 (unsatisfactory). If a pupil's level of achievement slips (e.g. from 4 to 5 or from 5 to 6), the school will send home an official letter three months before the end of the school year to warn parents that the pupil may have to sit the year again. Pupils refer to such a letter as ein blauer Brief.

Brieffreund, in *der, die* pen pal.

Briefkasten *der* **- 1.** [bei der Post] postbox *Br*, mailbox *Am* **- 2.** [am Hauseingang] letterbox *Br*, mailbox *Am*.

Briefkopf *der* letterhead.

Briefmarke *die* stamp.

Brieftasche *die* wallet.

Briefträger, in *der, die* postman (*f* postwoman).

Briefumschlag *der* envelope.

briet *prät* ▷ braten.

Brillant [brɪlˈjant] (*pl* -en) *der* brilliant.

Brille (*pl* -n) *die* **- 1.** [Sehhilfe, Augengläser] glasses (*pl*); **eine ~ tragen** to wear glasses **- 2.** *fam* [Klosettbrille] toilet seat.

bringen (*prät* brachte; *perf* hat gebracht) *vt* **- 1.** [herbringen] to bring; **jm etw ~** to bring sb sthg **- 2.** [holen] to get, to fetch; **jm etw ~** to get *ODER* fetch sb sthg **- 3.** [befördern] to take, to give a lift to; **ich bringe Sie zum Bahnhof** I'll take you *ODER* give you a lift to the station **- 4.** [begleiten] to see; **jn zur Tür ~** to see sb to the door **- 5.** *fig* [lenken]: **die Rede auf etw ~** to bring the conversation round to sthg; **jn auf die Idee ~, etw zu tun** to give sb the idea of doing sthg; **jn in Gefahr ~** to put sb in danger **- 6.** [Ergebnis]: **das bringt nur Ärger** that'll cause nothing but trouble; **jn dazu ~, dass er etw tut** to make sb do sthg, to get sb to do sthg; **Gewinn ~** to yield a profit; **das bringt nichts** *fam* that won't achieve anything - **7.** [leisten]: **es weit ~ to go far** ODER a long way; **er brachte es bis zum Minister** he made it to minister - **8.** [veröffentlichen - in einer Zeitung] to publish; [- im Fernsehen, Radio] to broadcast; [- Film] to screen - **9.** *RW*: **etw hinter sich** (A) ~ to get sthg over and done with; **ich kann es nicht über mich ~, so etwas zu tun** I can't bring myself to do such a thing; **jn um etw ~ to do sb out of sthg; du bringst mich noch mal um den Verstand!** you're driving me mad!

brisant *adj* [heikel] explosive.

Brise (*pl* -n) *die* breeze.

Brite (*pl* -n) *der* Briton, British person; **die ~n** the British; **ich bin ~** I'm British.

Britin (*pl* -nen) *die* Briton, British person.

britisch *adj* British.

Britische Inseln *pl* British Isles.

Broccoli, Brokkoli ['brɔkoli] *der* broccoli.

bröckeln (*perf* hat/ist gebröckelt) *vi* - **1.** (*hat*) [zerfallen] to crumble - **2.** (*ist*) [sich lösen]: **der Putz bröckelt von den Wänden** the plaster is flaking off the walls.

Brocken (*pl* -) *der* - **1.** [von Brot, Fleisch] bit, chunk; [von Lehm] lump - **2.** *fam* [dicker Mensch] hefty fellow - **3.** *RW*: **ein paar ~ einer Sprache sprechen** to speak a few words of a language.

brodeln *vi* [Wasser, Suppe, Lava] to bubble.

Brokkoli = Broccoli.

Brombeere *die* blackberry.

Bronchien ['brɔnçiən] *pl* bronchial tubes.

Bronchitis [brɔn'çi:tɪs] *die* bronchitis (U).

Bronze ['brɔ̃sə] *die* bronze.

Brosche (*pl* -n) *die* brooch.

Broschüre (*pl* -n) *die* brochure.

Brot (*pl* -e) *das* - **1.** [als Laib] bread; **ein Laib ~** a loaf of bread - **2.** [als Scheibe] slice of bread; **ein belegtes ~** an open sandwich; **ein ~ mit Schinken** a slice of bread with ham on it - **3.** [Lebensunterhalt]: **sich sein ~ verdienen** to earn a living.

Brötchen (*pl* -) *das* (bread) roll.

Browser ['braʊzɐ] (*pl* -) *der* EDV browser.

Bruch (*pl* Brüche) *der* - **1.** (*ohne pl*) [Brechen] breaking; [von Damm] bursting; **zu ~ gehen** [Glas] to smash, to shatter - **2.** [von Versprechen, Wort] breaking; [von Vertrag] breach - **3.** [Trennung]: **ein ~ mit der Tradition** a break with tradition; **es kam zum ~ mit seiner Familie** he broke off contact with his family - **4.** [MED - von Knochen] fracture; [- von Eingeweide] hernia; **sich einen ~ heben** to have ODER suffer a hernia - **5.** MATH fraction.

brüchig *adj* [Material] brittle; [Teig] crumbly; [Beziehung] fragile; [Stimme] cracked.

Bruchlandung *die* crash landing.

Bruchrechnung *die* (*ohne pl*) fractions (*pl*).

Bruchstrich *der* line (*of a fraction*).

Bruchstück *das* [von Vase, Werk] fragment.

bruchstückhaft ['brʊxʃtykhaft] ◇ *adj* fragmentary ◇ *adv* in fragments.

Bruchteil *der* fraction.

Brücke (*pl* -n) *die* - **1.** [gen] bridge; **eine ~ schlagen** [Turnübung] to make a bridge - **2.** [Teppich] rug.

Bruder (*pl* Brüder) *der* - **1.** [Geschwister, Mönch] brother - **2.** *fam* [Kerl] guy,

brüderlich ◇ *adj* brotherly ◇ *adv* like brothers.

Brühe (*pl* -n) *die* - **1.** [Suppe] broth; [zum Kochen] stock - **2.** [Wasser] dirty water - **3.** *abw* [Tee, Kaffee] dishwater.

Brühwürfel *der* stock cube.

brüllen ◇ *vt* to roar ◇ *vi* [Löwe, Person] to roar; [Stier] to bellow; [Baby, Affe] to screech; **vor Schmerz ~** to howl with pain.

brummen *vi* - **1.** [Hummel] to buzz; [Bär] to growl - **2.** [Person, Motor] to drone.

brummig ◇ *adj* [Person] grumpy; [Antwort] bad-tempered, surly ◇ *adv* grumpily.

brünett *adj*: **eine ~e Frau** a brunette.

Brunnen (*pl* -) *der* - **1.** [zum Wasserholen] well - **2.** [Springbrunnen] fountain - **3.** [Wasser] mineral water.

Brunst (*pl* Brünste) *die* [von Reh] heat; [von Hirsch] rut.

brüsk ◇ *adj* brusque ◇ *adv* brusquely.

Brüssel *nt* Brussels.

Brust (*pl* Brüste) *die* - **1.** (*ohne pl*) [Thorax] chest - **2.** [Busen] breast.

brüsten ➡ sich brüsten *ref abw*: **sich mit etw ~** to boast about sthg.

Brustkorb *der* thorax.

Brustschwimmen *das* breaststroke.

Brüstung (*pl* -en) *die* parapet.

Brustwarze *die* nipple.

brutal ◇ *adj* brutal ◇ *adv* brutally.

Brutalität (*pl* -en) *die* brutality.

brüten *vi* - **1.** [Vögel] to brood - **2.** [nachdenken]: **über etw** (A) ~ to ponder sthg.

brutto *adv* gross.

Bruttosozialprodukt *das* gross national product, GNP.

brutzeln ◇ *vi* to sizzle ◇ *vt* *fam* to fry (up).

BSE (*abk für* Bovine Spongiforme Enzephalopathie) *die* BSE.

Bube (*pl* -n) *der* - **1.** [Junge] boy - **2.** [Spielkarte] jack.

Buch (*pl* Bücher) *das* book; **die Bücher führen** to keep the books; **über etw** (A) ~ **führen** to keep a record of sthg.

Buchbinder, in (*mpl* -; *fpl* -nen) *der, die* bookbinder.

Buche (*pl* -n) *die* beech.

buchen *vt* - **1.** [verbuchen] to enter - **2.** [reservieren] to book.

Bücherei (*pl* -en) *die* library.

Bücherregal *das* bookshelves (*pl*).

Bücher|schrank der bookcase.
Buch|führung die bookkeeping.
Buchhalter, in (mpl -; fpl -nen) der, die accountant, bookkeeper.
Buch|haltung die accountancy, bookkeeping.
Buch|händler, in der, die bookseller.
Buch|handlung die, -laden der bookshop Br, bookstore Am.
Buchse ['bʊksə] (pl -n) die socket.
Büchse ['bʏksə] (pl -n) die - 1. [Dose] can, tin Br - 2. [Gewehr] shotgun.
Büchsen|milch die tinned milk Br, canned milk Am.
Büchsen|öffner der can opener, tin opener Br.
Buchstabe ['buːxʃtaːbə] (pl -n) der letter; **grosser ~** capital (letter); **kleiner ~** lowercase letter; **in fetten ~n** in bold.
buchstabieren [buːxʃtaˈbiːrən] vt to spell.
buchstäblich ['buːxʃtɛːplɪç] adv literally.
Bucht (pl -en) die bay.
Buchung (pl -en) die - 1. [Verbuchung] entry - 2. [Reservierung] booking.
Buchweizen der buckwheat.
Buckel (pl -) der [Rücken] hump; **einen ~ haben** to be a hunchback; **rutsch mir den ~ runter!** fam abw get lost ODER stuffed!
bucklig adj [Person] hunchbacked; [Oberfläche, Straße] bumpy.
Bückling (pl -e) der - 1. hum [Verbeugung] bow - 2. [Hering] smoked herring.
Budapest nt Budapest.
buddeln vt & vi to dig.
buddhistisch adj Buddhist.
Bude (pl -n) die - 1. [Verkaufsstand] stall - 2. fam [kleine Wohnung, möbliertes Zimmer] pad; **die Leute rennen ihr die ~ ein** she has people queuing on her doorstep - 3. fam abw [Wohnung] dump.
Budget [byˈdʒeː] (pl -s) das budget.
Büfett [byˈfɛt], **buffet** [byˈfeː] (pl -s) das - 1. [Verkaufstisch] counter - 2. [Speisen]: **kaltes ~** cold buffet - 3. [Geschirrschrank] sideboard.
Büffel (pl -) der buffalo.
Buffet [byˈfeː] (pl -s) das Österr & Schweiz = Büfett.
Bug (pl -e) der [von Schiff] bow; [von Flugzeug] nose.
Bügel (pl -) der - 1. [Kleiderbügel] (coat) hanger - 2. [Griff] handle - 3. [Steigbügel] stirrup - 4. [Brillenbügel] side-piece.
Bügel|brett das ironing board.
Bügel|eisen das iron.
Bügel|falte die crease.
bügeln vt & vi to iron.
Buggy (pl -s) der buggy.
Bühne (pl -n) die - 1. [Theaterraum] stage - 2. [Theater] theatre.

Bühnen|bild das set.
buk prät ⊳ backen.
Bukarest nt Bucharest.
Bulette, Boulette (pl -n) die rissole.
Bulgarien nt Bulgaria.
bulgarisch adj Bulgarian.
Bull|auge das porthole.
Bull|dogge die bulldog.
Bulldozer ['bʊldoːzɐ] (pl -) der bulldozer.
Bulle (pl -n) der - 1. [Tier] bull - 2. salopp abw [Polizist] pig, cop.
Bummel (pl -) der stroll; **einen ~ machen** to go for a stroll.
bummeln (perf hat/ist gebummelt) vi - 1. (ist) [spazieren] to stroll - 2. (hat) [langsam sein] to dawdle.
Bummel|zug der slow train.
bumsen (perf hat/ist gebumst) ◇ vi - 1. (hat) fam [knallen] to bang; **es hat gebumst** [Lärm] there was a bang; [bei Unfall] there was a crash - 2. (ist) fam [prallen]: **gegen** ODER **an etw** (A) ~ to bang into sthg - 3. (hat) fam [koitieren] to get laid, to have it off Br ◇ vt (hat) fam to lay, to have it off with Br.
Bund (pl Bünde ODER -e) ◇ der - 1. (pl Bünde) [Zusammenschluss] association - 2. [Bundesrepublik] central government - 3. fam [Bundeswehr]: **der ~** the army - 4. (pl Bünde) [an Kleidung] waistband ◇ das (pl Bunde) [von Gemüse] bunch.
Bündel (pl -) das - 1. [von Wäsche, Anträgen] bundle; [von Geldscheinen] wad - 2. [aus Stroh] bale.
bündeln vt - 1. [Heu, Stroh] to bale - 2. [Kleidung, Papier, Banknoten] to tie into bundles - 3. [Produkte] to combine.
Bundes|bahn ⊳ Deutsche Bahn.
Bundes|bürger, in der, die German citizen.
Bundesgrenz|schutz der (ohne pl) German border police.
Bundes|kanzler, in der, die German chancellor.
Bundes|land das federal state; **die alten/ neuen Bundesländer** the old/new federal states.
Bundes|liga die German national league for football, ice hockey etc.
Bundes|post ⊳ Deutsche Bundespost.
Bundes|präsident, in der, die - 1. [in Deutschland, Österreich] president - 2. [in der Schweiz] chair of the 'Bundesrat'.
Bundes|rat der (ohne pl) [Parlament] Bundesrat, upper house of German parliament, where federal states are represented.
Bundes|regierung die German ODER federal government.
Bundes|republik die - 1. [Föderation] federal republic - 2. ⊳ Bundesrepublik Deutschland.

Bundesrepublik Deutschland *die* Federal Republic of Germany.

Bundes|staat *der* federal state.

Bundes|straße *die* ≃ A road *Br,* ≃ state highway *Am.*

Bundes|tag ▷ Deutsche Bundestag.

Bundes|wehr *die* German army.

bundesweit *adj & adv* nationwide *(in Germany, Austria).*

bündig ◇ *adj* [kurz] concise ◇ *adv* [kurz] concisely.

Bündnis *(pl -se) das* alliance.

Bungalow ['bʊŋgalo] *(pl -s) der* bungalow.

Bunker *(pl -) der* [Schutzraum] bunker.

bunt ◇ *adj* - 1. [vielfarbig] colourful - 2. [abwechslungsreich - Programm] varied; **eine ~ Mischung** a motley assortment; **ein ~er Abend** a social evening - 3. [durcheinander] mixed-up; **jetzt wirds mir zu ~** I've had enough ◇ *adv* - 1. [vielfarbig] colourfully - 2. [abwechslungsreich]: **~ gemischt** assorted; **es zu ~ treiben** to overdo it.

Bunt|stift *der* coloured pencil.

Burg *(pl -en) die* - 1. [Gebäude] castle - 2. [Sandburg] *circular wall of sand built on beach by holidaymakers to mark off the area where they are sitting.*

Bürge *(pl -n) der* guarantee.

bürgen *vi*: **für jn/etw** ~ *fig* to vouch for sb/sthg; **für jn** ~ WIRTSCH to stand surety for sb.

Bürger, in *(mpl -; fpl -nen) der, die* - 1. [Einwohner] citizen - 2. [Mittelständler] middle-class person.

Bürger|initiative *die* [Gruppe] grass-roots pressure group.

Bürger|krieg *der* civil war.

bürgerlich ◇ *adj* - 1. [staatlich] civil - 2. [des Bürgertums - Partei, Familie] middle-class; [- Küche] traditional - 3. HIST & POL [spießig] bourgeois ◇ *adv* [wie das Bürgertum]: **Ulm ist eine ~ geprägte Stadt** Ulm is a middle-class city.

Bürger|meister, in *der, die* mayor. ◆ **Regierende Bürgermeister** *der mayor and leader of local government.*

Bürgersteig *(pl -e) der* pavement *Br,* sidewalk *Am.*

Bürgertum *das* bourgeoisie.

Bürgschaft *(pl -en) die* surety.

Büro [by'ro:] *(pl -s) das* office.

Büro|klammer *die* paper clip.

bürokratisch ◇ *adj* bureaucratic ◇ *adv* bureaucratically.

Bursche *(pl -n) der* - 1. [Junge] lad - 2. [Prachtexemplar]: **ein prächtiger ~** a magnificent specimen.

burschikos *adj* [Frau] mannish; [Mädchen] boyish.

Bürste *(pl -n) die* [Gerät] brush.

bürsten *vt* to brush; **sich** (D) **die Haare ~** to brush one's hair.

Bus *(pl -se) der* - 1. [Omnibus] bus - 2. [Reisebus] coach.

Busch *(pl Büsche) der* [Strauch, Zone] bush.

Büschel *(pl -) das* [von Gras, Haaren] tuft; [von Stroh] bundle.

buschig *adj* bushy.

Busen *(pl -) der* bosom.

Bus|fahrer, in *der, die* - 1. [von Omnibus] bus driver - 2. [von Reisebus] coach driver.

Bushalte|stelle *die* bus stop.

Business Class *die (ohne pl)* business class.

Bussard *(pl -e) der* buzzard.

büßen ◇ *vt* - 1. [Sünden] to atone for - 2. [Untat] to pay for ◇ *vi* - 1. REL: **für etw ~** to atone for sthg - 2. [bestraft werden]: **für etw ~** to pay for sthg.

Buß|geld *das* fine.

Buß- und Bet|tag *der* Day of Prayer and Repentance, *German public holiday in November.*

Büste *(pl -n) die* bust.

Büsten|halter *der* bra.

Butike = Boutique.

Butter *die* butter.

Butter|brot *das* slice of bread and butter.

Butter|dose *die* butter dish.

Butter|milch *die* buttermilk.

BWL [be:ve:'ɛl] *(abk für Betriebswirtschaftslehre) die business studies.*

Byzanz *nt* HIST Byzantium.

bzg. *(abk für bezüglich)* re.

bzw. *abk für* beziehungsweise.

C

c, C [tse:] *(pl - ODER -s) das* - 1. [Buchstabe] c, C - 2. MUS C. ◆ **C** *(abk für Celsius)* C.

ca. *(abk für circa)* approx.

Cabaret [kaba're:] *(pl -s) das* cabaret.

Cabrio ['ka:brio] *(pl -s) das* = Kabrio.

Café [ka'fe:] *(pl -s) das* cafe.

Cafeteria [kafetə'ri:a] *(pl -s) die* cafeteria.

Callcenter ['kɔ:lsɛntɐ] *(pl -s) das* TELEKOM call centre.

Calzium ['kaltsjʊm] *das* = Kalzium.

campen ['kɛmpn̩] *vi* to camp.

Camping ['kɛmpɪŋ] *das* camping; **zum ~ fahren** to go camping.

canceln ['kɛnsl̩n] *(präs* cancelt; *prät* cancelte; *perf* hat gecancelt) *vt* to cancel.

Cape [ke:p] (pl -s) das cape.

Carsharing das car sharing.

CB-|Funker [tse:'be:fʊŋkɐ] der CB ham.

CD [tse:'de:] (pl -s) (abk für Compactdisc) die CD.

CD-Spieler [tse:'de:ʃpi:lɐ] (pl -) der CD player.

CDU [tse:de:'u:] (abk für Christlich-Demokratische Union) die Christian Democratic Union, major German political party to the right of the political spectrum.

C-Dur ['tse:du:ɐ] das C major.

Cello ['tʃɛlo] (pl -s) das cello.

Celsius ['tsɛlzjʊs] Celsius, centigrade; **10 Grad ~** 10 degrees Celsius ODER centigrade.

Cent [(t)sɛnt] (pl -s ODER -) der - **1.** [in EU] cent - **2.** (pl Cents) [in USA] cent.

Chamäleon [ka'mɛ:leɔn] (pl -s) das chameleon.

Champagner [ʃam'panjɐ] (pl -) der champagne.

Champignon ['ʃampɪnjɔn] (pl -s) der mushroom.

Chance ['ʃã:s(ə)] (pl -n) die [Möglichkeit] chance; **jm eine ~ geben** to give sb a chance.

Chaos ['ka:ɔs] das chaos.

chaotisch [ka'o:tɪʃ] ◇ adj chaotic ◇ adv chaotically.

Charakter [ka'raktɐ] (pl -tere) der character.

charakterisieren [karakteri'zi:rən] vt to characterize.

Charakteristik [karakte'rɪstɪk] (pl -en) die characteristic.

charakteristisch [karakte'rɪstɪʃ] ◇ adj characteristic; **für jn/etw ~ sein** to be characteristic of sb/sthg ◇ adv characteristically.

charakterlich [ka'raktɐlɪç] adj: **~e Schwäche** weakness of character.

charakterlos [ka'raktɐlo:s] ◇ adj unprincipled ◇ adv without principle.

charmant, scharmant [ʃar'mant] ◇ adj charming ◇ adv charmingly.

Charme, Scharm [ʃarm] der charm.

Charter|flug ['tʃartɐflu:k] der charter flight.

Charter|maschine die charter plane.

chartern ['tʃartɐn] vt to charter.

Chat [tʃɛt] (pl -s) der EDV chat.

Chatroom ['tʃɛt‿ru:m] (pl -s) der EDV chatroom.

Chauvinismus [ʃovi'nɪsmʊs] der abw chauvinism.

chauvinistisch [ʃovi'nɪstɪʃ] abw ◇ adj chauvinist ◇ adv chauvinistically.

checken ['tʃɛkn] vt - **1.** [untersuchen] to check - **2.** salopp [verstehen]: **sie checkt es einfach nicht!** she just doesn't get it!

Chef [ʃɛf] (pl -s) der [von Firma, Mafiosi] boss; [von Organisation] head.

Chef

The German word Chef is a common false friend which has nothing to do with cooking. A Chef is a "boss" or "head" of an organization, and a woman in this role is a Chefin. The question Wer ist hier der Chef? could be translated into English as "Who's in charge around here?"

A professional "chef" working in a restaurant is referred to in German as a Koch, and a head chef would be a Chefkoch. The sentence "It's the chef's day off today" could be rendered in German as Der Koch hat heute frei.

Chef|arzt der senior consultant Br, specialist Am.

Chef|ärztin die senior consultant Br, specialist Am.

Chefin (pl -nen) die [von Firma] boss; [von Organisation] head.

Chef|redakteur, in der, die editor-in-chief.

Chemie [çe'mi:] die (ohne pl) - **1.** [Wissenschaft] chemistry - **2.** fam [Chemikalien] chemicals (pl).

Chemikalie [çemi'ka:ljə] (pl -n) die chemical.

Chemiker, in ['çe:mikɐ, rɪn] (mpl -; fpl -nen) der, die chemist.

chemisch ['çe:mɪʃ] ◇ adj [Reaktion, Zusammensetzung] chemical; **~es Labor** chemistry lab; **~e Reinigung** dry-cleaning ◇ adv chemically; **~ reinigen** to dry-clean.

Chemo|therapie [çemotera'pi:] die chemotherapy.

Chicorée, Schikoree ['ʃikore] (pl -s) die ODER der chicory.

Chiffre ['ʃifrə] (pl -n) die - **1.** [Zeichen] (code) symbol - **2.** [von Anzeigen] box number.

chiffrieren [ʃi'fri:rən] vt to encode.

Chile ['tʃi:le] nt Chile.

Chili ['tʃi:li] (pl -s) der - **1.** [Schote] chilli (pepper) - **2.** [Gewürz] chilli (powder).

China ['çi:na] nt China.

Chinakohl der (ohne pl) Chinese leaves (pl) Br, bok choy Am.

Chinese [çi'ne:zə] (pl -n) der Chinese (man).

Chinesin [çi'ne:zin] (pl -nen) die Chinese (woman).

chinesisch [çi'ne:zɪʃ] adj Chinese.

Chinin [çi'ni:n] das quinine.

Chip [tʃɪp] (pl -s) der [beim Spiel & ELEKTR & EDV] chip.

Chips [tʃɪps] pl crisps Br, chips Am.

Chirurg [çi'rʊrk] (pl -en) der surgeon.

Chirurgie [çiruɐˈgiː] (*pl* -n) *die* - **1.** [Wissenschaft] surgery - **2.** [Krankenhausabteilung] surgical unit; **auf der ~ liegen** to be in surgery.

Chirurgin [çiˈrʊrgɪn] (*pl* -nen) *die* surgeon.

chirurgisch [çiˈrʊrgɪʃ] <> *adj* surgical <> *adv* surgically.

Chlor [kloːɐ] *das* chlorine.

Cholesterin [kolesteˈriːn] *das* cholesterol.

Chor [koːɐ] (*pl* Chöre) *der* MUS & ARCHIT choir; **im ~** in chorus.

Choreografie, Choreographie [koreograˈfiː] (*pl* -n) *die* choreography.

Christ [ˈkrɪst] (*pl* -en) *der* Christian.

Christbaum *der* Christmas tree.

Christdemokrat, in *der, die* Christian Democrat.

Christentum [ˈkrɪstn̩tuːm] *das* Christianity.

Christi Himmelfahrt (*ohne Artikel*) [Feiertag] Ascension Day.

Christin [ˈkrɪstɪn] (*pl* -nen) *die* Christian.

Christkind *das* - **1.** [Jesuskind] baby Jesus, Christ Child - **2.** [zu Weihnachten] ≃ Santa Claus.

christlich [ˈkrɪstlɪç] <> *adj* Christian <> *adv*: **~ handeln** to act like a Christian.

Christus [ˈkrɪstʊs] *der* Christ.

Chrom [kroːm] *das* [als Überzug] chrome; CHEM chromium.

Chromosom [kromoˈzoːm] (*pl* -en) *das* chromosome.

Chronik [ˈkroːnɪk] (*pl* -en) *die* chronicle.

chronisch [ˈkroːnɪʃ] *adj* chronic.

chronologisch [kronoˈloːgɪʃ] <> *adj* chronological <> *adv* chronologically.

circa [ˈtsɪrka] *adv* = zirka.

clever [ˈklɛvɐ] <> *adj* clever, smart <> *adv* cleverly, smartly.

Clique [ˈklɪka] (*pl* -n) *die* - **1.** [Gruppe] group of friends - **2.** *abw* [Interessengemeinschaft] clique; [von Verbrechern] gang.

Clown, in [klaun, ɪn] (*mpl* -s; *fpl* -nen) *der, die* clown.

Club = Klub.

cm (*abk für* Zentimeter) cm.

c-Moll [ˈtseːmɔl] *das* MUS C minor.

Cocktail [ˈkɔkteːl] (*pl* -s) *der* cocktail.

Code [ˈkoːt] (*pl* -s) *der* = Kode.

Cognac® [ˈkɔnjak] (*pl* -s) *der* cognac.

Cola [ˈkoːla] (*pl* -s) *die* ODER *das* Coke®.

Comer See [ˈkoːmɐ ˈzeː] *der* Lake Como.

Comic [ˈkɔmɪk] (*pl* -s) *der* - **1.** [Geschichte] cartoon - **2.** [Heft] comic.

Computer [kɔmˈpjuːtɐ] (*pl* -) *der* computer.

Container [kɔnˈteːnɐ] (*pl* -) *der* [gen] container; [für Altglas, Papier] bank.

contra [ˈkɔntra] *präp* = kontra.

Cord [kɔrt] *der* = Kord.

Couch [kautʃ] (*pl* -s ODER -en) *die* couch.

Count-down [ˈkauntˈdaun] (*pl* -s) *das* ODER *der* countdown.

Cousin [kuˈzɛ̃] (*pl* -s) *der* cousin.

Cousine, Kusine [kuˈziːna] (*pl* -n) *die* cousin.

Cowboy [ˈkaubɔy] (*pl* -s) *der* cowboy.

Creme, Krem [kreːm, krɛːm] (*pl* -s ODER -n) *die* - **1.** [Hautcreme] cream - **2.** [Speise] confectioner's custard.

cremig, kremig [ˈkreːmɪç] <> *adj* creamy <> *adv*: **etw ~ schlagen** to cream sthg.

Crew [kruː] (*pl* -s) *die* [Besatzung] crew.

CSU [tseːɛsˈuː] (*abk für* Christlich-Soziale Union) *die* Christian Social Union, *Bavarian political party to the right of the political spectrum, long-time alliance partners of the CDU.*

Cup [kap] (*pl* -s) *der* SPORT cup.

Curry [ˈkœri] (*pl* -s) *das* - **1.** [Gewürz] curry powder - **2.** [Gericht] curry.

Currywurst *die* sausage with curry sauce.

CVP [tseːfauˈpeː] (*abk für* Christliche Volkspartei (der Schweiz)) *die* Popular Christian Democratic Party, *right-wing political party in Switzerland.*

Cyberspace [ˈsaibɐspeɪs] *der* (*ohne pl*) cyberspace.

D

d, D [deː] (*pl* - ODER -s) *das* - **1.** [Buchstabe] d, D - **2.** MUS D.

da <> *adv* - **1.** [dort] there; **guck mal ~!** look over there!; **~ kommt der Bus!** here comes the bus!; **das ~ gefällt mir am besten** I like that one best; **~ drüben** over there - **2.** [hier] here; **~ bin ich!** here I am!; **ist noch etwas Brot ~?** is there any bread left?; **ich bin gleich wieder ~** I'll be back in a minute - **3.** [in diesem Zusammenhang]: **~ fällt mir ein ...** I've just thought ... - **4.** [in dieser Beziehung] there; **~ irren Sie sich** you're wrong there - **5.** [unter dieser Bedingung] in that case; **~ gehe ich lieber gleich** in that case I'd rather go straight away <> *konj* [weil] as, since; **~ ihr Vater krank war, musste sie zu Hause bleiben** as her father was ill, she had to stay at home.

DAAD [deːaːaːˈdeː] (*abk für* Deutscher Akademischer Austauschdienst) *der* German

Academic Exchange Service, *cultural body which organizes academic exchanges for students and staff.*

da|behalten vt *(unreg)* to keep (in ODER back).

dabei, dabei adv - **1.** [räumlich]: waren Sie bei der Auktion ~? were you at the auction?; hast du zufällig eine Briefmarke ~? do you happen to have a stamp on you?; **nicht ~ sein** to be missing; **ich bin ~!** *fig* count me in! - **2.** [zeitlich] at the same time; **sie waren gerade ~, das Haus zu verlassen** they were just leaving the house - **3.** [bei dieser Sache]: ~ **kam heraus, dass ...** in the process it came out that ...; **mir ist nicht ganz wohl ~ (zumu-te)** I don't really feel happy about it; **und ~ bleibts!** and that's the end of it!; **es ist nichts ~** *fam fig* there's nothing wrong with it - **4.** [obwohl] although - **5.** [überdies]: **und ~ ist sie auch noch intelligent** and (what is more) she's clever too; *siehe auch* **dabei sein.**

dabei|haben vt *(unreg)* [Person] to have with one; [Gegenstand] to have on one; **sie wollten ihn nicht ~** they didn't want him there.

dabei sein *(perf* ist **dabei gewesen**) vi *(un-reg)* - **1.** [anwesend sein] to be present ODER there - **2.** [im Begriff sein]: ~, **etw zu tun** to be just doing sthg.

da|bleiben *(perf* ist **dagebliebén**) vi *(unreg)* to stay.

Dach *(pl* **Dächer)** das roof; **das ~ decken** to roof the house; **unterm ~ wohnen** to live in the attic.

Dach|boden der attic; **auf dem ~** in the at-tic.

Dach|luke die skylight.

Dach|rinne die gutter.

Dachs [daks] *(pl -e)* der badger.

dachte *prät* ⊳ **denken.**

Dach|ziegel der roof tile.

Dackel *(pl -)* der dachshund.

Dadaismus [dada'ısmʊs] der Dadaism.

dadurch, dadurch adv - **1.** [auf diese Art] because of this; ~, **dass** because; ~, **dass wir uns viel Mühe gaben ...** because we tried very hard ...; ~ **kam es, dass ...** that was why ... - **2.** [räumlich] through it.

dafür, dafür adv - **1.** [für etwas] for it; **200 DM ~ bezahlen** to pay 200 marks for it; **er kann nichts ~** it's not his fault; **er hat kein Verständnis ~** he has no feeling for that - **2.** [bejahend] for it, in favour of it; ~ **spricht, dass ...** this is confirmed by the fact that ... - **3.** [als Ausgleich]: **er arbeitet langsam, ~ aber gründlich** he works slowly yet thor-oughly - **4.** [im Tausch] in exchange.

dafür|können vt *(unreg)*: **nichts ~** not to be able to help it; **ich kann doch nichts dafür,**

dass der Zug zu spät kommt! it's not my fault if the train is late!

DAG [deːaːˈgeː] *(abk für* **Deutsche Angestellten-Gewerkschaft)** *die* German white-collar union.

dagegen, dagegen adv - **1.** [räumlich] against it; **das Auto fuhr ~** the car drove into it - **2.** [ablehnend] against it; **etwas ~ haben** to object; **hast du etwas ~, wenn ich rauche?** do you mind if I smoke?; ~ **lässt sich nichts machen** nothing can be done about it - **3.** [im Gegensatz] in comparison; **sie ist groß, er ~ ist klein** she's tall, whereas he is short; **die-ser ist nichts ~!** this is nothing in compari-son!

da gewesen ⇔ *pp* ⊳ **da sein** ⇔ *adj*: **noch nie ~** unheard of.

Daheim *das Süddt, Österr & Schweiz* home.

daher, daher adv - **1.** [aus dieser Richtung] from there; **ach, ~ weht (also) der Wind!** *fig* so that's the way the wind is blowing! - **2.** [deswegen] that is why; ~ **(auch) der Name** hence the name; ~ **der ganze Ärger** that's the reason for all the hassle; ~ **kommt es, dass ...** that is why/how ...

dahin, dahin ⇔ adv - **1.** [räumlich] there - **2.** [zeitlich]: **bis ~** until then; **bis ~ sind wir fertig** we'll be ready by then - **3.** [als Ziel]: **seine Bemühungen gehen ~, sich selbst-ständig zu machen** he's trying to set up his own business ⇔ *adj fam* [kaputt, beendet, weg]: **das Kleid ist ~!** the dress has had it!; **meine Träume sind ~** my dreams have been shattered.

dahingestellt *pp*: **es bleibt** ODER **sei ~** it re-mains to be seen.

dahinten adv back there, over there.

dahinter adv *eigtl & fig* behind it.

dahinter kommen *(perf* ist **dahinter ge-kommen)** vi *(unreg) fam* to find out.

dahinter stecken vi to be behind it.

dahinter stehen vi *(unreg)* to be behind it.

damalig adj [Bedingungen, Zustände] at that time; **der ~e Präsident** the then presi-dent.

damals adv then, in those days; **als ich ~ krank wurde** when I got ill; **seit ~** since then.

Damast *(pl -e)* der damask.

Dame *(pl -n)* die - **1.** [Frau] lady; **der Wettbe-werb der ~n** the women's competition; **mei-ne (sehr verehrten) ~n und Herren** ladies and gentlemen - **2.** [Spielkarte] queen - **3.** [Spiel] draughts *(U)*. ▶ **Damen** *pl* [Toi-lette] ladies *(sg)*.

Damen|binde die sanitary towel *Br*, sani-tary napkin *Am*.

damenhaft ⇔ *adj* ladylike ⇔ *adv* like a lady.

Damen|toilette die ladies (toilet).

damit, damit <> *konj* so that <> *adv* - **1.** [mit dieser Sache]: **was soll ich ~?** what am I supposed to do with this?; **sie war ~ einverstanden** she agreed to it; **was meinst du ~?** what do you mean by that?; **her ~!** *fam* hand it over!; **hör auf ~!** *fam* stop it! - **2.** [somit] because of that.

dämlich *fam abw* <> *adj* stupid <> *adv* stupidly.

Damm (*pl* Dämme) *der* [Deich] dam; **wieder auf dem ~ sein** *fam fig* to be up and about again.

dämmern *vi* - **1.** [einsetzen]: **es dämmert** [am Morgen] it's getting light, day is breaking; [am Abend] it's getting dark, night is falling - **2.** [halb schlafen]: **(vor sich hin) ~** to doze - **3.** *fam* [bewusst werden]: **eine Ahnung dämmerte ihm** a suspicion dawned on him.

Dämmerung (*pl* -en) *die* [am Morgen] dawn; [am Abend] dusk.

dämmrig, dämmerig *adj* [Licht] dim; [Tag] gloomy, dull.

Dämon (*pl* Dämonen) *der* demon.

dämonisch *adj* demonic.

Dampf (*pl* Dämpfe) *der* [Dunst] steam; **giftige Dämpfe** poisonous fumes; **jm ~ machen** *fam* to make sb get a move on.

Dampf|bad *das* steam bath, Turkish bath.

dampfen *vi* to steam.

dämpfen *vt* - **1.** [dünsten] to steam - **2.** [Geräusch, Schritte] to muffle; [Instrument, Farbton] to mute; [Licht] to dim; [Stoß] to cushion; [Stimme] to lower - **3.** [Wut, Aufregung] to calm; [Begeisterung] to dampen - **4.** [verringern] to curb.

Dampfer (*pl* -) *der* steamship, steamer.

Dämpfer (*pl* -) *der:* **jm einen ~ aufsetzen** ODER **verpassen** to dampen sb's spirits.

Dampf|maschine *die* steam engine.

Dampf|walze *die* steamroller.

danach, danach *adv* - **1.** [zeitlich] after, afterwards; **zwei Stunden ~** two hours later; **wir können doch erst ins Theater gehen und ~ etwas essen** why don't we go to the theatre first and eat afterwards? - **2.** [nach etwas]: **~ schnappen/greifen** to snap/grab at it; **sich ~ sehnen** to long for it; **ich habe ~ gefragt** I asked about it - **3.** [entsprechend]: **es sieht ganz ~ aus** it looks like it; **mir ist jetzt nicht ~ (zumute)** I don't feel like it at the moment.

Däne (*pl* -n) *der* Dane.

daneben *adv* - **1.** [räumlich] next to it/him/*etc*, beside it/him/*etc*; **gleich ~** right next to it - **2.** [vergleichend] in comparison - **3.** [außerdem] in addition (to that).

daneben|benehmen ◆ **sich danebenbenehmen** *ref (unreg)* to make an exhibition of o.s.

daneben|gehen (*perf* ist danebengegangen) *vi (unreg)* - **1.** [danebenzielen] to miss (the target) - **2.** *fam* [misslingen] to fail.

Dänemark *nt* Denmark.

Dänin (*pl* -nen) *die* Dane.

dänisch *adj* Danish.

dank *präp:* **~ einer Sache** (G) thanks to sthg.

Dank *der* (ohne *pl*) thanks (*pl*); **zum ~ dafür** as a reward, by way of saying thank you; **vielen ~!** thank you (very much)!; **schönen** ODER **besten ~ auch!** thank you (very much)!

dankbar <> *adj* - **1.** [voller Dank] grateful; **jm (für etw) ~ sein** to be grateful to sb (for sthg) - **2.** [lohnend] rewarding <> *adv* [voller Dank] gratefully.

Dankbarkeit *die* gratitude.

danke *interj* thanks!, thank you!; **~, dass du gekommen bist!** thanks ODER thank you for coming!; **~ keinen Kaffee? - ~, gern/im Moment nicht** would you like another coffee? - yes, please/no thanks ODER no thank you, not just now; **~ gleichfalls!** thanks, you too!; **~ sehr** ODER **schön!** thanks (very much)!, thank you (very much)!

danken *vi:* **jm (für etw) ~** to thank sb (for sthg); **na, ich danke!** *fam* no thanks!, no thank you!; **nichts zu ~!** don't mention it!

Dankeschön *das* thank you.

Dank|schreiben *das* letter of thanks.

dann *adv* - **1.** [gen] then; **bis ~** see you (then) - **2.** [außerdem] then; **und ~ (noch) ...** and, on top of that ... - **3.** [konditional] in that case, then. ◆ **also dann** *interj* all right then. ◆ **dann und dann** *adv* at such and such time. ◆ **dann und wann** *adv* now and then.

daran, daran *adv* - **1.** [an diese Sache]: **ich denke gerade ~** I'm just thinking about it; **er arbeitete lange ~** he worked at ODER on it for a long time; **es ist nichts Wahres ~** there is no truth in it; **mir liegt viel ~** it is very important to me; **er war schuld ~** it was his fault - **2.** [räumlich]: **er klebte Papier ~** he stuck paper (on)to it; **wir gingen ~ vorbei** we went past it; **nahe ~** close to it - **3.** [deshalb]: **sie ist ~ gestorben** she died of it; **es liegt ~, dass ...** it is because ...

daran|setzen *vt* [Energie, Kraft] to use; **alles ~** to do one's utmost.

darauf, darauf *adv* - **1.** [räumlich] on it - **2.** [Richtung]: **~ zielen** to aim at it; **das deutet ~ hin, dass ...** *fig* this implies that ... - **3.** [zeitlich] after that; **am Tag ~** the day after, the next day; **bald ~** soon after(wards) - **4.** [als Reaktion] to it; **~ steht die Todesstrafe** the penalty for that is death - **5.** [zum Ausdruck einer Intention]: **sie ist ~ aus, einen Mann zu bekommen** she's out to get a husband; **sie bestand ~** she was most particular about it; **besonders ~ achten, dass ...** to take particular care to ...

daraufhin adv - 1. [aus einem Grund] as a result - 2. [zu einem Zweck]: **das Produkt ~ prüfen, ob es den Normen entspricht** to test the product (in order) to see if it meets the standards.

daraus, daraus adv - 1. [räumlich] from it, out of it - 2. [aus dieser Sache] from it; **~ folgt, dass ...** from this it follows that ...; **mach dir nichts ~!** don't let it bother you!; **ich mache mir nichts!** I'm not very keen on it; **~ wird nichts!** fam nothing doing! - 3. [aus einem Material] from it, out of it.

darf präs ▷ **dürfen**.

darin, darin adv - 1. [in etwas] in it, inside - 2. [in diesem Sachverhalt] there.

dar|legen vt to explain.

Darlehen (pl -) das loan.

Darm (pl Därme) der - 1. [Organ] intestine - 2. [Material] gut.

Darm|infektion die bowel infection.

dar|stellen vt - 1. [Subj: Bild] to portray, to depict - 2. [beschreiben] to describe - 3. [Subj: Schauspieler] to play - 4. [sein] to represent, to constitute; **als Wissenschaftler stellt er etwas dar** he is an impressive scientist.

Darsteller, in (mpl -; fpl -nen) der, die actor (f actress); **der ~ des Hamlet** the actor playing Hamlet.

Darstellung die - 1. [als Bild] depiction, portrayal; **eine grafische ~** a graphic representation - 2. [Bericht] account.

darüber, darüber adv - 1. [räumlich - über etw] above it, over it; [- über etw hinweg] across it, over it; **~ hinaus** fig in addition; **~ sind wir schon hinaus** we have already passed that stage - 2. [über diese Sache] about it; **hast du ~ nachgedacht?** did you think about it?; **ich komme nicht ~ hinweg** I can't get over it; **~ hinwegsehen** to ignore it - 3. [mehr] above that, over that; **nichts geht ~!** fig there is nothing to beat it.

darum, darum adv - 1. [räumlich] round it - 2. [um diese Sache] about it; **jn ~ bitten, etw zu tun** to ask sb to do sthg; **~ geht es nicht** that's not the point; **es geht ~, dass ...** the thing is that ... - 3. [deswegen] that's why; **ach ~!** so that's why!; **eben ~** for that very reason; **warum? – ~!** fam why? – because!

darunter, darunter adv - 1. [räumlich] under it; **sie hob das Kissen und fand ihre Kette ~** she lifted the cushion and found her necklace underneath - 2. [unter dieser Sache]: **er leidet ~** he suffers from it; **was verstehst du ~?** what do you understand by that?; **~ kann ich mir nichts vorstellen** that doesn't mean anything to me - 3. [weniger]: **30 Meter oder etwas ~** 30 metres or a little less - 4. [in dieser Menge] among(st) them; **viele Besucher, ~ auch einige aus dem Ausland** many visitors, including some foreigners.

das ◇ det the; **~ Rauchen** smoking ◇ pron - 1. [Demonstrativpronomen] that; **da** that one there; **unser Haus? – ~ haben wir verkauft** our house? – we've sold it; **~ regnet heute wieder wie verrückt** it's raining like mad again today - 2. [Relativpronomen - Person] who, that; [- Sache] which, that.

da sein (perf ist da gewesen) vi (unreg) - 1. [vorhanden sein, anwesend sein] to be there; **es ist keine Milch mehr da** there's no more milk, there's no milk left; **ich bin gleich wieder da** I'll be back in a second - 2. [eingetreten sein - Situation] to arise; [- Augenblick] to arrive; **er überbot alles, was bisher da gewesen war** he surpassed everything which had gone before - 3. [leben] to live - 4. fam [wach sein] to be with it; **geistig voll ~** to be all there.

da|sitzen vi (unreg) - 1. [an einer Stelle] to sit (there) - 2. fam [in einer Situation] to be left (there).

dasjenige ◇ det the; **~ Kind, das hingefallen ist** the child who fell ◇ pron: **~, was sie am liebsten tut** the thing she likes to do most; **~, das ...** the one which ...

dass konj - 1. [im Objektsatz] that; **ich weiß, ~ du gern angelst** I know (that) you like fishing - 2. [im Subjektsatz] the fact that; **du musst bedenken, ~ er nicht mehr klein ist** you must remember (that) he's not young anymore - 3. [im Attributsatz] that; **unter der Bedingung, ~ ...** on (the) condition that ...; **es war eine Dummheit, ~ er das gesagt hat** it was stupid of him to say that - 4. [in festen Verbindungen]: **anstatt, ~ er selbst kam, ...** instead of coming himself, ...; **ohne ~ sie etwas gemerkt hat** without her noticing anything.

dasselbe ◇ det the same ◇ pron the same one; **genau ~ hast du gestern gesagt** you said exactly the same thing yesterday.

da|stehen vi (unreg) - 1. [an Stelle] to stand (there) - 2. [in Situation] to find o.s.; **mit leeren Händen ~** to be left empty-handed; **gut** ODER **glänzend ~** to be in a good ODER splendid position.

Datei (pl -en) die EDV file.

Daten pl - 1. [Zeiten] ▷ **Datum** - 2. [Informationen] data; **~ verarbeitend** data-processing.

Datenautolbahn die EDV information superhighway.

Datenbank (pl -en) die databank.

Datenlnetz das: **das ~** the Net; **im ~** on the Net.

Datenschutzlgesetz das data protection law.

Datentypist, in (mpl -en; fpl -nen) der, die data inputter.

Datenlverarbeitung die data processing.

datieren vt to date.

Dativ (pl -e) der dative.

Datum (pl Daten) das date; **welches ~ haben wir heute?** what's today's date?

Datum

In written German, the date is given as a number followed by a full stop (10. Mai 2000). However, when reading the date aloud, or if writing the date out in full, ordinal numbers are used (zehnter Mai 2000 or zehnter fünfter 2000). In abbreviated form, the day, month and year are separated by full stops (10.05.00). When referring to something happening on a particular date, the ordinal number is always preceded by am and has the dative ending -en (am zehnten Mai).

Dauer die length; **dieses Glück hatte keine ~ this** happiness did not last; **auf (die) ~** in the long term; **seine Ehe war nicht von ~** his marriage was short-lived.

dauerhaft <> adj [Friede, Freundschaft] lasting; [Material] durable <> adv: **das Problem ~ lösen** to find a lasting solution to the problem.

Dauer|karte die season ticket.

Dauer|lauf der jog.

dauern vi to last; **es dauert zu lange** it's taking too long; **eine Weile wird es schon noch ~, bis ich fertig bin** it will still be a while before I'm finished.

dauernd <> adj constant <> adv constantly.

Dauer|welle die perm.

Dauer|zustand der permanent state.

Däumchen (pl -) das: **~ drehen** fam to twiddle one's thumbs.

Daumen (pl -) der thumb; **am ~ lutschen** to suck one's thumb; **jm die ~ drücken** ODER **halten** fig to keep one's fingers crossed for sb.

Daune (pl -n) die: **~n** down (U).

Daunen|decke die eiderdown.

davon, davon adv - **1.** [räumlich] from it - **2.** [von diesem Gegenstand, aus dieser Menge] of it - **3.** [von dieser Sache] about it - **4.** [dadurch]: **er ist nicht ~ betroffen** he is not affected by it; **sie ist ~ krank geworden** it made her ill; **das kommt ~!** that's what happens!

davon|kommen (perf ist davongekommen) vi (unreg) to escape.

davon|laufen (perf ist davongelaufen) vi (unreg) to run away; **jm ~** [Ehepartner, Hausmädchen] to walk out on sb; [Verfolger] to shake sb off.

davor, davor adv - **1.** [räumlich] in front of it - **2.** [zeitlich] beforehand; **kurz ~ sein, etw**

zu tun to be on the point of doing sthg - **3.** [vor dieser Sache]: **jn ~ warnen** to warn sb of it; **ich habe Angst ~** I'm scared of it.

dazu, dazu adv - **1.** [außerdem] in addition, into the bargain; **es schneit und es ist noch kalt ~** it's snowing, and it's cold too - **2.** [zu dieser Sache]: **er hat nicht die Zeit ~** he hasn't got time for it; **ich habe keine Lust ~** I don't feel like it; **ich bin nicht ~ gekommen** I didn't get round to it.

dazu|geben vt (unreg) to add.

dazu|gehören vi - **1.** [zu etwas gehören] to belong; **gehört der Drucker dazu?** is the printer included? - **2.** [nötig sein]: **es gehört Mut dazu, das zu tun** it takes courage to do that.

dazu|kommen (perf ist dazugekommen) vi (unreg) - **1.** [ankommen] to arrive - **2.** [hinzukommen]: **sie ist neu dazugekommen** she's a recent arrival; **kommt noch etwas dazu?** would you like anything else?

dazu|tun vt (unreg) to add.

dazwischen adv - **1.** [örtlich, zeitlich] in between - **2.** [dabei] among them.

dazwischen|kommen (perf ist dazwischengekommen) vi (unreg) - **1.** [dazwischengeraten]: **er kam mit dem Finger dazwischen** he got his finger caught in it - **2.** [ungeplant passieren]: **mir ist etw dazwischengekommen** sthg has cropped up.

dazwischen|rufen (unreg) <> vt: **etw ~** interrupt by shouting sthg <> vi to interrupt by shouting.

DB (abk für Deutsche Bahn) German railway company.

DDR [de:de:'ɛr] (abk für Deutsche Demokratische Republik) die GDR.

Dealer, in ['di:lɐ, rɪn] (mpl -; fpl -nen) der, die fam pusher.

Debatte (pl -n) die debate; **zur ~ stehen** to be on the agenda.

debattieren <> vt to debate <> vi: **über etw (A) ~** to debate sthg.

Deck (pl -s) das deck; **unter ~ gehen** to go below. <> **an Deck** on deck.

Deck|blatt das title page.

Decke (pl -n) die - **1.** [Tischdecke] tablecloth - **2.** [zum Zudecken - Wolldecke] blanket; [- Steppdecke] quilt, duvet - **3.** [Zimmerdecke] ceiling - **4.** RW: **(mit jm) unter einer ~ stecken** to be in cahoots (with sb).

Deckel (pl -) der - **1.** [von Gefäßen] lid - **2.** [von Büchern] cover.

decken <> vt - **1.** [bedecken - Haus] to roof; **das Dach ~** [mit Ziegeln] to tile the roof; [mit Stroh] to thatch the roof - **2.** [Tisch] to lay, to set - **3.** [legen]: **die Hand über die Augen ~** to cover one's eyes with one's hand - **4.** [schützen - Kind, Körperteil, Rückzug] to cover; [- Komplizen] to cover up for - **5.** SPORT to

mark - **6.** [Bedarf] to meet - **7.** WIRTSCH & ZO-
OL to cover ◇ *vi* - **1.** [den Tisch decken] to
lay ODER set the table - **2.** [Farbe] to cover.
◆ **sich decken** *ref* [Dreiecke] to be congruent; [Meinungen] to coincide; [Aussagen] to
tally.

Deckname *der* assumed name.

Deckung (*pl* -en) *die* - **1.** [Schutz] cover; **in
~ gehen** to take cover - **2.** SPORT [beim Boxen]
guard; [Manndeckung] marking; [Verteidi-
gung] defence - **3.** [Befriedigung - von Bedarf]
covering; **zur ~ der Nachfrage** in order to
meet demand - **4.** [Versicherungsschutz, von
Scheck] cover - **5.** MATH congruence.

deckungsgleich *adj* [Dreiecke] congruent;
[Ansichten, Theorien] matching.

Decoder [de'ko:dɐ] (*pl* -) *der* ELEKTR decoder.

decodieren = dekodieren.

defekt *adj* faulty, defective.

Defekt (*pl* -e) *der* fault, defect.

defensiv [defen'zi:f] ◇ *adj* defensive;
[Fahrweise] safe, careful ◇ *adv* defensively;
[fahren] safely, carefully.

definieren *vt* to define. ◆ **sich definieren** *ref* to be defined.

Definition (*pl* -en) *die* definition.

definitiv ◇ *adj* final ◇ *adv*: **sich ~ entscheiden** to make a final decision; **kannst du
mir ~ sagen, ob du kommst?** can you let me
know for sure whether you're coming?

Defizit (*pl* -e) *das* - **1.** [Fehlbetrag] deficit
- **2.** [Fehlen] shortage.

deformieren *vt* to deform.

deftig *adj* - **1.** [nahrhaft] substantial, hearty
- **2.** [derb] coarse.

Degen (*pl* -) *der* rapier.

dehnbar *adj* [Stoff, Gummi, Begriff] elastic;
[Metall] ductile.

dehnen *vt* - **1.** [Substanz, Glieder] to stretch
- **2.** [Laut] to draw out. ◆ **sich dehnen** *ref*
- **1.** [gen] to stretch - **2.** [Gespräch, Warten] to
drag on.

Deich (*pl* -e) *der* dyke.

Deichsel ['daɪksl] (*pl* -n) *die* shafts (*pl*).

dein, e *det* your.

deine, r, s ODER **deins** *pron* yours.

deiner *pron* (*Genitiv von du*) of you; **ich erin-
nere mich ~** I remember you.

deinerseits *adv* - **1.** [du selbst] for your part
- **2.** [von dir] on your part.

deinesgleichen *pron* people like you; **du
und ~** you and your like.

deinetwegen *adv* - **1.** [dir zuliebe] for your
sake - **2.** [wegen dir] because of you.

deinetwillen ◆ **um deinetwillen** *adv*
for your sake.

dekadent *adj* decadent.

Deklination (*pl* -en) *die* declension.

deklinieren *vt* to decline.

dekodieren, decodieren [deko'di:rən] *vt*
to decode.

Dekolletee, Dekolletté [dekɔl'te:] (*pl* -s)
das décolleté.

Dekor (*pl* -s ODER -e) ◇ *das* ODER *der* [Verzie-
rung] pattern ◇ *das* [im Theater, Film] dé-
cor.

Dekoration (*pl* -en) *die* - **1.** [Ausschmü-
ckung, Auszeichnung] decoration; [von
Schaufenster] window-dressing - **2.** [Kulisse]
set.

dekorativ *adj* decorative.

dekorieren *vt* [schmücken, auszeichnen] to
decorate; [Schaufenster] to dress.

Delegation (*pl* -en) *die* delegation.

Delegierte (*pl* -n) *der, die* delegate.

Delfin (*pl* -e) *der* = Delphin.

delikat ◇ *adj* - **1.** [Speise] delicious
- **2.** [Person, Angelegenheit, Lage] delicate
◇ *adv* [behutsam] delicately.

Delikatesse (*pl* -n) *die* [Leckerbissen] delicacy.

Delikt (*pl* -e) *das* offence; **ein ~ begehen** to
commit an offence.

Delle (*pl* -n) *die* dent.

Delphin, Delfin (*pl* -e) ◇ *der* [Säugetier]
dolphin ◇ *das* (*ohne Pl*) [Sportart] butterfly.

Delta (*pl* -s) *das* delta.

dem ◇ *det* (*Dativ Singular von der, das*): **mit
~ Kind** with the child ◇ *pron* (*Dativ Singular*)
- **1.** [Demonstrativ von der, das - Person] to
him; [- Sache] to that one; **mit ~** [Person]
with him; [Sache] with that one - **2.** [Relativ-
pronomen von der, das - Person] to whom;
[- Sache] to which; **mit ~** [Person] with
whom; [Sache] which.

demaskieren *vt* [entlarven] to unmask.

dementsprechend ◇ *adj* appropriate
◇ *adv* accordingly.

demgegenüber *adv* on the other hand.

demgemäß *adv* accordingly.

demnach *adv* so.

demnächst [de:m'nɛːst] *adv* soon.

Demokrat (*pl* -en) *der* democrat.

Demokratie (*pl* -n) *die* democracy.

Demokratin (*pl* -nen) *die* democrat.

demokratisch ◇ *adj* democratic ◇ *adv*
democratically.

demolieren *vt* to wreck.

Demonstrant, in (*mpl* -en; *fpl* -nen) *der,
die* demonstrator.

Demonstration (*pl* -en) *die* demonstration.

demonstrativ *adj* - **1.** [betont auffällig]
pointed - **2.** [anschaulich] revealing.

Demonstrativ|pronomen *das* GRAM demonstrative pronoun.

demonstrieren ⬦ *vi* to demonstrate; **gegen/für etw ~** to demonstrate against/in support of sthg ⬦ *vt* to demonstrate.

demoskopisch ⬦ *adj* opinion poll *(vor Subst)*; **-e Untersuchung** opinion poll ⬦ *adv* through opinion polls.

demütig *adj* - 1. [ergeben] humble - 2. [unterwürfig] submissive.

demütigen *vt* to humiliate. ⬦ **sich demütigen** *ref* to humiliate o.s.

Demütigung *(pl -en) die* humiliation.

demzufolge *adv* consequently.

den ⬦ *det* - 1. *(Akkusativ Singular von der)* the - 2. *(Dativ Plural von der, die, das)* to the; **mit ~ Kindern** with the children ⬦ *pron (Akkusativ Singular)* - 1. [Demonstrativ von der - Person] him; [- Sache] that one - 2. [Relativpronomen von der - Person] whom; [- Sache] which.

denen *pron (Dativ Plural)* - 1. [Demonstrativ von der, die, das] to them; **mit ~** with them - 2. [Relativpronomen von der, die, das - Personen] to whom; [- Sachen] to which; **mit ~ Personen**] with whom; [Sachen] with which.

Den Haag *nt* The Hague.

denkbar ⬦ *adj* [vorstellbar] conceivable; **nicht ~** unthinkable ⬦ *adv* [äußerst] extremely; **die ~ besten/schlechtesten Bedingungen** the best/worst conditions imaginable.

denken *(prät* **dachte***; perf* **hat gedacht)** ⬦ *vi* - 1. [gen] to think; **es gab mir zu ~** it made me think; **ich denke nicht** I don't think so; **denkst du, er schafft das?** do you think he'll manage?; **an jn/etw ~** to think of sb/ sthg; **denk an den Kaffee!** don't forget the coffee!; **er denkt immer nur an sich** he always thinks about himself - 2. [planen] **an etw (A) ~** to think about sthg; **ich denke nicht daran, das zu tun** I have no intention of doing it ⬦ *vt* - 1. [gen] to think; **wer hätte das gedacht!** who would have thought it! - 2. [sich vorstellen]: **das hätte ich mir ~ können** I might have known; **das habe ich mir schon gedacht!** I thought as much!

denkfaul *adj* mentally lazy; **sei nicht so ~** use your brain.

Denk|fehler *der* mistake in one's reasoning; **einen ~ machen** to make a mistake in one's reasoning.

Denkmal *(pl* -mäler ODER -e) *das* [Monument] monument; **sich (D) ein ~ setzen** to ensure one's place in history.

Denkmalspflege, Denkmalpflege *die* preservation of historical monuments.

Denkmalsschutz, Denkmalschutz *der* protection of historical monuments.

Denk|weise *die* way of thinking.

denkwürdig *adj* memorable.

Denk|zettel *der* lesson; **jm einen ~ geben** ODER **verpassen** to teach sb a lesson.

denn ⬦ *konj* [weil] because ⬦ *adv* - 1. [verstärkend] **was hast du ~?** what's wrong?; **warum ~ nicht?** why not?; **was ist ~ eigentlich passiert?** so what ACTUALLY happened? - 2. [dann] then.

dennoch *adv* nevertheless.

Deo *(pl* -s) *das* deodorant.

Deodorant *(pl* -s ODER -e) *das* deodorant.

Deponie *(pl* -n) *die* dump.

deponieren *vt* to deposit.

Depp [dɛp] *(pl* -en) *der fam Österr, Schweiz & Süddt* twit.

Depression *(pl* -en) *die* depression; **an** ODER **unter ~en (D) leiden** to suffer from depression.

depressiv *adj* - 1. MED depressive - 2. [Situation, Stimmung] depressing.

der ⬦ *det* - 1. [Nominativ] the; **~ Tod** death - 2. [Genitiv] of the; **der Hut ~ Frau** the woman's hat; **der Duft ~ Rosen** the fragrance of the roses - 3. [Dativ] the ⬦ *pron* - 1. [Demonstrativpronomen - Person] he; **~ war es** it was him; **~ hat es getan** he did it; **unser Sohn? - ~ geht schon längst in die Schule** our son? - he's been at school for a long time - 2. [Demonstrativpronomen - Sache] that one; **der Wein? - ~ war fantastisch** the wine? - it was great; **~ und ~** so-and-so - 3. [Relativpronomen - Person] who, that; [- Sache] which, that; **die Frau, ~ ich das Buch gab** the woman I gave the book to, the woman to whom I gave the book.

derart *adv* so; **es hat lange nicht mehr ~ geregnet** it's a long time since it rained so much; **ein ~ teures Auto kann ich mir nicht leisten** I can't afford such an expensive car. ⬦ **derart ..., dass** *konj* so ... that.

derartig *adj* such; **eine ~e Frechheit** such (a) cheek.

derb ⬦ *adj* - 1. [kräftig - Stoß, Schlag] hefty; [- Leder] tough - 2. [grob] coarse, crude ⬦ *adv* - 1. [fest] roughly - 2. [grob] crudely.

deren *det* - 1. [Genitiv Singular von die - Person] her; [- Sache] its - 2. [Genitiv Plural von der, die, das] their - 3. [Relativpronomen - Person] whose; [- Sache] of which.

derentwegen ⬦ *adv* - 1. [ihr zuliebe] for her sake; [ihnen zuliebe] for their sake - 2. [wegen ihr] because of her; [wegen ihnen] because of them ⬦ *rel pron* - 1. [der, denen zuliebe - Person] for whose sake; [- Sache] for the sake of which - 2. [wegen der, denen - Person] because of whom; [- Sache] because of which.

dergleichen *pron* that sort of thing.

derjenige ⬦ *det:* **~ Mensch, der ...** the person who ... <> *pron:* ~, **der das getan hat** whoever did this; **von allen Posten erfordert** – **des Vorsitzenden besonders viel Einsatz** of all the jobs, the chairman's is the one which requires the most effort; **von allen Teilnehmern erhält** ~ **den Preis, der** ... the prize goes to the contestant who ....

dermaßen ◆ **dermaßen ..., dass** *konj* so ... that.

derselbe <> *det* the same <> *pron* the same one.

derzeit *adv* at the moment, at present.

derzeitig *adj* current.

des *det (Genitiv Singular von der, das)* of the; **der Schwanz** ~ **Hundes** the dog's tail.

desertieren *(perf* ist desertiert*) vi* to desert.

desgleichen *adv* likewise.

deshalb *adv* therefore. ◆ **deshalb, weil** *konj* because.

Desinfektionsmittel *das* disinfectant.

desinfizieren *vt* to disinfect.

Desktop-Publishing ['dɛsktɔppʌbliʃɪŋ] *das (ohne pl)* EDV desktop publishing.

dessen *pron* - 1. [Genitiv Singular von der, das - Person] his; [- Sache] its - 2. [Relativpronomen von der, das - Person] whose; [- Sache] of which.

Dessert [dɛ'seːɐ] *(pl -s) das* dessert; **zum** ~ for dessert.

destillieren *vt* to distil.

desto *konj:* **je eher,** ~ **besser!** the sooner, the better!

deswegen *adv* therefore; **er ist krank und kann** ~ **nicht kommen** he's ill, which is why he can't come; **er ist gerade** ~ **nicht gekommen** that's precisely the reason he didn't come; **ach,** ~**!** oh, that's why! ODER the reason!; ~, **weil** because.

Detail [de'tai] *(pl -s) das* detail. ◆ **im Detail** *adv* [detailliert] in detail.

detailliert <> *adj* detailed <> *adv* in detail.

Detektiv, in *(mpl -e; fpl -nen) der, die* detective.

deuten <> *vt* [auslegen] to interpret; [Sterne] to read <> *vi* - 1. [zeigen]: **auf jn/etw** ~ to point at sb/sthg - 2. [schließen lassen]: **auf etw** *(A)* ~ to point to sthg, to indicate sthg.

deutlich <> *adj* - 1. [klar erkennbar, leicht verständlich] clear; **jm etw** ~ **machen** to make sthg clear to sb - 2. [rücksichtslos offen] blunt; ~ **werden** to speak one's mind <> *adv* - 1. [klar, verständlich] clearly - 2. [rücksichtslos offen] bluntly.

Deutlichkeit *die* - 1. [Klarheit] clarity - 2. [Offenheit] bluntness. ◆ **mit aller Deutlichkeit** *adv* [nachdrücklich] quite clearly.

deutsch <> *adj* German <> *adv* [in deutscher Sprache] in German; *siehe auch* englisch.

Deutsch *das* German.

Deutsche *(pl -n)* <> *der, die* [Person] German; **die** ~**n** the Germans <> *das* - 1. [deutsche Sprache] German - 2. [deutsche Wesensart]: **das ist das typisch** ~ **an ihm** that is what is typically German about him; *siehe auch* Englische.

Deutsche Bahn *die (ohne pl)* German railway company.

Deutsche Bundesbahn *die (ohne pl)* = Deutsche Bahn.

Deutsche Bundesbank *die* Bundesbank.

Deutsche Bundespost *die (ohne pl)* = Deutsche Post.

Deutsche Bundestag *der (ohne pl)* Bundestag, *lower house of the German Parliament.*

Deutsche Demokratische Republik *die* German Democratic Republic.

Deutsche Gewerkschaftsbund *der* German Trade Union Federation.

Deutsche Mark *die (pl -)* German mark, Deutschmark.

Deutsche Post *die* German postal service.

Deutsche Reich *das* German Reich.

Deutschland *nt* Germany.

Deutschlandlied *das* German national anthem.

deutschsprachig ['dɔytʃʃpraːxɪç] *adj* - 1. [Bevölkerung] German-speaking - 2. [Unterricht]: ~**en Unterricht erteilen** to teach in German.

Deutschunterricht *der (ohne pl)* German lessons *(pl);* ~ **geben** to teach German.

Devise [de'viːzə] *(pl -n) die* motto. ◆ **Devisen** *pl* foreign currency *(U).*

Devisenkurs *der* exchange rate.

Dezember *der* December; *siehe auch* September.

dezent <> *adj* - 1. [taktvoll] discreet - 2. [unaufdringlich] tasteful <> *adv* - 1. [taktvoll] discreetly - 2. [unaufdringlich] tastefully.

dezimal *adj* decimal.

Dezimalsystem *das* decimal system.

Dezimalzahl *die* decimal.

DGB [deːgeːˈbeː] *(abk für Deutscher Gewerkschaftsbund) der Federation of German Trade Unions.*

dgl. *abk für* dergleichen.

d. h. *(abk für* das heißt*)* i.e.

Dia *(pl -s) das* slide.

Diabetes *der* diabetes *(U).*

Diabetiker, in *(mpl -; fpl -nen) der, die* diabetic.

Diagnose *(pl -n) die* MED & *fig* diagnosis; **die** ~ **auf etw** *(A)* **stellen** to diagnose sthg.

77 Dienstag

diagonal <> adj diagonal <> adv: **etw ~ lesen** to skim-read sthg.

Diagonale (pl -n) die diagonal; **eine ~ zeichnen** to draw a diagonal line.

Diakon (pl -e ODER -en) der - **1.** [evangelisch] Church welfare worker - **2.** [katholisch] deacon.

Diakonisse (pl -n) die - **1.** [evangelisch] community nurse (working for the Church) - **2.** [katholisch] deaconess.

Dialekt (pl -e) der dialect.

Dialog (pl -e) der dialogue.

Diamant (pl -en) der diamond.

Diaprojektor der slide projector.

Diät (pl -en) die diet; **~ halten** to be on a diet; **eine ~ machen** to go on a diet; **~ kochen** to cook dietary meals; **(nach einer) ~ leben** to follow a diet.

Diäten pl [in der Politik] allowance (sg).

dich pron (Akkusativ von du) - **1.** [Personalpronomen] you - **2.** [Reflexivpronomen] yourself; **hast du ~ umgezogen?** have you changed?; **beeil ~!** hurry up!

dicht <> adj - **1.** [gegen Luft] airtight; [gegen Wasser] watertight; [Schuhe, Stoff] waterproof; **nicht ~ sein** [Dach] to be leaking; [Schuh] to be letting water in; **nicht ODER nicht mehr ganz ~ sein** fam fig & abw to be funny in the head - **2.** [Wald, Nebel] dense - **3.** [Haar, Gefieder] thick; [Verkehr] heavy <> adv - **1.** [undurchlässig]: **~ schließen** to close tight - **2.** [gedrängt] tightly; [bevölkert] densely; **er ist ~ behaart** he is very hairy - **3.** [ganz nahe]: **~ dahinter/daneben** right behind/next to it.

Dichte die - **1.** [Undurchlässigkeit] impermeability - **2.** [von Wald, Nebel] denseness - **3.** [von Bevölkerung & PHYS] density; [von Verkehr] heaviness.

dichten <> vt - **1.** [in Verse fassen] to write - **2.** [gegen Wasser] to make watertight; [gegen Luft] to make airtight; [Fugen] to seal; [Leck] to stop <> vi - **1.** [dicht machen] to seal - **2.** [Verse schreiben] to write (poetry).

Dichter, in (mpl -; fpl -nen) der, die poet; [von Dramen] writer.

dichterisch <> adj poetic <> adv poetically.

Dichtung (pl -en) die - **1.** [Kunstwerk] poem - **2.** [Literatur] literature - **3.** [für Wasserhahn] washer; [im Maschinenbau] gasket.

dick <> adj - **1.** [gen] thick; [Person, Bauch] fat - **2.** [geschwollen] swollen - **3.** fam [groß, bedeutend - Auto, Gehalt, Fehler] whacking great; **ein ~es Lob** a big pat on the back; **sie sind ~e Freunde** they're as thick as thieves <> adv - **1.** [stark] thickly - **2.** fam [sehr] really; **mit jm ~ befreundet sein** to be as thick as thieves with sb - **3.** RW: **jn/etw ~(e) haben** fam to have had one's fill of sb/sthg; **mit jm**

durch ~ und dünn gehen to go through thick and thin with sb.

Dicke (pl -n) <> die [gen] thickness; [von Person, Bauch] fatness; **die Wand hat eine ~ von 20 cm** the wall is 20 cm thick <> der, die [Person] fatty.

dickflüssig adj thick.

Dickicht (pl -e) das thicket.

Dickkopf der - **1.** [Person] pig-headed person - **2.** [Haltung]: **einen ~ haben** to be pig-headed.

dickköpfig adj pig-headed.

Dickmilch die sour milk.

die <> det die; **sich** (D) **~ Hände waschen** to wash one's hands; **~ Natur** nature <> pron - **1.** [Demonstrativpronomen - Person] she; **~ war es** it was her; **~ hat es getan** she did it; **meine Tochter? - ~ geht schon längst in die Schule** my daughter? – she's been at school for a long time - **2.** [Demonstrativpronomen - Sache] that one; **meine Lehre? - ~ habe ich abgebrochen** my training? – I've given it up - **3.** [Relativpronomen - Person] who, that; [- Sache] which, that.

Dieb (pl -e) der thief.

Diebin (pl -nen) die thief.

diebisch <> adj - **1.** [schadenfroh] gloating - **2.** [stehlend] thieving <> adv: **sich ~ freuen** to gloat.

Diebstahl (pl -stähle) der theft.

diejenige <> det: **~ Frau, die ...** the woman who ... <> pron: **unter allen Bewerbungen wurde ~ ausgewählt, die am originellsten war** the application that was chosen was the most original one.

Diele (pl -n) die - **1.** [Flur] hall - **2.** [Brett] floorboard.

dienen vi - **1.** [nützen]: **einer Sache** (D) **~** to help with sthg; **jm ~** to be of use to sb; **als etw ~** to serve as sthg; **der Teppich dient nur zur Zierde** the carpet is only for decoration - **2.** [behilflich sein] to be of help - **3.** [für etw wirken]: **jm/einer Sache ~** to serve sb/sthg - **4.** [Subj: Butler]: **jm ~** to serve sb - **5.** [Soldat sein] to serve.

Diener, in (mpl -; fpl -nen) der, die eigtl & fig servant.

Dienst (pl -e) der - **1.** [gen] service; **der öffentliche ~** the civil service; **jm seine ~e anbieten** to offer sb one's services; **jm einen (guten) ~ erweisen** to serve sb well - **2.** [Arbeit, Pflicht] work; [von Arzt, Soldat] duty; **zum ~ gehen** to go to work; [Arzt, Soldat] to go on duty; **~ haben** to be working; [Arzt, Soldat] to be on duty; **~ habend** on duty; **~ nach Vorschrift** work-to-rule - **3.** [Arbeitsverhältnis] post.

Dienstag (pl -e) der Tuesday; siehe auch Samstag.

dienstags *adv* on Tuesdays; *siehe auch* samstags.

Dienst|geheimnis *das* official secret.

Dienst|grad *der* rank.

diensthabend *adj* = Dienst habend.

Dienst|leistung *die* service.

dienstlich <> *adj* - **1.** *amt* [den Dienst betreffend] business *(vor Subst)*; [Befehl] official - **2.** [unpersönlich] impersonal <> *adv amt* [verreisen] on business.

Dienst|reise *die* business trip; **auf ~ sein** [geschäftlich] to be away on business; [Politiker] to be away on official business.

Dienst|stelle *die*: **die oberste ~** the highest authority.

Dienst|wagen *der* company car.

Dienst|weg *der*: **den ~ einhalten** to go through the proper channels.

Dienst|zeit *die* - **1.** [Dienststunden] working hours *(pl)* - **2.** [Soldatenzeit] term of service.

dies *pron* this; **~ und das** ODER **jenes** *fig* this and that.

diesbezüglich <> *adj* related (to this) <> *adv* regarding this (matter).

diese, r, s ODER **dies** <> *det* this; [jene] that; **am 9. ~s Monats** on the 9th of this month <> *pron* this one; [jene] that one.

Diesel *(pl -)* *der* diesel.

dieselbe <> *det* the same <> *pron* the same one.

diesig *adj* misty.

diesjährig *adj*: **die ~e Ernte** this year's harvest.

diesmal *adv* this time.

diesseits *präp* [auf dieser Seite]: **~ eines Ortes** *(G)* on this side of a place.

Dietrich *(pl -e)* *der* skeleton key.

Differenz *(pl -en)* *die* - **1.** [gen] difference - **2.** [Fehlbetrag] deficit. ◆ **Differenzen** *pl* [Meinungsverschiedenheiten] differences.

differenzieren <> *vt* to differentiate between <> *vi* to make distinctions.

digital *adj* digital.

Digital|anzeige *die* digital display.

Diktat *(pl -e)* *das* - **1.** [Nachschrift] dictation - **2.** *geh* [Zwang] dictate.

Diktator *(pl -toren)* *der* dictator.

Diktatorin *(pl -nen)* *die* dictator.

Diktatur *(pl -en)* *die abw* dictatorship.

diktieren *vt* to dictate; **jm etw ~** to dictate sthg to sb.

Dill *der* dill.

Dimension *(pl -en)* *die eigtl & fig* dimension; **ungeahnte ~en annehmen** to take on unprecedented proportions.

DIN [di:n] *(abk für Deutsche Industrienorm)* *die* DIN.

Ding *(pl -e* ODER *-er)* *das* - **1.** *(pl Dinge)* [Gegenstand, Angelegenheit] thing; **vor allen ~en** above all; **über den ~en stehen** to be above it all; **den ~en ihren Lauf lassen** to let things take their course; **es ist nicht mit rechten ~en zugegangen** there was something odd about it; **wie die ~e liegen** as things stand - **2.** *(pl Dinger)* *fam* [Sache] thing - **3.** *(pl Dinger)* [Mädchen]: **ein junges/dummes ~** a young/stupid thing - **4.** *(pl Dinger)* *RW*: **das is (ja) 'n ~!** *fam* would you believe it!, there's a thing!; **ein ~ drehen** *fam* to do a job.

Dings *fam* <> *der, die* [Person] thingy, thingummy <> *das* [Gegenstand, Ort] thingy, thingummy.

Dino|saurier *der* dinosaur.

Diözese *(pl -n)* *die* diocese.

Diplom *(pl -e)* *das* - **1.** [akademischer Grad] degree *(in science or technology)* - **2.** [Urkunde] diploma.

Diplom|arbeit *die* dissertation *(submitted for a degree)*.

Diplomat *(pl -en)* *der* diplomat.

Diplomatie *die* diplomacy.

Diplomatin *(pl -nen)* *die* diplomat.

diplomatisch <> *adj* diplomatic <> *adv* diplomatically.

Diplom|ingenieur, in *der, die* qualified engineer.

dir *pron (Dativ von du)* (to) you; **das gehört ~** it belongs to you, it's yours; **ich komme mit ~** I'm coming with you; **tun ~ die Füße weh?** do your feet hurt?

direkt <> *adj* direct <> *adv* - **1.** [sofort] straight; *TV* live - **2.** [nahe] right; **~ neben** right next to - **3.** [unmittelbar]: **sie kaufen ihre Milch ~ beim Bauern** they buy their milk direct from the farmer - **4.** [unverblümt] directly.

Direktor *(pl -toren)* *der* [von Schule] headmaster *Br*, principal *Am*; [von Museum] director; [von Strafanstalt] governor *Br*, warden *Am*; [von Abteilung] manager.

Direktorin *(pl -nen)* *die* [von Schule] headmistress *Br*, principal *Am*; [von Museum] director; [von Strafanstalt] governor *Br*, warden *Am*; [von Abteilung] manager.

Direktübertragung *die* live broadcast.

Dirigent, in *(mpl -en; fpl -nen)* *der, die* conductor.

dirigieren <> *vt* - **1.** *MUS* to conduct - **2.** [Unternehmen] to manage, to run; [Verkehr] to direct <> *vi* to conduct.

Disketten|laufwerk *das* *EDV* disk drive.

Disko *(pl -s)* *die fam* disco.

Diskont|satz *der* *WIRTSCH* discount rate.

Diskothek *(pl -en)* *die* discotheque.

Diskretion *die* discretion; **in Bezug auf etw ~ wahren** to treat sthg in confidence.

diskriminieren *vt* - 1. [benachteiligen] to discriminate against - 2. [herabwürdigen] to disparage.

Diskussion (*pl* -en) *die* discussion.

Diskuswerfen *das* SPORT discus.

diskutieren ◇ *vi* to discuss; **über jn/etw** ~ to discuss sb/sthg ◇ *vt* to discuss.

disqualifizieren *vt* to disqualify.

Dissertation (*pl* -en) *die* (doctoral) thesis.

Distanz (*pl* -en) *die* - 1. [Entfernung] distance - 2. [persönlicher Abstand] detachment; **etw aus der ~ heraus beurteilen** to judge sthg from a distance; **jm gegenüber auf ~ gehen/ bleiben** to distance o.s./keep one's distance from sb.

distanziert ◇ *adj* detached ◇ *adv:* ~ **wirken** to seem distant.

Distel (*pl* -n) *die* thistle.

Disziplin (*pl* -en) *die* discipline.

disziplinarisch ◇ *adj* disciplinary ◇ *adv:* **gegen jn ~ vorgehen** to take disciplinary action against sb.

diszipliniert ◇ *adj* disciplined ◇ *adv* in a disciplined way.

diverse [di'vɛrzə] *adj pl* various.

Dividende [divi'dɛndə] (*pl* -n) *die* dividend.

dividieren [divi'di:rən] *vt:* **etw (durch etw) ~** to divide sthg (by sthg).

Division [divi'zjo:n] (*pl* -en) *die* MATH & MIL division.

Diwan (*pl* -e) *der* divan.

DM (*abk für* Deutsche Mark) DM.

D-Mark ['de:mark] (*pl* -) (*abk für* Deutsche Mark) *die* German mark, Deutschmark.

d-Moll *das* D minor.

DNA (*abk für* deoxyribonucleic acid) *die* DNA.

DNS (*abk für* Desoxyribonukleinsäure) *die* = DNA.

doch ◇ *konj* [aber] yet, but ◇ *adv* - 1. [trotzdem] anyway; **er wollte erst nicht, aber dann hat er es ~ gemacht** at first he didn't want to, but then he did it anyway; **willst du nicht? - ~ don't you want to? - yes, I do; ~ noch** after all - 2. [verstärkend]: **setzen Sie sich ~!** do sit down!; **das kann ~ nicht wahr sein!** I don't believe it!; **aber das konnte ich ~ nicht wissen!** but how could I have known! ➥ **nicht doch** *interj* don't do that!

Docht (*pl* -e) *der* wick.

Dock (*pl* -s) *das* dock.

Dogge (*pl* -n) *die* mastiff.

Doktor (*pl* -toren) *der* - 1. [Titel] doctorate; **seinen ~ machen** to do one's doctorate - 2. [Träger des Doktortitels, Arzt] doctor.

Doktorand, in (*mpl* -en; *fpl* -nen) *der, die* PhD student.

Doktorarbeit *die* doctoral thesis.

Doktorin (*pl* -nen) *die* doctor.

Doktrin (*pl* -en) *die* doctrine.

Dokument (*pl* -e) *das* document.

Dokumentarfilm *der* documentary.

Dokumentation (*pl* -en) *die* - 1. [Informationsmaterial] documentation (U) - 2. [Darstellung]: **eine ~ über etw** (A) **machen** to document sthg.

Dolch (*pl* -e) *der* dagger.

Dollar (*pl* -s ODER -) *der* dollar.

dolmetschen *vt* & *vi* to interpret.

Dolmetscher, in (*mpl* -; *fpl* -nen) *der, die* interpreter.

Dolomiten *pl* Dolomites.

Dom (*pl* -e) *der* cathedral.

dominant *adj* dominant.

Dominanz (*pl* -en) *die* dominance.

dominieren ◇ *vi* to predominate ◇ *vt* to dominate.

Dominikaner, in (*mpl* -; *fpl* -nen) *der, die* GEOGR & REL Dominican.

Dominikanische Republik *die* Dominican Republic.

Donau *die:* **die ~** the Danube.

Donner *der* thunder.

donnern (*perf* hat/ist gedonnert) ◇ *vi* - 1. (hat) [beim Gewitter]: **es donnert** it is thundering - 2. (ist) [sich bewegen] to thunder - 3. (hat) *fam* [schlagen] to hammer - 4. (ist) *fam* [prallen]: **gegen etw ~** to slam into sthg ◇ *vt* (hat) *fam* to hurl.

Donnerstag (*pl* -e) *der* Thursday; *siehe auch* Samstag.

donnerstags *adv* on Thursdays; *siehe auch* samstags.

Donnerwetter *das* (*ohne pl*) *fam* almighty row; **Donnerwetter!** my goodness!

doof *fam* ◇ *adj* stupid ◇ *adv* stupidly.

dopen ['do:pn] *vt* [Pferd] to dope. ➥ **sich dopen** *ref* [Sportler] to take drugs.

Doping ['do:pɪŋ] (*pl* -s) *das* drug-taking.

Doppel (*pl* -) *das* - 1. [Kopie] duplicate - 2. SPORT doubles (U).

Doppelbett *das* double bed.

Doppeldecker (*pl* -) *der* - 1. FLUG biplane - 2. [Omnibus] double-decker (bus).

doppeldeutig *adj* ambiguous; **~er Witz** double entendre.

Doppelgänger, in (*mpl* -; *fpl* -nen) *der, die* double.

Doppelhaus *das* pair of semi-detached houses.

Doppelkinn *das* double chin.

Doppelklick (*pl* -s) *der* EDV double click.

Doppelname *der* double-barrelled name.

Doppelpunkt *der* colon.

doppelseitig *adj* - 1. [Lungenentzündung] double - 2. [zwei Seiten umfassend] two-page.

doppelt ◇ *adj* - 1. [zweifach] double

- 2. [gesteigert] twice as much ⇔ *adv* twice; **~ so viel** twice as much.

Doppelzimmer *das* double room.

Dorf (*pl* -) *das* [Ort] village; **auf dem ~** in the country.

Dorf|bewohner, in *der, die* villager.

dörflich *adj* village (vor Subst); [Gegend] rural.

Dorn (*pl* -en) *der* [von Rose] thorn; [von Schnalle] prong.

Dornröschen *das* Sleeping Beauty.

Dörrobst *das* dried fruit.

Dorsch (*pl* -e) *der* cod.

dort *adv* there; **~ drüben** over there; **~, wo wir Fußball spielen** where we play football.

dorther *adv* from there.

dorthin *adv* there.

dortig *adj* local.

Dose (*pl* -n) *die* **- 1.** [Behälter] box; [für Zucker] bowl; [für Butter] dish **- 2.** [Konservendose] can, tin *Br*; [Bierdose] can; **Erbsen aus der ~** tinned ODER canned peas.

dösen *vi* to doze.

Dosen|milch *die* condensed ODER evaporated milk.

Dosen|öffner *der* can ODER tin *Br* opener.

dosieren *vt* to measure out.

Dosierung (*pl* -en) *die* dosage.

Dosis (*pl* Dosen) *die* dose.

Dotter (*pl* -) *das* ODER *der* yolk.

Double ['du:bl] (*pl* -s) *das* double.

down [daʊn] *adj fam*: **~ sein** to be down.

down|loaden [präs loadet down; prät loadete down; perf hat downgeloadet] *vt* EDV to download.

Dozent, in (*mpl* -en; *fpl* -nen) *der, die* lecturer *Br*, assistant professor *Am*.

dpa [de:pe'a:] (*abk für* Deutsche Presseagentur) *die* German Press Agency.

Dr. (*abk für* Doktor) Dr.

Drache (*pl* -n) *der* dragon.

Drachen (*pl* -) *der* **- 1.** [Spielzeug] kite **- 2.** abw [Frau] dragon.

Draht (*pl* Drähte) *der* **- 1.** [gen] wire **- 2.** *RW*: **auf ~ sein** *fam* to be on the ball; **einen guten ~ zu jm haben** to be well in with sb.

Drahtseil|bahn *die* cable railway.

Drahtzieher, in (*mpl* -; *fpl* -nen) *der, die* [Hintermann] string-puller.

Drama (*pl* Dramen) *das* drama.

dramatisch *adj* dramatic.

dramatisieren *vt* [hochspielen] to play up, to make a big thing of.

Dramaturg, in (*mpl* -en; *fpl* -nen) *der, die* person who selects and adapts plays for the stage.

dran *adv* **- 1.** *fam* = daran **- 2.** [an der Reihe]: **ich bin jetzt ~** it's my turn; **wer ist als Näch-** ster **~?** who's next?, whose turn is it? **- 3.** *RW*: **~ sein** to be for it.

drang *prät* ▷ dringen.

Drängelei (*pl* -en) *die* **- 1.** abw [durch Schieben] pushing (and shoving) **- 2.** [durch Reden] pestering.

drängeln ⇔ *vi* **- 1.** [durch Schieben] to push **- 2.** [durch Reden] to go on (and on) ⇔ *vt* **- 1.** [durch Schieben] to push **- 2.** [durch Reden] to pester. ◆ **sich drängeln** *ref*: **sich nach vorn ~** to push one's way to the front.

drängen ⇔ *vi* **- 1.** [schieben] to push **- 2.** [nicht warten]: **zum Aufbruch ~** to insist on leaving; **zur Eile ~** to urge haste; **auf etw** (A) **~** to push ODER press for sthg ⇔ *vt* **- 1.** [schieben] to push **- 2.** [antreiben] to urge.

dran|halten ◆ **sich dranhalten** *ref* (unreg) *fam* to get a move on.

dran|kommen (*perf* ist drangekommen) *vi* (unreg) *fam* **- 1.** [an die Reihe kommen] to have one's turn; **ich bin als Letzter drangekommen** I was last **- 2.** [heranreichen] to reach.

drastisch ⇔ *adj* **- 1.** [einschneidend] drastic **- 2.** [sehr deutlich] graphic ⇔ *adv* **- 1.** [stark] drastically **- 2.** [sehr deutlich] graphically.

drauf *adv fam* **- 1.** = darauf **- 2.** *RW*: **es kommt ~ an** it depends; **etw ~ haben** [Fähigkeit] to be really good at sthg; **er hatte hundert Sachen ~** AUTO he was doing a hundred; **gut ~ sein** to be in a good mood; **~ und dran sein, etw zu tun** to be on the point of doing sthg.

Draufgänger, in (*mpl* -; *fpl* -nen) *der, die* daredevil.

drauf|gehen (*perf* ist draufgegangen) *vi* (unreg) *fam* **- 1.** [umkommen] to buy it **- 2.** [verbraucht werden] to be used up.

draußen *adv* outside. ◆ **nach draußen** *adv* outside. ◆ **von draußen** *adv* from outside.

Dreck *der fam* **- 1.** [Schmutz] muck, dirt; **~ machen** to make a mess **- 2.** *RW*: **das geht dich einen ~ an** it's none of your damn business; **jn/etw in den ~ ziehen** to drag sb/sthg through the mud.

Dreck|arbeit *die fam* **- 1.** [schmutzige Arbeit] dirty work **- 2.** [niedere Arbeit] menial jobs (*pl*).

dreckig ⇔ *adj* **- 1.** [schmutzig, unverschämt] dirty; **sich ~ machen** to get dirty **- 2.** *fam abw* [gemein]: **du ~es Schwein!** you filthy swine! ⇔ *adv fam* **- 1.** abw [unverschämt] dirtily **- 2.** [schlecht]: **ihr geht es ~** she is in a bad way.

Dreck|spatz *der fam* mucky pup.

Dreh|buch *das* screenplay.

drehen ⇔ *vt* **- 1.** [im Kreis bewegen] to turn **- 2.** [einstellen]: **das Radio laut/leise ~** to turn the radio up/down **- 3.** [formen - Seil] to

twist; [~ Zigarette, Pillen] to roll - **4.** TV to film, to shoot ◇ vi - **1.** [wenden] to turn - **2.** [am Knopf, Schalter]: **an etw** (D) **~** to turn sthg; **am Radio ~** to turn the knob on the radio.
◆ **sich drehen** ref - **1.** [sich wenden] to turn; **mir dreht sich alles** fam my head is spinning - **2.** RW: **sich um jn/etw ~** to be about sb/sthg; **es dreht sich darum, dass ...** the thing is ...

Drehlorgel die barrel organ.

Drehlscheibe die [Knotenpunkt] hub.

Drehlstuhl der swivel chair.

Drehltür die revolving door.

Drehung (pl -en) die turn.

Drehlzahl die revs (pl).

drei num - **1.** [Zahl] three - **2.** RW: **für ~ essen** to eat like a horse; siehe auch sechs.

Drei (pl -en) die - **1.** [Zahl] three - **2.** [Schulnote] ≃ C, mark of 3 on a scale from 1 to 6; siehe auch Sechs.

dreidimensional ◇ adj three-dimensional ◇ adv three-dimensionally.

Dreieck (pl -e) das triangle.

dreieckig adj triangular.

Dreier (pl -) der - **1.** [Drei] three - **2.** [beim Lotto] three correct numbers (pl) - **3.** fam [Sprungbrett] three-metre board.

dreierlei adj (unver) three different; **auf ~ Weise** in three different ways.

dreifach ◇ adj triple; **die ~e Menge** three times as much; **in ~er Größe** three times as big; **in ~er Ausfertigung** in triplicate; **der ~e Gewinner** the three times ODER triple winner ◇ adv three times.

dreihundert num three hundred.

Dreikönigslfest das Epiphany.

dreimal adv three times.

Dreilsatz der rule of three.

dreißig num thirty; siehe auch sechs.

Dreißig die thirty; siehe auch Sechs.

Dreißigerjahre, dreißiger Jahre pl: **die ~** the thirties.

dreist ◇ adj impudent ◇ adv impudently.

Dreistigkeit (pl -en) die [Wesen, Verhalten] impudence.

dreistöckig adj - **1.** [Haus] three-storeyed - **2.** [Torte] three-tiered.

dreitausend num three thousand.

dreiteilig adj three-part; [Kostüm, Anzug] three-piece.

drei viertel num three quarters; **~ Liter** three-quarters of a litre; **~ acht** a quarter to Br ODER of Am eight.

Dreivierteltakt der three-four time.

dreizehn num thirteen; siehe auch sechs.

Dreizimmerlwohnung die three-roomed flat Br ODER apartment Am.

dreschen (präs drischt; prät drosch; perf hat gedroschen) ◇ vt - **1.** [Getreide] to thresh - **2.** fam [prügeln] to thrash ◇ vi fam [schlagen] to bang.

Dresden nt Dresden.

Dress (pl -e) der - **1.** SPORT kit - **2.** fam [Kleidung] outfit.

dressieren vt to train.

Dressing (pl -s) das dressing.

Dressur (pl -en) die - **1.** [Dressieren] training - **2.** [Pferdedressur] dressage.

drillen vt to drill.

drin adv fam - **1.** = darin - **2.** [möglich]: **~ sein** to be on the cards; **bei diesem Spiel ist noch alles ~** there is still everything to play for in this game - **3.** [gewöhnt]: **~ sein** to have got into the swing of things.

dringen (prät drang; perf hat/ist gedrungen) vi - **1.** (ist) [eindringen]: **durch** ODER **in etw** (A) **~** to penetrate sthg; **Wasser dringt durch die Decke** water is leaking through the ceiling; **Gas drang in den Raum** gas seeped into the room - **2.** (hat) [drängen]: **auf etw** (A) **~** to insist on sthg.

dringend ◇ adj urgent ◇ adv urgently.

Dringlichkeit die urgency.

drinnen adv inside; **nach ~ gehen** to go inside.

drischt präs ⊏⊐ dreschen.

dritt ◆ **zu dritt** num: **wir sind zu ~** there are three of us; **wir sind zu ~ ins Kino gegangen** three of us went to the cinema.

dritte, r, s adj third; siehe auch sechste.

Dritte der, die, das third; [außenstehende Person] third party; siehe auch Sechste.

drittel adj (unver) third of a; siehe auch sechstel.

Drittel (pl -) das third; siehe auch Sechstel.

dritteln vt to divide into three.

drittens adv thirdly.

Dritte Reich das: **das ~** the Third Reich.

Droge (pl -n) die drug.

drogenabhängig adj: **~ sein** to be a drug addict.

Drogenlabhängige (pl -n) der, die drug addict.

Drogenlhändler, in der, die drug dealer.

Drogerie (pl -n) die chemist's (shop) (non-dispensing) Br, drugstore Am.

drohen vi to threaten; **~, etw zu tun** to threaten to do sthg; **jm (mit etw) ~** to threaten sb (with sthg).

dröhnen vi - **1.** [hallen] to boom - **2.** salopp [berauschen] to give you a high.

Drohung (pl -en) die threat.

Dromedar (pl -e) das dromedary.

drosch prät ⊏⊐ dreschen.

Drossel (pl -n) die thrush.

drosseln vt [Geschwindigkeit, Leistung] to reduce; [Heizung] to turn down.

drüben adv [nebenan] over there.

drüber = darüber.

Druck (pl -e) der - **1.** [Kraft, Zwang] pressure; ~ **hinter etw** (A) **machen** fam fig to put pressure on regarding sthg; ~ **auf jn ausüben, jn unter ~ setzen** to put pressure on sb; ~ **machen** to put pressure on; **unter ~ stehen** to be under pressure - **2.** [Drucken] printing - **3.** [Gravur] print.

Druck|buchstabe der printed letter; **in ~n schreiben** to print.

Drückeberger, in (mpl -; fpl -nen) der, die abw shirker.

druckempfindlich adj [Körperstelle] sensitive to pressure; **Pfirsiche sind ~** peaches bruise easily.

drucken vt to print.

drücken <> vt - **1.** [pressen] to press; **jn/etw an sich** (A) ~ to hold sb/sthg to one - **2.** fam [umarmen] to hug, to squeeze - **3.** [mindern] to lower <> vi - **1.** [pressen]: **auf etw** (A) ~ to press sthg; **es drückt auf die Laune** it gets you down - **2.** [Schuhe] to pinch - **3.** salopp [fixen] to shoot up. ➤ **sich drücken** ref - **1.** [sich pressen]: **sich an etw** (A) ~ to flatten o.s. against sthg - **2.** [sich entziehen]: **sich vor etw** (D) ~ abw to get out of sthg.

drückend adj - **1.** [Probleme, Sorgen] serious; [Verantwortung, Schulden] heavy; [Armut] grinding - **2.** [Hitze] oppressive.

Drucker (pl -) der printer.

Drücker (pl -) der - **1.** [Türdrücker] handle - **2.** [Hausierer] door-to-door salesman - **3.** RW: **am ~ sitzen** fam to call the shots.

Druckerei (pl -en) die printing works, printer's.

Druck|fehler der misprint.

Druck|knopf der press stud Br, snap fastener Am.

Druck|sache die printed matter (U).

Druck|schrift die block capitals (pl).

drum fam = darum.

drunter adv fam - **1.** = darunter - **2.** RW: **alles** ODER **es geht ~ und drüber** everything is going haywire.

Drüse (pl -n) die gland.

Dschungel (pl -) der jungle.

dt. (abk für deutsch) Ger.

DTP (abk für Desktop-Publishing) das (ohne pl) EDV DTP.

du pron du; **ach, ~ bists!** oh, it's you!; ~ **sagen** to use the "du" form of address; **mit jm per ~ sein** ≃ to be on first name terms with sb.

Duale System das privately run waste disposal and recycling system.

Dübel (pl -) der Rawlplug®.

Dublin ['dablin] nt Dublin.

ducken ➤ **sich ducken** ref to duck.

dudeln fam abw <> vi [Plattenspieler, Radio] to drone; [auf Instrument] to tootle <> vt [auf Blasinstrument] to tootle on.

Dudel|sack der bagpipes (pl).

Duell [du'ɛl] (pl -e) das duel.

Duett [du'ɛt] (pl -e) das duet.

Duft (pl Düfte) der scent.

duften vi to smell nice; **nach etw ~** to smell of sthg.

dulden vt geh to tolerate.

dumm (kompar dümmer; superl dümmste) <> adj - **1.** [gen] stupid; **~es Zeug** rubbish, nonsense; **es ist** ODER **wird mir zu ~** I've had enough of it - **2.** [unangenehm - Fehler, Zufall] annoying <> adv stupidly.

Dumme (pl -n) der, die: **der ~ sein** to be the one who loses out.

dummerweise adv - **1.** [ärgerlicherweise] unfortunately - **2.** [aus Dummheit] stupidly.

Dummheit (pl -en) die - **1.** [fehlende Klugheit] stupidity - **2.** [Handlung] stupid thing; **mach keine ~en** don't do anything stupid.

Dummkopf der idiot.

dümmlich <> adj stupid <> adv stupidly.

dumpf <> adj - **1.** [Klang] dull, muffled - **2.** [Schmerz] dull; [Befürchtung, Verdacht] vague - **3.** [stumpfsinnig] apathetic <> adv - **1.** [dunkel] dully - **2.** [stumpfsinnig] apathetically.

Düne (pl -n) die dune.

düngen <> vt to fertilize <> vi - **1.** [Dung] to act as a fertilizer - **2.** [Person] to fertilize one's land/garden/etc.

Dünger (pl -) der fertilizer.

dunkel <> adj - **1.** [gen] dark; **im Dunkeln tappen** fig to grope around in the dark - **2.** [Ton, Stimme] deep - **3.** [vage] vague; **jn über etw** (A) **im Dunkeln lassen** to keep sb in the dark about sthg - **4.** [dubios] shady <> adv - **1.** [streichen, färben] in dark colours/a dark colour - **2.** [klingen] deep - **3.** [unklar] vaguely.

dunkelblau adj & adv dark blue.

dunkelblond <> adj light brown; [Person] with light brown hair <> adv light brown.

dunkelhaarig adj dark-haired.

Dunkelheit die darkness.

Dunkel|ziffer die number of unreported incidents.

dünn <> adj - **1.** [gen] thin; **sich ~ machen** [wenig Platz brauchen] to squeeze up - **2.** [Getränk, Stimme] weak - **3.** [Haare, Bewuchs] sparse <> adv - **1.** [bevölkert, bewachsen] sparsely - **2.** [auftragen] thinly.

dünnflüssig adj thin.

Dunst (pl Dünste) der - **1.** [Nebel] haze, mist - **2.** [von Zigaretten] smoke; [in der Küche]

steam - **3.** *RW:* **keinen (blassen) ~ von etw haben** *fam* not to have the foggiest (idea) about sthg.

dünsten *vt* to steam.

dunstig *adj* [neblig] hazy, misty.

Duo (*pl* -s) *das* duo.

Dur *das* major; **eine Sonate in ~** a sonata in a major key.

durch <> *präp* (+ A) - **1.** [räumlich, zeitlich] through; **darf ich mal bitte ~?** excuse me, please!; **~ die Schweiz reisen** to travel across Switzerland; **die ganze Nacht ~** throughout the night - **2.** [mittels] by; **~ eigene Schuld** through one's own fault; **~ Ihre Hilfe** with your help; **das Haus wurde ~ ein Erdbeben zerstört** the house was destroyed by an earthquake - **3.** MATH divided by; **sechs ~ drei** six divided by three <> *adv* - **1.** *fam* [später als]: **es ist schon zwölf ~** it's gone ODER past twelve - **2.** *fam* [durchgebraten] well done - **3.** *fam* [beendet]: **bis morgen muss ich mit dem Buch ~ sein** I have to finish the book by tomorrow - **4.** *RW:* **~ und ~** through and through; **~ und ~ nass** wet through.

durcharbeiten <> *vt* to work through <> *vi* to work without a break. ◆ **sich durcharbeiten** *ref:* **sich durch etw ~** [Menschenmenge, Text] to work one's way through sthg.

durchatmen *vi* to breathe deeply.

durchaus, durchaus *adv* - **1.** [gut, ohne weiteres] perfectly; **es kann ~ sein** it is perfectly possible - **2.** [unbedingt] absolutely - **3.** [absolut, überhaupt]: **~ nicht** definitely not, not at all.

durchblättern *vt* to flick through.

Durchblick *der fam* overview; **den ~ verlieren** to lose track of things.

durchblicken *vt* to see through.

Durchblutung *die* circulation.

durchbohren[1] <> *vt* [Brett] to drill through; [Loch] to drill <> *vi* to drill through.

durchbohren[2] *vt* [Subj: Kugel] to go through; **jn mit Blicken ~** to fix sb with a piercing gaze.

durchbraten *vt* (*unreg*) to cook well ODER through.

durchbrechen[1] (*perf* hat/ist durchgebrochen) (*unreg*) <> *vt* (*hat*) - **1.** [zerbrechen] to break in two - **2.** [einreißen - Wand] to knock in <> *vi* (*ist*) - **1.** [zerbrechen] to break in two; [Boden] to give way - **2.** [durchdringen] to break through; [Geschwür, Abszess] to perforate.

durchbrechen[2] (*präs* durchbricht; *prät* durchbrach; *perf* hat durchbrochen) *vt* to break through.

durchbrennen (*perf* ist durchgebrannt) *vi*

(*unreg*) - **1.** [Draht] to blow, to go - **2.** *fam* [weglaufen] to run away.

Durchbruch *der* - **1.** [Erfolg] breakthrough - **2.** [Öffnung] opening.

durchchecken ['dʊrçtʃɛkn] *vt* to check over.

durchdacht *adj* well thought out; **gut/schlecht ~** well/badly thought out.

durchdenken[1] *vt* (*unreg*) to think through.

durchdenken[2] (*prät* durchdachte; *perf* hat durchdacht) *vt* to think out.

durchdiskutieren *vt* to talk through.

durchdrehen (*perf* hat/ist durchgedreht) <> *vi* - **1.** (*ist*) *fam* [verrückt werden] to crack up - **2.** (*hat*) [Räder] to spin <> *vt* (*hat*) to mince.

durchdringen (*perf* ist durchgedrungen) *vi* (*unreg*) [Geräusch, Licht, Nachricht] to get through; [Wasser] to seep through.

durchdrücken *vt* - **1.** *fam* [durchsetzen] to push through - **2.** [Gelenk] to straighten - **3.** [passieren] to press through.

Durcheinander *das* [von Menschen] confusion; [von Dingen] chaos.

durcheinander bringen *vt* (*unreg*) - **1.** [Person] to confuse - **2.** [Dinge] to muddle up - **3.** [verwechseln] to mix up.

durchexerzieren *vt* to go through.

durchfahren (*perf* ist durchgefahren) *vi* (*unreg*) - **1.** [durchqueren] to go ODER drive through - **2.** [durchgehend fahren] to go ODER drive non-stop.

Durchfahrt *die* - **1.** [Durchfahren]: **die ~ freigeben** to open the road (again), 'no outlet' *Am* - **2.** [Durchreise] way through; **auf der ~ sein** to be travelling through - **3.** [Weg] access road.

Durchfall *der* - **1.** [Diarrhöe] diarrhoea - **2.** *fam* [Misserfolg] flop; [bei einer Prüfung] failure.

durchfallen (*perf* ist durchgefallen) *vi* (*unreg*) - **1.** *fam* [versagen] to flop; [bei einer Prüfung] to fail - **2.** [durch eine Öffnung] to fall through.

durchforsten *vt* - **1.** [durchsuchen - Gelände] to search; [- Textmaterial] to search through - **2.** [ausdünnen - Wald] to thin out.

durchfragen ◆ **sich durchfragen** *ref* to ask one's way.

durchführbar *adj* practicable.

durchführen <> *vt* to carry out; [Veranstaltung] to hold <> *vi* to go through.

Durchgang *der* - **1.** [Durchgehen]: **'~ verboten'** 'no right of way' - **2.** [Weg] passage - **3.** [Phase] stage; [von Wahl] round.

durchgängig <> *adj* [Auffassung] general; **ein ~ Motiv in seinen Werken** a motif that runs through his works <> *adv* universally;

~ gute Leistungen bringen to achieve consistently good results.

Durchgangsverkehr *der* through traffic.

durch|geben *vt (unreg)* to pass on; TV & RAD to broadcast.

durchgebraten ◇ *pp* ▷ **durchbraten** ◇ *adj:* **gut ~** well done.

durchgefroren *adj* frozen through.

durch|gehen *(perf* ist durchgegangen) *(unreg)* ◇ *vi* - **1.** [gen] to go through; **bitte ~!** [im Bus] please move to the back of the bus! - **2.** [durchdringen] to get through - **3.** [Pferd] to bolt; **mit jm ~** [Gefühle] to run away with sb - **4.** [andauern - Sitzung, Veranstaltung] to go on non-stop - **5.** [akzeptiert werden - Fehler, Gesetzesvorlage] to get through; **jm etw ~ lassen** to let sb get away with sthg ◇ *vt* to go through.

durch|greifen *vi (unreg)* - **1.** [einschreiten] to take action - **2.** [durch eine Öffnung]: **durch etw ~** to reach through sthg.

durch|halten *(unreg)* ◇ *vi* to hold out ◇ *vt* [Belastung] to withstand; [Strecke, Wettkampf] to make it to the end of.

Durchhaltevermögen *das* stamina.

durchkämmen *vt* to comb.

durch|kommen *(perf* ist durchgekommen) *vi (unreg)* - **1.** [durch etw gelangen]: **durch etw ~** to get through sthg - **2.** [am Telefon, bei Prüfung] to get through - **3.** [Nachricht] to be announced - **4.** [durchfahren] to pass through - **5.** [durchdringen - Wasser, Sonne] to come through - **6.** [überleben] to pull through - **7.** [erfolgreich sein]: **mit dieser Idee wirst du beim Chef kaum ~** you won't get anywhere with the boss with that idea.

durch|lassen *vt (unreg)* to let through.

durchlässig *adj* [Boden] porous; [Material] permeable; [Grenze] open.

durch|lesen *vt (unreg)* to read through.

durchleuchten *vt* - **1.** [röntgen] to X-ray - **2.** [untersuchen] to examine, to investigate.

durch|machen ◇ *vt* - **1.** [Schwierigkeiten, schwere Zeiten] to go through; **sie hat viel durchgemacht** she's been through a lot - **2.** *fam* [feiern]: **eine Nacht ~** to party all night ◇ *vi fam* to stay up.

Durch|messer *der* diameter.

durch|nehmen *vt (unreg)* to do.

durchqueren *vt* [Zimmer, Fluss] to cross; [Land] to go across; [Gegend] to go through.

durch|rechnen *vt* to calculate.

Durch|reise *die:* **~ (durch)** journey through; **auf der ~** passing through.

durch|reißen *(perf* hat/ist durchgerissen) *(unreg)* ◇ *vt (hat)* [Papier, Stoff] to tear in two; [Faden] to break in two ◇ *vi (ist)* [Stoff] to tear in two; [Faden, Draht] to break in two.

durch|ringen ◆ **sich durchringen** *ref (unreg):* **sich zu etw ~** to make up one's mind finally to do sthg.

durch|rosten *(perf* ist durchgerostet) *vi* to rust through.

durch|sagen *vt* to announce.

durch|schauen¹ *vt* to look through.

durch|schauen² *vt* to see through.

Durch|schlag *der* - **1.** [Kopie] carbon copy - **2.** [Sieb] strainer.

durch|schlagen *(perf* hat/ist durchgeschlagen) *(unreg)* ◇ *vt (hat)* [Glas] to smash through; [Stein, Holz] to split; [Wand] to knock through; **etw durch etw ~** to knock sthg through sthg ◇ *vi (ist)* to show through. ◆ **sich durchschlagen** *ref* - **1.** [durch Gegend] to make it - **2.** [durch Zeit] to struggle through.

durch|schneiden *vt (unreg)* [Faden, Stoff] to cut through; [Brot, Blatt Papier] to cut in half; [Kehle] to cut.

Durch|schnitt *der* average.

durchschnittlich ◇ *adj* average ◇ *adv* [im Durchschnitt] on average; *abw* [mittelmäßig] averagely.

durch|schütteln *vt* to shake well; **im Bus durchgeschüttelt werden** to be shaken about on the bus.

durch|schwitzen *vt* to soak with sweat.

durch|sehen *(unreg)* ◇ *vt* to look through ◇ *vi:* **durch etw ~** to see through sthg.

durch sein *(perf* ist durch gewesen) *vi (unreg)* *fam* - **1.** [Zug, Kontrolleur] to have come through; **bei jm unten ~** *fig & abw* to be in sb's bad books - **2.** [mit Buch, Arbeit] to have finished - **3.** [Braten, Kartoffeln] to be done - **4.** [Sohle, Ärmel] to be worn out - **5.** [Gesetz] to have gone through.

durch|setzen *vt* [Plan, Vorhaben, Reform] to push through; [Anspruch] to assert. ◆ **sich durchsetzen** *ref* to assert o.s.; [Erfindung] to gain acceptance.

durchsichtig *adj* [Stoff, Folie] transparent.

durch|sprechen *vt (unreg)* to talk over.

durch|stehen *vt (unreg)* to come through.

durch|stellen *vt* to put through.

durch|stöbern *vt* to rummage through.

durch|stoßen¹ *vt (unreg):* **etw durch etw ~** to push sthg through sthg.

durchstoßen² *(präs* durchstößt; *prät* durchstieß; *perf* hat durchstoßen) *vt* to break through.

durch|streichen *vt (unreg)* to cross out.

durchsuchen *vt* to search.

durchtrainiert ['dʊrçtrɛniːɐt] *adj* in peak condition.

durch|trennen¹ *vt* to sever.

durchtrennen² *vt* to sever.

durchtrieben ◇ *adj* cunning ◇ *adv* cunningly.

Durchwahl *die (ohne pl)* extension.

durchweg *adv* without exception.

durchwühlen[1] *vt* [Schublade] to rummage through; [Zimmer] to ransack.

durch|wühlen[2] *vt* [Schublade] to rummage through; [Zimmer] to ransack.

durch|zählen *vt* to count.

durch|ziehen[1] (*perf* hat/ist durchgezogen) (*unreg*) ◇ *vt* (hat) - **1.** [durch Öffnung] to pull through; **etw durch etw ~** to pull sthg through sthg - **2.** *fam* [Plan] to see through ◇ *vi* (ist) - **1.** [durch Gegend] to pass through - **2.** [in Marinade - Fleisch] to marinate; [- Gemüse] to steep.

durch|ziehen[2] *vt* (*unreg*) to pass through.

Durch|zug *der* - **1.** [von Wetter] passage - **2.** (*ohne pl*) [Zugluft] draught.

dürfen (*präs* darf; *prät* durfte; *perf* hat gedurft ODER -) ◇ *aux* (*perf* hat dürfen) - **1.** [als Erlaubnis]: **etw tun** ~ to be allowed to do sthg; **darf ich mich setzen?** may I sit down?; **darf ich fragen ...?** may I ask ...?; **darf ich Ihnen behilflich sein?** can I be of help? - **2.** [als Überzeugung, Wunsch]: **das ~ wir nicht vergessen** we mustn't forget that; **so etwas darf einfach nicht passieren** such a thing simply must not happen; **du darfst nicht traurig sein!** don't be sad! - **3.** [Veranlassung haben]: **man darf davon ausgehen, dass ...** we can assume that ... - **4.** [als Annahme]: **das dürfte genügen** that should be enough ◇ *vi* (*perf* hat gedurft): **sie darf nicht ins Schwimmbad** she's not allowed to go swimming ◇ *vt* (*perf* hat gedurft) *fam*: **das darf man nicht!** you're not allowed to do that!; **was darf es sein?** what can I get you?

dürftig ◇ *adj* - **1.** [Einkünfte, Bezahlung] meagre - **2.** *abw* [Ergebnis] poor; [Bearbeitung] sketchy; [Bewuchs] sparse ◇ *adv* - **1.** [entlohnt] meagrely; [bekleidet] scantily - **2.** *abw* [unzureichend] poorly; [sich entschuldigen] lamely.

dürr *adj* - **1.** [Person] scrawny - **2.** [Blatt] dry - **3.** [Worte] blunt.

Dürre (*pl* -n) *die* drought.

Durst *der* [Gefühl] thirst; **~ haben** to be thirsty.

durstig ◇ *adj* thirsty ◇ *adv* thirstily.

Durst|strecke *die* lean period.

Dusche (*pl* -n) *die* shower.

duschen ◇ *vi* to have a shower ◇ *vt* to shower. ◆ **sich duschen** *ref* to have a shower.

Dusch|raum *der* shower room.

Düse (*pl* -n) *die* nozzle.

düsen (*perf* ist gedüst) *vi fam* to rush.

Düsen|flugzeug *das* jet aircraft.

Dussel (*pl* -) *der fam* dope.

düster ◇ *adj* gloomy ◇ *adv* gloomily.

Dutzend (*pl* -) *das* [zwölf] dozen; **im ~** by the dozen. ◆ **Dutzende** *pl* [viele] dozens; **zu ~en** in their dozens.

dutzendmal *adv* a dozen times.

dutzendweise *adv* by the dozen.

duzen *vt* to address someone using the familiar *'du'* form. ◆ **sich duzen** *ref* to address each other using the familiar *'du'* form.

DVD (*pl* -s) (*abk für* Digital Versatile Disc) *die* EDV DVD.

Dynamit *das* dynamite.

DZ *abk für* Doppelzimmer.

E

e, E [e:] (*pl* - ODER -s) *das* - **1.** [Buchstabe] e, E - **2.** MUS E. ◆ **E** *der abk für* Eilzug.

Ebbe (*pl* -n) *die* tide (*outgoing*); **es ist ~** it is low tide; **bei Eintritt der ~** when the tide is going out.

eben ◇ *adj* [flach - Gegend, Weg] flat; [glatt - Brett, Boden] smooth ◇ *adv* - **1.** just; **kannst du mal ~ vorbeikommen?** can you just come round for a minute? - **2.** [genau]: **er hat ihn nur so ~ berührt** he just touched him; **ich mache das ~ zu Ende** I'll just finish it off - **3.** [genau]: **~ den Anwalt meine ich** he's the very lawyer I mean; **~ das war es, was ich sagen wollte!** that was exactly what I wanted to say! ◇ *interj* - **1.** [zum Ausdruck von Einverständnis]: **exactly** - **2.** [zum Ausdruck von Widerspruch]: **aber du hast doch dein Geld! - ~ nicht!** but you've got your money, haven't you! – no I haven't!

Eben|bild *das* image.

ebenbürtig *adj* equal; **jm ~ sein** to be sb's equal; **einer Sache ~ sein** to be equal to sthg.

Ebene (*pl* -n) *die* - **1.** [Flachland] plain - **2.** PHYS & MATH plane - **3.** [Niveau] level; **auf gleicher** ODER **der gleichen ~** on the same level; **auf höchster ~** at the highest level.

ebenfalls *adv* as well; **danke, ~** thanks, same to you.

ebenso *adv* just as.

ebenso gut *adv* just as well.

Eber (*pl* -) *der* boar.

ebnen *vt* to level; **jm den Weg ~** to smooth sb's path.

Echo (*pl* -s) *das* echo.

Echse ['ɛksə] (*pl* -n) *die* lizard.

echt ◇ *adj* - **1.** [unverfälscht] genuine - **2.** [wahr, typisch] real ◇ *adv* - **1.** [rein] real; **~ italienisch essen** to eat real Italian food - **2.** *fam* [wirklich] really.

Echtheit *die* genuineness.

Ecke (*pl* -n) *die* - **1.** [gen] corner - **2.** *fam* [Gegend] area; **eine hübsche ~!** a pretty spot!; **das ist noch eine ganze ~!** it's still quite a way! - **3.** *RW*: **um die ~** *fam* round the corner, ; **es fehlt (bei uns) an allen ~n und Enden** we are short of everything.

eckig ◇ *adj* - **1.** [Form] square - **2.** [Bewegung] awkward ◇ *adv* [ungelenk] awkwardly.

Eck|zahn *der* canine tooth.

edel *adj* - **1.** *geh* [Person, Geste] noble - **2.** *geh* [Form] well-formed - **3.** [Holz, Wein] fine.

Edel|metall *das* precious metal.

Edel|stahl *der* stainless steel.

Edel|stein *der* precious stone.

EDV [eːdeːˈfau] (*abk für* elektronische Datenverarbeitung) *die* data-processing.

Efeu *der* (*ohne pl*) ivy.

Effeff *das*: **etw aus dem ~ beherrschen** *fam* to know sthg inside out.

Effekt (*pl* -e) *der* effect.

effektiv ◇ *adj* effective; [Gewinn, Leistung] net ◇ *adv* effectively.

Effektivität [ɛfɛktiviˈtɛːt] *die* effectiveness.

effektvoll ◇ *adj* effective ◇ *adv* effectively.

egal *adj*: **es ist mir ~** it's all the same to me; **das kann dir doch ~ sein** that's no concern of yours; **das ist ~** it doesn't matter. ◆ **egal ob** *adv* no matter whether.

egal sein

I don't mind either way. Mir ist beides recht.
I don't care one way or the other. Wie auch immer.
I don't mind, you choose. Mir ist das gleich, du hast die Wahl.
You decide, it's all the same to me. Mir ist das gleich, entscheide du.
Chocolate? I can take it or leave it. Ich mache mir nicht so viel aus Schokolade.

Egoismus *der* egoism.

eh ◇ *interj fam* hey ◇ *adv* - **1.** [immer]: **wie ~ und je** as always - **2.** *fam Süddt & Österr* [sowieso] anyway.

Ehe (*pl* -n) *die* marriage.

Ehe|bett *das* double bed.

Ehe|bruch *der* adultery (*U*).

Ehe|frau *die* wife.

Ehe|leute *pl* married couple.

ehelich *adj* marital; [Recht] conjugal.

ehemalig *adj* former.

ehemals *adv* formerly.

Ehe|mann (*pl* -männer) *der* husband.

Ehe|paar *das* married couple.

Ehe|partner *der* marriage partner.

eher *adv* - **1.** [vorher] earlier, sooner - **2.** [lieber] rather - **3.**: **das ist schon ~ möglich** that is more likely - **4.** [vielmehr] more.

Ehe|ring *der* wedding ring.

Ehe|schließung *die* marriage ceremony.

Ehre *die* honour; **jm zu ~n** in sb's honour.

ehren *vt* [Achtung erweisen] to honour; **deine Großmut ehrt dich** your generosity does you credit; **dieses Angebot ehrt mich** I am honoured by this offer.

ehrenamtlich ◇ *adj* honorary ◇ *adv* in an honorary capacity.

Ehren|bürger, in *der, die* honorary citizen.

Ehren|gast *der* guest of honour.

ehrenhaft ◇ *adj* honourable ◇ *adv* honourably.

Ehren|mann (*pl* -männer) *der* man of honour.

Ehren|mitglied *das* honorary member.

Ehren|sache *die* point of honour; **das ist doch ~, dass ich bald wieder zurück bin** you can count on me to be back soon.

Ehrenwort (*pl* -e) *das* word of honour; **(großes) ~!** *fam* I/we promise!

Ehrfurcht *die* [Verehrung] reverence; [Scheu] awe.

ehrfürchtig ◇ *adj* reverent ◇ *adv* reverently.

Ehrgeiz *der* ambition.

ehrgeizig ◇ *adj* ambitious ◇ *adv* ambitiously.

ehrlich ◇ *adj* honest ◇ *adv* fairly; **~ gesagt** to be honest.

Ehrlichkeit *die* honesty.

Ehrung (*pl* -en) *die* [das Ehren] honouring (*U*); [Ehre] honour.

ehrwürdig *adj* venerable.

Ei (*pl* -er) *das* - **1.** [gen] egg; **jn/etw wie ein rohes ~ behandeln** to treat sb/sthg with kid gloves - **2.** *vulg* [Hoden] ball.

Eiche (*pl* -n) *die* oak.

Eichel (*pl* -n) *die* - **1.** [Frucht] acorn - **2.** [des männlichen Gliedes] glans (penis).

Eichhörnchen (*pl* -) *das* squirrel.

Eid (*pl* -e) *der* oath. ◆ **unter Eid** *adv* under oath.

Eidechse [ˈaidɛksə] (*pl* -n) *die* lizard.

eidesstattlich ◇ *adj* sworn ◇ *adv* solemnly.

Eid|genosse *der* Swiss citizen.

Eid|genossin *die* Swiss citizen.

Ei|dotter *das* ODER *der* egg yolk.

Eier|becher *der* egg cup.

Eier|kuchen der pancake.

Eier|schale die eggshell.

Eier|stock der ovary.

Eifer der eagerness.

Eifersucht die jealousy.

eifersüchtig <> adj jealous; **auf jn ~ sein** to be jealous of sb <> adv jealously.

eifrig <> adj eager <> adv eagerly.

Eigelb (pl - ODER -e) das egg yolk.

eigen adj - 1. [jm gehörend] own - 2. [typisch] typical. ◆ **Eigen** das: **sich** (D) **etw zu Eigen machen** to make sthg one's own.

Eigen|art die characteristic.

eigenartig <> adj strange <> adv strangely.

Eigenbedarf der (ohne pl) personal requirements (pl); **für den ~** for one's own use.

eigenbrötlerisch <> adj reclusive <> adv like a recluse.

eigenhändig <> adj own <> adv with one's own hands.

eigenmächtig <> adj unauthorized <> adv on one's own authority.

Eigen|name der proper name.

eigennützig <> adj selfish <> adv selfishly.

eigens adv specially.

Eigenschaft (pl -en) die characteristic; [von Auto] feature; **in seiner ~ als etw** in one's capacity as sthg.

Eigenschaftswort (pl -wörter) das adjective.

eigensinnig <> adj stubborn <> adv stubbornly.

eigenständig <> adj independent <> adv independently.

eigentlich <> adv - 1. [im Grunde, wirklich] really - 2. [übrigens] by the way; **wer ist ~ Petra?** who is Petra(, by the way)? - 3. [zum Ausdruck von Ärger]: **was erlauben Sie sich ~?** what do you think you're doing? <> adj [wirklich] real.

Eigen|tor das own goal.

Eigentum das - 1. [Besitz] property - 2. [Besitzerrecht] ownership.

Eigentümer, in (mpl -; fpl -nen) der, die owner.

eigentümlich adj peculiar.

eigenwillig adj - 1. [eigen] original - 2. [starrsinnig] obstinate.

eignen ◆ **sich eignen** ref to be suitable; **sich zu** ODER **für etw ~** to be suitable for sthg.

Eignungs|prüfung die aptitude test.

Eil|brief der express letter.

Eile die hurry; **in ~ sein** to be in a hurry; **etw hat -/keine ~** sthg is/is not urgent.

eilen (perf hat/ist geeilt) vi - 1. (ist) [Person] to hurry - 2. (hat) [Angelegenheit] to be urgent; **eilt! urgent!**; **mit etw eilt es/eilt es nicht** sthg is/is not urgent.

eilig <> adj - 1. [Bewegung] hurried; **es ~ haben** to be in a hurry - 2. [Angelegenheit, Brief] urgent <> adv hurriedly.

Eimer (pl -) der bucket.

ein, e <> num one; **~e einzelne Rose** a single rose; **~ Uhr** one o'clock; **~er Meinung sein** to have the same opinion; **für alle Mal** fam fig once and for all; **in ~em fort** fig nonstop; **js ~ und alles sein** fig to mean everything to sb <> det a, an (vor Vokal); **~ Hund** a dog; **~e Idee** an idea; **~ Mädchen** a girl; **~es Tages** one day; **da ist ~e Frau Schmidt am Apparat** there's a Mrs Schmidt on the phone <> pron - 1. [als Teil einer Menge] one; **hier ist noch ~s/-e** here's another one; **~ und dasselbe** one and the same - 2. fam [jemand] someone, somebody; **sieh mal ~en an!** well I never!; **das kann ~em schon mal passieren** these things can happen to you <> adv: **~-aus** on-off; **~ und aus gehen** fig to come and go; **nicht ~ noch aus wissen** fig not to know whether one is coming or going.

ein|arbeiten vt [an die Arbeit gewöhnen] to train. ◆ **sich einarbeiten** ref to settle in.

ein|atmen vt & vi to breathe in.

Einbahn|straße die one-way street.

Einband (pl -bände) der book cover.

ein|bauen vt - 1. [Schrank, Bad] to fit; [Motor] to install - 2. [in Text] to incorporate.

Einbau|küche die fitted kitchen.

ein|berufen vt (unreg) - 1. [Sitzung] to summon - 2. [Wehrpflichtige] to call up Br, to draft Am.

Ein|berufung die - 1. [einer Sitzung] summoning (U) - 2. [von Wehrpflichtigen] call-up Br, draft Am.

ein|betten vt to wrap.

ein|beziehen vt (unreg): **jn/etw in etw** (A) **~** to include sb/sthg in sthg.

ein|biegen (perf hat/ist eingebogen) (unreg) <> vi (ist) [abbiegen] to turn; **nach rechts/links ~** to turn right/left <> vt (hat) [verbiegen] to bend.

ein|bilden vt - 1. [sich einreden]: **sich** (D) **etw ~** to imagine sthg; **was bildest du dir eigentlich ein, wer du bist?** who do you think you are? - 2. [stolz sein]: **er bildet sich ganz schön viel ein** he is really full of himself; **sich** (D) **viel auf etw** (A) **~** to be conceited about sthg; **darauf brauchst du dir nichts einzubilden** that's nothing to be proud of.

Einbildung (pl -en) die - 1. [Fantasie] imagination - 2. [Hochmut] conceit.

Einbildungskraft die imagination.

ein|binden vt (unreg) - 1. [einschlagen] to bind - 2. [einbeziehen]: **jn/etw in etw** (A) **~** to integrate sb/sthg into sthg.

ein|bläuen vt: **jm etw ~** to drum sthg into sb.

einbleuen = einbläuen.

Ein|blick der - 1. [Blick]: **~ in die Dokumente**

bekommen to get a look at the documents; **~ in etw** (A) **nehmen** to examine sthg; **jm ~ in etw** (A) **gewähren** to allow sb to examine sthg - 2. [Einsicht] insight.

ein|brechen (perf hat/ist eingebrochen) vi (unreg) - 1. (hat) [gewaltsam eindringen] to break in; **bei jm ~** to burgle sb - 2. (ist) [einstürzen] to fall in - 3. (ist) [Partei, Mannschaft] to come unstuck - 4. (ist) [durchbrechen] to fall through - 5. (ist) [eindringen]: **(in ein Land) ~** to invade a (country) - 6. (ist) geh [Nacht, Dunkelheit] to fall; [Winter] to set in.

Einbrecher, in (mpl -; fpl -nen) der burglar.

ein|bringen vt (unreg) - 1. [Ernte] to bring in - 2. [Gewinn] to bring in; [Anerkennung] to bring; [Erfahrung] to give; **das bringt nichts ein** that's not worth it - 3. [vorlegen] to introduce - 4. amt [einsetzen - Geld, Vermögen] to invest; [- in eine Ehe] to put in.

ein|brocken vt fam: **jm/sich etwas ~** to land sb/o.s. in it; **dieses Problem hast du dir selbst eingebrockt!** you brought this problem on yourself!

Ein|bruch der - 1. [Straftat] break-in; **einen ~ begehen** to commit a burglary - 2. [Zusammenbruch] collapse - 3. [Eindringen] penetration - 4. fam [bei Wahl] drubbing - 5. [Beginn - von Winter] onset; **vor ~ der Nacht** before nightfall.

einbürgern vt [eine Staatsangehörigkeit verleihen] to naturalize. ➡ **sich einbürgern** ref [üblich werden] to become established.

Ein|buße die loss.

ein|büßen ⬦ vt to lose ⬦ vi: **an etw** (D) **~** to lose sthg.

ein|checken ['aɪntʃɛkn] vt & vi to check in.

ein|cremen, einkremen vt to put cream on. ➡ **sich eincremen** ref to put cream on.

ein|dämmen vt - 1. [stauen] to dam - 2. [zurückhalten] to contain.

ein|decken vt fam [überhäufen]: **jn mit etw ~** to swamp sb with sthg.

eindeutig ⬦ adj clear ⬦ adv clearly.

ein|dringen (perf ist eingedrungen) vi (unreg) - 1. [hineingelangen]: **in etw** (A) **~** [Wasser] to get into sthg; [Messer] to enter sthg - 2. [einbrechen]: **in etw** (A) **~** [Gebäude] to break into sthg; [Land] to invade sthg.

eindringlich ⬦ adj insistent ⬦ adv insistently.

Eindringling (pl -e) der intruder.

Eindruck (pl -drücke) der impression; **~ auf jn machen** to make an impression on sb; **einen ~ von etw bekommen** ODER **erhalten** to get an impression of sthg; **einen guten/schlechten ~ (auf jn) machen** to make a good/bad impression (on sb).

ein|drücken vt - 1. [beschädigen - Kotflügel, Fensterscheibe] to smash in; [- Nase, Kissen] to flatten - 2. [in etw hineindrücken] to press.

eindrucksvoll ⬦ adj impressive ⬦ adv impressively.

ein|ebnen vt to level.

eineiig ['aɪnaɪɪç] adj: **~e Zwillinge** identical twins.

eineinhalb num one and a half.

ein|engen vt - 1. [beschränken] to constrict - 2. [einschränken] to restrict; **jn in seiner Freiheit ~** to curb sb's freedom.

einerlei adj immaterial; **das ist mir ~** that's all the same to me.

einerseits adv: **~ ... andererseits** on the one hand ... on the other (hand).

einfach ⬦ adj - 1. [leicht, schlicht] simple - 2. [Fahrkarte, Knoten] single ⬦ adv - 1. [leicht, schlicht] simply; **ich komme ~ mit** I'll just come with you; **es sich ~ machen** to make it easy for o.s. - 2. [nicht mehrfach]: **etw ~ falten** to fold sthg once.

Einfachheit die simplicity.

ein|fädeln vt - 1. [Faden, Nadel] to thread - 2. [bewerkstelligen]: **sie hat die Sache schlau eingefädelt** she worked things very cleverly.

ein|fahren (perf hat/ist eingefahren) (unreg) ⬦ vi (ist) [Zug] to arrive ⬦ vt (hat) - 1. [hineinschaffen - Ernte] to bring in - 2. [beschädigen - Tor, Mauer] to knock down; [- Kotflügel] to smash in - 3. AUTO to run in Br, to break in Am - 4. [einziehen - Fahrwerk] to retract.

Ein|fahrt die - 1. [Einfahren] arrival; **der Zug hat noch keine ~** the train still hasn't arrived - 2. [Stelle zum Hineinfahren] entrance.

Ein|fall der - 1. [Idee] idea; **jm kam ein ~** he had an idea - 2. [Einfallen]: **der ~ von Sonnenstrahlen** the sun's rays shining in - 3. [Eindringen] invasion; **der ~ der Römer in Gallien** the invasion of Gaul by the Romans.

ein|fallen (perf ist eingefallen) vi (unreg) - 1. [in den Sinn kommen]: **ihm fiel nichts Besseres ein** no better idea occurred to him; **ihm fällt immer eine passende Ausrede ein** he always thinks of a suitable excuse; **mir fällt nichts ein, was ich kochen könnte** I can't think of anything that I could cook; **sich** (D) **etwas ~ lassen** to think of something; **was fällt dir/Ihnen ein!** what (ever) are you thinking of! - 2. [wieder in den Sinn kommen] to remember; **da fällt mir ein ...** that reminds me ... - 3. [hereinkommen] to shine in - 4. MIL: **in etw** (A) **~** to invade sthg - 5. [einstimmen] to join in - 6. [einstürzen] to collapse.

einfallslos adj unimaginative.

einfallsreich adj imaginative.

einfältig adj - 1. [arglos] naive; [Lächeln] innocent - 2. [beschränkt] simple-minded.

Einfamilien|haus das house designed for one family.

ein|fangen vt (unreg) - 1. [fangen und fest

halten] to capture - **2.** *fam* [bekommen]: **sich (D) etw ~** to get sthg.

einfarbig *adj* all one colour.

ein|fassen *vt* - **1.** [Stoff] to edge - **2.** [mit Mauer] to enclose - **3.** [Edelstein] to set.

ein|fliegen *vt (unreg)* to fly in; **jn/etw ~ lassen** to fly sb/sthg in.

ein|fließen *(perf* ist eingeflossen) *vi (unreg)* [Wasser, Luft] to flow in; **eine Kritik ~ lassen** to slip in a criticism.

ein|flößen *vt* - **1.** [zu trinken geben] to help to drink - **2.** [erregen]: **jm etw ~** [Ehrfurcht, Vertrauen, Angst] to inspire sthg in sb.

Einfluss *der* influence; **unter ~ von Alkohol** under the influence of alcohol; **auf jn/etw ~ haben** [Macht] to have influence over sb/ sthg; [Effekt] to influence sthg/sb; **auf jn/ etw ~ nehmen** to influence sthg/sb.

einflussreich *adj* influential.

einförmig *adj* monotonous.

ein|frieren *(perf* hat/ist eingefroren) *(unreg)* <> *vt (hat)* to freeze; [Beziehungen] to suspend <> *vi (ist)* [Wasserleitung] to freeze; [Teich] to freeze over.

ein|fügen *vt* [gen & EDV] to insert. <> **sich einfügen** *ref* [sich anpassen] to fit in.

einfühlsam *adj* sensitive.

Einfuhr *(pl* -en) *die* - **1.** [Einführen] importation - **2.** [Ware] import.

ein|führen *vt* - **1.** [gen] to introduce; **jn in etw** *(A)* **~** to introduce sb to sthg - **2.** [importieren] to import - **3.** [hineinschieben] to insert, to introduce.

Einführung *die* introduction.

ein|füllen *vt* to pour in; **etw in etw** *(A)* **~** to pour sthg into sthg.

Eingang *der* - **1.** [Eingangstür] entrance - **2.** [von Geld, Post] receipt.

eingangs *adv* at the beginning.

Eingangshalle *die* entrance hall.

ein|geben *vt* [unreg] EDV to enter.

eingebildet *adj* - **1.** [nicht wirklich] imaginary - **2.** [hochmütig] arrogant.

Eingeborene, Eingeborne *(pl* -n) *der, die* native.

eingefleischt *adj* ➞ Junggeselle.

ein|gehen *(perf* ist eingegangen) *(unreg)* <> *vi* - **1.** [ankommen] to arrive; **bei uns ist noch keine Antwort eingegangen** we have not yet received a reply - **2.** [Tier, Pflanze] to perish - **3.** [Firma] to close down - **4.** [beachten]: **auf jn/etw ~** to respond to sb/sthg; **auf etw** *(A)* **~** [Angebot, Vorschlag] to agree to sthg - **5.** [Kleidung] to shrink - **6.** *geh* [Einzug halten]: **in die Geschichte ~** to go down in history <> *vt* [Bündnis, Ehe, Verpflichtung] to enter into; [Risiko] to take; [Wette] to make.

eingehend <> *adj* detailed <> *adv* in detail.

eingenommen <> *pp* ➞ einnehmen

<> *adj*: **von sich ~ sein** to have a high opinion of o.s.; **für/gegen etw ~ sein** to be taken with/biased against sthg; **von jm/etw ~ sein** to be taken with sb/sthg.

eingeschlossen *pp* ➞ einschließen.

eingetragen <> *pp* ➞ eintragen <> *adj* registered ➞ Verein; *siehe auch* Warenzeichen.

Eingeweide *pl* entrails.

ein|gewöhnen ➞ **sich eingewöhnen** *ref* to settle in.

ein|gießen *vt (unreg)* [Tasse, Glas] to pour; **jm etw ~** to pour sb sthg.

ein|gliedern *vt*: **jn/etw in etw** *(A)* **~** to integrate sb/sthg into sthg. ➞ **sich eingliedern** *ref*: **sich in etw** *(A)* **~** to integrate into sthg.

ein|graben *vt (unreg)* - **1.** [in den Boden] to bury - **2.** [eindrücken - Spuren] to carve. ➞ **sich eingraben** *ref*: **sich in etw** *(A)* **~** [Tier] to burrow into sthg; [Fluss] to carve (itself) a channel into sthg.

ein|greifen *vi (unreg)*: **(in etw** *(A)***) ~** to intervene (in sthg).

Eingriff *der* - **1.** [Intervention] intervention - **2.** MED operation.

ein|haken <> *vt* to fasten <> *vi* to interrupt.

ein|halten *(unreg)* <> *vt* [befolgen, erfüllen - Termin] to keep; [- Plan] to keep to; [- Vorschrift] to observe <> *vi* [innehalten]: **in** ODER **mit seinem Tun ~** to interrupt what one is doing.

einhändig *adv* one-handed.

ein|hängen <> *vt* - **1.** [in ein Scharnier - Tür] to hang; [- Fenster] to put in - **2.** [auflegen - Telefonhörer] to put down <> *vi* to hang up.

einheimisch *adj* local.

Einheit *(pl* -en) *die* - **1.** [Geschlossenheit] unity - **2.** MIL [Maßeinheit] unit.

einheitlich <> *adj* - **1.** [geschlossen] unified - **2.** [gleich] uniform; [Standard] standardized <> *adv* uniformly; [sich kleiden] in the same way.

einhellig <> *adj* unanimous <> *adv* unanimously.

ein|holen <> *vt* - **1.** [Person, Wagen] to catch up with; [verlorene Zeit] to make up for - **2.** [holen] to obtain - **3.** [einziehen - Netz] to haul in; [- Leine] to reel in - **4.** [einkaufen] to get <> *vi*: **~ gehen** to go shopping.

einig *adj* [einer Meinung]: **(sich) über jn/etw ~ sein** to agree about sb/sthg; [vereint] united.

einige <> *det* - **1.** [eine gewisse Menge] a few, some; **nach ~r Zeit** after some time; **~ Probleme** a few problems; **nur ~ waren da** there were only a few people there - **2.** [beträchtlich] quite a few; **das brachte so ~ Probleme mit sich** this caused quite a lot of problems; **so ~ waren da** there were quite a lot of people there ◇ *pron* a few, some. ◆ **einiges** *pron* something; **das hat ~s für sich** there is something to be said for it; **ich könnte dir ~s erzählen** I could tell you a thing or two.

einigen *vt* to unite. ◆ **sich einigen** *ref*: **sich (mit jm) ~** to reach an agreement (with sb); **sich auf etw** (A) **~** to agree on sthg.

einigermaßen *adv* fairly.

Einigkeit *die* - 1. [Eintracht] unity - 2. [Übereinstimmung] agreement.

Einigung (*pl* -en) *die* - 1. [Übereinkunft] agreement - 2. [Vereinigung] unification.

Einkauf *der* - 1. [Einkaufen] shopping - 2. [eingekaufte Ware] purchase; **die Einkäufe aus dem Wagen holen** to get the shopping out of the car - 3. WIRTSCH purchasing.

einkaufen ◇ *vt* to buy ◇ *vi*: **~ gehen** to go shopping.

Einkaufsbummel *der* shopping expedition; **einen ~ machen** to go on a shopping expedition.

Einkaufstasche *die* shopping bag.

einkehren (*perf* ist **ein**gekehrt) *vi* to stop off.

einklammern *vt* to put in brackets, to bracket.

Einklang *der* harmony.

einkleiden *vt* to kit out. ◆ **sich einkleiden** *ref*: **sich neu ~** to buy o.s. a new wardrobe.

Einkommen (*pl* -) *das* income.

Einkommensteuer *die* income tax.

einkreisen *vt* - 1. [umzingeln] to surround - 2. [eingrenzen] to pin down - 3. [mit Stift] to circle.

einkremen = eincremen.

Einkünfte *pl* income (U).

einladen *vt* (*unreg*) - 1. [Gast] to invite; **jn zu etw ~** [Hochzeit, Party] to invite sb to sthg; **darf ich Sie zu einem Kaffee ~?** can I buy you a coffee?; **jn in ein Restaurant ~** to take sb out for a meal - 2. [Last] to load.

 einladen

Would you like to play tennis next week? Hast du Lust, nächste Woche Tennis zu spielen?

Let's have lunch some time. Wir sollten mal zusammen Mittag essen.

How about going to see a play? Wir könnten uns zum Beispiel ein Theaterstück anschauen.

Do you feel like a drink? Wie wärs mit etwas zu trinken?

Do you fancy going for a drive? Hast du Lust auf eine Spritztour?

einladend ◇ *adj* inviting ◇ *adv* invitingly.

Einladung *die* invitation.

Einlage *die* - 1. [im Schuh] insole - 2. KÜCHE vegetables, noodles, meat etc added to a clear soup - 3. [im Programm] interlude - 4. WIRTSCH [bei Bank] deposit; [bei Firma] investment.

Einlass *der* admission.

einlassen *vt* (*unreg*) - 1. [hereinlassen] to admit - 2. [Wasser] to run - 3. [einsetzen] to set. ◆ **sich einlassen** *ref*: **sich mit jm/auf etw** (A) **~** to get involved with sb/in sthg.

einlaufen (*perf* hat/ist **ein**gelaufen) (*unreg*) ◇ *vi* (ist) - 1. SPORT: **ins Stadion ~** to enter the stadium; **ins Ziel ~** to cross the finishing line - 2. [Wasser] to run in - 3. [eingelaufen] to come in - 4. [Stoff] to shrink ◇ *vt* (hat) [Schuhe] to wear in. ◆ **sich einlaufen** *ref* to warm up.

einleben ◆ **sich einleben** *ref* to settle in.

einlegen *vt* - 1. [hineintun] to put in; **den ersten Gang ~** to go into first gear - 2. KÜCHE to preserve; [in Essig] to pickle - 3. [Pause] to have, to take - 4. [Berufung, Bitte] to lodge; **ein gutes Wort für jn ~** to put in a good word for sb.

einleiten *vt* - 1. [beginnen - Untersuchung, Verfahren] to start; [- Schritte] to take; [- Geburt] to induce - 2. [einführen] to open - 3. [einlassen]: **Abwässer in den Fluss ~** to let effluent into the river.

einleitend ◇ *adj* introductory ◇ *adv* by way of introduction.

Einleitung *die* - 1. [Einführung] introduction - 2. [Beginn - von Untersuchung] start.

einlenken *vi* to give way.

einleuchten *vi*: **es leuchtet mir ein, dass ...** I can see that ...

einleuchtend ◇ *adj* convincing ◇ *adv* convincingly.

einliefern *vt* [bringen - in psychiatrische Anstalt] to commit; **jn in ein Krankenhaus ~** to take sb to hospital.

einloggen ◆ **sich einloggen** *ref* EDV to log on; **sich ins Internet ~** to log on to the Internet.

einlösen *vt* - 1. [Scheck] to cash; [Gutschein] to redeem - 2. [Versprechen] to keep.

Einlösung *die* [von Scheck] cashing; [von Gutschein] redemption.

einmachen *vt* to preserve.

einmal *adv* - 1. [ein einzelnes Mal] once; **noch ~** (once) again - 2. [irgendwann - zuvor] before; [- in Zukunft] sometime; **haben wir uns nicht schon ~ gesehen?** haven't we met before?; **irgendwann ~ möchte sie nach England ziehen** she'd like to move to England someday - 3. [mal, bitte]: **komm ~ her!** come here, will you!; **hör mir ~ gut zu!** now listen to me carefully! ◆ **auf einmal** *adv* - 1. [plötzlich] suddenly - 2. [zusammen, gleichzeitig] at once. ➡ **nicht einmal** *adv* not even.

Einmaleins *das (ohne pl)* - **1.** [Zahlenreihe] multiplication tables *(pl)* - **2.** [Grundwissen] ABC.

einmalig *adj* - **1.** [einzeln - Zahlung] one-off - **2.** [außergewöhnlich] unique - **3.** [wunderbar] fantastic.

einlmarschieren *(perf* ist einmarschiert) *vi* to invade.

einlmischen ➡ **sich einmischen** *ref:* **sich (in etw** *(A)*) ~ to interfere (in sthg).

Einmischung *die* interference.

einlmünden *(perf* hat/ist eingemündet) *vi:* **in etw** *(A)* ~ [Fluss] to flow into sthg; [Straße] to lead into sthg.

einmütig ◇ *adj* unanimous ◇ *adv* unanimously.

Einnahme *(pl -n) die* - **1.** [Einkommen] income; [an einer Kasse] takings *(pl);* [vom Staat] revenue - **2.** [von Medikament] taking - **3.** [Eroberung] capture.

einlnehmen *vt (unreg)* - **1.** [Geld, Medikament, Platz] to take; **viel Raum** ~ to take up a lot of room - **2.** [erobern] to capture; **jn für sich** ~ *fig* to win sb over.

einnehmend *adj* captivating.

einlordnen *vt* to put in its place; [Akten] to file; [Dichter, Politiker] to categorize. ➡ **sich einordnen** *ref* [Auto] to get into the correct lane; [Person] to fit in.

einlpacken *vt* - **1.** [verpacken - Kleidung] to pack; [- Geschenk] to wrap - **2.** *fam* [anziehen] to wrap up.

einlparken ◇ *vt* to park ◇ *vi* to park.

einlpassen *vt* to fit.

einlpflanzen *vt* - **1.** [pflanzen] to plant - **2.** MED to implant.

einlplanen *vt* [Verlust, Verzögerung] to allow for; [Person] to count in.

einlprägen *vt* - **1.** [eingravieren] to imprint - **2.** [einschärfen]: **sich** *(D)* **etw** ~ to memorize sthg; **jm etw** ~ to impress sthg on sb.

einprägsam *adj* easily remembered; [Melodie] catchy.

einlrahmen *vt* to frame.

einlräumen *vt* - **1.** [einordnen, ordnen - Kleidung, Geschirr] to put away; **den Schrank** ~ to put things away in the cupboard - **2.** [Frist, Kredit] to grant - **3.** [zugeben] to admit.

einlreden ◇ *vi:* **auf jn** ~ to keep on at sb ◇ *vt:* **jm etw** ~ to talk sb into sthg.

einlreiben *vt (unreg)* to rub in.

einlreichen *vt* [Antrag] to submit; [Beschwerde] to lodge.

Einlreise *die* entry.

einlreisen *(perf* ist eingereist) *vi* to enter; **nach Deutschland** ~ to enter Germany.

Einreiselvisum *das* entry visa.

einlreißen *(perf* hat/ist eingerissen) *(unreg)* ◇ *vt (hat)* - **1.** [Gebäude] to pull down - **2.** [Papier, Stoff] to tear ◇ *vi (ist)* - **1.** [Papier, Stoff] to tear - **2.** *abw* [Unsitte] to become a habit.

einlrenken *vt* - **1.** MED to put back in its socket - **2.** [bereinigen] to sort out. ➡ **sich einrenken** *ref* to sort itself out.

einlrichten *vt* - **1.** [möblieren] to furnish - **2.** [organisieren]: **etw so** ~, **dass** ... to organize sthg in such a way that ... - **3.** [Stelle, Institution] to set up. ➡ **sich einrichten** *ref* - **1.** [mit Möbeln] to furnish one's home - **2.** [sich einstellen]: **sich auf etw** *(A)* ~ to prepare for sthg.

Einlrichtung *die* - **1.** [Möbel] furnishings *(pl)* - **2.** [Einrichten] furnishing - **3.** [Schaffung] setting up - **4.** [Institution] institution.

einlrücken *(perf* hat/ist eingerückt) ◇ *vi (ist)* to enter ◇ *vt (hat)* TYPO to indent.

eins ◇ *num* [als Zahl] one; ~ **A** top-quality, A-1 ◇ *pron* one; *siehe auch* **sechs.**

Eins *(pl -en) die* - **1.** [Zahl] one - **2.** [Schulnote] ≃ A, mark of 1 on a scale from 1 to 6; *siehe auch* **Sechs.**

einsam *adj* - **1.** [Person] lonely - **2.** [Haus, Gegend] isolated.

Einsamkeit *die* - **1.** [von Person] loneliness - **2.** [von Haus, Gegend] isolation.

einlsammeln *vt* [Werkzeug, Spielzeug] to gather up; [Kinder] to pick up; [Klassenarbeiten] to collect in; [Geld] to collect.

Einlsatz *der* - **1.** [Geld] stake - **2.** [Einsetzen] use; **unter** ~ **aller Kräfte** with a huge effort; **zum** ~ **kommen** to be used - **3.** [Engagement] commitment - **4.** MIL mission; **im** ~ **sein** to be in action - **5.** [Fach] compartment - **6.** MUS entry.

einsatzbereit *adj* [Truppe] ready for action; [Maschine] ready for use.

einlschalten *vt* - **1.** [anstellen] to switch on - **2.** [hinzuziehen] to call in. ➡ **sich einschalten** *ref* - **1.** [von selbst angehen] to switch on - **2.** [eingreifen] to intervene.

einlschärfen *vt:* **jm etw** ~ to impress sthg upon sb.

einlschätzen *vt* [Gefahr, Lage] to assess; [Vermögen, Umsatz] to estimate; [Person] to judge; **jn/etw falsch** ~ to misjudge sb/sthg.

Einlschätzung *die* [von Gefahr, Lage] assessment; [von Vermögen, Umsatz] estimation; [von Person] judgement.

einlschenken *vt:* **jm etw** ~ to pour sb sthg.

einlschicken *vt* to send in.

einlschieben *vt (unreg)* - **1.** [hineinschieben] to insert - **2.** [einfügen] to fit in.

einlschlafen *(perf* ist eingeschlafen) *vi (unreg)* - **1.** [aus Müdigkeit] to fall asleep - **2.** [Körperteil] to go to sleep - **3.** [aufhören] to peter out - **4.** [sterben] to pass away.

ein|schläfern vt - **1.** [töten] to put to sleep - **2.** [in Schlaf versetzen] to send to sleep.

einschläfernd adj soporific.

ein|schlagen (perf hat/ist eingeschlagen) (unreg) <> vi - **1.** (ist) [treffen] to strike - **2.** (hat) [zustimmen] to agree; [mit Händedruck] to shake on it - **3.** (hat) [lenken] to steer; **nach rechts ~** to turn right - **4.** (hat) [Furore machen - Schallplatte] to be a hit; [- Erfindung] to be a success; [- Enthüllungen] to cause a furore - **5.** (hat) [schlagen]: **auf jn ~** to beat sb <> vt (hat) - **1.** [Nagel] to knock in - **2.** [Glas, Tür] to smash in - **3.** [Buch, Geschenk] to wrap (up) - **4.** [Weg] to take.

einschlägig <> adj [Literatur] relevant; [Methode] appropriate <> adv: **~ vorbestraft sein** to have a previous conviction for a similar offence.

ein|schleichen ← **sich einschleichen** ref (unreg) eigtl & fig to creep in.

ein|schleusen vt [Waffen] to smuggle in; [V-Leute] to infiltrate.

ein|schließen vt (unreg) - **1.** [einsperren] to lock up - **2.** [aufbewahren] to lock away - **3.** [umzingeln] to surround - **4.** [beinhalten] to include.

einschließlich <> präp (+ G) including; **vom 1,3 bis ~ 5,5** from 1.3 to 5.5 inclusive <> adv: **bis Montag ~** up to and including Monday.

ein|schmeicheln ← **sich einschmeicheln** ref: **sich bei jm ~** abw to curry favour with sb.

einschneidend <> adj drastic <> adv drastically.

ein|schneien (perf ist eingeschneit) vi to get snowed in.

Ein|schnitt der - **1.** [Schnitt] cut; [bei Operation] incision - **2.** [Zäsur] turning point.

ein|schränken vt to limit; [Rauchen, Trinken] to cut down on; [Menge, Anzahl] to reduce. ← **sich einschränken** ref to economize.

Einschränkung (pl -en) die - **1.** [Einschränken] limitation; [von Kosten] reduction - **2.** [Vorbehalt] reservation.

ein|schreiben vt (unreg) - **1.** [hineinschreiben]: **eingeschrieben sein** to be registered - **2.** [Brief]: **etw ~ lassen** ODER **eingeschrieben schicken** to send sthg recorded delivery. ← **sich einschreiben** ref [sich anmelden] to register.

Ein|schreiben das: **etw per ~ schicken** to send sthg recorded delivery.

ein|schreiten (perf ist eingeschritten) vi (unreg) to intervene.

ein|schüchtern vt to intimidate.

Einschüchterung (pl -en) die intimidation.

ein|schulen vt: **eingeschult werden** to start school.

Ein|schulung die [Tag] first day at school.

ein|sehen vt (unreg) - **1.** [Fehler, Schuld] to recognize, to admit - **2.** [Papiere] to examine.

einseitig <> adj - **1.** [subjektiv] one-sided - **2.** [auf einer Seite] on one side - **3.** [Beziehung] unilateral <> adv - **1.** [subjektiv] one-sidedly - **2.** [auf einer Seite] on one side - **3.** [unausgewogen]: **sich ~ ernähren** to eat an unbalanced diet.

ein|senden (prät sendete ein ODER sandte ein; perf hat eingesendet ODER eingesandt) vt to send in.

ein|setzen <> vt - **1.** [hineinsetzen] to put in - **2.** [gebrauchen] to use; **die Polizei/das Militär ~** to bring in the police/army - **3.** [in Amt] to appoint - **4.** [Leben] to risk; [Geld] to stake <> vi to begin; [Sturm] to break. ← **sich einsetzen** ref to be committed; **sich für jn ~** to stand up for sb; **sich für etw ~** to support sthg.

Ein|sicht die - **1.** [Erkenntnis] insight; **zu der ~ kommen, dass ...** to come to realize that ... - **2.** [Einblick]: **in etw (A) ~ bekommen** to get a look at sthg.

einsichtig <> adj - **1.** [vernünftig] sensible - **2.** [verständlich] clear <> adv - **1.** [vernünftig] sensibly - **2.** [verständlich] clearly.

Ein|siedler, in der, die hermit.

einsilbig <> adj - **1.** [Person] taciturn - **2.** [Wort, Antwort] monosyllabic <> adv [antworten] in monosyllables.

ein|sinken (perf ist eingesunken) vi (unreg) to sink (in).

ein|spannen vt - **1.** [Pferd] to harness - **2.** [zur Arbeit] to rope in - **3.** [in Schreibmaschine] to insert.

ein|sparen vt to save; [Personal] to cut back on.

ein|sperren vt to lock up.

ein|spielen vt - **1.** [Geld] to bring in; [Unkosten] to cover - **2.** [Instrument] to play in - **3.** [einfügen] to fit in. ← **sich einspielen** ref - **1.** [sich aufwärmen] to warm up - **2.** [sich abstimmen] to settle down; **die Kollegen haben sich aufeinander eingespielt** the colleagues are now working well together.

ein|springen (perf ist eingesprungen) vi (unreg): **(für jn) ~** to stand in (for sb).

Ein|spruch der objection; **~ (gegen etw) erheben** to object (to sthg).

einspurig <> adj single-lane <> adv: **'nur ~ befahrbar'** 'single-lane traffic only'.

ein|stecken vt - **1.** [in Tasche] to put in one's pocket; **vergiss nicht, Geld einzustecken!** don't forget to take some money with you! - **2.** [Kritik, Niederlage, Verlust] to take - **3.** [Stecker] to plug in - **4.** [Brief] to post Br, to mail Am - **5.** [stehlen] to pocket.

ein|steigen (perf ist eingestiegen) vi (unreg) - **1.** [in Auto] to get in; [in Bus, Zug] to get on; **ins Auto/in den Zug ~** to get in the car/on the train - **2.** [anfangen]: **in etw** *(A)* ~ [Beruf, Politik] to go into sthg - **3.** [sich einkaufen]: **bei RTL/in eine Firma** ~ to buy a share in RTL/a company.

einstellbar *adj* adjustable.

ein|stellen *vt* - **1.** [Angestellte] to take on - **2.** [Gerät, Lautstärke - zum ersten Mal] to set; [- genauer] to adjust; [Sender] to tune into - **3.** [anmachen] to switch on - **4.** [beenden] to stop. ◆ **sich einstellen** *ref* - **1.** [sich vorbereiten]: **sich auf jn/etw** ~ to prepare for sb/ sthg; [sich anpassen] to get used to sb/sthg - **2.** *geh* [anfangen] to begin.

Ein|stellung *die* - **1.** [von Angestellten] appointment - **2.** [von Gerät, Lautstärke - zum ersten Mal] setting; [- genauer] adjustment; [von Sender] tuning - **3.** [Beendigung - von Verfahren, Zahlungen] termination, stopping - **4.** [Meinung, Haltung] attitude - **5.** [Szene] take.

Einstellungs|gespräch *das* interview.

Einstieg *(pl* -e) *der* - **1.** [Beginn] entry - **2.** [in Bus, Zug] boarding.

ein|stimmen *vi* - **1.** [mitsingen, mitspielen]: **(in etw** *(A))* ~ to join in (sthg) - **2.** [vorbereiten]: **jn auf etw** *(A)* ~ to get sb in the right mood for sthg.

einstimmig ◇ *adj* - **1.** MUS for one voice - **2.** [übereinstimmend] unanimous ◇ *adv* - **1.** MUS in unison - **2.** [übereinstimmend] unanimously.

einstöckig *adj* single-storey.

ein|studieren *vt* to rehearse.

ein|stufen *vt* to categorize; **jn in eine Gehaltsgruppe** ~ to put sb in an income bracket.

einstündig *adj* one-hour.

Ein|sturz *der* collapse.

ein|stürzen *(perf* ist **eingestürzt)** *vi* - **1.** [Haus, Mauer] to collapse - **2.** [hereinbrechen]: **neue Eindrücke stürzten auf sie ein** she was overwhelmed by new impressions.

Einsturz|gefahr *die:* '**Vorsicht, ~!**' 'danger, building unsafe!'.

einstweilig *amt* ◇ *adj* temporary ◇ *adv* temporarily.

eintägig *adj* one-day.

ein|tauchen *(perf* hat/ist **eingetaucht)** ◇ *vt (hat)* to dip; [völlig] to immerse; [Keks] to dunk ◇ *vi (ist)* to dive in.

ein|tauschen *vt:* **etw gegen etw** ~ to exchange sthg for sthg.

eintausend *num* a ODER one thousand.

ein|teilen *vt* - **1.** [klassifizieren] to classify - **2.** [unterteilen] to divide up - **3.** [Arbeit, Zeit] to organize - **4.** [einplanen]: **jn für** ODER **zu etw** ~ to assign sb to sthg.

einteilig *adj* one-piece.

Ein|teilung *die* - **1.** [Klassifizierung] classifi-

cation - **2.** [Unterteilung] division - **3.** [von Arbeit, Zeit] organization.

eintönig ◇ *adj* monotonous ◇ *adv* monotonously.

Ein|topf *der* stew.

einträchtig *adv* harmoniously.

Eintrag *(pl* -träge) *der* [Notiz] entry.

ein|tragen *vt (unreg)* - **1.** [notieren] to write down - **2.** *amt* [registrieren] to register - **3.** [Geld] to bring in; [Ärger, Sympathie] to bring. ◆ **sich eintragen** *ref* to put one's name down.

einträglich *adj* lucrative.

ein|treffen *(perf* ist **eingetroffen)** *vi (unreg)* - **1.** [ankommen] to arrive - **2.** [wahr werden] to come true.

ein|treiben *vt (unreg)* to collect.

ein|treten *(perf* hat/ist **eingetreten)** *(unreg)* ◇ *vi (ist)* - **1.** [in Raum, Phase] to enter; **in etw** *(A)* ~ to enter sthg - **2.** [in Gruppe, Verein]: **in etw** *(A)* ~ to join sthg - **3.** [sich einsetzen]: **für jn/etw** ~ to stand up for sb/sthg - **4.** [Tod] to occur; [Fall, Umstände] to arise ◇ *vt (hat)* to kick in.

Ein|tritt *der* - **1.** [in Raum, Phase] entry; '**~ frei**' 'admission free'; '**~ verboten'** 'no entry' - **2.** [Eintrittspreis] admission - **3.** [in Gruppe, Verein] joining - **4.** [Anfang]: **bei ~ der Dämmerung** at dawn.

Eintritts|geld *das* admission fee.

Eintritts|karte *die* ticket.

ein|üben *vt* to rehearse.

einverstanden ◇ *adj:* **mit jm/etw** ~ **sein** to agree with sb/sthg; **sich mit etw** ~ **erklären** to agree to sthg ◇ *interj* OK!

Ein|verständnis *das* - **1.** [Übereinstimmung] agreement - **2.** [Billigung] consent.

Ein|wand *der* objection; **~ (gegen etw) erheben** to object (to sthg).

ein|wandern *(perf* ist **eingewandert)** *vi* to immigrate.

Einwanderung *die* immigration.

einwandfrei ◇ *adj* perfect; [Material] flawless; [Nachweis] irrefutable ◇ *adv* perfectly.

einwärts *adv* inwards.

Einweg|flasche *die* non-returnable bottle.

ein|weichen *vt* to soak.

ein|weihen *vt* - **1.** [Gebäude] to open - **2.** [Wagen, Sofa] to christen, to use for the first time.

Ein|weihung *die* [von Gebäude] opening; [von Wohnung] housewarming party.

ein|weisen *vt (unreg)* - **1.** [Patienten] to admit - **2.** [Anfänger]: **jn in etw** *(A)* ~ to introduce sb to sthg.

Ein|weisung *die* - **1.** [von Patienten] admission - **2.** [von Anfänger] introduction.

ein|wenden *vt:* **~, dass ...** to object that ...;

dagegen ist nichts einzuwenden there's no reason why not.

ein|werfen vt (unreg) - **1.** [Münze] to insert; [Brief] to post Br, to mail Am - **2.** [Ball, Frage, Bemerkung] to throw in - **3.** [kaputtwerfen] to smash.

ein|wickeln vt - **1.** [einpacken] to wrap up - **2.** fam abw [überreden] to take in.

ein|willigen vi: **(in etw** (A)**)** ~ to agree (to sthg).

Einwilligung (pl -en) die consent.

ein|wirken vi - **1.** [Salbe] to take effect - **2.** [Person]: **auf jn beruhigend** ~ to have a calming influence on sb.

Einwohner, in (mpl -; fpl -nen) der, die inhabitant.

Einwohnermelde|amt das local government office at which inhabitants of a town must register at the beginning and end of their residency.

Ein|wurf der - **1.** [Ausspruch] comment - **2.** [von Ball] throw-in - **3.** [von Münze] insertion; [von Brief] posting Br, mailing Am - **4.** [Schlitz] slot.

Einzahl die singular.

ein|zahlen vt to pay in.

Ein|zahlung die deposit.

ein|zeichnen vt to mark.

Einzel (pl -) das singles (pl).

Einzel|fall der isolated case.

Einzel|gänger, in (mpl -; fpl -nen) der, die loner.

Einzel|handel der retail trade.

Einzelheit, en die detail; **in allen ~en** down to the last detail.

Einzel|kind das only child.

einzeln <> adj - **1.** [speziell] individual - **2.** [isoliert] single; **jedes ~e Exemplar** every single copy - **3.** [Schuh, Socke] odd <> adv individually; [ankommen, abholen] separately; ~ **stehend** solitary <> det (nur pl) a few.

Einzelne <> pron sg - **1.** [Person]: **jede/jeder** ~ (each and) every one - **2.** [Sache]: **jede/jeder/jedes** ~ every single one <> pron pl - **1.** [Personen] some (people) - **2.** [Sachen] some <> der, die [Mensch] individual <> das: **ins** ~ **gehen** to go into detail; **im ~n** in detail. <> **Einzelnes** pron some things (pl).

Einzel|person die single person.

Einzel|stück das [Kunstgegenstand] piece.

Einzel|zimmer das single room.

ein|ziehen (perf hat/ist eingezogen) (unreg) <> vt (hat) - **1.** [Bauch, Netz] to pull in; [Krallen, Fahrgestell] to retract - **2.** [Faden, Band] to thread in - **3.** [Wand] to put in - **4.** [zur Armee] to call up - **5.** [Geld, Steuern] to collect - **6.** [beschlagnahmen] to confiscate - **7.** [Banknoten, Münzen] to withdraw (from circulation) - **8.** amt [Informationen] to gather <> vi (ist) - **1.** [in Wohnung] to move in

- **2.** [Einzug halten] to enter - **3.** [Fett, Creme, Flüssigkeit] to be absorbed.

einzig <> adj (ohne Kompar) - **1.** [alleinig] only; **nur noch ein ~es Mal** just one more time; **ein ~er Besucher** a single visitor - **2.** geh [einzigartig] unique - **3.** [total] complete <> adv only; ~ **und allein** entirely.

einzigartig adj unique.

Einzige der, die, das: **der/die/das** ~ [Person] the only one; [Sache] the only thing; **das** ~, **was ...** the only thing that ...; **nur ein ~r er-hob sich** only one person stood up.

Einzimmer|wohnung die one-room flat Br ODER apartment Am.

Ein|zug der - **1.** [von Jahreszeit] arrival - **2.** [von Sportler, Sieger] entrance - **3.** MIL entry - **4.** [in Wohnung] move - **5.** [von Geld, Steuern] collection.

Eis (pl -) das - **1.** [Gefrorenes] ice; **etw auf** ~ **legen** eigtl & fig to put sthg on ice - **2.** [Eiscreme] ice cream.

Eis|bahn die ice rink.

Eis|bär der polar bear.

Eis|becher der (ice-cream) sundae.

Eis|bein das knuckle of pork.

Eis|berg der iceberg.

Eis|café ['aiskafe:] das ice-cream parlour.

Eischnee der: **das Eiweiß zu** ~ **schlagen** to beat the egg white until stiff.

Eiscreme ['aiskre:m], **Eiskrem** die ice cream.

Eis|diele die ice-cream parlour.

Eisen (pl -) das [gen] iron.

Eisen|bahn die - **1.** [Zug] train; **mit der** ~ **fahren** to travel by train - **2.** [Institution] railway Br, railroad Am - **3.** [Modelleisenbahn] train set.

Eisenbahn|netz das rail network.

Eisen|erz das iron ore.

eisenhaltig adj [Erz] iron-bearing, ferrous; [Nahrung] containing iron.

eisern <> adj eigtl & fig iron; ~ **bleiben** to remain resolute <> adv (unnachgiebig) resolutely.

eisgekühlt adj chilled.

Eis|hockey das ice hockey.

eisig <> adj - **1.** [eiskalt] freezing - **2.** [abweisend] icy, frosty <> adv - **1.** [eiskalt]: ~ **kalt** freezing cold - **2.** [abweisend]: ~ **lächeln** to give a frosty smile.

eiskalt <> adj - **1.** [Körperteil, Getränk, Wind] ice-cold - **2.** [Mensch, Mord] coldblooded; [Blick] frosty <> adv - **1.** [sehr kalt] ice-cold - **2.** [herzlos] in cold blood.

Eiskrem = Eiscreme.

Eiskunstlauf der figure skating.

Eis|zapfen der icicle.

Eis|zeit die Ice Age.

eitel adj abw vain.

Eitelkeit (pl -en) die abw vanity.

Eiter *der* pus.

eitern *vi* to fester.

eitrig, eiterig *adj* [Wunde] festering; [Geschwür] suppurating.

Eiweiß (*pl* -e) *das* - 1. [im Hühnerei] egg white - 2. BIOL & CHEM protein.

Eilzelle *die* ovum.

EKD [e:'ka:'de:] (*abk für Evangelische Kirche in Deutschland*) *die Protestant Church in Germany.*

Ekel (*pl* -) ◇ *der* [Abscheu] disgust; ~ **vor etw** (*D*) **empfinden** to find sthg disgusting ◇ *das fam abw* [Person] horror.

ekelhaft ◇ *adj* - 1. [Ekel erregend] disgusting - 2. [Arbeit, Chef] nasty ◇ *adv* [Ekel erregend] disgustingly.

ekeln *vt*: **das ekelt mich** I find that disgusting. ◆ **sich ekeln** *ref*: **sich (vor jm/etw)** ~ to be disgusted (by sb/sthg).

eklig, ekelig *adj* - 1. [Ekel erregend] disgusting - 2. *fam* [gemein] nasty.

Ekzem (*pl* -e) *das* eczema (*U*).

elastisch *adj* - 1. [Gummi] elastic - 2. [Körper] supple; [Gang] springy.

Elbe *die*: **die** ~ the (River) Elbe.

Elch (*pl* -e) *der* elk.

Elefant (*pl* -en) *der* elephant; **wie ein** ~ **im Porzellanladen** *fam* like a bull in a china shop.

elegant ◇ *adj* elegant ◇ *adv* elegantly.

Eleganz *die* elegance.

Elektriker, in (*mpl* -; *fpl* -nen) *der, die* electrician.

elektrisch ◇ *adj* - 1. [elektrisch betrieben - Licht, Rasierapparat, *etc*] electric; **~es Gerät** electrical appliance - 2. [mit Elektrizität zusammenhängend - Widerstand, Ladung] electrical ◇ *adv* electrically.

Elektrizitätslwerk *das* power station.

Elektrode (*pl* -n) *die* electrode.

Elektrolgerät *das* electrical appliance.

Elektrolgeschäft *das* electrical goods store.

Elektrolherd *der* electric oven.

Elektrolmotor *der* electric motor.

Elektronik *die* (*ohne pl*) - 1. [Wissenschaft] electronics (*U*) - 2. [Teile] electronics (*pl*).

elektronisch ◇ *adj* electronic ◇ *adv* electronically.

Elektrotechnik *die* electrical engineering.

Element (*pl* -e) *das* element; **in seinem** ~ **sein** to be in one's element; **dunkle** ODER **zwielichtige ~e** shady characters.

elend ◇ *adj* - 1. [erbärmlich] miserable - 2. [krank] wretched ◇ *adv* - 1. [erbärmlich] miserably - 2. [schlecht] wretchedly; **sich ~ fühlen** to feel wretched.

Elend *das* - 1. [Unglück] misery - 2. [Ärmlichkeit] poverty.

Elendslviertel *das* slum.

elf *num* eleven; *siehe auch* **sechs**.

Elf (*pl* -en) ◇ *die* [Zahl & SPORT] eleven ◇ *der* elf; *siehe auch* **Sechs**.

Elfenbein *das* ivory.

elfhundert *num* one thousand one hundred.

Elflmeter *der* penalty.

elfte, r, s *adj* eleventh; *siehe auch* **sechste**.

Elfte (*pl* -n) *der, die, das* eleventh; *siehe auch* **Sechste**.

elftel *adj* (*unver*) eleventh; *siehe auch* **sechstel**.

Elftel (*pl* -) *das* eleventh; *siehe auch* **Sechstel**.

Elite (*pl* -n) *die* elite.

Elitelschule *die* prestigious school.

Ellbogen, Ellenbogen (*pl* -) *der* elbow.

Elle (*pl* -n) *die* - 1. [Knochen] ulna - 2. [Maßeinheit] cubit.

Ellenbogen = **Ellbogen**.

Elsass *das* Alsace.

elsässisch *adj* Alsatian.

Elster (*pl* -n) *die* magpie.

elterlich *adj* parental.

Eltern *pl* parents.

Elternlabend *der* SCHULE parents' evening.

Elternlhaus *das* home.

Elternlteil *der* parent.

Email [e'mai] *das* enamel.

E-Mail ['i:meil] (*pl* -s) *die* EDV e-mail; **jm eine ~ schicken** to send sb an e-mail, to e-mail sb.

E-Mail-lAdresse *die* e-mail address.

Emanzipation (*pl* -en) *die* emancipation.

emanzipieren ◆ **sich emanzipieren** *ref* to become emancipated.

Embargo (*pl* -s) *das* embargo.

Embryo (*pl* -s ODER -onen) *der* embryo.

Emigrant, in (*mpl* -en; *fpl* -nen) *der, die* émigré.

emigrieren (*perf* ist emigriert) *vi* to go into (voluntary) exile, to leave the country.

Emission (*pl* -en) *die* emission.

emotional ◇ *adj* emotional ◇ *adv* emotionally.

empfahl *prät* ▷ **empfehlen**.

empfand *prät* ▷ **empfinden**.

Empfang (*pl* Empfänge) *der* - 1. [Erhalt - von Brief, Ware] receipt; **ein Paket für die Nachbarn in ~ nehmen** to take a parcel for the neighbours - 2. [Begrüßung] welcome - 3. [Veranstaltung, Rezeption & TV] reception.

empfangen (*präs* empfängt; *prät* empfing; *perf* hat empfangen) *vt* - 1. [gen] to receive - 2. [begrüßen] to greet; **Gäste ~** to receive visitors.

Empfänger (*pl* -) *der* - 1. [Gerät] receiver - 2. [Adressat] addressee; [von Arbeitslosengeld] recipient.

Empfängerin (*pl* -nen) *die* [Adressat] addressee; [von Arbeitslosengeld] recipient.
empfänglich *adj*: **(für etw) ~ sein** to be susceptible (to sthg).
Empfängnis *die* conception.
Empfängnisverhütung *die* contraception.
Empfangs|bescheinigung *die* acknowledgement of receipt.
empfängt *präs* ⊳ empfangen.
empfehlen (*präs* empfiehlt; *prät* empfahl; *perf* hat empfohlen) *vt* to recommend; **jm ~, etw zu tun** to recommend that sb do sthg. ➡ **sich empfehlen** *ref* - **1.** [sich anbieten] to be recommended; **es empfiehlt sich, etw zu tun** it is advisable to do sthg - **2.** *geh* [sich verabschieden] to take one's leave.
empfehlenswert *adj* - **1.** [gut] recommendable - **2.** [ratsam] advisable.
Empfehlung (*pl* -en) *die* - **1.** [Ratschlag] recommendation; **auf js ~ hin, auf ~ von jm** on sb's recommendation - **2.** [Beurteilung] reference - **3.** *geh* [Gruß] regards (*pl*).
Empfehlungs|schreiben *das* reference.
empfiehlt *präs* ⊳ empfehlen.
empfinden (*prät* empfand; *perf* hat empfunden) *vt* to feel; **etw als Kränkung ~** to take offence at sthg.
Empfinden *das* feeling; **das ~ für Gut und Böse** the sense of good and evil; **für** ODER **nach mein ~** if you ask me.
empfindlich ⟨⟩ *adj* - **1.** [Haut, Film, Gemüt] sensitive - **2.** [Gesundheit, Person] delicate - **3.** [Strafe, Verlust] severe ⟨⟩ *adv* - **1.** [verletzlich] sensitively - **2.** [merklich] severely; **jn ~ treffen** to hurt sb badly - **3.** [sehr - kalt] bitterly.
Empfindlichkeit *die* - **1.** [von Haut, Film, Gemüt] sensitivity - **2.** [von Person] susceptibility - **3.** [von Material, Gemüt] delicacy.
Empfindung (*pl* -en) *die* - **1.** [Wahrnehmung] sensation - **2.** [Emotion] feeling.
empfing *prät* ⊳ empfangen.
empfohlen *pp* ⊳ empfehlen.
empfunden *pp* ⊳ empfinden.
empören *vt* to outrage. ➡ **sich empören** *ref*: **sich über etw** (*A*) **~** to be outraged by sthg.
empört *adj* outraged.
Empörung *die* outrage.
emsig ⟨⟩ *adj* industrious; [Biene] busy; [Treiben] bustling ⟨⟩ *adv* industriously.
Ende (*pl* -n) *das* - **1.** [gen] end; **~ März** at the end of March; **zu ~ sein** to be over; **zu ~ gehen** to come to an end; **ein ~ nehmen** to be over; **kein ~ nehmen** to go on and on - **2.** *fam* [Wegstrecke]: **es ist noch ein ganzes ~** it's still quite a way - **3.** *RW*: **am ~ sein** [körperlich] to be completely exhausted; [nervlich] to be at the end of one's tether *Br* ODER rope *Am*; **mit**

seiner Geduld am ~ sein to have run out of patience; **mit seiner Weisheit am ~ sein** to be at one's wit's end. ➡ **am Ende** *adv* in the end. ➡ **letzten Endes** *adv* - **1.** [am Schluss] in the end - **2.** [im Grunde genommen] ultimately, in the final analysis.
Endeffekt *der*: **im ~** in the end.
enden (*perf* hat/ist geendet) *vi* - **1.** (*hat*) [zu Ende gehen] to end; **der Zug endet in Köln** the train terminates in Cologne; **gut/schlecht ~** to have a happy/an unhappy ending; **nicht ~ wollend** unending - **2.** (*hat*, *ist*) [sterben] to meet one's end; [schließlich landen]: **im Gefängnis ~** to end up in prison.
End|ergebnis *das* end result.
endgültig ⟨⟩ *adj* final; [Antwort] definitive; [Beweis] conclusive ⟨⟩ *adv* finally; [erklären] definitively.
Endivie [ɛnˈdiːvjə] (*pl* -n) *die* endive.
endlich ⟨⟩ *adv* - **1.** [nach langem Warten] at last; **wann kommst du denn ~?** so when are you finally going to come?. - **2.** [am Ende] finally; **um neun erreichten wir ~ das Ziel** we eventually got there at nine ⟨⟩ *adj* finite.
endlos ⟨⟩ *adj* endless ⟨⟩ *adv* interminably; [dauern] for ages.
End|spurt *der* final spurt.
End|station *die* terminus.
Endung (*pl* -en) *die* ending.
Energie (*pl* -n) *die* energy.
Energie|bedarf *der* (*ohne pl*) energy requirements (*pl*).
Energie|krise *die* energy crisis.
Energie|verbrauch *der* energy consumption.
energisch ⟨⟩ *adj* forceful ⟨⟩ *adv* forcefully.
eng ⟨⟩ *adj* - **1.** [Raum] narrow; **im Auto ist es ~** it's cramped in the car - **2.** [Kleidung] tight - **3.** [Auslegung, Interpretation] narrow; **im ~eren Sinn (des Wortes)** in the narrowest sense (of the word) - **4.** [Beziehung, Freund, Verwandte] close ⟨⟩ *adv* - **1.** [dicht gedrängt] close together - **2.** [anliegen] tightly - **3.** [auslegen, interpretieren] narrowly - **4.** [nah] close; **~ mit jm befreundet sein** to be close friends with sb.
engagieren [ɑ̃gaˈʒiːrən] *vt* to engage. ➡ **sich engagieren** *ref*: **sie engagiert sich politisch** she's very involved in politics; **sich für jn/etw ~** to show commitment to sb/sthg.
Enge *die* - **1.** [Schmalheit] narrowness - **2.** [Platzmangel] crampedness.
Engel (*pl* -) *der* angel.
England *nt* England.
Engländer, in (*mpl* -; *fpl* -nen) *der*, *die* Englishman (*f* Englishwoman); **die ~** the English.

englisch ⬦ *adj* English ⬦ *adv* [sprechen] in English.

Englisch(e) *das* English; **auf/in ~** in English.

engstirnig *abw* ⬦ *adj* narrow-minded ⬦ *adv* narrow-mindedly.

Enkel, in (*mpl -*; *fpl -nen*) *der, die* grandson (*f* granddaughter); **unsere ~** our grandchildren.

Enkelkind *das* grandchild.

enorm ⬦ *adj* enormous, immense ⬦ *adv* tremendously, terribly; **sich ~ anstrengen** to make a tremendous effort.

entarten (*perf* ist entartet) *vi* to degenerate.

entbehren ⬦ *vt* - 1. [verzichten auf] to do without - 2. *geh* [vermissen] to miss ⬦ *vi*: **einer Sache** (*G*) ~ *geh* to lack sthg.

entbehrlich *adj* dispensable.

Entbehrung (*pl -en*) *die* privation.

Entbindung (*pl -en*) *die* - 1. [Befreiung] discharge - 2. [Gebären] delivery.

entblößen ➧ **sich entblößen** *ref* [sich ausziehen] to undress; [Exhibitionist] to expose o.s.

entdecken *vt* - 1. [gen] to discover - 2. [Fehler] to detect; [Urheber] to identify; **kannst du ihn ~?** can you make him out?

Entdecker, in (*mpl -*; *fpl -nen*) *der, die* discoverer.

Entdeckung *die* discovery.

Ente (*pl -n*) *die* - 1. [Tier] duck - 2. [Zeitungsmeldung] hoax - 3. *fam* [Auto] Citroën 2 CV.

enteignen *vt* [Mensch] to dispossess; [Vermögen] to expropriate.

enterben *vt* to disinherit.

entfallen (*präs* entfällt; *prät* entfiel; *perf* ist entfallen) *vi* - 1. [vergessen]: **ihr Name ist mir ~** her name has slipped my mind - 2. [sich verteilen]: **auf jn ~** to fall ODER to sb on sb.

entfalten *vt* - 1. [öffnen] to unfold - 2. [entwickeln] to develop - 3. [zeigen] to display, to show; [Aktivität] to launch into - 4. [erläutern] to set out. ➧ **sich entfalten** *ref* - 1. [Blüte, Fallschirm] to open; [Segel] to unfurl - 2. [sich verwirklichen] to develop.

Entfaltung (*pl -en*) *die* - 1. [von Persönlichkeit] development; [von Aktivität] launching into; **etw zur ~ bringen** to develop sthg to its full potential - 2. [von Blüte] opening.

entfernen *vt* [beseitigen] to remove; **ein Kind von seiner Mutter ~** to take a child away from its mother. ➧ **sich entfernen** *ref* [sich wegbegeben] to leave; **sich von etw ~** [weggehen] to leave sthg; [von Pfad, Thema] to stray from sthg.

entfernt ⬦ *adj* - 1. [fort]: **wenige Kilometer von hier ~** a few kilometres away ODER from here; **weit ~** a long way away - 2. [abgelegen] remote; **weit davon ~ sein, etw zu tun**

not to have the slightest intention of doing sthg - 3. [Verwandte] distant; [Ähnlichkeit] vague - 4. [Ahnung] faint, vague ⬦ *adv* - 1. [weitläufig] distantly, remotely - 2. [blass, gering] vaguely, faintly. ➧ **Entfernteste** *das*: **nicht im Entferntesten hatte ich daran gedacht** I didn't have the slightest intention of doing it.

Entfernung (*pl -en*) *die* - 1. [Distanz] distance; **in einer ~ von 2 km** at a distance of 2 km; **aus der ~ zugucken** to look on from afar - 2. [Beseitigung] removal - 3. [Weggehen] departure.

entfremden *vt* [Person] to alienate; **jn jm/einer Sache ~** to alienate ODER estrange sb from sb/sthg.

entführen *vt* [Mensch] to kidnap; [Flugzeug] to hijack.

Entführer, in *der, die* [von Menschen] kidnapper; [von Flugzeug] hijacker.

Entführung *die* [von Menschen] kidnapping; [von Flugzeug] hijacking.

entgegen *präp* (+ *D*) contrary to; **sie kam ihm ~** she was coming towards him.

entgegengehen (*perf* ist entgegengegangen) *vi* (*unreg*): **jm/einer Sache ~** to approach sb/sthg; **dem Ende ~** to draw to a close.

entgegengesetzt *adj* [Richtung, Seite, Meinung] opposite; **~e Ansichten** conflicting ODER opposing opinions.

entgegenkommen (*perf* ist entgegengekommen) *vi* (*unreg*) - 1. [herankommen]: **jm ~** to approach sb - 2. [auf Wünsche eingehen]: **js Wünschen/Erwartungen ~** to meet sb's wishes/expectations.

Entgegenkommen *das* goodwill; **zu großem ~ bereit sein** to be ready to make major concessions.

entgegenkommend ⬦ *adj* [Mensch, Verhalten] accommodating, obliging ⬦ *adv* accommodatingly, obligingly.

entgegennehmen *vt* (*unreg*) to accept.

entgegensetzen *vt*: **jm/etw Widerstand ~** to resist sb/sthg; **einer Behauptung Beweise ~** to produce evidence that contradicts a statement; **diesen Vorwürfen habe ich nichts entgegenzusetzen** I have no answer to these reproaches.

entgegenstehen *vi* (*unreg*): **einer Sache** (*D*) ~ to stand in sthg's way; **dem steht nichts entgegen** there is no objection to that.

entgegnen *vt* [antworten] to reply; [barsch] to retort.

entgehen (*prät* entging; *perf* ist entgangen) *vi* - 1. [entkommen]: **einer Sache** (*D*) ~ to escape sthg - 2. [unbemerkt bleiben]: **dieser Fehler ist mir entgangen** this mistake escaped my notice.

entgleisen (*perf* ist entgleist) *vi* - 1. [Zug] to

be derailed - **2**. [taktlos sein] to commit a faux pas.

entgleiten (*prät* entglitt; *perf* ist entglitten) *vi:* **jm** ODER **js Händen ~** to slip from sb's hands.

enthalten (*präs* enthält; *prät* enthielt; *perf* hat enthalten) *vt* to contain. ◆ **sich enthalten** *ref* - **1**. [nicht abstimmen]: **sich der Stimme ~** to abstain - **2**. *geh* [auf etw verzichten] **~** to abstain; **sich einer Sache** *(G)* **~** to abstain from sth.

enthaltsam *adj* abstemious; **sexuell ~ sein** to abstain from sex.

Enthaltsamkeit *die* abstinence.

Enthaltung *die* abstention.

enthüllen *vt* - **1**. [Denkmal, Gemälde] to unveil - **2**. [Wahrheit, Geheimnis] to reveal.

entkommen (*prät* entkam; *perf* ist entkommen) *vi* to escape; **jm ~** to elude sb.

entkräftet *adj* [kraftlos] exhausted.

entladen (*präs* entlädt; *prät* entlud; *perf* hat entladen) *vt* [Lkw, Waffe] to unload. ◆ **sich entladen** *ref* - **1**. [Gewitter] to break - **2**. [Wut, Aggressionen] to erupt - **3**. [Batterie] to discharge.

entlang ⟨⟩ *präp* along; **die Straße ~, der Straße ~** along the road ⟨⟩ *adv:* **am Fluss ~** along the river.

entlang|gehen (*perf* ist entlanggegangen) *vi & vt* (unreg): **etw** *(A)* ODER **an etw** *(D)* **~** to go along sthg.

entlarven [ɛntˈlarfn] *vt* to expose.

entlassen (*präs* entlässt; *prät* entließ; *perf* hat entlassen) *vt* - **1**. [Kranken, Soldat] to discharge; [Gefangenen] to release - **2**. [kündigen] to sack.

Entlassung (*pl* -en) *die* - **1**. [aus dem Krankenhaus, aus der Armee] discharge; [aus dem Gefängnis] release - **2**. [Kündigung] redundancy; [Aktion] sacking.

entlasten *vt* - **1**. [von einer Belastung befreien] to relieve the strain on; [Gewissen] to ease - **2**. RECHT to exonerate - **3**. WIRTSCH: **sein Konto ~** to reduce one's overdraft.

entleeren *vt* to empty. ◆ **sich entleeren** *ref* to empty.

entlegen *adj* remote.

entleihen (*prät* entlieh; *perf* hat entliehen) *vt* to borrow; **etw von jm ~** to borrow sthg from sb.

entlocken *vt:* **jm etw ~** to coax sthg out of sb.

entlüften *vt* to ventilate.

Entmachtung (*pl* -en) *die* removal from power.

entmilitarisieren *vt* to demilitarize.

entmündigen *vt:* **jn ~** to declare sb unfit to manage his/her own affairs.

entmutigen *vt* to discourage, to dishearten.

entnervt *adj:* **~ sein** to have reached the end of one's tether *Br* ODER rope *Am.*

entreißen (*prät* entriss; *perf* hat entrissen) *vt* [wegnehmen] to snatch away.

entrüsten *vt* to incense. ◆ **sich entrüsten** *ref:* **sich über jn/etw ~** to be incensed by sb/sthg.

Entrüstung *die* indignation.

entschädigen *vt* to compensate; **jn für etw ~** to compensate sb for sthg.

Entschädigung *die* compensation.

entschärfen *vt* - **1**. [Bombe, Debatte] to defuse - **2**. [Kritik] to take the sting out of.

entscheiden (*prät* entschied; *perf* hat entschieden) ⟨⟩ *vi:* **über etw** *(A)* **~** to decide on sthg ⟨⟩ *vt* [Streit] to settle; [Fußballspiel] to decide. ◆ **sich entscheiden** *ref* [sich entschließen] to decide; **sich für/gegen jn/etw ~** to decide on/against sth/sthg.

entscheidend ⟨⟩ *adj* [Problem, Frage] decisive; [Stimme, Tor] deciding ⟨⟩ *adv* decisively.

Entscheidung *die* decision; [von Jury] verdict; [von Gericht, Ausschuss] ruling; **eine ~ treffen** to make ODER take a decision.

entschieden ⟨⟩ *pp* ▷ entscheiden ⟨⟩ *adj* [Verteidiger] staunch, steadfast; [Gegner] firm, strong ⟨⟩ *adv* firmly, emphatically; **das geht ~ zu weit!** that's going far too far!

entschließen (*prät* entschloss; *perf* hat entschlossen) ◆ **sich entschließen** *ref* to decide; **sich zur Annahme des Angebots ~** to decide to accept the offer.

entschlossen ⟨⟩ *pp* ▷ entschließen ⟨⟩ *adj* determined, resolute ⟨⟩ *adv* without hesitation.

Entschlossenheit *die* determination, resolution.

Entschluss *der* decision; **einen ~ fassen** to make ODER take a decision.

entschlüsseln *vt* to decipher.

entschuldigen *vt* to excuse; **entschuldige bitte!** (I'm) sorry!; **~ Sie bitte!** [vor Frage, bitte] excuse me!; [tut mir leid!] (I'm) sorry!

Entschuldigung (*pl* -en) ⟨⟩ *die* - **1**. [Rechtfertigung] excuse - **2**. SCHULE note (from one's parents or a doctor) - **3**. [Bitte um Verzeihung] apology - **4**. [Nachsicht]: **jn um ~ bitten** to beg sb's pardon ⟨⟩ *interj* [vor Frage, Bitte] excuse me!; [tut mir leid!] (I'm) sorry!

Entsetzen *das* horror; **zu js ~** to sb's horror.

entsetzlich ⟨⟩ *adj* - **1**. [schrecklich] horrible - **2**. [stark] terrible ⟨⟩ *adv* [sehr] terribly.

entsetzt ⟨⟩ *adj* horrified; **über etw** *(A)* **~ sein** to be horrified at sthg ⟨⟩ *adv* in horror, aghast.

entsichern *vt* to release the safety catch of.

Entsorgung (*pl* -en) *die* waste disposal.

entspannen *vt* to relax. ◆ **sich entspan-**

nen ref - **1.** [Person] to relax - **2.** [Situation] to ease.

Entspannung die - **1.** [Erholung] relaxation - **2.** [von Situationen] reduction of tension.

Entspannungs|politik die policy of détente.

entsprechen (präs entspricht; prät entsprach; perf hat entsprochen) vi - **1.** [genügen]: **einer Sache (D) ~** to correspond to sthg; [Erwartungen, Anforderungen] to meet sthg; **100° Celsius ~ 212° Fahrenheit** 100° Celsius is equivalent to 212° Fahrenheit; **einem Zweck ~** to fulfil a purpose - **2.** [nachkommen]: **einer Sache (D) ~** to comply with sthg.

entsprechend <> adj - **1.** [angemessen, zuständig] appropriate - **2.** [dementsprechend] corresponding <> adv [angemessen] appropriately; [dementsprechend] correspondingly <> präp: **einer Sache (D) ~, ~ einer Sache (D)** in accordance with sthg.

entspringen (prät entsprang; perf ist entsprungen) vi - **1.** [Fluss] to rise - **2.** [entstehen aus]: **einer Sache (D) ~** to arise from sthg.

entstehen (prät entstand; perf ist entstanden) vi - **1.** [geschaffen werden] to come into being; [Gebäude] to be built; [Kunstwerk] to be created; [Beziehung] to develop; [Roman] to be written; [Streit] to arise; **aus etw** ODER **durch etw ~** to come about as a result of sthg - **2.** [Schaden, Kosten] to be incurred.

Entstehung (pl -en) die - **1.** [eines Gebäudes] building; [eines Kunstwerkes] creation; [des Lebens] origins (pl) - **2.** [von Kosten, Schaden] incurring.

entstellen vt - **1.** [Person] to disfigure - **2.** [Sachverhalt] to distort.

enttäuschen <> vt to disappoint; [Hoffnungen] to dash <> vi to be disappointing.

enttäuscht <> adj disappointed; [Hoffnungen] dashed; **von jm ~ sein** to be disappointed in ODER with sb <> adv disappointedly.

Ent|täuschung die disappointment.

entwaffnen vt eigtl & fig to disarm.

Ent|warnung die all-clear (signal).

entwässern vt to drain; MED to dehydrate.

entweder ◆ **entweder ... oder** konj either ... or.

entweichen (prät entwich; perf ist entwichen) vi to escape.

entwerfen (präs entwirft; prät entwarf; perf hat entworfen) vt [Möbelstück, Kleidungsstück] to design; [Text] to draft; [Programm] to plan.

entwerten vt - **1.** [Fahrkarte] to cancel, to validate - **2.** [Geld] to devalue.

entwickeln vt to develop; [Gase] to produce. ◆ **sich entwickeln** ref to develop; [Gase] to be produced; **sich aus etw ~** to de-

velop out of sthg; **sich zu etw ~** to develop into sthg, to become sthg.

Entwicklung (pl -en) die - **1.** [Entfaltung, Ausarbeitung] development; **in der ~ (sein)** (to be) at the development stage - **2.** FOTO developing - **3.** [von Gasen] production.

Entwicklungs|helfer, in der, die overseas aid worker.

Entwicklungs|hilfe die development aid.

Entwicklungs|land das developing country.

entwirren vt eigtl & fig to unravel.

entwischen (perf ist entwischt) vi fam to make off; **jm ~** to give sb the slip.

entwöhnen vt to wean.

entwürdigend <> adj degrading <> adv degradingly.

Ent|wurf der - **1.** [Zeichnung] blueprint - **2.** [Konzept] draft.

entwurzeln vt eigtl & fig to uproot.

entziehen (prät entzog; perf hat entzogen) vt: **jm etw ~** to withdraw sthg from sb; **einer Sache (D) etw ~** to draw ODER extract sthg from sthg. ◆ **sich entziehen** ref: **sich jm/einer Sache ~** to escape sb/sthg; **sich der Verantwortung ~** to evade responsibility; **das entzieht sich meiner Kenntnis** I don't know anything about that.

Entziehungs|kur die detox.

entziffern vt to decipher.

entzücken vt to delight; **sie war von dem Gemälde entzückt** she thought the painting was delightful.

entzückend adj delightful, charming.

Entzug der withdrawal; **im ~ sein** to be in detox.

Entzugs|erscheinung die withdrawal symptom.

ent|zünden vt to light. ◆ **sich entzünden** ref - **1.** [brennen] to catch fire; TECH to ignite - **2.** MED to become inflamed - **3.** [entstehen]: **sich an etw (D) ~** to be ignited by sthg.

Ent|zündung die inflammation.

Enzian (pl -e) der [Pflanze] gentian.

Enzyklopädie (pl -n) die encyclopedia.

Enzym (pl -e) das enzyme.

Epidemie (pl -n) die epidemic.

Epik die [Gattung] narrative literature.

Epilepsie (pl -n) die epilepsy.

Episode (pl -n) die episode.

Epoche (pl -n) die period, era.

Epos (pl Epen) das epic.

er pron he; [bei Sachen, Tieren] it; **~ wars!** it was him!

erachten vt: **jn/etw als** ODER **für etw ~** to consider sb/sthg (to be) sthg.

Erachten das: **meines ~s** in my opinion.

erahnen vt [im Dämmerlicht] to barely make out; [Absicht] to get an inkling of.

erarbeiten vt - **1.** [Stellung, Wissen] to acquire *(through one's own efforts)* - **2.** [Bericht, Programm] to draw up.

Erbarmen *das* mercy, compassion; **mit jm/ etw ~ haben** to take pity on sb/sthg.

erbärmlich <> *adj* - **1.** [armselig, unzureichend] wretched, terrible - **2.** *abw* [gemein] despicable - **3.** [sehr groß] terrible <> *adv* [sehr] terribly.

erbarmungslos <> *adj* merciless <> *adv* mercilessly.

erbauen *vt* - **1.** [errichten] to build - **2.** *geh* [erheben] to uplift.

Erbauer, in *(mpl -; fpl -nen) der, die* builder.

Erbe *(pl -n)* <> *das* - **1.** [Vermögen] inheritance - **2.** [geistiges Vermächtnis] legacy <> *der* heir.

erben<> *vt* to inherit <> *vi* to come into an inheritance.

erbeuten *vt* to capture *(as booty)*.

Erbfolge *die* succession.

Erbgut *das* BIOL genetic make-up.

Erbin *(pl -nen) die* heiress.

erbittert <> *adj* [Kampf] fierce; [Feind] bitter <> *adv* fiercely.

Erbkrankheit *die* hereditary disease.

erblich <> *adj* hereditary <> *adv:* **~ belastet sein** to have a hereditary condition.

erblinden *(perf* ist erblindet*) vi* to go blind.

erbrechen *(präs* erbricht; *prät* erbrach; *perf* hat erbrochen*) vt* to vomit (up). ◆ **sich erbrechen** *ref* to vomit.

Erbrechen *das* vomiting.

erbringen *(prät* erbrachte; *perf* hat erbracht*) vt* - **1.** [ergeben] to result in; [Geldsumme] to bring in; **Leistung ~** to produce; **eine notwendige Leistung ~** to do some necessary work - **2.** [Nachweis] to produce.

Erbschaft *(pl -en) die* inheritance.

Erbse *(pl -n) die* pea.

Erbstück *das* heirloom.

Erdball *der* globe.

Erdbeben *das* earthquake.

Erdbeere *die* strawberry.

Erdboden *der* - **1.** [Boden] ground, earth - **2.** *RW:* **etw dem ~ gleichmachen** to raze sthg to the ground; **wie vom ~ verschluckt sein** to seem to have vanished from the face of the earth.

Erde *die* - **1.** [Erdreich] soil, earth - **2.** [fester Boden] ground; **etw aus der ~ stampfen** *fam* [Gebäude] to build sthg overnight; **jn unter die ~ bringen** *fam* [begraben] to bury sb; **du bringst mich noch unter die ~!** you'll be the death of me! - **3.** [Welt] world; **auf der ganzen ~** in the whole world - **4.** [Planet] Earth.

erden *vt* ELEKTR to earth.

erdenklich *adj* conceivable, imaginable. ◆ **alles Erdenkliche** *adv:* **alles Erdenkliche tun** to do one's utmost.

Erdgas *das* natural gas.

Erdgeschoss *das* ground floor *Br,* first floor *Am.*

Erdkugel *die* globe.

Erdkunde *die* geography.

Erdnuss *die* peanut.

Erdöl *das* (mineral) oil.

erdrosseln *vt* to strangle.

erdrücken *vt* - **1.** [zu Tode drücken] to crush to death - **2.** [belasten] to overwhelm.

Erdrutsch *der* landslide.

Erdteil *der* continent.

erdulden *vt* to endure.

ereifern ◆ **sich ereifern** *ref* to get worked up.

ereignen ◆ **sich ereignen** *ref* to happen; [Unfall] to occur.

Ereignis *(pl -se) das* event.

ereignisreich *adj* eventful.

erfahren *(präs* erfährt; *prät* erfuhr; *perf* hat erfahren*)* <> *vt* - **1.** [Kenntnis erhalten von] to learn; [hören] to hear; **etw von jm ~** to hear sthg from sb; **etw über jn/etw ~** to find out sthg about sb/sthg; **etw durch jn/etw ~** to find out about sthg from sb/sthg - **2.** *geh* [erleben - Glück, Leid] to experience; [- Veränderung] to undergo <> *adj* experienced.

Erfahrung *(pl -en) die* - **1.** [Kenntnis] experience *(U)* - **2.** [durch Nachforschen]: **etw in ~ bringen** to find sthg out.

erfahrungsgemäß *adv* judging from experience.

erfassen *vt* - **1.** [Bedeutung] to grasp, to understand - **2.** [Daten, Zahlen] to record - **3.** [mitreißen - von Fahrzeug] to drag along; [- Wasser] to sweep along - **4.** [überkommen]: **Angst erfasste sie** she was overcome with fear.

erfinden *(prät* erfand; *perf* hat erfunden*) vt* to invent.

Erfinder, in *(mpl -; fpl -nen) der, die* inventor.

Erfindung *(pl -en) die* - **1.** [Entwicklung] invention; **eine ~ machen** to invent something - **2.** [Ausgedachtes] fabrication.

Erfolg *(pl -e) der* success; **~ haben** to be successful; **mit ~** successfully. ◆ **Erfolg versprechend** *adj* promising. ◆ **viel Erfolg** *interj* good luck!

erfolglos <> *adj* unsuccessful <> *adv* unsuccessfully.

erfolgreich <> *adj* successful <> *adv* successfully.

Erfolgserlebnis *das* feeling of success.

erforderlich *adj* required; **für** ODER **zu etw ~ sein** to be required for sthg.

erfordern *vt* to require.

Erfordernis *(pl -se) das* requirement.

erforschen *vt* [Wissensgebiet] to study; [Land, Gelände] to explore; [Möglichkeiten] to investigate.

Er|forschung *die* [von Wissensgebiet] study; [von Land, Gelände] exploration; [von Möglichkeiten] investigation.

erfreuen *vt* to please. ► **sich erfreuen** *ref*: **sich an etw** *(D)* ~ to take pleasure in sthg. ► **sehr erfreut** *interj* pleased to meet you!

erfreulich *adj* pleasing.

erfreulicherweise *adv* luckily.

erfrieren (*prät* erfror; *perf* ist erfroren) *vi* to freeze to death; [Blüten] to be killed by frost; **sich die Hände/Füße** ~ to suffer frostbite in one's hands/feet.

erfrischen *vt* to refresh; [geistig] to stimulate. ► **sich erfrischen** *ref* to refresh o.s.

erfrischend *adj* refreshing; [Gespräch] stimulating.

Erfrischung (*pl* -en) *die* refreshment.

erfüllen *vt* - **1.** [Wunsch, Vertrag, Pflicht, Bedingungen] to fulfil - **2.** [füllen, ausfüllen] to fill. ► **sich erfüllen** *ref* [Wunsch] to come true.

ergänzen *vt* - **1.** [vervollständigen] to complete - **2.** [hinzufügen] to add. ► **sich ergänzen** *ref* to complement one another.

Ergänzung (*pl* -en) *die* - **1.** [Vervollständigung] completion *(U)* - **2.** [Zusatz] supplement; [zu Gesetz] amendment.

ergeben (*präs* ergibt; *prät* ergab; *perf* hat ergeben) *vt* [Ertrag] to produce; [herausfinden] to show; **eins mal eins ergibt eins** one times one is ODER makes one; **das ergibt keinen Sinn** that doesn't make any sense. ► **sich ergeben** *ref* - **1.** [erfolgen] to arise; **sich aus etw** ~ to result from ODER be the result of sthg - **2.** [kapitulieren] to surrender.

Ergebenheit *die* devotion.

Ergebnis (*pl* -se) *das* result.

ergebnislos *adj* unsuccessful.

ergiebig *adj* [Quelle] rich; [Thema] fertile; [Gespräch] productive.

ergießen (*prät* ergoss; *perf* hat ergossen) ► **sich ergießen** *ref* to pour.

ergreifen (*prät* ergriff; *perf* hat ergriffen) *vt* - **1.** [packen, Macht] to seize - **2.** [festnehmen] to capture - **3.** [Initiative, Gelegenheit] to take; [Beruf] to take up; [Maßnahmen] to adopt - **4.** [erfassen] to overcome.

ergreifend ◇ *adj* moving ◇ *adv* movingly.

ergriffen ◇ *pp* ▷ ergreifen ◇ *adj*: ~ **sein** to be (deeply) moved.

ergründen *vt* to discover.

erhalten (*präs* erhält; *prät* erhielt; *perf* hat erhalten) *vt* - **1.** [bekommen] to receive, to get - **2.** [bewahren] to preserve; **gut** ~ in good condition.

erhältlich *adj* available.

Erhaltung *die* preservation; [von Tierarten] conservation.

erhängen *vt* to hang. ► **sich erhängen** *ref* to hang o.s.

erheben (*prät* erhob; *perf* hat erhoben) *vt* - **1.** [Arm, Stimme, Glas] to raise - **2.** [Gebühren] to charge; [Steuern] to levy - **3.** [Daten] to gather - **4.** [vorbringen]: **Anklage** ~ to bring charges; **auf etw** *(A)* **Anspruch** ~ to make a claim for sthg; **Einspruch** ~ to raise an objection; **etw zum Prinzip** ~ to make sthg a principle. ► **sich erheben** *ref* - **1.** [aufstehen] to rise, to get up - **2.** [losfliegen] to rise - **3.** [rebellieren]: **sich gegen jn/etw** ~ to rise up against sb/sthg - **4.** [überragen]: **sich über jn/ etw** ~ to rise above sb/sthg.

erheblich ◇ *adj* considerable ◇ *adv* considerably.

Er|hebung *die* - **1.** [Hügel] rise - **2.** [Aufstand] uprising - **3.** [Untersuchung] survey.

erhitzen *vt* - **1.** [heiß machen] to heat - **2.** [erregen] to excite.

erhoffen *vt* to anticipate; **sich** *(D)* **etw von jm** ~ to expect sthg from sb.

erhöhen *vt* - **1.** [Preis, Einsatz, Geschwindigkeit] to increase - **2.** [Mauer] to raise. ► **sich erhöhen** *ref* [steigen] to increase.

Erhöhung (*pl* -en) *die* increase.

erholen ► **sich erholen** *ref*: **sich (von etw)** ~ to recover (from sthg).

erholsam *adj* relaxing.

Erholung *die* [von Krankheit] recovery; [von Anstrengung] rest.

erinnern *vt* - **1.** [an Aufgabe, Termin]: **jn an etw** *(A)* ~ to remind sb about ODER of sthg - **2.** [an Vergangenheit]: **jn an jn/etw** ~ to remind sb of sb/sthg ◇ *vi* - **1.** [an Aufgabe, Termin]: **ich muss daran ~, dass ...** I must remind you that ... - **2.** [an Vergangenes]: **an jn/ etw** ~ to be reminiscent of sb/sthg. ► **sich erinnern** *ref* to remember; **sich an jn/etw** ~ to remember sb/sthg.

Erinnerung (*pl* -en) *die* - **1.** [Eindruck] memory; ~ **an etw** *(A)* memory of sthg - **2.** [Gedenken]: **zur** ~ **an jn** in memory of sb; **jn/etw in guter/schlechter** ~ **behalten** to have fond/ bad memories of sb/sthg - **3.** [Gedächtnis] memory - **4.** [Andenken] memento.

erkälten ► **sich erkälten** *ref* to catch (a) cold.

Erkältung (*pl* -en) *die* cold.

erkennbar *adj* recognizable.

erkennen (*prät* erkannte; *perf* hat erkannt) *vt* - **1.** [sehen können] to make out - **2.** [Person, Fehler] to recognize; **etw zu** ~ **geben** to reveal sthg - **3.** [Irrtum] to acknowledge.

erkenntlich *adj*: **sich** ~ **zeigen** to show one's gratitude.

Erkenntnis (*pl* -se) *die* - **1.** [Entdeckung, Einsicht] realization; **wissenschaftliche** ~**e** scientific discoveries; **zu der** ~ **kommen, dass ...** to realize that ... - **2.** [Erkennen] knowledge.

Erker (*pl* -) *der* bay window.

erklärbar *adj* explicable; **nicht ~** inexplicable; **leicht ~** easily explained.

erklären *vt* - **1.** [erläutern] to explain; **ich kann es mir nicht ~** I can't explain it - **2.** [bezeichnen] to declare; [Absicht] to state; [Rücktritt] to announce; **etw für ungültig ~** to declare sthg invalid; **jn für vermisst ~** to declare sb missing. ➣ **sich erklären** *ref* [sich äußern]: **sich (mit etw) einverstanden ~** to declare that one is in agreement (with sthg); **er erklärte sich bereit, es zu tun** he said he was willing to do it.

Erklärung (*pl* -en) *die* - **1.** [Erläuterung] explanation - **2.** [Mitteilung] statement.

erklingen (*prät* erklang; *perf* ist erklungen) *vi* [Ton, Instrument] to sound; **am Schluss erklang die Nationalhymne** at the end the national anthem was played.

erkranken (*perf* ist erkrankt) *vi* to fall ill.

Erkrankung (*pl* -en) *die* illness.

erkundigen ➣ **sich erkundigen** *ref* to enquire; **sich nach jm ~** to ask after sb; **sich nach etw ~** to ask about sthg.

Erkundigung (*pl* -en) *die* enquiry; **~en über jn/etw einziehen** ODER **einholen** to make enquiries about sb/sthg.

erlangen *vt* to obtain.

Erlass (*pl* -e ODER Erlässe) *der* - **1.** [von Befehl] decree - **2.** [von Schulden] remission.

erlassen (*präs* erlässt; *prät* erließ; *perf* hat erlassen) *vt* - **1.** [Befehl] to issue; [Gesetz] to enact - **2.** [Strafe, Schulden]: **jm etw ~** to let sb off sthg.

erlauben *vt* to allow; **jm etw ~** to allow sb sthg; **sich** (*D*) **etw ~** [sich herausnehmen] to take the liberty of doing sthg; [sich gönnen] to allow o.s. sthg. ➣ **erlaube mal** *interj* how dare you!

Erlaubnis *die* permission.

---

um Erlaubnis bitten

Could I use your mobile phone? Könnte ich mal von deinem Handy aus anrufen?

May I open the window? Darf ich das Fenster öffnen?

Do you mind if I smoke? Macht es dir etwas aus, wenn ich rauche?

Would it be all right if I left now? Ist es in Ordnung, wenn ich jetzt gehe?

I wonder if I might have a little more wine? Kann ich vielleicht noch ein kleines bisschen Wein haben?

---

erläutern *vt* to explain.

Erläuterung (*pl* -en) *die* explanation.

Erle (*pl* -n) *die* alder.

erleben *vt* - **1.** [erfahren, kennen lernen] to experience; [Abenteuer] to have - **2.** [Geburtstag, Jubiläum] to live to see.

Erlebnis (*pl* -se) *das* experience.

erledigen *vt* - **1.** [Frage, Angelegenheit, Auftrag] to deal with; [Arbeit] to get through; [Einkäufe, Hausaufgaben] to do - **2.** *fam* [töten] to bump off - **3.** *fam* [besiegen] to wipe out. ➣ **sich erledigen** *ref* [sich erübrigen]: **etw erledigt sich (von selbst)** sthg takes care of itself.

erledigt *adj* - **1.** [ausgeführt, beendet - Angelegenheit] settled; [- Auftrag] carried out; [- Arbeit] done - **2.** *fam* [erschöpft]: **~ sein** to be worn out.

erleichtern *vt* - **1.** [leichter machen - Arbeit, Situation] to make easier; [- Gepäck] to make lighter; **jm das Verständnis ~** to make it easier for sb to understand - **2.** [Gewissen] to ease.

erleichtert ◇ *adj*: **~ sein** to be relieved ◇ *adv*: **~ aufatmen** to breathe a sigh of relief.

Erleichterung (*pl* -en) *die* - **1.** [Befreiung] relief - **2.** [von Aufgabe] facilitation (*U*); [von Last] easing (*U*).

erleiden (*prät* erlitt; *perf* hat erlitten) *vt* to suffer.

erlernen *vt* to learn.

erlesen *adj geh* [Gemälde, Porzellan, Wein] fine; [Mahl] choice.

erleuchten *vt* - **1.** [erhellen] to light up - **2.** *geh* [inspirieren] to inspire.

erlischt *präs* ⊏⊐ erlöschen.

Erlös (*pl* -e) *der* proceeds (*pl*).

erlöschen (*präs* erlischt; *prät* erlosch; *perf* ist erloschen) *vi* - **1.** [Feuer, Licht] to go out; [Vulkan] to become extinct - **2.** [Gefühle] to die; [Anspruch, Mitgliedschaft] to lapse.

erlösen *vt* to rescue; **jn von etw ~** [Leid, Schmerz] to release sb from sthg; REL to deliver sb from sthg.

ermächtigen *vt*: **jn zu etw ~** to authorize sb to do sthg.

ermahnen *vt* to remind; **jn zu mehr Vorsicht ~** to remind sb to be more careful.

Ermahnung *die* reminder.

ermäßigt *adj* reduced.

Ermäßigung (*pl* -en) *die* reduction.

Ermessen *das* judgement; **das liegt ganz in Ihrem ~** that is entirely up to you.

ermitteln ◇ *vt* to determine; [Schuldige, Täter] to identify; [Sieger] to decide ◇ *vi* to investigate.

Ermittlung (*pl* -en) *die* [Erkundigung] enquiries (*pl*); [Entdeckung] identification (*U*).

ermöglichen *vt* to make possible.

ermorden *vt* to murder.

Ermordung (*pl* -en) *die* murder; [von Politiker] assassination.

ermüden *(perf* hat/ist ermüdet) *vt (hat) vi (ist)* to tire.

Ermüdung *die* tiredness.

ermuntern *vt* to encourage.

ermutigen *vt* to encourage.

ernähren *vt* - 1. [beköstigen] to feed - 2. [unterhalten] to support. ◆ **sich ernähren** *ref* to eat; **sich vegetarisch ~** to eat a vegetarian diet; **sich mit** ODER **von etw ~** [Person] to live on sthg; [Tier] to feed on sthg.

Ernährung *die* - 1. [Ernähren] feeding - 2. [Mahlzeit] diet; **gesunde ~** a healthy diet.

ernennen *(prät* ernannte; *perf* hat ernannt) *vt* to appoint; **jn zu etw ~** to appoint sb (as) sthg.

erneuern [ɛɐˈnɔyɐn] *vt* - 1. [ersetzen] to replace - 2. [ausbessern - Gebäude] to renovate; [- Gemälde] to restore; [- kaputten Zaun] to repair - 3. [Vertrag, Angebot] to renew.

Erneuerung [ɛɐˈnɔyɐrʊŋ] *die* - 1. [Ersatz] replacement *(U)* - 2. [Ausbesserung - von Gebäude] renovation *(U)*; [- von Gemälde] restoration *(U)* - 3. [von Vertrag, Angebot] renewal.

erneut ◇ *adj* [Angebot, Vorschlag] new; [Kraft] renewed; [Weigerung] further ◇ *adv* again.

erniedrigen *vt* to humiliate. ◆ **sich erniedrigen** *ref* [sich demütigen] to lower o.s.

Erniedrigung *(pl* -en) *die* humiliation *(U)*.

ernst ◇ *adj* - 1. [gen] serious; [Verhalten] solemn - 2. [Absicht, Vorschlag] sincere ◇ *adv* - 1. [gen] seriously - 2. [Absicht, Vorschlag] sincerely; **es mit etw ~ meinen** to be serious about sthg; **jn/etw ~ nehmen** to take sb/sthg seriously.

Ernst *der* seriousness; **mit etw ~ machen** to be serious about sthg; **im ~?** really?

Ernstfall *der* (case of) emergency.

ernsthaft ◇ *adj* serious; [Verhalten] solemn ◇ *adv* - 1. [gen] seriously - 2. [aufrichtig] sincerely.

ernstlich *adv* - 1. [gen] seriously - 2. [beabsichtigen, bereuen] sincerely.

Ernte *(pl* -n) *die* harvest.

ernten *vt* - 1. [Früchte] to harvest; [Obst] to pick - 2. [Beifall] to earn; [Undank] to receive.

ernüchtern *vt* [desillusionieren] to bring down to earth.

Ernüchterung *(pl* -en) *die* [Desillusion] disillusionment *(U)*.

erobern *vt* - 1. [erkämpfen] to conquer - 2. [gewinnen] to capture.

Eroberung *(pl* -en) *die* conquest.

eröffnen *vt* - 1. [gen] to open - 2. [bekannt geben]: **jm etw ~** to reveal sthg to sb - 3. [Gerichtsverfahren] to institute - 4. [von Möglichkeit] to open up. ◆ **sich eröffnen** *ref*: **sich jm ~** to open up to sb.

Eröffnung *die* - 1. [gen] opening *(U)* - 2. [Bekanntgabe - unerwartet] revelation *(U)*;

[- von Plan] disclosure *(U)* - 3. [von Gerichtsverfahren] institution - 4. [Möglichkeit] opening up *(U)*.

erörtern *vt* to discuss.

Erörterung *(pl* -en) *die* discussion.

Erotik *die* eroticism.

erotisch *adj* erotic.

erpressen *vt*: **jn (mit etw) ~** to blackmail sb (with sthg).

Erpresser, in *(mpl* -; *fpl* -nen) *der, die* blackmailer.

Erpressung *(pl* -en) *die* blackmail *(U)*.

erproben *vt* [Maschine, Mittel] to test; [Ausdauer, Zuverlässigkeit] to put to the test; [Methode] to try out.

erraten *(präs* errät; *prät* erriet; *perf* hat erraten) *vt* to guess.

erregen *vt* - 1. [aufregen - Person] to excite; [- Gemüt, sexuell] to arouse - 2. [anregen] to stimulate - 3. [verursachen - Aufmerksamkeit, Aufsehen] to attract; [- Widerspruch] to give rise to; [- Mitleid, Neid] to arouse.

Erreger *(pl* -) *der* MED pathogen.

Erregung *die* - 1. [von Person] excitement *(U)*; [sexuelle] arousal *(U)* - 2. [von Nerven] stimulation *(U)* - 3. [Verursachen - von Mitleid, Neid] arousing *(U)*; [- von Aufmerksamkeit] attracting *(U)*.

erreichbar *adj* [Person] available; [Ort] within reach.

erreichen *vt* - 1. [Ort, Person, Geschwindigkeit] to reach; [Ziel] to achieve; [Bahn] to catch - 2. [telefonisch] to contact; **wo/wann sind Sie zu ~?** where/when can you be contacted? - 3. [durchsetzen] to achieve; **bei ihm kann man nichts ~** you'll not get anywhere with him.

errichten *vt* - 1. [bauen, aufbauen] to erect - 2. [Herrschaft] to establish.

Errichtung *die* - 1. [Bau, Aufbau] erection - 2. [von Herrschaft] establishment.

erringen *(prät* errang; *perf* hat errungen) *vt* [Sieg, Freundschaft] to win; [Vorteil, Mehrheit] to gain.

erröten *(perf* ist errötet) *vi* to blush; **vor Wut ~** to flush with anger.

Errungenschaft *(pl* -en) *die* achievement; **technische ~en** technical advances; **meine neueste ~** my latest acquisition.

Ersatz *der* - 1. [Ausgleich] substitute - 2. [Entschädigung] compensation.

Ersatzdienst *der* community work done by conscientious objectors instead of military service.

ersatzlos *adv* without substitution; **~ gestrichen** abolished.

Ersatzmann *(pl* -männer ODER -leute) *der* [beim Fußball] substitute; [bei der Arbeit] replacement.

Ersatzrad *das* spare wheel.

Ersatzteil *das* spare part.

erscheinen *(prät* erschien; *perf* ist erschienen) *vi* - **1.** [kommen, sich zeigen] to appear - **2.** [Buch, Zeitung] to come out - **3.** [wirken] to seem.

Erscheinung (*pl* -en) *die* - **1.** [Ereignis] phenomenon - **2.** [Gestalt] appearance - **3.** [Vision] apparition.

erschießen (*prät* erschoss; *perf* hat erschossen) *vt* to shoot. ⬥ **sich erschießen** *ref* to shoot o.s.

erschlagen (*präs* erschlägt; *prät* erschlug; *perf* hat erschlagen) *vt* to kill; **vom Blitz ~ werden** to be struck by lightning.

erschöpft ◇ *adj* exhausted ◇ *adv* [müde] wearily.

Erschöpfung *die* exhaustion.

erschrak *prät* ⬛ erschrecken.

erschrecken (*präs* erschreckt ODER erschrickt; *prät* erschreckte ODER erschrak; *perf* hat erschreckt ODER ist erschrocken) ◇ *vt* (*hat*) (*reg*) [überraschen] to startle; [ängstigen] to frighten ◇ *vi* (*ist*) (*unreg*) [überrascht sein] to be startled; [Angst haben] to be frightened; **über etw** (*A*) ~ to be alarmed by sthg. ⬥ **sich erschrecken** *ref* (*unreg*) to get a fright.

erschreckend ◇ *adj* alarming ◇ *adv* alarmingly.

erschrickt *präs* ⬛ erschrecken.

erschrocken *pp* ⬛ erschrecken.

erschüttern *vt* - **1.** [Haus, Person] to shake; **er lässt sich durch nichts ~** he's unflappable - **2.** [Vertrauen, Ruf] to shatter.

erschütternd *adj* distressing.

Erschütterung (*pl* -en) *die* - **1.** [von Haus] shaking (*U*) - **2.** [von Person] (state of) shock - **3.** [von Vertrauen, Ruf] shattering.

erschweren *vt* to make (more) difficult.

erschwinglich *adj* affordable.

ersetzbar *adj* replaceable.

ersetzen *vt* - **1.** [auswechseln, ausgleichen] to replace - **2.** [erstatten - Auslagen] to reimburse; [- Schaden] to make good.

ersichtlich *adj* obvious.

ersparen *vt* to save; **jm/sich etw Unangenehmes ~** to spare sb/o.s. sthg unpleasant.

Ersparnis (*pl* -se) *die* saving. ⬥ **Ersparnisse** *pl* savings.

erst *adv* - **1.** [nicht eher] not until; **er fährt ~ morgen los** he's not going until tomorrow; **~ als** only when - **2.** [vor kurzem] (only) just; **sie war ~ gestern hier** she was here only yesterday - **3.** [zuerst] first; [anfänglich] at first - **4.** [emphatisierend]: **sie ist ja schon groß, aber ihr Bruder ~!** she is tall but her brother is even taller; **jetzt werde ich es ~ recht/nicht recht tun!** now I'm definitely going/not going to do it! ⬥ **erst einmal** *adv* - **1.** [nur einmal] only once - **2.** [zuerst] at first.

erstarren (*perf* ist erstarrt) *vi* [vor Kälte] to

go numb; [vor Schreck] to become paralysed; [Gips] to harden.

erstatten *vt* - **1.** [Betrag] to reimburse - **2.** [vorbringen]: **gegen jn Anzeige ~** to report sb (to the authorities); **Bericht ~** to (make a) report.

Erstaufführung *die* première.

erstaunen (*perf* hat/ist erstaunt) ◇ *vt* (*hat*) to astonish, to amaze ◇ *vi* (*ist*): **über etw** (*A*) ~ to be astonished ODER amazed at sthg.

Erstaunen *das* astonishment; **jn in ~ (ver)setzen** to astonish ODER amaze sb.

erstaunlich *adj* astonishing, amazing.

erstaunt *adj* [Person] astonished, amazed; [Gesicht, Miene] surprised; **über etw** (*A*) ~ **sein** to be astonished by sthg.

erstbeste, r, s *adj*: **kaufe nicht gleich den ~n Wagen!** don't simply buy the first car you look at! ⬥ **Erstbeste** *der, die, das* first thing to come along.

erste, r, s *adj* - **1.** [anfänglich] first - **2.** [beste - Qualität, Wahl] top; [- Liga, Geige] first - **3.** [Ergebnis, Erfolg] initial.

Erste *der, die, das* first; *siehe auch* Sechste. ⬥ **als Erstes** *adv* first (of all). ⬥ **fürs Erste** *adv* for the time being.

erstechen (*präs* ersticht; *prät* erstach; *perf* hat erstochen) *vt* to stab to death.

erste Hilfe *die* first aid.

erstens *adv* firstly, in the first place.

ersticken (*perf* hat/ist erstickt) ◇ *vi* (*ist*) to suffocate; **wir ~ zurzeit in Arbeit** we're up to our eyes in work at the moment ◇ *vt* (*hat*) [Person, Tier] to suffocate; [Feuer] to put out; **etw im Keim ~** to nip sthg in the bud.

erstklassig ◇ *adj* first-class ◇ *adv* excellently.

erstmalig ◇ *adj* first ◇ *adv* for the first time.

erstmals *adv* for the first time.

erstrangig ◇ *adj* - **1.** [vorrangig] of prime importance - **2.** [erstklassig] first-rate ◇ *adv* as a matter of priority.

erstrebenswert *adj* worthwhile.

erstrecken ⬥ **sich erstrecken** *ref* - **1.** [jn/ etw betreffen]: **sich auf jn/etw ~** to apply to sb/sthg - **2.** [sich ausdehnen]: **sich ~ bis** [räumlich] to extend as far as; **sich über etw** (*A*) ~ [zeitlich] to last for sthg; [räumlich] to extend over sthg.

ertappen *vt* to catch; **jn bei etw ~** to catch sb doing sthg; **jn auf frischer Tat ~** to catch sb red-handed.

erteilen *vt*: **jm etw ~** to give sb sthg.

ertönen (*perf* ist ertönt) *vi* [Instrument] to sound; [Stimme] to ring out; [Geräusch] to be heard.

Ertrag (*pl* -träge) *der* [an Gemüse, Getreide] yield; [finanziell] profits (*pl*).

ertragen (*präs* erträgt; *prät* ertrug; *perf* hat ertragen) *vt* to bear.

erträglich *adj* [Zustände] tolerable; [Schmerz] bearable.

ertränken *vt* to drown.

ertrinken (*prät* ertrank; *perf* ist ertrunken) *vi* to drown.

erübrigen *vt* to spare. **◆ sich erübrigen** *ref* to be unnecessary.

Erw. (*abk für* Erwachsene) adult.

Erwachen *das* awakening; **das gab ein böses ~** *fig* it was a rude awakening.

Erwachsene [ɛɐ'vaksnə] (*pl* -n) *der, die* adult.

Erwachsenenbildung *die* adult education.

erwägen (*prät* erwog; *perf* hat erwogen) *vt* to consider.

erwähnen *vt* to mention.

erwähnenswert *adj* worth mentioning.

Erwähnung (*pl* -en) *die* mention (U).

erwärmen [wärmen] to warm. **◆ sich erwärmen** *ref* - **1.** [sich aufwärmen] to warm up - **2.** [sich begeistern]: **ich kann mich für deine Idee nicht ~!** I can't generate any enthusiasm for your idea.

erwarten *vt* - **1.** [warten auf] to wait for; **ich kann es kaum ~!** I can hardly wait! - **2.** [mit etw rechnen, erhoffen] to expect.

Erwartung (*pl* -en) *die* expectation. **◆ Erwartungen** *pl* expectations; [Anforderung] requirements.

erwartungsvoll ◇ *adj* expectant ◇ *adv* expectantly.

erwecken *vt* - **1.** [Ehrgeiz, Misstrauen] to arouse; [Hoffnungen] to raise - **2.** [Tote] to awaken.

erweisen (*prät* erwies; *perf* hat erwiesen) *vt* [Schuld] to prove; **jm einen Dienst ODER Gefallen ~** to do sb a favour; **es ist erwiesen, dass ...** it has been proved that ... **◆ sich erweisen** *ref* [sich zeigen]: **sich als etw ~** to prove to be sthg.

erweitern *vt* [Raum, Angebot, Umfang] to extend; [Bekanntenkreis, Wissen] to expand. **◆ sich erweitern** *ref* [Straße, Angebot] to extend; [Bekanntenkreis, Produktion] to expand; [Pupillen] to dilate.

Erweiterung (*pl* -en) *die* [von Raum, Angebot] extension (U); [von Bekanntenkreis, Wissen] expansion (U); [von Pupillen] dilation (U).

Erwerb *der* - **1.** [von Haus, Grundstück] purchase - **2.** [von Kenntnissen] acquisition - **3.** [aus Geschäft] earnings (pl).

erwerben (*präs* erwirbt; *prät* erwarb; *perf* hat erworben) *vt* - **1.** [kaufen] to purchase - **2.** [erlangen] to acquire.

erwerbslos *adj* unemployed.

erwerbstätig *adj* employed; **die ~e Bevölkerung** the working population.

erwidern *vt* - **1.** [antworten] to reply - **2.** [Besuch, Gruß, Gefälligkeit] to return.

erwiesen ◇ *pp* ▷ erweisen ◇ *adj* proven.

erwischen *vt* - **1.** [ertappen] **jn (bei etw) ~** to catch sb (doing sthg) - **2.** [rechtzeitig erreichen] to catch - **3.** [bekommen] to get - **4.** *RW:* **ihn hat es erwischt** *fam* [krank sein] he's got it; [verletzt sein] he's hurt; [verliebt sein] he's got it bad; [tot sein] he's dead.

erwog *prät* ▷ erwägen.

erwogen *pp* ▷ erwägen.

erwünscht *adj* [Gäste, Entwicklung] welcome; [Ergebnis] desired; **nicht ~ sein** not to be welcome.

erwürgen *vt* to strangle.

Erz (*pl* -e) *das* ore.

erzählen *vt* - **1.** [Geschichte, Witz] to tell - **2.** *RW:* **dem werde ich was ~!** *fam* I'll give him a piece of my mind!

Erzählung (*pl* -en) *die* - **1.** [Bericht] account - **2.** [Dichtung] story.

Erzbischof *der* archbishop.

Erzengel *der* archangel.

erzeugen *vt* [Produkt] to produce; [Energie, Angst, Druck] to generate.

Erzeugnis *das* product.

Erzeugung *die* [von Produkten] production; [von Energie, Druck] generation.

erziehen (*prät* erzog; *perf* hat erzogen) *vt* [Kinder - in der Familie] to bring up; [- in der Schule] to educate; [Tier] to train; **jn zu jm/etw ~** to bring sb up to be sb/sthg.

Erzieher, in (*mpl* -; *fpl* -nen) *der, die* - **1.** [Berufsbezeichnung] teacher - **2.** [Eltern, Lehrer] educator.

erzieherisch ◇ *adj* educational ◇ *adv* educationally.

Erziehung *die* [in der Familie] upbringing; [in der Schule] education.

Erziehungsberechtigte *der, die* amt parent ODER guardian.

erzielen *vt* [Kompromiss] to reach; [Ertrag, Gewinn] to make.

erzogen ◇ *pp* ▷ erziehen ◇ *adj:* **gut/schlecht ~** well/badly brought up.

erzwingen (*prät* erzwang; *perf* hat erzwungen) *vt* to force.

es *pron* - **1.** [Personalpronomen im Nominativ - bei Sachen] it; [- bei Personen] he (*f* she) - **2.** [Personalpronomen im Akkusativ - bei Sachen] it; [- bei Personen] him (*f* her); **ich hoffe ~** I hope so; **ich weiß ~** I know - **3.** [unpersönliches Pronomen] it; **~ ist drei Uhr** it's three o'clock; **~ regnet/schneit** it's raining/snowing; **~ freut mich, dass ...** I'm pleased that ...; **gestern gab ~ Nudeln** yesterday we had pasta; **~ ist sehr interessant, sich mit Jill zu unterhalten** Jill is very interesting to talk to; **~ geht mir gut** I'm fine; **wer war ~?** who was it?

Es (*pl* -) *das* - **1.** MUS E flat - **2.** PSYCHOL id.

Esche (*pl* -n) *die* ash.

Esel (*pl* -) *der* - **1.** [Tier] donkey - **2.** *fam* [Schimpfwort] ass; **ich ~!** stupid me!

Eselin (*pl* -nen) *die* she-ass.

Eskimo (*pl* -s) *der* Eskimo.

Espe (*pl* -n) *die* aspen.

Espresso [ɛsˈprɛso] (*pl* - ODER -s) ⇔ *der* espresso ⇔ *das* [Lokal] coffee bar.

Essay [ˈɛse] (*pl* -s) *das* ODER *der* essay.

essbar *adj* edible.

essen (*präs* isst; *prät* aß; *perf* hat gegessen) ⇔ *vi* to eat; **~ gehen** to go out for a meal; **warm/kalt ~** to have a hot/cold meal ⇔ *vt* to eat; **seinen Teller leer ~** to eat everything on one's plate.

Essen (*pl* -) *das* meal; **~ machen** ODER **kochen** to make ODER cook a meal.

Essig (*pl* -e) *der* vinegar.

Ess|löffel *der* dessertspoon.

Ess|zimmer *das* dining room.

Estland *nt* Estonia.

estnisch *adj* Estonian.

Estragon *der* tarragon.

Etage [eˈtaːʒə] (*pl* -n) *die* floor.

Etagen|wohnung *die* flat *Br*, apartment *Am* (in a block).

Etappe (*pl* -n) *die* stage.

Etat [eˈtaː] (*pl* -s) *der* budget.

Ethik (*pl* -en) *die* - **1.** [Lehre] ethics (*U*) - **2.** (*ohne pl*) [Moral] ethics (*pl*).

ethnisch *adj* ethnic.

Etikett (*pl* -e(n) ODER -s) *das* label.

etliche, r, s *det* several, quite a few; **~ Male** several times. ⬥ **etliches** *pron* - **~s zahlen** to pay quite a lot; **es gibt ~s zu erwähnen** there are quite a few things to mention.

Etui [ɛtˈviː] (*pl* -s) *das* case.

etwa *adv* - **1.** [zirka, ungefähr] about; **es funktioniert ~ so** it works roughly like this - **2.** [zum Beispiel] for example - **3.** [zum Ausdruck der Beunruhigung, eines Vorwurfs in Fragen]: **ist es ~ schon 24 Uhr?** don't tell me it's 12 o'clock already - **4.** [zur Bekräftigung]: **Edinburgh ist nicht ~ groß, aber schön** Edinburgh is certainly not big but it is beautiful.

etwaig *adj* possible; **~e Fragen** any questions that might arise.

etwas ⇔ *det* - **1.** [gen] something; [in Fragen] anything; **~ Anderes/Schönes** something else/nice - **2.** [ein wenig] some ⇔ *pron* something; [in Fragen] anything; **hast du ~ für mich?** have you got anything for me?; **das ist doch wenigstens ~!** that's something at least!; **so ~** such a thing ⇔ *adv* a little; **~ spät** rather late.

EU (*abk für* Europäische Union) *die* EU.

euch *pron* (*Akkusativ und Dativ von ihr*) - **1.** [Personalpronomen] you; **wir haben es ~ gesagt** we told you; **das gehört ~** this is yours, this belongs to you; **mit ~** with you - **2.** [Reflexivpronomen] yourselves; **könnt**

ihr ~ das vorstellen? can you imagine that? - **3.** [einander] each other.

euer, e ODER **eure** *det* your; **alles Gute, Euer Thomas** yours, Thomas.

eure, r, s *pron* yours.

eurer *pron* (*Genitiv von ihr*): **wir gedenken ~** we remember you.

eurerseits *adv* - **1.** [Ihr selbst] for your part - **2.** [von Euch] on your part.

euretwegen *adv* - **1.** [euch zuliebe] for your sake - **2.** [wegen euch] because of you.

Euro [ˈɔyro] (*pl* -) *der* euro.

Eurocent [ˈɔyrosɛnt] (*pl* -s) *der* euro cent.

Eurocheque, Euro|scheck [ˈɔyroʃɛk] (*pl* -s) *der* Eurocheque.

Eurocheque-|Karte, Euroscheckkarte *die* Eurocheque card.

Eurocity [ˈɔyrositi] (*pl* -s) *der international train linking two or more major European cities.*

Euro|land *das* Euroland.

Europa *nt* Europe.

Europäer, in (*mpl* -; *fpl* -nen) *der, die* European.

europäisch *adj* European.

Europa|parlament *das* European Parliament.

Europa|rat *der* European Council.

Euro|scheck = Eurocheque.

Euro|zone *die* euro zone.

ev. *abk für* evangelisch.

e. V. (*abk für* eingetragener Verein) *registered society.*

evakuieren [evakuˈiːrən] *vt* to evacuate.

evangelisch [evaŋˈgeːlɪʃ] *adj* Protestant.

Evangelium [evaŋˈgeːljʊm] (*pl* -ien) *das* gospel.

eventuell [evɛnˈtuɛl] ⇔ *adj* possible ⇔ *adv* maybe, perhaps.

📖 **eventuell**

The German word eventuell looks as though it should mean "eventual" or "eventually", but it is a false friend which actually means "possible", "perhaps" or "maybe". So the phrase Ich werde <u>eventuell</u> auch mitspielen, wenn es nicht regnet could be rendered in English as "I might play too, if it doesn't rain".
It is normally possible to translate the English "eventual" or "eventually" using schließlich or letztendlich. So the sentence "You'll get used to it <u>eventually</u>" could be translated as Du wirst dich <u>letztendlich</u> daran gewöhnen.

---

ewig ⇔ *adj* - **1.** [nie endend] eternal - **2.** *fam abw* [andauernd] constant ⇔ *adv* - **1.** [endlos] eternally - **2.** *fam abw* [zu lange] constantly. ⬥ **auf ewig** *adv* [für immer] forever.

Ewigkeit (*pl* -en) *die* eternity.

EWS [eː'veːˈɛs] (*abk für* Europäisches Währungssystem) *das* EMS.

exakt ⬦ *adj* exact; [Arbeit] precise ⬦ *adv* exactly; [arbeiten] with precision.

Exaktheit *die* precision.

Examen (*pl* -) *das* examination; ~ **machen** to take one's examinations.

Exekutive [ɛkseku'tiːvə] *die* (*ohne pl*) executive.

Exempel (*pl* -) *das* example; **an jm ein ~ statuieren** to make an example of sb.

Exemplar (*pl* -e) *das* example; [von Buch] copy.

Exil (*pl* -e) *das* exile (*U*).

existent *adj* existing.

Existenz (*pl* -en) *die* - **1.** [Bestehen] existence - **2.** [Existenzgrundlage] livelihood - **3.** *abw* [Person] character.

Existenzminimum *das* (*ohne pl*) subsistence level.

existieren *vi* - **1.** [bestehen] to exist - **2.** [auskommen] to live.

exklusiv ⬦ *adj* exclusive ⬦ *adv* - **1.** [vornehm, abgesondert]: ~ **leben** to live an exclusive lifestyle - **2.** [ausschließlich] exclusively.

Exkursion (*pl* -en) *die* study trip.

Exmatrikulation (*pl* -en) *die* UNI removal of someone's name from a university register.

Exot (*pl* -en), **Exote** (*pl* -n) *der* [Mensch] exotic person; [Tier] exotic animal.

exotisch ⬦ *adj* exotic ⬦ *adv* exotically.

Expedition (*pl* -en) *die* expedition.

Experiment (*pl* -e) *das* - **1.** [Versuch] experiment - **2.** [Wagnis] experimentation.

experimentell ⬦ *adj* experimental ⬦ *adv* experimentally.

experimentieren *vi* to experiment; **mit etw ~** to experiment on sthg.

Experte (*pl* -n) *der* expert.

Expertin (*pl* -nen) *die* expert.

explodieren (*perf* ist explodiert) *vi* to explode.

Explosion (*pl* -en) *die* explosion.

explosiv *adj* explosive.

Export (*pl* -e) *der* export.

Exporteur [ɛkspɔr'tøːɐ] (*pl* -e) *der* exporter.

Expressionismus *der* expressionism.

extra ⬦ *adv* - **1.** [separat] separately - **2.** [zusätzlich] extra - **3.** [speziell] specially ⬦ *adj* (*unver*) extra.

Extrakt (*pl* -e) *der* extract.

extrem ⬦ *adj* extreme ⬦ *adv* [billig, auffällig] extremely; [reagieren, denken] in an extreme way; **~ rechts stehen** to be on the extreme right.

Extremfall *der* extreme case.

Extremist, in (*mpl* -en; *fpl* -nen) *der, die* extremist.

Extremsport *der* extreme sports (*pl*).

exzellent ⬦ *adj* excellent ⬦ *adv* excellently.

Exzess (*pl* -e) *der* excess.

EZ *abk für* Einzelzimmer.

EZB (*abk für* Europäische Zentralbank) *die* ECB.

F

f, F [ɛf] (*pl* -ODER -s) *das* - **1.** [Buchstabe] f, F - **2.** MUS F. ⬥ **F** (*abk für* Fahrenheit) F.

Fa. (*abk für* Firma) Co.

fabelhaft ⬦ *adj* fantastic ⬦ *adv* fantastically.

Fabrik (*pl* -en) *die* factory.

Fabrikant, in (*mpl* -en; *fpl* -nen) *der, die* factory owner.

Fabrikarbeiter, in *der, die* factory worker.

fabrikneu *adj* brand new.

fabrizieren *vt fam abw* [machen] to throw together.

Facette, Fassette [fa'sɛtə] (*pl* -n) *die* facet.

Fach (*pl* Fächer) *das* - **1.** [in Möbel, Behälter] compartment; [für Brief, Schlüssel] pigeonhole - **2.** [in Schule, Studium] subject; **vom ~ sein** to be an expert.

Fachabitur *das exam taken at the end of a secondary vocational school which enables students to enter a 'Fachhochschule' but not university.*

Facharbeiter, in *der, die* skilled worker.

Facharzt, ärztin *der, die* specialist.

Fachausdruck *der* technical term.

Fächer (*pl* -) *der* fan.

Fachgeschäft *das* specialist shop *Br* ODER store *Am*.

Fachhochschule *die college offering primarily vocational courses to the equivalent of bachelor level.*

Fachkenntnis *die* specialist knowledge (*U*).

Fachkraft *die* skilled worker.

fachkundig ⬦ *adj* expert ⬦ *adv* expertly.

fachlich ⬦ *adj* [Problem] technical; [beruflich] professional ⬦ *adv* technically; [beruflich] professionally; **sich ~ weiterbilden** to gain professional qualifications.

Fachmann (*pl* -leute) *der* expert.

fachmännisch ⬦ *adj* expert ⬦ *adv* expertly.

fachsimpeln [faxzɪmpl̩n] *vi fam* to talk shop.

Fach|wissen *das* specialist knowledge.
Fackel (*pl* -n) *die* torch.
Faden (*pl* Fäden) *der* - **1.** [Faser] thread
- **2.** MED stitch - **3.** *RW:* **den ~ verlieren** to lose
the thread.
fähig *adj* capable; **zu etw ~ sein** to be capable of sthg.
Fähigkeit (*pl* -en) *die* - **1.** [Begabung] talent
- **2.** [Können] ability.
fahnden *vi:* **nach jm/etw ~** to search for sb/
sthg.
Fahndung (*pl* -en) *die* search.
Fahne (*pl* -n) *die* flag; **eine ~ haben** *fam fig* to
smell of drink.
Fahnen|flucht *die* MIL desertion.
Fahr|ausweis *der* - **1.** [Fahrschein] ticket
- **2.** *Schweiz* [Führerschein] driving licence *Br*,
driver's license *Am*.
Fahr|bahn *die* road.
Fähre (*pl* -n) *die* ferry.
fahren (*präs* fährt; *prät* fuhr; *perf* hat/ist gefahren) <> *vi* (ist) - **1.** [Person - gen] to go;
[- mit Auto] to drive; [- mit Fahrrad] to ride;
mit dem Zug/Bus ~ to go by train/bus; **ins
Gebirge ~** to go to the mountains; **wir ~ nach
England** we're going to England; **durch
Wien ~** to drive through Vienna; **langsam/
zu schnell ~** to drive slowly/too fast; **120
km/h ~** to drive at 120 km/h; **ein Gedanke
fuhr ihm durch den Kopf** a thought flashed
through his mind; **was ist denn in dich gefahren?** *fig* what's got into you? - **2.** [Fahrzeug] to go; [Schiff] to sail - **3.** [abfahren] to
leave; **wann fährst du?** when are you leaving ODER going?; **der Bus fährt alle 30 Minuten** the bus leaves ODER runs every half hour
- **4.** *RW:* **einen ~ lassen** *fam* to fart <> *vt*
- **1.** (hat) [Fahrzeug] to drive; [Fahrrad] to ride
- **2.** (ist) [Entfernung, Strecke] to drive; **ich fahre diese Strecke jeden Tag** I drive ODER come
this way every day - **3.** (ist) SPORT: **Rollschuh
~** to rollerskate; **Ski ~** to ski; **Schlitten ~** to go
sledging.
Fahrenheit *nt* Fahrenheit.
Fahrer (*pl* -) *der* driver.
Fahrerflucht *die* failure to stop after an accident.
Fahrerin (*pl* -nen) *die* driver.
Fahr|gast *der* passenger.
Fahr|geld *das* fare.
Fahr|karte *die* ticket.
Fahrkarten|schalter *der* ticket desk.
fahrlässig <> *adj* negligent; **~e Tötung**
manslaughter *Br*, murder in the second degree *Am* <> *adv* negligently.
Fahrlässigkeit *die* negligence.
Fahr|plan *der* timetable.
fahrplanmäßig <> *adj* scheduled <> *adv*
on schedule.
Fahr|preis *der* fare.
Fahr|prüfung *die* driving test.

Fahr|rad *das* bicycle; **mit dem ~ fahren** to
cycle.
Fahr|schein *der* ticket.
Fahr|schule *die* driving school.
Fahr|stuhl *der* lift *Br*, elevator *Am*.
Fahrt (*pl* -en) *die* - **1.** [gen] journey; [kurzer
Ausflug] trip; **auf der ~ nach Berlin** on the
way to Berlin; **freie ~ haben** to have a clear
run - **2.** (ohne pl) [Geschwindigkeit] speed
- **3.** *RW:* **in ~ kommen** ODER **geraten** [in
Schwung kommen] to get going. <> **gute
Fahrt** *interj* have a good journey!
fährt *präs* > fahren.
Fährte (*pl* -n) *die* trail.
Fahrtkosten, Fahrkosten *pl* travelling
expenses.
Fahrt|richtung *die* [im Verkehr] direction;
[im Zug] direction of travel; **die A9 in
~ Berlin/München** the northbound/
southbound section of the A9.
fahrtüchtig *adj* [Person] fit to drive; [Fahrzeug] roadworthy.
Fahr|verbot *das* driving ban.
Fahr|zeug (*pl* -e) *das* vehicle.
Fahrzeughalter, in (*mpl* -; *fpl* -nen) *der*,
die registered owner.
fair [feːɐ̯] <> *adj* fair <> *adv* fairly.
Fairness ['feːɐ̯nɛs] *die* fairness.
Faktor (*pl* -toren) *der* factor.
Fakultät (*pl* -en) *die* UNI faculty.
Falke (*pl* -n) *der* falcon.
Fall (*pl* Fälle) *der* - **1.** [gen] case; **für alle Fälle**
for all eventualities; **klarer ~!** sure thing!; **jd/
etw ist ganz sein ~** *fam fig* one is very keen
on sb/sthg - **2.** (ohne pl) [Sturz] fall; **zu ~ kommen** to fall; **jn zu ~ bringen** *fig* to bring sb
down; **etw zu ~ bringen** *fig* to thwart sthg.
<> **auf alle Fälle** *adv* - **1.** [unbedingt] definitely - **2.** [vorsichtshalber] in any case. <> **auf
jeden Fall** *adv* in any case. <> **auf
keinen Fall** *adv* under no circumstances.
<> **für den Fall, dass** *konj* in case.
Falle (*pl* -n) *die* - **1.** [zum Fangen] trap; **(jm)
eine ~ stellen** to set a trap (for sb); **in eine
~ geraten** *fig* to fall into a trap - **2.** *fam* [Bett]
bed.
fallen (*präs* fällt; *prät* fiel; *perf* ist gefallen) *vi*
- **1.** [gen] to fall; [Preise, Niveau, Temperatur]
to drop; [Haare, Stoff] to hang - **2.** [Urteil] to
be passed; [Entscheidung] to be made; [Wort]
to be spoken; [Schuss] to be fired; **die Würfel
sind gefallen** the die is cast; **in Ungnade ~** to
fall out of favour; **durch eine Prüfung ~** to
fail an exam.
fällen *vt* - **1.** [Baum] to fell - **2.** [Urteil] to
pass; [Entscheidung] to make.
fällig *adj* due.
Fallobst *das* (ohne pl) windfalls (*pl*).
falls *konj* if; **~ es dir nicht gefällt** in case ODER
if you don't like it.
Fall|schirm *der* parachute.

Fallschirm|springer, in *der, die* parachutist.

fällt *präs* ▷ fallen.

Fall|tür *die* trapdoor.

falsch ◇ *adj* - **1.** [nicht korrekt, nicht passend] wrong - **2.** [imitiert, gefälscht, irreführend - Gebiss, Stolz, Angaben] false; [- Pass, Geldschein] forged ◇ *adv* - **1.** [nicht korrekt] wrongly; **etw ~ verstehen** to misunderstand sthg; **~ singen** to sing out of tune; **~ abbiegen** to take the wrong turning - **2.** [hinterhältig] falsely.

Falsche (*pl -n*) *der, die, das* [Person] wrong person; [Sache] wrong thing; **an den ~n** ODER **die ~ geraten** *fam* to come to the wrong person.

fälschen *vt* to forge.

Fälscher, in (*mpl -; fpl -nen*) *der, die* forger.

Falsch|fahrer, in *der, die* person who drives into oncoming traffic on a motorway.

Falschgeld *das* counterfeit money.

fälschlich ◇ *adj* false ◇ *adv* falsely.

Fälschung (*pl -en*) *die* - **1.** [Fälschen] forging - **2.** [Gefälschtes] forgery.

Falte (*pl -n*) *die* [in Stoff, Papier] fold; [in Hose, Hemd] crease; [in Haut] wrinkle.

falten *vt* [Stoff, Papier, Hände] to fold.

Falter (*pl -*) *der* butterfly.

faltig *adj* [Haut, Hände] wrinkled; [Hemd, Tischtuch] creased.

familiär ◇ *adj* [die Familie betreffend] family (*vor Subst*) ◇ *adv* [zwanglos] informally.

Familie [fa'mi:liǝ] (*pl -n*) *die* family; **~ haben** to have a family.

Familien|betrieb *der* family business.

Familien|feier *die* family celebration.

Familien|kreis *der* (*ohne pl*) family circle.

Familien|name *der* surname.

Familien|stand *der* marital status.

famos [fa'mo:s] *fam adj* marvellous.

famos

The German *famos* should not be confused with the normal sense of the English word "famous" – it actually means "marvellous". Eine *famose* Erfindung might therefore be translated as "a <u>marvellous</u> invention".
"Famous" when used to describe people or places is usually *berühmt*, so "the <u>famous</u> pyramids of Giza" can be rendered as die <u>berühmten</u> Pyramiden von Gizeh.

Fan (*pl -s*) *der* fan.

Fanatiker, in (*mpl -; fpl -nen*) *der, die* fanatic.

fand *prät* ▷ finden.

Fanfare (*pl -n*) *die* fanfare.

Fang *der* - **1.** [Fangen] catching - **2.** [Beute] catch.

fangen (*präs* fängt; *prät* fing; *perf* hat gefangen) *vt* to catch. ◆ **sich fangen** *ref* - **1.** [in Falle, Netz] to get caught - **2.** [nach Schwierigkeiten] to regain one's composure.

fängt *präs* ▷ fangen.

Fantasie, Phantasie [fanta'zi:] (*pl -n*) *die* - **1.** (*ohne pl*) [Vorstellungskraft] imagination - **2.** [Vorstellung] fantasy.

Fantasie

The German *Fantasie* corresponds to the English "imagination" and only in some cases to the word "fantasy". So the phrase Dieses Kind hat eine lebhafte <u>Fantasie</u> may be translated as "The child has a vivid <u>imagination</u>".

fantasielos, phantasielos ◇ *adj* unimaginative ◇ *adv* unimaginatively.

fantasieren, phantasieren *vi* - **1.** [irrereden] to be delirious - **2.** [träumen] to fantasize.

fantasievoll, phantasievoll ◇ *adj* imaginative ◇ *adv* imaginatively.

fantastisch, phantastisch ◇ *adj* fantastic ◇ *adv* fantastically.

Farb|aufnahme *die* colour photograph.

Farbband (*pl -bänder*) *das* (typewriter) ribbon.

Farb|drucker *der* EDV colour printer.

Farbe (*pl -n*) *die* - **1.** [Licht, Buntheit] colour; **~ bekommen** *fig* to get some colour - **2.** [Material] paint - **3.** [in Kartenspiel] suit.

farbecht *adj* colourfast.

färben ◇ *vt* to dye ◇ *vi* to run. ◆ **sich färben** *ref* to change colour; **sich rosa ~** to turn pink.

farbenblind *adj* colour-blind.

Farb|fernsehen *das* colour television.

Farb|fernseher *der* colour television.

Farb|film *der* colour film.

Farb|foto *das* colour photo.

farbig ◇ *adj* - **1.** [Druck, Fernsehen] colour - **2.** [bunt, lebhaft] colourful - **3.** [Person, Papier] coloured ◇ *adv* colourfully.

Farbige (*pl -n*) *der, die* coloured person.

farblich *adv* as regards colour.

farblos *adj* colourless.

Farb|stoff *der* colouring.

Färbung (*pl -en*) *die* - **1.** [Farbgebung] tinge - **2.** [Tendenz] slant.

Farn (*pl -e*) *der* fern.

Fasan (*pl -e* ODER *-en*) *der* pheasant.

Fasching (*pl -e* ODER *-s*) *der* carnival before Lent.

Faschismus *der* fascism.

Faschist, in (*mpl -en; fpl -nen*) *der, die* fascist.

Faser (*pl* -n) *die* fibre.

faserig *adj* [Fleisch] stringy; [Holz] coarse.

Fass (*pl* Fässer) *das* barrel. ◆ **vom Fass** *adj* & *adv* draught.

Fassade (*pl* -n) *die* facade.

fassen (*präs* fasst; *prät* fasste; *perf* hat gefasst) ⬦ *vt* - **1.** [anfassen] to take hold of; **jn/etw zu ~ bekommen** to catch hold of sb/sthg - **2.** [Dieb] to catch - **3.** [Entschluss] to make - **4.** [begreifen]: **ich kann es nicht ~** I can't take it in - **5.** [als Inhalt] to hold ⬦ *vi*: **an** ODER **in etw** (A) **~** [kurz] to touch sthg; [lang] to feel sthg. ◆ **sich fassen** *ref* to pull o.s. together; **sich auf etw** (A) **gefasst machen** *fig* to prepare o.s. for sthg; **sich kurz ~** to keep it short.

Fassette *die* = Facette.

Fassung (*pl* -en) *die* - **1.** [von Glühbirne] socket; [von Perle] setting - **2.** [von Text] version - **3.** [Selbstbeherrschung]: **jn aus der ~ bringen** to put sb out.

fassungslos ⬦ *adj* [Person] speechless; [Gesicht] astounded ⬦ *adv* speechlessly.

Fassungsvermögen *das* capacity.

fast *adv* nearly, almost.

fasten *vi* to fast.

📖 fasten

Particular care is required with the German verb **fasten**, as it has a different meaning as well as a different pronunciation to the identical English verb "to fasten". In the German word the **t** is pronounced and has the meaning "to fast". The traditional fasting period of Lent is called in German die Fastenzeit.

The English verb "to fasten" meaning "to secure" or "to attach" creates two problems for the German speaker, as it resembles both **fasten** and **fassen**, but can be translated by neither of these. Instead a verb such as **befestigen** or **festmachen** is needed. So the sentence "I <u>fastened</u> the bookshelves to the wall" could be rendered as Ich habe das Bücherregal an der Wand <u>befestigt</u>.

Fasten|zeit *die* - **1.** [Zeit religiösen Fastens] fasting period - **2.** [vor Ostern] Lent.

Fastnacht *die* carnival before Lent.

fatal *adj* [verhängnisvoll] fatal.

fauchen *vi* to hiss.

faul ⬦ *adj* - **1.** [Lebensmittel, Holz] rotten - **2.** [Person] lazy - **3.** *fam* [Witz, Ausrede] dubious ⬦ *adv* [träge] lazily.

faulen (*perf* hat/ist gefault) *vi* [Holz, Fleisch] to rot; [Zahn] to decay.

faulenzen *vi* to laze around.

Faulheit *die* laziness.

faulig *adj* [Obst] rotten; [Wasser] stagnant.

Fäulnis *die* rot.

Fauna *die* BIOL fauna.

Faust (*pl* Fäuste) *die* fist; **auf eigene ~** *fig* off one's own bat.

Faust|regel *die* rule of thumb.

Faust|schlag *der* punch.

Fax (*pl* -ODER -e) *das* fax.

faxen *vt* to fax.

Faxen *pl fam*: **die ~ dick** ODER **satt haben** to have had enough.

FAZ ['efaːtset] (*abk für* Frankfurter Allgemeine Zeitung) *die* German newspaper, renowned for its business and financial news.

Fazit (*pl* -s ODER -e) *das* result.

FCKW [ɛfˈtseːkaːveː] (*abk für* Fluorchlorkohlenwasserstoff) *der* (*ohne pl*) CFC.

F.D.P. [ɛfdeːˈpeː] (*abk für* Freie Demokratische Partei) *die* German liberal party.

Februar *der* February; *siehe auch* September.

fechten (*präs* ficht; *prät* focht; *perf* hat gefochten) *vi* to fence.

Fechter, in (*mpl* -; *fpl* -nen) *der*, *die* fencer.

Feder (*pl* -n) *die* - **1.** [von Vogel] feather - **2.** [zum Schreiben] nib; **zur ~ greifen** to take up one's pen - **3.** [in Maschine, Matratze] spring. ◆ **Federn** *pl*: **(noch) in den ~n liegen** *fam* to be (still) in bed.

Feder|ball *der* - **1.** [Spiel] badminton - **2.** [Ball] shuttlecock.

Feder|bett *das* quilt.

federn ⬦ *vi* [elastisch sein] to be springy; [bei Sprung, Druck] to spring back; **in den Knien ~** to give at the knees ⬦ *vt* [Fahrzeug]: **gut gefedert sein** [Auto] to have good suspension; [Matratze] to be well sprung.

Federung (*pl* -en) *die* [von Wagen] suspension (*U*); [von Bett] springs (*pl*).

Fee (*pl* -n) *die* fairy.

fegen (*perf* hat/ist gefegt) ⬦ *vt* (hat) to sweep ⬦ *vi* - **1.** (hat) Norddt [säubern] to sweep up - **2.** (ist) [rasen] to sweep.

fehl *adv*: **~ am Platz sein** to be out of place.

Fehl|betrag *der* shortfall.

fehlen *vi* - **1.** [nicht vorhanden sein] to be missing; **für ein Hobby fehlt ihr die Zeit** she doesn't have time for a hobby; **(in der Schule) ~** to miss school; **es fehlt an etw** (D) there is a lack of sthg; **es fehlt ihm einiges an Erfahrung** he is somewhat lacking in experience - **2.** [vermisst werden]: **sie fehlt mir** I miss her - **3.** [irren]: **weit gefehlt!** far from it! - **4.** [erkrankt sein]: **was fehlt dir/Ihnen?** what is the matter with you?

Fehl|entscheidung *die* wrong decision.

Fehler (*pl* -) *der* - **1.** [Unrichtigkeit] mistake - **2.** [Schwäche] fault; **ist es mein ~, dass er geht?** is it my fault that he's leaving? - **3.** [Mangel] defect.

fehlerfrei ⬦ *adj* perfect ⬦ *adv* perfectly.

fehlerhaft <> *adj* [Maschine] defective; [Aussprache] poor <> *adv* [schreiben, arbeiten] poorly; [verarbeitet] defectively.

Fehllgeburt *die* miscarriage.

Fehllgriff *der* mistake.

fehllschlagen (*perf ist* fehlgeschlagen) *vi* (*unreg*) to fail.

Fehllstart *der* - 1. [von Sportlern] false start - 2. [von Rakete] abortive launch.

Fehllurteil *das* - 1. [Rechtspruch - von Richter] wrong judgement; [- von Geschworenen] wrong verdict - 2. [Beurteilung] misjudgement.

Feier (*pl* -n) *die* party.

Feierlabend *der evening after work;* ~ **machen** to finish work; **nach** ~ after work; **mit etw ist** ~ *fam* it's all over with sthg.

feierlich <> *adj* - 1. [Akt, Handlung, Stille] dignified - 2. [Erklärung] solemn *RW:* **das ist schon nicht mehr** ~ *fam* that really is too much <> *adv* - 1. [verabschieden, begehen] in a dignified manner - 2. [erklären] solemnly.

Feierlichkeit (*pl* -en) *die* [Würde] solemnity. ◆ **Feierlichkeiten** *pl* celebrations.

feiern <> *vt* - 1. [Fest, Feiertag] to celebrate - 2. [Person] to fête <> *vi* to celebrate.

Feierltag *der* holiday; **kirchlicher** ~ feast day.

feige *adj* cowardly.

Feige (*pl* -n) *die* fig.

Feigheit *die* cowardice.

Feigling (*pl* -e) *der* coward.

Feile (*pl* -n) *die* file.

feilen <> *vt* to file <> *vi:* **an etw** (*D*) ~ *fig* to polish sthg up.

feilschen *vi:* **um etw** ~ to haggle over sthg.

fein <> *adj* - 1. [Haar, Spitze, Pulver] fine - 2. *fam* [erfreulich, sympathisch] great - 3. [Gesicht] delicate - 4. [Material, Zutat, Küche] top-quality - 5. [Sinne] keen - 6. [Spott, Nuance] subtle - 7. [Leute] refined; **sich ~ machen** to make o.s. smart <> *adv* - 1. [gemahlen, gezeichnet] finely - 2. *fam* [schön, erfreulich]: ~ **gemacht!** well done!; ~ **heraus sein** *fig* to have done well for o.s. - 3. [sich verhalten] nicely - 4. [vornehm, elegant] elegantly. ◆ **vom Feinsten** *adj* top-quality.

Feind (*pl* -e) *der* enemy; **sich** (*D*) ~**e machen** to make enemies.

Feindin (*pl* -nen) *die* enemy.

feindlich <> *adj* - 1. [Haltung, Nachbarn] hostile - 2. [Soldaten] enemy (*vor Subst*) <> *adv* hostilely.

Feindlichkeit *die* [Gesinnung] hostility.

Feindschaft (*pl* -en) *die* enmity (*U*).

feindselig <> *adj* hostile <> *adv* hostilely.

Feindseligkeit (*pl* -en) *die* hostility. ◆ **Feindseligkeiten** *pl* hostilities.

feinfühlig *adj* sensitive.

Feinheit (*pl* -en) *die* - 1. [Beschaffenheit]

fineness - 2. [Vornehmheit] refinement. ◆ **Feinheiten** *pl* subtleties.

Feinkostlgeschäft *das* delicatessen.

Feinlschmecker, in (*mpl* -; *fpl* -nen) *der, die* gourmet.

Feld (*pl* -er) *das* - 1. [gen] field - 2. [Teil - von Formular] box; [- von Brettspiel] square - 3. *RW:* **das ~ räumen** to bow out; **jm das ~ überlassen** to make way for sb.

Feldlbett *das* camp bed *Br*, cot *Am*.

Feldlflasche *die* water bottle.

Feldlsalat *der* (*ohne pl*) lamb's lettuce.

Feldlweg *der* footpath (*between fields*).

Feldlzug *der* campaign.

Felge (*pl* -n) *die* - 1. [Teil des Rades] (wheel) rim - 2. [Turnübung] circle.

Fell (*pl* -e) *das* [Haarkleid] fur; [von Hund, Pferd] coat; [von Schaf] fleece.

Fels (*pl* -en) *der* - 1. (*ohne pl*) [Gestein] rock - 2. *geh* [Felsen] cliff.

Felsen (*pl* -) *der* cliff.

felsenfest <> *adj* firm <> *adv* firmly.

felsig *adj* rocky.

feminin <> *adj* - 1. [gen] feminine - 2. *abw* [unmännlich] effeminate <> *adv* - 1. [weiblich] femininely - 2. *abw* [unmännlich] effeminately.

Femininum (*pl* -nina) *das* GRAM feminine noun.

Feminismus *der* [Frauenbewegung] feminism.

Feminist, in (*mpl* -en; *fpl* -nen) *der, die* feminist.

feministisch <> *adj* feminist <> *adv* in a feminist way.

Fenchel *der* fennel.

Fenster (*pl* -) *das* window; **weg vom** ~ **sein** *fam fig* to be out of it.

Fensterlladen *der* shutter.

Fensterlplatz *der* window seat.

Fensterlscheibe *die* window pane.

Ferien *pl* holiday (*sg*) *Br*, vacation (*sg*) *Am*; **die großen** ~ the summer holidays *Br*, the summer vacation *Am*; **in die** ~ **fahren**, ~ **machen** to go on holiday *Br*, to go on vacation *Am*.

Ferienllager *das* summer camp.

Ferienlort *der* resort.

Ferkel (*pl* -) *das* - 1. [Tier] piglet - 2. *fam* [dreckiger Mensch] mucky pup - 3. *fam* [unanständiger Mensch] filthy swine.

fern <> *adj* - 1. [räumlich] far-off - 2. [zeitlich] distant <> *adv* far; **von** ~ from a distance <> *präp geh:* ~ **einer Sache** (*D*) far from sthg.

Fernlbedienung *die* remote control.

Ferne *die* (*ohne pl*) [räumlich]: **ihr Blick schweifte in die** ~ she stared off into the distance; **in der** ~ in the distance; **aus der** ~ [betrachten] from a distance; [Gruß] from far-off lands.

Ferne Osten der Far East.

ferner <> konj in addition <> adv geh in future <> adj (Kompar) ⊳ **fern**.

Fern|gespräch das long-distance call.

ferngesteuert adj remote-controlled.

Fern|glas das binoculars (pl).

fern halten vt (unreg): **jn/etw von jm/etw ~** to keep sb/sthg away from sb/sthg. ➤ **sich fern halten** ref: **sich von jm/etw ~** to keep away from sb/sthg.

Fernlicht das full beam Br, high beam Am.

Fern|rohr das telescope.

Fernseh|apparat der television set.

fern|sehen vi (unreg) to watch television.

Fernsehen das television; **im ~** on television, on TV.

Fernseher (pl -) der - **1.** [Gerät] television, TV - **2.** [Fernsehzuschauer] viewer.

Fernseh|film der television ODER TV film.

Fernseh|programm das - **1.** [Sendungen] television ODER TV programmes (pl) - **2.** [Programmheft] television ODER TV guide.

Fern|steuerung die remote control.

Fern|straße die trunk road Br, highway Am.

Fern|verkehr der long-distance traffic.

Ferse (pl -n) die heel; **jm auf den ~n sein/bleiben** fig to be/stay on sb's heels.

fertig adj - **1.** [vollendet - gen] finished; [- Essen] ready - **2.** [bereit]: **~ sein** to be ready - **3.** [am/zu Ende]: **(mit etw) ~ sein** to have finished (sthg) - **4.** [müde]: **~ sein** fam [körperlich] to be worn out; [psychisch] to be shattered; **mit den Nerven ~ sein** to be at the end of one's tether Br ODER rope Am - **5.** RW: **mit jm ~ sein** fam to be finished ODER through with sb; **mit etw ~/nicht ~ werden** to cope/not cope with sthg; **mit jm schon/nicht ~ werden** fam to cope/not cope with sb.

fertig bringen vt (unreg) [zustande bringen]: **er hat es fertig gebracht, dass die Familien wieder miteinander reden** he has managed to get the families to talking to each other again.

Fertig|haus das prefabricated house.

Fertigkeit (pl -en) die skill. ➤ **Fertigkeiten** pl skills.

fertig|machen vt - **1.** fam [zurechtweisen] to lay into - **2.** fam [zur Verzweiflung bringen]: **der macht mich fertig** he does my head in - **3.** fam [erschöpfen] to wear out.

fertig machen vt - **1.** [abschließen] to finish - **2.** [bereitmachen] to get ready - **3.** fam [erledigen] to sort out; [zusammenschlagen] to do in. ➤ **sich fertig machen** ref [sich bereitmachen] to get ready.

fertig stellen vt to complete.

Fessel (pl -n) die - **1.** [Strick, Zwang] bond - **2.** [Körperteil - bei Tieren] pastern; [- bei Menschen] ankle.

fesseln vt - **1.** [anketten, binden] to tie up; **jm die Hände ~** to tie sb's hands up - **2.** [faszinieren] to grip.

fesselnd <> adj gripping <> adv grippingly.

fest <> adj - **1.** [gut befestigt - Knoten, Verband] tight - **2.** [Griff, Druck, Meinung] firm - **3.** [Wohnsitz, Angestellte] permanent; [Arbeitszeiten, Gehalt, Termin] fixed - **4.** [Stoff, Schuhe] strong - **5.** [verbindlich - Vereinbarung, Vorgabe] binding; [- Zusage] definite - **6.** [Nahrung] solid - **7.** [entschlossen - Blick, Stimme] steady <> adv - **1.** [haltbar, straff] tightly - **2.** [drücken, ziehen] hard - **3.** [überzeugt - glauben] firmly - **4.** [verbindlich - zusagen, vereinbaren] definitely - **5.** [angestellt] permanently - **6.** [schlafen] soundly - **7.** fam [tüchtig - zugreifen] with a will.

Fest (pl -e) das - **1.** [Veranstaltung] party - **2.** [Feiertag] festival. ➤ **frohes Fest** interj happy Christmas!

festangestellt ⊳ **fest**.

Fest|betrag der fixed amount.

fest|binden vt (unreg) to tie up.

Fest|essen das banquet.

fest|halten (unreg) <> vt - **1.** [aufzeichnen] to record - **2.** [feststellen]: **wir können ~, dass ... it is clear that ...** <> vi: **an jm ~** to stand by sb; **an etw ~** to stick to sthg.

fest halten (unreg) vt [halten] to hold on to. ➤ **sich fest halten** ref: **sich an jm/etw ~** to hold on to sb/sthg.

festigen vt to strengthen. ➤ **sich festigen** ref to become stronger.

Festiger (pl -) der [Schaum] styling mousse; [Spray] hairspray.

Festigkeit die - **1.** [Widerstandsfähigkeit] strength - **2.** [Standhaftigkeit] steadfastness.

Festival ['festival] (pl -s) das festival.

Festland das mainland.

fest|legen vt - **1.** [bestimmen] to fix - **2.** [verpflichten]: **jn auf etw (A) ~** to pin sb down to sthg. ➤ **sich festlegen** ref [sich binden] to commit o.s.; **sich auf etw (A) ~** to commit o.s. to sthg.

festlich <> adj [Essen, Veranstaltung] festive; [Kleidung] formal <> adv festively.

Festlichkeit (pl -en) die [Atmosphäre] festiveness. ➤ **Festlichkeiten** pl festivities.

fest|machen vt - **1.** [befestigen] to fix; [Boot] to moor - **2.** [vereinbaren - Termin] to fix; [- Geschäft] to secure.

Festnahme (pl -n) die arrest.

fest|nehmen vt (unreg) to arrest.

Fest|netz das TELEKOM land-line telephone network (as opposed to mobile phones).

Fest|platte die EDV hard disk.

fest|setzen vt - **1.** [bestimmen] to fix

- **2.** [verhaften] to arrest. ➤ **sich festsetzen** *ref* [Dreck] to collect.

fest sitzen *vi (unreg):* **es sitzt fest** [Dübel] it won't come out; [Farbe] it won't come off.

Festspiele *pl* festival *(sg).*

fest stehen *vi (unreg)* - **1.** [bestimmt sein] to have been fixed - **2.** [sicher sein] to be definite.

fest stellen *vt* - **1.** [in Erfahrung bringen] to find out; [diagnostizieren] to establish - **2.** [beobachten] to notice; **sie stellte fest, dass er Recht hatte** she realized that he was right - **3.** [anmerken] to state.

Fest stellung *die* - **1.** [Ermittlung] establishing - **2.** [Wahrnehmung] realization; **ich machte die ~, dass ...** I realized that ... - **3.** [Erklärung] remark.

Festung *(pl -en) die* fortress.

Fete ['fe:tə] *(pl -n) die fam* party.

fett ◇ *adj* - **1.** [Fleisch, Gericht] fatty - **2.** [Person, Tier, Erbe, Beute] fat ◇ *adv* [mit viel Fett]: **~ essen** to eat fatty food.

Fett *(pl -e) das* fat; **er hat sein ~ weg** *fam fig* he got what was coming to him.

fettarm *adj* low-fat.

fetten ◇ *vt* to grease ◇ *vi* to be greasy.

fett gedruckt *adj* in bold (type).

fettig *adj* greasy.

Fettnäpfchen *das:* **ins ~ treten** *fam* to put one's foot in it.

Fetzen *(pl -) der* scrap; **etw in ~ zerreißen** to tear sthg to pieces; **das Kleid ist ein billiger ~!** that dress is just cheap rubbish!

fetzig *adj fam* [toll] cool.

feucht *adj* [Wand, Tuch, Haar] damp; [Hände, Augen] moist; [Klima] humid ◇ *adv* [wischen] with a damp cloth.

Feuchtigkeit *die* - **1.** [leichte Nässe] moisture - **2.** [Feuchtsein - von Wand, Tuch, Haar] dampness; [- von Händen, Augen] moistness; [- von Klima] humidity.

feudal ◇ *adj* - **1.** [den Feudalismus betreffend] feudal - **2.** [aristokratisch] aristocratic - **3.** *fam* [vornehm] grand ◇ *adv fam* [vornehm] grandly.

Feuer *(pl -) ◇ das* - **1.** [gen] fire; **auf offenem ~ kochen** to cook over an open fire; **~ machen** to light a fire; **im Ofen ~ machen** to light the oven; **jm ~ geben** to give sb a light; **~ legen** to start a fire; **~ fangen** to catch fire; **das ~ einstellen/eröffnen** to cease/open fire - **2.** *(ohne pl)* [Schwung, Temperament - von Person] passion; [- von Begeisterung, Leidenschaft] fervour - **3.** *RW:* **(für jn/etw) ~ und Flamme sein** *fam* to be really keen (on sb/ sthg) ◇ *interj* fire!

Feueralarm *der* fire alarm.

feuerfest *adj* fireproof; [Backform] ovenproof.

feuergefährlich *adj* flammable.

Feuer löscher *(pl -) der* fire extinguisher.

feuern ◇ *vt fam* - **1.** [entlassen, heizen] to fire - **2.** [schleudern] to fling ◇ *vi* [schießen]: **auf jn/etw ~** to fire at sb/sthg.

Feuer wehr *(pl -en) die* fire brigade.

Feuer wehrmann *(pl -männer ODER -leute) der* fireman.

Feuer werk *das* - **1.** [Veranstaltung] firework display - **2.** [Raketen] fireworks *(pl).*

Feuer zeug *das* lighter.

Feuilleton [fœjə'tõ] *(pl -s) das* - **1.** [literarischer Teil einer Zeitung] arts section - **2.** [literarischer Beitrag] arts feature.

ff. *(abk für folgende Seiten)* ff.

FH [ɛf'ha:] *(pl -s) die* 🠖 **Fachhochschule.**

ficht *präs* 🠖 **fechten.**

Fichte *(pl -n) die* spruce.

Fieber *das* - **1.** [hohe Körpertemperatur] temperature; **~ haben** to have a temperature; **bei jm ~ messen** to take sb's temperature - **2.** *geh* [Besessenheit] fever.

fieberhaft ◇ *adj* feverish ◇ *adv* feverishly.

fiebern *vi* - **1.** [Fieber haben] to have a temperature - **2.** [angespannt warten]: **vor Erregung ~** to be in a fever of excitement; **nach etw ~** to yearn for sthg.

Fieber thermometer *das* thermometer.

fiel *prät* 🠖 **fallen.**

fies *fam abw* ◇ *adj* nasty ◇ *adv* - **1.** [gemein] nastily - **2.** [ekelhaft]: **~ schmecken** to taste horrible.

Figur *(pl -en) die* - **1.** [gen] figure; [männlich] physique - **2.** [literarische Darstellung] character - **3.** [Spielstein] piece - **4.** *RW:* **eine gute/ schlechte ~ abgeben** ODER **machen** to cut a good/poor figure.

Filet [fi'le:] *(pl -s) das* fillet.

Filiale *(pl -n) die* branch.

Film *(pl -e) der* film; **beim ~ sein** ODER **arbeiten** to be in the movies.

filmen *vt & vi* to film.

Film kamera *die* film camera, movie camera *Am.*

Film star ['fɪlmʃta:ɐ] *der* film star, movie star.

Filter *(pl -) das* ODER *der* filter.

filtern *vt* to filter.

Filter tüte *die* filter (paper).

Filter zigarette *die* filter cigarette.

Filz *(pl -e) der* - **1.** [Stoff] felt - **2.** *abw* [Vetternwirtschaft] jobs *(pl)* for the boys.

filzen *vt fam* [Person] to frisk; [Haus, Koffer] to search.

Filz stift *der* felt-tip (pen).

Finale *(pl -) das* - **1.** [Endkampf, Endspiel] final - **2.** *MUS* finale.

Finanz amt *das* tax office.

Finanz beamte *der* tax inspector.

Finanz beamtin *die* tax inspector.

114

Finanz|bedarf *der (ohne pl)* financial needs *(pl).*

Finanzen *pl* finances.

finanziell [finan'tsjɛl] <> *adj* financial <> *adv* financially.

finanzieren *vt* to finance.

Finanzierung *(pl -en) die* financing.

Finanz|ministerium *das* finance ministry, ≃ Treasury *Br*, ≃ Department of the Treasury *Am.*

finden *(prät* fand; *perf* hat gefunden) <> *vt* - **1.** [gen] to find; **wo finde ich die Post?** where is the post office?; **er fand die Kinder schlafend** he found the children sleeping; **an etw Gefallen ~** to get ODER come to like sthg - **2.** [erhalten]: **Verwendung ~** to be used; **Anerkennung ~** to receive recognition - **3.** [beurteilen]: **ich finde sie nett** I think she's nice; **wie findest du ...?** what do you think of ...? <> *vi* - **1.** [erfolgreich suchen]: **er hat nicht zu uns gefunden** he couldn't find his way to our place - **2.** [beurteilen]: **ich finde, dass ...** I think (that) ...; **ich finde nichts dabei** I don't see anything wrong with it. ◆ **sich finden** *ref* - **1.** [wieder auftauchen]: **der Schlüssel hat sich gefunden** I/we found the key - **2.** *RW*: **das wird sich (schon) alles ~!** everything will be all right.

Finder, in *(mpl -; fpl -nen) der* finder.

Finder|lohn *der* reward *(for finding something).*

fing *prät* ⌁ fangen.

Finger *(pl -) der* - **1.** [Glied] finger - **2.** *RW*: **jn in die ~ kriegen** ODER **bekommen** *fam* to get one's hands on sb; **etw in die ~ kriegen** ODER **bekommen** *fam* to get hold of sthg; **lange ~ machen** *fam abw* to be light-fingered.

Finger|abdruck *der* fingerprint.

Finger|hut *der* - **1.** [zum Nähen] thimble - **2.** [Blume] foxglove.

Finger|nagel *der* fingernail.

Finger|spitze *die* fingertip.

Finger|spitzengefühl *das* sensitivity; **~ haben** ODER **besitzen** ODER **beweisen** to show sensitivity.

Fink *(pl -en) der* finch.

finnisch *adj* Finnish; *siehe auch* englisch.

Finnisch(e) *das* Finnish; *siehe auch* Englisch(e).

Finnland *nt* Finland.

finster <> *adj* - **1.** [Nacht, Straße, Zimmer, Zeiten] dark - **2.** [Person, Miene] grim, sombre - **3.** [Gegend, Gestalt] sinister <> *adv* [unfreundlich] grimly.

Finsternis *(pl -se) die* darkness.

Finte *(pl -n) die* ruse.

Firma *(pl* Firmen) *die* firm, company.

Firmen|name *der* company name.

Firmen|wagen *der* company car.

Firmung *(pl -en) die* REL confirmation.

First Class *die* first class.

Fisch *(pl -e) der* - **1.** [Tier, Gericht] fish - **2.** ASTROL Pisces; **~ sein** to be a Pisces. ◆ **Fische** *pl* ASTROL Pisces *(U).*

Fisch|besteck *das* fish knives and forks *(pl).*

fischen <> *vt* - **1.** [fangen] to catch - **2.** [angeln] to fish for - **3.** [holen] to fish out <> *vi* - **1.** [Fische fangen] to fish; **~ gehen** to go fishing - **2.** *fam* [greifen]: **nach etw ~** to fish for sthg.

Fischer, in *(mpl -; fpl -nen) der, die* fisherman *(f* fisherwoman).

Fischer|boot *das* fishing boat.

Fischerei *die* fishing.

Fischfang *der* fishing.

Fisch|händler, in *der, die* fishmonger *Br*, fish seller *Am.*

Fisch|stäbchen ['fɪʃʃtɛːpçən] *das* fish finger *Br*, fish stick *Am.*

Fiskus *der* treasury.

fit *adj* [körperlich] fit; [geistig] sharp, mentally alert; **~ in Chemie sein** *fam* to be good at chemistry.

Fitness ['fɪtnɛs] *die* [körperliche] fitness; [geistige] sharpness, mental alertness.

Fitness|center *das* fitness centre.

fix <> *adj* - **1.** *fam* [schnell] quick - **2.** [Kosten] fixed - **3.** [erschöpft]: **~ und fertig sein** *fam* to be beat ODER knackered *Br* <> *adv* [schnell] quickly.

Fixer, in *(mpl -; fpl -nen) der, die fam* junkie.

fixieren *vt* - **1.** [anstarren] to stare fixedly at - **2.** [befestigen, konservieren] to fix - **3.** *geh* [festhalten] to record.

FKK [ɛf'kaːˈkaː] *(abk für* Freikörperkultur) *das* nudism; **am Strand ~ machen** to sunbathe in the nude.

◆ **FKK**

The cult of nudism in public places in Germany has a history dating back to the beginning of the 20th century and the growth in popularity of the bathing resorts on the Baltic and North Sea coasts. Today, many Germans still have a liberal attitude towards nudity, and it is not uncommon for visitors to Munich's Englischer Garten, for example, to be confronted with office workers stripping off at lunchtime to enjoy the sun and the cooling waters of the fast-flowing river Isar.

flach <> *adj* - **1.** [eben] flat - **2.** [niedrig, dünn - Gebäude, Absätze] low; [- Stein, Schuhe] flat; [- Teller] shallow - **3.** [seicht, oberflächlich] shallow <> *adv*: **~ atmen** to take shallow breaths.

Fläche *(pl -n) die* - **1.** [Gebiet] area - **2.** [geometrisch] plane - **3.** [Seite] surface.

flach|fallen (*perf* ist flachgefallen) *vi* (*unreg*) *fam:* **die Party fällt flach** the party's off; **23 Stellen fallen flach** 23 people are getting the boot.

Flachland *das* (*ohne pl*) lowlands (*pl*).

flackern *vi* to flicker.

Fladen (*pl* -) *der* - **1.** [Brotfladen] *flat, round loaf* - **2.** [Kuchen] pancake - **3.** [Kuhfladen] cowpat.

Flagge (*pl* -n) *die* flag.

flambieren *vt* to flambé.

Flamingo (*pl* -s) *der* flamingo.

flämisch *adj* Flemish.

Flamme (*pl* -n) *die* - **1.** [Feuer] flame - **2.** [zum Kochen] burner.

Flandern *nt* Flanders (*sg*).

Flanell (*pl* -e) *der* flannel.

Flanke (*pl* -n) *die* flank.

Flasche (*pl* -n) *die* - **1.** [Gefäß] bottle; **eine ~ Sekt** a bottle of champagne - **2.** *salopp abw* [Versager] drip.

Flaschen|bier *das* bottled beer.

Flaschen|öffner *der* bottle opener.

Flaschen|zug *der* block and tackle.

flattern (*perf* ist/hat geflattert) *vi* - **1.** [gen] to flutter - **2.** [schlagen]: **mit den Flügeln ~** to flutter its wings.

Flaum *der* down.

flauschig *adj* fleecy.

Flausen *pl:* **~ im Kopf haben** always to be up to some trick or other.

Flaute (*pl* -n) *die* - **1.** [wirtschaftlich] slack period - **2.** [Windstille] calm.

Flechte (*pl* -n) *die* - **1.** [Pflanze] lichen - **2.** [Hautausschlag] eczema.

flechten (*präs* flicht; *prät* flocht; *perf* hat geflochten) *vt* [Haare, Zopf] to plait *Br*, to braid *Am*; [Korb] to weave.

Fleck (*pl* -e ODER -en) *der* - **1.** [Klecks] stain - **2.** [Stelle] patch; **blauer ~** bruise - **3.** [Ort] spot.

fleckenlos ⬦ *adj* spotless ⬦ *adv* spotlessly.

Fleck|entferner *der* stain remover.

fleckig *adj* - **1.** [schmutzig] stained - **2.** [gefleckt - Haut] blotchy; [- Obst] blemished.

Fleder|maus *die* bat.

Flegel (*pl* -) *der* lout.

flegelhaft ⬦ *adj* loutish ⬦ *adv* loutishly.

flehen *vi:* **(um etw) ~** to plead (for sthg).

Fleisch *das* - **1.** [Nahrungsmittel] meat - **2.** [Muskelgewebe, Fruchtfleisch] flesh; **~ fressend** carnivorous.

Fleisch|brühe *die* meat stock.

Fleischer (*pl* -) *der* butcher.

Fleischerei (*pl* -en) *die* butcher's (shop).

Fleischerin (*pl* -nen) *die* butcher.

fleischfressend = Fleisch.

fleischig *adj* fleshy.

Fleisch|wolf *der* mincer *Br*, meat grinder *Am*.

Fleisch|wurst *die* type of cold pork sausage similar to mortadella.

Fleiß *der* diligence; **viel ~ auf etw** (*A*) **verwenden** to put a lot of work into sthg.

fleißig ⬦ *adj* [eifrig, arbeitsam] hardworking ⬦ *adv* - **1.** [eifrig, arbeitsam] hard - **2.** *fam* [oft, viel] a lot; **~ bezahlen** to fork out money.

fletschen *vt:* **die Zähne ~** to bare its teeth.

flicht *präs* ⮞ flechten.

flicken *vt* to mend.

Flicken (*pl* -) *der* patch.

Flickzeug *das* (*ohne pl*) [für Reifen] repair kit; [für Kleidung] sewing kit.

Flieder (*pl* -) *der* lilac.

Fliege (*pl* -n) *die* - **1.** [Insekt] fly - **2.** [Schleife] bow tie.

fliegen (*prät* flog; *perf* hat/ist geflogen) ⬦ *vi* (ist) - **1.** [gen] to fly - **2.** *fam* [stürzen] to fall - **3.** *fam* [entlassen werden] to get fired, to get the sack *Br* - **4.** [attraktiv finden]: **auf jn/ etw ~** to be crazy about sb/sthg ⬦ *vt* (*hat*) to fly.

Fliegen|pilz *der* fly agaric.

Flieger (*pl* -) *der* - **1.** [Pilot] pilot - **2.** *fam* [Flugzeug] plane.

Fliegerin (*pl* -nen) *die* pilot.

fliehen (*prät* floh; *perf* hat/ist geflohen) ⬦ *vi* (ist): **aus dem Gefängnis ~** to escape from jail; **vor jm/etw ~** to flee from sb/sthg ⬦ *vt* (*hat*) to shun.

Fliese (*pl* -n) *die* tile.

Fließband (*pl* -bänder) *das* conveyor belt; **am ~ arbeiten** to be an assembly-line ODER a production-line worker.

fließen (*prät* floss; *perf* ist geflossen) *vi* to flow; **das Blut fließt aus der Wunde** the blood is flowing from the wound.

fließend ⬦ *adj* - **1.** [perfekt] fluent - **2.** [ungenau, unscharf - Grenzen, Übergang] fluid - **3.** [Verkehr, Material] flowing; [Wasser] running ⬦ *adv* [sprechen] fluently.

flimmern *vi* - **1.** [Luft, Wasser, Oberflächen] to shimmer - **2.** [Fernsehbild] to flicker.

flink ⬦ *adj* - **1.** [geschickt] nimble - **2.** [schnell] quick ⬦ *adv* - **1.** [geschickt] nimbly - **2.** [schnell] quickly.

Flinte (*pl* -n) *die* shotgun.

flirten ['flœrtn] *vi:* **(mit jm) ~** to flirt (with sb).

Flitterwochen *pl* honeymoon (*sg*); **in die ~ fahren** to go on honeymoon.

flitzen (*perf* ist geflitzt) *vi fam* [Person, Wagen] to whizz.

flocht *prät* ⮞ flechten.

Flocke (*pl* -n) *die* [von Schnee, Getreide] flake; [von Staub] ball; [von Schaum] blob.

flog *prät* ⮞ fliegen.

floh *prät* ⊳ fliehen.

Floh *(pl Flöhe) der* flea.

Floh|markt *der* flea market.

Flora *die* flora.

florieren *vi* to flourish.

Floskel *(pl -n) die* cliché.

floss *prät* ⊳ fließen.

Floß *(pl Flöße) das* raft.

Flosse *(pl -n) die* - 1. [von Fisch, Rückenflosse von Delfin] fin; [Bauchflosse von Delfin und Robbe] flipper - 2. [Schwimmflosse] flipper - 3. *salopp abw* [Hand] paw.

Flöte *(pl -n) die* [Querflöte] flute; [Blockflöte] recorder.

flöten ⟨⟩ *vi* - 1. [Flöte spielen] to play the flute/recorder - 2. [pfeifen - Person] to whistle - 3. *fam abw* [einschmeichelnd sprechen] to speak in honeyed tones ⟨⟩ *vt* - 1. [spielen] to play on the flute/recorder - 2. [pfeifen] to whistle - 3. *fam abw* [einschmeichelnd sagen]: **sie flötete mir Schmeicheleien ins Ohr** she murmured flattering remarks into my ear.

flott ⟨⟩ *adj* - 1. [schick] smart, stylish - 2. [lebhaft, schnell - Musik, Person] lively; [- Service] speedy; [- Auto] fast - 3. [fahrtüchtig - Wagen] roadworthy; [- Kahn] seaworthy ⟨⟩ *adv* - 1. [schnell, lebhaft - arbeiten, laufen] quickly; [- tanzen, spielen] in a lively manner; **mach ~!** make it snappy! - 2. [schick] smartly.

Flotte *(pl -n) die* fleet.

Fluch *(pl Flüche) der* - 1. [Schimpfwort] curse - 2. *(ohne pl)* [Verwünschung] curse.

fluchen *vi* to swear.

Flucht *die* [aus dem Gefängnis] escape; **sie sind auf der ~** they are fleeing; **die ~ ergreifen** to take flight.

fluchtartig ⟨⟩ *adj* hurried ⟨⟩ *adv* hurriedly.

flüchten *(perf hat/ist geflüchtet) vi (ist)* to flee; **vor jm/etw ~** to flee from sb/sthg.
➨ **sich flüchten** *ref (hat)*: **sich in etw (A) ~** to take refuge in sthg.

flüchtig ⟨⟩ *adj* - 1. [kurz] fleeting; [Gruß, Abschied] brief - 2. [ungenau - Eindruck] superficial; [- Arbeit] hurried - 3. [flüchtend - Gefangene] escaped; [- Mörder] wanted ⟨⟩ *adv* - 1. [ungenau] superficially; [arbeiten] hurriedly - 2. [kurz] briefly.

Flüchtigkeits|fehler *der* careless mistake.

Flüchtling *(pl -e) der* refugee.

Flucht|weg *der* escape route.

Flug *(pl Flüge) der* of flight.

Flug|bahn *die* [von Rakete] trajectory.

Flug|blatt *das* leaflet.

Flügel *(pl -) der* - 1. [gen] wing - 2. [Musikinstrument] grand piano.

Flug|gast *der* passenger *(on plane)*.

flügge *adj* [Vogeljunge] fully-fledged;

~ **werden** [Kind] to be ready to leave the nest.

Flug|gesellschaft *die* airline.

Flug|hafen *der* airport.

Flug|lotse *der* air traffic controller.

Flug|platz *der* airfield.

Flug|verkehr *der* air traffic.

Flug|zeug *das* aeroplane, plane, airplane *Am*; **mit dem ~ fliegen** to fly.

Flugzeug|träger *der* aircraft carrier.

Flunder *(pl -n) die* flounder.

flunkern *vi* to tell stories.

Fluor *das* fluorine.

Flur *(pl -e ODER -en)* ⟨⟩ *der (pl Flure)* [Korridor] corridor; [am Eingang] hallway ⟨⟩ *die (pl Fluren)* [Gelände] fields *(pl)*.

Fluss *(pl Flüsse) der* - 1. [Wasserlauf] river - 2. [Bewegung] flow.

flussabwärts *adv* downstream.

flussaufwärts *adv* upstream.

Fluss|bett *das* river bed.

flüssig ⟨⟩ *adj* - 1. [nicht fest] liquid; [Metall] molten; [Butter] melted - 2. [Stil, Verkehr] flowing; [Ausdruck] fluent - 3. [zahlungsfähig, verfügbar]: ~ **sein** to be solvent; **nicht ~ sein** to be short of money ⟨⟩ *adv* [sprechen] fluently.

Flüssigkeit *(pl -en) die* liquid.

Fluss|lauf *der* course *(of a river)*.

Fluss|pferd *das* hippopotamus.

flüstern ⟨⟩ *vi* to whisper ⟨⟩ *vt* to whisper; **jm etw ins Ohr ~** to whisper sthg into sb's ear; **jm was ~** *fam fig* to tell sb a thing or two.

Flut *(pl -en) die* - 1. *(ohne pl)* [Ansteigen des Wasserstandes] tide *(incoming)*; **die ~ kommt** the tide is coming in; **bei ~** at high tide; **eine ~ von etw** *fig* a flood of sthg - 2. *geh* [Wassermasse] waters *(pl)*.

Flut|licht *das (ohne pl)*: **bei ~ spielen** to play under floodlights.

focht *prät* ⊳ fechten.

Fohlen *(pl -) das* foal.

Föhn *(pl -e) der* - 1. [Wind] *hot, dry wind typical of the Alps* - 2. [Haartrockner] hairdryer.

föhnen *vt*: **jm/sich die Haare ~** [zum Trocknen] to dry sb's/one's hair; **jm die Haare ~** [zum Frisieren] to blow-dry sb's hair.

Folge *(pl -n) die* - 1. [Konsequenz] consequence; **etw zur ~ haben** to result in sthg - 2. [Fortsetzung] episode - 3. [Serie] succession - 4. *amt* [Befolgung]: **jm/einem Befehl ~ leisten** to obey sb/an order; **einer Einladung ~ leisten** to accept an invitation.

folgen *(perf ist gefolgt) vi* - 1. [nachfolgen, verstehen, sich richten nach]: **jm/einer Sache ~** to follow sb/sthg - 2. [sich anschließen]: **auf etw (A) ~** to follow sthg; **wie folgt** as follows - 3. [gehorchen]: **(jm/einer Sache) ~** to obey (sb/sthg) - 4. [sich logisch ergeben]: **aus etw ~** to follow from sthg.

folgend *adj* following. ➤ **Folgende** *das:* **das Folgende** the following. ➤ **Folgendes** *nt* the following.

folgendermaßen *adv* as follows.

folgern *vt:* **aus etw ~, dass ...** to conclude from sthg that ...

Folgerung *(pl -en) die* conclusion.

folglich *adv* consequently.

folgsam ◇ *adj* obedient ◇ *adv* obediently.

Folie ['fo:ljə] *(pl -n) die* - **1.** [Verpackung - aus Plastik] film; [- aus Metall] foil - **2.** [für Overheadprojektor] transparency.

Folklore *die* - **1.** [Musik] folk music - **2.** [Brauchtum] folklore.

folkloristisch *adj* folkloric; [Musik] folk.

Folter *(pl -n) die* torture; **jn auf die ~ spannen** *fig* to keep sb on tenterhooks.

foltern *vt* to torture.

Fön® *(pl -e) der* = Föhn.

fönen = föhnen.

Fonetik, Phonetik *die (ohne pl)* phonetics.

fonetisch, phonetisch ◇ *adj* phonetic ◇ *adv* phonetically.

Fontäne *(pl -n) die* - **1.** [von Wasser] jet - **2.** [Springbrunnen] fountain.

Förderkurs *der* SCHULE extra classes *(pl)*.

fordern *vt* - **1.** [verlangen] to demand - **2.** [beanspruchen] to make demands on.

fördern *vt* - **1.** [unterstützen] to support; [Handel, Frieden] to promote; [Begabung] to foster - **2.** [Bodenschätze] to mine.

Forderung *(pl -en) die* - **1.** [Verlangen] demand - **2.** [finanzieller Anspruch] claim.

Förderung *(pl -en) die* - **1.** [Unterstützung] support; [von Handel, Frieden] promotion; [von Begabung] fostering - **2.** [von Bodenschätzen] mining.

Forelle *(pl -n) die* trout.

Form *(pl -en) die* - **1.** [gen] form; **in ~ einer Sache** in the form of sthg; **in ~ sein** to be in good form; **sich/jn in ~ bringen** to get o.s./sb into shape; **die ~ wahren** to observe the proprieties - **2.** [Gestalt] shape - **3.** [für Kuchen] baking tin.

formal ◇ *adj* formal ◇ *adv* formally.

Formalität *(pl -en) die* formality.

Format *(pl -e) das* - **1.** [Größe] size; **im ~ DIN A 3** in A3 format - **2.** [Niveau - von Person] stature; **die Frau hat ~** she's a woman of stature.

formatieren *vt* EDV to format.

Formation *(pl -en) die* - **1.** [gen] formation - **2.** [Gruppe] group.

Formel *(pl -n) die* formula; **~ 1** SPORT Formula One.

formell ◇ *adj* formal ◇ *adv* formally.

formen *vt* - **1.** [Material] to shape - **2.** [Person] to mould. ➤ **sich formen** *ref* [sich bilden] to take shape.

formieren *vt* to form. ➤ **sich formieren** *ref* [sich aufstellen] to get into formation; [Organisation] to form.

förmlich ◇ *adj* formal ◇ *adv* - **1.** [gen] formally - **2.** [regelrecht] really.

formlos ◇ *adj* - **1.** [nicht formal] informal - **2.** [amorph] shapeless - **3.** [ungezwungen] casual ◇ *adv* - **1.** [nicht formal] informally - **2.** [ungezwungen] casually.

Formular *(pl -e) das* form.

formulieren *vt* to formulate.

Formulierung *(pl -en) die* - **1.** [Formulieren] formulation - **2.** [Textstelle] wording.

forsch ◇ *adj* self-confident ◇ *adv* self-confidently.

forschen *vi* - **1.** [wissenschaftlich untersuchen] to do research - **2.** [ermitteln]: **in js Augen ~** to search sb's eyes; **nach jm/etw ~** to search for sb/sthg.

Forscher, in *(mpl -; fpl -nen) der, die* researcher.

Forschung *(pl -en) die* research; **~en** research.

Förster, in *(mpl -; fpl -nen) der, die* forest ranger.

fort *adv* [weg] away; **~ sein** to be gone. ➤ **und so fort**

fortbestehen *vi (unreg)* to continue; [trotz Bedrohung] to continue to exist.

fortbewegen *vt* to move. ➤ **sich fortbewegen** *ref* to move.

Fortbildung *(pl -en) die* - **1.** [Weiterbildung] training; **~ zur Bekämpfung der Arbeitslosigkeit** lifelong learning as a means of combatting unemployment - **2.** [Kurs] training course.

fortfahren *(perf hat/ist fortgefahren) (unreg)* ◇ *vi* - **1.** *(ist)* [wegfahren] to leave - **2.** [nicht aufhören] to continue ◇ *vt (hat)* [wegfahren] to take away.

fortführen *vt* - **1.** [weitermachen] to carry on - **2.** [fortbringen] to take away.

fortgehen *(perf ist fortgegangen) vi (unreg)* - **1.** [weggehen] to leave - **2.** [weitergehen] to continue.

fortgeschritten ◇ *pp* ⬑ **fortschreiten** ◇ *adj* advanced; **zu ~er Stunde** at a late hour.

Fortgeschrittene *(pl -n) der, die* advanced student.

fortkommen *(perf ist fortgekommen) vi (unreg)* - **1.** [wegkommen] to get away - **2.** [fortgebracht werden] to be taken away - **3.** [abhanden kommen] to disappear.

fortlaufend *adv* [ständig] continually; [nummerieren] consecutively.

fortpflanzen ➤ **sich fortpflanzen** *ref* - **1.** [sich reproduzieren] to reproduce - **2.** [sich ausbreiten] to spread.

Fortpflanzung *die* reproduction.

fort|schreiten (*perf* ist fortgeschritten) *vi* (*unreg*) to progress; [Zeit] to move on; [Krankheit, Prozess] to advance.

Fort|schritt *der* progress (*U*); ~e progress; ~e machen to make progress.

fortschrittlich <> *adj* progressive <> *adv* progressively.

fort|setzen *vt* to continue.

Fortsetzung (*pl* -en) *die* continuation; [von Film] sequel.

Fossil (*pl* -ien) *das* fossil.

Foto, Photo (*pl* -s) *das* photo; ein ~ machen to take a photo.

Fotoapparat *der* camera.

Fotograf (*pl* -en) *der* photographer.

Fotograf

Fotograf is a false friend because it refers to the person holding the camera – the "photographer" – rather than the photo itself. (N.B. a "female photographer" is eine Fotografin – not eine Fotográfin!) The English word "photograph" is usually translated by Foto(grafie) or Aufnahme. So to ask someone if you can take their photograph, you might say Darf ich ein Foto von dir machen?

Fotografie (*pl* -n) *die* - **1.** [Fotografieren] photography - **2.** [Foto] photograph.

fotografieren <> *vt* to photograph <> *vi* to take photographs.

Fotografin (*pl* -nen) *die* photographer.

Fotokopie *die* photocopy.

fotokopieren <> *vt* to photocopy <> *vi* to make photocopies.

Fotomodell *das* (photographic) model.

Fotozelle, Photozelle *die* photoelectric cell, photocell.

Fötus (*pl* -se ODER -ten) *der* foetus.

foulen ['faulən] SPORT <> *vt* to foul <> *vi* to commit a foul.

FPÖ [ɛf'peː'øː] (*abk für* Freiheitliche Partei Österreichs) *die* Austrian Freedom Party.

Fr. - **1.** (*abk für* Frau) [verheiratet] Mrs; [unverheiratet] Ms, Miss - **2.** (*abk für* Freitag) Fri.

Fracht (*pl* -en) *die* freight; [mit Schiff] cargo.

Frachter (*pl* -) *der* freighter.

Frachtgut *das* freight.

Frack (*pl* Fräcke) *der* tails (*pl*); im ~ in tails.

Frage (*pl* -n) *die* question; eine rhetorische ~ a rhetorical question; jm ~n stellen to ask sb questions; in diesen ~n weiß er am besten Bescheid he knows most about these issues ODER matters; das kommt nicht in ~ that's out of the question; etw in ~ stellen [bezweifeln] to question sthg; [gefährden] to jeopardize sthg.

Fragebogen *der* questionnaire.

fragen <> *vt* to ask; jn um Rat ~ to ask sb for advice; jn nach jm/etw ~ to ask sb about sb/sthg; jn nach seinem Namen/der Uhrzeit ~ to ask sb his name/the time <> *vi* to ask; nach jm ~ - [sich erkundigen] to ask about sb; [Treffen] to ask to see sb; der Polizist fragte nach dem genauen Hergang the policeman asked for a precise description of events; da fragst du noch! you need to ASK? ◆ sich fragen *ref* to wonder; ich frage mich, ob ... I wonder if ODER whether ...; es fragt sich noch, ob ... it is debatable whether ...

Fragewort (*pl* -wörter) *das* interrogative pronoun.

Fragezeichen *das* question mark.

fraglich *adj* - **1.** [zweifelhaft]: es ist ~, ob ... it is doubtful whether ... - **2.** [in Frage kommend] in question.

fragwürdig *adj* dubious.

Fraktion [frakˈtsi̯oːn] (*pl* -en) *die* - **1.** [im Parlament] (parliamentary) party - **2.** [innerhalb einer Partei] faction.

Fraktion

Care is required with the German word Fraktion, a false friend which has come to mean a "political group". So der Fraktionsvorsitzende der Grünen would be the equivalent of "the leader of the parliamentary Green Party".
The English word "fraction", meaning a small amount or a part of a whole, corresponds to the German Bruchteil. For example, the phrase "It was all over in a fraction of a second" can be translated as Im Bruchteil einer Sekunde war alles vorbei.

Franc [frãː] (*pl* -s ODER -) *der* franc.

Franken (*pl* -) <> *nt* Franconia <> *der* Swiss franc.

Frankfurt *nt:* ~ am Main/an der Oder Frankfurt (am Main)/an der Oder.

frankieren *vt* to stamp.

fränkisch *adj* - **1.** [aus Franken] Franconian - **2.** HIST [westgermanisch] Frankish.

Frankreich *nt* France.

Franse (*pl* -n) *die* strand; ein Schal mit ~n a scarf with a fringe.

Franziskaner, in (*mpl* -; *fpl* -nen) *der, die* Franciscan.

Franzose (*pl* -n) *der* Frenchman; die ~n the French.

Französin (*pl* -nen) *die* Frenchwoman.

französisch *adj* French; *siehe auch* englisch.

Französisch(e) *das* French; *siehe auch* Englisch(e).

fraß *prät* ▷ fressen.

Fratze (*pl* -n) *die* [Grimasse] grotesque face; [aus Schmerz, Widerwille] grimace.

Frau (*pl* -en) *die* - **1.** [Erwachsene] woman - **2.** [Gattin] wife - **3.** [als Anrede - verheiratet] Mrs; [- neutral] Ms; ~ **Doktor** Doctor.

Frauen|arzt, ärztin *der, die* gynaecologist.

frauenfeindlich <> *adj* misogynistic <> *adv* in a misogynistic way.

fraulich <> *adj* feminine <> *adv* in a feminine way.

frdl. ⊳ freundlich.

frech <> *adj* - **1.** [gen] cheeky; [unartig] naughty; [Lüge] barefaced - **2.** [Minirock] saucy <> *adv* [gen] cheekily; [unartig] naughtily.

Frechheit (*pl* -en) *die* - **1.** [freches Verhalten] cheek - **2.** [freche Bemerkung] cheeky remark.

frei <> *adj* - **1.** [gen] free; ~ **von etw** free of sthg; **ist dieser Stuhl** ~? is this seat free?; **drei Wochen** ~ **haben** to have three weeks off; **bei der Reaktion wird Energie** ~ energy is released during the reaction - **2.** [Mitarbeiter] freelance - **3.** [nackt] bare; **machen Sie sich bitte** ~ would you mind undressing? <> *adv* - **1.** [gen] freely; ~ **lebende Tiere** animals living in the wild; ~ **sprechen** to speak without notes - **2.** [gratis] for free; **etw** ~ **Haus liefern** to deliver sthg free. ◆ **im Freien** *adv* in the open air.

Frei|bad *das* open-air swimming pool.

Freiberufler, in (*mpl* -; *fpl* -nen) *der, die* - **1.** [Mitarbeiter] freelancer - **2.** [Arzt, Anwalt] doctor/lawyer in private practice.

freiberuflich <> *adj* [Journalist, Übersetzer, Fotograf] freelance; **-er Mitarbeiter** freelancer <> *adv:* ~ **tätig sein** to be self-employed.

Frei|bier *das* free beer.

frei|geben (*unreg*) <> *vt* - **1.** [gen] to release - **2.** [genehmigen - Film] to pass as fit for public viewing; [- Straße, Brücke] to open; **jm einen Tag** ~ to give sb a day off <> *vi* [Freizeit genehmigen]: **jm** ~ to give sb time off.

freigebig *adj* generous.

Freiheit (*pl* -en) *die* - **1.** [Ungebundenheit] freedom; **ein Tier in die** ~ **entlassen** to set an animal free - **2.** [Privileg] liberty.

Freiheits|strafe *die* prison sentence.

freiheraus *adv* freely.

Frei|karte *die* free ticket.

Freikörperkultur *die* naturism.

frei|lassen *vt* (*unreg*) [Gefangene] to release; [Tier] to set free.

freilich *adv* - **1.** [jedoch] admittedly - **2.** *Süddt* [sicher] of course.

Freilicht|bühne *die* open-air theatre.

frei|machen <> *vt* - **1.** [Brief] to stamp - **2.** [ausziehen]: **den Oberkörper** ~ to take one's top off, to strip to the waist <> *vi* to

take time off. ◆ **sich freimachen** *ref* - **1.** *fam* [als Urlaub] to take time off - **2.** [sich ausziehen] to take one's clothes off.

freimütig <> *adj* frank <> *adv* frankly.

frei|sprechen *vt* (*unreg*) to acquit.

frei|stehen *vi* (*unreg*) - **1.** [Wohnung] to stand ODER be empty - **2.** [Entscheidung]: **es steht ihm frei, zu gehen oder zu bleiben** it's up to him whether he stays or goes.

frei|stellen *vt* - **1.** [entbinden]: **jn von etw** ~ to exempt sb from sthg - **2.** [überlassen]: **jm etw** ~ to leave sthg up to sb.

Frei|stoß *der* SPORT free kick.

Frei|stunde *die* free period.

Freitag (*pl* -e) *der* Friday; *siehe auch* Samstag.

freitags *adv* on Fridays; *siehe auch* samstags.

freiwillig <> *adj* voluntary <> *adv* voluntarily.

Freiwillige (*pl* -n) *der, die* volunteer.

Frei|zeichen *das* dial tone.

Frei|zeit *die* - **1.** (*ohne pl*) [Mußezeit] free time - **2.** [Gruppenreise - für Kinder] holiday camp.

freizügig <> *adj* - **1.** [gewagt] daring - **2.** [großzügig] generous - **3.** [frei] liberal <> *adv* - **1.** [gewagt] daringly - **2.** [großzügig] generously - **3.** [frei] liberally.

fremd *adj* - **1.** [ausländisch] foreign - **2.** [nicht einem selbst gehörend]: **~e Angelegenheiten** other people's business; **in einer ~en Wohnung übernachten** to spend the night in someone else's flat - **3.** [unvertraut] strange; **er ist ~ in dieser Stadt** he is a stranger to this town.

fremdartig *adj* strange.

Fremde (*pl* -n) <> *der, die* stranger <> *die* (*ohne plural*) foreign parts (*pl*).

Fremden|führer, in *der, die* tourist guide.

Fremden|hass *der* xenophobia.

Fremden|verkehr *der* tourism.

Fremdenverkehrs|büro *das* tourist information office.

Fremden|zimmer *das* (guest) room.

Fremd|körper *der* foreign body.

Fremd|sprache *die* foreign language.

fremdsprachig *adj* in a foreign language.

Fremd|wort (*pl* -wörter) *das* foreign word.

Frequenz (*pl* -en) *die* - **1.** PHYS frequency - **2.** MED rate.

fressen (*präs* frisst; *prät* fraß; *perf* hat gefressen) <> *vt* - **1.** [beim Tier] to eat - **2.** *fam abw* [essen] to guzzle, to scoff *Br* - **3.** *fam* [Strom, Geld] to eat up - **4.** *RW:* **jn gefressen haben** *fam* not to be able to stand sb, to hate sb's guts <> *vi* - **1.** [Tier] to feed; **der Vogel frisst einem aus der Hand** the bird will eat out of your hand - **2.** *salopp abw* [Mensch] to stuff one's face - 3. [zehren, nagen]: **an etw** (D) ~ to eat away at sthg.

Freude (*pl* -n) *die* joy; **es ist mir eine ~ zu kommen** it would be a pleasure for me to come; **jm die ~ an etw verderben** to spoil sb's enjoyment of sthg; **an etw ~ haben** to take pleasure in sthg; **jm eine ~ machen** to make sb happy.

freudig ◇ *adj* - 1. [Begrüßung] joyful - 2. [Überraschung] pleasant ◇ *adv* - 1. [begrüßen] joyfully - 2. [überrascht] pleasantly.

freuen *vt* to please. ◆ **sich freuen** *ref* to be pleased; **es freut mich, dass ...** I'm pleased that ...; **freut mich sehr!** pleased to meet you!; **sich an etw** (D) ~ to get a lot of pleasure from sthg; **sich über etw** (A) ~ to be pleased about sthg; **sich auf etw** (A) ~ to be looking forward to sthg.

Freund (*pl* -e) *der* - 1. [guter Bekannter] friend - 2. [Liebhaber] boyfriend - 3. [Anhänger] lover; **ein ~ klassischer Musik** a classical music lover.

Freundin (*pl* -nen) *die* - 1. [gute Bekannte] friend - 2. [Geliebte] girlfriend.

freundlich ◇ *adj* - 1. [Mensch, Geste, Rat] friendly; **danke für die ~e Begrüßung** thank you for your kind welcome; **bist du so ~ und begleitest mich?** would you be so kind as to accompany me? - 2. [Umgebung, Stimmung] nice ◇ *adv* [nett] in a friendly way; **jm ~ gesinnt sein** to be well-disposed towards sb.

Freundlichkeit (*pl* -en) *die* - 1. (*ohne pl*) [nette Art] friendliness - 2. [Gefälligkeit] favour.

Freundschaft (*pl* -en) *die* friendship; **mit jm ~ schließen** to make friends with sb.

freundschaftlich ◇ *adj* friendly ◇ *adv* in a friendly way; **jm ~ verbunden sein** to be friends with sb.

Frieden, Friede *der* peace; **jn in ~ lassen** to leave sb in peace; **mit jm ~ schließen** to make peace with sb.

Friedens|bewegung *die* peace movement.

Friedens|vertrag *der* peace treaty.

Fried|hof *der* cemetery.

friedlich ◇ *adj* peaceful ◇ *adv* peacefully.

frieren (*prät* fror; *perf* hat/ist gefroren) *vi* - 1. (*hat*) [an Kälte leiden] to be cold; **es friert ihn** he is cold; **an den Füßen ~** to have cold feet; **es friert mich an den Händen** my hands are cold - 2. (*hat*) [sehr kalt sein]: **es friert** it is freezing - 3. (*ist*) [gefrieren] to freeze.

Frikadelle (*pl* -n) *die* rissole.

frisch ◇ *adj* - 1. [gen] fresh; [Verletzung] recent; [Farbe] wet; [Kraft] renewed; **diese Erinnerung ist noch ~** it's still fresh in my memory - 2. [sauber] clean; **sich ~ machen** to freshen up - 3. [kühl - unangenehm] chilly; [- angenehm] cool - 4. [in Form] refreshed;

~ **und munter sein** to be bright and cheery ◇ *adv* [gewaschen, zubereitet] freshly; [renoviert] newly; **das Brot kommt ~ vom Bäcker** the bread is fresh from the baker's; **'~ gestrichen'** 'wet paint'.

Frische *die* - 1. [gen] freshness; **in alter ~** as fresh as ever - 2. [Kühle - unangenehm] chilliness; [- angenehm] coolness.

Frisch|käse *der* soft cream cheese.

Friseur, Frisör, in [fri'zøːɐ̯, rɪn] (*mpl* -e; *fpl* -nen) *der, die* hairdresser.

Friseuse, Frisöse [fri'zøːzə] (*pl* -n) *die* hairdresser.

frisieren *vt* - 1. [Person]: **jn ~** to do sb's hair; **sie ist schick frisiert** she has a trendy hairstyle - 2. *fam* [Zahlen] to fiddle; **die Bilanzen ~** to cook the books - 3. *fam* AUTO to soup up. ◆ **sich frisieren** *ref* [sich kämmen] to do one's hair.

Frisör, in = Friseur.

Frisöse = Friseuse.

frisst *präs* ➭ fressen.

Frist (*pl* -en) *die*: **jm eine ~ von einer Woche geben** to give sb a week; **bis zur Prüfung bleibt dir noch eine ~ von drei Tagen** you still have three days to go until the exam; **die ~ wird nicht verlängert** the deadline is not being extended; **eine ~ einhalten** to meet a deadline; **innerhalb kürzester ~** in a very short space of time.

fristlos ◇ *adj* immediate ◇ *adv* without notice, with immediate effect.

Frisur (*pl* -en) *die* hairstyle.

froh *adj* - 1. [vergnügt] happy - 2. [erleichtert] glad; **über etw** (A) ~ **sein** to be pleased ODER glad about sthg - 3. [Nachricht] good.

fröhlich ◇ *adj* - 1. [Mensch, Lachen] cheerful - 2. [Fest] jolly ◇ *adv* [vergnügt] cheerfully.

Fröhlichkeit *die* cheerfulness.

fromm (*kompar* frommer ODER frömmer; *superl* frommste ODER frömmste) *adj* - 1. [Mensch, Christ] devout; [Worte, Einstellung] pious - 2. [heuchlerisch] sanctimonious, pious.

Fronleichnam (*ohne Artikel*) Corpus Christi.

Front (*pl* -en) *die* front.

frontal ◇ *adj* - 1. [Zusammenstoß] head-on - 2. [Angriff, Darstellung] frontal ◇ *adv* - 1. [von vorn] head-on - 2. [angreifen] from the front.

fror *prät* ➭ frieren.

Frosch (*pl* Frösche) *der* frog.

Frost (*pl* Fröste) *der* frost.

frösteln *vi* to shiver.

frostig ◇ *adj* eigtl & fig frosty ◇ *adv* frostily.

Frottee [frɔ'teː] (*pl* -s) *der* ODER *das* towelling.

Frucht (*pl* Früchte) *die* fruit; **Früchte** fruit (*U*).

fruchtbar *adj* - **1.** [Erde, Lebewesen] fertile - **2.** [Gespräch, Idee] fruitful.

Fruchtbarkeit *die* fertility.

fruchtig *adj* fruity.

Frucht|saft *der* fruit juice.

früh <> *adj* early; **am ~en Morgen/Abend** early in the morning/evening; [Tat] premature <> *adv* early; **~ am Abend/Morgen** early in the evening/morning; **er ist ~ gestorben** he died young; **gestern/heute/morgen ~** yesterday/this/tomorrow morning; **etw zu ~ verkaufen** to sell sthg too soon.

früher <> *adv* formerly <> *adj* former; **in ~en Zeiten** in the past.

frühestens *adv* at the earliest.

Früh|geburt *die* - **1.** [Geburt] premature birth; **eine ~ haben** to give birth prematurely - **2.** [Baby] premature baby.

Früh|jahr *das* spring; **im ~** in spring.

Frühling (*pl* -e) *der* spring; **im ~** in spring.

frühreif *adj* [Kind] precocious.

Früh|rentner, in *der, die* person who has taken early retirement.

Früh|stück *das* breakfast; **nach dem ~** after breakfast; **zum ~** for breakfast.

frühstücken <> *vi* to have breakfast <> *vt* to have for breakfast.

frustrieren *vt* to frustrate.

Fuchs [fʊks] (*pl* Füchse) *der* - **1.** [Tier] fox - **2.** [Pelz] fox fur - **3.** *fam* [Mensch]: **ein schlauer ~** a cunning devil.

Fuchsie ['fʊksjə] (*pl* -n) *die* fuchsia.

Füchsin ['fʏksɪn] (*pl* -nen) *die* vixen.

fuchteln *vi*: **mit etw ~** to wave sthg around.

Fuge (*pl* -n) *die* - **1.** [Ritze] gap - **2.** MUS fugue.

fügen *vt* [einfügen]: **etw an etw** (*A*) **~** to join sthg to sthg; **etw in etw** (*A*) **~** to fit sthg into sthg; **fest gefügt** firmly established. <> **sich fügen** *ref* - **1.** [hineinpassen] to fit - **2.** [sich unterordnen]: **sich einer Sache** (*D*) **~** to obey sthg.

fühlbar <> *adj* noticeable <> *adv* noticeably.

fühlen <> *vt* to feel <> *vi* to feel; **nach etw ~** to feel for sthg. <> **sich fühlen** *ref* to feel; **sich krank ~** to feel ill.

Fühler (*pl* -) *der* feeler, antenna.

fuhr *prät* <> fahren.

Fuhre (*pl* -n) *die* load; [von Taxi] fare.

führen <> *vt* - **1.** [Person, Tier] to lead; **jn zu einem Versteck ~** to show ODER lead sb to a hiding-place - **2.** [leiten - Firma, Hotel] to run, to manage; [- Partei] to lead; [- Haushalt] to run; [- Truppen] to command; [- Krieg, Kampf] to wage; **den Vorsitz ~** to be the chairperson - **3.** [durchführen - Gespräch] to hold; **ein Ferngespräch ~** to make a long-distance call; **das Protokoll ~** to take the mi-

nutes; **ein langes Gespräch geführt haben** to have had a long conversation; **einen Prozess gegen jn ~** to take legal action against sb - **4.** [Gegenstand]: **etw mit sich** ODER **bei sich ~** to carry sthg - **5.** [Ware] to stock - **6.** [Liste] to keep; **sie wird als Mitglied geführt** she is listed as a member - **7.** [Touristen] to show around - **8.** [Name, Titel] to have - **9.** [bewegen] to handle <> *vi* - **1.** SPORT to lead; **knapp ~** to be just in the lead; **mit 1:0 ~** to be leading 1-0, to be 1-0 up - **2.** [Straße] to lead - **3.** [zu einem Ergebnis]: **zu etw ~** to lead to sthg; **zum Erfolg ~** to bring success; **das führt zu nichts** that won't get us anywhere. <> **sich führen** *ref* to behave.

führend *adj* leading.

Führer, in (*mpl* -/ *fpl* -nen) *der, die* - **1.** [Anführer] leader; **der ~** [Hitler] the Führer - **2.** [Fremdenführer, Buch] guide.

Führer|schein *der* driving licence *Br*, driver's license *Am*.

Führung (*pl* -en) *die* - **1.** [das Führen - von Firma, Hotel] running, management; [- von Truppen] command; [- von Partei] leadership; [- von Haushalt] running; **unter (der) ~ von** under the direction of - **2.** [Personen - von Firma] management; [- von Partei] leadership - **3.** [führende Stellung] lead; **in ~ liegen** to be in the lead ODER ahead; **in ~ gehen** to take the lead - **4.** [Besichtigung] guided tour - **5.** [Verhalten]: **wegen guter ~** on the grounds of good conduct - **6.** [Handhabung, Steuerung] operation.

Führungs|zeugnis *das*: **polizeiliches ~** *police certificate stating that holder has no criminal record.*

Fülle *die* (*ohne pl*) [Menge, Übermaß] abundance.

füllen *vt* - **1.** [gen] to fill; [Geflügel, Tomate] to stuff - **2.** [hineingeben]: **etw in etw** (*A*) **~** to put sthg into sthg; **den Saft in Flaschen ~** to fill the bottles with juice. <> **sich füllen** *ref* [voll werden]: **sich mit etw ~** to fill up with sthg.

Füller (*pl* -) *der* fountain pen.

Füllfeder|halter *der* fountain pen.

füllig *adj* plump.

Füllung (*pl* -en) *die* [von Geflügel, Tomate] stuffing; [von Gebäck, in Zahn] filling.

fummeln *vi* - **1.** *fam* [tasten]: **nach etw ~** to fumble about for sthg; **an etw** (*D*) **~** to fumble around with sthg - **2.** *salopp* [sexuell berühren] to make out.

Fund (*pl* -e) *der* - **1.** [Objekt] find - **2.** [Handlung] discovery.

Fundament (*pl* -e) *das* - **1.** [Grundmauer] foundations (*pl*); **bis auf die ~e abgerissen** to be razed to the ground - **2.** [Grundlage] basis.

Fund|büro *das* lost property office *Br*, lost-and-found office *Am*.

Fund|grube *die* treasure trove.

fundiert adj [Wissen, Firma] sound; [Kritik, Überlegungen] well-founded; [Vortrag, Bericht] well-reasoned.

fündig adj: ~ **werden** to make a find.

Fund|sache die: ~n lost property (U).

fünf num five; siehe auch Sechs.

Fünf (pl -en) die - 1. [Zahl] five - 2. [Schulnote] ≃ E, mark of 5 on a scale from 1 to 6; siehe auch Sechs.

fünffach <> adj: die ~e **Menge** five times as much; in ~er **Größe** five times as big; der ~e **Gewinner** the five-times winner <> adv [auffordern] five times; ~ **gelagert** with five bearings.

fünfhundert num five hundred.

Fünf|kampf der pentathlon.

fünfmal adv five times.

fünftausend num five thousand.

fünfte num fifth; siehe auch sechste.

Fünfte (pl -n) der, die, das fifth; siehe auch Sechste.

fünftel adj (unver) fifth; siehe auch sechstel.

Fünftel (pl -) das fifth; siehe auch Sechstel.

fünfzehn num fifteen; siehe auch sechs.

Fünfzehn (pl -en) die fifteen; siehe auch Sechs.

fünfzig num fifty; siehe auch sechs.

Fünfzig die fifty; siehe auch sechs.

Fünfzigerjahre, fünfziger Jahre pl: die ~ the fifties.

Funk der [Übermittlung] radio.

Funke (pl -n), **Funken** (pl -) der spark; **keinen ~n von etw haben** ODER **besitzen** not to have a scrap of sthg.

funkeln vi [Licht] to sparkle; [Stern] to twinkle; [Gold] to glitter.

funken <> vt to radio <> vi: **bei ihm hat es endlich gefunkt** fam [er versteht] he finally got it; **bei den beiden hat es gefunkt** fam [sie sind verliebt] they've fallen for each other.

Funken = Funke.

Funk|gerät das radio set; [tragbar] walkie-talkie.

Funk|haus das broadcasting centre.

Funktion [fʊnk'tsjoːn] (pl -en) die - 1. MATH [Aufgabe] function; [Tätigkeit] functioning - 2. [Position] position.

Funktionär, in (mpl -e; fpl -nen) der, die official.

funktionieren vi to work.

für präp (+ A) - 1. [gen] for; **sich ~ etw entschuldigen** to apologize for sthg; **sich ~ Geschichte interessieren** to be interested in history; **~ jn einspringen** to stand in for sb; **jn ~ dumm halten** to think sb is stupid; **einen Mantel ~ 700 Euro kaufen** to buy a coat for 700 euros; **~ ein halbes Jahr** for half a year; **~ immer** for ever, for good; **~ sein Alter ist er noch recht munter** he's still very sprightly for his age - 2. [Unterstützung - ausdrückend]

in favour of; **~ die Abschaffung der Todesstrafe sein** to be in favour of abolishing the death penalty; **früh aufstehen hat etwas ~ sich** getting up early has something to be said for - 3. [zur Angabe der Folge]: **Wort ~ Wort** word by word; **Tag ~ Tag** day after day.

Furcht die fear; ~ **haben (vor jm/etw)** to be afraid (of sb/sthg); **aus ~ vor jm/etw** for fear of sb/sthg. ◆ **Furcht erregend** <> adj frightening <> adv frighteningly.

furchtbar <> adj terrible <> adv [sehr] terribly; **sich ~ anstrengen** to make an enormous effort.

fürchten <> vt to fear; **ich fürchte, dass der Wagen kaputt ist** I'm afraid the car is out of action; **er fürchtet, zu spät zu kommen** he's afraid of arriving late <> vi: **um etw ~** to fear for sthg. ◆ **sich fürchten** ref: **sich (vor jm/etw) ~** to be afraid (of sb/sthg).

fürchterlich <> adj terrible <> adv [sehr] terribly; **sich ~ anstrengen** to make an enormous effort.

furchtsam adj [Person, Tier] easily frightened; [Blick] fearful.

füreinander adv for each other.

Furnier (pl -e) das veneer.

fürs präp (für + das) ☞ für.

Fürsorge die - 1. [menschliche Unterstützung] care - 2. [Sozialhilfe] social security Br, welfare Am - 3. [Sozialamt] social services (pl) Br, welfare services (pl) Am.

fürsorglich <> adj attentive <> adv attentively.

Für|sprecher, in der, die advocate.

Fürst (pl -en) der prince.

Fürstentum (pl -tümer) das principality.

Fürstin (pl -nen) die princess.

fürstlich <> adj - 1. [von einem Fürsten]: **das ~e Schloss** the prince's castle - 2. [Bezahlung] handsome <> adv [bezahlen] handsomely; **~ leben** to live like a prince.

Fuß (pl Füße) der - 1. [Körperteil, von Berg] foot - 2. [tragender Teil - von Lampe, Gefäß] base; [- von Möbeln] leg - 3. RW: **auf eigenen Füßen stehen** to stand on one's own two feet; **(festen) ~ fassen** to find one's feet. ◆ **zu Fuß** adv on foot; **ich gehe oft zu ~ zur Arbeit** I often walk to work.

Fuß|ball der - 1. SPORT football Br, soccer Am - 2. [Ball] football Br, soccer ball Am.

Fußballer, in (mpl -; fpl -nen) der, die footballer Br, soccer player Am.

Fußball|mannschaft die football team Br, soccer team Am.

Fußball|platz der football ground Br, soccer ground Am.

Fußball|spiel das football match Br, soccer game Am.

Fußball|spieler, in *der, die* football player *Br,* soccer player *Am.*

Fuß|boden *der* floor.

Fussel *(pl* - ODER -n) *die* ODER *der* fluff *(U).*

fusseln *vi* to go bobbly.

Fußgänger *(pl* -) *der* pedestrian.

Fußgängerin *(pl* -nen) *die* pedestrian.

Fußgängerüber|weg *der* pedestrian crossing *Br,* crosswalk *Am.*

Fußgänger|zone *die* pedestrian precinct *Br* ODER zone *Am.*

Fuß|gelenk *das* ankle.

Fuß|note *die* footnote.

Fuß|sohle *die* sole *(of the foot).*

Fuß|spur *die* footprint.

Fuß|tritt *der* kick.

Fuß|weg *der* footpath.

futsch *adj fam:* ~ **sein** [fort] to have all gone; [kaputt] to be bust.

Futter *(pl* -) *das* - **1.** [für Haustiere] food; [für Vieh] feed; [Heu] fodder - **2.** [Stoff] lining.

futtern *fam* ⟨⟩ *vt* to feed ⟨⟩ *vi:* **sie kann viel ~** she can put away a lot of food.

füttern *vt* - **1.** [gen] to feed - **2.** [Kleidung] to line.

Futur *(pl* -e) *das* GRAM future (tense).

G

g, G [geː] *(pl* - ODER -s) *das* - **1.** [Buchstabe] g, G - **2.** MUS G. ◆ **g** *(abk für* Gramm) g.

gab *prät* ▷ geben.

Gabe *(pl* -n) *die* [Geschenk, Talent] gift.

Gabel *(pl* -n) *die* - **1.** [Besteckteil, beim Fahrrad] fork - **2.** [in der Landwirtschaft] pitchfork - **3.** [vom Telefon] cradle; **den Hörer auf die ~ legen** to hang up.

Gabelung, Gablung *(pl* -en) *die* fork.

gackern *vi eigtl & fig* to cackle.

gaffen *vi fam abw* to gawp.

Gag [gɛ(ː)k] *(pl* -s) *der* - **1.** *fam* [Witz] gag - **2.** [Besonderheit] gimmick.

Gage ['gaːʒə] *(pl* -n) *die* fee.

gähnen *vi eigtl & fig* to yawn.

Gala *(pl* -s) *die* - **1.** [Galavorstellung] gala - **2.** [Kleidung] formal dress.

Galaxis *(pl* -xien) *die* - **1.** [Milchstraße]: **die ~** the Galaxy - **2.** [Sternsystem] galaxy.

Galerie *(pl* -n) *die* gallery.

Galgen *(pl* -) *der* gallows *(sg).*

Galgenfrist *die* grace.

Galle *(pl* -n) *die* - **1.** [Organ] gall bladder

- **2.** [Flüssigkeit] bile; **mir kommt die ~ hoch** *fam* it makes my blood boil.

Galopp *(pl* -s ODER -e) *der* gallop; **im ~** [beim Pferd] at a gallop; *fam* [schnell] at top speed.

galoppieren *(perf* hat/ist galoppiert) *vi* to gallop.

galt *prät* ▷ gelten.

gammeln *vi fam* - **1.** *abw* [nichts tun] to loaf around - **2.** [verderben] to go off.

Gämse *(pl* -n) *die* chamois.

Gang¹ [gaŋ] *(pl* Gänge) *der* - **1.** [Gangart] gait; **er hat einen ~ wie John Wayne** he walks like John Wayne - **2.** [Spaziergang, Ausgang] walk - **3.** [Flur, Weg] corridor; [in Flugzeug] aisle; **unterirdischer ~** underground passage - **4.** [beim Kfz] gear; **im ersten ~** in first gear - **5.** [Bewegung]: **etw in ~ bringen** ODER **setzen** [gen] to get sthg going; [Maschine] to start sthg up; **der Motor ist/kam in ~** the engine is running/started up; **die Diskussion kam erst nach einer Stunde in ~** it was an hour before the discussion got going - **6.** [Ablauf] course; **im ~e sein** to be going on - **7.** [Speisegang] course.

Gang² [gɛŋ] *(pl* -s) *die* gang.

gängig *adj* - **1.** [üblich] common - **2.** [aktuell] current - **3.** [handelsüblich] popular.

Gangway ['gɛŋweː] *(pl* -s) *die* [von Schiff] gangway; [von Flugzeug] steps *(pl).*

Ganove [ga'noːvə] *(pl* -n) *der* crook.

Gans *(pl* Gänse) *die* goose.

Gänse|blümchen *das* daisy.

Gänse|braten *der* roast goose.

Gänse|füßchen *pl fam* quotation marks.

Gänse|haut *die (ohne pl)* goose-pimples *(pl) Br,* goosebumps *Am.*

Gänse|marsch *der:* **im ~** in single file.

Gänserich *(pl* -e) *der* gander.

ganz ⟨⟩ *adj* - **1.** [komplett] whole, entire; **den ~en Tag** all day, the whole day; **eine ~e Zahl** a whole number; **~e Note** MUS semibreve *Br,* whole note *Am* - **2.** [alle] all; **der ~e Kaffee** all the coffee; **~ Paris** the whole of Paris - **3.** *fam* [heil] whole, intact; **die Tasse ist noch ~** the cup is still intact ODER in one piece - **4.** [nur]: **wir haben ~ zehn Minuten dafür gebraucht** it took us no more than ten minutes - **5.** [verstärkend]: **eine ~e Menge** quite a lot; **was soll der ~e Quatsch!** what's all this nonsense about! ⟨⟩ *adv* - **1.** [sehr] really; **er ist ein ~ seltsamer Mensch** he's a very strange person; **~ viel/wenig** very much/little - **2.** [völlig] completely; **er kommt ~ bestimmt** he is sure to come; **~ und gar** completely; **~ und gar nicht** not at all - **3.** [einschränkend] quite; **der Film war ~ gut** the film was quite good.

Ganze *das* - **1.** [Einheit] whole; **eine Sache als ~s beurteilen** to judge sthg as a whole

-2. [alles] whole thing; **das ~ war eine Farce** the whole thing was a farce; **aufs ~ gehen** to go for it; **es geht ums ~** it's all or nothing.

gänzlich <> *adj* complete <> *adv* completely.

ganztägig <> *adj* all-day; **ein ~er Ausflug** a day trip <> *adv* [geöffnet] all day; [arbeiten] full-time.

ganztags *adv*: **~ arbeiten** to work full-time.

Ganztags|schule *die school attended in the morning and afternoon, rather than just in the morning as with most German schools.*

gar <> *adv*: **~ kein** ... no/not ... at all; **es war ~ keiner da** there was no one there at all; **auf ~ keinen Fall** under no circumstances at all; **~ nicht** not at all; **aber du hast doch ~ nicht gefragt!** but you didn't even ask!; **~ nichts** nothing at all <> *adj* [Speise] done.

Garage (*pl* -n) *die* garage.

Garantie (*pl* -n) *die* guarantee.

garantieren <> *vt* to guarantee <> *vi*: **für etw ~** to guarantee sthg.

garantiert <> *adv fam*: **er hat ~ verschlafen** I bet he's overslept; **wir werden ~ gewinnen** we're bound to win <> *adj* guaranteed.

Garderobe (*pl* -n) *die* **- 1.** [in der Wohnung] hallstand **- 2.** [in öffentlichen Räumen] cloakroom *Br*, coatroom *Am* **- 3.** (*ohne pl*) [Kleidung] clothes (*pl*) (*except underwear*); **eine neue ~ kaufen** to buy a new wardrobe **- 4.** [für Künstler] dressing room.

Garderoben|ständer *der* coatstand.

Gardine (*pl* -n) *die* net curtain; **hinter schwedischen ~n** *fam* behind bars.

garen *vt* to cook.

gären (*prät* gor ODER gärte; *perf* hat/ist gegoren ODER gegärt) *vi* **- 1.** (*ist*) (*unreg*) [in Gärung sein] to ferment **- 2.** (*hat*) (*reg*) [Unzufriedenheit, Ärger]: **es gärte im Volk** the people were growing restless.

Garn (*pl* -e) *das* [zum Nähen] thread; [zum Weben] yarn.

Garnele (*pl* -n) *die* shrimp.

garnieren *vt* to garnish.

Garnitur (*pl* -en) *die* **- 1.** [Satz] set; **eine Polstermöbel ~** a three-piece suite **- 2.** [Garnierung] garnish.

Garten (*pl* Gärten) *der* garden. ● **botanische Garten** *der* botanical gardens (*pl*), botanical garden. ● **zoologische Garten** *der* zoo.

Garten|arbeit *die* gardening.

Garten|bau *der* horticulture.

Garten|schere *die* [klein] secateurs (*pl*); [Heckenschere] shears (*pl*).

Gärtner (*pl* -) *der* gardener.

Gärtnerei (*pl* -en) *die* **- 1.** [Betrieb] nursery **- 2.** [Gartenarbeit] gardening.

Gärtnerin (*pl* -nen) *die* gardener.

Gar|zeit *die* cooking time.

Gas (*pl* -e) *das* **- 1.** [gen] gas **- 2.** [Gaspedal] accelerator *Br*, gas pedal *Am*; [Treibstoff] petrol *Br*, gas *Am*; **(das) ~ wegnehmen** to take one's foot off the accelerator *Br* ODER gas *Am*; **~ geben** to accelerate.

Gas|flasche *die* gas cylinder.

gasförmig *adj* gaseous.

Gas|hahn *der* gas tap.

Gas|heizung *die* gas heating.

Gas|herd *der* gas cooker *Br*, gas stove *Am*.

Gas|kocher *der* camping stove, Primus stove.®

Gas|maske *die* gas mask.

Gas|pedal *das* accelerator *Br*, gas pedal *Am*.

Gas|pistole *die pistol that fires gas cartridges.*

Gasse (*pl* -n) *die* alley; **die Menschenmenge bildete eine ~ für das Fahrzeug** the crowd parted to let the vehicle through.

Gast (*pl* Gäste) *der* **- 1.** [Eingeladene] guest; **bei jm zu ~ sein** to be sb's guest; **Gäste haben** to have guests; **wir haben heute Abend Freunde zu ~** we are having some friends round ODER over this evening **- 2.** [im Hotel] guest; [im Lokal] customer **- 3.** [Tourist] visitor.

Gast|arbeiter, in *der, die* foreign worker.

Gäste|buch *das* visitors' book.

Gäste|zimmer *das* guest room.

gastfreundlich *adj* hospitable.

Gast|geber, in (*mpl* -; *fpl* -nen) *der, die* **- 1.** [Einladende] host **- 2.** [heimische Mannschaft] home team.

Gast|haus *das* inn.

Gast|hof *der* inn.

Gast|hörer, in *der, die* UNI auditor *Am, person permitted to attend university lectures without being registered as a student.*

gastieren *vi* to give a guest performance.

Gast|land *das* [für Veranstaltung] host country.

Gast|mannschaft *die* away team.

Gastronomie *die* **- 1.** [Gewerbe] catering **- 2.** [Kochkunst] gastronomy.

Gast|spiel *das* guest performance.

Gast|stätte *die rustic restaurant with pub attached.*

Gatter (*pl* -) *das* **- 1.** [Tor] gate **- 2.** [Zaun] fence.

Gattung (*pl* -en) *die* **- 1.** BIOL genus **- 2.** [Art, Untergruppe] kind, type; [von Literatur, Kunst, Musik] genre.

GAU [gau] (*pl* -s) (*abk für* Größter anzunehmender Unfall) *der* MCA, *maximum credible accident.*

Gaumen (*pl* -) *der* palate.

Gauner (*pl* -) *der* - **1.** [Betrüger] crook - **2.** *fam* [Spitzbube] cunning devil.

Gaunerin (*pl* -nen) *die* crook.

Gazelle (*pl* -n) *die* gazelle.

geb. - **1.** (*abk für* geborene) née - **2.** (*abk für* geboren) b.

Gebäck (*pl* -e) *das* pastries (*pl*).

gebacken ◇ *pp* ▷ backen ◇ *adj* baked.

gebar *prät* ▷ gebären.

gebären (*präs* gebärt ODER gebiert; *prät* gebar; *perf* hat geboren) *vt* to give birth to.

Gebär|mutter *die* womb.

Gebäude (*pl* -) *das* - **1.** [Bauwerk] building - **2.** [gedanklich] structure; [aus Lügen] web.

geben (*präs* gibt; *prät* gab; *perf* hat gegeben) ◇ *vt* - **1.** [gen]: **jm etw ~** to give sb sthg, to give sthg to sb; **jm einen Kuss ~** to give sb a kiss, to kiss sb; **Unterricht ~** to teach; **eine Party ~** to have a party; **sein Einverständnis ~** to agree, to give one's consent - **2.** [platzieren]: **den Teig in die Kuchenform ~** to put the dough in the baking tin - **3.** [eine Bedeutung beimessen]: **viel/wenig auf etw** (*A*) **~** *fam* to set a lot of/little store by sthg - **4.** [telefonisch]: **~ Sie mir bitte die Personalabteilung!** can you put me through to the personnel department, please? - **5.** [kausal]: **die Kuh gibt Milch** the cow produces milk; **das gibt doch nie etwas** nothing will ever come of that; *fam* **das Buch gibt mir nichts** I didn't get much out of the book ◇ *v impers:* **es gibt** there is/are; **hier gibt es viele Studenten** there are a lot of students here; **die schönsten Fresken gibt es in Italien** the most beautiful frescoes can be found in Italy; **was gibt es heute zum Mittagessen?** what's for lunch today?; **was gibts?** *fam* what's up?; **das gibts doch nicht!** *fam* *fig* I don't believe it! ◇ *vi* [beim Kartenspielen] to deal; **du gibst!** it's your deal.

Gebet (*pl* -e) *das* prayer; **ein ~ sprechen** to say a prayer.

gebeten *pp* ▷ bitten.

Gebiet (*pl* -e) *das* - **1.** [Region, Gegend] area - **2.** [Bereich] field, area.

gebieten (*prät* gebot; *perf* hat geboten) *vt* - **1.** [befehlen]: **jm ~, etw zu tun** to command sb to do sthg - **2.** [verlangen] to call for; **Vorsicht ist geboten** caution is called for.

gebieterisch ◇ *adj* imperious ◇ *adv* imperiously.

Gebilde (*pl* -) *das* structure.

gebildet ◇ *adj* educated ◇ *adv* eruditely.

Gebirge (*pl* -) *das* mountains (*pl*); [Bergkette] mountain range; **im ~** in the mountains.

gebirgig *adj* mountainous.

Gebirgs|pass *der* mountain pass.

Gebiss (*pl* -e) *das* - **1.** [Zähne] teeth (*pl*) - **2.** [Zahnersatz] dentures (*pl*).

gebissen *pp* ▷ beißen.

Gebläse (*pl* -) *das* fan.

geblasen *pp* ▷ blasen.

geblieben *pp* ▷ bleiben.

geblümt *adj* [Kleid, Stil] flowery.

gebogen ◇ *pp* ▷ biegen ◇ *adj* curved.

geboren ◇ *pp* ▷ gebären ◇ *adj* born; **Frau Maier, ~ Müller** Mrs. Maier, née Müller; **dazu ~ sein, etw zu tun** *fig* to be born to do sthg.

geborgen ◇ *pp* ▷ bergen ◇ *adj* safe; **sich (bei jm) ~ fühlen** to feel secure ODER safe with sb.

Geborgenheit *die* security.

geborsten *pp* ▷ bersten.

Gebot (*pl* -e) *das* - **1.** [Befehl] directive; [moralisch] precept; [göttlich] commandment - **2.** [Erfordernis] requirement; **das ~ der Stunde** the needs of the moment - **3.** [Angebot] bid.

geboten ◇ *pp* ▷ bieten ▷ gebieten; **etw für sein Geld ~ bekommen** to get sthg for one's money ◇ *adj* necessary, requisite.

gebracht *pp* ▷ bringen.

gebrannt ◇ *pp* ▷ brennen ◇ *adj* burnt; **~e Mandeln** toasted almonds.

gebraten ◇ *pp* ▷ braten ◇ *adj* [in der Pfanne] fried; [im Backofen] roast.

Gebrauch [gə'braux] (*pl* -bräuche) *der* use; **etw in ~ nehmen** to start using sthg.

gebrauchen *vt* to use; **ich könnte etwas zu essen ~** I could use something to eat.

gebräuchlich *adj* - **1.** [verbreitet] common - **2.** [üblich] usual.

Gebrauchs|anweisung [gə'brauxsanvaizʊŋ] *die* instructions (*pl*).

gebrauchsfertig [gə'brauxsfɛrtɪç] *adj* ready-to-use.

Gebrauchs|gegenstand [gə'brauxsge:gŋʃtant] *der* everyday object.

gebraucht *adj* second-hand.

Gebraucht|wagen *der* used ODER second-hand car.

gebrochen ◇ *pp* ▷ brechen ◇ *adj* broken ◇ *adv* [unvollkommen]: **er spricht ~ Italienisch** he speaks broken Italian.

Gebrüll *das* (*ohne pl*) [von Löwe, Menschenmenge] roaring; [von Stier] bellowing; [von Kind, Affe] screeching.

Gebühr (*pl* -en) *die* charge; [für Arzt, Anwalt] fee; [für Autobahn] toll; [für Post] postage.

gebührend ◇ *adj* [Strafe, Belohnung] suitable; [Sorgfalt] due ◇ *adv* [strafen, belohnen] suitably; **etw ~ sorgfältig machen** to do sthg with due care.

Gebühren|einheit *die* TELEKOM unit.

gebührenfrei *adj & adv* free of charge.

gebührenpflichtig *adj* subject to a charge.

Geburt *(pl -en) die* birth; **er ist von ~ kein Deutscher** he is not German by birth.

gebürtig *adj:* **sie ist ~e Bayerin, sie ist aus Bayern ~** she's Bavarian by birth.

Geburts|datum *das* date of birth.

Geburts|ort *der* place of birth.

Geburts|tag *der* - **1.** [Jahrestag] birthday; **wann hast du ~?** when is your birthday?; **jm zum ~ gratulieren** to wish sb a happy birthday; **alles Gute zum ~!** happy birthday! - **2.** *amt* [Geburtsdatum] date of birth.

Geburtstags|feier *die* birthday party.

Geburtstags|kind *das* birthday boy/girl.

Geburts|urkunde *die* birth certificate.

Gebüsch *(pl -e) das* bushes *(pl).*

gedacht ⇔ *pp* ⊳ denken. ⇔ *adj:* **das Geschenk ist als Trost ~** the present is meant to be a consolation; **eigentlich war das anders ~** actually that's not what was intended.

Gedächtnis *(pl -se) das* memory; **kein ~ für Zahlen haben** to have no head for numbers; **zum ~ an jn** in memory of sb.

Gedächtnis|feier *die* commemoration.

gedämpft *adj* [Licht, Musik, Stimmung] subdued; [Geräusch, Schritte] muffled; [Farbton, Musikinstrument] muted; [Stimme] low.

Gedanke *(pl -n) der* - **1.** [Gedachte, Überlegung] thought; **sich** *(D)* **~ über etw** *(A)* **machen** to think about sthg; **js ~n lesen können** to be able to read sb's mind; **er hat sich entschlossen, keinen ~n daran zu verschwenden** he decided not to waste any time thinking about it; **der bloße ~, dass ...** the very idea that ... - **2.** [Vorstellung, Vorhaben] idea; **mit dem ~n spielen, etw zu tun** to toy with the idea of doing sthg - **3.** [Sorge]: **sich** *(D)* **~n über jn/etw machen** to be worried about sb/sthg.

gedanken|los ⇔ *adj* [ohne nachzudenken] thoughtless; [unaufmerksam] absent-minded ⇔ *adv* [ohne nachzudenken] without thinking; [unaufmerksam] absent-mindedly.

Gedanken|strich *der* dash.

gedankenverloren *adv* lost in thought.

Gedeck *(pl -e) das* - **1.** [Geschirr und Besteck] place setting - **2.** [Speisenfolge] set meal.

Gedenk|minute *die* minute's silence.

Gedenk|stätte *die* memorial.

Gedenk|tafel *die* plaque.

Gedicht *(pl -e) das* poem.

Gedränge *das* crush.

gedrängt ⇔ *adj* [Bericht, Beschreibung] succinct; [Zeitplan] busy ⇔ *adv* succinctly.

gedroschen *pp* ⊳ dreschen.

gedrückt *adj* depressed.

gedrungen ⇔ *pp* ⊳ dringen ⇔ *adj* stocky.

Geduld *die* patience; **mit jm ~ haben** to be patient with sb; **die ~ verlieren** to lose one's patience.

geduldig ⇔ *adj* patient ⇔ *adv* patiently.

Geduldsfaden *der:* **ihm reißt (gleich) der ~** he's losing his patience.

gedurft *pp* ⊳ dürfen.

geeignet *adj* suitable; **für etw ~ sein** to be suitable for sthg; **nicht ~** unsuitable; **er ist zum Lehrer ~** he'd make a good teacher.

Gefahr *(pl -en) die* danger; **es besteht die ~ eines Unfalls** there's the risk of an accident; **außer ~ sein** no longer to be in danger; **~ laufen, etw zu tun** to be in danger of doing sthg.

gefährden *vt* [Gesundheit, Leben, Mensch] to endanger; [Unternehmen, Projekt] to jeopardize.

gefahren *pp* ⊳ fahren.

gefährlich ⇔ *adj* dangerous ⇔ *adv* dangerously.

gefahrlos ⇔ *adj* safe ⇔ *adv* safely.

Gefälle *(pl -) das* - **1.** [von Straße, Dach] slope - **2.** [Unterschied] difference.

gefallen *(präs gefällt, prät gefiel, perf hat gefallen) vi* - **1.** [gut finden]: **er/es gefällt mir** I like him/it - **2.** [ertragen]: **sich** *(D)* **etw ~ lassen** to put up with sthg; **sich** *(D)* **nichts ~ lassen** not to put up with any nonsense; **das lasse ich mir ~!** *fam* I can handle this!

Gefallen *(pl -) der* favour; **jm einen ~ tun** to do sb a favour; **jn um einen ~ bitten** to ask sb a favour.

gefällig *adj* - **1.** [entkommend] helpful; **jm ~ sein** to be of help to sb - **2.** [angenehm] pleasant - **3.** [genehm]: **noch ein Bier ~?** would you like another beer?

Gefälligkeit *(pl -en) die* [Gefallen] favour.

gefälligst *adv* kindly.

Gefangene *(pl -n) der, die* prisoner.

gefangen nehmen *vt (unreg)* - **1.** [festnehmen] to capture - **2.** [in Bann ziehen] to captivate.

Gefangenschaft *die* captivity.

Gefängnis *(pl -se) das* - **1.** [Haftanstalt] prison - **2.** [Haftstrafe] imprisonment.

Gefängnis|strafe *die* prison sentence.

gefärbt *adj* dyed.

Gefäß *(pl -e) das* - **1.** [Behältnis] container - **2.** [von Lebewesen] blood vessel.

gefasst *adj* - **1.** [gelassen] composed - **2.** [vorbereitet]: **auf etw** *(A)* **~ sein** to be prepared for sthg; **du kannst dich darauf ~ ma-**

chen, dass ... *fam* you'd better start getting used to the idea that ...; **sonst kannst du dich auf was ~ machen** *fam* otherwise you're in for it ⬦ *adv* [gelassen] calmly.

Gefecht (*pl* -e) *das* skirmish.

Gefieder (*pl* -) *das* feathers (*pl*).

geflogen *pp* ⬦ fliegen.

geflohen *pp* ⬦ fliehen.

geflossen *pp* ⬦ fließen.

Geflügel *das* poultry.

Geflüster *das* whispering.

gefochten *pp* ⬦ fechten.

Gefolge *das* entourage; [bei Beerdigung] cortege.

Gefolgschaft (*pl* -en) *die* - 1. (*ohne pl*) [Loyalität] allegiance; **jm die ~ verweigern** to stop supporting sb - 2. [Anhängerschaft] followers (*pl*).

gefragt *adj* popular; **sehr ~ sein** to be very much in demand.

gefräßig *adj abw* greedy.

Gefreite (*pl* -n) *der* lance corporal *Br*, private first class *Am*.

gefressen *pp* ⬦ fressen.

gefrieren (*prät* gefror; *perf* hat/ist gefroren) *vi* (ist) to freeze; **es hat gefroren** there has been a frost.

Gefrierfach *das* freezer (compartment).

Gefriertruhe *die* (chest) freezer.

gefroren ⬦ *pp* ⬦ frieren ⬦ gefrieren ⬦ *adj* frozen.

Gefühl (*pl* -e) *das* - 1. [gen] feeling; **seine Beine sind ohne ~** he's got no feeling in his legs; **er kennt keine ~e** he doesn't have any feelings; **etw im ~ haben** to know sthg instinctively - 2. [Gespür] sense; **ein ~ für etw** a sense of sthg.

gefühllos ⬦ *adj* - 1. [taub] numb - 2. [herzlos] callous ⬦ *adv* [herzlos] callously.

Gefühlsleben *das* emotional life.

gefühlsmäßig ⬦ *adj* emotional ⬦ *adv* emotionally.

gefunden *pp* ⬦ finden.

gegangen *pp* ⬦ gehen.

gegebenenfalls *adv* if necessary.

Gegebenheit (*pl* -en) *die* condition, circumstance.

gegen *präp* (+ A) - 1. [gen] against; **~ die Tür hämmern** to bang on the door; **das Schiff fährt ~ die Strömung** the ship is sailing upstream; **~ etw sein** to be opposed to ODER against sthg; **heute spielt Leipzig ~ Bremen** Leipzig are playing Bremen today; **ein Mittel ~ Grippe** a flu remedy, a medicine for flu - 2. [zeitlich]: **~ fünf Uhr** at about five o'clock; **~ Abend wurde es kühler** it cooled down towards evening - 3. [im Austausch für] for; **~ bar** for cash - 4. [im Vergleich zu] in comparison to, compared with.

Gegenargument *das* counterargument.

Gegend (*pl* -en) *die* - 1. [Gebiet, Bereich] area; **in der ~** nearby; **in der ~ von** near; **in der Nierengegend** in the region of the kidneys; **hier in der ~** round here - 2. [Nachbarschaft] neighbourhood - 3. *RW*: **so in der ~** *fam* thereabouts.

Gegendarstellung *die* conflicting account.

gegeneinander *adv* against one another ODER each other.

Gegenfahrbahn *die* opposite side of the road.

Gegengewicht *das* counterbalance; **ein** ODER **das ~ zu etw bilden** to counterbalance sthg.

Gegengift *das* antidote.

gegenläufig ⬦ *adj* opposite ⬦ *adv* in the opposite direction.

Gegenleistung *die*: **als ~ (für etw)** in return (for sthg).

Gegenmaßnahme *die* countermeasure.

Gegenmittel *das* antidote.

Gegenrichtung *die* opposite direction.

Gegensatz *der* contrast; **im ~ zu** in contrast to; **im ~ zu etw stehen** to contrast with sthg.

gegensätzlich ⬦ *adj* conflicting ⬦ *adv* completely differently.

Gegenseite *die* - 1. [Gegenpartei] opposing side; [vor Gericht] opposing party; SPORT opposition - 2. [andere Seite] other side.

gegenseitig ⬦ *adj* mutual ⬦ *adv* each other, one another; **sich ~ helfen** to help each other ODER one another.

Gegenspieler, in *der, die* - 1. [Gegner] opponent - 2. [im Theater] antagonist.

Gegensprechanlage *die* intercom.

Gegenstand *der* - 1. [Ding, Objekt] object - 2. [Thema] subject.

gegenständlich *adj* [Kunst] representational.

Gegenstimme *die* - 1. [Stimme dagegen] vote against - 2. [abweichende Meinung] dissenting voice.

Gegenteil *das* opposite; **das ~ von jm/etw sein** to be the opposite of sb/sthg. ⬅ **im Gegenteil** *adv* on the contrary; **ganz im ~** quite the reverse ODER opposite.

gegenteilig *adj* opposite.

gegenüber ⬦ *präp* (+ D) - 1. [räumlich] opposite; **~ der Kirche** opposite the church; **mir ~** opposite me - 2. [zur Angabe einer Beziehung] towards; **so kannst du dich den Schülern ~ nicht verhalten** you can't behave like that towards the pupils - 3. [zur Angabe eines Vergleichs] compared with; **~ der alten Wohnung** compared with the old flat *Br* ODER apartment Am ⬦ adv opposite; **der Garten ~** the garden over ODER across the road.

Gegenüber das person sitting opposite.

gegenüber|liegen vi (unreg) to be opposite; **das ~de Gebäude** the building opposite; **einander ~** to face one another ODER each other. ➡ **sich gegenüberliegen** ref to face one another ODER each other.

gegenüber|stehen vi (unreg) - **1.** [zugewandt stehen]: **jm/einer Sache ~** to be facing sb/sthg - **2.** [gegenübergestellt sein]: **einer Sache** (D) **~** to be faced with sthg; **jm feindlich ~** to have a hostile attitude towards sb. ➡ **sich gegenüberstehen** ref - **1.** [sich zugewandt stehen, gegeneinander spielen] to face one another ODER each other - **2.** [in Konflikt stehen] to clash.

gegenüber|stellen vt - **1.** [mit jm konfrontieren]: **dem Zeugen die Verdächtigen ~** to line the suspects up in front of the witness - **2.** [nebeneinander halten]: **das Alterswerk eines Autors seinen frühen Romanen ~** to compare the late works of an author with his early novels.

gegenüber|treten (perf ist gegenübergetreten) vi (unreg): **jm ~** to face sb.

Gegenverkehr der oncoming traffic.

Gegenwart die - **1.** [Zeitpunkt] present; **die Kunst der ~** contemporary art; **bis in die ~** up to the present day - **2.** [Präsenz] presence; **in js ~** in sb's presence - **3.** GRAM present (tense).

Gegen|wert der equivalent amount.

Gegen|wind der headwind.

gegessen pp ▷ essen.

geglichen pp ▷ gleichen.

geglitten pp ▷ gleiten.

geglommen pp ▷ glimmen.

Gegner, in (mpl -; fpl -nen) der, die - **1.** [Widersacher, im Sport] opponent - **2.** [Feind] enemy.

gegnerisch adj opposing.

gegolten pp ▷ gelten.

gegoren ⬦ pp ▷ gären ⬦ adj fermented.

gegossen pp ▷ gießen.

gegraben pp ▷ graben.

gegriffen pp ▷ greifen.

Gehabe das abw affected behaviour.

gehabt pp ▷ haben.

Gehackte das mince Br, mincemeat Am.

Gehalt (pl Gehälter) ⬦ das salary ⬦ der - **1.** [Inhalt] content - **2.** [Anteil]: **ein geringer ~ an Gold** a low gold content.

gehalten pp ▷ halten.

Gehaltsab|rechnung die salary statement.

gehandikapt [gəˈhɛndɪkɛpt] adj handicapped.

gehangen pp ▷ hängen.

gehässig ⬦ adj spiteful ⬦ adv spitefully.

Gehäuse (pl -) das - **1.** [von Uhr, Fotoapparat, Radio] casing; [von Schnecke] shell - **2.** [von Apfel, Birne] core.

gehbehindert adj disabled (used of people who have difficulty walking).

Gehege (pl -) das reserve; [im Zoo] enclosure.

geheim ⬦ adj - **1.** [heimlich] secret - **2.** [geheimnisvoll] mysterious ⬦ adv [nicht offen] in secret; **~ abstimmen** to vote by secret ballot. ➡ **im Geheimen** adv secretly.

Geheim|dienst der secret service.

geheim halten vt (unreg) to keep secret.

Geheimnis (pl -se) das - **1.** [Geheimgehaltenes] secret - **2.** [Unbekanntes] mystery.

geheimnisvoll ⬦ adj mysterious ⬦ adv mysteriously.

Geheim|nummer die [von Telefon] ex-directory number Br, unlisted number Am; [von Scheckkarte] PIN (number); [von Tresor] combination.

Geheim|polizei die secret police.

geheißen pp ▷ heißen.

gehen (prät ging; perf ist gegangen) ⬦ vi - **1.** [Fortbewegung] to go; **einkaufen ~** to go shopping; **in die Stadt ~** to go into town; **zur Armee ~** to join the army; **in Serienproduktion ~** to go into mass production - **2.** [weggehen, abfahren] to go; **ich gehe jetzt** I'm off now; **mein Zug geht um acht Uhr** my train leaves ODER goes at eight o'clock - **3.** [zu Fuß gehen] to walk; **mit jm ~** fam [eine Beziehung haben] to go out with sb - **4.** [verkehren] to go; **der Bus geht drei Mal täglich** the bus goes ODER runs three times a day - **5.** [funktionieren - gen] to work; [- Uhr, Auto] to go; **das Geschäft geht gut** business is going well - **6.** [zur Beschreibung von Vorgängen]: **wie geht das mit der Anmeldung?** how's the application going?; **das geht doch ganz einfach** it's quite simple; **was geht denn hier vor sich?** what's going on here, then? - **7.** [möglich, erlaubt sein] to be OK; **aber das geht doch nicht!** you can't do that!; **ginge es vielleicht, dass wir ...?** do you think we could possibly ...? - **8.** [sich erstrecken]: **das Wasser ging ihm bis zu den Knien** the water came up to his knees; **die Straße geht bis zum Rathaus** the street goes as far as the townhall; **das geht über unsere Mittel** that's beyond our means - **9.** [passen]: **in/durch etw ~** to go in/through sthg - **10.** [sich erstrecken]: **es kann nicht immer nur nach dir ~** you can't always have things your own way; **wenn es nach mir ginge, ...** if I had my way, ... - **11.** [ein Arbeitsverhältnis beenden] to leave - **12.** [Teig] to rise ⬦ v impers - **1.** [ergehen]: **wie geht es dir/Ihnen?** how are you?;

es geht mir gut/schlecht I'm well/not very well; **der Firma geht es gut/schlecht** the company is doing well/badly - **2.** [sich handeln um]: **es geht um deine Mutter** it's about your mother; **worum geht es in diesem Buch?** what's this book about?; **es geht darum, alle Karten loszuwerden** the idea is to get rid of all your cards; **darum geht es nicht** that's not the point - **3.** [annehmbar sein]: **wie gefällt es dir? – es geht** how do you like it? – it's OK ◇ *vt* to walk. ◆ **sich gehen** *ref*: **~ lassen** to let o.s. go.

geheuer *adj*: **das ist mir nicht (ganz) ~** [Furcht einflößend] I find that (rather) eerie; [unwohl] I'm not (too) sure about that; [verdächtig] I find that (rather) odd ODER suspicious.

Geheul, Geheule das - **1.** [Heulen] howling - **2.** *fam abw* [Heulerei] wailing.

Gehilfe (*pl* -n) der - **1.** [Ausgebildeter] qualified assistant (*who has successfully completed an apprenticeship*) - **2.** [Helfer] assistant.

Gehilfin (*pl* -nen) die - **1.** [Ausgebildete] qualified assistant (*who has successfully completed an apprenticeship*) - **2.** [Helferin] assistant.

Gehirn (*pl* -e) das - **1.** [Hirn] brain - **2.** (*ohne pl*) *fam* [Verstand] brain, brains (*pl*); **sich das ~ zermartern** to rack one's brain ODER brains.

Gehirnlerschütterung die concussion (*U*).

gehoben ◇ *pp* ⊳ heben ◇ *adj* - **1.** [höher - Position, Stellung] senior; [- Einkommen, Erwartung] higher - **2.** [exklusiv] sophisticated - **3.**: **in ~er Stimmung** in high spirits.

geholfen *pp* ⊳ helfen.

Gehör (*pl* -e) das hearing; **ein schlechtes ~ haben** to be hard of hearing; **nach dem ~** by ear; **jm/einer Sache ~/kein ~ schenken** to listen/not to listen to sb/sthg.

gehorchen *vi* to obey; **jm ~** to obey sb; **der Vernunft ~** to listen to reason.

gehören *vi* - **1.** [einer Person]: **jm ~** to belong to sb - **2.** [an Ort] to belong; **wohin gehört das Werkzeug?** where does this tool belong? - **3.** [als Bestandteil]: **zu etw ~** to be part of sthg; **sie gehört zum Krankenhauspersonal** she's a member of the hospital staff - **4.** [als Notwendigkeit]: **zum Reiten gehört viel Geschick** riding requires a lot of skill; **es gehört Mut dazu, dies zu tun** it takes a lot of courage to do it - **5.** [müssen]: **solche Leute ~ eingesperrt** such people ought to be locked up. ◆ **sich gehören** *ref*: **es** ODER **das gehört sich nicht** it's not the done thing.

gehörig ◇ *adj* - **1.** [gebührend] proper - **2.** [beachtlich] considerable; **mit einer ~en Portion Mut** with a good deal of courage ◇ *adv* - **1.** [gebührend] properly - **2.** [beachtlich - steigen, erhöhen] considerably; **jn ~ durchprügeln** to give sb a good thrashing.

Gehörlose (*pl* -n) der, die deaf person; **die ~n** the deaf.

gehorsam *adj* obedient.

Gehorsam der obedience; **jm den ~ verweigern** to refuse to obey sb.

Gehorsamkeit die obedience.

Gehlweg der - **1.** [Gehsteig] pavement *Br*, sidewalk *Am* - **2.** [Weg] footpath.

Geige (*pl* -n) die [im Orchester] violin; [in Folk] fiddle.

geil *adj* - **1.** *fam* [begierig auf Sex] horny; **er war ~ auf sie** he wanted to get into her knickers - **2.** *abw* [lüstern - Mann] lecherous; [- Blick, Gedanke] lewd - **3.** *fam* [toll] wicked.

Geisel (*pl* -n) die hostage.

Geisellnahme (*pl* -n) die hostage-taking.

Geist (*pl* -e ODER -er) der - **1.** [Verstandeskraft] mind; **den ~ aufgeben** *fam* to give up the ghost; **jm auf den ~ gehen** *fam* to get on sb's nerves - **2.** [Intellekt] intellect - **3.** [Gesinnung] spirit - **4.** (*pl Geiste*) [Spirituose] *schnapps distilled from fruit, especially berries* - **5.** (*pl Geister*) [Person, Genie] mind - **6.** (*pl Geister*) [überirdische Wesenheit]: **der Heilige ~** the Holy Ghost - **7.** (*pl Geister*) [Gespenst] ghost.

Geisterlfahrer, in der, die *person who drives into oncoming traffic on a motorway*.

geistesabwesend ◇ *adj* absent-minded ◇ *adv* absent-mindedly.

Geisteslblitz der flash of inspiration.

geistesgegenwärtig ◇ *adj* quick-witted ◇ *adv* with great presence of mind.

geistesgestört *adj* mentally disturbed ODER unbalanced.

geisteskrank *adj* mentally ill.

Geisteslkranke der, die mentally ill person; [im Krankenhaus] mental patient.

Geisteslwissenschaft die arts subject; **die ~en** the arts.

geistig ◇ *adj* - **1.** [intellektuell - Mensch, Freiheit, Vermächtnis] intellectual; [- Anstrengung, Kraft, Fähigkeit] mental - **2.** [alkoholisch] alcoholic ◇ *adv* - **1.** [intellektuell - frei, überlegen] intellectually; [- fit, frisch, behindert] mentally; **sich ~ anstrengen** to make a mental effort.

geistlich ◇ *adj* [gen] religious; [Beistand] spiritual ◇ *adv*: **jm ~ beistehen** to lend sb spiritual guidance.

Geistliche (*pl* -n) der clergyman.

geistlos ◇ *adj* inane ◇ *adv* inanely.

geistreich ◇ *adj* intelligent ◇ *adv* intelligently.

Geiz der meanness.

geizen *vi*: **mit etw ~** [Geld] to be mean with sthg; [Lob] to be sparing with sthg.

Geizlhals der *fam abw* skinflint.

geizig ◇ *adj* mean ◇ *adv* meanly.

Geizlkragen der *fam abw* skinflint.

Gejammer das fam abw moaning.

gekannt pp ▷ kennen.

Gekicher das giggling.

geklungen pp ▷ klingen.

gekniffen pp ▷ kneifen.

gekommen pp ▷ kommen.

gekonnt ⬦ pp ▷ können ⬦ adj masterful ⬦ adv masterfully.

gekrochen pp ▷ kriechen.

gekünstelt abw ⬦ adj artificial ⬦ adv artificially.

Gel (pl -e) das gel.

Gelächter (pl -) das laughter.

geladen ⬦ pp ▷ laden ⬦ adj loaded; **~ sein** fam fig to be fuming.

gelähmt adj paralysed.

Gelähmte (pl -n) der, die paralysed man (f woman).

Gelände (pl -) das - **1.** [Land] country; **ein bergiges ~** mountainous terrain; **auf freiem ~** in the open country - **2.** [Gebiet] area - **3.** [Grundstück - zum Bau] site; [- um Haus] grounds (pl).

Geländelauf der - **1.** SPORT cross-country (running) - **2.** [Wettkampf] cross-country run.

Geländer (pl -) das [von Treppe] banister; [von Brücke] parapet; [von Balkon] railing.

gelang prät ▷ gelingen.

gelangen (perf ist gelangt) vi: **an etw (A) ~** to arrive at sthg; **an die Öffentlichkeit ~** to become public; **in js Besitz ~** to come into sb's possession; **zu etw ~** [Ruhm, Ansehen] to gain sthg; [Verständigung] to come to sthg; **zu Geld ~** [durch Erbe] to come into money; [durch Arbeit] to make money.

gelassen ⬦ pp ▷ lassen ⬦ adj calm ⬦ adv calmly.

Gelassenheit die composure.

gelaufen pp ▷ laufen.

geläufig adj [vertraut] common; **es ist mir ~** it is familiar to me.

gelb adj & adv yellow.

Gelb das yellow. ◆ **bei Gelb** adv on amber Br, on yellow Am.

Gelbe Sack der yellow refuse bag used for recyclable packaging.

gelblich adj [Tapete, Papier] yellowish; [Haut] sallow.

Gelbsucht die jaundice.

Geld (pl -er) das money; **großes ~** notes (pl); **kleines ~** change, coins (pl); **ins ~ gehen** to be expensive; **es ist sein ~ wert** it is worth every penny. ◆ **Gelder** pl funds.

Geldautomat der cash machine ODER dispenser.

Geldgeber, in der, die financial backer.

geldgierig adj greedy (for money).

Geldkarte die Switch card®Br, smart card which charges payments straight to one's bank account.

Geldmittel pl funds.

Geldschein der banknote Br, bill Am.

Geldschrank der safe.

Geldstrafe die fine.

Geldstück das coin.

Gelee [ʒəˈleː] (pl -s) das ODER der jelly.

gelegen ⬦ pp ▷ liegen ⬦ adj - **1.** [befindlich] situated - **2.** [bedeutsam]: **mir ist an deinem Besuch viel ~** geh your visit means a great deal to me.

Gelegenheit (pl -en) die - **1.** [geeignete Möglichkeit] opportunity - **2.** [Anlass] occasion - **3.** [Angebot] bargain. ◆ **bei Gelegenheit** adv when the opportunity arises.

gelegentlich ⬦ adj occasional ⬦ adv - **1.** [manchmal] occasionally - **2.** [bei Gelegenheit] some time.

gelehrt ⬦ adj learned ⬦ adv learnedly.

Gelehrte (pl -n) der, die scholar.

Gelenk (pl -e) das [beim Menschen] joint.

gelenkig adj supple.

gelernt adj trained.

gelesen pp ▷ lesen.

Geliebte (pl -n) der, die lover.

geliehen pp ▷ leihen.

gelingen (prät gelang; perf ist gelungen) vi: **die Zeichnung ist mir gut gelungen** my drawing turned out well; **es gelang mir, den Brief zu schreiben** I managed to write the letter; **es gelang ihm, das Buch zu finden** he succeeded in finding the book.

gelitten pp ▷ leiden.

gelockt adj: **~es Haar** curly hair.

gelogen pp ▷ lügen.

gelöst adj relaxed.

gelten (präs gilt; prät galt; perf hat gegolten) vi - **1.** [gültig sein] to be valid; **für jn/etw ~** to apply to sb/sthg - **2.** SPORT to count - **3.** [anerkannt sein]: **als etw ~** to be considered to be sthg - **4.** [korrekt sein]: **das gilt nicht!** fam [gen] that doesn't count!; [schummeln] that's cheating! - **5.** [akzeptieren]: **etw ~ lassen** to accept sthg - **6.** [wert sein] to count; **Kreativität gilt hier nichts** creativity counts for nothing here - **7.** [adressiert sein an]: **seine Bemerkung galt nicht allein dir** his remark was not only directed at you, his remark didn't only apply to you - **8.** [müssen]: **in dieser Lage gilt es, einen kühlen Kopf zu bewahren** in this situation you need to ODER it is necessary to keep a cool head.

geltend adj current; **etw ~ machen** [Forderung] to make sthg; [Einwand] to raise/put forward sthg.

Geltung die - **1.** [Gültigkeit] validity; **dieses**

Gesetz hat keine ~ mehr this law is no longer valid **- 2.** [Wirkung] prominence; **zur ~ kommen** to be shown to its best advantage.

gelungen <> *pp* ▷ gelingen <> *adj* successful.

gemächlich <> *adj* leisurely <> *adv:* **im Wald spazieren gehen** to go for a leisurely walk in the woods.

Gemälde (*pl* -) *das* painting.

gemäß *präp:* **~ einer Sache** (D), **einer Sache** (D) **~** in accordance with sthg.

gemäßigt *adj* [Politiker] moderate; [Klima] temperate.

Gemecker, Gemeckere *das* **- 1.** [von Ziegen] bleating **- 2.** *fam abw* [Nörgelei] moaning.

gemein <> *adj* **- 1.** [niederträchtig - Person, Verhalten] mean; [- Trick, Lüge] nasty; [- Witz] dirty **- 2.** *fam* [unfair]: **das ist ~!** that's not fair! <> *adv* **- 1.** [gemeinsam]: **etw mit jm/etw ~ haben** to have sthg in common with sb/sthg **- 2.** [niederträchtig] meanly **- 3.** *fam* [sehr]: **die Verletzung hat ~ wehgetan** the injury hurt like hell.

Gemeinde|zentrum *das* community centre.

gemeingefährlich <> *adj.* dangerous <> *adv* dangerously.

Gemeinheit (*pl* -en) *die* **- 1.** [verwerfliche Art] meanness **- 2.** [Handlung] mean trick **- 3.** *fam* [Ärgernis]: **so eine ~!** it's not fair!

gemeinnützig <> *adj* for the benefit of the community; [Verein] charitable, non-profit-making <> *adv* for the benefit of the community.

gemeinsam <> *adv* **- 1.** [zusammen] together; **~ verantwortlich** jointly responsible **- 2.** [gleich]: **etw ~ haben** to have sthg in common <> *adj* [Weg, Interessen] joint; [Verantwortung] joint; **ein ~er Urlaub/ Spaziergang** a holiday/walk together.

Gemeinsamkeit (*pl* -en) *die* **- 1.** [gleiche Eigenschaft] common feature; **sie haben viele ~en** they have a lot in common **- 2.** (*ohne pl*) [Zusammengehörigkeit]: **Gefühl der ~** sense of community.

Gemeinschaft (*pl* -en) *die* **- 1.** [Gruppe] community **- 2.** [Verbundenheit] company; **in unserer Klasse haben wir eine gute ~** in our class we have a good sense of community; **in js ~** in sb's company.

gemeinschaftlich <> *adj* joint; [Interessen] common <> *adv* jointly.

Gemeinschafts|kunde *die* (*ohne pl*) SCHULE social studies (*pl*).

Gemeinschafts|raum *der* common room.

gemeint *adj* meant; **das war nicht so ~!** I didn't mean it like that!; **mein Rat war gut ~** my advice was well-intentioned.

Gemetzel (*pl* -) *das* bloodbath.

Gemisch (*pl* -e) *das* mixture.

gemischt *adj* mixed.

gemocht *pp* ▷ mögen.

gemolken *pp* ▷ melken.

Gemurmel *das* murmuring.

Gemüse (*pl* -) *das* vegetables (*pl*).

Gemüse|eintopf *der* vegetable stew.

Gemüse|händler, in *der, die* greengrocer.

gemusst *pp* ▷ müssen.

Gemüt (*pl* -er) *das* **- 1.** [Wesen] disposition **- 2.** (*ohne pl*) [Empfindungsvermögen] heart; **dieses Buch ist etwas fürs ~** this is a moving book; **der Film ist ihr aufs ~ geschlagen** the film really got her down; [Text] to study sthg. ◆ **Gemüter** *pl* feelings; **der Skandal hat die ~er erregt** the scandal has caused feelings to run high.

gemütlich <> *adj* **- 1.** [behaglich] cosy; **es sich** (D) **~ machen** to make o.s. at home **- 2.** [Beisammensein] informal; [Abend] pleasant; [Fahrt] leisurely **- 3.** [Person] friendly <> *adv* **- 1.** [behaglich] cosily **- 2.** [zusammensitzen, sich unterhalten] pleasantly; [arbeiten] at a leisurely pace.

Gemütlichkeit *die* **- 1.** [Behaglichkeit] cosiness **- 2.** [Zwanglosigkeit, Ruhe] pleasant atmosphere; **in aller ~** at one's leisure.

Gen (*pl* -e) *das* gene.

genannt *pp* ▷ nennen.

genau <> *adj* **- 1.** [exakt] exact; [Waage, Voraussage, Arbeit] accurate **- 2.** [gründlich] thorough <> *adv* **- 1.** [exakt] precisely, exactly; **genau!** precisely!, exactly!; **~ um zehn Uhr** at exactly ten o'clock; **auf die Minute/ Sekunde** to the very minute/second; **die Uhr geht ~** the clock keeps perfect time **- 2.** [hören, hinsehen] carefully; **ich kenne ihn ~** I know exactly what he's like.

genau genommen *adv* strictly speaking.

Genauigkeit *die* **- 1.** [Exaktheit] exactness; [von Waage, Voraussage, Arbeit] accuracy **- 2.** [Gründlichkeit] thoroughness.

genauso *adv* just as; **er sieht ~ aus** he looks just the same.

Gen|datei *die* DNA database.

genehmigen *vt* [Antrag, Plan] to approve; [Demonstration, Aufenthalt] to authorize; **sich** (D) **etw ~** *fam* to treat o.s. to ODER allow o.s. sthg.

Genehmigung (*pl* -en) *die* **- 1.** [von Antrag, Plan] approval; [von Demonstration, Aufenthalt] authorization **- 2.** [Dokument] permit.

General (*pl* -räle ODER -räle) *der* general.

General|probe *die eigtl & fig* dress rehearsal.

generalüberholen vt to give a complete overhaul.

Generalver|sammlung die annual general meeting.

Generation (pl -en) die generation.

Generations|konflikt der conflict between the generations.

Generator (pl -toren) der generator.

generell ⬦ adj general ⬦ adv generally.

Genetik die genetics (U).

Genf nt Geneva.

Genfer See der Lake Geneva.

genial ⬦ adj brilliant ⬦ adv brilliantly.

Genick (pl -e) das (back of the) neck.

Genie [ʒe'niː] (pl -s) das genius.

genieren [ʒe'niːrən] vt to bother. ⬥ **sich genieren** ref to be embarrassed; **sich vor jm ~** to be shy of sb, to get embarrassed in sb's presence.

genießbar adj [essbar] edible; [trinkbar] drinkable.

genießen (prät genoss; perf hat genossen) vt - 1. [gen] to enjoy - 2. [essen] to eat; [trinken] to drink.

Genießer, in (mpl -; fpl -nen) der, die pleasure lover, bon vivant; [beim Essen] gourmet.

genießerisch ⬦ adj [Mensch] appreciative; [Leben] pleasurable ⬦ adv with relish.

Genitalien pl genitals.

Genitiv (pl -e) der GRAM genitive.

genommen pp ⬥ nehmen.

genormt adj standardized.

genoss prät ⬥ genießen.

genossen pp ⬥ genießen.

Genossenschaft (pl -en) die cooperative.

gentechnisch ⬦ adj: **~e Änderungen** genetic modifications ⬦ adv: **~ veränderte Lebensmittel** genetically modified foods, GM foods.

genug adv enough; **~ (von etw) haben** to have had enough (of sthg).

Genüge die: **einer Sache** (D) **~ tun** geh to satisfy sthg; **zur ~** abw only too well.

genügen vi - 1. [ausreichen] to be enough; **ein Glas Wein genügt mir** a glass of wine is enough for me; **das genügt!** that's enough! - 2. [entsprechen]: **einer Sache** (D) **~** [Anforderungen] to meet sthg; [Vorschriften] to comply with sthg.

genügend adj & adv enough.

genügsam ⬦ adj [Mensch] modest ⬦ adv modestly.

Genugtuung die satisfaction; **~ für etw** satisfaction for sthg; **mit ~** with satisfaction.

Genus (pl Genera) das GRAM gender.

Genuss (pl Genüsse) der - 1. [Konsum] consumption; **in den ~ von etw kommen** fig to receive sthg - 2. [Befriedigung] pleasure; **das Konzert war ein ~** the concert was a delight.

Geografie, Geographie die geography.

geografisch, geographisch ⬦ adj geographical ⬦ adv geographically.

Geologie die geology.

geologisch ⬦ adj geological ⬦ adv geologically.

Geometrie die geometry.

geordnet adj orderly.

Gepäck das luggage.

Gepäck|abfertigung die - 1. [Handlung] luggage check-in - 2. [Schalter - am Flughafen] (baggage) check-in; [- am Bahnhof] luggage office.

Gepäck|ablage die luggage rack.

Gepäck|annahme die [am Flughafen] (baggage) check-in.

Gepäck|aufbewahrung die [Schalter] left-luggage office Br, baggage room Am.

Gepäck|ausgabe die [am Flughafen] baggage reclaim.

Gepäck|schein der luggage ticket.

Gepäck|stück das item of luggage.

Gepäck|träger der - 1. [von Fahrrad] carrier; [von Auto] luggage rack - 2. [Person] porter.

Gepäck|wagen der luggage van Br, baggage car Am.

gepfiffen pp ⬥ pfeifen.

gepflegt ⬦ adj - 1. [Äußeres] well-groomed; [Hände] well-cared-for; [Haare, Kleidung] neat; [Garten, Haus] well-kept - 2. [von Qualität] quality (vor Subst) - 3. [Stil, Ausdruck] refined ⬦ adv - 1. [essen] well - 2. [gewählt]: **sie drückt sich sehr ~ aus** she has a very refined way of speaking.

gepriesen pp ⬥ preisen.

gequollen pp ⬥ quellen.

gerade ⬦ adv - 1. [vor kurzem] just; **ich bin ~ gekommen** I've just arrived; **~ erst** only just - 2. [jetzt] at the moment; **ich bin ~ beim Saubermachen** I'm just tidying up at the moment - 3. [in jenem Moment] just; **er wollte ~ gehen** he was just about to go - 4. [nicht schief oder gekrümmt] straight - 5. [besonders] exactly; **~ deshalb** precisely for that reason; **er war nicht ~ erfreut** he wasn't exactly pleased - 6. [ausgerechnet]: **warum ~ ich?** why me of all people?; **dass das ~ jetzt passieren musste!** why did it have to happen now of all times?; **das hat mir ~ noch gefehlt!** that's all I needed! - 7. [knapp]: **~ noch** only just ⬦ adj - 1. [nicht gekrümmt] straight - 2. [Haltung] upright.

Gerade (pl -n) die - 1. MATH straight line - 2. SPORT straight.

geradeaus adv straight ahead.

gerade|biegen vt (unreg) fam [bereinigen] to straighten out.

geradeheraus <> adj: ~ **sein** to be frank <> adv frankly.

gerade|stehen vi (unreg) [einstehen]: **für jn/ etw** ~ to take responsibility for sb/sthg.

gerade stehen vi (unreg) [aufrecht stehen] to stand up straight.

geradewegs adv - **1.** [ohne Umweg] directly - **2.** [unmittelbar] immediately.

geradezu adv downright; **es wäre ~ ein Wunder, wenn ...** it would be downright incredible if ...

geradlinig <> adj straight <> adv in a straight line.

Gerangel das - **1.** [Rauferei] scrapping - **2.** abw [Kampf] scramble.

Geranie (pl -n) die geranium.

gerannt pp <> rennen.

gerät präs <> geraten.

Gerät (pl -e) das [Apparat] device; [Werkzeug] tool; [in der Küche] utensil; **elektrisches** ~ (electrical) appliance; **schalt das ~ ab!** switch off the set!

geraten (präs gerät; prät geriet; perf ist geraten) <> vi - **1.** [gelangen]: **an eine unfreundliche Verkäuferin** ~ to get an unfriendly shop assistant; **in etw** (A) ~ [Schwierigkeiten, Not] to get into sthg; [Verdacht] to come under sthg; [Sturm] to be caught in sthg; **in Vergessenheit** ~ to be forgotten - **2.** [gelingen] to turn out; **das Bild ist mir gut** ~ my picture turned out well - **3.** [ähneln]: **nach jm** ~ to take after sb <> pp <> raten.

Geräteturnen das: **im** ~ on the apparatus.

Geratewohl das: **sie bewarb sich aufs** ~ she applied on the off-chance; **er nahm aufs** ~ **ein Buch aus dem Regal** he randomly selected a book from the shelf.

geräumig adj roomy.

Geräusch (pl -e) das noise.

geräuschempfindlich adj sensitive to noise.

geräuschlos <> adj silent <> adv silently.

gerecht <> adj fair; [Belohnung] just; **jm/ einer Sache** ~ **werden** to do sb/sthg justice; **er konnte den Ansprüchen des Chefs nicht** ~ **werden** he couldn't match up to the boss's expectations <> adv fairly.

Gerechtigkeit die justice.

Gerede das abw - **1.** [Geschwätz] chatter - **2.** [Klatsch]: **ins** ~ **kommen** to get o.s. talked about.

geregelt adj [Arbeit] steady; [Leben] orderly.

gereizt <> adj [Person] irritable; [Stimmung] strained <> adv irritably.

Gericht (pl -e) das - **1.** [Speise] dish - **2.** [Insti-

tution] court; **vor** ~ **gehen** to go to court; **vor** ~ **stehen** to stand trial - **3.** [Richter]: **das** ~ the bench - **4.** [Gebäude] court Br, courthouse Am - **5.** (ohne pl) [Richten] judgement; **über jn** ~ **halten** to sit in judgement on sb.

gerichtlich <> adj [Verfahren, Akte] legal; [Untersuchung] judicial <> adv: **gegen jn** ~ **vorgehen** to start legal proceedings against sb.

Gerichts|hof der Court of Justice.

Gerichts|verhandlung die hearing.

Gerichtsvollzieher, in (mpl -; fpl -nen) der, die bailiff.

gerieben pp <> reiben.

geriet prät <> geraten.

gering adj [Gewicht, Preis, Temperatur] low; [Menge] small; [Problem, Chance] slight; [Bedeutung, Rolle] minor; [Dauer] short. <> **nicht im Geringsten** adv not in the least.

geringfügig <> adj slight, minor <> adv slightly.

gering schätzen vt to have a low opinion of.

gerinnen (prät gerann; perf ist geronnen) vi [Milch] to curdle; [Blut] to coagulate.

Gerippe (pl -) das skeleton.

gerissen <> pp <> reißen <> adj crafty <> adv craftily.

geritten pp <> reiten.

Germane (pl -n) der Germanic man.

Germanin (pl -nen) die Germanic woman.

germanisch adj Germanic.

Germanistik die (ohne pl) German language and literature.

gern, gerne (kompar lieber; superl am liebsten) adv - **1.** [gen] with pleasure; **jn/etw** ~ **haben** to like sb/sthg; **etw** ~ **tun** to like to do sthg; **das kann ich** ~ **machen** I'll gladly do it; **aber** ~ !, **ja** ~ ! I'd love to!; ~ **geschehen!** don't mention it!; **ich möchte** ~ **wissen ...** I'd like to know ... - **2.** [oft]: **der Computer stürzt** ~ **ab** the computer tends to crash.

gerochen pp <> riechen.

Geröll das (ohne pl) [im Gebirge] scree; [im Bach] (loose) pebbles (pl).

geronnen pp <> rinnen.

Gerste die barley.

Gerte (pl -n) die switch.

Geruch (pl Gerüche) der smell.

geruchlos adj odourless.

Geruchs|sinn [gə'rʊxszɪn] der sense of smell.

Gerücht (pl -e) das rumour.

gerufen pp <> rufen.

geruhsam <> adj leisurely <> adv: ~ **durch den Garten gehen** to go for a leisurely walk round the garden.

Gerümpel das abw junk.

Gerundium (*pl* -dien) *das* GRAM gerund.

gerungen *pp* ⊳ ringen.

Gerüst (*pl* -e) *das* - 1. [beim Bauen] scaffolding - 2. [von Text] framework.

gesalzen ⬦ *pp* ⊳ salzen ⬦ *adj fam* [Preis, Miete] steep; [Beschwerde] harsh.

gesamt ⬦ *adj* whole, entire; [Einkommen, Kosten] total ⬦ *adv* entirely.

Gesamtausgabe *die* complete edition.

gesamtdeutsch *adj* relating to both eastern and western Germany.

Gesamteindruck *der* overall impression.

Gesamtschule *die* ≈ comprehensive school.

Gesamtschule

The comprehensive school caters for pupils between the ages of 10 and 16 and offers a curriculum comprising core and non-core subjects. Teaching in the core subjects is the same for all pupils, but the programme of study in the non-core subjects is adapted to match the learning needs of individual pupils. Gesamtschulen also offer courses leading to the Abitur.

---

gesandt *pp* ⊳ senden.

Gesandte, tin (*mpl* -n; *fpl* -nen) *der, die* envoy.

Gesang (*pl* Gesänge) *der* - 1. [Singen] singing - 2. [Lied, von Vogel] song.

Gesäß (*pl* -e) *das geh* buttocks (*pl*).

Geschädigte (*pl* -n) *der, die* injured party.

geschaffen *pp* ⊳ schaffen.

Geschäft (*pl* -e) *das* - 1. [Handel] business; **die ~e gehen schlecht** business is slack; **ein ~ abschließen** to close a deal; **du hast damit ein gutes/schlechtes ~ gemacht** that was a good/bad deal (for you); **mit jm ~e machen** to do business with sb - 2. [Laden] shop, store; [Firma] business - 3. [Gewinn] profit - 4. [Angelegenheit] task; **sich um seine ~e kümmern** to go about one's business.

geschäftig ⬦ *adj* [Treiben] bustling; [Person] busy ⬦ *adv* busily.

geschäftlich ⬦ *adj* - 1. [beruflich] business (*vor Subst*) - 2. [unpersönlich] businesslike ⬦ *adv* - 1. [verreisen, fliegen] on business - 2. [unpersönlich] in a businesslike manner.

Geschäftsbedingungen *pl* terms (and conditions).

Geschäftsbeziehungen *pl* business contacts.

Geschäftsfrau *die* businesswoman.

Geschäftsführer, in *der, die* - 1. [von Unternehmen] manager; [von GmbH] managing director - 2. [von Organisation] secretary.

Geschäftsführung *die* management.

Geschäftslage *die* - 1. [wirtschaftlich] commercial situation - 2. [örtlich] business location.

Geschäftsleute *pl* businessmen.

Geschäftsmann (*pl* -leute ODER -männer) *der* businessman.

Geschäftsreise *die* business trip.

Geschäftsschluss *der* closing time.

Geschäftsstelle *die* office; [von Bank] branch.

Geschäftsstraße *die* high street *Br,* main (shopping) street *Am.*

geschäftstüchtig *adj* with good business acumen.

Geschäftszeit *die* [von Laden] opening hours (*pl*); [von Firma] office hours (*pl*).

geschah *prät* ⊳ geschehen.

gescheckt *adj* [Hund, Katze, Stoff] spotted; [Pferd - braunweiß] skewbald; [- schwarzweiß] piebald.

geschehen (*präs* geschieht; *prät* geschah; *perf* ist geschehen) *vi* - 1. [sich ereignen] to happen - 2. [widerfahren]: **es kann dir nichts ~** nothing can happen to you; **ihm ist ein Unrecht ~** he has been wronged; **das geschieht dir/ihm (ganz) recht!** *abw* that serves you/him right! - 3. [verloren sein]: **es ist um seine Zukunft ~** he has no future.

gescheit ⬦ *adj* - 1. [klug] clever - 2. [vernünftig] sensible ⬦ *adv* - 1. [klug] cleverly - 2. [vernünftig] sensibly.

Geschenk (*pl* -e) *das* present.

Geschichte (*pl* -n) *die* - 1. [geschichtliche Entwicklung, Fach] history; **~ machen** to make history - 2. [Erzählung, Bericht] story - 3. [Begebenheit]: **es ist wieder die alte ~** it's the same old story; **mir ist heute eine seltsame ~ passiert** a strange thing happened to me today; **du machst ja ~n!** *hum* you are a one!

geschichtlich ⬦ *adj* historical ⬦ *adv* historically.

Geschichtsunterricht *der* (*ohne pl*) [Schulstunden] history lessons (*pl*).

Geschick (*pl* -e) *das* (*ohne pl*) [Talent, Können] skill.

Geschicklichkeit *die* skilfulness.

geschickt ⬦ *adj* - 1. [fingerfertig] skilful - 2. [raffiniert, gewandt] clever ⬦ *adv* - 1. [fingerfertig] skilfully - 2. [raffiniert, gewandt] cleverly.

geschieden ⬦ *pp* ⊳ scheiden ⬦ *adj* divorced.

geschieht *präs* ⊳ geschehen.

geschienen *pp* ⊳ scheinen.

Geschirr (*pl* -e) *das* - 1. (*ohne pl*) [Gefäße, Service] crockery; [benutzt] dishes (*pl*); **ein ~ für sechs Personen** a dinner/tea service for six people; **~ spülen** ODER **abwaschen** to do the dishes, to wash up *Br* - **2.** [für Zugtiere] harness.

Geschirrspül|maschine *die* dishwasher.

Geschirr|tuch *das* tea towel *Br*, dish towel *Am*.

geschissen *pp* ⊳ scheißen.

geschlafen *pp* ⊳ schlafen.

Geschlecht (*pl* -er) *das* - **1.** [biologische Einteilung] sex - **2.** *(ohne pl)* [Geschlechtsteil] genitals *(pl)* - **3.** [Familie] lineage - **4.** [Genus] der.

Geschlechts|krankheit *die* sexually transmitted disease.

Geschlechts|organ *das* sexual organ.

geschlechtsreif *adj* sexually mature.

Geschlechtsverkehr *der* sexual intercourse.

geschlichen *pp* ⊳ schleichen.

geschlungen *pp* ⊳ schlingen.

Geschmack (*pl* Geschmäcke ODER Geschmäcker) *der* - **1.** [gen] taste; ~ **haben** to have taste; **guten/schlechten** ~ **haben** to have good/bad taste; **an etw** ~ **finden** to acquire a taste for sthg - **2.** [Geschmackssinn] sense of taste.

geschmacklos ⬦ *adj* tasteless ⬦ *adv* tastelessly.

Geschmack|sache = Geschmackssache.

Geschmacks|richtung *die* - **1.** [von Nahrungsmitteln] flavour - **2.** [Stilrichtung, Vorliebe] taste.

Geschmackssache, Geschmacksache *die*: **das ist** ~ that is a matter of taste.

Geschmackssinn *der* sense of taste.

geschmackvoll ⬦ *adj* tasteful ⬦ *adv* tastefully.

geschmeidig ⬦ *adj* [Material, Bewegung] supple ⬦ *adv* [gewandt] supplely.

geschmissen *pp* ⊳ schmeißen.

geschmolzen *pp* ⊳ schmelzen.

Geschnetzelte *das (ohne pl)* small, thin strips of meat cooked in a sauce.

geschnitten ⬦ *pp* ⊳ schneiden ⬦ *adj* - **1.** [Fleisch] sliced - **2.** [Kleid] cut; **ihr Gesicht ist hübsch** ~ she has pretty features.

geschoben *pp* ⊳ schieben.

Geschöpf (*pl* -e) *das* - **1.** [Lebewesen, Person] creature - **2.** [Erfindung] creation.

geschoren *pp* ⊳ scheren.

Geschoss (*pl* -e) *das* - **1.** [Kugel] bullet; [Granate] shell - **2.** [Stockwerk] floor.

geschossen *pp* ⊳ schießen.

Geschrei *das abw* - **1.** [Schreien] shouting - **2.** [Gezeter] fuss.

geschrieben *pp* ⊳ schreiben.

geschrien *pp* ⊳ schreien.

Geschütz (*pl* -e) *das* (big) gun; ~e artillery (U).

Geschwätz *das abw* - **1.** [Gerede] prattle - **2.** [Tratsch] gossip.

geschwätzig *adj abw* prattling; [tratschend] gossipy.

geschweige *konj*: ~ **denn** let alone.

geschwiegen *pp* ⊳ schweigen.

geschwind *Süddt* ⬦ *adj* quick ⬦ *adv* quickly.

Geschwindigkeit (*pl* -en) *die* speed.

Geschwister *pl* brothers and sisters.

geschwollen ⬦ *pp* ⊳ schwellen ⬦ *adj* - **1.** [Finger, Gesicht] swollen - **2.** *abw* [Sätze, Ausdruck] pompous ⬦ *adv abw* [pompös] pompously.

geschwommen *pp* ⊳ schwimmen.

geschworen *pp* ⊳ schwören.

Geschworene (*pl* -n) *der, die* juror.

Geschwulst (*pl* Geschwülste) *die* tumour.

Geschwür (*pl* -e) *das* ulcer.

gesehen *pp* ⊳ sehen.

Geselle (*pl* -n) *der* - **1.** [Handwerker] qualified craftsman - **2.** [Kerl] fellow.

gesellig *adj* - **1.** [kontaktfreudig - Person] sociable; [- Tier] gregarious - **2.** [anregend] convivial.

Geselligkeit *die* conviviality; ~ **brauchen** to need company.

Gesellin (*pl* -nen) *die* qualified craftswoman.

Gesellschaft (*pl* -en) *die* - **1.** [Gemeinschaft] society - **2.** [Anwesenheit, Umgang] company; **jm** ~ **leisten** to keep sb company - **3.** [Fest] party; **geschlossene** ~ private party - **4.** [Gruppe] group (of people) - **5.** [Wirtschaftsunternehmen] company.

gesessen *pp* ⊳ sitzen.

Gesetz (*pl* -e) *das* [staatliche Vorschrift, Regel] law.

Gesetz|buch *das* statute book.

gesetzgebend *adj* legislative.

Gesetz|geber *der* legislature.

Gesetzgebung *die* legislation.

gesetzlich ⬦ *adj* legal; ~**er Feiertag** public holiday; **ein** ~**er Anspruch** a legitimate claim ⬦ *adv* legally; ~ **verankert** established in law.

gesetzmäßig *adj* - **1.**: **ein** ~**er Prozess** a process governed by a natural law - **2.** [Macht] legal; [Inhaber] lawful.

gesetzt *adj* sedate; ~ **den Fall, dass ...** assuming that ...

Gesicht (*pl* -er ODER -e) *das* face; **jm etw ins** ~ **sagen** *fig* to say sthg to sb's face.

Gesichts|punkt *der* point of view.

Gesichts|züge *pl* features.

Gesinnung (*pl* -en) *die* [Überzeugungen] convictions *(pl)*; [Einstellung] outlook (U).

gesittet ⬦ *adj* civilized ⬦ *adv* in a civilized manner.

gesoffen *pp* ⊳ saufen.

gesogen *pp* ⊳ saugen.

gesondert <> adj separate <> adv separately.

gespannt <> adj - **1.** [Stoff, Saite] taut - **2.** [Person] eager; **ich bin ~ auf seine neue Freundin** I can't wait to see his new girlfriend - **3.** [Situation] tense <> adv [erwartungsvoll, aufgeregt] eagerly.

Gespenst (pl -er) das ghost; [Bedrohung] spectre.

gespien pp [> speien.

gesponnen pp [> spinnen.

Gespött das mockery; **jn/sich zum ~ der Leute machen** to make sb/o.s. a laughing stock.

Gespräch (pl -e) das - **1.** [Konversation] conversation, talk; **etw ist im ~** fig sthg is under discussion - **2.** [Telefonanruf] call.

gesprächig adj talkative.

Gesprächs|partner, in [gə'ʃprɛːçspartnɐ] der, die; **mein ~** the person I am/was talking to; **seine ~ bei den Verhandlungen** his partners in the negotiations.

Gesprächs|thema [gə'ʃprɛːçsteːma] das topic of conversation.

gesprochen pp [> sprechen.

gesprossen pp [> sprießen.

gesprungen pp [> springen.

Gespür das feel; **ein/kein ~ für etw haben** to have a/no feel for sthg.

Gestalt (pl -en) die - **1.** [Person] figure - **2.** (ohne pl) [Körperform] build - **3.** [in Literatur] character - **4.** (ohne pl) [Form] shape; **unser Plan nimmt ~ an** our plan is taking shape.
⇒ **in Gestalt** präp: **in ~ einer Sache** (G) in the shape of sthg.

gestalten vt [Fest] to organize; [Schaufenster, Garten] to design. ⇒ **sich gestalten** ref to turn out.

Gestaltung die [von Fest] organizing; [von Schaufenster, Garten] designing.

Geständnis (pl -se) das confession; **ein ~ ablegen** to make a confession.

Gestank der (ohne pl) abw stench.

gestatten vt: **jm etw ~** to allow sb sthg.
⇒ **gestatten Sie** interj: **~ Sie?** may I?; **~ Sie, dass ich rauche?** do you mind if I smoke?

Geste (pl -n) die gesture.

gestehen (prät gestand; perf hat gestanden) <> vt: **ein Verbrechen/einen Mord ~** to confess to a crime/murder; **jm die Wahrheit ~** to confess the truth to sb <> vi [aussagen] to confess.

Gestein (pl -e) das rock.

Gestell (pl -e) das stand.

gestern adv yesterday; **~ früh** first thing yesterday; **~ Morgen/Mittag/Abend** yesterday morning/lunchtime/evening; **von ~ sein** fig to be behind the times.

gestiegen pp [> steigen.

gestochen pp [> stechen.

gestohlen pp [> stehlen.

gestorben pp [> sterben.

gestoßen pp [> stoßen.

gestreift adj striped.

gestrig adj yesterday's; **am ~en Abend** yesterday evening.

gestritten pp [> streiten.

Gestrüpp das undergrowth.

gestunken pp [> stinken.

Gestüt (pl -e) das stud.

Gesuch (pl -e) das request.

gesund (kompar gesünder ODER gesunder; superl gesündeste ODER gesundeste) <> adj healthy; **~er Menschenverstand** common sense <> adv healthily; **jn ~ schreiben** to certify sb fit; **jn ~ pflegen** to nurse sb back to health.

Gesundheit die health.

gesundheitlich <> adj health; **ihr ~er Zustand** the state of her health <> adv healthwise.

Gesundheits|amt das public health department.

gesundheitsschädlich adj damaging to one's health.

Gesundheitszu|stand der state of health.

gesungen pp [> singen.

gesunken pp [> sinken.

getan pp [> tun.

Getöse das roar.

getragen pp [> tragen.

Getränk (pl -e) das drink.

Getreide das cereals (pl), grain.

Getreidean|bau der cereal growing.

getrennt <> adj separate <> adv separately; **(von jm) ~ leben** to be separated (from sb).

getreten pp [> treten.

Getriebe (pl -) das gearbox.

getrieben pp [> treiben.

getrogen pp [> trügen.

getrost adv without any problem.

getrunken pp [> trinken.

Getto, Ghetto (pl -s) das ghetto.

Getue [gə'tuːə] das abw fuss.

Getümmel das: **sich ins ~ stürzen** to throw o.s. into the fray.

Gewächs [gə'vɛks] (pl -e) das plant.

gewachsen [gə'vaksn] <> pp [> wachsen <> adj: **jm ~ sein** to be a match for sb; **etw ~ sein** to be up to sthg.

Gewächs|haus das greenhouse.

gewagt <> adj daring <> adv [freizügig] daringly.

gewählt <> adj - **1.** [durch Abstimmung bestimmt] elected - **2.** [gehoben] refined <> adv [gehoben] in a refined manner.

Gewähr die (ohne pl) guarantee; **~ leisten** to

guarantee. **ohne Gewähr** *adv* subject to alteration.

gewähren *vt* to give; **jm etw ~** to grant sb sthg; **jn ~ lassen** to let sb do as he/she likes.

gewährleisten *vt* ▷ Gewähr.

Gewalt (*pl* -en) *die* - **1.** [Brutalität, Willkür] violence; **etw mit ~ öffnen** to force sthg open; **jn mit ~ zu etw zwingen** to compel sb to do sthg by (using) force; **etw mit aller ~ machen** to do sthg with all one's might - **2.** [Macht, Beherrschung] power; **jn/sich/ etw in der ~ haben** to be in control of sb/ o.s./sthg - **3.** [Naturgewalt] force, power.

Gewaltlherrschaft *die* tyranny.

gewaltig ⬦ *adj* [Kraft, Größe] enormous, huge; [Schönheit] tremendous ⬦ *adv* enormously.

gewaltsam ⬦ *adj* violent; **~e Vertreibung** forcible expulsion ⬦ *adv* forcibly; [schließen] by force; **jn ~ an etw hindern** to prevent sb forcibly from doing sthg.

gewalttätig ⬦ *adj* violent ⬦ *adv* violently.

Gewaltlverbrechen *das* crime of violence.

gewandt ⬦ *pp* ▷ wenden ⬦ *adj* - **1.** [Ausdrucksweise, Redner] skilful - **2.** [Auftreten] confident - **3.** [Bewegung] agile ⬦ *adv* - **1.** [sich ausdrücken] skilfully - **2.** [auftreten] confidently - **3.** [sich bewegen] agilely.

Gewandtheit *die* - **1.** [von Redner] skilfulness - **2.** [von Umgangsformen] confidence - **3.** [von Bewegungen] agility.

gewann *prät* ▷ gewinnen.

gewaschen *pp* ▷ waschen.

Gewässer (*pl* -) *das* stretch of water. **Gewässer** *pl* waters.

Gewebe (*pl* -) *das* - **1.** [Stoff] fabric - **2.** [im Körper] tissue.

Gewehr (*pl* -e) *das* rifle.

Geweih (*pl* -e) *das* antlers (*pl*); [Trophäe] set of antlers.

Gewerbe (*pl* -) *das* - **1.** [Beruf] trade - **2.** (*ohne pl*) [Bereich] trade.

Gewerbelschein *der* trading licence.

gewerblich ⬦ *adj* commercial ⬦ *adv* commercially.

Gewerkschaft (*pl* -en) *die* trade union *Br*, labor union *Am*.

Gewerkschaft(l)er, in (*mpl* -; *fpl* -nen) *der, die* trade *Br* ODER labor *Am* unionist.

Gewerkschaftsbund *der* trade union federation.

gewesen *pp* ▷ sein.

Gewicht (*pl* -e) *das* weight; **etw fällt ins ~** *fig* sthg is of consequence.

Gewichtheben *das* weightlifting.

Gewinde (*pl* -) *das* thread.

Gewinn (*pl* -e) *der* - **1.** [Profit] profit - **2.** (*ohne pl*) [Nutzen] benefit - **3.** [Preis] prize. **Gewinn bringend** ⬦ *adj* profitable ⬦ *adv* profitably.

gewinnen (*prät* gewann; *perf* hat gewonnen) ⬦ *vi* - **1.** [siegen] to win - **2.** [wachsen]: **an etw** (*D*) **~** to gain in sthg - **3.** [besser werden]: **durch etw ~** to benefit from sthg ⬦ *vt* - **1.** [Wettkampf, Preis] to win - **2.** [Ansehen] to gain; **jn für etw ~** to win sb over to sthg - **3.** [Produkt] to produce.

gewinnend *adj* winning.

Gewinner, in (*mpl* -; *fpl* -nen) *der, die* winner.

Gewinnung *die* extraction.

Gewirr, Gewirre *das* [von Kabeln] tangle; [von Stimmen] confusion.

gewiss ⬦ *adj* certain; **sich** (*D*) **einer Sache** (*G*) **~ sein** to be certain of sthg; **der Sieg ist uns ~** we are certain of victory ⬦ *adv* [sicherlich] certainly.

Gewissen *das* (*ohne pl*) [seelische Instanz] conscience; **gutes/schlechtes ~** clear/bad conscience.

gewissenhaft ⬦ *adj* conscientious ⬦ *adv* conscientiously.

Gewissenslbisse *pl* pangs of conscience.

Gewissenslkonflikt *der* moral dilemma; **in einen ~ geraten** to be faced with a moral dilemma.

gewissermaßen *adv* as it were.

Gewissheit *die* (*ohne pl*) certainty; **~ erlangen** to find out for certain; **etw mit ~ sagen/ wissen** to say/know sthg for certain.

Gewitter (*pl* -) *das* thunderstorm.

gewittrig *adj* thundery.

gewitzt ⬦ *adj* shrewd ⬦ *adv* shrewdly.

gewogen *pp* ▷ wiegen.

gewöhnen *vt*: **jn an jn/etw ~** to accustom sb to sb/sthg. **sich gewöhnen** *ref*: **sich an jn/etw ~** to get used to sb/sthg; **sich daran ~, etw zu tun** to get used to doing sthg.

Gewohnheit (*pl* -en) *die* habit; **jm zur ~ werden** to become a habit with sb.

gewöhnlich ⬦ *adj* - **1.** [normal] normal, ordinary - **2.** [gewohnt] usual - **3.** *abw* [primitiv] common ⬦ *adv* - **1.** [normalerweise] normally, usually - **2.** *abw* [primitiv] in a common way. **wie gewöhnlich** *adv* as usual.

gewohnt *adj* usual; **etw ~ sein** to be used to sthg.

gewöhnt *adj*: **an etw** (*A*) **~ sein** to be used to sthg.

Gewölbe (*pl* -) *das* vault.

gewonnen *pp* ▷ gewinnen.

geworben *pp* ▷ werben.

geworden *pp* ▷ werden.

geworfen *pp* ▷ werfen.

Gewühl das - **1.** [Menschenmenge] crush - **2.** [Wühlen] rummaging.

gewunden ◇ pp ▷ winden ◇ adj - **1.** [Weg] winding - **2.** [Sätze] tortuous.

Gewürz (pl -e) das spice.

Gewürzlgurke die pickled gherkin.

gewusst pp ▷ wissen.

Gezeiten pl tides.

Gezeter das abw scolding.

gezielt ◇ adj specific; **eine ~e Frage/Antwort** a specific question/answer ◇ adv: **~ vorgehen** to take specific action; **jn ~ auf etw ansprechen** to ask sb specifically about sthg.

geziert abw ◇ adj affected ◇ adv affectedly.

gezogen pp ▷ ziehen.

gezwungen ◇ pp ▷ zwingen ◇ adj forced ◇ adv in a forced way.

gezwungenermaßen adv: **etw ~ machen** to be forced to do sthg.

ggf. abk für gegebenenfalls.

Ghetto das = Getto.

gibt präs ▷ geben.

Gicht die gout.

Giebel (pl -) der - **1.** [auf Dach] gable - **2.** [über Tor] pediment.

Gier die greed; **~ nach etw** craving for sthg.

gierig ◇ adj greedy; **~ nach** ODER **auf etw** (A) **sein** to have a craving for sthg ◇ adv greedily.

gießen (prät goss, perf hat gegossen) ◇ vt - **1.** [schütten] to pour - **2.** [verschütten] to spill - **3.** [Blumen] to water - **4.** [Glocke, Blei] to cast; [Kerzen] to mould ◇ vi [regnen]: **es gießt** it's pouring.

Gift (pl -e) das [schädliche Substanz] poison.

📖 Gift

Care is required with the German word Gift, a false friend which corresponds to the English "poison" rather than "gift" or "present". So the sentence *Wegen der Mäuse haben wir Gift ausgelegt* means "We put poison down for the mice".
The English "gift", on the other hand, has the German equivalent Geschenk. So the sentence "I got a really nice gift for my birthday" can be rendered as *Zu meinem Geburtstag habe ich ein besonders schönes Geschenk bekommen.*

---

giftgrün adj lurid green.

giftig ◇ adj - **1.** [Gift enthaltend, gesundheitsschädlich] poisonous - **2.** fam abw [gehässig] venomous - **3.** [grell] lurid ◇ adv fam abw [gehässig] venomously.

Giftlmüll der toxic waste.

Gigant, in (mpl -en; fpl -nen) der, die giant.

gilt präs ▷ gelten.

Gin [dʒɪn] der gin.

ging prät ▷ gehen.

Ginster (pl -) der broom (U); [Stechginster] gorse (U).

Gipfel (pl -) der - **1.** [von Bergen] summit, peak - **2.** [Höhepunkt] height - **3.** [Gipfeltreffen] summit.

Gipfelltreffen das summit meeting.

Gips der - **1.** [Material] plaster - **2.** [Gipsverband] plaster cast.

Gipslbein das: **ein ~ haben** to have a leg in plaster.

Gipslverband der plaster cast.

Giraffe (pl -n) die giraffe.

Girlande (pl -n) die garland.

Girolkonto ['ʒiːrokɔnto] das current account Br, checking account Am.

Gischt die ODER der spray.

Gitarre (pl -n) die guitar.

Gitarrist, in (mpl -en; fpl -nen) der, die guitarist.

Gitter (pl -) das [aus Eisen] bars (pl); [gekreuzt] grille; [aus Holz] trellis; [Geländer] railings (pl). ➤ **hinter Gittern** adv fam behind bars.

Glanz der - **1.** [von Stern] brightness - **2.** [von Perl] gleam - **3.** [von Augen] sparkle.

glänzen vi - **1.** [gen] to shine, to gleam; [Augen, Edelsteine] to sparkle; [Farbe] to be shiny - **2.** [herausragen] to shine.

glänzend ◇ adj - **1.** [mit Glanz] shiny; [Lack] gloss - **2.** [sehr gut] brilliant ◇ adv [sehr gut] brilliantly.

Glas (pl Gläser) das - **1.** [Material, Trinkglas] glass; **eine Kanne aus ~** a glass pot; **ein ~ Saft** a glass of juice; **ein ~ über den Durst trinken** fig to have one too many - **2.** [für Marmelade] jar - **3.** [Brillenglas] lens.

Glaser, in (mpl -; fpl -nen) der, die glazier.

glasig adj - **1.** [Blick, Ausdruck] glazed - **2.** [beim Braten] transparent.

glasklar adj crystal clear.

Glaslscheibe die pane (of glass).

Glasur (pl -en) die - **1.** [für Keramik] glaze - **2.** [für Speisen] icing Br, frosting Am.

glatt ◇ adj - **1.** [Oberfläche] smooth; **~e Haare** straight hair - **2.** [rutschig] slippery - **3.** [reibungslos] smooth - **4.** fam [eindeutig]: **eine ~e Lüge** a downright lie; **eine ~e Ablehnung** a flat refusal; **das ist ~er Wahnsinn!** that's utter madness! ◇ adv - **1.**: **etw ~ streichen** to smooth sthg - **2.** [verlaufen] smoothly - **3.** fam [eindeutig]: **das haute ihn ~ um** that completely floored him.

Glätte die - **1.** [Ebenheit] smoothness - **2.** [Schlüpfrigkeit] slipperiness.

Glatteis das (ohne pl) black ice.

glätten vt [Decke] to smooth; [Falte] to smooth out. ➤ **sich glätten** ref [Meer] to become calm.

Glatze (*pl* -n) *die* - **1.** [kahler Kopf] bald head; **eine ~ haben** to be bald - **2.** [kahle Stelle] bald patch; **eine ~ haben** to be going bald.

Glaube *der* - **1.** [Annahme] belief; **~ an etw** *(A)* belief in sthg; **in gutem** ODER **im guten ~n** in good faith; **jm/einer Sache ~n/keinen ~n schenken** to/not to believe sb/sthg - **2.** [Religion] faith.

glauben <> *vt* - **1.** [denken] to think - **2.** [für richtig halten] to believe; **jm ~** to believe sb; **ich glaube ihm nichts mehr** I don't believe anything he says any more <> *vi* - **1.** [für wahr halten]: **an jn/etw ~** to believe in sb/sthg; **jm ~** to believe sb - **2.** [gläubig sein] to believe - **3.** RW: **dran ~ müssen** [umkommen] to bite the dust.

Glaubens|bekenntnis *das* (*ohne pl*) REL creed.

glaubhaft <> *adj* credible <> *adv* convincingly.

gläubig <> *adj* - **1.** [fromm] devout - **2.** [vertrauensselig] trusting <> *adv* - **1.** [fromm] devoutly - **2.** [vertrauensselig] trustingly.

Gläubige (*pl* -n) *der, die* believer.

Gläubiger, in (*mpl* -; *fpl* -nen) *der, die* creditor.

glaubwürdig <> *adj* credible <> *adv* convincingly.

gleich <> *adj* - **1.** [übereinstimmend] same; **den ~en Namen haben** to have the same name; **zwei ~e Tassen** two identical cups - **2.** [egal]: **das ist mir ~** it's all the same to me <> *adv* - **1.** [ebenso] equally; **~ groß/alt sein** to be the same size/age - **2.** [auf gleiche Weise] the same; **die beiden Wörter werden ~ ausgesprochen** the two words are pronounced the same - **3.** [egal]: **das bleibt sich ~, ob du nun ...** it makes no difference whether you ... - **4.** [zeitlich] straight away, immediately; **ich komme ~** I'm just coming; **ich komme ~ wieder** I'll be right back; **bis ~!** see you soon! - **5.** [räumlich] right; **~ daneben** right next to it - **6.** [in Fragesätzen] again; **wie hieß er doch ~?** what's his name again? - **7.** [ebensogut] just as well; **bei dem Reparaturpreis können wir doch ~ ein neues kaufen** if it's going to cost that much to repair it, we might as well buy a new one <> *präp* (+ D) *geh* like.

gleichaltrig, gleichalterig *adj* of the same age; **~ sein** to be the same age.

gleichberechtigt *adj* with equal rights; **~ sein** to have equal rights.

Gleichberechtigung *die* (*ohne pl*) equality, equal rights (*pl*).

gleichen (*prät* glich; *perf* hat geglichen) *vi*: **jm/einer Sache ~** to be like ODER resemble sb/sthg; **sich** *(D)* **~** to resemble each other.

gleichfalls *adv* also, as well; **danke ~!** you too!

Gleichgewicht *das* - **1.** [Balance] balance;

im ~ balanced; **das ~ halten/verlieren** to keep/lose one's balance - **2.** [Harmonie] equilibrium; **die Veränderungen brachten sie völlig aus dem ~** the changes threw her completely off balance.

gleichgültig <> *adj* - **1.** [desinteressiert] indifferent - **2.** [einerlei - Themen] trivial; **es ist ~, ob er kommt oder nicht** it's all the same whether he comes or not; **sie ist mir ~** she means nothing to me; **Politik ist ihm völlig ~** he's completely indifferent about politics <> *adv* [desinteressiert] indifferently; **~ was er macht ...** no matter what he does ...

Gleichheit *die* - **1.** [Übereinstimmung] similarity - **2.** [Gleichberechtigung] equality.

gleich|kommen (*perf* ist gleichgekommen) *vi* (*unregl*): **jm an etw** *(D)* **~** to match sb for sthg.

gleich lautend *adj* identical.

gleichmäßig <> *adj* - **1.** [Atmung, Schritte, Schichten] even - **2.** [Geschwindigkeit, Rhythmus] steady - **3.** [Abstände] regular <> *adv* - **1.** [atmen, anordnen, verteilen] evenly - **2.** [sich vorwärts bewegen] steadily - **3.** [wiederkehrend]: **~ hohe Punktzahlen** consistently high scores.

Gleichnis (*pl* -se) *das* parable.

gleichschenklig ['glaɪçʃɛŋk(ə)lɪç], **gleichschenkelig** *adj* MATH: **~es Dreieck** isosceles triangle.

Gleichschritt *der*: **im ~** in step.

gleich stellen ['glaɪçʃtɛlən] *vt* to treat equally.

Gleichstrom *der* direct current.

Gleichung (*pl* -en) *die* equation.

gleichzeitig <> *adj* simultaneous <> *adv* at the same time.

gleich ziehen *vi* (*unregl*): **mit jm ~** to draw level with sb, to catch up with sb.

Gleis (*pl* -e) *das* [Schienen] track; [Bahnsteig] platform.

gleiten (*prät* glitt; *perf* hat/ist geglitten) *vi* - **1.** (*ist*) [sich bewegen] to glide; [rutschen] to slip - **2.** (*hat*) *fam* [Arbeitnehmer] to work flexitime *Br* ODER flextime *Am*.

Gleit|zeit *die* flexitime *Br*, flextime *Am*.

Gletscher (*pl* -) *der* glacier.

glich *prät* [> gleichen.

Glied (*pl* -er) *das* - **1.** [Gelenk] joint - **2.** [Körperteil] limb - **3.** [Penis] (male) member - **4.** [Bindeglied - von Kette] link - **5.** [Einzelteil] part; [von Satz] clause.

gliedern *vt* to organize, to structure.
➤ sich gliedern *ref*: **sich in etw** *(A)* **~** to be divided into sthg.

Gliederung (*pl* -en) *die* - **1.** [Gliedern] organization, structuring - **2.** [Struktur] structure.

Gliedmaßen *pl* limbs.

glimmen (*prät* glimmte ODER glomm; *perf* hat geglimmt ODER geglommen) *vi* to glow.

glimpflich <> *adj* [ohne Schaden]: **die Entführung nahm ein ~es Ende** the kidnapping was resolved without anyone being seriously hurt <> *adv* [ohne Schaden]: **~ davonkommen** to get off lightly.

glitschig *adj* slippery.

glitt *prät* ▷ gleiten.

glitzern *vi* [Sterne] to twinkle; [Schmuck, Augen] to sparkle; [Schnee, Tränen] to glisten; [Silber, Gold] to glitter.

global <> *adj* - **1.** [weltumfassend] global; [Frieden] world (*vor Subst*) - **2.** [vielseitig, allgemein] general <> *adv* - **1.** [weltumfassend] globally - **2.** [vielseitig, allgemein] generally.

Globalisierung *die* globalization.

Globus (*pl* -se ODER Globen) *der* globe.

Glocke (*pl* -n) *die* bell.

Glocken|spiel *das* - **1.** [von Türmen] carillon - **2.** [Musikinstrument] glockenspiel.

Glocken|turm *der* belfry, bell tower.

glomm *prät* ▷ glimmen.

glorreich <> *adj* [Sieg, Geschichte, Ergebnis] glorious; [Einfall] brilliant <> *adv* triumphantly.

Glossar (*pl* -e) *das* glossary.

glotzen *vi fam abw* to gawk, to gawp *Br.*

Glück *das* - **1.** [Glücksfall] luck; **ein ~, dass ...** it's lucky that ...; **~ bringen** to bring luck, to be lucky; **~ haben** to be lucky; **bei jm (mit etw (D))** **kein ~ haben** to get no joy out of sb (with sthg); **er hatte mit dem Auto kein ~** he had no luck with the car - **2.** [Fortuna] fortune; **das ~ verließ ihn** *geh* fortune ODER luck abandoned him - **3.** [Segen] happiness; **das Kind war ihr ganzes ~** the child meant everything to her. **⬤ auf gut Glück** *adv* on the off chance. **⬤ viel Glück** *interj* good luck! **⬤ zum Glück** *adv* luckily, fortunately.

glücken (*perf* ist geglückt) *vi* to be successful; **ihm glückt alles, was er in Angriff nimmt** he succeeds at everything he does.

gluckern *vi* [Wasser, Flüssigkeit] to gurgle; [Wein] to glug.

glücklich <> *adj* - **1.** [Person, Ehe, Ende] happy - **2.** [Zufall] happy, lucky; [Zeitpunkt, Reise] good - **3.** [Sieger, Sieg] lucky <> *adv* - **1.** [verheiratet, enden] happily - **2.** [letztendlich] eventually.

glücklicherweise *adv* luckily, fortunately.

Glücksbringer (*pl* -) *der* [Sache] lucky charm; [Person] lucky mascot.

Glücks|fall *der* stroke of luck.

Glücks|spiel *das* - **1.** [um Geld] game of chance - **2.** [Glückssache] lottery.

Glücks|strähne *die* lucky streak.

Glück|wunsch *der* congratulations (*pl*); **jm seine Glückwünsche aussprechen** to congratulate sb, to offer sb one's congratulations; **herzlichen ~ zum Geburtstag!** happy birthday!; **herzliche Glückwünsche!** congratulations!

Glucose = Glukose.

Glüh|birne *die* light bulb.

glühen *vi* - **1.** [brennen] to glow - **2.** *geh* [bewegt sein] to burn.

glühend <> *adj* - **1.** [brennend] glowing; [Metall, Nadel] red-hot; [Hitze] scorching - **2.** [leidenschaftlich] passionate; [Neid] deep <> *adv* [leidenschaftlich] passionately.

Glüh|wein *der* mulled wine.

Glukose, Glucose *die* glucose.

Glut (*pl* -en) *die* - **1.** [in Feuer] embers (*pl*) - **2.** *geh* [Inbrunst] ardour.

GmbH [geːɛmbeːˈhaː] (*pl* -s) (*abk für* Gesellschaft mit beschränkter Haftung) *die* ≃ Ltd *Br*, ≃ Inc *Am*.

Gnade *die* - **1.** [Gunst] favour - **2.** [Erbarmen - menschlich] mercy; [- göttlich] grace.

gnadenlos <> *adj* merciless; [Hitze, Druck, Stress] unrelenting <> *adv* mercilessly; [heiß] mercilessly, unrelentingly.

gnädig <> *adj* - **1.** [wohlmeinend] kind - **2.** [nachsichtig] lenient - **3.** [barmherzig] merciful <> *adv* - **1.** [wohlmeinend] kindly - **2.** [nachsichtig] leniently. **⬤ gnädige Frau** *interj* Madam!

Gold *das* gold; **eine Uhr aus ~** a gold watch.

Gold|barren *der* gold bar ODER ingot.

golden <> *adj* - **1.** [aus Gold] gold - **2.** [goldfarben] golden - **3.** [großartig - Jahre, Zeit] golden; [- Freiheit, Moment] glorious <> *adv* [glänzen] like gold.

Gold|fisch *der* goldfish.

goldgelb *adj & adv* golden yellow.

Gold|medaille *die* gold medal.

Gold|schmied, -in *der, die* goldsmith.

Golf (*pl* -e) <> *der* gulf <> *das* golf.

Golf|platz *der* golf course.

Golf|strom *der* Gulf Stream.

gönnen *vt*: **jm etw ~** not to begrudge sb sthg; **sich** (D) **etw ~** to allow o.s. sthg.

Gönner (*pl* -) *der* patron.

gönnerhaft *abw* <> *adj* patronizing <> *adv* patronizingly.

Gönnerin (*pl* -nen) *die* patron, patroness.

Gorilla (*pl* -s) *der eigtl & fig* gorilla.

goss *prät* ▷ gießen.

Gosse (*pl* -n) *die* gutter.

Gotik *die* (ohne *pl*) [Stil] Gothic (style); [Epoche] Gothic period.

gotisch *adj* Gothic.

Gott (*pl* Götter) *der* - **1.** [christlich] God; **um ~es Willen!** [Schrecken ausdrückend] oh my God!; [flehend] for heaven's sake! - **2.** [Gottheit] god. **⬤ Gott sei Dank** *adv* thank goodness. **⬤ grüß Gott** *interj Südd, Österr* hello!

Gottes|dienst *der* service; **zum ~ gehen** to go to church.

Göttin (*pl* -nen) *die* goddess.

göttlich <> *adj* eigtl & *fig* divine <> *adv* [wunderbar] divinely.

gottlos <> *adj* - **1.** [respektlos, gottvergessen] ungodly - **2.** [ungläubig] godless <> *adv* [respektlos, gottvergessen] in an ungodly manner.

Gouverneur, in [guvɐˈnøːɐ̯, rɪn] (*mpl* -e; *fpl* -nen) *der, die* governor.

GPS [geːpeːˈʔɛs] (*abk für* Grüne Partei der Schweiz) *die* Swiss Green Party.

Grab (*pl* Gräber) *das* grave.

graben (*präs* gräbt; *prät* grub; *perf* hat gegraben) *vt* & *vi* to dig.

Graben (*pl* Gräben) *der* ditch; [um eine Festung] moat; [Schützengraben] trench.

Grab|stein *der* gravestone, tombstone.

gräbt *präs* ⫐ graben.

Grabung (*pl* -en) *die* excavation.

Grad (*pl* -e) *der* - **1.** [gen] degree; **es hängt in hohem ~ davon ab, ob ...** it depends to a large extent on whether ...; **die Temperatur beträgt 25 ~** the temperature is 25 degrees; **in hohem ~ verschmutzt** highly polluted - **2.** MIL rank.

grad|weise *adv* gradually.

Graf (*pl* -en) *der* count.

Grafik, Graphik (*pl* -en) *die* - **1.** [Kunst] graphic art; [Technik] graphics (*U*) - **2.** [Kunstwerk] graphic artwork - **3.** [Schema] diagram.

Gräfin (*pl* -nen) *die* countess.

grafisch, graphisch <> *adj* - **1.** [die Kunst betreffend] graphic - **2.** [schematisch] diagrammatic <> *adv* - **1.** [künstlerisch] graphically - **2.** [schematisch] diagrammatically.

Grafschaft (*pl* -en) *die* - **1.** [von Graf] count's lands (*pl*) - **2.** [Verwaltungsbezirk] county.

Gramm (*pl* -e ODER -) *das* gram; **500 ~** 500 grams.

Grammatik (*pl* -en) *die* grammar.

grammatikalisch, grammatisch <> *adj* grammatical <> *adv* grammatically.

Granate (*pl* -n) *die* shell; [Handgranate] grenade.

grandios <> *adj* superb <> *adv* superbly.

Granit *der* granite.

Grapefruit [ˈɡreːpfruːt] (*pl* -s) *die* grapefruit.

Graphik = Grafik.

graphisch = grafisch.

Gras (*pl* Gräser) *das* grass; **wir sollten warten bis ~ über die Sache gewachsen ist** we should wait until the dust has settled.

grasen *vi* to graze; **Kühe ~ lassen** to graze cattle.

Gras|halm *der* blade of grass.

grassieren *vi* [Krankheit, Pest] to rage; [Mode] to be all the rage.

grässlich <> *adj* terrible <> *adv* terribly.

Grat (*pl* -e) *der* ridge.

Gräte (*pl* -n) *die* (fish) bone.

gratis *adj* & *adv* free (of charge).

Grätsche (*pl* -n) *die*: **eine ~ über etw** (A) **machen** to hurdle sthg; **in der ~ stehen** to stand with one's legs astride.

gratulieren *vi* to offer one's congratulations; **jm (zu etw) ~** to congratulate sb (on sthg); **jm zum Geburtstag ~** to wish sb a happy birthday.

gratulieren

Congratulations! Gratuliere!

Well done! (Br), Good job! (Am) Gut gemacht!

Well played! Gut gespielt!

That's great news! Das sind tolle Neuigkeiten!

I'm really pleased for you! Ich freue mich riesig für dich!

grau *adj* grey; **~ meliert** [Haar] greying; [Wolle, Stoff] flecked with grey.

Grau *das* - **1.** [graue Farbe] grey - **2.** [Tristheit] greyness.

Grau|brot *das* bread made from mixed wholemeal, rye and wheat flour.

Graubünden *nt* Graubünden.

grauhaarig *adj* grey-haired.

grausam <> *adj* - **1.** [brutal] cruel - **2.** [fürchterlich, schlimm] terrible <> *adv* - **1.** [brutal] cruelly - **2.** [fürchterlich, äußerst] terribly.

Grausamkeit (*pl* -en) *die* - **1.** (ohne *pl*) [grausames Wesen] cruelty - **2.** [grausame Tat] atrocity.

grausig <> *adj* terrible <> *adv* terribly.

Gravur [ɡraˈvuːɐ̯] (*pl* -en) *die* engraving.

Graz *nt* Graz.

Grazie (*pl* -n) *die* grace; **mit ~** gracefully. ➤ **Grazien** *pl* MYTH Graces.

graziös <> *adj* graceful <> *adv* gracefully.

greifbar <> *adj* - **1.** [in Reichweite] to hand, handy - **2.** [parat] available - **3.** [absehbar] tangible <> *adv* [sehr]: **~ nahe** within reach.

greifen (*prät* griff; *perf* hat gegriffen) <> *vt* - **1.** [fassen] to take hold of - **2.** [erwischen] to catch - **3.** [Akkord] to play <> *vi* - **1.** [fassen]: **zur Flasche/Zigarette ~** *fig* to reach for the bottle/cigarettes; **nach etw ~** to reach for sthg; [Macht] to strive for sthg - **2.** [langen] to reach; **in etw** (A) **~** to reach into sthg - **3.** [Halt finden] to grip; [Zahnrad] to catch - **4.** [funktionieren] to work - **5.** *RW*: **um sich ~** to spread; **die Zahl ist zu hoch/niedrig gegriffen** the number is an overestimate/underestimate; **ihre Erwartungen sind zu hoch/niedrig gegriffen** she has set her sights too high/low.

Greif|vogel *der* bird of prey.

Greis, in (*mpl* -e; *fpl* -nen) *der, die* old man (*f* old woman).

grell ⟨⟩ *adj* - **1.** [Licht, Sonne, Lampe] glaring; [Farbe, Muster] garish - **2.** [Geräusch] shrill ⟨⟩ *adv* - **1.** [scheinen, leuchten] glaringly; [bunt, gefärbt] garishly - **2.** [klingen, rufen] shrilly.

Grenz|bereich *der* - **1.** (*ohne pl*) [von Ländern] border area - **2.** [Begrenzung] limits (*pl*).

Grenze (*pl* -n) *die* - **1.** [Staatsgrenze] border - **2.** [Gebietsgrenze] boundary - **3.** [Trennlinie] dividing line, boundary - **4.** [Beschränkung] limit. ➡ **grüne Grenze** *die*: **über die grüne ~ gehen** to cross the border at a point in the countryside where there is no border control.

grenzen *vi*: **an etw** (*A*) ~ [Gebiet, Land] to border sthg; [Betrug, Tollkühnheit] to border ODER verge on sthg; **aneinander ~** to have a common border.

grenzenlos ⟨⟩ *adj* [Landschaft, Vertrauen, Liebe] boundless; [Verlegenheit, Sorge, Ekel] extreme ⟨⟩ *adv* [weit, lieben, begeistert] boundlessly; [verlegen, erstaunt, traurig] extremely.

Grenz|fall *der* borderline case.

Grenz|kontrolle *die* border check.

Grenz|posten *der* border guard.

Grenz|schutz *der* (*ohne pl*) border police; [in Deutschland] ➡ **Bundesgrenzschutz**.

Grenzüber|gang *der* [Grenzkontrollstelle] border crossing.

grenzüberschreitend ⟨⟩ *adj* cross-border ⟨⟩ *adv* at a cross-border level.

Grenzverkehr *der* cross-border traffic.

Grenz|wert *der* limit.

Grieche (*pl* -n) *der* Greek.

Griechenland *nt* Greece.

Griechin (*pl* -nen) *die* Greek.

griechisch *adj* Greek.

griesgrämig ⟨⟩ *adj* grumpy ⟨⟩ *adv* grumpily.

Grieß *der* semolina.

griff *prät* ➡ **greifen**.

Griff (*pl* -e) *der* - **1.** [Greifen] grip; [von Ringer] hold; **beim ~ in die Tasche** on reaching into the pocket; **der ~ nach der Flasche** reaching for the bottle; **etw mit einem ~ tun** to do sthg in next to no time; **etw im ~ haben/bekommen** *fig* to be/get on top of sthg; **jn in den ~ bekommen** ODER **kriegen** *fig* to gain control of sb - **2.** [Teil, Henkel] handle.

griffbereit *adj* & *adv* ready to hand.

griffig *adj* - **1.** [handlich] easy to use - **2.** [gut greifend] with a good grip.

Grill (*pl* -s) *der* grill.

Grille (*pl* -n) *die* - **1.** [Insekt] cricket - **2.** [verrückte Idee] whim.

grillen ⟨⟩ *vt* to grill ⟨⟩ *vi* to have a barbecue.

Grimasse (*pl* -n) *die* grimace.

grimmig ⟨⟩ *adj* - **1.** [Gesicht, Ausdruck] grim; [Feind] fierce - **2.** [Kälte, Hunger] terrible ⟨⟩ *adv* [lachen] grimly.

grinsen *vi* to grin.

Grippe (*pl* -n) *die* flu.

Grips *der* (*ohne pl*) *fam* brains (*pl*).

grob (*kompar* gröber; *superl* gröbste) ⟨⟩ *adj* - **1.** [Sand, Salz, Züge] coarse - **2.** [Leinen, Haut, Papier, Übersicht, Skizze] rough - **3.** [unhöflich] crude - **4.** [schlimm] serious; **aus dem Gröbsten heraus sein** [Kind] to be old enough to look after oneself ⟨⟩ *adv* - **1.** [mahlen, hacken] coarsely - **2.** [planen, schätzen] roughly - **3.** [schwer wiegend]: **~ fahrlässig handeln** to be grossly negligent - **4.** [unhöflich] crudely.

Grobheit (*pl* -en) *die* - **1.** [grobe Wesensart] crudeness - **2.** [Äußerung] crude remark.

grölen *abw* *vi* & *vt* to bawl.

Grönland *nt* Greenland.

Groschen (*pl* -) *der* - **1.** [10 deutsche Pfennig] ten-pfennig coin; **bei ihm ist der ~ gefallen** *fam fig* the penny dropped *Br*, he got it - **2.** [österreichische Münze] groschen.

groß (*kompar* größer; *superl* größte) ⟨⟩ *adj* - **1.** [räumlich] big, large; [Person] tall; **sie ist 1,80 ~** she's 1.80 m (tall) - **2.** [Angebot] wide; **eine ~e Vielfalt** a wide variety - **3.** [intensiv] great; **eine ~e Enttäuschung** a great disappointment; **sich ~e Mühe geben** to try hard - **4.** [älter] big; **mein ~er Bruder** my big brother - **5.** [erwachsen] grown-up - **6.** [Buchstabe] capital - **7.** [bedeutend] great; **ein ~er Dichter** a great poet; **heute kommt meine ~e Stunde** it's my big moment today ⟨⟩ *adv* (*kompar* größer; *superl* am größten*) - **1.** [räumlich]: **ein ~ angelegtes Projekt** a large-scale project - **2.** [sehr] a lot; **wir haben dann nicht mehr ~ gearbeitet** we didn't do a lot of work afterwards; **~ und breit** *fam* at great length - **3.** [im großen Stil] in style; **der Sänger ist ~ herausgekommen** the singer became a big success - **4.** [erstaunt]: **jn ~ ansehen** to stare at sb wide-eyed - **5.** [Buchstabe]: **es wird ~ geschrieben** it's written with a capital letter. ➡ **Groß und Klein** *pron*: **ein Buch für Groß und Klein** a book for young and old. ➡ **im Großen und Ganzen** *pron*: **im Großen und Ganzen** on the whole, by and large.

großartig ⟨⟩ *adj* - **1.** [gut] marvellous - **2.** [angeberisch] showy ⟨⟩ *adv* - **1.** [gut] marvellously - **2.** [angeberisch] showily.

Groß|aufnahme *die* close-up.

Großbritannien *nt* Great Britain.

Groß|buchstabe *der* capital (letter).

Größe (*pl* -n) *die* - **1.** [von Gegenständen, Baby, Kleidern] size - **2.** [von Personen] height - **3.** [Wichtigkeit] greatness - **4.** [Person] leading figure.

großenteils *adv* largely.

Größenwahn der abw megalomania.

größenwahnsinnig adj megalomaniac.

größer adj bigger, larger; **eine ~e Summe** quite a large sum; **ohne ~e Schwierigkeiten** without any great difficulty.

Großfamilie die extended family.

Großhandel der wholesale trade; **etw im ~ beziehen** to get sthg wholesale.

Großhändler, in der, die wholesaler.

Großmacht die great power.

Großmaul das fam abw big mouth.

großmütig <> adj generous <> adv generously.

Großmutter die grandmother.

Großrechner der EDV mainframe.

großschreiben vt (unreg) [mit großem Anfangsbuchstaben] to write with a capital letter, to capitalize.

Großschreibung die capitalization.

großspurig abw <> adj pretentious <> adv pretentiously.

Großstadt die city (vor Subst).

größtenteils adv for the most part.

größtmöglich adj greatest possible.

großtun vi (unreg) abw to boast.

Großvater der grandfather.

Großverdiener, in der, die (mpl -; fpl -nen) high earner.

großziehen vt (unreg) [Kind] to bring up; [Tier] to rear.

großzügig <> adj - 1. [Person, Geste] generous - 2. [Raum] spacious <> adv - 1. [freigebig, großmütig] generously - 2. [weiträumig] spaciously.

Grotte (pl -n) die grotto.

grub prät ▷ graben.

Grübchen (pl -) das dimple.

Grube (pl -n) die pit.

grübeln vi to ponder.

Grübeln das: **ins ~ kommen** to start to ponder.

Gruft (pl Grüfte) die crypt.

grün <> adj [farbig, unreif, ökologisch] green <> adv [ökologisch]: **~ wählen** to vote Green.

Grün (pl - ODER -s) das - 1. green - 2. (ohne pl) [Pflanzen] greenery. ◆ **bei Grün** adv on green.

Grünanlage die park.

Grund (pl Gründe) der - 1. [Ursache] reason - 2. (ohne pl) [Boden] ground; [von Meer, Bach, Glas] bottom; **auf ~ laufen** to run aground - 3. RW: **einer Sache** (D) **auf den ~ gehen** to try to get to the bottom of sthg; **jn in ~ und Boden reden** not to let sb get a word in edgeways. ◆ **im Grunde** adv basically. ◆ **von Grund auf** adv thoroughly. ◆ **zu Grunde** adv = zugrunde.

Grundausstattung die basic equipment.

Grundbedürfnis das basic need.

Grundbegriff der basic principle.

Grundbesitz der land.

gründen <> vt [Partei, Unternehmen] to found; [Familie] to start; [Stiftung] to set up <> vi [basieren auf]: **auf etw** (D) **~** to be based on sthg. ◆ **sich gründen** ref: **sich auf etw** (A) **~** to be based on sthg.

Gründer, in (mpl -; fpl -nen) der, die founder.

Grundgebühr die standing charge.

Grundgedanke der basic idea.

Grundgesetz das Basic Law.

Grundgesetz

The written constitution of the Federal Republic of Germany, proclaimed on 23rd May 1949, is known as the Grundgesetz (Basic Law). It sets down the legal framework for the state, the rights of each citizen, and it defines the relationship between the Bund (central government) and the Länder (the federal states). The original Grundgesetz was always considered to be a temporary framework rather than a definitive constitution, as it allowed for the possibility of re-unification with the German Democratic Republic. When this was achieved on 3rd October 1990, parts of the Basic Law were amended accordingly.

Grundkurs der basic course.

Grundkurs

These are the compulsory or optional courses offered at sixth form level in the senior high school (Gymnasium) with the aim of providing a basic knowledge of a given subject. All pupils have to choose two courses out of German, mathematics and a foreign language. These will be tested as part of the final leaving certificate (Abitur).

Grundlage die basis.

grundlegend <> adj fundamental <> adv fundamentally.

gründlich <> adj thorough <> adv thoroughly; **sich ~ blamieren** to make a complete fool of o.s.

Grundlohn der basic wage.

grundlos <> adj unfounded <> adv without reason; **~ lachen** to laugh for no reason.

Grundnahrungsmittel das basic foodstuff.

Gründonnerstag der Maundy Thursday.

Grundrecht das basic right.

Grundriss der [von Gebäude] ground plan; [Schema] outline.

Grund|satz der principle.

grundsätzlich <> adj - **1.** [wichtig] fundamental - **2.** [allgemein] basic - **3.** [bedingungslos] on principle <> adv - **1.** [allgemein] basically - **2.** [bedingungslos] on principle - **3.** [grundlegend] fundamentally; **sich ~ äußern** to state one's principles.

Grund|schule die primary school Br, elementary school Am (for pupils aged 6 to 10).

Grund|stück das plot of land.

Gründung (pl -en) die [von Partei, Verein] foundation (sg); [von Familie] starting (U); [von Stiftung] setting up (U).

grundverschieden adj completely different.

Grund|wasser das ground water.

Grüne (pl -n) das - **1.** [Farbe] green - **2.** [Natur]: **im ~n/ins ~** in/into the country.

Grünen pl: **die ~** the Greens.

Grüne Punkt der (ohne pl) symbol on product packaging indicating that it is suitable for recycling.

Grün|fläche die green area.

Grün|kohl der kale.

grünlich <> adj greenish <> adv with a greenish colour.

grunzen vi to grunt.

Gruppe (pl -n) die group.

Gruppen|arbeit die [im Unterricht] group work.

Gruppen|reise die group tour.

gruppieren vt to arrange. ◆ **sich gruppieren** ref to form a group/groups.

gruselig adj [von Film] spine-chilling; [von Erscheinung] eerie.

gruseln vt: **es gruselt jm** ODER **jn vor jm/etw** sb/sthg makes sb's flesh creep. ◆ **sich gruseln** ref to be frightened; **sich vor jm/etw ~** sb/sthg makes one's flesh creep.

Gruß (pl Grüße) der greeting; **jm Grüße von jm bestellen** ODER **ausrichten** to give sb sb's regards ODER best wishes; **herzliche Grüße!** greetings!; **viele Grüße!** best wishes!; **mit freundlichen Grüßen** yours sincerely.

grüßen <> vt - **1.** [begrüßen] to greet - **2.** [Gruß senden]: **jn von jm ~** to give sb sb's regards ODER best wishes <> vi [begrüßen] to say hello. ◆ **grüß dich** interj hello! **grüß Gott** interj Süddt hello!

Grütze (pl -n) die gruel; **rote ~** jelly-like dessert made of red berries, fruit juice and sugar.

gucken fam <> vi to look <> vt [Fotos, Zeitschriften] to look at; [Fernsehen] to watch.

Guillotine [gijo'ti:nə] (pl -n) die guillotine.

Gulasch (pl -e ODER -s) das ODER der goulash.

Gulasch|kanone die large tureen used to serve hot food at outdoor public events.

Gulden (pl -) der guilder.

Gully (pl -s) der drain.

gültig adj valid; **nicht mehr ~ sein** [Kreditkarte, Reisepass] to be no longer valid.

Gültigkeit die validity; **seine ~ verlieren** [Kreditkarte, Reisepass] to become invalid.

Gummi (pl -s) <> das ODER der - **1.** [Material] rubber - **2.** fam [Band] rubber band <> der rubber.

Gummi|band (pl -bänder) das (piece of) elastic.

Gummi|knüppel der rubber truncheon.

Gummi|stiefel der rubber boot, wellington Br.

Gunst die favour; **die ~ der Stunde nutzen** to seize the moment; siehe auch zugunsten.

günstig <> adj - **1.** [Gelegenheit, Umstände] favourable - **2.** [Preis] good <> adv - **1.** [beeinflussen] favourably - **2.** [kaufen] for a good price.

Gurgel (pl -n) die throat.

gurgeln vi to gurgle; [mit Mundwasser] to gargle.

Gurke (pl -n) die - **1.** [Salatgurke] cucumber - **2.** [Gewürzgurke] gherkin.

Gurt (pl -e) der - **1.** [Sicherheitsgurt] belt - **2.** [Band] strap.

Gürtel (pl -) der belt.

Gürtel|linie die: **unter der ~** [unfair] below the belt; [anzüglich] near the bone.

Gurtpflicht die obligatory use of seat belts.

Guss (pl Güsse) der - **1.** [Gießen] casting (U) - **2.** [Wasserstrahl] stream - **3.** [Regen] downpour - **4.** [Zuckerguss] icing (U) Br, frosting (U) Am.

Gusseisen das cast iron.

gut (kompar besser; superl beste) <> adj [gen] good; **in etw ~ sein** [fähig] to be good at sthg; **für etw ~ sein** [günstig] to be good for sthg; **das Mittel ist ~ gegen Magendrücken** this medicine is good for stomach ache; **du hast es ~!** you've got it easy!; **etw ~ sein lassen** fig to leave ODER drop sthg <> adv (kompar besser; superl am besten) - **1.** [gen] well; **~ kochen können** to be able to cook well, to be a good cook; **~ befreundet sein mit jm** to be good friends with sb - **2.** [Geschmack, Geruch]: **~ schmecken/aussehen** to taste/look good; **~ gelaunt sein** to be in a good mood; **ihr ist nicht ~** she's not well - **3.** [leicht] easily; **du hast ~ reden!** it's easy for you to talk! - **4.** RW: **so ~ wie** as good as.

Gut (pl Güter) das - **1.** [Bauernhof] estate - **2.** [Ware] goods (pl).

Gutachten (pl -) das report.

Gutachter, in (mpl -; fpl -nen) der, die expert.

gutartig adj - **1.** [Hund, Charakter] good-natured - **2.** [Geschwulst, Tumor] benign.

gutbürgerlich adj: **~e Küche** traditional cooking.

Gute das good. ◆ **alles Gute** interj all the

best! ◆ im Guten adv [versuchen] amicably; [sagen] nicely.

Güte die - 1. [Milde] goodness; **(ach) du meine** ODER **liebe ~!** (oh) my goodness! - 2. [Qualität] quality.

Güte|klasse die grade.

Güter|bahnhof der freight depot.

Güter|verkehr der freight traffic.

Güter|zug der freight train.

Güte|zeichen das quality mark.

gut gehen (perf ist gut gegangen) vi (unreg) - 1. [gesundheitlich]: **es geht ihr gut** she is doing well - 2. [glücken] to turn out well - 3. [Geschäft] to do well - 4. [Ware] to go well.

gut gelaunt adj cheerful.

gut gemeint adj well-meant.

gutgläubig adj trusting.

Guthaben (pl -) das (credit) balance.

gütig ◇ adj kind ◇ adv kindly.

gütlich adj amicable.

gutmütig adj good-natured.

Gutmütigkeit die (ohne pl) good nature.

Gut|schein der voucher.

gut|schreiben vt (unreg): **jm etw ~** to credit sthg to sb.

Gut|schrift die - 1. [Handlung] crediting - 2. [Quittung] credit slip.

gut tun vi (unreg): **ein heißes Bad wird dir ~** a hot bath will do you good.

gutwillig adj willing.

Gymnasial|lehrer, in der, die ≈ grammar-school teacher Br.

Gymnasiast, in (mpl -en; fpl -nen) der, die ≈ grammar-school pupil Br.

Gymnasium (pl Gymnasien) das ≈ grammar school Br, selective secondary school attended by 10- to 19-year-olds; **altsprachliches/neusprachliches ~** 'Gymnasium' with focus on classical/modern languages.

📖 Gymnasium

This false friend has developed a meaning very different to the English term "gymnasium". Gymnasium is the name given to the traditional grammar school or senior high school in Germany, which provides a broad-based academic education for pupils aged 10 to 19. There are a number of other types of school in Germany, including the Hauptschule, Realschule and Gesamtschule.
The English word "gymnasium", on the other hand, is translated by the German Turnhalle, or, in case of a health club, by the word Fitnessstudio.

Gymnastik die keep-fit.

Gynäkologe (pl -n) der gynaecologist.

Gynäkologin (pl -nen) die gynaecologist.

H

h, H [ha:] (pl - ODER -s) das - 1. [Buchstabe] h, H - 2. MUS B. ◆ h (abk für Stunde, Uhr) h, hr.

ha¹ (abk für Hektar) ha.

ha² interj ha!

Haar (pl -e) das - 1. [Behaarung] hair; **graues ~** ODER **graue ~e haben** to have grey hair; **ein paar graue ~e haben** to have a few grey hairs; **sich** (D) **die ~e schneiden lassen** to have one's hair cut - 2. RW: **jm aufs ~ gleichen** to be the spitting image of sb; **etw aufs ~ gleichen** to be an exact copy of sthg; **der Hund hat ihm kein ~ gekrümmt** the dog didn't touch a hair on his head; **sich in die ~e kriegen** ODER **geraten** fam to start squabbling.

Haar|bürste die hairbrush.

haaren vi to moult.

Haaresbreite die: **um ~** by a hair's breadth; **um ~ hätte es einen Unfall gegeben** there was very nearly an accident.

Haar|festiger der setting lotion.

haargenau ◇ adj exact ◇ adv exactly.

haarig adj hairy.

haarklein adv in minute detail.

haarscharf ◇ adj precise; [Beobachtung] very close ◇ adv - 1. [knapp]: **das Auto fuhr ~ an ihr vorbei** the car only just missed her - 2. [sehr genau] precisely; [beobachten] very closely.

Haar|schnitt der haircut.

Haar|spange die hairclip.

Haar|spray das ODER der hairspray.

haarsträubend adj - 1. [empörend] shocking - 2. [grauenhaft] horrifying.

Haarwasch|mittel das shampoo.

haben (präs hat; prät hatte; perf hat gehabt) ◇ aux to have; **sie hat gegessen** she has eaten ◇ vt - 1. [besitzen] to have; **ich hätte gerne ...** [im Restaurant, Geschäft] I'd like ...; **er hat zwei kleine Schwestern** he's got ODER he has two younger sisters; **das Buch hat 600 Seiten** the book has (got) 600 pages; **sie hat blaue Augen** she has (got) blue eyes - 2. [zur Verfügung haben] to have; **hast du Geld dabei?** have you got any money on you?; **das Haus ist noch zu ~** the house is still available - 3. [erleben] to have; **Angst/Durst/Hunger ~** to be afraid/thirsty/hungry; **sie hatte es schwer im Leben** she's had a hard life - 4. [an etw leiden] to have; **Kopfschmerzen ~** to have a headache; **was hast du denn?** what's wrong? - 5. [mit Zeitangaben]: **wie spät ~ wir (es)?** fam what's the time?; **wir ~ (jetzt) zehn Uhr** fam it's ten o'clock; **wir**

~ **heute Dienstag** *fam* it's Tuesday today - **6**. *RW*: **... und damit hat es sich!** ... and that's that!; **was hast du davon?** what do you get out of it?; **der hat sie wohl nicht mehr alle!** *fam* he's not all there!; ~ **Sie etwas dagegen, wenn ...?** do ODER would you mind if ...?; **sie scheint was gegen dich zu** ~ she seems to have something against you; **sie** ~ **hier nichts zu suchen!** they've no business here; **ich habe zu tun** I'm busy. ◆ **sich haben** *ref fam* to make a fuss.

Habenichts (*pl* -e) *der abw* pauper.

Habseligkeiten *pl* belongings.

habsüchtig *adj* greedy.

Hacklbraten *der* meat loaf.

Hacke (*pl* -n) die - **1**. [Ferse, Absatz] heel - **2**. [Gartengerät] hoe.

hacken ['hakən] ◇ *vt* - **1**. [zerkleinern] to chop - **2**. [schlagen] to hack - **3**. [bearbeiten] to hoe ◇ *vi* [mit dem Schnabel]: **nach jm/etw** ~ to peck at sb/sthg.

Hackfleisch *das* mince *Br*, mincemeat *Am*.

Hafen (*pl* Häfen) *der* [klein] harbour; [groß] port.

Hafenlarbeiter, in *der, die* docker, dock worker.

Hafenlstadt *die* port.

Hafer *der (ohne pl)* oats (*pl*).

Haferlflocken *pl* rolled oats.

Haft *die* [Gewahrsam] custody; [Strafe] imprisonment.

Haftlanstalt *die* prison.

haftbar *adj*: **für etw** ~ **sein** to be liable for sthg.

Haftlbefehl *der* warrant.

haften *vi* - **1**. [kleben] to stick - **2**. [bürgen]: **für jn** ~ to be responsible for sb.

Häftling (*pl* -e) *der* prisoner.

Haftpflichtlversicherung *die* third party insurance.

Haftlstrafe *die* prison sentence.

Haftung *die* [Verantwortung] liability; **Gesellschaft mit beschränkter** ~ limited company.

Hagebutte (*pl* -n) *die* - **1**. [Frucht] rose hip - **2**. [Strauch] dog rose.

Hagel *der* hail.

Hagellkorn *das* hailstone.

hageln ◇ *vi*: **es hagelt** it is hailing ◇ *vt*: **es hagelte Beschwerden** *fig* there was a stream of complaints.

Hahn (*pl* Hähne) *der* - **1**. [Vogel] cock - **2**. [an der Leitung] tap *Br*, faucet *Am*.

Hähnchen (*pl* -) *das* - **1**. [Brathähnchen] chicken - **2**. [kleiner Hahn] cockerel.

Hai (*pl* -e) *der* shark.

Hailfisch *der* shark.

häkeln *vt & vi* to crochet.

Häkellnadel *die* crochet hook.

Haken (*pl* -) *der* - **1**. [Aufhänger] hook - **2**. [Zeichen] tick - **3**. [Problem] catch, snag.

halb ◇ *adj (ohne kompar)* half; **ein** ~**er Liter** half a litre; **der** ~**e Tag** half the day; ~ **und** ~ *fam* half and half; **es ist** ~ **drei** it is half past two; **keine** ~**en Sachen machen** not to do things by halves; ~ **Düsseldorf** half of Düsseldorf ◇ *adv* half; ~ **lange Haare** mid-length hair.

Halblbruder *der* half-brother.

Halbdunkel *das* semi-darkness.

Halbe (*pl* -n) *das* ODER *der* half litre; **ein** ~**s** [Bier] a half litre.

Halblfinale *das* semi-final.

halbherzig ◇ *adj* half-hearted ◇ *adv* half-heartedly.

halbieren *vt* - **1**. [Kuchen, Apfel] to cut in half, to halve - **2**. [Linie] to bisect - **3**. [Geldsumme, Zahl] to halve. ◆ **sich halbieren** *ref* to halve.

Halblinsel *die* peninsula.

Halbljahr *das* six months (*pl*); [Schule] ≃ term.

halbjährlich ◇ *adj* six-monthly, half-yearly ◇ *adv* every six months, twice a year.

Halblkreis *der* semi-circle.

Halblkugel *die* hemisphere.

halblaut ◇ *adj* low ◇ *adv* in a low voice.

halbmast *adv*: **auf** ~ at half-mast.

Halbmond *der* [Mondsichel] half-moon.

halb offen *adj* half-open.

Halbpension ['halppanzjo:n] *die* half board.

Halblschuh *der* shoe.

Halbtagslarbeit *die* part-time work.

Halbton (*pl* -töne) *der* MUS semitone.

halbtrocken *adj* medium-dry.

halb voll *adj* half-full.

Halblwahrheit *die* half-truth.

Halblwaise *die child with only one living parent.*

halbwegs *adv* reasonably, fairly.

Halblzeit *die* SPORT - **1**. [Hälfte] half - **2**. [Pause] half-time.

Halde (*pl* -n) *die* [Kohlenhalde] slag heap.

half *prät* ▷ helfen.

Hälfte (*pl* -n) *die* half; **die** ~ **der Angestellten** half (of) the employees. ◆ **zur Hälfte** *adv*: **zur** ~ **gefüllt** half-full; **etw zur** ~ **tun** to half-do sthg; **der Erlös ging zur** ~ **ans Rote Kreuz** half the proceeds went to the Red Cross.

Halfter (*pl* -) ◇ *das* ODER *der* [für Pferde] halter ◇ *das* [für Pistole] holster.

Halle (*pl* -n) *die* [gen] hall; [von Hotel] lobby; [zum Reiten] arena; [zum Turnen] gym; [zum Tennisspielen] covered court.

hallen *vi* to resound, to ring out.

Hallenlbad *das* indoor swimming pool.

hallo *interj* hello.

Halm (*pl* -e) *der* [von Gras] blade; [von Getreide] stalk.

Halogen|lampe *die* halogen lamp.

Hals (*pl* Hälse) *der* - **1.** [Körperteil - außen] neck; [- innen] throat - **2.** [von Flasche, Instrument] neck - **3.** *RW:* **aus vollem ~** at the top of one's voice; **es hängt mir zum ~ heraus** *fam abw* I'm sick of it; **etw in den falschen ~ bekommen** *fam* to take sthg the wrong way; **~ über Kopf** in a rush *ODER* hurry; **jm um den ~ fallen** to fling one's arms around sb's neck.

Hals|aus|schnitt *der* neckline.

Hals|band (*pl* -bänder) *das* - **1.** [für Tiere] collar - **2.** [Samtband] choker.

hals|brecherisch ◇ *adj* [Geschwindigkeit] breakneck; [Fahrt] madcap ◇ *adv* [fahren] at breakneck speed.

Hals|entzündung *die* sore throat.

Hals|kette *die* necklace.

Hals-Nasen-Ohren-|Arzt, Ärztin *der, die* ear, nose and throat specialist.

Hals|schlag|ader *die* carotid artery.

Hals|schmerzen *pl* sore throat *(sg)*; **~ haben** to have a sore throat.

Hals|tuch *das* scarf.

halt ◇ *interj* stop!; MIL halt!; **sag ~, wenn ich aufhören soll!** tell me when to stop ◇ *adv Südtt, Österr & Schweiz* just, simply.

Halt (*pl* -e *ODER* -s) *der* - **1.** [Stütze] hold, grip; **die Leiter hat keinen ~** the ladder is unstable; **den ~ verlieren** to lose one's hold - **2.** [Haltestelle] stop - **3.** [Stopp]: **~ machen** to stop; **vor jm/etw nicht ~ machen** *fig* to spare no one/nothing.

halt|bar *adj* - **1.** [konserviert]: **~ sein** to keep well - **2.** [strapazierfähig] hard-wearing, durable - **3.** [glaubhaft] tenable.

Halt|barkeit *die* [von Lebensmitteln] life; [von Material] durability.

Haltbarkeits|datum *das* 'best before' date.

halten (*präs* hält; *prät* hielt; *perf* hat gehalten) ◇ *vt* - **1.** [fest halten] to hold - **2.** [beibehalten] to keep; **die dicken Wände ~ die Wärme** the thick walls keep the heat in; **Kontakt ~** to keep in touch - **3.** [binden] to keep - **4.** SPORT to save - **5.** [behalten] to hold on to - **6.** [Rede] to make; [Vortrag, Predigt] to give; [Plädoyer] to present - **7.** [einhalten - Versprechen] to keep - **8.** [Tier] to keep - **9.** [verteidigen] to hold - **10.** [ausführen, komponieren]: **die Wohnung ist ganz in Blau gehalten** the flat is decorated entirely in blue; **das Kleid ist sehr schlicht gehalten** the dress is very simple in style - **11.** *RW:* **jeder, der etw auf sich hält** any self-respecting person; **jn/etw für jn/etw ~** to take sb/sthg to be sb/sthg; **ich habe ihn für klüger gehalten** I thought he was cleverer than that; **er war nicht zu ~** there was no holding him; **viel/wenig von jm/etw ~** to have a high/low

opinion of sb/sthg; **was hältst du von ihr?** what do you think of her? ◇ *vi* - **1.** [anhalten, stoppen] to stop - **2.** [ganz bleiben - Gegenstand] to hold; [- Freundschaft] to last; **zu jm ~** to stand by sb. ◆ **sich halten** *ref* - **1.** [in einem Zustand - Lebensmittel] to keep; **für sein Alter hält er sich gut** he's keeping well for his age; **sich fit ~** to keep fit - **2.** [in einer Position] to stay, to remain - **3.** [an einem Ort - sich fest halten] to hold on; [- bleiben] to stay; **sich rechts/links ~** to keep (to the) right/left - **4.** [in einer Körperhaltung]: **sich gerade ~** to stand up straight - **5.** [bei einer Herausforderung] to hold one's own.

Halterung (*pl* -en) *die* holder.

Halte|stelle *die* stop.

Halteverbot *das* [Stelle] no waiting zone, clearway *Br;* **'hier herrscht ~'** 'there is no waiting here'.

halt|los ◇ *adj* [grundlos] unfounded ◇ *adv* [unbeherrscht] uncontrollably.

halt|machen *vi* ▷ Halt.

Haltung (*pl* -en) *die* - **1.** [Körperhaltung] posture - **2.** [Meinung, Einstellung] attitude - **3.** [Beherrschung] composure; **~ bewahren/verlieren** to keep/lose one's composure - **4.** [von Tieren] keeping.

Halunke (*pl* -n) *der* - **1.** [Gauner] scoundrel - **2.** *hum* [Lausejunge] young rascal.

Hamburg *nt* Hamburg.

hämisch ◇ *adj* gloating; [Grinsen, Lachen] malicious ◇ *adv* gloatingly; [grinsen, lachen] maliciously.

Hammel (*pl* -) *der* - **1.** [Tier] castrated ram - **2.** [Fleisch] mutton - **3.** *fam abw* [Schimpfwort] ass, twit *Br.*

Hammer (*pl* Hämmer) *der* [Werkzeug & SPORT] hammer.

hämmern ◇ *vi* - **1.** [mit Hammer, Faust] to hammer - **2.** [schlagen - Herz, Puls] to pound, to throb ◇ *vt* - **1.** [mit Hammer] to hammer - **2.: auf dem Klavier ~** to pound away at the piano.

Hampelmann (*pl* -männer) *der* - **1.** [Spielzeug] jumping jack - **2.** *salopp abw* [Person] spineless person.

Hamster (*pl* -) *der* hamster.

hamstern *vt* to hoard.

Hand (*pl* Hände) *die* - **1.** [Körperteil] hand; **per ~** manually; **Hände hoch!** hands up!; **jn an die ~ nehmen** to take sb by the hand; **etw in die ~ nehmen** [ergreifen] to take sthg in one's hand; [initiativ werden] to take sthg in hand - **2.** SPORT handball - **3.** *RW:* **alle Hände voll zu tun haben** to have one's hands full; **eine ~ voll** a handful; **aus erster ~** secondhand *(with one previous owner)*; **aus zweiter ~** second-hand *(with two previous owners)*; **von der öffentlichen ~ bezahlt** paid for out of public funds; **etw aus der ~ geben** to give sthg up; **freie ~ haben** to have a free hand; **in**

festen Händen sein to be spoken for; **in js ~ sein** to be at sb's mercy; **er ist die rechte ~ des Chefs** he's the boss's right-hand man; **linker/rechter ~** on the left/right, on the left-hand/right-hand side; **unter der ~** secretly.
➤ **an Hand** = anhand.

Handarbeit die - 1. [Herstellung]: **in ~ hergestellte Töpferwaren** handmade pottery - 2. [Artikel] handmade article - 3. [Textilien]: **~en** needlework (U); **eine ~** a piece of needlework - 4. fam [Unterricht] needlework.

Handball der handball.

Handbewegung die gesture.

handbreit <> adj about 10 cm, distance of a hand's breadth <> adv: **~ offen stehen** to be ajar.

Handbremse die handbrake Br, parking brake Am.

Handbuch das [Lehrbuch] handbook.

Händedruck der handshake.

Handel der - 1. [Handeln] trade; **mit jm ~ treiben** to do business with sb; **mit etw ~ treiben** to deal in sthg - 2. [Geschäftsleben, Laden] business.

handeln <> vi - 1. [Handel treiben]: **mit etw ~ to trade** ODER deal in sthg; **mit jm ~** to do business with sb - 2. [feilschen] to bargain, to haggle; **mit jm um etw ~** to bargain ODER haggle with sb over sthg - 3. [agieren] to act - 4. [behandeln]: **von etw ~** to be about sthg <> vt [verkaufen] to trade. ➤ **sich handeln** ref: **worum handelt es sich?** what is it about?; **bei diesem Buch handelt es sich um einen Roman** this book is a novel.

Handelsbeziehungen pl trade relations.

Handelskammer die chamber of commerce.

Handelspartner der trading partner.

Handelsschule die college attended by people who left school at 16 and wish to obtain a commercial qualification.

handelsüblich adj standard, customary.

Handelsvertreter, in der, die commercial representative, rep.

händeringend adv desperately.

Handfeger der brush.

handfest adj - 1. [bodenständig] sturdy - 2. [klar, stark] solid, firm.

Handfläche die palm.

Handgelenk das wrist.

Handgemenge das scuffle.

Handgepäck das hand luggage.

handgeschrieben adj handwritten.

Handgranate die hand grenade.

handgreiflich adj: **~ werden** to become violent.

Handgreiflichkeit (pl -en) die violence; **es kam zu ~en** they came to blows.

Handgriff der - 1. [Handbewegung] movement (of the hand); **mit ein paar ~en** in no time - 2. [Haltegriff] handle.

Handhabe die: **keine ~ gegen jn haben** RECHT to have no evidence against sb.

handhaben vt - 1. [Werkzeug] to use; [Maschine] to operate; [Gesetze, Vorschriften] to apply - 2. [Fall] to handle.

Handicap, Handikap ['hɛndikɛp] (pl -s) das handicap.

Handlanger (pl -) der - 1. [Hilfsarbeiter] labourer - 2. abw [Zuarbeiter] dogsbody; [von Geheimpolizei] henchman.

Händler, in (mpl -; fpl -nen) der, die dealer.

handlich adj handy.

Handlung (pl -en) die - 1. [Tat] act - 2. [in Texten] plot - 3. [Laden] shop, business.

Handlungsfreiheit die freedom of action.

Handlungsweise die conduct.

Handschellen pl handcuffs; **jm ~ anlegen** to handcuff sb.

Handschrift die - 1. [Schrift] handwriting - 2. [Text] manuscript.

handschriftlich adj handwritten.

Handschuh der glove.

Handschuhfach das glove compartment.

Handstand der handstand.

Handtasche die handbag.

Handtuch das towel.

Handumdrehen das: **im ~** in (next to) no time.

Handwerk das - 1. [Beruf] trade; [künstlerisch] craft; **jm das ~ legen** to put an end to sb's misdemeanours - 2. (ohne pl) [Berufsstand] trade and crafts sector.

Handwerker, in (mpl -; fpl -nen) der, die tradesman (f tradeswoman).

handwerklich <> adj [Beruf] skilled; [künstlerisch] as a craftsman/craftswoman <> adv: **~ gut gearbeitet** well-crafted; **~ geschickt sein** to be good with one's hands.

Handwerkszeug das (ohne pl) tools (pl) of the trade.

Handy ['hɛndi] (pl -s) das mobile (phone); **er nahm sein ~ mit** he took his mobile with him.

📖 Handy

The relatively new false friend Handy is the normal word in German for "mobile phone". Zum Glück hatte ich mein Handy dabei might therefore be translated as "Fortunately I had my mobile phone with me".
The German, however, has nothing to do with the English word "handy" meaning "convenient" or "useful". This adjective is best translated by the word praktisch in German. So you might translate the sentence "a mobile phone comes in very handy these days" by Ein Handy ist heute sehr praktisch.

Handzeichen *das* signal (with one's hand); **durch ~ abstimmen** to decide by a show of hands.

Hanf *der* hemp.

Hang (*pl* Hänge) *der* - 1. [Abhang] slope - 2. [Vorliebe]: **einen ~ zum Selbstmitleid haben** to be inclined to be self-pitying.

Hängebrücke *die* suspension bridge.

hangeln (*perf* hat/ist gehangelt) *vi* (*ist*): **an etw** (*D*) **~** to move along sthg hand over hand. ◆ **sich hangeln** *ref* (*hat*): **sich nach unten/oben ~** to let o.s. down/pull o.s. up hand over hand.

Hängematte *die* hammock.

hängen (*prät* hing ODER hängte; *perf* hat gehangen ODER hat gehängt) <> *vt* (*reg*) - 1. [anbringen] to hang; **etw an etw** (*A*) **~** to hang sthg on sthg; **sich einen Pullover um die Schultern ~** to drape a pullover over one's shoulders - 2. [Körperteil] to dangle - 3. [töten] to hang <> *vi* (*unreg*) - 1. [gen] to hang - 2. [emotional]: **an jm/etw ~** to be attached to sb/sthg - 3. [haften] to be stuck. ◆ **sich hängen** *ref* (*reg*): **sich an etw** (*A*) **~** to hang onto sthg.

hängen bleiben (*perf* ist hängen geblieben) *vi* (*unreg*) - 1. [festhängen]: **mit dem Ärmel an der Türklinke ~** to catch one's sleeve on the doorhandle - 2. [bleiben] to stay longer than one intended - 3. [übrig bleiben]: **von dem Gelernten blieb nichts hängen** she didn't remember any of what she'd learned; **diese Arbeit bleibt immer an mir hängen** it is always me who ends up having to do this job - 4. *fam* [sitzen bleiben] to have to repeat the year.

hängen lassen *vt* (*unreg*) - 1. [vergessen] to leave (behind) - 2. [Person] to let down, to leave in the lurch - 3. [Körperteil]: **die Schultern ~** to let one's shoulders droop. ◆ **sich hängen lassen** *ref* [vernachlässigen] to let o.s. go.

Hannover *nt* Hanover.

Hanse *die* Hanseatic League.

hänseln *vt*: **jn (wegen etw) ~** to tease sb (about sthg).

Hansestadt *die* Hanseatic town.

Hantel (*pl* -n) *die* dumbbell.

Häppchen (*pl* -) *das* canapé.

happig *fam* <> *adj* [Preis] steep <> *adv* greedily.

Hardware ['ha:(r)dwεɐ] *die* EDV hardware.

Harfe (*pl* -n) *die* harp.

Harke (*pl* -n) *die* rake.

harken *vt* to rake.

harmlos <> *adj* [Tier, Person, Bemerkung] harmless; [Eingriff, Verletzung] minor; [Vergnügen] innocent <> *adv* [lachen, tun] innocently.

Harmlosigkeit (*pl* -en) *die* [von Tier, Per-son, Bemerkung] harmlessness; [von Krankheit] mildness; [von Verletzung] minor nature; [von Vergnügen] innocence.

Harmonie (*pl* -n) *die* harmony.

harmonieren *vi*: **miteinander ~** [Farben] to go (well) together; [Töne] to be in harmony.

harmonisch <> *adj* harmonious <> *adv* - 1. [passend] harmoniously - 2. MUS: **~ klingen** to be harmonious.

Harn (*pl* -e) *der* urine.

Harnblase *die* bladder.

Harpune (*pl* -n) *die* harpoon.

hart (*kompar* härter; *superl* härteste) <> *adj* - 1. [nicht weich - gen] hard; [- Ei] hard-boiled; **~e Währung** hard currency - 2. [widerstandsfähig] tough; **~ im Nehmen sein** to be tough - 3. [streng - Urteil, Strafe, Winter] harsh; [- Drogen] hard; [- Aufprall] violent - 4.: **es geht ~ auf ~** *fig* it's a pitched battle <> *adv* (*kompar* härter; *superl* am härtesten) - 1. [nicht weich] hard; **das Ei ~ kochen** to hard-boil the egg - 2. [streng - bestrafen, urteilen] harshly; [- arbeiten, aufschlagen] hard - 3. [räumlich]: **~ an** (+ *D*) close to; **das war ~ an der Grenze des Erlaubten** *fig* it was right on the limit of what is allowed.

Härte (*pl* -n) *die* - 1. [gen] hardness - 2. [Belastung] hardship - 3. [von Urteil, Strafe, Worte, Farbe, Aussprache] harshness - 4. *fam abw* [Zumutung]: **das ist die ~!** that's a bit much!

hart gekocht *adj* hard-boiled.

hartherzig *adj* hard-hearted.

hartnäckig <> *adj* [Person] stubborn; [Verfolger, Krankheit] persistent <> *adv* [schweigen, sich weigern] stubbornly; [verfolgen, nachfragen] persistently.

haschen *vi* - 1. [fangen wollen]: **nach jm/ etw ~** to snatch at sb/sthg - 2. *fam* [Haschisch rauchen] to smoke hash.

Haschisch *das* ODER *der* hashish.

Hase (*pl* -n) *der* hare; [Kaninchen] rabbit.

Haselnuss *die* hazelnut.

Hass *der*: **~ (auf jn/etw)** hatred (of sb/sthg).

hassen *vt* to hate.

hässlich <> *adj* - 1. [unattraktiv] ugly - 2. [gemein] nasty <> *adv* - 1. [unattraktiv] tastelessly; **sich ~ kleiden** to wear ugly clothes - 2. [gemein] nastily.

Hässlichkeit *die* [von Person, Einrichtung] ugliness.

hast *präs* ⊳ haben.

Hast *die* haste; **etw in ~ tun** to do sthg hastily.

hasten (*perf* ist gehastet) *vi* to hurry.

hastig <> *adv* hastily, hurriedly; **~ laufen** to rush <> *adj* hasty.

hat *präs* ⊳ haben.

hätscheln *vt* to pet.

hatschi *interj fam* atishoo!

hatte *prät* ⊳ haben.

Haube (*pl* -n) *die* - **1.** [von Krankenschwester] cap; [von Nonne] veil - **2.** [Motorhaube] bonnet *Br*, hood *Am* - **3.** [Trockenhaube] hairdryer.

Hauch *der* - **1.** [leichter Wind] gentle breeze - **2.** [Spur]: **ein ~ von etw** a hint of sthg.

hauchdünn ⊳ *adj* wafer-thin ⊳ *adv* [auftragen] very sparingly; [schneiden] into very thin slices.

hauchen *vt & vi* to breathe.

hauen (*prät haute* ODER *hieb*; *perf* hat gehauen) ⊳ *vt* - **1.** (*prät haute*) *fam* [Person] to hit - **2.** [Gegenstand]: **einen Pfahl in den Boden ~** to bang a post into the ground - **3.** (*prät haute*) *salopp* [werfen] to chuck, to bung *Br* ⊳ *vi* *fam* [auf Tisch, gegen Wand] to bang; **jm ins Gesicht ~** to smack sb in the mouth.

Haufen (*pl* -) *der* - **1.** [Anhäufung]: **alles auf einen ~ legen** to pile everything up - **2.** *fam* [Menge]: **ein ~ Freunde/Geld** loads of friends/money.

häufen *vt* to pile up. ◆ **sich häufen** *ref* [Briefe, Abfälle] to pile up; [Beweise] to accumulate; [Vorfall] to be on the increase.

haufenweise *adv fam*: **~ Geld verdienen** to earn heaps ODER loads of money.

häufig ⊳ *adj* [gen] frequent; [Fehler] common ⊳ *adv* often.

Häufigkeit (*pl* -en) *die* frequency.

Häufung (*pl* -en) *die* [von Gegenständen] accumulation; [von Vorfällen] mounting frequency.

Hauptbahnhof *der* main station; **Leipzig ~** Leipzig central (station).

hauptberuflich ⊳ *adj*: **~e Tätigkeit** main job ⊳ *adv*: **~ ist er Landwirt** farming is his principal occupation.

Hauptbeschäftigung *die* main occupation.

Hauptbestandteil *der* main component.

Hauptdarsteller, in *der, die* leading man (*f* leading lady).

Haupteingang *der* main entrance.

Hauptfach *das* main subject; **etw im ~ studieren** to study sthg as one's main subject.

Hauptfigur *die* central figure.

Hauptgericht *das* main course.

Hauptgewinn *der* first prize.

Hauptgrund *der* main reason.

Häuptling (*pl* -e) *der* chief.

Hauptperson *die* - **1.** [von Buch, Film] main character - **2.** [wichtigste Person]: **die ~ sein** to be the star of the show.

Hauptpost *die* main post office.

Hauptquartier *das* headquarters (*pl*).

Hauptrolle *die* [in Film] starring role; **Tennis spielt in ihrem Leben die ~** tennis is the most important thing in her life.

Hauptsache *die* main ODER most important

thing; **~, ich bestehe** the main thing is for me to pass. ◆ **in der Hauptsache** *adv* mainly, in the main.

hauptsächlich ⊳ *adv* principally, mainly ⊳ *adj* main, chief.

Hauptsaison ['hauptzezoːn] *die* high season.

Hauptsatz *der* main clause.

Hauptschule *die* secondary school attended by less academically gifted pupils aged between 10 and 15.

Hauptschule

The junior secondary school caters for pupils aged between 10 and 15. Whilst providing a general education, a certain emphasis is also placed on vocational training. Most pupils leave with a qualification to go on into apprenticeships in areas as diverse as small business, commerce, agriculture and the economic or social sectors.

Hauptstadt *die* capital.

Hauptstraße *die* main road ODER street.

Hauptteil *der* [von Text, Rede] main body; **der ~ der Fracht war beschädigt** most of the cargo was damaged.

Hauptverkehrsstraße *die* main thoroughfare.

Hauptverkehrszeit *die* rush hour.

Hauptwohnsitz *der* main place of residence.

Hauptwort (*pl* -wörter) *das* noun.

Haus (*pl* Häuser) *das* - **1.** [Wohnhaus] house - **2.** [Betrieb] firm; **er ist zurzeit nicht im ~** he is not on the premises just now; **mit den besten Empfehlungen des ~es** with the compliments of the house - **3.** [Familie] family - **4.** [Theater] auditorium; **volles ~ haben** to have a full house - **5.** *RW*: **~ halten** [sparen] to budget; **mit etw ~ halten** to be careful with sthg; **mit seinen Kräften ~ halten** to conserve one's energy; **die Kinder sind von ~ aus gewöhnt mitzuhelfen** the children have been brought up to be helpful.

Hausapotheke *die* - **1.** [Medikamente] first-aid kit - **2.** [Schränkchen] medicine cabinet.

Hausarbeit *die* - **1.** [im Haushalt] housework - **2.** [für die Schule, für die Universität] homework.

Hausarzt, ärztin *der, die* family doctor.

Hausaufgabe *die*: **als ~ für Morgen ...** for tomorrow's homework ...; **~n** homework (*U*).

Hausbesetzer, in (*mpl* -; *fpl* -nen) *der, die* squatter.

Hausbewohner, in *der, die* occupant.

Häuschen ['hɔyççən] (*pl* -) *das* [Haus] cottage; **vor Freude ganz aus dem ~ sein** *fam* to be beside o.s. with joy.

Haus|eigentümer, in *der, die* homeowner; [Vermieter] landlord (*f* landlady).

hausen *vi* - **1.** [wohnen] to live - **2.** *fam* [toben - Sturm, Krieg] to rage; [- Eroberer, Besatzer] to rampage.

Häuserblock (*pl* -blöcke) *der* block.

Haus|flur *der* (entrance) hall, hallway.

Haus|frau *die* housewife.

hausgemacht *adj* home-made.

Haushalt (*pl* -e) *der* - **1.** [Hausarbeit] housework; **im ~ helfen** to help around the house - **2.** [Hausstand] estate - **3.** [Familie] household; **einen ~ gründen** to set up home - **4.** WIRTSCH budget.

haus|halten *vi* (*unreg*) ⊳ Haus.

Haushälter, in (*mpl* -; *fpl* -nen) *der, die* housekeeper.

Haushalts|artikel *der* household article.

Haus|herr, in *der, die* host (*f* hostess).

haushoch ⬦ *adj* [Flammen, Wellen] towering; [Favorit, Sieg, Überlegenheit] overwhelming ⬦ *adv* [wachsen] as high as a house; [gewinnen] by a street; **jm ~ überlegen sein** to be head and shoulders above sb; **~ verlieren** to be hammered.

hausieren *vi*: **mit etw ~ (gehen)** [verkaufen] to sell sthg from door to door; *fam* [sprechen über] to go on about sthg.

häuslich ⬦ *adj* - **1.** [im Haus - Arbeiten, Probleme, Frieden] domestic; [- Angelegenheit] family (*vor Subst*); [- Pflege] home (*vor Subst*) - **2.** [Person]: **sie ist sehr ~** she's a real home bird ⬦ *adv*: **sich ~ niederlassen** *fam* to make o.s. at home; **sich ~ einrichten** *fam* to settle in.

Haus|mann *der* house husband.

Hausmannskost *die* traditional, simple fare.

Haus|marke *die* - **1.** [Wein] house wine - **2.** [von Geschäft] own-brand product - **3.** [Lieblingsmarke] favourite brand.

Haus|meister, in *der, die* caretaker *Br*, janitor *Am*.

Haus|mittel *das* home remedy.

Haus|nummer *die* house number.

Haus|ordnung *die* house rules (*pl*).

Haus|rat *der* (*ohne pl*) household contents (*pl*).

Haus|schuh *der* slipper.

Haus|tier *das* pet.

Haus|tür *die* front door.

Haus|verwaltung *die* property managers (*pl*).

Haus|wirt, in *der, die* landlord (*f* landlady).

Haut (*pl* Häute) *die* - **1.** [gen] skin; [von Tier] hide - **2.** *RW*: **es ging mir unter die ~** it got under my skin; **ihm war nicht wohl in seiner ~** he felt uncomfortable.

Haut|abschürfung (*pl* -en) *die* graze.

Haut|arzt, ärztin *der, die* dermatologist.

Haut|ausschlag *der* (skin) rash.

Haut|creme ['hautkre:m] *die* skin cream.

häuten *vt* [Früchte] to peel; [Tier] to skin. ⬥ **sich häuten** *ref* to shed its skin.

hauteng *adj* skintight.

Haut|farbe *die* skin colour.

hautnah ⬦ *adj* [Bild, Darstellung] graphic ⬦ *adv* [tanzen] very closely; **~ mit etw in Kontakt kommen** to come into close contact with sthg; **~ an etw** (*D*) **teilnehmen** to be closely involved in sthg.

Hbf. *abk für* Hauptbahnhof.

Headhunter (*pl* -) *der* headhunter.

Hebamme (*pl* -n) *die* midwife.

Hebel (*pl* -) *der* lever.

heben (*prät* hob; *perf* hat gehoben) *vt* - **1.** [hochnehmen] to lift; [Arm, Glas] to raise; **einen ~** *fam* to have a drink - **2.** [Niveau] to raise; [Umsatz, Selbstsicherheit] to boost, to improve; [Stimmung, Laune] to improve - **3.** [Wrack] to hoist, to salvage. ⬥ **sich heben** *ref* - **1.** [hochgehen - Vorhang, Flugzeug, Ballon] to rise; [- Nebel] to lift - **2.** [Niveau] to rise; [Umsatz, Laune] to improve.

hebräisch *adj* Hebrew.

hecheln *vi* [atmen] to pant.

Hecht (*pl* -e) *der* pike.

Heck (*pl* -e ODER -s) *das* [von Auto, Flugzeug] rear; [von Schiff] stern.

Hecke (*pl* -n) *die* hedge.

Hecken|schütze *der* sniper.

Heck|klappe *die* tailgate.

Heck|scheibe *die* rear windscreen *Br* ODER windshield *Am*.

Heer (*pl* -e) *das* army.

Hefe (*pl* -n) *die* yeast.

Hefe|teig *der* leavened dough (*U*).

Heft (*pl* -e) *das* - **1.** [Schulheft] exercise book - **2.** [geheftetes Büchlein] booklet - **3.** [von Zeitschriften] issue.

heften *vt* - **1.** [befestigen]: **etw an etw** (*A*) **~** [gen] to attach sthg to sthg; [mit Heftmaschine] to staple sthg to sthg - **2.** [nähen] to tack - **3.** [richten]: **die Augen auf etw** (*A*) **~** to fix one's eyes on sthg. ⬥ **sich heften** *ref* [sich richten]: **sich auf etw** (*A*) **~** to fix onto sthg.

Hefter (*pl* -) *der* folder.

heftig ⬦ *adj* violent ⬦ *adv* violently.

Heft|klammer *die* staple.

Heft|pflaster *das* (sticking) plaster *Br*, Band-Aid® *Am*.

Heft|zwecke (*pl* -n) *die* drawing pin *Br*, thumbtack *Am*.

hegen *vt* - **1.** [Verdacht, Gefühle, Hoffnung] to harbour; [Abneigung, Misstrauen, Achtung] to feel - **2.** [Wald, Wild, Garten] to tend;

jn/etw ~ **und pflegen** to lavish care on sb/sthg.

Hehl *das* ODER *der:* **kein** ODER **keinen ~ aus etw machen** to make no secret of sthg.

Hehlerei (*pl* -en) *die* receiving (stolen goods).

Heide (*pl* -n) <> *die* heath <> *der* heathen, pagan.

Heidekraut *das* heather.

Heidelbeere *die* bilberry.

Heidenlangst *die fam:* **eine ~ haben** to be scared stiff.

Heidenlgeld *das fam* fortune.

Heidenlspaß *der fam* great fun.

Heidin (*pl* -nen) *die* heathen, pagan.

heidnisch *adj* heathen, pagan.

heikel (*kompar* heikler; *superl* heikelste) *adj* - **1.** [kompliziert] awkward, tricky - **2.** [anspruchsvoll] fussy.

heil *adj* - **1.** [unzerstört] intact; [Welt] perfect - **2.** [geheilt] healed.

Heiland *der* Saviour.

Heillbad *das* - **1.** [Kurort] spa - **2.** [Baden] medicinal bath.

heilbar *adj* [Krankheit, Patient] curable; [Wunde] healable.

heilen (*perf* hat/ist geheilt) <> *vt (hat)* to cure; **jn von etw ~** [Idee] to cure sb of sthg; **jn von seinen Zweifeln ~** to allay sb's doubts <> *vi (ist)* to heal.

heilfroh *adj* relieved; **~ über etw** *(A)* **sein** to be relieved about sthg.

heilig *adj* - **1.** [geheiligt] holy; **der ~e Christopherus** Saint Christopher; **denen ist nichts ~** nothing is sacred to them - **2.** [Schrecken] almighty.

Heiliglabend *der* Christmas Eve.

Heilige (*pl* -n) *der*, *die* saint.

Heiligenlschein *der* halo.

Heiligtum (*pl* -tümer) *das* - **1.** [Ort] shrine - **2.** [Gegenstand] relic.

Heillkraft *die* healing power.

Heillkraut *das* medicinal herb.

heillos <> *adj* terrible <> *adv* terribly.

Heillmittel *das* remedy, cure.

Heillpflanze *die* medicinal plant.

Heillpraktiker, in *der*, *die* alternative therapist.

heilsam *adj* salutary.

Heilsarmee *die* Salvation Army.

Heilung (*pl* -en) *die* [von Patient, Krankheit] curing; [von Wunde] healing.

heim *adv* home.

Heim (*pl* -e) *das* home.

Heimarbeit *die:* **etw in ~ anfertigen** to make sthg at home; **~ machen** to work from home.

Heimat *die* [von Person] home, native country/region; [von Tier] original habitat.

Heimatlanschrift *die* home address.

Heimatlhafen *der* home port, port of registration.

Heimatlkunde *die* primary school subject covering local history, natural history and geography.

Heimatland *das* native country.

heimatlich *adj* of/from one's native country/region; **jm ein ~es Gefühl geben** to remind sb of home.

heimatlos *adj* [Mensch] homeless; [Tier] stray.

Heimatmuseum *das* local history museum.

Heimlcomputer *der* home computer.

Heimlfahrt *die* journey home.

heimisch *adj* - **1.** [Bevölkerung, Industrie, Sitte] local; [Pflanze, Tier] indigenous - **2.** [zu Hause]: **~ werden** to become acclimatized; **sich ~ fühlen** to feel at home.

Heimkehr *die* return journey.

heimlkehren (*perf* ist heimgekehrt) *vi* to return home.

heimlkommen (*perf* ist heimgekommen) *vi* (*unreg*) to come home.

heimlich <> *adj* secret <> *adv* secretly.

Heimlichkeit (*pl* -en) *die* secrecy.
◆ **Heimlichkeiten** *pl* secrets.

Heimlreise *die* journey home.

Heimlspiel *das* home game.

heimlsuchen *vt* - **1.** [Pest, Alptraum, Krankheit] to afflict; [Erdbeben] to hit - **2.** *hum* [belästigen] to descend on.

Heimltrainer [haim'tre:nɐ] *der* exercise bike.

heimtückisch <> *adj* [Mensch, Verbrechen] malicious; [Krankheit] insidious <> *adv* maliciously.

Heimlweg *der* way home.

Heimweh *das* homesickness; **(nach jm/etw) ~ haben** to be homesick (for sb/sthg).

heimlzahlen *vt:* **jm etw ~** to pay sb back for sthg.

Heirat (*pl* -en) *die* marriage.

heiraten <> *vi* to marry, to get married; **kirchlich ~** to have a church wedding <> *vt* to marry.

Heiratslannonce *die* advertisement seeking a marriage partner.

Heiratslantrag *der* proposal (of marriage).

Heiratslvermittlung *die* [Ort] marriage bureau.

heiser <> *adj* hoarse <> *adv* hoarsely; **sie hat sich ~ geschrien** she shouted until she was hoarse.

Heiserkeit (*pl* -en) *die* hoarseness.

heiß <> *adj* - **1.** [warm] [gen] hot; **mir ist ~** I'm hot; **es überläuft mich ~ und kalt** I feel hot and cold all over; **~ auf jn sein** *fam* to have the hots for sb - **2.** [heftig - Diskussion, Auseinandersetzung] heated; [~ Liebe,

Wunsch] ardent, burning - **3.** *fam* [gut] brilliant ⟨⟩ *adv* - **1.** [warm]: **~ baden** to have a hot bath - **2.** [heftig]: **~ umstritten** hotly contested; **jn ~ lieben** to love sb passionately; **es ging ~ her** things got a bit heated.

heißblütig *adj* hot-blooded.

heißen (*prät* hieß; *perf* hat geheißen) *vi* - **1.** [mit Namen] to be called; **er heißt Tom** he's called Tom, his name is Tom; **wie heißt du?** what's your name? - **2.** [bedeuten] to mean; **was heißt das auf Deutsch?** how do you say that in German?; **das will was ~!** that's quite something!; **... das heißt, wenn du willst ...** if you want, that is - **3.** [lauten] to be; **wie heißt der Titel?** what's the title?

Heißhunger *der* voracious appetite.

heiß laufen (*perf* hat/ist heiß gelaufen) *vi* (*unreg*) (ist) [Motor] to overheat; [Telefon] to buzz.

Heißluft|ballon *der* hot-air balloon.

heiter *adj* - **1.** [fröhlich] cheerful - **2.** [sonnig] fine.

Heiterkeit *die* - **1.** [Fröhlichkeit] cheerfulness - **2.** [vom Wetter] fineness.

heizen ⟨⟩ *vi* to turn on the heating; **wir ~ mit Gas/elektrisch** we have gas/electric heating ⟨⟩ *vt* to heat.

Heiz|kessel *der* boiler.

Heiz|kissen *das* heated pad *(for back pain etc)*.

Heiz|körper *der* radiator.

Heiz|öl *das* fuel oil.

Heizung (*pl* -en) *die* - **1.** [System] heating - **2.** [Heizkörper] radiator.

Heizungs|keller *der* boiler room.

Hektar (*pl* -e ODER -) *das* ODER *der* hectare.

Hektik *die* hectic pace; **bloß keine ~!** *fam* don't panic!

hektisch ⟨⟩ *adj* - **1.** [Person, Bewegung] frantic; **~ werden** to panic - **2.** [Ort] hectic ⟨⟩ *adv* frantically.

Hekto|liter *das* ODER *der* hectolitre.

Held (*pl* -en) *der* hero.

heldenhaft ⟨⟩ *adj* heroic ⟨⟩ *adv* heroically.

Helden|tat *die* heroic deed.

Heldin (*pl* -nen) *die* heroine.

helfen (*präs* hilft; *prät* half; *perf* hat geholfen) *vi* - **1.** [Hilfe leisten] to help; **jm (bei etw) ~** to help sb (with sthg); **sich** *(D)* **zu ~ wissen** to know what to do - **2.** [nützlich sein] to help; **es hilft nichts** it's no use ODER good; **das hilft gegen Zahnschmerzen** it's good for toothache; **es hilft kein Weinen** it's no good crying.

Helfer, in *der* (*mpl* -; *fpl* -nen) *der, die* helper.

Helium *das* helium.

hell ⟨⟩ *adj* - **1.** [Zimmer, Licht, Tag] bright; **es wird ~** it's getting light - **2.** [Farbe] light; [Haar, Haut] fair - **3.** [Stimme] high *(esp of*

child's voice) - **4.** [schlau] lucid - **5.** [groß, intensiv - Freude, Begeisterung] sheer; [- Empörung, Wahnsinn] utter ⟨⟩ *adv* - **1.** [leuchtend] brightly - **2.** [hoch]: **~ klingen** to ring out clearly - **3.** [sehr] totally.

hellblau *adj* light blue.

hellblond *adj* very fair.

hellhörig *adj* - **1.** [misstrauisch]: **sie wurde ~** her suspicions were aroused; **jn ~ machen** to arouse sb's suspicions - **2.** [Raum]: **die Wohnung ist sehr ~** you can hear everything through the walls in this flat.

Helligkeit (*pl* -en) *die* [von Licht] brightness.

hell|sehen *vi* (*unreg*) to see into the future.

Hellseher, in (*mpl* -; *fpl* -nen) *der, die* clairvoyant.

hellwach *adj* - **1.** [wach] wide awake - **2.** *fam* [rege] on the ball.

Helm (*pl* -e) *der* helmet.

Hemd (*pl* -en) *das* - **1.** [Oberhemd] shirt - **2.** [Unterhemd] vest *Br*, undershirt *Am*; **jn bis aufs ~ ausziehen** *fam* to have the shirt off sb's back.

hemdsärmelig *adj* casual.

hemmen *vt* - **1.** [bremsen - Bewegung, Geschwindigkeit] to slow down; [Fluss] to stem - **2.** [behindern] to impede, to hinder.

Hemm|schwelle *die* mental block.

Hemmung (*pl* -en) *die* [Behinderung] hindrance. ◆ **Hemmungen** *pl* inhibitions; **~en haben** to feel inhibited.

hemmungslos ⟨⟩ *adj* uninhibited ⟨⟩ *adv* uninhibitedly.

Hengst (*pl* -e) *der* [Pferd] stallion.

Henkel (*pl* -) *der* handle.

Henker (*pl* -) *der* [gen] executioner; [beim Erhängen] hangman.

Henne (*pl* -n) *die* hen.

her *adv* - **1.** [räumlich]: **komm ~!** come here!; **~ damit!** give me that!; **von Norden ~** from the north; **von weit ~** from a long way away - **2.** [zeitlich]: **das ist zehn Jahre ~** that was ten years ago; **ich kenne sie von früher ~** I know her from before - **3.** [unter dem Aspekt]: **von der Größe ~** as far as size is concerned; *siehe auch* her sein.

herab|lassen *vt* (*unreg*) to lower. ◆ **sich herablassen** *ref*: **sich ~, etw zu tun** to condescend to do sthg.

herablassend ⟨⟩ *adj* condescending, patronizing ⟨⟩ *adv* condescendingly, patronizingly.

herab|setzen *vt* - **1.** [Betrag] to reduce - **2.** [Person] to put down.

heran, ran *adv*: **nur ~!** come closer!

heran|kommen (*perf* ist herangekommen) *vi* (*unreg*) - **1.** [kommen] to approach; **sie lässt nichts an sich** *(A)* **~** she doesn't let anything bother her; **an jn ~** [erreichen] to get hold of

sb; [entsprechen] to match up to sb; **an etw**
(A) ~ to be able to reach sthg - **2.** [bekom-
men]: **an etw** *(A)* ~ to get hold of sthg.
heran|machen ➡ **sich heranmachen**
ref: **sich an etw** *(A)* ~ to get down to sthg.
heran|treten *(perf* ist herangetreten) *vi*
(unreg): **an jn** ~ to approach sb.
heran|wachsen [hɛ'ranvaksn̩] *(perf* ist he-
rangewachsen) *vi (unreg)* to grow up.
Heranwachsende [hɛ'ranvaksn̩də] *(pl* -n)
der, die adolescent.
heran|ziehen *(perf* hat/ist herangezogen)
(unreg) <> *vt (hat)* - **1.** [ziehen]: **etw an etw** *(A)*
~ to pull sthg up to sthg - **2.** [befragen] to consult - **3.** [erziehen] to teach <> *vi (ist)* [kom-
men] to draw near.
herauf, rauf *adv* up; **die Treppe** ~ up the
stairs; **vom Tal** ~ up from the valley.
herauf|beschwören *vt (unreg)* - **1.** [verur-
sachen] to cause - **2.** [Vergangenes] to evoke.
herauf|kommen *(perf* ist heraufgekom-
men) *vi (unreg)* to come up/upstairs.
heraus, raus *adv* out; ~ aus dem Bett! (get)
out of bed!; ~ **mit der Sprache!** spit it out!,
out with it!; **aus dieser Überlegung** ~ as a result of these reflections; **es ist noch nicht** ~,
wer das Rennen gewonnen hat it's still unclear who won the race; *siehe auch* **heraus
sein.**
heraus|bekommen *vt (unreg)* - **1.** [Geheim-
nis] to find out; [Lösung] to work out
- **2.** [entfernen] to get out - **3.** [Wechselgeld] to
get back.
heraus|bringen *vt (unreg)* - **1.** [bringen] to
bring/take out - **2.** [veröffentlichen, verkau-
fen] to bring out; **etw (ganz) groß** ~ to
launch sthg amid a fanfare of publicity
- **3.** *fam* [entlocken]: **etw aus jm** ~ to get sthg
out of sb - **4.** [aussprechen, artikulieren] to utter.
heraus|finden *(unreg)* <> *vt* [entdecken] to
find out <> *vi* [herauskommen]: **aus etw** ~ to
find a way out of sthg.
heraus|fliegen *(perf* hat/ist herausgeflo-
gen) *(unreg)* <> *vt (hat)* [fliegen] to fly out
<> *vi (ist)* - **1.** [fliegen - Tier, Gegenstand]: **aus**
etw ~ to fly out of sthg - **2.** *fam* [zur Strafe] to
be thrown out - **3.** *fam* [herausfallen]: **aus etw**
~ to fall out of sthg.
heraus|fordern *vt* - **1.** SPORT [Feind] to
challenge; **jn** ~, **etw zu tun** to challenge sb to
do sthg - **2.** [provozieren] to provoke; **das
Schicksal** ~ to tempt fate.
herausfordernd <> *adj* provocative; [Fra-
ge] challenging <> *adv* provocatively.
Heraus|forderung *die* - **1.** SPORT [Aufgabe]
challenge - **2.** [Provokation] provocation;
[von Schicksal] tempting.
heraus|geben *vt (unreg)* - **1.** [veröffentli-
chen] to publish - **2.** [geben]: **jm etw** ~ to pass
ODER hand sthg out to sb - **3.** [freilassen] to re-

turn - **4.** [Wechselgeld] to give back; **auf 100
Euro** ~ to give change from 100 euros.
Herausgeber, in *(mpl* -; *fpl* -nen) *der, die*
- **1.** [Redakteur] editor - **2.** [Verleger] publisher.
heraus|gehen *(perf* ist herausgegangen) *vi*
(unreg) - **1.** [nach draußen] to go out; **aus sich**
~ *fig* to come out of one's shell - **2.** [Fleck,
Schraube] to come out.
heraus|halten *(unreg) vt* - **1.** [nach draußen]
to hold out - **2.** *fam* [fern halten]: **jn aus etw** ~
to keep sb out of sthg. ➡ **sich heraushal-
ten** *ref:* **sich aus etw** ~ to keep out of sthg.
heraus|holen *vt* - **1.** [holen]: **jn/etw aus
etw** ~ to get sb/sthg out of sthg - **2.** [Informa-
tion]: **etw aus jm** ~ to get sthg out of sb
- **3.** [Leistung] to get ODER squeeze out
- **4.** [Geld, Gewinn] to make - **5.** SPORT to
make up.
heraus|hören *vt:* **etw aus etw** ~ [erahnen]
to detect sthg from sthg; [hören] to make out
sthg amid sthg.
heraus|kommen *(perf* ist herausgekom-
men) *vi (unreg)* - **1.** [nach draußen]: **(aus etw)**
~ to come out (from sthg) - **2.** [Resultat]: **was
kommt dabei heraus?** what's that going to
achieve?; **das kommt auf dasselbe heraus** it
amounts to the same thing, it makes no difference - **3.** [auf den Markt kommen] to come
out; **(ganz) groß** ~ *fig* to make a real splash
- **4.** [Verbrechen] to come to light - **5.** [ent-
kommen]: **aus etw** ~ to come out ODER
emerge from sthg - **6.** [deutlich werden] to
stand out - **7.** [aus dem Takt kommen] to get
out of time - **8.** [beim Kartenspiel] to lead
- **9.** *fam* [sagen]: **mit etw** ~ to come out with
sthg.
heraus|nehmen *vt (unreg)* - **1.** [entfernen]:
etw (aus etw) ~ to take sthg out (of sthg)
- **2.** [wagen]: **sich** *(D)* **Freiheiten** ~ to take liberties.
heraus|ragen *vi* - **1.** [hervorstechen] to
stand out - **2.** [heraussstehen] to jut out.
heraus|reden ➡ **sich herausreden** *ref:*
sich damit ~, **dass** ... to make excuses for o.s.
by saying that ...
heraus|rücken *(perf* hat/ist herausge-
rückt)* <> *vt (hat) fam* [Geld] to cough up
<> *vi (ist)* [sagen]: **mit etw** ~ to come out
with sthg.
heraus|schlagen *(perf* hat/ist herausge-
schlagen) *(unreg)* <> *vt (hat)* - **1.** [schlagen] to
knock out - **2.** [Gewinn] to make <> *vi (ist)*
[Feuer]: **aus etw** ~ to leap out of sthg.
heraus sein *(perf* ist heraus gewesen) *vi*
(unreg) - **1.** [entlassen sein]: **aus etw** ~ to be
out of sthg, to have left sthg - **2.** [entkommen
sein]: **fein** ~ to be sitting pretty - **3.** [Produkt]
to be out - **4.** [herausgegangen sein]: **aus einer
Phase** ~ to be past a phase - **5.** [entfernt sein]
to be out - **6.** [klar sein] to be known.

heraus|stellen vt - **1.** [nach draußen] to put out - **2.** [hervorheben] to highlight. ◆ **sich herausstellen** ref [klar werden] to become clear; **wer gelogen hat, wird sich noch ~** we'll soon see who has been lying; **sich als falsch/richtig ~** to turn out to be wrong/right.

heraus|strecken vt to stick out.

heraus|suchen vt to pick up; **jm etw ~** to find sthg for sb.

herbei adv here; **komm ~!** come here!

her|bitten vt (unreg) to ask to come.

her|bringen vt (unreg) to bring here.

Herbst (pl -e) der autumn Br, fall Am; **im ~** in the autumn Br, in the fall Am.

herbstlich adj autumnal.

Herd (pl -e) der - **1.** [Ofen] cooker - **2.** [von Revolte] seat; [von Krankheit] focus.

Herde (pl -n) die - **1.** [von Rindern, Elefanten] herd; [von Schafen] flock - **2.** abw [von Menschen] gang.

Herd|platte die hotplate.

herein, rein adv in; **herein!** come in!

herein|brechen (perf ist hereingebrochen) vi (unreg) geh - **1.** [Nacht] to fall - **2.** [Unglück]: **über jn ~** to befall sb.

herein|fallen (perf ist hereingefallen) vi (unreg) - **1.** [getäuscht werden] to be conned; **auf jn/etw ~** to be taken in by sb/sthg - **2.** [fallen] to fall in - **3.** [Licht] to come in, to enter.

herein|kommen (perf ist hereingekommen) vi (unreg) to come in.

herein|lassen vt (unreg) to let in.

herein|legen vt [täuschen] to take for a ride.

Her|fahrt die journey here.

her|fallen (perf ist hergefallen) vi (unreg): **über jn ~** [angreifen] to attack sb; **über etw** (A) **~** [essen] to attack sthg.

Her|gang der: **der ~ der Tat** the course of events leading to the crime.

her|geben vt (unreg) - **1.** [geben] to give; [überreichen] to hand over - **2.** [verschenken] to give away - **3.** [verzichten auf] to give up - **4.** [erbringen]: **der Text gibt für unser Thema nichts her** the text is of no use for our topic. ◆ **sich hergeben** ref: **sich zu etw ~** abw to allow o.s. to get involved in sthg.

hergeholt adj: **weit ~** far-fetched.

her|haben vt (unreg) fam: **wo hast du das her?** where did you get this?

her|halten (unreg) vi abw [dienen]: **als etw ~** to be used as sthg; **für jn ~** to have to take the blame for sb.

her|hören vi to listen.

Hering (pl -e) der - **1.** [Fisch] herring - **2.** [am Zelt] tent peg.

her|kommen (perf ist hergekommen) vi (unreg) - **1.** [kommen] to come here; **wo**

kommst du denn jetzt her? where have you just been? - **2.** [entstehen, stammen] to come from; **wo kommen Sie her?** where do you come from?

herkömmlich adj conventional.

Herkunft die (ohne pl) [von Person] origins (pl); [von Sache] origin.

Herkunfts|land das country of origin.

her|machen vi: **viel ~** to look impressive; **wenig ~** not to look very impressive; **nichts ~** not to be up to much. ◆ **sich herma-chen** ref fam: **sich über etw** (A) **~** to set about sthg.

her|nehmen vt (unreg) [nehmen, bekommen] to get.

Heroin das heroin.

Herr (pl -en) der - **1.** [Mann] gentleman; **meine ~en!** gentlemen!; **'~en'** [WC] 'gents' - **2.** [Anrede] Mr; **an ~n Müller** to Mr Müller; **~ Doktor** Doctor - **3.** [Gott] Lord - **4.** [Oberhaupt, Gebieter] lord; **der ~ des Hauses** the master of the house.

herrenlos adj [Tier] stray; [Koffer] abandoned.

her|richten vt - **1.** [vorbereiten] to get ready - **2.** [reparieren] to renovate.

Herrin (pl -nen) die mistress.

herrisch ◇ adj [Person, Worte] overbearing; [Blick] imperious ◇ adv in an overbearing manner.

herrlich adj wonderful.

Herrschaft (pl -en) die [über Staat, Volk] rule. ◆ **Herrschaften** pl people; **meine ~en!** ladies and gentlemen!

herrschen vi - **1.** [regieren]: **(über jn/etw)** ~ to rule (over sb/sthg) - **2.** [bestehen] to prevail; **es herrschte allgemeine Unruhe** there was general unrest.

Herrscher, in (mpl -; fpl -nen) der, die ruler.

her|schieben vt (unreg) to push here; **etw vor sich** (D) **~** [schieben] to push sthg along ahead of one; [vertagen] to put sthg off.

her sein (perf ist her gewesen) vi (unreg) - **1.** [vergangen sein]: **es ist drei Tage her, dass wir telefoniert haben** it is three days since we phoned - **2.** [herkommen] to come from - **3.** RW: **hinter jm/etw ~** to be after sb/sthg.

her|stellen vt - **1.** [produzieren] to produce, to make; [industriell] to manufacture - **2.** [Ruhe, Ordnung] to establish; **ihre Gesundheit ist wieder hergestellt** she has recovered, her health has been restored - **3.** [näher rücken] to put (over) here.

Hersteller, in (mpl -; fpl -nen) der, die manufacturer.

Her|stellung die [Produktion] production; [industriell] manufacture.

herüber, rüber adv over.

herum adv - **1.** [räumlich] round; **um etw ~** around sthg; **um den Tisch ~** around the table; **das Gerücht ist schon in der ganzen Nachbarschaft ~** the rumour has already got around the whole neighbourhood; **du trägst den Pullover verkehrt ~** your pullover is on the wrong way round; **was um sie ~ geschieht** what's going on around her - **2.** [ungefähr] around, about; **um die 50 Euro ~** around ODER about 50 euros.

herum|drehen ⟨⟩ vt [Blatt, Decke] to turn over; [Schlüssel] to turn; [Pfannkuchen] to toss ⟨⟩ vi [drehen]: **an etw** (D) **~** to turn sthg. ➡ **sich herumdrehen** ref [sich umdrehen] to turn round.

herum|fahren (perf hat/ist herumgefahren) (unreg) ⟨⟩ vi (ist) - **1.** [im Kreis]: **um etw ~** to go round sthg - **2.** [umherfahren] to drive around - **3.** [sich umdrehen] to turn round - **4.** [wischen] to wipe around ⟨⟩ vt (hat) to drive around.

herum|geben vt (unreg) to pass round.

herum|gehen (perf ist herumgegangen) vi (unreg) - **1.** [spazieren] to walk around - **2.** [zwischen Personen] to go around - **3.** [im Kreis]: **um etw ~** to go round sthg - **4.** [Gerücht] to go around - **5.** [Zeit] to pass.

herum|kommen (perf ist herumgekommen) vi (unreg) fam - **1.** [reisen] to get around - **2.** [gehen, fahren]: **um etw ~** to get round sthg - **3.** [vermeiden]: **um etw ~/nicht ~** to get out of/not to get out of sthg.

herum|kriegen vt fam - **1.** [überreden]: **sie hat mich doch noch herumgekriegt** she talked me into it in the end - **2.** [verbringen]: **die Zeit ~** to kill time - **3.** [räumlich]: **etw um etw ~** to get sthg round sthg.

herum|liegen vi (unreg) to lie around.

herum|lungern (perf hat/ist herumgelungert) vi fam [in der Stadt] to hang around; [auf dem Sofa] to lounge around.

herum|sprechen ➡ **sich herumsprechen** ref (unreg) to get around.

herum|treiben ➡ **sich herumtreiben** ref (unreg) fam to hang around.

herum|zeigen vt to show round.

herum|ziehen (perf hat/ist herumgezogen) (unreg) ⟨⟩ vi (ist) - **1.** [herumfahren] to wander about; **in der Welt ~** to roam the world - **2.** [im Kreis]: **um etw ~** to go round sthg ⟨⟩ vt (hat): **etw um etw ~** to put sthg round sthg.

herunter, runter adv down; **~ vom Dach!** get down from the roof!; **auf der Fahrt von Hamburg ~** on the journey down from Hamburg.

herunter|bekommen vt (unreg) fam - **1.** [schlucken können, nach unten bekommen] to get down - **2.** [entfernen können] to get off; **den Schmutz vom Teppich ~** to get the dirt out of the carpet.

herunter|fahren vt (unreg) - **1.** [reduzie-

ren - Produktion] to scale down; [- Temperatur] to reduce - **2.** EDV to shut down.

heruntergekommen adj - **1.** [Haus] dilapidated - **2.** [Person] down-at-heel.

herunter|holen vt to bring down, to have a wank Br.

herunter|laden vt (unreg) EDV to download.

herunter|lassen vt (unreg) - **1.** [senken] to lower - **2.** [gehen lassen] to let down.

herunter|machen vt: **jn/etw ~** fam to pull sb/sthg to pieces, to knock sb/sthg.

herunter|schlucken vt to swallow.

hervor adv: **~ mit euch!** out you come!

hervor|bringen vt (unreg) - **1.** [Ton] to utter - **2.** [entwickeln] to produce.

hervor|gehen (perf ist hervorgegangen) vi (unreg): **aus etw ~** [zu entnehmen sein] to be clear from sthg; **aus dieser Familie sind mehrere Künstler hervorgegangen** this family has produced several artists; **aus etw als Sieger ~** to emerge victorious from sthg.

hervor|heben vt (unreg) to emphasize; **js Leistung ~** to single out sb's performance.

hervor|holen vt to bring out.

hervorragend ⟨⟩ adj excellent ⟨⟩ adv excellently; **~ angezogen sein** to be extremely well-dressed; **~ schmecken** to taste excellent.

hervor|rufen vt (unreg) - **1.** [verursachen] to cause - **2.** [rufen] to call out.

hervor|stechen vi (unreg) to stand out.

hervor|tun ➡ **sich hervortun** ref (unreg) - **1.** [auffallen] to distinguish o.s. - **2.** abw [angeben] to show off.

Herz (pl ren ODER -) das - **1.** [gen] heart - **2.** (ohne Artikel) (ohne pl) [Spielkartenfarbe] hearts (pl); **die ~sechs** the six of hearts - **3.** RW: **ein ~ für jn/etw haben** to be fond of sb/sthg; **es nicht übers ~ bringen, etw zu tun** not to have the heart to do sthg; **etwas auf dem ~en haben** to have sthg on one's mind; **jm das ~ brechen** to break sb's heart; **ich möchte dir etwas ans ~ legen** allow me to give you a piece of advice; **sie/es liegt ihm am ~en** she/it matters to him; **kein ~ haben** to be heartless. ➡ **von ganzem Herzen** adv wholeheartedly.

Herzenslust die: **nach ~** to one's heart's content.

herzerfrischend ⟨⟩ adj refreshing ⟨⟩ adv refreshingly.

herzergreifend ⟨⟩ adj heartrending ⟨⟩ adv heartrendingly.

herzhaft ⟨⟩ adj - **1.** [fest] hearty - **2.** [nahrhaft] hearty and tasty ⟨⟩ adv - **1.** [fest] heartily - **2.** [nahrhaft]: **~ schmecken** to be hearty and tasty.

her|ziehen (perf hat/ist hergezogen) (unreg) ⟨⟩ vt (hat) [heranziehen] to pull up; **jn/**

etw hinter sich (D) ~ to drag sb/sthg along behind one ◇ *vi* - **1.** *abw* [lästern]: **über jn** ~ to pull sb to pieces - **2.** *(ist)* [umziehen] to move here - **3.** *(ist)* [gehen] to walk along.

Herz|infarkt *der* heart attack.

Herz|klopfen *das*: **ich habe** ~ my heart is pounding.

herzlich ◇ *adj* - **1.** [freundlich] warm - **2.** [aufrichtig] sincere ◇ *adv* - **1.** [freundlich] warmly - **2.** [aufrichtig] sincerely - **3.** [sehr] really; ~ **wenig** very little.

Herzog, in (*mpl* Herzöge; *fpl* -nen) *der, die* duke (*f* duchess).

Herz|schlag *der* - **1.** [Herzrhythmus] heartbeat - **2.** [Herzstillstand] heart failure *(U)*.

Herz|schrittmacher (*pl* -) *der* pacemaker.

Herz|stillstand *der* cardiac arrest.

herzzerreißend ◇ *adj* heartrending ◇ *adv* heartrendingly.

Hessen *nt* Hesse.

hessisch *adj* Hessian.

Hetze *die* - **1.** [Hast] (mad) rush - **2.** [Lästern] hate campaign.

hetzen (*perf* hat/ist gehetzt) ◇ *vi* - **1.** *(ist)* [rennen] to rush - **2.** *(hat)* [lästern]: **gegen jn** ~ to stir up hatred against sb ◇ *vt (hat)*: **jn/ etw auf jn** ~ to set sb/sthg on sb.

Heu *das* - **1.** [getrocknetes Gras] hay - **2.** *fam* [Geld] dough, dosh *Br*.

Heuchelei (*pl* -en) *die abw* - **1.** [Vortäuschen] hypocrisy - **2.** [Tat] piece of hypocrisy; [Äußerung] hypocritical remark.

heucheln ◇ *vt* to feign ◇ *vi* to be a hypocrite.

Heuchler, in (*mpl* -; *fpl* -nen) *der, die* hypocrite.

heulen *vi* - **1.** [Person, Tier] to howl - **2.** [Sirene] to wail.

Heuschnupfen *der* hay fever.

heute *adv* - **1.** [als ein Tag] today; ~ **früh** early this morning; ~ **Morgen/Mittag/Abend** this morning/lunchtime/evening; ~ **in vierzehn Tagen/einer Woche** a fortnight/a week today; **lieber** ~ **als morgen** sooner rather than later; **von** ~ **auf morgen** from one day to the next, overnight - **2.** [gegenwärtig] nowadays.

heutig *adj* today's; **der** ~**e Tag** today.

heutzutage *adv* nowadays.

Hexe (*pl* -n) *die* witch.

Hexenschuss *der*: **einen** ~ **haben** to have lumbago.

Hexerei (*pl* -en) *die* witchcraft.

Hieb (*pl* -e) *der* [Schlag] blow. ◆ **Hiebe** *pl fam* [Prügel]: ~**e bekommen** to get a beating.

hiebfest *adj*: **hieb- und stichfest** watertight.

hielt *prät* ⊳ halten.

hier *adv* - **1.** [räumlich] here; [in der Schule]: **hier!** here!, present!; **der/die/das** ~ this one

here; **ab** ~ from here; **von** ~ **aus** from here; ~ **und da** here and there; **„**~ **spricht Stefan"** [beim Telefon] 'Stefan speaking'; **ich bin nicht von** ~ I'm not from around here; ~, **nimm schon!** here, take it! - **2.** [zeitlich] now; ~ **brach sie in Tränen aus** then she broke into tears; **von** ~ **an** from now on; ~ **und da** now and then - **3.** [in dieser Sache]: ~ **täuschst du dich aber!** but that's where you're wrong.

hieran *adv* - **1.** [an dieser/diese Sache]: **die Erinnerung** ~ **fällt ihm schwer** he has difficulty remembering this - **2.** [an diesem/diesen Platz]: ~ **sind wir schon vorbeigekommen** we've already come past here.

Hierarchie (*pl* -n) *die* hierarchy.

hierauf *adv* - **1.** [auf dieser/diese Sache]: ~ **beharren** to insist on this; ~ **keine Antwort finden** to find no answer to this - **2.** [auf diesem/diesen Platz] on here - **3.** [daraufhin] hereupon.

hieraus *adv* out of this.

hier behalten *vt (unreg)* to keep here.

hierbei *adv* - **1.** [zeitlich] on this occasion - **2.** [bei dieser Sache]: ~ **ist Konzentration nötig** you need to concentrate whilst doing this.

hier bleiben (*perf* ist hier geblieben) *vi (unreg)* to stay here.

hierdurch *adv* - **1.** [örtlich] through here - **2.** [ursächlich] as a result of this - **3.** [hiermit] hereby.

hierfür *adv* for this.

hierher *adv* here.

hierhin *adv* here.

hierin *adv* - **1.** [örtlich] in here - **2.** [in dieser Angelegenheit] in this.

hiermit *adv* - **1.** [mit diesem Gegenstand, mit dieser Angelegenheit] with this - **2.** [mit dieser Handlung] hereby.

hiernach *adv* - **1.** [zeitlich] after this - **2.** [dieser Aussage folgend] according to this.

hier sein (*perf* ist hier gewesen) *vi (unreg)* to be here.

hierüber *adv* - **1.** [räumlich] over here - **2.** [über diese Angelegenheit] about this - **3.** *geh* [zeitlich]: ~ **vergingen mehrere Monate** this took several months.

hierum *adv* - **1.** [örtlich] around here - **2.** [um diese Sache] about this.

hierunter *adv* - **1.** [räumlich] under here - **2.** [unter dieser Sache] by this - **3.** [bei Menge] among these.

hiervon *adv* - **1.** [von diesem Gegenstand] of this - **2.** [von dieser Angelegenheit]: ~ **hängt es ab** it depends on this; ~ **halte ich viel** I think very highly of this - **3.** [örtlich] from here - **4.** [ursächlich] from this - **5.** [von dieser Menge] of these.

hierzu *adv* - **1.** [zu dieser Angelegenheit] to this; **ich rate dir dringend** ~ I urge you to do this - **2.** [zu diesem Gegenstand] with this

- 3. [zu dieser Menge]: **stellen Sie sich bitte ~** please stand with these people here; **legen Sie die Zeitungen bitte ~** please add your newspapers to these.

hierzulande adv in this country.

hiesig adj local.

hieß prät ⟾ heißen.

Hilfe (pl -n) ⟺ die **- 1.** [Helfen] help; **mit js ~** with sb's help; **jn/etw zu ~ nehmen** to use sb/sthg **- 2.** [Geld - freiwillig] aid; [- rechtlich garantiert] benefit **- 3.** [Haushaltshilfe] cleaner ⟺ interj help! ⟾ **Hilfe suchend** ⟺ adj [Blick] beseeching ⟺ adv beseechingly. ⟾ **mit Hilfe** adv = mithilfe.

Hilfe|leistung die aid (U).

Hilfe|ruf der call for help.

hilflos ⟺ adj **- 1.** [hilfsbedürftig] helpless **- 2.** [ratlos] clueless **- 3.** [unbeholfen] awkward ⟺ adv **- 1.** [hilfsbedürftig] helplessly **- 2.** [ratlos] cluelessly **- 3.** [unbeholfen] awkwardly.

hilfreich ⟺ adj helpful; **eine ~e Hand** a helping hand ⟺ adv: **jm ~ zur Seite stehen** to be a big help to sb.

Hilfs|arbeiter, in der, die [in der Fabrik] unskilled worker; [beim Bau] labourer.

hilfsbedürftig adj in need (of help).

hilfsbereit adj helpful.

Hilfs|kraft die assistant.

Hilfs|mittel das aid.

Hilfs|verb das GRAM auxiliary verb.

hilft präs ⟾ helfen.

Himalaya die: **der ~** the Himalayas.

Him|beere die raspberry.

Himmel (pl -) der **- 1.** [Firmament] sky; **am ~** in the sky; **unter freiem ~** in the open, out of doors **- 2.** [Jenseits] heaven **- 3.** [Vorsehung]: **der ~ weiß, wann er endlich zurückkommt** heaven (only) knows when he will finally come back **- 4.** [Baldachin] canopy **- 5.** RW: **aus heiterem ~** out of the blue; **im siebenten ~ sein** to be in seventh heaven.

himmelblau adj sky-blue.

Himmel|fahrt die Ascension Day.

Himmels|richtung die direction; **die vier ~en** the four points of the compass.

himmlisch ⟺ adj heavenly; **eine ~e Fügung** divine providence ⟺ adv [leicht, bequem, schön] wonderfully; **~ schmecken/aussehen** to taste/look divine.

hin adv **- 1.** [räumlich]: **bis zum Baum ~** up to the tree; **zur Straße ~** towards the street; **zum Norden ~** (towards the north); **wo ist er ~?** where has he gone?; **~ und her** back and forth; **der Weg ~** the way there; **zweimal London ~ und zurück** two returns Br ODER round-trip tickets Am to London; **einmal London – nur ~, bitte!** one for London – just a single please **- 2.** [zeitlich]: **zum Abend ~** towards evening; **über viele Jahre ~** for many

years; **~ und wieder** now and then **- 3.** fig: **er brabbelte da was vor sich ~** he was mumbling something to himself; **nach außen ~** outwardly; **auf deinen Rat ~** on your advice; **auf den Verdacht ~, dass ...** on the suspicion that ...; **ihr Kleid/Ruf ist ~** her dress/ reputation is ruined; **er war von dem Mädchen ganz ~ (und weg)** he was completely taken with the girl.

hinab adv = hinunter.

hinab|gehen (perf ist hinabgegangen) (unreg) vt & vi geh to go down.

hin|arbeiten vi: **auf etw** (A) **~** to work towards sthg.

hinauf adv up; **den Berg ~** up the mountain; **von den Alpen bis an die Ostsee ~** from the Alps right up to the Baltic.

hinauf|gehen (perf ist hinaufgegangen) (unreg) ⟺ vi to go up; **es geht hinauf the** road climbs ⟺ vt to go up.

hinauf|sehen vi (unreg): **zu jm/etw ~** to look up at sb/sthg.

hinauf|steigen (perf ist hinaufgestiegen) vi & vt (unreg) to climb.

hinaus adv **- 1.** [räumlich] out; **das Fenster geht zur Straße ~** the window looks (out) onto the street; **~ mit dir!** get out!; **über unsere Grenzen ~ bekannt** known beyond our borders **- 2.** [zeitlich]: **über das Abendbrot ~ bleiben** to stay over dinner; **auf Monate ~** for months to come.

hinaus|begleiten vt to see out.

hinaus|gehen (perf ist hinausgegangen) vi (unreg) **- 1.** [nach draußen] to go out **- 2.**: **auf etw** (A) **~** [gerichtet sein - Zimmer, Fenster] to look onto sthg; [- Tür, Gang] to lead into sthg; [- in eine Richtung] to face sthg **- 3.** [überschreiten]: **über etw** (A) **~** to go beyond sthg.

hinaus|laufen (perf ist hinausgelaufen) vi (unreg) **- 1.** [nach draußen] to run outside **- 2.** [abzielen]: **auf etw** (A) **~** to amount to sthg; **das läuft auf dasselbe hinaus** it amounts to the same thing.

hinaus|schieben vt (unreg) **- 1.** [nach draußen] to push outside **- 2.** [zeitlich] to put off, to postpone. ⟾ **sich hinausschieben** ref [örtlich] to push one's way out.

hinaus|werfen vt (unreg) to throw out.

hinaus|zögern vt to put off. ⟾ **sich hinauszögern** ref to be delayed.

hin|bekommen vt (unreg): **wie willst du denn das ~?** how do you intend to do ODER manage that?; **etw wieder ~** to mend sthg.

hin|bestellen vt to tell to come/go.

Hinblick der: **in** ODER **im ~ auf jn/etw** [in Bezug auf] with regard to sb/sthg; **in** ODER **im ~ auf etw** (A) [wegen] in view of sthg.

hinderlich adj: **jm/einer Sache ~ sein** to get in sb's/sthg's way.

hindern vt to prevent; **was hindert dich zu**

bleiben? what is preventing you from staying?

Hindernis (*pl* -se) *das* obstacle; [in Leichtathletik] hurdle; [in Springreiten] jump.

hin|deuten *vi* to point; **auf jn/etw** ~ [zeigen] to point at sb/sthg; [in einer Menge] to point sb/sthg out; [erkennen lassen] to point to sb/sthg.

Hindi *das* Hindi; *siehe auch* Englisch(e).

Hindu (*pl* -s) *der* Hindu.

hindurch *adv* - 1. [zeitlich]: **den ganzen Tag** ~ throughout the whole day - 2. [örtlich]: **durch den Berg** ~ through the mountain.

hinein *adv* - 1. [räumlich] in; ~ **ins Bett!** get into bed! - 2. [zeitlich]: **bis tief in die Nacht** ~ **arbeiten** to work late into the night.

hinein|denken ◆ **sich hineindenken** *ref* (*unreg*): **sich in jn/etw** ~ to put o.s. in sb's/sthg's position.

hinein|fressen *vt* (*unreg*): **etw in sich** (*A*) ~ to gobble sthg up; *fam* [Sorgen] to bottle sthg up.

hinein|gehen (*perf* ist hineingegangen) *vi* (*unreg*) - 1. [nach drinnen] to go inside - 2. [hineinpassen]: **in diese Flasche geht nicht mehr als ein Liter hinein** this bottle won't hold more than a litre.

hinein|geraten (*perf* ist hineingeraten) *vi* (*unreg*): **in etw** (*A*) ~ to get into sthg; **in einen einsamen Wald** ~ to find o.s. in a lonely wood.

hinein|steigern ◆ **sich hineinsteigern** *ref*: **sie hat sich in diese Sache hineingesteigert** she has become completely caught up in this affair.

hinein|versetzen ◆ **sich hineinversetzen** *ref*: **sich in jn** ODER **in js Lage** ~ to put o.s. in sb's position.

hinein|ziehen (*perf* hat/ist hineingezogen) (*unreg*) ◇ *vt* (*hat*) - 1. [nach drinnen] to pull in - 2. [verwickeln]: **jn in etw** (*A*) ~ to draw sb into sthg ◇ *vi* (*ist*) - 1. [umziehen] to move in - 2. [gehen] to go in.

hin|fahren (*perf* hat/ist hingefahren) (*unreg*) ◇ *vi* (*ist*) to go there; [mit Auto] to drive there; **wo ist er hingefahren?** where did he go (to)? ◇ *vt* (*hat*) to take there.

Hin|fahrt *die* [mit dem Auto] journey there; [mit dem Zug] outward journey.

hin|fallen (*perf* ist hingefallen) *vi* (*unreg*) to fall (down); **sie hat die Vase** ~ **lassen** she dropped the vase.

hinfällig *adj* - 1. [altersschwach] frail - 2. [ungültig] invalid.

Hin|flug *der* outward flight.

hin|führen ◇ *vt* to lead there ◇ *vi* to lead there; **zu etw** ~ to lead to sthg.

hing *prät* ⊳ **hängen**.

hin|geben *vt* (*unreg*) *geh* to give up. ◆ **sich hingeben** *ref*: **sich einer Sache** (*D*)

~ to devote o.s. to sthg; **sich einer Illusion** ~ to cherish an illusion; **sich jm** ~ to give o.s. to sb.

hingegen *konj* on the other hand.

hin|gehen (*perf* ist hingegangen) *vi* (*unreg*) [gehen] to go there; **zu etw** ~ to go to sthg.

hin|halten *vt* (*unreg*) - 1. [reichen] to hold out - 2. [vertrösten] to keep waiting.

hin|hocken ◆ **sich hinhocken** *ref* to crouch down.

hinken (*perf* hat/ist gehinkt) *vi* - 1. (*hat*) [humpeln] to (have a) limp - 2. (*ist*) [an einen Ort] to limp, to hobble.

hin|knien ◆ **sich hinknien** *ref* to kneel down.

hin|kommen (*perf* ist hingekommen) *vi* (*unreg*) - 1. [ankommen] to get there; **zu etw** ~ to get to sthg - 2. [hingehören] to belong, to go - 3. [hingeraten]: **wenn ich wüsste, wo meine Brille hingekommen ist** if I knew where my glasses had gone - 4. [auskommen]: **mit etw** ~ to manage with sthg - 5. [zutreffen] to work out; **das kommt hin/nicht hin!** that is right/wrong!

hin|kriegen *vt fam* to manage; **sie hat das gut hingekriegt** she made a good job of that; **etw wieder** ~ to fix sthg.

hinlänglich ◇ *adj* sufficient ◇ *adv* sufficiently.

hin|legen *vt* - 1. [Gegenstand] to put down; [Zettel] to leave - 2. [ins Bett] to put to bed - 3. *fam* [bezahlen] to fork out - 4. *fam* [Darbietung] to turn in; [Prüfung] to do. ◆ **sich hinlegen** *ref* - 1. [sich legen] to lie down - 2. *fam* [stürzen] to come a cropper.

hin|nehmen *vt* (*unreg*) - 1. [ertragen] to take - 2. *fam* [mitnehmen]: **jn/etw (zu jm) mit** ~ to take sb/sthg (to sb).

hin|pflanzen ◆ **sich hinpflanzen** *ref fam* [sich hinstellen]: **sich (vor jn)** ~ to plant o.s. (in front of sb).

hin|reichen ◇ *vt* [zureichen]: **jm etw** ~ to hand sb sthg ◇ *vi* - 1. [sich erstrecken] to reach - 2. [ausreichen] to be enough.

Hinreise *die* journey there.

hin|reißen *vt* (*unreg*) - 1. [ziehen] to pull - 2. [begeistern] to captivate - 3. [verleiten]: **sich zu etw** ~ **lassen** [überzeugen] to let o.s. be carried away into doing sthg; [provozieren] to be driven to do sthg.

hinreißend *adj* captivating.

hin|richten *vt* to execute.

Hin|richtung *die* execution.

hin sein (*perf* ist hin gewesen) *vi* (*unreg*) *fam* [kaputt] to have had it; [ruiniert] to be shattered; [vor Glück] to be overjoyed.

hin|setzen *vt* [Gegenstand] to put down; [Baby] to sit down. ◆ **sich hinsetzen** *ref* - 1. [sich setzen] to sit down - 2. *fam* [stürzen] to land on one's backside.

Hinsicht *die (ohne pl):* **in dieser/jeder ~** in this/every respect; **in doppelter ~** in two respects.

hin|stellen *vt* - 1. [stellen] to put - 2. [absetzen] to put down - 3. [darstellen]: **jn/etw als etw ~** to describe sb/sthg as sthg. ◆ **sich hinstellen** *ref* - 1. [sich stellen] to stand - 2. [darstellen]: **sich als jn/etw ~** to pretend to be sb/sthg.

hinten *adv* - 1. [am Ende] at the back; **da** ODER **dort ~** back there; **sie ist ~ im Garten** she's out the back (in the garden); **im Auto ~ sitzen** to sit in the back of the car; **das dritte Haus von ~** the third house from the end - 2. [weit entfernt]: **weit ~** a long way behind - 3. [an der Rückseite] on the back; **das Haus hat ~ einen Balkon** the house has a balcony at the back - 4. [als Richtungsangabe] back; **von ~** from behind.

hintenherum *adv fam* - 1. [um etw herum] round the back - 2. [indirekt] indirectly.

hinter *präp* - 1. (+ *D, A*) [räumlich] behind; **~ dem Haus** behind the house, in back of the house *Am;* **jm herlaufen** to run after sb; **3 km ~ Köln** 3 km after Cologne - 2. [zeitlich]: **etw ~ sich** (*A*) **bringen** to put sthg behind one; **das hätten wir endlich ~ uns!** thank God that's behind us!

Hinter|ausgang *der* rear exit.

Hinterbliebene (*pl* -n) *der, die* surviving dependant.

hintere, r, s *adj* back.

Hintere (*pl* -n) *der, die, das:* **der/die/das ~** the one at the back.

hintereinander *adv* - 1. [räumlich] behind each other - 2. [zeitlich] in a row.

Hinter|eingang *der* rear entrance.

Hinter|gedanke *der* ulterior motive.

hintergehen (*prät* hinterging; *perf* hat hintergangen) *vt* to deceive.

Hinter|grund *der* background; **im ~ bleiben** to remain in the background; **jn/etw in den ~ drängen** to push sb/sthg into the background.

hinterhältig ◇ *adj* devious ◇ *adv* deviously.

hinterher[1] *adv* [räumlich] behind.

hinterher[2] *adv* [zeitlich] afterwards.

hinterher|fahren (*perf* ist hinterhergefahren) *vi (unreg):* **jm/etw ~** to drive behind sb/sthg; [verfolgen] to drive after sb/sthg.

hinterher|gehen (*perf* ist hinterhergegangen) *vi (unreg):* **jm ~** to follow sb.

Hinter|kopf *der* back of the head; **etw im ~ haben/behalten** *fig* to have/keep sthg at the back of one's mind.

hinterlassen (*präs* hinterlässt; *prät* hinterließ; *perf* hat hinterlassen) *vt* to leave; **jm etw ~** to leave sb sthg.

hinterlegen *vt:* **etw bei jm ~** to leave sthg with sb.

Hinterlist *die* cunning.

hinterlistig ◇ *adj* cunning ◇ *adv* cunningly.

Hintern (*pl* -) *der fam* backside.

Hinter|rad *das* back wheel.

Hinter|seite *die* back.

Hinter|teil *das fam* backside.

Hintertreffen *das (ohne pl):* **ins ~ geraten** to fall behind.

hintertreiben (*prät* hintertrieb; *perf* hat hintertrieben) *vt* [Plan] to thwart; [Heirat] to prevent; [Gesetz, Reform] to block.

Hinter|tür *die* back door.

hinterziehen (*prät* hinterzog; *perf* hat hinterzogen) *vt:* **Steuern ~** to evade tax.

hin|treten (*perf* hat/ist hingetreten) *vi (unreg)* - 1. *(ist)* [an einen Ort]: **zu jm/etw ~** to step over to sb/sthg; **vor jn ~** to go up to sb - 2. *(hat)* [mit Fuß] to kick.

hinüber *adv* over, across; **da ~** over there; **gehen Sie links/rechts ~** go left/right; *siehe auch* hinüber sein.

hinüber sein (*perf* ist hinüber gewesen) *vi (unreg) fam* - 1. [kaputt] to have had it; [erschöpft] to be done in; [betrunken] to be well away - 2. [gehen] to have gone over.

hinunter *adv* down; **die Treppe ~** down the stairs; **vom General bis ~ zum einfachen Soldat** from the general down to the private.

hinunter|blicken *vi:* **in etw** (*A*) **~** to look down into sthg; **an sich** (*D*) **~** to look down at o.s.

hinunter|schlucken *vt eigtl & fig* to swallow.

hinunter|stürzen (*perf* hat/ist hinuntergestürzt) *vt* - 1. *(ist)* [hinunterfallen] to fall down - 2. *(hat)* [werfen] to throw down - 3. *(hat) fam* [schnell trinken] to gulp down. ◆ **sich hinunterstürzen** *ref* [sich hinunterwerfen]: **sich (von etw) ~** to throw o.s. off (sthg).

hinweg *adv geh* away; **über jn/etw ~** over sb/sthg; **über Jahre ~** for many years.

Hinweg *der* way there; **auf dem ~** on the way there.

hinweg|gehen (*perf* ist hinweggegangen) *vi (unreg):* **über etw** (*A*) **~** to pass over sthg.

hinweg|kommen (*perf* ist hinweggekommen) *vi (unreg):* **über etw** (*A*) **~** to get over sthg.

hinweg|sehen *vi (unreg):* **über jn/etw ~** to see over sb/sthg; **über etw** (*A*) **~** *fig* to overlook sthg.

hinweg|setzen ◆ **sich hinwegsetzen** *ref:* **sich über etw** (*A*) **~** to disregard sthg.

Hinweis (*pl* -e) *der* [Tip, Fingerzeig] tip; [Anleitung] instruction; [Indiz] sign.

hin|weisen *(unreg)* ⟨⟩ *vi* - **1.** [auf etw schließen lassen]: **auf etw** *(A)* ~ to point to sthg - **2.** [zeigen]: **auf jn/etw** ~ to point to sb/sthg ⟨⟩ *vt*: **jn auf etw** *(A)* ~ to point sthg out to sb.

hin|wenden *vt* to turn. ➡ **sich hinwenden** *ref* to turn.

hin|werfen *vt (unreg)* - **1.** [werfen] to throw down - **2.** *fam* [Arbeit, Projekt] to chuck in - **3.** [Skizze] to dash off - **4.** [Bemerkung] to drop casually; [Frage] to ask casually - **5.** *fam* [fallen lassen] to drop. ➡ **sich hinwerfen** *ref* to throw o.s. down.

hin|ziehen *(perf hat/ist hingezogen) (unreg)* ⟨⟩ *vt (hat)* - **1.** [anziehen]: **jn/etw zu sich** ~ to attract sb/sthg - **2.** [zeitlich] to draw out ⟨⟩ *vi (ist)* [umziehen] to move. ➡ **sich hinziehen** *ref* [lange dauern] to drag on.

hinzu *adv* in addition; ~ **kommt noch ...** (and) what is more ...

hinzu|fügen *vt* to add; **etw zu etw** ~ to add sthg to sthg.

hinzu|kommen *(perf ist hinzugekommen) vi (unreg)* - **1.** [ankommen]: **zu jm/etw** ~ to join sb/sthg - **2.** [sich ergeben] to be added on.

hinzu|ziehen *vt (unreg)* to call in.

Hirn *(pl -e) das* - **1.** [Gehirn] brain - **2.** *fam* [Denkvermögen] brains *(pl).*

Hirngespinst *(pl -e) das abw* figment of one's imagination.

Hirsch *(pl -e) der* [Tier] deer; [männlich] stag; [Fleisch] venison.

Hirse *die* millet.

Hirte *(pl -n)*, **Hirt** *(pl -en) der* shepherd.

Hirtin *(pl -nen) die* shepherdess.

hissen *vt* to hoist.

Historiker, in *(mpl -; fpl -nen) der, die* historian.

historisch ⟨⟩ *adj* - **1.** [geschichtlich] historical - **2.** [entscheidend] historic ⟨⟩ *adv* [geschichtlich] historically; **etw ~ betrachten** to look at sthg in historical terms.

Hit *(pl -s) der* hit.

Hit|parade *die* charts *(pl).*

Hitze *die* heat.

hitzebeständig *adj* heat-resistant.

hitzefrei *adj*: ~ **haben** to have the rest of the day off *school because of hot weather.*

Hitze|welle *die* heatwave.

hitzig ⟨⟩ *adj* - **1.** [Person] hot-blooded; [Temperament] fiery - **2.** [Diskussion, Streit] heated ⟨⟩ *adv* [lebhaft] heatedly.

hitzköpfig *adj* [Person] hot-tempered.

Hitz|schlag *der* heat stroke.

HIV-positiv *adj* MED HIV-positive.

H-Milch *die* long-life milk.

hob *prät* ⟹ heben.

Hobby ['hɔbi] *(pl -s) das* hobby.

Hobby|koch *der* amateur cook.

Hobby|köchin *die* amateur cook.

Hobel *(pl -) der* - **1.** [Werkzeug] plane - **2.** [Küchengerät] slicer.

Hobelbank *(pl -bänke) die* carpenter's bench.

hobeln ⟨⟩ *vt* [Holz] to plane; [Gemüse] to slice ⟨⟩ *vi* to plane; **an etw** *(D)* ~ to plane sthg.

hoch *(kompar höher; superl höchste)* ⟨⟩ *adj* - **1.** [räumlich] high; [Baum, Gebäude] tall; [Schnee] deep; **drei Meter** ~ three metres high/tall/deep; **im hohen Norden** in the far north - **2.** [bezeichnet Ausmass - Blutdruck, Tempo, Mieten, Preis *etc*] high; [- Gewicht, Strafe] heavy; [- Anzahl, Summe] large; **in hohem Grade** to a large extent; **wenn es ~ kommt** at the most - **3.** [bezeichnet Qualität - Position, Ansprüche] high; [- Ehre, Begabung] great; **das ist mir zu** ~ *fam fig* that's beyond me - **4.** [gesellschaftlich gehoben]: **von hoher Geburt** of noble birth; **von hohem Ansehen** highly regarded; **ein hoher Beamter** a high-ranking official - **5.** MUS high; **jn in den höchsten Tönen loben** *fig* to praise sb to the skies ⟨⟩ *adv (kompar höher; superl am höchsten)* - **1.** [räumlich] high; **das Dorf ist ~ gelegen** the village is situated high up; **zwei Treppen** ~ two floors up; **das Flugzeug fliegt 3000 Meter** ~ the plane is flying at (a height of) 3,000 metres; **ein ~ aufgeschossener Junge** a tall boy - **2.** [bezeichnet Ausmass, Qualität] highly; **~ verlieren** to lose heavily; **~ zufrieden** very content; **~ und heilig versprechen** to promise solemnly - **3.** MUS high; **du singst zu ~!** you're singing sharp!

Hoch *(pl -s) das* - **1.** [Jubelruf] cheer; **jm ein dreifaches ~ ausbringen** to give three cheers for sb - **2.** [Hochdruckgebiet] high.

Hochachtung *die* great respect.

hochachtungsvoll *adv* Yours faithfully *(nach Dear Sir/Madam);* Yours sincerely *(nach Dear Mr/Mrs X).*

hoch|arbeiten ➡ **sich hocharbeiten** *ref* to work one's way up.

hoch begabt *adj* highly talented.

Hochbetrieb *der*: **im Büro herrscht** ~ it's very busy in the office.

hoch bezahlt *adj* highly-paid.

Hoch|burg *die* stronghold.

hochdeutsch ⟨⟩ *adj* standard German ⟨⟩ *adv* in standard German.

Hochdruck *der* - **1.** [technisch, meteorologisch] high pressure; **unter ~ stehen** to be under high pressure - **2.** *fam fig* [Hochbetrieb]: **unter ~ stehen** to be at full stretch.

Hochdruck|gebiet *das* high-pressure area.

hoch empfindlich *adj* highly sensitive.

hocherfreut ⟨⟩ *adj* highly delighted ⟨⟩ *adv* with great delight.

hoch|fahren *(perf hat/ist hochgefahren) (unreg)* ⟨⟩ *vi (ist)* - **1.** [nach oben] to go up; [in

Auto] to drive up - **2.** [erschrecken] to start; **aus dem Schlaf ~** to wake up with a start - **3.** [zornig] to flare up <> vt (hat) fam [nach oben] to take up.

hoch|fliegen (perf ist hochgeflogen) vi (unreg) [Vogel, Flugzeug] to fly up.

Hoch|form die: **in ~ sein** to be on top form.

Hoch|frequenz die PHYS high frequency.

Hoch|gebirge das high mountains (pl).

Hoch|gefühl das: **im ~ einer Sache** (G) elated by sthg.

hoch|gehen (perf ist hochgegangen) vi (unreg) - **1.** [gehen, sich heben] to go up - **2.** [Mine, Bombe] to go off; [Gebäude] to blow up; **etw ~ lassen** to blow sthg up - **3.** fam [wütend werden] to hit the roof - **4.** [aufgedeckt werden] to be uncovered; **jn ~ lassen** fam to squeal on sb.

hochgestellt adj [Zahl] superscript.

Hochglanz der: **ein Fotoabzug in ~** a gloss print; **auf ~ poliert** polished until it shines; **etw auf ~ bringen** fig to make sthg spick-and-span.

hochgradig <> adj extreme <> adv extremely.

hoch|halten vt (unreg) [bewahren] to uphold.

hoch halten vt (unreg) [nach oben] to hold up.

Hoch|haus das high-rise building.

hoch|heben vt (unreg): **jn/etw ~** to lift sb/sthg (up).

hochkant adv on end.

hoch|klappen (perf hat/ist hochgeklappt) <> vt (hat) [Klapptisch] to fold up; [Verdeck, Armlehne] to fold back; [Kragen] to turn up; [Sitz] to tip up <> vi (ist) [Kragen, Hutkrempe] to turn up; [Sitz] to tip up.

hoch|klettern (perf ist hochgeklettert) vi: **an etw** (D) **~** to climb (up) sthg.

hoch|kommen (perf ist hochgekommen) vi (unreg) - **1.** [nach oben] to come up - **2.** [aufstehen] to get up - **3.** [beruflich] to get on - **4.** [erbrechen] **es kommt ihr bei dem Gedanken daran heute noch hoch** the thought of it still makes her feel sick today.

Hoch|konjunktur die boom.

hoch|krempeln vt to roll up.

Hoch|land das uplands (pl).

hoch|leben vi: **jn/etw ~ lassen** to give three cheers for sb/sthg.

Hochleistungssport der top-level sport.

Hochmut der arrogance.

hochmütig <> adj arrogant <> adv arrogantly.

hochnäsig abw adj conceited.

hoch nehmen vt (unreg) [Teppich] to lift up; [Baby] to pick up.

Hoch|ofen der blast furnace.

hochprozentig adj [Getränk, Spirituose] high-proof; [Lösung] highly concentrated.

Hoch|rechnung die projection.

hochrot adj bright red.

Hoch|saison die high season.

hoch|schlagen ['hoːxʃlaːgn̩] (perf hat/ist hochgeschlagen) (unreg) <> vt (hat) to turn up <> vi (ist) to leap up.

hoch|schrecken ['hoːxʃrɛkn̩] (prät schreckte ODER schrak hoch; perf hat/ist hochgeschreckt) <> vt (hat) (reg) to startle <> vi (ist) to start; **er ist aus dem Schlaf hochgeschreckt** he was startled out of sleep.

Hochschul|abschluss der (university) degree.

Hoch|schule die college; [Universität] university.

Hochschul|lehrer, in der, die college lecturer; [an der Universität] university lecturer.

Hochschul|reife die qualification required by school-leavers for university entrance.

hochschwanger ['hoːxʃvaŋɐ] adj heavily pregnant.

Hoch|sommer der midsummer.

Hoch|spannung die - **1.** [Strom] high voltage - **2.** [Stimmung] great tension.

hoch|spielen ['hoːxʃpiːlən] vt to blow up.

Hoch|springer, in der, die SPORT high jumper.

Hochsprung der SPORT high jump.

höchst ['høːçst] adv highly.

Hochstapler, in ['hoːxʃtaːplɐ, ərɪn] (mpl -; fpl -nen) der, die con artist.

Höchst|belastung die extreme pressure; [eines Materials, einer Konstruktion] maximum load.

höchstens ['høːçstn̩s] adv - **1.** [im äußersten Fall] at best - **2.** [außer] except.

Höchstfall der (ohne pl): **im ~** at (the) most.

Höchstform die: **in ~ sein** to be on top form.

Höchst|geschwindigkeit die speed limit.

Höchst|grenze die upper limit.

Hochstimmung die festive mood.

höchstmöglich ['høːçstmøːklɪç] adj highest possible.

höchstwahrscheinlich ['høːçstvaːɐ̯ʃainlɪç] adv most probably.

Hoch|tour die: **auf ~en laufen** [Maschine] to run at top speed; [Vorbereitungen] to be in full swing.

hochtrabend abw <> adj pompous <> adv pompously.

Hochwasser das high water; **~ haben** to be in spate; fam fig to be at half-mast.

hochwertig adj [Produkte] high-quality; [Eiweiß] highly nutritious.

Hoch|zeit die wedding; **silberne/goldene ~** silver/golden wedding.

Hochzeits|kleid das wedding dress.

Hochzeits|nacht *die* wedding night.

Hochzeits|paar *das* bride and groom.

Hochzeits|reise *die* honeymoon.

Hochzeits|tag *der* [Tag der Hochzeit] wedding day; [Jubiläum] wedding anniversary.

hoch|ziehen *vt (unreg)* - **1.** [Rollladen, Hose] to pull up; [Segel, Flagge] to hoist - **2.** [heben] to raise; **die Nase ~** to sniff - **3.** [bauen] to put up. ➡ **sich hochziehen** *ref*: **sich an etw** *(D)* **~** to pull o.s. up by holding on to sthg; *fig* to take pleasure in sthg.

Hocke *(pl -n) die* - **1.** [Haltung]: **in die ~ gehen** to crouch down - **2.** [Sprung] squat vault.

hocken *vi* - **1.** [kauern] to crouch - **2.** *fam* [sitzen] to sit. ➡ **sich hocken** *ref* - **1.** [sich kauern] to crouch - **2.** *fam* [sich setzen] to sit o.s. down.

Hocker *(pl -) der* stool.

Höcker *(pl -) der* - **1.** [Ausbuchtung] bump - **2.** [von Kamel] hump.

Hockey *das* hockey.

Hoden *(pl -) der* testicle.

Hof *(pl Höfe) der* - **1.** [von Häusern] courtyard - **2.** [Bauernhof] farm - **3.** [Schulhof] playground - **4.** [von Gefängnissen] yard - **5.** [von Königen] court; **jm den ~ machen** *fig* to court sb.

Hofbräuhaus *das large beer hall in Munich.*

hoffen ◇ *vt* to hope; **~ wir das Beste!** let's hope for the best! ◇ *vi*: **auf etw ~** to hope for sthg; **auf jn ~** to pin one's hopes on sb; **auf Gott ~** to trust in God.

hoffentlich *adv* hopefully; **kommt er? – ja, ~!** is he coming? – I hope so!

Hoffnung *(pl -en) die* hope; **die ~ aufgeben/nicht aufgeben** to give up/not to give up hope; **seine ~en auf jn/etw setzen** to pin one's hopes on sb/sthg.

hoffnungslos ◇ *adj* hopeless ◇ *adv* hopelessly.

Hoffnungslosigkeit *die* hopelessness.

hoffnungsvoll ◇ *adj* - **1.** [optimistisch] hopeful - **2.** [Erfolg versprechend] promising ◇ *adv* - **1.** [optimistisch] hopefully - **2.** [Erfolg versprechend] promisingly.

höflich ◇ *adj* polite ◇ *adv* politely.

Höflichkeit *(pl -en) die* - **1.** [im Auftreten] politeness - **2.** [Floskel] polite remark.

Höhe *(pl -n) die* - **1.** [von Schrank, Berg] height; [von Dreieck] altitude - **2.** [von Preis, Temperatur] level; **ein Bußgeld in ~ von 50 Euro** a fine of 50 euros - **3.** [Richtung]: **in die ~ up** - **4.** [Linie]: **auf der** ODER **in ~ von etw** level with sthg; **auf gleicher ~** level - **5.** *RW:* **das ist die ~!** *fam* that's the limit!

Hoheit *(pl -en) die* - **1.** [Herrschaft] sovereignty - **2.** [als Anrede] Your Highness.

Hoheits|gebiet *das* sovereign territory.

Höhen|lage *die* altitude; **in ~** at high altitude.

Höhen|sonne *die* sun lamp.

Höhe|punkt *der* high point.

hohl ◇ *adj* - **1.** [gen] hollow; [Augen] sunken; **in der ~en Hand** in the hollow of one's hand - **2.** *fam abw* [dumm - Phrase] empty; [- Person] empty-headed ◇ *adv* - **1.** [dumpf] hollowly - **2.** *fam abw* [geistlos] emptily.

Höhle *(pl -n) die* - **1.** [Grotte] cave - **2.** [von Dachs] sett; [von Löwe] den; [von Fuchs] lair.

Hohl|kreuz *das (ohne pl)* hollow back.

Hohl|raum *der* cavity.

höhnisch ◇ *adj* scornful ◇ *adv* scornfully.

holen *vt* - **1.** [herbeischaffen] to fetch, to get; **sich** *(D)* **bei jm Rat ~** to ask sb for advice; **in der ~en Hand** to come for sthg; **sich** *(D)* **etw ~** [gen] to get sthg; [Krankheit] to catch sthg - **2.** [kaufen] to get - **3.** [herausnehmen]: **etw aus etw ~** to take sthg out of sthg - **4.** [Arzt, Polizei, Handwerker] to call.

Holland *nt* Holland.

Holländer *(pl -) der* Dutchman; **die ~** the Dutch ◇ *adj (unver)* Dutch.

Holländerin *(pl -nen) die* Dutchwoman.

holländisch *adj* Dutch.

Hölle *die* hell; **die ~ ist los!** *fam fig* all hell has broken loose!; **jm die ~ heiß machen** *fam fig* to give sb hell.

höllisch ◇ *adj* - **1.** [schrecklich] appalling - **2.** *fam* [intensiv] infernal ◇ *adv fam* [sehr]: **die Wunde tut ~ weh** the wound hurts like hell; **~ aufpassen** to be incredibly careful.

Holm *(pl -e) der* SPORT bar.

holpern *(perf hat/ist geholpert) vi* - **1.** *(ist)* [beim Fahren] to jolt - **2.** *(hat)* [beim Sprechen] to stumble.

holprig ◇ *adj* - **1.** [Weg] bumpy - **2.** [Fremdsprache] halting - **3.** [Stil] clumsy ◇ *adv* [sprechen, lesen] haltingly.

Holunder *(pl -) der* - **1.** [Baum] elder - **2.** [Beere] elderberry.

Holz *(pl Hölzer) das* wood; [Bauholz] timber *Br,* lumber *Am;* **aus dem gleichen** ODER **demselben ~ (geschnitzt) sein** *fig* to be cast from the same mould. ➡ **Holz verarbeitend** *adj* timber-processing.

Holzfäller, in *(mpl -; fpl -nen) der, die* woodcutter *Br,* lumberjack *Am.*

holzig *adj* woody.

Holz|kohle *die* charcoal.

Holz|schuh *der* clog.

Holz|weg *der*: **auf dem ~ sein** to be barking up the wrong tree.

Homebanking ['hoːmbɛŋkɪŋ] *das* home banking.

Homepage ['hoːmpeːdʒ] *(pl -s) die* EDV home page.

Homeshopping *das (ohne pl)* home shopping.
Homöopathie *die* homeopathy.
Homosexualität *die* homosexuality.
homosexuell *adj* homosexual.
Honig *der* honey.
Honorar (*pl* -e) *das* fee.
Hopfen (*pl* -) *der* hops (*pl*); **bei ihm ist ~ und Malz verloren** he's a hopeless case.
hörbar ◇ *adj* audible ◇ *adv* audibly.
hörbehindert *adj* hard of hearing.
horchen *vi* to listen.
Horde (*pl* -n) *die* horde.
hören ◇ *vt* - **1.** [wahrnehmen, erfahren] to hear; **er hat lange nichts von sich ~ lassen** we haven't heard from him for ages; **von ihm hört man nur Gutes** you only hear good things about him - **2.** [willkürlich] to listen to ◇ *vi* - **1.** [unwillkürlich, erfahren] to hear; **schwer ~** to be hard of hearing; **Sie werden noch von mir ~!** you haven't heard the last of this! - **2.** [zuhören, gehorchen] to listen; **hör mal!** listen!; **~ auf** (+ A) to listen to; **hätte ich doch auf ihren Rat gehört!** if only I'd listened to her advice!
Hörensagen *das:* **etw vom ~ kennen** to know sthg from hearsay.
Hörer (*pl* -) *der* - **1.** [Zuhörer] listener - **2.** [Telefonhörer] receiver.
Hörerin (*pl* -nen) *die* listener.
Hörerschaft *die* listeners (*pl*).
Hörlfehler *der* hearing defect.
Hörlfunk *der* radio.
Hörlgerät *das* hearing aid.
hörgeschädigt *adj* hard of hearing.
Horizont (*pl* -e) *der* horizon; **das geht über meinen ~** *fig* that's right over the top of my head; **seinen ~ erweitern** *fig* to broaden one's horizons.
horizontal ◇ *adj* horizontal ◇ *adv* horizontally.
Hormon (*pl* -e) *das* hormone.
Horn (*pl* Hörner ODER -e) *das* horn.
Hörnchen (*pl* -) *das* - **1.** [Gebäck] croissant - **2.** [Horn] small horn.
Hornlhaut *die* - **1.** [Hautschicht] patch of hard skin, callus - **2.** [des Auges] cornea.
Hornisse (*pl* -n) *die* hornet.
Horoskop (*pl* -e) *das* horoscope.
horrend *adj* horrendous.
Horror *der* - **1.** [Entsetzen] horror; **einen ~ vor jm/etw haben** to be terrified of sb/sthg - **2.** *fam* [Unangenehmes]: **das war der (reine) ~** it was a (total) nightmare.
Hörlsaal *der* lecture hall.
Hörlspiel *das* radio play.
Hort (*pl* -e) *der* - **1.** [Kinderhort] *day-centre where children can spend the afternoon after lessons have finished* - **2.** *geh* [Schutz] refuge.
horten *vt* to hoard.

Hörweite *die:* **in/außer ~** in/out of earshot.
Hose (*pl* -n) *die* trousers (*pl*) *Br*, pants (*pl*) *Am*; [Unterhose - von Männern] pants (*pl*) *Br*, shorts (*pl*) *Am*; [- von Frauen] knickers (*pl*) *Br*, panties (*pl*) *Am*; **eine neue ~ kaufen** to buy a new pair of trousers *Br* ODER pants *Am*, to buy some new trousers *Br* ODER pants *Am*; **sich** (*D*) **die ~ anziehen** to put one's trousers on; **kurze ~** shorts (*pl*); **die ~ anhaben** *fam fig* to wear the trousers; **die ~n voll haben** *fam fig* to be crapping o.s.; **in die ~ gehen** *fam* to be a flop; **da ist tote ~** *fam* it's totally dead there.
Hosenlbein *das* trouser leg.
Hosenlschlitz *der* fly, flies (*pl*) *Br*.
Hosenlträger *der* braces (*pl*) *Br*, suspenders (*pl*) *Am*.
Hospital (*pl* -e ODER -täler) *das* hospital.
Hostess (*pl* -en) *die* hostess.
Hostie (*pl* -n) *die* REL host.
Hotdog ['hɔt'dɔk] (*pl* -s) *das* ODER *der* hot dog.
Hotel (*pl* -s) *das* hotel; **~ garni** ≃ bed and breakfast.
Hotellzimmer *das* hotel room.
Hotline ['hotlain] (*pl* -s) *die* hotline.
Hr. (*abk für* Herr) Mr.
hrsg. (*abk für* herausgegeben) ed.
Hubraum *der* cubic capacity.
hübsch ◇ *adj* - **1.** [Person, Anblick, Kleid, Blumen] pretty - **2.** [Idee, Umgebung] nice - **3.** *fam* [groß - Summe] tidy - **4.** *fam iron* [unangenehm]: **das ist ja eine ~e Überraschung!** what a pleasant surprise! ◇ *adv* - **1.** [schön] prettily - **2.** *fam* [sehr] jolly; **sei ~ brav!** be really good!
Hubschrauber (*pl* -) *der* helicopter.
huckepack *adv:* **jn ~ nehmen** ODER **tragen** *fam* to give sb a piggyback.
Huf (*pl* -e) *der* hoof.
Hufleisen *das* horseshoe.
Hüfte (*pl* -n) *die* hip.
Hufltier *das* hoofed animal.
Hügel (*pl* -) *der* - **1.** [Berg] hill - **2.** [Haufen] mound.
hügelig *adj* hilly.
Huhn (*pl* Hühner) *das* - **1.** [Vogel] chicken - **2.** *fam* [Mädchen, Frau]: **ein dummes ~** a silly cow; **ein verrücktes ~** a queer fish.
Hühnchen (*pl* -) *das* chicken.
Hühnerlauge *das* corn.
Hühnerlbrühe *die* chicken broth.
Hühnerlei *das* hen's egg.
Hülle (*pl* -n) *die* cover; [Verpackung] wrapping; [von Schallplatte] sleeve; **etw in ~ und Fülle haben** to have plenty of sthg.
hüllen *vt:* **jn/sich/etw in etw** (*A*) **~** to wrap sb/o.s./sthg in sthg.
Hülse (*pl* -n) *die* - **1.** [Hülle] case; [von Film, Zigarre] tube - **2.** [bei Pflanzen] pod.

Hülsen|frucht die pulse.

Hummel (pl -n) die bumblebee.

Hummer (pl -) der lobster.

Humor der humour; **viel ~ haben** to have a great sense of humour; **etw mit ~ nehmen** ODER **tragen** to bear sthg with great humour.

humoristisch <> adj humorous <> adv humorously.

humorvoll <> adj humorous <> adv humorously.

humpeln (perf hat/ist gehumpelt) vi - **1.** (hat, ist) [hinken] to walk with ODER have a limp - **2.** (ist) [in eine Richtung] to limp.

Hund (pl -e) der - **1.** [Tier] dog; **'vorsicht, bissiger ~!'** 'beware of the dog' - **2.** salopp [Mann]: **er ist ein blöder ~** he's a stupid git - **3.** RW: **vor die ~e gehen** fam to go to the dogs.

Hunde|hütte die kennel.

Hunde|leine die lead Br, leash Am.

hundemüde adj dog-tired.

hundert num - **1.** [Zahl] a ODER one hundred; **auf ~ kommen** fam to hit the roof - **2.** fam [sehr viele] hundreds of; siehe auch **sechs**.

Hundert (pl -e) die ODER das hundred.
◆ **Hunderte** pl [große Anzahl]: **~e von** hundreds of. ◆ **zu Hunderten** adv: **zu ~ kommen** to come in their hundreds; siehe auch **Sechs**.

hundertfach adv a hundred times.

Hundertjahr|feier die centenary.

hundertjährig adj hundred-year-old.

Hunderteuroschein der hundred mark note Br ODER bill Am.

hundertprozentig <> adj - **1.** [von hundert Prozent] one hundred percent - **2.** [vollkommen] complete; **er ist ein ~er Bayer** he's a Bavarian through and through <> adv fam [völlig] completely; **etw ~ wissen** to know sthg for certain.

hundertste, r, s adj hundredth; siehe auch **sechste**.

Hundertste (pl -n) der, die, das hundredth; siehe auch **Sechste**.

Hundertstel adj (unver) hundredth; **eine ~ Sekunde** a hundredth of a second; siehe auch **sechstel**.

Hundertstel (pl -) das hundredth; siehe auch **Sechstel**.

hunderttausend num a ODER one hundred thousand.

Hunde|steuer die dog licence fee.

Hunde|zwinger der dog cage.

Hündin (pl -nen) die bitch.

Hunger der eigtl & fig hunger; **auf etw** (A) **~ haben** to feel like eating sthg.

Hunger|lohn der abw starvation wage, pittance.

hungern vi - **1.** [nach Nahrung] to go hun-

gry - **2.** geh [verlangen]: **nach etw ~** to be hungry for sthg, to crave sthg.

Hungers|not die famine.

Hunger|streik der hunger strike.

hungrig <> adj hungry <> adv hungrily.

Hupe (pl -n) die horn.

hupen vi to sound one's horn.

hüpfen (perf ist gehüpft) vi to hop.

Hürde (pl -n) die hurdle.

Hürden|lauf der: **der ~** the hurdles.

Hure (pl -n) die abw whore.

hurra interj hurray!

huschen (perf ist gehuscht) vi to dart; [Lächeln] to flit.

hüsteln vi to give a slight cough.

husten <> vi to cough; **auf dieses Angebot huste ich!** fam you can keep your offer! <> vt [Blut, Schleim] to cough up; **jm eins** ODER **was ~ fam** to tell sb to get lost.

Husten der (ohne pl) cough; **~ haben** to have a cough.

Husten|saft der cough mixture.

Hut (pl Hüte) <> der - **1.** [Kleidungsstück] hat - **2.** RW: **das ist ein alter ~** that's old hat; **mit jm/etw nichts am ~ haben** fam to have no time for sb/sthg; **seinen ~ nehmen** to pack one's bags; **dein Geld kannst du dir an den ~ stecken!** fam you can keep your money!; **verschiedene Interessen unter einen ~ bringen** to reconcile different interests <> die: (vor jm) **auf der ~ sein** to be on one's guard (with sb); **beim Autofahren bin ich auf der ~** I'm on the alert when I'm driving.
◆ **Hut ab** interj: **das hätte ich dir gar nicht zugetraut - ~ ab!** I wouldn't have thought you capable of that – hats off to you!

hüten vt [Kinder] to look after; [Geheimnis] to keep; [Tiere] to watch over. ◆ **sich hüten** ref: **sich vor jm/etw ~** to be on one's guard against sb/sthg; **sich ~, etw zu tun** to take care not to do sthg.

Hütte (pl -n) die - **1.** [Haus] hut; [bewirtschaftete Berghütte] mountain lodge - **2.** [Eisenhütte] iron and steel works (sg).

Hütten|käse der cottage cheese.

Hyäne (pl -n) die hyena.

Hyazinthe (pl -n) die hyacinth.

Hydrant (pl -en) der hydrant.

Hydraulik die hydraulics (pl).

hydraulisch <> adj hydraulic <> adv hydraulically.

Hydrokultur die hydroponics (U).

Hygiene [hy'gie:nə] die hygiene.

hygienisch [hy'gie:nɪʃ] <> adj hygienic <> adv hygienically.

Hymne (pl -n) die hymn.

hypnotisieren vt to hypnotize.

Hypothek (pl -en) die mortgage.

Hypo|these die hypothesis.

Hysterie [hyste'ri:] (pl -n) die hysteria.

hysterisch <> *adj* hysterical; **~er Anfall** (fit of) hysterics <> *adv* hysterically.

I

i, I [iː] (*pl* - ODER -s) *das* i, I.

i.A. (*abk für* im Auftrag) pp.

IC [iː'tseː] (*pl* -s) (*abk für* Intercity) *der* intercity train.

ICE [iːtseː'eː] (*pl* -s) (*abk für* Intercity Express) *der* intercity express train.

ich *pron* I; **~ bins** it's me.

ideal <> *adj* ideal <> *adv* ideally.

Ideal (*pl* -e) *das* ideal.

Idealfall *der* ideal case.

Idealismus *der* idealism.

Idee (*pl* -n) *die* - **1.** [gen] idea; **eine fixe ~** an obsession - **2.** [Kleinigkeit] bit.

identifizieren *vt* to identify; **jn/etw mit etw ~** to identify sb/sthg with sthg. <> **sich identifizieren** *ref:* **sich mit jm/etw ~** to identify with sb/sthg.

Identifizierung (*pl* -en) *die* identification.

identisch *adj* identical.

Identität *die* identity.

Ideologie (*pl* -n) *die* ideology.

Idiot (*pl* -en) *der fam abw* [Dummkopf] idiot.

Idiotin (*pl* -nen) *die* idiot.

idiotisch *fam abw* <> *adj* [dumm, unsinnig] idiotic <> *adv* [unsinnig] idiotically.

Idol (*pl* -e) *das* idol.

Idylle (*pl* -n) *die* idyll.

idyllisch <> *adj* idyllic <> *adv* idyllically.

Igel (*pl* -) *der* hedgehog.

ignorieren *vt* to ignore.

IHK [iːhaː'kaː] (*abk für* Industrie- und Handelskammer) *die* chamber of commerce and industry.

ihm *pron* (*Dativ von er*) - **1.** [Person] (to) him; **sie sagte es ~** she told him; **das gehört ~** this is his, this belongs to him - **2.** [Sache] (to) it.

ihn *pron* (*Akkusativ von er*) - **1.** [Person] him - **2.** [Sache] it.

ihnen *pron* (*Dativ Plural von er/sie*) (to) them; **er ist von ~** it's theirs, it belongs to them; **gib ~ den Schlüssel** give them the key.

Ihnen *pron* (*Dativ von Sie*) (to) you; **gehört das ~?** is this yours?, does this belong to you?; **wer hat es ~ gegeben?** who gave you it?, who gave it to you?; **entschuldigen Sie, meine Herren, ist der Platz neben ~ frei?** excuse me gentlemen, is the seat next to you free?

ihr, e *det* - **1.** (*Singular*) her - **2.** (*Plural*) their.

ihr *pron* - **1.** [Nominativ Plural] you - **2.** [Dativ von sie - Person] (to) her; [- Sache] (to) it; **er sagte es ~** he told her; **das gehört ~** this is hers, this belongs to her; **mit ~** with her.

Ihr, e *det* your.

ihre, r, s *pron* - **1.** [Singular - von Person] hers; [- von Ding] its - **2.** [Plural] theirs.

Ihre, r, s *pron* yours.

ihrer *pron* (*Genitiv von sie*) [Singular von Person] (of) her; [Plural] (of) them; [Singular von Ding] (of) it.

ihrerseits *adv* - **1.** [sie selbst - Singular] for her part; [- Plural] for their part - **2.** [von ihr - Person] on her part; [- Tier, Sache] on its part; [- Plural] on their part.

Ihrerseits *adv* on your part.

ihretwegen *adv* - **1.** [ihr zuliebe - von Person] for her sake; [- von Ding] for its sake; [ihnen zuliebe] for their sake - **2.** [wegen ihr - Person] because of her; [- Ding] because of it; [wegen ihnen] because of them.

Ihretwegen *adv* - **1.** [Ihnen zuliebe] for your sake - **2.** [wegen Ihnen] because of you.

ihretwillen ➡ **um ihretwillen** *adv* [Singular - Person] for her sake; [- Ding] for its sake; [Plural] for them.

Ihretwillen ➡ **um Ihretwillen** *adv* for your sake.

ihrige (*pl* -n) *pron geh:* **der/die/das ~** [Singular - von Person] hers; [- von Ding] its; [Plural] theirs.

illegal <> *adj* illegal <> *adv* illegally.

Illusion (*pl* -en) *die* illusion.

Illustration (*pl* -en) *die* illustration.

illustrieren *vt* to illustrate.

Illustrierte (*pl* -n) *die* magazine.

im *präp* (*in + dem*) ➡ in.

Image ['ɪmɪtʃ] (*pl* -s) *das* image.

Imbiss (*pl* -e) *der* - **1.** [Mahlzeit] snack - **2.** [Imbissbude] snack bar.

Imbissbude *die fam* snack bar.

Imitation (*pl* -en) *die* imitation.

imitieren *vt* to imitate.

Immatrikulation (*pl* -en) *die* - **1.** UNI matriculation - **2.** *Schweiz* [Kfz-Zulassung] registration.

immatrikulieren *vt* - **1.** UNI to enrol - **2.** *Schweiz* [zulassen] to register. ➡ **sich immatrikulieren** *ref* UNI to matriculate.

immens <> *adj* immense <> *adv* immensely; **~ viel** an immense amount.

immer *adv* - **1.** [zeitlich] always; **für ~ und ewig** for ever and ever; **~ wieder** again and again, time and again; **~ wenn** whenever; **~ geradeaus!** keep going straight ahead!; **~ mit der Ruhe!** take it easy!; **~ noch** still - **2.** [mit Komparativ]: **~ schwieriger** more and more difficult; **~ stärker** stronger and stronger - **3.** [egal]: **was (auch) ~** whatever; **wer (auch) ~** whoever; **wie (auch) ~** however; **wo (auch) ~** wherever.

immerfort *adv* constantly.

immerhin *adv* - **1.** [wenigstens] at least - **2.** [schließlich] after all - **3.** [trotzdem] nevertheless.

immerzu *adv* constantly.

Immigrant, in (*mpl* -en; *fpl* -nen) *der, die* immigrant.

Immigration (*pl* -en) *die* immigration.

Immobilien [ɪmo'biːljən] *pl* property (*U*).

immun *adj*: **gegen etw ~ sein** to be immune to sthg.

Immunität *die* immunity.

Imperativ (*pl* -e) *der* GRAM imperative.

Imperfekt (*pl* -e) *das* GRAM imperfect.

impfen *vt* to vaccinate; **jn gegen etw ~** to vaccinate sb against sthg.

Impfstoff *der* vaccine.

Impfung (*pl* -en) *die* vaccination.

imponieren *vi* to impress; **jm (durch etw) ~** to impress sb (with sthg).

imponierend ⬦ *adj* impressive ⬦ *adv* impressively.

Import (*pl* -e) *der* - **1.** [Ware] import - **2.** [Einfuhr] importation.

importieren *vt* to import.

impotent *adj* impotent.

Impotenz *die* impotence.

imprägnieren *vt* to impregnate; [gegen Wasser] to waterproof.

improvisieren [ɪmprovi'ziːrən] *vt & vi* to improvise.

Impuls (*pl* -e) *der* - **1.** [Anregung] stimulus; [innere Regung] impulse; **einer Sache (D) neue ~e geben** to breathe new life into sthg - **2.** [Stoß] impulse.

impulsiv ⬦ *adj* impulsive ⬦ *adv* impulsively.

imstande, im Stande *adj*: **zu etw ~ sein** to be capable of sthg.

in ⬦ *präp* - **1.** (+ *D*) [räumlich] in; **im Bett liegen** to be in bed; **~ der Schule** at school - **2.** (+ *A*) [räumlich] into; **~ den Fluss fallen** to fall into the river; **~ die Stadt fahren** to go to ODER into town; **~ die Schule gehen** to go to school; **sich ~ jn verlieben** to fall in love with sb - **3.** (+ *D*) [zeitlich] in; **~ dieser Woche** this week; **im Moment** at the moment; **wir fahren ~ einer Stunde** we're going in an hour - **4.** (+ *A*) [zeitlich] into; **wir arbeiteten bis spät ~ die Nacht** we worked late into the night - **5.** (+ *D*) [modal]: **~ aller Eile** hurriedly; **~ Betrieb sein** to be working; **ich habe mich ~ der Zeit geirrt** I got the time wrong - **6.** (+ *A*) [modal]: **etw ~ seine Einzelteile zerlegen** to take sthg to pieces - **7.** (+ *D*) [mit Maß- oder Mengenangaben] in; **~ Millimetern** in millimetres ⬦ *adj*: **~ sein** *fam* to be in.

Inbegriff *der* embodiment, epitome.

inbegriffen ⬦ *adj*: **in etw (D) ~ sein** to be included in sthg ⬦ *adv*: **Steuern ~** including tax.

Inbetriebnahme (*pl* -n) *die* - **1.** [von Maschine, Kraftwerk] commissioning; **vor ~ des Gerätes die Gebrauchsanweisung lesen** read the instructions before switching the appliance on for the first time - **2.** [von Flughafen, Schwimmbad] opening.

Indefinitpronomen *das* GRAM indefinite pronoun.

indem *konj* - **1.** [instrumental] by; **er vernichtete die Unterlagen, ~ er sie in den Reißwolf steckte** he destroyed the documents by putting them through the shredder - **2.** [während] while.

Inder, in (*mpl* -; *fpl* -nen) *der, die* Indian.

Indianer, in (*mpl* -; *fpl* -nen) *der, die abw* (Red) Indian.

indianisch *adj* Indian.

Indien *nt* India.

Indikativ (*pl* -e) *der* GRAM indicative (mood).

indirekt ⬦ *adj* indirect ⬦ *adv* indirectly.

indisch *adj* Indian.

Indischer Ozean *der* Indian Ocean.

indiskret ⬦ *adj* indiscreet ⬦ *adv* indiscreetly.

indiskutabel *adj abw* out of the question.

Individualist, in [ɪndividuaˈlɪst, ɪn] (*mpl* -en; *fpl* -nen) *der, die* individualist.

individuell [ɪndivi'dʊɛl] ⬦ *adj* individual ⬦ *adv* individually; **~ verschieden sein** to vary from case to case.

Individuum [ɪndi'viːduɔm] (*pl* -viduen) *das* individual.

Indiz [ɪn'diːts] (*pl* -ien) *das* - **1.** RECHT piece of circumstantial evidence; **~ien** circumstantial evidence - **2.** [Anzeichen] indication.

Indonesien *nt* Indonesia.

Industrie (*pl* -n) *die* industry.

Industriegebiet *das* industrial area.

industriell ⬦ *adj* industrial ⬦ *adv* industrially.

ineinander *adv* in/into one another; **~ verliebt sein** to be in love (with one another); **~ verwickelt** tangled up (in each other).

ineinander fügen *vt* to fit together. ➧ **sich ineinander fügen** *ref* to fit together.

Infanterie ['ɪnfantəriː] *die* infantry.

Infarkt (*pl* -e) *der* heart attack.

Infekt (*pl* -e) *der* MED infection.

Infektion (*pl* -en) *die* infection.

Infektionskrankheit *die* infectious disease.

Infinitiv (*pl* -e) *der* GRAM infinitive.

infizieren *vt*: **jn (mit etw) ~** to infect sb (with sthg). ➧ **sich infizieren** *ref*: **sich (mit etw) ~** to become infected (with sthg).

Inflation (*pl* -en) *die* inflation.

Inflationsrate *die* rate of inflation.

infolge *präp*: **~ einer Sache (G)** ODER **von etw** as a result of sthg.

infolgedessen *adv* consequently.

Informatik *die* computer science.

Informatiker, in *(mpl -; fpl -nen) der, die* computer scientist.

Information *(pl -en) die* - **1.** information *(U);* -en information; **eine ~ über jn/etw** (a piece of) information about sb/sthg - **2.** *(ohne pl)* [in Kaufhaus, Bahnhof] information desk.

Informations|material *das* information.

Informations|stand *der* information stand.

informativ *adj* informative.

informieren *vt:* **jn über jn/etw ~** to inform sb about sb/sthg. ➤ **sich informieren** *ref:* **sich (über jn/etw) ~** to find out (about sb/ sthg).

Infrarot *das* infra-red.

Infra|struktur *die* infrastructure.

Infusion *(pl -en) die* MED infusion.

Ingenieur, in [ɪnʒe'njoːɐ̯, rɪn] *(mpl -e; fpl -nen) der, die* engineer.

Ingwer *der* ginger.

Inh. *(abk für* Inhaber) prop.

Inhaber, in *(mpl -; fpl -nen) der, die* - **1.** [von Geschäft] owner - **2.** [von Amt, Titel] holder.

inhaftieren *vt* to take into custody.

inhalieren ◇ *vt* to inhale ◇ *vi* - **1.** MED to use an inhalant - **2.** *fam* [einen Lungenzug machen] to inhale.

Inhalt *(pl -e) der* - **1.** [von Gefäß, Behälter] contents *(pl)* - **2.** [von Text, Gespräch] content; **Form und ~** form and content - **3.** [Größe - von Fläche] area; [- von Raum] volume - **4.** [Sinn] meaning.

inhaltlich ◇ *adj:* **der ~e Aufbau eines Textes** the way the content of a text is structured ◇ *adv* as far as content is concerned.

Inhalts|angabe *die* - **1.** [von Text] summary - **2.** [von Paket] description of contents.

Inhalts|verzeichnis *das* [von Buch] table of contents; [von Paket] list of contents.

Initiative [initsja'tiːvə] *(pl -n) die* - **1.** [gen] initiative; **die ~ ergreifen** to take the initiative; **aus eigener ~** on one's own initiative - **2.** [Gruppe] local action group.

Injektion *(pl -en) die* injection.

inkl. *(abk für* inklusive) incl.

inklusive [ɪnkluˈziːvə] ◇ *präp:* **~ einer Sache** *(G)* including sthg ◇ *adv:* **bis zum 10. August ~** until 10 August inclusive.

inkompatibel *adj* incompatible.

inkompetent ◇ *adj* incompetent ◇ *adv* incompetently.

inkonsequent ◇ *adj* inconsistent ◇ *adv* inconsistently.

Inland *das:* **im ~** at home; **die Waren sind für das ~ bestimmt** the goods are for the domestic market; **die Reaktionen des In- und Auslandes** the reactions at home and abroad.

inländisch *adj* - **1.** [Waren, Produkte] domestic - **2.** [Presse] national.

Inlineskates ['ɪnlainskeɪts] *pl* rollerblades, inline skates; **auf/mit ~ fahren** to go rollerblading.

inmitten ◇ *präp:* **~ einer Sache/Gruppe** *(G)* in the midst of sthg/a group ◇ *adv:* **~ von jm/etw** amidst sb/sthg.

innen *adv* inside; **die Schale ist ~ versilbert** the bowl is silver-plated on the inside. ➤ **nach innen** *adv* inwards. ➤ **von innen** *adv* from inside; **etw von ~ nach außen kehren** to turn sthg inside out.

Innen|leben *das (ohne pl)* - **1.** [Seele]: **sein ~ vor jm ausbreiten** to tell sb one's innermost thoughts - **2.** [von Gerät] insides *(pl)*.

Innen|minister, in *der, die* Minister of the Interior, ≃ Home Secretary *Br,* ≃ Secretary of the Interior *Am.*

Innen|politik *die (ohne pl)* - **1.** [Handeln] domestic policy - **2.** [Bereich der Politik] home affairs *(pl)*.

Innen|seite *die* inside.

Innen|stadt *die* town centre; [in Großstadt] city centre.

innere, r, s *adj* - **1.** [innen befindlich, persönlich] inner - **2.** [Struktur, Angelegenheit & MED] internal.

Innere *das (ohne pl)* - **1.** [Inhalt] inside - **2.** [von Raum] inside, interior; [von Land] interior; **Ministerium des ~n** Ministry of the Interior - **3.** [Geist, Seele, Basis] heart; **im tiefsten ~n** deep down (inside).

innerhalb ◇ *präp:* **~ einer Sache** *(G)* within sthg ◇ *adv:* **~ von** within.

innerlich ◇ *adj* [Erregung] inner ◇ *adv* inwardly.

innig ◇ *adj* - **1.** [Verehrung, Wunsch, Beileid] heartfelt - **2.** [Dank] sincere - **3.** [Freundschaft] intimate ◇ *adv* [verbunden] closely.

inoffiziell ◇ *adj* unofficial ◇ *adv* unofficially.

Input *(pl -s) das* ODER *der* EDV & WIRTSCH input.

ins *präp (in + das)* [räumlich]: **~ Wohnzimmer gehen** to go into the living room; **~ Kino gehen** to go to the cinema; *siehe auch* in.

Insasse *(pl -n) der* - **1.** [im Fahrzeug] passenger - **2.** [von Gefängnis, psychiatrischer Anstalt] inmate.

Insassin *(pl -nen) die* - **1.** [im Fahrzeug] passenger - **2.** [von Gefängnis, psychiatrischer Anstalt] inmate.

insbes. *(abk für* insbesondere) esp.

insbesondere, insbesondre *adv* especially, particularly.

In|schrift *die* inscription.

Insekt *(pl -en) das* insect.

Insektenschutz|mittel *das* insect repellent.

Insekten|stich der [von Wespe] insect sting; [von Mücke] insect bite.

Insel (pl -n) die island; **die ~ Sylt** the island of Sylt.

Inserat (pl -e) das advertisement; **ein ~ aufgeben** to put an advertisement in the paper.

insgeheim adv secretly.

insgesamt adv - **1.** [in der Summe] in total - **2.** [im Großen und Ganzen] overall; **sie hat ~ einen guten Eindruck hinterlassen** she made a good overall impression.

insofern[1] adv in this respect.

insofern[2] konj provided that, so long as. ◆ **insofern als** konj insofar as.

in spe [ɪnˈspeː] adj to be; **der Bürgermeister ~ the** mayor-elect.

Inspektion (pl -en) die - **1.** [von Anlage, Schule] inspection - **2.** [von Auto] service.

inspizieren vt to inspect.

installieren vt [gen & EDV] to install.

inständig <> adv urgently <> adj urgent.

Instanz (pl -en) die - **1.** [im Gerichtsverfahren] court - **2.** [Dienststelle] authority.

Instinkt (pl -e) der instinct.

instinktiv <> adj instinctive <> adv instinctively.

Institut (pl -e) das institute.

Institution (pl -en) die institution.

Instrument (pl -e) das instrument.

inszenieren vt - **1.** [Theaterstück] to direct; TV & RADIO to produce - **2.** [Skandal] to engineer; [Kampagne] to stage - **3.** [vortäuschen - Protest] abw to stage-manage.

Inszenierung (pl -en) die - **1.** [Aufführung] production - **2.** [Aufführen - von Theaterstück] direction; [- TV & RADIO] production - **3.** [von Skandal] engineering; [von Kampagne] staging - **4.** [Vortäuschung - von Protest] abw stage-managing.

intakt adj [Gerät, Organ] intact; [Beziehung] healthy.

Integral|rechnung die integral calculus.

integrieren vt to integrate.

intellektuell [ɪntɛlɛkˈtu̯ɛl] <> adj intellectual <> adv intellectually.

Intellektuelle [ɪntɛlɛkˈtu̯ɛlə] (pl -n) der, die intellectual.

intelligent <> adj intelligent <> adv intelligently.

Intelligenz die - **1.** [Verstand, Klugheit] intelligence - **2.** [Intellektuelle] intelligentsia.

Intendant, in (mpl -en; fpl -nen) der, die - **1.** [von Theater] artistic director and theatre manager - **2.** [von Fernsehanstalt] director general.

intensiv <> adj - **1.** [Gefühl, Farbe] strong - **2.** [Licht] intense - **3.** [Arbeit] intensive <> adv - **1.** [fühlen] strongly - **2.** [leuchten] intensely - **3.** [arbeiten] intensively.

Intensiv|kurs der crash course.

Intensiv|station die intensive care unit.

interaktiv adj EDV interactive.

Inter|City der intercity train.

interessant <> adj interesting <> adv interestingly; **sich ~ machen** abw to attract attention (to o.s.).

Interesse (pl -n) das interest; **an jm/etw ~ haben** to be interested in sb/sthg; **~ für jn/etw zeigen** to show an interest in sb/sthg; **in js eigenem ~** in sb's own interest. ◆ **Interessen** pl [Neigung] interests.

Interessent, in (mpl -en; fpl -nen) der, die - **1.** [Interessierte] interested person - **2.** [Kunde] prospective customer.

interessieren vt to interest. ◆ **sich interessieren** ref: **sich für jn/etw ~** to be interested in sb/sthg.

interessiert <> adj interested; **an jm/etw ~ sein** to be interested in sb/sthg <> adv with interest.

intern <> adj internal <> adv internally.

Internat (pl -e) das boarding school.

international <> adj international <> adv internationally.

Internet [ˈɪntɐ(r)nɛt] das Internet; **im ~** on the Internet; **im ~ surfen** to surf the Net; **etw über das ~ verkaufen** to sell sthg on ODER over the Internet.

Internet|café das Internet cafe, cybercafe.

Interpretation (pl -en) die - **1.** [Deutung] interpretation - **2.** MUS performance.

interpretieren vt - **1.** [deuten] to interpret - **2.** MUS to perform.

Interpunktion die punctuation.

InterRegio (pl -s) der train which covers medium distances and makes frequent stops.

Intervall [ɪntɐˈval] (pl -e) das [gen & MUS] interval.

Interview [ɪntɐˈvjuː] (pl -s) das interview.

interviewen [ɪntɐˈvjuːən] vt to interview.

intim adj intimate; **mit jm ~ werden** amt to become intimate with sb.

Intimität (pl -en) die intimacy.

intolerant adj intolerant; **jm/etw gegenüber ~ sein** to be intolerant of sb/sthg.

Intrige (pl -n) die intrigue, plot.

Intuition (pl -en) die intuition.

intuitiv <> adj intuitive <> adv intuitively.

Invalide [ɪnvaˈliːdə] (pl -n) der, die invalid.

Invasion [ɪnvaˈzjoːn] (pl -en) die eigtl & fig invasion.

Inventar [ɪnvɛnˈtaːɐ] (pl -e) das - **1.** [von Geschäft] fittings (pl) and equipment; [von Haus] fixtures and fittings (pl) - **2.** [von Betrieb] machinery and equipment - **3.** [Verzeichnis] inventory.

Inventur [ɪnvɛnˈtuːɐ] (pl -en) die stocktaking; **~ machen** to stocktake.

investieren [ɪnvɛsˈtiːrən] vt: **(in etw (A)) ~** to invest (in sthg).

Investition [ɪnvɛstiˈtsi̯oːn] (pl -en) die investment.

inwiefern *adv & konj* [in welcher Hinsicht] in what way; [bis zu welchem Grad] to what extent.

inwieweit *adv & konj* to what extent.

Inzest (*pl* -e) *der* incest.

inzwischen *adv* - **1.** [gleichzeitig] in the meantime - **2.** [mittlerweile, jetzt] now; **~ war es Winter geworden** by now winter had arrived.

Ion [joːn] (*pl* -en) *das* ion.

IQ [iːˈkuː, aiˈkjuː] (*pl* -s) (*abk für* Intelligenzquotient) *der* IQ.

i.R. (*abk für* im Ruhestand) retd.

Irak *der* Iraq.

Iran *der* Iran.

irdisch *adj* earthly, worldly.

Ire (*pl* -n) *der* Irishman.

irgend *adv* [irgendwie]: **wenn es ~ möglich ist** if (it's) at all possible; **wenn ich es ~ schaffe, komme ich** I'll come if I possibly can.
➤ **irgend so ein** *det fam* some.

irgendein, e *det* - **1.** [unbekannt] some - **2.** [beliebig] any.

irgendeine (*m* -r; *nt* -s) *pron* - **1.** [Person] someone, somebody; [in Fragen] anyone; **~r von uns muss es tun** one of us has to do it - **2.** [Sache] any (one); **irgendeins von den Büchern** one or other of the books.

irgendetwas *pron* [unbekannte Sache] something; [beliebige Sache, in Fragen] anything.

irgendjemand *pron* [unbekannte Person] someone; [beliebige Person, in Fragen] anyone.

irgendwann *adv* [zu unbekannter Zeit] sometime; [zu beliebiger Zeit] any time.

irgendwas *adv* [unbekannte Sache] something; [beliebige Sache, in Fragen] anything.

irgendwer *pron fam* - **1.** [unbekannte Person] someone, somebody - **2.** [beliebige Person, in Fragen] anyone.

irgendwie *adv* [auf unbekannte Weise] somehow; [auf beliebige Weise] anyhow.

irgendwo *adv* [an unbekanntem Ort] somewhere; [an beliebigem Ort] anywhere.

Irin (*pl* -nen) *die* Irishwoman.

Iris (*pl* -) *die* iris.

irisch *adj* Irish.

Irland *nt* Ireland.

Ironie *die* irony.

ironisch <> *adj* ironic <> *adv* ironically.

Irre (*pl* -n) <> *der, die* (*pl* Irren) [Person] lunatic <> *die* (*ohne pl*) [Ungewissheit]: **in die ~ führen** to be misleading.

irreführen *vt* - **1.** [belügen] to mislead - **2.** [auf einem Weg] to cause to get lost.

irren (*perf* hat/ist geirrt) *vi* (*ist*) to wander.
➤ **sich irren** *ref* (*hat*): **sich (in jm/etw (D)) ~** to be wrong (about sb/sthg); **wenn ich mich nicht irre** if I am not mistaken.

irritieren *vt* [stören] to annoy; **ihr Verhal-** **ten irritiert mich** I find her behaviour disconcerting ODER confusing.

Irrtum (*pl* -tümer) *der* mistake.

irrtümlich <> *adj* mistaken <> *adv* [verwechseln, mitnehmen] by mistake.

ISDN-Anschluss *der* TELEKOM ISDN link.

Islam *der* Islam.

islamisch *adj* Islamic.

Island *nt* Iceland.

Isländer, in (*mpl* -; *fpl* -nen) *der, die* Icelander.

isländisch *adj* Icelandic.

Isolation (*pl* -en) *die* - **1.** [von Person] isolation - **2.** [Material, Abdichtung] insulation; [von Rohr, Boiler] lagging.

Isolierband (*pl* -bänder) *das* insulating tape.

isolieren *vt* - **1.** [Person & CHEM] to isolate - **2.** [Leitung, Wand] to insulate.

Israel *nt* Israel.

Israeli (*pl* - ODER -s) *der, die* Israeli.

israelisch *adj* Israeli.

isst *präs* ⊳ essen.

ist *präs* ⊳ sein.

Istanbul *nt* Istanbul.

Italien *nt* Italy.

Italiener, in [itaˈljeːnɐ, rin] (*mpl* -; *fpl* -nen) *der, die* Italian.

italienisch [itaˈljeːnɪʃ] *adj* Italian.

Italienisch(e) *das* Italian; *siehe auch* Englisch(e).

J

j, J [jɔt] (*pl* - ODER -s) *das* j, J.

ja *interj* - **1.** [zum Ausdruck der Zustimmung] yes - **2.** [einschränkend]: **ich würde ~ gerne, aber ...** I'd love to, but ...; **ich kann es ~ versuchen, aber ...** I can always try, but ... - **3.** [emphatisierend]: **da bist du ~!** there you are!; **das ist ~ großartig!** that's really great!; **ich habe es dir ~ gesagt!** I TOLD you so!; **das ist es ~ (eben)!** that's just it! - **4.** [als rhetorisches Element] well; **~, wenn das so ist ...** well, if that's the case ... - **5.** [zum Ausdruck einer Drohung]: **sag ~ nichts!** don't you dare say anything!; **dass du mir ~ pünktlich kommst!** you'd better be on time! - **6.** [zum Ausdruck einer Bitte]: **du bleibst doch, ~?** you will stay, won't you? - **7.** [drückt Überraschung aus]: **(ach) ~?** really?

Jacht, Yacht [jaxt] (*pl* -en) *die* yacht.

Jacke (*pl* -n) *die* - **1.** [Mantel, Jackett] jacket - **2.** [Strickjacke] cardigan.

Jackett [ʒa'kɛt] (pl -s) das jacket.

Jagd (pl -en) die - 1. [auf Tiere] hunting; **auf die ~ gehen** to go hunting - 2. [auf Personen, Dinge]: **~ nach jm/etw** hunt for sb/sthg.

jagen (perf hat/ist gejagt) <> vt (hat) to hunt; **der Dieb wurde aus der Stadt gejagt** the thief was driven out of town; **sich** (D) **eine Kugel in den Kopf ~** to shoot o.s. in the head <> vi - 1. (hat) [als Sport] to hunt - 2. (ist) [hetzen] to race.

Jäger (pl -) der - 1. [von Tieren] hunter - 2. [Flugzeug] fighter (plane).

Jägerin (pl -nen) die hunter.

Jägerschnitzel (pl -) das escalope of pork or beef with mushroom sauce.

jäh <> adj sudden <> adv suddenly.

Jahr (pl -e) das year; **im ~(e) 1992** in 1992; **die 90er ~e** the nineties; **seit ~en** for years; **(ein) gutes neues ~!** Happy New Year!; **~ für ~** year after year; **in jungen ~en** at an early age.

jahrelang <> adj: **~e Arbeit** years of work <> adv for years.

Jahres|tag der anniversary.

Jahres|zeit die season.

Jahr|gang der - 1. [Geburtsjahr]: **der ~ 1967** the people who were born in 1967; **er ist mein ~** he was born in the same year as me - 2. [an der Schule] year - 3. [von Wein] vintage, year - 4. [von Zeitschrift] year's issues (pl).

Jahr|hundert (pl -e) das century; **im 19. ~** in the 19th century.

Jahrhundert|wende die turn of the century; **um die ~** at the turn of the century.

jährlich <> adj annual <> adv annually; **dreimal ~** three times a year.

Jahr|markt der fair.

Jahr|tausend (pl -e) das millennium.

Jahr|zehnt (pl -e) das decade.

jähzornig <> adj irascible <> adv in a violent temper.

Jalousie [ʒalu'ziː] (pl -n) die Venetian blind.

Jammer der misery; **es ist ein ~** it's a crying shame.

jämmerlich <> adj - 1. [traurig] miserable - 2. abw [würdelos, schlecht] pathetic <> adv - 1. [traurig] miserably - 2. abw [würdelos, schlecht] pathetically - 3. [sehr]: **~ frieren** to be frozen stiff.

jammern vi to moan.

Januar der January; siehe auch September.

Japan nt Japan.

Japaner, in (mpl -; fpl -nen) der, die Japanese.

japanisch adj Japanese.

Japanisch(e) das Japanese; siehe auch Englisch(e).

Jargon [ʒar'gõ] (pl -s) der jargon.

jäten vt [Garten] to weed; [Unkraut] to pull up.

jaulen vi to howl.

jawohl interj certainly!

Ja|wort das: **jm sein ~ geben** to tie the knot with sb.

Jazz [dʒɛs] der jazz.

je <> adv - 1. [jeweils] each; **drei Gruppen mit ~ fünf Personen** three groups, each of five people; **die drei Tore sind mit ~ zwei Schlössern gesichert** the three gates each have two locks - 2. [jemals] ever; **seit eh und ~** since time immemorial; **sie ist schöner denn ~** she is more beautiful than ever <> präp [pro] per; **~ nach** depending on <> konj: **~ schneller, desto besser** the quicker the better; **~ nachdem** it depends; **~ nachdem, ob ...** depending on whether ... <> interj: **oh ~!** oh no!, oh dear!

Jeans [dʒiːnz] (pl -) die jeans (pl); **eine ~** a pair of jeans.

jede, r, s det every, each; [in negativen Konstruktionen] any; **ohne ~n Zweifel** without any doubt; **~n zweiten Tag** every second day <> pron - 1. [Person] everyone, everybody; **~ von ihnen** each of them; **~r Zweite** every second OR other one; **~r kann teilnehmen** anyone can take part - 2. [Sache] each (one).

jedenfalls adv - 1. [wenigstens] at least; **ich ~ habe keine Lust** I at any rate don't want to - 2. [auf jeden Fall] in any case.

jedermann pron everybody, everyone.

jederzeit adv at any time.

jedesmal adv ▷ Mal.

jedoch adv & konj however.

jegliche, r, s pron: **hier kommt ~ Hilfe zu spät** all help will come too late here; **ohne ~s Risiko** with no risk.

jeher adv: **von ~** always.

jemals adv ever.

jemand pron someone, somebody; [in Fragen] anyone, anybody.

jene, r, s geh <> det that <> pron that one.

jenseits präp: **~ einer Sache** (G) OR **von etw** [räumlich] on the other side of sthg; [ideell] beyond sthg.

Jerusalem nt Jerusalem.

Jetlag ['dʒɛtlɛg] (pl -s) der jet lag.

jetzig adj current.

jetzt adv - 1. [momentan, mittlerweile] now; **bis ~** so far; **von ~ an** from now on; **erst ~** only just; **schon ~** already - 2. [gegenwärtig, heute] nowadays; **das gibt es ~ nicht mehr** you don't get that any more (nowadays) - 3. [gleich, sofort] in a moment; **~ gleich** right away; **von ~ auf gleich** on the spur of the moment - 4. [damals] then - 5. [zum Ausdruck des Ärgers]: **das ist doch ~ kein Argu-**

ment! that's no argument!; **~ mach endlich voran!** get a move on, will you!

jeweilig adj - **1.** [zeitlich]: **nach der ~en Mode angezogen sein** to be dressed in the fashion of the day; **die Stimmung ändert sich mit der ~en Laune des Chefs** the atmosphere changes depending on what mood the boss happens to be in - **2.** [zugehörig] respective.

jeweils adv - **1.** [jedes Mal] each time - **2.** [jeder] each; **~ drei Karten** three cards each - **3.** [momentan] at the time.

Jh. (abk für Jahrhundert) C.

Jiddisch(e) das Yiddish; siehe auch Englisch(e).

Job [dʒɔp] (pl -s) der - **1.** [als Aushilfe] (temporary) job - **2.** [Arbeit] job.

jobben [dʒɔbn] vi to work.

Jockey ['dʒɔke, 'dʒɔki] (pl -s) der jockey.

Jod das iodine.

jodeln vi to yodel.

Joga, Yoga ['jo:ga] = Yoga.

Jogging ['dʒɔgɪŋ] das jogging.

Joghurt, Yoghurt, Jogurt (pl - ODER -s) das ODER der yoghurt.

Johannisbeere die: **Rote ~** redcurrant; **Schwarze ~** blackcurrant.

Joker ['dʒo:kɐ] (pl -) der joker.

jonglieren [ʒɔŋ'liːrən] vi to juggle; **mit etw ~** eigtl & fig to juggle sthg <> vt [balancieren] to juggle.

Journalist, in [ʒʊrna'lɪst, ɪn] (mpl -en; fpl -nen) der, die journalist.

Jubel der - **1.** [Freude] jubilation - **2.** [Rufen] cheering.

jubeln vi - **1.** [sich freuen] to rejoice - **2.** [rufen] to cheer.

Jubiläum [jubi'lɛːʊm] (pl Jubiläen) das anniversary; **ein ~ feiern** to celebrate an anniversary.

jucken <> vi - **1.** [Haut] to itch - **2.** [Material] to be itchy <> vt - **1.** [kratzen]: **die Narbe juckt ihn** his scar is itchy - **2.** fam [beeinflussen]: **es juckt mich, es zu versuchen** I'm itching to try; **das juckt mich nicht** I don't care.

Juckreiz der itching; **~ verspüren** to have an itch.

Jude (pl -n) der Jew.

Jüdin (pl -nen) die Jew.

jüdisch adj Jewish.

Judo das judo.

Jugend die (ohne pl) - **1.** [junges Alter] youth - **2.** [junge Personen] young people (pl); **die ~ von heute** today's youth, young people today.

Jugendamt das local authority service responsible for the welfare of young people.

Jugendarbeit die youth work.

jugendfrei adj: **'nicht ~'** 'not suitable for persons under 18'.

Jugendherberge die youth hostel.

jugendlich <> adj - **1.** [jung] young - **2.** [jung wirkend] youthful <> adv: **sich ~ geben/kleiden** to act/dress young.

Jugendliche (pl -n) der, die young person.

Jugendstil der art nouveau.

Jugoslawien nt Yugoslavia.

Juli der July; siehe auch September.

jung (kompar jünger; superl jüngste) <> adj - **1.** [gen] young; [Aussehen, Stil] young, youthful; **meine jüngere Schwester** my younger sister - **2.** [nicht lange zurückliegend]: **die jüngsten Ereignisse** recent events <> adv (kompar jünger; superl am jüngsten): **~ sterben** to die young.

Junge (pl -n ODER Jungs) <> der (pl Jungen, Jungs) [Knabe, Mann] boy; **hallo, alter ~** hello, my old pal; **ein schwerer ~** fam fig a thug <> das (pl Jungen) [Tier] young animal; **die ~n** the young; **~ kriegen** ODER **werfen** to give birth to young.

Jünger, in (mpl -; fpl -nen) der, die disciple.

Jungfer (pl -n) die: **alte ~** abw old maid.

Jungfrau die - **1.** [Frau] virgin - **2.** ASTROL Virgo; **~ sein** to be a Virgo.

Junggeselle der bachelor; **ein eingefleischter ~** a confirmed bachelor.

jüngste adj ▷ jung.

Jüngste (pl -n) der, die, das youngest; **er ist nicht mehr der ~** he's not as young as he used to be.

Juni der June; siehe auch September.

Junior (pl Junioren) der - **1.** [gen] junior - **2.** [im Geschäft] junior partner.

Juniorin (pl -nen) die - **1.** [Tochter] daughter - **2.** [im Geschäft] junior partner - **3.** SPORT junior.

Jura der - **1.** (ohne Artikel) [Studienfach] law - **2.** [Gebirge]: **der ~** the Jura - **3.** [Erdzeitalter] Jurassic period.

Jurist, in (mpl -en; fpl -nen) der, die lawyer.

juristisch <> adj legal <> adv legally.

Jury [ʒy'riː] (pl -s) die jury.

Justiz die - **1.** [Behörde]: **jn der deutschen ~ ausliefern** to hand sb over to the German courts; **unabhängige ~** independent judiciary - **2.** [Rechtsprechung]: **nach irischer ~** under Irish law.

Justizministerium das Ministry of Justice.

Justizvollzugsanstalt die amt penal institution, penitentiary Am.

Juwel (pl -en) das ODER der - **1.** (der) [Schmuck] piece of jewellery - **2.** [Edelstein, Prachtstück] jewel; **sie ist ein ~** she is a gem.

Juwelier (pl -e) der jeweller.

Juwelierin (pl -nen) die jeweller.

K

k, K [ka:] (*pl* - ODER -s) *das* k, K.

Kabarett, Cabaret [kaba'rɛt, kaba're:] (*pl* -s ODER -e) *das* - **1.** [Aufführung] satirical revue - **2.** [Institution] *theatre where satirical revues are performed.*

Kabarettist, in (*mpl* -en; *fpl* -nen) *der, die* satirical revue artist.

Kabel (*pl* -) *das* cable.

Kabelanschluss *der:* ~ **haben** to have cable television.

Kabelfernsehen *das* cable television.

Kabeljau (*pl* -s) *der* cod.

Kabine (*pl* -n) *die* - **1.** [von Schiff, Flugzeug] cabin - **2.** [in Schwimmbad] cubicle; [in Kleidergeschäft] fitting room.

Kabinett (*pl* -e) *das* - **1.** [aus Ministern] cabinet - **2.** [Wein] *term designating a high-quality German wine.*

Kabrio, Cabrio (*pl* -s) *das* convertible.

Kachel (*pl* -n) *die* tile.

kacheln (*perf* hat/ist gekachelt) <> *vt* (*hat*) [auslegen] to tile <> *vi* (*ist*) *fam* [rasen] to zoom along.

Kadaver [ka'da:vɐ] (*pl* -) *der* carcass.

Käfer (*pl* -) *der* [Insekt, Auto] beetle.

Kaff (*pl* -s ODER -e) *das fam* dump.

Kaffee, Kaffee ['kafe, ka'fe:] (*pl* -s) *der* - **1.** [gen] coffee; **eine Tasse** ~ a cup of coffee; ~ **mit Milch** white coffee; **schwarzer** ~ black coffee - **2.** [Mahlzeit] afternoon coffee and cake; ~ **trinken** [am Nachmittag] to have afternoon coffee; [in der Pause] to have a coffee break.

📖 **Kaffee und Kuchen**

Germans often like to sit down to a cup of strong coffee and a piece of cake midafternoon. On Sundays Kaffee und Kuchen usually takes place at home or with friends, but it is common also to go out to a café (Kaffeehaus or Konditorei), where you first choose a cake from a glass counter before sitting down to order a drink. The atmosphere in such places is generally quiet, with newspapers provided for the use of customers, and although there is a good mix amongst the clientele, older people tend to outnumber the young.

Kaffeefilter *der* filter (paper).

Kaffeekanne *die* coffeepot.

Kaffeeklatsch (*pl* -e) *der:* **sich zum ~ treffen** to meet for a chat over a cup of coffee.

Kaffeelöffel *der* coffee spoon.

Kaffeemaschine *die* coffee machine.

Kaffeetasse *die* coffee cup.

Käfig (*pl* -e) *der* cage.

kahl *adj* - **1.** [ohne Haare] bald; ~ **werden** to go bald - **2.** [Berg, Baum] bare.

Kahn (*pl* Kähne) *der* - **1.** [Ruderboot] rowing boat *Br*, rowboat *Am* - **2.** [Stechkahn] punt - **3.** [Lastkahn] barge.

Kai (*pl* -s ODER -e) *der* quay.

Kairo *nt* Cairo.

Kaiser (*pl* -) *der* emperor.

Kaiserin (*pl* -nen) *die* empress.

kaiserlich *adj* imperial.

Kaiserreich *das* empire.

Kaiserschmarrn (*pl* -) *der pancake torn into thin strips.*

Kaiserschnitt *der* MED caesarean (section).

Kajak (*pl* -s) *das* ODER *der* kayak.

Kajüte (*pl* -n) *die* cabin.

Kakao [ka'kau] *der* cocoa; **jn/etw durch den** ~ **ziehen** *fam* to take the mickey out of sb/sthg.

Kakerlake (*pl* -n) *die* cockroach.

Kaktee = Kaktus.

Kaktus (*pl* Kakteen ODER -se) *der* cactus.

Kalb (*pl* Kälber) *das* - **1.** [Tier] calf - **2.** [Fleisch] veal.

Kalbfleisch *das* veal.

Kalender (*pl* -) *der* - **1.** [Wandkalender] calendar - **2.** [Taschenkalender] diary; **sich** (*D*) **etw im** ~ **rot anstreichen** *fig* to make sthg a red-letter day.

Kaliber (*pl* -) *das* - **1.** [von einem Geschütz] calibre - **2.** [Art, Sorte] kind, ilk.

Kalium *das* potassium.

Kalk *der* (*ohne pl*) - **1.** [Kalkstein] limestone - **2.** [in Wasserkessel] lime - **3.** [zum Tünchen] whitewash.

Kalkstein *der* limestone.

kalkulieren <> *vt* [berechnen] to calculate <> *vi* to calculate; **genau/scharf** ~ to make precise calculations.

Kalorie [kalo'ri:] (*pl* -n) *die* calorie.

kalorienarm [kalo'ri:ʔarm] <> *adj* lowcalorie <> *adv:* ~ **essen** to eat low-calorie food.

kalt (*kompar* kälter; *superl* kälteste) <> *adj* cold; **es ist** ~ it's cold; **mir ist** ~ I'm cold; ~**e Füße kriegen** *fig* to get cold feet <> *adv* (*kompar* kälter; *superl* am kältesten): ~ **duschen** to have a cold shower; **das Bier** ~ **stellen** to chill the beer; ~ **lächeln** to smile coldly.

kaltblütig <> *adj* cold-blooded <> *adv* in cold blood.

Kälte *die* (*ohne pl*) - **1.** [gen] coldness - **2.** [Wetter] cold; **bei** ~ in cold weather.

Kälteeinbruch *der* cold snap.

Kalte Krieg der cold war.

Kaltmiete die rent not including bills.

Kalzium das calcium.

kam prät ⊏⟹ kommen.

Kambodscha nt Cambodia.

Kamel (pl -e) das - 1. [Tier] camel - 2. fig [Trottel] idiot.

Kamera (pl -s) die camera.

Kamerad, in (mpl -en; fpl -nen) der, die friend.

kameradschaftlich ◇ adj friendly ◇ adv in a friendly way.

Kamerun nt Cameroon.

Kamille (pl -n) die camomile.

Kamillentee der camomile tea.

Kamin (pl -e) der - 1. [Schornstein] chimney - 2. [Feuerstelle] fireplace; **offener ~** open fireplace.

Kamm (pl Kämme) der - 1. [Haarkamm, Hahnenkamm] comb; **alles über einen ~ scheren** fig [keinen Unterschied machen] to lump everything together - 2. [Bergkamm] ridge.

kämmen vt to comb.

Kammer (pl -n) die - 1. [kleines Zimmer] cubbyhole - 2. POL chamber.

Kammermusik die chamber music.

Kampagne (pl -n) die campaign.

Kampf (pl Kämpfe) der - 1. [Streit] fight; [politisch, sozial] struggle, fight; [in Sport] contest; [in Krieg] battle; **~ um etw** fight for sthg; **~ gegen jn/etw** fight against sb/sthg; **jm/ einer Sache den ~ ansagen** to declare war on sb/sthg - 2. MIL fighting (U).

kämpfen vi to fight; **gegen jn/etw ~** to fight against sb/sthg; **für jn/etw ~** to fight for sb/sthg; **um jn/etw ~** to fight for sb/sthg; **mit etw ~** fig [Schlaf, Tod] to fight sthg off; [Tränen] to fight shg back.

Kampfgebiet das combat zone.

kampflos ◇ adj MIL peaceful ◇ adv without a fight.

Kampfrichter, in der, die SPORT referee.

Kanada nt Canada.

Kanadier [ka'na:diɐ] (pl -) der - 1. [Einwohner Kanadas] Canadian - 2. [Sportboot] Canadian canoe.

Kanadierin [ka'na:dʒərn] (pl -nen) die Canadian.

kanadisch adj Canadian.

Kanal (pl Kanäle) der - 1. [Wasserweg] canal - 2. TELEKOM channel - 3. RW: **den ~ voll haben** [betrunken sein] to be plastered; fam [es satt haben] to be fed up to the back teeth.

Kanalisation (pl -en) die - 1. [für Abwässer] sewers (pl) - 2. [Ausbau eines natürlichen Wasserweges] canalization (U).

Kanaltunnel der Channel Tunnel.

Kanarienvogel der canary.

Kanarische Inseln pl Canary Islands.

Kandidat, in (mpl -en; fpl -nen) der, die can-

didate; **jn als ~en aufstellen** ODER **nominieren** to put sb forward as a candidate.

Kandiszucker der sugar candy.

Känguru (pl -s) das kangaroo.

Kaninchen (pl -) das rabbit.

Kanister (pl -) der can.

kann präs ⊏⟹ können.

Kanne (pl -n) die pot.

Kannibale (pl -n) der cannibal.

Kannibalin (pl -nen) die cannibal.

kannte prät ⊏⟹ kennen.

Kanon (pl -s) der MUS canon.

Kanone (pl -n) die - 1. [Geschütz] cannon - 2. RW: **unter aller ~ sein** fam [miserabel] to be the pits.

Kante (pl -n) die edge.

Kantine (pl -n) die canteen.

Kanton (pl -e) der canton.

Kantor (pl -toren) der choirmaster and organist.

Kantorin (pl -nen) die choirmistress and organist.

Kanu (pl -s) das canoe.

Kanzel (pl -n) die - 1. [von Kirchen] pulpit - 2. [von Flugzeugen] cockpit.

Kanzlei (pl -en) die office.

Kanzler (pl -) der - 1. [Bundeskanzler] chancellor - 2. UNI vice-chancellor Br, chancellor Am.

Kanzleramt das [Amtssitz des Bundeskanzlers] chancellery.

Kap (pl -s) das cape.

Kapazität (pl -en) die - 1. [gen] capacity - 2. [Experte] authority.

Kapelle (pl -n) die - 1. [kleine Kirche] chapel - 2. MUS band.

Kapellmeister, in der, die [Leiter - einer Musikkapelle] bandmaster; [- eines Orchesters] conductor.

Kaper (pl -n) die caper.

kapieren vt fam to get.

kapital [kapi'ta:l] adj - 1. [Irrtum] serious - 2. [Hirsch] magnificent.

Kapital (pl -ien ODER -e) das - 1. [gen] capital - 2. RW: **aus etw ~ schlagen** to make capital out of sthg; **geistiges ~** intellectual assets (pl); **totes ~** unused skills (pl).

Kapitalanlage die capital investment.

Kapitalismus der capitalism.

Kapitalist, in (mpl -en; fpl -nen) der, die capitalist.

kapitalistisch adj capitalist.

Kapitän (pl -e) der captain.

Kapitel (pl -) das chapter; **ein ~ für sich sein** fig to be an awkward business; **das ist ein anderes ~** that's another story.

Kapitulation (pl -en) die [Aufgabe] surrender (U); **bedingungslose ~** unconditional surrender (U).

kapitulieren vi to surrender; **vor etw** (D) **~** to give up in the face of sthg.

Kaplan (*pl* Kapläne) *der* curate.

Kappe (*pl* -n) *die* cap.

kappen *vt* - **1.** [beschneiden] to cut back - **2.** [durchschneiden] to cut through.

Kapsel (*pl* -n) *die* - **1.** [kleiner Behälter] box - **2.** [von Medikament, von Blüten] capsule.

kaputt *adj fam* - **1.** [Vase, Gerät] broken; [Beziehung, Gesundheit] ruined - **2.** *fig* [erschöpft] ~ **sein** to be done in.

kaputtgehen (*perf* ist kaputtgegangen) *vi* (*unreg*) *fam* - **1.** [Gerät, Gegenstand] to break; [Beziehungen, Geschäfte] to be ruined - **2.** [eingehen] to die.

kaputtlachen ◆ **sich kaputtlachen** *ref fam* to kill o.s. laughing; **sich über jn/etw ~** to kill o.s. laughing at sb/sthg.

Kapuze (*pl* -n) *die* hood.

Karaffe (*pl* -e ODER -s) *die* - **1.** [mit Stöpsel] decanter - **2.** [ohne Stöpsel] carafe.

Karamell *der* caramel.

Karamell|bonbon *das* ODER *der* toffee.

Karat (*pl* -e ODER -s) *das* - **1.** [Edelsteingewicht] carat - **2.** [Einheit]: **dieser Ring hat 20 ~** this ring is 20 carats.

Karate *das* karate.

Karawane (*pl* -n) *die* caravan.

Kardinal (*pl* Kardinäle) *der* cardinal.

Kar|freitag *der* Good Friday.

karg *adj* - **1.** [Mahlzeit, Lohn] meagre - **2.** [Raum] bare - **3.** [Boden] barren.

Karibik *die* Caribbean.

karibisch *adj* Caribbean.

kariert <> *adj* - **1.** [Stoff] checked - **2.** [Papier] squared <> *adv fam* [verwirrt]: ~ **schauen** to look bewildered.

Karies ['kaːriəs] *die* MED tooth decay.

Karikatur (*pl* -en) *die* cartoon; [Porträt] caricature.

kariös *adj* decayed.

Karlsruhe *nt* - **1.** [Stadt] Karlsruhe - **2.** [Gericht] the Federal Constitutional Court.

Karneval ['karnəval] (*pl* -e ODER -s) *der* carnival.

🎭 Karneval

The biggest Karneval celebrations take place in the Rhineland (Cologne, Düsseldorf and Mainz), although the tradition is also associated with Bavaria (where it is known as Fasching) and Swabia (where it is known as Fasenacht or Fasnet). The Karneval period officially begins at eleven minutes past eleven on the 11th November and ends on Ash Wednesday. On the Monday before Ash Wednesday (Rosenmontag), there are processions with floats carrying figures that caricature social and political life.

---

karnevalistisch [karnəva'lɪstɪʃ] *adj* carnival (*vor Subst*).

Karnevals|zug *der* carnival procession.

Kärnten *nt* Carinthia.

Karo (*pl* -s) *das* - **1.** [Raute] diamond - **2.** (*ohne Artikel, ohne pl*) [Spielfarbe] diamonds (*pl*) - **3.** [Spielkarte] diamond; **die ~sechs** the six of diamonds.

Karosserie (*pl* -n) *die* bodywork (*U*).

Karotte (*pl* -n) *die* carrot.

Karpfen (*pl* -) *der* carp.

Karre (*pl* -n) *die* - **1.** [Handkarre] cart - **2.** *fam* [Auto] jalopy, banger *Br*.

Karren (*pl* -) *der* [kleiner Wagen] cart.

Karriere [ka'rjeːrə] (*pl* -n) *die* career; ~ **machen** to make a career for o.s.

Karte (*pl* -n) *die* - **1.** [Postkarte, Spielkarte] card - **2.** [Landkarte] map - **3.** *RW*: **jm die gelbe/rote ~ zeigen** to show sb the yellow/red card; **mit offenen ~n spielen** to put one's cards on the table; **alles auf eine ~ setzen** to stake everything on one chance; **schlechte ~n haben** to have been dealt a bad hand.

Kartei (*pl* -en) *die* card index.

Kartei|karte *die* index card.

Kartei|kasten *der* index-card box.

Kartell (*pl* -e) *das* WIRTSCH cartel.

Karten|spiel *das* - **1.** [Gesellschaftsspiel] card game - **2.** [Spielkarten] pack *Br* ODER deck *Am* of cards.

Karten|telefon *das* cardphone.

Karten|vorverkauf *der* advance booking.

Kartoffel (*pl* -n) *die* potato.

Kartoffel|brei *der* KÜCHE mashed potatoes (*pl*).

Kartoffel|chips *pl* crisps *Br*, chips *Am*.

Kartoffel|puffer *der* KÜCHE potato pancake (*made from grated potatoes*).

Kartoffel|püree *das* KÜCHE mashed potatoes (*pl*).

Kartoffel|salat *der* KÜCHE potato salad.

Karton (*pl* -s) *der* - **1.** [Pappe] card - **2.** [Kiste] (cardboard) box.

Karussell (*pl* -s) *das* merry-go-round; ~ **fahren** to go on the merry-go-round.

Kar|woche *die* Holy Week.

Käse (*pl* -) *der* cheese; **das ist ~!** *abw* & *fig* that's rubbish!

Käse|fondue *das* KÜCHE cheese fondue.

Käse|kuchen *der* KÜCHE cheesecake.

Kaserne (*pl* -n) *die* MIL barracks (*pl*).

käsig *adj* pale.

Kasino (*pl* -s) *das* - **1.** [Spielkasino] casino - **2.** MIL (officers') mess.

Kasperle|theater *das* [Vorstellung] Punch and Judy show; [Gebäude] Punch and Judy theatre.

Kasse (*pl* -n) *die* - **1.** [Kassette] cashbox - **2.** [im Laden] till - **3.** [im Supermarkt] checkout - **4.** [im Theater, Kino] box office - **5.** *fam* [Krankenkasse] (health) insurance (*U*)

- 6. *RW:* ~ **machen** to cash up; **knapp bei ~ sein** *fam* to be short of cash.

Kassen|arzt, ärztin *der, die* doctor who treats *patients with health insurance.*

Kassen|bon *der* receipt.

Kassen|patient, in *der, die* patient with *health insurance.*

Kassen|zettel *der* receipt.

Kassette (*pl* -n) *die* - **1.** [Musik- und Videokassette] cassette, tape; **etw auf ~ aufnehmen** to record sthg on cassette ODER tape - **2.** [für Schmuck, Schallplatten, Bücher] box.

Kassetten|rekorder *der* cassette recorder.

kassieren *vt* - **1.** [einziehen] to collect - **2.** *fam* [einnehmen] to pocket - **3.** *fam* [einheimsen - Lob, Kritik] to get; [- Niederlage] to suffer - **4.** *fam* [Führerschein] to take away.

Kassierer, in (*mpl* -; *fpl* -nen) *der, die* - **1.** [von Geschäft, Bank] cashier - **2.** [von Verein] treasurer.

Kastanie [kas'ta:njə] (*pl* -n) *die* chestnut.

Kasten (*pl* Kästen) *der* - **1.** [Kiste] box - **2.** [für Flaschen] crate - **3.** [Briefkasten] postbox *Br*, mailbox *Am* - **4.** *fam* [Gebäude] great box of a building - **5.** SPORT box - **6.** *fam* [Kopf]: **etwas/viel auf dem ~ haben** [intelligent sein] to be brainy/very brainy.

kastrieren *vt* MED to castrate.

Kasus (*pl* -) *der* GRAM case.

Kat [kat] (*pl* -s) (*abk für* Katalysator) *der* AUTO cat.

Katalanisch(e) *das* Catalan; *siehe auch* Englisch(e).

Katalog (*pl* -e) *der* catalogue.

Katalysator (*pl* -toren) *der* [am Auto] catalytic converter; [in Chemie] catalyst.

Katamaran (*pl* -e) *der* catamaran.

katastrophal [katastro'fa:l] ⇔ *adj* disastrous ⇔ *adv* disastrously.

Katastrophe [katas'tro:fə] (*pl* -n) *die* disaster; **eine ~ sein** *fam* to be a disaster.

Katastrophen|gebiet [katas'tro:fəngəbi:t] *das* disaster area.

Katechismus (*pl* -men) *der* catechism.

Kategorie (*pl* -n) *die* category.

kategorisch ⇔ *adj* categorical ⇔ *adv* categorically.

Kater (*pl* -) *der* - **1.** [Tier] tomcat - **2.** *fam* [von Alkohol] hangover; **einen ~ haben** to have a hangover.

kath. (*abk für* katholisch) Cath.

Kathedrale (*pl* -n) *die* cathedral.

Kathode (*pl* -n) *die* PHYS cathode.

Katholik (*pl* -en) *der* Catholic.

Katholiken|tag *der biannual congress of German Catholics.*

Katholikin (*pl* -nen) *die* Catholic.

katholisch *adj* Catholic.

Katholizismus *der* Catholicism.

Katz *die:* ~ **und Maus spielen** to play cat and mouse; **für die ~ sein** *fam* to be a waste of time.

Katze (*pl* -n) *die* - **1.** [Tier] cat - **2.** [weibliches Tier] she-cat.

Katzen|sprung *der:* **etw ist nur ein ~ von etw entfernt** sthg is only a stone's throw away from sthg.

Kauderwelsch *das* gibberish.

kauen ⇔ *vi* to chew; **an etw** (*D*) ~ [herumkauen] to chew sthg; [bewältigen] to grapple with sthg ⇔ *vt* to chew.

kauern *vi* to crouch.

Kauf (*pl* Käufe) *der* purchase; **einen ~ abschließen** to complete a purchase; **etw in ~ nehmen** *fig* to accept sthg.

kaufen *vt* to buy; **jm/sich etw ~** to buy sb/o.s. sthg.

Käufer, in (*mpl* -; *fpl* -nen) *der, die* buyer.

Kauf|frau *die* businesswoman.

Kauf|haus *das* department store.

Kauf|kraft *die* purchasing power.

Kauf|leute *pl* business people.

käuflich *adj* - **1.** [zu erwerben]: **etw ~ erwerben** *amt* to purchase sthg; ~ **sein** [Ware] to be for sale; [Person] to be easily bought; **nicht ~ sein** [Ware] not to be for sale; [Person] not to be easily bought - **2.** [prostituiert]: ~**es Mädchen** prostitute; ~**e Liebe** prostitution.

Kaufmann (*pl* -leute) *der* businessman.

kaufmännisch *adj* commercial.

Kauf|preis *der* purchase price.

Kau|gummi *das* ODER *der* chewing gum.

kaum *adv* - **1.** [gen] hardly; **das ist ~ zu glauben** that's hard to believe; ~ **dass ich angerufen hatte, standen sie schon vor der Tür** no sooner had I rung than they were at the door - **2.** [höchstens] barely.

Kaution (*pl* -en) *die* - **1.** [für Wohnung] deposit - **2.** [für Häftling] bail; **gegen ~ freikommen** to be released on bail.

Kautschuk *der* (India) rubber.

Kauz (*pl* Käuze) *der:* **ein komischer ~** *fig* an odd bird.

Kavalier [kava'li:ɐ] (*pl* -e) *der* gentleman.

Kaviar [ka:vjar] (*pl* -e) *der* caviar.

Kegel (*pl* -) *der* - **1.** MATH cone - **2.** [zum Spielen] skittle.

Kegel|klub *der* bowling club.

kegeln *vi* to bowl.

Kehle (*pl* -n) *die* - **1.** [gen] throat - **2.** *RW:* **etw in die falsche ~ bekommen** *fam* to take sthg the wrong way; **aus voller ~ singen/schreien** to sing/shout at the top of one's voice.

Kehl|kopf *der* larynx.

kehren *vt* - **1.** [fegen] to sweep - **2.** [wenden] to turn; **den starken Mann nach außen ~** to act the tough guy; **in sich gekehrt** lost in one's own world. ⬥ **sich kehren** *ref* - **1.** [sich kümmern]: **sich nicht an** ODER **um etw**

~ not to care about sthg - **2.** [sich richten]: **sich gegen jn** ~ to turn against sb.

Kehr|reim der refrain.

Kehr|seite die drawback, downside; **die ~ der Medaille** the downside.

kehrt|machen vi to turn round.

Kehrt|wendung die: **eine ~ machen** to turn round; [politisch] to do a U-turn.

keifen vi abw to nag.

Keil (pl -e) der wedge.

Keil|riemen der fan belt.

Keim (pl -e) der - **1.** [Pflanzentrieb] shoot; **etw im ~ ersticken** fig to nip sthg in the bud - **2.** [Bakterie] germ.

keimen vi [Saat] to germinate; [Kartoffeln, Zwiebeln] to sprout.

keimfrei <> adj [Instrumente, Milch] sterilized; [Bedingungen] sterile <> adv [arbeiten] in a sterile environment.

keimtötend adj germicidal, antiseptic.

Keim|zelle die - **1.** BIOL sex cell - **2.** [Ausgangspunkt] germ.

kein, e det no, not ... any; **~ Mensch** no one; **es gibt ~e Bananen** there are no bananas, there aren't any bananas; **ich habe ~ Geld/~e Zeit** I haven't got any money/time; **das ist doch ~e Schande** it's no disgrace; **~ Wunder, dass ...** it's no wonder (that) ...

keine, r, s pron - **1.** [Person] no one, nobody; **~r weiß, dass ...** no one ODER nobody knows that ...; **~r der Schüler** ODER **von den Schülern** none of the pupils - **2.** [Gegenstand] none; **welchen nehmen Sie? – ~n** which do you want? – neither.

keinerlei adj (unver) no ... at all; **~ Bedenken haben** to have no scruples at all.

keinesfalls adv on no account; **das ist ~ schwer** that's not at all difficult.

keineswegs adv not at all; **~ besser** in no way better.

Keks (pl -e) der biscuit Br, cookie Am.

Kelle (pl -n) die [Schöpflöffel] ladle.

Keller (pl -) der cellar.

Kellner, in (mpl -; fpl -nen) der, die waiter (f waitress).

Kelte (pl -n) der Celt.

keltern vt to press.

Keltin (pl -nen) die Celt.

keltisch adj Celtic.

Kenia nt Kenya.

kennen (prät kannte; perf hat gekannt) vt to know; **jn/etw gut ~** to know sb/sthg well; **ich kenne mich** I know what I'm like; **~ wir uns nicht?** haven't we met somewhere before?; **da kennst du ihn aber schlecht!** you don't know what he's like!

kennen lernen vt - **1.** [Person] to get to know, to meet; **freut mich, Sie kennen zu lernen!** pleased to meet you! - **2.** [Sache] to get to know, to familiarize o.s. with.

➡ **sich kennen lernen** ref [sich begegnen] to meet.

Kenntnis (pl -nisse) die knowledge; **etw zur ~ nehmen** to take note of sthg, to note sthg; **jn von etw in ~ setzen** to inform sb of sthg; **dieser Vorfall entzieht sich meiner ~** geh I don't know anything about this incident. ➡ **Kenntnisse** pl knowledge (U).

Kennwort (pl -wörter) das password.

Kenn|zahl die code number.

Kenn|zeichen das - **1.** [Merkmal] symbol, sign; **besondere ~** distinguishing features - **2.** [an Kfz]: **amtliches ~** registration number Br, license number Am.

kennzeichnen vt [markieren]: **etw (mit** ODER **durch etw) ~** to mark sthg (with sthg); **etw als etw ~** [Produkt, Ware] to label sthg as sthg; **jn als etw ~** to describe sb as sthg.

kennzeichnend adj: **für jn/etw ~ sein** to be typical ODER characteristic of sb/sthg.

Kenn|zeichnung die labelling.

Kenn|ziffer die reference number.

kentern (perf ist gekentert) vi to capsize.

Keramik (pl -en) die - **1.** [Gefäß]: **eine ~ a** piece of pottery - **2.** (ohne pl) [Ton] pottery, ceramics (pl).

Kerbe (pl -n) die notch.

Kerbel der chervil.

Kerker (pl -) der dungeon.

Kerl (pl -e) der fam guy, bloke Br; **ein netter ~** a nice guy; **ein gemeiner ~** a swine.

Kern (pl -e) der - **1.** [von Apfel, Birne, Zitrusfrucht] pip; [von Pfirsich, Kirsche] stone, pit Am; [von Nuß] kernel - **2.** [Wichtigstes] core, crux - **3.** PHYS nucleus.

Kern|energie die nuclear power.

kerngesund adj as fit as a fiddle.

Kernkraft|gegner, in der, die opponent of nuclear power.

Kernkraft|werk das nuclear power station.

Kern|punkt der [eines Vortrags] central point; [eines Problems] crux.

Kern|stück das centrepiece.

Kern|waffe die nuclear weapon.

Kerze (pl -n) die - **1.** [zur Beleuchtung] candle - **2.** [Turnübung] shoulder stand.

kerzengerade adj & adv bolt upright.

Kerzenlicht das candlelight.

kess (kompar kesser; superl kesseste) <> adj - **1.** [Person, Verhalten] cheeky - **2.** [Kleidung] jaunty <> adv [frech] cheekily.

Kessel (pl -) der - **1.** [Topf] kettle; [groß] cauldron - **2.** [Tal] basin, basin-shaped valley.

Ketchup ['kɛtʃap], **Ketschup** das ODER der ketchup.

Kette (pl -n) die chain; [aus Perlen] string; [von Polizisten] cordon; [von Unfällen, Ereignissen] string, series.

ketten vt: jn/etw an etw (A) ~ to chain sb/sthg to sthg.

Ketten|fahrzeug das tracked vehicle.

Ketten|reaktion die chain reaction.

Ketten|säge die chain saw.

Ketzer (pl -) der heretic.

Ketzerin (pl -nen) die heretic.

keuchen (perf hat/ist gekeucht) vi to pant.

Keuchhusten der whooping cough.

Keule (pl -n) die - 1. KÜCHE leg - 2. [Waffe & SPORT] club.

keusch <> adj chaste <> adv chastely.

Keuschheit die chastity.

Keyboard ['ki:bɔːd] (pl -s) das [Musikinstrument & EDV] keyboard.

Kfz [ka:ɛf'tsɛt] (pl -) das abk für Kraftfahrzeug.

Kfz-|Steuer die road tax.

kg (abk für Kilogramm) kg.

kichern vi to giggle.

kicken <> vi to play (football) <> vt to kick.

kidnappen ['kɪtnɛpn] vt to kidnap.

Kidnapper, in ['kɪtnɛpɐ, rɪn] (mpl -; fpl -nen) der, die kidnapper.

Kiefer (pl - ODER -n) <> der (pl Kiefer) jaw <> die (pl Kiefern) pine.

Kiel (pl -e) der - 1. [von Schiff] keel - 2. [von Federn] quill.

Kieme (pl -n) die gill.

Kies der - 1. [auf Weg] gravel; [am Ufer] shingle - 2. salopp [Geld] cash, dosh Br.

Kiesel|stein der pebble.

Kies|grube die gravel pit.

Kiew ['ki:ɛf] nt Kiev.

kikeriki interj cock-a-doodle-doo!

Killer, in (mpl -; fpl -nen) der, die killer.

Kilo (pl - ODER -s) das kilo.

Kilo|gramm das kilogram.

Kilo|hertz das kilohertz.

Kilo|kalorie die kilocalorie.

Kilo|meter der kilometre; ~ pro Stunde kilometres per hour.

kilometerlang adj ≃ miles long; ~e Strände miles and miles of beaches.

Kilometer|stand der ≃ mileage; bei ~ 10.000 when there are 10,000 km on the clock.

Kilometer|zähler der ≃ mileometer.

Kilo|watt das kilowatt.

Kilowatt|stunde die kilowatt hour.

Kind (pl -er) das child; von ~ auf ODER an from childhood; ein ~ erwarten to be expecting (a baby); ein ~ bekommen ODER kriegen to have a baby; mit ~ und Kegel with the whole tribe.

Kinder|arzt, ärztin der, die paediatrician.

Kinder|buch das children's book.

Kinder|garten der nursery school.

Kinder|gärtner, in der, die = Erzieher.

Kinder|geld das child benefit.

Kinder|heim das children's home.

Kinder|hort der day centre where children can spend the afternoon after lessons have finished.

Kinder|krankheit die illness affecting children.

Kinder|krippe die crèche.

Kinder|lähmung die polio.

kinderleicht adj fam dead easy; es war ~ it was child's play.

kinderlieb adj fond of children.

Kinder|lied das nursery rhyme.

Kinder|mädchen das nursemaid.

kinderreich adj: eine ~e Familie a large family, a family with lots of children.

Kinderschutz|bund der child protection league.

Kinder|sicherung die [an Auto] childproof lock.

Kinder|sitz der child seat.

Kinder|spiel das children's game; ein ~ sein to be child's play.

Kinder|stube die: eine gute/schlechte ~ haben to have been well/badly brought up.

Kindertages|stätte die day nursery.

Kinder|wagen der pram Br, baby carriage Am.

Kinder|zimmer das children's bedroom.

Kindes|alter das childhood; im ~ as a child, at an early age.

Kindes|misshandlung die child abuse.

Kindheit die childhood; von ~ an from an early age.

kindisch abw <> adj childish <> adv childishly.

kindlich <> adj childlike <> adv like a child.

Kinn (pl -e) das chin.

Kinn|haken der hook (to the chin).

Kino (pl -s) das cinema, movie theater Am; ins ~ gehen to go to the movies, to go to the cinema.

Kino|besucher, in der, die moviegoer, cinemagoer.

Kino|programm das movie guide, cinema guide.

Kiosk (pl -e) der kiosk.

Kippe (pl -n) die - 1. fam [Zigarette] ciggy, fag Br - 2. fam [Zigarettenstummel] cigarette butt, fag end Br - 3. RW: auf der ~ stehen [zu fallen drohen] to be precariously balanced; [gefährdet oder unsicher sein] to be in the balance.

kippen (perf hat/ist gekippt) <> vi (ist) to topple <> vt (hat) - 1. [Fenster, Möbel] to tilt - 2. [Flüssigkeit] to tip - 3. fam [Schnaps] to knock back.

Kirche (pl -n) die church; in die ~ gehen to go to church.

Kirchen|chor *der* church choir.
Kirchen|gemeinde *die* [Bezirk] parish; [Gottesdienstteilnehmer] congregation.
Kirchen|musik *die* church music.
Kirchen|schiff *das* ARCHIT nave.
Kirchen|steuer *die* church tax.
kirchlich <> *adj* church (*vor Subst*) <> *adv*: **sich ~ trauen lassen** to have a church wedding.
Kirch|turm *der* [mit Spitze] steeple; [ohne Spitze] church tower.
Kirmes *die* fair.
Kirsch|baum *der* cherry tree.
Kirsche (*pl* -n) *die* cherry.
Kirsch|torte *die*: **Schwarzwälder ~** Black Forest gâteau.
Kissen (*pl* -) *das* [auf Stuhl, Sofa] cushion; [für Bett] pillow.
Kiste (*pl* -n) *die* - **1.** [Behälter] crate, box - **2.** *fam* [Auto] jalopy, banger *Br*.
kitschig *adj* kitschy.
Kitt *der* putty.
Kittchen (*pl* -) *das fam* nick *Br*, can *Am*; **im ~ sein** ODER **sitzen** *fam* to be in the nick *Br* ODER can *Am*.
Kittel (*pl* -) *der* [für Werkstatt] overalls (*pl*); [für Arzt] white coat; [für Labor] lab coat.
Kittel|schürze (*pl* -n) *die* housecoat.
kitten *vt* - **1.** [kleben] to glue together - **2.** [Ehe] to patch up.
Kitzel (*pl* -) *der* thrill.
kitzelig = kitzlig.
kitzeln *vt* - **1.** [krabbeln] to tickle; **jn an den Füßen ~** to tickle sb's feet - **2.** [reizen - Ehrgeiz] *fam* to arouse.
kitzlig, kitzelig *adj* - **1.** [empfindlich] ticklish - **2.** [heikel] tricky.
Kiwi (*pl* -s) *die* kiwi fruit.
klaffen *vi* to gape.
kläffen *vi abw* to yap.
Klage (*pl* -n) *die* - **1.** [Beschwerde] complaint - **2.** RECHT action, suit; **gegen jn ~ einreichen** to bring an action against sb.
klagen <> *vi* - **1.** [jammern] to complain; **über jn/etw ~** to complain about sb/sthg; **über Rückenschmerzen ~** to complain of backache - **2.** [vor Gericht]: **gegen jn ~** to take legal action against sb; **auf Schadenersatz ~** to sue for damages <> *vt*: **jm seine Not ~** to pour out one's troubles to sb.
Kläger, in (*mpl* -; *fpl* -nen) *der, die* RECHT plaintiff.
klaglos *adv* uncomplainingly.
Klammer (*pl* -n) *die* - **1.** [für Blätter] paper clip; [für Wäsche] (clothes) peg *Br*, clothespin *Am*; [für Wunde, von Heftmaschine] staple; [für Zähne] brace - **2.** [Symbol] bracket; **etw in ~n setzen** to bracket sthg; **in ~n stehen** to be in brackets.
Klammer|affe *der fam* EDV at-sign.

klammern *vt*: **etw an etw** (A) **~** to attach sthg to sthg. ◆ **sich klammern** *ref*: **sich an jn/etw ~** to cling to sb/sthg.
Klamotten *pl fam* gear (*U*), clothes.
klang *prät* ▷ klingen.
Klang (*pl* Klänge) *der* sound.
Klapp|bett *das* folding bed.
Klappe (*pl* -n) *die* - **1.** [Gegenstand] flap; [bei Blasinstrument, Motor] valve; [bei Film] clapperboard; „**~ die Fünfte**" 'take five' - **2.** *fam* [Mund] trap.
klappen <> *vt*: **etw nach oben/unten ~** [Sitz] to tip sthg forward/back <> *vi* [gelingen] to work, to come off; **hat alles geklappt?** did everything go OK?; **es klappt (gut)** it works; **es klappt nicht** it doesn't work.
klapperig = klapprig.
klappern *vi* [Tür, Fensterladen] to rattle; [Kastagnette] to clack (together); **ich klappere mit den Zähnen** my teeth are chattering.
Klapp|rad, Klappfahrrad *das* folding bicycle.
klapprig, klapperig *adj* - **1.** [Gegenstand] rickety - **2.** [Person] doddery.
Klapp|sitz *der* folding seat.
Klaps (*pl* -e) *der* [leichter Schlag] pat.
klar <> *adj* - **1.** [gen] clear; **mir ist nicht ~, wie das funktioniert** I'm not clear how it works; **ist dir das jetzt ~?** do you understand now?; **na ~!** of course! - **2.** [bewusst]: **sich** (*D*) **über etw im Klaren sein** to be aware of sthg <> *adv* - **1.** [deutlich] clearly - **2.** [fertig]: **~ zu etw** ready for sthg. ◆ **alles klar** *interj*: **alles ~?** OK?; **alles ~!** OK! ◆ **klar und deutlich** <> *adj* perfectly clear <> *adv* quite clearly.
Klär|anlage *die* sewage works (*sg*).
Klare (*pl* -n) *der* schnapps.
klären *vt* [Problem, Angelegenheit] to clear up.
klar|gehen (*perf* ist klargegangen) *vi* (*unreg*) *fam* to go OK.
Klarheit *die* [Gewissheit, Deutlichkeit] clarity; **über etw** (*A*) **~ gewinnen** ODER **bekommen** to clarify sthg; **sich** (*D*) **~ verschaffen** to get sthg clear.
Klarinette (*pl* -n) *die* clarinet.
klar|kommen (*perf* ist klargekommen) *vi* (*unreg*): **mit jm/etw ~** to be able to cope with sb/sthg.
klar machen *vt*: **jm etw ~** to explain sthg to sb, to make sthg clear to sb.
Klarsicht|folie *die* transparent film, cling-film *Br*.
Klarsicht|hülle *die* plastic cover.
klar|stellen *vt* [Problem, Frage] to clear up; **~, dass ...** to make it clear that ...
Klärung (*pl* -en) *die* clearing up.
klar werden (*perf* ist klar geworden) *vi* (*un-*

reg): **jm ~** to become clear to sb; **sich** *(D)* **über etw ~** to be able to understand sthg.

klasse *adj* fam great, neat Am.

Klasse *(pl* -n) die - 1. [gen] class; **erster/ zweiter ~** first/second class - 2. [Zimmer] classroom - 3. [Schuljahr] form *Br,* grade *Am;* **eine ~ wiederholen** to repeat a year.

Klassen|arbeit die class test.

Klassen|kamerad, in der, die classmate.

Klassen|lehrer, in der, die class teacher.

Klassen|zimmer das classroom.

Klassik die *(ohne pl)* - 1. [Epoche] classical period - 2. [Antike]: **die ~** classical antiquity - 3. [Musik] classical music - 4. [Literatur] classical literature.

Klassiker, in *(mpl* -; *fpl* -nen) der, die - 1. [Dichter] classical author; **die ~ lesen** to read the classics - 2. [Referenz] classic.

klassisch *adj* - 1. [Kunst, Kultur] classical - 2. [Fehler] classic.

Klatsch der fam [Gerede] gossip.

klatschen *(perf* hat/ist geklatscht) <> *vi* - 1. *(hat)* [schlagen] to slap; **in die Hände ~** to clap (one's hands) - 2. *(hat)* [Publikum] to clap - 3. *(ist)* [Regen] to drum; [Wellen] to slap - 4. *(hat)* fam [tratschen]: **über jn/etw ~** to gossip about sb/sthg <> *vt:* **Beifall ~** to applaud; **jm eine ~** fam to give sb a slap.

Klaue *(pl* -n) die - 1. [von Adler, Löwen] claw - 2. fam [Schrift] scrawl.

klauen fam <> *vt* to pinch, to nick *Br;* **jm etw ~** to pinch sthg from sb, to nick sthg off sb *Br* <> *vi* [stehlen]: **hier wird viel geklaut** a lot of stuff gets pinched ODER nicked *Br* round here.

Klausel *(pl* -n) die clause.

Klausur *(pl* -en) die UNI exam.

Klavier [kla'viːɐ] *(pl* -e) das piano; **~ spielen** to play the piano.

Klavier|konzert das - 1. [Musikstück] piano concerto - 2. [Konzert] piano recital.

kleben <> *vt* [ankleben] to stick, to glue; [reparieren] to stick ODER glue together <> *vi* [halten]: **an etw** *(D)* **~** eigtl & fig to stick to sthg.

Kleber *(pl* -) der adhesive.

Klebe|streifen der adhesive tape.

klebrig *adj* sticky.

Klebe|stoff der adhesive, glue.

kleckern <> *vi* [verschütten] to make a mess; **du hast gekleckert** [beim Essen] you've spilt your food <> *vt* [verschütten] to spill.

Klecks *(pl* -e) der [von Farbe, Senf] blob; [von Tinte] blot.

Klee der clover.

Klee|blatt das clover leaf.

Kleid *(pl* -er) das [Frauenkleid] dress. ◆ **Kleider** pl [Kleidungsstücke] clothes.

Kleider|bügel der coathanger.

Kleider|schrank der - 1. [Möbelstück] wardrobe, closet *Am* - 2. fam [Mann] man mountain.

Kleidung *(pl* -en) die clothes *(pl),* clothing.

Kleie *(pl* -n) die bran.

klein <> *adj* - 1. [gen] small, little; **mein ~er Finger** my little finger - 2. [temporal] short; **eine ~e Pause** a short break - 3. [unerheblich] little; **meine ~ste Sorge** the least of my worries; **~e Leute** ordinary people; **aus ~en Verhältnissen stammen** to come from a humble background <> *adv* - 1.: **ein ~ wenig** a little bit - 2. *RW:* **haben Sie es nicht ~er?** don't you have anything smaller?

Klein|anzeige die small ad *Br,* want ad *Am.*

kleinbürgerlich abw <> *adj* petty bourgeois <> *adv* in a petty bourgeois way.

Kleine *(pl* -n) <> der, die - 1. [Kind] little one - 2. [als Anrede - nett] little one; [- beleidigend] shorty <> das [Baby] little one.

klein gedruckt *adj* in small print.

Kleingeld das change.

Kleinigkeit *(pl* -en) die - 1. [unwichtig] trifle; **für jn eine/keine ~** sein to be an/no easy matter for sb - 2. [klein, wenig]: **ein paar ~en einkaufen** to buy a few little things - 3. [zu essen] snack.

Klein|kind das small child.

Kleinkram der *(ohne pl)* fam - 1. [Gegenstände] bits and pieces *(pl)* - 2. [Angelegenheiten] trifling things *(pl).*

klein|kriegen *vt* - 1. [Person]: **jn ~** to bring sb into line; **lass dich davon nicht ~** don't let that get you down - 2. [Gegenstand]: **etw ist nicht kleinzukriegen** sthg will last forever - 3. [zerkleinern mit Messer] to chop up.

kleinlaut <> *adj* subdued <> *adv* in a subdued manner.

kleinlich *adj* abw petty.

klein machen *vt* - 1. [Holz, Pappe] to chop up - 2. [Geldschein] fam to change.

klein schneiden *vt (unreg)* to chop into small pieces.

klein|schreiben *vt (unreg)* [mit kleinem Anfangsbuchstaben] to write with a small initial letter.

Klein|schreibung die use of small initial letters.

Klein|stadt die small town.

Kleister *(pl* -) der paste.

Klemme *(pl* -n) die - 1. *(ohne pl)* fam [Bedrängnis] tight spot; **jm aus der ~ helfen** to help sb out of a tight spot; **in der ~ stecken** ODER **sitzen** ODER **sein** to be in a tight spot - 2. ELEKTR terminal.

klemmen <> *vt* - 1. [feststecken] to jam - 2. [Finger]: **sich** *(D)* **etw ~** to get sthg caught <> *vi* [Tür, Schublade] to jam. ◆ **sich klemmen** ref fam: **sich dahinter ~** to get stuck in.

Klempner, in *(mpl -; fpl -nen) der, die* plumber.

Klerus *der (ohne pl)* clergy *(pl)*.

Klette *(pl -n) die* - **1.** *fam* [Mensch] limpet - **2.** [Pflanze] burdock.

klettern *(perf hat/ist geklettert) vi* - **1.** *(ist)* [gen] to climb - **2.** *(hat)* SPORT to climb.

klicken *vi* to click.

Klient *(pl -en) der* client.

Klientin *(pl -nen) die* client.

Kliff *(pl -e) das* cliff.

Klima *(pl -s) das* climate.

Klimaanlage *die* air conditioning *(U)*.

klimpern *vi* [spielen - auf Klavier] to tinkle away; [- auf Gitarre] to strum.

Klinge *(pl -n) die* blade.

Klingel *(pl -n) die* bell.

klingeln *vi* to ring (the bell); **es hat geklingelt** [an der Tür] there's someone at the door; [in der Schule] the bell has gone; **bei jm ~** to ring sb's bell; **nach jm ~** to ring for sb.

klingen *(prät klang; perf hat geklungen) vi* - **1.** [gen] to sound - **2.** [Glocken, Gläser] to ring.

Klinik *(pl -en) die* clinic.

klinisch *<> adj* clinical *<> adv* clinically.

Klinke *(pl -n) die* (door) handle.

Klipp, Clip *(pl -s) der* clip.

Klippe *(pl -n) die* rock; **alle ~n umfahren** to negotiate all obstacles.

klirren *vi* [Scheiben] to rattle; [Gläser] to clink.

klirrend *adj:* **~e Kälte** freezing cold.

Klischee *(pl -s) das* cliché.

Klo *(pl -s) das fam* loo *Br,* john *Am;* **aufs ~ gehen** to go to the loo *Br* OR john *Am*.

klobig *adj* - **1.** [ungeschliffen] clumsy - **2.** [massig - Hände] massive; [- Stuhl, Bau, Schuhe] clunky.

Klofrau *die fam* toilet attendant.

Klopapier *das fam* toilet paper.

klopfen *<> vi* - **1.** [Person - an die Tür] to knock; [- auf den Tisch] to rap; **es hat geklopft** there's someone at the door - **2.** [Herz] to beat *<> vt* [Teppich, Kissen] to beat.

Klops *(pl -e) der* meatball.

Klosett *(pl -e) das* toilet.

Kloß *(pl Klöße) der* dumpling; **einen ~ im Hals haben** *fig* to have a lump in one's throat.

Kloster *(pl Klöster) das* [für Nonnen] convent; [für Mönche] monastery.

Klotz *(pl Klötze) der* - **1.** block - **2.** [Scheit] log - **3.** *abw* [Gebäude] concrete block - **4.** *RW:* **einen ~ am Bein haben** to have a millstone round one's neck.

klotzig *fam <> adj* [groß] clunky *<> adv:* **~ verdienen** to earn a packet.

Klub, Club *(pl -s) der* club.

Kluft *(pl -en* ODER **Klüfte) die** - **1.** *(pl Klüfte)* [zwischen Gegensätzen] gulf - **2.** *(pl Klüfte)* [im Fels] cleft - **3.** *(pl Kluften)* [Kleidung] outfit.

klug *(kompar klüger; superl klügste) <> adj* - **1.** [schlau] clever - **2.** [weise] wise - **3.** *RW:* **jd wird aus jm/etw nicht ~** sb can't make sb/sthg out; **der Klügere gibt nach** discretion is the better part of valour *<> adv* [umsichtig] wisely.

Klugheit *(pl -en) die* - **1.** [Schläue] cleverness - **2.** [Weisheit] wisdom.

Klumpen *(pl -) der* lump.

km *(abk für Kilometer)* km.

km/h *(abk für Stundenkilometer)* kph.

knabbern *<> vt* to nibble *<> vi:* **an etw** *(D)* **~** to nibble sthg.

Knabe *(pl -n) der* - **1.** *geh* [Junge] boy - **2.** *fam* [Mann] chap.

Knäckebrot *das* crispbread.

knacken *<> vt* - **1.** [Nüsse, Finger] to crack - **2.** [mit Gewalt - Schloss] to force; [- Bank] to break into - **3.** [Code] to crack *<> vi* - **1.** [Holz, Finger] to crack; [Feuer, im Radio, Telefon] to crackle - **2.** *salopp* [schlafen] to crash out - **3.** [an Problemen]: **an etw** *(D)* **zu ~ haben** *fig* [sich bemühen] to have one's work cut out with sthg; [die Folgen spüren] to have a hard time getting over sthg.

knackig *adj* - **1.** [Salat] crisp - **2.** *salopp* [Po] sexy.

Knacks *(pl -e) der fam* [psychischer Schaden]: **einen ~ haben/bekommen** to be/get screwed up.

Knall *(pl -e) der* [von Schuss, Tür] bang; [von Korken] pop.

knallen *(perf hat/ist geknallt) <> vi* - **1.** *(hat)* [Schuss] to ring out; [Peitsche] to crack; [Korken] to pop - **2.** *(ist) fam* [aufprallen] to crash; **mit dem Kopf auf den Boden ~** to bang one's head on the floor - **3.** *(hat)* [Sonne] to beat down *<> vt* - **1.** [werfen] to fling; **die Tür ins Schloss ~** to slam the door - **2.** [ohrfeigen]: **jm eine ~** *fam* to clout sb.

knapp *<> adj* - **1.** [Ergebnis, Rennen] close; [Vorsprung, Stimmenmehrheit] narrow - **2.** [Kleid, Schuhe] tight - **3.** [fast ganz]: **eine ~e Stunde** just under an hour; **das war ~** that was close - **4.** [wenig]: **~ bei Kasse sein** to be short of money; **~ werden** to be running short *<> adv* - **1.** [um weniges] narrowly - **2.** [eng] tightly.

knarren *vi* to creak.

Knast *(pl Knäste) der fam* clink.

Knatsch *der (ohne pl) fam* row.

knattern *vi* [Motor] to roar; [Maschinengewehr] to rattle; [Fahne] to flap.

Knäuel *(pl -) das* ball.

Knauf *(pl Knäufe) der* knob.

knauserig *adj* stingy.

knausern *vi*: **mit etw ~** to be stingy with sthg.

knautschen *vt & vi* to crumple.

Knebel (*pl* -) *der* gag.

knebeln *vt* to gag.

Knecht (*pl* -e) *der* [auf Bauernhof] farmhand; [Diener] servant.

kneifen (*prät* **kniff**; *perf* **hat gekniffen**) <> *vi* - **1.** [Kleidung] to pinch - **2.** *fam abw* [sich drücken]: **(vor etw** (*D*)) **~** to duck out (of sthg) <> *vt* to pinch.

Kneifzange *die* pincers (*pl*).

Kneipe (*pl* -n) *die fam* bar, pub *Br.*

kneten *vt* [Teig, Muskeln] to knead; [Figur] to model.

Knick (*pl* -e ODER -s) *der* - **1.** (*pl* Knicke) [Falte] crease - **2.** (*pl* Knicke) [in Straße] sharp bend.

knicken *vt* - **1.** [falten] to fold - **2.** [Äste, Blumen] to bend.

Knicks (*pl* -e) *der* curtsey.

Knie (*pl* -) *das* - **1.** [Körperteil] knee - **2.** *RW*: **etw übers ~ brechen** to rush sthg.

Kniebeuge (*pl* -n) *die* knee-bend.

Kniegelenk *das* knee joint.

Kniekehle *die* hollow of the knee.

knien *vi* to kneel. ◆ **sich knien** *ref* to kneel; **sich in etw** (*A*) **~** *fig* to buckle down to sthg.

Kniescheibe *die* kneecap.

Kniestrumpf *der* knee-length sock.

kniff *prät* ⊳ kneifen.

Kniff (*pl* -e) *der* [Trick] trick.

knifflig *adj* tricky.

knipsen *fam* <> *vi* [fotografieren] to take snaps <> *vt* - **1.** [Fahrkarte] to punch - **2.** [fotografieren]: **jn/etw ~** to snap sb/sthg.

Knirps (*pl* -e) *der* [Kind] little lad.

knirschen *vi* - **1.**: **mit den Zähnen ~** to grind one's teeth - **2.** [Schnee, Sand] to crunch.

knistern *vi* [Feuer, brennendes Holz] to crackle; [Papier] to rustle; **mit etw ~** to rustle sthg.

knitterfrei *adj* crease-resistant.

knittern *vi* to crease.

knobeln *vi* - **1.** [losen] to toss - **2.** [spielen] to play dice - **3.** [tüfteln]: **an etw** (*D*) **~** to puzzle over sthg.

Knoblauch *der* garlic.

Knöchel (*pl* -) *der* ankle.

Knochen (*pl* -) *der* bone.

Knochenbruch *der* fracture.

Knochenmark *das* bone marrow.

knochig *adj* bony.

Knödel (*pl* -) *der* dumpling.

Knolle (*pl* -n) *die* BIOL tuber.

Knopf (*pl* Knöpfe) *der* button.

Knopfdruck *der*: **auf ~** at the push of a button.

knöpfen *vt* to button.

Knopfloch *das* buttonhole.

Knorpel (*pl* -) *der* cartilage.

Knospe (*pl* -n) *die* bud.

knoten *vt* to tie.

Knoten (*pl* -) *der* - **1.** [gen] knot - **2.** MED lump.

Knotenpunkt *der* - **1.** [von Straßen] junction - **2.** [wichtiger Ort] centre.

Know-how ['noʊhaʊ] (*pl* -s) *das* know-how (*U*).

knüllen *vt* to crumple.

Knüller (*pl* -) *der fam* sensation.

knüpfen *vt* to knot; [Netz] to make; **etw an etw** (*A*) **~** [mit Faden] to tie sthg to sthg; *fig* [Erwartungen, Bedingungen] to attach sthg to sthg.

Knüppel (*pl* -) *der* club; **jm einen ~ zwischen die Beine werfen** *fig* to put a spoke in sb's wheel.

knurren *vi* - **1.** [Magen] to rumble - **2.** [Hund] to growl - **3.** [Person] to grumble.

knusprig, knusperig <> *adj* crisp <> *adv*: **~ braun** crisp and brown.

knutschen *fam* <> *vt* to smooch with <> *vi* to smooch.

K. o. (*pl* -) *der* knockout.

Kobalt *das* CHEM cobalt.

Koch [kɔx] (*pl* Köche ['kœçə]) *der* cook.

Kochbuch *das* cookbook.

kochen <> *vt* - **1.** [Essen] to cook; [Kaffee] to make; **jm/sich etw ~** to cook sb/o.s. sthg - **2.** [Wäsche] to boil <> *vi* - **1.** [Wasser, Person] to boil - **2.** [Koch]: **gut/schlecht ~** to be a good/bad cook.

Kochgelegenheit *die* cooking facilities (*pl*).

Köchin [kœçɪn] (*pl* -nen) *die* cook.

Kochlöffel *der* wooden spoon.

Kochrezept *das* recipe.

Kochsalz *das* cooking salt.

Kochtopf *der* saucepan.

Kochwäsche *die washing that needs to be boiled.*

Kode, Code ['koːt] (*pl* -s) *der* code.

Köder (*pl* -) *der* bait.

ködern *vt* to lure.

kodieren, codieren [ko'diːrən] *vt* to encode.

Koffein *das* caffeine.

koffeinfrei *adj* decaffeinated.

Koffer (*pl* -) *der* suitcase; **die ~ packen** to pack one's bags.

Kofferraum *der* boot *Br*, trunk *Am*.

Kognak ['kɔnjak] (*pl* -s) *der* brandy.

Kohl *der* cabbage.

Kohle (*pl* -n) *die* - **1.** [Brennstoff] coal (*U*); **wie auf glühenden ~n sitzen** *fig* to be like a cat on hot bricks - **2.** *fam* [Geld] cash.

Kohlenhydrat (*pl* -e) *das* carbohydrate.

Kohlen|säure *die:* Mineralwasser mit/ohne ~ sparkling/still mineral water.

Kohle|zeichnung *die* KUNST charcoal drawing.

Kohlrabi (*pl* - ODER -s) *der* kohlrabi.

Kohl|roulade *die* stuffed cabbage leaves (*pl*).

Koje (*pl* -n) *die* - 1. *fam* [Bett] bed - 2. [Schiffsbett] bunk.

Kokain *das* cocaine.

Kokos|nuss *die* coconut.

Koks *der* coke.

Kolben (*pl* -) *der* - 1. TECH piston - 2. CHEM flask.

Kolik, Kolik (*pl* -en) *die* colic (*U*).

Kollaps, Kollaps (*pl* -e) *der* collapse (*sg*).

Kollege (*pl* -n) *der* colleague.

Kollegin (*pl* -nen) *die* colleague.

Kollegium [kɔ'leːgjʊm] (*pl* -gien) *das* [in Schule] teaching staff.

Kollektion (*pl* -en) *die* collection.

kollidieren (*perf* ist kollidiert) *vi* - 1. [Fahrzeuge] to collide - 2. [Interessen] to clash.

Kollision (*pl* -en) *die* collision.

Köln *nt* Cologne.

Kolonie [kolo'niː] (*pl* -n) *die* colony.

Kolonne (*pl* -n) *die* column; (in) ~ fahren to drive in convoy.

kolossal *adj* colossal; **ein ~er Irrtum** a huge mistake.

Kolumbien *nt* Colombia.

Koma (*pl* -s) *das* coma.

Kombination (*pl* -en) *die* - 1. [Zusammenfügung] combination - 2. [Schlussfolgerung] deduction - 3. [Arbeitsanzug] overalls (*pl*).

kombinieren <> *vi* to reason <> *vt* to combine; **etw mit etw ~** to combine sthg with sthg.

Komet (*pl* -en) *der* ASTRON comet.

Komfort [kɔm'foːg] *der:* **mit allem ~** with all mod cons.

komfortabel <> *adj* comfortable <> *adv* [bequem] comfortably.

Komik *die* comic effect.

Komiker, in (*mpl* -; *fpl* -nen) *der, die* comedian.

komisch *adj* funny.

Komitee (*pl* -s) *das* committee.

Komma (*pl* -s ODER -ta) *das* - 1. [Satzzeichen] comma - 2. [mathematisches Zeichen] decimal point.

Kommandeur, in [kɔman'døːg, rɪn] (*mpl* -e; *fpl* -nen) *der, die* commander.

kommandieren *vt* [Soldaten] to command.

Kommando (*pl* -s) *das* - 1. [gen] command; **auf ~** on command; **das ~ haben/übernehmen** to be in/take command - 2. [kleine Einheit] detachment.

kommen (*prät* kam; *perf* ist gekommen) <> *vi* - 1. [herkommen] to come; **den Arzt ~ lassen** to call the doctor - 2. [ein Ziel erreichen] to get; **wie komme ich zum Markt?** how do I get to the market?; **nach Hause ~** to get home; **an die Macht ~** to come to power - 3. [mit Institutionen] to go; **ins/aus dem Krankenhaus ~** to go to/leave hospital; **in die Schule ~** to start school - 4. [stammen] to come; **aus Deutschland ~** to come from Germany - 5. [folgen] to come; **rechts kommt der Bahnhof** the station's coming up on the right - 6. [resultieren]: **von etw ~** to result from sthg; **das kommt daher, dass ...** it's because ...; **das kommt davon!** see what happens!; **wie kommt es, dass ...?** how is it that ...? - 7. [passieren] to happen; **das musste ja so ~!** it had to happen!; **überraschend ~** to come as a surprise - 8. [Programm, Film]: **im Fernsehen ~** to be on (the) television; **im Kino ~** to be on at the cinema *Br* ODER the movies *Am* - 9. *fam* [einen Orgasmus haben] to come - 10. [hingehören] to go, to belong; **die Kisten ~ in den Keller** the crates go underneath the cellar - 11. [anfangen]: **ins Schleudern ~** to skid; **auf etw (A) zu sprechen ~** to get around to talking about sthg - 12. [mit Dativ]: **mir kam eine Idee** an idea came to me; **jm frech ~** *fam* to be cheeky to sb - 13. [figurative Verwendungen mit Präposition]: **auf eine Idee ~** to think of an idea; **hinter etw (A) ~** to get to the bottom of sthg; **ums Leben ~** to lose one's life, to die; **zu sich ~** to come round; **dazu ~, etw zu tun** to get round to doing sthg <> *v impers:* **es kam zu einem Streit** there was a quarrel <> *vt fam:* **welchen Weg bist du gekommen?** which way did you come?

kommend *adj* - 1. [Woche] coming - 2. [Generation, Mode] future.

Kommentar (*pl* -e) *der* - 1. [in Zeitung, Buch, Radio] commentary - 2. *fam* [Bemerkung] comment; **kein ~** no comment.

kommentieren *vt* - 1. [Ereignis] to comment on - 2. [Text, Buch] to provide a commentary on.

kommerziell <> *adj* commercial <> *adv* commercially.

Kommilitone (*pl* -n) *der* UNI fellow student.

Kommilitonin (*pl* -nen) *die* UNI fellow student.

Kommissar, in (*mpl* -e; *fpl* -nen) *der, die* [bei der Polizei] superintendent *Br*, captain *Am*.

kommunal *adj* local.

Kommune (*pl* -n) *die* - 1. [Gemeinde] local authority - 2. [Wohngemeinschaft] commune.

Kommunikation (*pl* -en) *die* communication.

Kommunion (*pl* -en) *die* REL Communion (*U*).

Kommunismus *der* Communism.

Kommunist, in (*mpl* -en; *fpl* -nen) *der, die* Communist.

kommunistisch *adj* Communist.

Komödie [ko'mø:djə] (*pl* -n) *die* comedy; **jm eine ~ vorspielen** to put on an act for sb.

kompakt <> *adj* compact <> *adv* compactly.

Kompanie [kɔmpa'ni:] (*pl* -n) *die* MIL company.

Komparativ (*pl* -e) *der* GRAM comparative.

Kompass (*pl* -e) *der* compass.

kompatibel *adj* EDV compatible; **mit etw ~ sein** to be compatible with sthg.

kompetent <> *adj* competent <> *adv* competently.

Kompetenz (*pl* -en) *die* competence (*U*).

komplett <> *adj* complete <> *adv* - **1.** [vollständig] fully - **2.** *fam* [völlig] completely.

Komplex (*pl* -e) *der* [gen & PSYCH] complex; **-e haben** to have a complex.

Kompliment (*pl* -e) *das* compliment; **mein ~!** my compliments!; **jm ein ~ machen** to pay sb a compliment.

Komplize (*pl* -n) *der* accomplice.

kompliziert <> *adj* complicated <> *adv* in a complicated way.

Komplizin (*pl* -nen) *die* accomplice.

Komplott (*pl* -e) *das* plot.

komponieren *vt* [zusammenstellen & MUS] to compose.

Komponist, in (*mpl* -en; *fpl* -nen) *der, die* composer.

Komposition *die* [Zusammenstellung & MUS] composition.

Kompost, Kompost (*pl* -e) *der* compost (*U*).

Kompott (*pl* -e) *das* stewed fruit.

Kompromiss (*pl* -e) *der* compromise.

kompromissbereit *adj* ready to compromise.

kondensieren *vt* & *vi* to condense.

Kondensmilch *die* condensed milk.

Kondenswasser *das* condensation.

Konditional (*pl* -e) *der* GRAM conditional.

Konditionstraining *das* fitness training.

Konditorei (*pl* -en) *die* cake shop.

Kondom (*pl* -e) *das* condom.

Konfekt (*pl* -e) *das* confectionery (*U*).

Konfektion (*pl* -en) *die* - **1.** [Kleidung] ready-to-wear clothes (*pl*) - **2.** [Herstellung] manufacture of ready-to-wear clothes.

Konferenz (*pl* -en) *die* - **1.** [Tagung] conference - **2.** [Besprechung] meeting.

Konfession (*pl* -en) *die* REL denomination.

Konfirmation (*pl* -en) *die* REL confirmation.

konfirmieren *vt* REL to confirm.

Konfitüre (*pl* -n) *die* geh jam.

Konflikt (*pl* -e) *der* conflict; **mit etw in ~ geraten** ODER **kommen** to come into conflict with sthg.

konform <> *adj* concurrent; **mit jm/etw ~ gehen** *geh* to concur with sb/sthg <> *adv*: **sich ~ verhalten** to behave like everyone else.

Konfrontation (*pl* -en) *die* confrontation.

konfrontieren *vt*: **jn mit jm/etw ~** to confront sb with sb/sthg.

konfus <> *adj* confused <> *adv* confusedly.

Kongo *der*: **der ~** the Congo.

Kongress (*pl* -e) *der* - **1.** [Tagung] conference - **2.** POL Congress.

König (*pl* -e) *der* - **1.** [gen] king - **2.** [Feiertag]: **Heilige Drei ~e** Epiphany.

Königin (*pl* -nen) *die* queen.

königlich <> *adj* - **1.** [des Monarchen] royal - **2.** [reichlich - Mahl] lavish; [- Trinkgeld, Geschenk] handsome; [- Vergnügen] tremendous <> *adv* - **1.** [riesig] tremendously - **2.** [bewirten] lavishly.

Königreich *das* kingdom.

Konjugation (*pl* -en) *die* GRAM conjugation.

konjugieren *vt* GRAM to conjugate.

Konjunktiv (*pl* -e) *der* GRAM subjunctive.

Konjunktur (*pl* -en) *die* economic situation; **rückläufige ~** declining economic activity; **~ haben** to be in demand.

konkret <> *adj* concrete <> *adv* concretely.

Konkurrent, in (*mpl* -en; *fpl* -nen) *der, die* competitor.

Konkurrenz (*pl* -en) *die* competition; **jm ~ machen** to compete with sb. ◆ **außer Konkurrenz** *adv* as an unofficial competitor.

konkurrenzfähig <> *adj* competitive <> *adv* competitively.

Konkurrenzkampf *der* competition.

Konkurs (*pl* -e) *der* - **1.** [Zahlungsunfähigkeit] bankruptcy - **2.** [Verfahren] bankruptcy proceedings (*pl*).

können (*präs* kann; *prät* konnte; *perf* hat können ODER hat gekonnt) <> *aux* - **1.** [vermögen, dürfen] can; **etw tun ~** to be able to do sthg; **er kann Klavier spielen** he can play the piano; **kann ich noch ein Eis haben?** can I have another ice cream?; **könnte ich mal telefonieren?** could I use the telephone? - **2.** [zum Ausdruck der Möglichkeit] can; **es könnte verloren gegangen sein** it could ODER might have got lost; **sie kann nicht kommen** she can't come; **wir können es versuchen**

we can try; **das kann schon sein** that's quite possible; **man kann nie wissen** you never know <> *vi:* **fahren, so schnell man kann** to drive as fast as you can; **kann ich ins Kino?** can I go to the cinema?; **ich kann nicht mehr** *fam* I've had it, I'm exhausted <> *vt (perf hat gekonnt)* - **1.** [vermögen]: **kannst du Deutsch?** can ODER do you speak German?; **etw auswendig ~** to know sthg by heart; **der kann nichts** he's useless - **2.** *RW:* **du kannst mich mal!** *vulg* piss off!

Können *das (ohne pl)* ability; **sein ~ unter Beweis stellen** to prove one's ability.

Könner, in (*mpl* -; *fpl* -nen) *der, die* expert.

konnte *prät* ▷ können.

konsequent <> *adj* - **1.** [folgerichtig] consistent - **2.** [Gegner] resolute; [Nichtraucher, Christ] strict <> *adv* - **1.** [folgerichtig] consistently - **2.** [bekämpfend] resolutely.

Konsequenz (*pl* -en) *die* - **1.** [Folge] consequence; **aus etw die ~en ziehen** to draw the obvious conclusion from sthg - **2.** [Unbeirrbarkeit] resolution.

konservativ [kɔnzɛrva'tiːf] <> *adj* conservative <> *adv* conservatively.

Konservative [kɔnzɛrva'tiːvə] (*pl* -n) *der, die* Conservative.

Konserve [kɔn'zɛrvə] (*pl* -n) *die* [Dose] can, tin *Br;* **sich nur von ~n ernähren** to live only on tinned ODER canned *Am* food.

Konserven|dose *die* can, tin *Br.*

konservieren [kɔnzɛr'viːrən] *vt* to preserve.

Konservierungsstoffe [kɔnzɛr'viːrʊŋsˌʃtɔfə] *pl* preservatives.

Konsonant (*pl* -en) *der* consonant.

konstant <> *adj* constant <> *adv* constantly.

konstruieren [kɔnstru'iːrən] *vt* - **1.** [bauen] to construct - **2.** *abw* [erfinden] to fabricate.

Konstrukteur, in [kɔnstrʊk'tøːɐ̯, rɪn] (*mpl* -e; *fpl* -nen) *der, die* designer.

Konstruktion (*pl* -en) *die* construction.

Konsulat (*pl* -e) *das* POL consulate.

Konsum *der* [Verbrauch] consumption.

Konsument, in (*mpl* -en; *fpl* -nen) *der, die* consumer.

konsumieren *vt* to consume.

Kontakt (*pl* -e) *der* contact; **mit jm ~ aufnehmen** to get in touch with sb; **zu** ODER **mit jm/etw ~ haben** to be in contact with sb/sthg.

kontaktarm *adj:* **er ist ~** he finds it difficult to make friends.

kontaktfreudig *adj* sociable.

Kontakt|linse *die* contact lens.

Kontinent, Kontinent (*pl* -e) *der* continent.

Konto (*pl* Konten) *das* [Bankkonto] account; **ein ~ eröffnen/auflösen** to open/close an

account; **etw geht auf js ~** sb is to blame for sthg.

Konto|auszug *der* bank statement.

Konto|stand *der* bank balance.

kontra, contra <> *präp* versus <> *adv:* **~ eingestellt sein** to be against.

Kontra (*pl* -s) *das* double; **jm ~ geben** *fam* to contradict sb.

Kontra|bass *der* double bass.

Kontrast (*pl* -e) *der* contrast; **einen ~ zu etw bilden** to contrast with sthg.

Kontrolle (*pl* -n) *die* - **1.** [Überwachung] check; **jn/etw unter ~ halten** to keep a check on sb/sthg - **2.** [Beherrschung] control; **jn/etw unter ~ bekommen/haben** to get/have sb/sthg under control; **die ~ über sich verlieren** to lose control.

kontrollieren *vt* - **1.** [überprüfen] to check - **2.** [überwachen] to keep a check on - **3.** [beherrschen] to control.

Kontur (*pl* -en) *die* contour; [von Politiker] profile; **~ gewinnen/verlieren** to take/lose shape.

konventionell [kɔnvɛntsɪo'nɛl] <> *adj* conventional <> *adv* conventionally.

Konversation [kɔnvɛrza'tsɪoːn] (*pl* -en) *die geh* conversation.

Konzentrat (*pl* -e) *das* concentrate.

Konzentration (*pl* -en) *die* concentration.

Konzentrations|lager *das* concentration camp.

konzentrieren *vt* - **1.** [richten]: **etw auf etw** *(A)* **~** to concentrate sthg on sthg - **2.** [vereinigen] to concentrate. ◆ **sich konzentrieren** *ref* to concentrate; **sich auf etw** *(A)* **~** to concentrate on sthg.

konzentriert <> *adj* concentrated <> *adv* with concentration; **~ nachdenken** to concentrate.

Konzept (*pl* -e) *das* - **1.** [Entwurf] draft - **2.** [Plan] plan - **3.** *RW:* **jn aus dem ~ bringen** to put sb off his/her stride.

Konzern (*pl* -e) *der* group (of companies).

Konzert (*pl* -e) *das* [Veranstaltung] concert; [Musikstück] concerto.

Konzession (*pl* -en) *die* - **1.** WIRTSCH licence - **2.** [Zugeständnis] concession.

Koordinate (*pl* -n) *die* coordinate.

koordinieren *vt* to coordinate.

Kopenhagen *nt* Copenhagen.

Kopf (*pl* Köpfe) *der* - **1.** [gen] head; **mit dem** ODER **den ~ schütteln** to shake one's head; **jm etw an den ~ werfen** *eigtl* & *fig* to hurl sthg at sb - **2.** [Anführer] leader - **3.** *RW:* **den ~ hängen lassen** to be downhearted; **jm über den ~ wachsen** to overwhelm sb; **jm zu ~ steigen** to go to sb's head; **etw auf den ~ stellen** *fam* to turn sthg upside down; **und wenn du dich auf den ~ stellst** you're wasting your breath; **sich** *(D)* **etw durch den ~ gehen lassen** to think sthg over; **sich** *(D)* **(über etw** *(A)***) den ~ zerbrechen** to rack one's brains (over sthg). ➤ **aus dem Kopf** *adv* off the top of one's head. ➤ **Kopf an Kopf** *adv* neck and neck. ➤ **pro Kopf** *adv* per head. ➤ **von Kopf bis Fuß** *adv* from head to toe.

Köpfchen *(pl -) das* little head; **~ haben** *fam fig* to have brains.

köpfen *vt* - 1. SPORT to head - 2. [hinrichten] to behead - 3. *fam* [öffnen - Flasche] to crack open; [- Ei] to slice the top off ◇ *vi* SPORT to head.

Kopf|haut *die* scalp.

Kopf|hörer *der* headphones *(pl)*.

Kopf|kissen *das* pillow.

kopflos ◇ *adj* - 1. [ohne Kopf] headless - 2. [wirr] panicky ◇ *adv* in a state of panic.

Kopf|rechnen *das* mental arithmetic.

Kopf|salat *der* lettuce.

Kopf|schmerzen *pl* headache *(sg)*; **~ haben** to have a headache.

Kopf|sprung *der* dive.

Kopf|stand *der* headstand.

Kopf|stütze *die* headrest.

Kopf|tuch *das* headscarf.

Kopfzerbrechen *das*: **jm ~ machen** ODER **bereiten** to be a real headache for sb.

Kopie [ko'piː] *(pl -n) die* copy.

kopieren *vt* to copy.

Kopierer *(pl -) der* photocopier.

Kopier|gerät *das* photocopier.

Ko|pilot, in, -pilot ['koːpiloːt, ɪn] *der, die* co-pilot.

koppeln *vt* - 1. [knüpfen] to attach - 2. [anschließen] to couple.

Koppelung, Kopplung *(pl -en) die* coupling.

Koralle *(pl -n) die* coral.

Koran *(pl -e) der* Koran.

Korb *(pl Körbe) der* - 1. [Behälter & SPORT] basket - 2. [Abfuhr] rebuff; **jm einen ~ geben** to turn sb down.

Korb|stuhl *der* wicker chair.

Kord, Cord [kɔrt] *der* corduroy.

Kordel *(pl -n) die* cord.

Kork *der* cork.

Korken *(pl -) der* cork.

Korkenzieher *(pl -) der* corkscrew.

Korn *(pl Körner* ODER *-)* ◇ *das* - 1. [Getreide] grain, corn *Br* - 2. *(pl Körner)* [Pflanzenfrucht, kleines Partikel] grain - 3. *RW*: **jn/etw aufs ~ nehmen** *fam fig* to hit out at sb/sthg ◇ *der (pl Korn)* [Schnaps] schnapps.

Korn|blume *die* cornflower.

Körper *(pl -) der* body.

Körperbau *der* build.

körperbehindert *adj* disabled.

Körper|gewicht *das amt* weight.

Körper|größe *die amt* height.

körperlich ◇ *adj* physical ◇ *adv* physically.

Körperpflege *die* personal hygiene.

Körperschaft *(pl -en) die* RECHT corporation.

Körper|teil *der* part of the body.

Körper|verletzung *die* bodily harm.

korpulent *adj* corpulent.

korrekt ◇ *adj* correct ◇ *adv* correctly.

Korrektur *(pl -en) die* correction; **~ lesen** to read the proofs.

Korrespondent, in *(mpl -en; fpl -nen) der, die* [Berichterstatter] correspondent.

Korrespondenz *die* correspondence.

Korridor *(pl -e) der* corridor.

korrigieren *vt* to correct.

korrupt *adj* corrupt.

Korruption *(pl -en) die* corruption *(U)*.

Kosmetik *(pl -ka) die* [Pflege] beauty care.

Kosmetiker, in *(mpl -; fpl -nen) der, die* beautician.

kosmetisch ◇ *adj* cosmetic ◇ *adv* cosmetically.

Kosmos *der* cosmos.

Kost *die* food.

kostbar *adj* - 1. [wertvoll, erlesen] valuable - 2. [wichtig] precious.

Kostbarkeit *(pl -en) die* - 1. [Wert] value - 2. [Gegenstand] treasure.

kosten ◇ *vi* [probieren] to have a taste; **von der Suppe ~** to taste the soup ◇ *vt* - 1. [gen] to cost; **was** ODER **wieviel kostet das?** how much is it?, how much does it cost?; **Fragen kostet nichts** there's no harm in asking - 2. [probieren] to taste, to try.

Kosten *pl* costs; **auf js ~** *(A)* at sb's expense; **auf js ~ gehen** to be at sb's expense; **auf ~ einer Sache** *(G)* **gehen** to be at the expense of sthg; **auf seine ~ kommen** to get one's money's worth; [bei einer Party] to have a good time.

kostenlos ◇ *adj* free ◇ *adv* free of charge.

Kosten|voranschlag *der* estimate.

köstlich ◇ *adj* - 1. [im Geschmack] delicious - 2. [amüsant] delightful ◇ *adv* - 1.: **~ speisen** to have a delicious meal - 2.: **sich ~ amüsieren** to enjoy o.s. enormously.

Kost|probe *die* [von Speise] taste; [von js Können] sample.

kostspielig *adj* costly.

Kostüm *(pl -e) das* - 1. [Rock und Jacke] suit - 2. [im Theater, zu Fasching] costume.

kostümieren ➤ **sich kostümieren** *ref* to dress up *(in fancy dress)*.

Kot *der* excrement.

Kotelett *(pl -s) das* chop, cutlet.

Koteletten *pl* sideboards *Br*, sideburns *Am*.

Kot|flügel *der* wing.

kotzen *vi salopp* to puke.

Krabbe (*pl* -n) *die* [Krebs] crab; [Garnele] shrimp.

krabbeln (*perf* hat/ist gekrabbelt) <> *vi* (*ist*) to crawl <> *vt* (*hat*) *fam* [kratzen] to scratch; [kitzeln] to tickle.

Krach (*pl* Kräche) *der* - **1.** [Lärm] racket; **~ machen** to make a racket - **2.** *fam* [Ärger] row; **er hat ~ mit seiner Freundin** he's rowing with his girlfriend - **3.** [Zusammenbruch] crash.

krachen (*perf* hat/ist gekracht) <> *vi* - **1.** (*hat*) [lärmen - Donner] to crash; [- Schuss] to ring out; [- Gewehr] to bang; **dann krachts!** there'll be trouble!; **an der Ecke hat es gekracht** there's been a crash on the corner - **2.** (*ist*) *fam* [kaputtgehen - Bett, Stuhl] to collapse; [- Reißverschluss, Brett] to split; [- Eis] to crack <> *vt* (*hat*) *fam* to bang.

krächzen <> *vi* [Rabe] to caw; [Person] to croak <> *vt* to croak out.

Kraft (*pl* Kräfte) *die* - **1.** [Körperkraft] strength (*U*); **am Ende seiner Kräfte sein** to be completely exhausted; **~/keine ~ haben** to be strong/weak - **2.** [Fähigkeit, Wirksamkeit] power; **aus eigener ~** by oneself; **mit vereinten Kräften** by joining forces - **3.** [Hilfskraft] helper. ➤ **Kräfte** *pl* [politisch] forces. ➤ **außer Kraft** *adv:* **außer ~ treten/sein** to cease to be/be no longer in force. ➤ **in Kraft** *adv:* **in ~ treten/setzen/sein** to come into/put into/be in force.

Kraft|fahrzeug *das amt* motor vehicle.

Kraft|fahrzeug|steuer *die amt* road tax *Br*, vehicle tax *Am*.

kräftig <> *adj* - **1.** [stark - Person] strong; [- Schlag] powerful; [- Körperbau, Stimme] powerful, strong - **2.** [Hunger, Farben] intense - **3.** [Mahlzeit] nourishing - **4.** [Fluch] coarse <> *adv* - **1.** [stark] hard - **2.** [fluchen] violently.

kräftigen *vt* to strengthen.

kraftlos <> *adj* weak <> *adv* [wanken] weakly; [herabhängen] limply.

Kraft|probe *die* trial of strength.

Kraft|stoff *der* fuel.

kraftvoll <> *adj* powerful <> *adv* powerfully.

Kraft|werk *das* power station.

Kragen (*pl* - ODER Krägen) *der* collar; **es geht jm an den ~** *fam fig* sb is in for it; **ihr platzte der ~** *fam fig* she blew her top.

Krähe (*pl* -n) *die* crow.

krähen *vi* to crow.

Kralle (*pl* -n) *die* claw.

Kram *der fam* - **1.** [Zeug] stuff; **jm nicht in den ~ passen** *fam fig* not to fit in with sb's plans - **2.** [Arbeit] business.

kramen *vi* to rummage about.

Krampf (*pl* Krämpfe) *der* cramp; **einen ~ bekommen/haben** to get/have cramp.

Krampf|ader *die* varicose vein.

krampfhaft <> *adj* [Husten, Verrenkungen] convulsive; [Anstrengungen] strenuous <> *adv* [zucken] convulsively; [lächeln] in a strained way; **sich ~ bemühen** to make strenuous efforts; **~ nachdenken** to rack one's brains.

Kran (*pl* Kräne) *der* crane.

krank (*kompar* kränker; *superl* am kränksten) *adj* sick, ill; **er ist ~** he is ill ODER sick; **~ werden** to be taken ill; **diese ständigen Streitereien machen mich ~** these constant arguments are getting on my nerves.

Kranke (*pl* -n) *der, die* sick person; [im Krankenhaus] patient.

kranken *vi*: **an etw** (*D*) **~** to suffer from sthg.

kränken *vt* to hurt.

Kranken|geld *das* (*ohne pl*) sickness benefit.

Kranken|gymnastik *die* physiotherapy.

Kranken|haus *das* hospital.

Kranken|kasse *die* health insurance association.

Kranken|pfleger *der* (male) nurse.

Kranken|schwester *die* nurse.

Kranken|versicherung *die* health insurance.

Kranken|wagen *der* ambulance.

krankhaft <> *adj* pathological <> *adv* [übertrieben] pathologically.

Krankheit (*pl* -en) *die* - **1.** [Zustand] illness - **2.** [bestimmte Krankheit] disease.

kränklich *adj* sickly.

krank|melden ➤ **sich krankmelden** *ref* to report sick.

Kränkung (*pl* -en) *die* hurt.

Kranz (*pl* Kränze) *der* - **1.** [Schmuck] wreath - **2.** [Kuchen] ring.

krass <> *adj* [Gegensatz] stark; [Verstoß, Fall] blatant <> *adv* [ausdrücken] bluntly.

Krater (*pl* -) *der* crater.

kratzen <> *vi* - **1.** [verletzen] to scratch - **2.** [schaben] to scrape - **3.** [jucken] to itch; **es kratzt im Hals** I've got a tickle in my throat <> *vt* - **1.** [verletzen] to scratch - **2.** [schaben] to scrape - **3.** [jucken]: **jn ~** to make sb itch. ➤ **sich kratzen** *ref* to scratch o.s.

Kratzer (*pl* -) *der* scratch.

kratzig *adj* - **1.** [rau] scratchy - **2.** [heiser] rough.

Kraul *das* SPORT crawl.

kraulen (*perf* hat/ist gekrault) <> *vi* (*ist*) SPORT to do the crawl <> *vt* (*hat*) [streicheln] to tickle.

kraus *adj* - **1.** [lockig] frizzy - **2.** [gerunzelt] wrinkled - **3.** [wirr] confused.

kräuseln *vt* - **1.** [in Locken] to frizz - **2.** [in Wellen] to ripple. ➤ **sich kräuseln** *ref* [in Locken] to go frizzy.

Kraut (*pl* Kräuter) *das* - **1.** (*ohne pl*) [Kohl] cabbage - **2.** (*ohne pl*) [Grünes] leaves (*pl*) - **3.** *fam* [Tabak] weed - **4.** *RW:* **dagegen ist kein ~ gewachsen** there is no cure for it. ◆ **Kräuter** *pl* herbs.

Kräuter|tee *der* herbal tea.

Krawall (*pl* -e) *der* [Krach, Lärm] row; **~ machen** to make a row. ◆ **Krawalle** *pl* [Unruhen] riots.

Krawatte (*pl* -n) *die* tie.

kreativ *adj* creative.

Kreativität [kreativi'tɛːt] *die* creativity.

Kreatur (*pl* -en) *die* creature.

Krebs (*pl* -e) *der* - **1.** [Tier] crab - **2.** (*ohne pl*) [Tumor] cancer; **~ haben** to have cancer - **3.** ASTROL Cancer; **~ sein** to be a Cancer.

Kredit (*pl* -e) *der* [Darlehen] credit (*U*); **einen ~ aufnehmen/gewähren** to take out/grant credit.

Kredit|karte *die* credit card.

Kreide (*pl* -n) *die* chalk; **bei jm in der ~ stehen** *fig* to be in debt to sb.

kreideweiß *adj* as white as a sheet.

kreieren [kre'iːrən] *vt* to create.

Kreis (*pl* -e) *der* - **1.** [Form, Personenkreis] circle; **im ~** in a circle - **2.** [Verwaltungsbezirk] district - **3.** *RW:* **-e ziehen** to have repercussions; **sich im ~ drehen** to go round in circles.

kreischen *vi* [Person] to shriek; [Tier, Säge, Bremsen] to screech.

kreisen (*perf* hat/ist gekreist) *vi* - **1.** [sich drehen] to circle; **die Erde kreist um die Sonne** the earth goes round the sun - **2.** [Gedanken]: **um etw ~** to revolve aroung sthg.

Kreis|lauf *der* - **1.** [Zyklus] cycle - **2.** [Blutkreislauf] circulation.

Kreis|laufstörungen *pl* circulatory trouble (*U*).

Kreis|säge *die* - **1.** [Säge] circular saw - **2.** [Hut] boater.

Kreis|stadt *die* chief town of a district.

Kreis|verkehr *der* roundabout *Br,* traffic circle *Am.*

Krem (*pl* -s) *die* = Creme.

Kreme (*pl* -s ODER -n) *die* = Creme.

kremig *adj* = cremig.

Krempe (*pl* -n) *die* brim.

Krempel *der* *fam* junk.

Krepppapier *das* crepe paper.

Kresse (*pl* -n) *die* cress (*U*).

Kreta *nt* Crete.

Kreuz (*pl* -e) *das* - **1.** [Zeichen & REL] cross; **über ~** crosswise - **2.** [Rücken] small of the back; **mir tut das ~ weh** my back aches; **jn aufs ~ legen** *fam* *fig* to take sb for a ride - **3.** [Autobahnkreuz] intersection - **4.** (*ohne pl*) [Qual] burden - **5.** (*ohne Artikel, ohne pl*) [Spielfarbe] clubs (*pl*) - **6.** [Spielkarte] club; **die ~sechs** the six of clubs.

kreuzen (*perf* hat/ist gekreuzt) ◇ *vt* (hat)

to cross ◇ *vi* (hat, ist) - **1.** [Boot - hin und her fahren] to cruise - **2.** [gegen den Wind segeln] to tack. ◆ **sich kreuzen** *ref* - **1.** [Weg, Brief, Linie] to cross - **2.** [Ansichten] to clash.

Kreuz|fahrt *die* cruise.

Kreuz|gang *der* cloister.

kreuzigen *vt* to crucify.

Kreuzigung (*pl* -en) *die* crucifixion.

Kreuzung (*pl* -en) *die* - **1.** [Straßenkreuzung] crossroads (*sg*) - **2.** [Züchtung] cross.

Kreuzwort|rätsel *das* crossword (puzzle).

kriechen (*prät* kroch; *perf* ist gekrochen) *vi* - **1.** [Wurm, Verkehr, Kind] to crawl - **2.** [Zeit] to creep by - **3.** *abw* [unterwürfig sein]: **vor jm ~** to crawl to sb.

Kriech|spur *die* crawler lane.

Krieg (*pl* -e) *der* war; **jm/einer Sache den ~ erklären** to declare war on sb/sthg.

kriegen *vt* *fam* [bekommen] to get; [Zug, Bus, Straßenbahn] to catch; [gebären - Kind] to have; **wenn wir den ~!** just wait till we get hold of him!

Kriegs|dienstverweigerer (*pl* -) *der* conscientious objector.

Kriegs|gefangene *der, die* prisoner of war.

Krimi (*pl* -s) *der* *fam* thriller.

Kriminal|beamte *der* detective.

Kriminal|beamtin *die* detective.

Kriminalität *die* crime.

Kriminalpolizei *die* ≃ Criminal Investigation Department *Br,* ≃ Federal Bureau of Investigation *Am.*

kriminell *adj* criminal; **~ werden** to turn to crime.

Kripo (*abk für* Kriminalpolizei) *die* ≃ CID *Br,* ≃ FBI *Am.*

Krippe (*pl* -n) *die* - **1.** [Kinderkrippe] crèche *Br,* day nursery *Am* - **2.** [Futterkrippe] manger - **3.** [Weihnachtskrippe] crib.

Krise (*pl* -n) *die* crisis; **in einer ~ stecken** to be in (a) crisis.

Krisen|herd *der* trouble spot.

Kristall (*pl* -e) *das* ODER *der* crystal.

Kriterium (*pl* Kriterien) *das* criterion.

Kritik (*pl* -en) *die* - **1.** [Beurteilung] criticism; **an jm/etw ~ üben** to criticize sb/sthg - **2.** [Rezension] review.

Kritiker, in (*mpl* -; *fpl* -nen) *der, die* critic.

kritisch ◇ *adj* critical ◇ *adv* - **1.** [prüfend, negativ] critically - **2.** [gefährlich]: **es steht ~ um den Kranken** the patient is critical.

kritisieren *vt* to criticize.

kritzeln *vt* to scribble.

Kroatien [kro'aːtsjən] *nt* Croatia.

kroatisch [kro'aːtɪʃ] *adj* Croatian.

kroch *prät* ▷ kriechen.

Krokant *der* (*ohne pl*) praline.

Krokodil (*pl* -e) *das* crocodile.

Krokus (*pl* -se) *der* crocus.

Krone (*pl* -n) *die* - **1.** [gen] crown - **2.** [Herrschaft] Crown - **3.** [Währung · dänische] krone; [- schwedische] krona - **4.** *RW*: **einer Sache** (*D*) **die ~ aufsetzen** to cap sthg.

krönen *vt* to crown; **jn zum König ~** to crown sb king.

Kronlleuchter *der* chandelier.

Krönung (*pl* -en) *die* - **1.** [das Krönen] coronation - **2.** [Höhepunkt] culmination.

Kropf (*pl* Kröpfe) *der* goitre.

Kröte (*pl* -n) *die* toad.

Krücke (*pl* -n) *die* - **1.** [Stock] crutch - **2.** *fam abw* [Person] clown.

Krug (*pl* Krüge) *der* [für Milch, Wein] jug; [für Bier] mug.

Krümel (*pl* -) *der* crumb.

krumm <> *adj* - **1.** [Linie] curved; [Nagel, Rücken] bent; [Nase] hooked; [Finger, Beine] crooked - **2.** *fam* [unehrlich] crooked; **auf eine ~e Tour** by crooked means <> *adv* [gehen, stehen] with a stoop; [sitzen] bent over.

krümmen *vt* to bend. ⇒ **sich krümmen** *ref* to bend; [vor Schmerzen] to double up.

krumm nehmen *vt* (*unreg*) *fam* to take offence at; **jm etw ~** to hold sthg against sb.

Krümmung (*pl* -en) *die* [von Horizont, Rücken] curve; [von Straße, Fluss] bend.

Krüppel (*pl* -) *der* cripple.

Kruste (*pl* -n) *die* - **1.** [Rinde] crust - **2.** [Schicht] scab.

Kruzifix (*pl* -e) *das* crucifix.

Kto. (*abk für* Konto) a/c.

Kuba *nt* Cuba; **auf ~** in Cuba.

Kübel (*pl* -) *der* [für Abfälle] bin; [für Pflanzen] tub.

Kubiklmeter *der* cubic metre.

Küche (*pl* -n) *die* - **1.** [Raum] kitchen - **2.** [Kochen] cooking; **kalte/warme ~** cold/hot food.

Kuchen (*pl* -) *der* cake.

Kuchenlblech *das* baking sheet.

Kuchenlform *die* cake tin *Br* ODER pan *Am*.

Kuchenlgabel *die* cake fork.

Küchenlschabe *die* cockroach.

Kuckuck (*pl* -e) *der* cuckoo.

Kufe (*pl* -n) *die* runner.

Kugel (*pl* -n) *die* - **1.** [gen & SPORT] ball; [am Weihnachtsbaum] bauble; [beim Kugelstoßen] shot - **2.** [Form] sphere - **3.** [Geschoss] bullet - **4.** *RW*: **eine ruhige ~ schieben** *fam fig* to have it easy.

Kugellager *das* ball bearing.

Kugelschreiber (*pl* -) *der* ballpoint (pen), Biro.®

kugelsicher *adj* bullet-proof.

Kugelstoßen *das* SPORT shot put.

Kuh (*pl* Kühe) *die* cow.

kühl <> *adj* cool <> *adv* coolly; **~ servieren**

serve chilled; **~ und trocken lagern** keep in a cool, dry place.

kühlen *vt* to cool.

Kühler (*pl* -) *der* - **1.** AUTO radiator - **2.** [für Getränke] cooler.

Kühlerlhaube *die* bonnet *Br*, hood *Am*.

Kühllschrank *der* fridge.

Kühltruhe *die* freezer.

Kühlung (*pl* -en) *die* - **1.** [Erfrischung] coolness - **2.** TECH cooling.

kühn *adj* bold.

Küken (*pl* -) *das* - **1.** [Tier] chick - **2.** *fam fig* [Nesthäkchen] baby; [Mädchen] little girl.

kulant *adj* [Verkäufer, Geschäftspartner] obliging; [Preis] reasonable.

Kuli (*pl* -s) *der* - **1.** [Mensch] coolie - **2.** *fam* [Schreiber] Biro.®

Kulisse (*pl* -n) *die* - **1.** [Bühnenbild] scenery (*U*) - **2.** [Hintergrund] background.

kullern (*perf* ist gekullert) *vi* to roll.

Kult (*pl* -e) *der* cult.

kultivieren [kulti'vi:rən] *vt* to cultivate.

kultiviert [kulti'vi:ɐt] <> *adj* refined <> *adv* in a refined manner.

Kultur (*pl* -en) *die* culture.

Kulturlbeutel *der* toilet bag.

kulturell <> *adj* cultural <> *adv* culturally.

Kultuslminister, in *der, die* minister of a German Federal state responsible for education and cultural affairs.

Kümmel (*pl* -) *der* - **1.** (ohne *pl*) [Gewürzpflanze] caraway - **2.** [Schnaps] kümmel.

Kummer *der* worries (*pl*); **~ mit jm haben** to worry about sb; **jm ~ machen** to worry sb.

kümmerlich *adj* miserable.

kümmern *vt* to concern; **das kümmert sie nicht** she doesn't care about that; **was kümmert es ihn?** what is it to him? ⇒ **kümmern** *ref*: **sich um jn ~** [helfen] to look after sb; **sich um etw ~** [organisieren, zubereiten] to see to sthg; [beachten] to worry about sthg; **kümmere dich um deine eigenen Angelegenheiten!** mind your own business!

Kumpel (*pl* -) *der* - **1.** [Bergarbeiter] miner - **2.** *fam* [Kamerad] pal.

kündbar *adj* [Stellung, Vertrag] terminable; [Mitarbeiter] dismissible.

Kunde (*pl* -n) *der* customer.

Kundenldienst *der* - **1.** [Service] customer service - **2.** [Servicestelle] customer service department.

Kundgebung (*pl* -en) *die* rally.

kündigen <> *vi* [Arbeitnehmer] to hand in one's notice; [Mieter] to give notice that one is leaving; **jm ~** [Firma] to give sb his/her notice; [Vermieter] to give sb notice to quit <> *vt* [Vertrag, Kredit] to terminate; **seine Arbeitsstelle ~** to hand in one's notice; **seine Wohnung ~** to give notice that one is leaving; **jm die Freundschaft ~** to break off one's friendship with sb.

Kündigung (*pl* -en) *die* [von Vertrag] termination; [von Arbeitsstelle] notice; [von Wohnung] notice to quit; **jm die ~ aussprechen** to give sb his/her notice.

Kündigungsfrist *die* period of notice.

Kündigungsschutz *der* [für Mieter] protection against wrongful eviction; [für Arbeitnehmer] protection against wrongful dismissal.

Kundin (*pl* -nen) *die* customer.

Kundschaft *die* (*ohne pl*) customers (*pl*).

künftig <> *adj* future <> *adv* in future.

Kunst (*pl* Künste) *die* art; **das ist keine ~!** there is nothing to it!

Kunstdünger *der* artificial fertilizer.

Kunsterziehung *die* (*ohne pl*) art lessons (*pl*).

Kunstfaser *die* synthetic fibre.

Kunstfehler *der* professional error.

kunstfertig <> *adj* skilful <> *adv* skilfully.

Kunstgegenstand *der* objet d'art.

Kunstgeschichte *die* history of art.

Kunstgewerbe *das* (*ohne pl*) arts and crafts (*pl*).

Kunsthandwerk *das* craft.

Künstler, in (*mpl* -; *fpl* -nen) *der, die* - **1.** [Kunstschaffende] artist - **2.** [Könner] master.

künstlerisch <> *adj* artistic <> *adv* artistically.

Künstlername *der* pseudonym.

künstlich <> *adj* - **1.** [nicht natürlich] artificial - **2.** [übertrieben] forced <> *adv* - **1.** [nicht natürlich] artificially - **2.** [übertrieben] in a forced way.

Kunststoff *der* plastic.

Kunststück *das* - **1.** [Trick] trick - **2.** [Leistung] feat.

Kunstwerk *das* work of art.

kunterbunt <> *adj* varied <> *adv* in a jumble.

Kupfer *das* copper.

Kuppe (*pl* -n) *die* - **1.** [landschaftlich] (hill)top - **2.** [von Fingern] tip.

Kuppel (*pl* -n) *die* dome.

Kupplung (*pl* -en) *die* - **1.** [in Auto] clutch - **2.** [für Anhänger] coupling.

Kur (*pl* -en) *die* health cure; **auf** ODER **zur ~ sein/gehen** to be/go on a health cure.

Kür (*pl* -en) *die* free programme.

Kurbel (*pl* -n) *die* [von Fenster, Rollo] winder; [von Drehorgel, Spieluhr] handle; [von Maschine, zum Aufziehen] crank.

Kürbis (*pl* -se) *der* pumpkin.

Kurdistan *nt* Kurdistan.

Kurgast *der* visitor to a health resort.

Kurier (*pl* -e) *der* courier.

kurieren *vt* to cure; **von etw kuriert sein** *fam fig* to be cured of sthg.

kurios *adj* curious.

Kuriosität (*pl* -en) *die* curiosity.

Kurort *der* health resort.

Kurs (*pl* -e) *der* - **1.** [Fahrtrichtung, Lehrgang] course - **2.** [Teilnehmer] course members (*pl*) - **3.** [Marktpreis - von Aktien] price; [- von Währung] exchange rate; **hoch im ~ stehen** to be very popular.

Kursbuch *das* timetable.

kursieren *vi* to circulate.

Kursus (*pl* Kurse) *der* course.

Kurtaxe *die* tax paid by visitors to health resorts.

Kurve ['kʊrvə] (*pl* -n) *die* - **1.** [Straßenkrümmung] bend; **die Straße macht eine ~** the road bends - **2.** [Bogenlinie] curve.

kurvenreich *adj* [Straße] winding; [Frau] curvaceous.

kurz (*kompar* kürzer; *superl* kürzeste) <> *adj* - **1.** [räumlich] short; **was ist der kürzeste Weg zum Bahnhof?** what's the quickest way to the station? - **2.** [zeitlich] short, brief; **innerhalb ~er Zeit** within a short space of time; **vor ~em** recently; **über ~ oder lang** sooner or later <> *adv* - **1.** [räumlich]: **vor/hinter** just in front of/behind; **alles ~ und klein schlagen** *fam* to smash everything to pieces - **2.** [zeitlich] briefly; **ich gehe mal ~ in das Geschäft dort** I'm just popping into that shop; **~ vor dem Konzert** shortly before the concert.

kurzärmelig, kurzärmlig <> *adj* short-sleeved <> *adv* in short sleeves.

Kürze *die* shortness. **➠ in Kürze** *adv* shortly.

kürzen *vt* - **1.** [Haare, Nägel, Film, Text] to cut; [Rock, Kabel] to shorten - **2.** [finanziell] to cut - **3.** MATH to cancel.

kurzerhand *adv* without further ado.

kurzfristig <> *adj* - **1.** [unangemeldet] sudden - **2.** [kurz dauernd] short-term - **3.** [rasch] quick <> *adv* - **1.** [unangemeldet] at short notice - **2.** [kurz dauernd] for a short time - **3.** [rasch] quickly.

Kurzgeschichte *die* short story.

kurzhaarig *adj* short-haired.

kürzlich *adv* recently.

kurzschließen *vt* (*unreg*) to short-circuit. **➠ sich kurzschließen** *ref* to get in touch.

Kurzschluss *der* - **1.** [elektrisch] short-circuit - **2.** [seelisch]: **er muss es aus einem ~ heraus getan haben** something must have snapped to make him do that.

kurzsichtig <> *adj* *eigtl* & *fig* short-sighted <> *adv* short-sightedly.

Kürzung (*pl* -en) *die* cut.

Kurzwahltaste *die* EDV speed-dial button.

Kurzwelle *die* short wave.

kuschelig *adj* cosy.

kuscheln *vi* to cuddle up; **mit jm** ~ to cuddle sb. ◆ **sich kuscheln** *ref* to cuddle up; **sich an jn** ~ to cuddle up to sb.

Kusine (*pl* -n) *die* cousin.

Kuss (*pl* Küsse) *der* kiss.

küssen *vt & vi* to kiss. ◆ **sich küssen** *ref* to kiss.

Küste (*pl* -n) *die* coast.

Küster, in (*mpl* -; *fpl* -nen) *der, die* verger.

Kutsche (*pl* -n) *die* - **1.** [Pferdewagen] coach - **2.** *fam* [Auto] jalopy, motor *Br*.

Kuvert [ku'vɛːɐ̯] (*pl* -e) *das* envelope.

KZ [kaː'tsɛt] (*pl* -s) *das abk für* Konzentrationslager.

L

l, L [ɛl] (*pl* - ODER -s) *das* l, L. ◆ **l** (*abk für* Liter) l.

labil *adj* unstable; [Kreislauf] bad; [Konstitution, Gleichgewicht] delicate.

Labor (*pl* -s ODER -e) *das* laboratory.

Laborant, in (*mpl* -en; *fpl* -nen) *der, die* laboratory technician.

Labyrinth (*pl* -e) *das* maze.

Lache (*pl* -n) *die* [von Wasser] puddle; [von Blut, Öl] pool.

lächeln *vi* to smile; **über jn/etw** ~ to smile about sb/at sthg.

Lächeln *das (ohne pl)* smile.

lachen *vi* to laugh; **über jn/etw** ~ to laugh at sb/sthg; **es** ODER **das wäre doch gelacht, wenn ...** *fig* it would be ridiculous if ...; **du hast gut** ~! *fig* it's all right for you!

Lachen *das* laughter; **ein leises** ~ a quiet laugh; **jn zum** ~ **bringen** to make sb laugh; **etw ist zum** ~ *fam fig* sthg is laughable; **ihm wird das** ~ **schon noch vergehen** he'll soon be laughing on the other side of his face.

lächerlich *adj* [komisch] ridiculous; **jn/sich** ~ **machen** to make a fool of sb/o.s.

Lächerliche *das*: **etw ins** ~ **ziehen** to make a joke out of sthg.

lachhaft *adj* ludicrous.

Lachs [laks] (*pl* -e) *der* salmon.

Lack (*pl* -e) *der* [farblos] varnish; [farbig] paint; [Nagellack] varnish *Br*, polish *Am*.

lackieren *vt* - **1.** [Holz] to varnish; [Auto] to spray - **2.** [mit Nagellack] to paint.

Lackierung (*pl* -en) *die* - **1.** [Lackieren - von

Holz] varnishing; [- von Auto] spraying - **2.** [Lack - farblos] varnish; [- farbig] paint.

Ladefläche *die* load area.

laden (*präs* lädt; *prät* lud; *perf* hat geladen) ◇ *vt* - **1.** [Fracht, Waffe & EDV] to load; **der LKW hat Kies geladen** the lorry has loaded up with gravel; **etw auf/in etw** (*A*) ~ to load sthg onto/into sthg - **2.** [mit Elektrizität] to charge - **3.** *geh* [vorladen] to summon ◇ *vi* [mit einer Last] to load up; **der Laster hat schwer geladen** the truck is heavily laden.

Laden (*pl* Läden) *der* - **1.** [Geschäft] shop *Br*, store *Am* - **2.** *fam* [Angelegenheit] business - **3.** *fam* [Betrieb] outfit.

Ladendieb, in *der, die* shoplifter.

Ladenschluss *der* closing time.

Ladentisch *der* counter.

Laderampe *die* loading platform.

lädieren *vt* to damage.

lädt *präs* ▷ laden.

Ladung (*pl* -en) *die* - **1.** [gen] load - **2.** [zum Schießen] charge - **3.** PHYS: **positive/negative** ~ positive/negative charge.

lag *prät* ▷ liegen.

Lage (*pl* -n) *die* - **1.** [Stelle, Stellung] position - **2.** [Situation] situation; **zu etw in der** ~ **sein** to be able to do sthg; **in der** ~ **sein, etw zu tun** to be able to do sthg; **sich in js** (*A*) **versetzen** to put o.s. in sb's position - **3.** [Schicht] layer.

Lager (*pl* -) *das* - **1.** *eigtl & fig* [Feldlager, Gesinnung] camp - **2.** [für Waren] store; **etw auf** ~ **haben** [als Ware] to have sthg in stock; [zur Unterhaltung] to be ready with sthg - **3.** TECH bearing.

Lagerbestand *der* stock.

Lagerfeuer *das* camp fire.

Lagerhaus *das* warehouse.

lagern ◇ *vt* - **1.** [aufbewahren] to store - **2.**: **einen Kranken bequem** ~ to make an ill person comfortable; **den Arm hoch** ~ to put one's arm in a raised position ◇ *vi* [kampieren] to camp.

Lagerung (*pl* -en) *die* storage (*U*).

lahm ◇ *adj* - **1.** [gelähmt, Ausrede] lame - **2.** [ermüdet] stiff - **3.** [matt - Mensch] dull; [- Bewegung] sluggish ◇ *adv fam* [sich bewegen] sluggishly; [sich entschuldigen] lamely.

lähmen *vt eigtl & fig* to paralyse.

lahm legen *vt* to bring to a standstill.

Lähmung (*pl* -en) *die eigtl & fig* paralysis.

Laib (*pl* -e) *der*: **ein** ~ **Brot** a loaf of bread; **ein** ~ **Käse** a cheese.

Laie ['laiə] (*pl* -n) *der* layman (*f* laywoman); **ein medizinischer** ~ a layman when it comes to medicine.

laienhaft ['laiənhaft] ◇ *adj* inexpert ◇ *adv* inexpertly.

Laken (*pl* -) *das* sheet.

Lakritz (*pl* -e) *das* ODER *der* liquorice.
lallen *vt* & *vi* to babble.
Lama (*pl* -s) *das* llama.
Lamelle (*pl* -n) *die* - **1.** [von Jalousie] slat
- **2.** [von Heizkörper] fin - **3.** [von Pilzen] gill.
Lamm (*pl* Lämmer) *das* lamb.
Lampe (*pl* -n) *die* light; [Bürolampe, Steh-
lampe] lamp.
Lampenfieber *das* stage fright.
Lampen|schirm *der* lampshade.
Land (*pl* Länder) *das* - **1.** [Staatsgebiet, ländli-
che Gegend] country; **jn des ~es verweisen**
to deport sb; **auf dem ~** in the country
- **2.** [Gelände, Festland] land; **an ~ gehen** to go
ashore - **3.** [Bundesland - in Deutschland]
state; [- in Österreich] province - **4.** *RW:* **wieder im ~(e) sein** to be back. ➡ **hier zu Lande** *adv* = hierzulande.
Land|bevölkerung *die* rural population.
Lande|bahn *die* runway.
landen (*perf* hat/ist gelandet) ⬦ *vi (ist)*
- **1.** [nach einem Flug] to land - **2.** *fam* [ankom-
men] to land up; **bei jm (mit etw) nicht
~ können** *fam* not to be able to get anywhere
with sb (by using sthg) ⬦ *vt (hat) eigtl* & *fig*
to land.
Lande|platz *der* landing strip.
Länder|spiel *das* international match.
Landes|ebene *die:* **auf ~** at state level.
Landeshaupt|mann *der* Österr head of a re-
gional government in Austria.
Landes|innere *das* interior (of the country).
Landes|kunde *die* study of a country and its
culture.
Landes|regierung *die* state government.
Landes|sprache *die* national language.
Landesverrat *der* treason.
Landes|währung *die* national currency.
Land|haus *das* country house.
Land|karte *die* map.
Land|kreis *der* district.
landläufig *adj* popular.
Landleben *das* country life.
ländlich *adj* rural.
Landschaft (*pl* -en) *die* [Gelände] countryside; [Abbildung] landscape.
landschaftlich ⬦ *adj* [Schönheit, Beson-
derheit] of the countryside; [Sitte] regional
⬦ *adv:* **der Schwarzwald ist ~ schön** the
Black Forest countryside is beautiful.
Landsleute *pl* compatriots.
Land|straße *die* country road.
Land|streicher, in (*mpl* -; *fpl* -nen) *der, die*
tramp.
Land|strich *der* area.
Land|tag *der* - **1.** [Volksvertretung] state par-
liament - **2.** [Gebäude] state parliament
building.
Landung (*pl* -en) *die* landing.

Land|weg *der* overland route.
Land|wirt, in *der, die* farmer.
Land|wirtschaft *die* [Agrarwesen] agricul-
ture.
lang (*kompar* länger; *superl* längste) ⬦ *adj*
long; [Person] tall; **drei Meter ~** three metres
long; **vor ~er Zeit** a long time ago; **vor nicht
zu ~er Zeit** not (so) long ago; **drei ~e Jahre**
three long years ⬦ *adv fam* - **1.** [entlang]
along; **hier/dort ~** this/that way - **2.** [zeitlich]:
drei Jahre ~ for three years; **den ganzen Tag
~** all day.
langärmelig, langärmlig *adj* long-
sleeved.
langatmig ⬦ *adj* long-winded ⬦ *adv*
long-windedly.
lange (*kompar* länger; *superl* am längsten)
adv [während langer Zeit] a long time; [seit
langer Zeit] for a long time; **es dauert nicht
mehr ~** it won't be long; **das mache ich nicht
mehr länger** I won't be doing this for much
longer; **das ist noch ~ nicht alles** that's not all
by any means; **ich war schon ~ nicht mehr zu
Hause** I haven't been home for a long time;
etw ist ~ her sthg was a long time ago.
Länge (*pl* -n) *die* - **1.** [von Brett, Brief] length;
ein Stau von 5 km ~ a 5 km-long traffic jam;
der ~ nach [teilen] lengthways; [hinstürzen]
flat on one's face - **2.** (*ohne pl*) [Körpergröße]
height - **3.** GEOGR longitude - **4.** (*ohne pl*) [Dau-
er] length; **in die ~ ziehen** to drag out.
➡ **Längen** *pl* [von Film] tedious scenes;
[von Buch] tedious passages.
langen *vi fam* - **1.** [ausreichen] to be enough;
mir langt es! *fam* that's enough! - **2.** [greifen]
to reach.
Längen|grad *der* degree of longitude.
Längen|maß *das* unit of length.
längerfristig ⬦ *adj* longer-term ⬦ *adv*
on a longer-term basis.
Langeweile, Langeweile *die* boredom;
aus ~ out of boredom.
langfristig ⬦ *adj* long-term ⬦ *adv* on a
long-term basis.
Langlauf *der* SPORT cross-country skiing.
langlebig *adj* - **1.** [lange lebend] long-lived
- **2.** [lange gebrauchsfähig] durable.
länglich *adj* oblong.
längs ⬦ *präp:* **~ einer Sache** (*G*) along sthg
⬦ *adv* lengthways.
Längs|achse ['lɛŋsaksə] *die* longitudinal
axis.
langsam ⬦ *adj* - **1.** [nicht schnell] slow
- **2.** [allmählich] gradual ⬦ *adv* - **1.** [nicht
schnell] slowly - **2.** [nach und nach] gradually; **das wird ja ~ Zeit!** it's about time!
Langschläfer, in (*mpl* -; *fpl* -nen) *der, die*
late riser.
Längs|richtung *die:* **in ~** lengthways.
Längs|seite *die* long side.

längst *adv* for a long time; **sie war ~ tot** she was long since dead, she had died a long time ago; **~ nicht** nowhere near.

längstens *adv fam* - **1.** [höchstens] at (the) most - **2.** [seit langem] for a long time; **es war ~ entschieden** it was long since agreed, it had been agreed a long time ago.

Langstrecken|lauf *der* [Wettbewerb] long-distance race; [Sportart] long-distance running (U).

Languste [laŋˈgʊstə] (*pl -n*) *die* crayfish.

langweilen *vt* to bore. ◆ **sich langweilen** *ref* to be bored.

langweilig ◇ *adj* - **1.** [uninteressant] boring - **2.** *fam* [Zeit raubend] slow ◇ *adv* boringly.

Langwelle *die* long wave.

langwierig *adj* lengthy.

Lanze (*pl -n*) *die* spear.

Lappalie [laˈpaːliə] (*pl -n*) *die* trifle.

Lappen (*pl -*) *der* cloth; **etw geht jm durch die ~** *fam* fig sthg slips through sb's fingers.

läppern ◆ **sich läppern** *ref*: **das** ODER **es läppert sich** it mounts up.

läppisch *adj abw* - **1.** [albern] silly - **2.** [lächerlich] ridiculous.

Laptop [ˈlɛptɔp] (*pl -s*) *der* EDV laptop.

Lärche (*pl -n*) *die* larch.

Lärm *der* noise; **~ schlagen** *fam* fig to kick up a fuss.

lärmen *vi* to make a noise; [Radio] to blare.

Larve [ˈlarfə] (*pl -n*) *die* larva.

las *prät* ▷ lesen.

lasch ▷ *adj* - **1.** [Bewegung, Spiel] listless; [Händedruck] limp - **2.** [fade] insipid - **3.** [nachlässig] lax ◇ *adv* - **1.** [schlaff] listlessly - **2.** [fade] insipidly - **3.** [nachlässig] laxly.

Lasche (*pl -n*) *die* [von Umschlag] flap; [von Schuh] tongue.

Laser [ˈleːzɐ] (*pl -*) *der* laser.

Laser|drucker *der* EDV laser printer.

lassen (*präs* lässt; *prät* ließ; *perf hat gelassen* ODER *-*) ◇ *vt* - **1.** [geschehen lassen] to let; **jn nicht ins Haus ~** not to let sb in the house; **Wasser in die Badewanne ~** to run a bath - **2.** [unterlassen] to stop; **das Rauchen ~** to stop smoking; **lass das!** stop it! - **3.** [überlassen]: **jm etw ~** to let sb have sthg; **eines muss man dir ~** ... *fig* I'll say this much for you ... - **4.** [belassen, zurücklassen] to leave; **lass mich!** let me go!; **lass alles so, wie es ist** leave everything as it is ◇ *vi* (*perf hat gelassen*) - **1.** [belassen]: **von jm/etw ~** *geh* to abandon sb/sthg - **2.** [geschehen lassen]: **lass mal, ich mach das schon!** leave it, I'll do it ◇ *aux* - **1.** [veranlassen]: **etw machen** ODER **tun ~** to have sthg done; **jn etw tun ~** to have sb do sthg; **sich** (*D*) **die Haare schneiden ~** to get ODER have one's hair cut; **sich** (*D*) **einen An-**

zug machen ~ to have a suit made - **2.** [belassen] leave; **lass die Vase auf dem Tisch stehen** leave the vase on the table - **3.** [geschehen lassen]: **jn etw tun ~** to let sb do sthg; **ich lasse mich überraschen** I want it to be a surprise; **etw mit sich/nicht mit sich machen ~** to put up/not to put up with sthg; **die Vase fallen ~** to drop the vase; **jn warten ~** to keep sb waiting. ◆ **sich lassen** *ref* (*perf hat lassen*): **das lässt sich machen** it can be done; **die Fenster ~ sich nicht öffnen** the windows don't open.

lässig ◇ *adj* casual ◇ *adv* - **1.** [salopp] casually - **2.** *fam* [leicht] easily.

Lässigkeit *die* [Lockerheit] casualness; [Leichtigkeit] ease.

lässt *präs* ▷ lassen.

Last (*pl -en*) *die* - **1.** [Gewicht] load - **2.** *geh* [Bürde] burden - **3.** *RW:* **jm zur ~ fallen** to be a burden on sb; **jm etw zur ~ legen** to accuse sb of sthg. ◆ **Lasten** *pl* [Kosten] costs; **zu js ~en** chargeable to sb.

lasten *vi* - **1.** [Gewicht]: **auf jm ~** to weigh sb down; **auf etw** (*D*) **~** [auf Schultern] to weigh down on sthg; [auf Pfeilern] to bear down on sthg - **2.** [Verantwortung]: **auf jm ~** to weigh on sb - **3.** [finanziell]: **auf jm/etw ~** to be a burden on sb/sthg.

Laster (*pl -*) ◇ *das* [Untugend] vice ◇ *der* *fam* [Lastwagen] truck, lorry *Br*.

lästern *vi*: **über jn/etw ~** to make nasty remarks about sb/sthg.

lästig *adj* annoying; **jm ~ werden/sein** to become/be a nuisance to sb.

Lastkraft|wagen *der amt* heavy goods vehicle.

Last-Minute-|Flug [laːstˈmɪnɪtfluːk] *der* last-minute flight.

Last|schrift *die* [Abbuchung] debit; [Mitteilung] debit advice.

Last|wagen *der* truck, lorry *Br*.

Latein *das* Latin; *siehe auch* Englisch(e).

Lateinamerika *nt* Latin America.

lateinisch *adj* Latin.

latent ◇ *adj* latent ◇ *adv* latently.

Laterne (*pl -n*) *die* - **1.** [Lampion] Chinese lantern - **2.** [Straßenlaterne] streetlamp.

Latinum *das*: **großes/kleines ~** *school examination in Latin taken after at least six/three years*.

latschen (*perf hat/ist gelatscht*) *fam* ◇ *vi* (*ist*) to traipse ◇ *vt* (*hat*): **jm eine** ODER **ein paar ~** to give sb a clout.

Latschen (*pl -*) *der fam* [Schuh] worn-out shoe; [Hausschuh] worn-out slipper.

Latte (*pl -n*) *die* [Brett] slat; [bei Hochsprung] bar; [von Tor] crossbar; **lange ~** *fam* beanpole.

Latten|rost *der* slatted base.

Latz (*pl* Lätze) *der* bib.

Latz|hose *die* dungarees (*pl*).

lau ⬦ adj - **1.** [mäßig warm, zurückhaltend] lukewarm - **2.** [mild] mild - **3.** [mäßig] moderate ⬦ adv - **1.** [zurückhaltend] lukewarmly - **2.** [mäßig] moderately well.

Laub das (ohne pl) leaves (pl).

Laub|baum der deciduous tree.

Laub|frosch der tree frog.

Laub|säge die fretsaw.

Laub|wald der deciduous forest.

Lauch der leek.

Lauer die: auf der ~ sitzen ODER liegen fam to be on the lookout.

lauern vi: auf jn/etw ~ [warten] to lie in wait for sb/sthg.

Lauf (pl Läufe) der - **1.** (ohne pl) [Laufen] - **2.** [Betrieb] running - **3.** (ohne pl) [Verlauf, von Fluss] course; **im ~e des Tages** during the day; **etw nimmt seinen ~** sthg takes its course; **im ~(e) der Zeit** in the course of time; **einer Sache** (D) **freien** ODER **ihren ~ lassen** [Tränen, Gefühlen] to give free rein to sthg - **4.** [von Gewehren] barrel.

Lauf|bahn die career.

laufen (präs läuft; prät lief; perf hat/ist gelaufen) ⬦ vi (ist) - **1.** [schnell] to run - **2.** fam [gehen] to walk; **jn ~ lassen** to let sb go; **er läuft dauernd zum Arzt** he's always going to the doctor's - **3.** [zugange sein] to go on; **die Verhandlungen ~ noch** negotiations are still going on; **was läuft im Kino?** what's on at the cinema Br ODER movies? - **4.** [einen bestimmten Verlauf nehmen] to go; **es läuft gut** it's going well - **5.** [Motor, Maschine] to run, to be on; **ihr Radio läuft schon stundenlang** their radio has been on for hours; **bei ~der Maschine** when the machine is running ODER on - **6.** [funktionieren] to work - **7.** [fließen] to run; **mir läuft die Nase** my nose is running - **8.** [amtlich geführt werden]: **das Konto läuft auf ihren Namen** the account is in her name - **9.** [juristisch gültig sein] to run; **der Vertrag läuft bis zum 31.12** the contract runs ODER is valid until 31 December ⬦ vt - **1.** (hat, ist) SPORT to run; **er ist eine neue Bestzeit gelaufen** he ran a new record; **Marathon ~** to run the marathon - **2.** (ist) [gehen] to walk - **3.** (ist) [mit Sportgerät]: **Ski ~** to ski; **Schlittschuh ~** to skate. ⬥ **sich laufen** ref: **sich warm ~** to warm up.

laufend ⬦ adj - **1.** [Kosten] regular; [Beschwerden, Störungen] continual - **2.** [gerade ablaufend] current - **3.** [in Betrieb] running - **4.** RW: **auf dem Laufenden sein/bleiben** to be/keep up-to-date ⬦ adv [ständig] continually.

Läufer (pl -) der - **1.** SPORT runner - **2.** [Schachfigur] bishop.

Läuferin (pl -nen) die runner.

läufig adj on heat.

Lauf|masche die ladder Br, run Am.

Lauf|schritt der running step; **im ~** at a run.

läuft präs ⬡> laufen.

Lauf|werk das EDV drive.

Lauge (pl -n) die - **1.** CHEM alkaline solution - **2.** [Waschlauge] soapy water (U).

Laugen|brezel die pretzel.

Laune (pl -n) die - **1.** (ohne pl) [Stimmung] mood; **gute/schlechte ~ haben** to be in a good/bad mood - **2.** [Einfall] whim; **etw aus einer ~ heraus tun** to do sthg on a whim. ⬥ **Launen** pl [von Person] moods; [von Wetter] vagaries.

launisch adj moody.

Laus (pl Läuse) die louse.

Lausbub (pl -en), **Lausbube** (pl -n) der little rascal.

lauschen vi [horchen] to listen; [heimlich] to eavesdrop.

lausig fam ⬦ adj - **1.** [schlecht, Geld] lousy - **2.** [groß] terrible ⬦ adv lousily; **~ kalt** fam freezing (cold).

laut ⬦ adj loud; [lärmend] noisy; **es wurden ~ Zweifel** ~ doubts were voiced; **~er sprechen** to speak up, to speak louder ⬦ adv loudly; [lärmend] noisily ⬦ präp (+ G or D) amt according to.

Laut (pl -e) der sound.

lauten vi: **die Anweisung lautet folgendermaßen** ... the instructions are as follows ...; **auf etw** (A) ~: **die Anklage lautet auf versuchten Mord** the charge is attempted murder.

läuten vi to ring; **bei jm** ~ to ring sb's bell; **es läutet** there is someone at the door; **von etw ~ hören** to hear something about sthg.

lauter adv nothing but; **vor ~ Lärm** because of all the noise.

lauthals adv at the top of one's voice.

lautlos ⬦ adj silent; [Stille] complete ⬦ adv silently.

Laut|schrift die phonetic alphabet.

Laut|sprecher der - **1.** [Tonverstärker] (loud)speaker - **2.** [Megafon] loudspeaker.

lautstark ⬦ adj loud ⬦ adv loudly.

Laut|stärke die volume.

lauwarm ⬦ adj lukewarm ⬦ adv [baden] in lukewarm water; **etw ~ essen/trinken** to eat/drink sthg lukewarm.

Lava ['laːva] (pl Laven) die lava.

Lavendel [la'vɛndl] der lavender.

Lawine (pl -n) die eigtl & fig avalanche.

lax ⬦ adj lax ⬦ adv laxly.

Leasing ['liːzɪŋ] das leasing (U).

leben vi to live; **seine Mutter lebt noch** his mother is still alive; **von etw ~** to live off ODER on sthg; **vom Schreiben ~** to make one's living by ODER from writing; **es lebe der Präsident!** long live the president!; **damit kann**

ich ~ I can live with that <> *vt* to live; **sie leb-te ein erfülltes Leben** she lived a full life.

Leben (*pl* -) *das* - **1.** [gen] life; **jm das ~ schwer machen** to make life difficult for sb; **sich** (*D*) **das ~ nehmen** to take one's (own) life; **ums ~ kommen** to die - **2.** [Treiben] activity - **3.** *RW:* **etw ins ~ rufen** to bring sthg into being.

lebendig <> *adj* - **1.** [lebend, fortwirkend] living - **2.** [lebhaft] lively <> *adv* [lebhaft] in a lively manner.

lebensfähig *adj* capable of survival.

Lebensgefahr *die* mortal danger; **außer ~ sein** to be out of danger; **Vorsicht, ~!** danger of death!

lebensgefährlich <> *adj* [Situation, Handlung] extremely dangerous; [Verletzung] critical <> *adv* [handeln] extremely dangerously; [sich verletzen] critically.

Lebens|gefährte *der* partner.

Lebens|gefährtin *die* partner.

Lebens|haltungskosten *pl* cost of living (*U*).

lebenslänglich *adj & adv* for life.

Lebens|lauf *der* curriculum vitae *Br*, CV *Br*, resumé *Am*.

lebenslustig *adj* full of life.

Lebens|mittel *das* food.

Lebensmittel|geschäft *das* grocer's (shop).

lebensmüde *adj* - **1.** [den Tod herbeisehnend] tired of life - **2.** [leichtsinnig]: **du bist wohl ~** you're out of your mind.

Lebens|standard *der* standard of living.

Lebens|unterhalt *der* maintenance; **seinen ~ verdienen** to earn one's living.

Lebens|versicherung *die* life insurance (*U*).

Lebens|wandel *der* (*ohne pl*) lifestyle.

Lebens|weise *die* way of life.

lebenswichtig *adj* essential.

Lebens|zeichen *das* eigtl & fig sign of life.

Leber (*pl* -n) *die* liver.

Leber|fleck *der* mole.

Leber|käse *der* spiced meat loaf, sliced and often fried.

Leber|tran *der* cod-liver oil.

Leber|wurst *die* liver sausage.

Lebe|wesen *das* living being; [tierisch, pflanzlich] living thing.

lebhaft <> *adj* - **1.** [gen] lively - **2.** [Auseinandersetzung] vigorous; [Interesse] keen; [Bedauern] deep <> *adv* - **1.** [angeregt] in a lively manner - **2.** [sich widersetzen] vigorously; [sich interessieren] keenly; [bedauern] deeply - **3.** [gut] well.

Leb|kuchen *der* gingerbread (*U*).

leblos <> *adj* lifeless <> *adv* lifelessly.

leck *adj* leaky.

Leck (*pl* -s) *das* leak.

lecken <> *vt* to lick; **sich die Lippen ~** to lick one's lips; **die Katze leckte sich das Fell** the cat licked its coat <> *vi* - **1.** [schlecken]: **an etw** (*D*) **~** to lick sthg - **2.** [undicht sein] to leak. ◆ **sich lecken** *ref* to lick o.s.

lecker *adj* delicious.

Lecker|bissen *der* - **1.** [essbar] delicacy - **2.** [Genuss] treat.

Leder (*pl* -) *das* leather (*U*); **jm ans ~ gehen/wollen** *fam fig* to go for/want to go for sb.

Leder|hose *die* lederhosen (*pl*).

Leder|waren *pl* leather goods.

ledig *adj* single.

lediglich *adv* only.

leer *adj* - **1.** [gen] empty; **~ ausgehen** to come away empty-handed - **2.** [unbeschrieben] blank.

Leere *die* emptiness; **sein Schlag ging ins ~** his punch missed; **ins ~ starren** to stare into space.

leeren *vt* to empty. ◆ **sich leeren** *ref* to empty.

Leer|gut *das* (*ohne pl*) empties (*pl*).

Leer|lauf *der* - **1.** TECH neutral; **im ~** in neutral - **2.** [unproduktive Phase] slack period.

leer stehend *adj* empty.

Leerung (*pl* -en) *die* emptying (*U*); [von Briefkasten] collection.

legal <> *adj* legal <> *adv* legally.

legalisieren *vt* - **1.** [legal machen] to legalize - **2.** RECHT to authenticate.

Legalität *die* legality.

legen *vt* - **1.** [ablegen] to put; **leg den Schlüssel auf den Tisch** put the key on the table - **2.** [in horizontale Position bringen] to lay; **du musst die Flaschen ins Regal ~, nicht stellen** you should lay the bottles flat in the rack, not put them upright - **3.** [Termin] to arrange; **den Urlaub auf Juli ~** to arrange one's holidays for July - **4.** [installieren - Rohre, Kabel] to lay; **Minen ~** to lay mines; **Feuer ~** to lay a fire - **5.** [Ei] to lay. ◆ **sich legen** *ref* - **1.** [sich hinlegen] to lie down; **sich schlafen ~** to lie down to sleep - **2.** [Staub, Nebel] to settle - **3.** [Aufregung, Sturm] to die down.

Legende (*pl* -n) *die* - **1.** [gen] legend - **2.** [Irrglaube] myth.

leger [le'ʒeːɐ] <> *adj* casual <> *adv* casually.

Legierung (*pl* -en) *die* alloy.

Legislative [leɡɪsla'tiːvə] (*pl* -n) *die* legislature.

legitim *adj* legitimate.

Lehm *der* clay.

lehmig *adj* clayey.

Lehne (*pl* -n) *die* [Rückenlehne] back; [Armlehne] arm.

lehnen <> *vt*: **etw gegen** ODER **an etw** (*A*) **~**

to lean sthg against sthg ◇ *vi*: **an etw** *(D)* ~ to lean against sthg. ◆ **sich lehnen** *ref* - **1.** [stützen]: **sich gegen** ODER **an jn/etw** ~ to lean against sb/sthg - **2.** [sich beugen] to lean.

Lehr|amt *das amt* teaching *(U).*

Lehr|buch *das* textbook.

Lehre *(pl* -n) *die* - **1.** [Ausbildung] apprenticeship; **in der** ~ **sein** to be serving one's apprenticeship - **2.** [lehrreiche Erfahrung] lesson - **3.** [Ideologie - von Propheten, Philosophen] teachings *(pl);* [- katholisch, marxistisch] doctrine.

lehren ◇ *vi* to teach ◇ *vt* to teach; **jn etw** ~ to teach sb sthg.

Lehrer, in *(mpl* -; *fpl* -nen) *der, die* [in Schule] teacher; [in Sportverein] instructor.

Lehr|gang *der* course.

Lehr|ling *(pl* -e) *der* apprentice.

Lehr|plan *der* syllabus.

lehrreich *adj* instructive.

Lehr|stelle *die* apprenticeship.

Lehr|stuhl *der amt* chair.

Lehr|zeit *die* apprenticeship.

Leib *(pl* -er) *der* - **1.** *geh* [Körper] body - **2.** *RW*: **sie ist mit** ~ **und Seele Krankenschwester** she is a dedicated nurse; **mit** ~ **und Seele dabei sein** to put one's whole heart into it; **jm jn/etw vom** ~ **halten** *fam* to keep sb/sthg away from sb; **sich** *(D)* **jn/etw vom** ~ **halten** *fam* to keep sb/sthg at bay.

Leibeskräfte *pl*: **aus** ~**n** with all one's might.

Leib|gericht *das* favourite dish.

leiblich *adj* - **1.** [körperlich] physical - **2.** [blutsverwandt] natural.

Leiche *(pl* -n) *die* corpse; **über** ~**n gehen** *fam fig* to stop at nothing.

Leichen|halle *die* mortuary.

Leichnam *(pl* -e) *der geh* body.

leicht ◇ *adj* - **1.** [an Gewicht] light - **2.** [geringfügig] slight; ~**e Kopfschmerzen** a slight headache; **eine** ~**e Grippe** a mild attack of flu - **3.** [einfach] easy; **es** ~ **haben** to have it easy; **er hat es nicht** ~ he is having a hard time - **4.** [kalorienarm] diet, low-fat; [Mahlzeit] light; [Zigarette] mild ◇ *adv* - **1.** [einfach, schnell] easily; **das ist sehr** ~ **möglich** that's perfectly possible; **er ist** ~ **beleidigt** he is quick to take offence - **2.** [geringfügig] slightly; ~ **nicken** to give a little nod; **es riecht** ~ **angebrannt** there's a slight smell of burning; ~ **bekleidet** scantily clad - **3.** [unbeschwert] lightly.

Leicht|athletik *die* athletics *(U).*

leicht fallen *(perf* ist leicht gefallen) *vi (unreg)*: **es fällt ihm leicht/nicht leicht** it comes/ doesn't come easy to him.

leichtfertig *abw* ◇ *adj* rash ◇ *adv* rashly.

leichtgläubig *adj* credulous.

Leichtigkeit *die* - **1.** [geringes Gewicht] lightness - **2.** [Mühelosigkeit] ease.

leicht machen *vt* to make easy; **jm etw** ~ to make sthg easy for sb.

Leicht|metall *das* light metal.

leicht nehmen *vt (unreg)* not to take seriously.

Leichtsinn *der* recklessness.

leichtsinnig ◇ *adj* reckless ◇ *adv* recklessly.

leid *adj*: **jn/etw** ~ **sein** ODER **haben** to be tired of sb/etw.

Leid *das* sorrow; **sie tut mir** ~ I feel sorry for her; **es tut mir** ~ I'm sorry.

leiden *(prät* litt; *perf* hat gelitten) ◇ *vi* to suffer; **an/unter etw** *(D)* ~ to suffer from sthg ◇ *vt* - **1.** [erdulden] to suffer - **2.** [mögen]: **jn gut/nicht** ~ **können** to like/not to like sb.

Leiden *(pl* -) *das* illness.

Leidenschaft *(pl* -en) *die* passion.

leidenschaftlich ◇ *adj* passionate ◇ *adv* passionately; ~ **gern tanzen** to adore dancing.

leider *adv* unfortunately.

Leidtragende *(pl* -n) *der, die*: **die Kinder sind immer die** ~**n** the children are always the ones to suffer.

Leih|bücherei *die* lending library.

leihen *(prät* lieh; *perf* hat geliehen) *vt* - **1.** [leihweise geben]: **jm etw** ~ to lend sb sthg - **2.** [ausleihen]: **sich** *(D)* **etw (von jm)** ~ to borrow sthg (from sb); [mieten] to hire *Br* ODER **rent** *Am* sthg (from sb).

Leih|gebühr *die* [für Auto] hire *Br* ODER rental *Am* charge; [für Buch] lending charge.

Leih|wagen *der* hire *Br* ODER rental *Am* car.

Leim *(pl* -e) *der* glue; **aus dem** ~ **gehen** *fam* [kaputtgehen] to fall to pieces.

leimen *vt* - **1.** [zusammenfügen] to glue together - **2.** [ankleben] to glue.

Leine *(pl* -n) *die* - **1.** [Seil] cord; ~ **ziehen** *salopp fig* to scram - **2.** [Wäscheleine] line - **3.** [Hundeleine] lead *Br*, leash *Am*.

Leinen *das* linen.

Lein|samen *der* linseed.

Lein|wand *die* [Projektionswand] screen.

leise ◇ *adj* - **1.** [nicht laut] quiet - **2.** [schwach] slight ◇ *adv* quietly.

Leiste *(pl* -n) *die* - **1.** [Latte] edging strip - **2.** [Körperteil] groin.

leisten *vt* - **1.** [vollbringen] to achieve - **2.** [machen] to do - **3.** [Beitrag, Anzahlung] to make.

Leistung *(pl* -en) *die* - **1.** TECH [das Geleistete] performance - **2.** [Ergebnis] achievement - **3.** [Bezahlung] payment.

Leistungsdruck *der* pressure to do well.

Leistungs|kurs der one of two specialist subjects chosen by pupils for their 'Abitur'.

📖 Leistungskurs

A Leistungskurs forms part of a student's sixth form programme of study. However, unlike the teaching given in a Grundkurs, the subject chosen for a Leistungskurs is explored in much greater depth and detail. Four subjects are offered for the final leaving certificate (Abitur), of which two are Leistungskurse carrying double the weighting.

Leistungs|sport der competitive sport.

Leit|artikel der editorial.

leiten ⬦ vt - 1. [anführen - Unternehmen, Projekt] to run; [- Gruppe, Diskussion] to lead - 2. PHYS to conduct - 3. [lenken - Bach, Verkehr] to divert; [- Antrag] to forward; **sich von etw ~ lassen** fig to let o.s. be guided by sthg ⬦ vi to conduct.

leitend adj - 1. [Stellung] managerial; [Direktor] managing; [Architekt] chief; **~er Angestellter** manager - 2. [führend] guiding - 3. [weiterleitend] conductive.

Leiter (pl -n ODER -) ⬦ die (pl Leitern) ladder ⬦ der (pl Leiter) [von Firma, Abteilung] manager; [von Gruppe, Projekt] leader.

Leiterin (pl -nen) die [von Firma, Abteilung] manager; [von Gruppe, Projekt] leader.

Leit|faden der introductory guide.

Leit|planke die crash barrier Br, guardrail Am.

Leitung (pl -en) die - 1. [Führung] running; **unter der ~ von jm** conducted by sb - 2. [Führungsgruppe] management (U) - 3. [Rohr] pipe - 4. [Draht] wire; [Kabel] cable - 5. [Telefonleitung] line; **eine lange ~ haben** fam fig to be slow on the uptake.

Leitungs|rohr das pipe.

Leitungs|wasser das tap water.

Lektion (pl -en) die eigtl & fig lesson.

Lektor, in (mpl -toren; fpl -nen) der, die - 1. [bei Verlag] editor - 2. [an Hochschulen] language assistant.

Lektüre (pl -n) die - 1. [das Lesen] reading - 2. [Lesestoff] reading matter.

Lende (pl -n) die loin.

lenken vt - 1. [Fahrzeug, Gespräch] to steer - 2. [richten]: **die Aufmerksamkeit auf jn/etw ~ lenken** to draw attention to sb/sthg; **er lenkte den Verdacht auf sich** he attracted suspicion - 3. [führen] to control.

Lenker (pl -) der - 1. [Lenkstange] handlebars (pl) - 2. [Person] driver.

Lenkerin (pl -nen) die driver.

Lenk|rad das steering wheel.

Lenkung (pl -en) die - 1. [Steuerung] steering (U) - 2. [Beeinflussung] control.

Leopard (pl -en) der leopard.

Lepra die leprosy.

Lerche (pl -n) die lark.

lernen ⬦ vt to learn; **Klavier spielen ~** to learn to play the piano; **Bäcker ~** to train to be a baker ⬦ vi - 1. [gen] to learn; **aus der Geschichte ~** to learn from history - 2. [für Prüfung] to study, to revise.

Lesbierin ['lɛsbjərɪn] (pl -nen) die lesbian.

lesbisch adj lesbian.

lesen (präs liest; prät las; perf hat gelesen) ⬦ vt - 1. [gen] to read - 2. [Früchte, Trauben] to pick ⬦ vi - 1. [gen] to read; **in seiner Miene war die Verzweiflung zu ~** despair was written all over his face - 2. [einen Vortrag halten] to lecture.

Leser (pl -) der reader.

Leser|brief der reader's letter, letter to the editor.

Leserin (pl -nen) die reader.

leserlich ⬦ adj legible ⬦ adv legibly.

Lese|zeichen das bookmark.

Lettland nt Latvia.

Letzt ⬦ **zu guter Letzt** adv in the end.

letzte, r, s adj last; **das ist mein ~s Geld** that's the last of my money; **~s Jahr** last year.

Letzte (pl -n) ⬦ der, die [Person] last; **~r werden** to come last; **sie kam als ~ an die Reihe** she had her turn last ⬦ der [Tag] last day ⬦ das - 1.: **er ist das ~** fam he's scum; **der Film ist das ~** fam the film is the pits - 2.: **bis ins ~** down to the last detail.

letztemal adv ⬦ Mal.

letztendlich adv - 1. [am Schluss] in the end - 2. [im Grunde genommen] ultimately, in the final analysis.

letztenmal adv ⬦ Mal.

letztens adv - 1. [an letzter Stelle] lastly - 2. [vor kurzem] recently.

letztere, r, s adj the latter; **in ~m Fall** in the latter case ⬦ pron the latter.

Letztere die, das ODER der: **der/die/das ~** the latter.

letztgenannte, r, s adj: **die ~ Alternative** the last alternative mentioned.

letztlich adv - 1. [am Schluss] in the end - 2. [im Grunde genommen] ultimately, in the final analysis.

leuchten vi to shine; [Feuer, Himmel] to glow.

leuchtend ⬦ adj - 1. [Farbe] bright; **sie bekam ~e Augen** her eyes lit up - 2. [Vorbild, Beispiel] shining ⬦ adv: **~ blau/rot** bright blue/red.

Leuchter (pl -) der candelabrum; [für eine Kerze] candlestick.

Leucht|farbe die luminous paint.

Leuchtstoff|röhre die fluorescent tube.

Leucht|turm der lighthouse.

leugnen ⬦ *vt* to deny ⬦ *vi* to deny everything.

Leukämie *die* leukaemia.

Leute *pl* - **1.** [Menschen] people; **die jungen ~ young people; die ~ sagen** what people say - **2.** *RW:* **etw unter die ~ bringen** *fam* to spread sthg around; **unter (die) ~ gehen** *fam* to get out and meet people.

Leutnant (*pl* -s) *der* second lieutenant.

Lexikon (*pl* -ka ODER -ken) *das* [Enzyklopädie] encyclopaedia.

Libanon *der:* **(der) ~** (the) Lebanon.

Libelle (*pl* -n) *die* [Insekt] dragonfly.

liberal ⬦ *adj* liberal ⬦ *adv* - **1.** [tolerant]: **~ eingestellt sein** to be liberal-minded - **2.** POL.: **~ wählen** to vote Liberal.

Libyen *nt* Libya.

Licht (*pl* -er) *das* - **1.** [Helligkeit, Lampe] light; **~ machen** to put the light on - **2.** [Kerze] candle - **3.** *RW:* **ans ~ kommen** to come to light; **grünes ~ geben** to give the green light; **jetzt geht mir ein ~ auf** now I see; **jn hinters ~ führen** to pull the wool over sb's eyes.

Lichtblick *der* bright spot.

lichten *vt* to thin out. ⬤ **sich lichten** *ref* to thin out.

lichterloh *adv:* **~ brennen** to blaze fiercely.

Lichthupe *die* AUTO: **die ~ betätigen** to flash one's headlights.

Lichtmaschine *die* AUTO alternator.

Lichtschalter *der* light switch.

Lichtschranke *die* photoelectric beam.

Lichtschutzfaktor *der* (protection) factor; **~ 10** factor 10.

Lichtstrahl *der* beam (of light).

Lichtung (*pl* -en) *die* clearing.

Lid (*pl* -er) *das* eyelid.

Lidschatten *der* eye shadow.

lieb ⬦ *adj* - **1.** [nett] kind, nice; **wie ~ von Ihnen, dass Sie daran gedacht haben!** how kind ODER nice of you to remember! - **2.** [als Anrede] dear; **Liebe Sue!** Dear Sue,; **~ Kollegen!** colleagues! - **3.** [brav] good; **sei schön ~!** be a good boy/girl! ⬦ *adv* nicely; *siehe auch* **lieb gewinnen;** *siehe auch* **lieb haben.**

liebäugeln *vi:* **mit etw ~** [Gegenstand, Kauf, Arbeitsstelle] to have one's eye on sthg; [Idee, Plan] to be thinking about sthg.

Liebe *die* - **1.** [gen] love; **die ~ zur Kunst** love of art; **sie war seine erste ~** she was his first love - **2.** [Sex] sex; **käufliche ~** prostitution; **~ machen** to make love - **3.** *RW:* **~ auf den ersten Blick** love at first sight.

lieben *vt* to love. ⬤ **sich lieben** *ref* - **1.** [lieb haben] to be in love - **2.** [sexuell] to make love.

liebenswert *adj* [Art, Geste] endearing; [Person] likable.

liebenswürdig *adj* kind.

lieber ⬦ *kompar* ▷ **gern** ⬦ *adv* better;

das hättest du ~ nicht sagen sollen it would have been better if you hadn't said that; **~ nicht** maybe we shouldn't, maybe not ⬦ *adj:* **das wäre mir ~** I'd prefer that.

Liebesbrief *der* love letter.

Liebeskummer *der:* **~ haben** to be lovesick.

Liebespaar *das* lovers (*pl*).

liebevoll ⬦ *adj* loving ⬦ *adv* lovingly.

lieb gewinnen *vt* (*unreg*): **jn/etw ~** to grow fond of sb/sthg.

lieb haben *vt* (*unreg*) to love; [gern haben] to be fond of. ⬤ **sich lieb haben** *ref* to be in love.

Liebhaber (*pl* -) *der* - **1.** [gen] lover - **2.** [Sammler] collector.

Liebhaberin (*pl* -nen) *die* - **1.** [gen] lover - **2.** [Sammler] collector.

Liebling (*pl* -e) *der* - **1.** [als Anrede, der Oma] darling - **2.** [Bevorzugte] favourite.

Lieblingsgericht *das* favourite dish.

lieblos ⬦ *adj* unaffectionate ⬦ *adv* - **1.** [ohne Liebe] unaffectionately - **2.** [nachlässig]: **sie hat das Essen ~ zubereitet** she carelessly threw the meal together.

Liebschaft (*pl* -en) *die* *abw* casual affair.

liebsten *superl* ▷ **gern.** ⬤ **am liebsten** *adv:* **am ~ würde ich jetzt nach Hause gehen** what I'd really like to do now would be to go home; **das ist mir am ~** I like it best of all.

Liechtenstein *nt* Liechtenstein.

Lied (*pl* -er) *das* song; REL hymn.

liederlich *adj* [Person] slovenly; [Arbeit] sloppy; [Lebenswandel] dissolute.

lief *prät* ▷ **laufen.**

Lieferant, in (*mpl* -en; *fpl* -nen) *der, die* supplier.

lieferbar *adj* available.

liefern ⬦ *vt* - **1.** [Ware - zustellen] to deliver; [- verkaufen] to supply; **jetzt bin ich geliefert** *fam* I've had it now - **2.** [Ernte, Eier] to produce - **3.** [Beispiel, Beweis] to provide; **sie lieferten sich ein spannendes Match** they battled out an exciting match ⬦ *vi* to deliver.

Lieferung (*pl* -en) *die* [Versand] delivery; [Versorgung] supply.

Lieferwagen *der* van.

Liege (*pl* -n) *die* [für Garten] sun lounger; [zum Übernachten] camp bed *Br*, cot *Am*.

liegen (*prät* lag; *perf* hat gelegen) *vi* - **1.** [gen] to lie; **das Schiff liegt im Hafen** the ship is docked; **in den Bergen liegt viel Schnee** there's a lot of snow on the hills - **2.** [angelehnt sein]: **an etw** (*A*) **~** to rest on sthg - **3.** [sich befinden]: **Dresden liegt an der Elbe** Dresden is on the Elbe - **4.** [in Reihenfolge] to lie; **sie liegt auf dem vierten Platz** she's (lying) in fourth place; **an der Spitze ~** to be in the lead - **5.** [mit Dativ]:

Physik liegt mir nicht physics isn't my thing; **es liegt mir viel daran** it matters a lot to me **- 6.** [mit Präpositionen]: **an mir soll es nicht ~!** don't let me stop you!; **es liegt nicht an dir** it's not your fault; **die Entscheidung liegt bei Ihnen** it's your decision; **das liegt daran, dass …** this is because …

liegen bleiben *(perf* ist *liegen geblieben) vi (unreg)* **- 1.** [nicht aufstehen] to remain lying down; **(im Bett) ~** to stay in bed **- 2.** [Schnee, Laub] to lie **- 3.** [vergessen werden] to be left behind **- 4.** [unerledigt bleiben] to be left undone **- 5.** [eine Panne haben] to break down.

liegen lassen *(perf* hat *liegen gelassen* ODER -) *vt (unreg)* to leave; **jn/etw links ~** *fam fig* to ignore sb/sthg.

Liege|sitz *der* reclining seat.

Liege|stuhl *der* [am Strand] deckchair; [im Garten] sun lounger.

Liege|stütz *(pl -e) der* press-up.

Liege|wagen *der* couchette car.

lieh *prät* ⊳ leihen.

ließ *prät* ⊳ lassen.

liest *präs* ⊳ lesen.

Lifestyle ['laɪfstaɪl] *der (ohne pl)* lifestyle.

Lift *(pl -e* ODER *-s) der* **- 1.** [Aufzug] lift *Br*, elevator *Am* **- 2.** *(pl Lifte)* [Skilift] ski lift.

Likör *(pl -e) der* liqueur.

lila *adj (unver)* lavender; [dunkler] mauve.

Lila *das* purple; [Zartlila] lilac; [Tieflila] mauve.

Lilie ['liːljə] *(pl -n) die* lily.

Limit *(pl -s) das* limit.

Limonade *(pl -n) die* fizzy drink *Br*, soda *Am*; [mit Zitronengeschmack] lemonade; [mit Orangengeschmack] orangeade.

Linde *(pl -n) die* lime tree.

lindern *vt* [Schmerzen] to relieve; [Not] to alleviate.

Lineal *(pl -e) das* ruler.

Linguistik *die* linguistics *(U)*.

Linie ['liːnjə] *(pl -n) die* **- 1.** [Strich, Verwandtschaftslinie] line; **sie stammt in direkter ~ vom Kaiser Karl ab** she is directly descended from Emperor Charles **- 2.** [Denkrichtung] policy **- 3.** [von Verkehrsmittel] number; **die ~ 3** the number 3 **- 4.** [Figur]: **auf die schlanke ~ achten** to watch one's figure **- 5.** *RW*: **in erster ~** first and foremost.

Linien|bus *der* bus *(forming part of public transport network).*

Linien|flug *der* scheduled flight.

Linienverkehr *der (ohne pl)* [Flugverkehr] scheduled flights *(pl);* [Omnibusverkehr] buses *(forming part of public transport network).*

linieren, liniieren *vt* to rule (lines on).

link *adj fam abw* shady.

linke, r, s *adj* **- 1.** [Seitenangabe] left **- 2.** [linkspolitisch] left-wing.

Linke *(pl -n) ⟨⟩ die* **- 1.** [Hand] left hand; **zur**

~n to the left **- 2.** POL: **die ~** the Left **- 3.** [Schlag] left ⟨⟩ *der, die* [Person] left-winger.

links ⟨⟩ *adv* **- 1.** [Angabe der Seite] on the left; [Angabe der Richtung] left; **~ von jm/etw** on sb's/sthg's left; **nach ~ fahren** to turn left; **von ~** from the left; **etw mit ~ machen** *fam fig* to do sthg easily **- 2.** [verkehrt herum] inside out; **etw von ~ bügeln** to iron sthg on the wrong side **- 3.** [linkspolitisch]: **~ wählen** to vote for the Left ⟨⟩ *präp (+ G)* **- 1.** [Angabe der Seite] on the left-hand side of **- 2.** [politisch] to the left of.

Links|abbieger *der* car turning left.

Links|außen *(pl -) der* outside left.

linksextrem *adj* extreme left-wing.

Links|extremist, in *der, die* left-wing extremist.

linksgerichtet *adj* left-wing.

Links|händer, in *(mpl -; fpl -nen) der, die* left-hander.

linksherum *adv* **- 1.** [nach links] round to the left **- 2.** [falsch herum] inside out.

Links|kurve *die* left hand bend.

linksradikal *adj* radical left-wing.

Linksverkehr *der*: **in Großbritannien herrscht ~** people drive on the left in Great Britain.

Linse *(pl -n) die* **- 1.** [Nahrungsmittel] lentil **- 2.** [optisch] lens.

Lippe *(pl -n) die* lip; **keine Klage kam über ihre ~n** she didn't utter a word of complaint.

Lippen|stift *der* lipstick.

lispeln *vi* to lisp.

Lissabon *nt* Lisbon.

List *(pl -en) die* **- 1.** [listiges Verhalten] cunning **- 2.** [listige Handlung] cunning trick.

Liste *(pl -n) die* list; **auf der schwarzen ~ stehen** to be on the blacklist.

listig ⟨⟩ *adj* cunning ⟨⟩ *adv* cunningly.

Litauen *nt* Lithuania.

litauisch *adj* Lithuanian.

Liter *(pl -) der* ODER *das* litre; **ein ~ Milch** a litre of milk.

literarisch ⟨⟩ *adj* literary ⟨⟩ *adv* **- 1.** [Literatur betreffend]: **~ interessiert sein** to be interested in literature; **~ gebildet sein** to have studied literature **- 2.** [gewählt] in a literary manner.

Literatur *(pl -en) die* literature.

Literatur|wissenschaft *die* literary studies *(pl).*

Liter|flasche *die* litre bottle.

Litfaß|säule *die* advertising column.

litt *prät* ⊳ leiden.

Lizenz *(pl -en) die* licence.

Lkw, LKW [ɛlkaːˈveː] *(pl -s) (abk für Lastkraftwagen) der* truck, HGV *Br*, lorry *Br*.

Lob *das* praise; **ein hohes ~** high praise.

loben *vt* to praise; **das lobe ich mir!** [sehr

gut]: **da lobe ich mir doch meine alte Schreibmaschine!** give me my old typewriter any day!

lobenswert adj commendable, praiseworthy.

Loch (pl Löcher) das hole; [im Zahn] cavity.

lochen vt to punch a hole/holes in.

Locher (pl -) der hole punch.

löchern vt fam to pester.

löchrig adj full of holes.

Locke (pl -n) die curl; **~n haben** to have curly hair.

locken vt - 1. [anlocken] to entice; **jn in eine Falle ~** to lure sb into a trap - 2. [wellen] to curl.

Lockenwickler (pl -) der curler.

locker <> adj - 1. [gen] loose; **ein ~es Mundwerk haben** to have a loose tongue - 2. [Beziehung] casual; [Haltung] laid-back <> adv - 1. [nicht fest] loosely - 2. [zwanglos] casually - 3. fam [mit Leichtigkeit] no sweat.

locker|lassen vi (unreg): **nicht ~** not to give up.

lockern vt - 1. [Schraube, Griff, Erde, Krawatte] to loosen; **die Muskeln ~** to limber up - 2. [Gesetze, Vorschriften] to relax. ◆ **sich lockern** ref - 1. [Schraube, Zahn] to work itself loose - 2. [Stimmung] to become more relaxed; [Muskeln, Griff] to relax.

lockig adj [Haare] curly; [Mensch] curly-haired.

Lock|vogel der decoy.

lodern vi [Feuer] to blaze.

Löffel (pl -) der spoon.

löffeln vt to spoon.

log prät ⮕ lügen.

Logarithmus (pl -ithmen) der logarithm.

Loge ['lo:ʒə] (pl -n) die - 1. [im Theater] box - 2. [von Freimaurern, Portier] lodge.

Logik die logic.

logisch <> adj logical <> adv logically.

Lohn (pl Löhne) der - 1. [Bezahlung] wages (pl), pay - 2. [Belohnung] reward.

lohnen vt - 1. [rechtfertigen] to be worth; **es lohnt eine Renovierung nicht mehr** it's no longer worth repairing - 2. geh [vergelten]: **jm etw ~** to repay sb for sthg. ◆ **sich lohnen** ref to be worth it; **es lohnt sich, etw zu tun** it's worth doing sthg.

lohnend adj worthwhile.

Lohn|steuer die income tax (paid by employees). ⮕ PAYE Br.

Lohnsteuerjahres|ausgleich der annual adjustment of income tax.

Lohnsteuer|karte die form filled in by employer stating employee's annual income and tax paid.

Lok (pl -s) die (railway) engine.

lokal adj local.

Lokal (pl -e) das bar, pub Br; [Restaurant] restaurant.

📖 Lokal

Although the German Lokal can be a place to drink, ("bar" or "pub"), it can also be translated by "restaurant". So the phrase Abends waren wir in einem netten Lokal might be translated as "In the evening we went to a nice restaurant".
Lokal does not have the familiar sense of the English word "local", meaning "a favourite or regular place to eat or drink". This would have to be translated as Stammkneipe. So the phrase "Our local is only two minutes' walk from here" might be rendered as Unsere Stammkneipe ist nur zwei Gehminuten von hier entfernt.
In English the word "local" has several other significant meanings, both as a noun and an adjective: "somebody born in the area" (ein Einheimischer); "nearby" or "belonging to the community" (örtlich/am Ort/kommunal)

Lokal|nachrichten pl local news (U).

Lokomotive [lokomo'ti:və] (pl -n) die (railway) engine.

London nt London.

Lorbeer (pl -en) der [Gewürz] bay leaf.

Lorbeer|blatt das bay leaf.

los <> adj - 1. [lose] loose - 2. RW: **jn/etw ~ sein** fam to have got rid of sb/sthg; **es ist viel/wenig/nichts ~** fam there is a lot/not much/nothing going on; **was ist ~?** fam what's the matter?, what's wrong?; **was ist hier ~?** fam what's going on here? <> interj come on!

Los (pl -e) das - 1. [Losentscheid]: **durch das ~ bestimmen** to decide by drawing lots - 2. [in der Lotterie] ticket; **das große ~** the jackpot - 3. geh [Schicksal] lot.

lösbar adj solvable.

los|binden vt (unreg) to untie.

löschen vt - 1. [Kerze, Feuer] to extinguish, to put out - 2. [Konto] to close; [Schuld, Hypothek] to pay off - 3. [Tonträger] to erase - 4. [Schiff, Ladung] to unload - 5. EDV to delete.

Löschen das - 1. [von Feuer] extinguishing - 2. [von Konto] closing; [von Schuld, Hypothek] paying off - 3. [von Tonträger] erasure - 4. [von Schiff, Ladung] unloading - 5. EDV deletion.

Löschpapier das blotting paper.

lose <> adj loose; **ein ~s Mundwerk haben** to have a loose tongue <> adv [locker] loosely.

Löse|geld das ransom.

losen vi [mit einem Los] to draw lots; **darum**

~, wer/wann/was ... to draw lots to see who/when/what ...

lösen vt - **1.** [trennen - Knoten] to undo; [- Bremse] to release; [- Schraube] to unscrew; [- Haare] to let down - **2.** [locker machen] to loosen - **3.** [abmachen]: **etw von etw ~** to remove sthg from sthg - **4.** [rechnen] to work out - **5.** [klären - Aufgabe, Rätsel] to solve - **6.** [Vertrag] to cancel; [Verlobung] to break off; [Ehe] to dissolve - **7.** [Fahrkarte] to buy - **8.** [auflösen] to dissolve - **9.** [Husten, Schleim] to loosen; [Krampf] to ease.
➡ **sich lösen** ref - **1.** [aus Versehen] to break free; [Schuss] to go off; [Lawine] to start; **sich aus etw ~** to break away from sthg - **2.** [Tapete, Briefmarke] to come off; [Knoten] to come undone; [Schraube] to work loose - **3.** [sich auflösen] to dissolve; [Schleim] to loosen - **4.** [umdenken]: **sich von etw ~** [von Vorurteilen, Vorstellung] to rid o.s. of sthg - **5.** [sich trennen]: **sich von jm ~** to break away from sb - **6.** [Muskeln] to relax; [Verkrampfung, Spannung] to ease - **7.** [Problem, Rätsel] to be solved.

los|fahren (perf ist losgefahren) vi (unreg) to set off.

los|gehen (perf ist losgegangen) vi (unreg) - **1.** [weggehen] to set off; **auf jn ~** fig to go for sb; **auf ein Ziel ~** to pursue a goal - **2.** [anfangen] to start; **gleich gehts los** it's just about to start; **jetzt geht das schon wieder los!** here we go again!; **los gehts!** off we go!

los|kommen (perf ist losgekommen) vi (unreg) to get away; **(nicht) von jm/etw ~** (not) to get away from sb/sthg.

los|lassen vt (unreg) - **1.** [Person, Gegenstand] to let go of; **lass mich los!** let go of me!, let me go! - **2.** [Tier]: **ein Hund auf jn ~** to set a dog on sb; **den Hund ~** to let the dog off the lead Br ODER leash Am - **3.** [Schrei, Fluch] to let out - **4.** [Subj: Gedanke, Problem]: **der Gedanke lässt mich nicht los** I can't get the thought out of my head.

los|legen vi fam to get started; **mit Fragen ~** to start firing questions; **na, denn leg mal los!** fire away, then!

löslich adj soluble; [Kaffeepulver, Milchpulver] instant.

los|machen vt to undo; [Hund] to let off the lead Br ODER leash Am. ➡ **sich losmachen** ref to free o.s.

Losung (pl -en) die - **1.** [Motto] motto; [Spruch] slogan - **2.** [Kennwort] password.

Lösung (pl -en) die - **1.** [gen] solution; [von Konflikt] resolution - **2.** [von Eltern, Tradition] breaking away - **3.** [von Ehe, Bündnis] break-up; [von Arbeitsverhältnis] termination.

los|werden (perf ist losgeworden) vt (unreg) fam - **1.** [gen] to get rid of; **ich werde das Gefühl nicht los, dass ...** I can't escape the feeling that ... - **2.** [Vermögen] to lose.

Lot (pl -e) das - **1.** [Senkblei] plumb line; **etw wieder ins ~ bringen** fig to put sthg right - **2.** SCHIFF sounding line - **3.** MATH perpendicular.

löten vt to solder.

Lothringen nt Lorraine.

Lotion [loˈtsi̯oːn] (pl -en) die lotion.

Lotse (pl -n) der - **1.** [von Schiff] pilot - **2.** [Fluglotse] air traffic controller.

lotsen vt to guide.

Lotterie [lɔtəˈriː] (pl -n) die lottery.

Lotto das - **1.** [Glücksspiel] (national) lottery; **im ~ gewinnen** to win the (national) lottery - **2.** [Gesellschaftsspiel] lotto.

Lotto|schein der (national) lottery ticket.

Loveparade [ˈlavpəɾɛjd] die Love Parade, annual open-air mass rave and procession in the centre of Berlin.

Löwe (pl -n) der - **1.** [Tier] lion - **2.** [Sternzeichen, Person] Leo; **~ sein** to be a Leo.

Löwenzahn der dandelion.

Löwin (pl -nen) die lioness.

Luchs [lʊks] (pl -e) der lynx.

Lücke (pl -n) die - **1.** [gen] gap; [zum Parken] space - **2.** [in Gesetz] loophole.

lückenhaft ◇ adj [Erinnerung, Beweisführung, Wissen] sketchy; **sein Lebenslauf ist ~** he has gaps in his CV Br ODER resumé Am ◇ adv [sich erinnern] sketchily.

lud prät ⟶ laden.

Luft (pl Lüfte) die - **1.** [gen] air; **freie ~** open air; **die ~ anhalten** to hold one's breath; **~ holen** [atmen] to take a breath; [eine Pause machen] to catch one's breath; **frische ~ schöpfen** to get some fresh air; **nach ~ schnappen** to gasp - **2.** [Platz] room - **3.** RW: **die ~ ist rein** fam the coast is clear; **in der ~ liegen** to be in the air; **jn in der ~ hängen lassen** to leave sb hanging in the air; **in die ~ gehen** fam to blow one's top; **mir blieb die ~ weg** fam I was gobsmacked.

Luft|angriff der air raid.

Luft|ballon der balloon.

Luft|brücke die airlift.

luftdicht ◇ adj airtight ◇ adv [verschließen] hermetically.

Luftdruck der air pressure.

lüften ◇ vt - **1.** [Zimmer, Wäsche] to air - **2.** [Geheimnis] to reveal ◇ vi to let some air in.

Luftfahrt die aviation.

luftig ◇ adj - **1.** [Kleidung] light - **2.** [hochgelegen]: **in ~er Höhe** high up - **3.** [Raum] airy ◇ adv [leicht] lightly.

Luft|linie die: **600 km ~** 600 km as the crow flies.

Luft|matratze die airbed.

Luft|pirat, in der, die (aircraft) hijacker.

Luft|post die airmail; **mit** ODER **per ~** (by) airmail.

Luft|pumpe *die* air pump.

Luft|röhre *die* windpipe.

Luft|schlange *die* streamer.

Lüftung (*pl* -en) *die* - **1.** [Gerät] ventilation (system) - **2.** [Lüften] ventilation.

Luft|verkehr *der* air traffic.

Luft|verschmutzung *die* air pollution.

Luft|waffe *die* airforce; HIST Luftwaffe.

Luft|zug *der* [in Gebäude] draught; [im Freien] breath of wind.

Lüge (*pl* -n) *die* lie.

lügen (*prät* log; *perf* hat gelogen) *vi* to lie; **das ist gelogen!** that's a lie!

Lügner, in (*mpl* -; *fpl* -nen) *der, die* liar.

Lümmel (*pl* -) *der fam* - **1.** [Kind] rascal - **2.** *abw* [Rüpel] lout.

lümmeln ➡ **sich lümmeln** *ref fam abw* to sprawl.

Lump (*pl* -en) *der abw* scoundrel.

Lumpen (*pl* -) *der* rag.

Lunge (*pl* -n) *die* lungs (*pl*).

Lungenent|zündung *die* pneumonia.

Lunte (*pl* -n) *die* fuse.

Lupe (*pl* -n) *die* magnifying glass; **jn/etw unter die ~ nehmen** *fam fig* to examine sb/sthg very closely.

Lust (*pl* Lüste) *die* - **1.** [Bedürfnis] desire; **die ~ am Reisen ist mir vergangen** I don't feel like travelling any more; **~ bekommen/haben, etw zu tun** to feel like doing sthg; **ich habe keine ~ zum Spazierengehen** I don't feel like going for a walk; **~/keine ~ auf etw** (*A*) **haben** to fancy/not to feel like sthg; **ich hätte jetzt ~ auf ein Eis** I fancy an ice cream; **er arbeitet ganz nach ~ und Laune** he works as and when he feels like it - **2.** [Freude] pleasure; **die ~ an etw** (*D*) **verlieren** no longer to take any pleasure in sthg - **3.** [Begierde] desires (*pl*), lust.

lüstern <> *adj* lascivious <> *adv:* **~ blicken** to leer.

lustig <> *adj* - **1.** [komisch] funny; [unterhaltsam] entertaining; **sich über jn/etw ~ machen** to make fun of sb/sthg - **2.** [fröhlich - Person, Augen] merry; [- Abend] fun, enjoyable <> *adv* - **1.** [komisch] funnily; [unterhaltsam] entertainingly - **2.** [unbekümmert] merrily.

lustlos <> *adj* unenthusiastic <> *adv* unenthusiastically.

lutschen <> *vt* to suck <> *vi:* **an etw** (*D*) **~** to suck sthg.

Lutscher (*pl* -) *der* [Süßigkeit] lollipop.

Luxemburg *nt* Luxembourg.

luxemburgisch *adj* of/from Luxembourg.

luxuriös <> *adj* luxurious <> *adv* luxuriously.

Luxus *der* luxury.

Luzern *nt* Lucerne.

Lyrik *die* lyric poetry.

lyrisch <> *adj* [Dichtung] lyric; [Stil] lyrical <> *adv* lyrically.

m, M [ɛm] (*pl* - ODER -s) *das* m, M.

m. *abk für* mit.

MA *abk für* Mittelalter.

machbar *adj* feasible.

machen <> *vt* - **1.** [tun] to do; **so was macht man nicht!** you can't ODER mustn't do that! - **2.** [herstellen] to make; **ein Foto ~** to take a photo; **etw aus etw ~** to make sthg out of sthg; **sich** (*D*) **etw ~ lassen** to have sthg made - **3.** [Summe, Ergebnis] to be; **zwei mal drei macht sechs** two times three is six; **das macht fünf Euro** that comes to five euros - **4.** [mit Substantiv]: **das Abendessen ~** to make dinner; **mach bloß keine Dummheiten!** don't do anything silly!; **eine Prüfung ~** to take an exam; **den Doktor ~** to do a doctorate; **einen Handstand ~** to do a handstand; **täglich 1000 Euro Umsatz ~** to turn over 1000 euros a day - **5.** [erledigen] to do; **Einkäufe ~** to go shopping; **(seine) Hausaufgaben ~** to do one's homework; **sich** (*D*) **die Haare ~** to do one's hair; **da ist nichts zu ~** there's nothing we can do about it - **6.** [durchführen]: **eine Party ~** to have a party; **eine Reise/einen Spaziergang ~** to go on a journey/for a walk; **eine Pause ~** to have a break - **7.** [verursachen]: **Licht ~** to switch on the light; **was macht das schon!** so what!; **jm Angst/Freude ~** to make afraid/happy; **jm Hoffnung ~** to raise sb's hopes - **8.** [mit Adjektiv] to make; **sich bemerkbar ~** to become noticeable; **mach die Musik leiser** turn the music down; **jn krank/glücklich ~** to make sb ill/happy; **machs gut!** take care! - **9.** [mit Präposition]: **sie haben aus dem alten Häuschen etwas gemacht** they've really made something out of that old cottage; **sie lässt alles mit sich ~** she is very long-suffering <> *vi* - **1.** [verursachen]: **macht, dass ihr bald zurück seid!** make sure you're back soon; **mach schon** ODER **doch!** *fam* get a move on! - **2.** *fam* [Toilette verrichten]: **der Hund hat vor die Haustür gemacht** the dog made a mess outside the front door; **in die Hosen ~** to wet/dirty one's pants - **3.** [mit Adjektiv]: **Joggen macht schlank** jogging helps you lose weight; **mach schnell!** hurry up! ➡ **sich machen** *ref* - **1.** *fam* [sich entwickeln] to come on; **du machst dich!** you're coming on very well - **2**. [mit Adjektiv]: **sich beliebt/verständlich** ~ to make o.s. popular/understood; **der Hut macht sich gut zu Ihrem Kleid** the hat goes well with your dress - **3**. [mit Präposition]: **sich an die Arbeit** ~ to get down to work; **sich auf den Weg** ~ to set off; **sich** *(D)* **aus etw nichts** ~ not to be keen on sthg; **mach dir nichts draus!** don't let it bother you!

Machenschaft *(pl -en) die abw* intrigue.

Macht *(pl* Mächte) *die* power; **an die ~ kommen** to come to power; **an der ~ sein** to be in power; **die ~ der Gewohnheit** force of habit; **~ über jn haben** to have a hold on sb; **mit aller** ~ with all one's might.

Machthaber, in *(mpl -; fpl -nen) der, die:* **die ~** those in power.

mächtig *<> adj* - **1**. [einflussreich] powerful - **2**. [Stimme, Hieb, Stamm] mighty; [Hunger, Angst] terrible; [Gebäude] enormous *<> adv* [enorm] terribly.

machtlos *adj* powerless; **gegen etw ~ sein** to be powerless in the face of sthg.

Machtprobe *die* trial of strength.

Machtwort *(pl -e) das:* **ein ~ sprechen** to put one's foot down, to exercise one's authority.

Macke *(pl -n) die fam* - **1**. [Tick] quirk - **2**. [Fehler]: **mein Auto hat eine ~** there's something up ODER wrong with my car.

Madagaskar *nt* Madagascar.

Mädchen *(pl -) das* - **1**. [gen] girl - **2**. [Hausangestellte] maid.

Mädchenname *der* maiden name.

Made *(pl -n) die* maggot.

madig *adj* maggoty, full of maggots; **jm etw ~ machen** *fam* fig to spoil sthg for sb.

Madonna *(pl* Madonnen) *die* - **1**. [Muttergottes] Madonna - **2**. [Bild, Plastik] madonna.

mag *präs* ▷ mögen.

Magazin *(pl -e) das* - **1**. [Illustrierte, Behälter für Patronen] magazine - **2**. [Lager] storeroom - **3**. [Fernsehsendung] magazine (programme).

Magd *(pl* Mägde) *die* - **1**. [Dienstmagd] maid - **2**. [Landarbeiterin] farmhand.

Magen *(pl* Mägen ODER -) *der* stomach; **jm auf den ~ schlagen** *fam* to upset sb; **sich** *(D)* **den ~ verderben** to get an upset stomach; **mir knurrt der ~** *fam* my stomach is rumbling.

Magenbeschwerden *pl* stomach trouble *(U)*.

Magengeschwür *das* stomach ulcer.

Magenschmerzen *pl* stomachache *(U)*.

mager *<> adj* - **1**. [Person, Tier, Gesicht] thin - **2**. [Fleisch] lean; [Quark] low-fat - **3**. [Ergebnis, Ernte] meagre *<> adv* [fettarm]: **~ essen** to eat a low-fat diet.

Magermilch *die* skimmed milk.

magersüchtig *adj* anorexic.

Magie [ma'giː] *die* magic.

magisch *<> adj* magical; [Kräfte] magic *<> adv* magically.

Magister *(pl -) der* [Titel] ≃ Master's degree.

Magnesium *das* magnesium.

Magnet *(pl -e* ODER *-en) der* magnet.

magnetisch *<> adj* magnetic *<> adv* magnetically.

Mahagoni *das* mahogany.

mähen *<> vt* [Rasen] to mow; [Getreide] to reap *<> vi* - **1**. [mit Mäher] to mow; [mit Sense] to reap - **2**. [blöken] to bleat.

mahlen *vt & vi* to grind.

Mahlzeit *<> die* meal *<> interj* hello! *(said around lunchtime to work colleagues).*

Mähne *(pl -n) die* mane.

mahnen *<> vt* - **1**. [ermahnen] to urge; **jn ~, etw zu tun** to urge sb to do sthg - **2**. [erinnern]: **jn an etw** *(A)* ~ to remind sb of sthg *<> vi* [ermahnen]: **das Ozonloch mahnt zur Vorsicht beim Sonnen** because of the hole in the ozone layer it is advisable to take care whilst sunbathing.

Mahnmal *das* memorial.

Mahnung *(pl -en) die* - **1**. [Ermahnung] exhortation - **2**. [Schreiben] reminder.

Mai *der* May; **der Erste ~** May Day; *siehe auch* September.

Maiglöckchen *(pl -) das* lily of the valley.

Maikäfer *der* cockchafer.

Mailand *nt* Milan.

Main *der:* **der ~** the (River) Main.

Mainz *nt* Mainz.

Mais *der* [als Konserve] sweetcorn; [Pflanze] maize.

Maiskolben *der* corn on the cob.

Majestät *(pl -en) die* Majesty.

majestätisch *<> adj* majestic *<> adv* majestically.

Majonäse, Mayonnaise [majo'nɛːzə] *(pl -n) die* mayonnaise.

Major *(pl -e) der* major.

Majoran *der* marjoram.

makaber *adj* macabre.

makellos *<> adj* - **1**. [tadellos] impeccable; [Figur] perfect - **2**. [fehlerlos] flawless *<> adv* - **1**. [tadellos] impeccably - **2**. [sauber] spotlessly.

Make-up [meːkˈap] *(pl -s) das* - **1**. [Schminken] make-up - **2**. [Creme] foundation.

Makler, in *(mpl -; fpl -nen) der, die* [für Immobilien] estate agent *Br*, realtor *Am*; [an Börse] broker.

Makrele *(pl -n) die* mackerel.

mal *<> adv fam* - **1**. [irgendwann - in Zukunft] sometime, someday; [- in Vergangenheit] once; **hier stand ~ ein Gebäude** there was a building here once; **aus ihr wird ~ was werden** she'll be someone some ODER one day - **2.** [zum Ausdruck der Verbindlichkeit]: **ich komme um neun Uhr ~ vorbei** I'll drop by at nine o'clock; **wir müssen das am Sonntag ~ besprechen** we ought to discuss this on Sunday - **3.** [als Aufforderung]: **hör mir ~ gut zu!** now listen to me carefully!; **gib mir ~ bitte den Schlüssel!** would you give me the key?; **beruhige dich ~!** calm down, will you!; **sag ~!** tell me!; **hör ~!** listen! listen! - **4.** [zur Verstärkung eines Adverbs]: **nimm schon ~ Platz, ich komme gleich** just take a seat, I'll be here in a minute; **vielleicht ~** maybe; **höchstens ~** at the very most - **5.** [einmal]: **er redet ~ so, ~ so** he says one thing one minute and another thing the next <> *konj* [zur Multiplikation] times.

Mal (*pl* -e ODER **Mäler**) *das* - **1.** (*pl* **Male**) [Zeitpunkt] time; **letztes/nächstes ~** last/next time; **jedes ~** every time; **mit einem ~(e)** all of a sudden; **von ~ zu ~** [immer mehr] more and more; [jedes Mal] every time; **beim ersten ~** the first time; **beim letzten ~** last time; **zum ersten/letzten ~** for the first/last time - **2.** (*pl* **Male**, **Mäler**) [Fleck] mark; [Muttermal] birthmark; [Pigmentmal] mole.

Malbuch *das* colouring book.

malen *vt & vi* to paint.

Maler (*pl* -) *der* - **1.** [Künstler] painter, artist - **2.** [Handwerker] painter.

Malerei (*pl* -en) *die* painting.

Malerin (*pl* -nen) *die* - **1.** [Künstlerin] painter, artist - **2.** [Handwerkerin] painter.

malerisch <> *adj* [idyllisch] picturesque <> *adv* [schön] picturesquely.

malnehmen *vt* (*unreg*): **etw mit etw ~** to multiply sthg by sthg.

Malta *nt* Malta.

Malz *das* malt.

Malzbier *das* malt beer.

Mama (*pl* -s) *die fam* mummy *Br*, mommy *Am*.

man *pron* - **1.** [jemand]: **~ sagte mir ...** I was told ...; **~ hat ihm eine Stelle angeboten** he was offered a job - **2.** [generalisierend] you; **wie sagt ~ das auf Deutsch?** how do you say that in German?; **das sagt ~ nicht** you don't say that; **~ sagt, dass ...** people say that ...

manche, r, s <> *pron* - **1.** [bei Dingen - einige] some; [- viele] many (things) - **2.** [bei Personen - einige] some people; [- viele] many (people); **manch einer** many a person <> *det* - **1.** [einige] some - **2.** [viele] many. **so manche, r, s** *pron & det* quite a few.

manchmal *adv* sometimes.

Mandarine (*pl* -n) *die* mandarin.

Mandat (*pl* -e) *das* - **1.** [gen] mandate; [von Anwalt] brief - **2.** [POL - Amt] seat.

Mandel (*pl* -n) *die* almond. **Mandeln** *pl* [im Hals] tonsils.

Mandelentzündung *die* tonsillitis (*U*).

Manege [ma'ne:ʒə] (*pl* -n) *die* (circus) ring.

Mangel (*pl* **Mängel** ODER -n) <> *der* (*pl* **Mängel**) - **1.** [an Verantwortungsbewusstsein, Geistesgegenwart] lack; [an Lebensmitteln, Medikamenten] shortage; **aus ~ an etw** (*D*) for lack of sthg; **es herrscht ~ an etw** (*D*) there is a shortage of sthg - **2.** [Fehler] fault; **Mängel beheben** ODER **beseitigen** to rectify faults - **3.** [Not] hardship <> *die* (*pl* **Mangeln**) mangle.

Mangelerscheinung *die* deficiency symptom.

mangelhaft <> *adj* [unzureichend Schulnote] poor <> *adv* poorly.

mangeln <> *vi*: **es mangelt jm an etw** (*D*) sb lacks sthg; **es mangelt an etw** (*D*) [nicht genug sein] there is a shortage of sthg; [fehlen] there is a lack of sthg <> *vt* to mangle.

mangelnd *adj* inadequate.

mangels *präp*: **~ einer Sache** (*G*) for lack of sthg.

Mangelware *die*: **~ sein** to be a scarce commodity; *fam fig* to be thin on the ground.

Mango (*pl* -s) *die* mango.

Manie (*pl* -n) *die* - **1.** [Tick] obsession - **2.** MED mania.

Manier (*pl* -en) *die* manner. **Manieren** *pl* manners.

manisch <> *adj* manic <> *adv* [krankhaft] manically.

Manko (*pl* -s) *das* - **1.** [Fehler] drawback - **2.** [Geldsumme] deficit.

Mann (*pl* **Männer** ODER **Leute** ODER -en) *der* - **1.** [gen] man; **von ~ zu ~** man to man - **2.** [Ehemann] husband - **3.** *RW*: **seinen ~ stehen** to hold one's own. **alle Mann** *pron fam* everyone; **alle ~ an Deck!** all hands on deck! **kleine Mann** *der fam*: **der kleine ~** the ordinary man.

Männchen (*pl* -) *das* - **1.** [Tier] male - **2.** *fam* [kleiner Mann] little man.

männlich <> *adj* - **1.** [Lebewesen] male - **2.** [viril] manly - **3.** [zum Mann gehörig] man's - **4.** GRAM [Substantiv] masculine <> *adv* [viril] in a manly way.

Mannschaft (*pl* -en) *die* - **1.** [im Sport, Team] team; **vor versammelter ~** *fam* in front of everybody - **2.** [Besatzung] crew - **3.** [Soldaten] men (*pl*).

Mannschaftsgeist *der* team spirit.

Mannschaftssport *der* team sport.

Manöver [ma'nø:vɐ] (*pl* -) *das* manoeuvre.

manövrieren [manø'vri:rən] *vt & vi eigtl & fig* to manoeuvre. **sich manövrieren** *ref* [sich bringen] to manoeuvre o.s.

Manschettenknopf *der* cufflink.

Mantel (*pl* **Mäntel**) *der* - **1.** [Kleidungsstück] coat - **2.** *fig* [Deckmantel] cloak - **3.** TECH casing; [von Kabel] sheath.

manuell ⬦ *adj* manual ⬦ *adv* manually.

Manuskript (*pl* -e) *das* - **1.** [Entwurf] notes (*pl*) - **2.** [Handschrift, Satzvorlage] manuscript.

Mappe (*pl* -n) *die* - **1.** [Hülle] folder - **2.** [Tasche] briefcase.

Marathon (*pl* -s) *der* ODER *das* marathon.

Marathon|läufer, in *der, die* marathon runner.

Märchen (*pl* -) *das* - **1.** [Erzählung] fairy tale - **2.** [Lüge] tall story.

märchenhaft ⬦ *adj* - **1.** [sagenhaft] fairytale - **2.** [wunderschön] wonderful - **3.** [unglaublich] fantastic ⬦ *adv* - **1.** [wunderbar] wonderfully - **2.** [unglaublich] fantastically.

Marder (*pl* -) *der* marten.

Margarine *die* margarine.

Margerite (*pl* -n) *die* daisy.

Mariä Himmelfahrt (*ohne Artikel*) Assumption.

Marien|käfer *der* ladybird *Br*, ladybug *Am*.

Marihuana *das* marijuana.

Marine *die* (*ohne pl*) MIL navy.

marineblau *adj* navy blue.

Marionette (*pl* -n) *die* - **1.** [Puppe] marionette, puppet - **2.** *fig* [Person] puppet.

Mark (*pl* -) ⬦ *die* mark ⬦ *das* (*ohne pl*) - **1.** [im Knochen] marrow; **es geht mir durch ~ und Bein** *fig* it goes right through me - **2.** [Konzentrat] purée.

markant *adj* striking; [Kinn, Nase] prominent.

Marke (*pl* -n) *die* - **1.** [Lebensmittel, Verbrauchsgüter] brand; [Auto, Gebrauchsgegenstände] make - **2.** [Briefmarke] stamp - **3.** [Erkennungszeichen - von Hund] identity disc; [- von Polizist] badge - **4.** [Wertzeichen - für Lebensmittel] coupon; [- für Garderobe] ticket *Br*, check *Am* - **5.** *fam* [Person] character.

Marken|artikel *der* branded item.

Marken|zeichen *das* trademark.

markieren ⬦ *vt* - **1.** [kennzeichnen] to mark - **2.** [hervorheben] to highlight - **3.** *fam* [vortäuschen] to play ⬦ *vi fam* [vortäuschen] to fake.

Markise (*pl* -n) *die* awning.

Mark|stück *das* one-mark piece.

Markt (*pl* Märkte) *der* - **1.** [gen] market; **auf den** ODER **zum ~ gehen** to go to the market; **auf den ~ bringen** to put on the market - **2.** [Platz] marketplace.

Markt|forschung *die* market research.

Markt|halle *die* covered market.

Markt|lücke *die* gap in the market.

Markt|platz *der* marketplace.

Markt|preis *der* market price.

Markt|wert *der* market value.

Markt|wirtschaft *die* market economy.

Marmelade (*pl* -n) *die* jam.

> ## Marmelade
>
> Marmelade is a false friend because it means "jam", which can be made from any type of fruit, as opposed to "marmalade", which is made from citrus fruits. (Note also the difference in spelling.) If you specifically wanted to ask "Do you sell marmalade?" in Germany, then you would need to say Haben Sie Orangenmarmelade?

Marmor *der* marble.

Marokkaner, in (*mpl* -; *fpl* -nen) *der, die* Moroccan.

marokkanisch *adj* Moroccan.

Marokko *nt* Morocco.

Marone (*pl* -n) *die* (sweet) chestnut.

marsch *interj* - **1.**, **an die Arbeit/ins Bett!** off to work/to bed!; **vorwärts ~!** forward march!

Marsch (*pl* Märsche) *der* - **1.** [Gehen] walk; **sich in ~ setzen** to set off - **2.** [beim Militär, Musikstück] march.

marschieren (*perf* ist marschiert) *vi* - **1.** [Soldaten] to march - **2.** [gehen] to walk.

Marschmusik *die* marching music.

Märtyrer, in (*mpl* -; *fpl* -nen) *der, die* martyr.

marxistisch ⬦ *adj* Marxist ⬦ *adv* in a Marxist way.

März *der* March; *siehe auch* September.

Marzipan, Marzipan (*pl* -e) *das* marzipan (*U*).

Masche (*pl* -n) *die* - **1.** [beim Stricken, Häkeln] stitch - **2.** [Art und Weise] trick; **die neueste ~** *fam* [Marotte] the latest fad; *fam* [Mode] the latest thing.

Maschine (*pl* -n) *die* - **1.** [Gerät, Motorrad] machine - **2.** *fam* [Motor] engine - **3.** [Flugzeug] plane - **4.** [Schreibmaschine] **~ schreiben** to type.

maschinell ⬦ *adj* [Herstellung, Bearbeitung] machine (*vor Subst*); [Vorgang] mechanical ⬦ *adv* by machine.

Maschinenbau *der* mechanical engineering.

Maschinen|gewehr *das* machine gun.

Maschinen|pistole *die* submachine gun.

Maschinen|schaden *der* engine trouble (*U*).

maschineschreiben, maschinenschreiben *vi* (*unreg*) ▷ Maschine.

Masern *pl* measles (*U*).

Maske (*pl* -n) *die* - **1.** [zum Verkleiden & EDV] mask - **2.** [beim Theater] make-up.

Masken|ball der masked ball.

maskieren vt eigtl & fig to mask. ◆ **sich maskieren** ref - 1. [sich verdecken] to disguise o.s. - 2. [sich verkleiden] to dress up.

Maskottchen (pl -) das mascot.

maskulin, maskulin adj masculine.

Maskulinum (pl Maskulina) das GRAM masculine noun.

maß prät ⊏▷ messen.

Maß (pl -e ODER -) ◇ das (pl Maße) - 1. [Maßeinheit] measure - 2. [Messgerät] (tape) measure - 3. [Körpermaß]: ~ **nehmen** to take measurements - 4. [Umfang, Verhältnis] degree; **in demselben/höherem** ~ **als** to the same/a greater degree as/than; ~ **halten** to be moderate ◇ die (pl Maß) Süddt & Österr [Krug] litre (of beer). ◆ **in Maßen** adv in moderation. ◆ **nach Maß** adv [Anzug] made-to-measure; [Urlaub] tailor-made. ◆ **Maße** pl - 1. [von Räumen] dimensions - 2. [von Personen] measurements.

Massage [ma'sa:ʒə] (pl -n) die massage.

Massaker (pl -) das massacre.

Maßarbeit die: ~ **sein** to be made-to-measure.

Masse (pl -n) die mass; **die breite** ~ abw the masses (pl). ◆ **in Massen** adv [einkaufen] in bulk; **die Leute kamen in** ~**n** masses of people came.

Maß|einheit die unit of measurement.

massenhaft ◇ adj in great numbers; **die** ~**e Hinrichtungen** the great number of executions ◇ adv in great numbers.

Massen|medien pl mass media.

Massen|mord der mass murder.

maßgebend, maßgeblich ◇ adj [Person] influential; [Meinung] authoritative; [Urteil, Argument] decisive ◇ adv: **an etw** (D) ~ **beteiligt sein** to play a decisive role in sthg.

maßgeschneidert adj made-to-measure.

massieren vt to massage.

massig ◇ adj massive ◇ adv fam: ~ **zu essen** loads to eat; ~ **Arbeit** loads of work.

mäßig ◇ adj - 1. [gen] moderate - 2. [mittelmäßig - Leistung, Wetter, Schüler] average ◇ adv - 1. [maßvoll] in moderation - 2. [wenig] moderately.

mäßigen vt [Wut] to curb; [Worte] to moderate. ◆ **sich mäßigen** ref [Person] to restrain o.s.; [Unwetter] to die down.

massiv ◇ adj - 1. [Holz, Metall] solid - 2. [wuchtig] massive - 3. [heftig] strong ◇ adv - 1. [wuchtig] massively - 2. [heftig] strongly.

Massiv (pl -e) das massif.

Maß|krug der Süddt & Österr litre beer mug.

maßlos ◇ adj extreme ◇ adv extremely.

Maßnahme (pl -n) die measure; ~**n einlei-**ten to introduce measures; ~**n ergreifen** ODER **treffen** to take measures.

Maßstab der - 1. [auf Landkarten] scale - 2. [Richtlinie] standard. ◆ **im Maßstab** adv: **im** ~ **1:25000** to a scale of 1:25,000.

maßstabgetreu, maßstabsgetreu adj & adv to scale.

Mast (pl -en ODER -e) ◇ der (pl Maste, Masten) - 1. [auf Schiffen, für Antenne] mast - 2. [Stange - für Fahne, Leitungen] pole; [- für Hochspannungsleitungen] pylon ◇ die (pl Masten) [Mästen] fattening (U).

mästen vt to fatten.

masturbieren vi & vt to masturbate.

Material [mate'ria:l] (pl -ien) das - 1. [Werkstoff, Unterlagen] material - 2. [Gerät] equipment.

materialistisch adj materialistic.

Materie [ma'te:rjə] (pl -n) die - 1. matter - 2. geh [Themenbereich] subject matter.

materiell ◇ adj - 1. [wirtschaftlich] financial - 2. [materialistisch] materialistic - 3. [stofflich] material ◇ adv - 1. [materialistisch] materialistically - 2. [wirtschaftlich] financially.

Mathematik, Mathematik die mathematics (U).

Mathematiker, in (mpl -; fpl -nen) der, die mathematician.

mathematisch ◇ adj mathematical ◇ adv mathematically.

Matjes|hering der salted herring.

Matratze (pl -n) die mattress.

Matrose (pl -n) der sailor.

Matsch der - 1. [Schlamm] mud; [von Schnee] slush - 2. fam [Brei] mush.

matschen vi fam [in Pfütze] to splash around; [in Schlamm] to squelch around; **mit etw** ~ [beim Essen] to make a mush of sthg.

matt ◇ adj - 1. [kraftlos] weak; [Händedruck, Reaktion] feeble - 2. [nicht glänzend] matt - 3. [trübe - Licht] dim; [- Augen, Farbe, Glanz] dull; [- Glühbirne] pearl; [- Glas] frosted - 4. [im Schach]: ~ **sein** to be checkmated ◇ adv - 1. [im Schach]: **jn** ~ **setzen** to checkmate sb - 2. [trübe] dimly - 3. [kraftlos] weakly; [reagieren] feebly.

Matte (pl -n) die mat.

Mauer (pl -n) die wall.

mauern ◇ vi - 1. [bauen] to build - 2. SPORT to play defensively ◇ vt [bauen] to build.

Mauerwerk das masonry.

Maul (pl Mäuler) das - 1. [bei Tieren] mouth - 2. salopp [Mundwerk] trap; **halts** ~! shut your trap!; **böses** ~ malicious tongue.

maulen vi fam abw to moan.

Maul|korb der muzzle.

Maul- und Klauen|seuche die (ohne Pl) foot-and-mouth (disease).

Maul|wurf der mole.

Maulwurfs|hügel der molehill.

Maurer, in (*mpl* -; *fpl* -nen) *der, die* bricklayer.

Mauritius *nt* Mauritius.

Maus (*pl* Mäuse) *die* - **1.** EDV [Tier] mouse
- **2.** *fam* [Mädchen] cutie - **3.** *RW:* **eine graue**
~ *fam abw* a nondescript kind of woman.

Mauselfalle *die* mousetrap.

mausern ⬥ **sich mausern** *ref* - **1.** [Vögel]
to moult - **2.** [Person] to blossom.

mausetot *adj fam* as dead as a doornail.

Mausklick (*pl* -s) *der* EDV mouse click; **per**
~ **die Adresse einfügen** to add the address
by clicking the mouse.

Mauspad (*pl* -s) *das* mouse mat.

Mautlgebühr *die* Österr toll.

Mautlstelle *die* Österr tollgate.

max. (*abk für* maximal) max.

maximal ⬦ *adj* maximum ⬦ *adv:* **das**
~ **zulässige Gewicht** the maximum permitted weight.

Maximum (*pl* Maxima) *das* maximum.

Mayonnaise *die* = Majonäse.

Mazedonien [maze'do:njən] *nt* Macedo-
nia.

MB (*abk für* Megabyte) MB, Mb.

MdB (*abk für* Mitglied des Bundestags)
Member of the 'Bundestag'.

Mechanik (*pl* -en) *die* - **1.** [Fach] mechanics
(*U*) - **2.** [Mechanismus] mechanism.

Mechaniker, in (*mpl* -; *fpl* -nen) *der, die*
mechanic.

mechanisch ⬦ *adj* mechanical ⬦ *adv*
mechanically.

Mechanismus (*pl* Mechanismen) *der*
mechanism.

meckern *vi* - **1.** [Ziege] to bleat - **2.** *fam* [nör-
geln]: **über jn/etw** ~ to moan about sb/sthg.

Mecklenburg-Vorpommern   *nt*
Mecklenburg-West Pomerania.

Medaille [me'daljə] (*pl* -n) *die* medal.

Medaillon [medalj'õ] (*pl* -s) *das*
- **1.** [Schmuck] locket - **2.** [Fleisch, Fisch] medallion.

Medien *pl* media.

Medikament (*pl* -e) *das* medicine; **ein**
~ **gegen etw** a medicine for sthg.

Meditation (*pl* -en) *die* meditation.

meditieren *vi* - **1.** [versunken sein] to meditate - **2.** [nachdenken]: **über etw** (*A*) ~ to meditate on sthg.

Medium ['me:djʊm] (*pl* Medien) *das* medium.

Medizin (*pl* -en) *die* medicine.

Mediziner, in (*mpl* -; *fpl* -nen) *der, die* [Arzt]
doctor; [Student] medical student.

medizinisch ⬦ *adj* - **1.** [heilkundlich, ärzt-
lich] medical - **2.** [heilend] medicinal ⬦ *adv*
medically.

Meer (*pl* -e) *das eigtl & fig* sea; **ans** ~ **fahren**
to go to the seaside; **am** ~ **by** the sea.

Meerlenge *die* strait.

Meereslfrüchte *pl* seafood (*U*).

Meereslgrund *der* seabed.

Meereslspiegel *der* sea level.

Meerlrettich *der* horseradish.

Meerlschweinchen (*pl* -) *das* guinea pig.

Meerlwasser *das* seawater.

Megafon, Megaphon [mega'fo:n] (*pl* -e)
das megaphone.

Mehl *das* - **1.** [zum Backen] flour - **2.** [Pul-
ver - von Holz] sawdust; [- von Knochen]
meal; [- von Gestein] powder.

Mehllschwitze (*pl* -n) *die* roux.

mehr ⬦ *pron* [komparativ von viel] more
⬦ *adv* - **1.** [komparativ von viel] more; **50**
Euro, ~ nicht? 50 euros, no more than that?;
er ist ~ Gelehrter als Künstler he is more of a
scholar than an artist - **2.** [übrig] more;
~ **denn je** more than ever; **es ist keiner ~ da**
there is no one left; **nichts** ~ nothing more
- **3.** [zeitlich]: **nicht** ~ not any longer; **du bist**
doch kein Kind ~! you are not a child any
more - **4.** *RW:* **immer ~, und ~** more and
more; **oder weniger** more or less.

Mehrlaufwand *der* extra expenditure.

mehrdeutig *adj* ambiguous.

mehrere *det & pron* several. ⬥ **mehre-**
res *pron* several things. ⬥ **zu mehreren**
adv: **sie kommen** ~ several (of them) are
coming.

mehrfach ⬦ *adj* multiple; [Olympiasieger]
several times over; **ein Bericht in ~er Ausfer-**
tigung several copies of a report; **in ~er Hin-**
sicht in more than one respect ⬦ *adv* several times.

mehrfarbig ⬦ *adj* multicoloured ⬦ *adv*
in many colours.

Mehrheit (*pl* -en) *die* majority; **mit großer/**
knapper ~ by a large/narrow majority; **die**
absolute ~ an absolute majority.

mehrheitlich ⬦ *adj* majority ⬦ *adv* by a
majority.

mehrmalig *adj* repeated.

mehrmals *adv* several times.

mehrsprachig ⬦ *adj* [Wörterbuch, Ausgabe, Person] multilingual; [Unterhaltung] in
several languages ⬦ *adv:* ~ **aufwachsen** to
grow up multilingual.

mehrstimmig ⬦ *adj* for several voices
⬦ *adv* in harmony.

Mehrwertsteuer *die* VAT *Br*, sales tax
Am.

Mehrzahl *die* - **1.** [größerer Anteil] majority
- **2.** [Plural] plural.

Mehrzwecklhalle *die* multipurpose hall.

Meile (*pl* -n) *die* mile.

meilenweit adv for miles; **~ entfernt** miles away.

mein, e ◇ det my; **~e Damen und Herren** ladies and gentlemen ◇ pron mine.

meine, r, s ODER **meins** pron mine.

Meineid der perjury (U).

meinen ◇ vt - **1**. [denken, glauben] to think; **was meinst du dazu?** what do you think? - **2**. [sagen] to say; **was meint er?** fam what did he say? - **3**. [zum Ausdruck einer Intention] to mean; **etw ironisch ~** to mean sthg ironically; **wie ~ Sie das?** what do you mean by that?; **das war nicht so gemeint** it wasn't meant like that; **gut gemeint** well-intentioned ◇ vi to think; **ich meine ja nur!** it was just a suggestion; **~ Sie?** do you think so?; **wie ~ Sie?** what did you say?; **wie Sie ~!** as you wish!

meiner pron (Genitiv von ich) of me; **er erinnert sich ~** he remembers me.

meinetwegen adv - **1**. [mir zuliebe] for my sake - **2**. [wegen mir] because of me - **3**. [von mir aus] as far as I'm concerned; **(also) ~!** if you like.

meinetwillen ◆ **um meinetwillen** adv for my sake.

Meinung (pl -en) die opinion; **eine vorgefasste ~** a preconceived idea; **anderer ~ sein** to be of a different opinion; **der ~ sein, dass** to be of the opinion that; **einer derselben ~ sein** to agree; **jm die ~ sagen** fam fig to give sb a piece of one's mind; **meiner ~ nach** in my opinion.

Meinungs|austausch der exchange of views.

Meinungs|freiheit die freedom of expression.

Meinungs|umfrage die opinion poll.

Meinungs|verschiedenheit die difference of opinion.

Meise (pl -n) die tit.

Meißel (pl -) der chisel.

meißeln vi & vt to chisel.

meist adv usually, mostly. ◆ **am meisten** adv most; **die am ~en besuchte Ausstellung** the most visited exhibition.

meiste ◇ adj (the) most; **die ~n Leute** most people; **er hat das ~ Geld** he has the most money ◇ pron: **das/die ~** (the) most. ◆ **die meisten** pron most people.

meistens adv usually, mostly.

Meister (pl -) der - **1**. [Handwerker] master craftsman; **seinen ~ machen** fam to get one's master craftsman's certificate - **2**. [Experte, Künstler] master - **3**. [im Sport] champion.

Meisterin (pl -nen) die [Handwerkerin] master craftswoman; [Expertin, Künstlerin] master; [im Sport] champion.

meistern vt - **1**. [bewältigen] to master - **2**. geh [zügeln] to control.

Meisterschaft (pl -en) die - **1**. SPORT championship - **2**. [Können] mastery.

Meister|werk das masterpiece.

Mekka nt Mecca.

melancholisch [melaŋ'ko:lɪʃ] ◇ adj melancholy ◇ adv in a melancholy way.

melden vt - **1**. [anzeigen, berichten] to report; [Geburt] to register; **(bei jm) nichts/nicht viel zu ~ haben** fam fig to have no/little say (with sb) - **2**. [anmelden] to announce. ◆ **sich melden** ref - **1**. [sich bemerkbar machen - im Unterricht] to put one's hand up; [- Finder] to make o.s. known - **2**. [Nachricht geben]: **melde dich mal wieder!** keep in touch!; **sich bei jm ~** [bei Freunden] to get in touch with sb; [bei Polizei] to report to sb - **3**. [am Telefon] to answer; **es meldet sich niemand** there's no answer - **4**. [sich anmelden] to register; **sich freiwillig zu etw ~** to volunteer for sthg.

Meldung (pl -en) die - **1**. [Nachricht, Anzeige] report - **2**. [Mitteilung] announcement - **3**. [Anmeldung] entry.

melken (prät melkte ODER molk; perf hat gemolken) vt & vi to milk.

Melodie [melo'di:] (pl -n) die tune.

melodisch ◇ adj melodic ◇ adv melodically.

Melone (pl -n) die - **1**. [Frucht] melon - **2**. [Hut] bowler (hat).

Membran (pl -en) die - **1**. TECH diaphragm - **2**. BIOL, CHEM & PHYS membrane.

Memoiren [me'mǫaːrən] pl memoirs.

Menge (pl -n) die - **1**. [Anzahl] amount; **die doppelte/dreifache ~** twice/three times the amount; **in rauen ~n** fam: **die Leute kamen in rauen ~n** loads of people came - **2**. [Vielzahl] **a lot** ODER **lots**; **eine ~ Bücher** a lot ODER lots of books - **3**. (ohne pl) [Menschenmasse] crowd - **4**. MATH set. ◆ **eine ganze Menge** adv quite a lot; **eine ganze ~ Geld** quite a lot of money. ◆ **jede Menge** adv fam loads; **jede ~ Arbeit** loads of work.

Mengenlehre die MATH set theory.

mengenmäßig ◇ adj quantitative ◇ adv quantitatively.

Mengen|rabatt der bulk discount.

Mensa (pl Mensen) die UNI university canteen.

Mensch (pl -en) ◇ der - **1**. [Art, Lebewesen] human (being); **der ~ ist ein vernunftbegabtes Tier** man is a rational animal - **2**. [Person] person ◇ interj [wütend] for heaven's sake!; [begeistert] wow! ◆ **kein Mensch** pron no one.

Menschen|kenntnis die knowledge of human nature.

menschenleer adj deserted.

Menschen|menge die crowd.

Menschenrechte pl human rights.

Menschen|seele *die:* **keine ~** not a soul.

menschenunwürdig *adj* inhumane.

Menschenverstand *der:* **der gesunde ~** common sense.

Menschenwürde *die* human dignity.

Menschheit *die* humanity, mankind.

menschlich <> *adj* - **1.** [des Menschen] human - **2.** [human] humane <> *adv* [human] humanely.

Menstruation (*pl* -en) *die* MED menstruation.

Mentalität (*pl* -en) *die* mentality.

Menthol *das* menthol.

Menü (*pl* -s) *das* - **1.** [Speisenfolge] set menu - **2.** EDV menu.

merken *vt* to notice; **sich** (D) **etw ~** to remember sthg; **du merkst aber auch alles!** *fam iron* how observant of you!

Merkmal (*pl* -e) *das* feature.

Merk|satz *der* mnemonic.

merkwürdig <> *adj* strange <> *adv* strangely.

Messe (*pl* -n) *die* - **1.** [Gottesdienst] mass - **2.** [Ausstellung] (trade) fair.

messen (*präs* misst; *prät* maß; *perf* hat gemessen) <> *vt* to measure; [Temperatur] to take <> *vi* [eine bestimmte Größe haben] to measure; **er misst 1,76 m** he is 1.76m tall.

Messer (*pl* -) *das* [zum Schneiden] knife; [zum Rasieren] razor. **➤ bis aufs Messer** *adv* to the bitter end.

messerscharf <> *adj* razor-sharp <> *adv* [scharfsinnig] incisively.

Messe|stand *der* stand at a (trade) fair.

Messing *das* brass.

Messung (*pl* -en) *die* measurement.

Metall (*pl* -e) *das* metal.

Metall|arbeiter, in *der, die* metalworker.

Metall|industrie *die* metalworking industry.

metallisch <> *adj* metallic <> *adv:* **~ schimmern** to have a metallic gleam.

Metapher [me'tafɐ] (*pl* -n) *die* metaphor.

Meteor (*pl* -e) *der* meteor.

Meteorologe (*pl* -n) *der* weather forecaster.

Meteorologin (*pl* -nen) *die* weather forecaster.

Meter (*pl* -) *das* ODER *der* metre; **zwei ~ breit/hoch/lang/tief sein** to be two metres wide/high/long/deep.

Meter|maß *das* tape measure.

Methan *das* methane.

Methode (*pl* -n) *die* method.

methodisch <> *adj* methodical <> *adv* methodically.

Mett|wurst *die* soft, smoked pork or beef sausage, usually spread on bread.

Metzger (*pl* -) *der* butcher.

Metzgerei (*pl* -en) *die* butcher's.

Metzgerin (*pl* -nen) *die* butcher.

Meute (*pl* -n) *die* - **1.** [Hunde] pack - **2.** *fam* [Menschen] mob.

Meuterei (*pl* -en) *die* [auf Schiff] mutiny; [in Gefängnis] revolt.

meutern *vi* - **1.** [sich auflehnen - Besatzung] to mutiny; [- Strafgefangene] to revolt - **2.** *fam* [sich weigern] to protest.

Mexiko *nt* Mexico.

MEZ [em'e:'tsɛt] (*abk für mitteleuropäische Zeit*) *die* CET.

MFG [em'ɛf'geː] (*pl* -s) *die abk für* Mitfahrgelegenheit.

mg (*abk für* Milligramm) mg.

miauen *vi* to miaow.

mich *pron* (*Akkusativ von ich*) - **1.** [Personalpronomen] me - **2.** [Reflexivpronomen] myself; **ich entschied ~ zu kündigen** I decided to hand in my notice.

Miene (*pl* -n) *die* expression; **keine ~ verziehen** not to bat an eyelid.

mies *fam abw* <> *adj* lousy <> *adv:* **~ gelaunt sein** to be in a foul mood.

Miese *pl fam:* **in den ~n sein, ~ haben** to be in the red; **~ machen** to make a loss.

Mies|muschel *die* mussel.

Miete (*pl* -n) *die* [für Wohnung, Geschäftsfläche, Garage] rent; [für Fahrzeug] hire charge *Br*, rental *Am*; **zur ~ wohnen** to live in rented accommodation.

mieten *vt:* **(sich** (D)) **etw ~** [Wohnung, Geschäftsfläche, Garage] to rent; [Fahrzeug] to hire *Br*, to rent *Am*.

Mieter, in (*mpl* -; *fpl* -nen) *der, die* tenant.

Miet|preis *der* rent.

Miets|haus *das* block of flats *Br*, apartment building *Am*.

Miet|vertrag *der* [für Wohnung, Geschäftsfläche] lease; [für Fahrzeug] hire *Br* ODER rental *Am* agreement.

Migräne *die* migraine.

Mikro|chip *der* microchip.

Mikrofon, Mikrophon (*pl* -e) *das* microphone.

Mikroskop (*pl* -e) *das* microscope.

mikroskopisch <> *adj* microscopic <> *adv* - **1.** [mit einem Mikroskop] under the microscope - **2.** [winzig] microscopically.

Mikrowellen|herd *der* microwave (oven).

Milch *die* milk.

Milch|flasche *die* [für Säuglinge] feeding bottle; [von Molkerei] milk bottle.

milchig <> *adj* milky <> *adv:* **~ trüb** milky and cloudy.

Milch|produkt *das* dairy product.

Milch|pulver *das* powdered milk.

Milch|reis *der (ohne pl)* rice pudding.

Milch|straße *die* ASTRON Milky Way.

Milch|zahn *der* milk tooth.

mild, milde <> *adj* - 1. [gen] mild - 2. [Licht, Worte, Lächeln] gentle - 3. [Strafe, Urteil] lenient; [Herrscher] benevolent <> *adv* - 1. [urteilen, strafen] leniently - 2. [scheinen, wehen, lächeln] gently - 3. [nicht scharf - würzen] lightly.

Milde *die* - 1. [von Urteil] leniency - 2. [von Licht] gentleness; [von Abend, Klima, Aroma] mildness.

mildern *vt* - 1. [abschwächen - Wut, Worte, Urteil] to moderate; [- Schärfe] to reduce; [- Aufprall] to soften - 2. [lindern] to alleviate, to relieve. ◆ **sich mildern** *ref* - 1. [Wut, Zorn] to abate - 2. [Klima] to become milder.

Milieu [mi'ljø:] *(pl -s) das* - 1. [Umfeld, Umwelt] environment - 2. [Unterwelt] world of prostitution.

militant <> *adj* militant <> *adv* militantly.

Militär *(pl -s)* <> *das:* **das ~ the** military <> *der* army officer.

Militärdienst *der* military service.

militärisch <> *adj* military <> *adv* militarily.

Militär|regierung *die* military government.

Milliardär, in *(mpl -e; fpl -nen) der, die* billionaire.

Milliarde *(pl -n) die* billion.

Milli|gramm *das* milligram.

Milli|liter *der* millilitre.

Milli|meter *der* millimetre.

Milli|meterpapier *das* graph paper.

Million *(pl -en) die* million.

Millionär, in *(mpl -e; fpl -nen) der, die* millionaire.

Millionen|stadt *die* city with a population of over one million.

Milz *(pl -en) die* spleen.

Milz|brand *der (ohne Pl)* anthrax.

Mimik *die (ohne pl)* facial expressions and gestures.

Minderheit *(pl -en) die* minority; **in der ~ sein** to be in a/the minority.

minderjährig *adj* underage.

Minderjährige *(pl -n) der, die* minor.

mindern *vt* [Strafmaß, Preis, Wert] to reduce; [Ansehen] to diminish.

minderwertig <> *adj* inferior <> *adv* [herstellen] poorly.

Mindestalter *das* minimum age.

mindeste *adj* slightest; **das ist das Mindeste, was man erwarten kann** that is the least you can expect. ◆ **nicht im Mindesten** *adv* not in the slightest.

mindestens *adv* at least.

Mindest|lohn *der* minimum wage.

Mine *(pl -n) die* - 1. [Schreibutensil - von Kugelschreiber] refill; [- von Bleistift] lead - 2. [Bergwerk, Sprengsatz] mine; [Stollen] tunnel.

Mineral *(pl -e ODER -ien) das* mineral.

Mineral|öl *das* mineral oil.

Mineralöl|steuer *die* tax on oil.

Mineral|wasser *das* mineral water.

mini *adv:* ~ **tragen** to wear a mini.

Mini *(pl -s)* <> *das* - 1. *(ohne pl, ohne Artikel)* [Mode] miniskirts *(pl)* - 2. *fam* [Kleid] mini <> *der fam* [Rock] mini.

minimal <> *adj* minimal <> *adv* minimally.

Minimum *(pl Minima) das* minimum *(U)*.

Minister *(pl -) der* minister.

ministeriell <> *adj* ministerial <> *adv* ministerially.

Ministerin *(pl -nen) die* minister.

Ministerium [minɪs'te:rjʊm] *(pl Ministerien) das* ministry; ~ **des Inneren/der Finanzen** interior/finance ministry.

Minister|präsident, in *der, die* - 1. [von Bundesländern] minister president, *title given to leader of government in the German federal states* - 2. [Premierminister] prime minister.

Minister|rat *der* Council of Ministers.

minus <> *präp* minus <> *adv:* ~ **dreizehn Grad** minus thirteen degrees <> *konj:* **zehn ~ drei** ten minus three.

Minus *das (ohne pl)* - 1. [Fehlbetrag] deficit; **im ~ stehen** to be in the red - 2. [Zeichen] minus (sign).

Minute *(pl -n) die* minute; **auf die ~ pünktlich** on the dot.

Minze *(pl -n) die* mint.

Mio. *(abk für Million)* m.

mir *pron (Dativ von ich)* - 1. (to) me; **er sagte es ~** he told me; **das gehört ~ this is mine,** this belongs to me; **mit ~** with me - 2. [Reflexivpronomen] myself.

Misch|brot *das* bread made from a mixture of *rye and wheat flour.*

mischen *vt* [Farben, Zutaten] to mix; [Karten] to shuffle; **etw mit etw ~** to mix sthg with sthg. ◆ **sich mischen** *ref:* **sich unter etw** *(A)* ~ to mix with sthg.

Mischling *(pl -e) der* [Tier] half-breed.

Mischung *(pl -en) die* mixture.

missachten *vt* - 1. [nicht befolgen] to disregard - 2. [verachten] to despise.

missbilligen *vt* to disapprove of.

Miss|brauch *der* - 1. [sexuell, von Medikamenten, von Drogen] abuse - 2. [schlechter Gebrauch] misuse.

missbrauchen *vt* - 1. [ausnutzen - Macht, Mittel] to misuse; [- Vertrauen] to abuse; [- Gutmütigkeit] to take advantage of - 2. [übermäßig nutzen, sexuell] to abuse.

missen *vt* to do without; **etw nicht (mehr) ~ wollen** not to want to be without sthg.

Misserfolg *der* failure.

missfallen (*präs* missfällt; *prät* missfiel; *perf* hat missfallen) *vi*: **es missfällt mir, wie sie ...** I dislike the way she ...; **der Plan missfiel ihm** he disliked the plan.

Missfallen *das* displeasure.

missgebildet *adj* deformed.

Missgeschick *das* mishap; **jm passiert ein ~ sb** has a mishap.

missglücken (*perf* ist missglückt) *vi* to be unsuccessful; **der Versuch ist mir missglückt** my attempt was unsuccessful.

missgönnen *vt*: **jm etw ~** to begrudge sb sthg.

Missgunst *die* resentment.

misshandeln *vt* to ill-treat.

Misshandlung *die* ill-treatment *(U)*.

Mission (*pl* -en) *die* mission.

Misskredit *der*: **jn in ~ bringen** to discredit sb; **in ~ geraten** ODER **kommen** to be discredited.

misslang *prät* ⊳ misslingen.

misslingen (*prät* misslang; *perf* ist misslungen) *vi* to fail; **das Experiment ist mir misslungen** my experiment was a failure; **ein misslungener Versuch** an unsuccessful attempt.

misslungen *pp* ⊳ misslingen.

missmutig ⋄ *adj* [Person, Charakter] bad-tempered; [Gesicht, Laune] sullen; **~ sein** to be in a bad mood ⋄ *adv* bad-temperedly; [ansehen] sullenly.

missraten (*präs* missrät; *prät* missriet; *perf* ist missraten) ⋄ *vi*: **der Braten war ihr ~** her roast had turned out badly ⋄ *adj* which/who turned out badly.

misst *präs* ⊳ messen.

misstrauen *vi*: **jm/etw ~** to mistrust sb/sthg.

Misstrauen *das* mistrust.

misstrauisch ⋄ *adj* mistrustful; **jm gegenüber ~ sein** to be mistrustful of sb ⋄ *adv* mistrustfully.

Missverhältnis *das* discrepancy.

Missverständnis (*pl* -nisse) *das* misunderstanding.

missverstehen (*prät* missverstand; *perf* hat missverstanden) *vt* to misunderstand.

Misswirtschaft *die* mismanagement.

Mist *der* - **1.** [Dung] dung; [Düngemittel] manure - **2.** *fam fig & abw* [Plunder, Blödsinn] rubbish; **~ machen** ODER **bauen** to make a mess of things - **3.** *fam* [als Ausruf]: **(so ein) ~!** damn it!

mit ⋄ *präp* (+ *D*) - **1.** [zusammen mit] with; **er kommt ~ seiner Frau** he's coming with his wife; **Kaffee ~ Zucker** coffee with sugar; **ein**

Haus ~ Garten a house with a garden; **eine Scheibe Brot ~ Butter** a slice of bread and butter; **sich ~ jm unterhalten** to talk to sb - **2.** [modal]: **~ lauter Stimme** in a loud voice; **~ Nachdruck** emphatically; **~ 100 Stundenkilometern** at 100 kilometres per hour; **~ Verspätung eintreffen** to arrive late - **3.** [mittels] with; **~ dem Hammer** with a hammer; **~ dem Zug** by train; **~ der Post** by post; **~ Scheck bezahlen** to pay by cheque - **4.** [stellt Bezug her]: **wie weit bist du ~ deiner Arbeit?** how far have you got with your work?; **wie wäre es ~ einer Tasse Kaffee?** how about a cup of coffee?; **er hat es ~ dem Magen** he has stomach trouble - **5.** [temporal] at; **~ jedem Tag** every day; **~ 16 Jahren** at (the age of) 16; **~ der Zeit** in (the course of) time ⋄ *adv* - **1.** [auch] too; **sie war nicht ~ dabei** she wasn't there - **2.** [unter anderen]: **er ist ~ der beste Schüler seiner Klasse** he is one of the best pupils in his class.

Mitarbeit *die* [an Projekt] collaboration; [von Schülern, Bevölkerung] participation;

mitarbeiten *vi* - **1.** [in Projekt] to collaborate; [im Haushalt] to help out; **bei/an etw** *(D)* **~** to collaborate on sthg - **2.** [in der Schule] to participate.

Mitarbeiter, in *der, die* [Betriebsangehörige] colleague, co-worker *Am*.

mitbekommen *vt* (*unreg*) - **1.** [verstehen] to follow - **2.** [aufschnappen]: **etw von etw ~** to hear sthg about sthg; **(von etw) nicht viel ~** not to take much (of sthg) in - **3.** [bekommen]: **etw ~** to get sthg to take with one.

Mitbestimmung *die* codetermination.

Mitbewohner, in *der, die* [in Haus] other occupant; [in Wohnung] flatmate *Br*, roommate *Am*.

mitbringen *vt* (*unreg*) - **1.** [Geschenk, Personen] to bring (with one); [von Reise] to bring back; **jm etw ~** to bring sthg for sb - **2.** [Fähigkeiten] to have.

Mitbürger, in *der, die* fellow citizen.

miteinander *adv* [auskommen, streiten, flirten] with each other; [reden, verbinden] to each other; [gemeinsam] together. ◆ **alle miteinander** *pron* all (together).

miterleben *vt* to witness.

Mitesser (*pl* -) *der* blackhead.

mitfahren (*perf* ist mitgefahren) *vi* (*unreg*) to go/come along; **mit** ODER **bei jm ~** to get a lift *Br* ODER **ride** *Am* with sb.

Mitfahrgelegenheit *die* lift *Br*, ride *Am*.

Mitfahrzentrale, Mitfahrerzentrale *die agency which organizes lifts, with passengers contributing to costs.*

mitfühlen ⋄ *vi*: **mit jm ~** to sympathize with sb ⋄ *vt* to share.

mitgeben *vt* (*unreg*): **jm etw ~** to give sb sthg.

Mitgefühl *das* sympathy.

Mitgefühl zeigen

I'm so sorry. Es tut mir sehr Leid.
How awful for you! Wie furchtbar für dich!
If there's anything I can do … Falls ich irgendetwas tun kann …
You poor thing! Du Ärmste/Ärmster!
Get well soon! Gute Besserung!

---

mit|gehen (*perf* ist mitgegangen) *vi* (*unreg*) - 1. [mitkommen] to go/come along; **mit jm** ~ to go/come with sb - 2. [teilhaben] to be carried along - 3. *fam* [stehlen]: **etw** ~ **lassen** to pinch sthg.

mitgenommen ◇ *pp* ⊳ mitnehmen ◇ *adj* worn out; ~ **aussehen** to look worn out.

Mitgift (*pl* -en) *die* dowry.

Mitglied *das* member.

Mitglieds|beitrag *der* membership fee.

Mitgliedschaft (*pl* -en) *die* membership (*U*).

mit|halten *vi* (*unreg*): **bei etw (nicht)** ~ **können** (not) to be able to keep up in sthg; **mit jm/etw (nicht)** ~ **können** (not) to be able to keep up with sb/sthg.

mithilfe ◇ *adv*: ~ **von etw/** with the help of sthg/sb ◇ *präp*: ~ **js/einer Sache** with the help of sb/sthg.

mit|hören ◇ *vi* [zufällig] to overhear; [heimlich] to listen in ◇ *vt* [zufällig] to overhear; [heimlich] to listen in.

mit|kommen (*perf* ist mitgekommen) *vi* (*unreg*) - 1. [auch kommen] to come along; **kommst du mit?** are you coming? - 2. [folgen können] to keep up; **da komme ich nicht (mehr) mit!** *fam* it's beyond me! - 3. [eintreffen] to arrive.

Mitleid *das* pity; **mit jm** ~ **haben** ODER **empfinden** to feel pity for sb.

Mitleidenschaft *die*: **jn/etw in** ~ **ziehen** to affect sb/sthg.

mitleidig ◇ *adj* pitying ◇ *adv* pityingly.

mit|machen ◇ *vt* - 1. [Spiel, Kurs] to take part in; [Mode] to follow; **das mache ich nicht mehr länger mit** I'm not going to put up with this any longer - 2. [erledigen]: **etw für jn** ~ to do sthg for sb - 3. [aushalten]: **sie hat schon viel mitgemacht** she has been through a lot ◇ *vi* [sich beteiligen] to take part; **bei etw (nicht)** ~ (not) to take part in sthg.

Mitmenschen *pl* fellow human beings ODER men.

mit|mischen *vi fam*: **bei etw** ~ [sich einmischen] to interfere in sthg; [teilnehmen] to get involved in sthg.

mit|nehmen *vt* (*unreg*) - 1. [mit sich nehmen] to take (with one); **ich kann dich bis zum Bahnhof** ~ I can give you a lift *Br* ODER ride *Am* to the station; **sich** (*D*) **etw** ~ to take sthg (with one) - 2. [strapazieren] to take it out of - 3. [kaufen] to buy - 4. [stehlen] to make off with - 5. *fam* [wahrnehmen, besuchen] to take in.

Mit|reisende *der, die* fellow passenger.

mit|reißen *vt* (*unreg*) - 1. [begeistern] to carry away - 2. [fortreißen - bei Sturz] to pull down; [- bei Lawine] to sweep away.

mitsamt *präp*: ~ **einer Sache** (*D*) together with sthg.

mit|schreiben (*unreg*) ◇ *vt* - 1. [festhalten] to take down - 2. [Klassenarbeit, Prüfung] to do ◇ *vi* [festhalten] to take notes.

Mitschuld *die* share of the blame.

mitschuldig *adj*: **(an etw** (*D*)) ~ **sein** to be partly to blame (for sthg).

Mit|schüler, in *der, die* schoolmate.

mit|spielen ◇ *vi* - 1. [auch spielen]: **bei/in etw** (*D*) ~ [Spiel] to join in sthg; [Mannschaft, Orchester] to play in sthg; [Theatergruppe, Film] to act in sthg - 2. [wichtig sein]: **bei etw** ~ to play a part in sthg - 3. [mitmachen] to play along; **bei etw** ~ to go along with sthg - 4. [schaden]: **jm übel** ~ to give sb a hard time ◇ *vt* [Spiel] to play.

Mit|spieler, in *der, die* [bei Spiel, in Mannschaft] other player.

Mittag (*pl* -e) *der* midday; **am** ~ at midday; **über** ~ at lunchtime; **zu** ~ **essen** to have lunch; **gestern/heute/morgen** ~ at midday yesterday/today/tomorrow.

Mittag|essen *das* lunch.

mittags *adv* at midday.

Mittags|pause *die* lunch break.

Mittags|schlaf *der* (*ohne pl*) afternoon nap.

Mitte (*pl* -n) *die* middle; **in der** ~ in the middle; ~ **vierzig** in one's mid-forties; ~ **nächster Woche** in the middle of next week.

mit|teilen *vt*: **jm etw** ~ to tell sb sthg.

Mit|teilung *die* communication; [an Presse] statement; **jm eine** ~ **machen** to inform sb; **eine schriftliche** ~ a written communication.

Mittel (*pl* -) *das* - 1. [Hilfsmittel] means (*sg*); **mit allen** ~**n** by every means - 2. [Medikament] medicine; **ein** ~ **gegen etw** a remedy for sthg - 3. [zur Reinigung] cleaning agent. ➡ **Mittel** *pl* [Geldmittel] means; **öffentliche** ~ public funds.

Mittelalter *das* (*ohne pl*) Middle Ages (*pl*).

mittelalterlich ◇ *adj* medieval ◇ *adv* like in medieval times.

Mittelamerika *nt* Central America.

Mittel|europa *nt* Central Europe.

Mittel|finger *der* middle finger.

Mittel|gebirge *das* low-lying mountain range.

mittelgroß *adj* medium-sized; [Person] of medium height.

mittellos *adj* penniless.

mittelmäßig *abw* ◇ *adj* average ◇ *adv* averagely.

Mittelmeer *das:* **das ~** the Mediterranean (Sea).

Mittel|punkt *der* centre; **im ~ stehen** to be the centre of attention.

Mittel|streifen *der* central reservation *Br,* median *Am.*

Mittel|weg *der* middle way.

Mittel|wert *der* mean.

mitten *adv:* **~ auf** in the middle of; **~ durch** through the middle of; **~ in etw** (*D*) in the middle of sthg; **~ in etw** (*A*) into the middle of sthg; **~ unter** among; **~ am Tag/in der Nacht** in the middle of the day/night.

mittendrin *adv* in the middle.

mittendurch *adv* through the middle.

Mitternacht *die* midnight.

mittlere, r, s *adj* - **1.** [zwischen den Extremen] average; **im ~n Alter** middle-aged - **2.** [in der Mitte liegend] middle.

Mittlere Osten *der:* **der ~** the Middle East.

mittlerweile *adv* [inzwischen] in the meantime; [jetzt] now.

Mittwoch (*pl* -e) *der* Wednesday; *siehe auch* **Samstag.**

mittwochs ['mɪtvɔxs] *adv* on Wednesdays; *siehe auch* **samstags.**

mitunter *adv* occasionally.

mitverantwortlich *adj* jointly responsible.

mit|verdienen *vi* to earn money as well.

mit|wirken *vi:* **(bei etw) ~** [mitarbeiten] to contribute (to sthg); [mitspielen] to take part (in sthg).

mixen *vt* to mix.

MKS (*abk für* Maul- und Klauenseuche) *die* (*ohne Pl*) foot-and-mouth (disease).

Möbel (*pl* -) *das* piece of furniture; **die ~** the furniture.

Möbel|wagen *der* removal *Br* ODER moving *Am* van.

mobil *adj* - **1.** [beweglich] mobile - **2.** [munter] lively; **~ machen** MIL to mobilize; **jn ~ machen** [munter machen] to liven sb up.

Mobil|funk *der (ohne pl)* TELEKOM cellphone ODER mobile phone network.

Mobil|telefon *das* mobile phone.

möblieren *vt* to furnish.

möbliert ◇ *adj* furnished ◇ *adv:* **~ wohnen** to live in furnished accommodation.

mochte *prät* ▷ **mögen.**

Mode (*pl* -n) *die* [Kleidungsstil, Zeitgeschmack] fashion; **es ist jetzt groß in ~** it is very fashionable now; **mit der ~ gehen** to follow the fashion.

Mode|haus *das* - **1.** [Einzelgeschäft] fashion store - **2.** [Unternehmen] fashion house.

Modell (*pl* -e) *das* model; **~ stehen** [für Maler] to model.

modellieren *vt* to model.

Modem (*pl* -s) *das* EDV modem.

Moden|schau *die* fashion show.

Moderator (*pl* -en) *der* presenter.

Moderatorin (*pl* -nen) *die* presenter.

moderig = modrig.

modern¹ (*perf* hat/ist gemodert) *vi* to moulder.

modern² ◇ *adj* modern; [modisch] fashionable ◇ *adv* - **1.** [zeitgemäß] in a modern way; **~ denken** to have modern ideas - **2.** [zeitgenössisch] in a modern style.

modernisieren *vt* to modernize.

Mode|schmuck *der* costume jewellery.

modisch ◇ *adj* fashionable ◇ *adv* fashionably.

modrig, moderig *adj & adv* musty.

Mofa (*pl* -s) *das* moped.

mogeln *vi* to cheat.

mögen (*präs* mag; *prät* mochte; *perf* hat gemocht ODER -) ◇ *vt* (*perf* hat gemocht) - **1.** [gern haben] to like; **jn/etw (nicht) ~** (not) to like sb/sthg - **2.** [wollen]: **ich möchte bitte ein Eis** I'd like an ice-cream please; **was möchten Sie?** what would you like? ◇ *vi* (*perf* hat gemocht) [wollen]: **er möchte nach Hause** he wants to go home ◇ *aux* (*perf* hat mögen): **ich möchte etwas trinken** I'd like something to drink; **möchtest du mitkommen?** would you like to come?; **mag sein** that may well be.

möglich *adj & adv* possible; **ich habe es so gut wie ~ gemacht** I did it as well as I could; **jm ist es (nicht) ~, etw zu tun** it is (not) possible for sb to do sthg. ◆ **alles Mögliche** *pron* absolutely everything.

möglicherweise *adv* possibly.

Möglichkeit (*pl* -en) *die* - **1.** [das Mögliche] possibility; **es besteht die ~, dass ...** it is possible that ...; **nach ~** if possible - **2.** [Chance] opportunity. ◆ **Möglichkeiten** *pl* [Fähigkeiten] capabilities.

möglichst ['møːklɪçst] *adv* - **1.** [wenn möglich] if possible - **2.** [so viel wie möglich]: **~ groß/stark/viel** as big/strong/much as possible.

Mohammedaner, in (*mpl* -; *fpl* -nen) *der, die* Muslim.

mohammedanisch *adj* Muslim.

Mohn (*pl* -e) *der* - **1.** [Pflanze] poppy - **2.** [Samen] poppy seeds (*pl*).

Mohn|blume *die* poppy.

Möhre (*pl* -n) *die* carrot.

Mohren|kopf *der* KÜCHE chocolate-covered marshmallow.

Mokka (*pl* -s) *der* mocha.

Molekül (*pl* -e) *das* molecule.

molk *prät* ▭ melken.

Molke *die* whey.

Molkerei (*pl* -en) *die* dairy.

Moll *das* minor (key).

mollig *adj* plump.

Moment (*pl* -e) ⬦ *der* moment; **im** ~ at the moment; **jeden** ~ (at) any moment; **(einen)** ~, **bitte!** just a moment, please!; ~ **mal!** *fam* wait a moment! ⬦ *das* element.

momentan ⬦ *adj* present ⬦ *adv* at the moment.

Monaco *nt* Monaco.

Monarchie (*pl* -n) *die* monarchy.

Monat (*pl* -e) *der* month; **diesen/nächsten/ vorigen** ~ this/next/last month; **sie ist im fünften** ~ **(schwanger)** she is over four months pregnant.

monatelang ⬦ *adj* lasting for months ⬦ *adv* for months.

monatlich *adj* & *adv* monthly.

Monats|karte *die* monthly season ticket.

Mönch (*pl* -e) *der* monk.

Mond (*pl* -e) *der* moon.

Mond|finsternis *die* eclipse of the moon.

Mond|landung *die* moon landing.

Mond|schein *der* moonlight.

Monitor (*pl* -en ODER -e) *der* monitor.

Monogramm (*pl* -e) *das* monogram.

Monolog (*pl* -e) *der* monologue.

Monopol (*pl* -e) *das* monopoly; **das** ~ **auf etw** (A) **haben** to have a monopoly on sthg.

monoton ⬦ *adj* monotonous ⬦ *adv* monotonously.

Monster (*pl* -) *das* monster.

Monsun (*pl* -e) *der* monsoon.

Montag (*pl* -e) *der* Monday; *siehe auch* Samstag.

Montage [mɔn'taːʒə] (*pl* -n) *die* - **1.** TECH [Zusammenbau] assembly (U); [Einbau] installation (U); **auf** ~ **sein** to be away on assembly/installation work - **2.** [Schnitt] editing (U) - **3.** KUNST montage.

montags *adv* on Mondays; *siehe auch* samstags.

Montblanc [mõ'blãː] *der* Mont Blanc.

montieren *vt* - **1.** TECH [zusammenbauen] to assemble; [einbauen] to install; [festmachen] to fix - **2.** [schneiden] to edit.

Monument (*pl* -e) *das* monument.

monumental ⬦ *adj* monumental ⬦ *adv* on a monumental scale.

Moor (*pl* -e) *das* bog.

Moos (*pl* -e) *das* - **1.** [Pflanze, Pflanzengattung] moss - **2.** [Geld] dough.

Moped (*pl* -s) *das* moped.

Mops (*pl* Möpse) *der* - **1.** [Hund] pug (dog) - **2.** *fam fig* [Mensch] roly-poly.

Moral *die* - **1.** [Normen] morals (*pl*) - **2.** [Stim-

mung] morale - **3.** [das Lehrreiche] moral - **4.** [Ethik] morality.

moralisch ⬦ *adj* moral ⬦ *adv* morally.

Morast (*pl* -e) *der* quagmire.

Morchel (*pl* -n) *die* morel.

Mord (*pl* -e) *der* murder, homicide *Am*; [durch Attentat] assassination; **einen** ~ **begehen** to commit murder.

Mörder, in (*mpl* -; *fpl* -nen) *der, die* murderer; [durch Attentat] assassin.

mörderisch ⬦ *adj* - **1.** [lebensgefährlich] deadly; [Tempo] breakneck - **2.** [Verbrechen, Absicht] murderous - **3.** *fam* [groß] terrible ⬦ *adv* - **1.** [steil, schnell] murderously - **2.** *fam* [sehr] terribly.

morgen *adv* - **1.** [am Tag nach heute, zukünftig] tomorrow; **bis** ~! see you tomorrow!; ~ **früh** tomorrow morning - **2.** [vormittag] morning.

Morgen (*pl* -) *der* morning; **am** ~ in the morning; **gestern/heute** ~ yesterday/this morning. ➡ **guten Morgen** *interj* good morning!

Morgen|grauen *das* dawn.

Morgen|rot *das* red dawn sky.

morgens *adv* in the morning; [jeden Morgen] every morning; **von** ~ **bis abends** from dawn till dusk.

morgig *adj* [Treffen] tomorrow's; **der** ~**e Tag** tomorrow.

Morphium *das* morphine.

morsch *adj* rotten.

morsen ⬦ *vt* to send in Morse (code) ⬦ *vi* to use Morse (code).

Mörtel (*pl* -) *der* mortar.

Mosaik (*pl* -e ODER -en) *das* mosaic.

Moschee [mɔ'ʃeː] (*pl* -n) *die* mosque.

Mosel *die* Moselle.

Moskau *nt* Moscow.

Moskauer (*pl* -) ⬦ *der* Muscovite ⬦ *adj* (*unver*) of/from Moscow.

Moskauerin (*pl* -nen) *die* Muscovite.

Moskito (*pl* -s) *der* mosquito.

Moslem (*pl* -s) *der* Muslim.

Moslime (*pl* -n) *die* Muslim.

Most (*pl* -e) *der* - **1.** [Fruchtsaft] (cloudy) fruit juice - **2.** *Süddt* [Apfelwein] cider.

Motiv (*pl* -e) *das* - **1.** [von Handlung] motive - **2.** [von Bild] subject - **3.** [Thema] motif.

motivieren [moti'viːrən] *vt* to motivate; **jn** ~, **etw zu tun** to motivate sb to do sthg.

Motor, Motor (*pl* -toren) *der* - **1.** [von Fahrzeug] engine; [von Gerät] motor - **2.** *fig* [Triebfeder] driving force.

Motor|rad *das* motorcycle, motorbike.

Motor|schaden *der* engine trouble (U).

Motte (*pl* -n) *die* moth.

Motto (*pl* -s) *das* motto; **unter dem** ~ „keine

Steuererhöhung" stehen to have 'no tax increases' as its motto.

Möwe (pl -n) die seagull.

Mrd. abk für Milliarde.

Mücke (pl -n) die [in Tropen] mosquito; [kleiner] midge, gnat.

Mückenǀstich der mosquito bite.

müde <> adj tired; **einer Sache** (G) **~ sein** geh to be tired of sthg; **nicht ~ werden, etw zu tun** never to tire of doing sthg <> adv wearily.

Müdigkeit die tiredness.

muffig <> adj - 1. [modrig] musty - 2. fam [schlecht gelaunt] grumpy <> adv: **~ riechen** to smell musty.

Mühe (pl -n) die effort; **es macht mir eine ~** it's no trouble (to me); **sich** (D) **~ machen (mit etw)** to go to trouble (over sthg); **sich** (D) **~ geben** to make an effort; **gib dir keine ~ don't** bother; **mit Müh und Not** by the skin of one's teeth.

mühelos <> adj effortless <> adv effortlessly.

mühevoll <> adj laborious, painstaking <> adv laboriously, painstakingly.

Mühle (pl -n) die - 1. [Mahlwerk - für Getreide] mill; [- für Kaffee] grinder - 2. [Gebäude] mill - 3. [Spiel] nine men's morris - 4. fam [Fahrzeug] jalopy, banger Br.

mühsam <> adj laborious <> adv laboriously.

mühselig <> adj [Arbeit, Tun] laborious; [Leben] arduous <> adv laboriously.

Mulde (pl -n) die GEOGR hollow; [Griffmulde] grip.

Mull (pl -e) der [Material] muslin; [für Verband] gauze.

Müll der rubbish Br, garbage Am; **[radioaktiv] waste; etw in den ~ werfen** ODER **tun** to throw sthg out ODER away.

Müllǀabfuhr die - 1. [Transport] refuse Br ODER garbage Am collection - 2. [Unternehmen] refuse Br ODER garbage Am collection service.

Müllǀbinde die gauze dressing.

Müllǀdeponie die refuse disposal site.

Müllǀeimer der dustbin Br, garbage ODER trash can Am.

Müller, in (mpl -; fpl -nen) der, die miller.

Müllǀschlucker der rubbish Br ODER garbage Am chute.

Müllǀtonne die dustbin Br, garbage ODER trash can Am.

Müllǀtrennung die separation of household waste for recycling purposes.

Müllǀwagen der dustcart Br, garbage truck Am.

mulmig adj uncomfortable; **mir wird ~** [körperlich] I feel queasy.

multikulturell adj multicultural.

Multiplexǀkino das multiplex (cinema).

multiplizieren vt: **etw mit etw ~** to multiply sthg by sthg.

Mumie ['mu:mjə] (pl -n) die mummy.

Mumm der (ohne pl) fam guts (pl); **(keinen) ~ haben** to have (no) guts.

Mumps der MED mumps (U).

München nt Munich.

Mund (pl Münder) der mouth; **jn von ~ zu ~ beatmen** to give sb mouth-to-mouth resuscitation; **halt den ~!** fam shut up!

Mundǀart die amt dialect.

münden (perf hat/ist gemündet) vi - 1. [einmünden]: **(in etw** (A)) **~** [Fluss] to flow (into sthg); [Straße] to lead (to sthg) - 2. geh [enden]: **in etw** (D) **~** [Vorgang] to end in sthg.

Mundǀharmonika die harmonica, mouthorgan.

mündig adj - 1. [volljährig] of age; **~ werden** to come of age - 2. [urteilsfähig] responsible.

mündlich <> adj [Vereinbarung, Versprechung] verbal; [Prüfung] oral <> adv verbally.

mundtot adj: **jn ~ machen** to silence sb.

Mündung (pl -en) die - 1. [von Fluss] mouth; GEOGR estuary - 2. [von Straße] end - 3. [von Gewehr] muzzle.

Mundwerk das fam: **ein großes ~ haben** to be a bigmouth; **ein loses ~ haben** to be cheeky.

Munition (pl -en) die ammunition.

munkeln <> vi: **es wurde schon lange darüber gemunkelt** there had already been rumours about it for some time <> vt: **man munkelt, dass …** it is rumoured that …

Münster (pl -) das cathedral, minster.

munter <> adj - 1. [wach]: **~ sein** to be (wide) awake - 2. [lebhaft - Mensch, Tier, Spiel] lively - 3. [fröhlich] cheerful <> adv cheerfully.

Münze (pl -n) die coin.

münzen vt [Geld] to mint; **auf jn/etw gemünzt sein** fig to refer to sb/sthg.

Münzfernǀsprecher der amt pay phone Br, pay station Am.

mürbe adj - 1. [Kuchen, Teig] crumbly; [Fleisch] tender; [Obst] soft - 2. [Material] rotten, crumbling - 3. [zermürbt]: **jn ~ machen** to wear sb down.

Mürbeǀteig der shortcrust pastry.

murmeln vt & vi to murmur.

murren vi: **(über etw** (A)) **~** to grumble (about sthg).

mürrisch <> adj sullen, surly <> adv in a sullen ODER surly manner.

Mus (pl -e) das puree.

Muschel (pl -n) die - 1. [Tier] mussel - 2. [Schale] shell.

Museum [mu'ze:ʊm] (pl Museen) das museum.

Musical ['mju:zik(ə)l] (*pl* -s) *das* musical.

Musik (*pl* -en) *die* music.

musikalisch <> *adj* musical <> *adv* musically.

Musiker, in (*mpl* -; *fpl* -nen) *der, die* musician.

Musik|unterricht *der* (*ohne pl*) [Schulfach] music; [Musikstunden] music lessons (*pl*).

musizieren *vi* to make music.

Muskatnuss *die* nutmeg.

Muskel (*pl* -n) *der* muscle.

Muskelkater *der*: **(einen) ~ haben** to be stiff.

Muskulatur (*pl* -en) *die* muscles (*pl*).

muskulös *adj* muscular.

Müsli (*pl* -) *das* muesli.

muss *präs* ⟼ müssen.

Muss *das* (*ohne pl*) necessity, must.

Muße *die* leisure; **Zeit und ~ haben, etw zu tun** to have enough time to do sthg at one's leisure.

müssen (*präs* muss; *prät* musste; *perf* hat gemusst ODER -) <> *aux* (*perf hat müssen*) - **1.** [gezwungen sein] must; **etw tun ~** to have to do sthg; **du musst aufstehen** you must get up; **sie musste lachen/niesen** she had to laugh/sneeze; **etw nicht tun ~** not to need to do sthg - **2.** [nötig sein]: **der Brief muss noch heute weg** the letter has to go today; **muss das sein?** is that really necessary? - **3.** [wahrscheinlich sein]: **du musst Hunger haben nach der langen Reise** you must be hungry after your long journey; **das müsste alles sein** that should be all <> *vi* (*perf hat gemusst*) to have to; **ich muss ins Büro (gehen)** I have to go to the office; **ich muss mal** *fam* I need the toilet.

musste *prät* ⟼ müssen.

Muster (*pl* -) *das* - **1.** [Vorlage, Beispiel] model; **ein ~ an etw** (*D*) a model of sthg - **2.** [Musterung] pattern - **3.** [Warenprobe] sample.

mustern *vt* - **1.** [betrachten] to study, to scrutinize - **2.** [Wehrpflichtigen] to inspect.

Musterung (*pl* -en) *die* - **1.** [von Wehrpflichtigen] inspection - **2.** [Betrachtung] scrutiny.

Mut *der* courage; **jm ~ machen** to encourage sb. ➤ **nur Mut** *interj* chin up! ➤ **zu Mute** ⟶ mutig <> *adj* brave, courageous <> *adv* bravely, courageously.

mutmaßlich *adj* suspected.

Mutter (*pl* Mütter ODER -n) *die* - **1.** (*pl* Mütter) [gen] mother - **2.** (*pl* Muttern) [von Schraube] nut.

mütterlich <> *adj* [Liebe, Frau] motherly; [Eigenschaft, Erbe] maternal <> *adv* [fürsorgend] in a motherly fashion.

mütterlicherseits *adv* on one's mother's side.

Mutter|mal *das* mole.

Mutter|sprache *die* mother tongue, native language.

Mutterltag *der* Mother's Day.

mutwillig <> *adj* wilful <> *adv* wilfully.

Mütze (*pl* -n) *die* cap; [aus Wolle] hat.

MwSt. (*abk für* Mehrwertsteuer) VAT *Br*, sales tax *Am*.

Mythos (*pl* Mythen) *der* myth; **er ist schon jetzt ein ~** he is already a legend.

N

n, N [ɛn] (*pl* - ODER -s) *das* n, N. ➤ **N** (*abk für* Nord) N.

na *interj* well?; **~, wie gehts?** so how's it going, then?; **~ los, mach schon!** well go on then, do it!; **~, lass das sein!** hey, leave that alone! ➤ **na also** *interj* there you are! ➤ **na gut** *interj* all right, then! ➤ **na ja** *interj* well! ➤ **na und** *interj*: **na und?** so (what)?

Nabel (*pl* -) *der* navel.

Nabel|schnur *die* umbilical cord.

nach *präp* (+ *D*) - **1.** [zeitlich, zur Angabe einer Reihenfolge] after; **~ dem Essen** after the meal; **fünf (Minuten) ~ drei** five (minutes) past three *Br*, five (minutes) after three *Am*; **~ Ihnen!** after you! - **2.** [räumlich] to; **~ Frankfurt** to Frankfurt; **~ Hause gehen** to go home; **~ Süden** south, southwards; **~ links/rechts abbiegen** to turn left/right - **3.** [gemäß] according to; **~ Angaben der Polizei** according to the police - **4.** [stellt Bezug her]: **seinem Akzent ~ ist er kein Deutscher** judging by his accent, he is not German; **meiner Meinung ~** in my opinion. ➤ **nach und nach** *adv* little by little. ➤ **nach wie vor** *adv* as before.

nachlahmen *vt* to imitate, to copy.

Nachbar, in (*mpl* -n; *fpl* -nen) *der, die* neighbour.

Nachbarschaft *die* neighbourhood.

nachlbessern *vt* [Vorschlag, Entwurf] to amend; [Preisangebot] to raise; **sie musste ihre Arbeit ~** she had to redo the bits she had got wrong.

nachdem *konj* after. ➤ **je nachdem** *konj* depending on.

nachldenken *vi* (*unreg*): **(über jn/etw) ~** to think (about sb/sthg).

nachdenklich <> *adj* thoughtful, pensive; **jn ~ machen** to set sb thinking <> *adv* thoughtfully, pensively.

Nachdruck (*pl* -e) *der* - **1.** [Eindringlichkeit] emphasis; **einer Sache** (*D*) **~ verleihen** to reinforce sthg; **mit ~** emphatically - **2.** [Nachdrucken - von Buch] reprinting; [- von Druck] reproduction - 3. [Ausgabe] reprint.

nachdrücklich <> adj emphatic, forceful <> adv emphatically.

nach|eifern vi: jm (in etw (D)) ~ to seek to emulate sb (in sthg).

nacheinander adv - 1. [der Reihe nach] one after the other - 2. [gegenseitig] one another.

nach|empfinden vt (unreg) [nachfühlen]: js Schmerz ~ to share sb's pain; **ich kann dir ~, wie du dich jetzt fühlst** I can understand how you feel.

Nacher|zählung die retelling (in one's own words).

Nachfolge die succession.

nach|folgen (perf ist nachgefolgt) vi - 1. [Nachfolge antreten]: **jm (in einem Amt)** ~ to succeed sb (in a position) - 2. [nachkommen] to follow; **das ~de Fahrzeug** the vehicle behind.

Nachfolger, in (mpl -; fpl -nen) der, die successor.

nach|forschen vi to make enquiries; **jm/einer Sache** ~ geh to investigate sb/sthg.

Nachfrage die WIRTSCH demand.

nach|fragen vi - 1. [nachhaken] to ask repeatedly - 2. [fragen] to enquire.

nach|füllen vt - 1. [füllen] to refill - 2. [nachgießen] to top up with.

nach|geben vi (unreg) - 1. [bei Streit] to give in - 2. [Brücke, Boden] to give way; [Preise, Kurse] to fall.

nach|gehen (perf ist nachgegangen) vi (unreg) - 1. [folgen]: **jm/einer Sache** ~ to follow sb/sthg - 2. [etw prüfen]: **einer Sache** (D) ~ to look into sthg - 3. [Uhr] to be slow; **meine Uhr geht zehn Minuten nach** my watch is ten minutes slow - 4. [nachwirken]: **jm** ~ to stick in sb's mind - 5. [sich widmen]: **einer Sache** (D) ~ to pursue sthg.

Nachgeschmack der aftertaste.

nachgiebig adj compliant; [Eltern] indulgent.

nach|haken vi to return to the same question.

nachhaltig <> adj lasting <> adv: ~ **wirken** to have a lasting effect.

nach|hängen vi (unreg) - 1. [sich erinnern]: **einer Sache** (D) ~ to dwell on sthg - 2. fam [zurückliegen]: **in etw** (D) ~ to lag behind in sthg.

Nachhause|weg der way home.

nach|helfen vi (unreg) - 1. [antreiben]: **bei jm** ~ **müssen** to have to chivvy sb along - 2. [helfen]: **(jm)** ~ to lend (sb) a hand.

nachher, nachher adv - 1. [später] later (on) - 2. [anschließend] afterwards. **bis nachher** interj see you later!

Nachhilfe die extra tuition.

Nachhinein adv: **im** ~ with hindsight; **im**

~ **zeigte sich, dass er gelogen hatte** it later turned out that he had lied.

nach|holen vt - 1. [nachträglich machen]: **etw** ~ [Versäumtes] to catch up on sthg; [Prüfung] to do sthg later - 2. [nachziehen lassen]: **er holte seine Familie nach** his family joined him later.

nach|jagen (perf ist nachgejagt) vi: **jm/einer Sache** ~ to chase after sb/sthg.

Nachkomme (pl -n) der descendant.

nach|kommen (perf ist nachgekommen) vi (unreg) - 1. [später kommen] to come (along) later - 2. geh [entsprechen]: **einer Sache** (D) ~ to comply with sthg.

Nachkriegs|zeit die post-war period.

nach|lassen (unreg) <> vi [Schmerz, Spannung] to ease; [Regen] to ease off; [Augen, Gehör] to fail; [Geschäft, Anstrengung] to slacken; [Qualität] to drop off <> vt [Preis]: **jm** ~ % to give sb a 10% discount.

nachlässig <> adj careless <> adv carelessly.

nach|laufen (perf ist nachgelaufen) vi (unreg): **jm/einer Sache** ~ [laufen nach] to run after sb/sthg; [folgen] to follow sb/sthg; fam [sich bemühen um] to pursue sb/sthg.

nach|machen vt - 1. [nachahmen, kopieren] to copy; [nachäffen] to mimic; [fälschen] to forge; **jm etw** ~ to copy sthg off sb; **etw** ~ **lassen** to have sthg copied - 2. [nachholen]: **etw** (A) ~ to catch up on sthg later.

Nach|mittag der afternoon; **am** ~ in the afternoon; **gestern/heute/morgen** ~ yesterday/this/tomorrow afternoon; **Dienstag** ~ on Tuesday afternoon.

nachmittags adv in the afternoon.

Nachnahme (pl -n) die: **etw als** ~ **versenden** to send sthg cash on delivery; **per** ODER **gegen** ~ cash on delivery.

Nach|name der surname.

nach|prüfen vt - 1. [kontrollieren] to check - 2. [erneut prüfen] to re-examine.

nach|rechnen <> vt - 1. [nochmals rechnen] to check - 2. [nachzählen] to work out <> vi - 1. [nochmals rechnen] to check - 2. [nachzählen] to work it out.

Nach|rede die: **üble** ~ slander.

Nachricht (pl -en) die [Neuigkeit] piece of news; [Mitteilung] message; **eine gute** ~ **haben** to have (some) good news; **die** ~, **dass** ... the news that ...; **eine** ~ **von jm** [Neuigkeit] news of sb; [Mitteilung] a message from sb. **Nachrichten** pl: **die** ~**en** the news (sg).

Nachrichten|agentur die news agency.

Nachrichten|sprecher, in der, die newsreader.

nach|rücken (perf ist nachgerückt) vi to move up.

Nach|ruf der obituary.

nach|rüsten ⟨⟩ *vt* EDV to upgrade ⟨⟩ *vi* MIL to rearm.

nach|sagen *vt* [behaupten]: **jm etw ~** to say sthg of sb.

Nachsaison *die* low season.

nach|schicken *vt* to forward.

Nach|schlag *der* second helping.

nach|schlagen (*perf* hat/ist nachgeschlagen) ⟨⟩ *vi* - **1.** (*hat*) [nachlesen]: **in einem Wörterbuch ~** to consult a dictionary - **2.** (*ist*) [ähneln]: **jm ~** to take after sb ⟨⟩ *vt* (*hat*) [nachlesen] to look up.

Nachschlage|werk *das* reference work.

Nach|schlüssel *der* duplicate key.

Nachschub *der* (*ohne pl*) supplies (*pl*).

nach|sehen (*unreg*) ⟨⟩ *vi* - **1.** [hinterhersehen]: **jm/einer Sache ~** to gaze after sb/sthg - **2.** [suchen] to look - **3.** [prüfen] to check - **4.** [nachschlagen]: **in etw** (*D*) **~** to consult sthg ⟨⟩ *vt* - **1.** [nachschlagen]: **etw in etw** (*D*) **~** to look sthg up in sthg - **2.** [prüfen] to check - **3.** [verzeihen]: **jm seine Fehler ~** to overlook sb's mistakes.

Nachsehen *das*: **das ~ haben** [unterlegen sein] to come off badly; [etw nicht bekommen] to be left empty-handed.

nach|senden *vt* (*unreg*) to forward.

nach|sitzen *vi* (*unreg*): **~ müssen** to get detention.

Nach|speise *die* dessert.

Nach|spiel *das* [Folgen] consequences (*pl*); [Theaterstück] epilogue; **es wird ein ~ haben** it will have consequences.

nach|sprechen *vt & vi* (*unreg*) to repeat.

nächstbeste, r, s *adj*: **bei der ~n Gelegenheit** at the first available opportunity. ➤ **Nächstbeste** *der, die, das*: **der/die/das Nächstbeste** *fig* the first available one.

nächste, r, s ['nɛːçstə, ɐ, əs] *adj* - **1.** [nah] nearest, closest - **2.** [folgend] next; **der Nächste bitte!** next, please!; **wie heißt die ~ Haltestelle?** what's the next stop?; **die ~ Straße links** the next road on the left.

Nächstenliebe ['nɛːçstənliːbə] *die* charity.

nächstens ['nɛːçstn̩s] *adv* shortly, soon.

nächstliegend ['nɛːçstliːgn̩t] *adj* most obvious.

nächstmöglich ['nɛːçstmøːklɪç] *adj* next possible.

Nacht (*pl* Nächte) *die* night; **gestern/morgen ~** last/tomorrow night; **heute ~** tonight. ➤ **gute Nacht** *interj* good night!

Nach|teil *der* disadvantage; **zu js ~** to sb's disadvantage.

nächtelang ⟨⟩ *adj* lasting several nights ⟨⟩ *adv* night after night.

Nacht|frost *der* night frost.

Nacht|hemd *das* [für Frauen] nightdress; [für Männer] nightshirt.

Nachtigall (*pl* -en) *die* nightingale.

Nachtisch *der* (*ohne pl*) dessert.

nächtlich *adj* nocturnal; [Stille] of the night.

nach|tragen *vt* (*unreg*) - **1.** [übel nehmen]: **jm etw ~** to hold sthg against sb - **2.** [ergänzen] to add - **3.** [hinterhertragen]: **jm etw ~** to follow behind sb carrying sthg.

nachträglich ⟨⟩ *adj* [Glückwunsch] belated; [Beweis] subsequent ⟨⟩ *adv* [beglückwünschen] belatedly; [beweisen] subsequently.

nach|trauern *vi*: **jm/einer Sache ~** to miss sb/sthg.

Nachtruhe *die* night's sleep.

nachts *adv* at night; **um vier Uhr ~** at four in the morning.

Nacht|schicht *die* night shift.

Nacht|wache *die* - **1.** [Dienst] night watch - **2.** [Person] person on night watch.

Nacht|wächter, in *der, die* night watchman (*f* -woman).

nach|vollziehen *vt* (*unreg*) to comprehend.

nach|wachsen ['naːxvaksn̩] (*perf* ist nachgewachsen) *vi* (*unreg*) to grow again.

Nachweis (*pl* -e) *der* proof (*U*).

nach|weisen *vt* (*unreg*) - **1.** [Fehler] to prove - **2.** [Substanz] to detect.

Nach|welt *die* posterity.

Nach|wirkung *die* aftereffect.

Nach|wuchs ['naːxvuːks] *der* - **1.** [Kind(er)] offspring - **2.** [im Beruf]: **künstlerischer/wissenschaftlicher ~** rising generation of artists/scientists; **es fehlt an ~** there is a lack of new blood.

nach|zahlen ⟨⟩ *vi* to pay the extra ⟨⟩ *vt*: **3 Euro ~** to pay 3 euros extra.

nach|zählen *vt* to check.

Nacken (*pl* -) *der* back ODER nape of the neck; **ihm sitzt die Angst im ~** he is afraid.

nackt ⟨⟩ *adj* - **1.** [ohne Kleider/Fell] naked; [Körperteil] bare - **2.** [bloß] bare; **die ~e Wahrheit** the plain truth; **~e Tatsachen** hard facts ⟨⟩ *adv* naked.

Nadel (*pl* -n) *die* [gen] needle; [Stecknadel] pin.

Nadel|baum *der* conifer.

Nadel|öhr *das* - **1.** [von Nadeln] eye - **2.** *fig* [enge Stelle] bottleneck.

Nadel|wald *der* coniferous forest.

Nagel (*pl* Nägel) *der* - **1.** nail - **2.** *RW*: **den ~ auf den Kopf treffen** to hit the nail on the head; **etw an den ~ hängen** to give sthg up; **sich** (*D*) **etw unter den ~ reißen** *fam abw* to pinch sthg for o.s.

Nagel|feile *die* nail file.

Nagel|lack *der* nail varnish.

nageln *vt* to nail; [Knochen] to pin.

nagelneu *adj* brand-new.

nagen ⟨⟩ *vi* - **1.** [knabbern]: **an etw** (*D*) **~** to gnaw at sthg - **2.** [jn beunruhigen]: **an jm ~** [Zweifel] to prey on sb; [Hunger] to gnaw at sb ⟨⟩ *vt* to gnaw.

Nageltier *das* rodent.

nah, nahe (*kompar* näher; *superl* nächste) <> *adj* near; **~ an/bei jm/etw** close to ODER near sb/sthg; **zu ~** too close; **in ~er Zukunft** in the near future; **den Tränen/dem Wahnsinn ~ sein** to be on the verge of tears/madness; **~ daran sein, etw zu tun** to be on the point ODER verge of doing sthg <> *adv* - 1. [räumlich]: **eine ~e gelegene Stadt** a nearby town; **komm mir nicht zu ~e!** keep your distance!; **von ~em** from close up; **von ~ und fern** from near and far - 2. [vertraut] closely; **~e verwandt** closely related; **jm zu ~ treten** *fig* to offend sb.

Nahlaufnahme *die* close-up.

Nähe *die* - 1. [räumlich, zeitlich] closeness; **in meiner ~** near me; **aus der ~** from close-up; **in der ~** nearby; **in greifbarer ~** within reach - 2. [emotional] closeness, intimacy; **js ~ suchen** to seek sb's company.

nahe gehen (*perf* ist nahe gegangen) *vi* (*unreg*): **jm ~** to affect sb deeply.

nahe legen *vt* - 1. [Verdacht, Vermutung] to give rise to - 2. [jn auffordern]: **jm ~, etw zu tun** to advise sb to do sthg.

nahe liegen *vi* (*unreg*) [Idee, Plan] to suggest itself; **der Verdacht/die Vermutung liegt nahe, dass ...** it seems reasonable to suspect/suppose that ...

nähen <> *vt* - 1. [Kleid, Hose] to make - 2. [Riss] to mend - 3. [Wunde] to stitch <> *vi* [schneidern] to sew.

Nahe Osten *der*: **der ~** the Middle East.

näher <> *adj* - 1. [Komparativ von nahe] closer, nearer - 2. [Umstände, Angaben] more precise <> *adv* - 1. [Komparativ von nahe] closer, nearer - 2. [betrachten] more closely; [erklären] more precisely.

Naherholungslgebiet *das amt area close to a town, offering recreational facilities.*

näher kommen (*perf* ist näher gekommen) *vi* (*unreg*) - 1. [nahe kommen]: **jm ~** to get to know sb better - 2. [entsprechen]: **einer Sache** (*D*) **~** to get closer to sthg. **⮞ sich näher kommen** *ref* [sich nahe kommen] to get to know one another better.

nähern ⮞ sich nähern *ref* to approach.

nahe stehen *vi* (*unreg*): **sich/jm ~** to be close to one another/sb.

nahe stehend *adj* - 1.: **jm ~** [persönlich] close to sb; **einer Sache** (*D*) **~** [politisch] sympathetic to sthg - 2. [in der Nähe] nearby.

nahezu *adv* nearly, almost.

nahm *prät* ⮕ nehmen.

Nählmaschine *die* sewing machine.

Nählnadel *die* (sewing) needle.

Nahost (*ohne Artikel*) the Middle East.

nahrhaft *adj* nourishing, nutritious.

Nährlstoff *der* nutrient.

Nahrung *die* food; **feste ~** solids (*pl*).

Nahrungslmittel *das* food.

Naht (*pl* Nähte) *die* - 1. [an Kleidung] seam; **aus allen Nähten platzen** *fig* to burst at the seams - 2. [in der Medizin] suture - 3. [in der Technik] join.

nahtlos <> *adj* seamless; **~e Bräune** all-over tan <> *adv* [ununterbrochen] seamlessly.

Nahverkehr *der* local traffic.

Nähzeug *das* (*ohne pl*) sewing things (*pl*).

naiv [na'i:f] <> *adj* naive <> *adv* naively.

Naivität [naivi'tɛ:t] *die* naivety.

Name (*pl* -n) *der* name; **im ~n von jm** in the name of sb; **jn/etw (nur) dem ~n nach kennen** to know sb/sthg (only) by name.

namhaft *adj* renowned.

Namibia *nt* Namibia.

nämlich *adv* because; **zwei von ihnen, ~ Anna und Berthold** two of them, namely Anna and Berthold; **übermorgen, ~ am Donnerstag** the day after tomorrow, that is, on Thursday; **wir treffen uns jetzt ~ am Freitag** we'll now actually be meeting on Friday.

nanu *interj* well (I never)!

Napf (*pl* Näpfe) *der* dish, bowl.

Narbe (*pl* -n) *die* scar.

narbig *adj* scarred.

Narkose (*pl* -n) *die* anaesthetic.

närrisch <> *adj* - 1. [verrückt] mad, crazy; **das ~e Treiben** [im Karneval] carnival festivities - 2. *fam* [unglaublich] terrific <> *adv* - 1. [verrückt]: **sich ~ gebärden** to act crazy - 2. *fam* [unglaublich] terribly.

Narzisse (*pl* -n) *die* narcissus.

naschen *vt* & *vi* to nibble.

Nase (*pl* -n) *die* - 1. nose; **sich** (*D*) **die ~ putzen** to blow one's nose; **jm läuft die ~** sb's nose is running - 2. *RW*: **über etw die ~ rümpfen** to turn one's nose up at sthg; **jn an der ~ herumführen** to pull the wool over sb's eyes.

Nasenlbluten *das* (*ohne pl*) nosebleed.

Nasenlloch *das* nostril.

Nashorn (*pl* -hörner) *das* rhinoceros.

nass <> *adj* wet <> *adv*: **~ machen** to wet.

Nässe *die* wet; **vor ~ triefen** to be dripping wet.

Nation (*pl* -en) *die* nation.

national <> *adj* national <> *adv*: **~ denken** to think in national terms.

Nationalfeiertag *der* national day.

Nationallhymne *die* national anthem.

Nationalismus *der* nationalism.

nationalistisch <> *adj* nationalistic <> *adv*: **~ orientiert** with nationalistic leanings.

Nationalität (*pl* -en) *die* nationality.

Nationalsozialismus *der* National Socialism, Nazism.

NATO ['na:to:] (*abk für North Atlantic Treaty Organization*) *die* NATO.

Natron *das* CHEM soda.

Natur (*pl* -en) *die* nature; **Tiere in der freien ~ animals** in the wild; **hinaus in die ~ fahren** to go out into the countryside. ◆ **von Natur aus** *adv* by nature.

Naturalien [natu'ra:ljən] *pl*: **in ~ bezahlen** to pay in kind.

Naturalismus *der* naturalism.

naturbelassen *adj* natural; [Obst, Gemüse] organic.

Naturereignis *das* natural phenomenon.

naturgemäß ◇ *adj* natural ◇ *adv* - **1.** [gemäß der Natur] in accordance with natural laws - **2.** [grundsätzlich] by its very nature.

naturgetreu ◇ *adj* [Abbildung] lifelike ◇ *adv* in a lifelike manner.

Naturheilkunde *die* naturopathy.

natürlich ◇ *adj* natural ◇ *adv* - **1.** [nicht künstlich] naturally - **2.** [selbstverständlich] of course, naturally; **~ war er wieder zu spät** naturally he was too late again; **~ stimmt das, aber ...** of course that's correct but ... ◇ *interj* (but) of course!

naturrein *adj* pure.

Naturschutz *der* nature conservation; **unter ~ stehen** to be protected.

Naturschutzgebiet *das* nature reserve.

Naturwissenschaft *die* natural science.

Naturwissenschaftler, in *der, die* scientist.

Nazi (*pl* -s) *der abw* Nazi.

n. Chr. (*abk für* nach Christus) AD.

NDR [ɛn'de:'ɛr] (*abk für* Norddeutscher Rundfunk) *der* North German Radio.

Neapel *nt* Naples.

Nebel (*pl* -) *der* fog; **leichter ~** mist.

nebelig = neblig.

Nebelscheinwerfer *der* fog lamp.

Nebelschwaden *pl* swathes of mist.

neben *präp* - **1.** (*+ D*) [lokal] beside, next to - **2.** (*+ D*) [außer] apart from, as well as - **3.** (*+ D*) [verglichen mit] compared to ODER with - **4.** (*+ A*) beside, next to.

nebenan *adv* next door.

nebenbei *adv* - **1.** [außerdem] in addition, as well; **etw ~ erledigen** to do sthg on the side - **2.** [beiläufig] in passing; **~ bemerkt** by the way.

nebenberuflich ◇ *adj*: **-e Tätigkeit** second job ◇ *adv*: **~ tätig sein** to have a second job.

nebeneinander *adv* - **1.** [neben jm/etw] next to each other - **2.** [gleichzeitig] simultaneously.

Nebenfach *das* SCHULE subsidiary subject.

Nebenfluss *der* tributary.

Nebengeräusch *das* background noise.

nebenher *adv* in addition, as well; **~ arbeiten** to work on the side.

Nebenjob *der* second job.

Nebenkosten *pl* - **1.** [bei Miete] additional charges - **2.** [zusätzliche Auslagen] additional costs.

Nebenrolle *die* minor part.

Nebensache *die* minor issue.

nebensächlich *adj* of secondary importance.

Nebensatz *der* GRAM subordinate clause.

Nebenstraße *die* side street.

neblig, nebelig *adj* foggy; **leicht ~** misty.

necken *vt* to tease; **jn mit jm/etw ~** to tease sb about sb/sthg. ◆ **sich necken** *ref* to tease each other.

neckisch *adj* - **1.** [verschmitzt] teasing - **2.** [frech] coquettish.

Neffe (*pl* -n) *der* nephew.

negativ ◇ *adj* negative ◇ *adv* negatively; **jm/etw ~ beeinflussen** to have a negative influence on sb/sthg.

Negativ (*pl* -e) *das* negative.

Neger, in (*mpl* -; *fpl* -nen) *der, die abw* negro (*f* negress).

nehmen (*präs* nimmt; *prät* nahm; *perf* hat genommen) *vt* - **1.** [gen] to take; **für etw fünf Euro ~** to charge five euros for sthg; **ich nehme ein Omelett** I'll have an omelette; **sich** (*D*) **etw ~** to help o.s. to sthg; **jn/etw für voll ~** to take sb/sthg seriously; **es leicht/schwer nehmen** to take it lightly/hard; **wie mans nimmt** it depends (how you look at it); **etw zu sich ~** [Nahrung] to take sthg, to eat sthg; **etw an sich** (*A*) **~** to look after sthg; **etw auf sich** (*A*) **~** to take sthg on - **2.** [wegnehmen] to take away; **jm den Glauben/die Illusionen ~** to destroy sb's faith/illusions; **jm seine/ihre Freiheit ~** to deprive sb of his/her freedom - **3.** [einstellen] to take on - **4.** [verwenden] to use; **den Zug ~** to take the train; **sich** (*D*) **einen Anwalt ~** to get o.s. a lawyer.

Neid *der* envy.

neidisch ◇ *adj* envious ◇ *adv* enviously.

neigen ◇ *vi*: **zu etw ~** [tendieren] to have a tendency ODER be inclined to sthg; [anfällig sein] to be prone to sthg ◇ *vt* [beugen - Körper] to bend; [- Kopf] to bow. ◆ **sich neigen** *ref* [sich beugen - Gegenstand] to bend; [- Mensch] to lean.

Neigung (*pl* -en) *die* - **1.** [Veranlagung] inclination; **künstlerische ~en** artistic leanings - **2.** (*ohne pl*) [Anfälligsein] susceptibility - **3.** (*ohne pl*) [Tendenz] tendency - **4.** [von Linie, Fläche] inclination.

nein *adv* no; **~, danke!** no thank you!; **regnet es? – ich glaube** is it raining? – I don't think so; **aber ~!** certainly not!; **zu etw ~ sagen** to say no to sthg; **~ sowas!** well I never!

Nektar (*pl* -e) *der* - **1.** [Pflanzensaft] nectar (*U*) - **2.** [Getränk] fruit drink.

Nelke (*pl* -n) *die* - **1.** [Blume] carnation - **2.** [Gewürz] clove.

nennen (*prät* nannte; *perf* hat genannt) *vt* - **1.** [benennen, bezeichnen] to call - **2.** [anführen] to name; [Adresse, Name] to give. ◆ **sich nennen** *ref* - **1.** [heißen] to be called - **2.** [sich bezeichnen] to call o.s.

nennenswert ◇ *adj* significant ◇ *adv* significantly.

Nenner (*pl* -) *der* MATH denominator.

Neon *das* CHEM neon.

Neon|licht (*pl* -er) *das* neon light.

Nerv (*pl* -en) *der* nerve. ◆ **Nerven** *pl* nerves; **die ~en verlieren/behalten** to lose/keep one's cool; **jm auf die ~en gehen** ODER **fallen** to get on sb's nerves.

Nervenzusammen|bruch *der* nervous breakdown.

nervlich ◇ *adj* nervous ◇ *adv:* **~ völlig am Ende sein** to be a nervous wreck.

nervös ◇ *adj* nervous; **jn ~ machen** to make sb nervous ◇ *adv* nervously.

Nervosität *die* nervousness.

Nerz (*pl* -e) *der* - **1.** [Pelz] mink coat - **2.** [Tier] mink.

Nest (*pl* -er) *das* - **1.** [von Vögeln] nest - **2.** *fam abw* [Ortschaft] little place; **ein trostloses ~** a miserable hole - **3.** *fam* [Bett] bed.

nett ◇ *adj* nice; **wären Sie so ~ mir zu helfen?** would you mind helping me?; **eine ~e Summe** a tidy sum; **das ist ja eine ~e Bescherung!** what a nice mess! ◇ *adv* - **1.** [ansprechend] nicely; **sich ~ unterhalten** to have a nice chat - **2.** *fam* [ziemlich]: **ganz ~ verdienen** to earn pretty well.

netterweise *adv* kindly.

netto *adv* net.

Netz (*pl* -e) *das* - **1.** [zum Fischen, für Haare, im Sport] net; **jm ins ~ gehen** *fig* [gefasst werden] to fall into sb's trap - **2.** [System] network; [Strom] grid; [Internet] Web; **ins ~ gehen** to go on the Web - **3.** [für Akrobaten] safety net - **4.** [von Spinnen] web - **5.** [Einkaufstasche] string bag.

Netz|haut *die* retina.

neu ◇ *adj* - **1.** [gen] new; **das ist mir ~** that's news to me; **ich bin hier ~** I'm new here - **2.** [erneuert] fresh; **eine ~e Flasche holen** to fetch another bottle - **3.** [aktuell]: **die ~esten Nachrichten** the latest news; **was gibts Neues?** what's new?; **seit ~estem** just lately ODER recently ◇ *adv* newly; **sie sind ~ eingezogen** they have just (recently) moved in; **~ anfangen** to start (all over) again; **etw noch mal ~ machen** to redo sthg; **~ streichen** to repaint. ◆ **aufs Neue** *adv* again. ◆ **von neuem** *adv* again.

neuartig *adj* new; **ein ~ Produkt** a new kind of product.

Neubau (*pl* -ten) *der* new building.

neuerdings *adv* recently, lately.

Neuerung (*pl* -en) *die* innovation; **~en einführen** to make changes.

Neugier, Neugierde *die* curiosity.

neugierig ◇ *adj* inquisitive; **sie ist ~, ob**

... she is curious to see whether ... ◇ *adv* inquisitively.

Neuheit (*pl* -en) *die* - **1.** [Produkt] innovation - **2.** [Originalität] innovativeness - **3.** [Neusein] newness.

Neuigkeit (*pl* -en) *die* news (*U*); **~ en** news; **ich habe gute ~en** I have some good news.

Neu|jahr (*ohne Artikel*) New Year. ◆ **prost Neujahr!** *interj* Happy New Year!

neulich *adv* recently.

Neuling (*pl* -e) *der* novice.

Neumond *der* new moon.

neun *num* nine; *siehe auch* **sechs**.

Neun (*pl* -en) *die* nine; *siehe auch* **Sechs**.

neunfach ◇ *adj* ninefold ◇ *adv* nine times.

neunhundert *num* nine hundred.

neunmal *adv* nine times.

neuntausend *num* nine thousand.

neunte, r, s *adj* ninth; *siehe auch* **sechste**.

Neunte (*pl* -n) *der, die, das* ninth; *siehe auch* **Sechste**.

neuntel *adj* (*unver*) ninth; *siehe auch* **sechstel**.

Neuntel (*pl* -) *das* ninth; *siehe auch* **Sechstel**.

neunzehn *num* nineteen; *siehe auch* **sechs**.

Neunzehn (*pl* -en) *die* nineteen; *siehe auch* **Sechs**.

neunzig *num* ninety; *siehe auch* **sechs**.

Neunzig *die* ninety; *siehe auch* **Sechs**.

Neunzigerjahre, neunziger Jahre *pl:* **die ~** the nineties.

neureich *adj abw* nouveau riche.

Neurose (*pl* -n) *die* neurosis.

neurotisch *adj* neurotic.

Neuseeland *nt* New Zealand.

neusprachlich *adj* ☞ **Gymnasium**.

neutral ◇ *adj* neutral ◇ *adv* neutrally.

Neutralität *die* neutrality.

Neutron (*pl* -en) *das* neutron.

Neutrum (*pl* **Neutra** ODER **Neutren**) *das* - **1.** GRAM neuter - **2.** *abw* [Mensch] asexual creature.

neuwertig *adj* nearly new.

Neuzeit (*ohne -pl*) modern times (*pl*).

Newsgroup (*pl* -s) *die* EDV newsgroup.

Nicaragua *nt* Nicaragua.

nicht ◇ *adv* - **1.** [gen] not; **sie raucht ~** she doesn't smoke; **sie mag kein Marzipan – ich auch ~** she doesn't like marzipan – neither do I; **warum ~?** why not? - **2.** [als Bestätigungsfrage]: **der Film war großartig, ~ wahr?** the film was great, wasn't it?; **du wusstest es schon länger, ~ (wahr)?** you've known for a while, haven't you?; **ist das ~ schön?** isn't that nice? - **3.** [verstärkend]: **was habe ich ~ alles für dich getan!** all the things I've done for you! ◇ *konj:* **~ dass ich ...** it's not that I ...; **~ nur ..., sondern auch ...** not only ..., but also ... ◆ **nicht einmal** *adv* not ...

even; **er kann ~ einmal Englisch** he can't even speak English.

Nichte (*pl* **-n**) *die* niece.

Nicht|raucher *der* - **1.** [Person] non-smoker - **2.** [Abteil] no-smoking compartment.

Nicht|raucherin *die* non-smoker.

nichts *pron* nothing; **ich weiß ~ darüber** I don't know anything about it; **das macht ~ fig** it doesn't matter; **~ zu danken** don't mention it; **das ist ~ für dich** it's not your kind of thing. **nichts als** *pron* nothing but. **nichts anderes** *pron* nothing else. **nichts da** *interj fam* no way!

nichts ahnend <> *adj* unsuspecting <> *adv* unsuspectingly.

Nicht|schwimmer, in *der, die* non-swimmer.

nichts sagend *adj* [Worte, Geschwätz] empty.

Nichtstun *das* inactivity; **ich hasse dieses ~** I hate all this sitting around doing nothing.

Nickel *das* nickel.

nicken *vi* - **1.** [zustimmen] to nod; **mit dem Kopf ~** to nod (one's head) - **2.** [dösen] to doze.

Nickerchen (*pl* -) *das:* **ein ~ machen** to have a nap.

nie *adv* never; **~ im Leben!** not on your life! **nie mehr** *adv* never again. **nie und nimmer** *adv* not on your life.

nieder *adv:* **mit ...!** down with ...!

niedere, r, s *adj* [Einkommen, Lohn, Steuerklasse] low; [Arbeit] lowly; [Motive, Triebe] base; [Adel] lesser.

Niedergang *der* decline.

niedergeschlagen <> *pp* ▷ **niederschlagen** <> *adj* dejected <> *adv* dejectedly.

Nieder|lage *die* defeat.

Niederlande *pl:* **die ~** the Netherlands.

Niederländer, in (*mpl* -; *fpl* -nen) *der, die* Dutchman (*f* Dutchwoman).

niederländisch *adj* Dutch.

Niederländisch(e) *das* Dutch; *siehe auch* Englisch(e).

nieder|lassen **sich niederlassen** *ref* (*unreg*) - **1.** [sich setzen] to sit down - **2.** [beruflich]: **sich als etw ~** to set up as sthg - **3.** [sich ansiedeln] to settle.

Niederlassung (*pl* -en) *die* - **1.** [Unternehmen] branch - **2.** [als Arzt, Rechtsanwalt] setting up in practice.

nieder|legen *vt* - **1.** [Amt, Mandat] to resign from - **2.** geh [aufzeichnen] to put down - **3.** geh [hinlegen] to lay.

Niederösterreich *nt* Lower Austria.

Niedersachsen ['niːdɐzaksn] *nt* Lower Saxony.

niedersächsisch ['niːdɐ'zɛksɪʃ] *adj* of/from Lower Saxony.

Nieder|schlag *der* precipitation.

nieder|schlagen *vt* (*unreg*) - **1.** [zusammen-schlagen] to knock down - **2.** [Blick, Augen] to lower - **3.** [Revolution] to put down. **sich niederschlagen** *ref* - **1.** [sich auswirken]: **sich in etw** (*D*) ODER **auf etw** (*A*) **~** to be reflected in sthg - **2.** [sich ablagern] to condense.

niederträchtig <> *adj* malicious <> *adv* maliciously.

niedlich <> *adj* cute <> *adv* cutely.

niedrig <> *adj* low; [Arbeit] lowly <> *adv:* **~ fliegen** to fly low; **die Preise ~ halten** to keep prices low.

niemals <> *adv* never <> *interj* never!

niemand *pron* nobody, no one; **ich habe ~en gesehen** I didn't see anybody; **~ von uns spricht Französisch** none of us speaks French; **~ anders, sonst ~** nobody else.

Niere (*pl* -n) *die* kidney.

nieseln *vi:* **es nieselt** it's drizzling.

Nieselregen *der* drizzle.

niesen *vi* to sneeze.

Niete (*pl* -n) *die* - **1.** [Los] losing ticket - **2.** [Bolzen, Knopf] stud - **3.** *fam* [Mensch] dead loss.

niet- und nagelfest *adj:* **sie haben alles, was nicht ~ war, mitgenommen** they took everything that wasn't nailed down.

Nigeria *nt* Nigeria.

Nikolaus (*pl* -läuse) *der* - **1.** [Person]: **der ~** St Nicholas (*who brings children presents on 6 December*), ≃ Santa Claus - **2.** [aus Schokolade] chocolate Santa Claus.

Nikolaustag *der* St Nicholas' Day (*6 December*).

Nikotin *das* nicotine.

Nil *der:* **der ~** the (River) Nile.

Nil|pferd *das* hippopotamus.

nimmt *präs* ▷ nehmen.

nirgends, nirgendwo *adv* nowhere.

Nische (*pl* -n) *die* - **1.** [in der Wand - klein] niche; [- groß] recess - **2.** [für Produkt, Lebewesen] niche.

nisten *vi* to nest.

Niveau [ni'voː] (*pl* -s) *das* level; **~ haben** [Person] to be cultured; **der Krimi hat ~** the detective story is quality literature.

Nixe (*pl* -n) *die* water nymph.

nobel <> *adj* - **1.** [kostspielig] luxurious - **2.** *hum* [vornehm] posh - **3.** *geh* [großzügig] noble <> *adv* - **1.** [kostspielig] luxuriously - **2.** *geh* [großzügig] nobly - **3.** *hum* [vornehm]: **sich ~ kleiden** to dress posh.

noch <> *adv* - **1.** [immer noch] still; **wir haben ~ Zeit** we still have time; **er hat ~ nichts gesagt** he still hasn't said anything; **hast du ~ Geld?** have you got any money left? - **2.** [nicht später] only; **das muss ~ heute gemacht werden** it has to be done today; **schafft ihr das ~ bis Freitag?** do you think you'll manage it by Friday? - **3.** [zur Warnung]: **du wirst ~ an meine Worte denken!**

mark my words! **- 4.** [zusätzlich]: **~ einen Kaffee, bitte!** another coffee, please!; **ich muss ~ ein paar Einkäufe machen** I have to buy a few more things; **wer ~?** who else? **- 5.** (+ kompar) even; **~ schneller** even quicker; **~ komplizierter** even more complicated **- 6.** [rhetorisch]: **wie war ~ sein Name?** what was his name again?; **man wird ja wohl ~ fragen dürfen** I was only asking ◇ konj: **weder ... ~ ...** neither ... nor ... ◆ **noch einmal, noch mal** adv again. ◆ **noch immer, immer noch** adv still. ◆ **noch mehr** adv even more. ◆ **noch nicht** adv not yet. ◆ **noch und noch** adv: **Leute ~ und ~** lots and lots of people; **es regnete ~ und ~** it rained for hours on end. ◆ **noch so** adv: **sei es auch ~ so klein** however small it may be; **es kann ~ so regnen** however much it rains.

nochmals adv again.

Nomade (pl -n) der nomad.

Nomadin (pl -nen) die nomad.

Nominativ (pl -e) der nominative.

Nonne (pl -n) die nun.

Nordamerika nt North America.

norddeutsch adj Northern German.

Norden der north; **nach ~** north; **im ~** in the north.

Nordeuropa nt Northern Europe.

Nordirland nt Northern Ireland.

nordisch adj Nordic.

Nordkap das North Cape.

Nordkorea nt North Korea.

nördlich ◇ adj northern; [Wind] northerly ◇ präp: **~ einer Sache** (G) ODER **von etw** to the north of sthg.

Nordosten der northeast.

Nordpol der **- 1.** GEOGR North Pole **- 2.** PHYS north pole.

Nordrhein-Westfalen nt North Rhine-Westphalia.

Nordsee die North Sea.

Nordwesten der northwest.

nörgeln vi: **(über jn/etw) ~** to moan (about sb/sthg).

Norm (pl -en) die **- 1.** TECH [Regel] norm **- 2.** [Leistung] standard.

normal ◇ adj normal ◇ adv normally.

Normalbenzin das regular petrol Br, regular gas Am.

normalerweise adv normally, usually.

normalisieren vt to normalize. ◆ **sich normalisieren** ref to return to normal.

normen vt to standardize.

Norwegen nt Norway.

Norweger, in (mpl -; fpl -nen) der, die Norwegian.

norwegisch adj Norwegian.

Norwegisch(e) das Norwegian; siehe auch Englisch(e).

Not (pl Nöte) die **- 1.** [Notlage, Armut] need;

in ~ sein to be in need; **~ leidend** needy **- 2.** [Verzweiflung] despair; **Nöte** [Sorgen] troubles **- 3.** RW: **~ tun** to be needed; **zur ~ fam** if needs be.

Notar (pl -e) der notary.

notariell ◇ adj notarial, notary's ◇ adv by a notary.

Notarin (pl -nen) die notary.

Notarzt, ärztin der, die emergency doctor.

Notausgang der emergency exit.

Notbremse die emergency brake.

notdürftig ◇ adj makeshift ◇ adv provisionally; [bekleidet] scantily.

Note (pl -n) die **- 1.** [Beurteilung] mark Br, grade Am **- 2.** MUS note; **nach ~n** with music ODER a score **- 3.** [Eigenschaft] touch.

📖 Note

Throughout the German education system a common marking scale is used (1–6), so if a pupil changes school the grades are easily transferable. The grades range from 1 (highest) to 6 (lowest), and each grade is defined as follows: 1 = sehr gut (excellent); 2 = gut (good); 3 = befriedigend (satisfactory); 4 = ausreichend (adequate); 5 = mangelhaft (poor); 6 = ungenügend (unsatisfactory).

Notfall der emergency. ◆ **im Notfall** adv in an emergency.

notfalls adv if necessary.

notgedrungen adv out of necessity.

notieren ◇ vt **- 1.** [aufschreiben] to note down; **sich** (D) **etw ~** to make a note of sthg **- 2.** [Aktie] to quote ◇ vi WIRTSCH: **höher/niedriger ~** to rise/fall.

nötig ◇ adj necessary; **etw ~ haben** to need sthg; **du hast es gerade ~!** iron you can talk!; **sie hat es nicht ~ zu putzen** ha, she doesn't have ODER need to do the cleaning! ◇ adv fam urgently.

Notiz (pl -en) die note; [in der Zeitung] notice; **keine ~ von jm/etw nehmen** to take no notice of sb/sthg. ◆ **Notizen** pl notes.

Notizbuch das notebook.

Notlage die crisis.

Notlösung die temporary solution.

Notruf der emergency call; [Nummer] emergency number.

Notrufsäule die emergency phone.

notwendig, notwendig ◇ adj **- 1.** [nötig] necessary **- 2.** [logisch] inevitable ◇ adv necessarily.

Novelle [no'vɛlə] (pl -n) die **- 1.** [Literatur] novella **- 2.** RECHT amendment.

November [no'vɛmbɐ] der November; siehe auch September.

Nr. (abk für Nummer) no.

NRW *abk für* Nordrhein-Westfalen.

nüchtern <> *adj* - **1.** [nicht betrunken] so-ber - **2.** [sachlich] matter-of-fact - **3.** [mit leerem Magen]: **~ sein** to have an empty stomach; **auf ~en Magen** on an empty stomach <> *adv* - **1.** [nicht betrunken] soberly - **2.** [sachlich] matter-of-factly - **3.** [mit leerem Magen] on an empty stomach.

Nudel (*pl -n*) *die* noodle; **~n** [italienisch] pasta; [chinesisch, in Suppe] noodles.

null <> *num* zero; **~ Komma fünf** zero ODER nought *Br* point five; **eins zu ~** one-zero, one-nil *Br*; **~ und nichtig** *fig* null and void <> *adj* (*unver*) *fam* no; *siehe auch* sechs.

Null (*pl -en*) *die* - **1.** [Zahl] zero - **2.** *fam abw* [Mensch] dead loss.

Null|punkt *der* - **1.** [Tiefpunkt]: **auf den ~ sinken** to hit rock-bottom - **2.** PHYS zero.

numerieren = nummerieren.

Nummer (*pl -n*) *die* - **1.** [Zahl] number - **2.** [Größe] size - **3.** [im Zirkus] act - **4.** *fam* [Mensch] character - **5.** *salopp* [Geschlechtsakt] shag.

nummerieren *vt* to number.

Nummern|schild *das* numberplate *Br*, license plate *Am*.

nun <> *adv* - **1.** [gen] now; **von ~ an** from now on - **2.** [Ausdruck der Ungeduld]: **bist du ~ zufrieden?** are you happy now?; **was denn ~?** so what happens now? <> *interj* now; **~ denn** right ODER well then; **~ gut** oh well. ➤ **nun mal** *adv* now; **das ist ~ mal so!** that's just the way it is!

nur *adv* - **1.** [lediglich] only, just; **ich bin nicht krank, ~ müde** I'm not ill, just tired - **2.** [jedoch] but, yet - **3.** [verstärkend]: **was meint er ~?** what does he mean?; **wenn sie ~ käme!** if only she would come!; **kommen Sie ~ herein!** do come in!; **~ keine Panik!** don't panic!; **hätte ich ~ auf dich gehört!** if only I'd listened to you! ➤ **nur noch** *adv*: **ich habe ~ noch 10 Euro** I've only got 10 euros left. ➤ **nur so** *adv*: **das sagt er ~ so** *fam* he's just saying that; **der Putz bröckelt ~ so** the plaster is crumbling really badly. ➤ **nur zu** *interj* go on!

nuscheln *vi* to mumble.

Nuss (*pl* Nüsse) *die* - **1.** [Frucht] nut - **2.** *fam abw* [Mensch]: **du dumme ~!** you stupid idiot!

Nuss|baum *der* - **1.** [Baum] walnut tree - **2.** [Holz] walnut.

Nussknacker (*pl -*) *der* [Gerät] nut-cracker.

Nutte (*pl -n*) *die salopp* - **1.** [Prostituierte] tart, hooker *Am* - **2.** *abw* [Frau] slut.

nutzbar *adj* usable; **(sich (D)) etw ~ machen** [Energiequelle] to harness sthg; [Boden, Land] to cultivate sthg.

nütze *adj* (*unver*): **zu etwas/nichts ~ sein** to be of some/no use.

nutzen, nützen <> *vt* to use; **das nützt nichts/nicht viel** that's no/not much use <> *vi*: **jm ~** to be of use to sb.

Nutzen *der* benefit.

nützlich *adj* useful; **sich ~ machen** to make o.s. useful.

nutzlos <> *adj* useless <> *adv* uselessly.

Nutzung (*pl -en*) *die* [von Bodenschätzen] exploitation; [von Energiequelle] harnessing.

NW (*abk für* Nordwest) NW.

Nylon® ['nailɔn] *das* nylon.

o, O [oː] (*pl* o ODER -s) *das* o, O. ➤ **O** (*abk für* Ost) E.

Oase (*pl -n*) *die* oasis.

ob *konj* whether; **ich weiß nicht, ~ er kommt** I don't know whether ODER if he'll come; **~ er wohl kommt?** I wonder if he'll come?; **und ~!** you bet! ➤ **als ob** *konj* as if, as though; **(so) tun als ~ ...** to pretend (that) ...; **er tat, als ~ er sie nicht gesehen hätte** he pretended not to have seen her.

ÖBB (*abk für* Österreichische Bundesbahn) *Austrian Railways*.

Obelisk (*pl -en*) *der* obelisk.

oben *adv* - **1.** [räumlich] up; [obenauf] at the top; **hier/dort ~** up here/there; **links/rechts ~ im Bild** in the top left-hand/right-hand corner of the picture; **bis ~ hin** up to the top; **nach ~** up; [im Haus] upstairs; **mit dem Gesicht nach ~** face up; **von ~** down; **von ~ bis unten** from top to bottom; **von ~ herab** *fig* condescendingly; **weiter ~** further up; **~ ohne** *fig* topless - **2.** [im Text] above; **siehe ~** see above; **~ erwähnt** above-mentioned.

Ober (*pl -*) *der* waiter; **Herr ~!** waiter!

Ober|arm der upper arm.

obere, r, s adj upper.

Ober|fläche die **- 1.** [Außenfläche] surface **- 2.** MATH (surface) area.

oberflächlich <> adj superficial <> adv superficially.

Ober|geschoss das top floor; **im dritten ~** on the third Br ODER fourth Am floor.

Ober|haupt das head.

Ober|hemd das shirt.

Ober|körper der upper body; **den ~ freimachen** to strip to the waist, to take one's top off.

Ober|lippe die upper lip.

Ober|österreich nt Upper Austria.

Ober|schenkel der thigh.

Ober|schicht die: **die ~** the upper classes (pl).

Oberst (pl -en ODER -e) der colonel.

oberste, r, s adj top; [Gericht] supreme; **die ~ Heeresleitung** the military high command.

Ober|stufe die SCHULE final three years of secondary education.

Ober|teil das top.

Ober|weite die bust (measurement).

Objekt (pl -e) das **- 1.** [Gegenstand, KUNST & GRAM] object **- 2.** [Immobilie] property.

objektiv [ɔpjɛk'tiːf] <> adj objective <> adv objectively.

Objektiv (pl -e) das FOTO lens.

Oboe (pl -n) die oboe.

Obst das fruit.

Obst|baum der fruit tree.

obszön <> adj obscene <> adv obscenely.

obwohl konj although.

Ochse ['ɔksə] (pl -n) der [Rind] ox.

öde adj **- 1.** [trostlos] desolate **- 2.** fam [langweilig] dreary.

oder konj **- 1.** [gen] or **- 2.** fam [als Bestätigungsfrage]: **du kommst doch mit, ~?** you're going to come, aren't you?; **du hast doch kein Auto, ~?** you haven't got a car, have you? ◆ **oder aber** konj or (else). ◆ **oder auch** konj or. ◆ **oder so** adv or something like that.

Oder die: **die ~** the (River) Oder.

Ofen (pl Öfen) der **- 1.** [Wärmespender] stove; **elektrischer ~** (electric) heater **- 2.** [Backofen] oven **- 3.** fam [Motorrad] bike.

offen <> adj **- 1.** [gen] open; **das Geschäft hat bis 6 Uhr ~** the shop is open until 6 o'clock; **sperrangelweit ~** wide open; **mit ~en Augen** with one's eyes open; **auf ~em Meer** on the open sea; **für etw ~ sein** to have an open mind about sthg; **~ zu jm sein, jm gegenüber ~ sein** to be frank ODER open with sb **- 2.** [unverpackt] loose, unpacked; **~e Wei-**

ne wine by the glass/carafe **- 3.** [lose] undone; **der Knopf ist ~** the button has come undone; **mit ~n Haaren** with one's hair down **- 4.** [Rechnung] outstanding <> adv openly; **etw ~ zugeben** to admit sthg openly; **~ gesagt** quite honestly.

offenbar adv obviously, clearly.

offen bleiben (perf ist offen geblieben) vi (unreg) **- 1.** [Tür, Geschäft] to stay open **- 2.** [Frage, Problem] to remain unresolved.

Offenheit (pl -en) die **- 1.** [Ehrlichkeit] frankness; **in aller ~** in all honesty **- 2.** [Aufgeschlossenheit] openness.

offenherzig adj **- 1.** [Mensch] openhearted **- 2.** fam hum [Kleidung] revealing.

offen lassen vt (unreg) eigtl & fig to leave open.

offensichtlich <> adj [Lüge, Betrug, Bevorzugung] blatant; [Wohlstand, Begabung] obvious; **es ist ~, dass ...** [eindeutig] it is clear that ... <> adv obviously, clearly; [lügen] blatantly.

offen stehen vi (unreg) **- 1.** [Tür, Fenster] to be open **- 2.** [zugänglich sein]: **jm ~** to be open to sb **- 3.** [Rechnung] to be outstanding.

öffentlich <> adj public <> adv publicly; [auftreten] in public.

Öffentlichkeit die public; **etw an die ~ bringen** to make sthg public; **in aller ~** in front of everyone.

offiziell <> adj official <> adv officially.

Offizier (pl -e) der officer.

offline ['ɔflaɪn] adv EDV offline; **~ gehen** to go offline.

öffnen <> vt **- 1.** [gen] to open **- 2.** [lösen] to undo <> vi to open; **jm ~** to open the door to sb. ◆ **sich öffnen** ref to open; [neue Märkte etc] to open up.

Öffnung (pl -en) die opening; [von Körper] orifice; [von Flasche] mouth; [in Mauer] gap.

Öffnungszeiten pl opening hours.

oft (kompar öfter; superl am öftesten) adv often; **wie ~?** how often?, how many times?

öfter, öfters adv quite often; **warst du schon ~ hier?** have you been here often?; **~ als mir lieb ist** more often than I'd like.

ohne <> präp (+ A) without; **ein Ehepaar ~ Kinder** a couple with no children; **das ist ~ weiteres möglich** it's perfectly possible <> konj without; **sie tat es, ~ dass er es merkte** she did it without him noticing; **~ zu fragen** without asking. ◆ **ohne mich** interj count me out!

ohnehin adv anyway.

Ohnmacht (pl -en) die **- 1.** [Bewusstlosigkeit] unconsciousness; **in ~ fallen** to faint **- 2.** [Machtlosigkeit] impotence.

ohnmächtig <> adj **- 1.** [bewusstlos] unconscious; **~ werden** to faint **- 2.** [machtlos]

impotent <> *adv* - **1.** [bewusstlos]: **~ daliegen** to lie there unconscious - **2.** [zusehen, ausgeliefert] helplessly.

Ohr (*pl* -en) *das* - **1.** [von Person, Tier] ear - **2.** *RW:* **halt die ~en steif!** *fam* chin up!; **jn übers ~ hauen** *fam* to take sb for a ride.

ohrenbetäubend <> *adj* deafening <> *adv* deafeningly.

Ohr|feige *die* slap (in the face).

ohrfeigen *vt* to slap (in the face).

Ohr|läppchen (*pl* -) *das* earlobe.

Ohr|ring *der* earring.

Ohr|wurm *der* catchy tune; **ein ~ sein** to be catchy.

Öko|laden *der* wholefood store.

ökologisch <> *adj* ecological <> *adv* ecologically.

ökonomisch <> *adj* - **1.** WIRTSCH economic - **2.** [sparsam] economical <> *adv* economically.

Öko|steuer *die* ecotax.

Öko|system *das* ecosystem.

Oktan (*pl* -e) *das* octane.

Oktave [ɔk'taːvə] (*pl* -n) *die* octave.

Oktober *der* October; **der 3. ~** German national holiday commemorating reunification on 3 October 1990; *siehe auch* September.

Oktober|fest *das* Munich beer festival.

Öl (*pl* -e) *das* - **1.** [gen] oil - **2.** KUNST oils (*pl*).

ölen *vt* to oil.

Öl|farbe *die* - **1.** KUNST oil paint; **mit ~n malen** to paint in oils - **2.** [Streichmittel] oil-based paint.

Öl|gemälde *das* oil painting.

Öl|heizung *die* oil-fired central heating.

ölig <> *adj* oily <> *adv:* **~ glänzen** to have an oily sheen.

Olive [o'liːvə] (*pl* -n) *die* olive.

Öl|pest *die* oil slick.

Öl|quelle *die* oil well.

olympisch *adj* SPORT Olympic.

Olympische Spiele *pl* Olympic Games.

Oma (*pl* -s) *die* - **1.** [Großmutter] grandma, granny - **2.** *fam abw* [Frau] grandma; **die ~ vor mir** the old dear in front of me.

Omelett [ɔm(ə)'lɛt] (*pl* -e ODER -s) *das* omelette.

Omni|bus *der* [Linienbus] bus; [Reisebus] coach.

Onkel (*pl* -) *der* - **1.** [Verwandter, Freund] uncle - **2.** *fam* [Mann]: **gib dem ~ die Hand** give the nice man your hand.

online ['ɔnlain] <> *adj* EDV [angeschlossen] online; **~ sein** to be online <> *adv* online.

Online-Banking ['ɔnlainbɛŋkiŋ] *das* online ODER Internet banking.

Online-|Dienst ['ɔnlaindiːnst] *der* EDV online service.

OP [oː'peː] (*pl* -s) (*abk für* Operationssaal) *der* OR *Am*, operating theatre *Br*.

Opa (*pl* -s) *der* - **1.** [Großvater] grandpa, grandad - **2.** *fam abw* [Mann] grandpa, grandad.

Open-Air-|Konzert *das* open-air concert.

Oper (*pl* -n) *die* - **1.** MUS opera - **2.** [Opernhaus] opera house; **in die ~ gehen** to go to the opera.

Operation (*pl* -en) *die* operation.

Operette (*pl* -n) *die* operetta.

operieren (*pl* -s) *der* - **1.** [Großvater] to operate on; **jn am Blinddarm ~** to operate on sb's appendix; **sich ~ lassen** to have an operation <> *vi* to operate; **behutsam ~** to proceed carefully.

Opfer (*pl* -) *das* - **1.** [Mensch - von Unglück, Leidenschaften] victim - **2.** [Verzicht & REL] sacrifice - **3.** *RW:* **jm/einer Sache zum ~ fallen** to fall victim to sb/sthg.

opfern *vt* to sacrifice; **jm etw ~** to sacrifice sthg for sb; **jetzt habe ich dir so viel Zeit geopfert** now I've given up so much time for you. **~ sich opfern** *ref* - **1.** [sich aufopfern] to sacrifice o.s. - **2.** *fam hum* [sich bereit erklären]: **wer opfert sich freiwillig und geht zum Chef?** who's going to volunteer to go to the boss?

Opium *das* opium.

Opposition (*pl* -en) *die* opposition; **in ~ zu etw stehen** to be opposed to sthg.

Optik *die* - **1.** PHYS optics (*U*) - **2.** [Sichtweise] point of view - **3.** [Erscheinungsbild] appearance.

Optiker, in (*mpl* -; *fpl* -nen) *der, die* optician.

optimal <> *adj* optimal <> *adv* optimally.

Optimismus *der* optimism.

optimistisch <> *adj* optimistic <> *adv* optimistically.

optisch <> *adj* - **1.** PHYS optical - **2.** [visuell] visual <> *adv* [visuell] visually.

orange [o'rɑ̃ːʒə] *adj* orange.

Orange[1] [o'rɑŋːʒə] (*pl* -n) *die* [Frucht] orange.

Orange[2] [o'rɑ̃ːʒ] (*pl* -) *das* [Farbe] orange.

Orangen|saft *der* orange juice.

Orchester [ɔr'kɛstɐ] (*pl* -) *das* orchestra.

Orchidee [ɔrçi'deːə] (*pl* -n) *die* orchid.

Orden (*pl* -) *der* - **1.** [Auszeichnung] decoration; [Medaille] medal; **jm einen ~ verleihen** to decorate sb - **2.** REL order.

ordentlich <> *adj* - **1.** [Person, Schreibtisch, Wohnung] tidy; [Schrift, Hausaufgabe] neat; [Leben] orderly - **2.** [regelgerecht - Mitglied] full; **~es Gericht** court for civil and criminal cases - **3.** [Note, Ergebnis] respectable - **4.** [Verdienst, Schluck] good; [Portion] good-sized; **einen ~en Schreck kriegen** to get a real fright - **5.** [anständig] proper <> *adv* - **1.** [sauber] tidily; [schreiben, gekleidet] neatly - **2.** [nach Regeln] correctly, in accordance with correct procedures - 3. [viel] really well; ~ **verdienen** to earn good money; **sie hat mit mir ~ geschimpft** she gave me a real telling-off.

ordinär ⬦ adj - 1. abw [vulgär - Person, Witz] crude; [- Benehmen, Kleidung] vulgar, common - 2. [normal] ordinary ⬦ adv abw [vulgär - lachen, fluchen] crudely; [- sich verhalten, sich kleiden] vulgarly, commonly.

📖 ordinär

The German adjective ordinär is a false friend, as its primary meaning in English is "vulgar" or "crude". Sein Benehmen gestern war ganz ordinär might therefore be translated as "His behaviour yesterday was very vulgar".
The English adjective "ordinary", however, would usually be translated by gewöhnlich or normal, so "This is no ordinary computer" would be rendered as Dies ist kein gewöhnlicher Computer.

ordnen vt - 1. [sortieren] to sort out; [Gedanken] to organize; **etw nach Datum ~** to arrange stvg according to date - 2. [aufräumen] to tidy up - 3. [regeln - Finanzen, Affären, Privatleben] to put in order. ➡ **sich ordnen** ref: **sich zu etw ~** to form stvg.

Ordner (pl -) der - 1. [Hefter] file - 2. [Person] steward.

Ordnerin (pl -nen) die steward.

Ordnung (pl -en) die - 1. [geordneter Zustand] tidiness; **~ schaffen** to tidy up - 2. [Disziplin, Gesetzmäßigkeit] order; **für ~ sorgen** to keep order - 3. [Anordnung] order; **in alphabetischer ~** in alphabetical order - 4. [Grad]: **eine Dummheit erster ~** an extremely stupid thing to do - 5. RW: **etw in ~ bringen** [ordnen, erledigen] to sort stvg out; **in ~ sein** fam to be okay; **sie lässt ihre Tochter allein zu Hause? – das ist nicht in ~** she leaves her daughter alone at home? – that's not right; **der Computer ist nicht in ~** there's something wrong with the computer. ➡ **in Ordnung** interj okay!

ordnungsgemäß adj & adv in accordance with the regulations.

ordnungswidrig amt ⬦ adj [Parken] illegal; **~es Verhalten im Straßenverkehr** minor traffic offence ⬦ adv [parken] illegally; **sich ~ verhalten** to contravene the regulations.

Oregano der oregano.

ÖRF (abk für Österreichischer Rundfunk) Austrian radio and television corporation.

Organ (pl -e) das - 1. [gen] organ - 2. [Stimme] voice.

Organisation (pl -en) die organization.

organisatorisch ⬦ adj organizational ⬦ adv organizationally.

organisch adj - 1. [eines Körperteils] physical - 2. [natürlich & CHEM] organic.

organisieren vt - 1. [veranstalten, ordnen] to organize - 2. [gründen] to form - 3. fam [beschaffen] to get hold of - 4. fam [stehlen] to pinch. ➡ **sich organisieren** ref - 1. [sich zusammenschließen] to organize - 2. [sich bilden] to develop.

Organismus (pl -men) der organism.

Organizer der (electronic) organizer.

Organ|spende die organ donation.

Orgasmus (pl -men) der orgasm.

Orgel (pl -n) die organ.

Orient ['ɔːrjɛnt] der - 1. [der Nahe Osten] Middle East - 2. [Asien] Orient.

orientalisch adj - 1. [vom Nahen Osten] Middle Eastern - 2. [vom Morgenland] oriental.

orientieren [ɔrjɛn'tiːrən] vt - 1. [ausrichten]: **etw nach** ODER **an etw** (D) **~** to base stvg on stvg - 2. [informieren]: **jn über etw** (A) **~** to inform sb about stvg. ➡ **sich orientieren** ref - 1. [sich zurechtfinden] to orientate o.s., to get one's bearings - 2. [sich informieren]: **sich über etw** (A) **~** to inform o.s. about stvg - 3. [sich ausrichten]: **sich nach** ODER **an etw** (D) **~** to be orientated towards stvg; **sich nach der Mutter ~** to follow the example of one's mother.

Orientierung die (ohne pl) - 1. [Zurechtfinden]: **die ~ in der Wüste ist nicht einfach** it's not easy to get one's bearings in the desert; **dieser Stadtplan ist zur Ihrer ~** this city map is to help you find your way around; **die ~ verlieren** to lose one's bearings - 2. [Information] information - 3. [Ausrichtung]: **~ nach** ODER **an etw** (D) orientation towards stvg; [nach Vorgaben, Richtlinien] conformance to stvg; **vielen Jugendlichen fehlt die ~ an religiösen Werten** many young people have no orientation towards religious values.

Orientierungs|sinn der sense of direction.

original ⬦ adj - 1. [ursprünglich] original - 2. [unverfälscht] genuine ⬦ adv - 1. [echt]: **eine ~ chinesische Tasse** a genuine Chinese tea cup - 2. [direkt] live.

Original (pl -e) das - 1. [Urform] original - 2. [Person] character.

Orkan (pl -e) der hurricane.

Ort (pl -e) der - 1. [gen] place; [von Verbrechen] scene; **an ~ und Stelle** on the spot - 2. [Ortschaft - Dorf] village; [- Stadt] small town. ➡ **vor Ort** on the spot.

Orthografie, Orthographie [ɔrtogra'fiː] (pl -n) die spelling, orthography.

Orthopädie die orthopaedics (U).

orthopädisch ⬦ adj orthopaedic ⬦ adv orthopaedically.

ortsansässig adj local.

Ortschaft (pl -en) die village.

Ortsıgespräch *das* TELEKOM local call.

ortskundig *adj:* **ich bin hier ~** I'm familiar with this area.

Ortsınetz *das* - **1.** TELEKOM local (telephone) exchange - **2.** ELEKTR local grid.

öS (*abk für* österreichischer Schilling) Sch.

Öse (*pl* -n) *die* eye; [von Schuh] eyelet.

Oslo *nt* Oslo.

Ossi (*pl* -s) *der fam* term used to describe citizen of the former GDR.

Ostblock *der* Eastern bloc.

ostdeutsch *adj* [Gebiet] Eastern German; POL East German.

Ostdeutschland *nt* [Gebiet] Eastern Germany; [DDR] East Germany.

Osten *der* - **1.** [Richtung] east; **nach ~** east - **2.** [Gegend] East; **im ~** in the East - **3.** POL: **der ~** the East.

Osterıei *das* Easter egg.

Osterıhase *der* Easter Bunny.

Ostern *nt* Easter; **an** ODER **zu ~** at Easter. ◆ **frohe Ostern** *interj* Happy Easter!

Österreich *nt* Austria.

Österreicher, in (*mpl* -; *fpl* -nen) *der, die* Austrian.

österreichisch *adj* Austrian.

Osterısonntag *der* Easter Sunday.

Osteuropa *nt* Eastern Europe.

Ostfriesland *nt* East Frisia.

Ostıküste *die* east coast.

östlich ◇ *adj* eastern; [Wind] east ◇ *adv:* **~ einer Sache** (*G*) ODER **von etw** to the east of sthg.

Ostıpolitik *die* Ostpolitik.

Ostıpreußen *nt* East Prussia.

Ostsee *die:* **die ~ the** Baltic (Sea).

Otter (*pl* - ODER -n) ◇ *der* (*pl* Otter) otter ◇ *die* (*pl* Ottern) viper.

ÖTV [øː'teː'fau] (*abk für* Gewerkschaft Öffentliche Dienste, Transport und Verkehr) *die German public services and transport workers' union.*

Outdoor-Aktivitäten *pl* outdoor pursuits.

outen *vt* to out. ◆ **sich outen** *ref* to come out.

oval [o'vaːl] ◇ *adj* oval ◇ *adv* in/into an oval.

ÖVP [øː'fau'peː] (*abk für* Österreichische Volkspartei) *die* Austrian People's Party, *Christian Democratic political party in Austria.*

oxidieren, oxydieren (*perf* hat/ist oxidiert ODER oxydiert) *vt* (*hat*) *vi* (*ist*) to oxidize.

Ozean (*pl* -e) *der* ocean.

Ozon *der* ODER *das* ozone.

P

p, P [peː] (*pl* - ODER -s) *das* p, P.

paar *adj* few. ◆ **ein paar** *det* a few; **kannst du mal ein ~ Minuten rüberkommen?** can you come over here for a couple of minutes?

Paar (*pl* -e ODER -) *das* - **1.** (*pl* Paare) [zwei Personen] couple - **2.** (*pl* Paar) [zwei Dinge] pair; **ein ~ Strümpfe** a pair of socks.

paaren *vt* - **1.** [Tiere] to mate - **2.** [kombinieren] to combine. ◆ **sich paaren** *ref* [kopulieren] to mate.

paarmal ◆ **ein paarmal** *adv* a few times; **den Film habe ich ein ~ gesehen** I've seen the film a couple of times.

Paarung (*pl* -en) *die* - **1.** [von Tieren] mating - **2.** [von Spielern, Mannschaften] pairing.

paarweise *adv* in pairs.

Pacht (*pl* -en) *die* - **1.** [das Pachten, Vertrag] lease; **etw in ~ haben** to lease sthg - **2.** [Geld] rent.

Pächter, in (*mpl* -; *fpl* -nen) *der, die* - **1.** [von Geschäft] leaseholder - **2.** [von Grundstück] tenant.

Pack *das abw* rabble.

Päckchen (*pl* -) *das* - **1.** [Paket] small parcel - **2.** [Packung] packet.

packen ◇ *vt* - **1.** [voll packen] to pack; **seine Sachen ~** to pack one's things - **2.** [legen, stellen]: **etw auf/unter etw** (*A*) **~** to put sthg on/under sthg; **etw aus etw ~** to take sthg out of sthg - **3.** [fassen] to seize - **4.** [überkommen]: **mich packt das Grauen** I am filled with horror - **5.** [emotional bewegen] to grip - **6.** *fam* [schaffen - Studium, Prüfung] to get through; **glaubst du, du packst es?** do you think you can manage?; **sie hat den Bus noch gepackt** she managed to catch the bus - **7.** *salopp* [begreifen] to get ◇ *vi* [vor Reisen] to pack.

Packen (*pl* -) ◇ *der* pile; [zusammengeschnürt] bundle ◇ *das* packing.

packend ◇ *adj* gripping ◇ *adv* grippingly.

Packpapier *das* brown paper.

Packung (*pl* -en) *die* - **1.** [für Waren] packet - **2.** MED compress; [aus Eis] ice pack - **3.** [Gesichtspackung] face pack.

Pädagogik *die* education.

pädagogisch ◇ *adj* educational; **ihre ~en Fähigkeiten** her teaching ability; **meine ~e Ausbildung** my training in education ◇ *adv* educationally.

Paddel (pl -) das paddle.
Paddel|boot das canoe.

paddeln (perf hat/ist gepaddelt) vi - 1. (hat) [rudern] to paddle - 2. (ist) [Boot fahren] to canoe.

paffen fam <> vt [rauchen] to puff at <> vi - 1. abw [rauchen] to puff away - 2. [nicht Lunge rauchen]: **du paffst ja nur!** you're not inhaling!

Page ['pa:ʒə] (pl -n) der [im Hotel] bellboy Br, bellhop Am.

Paket (pl -e) das - 1. [Postsendung] parcel - 2. [Packung] packet - 3. [Packen] bundle - 4. [Zusammenstellung] package.

Pakistan nt Pakistan.

Pakt (pl -e) der pact; **einen ~ schließen** to make a pact.

Palast (pl Paläste) der palace.

Palästina nt Palestine.

Palästinenser, in (mpl -; fpl -nen) der, die Palestinian.

palästinensisch adj Palestinian.

Palette (pl -n) die - 1. [für Farben] palette - 2. [zum Transport] pallet - 3. [Vielfalt] range.

Palme (pl -n) die palm (tree).

Palm|sonntag der Palm Sunday.

Pampelmuse (pl -n) die grapefruit.

pampig fam <> adj - 1. [frech] insolent - 2. [breiig] mushy <> adv [frech] insolently.

Panamakanal der Panama Canal.

panieren vt to coat with breadcrumbs; **paniertes Schnitzel** breaded escalope of pork.

Paniermehl das (ohne pl) breadcrumbs (pl).

Panik die panic; **in ~ geraten** to panic.

panisch <> adj [Reaktion] panic-stricken; **eine ~e Angst vor etw** (D) **haben** to be terrified of sthg <> adv [reagieren] with panic; **sich ~ fürchten** to be terrified.

Panne (pl -n) die - 1. [mit Auto, Maschine] breakdown; **eine ~ haben** to break down - 2. [Fehler] slip-up; [Versprecher] slip; **die Veranstaltung verlief ohne jede ~** the event went off without a hitch.

Pannen|dienst der breakdown service.

panschen <> vt [mit Chemikalien] to adulterate; [mit Wasser] to water down <> vi [mit Chemikalien] to adulterate the drinks; [mit Wasser] to water down the drinks.

Panther, Panter (pl -) der panther.

Pantoffel (pl -n) der slipper.

Pantomime (pl -n) <> die mime <> der mime artist.

Panzer (pl -) der - 1. [Fahrzeug] tank - 2. [von Insekt, Schildkröte] shell; [von Krokodil] armour - 3. [Schutzplatte] armour plating.

Papa (pl -s) der fam dad, daddy.

Papagei (pl -en) der parrot.

Papier (pl -e) das - 1. [gen] paper - 2. [Wertpapier] security. ➡ **Papiere** pl [Ausweis,

persönliches Dokument] documents; **Ihre ~e bitte** your papers, please; **seine ~e bekommen** ODER **kriegen** fam fig to get fired, to get the sack Br.

Papier|geld das paper money.

Papier|korb der wastepaper basket Br, wastebasket Am.

Papier|kram der fam abw paperwork.

Papierwaren|geschäft das stationer's.

Papp|becher der paper cup.

Pappe (pl -n) die cardboard.

Papp|karton der cardboard box.

Paprika (pl - ODER -s) der - 1. [Gemüse] pepper - 2. [Gewürz] paprika.

Paprika|schote die pepper.

Papst (pl Päpste) der pope.

Parabel (pl -n) die - 1. MATH parabola - 2. [Gleichnis] parable.

Parade (pl -n) die - 1. [Aufmarsch] parade - 2. [bei Fechten] parry; [bei Ballspiel] save.

Paradies (pl -e) das paradise.

paradiesisch adj heavenly.

Paragraf, Paragraph (pl -en) der - 1. [in Vertrag, Gesetz] section; [in Verfassung] article - 2. [typografisches Zeichen] paragraph.

parallel <> adj parallel <> adv - 1. [gleichzeitig]: **~ zu etw** at the same time as sthg - 2. [in gleichem Abstand]: **~ zu etw verlaufen** to run parallel to sthg.

Parallele (pl -n) die - 1. MATH parallel line - 2. [Entsprechung] parallel; **~n zu etw ziehen** to draw parallels with sthg.

Parallelogramm (pl -e) das parallelogram.

Paral|nuss die brazil nut.

Parasit (pl -en) der eigtl & fig parasite.

parat <> adv: **etw ~ haben/halten** to have/keep sthg ready; **auf diese Frage habe ich keine passende Antwort ~** I don't have a ready answer to this question <> adj (unver): **~ sein** to be ready.

Pärchen (pl -) das couple.

Parfüm (pl -e ODER -s) das perfume.

Parfümerie [parfymə'ri:] (pl -n) die perfumery.

parfümieren vt to perfume. ➡ **sich parfümieren** ref: **sich stark ~** [Frau] to wear a lot of perfume; [Mann] to wear a lot of aftershave.

Pariser (pl -) der fam [Kondom] rubber.

Park (pl -s) der park.

Parka (pl -s) der parka.

Parkan|lage die [von Stadt] park; [von Schloss] grounds (pl).

parken <> vt to park <> vi - 1. [Person] to park; **falsch ~** to park illegally - 2. [Fahrzeug]: **ein parkendes Auto** a parked car.

Parken das parking.

Parkett (pl -e ODER -s) das - 1. [Fußbodenbe-

lag] parquet - 2. [im Kino, Theater] stalls *(pl)*
Br, parquet *Am*.

Park|gebühr *die* parking fee.

Park|haus *das* multi-storey car park *Br*,
parking garage *Am*.

Park|lücke *die* parking space.

Park|platz *der* - 1. [Platz] car park *Br*, park-
ing lot *Am* - 2. [Parklücke] parking space.

Park|scheibe *die* parking disc.

Park|schein *der* (car park) ticket.

Park|uhr *die* parking meter.

Park|verbot *das*: **im ~ stehen** to be in a no-
parking zone.

Parlament *(pl -e) das* parliament.

Parlamentarier, in [parlamɛn'taːrjɐ, rɪn]
(mpl -; fpl -nen) der, die Member of Parliament.

parlamentarisch <> *adj* parliamentary
<> *adv* in parliament.

Parmesan *der* Parmesan.

Parodie [paro'diː] *(pl -n) die* parody; **eine
~ auf etw** a parody of sthg; **eine ~ auf jn** a
take-off of sb.

Parole *(pl -n) die* - 1. [Kennwort] password
- 2. [Leitspruch] slogan - 3. *abw* [Behauptung]:
eine ausländerfeindliche ~ a racial stereotype.

Partei *(pl -en) die* - 1. [gen] party; **für jn ~ ergreifen** *fig* to side with sb - 2. [bei Streit] side.

parteiisch <> *adj* biased <> *adv*: **~ urteilen**
to make a biased judgement.

Parterre [par'tɛr] *(pl -s) das* ground floor *Br*,
first floor *Am*. ◆ **im Parterre** *adv* on the
ground floor *Br* ODER first floor *Am*.

Partie [par'tiː] *(pl -n) die* - 1. [Teil] part
- 2. [Spiel] game; **eine ~ Schach/Tennis spielen** to play a game of chess/tennis - 3. *RW*:
da bin ich mit von der ~! count me in!

Partitur *(pl -en) die* score.

Partizip *(pl -ien) das* participle. ◆ **Partizip Perfekt** *das* past participle. ◆ **Partizip
Präsens** *das* present participle.

Partner, in *(mpl -; fpl -nen) der, die* partner;
[in Film] co-star.

Partnerschaft *(pl -en) die* - 1. [zwischen
Personen] partnership - 2. [zwischen Städten]
twinning.

partnerschaftlich <> *adj* [Verhältnis]
based on partnership; **~e Beziehung** partnership; **~e Zusammenarbeit** cooperation
<> *adv* - 1. [freundschaftlich] in a spirit of
partnership; [zusammenleben] as partners
- 2. [kollegial] in partnership.

Partner|stadt *die* twin town.

partout [par'tuː] *adv fam* at all costs; **sie
will ~ nicht gehorchen!** she simply refuses
to obey!

Party ['paːɐti] *(pl -s) die* party.

Pass *(pl Pässe) der* - 1. [Dokument] passport
- 2. [Gebirgspass, beim Fußball] pass.

Passage [pa'saːʒə] *(pl -n) die* - 1. [gen] passage - 2. [Geschäftsstraße] arcade.

Passagier [pasa'ʒiːɐ] *(pl -e) der* passenger;
blinder ~ [auf Schiff] stowaway; [im Zug]
fare dodger.

Passagierin [pasa'ʒiːrɪn] *(pl -nen) die* passenger.

Passant, in *(mpl -en; fpl -nen) der, die* passerby.

Pass|bild *das* passport photo.

passen *vi* - 1. [die richtige Größe haben] to
fit; **die Schuhe ~ mir nicht** my shoes don't fit;
in etw *(A)* **~** to fit in sthg - 2. [angenehm sein]:
passt es (dir) morgen besser? does tomor-
row suit you better?; **das passt mir nicht**
that doesn't suit me; **das könnte dir so ~!** no
way!; **das könnte ihm so ~!** he should be so
lucky! - 3. [zusammenpassen - Farben] to
match; **zu jm ~** to suit sb; **sie passt in keins-
ter Weise zu ihm** she isn't at all suited to
him; **diese Schuhe ~ nicht zu dem Rock** these
shoes don't go with the skirt - 4. [nicht kön-
nen] to pass; **da muss ich ~!** I pass!

passend <> *adj* - 1. [Gelegenheit, Methode,
Kleidung] suitable; [Worte] right; **der ~e
Schlüssel** the right key - 2. [Farbe] matching
<> *adv* suitably; **~ antworten** to give a fit-
ting reply; **haben Sie es ~?** do you have the
exact amount?

Pass|foto *das* passport photo.

passieren *(perf* hat/ist passiert) <> *vt (hat)*
- 1. [überschreiten, durchschreiten] to cross
- 2. [Zollkontrolle] to go through - 3. SPORT to
pass - 4. KÜCHE to pass through a sieve <> *vi
(ist)* to happen; **es ist ein Unglück passiert**
there's been an accident; **mir ist etwas un-
glaubliches passiert** something incredible
happened to me; **bei dem Unfall ist zum
Glück nichts passiert** fortunately, nobody
was hurt in the accident.

passiv, passiv <> *adj* - 1. [untätig] passive
- 2. [Mitglied] non-active <> *adv* passively.

Passiv ['pasif] *(pl -e) das* GRAM passive
(voice).

Pass|kontrolle *die* - 1. [Kontrollieren] pass-
port check - 2. [Kontrollstelle] passport control.

Paste *(pl -n) die* paste.

Pastell|farbe *die* pastel colour.

Pastete *(pl -n) die* - 1. [mit Blätterteig] vol-
au-vent - 2. [ohne Blätterteig] pâté.

Pastor *(pl -toren) der* [katholisch] priest;
[evangelisch] vicar.

Pastorin *(pl -nen) die* - 1. [Pfarrerin] vicar
- 2. [Ehefrau des Pastors] vicar's wife.

Pate *(pl -n) der* godfather; **bei etw ~ stehen**
to be the influence behind sthg.

Paten|kind *das* godchild.

Paten|onkel *der* godfather.

Patenschaft *(pl -en) die:* **die ~ für etw übernehmen** to sponsor sthg; **die ~ für jn übernehmen** to become sb's godparent.

patent <> *adj* - **1.** [lebenstüchtig] capable - **2.** [praktisch] neat - **3.** *fam* [nett] great <> *adv* [tüchtig] capably.

Patent *(pl -e) das* patent; **auf etw** *(A)* **ein ~ anmelden** to apply for a patent for sthg.

Paten|tante *die* godmother.

patentieren *vt* to patent; **sich** *(D)* **etw ~ lassen** to take out a patent on sthg.

Pater *(pl -) der* father *(priest).*

Patient, in *(mpl -en; fpl -nen) der, die* patient.

Patin *(pl -nen) die* godmother.

Patina *die* patina.

Patriot, in *(mpl -en; fpl -nen) der, die* patriot.

patriotisch <> *adj* patriotic <> *adv* patriotically.

Patron, in *(mpl -e; fpl -nen) der, die* patron saint.

Patrone *(pl -n) die* cartridge.

patrouillieren [patrul'(j)iːrən] *(perf hat/ist patrouilliert) vi* to patrol.

Patsche *(pl -n) die fam* - **1.** [Not]: **in der ~ sitzen** to be in a fix; **jm aus der ~ helfen** to help sb out of a tight spot - **2.** [Hand] paw.

patschnass *adj fam* soaking wet.

patzig <> *adj* nasty <> *adv* nastily.

Pauke *(pl -n) die* kettledrum; **auf die ~ hauen** *fam fig* to paint the town red.

pauken *fam* <> *vi* to swot *Br,* to grind *Am* <> *vt* to swot up on *Br,* to bone up on *Am.*

pauschal <> *adj* - **1.** [Preis, Versicherung] all-inclusive - **2.** [Urteil] sweeping <> *adv* - **1.** [beurteilen] sweepingly - **2.** [abrechnen] altogether.

Pauschale *(pl -n) die* flat rate.

Pauschal|reise *die* package tour.

Pauschal|urteil *das* sweeping judgement.

Päuschen ['pɔyscən] *(pl -) das fam* breather.

Pause *(pl -n) die* - **1.** [Unterbrechung] break; [im Theater, Konzert] interval - **2.** MUS rest.

Pausen|brot *das* snack (for the break).

pausenlos *adj & adv* non-stop.

Pavian ['paːvjaːn] *(pl -e) der* baboon.

Pazifik *der:* **der ~** the Pacific.

Pazifische Ozean *der* Pacific Ocean.

Pazifist, in *(mpl -en; fpl -nen) der, die* pacifist.

pazifistisch <> *adj* pacifist <> *adv* in a pacifist way.

PC [peː'tseː] *(pl -* ODER *-s) (abk für Personal Computer) der* PC.

PDS [peːdeː'ɛs] *(abk für Partei des Demokra*

tischen Sozialismus) die Democratic Socialist Party.

Pech *(pl -e) das* - **1.** [Unglück] bad luck; **~ haben** to be unlucky - **2.** [Erdölprodukt] pitch.

Pech|strähne *die* run of bad luck.

Pech|vogel *der* unlucky person.

Pedal *(pl -e) das* pedal.

pedantisch *abw* <> *adj* fastidious <> *adv* fastidiously.

Pegel *(pl -) der* [von Fluss] water level; [von Lärm] level.

peilen <> *vt* to take a bearing on; **die Lage ~** to see how the land lies <> *vi fam:* **über den Daumen ~** to make a rough guess.

peinlich <> *adj* - **1.** [unangenehm] embarrassing; **das ist mir sehr ~** I feel very embarrassed about it - **2.** [sorgfältig] scrupulous <> *adv* - **1.** [unangenehm] embarrassingly - **2.** [sorgfältig] scrupulously.

Peitsche *(pl -n) die* whip.

peitschen *(perf hat/ist gepeitscht)* <> *vt (hat)* to whip <> *vi (ist)* [Wind, Regen] to lash; [Schuss] to ring out.

Peking *nt* Peking.

Pelikan *(pl -e) der* pelican.

Pelle *(pl -n) die Norddt* [von Kartoffel] peel; [von Wurst] skin.

pellen *vt Norddt* [Kartoffel] to peel; [Wurst] to skin. ◆ **sich pellen** *ref* to peel.

Pell|kartoffel *die* unpeeled boiled potato.

Pelz *(pl -e) der* - **1.** [Fell] fur *(U);* **jm auf den ~ rücken** *fam fig* to pester sb - **2.** [Pelzmantel] fur (coat).

pelzig *adj* - **1.** [taub] numb - **2.** [pelzartig] furry.

Pelz|mantel *der* fur coat.

Pendel *(pl -) das* pendulum.

pendeln *(perf ist/hat gependelt) vi* - **1.** *(ist)* [fahren] to commute - **2.** *(hat)* [schwingen - Glocken] to swing; [- Beine] to dangle.

Pendelverkehr *der* [für Pendler] commuter traffic; [Hin- und Herfahren] shuttle service.

Pendler, in *(mpl -; fpl -nen) der, die* commuter.

penetrant *abw* <> *adj* [Mensch, Fragerei] obtrusive; [Geruch, Geklingel] penetrating <> *adv* [nach etw riechen] penetratingly; [auf jn einreden] obtrusively.

Penis *(pl -se) der* penis.

Penizillin *das* penicillin.

pennen *vi fam* - **1.** [schlafen] to sleep, to kip *Br* - **2.** [nicht aufpassen] to be half-asleep - **3.** [mit jm schlafen]: **mit jm ~** *salopp* to do it with sb.

Penner, in *(mpl -; fpl -nen) der, die fam* - **1.** [Stadtstreicher] tramp, bum *Am* - **2.** [Schlafmütze] sleepyhead.

Pension [paŋ'zjoːn] *(pl -en) die* - **1.** [Hotel] guesthouse - **2.** [Ruhestand]: **in ~ gehen** to re tire; **in ~ sein** to be retired - **3.** *(ohne pl)* [Bezüge] pension.

Pensionär, in [pɑ̃zjon'ɛːɐ̯, rɪn] *(mpl -e; fpl -nen) der, die* pensioner *(retired civil servant)*.

pensionieren [pɑ̃zjo'niːrən] *vt* to pension off.

Pensum *(pl* Pensen) *das* quota.

Peperoni *(pl -) die* chilli (pepper).

per *präp (+A)* by.

perfekt <> *adj* - **1.** [vollkommen] perfect - **2.** [abgeschlossen]: **~ sein** [Vertrag, Kauf] to be finalized; [Niederlage, Sieg] to be complete; **~ machen** to finalize <> *adv* [vollkommen] perfectly.

Perfekt *(pl -e) das* GRAM perfect.

Perfektion *die* perfection.

Pergament *(pl -e) das* parchment.

Pergamentpapier *das* greaseproof paper.

Periode *(pl -n) die* - **1.** [Epoche, Menstruation] period - **2.** MATH repetend; **1,6** ~ 1.6 recurring.

periodisch <> *adj* periodic <> *adv* periodically.

Perle *(pl -n) die* - **1.** [Schmuck - aus Muschel] pearl; [- aus Holz, Glas] bead - **2.** *geh* [Kostbarkeit] gem.

perlen *(perf* hat/ist geperlt) *vi* - **1.** *(hat)* [sprudeln] to bubble - **2.** *(ist) geh* [abperlen]: **Schweiß perlt ihm auf der Stirn** beads of sweat are forming on his brow.

Perlenkette *die* pearl necklace.

Perlmutt, Perlmutt *das* mother of pearl.

Perlon® *das* ≈ nylon.

permanent <> *adj* permanent <> *adv* permanently.

perplex *adj*: **(ganz) ~ sein** to be stunned.

Persien *nt* Persia.

Person *(pl -en) die* - **1.** [Mensch & GRAM] person; **sie ist Köchin und Inhaberin in einer ~** she is chef and owner rolled into one; **etw in ~ sein** *fig* to be sthg personified - **2.** [Figur] character.

Personal *das* staff.

Personalabteilung *die* personnel department.

Personalausweis *der* identity card.

Personalchef, in *der, die* personnel manager.

Personalcomputer *der* EDV personal computer.

Personalien [pɛrzo'naːljən] *pl* personal details.

Personalpronomen *das* GRAM personal pronoun.

Personalrat *der* - **1.** [Gremium] staff council *(for civil servants)* - **2.** [Vertreter] staff council representative *(for civil servants)*.

Personalrätin *die* staff council representative *(for civil servants)*.

personell <> *adj* staff *(vor Subst)* <> *adv* with regard to staff; **~ unterbesetzt** understaffed.

Personenwagen *der* car.

persönlich <> *adj* personal; **~ werden** to get personal <> *adv* personally; **etw ~ nehmen** to take sthg personally.

Persönlichkeit *(pl -en) die* personality.

Perspektive [perspɛk'tiːvə] *(pl -n) die* - **1.** [Bildaufbau, Sichtweise] perspective; **aus js ~** from sb's perspective - **2.** [Aussicht] prospect.

Peru *nt* Peru.

Perücke *(pl -n) die* wig.

Pessimismus *der* pessimism.

pessimistisch <> *adj* pessimistic <> *adv* pessimistically.

Pest *die (ohne pl)* [Seuche] plague; **jn/etw meiden wie die** ~ *fam fig* to avoid sb/sthg like the plague; **stinken wie die** ~ *fam fig* to stink to high heaven.

Petersilie [petɐ'ziːljə] *die* parsley.

Petroleum [pe'troːleʊm] *das* paraffin *Br*, kerosene *Am*.

petzen *vi fam* to tell tales.

Pf. *(abk für Pfennig)* pf.

Pfad *(pl -e) der* [gen & EDV] path.

Pfadfinder, in *(mpl -; fpl -nen) der, die* boy scout *(f girl guide Br, girl scout Am)*.

Pfahl *(pl Pfähle) der* post.

Pfalz *die*: **die ~** the Palatinate.

pfälzisch *adj* of/from the Palatinate.

Pfand *(pl Pfänder) das* [von Flasche] deposit; [als Sicherheit] security; [beim Pfänderspiel] token; **etw als ~ nehmen** to take sthg as security.

pfänden *vt* to seize.

Pfandflasche *die* returnable bottle.

Pfandhaus *das* pawnshop.

Pfändung *(pl -en) die* seizure *(U)*.

Pfanne *(pl -n) die* (frying) pan.

Pfannkuchen *der* pancake.

Pfarrei *(pl -en) die* parish.

Pfarrer *(pl -) der* [katholisch] priest; [evangelisch] minister.

Pfarrerin *(pl -nen) die* minister.

Pfau *(pl -en) der* peacock.

Pfeffer *der* pepper.

Pfefferminze, Pfefferminze *die* peppermint.

pfeffern *vt* - **1.** [würzen] to put pepper on/in - **2.** *fam* [werfen] to chuck - **3.** *fam* [ohrfeigen]: **jm eine ~** to give sb a clout.

Pfeife *(pl -n) die* - **1.** [zum Rauchen, Musikinstrument] pipe; **nach js ~ tanzen** *fam fig* to dance to sb's tune; **~ rauchen** to smoke a pipe - **2.** [zum Pfeifen] whistle - **3.** *fam abw* [Mensch] dead loss.

pfeifen (*prät* pfiff; *perf* hat gepfiffen) ⬦ *vi* to whistle; **auf jn/etw ~** *fam fig* not to give a damn about sb/sthg ⬦ *vt* - **1.** [Lied] to whistle - **2.** [Spiel] to referee.

Pfeil (*pl* -e) der - **1.** [Waffe, Hinweiszeichen] arrow; **grüner ~** filter arrow - **2.** *fam* [Stichelei] barb.

Pfeiler (*pl* -) der pillar.

Pfennig (*pl* -e ODER -) der pfennig; **keinen ~ haben** *fam* not to have a penny.

Pferd (*pl* -e) das horse; **aufs falsche/richtige ~ setzen** to back the wrong/right horse.

Pferdeäpfel *pl* horse droppings.

Pferde|rennen das horse race.

Pferde|schwanz der [Frisur] ponytail.

Pferde|sport der (*ohne pl*) equestrian sports (*pl*).

Pferde|stall der stable.

Pferde|stärke die horsepower (*U*).

pfiff *prät* ⬦ pfeifen.

Pfiff (*pl* -e) der - **1.** [Ton] whistle - **2.** *fig* [Reiz] style; **mit ~** stylish.

Pfifferling (*pl* -e) der chanterelle; **nicht einen** ODER **keinen ~** *fam fig* not a thing.

pfiffig ⬦ *adj* [Mensch, Idee] smart; [Gesicht] knowing ⬦ *adv* cleverly.

Pfingsten (*ohne Artikel*) Whitsun.

Pfirsich (*pl* -e) der peach.

Pflanze (*pl* -n) die plant.

pflanzen *vt* to plant.

pflanzlich ⬦ *adj* [Nährstoffe, Fasern] plant (*vor Subst*); [Öl] vegetable (*vor Subst*); **~e Ernährung** [von Person] vegetarian diet; [von Tier] herbivorous diet ⬦ *adv*: **sich ~ ernähren** [Person] to be a vegetarian; [Tier] to be a herbivore.

Pflaster (*pl* -) das - **1.** [Verband] plaster - **2.** (*ohne pl*) [Straßenbelag] (road) surface; **ein teures ~ sein** *fig* to be an expensive place.

Pflaume (*pl* -n) die - **1.** [Frucht] plum - **2.** *fam* [Mensch] drip.

Pflaumen|baum der plum tree.

Pflaumen|mus das *thick plum purée, used like jam*.

Pflege die - **1.** [von Lebewesen] care; **bei jm in ~ sein** to be looked after by sb; **jn in ~ nehmen/haben** to look after sb; **ein Kind in ~ nehmen** to foster a child - **2.** [von Sprache, Beziehung] cultivation; [von Garten, Tradition] maintenance.

Pflege|eltern *pl* foster parents.

Pflege|heim das nursing home.

Pflege|kind das foster child.

pflegeleicht *adj* - **1.** [Material] easy-care - **2.** *fam* [Person] easy to deal with.

pflegen *vt* - **1.** [versorgen] to look after; **jn gesund ~** to nurse sb back to health - **2.** [schonen] to take care of - **3.** [gewohnt

sein]: **etw zu tun ~** *geh* to be in the habit of doing sthg.

Pflegepersonal das nursing staff.

Pfleger, in (*mpl* -; *fpl* -nen) der, die nurse.

Pflicht (*pl* -en) die - **1.** [Aufgabe] duty; **etw ist ~** sthg is compulsory - **2.** (*ohne pl*) SPORT compulsories (*pl*).

pflichtbewusst ⬦ *adj* conscientious ⬦ *adv* conscientiously.

Pflicht|fach das compulsory subject.

Pflicht|gefühl das sense of duty.

Pflicht|versicherung die compulsory insurance.

Pflock (*pl* Pflöcke) der [für Tier] stake; [für Zelt] peg.

pflücken *vt* to pick.

Pflug (*pl* Pflüge) der plough.

pflügen *vt & vi* to plough.

Pforte (*pl* -n) die - **1.** [von Krankenhaus, Firma - Tor] gate; [- Eingang] entrance - **2.** *geh* [kleine Tür] door.

Pförtner, in (*mpl* -; *fpl* -nen) der, die porter.

Pfosten (*pl* -) der post.

Pfote (*pl* -n) die paw.

Pfropf (*pl* -e) der blockage; [in Ader] clot.

Pfropfen (*pl* -) der stopper.

pfui *interj* ugh!

Pfund (*pl* -e) das - **1.** [Gewicht] 500 grams, ≃ pound - **2.** [Währung] pound.

Pfusch der (*ohne pl*) *fam abw* botched job.

Pfuscher, in (*mpl* -; *fpl* -nen) der, die *fam abw* bungler.

Pfütze (*pl* -n) die puddle.

Phantasie = Fantasie.

phantasieren = fantasieren.

phantastisch = fantastisch.

Pharao (*pl* -s ODER -aonen) der Pharaoh.

Phase (*pl* -n) die phase.

Philharmoniker *pl* Philharmonic (Orchestra) (*sg*).

Philippinen *pl*: **die ~** the Philippines.

Philosoph, in (*mpl* -en; *fpl* -nen) der, die philosopher.

Philosophie (*fɪlozo'fiː*) (*pl* -n) die philosophy.

philosophisch ⬦ *adj* philosophical ⬦ *adv* philosophically.

Phonetik = Fonetik.

Phosphat (*pl* -e) das phosphate.

Phosphor der phosphorus.

phosphoreszieren *vi* to phosphoresce.

Phrase (*pl* -n) die cliché; **leere ~n** empty phrases; **~n dreschen** *fam fig* to spout clichés.

pH-Wert [peːˈhaːveːɐt] der pH-value.

Physik die physics (*U*).

physikalisch ⬦ *adj* - **1.** [gen] physical - **2.** [Forschung, Institut] physics (*vor Subst*) ⬦ *adv* in terms of physics.

Physiker, in (*mpl* -; *fpl* -nen) *der, die* physicist.

physisch <> *adj* physical <> *adv* physically.

Pianist, in (*mpl* -en; *fpl* -nen) *der, die* pianist.

Pickel (*pl* -) *der* - **1.** [Entzündung] spot - **2.** [Gerät] pickaxe; [für Eis] ice-pick.

pickelig, picklig *adj* spotty.

picken *vt & vi* to peck.

Picknick (*pl* -s ODER -e) *das* picnic; **ein ~ machen** to have a picnic.

pieken *vi* to prick.

piepen *vi* [Vogel] to cheep; [Maus] to squeak; [Piepser] to bleep; **bei dir piepts wohl!** *fam fig* you're off your head!

piercen ◆ **sich piercen** *vpr*: **sich die Nase ~** to have one's nose pierced.

Piercing ['pi:rsɪŋ] (*pl* -s) *das* body piercing; **ein ~ in der Zunge/Augenbraue haben** to have a pierced tongue/eyebrow.

piesacken *vt fam* to torment.

Pigment (*pl* -e) *das* pigment.

Pik (*pl* -) *das* - **1.** (*ohne Artikel, ohne pl*) [Spielfarbe] spades (*pl*) - **2.** (*pl* Pik) [Spielkarte] spade; **die ~sechs** the six of spades.

pikant <> *adj* spicy <> *adv* - **1.** [scharf]: **etw ~ würzen** to spice sthg well - **2.** [frivol] spicily.

Pike (*pl* -n) *die*: **etw von der ~ auf lernen** *fam fig* to learn sthg by working one's way up from the bottom.

Pilger (*pl* -) *der* pilgrim.

Pilger|fahrt *die* pilgrimage.

Pilgerin (*pl* -nen) *die* pilgrim.

pilgern (*perf* ist gepilgert) *vi* - **1.** [wallfahren] to go on a pilgrimage - **2.** *fam* [laufen] to trek.

Pille (*pl* -n) *die* - **1.** [Verhütungsmittel]: **die ~** the pill; **die ~ nehmen** to be on the pill - **2.** *fam* [Tablette] pill.

Pilot (*pl* -en) *der* [von Flugzeug] pilot; [von Rennwagen] driver.

Pilotin (*pl* -nen) *die* [von Flugzeug] pilot; [von Rennwagen] driver.

Pils (*pl* -) *das* Pilsner.

Pilz (*pl* -e) *der* - **1.** [Pflanze - essbar] mushroom; [- giftig] toadstool - **2.** (*ohne pl*) [Hautpilz] fungal infection.

PIN (*pl* -s) (*abk für* persönliche Identifikationsnummer) *die* PIN (number).

pingelig *fam* <> *adj* fussy <> *adv* fussily.

Pinguin ['pɪŋɡuiːn] (*pl* -e) *der* penguin.

Pinie ['pi:niə] (*pl* -n) *die* stone pine.

pink *adj* (*unver*) bright pink.

Pink *das* bright pink.

pinkeln *vi fam* to pee.

Pinsel (*pl* -) *der* brush.

pinseln *vt & vi* to paint.

Pinzette (*pl* -n) *die* tweezers (*pl*).

Pionier (*pl* -e) *der* - **1.** [Vorkämpfer] pioneer - **2.** [Soldat] engineer.

Pionierin (*pl* -nen) *die* pioneer.

Pipi *das fam*: **~ machen** to do a wee-wee.

Pirat (*pl* -en) *der* pirate.

Piraten|sender *der* pirate radio station.

Piratin (*pl* -nen) *die* pirate.

Pirsch *die*: **auf die ~ gehen** to go stalking.

Pistazie [pɪs'ta:tsiə] (*pl* -n) *die* pistachio.

Piste (*pl* -n) *die* - **1.** [für Flugzeuge] runway - **2.** [Skipiste] piste - **3.** [für Fahrzeuge] track.

Pistole (*pl* -n) *die* pistol; **wie aus der ~ geschossen** *fam fig* like a shot.

Pizza ['pɪtsa] (*pl* -s) *die* pizza.

Pizzeria [pɪtse'ri:a] (*pl* Pizzerien ODER -s) *die* pizzeria.

Pkw ['pe:ka:ve:] (*pl* -s) (*abk für* Personenkraftwagen) *der* car, automobile *Am*.

plädieren *vi* - **1.** *geh* [stimmen]: **für etw ~** to argue for sthg - **2.** RECHT: **für** ODER **auf etw** (A) **~** to plead for sthg.

Plage (*pl* -n) *die* nuisance.

plagen *vt* to torment; **von etw geplagt sein** to be tormented by sthg. ◆ **sich plagen** *ref* to slave away; **sich mit etw ~** to slave away at sthg.

Plakat (*pl* -e) *das* poster.

Plakette (*pl* -n) *die* [Tafel] plaque; [Abzeichen] badge.

Plan (*pl* Pläne) *der* - **1.** [Vorgehensweise, Vorhaben] plan; **Pläne schmieden** to make plans - **2.** [Karte] map. ◆ **nach Plan** *adv* according to plan.

Plane (*pl* -n) *die* tarpaulin.

planen *vt* to plan.

Planet (*pl* -en) *der* planet.

planieren *vt* to level.

Planke (*pl* -n) *die* plank.

planlos <> *adj* unsystematic <> *adv* unsystematically.

planmäßig <> *adj* - **1.** [nach Plan] scheduled - **2.** [systematisch] systematic <> *adv* - **1.** [nach Plan] on time - **2.** [systematisch] systematically.

planschen, plantschen *vi* to splash about.

Plantage [plan'ta:ʒə] (*pl* -n) *die* plantation.

Planung (*pl* -en) *die* - **1.** [Vorbereitung] planning (*U*) - **2.** [Ergebnis] plan.

plappern *vi* to prattle.

plärren *vi abw* - **1.** [weinen] to wail - **2.** [rufen] to yell - **3.** [Krach machen] to blare.

Plastik (*pl* -en) <> *das* (*ohne pl*) plastic <> *die* sculpture.

Plastik|tüte *die* plastic bag.

plastisch <> *adj* [dreidimensional] three-dimensional; **eine ~e Darstellung** a vivid description ⬦ *adv* - **1.** [dreidimensional] three-dimensionally - **2.** [lebendig] vividly.

Platane (*pl* -n) *die* plane tree.

Platin *das* platinum.

platonisch *adj* platonic.

plätschern (*perf* hat/ist geplätschert) *vi* - **1.** (ist) [fließen] to splash; [Bach] to babble - **2.** (hat) [Geräusch machen] to splash.

platt ⬦ *adj* - **1.** [flach] flat (tyre); **einen Platten haben** *fam* to have a flat; **~ sein** *fam fig* to be flabbergasted - **2.** [nichts sagend] trite ⬦ *adv* - **1.** [flach] flat - **2.** [nichts sagend] tritely.

Platt *das* Low German, *dialect spoken in northern Germany;* **~ sprechen** to speak Low German.

Plattdeutsch(e) *das* Low German, *dialect spoken in northern Germany; siehe auch* Englisch(e).

Platte (*pl* -n) *die* - **1.** [Bauelement - aus Metall, Glas] sheet; [- aus Stein, Beton] slab; [- aus Holz] board - **2.** [Servierplatte] plate - **3.** [Schallplatte] record; **eine ~ auflegen** ODER **spielen** to put on ODER play a record - **4.** [Herdplatte] ring - **5.** *fam* [Glatze] bald patch. ➡ **kalte Platte** *die* meal of cold meats, cheese, salad etc.

Platten ➪ platt.

plätten *vt Norddt* [bügeln] to iron.

Platten|spieler *der* record player.

Platt|fuß *der* (*ohne pl*) *fam* flat. ➡ **Plattfüße** *pl:* **Plattfüße haben** to have flat feet.

Platz (*pl* Plätze) *der* - **1.** [Sitzplatz] seat; **~ nehmen** *geh* to take a seat - **2.** [Freiraum] room, space; **jm/etw ~ machen** [zur Seite gehen] to make room for sb/sthg; [weichen] to make way for sb/sthg; **keinen/genug ~ haben** to have no/enough room - **3.** [Stelle, Rang] place; **auf die Plätze, fertig, los!** on your marks, get set, go! - **4.** [in Stadt] square - **5.** [bei Fußball, Hockey] pitch; [bei Tennis, Volleyball] court. ➡ **fehl am Platz** *adj* out of place. ➡ **Platz sparend** ⬦ *adj* space-saving ⬦ *adv* in order to save space.

Platzanweiser, in (*mpl* -; *fpl* -nen) *der, die* usher (*f* usherette).

Plätzchen (*pl* -) *das* - **1.** [Platz] spot - **2.** [Gebäck] biscuit *Br*, cookie *Am*.

platzen (*perf* ist geplatzt) *vi* - **1.** [bersten] to burst - **2.** *fam* [ausfallen, scheitern - Termin, Vorstellung] to be cancelled; [- Projekt, Vertrag] to fall through; **etw ~ lassen** to cancel sthg; **vor etw** (*D*) **~ to** be seething with sthg.

platzieren *vt* to place. ➡ **sich platzieren** *ref* [Platz belegen] to be placed.

Platz|karte *die* seat reservation.

Platz|mangel *der* lack of space.

platzsparend *adj* ➪ Platz.

Platz|wunde *die* laceration.

plaudern *vi* to chat.

plausibel ⬦ *adj* plausible; **jm etw ~ machen** to make sthg clear to sb ⬦ *adv* plausibly.

plazieren *vt* = platzieren.

pleite *adj fam:* **~ sein** to be broke.

Pleite (*pl* -n) *die fam* - **1.** [Ruin] bankruptcy; **~ gehen/machen** to go bankrupt; **vor der ~ stehen** *fam* to be faced with bankruptcy - **2.** [Reinfall] flop.

Plombe (*pl* -n) *die* - **1.** [Zahnfüllung] filling - **2.** [Siegel] lead seal.

plombieren *vt* - **1.** [füllen] to fill - **2.** [versiegeln] to put a lead seal on.

plötzlich ⬦ *adj* sudden; **ganz ~** all of a sudden ⬦ *adv* suddenly; **aber ein bisschen ~!** *fam* get a move on!

plump *abw* ⬦ *adj* clumsy ⬦ *adv* clumsily.

plumpsen (*perf* ist geplumpst) *vi* to crash; [ins Wasser] to splash.

Plunder *der fam abw* junk.

plündern ⬦ *vt* - **1.** [ausrauben] to loot - **2.** [leeren] to raid ⬦ *vi* to loot.

Plural (*pl* -e) *der* GRAM plural; **im ~** in the plural.

plus *adv, präp & konj* plus.

Plus *das* (*ohne pl*) - **1.** [Mehrbetrag]: **(ein) ~ (von 100 DM) machen** to make a profit (of 100 marks); **im ~ stehen** to be in credit - **2.** [Vorteil] advantage.

Plüsch *der* plush.

Plus|pol *der* positive pole.

Plus|punkt *der* - **1.** [Vorteil] plus point - **2.** [Punkt] point.

Plusquam|perfekt *das* GRAM pluperfect.

Plutonium *das* CHEM plutonium.

PLZ *abk für* Postleitzahl.

Po (*pl* -s) *der* bottom.

pochen *vi* - **1.** [klopfen] to knock; **auf etw** (*A*) **~** *fig* to insist on sthg - **2.** [pulsieren - Herz] to pound; [- Blut] to throb.

Pocken *pl* MED smallpox (*U*).

Podest (*pl* -e) *das* [für Redner] rostrum; [für Orchester, Chor] platform.

Podium ['po:djʊm] (*pl* Podien) *das* podium.

Podiums|diskussion *die* panel discussion.

Poesie *die geh* poetry.

poetisch ⬦ *adj* poetic ⬦ *adv* poetically.

Pointe ['pо̃ɛ̃:tə] (*pl* -n) *die* punchline.

Pokal (*pl* -e) *der* - **1.** [Trophäe] cup - **2.** [Gefäß] goblet.

Poker *der* ODER *das* poker.

pokern *vi* to play poker.

Pol (*pl* -e) *der* pole; **er ist in der Familie der ruhende ~** he is the calming influence in the family.

polar *adj* polar.

Polar|kreis *der* polar circle.

Pole (*pl* -n) *der* Pole.

polemisch ◇ *adj* polemical ◇ *adv* polemically.

Polen *nt* Poland.

polieren *vt* to polish.

Polin (*pl* -nen) *die* Pole.

Politesse (*pl* -n) *die* traffic warden.

Politik *die* (*ohne pl*) - **1.** [des Staates] politics (*U*) - **2.** [Vorgehensweise] policy.

Politiker, in (*mpl* -; *fpl* -nen) *der, die* politician.

politisch ◇ *adj* political ◇ *adv* politically.

Politur (*pl* -en) *die* polish.

Polizei *die* (*ohne pl*) *die* police (*pl*).

Polizei‖beamte *der* police officer.

Polizei‖beamtin *die* police officer.

polizeilich ◇ *adj* police (*vor Subst*); ~**es Kennzeichen** registration *Br* ODER license *Am* number ◇ *adv* by the police.

Polizei‖revier *das* - **1.** [Polizeiwache] police station - **2.** [Bereich] police district.

Polizei‖stunde *die* (*ohne pl*) closing time.

Polizei‖wache *die* police station.

Polizist, in (*mpl* -en; *fpl* -nen) *der, die* policeman (*f* policewoman).

Pollen (*pl* -) *der* pollen (*U*).

polnisch *adj* Polish.

Polnisch(e) *das* Polish; *siehe auch* Englisch(e).

Polo *das* polo.

Polster (*pl* -) *das* - **1.** [zum Sitzen, finanziell] cushion - **2.** [Schulterpolster] shoulder pad - **3.** *fam* [Fettpolster] wad of fat.

Polstermöbel *pl* upholstered furniture (*U*).

polstern *vt* - **1.** [Möbel] to upholster - **2.** [Kleidung] to pad.

Polsterung (*pl* -en) *die* - **1.** [Polstern] upholstering - **2.** [Polster] upholstery (*U*).

Polter‖abend *der celebration usually held on the evening before a wedding, when crockery is broken to bring good luck.*

poltern (*perf* hat/ist gepoltert) *vi* - **1.** (ist) [sich laut bewegen] to crash - **2.** (hat) [Krach machen] to make a racket; **draußen hat etwas gepoltert** there was a crash outside - **3.** (hat) [am Polterabend] *to celebrate a 'Polterabend'.*

Polyester [poli'ɛstɐ] *das* polyester.

Pommes frites [pɔm'frits] *pl* chips *Br*, French fries *Am*.

Pomp *der* pomp.

pompös ◇ *adj* lavish ◇ *adv* lavishly.

Pony ['pɔni] (*pl* -s) ◇ *das* pony ◇ *der* fringe *Br*, bangs *Am*.

popelig, poplig *fam abw* ◇ *adj* - **1.** [minderwertig] lousy - **2.** [geizig] stingy - **3.** [gewöhnlich] ordinary ◇ *adv* - **1.** [geizig] stingily - **2.** [billig] cheaply.

poplig = popelig.

Popmusik *die* pop music.

Popo (*pl* -s) *der fam* bottom.

populär ◇ *adj* popular ◇ *adv:* ~ **schreiben** to write in an accessible way.

Popularität *die* popularity.

Pore (*pl* -n) *die* pore.

Porno (*pl* -s) *der fam* [Film] porn film; [Pornoheft] porn mag.

Pornografie, Pornographie *die* pornography.

porös *adj* porous.

Porree *der* (*ohne pl*) leek.

Portal (*pl* -e) *das* portal.

Portier [pɔr'tje:] (*pl* -s) *der* porter.

Portion (*pl* -en) *die* - **1.** [von Essen] portion - **2.** [viel] amount.

Portmonee, Portemonnaie [pɔrtmɔ'ne:] (*pl* -s) *das* purse.

Porto (*pl* -s) *das* postage (*U*).

portofrei *adj* & *adv* post-free *Br*, postpaid *Am*.

Porträt [pɔr'trɛ:] (*pl* -s) *das* portrait.

porträtieren *vt* to do a portrait of.

Portugal *nt* Portugal.

Portugiese (*pl* -n) *der* Portuguese.

Portugiesin (*pl* -nen) *die* Portuguese.

portugiesisch *adj* Portuguese.

Portugiesisch(e) *das* Portuguese; *siehe auch* Englisch(e).

Port‖wein *der* port.

Porzellan (*pl* -e) *das* - **1.** [Material] porcelain - **2.** [Geschirr] china.

Posaune (*pl* -n) *die* trombone.

posieren *vi* to pose.

Position (*pl* -en) *die* position.

positiv ◇ *adj* positive ◇ *adv* positively.

Possessiv‖pronomen *das* GRAM possessive pronoun.

Post *die* (*ohne pl*) - **1.** [Institution, Amt] post office; **etw mit der** ~ **schicken** to send sthg by post *Br* ODER mail *Am*; **auf die** ODER **zur** ~ **gehen** to go to the post office - **2.** [Postsendung] post *Br*, mail *Am*.

Post‖amt *das* post office.

Post‖anweisung *die* ≃ postal order *Br*, ≃ money order *Am*.

Post‖bote *der* postman *Br*, mailman *Am*.

Post‖botin *die* postwoman *Br*, mailwoman *Am*.

Posten (*pl* -) *der* - **1.** [Ware] item - **2.** [Arbeitsstelle, Wachposten] post - **3.** *RW:* **auf dem** ~ **sein** *fam* to be fit; **nicht auf dem** ~ **sein** *fam* to be under the weather.

Poster (*pl* -) *der* ODER *das* poster.

Postf. *abk für* Postfach.

Post∣fach *das* PO box.

Post∣karte *die* postcard.

postlagernd *adj & adv* poste restante *Br,* general delivery *Am.*

Postleit∣zahl *die* postcode *Br,* zip code *Am.*

Postspar∣buch *das* post office savings book.

Postspar∣kasse *die* post office savings bank.

Post∣stempel *der* postmark.

Post∣weg *der:* **auf dem ~ verloren gehen** to get lost in the post *Br* ODER mail *Am.*

postwendend *adv* by return (of post) *Br,* by return mail *Am.*

potent *adj* - **1.** [Mann] potent - **2.** *geh* [solvent] financially strong - **3.** *geh* [mächtig] powerful.

Potenz (*pl* -en) *die* - **1.** [sexuelle] potency - **2.** [Kraft & MATH] power; **die zweite/dritte ~ von fünf** the square/cube of five.

Potenzial, Potential [potɛn'tsjaːl] (*pl* -e) *das* potential.

Pott (*pl* Pötte) *der Norddt fam* pot.

Pracht *die* magnificence; **eine wahre ~ sein** *fam* to be magnificent.

Pracht∣exemplar *das* [Gegenstand] magnificent example; [Person] magnificent specimen.

prächtig ◇ *adj* - **1.** [wunderschön] magnificent - **2.** [hervorragend] marvellous ◇ *adv* - **1.** [wunderschön] magnificently - **2.** [hervorragend] marvellously.

prachtvoll ◇ *adj* magnificent ◇ *adv* magnificently.

Prädikat (*pl* -e) *das* - **1.** [Gütezeichen] rating - **2.** GRAM predicate.

Prag *nt* Prague.

prägen *vt* - **1.** [in der Entwicklung] to influence; **von etw geprägt sein** to be influenced by sthg - **2.** [von Anfang an] to shape - **3.** [Wort] to coin - **4.** [Münzen] to mint; [Metall, Leder] to emboss.

prägnant ◇ *adj* concise ◇ *adv* concisely.

Prägung (*pl* -en) *die* - **1.** [Muster] impression - **2.** [in der Entwicklung] influence; **gesellschaftliche ~** social influence - **3.** [von Anfang an] shaping - **4.** [von Worten] coining (*U*).

prahlen *vi* to boast; **mit etw ~** to boast about sthg.

Praktik (*pl* -en) *die* practice. ➠ **Praktiken** *pl abw* practices.

praktikabel ◇ *adj* practicable ◇ *adv* practicably.

Praktikant, in (*mpl* -en; *fpl* -nen) *der, die* trainee.

Praktikum (*pl* Praktika) *das* work place-

ment; **ein ~ machen** ODER **absolvieren** to be on a work placement.

praktisch ◇ *adj* practical ◇ *adv* - **1.** [gen] practically; **~ alles** practically everything - **2.** [nicht theoretisch] in practice.

praktizieren *vt & vi* to practise.

Praline (*pl* -n) *die* chocolate.

prall ◇ *adj* [Po, Busen] well-rounded; [Sack] bulging; [Tomate] firm; **in der ~en Sonne** under the blazing sun ◇ *adv:* **~ gefüllt** filled to bursting.

prallen (*perf* hat/ist geprallt) *vi* - **1.** *(ist)* [stoßen]: **gegen/auf etw** (*A*) **~** to crash into sthg; **er ist mit dem Kopf auf den Boden geprallt** he banged his head on the floor - **2.** *(hat)* [Sonne] to blaze down.

Prämie ['prɛːmjə] (*pl* -n) *die* - **1.** [Beitrag] premium - **2.** [Belohnung] reward - **3.** [Sonderzahlung] bonus.

prämieren *vt* to give an award to.

Pranger (*pl* -) *der:* **jn/etw an den ~ stellen** *fig* to pillory sb/sthg.

Pranke (*pl* -n) *die* paw.

Präparat (*pl* -e) *das geh* preparation.

Präposition (*pl* -en) *die* GRAM preposition.

Prärie [prɛ'riː] (*pl* -n) *die* prairie.

Präsens ['prɛːzɛns] *das* GRAM present (tense).

Präservativ [prɛzɛrva'tiːf] (*pl* -e) *das* condom.

Präsident, in (*mpl* -en; *fpl* -nen) *der, die* president.

Präsidentschaft (*pl* -en) *die* presidency.

Präsidium [prɛ'ziːdjʊm] (*pl* -dien) *das* - **1.** [von Verein] committee - **2.** [Polizeipräsidium] headquarters (*pl*).

prasseln (*perf* hat/ist geprasselt) *vi* - **1.** *(ist)* [Regen] to drum - **2.** *(hat)* [Feuer] to crackle.

Präteritum *das* GRAM preterite.

Praxis (*pl* Praxen) *die* - **1.** [Wirklichkeit] practice; **etw in die ~ umsetzen** to put sthg into practice - **2.** [Erfahrung] experience - **3.** [Räumlichkeit - von Anwalt] office; [- von Arzt] surgery *Br,* office *Am.* ➠ **in der Praxis** *adv* in practice.

präzis, präzise ◇ *adj* precise ◇ *adv* precisely.

predigen *vt & vi* to preach.

Prediger, in (*mpl* -; *fpl* -nen) *der, die* preacher.

Predigt (*pl* -en) *die* sermon; **(jm) eine ~ halten** to give (sb) a sermon.

Preis (*pl* -e) *der* - **1.** [Geldbetrag] price - **2.** [ausgesetzte Prämie] prize - **3.** RW: **der ~ für etw** the price of sthg; **um jeden/keinen ~** at any/not at any price. ➠ **zum halben Preis** *adv* at half-price.

Preisaus∣schreiben *das* competition.

preisbewusst ◇ *adj* price-conscious ◇ *adv* price-consciously.

Preiselbeere *die* cranberry.

preisen (*prät* pries; *perf* hat gepriesen) *vt* geh to praise; **sich glücklich ~** to count o.s. lucky.

preisgünstig ◇ *adj* cheap ◇ *adv* cheaply.

preislich ◇ *adj* price (*vor Subst*) ◇ *adv* with regard to price.

Preislrichter, in *der, die* judge.

Preislschild (*pl* -er) *das* price tag.

Preislträger, in *der, die* prizewinner.

Preislverleihung *die* prize ceremony.

preiswert ◇ *adj* cheap ◇ *adv* cheaply.

prellen *vt* - **1.** [betrügen] to cheat - **2.** [stoßen]: **sich** (*D*) **den Schenkel/Arm ~** to bruise one's thigh/arm - **3.** [Ball] to bounce.

Prellung (*pl* -en) *die* bruise.

Premiere [prə'mjɛːrə] (*pl* -n) *die* premiere.

Premierlminister, in [prə'mjeːminɪs-tɐ, rɪn] *der, die* prime minister.

Presse (*pl* -n) *die* press.

Presselagentur *die* press agency.

Presselbericht *der* press report.

Presselfreiheit *die* freedom of the press.

Presselkonferenz *die* press conference.

Presselmeldung *die* press report.

pressen ◇ *vt* to press ◇ *vi* [Schwangere] to push.

Presselsprecher, in *der, die* press officer.

Presselstelle *die* press office.

Preuße (*pl* -n) *der* HIST Prussian.

Preußin (*pl* -nen) *die* HIST Prussian.

preußisch *adj* HIST Prussian.

prickeln *vi* - **1.** [kitzeln] to tingle - **2.** [perlen] to sparkle.

prickelnd *adj* [Gefühl] thrilling; [Wein, Wasser] sparkling.

pries *prät* ▷ preisen.

Priester, in (*mpl* -; *fpl* -nen) *der, die* - **1.** [ka-tholischer] priest - **2.** [heidnischer] priest (*f* priestess).

prima *fam* ◇ *adj* (*unver*) fantastic ◇ *adv* fantastically.

Primel (*pl* -n) *die* primula.

primitiv ◇ *adj* - **1.** [gen] primitive - **2.** [Re-geln, Bedürfnisse] basic ◇ *adv* primitively.

Prinz (*pl* -en) *der* prince.

Prinzessin (*pl* -nen) *die* princess.

Prinzip (*pl* -ien) *das* principle. ◆ **aus Prin-zip** *adv* on principle. ◆ **im Prinzip** *adv* in principle.

prinzipiell ◇ *adj* basic ◇ *adv* - **1.** [aus Prinzip] on principle; [im Prinzip] in principle - **2.** [grundsätzlich] basically.

Priorität (*pl* -en) *die* priority. ◆ **Prioritä-ten** *pl* priorities.

Prise (*pl* -n) *die*: **eine ~ Salz/Pfeffer** a pinch of salt/pepper.

pritschen *vt* SPORT to flick.

privat [pri'vaːt] ◇ *adj* private ◇ *adv* pri-vately.

Privatladresse *die* home address.

Privatanlgelegenheit *die* private matter; **das ist meine ~** that is a private matter.

Privatleigentum *das* private property.

Privatlinitiative *die* private initiative.

Privatlleben *das* (*ohne pl*) private life.

Privatlperson *die* private person.

Privatlunterricht *der* private tuition.

Privileg [privi'leːk] (*pl* -ien) *das* privilege.

pro ◇ *präp* per; **einmal ~ Tag** once a day ◇ *adv*: **~ und kontra argumentieren** to ar-gue for and against.

Pro (*pl* -s) *das*: **das ~ und Kontra** the pros and cons (*pl*).

Probe (*pl* -n) *die* - **1.** [Test] test; **jn/etw auf die ~ stellen** to put sb/sthg to the test - **2.** [Stichprobe, Warenprobe] sample - **3.** [Übung] rehearsal. ◆ **auf Probe** *adv* on a trial basis.

Probelexemplar *das* specimen copy.

proben *vt* & *vi* to rehearse.

probeweise *adv* on a trial basis.

probieren *vt* to try.

Problem (*pl* -e) *das* problem; **~e mit jm/etw haben** to have problems with sb/sthg. ◆ **kein Problem** *interj* no problem!

problematisch *adj* problematic.

problemlos ◇ *adj* problem-free ◇ *adv* without any problems.

Produkt (*pl* -e) *das* product.

Produktion (*pl* -en) *die* - **1.** [Herstellung] production - **2.** [Erzeugnis] product; [Film, Sendung] production.

produktiv ◇ *adj* productive ◇ *adv* pro-ductively.

Produktivität [produktivi'tɛːt] *die* pro-ductivity.

Produzent, in (*mpl* -en; *fpl* -nen) *der, die* producer.

produzieren *vt* - **1.** [Ware, Film] to produce - **2.** *fam abw* [machen] to make.

professionell ◇ *adj* professional ◇ *adv* professionally.

Professor (*pl* -oren) *der* professor.

Professorin (*pl* -nen) *die* professor.

Profi (*pl* -s) *der* professional.

Profil (*pl* -e) *das* - **1.** [Persönlichkeit] image - **2.** [Seitenansicht] profile - **3.** [von Reifen, Sohle] tread.

Profit (*pl* -e) *der* profit; **aus etw ~ schlagen** ODER **ziehen** *fig* to profit from sthg; *eigtl* to make a profit out of sthg; **~ machen** to make a profit.

profitieren *vi:* **von etw ~** to profit from sthg.

pro forma *adv* for form's sake.

Prognose (*pl* -n) *die* prognosis.

Programm (*pl* -e) *das* - **1.** [Programmvorschau] listings (*pl*) - **2.** [Sendungen] programmes (*pl*) - **3.** [Sender] channel - **4.** [Programmheft, Veranstaltungsablauf, Konzeption] programme; **auf dem ~ stehen** to be on the programme - **5.** [Tagesablauf] schedule; **auf dem ~ stehen** to be on the agenda - **6.** EDV program.

Programm|heft *das* programme.

Programm|hinweis *der* programme announcement.

programmieren *vt* - **1.** [Computer] to program - **2.** [Videorecorder] to programme.

Programmierer, in (*mpl* -; *fpl* -nen) *der, die* EDV programmer.

Programm|punkt *der* item (*on programme/agenda*).

progressiv <> *adj* progressive <> *adv* progressively.

Projekt (*pl* -e) *das* project.

Projektwoche

For one week of the school year all pupils take part in a project week. During this period there are no formal lessons, and teachers set up group work activities of a more practical nature. The aim of this kind of work is to stimulate in the students independence and a sense of initiative, as well as allowing them to discover abilities as yet undeveloped. Activities may vary from photography and sport to handicrafts and furniture restoring.

Projektor (*pl* -toren) *der* projector.

projizieren *vt* to project.

Prolet (*pl* -en) *der* *abw* peasant.

Promenade (*pl* -n) *die* promenade.

Promille (*pl* -) *das* - **1.** MATH thousandth - **2.** [Alkoholgehalt] alcohol level; **er hatte 1,5 ~** he had a blood alcohol level of 1.5 parts per thousand.

prominent *adj* prominent.

Prominenz *die* (*ohne pl*) prominent figures (*pl*).

Promotion [promo'tsi̯oːn] (*pl* -en) *die* UNI doctorate.

promovieren [promo'viːrən] *vi* to gain a doctorate.

prompt <> *adj* prompt <> *adv* [erwartungsgemäß] of course; [sofort] promptly.

Pronomen (*pl* - ODER **Pronomina**) *das* GRAM pronoun.

Propaganda *die* - **1.** [Verbreitung] propa-

ganda - **2.** [Werbung]: **für jn/etw ~ machen** to publicize sb/sthg.

Propangas *das* propane (gas).

Propeller (*pl* -) *der* propeller.

Prophet, in (*mpl* -en; *fpl* -nen) *der, die* prophet (*f* prophetess).

prophezeien *vt* to predict; [Subj: prophet] to prophesy; **jm etw ~** to predict sthg for sb.

Proportion (*pl* -en) *die* proportion.

proportional <> *adj* proportional <> *adv* proportionally.

Prosa *die* prose.

prosit, prost *interj* cheers! ➡ **prost Neujahr** *interj* Happy New Year!

Prospekt (*pl* -e) *der* brochure.

Prospekt

Be careful when using the German word Prospekt as it means "brochure" rather than "prospect". Ich habe Prospekte von der Touristeninformation geholt is equivalent to the English "I picked up some brochures at the tourist office".
"Prospect" in the sense of "future potential" corresponds to the German Aussicht, so "A job with good prospects" would be Ein Job mit guten Aussichten.

Prostituierte (*pl* -n) *die* prostitute.

Prostitution *die* prostitution.

Protest (*pl* -e) *der* protest; **gegen etw ~ einlegen** ODER **erheben** to make a protest against sthg.

Protestant, in (*mpl* -en; *fpl* -nen) *der, die* Protestant.

protestantisch <> *adj* Protestant <> *adv*

protestieren *vi* to protest; **gegen etw ~** to protest against ODER about sthg.

Protest|kundgebung *die* protest rally.

Prothese (*pl* -n) *die* [für Arm, Bein] artificial limb; [für Zähne] dentures (*pl*).

Protokoll (*pl* -e) *das* - **1.** [gen] record; [Aufzeichnung - wortgetreu] transcript; [- von Sitzung] minutes (*pl*); [- polizeilich] statement; **etw zu ~ geben** to put sthg on the record; [polizeilich] to say sthg in one's statement; **eine Aussage zu ~ nehmen** to take down a statement; **~ führen** to take the minutes; [wortgetreu] to make a transcript - **2.** [Zeremoniell] protocol.

Protokoll|führer, in *der, die* [von Sitzung] minute-taker; [im Gericht] clerk.

protokollieren <> *vt* to take down; [Sitzung] to minute <> *vi* to keep a record; [bei Sitzung] to take the minutes.

protzig *abw adj fam* showy.

Proviant [pro'vi̯ant] *der* (*ohne pl*) provisions (*pl*).

Provider [pro'vaidɐ] (*pl -*) *der* EDV Internet Service Provider.

Provinz [pro'vɪnts] (*pl -*en) *die* - **1.** [Verwaltungsbezirk] province - **2.** (*ohne pl*) *abw* [Gegend] provinces (*pl*).

provinziell [provɪn'tsjɛl] *abw* ◇ *adj* provincial ◇ *adv* provincially.

Provision [provi'zjoːn] (*pl -*en) *die* commission.

provisorisch [provi'zoːrɪʃ] ◇ *adj* temporary ◇ *adv* temporarily.

Provokation [provoka'tsjoːn] (*pl -*en) *die* provocation.

provozieren [provo'tsiːrən] ◇ *vt* to provoke ◇ *vi* to be provocative.

Prozent (*pl -* ODER -e) *das* percent; **~e bekommen** to get a discount.

Prozent|satz *der* percentage.

prozentual ◇ *adj* percentage (*vor Subst*) ◇ *adv* in percentage terms.

Prozess (*pl -*e) *der* - **1.** [Rechtsstreit] trial; **jm den ~ machen** to put sb on trial - **2.** [Vorgang] process.

prozessieren *vi* to go to court; **gegen jn ~** to take sb to court.

Prozession (*pl -*en) *die* - **1.** [kirchliche] procession - **2.** *fam* [Schlange] line.

prüde ◇ *adj* prudish ◇ *adv* prudishly.

prüfen ◇ *vt* - **1.** [Gerät, Material] to test; [bei Examen] to examine; **jn auf etw** (*A*) **~** to examine sb on sthg; **jn in etw** (*D*) **~** to examine sb in sthg; **etw auf etw** (*A*) **~** to test sthg for sthg - **2.** [Rechnung, Aussage, Unterschrift] to check - **3.** [Angebot] to consider ◇ *vi* [examinieren] to be an/the examiner.

Prüfer, in (*mpl -*; *fpl -*nen) *der, die* - **1.** [Lehrer] examiner - **2.** [Tester] tester.

Prüfling (*pl -*e) *der* candidate.

Prüfung (*pl -*en) *die* - **1.** [Kontrolle] check - **2.** [Examen] exam, examination; **eine ~ machen** ODER **haben** to take an exam; **eine mündliche/schriftliche ~** an oral/a written exam; **eine ~ bestehen** to pass an exam - **3.** *geh* [Belastung] trial - **4.** [im Sport] test.

Prügel (*pl -*) *der* club. ◆ **Prügel** *pl* thrashing (*U*).

Prügelei (*pl -*en) *die* fight.

prügeln *vt* to beat. ◆ **sich prügeln** *ref* to fight.

Prunk *der* *abw* splendour.

prunkvoll ◇ *adj* magnificent ◇ *adv* magnificently.

Psalm (*pl -*en) *der* psalm.

Psychiater, in (*mpl -*; *fpl -*nen) *der, die* psychiatrist.

psychisch ◇ *adj* [Wohlbefinden, Probleme] psychological; [Krankheit] mental ◇ *adv* mentally.

Psychoanalyse *die* psychoanalysis.

Psychologe (*pl -*n) *der* psychologist.

Psychologie *die* psychology.

Psychologin (*pl -*nen) *die* psychologist.

psychologisch ◇ *adj* psychological ◇ *adv* - **1.** [als Psychologe]: **jn ~ begutachten** to give sb a psychological examination - **2.** [mit Menschenkenntnis] psychologically.

Psycho|therapie *die* psychotherapy.

Pubertät *die* puberty.

publik *adj*: **etw ~ machen** to make sthg public.

Publikation [publika'tsjoːn] (*pl -*en) *die* publication.

Publikum *das* (*ohne pl*) - **1.** [Zuhörer, Zuschauer] audience - **2.** [Gäste] clientele - **3.** [Anhänger] public; [von Schriftsteller] readership.

Pudding (*pl -*e ODER -s) *der* blancmange.

Pudel (*pl -*) *der* poodle.

Puder (*pl -*) *der* ODER *das* powder.

Puder|dose *die* (powder) compact.

pudern *vt* to powder. ◆ **sich pudern** *ref* to powder o.s.

Puderzucker *der* icing sugar.

Puff (*pl -*s) *der* ODER *das* *fam* brothel.

Puffer (*pl -*) *der* - **1.** [von Bahnen] buffer - **2.** [Kartoffelpuffer] potato pancake.

Pulli (*pl -*s) *der* *fam* sweater, jumper *Br*.

Pullover [pʊ'loːvɐ] (*pl -*) *der* sweater, jumper *Br*.

Puls (*pl -*e) *der* pulse; **am ~ von etw sein** to have one's finger on the pulse of sthg.

Puls|ader *die* artery; **sich** (*D*) **die ~ aufschneiden** to slit one's wrists.

pulsieren *vi* to pulsate; [Blut] to pulse.

Pult (*pl -*e) *das* desk; [Stehpult] lectern.

Pulver ['pʊlfɐ, 'pʊlvɐ] (*pl -*) *das* - **1.** [Stoff] powder - **2.** [Schießpulver] gunpowder (*U*).

Pulver|kaffee *der* instant coffee.

Pulver|schnee *der* powder snow.

Puma (*pl -*s) *der* puma.

pummelig *adj* chubby.

Pumpe (*pl -*n) *die* - **1.** [Gerät] pump - **2.** *salopp* [Herz] ticker.

pumpen ◇ *vt* - **1.** [saugen] to pump - **2.** *fam* [leihen]: **jm etw ~** to lend sb sthg; **(sich** (*D*)**) etw von jm ~** to borrow sthg from sb - **3.** [investieren]: **Geld in etw ~** to pump money into sthg ◇ *vi* [saugen] to pump.

Pumps [pœmps] (*pl -*) *der* court shoe *Br*, pump *Am*.

Punker, in ['paŋkɐ, rɪn] (*mpl -*; *fpl -*nen) *der, die* punk.

Punkt (*pl -*e) *der* - **1.** [gen] point - **2.** [Fleck, typografisches Zeichen] dot; [am Satzende] full stop *Br*, period *Am* - **3.** [Zeitpunkt]: **~ ein Uhr** one o'clock on the dot - **4.** *RW*: **der springende ~** the crux of the matter; **an einem toten ~ angelangt** [Verhandlungen] to have reached deadlock; **ein wunder** ODER **schwa-**

cher ~ [Schwäche] a weak point; [heikles Thema] a sore point.

pünktlich <> adj punctual <> adv punctually, on time.

Pünktlichkeit die punctuality.

Pupille (pl -n) die pupil.

Puppe (pl -n) die - **1.** [Figur] doll - **2.** salopp [Frau, Mädchen] bird Br, doll Am; [als Anrede] baby.

pur adj - **1.** [rein] pure - **2.** [Whisky] neat.

Püree (pl -s) das puree.

Purzelbaum der: **einen ~ machen** ODER **schlagen** to do a somersault.

Puste die fam puff; **aus der** ODER **außer ~ sein** to be out of puff.

pusten vt & vi to blow.

Pute (pl -n) die - **1.** [Tier] turkey (hen) - **2.** salopp abw [Frau] cow.

Puter (pl -) der turkey (cock).

Putsch (pl -e) der putsch.

Putz der plaster.

putzen <> vt to clean; [Gemüse] to wash; **jm die Nase ~** to wipe sb's nose; **sich** (D) **die Zähne putzen** to clean ODER brush one's teeth; **sich** (D) **die Nase putzen** to blow one's nose <> vi to clean. ◆ **sich putzen** ref to wash o.s.; [Vogel] to preen o.s.

Putzfrau die cleaner.

Putzlappen der cloth.

Putzmittel das cleaning fluid.

Puzzle ['paz!] (pl -s) das jigsaw (puzzle).

Pyramide (pl -n) die pyramid.

Pyrenäen pl: **die ~** the Pyrenees.

Q

q, Q [ku:] (pl -ODER -s) das q, Q.

qm (abk für Quadratmeter) m².

Quader (pl -) der - **1.** MATH rectangular solid - **2.** [Block] stone block.

Quadrat (pl -e) das square.

quadratisch <> adj square <> adv in squares.

Quadratmeter der square metre.

quaken vi - **1.** [Frosch] to croak; [Ente] to quack - **2.** fam abw [reden] to squawk.

Qual (pl -en) die agony; [seelisch] torment; **jm das Leben zur ~ machen** to make sb's life a misery. ◆ **Qualen** pl suffering (sg), agony (sg); [seelisch] torment (sg); **jn von seinen/ ihren ~ erlösen** to put sb out of his/her misery.

quälen vt - **1.** [gen] to torment; [foltern] to torture - **2.** fam [bedrängen] to pester; **jn mit etw ~** to plague sb with sthg. ◆ **sich quälen** ref - **1.** [leiden] to suffer - **2.** [sich abmühen] to struggle.

Quälerei (pl -en) die - **1.** [Peinigung] torment; [Folter] torture; [Grausamkeit] cruelty; **~ der Tiere** cruelty to animals - **2.** (ohne pl) [Anstrengung] struggle.

qualifizieren vt - **1.** [befähigen] to qualify - **2.** [beurteilen] to classify. ◆ **sich qualifizieren** ref [sich befähigen] to obtain qualifications; [für Wettbewerb] to qualify.

Qualität (pl -en) die quality.

Qualle (pl -n) die jellyfish.

Qualm der - **1.** [von Feuer] thick smoke - **2.** fam abw [von Zigaretten] fug.

qualmen <> vi to smoke <> vt salopp [Zigaretten] to puff away at.

qualvoll <> adj agonizing <> adv in agony.

Quantität die (ohne pl) quantity.

Quarantäne [karan'tɛ:nə] (pl -n) die quarantine (U).

Quark der quark, type of soft cheese.

Quartal (pl -e) das quarter.

Quartett (pl -e) das - **1.** MUS quartet - **2.** (ohne pl) [Kartenspiel] children's card game where players have to collect four of a kind.

Quartier (pl -e) das accommodation (U).

Quarzuhr die quartz watch.

quasi adv virtually.

Quatsch der fam rubbish.

quatschen fam <> vi - **1.** [reden] to chat - **2.** abw [quasseln] to chatter <> vt [reden] to talk.

Quecksilber das CHEM mercury.

Quelle (pl -n) die - **1.** [Wasserquelle] spring - **2.** [Informant(en), Fundstelle] source.

quellen (präs quillt; prät quoll; perf ist gequollen) vi - **1.** [austreten - Flüssigkeit] to stream; [- Rauch] to billow - **2.** [hervortreten] to swell; [Augen] to bulge - **3.** [Feuchtigkeit aufnehmen] to soak.

quengeln vi fam to whine.

quer adv diagonally; **~ durch etw** straight through sthg; **~ über etw** (A), **~ auf etw** (D) across sthg; **~ zu etw** at right angles to sthg.

Quere die: **jm in die ~ kommen** fig [behindern] to get in sb's way; [Weg abschneiden] to block sb's path; [treffen] to bump into sb.

querfeldein adv cross-country.

Querflöte die flute.

Querschnitt der - **1.** [Auswahl, Abbildung] cross-section - **2.** [Schnitt] cut.

querschnittsgelähmt adj paraplegic.

Querstraße die: **die nächste ~ rechts** the next turning on the right.

quetschen vt - **1.** [unterbringen, drängen] to squeeze - **2.** [zerdrücken] to crush - **3.** [verlet-

zen]: **der Baum hat mir das Bein gequetscht**
the tree crushed my leg. ➡ **sich quetschen** *ref* [sich zwängen] to squeeze.

Quetschung (*pl* -en) *die* bruise.

quieken *vi* [Ferkel] to squeal; [Maus] to
squeak.

quietschen *vi* - **1.** [Tür, Bremse] to squeak
- **2.** *fam* [juchzen] to squeal.

quillt *präs* ▷ quellen.

Quirl (*pl* -e) *der* whisk.

quitt *adj* (*unver*): **mit jm ~ sein** *fam* to be quits
with sb.

quittieren ◇ *vt* - **1.** [bestätigen] to sign for;
etw ~ lassen to get a receipt for sthg - **2.** [er-
widern] to respond to - **3.** [kündigen]: **den
Dienst ~** to resign ◇ *vi* [Empfang bestätigen]
to sign.

Quittung (*pl* -en) *die* - **1.** [Beleg] receipt
- **2.** *fig* [Konsequenz]: **da hast du die ~!** that's
the price you pay!

Quiz [kvis] (*pl* -) *das* quiz.

quoll *prät* ▷ quellen.

Quote (*pl* -n) *die* [Anteil] proportion; [festge-
schriebene Zielmenge] quota; [Einschaltquo-
te] viewing figures (*pl*).

R

r, R [ɛr] (*pl* - ODER -s) *das* r, R.

Rabatt (*pl* -e) *der* discount.

Rabbi (*pl* -s) *der* rabbi.

Rabe (*pl* -n) *der* raven.

rabiat ◇ *adj* [gewalttätig] brutal; [wütend]
furious ◇ *adv* [gewalttätig] brutally; [wü-
tend] furiously.

Rache *die* revenge.

Rachen (*pl* -) *der* throat.

rächen *vt* to avenge. ➡ **sich rächen** *ref*
- **1.** [Rache nehmen] to get one's revenge;
sich an jm (für ODER **wegen etw) ~** to take revenge on sb (for sthg) - **2.** [Konsequenzen ha-
ben]: **seine Faulheit wird sich ~** he'll pay for
his laziness.

Rad (*pl* Räder) *das* - **1.** [von Fahrzeug] wheel
- **2.** [Fahrrad] bike; **~ fahren** to cycle - **3.** [von
Maschine] cog.

Radar *der* ODER *das* radar.

Radarkontrolle *die* radar speed check.

Radau *der* racket.

radebrechen ◇ *vt*: **Englisch/Deutsch ~** to
speak broken English/German ◇ *vi*: **er ra-
debrechte in Englisch** he spoke broken English.

radeln (*perf* ist geradelt) *vi* to cycle.

radfahren *vi* (*unreg*) ▷ Rad.

Radfahrer, in *der, die* cyclist.

Radfahrweg *der* cycle track.

radieren *vt* & *vi* [mit Radiergummi] to
erase.

Radiergummi *der* rubber *Br*, eraser *Am*.

Radieschen [ra'diːsçən] (*pl* -) *das* radish.

radikal ◇ *adj* radical ◇ *adv* radically.

Radio (*pl* -s) *das* - **1.** [gen] radio; **~ hören** to
listen to the radio - **2.** (*ohne pl*) [Anstalt] radio
station.

Radioaktivität *die* radioactivity.

Radiorekorder (*pl* -) *der* radio cassette recorder.

Radiosendung *die* radio programme.

Radiowecker *der* radio alarm.

Radius (*pl* Radien) *der* radius.

Radrennen *das* cycle race.

Radsport *der* cycling.

Radtour *die* cycling tour.

Radweg *der* cycle path.

raffen *vt* - **1.** *abw* [nehmen] to stuff; **etw an
sich** (*A*) **~** to grab sthg - **2.** [Stoff] to gather
- **3.** *salopp* [begreifen] to get.

Raffinerie [rafinə'riː] (*pl* -n) *die* refinery.

raffiniert ◇ *adj* - **1.** [Person, Plan, System]
ingenious; [Geschmack, Farbe] subtle; [Klei-
derschnitt] sophisticated - **2.** [gerissen] cunning ◇ *adv* - **1.** [planen, arrangieren] ingeni-
ously; [würzen] subtly; **~ kochen** to be a
sophisticated cook - **2.** [gerissen] cunningly.

ragen (*perf* hat/ist geragt) *vi*: **aus etw ~** to
stick out of sthg; [Berg, Baum, Gebäude] to
rise up out of sthg.

Ragout [ra'guː] (*pl* -s) *das* stew.

Rahm *der* cream.

rahmen *vt* to frame.

Rahmen (*pl* -) *der* - **1.** [von Bild, Fenster,
Fahrrad] frame - **2.** [von Fahrzeugen] chassis
- **3.** (*ohne pl*) [Umgebung] setting; [Kontext]
context - **4.** *RW*: **aus dem ~ fallen** to be out of
place. ➡ **im Rahmen** *adv*: **im ~ einer Sache
(G)** [Zusammenhang] in the context of sthg;
[Verlauf] in the course of sthg; [innerhalb der
Grenzen] within the bounds of sthg; [als
Teil] as part of sthg.

räkeln, rekeln ➡ **sich räkeln, sich rekeln** *ref* to stretch out.

Rakete (*pl* -n) *die* rocket; MIL missile.

rammen *vt* to ram.

Rampe (*pl* -n) *die* - **1.** [Laderampe, Auffahrt]
ramp - **2.** [in Theater] apron.

Rampenlicht *das* (*ohne pl*) footlights (*pl*);
im ~ stehen *fig* to be in the limelight.

ramponiert *adj fam* battered.

Ramsch *der fam abw* junk.

ran *fam* = heran.

Rand (*pl* Ränder) *der* - **1.** [von Stadt, Tisch,
Teich] edge - **2.** [von Gefäßen] rim - **3.** [von

Buchseite] margin - **4.** [Umrandung] edging (U); **(dunkle) Ränder um die Augen haben** to have dark rings around one's eyes - **5.** RW: **mit jm/etw (nicht) zu ~ kommen** fam (not) to be able to cope with sb/sthg. ◆ **am Rande** adv - **1.** [nebenbei] in passing; **sich am ~e abspielen** to take place on the sidelines - **2.** [nahe]: **am ~e der Verzweiflung sein** to be close to despair.

randalieren vi to rampage.

Randlbezirk der suburb.

Randlgruppe die marginal group.

randvoll ⬦ adj full to the brim ⬦ adv to the brim.

rang prät ▷ ringen.

Rang (pl Ränge) der - **1.** [Position] rank - **2.** [Ansehen] class; **ein Wissenschaftler von ~** a renowned scientist - **3.** [in Theater, Stadion] circle; **der erste/zweite ~** [in Theater] the dress/upper circle; [im Wettbewerb] first/second place.

rangieren [raŋˈʒiːrən] ⬦ vt to shunt ⬦ vi to be ranked.

Ranglliste die (army/navy/civil service) list.

Ranglordnung die order of precedence.

ranlhalten ◆ **sich ranhalten** ref (unreg) fam to get on with it.

Ranke (pl -n) die tendril.

ranken (perf hat/ist gerankt) vi (ist) to climb. ◆ **sich ranken** ref to climb; **sich um etw ~** [wachsen] to entwine itself around sthg; fig & geh [spinnen] to grow up around sthg.

rann prät ▷ rinnen.

rannte prät ▷ rennen.

ranzig adj rancid.

Raps der rape.

rar adj rare.

Rarität (pl -en) die rarity.

rasant ⬦ adj - **1.** [schnell] rapid - **2.** fam [imponierend] stunning ⬦ adv [schnell] rapidly.

rasch ⬦ adj quick ⬦ adv quickly.

rascheln vi to rustle.

rasen (perf hat/ist gerast) vi - **1.** (ist) [fahren] to race; **gegen etw ~** to crash into sthg - **2.** (hat) [toben] to rage; **das Publikum raste vor Begeisterung** the audience went wild with enthusiasm.

Rasen (pl -) der [Rasenfläche] lawn; [Gras] grass.

rasend ⬦ adj - **1.** [Entwicklung] rapid; [Geschwindigkeit] lightning (vor Subst); [Eile] great - **2.** [gewaltig] raging - **3.** [wütend]: **jn ~ machen** fam to drive sb mad ⬦ adv - **1.**: **~ schnell** incredibly quickly - **2.** [enorm] terribly; **~ verliebt sein** to be madly in love.

Rasenlmäher der lawnmower.

Raserei die (ohne pl) - **1.** [Toben] rage; **jn zur**

~ **bringen** to drive sb mad - **2.** abw [Schnelligkeit] speeding.

Rasierlapparat der shaver.

rasieren vt to shave. ◆ **sich rasieren** ref to shave; **sich nass/trocken ~** to have a wet/dry shave.

Rasierer (pl -) der fam shaver.

Rasierlklinge die razor blade.

Rasierlschaum der shaving foam.

Rasierlwasser das aftershave.

raspeln vt [reiben] to grate.

Rasse (pl -n) die - **1.** [bei Tieren] breed - **2.** [bei Menschen] race.

Rassel (pl -n) die rattle.

rasseln (perf hat/ist gerasselt) vi - **1.** (hat) [Geräusch erzeugen] to rattle - **2.** (ist) fam [durchfallen]: **durch eine Prüfung ~** to flunk an exam.

Rassismus der racism.

rassistisch adj racist.

Rast (pl -en) die rest; **~ machen** [beim Fahren] to stop for a break; [beim Gehen] to stop for a rest.

rasten vi [beim Fahren] to stop for a break; [beim Gehen] to stop for a rest.

Raster (pl -) das TECH screen; [System] framework.

Rastlhof der [an Autobahnen] services (pl).

rastlos ⬦ adj tireless ⬦ adv tirelessly.

Rastlplatz der picnic area (with toilet facilities).

Rastlstätte die [auf Autobahnen] services (pl).

Rasur (pl -en) die shave.

Rat (pl Räte) der - **1.** [Ratschlag] advice (U); **jm einen ~ geben** to give sb a piece of advice; **jn/etw zu ~e ziehen** to consult sb/sthg; **jn um ~ fragen** ODER **bitten** to ask sb for advice; **sich** (D) **keinen ~ (mehr) wissen** to be at one's wits' end - **2.** [Versammlung] council - **3.** [Person] councillor.

rät präs ▷ raten.

Rate (pl -n) die - **1.** [Teilzahlung] instalment; **etw auf ~n kaufen** to buy sthg on hire purchase - **2.** [statistische] rate.

raten (präs rät; prät riet; perf hat geraten) ⬦ vt - **1.** [erraten] to guess - **2.** [empfehlen] to advise ⬦ vi - **1.** [erraten] to guess - **2.** [Rat geben]: **jm zu etw ~** to advise sb to do sthg.

Ratenlzahlung die payment by instalments.

Ratgeber (pl -) der - **1.** [Mensch] adviser - **2.** [Buch] guide.

Ratgeberin (pl -nen) die adviser.

Rathaus das town hall.

Ration (pl -en) die ration.

rational ⬦ adj rational ⬦ adv rationally.

rationalisieren vt to rationalize.

rationell ⟨⟩ *adj* efficient ⟨⟩ *adv* efficiently.

rationieren *vt* to ration.

ratlos ⟨⟩ *adj* helpless ⟨⟩ *adv* helplessly.

Rätoromanisch(e) *das* Rhaeto-Romanic; *siehe auch* Englisch(e).

ratsam *adj* advisable.

Rat|schlag *der* piece of advice.

Rätsel (*pl* -) *das* - 1. [Aufgabe] puzzle; **jm ein ~ aufgeben** to ask sb a riddle - 2. [Geheimnis] mystery; **etw ist jm ein ~** sthg is a mystery to sb; **vor einem ~ stehen** to be faced with a mystery.

rätselhaft *adj* mysterious; **es ist mir ~** it's a mystery to me.

rätseln *vi*: **über etw** (A) **~** to puzzle over sthg.

Ratte (*pl* -n) *die* rat.

rau *adj* - 1. [Oberfläche, Person, Sitten] rough - 2. [Klima, Leben] harsh - 3. [angegriffen - Stimme] hoarse; [- Hals] sore.

Raub *der* robbery.

Raubbau *der* overexploitation.

rauben *vt* - 1. [stehlen] to steal - 2. [kosten]: **jm etw ~** to rob sb of sthg; **jm den Schlaf ~** to deprive sb of their sleep.

Räuber, in (*mpl* -; *fpl* -nen) *der, die* robber.

Raub|mord *der* robbery with murder.

Raub|tier *das* predator.

Raub|über|fall *der* robbery.

Raub|vogel *der* bird of prey.

Rauch *der* smoke.

rauchen *vt* & *vi* to smoke.

Raucher (*pl* -) *der* smoker.

Raucherin (*pl* -nen) *die* smoker.

räuchern *vt* to smoke.

Rauch|verbot *das* ban on smoking.

rauf *fam* = herauf.

raufen *vi* to fight. ◆ **sich raufen** *ref* to fight.

Rauferei (*pl* -en) *die* fight.

rauh = rau.

Rauhreif *der* = Raureif.

Raum (*pl* Räume) *der* - 1. [Zimmer] room - 2. [Platz & PHYS] space - 3. (*ohne pl*) GEOGR area.

räumen *vt* - 1. [Wohnung] to vacate - 2. [Platz, Posten] to clear.

Raum|fahrt *die* space travel.

Raum|inhalt *der* volume.

räumlich ⟨⟩ *adj* spatial ⟨⟩ *adv* spatially.

Raum|schiff *das* spaceship.

Räumung (*pl* -en) *die* clearing (U); [von Wohnung] vacation (U); [vor Gefahr] evacuation.

Raupe (*pl* -n) *die* [Insekt] caterpillar.

Raureif *der* hoarfrost.

raus *adv fam* - 1. = heraus - 2. [hinaus] out; **~ hier!** get out!

Rausch (*pl* Räusche) *der* - 1. [das Betrunkensein] intoxication; **einen ~ haben** to be drunk - 2. [Ekstase] ecstasy; **im ~ sein** in ecstasy.

rauschen (*perf* hat/ist gerauscht) *vi* - 1. (hat) [Bäume] to rustle; [Bach] to murmur; **es rauscht** [im Telefon] there's a crackle; [in den Ohren] there's a buzz - 2. (ist) *fam* [gehen] to rush.

rauschend *adj*: **ein ~es Fest** a glittering party; **~er Beifall** loud applause.

Rausch|gift *das* drug.

rauschgiftsüchtig *adj* addicted to drugs.

raus|fliegen (*perf* ist rausgeflogen) *vi* (*unreg*) *fam* [aus Schule] to be thrown out; [aus Firma] to be fired.

raus|halten *vt* (*unreg*) *fam* [nach draußen] to hold out. ◆ **sich raushalten** *ref fam*: **sich aus etw ~** to keep out of sthg.

raus|kriegen *vt fam* to find out.

räuspern ◆ **sich räuspern** *ref* to clear one's throat.

raus|rücken (*perf* hat/ist rausgerückt) *fam* ⟨⟩ *vi* (*ist*): **mit etw ~** [ausdrücken] to come out with sthg; [herausgeben] to hand over sthg ⟨⟩ *vt* (*hat*) [herausgeben] to hand over.

raus|schmeißen *vt* (*unreg*) *fam* to throw out.

Raute (*pl* -n) *die* diamond (shape).

Razzia (*pl* Razzien) *die* (police) raid.

rd. *abk für* rund.

reagieren *vi* to react; **auf etw** (A) **~** to react to sthg.

Reaktion (*pl* -en) *die* reaction; **die ~ auf etw** (A) the reaction to sthg.

Reaktor (*pl* -toren) *der* (nuclear) reactor.

realistisch ⟨⟩ *adj* realistic ⟨⟩ *adv* realistically.

Realität (*pl* -en) *die* reality.

Real|schule *die* secondary school for pupils up to the age of 16.

📖 Realschule

This intermediate school caters for pupils aged between 10 and 16 and leads to a qualification for further vocational training at a technical school (Berufsschule or Fachschule). Pupils receive a general education covering technical subjects as well as one modern foreign language.

Rebe (*pl* -n) *die* vine.

rebellieren *vi* to rebel; **gegen jn/etw ~** to rebel against sb/sthg.

Rebellion (*pl* -en) *die* rebellion.

rebellisch *adj* rebellious.

Reb|huhn *das* partridge.

Reb|stock *der* vine.

Rechen (*pl* -) *der* rake.

Rechen|aufgabe *die* sum.

Rechen|fehler der miscalculation.

rechnen ⟨⟩ vi - **1.** [berechnen] to calculate - **2.** [schätzen] to estimate - **3.** [erwarten]: **mit jm/etw ~** to expect sb/sthg - **4.** [sich verlassen]: **auf jn/etw ~** to count on sb/sthg; **mit jm ~** to rely on sb - **5.** [bedenken]: **mit jm/etw ~** to reckon with sb/sthg; **im Urlaub mit gutem Wetter ~** to reckon on having good weather on holiday ⟨⟩ vt [berechnen] to work out. ◆ **sich rechnen** ref to be profitable.

Rechner (pl -) der EDV computer.

Rechnung (pl -en) die - **1.** WIRTSCH bill; [im Restaurant] bill Br, check Am; **eine ~ begleichen** to pay a bill - **2.** [Rechenaufgabe] calculation - **3.** RW: **eine ~ begleichen** to settle a score.

recht ⟨⟩ adj - **1.** [korrekt, passend] right; **~ und billig** fig right and proper; **zur ~en Zeit am ~en Ort** at the right place at the right time; **ist es dir ~, wenn ich morgen vorbeikomme?** is it all right with you if I come by tomorrow? - **2.** [besonders] particular; **es macht keinen ~en Spaß** it's not really much fun ⟨⟩ adv - **1.** [ziemlich] quite - **2.** RW: **man kann ihm nichts ~ machen** there's no pleasing him; **jetzt erst ~** even more.

Recht (pl -e) das - **1.** RECHT law; **~ sprechen** to administer justice; **im ~ sein** to be in the right; **jm ~ geben** to admit sb is right - **2.** [Anrecht] right; **ein ~ auf etw** (A) **haben** to have a right to sthg. ◆ **mit** ODER **zu Recht** adv rightly.

rechte, r, s adj - **1.** [Seitenangabe] right - **2.** [rechtspolitisch] right-wing.

Rechte (pl -n) ⟨⟩ die - **1.** [rechte Hand] right hand; **zur ~n** on the right - **2.** POL: **die ~** the Right ⟨⟩ der, die right-winger ⟨⟩ das: **nach dem ~n sehen** to see to things.

Rechteck (pl -e) das rectangle.

rechteckig adj rectangular.

rechtfertigen vt to justify; **etw vor jm ~** to justify sthg to sb. ◆ **sich rechtfertigen** ref: **sich (vor jm) ~** to justify o.s. (to sb).

Rechtfertigung (pl -en) die justification.

rechthaberisch adj abw opinionated; **er ist immer so ~** he always thinks he's right.

rechtlich ⟨⟩ adj legal ⟨⟩ adv legally.

rechtmäßig ⟨⟩ adj lawful ⟨⟩ adv lawfully.

rechts ⟨⟩ adv - **1.** [Angabe der Seite, Richtung] on the right; **~ abbiegen** turn right; **nach/von ~** to/from the right; **~ von jm** to one's right; **~ von etw** to the right of sthg - **2.** [Angabe der politischen Richtung] right wing; **~ eingestellt sein** to have right-wing leanings ⟨⟩ präp (+ G) [Angabe der Seite] to the right of.

Rechts|anwalt der lawyer.

Rechts|anwältin die lawyer.

rechtsbündig adj right justified.

Rechtschreib|fehler der spelling mistake.

Recht|schreibung die spelling.

rechtsextrem adj: **~e Jugendliche** young right-wing extremists.

Rechts|extremist, in der, die abw right-wing extremist.

rechtsgerichtet adj right-wing.

rechtsgültig adj legally valid.

Rechtshänder, in (mpl -; fpl -nen) der, die right-hander.

rechtsherum adv to the right.

rechtskräftig ⟨⟩ adj final; **~ sein** to be legally effective ⟨⟩ adv: **jn ~ verurteilen** to pass a final sentence on sb.

Rechts|kurve die right-hand bend.

Rechts|lage die legal situation.

Rechtsprechung (pl -en) die administration of justice (U).

rechtsradikal adj extreme right-wing.

Rechts|radikale der, die right-wing extremist.

rechtsseitig adj of the right side.

Rechts|staat der state based upon the rule of law.

Rechts|verkehr der - **1.** [Straßenverkehr] driving on the right - **2.** RECHT law.

Rechts|weg der legal action; **der ~ ist ausgeschlossen** no legal action may be taken.

rechtwinklig, rechtwinkelig ⟨⟩ adj right-angled ⟨⟩ adv at a right angle.

rechtzeitig ⟨⟩ adj timely ⟨⟩ adv in time; **~ da sein/eintreffen** to be/get there in time.

Reck (pl -e ODER -s) das horizontal bar.

recyceln [ri'saikəln] vt to recycle.

Recycling [ri'saiklɪŋ] das recycling.

Recyclingpapier das recycled paper.

Redakteur, in [redak'tø:ɐ, rɪn] (mpl -e; fpl -nen) der, die editor.

Redaktion (pl -en) die - **1.** [Team] editorial staff - **2.** [von Texten] editing.

Rede (pl -n) die - **1.** [Ansprache] speech; **eine ~ halten** to make a speech - **2.** (ohne pl) [das Reden] talk; **die ~ ist von jm/etw** we are talking about sb/sthg - **3.** GRAM [gebundene] verse; [ungebundene] prose; **wörtliche/indirekte ~** direct/indirect speech - **4.** RW: **jn zur ~ stellen** to demand an explanation from sb.

Redefreiheit die freedom of speech.

reden ⟨⟩ vi - **1.** [gen] to talk; **deutlich/langsam ~** to speak clearly/slowly; **(mit jm) über jn/etw ~** to talk (to sb) about sb/sthg - **2.** [eine Rede halten] to speak - **3.** RW: **du hast gut ~** fam it's easy for you to talk; **jn zum Reden bringen** to get sb to talk; **von sich ~ machen** to cause a stir ⟨⟩ vt: **Unsinn ~** to talk nonsense.

Redens|art die saying; **das ist doch nur eine ~** it's just an expression.

Rede|wendung die idiom.

Redner, in (mpl -; fpl -nen) der, die speaker.

redselig adj talkative.

reduzieren vt - **1.** [verringern] to reduce - **2.** [vereinfachen]: **etw auf etw** (A) ~ to reduce sthg to sthg. ◆ **sich reduzieren** ref to decrease.

Reederei (pl -en) die shipping company.

Referat (pl -e) das - **1.** [Abhandlung] paper; **ein ~ halten** to give a paper - **2.** [Abteilung] department.

Referendar (pl -e) der person undergoing 'Referendariat'; [in Schule] student teacher.

Referendarin (pl -nen) die person undergoing 'Referendariat'; [in Schule] student teacher.

Referenz (pl -en) die reference.

reflektieren ⇔ vt - **1.** [Licht] to reflect - **2.** geh [Problem] to reflect on ⇔ vi geh: **über etw** (A) ~ to reflect on sthg.

Reflex (pl -e) der - **1.** [Reaktion] reflex - **2.** [Lichtreflex] reflection.

Reflexion (pl -en) die reflection.

reflexiv GRAM ⇔ adj reflexive ⇔ adv reflexively.

Reflexivpronomen das GRAM reflexive pronoun.

Reform (pl -en) die reform.

Reformationstag der REL Reformation Day, 31 October, day on which the Reformation is celebrated.

Reformhaus das health food shop.

reformieren vt to reform.

Reformkost die health food.

Refrain [rəˈfrɛ̃ː] (pl -s) der refrain.

Regal (pl -e) das shelves (pl).

Regatta (pl Regatten) die regatta.

rege ⇔ adj lively; [Verkehr] busy; [Handel] brisk ⇔ adv: **sich ~ an etw** (D) **beteiligen** to take a lively interest in sthg.

Regel (pl -n) die - **1.** [Norm] rule; **in aller** ODER **der ~** as a rule - **2.** [Periode] period.

Regelblutung die period.

Regelfall der rule.

regelmäßig ⇔ adj regular ⇔ adv regularly.

Regelmäßigkeit (pl -en) die regularity.

regeln vt [Temperatur, Geschwindigkeit] to regulate; [Angelegenheit] to settle; [Nachlass] to put in order; [Verkehr] to direct. ◆ **sich regeln** ref to sort itself out; **sich von selbst ~** to sort itself out.

regelrecht adj - **1.** fam [richtig] proper - **2.** [ordnungsgemäß] correct.

Regelung (pl -en) die regulation.

regen vt to move. ◆ **sich regen** ref to move; [Gefühl, Hoffnung] to stir.

Regen der rain; **saurer ~** acid rain.

Regenbogen der rainbow.

Regenmantel der raincoat.

Regenrinne die gutter.

Regenschauer der shower.

Regenschirm der umbrella.

Regentropfen der raindrop.

Regenwald der rain forest.

Regenwurm der earthworm.

Regie [reˈʒiː] die direction; ~ **führen** to direct; **etw in eigener ~ tun** ODER **durchführen** to do sthg on one's own account.

regieren ⇔ vt to rule ⇔ vi to rule; **über jn/etw** ~ to rule over sb/sthg.

Regierung (pl -en) die government.

Regierungschef, in der, die head of government.

Regierungssitz der seat of government.

Regierungssprecher, in der, die government spokesperson.

Regime [reˈʒiːm] (pl -) das regime.

Regiment (pl -e ODER -er) das - **1.** (pl Regimenter) MIL regiment - **2.** (pl Regimente) [Leitung] rule; **ein strenges ~ führen** to be strict.

Region (pl -en) die region.

regional ⇔ adj regional ⇔ adv regionally; ~ **verschieden** different from region to region.

Regisseur, in [reʒɪˈsøːɐ̯, rɪn] (mpl -e; fpl -nen) der, die director.

Register (pl -) das - **1.** [Verzeichnis - in Buch] index; [- amtlich] register - **2.** [MUS - von Orgel] stop; [- von Stimme] register.

registrieren vt - **1.** [wahrnehmen] to notice - **2.** [eintragen] to register.

reglos ⇔ adj motionless ⇔ adv motionlessly.

regnen ⇔ vi: **es regnet** it's raining ⇔ vt: **es regnet Konfetti** confetti is raining down.

regnerisch adj rainy.

regulär ⇔ adj - **1.** [Preis, Arbeit] normal; [Wahl, Spiel] in accordance with the rules - **2.** MIL regular ⇔ adv [arbeiten] normally; [zum normalen Preis] at the normal price.

regulieren vt - **1.** [regeln - Preis, Schaden, Verkehr] to regulate - **2.** [Temperatur, Lautstärke] to adjust - **3.** [Gewässer] to straighten.

Regung (pl -en) die - **1.** [Bewegung] movement - **2.** geh [Gefühl] stirring.

regungslos ⇔ adj motionless ⇔ adv motionlessly.

Reh (pl -e) das deer.

Reha-Klinik die rehab clinic.

Rehbock der roebuck.

Rehkitz (pl -e) das fawn.

Reibe (pl -n) die grater.

Reibekuchen der small pancake made from grated potatoes.

reiben (prät rieb; perf hat gerieben) ⇔ vt - **1.** [Körperteile] to rub; **sich** (D) **die Hände/die Nase/das Auge** ~ to rub one's hands/nose/eye; **jm die Hände/Wangen** ~ to rub sb's hands/cheeks - **2.** [Käse, Karotten] to grate ⇔ vi to rub.

Reiberei (pl -en) die friction.

Reibung die - 1. PHYS friction - 2. [das Reiben] rubbing.

reibungslos ⬦ adj smooth ⬦ adv smoothly.

reich ⬦ adj - 1. [wohlhabend] rich; ~ an etw (D) sein [Bodenschätzen] to be rich in sthg; [Erfahrungen] to have a wealth of sthg - 2. [Erdölvorkommen, Ernte] rich; [Erfahrung] extensive ⬦ adv [geschmückt] richly.

Reich (pl -e) das - 1. POL empire - 2. [Bereich] world.

Reiche (pl -n) der, die rich person.

reichen ⬦ vi - 1. [Geld, Zeit] to be enough; [Vorrat] to last; **das reicht!** that's enough!; **mir reichts** fam fig I've had enough - 2.: **(von … bis zu …) ~** [Grundstück, Gebiet] to extend (from … to …); [Kleidungsstück] to reach (from … to …) ⬦ vt: **jm etw ~** to pass sb sthg; **sich** (D) **die Hände ~** to shake hands.

reichhaltig adj rich.

reichlich ⬦ adj [Essen, Zeit] ample; [Trinkgeld] generous ⬦ adv - 1. [viel] amply - 2. [ziemlich] rather.

Reichstag ['raiçsta:k] der [Gebäude] Reichstag.

📖 **Reichstag**

The Reichstag was built between 1884 and 1894. Until 27 February 1933, when the building was burnt down, the German parliament (deutsche Reichstag) met in session there. The fire gave the National Socialists (who had in fact orchestrated the fire) an excuse to persecute their political opponents; this marked the end of democracy in the Weimar Republic. The Reichstag was badly damaged during the Second World War and, after it was rebuilt, the Bundestag only used it for special occasions. After the reunification of Germany in 1990, the restoration of the Reichstag was completed and the building was surmounted by a glass dome. The Reichstag has been the seat of the German parliament again since 1999.

Reichtum (pl -tümer) der - 1. [Vermögen] wealth - 2. [Fülle]: **der ~ an etw** (D) the abundance of sthg. ➡ **Reichtümer** pl riches.

Reichweite die - 1. [greifbare Nähe, von Boxern] reach - 2. TECH range. ➡ **außer Reichweite** adv out of reach. ➡ **in Reichweite** adv within reach.

reif adj - 1. [gen] ripe; **~ für etw sein** fam fig to be ready for sthg; **~ fürs Irrenhaus sein** to belong in the madhouse - 2. [erwachsen] mature.

Reife die - 1. [von Person] maturity; **mittlere ~** SCHULE intermediate school-leaving certif-

icate (for those leaving at 16) - 2. [von Obst] ripeness.

Reifen (pl -) der - 1. [von Fahrzeugen] tyre - 2. [Ring] hoop.

Reifen|druck der tyre pressure.

Reifen|panne die flat tyre.

Reife|prüfung die final examination at a German 'Gymnasium', required for university entrance.

Reife|zeugnis das certificate awarded to people who have passed the 'Reifeprüfung'.

reiflich ⬦ adj very careful ⬦ adv very carefully.

Reihe (pl -n) die - 1. [Linie, Sitzreihe] row - 2. [Menge]: **eine ~ von etw** a number of sthg - 3. [Reihenfolge]: **du bist an der ~** it's your turn; **jn außer der ~ drannehmen** to take sb out of turn; **er kommt an die ~** it is his turn. ➡ **der Reihe nach** adv in turn.

reihen vt - 1. [nebeneinander stellen] to line up - 2. [auffädeln]: **etw auf etw** (A) **~** to string sthg on sthg - 3. [nähen] to tack.

Reihen|folge die order; **alphabetische ~** alphabetical order.

Reihen|haus das terraced house Br, row house Am.

Reiher (pl -) der heron.

Reim (pl -e) der rhyme.

reimen ⬦ vt to rhyme ⬦ vi to make up rhymes. ➡ **sich reimen** ref to rhyme; **'Bein' reimt sich auf 'klein'** 'Bein' rhymes with 'klein'.

rein ⬦ adj - 1. [ohne Zusätze, nicht gemischt] pure; **eine ~e Arbeitergegend** a wholly working-class area - 2. [nicht als] sheer - 3. [sauber] clean - 4. RW: **etw ins Reine bringen** to clear sthg up; **mit jm ins Reine kommen** to sort things out with sb ⬦ adv - 1. [ausschließlich] purely; **zeitlich geht es nicht** there's simply not enough time to do it - 2. fam [völlig] absolutely; **er wusste auch ~ gar nichts** he didn't know anything - 3. fam = **herein**.

Rein|fall der fam disaster.

rein|fallen (perf ist reingefallen) vi (unreg) fam - 1. [hineinfallen] to fall in - 2. [getäuscht werden] to fall for it; **auf jn/etw ~** to be taken in by sb/sthg; **mit jm/etw ~** to have nothing but trouble with sb/sthg.

reinigen vt to clean; **ein Kleidungsstück chemisch ~ lassen** to have a garment drycleaned. ➡ **sich reinigen** ref to clean o.s.

Reinigung (pl -en) die - 1.: **die (chemische) ~** the (dry) cleaner's - 2. [Säubern] cleaning.

Reinigungs|mittel das cleaner.

rein|legen vt fam - 1. [hineinlegen] to put in - 2. [übertölpeln] to take for a ride.

reinrassig adj purebred; [Pferd] thoroughbred.

rein|reden vi fam - 1. [ins Wort fallen] to

butt in - 2. [sich einmischen]: **jm ~ to tread on sb's toes; sich von niemandem ~ lassen** not to take orders from anybody.

Reis der rice.

Reise (pl -n) die [lang] journey; [kurz] trip; **auf ~n sein/gehen** to be/go away; **eine ~ machen** to go on a journey/trip. **➤ gute Reise** interj have a good journey/trip!

Reise|apotheke die first-aid kit.

Reise|begleiter, in der, die travelling companion.

Reise|büro das travel agent's.

Reise|bus der coach.

Reise|führer der - 1. [Mensch] guide, courier - 2. [Buch] guide book.

Reise|führerin die guide, courier.

Reise|gepäck das luggage.

Reise|gesellschaft die - 1. [Reisegruppe] group of tourists - 2. [Veranstalter] tour operator.

Reise|gruppe die group of tourists.

Reise|leiter, in der, die guide, courier.

reisen (perf ist gereist) vi to travel; **nach Athen/Schottland ~** to go to Athens/Scotland.

Reisende (pl -n) der, die [Fahrgast] passenger.

Reise|pass der passport.

Reise|route die route.

Reise|ruf der emergency message for a driver, broadcast over the radio.

Reise|tasche die travel bag.

Reise|verkehr der holiday traffic.

Reisever|sicherung die travel insurance.

Reise|zeit die - 1. [Fahrtdauer] journey time - 2. [Saison] holiday season.

Reise|ziel das destination.

Reiß|brett das drawing board.

reißen (prät riss; perf hat/ist gerissen) <> vi - 1. (ist) [abreißen - Papier, Stoff] to tear; [- Seil, Kette] to snap - 2. (hat) [ziehen]: **an etw** (D) **~** to pull at sthg <> vt (hat) - 1. [zerreißen]: **etw in Stücke ~** to tear sthg into pieces - 2. [herunterreißen] to pull - 3. [herausreißen]: **sie wurde aus dem Schlaf gerissen** she was rudely awakened; **etw aus dem Zusammenhang ~** to take sthg out of context - 4. [wegreißen]: **jm etw aus der Hand ~** to snatch sthg from sb; **etw an sich** (A) **~** [Paket, Macht] to seize sthg; [Gespräch] to monopolize sthg; **hin und her gerissen sein** fig to be torn - 5. [töten] to kill. **➤ sich reißen** ref: **sich um etw ~** to fight to get sthg.

reißend adj - 1. [Gewässer] raging - 2. [schnell]: **~en Absatz finden** to sell like hot cakes - 3. [Tier] rapacious - 4. [Schmerzen] searing.

Reißver|schluss der zip Br, zipper Am.

Reiß|zwecke die drawing pin Br, thumbtack Am.

reiten (prät ritt; perf hat/ist geritten) <> vi (ist) to ride; **im Schritt/Trab/Galopp ~** to ride at a walk/trot/gallop <> vt (hat) to ride.

Reiter, in (mpl -; fpl -nen) der, die rider.

Reit|hose die jodhpurs (pl).

Reit|pferd das horse (for riding).

Reit|sport der riding.

Reit|stiefel der riding boot.

Reit|weg der bridle path.

Reiz (pl -e) der - 1. [Impuls] stimulus - 2. [Verlockung, Schönheit] appeal (U); **die ~e einer schönen Frau** the charms of a beautiful woman.

reizbar adj irritable; **sie ist leicht ~** she is very irritable.

reizen vt - 1. [interessieren] to appeal to - 2. [provozieren] to provoke - 3. [Augen, Magen] to irritate - 4. [Neugier] to arouse.

reizend <> adj charming <> adv charmingly.

reizlos <> adj unattractive <> adv unattractively.

Reizung (pl -en) die irritation.

reizvoll <> adj [verlockend] attractive; [reizend] charming <> adv attractively.

rekeln = räkeln.

Reklamation (pl -en) die complaint.

Reklame die - 1. [Werbung] advertising; **für jn/etw ~ machen** to advertise sb/sthg, fig to sing sb's/sthg's praises - 2. [Werbemittel] advertisement.

reklamieren <> vt - 1. [beanstanden] to complain about - 2. [einklagen] to claim <> vi [Einspruch erheben]: **gegen etw ~** to object to sthg.

rekonstruieren vt to reconstruct.

Rekord (pl -e) der [Bestleistung, Spitzenwert] record; **einen ~ aufstellen/brechen** to set/break a record.

Rekrut (pl -en) der MIL recruit.

rekrutieren vt to recruit.

Rektor (pl -toren) der - 1. [von Schulen] head teacher Br, principal Am - 2. [von Hochschulen] vice-chancellor Br, president Am.

relativ, relativ <> adj relative <> adv relatively.

Relativ|pronomen das GRAM relative pronoun.

Relativ|satz der GRAM relative clause.

relaxen [ri'leksn] vi fam to take it easy.

relevant [rele'vant] adj relevant.

Religion (pl -en) die - 1. [Anschauung] religion - 2. (ohne pl) [Schulfach] religious education.

religiös <> adj religious <> adv in a religious way; **jn ~ erziehen** to give sb a religious upbringing.

Relikt (pl -e) das relic.

Reling (pl -s ODER -e) die SCHIFF rail.

remis [rə'mi:] *adv* SPORT: ~ **enden** to end in a draw.

Remoulade (*pl* -n) *die* remoulade.

Renaissance [rənɛ'sɑ̃:s] *die* Renaissance.

Rennibahn *die* SPORT racetrack; [Pferdesport] racecourse.

rennen (*prät* rannte; *perf* ist gerannt) *vi* to run; **sie kommt immer zu mir gerannt, wenn sie etwas braucht** she's always running to me when she needs something; **gegen etw ~ to** run into sthg.

Rennen (*pl* -) *das* - **1.** [Wettkampf] race - **2.** *RW:* **das ~ machen** to win.

Renner (*pl* -) *der fam* in-thing.

Rennifahrer, in *der, die* racing driver.

Rennirad *das* racing bike.

Rennisport *der* racing.

Renniwagen *der* racing car.

renovieren [reno'vi:rən] *vt* to renovate.

Renovierung [reno'vi:rʊŋ] (*pl* -en) *die* renovation.

Rente (*pl* -n) *die* pension; **auf** ODER **in ~ gehen** to retire.

Rente

Rente is a false friend which has nothing to do with the English words "rent" or "rental"; it refers to a person's "pension". So the phrase Meine Mutter ist letztes Jahr in Rente gegangen can be translated as "My mother began drawing her pension last year".
In German, the money one pays in "rent" for a flat is die Miete, and a "car rental company" is ein Autoverleih.

Rentenverisicherung *die* pension scheme.

Renitier, Rentier *das* reindeer.

rentieren ➔ sich rentieren *ref* [rentabel sein] to be profitable; [sich lohnen] to be worthwhile.

Rentner, in (*mpl* -; *fpl* -nen) *der, die* pensioner.

Reparatur (*pl* -en) *die* repair; **in ~ sein** to be being repaired.

Reparaturiwerkstatt *die* [für Autos] garage.

reparieren *vt* to repair.

Reportage [repɔr'ta:ʒə] (*pl* -n) *die* report.

Reporter, in (*mpl* -; *fpl* -nen) *der, die* reporter.

Repräsentant, in (*mpl* -en; *fpl* -nen) *der, die* representative.

repräsentativ ◇ *adj* - **1.** [ausgewogen, stellvertretend] representative - **2.** [vorzeigbar] imposing ◇ *adv* - **1.** [ausgewogen, stellvertretend] representatively - **2.** [vorzeigbar] imposingly.

repräsentieren ◇ *vt* to represent ◇ *vi* [öffentlich] to perform official duties.

Reiproduktion *die* reproduction.

reproduzieren *vt* to reproduce.

Reptil (*pl* -ien ODER -e) *das* reptile.

Republik (*pl* -en) *die* republic.

Republikaner, in (*mpl* -; *fpl* -en) *der, die* [Anhänger der Republik] republican.

Requiem ['re:kvi̯ɛm] (*pl* -s ODER Requien) *das* requiem.

Reserve [re'zɛrvə] (*pl* -n) *die* - **1.** [Vorrat] reserve; **jn/etw in ~ haben** ODER **halten** to have sb/sthg in reserve - **2.** (*ohne pl*) [Zurückhaltung] reserve - **3.** (*ohne pl*) [beim Militär] reserves (*pl*).

Reserveikanister *der* spare can.

Reserveirad *das* spare wheel.

Reserveireifen *der* spare tyre.

Reserveispieler, in *der, die* substitute.

reservieren [rezɛr'vi:rən] *vt* to reserve.

reserviert [rezɛr'vi:ɐ̯t] *adj* reserved.

Reservierung [rezɛr'vi:rʊŋ] (*pl* -en) *die* reservation.

Residenz (*pl* -en) *die* [Wohnsitz] residence; [Stadt] royal seat.

Resignation (*pl* -en) *die* resignation (*U*).

resignieren *vi* to give up.

Resonanz (*pl* -en) *die* - **1.** [Widerhall] response; **die ~ auf etw** (*A*) the response to sthg - **2.** [akustisch] resonance.

Respekt *der* respect; **~ vor jm haben** to have respect for sb; **Respekt!** well done!; **sich** (*D*) **~ verschaffen** to make o.s. respected.

respektieren *vt* to respect.

respektlos ◇ *adj* disrespectful ◇ *adv* disrespectfully.

respektvoll ◇ *adj* respectful ◇ *adv* respectfully.

Rest (*pl* -e) *der* - **1.** [von Mahlzeit, Gebäude, Leichnam] remains (*pl*); [von Stoff] remnant - **2.** [von Tag, Urlaub, Erzählung] rest; **jm/etw den ~ geben** *fam fig* to finish sb/sthg off.

Restaurant [rɛsto'rɑ̃:] (*pl* -s) *das* restaurant.

restaurieren *vt* to restore.

Restaurierung (*pl* -en) *die* restoration.

Restibetrag *der* balance.

restlich *adj* remaining.

restlos *adv* totally.

Resultat (*pl* -e) *das* result.

Retorte (*pl* -n) *die* CHEM retort; **aus der ~** *abw* artificial; **ein Kind aus der ~** a test-tube baby.

Retortenibaby *das* test-tube baby.

Retrospektive [retrospɛk'ti:və] (*pl* -n) *die* - **1.** *geh* [Rückblick] retrospective view - **2.** [Ausstellung] retrospective.

retten *vt* to save; [aus einer Gefahr] to rescue; **jn/etw vor jm/etw ~ to** save sb/sthg

from sb/sthg. ← **sich retten** ref to escape;
sich vor jm/etw nicht mehr ~ können fam fig
to be besieged by sb/swamped with sthg.
Retter, in (mpl -; fpl -nen) der, die rescuer.
Rettich (pl -e) der radish (of large red or white
variety).
Rettung die (ohne pl) rescue; **jd/etw ist js
(letzte) ~** fig sb/sthg is sb's salvation.
Rettungslboot das lifeboat.
Rettungsldienst der rescue service.
Rettungslring der lifebelt.
Rettungslwagen der ambulance.
Revanche [re'vãː∫(ə)] (pl -n) die - **1.** [Gegen-
leistung]: **als ~ für etw** in return for sthg
- **2.** [Vergeltung] revenge (U) - **3.** [beim Spiel]
return game.
Revier [re'viːɐ] (pl -e) das - **1.** [von Tieren]
territory - **2.** [Polizeirevier - Wache] (police)
station; [- Bezirk] district - **3.** [Bereich] do-
main - **4.** [von Jäger, Förster] area.
Revolte [re'vɔltə] (pl -n) die revolt.
Revolution [revolu'tsjoːn] (pl -en) die revolution.
revolutionär [revolutsjo'nɛːɐ] adj revolutionary.
Revolutionär, in [revolutsjo'nɛːɐ, rɪn]
(mpl -e; fpl -nen) der, die revolutionary.
Revolver [re'vɔlvɐ] (pl -) der revolver.
Revue [re'vyː] (pl -n) die - **1.** [Show] revue
- **2.** [Zeitschrift] review.
Rezension (pl -en) die review.
Rezept (pl -e) das - **1.** [ärztlich] prescription
- **2.** [für Speisen] recipe.

📖 **Rezept**

Care is needed with the German word
Rezept – it does not mean "receipt". Depending on the circumstances it can
mean both "recipe" and "prescription".
So the phrase nur auf Rezept erhältlich is
translated as "only available on prescription", whereas ein Rezept für Hähnchen
mit Bratkartoffeln is "a recipe for chicken
and roast potatoes".
The English word "receipt" is normally
translated by Quittung. The question
"Should I write you out a receipt?" could
be rendered in German as Soll ich Ihnen
eine Quittung ausstellen?

rezeptfrei adj available without a pre-
scription.
Rezeption (pl -en) die reception.
rezeptpflichtig adj available only on pre-
scription.
R-lGespräch das TELEKOM reverse charge Br
ODER collect Am call.
Rhabarber der rhubarb.
Rhein der: **der ~** the (River) Rhine.

rheinisch adj Rhenish.
Rheinland das: **das ~** the Rhineland.
Rheinland-Pfalz nt Rhineland-Palatinate.
Rhesusfaktor der MED rhesus factor.
rhetorisch adj rhetorical.
Rheuma das rheumatism.
Rheumatismus (pl -tismen) der rheumatism (U).
Rhododendron (pl -dendren) der rhododendron.
rhythmisch ⟨⟩ adj rhythmic ⟨⟩ adv
rhythmically.
Rhythmus (pl Rhythmen) der rhythm.
richten ⟨⟩ vt - **1.** [hinwenden] to point; **etw
auf jn/etw ~** [Waffe] to point sthg at sb/etw;
[Aufmerksamkeit] to turn sthg to sb/sthg
- **2.** [Brief, Appell]: **etw an jn ~** to address sthg
to sb - **3.** [reparieren] to fix - **4.** [Essen, Zim-
mer] to prepare ⟨⟩ vi [urteilen] to judge;
über jn/etw ~ geh to judge sb/sthg. ← **sich
richten** ref - **1.** [sich einstellen auf]: **sich nach
jm/etw ~** to fit in with sb/sthg - **2.** [abhängen
von]: **sich nach etw ~** to depend on sthg
- **3.** [sich wenden]: **sich gegen jn/etw ~** to be
directed at sb/sthg.
Richter, in (mpl -; fpl -nen) der, die judge.
richterlich adj judicial.
richtig ⟨⟩ adj - **1.** [nicht falsch, passend]
right; **bin ich hier ~?** am I in the right place?;
sehr ~! quite right! - **2.** [echt - Person] real,
true; [- Sache] real - **3.** [vollwertig] proper
⟨⟩ adv - **1.** [nicht falsch] correctly; **meine Uhr
geht ~** my watch is right ODER accurate; **das
hast du ~ gemacht!** you were right to do it!
- **2.** [passend]: **er kam gerade ~** he came at
just the right moment - **3.** fam [wirklich] really.
Richtige (pl -n) ⟨⟩ das right thing; **genau
das ~** just the right thing; **nichts ~s** nothing
much ⟨⟩ der, die right person.
richtig gehend adj [Uhr] accurate.
Richtigkeit die correctness.
rieb prät ⟩ reiben.
riechen (prät roch; perf hat gerochen) ⟨⟩ vi
to smell ⟨⟩ vt [Duft] to smell.
rief prät ⟩ rufen.
Riemen (pl -) der - **1.** [Band] strap; **sich am
~ reißen** fam fig to pull o.s. together - **2.** [Ru-
der] oar.
Riese (pl -n) der giant.
rieseln (perf ist gerieselt) vi [Flüssigkeit] to
trickle; [Schnee] to float down; [Putz, Kalk]
to crumble.
Riesenlerfolg der huge success.
riesengroß adj enormous.
Riesenlrad das big wheel.
Riesenlslalom der giant slalom.
riesig ⟨⟩ adj - **1.** [groß] enormous - **2.** fam
[toll] fantastic ⟨⟩ adv fam [sehr] enormously.
riet prät ⟩ raten.

Riff (*pl* -e) *das* reef.

Rille (*pl* -n) *die* groove.

Rind (*pl* -er) *das* - **1.** [Tier] cow - **2.** [Fleisch] beef.

Rinde (*pl* -n) *die* - **1.** [von Bäumen] bark - **2.** [von Käse] rind - **3.** [von Brot] crust.

Rinder|braten *der* [roh] joint of beef; [gebraten] roast beef.

Rindfleisch *das* beef.

Ring (*pl* -e) *der* - **1.** [gen] ring - **2.** [Gruppe] group - **3.** [Straße] ring road. **Ringe** *pl* SPORT rings.

Ring|buch *das* ring binder.

Ringel|natter *die* grass snake.

ringen (*prät* rang; *perf* hat gerungen) *vi* - **1.** SPORT to wrestle - **2.** [sich anstrengen] to struggle; **mit etw ~** *geh* to wrestle with sthg *vt:* **die Hände ~** to wring one's hands.

Ringer, in (*mpl* -; *fpl* -nen) *der, die* wrestler.

Ring|finger *der* ring finger.

Ring|kampf *der* SPORT wrestling match.

Ring|richter, in *der, die* referee.

rings *adv:* **~ um jn/etw (herum)** all around sb/sthg.

ringsherum *adv* all around.

ringsumher *adv* all around.

Rinne (*pl* -n) *die* - **1.** [Vertiefung] channel - **2.** [Abflussrinne] gutter.

rinnen (*prät* rann; *perf* ist geronnen) *vi geh* to flow.

Rinn|stein *der* gutter.

Rippchen (*pl* -) *das* KÜCHE lightly smoked pork rib.

Rippe (*pl* -n) *die* - **1.** [Knochen] rib - **2.** [von Heizkörper] fin.

Risiko (*pl* Risiken) *das* risk; **auf eigenes ~** at one's own risk; **ein ~ eingehen** to take a risk.

riskant *adj* risky *adv* riskily.

riskieren *vt* to risk.

riss *prät* reißen.

Riss (*pl* -e) *der* [in Stoff, Kleidungsstück] tear; [in Gestein, Wand] crack; [in Gesellschaft] rift.

rissig *adj* cracked.

ritt *prät* reiten.

Ritt (*pl* -e) *der* ride.

Ritter (*pl* -) *der* knight.

Ritual (*pl* -e) *das* ritual.

rituell *adj* ritual.

Ritze (*pl* -n) *die* crack.

ritzen *vt* [gravieren] to carve. **sich ritzen** *ref* [verletzen] to scratch o.s.

Rivale [ri'vaːlə] (*pl* -n) *der* rival.

Rivalin [ri'vaːlɪn] (*pl* -nen) *die* rival.

Rivalität [rivaliˈtɛːt] (*pl* -en) *die* rivalry.

Robbe (*pl* -n) *die* seal.

robben (*perf* ist gerobbt) *vi* to crawl.

Roboter (*pl* -) *der* robot.

robust *adj* robust.

roch *prät* riechen.

röcheln *vi* to breathe with a wheezing sound; [Sterbender] to give the death rattle.

Rock *der* rock.

Rocker, in (*mpl* -; *fpl* -nen) *der, die abw* rocker.

Rock|musik *die* rock music.

Rodel|bahn *die* toboggan run.

rodeln (*perf* hat/ist gerodelt) *vi* to toboggan.

roden *vt* to clear.

Roggen *der* rye.

Roggen|brot *das* rye bread *(U)*.

roh *adj* - **1.** [ungekocht] raw - **2.** [grob, unbearbeitet] rough; **~e Gewalt** brute force *adv* - **1.** [ungekocht]: **etw ~ essen** to eat sthg raw - **2.** [behandeln, entwerfen] roughly.

Roh|bau (*pl* -ten) *der* shell.

Roh|kost *die* (*ohne pl*) raw fruit and vegetables (*pl*).

Roh|material *das* raw material.

Rohr (*pl* -e) *das* - **1.** [Röhre] pipe - **2.** [Pflanze] reed.

Rohr|bruch *der* burst pipe.

Röhre (*pl* -n) *die* - **1.** TECH pipe - **2.** ELEKTR valve *Br*, tube *Am* - **3.** [Backofen] oven.

Rohr|zucker *der* cane sugar.

Roh|stoff *der* raw material.

Rokoko *das* rococo.

Rolladen *der* = Rollladen.

Roll|bahn *die* runway.

Rolle (*pl* -n) *die* - **1.** [in Theater, in Gesellschaft] role - **2.** [von Garn] reel *Br*, spool *Am* - **3.** [von Möbeln] castor - **4.** SPORT roll - **5.** *RW:* **eine/keine ~ spielen** to/not to matter.

rollen (*perf* hat/ist gerollt) *vi* (ist) to roll *vt* (hat) - **1.** [Zigarette] to roll; [Teig] to roll out; [Papier, Fleisch] to roll up - **2.** [fortbewegen] to roll. **sich rollen** *ref* [Papier, Foto] to curl up; [sich wälzen] to roll around.

Roller (*pl* -) *der* scooter.

Roller|blades® (*pl* -) *pl* roller blades, inline skates.

Roll|kragen *der* polo neck.

Rollladen (*pl* -läden) *der* (rolling) shutters (*pl*).

Roll|mops *der* rollmop, rolled-up pickled herring.

Rollo (*pl* -s) *das* roller blind.

Roll|schuh *der* roller skate; **~ laufen** to roller-skate.

Roll|splitt *der* (*ohne pl*) loose chippings (*pl*).

Roll|stuhl *der* wheelchair.

Rollstuhl|fahrer, in *der, die* wheelchair user.

Roll|treppe *die* escalator.

Rom *nt* Rome.

Roma *pl* Romanies.

Roman (*pl* -e) *der* - **1.** [Buch] novel - **2.** *fam* [lange Geschichte] long rigmarole.

romanisch *adj* - **1.** [in Bezug auf Sprache] Romance - **2.** [der Romanik] Romanesque.

Romanistik *die* Romance languages and literature.

Romantik *die* - **1.** [Gefühl] romance - **2.** [Epoche] Romantic period.

romantisch <> *adj* - **1.** [gefühlvoll] romantic - **2.** KUNST & MUS Romantic <> *adv* romantically.

Romanze (*pl* -n) *die* romance.

Römer, in (*mpl* -; *fpl* -nen) *der, die* Roman.

römisch *adj* Roman.

römisch-katholisch *adj* Roman Catholic.

Rommee, Rommé (*pl* -s) *das* rummy (U).

röntgen *vt* to X-ray.

Röntgen|aufnahme *die*, **-bild** *das* (*pl* -bilder) X-ray.

Röntgenstrahlen *pl* X-rays.

rosa *adj* (*unver*) pink.

Rosa *das* pink.

Rose (*pl* -n) *die* rose.

Rosen|kohl *der* (*ohne pl*) (Brussels) sprouts (*pl*).

Rosen|montag *der* day before Shrove Tuesday which marks the height of the carnival season.

rosig *adj* rosy.

Rosine (*pl* -n) *die* raisin.

Rosmarin *der* rosemary.

Rost (*pl* -e) *der* - **1.** [Eisenoxyd] rust - **2.** [Gitter - zum Braten] grill; [- zum Abdecken] grating.

Rostbrat|wurst *die*: **Nürnberger ~** Nuremberg grilled sausage.

rosten (*perf* hat/ist gerostet) *vi* to rust.

rösten *vt* & *vi* to roast.

rostfrei *adj* [Stahl] stainless; [Messer] stainless steel; [Blech] rustproof.

Rösti *pl* Schweiz potato pancake made from grated fried potatoes.

rostig *adj* rusty.

rot (*kompar* röter ODER roter; *superl* röteste ODER roteste) *adj* - **1.** [Farbe] red; **~ werden** to blush - **2.** *fam* POL Red.

Rot *das* (*ohne pl*) red. ⬤ **bei Rot** *adv* at red.

Röte *die* redness.

Rote Kreuz *das*: **das ~** the Red Cross.

Röteln *pl* MED German measles (U).

Rote Meer *das*: **das ~** the Red Sea.

rothaarig *adj* red-haired.

rotieren (*perf* hat/ist rotiert) *vi* - **1.** (hat) [sich drehen, wechseln] to rotate - **2.** (hat, ist) *fam* [durchdrehen] to be in a flap.

Rot|käppchen *das* Little Red Riding Hood.

Rot|kehlchen (*pl* -) *das* robin.

Rot|kohl *der* red cabbage.

rötlich *adj* reddish.

Rötung (*pl* -en) *die* reddening.

Rot|wein *der* red wine.

Rotwild *das* red deer (*pl*).

Roulade [ru'la:də] (*pl* -n) *die* ≃ beef olive.

Roulette [ru'lɛ:t] (*pl* -s) *das* roulette (U).

Route ['ru:tə] (*pl* -n) *die* route.

Routine [ru'ti:nə] (*pl* -n) *die* - **1.** [Gewohnheit] routine; **zur ~ werden** to become routine - **2.** [Erfahrung]: **~ haben** to have experience.

routiniert [ruti'ni:ɐt] <> *adj* [Autofahrer, Redner] experienced; [Betrüger, Stil] skilful <> *adv* skilfully.

rubbeln *vt* [abrubbeln] to rub.

Rübe (*pl* -n) *die* - **1.** [Pflanze] turnip - **2.** *fam* [Kopf] nut.

Rubel (*pl* -) *der* rouble.

rüber *fam* - **1.** = herüber - **2.** = hinüber.

Rubin (*pl* -e) *der* ruby.

Rubrik (*pl* -en) *die* - **1.** [Kategorie] category - **2.** [von Zeitung] section.

Ruck (*pl* -e) *der* - **1.** [Bewegung] jerk; **sich** (D) **einen ~ geben** *fam fig* to make the effort - **2.** [politisch] swing.

Rück|antwort *die* reply.

Rück|blick *der* look back; **im ~** looking back; **ein ~ auf etw** (A) a look back at sthg.

rücken (*perf* hat/ist gerückt) *vt* (hat) *vi* (ist) to move.

Rücken (*pl* -) *der* - **1.** [gen] back; [von Buch] spine; [von Nase] bridge - **2.** SPORT [Schwimmen] backstroke.

Rücken|lehne *die* backrest.

Rücken|mark *das* (*ohne pl*) spinal cord.

Rücken|schmerzen *pl* backache (sg).

Rücken|schwimmen *das* backstroke.

Rücken|wind *der*: **~ haben** to have a following wind.

rück|erstatten *vt* to reimburse; **jm etw ~** to reimburse sb for sthg.

Rückfahr|karte *die* return (ticket) Br, round-trip ticket Am.

Rück|fahrt *die* return journey.

rückfällig *adj*: **~ werden** to relapse.

Rück|flug *der* return flight.

Rück|frage *die* query.

Rück|gabe *die* return (U).

Rück|gang *der* decrease.

rückgängig <> *adj* decreasing <> *adv*: **etw ~ machen** [Geschäft] to cancel sthg; [Entschluss] to reverse sthg.

Rück|gewinnung *die* recovery.

Rück|grat *das* spine; **jm das ~ brechen** *fig* [Widerstand brechen] to break sb; **~ haben** *fig* to have fight in one; **~ zeigen** to show fight.

Rück|griff *der*: **~ auf etw** (A) [Methode] recourse to sthg; [Mode, Musik] throwback to sthg.

Rückkehr *die* return.

Rück|kopplung, Rückkoppelung *die* feedback (U).

rückläufig <> *adj* declining; [Trend]

downward; **~e Entwicklung** decline ◇ *adv:* **sich ~ entwickeln** to decline.

Rück|licht *(pl -er) das* rear light.

Rück|reise *die* return journey.

Rück|ruf *der* return call.

Rück|sack *der* rucksack, pack; [für Reisen] backpack.

Rück|schlag *der* setback.

Rück|schluss *der* conclusion; **aus etw Rückschlüsse ziehen** to draw conclusions from sthg.

Rück|schritt *der* backward step.

Rück|seite *die* back.

Rück|sicht *die* - 1. [auf Person, Umstand] consideration; **aus ~ auf jn/etw** out of consideration for sb/sthg; **auf jn/etw ~ nehmen** to show consideration for sb/sthg - 2. [nach hinten] rear view.

rücksichtslos ◇ *adj* [unhöflich] inconsiderate; [verantwortungslos] reckless; [erbarmungslos] ruthless ◇ *adv* [unhöflich] inconsiderately; [verantwortungslos] recklessly; [erbarmungslos] ruthlessly.

rücksichtsvoll ◇ *adj* considerate ◇ *adv* considerately.

Rück|sitz *der* back seat.

Rück|spiegel *der* rear-view mirror.

Rück|spiel *das* SPORT return game.

Rück|stand *der* - 1. WIRTSCH arrears *(pl)*; **(mit etw) im ~ sein** to be in arrears (with sthg) - 2. SPORT: **in ~ geraten** to fall behind; **(mit etw) im ~ sein** to be trailing (by sthg) - 3. [von Gift] residue - 4. [Abstand] gap; **den ~ aufholen** to close the gap.

rückständig *abw adj* - 1. [Person, Politik] outdated - 2. [Land, Technik] backward.

Rück|stau *der* [von Autos] tailback *Br*, backup *Am*; [von Flüssigkeiten] backing up *(U)*.

Rück|stoß *der* - 1. PHYS thrust *(U)* - 2. [von Gewehr] recoil.

Rück|tritt *der* - 1. [aus Amt] resignation - 2. *fam* [von Fahrrad] backpedal brake.

Rück|wand *die* back.

rückwärts *adv* backwards; **~ einparken** to reverse into a parking space.

Rückwärts|gang *der* reverse gear; **im ~** in reverse.

Rück|weg *der* way back.

rückwirkend ◇ *adj* [Zahlung] backdated; [Datierung, Gesetz] retrospective ◇ *adv:* **die Gehaltserhöhung ist~ vom 1.1. wirksam** the salary increase is backdated to 1 January.

Rück|zahlung *die* repayment.

Rück|zug *der (ohne pl)* retreat.

Rudel *(pl -) das* [von Wölfen] pack; [von Hirschen] herd.

Ruder *(pl -) das* - 1. [zum Rudern] oar - 2. [zum Steuern] rudder.

Ruder|boot *das* rowing boat *Br*, rowboat *Am*.

Ruderer, in *(mpl -; fpl -nen) der, die* oarsman *(f oarswoman)*.

rudern *(perf hat/ist gerudert)* ◇ *vi* - 1. *(hat)* SPORT to row; **mit den Armen ~** to flail one's arms - 2. *(ist)* [in bestimmte Richtung] to row ◇ *vt (hat)* to row.

Ruf *(pl -e) der* - 1. *(ohne pl)* [Leumund] reputation - 2. *(ohne pl)* [Aufruf] call - 3. UNI offer of a chair - 4. [von Tier] call.

rufen *(prät rief; perf hat gerufen)* ◇ *vi* to call; **nach jm/etw ~** to call for sb/sthg ◇ *vt* - 1. [herbeirufen, nennen] to call; **jd/etw kommt (jm) wie gerufen** sb/sthg comes at just the right moment; **jn zu Hilfe ~** to call on sb to help - 2. [schreien] to shout.

Ruf|nummer *die amt* telephone number.

Rüge *(pl -n) die* reprimand.

rügen *vt* - 1. [Person] to reprimand - 2. [Mängel] to complain about.

Rügen *nt* Rügen.

Ruhe *die* - 1. [Stille] silence; **~ bitte!** quiet please! - 2. [Erholung] rest - 3. [das Ungestörtsein] peace; **ich will jetzt meine ~ (haben)** I want a bit of peace and quiet; **in ~** in peace; **jn (mit etw) in ~ lassen** *fam* to stop bothering sb (with sthg); **keine ~ geben** to keep pestering - 4. [Gelassenheit] calm; **sie ist durch nichts aus der ~ zu bringen** she won't let anything disturb her composure; **(die) ~ bewahren** to keep calm - 5. *RW*: **zur ~ kommen** to calm down.

ruhen *vi* - 1. [stillstehen - Verkehr, Arbeit, Maschinen] to be at a standstill; [- Waffen] to be silent - 2. *geh* [liegen] to lie; [schlafen] sleep - 3. [lasten, verweilen] to rest.

Ruhe|stand *der* retirement; **in den ~ gehen** ODER **treten** to retire; **in den ~ versetzt werden** to be retired.

Ruhe|störung *die:* **jn wegen ~ anzeigen** to report sb for disturbing the peace; **nächtliche ~** disturbance of the peace *(at night)*.

Ruhe|tag *der* closing day; **'montags ~!'** 'closed on Mondays'.

ruhig ◇ *adj* - 1. [still] quiet - 2. [unbewegt] calm - 3. [gelassen - Mensch, Stimme] calm; [- Hand] steady; [- Gewissen] clear - 4. [geruhsam] peaceful ◇ *adv* - 1. [still - liegen] still; [- wohnen] in a quiet area; **sich ~ verhalten** to keep quiet - 2. [gelassen] calmly - 3. *fam* [gerne]: **mach ~ mit!** join in if you like!

Ruhm *der* fame.

Ruhr *die (ohne pl)* [Krankheit] dysentery.

Rühr|ei *das* scrambled eggs *(pl)*.

rühren ◇ *vt* - 1. [gen] to move; **sie war gerührt** she was moved - 2. [umrühren] to stir ◇ *vi* [ansprechen]: **an etw (A) ~** to touch on sthg. ◆ **sich rühren** *ref* - 1. [sich bewegen] to move; **rührt euch!** stand at ease! - 2. *fam* [sich melden] to be in touch.

Ruhrgebiet *das:* **das ~** the Ruhr.

Rührteig *der* cake mixture.

Ruin der ruin.

Ruine (pl -n) die ruin.

ruinieren vt to ruin. ◆ **sich ruinieren** ref to ruin o.s.

rülpsen vi to burp.

Rülpser (pl -) der burp.

rum fam = herum.

Rum (pl -s) der rum.

Rumäne (pl -n) der Romanian.

Rumänien nt Romania.

Rumänin (pl -nen) die Romanian.

rumänisch adj Romanian.

rum|gammeln vi fam to laze about.

rum|hängen vi (unreg) fam to hang around.

rum|kriegen vt fam - **1.** [Person] to talk round - **2.** [Zeit] to get through.

Rummel (pl -) der - **1.** [Jahrmarkt] fair - **2.** fam [Umstände]: **um jn/etw viel ~ machen** to make a big fuss about sb/sthg.

Rumpf (pl Rümpfe) der - **1.** [Oberkörper] trunk - **2.** TECH [von Schiff] hull; [von Flugzeug] fuselage - **3.** [Rest] remnant.

rümpfen vt ▷ Nase.

Rump|steak ['rumpste:k] das rump steak.

rund ◇ adj - **1.** [Form, Summe] round - **2.** [ungefähr]: **eine ~e Woche** a good week ◇ adv - **1.** [ungefähr] about; **~ gerechnet** at a rough estimate - **2.** [ohne Ecken] in a round shape; [laufen] smoothly - **3.** [um ... herum]: **~ um jn/etw** [räumlich] round sb/sthg; [thematisch] all about sb/sthg.

Runde (pl -n) die - **1.** [gen] round - **2.** SPORT [bei Rennen] lap; [bei Boxkampf] round - **3.** [Personen] group - **4.** RW: **etw macht die ~** sthg is doing the rounds; **über die ~n kommen** fam to get by.

Rund|fahrt die tour.

Rund|flug der sightseeing flight.

Rund|funk der - **1.** [Institution] radio - **2.** [Radiosender] radio station.

Rundfunk|gebühr die radio licence fee.

Rund|gang der [Spaziergang] walk; [von Wächter] round.

rund|gehen (perf ist rundgegangen) vi (unreg): **es geht rund** it's all go.

rundheraus adv straight out.

rundherum adv - **1.** [ganz] completely - **2.** [ringsherum] all round.

rundlich adj [Mensch] plump.

Rund|reise die tour.

rundum adv completely.

rundweg adv flatly.

runter fam = herunter, hinunter.

runter|hauen fam vt: **jm eine ~** to slap sb.

runzeln vt ▷ Stirn.

rupfen vt [Unkraut] to pull up; [Blätter] to pull off; [Huhn] to pluck.

ruppig ◇ adj [unfreundlich] gruff ◇ adv [unfreundlich] gruffly.

Rüsche (pl -n) die frill.

Ruß der soot.

Russe (pl -n) der Russian.

Rüssel (pl -) der [von Elefant] trunk; [von Schwein] snout; [von Fliege] proboscis.

rußig adj sooty.

Russin (pl -nen) die Russian.

russisch adj Russian.

Russisch(e) das Russian; siehe auch Englisch(e).

Russland nt Russia.

rüstig adj sprightly.

rustikal adj rustic.

Rüstung (pl -en) die - **1.** (ohne pl) [von Staat] armaments (pl) - **2.** [von Ritter] armour.

Rutsch (pl -e) der: **in einem** ODER **auf einen ~** in one go. ◆ **guten Rutsch** interj Happy New Year!

Rutsch|bahn die [auf dem Spielplatz] slide; [spiralförmig] helter-skelter; [Wasserröhre] flume.

Rutsche (pl -n) die - **1.** [Rutschbahn] slide - **2.** [zum Schütten] chute.

rutschen (perf ist gerutscht) vi [gleiten - ausrutschen, fallen] to slip; [- mit dem Auto] to skid; **auf dem Stuhl hin und her ~** to shift around on one's chair; **rutsch mal ein Stück** move up a bit.

rutschfest adj non-slip.

rutschig adj slippery.

rütteln ◇ vt to shake ◇ vi: **an etw** (D) **~** to rattle sthg.

S

s, S [ɛs] (pl -) das s, S. ◆ **S** (abk für Süd) S.

Saal (pl Säle) der hall.

Saar die: **die ~** the (River) Saar.

Saarbrücken nt Saarbrücken.

Saarland das Saarland.

saarländisch adj of/from Saarland.

Saat (pl -en) die - **1.** [das Säen] sowing - **2.** [Körner] seed.

Säbel (pl -) der sabre.

Sabotage [sabo'ta:ʒə] (pl -n) die sabotage (U).

sabotieren vt to sabotage.

Sach|bearbeiter, in der, die employee in charge of a particular matter.

Sach|buch das non-fiction book.

Sache (pl -n) die - **1.** (ohne pl) [Angelegenheit] matter; **das ist (nicht) deine ~** that's (none

sammeln

of) your business; **bei der ~ bleiben** to keep to the point; **zur ~ kommen** to get to the point; **nicht bei der ~ sein** not to be with it; **das tut nichts zur ~** *fig* that is beside the point - **2.** *(ohne pl)* RECHT [Rechtssache] case - **3.** RW: **das ist so eine ~** *fam* it's a bit of a problem; **mit jm gemeinsame ~ machen** *fam* to join forces with sb; **seiner ~ sicher sein** to know what one is doing. ➡ **Sachen** *pl* - **1.** [gen] things - **2.** *fam* [Stundenkilometer]: **100 ~n draufhaben** to be doing a hundred; **mit 180 ~n** *salopp* at 180 - **3.** RW: **du machst vielleicht ~n!** the things you do!; **in ~n** in the matter of.

Sach|gebiet *das* subject area.

Sach|kenntnis *die* expertise *(U)*.

sachkundig ◇ *adj* knowledgeable ◇ *adv* knowledgeably.

Sachlage *die (ohne pl)* situation.

sachlich ◇ *adj* - **1.** [Person, Diskussion] objective - **2.** [Fehler, Unterschied] factual ◇ *adv* - **1.** [diskutieren, bleiben] objectively - **2.** [richtig, falsch] factually.

Sach|schaden *der* material damage.

Sachsen ['zaksn] *nt* Saxony.

Sachsen-Anhalt [zaksn'anhalt] *nt* Saxony-Anhalt.

sächsisch ['zɛksɪʃ] *adj* Saxon.

sacht, sachte ◇ *adj* - **1.** [sanft, langsam] gentle - **2.** [vorsichtig] cautious ◇ *adv* gently; **sachte!** *fam* steady on!

Sachverstand *der* expertise.

Sach|verständige *(pl -n) der, die* expert.

Sack *(pl Säcke oder -) der* - **1.** *(pl Säcke, Sack)* [Behälter] sack - **2.** *(pl Säcke) salopp* [Mensch] bastard - **3.** *(pl Säcke) salopp* [Hodensack] balls *(pl)*.

Sack|gasse *die* dead end; [in Wohngebiet] cul-de-sac.

Sadismus *der* sadism.

säen *vt* to sow.

Safe [se:f] *(pl -s) der* safe.

Saft *(pl Säfte) der* - **1.** [Fruchtsaft, Strom] juice - **2.** [Pflanzensaft] sap.

saftig *adj* - **1.** [Obst, Fleisch] juicy - **2.** *fam* [Rechnung, Ohrfeige] hefty.

Sage *(pl -n) die* legend.

Säge *(pl -n) die* saw.

sagen *vt* - **1.** [gen] to say; **jm etw ~** to tell sb sthg; **sich** *(D)* **etw ~** to tell o.s. sthg; **das kann jeder ~!** that's easy to say!; **das hat nichts zu ~** that doesn't mean anything; **was sagst du (denn) dazu?** (so) what do you think about it? - **2.** [befehlen]: **etwas/nichts zu ~ haben** to have a/no say in things; **jm etwas/nichts zu ~ haben** to have sthg/nothing to say to sb; **er lässt sich nichts ~** you can't tell him anything; **das Sagen haben** to be in charge - **3.** RW: **das sage ich dir** *fam* I'm telling you; **das kann man wohl ~!** *fam* you can say that

again!; **dagegen ist nichts zu ~** it's perfectly all right; **man sagt ...** it is said ...; **wem sagst du das!** you're telling me! ➡ **du sagst es** *interj* you said it! ➡ **sag bloß** *interj* you don't say. ➡ **sag mal** *interj* tell me. ➡ **wie gesagt** *interj* as I've said.

sägen *vt* & *vi* to saw.

sagenhaft ◇ *adj* fantastic ◇ *adv* fantastically.

Sägespäne *pl* wood shavings.

sah *prät* ➪ sehen.

Sahne *die* cream.

Sahne|torte *die* gâteau.

sahnig *adj* creamy.

Saison [sɛ'zõ] *(pl -s) die* season.

Saite *(pl -n) die* string.

Saiten|instrument *das* stringed instrument.

Sakko *(pl -s) der* jacket.

Sakrament *(pl -e) das* REL sacrament.

Sakristei *(pl -en) die* sacristy.

Salamander *(pl -) der* salamander.

Salami *(pl -s) die* salami.

Salat *(pl -e) der* - **1.** [Gericht] salad; **grüner ~** green salad - **2.** [Produkt] lettuce - **3.** *fam* : **da haben wir den ~!** *fam* I said we'd end up in this mess!

Salat|schüssel *die* salad bowl.

Salat|soße *die* salad dressing.

Salbe *(pl -n) die* ointment.

Salbei *der* sage.

Salmonellen|vergiftung *die* salmonella poisoning.

Salon [sa'lõ] *(pl -s) der* [Zimmer] drawing room.

salopp ◇ *adj* casual; [Ausdrucksweise] slangy ◇ *adv* casually; [sich ausdrücken] slangily.

Salto *(pl -s) der* somersault.

Salz *(pl -e) das* salt.

Salzburg *nt* Salzburg.

salzen *(perf hat gesalzen) vt* to put salt in/on.

salzig *adj* salty.

Salzkartoffeln *pl* boiled potatoes.

Salz|säure *die* hydrochloric acid.

Salz|stange *die* pretzel stick.

Salz|streuer *(pl -) der* salt cellar.

Salz|wasser *das* - **1.** [Meerwasser] saltwater - **2.** [Kochwasser] salted water.

Samen *(pl -) der* - **1.** [Sperma] sperm - **2.** [Pflanzensamen] seed.

sämig *adj* thick.

Sammel|band *(pl -bände) der* omnibus edition.

sammeln *vt* - **1.** [Eindrücke, Anhänger, Kräuter] to gather - **2.** [Geld, Briefmarken] to collect. ➡ **sich sammeln** *ref* [sich konzentrieren] to collect one's thoughts.

Sammel|stelle die collection point.

Sammler, in (mpl -; fpl -nen) der, die collector.

Sammlung (pl -en) die - **1.** [gen] collection - **2.** [Ruhe] composure.

Samstag (pl -e) der Saturday; **am ~** on Saturday; **(am) nächsten ~ kommt sie** she's coming next Saturday; **~, den 31. Dezember** Saturday, 31 December.

Samstag|abend (pl -e) der Saturday evening; **~ muss ich nach Köln** I have to go to Cologne on Saturday evening.

Samstag|morgen (pl -) der Saturday morning; **~ muss ich nach Köln** I have to go to Cologne on Saturday morning.

Samstag|nacht die Saturday night; **~ hat es stark geregnet** it rained hard on Saturday night.

samstags adv on Saturdays; **~ morgens/abends** on Saturday mornings/evenings.

samt präp: **~ jm/einer Sache** (together) with sb/sthg.

Samt (pl -e) der velvet.

sämtlich <> adj all; **~e Fehler verbessern** to correct all the mistakes; **er hat ~en Mut verloren** he lost all his courage <> adv: **sie waren ~ erschienen** they all turned up.

Sanatorium [zana'to:rjʊm] (pl -torien) das sanatorium.

Sand der sand; **die Straßen mit ~ streuen** to grit the roads; **im ~ verlaufen** fig to come to nothing.

Sandale (pl -n) die sandal.

Sandbank (pl -bänke) die sandbank.

sandig adj sandy.

Sand|kasten der sandpit Br, sandbox Am.

Sand|korn (pl -körner) das grain of sand.

Sand|männchen das sandman.

Sand|papier das sandpaper.

Sand|stein der sandstone.

Sand|strand der sandy beach.

sandte prät ⊳ senden.

Sand|uhr die hourglass.

sanft <> adj - **1.** [gen] gentle - **2.** [Hände, Stimme, Licht] soft - **3.** [Geburt] natural; [Energie, Tourismus] sustainable; [Tod] peaceful <> adv - **1.** [gen] gently - **2.** [entschlafen] peacefully.

sanftmütig <> adj gentle <> adv gently.

sang prät ⊳ singen.

Sänger, in (mpl -; fpl -nen) der, die singer.

sanieren vt - **1.** [Gebäude, Viertel] to renovate - **2.** [Firma] to turn around - **3.** [Finanzen] to sort out. ◆ **sich sanieren** ref [Person] to get o.s. out of the red.

Sanierung (pl -en) die - **1.** [von Gebäude, Viertel] renovation - **2.** [von Firma] turning round - **3.** [von Finanzen] sorting out.

sanitär adj sanitary; **~e Anlagen** sanitation (U).

Sanitäter, in (mpl -; fpl -nen) der, die - **1.** MED paramedic - **2.** MIL medical orderly.

sank prät ⊳ sinken.

Sankt Gallen nt St Gallen.

Sankt Gotthard der St Gotthard.

Sanktion (pl -en) die sanction; **~en verhängen** to impose sanctions.

Sankt Petersburg nt St Petersburg.

Saphir, Saphir (pl -e) der sapphire.

Sardelle (pl -n) die anchovy.

Sardine (pl -n) die sardine.

Sardinien [zar'di:njən] nt Sardinia.

Sarg (pl Särge) der coffin, casket Am.

Sarkasmus (pl -men) der - **1.** [Spott] sarcasm - **2.** [spöttische Bemerkung] sarcastic comment.

saß prät ⊳ sitzen.

Satan (pl -e) der - **1.** [Teufel] Satan - **2.** abw [Mensch] fiend.

Satellit (pl -en) der satellite.

Satelliten|schüssel die satellite dish.

Satire (pl -n) die satire.

satt <> adj - **1.** [Mensch, Tier] full; **~ sein** to be full (up); **bist du ~?** have you had enough (to eat)?; **diese Knödel machen ~** these dumplings are filling; **davon werde ich nicht ~** I won't have enough to eat with that - **2.** [Farbe, Klang] rich <> adv: **sich ~ essen** to eat one's fill; **jn/etw ~ haben** fam to be fed up with sb/sthg.

Sattel (pl Sättel) der saddle.

satteln vt to saddle.

Satz (pl Sätze) der - **1.** [grammatikalische Einheit] sentence - **2.** [Sprung] leap - **3.** [SPORT - bei Tennis] set; [- bei Badminton, Tischtennis] game - **4.** [von Text - das Setzen] setting; [- das Gesetzte] type - **5.** MUS movement - **6.** MATH theorem - **7.** [von Reifen, Unterwäsche] set - **8.** [Tarif] rate.

Satz|bau der syntax.

Satz|teil der sentence part.

Satzung (pl -en) die statutes (pl).

Satz|zeichen das punctuation mark.

Sau (pl Säue ODER -en) die - **1.** (pl Säue) [Schwein] sow - **2.** (pl Sauen) [Wildschwein] female wild boar - **3.** (pl Säue) salopp abw [Mensch] pig.

sauber <> adj - **1.** [rein] clean - **2.** fam iron [fein] fine - **3.** [Arbeit] neat; [Darbietung] faultless <> adv - **1.** [gut] neatly - **2.** [fehlerfrei] faultlessly.

Sauberkeit die cleanliness.

sauber machen vt to clean.

säubern vt - **1.** [reinigen] to clean - **2.** [Institution] to purge.

Sauce ['zo:sə] (pl -n) die sauce; [Bratensoße] gravy.

Saudi (pl -s) der Saudi.

Saudi-Arabien nt Saudi Arabia.

sauer <> adj - **1.** [Essen] sour; **saure Gurken**

(pickled) gherkins; **ein saurer Wein** an acidic wine - **2.** [Stimmung] annoyed, cross; **~ auf jn sein** *fam* to be annoyed ODER cross with sb; **ein saures Gesicht machen** to pull a sour face - **3.** CHEM acidic ◇ *adv* - **1.** [reagieren] crossly - **2.** [nicht süß] **~ schmecken** to taste sour - **3.** CHEM acidically.

Sauer|braten *der* sauerbraten, *braised beef marinated in vinegar.*

Sauerei (*pl* -en) *die* salopp - **1.** [Schmutz] damn mess - **2.** [Gemeinheit] damn disgrace.

Sauer|kirsche *die* sour cherry.

Sauerkraut *das* sauerkraut.

säuerlich ◇ *adj* - **1.** [Essen] slightly sour - **2.** [Stimmung] annoyed, cross ◇ *adv* - **1.** [nicht süß] **~ schmecken** to taste slightly sour - **2.** [reagieren] crossly.

Sauer|stoff *der* oxygen.

saufen (*präs* säuft; *prät* soff; *perf* hat gesoffen) ◇ *vt* - **1.** [Subj: Tier] to drink - **2.** *salopp* [trinken] to knock back; **sie gehen einen ~** they're going on the booze - **3.** *fam* [verbrauchen]: **mein Auto säuft zu viel** my car's a real gas-guzzler ◇ *vi* - **1.** [Tier] to drink - **2.** *salopp* [Mensch] to booze.

Säufer (*pl* -) *der* salopp abw boozer.

Sauferei (*pl* -en) *die* salopp abw booze-up.

Säuferin (*pl* -nen) *die* salopp abw boozer.

säuft *präs* ⌐⊃ saufen.

saugen (*prät* sog ODER saugte; *perf* hat gesogen ODER gesaugt) ◇ *vt* - **1.** [heraussaugen] to suck; **etw aus etw ~** to suck sth out of sth - **2.** (*reg*) [mit Staubsauger] to vacuum ◇ *vi* - **1.** [ziehen] to suck; **an etw** (*D*) **~** to suck at sth - **2.** (*reg*) [mit Staubsauger] to vacuum.

säugen *vt* to suckle.

Säuge|tier *das* mammal.

Säugling (*pl* -e) *der* baby.

Säule (*pl* -n) *die* eigtl & fig pillar.

Saum (*pl* Säume) *der* hem.

säumen *vt* - **1.** [Stoff] to hem - **2.** geh [Weg] to line.

Sauna (*pl* -s ODER Saunen) *die* sauna.

Säure (*pl* -n) *die* - **1.** CHEM acid - **2.** [von Wein] acidity; [von Zitrone] sourness.

Saurier ['zaʊʁiɐ] (*pl* -) *der* dinosaur.

säuseln ◇ *vi* [Wind] to murmur ◇ *vt* [sprechen] to purr.

sausen (*perf* hat/ist gesaust) *vi* (*ist*) *fam* [schnell]: **zum Bäcker ~** to dash over to the baker's; **mit dem Fahrrad um die Ecke ~** to hurtle round the corner on one's bike.

Saxofon, Saxophon (*pl* -e) *das* saxophone.

SB *abk für* Selbstbedienung.

S-|Bahn *die* suburban railway.

S-Bahn|hof *der* suburban railway station.

SBB (*abk für* Schweizerische Bundesbahn) *Swiss federal railway company.*

Schabe (*pl* -n) *die* cockroach.

schaben *vt* & *vi* to scrape.

schäbig *abw* ◇ *adj* - **1.** [Kleidung, Möbel] shabby - **2.** [Bezahlung] paltry - **3.** [Person] mean ◇ *adv* - **1.** [angezogen, eingerichtet] shabbily - **2.** [ausnützen] shamelessly.

Schablone (*pl* -n) *die* - **1.** [zum Ausmalen] stencil; [zum Rundherummalen] template - **2.** [Schema] mould.

Schach (*pl* -s) *das* chess; **Schach!** check!

Schach|brett *das* chessboard.

schachmatt *adj* [beim Spiel] checkmate.

Schacht (*pl* Schächte) *der* shaft.

Schachtel (*pl* -n) *die* - **1.** [Behälter] box; **eine ~ Zigaretten** a packet *Br* ODER pack *Am* of cigarettes - **2.** *salopp abw* [Frau] bag.

Schach|zug *der* eigtl & fig move.

schade *adj*: **es ist ~ (um jn/etw)** it's a shame (about sb/sth); **(wie) ~!** what a shame!; **zu ~ für jn/etw sein** to be too good for sb/sth.

Schädel (*pl* -) *der* - **1.** [Knochen] skull - **2.** *fam* [Kopf] nut; **mir brummt der ~** *fam* my head is killing me.

Schädel|bruch *der* skull fracture.

schaden *vi* [Sache] to damage; [Person] to harm; **das schadet nichts** it won't do any harm.

Schaden (*pl* Schäden) *der* - **1.** [an Sachen] damage (*U*) - **2.** [an Menschen] injury; **jm (einen) ~ zufügen** to cause sb harm - **3.** [Nachteil]: **es soll dein ~ nicht sein** I'll make it worth your while.

Schaden|ersatz *der* compensation.

Schaden|freude *die* malicious pleasure.

schadenfroh *adj* gloating; **~ sein** to gloat.

Schadens|fall *der*: **einen ~ melden** to make a claim; **im ~** in the event of damage.

schadhaft *adj* [mit Fabrikationsfehler] defective; [beschädigt] damaged.

schädigen *vt* to damage; [Person] to harm.

schädlich *adj* harmful; **Rauchen ist ~ für die Gesundheit** smoking damages your health.

Schädling (*pl* -e) *der* pest.

Schad|stoff *der* [im Boden, in der Luft] pollutant; [im Essen] harmful substance.

Schaf (*pl* -e) *das* - **1.** [Tier] sheep - **2.** *fam abw* [Mensch] dope; **ein schwarzes ~** abw a black sheep.

Schäfer (*pl* -) *der* shepherd.

Schäfer|hund *der* [Hirtenhund] sheepdog.

Schäferin (*pl* -nen) *die* shepherdess.

schaffen[1] ◇ *vt* - **1.** [beenden, bewältigen] to manage; **es ~, etw zu tun** to manage to do sthg; **er schafft drei Teller Spaghetti zum Abendbrot** he gets through three plates of spaghetti for his dinner; **bis wann schaffst du das?** when can you have it ready by?; **du schaffst es!** you can do it!; **das wäre geschafft!** that's that done! - **2.** [Prüfung] to get through - **3.** [Ärger, Unruhe] to cause

- 4. [transportieren]: **etw an einen Ort ~** to take sthg somewhere; **jn ins Bett ~** to put sb to bed; **den Verletzten vom Spielfeld ~** to carry the injured player off the pitch - 5. [erschöpfen] to wear out; **du schaffst mich!** you'll be the death of me! - 6. [erreichen] *fam:* **den Bus gerade noch ~** only just to make it in time for the bus ⬦ *vi* - 1. [tun]: **mit jm/ etw nichts zu ~ haben** to have nothing to do with sb/sthg; **jm zu ~ machen** to give sb trouble; **sich an etw** *(D)* **zu ~ machen** to busy o.s. with sthg - 2. *Südd* [arbeiten] to work. ◆ **geschafft** *interj* that's it!; [geglückt] done it!

schaffen² (*prät* schuf; *perf* hat geschaffen) *vt* to create; **Platz ~** to make room; **Ordnung ~** to restore order; **wie geschaffen für jn sein** to be made for sb.

Schaffner, in (*mpl* -; *fpl* -nen) *der, die* [in Bus] conductor; [in Zug] ticket collector.

Schafs|fell *das* - 1. [an Tier] fleece - 2. [Material, Teppich] sheepskin.

Schafskäse *der* ewe's milk cheese.

Schaft (*pl* Schäfte) *der* - 1. [von Speer, Pfeil] shaft; [von Messer] handle - 2. [von Stiefel] leg.

Schakal (*pl* -e) *der* jackal.

schäkern *vi fam* [flirten] to flirt.

schal *adj* [Bier] flat; [Geschmack] stale.

Schal (*pl* -s ODER -e) *der* scarf.

Schale (*pl* -n) *die* - 1. [von Zwiebel, Banane, Tomate] skin; [von Apfel, Orange, Kartoffel] peel; **Kartoffel ~n** potato peelings - 2. [von Krebs, Ei, Kokosnuss] shell - 3. [Gefäß] bowl; [flach] dish.

schälen *vt* to peel; [Ei, Nüsse, Erbsen] to shell. ◆ **sich schälen** *ref* to peel.

Schall (*pl* -e ODER Schälle) *der* sound.

Schall|dämpfer *der* - 1. [von Auto] silencer *Br*, muffler *Am* - 2. [von Waffe] silencer - 3. [von Musikinstrument] mute.

schalldicht *adj* soundproof; **etw ~ machen** to soundproof sthg.

schallen (*prät* schallte ODER scholl; *perf* hat geschallt) *vi* to resound.

schallend ⬦ *adj* resounding ⬦ *adv:* **~ lachen** to roar with laughter.

Schall|mauer *die* sound barrier.

Schall|platte *die* record.

schalten ⬦ *vi* - 1. [den Gang wechseln] to change gear; **in den vierten Gang ~** to change into fourth gear - 2. [umschalten]: **auf das zweite Programm ~** to turn to channel two; **wir ~ jetzt nach Hamburg** we're now going over to Hamburg - 3. *fam* [reagieren] to catch on - 4. [tun]: **~ und walten** to do as one pleases ⬦ *vt* [anschließen] to connect; **etw parallel/in Serie ~** ELEKTR to connect sthg in parallel/series.

Schalter (*pl* -) *der* - 1. [Schaltknopf] switch - 2. [für Auskunft, Verkauf] counter.

Schalt|hebel *der* AUTO gear lever.

Schalt|jahr *das* leap year.

Schaltung (*pl* -en) *die* - 1. [Gangschaltung] gear change - 2. ELEKTR circuit - 3. TV link-up.

Scham *die* shame; **~ empfinden** to be ashamed.

schämen ◆ **sich schämen** *ref* to be ashamed; **schäm dich!** shame on you!; **sich für jn ~** to be ashamed for sb; **ich schäme mich seinetwegen** I'm ashamed of him.

schamlos ⬦ *adj* - 1. [gen] shameless - 2. [Lüge] barefaced ⬦ *adv* shamelessly.

Schande *die* disgrace; **zu js ~** to sb's shame.

schändlich ⬦ *adj* disgraceful ⬦ *adv* disgracefully.

Schandtat *die* - 1. [Verbrechen] heinous crime - 2. *fam hum* [Aktion]: **zu jeder ~ bereit sein** to be game for anything.

Schanze (*pl* -n) *die* ski jump.

Schar (*pl* -en) *die* [von Kindern] group; [von Vögeln] flock; **~en von ...** swarms of ... ◆ **in Scharen** *adv* [von Menschen] in droves; [von Tieren] in swarms.

scharen *vt*: **jn/etw um sich ~** to gather sb/ sthg around o.s. ◆ **sich scharen** *ref*: **sich um jn ~** to gather round sb.

scharf (*kompar* schärfer; *superl* schärfste) ⬦ *adj* - 1. [gen] sharp - 2. [Geschmack] hot, spicy - 3. *fam* [toll] great; [erotisch] hot; **auf etw sein** to be dead keen on sthg - 4. [Tempo] high; [Wind] biting - 5. [Geräusch] piercing; [Geruch] pungent - 6. [Säure] caustic - 7. [Hund, Angriff] fierce - 8. [Munition] live - 9. [Prüfer] tough ⬦ *adv* [gen] sharply; **~ geschliffen** keenly whetted; **~ gewürzt** hot, spicy; **~ riechen** to be pungent; **~ beobachten** to watch closely; **~ nachdenken** to think hard; **jn ~ angreifen** to attack sb fiercely.

Schärfe (*pl* -n) *die* - 1. [von Messer, Sinnen] sharpness; [von Verstand] keenness - 2. [Bildschärfe] focus - 3. [von Ton, Streit] severity - 4. [von Geschmack] spiciness - 5. [von Prüfer] toughness.

scharf|machen *vt fam* [aggressiv machen] to rouse.

Scharf|schütze, schützin *der, die* marksman (*f* markswoman).

Scharfsinn *der* astuteness.

Scharlach *der* scarlet fever.

Scharm *der* = Charme.

scharmant *adj* = charmant.

Scharnier (*pl* -e) *das* hinge.

scharren *vi* to scrape; [Hund, Pferd] to paw; **mit den Füßen ~** to shuffle one's feet.

Schaschlik (*pl* -s) *der* ODER *das* shish kebab.

Schatten (*pl* -) *der* - 1. [Bereich ohne Sonne] shade; **im ~** in the shade - 2. [Silhouette, Fleck] shadow - 3. *RW:* **über seinen ~ springen** to force o.s.

Schatten|seite *die* - **1.** [von Berg, Haus] side in shadow - **2.** [Nachteil] drawback.

Schattierung (*pl* -en) *die* - **1.** [dunkle Stelle] shading - **2.** [Farbe] shade.

schattig *adj* shady.

Schatz (*pl* Schätze) *der* - **1.** [Reichtum] treasure - **2.** *fam* [Liebling] darling.

schätzen *vt* - **1.** [Wert, Alter, Schaden] to estimate - **2.** [glauben, meinen] to think - **3.** [mögen]: **jn/etw ~ to value sb/sthg; jn/ etw zu ~ wissen** to appreciate sb/sthg.

Schatz|kammer *die* treasure chamber.

Schätzung (*pl* -en) *die* estimate; [das Schätzen] estimation; [von Gebäuden, Grundstücken] valuation.

schätzungsweise *adv* approximately.

Schätz|wert *der* estimated value.

Schau (*pl* -en) *die* show; **eine ~ abziehen** *fam* to put on a show; **jn zur ~ stellen** to exhibit sb.

Schauder (*pl* -) *der* shudder; [vor Kälte] shiver.

schauderhaft <> *adj* terrible <> *adv*: **~ aussehen** to look terrible.

schauen *vi* - **1.** [blicken] to look; **zu Boden ~** to stare at the ground; **auf jn/etw ~** to look at sb/sthg; **schau mal!** look! - **2.** [sich kümmern]: **nach jm/etw ~** to look after sb/sthg - **3.** [kontrollieren] to check.

Schauer (*pl* -) *der* - **1.** [Regen] shower - **2.** [vor Angst] shudder; [vor Kälte] shiver.

Schaufel (*pl* -n) *die* shovel.

schaufeln *vt* - **1.** [Erde, Kies] to shovel; [Loch] to dig - **2.** *fam* [essen] to shovel down.

Schau|fenster *das* shop window.

Schaufenster|bummel *der* window-shopping trip.

Schaufenster|puppe *die* mannequin.

Schau|kasten *der* display case.

Schaukel (*pl* -n) *die* swing.

schaukeln <> *vi* - **1.** [gen] to rock - **2.** [auf einer Schaukel] to swing <> *vt* - **1.** [Baby, Wiege] to rock - **2.** *fam* [erledigen]: **ich werde das schon ~** I'll sort it out.

Schaukel|stuhl *der* rocking chair.

Schaulustige (*pl* -n) *der, die* onlooker.

Schaum (*pl* Schäume) *der* foam; [von Bier] head; **~ vor dem Mund haben** to be foaming at the mouth.

schäumen *vi* - **1.** [Flüssigkeit] to foam; [Bier] to froth - **2.** *fam* [vor Wut] to fume.

Schaumgummi *der* foam rubber.

schaumig <> *adj* foamy <> *adv*: **etw ~ rühren** to beat sthg until light and fluffy.

Schaum|stoff *der* plastic foam.

Schaum|wein *der* sparkling wine.

Schau|platz *der* [von Ereignis] scene; [von Erzählung] setting.

Schau|spiel *das* - **1.** [Bühnenstück] play

- **2.** [Gattung] drama - **3.** *fam* [Spektakel] spectacle.

Schau|spieler, in *der, die* actor (*f* actress).

Schauspiel|haus *das* theatre.

Schau|steller, in (*mpl* -; *fpl* -nen) *der, die* showman (*f* showwoman).

Schau|tafel *die* wall chart (*often made of plastic, wood, etc*).

Scheck (*pl* -s) *der* cheque; **mit ~ bezahlen** to pay by cheque; **ungedeckter ~** bad cheque.

Scheck|heft *das* chequebook.

Scheck|karte *die* cheque card.

Scheibe (*pl* -n) *die* - **1.** [Glas] pane (of glass); [Fensterscheibe] window pane; [von Auto] window - **2.** [von Brot, Käse, Wurst] slice.

Scheiben|wischer (*pl* -) *der* windscreen *Br* ODER windshield *Am* wiper.

Scheich (*pl* -s ODER -e) *der* sheikh.

Scheide (*pl* -n) *die* - **1.** [Vagina] vagina - **2.** [von Messer] sheath.

scheiden (*prät* schied; *perf* hat/ist geschieden) <> *vt* (hat) [Ehe] to dissolve; **sich ~ lassen** to get divorced <> *vi* (ist) *geh* - **1.** [fortgehen] to part - **2.** [entlassen werden]: **aus dem Amt ~** to resign from office.

Scheidung (*pl* -en) *die* divorce; **die ~ einreichen** to file for divorce.

Schein (*pl* -e) *der* - **1.** [Lichtschein] light; **im ~ einer Taschenlampe** by torchlight - **2.** (*ohne pl*) [Anschein] appearances (*pl*); **der ~ trügt** appearances can be deceptive - **3.** UNI ≃ credit, certificate issued to students on successful completion of a course in a specific subject - **4.** [Geldschein] note.

scheinbar <> *adj* apparent <> *adv* apparently, seemingly.

scheinen (*prät* schien; *perf* hat geschienen) *vi* - **1.** [leuchten] to shine - **2.** [den Eindruck erwecken] to seem, to appear; **es scheint, dass ... it** seems ODER appears that ...; **mir scheint, dass ... it** seems to me that ...; **das scheint dir nur so** it just seems that way to you.

scheinheilig *adj* [heuchlerisch] hypocritical.

scheintot *adj* MED: **~ sein** to be apparently dead.

Scheinwerfer (*pl* -) *der* - **1.** [am Auto] headlight - **2.** [im Theater] spotlight; [Suchscheinwerfer] searchlight.

Scheinwerfer|licht *das* [von Autos] headlights (*pl*); [im Theater] spotlight; **im ~** in the spotlight.

Scheiß- *präfix salopp*: **~ computer** bloody computer.

Scheiße <> *die salopp* - **1.** [gen] shit - **2.** *RW*: **nur ~ im Kopf haben** to be a piss-artist; **in der ~ sitzen** to be in the shit <> *interj salopp* shit!

scheißen (*prät* schiss; *perf* hat geschissen) *vi salopp* to shit.

Scheitel (pl -) der [Frisur] parting Br, part Am.

scheitern (perf ist gescheitert) vi - 1. [Person - gen] to fail; [- Sport] to lose; **sie sind mit ihrem Plan am Widerstand der Bewohner gescheitert** their plan failed because of the opposition of the local population - 2. [Versuch, Vorhaben] to fail; **an etw** (D) ~ to fail because of sthg.

Schell|fisch der haddock.

Schema (pl -s ODER -ta ODER Schemen) das - 1. [Darstellung] diagram - 2. [Muster] routine.

schematisch <> adj - 1. [grob] schematic - 2. [routiniert] mechanical <> adv - 1. [grob] schematically - 2. [routiniert] mechanically.

schemenhaft <> adj shadowy <> adv: **etw ~ erkennen** to make out the silhouette of sthg.

Schenkel (pl -) der - 1. [Bein] thigh - 2. MATH side.

schenken vt - 1. [geben] to give (as a present); **jm etw ~** to give sb sthg - 2. [erlassen]: **jm etw ~** to let sb off sthg; **sich etw ~** to spare o.s. sthg.

Schenkung (pl -en) die gift.

scheppern vi to clatter.

Scherbe (pl -n) die piece, fragment; **die ~n zusammenkehren** to sweep up the broken pieces.

Schere (pl -n) die - 1. [Werkzeug] pair of scissors, scissors (pl) - 2. [von Krebs] pincer, claw.

scheren (prät scherte ODER schor; perf hat geschert ODER geschoren) vt (unreg) - 1. [Schaf] to shear; [Hund] to clip - 2. [Hecke] to clip; [Haare] to crop - 3. (reg) [kümmern]: **das schert mich nicht** I don't care. <> **sich scheren** ref (reg): **sich um jn/etw ~/nicht ~** to care/not to care about sb/sthg.

Scherereien pl trouble (U); **das gibt ~** that will lead to trouble.

Scherz (pl -e) der joke.

scherzen vi geh to joke.

scherzhaft adv jokingly.

scheu <> adj shy; **jn/etw ~ machen** to frighten sb/sthg <> adv shyly.

Scheu die shyness; **ohne ~** uninhibitedly.

scheuchen vt to shoo.

scheuen <> vt: **keine Mühen/Kosten ~** to spare no effort/expense <> vi [Pferd] to shy.

Scheuer|lappen der floorcloth.

scheuern <> vt - 1. [putzen - Boden] to scrub; [- Töpfe] to scour - 2. [reiben]: **sich** (D) **in seinen Schuhen die Fersen wund ~** to get sore heels because one's shoes are rubbing <> vi to rub.

Scheuklappen pl blinker.

Scheune (pl -n) die barn.

Scheusal (pl -e) das fam abw beast.

scheußlich abw <> adj - 1. [Verhalten, Anblick, Wetter] terrible - 2. [Aussehen, Geschmack] horrible <> adv - 1. [sich verhalten, kalt] terribly - 2. [einrichten, dekorieren] horribly.

Schi = Ski.

Schicht (pl -en) die - 1. [Lage] layer - 2. [Gesellschaftsschicht] (social) class; **alle ~en der Bevölkerung** all strata of society - 3. [Schichtarbeit] shift; **~ arbeiten** to work shifts.

schichten vt to stack.

schick adj - 1. [modisch] stylish - 2. [in] trendy - 3. [toll] great.

schicken vt to send; **jm etw ~, etw an jn ~** to send sb sthg, to send sthg to sb. <> **sich schicken** ref geh - 1. [sich gehören] to be proper - 2. [sich abfinden]: **sich in etw** (A) ~ to resign o.s. to sthg.

Schicksal (pl -e) das fate; **jn/etw seinem ~ überlassen** to leave sb/sthg to his/her/its fate.

Schiebe|dach das sunroof.

schieben (prät schob; perf hat geschoben) vt - 1. [wegschieben] to push; **die Schuld auf einen anderen ~** to put the blame on sb else; **ein schlechtes Ergebnis auf etw** (A) ~ to blame a poor result on sthg - 2. [hineinschieben] to put - 3. fam [schmuggeln] to traffic in. <> **sich schieben** ref to move; **sich durch das Gewühl ~** to push one's way through the crowd.

Schieber (pl -) der - 1. [an Gerät] slider - 2. fam [Mensch] black marketeer.

Schiebe|tür die sliding door.

Schiebung (pl -en) die fixing; **das ist ~!** it's a fix!

schied prät ⊏⊐ scheiden.

Schieds|richter, in der, die SPORT referee; [bei Tennis] umpire.

schief <> adj - 1. [krumm] crooked; [geneigt] leaning; [Blick] wry; [Absatz] worn - 2. [falsch - Vergleich] false; **ein ~es Bild abgeben** to present a lop-sided ODER distorted picture <> adv: **das Sofa steht ~** the sofa is at an angle; **das Bild hängt ~** the picture isn't straight; **jn ~ ansehen** to look at sb askance.

Schiefer (pl -) der slate.

schief gehen (perf ist schief gegangen) vi (unreg) to go wrong.

schief|lachen <> **sich schieflachen** ref fam to kill o.s. laughing.

schief liegen vi (unreg) fam: **mit einer Meinung ~** to be out in one's opinion.

schielen vi - 1. [wegen Augenfehler] to squint; **sie schielt mit einem Auge** she has a squint in one eye - 2. fam [schauen] to glance; **nach jm/etw ~** fig to have one's eye on sb/sthg.

schien prät ⊏⊐ scheinen.

Schien|bein *das* shin.

Schiene (*pl* -n) *die* - 1. [Gleis] rail - 2. MED splint - 3. [Führungsschiene] runner.

schießen (*prät* schoss; *perf* hat/ist geschossen) ⟨> *vi* - 1. (*hat*) [mit Gewehr] to shoot, to fire; **auf jn/etw ~** to shoot ODER fire at sb/sthg - 2. (*ist*) [wachsen] to shoot up - 3. (*ist*) [sich schnell bewegen] to shoot; [Flüssigkeit] to gush - 4. (*hat*) SPORT to shoot ⟨> *vt* (*hat*) - 1. [gen] to shoot - 2. [Tor] to score - 3. [Foto] to take.

Schießerei (*pl* -en) *die* shoot-out.

Schiff (*pl* -e) *das* - 1. [Wasserfahrzeug] ship; **mit dem ~** by ship - 2. [von Kirche] nave.

Schiffahrt *die* = Schifffahrt.

Schiff|bruch *der* shipwreck.

Schifffahrt *die* shipping.

Schiffs|reise *die* voyage.

Schiffs|verkehr *der* shipping traffic.

Schikane (*pl* -n) *die* harassment; **mit allen ~n** *fam fig* with all the extras.

schikanieren *vt abw* to harass.

Schikoree (*pl* -s) *die* ODER *der* = Chicorée.

Schild (*pl* -er ODER -e) ⟨> *das* (*pl* Schilder) sign; [an Auto] numberplate *Br*, license plate *Am*; [Namensschild] nameplate ⟨> *der* (*pl* Schilde) shield; **etw im ~e führen** *fig* to be up to sthg.

Schild|drüse *die* thyroid gland.

schildern *vt* to describe.

Schilderung (*pl* -en) *die* description.

Schild|kröte *die* [auf dem Land] tortoise; [im Wasser] turtle.

Schilf (*pl* -e) *das* - 1. [Pflanze] reed - 2. (*ohne pl*) [Gebiet] reedbed.

schillern *vi* to shimmer.

Schilling (*pl* -e ODER -) *der* schilling.

Schimmel (*pl* -) *der* - 1. [Pilz] mould - 2. [Pferd] white horse.

schimmelig, schimmlig *adj* mouldy.

schimmeln (*perf* hat/ist geschimmelt) *vi* to go mouldy.

Schimmer (*pl* -) *geh der* - 1. [Glanz] gleam - 2. [Spur] glimmer.

schimmern *vi* to glimmer.

schimmlig = schimmelig.

Schimpanse (*pl* -n) *der* chimpanzee.

schimpfen *vi* to grumble; **auf** ODER **über jn/ etw ~** to grumble about sb/sthg; **mit jm ~** to tell sb off.

Schimpfwort (*pl* -wörter ODER -e) *das* swearword.

schinden (*prät* schund; *perf* hat geschunden) *vt* - 1. [quälen] to maltreat - 2. [herausschlagen]: **Zeit ~** to play for time; **Applaus ~** to fish for applause; **Eindruck ~** to try to impress. ⟨> **sich schinden** *ref* to slave away.

Schinderei (*pl* -en) *die* - 1. [Quälerei] maltreatment - 2. [Strapaze] struggle.

Schinken (*pl* -) *der* - 1. [Fleisch] ham - 2. *fam* [Buch] enormous tome - 3. *fam* [Film] tacky epic saga.

Schirm (*pl* -e) *der* - 1. [Regenschirm] umbrella - 2. [Sonnenschirm] sunshade; [zum Tragen] parasol; [an Mütze] visor, peak.

schiss *prät* ▷ scheißen.

schlabberig, schlabbrig *abw adj* - 1. [wässrig] watery - 2. [Pullover] baggy.

Schlacht (*pl* -en) *die* battle.

schlachten *vt* to slaughter.

Schlachter (*pl* -) *der* butcher.

Schlacht|feld *das* [Kriegsschauplatz] battlefield.

Schlacht|hof *der* slaughterhouse.

Schlaf *der* sleep.

Schlafan|zug *der* pyjamas (*pl*).

Schläfe (*pl* -n) *die* temple.

schlafen (*präs* schläft; *prät* schlief; *perf* hat geschlafen) *vi* - 1. [eingeschlafen sein] to sleep; **~ gehen, sich ~ legen** to go to bed; **mit jm ~** to sleep with sb; **schlaf schön** ODER **gut!** sleep well! - 2. [übernachten]: **bei jm ~** to stay the night with sb - 3. *fam* [unaufmerksam sein] to be asleep.

schlaff ⟨> *adj* - 1. [nicht fest - Seil] slack; [- Penis, Händedruck] limp; [- Haut] loose; [- Muskeln] flabby - 2. [müde] listless; **Mensch, bist du ein ~er Typ!** you're such a drip! ⟨> *adv* - 1. [lose] slackly - 2. [energielos] listlessly.

Schlaf|lied *das* lullaby.

schlaflos ⟨> *adj* sleepless ⟨> *adv* sleeplessly.

Schlaf|mittel *das* sleeping pill.

schläfrig ⟨> *adj* sleepy ⟨> *adv* sleepily.

Schlaf|saal *der* dormitory.

Schlaf|sack *der* sleeping bag.

schläft *präs* ▷ schlafen.

Schlaf|tablette *die* sleeping pill.

schlaftrunken ⟨> *adj* drowsy ⟨> *adv* drowsily.

Schlaf|wagen *der* sleeper.

schlafwandeln (*perf* hat/ist schlafgewandelt) *vi* to sleepwalk.

Schlaf|zimmer *das* - 1. [Zimmer] bedroom - 2. [Möbel] bedroom suite.

Schlag (*pl* Schläge) *der* - 1. [Stoß] blow; [leicht] pat; [mit der Faust] punch; [mit der Hand] slap; **jm einen ~ versetzen** [Hieb] to hit sb; [Schock] to be a blow to sb - 2. [Geräusch - von Uhr] chime; *Süddt* [Knall] crash; [- von Trommel] bang; **~ zwölf** on the stroke of twelve o'clock - 3. *fam* [Stromstoß] (electric) shock - 4. *RW*: **auf einen ~** in one go; **alle erschienen auf einen ~** they all turned up at once; **mich trifft der ~** *fam* I'm flabbergasted.

➤ **Schläge** *pl*: **Schläge bekommen** to get a hiding.

Schlag|ader *die* artery.

Schlaganfall *der* stroke.

schlagartig <> *adj* sudden <> *adv* suddenly.

schlagen (*präs* schlägt; *prät* schlug; *perf* hat/ist geschlagen) <> *vt* (*hat*) - **1.** [prügeln] to hit; [regelmäßig] to beat; [mit der Faust] to punch; [mit der Hand] to slap; [leicht] to pat; **jm etw aus der Hand ~** to knock sthg out of sb's hand - **2.** [besiegen] to beat; **jn eins zu null ~** to beat sb one-zero - **3.** [befestigen]: **jn/etw an etw** (*A*) **~** [mit Nägeln] to nail sb/sthg to sthg; **einen Nagel in die Wand ~** to bang a nail into the wall - **4.** [Ball - bei Fußball] to kick - **5.** [Eier, Sahne, Trommel] to beat - **6.** [legen]: **die Hände vor das Gesicht ~** to cover one's face with one's hands - **7.** [hinzufügen]: **etw zu etw ~** [Gebiet] to annex sthg to sthg; **etw auf etw** (*A*) **~** to add sthg to sthg <> *vi* - **1.** (*ist*) [aufprallen]: **gegen etw ~** [Regen] to beat against sthg; [Wellen] to pound against sthg; **er schlug mit dem Kopf gegen die Wand** he banged his head against the wall - **2.** (*hat*) [hauen] to hit; **jm auf die Schulter ~** to slap sb on the back; **nach jm ~** to hit out at sb; **mit der Hand auf den Tisch ~** to bang one's hand on the table; **gegen etw ~** [Tür] to bang on sthg; **um sich ~** to lash out - **3.** (*ist*) [sich auswirken]: **das fette Essen schlägt mir auf den Magen** greasy food affects my stomach - **4.** (*hat*) [Uhr] to strike; [mit Glocke] to chime - **5.** (*ist*) [ähneln]: **nach jm ~** to take after sb - **6.** (*hat*) [Herz, Puls] to beat - **7.** (*hat, ist*) [einschlagen]: **in etw** (*A*) **~** to strike sthg - **8.** (*ist*) [Flammen] to leap. ➡ **sich schlagen** *ref* - **1.** [sich prügeln]: **sich (mit jm) ~** to fight (sb); **sich um etw ~** *fam* to fight for sthg; **die Gäste schlugen sich um das kalte Büfett** the guests fought over the cold buffet - **2.** [sich begeben]: **sich in die Büsche ~** to slip off into the bushes.

Schlager (*pl* -) *der* [Lied] hit.

Schläger (*pl* -) *der* - **1.** [für Tennis, Badminton] racquet; [für Tischtennis] bat; [für Golf] club; [für Hockey] stick - **2.** *abw* [Mensch] thug.

Schlägerei (*pl* -en) *die* fight.

schlagfertig <> *adj* quick-witted <> *adv*: **~ antworten** to give a quick-witted reply.

Schlag|loch *das* pothole.

Schlag|sahne *die* whipped cream.

Schlag|seite *die* (*ohne pl*) list; **~ bekommen** [Schiff] to start to list; **er hatte ~** *fam fig* he was swaying from side to side.

schlägt *präs* ⊳ schlagen.

Schlag|wort (*pl* -e ODER -wörter) *das* - **1.** (*pl* Schlagworte) *abw* [Gemeinplatz] catchword - **2.** (*pl* Schlagwörter) [Stichwort] key word.

Schlag|zeile *die* headline; **~n machen** to make the headlines.

Schlag|zeug (*pl* -e) *das* [in Band] drums (*pl*); [in Orchester] percussion.

Schlamassel *der fam* mess.

Schlamm (*pl* -e ODER Schlämme) *der* mud; [Ablagerung] sludge.

schlammig *adj* muddy.

Schlamperei (*pl* -en) *die fam* sloppiness.

schlampig *abw* <> *adj* - **1.** [Person] slovenly - **2.** [Arbeit] sloppy <> *adv* - **1.** [sich anziehen] in a slovenly way - **2.** [arbeiten] sloppily.

schlang *prät* ⊳ schlingen.

Schlange (*pl* -n) *die* - **1.** [Tier] snake - **2.** [Reihe] queue *Br*, line *Am*; **~ stehen** to queue *Br*, to stand in line *Am*.

schlängeln ➡ **sich schlängeln** *ref* to wind one's/its way.

schlank <> *adj* slim; [Hals, Beine] slender <> *adv*: **das macht ~** that's good for your figure.

schlapp <> *adj* [müde] tired out; [energielos] listless <> *adv* listlessly.

schlapp|machen *vi fam*: **kurz vor dem Ziel ~** to pull out just before the finishing line.

schlau <> *adj* clever; [listig] cunning; **aus jm/etw nicht ~ werden** not to be able to work sb/sthg out <> *adv* cleverly; [listig] cunningly.

Schlauch (*pl* Schläuche) *der* hose; [in Reifen] tube.

Schlauch|boot *das* rubber dinghy.

schlauchen *vt fam* to wear out.

Schlaufe (*pl* -n) *die* loop.

schlecht <> *adj* - **1.** [gen] bad, poor; [Zeiten] hard; **ein ~es Gedächtnis** a bad ODER poor memory; **(das ist) nicht ~!** *fam* (that's) not bad! - **2.** [gesundheitlich - Person] sick; **mir ist/wird ~** I feel sick; **~ aussehen** to look ill - **3.** [Lebensmittel] off; **~ werden** to go off <> *adv* - **1.** [gen] badly, poorly; **die Geschäfte gehen ~** business is bad; **er sieht ~** he's got bad eyesight; **das Essen ist mir ~ bekommen** the food didn't agree with me - **2.** [unangenehm - schmecken, riechen] bad - **3.** [kaum] hardly; **das kann ~ sein** that's hardly possible.

schlecht machen *vt* to run down.

schlecken <> *vt* [lecken] to lick <> *vi fam* [naschen] to eat sweet things.

schleichen (*prät* schlich; *perf* ist geschlichen) *vi* to creep; [Auto] to crawl. ➡ **sich schleichen** *ref* to creep.

schleichend <> *adj* - **1.** [vorsichtig] creeping - **2.** [allmählich - Inflation] creeping; [- Krankheit] insidious <> *adv* [langsam]: **die Autos bewegten sich ~ vorwärts** the cars crept forwards.

Schleier (*pl* -) *der* - **1.** [Stoff] veil - **2.** [von Dunst, Nebel] haze; **auf dem Foto ist ein ~** the photo is fogged.

schleierhaft *adj*: **es ist mir ~, wie du das gemacht hast** it's a mystery to me how you did that.

Schleife (*pl* -n) *die* - **1.** [Band] bow - **2.** [Biegung] bend.

schleifen (*prät* schliff ODER schleifte; *perf* hat geschliffen ODER hat/ist geschleift) ◇ *vt* - **1.** (*unreg*) (*hat*) [abschleifen - Diamanten, Glas] to cut; [- mit Sandpapier] to sand; [- optische Linsen] to grind - **2.** (*unreg*) (*hat*) [schärfen] to sharpen, to grind - **3.** (*unreg*) (*hat*) [drillen] to drill hard - **4.** (*reg*) (*hat*) [zerren] to drag ◇ *vi* (*reg*) (*hat, ist*) to drag.

Schleim (*pl* -e) *der* [in der Nase] mucus; [im Rachen] phlegm; [einer Schnecke] slime.

Schleimhaut *die* mucous membrane.

schlemmen ◇ *vt* to feast on ◇ *vi* to feast.

schlendern (*perf* ist geschlendert) *vi* to stroll.

schleppen *vt* - **1.** [tragen] to lug; [zerren] to drag - **2.** [Fahrzeug] to tow - **3.** *fam* [mitnehmen] to drag (along) - **4.** *fam abw* [schmuggeln] to smuggle. ◆ **sich schleppen** *ref* - **1.** [gehen] to drag o.s. - **2.** [sich hinziehen] to drag on.

Schlesien *nt* Silesia.

Schleswig-Holstein *nt* Schleswig-Holstein.

Schleuder (*pl* -n) *die* - **1.** [Steinschleuder] sling; [Wurfmaschine] catapult - **2.** [Wäscheschleuder] spin-dryer.

schleudern (*perf* hat/ist geschleudert) ◇ *vt* (*hat*) - **1.** *fam* [werfen] to hurl - **2.** [zentrifugieren - Wäsche] to spin; [- Honig] to extract ◇ *vi* (*ist*) to skid.

Schleudern *das*: ins ~ kommen ODER geraten [mit dem Fahrzeug] to go into a skid; *fam* [unsicher werden] to be thrown.

Schleudersitz *der* ejector seat.

schleunigst *adv fam* - **1.** [sofort] at once - **2.** [schnell] hastily.

Schleuse (*pl* -n) *die* - **1.** SCHIFF lock - **2.** [Zwischenkammer] airlock.

schlich *prät* ⮕ schleichen.

schlicht ◇ *adj* simple ◇ *adv* simply.

schlichten *vt* to settle.

schlief *prät* ⮕ schlafen.

schließen (*prät* schloss; *perf* hat geschlossen) ◇ *vt* - **1.** [gen] to close; [Umschlag] to seal; [Stromkreis] to complete - **2.** [Laden, Firma] to close down - **3.** [einschließen]: **jn/etw in etw** (*A*) ~ to lock sb/sthg in sthg - **4.** [schlussfolgern] to conclude - **5.** [befestigen]: **etw an etw** (*A*) ~ to lock sthg to sthg - **6.** [umarmen]: **er schloss sie in seine Arme** he embraced her - **7.** [Vertrag] to conclude, to sign; [Bündnis] to form ◇ *vi* - **1.** [zumachen] to close - **2.** [den Betrieb einstellen] to close down - **3.** [schlussfolgern] to conclude - **4.** [enden] to end. ◆ **sich schließen** *ref* - **1.** [anschließen]: **sich an etw** (*A*) ~ to follow sthg - **2.** [Wunde, Blüte, Kreis] to close.

Schließfach *das* [am Bahnhof] left-luggage

Br ODER baggage *Am* locker; [bei der Bank] safe-deposit box.

schließlich *adv* - **1.** [endlich] finally - **2.** [nun einmal] after all.

schliff *prät* ⮕ schleifen.

Schliff (*pl* -e) *der* - **1.** [Zuschleifen - Vorgang] cutting (*U*); [- Ergebnis] cut - **2.** [Schärfen - Vorgang] sharpening (*U*); [- Ergebnis] edge - **3.** [Vollkommenheit]: **ihm fehlt noch der** ~ he lacks polish - **4.** [Benehmen] refinement.

schlimm *adj* - **1.** [gen] bad; [Folgen] serious; **es ist ~, wie viele Leute jetzt arbeitslos werden** the number of people being made redundant at the moment is terrible; **halb so ~ sein** to be not too bad; **halb so ~!** never mind! - **2.** [böse, inakzeptabel] wicked; **es ist eine ~e Sache, wie er mit ihr umgeht** it's terrible the way he treats her.

schlimmstenfalls *adv* at worst.

Schlinge (*pl* -n) *die* - **1.** [Armschlinge] sling - **2.** [in Seil] loop; [zum Aufhängen] noose - **3.** [zum Jagen] snare.

Schlingel (*pl* -) *der fam* rascal.

schlingen (*prät* schlang; *perf* hat geschlungen) ◇ *vt* - **1.** [binden] to tie; **etw um/in etw** (*A*) ~ to tie sthg round/in sthg - **2.** *fam* [essen] to gobble down - **3.** [legen]: **die Arme um jn/etw** ~ to throw one's arms around sb/sthg ◇ *vi fam* [essen] to gobble. ◆ **sich schlingen** *ref*: **sich um etw** ~ to wind o.s./itself around sthg.

schlingern (*perf* hat/ist geschlingert) *vi* to roll.

Schlips (*pl* -e) *der* tie.

Schlitten (*pl* -) *der* - **1.** [Rodelschlitten] sledge *Br*, sled *Am* - **2.** [Pferdeschlitten] sleigh - **3.** *fam* [Auto] wheels (*pl*).

schlittern (*perf* ist geschlittert) *vi* - **1.** [Fahrzeug] to skid - **2.** [Mensch] to slide - **3.** [geraten]: **in den Konkurs** ~ to slide into bankruptcy.

Schlittschuh *der* ice skate; ~ **laufen** to ice-skate.

Schlitz (*pl* -e) *der* [für Geld, Briefe] slot; [Spalte] slit.

schloss *prät* ⮕ schließen.

Schloss (*pl* Schlösser) *das* - **1.** [Burg] castle; [Palast] palace - **2.** [Verschluss] lock.

Schlosser, in (*mpl* -/*fpl* -nen) *der, die* metalworker; [Autoschlosser] mechanic; [für Türschlösser] locksmith.

Schlot (*pl* -e) *der* chimney.

schlottern *vi* - **1.** [zittern] to tremble - **2.** [zu groß sein] to hang loose.

Schlucht (*pl* -en) *die* ravine.

schluchzen *vi* to sob.

Schluck (*pl* -e) *der* - **1.** [Menge] drop; **ein kleiner** ~ a sip; **einen** ~ **trinken** to have a drop (to drink); **einen ~ nehmen** ODER **tun** to take a gulp - **2.** [Schlucken] gulp.

Schluckauf *der:* **einen ~ haben** to have hiccups.

schlucken <> *vt* - **1.** [Essen, Gefühle] to swallow - **2.** [übernehmen - Firma] to swallow up - **3.** *fam* [Alkohol, Benzin] to guzzle <> *vi* to swallow.

schlug *prät* [> schlagen.

schlüpfen (*perf* ist geschlüpft) *vi* - **1.** [anziehen, ausziehen]: **aus etw ~** to slip sthg off; **in etw** (A) **~** to slip sthg on - **2.** [sich schnell bewegen] to slip; **aus etw ~** to slip out of sthg - **3.** [Küken]: **(aus etw) ~** to hatch (out of sthg).

Schlüpfer (*pl* -) *der* knickers (*pl*) *Br,* panties (*pl*) *Am.*

Schlupfloch *das* - **1.** [Öffnung] hole - **2.** [Versteck] hideout.

schlüpfrig *adj* - **1.** [anzüglich] lewd - **2.** [rutschig] slippery.

schlurfen (*perf* ist geschlurft) *vi fam* to shuffle.

schlürfen *vt* & *vi* to slurp.

Schluss (*pl* Schlüsse) *der* - **1.** [Ende] end; **zum ~** at the end; **mit etw ~ machen** to stop sthg; **mit jm ~ machen** *fam* to break up with sb; **jetzt ist aber ~ damit!** it's over now!; **damit mache ich ~ für heute** with that, I'll finish for today - **2.** [Schlussfolgerung] conclusion; **Schlüsse aus etw ziehen** to draw conclusions from sthg - **3.** [Schlussstück] ending.

Schlüssel (*pl* -) *der* - **1.** [für Schloss, Auflösung] key; **der ~ zu etw** *fig* the key to sthg - **2.** [Schraubenschlüssel] spanner - **3.** [Code] code - **4.** [Verteilungsschlüssel] allocation base.

Schlüsselbein *das* collar bone.

Schlüsselbund *der* bunch of keys.

Schlüsselloch *das* keyhole.

Schlussfolgerung *die* conclusion.

schlüssig <> *adj* conclusive <> *adv* conclusively.

Schlusslicht *das* - **1.** [Letzter]: **der Verein ist das ~ in der Tabelle** the club is bottom of the table - **2.** [Rücklicht] rear light, taillight.

Schlussstrich *der:* **einen ~ unter etw** (A) **ziehen** to draw a line under sthg.

Schlussverkauf *der* end-of-season sale.

schmächtig <> *adj* slight <> *adv* [gebaut] slightly.

schmackhaft <> *adj* tasty <> *adv* [kochen] appetizingly; **jm etw ~ machen** to make sthg palatable to sb.

schmal <> *adj* [Straße, Treppe, Hüften] narrow; [Person] thin; [Figur] slender <> *adv* [geschnitten] narrowly; [gebaut] slenderly; [zusammenkneifen] tightly.

schmälern *vt* to diminish.

Schmalz (*pl* -e) *der* - **1.** [Fett - zum Kochen] lard; [- zum Essen] dripping - **2.** *fam* [Gefühl] schmaltz.

schmalzig <> *adj* schmaltzy <> *adv* schmaltzily.

schmarotzen *vi* - **1.** *abw* [Person] to sponge - **2.** BIOL to live as a parasite.

Schmarotzer, in (*mpl* -; *fpl* -nen) *der, die abw* sponger.

schmatzen *vi* to eat noisily; **mit den Lippen ~** to smack one's lips.

schmecken <> *vi* to taste; **schmeckt es?** does it taste good?; **hat es geschmeckt?** did you enjoy your meal?; **es schmeckt mir** I like it; **nach etw ~** to taste of sthg; **es schmeckt gut/schlecht** it tastes good/bad; **lass es dir ~!** enjoy your meal! <> *vt* to taste.

Schmeichelei (*pl* -en) *die* flattery (*U*).

schmeicheln *vi:* **jm ~** to flatter sb.

schmeißen (*prät* schmiss; *perf* hat geschmissen) *fam* <> *vt* - **1.** [werfen] to chuck - **2.** [spendieren]: **eine Runde ~** to stand a round - **3.** [aufgeben] to pack in - **4.** [organisieren] to handle <> *vi:* **er schmiss mit dem Geschirr nach mir** he chucked the crockery at me.

schmelzen (*präs* schmilzt; *prät* schmolz; *perf* hat/ist geschmolzen) <> *vi* (*ist*) to melt <> *vt* (*hat*) to melt; [Erz] to smelt.

Schmelzpunkt *der* melting point.

Schmerz (*pl* -en) *der* - **1.** (*meist pl*) [körperlich] pain - **2.** [seelisch] grief.

schmerzen *vi* & *vt* to hurt.

schmerzhaft *adj* painful.

schmerzlos <> *adj* painless <> *adv* painlessly.

Schmerzmittel *das* painkiller.

Schmerztablette *die* painkiller.

Schmetterling (*pl* -e) *der* [Tier & SPORT] butterfly.

Schmied (*pl* -e) *der* blacksmith.

Schmiedeeisen *das* wrought iron.

schmieden *vt* - **1.** [bearbeiten] to forge - **2.** [befestigen]: **jn an etw** (A) **~** to chain sb to sthg - **3.** [Pläne] to make.

schmiegen *vt* to nestle. ◆ **sich schmiegen** *ref:* **sich an jn/etw ~** to snuggle up to sb/sthg.

Schmiere (*pl* -n) *die* - **1.** [Fett] grease - **2.** *fam* [Wache]: **~ stehen** to act as a lookout.

schmieren <> *vt* - **1.** [mit Fett] to grease; [mit Öl] to oil - **2.** *fam* TECH to lubricate; [bestechen] to bribe - **3.** [streichen] to spread; **ein Butterbrot ~** ≈ to make a sandwich - **4.** *RW:* **wie geschmiert** *fam* without a hitch <> *vi* - **1.** [schreiben] to scribble - **2.** [klecksen] to smudge.

Schmiergeld *das fam* bribe.

schmierig <> *adj* - **1.** [ölig] greasy - **2.** *abw* [Witz, Anspielung] smutty - **3.** *abw* [Typ]

smarmy ◇ *adv* [angrinsen] smarmily; [lachen, anmachen] smuttily.

Schmier|mittel *das* lubricant.

Schmier|seife *die* soft soap.

schmilzt *präs* ▭ schmelzen.

Schminke (*pl* -n) *die* make-up.

schminken *vt* to make up. ◆ **sich schminken** *ref* to put on one's make-up.

schmirgeln *vt* to sand.

Schmirgel|papier *das* sandpaper.

schmiss *prät* ▭ schmeißen.

Schmöker (*pl* -) *der* tome (*of lightweight reading*).

schmökern ◇ *vi*: **in einem Buch ~** to bury o.s. in a book ◇ *vt* to bury o.s. in.

schmollen *vi* to sulk.

schmolz *prät* ▭ schmelzen.

schmoren ◇ *vt* to braise ◇ *vi* - **1.** [braten] to braise - **2.** *fam* [in der Sonne] to roast - **3.** *fam* [warten]: **jn ~ lassen** to leave sb to stew (in his/her own juice).

Schmuck *der* - **1.** [Gegenstand] jewellery - **2.** [Dekoration] decoration.

schmücken *vt* to decorate. ◆ **sich schmücken** *ref* to adorn o.s.

schmucklos ◇ *adj* plain, unadorned ◇ *adv* plainly.

Schmuck|stück *das* - **1.** [Schmuck] piece of jewellery - **2.** [aus Sammlung, Ausstellung] jewel.

Schmuggel *der* smuggling.

schmuggeln *vt & vi* to smuggle.

Schmuggler, in (*mpl* -; *fpl* -nen) *der, die* smuggler.

schmunzeln *vi*: **(über etw** (*A*)**) ~** to smile to o.s. (at sthg).

schmusen *vi*: **(mit jm) ~** to cuddle (sb); [Liebespaar] to kiss and cuddle (with sb).

Schmutz *der* dirt; **~ abweisend** dirt-resistant.

schmutzen *vi* to get dirty.

Schmutz|fink *der* *fam* - **1.** [schmutziger Mensch - Erwachsener] dirty pig; [- Kind] mucky pup - **2.** [unsittlicher Mensch] creep.

schmutzig *adj* - **1.** [gen] dirty; **sich ~ machen** to get dirty - **2.** [Geschäftspraktiken] shady.

Schnabel (*pl* Schnäbel) *der* beak.

Schnalle (*pl* -n) *die* buckle.

schnallen *vt* - **1.** [festmachen] to strap; [Gürtel] to fasten, to buckle; **den Gürtel enger ~** to tighten one's belt; **etw auf etw** (*A*) **~** to strap sthg to sthg - **2.** *fam* [kapieren] to get.

schnalzen *vi*: **mit der Zunge/den Fingern ~** to click one's tongue/fingers; **mit der Peitsche ~** to crack the whip.

Schnäppchen (*pl* -) *das* snip, bargain; **mit dem Hemd habe ich ein ~ gemacht** the shirt was a real snip ODER bargain.

schnappen (*perf* hat/ist geschnappt) ◇ *vt*

(hat) - **1.** *fam* [festnehmen] to catch - **2.** *fam* [nehmen]: **sich** (*D*) **etw ~** to grab sthg - **3.** [packen] to grab ◇ *vi* - **1.** (hat) [beißen]: **nach jm/etw ~** to snap at sb/sthg - **2.** (ist) [federn] to spring up.

Schnapp|schuss *der* snapshot.

Schnaps (*pl* Schnäpse) *der* schnapps.

schnarchen *vi* [im Schlaf] to snore.

schnattern *vi* - **1.** [Gänse] to gabble; [Enten] to quack - **2.** *fam* [reden] to chatter - **3.** [zittern]: **er schnattert vor Kälte** his teeth are chattering with cold.

schnauben *vi eigtl & fig* to snort; **vor Wut ~** to snort with anger.

schnaufen *vi* to wheeze.

Schnauz|bart *der* - **1.** [Bart] moustache - **2.** *fam* [Mensch] guy with the 'tache.

Schnauze (*pl* -n) *die* - **1.** [Maul] muzzle; [von Schwein] snout - **2.** *salopp abw* [Mund] trap, gob *Br*; **jm eins auf die ~ hauen** to sock sb in the mouth - **3.** *RW*: **halt die ~!** *salopp* shut your trap!

schnäuzen ◆ **sich schnäuzen** *ref*: **sich (die Nase) ~** to blow one's nose.

Schnauzer (*pl* -) *der* - **1.** [Hunderasse] Schnauzer - **2.** [Schnurrbart] large moustache.

Schnecke (*pl* -n) *die* snail; [ohne Schneckenhaus] slug; **jn zur ~ machen** *fig* to give sb a dressing-down.

Schnecken|haus *das* snail shell.

Schnee *der* snow; **es liegt ~** there is snow (on the ground); **~ räumen** to clear snow.

Schnee|ball *der* snowball.

Schnee|besen *der* whisk.

Schnee|fall *der* snowfall.

Schnee|flocke *die* snowflake.

Schnee|gestöber (*pl* -) *das* [leicht] snow flurry; [stärker] snowstorm.

Schnee|glöckchen (*pl* -) *das* snowdrop.

Schnee|kette *die* snow chain.

Schnee|mann (*pl* -männer) *der* snowman.

Schnee|pflug *der* snowplough.

Schnee|schmelze *die* thaw.

Schnee|sturm *der* snowstorm.

Schnee|treiben *das* blizzard.

Schneewittchen *das* Snow White.

Schneide (*pl* -n) *die* [Klinge] blade.

schneiden (*prät* schnitt; *perf* hat geschnitten) ◇ *vt* - **1.** [gen] to cut; [Hecke] to trim; [Baum] to cut back; **sich** (*D*) **die Haare ~ lassen** to have one's hair cut - **2.** [klein schneiden - in Stücke] to chop; [- in Scheiben] to slice; [- Braten] to carve; **etw in Würfel ~** to cube sthg - **3.** [zurechtschneiden - Foto] to cut to size - **4.** [ausschneiden] to cut out - **5.** [beim Überholen] to cut in on; **eine Kurve ~** to cut a corner - **6.** [ignorieren]: **jn ~** to ignore sb - **7.** [überschneiden] to cut across, to cross; MATH to intersect - **8.** [hinzufügen]:

Schnittlauch in die Suppe ~ to chop some chives and add them to the soup **- 9.** SPORT [Ball] to put spin on ◇ *vi* **- 1.** [beschädigen]: **(mit etw) in etw** *(A)* **~** to cut sthg (with sthg) **- 2.** [Frisör, Messer, Schere] to cut. ◆ **sich schneiden** *ref* **- 1.** [sich verletzen] to cut o.s.; **sich in den Finger ~** to cut one's finger **- 2.** [sich überschneiden] to intersect **- 3.** *fam* [sich täuschen] **wenn du das glaubst, dann hast du dich aber geschnitten!** if you think that, you've got another think ODER thing coming!

schneidend ◇ *adj* **- 1.** [Wind, Kälte] biting **- 2.** [Stimme] piercing ◇ *adv* piercingly.

Schneider *(pl -) der* tailor; [für Damen] dressmaker.

Schneiderin *(pl -nen) die* tailor; [für Damen] dressmaker.

schneidern ◇ *vt:* **(sich** *(D)***) etw ~** to make sthg ◇ *vi* to make clothes.

Schneiderlsitz *der:* **im ~** cross-legged.

Schneidelzahn *der* incisor.

schneidig *adj* [Bursche] dashing; [Fahrstil] daring.

schneien *vi:* **es schneit** it's snowing.

schnell ◇ *adj* **- 1.** [gen] quick **- 2.** [Tempo] fast, quick **- 3.** [Person, Gefährt] fast ◇ *adv* **- 1.** [laufen] fast, quickly **- 2.** [zügig] quickly; **~ machen** to hurry up **- 3.** [bald] soon **- 4.** [gleich] **kannst du mal ~ vorbeikommen?** could you just pop round quickly?; **sag doch mal ~** just tell me again.

Schnelle *die:* **auf die ~** quickly.

Schnelllhefter *der* loose-leaf binder.

Schnelligkeit *die* speed.

Schnelllimbiss *der* snack bar.

schnellstens *adv* as quickly as possible.

Schnelllstraße *die* expressway.

Schnelllzug *der* express train.

schneuzen *ref* = schnäuzen.

schnippisch ◇ *adj* pert ◇ *adv* pertly.

Schnipsel *(pl -) der* scrap.

schnipsen ◇ *vt* to flick ◇ *vi* to snap.

schnitt *prät* ▭ schneiden.

Schnitt *(pl -e) der* **- 1.** [Öffnung] cut; [bei Operation] incision **- 2.** [von Haar, Kleidung] cut; [Schnittmuster] pattern **- 3.** [von Film] editing *(U)* **- 4.** [Schneiden - von Baum] cutting back; [- von Hecke] trimming **- 5.** *fam* [Durchschnitt] average; **im ~** on average **- 6.** *fam* [Gewinn] profit.

Schnitte *(pl -n) die* **- 1.** [Scheibe] slice **- 2.** [belegtes Brot] open sandwich.

Schnittlfläche *die* **- 1.** [angeschnittener Teil] cut end **- 2.** MATH section.

Schnittlauch *der (ohne pl)* chives *(pl).*

Schnittlpunkt *der* point of intersection.

Schnittlwunde *die* cut.

Schnitzel *(pl -) das* **- 1.** [Fleisch] escalope **- 2.** [aus Papier] scrap.

schnitzen *vt & vi* to carve.

Schnitzer *(pl -) der* **- 1.** [Fehler] blunder **- 2.** [Beruf] carver.

Schnitzerei *(pl -en) die* carving.

Schnorchel *(pl -) der* snorkel.

schnorcheln *vi* to snorkel.

schnüffeln ◇ *vi* **- 1.** [riechen]: **an etw** *(D)* **~** to sniff at sthg **- 2.** [durchsuchen] to snoop ◇ *vt fam* [einatmen] to sniff.

Schnuller *(pl -) der* dummy *Br,* pacifier *Am.*

Schnupfen *(pl -) der* cold; **einen ~ haben/ bekommen** to have/get a cold.

schnuppern ◇ *vi* **- 1.** [riechen]: **(an etw** *(D)***) ~** to smell (at sthg) **- 2.** [testen]: **einige Stunden ~** to try it out for a few classes ◇ *vt* to sniff.

Schnur *(pl Schnüre) die* string; [Zugschnur] cord; [Kabel] lead.

Schnürchen *das:* **wie am ~** *fam* without a hitch.

schnüren ◇ *vt* **- 1.** [gen] to tie; [Mieder] to lace up **- 2.** [Bündel, Paket] to tie up; **etw um etw ~** to tie sthg around sthg ◇ *vi:* **ins Fleisch ~** to bite into one's flesh.

Schnurrlbart *der* moustache.

schnurren *(perf hat geschnurrt) vi eigtl & fig* to purr.

Schnürsenkel *(pl -) der* shoelace.

schob *prät* ▭ schieben.

Schock *(pl -s) der* shock; **unter ~ stehen** to be in shock.

schockieren *vt* to shock.

schockiert ◇ *adj* shocked; **über etw** *(A)* **~ sein** to be shocked at sthg ◇ *adv:* **~ reagieren** to react with shock.

Schokolade *(pl -n) die* **- 1.** [Süßigkeit] chocolate **- 2.** [Getränk - heiß] hot chocolate; [- kalt] chocolate drink.

Scholle *(pl -n) die* [Fisch] plaice.

schon *adv* **- 1.** [bereits] already; **wir essen heute ~ um elf Uhr** we're eating earlier today, at eleven o'clock; **~ damals** even then; **~ 1914** as early as 1914; **er ist ~ lange hier** he's been here for a long time; **~ jetzt** already; **~ wieder** again **- 2.** [inzwischen] yet; **warst du ~ auf der Post?** have you been to the post office yet?; **~ längst** a long time ago; **~ oft** often **- 3.** [zwar] **es gefällt mir ~, aber ...** I DO like it, but ...; **ja ~, aber ...** yes of course, but ... **- 4.** [endlich]: **komm ~!** come on!; **nun rede ~!** come on — say something! **- 5.** [zur Beruhigung]: **du machst das ~** don't worry, I'm sure you'll manage it!; **es wird ~ gehen** it will work out all right; **~ gut!, ~ recht!** all right!, OK! **- 6.** [allein] just; **~ der Gedanke daran macht mich nervös** just thinking about it makes me nervous.

schön ◇ *adj* **- 1.** [Frau, Kind, Sache] beautiful; [Mann] handsome **- 2.** [angenehm] good; **~es Wochenende!** have a nice weekend!

- 3. [erheblich] considerable; **es ist noch ein ~es Stück** it's still quite a way **- 4.** *RW:* **~en Dank!** many thanks!, thanks a lot! ◇ *adv* **- 1.** [gen] well; [gekleidet] beautifully **- 2.** [verstärkend]: **~ langsam** nice and slowly; **sei ~ brav!** be a good boy/girl! ◆ **ganz schön** *adv fam* really. ◆ **na schön** *interj fam* all right!

Schöne (*pl* -n) *der, die, das:* **die ~** the beauty; **der ~** the handsome man; **das ~** the beautiful; **das ~ daran** the nice thing about it; **da hast du was ~s angerichtet!** *fam* you've gone and done it now!

schonen *vt* **- 1.** [pfleglich behandeln - Kleider, Auto, Möbel] to be careful with, to treat gently **- 2.** [schützen - Augen, Umwelt] to protect **- 3.** [weniger verlangen von] to go easy on; **er schont den Stürmer für das nächste Spiel** he's saving ODER resting the forward for the next game. ◆ **sich schonen** *ref* to take it easy.

schonend ◇ *adj* gentle ◇ *adv* gently; **jm etw ~ beibringen** to break sthg to sb gently.

Schon|frist *die* period of grace.

Schönheit (*pl* -en) *die* **- 1.** [gen] beauty **- 2.** [Sehenswürdigkeit] attraction.

schön machen *vt* **- 1.** [hübsch machen]: **etw ~** to make sthg look nice **- 2.** [angenehm machen] to make agreeable; **es sich** (D) **~** to make things nice. ◆ **sich schön machen** *ref* to do o.s. up.

Schonung (*pl* -en) *die* **- 1.** [Baumschule] young plantation **- 2.** [pflegliche Behandlung] careful ODER gentle treatment; [Schützen] protection; [verschonen] to spare; **jn um ~ bitten** [weniger verlangen von] to ask sb to go easy on one.

schonungslos ◇ *adj* ruthless; [Offenheit] brutal ◇ *adv* ruthlessly; [offen] brutally.

Schon|zeit *die* close season.

Schopf (*pl* Schöpfe) *der* [Haar] shock of hair; **die Gelegenheit beim ~ packen** to grasp the opportunity with both hands.

schöpfen *vt* **- 1.** [auftun] to scoop; [mit Löffel, Kelle] to ladle; **etw aus etw ~** to scoop/ladle sthg out of sthg **- 2.** [Mut, Kraft, Atem] to draw; **Verdacht ~** to become suspicious.

Schöpfer (*pl* -) *der* [Gott] Creator.

schöpferisch ◇ *adj* creative ◇ *adv* creatively; **~ veranlagt sein** to have creative tendencies.

Schöpf|kelle *die* ladle.

Schöpfung (*pl* -en) *die* **- 1.** [Welterschaffung] Creation **- 2.** *geh* [Werk] creation.

schor *prät* ▷ scheren.

Schorf *der (ohne pl)* scab.

Schorn|stein *der* chimney.

Schornsteinfeger, in (*mpl* -; *fpl* -nen) *der, die* chimney sweep.

schoss *prät* ▷ schießen.

Schoß (*pl* Schöße) *der* **- 1.** [Körperteil] lap; **auf js ~ sitzen** to sit on sb's lap; **der Erfolg ist mir nicht in den ~ gefallen** success wasn't handed to me on a plate **- 2.** *geh* [Schutz] bosom **- 3.** *geh* [Mutterleib] womb **- 4.** [von Jacke] tail.

Schotte (*pl* -n) *der* Scotsman, Scot.

Schottin (*pl* -nen) *die* Scotswoman, Scot.

schottisch *adj* Scottish.

Schottland *nt* Scotland.

schraffieren *vt* to hatch.

schräg ◇ *adj* **- 1.** [schief] sloping; [Linie] diagonal **- 2.** *fam* [eigenartig] offbeat **- 3.** *fam* [falsch] dodgy ◇ *adv* **- 1.** [schief] at an angle; [diagonal] diagonally; **jn ~ ansehen** *fam* to look askance at sb **- 2.** *fam* [falsch]: **das klingt ~** that sounds dodgy.

Schräge (*pl* -n) *die* slope; [Wand] sloping ceiling.

Schramme (*pl* -n) *die* scratch.

Schrank (*pl* Schränke) *der* [für Geschirr, Vorräte] cupboard; [für Kleider] wardrobe *Br*, closet *Am*; [für Bücher] bookcase.

Schranke (*pl* -n) *die* barrier. ◆ **Schranken** *pl* [Grenzen] limits.

schrankenlos *adj* [Freiheit] boundless.

Schrank|wand *die* wall unit.

Schraube (*pl* -n) *die* **- 1.** [zum Befestigen] screw; [ohne Spitze] bolt **- 2.** SPORT twist.

schrauben *vt:* **etw (auf/in etw** (A)) **~** to screw sthg (onto/into sthg); **etw an etw** (A) **~** to screw sthg to sthg; **etw aus** ODER **von etw ~** to unscrew sthg from sthg; **den Deckel von der Flasche ~** to screw the lid off the bottle; **etw nach oben/unten ~** *fig* to raise/lower sthg.

Schrauben|schlüssel *der* spanner *Br*, wrench *Am*.

Schrauben|zieher (*pl* -) *der* screwdriver.

Schreber|garten *der* ≈ allotment.

Schreck *der* fright; **vor ~** in fear ODER fright; **einen ~ kriegen** to get a fright; **jm einen ~ einjagen** to give sb a fright.

Schrecken (*pl* -) *der* terror; **die ~ des Krieges** the horrors of war; **er ist der ~ der Nachbarschaft** he's the terror of the neighbourhood.

schreckhaft *adj* easily scared.

schrecklich ◇ *adj* terrible ◇ *adv* terribly.

Schrei (*pl* -e) *der* shout; [von Tier, Baby] cry; [aus Angst, vor Schmerz, Lust] scream; **der letzte ~** *fam fig* the latest thing.

schreiben (*prät* schrieb; *perf* hat geschrieben) ◇ *vt* **- 1.** [gen] to write; [mit Schreibmaschine] to type **- 2.** [orthografisch] to spell; **wie schreibt man das?** how do you spell that?, how's that spelt? **- 3.** [Klassenarbeit, Test] to do **- 4.** [Rechnung] to make out; **die Firma schreibt rote Zahlen** the company is in the red ◇ *vi* **- 1.** [gen] to write; **an jn ~** to write to sb; **an etw** *(D)* ~ to be writing sthg - **2.** [tippen] to type; *siehe auch* **großschreiben, kleinschreiben.** ◆ **sich schreiben** *ref* - **1.** [korrespondieren] to correspond - **2.** [sich buchstabieren] to be spelt.

Schreiben *(pl -)* das letter.

Schreib|kraft die clerical assistant; [Stenotypistin] shorthand typist.

Schreib|maschine die typewriter.

Schreib|schrift die cursive script.

Schreib|tisch der desk.

Schreibtisch|lampe die desk lamp.

Schreibwaren|geschäft das stationery shop.

schreien *(prät* schrie; *perf* hat geschrie(e) n) *vi* [gen] to shout; [Tier, Baby] to cry; [aus Angst, vor Schmerz, Lust] to scream; **vor Schmerz ~** to scream with pain; **schrei nicht so!** stop shouting!; **nach etw ~** *eigtl & fig* to cry out for sthg.

Schreien das crying; [gellend] screaming; [Brüllen] shouting; **zum ~ sein** *fam* to be a scream.

Schrei|hals der *fam* bawler.

Schreiner, in *(mpl -; fpl -nen)* der, die joiner.

schrie *prät* ⏴ schreien.

schrieb *prät* ⏴ schreiben.

Schrift *(pl -en)* die - **1.** [Handschrift] handwriting *(U)* - **2.** [das Geschriebene] writing *(U)* - **3.** [Alphabet] script - **4.** TYPO type. ◆ **Schriften** *pl* texts; [kurze Abhandlungen] papers; [Werke] works.

schriftlich ◇ *adj* written ◇ *adv* in writing.

Schriftsteller, in *(mpl -; fpl -nen)* der, die writer.

schrill *adj* shrill.

Schrimp, Shrimp [ʃrɪmp] *(pl -s)* der shrimp.

Schritt *(pl -e)* der - **1.** [gen] step; **er ist mir immer einen ~ voraus** he's always a step ahead of me; **jn am ~ erkennen** to recognize sb's step - **2.** [von Hose] crotch - **3.** [zur Angabe der Entfernung] pace; **drei ~e von mir entfernt** three paces away from me - **4.** [Gangart] walk; **im ~ reiten** to ride at a walk - **5.** *RW*: **~ für ~** step by step; **mit jm/etw ~ halten** to keep up with sb/sthg.

Schritt|macher *(pl -)* der - **1.** [Vorreiter] pacesetter - **2.** [im Sport] pacemaker.

schrittweise *adv* gradually.

schroff ◇ *adj* - **1.** [Verhalten, Antwort, Wechsel] abrupt - **2.** [Felsen, Abhang] sheer - **3.** [Gegensatz] stark ◇ *adv* [abweisen, antworten] abruptly.

schröpfen *vt fam* [ausnehmen] to rip off.

Schrot der ODER das - **1.** [Munition] shot - **2.** [Getreide] meal; [von Weizen] wholemeal *Br*, wholewheat *Am*.

Schrott der - **1.** [altes Metall] scrap metal

- **2.** *fam* [Plunder] junk - **3.** *fam* [Blödsinn] rubbish.

Schrott|platz der scrapyard *Br*, junkyard *Am*.

schrottreif *adj* fit for the scrapheap.

schrubben *vt* to scrub.

Schrubber *(pl -)* der stiff brush *(for scrubbing floors)*.

schrumpelig, schrumplig *adj* [Haut] wrinkled; [Apfel] shrivelled.

schrumpfen *(perf* ist geschrumpft) *vi* to shrink.

schrumplig = schrumpelig.

Schub *(pl* Schübe) der - **1.** [Kraft] thrust - **2.** [Anfall] bout - **3.** [Ladung, Menschengruppe] batch.

Schub|karre die, **Schubkarren** der wheelbarrow.

Schub|lade *(pl -n)* die drawer.

Schubs *(pl -e)* der push.

schubsen *vt* to push.

schüchtern ◇ *adj* [Person, Blick] shy; [Versuch, Frage] timid ◇ *adv* [lächeln, schauen] shyly; [sich benehmen, fragen] timidly.

Schüchternheit die shyness.

schuf *prät* ⏴ schaffen.

Schuft *(pl -e)* der *abw* scoundrel.

schuften *vi fam* to slave away.

Schuh *(pl -e)* der shoe; **jm etw in die ~e schieben** *fig* to pin the blame for sthg on sb.

Schuh|creme, Schuhkrem die shoe polish.

Schuh|geschäft das shoe shop.

Schuh|größe die shoe size.

Schuh|macher, in *(mpl -; fpl -nen)* der, die cobbler, shoemaker.

Schulab|schluss der school-leaving qualification.

Schul|anfang der - **1.** [Einschulung] first day of school - **2.** [nach den Ferien] beginning of term.

Schul|aufgabe die homework *(U)*.

Schul|besuch der school attendance.

Schul|bildung die school education, schooling.

Schul|bus der school bus.

schuld *adj*: **an etw** *(D)* **~ sein** to be to blame for sthg; **er ist ~ daran** it's his fault.

Schuld *(pl -en)* die - **1.** [Verantwortung, Ursache] blame; **es war seine ~** it was his fault; **an etw ~ haben** to be to blame for sthg; **jm (an etw** *(D))* **~ geben** to blame sb (for sthg); *siehe auch* **zuschulden** - **2.** [Unrecht] guilt; **sich** *(D)* **keiner ~ bewusst sein** to be unaware of having done anything wrong. ◆ **Schulden** *pl* debts; **~en haben** to be in debt; **20 Milliarden Euro ~en haben** to have debts of 20 billion euro; **~en machen** to run up debts.

schuldbewusst ◇ *adj* guilty ◇ *adv* guiltily.

schulden *vt:* **jm etw ~** to owe sb sthg.

schuldig <> *adj -* **1.** [verantwortlich] guilty; **an etw** *(D)* **~ sein** to be to blame for sthg **- 2.** [nicht bezahlt] due; **jm etw ~ sein** ODER **bleiben** to owe sb sthg <> *adv:* **sich ~ bekennen** to admit one's guilt.

schuldlos *adj* innocent.

Schule *(pl -n) die* school; **in der ~** at school; **zur ~** ODER **in die ~ gehen** to go to school; **~ machen** *fig* to set a precedent.

schulen *vt* to train.

Schüler *(pl -) der* pupil.

Schüleraustausch *der* (school) exchange.

Schülerlausweis *der pupil's ID card entitling them to concessions etc.*

Schülerin *(pl -nen) die* pupil.

Schülerlkarte *die* school season ticket.

Schülervertretung *die* student council.

Schülervertretung

The aim of this initiative is to give pupils a say in the daily life of their school. In this way they can have some input into organising school trips and parties or putting together a class newspaper. Pupils can have a hand in the running of their school by sitting on school councils, attending meetings of student representatives or by taking part in the election of year group representatives. The pupils themselves decide how they wish to voice their feelings.

Schullferien *pl* school holidays.

Schulferien

In Germany the school year varies from one federal state (Land) to another, but all pupils have 75 days holiday per year. These take place in autumn, at Christmas, at Easter and at Whitsuntide, and the six week long summer holiday brings the school year to a close.

schulfrei *adj:* **morgen ist ~** there's no school tomorrow; **~ haben** to be off school.

Schullhof *der* school playground.

schulisch *adj & adv* at school.

Schulljahr *das -* **1.** [Jahr] school year **- 2.** [Klasse] year.

Schullklasse *die* class.

Schullleiter, in *der, die* headmaster (f headmistress) *Br,* principal *Am.*

schulpflichtig *adj* required to attend school; **im ~en Alter** of school age.

Schullschluss *der:* **nach ~** after school.

Schullstunde *die* period.

Schullttasche *die* schoolbag.

Schulter *(pl -n) die* shoulder.

Schulterlblatt *das* shoulder blade.

Schultüte *die* cornet of sweets.

Schultüte

It is traditional for children on their first day at school to be presented with a large paper cornet full of sweets.

Schulung *(pl -en) die -* **1.** [gen] training **- 2.** [Lehrveranstaltung] training course.

Schullzeit *die* schooldays *(pl).*

Schullzeugnis *das* school report.

schummeln *vi* to cheat.

Schund *der abw* trash.

schunkeln *(perf hat geschunkelt) vi* **- 1.** [sich wiegen] to link arms and sway in time to the music **- 2.** [Schiff] to rock.

Schuppe *(pl -n) die -* **1.** [von Fischen] scale **- 2.** [Hautstück] flake **- 3.** [Kopfschuppe] dandruff *(U).*

schuppen *vt* to scale. ➡ **sich schuppen** *ref* to flake.

schürfen <> *vi* [schleifen] to scrape <> *vt:* **sich** *(D)* **das Knie ~** to graze one's knee.

Schürflwunde *die* graze.

Schurke *(pl -n) der abw* villain.

Schürze *(pl -n) die* apron.

Schuss *(pl Schüsse) der -* **1.** [mit Schusswaffe, beim Fußball] shot **- 2.** [ein wenig] dash; **ein ~ Whisky** a dash of whisky **- 3.** [beim Skifahren]: **~ fahren** to schuss **- 4.** *RW:* **gut in ~ sein** *fam* to be in good shape.

Schüssel *(pl -n) die* bowl.

schusselig *adj fam* scatterbrained.

Schusslwaffe *die* firearm.

Schuster, in *(mpl -; fpl -nen) der, die* shoemaker.

Schutt *der* rubble.

Schuttabladelplatz *der* rubbish *Br* ODER garbage *Am* dump.

Schüttelfrost *der:* **~ haben** to be shivering.

schütteln *vt* to shake; **den Kopf ~** to shake one's head; **'vor Gebrauch ~'** 'shake before use'; **es schüttelte ihn bei dem Gedanken** the thought made him shudder. ➡ **sich schütteln** *ref* to shake o.s.; **sich vor etw** *(D)* **~** [Lachen, Kälte] to shake with sthg; [Ekel, Entsetzen] to be filled with sthg.

schütten <> *vt* [Flüssigkeit] to pour; [Mehl, Kartoffeln] to tip <> *vi:* **es schüttet** *fam* it's pouring (down).

Schutz *der* protection; **jn in ~ nehmen** to stand up for sb.

Schutzlblech *das* mudguard.

Schütze *(pl -n) der -* **1.** ASTROL Sagittarius; **~ sein** to be a Sagittarius **- 2.** [Sportschütze] marksman - **3**. [bei Ballsport] scorer - **4**. [Soldat] private.

schützen *vt:* **jn/etw (vor jm/etw) ~** to protect sb/sthg (from sb/sthg). ◆ **sich schützen** *ref:* **sich gegen etw** ODER **vor etw** (D) **~** to protect o.s. against sthg ODER from sthg.

Schützen|fest *das shooting festival.*

Schutz|gebiet *das* - **1**. [Naturschutzgebiet] protected area - **2**. [Kolonie] protectorate.

Schutz|impfung *die* vaccination.

Schützling *(pl -e) der* [Kind in Obhut] charge; [Protégé] protégé (f protégée).

schutzlos <> *adj* defenceless <> *adv:* **jm ~ ausgeliefert sein** to be completely at sb's mercy.

Schutz|maßnahme *die* precaution.

Schutz|patron, in *der, die* patron saint.

Schutzum|schlag *der* dust jacket.

schwabbelig *adj* [Körperteil] flabby; [Pudding] wobbly.

Schwabe *(pl -n) der* Swabian.

Schwaben *nt* Swabia.

Schwäbin *(pl -nen) die* Swabian.

schwäbisch *adj* Swabian.

schwach *(kompar* schwächer; *superl* schwächste) <> *adj* - **1**. [gen] weak; **bei Kuchen werde ich immer ~** I have no willpower when it comes to cakes - **2**. [Konstitution] delicate - **3**. [leicht - Brise, Wärme, Ahnung, Gefühl] faint; [- Druck] light; [- Versuch, Entschuldigung] feeble - **4**. [Selbstbewusstsein] low - **5**. [Film, Leistung, Schüler] weak, poor; [Gehör, Gedächtnis] poor; **ein ~er Trost sein** to be cold comfort - **6**. [Beteiligung] poor <> *adv* - **1**. [eingeschränkt, schlecht, wenig] poorly - **2**. [leicht - wehen, strahlen, sich erinnern] faintly; [- drücken] lightly; [- protestieren] feebly - **3**. GRAM: **das Verb wird ~ konjugiert** it is a weak verb.

Schwäche *(pl -n) die* - **1**. [gen] weakness; **eine ~ für jn/etw haben** to have a weakness for sb/sthg - **2**. [von Geräusch] faintness - **3**. [von Druck] lightness.

schwächen *vt* to weaken.

Schwach|kopf *der fam abw* dummy.

schwächlich *adj* delicate.

Schwächling *(pl -e) der abw* weakling.

Schwachsinn *der* - **1**. *fam* [Unsinn] nonsense - **2**. MED mental deficiency.

schwachsinnig <> *adj* - **1**. *fam* [unsinnig] stupid, ridiculous - **2**. MED mentally deficient <> *adv fam* stupidly.

Schwächung *(pl -en) die* weakening.

Schwaden *pl* clouds.

schwafeln *fam abw* <> *vi* to talk drivel <> *vt* to drivel on about.

Schwager *(pl Schwäger) der* brother-in-law.

Schwägerin *(pl -nen) die* sister-in-law.

Schwalbe *(pl -n) die* swallow.

schwamm *prät* ⟹ schwimmen.

Schwamm *(pl Schwämme) der* - **1**. [Tier, Haushaltsschwamm] sponge - **2**. [Schimmel] dry rot.

schwammig <> *adj* - **1**. [Definition, Worte] woolly; [Kontur] vague, blurred - **2**. [Gesicht] pasty - **3**. [Material] spongy <> *adv* [unklar] vaguely.

Schwan *(pl Schwäne) der* swan.

schwang *prät* ⟹ schwingen.

schwanger *adj* pregnant; **~ werden** to get pregnant; **im dritten Monat ~ sein** to be in the third month of pregnancy.

Schwangere *(pl -n) die* pregnant woman.

schwängern *vt* to make pregnant.

Schwangerschaft *(pl -en) die* pregnancy.

schwanken *(perf* hat/ist geschwankt) *vi* - **1**. *(ist)* [sich schwankend bewegen] to sway - **2**. *(hat)* [unentschlossen sein] to waver - **3**. *(hat)* [instabil sein] to fluctuate.

Schwankung *(pl -en) die* fluctuation.

Schwanz *(pl Schwänze) der* - **1**. [von Tieren] tail; **den ~ einziehen** *fig* to back down - **2**. *vulg* [männliches Glied] dick - **3**. *fam* [Serie] series.

schwänzen <> *vi fam* to skive Br, to play hookey Am <> *vt* [Unterricht, Stunde] to skip; **die Schule ~** to skive off Br ODER play hookey Am from school.

schwappen *(perf* hat/ist geschwappt) <> *vi* - **1**. *(ist)* [überlaufen] to spill - **2**. *(hat)* [sich bewegen] to slosh <> *vt (hat)* to splash.

Schwarm *(pl Schwärme) der* - **1**. [von Kindern, Bienen] swarm; [von Fischen] shoal; [von Vögeln] flock - **2**. *fam* [Idol] heartthrob.

schwärmen *(perf* hat/ist geschwärmt) *vi* - **1**. *(hat)* [begeistert sein]: **für jn/etw ~** to be mad about sb/sthg - **2**. *(hat)* [erzählen]: **von jm/etw ~** to rave about sb/sthg - **3**. *(ist)* [im Schwarm fliegen] to swarm.

Schwärmer, in *(mpl -; fpl -nen) der, die* dreamer.

Schwarte *(pl -n) die* - **1**. [von Speck] rind; [von Schweinebraten] crackling (U) - **2**. *fam abw* [Buch] tome.

schwarz *(kompar* schwärzer; *superl* schwärzeste) <> *adj* - **1**. [gen] black - **2**. POL pro-CDU/CSU - **3**. [Geschäfte] illicit <> *adv:* **der Stift schreibt ~** the pen writes in black; **~ auf weiß** *fig* in black and white; *siehe auch* schwarz sehen.

Schwarz *das* black.

Schwarzafrika *nt* Black Africa.

Schwarzarbeit *die* work on the black market; [als Nebentätigkeit] moonlighting.

Schwarz|brot *das* black bread.

Schwarze *(pl -n)* <> *der, die* black person <> *das (ohne pl)* black; **ins ~ treffen** to hit the bull's-eye.

Schwärze *die* blackness.

Schwarze Markt *der* black market.

Schwarze Meer *das* Black Sea.

schwärzen *vt* to blacken.

schwarzfahren *(perf* ist schwarzgefahren*)* *vi (unreg)* to travel without a ticket.

Schwarzhändler, in *der, die* black marketeer.

schwärzlich *adj* blackish.

Schwarzmarkt *der* black market.

schwarz sehen *vi (unreg):* **(für jn/etw) ~** to be pessimistic (about sb/sthg).

Schwarzwald *der* Black Forest.

schwarzweiß ◇ *adj* black and white ◇ *adv* in black and white.

Schwarzweißfilm *der* black and white film.

schwatzen, schwätzen ◇ *vi* **- 1.** [sich unterhalten] to chat **- 2.** [in der Schule] to talk ◇ *vt abw:* **dummes Zeug ~** to talk rubbish.

Schwätzer, in *(mpl -; fpl -nen) der, die abw:* **ein ~ sein** to talk a load of nonsense.

schwatzhaft *adj abw:* **ein ~er Mensch** a person who can't keep their mouth shut.

Schwebe *die:* **in der ~** in the balance.

Schwebebahn *die* overhead monorail.

Schwebebalken *der* SPORT beam.

schweben *vi* **- 1.** [fliegen, in Wasser] to float; [Vögel] to hover; [Staubteilchen] to hang **- 2.** [unentschieden sein] to hover **- 3.** [Duft, Verdacht] to hang.

Schwede *(pl -n) der* Swede.

Schweden *nt* Sweden.

Schwedin *(pl -nen) die* Swede.

schwedisch *adj* Swedish.

Schwedisch(e) *das* Swedish; *siehe auch* Englisch(e).

Schwefel *der* sulphur.

Schwefelsäure *die* sulphuric acid.

Schweif *(pl -e) der* tail.

schweigen *(prät* schwieg; *perf* hat geschwiegen*)* *vi* to be silent; **wenn du ~ kannst, verrate ich dir etwas** if you can keep a secret, I'll tell you something; **von jm/etw ganz zu ~** to say nothing of sb/sthg.

Schweigen *das* silence; **jn zum ~ bringen** to silence sb.

Schweigepflicht *die* professional duty to maintain confidentiality.

schweigsam *adj* taciturn; **du bist heute ~** you're rather quiet today.

Schwein *(pl -e) das* **- 1.** [Tier] pig **- 2.** [Schweinefleisch] pork **- 3.** *salopp abw* [Mensch] bastard **- 4.** *RW:* **armes ~** *salopp* poor bastard; **~ haben** *fam* to be jammy.

Schweinebraten *der* roast pork.

Schweinefleisch *das* pork.

Schweinerei *(pl -en) die fam* **- 1.** [schlimme Sache] goddamn scandal; **das neue Abtreibungsgesetz ist eine ~!** the new law on abortion is bloody *Br* ODER goddamn *Am* dis-

graceful! **- 2.** [Schmutz] mess **- 3.** [Unanständiges]: **~en** filth *(U).*

Schweinestall *der eigtl & fig* pigsty *Br,* pigpen *Am.*

Schweiß *der* sweat; **ihr brach der ~ aus** she broke out in a sweat.

schweißen *vt & vi* to weld.

schweißgebadet *adj & adv* bathed in sweat.

Schweißtropfen *der* drop of sweat.

Schweiz *die:* **die ~** Switzerland.

Schweizer *(pl -) der & adj (unver)* Swiss.

Schweizerdeutsch *das* Swiss German; *siehe auch* Englisch(e).

Schweizerin *(pl -nen) die* Swiss.

schweizerisch *adj* Swiss.

Schweizerische Eidgenossenschaft *die:* **die ~** the Swiss Confederation.

schwelen *vi* [Rauch entwickeln] to smoulder.

Schwelle *(pl -n) die* **- 1.** [Türschwelle] threshold; **an der ~ einer Sache** *(D) fig* on the threshold of sthg **- 2.** [der Eisenbahn] sleeper *Br,* tie *Am.*

schwellen *(präs* schwillt; *prät* schwoll; *perf* ist geschwollen*)* *vi* to swell.

Schwellung *(pl -en) die* swelling.

schwenken *vt* **- 1.** [Kran] to swing; [Kamera] to pan **- 2.** [Fahne] to wave **- 3.** KÜCHE to toss.

schwer ◇ *adj* **- 1.** [Gewicht] heavy; **wie ~ bist du/ist der Koffer?** how heavy are you/is the suitcase? **- 2.** [schwierig] difficult; [beschwerlich] hard; **es ~ haben mit ...** to have a hard time with ... **- 3.** [schlimm - Krankheit, Schaden, Unfall] serious; [- Enttäuschung] huge, great **- 4.** [stark - Mahlzeit, Sturm] heavy ◇ *adv* **- 1.** [an Gewicht] heavily **- 2.** [unter Mühen]: **~ atmen** to breathe with difficulty; **~ hören** to be hard of hearing **- 3.** [arbeiten] hard **- 4.** [schwerlich] hardly **- 5.** [schlimm - verletzt, krank] seriously; [- bestrafen] severely **- 6.** *fam* [sehr] really; **er ist ~ in Ordnung** he's all right.

Schwerarbeit *die* heavy work.

schwerbehindert, schwer behindert *adj* severely disabled.

schwer beschädigt *adj* [beschädigt] badly damaged.

schwer bewaffnet *adj* heavily armed.

Schwere ◇ *die* **- 1.** [gen] heaviness **- 2.** [von Krankheit, Schaden, Unfall] seriousness; [von Enttäuschung] enormity **- 3.** [Schwierigkeitsgrad] difficulty ◇ *das:* **~s durchmachen** to have a difficult time (of it).

schwerelos ◇ *adj* weightless ◇ *adv* weightlessly.

schwer erziehbar *adj* difficult.

schwer fallen *(perf* ist schwer gefallen*)* *vi (unreg):* **es fiel ihm schwer, Abschied zu nehmen** he found it difficult to say goodbye.

schwerfällig <> *adj* ponderous <> *adv* ponderously.

schwerhörig *adj* hard of hearing.

Schwer|industrie *die* heavy industry.

Schwerkraft *die* gravity.

schwer machen *vt*: **jm etw ~** to make sthg difficult for sb.

schwermütig <> *adj* melancholy <> *adv* in a melancholy way.

schwer nehmen *vt (unreg)*: **etw ~** to take sthg hard.

Schwer|punkt *der* - **1.** [Hauptsache] main focus - **2.** PHYS centre of gravity.

Schwert (*pl* -er) *das* sword.

schwer tun ⇒ **sich schwer tun** *ref (unreg)*: **sich mit etw ~** to have difficulty with sthg.

Schwer|verbrecher, in *der, die* person who has committed a serious crime.

schwer verletzt *adj* seriously injured.

schwerwiegend *adj* serious.

Schwester (*pl* -n) *die* - **1.** [Verwandte] sister - **2.** [Krankenschwester] nurse - **3.** [Ordensschwester] nun, sister.

schwieg *prät* ⊳ schweigen.

Schwieger|eltern *pl* parents-in-law.

Schwieger|mutter *die* mother-in-law.

Schwieger|sohn *der* son-in-law.

Schwieger|tochter *die* daughter-in-law.

Schwieger|vater *der* father-in-law.

Schwiele (*pl* -n) *die* callus.

schwierig <> *adj* difficult <> *adv* with difficulty.

Schwierigkeit (*pl* -en) *die* difficulty; **ohne ~en** without difficulty; **in ~en geraten/stecken** to get into/be in trouble.

schwillt *präs* ⊳ schwellen.

Schwimm|bad *das* swimming pool.

Schwimm|becken *das* (swimming) pool.

schwimmen (*prät* schwamm; *perf* hat/ist geschwommen) *vi & vt (hat, ist)* to swim.

Schwimmen *das* swimming.

Schwimmer, in (*mpl* -, *fpl* -nen) *der, die* swimmer.

Schwindel *der* - **1.** [Gleichgewichtsstörung] dizziness - **2.** *abw* [Betrug] swindle.

schwindelig, schwindlig *adj*: **mir wird (es) ~** I feel dizzy.

Schwindler, in (*mpl* -, *fpl* -nen) *der, die* - **1.** [Betrüger] swindler - **2.** [Lügner] liar.

schwindlig = schwindelig.

schwingen (*prät* schwang, *perf* hat/ist geschwungen) <> *vi* - **1.** *(hat)* [vibrieren] to vibrate - **2.** [pendeln] to swing. <> *vt (hat)* to wave.

schwitzen *vi* [Person] to sweat.

schwoll *prät* ⊳ schwellen.

schwor *prät* ⊳ schwören.

schwören (*prät* schwor; *perf* hat geschworen) *vt & vi* to swear.

schwul *adj fam* gay.

schwül *adj* [Wetter] close, muggy.

Schwung (*pl* Schwünge) *der* - **1.** [Bewegung] swing - **2.** [Elan] zest, verve - **3.** [Menge] stack.

Schwur (*pl* Schwüre) *der* oath.

scratchen *vi* to scratch.

sechs [zɛks] <> *num* [als Zahl, Anzahl] six; **~ Mal** six times; **um ~ (Uhr)** at six (o'clock); **fünf vor/nach ~** five to/past *Br* ODER after *Am* six; **mit ~ kommen die Kinder in die Schule** children start school at the age of six; **~ zu null** six-zero <> *pron* six; **sie waren ~** there were six of them; **ein Tisch für ~** a table for six.

Sechs (*pl* -en) *die* - **1.** [Zahl, Spielkarte] six - **2.** [Spieler, Bus] number six - **3.** [Schulnote] ≃ F, mark of 6 on a scale from 1 to 6.

sechsfach <> *adj*: **die ~e Menge** six times as much; **in ~er Größe** six times as big; **die Formulare in ~er Ausfertigung abgeben** to provide six copies of the forms; **der ~e Gewinner** the six-times winner <> *adv* sixfold.

sechshundert *num* six hundred.

sechsmal *adv* six times.

sechstausend *num* six thousand.

sechste, r, s [ˈzɛkstə, ɐ, s] *adj* sixth; **der ~ Juni** the sixth of June, June the sixth; **auf dem ~n Rang sein** to be sixth in the rankings.

Sechste (*pl* -n) *der, die, das* [in einer Reihenfolge] sixth; **Heinrich der ~** Henry the Sixth, Henry VI; **sie ist die ~ im Weitsprung** she is sixth in the long jump <> *der* [Angabe des Datums] sixth; **am ~n** on the sixth; **ich fahre Freitag, den ~n** I'm going on Friday the sixth.

sechstel *adj (unver)* sixth; **ein ~ Liter** a sixth of a litre.

Sechstel (*pl* -) *das* sixth; **etw in ~ teilen** to divide sthg in six ODER into sixths.

sechzehn *num* sixteen; *siehe auch* sechs.

sechzehntel *adj* sixteenth.

Sechzehntel (*pl* -) *das* sixteenth.

sechzig *num* sixty; *siehe auch* sechs.

Sechzig *die* sixty; *siehe auch* Sechs.

Sechzigerjahre, sechziger Jahre *pl*: **die ~** the sixties.

See (*pl* -n) <> *der* lake <> *die* sea; **an die ~ fahren** to go to the seaside; **auf hoher ~** out at sea.

See|gang *der*: **leichter/hoher ~** calm/rough seas *(pl)*.

See|hund *der* [Robbe] seal.

See|igel *der* sea urchin.

seekrank *adj* seasick.

Seele (*pl* -n) *die* - **1.** [gen] soul - **2.** RW: **etw auf der ~ haben** to have sthg on one's mind.

seelenruhig *adv* calmly.

Seeleute *pl* ⊳ Seemann.

seelisch <> *adj* psychological <> *adv* mentally.

See|löwe *der* sea lion.

Seelsorge *die* pastoral care.

See|mann *(pl -leute) der* sailor.

See|meile *die* nautical mile.

See|not *die:* in ~ geraten/sein to get into/be in distress.

See|räuber *der* pirate.

See|rose *die* [Pflanze] water lily.

seetüchtig *adj* seaworthy.

See|weg *der:* auf dem ~ by sea.

See|zunge *die* sole.

Segel *(pl -) das* sail.

Segel|boot *das* sailing boat.

segelfliegen *vi* to glide.

Segel|flugzeug *das* glider.

segeln *(perf* hat/ist gesegelt) *vi* to sail.

Segel|schiff *das* sailing ship.

Segen *(pl -) der* blessing.

segnen *vt* to bless.

sehbehindert *adj* visually impaired.

sehen *(präs* sieht; *prät* sah; *perf* hat gesehen) <> *vt* - 1. [gen] to see; [willkürlich] to watch; etw gerne/ungerne ~ to like/dislike sthg; das werden wir ja gleich ~ we'll soon see; das kann sich ~ lassen that's remarkable - 2. [treffen] to see, to meet <> *vi* - 1. [gen] to see; gut/schlecht ~ to have good/bad eyesight; sieh mal! look!; jm ähnlich ~ to look like sb - 2. [hervorstehen]: das Wrack sieht aus dem Wasser the wreck sticks out of the water - 3. [mit Präpositionen]: auf jn/etw ~ to look at sb/sthg; nach jm/etw ~ to look after sb/sthg. ◆ sich sehen *ref* - 1. [treffen] to meet - 2. [sich fühlen]: sich betrogen ~ to see o.s. cheated; sich gezwungen ~, etw zu tun to feel obliged to do sthg. ◆ mal sehen *interj* we'll see! ◆ sieh mal *interj* look! ◆ siehste, siehst du *interj* there you are!

sehenswert *adj* worth seeing.

Sehenswürdigkeit *(pl -en) die* attraction; ~en sights.

Sehkraft *die* sight.

Sehne *(pl -n) die* - 1. [vom Muskel] tendon - 2. [vom Bogen] string.

sehnen ◆ sich sehnen *ref:* sich nach jm/etw ~ to long for sb/sthg.

sehnig *adj* - 1. [Fleisch] stringy - 2. [Körper] sinewy.

Sehnsucht *(pl -süchte) die* longing; ~ nach jm/etw haben to long for sb/sthg.

sehnsüchtig <> *adj* [Blick] longing <> *adv* longingly.

sehr *adv* very; [mit Verben] a lot, very much; das gefällt mir ~ I like it a lot; zu ~ too much; ~ viel Geld an awful lot of money; bitte ~! you're welcome!; danke ~! thank you very much!

seicht *adj* shallow.

seid *präs* ➡ sein.

Seide *(pl -n) die* silk.

seidig *adj* silky.

Seife *(pl -n) die* soap.

Seifen|blase *die* soap bubble.

Seil *(pl -e) das* rope.

Seil|bahn *die* cable railway.

sein *(präs* ist; *prät* war; *perf* ist gewesen) <> *aux* - 1. [im Perfekt] to have; sie ist gegangen she has gone - 2. [im Konjunktiv]: sie wäre gegangen she would have gone <> *vi* - 1. [gen] to be; Lehrer ~ to be a teacher; aus etw ~ to be made of sthg; aus Indien/Zürich ~ to be from India/Zurich; du warst es! it was you! - 2. [mit Infinitiv, müssen]: mein Befehl ist sofort auszuführen my order is to be carried out immediately - 3. [mit Infinitiv, können]: das ist nicht zu ändern there's nothing that can be done about it; dieses Spiel ist noch zu gewinnen this game can still be won - 4. [mit Dativ]: mir ist schlecht/kalt I'm sick/cold - 5. [mit unpersönlichem Pronomen] to be; es ist zwölf Uhr it's twelve o'clock; es ist dunkel it's dark; wie wäre es mit ...? what about ...? - 6. *RW:* was ist? what's up?; das wärs that's all; etw ~ lassen to give sthg up; lass es gut ~! leave it!; ist was? is there anything wrong?

sein, e *det* his.

seine, r, s *pron* [bei Personen] his; [bei Sachen, Tieren] its.

Seine *(sɛːn(ə)) die:* die ~ the (River) Seine.

seiner *pron (Genitiv von er, es):* wir gedenken ~ we remember him.

seinerseits *adv* - 1. [er selbst] for his part; [es selbst] for its part - 2. [von ihm - Person] on his part; [- Tier, Sache] on its part.

seinerzeit *adv* at that time.

seinesgleichen *pron abw* [Person] the likes of him; [Tier, Sache] the likes of it.

seinetwegen *adv* - 1. [ihm zuliebe - Person] for his sake; [- Tier, Sache] for its sake - 2. [wegen ihm - Person] because of him; [- Tier, Sache] because of it - 3. [von ihm aus - Person] as far as he's concerned; [- Tier] as far as it's concerned.

seinetwillen ◆ um seinetwillen *adv* [Person] for his sake; [Tier] for its sake.

sein lassen *vt (unreg) fam:* lass das sein! stop that!; sie kann es einfach nicht ~ she just can't help herself.

seit <> *präp (+ D)* - 1. [zur Angabe des Zeitpunktes] since; ~ wann? since when? - 2. [zur Angabe der Dauer] since; ich wohne hier ~ drei Jahren I've lived here for three years; ~ langem for a long time <> *konj* since.

seitdem <> *adv* since then <> *konj* since.

Seite *(pl -n) die* - 1. [gen] side; etw zur ~ legen to put sthg to one side; zur ~ gehen ODER treten to move aside; auf der linken/ rechten ~ on the left-hand/right-hand side - 2. [von Buch, Heft, Zeitung] page; auf beiden ~n on both sides; jedes Ding hat seine guten und schlechten ~n there's a good and a bad side to everything - **3.** *RW:* **jm zur ~ ste-hen** to stand by sb; **jn von der ~ ansehen** to look at sb askance; **jn zur ~ nehmen** to take sb aside. ◆ **auf Seiten** *präp (+ G)* on the part of. ◆ **Seite an Seite** *adv* side by side. ◆ **von Seiten** *präp (+ G)* on the part of.

Seiten|sprung *der* affair; **einen ~ machen** to have an affair.

Seiten|stechen *das* stitch; **~ haben** to have a stitch.

Seiten|straße *die* side street.

seither *adv* since then.

seitlich *adj* [Fenster, Eingang] side; [Zusammenstoß] side-on; **ein ~er Wind** a crosswind.

seitwärts *adv* - **1.** [zur Seite] sideways - **2.** [auf der Seite] to one side.

Sekretär *(pl -e) der* - **1.** [Person] secretary - **2.** [Möbelstück] bureau.

Sekretariat *(pl -e) das* secretary's office.

Sekretärin *(pl -nen) die* secretary.

Sekt *(pl -e) der German sparkling wine similar to champagne.*

Sekte *(pl -n) die* sect.

Sekt|glas *das* champagne glass.

Sekundar|stufe *die* SCHULE secondary *Br* ODER high *Am* school level; **~ I** ≃ junior high school *Am;* **~ II** ≃ sixth form *Br,* ≃ senior high school *Am.*

Sekundarstufe

The term Sekundarstufe I refers to the first six years in secondary/high school (Gymnasium), for pupils aged 10 to 16, and Sekundarstufe II is applied to the sixth form level, also called the Oberstufe. The sixth form is a three-year programme of study leading to the final leaving certificate, for which students must choose main and subsidiary subjects. In general two or three foreign languages are taught at the Gymnasium.

Sekunde *(pl -n) die* second.

selber *pron (unver)* = selbst.

selbst ◇ *pron (unver):* **er ~** himself; **sie ~** herself, themselves *(pl);* **ich ~** myself; **wir ~** ourselves; **Sie ~** yourself, yourselves *(pl);* **ich ~** I myself; **du bist ~ schuld** it's your own fault; **das versteht sich von ~** that goes without saying ◇ *adv* even; **~ wenn** even if. ◆ **von selbst** *adv* - **1.** [freiwillig] of one's own accord - **2.** [automatisch] automatically, by itself.

Selbstachtung *die* self-respect.

selbständig = selbstständig.

Selbständigkeit = Selbstständigkeit.

Selbst|bedienung *die* self-service; **Restaurant mit ~** self-service restaurant.

Selbst|befriedigung *die* masturbation.

Selbst|beherrschung *die* self-control.

Selbst|beteiligung *die* [bei Versicherungen] excess.

selbstbewusst ◇ *adj* self-confident ◇ *adv* self-confidently.

Selbstbewusstsein *das* self-confidence.

Selbst|gespräch *das:* **~e führen** ODER **halten** to talk to o.s.

Selbstkosten|preis *der* cost price; **zum ~** at cost.

selbstlos ◇ *adj* unselfish, selfless ◇ *adv* unselfishly, selflessly.

Selbst|mord *der* suicide; **~ begehen** to commit suicide.

selbstsicher ◇ *adj* self-confident ◇ *adv* self-confidently.

selbstständig ◇ *adj* - **1.** [unabhängig] independent - **2.** [im Beruf] self-employed; **sich ~ machen** to set up on one's own ◇ *adv* [unabhängig] independently.

Selbstständigkeit *die* independence.

selbsttätig ◇ *adj* automatic ◇ *adv* automatically.

selbstverständlich ◇ *adj* natural; **das ist doch ~!** that goes without saying! ◇ *adv* naturally.

Selbst|verteidigung *die* self-defence.

Selbst|vertrauen *das* self-confidence.

Selbstzweck *der* end in itself.

selig ◇ *adj* - **1.** [glücklich - Person, Lächeln] blissfully happy; [- Schlummer] blissful - **2.** [heilig gesprochen] blessed - **3.** *geh* [tot] late ◇ *adv* [glücklich] blissfully.

Seligkeit *die* bliss.

Sellerie *der* celery.

selten ◇ *adj* rare ◇ *adv* - **1.** [kaum] rarely - **2.** [besonders] exceptionally.

Selters *(pl -) die* ODER *das* sparkling mineral water.

seltsam ◇ *adj* strange ◇ *adv* strangely.

Semester *(pl -) das* semester; **im achten ~ sein** to be in the second half of one's fourth year.

Semikolon *(pl -s) das* semicolon.

Semmel *(pl -n) die Österr & Süddt* (bread) roll.

Senat *(pl -e) der* - **1.** [gen & UNI] senate - **2.** [von Berlin, Bremen, Hamburg] *government of one of the three German cities that have 'Land' status* - **3.** RECHT panel of judges.

Senator *(pl -en) der* [gen & UNI] senator.

Senatorin *(pl -nen) die* [gen & UNI] senator.

senden *(prät sendete* ODER *sandte; perf hat gesendet* ODER *gesandt)* ◇ *vt* - **1.** *(reg)* [ausstrahlen] to broadcast - **2.** *(reg)* [funken] to transmit, to send - **3.** *(reg & unreg)* [schicken] to send; **etw an jn ~** to send sb sthg ◇ *vi (reg)* [übertragen] to broadcast.

Sende|pause *die* interval.

Sender *(pl -) der* - **1.** [Station] station - **2.** [Gerät] transmitter.

Sender

Sender is a false friend which has nothing to do with the English term "sender", meaning the person who sends a letter or parcel. Sender most commonly means a TV or radio broadcasting station such as ARD or ZDF in Germany and the BBC or ITV in Britain.
On the other hand, a person sending a letter would write Absender above their own address on the back of an envelope to show who the letter is from.

Sendung (pl -en) die - **1.** [das Senden] dispatch - **2.** [Postsendung - von Waren] consignment; [- Brief] letter; [- Paket] parcel - **3.** [ausgestrahltes Programm] programme - **4.** [Übertragung] broadcasting; **auf ~ gehen** to go on (the) air.
Senegal der Senegal.
Senf (pl -e) der mustard.
sengend adj scorching.
Senior (pl Senioren) der - **1.** [gen] senior - **2.** [von Mannschaft, Gruppe] oldest member. ➡ **Senioren** pl - **1.** [Alte] senior citizens - **2.** SPORT seniors.
Seniorenheim das old people's home.
Seniorin (pl -nen) die - **1.** [gen] senior - **2.** [von Mannschaft, Gruppe] oldest member.
senken vt - **1.** [gen] to lower; **beschämt senkte er den Kopf** he hung his head in shame - **2.** [Preis, Steuern] to cut. ➡ **sich senken** ref - **1.** [Wasserspiegel] to drop; [Erdreich] to subside - **2.** [Schranken, Vorhang] to come down.
senkrecht ◇ adj vertical ◇ adv vertically.
Senkrechte die - **1.** [Linie] vertical line - **2.** [Lot] perpendicular.
Sense (pl -n) die [Gerät] scythe.
sensibel ◇ adj sensitive ◇ adv sensitively.

---

sensibel

The German word sensibel is a false friend which has to do with feelings rather than the mind, and so it corresponds to the adjective "sensitive", not "sensible". Sie ist immer ein sensibles Kind gewesen therefore translates as "She has always been a sensitive child".
The English word "sensible" is most commonly translated by vernünftig. So if you want to tell someone in German: "Be sensible!" you could say Sei doch vernünftig!

---

sentimental ◇ adj sentimental ◇ adv sentimentally.

Seoul [se'uːl] nt Seoul.
separat ◇ adj separate; [Wohnung] self-contained ◇ adv separately.
September der September; **am siebten ~** on the seventh of September, on September the seventh; **Sonntag, den 1. ~** Sunday, 1 September; **im ~** in September; **Anfang/Ende ~** at the beginning/end of September; **Mitte ~** in mid-September.
Serbe (pl -n) der Serb.
Serbien nt Serbia.
Serbin (pl -nen) die Serb.
serbisch adj Serbian.
Serie ['zeːrjə] (pl -n) die - **1.** [Reihe, Senderei-he] series - **2.** [Satz] set - **3.** [von Produkten] line.
serienmäßig ◇ adj standard ◇ adv [konstruieren, anfertigen] on a mass scale; [mit etw ausgestattet] as standard.
seriös ◇ adj - **1.** [vertrauenswürdig] reliable - **2.** [würdevoll, solide] respectable ◇ adv [vertrauenswürdig] reliably; [würdevoll, solide] respectably.

---

seriös

The German adjective seriös should not be confused with the English "serious" – its primary meaning when used to describe people is "reliable" or "respectable". So you might translate the sentence Herr von Plato hat einen sehr seriösen Namen in der Textilbranche by the English "Herr von Plato has a very reliable reputation in the textile business."
The English adjective "serious" when used to describe people should be translated by ernst or ernsthaft – "Is he serious about her?" could be rendered as Meint er es ernst mit ihr? When referring to an accident, however, schwer is more commonly used. "He was in a serious car accident last week" would be translated as Er hat letzte Woche einen schweren Autounfall gehabt.

Serum (pl Seren) das serum.
servieren [zɛr'viːrən] vt [Speisen, Getränke] to serve.
Serviette [zɛr'vjɛtə] (pl -n) die serviette.
Servolenkung ['zɛrvolɛŋkʊŋ] die power steering (U).
Sesam der sesame seeds (pl).
Sessel (pl -) der armchair.
Sessellift der chairlift.
setzen (perf hat/ist gesetzt) ◇ vt (hat) - **1.** [gen] to put; **etw in jn/etw ~** to put sth in sb/sth/etw - **2.** [Denkmal, Grabmal] to put up - **3.** [Frist, Belohnung, Text] to set - **4.** [Pflanzen] to plant - **5.** [wetten]: **etw auf etw (A) ~** to put sth on sth - **6.** RW: **es setzt was** fam

there'll be trouble ⇔ *vi* - **1.** *(hat)* [wetten] to bet; **auf jn/etw ~** to bet on sb/sthg - **2.** *(hat, ist)* [befördern]: **über etw** *(A)* ~ [Fluss] to cross sthg; [Hindernis] to get over sthg. ◆ **sich setzen** *ref* - **1.** [hinsetzen] to sit down; **sich zu jm ~** to sit with sb - **2.** [Kaffeesatz] to settle.

Seuche *(pl* -n) *die* epidemic.

seufzen *vi* to sigh.

Seufzer *(pl* -) *der* sigh.

Sex *der* sex.

Sexualität *die* sexuality.

sexuell ⇔ *adj* sexual ⇔ *adv* sexually.

sexy *fam* ⇔ *adj (unver)* sexy ⇔ *adv* sexily.

sezieren *vt* & *vi* to dissect.

sfr. *(abk für Schweizer Franken)* Swiss francs.

Shampoo ['ʃampu] *(pl* -s) *das* shampoo.

Shareware *die* EDV shareware.

Sherry ['ʃɛri] *(pl* -s) *der* sherry.

Shorts ['ʃɔːɐts] *pl* shorts.

Show [ʃoː] *(pl* -s) *die* show.

Showmaster, in ['ʃoːmaːstɐ, rɪn] *(mpl* -; *fpl* -nen) *der, die* compere *Br,* emcee *Am.*

Shrimp *der* = Schrimp.

Sibirien [ziˈbiːrjən] *nt* Siberia.

sich *pron* - **1.** [Reflexivpronomen - unbestimmt] oneself; [- Person] himself (*f* herself), themselves *(pl);* [- Ding, Tier] itself, themselves *(pl);* [- bei Höflichkeitsform] yourself, yourselves *(pl);* **~** *(D)* **etw kaufen** to buy (o.s.) sthg - **2.** [reziprokes Pronomen] each other.

Sichel *(pl* -n) *die* sickle.

sicher ⇔ *adj* - **1.** [ungefährdet] safe; **in ~em Abstand** at a safe distance; **vor jm/etw ~ sein** to be safe from sb/sthg - **2.** [zuverlässig] reliable - **3.** [überzeugt, gewiss] sure, certain; **sich** *(D)* **einer Sache** *(G)* **~ sein** to be sure ODER certain about sthg - **4.** [selbstbewusst] self-confident ⇔ *adv* - **1.** [ungefährdet] safely - **2.** [zuverlässig] reliably; **etw ~ wissen** to know sthg for sure; **langsam aber ~** slowly but surely - **3.** [sicherlich] certainly, definitely; **das ist ~ richtig, aber** ... that may be true, but ...; **Sie haben es ~ gemerkt** you must have noticed it - **4.** [selbstbewusst] self-confidently. ◆ **aber sicher** *interj* of course!

sicher|gehen *(perf* ist sichergegangen) *vi (unreg)* to play safe.

Sicherheit *(pl* -en) *die* - **1.** [Schutz - persönliche, öffentliche, im Straßenverkehr] safety; [- soziale, wirtschaftliche, innere] security; **in ~ (vor jm/etw) sein** to be safe (from sb/sthg) - **2.** [Bestimmtheit] certainty - **3.** [Fundiertheit, Zuverlässigkeit] reliability - **4.** [Selbstbewusstsein] confidence - **5.** [Bürgschaft] surety.

Sicherheits|gurt *der* seat belt.

sicherheitshalber *adv* to be on the safe side.

Sicherheits|nadel *die* safety pin.

sicherlich *adv* certainly.

sichern *vt* to secure. ◆ **sich sichern** *ref* - **1.** [sich absichern] to secure o.s.; **sich gegen etw ~** to protect o.s. against sthg - **2.** [sich verschaffen]: **sich** *(D)* **etw ~** to secure sthg.

sicher|stellen *vt* - **1.** [beschlagnahmen - Geld, Fund] to seize; [- Spuren] to secure - **2.** [gewährleisten] to safeguard.

Sicherung *(pl* -en) *die* - **1.** [Schutz] safeguarding - **2.** ELEKTR fuse - **3.** [Schutzmaßnahme] safeguard.

Sicht *die* - **1.** [Aussicht] visibility; **außer ~** out of sight - **2.** [Betrachtungsweise] point of view; **aus meiner ~** from my point of view. ◆ **auf lange Sicht** *adv* long-term. ◆ **in Sicht** *adv* in sight; **Land in ~!** land ahoy!

sichtbar ⇔ *adj* - **1.** [deutlich] clear - **2.** [wahrnehmbar] visible ⇔ *adv* [deutlich] clearly.

sichten *vt* - **1.** [einsehen] to sift through - **2.** *geh* [sehen] to sight.

sichtlich ⇔ *adj* obvious ⇔ *adv* obviously.

Sicht|weite *die* visibility *(U);* **außer/in ~ sein** to be out of/in sight.

sickern *(perf* ist gesickert) *vi* [fließen] to seep.

sie *pron* - **1.** [Singular - Nominativ] she; [- Akkusativ] her; **~ wars!** it was her! - **2.** [Plural - Nominativ] they; [- Akkusativ] them - **3.** [Tier, Gegenstand] it.

Sie *pron (Singular und Plural)* you.

Sieb *(pl* -e) *das* [Küchensieb] sieve; [Teesieb] strainer.

sieben[1] ⇔ *vt* - **1.** [durchsieben] to sieve - **2.** [auswählen] to weed out ⇔ *vi* [auswählen] to pick and choose.

sieben[2] *num* seven; *siehe auch* sechs.

Sieben *(pl* - ODER -en) *die* seven; *siehe auch* Sechs.

siebenfach *adj* & *adv* sevenfold.

siebenhundert *num* seven hundred.

siebenmal *adv* seven times.

siebentausend *num* seven thousand.

siebte, siebente, r, s *adj* seventh; *siehe auch* sechste.

Siebte *(pl* -n) *der, die, das* seventh; *siehe auch* Sechste.

siebtel *adj (unver)* seventh; *siehe auch* sechstel.

Siebtel *(pl* -) *das* seventh; *siehe auch* Sechstel.

siebzehn *num* seventeen; *siehe auch* sechs.

Siebzehn *(pl* -en) *die* seventeen; *siehe auch* Sechs.

siebzig *num* seventy; *siehe auch* sechs.

Siebzigerjahre, siebziger Jahre *pl:* **die ~ seventies.

sieden *(prät* siedete ODER sott; *perf* hat gesie-

det ODER **hat gesotten** <> *vi (reg)* [Flüssigkeit] to boil <> *vt* to boil.

Siedler, in *(mpl -; fpl -nen) der, die* settler.

Siedlung *(pl -en) die* [Häusergruppe] housing estate *Br* ODER development *Am.*

Sieg *(pl -e) der* victory; **der ~ über jn/etw** the victory over sb/sthg.

Siegel *(pl -) das* seal.

siegen *vi* to win; **über jn/etw ~** to beat sb/sthg.

Sieger *(pl -) der* winner.

Siegerlehrung *die* medals ceremony.

Siegerin *(pl -nen) die* winner.

siehe *vi* [in Text]: **~ oben** see above; **~ Seite 15** see page 15.

sieht *präs* ▭ sehen.

siezen *vt* to address as 'Sie'. ◆ **sich siezen** *ref* to address each other as 'Sie'.

Signal *(pl -e) das* signal; **das ~ zu etw geben** to give the signal for sthg.

Silbe *(pl -n) die* syllable; **jn/etw mit keiner ~ erwähnen** *fig* not to say a word about sb/sthg.

Silbenltrennung *die* syllabification *(U).*

Silber *das* silver.

Silberhochlzeit *die* silver wedding (anniversary).

Silberlmedaille *die* silver medal.

silbern <> *adj* [aus Silber] silver <> *adv* [wie Silber - glänzen] with a silvery sheen.

Silo *(pl -s)* ODER *das* silo.

Silvester [zɪl'vɛstɐ] *(pl -) der* ODER *das* New Year's Eve; **~ feiern** to see the New Year in.

Simulation *(pl -en) die* EDV simulation.

simultan <> *adj* simultaneous <> *adv* simultaneously.

sind *präs* ▭ sein.

Sinfonie *die* = Symphonie.

Sinfoniker, in *der, die* = Symphoniker.

Singapur *nt* Singapore.

singen *(prät* sang; *perf* hat gesungen) <> *vi* - 1. [musizieren] to sing - 2. *salopp abw* [aussagen] to squeal <> *vt* to sing; **jn in den Schlaf ~** to sing sb to sleep.

Single ['sɪŋ(g)l] *(pl -* ODER *-s)* <> *der (pl Singles)* single person <> *die (pl Single(s))* single.

Singular *der* GRAM singular.

Singlvogel *der* songbird.

sinken *(prät* sank; *perf* ist gesunken) *vi* - 1. [einsinken, versinken] to sink - 2. [abnehmen, niedersinken] to fall.

Sinn *(pl -e) der* - 1. [Bedeutung, Wahrnehmungsfähigkeit] sense; **im übertragenen ~** figuratively - 2. [Gefühl]: **einen/keinen ~ für etw haben** to have a/no feeling for sthg; **er hat keinen ~ für Humor** he has no sense of humour.

Sinnlbild *das* symbol.

Sinneslorgan *das* sense organ.

sinngemäß <> *adj*: **eine ~e Übersetzung von etw** a translation which conveys the general meaning of sthg <> *adv*: **etw ~ wiedergeben** to give the gist of sthg.

sinnig <> *adj* clever <> *adv* cleverly.

sinnlich <> *adj* - 1. [körperlichen Genuss betreffend] sensual - 2. [Sinneswahrnehmung betreffend] sensory <> *adv* - 1. [körperlichen Genuss betreffend] sensually - 2. [Sinneswahrnehmung betreffend] through the senses.

sinnlos <> *adj* - 1. [unsinnig] pointless - 2. *abw* [maßlos] blind *(vor Subst)* <> *adv* - 1. [unsinnig] pointlessly - 2. *abw* [maßlos - zerstören] in a blind rage; **sich ~ betrinken** to get blind drunk.

Sinnlosigkeit *(pl -en) die* - 1. [Wesen] pointlessness - 2. [Handlung] pointless action.

sinnvoll <> *adj* - 1. [befriedigend] meaningful - 2. [zweckmäßig] sensible <> *adv* - 1. [befriedigend] meaningfully - 2. [zweckmäßig] sensibly.

Sintflut *die* - 1. [biblisch] Flood - 2. [Übermaß - von Post, Anrufen] flood.

Sippe *(pl -n) die* clan.

Sirene *(pl -n) die* siren.

Sirup *der* - 1. [für Saft] syrup - 2. [aus Zucker] treacle *Br,* molasses *Am.*

Sitte *(pl -n) die* - 1. [Gepflogenheit] custom; **etw ist (bei jm) ~** sthg is the custom (with sb) - 2. *(ohne pl) fam* [Sittenpolizei] vice squad. ◆ **Sitten** *pl* - 1. [Benehmen] manners - 2. [Moral] morals.

sittenwidrig <> *adj* morally offensive <> *adv* in a morally offensive way.

sittlich <> *adj* moral <> *adv* morally.

Situation *(pl -en) die* situation.

Sitz *(pl -e) der* - 1. [in Parlament, Möbelstück] seat - 2. *(ohne pl)* [von Institution, Firma] headquarters *(pl);* [von Regierung] seat - 3. *(ohne pl)* [von Kleidung] fit.

sitzen *(prät* saß; *perf* hat gesessen) *vi* - 1. [gen] to sit; **bleiben Sie doch bitte ~!** please don't get up!; **auf etw** *(D)* **~** to be sitting on sthg - 2. [Mitglied sein]: **im Vorstand ~** to sit on the board (of directors); **im Parlament ~** to have a seat in parliament - 3. [sich befinden] to be; [Firma] to be based - 4. [passen] to fit - 5. *fam* [im Gefängnis sein] to be inside - 6. *fam* [Gelerntes]: **das Gedicht sitzt** the poem has stuck; **bei dem Meister sitzt jeder Handgriff** the expert can do every move in his sleep - 7. *fam* [nicht loswerden]: **auf etw** *(D)* **~** to be stuck with sthg.

sitzen bleiben *(perf* ist sitzen geblieben) *vi (unreg)* - 1. [in Schule] to have to repeat a year - 2. [auf Waren]: **auf etw** *(D)* **~** to be stuck with sthg.

sitzen lassen *vt (unreg) fam* - 1. [Person]: **jn ~** [versetzen] to stand sb up; [verlassen] to walk out on sb.

Sitzlgelegenheit *die* seat.

Sitz|ordnung die seating plan.

Sitz|platz der seat.

Sitzung (pl -en) die [Konferenz - von Vorstand, Abteilung] meeting; [- von Bundestag] sitting.

Sizilien [zi'tsi:ljən] nt Sicily.

Skala (pl -s ODER -len) die scale; [von Farben] range.

Skalpell (pl -e) das scalpel.

Skandal (pl -e) der scandal.

skandalös <> adj scandalous <> adv scandalously.

Skandinavien [skandi'na:vjən] nt Scandinavia.

Skandinavier, in [skandi'na:vjɐ, rɪn] (mpl -; fpl -nen) der, die Scandinavian.

skandinavisch [skandi'na:vɪʃ] adj Scandinavian.

Skat der skat; ~ **spielen** to play skat.

Skelett (pl -e) das skeleton.

Skepsis die scepticism.

skeptisch <> adj sceptical <> adv sceptically.

Ski, Schi [ʃiː] (pl - ODER -er) der ski; **auf ~ern** on skis; ~ **fahren** ODER **laufen** to ski.

Ski|fahren das skiing.

Ski|gebiet das skiing area.

Ski|langlauf der cross-country skiing.

Ski|läufer, in der, die skier.

Ski|lehrer, in der, die skiing instructor.

Ski|lift der ski lift.

Ski|piste die ski run.

Ski|urlaub der skiing holiday Br ODER vacation Am.

Skizze (pl -n) die - 1. [Zeichnung] sketch - 2. [Text] outline.

skizzieren vt - 1. [zeichnen] to sketch - 2. [schreiben] to outline.

Sklave ['skla:və] (pl -n) der slave.

Sklavin ['skla:vɪn] (pl -nen) die slave.

Skorpion (pl -e) der - 1. [Tier] scorpion - 2. ASTROL [Sternzeichen, Person] Scorpio; ~ **sein** to be a Scorpio.

Skrupel (pl -) der scruple.

skrupellos <> adj unscrupulous <> adv unscrupulously.

Skulptur (pl -en) die sculpture.

Slalom (pl -s) der slalom (U).

Slawe (pl -n) der Slav.

Slawin (pl -nen) die Slav.

slawisch adj Slavonic.

Slip (pl -s) der briefs (pl).

Slowakei die Slovakia.

Slowenien nt Slovenia.

Smoking (pl -s) der dinner jacket Br, tuxedo Am.

SMS (abk für Short Message System) die (ohne Pl) SMS.

Snowboard (pl -s) das snowboard; ~ **fahren** to go snowboarding.

so <> adv - 1. [auf diese Art] like this; [auf jene Art] like that; **lass es ~, wie es ist** leave it

as it is; ~ **ist es!** fam that's right!; **weiter ~!** keep it up!; **gut ~!** fam good; ~ **was** something like that - 2. [mit Adjektiv, Adverb] so; **eine ~ schwierige Prüfung** such a difficult exam; ~ ... **wie** ... as ... as ...; **sie ist ~ alt wie du** she's as old as you - 3. [mit Substantiv, Pronomen]: ~ **einer/eine/eins** such a; ~ **ein Pech!** what bad luck!; ~ **ein Unsinn!** what nonsense!; ~ **eine Art Jacke** a sort of jacket; ~ **mancher** many (people) - 4. [mit Geste] this; **er war ~ groß** he was this big - 5. fam [etwa] about, around - 6. [bei Zitaten]: ..., ~ **der Minister** ..., said the minister - 7. fam [ohne etwas] as it is - 8. fam [kostenlos] for free - 9. fam [im Allgemeinen]: **was hast du sonst noch ~ gemacht?** what else did you do, then? <> konj as; **laufen, ~ schnell man kann** to run as fast as one can; ~ ..., **dass** so ... that <> interj: ~, **das wars** so, that's it; **ach ~!** oh, I see! **◆ so dass** konj = sodass. **◆ oder so** adv fam or so.

s. o. (abk für siehe oben) see above.

SO (abk für Südost) SE.

sobald konj as soon as.

Socke (pl -n) die sock.

Sockel (pl -) der [von Denkmal] plinth; [von Haus] base.

sodass, so dass konj so that.

soeben adv just.

Sofa (pl -s) das sofa.

soff prät ⊳ saufen.

sofort adv - 1. [unverzüglich] immediately, straight away - 2. fam [gleich] in a moment.

Software|paket das EDV bundled software (U), software package.

sog prät ⊳ saugen.

sogar adv even.

Sohle (pl -n) die [Fuß-, Schuhsohle] sole.

Sohn (pl Söhne) der son.

solang, solange konj as long as.

solche, r, s det such.

Soldat (pl -en) der soldier.

Solidaritäts|zuschlag der special tax levied to help finance the reconstruction of former East Germany.

Solist, in (mpl -en, fpl -nen) der, die soloist.

sollen (perf hat gesollt ODER -) <> aux (perf hat sollen) - 1. [als Aufforderung] to be supposed to; **soll ich das Fenster aufmachen?** shall I open the window? - 2. [als Vermutung]: **er soll 108 Jahre alt sein** he is said to be 108 years old; **was soll das heißen?** what's that supposed to mean? - 3. [konjunktivisch] should, ought to - 4. [als Bedingung]: **sollte sie noch kommen, sag ihr ...** if she should turn up, tell her ... <> vi (perf hat gesollt): **die Ware soll nach München** the goods are meant to go to Munich; **soll er doch!** fam let him!; **was soll das?** fam what's all this?; **was solls!** fam what the hell!

◇ vt (perf hat gesollt): **warum soll ich das?** why should I?

solo adv - **1.** [im Solo] solo - **2.** fam [allein] on one's own.

Somalia nt Somalia.

Sommer (pl -) der summer.

Sommer|ferien pl summer holiday Br ODER vacation Am.

Sommer|sprosse die freckle.

Sommer|zeit die summertime.

Sonate (pl -n) die MUS sonata.

Sonderan|gebot das special offer; **im ~** on special offer.

sonderbar ◇ adj strange ◇ adv strangely.

Sonder|fahrt die amt [Zugfahrt] special train; [Busfahrt] special bus.

Sonder|fall der special case.

sondergleichen adj unparalleled.

sonderlich ◇ adj - **1.** [besondere] particular - **2.** [sonderbar] peculiar ◇ adv: **nicht ~** not particularly.

Sondermüll der hazardous waste.

sondern konj but.

Sonder|schule die special school.

Sonett (pl -e) das sonnet.

Sonnabend (pl -e) der Saturday; siehe auch Samstag.

sonnabends adv on Saturdays; siehe auch samstags.

Sonne (pl -n) die sun; **die ~ geht auf/unter** the sun rises/sets; **die ~ scheint** the sun is shining; **in der prallen ~** in the blazing sun.

sonnen ➧ **sich sonnen** ref - **1.** [sich bräunen] to sun o.s. - **2.** [in Erfolg, Ruhm]: **sich in etw** (D) **~** fig to bask in sthg.

Sonnenauf|gang der sunrise.

Sonnen|blume die sunflower.

Sonnen|brand der sunburn (U).

Sonnen|brille die sunglasses (pl).

Sonnen|creme die sun cream.

Sonnen|energie die solar energy.

Sonnen|finsternis die solar eclipse.

Sonnen|licht das sunlight.

Sonnen|schein der sunshine.

Sonnen|schirm der sunshade.

Sonnen|schutz der protection against the sun.

Sonnen|stich der sunstroke.

Sonnen|strahl der sunbeam.

Sonnen|system das solar system.

Sonnen|uhr die sundial.

Sonnenunter|gang der sunset.

Sonnen|wende die solstice.

sonnig adj sunny.

Sonntag (pl -e) der Sunday; siehe auch Samstag.

sonntags adv on Sundays; siehe auch samstags.

sonst ◇ adv - **1.** [außerdem] else; **~ nichts** nothing else; **~ noch etwas/jemand?** fam anything/anybody else?; **~ noch Fragen?**

any more questions? - **2.** [abgesehen hiervon] otherwise, apart from that; **wer/was (denn) ~?** who/what else? - **3.** [gewöhnlich] usually ◇ konj or (else).

sonstig adj other.

sonst wo adv fam somewhere else; [in Fragen] anywhere else.

sonst woher adv fam somewhere else; [in Fragen] anywhere else; **die Leute kamen (von) ~** people came from all over; **das könnte ~ stammen** that could be from anywhere.

sonst wohin adv fam somewhere else; [in Fragen] anywhere else.

sooft konj whenever.

Sopran (pl -e) der - **1.** [Stimmlage - Frau] soprano; [- Knabe] treble - **2.** (ohne pl) [Stimme im Chor - Frauen] sopranos (pl); [- Knaben] trebles (pl) - **3.** [Sängerin] soprano; [Sänger] treble.

Sorge (pl -n) die - **1.** [Problem] worry; **sich um jn/etw ~n machen** to worry about sb/sthg - **2.** [Pflege] care; **dafür tragen, dass ...** to make sure that ... ➧ **keine Sorge** interj [keine Angst] don't worry!

sorgen vi: **für etw ~** to see to sthg; **für jn ~** to look after sb. ➧ **sich sorgen** ref: **sich um jn/etw ~** to be worried about sb/sthg.

Sorgen|kind das problem child.

Sorgerecht das custody.

Sorgfalt die care.

sorgfältig ◇ adj careful ◇ adv carefully.

sorglos ◇ adj carefree ◇ adv in a carefree way.

Sorte (pl -n) die sort, type. ➧ **Sorten** pl WIRTSCH foreign currency (sg).

sortieren vt to sort.

Sortiment (pl -e) das range.

sosehr konj however much.

Soße (pl -n) die [für Nudeln, Pudding] sauce; [für Braten] gravy; [für Salat] dressing.

Sound|karte die EDV sound card.

Souvenir [suvə'ni:ɐ] (pl -s) das souvenir.

souverän [zuvə'rɛ:n] ◇ adj - **1.** POL sovereign - **2.** [überlegen] masterful ◇ adv - **1.** POL: **~ herrschen** ODER **regieren** to have sovereign power - **2.** [überlegen] masterfully.

soviel konj as far as; **~ ich weiß** as far as I know.

so viel adv so much; **~ du willst** as much as you want; **noch einmal ~** as much again; **dreimal ~** three times as much; **~ wie** as much as; **halb ~ (wie)** half as much/many (as).

soweit konj as far as; **~ ich weiß** as far as I know.

so weit ◇ adj: **~ sein** to be ready; **es ist ~** it is time ◇ adv on the whole; **~ wie möglich** as far as possible; **~ ich weiß** as far as I know.

so wenig adv: **~ wie möglich** as little as possible.

sowie konj as well as.

sowieso adv anyway.

Sowjetunion die: **die ehemalige ~** the former Soviet Union.

sowohl konj: **~ A als auch B** A as well as B, both A and B.

sozial <> adj social; [Einstellung] socially aware; **~er Beruf** caring profession <> adv socially; [handeln] in a socially aware manner; **~ eingestellt** socially aware.

Sozialabgaben pl social security contributions.

Sozialamt das social security office.

Sozialarbeiter, in der, die social worker.

Sozialdemokrat, in der, die Social Democrat.

Sozialfall der: **ein ~ sein** to be dependent on state benefit.

Sozialhilfe die ≃ income support Br, ≃ welfare Am.

Sozialismus der socialism.

sozialkritisch adj socially critical.

Sozialleistungen pl social security benefits.

Sozialminister, in der, die social services minister.

Sozialpädagogik die social education.

Sozialpolitik die social policy.

Sozialstaat der welfare state.

Sozialversicherung die social security.

Sozialwohnung die ≃ council flat Br, ≃ low-rent apartment Am.

Soziologie die sociology.

sozusagen adv so to speak.

Spachtel (pl -) die ODER der spatula.

spachteln vt [mit Spachtelmasse] to fill.

Spagat (pl -e) der - 1. SPORT: **einen ~ machen** to do the splits - 2. fig balancing act.

Spagetti, Spaghetti pl spaghetti (U).

Spalt (pl -e) der crack; **etw einen ~ weit** ODER **breit öffnen** to open sthg a crack.

Spalte (pl -n) die - 1. [Öffnung] crack - 2. TYPO column.

spalten vt [gen, CHEM & PHYS] to split; [Substanz, Verbindung] to break down.

Spaltung (pl -en) die - 1. [Teilen - von Land, Partei] splitting up (U); [Teilung - von Land, Partei] split - 2. CHEM & PHYS splitting (U); [von Substanz] breaking down (U) - 3. MED split.

Span (pl Späne) der shaving.

Spanferkel das KÜCHE suckling pig.

Spange (pl -n) die - 1. [Schmuckstück] slide Br, barrette Am - 2. [Zahnspange] brace.

Spanien nt Spain.

Spanier, in ['ʃpa:niɐ, rɪn] (mpl -; fpl -nen) der, die Spaniard.

spanisch <> adj Spanish <> adv: **~ sprechen** to speak Spanish.

Spanisch(e) das Spanish; siehe auch Englisch(e).

spann prät ⊳ spinnen.

Spannbetttuch das fitted sheet.

Spanne (pl -n) die period; **in der/einer ~ von … bis** between … and …

spannen <> vt [Bogen] to draw; [Muskeln] to tense; [Schnur] to tighten; [Netz] to stretch out <> vi - 1. fam [heimlich zusehen] to take a peep - 2. [zu eng sein] to be too tight. **⇢ sich spannen** ref: **sich über etw** (A) **~** to span sthg.

spannend <> adj exciting <> adv excitingly.

Spannkraft die vigour.

Spannung (pl -en) die - 1. [gen] tension - 2. [elektrisch] voltage; **unter ~ stehen** to be live. **⇢ Spannungen** pl tension (sg).

Spannungsgebiet das area of tension.

Spannweite die wingspan.

Spanplatte die chipboard (U).

Sparbuch das savings book.

Sparbüchse die money box.

sparen <> vt to save; **spar dir deine dummen Bemerkungen** you can keep your silly remarks <> vi to save; **an etw** (D) **~** to save on sthg; **für** ODER **auf etw** (A) **~** to save (up) for sthg.

Spargel (pl -) der asparagus (U).

Sparkasse die savings bank.

spärlich <> adj [Haare] sparse; [Beifall, Maßnahmen] meagre <> adv [bekleidet] scantily; [bewachsen, wachsen] sparsely.

Sparprogramm das economy drive.

sparsam <> adj economical; **mit etw ~ sein** to be economical with sthg <> adv economically; **mit etw ~ umgehen** to be economical with sthg.

Sparsamkeit die economy.

Sparschwein das piggy bank.

Sparte (pl -n) die - 1. WIRTSCH line of business - 2. [in Zeitungen] section.

Spaß (pl Späße) der - 1. [Vergnügen] fun; **zum ~** for fun; **an etw** (D) **~ haben** to enjoy sthg; **jm den ~ verderben** to spoil sb's fun; **es macht mir ~** I enjoy it; **Auto fahren macht mir keinen ~** I don't enjoy driving; **viel ~!** have fun!; **da hört der ~ auf** I draw the line at that; **mir ist der ~ vergangen** it's no fun any more - 2. [Scherz] joke; [Streich] prank; **aus** ODER **im** ODER **zum ~** as a joke; **~ machen** [nicht ernst meinen] to be joking; **~/keinen ~ verstehen** to have a/no sense of humour.

spaßen vi to joke.

spät <> adj late; **bis in die ~e Nacht** until late at night; **wie ~ ist es?** what's the time? <> adv late; **sie kam mal wieder zu ~** she was late again; **von früh bis ~** from dawn to dusk.

Spaten (pl -) der spade.

später adj & adv later. **⇢ bis später** interj see you later!

spätestens adv at the latest.
Spätllese (pl -n) die [Wein] late vintage.
Spätnachlmittag der late afternoon.
Spätlsommer der late summer.
Spätvorlstellung die late show.
Spatz (pl -en) der - **1.** [Tier] sparrow - **2.** fam [Anrede] pet.
Spätzle pl Süddt small round noodles, similar to macaroni.
spazieren (perf ist spaziert) vi to stroll.
spazieren gehen (perf ist spazieren gegangen) vi (unreg) to go for a walk.
Spazierlgang der walk.
Spazierlgänger, in (mpl -; fpl -nen) der, die person going for a walk.
SPD [espe:'de:] (abk für Sozialdemokratische Partei Deutschlands) die SPD.
Specht (pl -e) der woodpecker.
Speck der - **1.** [tierisch - von Schwein] pork fat; [- geräuchert, durchwachsen] bacon; [- von Wal, Robbe] blubber - **2.** fam [menschlich] flab.
Spediteur, in [ʃpedi'tø:ɐ̯, rɪn] (mpl -e; fpl -nen) der, die haulier; [für Umzug] furniture mover.
Spedition [ʃpedi'tsjo:n] (pl -en) die haulage firm; [für Umzug] removal firm.
Speer (pl -e) der - **1.** SPORT javelin - **2.** [Waffe] spear.
Speiche (pl -n) die spoke.
Speichel der saliva.
Speicher (pl -) der - **1.** [Dachboden] loft - **2.** EDV memory.
speichern vt - **1.** [ansammeln, abspeichern] to store - **2.** EDV to save.
speien ['ʃpaɪən] (prät spie; perf hat gespie(e)n) ◇ vt [Feuer, Lava] to spew; [Wasser] to spout ◇ vi to vomit.
Speise (pl -n) die dish; **warme ~n** hot food; **~n und Getränke** meals and drinks.
speisen geh ◇ vt - **1.** [essen] to dine on - **2.** [zu essen geben] to feed ◇ vi to dine.
Speiselröhre die gullet.
Speiselsaal der dining room.
Speiselwagen der dining car.
Spektakel (pl -) ◇ das [Aufführung, Ereignis] spectacle ◇ der racket.
Spektrum (pl Spektren) das spectrum.
Spekulant, in (mpl -en; fpl -nen) der, die speculator.
Spekulation (pl -en) die speculation.
spekulieren vi - **1.** fam [hoffen]: **auf etw** (A) **~** to hope to get sthg - **2.** WIRTSCH: **(auf etw** (A)**) ~** to speculate (on sthg) - **3.** [mutmaßen]: **über etw** (A) **~** to speculate about sthg.
spendabel adj fam generous.
Spende (pl -n) die donation.
spenden ◇ vt to donate; [Blut] to give ◇ vi to give.

spenden

The German verb spenden is a false friend which might easily be taken to mean "to spend". In fact spenden means "to donate", often to a charitable cause — money or blood, for example. Ich habe letzte Woche Blut gespendet would best be translated as "I gave blood last week". The English verb "to spend" is used in a variety of contexts, of which the most important are: "to spend money" — Geld ausgeben, and "to spend the weekend" — das Wochenende verbringen.

Spender, in (mpl -; fpl -nen) der, die donor; **wer war der edle ~?** who do I/we have to thank for this?
spendieren vt: **(jm) etw ~** to buy (sb) sthg.
Sperling (pl -e) der sparrow.
Sperma (pl -ta ODER Spermen) das sperm.
Sperre (pl -n) die - **1.** [Verbot & SPORT] ban; **eine ~ verhängen/aufheben** to impose/lift a ban - **2.** [Absperrung] barrier - **3.** TECH locking device.
sperren vt - **1.** [einsperren]: **jn/etw in etw** (A) **~** to shut sb/sthg in sthg - **2.** [Konto, Kredit] to freeze; [Scheck] to stop - **3.** [Straße] to close - **4.** SPORT to ban. ◆ **sich sperren** ref: **sich (gegen etw) ~** to resist (sthg).
Sperrholz das plywood.
sperrig adj bulky.
Sperrlmüll der bulky refuse (collected separately from normal refuse).
Sperrlsitz der [in Zirkus] ringside seat.
Sperrlstunde die closing time.
Sperrung (pl -en) die - **1.** [von Straße] closing - **2.** [von Konto, Kredit] freezing; [von Scheck] stopping.
Spesen pl expenses; **auf ~** on expenses.
Spezi (pl -s) fam ◇ der Süddt mate ◇ das cola and orangeade.
spezialisieren ◆ **sich spezialisieren** ref: **sich auf etw** (A) **~** to specialize in sthg.
Spezialist, in (mpl -en; fpl -nen) der, die specialist.
Spezialität (pl -en) die speciality Br, specialty Am.
speziell ◇ adj special ◇ adv specially.
spicken ◇ vt - **1.** KÜCHE: **etw mit etw ~** to lard sthg with sthg - **2.** [ausstatten]: **etw mit etw ~** [Text, Rede] to pepper sthg with sthg ◇ vi to crib.
Spicklzettel der fam crib (sheet).
spie prät ▷ speien.
Spiegel (pl -) der - **1.** [Gegenstand] mirror - **2.** [von Gewässern] surface - **3.** MED level.
Spiegellbild das reflection.
Spiegellei das fried egg.
spiegelglatt adj very slippery.

spiegeln *vi* to shine. ◆ **sich spiegeln** *ref:* **sich in etw** *(D)* ~ to be reflected in sthg.

Spiegelreflexkamera *die* reflex camera.

Spiel *(pl* -e) *das* - **1.** [Vergnügen, Wettkampf] game; **machen wir noch ein ~?** shall we have another game?; **ein ~ mit jm treiben** to play games with sb - **2.** [von Musiker] playing; [von Schauspieler] acting; [von Sportler, Mannschaft] game - **3.** TECH play - **4.** [Glücksspiel] gambling - **5.** *RW:* **auf dem ~ stehen** to be at stake; **etw aufs ~ setzen** to risk sthg; **jn/etw aus dem ~ lassen** to leave sb/sthg out of it.

Spielautomat *der* slot machine, fruit machine *Br*.

spielen ◇ *vi* - **1.** [gen] to play; **mit jm/etw ~** to play with sb/sthg - **2.** [als Schauspieler] to act - **3.** [Roman, Film] to be set - **4.** [Glücksspiel machen] to gamble; **um etw ~** to play for sthg - **5.** [einsetzen]: **seine Beziehungen ~ lassen** to pull strings; **seinen Charme ~ lassen** to use one's charm ◇ *vt* to play; **Klavier/Saxophon ~** to play the piano/saxophone; **Lotto ~** to do the lottery; **den Unschuldigen ~** to act ODER play the innocent.

spielend *adv* - **1.** [einfach] easily - **2.** [beim Spielen] through play.

Spieler *(pl* -) *der* - **1.** [Mitspieler] player - **2.** [Glücksspieler] gambler.

Spielerin *(pl* -nen) *die* - **1.** [Mitspielerin] player - **2.** [Glücksspielerin] gambler.

spielerisch ◇ *adj* - **1.** [locker] effortless - **2.** [Fähigkeit - in Sport, Musik] as a player; [- in Theater] as an actor ◇ *adv* - **1.** [locker] effortlessly - **2.** [in Sport]: **eine ~ enttäuschende Mannschaft** a team that gave a disappointing performance.

Spielfeld *das* [für Fußball, Hockey] field, pitch *Br*; [für Tennis, Federball, Volleyball] court.

Spielfilm *der* feature film.

Spielkonsole *(pl* -n) *die* game ODER video console.

Spielplan *der* - **1.** [von Theatern] programme - **2.** SPORT fixture list.

Spielplatz *der* playground.

Spielraum *der* leeway.

Spielregel *die* rule.

Spielverderber, in *(mpl* -; *fpl* -nen) *der, die* spoilsport.

Spielwaren *pl* toys.

Spielzeug *das* - **1.** *(ohne pl)* [Spielsachen] toys *(pl)* - **2.** [einzelnes Spielgerät] toy.

Spieß *(pl* -e) *der* spit; **am ~** spit-roasted; **den ~ umdrehen** *fig* to turn the tables.

spießen *vt:* **etw auf etw** *(A)* ~ to skewer sthg with sthg.

Spießer, in *(mpl* -; *fpl* -nen) *der, die abw* (petit) bourgeois.

Spinat *(pl* -e) *der* spinach.

Spind *der* locker.

Spinne *(pl* -n) *die* spider.

spinnen *(prät* spann; *perf* hat gesponnen) ◇ *vt* to spin ◇ *vi* - **1.** *fam* [verrückt sein] to be crazy; **du spinnst!, spinnst du?** are you crazy? - **2.** [arbeiten] to spin.

Spinnwebe *(pl* -n) *die* cobweb.

Spion *(pl* -e) *der* - **1.** [Geheimagent] spy - **2.** [Türspion] peephole.

Spionage [ʃpio'na:ʒə] *die* spying; **~ betreiben** to spy.

spionieren *vi* - **1.** [Spionage treiben] to spy - **2.** *fam abw* [neugierig sein] to snoop.

Spionin *(pl* -nen) *die* spy.

Spirale *(pl* -n) *die* - **1.** [gewundene Linie] spiral - **2.** MED coil.

Spirituose *(pl* -n) *die amt* spirit.

Spiritus *(pl* -se) *der* spirit.

spitz ◇ *adj* - **1.** [Ende, Schuh, Bogen, Bemerkung] pointed; [Bleistift, Messer, Nadel] sharp - **2.** [Winkel] acute - **3.** *fam* [geil]: **auf jn ~ sein** to have the hots for sb; **~ darauf sein, etw zu tun** to be dying to do sthg ◇ *adv* - **1.** [zulaufen] to a point - **2.** [bemerken] pointedly.

Spitze *(pl* -n) *die* - **1.** [von Messer, Bleistift] point; [von Kirchturm, Baum] top; [von Berg] peak - **2.** [Führung]: **an der ~** [in Betrieb, Partei] at the top; [in Rennen] in the lead - **3.** [Höchstwert] maximum; **etw auf die ~ treiben** *fig* to take sthg too far - **4.** *fam* [besonders gut]: **~ sein** to be great - **5.** [Bemerkung] gibe.

Spitzel *(pl* -) *der* informer.

spitzen *vt* - **1.** [spitz machen] to sharpen - **2.** [Ohren] to prick up.

Spitzenreiter, in *der, die* leader.

spitzfindig *abw* ◇ *adj* hairsplitting ◇ *adv:* **~ argumentieren** to split hairs.

Spitzname *der* nickname.

Splitter *(pl* -) *der* [aus Holz, Glas] splinter; [von Bombe] fragment.

Splittergruppe *die* splinter group.

splittern *(perf* hat/ist gesplittert) *vi* to splinter.

splitternackt *adj & adv* stark naked.

SPÖ [ɛspeː'øː] *(abk für Sozialdemokratische Partei Österreichs) die* Austrian Social Democratic Party.

Sponsor *(pl* -soren) *der* sponsor.

Sponsorin *(pl* -nen) *die* sponsor.

spontan ◇ *adj* spontaneous ◇ *adv* spontaneously.

Sport *der* sport; **~ treiben** to do sport.

Sportart *die* sport.

Sporthalle *die* sports hall.

Sportlehrer, in *der, die* sports teacher.

Sportler, in *(mpl* -; *fpl* -nen) *der, die* sportsman (*f* sportswoman).

sportlich <> *adj* - **1.** [Leistung, Betätigung, Verhalten] sporting; [Person, Figur] sporty - **2.** [leger] casual <> *adv* - **1.** [den Sport betreffend]: **sich ~ betätigen** to do sport - **2.** [leger] casually - **3.** [fair] sportingly.

Sport|platz *der* playing field.

Sport|verein *der* sports club.

Sport|wagen *der* - **1.** [Auto] sports car - **2.** [Kinderwagen] pushchair *Br*, stroller *Am*.

Spott *der* mockery.

spottbillig *adj* & *adv* dirt-cheap.

spotten *vi*: **(über jn/etw)** ~ to mock (sb/sthg).

spöttisch <> *adj* mocking <> *adv* mockingly.

Spott|preis *der* knockdown price.

sprach *prät* |> sprechen.

Sprache (*pl* -n) *die* - **1.** [gen] language; **in deutscher ~** in German - **2.** *RW*: **jm die ~ verschlagen** to leave sb speechless; **raus mit der ~!** *fam* out with it!

Sprach|kenntnisse *pl* knowledge (U) of languages.

Sprach|kurs *der* language course.

Sprach|labor *das* language laboratory.

sprachlich <> *adj* linguistic <> *adv* linguistically.

sprachlos <> *adj* [Staunen] speechless; **~ sein** to be speechless <> *adv* [dastehen] speechlessly.

Sprach|reise *die* language trip.

sprang *prät* |> springen.

Spray [ʃpreː, spreː] (*pl* -s) *der* ODER *das* spray.

Sprech|anlage *die* intercom.

sprechen (*präs* spricht; *prät* sprach; *perf* hat gesprochen) <> *vi* - **1.** [gen] to talk, to speak; **wer spricht da, bitte?** [am Telefon] who's speaking?; **mit jm ~** to talk to sb; **über jn/etw ~, von jm/etw ~** to talk about sb/sthg; **er sprach davon, dass ...** he mentioned that ...; **zu jm ~** to speak to sb; **auf jn/etw zu ~ kommen** to discuss sb/sthg - **2.** [als Redner auftreten] to speak; **frei ~** to speak without notes - **3.** [urteilend]: **es spricht für ihn, dass ...** it's in his favour that ...; **alles spricht dafür, dass ...** there is every reason to believe that ... <> *vt* - **1.** [gen] to speak; **Deutsch ~** to speak German; **jn ~** to speak to sb - **2.** [Gebet] to say - **3.** [reden mit] to speak to.

Sprecher, in (*mpl* -; *fpl* -nen) *der, die* - **1.** [von Gruppe] spokesperson - **2.** [von Nachrichten] newsreader.

Sprech|stunde *die* [beim Arzt] surgery.

Sprechstunden|hilfe *die* (doctor's) receptionist.

Sprech|zimmer *das* consulting room.

spreizen *vt* to spread.

sprengen *vt* - **1.** [mit Sprengstoff - Brücke, Gebäude] to blow up; [- Tür] to blow open; **etw in die Luft ~** to blow sthg up - **2.** [mit

Wasser - Rasen, Garten] to water; [- Wäsche] to sprinkle with water.

Spreng|satz *der* explosive charge.

Spreng|stoff *der* explosive.

spricht *präs* |> sprechen.

Sprichwort (*pl* -wörter) *das* proverb.

sprießen (*prät* spross; *perf* ist gesprossen) *vi* to sprout.

Spring|brunnen *der* fountain.

springen (*prät* sprang; *perf* hat/ist gesprungen) <> *vi* - **1.** *(ist)* [hüpfen & SPORT] to jump; **auf etw** *(A)* **/aus etw/von etw ~** to jump onto/out of/from sthg - **2.** [Ball] to bounce - **3.** *(ist)* [kaputtgehen] to crack - **4.** *RW*: **mein Vater hat 20 Euro ~ lassen** *fam* my dad gave me 20 euros <> *vt (hat)* SPORT [Salto] to do.

Sprint (*pl* -s) *der* sprint.

Spritze (*pl* -n) *die* - **1.** [Injektion] injection - **2.** [Injektionsgerät, Küchengerät] syringe - **3.** [Wasserspritze] hose.

spritzen (*perf* hat/ist gespritzt) <> *vi* - **1.** *(hat)* [herumspritzen - Flüssigkeit, Person] to splash; [- Fett] to spit - **2.** *(ist)* [in bestimmte Richtung] to splash - **3.** *(hat)* [eine Spritze geben] to give an injection <> *vt (hat)* - **1.** [gen] to spray; **jn nass ~** to splash sb - **2.** [Medikament, Droge] to inject; **sich/jm ein Schmerzmittel ~** to inject o.s./sb with a painkiller.

Spritzer (*pl* -) *der* splash.

spröde <> *adj* - **1.** [trocken] dry - **2.** [brüchig] brittle - **3.** [Mensch, Art] standoffish <> *adv* [unzugänglich] standoffishly.

spross *prät* |> sprießen.

Sprosse (*pl* -n) *die* rung.

Spruch (*pl* Sprüche) *der* [Redensart] saying.

Sprudel (*pl* -) *der* sparkling mineral water.

sprudeln (*perf* hat/ist gesprudelt) *vi* - **1.** [gen] to bubble - **2.** [wenn Kohlensäure entweicht] to fizz.

Sprüh|dose *die* aerosol.

sprühen (*perf* hat/ist gesprüht) <> *vt (hat)* to spray <> *vi* - **1.** *(ist)* [fliegen] to spray - **2.** *(hat)* [glänzen]: **vor Ideen ~** to be bubbling over with ideas; **vor Witz ~** to be sparklingly witty.

Sprühregen *der* drizzle.

Sprung (*pl* Sprünge) *der* - **1.** [Bewegung] jump - **2.** [Riss] crack; **einen ~ haben** to be cracked.

Sprung|brett *das* springboard.

sprunghaft <> *adj* - **1.** [unstet] erratic - **2.** [abrupt steigend] rapid <> *adv* - **1.** [unstet] erratically - **2.** [abrupt steigend] rapidly.

SPS [ɛspeː ˈɛs] (*abk für* Sozialdemokratische Partei der Schweiz) *die* Swiss Social Democratic Party.

Spucke *die* spit.

spucken <> *vi* - **1.** [ausspucken] to spit

- 2. *fam* [sich übergeben] to puke ⟨⟩ *vt* [Olivenstein, Blut] to spit.

Spuk *der* haunting; **dem ~ ein Ende machen** *fig* to return things to normal.

spuken *vi:* **in einem Haus ~** to haunt a house; **spukt es hier?** is this place haunted?

Spule (*pl* -n) *die* **- 1.** [Rolle] spool **- 2.** ELEKTR coil.

Spüle (*pl* -n) *die* sink.

spülen ⟨⟩ *vt* **- 1.** [Geschirr] to wash **- 2.** [Wäsche] to rinse **- 3.** [hinwegtragen]: **über Bord gespült werden** to be washed overboard ⟨⟩ *vi* **- 1.** [Geschirr reinigen] to do the dishes, to wash up *Br* **- 2.** [Subj: Waschmaschine] to rinse **- 3.** [hinunterspülen] to flush.

Spülmaschine *die* dishwasher.

Spülmittel *das* washing-up liquid *Br*, dishwashing liquid *Am*.

Spur (*pl* -en) *die* **- 1.** [Anzeichen] clue **- 2.** [Abdruck] track **- 3.** [Fahrstreifen] lane; **die ~ wechseln** to change lanes **- 4.** [kleine Menge - von Zutat] hint; [- von Substanz] trace **- 5.** *RW:* **eine heiße ~** a strong lead; **jm/einer Sache auf der ~ sein** to be on sb's/sthg's track. ◆ **keine Spur** *interj* not at all!

spürbar ⟨⟩ *adj* **- 1.** [fühlbar] noticeable **- 2.** [deutlich] clear ⟨⟩ *adv* **- 1.** [fühlbar] noticeably **- 2.** [sichtlich] clearly.

spüren *vt* **- 1.** [fühlen] to feel; **du wirst die Konsequenzen zu ~ bekommen** you'll see what the consequences are **- 2.** [ahnen] to sense.

Spurenelement *das* trace element.

spurlos *adv* **- 1.** [verschwinden] without a trace **- 2.** [ohne negative Auswirkungen]: **die Trennung ist nicht ~ an ihr vorübergegangen** the separation has left its mark on her.

Spurt (*pl* -s ODER -e) *der* [Endspurt] sprint for the line; [Zwischenspurt] spurt.

sputen ◆ **sich sputen** *ref* to hurry up.

Squash [skvɔʃ] *das* squash.

Sri Lanka *nt* Sri Lanka.

s. S. (*abk für* siehe Seite) see p.

SS [ɛs'ɛs] (*abk für* Schutzstaffel) *die* MIL SS.

St. - 1. (*abk für* Sankt) St **- 2.** *abk für* Stück.

Staat (*pl* -en) *der* state; **die ~en** *fam* the States.

Staatenbund *der* Confederation.

staatenlos *adj* stateless.

staatlich ⟨⟩ *adj* state ⟨⟩ *adv* by the state; **~ anerkannt** government-approved; **~ geprüft** government-certified.

Staatsangehörigkeit *die* nationality; **doppelte ~** dual nationality.

Staatsanwalt, anwältin *der, die* public prosecutor *Br*, district attorney *Am*.

Staatsbesuch *der* state visit.

Staatsbürger, in *der, die* citizen.

Staatsdienst *der* civil service.

staatseigen *adj* state-owned.

Staatsexamen *das* final exam taken by law and arts students at university.

Staatsmann (*pl* -männer) *der* statesman.

Staatsoberhaupt *das* head of state.

Staatssekretär, in *der, die* ≃ permanent secretary.

Staatssicherheitsdienst *der* security service *in former GDR.*

Staatsstreich *der* coup (d'état).

staatstragend *adj* pro-government.

Staatsvertrag *der* international treaty.

Stab (*pl* Stäbe) *der* rod; [von Gitter] bar; [von Dirigent] baton; MIL [von Pilger] staff; [zum Stabhochsprung] pole.

Stäbchen (*pl* -) *das* stick; [Essstäbchen] chopstick.

Stabhochsprung *der* SPORT pole vault.

stabil *adj* **- 1.** [Haus, Währung, Wetter] stable **- 2.** [Person, Gesundheit] robust; [Möbel] solid.

stabilisieren *vt* to stabilize. ◆ **sich stabilisieren** *ref* to stabilize.

stach *prät* ⊏⟩ stechen.

Stachel (*pl* -n) *der* **- 1.** [von Tier] sting **- 2.** [von Pflanze] thorn.

Stachelbeere *die* gooseberry.

Stacheldraht *der* barbed wire *(U).*

stachelig, stachlig *adj* prickly.

Stadion ['ʃtaːdjɔn] (*pl* Stadien) *das* stadium.

Stadium ['ʃtaːdjʊm] (*pl* Stadien) *das* stage.

Stadt (*pl* Städte) *die* **- 1.** [Ort] town; [Großstadt] city; **die ~ Köln** the city of Cologne **- 2.** *fam* [Stadtverwaltung] town/city council.

stadtbekannt *adj* well-known throughout the town/city.

Stadtbummel *der* stroll through town.

Städtebau *der* urban development; [Planung] town planning.

Stadtgespräch *das:* **~ sein** to be the talk of the town.

städtisch *adj* **- 1.** [der Stadtverwaltung] municipal **- 2.** [der Stadt] urban.

Stadtkern *der* town/city centre.

Stadtplan *der* street map.

Stadtrand *der* outskirts *(pl).*

Stadtrat *der* **- 1.** [Versammlung] town/city council **- 2.** [Person] town/city councillor.

Stadträtin *die* town/city councillor.

Stadtrundfahrt *die* city tour.

Stadtstaat *der* city state.

Stadtteil *der* district.

Stadttor *das* city gate.

Stadtviertel *das* district, quarter.

Stadtzentrum *das* town/city centre, downtown area *Am*.

Staffel (*pl* -n) *die* SPORT relay race.

Staffelei (*pl* -en) *die* easel.

staffeln *vt* to grade.

stahl *prät* ⊳ **stehlen**.

Stahl *(pl* Stähle) *der* steel *(U).*

Stahl|industrie *die* steel industry.

Stall *(pl* Ställe) *der* [gen] barn; [für Kühe] cowshed; [für Pferde] stable; [für Kaninchen] hutch; [für Schweine] sty; [für Hühner] coop.

Stamm *(pl* Stämme) *der* **- 1.** [von Baum] trunk **- 2.** [Volk] tribe **- 3.** [Wortstamm] stem.

Stamm|baum *der* family tree; [von Tier] pedigree.

stammeln *vt* & *vi* to stammer.

stammen *vi* to come; **aus etw ~** to come from sthg; **von jm ~** [herrühren] to come from sb; [gemacht sein] to be made by sb; **das Bild stammt von meiner Nachbarin** the picture was painted by my neighbour; **aus etw ~** [zeitlich] to date from sthg.

Stamm|gast *der* regular.

stämmig *adj* stocky.

Stamm|platz *der* usual seat.

Stamm|tisch *der* **- 1.** [Personen] group of regular customers at a pub **- 2.** [Treffen] meeting of regular customers at a pub **- 3.** [Tisch] regulars' table at a pub.

stampfen *(perf* hat/ist gestampft) ◇ *vi* **- 1.** *(hat)* [auftreten] to stamp; **mit den Füßen ~** to stamp one's feet **- 2.** *(ist)* [gehen] to stomp ◇ *vt (hat)* [Kartoffeln] to mash.

stand *prät* ⊳ **stehen**.

Stand *(pl* Stände) *der* **- 1.** [auf Messe, Markt] stand **- 2.** *(ohne pl)* [das Stehen] standing position **- 3.** *(ohne pl)* [Stellung - von Sonne] position; [- von Zähler] reading; [- von Entwicklung] **der ~ der Dinge** the state of things; **auf dem neuesten ~ sein** to be right up-to-date **- 4.** *RW:* **einen schweren ~ (bei jm) haben** to have a tough time (with sb); *siehe auch* imstande.

Standard *(pl* -s) *der* standard.

Stand-by [stɛnt'bai] *(pl* -s) ◇ *das* [bei Elektrogeräten] standby mode; **in ~ sein** standby mode ◇ *der* [bei Flugreisen] standby flight.

Ständchen *(pl* -) *das* serenade; **jm ein ~ bringen** to serenade sb.

Ständer *(pl* -) *der* [Gestell] stand.

Standes|amt *das* registry office.

standesamtlich ◇ *adj* registry-office ◇ *adv* at the registry office.

standesgemäß ◇ *adj* in keeping with one's social status ◇ *adv* according to one's social status.

standhaft ◇ *adj* steadfast ◇ *adv:* **sich ~ weigern** to refuse consistently.

stand|halten *vi (unreg):* **einer Sache** *(D)* **~** to withstand sthg.

ständig ◇ *adj* [Schmerzen, Belästigung] constant; [Mitglied] permanent ◇ *adv* constantly.

Stand|ort *der* **- 1.** [von Firma] location; **der ~ Deutschland** Germany as an industrial location **- 2.** [von Person, Pflanze] position.

Stand|punkt *der* point of view.

Stand|spur *die* hard shoulder *Br,* shoulder *Am.*

Stange *(pl* -n) *die* pole; [aus Metall] rod; **eine ~ Zigaretten** a carton of cigarettes; **ein Anzug von der ~** an off-the-peg suit; **eine ~ Geld** *fam* fig a fortune.

Stängel *(pl* -) *der* stalk.

stank *prät* ⊳ **stinken**.

stanzen *vt* **- 1.** [Formen, Teile] to press **- 2.** [Löcher] to punch.

Stapel *(pl* -) *der* [Haufen] pile.

Stapel|lauf *der* launching (of a ship).

stapeln *vt* to pile up. ◆ **sich stapeln** *ref* [hingestellt werden] to be piled up; [sich türmen] to be piling up.

Star [ʃtaːɐ̯] *(pl* -e ODER -s) *der* **- 1.** *(pl* Stare) [Vogel] starling **- 2.** *(pl* Stars) [Person] star.

starb *prät* ⊳ **sterben**.

stark *(kompar* stärker; *superl* stärkste) ◇ *adj* **- 1.** [gen] strong **- 2.** [Sturm, Schnupfen, Verkehr] heavy **- 3.** *fam* [toll] great; **stark!** great! **- 4.** [dick - Brille, Wände, Träger] thick; [- Figur, Beine] large **- 5.** [mit Maßangabe] thick **- 6.** [Beteiligung] good; [Interesse] strong **- 7.** GRAM: **~e Verben** strong verbs **- 8.** *RW:* **sich für jn/etw ~ machen** to stand up for sb/sthg ◇ *adv* **- 1.** [intensiv - zuschlagen, schwanken, etw vermuten] strongly; [- regnen] heavily **- 2.** [viel] a lot.

Stärke *(pl* -n) *die* **- 1.** [gen] strength **- 2.** [von Brett, Platte, Papier] thickness **- 3.** [für Wäsche] starch; [Speisestärke] cornflour *Br,* cornstarch *Am.*

stärken *vt* **- 1.** [kräftigen] to strengthen **- 2.** [Wäsche] to starch. ◆ **sich stärken** *ref* to fortify o.s.

Stärkung *(pl* -en) *die* **- 1.** [Mahlzeit] refreshment **- 2.** [Aufbau] strengthening.

starr ◇ *adj* **- 1.** [unbeweglich - Glieder, Material] stiff; [- Blick] fixed **- 2.** [System, Regeln] fixed ◇ *adv* [unflexibel] doggedly.

starren *vi* **- 1.** [sehen] to stare; **auf jn/etw ~** to stare at sb/sthg **- 2.** [emporragen]: **aus etw ~** to rise up out of sthg; **vor** ODER **von Dreck ~** to be absolutely filthy.

starrsinnig *adj* obstinate.

Start *(pl* -s ODER -e) *der* **- 1.** [gen] start **- 2.** [von Flugzeug] takeoff; [von Rakete] launch.

Start|bahn *die* runway.

starten *(perf* hat/ist gestartet) ◇ *vi (ist)* **- 1.** [Läufer, Pferd, Rennauto] to start **- 2.** [Flugzeug] to take off **- 3.** [abreisen] to set off ◇ *vt (hat)* to start.

Stasi *(abk für* Staatssicherheit) *die* ODER *der* Stasi, security service in former GDR.

Statik *die* statics *(U).*

Station (pl -en) die - **1.** [im Krankenhaus] ward - **2.** [Haltestelle, Halt] stop - **3.** [für Forschung] plant.

stationär adv: ~ **behandeln** to treat as an in-patient.

Statistik (pl -en) die statistics (pl).

Statistin (pl -nen) die extra.

Stativ (pl -e) das tripod.

statt ⇔ konj instead of; ~ **früher aufzustehen**, ... instead of getting up earlier, ... ⇔ präp (+G) instead of.

stattdessen adv instead.

Stätte (pl -n) die geh place.

stattfinden vi (unreg) to take place.

stattlich ⇔ adj - **1.** [Erscheinung, Größe] imposing - **2.** [Summe, Anwesen] considerable ⇔ adv considerably.

Statue ['ʃtaːtuə, 'ʃtaːtuə] (pl -n) die statue.

Stau (pl -s ODER -e) der - **1.** [von Autos] traffic jam; **im** ~ **stehen** to be stuck in a traffic jam - **2.** (ohne pl) [von Wasser] build-up.

Staub der dust; ~ **wischen** to dust; **sich aus dem** ~ **machen** fam fig to make one's getaway.

stauben vi to be dusty.

staubig adj dusty.

staubsaugen vt & vi to vacuum.

Staubsauger (pl -) der vacuum cleaner.

Staudamm der dam.

Staude (pl -n) die perennial.

stauen vt [Wasser] to dam; [Blut] to staunch. ➤ **sich stauen** ref - **1.** [Autos] to form a tailback - **2.** [sich ansammeln - Wut, Hitze] to build up; [- Luft] to accumulate.

staunen vi to be amazed; **über jn/etw** ~ to be amazed at sb/sthg.

Staunen das amazement.

Stausee der reservoir.

Stauung (pl -en) die [von Wasser] damming (U); [von Blut] staunching (U).

Std. abk für Stunde.

Steak [ʃteːk, steːk] (pl -s) das KÜCHE steak.

stechen (präs sticht; prät stach; perf hat gestochen) ⇔ vt - **1.** [verletzen - mit Stachel] to sting; [- mit Nadel] to prick; [- mit Spritze] to stick; [- mit Messer] to stab - **2.** [Spargel] to cut ⇔ vi - **1.** [Nadel, Dorn, Stachel] to prick; **mit etw in etw** (A) ~ to stick sthg in sthg - **2.** [Sonne] to beat down. ➤ **sich stechen** ref [sich verletzen] to prick o.s.

stechend adj - **1.** [Blick] piercing - **2.** [Geruch] pungent - **3.** [Schmerz] stabbing - **4.** [Sonne] burning.

Steckbrief der description (of a criminal).

Steckdose die socket.

stecken ⇔ vt to put; **sich** (D) **etw in etw** (A) ~ to put sthg in sthg; **etw an etw** (A) ~ to put sthg on sthg; **die Kinder ins Bett** ~ fam to put the children to bed ⇔ vi - **1.** [gen] to be; **wo steckst du?** where have you got to? - **2.** RW: **hinter etw** (D) ~ fam to be behind sthg.

stecken bleiben (perf ist stecken geblieben) vi (unreg) to get stuck.

Stecker (pl -) der plug.

Stecknadel die pin.

Steg (pl -e) der - **1.** [über Bach, Fluss] footbridge - **2.** [zu Boot] jetty.

stehen (prät stand; perf hat gestanden) vi - **1.** [aufrecht sein] to stand - **2.** [sich befinden] to be; **die Vase steht auf dem Tisch** the vase is on the table; **du stehst mir im Weg** you're in the way; **vor Schwierigkeiten/einer Wahl** ~ to be faced with difficulties/a choice; **unter Alkohol** ~ to be under the influence (of alcohol); **es steht 15:3** the score is 15–3; **wie steht es mit deiner Gesundheit?** how is your health? - **3.** [geschrieben sein]: **auf dem Schild steht, dass ...** the notice says that ...; **in der Zeitung steht, dass ...** it says in the paper that ... - **4.** [Uhr, Motor, Zeiger] to have stopped - **5.** [Kleid, Farbe, Frisur]: **jm** ~ to suit sb; **jm gut/nicht** ~ to suit/not to suit sb - **6.** GRAMM.: **mit Akkusativ/Dativ** ~ to take the accusative/dative; **das Substantiv steht im Plural** the noun is in the plural - **7.** fam [mögen]: **auf jn** ~ to fancy sb; **auf etw** (A) ~ to be into sthg - **8.** [stellvertretend]: **für etw** ~ to stand for sthg - **9.** [verantwortlich]: **zu jm/etw** ~ to stand by sb/sthg - **10.** [beurteilend]: **wie stehst du dazu?** what do you think about that? - **11.** RW: **alles** ~ **und liegen lassen** to drop everything; **wie stehts?** fam how are things?; **die Arbeit steht mir bis hier** fam I've had it up to here with this job. ➤ **sich stehen** ref fam [verstehen]: **sich mit jm gut** ~ to get on with sb; **sich mit jm schlecht** ~ not to get on with sb.

Stehen das: **im** ~ **standing up**.

stehen bleiben (perf ist stehen geblieben) vi (unreg) - **1.** [anhalten] to stop; **wo waren wir stehen geblieben?** where were we?; **die Zeit ist stehen geblieben** time has stood still - **2.** [nach Schlag, Erschütterung] to be left standing - **3.** [Satz] to stay.

stehen lassen (perf hat stehen lassen ODER stehen gelassen) vt (unreg) to leave.

Stehlampe die standard lamp.

stehlen (präs stiehlt; prät stahl; perf hat gestohlen) vt [entwenden] to steal; **sie kann mir gestohlen bleiben** fam she can get lost.

Steiermark die Styria.

steif ⇔ adj stiff; [Sahne] thick ⇔ adv stiffly; **Sahne/Eiweiß** ~ **schlagen** to beat cream until thick/egg white until stiff; ~ **und fest behaupten** fig to swear blind.

Steigbügel der stirrup.

steigen (prät stieg; perf ist gestiegen) vi - **1.** [hinaufsteigen]: **auf etw** (A) ~ [auf Leiter, Berg, Baum] to climb sthg; [auf Stuhl, Pferd] to climb onto sthg; [auf Fahrrad, Motorrad] to get on sthg - **2.** [hineinsteigen]: **in etw** (A) ~ [Zug, Straßenbahn] to get on sthg; [Auto,

Taxi] to get into sthg - **3.** [aussteigen]: **aus etw ~** [Zug, Straßenbahn] to get off sthg; [Auto, Taxi] to get out of sthg - **4.** [absteigen]: **von etw ~** to get off sthg - **5.** [Flugzeug, Preis, Temperatur, Wasser] to rise; [Nebel] to lift; **einen Drachen ~ lassen** to fly a kite - **6.** [Spannung, Misstrauen] to grow - **7.** *fam* [Fest] to take place; **ein Fest ~ lassen** to have a party.

Steigerung (*pl* -en) *die* - **1.** [von Preis, von Dosis] increase - **2.** [von Leistung] improvement - **3.** GRAM comparison.

steil ⟨⟩ *adj* - **1.** [Wand, Berg, Weg] steep - **2.** [Karriere, Aufstieg] rapid ⟨⟩ *adv* - **1.** [senkrecht] steeply - **2.** [schnell] rapidly.

Steil|hang *der* steep slope.

Stein (*pl* -e) *der* stone; **bei jm einen ~ im Brett haben** to be in sb's good books.

Stein|bock *der* - **1.** [Tier] ibex - **2.** ASTROL Capricorn; **~ sein** to be a Capricorn.

Stein|bruch *der* quarry.

Steingut *das* earthenware.

steinig *adj* stony.

Stein|kohle *die* coal.

Stein|schlag *der* falling rocks (*pl*).

Stein|zeit *die* Stone Age.

steirisch *adj* Styrian.

Steiß (*pl* -e) *der* coccyx.

Stelle (*pl* -n) *die* - **1.** [Platz] place; [kleine Stelle] patch; [im Text] passage; **an vierter ~ in** fourth place - **2.** [Arbeitsplatz] job - **3.** [Amt] office - **4.** MATH figure; **eine Zahl mit vier ~n a** four-figure number; **zwei ~n nach/hinter dem Komma** two decimal places - **5.** *RW:* **an deiner ~** if I were you.

stellen *vt* - **1.** [hinstellen] to put - **2.** [aufrecht stellen] to place upright - **3.** [Gerät, Aufgabe] to set; **jm eine Frage ~** to ask sb a question; **der Wecker auf drei Uhr ~** to set the alarm clock for three o'clock; **das Radio lauter/leiser ~** to turn the radio up/down - **4.** [zur Verfügung stellen]: **jm etw ~** to provide sb with sthg - **5.** [Diagnose, Prognose, Bedingung] to make - **6.** [Forderung, Antrag] to submit - **7.** [Dieb, Täter] to catch - **8.** FOTO to pose - **9.** [konfrontieren mit]: **jn vor etw** (*A*) **~** to present sb with sthg - **10.** *RW:* **gut/schlecht gestellt sein** to be well/badly off; **auf sich** (*A*) **(selbst) gestellt sein** to have to fend for o.s. ➡ **sich stellen** *ref* - **1.** [sich hinstellen] to go and stand; **sich auf einen Stuhl ~** to stand on a chair - **2.** [nicht ausweichen]: **sich einer Sache** (*D*) **~** to face sthg - **3.** [ablehnen]: **sich gegen jn/etw ~** to be against sb/sthg - **4.** [unterstützen]: **sich hinter jn/etw ~** to back sb/sthg - **5.** [so tun als ob]: **sich krank/schlafend ~** to pretend to be ill/asleep - **6.** [sich melden] to give o.s. up - **7.** *RW:* **sich gut mit jm ~** to get on good terms with sb.

Stellen|angebot *das* job offer.

Stellen|gesuch *das* 'situation wanted' advertisement.

stellenweise *adv* in places.

Stellung (*pl* -en) *die* position; **in seiner ~ als Vorsitzender** in his capacity as chairman; **(zu etw) ~ nehmen** to comment (on sthg).

Stellungnahme (*pl* -n) *die* statement.

Stell|vertreter, in *der, die* deputy.

stemmen *vt* - **1.** [drücken] to press - **2.** SPORT to lift; **ein Gewicht ~** to lift a weight above one's head; **den Körper hoch ~** to push one's body up. ➡ **sich stemmen** *ref* [sich drücken] to push o.s. up; **sich gegen etw ~** [sich abstemmen] to brace o.s. against sthg; **sich gegen etw ~** [sich wehren] to resist sthg.

Stempel (*pl* -) *der* [Gerät, Abdruck] stamp; [auf Briefmarke] postmark; [in Schmuckstück] hallmark.

stempeln ⟨⟩ *vt* [Stempel anbringen] to stamp; [Briefmarke] to cancel; [Post] to postmark; [Schmuckstück] to hallmark; **jn zu etw ~** [klassifizieren] to brand sb sthg ⟨⟩ *vi:* **gehen** *fam* to be on the dole *Br* ODER welfare *Am.*

Stengel *der* = Stängel.

Stenografie, Stenographie (*pl* -n) *die* shorthand.

Stepp|decke *die* quilt.

Steppe (*pl* -n) *die* steppe.

steppen ⟨⟩ *vi* [tanzen] to tap dance ⟨⟩ *vt* [nähen] to backstitch.

sterben (*präs* stirbt; *prät* starb; *perf* ist gestorben) *vi* to die; **an etw** (*D*) **~** to die of sthg; **vor etw** (*D*) **~** *fig fam* to die of sthg.

sterblich *adj* mortal.

stereo ⟨⟩ *adj* (*unver*) stereo ⟨⟩ *adv* in stereo.

Stereoan|lage *die* stereo (system).

steril *adj* sterile.

sterilisieren *vt* to sterilize.

Stern (*pl* -e) *der* star.

Stern|bild *das* constellation.

Stern|schnuppe (*pl* -n) *die* shooting star.

Stern|warte (*pl* -n) *die* observatory.

Stern|zeichen *das* star sign, sign of the zodiac.

stetig ⟨⟩ *adj* steady; [Belästigungen, Wiederholung] constant ⟨⟩ *adv* steadily; [wiederholen] constantly.

stets *adv* always.

Steuer (*pl* -n ODER -) ⟨⟩ *die* - **1.** (*pl* -n) [Abgabe] tax; **etw von der ~ absetzen** to claim sthg against tax; **~n hinterziehen** to be guilty of tax evasion - **2.** (*pl* -) *fam* [Steuerbehörde]: **die ~ the taxman** ⟨⟩ *das* (*pl* -) [von Fahrzeug] (steering) wheel; [von Flugzeug] controls (*pl*); [von Schiff] helm.

Steuer|bord *das* starboard.

Steuerer|klärung *die* tax return.

Steuer|fahndung *die* [Behörde] *body responsible for carrying out investigations into cases of suspected tax evasion.*

Steuermann (*pl* -männer) *der* helmsman.

steuern vt - 1. [lenken - Schiff, Fahrzeug] to steer; [- Flugzeug] to fly; [- Spielzeugauto] to control - 2. [beeinflussen] to guide, to steer - 3. [organisieren] to organize - 4. [kontrollieren & TECH] to control.

Steuerloase die tax haven.

Steuerlrad das [von Auto] steering wheel; [von Flugzeug] wheel; [von Schiff] wheel, helm.

Steuerung (pl -en) die - 1. [Lenken - von Auto, Schiff] steering; [- von Flugzeug] flying; [- von Modellflugzeug] controlling - 2. [Steuergerät] controls (pl).

Steuerlzahler, in (mpl -; fpl -nen) der, die taxpayer.

Steward, Stewardess ['stju:ɐt, ʃtju:ɐt] ['stju:ɐdɛs, ʃtju:ɐdɛs] (mpl -s; fpl -en) der, die steward (f stewardess).

Stich (pl -e) der - 1. [Einstich - von Messer] stab; [- von Biene, Wespe] sting; [- von Mücke] bite - 2. [Färbung] tinge - 3. [beim Nähen & MED] stitch - 4. [Schmerz] stabbing pain; [in der Seite] stitch - 5. [Bemerkung] gibe - 6. [beim Kartenspiel] trick - 7. [Bild] engraving - 8. RW: einen ~ haben salopp [verrückt sein] to be nuts; [ungenießbar werden] to have gone ODER be off; jn/etw im ~ lassen [verlassen] to leave sb/sthg; [fallen lassen] to abandon sb/sthg; wenn mich mein Orientierungssinn nicht im ~ lässt if my sense of direction isn't deceiving me.

sticheln <> vt to tease <> vi to make snide remarks.

stichhaltig <> adj valid; [Beweis] conclusive <> adv validly; [beweisen, widerlegen] conclusively.

Stichlprobe die - 1. [Menge] (random) sample - 2. [Handlung] spot check.

sticht präs [➞] stechen.

Stichltag der effective date.

Stichlwahl die final ballot.

Stichlwort (pl -e ODER -wörter) das - 1. [Notiz] note - 2. [Eintrag] headword - 3. [Schlüsselwort] keyword - 4. [im Theater] fig: das ~ geben to give the cue.

sticken vt & vi to embroider.

Stickerei (pl -en) die embroidery.

stickig adj stuffy.

Stickstoff der nitrogen.

Stieflbruder der stepbrother.

Stiefel (pl -) der boot.

Stieflkind das stepchild.

Stieflmutter die stepmother.

Stieflmütterchen (pl -) das pansy.

Stieflschwester die stepsister.

Stieflvater der stepfather.

stieg prät [➞] steigen.

Stiel (pl -e) der - 1. [von Blume, Frucht, Trinkglas] stem - 2. [Griff] handle; [von Lutscher, Eis] stick.

Stier (pl -e) der - 1. [Tier] bull - 2. [Sternzeichen, Person] Taurus; ~ sein to be a Taurus.

stieß prät [➞] stoßen.

Stift (pl -e) der - 1. [Schreibutensil] pen; [Bleistift] pencil; [Buntstift] crayon - 2. fam [Lehrling] name given to apprentices during their first year - 3. TECH [aus Holz] peg; [aus Metall] pin.

stiften vt - 1. [gründen] to found - 2. [spenden] to donate; [ausgeben] to pay for - 3. [hervorrufen - Unruhe, Aufregung] to cause - 4. [spendieren] to buy.

Stiftung (pl -en) die - 1. [Institution] foundation - 2. [Schenkung] donation.

Stil (pl -e) der style; in diesem ~ kann es nicht weitergehen! it can't go on like this!; im großen ~ on a grand scale.

still <> adj - 1. [ruhig, lautlos, stressfrei] quiet; im Stillen secretly - 2. [bewegungslos] still - 3. [ohne Worte - Protest, Gebet, Leiden] silent - 4. [heimlich] secret <> adv - 1. [ruhig, lautlos, stressfrei] quietly - 2. [bewegungslos] still; sie stand ~ da she was standing still - 3. [ohne Worte - protestieren, beten, leiden] silently.

Stille die - 1. [Ruhe] quiet - 2. [Schweigen] silence; in aller ~ heiraten to get married in secret.

Stillleben das = Stillleben.

stilllegen vt = stilllegen.

stillen <> vt - 1. [die Brust geben] to breastfeed - 2. [Schmerz] to stop - 3. [Hunger, Bedürfnis] to satisfy; [Durst] to quench <> vi to breastfeed.

Stille Ozean der: der ~ the Pacific (Ocean).

stillgestanden pp [➞] stillstehen.

stilllhalten vi (unreg) [sich nicht wehren] to offer no resistance.

still halten vt & vi (unreg) to keep still.

Stilllleben (pl -) das still life.

stilllegen vt to close down.

stillschweigend <> adj tacit <> adv tacitly.

stilllsitzen vi (unreg) [ruhig sein] to sit still.

Stilllstand der stopping; [von Maschine] stoppage; [von Verhandlung] deadlock; [von Entwicklung] halt; zum ~ kommen [Verkehr, Produktion] to come to a standstill; [Verhandlungen] to reach a deadlock; [Blutungen] to stop.

stilllstehen vi (unreg) - 1. [Bewegung stoppen] to stand still; stillgestanden! MIL attention! - 2. [Telefon]: das Telefon stand keine Minute still the phone never stopped ringing - 3. [stillliegen - Verkehr, Produktion] to be at a standstill; [- Uhr, Maschine] to have stopped.

Stimmband (pl -bänder) das vocal cord.

stimmberechtigt adj entitled to vote.

Stimmlbruch der: er ist im ~ his voice is breaking.

strahlen

Stimme (*pl* -n) *die* - **1.** [gen] voice - **2.** [Wählerstimme] vote; **seine ~ abgeben** to vote; **sich der ~ enthalten** to abstain - **3.** MUS part.

stimmen <> *vi* - **1.** [richtig sein] to be right ODER correct; [Gerücht, Aussage] to be true ODER correct; **das stimmt nicht!** that's not true! - **2.** [wählen]: **für/gegen jn/etw ~** to vote for/against sb/sthg - **3.** [übereinstimmen] to be right; **stimmt so!** keep the change! <> *vt* MUS to tune.

Stimmlgabel *die* tuning fork.

stimmhaft <> *adj* voiced.

Stimmllage *die* voice; [beim Singen] register.

stimmlos <> *adj* voiceless, unvoiced.

Stimmlrecht *das* right to vote.

Stimmung (*pl* -en) *die* - **1.** [Laune] mood; **guter/schlechter ~ sein** to be in a good/bad mood - **2.** [Atmosphäre] atmosphere.

Stimmlzettel *der* ballot paper.

stinken (*prät* stank; *perf* hat gestunken) *vi* - **1.** *abw* [schlecht riechen]: **(nach etw) ~** to stink (of sthg) - **2.** *salopp* [reichen]: **mir stinkt es** I'm fed up to the back teeth.

Stipendium (*pl* -dien) *das* [als Unterstützung] grant; [als Auszeichnung] scholarship.

stirbt *präs* ⊏▷ sterben.

Stirn (*pl* -en) *die* forehead.

stöbern *vi* to rummage (around).

stochern *vi*: **(mit etw) in etw** (A) **~** to poke at sthg (with sthg); **im Essen ~** to pick at one's food.

Stock (*pl* Stöcke ODER -s) *der* - **1.** (*pl* Stöcke) [Stab] stick; [von Dirigent] baton - **2.** (*pl* -s) [Stockwerk] floor, storey.

stockdunkel *adj* pitch-dark.

stocken *vi* [zum Stillstand kommen - Verkehr] to be held up; [- Gespräch] to falter; [- Produktion] to be interrupted; [- Verhandlungen] to break off.

stockend <> *adj* faltering; **es herrscht ~er Verkehr** traffic is moving slowly <> *adv* falteringly.

Stockung (*pl* -en) *die* [Stillstand - von Verkehr] hold-up; [- von Verhandlungen] break; [- von Produktion] interruption.

Stocklwerk *das* floor, storey.

Stoff (*pl* -e) *der* - **1.** [Tuch] material - **2.** [Inhalt] subject matter; [zu Roman, Film] material - **3.** [Substanz] substance.

Stoffwechsel *der* metabolism.

stöhnen *vi* to groan.

Stollen (*pl* -) *der* - **1.** [Gang] gallery, tunnel - **2.** [Gebäck] stollen, *sweet bread loaf made with dried fruit and marzipan, eaten at Christmas*.

stolpern (*perf* ist gestolpert) *vi* to stumble; **über etw** (A) **~** to trip over sthg.

stolz <> *adj* proud; **auf jn/etw ~ sein** to be proud of sb/sthg <> *adv* proudly.

Stolz *der* pride.

stopfen <> *vt* - **1.** [ausbessern] to darn - **2.** [hineinstopfen] to stuff - **3.** [zustopfen] to plug - **4.** [füllen - Pfeife] to fill; [- Geflügel] to stuff. <> *vi* [Stuhlgang erschweren] to cause constipation.

stopp *interj* [halt] stop!

stoppen <> *vt* - **1.** [anhalten] to stop - **2.** [messen - Person, Lauf] to time. <> *vi* [anhalten] to stop.

Stopplschild *das* stop sign.

Stoppluhr *die* stopwatch.

Stöpsel (*pl* -) *der* [Gegenstand - von Becken] plug; [- von Flasche] stopper.

Storch (*pl* Störche) *der* stork.

stören <> *vt* - **1.** [belästigen] to disturb; [unterbrechen] to interrupt - **2.** [missfallen] to bother - **3.** [beeinträchtigen - Verhältnis] to spoil; [- Radioempfang, Fernsehempfang] to interfere with. <> *vi* [belästigend sein]: **darf ich mal kurz ~?** may I disturb you for a moment?; **'bitte nicht ~!'** 'do not disturb!'.

Störung (*pl* -en) *die* - **1.** [Belästigung] disturbance; [von Zeremonie] disruption - **2.** [Funktionsstörung - von Gerät] fault; [- von Organ] disorder.

Stoß (*pl* Stöße) *der* - **1.** [Schlag] push, shove; [mit dem Fuß] kick; [in Auto, Schiff, Zug] jolt - **2.** [Stapel] pile.

stoßen (*präs* stößt; *prät* stieß; *perf* hat/ist gestoßen) <> *vt* (hat) - **1.** [schubsen] to push; [mit der Faust] to punch; [mit dem Fuß] to kick - **2.** SPORT [Kugel] to put; [Gewichte] to press - **3.** [aufmerksam machen]: **jn auf etw** (A) **~** to point sthg out to sb <> *vi* - **1.** (ist) [berühren]: **an etw** (A) **~** to bang sthg; **gegen etw** (A) **~** to bang into sthg; [Fahrzeug] to crash into sthg - **2.** (ist) [angrenzen]: **an etw** (A) **~** [Grundstück] to border on sthg; [Zimmer] to be next to sthg - **3.** (ist) [finden]: **auf jn/etw ~** to come across sb/sthg; **auf Erdöl ~** to strike oil - **4.** (ist) [auf Reaktion]: **auf etw** (A) **~** to meet with sthg - **5.** (ist) [sich treffen mit]: **zu jm ~** to meet up with sb. ◆ **sich stoßen** *ref* - **1.** [sich wehtun] to bang o.s. - **2.** [nicht mögen]: **sich an etw** (D) **~** to take exception to sthg.

stößt *präs* ⊏▷ stoßen.

stottern *vi* [sprechen] to stutter, to stammer.

Str. (*abk für* Straße) St.

Strafe (*pl* -n) *die* - **1.** [Bestrafung] punishment - **2.** [Geldbuße] fine - **3.** [in Gefängnis] sentence.

strafen *vt* to punish.

Strafzettel *der* ticket.

Strahl (*pl* -en) *der* - **1.** [Wasserstrahl] jet - **2.** [Lichtstrahl] ray; [von Scheinwerfer, Licht, Laser] beam. ◆ **Strahlen** *pl* [Energiewellen] rays.

strahlen *vi* - **1.** [lachen] to beam

- **2.** [leuchten] to shine - **3.** [Strahlen abgeben] to radiate - **4.** [glänzen] to sparkle.

Strähne (*pl* -n) *die* strand.

Strand (*pl* Strände) *der* beach; **am ~** on the beach.

Straße (*pl* -n) *die* - **1.** [in Stadt] street - **2.** [Landstraße] road.

Straßen|bahn *die* tram *Br*, streetcar *Am*.

Straßen|karte *die* road map.

Straßen|schild *das* street sign.

Strategie (*pl* -n) *die* strategy.

sträuben ◆ **sich sträuben** *ref* - **1.** [Federn] to become ruffled; [Fell] to bristle - **2.** [sich wehren]: **sich gegen etw ~** to resist sthg.

Strauch (*pl* Sträucher) *der* bush.

Strauß (*pl* Sträuße ODER -e) *der* - **1.** (*pl* Sträuße) [Blumen] bunch of flowers - **2.** (*pl* Strauße) [Vogel] ostrich.

streben (*perf* hat/ist gestrebt) *vi* (hat) [trachten]: **nach etw ~** to strive for sthg.

Streber, in (*mpl* -; *fpl* -nen) *der, die abw* swot *Br*, grind *Am*.

Strecke (*pl* -n) *die* - **1.** [Weg] route; **diese ~ bin ich noch nie gefahren** I've never been this way before - **2.** [Entfernung] distance - **3.** [von Straße] stretch - **4.** [von Eisenbahn] line; [von Schienen] track - **5.** MATH (straight) line.

strecken *vt* - **1.** [ausstrecken] to stretch - **2.** [Hals] to crane - **3.** [verdünnen] to thin down; [Droge] to cut. ◆ **sich strecken** *ref* - **1.** [sich recken] to stretch - **2.** [sich hinlegen] to stretch out.

streckenweise *adv* in places.

Streich (*pl* -e) *der* [zum Ärgern] trick; **jm einen ~ spielen** *eigtl & fig* to play a trick on sb.

streicheln ⬦ *vt* to stroke ⬦ *vi*: **über etw** (*A*) **~** to stroke sthg.

streichen (*prät* strich; *perf* hat gestrichen) ⬦ *vt* (hat) - **1.** [mit Farbe] to paint; **'frisch gestrichen'** 'wet paint' - **2.** [Satz, Passage] to delete; **etw von einer Liste ~** to cross sthg off a list - **3.** [schmieren] to spread - **4.** [Subvention, Auftrag] to cancel ⬦ *vi* - **1.** (hat): **sich** (*D*) **über den Kopf ~** to stroke one's head - **2.** (hat) [mit Farbe] to paint.

Streicher, in (*mpl* -; *fpl* -nen) *der, die*: **die ~** the strings.

Streich|holz *das* match.

Streich|instrument *das* stringed instrument.

Streichung (*pl* -en) *die* - **1.** [von Subvention, Auftrag] cancellation; **~en** [an Etat] cuts - **2.** [im Text] deletion.

Streife (*pl* -n) *die* patrol.

streifen (*perf* hat/ist gestreift) ⬦ *vt* (hat) - **1.** [berühren] to brush against - **2.** [ziehen]: **etw über etw** (*A*) **~** to pull sthg over sthg;

etw von etw ~ to pull sthg off sthg - **3.** [Thema] to touch on.

Streifen (*pl* -) *der* - **1.** [Stück, Band] strip - **2.** [Strich] stripe; [auf Fahrbahn] line.

Streifen|wagen *der* patrol car.

Streik (*pl* -s) *der* strike; **in (den) ~ treten** to go on strike.

streiken *vi* - **1.** [im Streik stehen] to strike - **2.** [Motor, Maschine] to pack up.

Streit *der* argument; **~ mit jm haben** to argue with sb.

streiten (*prät* stritt; *perf* hat gestritten) *vi* - **1.** [sich auseinander setzen]: **(über etw** (*A*)**) ~** to argue (about sthg) - **2.** *geh* [kämpfen]: **gegen/für etw ~** to fight against/for sthg. ◆ **sich streiten** *ref*: **sich (mit jm/um etw) ~** to argue (with sb/about sthg).

Streit|frage *die* contentious issue.

Streitigkeiten *pl* disputes.

Streitkräfte *pl* armed forces.

streitsüchtig *adj* quarrelsome.

streng ⬦ *adj* - **1.** [Eltern, Kontrolle, Diät, Regel] strict; [Blick] stern; [Maßnahme] stringent - **2.** [Geruch, Geschmack] pungent - **3.** [Gesicht, Frisur, Winter] severe ⬦ *adv* - **1.** [erziehen, verbieten, einhalten] strictly; [überwachen] closely; [ansehen] sternly - **2.** [durchdringend]: **~ riechen** to smell pungent.

Strenge *die* [von Erziehung, Kontrolle, Gesetz] strictness; [von Blick] sternness; [von Maßnahme] stringency.

streng genommen *adv* strictly speaking.

strengstens *adv* strictly.

Stress *der* stress; **mach keinen ~!** *fam* stay cool!

Streu *die* [aus Stroh] straw.

streuen ⬦ *vt* [Salz, Gewürze] to sprinkle; [Dünger, Stroh, Gerüchte] to spread; [Futter, Samen] to scatter ⬦ *vi* [mit Sand] to grit; [mit Salz] to put down salt.

streunen (*perf* hat/ist gestreunt) *vi* - **1.** [irgendwo] to roam around; [Hund, Katze] to stray - **2.** (ist) [irgendwohin] to roam.

Streusel (*pl* -) *der* ODER *das* crumble topping.

strich *prät* ⊏⊐ **streichen**.

Strich (*pl* -e) *der* - **1.** [Linie] line; [Gedankenstrich] dash; [von Pinsel] stroke - **2.** [Streichen] stroke - **3.** [zur Prostitution] prostitution; **auf den ~ gehen** *fam* to walk the streets - **4.** *RW*: **jm einen ~ durch die Rechnung machen** to wreck sb's plans. ◆ **unter dem Strich** *adv* at the end of the day.

Strick (*pl* -e) *der* rope.

stricken *vt & vi* to knit.

Strick|jacke *die* cardigan.

Strick|leiter *die* rope ladder.

Strick|nadel *die* knitting needle.

Strickzeug das (ohne pl) [Handarbeit] knitting.

striegeln vt to groom.

Striemen (pl -) der weal.

Striptease ['ʃtriptiːs, 'striptiːs] der ODER das striptease.

stritt prät ⊳ streiten.

strittig adj contentious.

Stroh das straw.

Strohldach das thatched roof.

Strolch (pl -e) der - 1. abw [Mann] ruffian - 2. fam hum [Schlingel] rascal.

Strom (pl Ströme) der - 1. [elektrisch] electricity - 2. [Fluss] river - 3. [Strömung] current - 4. [Menge] stream - 5. RW: **es regnet** ODER **gießt in Strömen** it's pouring down; **gegen den ~ schwimmen** to swim against the tide.

strömen (perf ist geströmt) vi to stream.

Stromlkreis der (electrical) circuit.

Stromlstärke die current strength.

Strömung (pl -en) die - 1. [Strom] current - 2. [Bewegung] current of thought.

Stromlzähler der electricity meter.

Strophe (pl -n) die verse.

strotzen vi: **vor Gesundheit ~** to be bursting with health; **vor Dreck ~** to be filthy.

Strudel (pl -) der - 1. [Wirbel] whirlpool - 2. [Kuchen] strudel.

Struktur (pl -en) die - 1. [von Systemen] structure - 2. [von Material] texture.

Strumpf (pl Strümpfe) der - 1. [beinlang] stocking - 2. [Socke] sock.

Strumpflhose die tights (pl) Br, pantyhose (U) Am.

struppig adj shaggy.

Stube (pl -n) die - 1. fam [Wohnzimmer] living room - 2. [Raum] room.

stubenrein adj house-trained.

Stück (pl -e) das [gen] piece; [von Butter, Zucker] lump.

stückeln vi to add patches.

Student (pl -en) der student.

Studentenwohnlheim das hall of residence.

Studentin (pl -nen) die student.

Studie ['ʃtuːdjə] (pl -n) die study.

Studienablschluss der degree.

Studienlfach das subject.

Studienlplatz der university/college place.

Studienlrat der secondary school teacher.

Studienlrätin die secondary school teacher.

studieren ['ʃtuːdiːrən] vt & vi to study.

Studio (pl -s) das studio.

Studium ['ʃtuːdjʊm] (pl Studien) das - 1. [gen] study - 2. (ohne pl) [Ausbildung] studies (pl).

Stufe (pl -n) die - 1. [von Treppen] step; '**Vorsicht ~!**' 'mind the step!' - 2. [Stand] stage - 3. [in einer Hierarchie] level - 4. [Schaltstufe] setting - 5. [Abstufung] degree.

Stuhl (pl Stühle) der [Sitzmöbel] chair.

Stuhlgang der (ohne pl) stool.

stülpen vt: **etw nach außen ~** to turn sthg inside out; **etw auf/über etw** (A) **~** to put sthg onto/over sthg.

stumm ⟨⟩ adj - 1. [sprechunfähig] dumb - 2. [schweigend] silent ⟨⟩ adv - 1. [sprechunfähig] dumbly - 2. [schweigend] silently.

Stummel (pl -) der [von Arm, Bein, Schwanz] stump; [von Zigarette] butt; [von Kerze, Bleistift] stub.

Stummlfilm der silent movie.

Stümper (pl -) der abw bungler.

Stümperin (pl -nen) die abw bungler.

stumpf ⟨⟩ adj - 1. [Messer, Spitze] blunt - 2. [Fell, Haar, Lack] dull - 3. [Person, Ausdruck] apathetic - 4. MATH obtuse ⟨⟩ adv - 1. [leben, blicken] apathetically - 2. [nicht scharf, nicht spitz] bluntly - 3. [glanzlos] dully.

Stumpf (pl Stümpfe) der stump; [von Kerze] stub.

Stumpfsinn der - 1. [Monotonie] monotony - 2. [geistige Abwesenheit] apathy.

Stunde (pl -n) die - 1. [Zeiteinheit] hour - 2. [Unterrichtsstunde] lesson. ◆ **zu später Stunde** adv geh at a late hour.

stunden vt: **jm eine Zahlung ~** to give sb longer to make a payment.

Stundenlgeschwindigkeit die: **eine ~ von 100 km** a speed of 100 km/h.

Stundenkilometer pl kilometres per hour.

stundenlang ⟨⟩ adj lasting for hours; **nach ~em Warten** after waiting for hours ⟨⟩ adv for hours.

Stundenllohn der hourly rate.

Stundenlplan der timetable.

Stundenlzeiger der hour hand.

stündlich ⟨⟩ adv - 1. [jede Stunde] hourly, once an hour - 2. [jeden Augenblick] at any moment ⟨⟩ [jede Stunde] hourly.

Stups (pl -e) der nudge.

Stupslnase die snub nose.

stur abw ⟨⟩ adj pigheaded ⟨⟩ adv pigheadedly; **~ geradeaus fahren** to drive straight on.

Sturm (pl Stürme) der - 1. [Unwetter] storm - 2. [von Begeisterung, Entrüstung] wave - 3. [Andrang, Angriff] assault; **der ~ auf die Bastille** the storming of the Bastille - 4. [beim Fußball] forward line.

stürmen (perf hat/ist gestürmt) ⟨⟩ vt (hat) - 1. [Geschäfte, Büfett] to besiege - 2. [Festung, Stellung] to storm ⟨⟩ vi - 1. (ist) [rennen] to rush - 2. (hat) [beim Fußball] to attack

- 3. *(hat)* [Sturm herrschen]: **es stürmt** it's blowing a gale.

Stürmer, in *(mpl -; fpl -nen) der, die* forward.

Sturm|flut *die* storm tide.

stürmisch ◇ *adj* **- 1.** [windig] stormy **- 2.** [Applaus] tumultuous; [Begeisterung] wild; [Protest] vehement **- 3.** [leidenschaftlich] passionate ◇ *adv* **- 1.** [applaudieren] tumultuously **- 2.** [leidenschaftlich] passionately **- 3.** [wehen] stormily; [regnen] violently.

Sturz *(pl* Stürze) *der* fall.

stürzen *(perf* hat/ist gestürzt) ◇ *vi (ist)* **- 1.** [fallen, zurückgehen] to fall **- 2.** [eilen] to rush ◇ *vt (hat)* **- 1.** [Regierung, Herrscher] to bring down; [mit Gewalt] to overthrow **- 2.** [Kuchen, Pudding] to turn out **- 3.** [stoßen] to hurl. ◆ **sich stürzen** *ref* **- 1.** [springen] to jump **- 2.** [herfallen über]: **sich auf jn/etw ~** [bestürmen] to fall on sb/sthg; [angreifen] to pounce on sb/sthg **- 3.** [sich begeben]: **sich in etw** *(A)* **~** [springen] to plunge into sthg; [sich widmen] to throw o.s. into sthg.

Sturz|helm *der* crash helmet.

Stute *(pl -n) die* mare.

Stuttgart *nt* Stuttgart.

Stütze *(pl -n) die* [Vorrichtung] prop, support; [für Kopf, Rücken, Füße] rest.

stutzen ◇ *vt* [Bart, Haare, Hecke] to trim; [Pflanze, Baum] to cut back ◇ *vi* [innehalten] to stop short.

stützen *vt* to support; **den Kopf in die Hände ~** to prop one's head on one's hands; **die Ellbogen auf den Tisch ~** to prop one's elbows on the table. ◆ **sich stützen** *ref*: **sich auf jn/etw ~** [auf Stock, Möbel] to lean on sb/sthg; [auf Vermutung, Beweis] to be based on sb/sthg.

stutzig *adj*: **~ werden** to become suspicious.

Stütz|punkt *der* base.

Styropor® *das* polystyrene.

Subjekt *(pl -e) das* GRAM subject.

subjektiv ◇ *adj* subjective ◇ *adv* subjectively.

Substantiv *(pl -e) das* GRAM noun.

Substanz *(pl -en) die* substance; **das geht an die ~** it wears you down.

subtrahieren *vt & vi* to subtract.

subventionieren [zʊpvɛntsjoˈniːrən] *vt* to subsidize.

Suche *(pl -n) die* search; **auf der ~ nach jm/etw sein** to be looking for sb/sthg; [angestrengt] to be searching for sb/sthg; **sich auf die ~ (nach jm/etw) machen** to start looking (for sb/sthg).

suchen ◇ *vt* **- 1.** [finden wollen] to look for; [angestrengt] to search for; **er/es hat hier nichts zu ~** *fam* he/it has no business being here **- 2.** [sich wünschen] to seek ◇ *vi*: **(nach**

jm/etw) ~ to look (for sb/sthg); [angestrengt] to search (for sb/sthg).

Such|maschine *die* EDV search engine.

Sucht *(pl* Süchte) *die* addiction.

süchtig *adj*: **(nach etw) ~ sein** to be addicted (to sthg); **~ machen** to be addictive.

Such|trupp *der* search party.

Südafrika *nt* South Africa.

südafrikanisch *adj* South African.

Südamerika *nt* South America.

Süd|amerikaner, in *der, die* South American.

südamerikanisch *adj* South American.

süddeutsch *adj* South German.

Süden *der* south; **nach ~** south; **im ~** in the south.

Südeuropa *nt* Southern Europe.

Süd|frucht *die* ordinary citrus fruits and certain tropical fruits, e.g. bananas.

Südkorea *nt* South Korea.

südländisch *adj* Mediterranean.

südlich ◇ *adj* [Gegend] southern; [Richtung, Wind] southerly ◇ *präp*: **~ einer Sache** *(G)* ODER **von etw** to (the) south of sthg.

Südosten *der* south-east.

Süd|pol *der* **- 1.** GEOGR South Pole **- 2.** PHYS south pole.

Südsee *die*: **die ~** the South Seas *(pl)*.

Südtirol *nt* South Tyrol.

Südwesten *der* south-west.

Sueskanal [ˈzuːɛskanaːl] *der* Suez Canal.

süffig *adj* very drinkable.

Sulfat *(pl -e) das* CHEM sulphate.

Sultan *(pl -e) der* sultan.

Sultanine *(pl -n) die* sultana.

Sülze *(pl -n) die* brawn *(U)* *Br*, headcheese *(U) Am*.

Summe *(pl -n) die* sum.

summen *(perf* hat/ist gesummt) ◇ *vi (hat, ist)* to buzz ◇ *vt (hat)* to hum.

summieren *vt* to add. ◆ **sich summieren** *ref* to add up.

Sumpf *(pl* Sümpfe) *der* [Sumpfgelände] marsh; [in Tropen] swamp.

sumpfig *adj* marshy.

Sünde *(pl -n) die* sin.

Sünden|bock *der* scapegoat.

super *fam* ◇ *adj (unver)* great ◇ *adv* really well ◇ *interj* great!

Super *das* four-star (petrol) *Br*, premium (gas) *Am*.

Superlativ *(pl -e) der* GRAM superlative.

Super|markt *der* supermarket.

Suppe *(pl -n) die* **- 1.** [Essen] soup; **jm die ~ versalzen** *fam fig* to put a spoke in sb's wheel **- 2.** *fam* [Dunst, Nebel] pea souper.

Suppen|schüssel *die* tureen.

Suppen|teller *der* soup plate.

Suppen|würfel *der* stock cube.

Surf|brett ['sœːɐ̯fbrɛt] *das* - **1.** [zum Wellensurfen] surfboard - **2.** [zum Windsurfen] sailboard.

surfen ['sœːɐ̯fn̩] *(perf hat/ist gesurft) vi* - **1.** *(gen & EDV)* to surf - **2.** [mit Segel] to windsurf.

Surrealismus *der* surrealism.

surren *(perf hat/ist gesurrt) vi* - **1.** *(ist)* [Pfeil] to whizz - **2.** *(hat)* [Maschine] to whirr; [Insekt] to buzz.

suspekt *adj* suspicious; **jm ~ sein** to make sb suspicious.

süß <> *adj* sweet <> *adv:* **~ schmecken/ aussehen** to taste/look sweet; **träume ~!** sweet dreams!

süßen *vt* to sweeten.

Süßigkeiten *pl* sweets *Br,* candy *(U) Am.*

süßlich <> *adj* - **1.** [süß] sweetish - **2.** [übertrieben freundlich] syrupy <> *adv* - **1.** [süß]: **~ schmecken** to have a sweetish taste - **2.** [übertrieben freundlich] in a sickly-sweet way.

süß-sauer <> *adj* sweet and sour <> *adv:* **~ schmecken** to have a sweet and sour taste.

Süß|speise *die* dessert.

Süßwasser *das* fresh water.

SVP [ɛsfau̯'peː] *(abk für Schweizer Volkspartei) die (ohne pl) political party in Switzerland.*

SW *(abk für Südwest) abk für* SW.

Symbol *(pl -e) das* - **1.** [Zeichen] symbol - **2.** EDV [Icon] icon.

symbolisch <> *adj* symbolic <> *adv* symbolically.

Symmetrie *(pl -n) die* symmetry.

symmetrisch <> *adj* symmetrical <> *adv* symmetrically.

Sympathie *(pl -n) die* [Zuneigung] liking *(U); sich (D)* **viele ~n verscherzen** to lose a lot of sympathy.

sympathisch <> *adj* nice; **sie ist mir ~** I like her <> *adv* nicely.

📖 **sympathisch**

The German sympathisch closely resembles the English "sympathetic", but in fact it is a false friend which means "nice". So ein sympathischer Mensch is "a <u>nice</u> person".
The English word "sympathetic" can normally be translated by verständnisvoll. So the sentence "Our teacher is always <u>sympathetic</u> if we have a problem to discuss" could be translated as Unser Lehrer ist immer <u>verständnisvoll</u>, wenn wir Probleme zu besprechen haben.

---

sympathisieren *vi:* **mit jm ~** to sympathize with sb.

Symphonie = Sinfonie.

Symphoniker = Sinfoniker.

Symptom *(pl -e) das* - **1.** MED symptom - **2.** [Anzeichen] sign.

Synagoge *(pl -n) die* synagogue.

synchron <> *adj* synchronous <> *adv* synchronously.

synchronisieren *vt* [Film, Stimme] to dub; [Bewegungen, Abläufe] to synchronize.

Synonym *(pl -e) das* synonym.

Syntax *(pl -en) die* syntax.

Synthese *(pl -n) die:* **die ~ aus etw** the synthesis of sthg.

synthetisch <> *adj* synthetic <> *adv* synthetically.

Syrien *nt* Syria.

System [zʏsˈteːm] *(pl -e) das* system.

systematisch <> *adj* systematic <> *adv* systematically.

Szene *(pl -n) die* - **1.** [im Film, Theater] scene - **2.** [Vorfall] scene; **(jm) eine ~ machen** to make a scene (in front of sb) - **3.** [Milieu] scene.

T

t, T [teː] *(pl* t, T ODER -s) *das* t, T. ➤ **t** *abk für* Tonne.

Tabak, Tabak *(pl -e) der* tobacco *(U).*

Tabak|laden *der* tobacconist's.

tabellarisch <> *adj* tabular <> *adv* in tabular form.

Tabelle *(pl -n) die* - **1.** [Liste] table - **2.** SPORT (league) table.

Tablett *(pl -s* ODER -e) *das* tray.

📖 **Tablett**

The German Tablett is misleading as it means "tray" rather than "tablet". You would translate the phrase Sie servierte den Kaffee auf einem <u>Tablett</u> by "She brought in the coffee on a <u>tray</u>".
The English word "tablet" in the sense of "pill" is translated by Tablette, but "a <u>tablet</u> of soap" would be ein <u>Stück</u> Seife.

Tablette *(pl -n) die* tablet, pill.

tabu *adj (unver):* **etw ist ~** sthg is taboo.

Tabu *(pl -s) das* taboo.

Tacho|meter *der* speedometer.

Tadel *(pl -) der geh* rebuke.

tadellos <> *adj* impeccable <> *adv* impeccably.

tadeln *vt* to rebuke.

Tafel (*pl* -n) *die* - **1.** [Schreibtafel] blackboard - **2.** *geh* [Tisch] table - **3.** [Stück]: **eine ~ Schokolade** a bar of chocolate.

Tafelwasser (*pl* -wässer) *das* mineral water.

Tag (*pl* -e) *der* - **1.** [24 Stunden] day; **in vierzehn ~en** in a fortnight - **2.** [in seinem Verlauf] day - **3.** *RW*: **am helllichten ~** in broad daylight; **über/unter ~(e)** above/below ground. ➡ **eines Tages** *adv* [irgendwann] one day. ➡ **guten Tag** *interj* hello!; [am Morgen] good morning!; [am Nachmittag] good afternoon! ➡ **Tag für Tag** *adv* [immer] day after day. ➡ **von Tag zu Tag** *adv* [immer mehr] day by day. ➡ **Tage** *pl* - **1.** [Zeit] days; **js ~e sind gezählt** [muss sterben/weggehen] sb's days are numbered - **2.** *fam* [Periode] period (*sg*); **sie hat/bekommt ihre ~e** *fam* she's got her period; *siehe auch* zutage.

tagaus *adv*: **~, tagein** day in, day out.

Tag der Deutschen Einheit *der* Day of German Unity.

Tagebuch *das* diary.

tagelang ⬦ *adj* lasting for days; **~er Regen** days of rain ⬦ *adv* for days.

tagen *vi* - **1.** [Sitzung haben - gen] to meet; [- Gericht] to be in session - **2.** *geh* [hell werden]: **es tagt** day is breaking.

Tagesablauf *der* day.

Tagesanbruch *der* dawn.

Tagesbedarf *der* (*ohne pl*) daily requirement.

Tagesfahrt *die* day trip.

Tagesgericht *das* dish of the day.

Tagesgeschehen *das* day's events (*pl*).

Tageskarte *die* day ticket.

Tageslicht *das* daylight; **etw kommt ans ~** sthg comes to light.

Tagesordnung *die* agenda.

Tagesschau *die* news.

Tageszeit *die* time of day.

Tageszeitung *die* daily newspaper.

täglich ⬦ *adj* daily ⬦ *adv* every day; **dreimal ~** three times a day.

tagsüber *adv* during the day.

tagtäglich *adj* daily.

Tagung (*pl* -en) *die* conference.

Taifun (*pl* -e) *der* typhoon.

Taille ['taljə] (*pl* -n) *die* waist.

tailliert [ta'jiːɐt] *adj* fitted.

Taiwan *nt* Taiwan.

Takt (*pl* -e) *der* - **1.** [musikalische Einheit] bar - **2.** (*ohne pl*) [Feingefühl] tact - **3.** (*ohne pl*) [Rhythmus] time - **4.** *RW*: **jn aus dem ~ bringen** to put sb off.

Taktgefühl *das* tact.

Taktik (*pl* -en) *die* tactics (*pl*).

taktisch ⬦ *adj* [klug] tactical ⬦ *adv* tactically; **~ klug vorgehen** to use clever tactics.

taktlos ⬦ *adj* tactless ⬦ *adv* tactlessly.

Taktlosigkeit (*pl* -en) *die* tactlessness.

Taktstock *der* baton.

taktvoll ⬦ *adj* tactful ⬦ *adv* tactfully.

Tal (*pl* Täler) *das* valley.

Talent (*pl* -e) *das* talent.

talentiert ⬦ *adj* talented ⬦ *adv* with talent.

Talg (*pl* -e) *der* tallow; [von Menschen] sebum.

Talisman (*pl* -e) *der* talisman.

Talkshow ['tɔːkʃoː] (*pl* -s) *die* talk show.

Tampon ['tampɔn, tam'poːn] (*pl* -s) *der* tampon.

Tandem (*pl* -s) *das* tandem.

Tang (*pl* -e) *der* seaweed (U).

Tangente (*pl* -n) *die* MATH tangent.

Tango (*pl* -s) *der* tango.

Tank (*pl* -s) *der* tank.

Tankdeckel *der* fuel cap, petrol cap *Br*.

tanken ⬦ *vi* to get some petrol *Br* ODER gas *Am* ⬦ *vt* - **1.** [auftanken]: **Benzin ~** to get some petrol *Br* ODER gas *Am* - **2.** [genießen] to get one's fill of.

Tanker (*pl* -) *der* tanker.

Tankstelle *die* petrol station *Br*, gas station *Am*.

Tankwart, in (*mpl* -e; *fpl* -nen) *der, die* petrol *Br* ODER gas *Am* station attendant.

Tanne (*pl* -n) *die* - **1.** [Baum] fir tree - **2.** (*ohne pl*) [Holz] fir.

Tannenbaum *der* - **1.** [Tanne] fir tree - **2.** [Weihnachtsbaum] Christmas tree.

Tannenzapfen *der* fir cone.

Tansania *nt* Tanzania.

Tante (*pl* -n) *die* - **1.** [Verwandte] aunt - **2.** *fam* [als Anrede] auntie.

Tante-Emma-Laden *der* corner shop.

Tanz (*pl* Tänze) *der* dance.

Tanzbein *das* (*ohne pl*): **das ~ schwingen** *fam hum* to hit the floor.

tanzen *vt & vi* to dance; **komm, lass uns ~ gehen** let's go dancing; **willst du mit mir tanzen?** would you like to dance?

Tänzer, in (*mpl* -; *fpl* -nen) *der, die* dancer.

Tanzfläche *die* dance floor.

Tanzschule *die* dancing school.

Tanzstunde *die* - **1.** [Kurs] dancing lessons (*pl*) - **2.** [Unterrichtsstunde] dancing lesson.

Tapete (*pl* -n) *die* wallpaper (U).

Tapetenwechsel *der* *fig* change of scenery.

tapezieren *vt & vi* to wallpaper.

tapfer ⬦ *adj* brave ⬦ *adv* bravely.

Tapferkeit *die* bravery.

tappen (*perf* ist getappt) *vi*: **durch das Zimmer ~** to patter through the room.

tapsig ◇ *adj* awkward ◇ *adv* awkwardly.

Tarif (*pl* -e) *der* - **1.** WIRTSCH rate - **2.** [Gebühr] charge; [Verkehrstarif] fare.

Tarif|lohn *der* agreed rate of pay.

Tarif|ver|handlung *die* collective bargaining.

Tarif|vertrag *der* collective agreement.

tarnen *vt* to camouflage. ◆ **sich tarnen** *ref* to camouflage o.s.; **sich als etw ~** to disguise o.s. as sthg.

Tarnung *die* camouflage.

Tasche (*pl* -n) *die* - **1.** [Tragetasche, Handtasche] bag - **2.** [Hosentasche] pocket - **3.** *RW*: **etw aus eigener ~ bezahlen** to pay for sthg o.s.; **etw (schon) in der ~ haben** *fam* to have sthg in the bag; **jm auf der ~ liegen** *fam* to live off sb.

Taschen|buch *das* paperback.

Taschen|dieb, in *der, die* pickpocket.

Taschen|format *das*: **im ~** pocket-sized.

Taschen|geld *das* pocket money.

Taschen|lampe *die* torch *Br*, flashlight *Am*.

Taschen|messer *das* penknife, pocketknife.

Taschen|rechner *der* pocket calculator.

Taschentuch (*pl* -tücher) *das* [aus Stoff] handkerchief; [aus Papier] tissue.

Taschen|uhr *die* pocket watch.

Tasse (*pl* -n) *die* cup; **nicht alle ~n im Schrank haben** *fam fig & abw* to have a screw loose.

Tastatur (*pl* -en) *die* keyboard.

Taste (*pl* -n) *die* - **1.** [von Instrument, Computer] key - **2.** [von Geräten] button.

📖 **Taste**

Although Taste looks as if its meaning is clear, it is a false friend which has more to do with your sense of touch than your sense of taste. Taste is a "key" or "button" such as you might find on a computer keyboard or a musical instrument. Klicken Sie mit der rechten Maustaste darauf means "Click with the right mouse <u>button</u>". Remember also that the verb tasten means to "feel" or "grope" for something.

The concept of "taste" in English – whether in the sense of "flavour", "preference" or "ability to be discerning" – is translated by Geschmack. So the phrase "My girlfriend has good <u>taste</u>" can be translated as Meine Freundin hat einen gu-ten <u>Geschmack</u>.

---

tasten ◇ *vi* to feel one's way; **nach etw ~** to feel for sthg ◇ *vt* to feel. ◆ **sich tasten** *ref* to feel one's way.   ●

Tasten|instrument *das* keyboard instrument.

Tastsinn *der* sense of touch.

tat *prät* ⊏▷ tun.

Tat (*pl* -en) *die* action; **eine verbrecherische ~** a criminal act; **eine gute ~** a good deed; **jn auf frischer ~ ertappen** *fig* to catch sb in the act; **etw in die ~ umsetzen** to put sthg into action. ◆ **in der Tat** *adv* [tatsächlich] indeed.

Tat|be|stand *der* - **1.** RECHT: **der ~ der Bestechung** the offence of bribery; **den ~ des Betrugs erfüllen** to constitute fraud - **2.** [Tatsache] facts (*pl*) (of the matter).

tatenlos ◇ *adj* idle ◇ *adv* idly; **wir mussten ~ zusehen** we could only stand and watch.

Täter, in (*mpl* -; *fpl* -nen) *der, die* culprit.

tätig *adj* - **1.** [beschäftigt]: **~ sein** to work - **2.** [aktiv] active; **~ werden** to take action.

tätigen *vt geh* [von Geschäft] to transact.

Tätigkeit (*pl* -en) *die* [Arbeit] job; [Aktivität] activity.

tatkräftig ◇ *adj* active ◇ *adv* actively.

tätlich ◇ *adj* physical; **~ werden** to become violent ◇ *adv* physically.

Tat|ort *der* [von Verbrechen] scene of the crime.

Tätowierung (*pl* -en) *die* - **1.** [Vorgang] tattooing (*U*) - **2.** [Ergebnis] tattoo.

Tat|sache *die* fact; **jn vor vollendete ~n stellen** *fig* to present sb with a fait accompli ◇ *interj* it's true!

tatsächlich, tatsächlich ◇ *adj* real, actual ◇ *adv* really; **du bist ja ~ pünktlich!** you're actually on time!

tätscheln *vt* [liebkosen] to pat.

Tattoo [ta'tu:] (*pl* -s) *das* = Tätowierung.

Tatze (*pl* -n) *die* paw.

Tau (*pl* -e) ◇ *der* [Niederschlag] dew ◇ *das* [Seil] rope.

taub *adj* - **1.** [nichts hörend] deaf; **sich ~ stellen** *fam* to turn a deaf ear - **2.** [nichts fühlend] numb.

Taube (*pl* -n) ◇ *der, die* [Gehörlose] deaf person ◇ *die* [Tier - gewöhnlich] pigeon; [- weiße] dove.

taubstumm *adj* deaf and dumb.

tauchen (*perf* hat/ist getaucht) ◇ *vi* (hat, ist) to dive ◇ *vt* (hat) - **1.** [eintauchen] to dip - **2.** [drücken] to duck.

Taucher, in (*mpl* -; *fpl* -nen) *der, die* diver.

Taucher|brille *die* diving goggles (*pl*).

tauen (*perf* hat/ist getaut) ◇ *vi* (hat, ist) to melt; **es taut** it's thawing ◇ *vt* (hat) to thaw.

Taufe (*pl* -n) *die* - **1.** [Vorgang] christening - **2.** (*ohne pl*) [Sakrament] baptism.

taufen *vt* - **1.** REL [Menschen] to baptize - **2.** [Tiere, Gegenstände] to name.

Tauf|pate *der* godfather.

Tauf|patin *die* godmother.

taugen *vi:* **nichts/wenig ~** to be no/not much good; **zu** ODER **für etw ~** to be suitable for sthg.

tauglich *adj* - 1. [geeignet] suitable - 2. MIL fit (for service).

Taumel *der (ohne pl)* - 1. [Rausch] frenzy - 2. [Schwindel] (feeling of) dizziness.

taumeln *(perf hat/ist getaumelt) vi* - 1. *(ist)* [schwankend gehen] to stagger - 2. *(hat)* [schwanken] to reel.

Tausch *(pl -e) der* exchange.

tauschen <> *vt* to swap <> *vi:* **mit jm ~** [Arbeitszeit] to swap with sb; [an js Stelle sein, jd anderes sein] to swap places with sb.

täuschen <> *vt* to deceive; [Gegner] to trick <> *vi* to be deceptive. ➡ **sich täuschen** *ref* to be wrong; **sich in jm ~** to be wrong about sb.

täuschend <> *adj* deceptive <> *adv* deceptively.

Täuschung *(pl -en) die* - 1. [Irreführung] deception - 2. [Verwechslung] illusion.

Täuschungs|manöver *das* ploy.

tausend *num.* a ODER one thousand; *siehe auch* **sechs**.

Tausend *(pl -* ODER *-e) das* thousand. ➡ **Tausende** *pl* [sehr viele]: **zu ~en** by the thousand; *siehe auch* **Sechs**.

Tausender *(pl -) der* MATH thousand.

Tausendfüßler *(pl -) der* centipede.

tausendmal *adv* a thousand times.

tausendste, r, s *adj* thousandth; *siehe auch* **sechste**.

Tausendste *(pl -n) der, die, das* thousandth; *siehe auch* **Sechste**.

tausendstel *adj (unver)* thousandth; *siehe auch* **sechstel**.

Tausendstel *(pl -) das* thousandth; *siehe auch* **Sechstel**.

Tauwetter *das* thaw.

Tauziehen *das* tug-of-war.

Taxi *(pl -s) das* taxi.

Technik *(pl -en) die* - 1. *(ohne pl)* [Wissenschaft] technology - 2. [Methode] technique - 3. [Ausrüstung] equipment - 4. *(ohne pl)* [Funktionsweise] workings *(pl)*.

Techniker, in *(mpl -; fpl -nen) der, die* engineer; [im Sport, in Musik] technician.

technisch <> *adj* technical; [Fortschritt] technological <> *adv* technically; [fortgeschritten] technologically.

Technische Hoch|schule *die technical college.*

Technische Überwachungsverein *der amt institution charged with testing roadworthiness of cars and safety of consumer goods and installations.*

Techno *der* MUS techno.

Technologie *(pl -n) die* technology.

technologisch <> *adj* technological <> *adv* technologically.

Teddy *(pl -s)*, **Teddybär** *(pl -en) der* teddy bear.

Tee *(pl -s) der* - 1. [gen] tea; **schwarzer ~** black tea - 2. [Kräutertee] herbal tea.

Tee|beutel *der* teabag.

Tee|kanne *die* teapot.

Tee|löffel *der* teaspoon.

Teer *der* tar *(U)*.

teeren *vt* to tar.

Tee|sieb *das* tea strainer.

Teheran *nt* Teheran.

Teich *(pl -e) der* pond.

Teig *(pl -e) der* dough *(U)*.

Teigwaren *pl amt* pasta *(U)*.

Teil *(pl -e)* <> *der* [Teilmenge] part <> *der* ODER *das* [Anteil] share; **sich** *(D)* **seinen ~ denken** *fig* to keep one's thoughts to o.s. <> *das* [Bestandteil] part. ➡ **zum Teil** *adv* [teilweise] partly.

teilen <> *vt* [aufteilen] to share; [zerteilen] to divide; [etw mit jm] ~ to share sthg with sb; **sich** *(D)* **etw ~** to share sthg <> *vi* to share. ➡ **sich teilen** *ref* [Gruppe] to split up; [Straße] to fork; [Meinungen] to be divided.

teil|haben *vi (unreg):* **an etw** *(D)* **~** to share in sthg.

Teilhaber, in *(mpl -; fpl -nen) der, die* partner.

Teilnahme *(pl -n) die* - 1. [Aufmerksamkeit, Beteiligung] participation *(U)* - 2. [an Kurs] attendance - 3. [Mitgefühl] sympathy.

teilnahmslos <> *adj* apathetic <> *adv* apathetically.

teil|nehmen *vi (unreg)* - 1. [mitmachen]: **an etw** *(D)* **~** to take part in sthg - 2. [mitfühlen]: **an etw** *(D)* **~** *geh* to share in sthg.

Teilnehmer, in *(mpl -; fpl -nen) der, die* participant.

teils *adv fam* partly. ➡ **teils ..., teils ...** *adv* partly ..., partly ...

Teilung *(pl -en) die* division.

teilweise <> *adv* - 1. [zum Teil] partly - 2. [zeitweise] sometimes <> *adj* partial.

Tel. *(abk für Telefon)* tel.

Tele|arbeit *die* teleworking.

Telefon, Telefon *(pl -e) das* - 1. [Gerät] telephone; **am ~** on the telephone - 2. *fam* [Anruf]: **~ für dich** there's a call for you.

Telefonan|ruf *der* telephone call.

Telefonat *(pl -e) das* telephone call.

Telefon|buch *das* telephone book.

Telefon|gespräch *das* telephone conversation.

telefonieren *vi* to make a telephone call; **mit jm ~** to talk to sb on the telephone.

telefonisch <> *adj* telephone *(vor Subst)* <> *adv* by telephone; **ich bin ~ erreichbar** you can reach me by telephone.
Telefon|karte *die* phonecard.
Telefon|nummer *die* telephone number.
Telefonver|bindung *die* telephone line.
Telefon|zelle *die* telephone box.
Telefon|zentrale *die* switchboard.
telegrafieren *vt* to telegraph.
telegrafisch <> *adj* telegraphic <> *adv* by telegram.
Telegramm *(pl* -e) *das* telegram.
Telekom® *die German telecommunications company.*
Tele|objektiv *das* FOTO telephoto lens.
Telex *(pl* -e) *das* telex.
Teller *(pl* -) *der* [Gefäß] plate.
Tempel *(pl* -) *der* temple.
Temperament *(pl* -e) *das* - **1.** [Energie] liveliness; **~ haben** to be lively - **2.** [Wesen] temperament.
temperamentvoll *adj* lively.

📖 temperamentvoll

Caution is needed with the German temperamentvoll since it describes not a negative characteristic but a positive one: Ein temperamentvolles Pferd is "a lively horse", not a temperamental one.
The English word "temperamental", describing a person or a machine, is best translated by launenhaft or launisch. For example, the sentence "The children are always a bit temperamental first thing in the morning" could be translated as Die Kinder sind immer etwas launisch am frühen Morgen.

Temperatur *(pl* -en) *die* temperature.
Tempo[1] *(pl* -s ODER Tempi) *das* - **1.** *(pl Tempos)* [Geschwindigkeit] speed; **hier gilt ~ 30** there's a 30 km/h speed limit here - **2.** *(pl Tempi)* MUS tempo.
Tempo®[2] *(pl* -s) *das fam* [Papiertaschentuch] tissue.
Tempo|limit *das* speed limit.
Tempotaschen|tuch® *das fam* tissue.
Tendenz *(pl* -en) *die* - **1.** [Entwicklung] trend - **2.** [Neigung] tendency.
tendieren *vi* to tend; **zu etw ~** to tend towards sthg.
Tennis *das* tennis.
Tennis|platz *der* tennis court.
Tennis|schläger *der* tennis racquet.
Tenor *(pl* Tenöre) *der* MUS tenor.
Teppich *(pl* -e) *der* - **1.** [Einzelstück] rug - **2.** [Teppichboden] carpet.
Teppich|boden *der* carpet.

Termin *(pl* -e) *der* - **1.** [Zeitpunkt] date; [Vereinbarung] appointment - **2.** RECHT hearing.
Terminal ['tø:ɐminəl] *(pl* -s) <> *der* ODER *das* [Gebäude] terminal <> *das* EDV terminal.
Termin|kalender *der* diary.
Termin|plan *der* schedule.
Terpentin *(pl* -e) *das* turpentine *(U).*
Terrasse *(pl* -n) *die* - **1.** [am Haus] patio - **2.** [am Berg] terrace.
Terrier ['tɛrjɐ] *(pl* -) *der* terrier.
Territorium [tɛri'to:rjʊm] *(pl* -torien) *das* territory.
Terror *der* - **1.** [Gewalt] terrorism - **2.** [Angst] terror - **3.**: **~ machen** *fam* to raise hell.
Terroran|schlag *der* terrorist attack.
terrorisieren *vt* to terrorize.
Terrorismus *der* terrorism.
Terrorist, in *(mpl* -en; *fpl* -nen) *der, die* terrorist.
Terz *(pl* -en) *die* MUS third.
Tesa® *der* Sellotape® *Br,* Scotch tape® *Am.*
Tesafilm® *der* Sellotape® *Br,* Scotch tape® *Am.*
Tessin *das* Ticino.
Test *(pl* -e ODER -s) *der* test.
Testament *(pl* -e) *das* - **1.** [letzter Wille] will - **2.** REL: **das Alte/Neue ~** the Old/New Testament.
testamentarisch *adv:* **etw ~ verfügen** to put sthg in one's will.
testen *vt* to test.
Tetanus|impfung *die* tetanus vaccination.
teuer <> *adj* - **1.** [Preis] expensive - **2.** *geh* [Freund] dear <> *adv* dearly.
Teufel *(pl* -) *der* - **1.** [gen] devil - **2.** RW: **der ~ ist los** *fam* all hell has broken loose; **zum ~ mit ihr!** *fam* [Schluss damit] to hell with her!
Teufels|kreis *der* vicious circle.
teuflisch <> *adj* devilish <> *adv* devilishly.
Text *(pl* -e) *der* - **1.** [Geschriebenes] text; [von Lied] lyrics *(pl)* - **2.** [von Bild] caption.
Textilien *pl* textiles.
Textil|industrie *die* textile industry.
Text|verarbeitung *die* EDV word processing *(U).*
TH [te:'ha:] *die abk für* Technische Hochschule.
Thailand *nt* Thailand.
Theater *(pl* -) *das* - **1.** [gen] theatre; **~ spielen** to act - **2.** *fam* [Ärger] fuss; **~ machen** to make a fuss; **so ein ~!** such a fuss! - **3.** *fam* [Vortäuschung] play-acting; **~ spielen** to put on an act.
Theaterauf|führung *die* performance.
Theater|kasse *die* theatre box office.
Theater|stück *das* play.
theatralisch *adj* dramatic.

Theke (pl -n) die - **1.** [in Kneipe] bar - **2.** [in Geschäft] counter.

Thema (pl Themen) das subject; MUS theme; **etw ist für jn kein ~** fig sthg is not important to sb; **etw ist kein ~ mehr** fig sthg is of no interest any more.

 das Thema wechseln

Anyway, I'm going home now. Wie dem auch sei, ich gehe jetzt jedenfalls nach Hause.

Before I forget, who won the match? Ach ja, wer hat eigentlich das Spiel gewonnen?

While I remember, did you ever find your ring? Da fällt mir gerade ein, hast du eigentlich deinen Ring wiedergefunden?

By the way, you still owe me for the train ticket. Ach ja, du schuldest mir übrigens noch Geld für die Zugfahrkarte.

Talking of ghosts, did anyone see that film on TV last night? Apropos Geister, hat jemand gestern Abend den Film im Fernsehen gesehen?

Incidentally, has anyone heard from John recently? Ach übrigens, hat jemand in letzter Zeit etwas von John gehört?

Themse die: **die ~** the (River) Thames.
Theologe (pl -n) der theologian.
Theologie (pl -n) die theology.
Theologin (pl -nen) die theologian.
Theoretiker, in (mpl -; fpl -nen) der, die theorist.
theoretisch <> adj theoretical <> adv theoretically.
Theorie (pl -n) die theory.
therapeutisch <> adj therapeutic <> adv therapeutically.
Therapie (pl -n) die therapy.
Thermal|bad das thermal bath.
Thermo|meter das thermometer.
Thermos|flasche die Thermos® (flask).
Thermostat (pl -e ODER -en) der thermostat.
These (pl -n) die thesis.
Thron (pl -e) der throne.
thronen vi to sit imposingly.
Thronfolger, in (mpl -; fpl -nen) der, die heir to the throne.
Thun|fisch, Tunfisch der tuna.
Thüringen nt Thuringia.
Thüringer (pl -) <> der native/inhabitant of Thuringia <> adj (unver) of/from Thuringia.
Thüringerin (pl -nen) die native/inhabitant of Thuringia.
Thymian (pl -e) der thyme.
Tick (pl -s) der quirk; [nervös] tic.
ticken vi to tick.

tief <> adj - **1.** [gen] deep; **ein ~er Fall** a long fall; **zwei Meter ~** two metres deep; **im ~sten Winter** in the depths of winter - **2.** [niedrig] low <> adv - **1.** [nach unten] deep - **2.** [niedrig] low; **zu ~ singen** to sing flat - **3.** [zeitlich]: **bis ~ in die Nacht** far into the night - **4.** [verletzt, atmen, bewegt] deeply; **~ schlafen** to be in a deep sleep.
Tief (pl -s) das depression.
Tiefdruck|gebiet das area of low pressure.
Tiefe (pl -n) die depth.
tiefernst <> adj very serious <> adv very seriously.
Tief|garage die underground car park Br ODER parking lot Am.
tiefgefroren adj frozen.
tiefgekühlt <> adj frozen <> adv in a freezer.
tief greifend <> adj radical <> adv radically.
Tiefkühl|fach das freezer compartment.
Tiefkühl|kost die frozen food.
Tiefkühl|truhe die freezer.
Tief|punkt der low.
tief schürfend <> adj profound <> adv profoundly.
tiefsinnig adj profound.
Tiefstand der (ohne pl) low.
Tier (pl -e) das animal; **ein großes** ODER **hohes ~** fam fig a big shot.
Tier|art die species.
Tier|arzt, ärztin der, die vet.
Tier|garten der zoo.
Tier|handlung die pet shop.
Tier|heim das animal home.
tierisch <> adj - **1.** [von Tieren] animal - **2.** fam [groß]: **ich habe ~e Angst** I'm really frightened <> adv fam really.
Tierkreis|zeichen das ASTROL star sign.
tierlieb adj animal-loving; **~ sein** to be an animal lover.
Tier|park der zoo.
Tier|quälerei die cruelty to animals.
Tierschutz|verein der society for the prevention of cruelty to animals.
Tier|versuch der animal experiment.
Tiger, in (mpl -; fpl -nen) der, die tiger.
Tilde (pl -n) die tilde.
tilgen vt to repay.
Tinte (pl -n) die ink; **in der ~ sitzen** fam fig to be in the soup.
Tinten|fisch der octopus; [klein] squid; [Sepia] cuttlefish.
Tip = **Tipp.**
Tipp (pl -s) der - **1.** [Hinweis] tip - **2.** [Wette] bet.
tippen <> vi - **1.** [vorhersagen, wetten] to bet; **meistens tippe ich richtig** I'm usually

right; **auf etw** *(A)* ~ to bet on sthg; **ich tippe darauf, dass ...** I bet that ... **- 2.** *fam* [Maschine schreiben] to type <> *vt* **- 1.** *fam* [Schreibmaschine schreiben] to type **- 2.** [antippen] to tap.

tipptopp *adj (unver) fam* [von Person, Garten] immaculate; [von Haus] shipshape.

Tirol *nt* Tyrol.

Tiroler *(pl -)* der & adj *(unver)* Tyrolean.

Tirolerin *(pl -nen)* die Tyrolean.

tirolerisch *adj* Tyrolean.

Tisch *(pl -e)* der **- 1.** [Möbel] table; **den ~ decken** to set the table **- 2.** *RW:* **unter den ~ fallen** to fall by the wayside; **das ist vom ~** that's been done and dusted.

Tischldecke die tablecloth.

Tischler, in *(mpl -; fpl -nen)* der, die carpenter.

Tischltennis das table tennis.

Tischtuch *(pl -tücher)* das tablecloth.

Titel *(pl -)* der title.

Titellbild das cover picture.

Titellseite die front page.

Titellverteidiger, in der, die SPORT defending champion.

Toast [tɔːst] *(pl -e ODER -s)* der **- 1.** [Brot] toast; [Scheibe] slice of toast **- 2.** [Trinkspruch] toast.

Toastlbrot das sliced white bread *(U)*.

toasten ['tɔːstn̩] *vt* to toast.

Toaster ['tɔːstɐ] *(pl -)* der toaster.

toben *(perf* hat/ist getobt*) vi* **- 1.** (hat) [wild werden] to go berserk **- 2.** (ist) [rennen] to charge about **- 3.** (hat) [wüten] to rage.

Tochter *(pl Töchter)* die daughter.

Tod *(pl -e)* der death; **jn zum ~(e) verurteilen** to condemn sb to death; **zu ~e erschreckt** scared to death.

todernst <> *adj* deadly serious <> *adv* in a deadly serious way.

Todeslangst die: **eine ~ haben/ausstehen** to be scared to death.

Todeslanzeige die [in Zeitung] death notice.

Todeslfall der death.

Todeslkampf der death throes *(pl)*.

Todeslopfer das casualty, fatality.

Todeslstrafe die death penalty.

Todeslursache die cause of death.

Todeslurteil das death sentence.

todkrank *adj* terminally ill.

tödlich <> *adj* **- 1.** [Krankheit, Unfall] fatal; [Gift, Biss] lethal **- 2.** *fam* [Angst, Langeweile, Sicherheit] deadly; [Beleidigung] mortal <> *adv* **- 1.** [verlaufen] fatally; [wirken] lethally **- 2.** *fam* [langweilig] deadly; [beleidigt] mortally.

todmüde *adj* exhausted.

todschick *fam* <> *adj* dead smart <> *adv* dead smartly.

todsicher *fam* <> *adj* [Sache, Gewinn] sure-fire; **das ist ~** it's dead certain <> *adv* definitely.

Tofu der tofu.

toi, toi, toi ['tɔy 'tɔy 'tɔy] *interj* **- 1.** [unberufen] touch wood! **- 2.** [viel Glück] best of luck!

Toilette [tɔa'lɛtə] *(pl -n)* die toilet; **auf die ~ gehen** to go to the toilet.

Toilettenpapier das toilet paper.

Tokio *nt* Tokyo.

tolerant <> *adj* tolerant <> *adv* tolerantly.

Toleranz *(pl -en)* die tolerance.

tolerieren *vt* to tolerate.

toll *fam* <> *adj* **- 1.** [schön] fantastic, brilliant **- 2.** [unglaublich] far-out <> *adv* **- 1.** [wunderbar] fantastically, brilliantly **- 2.** [sehr] like crazy; **er hat sich ganz ~ gefreut** he was dead pleased.

tollen *(perf* ist getollt*) vi* to run around like crazy.

tollkühn <> *adj* reckless; **ein ~er Mensch** a daredevil <> *adv* recklessly.

Tollpatsch *(pl -e)* der clumsy devil.

Tollwut die rabies *(U)*.

Tomate *(pl -n)* die tomato.

Tomatenlmark das tomato purée.

Ton *(pl -e ODER Töne)* der **- 1.** *(pl* Tone*)* [Lehm] clay **- 2.** *(pl* Töne*)* [Laut] note **- 3.** *(pl* Töne*)* [Tonfall] tone; **hier herrscht ein rauer ~!** the atmosphere's terrible here!; **sich im ~ vergreifen** to adopt the wrong tone **- 4.** *(pl* Töne*)* [Farbton] shade, tone **- 5.** [von Platte, Film] sound **- 6.** *RW:* **den ~ angeben** to be extremely influential; **zum guten ~ gehören** to be the done thing.

Tonlart die **- 1.** MUS key **- 2.** [Tonfall] tone.

Tonauslfall der TV loss of sound.

Tonband *(pl -bänder)* das **- 1.** [Spule] tape **- 2.** [Gerät] tape recorder.

Tonbandlgerät das tape recorder.

tönen <> *vi* **- 1.** [klingen] to sound **- 2.** [prahlen] to boast <> *vt* [Haare] to tint.

Tonlfall der **- 1.** [Tonart] tone **- 2.** [Sprachmelodie] intonation.

Tonlfilm der sound film.

Tonllage die pitch.

Tonlleiter die scale.

Tonne *(pl -n)* die **- 1.** [Behälter] barrel **- 2.** [Gewicht] tonne.

top *fam* <> *adj (unver)*: **~ sein** to be brilliant <> *adv* brilliantly.

TOP [tɔp] *(pl -)* (abk für Tagesordnungspunkt) der item on the agenda.

Topf *(pl Töpfe)* der **- 1.** [zum Kochen] pan **- 2.** [für Vorräte, Blumen] pot **- 3.** *fam* [Klo] loo *Br*, john *Am*.

Töpfer *(pl -)* der potter.

Töpferei *(pl -en)* die pottery.

Töpferin (*pl* -nen) *die* potter.

töpfern <> *vt* to make (*pottery*) <> *vi* to do pottery.

Topf|lappen *der* oven cloth.

Tor (*pl* -e) *das* - 1. SPORT goal; **ein ~ schießen** to score a goal; **im ~ stehen** to be in goal - 2. [Tür] gate; [von Garage, Scheune] door.

Torein|fahrt *die* entrance gate.

Torf *der* peat.

Torhüter, in (*mpl* -; *fpl* -nen) *der, die* goalkeeper.

torkeln (*perf* hat/ist getorkelt) *vi* to stagger.

Torpedo (*pl* -s) *das* torpedo.

Tor|schütze, schützin *der, die* goalscorer.

Torte (*pl* -n) *die* gâteau.

Torten|guss *der* glaze (in fruit flan), jelly.

Tortur (*pl* -en) *die eigtl & fig* torture.

Torwart, in (*mpl* -e; *fpl* -nen) *der, die* goalkeeper.

tosen (*perf* hat/ist getost) *vi* to roar.

Toskana *die*: **die ~** Tuscany.

tot <> *adj eigtl & fig* dead; **ein ~er Punkt** a standstill; *fig* a deadlock <> *adv*: **~ umfallen** to drop dead; *siehe auch* **tot stellen**.

total <> *adj* total <> *adv fam* totally; **~ gut** dead good.

Total|schaden *der* write-off.

Tote (*pl* -n) *der, die* dead person; **es gab mehrere ~** several people were killed.

töten *vt & vi* to kill.

Toten|kopf *der* - 1. [auf Arzneimittel, Piratenflagge] skull and crossbones - 2. [Schädel] skull.

Toten|schädel *der* skull.

Toten|schein *der* death certificate.

Toten|sonntag *der* Sunday before Advent, day for commemoration of the dead in Protestant religion.

totenstill *adj* deathly silent.

tot|lachen ➞ **sich totlachen** *ref fam* to kill o.s. laughing.

Totschlag *der* RECHT manslaughter.

tot|schlagen *vt* (*unreg*) [töten] to beat to death.

tot|schweigen *vt* (*unreg*) to hush up.

tot stellen ➞ **sich tot stellen** *ref* to play dead.

Toupet [tu'pe:] (*pl* -s) *das* toupee.

toupieren [tu'pi:rən] *vt* to backcomb.

Tour [tu:ɐ̯] (*pl* -en) *die* - 1. [Ausflug] tour; [kürzere Fahrt] trip - 2. *fam* [Verhaltensweise] ploy; **es auf die sanfte ~ versuchen** *fam* to use the gentle approach - 3. [Strecke] route - 4. TECH revolution; **auf vollen ODER höchsten ~en laufen** [Motor, Maschine] to run at full speed - 5. *RW*: **auf ~en kommen** *fam* to get going.

Tourismus [tu'rɪsmʊs] *der* tourism.

Tourist [tu'rɪst] (*pl* -en) *der* tourist.

Touristin [tu'rɪstɪn] (*pl* -nen) *die* tourist.

Trab *der* trot; **auf ~ sein** *fig* to be on the go; **jn in ~ halten** *fam fig* to keep sb on the go; **sich in ~ setzen** *fam fig* to get going.

Trabant® (*pl* -s) *der* AUTO Trabant, small car formerly manufactured in the GDR.

traben (*perf* ist getrabt) *vi* to trot.

Trabi (*pl* -s) *der fam* colloquial name for a Trabant.

Trab|rennen *das* trotting.

Tracht (*pl* -en) *die* - 1. [Kleidung] traditional costume - 2. [Schläge]: **eine ~ Prügel** *fam* a beating.

trachten *vi*: **nach etw ~** to strive for sthg; **jm nach dem Leben ~** to be after sb's blood.

trächtig *adj* pregnant.

Trackball [tr'ɛkbɔ:l] (*pl* -s) *der* EDV trackball.

Tradition (*pl* -en) *die* tradition.

traditionell <> *adj* traditional <> *adv* traditionally.

traf *prät* ⊏⊐ **treffen**.

tragbar *adj* - 1. [Gerät] portable - 2. [Zustand, Verhalten] acceptable; **finanziell ~ sein** to be financially viable.

träge <> *adj* - 1. [müde] lethargic - 2. [langsam] sluggish <> *adv* - 1. [müde] lethargically - 2. [langsam] sluggishly.

tragen (*präs* trägt; *prät* trug; *perf* hat getragen) <> *vt* - 1. [schleppen] to carry - 2. [am Körper haben] to wear - 3. [bei sich haben]: **etw bei sich ~** to carry sthg (on one) - 4. [Früchte] to produce; [Zinsen] to yield - 5. [Kosten, Schicksal, Leid] to bear; [Anteil] to pay - 6. [Einrichtung, Schule] to support - 7. [Verantwortung] to take; [Folgen] to suffer - 8. [Namen, Unterschrift] to bear <> *vi* - 1. [Baum] to bear fruit - 2. [Gewicht]: **das Eis trägt noch nicht** the ice won't bear any weight yet - 3. [Reichweite haben] to carry - 4. [stützen] to support - 5. *RW*: **an etw** (*D*) **schwer ~** to find sthg hard to bear. ➞ **sich tragen** *ref fig* - 1. [zu tragen sein]: **dieser Stoff trägt sich sehr angenehm** this material is very pleasant to wear; **der Koffer trägt sich schlecht** the suitcase is difficult to carry - 2. [sich selbst finanzieren] to be self-supporting - 3. *geh* [planen]: **sich mit etw ~** to contemplate sthg. ➞ **Tragen** *das*: **zum Tragen kommen** to apply.

tragend *adj* load-bearing.

Träger, in (*mpl* -; *fpl* -nen) <> *der, die* - 1. [Lastenträger] porter - 2. [von Titel] holder - 3. [Geldgeber] sponsor <> *der* - 1. ARCHIT girder - 2. [an Kleidung] strap.

Trage|tasche *die* carrier bag.

tragfähig *adj* - 1. [Kompromiss, Politik] tenable - 2. [Konstruktion] solid, capable of supporting a load.

Trag|fläche *die* wing.

Trägheit die - 1. [Faulheit] lethargy - 2. PHYS inertia.

Tragik die tragedy.

tragisch ⟨⟩ adj tragic ⟨⟩ adv tragically.

Tragödie [tra'gø:djə] (pl -n) die tragedy.

trägt präs ⟶ tragen.

Tragweite die (ohne pl) consequences (pl); **von großer** ~ of great consequence.

Trainer, in ['trɛːnɐ, rɪn] (mpl -; fpl -nen) der, die coach.

trainieren [trɛ'niːrən] ⟨⟩ vt [Verein, Sportler] to coach; [Pferd] to train; [Salto, Elfmeterschießen] to practise ⟨⟩ vi to train.

Training ['trɛːnɪŋ] (pl -s) das training (U).

Trainingsanzug der tracksuit.

Traktor (pl -toren) der tractor.

trällern vt & vi to warble.

trampeln (perf hat/ist getrampelt) vi - 1. (ist) fam [gehen] to stamp - 2. (hat) [stampfen]: **mit den Füßen** ~ to stamp one's feet.

trampen ['trɛmpn] (perf hat/ist getrampt) vi (hat) [an der Straße stehen] to hitchhike.

Tramper, in ['trɛmpɐ, rɪn] (mpl -; fpl -nen) der, die hitchhiker.

Trampolin (pl -e) das trampoline.

Tran (pl -e) der train oil; **im** ~ **sein** fam [unaufmerksam] to be out of it.

Träne (pl -n) die tear; **in ~n ausbrechen** to burst into tears.

tränen vi to water.

Tränengas das tear gas.

trank prät ⟶ trinken.

tränken vt to water.

Transformator (pl -toren) der transformer.

Transfusion (pl -en) die transfusion.

transitiv adj GRAM transitive.

transparent adj transparent.

Transparent (pl -e) das banner.

Transport (pl -e) der transport.

transportabel adj portable.

transportfähig adj: **der Verletzte ist nicht** ~ the injured man cannot be moved.

transportieren ⟨⟩ vt - 1. [befördern] to transport - 2. [Film] to wind on ⟨⟩ vi [Kamera] to wind on; [Nähmaschine] to feed.

Transportmittel das means (sg) of transport.

Transvestit [tansvɛs'tiːt] (pl -en) der transvestite.

Trapez (pl -e) das - 1. [im Zirkus] trapeze - 2. MATH trapezium Br, trapezoid Am.

Trara das fam: **mit großem** ~ with a great hullabaloo; ~ **machen** to make a fuss.

trat prät ⟶ treten.

Tratsch der fam abw gossip.

Traube (pl -n) die - 1. [Obst] grape - 2. BIOL raceme - 3. [Menge] cluster.

Traubenzucker der glucose.

trauen ⟨⟩ vi: **jm/einer Sache** ~ to trust sb/sthg ⟨⟩ vt [Brautpaar] to marry; **sich ~ lassen** to be married. ⟶ **sich trauen** ref to dare.

Trauer die - 1. [Schmerz] sorrow - 2. [Staatstrauer, Trauerkleidung] mourning.

Trauerfall der death, bereavement.

trauern vi: **(um jn)** ~ to mourn (for sb).

Trauerspiel das: **es ist ein** ~ fam it's tragic.

Trauerzug der funeral procession.

Traufe (pl -n) die: **vom Regen in die** ~ **kommen** to jump out of the frying pan into the fire.

träufeln vt: **etw auf/in etw** (A) ~ to trickle sthg onto/into sthg.

Traum (pl Träume) der dream.

Trauma (pl -ta) das trauma.

träumen ⟨⟩ vi - 1. [gen] to dream; **schrecklich/schön** ~ to have terrible/ pleasant dreams; **von jm/etw** ~ eigtl & fig to dream about sb/sthg - 2. [abwesend sein] to dream, to daydream ⟨⟩ vt to dream about; **das hätte ich mir nicht** ~ **lassen** fig I'd never have imagined it possible.

Träumerei (pl -en) die daydream.

träumerisch ⟨⟩ adj [Mensch] dreamy; [Gedanken] wistful ⟨⟩ adv dreamily.

traumhaft ⟨⟩ adj - 1. [wunderschön] fabulous - 2. [souverän] amazing ⟨⟩ adv [wunderschön] fabulously.

traurig ⟨⟩ adj - 1. [betrüblich] sad - 2. [Rest, Zustand] sorry ⟨⟩ adv sadly.

Traurigkeit die sadness.

Trauschein der marriage certificate.

Trauung (pl -en) die wedding; **kirchliche/ standesamtliche** ~ church/civil wedding.

Trauzeuge der witness (at a wedding).

Trauzeugin die witness (at a wedding).

Travellerscheck ['trɛvələʃɛk] der traveller's cheque.

treffen (präs trifft; prät traf; perf hat/ist getroffen) ⟨⟩ vt (hat) - 1. [begegnen] to meet - 2. [Ziel] to hit; **auf dem Foto bist du gut getroffen** it's a good photo of you; **es gut/ schlecht getroffen haben** fig to have been lucky/unlucky - 3. [emotional verletzen] to affect - 4. [Verabredung, Entscheidung] to make; [Maßnahmen] to take; **eine Vereinbarung** ~ to come to an agreement ⟨⟩ vi - 1. (hat) [ins Ziel treffen] to score; **der Schuss traf nicht** the shot missed - 2. (ist) [begegnen]: **auf jn/etw** ~ to come across sb/sthg. ⟶ **sich treffen** ref to meet; **sich mit jm** ~ to meet sb; **es trifft sich gut/schlecht, dass ...** fig it's lucky/unlucky that ...

Treffen (pl -) das meeting.

treffend ⟨⟩ adj fitting ⟨⟩ adv fittingly.

Treffer (pl -) der - 1. [Tor] goal; [beim Basketball] basket - 2. [mit Schusswaffe] hit - 3. [Boxhieb] blow - 4. [Losgewinn] win.

Treffpunkt der meeting place.

treiben (*prät* trieb; *perf* hat/ist getrieben) ⟨⟩ *vt (hat)* - **1.** [gen] to drive; **jn in etw** *(A)* **/zu etw ~** to drive sb to sthg; **du treibst mich noch in den Wahnsinn** you're driving me mad; **die Strömung trieb das Boot an den Strand** the current carried the boat ashore; **durch Windkraft getrieben** wind-powered - **2.** *fam* [anstellen] to get up to; **was treibt ihr beiden denn da wieder?** what are you two up to now? - **3.** [ansetzen] to produce - **4.** [bohren - Schacht, Tunnel] to dig - **5.** *RW:* **es zu bunt ~** *fam* to overdo it ⟨⟩ *vi* - **1.** *(ist)* [im Wasser] to drift; **sich ~ lassen** *fig* to drift - **2.** *(hat)* [ansetzen - Blüten] to flower; [- Wurzeln] to root - **3.** *(hat)* [Harndrang verursachen] to be a diuretic, to have a diuretic effect.

Treiben *das* (*ohne pl*) - **1.** [Durcheinander] bustle - **2.** *abw* [Tun] activities (*pl*).

Treib|haus *das* greenhouse.

Treib|hauseffekt *der* greenhouse effect.

Treib|jagd *die* shoot (*in which game is beaten*).

Treib|stoff *der* fuel.

Trend (*pl* -s) *der* trend; **im ~ liegen** to be in vogue.

trennen *vt* - **1.** [gen] to separate - **2.** [unterscheiden] to distinguish. ◆ **sich trennen** *ref* - **1.** [Menschen] to separate; **sich von jm ~** to leave sb; **sich von etw ~** to part with sthg - **2.** [Wege, Leitungen *etc*] to divide.

Trennung (*pl* -en) *die* - **1.** [gen & CHEM] separation; **in ~ leben** to be separated - **2.** [Unterscheidung] distinction - **3.** GRAM end-of-line hyphenation.

Trenn|wand *die* partition.

Treppe (*pl* -n) *die* [in Gebäude] stairs (*pl*); [im Freien] steps (*pl*); **eine ~** [in Gebäude] a staircase; [im Freien] a flight of steps.

Treppen|ab|satz *der* half-landing.

Treppen|geländer *das* banister.

Treppen|haus *das* stairwell.·

Tresen (*pl* -) *der* [Ausschank] bar; [Ladentisch] counter.

Tresor (*pl* -e) *der* safe; [Raum] strong room.

Tret|boot *das* pedal boat.

treten (*präs* tritt; *prät* trat; *perf* hat/ist getreten) ⟨⟩ *vt (hat)* - **1.** [mit dem Fuß] to kick; **jm auf den Fuß ~** to tread on sb's foot - **2.** [Kupplung, Bremse] to step on, to put one's foot down on - **3.** *fam* [antreiben]: **jn ~** to push sb ⟨⟩ *vi* - **1.** *(hat)* [mit dem Fuß] to kick; **auf etw** *(A)* **~** to step on sthg - **2.** *(ist)* [gehen]: **ins Zimmer ~** to enter ODER come into the room; **zu jm ~** to go up to sb; **~ Sie näher!** come closer! - **3.** [betätigen]: **auf die Bremse ~** to step on the brake, to brake - **4.** *(ist)* [hervor]: **aus etw ~** to issue from sthg - **5.** [beginnen]: **in den Streik ~** to go on strike.

treu ⟨⟩ *adj* faithful; [Anhänger, Kunde] loyal; **einer Sache** *(D)* **~ sein** to be true to sthg; **jm ~ sein** [sexuell] to be faithful to sb; **jm/**

einer Sache ~ bleiben to remain faithful to sb/true to sthg ⟨⟩ *adv* [verlässlich] faithfully; [unterstützen] loyally.

Treue *die* - **1.** [gen] faithfulness; [von Anhänger, Kunde] loyalty; **jm die ~ halten** to keep faith with sb - **2.** [sexuell] fidelity.

treuherzig ⟨⟩ *adj* trusting ⟨⟩ *adv* trustingly.

treulos ⟨⟩ *adj* disloyal; [Liebhaber] unfaithful ⟨⟩ *adv* disloyally; [Liebhaber] unfaithfully.

Tribüne (*pl* -n) *die* - **1.** [Sitzplätze] stand - **2.** [Rednertribüne] rostrum.

Trichine (*pl* -n) *die* trichina.

Trichter (*pl* -) *der* - **1.** [Gerät] funnel - **2.** [nach Explosion] crater.

Trick (*pl* -s) *der* trick.

Trick|film *der* cartoon.

trieb *prät* ▭ treiben.

Trieb (*pl* -e) *der* - **1.** [biologisch] instinct - **2.** [psychologisch] urge - **3.** [pflanzlich] shoot.

triebhaft ⟨⟩ *adj* compulsive ⟨⟩ *adv* compulsively.

Trieb|kraft *die* driving force; [von Handeln] motive.

Trieb|wagen *der* railcar.

Trieb|werk *das* FLUG engine.

triefen (*prät* triefte ODER troff; *perf* hat/ist getrieft) *vi* - **1.** *(hat)* [nass sein]: **von** ODER **vor etw** *(D)* **~** *eigtl & fig* to drip with sthg; **eure Kleider ~ vor Nässe** your clothes are dripping wet - **2.** *(ist)* [fließen - in Tropfen] to drip; [- in Rinnsalen] to run.

trifft *präs* ▭ treffen.

triftig *adj* [Grund] good; [Argumente] valid.

Trikot, Trikot [tri'ko:, 'triko] (*pl* -s) *das* [von Radrennfahrer] jersey; [von Fußballspieler] shirt; [von Tänzer] leotard.

trillern *vt & vi* to warble.

Triller|pfeife *die* whistle.

Trimester (*pl* -) *das* [von Studienjahr] term; WIRTSCH quarter.

trinkbar *adj* drinkable.

trinken (*prät* trank; *perf* hat getrunken) ⟨⟩ *vt* to drink; **einen ~** *fam* to have a drink; **einen ~ gehen** *fam* to go for a drink ⟨⟩ *vi* to drink; **auf jn/etw ~** to drink to sb/sthg.

Trinker, in (*mpl* -; *fpl* -nen) *der, die* alcoholic.

Trink|geld *das* tip.

Trink|halm *der* (drinking) straw.

Trink|wasser *das* drinking water.

Trio (*pl* -s) *das* trio.

trippeln (*perf* ist getrippelt) *vi* to trip along.

Tripper (*pl* -) *der* gonorrhoea.

tritt *präs* ▭ treten.

Tritt (*pl* -e) *der* - **1.** [Fußtritt] kick; **jm einen ~ (in den Bauch) versetzen** to kick sb (in the stomach) - **2.** [Schritt, Gang] step; **im ~** in step.

Trittlbrett *das* step; [von Auto] running board.

Triumph (*pl* -e) *der* triumph.

triumphieren *vi* - **1.** [siegen]: **über jn/etw ~** to triumph over sb/sthg - **2.** [frohlocken]: **innerlich ~** to be inwardly triumphant.

trivial [tri'vja:l] *geh <> adj* - **1.** [banal] trite - **2.** [unbedeutend] trivial <> *adv* - **1.** [banal] tritely - **2.** [unbedeutend] trivially.

trocken <> *adj* - **1.** [gen] dry - **2.** [ohne Beilage] plain; [Brot] dry - **3.** *RW*: **auf dem Trockenen sitzen** *fam* [keinen Alkohol mehr haben] to have nothing to drink; [kein Geld haben] to be broke <> *adv* drily.

Trockenheit (*pl* -en) *die* - **1.** [regenlose Zeit] drought - **2.** [Zustand] dryness.

trockenllegen *vt* - **1.** [entwässern] to drain - **2.** [Windeln wechseln] to change.

trocknen (*perf* hat/ist getrocknet) <> *vt* (hat) to dry; **sich** (*D*) **die Tränen/Hände ~** to dry one's tears/hands <> *vi* (ist) to dry.

Trockner (*pl* -) *der* dryer.

Trödel *der* junk.

trödeln (*perf* hat/ist getrödelt) *vi* to dawdle.

troff *prät* ⤳ triefen.

trog *prät* ⤳ trügen.

Trog (*pl* Tröge) *der* trough.

Trommel (*pl* -n) *die* drum; [von Revolver] cylinder; [für Kabel] reel.

Trommellfell *das* MED eardrum.

trommeln <> *vi* - **1.** [Musik machen, Lärm machen] to drum; **sie trommelt sehr gut** she plays the drums very well - **2.** [schlagen] to beat <> *vt* - **1.** [Rhythmus] to beat out - **2.** [mit Lärm wecken]: **jn aus dem Bett ~** to get sb up by hammering on the door.

Trommler, in (*mpl* -; *fpl* -nen) *der, die* drummer.

Trompete (*pl* -n) *die* trumpet.

Trompeter, in (*mpl* -; *fpl* -nen) *der, die* trumpeter.

Tropen *pl*: **die ~** the tropics.

Tropf (*pl* -e ODER Tröpfe) *der* - **1.** (*pl* Tropfe) MED drip - **2.** (*pl* Tröpfe) [Mensch]: **armer ~!** poor devil!

tröpfeln (*perf* hat/ist getröpfelt) <> *vi* - **1.** (*ist*) [tropfen] to drip - **2.** (*hat*) *fam* [regnen]: **es tröpfelt** it's spitting <> *vt* (*hat*) to drip.

tropfen (*perf* hat/ist getropft) <> *vi* to drip; **es tropft** it's spitting <> *vt* (*hat*) to drip.

Tropfen (*pl* -) *der* drop. ⤳ **Tropfen** *pl* MED drops.

Trophäe (*pl* -n) *die* [Jagdtrophäe] trophy.

tropisch <> *adj* tropical <> *adv* tropically.

Trost *der* (ohne *pl*) consolation, comfort; **nicht ganz bei ~ sein** *fam* to be out of one's mind.

trösten *vt* to console, to comfort. ⤳ **sich trösten** *ref*: **sich (mit etw) ~** to console o.s. (with sthg); **sie tröstete sich mit ihrem Liebhaber** she found consolation in her lover; **tröste dich, mir geht es doch nicht besser!** if it's any consolation, I'm not much better!

tröstlich *adj* comforting.

trostlos *adj abw* - **1.** [deprimierend] dreary - **2.** [traurig] despairing.

Trostlpreis *der* consolation prize.

Trott (*pl* -e) *der* - **1.** [Gangart] trot - **2.** *fam* [Gewohnheit] routine.

Trottel (*pl* -) *der fam abw* idiot.

trotten (*perf* ist getrottet) *vi* to trot.

trotz *präp* (+ *G*) despite, in spite of.

trotzdem *adv* nevertheless.

trotzig <> *adj* [Kind] difficult; [aus gutem Grund] defiant; [Gesicht, Antwort] contrary <> *adv* [aus gutem Grund] defiantly; [uneinsichtig] contrarily.

Trotzlkopf *der* [sturer Mensch] pigheaded so-and-so.

trüb, trübe *adj* - **1.** [Flüssigkeit] cloudy; [Augen] dull - **2.** [Wetter, Tag, Stimmung] gloomy; **mit seinen Berufschancen siehts ~** it's looking bleak as far as his career prospects are concerned.

Trubel *der* hurly-burly.

trüben *vt* - **1.** [verschlechtern] to mar; [gute Laune] to dampen - **2.** [Flüssigkeit, Denken, Urteilskraft] to cloud. ⤳ **sich trüben** *ref* - **1.** [Wasser] to go cloudy; [Himmel] to cloud over - **2.** [Stimmung, Laune] to be dampened.

Trübsal *die geh* [Melancholie] melancholy; [Kummer] grief; **~ blasen** *fig* to mope.

trübselig <> *adj* gloomy <> *adv* gloomily.

trudeln (*perf* ist getrudelt) *vi* - **1.** [fliegen] to spin - **2.** [rollen] to roll.

Trüffel (*pl* -) *der* truffle.

trug *prät* ⤳ tragen.

trügen (*prät* trog; *perf* hat getrogen) <> *vi* to be deceptive <> *vt* to deceive.

trügerisch *adj* deceptive.

Truglschluss *der* misconception.

Truhe (*pl* -n) *die* chest.

Trümmer *pl* [Ruinen] ruins; [Schutt] rubble (*U*); [von Fahrzeug] wreckage (*U*); **in ~n** *eigtl* & *fig* in ruins.

Trumpf (*pl* Trümpfe) *der* trump (card); **Karo ist ~!** diamonds are trumps!; **Flexibilität ist ~** flexibility is the order of the day.

Trunkenheit *die amt* inebriation.

Trunksucht *die* alcoholism.

Trupp (*pl* -s) *der* [von Soldaten, Polizisten] detachment, squad; [von Arbeitern] group.

Truppe (*pl* -n) *die* - **1.** [Einheit] unit - **2.** (ohne *pl*) [Streitkräfte] forces (*pl*); [Heer] army - **3.** [Gruppe] troupe. ⤳ **Truppen** *pl* troops.

Trutlhahn *der* turkey.

Tscheche (*pl* -n) *der* Czech.

Tschechien *nt* Czech Republic.

Tschechin (*pl* -nen) *die* Czech.

tschechisch *adj* Czech.

Tschechisch(e) *das* Czech; *siehe auch* Englisch(e).

Tschechische Republik *die* Czech Republic.

Tschechoslowakei *die* HIST Czechoslovakia.

tschüs, tschüss *interj fam* bye!

Tsd. *abk für* Tausend.

T-Shirt ['tiːʃœːɐt] (*pl* -s) *das* T-shirt.

TU [teːˈuː] (*pl* -s) (*abk für* Technische Universität) *die* university specializing in science and technology.

Tuba (*pl* Tuben) *die* tuba.

Tube (*pl* -n) *die* tube.

Tuberkulose (*pl* -n) *die* tuberculosis.

Tuch (*pl* -e ODER Tücher) *das* [Stoffteil, Stoff] cloth; [Halstuch] scarf; **für jm ein rotes ~ sein** *fig* to make sb see red.

tüchtig <> *adj* - 1. [fleißig] hardworking; [fähig] competent - 2. [groß] big; **ein ~er Schreck** a real shock <> *adv* - 1. [fleißig] hard; [fähig] competently - 2. *fam* [viel]: **~ kalt** really cold.

Tücke (*pl* -n) *die* - 1. [Eigenschaft] deceit - 2. [Handlung] trick, ruse.

tückisch <> *adj* - 1. [hinterhältig - Person] deceitful; [- Plan, Idee] underhand - 2. [schwierig] devilishly difficult - 3. [Auto, Gerät] temperamental - 4. [gefährlich] treacherous <> *adv* - 1. [hinterhältig] deceitfully - 2. [gefährlich] treacherously.

Tugend (*pl* -en) *die* virtue.

tugendhaft <> *adj* virtuous <> *adv* virtuously.

Tulpe (*pl* -n) *die* tulip.

tummeln ➡ **sich tummeln** *ref* to romp around.

Tumor, Tumor (*pl* Tumore) *der* tumour.

Tümpel (*pl* -) *der* pond.

Tumult (*pl* -e) *der* commotion.

tun (*prät* tat; *perf* hat getan) <> *vt* - 1. [machen] to do; **was tust du denn da?** what are you doing?; **so etwas tut man nicht** you shouldn't do that; **was kann ich für Sie ~?** what can I do for you?; **das hat damit nichts zu ~** that's got nothing to do with it - 2. [stellen, legen] to put - 3. [antun]: **jm/sich etwas ~** to do something to sb/o.s. - 4. *fam* [hinreichend sein]: **ich denke, das tut es** I think that will do; **damit ist es nicht getan** that's not enough - 5. *fam* [funktionieren]: **das Auto tut es noch/nicht mehr** the car still works/has had it <> *vi* - 1. [machen]: **zu ~ haben** to be busy; **im gut ~** to do sb good - 2. [vortäuschen]: **so ~, als ob** *fam* to act as if; **er tut nur so** he's only pretending - 3. [Ausdruck einer Beziehung]: **du bekommst es mit mir zu ~, wenn ...** *fam* you'll have me to answer to if

...; **mit jm dienstlich zu ~ haben** to know sb professionally. ➡ **sich tun** *ref*: **es tut sich etwas/nichts** something/nothing is happening.

Tun *das* (*ohne pl*) actions (*pl*).

tünchen *vt* to whitewash.

Tunesien *nt* Tunisia.

Tunesier, in [tuˈneːziɐ, rɪn] (*mpl* -; *fpl* -nen) *der, die* Tunisian.

tunesisch *adj* Tunisian.

Tunfisch *der* = Thunfisch.

tunken *vt* to dip; [Brot, Keks] to dunk.

tunlichst ['tuːnlɪçst] *adv* [unbedingt] at all costs; [möglichst] as far as possible.

Tunnel (*pl* -) *der* tunnel.

Tüpfelchen (*pl* -) *das* dot; **das ~ auf dem i sein** to be the icing on the cake.

tupfen *vt* to dab; **etw auf etw** (*A*) **~** to dab sthg onto sthg.

Tupfen (*pl* -) *der* spot; [kleiner] dot.

Tür (*pl* -en) *die* - 1. [gen] door; **~ zu!** shut the door! - 2. *RW*: **jn vor die ~ setzen** *fam* [rauswerfen, entlassen] to kick sb out.

Turban (*pl* -e) *der* turban.

Turbine (*pl* -n) *die* turbine.

turbulent *adj* - 1. [ereignisreich] eventful - 2. [chaotisch] turbulent.

Türgriff *der* doorhandle.

Türke (*pl* -n) *der* Turk.

Türkei *die*: **die ~** Turkey.

Türkin (*pl* -nen) *die* Turk.

türkis *adj* turquoise.

Türkis (*pl* -e) *der* ODER *das* turquoise.

türkisch *adj* Turkish.

Türkisch(e) *das* Turkish; *siehe auch* Englisch(e).

Türklinke *die* door handle.

Turm (*pl* Türme) *der* - 1. [Bauwerk] tower - 2. [Schachfigur] rook, castle.

türmen (*perf* hat/ist getürmt) <> *vi* (*ist*) *fam* to beat it, to do a runner *Br* <> *vt* (*hat*) to pile up. ➡ **sich türmen** *ref* to be piled up.

Turmuhr *die* tower clock; [von Kirche] church clock.

turnen (*perf* hat/ist geturnt) <> *vt* (*hat*) to perform <> *vi* - 1. (*hat*) [an einem Sportgerät] to do gymnastics; **an den Ringen/am Barren ~** to exercise on the rings/on the parallel bars - 2. (*ist*) *fam* [klettern] to clamber about.

Turnen *das* [in der Schule] gym; [sport] gymnastics (*U*).

Turnhalle *die* gymnasium.

Turnhose *die* (gym) shorts (*pl*).

Turnier (*pl* -e) *das* tournament.

Turnschuh *der* gym shoe *Br*, sneaker *Am*.

Turnverein *der* sports club.

Türrahmen *der* doorframe.

Türschloss *das* lock.

Türschwelle *die* threshold.

Tusch (*pl* -e) *der* fanfare.

Tusche (*pl* -n) *die* Indian ink.

tuscheln *vt* & *vi* to whisper.

tut *präs* ⊳ tun.

Tütchen (*pl* -) *das* sachet.

Tüte (*pl* -n) *die* bag; [mit Backpulver] packet.

tuten *vi* - 1. [hupen] to toot; **das Schiff tutet** the ship sounds its horn - 2. [tönen] to beep.

Tutor (*pl* -toren) *der* tutor.

Tutorin (*pl* -nen) *die* tutor.

TÜV [tyf] (*abk für* Technischer Überwachungsverein) *der* (*ohne pl*): **ein Auto zum ~ bringen** ≃ to take a car for its MOT (test) Br.

TV (*abk für* Fernsehen) TV.

Typ (*pl* -en) *der* - 1. [Menschentyp, Art] type; **er ist der ~ eines Deutschen** he is a typical German; **(nicht) js ~ sein** *fam* (not) to be sb's type - 2. *fam* [Kerl] guy.

Typhus *der* MED typhoid.

typisch ⬦ *adj* typical; **etw ist ~ für jn** sthg is typical of sb ⬦ *adv* typically ⬦ *interj*: **typisch!** typical!

Tyrann, in (*mpl* -en; *fpl* -nen) *der, die* tyrant.

tyrannisieren *vt abw* to tyrannize.

U

u, U [u:] (*pl* - ODER -s) *das* u, U.

u. *abk für* und.

u. a. (*abk für* unter anderem) among other things.

u. a. m. (*abk für* und anderes mehr) etc.

U-Bahn *die* underground Br, subway Am.

übel (*kompar* übler; *superl* übelste) ⬦ *adj* - 1. [Essen, Laune] bad; **nicht ~ sein** *fam* to be not bad - 2. [moralisch] evil; **in übler Gesellschaft** in bad company - 3. [Zustand] nasty, bad; **~ dransein** *fam* to be in a bad way - 4. [unwohl]: **mir ist/wird ~** I feel sick ⬦ *adv* - 1. [schlimm] badly - 2. [unwirsch]: **~ gelaunt (sein)** (to be) in a bad mood ODER temper.

Übel (*pl* -) *das* evil; **von ~ sein** to be an evil.

übel nehmen *vt* (*unreg*): **jm etw ~** to hold sthg against sb.

üben ⬦ *vt* - 1. [trainieren] to practise - 2. *geh* [äußern]: **Nachsicht ~** to be lenient; **Kritik ~** to criticize ⬦ *vi* to practise.

über ⬦ *präp* - 1. (+ A) [eine Richtung anzeigen - oberhalb] over, above; [- quer über] over; [- bei Routen] via; **das Flugzeug flog ~ das Tal** the plane flew over the valley; **er breitete die Decke ~ das Bett** he spread the blanket over the bed; **~ die Straße gehen** to cross the road - 2. (+ D) [eine Position anzeigend] over, above; **die Lampe hängt ~ dem Tisch** the lamp hangs above ODER over the table - 3. (+ A) [zeitlich] over; **~ Wochen/Monate** for weeks/months; **~ Nacht** overnight - 4. (+ A) [mehr als] over; **~ eine Stunde** over an hour - 5. (+ D) [mehr als] above; **~ dem Durchschnitt liegen** to be above average; **Kinder ~ zehn Jahren** children over ten (years of age); **seit ~ einem Jahr** for more than a year - 6. (+ A) [mittels] through, via - 7. (+ A) [stellt Bezug her] about; **ein Buch ~ Mozart** a book about ODER on Mozart - 8. (+ A) [zur Angabe des Betrages] for; **eine Rechnung ~ 30 Euro** a bill for 30 euros - 9. (+ A) *RW*: **ich bringe es nicht ~ mich ...** *fig* I can't bring myself to ... ⬦ *adv* - 1. [mehr als] over - 2. [zeitlich]: **den Winter ~** all winter (long); **das ganze Jahr ~** all (the) year round ⬦ *adj fam* - 1. [überdrüssig]: **etw ~ haben** to have had enough of sthg - 2. [übrig] left (over); **ich habe noch fünf Euro ~** I still have five euros left.

überall, überall *adv* everywhere.

überanstrengen *vt* to overstrain. ⬦ **sich überanstrengen** *ref* to overexert o.s.

überarbeiten *vt* to revise. ⬦ **sich überarbeiten** *ref* to overwork.

überbacken (*präs* überbackt ODER überbäckt; *prät* überbackte ODER überbuk; *perf* hat überbacken) *vt* to brown; **etw mit Käse ~** to bake sthg with a cheese topping.

überbelichten *vt* to overexpose.

überbieten (*prät* überbot; *perf* hat überboten) *vt*: **einen Preis (um etw) ~** to exceed a price (by sthg); **jn (um 5.000 Euro) ~** to outbid sb (by 5,000 euros); **einen Rekord (um 10 cm) ~** to break a record (by 10 cm). ⬦ **sich überbieten** *ref* to surpass o.s.; [Konkurrenten] to vie with each other.

Überbleibsel (*pl* -) *das* [Spur] remnant; [Ruinen, Scherben] remains (*pl*).

Überblick *der* - 1.: **ein ~ über etw** (A) [Übersicht] an overall perspective of sthg; [Zusammenfassung] a summary of sthg; **den ~ verlieren** to lose perspective - 2. [Aussicht]: **ein ~ über etw** (A) a (panoramic) view of sthg.

überblicken *vt* - 1. [einschätzen] to assess - 2. [sehen] to overlook.

überbringen (*prät* überbrachte; *perf* hat überbracht) *vt*: **jm etw ~** to deliver sthg to sb.

überbrücken *vt* [Zeit] to fill in; [Gegensätze] to reconcile.

überdauern *vt geh* to survive.

überdehnen *vt* to strain.

überdenken (*prät* überdachte; *perf* hat überdacht) *vt* to think over.

Überdruss *der* weariness; **sie haben bis zum ~ Karten gespielt** *fam fig* they played cards till they got fed up with it.

übereilen vt to rush; **nur nichts ~** don't rush things, take your time.

übereilt ⬦ adj hasty ⬦ adv hastily.

übereinander adv - 1. [Dinge] on top of each other - 2. [Menschen - reden, nachdenken] about each other.

übereinander schlagen vt (unreg): **die Beine ~** to cross one's legs.

Übereinkunft (pl -künfte) die geh agreement.

übereinlstimmen vi - 1. geh [einig sein]: **mit jm (in etw (D)) ~** to agree with sb (about sthg) - 2. [gleich sein - Zahlen, Messwerte] to tally; [- Aussagen] to correspond.

Übereinlstimmung die - 1. [Einigung] agreement (U) - 2. [Gleichheit] correspondence (U); **etw (mit etw) in ~ bringen** to bring sthg into line (with sthg).

überfahren (präs überfährt; prät überfuhr; perf hat überfahren) vt - 1. [töten] to run over - 2. [Kreuzung, Schild] to drive through.

Überlfahrt die crossing.

Überlfall der attack; **~ auf jn/etw** attack on sb/sthg.

überfallen (präs überfällt; prät überfiel; perf hat überfallen) vt - 1. [ausrauben - gen] to attack; [- Bank] to raid; [- eine Frau] to assault - 2. fam [überraschen] to descend on.

überfällig adj overdue.

überfliegen (prät überflog; perf hat überflogen) vt - 1. [fliegen] to fly over - 2. fig [lesen] to glance over.

Überfluss der [viel] abundance; [zu viel] surplus; **im ~ leben** to live affluently; **etw im ~ haben** to have sthg in abundance.

überflüssig adj [überzählig] superfluous; [frei] spare; [unnötig] unnecessary.

überfordern vt to overtax; **jn (mit etw (D)) ~** to ask too much of sb (with sthg); **die junge Mutter war überfordert** the young mother couldn't cope.

überfragt adj: **da bin ich ~** I can't help you there.

Überlführung die - 1. [Transport] transfer; [von Toten] transportation - 2. [Brücke] bridge.

überfüllt adj overcrowded.

Überlgabe die - 1. [von Gegenstand, Besitz] handing over; **die ~ (einer Sache (G)) an jn** the handing over (of sthg) to sb - 2. MIL surrender.

Übergang (pl -gänge) der - 1. (ohne pl) [Provisorium] temporary arrangement - 2. [Kontrast] contrast - 3. [Weg] crossing; [Brücke] bridge - 4. [Phase] transition.

übergeben (präs übergibt; prät übergab; perf hat übergeben) vt - 1. [überreichen, weitergeben]: **jm etw ~** to hand sthg over to sb; [feierlich überreichen] to present sthg to sb - 2. [überantworten]: **jm etw/jn ~** to hand

sthg/sb over to sb - 3. [freigeben] to open. ⬦ **sich übergeben** ref to vomit.

übergehen[1] (prät überging; perf hat übergangen) vt - 1.: **jn/etw ~** [nicht beachten] to ignore sb/sthg; [überspringen] to skip sb/sthg - 2. [nicht berücksichtigen]: **jn bei etw ~** to pass sb over for sthg.

überlgehen[2] (perf ist übergegangen) vi (unreg) - 1. [wechseln]: **zu etw ~** to proceed to sthg; **dazu ~, etw zu tun** to proceed to do sthg - 2. [den Besitzer wechseln]: **an jn ~** to pass to sb.

Überlgewicht das - 1. [von Personen]: **~ haben** to be overweight - 2. [von Gegenständen] excess weight (U).

übergießen (prät übergoß; perf hat übergossen) vt: **jn/etw mit etw ~** to pour sthg over sb/sthg.

überlgreifen vi (unreg): **auf etw (A) ~** to spread to sthg.

überhand nehmen vi (unreg) to get out of hand.

überhäufen vt: **jn/etw mit etw ~** to inundate sb/sthg with sthg.

überhaupt ⬦ adv - 1. [verstärkend] at all; **gibt es ~ eine Hoffnung?** is there any hope at all?; **~ nicht** not at all; **~ nichts** nothing at all - 2. [eigentlich] anyway; **wie gehts dir ~?** so, how are you, anyway? - 3. [im Allgemeinen] on the whole ⬦ interj [Ausdruck der Ungeduld, des Missfallens]: **und ~** anyway.

überheblich ⬦ adj arrogant ⬦ adv arrogantly.

überholen ⬦ vt - 1. [vorbeifahren] to overtake - 2. fam [übertreffen] to leave behind - 3. [warten] to overhaul ⬦ vi to overtake.

überholt adj outdated.

überhören vt - 1. [nicht hören] not to hear - 2. [ignorieren] to ignore.

📖 **überhören**

The verb überhören is a false friend which looks as though it should correspond to the English verb "to overhear". In fact it means "to not hear" or sometimes "to ignore" – in other words, to fail to hear something either intentionally or unintentionally. The phrase Das habe ich leider überhört is equivalent to the English "I'm sorry, I didn't catch that".
The verb "to overhear" in the sense of hearing something by chance is best translated using the construction zufällig hören. "I overheard them plotting together" could be translated into German as Ich hörte zufällig, wie sie gemeinsam etwas ausheckten.

überirdisch adj supernatural.

überladen (*präs* überlädt; *prät* überlud; *perf* hat überladen) *vt* to overload.

überlassen (*präs* überläßt; *prät* überließ; *perf* hat überlassen) *vt* - **1.** [leihen]: **jm etw ~** to let sb have sthg - **2.** [sich nicht einmischen]: **jm etw ~** to leave sthg to sb - **3.** [allein lassen]: **jn sich** (*D*) **selbst ~** to leave sb to his/her own devices.

überlastet *adj* - **1.** [belastet] overloaded - **2.** [überfordert]: **mit etw ~ sein** to be overburdened with sthg.

überlaufen[1] (*perf* ist übergelaufen) *vi* (*unreg*) - **1.** [überfließen] to overflow - **2.** [überwechseln] to go over to the other side; **zu jm/etw ~** to go over to sb/sthg.

überlaufen[2] (*präs* überläuft; *prät* überlief; *perf* hat überlaufen) *vt* - **1.** [überkommen]: **es überläuft mich** shivers run down my spine - **2.** SPORT [hinter sich lassen] to outrun; [zu weit laufen] to overshoot.

überlaufen[3] *adj*: **~ sein** to be overcrowded; [Kurs] to be oversubscribed.

überleben ◇ *vt* - **1.** [lebend überstehen] to survive - **2.** [länger leben als]: **jn ~** to outlive sb ◇ *vi* to survive.

Überlebende (*pl* -n) *der, die* survivor.

überlegen[1] ◇ *vt* [nachsinnen] to think about, to consider; **sich** (*D*) **etw ~** [über etw nachdenken] to think sthg over; [sich etw ausdenken] to think of sthg ◇ *vi* to think.

überlegen[2] ◇ *adj* [besser] superior; [arrogant] patronizing; **jm ~ sein** to be superior to sb ◇ *adv* [siegen] convincingly; [lächeln] patronizingly.

Überlegenheit *die* superiority.

Überlegung (*pl* -en) *die* consideration (*U*); **ohne ~ handeln** to act without thinking.

überliefern *vt* to hand down.

Überlieferung *die* - **1.** [das Überliefern] handing down - **2.** [das Überlieferte] tradition.

Übermacht *die* superior strength; **in der ~ sein** to be stronger.

Übermaß *das* excess.

übermäßig ◇ *adj* excessive ◇ *adv* excessively; **sich ~ anstrengen** to overexert o.s.; **~ ehrgeizig** overambitious.

übermitteln *vt*: **jm etw ~** to pass sthg on to sb.

übermorgen *adv* the day after tomorrow.

übermüdet *adj* overtired.

Übermut *der* (*ohne pl*) high spirits (*pl*).

übernachten *vi* to stay ODER spend the night; **bei jm ~** to stay the night with sb.

übernächtigt *adj* bleary-eyed.

Übernachtung (*pl* -en) *die* overnight stay; **eine ~ mit Frühstück** bed and breakfast.

Übernahme (*pl* -n) *die* - **1.** [von Firma, Betrieb] takeover; [das Übernehmen] taking over (*U*) - **2.** [Eingliederung]: **die ~ in ein dau-**

erhaftes Arbeitsverhältnis the conversion to a permanent position - **3.** [von Kosten] meeting (*U*) - **4.** [von Wort, Brauch] adoption (*U*).

übernehmen (*präs* übernimmt; *prät* übernahm; *perf* hat übernommen) *vt* - **1.** [Firma, Betrieb] to take over; **etw von jm ~** to take sthg over from sb - **2.** [annehmen] to take on - **3.** [einstellen, weiterbeschäftigen] to keep on - **4.** [kopieren]: **etw von jm/etw ~** [Verhaltensweise, Konzept] to adopt sthg from sb/sthg; [Text] to copy sthg from sb/sthg. ◆ **sich übernehmen** *ref* to overdo it.

überprüfen *vt* to inspect, to check; [Verdächtigen] to screen.

Überprüfung *die* checking (*U*); [von Verdächtigen] screening (*U*).

überqueren *vt* to cross.

überragen *vt* - **1.** [größer sein] to tower above - **2.** [übertreffen] to surpass.

überragend ◇ *adj* outstanding ◇ *adv* superbly.

überraschen *vt* to surprise; **jn mit etw ~** to surprise sb with sthg; **jn bei etw ~** to catch sb doing sthg; **von jm/etw überrascht werden** to be taken by surprise by sb/sthg; **vom Regen überrascht werden** to get caught in the rain.

Überraschung (*pl* -en) *die* surprise.

überreden *vt* to persuade; **jn zu etw ~** to persuade sb to do sthg; **sich zu etw ~ lassen** to let o.s. be talked into (doing) sthg.

überreichen *vt*: **jm etw ~** to present sthg to sb.

überreizt ◇ *adj* tense; [nervös] edgy, jumpy ◇ *adv* nervously.

Überrest *der* remains (*pl*).

überrumpeln *vt*: **jn (mit etw) ~** to take sb by surprise (with sthg).

überrunden *vt* - **1.** SPORT to lap - **2.** [übertreffen] to outstrip.

übers *präp fam* (*über + das*): **der Vogel fliegt ~ Haus** the bird is flying over the house; **~ Jahr verteilt** spread over the year; **~ schlechte Wetter schimpfen** to complain about the bad weather.

übersät *adj*: **mit etw ~ sein** to be strewn with sthg.

Überschallgeschwindigkeit *die* supersonic speed.

überschatten *vt* to overshadow.

überschätzen *vt* to overestimate. ◆ **sich überschätzen** *ref* to overestimate o.s.

überschäumen (*perf* ist übergeschäumt) *vi* - **1.** [überfließen] to froth over - **2.** *fig* [emotional - vor Begeisterung, Lebenslust] to brim over; [- vor Wut, Zorn] to boil over.

überschlagen (*präs* überschlägt; *prät* überschlug; *perf* hat überschlagen) *vt* - **1.** [rechnen] to estimate (roughly) - **2.** [überblättern] to skip. ➤ **sich überschlagen** ref - **1.** [Auto] to overturn; [Person] to fall head over heels - **2.** [Ereignisse] to follow one another thick and fast - **3.** [Stimme] to crack.

über|schnappen (*perf* ist übergeschnappt) *vi fam* to go crazy.

überschneiden (*prät* überschnitt; *perf* hat überschnitten) ➤ **sich überschneiden** ref - **1.** [räumlich] to intersect - **2.** [zeitlich] to coincide - **3.** [inhaltlich] to overlap.

überschreiben (*prät* überschrieb; *perf* hat überschrieben) *vt* - **1.** [übereignen]: **jm etw ~** to make sthg over to sb - **2.** [betiteln] to head.

überschreiten (*prät* überschritt; *perf* hat überschritten) *vt* - **1.** [räumlich] to cross - **2.** [inhaltlich - gen] to exceed; [- Befugnis] to overstep - **3.** [zeitlich] to pass.

Über|schrift die heading; [in Fettdruck] headline.

Über|schuss der - **1.** [Gewinn] profit; **~ erzielen** to make a profit - **2.** [ein Zuviel] surplus.

überschüssig *adj* surplus.

überschütten *vt*: **jn/etw mit etw ~** to cover sb/sthg with sthg; **jn mit Lob ~** to shower sb with praise; **jn mit Vorwürfen ~** to heap criticism on sb.

überschwänglich <> *adj* effusive <> *adv* effusively.

überschwemmen *vt* - **1.** [nass machen] to flood - **2.** [überreich versehen]: **jn/etw mit etw ~** to inundate sb/sthg with sthg.

Überschwemmung (*pl* -en) die flood.

überschwenglich = überschwänglich.

übersehen (*präs* übersieht; *prät* übersah; *perf* hat übersehen) *vt* - **1.** [nicht sehen, ansehen] to overlook; [absichtlich] to ignore - **2.** [einschätzen] to assess.

übersetzen¹ *vt* [in Sprache] to translate; **in etw** (A) **~** to translate into sthg.

über|setzen² (*perf* hat/ist übergesetzt) <> *vi* (ist) [überqueren] to cross <> *vt* (hat) [befördern] to take across.

Über|setzer, in der, die translator.

Übersetzung (*pl* -en) die - **1.** [das Übersetzen] translation - **2.** TECH gear ratio.

Übersicht (*pl* -en) die - **1.** [Fähigkeit] overview - **2.** [Darstellung]: **eine ~ über etw** (A) an outline of sthg.

übersichtlich <> *adj* - **1.** [gut strukturiert] clear - **2.** [gut zu sehen] open <> *adv* clearly.

überspitzt <> *adj* exaggerated <> *adv* in an exaggerated way.

überspringen (*prät* übersprang; *perf* hat übersprungen) *vt* - **1.** [darüber hinwegspringen] to jump - **2.** [auslassen] to skip.

über|sprudeln (*perf* ist übergesprudelt) *vi* - **1.** [Person]: **vor etw** (D) **~** to bubble over with sthg - **2.** [Flüssigkeit] to bubble over.

überstehen¹ (*prät* überstand; *perf* hat

überstanden) *vt* [hinter sich bringen] to come through.

über|stehen² (*perf* hat/ist übergestanden) *vi* (*unreg*) [vorstehen] to jut out.

übersteigen (*prät* überstieg; *perf* hat überstiegen) *vt* - **1.** [zu viel sein] to exceed - **2.** [überklettern] to climb over.

überstimmen *vt* [Person] to outvote; [Antrag] to vote down.

Über|stunde die: **eine ~** an hour's overtime.

überstürzen *vt* to rush into. ➤ **sich überstürzen** ref [Ereignisse] to follow in rapid succession.

übertragbar *adj* - **1.** [Fahrkarte, Recht] transferable; **nicht ~** non-transferable - **2.** [anwendbar] applicable.

übertragen¹ (*präs* überträgt; *prät* übertrug; *perf* hat übertragen) *vt* - **1.** [anwenden]: **etw auf jn/etw ~** to apply sthg to sb/sthg - **2.** [senden] to broadcast - **3.** [übersetzen]: **etw in etw** (A) **~** to translate sthg into sthg - **4.** [Krankheit] to transmit - **5.** [überantworten]: **jm etw ~** to assign sthg to sb. ➤ **sich übertragen** ref: **sich auf jn ~** MED & fig to infect sb.

übertragen² <> *adj* [nicht wörtlich] figurative <> *adv* [nicht wörtlich] figuratively.

Übertragung (*pl* -en) die - **1.** [Sendung] broadcast; [das Senden] broadcasting - **2.** [von Krankheit] transmission - **3.** [Überantwortung] transfer.

übertreffen (*präs* übertrifft; *prät* übertraf; *perf* hat übertroffen) *vt* [Erwartungen] to surpass; [Rekord] to beat; **jn an Ausdauer/ Schnelligkeit ~** to have more stamina/be faster than sb.

übertreiben (*prät* übertrieb; *perf* hat übertrieben) <> *vt* [bei Darstellung] to exaggerate; [Handlung] to overdo <> *vi* [bei Darstellung] to exaggerate; [bei Handlung] to overdo it.

Übertreibung (*pl* -en) die exaggeration.

übertreten¹ (*präs* übertritt; *prät* übertrat; *perf* hat übertreten) *vt* to break.

über|treten² (*perf* hat/ist übergetreten) *vi* (*unreg*) - **1.** (ist) [beitreten]: **zu etw** (D) **~** [zu Partei] to go over to sthg; [zu Konfession] to convert to sthg - **2.** (hat) SPORT to overstep.

übertrieben <> *adj* [Darstellung] exaggerated; [Forderung, Ehrgeiz] excessive <> *adv* [darstellen] in an exaggerated manner; [ernst, höflich] excessively.

überwachen *vt* to keep under surveillance; [Arbeit] to oversee.

überwältigen *vt* - **1.** [besiegen] to overpower - **2.** [überkommen] to overwhelm.

überwältigend <> *adj* overwhelming <> *adv*: **~ aussehen** to look stunning; **~ viele Besucher** an overwhelming number of visitors.

überweisen (*prät* überwie**s**; *perf* hat überwiesen) *vt* - **1.** [bezahlen] to pay; **jm etw ~, etw an jn ~** to pay sthg to sb; **Geld auf ein anderes Konto ~** to transfer money to another account; **Ihr Gehalt bekommen Sie überwiesen** your salary will be paid into your account - **2.** MED: **einen Patienten ins Krankenhaus ~** to have a patient admitted to hospital.

Über|weisung *die* - **1.** [Zahlung] transfer; [Formular] money transfer form - **2.** MED referral.

überwiegen (*prät* überwog; *perf* hat überwogen) ◇ *vi* - **1.** [Skepsis, Zweifel] to prevail - **2.** [zahlenmäßig] to predominate ◇ *vt* to outweigh.

überwinden (*prät* überwand; *perf* hat überwunden) ◆ *vt* to overcome; [Krise] to get over. ◆ **sich überwinden** *ref*: **sich jn ~** to force o.s. to do sthg; **sich nicht ~ können, etw zu tun** not to be able to bring o.s. to do sthg.

Überwindung *die* - **1.** [gen] overcoming - **2.** [von Berg] conquering - **3.** [das Sichüberwinden]: **es ist für mich eine ~** ODER **es kostet mich ~, es zu tun** I have to force myself to do it.

überwintern *vi* - **1.** [Pflanze, Vogel] to spend the winter - **2.** [Winterschlaf halten] to hibernate - **3.** *hum* [Mensch] to winter.

Überzahl *die* majority; **in der ~ sein** SPORT to have a numerical advantage; [mehr sein] to be in the majority.

überzählig *adj* spare, surplus.

überzeugen *vt* to convince; **jn von etw ~** to convince sb of sthg. ◆ **sich überzeugen** *ref*: **sich (von etw) ~** to satisfy o.s. (of sthg); **~ Sie sich selbst!** see for yourself!

überzeugt *adj* convinced; **davon ~ sein, dass …** to be convinced that …

Über|zeugung *die* conviction; **gegen seine ~ handeln** to go against one's convictions; **zur ~ kommen** ODER **gelangen, dass …** to become convinced ODER come to believe that …

überziehen¹ (*prät* überzog; *perf* hat überzogen) ◇ *vi* - **1.** [bei Bank] to go overdrawn - **2.** [zeitlich] to overrun ◇ *vt* - **1.** [Konto] to overdraw - **2.** [nicht pünktlich beenden] to overrun - **3.** [übertreiben] to take too far.

über|ziehen² *vt* (*unreg*) [anziehen]: **sich** (D) **etw ~** to pull sthg on.

überzogen ◇ *adj* exaggerated ◇ *adv*: **~ reagieren** to overreact.

Über|zug *der* - **1.** [Bezug] cover - **2.** [Belag] coating.

üblich *adj* usual; **wie ~** as usual.

U-|Boot *das* submarine.

übrig ◇ *adj* remaining; **ist noch etwas ~?** is there any left?; **die ~en Autos** the rest of the cars, the remaining cars; **die Übrigen** the rest ◇ *adv*: **für jn/etw viel/nichts ~ haben** to have a lot of/no time for sb/sthg. ◆ **im Übrigen** in addition.

übrig bleiben (*perf* ist übrig geblieben) *vi* (*unreg*) to be left over; **uns blieb nichts anderes** ODER **weiter übrig, als zuzustimmen** we had no alternative but to agree.

übrigens *adv* by the way.

Übung (*pl* -en) *die* - **1.** [das Üben] practice; **aus der ~ kommen/sein** to get/be out of practice - **2.** SPORT, SCHULE, MIL & MUS exercise - **3.** UNI seminar.

UdSSR [u:de:εsεs'εr] (*abk für* Union der sozialistischen Sowjetrepubliken) *die* USSR.

UEFA-Pokal *der* UEFA Cup.

Ufer (*pl* -) *das* [von Fluss] bank; [von See, Meer] shore; **am ~** [von Fluss] on the bank; [von See, Meer] on the shore.

UFO, Ufo ['u:fo:] (*pl* -s) *das* UFO.

Uhr (*pl* -en) *die* - **1.** [Zeitanzeiger] clock - **2.** [Armbanduhr] watch - **3.** [Zeit]: **es ist 3 ~** it is 3 o'clock; **um 3 ~** at 3 o'clock; **um wie viel ~?** (at) what time?; **wie viel ~ ist es?** what time is it?; **rund um die ~** round the clock.

Uhrmacher, in (*mpl* -; *fpl* -nen) *der, die* [von Armbanduhren] watchmaker; [von größeren Uhren] clockmaker.

Uhr|zeiger *der* hand.

Uhr|zeiger|sinn *der*: **im ~** clockwise; **gegen den ~** anticlockwise.

Uhr|zeit *die* time.

Uhu (*pl* -s) *der* eagle owl.

Ukraine *die* Ukraine.

Ukrainer, in (*mpl* -; *fpl* -nen) *der, die* Ukrainian.

ukrainisch *adj* Ukrainian.

Ukrainisch(e) *das* Ukrainian; *siehe auch* **Englisch(e)**.

UKW [u:ka:'ve:] (*abk für* Ultrakurzwelle) *die* FM.

ulkig *adj* comical, funny.

Ulme (*pl* -n) *die* elm.

Ultimatum (*pl* -ten) *das* ultimatum; **jm ein ~ stellen** to give sb an ultimatum.

Ultraschall *der* ultrasound.

um ◇ *präp* (+ A) - **1.** [räumlich] (a)round; **~ jn/etw herum** around sb/sthg; **gleich ~ die Ecke** just around the corner; **~ sich blicken** to look around - **2.** [zur Angabe der Uhrzeit] at; **~ drei Uhr** at three o'clock - **3.** [zur Angabe einer Differenz] by; **die Preise steigen ~ 15%** prices are rising by 15% - **4.** [zur Angabe von Grund]: **~ etw kämpfen** to fight for sthg - **5.** [zur Angabe einer Folge] after; **Tag ~ Tag** day after day - **6.** [ungefähr] about, around; **es kostet ~ die 300 Euro** it costs about ODER around 300 euros ◇ *konj*: **~ zu** (in order) to; **zu stolz, ~ nachzugeben** too proud to give in ◇ *adv* [vorüber] up; **die zehn Minuten sind ~** the ten minutes are up. ◆ **um so** *konj* = umso.

umarmen vt to hug. **sich umarmen** ref to hug.

Umbau (pl -e ODER -ten) der renovation.

um|bauen <> vt [verändern] to renovate; **etw zu etw ~** to convert sthg to sthg <> vi to renovate.

um|binden vt (unreg): **sich** (D) **etw ~** to put sthg on.

um|blättern <> vt to turn over <> vi to turn over the page.

Um|bruch der - 1. [Veränderung] radical change - 2. [von Büchern] page make-up.

um|buchen vt: **einen Flug ~** to change one's flight booking.

um|denken vi (unreg) to change one's way of thinking.

um|drehen (perf hat/ist umgedreht) <> vt (hat) - 1. [Seite, Stein] to turn over; [Pulli] to turn round - 2. [Auto, Stuhl, Schlüssel] to turn <> vi (ist, hat) [umkehren] to turn back. **sich umdrehen** ref - 1. [im Stehen] to turn round; **sich nach jm/etw ~** to turn round to look at sb/sthg - 2. [im Liegen] to turn over.

Um|drehung die - 1. [um eigene Achse] turn - 2. TECH revolution.

umeinander, umeinander adv [sich kümmern] about each other; [wickeln] around each other.

um|fahren[1] vt (unreg) [überfahren] to knock down.

umfahren[2] (präs umfährt; prät umfuhr; perf hat umfahren) vt [ausweichen] to go round.

um|fallen (perf ist umgefallen) vi (unreg) - 1. [umkippen] to fall over; [auf den Boden] to fall down - 2. [zusammenbrechen] to collapse - 3. fam abw [nachgeben] to give in.

Umfang (pl -fänge) der - 1. [Maß] circumference - 2. [Ausmaß - von Projekt, Untersuchung] scale; [- von Buch, Zahlung] size; [- von Schaden] extent; [- von Stimme] range; **in vollem ~** fully.

umfangreich <> adj extensive <> adv extensively, at length.

umfassen (präs umfasst; prät umfasste; perf hat umfasst) vt - 1. [beinhalten] to contain; **das Buch umfasst 200 Seiten** the book contains 200 pages - 2. [umschlingen]: **jn ~** to put one's arm around sb; **etw ~** to clasp sthg.

umfassend, umfassend <> adj comprehensive <> adv comprehensively.

Um|feld das - 1. [Umgebung] surroundings (pl) - 2. [Milieu] environment, milieu.

Um|frage die survey.

um|funktionieren vt to convert.

Umgang der contact; **der ~ mit Kindern/ Tieren** working with children/animals; **das ist kein ~ für dich!** you shouldn't mix with

people like that; **mit jm ~ haben** ODER **pflegen** to associate with sb.

umgänglich adj [angenehm] friendly, affable; [gesellig] sociable.

Umgangsformen pl manners.

Umgangssprache die [informelle Sprache] colloquial speech; **in der ~** colloquially.

umgeben (präs umgibt; prät umgab; perf hat umgeben) vt to surround.

Umgebung (pl -en) die - 1. [Gebiet] surroundings (pl); **in der ~ von Heilbronn** in the vicinity of Heilbronn - 2. [Umfeld] environment.

umgehen[1] (präs umgeht; prät umging; perf hat umgangen) vt - 1. [Schwierigkeiten] to avoid; [Verordnung] to get round; [Antwort] to evade - 2. [Stau, Ortschaft] to bypass.

um|gehen[2] (perf ist umgegangen) vi (unreg) - 1. [Grippe, Gerücht, Nachricht] to go round - 2. [behandeln]: **mit jm/etw ~ (können)** [Maschine] to (know how to) handle sb/sthg; [Kind, Tier] to (know how to) treat sb/sthg; **kannst du mit einem Computer ~?** do you know how to use a computer?

umgehend <> adj immediate <> adv immediately.

Umgehungs|straße die bypass.

umgekehrt <> adj [Vorzeichen, Fall] opposite; [Verhältnis] inverse; [Reihenfolge] reverse; **nein, es ist genau ~!** no, the opposite is true! <> adv the other way round; **die Sache verhält sich genau ~** the opposite is true; **... und ~ ...** and vice versa.

um|graben vt (unreg) to dig over.

Um|hang der cape.

um|hängen vt - 1. [woandershin hängen] to hang somewhere else - 2. [umlegen]: **jm/sich etw ~** [Jacke, Decke] to put sthg round sb's/ one's shoulders; [Kette] to hang sthg round sb's/one's neck.

um|hauen vt (unreg) - 1. [fällen] to cut down - 2. fam [überraschen]: **es hat mich umgehauen, als ...** I was bowled over when ... - 3. salopp [Alkohol, Gestank] to knock out - 4. fam [niederschlagen] to knock for six - 5. fam [umwerfen] to knock over.

umher adv around.

umher|irren (perf ist umhergeirrt) vi to wander around.

um|hören **sich umhören** ref: **sich ~** to ask around.

Umkehr die turning back.

um|kehren (perf hat/ist umgekehrt) <> vi (ist) to turn back <> vt (hat) [Entwicklung, Reihenfolge, Situation] to reverse. **sich umkehren** ref to be reversed.

um|kippen (perf ist umgekippt) vi - 1. [umfallen] to fall over; [Auto] to overturn - 2. fam [bewusstlos werden] to keel over - 3. [ökologisch] to become uninhabitable - 4. [Stimmung] to take a turn for the worse.

Umkleide|kabine *die* [in Schwimmbad] changing cubicle; [auf Sportplatz] changing room; [in Kaufhaus] fitting room.

um|kommen *(perf* ist umgekommen) *vi (unreg)* to die; **vor Hunger** *(D)* ~ *fig* to be dying of hunger.

Um|kreis *der* - 1. *(ohne pl)* [Umgebung] vicinity; **im ~ von 50 km** within a 50 km radius - 2. MATH circumcircle.

um|krempeln *vt* - 1. [hochkrempeln] to roll up - 2. *fam* [verändern - Mensch] to reform; [- Geschäft] to reorganize completely - 3. *fam* [durchsuchen] to turn upside down.

Umland *das* surrounding area.

Um|lauf *der* [Zirkulation] circulation.

Umlauf|bahn *die* orbit.

Um|laut *der* umlaut.

um|legen *vt* - 1. *salopp* [erschießen] to bump off - 2. [verteilen - Kosten, Ausgaben]: **etw auf mehrere Personen** ~ to share sthg between several people - 3. [umhängen]: **sich/jm etw** ~ [Jacke, Decke] to put sthg round one's/sb's shoulders; [Kette] to put sthg round one's/sb's neck - 4. [verlegen - Termin] to change - 5. [umklappen] to fold down - 6. [Kippen] to knock down; [Baum] to fell.

um|leiten *vt* to divert.

Um|leitung *die* diversion.

umliegend *adj* surrounding.

um|rechnen *vt*: **etw (auf/in etw** *(A))* ~ to convert sthg (into sthg).

umringen *vt* to surround.

Um|riss *der* outline; **etw in groben ~en darstellen** to give a rough outline of sthg.

um|rühren *vt* to stir.

um|rüsten <> *vt* - 1. MIL to re-equip - 2. [ändern] to adapt <> *vi* to re-equip.

ums *präp (um + das)* round the; ~ **Viereck gehen** to go round the block; **ihm geht es dabei weniger** ~ **Geld, als** ... for him it is not so much a question of money, as ...

Um|satz *der* turnover; **wir müssen den** ~ **steigern** we have to boost our sales ODER turnover.

Um|schlag *der* - 1. [von Brief] envelope; [von Buch] dust jacket - 2. [Wechsel] sudden change - 3. MED compress - 4. [an Ärmel] cuff; [an Hose] turn-up - 5. [von Gütern] transfer - 6. [Verkauf] sale.

um|schlagen *(perf* hat/ist umgeschlagen) *(unreg)* <> *vi (ist)* [Wetter, Stimmung] to change suddenly <> *vt (hat)* - 1. [umlegen - Kragen] to turn down; [- Hosenbeine] to turn up - 2. [umblättern - Seite] to turn over - 3. WIRTSCH to transfer - 4. [verkaufen] to sell - 5. [Baum] to fell.

umschreiben¹ *(prät* umschrieb; *perf* hat umschrieben) *vt* - 1. [paraphrasieren] to para-

phrase - 2. [abgrenzen] to define - 3. [schildern] to describe.

um|schreiben² *vt (unreg)* - 1. [ändern] to rewrite - 2. [übertragen]: **etw auf jn** ~ **lassen** to have sthg transferred to sb.

um|schulen <> *vt* - 1. [ausbilden] to retrain - 2. [Schule wechseln lassen] to move (to another school) <> *vi* to retrain.

Umschwung *der* sudden change.

um|sehen ◆ **sich umsehen** *ref (unreg)*: **sich (nach jm/etw)** ~ [suchen] to look around (for sb/sthg); [sich umdrehen] to look round (at sb/sthg).

um sein *(perf* ist um gewesen) *vi (unreg) fam* to be over.

Umsicht *die* prudence.

umso *konj (+ kompar)*: ~ **schneller/mehr/wichtiger** all the faster/more/more important; ~ **besser** all the better!

umsonst <> *adj*: ~ **sein** [erfolglos] to be in vain; [gratis] to be free (of charge) <> *adv* - 1. [erfolglos] in vain - 2. [gratis] for free, for nothing.

Umstand *(pl* -stände) *der* - 1. [Mühe]: **Umstände** trouble *(U)*; **wir wollen dir keine Umstände machen** we don't want to put you to any trouble - 2. [Sachlage] circumstance; **unter Umständen** in certain circumstances; **unter allen Umständen** whatever happens; **in anderen Umständen sein** *fig* to be in the family way.

umständlich <> *adj* - 1. [Methode, Arbeit] laborious - 2. [im Denken] ponderous; [beim Sprechen] long-winded <> *adv* - 1. [mühevoll] laboriously - 2. [denken] ponderously; [sprechen] long-windedly.

Umstands|kleid *das* maternity dress.

Umstandswort *(pl* -wörter) *das* GRAM adverb.

umstehend *adj* - 1. [umgebend] standing round about; **die Umstehenden** the bystanders - 2. [umseitig] overleaf.

um|steigen *(perf* ist umgestiegen) *vi (unreg)* - 1. [beim Reisen] to change - 2. [wechseln]: **auf etw** *(A)* ~ to switch to sthg.

um|stellen¹ *vt* - 1. [anders ausrichten - Möbel] to switch round; [- Methode, Produktion, Weichen] to switch; [- Kabinett] to reshuffle; **heute Nacht werden die Uhren umgestellt** the clocks go forward/back tonight; **etw auf etw** *(A)* ~ to switch sthg to sthg; **einen Betrieb auf EDV** ~ to computerize a company - 2. [Leben, Fahrplan, Mannschaft, Programm] to change. ◆ **sich umstellen** *ref* to change; **sich in der Ernährung** ~ to change one's diet; **sich auf etw** *(A)* ~ [sich anpassen] to adapt to sthg.

um|stellen² *vt* [einkreisen] to surround.

Um|stellung *die* - 1. [von Methode, Produktion, Weichen] switch; ~ **auf EDV** computerization - 2. [Veränderung] change.

um|stimmen vt: **jn ~** to make sb change his/her mind.

um|stoßen vt (unreg) - **1.** [Stapel, Vase, Stuhl] to knock over - **2.** [Plan, Testament, Berechnungen] to wreck.

umstritten adj controversial; **es ist ~, ob …** it is disputed whether …

Umsturz der coup (d'état); **der ~ der Regierung** the overthrow of the government.

um|stürzen (perf hat/ist umgestürzt) ⟨⟩ vi (ist) to fall over; [Auto] to overturn ⟨⟩ vt (hat) - **1.** [umwerfen] to knock over; [Auto] to overturn - **2.** [vereiteln] to upset - **3.** [ablösen] to overthrow.

Umtausch der exchange; **'vom ~ ausgeschlossen'** 'no refunds or exchanges'.

um|tauschen vt - **1.** [auswechseln] to exchange; **etw gegen etw ~** to exchange sth for sth - **2.** [Währung tauschen] to change.

um|wandeln vt: **etw in etw** (A) **/zu etw ~** to convert sth into sthg.

Umweg der detour; **einen ~ über etw** (A) **machen** to make a detour via sthg; **auf ~en** fig in a roundabout way.

Umwelt die environment.

Umwelt|belastung die environmental pollution ODER damage.

umweltbewusst ⟨⟩ adj environmentally aware ⟨⟩ adv in an environmentally aware way.

umweltfreundlich ⟨⟩ adj environmentally friendly, eco-friendly ⟨⟩ adv in an environmentally friendly ODER eco-friendly way.

Umwelt|papier das recycled paper.

Umwelt|schäden pl ecological damage (U).

Umwelt|schutz der environmental protection.

Umweltschützer, in (mpl -; fpl -nen) der, die environmentalist.

Umwelt|verschmutzung die pollution (U).

um|werfen vt (unreg) - **1.** [umstürzen] to knock over - **2.** fam : **jn ~** [Alkohol] to knock sb out; [Nachricht] to stun sb - **3.** [umhängen]: **sich** (D) **etw ~** to put sthg round one's shoulders - **4.** [hinfällig machen] to upset.

um|ziehen (perf hat/ist umgezogen) (unreg) ⟨⟩ vi (ist) to move; **nach … ~** to move to … ⟨⟩ vt (hat) to change. ◆ **sich umziehen** ref to change, to get changed.

umzingeln vt to surround.

Umzug der - **1.** [Wohnungswechsel] move - **2.** [Festzug] parade.

unabhängig ⟨⟩ adj independent; **von jm/ etw ~ sein** to be independent of sb/sthg ⟨⟩ adv independently.

Unabhängigkeit die independence.

unabsichtlich ⟨⟩ adj unintentional ⟨⟩ adv unintentionally.

unachtsam ⟨⟩ adj - **1.** [unaufmerksam] inattentive - **2.** [nicht sorgsam] careless ⟨⟩ adv [nicht sorgsam] carelessly.

Unachtsamkeit (pl -en) die - **1.** [Unaufmerksamkeit] inattentiveness (U) - **2.** [fehlende Sorgfalt] carelessness (U).

unangebracht adj inappropriate.

unangemessen ⟨⟩ adj inappropriate ⟨⟩ adv inappropriately; **~ hoch** disproportionately high.

unangenehm ⟨⟩ adj unpleasant; **etw ist jm ~** sb feels embarrassed about sthg ⟨⟩ adv: **~ berührt** embarrassed; **~ auffallen** to make a bad impression.

Unannehmlichkeiten pl trouble (U).

unansehnlich adj unattractive.

unanständig ⟨⟩ adj [obszön] indecent; [Wort, Witz] rude; **es ist ~, mit vollem Mund zu reden** it's rude to talk with your mouth full ⟨⟩ adv [obszön] indecently; [unhöflich] rudely.

unauffällig ⟨⟩ adj unobtrusive ⟨⟩ adv - **1.** [nicht auffällig] unobtrusively - **2.** [heimlich] without anyone noticing.

unauffindbar, unauffindbar ⟨⟩ adj: **~ sein** to be nowhere to be found ⟨⟩ adv: **etw ~ verstecken** to hide sthg where it cannot be found.

unaufgefordert ⟨⟩ adj unasked-for ⟨⟩ adv without being asked.

unaufhaltsam, unaufhaltsam ⟨⟩ adj inexorable ⟨⟩ adv inexorably.

unaufhörlich, unaufhörlich ⟨⟩ adj constant ⟨⟩ adv constantly.

unaufmerksam ⟨⟩ adj inattentive ⟨⟩ adv inattentively.

unaufrichtig ⟨⟩ adj insincere; **jm gegenüber ~ sein** not to be open with sb ⟨⟩ adv insincerely.

unausstehlich, unausstehlich ⟨⟩ adj unbearable ⟨⟩ adv unbearably.

unbändig adj [Wut, Freude, Eifersucht] unbridled; [Temperament] boisterous.

unbeabsichtigt ⟨⟩ adj unintentional ⟨⟩ adv unintentionally.

unbeachtet ⟨⟩ adj unnoticed ⟨⟩ adv unnoticed.

unbedenklich ⟨⟩ adj safe ⟨⟩ adv [Medikament einnehmen] safely; [annehmen, zustimmen] without hesitation.

unbedeutend ⟨⟩ adj - **1.** [nicht bedeutend] unimportant - **2.** [belanglos] slight ⟨⟩ adv [belanglos] slightly.

unbedingt ⟨⟩ adj absolute ⟨⟩ adv - **1.** [auf jeden Fall] definitely; **er will ~ Ski fahren** he is determined to go skiing; **DU wolltest ja ~ Ski fahren** it was YOU that wanted to go skiing - **2.** [bedingungslos] absolutely.

unbefriedigend *adj* unsatisfactory.

unbefugt <> *adj* unauthorized <> *adv* without authorization.

unbegreiflich, unbegreiflich <> *adj* incomprehensible <> *adv* unbelievably.

unbegrenzt <> *adj* [Freiheit, Möglichkeiten] unlimited; [Vertrauen, Zustimmung] total <> *adv* [vertrauen, zustimmen] totally; [nutzen, wohnen] indefinitely.

unbegründet <> *adj* unfounded <> *adv* without foundation.

unbeholfen <> *adj* clumsy <> *adv* clumsily.

unbekannt <> *adj* [Künstler, Substanz, Krankheit] unknown; [Flugobjekt] unidentified; **er ist mir ~** I don't know him; **diese Änderung ist mir ~** I don't know about this change; **Anzeige gegen ~** RECHT charge against person or persons unknown <> *adv*: **'~ verzogen'** 'gone away', 'address unknown'.

unbekümmert, unbekümmert <> *adj* [unbeschwert] carefree; [ohne Bedenken] casual <> *adv* [unbeschwert] in a carefree way; [ohne Bedenken] casually.

unbeliebt *adj* unpopular.

unbequem <> *adj* - **1.** [nicht bequem] uncomfortable - **2.** [lästig] awkward <> *adv* [nicht bequem] uncomfortably.

unberechenbar, unberechenbar <> *adj* unpredictable <> *adv* unpredictably.

unberechtigt <> *adj* [Ansprüche, Vorwürfe] unjustified; [Zutritt] unauthorized <> *adv* [entlassen, bestrafen] without justification; [ohne Erlaubnis] without authorization.

unberührt *adj* - **1.** [nicht berührt - Essen, Gegenstand] untouched; [- Schnee] undisturbed; [- Natur] unspoilt - **2.** [ohne Regung] unmoved - **3.** [jungfräulich]: **~ sein** to be a virgin.

unbeschreiblich, unbeschreiblich <> *adj* indescribable <> *adv* indescribably; **sich ~ freuen** to be overjoyed.

unbeschwert <> *adj* carefree <> *adv* free from care.

unbeständig *adj* changeable.

unbestechlich, unbestechlich *adj* [durch Geld] incorruptible; [Kritiker] uncompromising; [Verfechter] unwavering.

unbestimmt <> *adj* [Zeitpunkt & GRAM] indefinite; [Vorstellung, Äußerung] vague <> *adv* vaguely.

unbeteiligt <> *adj* - **1.** [nicht verwickelt] uninvolved; **an etw** *(D)* **~ sein** not to be involved in sthg - **2.** [nicht interessiert] uninterested <> *adv* - **1.** [nicht verwickelt] without getting involved - **2.** [nicht interessiert] without taking an interest.

unbewacht *adj* [Haus, Gefangene] unguarded; [Gepäck, Parkplatz] unattended; **in einem ~en Moment** when no one was looking.

unbeweglich <> *adj* - **1.** [nicht beweglich, festgelegt] immovable - **2.** [unflexibel] inflexible - **3.** [steif] stiff - **4.** [unverändert] fixed <> *adv* - **1.** [regungslos] motionlessly - **2.** [unverändert] fixedly.

unbewusst <> *adj* unconscious <> *adv* unconsciously.

unbrauchbar *adj* useless.

und *konj* - **1.** [gen] and; **~ wenn** even if; **eins ~ eins ist zwei** one and one is two; **~ so weiter** and so on - **2.** [Ausdruck von Ironie]: **der ~ sich entschuldigen?** him, say he's sorry? ➤ **und ob** *interj* of course! ➤ **und wie** *interj* and how!

undankbar *adj* - **1.** [unhöflich] ungrateful - **2.** [schwer] thankless.

undenkbar, undenkbar *adj* inconceivable.

undeutlich <> *adj* unclear <> *adv* unclearly.

undicht *adj* leaky.

undurchsichtig *adj* - **1.** [Geschichte, Mensch] shady - **2.** [Glas, Strümpfe] opaque.

uneben *adj* uneven.

unehelich <> *adj*: **~es Kind** illegitimate child; **in einer ~en Beziehung leben** to live together <> *adv* illegitimately.

unehrlich <> *adj* dishonest <> *adv* dishonestly.

uneigennützig <> *adj* unselfish <> *adv* unselfishly.

uneinig *adj* in disagreement; **sich** *(D)* **über etw** *(A)* **~ sein** to disagree about sthg.

unempfindlich *adj* - **1.** [robust - Stoff, Material] hardwearing *Br*, longwearing *Am*; [- Gerät] sturdy; [- Pflanze] hardy - **2.** [nicht anfällig - Person] immune; [- Haut] insensitive.

unendlich <> *adj* [Raum, Mühe & MATH] infinite; [Weite, Arbeit, Wiederholung] endless; [Geschichte] never-ending <> *adv* enormously.

Unendlichkeit *die* - **1.** [von Raum, Universum] infinity; [von Weite, Wüste] endlessness - **2.** *fam* [zeitlich] eternity.

unentbehrlich, unentbehrlich *adj* indispensable.

unentgeltlich, unentgeltlich <> *adj* free <> *adv* [benutzen] free of charge; [arbeiten, helfen] for nothing.

unentschieden <> *adj* - **1.** [nicht entschieden - Spiel] drawn; [- Angelegenheit] undecided; **bei ~em Wahlausgang** if the election result is inconclusive - **2.** [vor Entscheidung] undecided; [nicht entschlussfreudig] indecisive <> *adv* - **1.** [nicht entschieden]: **~ spielen** to draw; **im Spiel steht es ~** so far the game is a draw - **2.** [unentschlossen] undecidedly.

unentschlossen <> *adj* [vor Entscheidung] undecided; [nicht entschlussfreudig] indecisive <> *adv* [vor Entscheidung] undecidedly; [nicht entschlussfreudig] indecisively.

unerbittlich, unerbittlich <> *adj* - 1. [unnachgiebig] unrelenting - 2. [gnadenlos] relentless <> *adv* - 1. [unnachgiebig] unrelentingly; **~ bleiben** to remain adamant - 2. [gnadenlos] relentlessly.

unerfahren *adj* inexperienced.

unerfreulich *adj* unpleasant.

unerhört <> *adj* - 1. [empörend] outrageous; **(das ist ja) ~!** that's outrageous! - 2. [Glück, Leistung] tremendous; [Preis] exorbitant <> *adv* - 1. [ungeheuer] tremendously; **~ viel** a tremendous amount - 2. [empörend] outrageously.

unerlässlich, unerlässlich *adj* essential.

unerlaubt <> *adj* unauthorized <> *adv* without authorization.

unermesslich, unermesslich *geh* <> *adj* - 1. [unendlich] immeasurable - 2. [ungeheuer] immense <> *adv* immensely.

unermüdlich, unermüdlich <> *adj* tireless <> *adv* tirelessly.

unerschütterlich, unerschütterlich <> *adj* [Überzeugung, Wille] unshakeable; [Person] unflinching <> *adv* unflinchingly.

unerschwinglich, unerschwinglich <> *adj* [Preis] prohibitive; [Luxusartikel] prohibitively expensive; **für jn ~ sein** to be beyond sb's means <> *adv* prohibitively.

unerträglich <> *adj* unbearable <> *adv* unbearably.

unerwartet <> *adj* unexpected <> *adv* unexpectedly.

unerwünscht *adj* [Gast] unwelcome; [Kind] unwanted; [Benehmen] undesirable.

UNESCO [u'nɛsko] *(abk für United Nations Educational, Scientific and Cultural Organization) die* UNESCO.

unfähig *adj* incompetent; **~ sein, etw zu tun** to be incapable of doing sthg.

Unfähigkeit *die* incompetence; **die ~, etw zu tun** the inability to do sthg.

unfair ['ʊnfɛːɐ̯] <> *adj* unfair <> *adv* unfairly.

Unfall *der* accident.

Unfallflucht *die* RECHT failure to stop after an accident.

Unfallstelle *die* scene of the/an accident.

Unfallversicherung *die* accident insurance.

unfehlbar, unfehlbar *adj* infallible.

unfreiwillig <> *adj* - 1. [nicht freiwillig] compulsory - 2. *hum* [unabsichtlich] unintentional <> *adv* - 1. [nicht freiwillig] without wanting to - 2. *hum* [unabsichtlich] unintentionally.

unfreundlich <> *adj* - 1. [nicht freundlich]

unfriendly; **zu jm ~ sein** to be unfriendly to sb - 2. [unangenehm] unpleasant <> *adv* [nicht freundlich] coldly.

unfruchtbar *adj* - 1. [steril, trocken] infertile - 2. [nutzlos] fruitless.

Ungar, in *(mpl -n; fpl -nen) der, die* Hungarian.

ungarisch *adj* Hungarian.

Ungarisch(e) *das* Hungarian; *siehe auch* Englisch(e).

Ungarn *nt* Hungary.

ungeahnt, ungeahnt ['ʊngeaːnt, ʊngeˈʔaːnt] *adj* undreamt-of; [Schwierigkeiten] unsuspected.

ungebeten <> *adj* uninvited <> *adv* without being invited.

ungebildet *adj* uneducated.

Ungeduld *die* impatience.

ungeduldig <> *adj* impatient <> *adv* impatiently.

ungeeignet *adj* unsuitable.

ungefähr, ungefähr *adv* about; **wann kommst du denn ~ wieder?** about when will you be back?; **die Wohnung sieht ~ so aus** the flat looks something like this; **sowas kommt nicht von ~** such a thing is no accident.

ungefährlich *adj* safe.

ungehalten <> *adj* indignant; **über jn/etw ~ sein** to be indignant about sb/sthg <> *adv* indignantly.

Ungeheuer *(pl -) das* monster.

ungehörig <> *adj* [Benehmen] improper; [Antwort] impertinent <> *adv* [sich benehmen] improperly.

ungehorsam *adj* disobedient.

Ungehorsam *der* disobedience.

ungeklärt *adj* - 1. [nicht entschieden - Problem, Mord] unsolved; [- Frage] unsettled - 2. [nicht gereinigt - Abwasser] untreated.

ungelegen <> *adj* inconvenient; **das kommt mir ~** that's inconvenient for me.

ungelogen *adv fam* honestly.

ungemein, ungemein <> *adj* tremendous <> *adv* tremendously.

ungemütlich <> *adj* - 1. [nicht behaglich] uncomfortable; [Mensch] unfriendly - 2. [unangenehm] unpleasant <> *adv* uncomfortably.

ungenau <> *adj* [Ausführungen, Erklärung] imprecise; [Übersetzung, Messung] inaccurate; [Vorstellung] vague <> *adv* [ausführen, erklären] imprecisely; [übersetzen, messen] inaccurately; [erkennbar] vaguely.

ungeniert, ungeniert <> *adj* uninhibited <> *adv* without any inhibition; [sich äußern] openly.

ungenießbar, ungenießbar *adj* - 1. [Essen] inedible; [Getränk] undrinkable - **2.** *fam* [schlecht gelaunt] unbearable.

ungenügend ◇ *adj* inadequate ◇ *adv* inadequately.

ungerade *adj* MATH odd.

ungerecht ◇ *adj* unjust ◇ *adv* unjustly.

Un|gerechtigkeit *die* injustice.

ungern *adv* reluctantly; **ich tue das nur ~** I don't like doing this.

ungeschehen *adj:* **etw ~ machen** to undo sthg.

ungeschickt ◇ *adj* - **1.** [nicht geschickt] clumsy; **es wäre ~, das jetzt schon zu erwähnen** it wouldn't be wise to mention that now - **2.** *fam Süddt* [ungelegen] inconvenient - **3.** *fam Süddt* [unpraktisch] impractical ◇ *adv* [nicht geschickt] clumsily.

ungeschminkt ◇ *adj* - **1.** [nicht geschminkt] without make-up - **2.** [unverhüllt] unvarnished ◇ *adv* - **1.** [nicht geschminkt] without make-up - **2.** [unverhüllt] openly.

ungestört *adj* & *adv* undisturbed.

ungesund ◇ *adj* unhealthy ◇ *adv* unhealthily.

ungetrübt *adj* - **1.** [Glück] perfect; [Zeit] blissful; [Zukunft] unclouded - **2.** [Glas, Wasser] clear.

ungewiss *adj* uncertain.

ungewöhnlich ◇ *adj* - **1.** [unüblich] unusual - **2.** [erstaunlich] exceptional ◇ *adv* - **1.** [unüblich] unusually - **2.** [erstaunlich] exceptionally.

ungewohnt ◇ *adj* [fremd] unfamiliar; [Tageszeit, Großzügigkeit] unaccustomed; **etw ist für jn ~** sb is not used to sthg ◇ *adv* unusually.

Ungeziefer *das (ohne pl)* pests *(pl)*; **der Hund hat ~** the dog has fleas.

ungezogen ◇ *adj* naughty; [Benehmen] bad; [frech] cheeky ◇ *adv* [frech] cheekily; [sich benehmen] badly.

ungezwungen ◇ *adj* [Atmosphäre, Unterhaltung] informal; [Verhalten, Art] natural; [Lachen] easy ◇ *adv* [sich verhalten] naturally; [sich unterhalten] informally; [sich bewegen] easily.

ungläubig ◇ *adj* - **1.** [nicht gläubig] unbelieving - **2.** [zweifelnd] disbelieving ◇ *adv* in disbelief.

unglaublich, unglaublich ◇ *adj* - **1.** [nicht zu glauben] unbelievable - **2.** [ungeheuer] incredible ◇ *adv* incredibly.

unglaubwürdig *adj* [Mensch] untrustworthy; [Geschichte] implausible.

ungleich ◇ *adj* unequal; [Brüder] different ◇ *adv* - **1.** [nicht gleich] unequally; [sich verhalten] differently - **2.** [bei weitem] far.

Un|glück *das* - **1.** [Vorfall] accident - **2.** [Pech] bad luck; **zu allem ~ brach er sich auch noch**

den Arm on top of everything he broke his arm as well.

unglücklich ◇ *adj* - **1.** [nicht glücklich] unhappy - **2.** [ungünstig] unfortunate - **3.** [ungeschickt] clumsy ◇ *adv* - **1.** [nicht glücklich] unhappily - **2.** [ungeschickt] awkwardly - **3.** [ungünstig] badly.

unglücklicherweise *adv* unfortunately.

ungültig *adj* invalid.

Ungunsten *pl:* **zu js ~** to sb's disadvantage.

ungünstig ◇ *adj* unfavourable; [Moment] inconvenient; [Witterung] bad ◇ *adv* unfavourably.

ungut ◇ *adj* bad ◇ *adv* badly; **nichts für ~!** *fig* no offence!

unhaltbar, unhaltbar *adj* - **1.** [Argument, Lage, These] untenable - **2.** [Schuss] unstoppable.

Unheil *das geh* disaster.

unheimlich, unheimlich ◇ *adj* - **1.** [gruselig] eerie; **dieser Typ ist mir ~** this guy makes my flesh creep; **mir wird ~** I have an eerie feeling - **2.** *fam* [groß] terrible; [Menge] huge ◇ *adv fam* [ungeheuer] dead; **~ viel Geld** loads of money; **sich ~ freuen** to be dead pleased.

unhöflich ◇ *adj* impolite ◇ *adv* impolitely.

Uni *(pl -s) die fam* uni.

Uniform (*pl -en*) *die* uniform.

Union (*pl -en*) *die* union.

Universität [univerzi'tɛːt] (*pl -en*) *die* university.

Universum [uni'verzum] *das* universe.

unkenntlich *adj* unrecognizable.

Unkenntnis *die:* **etw in ~ einer Sache** (G) **tun** to do sthg out of ignorance of sthg.

unklar ◇ *adj* unclear; **jn (über etw** (A)) **im Unklaren lassen** to leave sb in the dark (about sthg) ◇ *adv* - **1.** [unverständlich] unclearly - **2.** [vage] vaguely.

unklug ◇ *adj* unwise ◇ *adv* unwisely.

Unkosten *pl* expenses; **sich in ~ stürzen** *fig* to go to great expense.

Unkosten|beitrag *der* contribution towards expenses.

Un|kraut *das* - **1.** *(ohne pl)* [störende Pflanzen] weeds *(pl)* - **2.** [Unkrautart] weed.

unleserlich ◇ *adj* illegible ◇ *adv* illegibly.

unlogisch ◇ *adj* illogical ◇ *adv* illogically.

Un|menge *die* masses *(pl)*; **eine ~ Arbeit** masses of work.

Un|mensch *der abw* monster.

unmenschlich ◇ *adj* - **1.** [menschenunwürdig, brutal] inhuman - **2.** *fam* [unerträglich] terrible ◇ *adv* - **1.** [menschenunwürdig, brutal] inhumanly - **2.** *fam* [ungeheuer] terribly.

unmerklich, unmerklich <> *adj* imperceptible <> *adv* imperceptibly.

unmissverständlich <> *adj* unambiguous <> *adv* unambiguously.

unmittelbar <> *adj* immediate; [Verbindung] direct; **in ~er Nähe** in the immediate vicinity <> *adv* directly; **~ danach** immediately afterwards.

unmöglich, unmöglich <> *adj* [nicht möglich] impossible; **es ist mir ~, das zu tun** it is impossible for me to do that; **sich ~ machen** to make a fool of o.s. <> *adv* - 1. [nicht möglich, keinesfalls]: **das kann ~ stimmen** that can't possibly be right; **das kannst du ~ von ihm verlangen** you can't possibly ask that of him - 2. *fam* [sich benehmen] impossibly.

unmoralisch <> *adj* immoral <> *adv* immorally.

unnachgiebig <> *adj* inflexible <> *adv* inflexibly.

unnahbar, unnahbar *adj* unapproachable.

unnötig <> *adj* unnecessary <> *adv* unnecessarily.

unnütz <> *adj* useless <> *adv* [unnötig] needlessly.

UNO ['u:no] (*abk für* United Nations Organization) *die* UN.

unordentlich <> *adj* untidy <> *adv* untidily.

Unordnung *die* mess; **etw in ~ bringen** to mess sthg up; **in ~ geraten** to get messed up.

unparteiisch <> *adj* impartial <> *adv* impartially.

unpassend <> *adj* inappropriate <> *adv* inappropriately.

unpersönlich <> *adj* [gen & GRAM] impersonal <> *adv* [gen & GRAM] impersonally.

unpraktisch <> *adj* impractical <> *adv* impractically.

unpünktlich <> *adj* [Mensch] unpunctual; [Abfahrt, Zahlung] late <> *adv* late.

unrecht <> *adj* - 1. [Zeit, Moment] inconvenient - 2. *geh* [Tat, Gedanke] wicked; **es ist ~, so etw zu denken** it is wrong to think like that <> *adv* - 1. [ungelegen] inconveniently - 2. *geh* [handeln, sich benehmen] wrongly; **jm ~ tun** to wrong sb.

Unrecht *das* wrong; **~ haben, im ~ sein** to be wrong; **jn/sich ins ~ setzen** to put sb/o.s. in the wrong; **zu ~** wrongly.

unrechtmäßig <> *adj* illegal <> *adv* illegally.

unregelmäßig <> *adj* [gen & GRAM] irregular <> *adv* [gen & GRAM] irregularly.

unreif *adj* - 1. [Obst] unripe - 2. [Person] immature.

Unruhe *die* (*ohne pl*) - 1. [Treiben] commotion; **er sorgt ständig für ~** he's always caus-

ing a commotion; **~ stiften** to stir up trouble - 2. [Ruhelosigkeit] unease; **jn in ~ versetzen** to make sb uneasy - 3. [Aufregung] unrest, disquiet - 4. [Bewegung]: **in ~ sein** to be moving restlessly. ➡ **Unruhen** *pl* [Aufruhr] riots.

unruhig <> *adj* - 1. [nicht ruhig] restless - 2. [ruhelos] uneasy; **~ werden** to get anxious - 3. [gestört - Schlaf] fitful; [- Nacht] disturbed - 4. [Zeit] troubled - 5. [laut] noisy - 6. [Muster, Bild] busy <> *adv* - 1. [nicht ruhig] restlessly - 2. [ruhelos] uneasily - 3. [schlafen] fitfully.

uns *pron* - 1. [Personalpronomen - Akkusativ, Dativ] us; **er sagte es ~** he told us; **das gehört ~** this is ours, this belongs to us; **sie hat ~ gesehen** she has seen us - 2. [Reflexivpronomen] ourselves; **wir konnten ~ das nicht vorstellen** we couldn't imagine that; **wir setzten ~** we sat down - 3. [einander] each other, one another.

unsachlich <> *adj* subjective <> *adv* subjectively.

unsanft <> *adj* rough <> *adv* roughly.

unschädlich *adj* harmless; **jn/etw ~ machen** to put sb/sthg out of action.

unscharf <> *adj* - 1. [nicht scharf] blurred - 2. [ungenau] vague <> *adv*: **~ sehen** to have blurred vision.

unscheinbar *adj* inconspicuous.

unschlagbar, unschlagbar *adj* - 1. [nicht zu schlagen] unbeatable - 2. [nicht zu übertreffen] unsurpassable.

unschlüssig <> *adj* undecided; **(sich (D)) über etw (A) ~ sein** to be undecided about sthg <> *adv* indecisively.

Unschuld *die* - 1. [gen] innocence - 2. [Jungfräulichkeit] virginity.

unschuldig <> *adj* - 1. [gen] innocent; **an etw (D) ~ sein** not to be to blame for sthg - 2. [jungfräulich]: **ein ~es Mädchen** a virgin <> *adv* - 1. [gen] innocently - 2. [verurteilen] wrongly.

unselbstständig *adj* dependent.

unser, e *det* our.

unsere, r, s ODER **unsers** <> *pron* ours <> *det* = unser.

unsereins *pron fam* the likes of us.

unsererseits, unsrerseits *adv* - 1. [wir selbst] for our part - 2. [von uns] on our part.

unseretwegen, unsertwegen *adv* - 1. [uns zuliebe] for our sake - 2. [wegen uns] because of us - 3. [von uns aus] as far as we are concerned.

unsicher <> *adj* - 1. [gen] uncertain - 2. [Stimme, Hand] unsteady; **ich bin mir ~, ob ...** I'm uncertain whether ... - 3. [unzuverlässlich] unreliable - 4. [gefährdet] insecure - 5. [unbeständig] unsettled - 6. [gefährlich] unsafe; **etw ~ machen** *fam* [sich vergnügen] to hit sthg <> *adv* [nicht sicher - gehen fahren] unsteadily; [- reden, auftreten] uncertainly.

Un|sicherheit die - 1. [Ungewissheit] uncertainty; [Eigenschaft] insecurity - 2. [von Handlung] lapse.

unsichtbar <> adj invisible; **sich ~ machen** to make o.s. scarce <> adv invisibly.

Unsinn der nonsense.

unsinnig <> adj - 1. [blödsinnig] idiotic - 2. fam [ungeheuer] tremendous <> adv tremendously.

Un|sitte die abw bad habit.

unsportlich adj - 1. [Person] unsporty - 2. [Verhalten] unsporting.

unsterblich, unsterblich <> adj immortal; [Liebe] undying <> adv: ~ **verliebt** madly in love; **sich ~ blamieren** to make an absolute fool of o.s.

unstillbar adj insatiable.

Unstimmigkeiten pl - 1. [Differenzen] differences of opinion - 2. [Abweichungen] discrepancies.

Un|summe die huge amount of money.

unsympathisch adj unpleasant; **er/es ist mir ~** I don't like him/it.

Un|tat die evil crime.

untätig <> adj idle <> adv idly.

untauglich adj unsuitable; **für den Wehrdienst ~** unfit for military service.

unten adv - 1. [räumlich - im unteren Teil] at the bottom; [- tiefer gelegen] below; [- an der Unterseite] underneath; ~ **am Tisch** at the bottom of the table; **links/rechts ~ im Bild** in the bottom left-hand/right-hand corner of the picture; **hier/dort ~** down here/there; **von ~** from below; **nach ~** down; [im Haus] downstairs; **mit dem Gesicht nach ~** face down; **weiter ~** further down - 2. [im Text] below; **siehe ~** see below - 3. fam [im Süden]: **im Süden ~** down south - 4. fam [rangniedriger]: **die da ~** those at the bottom of the pile - 5. RW: **der ist bei mir ~ durch** fam fig I'm finished with him.

unter <> präp - 1. (+ D) [räumlich] under; [an der Unterseite von] underneath; ~ **dem Tisch liegen** to lie under the table; ~ **uns wohnt Herr Braun** Mr Braun lives below ODER beneath us - 2. (+ A) [räumlich] under; ~ **den Tisch kriechen** to crawl under the table - 3. (+ D) [weniger als] under; **Kinder ~ 12 Jahren** children under the age of 12 - 4. (+ A) [weniger als] below - 5. (+ D) [zur Angabe einer Teilmenge] among; **einer ~ vielen** one of many; ~ **uns (gesagt)** between you and me; ~ **anderem** among other things - 6. (+ D) [zwischen] between; **sie haben es ~ sich ausgemacht** they arranged it between themselves - 7. (+ A) [zwischen]: **sich ~ die Menge mischen** to mingle ODER mix with the crowd - 8. (+ D) [zur Angabe einer Hierarchie, einer Bezeichnung] under; ~ **der Aufsicht/Leitung**

von ... under the supervision/leadership of ...; ~ **dem Namen X bekannt sein** to be known by the name of X - 9. (+ D) [zur Angabe des Umstands] under; ~ **Umständen** under ODER in certain circumstances; ~ **Berücksichtigung von** taking into consideration; ~ **der Bedingung, dass ...** on the condition that ... <> adj lower; **der ~ste Knopf** the bottom button.

Unter|arm der forearm.

unterbelichtet adj - 1. [Foto, Film] underexposed - 2. salopp [Mensch] dim.

Unterbewusstsein das subconscious.

unterbieten (prät unterbot; perf hat unterboten) vt - 1. [Preis, Angebot, Konkurrenz] to undercut - 2. SPORT to beat.

unterbrechen (präs unterbricht; prät unterbrach; perf hat unterbrochen) vt - 1. [stören] to interrupt - 2. [aufhören - Arbeit, Behandlung, Urlaub] to break off.

Unter|brechung die - 1. [Störung] interruption - 2. [Aufhören - von Arbeit, Behandlung, Urlaub] breaking off.

unter|bringen vt (unreg) - 1. [an einem Platz] to fit - 2. [über Nacht] to put up - 3. [bei Firma] to get a job for - 4. [in Gedächtnis] to place.

Unterbringung die [Unterkunft] accommodation.

unterdessen adv meanwhile.

unterdrücken vt - 1. [Volk, Minderheit] to oppress - 2. [Gefühl, Bemerkung, Information] to suppress.

untereinander adv - 1. [unter sich] among ourselves/yourselves/themselves - 2. [unter das andere] one below the other.

unterentwickelt adj underdeveloped.

unterernährt adj undernourished.

Unter|führung die underpass, subway Br.

Untergang (pl -gänge) der - 1. [von Volk, Kultur] decline - 2. [von Schiff] sinking - 3. [von Sonne, Mond] setting.

Untergebene (pl -n) der, die subordinate.

unter|gehen (perf ist untergegangen) vi (unreg) - 1. [Sonne, Mond] to set - 2. [Schiff, Person] to sink - 3. [Kultur, Volk] to decline.

untergeordnet adj - 1. [unterstellt & GRAM] subordinate - 2. [Bedeutung, Rolle] secondary.

Unter|grenze die lower limit.

Unter|grund der - 1. [Boden] subsoil - 2. [Unterwelt] underground; **in den ~ gehen** to go underground - 3. [für Farbe, Stellfläche] surface.

Untergrund|bahn die underground Br, subway Am.

unter|haken vt to link arms with. **sich unterhaken** ref: **sich (bei jm) ~** to link arms (with sb).

unterhalb ◇ *adv:* ~ **von** below ◇ *präp:* ~ **einer Sache** (G) below sthg.

Unterhalt *der* - 1. [Zahlung] maintenance - 2. [von Familie, Kindern] keep - 3. [von Gebäude, Park] upkeep.

unterhalten (*präs* unterhält; *prät* unterhielt; *perf* hat unterhalten) *vt* - 1. [amüsieren] to entertain - 2. [Kosten übernehmen für - Familie] to support; [- Haus, Büro] to pay for the upkeep of - 3. [Kontakte] to maintain - 4. [betreiben] to run. ◆ **sich unterhalten** *ref* - 1. [reden]: **sich (mit jm/über etw** (A)**)** ~ to talk (with sb/about sthg) - 2. [sich amüsieren] to enjoy o.s.

unterhaltsam ◇ *adj* entertaining ◇ *adv* entertainingly.

Unterlhaltung *die* - 1. [Gespräch] conversation - 2. [Zeitvertreib] entertainment; **gute** ~! enjoy yourselves! - 3. [von Kontakten] maintenance - 4. [Betreibung] running.

Unterlhändler, in *der, die* negotiator.

Unterlhemd *das* vest *Br*, undershirt *Am*.

Unterlhose *die* [für Herren] underpants (pl); [für Frauen] briefs (pl).

unterirdisch *adj & adv* underground.

Unterlkiefer *der* lower jaw.

unterlkriegen *vt fam* to get down; **sich nicht ~ lassen** *fam* not to let things get one down.

unterkühlt ◇ *adj* - 1. [Reaktion, Verhalten] frosty - 2. [untertemperiert] suffering from hypothermia ◇ *adv* - 1. [reagieren, sich verhalten] frostily - 2. [untertemperiert] suffering from hypothermia.

Unterkunft (*pl* -künfte) *die* accommodation (U).

Unterllage *die* [für Gymnastik] mat; [zum Schreiben] something to rest on. ◆ **Unterlagen** *pl* [Urkunden] documents.

unterlassen (*präs* unterlässt; *prät* unterließ; *perf* hat unterlassen) *vt* to refrain from; **es ~, etw zu tun** to refrain from doing sthg.

unterlaufen (*präs* unterläuft; *prät* unterlief; *perf* ist unterlaufen) *vt* [passieren]: **mir ist ein Fehler ~** I made a mistake.

unterllegen[1] *vt* [drunter legen] to put underneath.

unterllegen[2] *vt* - 1. [Teppich] to underlay; [Kragen, Hosenbund] to line - 2. [Film]: **etw mit Musik ~** to add background music to sthg.

unterllegen[3] *adj* inferior.

Unterlleib *der* abdomen.

unterliegen (*prät* unterlag; *perf* hat/ist unterlegen) *vi* - 1. (hat) [ausgesetzt sein]: **einer Sache** (D) ~ to be subject to sthg - 2. (ist) [verlieren] to be defeated.

Unterllippe *die* lower lip.

Untermiete *die*: **in** ODER **zur ~ wohnen** to be a subtenant.

unternehmen (*präs* unternimmt; *prät* unternahm; *perf* hat unternommen) *vt* [Versuch, Anstrengung] to make; [Reise, Ausflug] to go on; **etwas/nichts ~** to do something/nothing.

Unternehmen (*pl* -) *das* - 1. [Betrieb] business, company - 2. [Vorhaben] undertaking.

Unternehmer, in (*mpl* -; *fpl* -nen) *der, die* entrepreneur.

unternehmungslustig *adj* enterprising.

unterlordnen *vt* to subordinate. ◆ **sich unterordnen** *ref:* **sich (jm/einer Sache)** ~ to subordinate o.s. (to sb/sthg).

Unterredung (*pl* -en) *die* discussion.

Unterricht (*pl* -e) *der* lessons (pl); **jm ~ geben** ODER **erteilen** to teach sb; **jm ~ in Englisch geben** to teach sb English; **hast du morgen ~?** do you have any classes tomorrow?; ~ **in Deutsch nehmen** to have German lessons.

unterrichten ◇ *vt* - 1. [Unterricht geben] to teach; **sie unterrichtet Kinder im Zeichnen** she teaches children drawing - 2. [informieren]: **sich/jn (über etw** (A)**)** ~ to inform o.s./sb (about sthg) ◇ *vi* to teach.

Unterrichtslfach *das* subject.

Unterlrock *der* slip.

untersagen *vt* to forbid; **jm ~, etw zu tun** to forbid sb to do sthg.

unterschätzen *vt* to underestimate.

unterscheiden (*prät* unterschied; *prät* hat unterschieden) ◇ *vt* - 1. [auseinander halten, bemerken] to distinguish; **jn/etw von jm/etw** ~ to tell sb/sthg from sb/sthg - 2. [abgrenzen] to distinguish between ◇ *vi* - 1. [abgrenzen] to distinguish - 2. [differenzieren] to make a distinction. ◆ **sich unterscheiden** *ref:* **sich (durch etw** ODER **in etw** (D)**)** ~ to differ (in sthg).

Unterlschenkel *der* lower leg.

Unterlschicht *die* lower classes (pl).

Unterschied (*pl* -e) *der* - 1. [Verschiedenheit] difference - 2. [Unterscheidung] distinction; **im ~ zu jm/etw** unlike sb/sthg.

unterschiedlich ◇ *adj* different ◇ *adv* differently; ~ **groß/schnell** of varying size/speed.

Unterschlagung (*pl* -en) *die* [von Geldern] misappropriation.

Unterschlupf (*pl* -e) *der* [Obdach] shelter; [Versteck] hiding place; ~ **suchen/finden** [Obdach] to seek/find shelter; [Versteck] to seek/find a hiding place.

unterschreiben (*prät* unterschrieb; *perf* hat unterschrieben) ◇ *vt* to sign ◇ *vi* to sign.

Unterlschrift *die* signature.

unterschwellig ◇ *adj* subliminal ◇ *adv* subliminally.

Unterseelboot *das* submarine.

Unterlseite *die* underside.

Untersetzer (*pl* -) *der* [für Glas] coaster; [für Topf] mat.

untersetzt *adj* stocky.

Unterstand *der* [vor Regen, Gefahr] shelter; [für Soldaten] dugout.

unterstellen[1] *vt* - 1. [zum Schutz] to store - 2. [unter Gegenstand] to put underneath. ➤ **sich unterstellen** *ref* [zum Schutz] to shelter.

unterstellen[2] *vt* - 1. [in Hierarchie]: **jm etw ~** to put sb in charge of sthg; **sie ist direkt dem Regierungspräsidenten unterstellt** she is directly answerable to the president - 2. [Behauptung] to assume.

unterstreichen (*prät* unterstrich; *perf* hat unterstrichen) *vt* to underline.

Unterstufe *die* SCHULE lower school.

unterstützen *vt* to support.

Unterstützung (*pl* -en) *die* support (*U*).

untersuchen *vt* to examine; [polizeilich] to investigate; **etw auf etw** (*A*) **(hin) ~** to examine sthg for sthg.

Untersuchung (*pl* -en) *die* - 1. [Untersuchen - ärztlich] examination; [- polizeilich] investigation - 2. [Studie] study.

Untersuchungsausschuss *der* committee of inquiry.

Untersuchungshaft *die* imprisonment whilst awaiting trial.

Untertan (*pl* -en) *der* subject.

Untertasse *die* saucer; **fliegende ~** *fig* flying saucer.

untertauchen (*perf* hat/ist untergetaucht) ⬦ *vi* (ist) - 1. [tauchen] to dive; [versinken] to sink - 2. *fig* [in der Menge] to disappear; [Verbrecher] to go to ground ⬦ *vt* (hat) to duck.

Unterteilung *die* division (*U*).

Untertitel *der* subtitle; **mit ~n** with subtitles.

Untertreibung (*pl* -en) *die* understatement.

untervermieten *vt* to sublet.

unterwandern *vt* to infiltrate.

Unterwäsche *die* underwear.

unterwegs *adv* on the way; **~ sein** to be away.

unterweisen (*prät* unterwies; *perf* hat unterwiesen) *vt geh*: **jn in etw** (*D*) **~** to instruct sb in sthg.

Unterwelt *die* underworld.

unterwerfen (*präs* unterwirft; *prät* unterwarf; *perf* hat unterworfen) *vt* to subjugate. ➤ **sich unterwerfen** *ref* to submit.

unterwürfig *abw* ⬦ *adj* servile ⬦ *adv* servilely.

unterzeichnen *vt* to sign.

unterziehen[1] (*prät* unterzog; *perf* hat unterzogen) *vt* [aussetzen] to subject. ➤ **sich**

unterziehen *ref* [über sich ergehen lassen]: **sich einer Sache** (*D*) **~** to undergo sthg.

Untiefe *die* - 1. [seichte Stelle] shallow - 2. [sehr große Tiefe] depth.

untreu *adj* - 1. [treulos] unfaithful; **jm ~ werden** to be unfaithful to sb - 2. *geh* [illoyal] disloyal.

Untreue *die* [zu Liebhaber] infidelity; [Illoyalität] disloyalty.

untröstlich *adj*: **über etw** (*A*) **~ sein** to be inconsolable about sthg.

untrüglich *adj* unmistakable.

unüberlegt ⬦ *adj* rash ⬦ *adv* rashly.

unübersehbar *adj* - 1. [Gebiet, Weite] vast; [Schild, Hinweis, Kratzer] obvious; [Folgen] inestimable ⬦ *adv* [groß] extremely; [aufgestellt] conspicuously.

unumgänglich *adj* unavoidable.

ununterbrochen ⬦ *adj* uninterrupted ⬦ *adv* nonstop.

unveränderlich *adj* unchanging.

unverantwortlich ⬦ *adj* irresponsible ⬦ *adv* irresponsibly.

unverbesserlich *adj* incorrigible.

unverbindlich ⬦ *adj* not binding ⬦ *adv* without obligation.

unverblümt ⬦ *adj* blunt ⬦ *adv* bluntly.

unverfänglich ⬦ *adj* harmless ⬦ *adv* harmlessly.

unverfroren ⬦ *adj* impudent ⬦ *adv* impudently.

unvergesslich *adj* unforgettable.

unverheiratet *adj* unmarried.

unverkennbar ⬦ *adj* unmistakable ⬦ *adv* unmistakably.

unvermeidlich *adj* unavoidable.

unvermittelt ⬦ *adj* sudden ⬦ *adv* suddenly.

unvermutet ⬦ *adj* unexpected ⬦ *adv* unexpectedly.

unvernünftig ⬦ *adj* stupid ⬦ *adv* stupidly.

unverrichtet *adj*: **~er Dinge** without having achieved anything.

unverschämt ⬦ *adj* - 1. [Mensch, Äußerung, Benehmen] impertinent; [Lüge] barefaced - 2. [enorm - Glück] incredible; [- Preis] outrageous ⬦ *adv* - 1. [taktlos] impertinently - 2. [sehr] incredibly.

Unverschämtheit (*pl* -en) *die* impertinence (*U*).

unversehrt ⬦ *adj* [Person] unscathed; [Sache] intact; **~ sein/bleiben** [Person] to be/remain unscathed; [Sache] to be/remain intact ⬦ *adv* unscathed.

unverständlich *adj* - 1. [nicht deutlich] unintelligible - 2. [unbegreiflich]: **es ist mir ~, wie ...** I don't understand how ...

unversucht *adj*: **nichts ~ lassen** to try everything.

unverwüstlich *adj* [Material] durable; [Mensch, Natur] resilient; [Gesundheit] robust; [Humor] irrepressible.

unverzeihlich *adj* inexcusable.

unverzüglich <> *adj* immediate <> *adv* immediately.

unvorbereitet *adj* unprepared; [Rede] improvised.

unvoreingenommen <> *adj* impartial <> *adv* impartially.

unvorhergesehen <> *adj* [Ereignis, Problem] unforeseen; [Besuch] unexpected <> *adv* unexpectedly.

unvorsichtig <> *adj* careless <> *adv* carelessly.

unvorstellbar <> *adj* unimaginable <> *adv* incredibly.

unvorteilhaft *adj* unflattering.

unwahrscheinlich <> *adj* **- 1.** [nicht wahrscheinlich] unlikely **- 2.** *fam* [enorm] incredible <> *adv fam* [sehr] incredibly.

unweigerlich <> *adj* inevitable <> *adv* inevitably.

Un|wetter *das* storm.

unwichtig *adj* unimportant.

unwiderruflich <> *adj* irrevocable <> *adv* irrevocably.

unwiderstehlich, unwiderstehlich <> *adj* irresistible <> *adv* irresistibly.

unwillig <> *adj* [widerwillig] reluctant; [verärgert] angry <> *adv* [widerwillig] reluctantly; [verärgert] angrily.

unwillkürlich <> *adj* involuntary <> *adv* involuntarily.

unwirsch <> *adj* surly <> *adv* in a surly way.

Unwissenheit *die* ignorance.

unwohl *adj*: **jm ist ~** [krank] sb feels unwell; [unbehaglich] sb feels uneasy; **sich ~ fühlen** [krank] to feel unwell; [unbehaglich] to feel uneasy.

Unwohlsein *das* indisposition.

unwürdig <> *adj* undignified; **einer Sache** *(G)* **~ sein** to be unworthy of sthg <> *adv* in an undignified manner.

unzählig, unzählig <> *adj* innumerable <> *adv*: **~ viele** a huge number (of).

Unze *(pl -n) die* ounce.

unzertrennlich, unzertrennlich *adj* inseparable.

unzüchtig <> *adj* indecent <> *adv* indecently.

unzufrieden *adj* dissatisfied; **mit etw ~ sein** to be dissatisfied with sthg.

Unzufriedenheit *die* dissatisfaction.

unzulässig <> *adj* inadmissible <> *adv* inadmissibly.

unzurechnungsfähig *adj* not responsible for one's actions; **jn für ~ erklären** to certify sb insane.

unzureichend <> *adj* insufficient <> *adv* insufficiently.

unzuverlässig *adj* unreliable.

üppig <> *adj* [Busen] full; [Frau] voluptuous; [Essen] lavish; [Haar] thick; [Vegetation] lush <> *adv* [bewachsen] thickly; [speisen, leben] lavishly; **~ geformt** voluptuous.

Ur|abstimmung *die* strike ballot.

Uran *das* CHEM uranium.

Urauf|führung *die* premiere.

urbar *adj*: **~ machen** [Sumpf] to reclaim; [Stück Land] to cultivate.

Ur|bevölkerung *die* original inhabitants *(pl)*.

Ur|einwohner, in *der, die* original inhabitant.

Ur|enkel, in *der, die* great-grandson (*f* great-granddaughter).

Urgroß|mutter *die* great-grandmother.

Urgroß|vater *der* great-grandfather.

Urheber, in *(mpl -; fpl -nen) der, die* [von Kunstwerk] creator; [von Verbrechen] perpetrator.

Urin *(pl -e) der* urine *(U)*.

Urkunde *(pl -n) die* certificate.

Urkundenfälschung *die* forging of documents.

Urlaub *(pl -e) der* holiday *Br*, vacation *Am*; **~ machen/haben** to have a holiday *Br* ODER vacation *Am*; **im** ODER **in ~ sein** to be on holiday *Br* ODER vacation *Am*.

Urlauber, in *(mpl -; fpl -nen) der, die* holidaymaker *Br*, vacationer *Am*.

Urlaubs|ort *der* holiday *Br* ODER vacation *Am* resort.

Urlaubs|zeit *die* holiday *Br* ODER vacation *Am* season.

Urne *(pl -n) die* **- 1.** [Graburne] urn **- 2.** [Wahlurne] ballot box.

Ur|sache *die* cause; **die ~ für etw** the cause of sthg. ◆ **keine Ursache** *interj* don't mention it!

Ur|sprung *der* origin.

ursprünglich <> *adj* **- 1.** [anfänglich] original **- 2.** [naturhaft] natural <> *adv* [zunächst] originally.

Ur|teil *das* **- 1.** RECHT verdict **- 2.** [Bewertung] opinion; **sich** *(D)* **ein ~ bilden** to form an opinion.

urteilen *vi* to judge; **über jn/etw ~** to judge sb/sthg.

Urteilskraft *die* judgement.

Urteils|spruch *der* verdict.

Uruguay *nt* Uruguay.

Ur|wald *der* primeval forest; [tropisch] jungle.

urwüchsig [ˈuːɐ̯vyːksɪç] *adj* [Garten, Gelände] natural; [Sprache, Humor] earthy; [Stärke] elemental.

USA [uːˈɛsfaː] (*abk für* United States of America) *die* USA.

User [ˈjuːzɐ] (*pl -*) *der* EDV user.

usw. (*abk für* und so weiter) etc.

Utensilien [utɛnˈziːljən] *pl* equipment (U).

Utopie [utoˈpiː] (*pl -n*) *die* utopia.

u. U. (*abk für* unter Umständen) possibly.

u. v. a. (*abk für* und viele(s) andere) and many others.

V

v, V [fau] (*pl -* ODER *-s*) *das* v, V. ← **V** (*abk für* Volt) V.

v. *abk für* von.

vage [ˈvaːɡə], **vag** [vaːk] (*kompar* vager; *superl* vagste) ◇ *adj* vague ◇ *adv* vaguely.

Vagina [vaˈɡiːna] (*pl -nen*) *die* MED vagina.

Vakuum [ˈvaːkuʊm] (*pl -kuen*) *das* vacuum.

vakuumverpackt [ˈvaːkuʊmfɛɐpakt] *adj* vacuum-packed.

Vampir [ˈvampiːɐ] (*pl -e*) *der* vampire.

Vanille [vaˈnɪljə, vaˈnɪlə] *die* vanilla.

Vanilleeis *das* vanilla ice cream.

variieren [variˈiːrən] *vt & vi* to vary.

Vase [ˈvaːzə] (*pl -n*) *die* vase.

Vater (*pl* Väter) *der* father.

Vaterland *das* homeland.

väterlich ◇ *adj* **- 1.** [des Vaters] paternal **- 2.** [wohlwollend] fatherly ◇ *adv* [wohlwollend] in a fatherly way.

väterlicherseits *adv* on one's father's side.

Vatertag *der* Father's Day.

Vaterunser (*pl -*) *das* REL: **das ~** the Lord's Prayer.

Vatikan [vatiˈkaːn] *der*: **der ~** the Vatican.

V-Ausschnitt *der* V-neck.

v. Chr. (*abk für* vor Christus) BC.

Veganer (*pl -*) *der* vegan.

Vegetarier, in [vegeˈtaːriɐ, rɪn] (*mpl -*; *fpl -nen*) *der, die* vegetarian.

vegetarisch [vegeˈtaːrɪʃ] ◇ *adj* vegetarian ◇ *adv*: **~ leben/essen** to be a vegetarian.

vegetieren [vegeˈtiːrən] *vi abw* to live from hand to mouth.

Veilchen [ˈfailçən] (*pl -*) *das* **- 1.** [Blume] violet **- 2.** *fam fig* [blaues Auge] black eye.

Vene [ˈveːnə] (*pl -n*) *die* MED vein.

Venedig [veˈneːdɪç] *nt* Venice.

Ventil [vɛnˈtiːl] (*pl -e*) *das* valve.

Ventilator [vɛntiˈlaːtoɐ] (*pl -toren*) *der* fan.

verabreden *vt* to arrange; **etw mit jm ~** to arrange sthg with sb. ← **sich verabreden** *ref* to arrange to meet; **sich mit jm ~** to arrange to meet sb.

sich verabreden

Why don't we go for a drink sometime? Lass/lasst uns doch bei Gelegenheit mal einen trinken gehen.
Are you free any time next week? Hast du irgendwann nächste Woche Zeit?
How about Friday at 10 o'clock? Wie wärs mit Freitag um 10 Uhr?
When would suit you best? Wann passt es dir am besten?
Let's say tomorrow outside the cinema at 7.30. Sagen wir morgen um halb acht vor dem Kino.

Verabredung (*pl -en*) *die* **- 1.** [Treffen - geschäftlich] appointment; [- mit Freund] date **- 2.** [Übereinkommen] arrangement.

verabreichen *vt* to administer; **jm etw ~ amt** to administer sthg to sb.

verabscheuen *vt* to detest.

verabschieden *vt* **- 1.** [zum Abschied] to say goodbye to **- 2.** [Gesetz] to pass. ← **sich verabschieden** *ref* [Auf Wiedersehen sagen] to say goodbye; **sich von jm ~** to say goodbye to sb.

sich verabschieden

Goodbye Mrs Jones! It was nice meeting you. Auf Wiedersehen, Frau Jones! Es hat mich gefreut, Sie kennen zu lernen.
See you again some time! Bis demnächst!
Right, then. See you on Monday. Ok, dann bis Montag.
Bye! Take care! Tschüs! Machs gut!
All the best! Alles Gute!

verachten *vt* to despise.

verächtlich ◇ *adj* **- 1.** [missbilligend] contemptuous **- 2.** [verachtenswert] despicable ◇ *adv* **- 1.** [missbilligend] contemptuously **- 2.** [verachtenswert] despicably.

Verachtung *die* contempt.

verallgemeinern *vt & vi* to generalize.

Verallgemeinerung (*pl -en*) *die* generalization.

veraltet *adj* obsolete.

Veranda [veˈranda] (*pl -den*) *die* veranda.

veränderlich *adj* [Wetter, Stimmung] changeable; [Größe] variable.

verändern *vt* to change. ← **sich verändern** *ref* **- 1.** [anders werden] to change **- 2.** [eine andere Stelle annehmen] to change one's job.

Ver|änderung *die* change.

verängstigt *adj* frightened.

Ver|ankerung *(pl -en) die* [das Anbringen] fixing *(U)*; [Befestigung] fixture; [von Schiff] anchoring *(U)*.

veranlagt *adj*: **melancholisch ~ sein** to have a melancholic disposition; **homosexuell ~ sein** to have homosexual tendencies *(pl)*.

Veranlagung *(pl -en) die* disposition; [künstlerisch] bent; **homosexuelle ~** homosexual tendencies *(pl)*.

veranlassen *vt*: **jn ~, etw zu tun, jn zu etw ~** to make sb do sthg; **etw ~** to arrange for sthg.

Veranlassung *(pl -en) die* - **1.** [Veranlassen] instigation; **auf js ~ (hin)** at sb's instigation - **2.** [Anlass] reason; **keine ~ haben, etw zu tun** to have no reason to do sthg.

veranschaulichen *vt* to illustrate.

veranstalten *vt* - **1.** [organisieren] to organize - **2.** *fam* [machen] to make.

Veranstalter, in *(mpl -; fpl -nen) der, die* organizer.

Veranstaltung *(pl -en) die* - **1.** [Ereignis] event - **2.** [Organisation] organization.

verantworten *vt* to take responsibility for. ➤ **sich verantworten** *ref*: **sich vor jm/etw ~** to answer to sb/sthg; **sich für** ODER **wegen etw ~** to answer for sthg.

verantwortlich *adj* responsible; **für jn/etw ~ sein** to be responsible for sb/sthg; **jn für etw ~ machen** to hold sb responsible for sthg.

Verantwortung *(pl -en) die* responsibility; **jn zur ~ ziehen** to call sb to account; **auf eigene ~** on one's own responsibility.

verantwortungslos ◇ *adj* irresponsible ◇ *adv* irresponsibly.

verarbeiten *vt* - **1.** [Material] to process; **etw zu etw ~** to make sthg into sthg - **2.** [Eindruck, Erlebnis] to digest; [Misserfolg] to come to terms with.

Verarbeitung *(pl -en) die* - **1.** [von Rohstoffen] processing *(U)* - **2.** [Qualität] quality - **3.** [psychisch] coming to terms with the past.

verärgern *vt* to annoy.

verarzten *vt* to treat.

Verb [vɛrp] *(pl -en) das* GRAM verb.

Verband *(pl -bände) der* - **1.** [für Wunden] bandage; **einen ~ anlegen** to apply a bandage - **2.** [Organisation] association - **3.** [Gruppe] unit.

Verband|kasten, Verbandskasten *der* first-aid box.

verbannen *vt* to exile.

verbarrikadieren *vt* to barricade. ➤ **sich verbarrikadieren** *ref* to barricade o.s. in.

verbergen *(präs verbirgt; prät verbarg; perf hat verborgen) vt* to hide; **etw vor jm ~** to hide sthg from sb. ➤ **sich verbergen** *ref* to hide.

verbessern *vt* - **1.** [Leistung] to improve - **2.** [Fehler] to correct. ➤ **sich verbessern** *ref* - **1.** [besser werden] to improve - **2.** [sich korrigieren] to correct o.s. - **3.** [sozial, finanziell] to better o.s.

Ver|besserung *die* - **1.** [gen] improvement - **2.** [Korrigieren, Text] correction - **3.** [Aufstieg] betterment.

verbeugen ➤ **sich verbeugen** *ref* to bow.

Verbeugung *(pl -en) die* bow.

verbiegen *(prät verbog; perf hat verbogen) vt* to bend. ➤ **sich verbiegen** *ref* to bend.

verbieten *(prät verbot; perf hat verboten) vt* [Handlung] to forbid; [Partei] to ban; **jm ~, etw zu tun** to forbid sb to do sthg.

verbieten

Smoking is not permitted in the office. Im Büro ist das Rauchen untersagt.

You're not meant to be in here at the weekend. Sie sollten am Wochenende gar nicht hier sein.

You're not allowed to run in the corridors. Auf den Korridoren darf man nicht laufen.

Don't ever do that again! Tu das ja nicht noch mal!

There's no way you're going out tonight! Du wirst heute Abend auf keinen Fall ausgehen!

verbilligt ◇ *adj* reduced ◇ *adv* at a reduced price.

verbinden *(prät verband; perf hat verbunden)* ◇ *vt* - **1.** [Wunde] to bandage - **2.** [Werkstücke, Material] to join - **3.** [Orte, Punkte] to connect - **4.** [am Telefon] to put through; **jn mit jm ~** to put sb through to sb - **5.** [zubinden]: **jm die Augen ~** to blindfold sb - **6.** [kombinieren]: **etw mit etw ~** to combine sthg with sthg - **7.** [Freunde, Bekannte] to unite - **8.** [Gedanken] to associate ◇ *vi* [am Telefon]: **ich verbinde** I'll put you through; **falsch verbunden!** wrong number! ➤ **sich verbinden** *ref* - **1.** [Stoffe, Materialien] to combine - **2.** [zusammentreffen] to be combined.

verbindlich ◇ *adj* - **1.** [Person] friendly - **2.** [Zusage] binding ◇ *adv* - **1.** [lächeln] in a friendly manner - **2.** [verpflichtend]: **er hat ~ zugesagt** he has firmly accepted.

Ver|bindung *die* - **1.** [Aneinanderfügen] joining *(U)* - **2.** [Kombination & CHEM] combination - **3.** [zwischen Orten, Punkten] link - **4.** [Zusammenhang, am Telefon, Verkehrsverbindung] connection - **5.** [mit Erinnerung] association - **6.** [zu Freund, Bekannten] contact; **sich mit jm in ~ setzen** to contact sb.

verbissen <> *adj* [Kampf, Person] dogged; [Miene] grim <> *adv* [arbeiten, kämpfen] doggedly; [betrachten] grimly.

verbittert <> *adj* bitter <> *adv* with bitterness.

verblassen (*präs* verblasst; *prät* verblasste; *perf* ist verblasst) *vi* to fade.

verbleiben (*prät* verblieb; *perf* ist verblieben) *vi* - **1.** [übereinkommen]: **wie seid ihr gestern verblieben?** what did you arrange yesterday? - **2.** [bleiben, übrig bleiben] to remain.

verbleit *adj*: **~es Benzin** leaded petrol; **~es Super** leaded.

verblöden (*perf* hat/ist verblödet) *vi* (ist) *vt* (hat) to turn into a moron.

verblüffen <> *vt* to amaze; **verblüfft sein** to be taken aback <> *vi* to be amazing.

verbluten (*perf* ist verblutet) *vi* to bleed to death.

verbohrt <> *adj* stubborn <> *adv* stubbornly.

verborgen <> *pp* ⊳ verbergen <> *adj* hidden.

Verbot (*pl* -e) *das* ban.

verboten <> *pp* ⊳ verbieten <> *adj* - **1.** [nicht erlaubt] banned; **~ sein** to be forbidden; **'streng ~!'** 'strictly prohibited!' - **2.** *fam* [schrecklich] horrendous; **~ aussehen** *fam* to look a real sight.

Verbotsschild (*pl* -er) *das* sign indicating a restriction, e.g. 'no parking', 'no entry'.

Verbrauch *der* consumption; **der ~ von** ODER **an etw** (*D*) the consumption of sthg.

verbrauchen *vt* to consume.

Verbraucher, in (*mpl* -; *fpl* -nen) *der, die* consumer.

Verbrechen (*pl* -) *das* crime; **ein ~ begehen** to commit a crime.

Verbrecher, in (*mpl* -; *fpl* -nen) *der, die* criminal.

verbrecherisch *adj* criminal.

verbreiten *vt* to spread. ← **sich verbreiten** *ref* - **1.** [sich ausbreiten] to spread - **2.** *abw* [sich auslassen]: **sich über etw** (*A*) **~** to hold forth about sthg.

verbreitern *vt* to widen. ← **sich verbreitern** *ref* to widen.

verbrennen (*prät* verbrannte; *perf* hat/ist verbrannt) <> *vt* (hat) - **1.** [durch Feuer] to burn - **2.** [Kalorien] to convert <> *vi* (ist) - **1.** [durch Feuer] to burn - **2.** [Kalorien] to be converted. ← **sich verbrennen** *ref* to burn o.s.

verbringen (*prät* verbrachte; *perf* hat verbracht) *vt* - **1.** [Zeit] to spend - **2.** *amt* [bringen] to take.

verbrüdern ← **sich verbrüdern** *ref*: **sich mit jm ~** to avow eternal brotherhood with sb; [mit Feind] to fraternize with sb.

verbrühen *vt* to scald. ← **sich verbrühen** *ref* to scald o.s.

verbuchen *vt* to enter; **einen Sieg für sich ~ können** to notch up a success; **der Betrag wurde auf ihren Konto verbucht** the sum was credited to her account.

verbünden ← **sich verbünden** *ref* to form an alliance; **sich mit jm ~** to form an alliance with sb.

Verbündete (*pl* -n) *der, die* ally.

verbürgen *vt* to guarantee. ← **sich verbürgen** *ref*: **sich für jn/etw ~** to vouch for sb/ sthg.

verbüßen *vt* to serve.

Verdacht (*pl* -e) *der* suspicion; **im ~ stehen** to be under suspicion; **jn im** ODER **in ~ haben** to suspect sb.

verdächtig <> *adj* suspicious <> *adv* suspiciously.

verdächtigen *vt* to suspect; **jn einer Sache** (*G*) **~** to suspect sb of sthg.

verdammt *adj & adv fam* [übel] damned.

verdampfen (*perf* ist verdampft) *vi* to vaporize.

verdanken *vt*: **jm etw ~** to owe sthg to sb.

verdarb *prät* ⊳ verderben.

verdauen *vt* to digest.

verdaulich *adj*: **leicht/schwer ~** easy/hard to digest.

Verdauung *die* digestion.

Verdeck (*pl* -e) *das* [von Autos] hood.

verdecken *vt* [zudecken] to cover; [verbergen] to conceal; **jm die Sicht ~** to block sb's view.

verderben (*präs* verdirbt; *prät* verdarb; *perf* hat/ist verdorben) <> *vi* (ist) to go off <> *vt* (hat) to spoil; [völlig] to ruin; **jm die Laune ~** to put sb in a bad mood; **es sich** (*D*) **mit niemandem nicht ~ wollen** *fig* not to want to fall out with anyone.

verderblich *adj* perishable.

verdeutlichen *vt*: **jm etw ~** to explain sthg to sb.

verdienen <> *vt* - **1.** [Gehalt, Gewinn] to earn - **2.** [Lob, Strafe] to deserve <> *vi* to earn; **gut/schlecht ~** to be well/poorly paid.

Verdienst <> *der* [Entgelt] earnings (*pl*) <> *das* [Leistung] achievement.

verdirbt *präs* ⊳ verderben.

verdoppeln *vt* [Gewinn, Einsatz] to double; [Anstrengungen] to redouble. ← **sich verdoppeln** *ref* to double.

verdorben *pp* ⊳ verderben.

verdrängen *vt* - **1.** [räumlich] to force out - **2.** [psychisch] to repress.

Verdrängung (*pl* -en) *die* - **1.** [psychisch]

repression (U) - 2. [Abdrängen - von Person] ousting.

verdrehen vt to twist; **die Augen ~** to roll one's eyes.

verdreifachen vt to triple. ◆ **sich verdreifachen** ref to triple.

Verdruss der annoyance.

verdünnen vt to dilute; [Farbe, Soße] to thin; [Kaffee, Wein] to water down.

verdunsten (perf ist verdunstet) vi to evaporate.

verdursten (perf ist verdurstet) vi to die of thirst.

verdutzt adj nonplussed.

verehren vt - 1. [Gottheit] to worship - 2. geh [Person] to admire - 3. iron [schenken]: **jm etw ~** to present sb with sthg.

Verehrer, in (mpl -; fpl -nen) der, die admirer.

Verehrung die - 1. [von Gottheit] worship - 2. geh [für Person] admiration.

vereidigen vt to swear in.

Verein (pl -e) der [für Sport und Hobby] club; [gemeinnützig] society.

vereinbaren vt - 1. [verabreden]: **etw mit jm ~** to agree sthg with sb; [Termin, Treffpunkt] to arrange sthg with sb - 2. [vereinen]: **etw mit etw ~** to reconcile sthg with sthg.

Vereinbarung (pl -en) die agreement; [von Termin, Treffpunkt] arrangement; **eine ~ treffen** to come to an agreement.

vereinen vt [Gruppen, Länder] to unite; [Meinungen] to reconcile; [Eigenschaften] to combine. ◆ **sich vereinen** ref [Gruppen, Länder] to unite; [Eigenschaften] to be combined.

vereinfachen vt to simplify.

vereinheitlichen vt to standardize.

vereinigen vt [Länder, Gebiete] to unite; [Firmen] to merge; **mehrere Titel auf sich ~** to hold several titles. ◆ **sich vereinigen** ref [Statten, Gruppen] to unite; [Flüsse] to join up.

Vereinigte Staaten (von Amerika) pl United States (of America).

Vereinigung die - 1. [Vereinigen - von Staaten] uniting (U); [- von Firmen] merging (U); - 2. [Gruppe] organization.

vereint <> adj united <> adv together.

Vereinte Nationen pl United Nations.

vereinzelt <> adj [Regen] occasional; [Person, Überreste] odd <> adv occasionally.

vereist adj icy.

vereiteln vt to thwart.

verenden (perf ist verendet) vi to perish.

vererben vt [Güter]: **jm etw ~** to leave sthg to sb.

Vererbung (pl -en) die heredity (U); **wir untersuchen die ~ von bestimmten Eigen**schaften we are investigating the way in which certain characteristics are passed on.

verewigen vt to immortalize. ◆ **sich verewigen** ref fam hum to immortalize o.s.

verfahren (präs verfährt; prät verfuhr; perf hat/ist verfahren) vi (ist) to proceed; **mit jm/etw ~** to deal with sb/sthg. ◆ **sich verfahren** ref to get lost.

Verfahren (pl -) das - 1. [Gerichtsverfahren] proceedings (pl) - 2. [Methode] procedure.

Verfall der - 1. [Niedergang - von Gebäude] decay; [- von Person, Gesundheit] decline - 2. [von Gutschein, Garantie] expiry.

verfallen (präs verfällt; prät verfiel; perf ist verfallen) vi - 1. [Gebäude] to decay; [Person] to decline - 2. [Gutschein, Garantie] to expire - 3. [auf etw kommen]: **auf jn/etw ~** to hit on sb/sthg - 4. [geraten]: **in etw (A) ~** to lapse into sthg - 5. [hörig werden]: **jm/einer Sache ~** to become a slave to sb/sthg.

Verfalls|datum das sell-by date.

verfälschen vt [Aussage, Tatsachen] to distort; [Geschmack] to adulterate.

verfänglich adj awkward.

verfärben vt to discolour. ◆ **sich verfärben** ref to change colour; **sich blau/schwarz ~** to turn blue/black.

verfassen vt to write.

Verfasser, in (mpl -; fpl -nen) der, die author.

Ver|fassung die - 1. [von Staaten] constitution - 2. [von Person] condition; **in guter/schlechter ~ sein** to be in good/poor shape.

verfaulen (perf ist verfault) vi to rot.

verfehlen vt to miss.

verfeinern vt to refine.

verfilmen vt: **einen Roman ~** to make a film of a novel.

verfliegen (prät verflog; perf hat/ist verflogen) vi (ist) - 1. [Geruch] to disappear; [Flüssigkeit] to evaporate - 2. [Zeit] to fly by.

verflixt fam <> adj - 1. [verdammt] damned - 2. [groß] incredible <> adv [sehr] damned.

verfluchen vt to curse.

verflüchtigen ◆ **sich verflüchtigen** ref [Geruch] to disappear; [Gas] to disperse.

verfolgen vt - 1. [folgen, beobachten] to follow - 2. [Verbrecher, Ziel, Plan] to pursue - 3. [unterdrücken] to persecute.

Verfolger, in (mpl -; fpl -nen) der, die pursuer.

Verfolgung (pl -en) die - 1. [gen] pursuit (U) - 2. [Unterdrückung] persecution.

Verfolgungswahn der persecution mania.

verfrachten vt - 1. [verladen] to transport - 2. fam hum [transportieren] to cart off.

verfrüht <> adj premature <> adv prematurely.

verfügbar adj available.

verfügen <> vt to order <> vi: **über jn/etw ~** [haben] to have sb/sthg at one's disposal; **über etw** (A) **(frei) ~ können** [bestimmen] to be able to do as one likes with sthg.

Ver|fügung die - **1.** [Zugriff]: **jm etw zur ~ stellen** to put sthg at sb's disposal - **2.** [Erlass] order.

verführen vt - **1.** [verleiten]: **jn zu etw ~** to tempt sb to do sthg; **jn zum Klauen ~** to encourage sb to steal - **2.** [zum Geschlechtsverkehr] to seduce.

verführerisch <> adj - **1.** [anziehend] tempting - **2.** [erotisch] seductive <> adv - **1.** [anziehend] temptingly - **2.** [erotisch] seductively.

Verführung (pl -en) die seduction (U).

vergammeln adj fam abw - **1.** [verdorben] spoilt - **2.** [heruntergekommen] scruffy.

vergangen <> pp ⊳ vergehen <> adj [Zeiten] past; **~en Dienstag** last Tuesday.

Vergangenheit die - **1.** [vergangene Zeit] past - **2.** GRAM past tense.

Vergaser (pl -) der carburettor.

vergaß prät ⊳ vergessen.

vergeben (präs vergibt; prät vergab; perf hat vergeben) <> vi: **jm ~** to forgive sb <> vt - **1.** [verzeihen]: **jm etw ~** to forgive sb sthg - **2.** [geben] to award - **3.** [verpassen] to miss.

vergebens adv in vain.

vergeblich <> adj futile <> adv in vain.

vergehen (prät verging; perf hat/ist vergangen) vi (ist) - **1.** [Zeit] to pass - **2.** [verschwinden] to disappear; **der Spaß ist mir vergangen** I'm not enjoying it any more; **vor etw** (D) **~** fig to die of sthg.

Vergeltung die retaliation.

vergessen (präs vergisst; prät vergaß; perf hat vergessen) vt to forget.

Vergessenheit die: **in ~ geraten** to fall into oblivion.

vergesslich adj forgetful.

vergeuden vt to waste.

vergewaltigen vt [sexuell] to rape; [allgemein] to violate.

Vergewaltigung (pl -en) die rape.

vergewissern ◆ **sich vergewissern** ref to make sure.

vergießen (prät vergoss; perf hat vergossen) vt - **1.** [verschütten] to spill - **2.** [Blut, Tränen] to shed.

vergiften vt to poison. ◆ **sich vergiften** ref to poison o.s.

Vergiftung (pl -en) die poisoning (U).

Vergissmeinnicht (pl -e) das forget-me-not.

vergisst präs ⊳ vergessen.

verglasen vt to glaze.

Vergleich (pl -e) der - **1.** [Gegenüberstellung] comparison; **im ~ mit** ODER **zu jm/etw** com-

pared to sb/sthg - **2.** RECHT settlement - **3.** SPORT friendly.

vergleichbar adj comparable.

vergleichen (prät verglich; perf hat verglichen) vt to compare; **jn/etw mit jm/etw ~** to compare sb/sthg to sb/sthg.

vergnügen ◆ **sich vergnügen** ref to enjoy o.s.

Vergnügen (pl -) das - **1.** [Freude] pleasure; **Tanzen macht ihr großes ~** she really enjoys dancing; **mit ~!** with pleasure! - **2.** [Unterhaltung] fun (U). ◆ **viel Vergnügen** interj have fun!

vergnügt <> adj - **1.** [Person] cheerful - **2.** [Stunden] enjoyable <> adv cheerfully.

vergoldet adj gold-plated.

vergraben (präs vergräbt; prät vergrub; perf hat vergraben) vt to bury.

vergreifen (prät vergriff; perf hat vergriffen) ◆ **sich vergreifen** ref: **sich an jm ~** [brutal werden] to assault sb; [sexuell] to assault sb (sexually); **sich an etw** (D) **~** [stehlen] to misappropriate sthg.

vergriffen <> pp ⊳ vergreifen <> adj out of print.

vergrößern <> vt to expand; [Foto] to enlarge; [Haus] to extend; [vermehren] to increase <> vi to magnify. ◆ **sich vergrößern** ref - **1.** [größer werden] to expand; [zunehmen] to increase; [Tumor] to increase in size - **2.** [mehr Raum benutzen] to get more space.

Vergrößerung (pl -en) die - **1.** [Vergrößern] expansion (U); [von Haus] extension (U); [von Tumor] increase in size; [Vermehrung] increase - **2.** [Foto] enlargement.

Vergrößerungs|glas das magnifying glass.

Vergünstigung (pl -en) die concession.

vergüten vt: **jm etw ~** [Unkosten] to reimburse sb for sthg; [Arbeit] to remunerate sb for sthg.

verhaften vt to arrest.

Ver|haftung die arrest.

verhallen (perf ist verhallt) vi to die away.

verhalten (präs verhält; prät verhielt; perf hat verhalten) ◆ **sich verhalten** ref - **1.** [sich benehmen] to behave - **2.** [sein] to be; **es verhält sich so** this is how matters stand.

Verhalten das behaviour.

Verhältnis (pl -se) das - **1.** [Relation] ratio; **im ~ zum letzten Jahr** compared to last year - **2.** [persönliche Beziehung] relationship; **ein gutes ~ zu jm haben** to have a good relationship with sb - **3.** [Liebesbeziehung] affair; **ein ~ mit jm haben** to have an affair with sb. ◆ **Verhältnisse** pl [Bedingungen] conditions; **über seine ~se leben** to live beyond one's means.

verhältnismäßig adv relatively.

verhandeln ⟨> vi - **1.** [beraten]: **mit jm ~** to negotiate with sb; **über etw** (A) **~** to negotiate sthg - **2.** [vor Gericht] to hear a case ⟨> vt - **1.** [aushandeln] to negotiate - **2.** [vor Gericht] to hear.

Verlhandlung die - **1.** [Beratung] negotiation - **2.** RECHT hearing.

verhängen vt - **1.** [zuhängen] to cover - **2.** [Urteil, Verbot] to impose; **etw über jn/ etw ~** to impose sthg on sb/sthg.

Verhängnis (pl -se) das: **jn zum ~ werden** to be sb's downfall.

verhängnisvoll ⟨> adj [Tag, Begegnung] fateful; [Fehler] disastrous ⟨> adv disastrously.

verharmlosen vt to play down.

verhärten (perf hat/ist verhärtet) ⟨> vi (ist) to harden ⟨> vt (hat) to harden. ◆ **sich verhärten** ref to harden.

verheerend ⟨> adj devastating ⟨> adv devastatingly.

verheilen (perf ist verheilt) vi to heal.

verheimlichen vt to keep secret; **jm etw ~** to keep sthg secret from sb.

verheiratet adj married; **mit jm ~ sein** [mit dem Ehepartner] to be married to sb; **mit etw ~ sein** fam hum [auf etw fixiert sein] to be married to sthg.

verhindern vt to prevent.

Verhör (pl -e) das interrogation.

verhören vt to interrogate. ◆ **sich verhören** ref to mishear.

verhungern (perf ist verhungert) vi to starve to death.

verhüten ⟨> vt to prevent ⟨> vi to take precautions.

Verhütungslmittel das contraceptive.

verirren ◆ **sich verirren** ref to get lost.

verjagen vt to chase away.

verjähren (perf ist verjährt) vi to come under the statute of limitations.

verjüngen vt [Aussehen, Haut] to rejuvenate; [Belegschaft] to introduce young blood into. ◆ **sich verjüngen** ref to taper.

verkalkt adj - **1.** [verstopft] furred up - **2.** fam [senil] senile; **~ sein** to be gaga.

Verlkauf der - **1.** [das Verkaufen] sale - **2.** [Abteilung] sales (U).

verkaufen vt - **1.** [Ware] to sell; **etw an jn ~** to sell sb sthg; **'zu ~!'** 'for sale' - **2.** fam [darstellen]: **(jm) etw als etw ~** to sell (sb) sthg as sthg. ◆ **sich verkaufen** ref: **sich gut/ schlecht** [Ware] to sell well/poorly; [sich darstellen] to sell o.s. well/poorly.

Verlkäufer, in der, die - **1.** [beruflich] sales assistant Br ODER clerk Am - **2.** [Verkaufende] seller.

verkäuflich adj: **~ sein** to be for sale; **schwer ~ sein** to be hard to sell.

Verkehr der - **1.** [Straßenverkehr] traffic; **dichter ~** heavy traffic - **2.** [Gebrauch]: **etw aus dem ~ ziehen** [Geld] to withdraw sthg from circulation; [Produkt] to withdraw sthg from sale - **3.** geh [Umgang] contact - **4.** [Geschlechtsverkehr] intercourse.

verkehren (perf hat/ist verkehrt) ⟨> vi - **1.** (hat) geh [Person]: **mit jm ~** to associate with sb; **in einem Lokal ~** to frequent a bar - **2.** [Zug, Bus] to run ⟨> vt (hat): **etw ins Gegenteil ~** to reverse sthg.

Verkehrslampel die traffic lights (pl).

Verkehrslaufkommen das: **dichtes** ODER **hohes ~** heavy traffic.

Verkehrslfunk der traffic bulletin service.

Verkehrslkontrolle die traffic check.

Verkehrslmittel das: **die öffentlichen ~** public transport (U).

Verkehrspolizei die (ohne pl) traffic police (pl).

Verkehrsunlfall der road accident.

Verkehrsverlbindung die connection.

Verkehrslzeichen das road sign.

verkehrt ⟨> adj wrong ⟨> adv wrongly; **~ fahren** to go the wrong way. ◆ **verkehrt herum** adv the wrong way round.

verkennen (prät verkannte; perf hat verkannt) vt [Situation] to misjudge; [Absicht] to mistake.

verklagen vt to sue.

verkleben (perf hat/ist verklebt) ⟨> vi (ist) to become sticky ⟨> vt (hat) - **1.** [beschmieren] to make sticky - **2.** [Riss] to stick something over.

verkleiden vt - **1.** [mit Kostüm] to dress up - **2.** [Innenwand] to cover; [Gebäude] to face. ◆ **sich verkleiden** ref to dress up.

Verlkleidung die - **1.** [Kostüm] costume - **2.** [das Verkleiden] dressing up - **3.** [von Innenwand] covering; [von Gebäude] facing.

verkleinern vt to reduce. ◆ **sich verkleinern** ref to decrease.

verklemmt adj inhibited.

verkneifen (prät verkniff; perf hat verkniffen) vt: **sich** (D) **etw ~** to suppress sthg.

verknoten vt to tie together. ◆ **sich verknoten** ref to become knotted.

verknüpfen vt - **1.** [verknoten] to tie together - **2.** [verbinden]: **etw mit etw ~** to connect sthg with sthg.

verkommen (prät verkam; perf ist verkommen) vi - **1.** [verfallen] to become run-down - **2.** [verderben] to go bad - **3.** [verwahrlosen]: **jn ~ lassen** to let sb go to the bad.

verkrachen ◆ **sich verkrachen** ref: **sich mit jm ~** to have a row with sb.

verkraften vt to cope with.

verkriechen (prät verkroch; perf hat verkrochen) ◆ **sich verkriechen** ref [kriechen] to crawl; [sich verstecken] to hide.

verkrüppelt *adj* - **1.** [Mensch] crippled - **2.** [Baum] twisted, gnarled.

verkümmern (*perf* ist verkümmert) *vi* to wither (away).

verkünden *vt* to announce; [Urteil] to pronounce; [Prophezeiung] to make.

verkürzen *vt* to shorten; [Leben, Urlaub] to cut short; [Arbeitszeit] to reduce; **die Zeit ~** to while away the time.

Verlag (*pl* -e) *der* publishing house.

verlagern *vt* [Gewicht, Schwerpunkt] to shift; [an einen anderen Ort] to move. ◆ **sich verlagern** *ref* to shift.

verlangen ◇ *vt* - **1.** [fordern] to demand; [bitten] to ask for; **viel von jm ~** to ask a lot of sb - **2.** [erfordern] to call for - **3.** [Lohn] to ask - **4.** [Ausweis] to ask to see - **5.** [am Telefon]: **jn am Telefon ~** to ask to speak to sb on the phone ◇ *vi*: **nach jm/etw ~** [um etw bitten] to ask for sb/sthg; *geh* [sich sehnen] to long for sb/sthg.

Verlangen *das* - **1.** [Wunsch] desire - **2.** [Forderung] request. ◆ **auf Verlangen** *adv* on demand.

verlängern *vt* - **1.** [zeitlich, räumlich] to extend; [Ausweis] to renew - **2.** [Rock, Ärmel] to lengthen - **3.** [Soße] to thin down. ◆ **sich verlängern** *ref* - **1.** [zeitlich] to be extended - **2.** [räumlich] to grow longer.

Verlängerung (*pl* -en) *die* - **1.** [von Zeitraum, Strecke] extension - **2.** [von Rock, Ärmel] lengthening; [von Ausweis] renewal - **3.** SPORT extra time.

Verlängerungs|schnur *die* ELEKTR extension lead *Br* ODER *Am*.

verlangsamen *vt* to slow down; **das Tempo ~** to reduce speed. ◆ **sich verlangsamen** *ref* to slow down.

verlassen (*präs* verlässt; *prät* verließ; *perf* hat verlassen) *vt* to leave. ◆ **sich verlassen** *ref*: **sich auf jn/etw ~** to rely on sb/sthg.

verlässlich *adj* reliable.

Ver|lauf *der* course; **im ~ von etw/einer Sache** (*G*) in the course of sthg.

verlaufen (*präs* verläuft; *prät* verlief; *perf* hat/ist verlaufen) *vi* (ist) - **1.** [Weg, Strecke, Farbe] to run - **2.** [Operation, Prüfung] to go. ◆ **sich verlaufen** *ref* - **1.** [sich verirren] to get lost - **2.** [Menge] to disperse.

verlegen¹ *vt* - **1.** [verlieren] to mislay - **2.** [Termin] to postpone - **3.** [an anderen Ort] to move, to transfer - **4.** [Kabel, Teppichboden] to lay - **5.** [Buch] to publish.

verlegen² ◇ *adj* embarrassed; **um etw nicht ~ sein** not to be short of sthg ◇ *adv* in embarrassment.

Verlegenheit (*pl* -en) *die* - **1.** [Befangenheit] embarrassment; **jn in ~ bringen** to embarrass sb - **2.** [Notlage] difficulty; **in finanzieller ~** in financial difficulties.

Verleih (*pl* -e) *der* - **1.** (*ohne pl*) [das Verleihen]

hiring (out) - **2.** [Firma - von Videos, Fahrrädern] rental shop; [- von Autos] car hire *Br* ODER rental *Am* company.

verleihen (*prät* verlieh; *perf* hat verliehen) *vt* - **1.** [leihen] to lend; [gegen Bezahlung] to hire out - **2.** [Orden, Titel]: **jm etw ~** to award sb sthg - **3.** [Reiz, Glanz] to give, to lend.

verleiten *vt*: **jn dazu ~, etw zu tun** to lead sb to do sthg.

verlernen *vt* to forget; **das Klavierspielen ~** to forget how to play the piano.

verletzen *vt* - **1.** [Mensch, Körperteil] to injure; **sich den Fuß ~** to injure one's foot - **2.** [Gefühle, Stolz] to hurt - **3.** [Grenze] to violate; [Abkommen] to break. ◆ **sich verletzen** *ref* to hurt o.s.; [schwer] to injure o.s.

verletzlich *adj* [verletzbar] vulnerable; [empfindlich] sensitive.

verletzt ◇ *pp* ▷ verletzen ◇ *adj*: **~ sein** [eine Wunde haben] to be injured; [gekränkt sein] to be hurt.

Verletzte (*pl* -n) *der, die* injured person; **ein Unfall mit vielen ~n** an accident in which several people were injured.

Verletzung (*pl* -en) *die* - **1.** [Wunde] injury - **2.** [von Grenzraum] violation; [von Gesetz, Abkommen] infringement.

verleugnen *vt* to deny; [Freund] to disown.

Verleumdung (*pl* -en) *die* [mündlich] slander; [schriftlich] libel.

verlieben ◆ **sich verlieben** *ref*: **sich (in jn/etw) ~** to fall in love (with sb/sthg).

verliebt ◇ *adj* [Person] in love; [Blicke] amorous; **in jn ~ sein** to be in love with sb ◇ *adv* amorously.

verlieren (*prät* verlor; *perf* hat verloren) ◇ *vt* to lose; **du hast hier nichts verloren** *fam* you've no business here ◇ *vi* - **1.** [nicht gewinnen] to lose; **gegen jn ~** to lose to sb - **2.** [einbüßen] to suffer; **an etw** (D) **~** [Reiz, Schönheit] to lose sthg. ◆ **sich verlieren** *ref* - **1.** [Personen] to lose one another - **2.** [Angst, Begeisterung] to evaporate.

Verlierer, in (*mpl* -/*fpl* -nen) *der, die* loser.

verloben ◆ **sich verloben** *ref*: **sich (mit jm) ~** to get engaged (to sb).

Verlobte (*pl* -n) *der, die* fiancé (*f* fiancée).

Verlobung (*pl* -en) *die* engagement.

verlockend *adj* tempting.

verlogen *adj* false.

verlor *prät* ▷ verlieren.

verloren ◇ *pp* ▷ verlieren ◇ *adj* lost.

verloren gehen (*perf* ist verloren gegangen) *vi* (*unreg*) to go missing, to disappear; **der Geschmack geht durch das Kochen verloren** it loses its taste when you boil it; **an ihm ist ein Lehrer verloren gegangen** he would have made a good teacher.

verlosen *vt* [kleine Preise] to raffle; [große Gewinne] to give away *(in a prize draw).*

Verlosung *(pl -en) die* [von kleinen Preisen] raffle; [von großen Gewinnen] prize draw.

Verlust *(pl -e) der* loss.

Vermächtnis *(pl -se) das* legacy.

vermasseln *vt fam:* **jm etw ~** to ruin sthg for sb.

vermehren *vt* to increase. ◆ **sich vermehren** *ref* - 1. [größer werden] to increase - 2. [sich fortpflanzen] to reproduce.

vermeiden *(prät vermied; perf hat vermieden) vt* to avoid.

vermerken *vt* - 1. [notieren] to make a note of - 2. [feststellen] to note.

vermessen[1] *(präs vermisst; prät vermaß; perf hat vermessen) vt* to measure; [Land, Wand] to survey.

vermessen[2] *adj* presumptuous.

vermieten *vt:* **etw (an jn) ~** to rent sthg out (to sb); **'zu ~!'** 'to let'.

Ver|mieter, in *der, die* landlord (*f* landlady).

vermindern *vt* to reduce.

Verminderung *(pl -en) die* reduction.

vermischen *vt* to mix. ◆ **sich vermischen** *ref* to mingle.

vermissen *vt* - 1. [sehnsüchtig] to miss - 2. [suchen]: **ich vermisse meinen Regenschirm** my umbrella is missing.

vermisst *adj* missing.

vermitteln ◇ *vi* to mediate ◇ *vt* - 1. [Ehe, Kontakt] to arrange - 2. [Job, Arbeitskraft]: **jm jn/etw ~** to find sb/sthg for sb - 3. [Gefühl, Eindruck] to convey; [Wissen, Erfahrung] to impart, to pass on.

Vermittlung *(pl -en) die* - 1. *(ohne pl)* [von Mitarbeitern, Jobs] finding; [von Kontakten, Ehen] arranging; **durch js ~ eine Stelle bekommen** to get a job through sb - 2. [Firma, Büro] agency - 3. [Telefonzentrale] exchange.

Vermögen *(pl -) das* - 1. [Besitz] fortune - 2. *geh* [Fähigkeit] ability.

vermögend *adj* wealthy.

vermuten *vt* - 1. [annehmen] to assume - 2. [für wahrscheinlich halten] to suspect.

vermutlich ◇ *adj* probable ◇ *adv* probably.

Vermutung *(pl -en) die* - 1. [Annahme] supposition - 2. [Verdacht] suspicion.

vernachlässigen *vt* - 1. [gen] to neglect - 2. [nicht beachten] to ignore.

vernehmen *(präs vernimmt; prät vernahm; perf hat vernommen) vt* - 1. [verhören] to question; [vor Gericht] to examine - 2. *geh* [hören] to hear.

Vernehmung *(pl -en) die* questioning; [vor Gericht] examination.

verneinen *vt* [Vorschlag] to reject; [Frage] to say no to.

vernetzen *vt* - 1. [gen] to connect, to link - 2. EDV to network, to connect to the Internet; **vernetzt sein** to be on the Internet ODER online.

vernichten *vt* to destroy; [Schädlinge] to exterminate.

vernichtend ◇ *adj* [Kritik, Niederlage] devastating; [Blick] withering ◇ *adv* [kritisieren] devastatingly; **jn ~ ansehen** to give sb a withering look.

Vernichtung *(pl -en) die* destruction; [von Insekten] extermination.

Vernunft *die* reason; **mit/ohne ~ handeln** to act sensibly/foolishly; **das widerspricht jeder Vernunft** that goes against all common sense; **zur ~ kommen** to come to one's senses; **jn zur ~ bringen** to bring sb to his/her senses.

vernünftig ◇ *adj* - 1. [klug] sensible - 2. [ordentlich] decent; [Preis] reasonable ◇ *adv* - 1. [klug] sensibly - 2. [ordentlich] decently.

veröffentlichen *vt* to publish.

Veröffentlichung *(pl -en) die* publication.

verordnen *vt:* **(jm) etw ~** to prescribe sthg (for sb).

Verordnung *(pl -en) die* - 1. [von Medikament] prescription - 2. [von Regel] regulation.

verpacken *vt* [Waren] to pack; [Geschenk] to wrap (up).

Ver|packung *die* - 1. [Hülle - von Ware] packaging; [- von Geschenk] wrapping paper - 2. [Verpacken] packing.

verpassen *vt* - 1. [Bus, Gelegenheit, Film] to miss - 2. *fam* [Schlag, Frisur] to give.

verpesten *vt abw* to pollute.

verpflanzen *vt* to transplant; [Haut] to graft.

verpflegen *vt* to cater for.

Verpflegung *die* - 1. [das Verpflegen] catering - 2. [Essen] food.

verpflichten ◇ *vt* - 1. [auf etw festlegen] to oblige; [durch Eid] to bind; **jn zu sechs Wochen gemeinnütziger Arbeit ~** to give sb six weeks' community service - 2. [Schauspieler] to engage; [Mannschaftssportler] to sign ◇ *vi:* **dieses Angebot verpflichtet nicht zum Kauf** no purchase necessary to take advantage of this offer. ◆ **sich verpflichten** *ref* to commit o.s.; **sich vertraglich ~** to sign a contract.

Verpflichtung *(pl -en) die* - 1. [Pflichten] obligation; **seine gesellschaftlichen ~en** his social commitments - 2. [von Schauspieler] engaging; [von Mannschaftssportler] signing - 3. [Schulden] commitment.

verprügeln *vt* to beat up.

Verrat *der* betrayal; [gegen Vaterland] treason.

verraten *(präs verrät; prät verriet; perf hat*

verraten) vt - **1.** [Person, Gedanken] to betray; [Geheimnis, Versteck] to give away, to betray - **2.** [Gefühle] to show - **3.** [mitteilen]: **er hat mir den Preis nicht ~** he didn't tell me the price. ➔ **sich verraten** ref to give o.s. away.

Verräter, in (mpl -; fpl -nen) der, die traitor.

verrechnen vt to include; **etw mit etw ~** to offset sthg against sthg. ➔ **sich verrechnen** ref - **1.** [falsch rechnen] to make a mistake; **sich um fünf Euro ~** to be five euros out - **2.** [sich täuschen] to miscalculate.

verregnet adj wet.

verreisen (perf ist verreist) vi to go away; **verreist sein** to be away.

verrenken vt: **sich** (D) **den Arm ~** to dislocate one's arm.

verriegeln vt to bolt.

verringern vt to reduce. ➔ **sich verringern** ref to decrease.

verrosten (perf ist verrostet) vi to rust.

verrücken vt to move.

verrückt ⟨⟩ adj - **1.** [geistesgestört] mad; **~ spielen** [Person] to act crazy; [Computer, Auto] to play up; **nach jm/etw ~ sein** fam to be crazy about sb/sthg - **2.** [ausgefallen] crazy ⟨⟩ adv [ausgefallen] crazily. ➔ **wie verrückt** adv fam like mad.

Verrückte (pl -n) der, die lunatic.

Verruf der: **in ~ bringen/kommen** to bring/fall into disrepute.

verrufen adj disreputable.

Vers (pl -e) der line; **in ~en** in verse.

versagen vi to fail.

Versagen das failure.

Versager (pl -) der failure.

Versagerin (pl -nen) die failure.

versammeln vt to assemble, to gather. ➔ **sich versammeln** ref to assemble, to gather.

Ver|sammlung die meeting; [im Freien] rally.

Versand der (ohne pl) - **1.** [Versenden] dispatch - **2.** [Abteilung] dispatch department.

Versand|haus das mail order firm.

versäumen vt - **1.** [Zug, Termin] to miss - **2.** [Pflicht] to neglect.

verschaffen vt: **jm etw ~** to get sb sthg; **sich** (D) **etw ~** to get (hold of) sthg; **sich** (D) **einen Vorteil ~** to gain an advantage; **sich** (D) **Respekt ~** to earn respect.

verschämt ⟨⟩ adj bashful ⟨⟩ adv bashfully.

verschärfen vt [Kontrolle] to tighten up; [Lage, Krise] to aggravate. ➔ **sich verschärfen** ref [Gegensätze] to intensify; [Lage, Krise] to get worse.

verschätzen ➔ **sich verschätzen** ref to miscalculate.

verschenken vt - **1.** [weg geben] to give

away - 2. [als Geschenk] to give (as present) - **3.** [Punkte] to throw away; [Raum] to waste.

verscherzen vt: **sich** (D) **etw ~** to throw sthg away.

verscheuchen vt [Tier] to chase away; [Angst machen] to scare away.

verschicken vt to send out.

verschieben (prät verschob; perf hat verschoben) vt - **1.** [Termin] to postpone - **2.** [Möbel] to move - **3.** [schmuggeln] to traffic in. ➔ **sich verschieben** ref - **1.** [Termin] to be postponed - **2.** [verrutschen] to slip.

Verschiebung (pl -en) die postponement.

verschieden ⟨⟩ adj - **1.** [unterschiedlich] different - **2.** [mehrere] various ⟨⟩ adv [unterschiedlich] differently; **~ groß sein** to be different sizes; **die Aufgaben waren ~ schwer** the tasks were of varying degrees of difficulty.

verschimmeln (perf ist verschimmelt) vi to go mouldy.

verschlafen (präs verschläft; prät verschlief; perf hat verschlafen) ⟨⟩ vi to oversleep ⟨⟩ vt - **1.** [schlafend verbringen] to sleep through - **2.** fam [vergessen] to forget.

verschlagen abw ⟨⟩ adj sly ⟨⟩ adv slyly.

verschlechtern vt to make worse. ➔ **sich verschlechtern** ref to get worse, to deteriorate.

Verschlechterung (pl -en) die deterioration.

Verschleiß der wear (and tear).

verschleißen (prät verschliss; perf hat/ist verschlissen) ⟨⟩ vi (ist) to wear out; **diese Teile sind verschlissen** these parts are worn out ⟨⟩ vt (hat) to wear out.

verschleppen vt - **1.** [Person] to take away (by force) - **2.** [Gegenstand] to hide - **3.** [Verhandlung] to draw out - **4.** [Krankheit] to allow to drag on.

verschleudern vt - **1.** [billig verkaufen] to give away - **2.** abw [verschwenden] to throw away.

verschließen (prät verschloss; perf hat verschlossen) vt - **1.** [Haus, Tür, Schrank] to lock - **2.** [Kunststoffbehälter] to seal; [Flasche] to stop up.

verschlimmern vt to make worse. ➔ **sich verschlimmern** ref to get worse.

verschlingen (prät verschlang; perf hat verschlungen) vt to devour; **viel Geld ~** to cost a fortune.

verschlossen adj [Mensch] reticent; [Raum, Tür] locked; [Umschlag] sealed.

verschlucken vt to swallow. ➔ **sich verschlucken** ref to choke.

Ver|schluss der fastener; [von Flasche] top. ➔ **unter Verschluss** adv under lock and key.

verschlüsseln vt to encode.

verschmelzen (präs verschmilzt; prät verschmolz; perf ist verschmolzen) vi: **mit etw ~** to blend with sthg.

verschmutzen (perf hat/ist verschmutzt) ◇ vi (ist) [Kleidung, Wohnung] to get dirty ◇ vt (hat) [Kleidung, Wohnung] to get dirty; [Umwelt] to pollute.

verschnaufen vi to have a breather.

verschneit adj snow-covered.

verschnupft adj: **~ sein** to have a cold.

verschollen adj missing.

verschonen vt to spare; **jn mit etw ~** to spare sb sthg.

verschränken vt: **die Arme ~** to fold one's arms; **die Beine ~** to cross one's legs.

verschreiben (prät verschrieb; perf hat verschrieben) vt: **jm etw ~** to prescribe sb sthg. ◆ **sich verschreiben** ref: **ich habe mich verschrieben** I've written it down wrong.

verschreibungspflichtig adj available on prescription only.

verschrieen adj notorious.

verschrotten vt to scrap.

verschuldet adj in debt.

verschütten vt - 1. [Wasser, Getränk] to spill - 2. [mit Erde] to bury.

verschweigen (prät verschwieg; perf hat verschwiegen) vt [Nachricht] to keep quiet about; [Wahrheit] to conceal; **jm etw ~** to conceal sthg from sb.

verschwenden vt to waste.

verschwenderisch ◇ adj [mit Geld] extravagant; [mit Energie] wasteful ◇ adv [mit Geld] extravagantly; [mit Energie] wastefully.

Verschwendung die squandering; **so eine ~!** what a waste!

verschwiegen ◇ pp ▷ verschweigen ◇ adj - 1. [Mensch] discreet - 2. [Winkel] secluded.

Verschwiegenheit die discretion.

verschwinden (prät verschwand; perf ist verschwunden) vi to disappear.

verschwommen ◇ adj blurred ◇ adv vaguely; **ohne Brille sieht sie alles ~** without her glasses everything looks blurred to her.

verschwören (prät verschwor; perf hat verschworen) ◆ **sich verschwören** ref: **sich gegen jn ~** to conspire against sb.

Verschwörung (pl -en) die conspiracy.

verschwunden ◇ pp ▷ verschwinden ◇ adj missing.

versehen (präs versieht; prät versah; perf hat versehen) vt - 1. [ausrüsten]: **etw mit etw ~** to equip sthg with sthg; **jn mit etw ~** to provide sb with sthg - 2. [erledigen] to perform.

Versehen (pl -) das accident. ◆ **aus Versehen** adv accidentally.

versehentlich ◇ adj accidental ◇ adv accidentally.

versenden (prät versandte ODER versendete; perf hat versandt ODER versendet) vt to send.

versengen vt to scorch.

versenken vt [Schiff] to sink.

versetzen vt - 1. [umstellen] to move; [Angestellten] to transfer, to move; [Schüler] to move up Br, to promote Am - 2. [in einen anderen Zustand]: **sich in die Lage eines anderen ~** to put o.s. in somebody else's position; **jn in Erstaunen/Angst ~** to astonish/frighten sb; **etw in Bewegung ~** to set sthg in motion - 3. [verpfänden] to pawn - 4. [bei einer Verabredung]: **jn ~** to stand sb up - 5. [austeilen]: **jm einen Stoß ~** to give sb a push; **jm einen Schlag ~** to hit sb - 6. [antworten] to retort.

Versetzung (pl -en) die - 1. [beruflich] transfer - 2. SCHULE moving up Br, promotion Am.

verseuchen vt to contaminate.

versichern vt - 1. [erklären] to affirm; **jm ~, dass ...** to assure sb that ... - 2. [bei Versicherung] to insure. ◆ **sich versichern** ref - 1. [bei Versicherung] to insure o.s. - 2. [Gewissheit]: **sich einer Sache** (G) **~** to assure o.s. of sthg.

Versicherung die - 1. [vertraglicher Schutz] insurance (U); [Vertrag] insurance policy; **eine ~ (über etw** (A)**) abschließen** to take out insurance ODER an insurance policy (for sthg) - 2. [Firma] insurance company - 3. [Angabe] assurance.

versinken (prät versank; perf ist versunken) vi - 1. [in Sumpf, Sand, Schnee]: **in etw** (A) **~** to sink into sthg - 2. [Schiff, Sonne] to sink - 3. [in Gedanken]: **in etw** (A) **~** to become immersed in sthg.

versöhnen vt [Feinde] to reconcile; [besänftigen] to appease. ◆ **sich versöhnen** ref to become reconciled; **sich mit jm ~** to make it up with sb.

versöhnlich ◇ adj - 1. [Antwort, Stimmung] conciliatory - 2. [Ende, Ausgang] optimistic ◇ adv in a conciliatory way.

Versöhnung (pl -en) die reconciliation; [Besänftigung] appeasement.

versorgen vt - 1. [versehen]: **jn/sich mit etw ~** to provide sb/o.s. with sthg - 2. [beliefern - mit Strom, Wasser] to supply - 3. [pflegen] to look after - 4. [ernähren] to provide for.

Versorgung (pl -en) die - 1. [mit Lebensmitteln] supply - 2. [von Patienten] care.

verspäten ◆ **sich verspäten** ref to be late; **sich um eine halbe Stunde ~** to be half an hour late.

verspätet ◇ adj late; [Gratulation] belated ◇ adv late.

Verspätung (pl -en) die delay; **mit ~ ankommen** to arrive late; **~ haben** to be delayed; **eine Stunde ~ haben** to be an hour late.

versperren vt to block; **jm den Weg/die Sicht ~** to block sb's way/view.

verspielen vt [Geld] to gamble away; [Glück, Chance] to throw away, to squander.

verspielt adj [Kind] playful; [Muster] fanciful.

versprechen (präs **verspricht**; prät **versprach**; perf **hat versprochen**) vt - **1.** [zusagen] to promise; **jm etw ~** to promise sb sthg - **2.** [erwarten]: **sich** (D) **etw von jm/etw ~** to hope for sthg from sb/sthg. ◆ **sich versprechen** ref [etw Falsches sagen] to trip over one's words.

Versprechen (pl -) das promise.

Verstand der (ohne pl) [Urteilsvermögen] reason; [Intellekt] mind; [Vernunft] sense; **den ~ verlieren** fam fig to go out of one's mind; **jn um den ~ bringen** fig to drive sb mad.

verständigen vt: **jn** (**von etw** ODER **über etw** (A)) **~** to notify sb (of sthg). ◆ **sich verständigen** ref - **1.** [kommunizieren] to make o.s. understood; **sich mit jm ~** to communicate with sb - **2.** [übereinkommen]: **sich über etw** (A) **~** to come to an agreement on sthg.

Verständigung (pl -en) die - **1.** [Benachrichtigung] notification - **2.** [Kommunikation] communication - **3.** [Übereinkunft] agreement.

verständlich ◇ adj - **1.** [klar - Worte, Antwort] audible - **2.** [begreiflich - Verhalten, Angst] understandable; [- Text] comprehensible; **sich ~ machen** to make o.s. understood ◇ adv [klar] clearly.

Verständnis das understanding.

verständnisvoll ◇ adj understanding ◇ adv understandingly.

verstärken vt - **1.** [stärker machen] to strengthen - **2.** [intensivieren] to increase; [Bemühungen] to intensify; [Strom] to boost; [Signal, Ton] to amplify - **3.** [Truppen, Team] to reinforce. ◆ **sich verstärken** ref [stärker werden] to intensify.

Verstärkung (pl -en) die reinforcement; **~ anfordern** to call for reinforcements.

verstauchen vt: **sich** (D) **den Fuß ~** to sprain one's ankle.

verstauen vt to pack.

Versteck (pl -e) das hiding place; [von Verbrechern] hideout.

verstecken vt to hide. ◆ **sich verstecken** ref: **sich** (**vor jm/etw**) **~** to hide (from sb/sthg).

verstehen (prät **verstand**; perf **hat verstanden**) ◇ vt - **1.** [gen] to understand; **ich konnte kein Wort ~** I couldn't understand ODER make out a single word; **etw unter etw**

(D) **~** to understand sthg by sthg; **versteh mich nicht falsch** don't get me wrong - **2.** [vermögen] to know; **etwas/nichts ~ von ...** to know a bit/nothing about ... ◇ vi to understand; **jm zu ~ geben, dass ...** to give sb to understand that ... ◆ **sich verstehen** ref [Personen] to get on; **sich** (**gut**) **mit jm ~** to get on well with sb; **das versteht sich von selbst!** that goes without saying!

versteigern vt to auction; **etw meistbietend ~** to sell sthg to the highest bidder.

verstellen vt - **1.** [verändern] to adjust - **2.** [falsch stellen] to set wrongly; [Stimme, Schrift] to disguise - **3.** [blockieren]: **jm den Weg/die Sicht ~** to block sb's path/view - **4.** [an einen falschen Ort] to put in the wrong place. ◆ **sich verstellen** ref - **1.** [zur Täuschung - im Wesen] to play-act - **2.** [anders einstellen] to be moved (out of position).

verstohlen ◇ adj furtive ◇ adv furtively.

verstopfen (perf **hat/ist verstopft**) ◇ vt (hat) to plug (up); [Abfluss] to block ◇ vi (ist) to be blocked (up).

verstört adj distraught.

Verstoß der infringement; **ein ~ gegen etw** [gegen Gesetz] an infringement of sthg; [gegen Anstand] an offence against sthg.

verstoßen (präs **verstößt**; prät **verstieß**; perf **hat verstoßen**) ◇ vi: **gegen etw ~** [Regel, Gesetz] to infringe sthg; [Anstand, Geschmack] to offend against sthg ◇ vt [Kind, Ehefrau] to disown; **jn aus einer Gruppe ~** to throw sb out of a group.

verstreichen (prät **verstrich**; perf **hat/ist verstrichen**) ◇ vt (hat) [Butter] to spread; [Farbe] to apply ◇ vi (ist) [Zeit] to pass.

verstreuen vt - **1.** [verteilen] to scatter - **2.** [verschütten] to spill - **3.** [Creme] to spread.

verstümmeln vt to mutilate.

Versuch (pl -e) der - **1.** [Handlung] attempt - **2.** [wissenschaftlich] experiment.

versuchen ◇ vt to try; [etwas Schwieriges] to attempt ◇ vi [kosten]: **von etw ~** to try sthg.

Versuchskaninchen [fɛɐ̯'tsuːxskaniːnçən] das guinea pig.

Versuchung (pl -en) die temptation.

versüßen vt [Leben, Befinden] to make more pleasant; [schlechte Situation] to sweeten.

vertagen vt [verschieben] to postpone; [später fortsetzen] to adjourn.

vertauschen vt [verwechseln] to mix up.

verteidigen vt to defend. ◆ **sich verteidigen** ref to defend o.s.

Verteidiger, in (mpl -; fpl -nen) der, die RECHT counsel for the defence.

Verteidigung (pl -en) die defence.

Verteidigungsǀminister, in *der, die* defence minister.

verteilen *vt* - **1.** [ausgeben] to distribute; [Prospekte] to hand out - **2.** [teilen] to share out - **3.** [Creme] to spread. ◆ **sich verteilen** *ref* to spread out.

Verǀteilung *die* distribution.

vertiefen *vt* to deepen. ◆ **sich vertiefen** *ref* - **1.** [Graben, Loch, Falten] to become deeper - **2.** [Gefühl, Freundschaft] to deepen - **3.** [sich konzentrieren]: **sich in etw** *(A)* ~ to become engrossed in sthg.

Vertrag (*pl* Verträge) *der* contract.

vertragen (*präs* verträgt; *prät* vertrug; *perf* hat vertragen) *vt* to stand, to bear; [Belastung, Kritik, Witz] to take; **sie verträgt keinen Kaffee** coffee doesn't agree with me. ◆ **sich vertragen** *ref*: **sich mit jm** ~ to get on with sb.

vertraglich ⟨⟩ *adj* contractual ⟨⟩ *adv* contractually.

verträglich *adj* [Person, Charakter] easy-going; **gut** ~ [Essen] easily digestible; [Medikament] with few side-effects.

vertrauen *vi*: **jm/einer Sache** ~ to trust sb/sthg; **auf etw** *(A)* ~ to put one's trust in sthg; **auf sein Glück** ~ to trust to luck.

Vertrauen *das* trust; **zu jm** ~ **haben** to trust sb. ◆ **im Vertrauen** *adv* in confidence. ◆ **Vertrauen erweckend** *adj*: **ein** ~ **erweckender Mensch** a person who inspires confidence.

Vertrauensǀlehrer, in *der, die* teacher who *represents the interests of the pupils.*

Vertrauenslehrer

Pupils at any stage in their school career, from entry until leaving, nominate a teacher to be their liaison/contact/tutor (der Vertrauenslehrer or der Verbindungslehrer). This teacher's role is to offer advice or counselling to his tutees, as well as to defend their interests within the school.

Vertrauensǀsache *die* matter of trust.

vertrauenswürdig *adj* trustworthy.

vertraulich ⟨⟩ *adj* - **1.** [geheim] confidential - **2.** [herzlich] familiar ⟨⟩ *adv* [geheim] confidentially.

verträumt ⟨⟩ *adj* dreamy ⟨⟩ *adv* dreamily.

vertraut *adj* familiar; [Freund] close; **jm** ~ **sein** to be familiar to sb; **mit etw** ~ **sein** to be familiar with sthg; **sich mit etw** ~ **machen** to familiarize o.s. with sthg.

vertreiben (*prät* vertrieb; *perf* hat vertrieben) *vt* - **1.** [verjagen] to drive away; [aus Land] to drive out; **jn aus einem Haus** ~ to

turn sb out of a house - **2.** [verkaufen] to sell - **3.** [Zeit] to pass.

vertretbar *adj* [Meinung] tenable; [Kosten, Risiko] justifiable.

vertreten (*präs* vertritt; *prät* vertrat; *perf* hat vertreten) *vt* - **1.** [bei Urlaub, Krankheit] to stand in for - **2.** [Interessen, Firma, Land] to represent - **3.** [Standpunkt, These, Prinzip] to support - **4.** [anwesend]: ~ **sein** to be present - **5.** [verletzen]: **sich** *(D)* **den Fuß** ~ to twist one's ankle.

Vertreter, in (*mpl* -; *fpl* -nen) *der, die* - **1.** [Stellvertreter] stand-in; [von Arzt] locum - **2.** [von Firma, Gruppe] representative - **3.** [von Meinung, Interessen] advocate.

Vertretung (*pl* -en) *die* - **1.** [bei Urlaub, Krankheit] replacement - **2.** [von Interessen, Firma, Land] representation - **3.** [Person] representative - **4.** [Filiale] branch; **diplomatische** ~ diplomatic mission.

Vertrieb *der* - **1.** [Verkauf] sale - **2.** [Abteilung] sales department; **im** ~ **arbeiten** to work in sales.

vertrocknen (*perf* ist vertrocknet) *vi* [Boden] to dry out; [Pflanze, Gras] to wither.

vertrödeln *vt* to waste.

vertrösten *vt* to put off; **jn auf später** ~ to put sb off until later.

vertun (*prät* vertat; *perf* hat vertan) *vt* to waste. ◆ **sich vertun** *ref* to get it wrong.

vertuschen *vt* [Skandal] to hush up; [Fehler, Wahrheit] to cover up.

verübeln *vt*: **jm etw** ~ to hold sthg against sb.

verüben *vt* to commit.

verunglücken (*perf* ist verunglückt) *vi* to have an accident; **mit dem Zug** ~ to be in a train crash.

verunsichern *vt* to make uneasy.

verunstalten *vt* to disfigure.

veruntreuen *vt* RECHT to embezzle.

verursachen *vt* to cause.

verurteilen *vt* - **1.** [vor Gericht]: **jn zu etw** ~ to sentence sb to sthg - **2.** [kritisieren] to condemn.

Verurǀteilung *die* - **1.** [vor Gericht] sentencing - **2.** [Missbilligung] condemnation.

vervielfachen *vt* to multiply. ◆ **sich vervielfachen** *ref* to multiply.

vervielfältigen *vt* to make copies of.

vervollkommnen *vt* to perfect.

vervollständigen *vt* to complete.

verwackelt *adj fam* blurred.

verwählen ◆ **sich verwählen** *ref* to dial the wrong number.

verwahren *vt* to keep (safe).

verwahrlosen (*perf* ist verwahrlost) *vi* to be neglected; [Garten] to run wild.

verwaist *adj* - **1.** [Kind] orphaned - **2.** [Ort] deserted.

verwalten *vt* [Gebäude, Besitz] to manage; [Altenheim, Geschäft] to run; [Amt] to hold; [Geld] to administer.

Verwalter, in (*mpl* -; *fpl* -nen) *der, die* manager; [von Geld] administrator.

Verwaltung (*pl* -en) *die* administration; [von Geschäft, Gebäude] management; **die städtische ~** the municipal authorities.

verwandeln *vt* to transform, to change; **etw in etw** (*A*) **~** to transform ODER change sthg into sthg. **◆ sich verwandeln** *ref* to change.

Verwandlung *die* transformation; ZOOL metamorphosis.

verwandt ◇ *pp* ▷ **verwenden** ◇ *adj* related; **mit jm ~ sein** to be related to sb.

Verwandte (*pl* -n) *der, die* relative.

Verwandtschaft (*pl* -en) *die* - **1.** [alle Verwandte] family - **2.** [Verwandtsein] relationship.

Verlwarnung *die* caution; **eine gebührenpflichtige ~** a fine.

verwechseln [fer'vɛksln] *vt* to mix up; **jn/ etw mit jm/etw ~** to mistake sb/sthg for sb/ sthg.

Verwechslung,   Verwechselung [fer'vɛks(ə)luŋ] (*pl* -en) *die* mixing up; **es gab eine ~** there was a mix-up.

verweigern ◇ *vt* to refuse; **die Annahme von etw ~** to refuse to take sthg; **einen Befehl ~** to refuse to obey an order; **den Kriegsdienst ~** to be a conscientious objector; **jm etw ~** to refuse sb sthg ◇ *vi fam* [den Wehrdienst verweigern] to be a conscientious objector.

Verlweigerung *die* refusal; **die ~ eines Befehls** refusal to obey an order.

Verweis (*pl* -e) *der* [Tadel] reprimand.

verweisen (*prät* verwies; *perf* hat verwiesen) ◇ *vt* - **1.** [weiterleiten]: **jn/etw auf jn/ etw ~** to refer sb/sthg to sb/sthg - **2.** [ausweisen - von Schule] to expel; [- aus Raum] to throw out ◇ *vi*: **auf etw** (*A*) **~** to refer to sthg; **eine Tafel verweist auf den Eingang** a sign points to the entrance.

verwelken (*perf* ist verwelkt) *vi* to wilt.

verwenden (*prät* verwendete ODER verwandte; *perf* hat verwendet ODER verwandt) *vt* - **1.** [benutzen] to use - **2.** [einsetzen - Zeit, Geld] to spend; ; **etw für** ODER **zu etw ~** to use sthg for sthg; **Kraft auf etw ~** to put energy into sthg.

Verlwendung *die* use.

verwerfen (*präs* verwirft; *prät* verwarf; *perf* hat verworfen) *vt* to reject.

verwerten *vt* - **1.** [Kenntnisse] to make use of - **2.** [Abfall, Altpapier] to re-use, to recycle.

verwest *adj* decomposed.

Verwesung *die* decomposition.

verwildern (*perf* ist verwildert) *vi* [Garten] to become overgrown; [Tier] to become wild.

verwirklichen *vt* [Traum] to realize; [Plan, Ziel] to achieve; [Idee] to put into practice. **◆ sich verwirklichen** *ref* - **1.** [Hoffnung, Traum, Befürchtung] to come true - **2.** [Person]: **sich selbst ~** to fulfil o.s.

Verwirklichung (*pl* -en) *die* [von Traum] realization; [von Plan, Ziel] achievement; [von Idee] putting into practice.

verwirren *vt* - **1.** [Fäden] to tangle up - **2.** [Person] to confuse.

Verwirrung (*pl* -en) *die* confusion.

verwischen *vt* [Spur] to cover over; [Schrift] to smudge; [Farbe] to smear; [Kontur] to blur.

verwitwet *adj* widowed.

verwöhnen *vt* to spoil.

verworren ◇ *adj* confused ◇ *adv* [erzählen] in a confusing manner.

verwunden *vt* to wound.

Verwunderung *die* surprise.

Verwundete (*pl* -n) *der, die* wounded person; **die ~n** the wounded.

Verwundung (*pl* -en) *die* [Wunde] wound.

verwünschen *vt* - **1.** [verfluchen] to curse - **2.** [verzaubern] to bewitch.

verwüsten *vt* to devastate.

Verwüstung (*pl* -en) *die* devastation (*U*).

verzählen ◆ sich verzählen *ref* to miscount.

verzaubern *vt* to enchant; **einen Prinz in einen Frosch ~** to turn a prince into a frog.

verzeichnen *vt* to record; [Erfolg] to notch up; **ist diese Stadt auf der Landkarte verzeichnet?** is this town (marked) on the map?

Verzeichnis (*pl* -se) *das* - **1.** [Liste] list; [Katalog] catalogue; [mit Namen] index - **2.** EDV directory.

verzeihen (*prät* verzieh; *perf* hat verziehen) *vt* to forgive; **jm etw ~** to forgive sb for sthg; **~ Sie bitte!** excuse me, please!; **~ Sie bitte, dass ich stören muss!** please forgive the intrusion!

Verzeihung *die* forgiveness; **jn um ~ bitten** to apologize to sb. **◆ Verzeihung** *interj* sorry!

verzerren *vt* - **1.** [Gesicht] to contort - **2.** [Bild, Klang] to distort. **◆ sich verzerren** *ref* [Gesicht] to contort.

Verzicht (*pl* -e) *der*: **der ~ auf Süßigkeiten fällt ihr schwer** she finds it hard to go without sweets.

verzichten *vi* to do without; **auf jn/etw ~** to do without sb/sthg; **wir werden zukünftig auf ihre Dienste ~** we will be dispensing with her services; **auf eine Bemerkung ~** not to make ODER to refrain from making a comment; **er verzichtete darauf, sich zu be-**

schweren he refrained from making a complaint; **zugunsten eines anderen auf eine Stelle ~** to let sb have a job instead of o.s.; **danke, ich verzichte** I'll pass (on that one), thanks.

verzieh *prät* ⊏⊳ verzeihen.

verziehen (*prät* verzog; *perf* hat/ist verzogen) ⟨⟩ *pp* ⊏⊳ verziehen ⟨⟩ *vt (hat)* - **1.** [Miene, Mund] to screw up; **das Gesicht ~** to pull a face - **2.** [Kind] to spoil ⟨⟩ *vi (ist)* [fortziehen] to move. ⟶ **sich verziehen** *ref* - **1.** [Gesicht, Mund] to contort - **2.** [Tür, Holz] to warp - **3.** [Nebel, Rauch] to disperse; [Unwetter] to pass - **4.** *fam* [fortgehen] to disappear; **verzieh dich** get lost!

verzieren *vt* to decorate.

verzögern *vt* - **1.** [verschieben] to delay - **2.** [verlangsamen] to slow down. ⟶ **sich verzögern** *ref* [sich verspäten] to be delayed.

Verzögerung (*pl* -en) *die* [Verspätung] delay.

verzollen *vt* to declare; **haben Sie etwas zu ~?** do you have anything to declare?

Verzug *der (ohne pl)* delay. ⟶ **im Verzug** *adv*: **mit etw im ~ sein** to be behind with sthg; **Gefahr ist im ~** danger is imminent.

verzweifeln (*perf* ist verzweifelt) *vi* to despair; **an etw** (*D*)/**über etw** (*A*) **~** to despair of/at sthg.

verzweifelt ⟨⟩ *adj* desperate; [Blick] despairing ⟨⟩ *adv* [kämpfen, versuchen] desperately; [sagen, anblicken] despairingly.

Verzweiflung (*pl* -en) *die* despair; **vor ~** in despair.

Veto ['ve:to] (*pl* -s) *das* veto.

Vetter (*pl* -n) *der* cousin.

vgl. (*abk für* vergleiche) cf.

VHS [fauha:'ʔɛs] *die abk für* Volkshochschule.

vibrieren [vi'bri:rən] *vi* to vibrate; [Stimme] to quiver.

Video ['vi:deo] (*pl* -s) *das* video.

Video|film *der* video.

Video|kamera *die* video camera.

Video|kassette *die* video (tape).

Video|rekorder *der* video (recorder) *Br*, VCR *Am*.

Video|spiel *das* video game.

Video|text *der* videotext.

Vieh *das* - **1.** [alle Tiere] livestock - **2.** [Rinder] cattle.

viel (*kompar* mehr; *superl* meiste), **vieles** ⟨⟩ *adj*: **das ~e Geld** all the money; **das Kleid mit den ~en Knöpfen** the dress with all the buttons; **~en Dank!** thank you very much! ⟨⟩ *det* - **1.** [Menge] much, a lot of; **zu ~** too much - **2.** [Anzahl] many, a lot of, lots of; **zu ~ too many; ~e Menschen** many ODER a lot of people ⟨⟩ *adv* - **1.** [intensiv, oft] a lot; **~ arbeiten** to work a lot; **sie ist ~ allein** she is alone a lot of the time - **2.** [zum Ausdruck der

Verstärkung] much; **~ mehr** much more; **~ zu** much too, far too; **nicht ~ anders** not very different ⟨⟩ *pron* a lot; **er sagt ~** he says a lot; **er sagt nicht ~** he doesn't say much. ⟶ **nicht viel** ⟨⟩ *det* not much ⟨⟩ *adv* not much; **er schläft nicht ~** he doesn't sleep much. ⟶ **nicht viele** *det* not many. ⟶ **vieles** *pron* a lot of things. ⟶ **viel zu** *viel det* & *adv* much too much. ⟶ **viele** *det* far too many; *siehe auch* **zu viel**.

vielfach ⟨⟩ *adj* [mehrfach, wiederholt] multiple; **auf ~en Wunsch** by popular demand; **das ~e Gewicht** many times the weight ⟨⟩ *adv* - **1.** [mehrfach, wiederholt] several times - **2.** [häufig] often.

Vielfache *das* [von Zahl] multiple; **um ein ~s** many times over.

Vielfalt *die* diversity, great variety.

vielfältig *adj* diverse.

vielleicht *adv* - **1.** [eventuell] perhaps - **2.** *fam* [wirklich, außerordentlich] really; **der ist ~ gerannt!** he didn't half run! - **3.** [Ausdruck der Höflichkeit]: **wären Sie ~ so freundlich, den Termin zu bestätigen?** could you possibly confirm the date for me? - **4.** [ungefähr] about - **5.** *fam* [etwa]: **hast du ~ gedacht, ich würde da mitmachen?** you didn't think I would join in, did you? - **6.** *fam* [Ausdruck der Ungeduld]: **~ kannst du dich mal beeilen!** do you think you could possibly get a move on!

vielmals *adv*: **danke ~** thank you very much.

vielsagend ⟨⟩ *adj* meaningful ⟨⟩ *adv* meaningfully.

vielseitig ⟨⟩ *adj* - **1.** [Person] versatile - **2.** [umfassend] varied ⟨⟩ *adv*: **~ begabt** multitalented; **~ einsetzbar** versatile.

vielversprechend ⟨⟩ *adj* promising ⟨⟩ *adv* promisingly.

vier [fi:ɐ] *num* four; **auf allen ~en** *fam* on all fours; *siehe auch* **sechs**.

Vier (*pl* -en) *die* - **1.** [Zahl] four - **2.** [Schulnote] ≃ D, mark of 4 on a scale from 1 to 6; *siehe auch* **Sechs**.

Viereck (*pl* -e) *das* four-sided figure; [Rechteck] rectangle; [Quadrat] square.

viereckig *adj* four-sided; [rechteckig] rectangular; [quadratisch] square.

vierfach ⟨⟩ *adj*: **die ~e Menge** four times as much; **in ~er Größe** four times as big; **der ~e Gewinner** the four-times winner ⟨⟩ *adv* four times.

vierhundert *num* four hundred.

viermal *adv* four times.

vierspurig *adj* four-lane.

viertausend *num* four thousand.

vierte, r, s *adj* fourth; *siehe auch* **sechste**.

Vierte (*pl* -n) *der, die, das* fourth; *siehe auch* **Sechste**.

viertel adj (unver) quarter; siehe auch sechstel.

Viertel (pl -) das - **1.** [Teil] quarter; ~ vor/nach drei a quarter to/past Br ODER after Am three; siehe auch Sechstel - **2.** MUS Br crotchet.

Viertel|finale das quarter-final.

Viertel|jahr das quarter.

Viertel|stunde die quarter of an hour.

vierzehn num fourteen; siehe auch sechs.

Vierzehn (pl -en) die fourteen; siehe auch Sechs.

vierzehntägig <> adv every fortnight, fortnightly <> adj - **1.** [alle zwei Wochen] fortnightly - **2.** [zwei Wochen lang] two-week, fortnight-long.

vierzig num forty; siehe auch sechs.

Vierzigerjahre, vierziger Jahre pl: **die ~** the forties.

Vierzimmer|wohnung die four-room flat Br ODER apartment Am.

Vietnam [vjɛt'nam] nt Vietnam.

Vikar, in [vi'kaːɐ̯, rɪn] (mpl -e; fpl -nen) der, die (evangelisch) ~ curate.

Villa ['vɪla] (pl Villen) die villa.

violett [vjo'lɛt] adj purple.

Violine [vjo'liːnə] (pl -n) die violin.

Violin|schlüssel der treble clef.

Viper ['viːpɐ] (pl -n) die viper.

virtuell <> adj virtual; ~e Realität virtual reality <> adv virtually.

Virus ['viːrʊs] (pl Viren) der ODER das MED & EDV virus.

Virus|infektion die viral infection.

Visier [vi'ziːɐ̯] (pl -e) das - **1.** [von Helm] visor - **2.** [von Gewehr] sight; **jn/etw im ~ haben** [es auf jn abgesehen haben] to have it in for sb/sthg; [anpeilen] to have one's eye on sb/sthg.

Visite [vi'ziːtə] (pl -n) die [privat, geschäftlich] visit; [Besuch des Arztes]: ~ **machen** to do one's rounds.

Visiten|karte die visiting card.

Viskose [vɪs'koːzə] die viscose.

Visum ['viːzʊm] (pl Visa ODER Visen) das visa.

Vitamin [vita'miːn] (pl -e) das vitamin.

Vitrine [vi'triːnə] (pl -n) die - **1.** [Schrank] display cabinet - **2.** [Ausstellungskasten] display case.

Vize|kanzler, in der, die vice-chancellor.

Vize|präsident, in der, die vice-president.

Vogel (pl Vögel) der - **1.** [Tier] bird - **2.** fam [Person]: **ein komischer ~** an odd customer - **3.** RW: **einen ~ haben** salopp abw to be off one's head; **jm einen ~ zeigen** fam to tap one's forehead at sb (to indicate that he/she is crazy).

Vogelscheuche (pl -n) die scarecrow.

Vokabel [vo'kaːbl] (pl -n) die word; ~**n** vocabulary (U).

Vokabular [vokabu'laːɐ̯] (pl -e) das vocabulary.

Vokal [vo'kaːl] (pl -e) der vowel.

Volk (pl Völker) das - **1.** [gen] people (pl); **das deutsche** ~ the German nation ODER people - **2.** (ohne pl) fam [viele Personen] crowd.

Völker|bund der HIST League of Nations.

Völker|kunde die ethnology.

Völker|recht das international law.

Völker|wanderung die HIST migration of the peoples.

Volksab|stimmung die referendum.

Volks|fest das festival.

Volkshoch|schule die ≃ college of adult education.

Volks|lied das folk song.

Volks|musik die folk music.

Volks|tanz der folk dance.

volkstümlich <> adj - **1.** [traditionell] traditional - **2.** [populär] popular <> adv [populär] in plain language.

Volks|wirtschaft die - **1.** [Wissenschaft] economics (U) - **2.** [Wirtschaft] economy.

voll <> adj - **1.** [gen] full; ~ **von** ODER **mit etw sein** to be full of sthg; **halb** ~ half full; **mit ~em Recht** with every justification; **in ~em Ernst** in all seriousness - **2.** fam [gesättigt]: ~ **sein** to be full (up) - **3.** salopp [betrunken]: ~ **sein** to be plastered - **4.** [vollwertig]: **jn nicht für** ~ **nehmen** fam fig not to take sb seriously <> adv - **1.** [völlig] totally, completely; ~ **und ganz** completely - **2.** salopp [verstärkend] really.

vollauf adv completely.

Voll|bart der full beard.

Voll|blut (pl -blüter) das thoroughbred.

vollenden vt to complete.

vollendet <> pp ▷ vollenden <> adj - **1.** [perfekt] perfect - **2.** [fertig] completed <> adv perfectly.

vollends adv completely.

Voll|endung die - **1.** [Perfektion] perfection - **2.** [Vollenden] completion.

voller adj (unver) full of.

Volley|ball ['vɔlibal] der volleyball.

Voll|gas das: **mit** ~ at full throttle; ~ **geben** to put one's foot down Br, to step on the gas Am.

völlig <> adj complete <> adv completely.

volljährig adj: ~ **sein** to be of age.

Vollkasko|ver|sicherung die comprehensive insurance.

vollkommen <> adj - **1.** [perfekt] perfect - **2.** [absolut] complete <> adv - **1.** [perfekt] perfectly - **2.** [absolut] completely.

Vollkorn|brot das wholemeal Br ODER whole wheat Am bread.

voll machen vt fam - **1.** [Bett] to wet; [Windel, Hose] to dirty - **2.** [füllen] to fill - **3.** [vervollständigen] to complete.

Voll|macht (pl -en) die - 1. (ohne pl) [Befugnis] authority; **RECHT** power of attorney; **jm (die) ~ geben** ODER **erteilen** to authorize sb; **RECHT** to give sb power of attorney - 2. [Schreiben] letter of authorization; **schriftliche ~** written authorization.

Voll|milch die full-fat milk.

Voll|mond der full moon.

Voll|pension die full board.

vollständig <> adj complete <> adv completely.

vollstrecken vt - 1. **RECHT** [Testament] to execute; [Urteil] to carry out - 2. **SPORT** to score from, to convert.

voll tanken vi to fill up; **bitte einmal ~!** fill it up, please!

Voll|treffer der - 1. [Schuss] direct hit - 2. RW: **ein ~ sein** to be a hit.

vollwertig adj - 1. [gleichwertig] fully-fledged - 2. [Speisen] wholefood.

Vollwertkost die wholefood.

vollzählig <> adj entire <> adv: **sie sind ~ erschienen** they all turned up.

Vollzug der - 1. [von Urteil, Beschlagnahmung] carrying out - 2. [von Ehe] consummation - 3. fam [Gefängnis] clink.

Vollzugs|anstalt die prison, penitentiary Am.

Volt [vɔlt] (pl -) das volt.

Volumen [voˈluːmən] (pl -) das volume.

vom präp - 1. (von + dem) from the; **~ Bahnhof** from the station - 2. (untrennbar): **~ Fach sein** to be an expert; **müde ~ Arbeiten sein** to be tired from working.

von präp (+ D) - 1. [räumlich] from; [von weg] off, from; **~ ... nach ...** from ... to ...; **etw vom Tisch nehmen** to take sth from ODER off the table - 2. [zeitlich] from; **~ Montag bis Freitag** from Monday to Friday, Monday through Friday Am; **~ heute an** from today - 3. [stellt Bezug her]: **die Zeitung ~ gestern** yesterday's paper; **~ wem hast du das?** who gave it to you?; **ist das Buch ~ dir?** is the book yours?; **das war dumm/nett ~ dir** that was stupid/nice of you - 4. [in Passivsätzen] by; **~ einem Hund gebissen werden** to be bitten by a dog; **~ Hand hergestellt** made by hand - 5. [zur Angabe der Ursache] from; **müde ~ der Reise** tired from the journey - 6. [drückt Eigenschaften aus] of; **ein Sack ~ 25 kg** a 25 kg bag; **eine Fahrt ~ 3 Stunden** a 3-hour journey - 7. [zur Angabe einer Teilmenge] of; **ein Stück ~ der Torte** a piece of the cake; **neun ~ zehn** nine out of ten - 8. RW: **~ mir aus** fam I don't mind; **~ sich aus** fam by oneself. ➡ **von ... an** präp from; **~ hier an** from here; **~ jetzt an** from now on. ➡ **von ... aus** präp from; **~ hier aus** from here.

voneinander adv from one another; **sie**

sind ~ unabhängig they are independent of one another.

vor <> präp - 1. (+ D) [räumlich] in front of; **~ dem Haus stehen** to stand in front of the house; **~ Gericht erscheinen** to appear before a court - 2. (+ A) [räumlich] in front of - 3. (+ D) [zeitlich - zuvor] ago; **heute ~ fünf Jahren** five years ago today; **~ kurzem** recently - 4. [zur Angabe der Uhrzeit] to Br; before Am; **fünf ~ zwölf** five to twelve Br, five before twelve Am; **fünf ~ halb neun** twenty-five past eight Br, twenty-five after eight Am - 5. (+ D) [wegen] with; **~ Kälte/Angst zittern** to tremble with cold/fear; **~ Freude in die Luft springen** to jump for joy; **~ Hunger sterben** to die of hunger - 6. [stellt Bezug her]: **Schutz ~ etw** protection from sthg; **jn ~ etw warnen** to warn sb about sthg - 7. RW: **~ sich hin murmeln/singen** to mutter/sing to oneself <> adv forwards. ➡ **vor allem** adv above all.

Vorabend der evening before.

voran adv - 1. [vorweg] at the front - 2. [vorwärts] forwards.

voran|gehen (perf ist vorangegangen) vi (unreg) - 1. [Arbeit, Projekt] to advance, to progress - 2. [vorne gehen] to go on ahead - 3. [vorher passieren]: **jm/etw ~** to precede sb/sthg.

voran|kommen (perf ist vorangekommen) vi (unreg) to make progress; [Arbeit, Projekt] to advance, to progress; **gut ~** to make good progress; **nicht ~** not to make any progress.

vor|arbeiten vi: **einen Tag ~** to work an extra day (in order to have a day off later). ➡ **sich vorarbeiten** ref to work one's way forward.

voraus adv in front; **jm in etw ~ sein** fig to be ahead of sb in sthg; **seiner Zeit ~** ahead of one's time.

voraus|gehen (perf ist vorausgegangen) vi (unreg) - 1. [vorher, früher gehen] to go on ahead - 2. [vorher passieren]: **einer Sache** (D) **~** to precede sthg.

vorausgesetzt <> pp ▷ voraussetzen <> konj provided (that).

voraus|haben vt (unreg): **jm etw ~** to have the advantage of sthg over sb.

voraus|sagen vt to predict.

voraus|sehen vt (unreg) to foresee; **es war vorauszusehen, dass ...** it was to be expected that ...

voraus|setzen vt - 1. [erfordern] to require - 2. [für selbstverständlich halten] to take for granted; **wir müssen ~, dass ...** we must assume that ...; **etw als bekannt ~** to assume sthg is known.

Voraussetzung (pl -en) die - 1. [Erfordernis] requirement; **ihm fehlen die nötigen ~en** he lacks the necessary qualifications; **unter der**

~, **dass** on condition that - **2.** [Annahme] assumption.

Voraussicht die foresight; **aller ~ nach** in all probability.

voraussichtlich <> adj expected <> adv probably.

Voraus|zahlung die advance payment.

Vorbehalt (pl -e) der reservation; **etw unter** ODER **mit ~ annehmen** to accept sthg with reservations.

vor|behalten vt (unreg): **sich etw ~** to reserve o.s. sthg; **der Swimmingpool ist den Hotelgästen ~** the swimming pool is reserved for hotel guests only.

vorbei adv - **1.** [räumlich] past, by; **an mir ~** past me - **2.** [zeitlich] over; **die Schmerzen sind ~** the pain has gone; **mit etw ist es ~** fam sthg is over.

vorbei|gehen (perf ist vorbeigegangen) vi (unreg) - **1.** [entlanggehen, vergehen] to pass; **an jm/etw ~** to pass sb/sthg - **2.** [hingehen] to drop in. **im Vorbeigehen** adv in passing.

vorbei|kommen (perf ist vorbeigekommen) vi (unreg) - **1.** [an etw vorüber]: **(an etw (D)) ~** to pass (sthg) - **2.** [besuchen]: **(bei jm) ~** to drop in (on sb); **komm mal vorbei!** come round some time! - **3.** [vorbeikönnen] to get past.

vorbei|reden vi: **aneinander ~** to talk at cross purposes.

vor|bereiten vt to prepare; **jn/etw auf etw (A) ~** to prepare sb/sthg for sthg. **sich vorbereiten** ref: **sich (auf etw (A)) ~** to prepare o.s. (for sthg).

Vor|bereitung die preparation; **in ~ sein** to be in preparation.

vor|bestellen vt to order in advance.

vorbestraft adj: **~ sein** to have previous convictions, to have a criminal record.

vor|beugen <> vi: **einer Sache (D) ~** to prevent sthg <> vt to bend forward. **sich vorbeugen** ref to lean forward.

Vor|beugung die prevention.

Vor|bild das model.

vorbildlich <> adj exemplary <> adv in exemplary fashion.

vor|bringen vt (unreg) - **1.** [Wunsch, Bedenken] to express; [Bitte, Beschwerde] to make; **etw gegen etw ~** to raise sthg as an objection to sthg; **etw gegen jn ~** to say sthg against sb - **2.** [Beweise] to produce.

vordere, r, s adj front.

Vorder|grund der foreground; **etw in den ~ stellen** ODER **rücken** to place special emphasis on sthg; **im ~ stehen** to be to the fore.

Vorder|mann der: **der Läufer überholte seinen ~** the runner overtook the man in front of him.

Vorder|rad das front wheel.

Vorder|sitz der front seat.

vor|drängen sich vordrängen ref to push in.

vor|dringen (perf ist vorgedrungen) vi (unreg) to advance; [in Menschenmenge] to push forward.

Vor|druck der form.

voreilig <> adj rash <> adv rashly.

voreinander adv - **1.** [in Bezug aufeinander]: **Angst ~ haben** to be afraid of one another - **2.** [räumlich] one in front of the other.

voreingenommen <> adj biased; **gegen jn/etw ~ sein** to be biased against sb/sthg <> adv in a biased way.

vor|enthalten vt (unreg): **jm etw ~** to withhold sthg from sb; [Nachricht] to keep sthg from sb.

vorerst adv for the time being.

Vorfahr (pl -en), **Vorfahre** (pl -n) der ancestor.

vor|fahren (perf hat/ist vorgefahren) <> vi (ist) - **1.** [nach vorn fahren] to drive forward - **2.** [vorausfahren] to drive on ahead - **3.** [vor Gebäude] to drive up <> vt (hat) - **1.** [nach vorn] to drive forward - **2.** [vor Gebäude] to drive up.

Vorfahrt die right of way; **~ haben** to have right of way.

Vorfahrts|straße die major road.

Vor|fall der [Geschehnis] occurrence, incident.

vor|fallen (perf ist vorgefallen) vi (unreg) to happen, to occur.

vor|finden vt (unreg) to find.

vor|führen vt - **1.** [zeigen - Film] to show; [- Kunststück] to perform; [- Funktionsweise] to demonstrate; **jm etw ~** to show sb sthg - **2.** fam [blamieren] to show up.

Vor|führung die - **1.** [im Theater, Kino, Zirkus] performance - **2.** [von Maschine] demonstration.

Vor|gang der event, occurrence.

Vorgänger, in (mpl -; fpl -nen) der, die predecessor.

vorgefertigt adj prefabricated.

vorgegeben adj set in advance.

vor|gehen (perf ist vorgegangen) vi (unreg) - **1.** [vorhergehen] to go on ahead - **2.** [passieren] to go on - **3.** [handeln] to proceed; **gegen jn/etw ~** to take action against sb/sthg - **4.** [Uhr] to be fast - **5.** [vorne gehen] to go first.

Vor|geschichte die - **1.** [vorherige Entwicklung] history - **2.** [Prähistorie] prehistory.

Vorgesetzte (pl -n) der, die superior.

vorgestern adv [vor zwei Tagen] the day before yesterday.

vor|haben vt (unreg) to plan; **was habt ihr am Wochenende vor?** what have you got planned for the weekend?

Vorhaben (*pl -*) *das* plan.

vor|halten (*unreg*) ◇ *vt*: **jm etw** ~ [halten] to hold sthg up to sb; [vorwerfen] to hold sthg against sb ◇ *vi* [ausreichen] to last.

vorhanden *adj* existing; [Vorräte, Mittel] available; ~ **sein** to exist; [Vorräte, Mittel] to be available; **davon ist nichts mehr** ~ there's none of it left.

Vor|hang *der* curtain; **der Eiserne** ~ the Iron Curtain.

Vorhänge|schloss *das* padlock.

Vor|haut *die* foreskin.

vorher *adv* - 1. [früher] before; **am Tag** ~ the day before - 2. [im Voraus] before(hand).

vorherig *adj* previous.

vor|herrschen *vi* to prevail.

Vorher|sage *die* - 1. [für Wetter] forecast - 2. [des Schicksals] prediction.

vorher|sehen *vt* (*unreg*) [wahrsagen] to foresee; [voraussehen] to predict; [Wetter] to forecast.

vorhin, vorhin *adv* just now.

vorig *adj* last.

Vorkehrungen *pl*: ~ **treffen** to take precautions.

Vorkenntnisse *pl* previous experience (*U*).

vor|kommen (*perf* ist **vorgekommen**) *vi* (*unreg*) - 1. [passieren] to happen - 2. [auftreten] to be found, to occur - 3. [scheinen] **jm verdächtig** ~ to seem suspicious to sb; **es kommt mir vor, als sei heute Sonntag** today feels like Sunday to me; **sich überflüssig** ~ to feel unwanted - 4. [nach vorne kommen] to come forward.

Vorkommen (*pl -*) *das* - 1. [an Bodenschätzen] deposit - 2. [Existieren] presence - 3. [Auftreten] occurrence.

Vor|ladung *die* summons (*sg*).

Vor|lage *die* - 1. [Muster] pattern - 2. [Vorlegen] presentation - 3. [Gesetzesvorlage] bill - 4. SPORT [bei Fußball] assist, pass (*leading to a goal*).

vor|lassen *vt* (*unreg*) **jn** ~ to let sb go first.

Vor|läufer, in *der, die* forerunner.

vorläufig ◇ *adj* provisional ◇ *adv* provisionally; **ich wohne** ~ **bei ihm** I'm staying with him for the time being; **die Polizei nahm sie** ~ **fest** the police held them.

vorlaut ◇ *adj*: ~ **sein** to make comments out of turn ◇ *adv* out of turn.

vor|legen *vt* to present; [Ausweis] to show; [Zeugnis] to submit; **jm etw** ~ to present sb with sthg.

vor|lesen *vt* (*unreg*) to read out; **jm etw** ~ to read sthg to sb.

Vor|lesung *die* UNI lecture.

vor|letzte, r, s *adj* penultimate, last but one.

Vorliebe (*pl -n*) *die* preference; **eine** ~ **für**

jn/etw haben to be particularly fond of sb/sthg.

vor|liegen *vi* (*unreg*) [vorgelegt sein]: **der Antrag liegt vor** the application has been received; **die Ergebnisse liegen noch nicht vor** the results are not yet available; **gegen ihn liegt nichts vor** no charges have been brought against him.

vor|machen *vt* - 1. *fam* [zeigen]: **jm etw** ~ to show sb how to do sthg - 2. [vortäuschen]: **jm etwas** ~ to fool sb.

Vormacht|stellung *die* supremacy (*U*).

Vor|marsch *der*: **auf dem** ~ **sein** *fig* to be gaining ground.

vor|merken *vt* - 1. [Termin] to make a note of - 2. [Person] **jn für einen Kurs** ~ to put sb's name down for a course.

Vor|mittag *der* morning; **gestern/heute/morgen** ~ yesterday/this/tomorrow morning.

vormittags *adv* in the morning.

Vormund (*pl -e* ODER *-münder*) *der* guardian.

vorn, vorne *adv* in front, at the front; **da** ~ over there; **nach** ~ forwards. ◆ **von vorn** *adv* [von Anfang an] from the beginning.

Vor|name *der* first name.

vornehm ◇ *adj* - 1. [fein - Charakter] noble; [der Oberschicht angehörend] distinguished - 2. [elegant] upmarket ◇ *adv* [elegant] elegantly.

vor|nehmen *vt* (*unreg*) - 1. [durchführen] to carry out; [Auswahl] to make - 2. [sich beschäftigen mit]: **sich** (*D*) **etw** ~ *fam* to tackle sthg - 3. [sich entschließen]: **sich** (*D*) ~, **etw zu tun** to resolve to do sthg; **sich** (*D*) **etw fest vorgenommen haben** to have made up one's mind to do sthg.

vornherein ◆ **von vornherein** *adv* from the start.

Vor|ort *der* suburb.

Vor|platz *der* forecourt.

Vorrang *der*: **vor jm** ~ **haben** to take precedence over sb.

vorrangig <> *adj* of prime importance <> *adv:* **etw ~ behandeln** to treat sthg as a matter of priority.

Vorrat (*pl* -räte) *der* supply; [Reserve] store; **Vorräte** [von Geschäft] stocks; **ein ~ an etw** (D) a supply/store of sthg. ◆ **auf Vorrat** *adv:* **etw auf ~ einkaufen** to stock up on sthg.

vorrätig *adj* in stock.

Vorraum *der* anteroom.

Vorrecht *das* privilege.

Vorrichtung *die* device.

vorrücken (*perf* hat/ist vorgerückt) <> *vt* (hat) to move forward <> *vi* (ist) - **1.** [räumlich] to move forward - **2.** [in Hierarchie] to move up.

Vorruhestand *der* early retirement; **in den ~ gehen** to take early retirement.

vorsagen <> *vt:* **jm etw ~** to tell sb sthg <> *vi:* **jm ~** to tell sb the answer.

Vorsaison *die* low season.

Vorsatz *der* resolution; **einen ~ fassen, etw zu tun** to resolve to do sthg.

vorsätzlich <> *adj* RECHT premeditated <> *adv* intentionally, on purpose.

Vorschau *die* preview.

Vorschein *der:* **zum ~ kommen** to turn up.

vorschieben *vt* (*unreg*) - **1.** [schieben] to push forward; [Riegel] to push across; **das Kinn ~** to stick one's chin out - **2.** [Vorwand] to put forward as an excuse - **3.** [Stellvertreter] to use as a front man.

Vorschlag *der* suggestion.

Vorschläge machen

Let's go swimming! Komm/Kommt, wir gehen schwimmen!

How about a game of chess? Wie wärs mit einer Partie Schach?

I suggest that we tell him. Ich schlage vor, wir erzählen es ihm.

You could always write to them. Du könntest ihnen doch schreiben.

Perhaps we could buy him a watch. Könnten wir ihm nicht eine Armbanduhr kaufen?

vorschlagen *vt* (*unreg*) to suggest; **jm etw ~** to suggest sthg to sb; **er schlug vor, ins Kino zu gehen** he suggested going to the cinema.

vorschnell <> *adj* rash <> *adv* rashly.

vorschreiben *vt* (*unreg*) [Subj: Gesetz] to stipulate; **sein Vater versucht ihm alles vorzuschreiben** his father is always trying to tell him what to do.

Vorschrift *die* regulation.

Vorschule *die* nursery school.

Vorschuss *der* advance.

vorsehen *vt* (*unreg*) - **1.** [planen] to plan; **die** Feier ist für nächste Woche vorgesehen the celebration is scheduled ODER planned for next week; **das ist nicht vorgesehen** there are no plans for that; **jn für etw ~** to have sb in mind for sthg - **2.** [vorschreiben] to provide for. ◆ **sich vorsehen** *ref:* **sich vor jm/etw ~** [achtsam sein] to beware of sb/sthg.

vorsetzen *vt:* **jm etw ~** to serve sb sthg.

Vorsicht <> *die* care <> *interj* look out!; **~, Stufe!** mind the step!

vorsichtig <> *adj* careful <> *adv* carefully.

vorsichtshalber *adv* as a precaution.

Vorsichtsmaßnahme *die* precaution; **~n treffen** to take precautions.

Vorsilbe *die* prefix.

Vorsitz *der* chairmanship.

Vorsitzende (*pl* -n) *der, die* chairperson.

Vorsorge *die* (ohne pl) [gegen Krankheit, Gefahr] precautions (pl); [für das Alter] provisions (pl); **~ treffen** to take precautions; [für das Alter] to make provisions.

vorsorgen *vi:* **für etw ~** to make provisions for sthg.

vorsorglich <> *adj* precautionary <> *adv* as a precaution.

Vorspeise *die* starter.

vorspielen <> *vt* - **1.** [auf einem Instrument]: **jm ein Stück ~** to play a piece for sb - **2.** [vortäuschen] to put on an act <> *vi* [auf einem Instrument]: **jm ~** to play for sb.

Vorsprung *der* - **1.** [von Läufer, Auto] lead - **2.** [von Wand] ledge.

Vorstadt *die* suburb.

Vorstand *der* [von Firma] board of directors; [von Verein] committee; [von Partei] executive.

vorstehen *vi* (*unreg*) - **1.** to jut out; [Backenknochen] to be prominent; [Zähne] to protrude - **2.** [einer Gruppe, Institution]: **jm/etw ~** to be in charge of sb/sthg.

vorstellen *vt* - **1.** [bekannt machen] to introduce; **jn jm ~** to introduce sb to sb - **2.** [sich ausdenken]: **sich** (D) **etw ~** to imagine sthg - **3.** [Uhr] to put forward. ◆ **sich vorstellen** *ref* - **1.** [bekannt machen]: **sich jm ~** to introduce o.s. to sb - **2.** [sich bewerben]: **sich bei jm ~** to go for an interview with sb.

Vorstellung *die* - **1.** [Idee] idea; **etw entspricht (nicht) js ~en** sthg is (not) as sb imagined it - **2.** [im Theater] performance - **3.** [das Vorstellen] presentation.

Vorstellungsgespräch *das* interview.

Vorstrafe *die* RECHT previous conviction.

vorstrecken *vt* - **1.** [Arme, Beine] to stretch out - **2.** [Geld] to advance to sb sthg.

vortäuschen *vt* to feign; **jm etw ~** to pretend sthg to sb.

Vorteil *der* advantage; **zu js ~** to sb's advantage; **jm gegenüber im ~ sein** to have an advantage over sb.

vorteilhaft adj [Geschäft, Lage] advantageous; [Haarschnitt] flattering.

Vortrag (pl -träge) der talk; **ein ~ über jn/etw** a talk about sb/sthg; **einen ~ halten** to give a talk.

vor|tragen vt (unreg) - **1.** [darbieten] to perform; [Gedicht] to recite - **2.** [darlegen] to present.

Vortritt der: **jm den ~ lassen** to let sb go first.

vorüber adj: **~ sein** to be over.

vorüber|gehen (perf ist vorübergegangen) vi (unreg) - **1.** [Person] to pass by; **an jm/etw ~** to pass by sb/sthg - **2.** [Schmerzen] to come to an end.

vorübergehend <> adj temporary <> adv temporarily.

Vorurteil das prejudice.

Vorverkauf der advance booking; **Karten im ~ bekommen** to buy tickets in advance.

Vorwahl die - **1.** [telefonisch] dialling code Br, area code Am - **2.** [von Wahlen] primary Am, candidate selection procedure.

Vorwand (pl -wände) der excuse; **unter dem ~** under the pretext.

vorwärts adv forwards.

vorwärts gehen (perf ist vorwärts gegangen) vi (unreg) to progress; **mit dem Experiment geht es nicht vorwärts** the experiment isn't getting anywhere.

vorwärts kommen (perf ist vorwärts gekommen) vi (unreg) to make progress.

vorweg adv - **1.** [vorher] beforehand - **2.** [voraus] in front.

vorweg|nehmen vt (unreg) to anticipate.

vor|weisen vt (unreg) - **1.** [vorzeigen] to show - **2.** [bieten]: **etw ~ können** to possess sthg.

vor|werfen vt (unreg): **jm etw ~** to accuse sb of sthg.

vorwiegend adv mainly.

Vorwort das preface.

Vorwurf der accusation.

vorwurfsvoll <> adj reproachful <> adv reproachfully.

Vor|zeichen das - **1.** [Anzeichen] omen - **2.** MATH sign - **3.** MUS key signature.

vor|zeigen vt: **(jm etw) ~** to show (sb sthg).

vorzeitig <> adj early; [Altern, Wehen] premature <> adv prematurely; **~ in Rente gehen** to take early retirement.

vor|ziehen vt (unreg) - **1.** [lieber mögen] to prefer; **etw einer Sache** (D) **~** to prefer sthg to sthg - **2.** [Termin] to bring forward - **3.** [nach vorn ziehen] to pull forward.

Vorzug der - **1.** [Vorrang] advantage; **jm/etw den ~ geben** to give sb/sthg preference - **2.** [gute Eigenschaft] virtue.

vorzüglich <> adj excellent <> adv excellently.

vorzugsweise adv mainly.

vulgär adj vulgar.

Vulkan (pl -e) der volcano.

w, W [ve:] (pl -ODER -s) das w, W. ➤ **W** (abk für West, Watt) W.

Waage (pl -n) die - **1.** [Gerät] scales (pl) - **2.** ASTROL Libra; **~ sein** to be Libra.

waagerecht, waagrecht <> adj horizontal <> adv horizontally.

Wabe (pl -n) die honeycomb.

wach adj - **1.** [nicht schlafend] awake; **jn ~ machen** to wake sb; **~ halten** [Person] to keep awake; [Erinnerung] to keep alive; **~ sein** to be awake; **~ werden** to wake up - **2.** [Geist] alert.

Wache (pl -n) die - **1.** (ohne pl) [Wachdienst] guard duty; **~ halten** to be on guard - **2.** [Wächter] guard - **3.** [Polizeiwache] police station.

Wachhund der guard dog.

Wacholder (pl -) der juniper.

Wachs [vaks] (pl -e) das wax (U).

wachsam ['vaxza:m] adj vigilant.

wachsen [vaksn] (präs wächst ODER wachst; prät wuchs ODER wachste; perf ist gewachsen ODER hat gewachst) <> vi (unreg) (ist) - **1.** [größer werden] to grow - **2.** [entsprechen]: **einer Sache** (D) **gewachsen sein** to be up to sthg <> vt (reg) (hat) [mit Wachs] to wax.

Wachsmal|stift ['vaksma:lʃtɪft] der wax crayon.

wächst [vɛkst] präs ⊳ wachsen.

Wachstuch das oilcloth.

Wachstum ['vakstu:m] das growth.

Wachtel (pl -n) die quail.

Wächter, in (mpl -; fpl -nen) der, die guard.

Wachtposten der guard.

Wachturm, Wachtturm der watchtower.

wackelig, wacklig adj - **1.** [nicht fest] wobbly - **2.** fam [gefährdet] shaky.

Wackelkontakt der ELEKTR loose contact.

wackeln (perf hat/ist gewackelt) vi - **1.** (hat) [nicht fest sein] to be wobbly - **2.** (hat) [hin und her bewegen]: **mit etw ~** to shake sthg - **3.** (ist) fam [gehen] to totter - **4.** (hat) fam [Posten] to be shaky.

wacker <> adj - **1.** [anständig] upright - **2.** [tüchtig] hearty <> adv valiantly.

Wade (*pl* -n) *die* calf.

Waffe (*pl* -n) *die* weapon.

Waffel (*pl* -n) *die* waffle.

Waffel|eisen *das* waffle iron.

Waffen|gewalt *die*: **mit ~** by force of arms.

Waffen|schein *der* firearms licence.

Waffenstill|stand *der* armistice.

wagen *vt* to risk; **einen Versuch ~** to risk an attempt; **es ~, etw zu tun** to dare to do sthg. ➤ **sich wagen** *ref* to dare; **sich nachts nicht auf die Straße ~** not to dare to go out on the street at night; **sich an etw** (*A*) **~** to attempt sthg.

Wagen (*pl* -) *der* - **1.** [Auto] car - **2.** [von Zug, Straßenbahn] carriage *Br*, car *Am* - **3.** [mit Pferd] carriage. ➤ **der Große Wagen** *der* ASTRON the Plough. ➤ **der Kleine Wagen** *der* ASTRON the Little Bear.

Wagen|heber (*pl* -) *der* jack.

Waggon, Wagon [vaˈɡɔŋ] (*pl* -s) *der* carriage *Br*, car *Am*.

waghalsig *adj* reckless.

Wagnis (*pl* -se) *das* risk.

Wagon = Waggon.

Wahl (*pl* -en) *die* - **1.** (*ohne pl*) [Auswahl] choice; **die ~ haben** to have the choice; **eine ~ treffen** to make a choice; **erste/zweite ~** first/second class; **in die engere ~ kommen** to be short-listed - **2.** [Abstimmung] election; **geheime ~** secret ballot; **zur ~ gehen** to vote.

wahlberechtigt *adj* entitled to vote.

wählen ◇ *vt* - **1.** [aussuchen] to choose - **2.** [am Telefon] to dial - **3.** [politisch] to elect ◇ *vi* - **1.** [aussuchen] to choose; **zwischen etw** (*D*) **und etw** (*D*) **~** to choose between sthg and sthg - **2.** [am Telefon] to dial - **3.** [politisch] to vote.

Wähler (*pl* -) *der* voter.

Wählerin (*pl* -nen) *die* voter.

wählerisch *adj* choosy.

Wähler|stimme *die* vote.

Wahl|fach *das* SCHULE optional subject.

Wahl|gang *der* ballot.

Wahl|heimat *die* adopted home.

Wahl|kabine *die* polling booth.

Wahl|kampf *der* election campaign.

Wahl|kreis *der* constituency.

Wahl|lokal *das* polling station.

wahllos *adv* at random.

Wahlnieder|lage *die* election defeat.

Wahl|recht *das* right to vote; **allgemeines ~** universal suffrage.

Wahl|rede *die* election speech.

Wahl|sieg *der* election victory.

Wahl|spruch *der* motto.

wahlweise *adv*: **zum Frühstück gibt es ~ Kaffee oder Tee** for breakfast there's a choice of coffee or tea.

Wahn *der* (*ohne pl*) delusion.

Wahnsinn *der* madness; **Wahnsinn!** amazing!

wahnsinnig ◇ *adj* - **1.** [verrückt] mad - **2.** [groß] incredible ◇ *adv fam* [sehr] incredibly.

wahr *adj* true; **~e Liebe/Freundschaft** true love/friendship; **das darf doch nicht ~ sein!** *fam* that can't be true!; **etw ~ machen** *fig* to carry out sthg. ➤ **nicht wahr** *interj*: **du warst doch gestern auch hier, nicht ~?** you were here yesterday too, weren't you?; **das stimmt doch, nicht ~?** that's right, isn't it?

während ◇ *konj* [zeitlich, gegensätzlich] while ◇ *präp* during.

währenddessen *adv* in the meantime.

wahrhaben *vt*: **etw nicht ~ wollen** not to want to accept sthg.

Wahrheit (*pl* -en) *die* truth (*U*). ➤ **in Wahrheit** *adv* in reality.

wahrheitsgemäß ◇ *adj* truthful ◇ *adv* truthfully.

wahr|nehmen *vt* (*unreg*) - **1.** [Veränderung, Geräusch] to notice - **2.** [Gelegenheit] to avail oneself of - **3.** [Interessen] to protect.

Wahrnehmung (*pl* -en) *die* - **1.** [Spüren] awareness (*U*) - **2.** [von Gelegenheit] seizing - **3.** [von Geschäft] representation.

wahr|sagen *vi* to predict the future.

Wahrsager, in (*mpl* -; *fpl* -nen) *der, die* fortune-teller.

wahrscheinlich ◇ *adj* probable ◇ *adv* probably.

Wahrscheinlichkeit (*pl* -en) *die* probability; **aller ~ nach** in all probability.

Wahrung *die* protection.

Währung (*pl* -en) *die* currency; **eine harte ~** a hard currency.

Währungs|einheit *die* currency unit.

Währungsre|form *die* HIST & WIRTSCH currency reform.

Währungs|system *das* monetary system.

Wahr|zeichen *das* symbol.

Waise (*pl* -n) *die* orphan.

Waisen|haus *das* orphanage.

Waisen|kind *das* orphan.

Wal (*pl* -e) *der* whale.

Wald (*pl* Wälder) *der* wood; [groß] forest.

Wald|brand *der* forest fire.

Wäldchen (*pl* -) *das* copse.

Wald|gebiet *das* wooded area.

Waldmeister *der* woodruff.

Wald|sterben *das* forest dieback.

Wald|weg *der* forest track.

Wales [ˈweːls] *nt* Wales.

Walkman® [ˈwɔːkmɛn] (*pl* -men) *der* Walkman®.

Wall (*pl* Wälle) *der* rampart.

Wall|fahrt *die* pilgrimage.

Wallis *das* Valais.

walliserisch *adj* of/from Valais.

Wallonien *nt* Wallonia.

wallonisch *adj* Walloon.

Wallnuss *die* walnut.

Wallross *das* walrus.

walten *vi geh* to reign; **etw ~ lassen** to exercise sthg.

Walze (*pl* -n) *die* roller.

walzen *vt* to roll.

wälzen *vt* - **1.** [rollen] to roll - **2.** [Buch] to pore over. ➡ **sich wälzen** *ref* to roll around.

Walzer (*pl* -) *der* waltz; **~ tanzen** to waltz.

Wälzer (*pl* -) *der fam* tome.

wand *prät* ▷ winden.

Wand (*pl* Wände) *die* - **1.** [Mauer] wall (*inside*) - **2.** [Felswand] rock face - **3.** [von Schrank] side - **4.** *RW:* **in den eigenen vier Wänden** in one's own home; **jn an die ~ stellen** *fam* to send sb before the firing squad.

Wandel *der* change; **im ~ begriffen** to be in a state of flux.

wandeln (*perf* hat/ist gewandelt) *geh* ◇ *vi* (*ist*) to stroll ◇ *vt* (*hat*) to change. ➡ **sich wandeln** *ref* to change.

Wanderer, Wandrer (*pl* -) *der* hiker.

Wanderin, Wandrerin (*pl* -nen) *die* hiker.

Wanderkarte *die* walking map.

wandern (*perf* ist gewandert) *vi* - **1.** [als Sport] to go hiking - **2.** [ziellos] to wander - **3.** *fam* [gebracht werden]: **ins Gefängnis ~** to end up in prison.

Wanderschuh *der* hiking ODER walking boot.

Wandertag *der* school outing.

Wanderung (*pl* -en) *die* hike.

Wanderweg *der* trail.

Wandgemälde *das* fresco.

Wandlung (*pl* -en) *die* change.

Wandmalerei *die* mural.

Wandrer = Wanderer.

Wandrerin = Wanderin.

Wandschrank *der* built-in cupboard *Br* ODER closet *Am;* [Kleiderschrank] built-in wardrobe *Br* ODER closet *Am.*

wandte *prät* ▷ wenden.

Wandteppich *der* tapestry.

Wanduhr *die* wall clock.

Wange (*pl* -n) *die geh* cheek.

wanken (*perf* hat/ist gewankt) *vi* - **1.** (*ist*) [Betrunkener] to stagger - **2.** (*hat*) [Boden, Mauer] to sway - **3.** (*hat*) geh [Macht] to be under threat; [Entschluss] to waver.

wann *adv* when; **bis ~?** until when?, till when?; **seit ~ lebst du schon hier?** how long have you been living here?; **von ~ bis ~?** when?; **~ du willst** whenever you want.

Wanne (*pl* -n) *die* - **1.** [Badewanne] bath - **2.** [Becken] tub.

Wanze (*pl* -n) *die* bug.

Wappen (*pl* -) *das* coat of arms.

war *prät* ▷ sein.

warb *prät* ▷ werben.

Ware (*pl* -n) *die* product.

Warenhaus *das* department store.

📖 **Warenhaus**

Be careful with the German false friend Warenhaus as it refers to a "department store" rather than a "warehouse". Herrenbekleidung befindet sich in diesem Warenhaus im ersten Obergeschoss can be rendered in English as "The men's clothing department in this store is on the first floor."
A "warehouse" for storing goods is translated by Lager(haus) in German.

Warenlager *das* warehouse.

Warenzeichen *das:* **eingetragenes ~** registered trademark.

warf *prät* ▷ werfen.

warm (*kompar* wärmer; *superl* wärmste) ◇ *adj* warm; **es ist ~** it's warm; **mir ist/wird ~** I'm warm/warming up; **draußen ist es 30°C ~** it's 30°C outside; **mit jm ~ werden** *fam fig* to get on well with sb; **~e Miete** *rent including heating bills* ◇ *adv* warmly; **~ essen** to have a hot meal.

Wärme *die* warmth.

wärmedämmend *adj* insulating.

wärmen *vt & vi* to warm. ➡ **sich wärmen** *ref:* **sich an etw** (*D*) ~ to warm o.s. at sthg.

Wärmflasche *die* hot-water bottle.

warmherzig *adj* warm-hearted.

warm laufen (*perf* hat/ist warm gelaufen) *vi* (*unreg*) (*ist*) to warm up. ➡ **sich warm laufen** *ref* to warm up.

Warmmiete *die* rent including heating bills.

Warmwasser *das* hot water.

Warnblinkanlage *die* AUTO hazard lights (*pl*).

Warndreieck *das* AUTO warning triangle.

warnen *vt* to warn; **jn vor jm/etw ~** to warn sb about sb/sthg.

Warnschild (*pl* -er) *das* warning sign.

Warnung (*pl* -en) *die* warning.

Warschau *nt* Warsaw.

warten ◇ *vi* to wait; **auf jn/etw ~** to wait for sb/sthg; **mit etw ~** to put sthg on hold ◇ *vt* TECH to service.

Wärter, in (*mpl* -; *fpl* -nen) *der, die* [im Zoo, Leuchtturm] keeper; [im Gefängnis] warder.

Wartesaal *der* waiting room.

Wartezimmer *das* waiting room.

Wartung (*pl* -en) *die* servicing *(U)*.

warum *adv* why.

Warze (*pl* -n) *die* wart.

was ◇ *pron* - **1.** [Interrogativpronomen] what; **~ ist?** what is it?; **~ ist sie (von Beruf)?** what does she do (for a living)? - **2.** [wieviel] how much, what; **~ kostet das?** how much is it? - **3.** *fam* [warum] why; **~ fragst du?** why do you ask? - **4.** *fam* [nicht wahr]: **da freust du dich, ~?** you're pleased, aren't you?; **es ist schön, ~?** it's nice, isn't it?; **gut, ~?** not bad, eh? - **5.** [Relativpronomen] which, that; **das, ~ ...** what ...; **alles, ~ ...** everything (that) ...; **das Beste, ~ ich je gehört habe** the best I've ever heard - **6.** *fam* [etwas] something - **7.** *RW:* **~ für** what sort *ODER* kind of; **~ sind das für Tiere?** what sort *ODER* kind of animals are those?; **~ für ein Lärm!** what a noise!; **~ weiß ich!** *fam* don't ask me! ◇ *interj fam* [wie bitte] what? ◇ **ach, was** *interj* no it's/etc not! ◆ **so was** *interj*: **na** *ODER* **also so ~!** really!

Waschanlage *die* carwash.

waschbar *adj* washable.

Waschbecken *das* washbasin.

Wäsche (*pl* -n) *die* - **1.** [schmutzige Wäsche] laundry - **2.** [Unterwäsche] underwear - **3.** [Waschen] wash.

waschecht *adj* - **1.** [Stoff] colourfast - **2.** [typisch] true.

Wäscheklammer *die* clothes peg *Br*, clothespin *Am*.

Wäschekorb *der* laundry basket.

Wäscheleine *die* washing line.

waschen (*präs* wäscht; *prät* wusch; *perf* hat gewaschen) *vt* to wash; **sich** (D) **die Haare/die Hände ~** to wash one's hair/hands. ◆ **sich waschen** *ref* to have a wash; **er bekam eine Abreibung, die sich gewaschen hatte** he got one hell of a hiding.

Wäscherei (*pl* -en) *die* laundrette.

Wäscheständer *der* clotheshorse.

Wäschetrockner *der* - **1.** [Maschine] tumble-dryer - **2.** [Wäscheständer] clotheshorse.

Waschgelegenheit *die* washing facilities *(pl)*.

Waschlappen *der* - **1.** [Lappen] facecloth - **2.** *fam abw* [Person] wimp.

Waschmaschine *die* washing machine.

Waschmittel *das* detergent.

Waschpulver *das* washing powder.

Waschraum *der* washroom.

Waschsalon *der* laundrette.

wäscht *präs* ▷ waschen.

Wasser (*pl* - *ODER* Wässer) *das* - **1.** [gen] water; **~ abstoßend** water-repellent; **unter ~ stehen** to be under water - **2.** *(ohne pl)* [Körperflüssigkeit] fluid; **mir läuft das ~ im Mund zusammen** my mouth is watering - **3.** *RW:*

sich über ~ halten to keep one's head above water. ◆ **am Wasser** *adv* by the water.

wasserabstoßend ▷ Wasser.

Wasserbad *das* KÜCHE bain-marie.

wasserdicht *adj* - **1.** [Bekleidung, Uhr] waterproof - **2.** *fam* [Alibi] watertight.

Wasserfarbe *die* watercolours *(pl)*.

Wassergraben *der* ditch; [Burggraben] moat.

Wasserhahn *der* tap *Br*, faucet *Am*.

Wasserkraftwerk *das* hydroelectric power station.

Wasserleitung *die* water pipe.

wasserlöslich *adj* water-soluble.

Wassermann (*pl* -männer) *der* ASTROL Aquarius; **~ sein** to be an Aquarius.

Wassermelone *die* watermelon.

wässern *vt* - **1.** [Pflanze, Beet] to water - **2.** KÜCHE to soak.

Wasserpflanze *die* aquatic plant.

Wasserratte *die* - **1.** [Tier] water rat - **2.** *fam* [Person] waterbaby.

wasserscheu *adj* scared of water.

Wasserschutzpolizei *die* river police.

Wasserski ◇ *der* [Gerät] water ski ◇ *nt* water-skiing.

Wasserspiegel *der* water level.

Wassersport *der* water sport.

Wasserspülung (*pl* -en) *die* flush.

Wasserstand *der* water level.

Wasserstoff *der* CHEM hydrogen.

Wasserversorgung *die* *(ohne pl)* water supply.

Wasserwaage *die* spirit level.

Wasserwerk *das* waterworks *(pl)*.

Wasserzeichen *das* watermark.

wässrig *adj* watery.

waten (*perf* ist gewatet) *vi* to wade.

watscheln (*perf* ist gewatschelt) *vi* to waddle.

Watt (*pl* -en *ODER* -) *das* - **1.** (*pl* Watten) [Küstengebiet] mudflats *(pl)* - **2.** (*pl* Watt) PHYS & TECH [Maßeinheit] watt.

Watte *die* cotton wool.

Wattebausch *der* wad of cotton wool.

Wattenmeer *das* mudflats *(pl)*.

Wattestäbchen *das* cotton bud.

wattiert *adj* padded.

WC [ve:ˈtseː] (*pl* -s) *(abk für* water closet) *das* WC.

weben (*prät* wob; *perf* hat gewoben) *vt* to weave.

Webseite [websaitə] *die* EDV web page, website.

Webstuhl *der* loom.

Wechsel [ˈvɛksl̩] (*pl* -) *der* - **1.** [Tausch] change - **2.** [Zahlungsmittel] exchange. ◆ **im Wechsel** *adv* in turns.

Wechsel|beziehung *die* correlation.

Wechsel|geld *das* change.

wechselhaft ['vɛkslhaft] *adj* changeable.

Wechseljahre *pl* menopause *(U)*.

Wechsel|kurs *der* exchange rate.

wechseln ['vɛksln] *(perf* hat/ist gewechselt*)* ◇ *vt (hat)* - **1.** [Thema, Kleidung, Arbeitsplatz, Geld] to change; **etw gegen** ODER **in etw** *(A)* **~** to change sthg for sthg - **2.** [tauschen] to exchange ◇ *vi* - **1.** *(hat)* [sich verändern] to change - **2.** *(ist)* [an anderen Ort] to move.

wechselseitig ◇ *adj* mutual ◇ *adv* mutually.

Wechsel|strom *der (ohne pl)* ELEKTR alternating current.

Wechsel|stube *die* bureau de change.

Wechsel|wirkung *die* interaction.

wecken *vt* - **1.** [Person] to wake - **2.** [Neugier, Wunsch] to awaken.

Wecker *(pl* -*)* *der* alarm clock; **jm auf den - fallen** *fam fig* to get on sb's nerves.

wedeln *(perf* hat/ist gewedelt*)* *vi*: **mit etw ~** to wave sthg; **mit dem Schwanz ~** to wag its tail.

weder ◆ **weder … noch** *konj* neither … nor.

weg *adv* away; **er ist schon ~** he has already gone; **nichts wie - hier!** *fam* let's get out of here!; **- damit!** *fam* take it away!; **Hände ~!** hands off!; **weit ~** far away; **über etw** *(A)* **~ sein** *fam fig* to have got over sthg.

Weg *(pl* -e*)* *der* - **1.** [Pfad] path - **2.** [Strecke, Methode] way; **ein weiter - a** long way; **jm im ~ stehen** ODER **sein** to be in sb's way; **jm über den ~ laufen** to bump into sb; **(jn) nach dem ~ fragen** to ask (sb) the way; **sich auf den ~ machen** to be on one's way - **3.** *RW*: **jm/etw aus dem ~ gehen** to avoid sb/sthg; **jm nicht über den ~ trauen** not to trust sb an inch.

wegen *präp* (+ *G, D*) because of; **~ Umbau geschlossen** closed for refurbishment. ◆ **von wegen** *interj fam* far from it!

weg|fahren *(perf* hat/ist weggefahren*)* *(unreg)* ◇ *vi (ist)* to leave; [verreisen] to go away; **er stieg ins Auto und fuhr weg** he got in the car and drove off ◇ *vt (hat)* [transportieren] to move; [entsorgen] to take away.

weg|gehen *(perf* ist weggegangen*)* *vi (unreg)* - **1.** [fortgehen] to leave; [ausgehen] to go out; **geh weg!** go away! - **2.** [verschwinden] to go away - **3.** [Ware] to sell well.

weg|jagen *vt* to chase away.

weg|kommen *(perf* ist weggekommen*)* *vi (unreg)* - **1.** [fortgehen können] to get away; **von etw ~** to get away from sthg; [Drogen] to get off sthg - **2.** [verschwinden] to disappear - **3.** [behandelt werden]: **gut/schlecht bei etw ~** to do well/badly out of sthg.

weg|lassen *vt (unreg)* - **1.** [Person] to let go - **2.** [Abschnitt, Teil] to leave out.

weg|laufen *(perf* ist weggelaufen*)* *vi (unreg)* to run away; **vor** ODER **von jm/etw ~** to run away from sb/sthg.

weg|legen *vt* to put down.

weg|machen *vt fam* to get rid of.

weg|müssen *vi (unreg)* to have to go.

weg|nehmen *vt (unreg)* to take away; **jm etw ~** to take sthg away from sb.

weg|räumen *vt* to clear away.

weg|schaffen *vt* [sich einer Sache entledigen] to get rid of; [woandershin bringen] to move.

weg|schicken *vt* [Person] to send away; [Päckchen] to send.

weg|sehen *vi (unreg)* to look away.

weg|tun *vt (unreg)* - **1.** [weglegen] to put away - **2.** [wegwerfen] to throw away.

Wegweiser *(pl* -*)* *der* signpost.

weg|werfen *vt (unreg)* to throw away.

Wegwerf|gesellschaft *die abw* throwaway society.

weg|wischen *vt* to wipe away.

weg|ziehen *(perf* hat/ist weggezogen*)* *(unreg)* ◇ *vi (ist)*: **aus etw ~** [Stadt] to move away from sthg; [Wohnung, Haus] to move out of sthg ◇ *vt (hat)* to pull away; [Vorhang, Decke] to pull back.

weh *adj* painful; *siehe auch* wehtun. ◆ **oh weh** *interj* oh dear!

wehen *(perf* hat/ist geweht*)* ◇ *vi* - **1.** *(hat)* [blasen] to blow; [flattern] to flutter - **2.** *(ist)* [geweht werden - Blatt, Schneeflocken] to blow about; [- Duft, Geruch] to waft ◇ *vt (hat)* to blow.

Wehen *pl* contractions.

wehleidig *adj abw* self-pitying.

wehmütig ◇ *adj* melancholy ◇ *adv* melancholically.

Wehr *(pl* -e*)* ◇ *die*: **sich zur ~ setzen** to defend o.s. ◇ *das (pl Wehre)* weir.

Wehr|dienst *der* military exercise.

Wehr|dienstverweigerer *(pl* -*)* *der* conscientious objector.

wehren ◆ **sich wehren** *ref* to defend o.s.

wehrlos ◇ *adj* defenceless ◇ *adv*: **jm ~ ausgeliefert sein** to be defenceless against sb.

Wehrpflicht *die* compulsory military service.

wehrpflichtig *adj* liable for military service.

weh|tun *vi*: **jm ~** to hurt sb; **mir tun die Füße ~** my feet hurt. ◆ **sich wehtun** *ref*: to hurt o.s.

Weib *(pl* -er*)* *das fam abw* [Frau] woman.

Weibchen *(pl* -*)* *das* female.

weiblich *adj* - **1.** [Person, Tier, Geschlecht]

female - 2. [Kleidung, Verhalten & GRAM] feminine.

weich <> *adj* soft; **~ werden** *fam* to soften <> *adv* [landen] softly; [bremsen] gently; [liegen] comfortably; **~ gekocht** soft-boiled; **jn ~ machen** to soften sb up.

Weiche (*pl* -n) *die* points (*pl*) *Br,* switch *Am.*

weichgekocht *adj* ⤳ weich.

Weich|käse *der* soft cheese.

weichlich *adj abw* weak.

Weichling (*pl* -e) *der abw* weakling.

Weichsel ['vaiksl] *die:* **die ~** the (River) Vistula.

Weichspüler ['vaiçʃpyːlɐ] (*pl* -) *der* fabric conditioner.

Weide (*pl* -n) *die* **- 1.** [für Vieh] meadow **- 2.** [Baum] willow tree.

weiden *vi* to graze.

weigern ⤳ **sich weigern** *ref:* **sich ~, etw zu tun** to refuse to do sthg.

---

sich weigern

I'm sorry but it's not up to me. Es tut mir Leid, aber das ist nicht meine Entscheidung.

It's out of the question! Das kommt nicht in Frage!

No, I (most certainly) will not! Nein, werde ich (ganz sicher) nicht!

Certainly not!, You must be joking! Kommt gar nicht in Frage!, Du machst wohl Witze!

No way!, Forget it! Vergiss es!, Auf keinen Fall!

Weigerung (*pl* -en) *die* refusal.

weihen *vt* to consecrate.

Weiher (*pl* -) *der* pond.

Weihnachten (*pl* -) (*ohne Artikel*) Christmas; **~ feiern** to celebrate Christmas. ⤳ **frohe Weihnachten** *interj* Merry Christmas!

weihnachtlich <> *adj* Christmassy <> *adv* for Christmas.

Weihnachts|abend *der* Christmas Eve.

Weihnachts|baum *der* Christmas tree.

Weihnachts|geld *das* (*ohne pl*) Christmas bonus.

Weihnachts|geschenk *das* Christmas present.

Weihnachts|lied *das* Christmas carol.

Weihnachts|mann (*pl* -männer) *der* Father Christmas.

Weihnachts|markt *der* Christmas market.

Weihnachts|tag *der:* **erster/zweiter ~** Christmas/Boxing Day.

Weih|rauch *der* incense.

Weih|wasser *das* holy water.

weil *konj* because.

Weile ⤳ **eine Weile** *adv* a while.

Weimarer Republik *die* Weimar Republic.

Wein (*pl* -e) *der* **- 1.** [Getränk] wine **- 2.** (*ohne pl*) [Pflanze] vine.

Wein|bau *der* wine-growing.

Wein|berg *der* vineyard.

Wein|brand *der* brandy.

weinen <> *vi* to cry; **über etw** (*A*) **~** to cry over sthg; **um jn ~** to cry for sb; **vor etw** (*D*) **~** to cry with sthg; **wegen etw ~** to cry because of sthg <> *vt* to cry.

weinerlich *adj* tearful.

Wein|flasche *die* wine bottle.

Wein|keller *der* wine cellar.

Wein|lese (*pl* -n) *die* grape harvest.

Wein|probe *die* wine tasting.

Wein|stube *die* wine bar.

Wein|traube *die* grape.

weise <> *adj* wise <> *adv* wisely.

Weise (*pl* -n) <> *die* **- 1.** [Art] way **- 2.** [Melodie] tune <> *der, die* wise man (*f* wise woman).

weisen (*prät* wies; *perf* hat gewiesen) *geh* <> *vt* [zeigen]: **jm etw ~** to show sb sthg <> *vi* to point.

Weisheit (*pl* -en) *die* wisdom; **kannst du deine ~en nicht für dich behalten?** can't you keep your pearls of wisdom to yourself?

Weisheits|zahn *der* wisdom tooth.

weis|machen *vt fam:* **jm etw ~** to make sb believe sthg.

weiß <> *präs* ⤳ wissen <> *adj* white.

Weiß *das* white.

Weiß|brot *das* white bread (*U*).

Weiße (*pl* -n) <> *der, die* [Person] white person <> *das* [Farbe] white <> *die:* **Berliner ~ mit Schuss** type of wheat beer, with a shot of raspberry syrup.

Weiß|glut *die:* **jn zur ~ bringen** *fam fig* to send sb into a rage.

Weiß|kohl *der* white cabbage.

Weiß|wein *der* white wine.

weit <> *adj* **- 1.** [gen] wide; [Reise, Fahrt] long; **wie ~ ist es bis ...?** how far is it to ...?; **ist es ~?** is it far?; **im ~esten Sinne** in the broadest sense **- 2.** *RW:* **mit seinen Kenntnissen ist es nicht ~ her** he doesn't know enough; **bist du so ~?** are you ready?; **es ist so ~** the time has come <> *adv* **- 1.** [beträchtlich] far; **~ besser** far better; **~ weg** far away; **ihre Meinungen gehen ~ auseinander** they differ widely in their opinions; **~ geöffnet** wide open; **~ verbreitet** widespread; **~ nach Mitternacht** long after midnight **- 2.** [gehen, fahren] a long way; **zwei Kilometer ~ fahren** ODER **gehen** to go two kilometres **- 3.** *RW:* **das**

geht zu ~! that's going too far!; **so ~, so gut** so far, so good. **bei weitem** *adv* by far; **bei ~em nicht genug** not nearly enough. **von weitem** *adv* from far away.

weitaus *adv* by far.

Weite (*pl* -n) *die* - **1.** *(ohne pl)* [weite Fläche] expanse; **das ~ suchen** *fig* to make o.s. scarce - **2.** SPORT distance - **3.** [von Kleidungsstücken] width.

weiter *adv* further; **was geschah ~?** what happened then?; **immer ~** further and further. **nicht weiter** *adv* [nicht weiter fort] no further; [nicht mehr] no longer; **es hat mich nicht ~ interessiert** I wasn't really interested in it. **und so weiter** *adv* and so on. **weiter nichts** *adv* nothing more.

weiterarbeiten *vi* to carry on working.

weitere, r, s *adj* further.

weiterempfehlen *vt* (*unreg*) to recommend; **jm etw ~** to recommend sthg to sb.

weitergeben *vt* (*unreg*) to pass on; **etw an jn ~** to pass on sthg to sb.

weitergehen (*perf* ist weitergegangen) *vi* (*unreg*) - **1.** [gehen] to go on - **2.** [sich fortsetzen] to continue.

weiterhin *adv* - **1.** [immer noch] still - **2.** [künftig] in future.

weitermachen *vi* to carry on.

weiterwissen *vi* (*unreg*): **nicht mehr ~** to be at one's wits' end.

weit gehend *adj* considerable.

weitläufig <> *adj* - **1.** [Haus, Grundstück] spacious - **2.** [Verwandtschaft] distant - **3.** [Schilderung] long-winded <> *adv* - **1.** [angelegt] spaciously - **2.** [verwandt] distantly - **3.** [schildern] at great length.

weiträumig <> *adj* spacious <> *adv*: **etw ~ umfahren** to give sthg a wide berth.

weitsichtig *adj* - **1.** [sehbehindert] longsighted - **2.** [umsichtig] farsighted.

Weitsprung *der* SPORT long jump.

weit verbreitet *adj* common.

Weizen *der* wheat.

Weizenbier *das* wheat beer.

welche, r, s <> *det* which <> *pron* - **1.** [Interrogativpronomen] which (one); **~r von ihnen?** which (one) of them? - **2.** [Relativpronomen - Person] who, that; [- Sache] which, that - **3.** [Indefinitpronomen - in Aussagesätzen] some; [- in Frage- und Konditionalsätzen] any; **hast du ~?** have you got any?

welk *adj* [Blumen] wilted; [Haut] withered.

welken (*perf* ist gewelkt) *vi* to wilt.

Wellblech *das* corrugated iron (*U*).

Welle (*pl* -n) *die* - **1.** [im Wasser] wave - **2.** [beim Rundfunk] wavelength - **3.** RW: **~n schlagen** to create a stir.

wellen **sich wellen** *ref* [Papier] to wrinkle; [Haar] to become wavy; [Teppich] to ruck up.

Wellenbereich *der* waveband.

Wellengang *der*: **hoher ~** heavy seas (*pl*).

Wellenlänge *die* PHYS wavelength.

Wellenlinie *die* wavy line.

Wellensittich *der* budgerigar.

wellig *adj* [Haar] wavy; [Papier] wrinkled; [Gelände] undulating.

Wellpappe *die* corrugated cardboard (*U*).

Welpe (*pl* -n) *der* [von Hund] puppy; [von Fuchs, Wolf] cub.

Welt (*pl* -en) *die* world; **auf der ~** in the world; **die Dritte ~** the Third World; **alle ~** the whole world; **auf die** ODER **zur ~ kommen** to come into the world.

Weltall *das* (*ohne pl*) universe.

Weltanschauung *die* world view.

Weltausstellung *die* world fair.

weltberühmt *adj* world-famous.

weltfremd *adj* unworldly.

Weltkrieg *der* HIST: **der Erste/Zweite ~** the First/Second World War.

weltlich *adj* worldly.

Weltmacht *die* world power.

Weltmeister, in *der, die* world champion.

Weltrang *der*: **von ~** world-class.

Weltrangliste *die* SPORT world rankings (*pl*).

Weltraum *der* space.

Weltreise *die* round-the-world trip.

Weltrekord *der* world record.

Weltstadt *die* cosmopolitan city.

Weltuntergang *der* end of the world.

weltweit *adj* worldwide.

wem *pron* (*Dativ von* wer) (to) who; **~ gehört die Tasche** whose bag is it?; **mit ~ spreche ich?** who's speaking?; **von ~ hast du das?** who did you get it from?

wen *pron* (*Akkusativ von* wer) who, whom; **für ~ ist das?** who is that for?

Wende (*pl* -n) *die* - **1.** [Veränderung] change - **2.** SPORT turn - **3.** HIST: **die ~** the fall of the Berlin Wall.

Wendekreis *der* - **1.** [von Auto] turning circle - **2.** GEOGR tropic.

Wendeltreppe *die* spiral staircase.

wenden (*prät* wendete ODER wandte; *perf* hat gewendet ODER gewandt) <> *vt* (*reg*) [umdrehen] to turn; [Kleidungsstück] to reverse <> *vi* (*reg*) to turn around; **'bitte ~'** 'please turn over'. **sich wenden** *ref* - **1.** (*reg*) [sich ändern]: **sich zum Besseren/Schlechteren ~** to take a turn for the better/worse - **2.** [sich richten]: **sich an jn/etw ~** [hilfesuchend] to turn to sb/sthg; [appellierend] to address sb/sthg; **sich gegen jn/etw ~** to oppose sb/sthg.

Wendepunkt *der* turning point.

Wendung (*pl* -en) *die* - **1.** [Redewendung] idiom - **2.** [Drehung] turn.

wenig ◇ *det* - **1.** [Anzahl] a few; **mit ~en Worten** in few words - **2.** [Menge] little ◇ *pron* - **1.** [Anzahl] a few; **es ist nur ~en bekannt, dass ...** only a few people know that ... - **2.** [Menge] little ◇ *adv* a little; **~ bekannt** little known; **~ erfreulich** not very pleasant. ◆ **ein wenig** *det, pron & adv* a little. ◆ **nur wenig** ◇ *det* - **1.** [Anzahl] only a few - **2.** [Menge] only a little; **er hat nur ~ Zeit** he hasn't got much time ◇ *adv* only a little. ◆ **zu wenig** ◇ *det* - **1.** [Anzahl] too few - **2.** [Menge] too little ◇ *adv & pron* too little.

weniger ◇ *adv* less ◇ *konj:* **sieben ~ drei** seven minus three.

wenigste ◆ **am wenigsten** *adv* least.

wenigstens *adv* at least.

wenn *konj* - **1.** [zeitlich] when - **2.** [konditional] if; **~ ich das gewusst hätte** if I had known, had I known; **~ er nur käme!** if only he would come! ◆ **wenn auch** *konj* even if. ◆ **wenn bloß** *konj* if only.

wer *pron* - **1.** [Interrogativpronomen] who; **~ von euch?** which of you? - **2.** [Relativpronomen] anyone ODER anybody who; **~ mitkommen will** anyone who wants to come - **3.** *fam* [Indefinitpronomen - in Aussagesätzen] somebody, someone; [- in Frage- und Konditionalsätzen] anybody, anyone; **ist da ~?** is there anyone there?

Werbelfernsehen *das* television advertising.

werben (*präs* wirbt; *prät* warb; *perf* hat geworben) ◇ *vi* to advertise ◇ *vt* to attract.

Werbung (*pl* -en) *die* advertising.

Werdelgang *der* development; **der berufliche ~** professional development.

werden (*präs* wird; *prät* wurde; *perf* ist geworden ODER worden) ◇ *aux* - **1.** [zur Bildung des Futurs] will; **sie wird kommen** she will come, she'll come; **sie wird nicht kommen** she won't come; **es wird warm werden** it is going to be warm - **2.** [zur Bildung des Konjunktivs] would; **würdest du/würden Sie ...?** would you ...?; **ich würde gerne ... I** would like to ...; **ich würde lieber noch bleiben** I would prefer to stay a bit longer - **3.** *(perf ist worden)* [zur Bildung des Passivs] to be; **sie wurde kritisiert** she was criticised; **nebenan wird gelacht** there's someone laughing next door ◇ *vi (perf ist geworden)* - **1.** [gen] to become; **Vater ~** to become a father; **er will Lehrer ~** he wants to be a teacher; **alt ~** to grow ODER get old; **rot ~** to turn ODER go red; **verrückt ~** to go mad; **krank ~** to fall ill; **schlecht ~** to go off; **ich werde morgen 25** I'll be 25 tomorrow; **es wird Nacht** it's getting dark; **daraus wird nichts** nothing will come of it; **zu Stein ~** to turn to stone;

zum Mann ~ to become a man; **(na,) wirds bald!** *fam* get a move on! - **2.** *fam* [gelingen, sich erholen]: **sind die Fotos was geworden?** did the photos come out?; **es wird schon wieder ~** *fam* it will be all right.

werfen (*präs* wirft; *prät* warf; *perf* hat geworfen) ◇ *vt* - **1.** [Ball, Stein] to throw - **2.** [Tor, Korb] to score ◇ *vi* to throw; **mit etw ~** to throw sthg. ◆ **sich werfen** *ref* to throw o.s.

Werft (*pl* -en) *die* shipyard.

Werk (*pl* -e) *das* - **1.** [gen] work - **2.** [Betrieb] plant.

Werklstatt (*pl* -stätten) *die* workshop.

Werkltag *der* working day.

werktags *adv* on working days.

werktätig *adj* working.

Werkzeug (*pl* -e) *das* tool.

Werkzeuglkasten *der* tool box.

Wermut (*pl* -s) *der* vermouth *(U)*.

wert *adj:* **~ sein** to be worth; **nichts ~ sein** to be worthless; **viel/tausend Euro ~ sein** to be worth a lot/a thousand euros; **~e Gäste!** dear guests!

Wert (*pl* -e) *der* value; **auf etw** *(A)* **~ legen** to attach importance to sthg; **im ~ steigen/fallen** to increase/decrease in value; **das hat keinen ~!** *fam* it's pointless.

werten *vt* [benoten] to rate; [beurteilen] to judge; [einschätzen]: **etw als Erfolg ~** to consider sthg a success.

Wertgegenlstand *der* valuable object.

wertlos *adj* worthless.

Wertlpapier *das* WIRTSCH bond.

Wertung (*pl* -en) *die* judgement.

wertvoll *adj* valuable.

Wesen (*pl* -) *das* - **1.** [Charakter] nature - **2.** [Mensch] being - **3.** [Lebewesen] creature.

wesentlich ◇ *adj* essential ◇ *adv* considerably. ◆ **im Wesentlichen** *adv* essentially.

weshalb *adv* why.

Wespe (*pl* -n) *die* wasp.

wessen *pron* *(Genitiv von wer)* whose.

Wessi (*pl* -s) *der fam citizen of the former West Germany.*

Westdeutschland *nt* western Germany; [frühere BRD] West Germany.

Weste (*pl* -n) *die* waistcoat *Br,* vest *Am.*

Westen *der* - **1.** [gen] west; **aus ~** from the west; **nach ~** west; **im ~** in the west; **der Wilde ~** the Wild West - **2.** POL West.

Westeuropa *nt* Western Europe.

Westfalen *nt* Westphalia.

Westlküste *die* West Coast.

westlich ◇ *adj* western ◇ *präp:* **~ einer Sache** *(G)* ODER **von etw** (to the) west of sthg.

weswegen *adv* why.

Wettbewerb (*pl* -e) *der* competition.

Wette (*pl* -n) *die* bet. ◆ **um die Wette** *adv:* **um die ~ laufen** to have a race; **um die ~ jodeln** to have a yodelling competition.

wetten ◇ *vi* to bet; **mit jm ~** to bet sb; **um etw ~** to bet sthg ◇ *vt* to bet. ◆ **wetten, dass?** *interj* do you want to bet?

Wetter (*pl* -) *das* [Klima] weather; **schönes/ schlechtes ~** good/bad weather.

Wetter|amt *das* meteorological office.

Wetter|bericht *der* weather report.

wetterfest *adj* weatherproof.

Wetter|karte *die* weather map.

Wetter|lage *die* general weather situation.

wettern *vi:* **gegen jn/etw ~** to curse sb/ sthg.

Wettervorher|sage *die* weather forecast.

Wett|kampf *der* contest.

Wett|lauf *der* race.

wett|machen *vt* to make up for.

Wett|rennen *das* race.

wetzen (*perf* hat gewetzt) *vt* to sharpen.

WG [ve:'ge:] (*pl* -s) *die abk für* Wohngemeinschaft.

Whg. *abk für* Wohnung.

Whirlpool ['wœrlpu:l] *der* Jacuzzi®.

Whisky, Whisky ['vɪski] (*pl* -s) *der* whisky.

wichtig *adj* important; **etw ~ nehmen** to take sthg seriously.

Wichtigkeit *die* importance.

Wichtigtuer (*pl* -) *der fam abw* bighead.

wickeln *vt* to wind; **etw um etw ~** to wrap sthg around sthg; **jn/etw in etw** (*A*) **~** to wrap sb/sthg in sthg; **ein Baby ~** to change a baby's nappy *Br* ODER diaper *Am*.

Widder (*pl* -) *der* - **1.** [Tier] ram - **2.** ASTROL Aries; **~ sein** to be an Aries.

wider *präp geh* against.

widerlegen *vt* [Argument, Behauptung] to refute; **jn ~** to prove sb wrong.

widerlich *adj abw* revolting.

widerrechtlich ◇ *adj* illegal ◇ *adv* illegally.

Wider|ruf *der* [von Aussage] retraction (*U*); [von Befehl] revocation. ◆ **bis auf Widerruf** *adv* until further notice.

widerrufen (*prät* widerrief; *perf* hat widerrufen) *vt* [von Aussage] to retract; [von Befehl] to revoke.

wider|setzen ◆ **sich widersetzen** *ref:* **sich einer Sache** (*D*) **~** to oppose sthg; **sich einem Befehl ~** to refuse to comply with an order.

widerspenstig ◇ *adj* unruly ◇ *adv* in an unruly manner.

wider|spiegeln *vt* to reflect. ◆ **sich widerspiegeln** *ref* to be reflected.

widersprechen (*präs* widerspricht; *prät* widersprach; *perf* hat widersprochen) *vi* to contradict; **jm ~** to contradict sb; **einer Sache/sich** (*D*) **~** to contradict sthg/o.s.

⬚ widersprechen

I don't agree/I disagree. Das finde ich nicht.
I'm not convinced. Das überzeugt mich nicht.
With respect, I think you're forgetting one important point. Verzeihung, aber ich glaube, Sie vergessen da einen wichtigen Punkt.
You have a point, but … Da gebe ich dir Recht, aber …
Nonsense!, Rubbish! (Br) Quatsch!, Blödsinn!

Wider|spruch *der* - **1.** [von Personen] protest - **2.** [in Aussage] contradiction.

Wider|stand *der* - **1.** [Ablehnung & ELEKTR] resistance (*U*); **~ gegen jn/etw** resistance against sb/sthg; **~ leisten** to put up resistance; **auf ~ stoßen** to meet with resistance - **2.** [Hindernis] obstacle.

widerstandsfähig *adj* resilient.

widerstehen (*prät* widerstand; *perf* hat widerstanden) *vi:* **jm/einer Sache ~** to resist sb/ sthg.

widerstrebend ◇ *adj* reluctant ◇ *adv* reluctantly.

widerwärtig ◇ *adj* revolting ◇ *adv:* **sich ~ verhalten** to behave offensively.

Widerwille, Widerwillen *der* reluctance; **~n gegen jn/etw empfinden** to be disgusted by sb/sthg.

widmen *vt* - **1.** [zueignen]: **jm etw ~** to dedicate sthg to sb - **2.** [aufwenden] to dedicate. ◆ **sich widmen** *ref* [sich zuwenden]: **sich jm/einer Sache ~** to devote o.s. to sb/sthg.

Widmung (*pl* -en) *die* dedication.

wie ◇ *adv* how; **~ heißen Sie?** what's your name?; **sie fragte ihn, ~ alt er sei** she asked him how old he was; **~ war das Wetter?** what was the weather like?; **~ gehts?** how are you?; **~ spät ist es?** what's the time?, what time is it?; **~ oft?** how often?; **~ bitte?** sorry?, excuse me?; **~ war das?** *fam* come again?; **~ nett von dir!** how kind of you!; **~ schade!** what a pity! ◇ *interj:* **er kam wohl nicht, ~?** he didn't come, did he? ◇ *konj* - **1.** [vergleichend - vor Substantiv] like; [- vor Adjektiv, Verb, Partikel] as; **~ sein Vater** like his father; **so … ~ … as … as …;** **so viel, ~ du willst** as much as you want; **so groß ~ du** as big as you; **weiß ~ Schnee** as white as snow - **2.** [zum Beispiel] such as, like - **3.** [dass]: **ich hörte, ~ mein Nachbar Klavier spielte** I heard my neighbour playing the piano.

wieder *adv* - **1.** [gen] again; **immer ~, ~ und ~** again and again; **hin und ~** now and again;

nie ~ never again; **was hast du denn (jetzt) ~ angestellt?** what have you done this time?; **er ist ~ da** he is back; **er ging ~ ins Haus** he went back into the house **- 2.** *fam* [wiederum] on the other hand.

wieder|bekommen *vt (unreg)* to get back.

wiederbeleben *vt* to revive.

wieder|bringen *vt (unreg)* to bring back.

wieder erkennen *vt (unreg)* to recognize.

Wieder|gabe *die* [Bericht] account; [von Bild, Ton, Farben] reproduction; [von Musikstück, Gedicht] rendition.

wieder|geben *vt (unreg)* **- 1.** [zurückgeben]: **jm etw ~** to give sth back to sb **- 2.** [mit Worten] to give an account of **- 3.** [technisch] to reproduce.

wieder gut|machen *vt* [Schaden] to compensate for; [Fehler] to put right; [Unrecht] to repair.

wiederher|stellen *vt* to restore; [Kontakt] to reestablish.

wiederholen *vt* **- 1.** [gen] to repeat **- 2.** [lernen] to revise. ◆ **sich wiederholen** *ref* **- 1.** [Sprecher] to repeat o.s. **- 2.** [Ereignis] to recur **- 3.** [Muster] to reappear.

Wiederholung *(pl -en) die* repetition.

Wiederhören ◆ **auf Wiederhören** *interj* goodbye! (on telephone).

wiedersehen *vt (unreg)* to see again.

Wiedersehen *(pl -)* das reunion. ◆ **auf Wiedersehen** *interj* goodbye!

wiederum *adv* **- 1.** [von neuem] again **- 2.** [andererseits] on the other hand.

Wiederver|einigung *die* HIST reunification *(U)*.

wieder verwerten *vt* to reuse.

Wiege *(pl -n) die* cradle.

wiegen *(prät wiegte ODER wog; perf hat gewiegt ODER gewogen) vt* **- 1.** *(unreg)* [abwiegen] to neigh **- 2.** *(reg)* [schaukeln] to rock.

Wiegen|lied *das* lullaby.

wiehern *vi* to weigh.

Wien *nt* Vienna.

Wiener *(pl -) <> der* Viennese <> *adj (unver):* **~ Schnitzel** Wiener schnitzel, *escalope of veal coated with breadcrumbs;* **~ Würstchen** Wiener, *small sausage made of beef, pork or veal.*

Wienerin *(pl -nen) die* Viennese.

wies *prät* ▷ weisen.

Wiese *(pl -n) die* meadow; **auf der grünen ~** outside town.

Wiesel *(pl -) das* weasel.

wieso *pron* why.

wie viel *pron* **- 1.** [Anzahl] how many **- 2.** [Menge] how much; **~ ist zwei mal drei?** what is two times three?; **~ Uhr ist es?** what's the time?, what time is it?; **~ älter/ schneller?** how much older/faster?; **~ Geld das kostet!** what a lot of money it costs!

wievielt *adj* which. ◆ **zu wievielt** *adv:* **zu ~ seid ihr in Urlaub gefahren?** how many of you went on holiday?

wieweit *konj* how far.

wild <> *adj* **- 1.** [gen] wild **- 2.** [unzivilisiert] savage **- 3.** [illegal] illegal <> *adv* **- 1.** [gen] wildly **- 2.** [illegal] illegally.

Wild *das* game.

wildern <> *vi* [jagen - Mensch] to poach; [- Tier] to hunt <> *vt* to poach.

wildfremd *adj* completely strange; **ein ~er Mensch** a complete stranger.

Wild|leder *das* suede *(U)*.

Wildnis *(pl -se) die* wilderness.

Wild|schwein *das* wild boar.

will *präs* ▷ wollen.

Wille *(pl -n)*, **Willen** *der* will; **beim besten ~n** with the best will in the world.

willen *präp:* **um js/einer Sache ~** for the sake of sb/sthg.

willenlos *adj & adv* with a total lack of will.

willensstark *adj* strong-willed.

willig <> *adj* willing <> *adv* willingly.

willkommen *adj* welcome; **ihr seid uns jederzeit ~** you are always welcome. ◆ **herzlich willkommen** *interj* welcome!

Willkommen *(pl -) das* welcome.

willkürlich <> *adj* arbitrary <> *adv* arbitrarily.

wimmeln *vi:* **es wimmelt von ...** it's crawling with ...

wimmern *vi* to whimper.

Wimper *(pl -n) die* eyelash; **ohne mit der ~ zu zucken** *fig* without batting an eyelid.

Wimpern|tusche *die* mascara *(U)*.

Wind *(pl -e) der* wind; **bei ~ und Wetter** in all weathers; **~ von etw bekommen** *fam fig* to get wind of sthg.

Winde *(pl -n) die* **- 1.** [Hebevorrichtung] winch **- 2.** [Pflanze] bindweed *(U)*.

Windel *(pl -n) die* nappy *Br*, diaper *Am*.

winden *(prät wand; perf hat gewunden) vt geh* [flechten] to wind; [Kranz] to make; **etw um etw ~** to wind sthg around sthg. ◆ **sich winden** *ref* **- 1.** [sich schlängeln - Schlange, Aal] to slither; [- vor Schmerz] to writhe **- 2.** *geh* [Pflanze] to wind o.s. **- 3.** [Weg] to wind **- 4.** [vor Verlegenheit] to squirm.

windig *adj* **- 1.** [Wetter] windy **- 2.** *fam abw* [Person, Ausrede] dodgy.

Wind|mühle *die* windmill.

Wind|pocken *pl* chickenpox *(U)*.

Windschutz|scheibe *die* windscreen *Br,* windshield *Am.*

windstill *adj* [Tag] still; [Ecke] sheltered.

Wind|stoß *der* gust of wind.

Windung *(pl -en) die* winding.

Wink (pl -e) der - **1.** [Geste] sign - **2.** [Bemerkung] hint; **jm einen ~ geben** to give sb a tip.

Winkel (pl -) der - **1.** MATH angle; **ein stumpfer/spitzer/rechter ~** an obtuse/an acute/a right angle; **toter ~** fig blind spot - **2.** [Ecke] corner - **3.** [Platz] spot.

winken (perf hat gewinkt ODER gewunken) <> vi - **1.** [zur Begrüßung, zum Abschied] to wave; **jm ~** to wave to sb - **2.** [als Aufforderung]: **einem Taxi ~** to hail a taxi; **dem Kellner ~** to call the waiter - **3.** [Belohnung] to get <> vt: **jn zu sich (hin) ~** to beckon sb over; **jn an einen Ort ~** to direct sb to a place.

winseln vi - **1.** [Tier] to whine - **2.** abw [Person] to whimper.

Winter (pl -) der winter; **den ~ über** for the winter; **im ~** in winter.

winterlich <> adj wintery; [Kleidung, Landschaft] winter <> adv: **~ kalt** cold and wintery.

Winter|reifen der winter tyre.

Winter|schlaf der hibernation.

Winterschlussver|kauf der January sale.

Winter|semester das UNI winter semester.

Winter|spiele pl: **Olympische ~** Winter Olympics.

Winter|sport der winter sport.

Winzer, in (mpl -; fpl -nen) der, die wine grower.

winzig adj tiny.

wippen vi to rock.

wir pron we; **~ beide** both of us; **~ waren es** it was us.

Wirbel (pl -) der - **1.** [von Wasser] whirlpool; [von Wind] whirlwind - **2.** [Aufregung] stir; **viel ~ um etw machen** to make a big fuss about sthg - **3.** [im Haar] cowlick - **4.** [im Rücken] vertebra.

wirbeln (perf hat/ist gewirbelt) <> vi (ist) to whirl; [Schneeflocken, Blätter] to swirl <> vt (hat) to whirl; [Schneeflocken, Blätter] to swirl.

Wirbel|säule die spine.

Wirbel|tier das BIOL vertebrate.

wirbt präs ⊳ werben.

wird präs ⊳ werden.

wirft präs ⊳ werfen.

wirken vi - **1.** [erscheinen] to seem; **sie wirkt auf jeden sympathisch** everybody finds her nice - **2.** [wirksam sein] to have an effect; **beruhigend ~** to have a calming effect; **gegen etw ~** to be effective against sthg - **3.** [beruflich, Bild, Muster] to work.

wirklich <> adj real <> adv really.

Wirklichkeit (pl -en) die reality.

wirksam <> adj effective <> adv effectively.

Wirkung (pl -en) die effect.

wirkungslos adj ineffective.

wirkungsvoll adj effective.

wirr <> adj - **1.** [unordentlich] tangled - **2.** [konfus] confused <> adv - **1.** [unordentlich] in a tangle - **2.** [konfus] in a confused way.

Wirrwarr der ODER das confusion.

Wirt, in (mpl -e; fpl -nen) der, die landlord (f landlady).

Wirtschaft (pl -en) die - **1.** [Ökonomie] economy; **die freie ~** the private sector - **2.** [Gaststätte] pub Br, bar Am.

wirtschaften vi [leiten]: **Gewinn bringend ~** to run things at a profit; **wer wirtschaftet auf diesem Gut?** who runs this estate?; **mit Geld ~** to manage finances.

wirtschaftlich <> adj - **1.** [materiell] economic - **2.** [sparsam] economical <> adv economically.

Wirtschafts|krise die economic crisis.

Wirtschafts|ministerium das Ministry of the Economy.

Wirtschafts|politik die (ohne pl) economic policy.

Wirtschafts|system das economic system.

Wirtschafts|zweig der economic sector.

Wirts|haus das pub, often with accommodation.

Wirts|leute pl landlord and landlady.

Wirts|stube die bar.

wischen <> vt [Boden, Mund] to wipe; [Dreck] to wipe away; [putzen] to clean <> vi: **mit der Hand über die Stirn ~** to wipe one's hand across one's brow.

wispern vt & vi to whisper.

wissbegierig adj thirsty for knowledge.

wissen (präs weiß; prät wusste; perf hat gewusst) <> vt to know; **etw über jn/etw ~** to know sthg about sb/sthg; **immer alles besser ~** to always know better; **weißt du was?** fam you know what?; **ich will nichts von ihm/davon ~** I don't want to have anything to do with him/it; **das musst du ~** it's up to you; **was weiß ich!** fam don't ask me! <> vi to know; **ich weiß!** I know!; **soviel** ODER **soweit ich weiß, ...** as far as I know ...; **nicht, dass ich wüsste** fam not as far as I know; **von/um etw ~** to know about sthg; **man kann nie ~** you never know.

Wissen das knowledge; **nach bestem ~ und Gewissen** to the best of one's knowledge and ability; **meines ~s** to my knowledge.

Wissenschaft (pl -en) die science.

Wissenschaftler, in (mpl -; fpl -nen) der, die scientist; [in Geisteswissenschaften] academic.

wissenschaftlich <> adj academic; [naturwissenschaftlich] scientific <> adv academically; [naturwissenschaftlich] scientific-ally.

wissenswert *adj* worth knowing; [Fakten] valuable.

Wissenswerte *das* useful knowledge.

wittern *vt* - **1.** [riechen] to scent - **2.** [vermuten] to sense.

Witterung (*pl* -en) *die* - **1.** [Wetter] weather - **2.** [Geruch] scent.

Witwe (*pl* -n) *die* widow.

Witwer (*pl* -) *der* widower.

Witz (*pl* -e) *der* - **1.** [Scherz] joke; **~e machen** ODER **reißen** *fam* to crack jokes; **du machst wohl ~e!** you can't be serious! - **2.** [Humor] wit.

Witzbold (*pl* -e) *der fam* joker.

witzeln *vi*: **über jn/etw ~** to make fun of sb/ sthg.

witzig ⬦ *adj* funny; [Idee] original ⬦ *adv* [lustig] funnily.

witzlos *adj* - **1.** [langweilig] dull - **2.** *fam* [überflüssig] pointless.

wo ⬦ *adv* where; **von ~ kam das Geräusch?** where did that noise come from? ⬦ *pron* where ⬦ *konj fam* - **1.** [obwohl] when - **2.** [da] since; **jetzt, ~ alles vorbei ist ...** now that it's all over ...

woanders *adv* somewhere else.

wob *prät* ⤳ weben.

wobei *pron* - **1.** [als Frage]: **~ ist es passiert?** how did it happen?; **~ hast du ihn gestört?** what was he doing when you disturbed him? - **2.** [zeitlich]: **sie stürzte von der Leiter, ~ sie sich ein Arm brach** she fell off the ladder and broke her arm - **3.** [allerdings] although.

Woche (*pl* -n) *die* week; **vorige** ODER **letzte ~** last week; **diese/nächste ~** this/next week.

Wochenende *das* weekend; **am ~** at the weekend. ➠ **schönes Wochenende** *interj* have a nice weekend!

Wochenkarte *die* weekly ticket.

wochenlang ⬦ *adj* lasting for weeks; **nach ~em Warten** after waiting for weeks ⬦ *adv* for weeks.

Wochenmarkt *der* weekly market.

Wochentag *der* weekday.

wöchentlich *adj & adv* weekly.

Wodka (*pl* -s) *der* vodka.

wodurch, wodurch *pron* - **1.** [als Frage] how - **2.** [Relativpronomen] as a result of which.

wofür, wofür *pron* - **1.** [als Frage] what ... for? - **2.** [Relativpronomen] for which.

wog *prät* ⤳ wiegen.

wogegen, wogegen ⬦ *pron* - **1.** [als Frage] against what - **2.** [Relativpronomen] against which ⬦ *konj* [wohingegen] where-as.

woher, woher *pron* - **1.** [als Frage] where ... from; **~ kommen Sie?** where do you come from?; **~ weißt du das?** how do you know that? - **2.** [Relativpronomen] from where.

wohin, wohin *pron* - **1.** [als Frage] where; **~ damit?** *fam* where shall I put it? - **2.** [Relativpronomen] where.

wohl (*kompar* wohler ODER besser; *superl* am wohlsten ODER besten) *adv* - **1.** (*kompar* wohler, *superl* am wohlsten) [zufrieden] well; **sich ~ fühlen** [gesundheitlich] to feel well; [angenehm] to feel at home; **~ oder übel** *fig* like it or not - **2.** [wahrscheinlich] probably; **das ist ~ möglich** quite possibly; **du bist ~ wahnsinnig!** you must be crazy! - **3.** [zum Ausdruck der Unbeantwortbarkeit]: **ob sie ~ gut angekommen sind?** I wonder if they have arrived safely - **4.** (*kompar* besser, *superl* am besten) geh [gut] well; **er weiß sehr ~, dass ...** he knows perfectly well that ... ➠ **wohl aber** *konj* but.

Wohl *das* well-being; **zum ~e der Allgemeinheit** for the common good; **zum ~!** cheers!

wohlbehalten *adv* safe and sound.

Wohlfahrt *die* welfare.

wohlhabend *adj* well-to-do.

wohlig ⬦ *adj* [Wärme, Gefühl] pleasant; [Seufzer] contented ⬦ *adv* contentedly.

Wohlstand *der* affluence.

wohltätig *adj* charitable.

wohlverdient *adj* well-earned.

wohlwollend ⬦ *adj* benevolent ⬦ *adv* benevolently.

wohnen *vi* to live; **wir ~ vorübergehend bei Freunden** we're staying with friends at the moment; **zur Miete ~** to rent, to live in rented accommodation.

Wohngemeinschaft *die* shared flat/ house; **in einer ~ wohnen** to share a flat/ house.

wohnhaft *adj amt* resident.

Wohnhaus *das* house.

Wohnheim *das* [für Studenten] hall of residence; [für Obdachlose] hostel.

wohnlich ⬦ *adj* homely ⬦ *adv* in a homely way.

Wohnmobil (*pl* -e) *das* camper *Br*, RV *Am*.

Wohnort *der* place of residence.

Wohnsitz *der* place of residence.

Wohnung (*pl* -en) *die* flat *Br*, apartment *Am*.

Wohnungsbau *der* housebuilding.

Wohnungsnot *die* housing shortage.

Wohnungssuche *die* flat-hunting.

Wohnviertel *das* residential area.

Wohnwagen *der* caravan *Br*, trailer *Am*.

Wohnzimmer *das* living room.

Wölbung (*pl* -en) *die* [von Himmel] dome; [von Oberfläche] curvature.

Wolf (*pl* Wölfe) *der* - **1.** [Tier] wolf - **2.** *fam* [Fleischwolf] mincer; **jn durch den ~ drehen** *fig* to give sb a hard time.

Wolke (*pl* -n) *die* cloud; **aus allen ~n fallen** *fig* to be astounded.

Wolken|bruch *der* cloudburst.

Wolken|kratzer *der* skyscraper.

wolkig *adj* cloudy.

Woll|decke *die* blanket.

Wolle *die* wool; **aus ~ woollen; sich in die ~ kriegen** *fam fig* to start arguing.

wollen (*präs* will; *prät* wollte; *perf* hat gewollt ODER -) <> *aux (perf hat wollen)*: **er will anrufen** he wants to make a call; **~ wir aufstehen?** shall we get up?; **ich wollte gerade gehen, da ...** I was just about to go when ...; **was willst du damit sagen?** what do you mean by that?; **diese Entscheidung will überlegt sein** this decision needs to be thought through <> *vi (perf hat gewollt):* **das Kind will nicht** the child doesn't want to; **sie will nach Hause** she wants to go home; **ich wollte, es wäre nur schon vorbei** I wish it were over; **dann ~ wir mal!** *fam* let's do it!; **ganz wie du willst** *fam* it's up to you! <> *vt (perf hat gewollt)* - **1.** [gen] to want; **ich will ein Eis** I want an ice-cream; **mach, was du willst** do as you like; **~, dass jd etw tut** to want sb to do sthg; **was willst du mit dem Messer?** what do you want a knife for?; **von jm etwas ~** *fam* to fancy sb - **2.** *fam* [brauchen] to need - **3.** *RW*: **da ist nichts (mehr) zu ~** *fam* there's nothing that we/*etc* can do about it.

Woll|knäuel *das* ball of wool.

womit *pron* [Interrogativpronomen] what ... with; **~ habe ich das verdient?** what did I do to deserve that?

womöglich *adv* possibly.

wonach *pron* [als Frage] for what; **~ suchst du?** what are you looking for?; **~ schmeckt es?** what does it taste of?

woran *pron* [Interrogativpronomen] what ... on; **~ denkst du?** what are you thinking about?

worauf *pron* [Interrogativpronomen] what ... on; **~ wartest du?** what are you waiting for?

woraus *pron* [Interrogativpronomen] what ... from; **~ ist die Tasche?** what is the bag made of?

worin *pron* [Interrogativpronomen] what ... in; **~ besteht der Unterschied?** what's the difference?

World Wide Web [wɜːld waɪd web] *das* EDV World Wide Web; **im ~ on** the (World Wide) Web.

Wort (*pl* -e ODER Wörter) *das* - **1.** (*pl* Wörter) [sprachliche Einheit] word; **~ für ~** word for word - **2.** (*pl* Worte) [Äußerung] word; **etw aufs ~ glauben** to believe every word of

sthg; **kein ~ sagen/glauben** not to say/ believe a word; **mir fehlen die ~e!** I'm speechless!; **mit anderen ~en** in other words; **sie ließ mich nicht zu ~ kommen** she wouldn't let me speak ODER have my say - **3.** (*pl* Worte) [Zitat] quotation - **4.** (*pl* Worte) *geh* [Text] words (*pl*) - **5.** (*ohne pl*) [Zusage] word; **jm sein ~ geben** to give sb one's word - **6.** *RW*: **das ~ haben/erteilen/ergreifen** to have/give/take the floor; **ein geflügeltes ~** a well-known quotation; **für jn ein gutes ~ einlegen** to put in a good word for sb.

Wort|art *die* GRAM part of speech.

wortbrüchig *adj*: **~ werden** to break one's word.

Wörter|buch *das* dictionary.

wortgewandt <> *adj* eloquent <> *adv* eloquently.

wortkarg <> *adj* laconic <> *adv* laconically.

wörtlich <> *adj* word-for-word <> *adv* [übersetzen] word for word; **etw ~ nehmen** to take sthg literally.

wortlos <> *adj* silent <> *adv* without a word.

Wort|spiel *das* pun.

worüber *pron* [Interrogativpronomen] what ... about; **~ lachst du?** what are you laughing about?

worum *pron* [Interrogativpronomen] what ... about; **~ geht es?** what's it about?

worunter *pron* [Interrogativpronomen] under what; **~ hat er gelitten?** what did he suffer from?

wovor *pron* [Interrogativpronomen] what ... of; **~ hast du Angst?** what are you frightened of?

wozu *pron* [Interrogativpronomen] why; **~ dient dieser Schalter?** what's this switch for?

Wrack (*pl* -s ODER -e) *das* wreck.

WS *abk für* Wintersemester.

WSV *abk für* Winterschlussverkauf.

Wucher *der abw* extortion; **5 Euro für ein Sandwich? das ist ~!** 5 euros for a sandwich? that's daylight robbery!

wuchern (*perf* hat/ist gewuchert) *vi* - **1.** (*ist*) [wild wachsen] to grow uncontrollably - **2.** (*hat*) [Wucher treiben] to profiteer.

Wucher|preis *der abw* extortionate price.

wuchs [vuːks] *prät* ⟶ wachsen.

Wuchs [vuːks] *der* - **1.** [Wachstum] growth - **2.** [Gestalt] stature.

Wucht *die* force; **mit voller ~ gegen einen Baum fahren** to smash into a tree.

wuchtig *adj* - **1.** [plump] massive - **2.** [Schlag, Stoß] violent.

wühlen *vi* - **1.** [graben] to dig - **2.** [stöbern] to rummage; **in etw** (*D*) **~** *fam* to rummage through sthg. ➤ **sich wühlen** *ref* [sich graben] to burrow; **sich in etw** *(A)* ~ to dig into sthg.

Wulst *(pl* Wülste*) der* roll.

wund ⬦ *adj* sore ⬦ *adv:* **sich die Füße** ~ **laufen** to walk until one's feet are sore.

Wunde *(pl* -n*) die* wound.

Wunder *(pl* -*) das* miracle; ~ **wirken** to work wonders; **kein** ~**!** no wonder!; **er glaubt, er sei** ~ **was für ein toller Kerl** *fam* he thinks he's God's gift.

wunderbar ⬦ *adj* - **1.** [großartig] wonderful - **2.** [übernatürlich] miraculous ⬦ *adv* [großartig] wonderfully.

Wunder|kind *das* child prodigy.

wunderlich ⬦ *adj* strange ⬦ *adv* strangely.

wundern *vt* to surprise. ➤ **sich wundern** *ref:* **sich (über jn/etw)** ~ to be surprised (at sb/sthg); **du wirst dich noch** ~ you're in for a nasty surprise.

wunderschön ⬦ *adj* beautiful ⬦ *adv* beautifully.

Wunsch *(pl* Wünsche*) der* wish; **nach** ~ **verlaufen** to go as planned; **die besten Wünsche für etw** best wishes for sthg.

wünschen *vt* - **1.** [haben wollen]: **sich** *(D)* **etw** ~ to want sthg; **was wünschst du dir zum Geburtstag?** what would you like for your birthday?; **wünsch dir etwas** make a wish; **(sich** *(D)*)) ~, **dass** to hope that; **ich wünschte, das wäre schon zu Ende** I wish it was already over - **2.** [erhoffen]: **jm etw** ~ to wish sb sthg - **3.** [verlangen] to want; **ich wünsche eine Auskunft** I would like some information; **wie viel Kilo** ~ **Sie?** how many kilos would you like?; **ich wünsche das nicht, dass du so spät heimkommst** I don't want you coming home so late; **was** ~ **Sie?** can I help you?; ~, **dass jd etw macht** to want sb to do sthg - **4.** [zu erhoffen]: **es ist zu** ~, **dass** it is to be hoped that - **5.** [an einen Ort]: **jn weit weg** ~ to wish sb far away - **6.** *RW:* **zu** ~ **übrig lassen** to leave a lot to be desired; **ganz wie Sie** ~**!** certainly!

wünschen

I'd love to meet them. Ich würde sie liebend gerne treffen.

Wouldn't it be wonderful if we could all go? Wäre es nicht toll, wenn wir alle hingehen könnten?

If only he were here! Wenn er nur hier wäre!

I wish I were on a Greek island ... Ich wäre jetzt am liebsten auf einer griechischen Insel ...

I just wish this was all over ... Wenn nur schon alles vorbei wäre ...

wünschenswert *adj* desirable.

Wunsch|traum *der* dream.

Wunsch|zettel *der* ≃ letter to Santa Claus *(asking for presents)*.

wurde *prät* ➡ werden.

Würde *(pl* -n*) die* [Selbstachtung] dignity; **unter js** ~ **sein** to be beneath sb.

würdig ⬦ *adj* - **1.** [würdevoll] dignified - **2.** [entsprechend] worthy; **einer Sache** *(G)* ~ **sein** to be worthy of sthg ⬦ *adv* - **1.** [würdevoll] with dignity - **2.** [entsprechend] appropriately.

würdigen *vt* - **1.** [mit Auszeichnung] to honour; [in Ansprache] to pay tribute to - **2.** [schätzen] to appreciate.

Wurf *(pl* Würfe*) der* - **1.** [Werfen] throw - **2.** [bei Säugetieren] litter.

Würfel *(pl* -*) der* - **1.** [Kubus] cube - **2.** [Spielwürfel] dice.

würfeln ⬦ *vi* [Würfel werfen] to throw the dice ⬦ *vt* - **1.** [mit dem Würfel] to throw - **2.** [in Würfel schneiden] to dice.

Würfelzucker *der (ohne pl)* sugar cubes *(pl)*.

würgen ⬦ *vt* [Subj: Person] to strangle; [Subj: Krawatte] to choke ⬦ *vi* - **1.** [schlucken]: **an etw** *(D)* ~ to choke on sthg - **2.** [Brechreiz haben] to retch.

Wurm *(pl* Würmer*) der* worm.

wurmstichig *adj* worm-ridden.

Wurst *(pl* Würste*) die* - **1.** [gen] sausage - **2.** [Aufschnitt] cold meats *(pl)* - **3.** *RW:* **es ist mir** ~ *fam* I couldn't care less.

Würstchen *(pl* -*) das* - **1.** [kleine Wurst] frankfurter-style sausage - **2.** *fam* [unwichtige Person] nobody; **ein armes** ~ a poor thing.

Würze *(pl* -n*) die* seasoning; *fig* spice.

Wurzel *(pl* -n*) die* [gen & MATH] root; **~n schlagen** *lit & fig* to put down roots.

würzen *vt* - **1.** [Speise] to season - **2.** [Bericht] to spice up.

würzig *adj* [gut gewürzt] well-seasoned; [Bier] rich; [stark duftend] aromatic.

wusch *prät* ➡ waschen.

wusste *prät* ➡ wissen.

wüst *adj* - **1.** [vereinsamt - Gegend] desolate - **2.** [wirr - Haare] wild; [- Durcheinander] chaotic - **3.** *abw* [Schlägerei, Beschimpfung] savage ⬦ *adv* - **1.** [wirr] chaotically - **2.** *abw* [fluchen, schimpfen] savagely.

Wüste *(pl* -n*) die* desert.

Wut *die* rage; **eine** ~ **auf jn haben** to be furious with sb; **seine** ~ **an jm/etw auslassen** to vent one's anger on sb/sthg.

wüten *vi* to rage.

wütend ⬦ *adj* furious; **auf** ODER **über jn** ~ **sein** to be furious with sb ⬦ *adv* furiously.

WWW *abk für* World Wide Web.

x, X [ɪks] (*pl* -) *das* x, X.
X-Beine *pl* knock-knees.
x-beliebig *adj fam* any old.
x-mal *adv fam* countless times.

y, Y ['ypsilɔn] (*pl* - ODER -s) *das* y, Y.
Yacht [jaxt] (*pl* -en) *die* = Jacht.
Yoga, Joga ['joːga] *der* ODER *das* yoga.

Z

z, Z [tsɛt] (*pl* - ODER -s) *das* z, Z.
zack *interj fam* pow!
Zacke (*pl* -n) *die* [von Gabel, Harke] prong; [von Stern] point.
zackig <> *adj* - **1.** [gezackt - Felsen, Kante, Blatt] jagged; [- Stern] pointed - **2.** *fam* [forsch] brisk <> *adv* - **1.** [gezackt] jaggedly - **2.** *fam* [forsch] briskly.
zaghaft <> *adj* hesitant <> *adv* hesitantly.
zäh <> *adj* - **1.** [widerstandsfähig] tough - **2.** [zähflüssig] thick - **3.** [hartnäckig] tenacious <> *adv* - **1.** [langsam] slowly - **2.** [hartnäckig] firmly.
Zähigkeit *die* - **1.** [von Material] toughness - **2.** [von Mensch] tenacity.
Zahl (*pl* -en) *die* number; **römische ~en** Roman numerals; **wir haben keine genauen ~en** we don't have exact figures; **eine gerade/ungerade ~** an even/odd number; **in den roten/schwarzen ~en sein** *fig* to be in the red/black.
zahlbar *adj* payable; **~ an/in** payable to/in.
zahlen <> *vt* - **1.** [gen] to pay - **2.** [Taxi, Hotelzimmer, Reparatur] to pay for <> *vi* to pay;

bitte ~! the bill, please! *Br,* the check, please! *Am.*
zählen <> *vt* - **1.** [die Anzahl ermitteln] to count - **2.** [rechnen]: **etw zu etw ~** to count sthg as sthg - **3.** [wert sein] to be worth <> *vi* - **1.** [gen] to count - **2.** [gehören]: **Monet zählt zu meinen Lieblingsmalern** Monet is one of my favourite painters - **3.** [vertrauen]: **auf jn/etw ~** to count on sb/sthg.
zahlenmäßig <> *adj* numerical <> *adv*: **~ überlegen sein** to have a numerical advantage.
Zähler (*pl* -) *der* - **1.** [Gerät] meter - **2.** MATH numerator.
Zahllgrenze *die* fare stage.
zahllos *adj* innumerable.
zahlreich <> *adj* numerous <> *adv* in great numbers.
Zahlung (*pl* -en) *die* payment.
Zählung (*pl* -en) *die* count; [der Bevölkerung] census.
Zahlungslanlweisung *die* money transfer order.
zahlungsfähig *adj* solvent.
Zahlwort (*pl* -wörter) *das* GRAM numeral.
zahm <> *adj* tame <> *adv* tamely.
zähmen *vt* - **1.** [Tier, Natur] to tame - **2.** *geh* [Neugier, Ungeduld] to curb; [Kinder] to control.
Zähmung (*pl* -en) *die* - **1.** [von Tier] taming - **2.** [von Neugier, Ungeduld] curbing.
Zahn (*pl* Zähne) *der* - **1.** [im Mund] tooth; **einen ~ ziehen** to extract a tooth; **sich einen ~ ziehen lassen** to have a tooth out; **sich** *(D)* **die Zähne putzen** to clean ODER brush one's teeth; **die dritten Zähne** [Gebiss] false teeth - **2.** *RW*: **die Zähne zusammenbeißen** *fam* to grit one's teeth; **jm einen ~ ziehen** to pour cold water on sb's idea.
Zahnlarzt *der* dentist.
Zahnlärztin *die* dentist.
Zahnlbürste *die* toothbrush.
Zahnlersatz *der* (*ohne pl*) false teeth (*pl*).
Zahnlfleisch *das* (*ohne pl*) gums (*pl*).
Zahnllücke *die* gap in one's teeth.
Zahnpasta (*pl* -ten), **Zahnpaste** (*pl* -n) *die* toothpaste.
Zahnlrad *das* cog.
Zahnlradlbahn *die* cog railway.
Zahnlschmelz *der* (tooth) enamel.
Zahnlschmerzen *pl* toothache (*U*); **~ haben** to have toothache.
Zahnlseide *die* dental floss.
Zahnlspange *die* brace.
Zahnlstein *der* tartar.
Zahnlstocher (*pl* -) *der* toothpick.
Zange (*pl* -n) *die* pliers (*pl*); [Beißzange, von Insekt] pincers (*pl*); [für Kohlen, Zucker] tongs (*pl*); MED forceps (*pl*); **jn in die ~ nehmen** *fam fig* to put the screws on sb.

zanken ◆ **sich zanken** ref: **sich (mit jm um etw)** ~ to quarrel (with sb about sthg).

Zäpfchen (pl -) das [Medikament] suppository.

zapfen vt: **ein großes Bier** ~ ≃ to pull a pint.

Zapfen (pl -) der - **1.** [aus Holz] tenon - **2.** [von Bäumen] cone - **3.** [aus Eis] icicle.

Zapfenstreich der: **um 23 Uhr ist** ~ lights out is at eleven o'clock.

Zapf|säule die petrol Br ODER gas Am pump.

zappeln vi to wriggle; **auf seinem Stuhl** ~ to fidget in one's chair; **jn** ~ **lassen** fam fig to let sb sweat.

zappen vi to channel-hop.

zart ◇ adj - **1.** [gen] delicate - **2.** [weich - Haut] soft; [- Fleisch, Gemüse, Pflänzchen] **tender** - **3.** [Gebäck] fine - **4.** [Berührung, Kuss] gentle; [Farbton] soft ◇ adv [berühren, küssen, lächeln] gently.

zart besaitet adj very sensitive.

zartbitter adj [Schokolade] dark.

zärtlich ◇ adj tender, affectionate; [Fürsorge] loving; **zu jm** ~ **sein** to be tender ODER affectionate towards sb ◇ adv tenderly, affectionately.

Zärtlichkeit (pl -en) die [Gefühl] tenderness. ◆ **Zärtlichkeiten** pl [Liebkosungen] caresses.

Zauber (pl -) der magic; **das ist doch fauler** ~! fam abw that's a con!

Zauberei (pl -en) die magic.

Zauberer (pl -) der magician.

Zauber|formel die [Zauberspruch] (magic) spell.

zauberhaft ◇ adj enchanting ◇ adv enchantingly.

Zauberin (pl -nen) die magician.

Zauber|künstler, in der, die magician.

Zauberkunst|stück das magic trick.

zaubern ◇ vi to do magic ◇ vt: **etw aus etw** ~ fig to conjure sthg from sthg.

Zauber|spruch der (magic) spell.

Zauber|stab der magic wand.

Zaum (pl Zäume) der bridle; **sich/etw im** ~ **halten** fig to keep o.s./sthg in check.

zäumen vt to bridle.

Zaumzeug (pl -e) das bridle.

Zaun (pl Zäune) der fence.

Zaun|pfahl der fencepost.

z. B. (abk für zum Beispiel) e.g.

ZDF [tsɛtdeːʔɛf] (abk für Zweites Deutsches Fernsehen) das second German public television channel.

Zebra (pl -s) das zebra.

Zebra|streifen der zebra crossing Br, crosswalk Am.

Zeder (pl -n) die cedar.

Zeh (pl -en) der toe.

Zehe (pl -n) die - **1.** [Fußglied] toe; **jm auf die** ~**n treten** fam fig to tread on sb's toes - **2.** [Knoblauchzehe] clove.

Zehen|nagel der toenail.

Zehen|spitze die tip of one's toes; **auf ~n** on tiptoe.

zehn num ten; siehe auch sechs.

Zehn (pl -en) die ten; siehe auch Sechs.

Zehner|karte die book of ten tickets.

zehnfach ◇ adj tenfold ◇ adv ten times.

Zehn|kampf der SPORT decathlon.

zehnmal adv ten times.

Zehneuro|schein der ten-euro note Br ODER bill Am .

zehntausend num ten thousand; siehe auch sechs.

zehnte, r, s adj tenth; siehe auch sechste.

Zehnte (pl -n) der, die, das tenth; siehe auch Sechste.

zehntel adj (unver) tenth; siehe auch sechstel.

Zehntel (pl -) das tenth; siehe auch Sechstel.

Zehntel|sekunde die tenth of a second.

zehren vi: **von etw** ~ to live on sthg.

Zeichen (pl -) das - **1.** [gen] sign; **jm ein** ~ **geben** to give sb a signal ODER sign; **zum** ~ **seiner Dankbarkeit** as a token of his appreciation; **zum** ~, **dass sie ihm folgen solle** to let her know that she should follow him - **2.** [Symbol] symbol - **3.** [Tierkreiszeichen] (star) sign - **4.** EDV character.

Zeichen|block (pl -blöcke ODER -s) der drawing pad.

Zeichener|klärung die key.

Zeichen|papier das drawing paper.

Zeichen|setzung die punctuation.

Zeichen|sprache die sign language.

Zeichentrick|film der cartoon.

zeichnen ◇ vt - **1.** [darstellen] to draw - **2.** [kennzeichnen] to mark; **das Fell ist interessant gezeichnet** its coat has interesting markings - **3.** [unterzeichnen - Scheck] to sign; [- Aktien, Anleihe] to subscribe ◇ vi to draw.

Zeichner, in (mpl -; fpl -nen) der, die draughtsman (f draughtswoman).

Zeichnung (pl -en) die - **1.** [Bild] drawing - **2.** [von Fell, Tier, Blüte] markings (pl).

Zeige|finger der index finger.

zeigen ◇ vt - **1.** [gen] to show; **jm etw** ~ to show sb sthg; **den Gästen die neue Wohnung** ~ to show the guests round the new flat; **der habe ich es gezeigt!** fam I showed her! - **2.** [Uhr] to say; [Waage] to read ◇ vi to point; **nach Südost** ~ to point south-east; **auf jn/etw** ~ to point at sb/sthg. ◆ **sich zeigen** ref - **1.** [sich verhalten] to show o.s.; **sich nachsichtig** ~ to show lenience, to show o.s. to be lenient - **2.** [sich präsentieren]: **sich in der Öffentlichkeit** ~ to appear in public - **3.** [erkennbar werden]: **schon** ~ **sich die ersten Fehler** the first mistakes are already starting to appear; **es hat sich gezeigt, dass ...** it has been shown ODER demonstrated that ...; **es wird sich ~, ob ...** time will tell whether ...

Zeiger (*pl* -) *der* hand.

Zeile (*pl* -n) *die* - **1.** [von Texten] line - **2.** [Nachricht]: **jm ein paar ~n schreiben** to drop sb a line.

Zeit (*pl* -en) *die* - **1.** [gen] time; **in letzter ~** lately; **im Laufe der ~** in the course of time; **von ~ zu ~** from time to time; **die ~ stoppen** to stop the clock; **~ raubend** time-consuming; **~ sparend** time-saving; **sich** (*D*) **für jn/etw ~ nehmen** to spend time on sb/sthg; **sich** (*D*) **die ~ (mit Kartenspielen) vertreiben** to pass the time (playing cards); **sich** (*D*) **~ lassen** to take one's time - **2.** GRAM tense - **3.** [Zeitung]: **Die ~** *weekly German newspaper.* ◆ **auf Zeit** *adv* temporarily. ◆ **eine Zeit lang** *adv* for a while. ◆ **mit der Zeit** *adv* - **1.** in time - **2.** = zurzeit.

Zeitlalter *das* age.

Zeitanlsage *die* speaking clock.

Zeitlarbeit *die* temporary work.

Zeitlbombe *die* eigtl & fig time bomb.

Zeitldruck *der*: **in ~ sein, unter ~ stehen** to be under time pressure.

Zeitlgeist *der* spirit of the times, zeitgeist.

zeitlgemäß *adj* contemporary, modern.

Zeitlgenosse *der* contemporary.

Zeitlgenossin *die* contemporary.

Zeitlgeschehen *das* (*ohne pl*) current affairs (*pl*).

zeitig *adj & adv* early.

zeitlebens *adv* all my/his/her/*etc* life.

zeitlich <> *adj* chronological <> *adv:* **~ begrenzt sein** to be of limited duration.

Zeitliche *das*: **das ~ segnen** to give up the ghost.

zeitlos *adj* timeless.

Zeitlupe ◆ **in Zeitlupe** *adv* TV in slow motion.

Zeitlpunkt *der* time; **etw zum richtigen ~ tun** to do sthg at the right moment ODER time; **zu diesem ~** at this point in time.

Zeitlraffer *der* time-lapse photography.

Zeitlraum *der* period.

Zeitlrechnung *die*: **vor unserer ~** Before Christ; **nach unserer ~** Anno Domini.

Zeitlschrift *die* [Illustrierte] magazine; [wissenschaftlich] journal.

Zeitlsoldat *der* soldier who enlists for a fixed period of time.

Zeitlspanne *die* timespan.

Zeitung (*pl* -en) *die* newspaper.

Zeitungslannonce *die* newspaper advertisement.

Zeitungsauslschnitt *der* newspaper cutting.

Zeitungslbericht *der* newspaper report.

Zeitungslkiosk *der* newspaper kiosk.

Zeitungslpapier *das* newspaper.

Zeitlunterschied *der* time difference.

Zeitlverlust *der* lost time.

Zeitlverschiebung *die* time difference.

Zeitlverschwendung *die* waste of time.

Zeitlvertrag *der* fixed-term ODER temporary contract.

Zeitlvertreib (*pl* -e) *der* pastime; **zum ~ to** pass the time.

zeitweilig <> *adj* temporary <> *adv* from time to time, on and off.

zeitweise *adv* - **1.** [gelegentlich] occasionally - **2.** [vorübergehend] temporarily.

Zelle (*pl* -n) *die* cell.

Zellstoff *der* cellulose.

Zelt (*pl* -e) *das* tent; **die ~e abbrechen** *fig* to up sticks; **die ~e aufschlagen** *fig* to settle.

zelten *vi* to camp.

Zeltllager *das* camp.

Zeltlplatz *der* campsite.

Zeltlstange *die* tent pole.

Zement *der* cement.

zensieren <> *vt* - **1.** [benoten] to mark - **2.** [kontrollieren] to censor <> *vi* to mark.

Zensur (*pl* -en) *die* - **1.** [Benotung] mark - **2.** [Kontrolle] censorship - **3.** [Behörde] censorship board, censors (*pl*).

Zentilliter *der* centilitre.

Zentilmeter *der* centimetre.

Zentimeterlmaß *das* tape measure.

Zentner (*pl* -) *der unit of measurement equivalent to 50 kg in Germany and 100 kg in Austria and Switzerland.*

zentral <> *adj* central <> *adv* [wohnen, gelegen] centrally.

Zentralafrika *nt* Central Africa.

Zentrale (*pl* -n) *die* - **1.** [zentrale Stelle] headquarters (*pl*) - **2.** [Telefonzentrale] switchboard.

Zentrallheizung *die* central heating.

Zentrifuge (*pl* -n) *die* centrifuge.

Zentrum (*pl* Zentren) *das* centre.

Zeppelin (*pl* -e) *der* zeppelin.

zerbrechen (*präs* zerbricht; *prät* zerbrach; *perf* hat/ist zerbrochen) <> *vi* (*ist*) [Glas, Vase] to break into pieces, to smash; [Freundschaft, Ehe] to break up; **an etw** (*D*) **~** *fig* to be broken by sthg <> *vt* (*hat*) to smash.

zerbrechlich *adj* fragile.

zerdrücken *vt* [Kartoffeln, Bananen] to mash; [Knoblauch, Insekt] to crush.

Zeremonie (*pl* -n) *die* ceremony.

Zerfall *der* [von Gebäude, Denkmal] decay; [von Moral, Diktatur] decline.

zerfallen (*präs* zerfällt; *prät* zerfiel; *perf* ist zerfallen) *vi* to disintegrate; [Mauer, Kuchen, Reich] to crumble; [Molekül] to decay; **in**

etw *(A)* ~ [Molekül] to decay into sthg; [Mauer, Kuchen] to crumble into sthg.

zerfetzen *vt* to tear to pieces; [Brief] to tear up.

zerfleddern *vt* to make tatty.

zerfließen *(prät* zerfloss; *perf* ist zerflossen) *vi* - **1.** [schmelzen] to melt - **2.** [auseinander fließen] to run.

zergehen *(prät* zerging; *perf* ist zergangen) *vi* to melt; **etw im Mund ~ lassen** to allow sthg to dissolve in one's mouth.

zerkleinern *vt* to cut up; [mit Gabel] to mash.

zerklüftet *adj* [Landschaft, Tal] rugged; [Felsen] jagged.

zerknirscht *adj* remorseful; **über etw** *(A)* **~ sein** to be full of remorse for sthg.

zerknittern *vt* to crumple.

zerkratzen *vt* to scratch.

zerlegen *vt* - **1.** [auseinander nehmen] to take apart; **etw in (seine) Einzelteile ~** to dismantle sthg into its constituent parts - **2.** [Geflügel, Wild] to carve up.

zermürben *vt* to wear down.

zerquetschen *vt* to crush; [Kartoffeln] to mash.

zerreißen *(prät* zerriss; *perf* hat/ist zerrissen) <> *vt (hat)* - **1.** [in Stücke] to tear to pieces; [Brief] to tear up - **2.** [Strümpfe, Hose] to tear <> *vi (ist)* to tear.

zerren <> *vt* to drag; **sich** *(D)* **einen Muskel ~** to pull a muscle <> *vi:* **an etw** *(D)* **~** to pull on sthg.

zerrinnen *(prät* zerronn; *perf* ist zerronnen) *vi* - **1.** [Butter] to melt - **2.** [Träume] to fade away - **3.** [Zeit] to slip by.

Zerrung *(pl* -en) *die* pulled muscle ODER ligament.

zerrüttet *adj* [Gesundheit] ruined; [Ehe] broken; **aus ~en Verhältnissen** from a broken home.

zerschlagen *adj* shattered.

zerschneiden *(prät* zerschnitt; *perf* hat zerschnitten) *vt* - **1.** [in Stücke] to cut up - **2.** [verletzen] to cut.

zersetzen *vt* - **1.** [Subj: Säure, Rost] to corrode; [Subj: Fäulnis] to decompose - **2.** [untergraben] to undermine. ◆ **sich zersetzen** *ref* [durch Säure, Rost] to corrode; [durch Fäulnis] to decompose.

zersplittern *(perf* ist zersplittert) *vi* [Holz, Knochen] to splinter; [Glas, Fenster] to shatter.

zerspringen *(prät* zersprang; *perf* ist zersprungen) *vi* to shatter.

zerstäuben *vt* to spray.

Zerstäuber *(pl* -) *der* atomizer.

zerstechen *(präs* zersticht; *prät* zerstach; *perf* hat zerstochen) *vt* - **1.** [beschädigen] to puncture - **2.** [Subj: Insekten] to bite all over.

zerstören *vt* to destroy.

zerstörerisch *adj* destructive.

Zerstörung *die* destruction.

zerstreuen *vt* - **1.** [Blätter] to scatter - **2.** [Demonstranten] to disperse - **3.** [vom Alltag ablenken] to distract - **4.** [Zweifel] to dispel. ◆ **sich zerstreuen** *ref* - **1.** [Menschenmenge] to disperse - **2.** [sich vom Alltag ablenken] to distract o.s.

zerstreut <> *adj* absent-minded <> *adv* absent-mindedly.

Zerstreuung *(pl* -en) *die* distraction.

Zertifikat *(pl* -e) *das* certificate.

zertreten *(präs* zertritt; *prät* zertrat; *perf* hat zertreten) *vt* [Insekt] to stamp on; [Zigarettenkippe] to stub out with one's foot.

zertrümmern *vt* [Schrank, Felsbrocken] to smash up; [Spiegel] to smash.

zerzaust *adj* [Haare] dishevelled.

Zettel *(pl* -) *der* piece of paper; [Nachricht] note; [Einkaufszettel] (shopping) list.

Zeug *das* fam [Sachen] stuff; [Kleidung] gear; **das ~ zu etw haben** fig to have the makings of sthg; **wir müssen uns ins ~ legen** we're going to have to put our backs into it. ◆ **dummes Zeug** *interj* fam rubbish!

Zeuge *(pl* -n) *der* witness.

zeugen <> *vi:* **von etw ~** geh to show sthg <> *vt* to father.

Zeugenaussage *die* statement.

Zeugin *(pl* -nen) *die* witness.

Zeugnis *(pl* -se) *das* - **1.** [von Arbeitgeber] reference - **2.** [von Prüfung] certificate - **3.** SCHULE report.

z. H. *(abk für* zu Händen) attn.

Zickzack *(pl* -e) *der* zigzag. ◆ **im Zickzack** *adv:* **im ~ laufen/fahren** to zigzag.

Ziege *(pl* -n) *die* - **1.** [Tier] goat - **2.** fam [als Schimpfwort] cow.

Ziegel *(pl* -) *der* - **1.** [Stein] brick - **2.** [Dachziegel] tile.

Ziegelstein *der* brick.

Ziegenbock *der* billy goat.

Ziegenkäse *der* goat's cheese.

ziehen *(prät* zog; *perf* hat/ist gezogen) <> *vt (hat)* - **1.** [gen] to pull; [Subj: Tier - Karren] to draw; **etw durch etw ~** to pull sthg through sthg; **etw von etw ~** to pull sthg off sthg; **jn am Armel ~** to tug sb's sleeve; **jn an den Haaren ~** to pull sb's hair - **2.** [herausziehen - Zahn, Korken] to pull out; [- Rüben, Unkraut] to pull up - **3.** MED [Fäden] to take out - **4.** [Brieftasche, Waffe] to take out; [Hut] to doff; **etw aus etw ~** to take sthg out of sthg - **5.** [zeichnen] to draw - **6.** [züchten - Pflanzen] to grow; [- Tiere] to breed - **7.** [anziehen]: **Aufmerksamkeit auf sich** *(A)* **~** to draw attention to o.s. - **8.** [zur Folge haben]: **etw nach sich ~** to lead to sthg; **Probleme nach sich ~** to cause problems - **9.** [aus dem Automaten] to get *(from a vending machine)* - **10.** [anlegen - Mauer, Zaun] to put up; [- Graben] to dig; [- Grenze] to draw ◇ *vi* - **1.** *(hat)* [zerren] to pull; **an etw** *(D)* **~** to pull sthg; **der Hund zog an der Leine** the dog was pulling on the lead *Br* ODER leash *Am* - **2.** *(ist)* [umziehen, sich bewegen] to move; **durch die Straßen ~** to wander through the streets; **eine Blaskapelle zog durchs Dorf** a brass band trooped through the village; **die Vögel ~ nach Süden** the birds are going ODER flying south - **3.** *(hat)* [saugen]: **an etw** *(D)* **~** [Pfeife, Zigarette] to puff on sthg - **4.** *(hat)* [Auto, Motor] to run - **5.** *(ist)* [dringen]: **der Duft zog durchs ganze Haus** the scent floated throughout the house; **in etw** *(A)* **~** [Flüssigkeit] to soak into sthg - **6.** *(hat)* [Kaffee, Tee] to brew - **7.** *(hat)* [bei Brettspiel] to move; **du musst ~!** it's your move! - **8.** *(hat) fam* [Eindruck machen] to go down well; **das zieht bei mir nicht!** that doesn't wash with me! - **9.** *(hat)* [Luftzug haben]: **es zieht** there's a draught. ◆ **sich ziehen** *ref* - **1.** [nicht enden wollen] to drag on - **2.** [sich erstrecken] to stretch.

Ziehharmonika die concertina.

Ziehung *(pl* -en) *die:* **die ~ der Lottozahlen** the lottery draw; **die ~ der Lose** the drawing of lots.

Ziel *(pl* -e) *das* - **1.** [Zielort] destination - **2.** SPORT finish - **3.** [Zweck] goal; **sich** *(D)* **ein ~ setzen** to set o.s. a goal ODER target.

zielen *vi* to aim; **auf jn/etw ~** to aim at sb/sthg.

Zielgruppe die target group.

ziellos ◇ *adj* aimless ◇ *adv* aimlessly.

Zielscheibe die - **1.** [beim Schießen] target - **2.** [Opfer] butt.

zielstrebig ◇ *adj* single-minded ◇ *adv* single-mindedly.

ziemlich ◇ *adj fam*: **mit ~er Genugtuung/Sicherheit** with some satisfaction/certainty; **das war eine ~e Gemeinheit** that was a rather mean thing to do ◇ *adv* - **1.** [sehr] quite; **~ viel** quite a lot - **2.** *fam* [fast] almost.

Zierde *(pl* -n) *die* decoration.

zieren ◆ **sich zieren** *ref* to be coy.

zierlich ◇ *adj* [Person] petite; [Hände] dainty; [Porzellanfigur] delicate ◇ *adv* daintily.

Zierpflanze die ornamental plant.

Ziffer *(pl* -n) *die* figure.

Zifferblatt das face.

zig *adj fam* umpteen.

Zigarette *(pl* -n) *die* cigarette.

Zigarettenautomat *der* cigarette machine.

Zigarettenschachtel *die* cigarette packet.

Zigarillo *(pl* -s) *der* ODER *das* cigarillo.

Zigarre *(pl* -n) *die* cigar.

Zigeuner, in *(mpl* -; *fpl* -nen) *der, die* gypsy.

zigmal *adv fam* umpteen times.

Zimmer *(pl* -) *das* room; **'~ frei!'** 'vacancies'.

Zimmerlautstärke *die:* **in ~** at low volume.

Zimmermädchen *das* chambermaid.

Zimmermann *(pl* -leute) *der* carpenter.

zimmern ◇ *vt* to make *(from wood)* ◇ *vi* to do carpentry.

Zimmerpflanze die house plant.

Zimmersuche *die:* **auf ~ sein** to be looking for a room.

Zimmervermittlung *die* accommodation service.

zimperlich *abw* ◇ *adj*: **sei nicht so ~!** I don't be such a wimp!; **sie ist nicht gerade ~** she doesn't exactly hold back ◇ *adv*: **nicht ~ mit jm umgehen** not to treat sb with kid gloves.

Zimt *der* cinnamon.

Zink *das* zinc.

Zinke *(pl* -n) *die* [von Gabel] prong; [von Kamm] tooth.

Zinn *das* - **1.** [Metall] tin - **2.** [Gegenstände] pewter.

Zins *(pl* -en) *der:* **~en** interest *(U)*.

zinslos *adj* interest-free.

Zinssatz *der* interest rate.

Zipfel *(pl* -) *der* corner.

Zipfelmütze *die* pointed hat.

zirka, circa ['tsɪrka] *adv* about, approximately; **~ 1900** circa 1900.

Zirkel *(pl* -) *der* - **1.** [Gerät] compasses *(pl)* - **2.** [Gruppe] circle.

Zirkus *(pl* -se) *der* circus.

zischen *(perf* hat/ist gezischt) ◇ *vi* - **1.** *(hat)* [Geräusch] to hiss - **2.** *(ist)* [Fahrzeug] to whizz ◇ *vt (hat)* - **1.** [sagen] to hiss - **2.** *salopp* [trinken] to knock back.

Zitat *(pl* -e) *das* quotation, quote.

zitieren ◇ *vt* - **1.** [wiedergeben] to quote - **2.** [rufen]: **jn zu jm/vor etw** *(A)* **~** to summon sb to sb/before sthg ◇ *vi*: **aus etw ~** to quote from sthg.

Zitronat *das* KÜCHE candied lemon peel.

Zitrone *(pl* -n) *die* lemon.

Zitronensaft *der* lemon juice.

zitterig, zittrig *adj* shaky.

zittern *vi* - **1.** [vibrieren - Hände, Körper] to tremble; [- Stimme] to shake; **vor Kälte ~** to shiver with cold - **2.** [Angst haben]: **vor jm/etw ~** to be terrified of sb/sthg - **3.** [sich sorgen]: **um** ODER **für jn/etw ~** to be very worried about sb/sthg.

Zivi ['tsiːvi] *(pl* -s) *der fam* man doing his 'Zivildienst'.

zivil [tsiˈviːl] ◇ *adj* - **1.** [Bevölkerung, Leben] civilian - **2.** [Preise] *fam* reasonable ◇ *adv fam* [anständig] reasonably.

Zivil [tsi'vi:l] ◆ **in Zivil** *adv* [Soldat] in civilian clothes; [Polizist] in plain clothes.

Zivil|bevölkerung *die* civilian population.

Zivil|courage *die* courage of one's convictions.

Zivil|dienst *der community service done by conscientious objectors.*

Zivilisation [tsiviliza'tsjo:n] *(pl -en) die* civilization.

zivilisiert [tsivili'zi:ɐt] *adj* civilized.

Zivilist, in [tsivi'lɪst, ɪn] *(mpl -en; fpl -nen) der, die* civilian.

Zivil|recht *das* RECHT civil law.

zog *prät* ▷ ziehen.

zögern *vi* to hesitate; **mit etw ~ to** delay sthg.

Zölibat *das ODER der* REL celibacy.

Zoll *(pl Zölle ODER -) der* **- 1.** *(pl Zölle)* [Abgabe] duty **- 2.** *(ohne pl)* [Behörde] customs *(pl)* **- 3.** *(pl Zoll)* [Maßeinheit] inch.

Zoll|abfertigung *die* customs clearance.

Zoll|amt *das* customs office.

Zoll|beamte *der* customs officer.

Zoll|beamtin *die* customs officer.

zollfrei *adj* duty-free.

Zoll|kontrolle *die* customs check.

Zöllner *(pl -) der* customs officer.

zollpflichtig *adj* liable for duty.

Zoll|stock *der* folding rule.

Zone *(pl -n) die* zone.

Zoo [tso:] *(pl -s) der* zoo.

Zoologie [tsoolo'gi:] *die* zoology.

Zopf *(pl Zöpfe) der* plait *Br,* braid *Am;* **Zöpfe flechten** to plait *Br ODER* braid *Am* one's hair.

Zorn *der* anger. ◆ **im Zorn** *adv* in anger.

zornig ◇ *adj* angry; **auf jn/über etw** *(A)* **~ sein** to be angry with sb/about sth ◇ *adv* angrily.

zottig *adj* shaggy.

z. T. *(abk für zum Teil)* partly.

zu ◇ *präp (+ D)* **- 1.** [räumlich - Richtung] to; [- Position] at; **~ jm/etw hin** towards sb/sthg; **~ Hause** (at) home; **~ beiden Seiten** on both sides - 2. [zeitlich] at; **~ Beginn** at the beginning; **~ Ostern/Weihnachten** at Easter/ Christmas - 3. [modal]; **~ Pferd** by horse; **~ Fuß** on foot; **~ Fuß gehen** to walk; **~ meiner großen Enttäuschung** to my great disappointment - 4. [stellt Bezug her] about - 5. [in Kombination mit] with; **stell das Glas ~ den anderen** put that glass with the others - 6. [für einen bestimmten Zweck] for - 7. [mit Nennung eines Endzustandes] into; **~ Eis werden** to turn into ice - 8. [aus einem bestimmten Anlass] on - 9. [in Mengenangaben]: **~ viert** in fours; **wir sind ~ viert** there are four of us; **~ Tausenden** in thousands; **Säcke ~ 50 kg** 50 kg bags; **Orangen ~ 25 Cent das Stück** oranges at 25 cents each - 10. SPORT: 3 ~ 2 3–2 ◇ *adv* **- 1.** [übermäßig] too; **~ alt**

too old; **~ sehr** too much - 2. *fam* [zumachen]: **Tür ~!** shut the door! - 3. [zur Angabe der Richtung] towards ◇ *konj* **- 1.** *(+ Infinitiv)* to; **etwas ~ essen** something to eat; **es fängt an ~ schneien** it's starting to snow; **~ verkaufen** for sale; **ohne ~ fragen** without asking - 2. *(+ pp)* to; **die ~ erledigende Sache** the matter to be dealt with. ◆ **nur zu** *interj* go ahead!; *siehe auch* zu sein.

zuallererst, zuallererst *adv* first of all.

zuallerletzt, zuallerletzt *adv* last of all.

Zubehör *(pl -e) das* accessories *(pl).*

zu|beißen *vi (unreg)* to bite.

zu|bekommen *vt (unreg)* [Tür, Koffer] to get shut.

zu|bereiten *vt* to prepare.

zu|bewegen *vt*: **etw auf jn/etw ~** to move sthg towards sb/sthg. ◆ **sich zubewegen** *ref*: **sich auf jn/etw ~** to make one's way towards sb/sthg.

zu|binden *vt (unreg)* to tie up.

zu|bleiben *(perf* ist zugeblieben) *vi (unreg) fam* to stay shut.

zu|blinzeln *vi*: **jm ~** to wink at sb.

Zubringer *(pl -) der* feeder road.

Zucchini [tsu'ki:ni] *(pl -s) die* courgette *Br,* zucchini *Am.*

Zucht *(pl -en) die* **- 1.** [Züchten - von Tieren] breeding; [- von Pflanzen] growing; [- von Perlen] cultivation **- 2.** *geh* [Disziplin] discipline.

züchten *vt* [Tiere] to breed; [Pflanzen] to grow; [Bakterien, Perlen] to cultivate.

Züchtung *(pl -en) die* [Züchten - von Tieren] breeding; [- von Pflanzen] growing; [- von Bakterien, Perlen] cultivation; [Zuchtergebnis - Tiere] breed; [- Pflanze] variety.

zucken *(perf* hat/ist gezuckt) *vi* **- 1.** *(hat)* [unwillkürlich] to twitch; **mit den Schultern ~** to shrug (one's shoulders) - 2. *(ist)* [in eine Richtung - Flamme] to leap up; [- Blitz] to flash.

zücken *vt* **- 1.** *geh* [Waffe] to draw - 2. *hum* [Portmonee, Notizbuch] to whip out.

Zucker *der* **- 1.** [Nahrungsmittel] sugar *(U)* - 2. *fam* [Krankheit] diabetes; **~ haben** to be diabetic.

Zucker|guss *der* icing.

zuckerkrank *adj* diabetic.

Zucker|rohr *das* sugarcane.

Zucker|rübe *die* sugar beet.

Zuckerwatte *die* candyfloss *Br,* cotton candy *Am.*

zu|decken *vt* to cover; **sich/jn/etw mit etw ~** to cover o.s./sb/sthg with sthg.

zu|drehen *vt* **- 1.** [schließen] to turn off - 2. [zuwenden]: **jm den Rücken ~** to turn one's back on sb.

zudringlich *adj* pushy.

zu|drücken *vt* [Auge, Koffer] to close; [Tür] to push shut.

zueinander *adv* to each other; **~ passen** to go together.

zueinander halten *vi (unreg)* to stick together.

zuerst *adv* - **1.** [als Erstes] first - **2.** [am Anfang] at first - **3.** [zum ersten Mal] for the first time.

zulfahren *(perf* ist zugefahren) *vi (unreg)* - **1.** [sich zubewegen]: **auf jn/etw ~** to drive towards sb/sthg - **2.** *fam*: **fahr zu!** get a move on!

Zulfahrt *die* [Zufahrtsweg] access road; [zu einem Haus] drive.

Zufahrtslstraße *die* access road.

Zulfall *der* coincidence; **etw dem ~ überlassen** to leave sthg to chance. ➠ **durch Zufall** *adv* by chance.

zulfallen *(perf* ist zugefallen) *vi (unreg)* - **1.** [Tür, Deckel] to slam shut; [Augen] to close - **2.**: **jm ~** [Preis] to go to sb; [Aufgabe] to fall to sb.

zufällig ◇ *adj* chance *(vor Subst)* ◇ *adv* by chance.

zulfassen *vi*: **fest ~** to grip tightly.

Zulflucht *die* refuge.

zulflüstern *vt*: **jm etw ~** to whisper sthg to sb.

zufolge *präp*: **jm/einer Sache ~** according to sb/sthg.

zufrieden ◇ *adj* contented; [mit Befriedigung] satisfied; **mit jm/etw ~ sein** to be satisfied with sb/sthg ◇ *adv* contentedly.

zufrieden geben ➠ **sich zufrieden geben** *ref (unreg)*: **sich mit etw ~** to be satisfied with sthg.

zufrieden lassen *vt (unreg)* to leave in peace.

zufrieden stellen *vt* to satisfy.

zulfügen *vt*: **jm Schaden/Unrecht ~** to do sb harm/an injustice.

Zufuhr *die* [von Energie] supply; [von Luft] influx.

Zug *(pl* Züge) *der* - **1.** [Bahn] train; **mit dem ~ fahren** to go by train - **2.** [Schar] procession - **3.** [Bewegung - von Vögeln] migration; [- von Wolken] drifting - **4.** [mit Spielfigur] move; **er ist am ~** *eigtl* & *fig* it is his move - **5.** [Schluck] gulp; **in einem ~** in one go - **6.** [beim Rauchen] puff - **7.** [Atemzug] breath; **in vollen Zügen** in deep breaths; *fig* to the full - **8.** *(ohne pl)* [Durchzug] draught - **9.** [Gesichtszug]: **Züge** features - **10.** [Charakterzug] characteristic - **11.** [beim Schwimmen] stroke - **12.** *RW*: **in groben Zügen** in broad outline; **zum ~(e) kommen** to get a chance.

Zulgabe ◇ *die* - **1.** [Zugeben] addition - **2.** [Zugegebenes] free gift. ◇ *interj* encore!

Zugablteil *das* compartment.

Zulgang *der* - **1.** [gen & EDV] access; **~ zu**

etw haben to have access to sthg - **2.** [Zugangsweg] entrance.

zugänglich *adj* - **1.** [Raum, Ort] accessible - **2.** [Information] available; **jm etw ~ machen** to make sthg available to sb - **3.** [Person] approachable.

Zuglbrücke *die* drawbridge.

zulgeben *vt (unreg)* - **1.** [hinzugeben] to add - **2.** [gestehen] to admit.

zulgehen *(perf* ist zugegangen) *vi (unreg)* - **1.** [sich zubewegen]: **auf jn/etw ~** to approach sb/sthg - **2.** [verlaufen]: **auf der Party gehts lustig zu** the party is going with a swing - **3.** *fam* [schneller gehen]: **geh zu!** get a move on! - **4.** [sich schließen - Tür, Koffer] to close; [- Knopf, Reißverschluss] to do up.

zugehörig *adj* that belongs with it/them; **sich jm/einer Sache ~ fühlen** to feel a part of sb/sthg.

Zugehörigkeit *die* [zu Verein, Familie] membership.

zugeknöpft *adj* buttoned up.

Zügel *(pl* -) *der* the reins *(pl)*.

zügellos ◇ *adj* unrestrained ◇ *adv* in an unrestrained manner.

zügeln *vt* - **1.** [Pferd] to rein in - **2.** [Gefühl] to restrain.

Zulgeständnis *das* concession.

zulgestehen *vt (unreg)*: **jm etw ~** [gestatten] to grant sb sthg; [zugeben] to admit sthg to sb.

Zuglführer, in *der, die* senior guard *Br* ODER conductor *Am*.

zugig *adj* draughty.

zügig ◇ *adj* rapid ◇ *adv* rapidly.

zugleich *adv* at the same time.

Zuglluft *die (ohne pl)* draught.

Zuglpersonal *das* train crew.

zulgreifen *vi (unreg)* - **1.** [zufassen] to grab it/them - **2.** [sich bedienen] to help o.s. - **3.** [mithelfen] to do one's bit.

zugrunde, zu Grunde *adv*: **an etw (D) ~ gehen** [sterben] to perish from sthg; [ruiniert werden] to be wrecked by sthg; **einer Sache (D) ~ liegen** to form the basis of sthg; **jn ~ richten** to ruin sb.

Zuglschaffner, in *der, die* ticket inspector.

Zuglunglück *das* train accident.

zugunsten, zu Gunsten ◇ *präp*: **~ js/ einer Sache** in favour of sb/sthg ◇ *adv*: **~ von jm/etw** in favour of sb/sthg.

zugute *adv*: **jm/etw ~ kommen** to prove beneficial to sb/sthg.

Zugverlbindung *die* train connection.

Zuglverkehr *der (ohne pl)* train services *(pl)*.

zulhaben *vi (unreg) fam* to be shut.

Zuhälter *(pl* -) *der* pimp.

zuhause *adv Schweiz* & *Österr* at home; *siehe auch* Haus.

Zuhause *das* home.

zu|hören vi to listen; **jm/einer Sache ~ to** listen to sb/sthg.

Zu|hörer, in der, die listener.

zu|kehren vt: **jm den Rücken ~ to turn one's** back on sb.

zu|knöpfen vt to button up.

zu|kommen (perf ist zugekommen) vi (unreg) - **1.** [sich bewegen]: **auf jn/etw ~ to approach sb/sthg; etw auf sich** (A) **~ lassen** fig to take sthg as it comes - **2.** [zustehen]: **jm ~** to befit sb - **3.** geh [zuteil werden]: **etw kommt jm zu** sb receives sthg; **jm etw ~ lassen** to send sb sthg.

Zukunft die [künftige Zeit & GRAM] future.
  ➡ **in Zukunft** adv in future.

zukünftig <> adj future <> adv in future.

zu|lächeln vi: **jm ~ to smile at sb.**

Zu|lage die bonus.

zu|lassen vt (unreg) - **1.** [erlauben] to allow - **2.** [amtlich - Medikament] to license; [- Auto] to register; **jn zu einer Prüfung ~ to permit sb to take an examination.**

zulässig adj permissible.

Zulassung (pl -en) die - **1.** [Zulassen - von Medikament] licensing; [- von Arzt, Auto] registration; **die ~ zum Studium** acceptance to study at university; **die ~ zur Prüfung** permission to take an examination - **2.** AUTO [Schein] vehicle registration document.

zu|laufen (perf ist zugelaufen) vi (unreg) - **1.** [sich bewegen]: **auf jn/etw ~ to run towards sb/sthg - 2.** [Tier]: **jm ~ to adopt sb** - **3.** [auslaufen] to taper; **spitz ~ to end in a point.**

zu|legen vt [anschaffen]: **sich** (D) **etw ~ to get o.s. sthg.**

zuletzt adv - **1.** [gen] last - **2.** [am Ende] in the end.

zuliebe präp: **jm ~ for sb's sake; einer Sache** (D) **~ for the sake of sthg.**

zum präp - **1.** (zu + dem) to the; **~ Friseur gehen** to go to the hairdresser's - **2.** (untrennbar): **~ Tanzen gehen** to go dancing; **~ Teil** partly; **~ Beispiel** for example; **~ Thema ... on** the subject of ...; **Fenster ~ Garten** window overlooking the garden; siehe auch zu.

zu|machen vt & vi to close; [Mantel] to do up.

zumindest adv at least.

zumutbar adj reasonable.

zu|muten vt: **jm etw ~ to expect sthg of sb; das kannst du ihr nicht ~ you can't ask her to** do that.

Zumutung (pl -en) die: **etw als ~ empfinden** to feel that sthg is unreasonable; **eine ~ sein** to be unreasonable.

zunächst [tsuˈnɛːçst] adv - **1.** [zuerst] first - **2.** [einstweilen] for the moment.

zu|nähen vt to sew up.

Zunahme (pl -n) die increase.

zünden <> vt [Bombe, Sprengladung] to detonate; [Triebwerk] to fire <> vi [Triebwerk] to fire; [Treibstoff] to ignite.

zündend adj fig [Aussprache] rousing; [Idee] exciting.

Zünder (pl -) der detonator.

Zünd|kerze die AUTO spark plug.

Zünd|schlüssel der AUTO ignition key.

Zünd|schnur die fuse.

Zünd|stoff der fig dynamite (U).

Zündung (pl -en) die - **1.** [Zünden] detonation - **2.** AUTO ignition.

zu|nehmen (unreg) <> vi - **1.** [gewinnen]: **an etw** (D) **~ to gain in sthg - 2.** [dicker werden] to put on weight <> vt: **5 Kilo ~ to put on 5** kilos.

Zuneigung die affection; **~ zu jm/etw** affection for sb/sthg.

Zunft (pl Zünfte) die HIST guild.

zünftig <> adj proper <> adv properly.

Zunge (pl -n) die tongue; **auf der ~ zergehen** to melt in the mouth; **die ~ herausstrecken** to stick one's tongue out; **es liegt mir auf der ~** fig it's on the tip of my tongue.

Zungen|spitze die tip of the tongue.

zunichte adj: **etw ~ machen** to ruin sthg.

zu|nicken vi: **jm ~ to nod to sb.**

zunutze, zu Nutze adj: **sich** (D) **etw ~ machen** to take advantage of sthg.

zuoberst adv on top.

zu|ordnen vt: **jn/etw jm/einer Sache ~ to** assign sb/sthg to sb/sthg; **Katzen werden den Raubtieren zugeordnet** cats are classified as carnivores.

zu|packen vi - **1.** [greifen] to grab it/them - **2.** [mitarbeiten] to knuckle down to it.

zu|pfen <> vi: **an etw** (D) **~ to tug at sthg** <> vt - **1.** [Unkraut] to pull up - **2.** [Instrument, Augenbrauen, Haar] to pluck.

zur präp - **1.** (zu + der) to the; **~ Post gehen** to go to the post office - **2.** (untrennbar): **~ Zeit** at the moment; **~ Straße liegen** to face the street; **~ allgemeinen Verwunderung** to everyone's amazement; siehe auch zu.

zurechnungsfähig adj of sound mind.

zurecht|finden ➡ **sich zurechtfinden** ref (unreg) to find one's way around.

zurecht|kommen (perf ist zurechtgekommen) vi (unreg) to get on; **mit jm ~ to get on** with sb; **mit etw ~ to cope with sthg.**

zurecht|legen vt - **1.** [Kleidung, Werkzeug] to lay out ready - **2.** [Ausrede] to get ready.

zurecht|machen vt [herrichten] to get ready. ➡ **sich zurechtmachen** ref [schminken] to put one's make-up on.

zurecht|weisen vt (unreg) to reprimand.

Zurecht|weisung die reprimand.

zu|reden vi: **jm ~ to persuade sb; jm gut ~ to** talk nicely to sb.

Zürich nt Zurich.

zu|richten *vt* to mess up; **jn übel ~** to beat sb up.

zurück *adv* - **1.** [gen] back; **ich bin um 5 Uhr ~** I'll be back at 5 o'clock; **einmal Berlin und ~** a return to Berlin *Br*, a round-trip ticket to Berlin *Am* - **2.** [im Rückstand] behind.

zurück|bekommen *vt (unreg)* to get back.

zurück|bleiben *(perf* ist zurückgeblieben) *vi (unreg)* - **1.** [nicht folgen] to stay behind; **hinter jm/etw ~** to fall behind sb/sthg - **2.** [sich nicht nähern] to keep back - **3.** [mit Leistung, Ergebnis] to fall behind - **4.** [Erinnerung, Schaden] to be left.

zurück|blicken *vi* to look back; **auf etw** *(A)* **~** to look back at sthg; *fig* to look back on sthg.

zurück|bringen *vt (unreg)* to bring/take back.

zurück|erhalten *vt (unreg)* to get back.

zurück|erstatten *vt:* **jm etw ~** to refund sb sthg.

zurück|fahren *(perf* hat/ist zurückgefahren) *(unreg)* ◇ *vi (ist)* - **1.** [zurückkehren] to go back - **2.** [rückwärts fahren] to drive back ◇ *vt (hat)* to drive back.

zurück|fallen *(perf* ist zurückgefallen) *vi (unreg)* - **1.** [gen] to fall back - **2.** [in Rückstand geraten] to fall behind - **3.** [zurückgegeben werden]: **an jn ~** to revert to sb - **4.** [zurückgeführt werden]: **auf jn ~** to reflect on sb.

zurück|fordern *vt:* **etw ~** to ask for sthg back.

zurück|führen ◇ *vt* - **1.** [von etwas herleiten]: **etw auf etw** *(A)* **~** to put sthg down to sthg - **2.** [Person, Sache] to take back ◇ *vi* [Weg] to lead back.

zurück|geben *vt (unreg)* - **1.** [wiedergeben - Geliehenes, Führerschein] to give back; [- Ware] to return; [- Mandat] to give up; **jm etw ~** to give sb sthg back - **2.** [antworten] to answer - **3.** [zurückspielen] to return.

zurückgeblieben *adj* retarded.

zurück|gehen *(perf* ist zurückgegangen) *vi (unreg)* - **1.** [gen] to go back - **2.** [weniger werden] to go down - **3.** [zurückzuführen sein]: **auf jn/etw ~** to go back to sb/sthg - **4.** [zurückgesandt werden]: **etw ~ lassen** to send sthg back.

zurückgezogen ◇ *adj* [Mensch] retiring; [Leben] secluded ◇ *adv* in seclusion.

zurück|greifen *vi (unreg):* **auf jn/etw ~** to fall back on sb/sthg.

zurück|halten *vt (unreg)* - **1.** [Person, Meinung, Gefühl] to hold back - **2.** [Nachricht, Sendung] to withhold - **3.** [an etw hindern]: **jn von etw ~** to stop sb from doing sthg. ➡ **sich zurückhalten** *ref* [sich bremsen] to restrain o.s.; **sich mit dem Trinken ~** to watch what one drinks.

zurückhaltend ◇ *adj* [Mensch] reserved; [Beifall, Äußerung] restrained ◇ *adv* with restraint.

Zurückhaltung *die* restraint.

zurück|holen *vt* to fetch back.

zurück|kehren *(perf* ist zurückgekehrt) *vi geh* to return.

zurück|kommen *(perf* ist zurückgekommen) *vi (unreg)* - **1.** [zurückkehren] to come back - **2.** [zurückgreifen]: **auf jn/etw ~** to come back to sb/sthg.

zurück|lassen *vt (unreg)* - **1.** [hinterlassen] to leave behind - **2.** [zurückgehen lassen] to let go back.

zurück|legen *vt* - **1.** [wieder hinlegen] to put back - **2.** [Kopf] to lean back - **3.** [Geld, Ware] to put aside - **4.** [Strecke] to cover. ➡ **sich zurücklegen** *ref* [sich zurücklehnen] to lie back.

zurück|liegen *vi (unreg)* - **1.** [vergangen sein]: **es liegt zwei Jahre zurück** it was two years ago - **2.** [im Rückstand sein] to be behind.

zurück|müssen *vi (unreg)* to have to go back.

zurück|nehmen *vt (unreg)* - **1.** [Ware] to take back - **2.** [widerrufen - Äußerung, Vorwurf] to take back; [- Antrag] to withdraw; [- Entscheidung, Befehl] to rescind.

zurück|rufen *(unreg)* ◇ *vt* to call back; **sich etw in Bewusstsein ~** to recall sthg ◇ *vi* [am Telefon] to call back.

zurück|schrecken *(perf* ist zurückgeschreckt) *vi* - **1.** [vor Schreck] to start back in fright - **2.** [sich scheuen]: **vor etw** *(D)* **~** to shy away from sthg; **vor nichts ~** to stop at nothing.

zurück|stellen *vt* - **1.** [wieder zurück] to put back - **2.** [nach hinten] to move back - **3.** [Heizung, Lautstärke] to turn down - **4.** [verschieben - Plan, Projekt] to put off; [- Wünsche, Zweifel] to set aside.

zurück|stoßen *vt (unreg)* - **1.** [wieder zurück] to push back - **2.** [wegstoßen] to push away.

zurück|treten *(perf* ist zurückgetreten) *vi (unreg)* - **1.** [nach hinten] to step back - **2.** [von Amt] to resign; **von etw ~** to resign from sthg.

zurück|weichen *(perf* ist zurückgewichen) *vi (unreg)* to shrink back; **vor jm/etw ~** to shrink away from sb/sthg.

zurück|weisen *vt (unreg)* - **1.** [abweisen] to reject - **2.** [Vorwurf] to repudiate.

zurück|zahlen *vt* to pay back; **jm etw ~** [Schulden] to pay sb back sthg; *fam* [aus Rache] to pay sb back for sthg.

zurück|ziehen *(perf* hat/ist zurückgezogen) *(unreg)* ◇ *vt (hat)* - **1.** [gen] to withdraw - **2.** [nach hinten] to pull back ◇ *vi (ist)* [umziehen] to move back. ➤ **sich zurückziehen** *ref* [sich isolieren] to withdraw.

Zu|ruf *der* shout.

zu|rufen *vt (unreg)* to shout.

zurzeit *adv* at present.

Zu|sage *die* - 1. [zu Einladung] acceptance *(U)* - 2. [Versprechen] promise.

zu|sagen ◇ *vt* [versprechen] to promise; **jm etw ~** to promise sb sthg ◇ *vi* - 1. [bei Einladung] to accept - 2. [gefallen]: **jm ~** to appeal to sb.

zusammen *adv* - 1. [gen] together - 2. [insgesamt] altogether; **das macht ~ 10 Euro** that's 10 euros altogether.

Zusammenarbeit *die* collaboration.

zusammen|arbeiten *vi* to work together.

zusammen|brauen *vt fam* to concoct. ➤ **sich zusammenbrauen** *ref* to be brewing.

zusammen|brechen *(perf* ist zusammengebrochen) *vi (unreg)* - 1. [gen] to collapse - 2. [Verkehr] to come to a standstill.

zusammen|bringen *vt (unreg)* - 1. [beschaffen] to get together - 2. [Personen] to bring together - 3. [Gelerntes] to manage.

Zusammen|bruch *der* collapse.

zusammen|fahren *(perf* ist zusammengefahren) *vi (unreg)* [erschrecken] to start.

zusammen|fallen *(perf* ist zusammengefallen) *vi (unreg)* - 1. [einsinken]: **(in sich) ~** to collapse - 2. [abmagern] to become emaciated - 3. [Termine, Flächen] to coincide.

zusammen|fassen *vt* to summarize.

 zusammenfassen

All in all, it was a very enjoyable day. Es war insgesamt ein sehr schöner Tag.

When all is said and done, she's still my sister! Schließlich ist sie immer noch meine Schwester!

Anyway, to cut a long story short, she's decided to come next week instead. Um es kurz zu machen, sie hat beschlossen, stattdessen nächste Woche zu kommen.

All of which goes to show that you were wrong. Was nichts anderes heißt, als dass du dich geirrt hast.

To put it in a nutshell, we can't go. Kurz gesagt, wir können nicht fahren.

Zusammen|fassung *die* summary.

zusammen|gehören *vi* to belong together.

zusammen|halten *(unreg)* ◇ *vi* - 1. [Personen] to stick together - 2. [Teile] to hold together ◇ *vt* - 1. [verbunden halten] to hold together - 2. [beisammenhalten - Herde,

Gruppe] to keep together; [- Geld] to hang on to.

Zusammen|hang *der* connection; **etw in ~ mit etw bringen** to make a connection between sthg and sthg; **im ~ mit etw stehen** to be connected with sthg.

zusammen|hängen *vi (unreg)* - 1. [befestigt sein] to be joined (together) - 2. [ursächlich]: **mit etw ~** to be connected with sthg.

zusammenhängend *adj* coherent.

zusammenhanglos,   zusammenhangslos ◇ *adj* incoherent ◇ *adv* incoherently.

zusammen|kommen *(perf* ist zusammengekommen) *vi (unreg)* - 1. [Personen] to meet - 2. [Ereignisse, Unglück] to happen together; **heute kam wirklich alles zusammen** everything that could go wrong today, did go wrong - 3. [sich sammeln - Spenden] to be collected; [- Unkosten, Verluste] to mount up.

zusammen|legen ◇ *vt* - 1. [sammeln, zusammen unterbringen] to put together - 2. [falten] to fold up - 3. [Termine, Gruppen] to combine ◇ *vi* [gemeinsam bezahlen] to club together.

zusammen|nehmen *vt (unreg)* to summon up. ➤ **sich zusammennehmen** *ref* to pull o.s. together.

zusammen|passen *vi* [Farben, Kleidungsstücke] to go together; [Menschen] to suit each other.

zusammen|prallen *(perf* ist zusammengeprallt) *vi* to collide.

zusammen|rechnen *vt* to add up.

zusammen|reißen ➤ **sich zusammenreißen** *ref (unreg) fam* to pull o.s. together.

zusammen|schlagen *(perf* hat/ist zusammengeschlagen) *(unreg)* ◇ *vt (hat)* - 1. [gegeneinanderschlagen - Hände] to clap; [- Absätze] to click - 2. *fam* [niederschlagen] to beat up ◇ *vi (ist)*: **über jm/etw ~** to engulf sb/sthg.

zusammen|schließen *vt (unreg)* to lock together. ➤ **sich zusammenschließen** *ref* to join forces.

Zusammen|schluss *der* joining together *(U)*.

Zusammensein *das* being together.

zusammen|setzen *vt* to put together. ➤ **sich zusammensetzen** *ref* - 1. [bestehen]: **sich aus etw ~** to be composed of sthg - 2. [zusammentreffen] to get together; **sich mit jm ~** to get together with sb.

Zusammensetzung *(pl -en) die* composition.

zusammen|stellen *vt* to put together.

Zusammen|stoß *der* [von Fahrzeugen] crash; *fig* [von Menschen] clash.

zusammen|stoßen *(perf* ist zusammengestoßen) *vi (unreg)* to crash.

zusammen|treffen (*perf* ist zusammengetroffen) *vi* (*unreg*) - **1.** [Personen] to meet; **mit jm ~** to meet sb - **2.** [Ereignisse] to coincide.

Zusammen|treffen *das* [mit Freunden] meeting; [von Ereignissen] coincidence.

zusammen|tun *vt* (*unreg*) *fam* to put together. ➤ **sich zusammentun** *ref* to get together; **sich mit jm ~** to get together with sb.

zusammen|zählen *vt* to count up.

zusammen|ziehen (*perf* hat/ist zusammengezogen) (*unreg*) ◇ *vt* (*hat*) - **1.** [enger machen - Schlinge, Netz] to pull tight; [- Augenbrauen] to knit - **2.** [sammeln] to mass ◇ *vi* (*ist*) [in eine Wohnung] to move in together; **mit jm ~** to move in with sb. ➤ **sich zusammenziehen** *ref* [enger, kleiner werden] to contract.

zusammen|zucken (*perf* ist zusammengezuckt) *vi* to give a start.

Zu|satz *der* addition; [in Nahrungsmittel] additive; [in Vertrag] rider.

Zusatz|gerät *das* attachment.

zusätzlich ◇ *adj* additional ◇ *adv* in addition.

Zuschauer, in (*mpl* -; *fpl* -nen) *der, die* [im Theater, Kino] member of the audience; [im Stadion] spectator; [bei Unfall, Prügelei] onlooker. ➤ **Zuschauer** *pl* [im Theater, Kino] audience (*sg*).

zu|schicken *vt*: **jm etw ~** to send sthg to sb.

zu|schieben *vt* (*unreg*) - **1.** [schließen] to push shut - **2.** [hinschieben]: **jm etw ~** to push sthg over to sb - **3.** [Schuld]: **jm etw ~** to push sthg onto sb.

Zu|schlag *der* - **1.** [zusätzlicher Betrag - auf Lohn] additional pay (*U*); [- auf Ware] surcharge - **2.** [zur Fahrkarte] supplement - **3.** [Zusage]: **den ~ erhalten** [Firma] to be awarded the contract; [Gebot] to be successful.

zu|schlagen (*perf* hat/ist zugeschlagen) (*unreg*) ◇ *vi* - **1.** (*ist*) [Tür, Deckel] to slam shut - **2.** (*hat*) [Person] to hit out - **3.** (*hat*) [Einsatztruppe, Terrorist] to strike - **4.** (*hat*) *fam* [kaufen] to go for it ◇ *vt* (*hat*) - **1.** [Tür, Deckel] to slam shut - **2.** [zusprechen]: **jm etw ~** [einem Bieter] to knock sthg down to sb; [einer Firma] to award sthg to sb.

zu|schließen (*unreg*) ◇ *vt* to lock ◇ *vi* to lock up.

zu|schnappen (*perf* hat/ist zugeschnappt) *vi* - **1.** (*hat*) [Hund] to snap - **2.** (*ist*) [Fälle, Tür] to click shut.

zu|schneiden *vt* (*unreg*) [Stoff, Kleidungsstück] to cut out; [Brett] to cut to size.

zu|schrauben *vt* [Flasche, Glas] to screw the top on; [Deckel] to screw on.

zu|schreiben *vt* (*unreg*): **jm etw ~** to attribute sthg to sb.

Zu|schrift *die* reply.

zuschulden, zu Schulden *adv*: **sich** (*D*) **etwas ~ kommen lassen** to do wrong.

Zu|schuss *der* [öffentlich] grant; [privat] contribution.

zu|sehen *vi* (*unreg*) - **1.** [zuschauen] to watch; **jm bei etw ~** to watch sb doing sthg; **bei etw ~** to watch sthg - **2.** [veranlassen]: **~, dass ...** to make sure that ...; **sieh zu, dass du wegkommst!** *fam* go away!

zu sein (*perf* ist zu gewesen) *vi* (*unreg*) to be closed.

zu|setzen ◇ *vt* - **1.** [Zutat] to add - **2.** [Geld] to pay out ◇ *vi* [schaden]: **jm ~** to take it out of sb.

zu|sichern *vt*: **jm etw ~** to assure sb of sthg.

zu|spitzen ➤ **sich zuspitzen** *ref* to intensify.

Zu|stand *der* state; [Gesundheitszustand] condition; **in gutem/schlechtem ~** in good/bad condition. ➤ **Zustände** *pl* situation.

zustande, zu Stande *adv*: **etw ~ bringen** to bring sthg about; **~ kommen** to come about.

zuständig *adj* [verantwortlich] responsible; [Amtssprache] relevant.

zu|stehen *vi* (*unreg*): **etw steht jm zu** sb is entitled to sthg.

zu|steigen (*perf* ist zugestiegen) *vi* (*unreg*) to get on.

zu|stimmen *vi* to agree; **jm ~** to agree with sb.

 zustimmen

I quite agree. Das finde ich auch.
That's exactly what I was thinking. Genau das habe ich auch gedacht.
I couldn't have put it better myself. Das hätte ich nicht besser sagen können.
I don't see why. Ich wüsste nicht, wieso.
That's fine by me. Ich habe nichts dagegen.

Zu|stimmung *die* agreement; **zu etw seine ~ geben** to give one's consent to sthg.

zu|stoßen (*perf* hat/ist zugestoßen) (*unreg*) ◇ *vt* (*hat*) [schließen] to push shut ◇ *vi* - **1.** (*hat*) [mit Waffe] to make a stab - **2.** (*ist*) [geschehen]: **jm ~** to happen to sb.

Zu|strom *der* (*ohne pl*) stream.

zutage, zu Tage *adv*: **~ treten** ODER **kommen** to come to the surface; *fig* to come to light.

Zutaten *pl* ingredients.

zutiefst *adv* deeply.

zu|trauen *vt*: **jm/sich etw ~** to think sb/one is capable of sthg; **ich hätte ihm mehr Geschick zugetraut** I would have expected him to show more skill.

zutraulich ◇ *adj* trusting ◇ *adv* trustingly.

zu|treffen *vi (unreg)* to be correct; **auf jn/
etw ~** to apply to sb/sthg.

Zutritt *der* entry; **~ haben** to have access;
'~ verboten!' 'no entry'.

Zutun *das:* **ohne js ~** without sb's involvement.

zuverlässig ◇ *adj* reliable ◇ *adv* reliably.

Zuverlässigkeit *die* reliability.

Zuversicht *die* confidence.

zuversichtlich ◇ *adj* confident ◇ *adv*
confidently.

zu viel *pron* too much.

zuvor *adv* before.

zuvor|kommen (*perf* ist zuvorgekommen)
vi (unreg): **jm ~** to beat sb to it.

zuvorkommend *adj* obliging.

Zuwachs ['tsu:vaks] *der* growth; **etw auf
~ kaufen** to buy sthg big enough to allow
room for growth.

zu|wachsen ['tsu:vaksn̩] (*perf* ist zuge-
wachsen) *vi (unreg)* to become overgrown.

zuwege, zu Wege *adv:* **etw ~ bringen** to
bring sthg about.

zu|weisen *vt (unreg):* **jm etw ~** to allocate
sthg to sb.

zu|wenden *vt:* **jm den Rücken ~** to turn
one's back on sb. ◆ **sich zuwenden** *ref:*
sich jm/etw ~ to turn to sb/sthg.

Zuwendung *die* **- 1.** [Aufmerksamkeit] attention **- 2.** [Geld] contribution.

zu wenig *pron* not enough.

zuwider *adv:* **mir sind Würmer ~** I find
worms revolting.

zu|winken *vi:* **jm ~** to wave to sb.

zu|ziehen (*perf* hat/ist zugezogen) (*unreg*)
◇ *vt (hat)* **- 1.** [schließen - Tür, Fenster] to pull
shut; [- Vorhang, Reißverschluss] to close;
[- Schlinge, Knoten] to pull tight **- 2.** [Spezia-
list] to bring in **- 3.** [verschaffen]: **sich** (D) **etw
~** [Erkältung] to catch sthg; [Zorn, Neid] to
incur sthg ◇ *vi (ist)* [an einen Ort ziehen] to
move into the area/town/*etc*.

zuzüglich *präp* (+G, D) plus.

ZVS [tsɛtfauˈʔɛs] (*abk für* Zentralstelle für die
Vergabe von Studienplätzen) *die* ≃ UCAS
*Br, German organization responsible for the allo-
cation of student places.*

zwang *prät* ▷ zwingen.

Zwang (*pl* Zwänge) *der* [körperlich] force;
[Druck] pressure; [gesellschaftlich] constraint; [innerer] compulsion.

zwängen *vt* to force; **sich/etw in etw** (A) **~**
to force o.s./sthg into sthg.

zwanglos ◇ *adj* informal ◇ *adv* informally.

Zwangs|lage *die* predicament.

zwangsläufig ◇ *adj* inevitable ◇ *adv*
inevitably; **etw ~ tun müssen** to be bound to
do sthg.

zwanzig *num* twenty; *siehe auch* sechs.

Zwanzig *die* (*ohne pl*) twenty; *siehe auch*
Sechs.

Zwanzigeuro|schein *der* twenty-euro
note *Br* ODER bill *Am.*

zwanzigste, r, s *adj* twentieth; *siehe auch*
sechste.

Zwanzigste (*pl* -n) *der, die, das* twentieth;
siehe auch Sechste.

zwar *adv:* das ist **~** schön, aber viel zu teuer
it's nice but far too expensive; **und ~ ... ...** to
be exact; **ihr geht jetzt ins Bett, und ~ sofort!**
go to bed right now, and I mean right now!

Zweck (*pl* -e) *der* **- 1.** [Ziel] purpose; **für einen guten ~** for a good cause; **seinen ~ erfüllen** to serve its purpose; **zu diesem ~** for this
purpose **- 2.** [Sinn] point.

zwecklos *adj* pointless.

zwei *num* two; **für ~ essen** *fig* to eat enough
for two; *siehe auch* sechs.

Zwei (*pl* -en) *die* **- 1.** [Zahl] two **- 2.** [Schulno-
te] ≃ B, *mark of 2 on a scale from 1 to 6; siehe
auch* Sechs.

Zweibett|zimmer *das* twin room.

zweideutig ◇ *adj* **- 1.** [mehrdeutig] ambiguous **- 2.** [frivol] suggestive ◇ *adv*
- 1. [mehrdeutig] ambiguously **- 2.** [frivol]
suggestively.

zweierlei *num* **- 1.** [zwei verschiedene] odd
- 2. [etwas anderes]: **es ist ~** it is two different
things.

Zweieuro|stück *das* two-euro piece.

zweifach ◇ *adj* double; **die ~e Menge**
twice as much; **in ~er Ausfertigung** in duplicate; **der ~e Gewinner** the two-times winner ◇ *adv* twice.

Zweifel (*pl* -) *der* doubt; **~ an etw** (D)
doubts (*pl*) about sthg; **ohne ~** without
doubt.

zweifelhaft *adj* **- 1.** [unsicher] doubtful
- 2. [anrüchig] dubious.

zweifellos *adv* undoubtedly.

zweifeln *vi* to doubt; **an etw** (D) **~** to doubt
sthg.

Zweifels|fall *der:* **im ~** in case of doubt.

Zweig (*pl* -e) *der* branch.

Zweig|stelle *die* branch.

zweihundert *num* two hundred.

zweimal *adv* twice.

Zwei|rad *das* two-wheeler.

zweiseitig *adj* **- 1.** [zwei Seiten umfassend]
two-page (*vor Subst*) **- 2.** [gegenseitig] bilat-
eral.

zweisprachig ◇ *adj* bilingual ◇ *adv*
[aufwachsen] bilingually; [geschrieben] in
two languages.

zweistellig *adj* two-figure (*vor Subst*).

zweistöckig *adj* two-storey (*vor Subst*).

zweit ◆ **zu zweit** *adv:* sie waren zu ~

there were two of them; **wir sind zu ~ ins Kino gegangen** two of us went to the cinema.

zweitausend *num* two thousand.

zweitbeste, r, s *adj* second best.

zweite, r, s *adj* second; *siehe auch* sechste.

Zweite (*pl* -n) *der, die, das* second; **wie kein ~r** like nobody else; *siehe auch* Sechste.

zweiteilig *adj* [Kleid, Badeanzug] two-piece (*vor Subst*); [Film] two-part (*vor Subst*); [Ausgabe] two-volume (*vor Subst*).

zweitens *adv* secondly.

zweitrangig *adj* [Frage, Aufgabe] of secondary importance; [Bedeutung] secondary.

Zweitwagen *der* second car.

Zweizimmerwohnung *die* two-room flat *Br* ODER apartment *Am*.

Zwerchfell *das* diaphragm.

Zwerg (*pl* -e) *der* dwarf.

Zwetsche, Zwetschge (*pl* -n) *die* plum.

zwicken *vt & vi* to pinch.

Zwieback (*pl* Zwiebäcke ODER -e) *der* rusk.

Zwiebel (*pl* -n) *die* onion.

zwielichtig *adj* shady.

zwiespältig *adj* [Gefühle] conflicting; [Charakter] contradictory.

Zwilling (*pl* -e) *der* - **1.** [Person] twin - **2.** ASTROL Gemini; **~ sein** to be a Gemini. **◆ Zwillinge** *pl* ASTROL Gemini (*sg*).

Zwillingsbruder *der* twin brother.

Zwillingsschwester *die* twin sister.

zwingen (*prät* zwang; *perf* hat gezwungen) *vt* to force; **jn zu etw ~** to force sb to do sthg. **◆ sich zwingen** *ref* to force o.s.; **sich zu etw ~** to force o.s. to do sthg.

zwinkern *vi* [als Reflex] to blink; [als Zeichen] to wink.

Zwirn (*pl* -e) *der* thread.

zwischen *präp* (+D, A) - **1.** [gen] between - **2.** [inmitten] amongst.

zwischendurch *adv* - **1.** [zeitlich] in the meantime - **2.** [räumlich] here and there.

Zwischenfall *der* incident. **◆ Zwischenfälle** *pl* clashes.

Zwischenlandung *die* stopover.

Zwischenprüfung *die* UNI intermediate examination.

Zwischenraum *der* gap.

Zwischenruf *der* interjection.

Zwischenzeit *die* time in between; **in der ~** in the meantime.

zwitschern *vi* to twitter.

zwölf *num* twelve; *siehe auch* sechs.

Zwölf (*pl* -en) *die* twelve; *siehe auch* Sechs.

zwölfte, r, s *adj* twelfth; *siehe auch* sechste.

Zwölfte (*pl* -n) *der, die, das* twelfth; *siehe auch* Sechste.

zwölftel *adj* (*unver*) twelfth; *siehe auch* sechstel.

Zwölftel (*pl* -) *das* twelfth; *siehe auch* Sechstel.

Zyankali [tsya:n'ka:li] *das* potassium cyanide.

Zylinder [tsi'lɪndɐ] (*pl* -) *der* - **1.** [Hut] top hat - **2.** MATH & TECH cylinder.

Zynismus [tsy'nɪsmʊs] *der* cynicism.

Zypern *nt* Cyprus.

Zypresse [tsy'prɛsə] (*pl* -n) *die* cypress.

Zyste ['tsʏstə] (*pl* -n) *die* MED cyst.

z. Z. (*abk für* zur Zeit) = zurzeit.

a¹ (*pl* **a's** OR **a's**), **A** (*pl* **As** OR **A's**) [eɪ] *n* [letter] a *das*, A *das*; **to get from A to B** von A nach B kommen. **◆ A** *n* **- 1.** MUS [note] A *das* **- 2.** SCH [mark] ≃ eins.

a² [stressed eɪ, unstressed ə] (before vowel or silent "h" **an** [stressed æn, unstressed ən]) *indef art* **- 1.** [gen] ein, -e; **~ woman** eine Frau; **~ restaurant** ein Restaurant; **~ friend** ein Freund, eine Freundin; **an apple** ein Apfel **- 2.** [referring to occupation]: **I'm ~ doctor** ich bin Arzt **- 3.** [instead of the number one] ein, -e; **~ hundred** hundert; **~ hundred and twenty** hundertzwanzig; **for ~ week** eine Woche lang **- 4.** [in prices, ratios] pro; **£2 ~ kilo** £2 pro Kilo; **£10 ~ head** £10 pro Kopf; **twice ~ week/year** zweimal in der Woche/im OR pro Jahr; **50 km an hour** 50 km pro Stunde **- 5.**: **not ~ kein**, -e; **not ~ soul** kein Mensch; **I haven't understood ~ (single) word** ich habe kein (einziges) Wort verstanden.

AA *n* (*abbr of* Automobile Association) ≃ ADAC *der*.

AAA *n* (*abbr of* American Automobile Association) ≃ ADAC *der*.

AB *n Am* (*abbr of* Bachelor of Arts) *Hochschulabschluss in einem geisteswissenschaftlichen Fach nach drei- oder vierjährigem Studium.*

aback [ə'bæk] *adv*: **to be taken ~ (by sthg)** schockiert sein (über etw (A)).

abandon [ə'bændən] ◇ *vt* **- 1.** [leave, desert] verlassen **- 2.** [give up] aufgeben ◇ *n* (U): **with ~** ausgelassen.

abashed [ə'bæʃt] *adj* verlegen, beschämt.

abate [ə'beɪt] *vi fml* nachlassen.

abattoir ['æbətwɑː'] *n* Schlachthaus *das*.

abbey ['æbɪ] *n* Abtei *die*.

abbot ['æbət] *n* Abt *der*.

abbreviate [ə'briːvɪeɪt] *vt* abkürzen.

abbreviation [ə,briːvɪ'eɪʃn] *n* Abkürzung *die*.

ABC *n* **- 1.** [alphabet] ABC *das* **- 2.** *fig* [basics]: **the ~ of** das ABC (+ G).

abdicate ['æbdɪkeɪt] ◇ *vi* abdanken ◇ *vt* [responsibility] von sich schieben.

abdomen ['æbdəmən] *n* [of person] Unterleib *der*; [of animal, insect] Hinterleib *der*.

abduct [əb'dʌkt] *vt* entführen.

aberration [,æbə'reɪʃn] *n* Abweichung *die*.

abet [ə'bet] *vt* ➪ aid.

abeyance [ə'beɪəns] *n fml*: **to be in ~** [law] außer Kraft sein.

abhor [əb'hɔː'] *vt* verabscheuen.

abide [ə'baɪd] *vt* ausstehen. **◆ abide by** *vt fus* sich halten an (+ A).

ability [ə'bɪlətɪ] *n* **- 1.** (U) [capability] Fähigkeit *die* **- 2.** [capability] Fähigkeit *die*, Gabe *die*; [talent] Begabung *die*.

abject ['æbdʒekt] *adj* **- 1.** [poverty] bitter; **~ misery** tiefes Elend **- 2.** [person] unterwürfig, demütig; **to offer an ~ apology** unterwürfig um Entschuldigung bitten.

ablaze [ə'bleɪz] *adj* [on fire] in Flammen.

able ['eɪbl] *adj* **- 1.** [capable] fähig; **to be ~ to do sthg** etw tun können; [due to circumstances] imstande OR in der Lage sein, etw zu tun **- 2.** [competent] tüchtig; [gifted] begabt.

ably ['eɪblɪ] *adv* geschickt, gekonnt.

abnormal [æb'nɔːml] *adj* [behaviour] abnorm; [interest] krankhaft; [workload] übermäßig.

aboard [ə'bɔːd] ◇ *adv* [on ship, plane] an Bord; **to go ~** an Bord gehen ◇ *prep*: **~ the ship/plane** an Bord des Schiffes/Flugzeugs; **~ the bus/train** im Bus/Zug.

abode [ə'bəʊd] *n fml*: **of no fixed ~** ohne festen Wohnsitz.

abolish [ə'bɒlɪʃ] *vt* abschaffen.

abolition [,æbə'lɪʃn] *n* Abschaffung *die*.

abominable [ə'bɒmɪnəbl] *adj* [behaviour, treatment] abscheulich; [performance] furchtbar.

aborigine [,æbə'rɪdʒənɪ] *n* Ureinwohner *der*, -in *die* Australiens, Aborigine *der*.

abort [ə'bɔːt] *vt* **- 1.** [pregnancy] abbrechen; [baby] abtreiben **- 2.** *fig* [plan, mission] abbrechen **- 3.** COMPUT abbrechen.

abortion [ə'bɔːʃn] *n* [of pregnancy] Abtreibung *die*; **she's going to have an ~** sie wird eine Abtreibung vornehmen lassen.

abortive [ə'bɔːtɪv] *adj* misslungen.

abound [ə'baʊnd] *vi* **- 1.** [be plentiful] in

großer Fülle vorhanden sein - **2.** [be full]: **to ~ with** OR **in sthg** reich an etw (D) sein.

about [ə'baʊt] <> *adv* - **1.** [approximately] ungefähr, etwa; **~ 50** ungefähr 50; **at ~ six o'clock** gegen sechs Uhr - **2.** [referring to place] herum; **to walk ~** herumllaufen; **is Mr Smith ~?** ist Herr Smith da?; **there's a lot of flu ~** die Grippe geht um - **3.** [on the point of]: **to be ~ to do sthg** im Begriff sein, etw zu tun <> *prep* - **1.** [concerning] um, über (+ A); **a book ~ Scotland** ein Buch über Schottland; **what's it ~?** worum gehts?; **to talk ~ sthg** über etw sprechen; **to quarrel ~ sthg** sich wegen etw streiten; **what ~ a drink?** wie wärs mit etwas zu trinken? - **2.** [referring to place] herum; **to wander ~ the streets** in den Straßen umherschlendern.

about-turn *esp Br*, **about-face** *esp Am n* - **1.** MIL Kehrtwendung *die* - **2.** *fig* [change of attitude] Wendung *die* um hundertachtzig Grad.

above [ə'bʌv] <> *prep* - **1.** [higher than] über (+ A, D); **to fly ~ the clouds** über den Wolken fliegen - **2.** [more than] über (+ A); **children ~ the age of twelve** Kinder über zwölf Jahre <> *adv* - **1.** [on top, higher up] oben; **the flat ~** die Wohnung oben; **see ~** [in text] siehe oben - **2.** [more]: **children aged ten and ~** Kinder ab zehn Jahren. ◆ **above all** *adv* vor allem.

aboveboard [ə,bʌv'bɔːd] *adj* ehrlich.

abrasive [ə'breɪsɪv] *adj* - **1.** [for cleaning] Scheuer- - **2.** *fig* [person] ungehobelt; [manner] grob.

abreast [ə'brest] *adv* nebeneinander. ◆ **abreast of** *prep*: **to keep ~ of sthg** in Bezug auf etw (A) auf dem Laufenden bleiben.

abridged [ə'brɪdʒd] *adj* gekürzt.

abroad [ə'brɔːd] *adv* [live] im Ausland; [travel, go] ins Ausland.

abrupt [ə'brʌpt] *adj* - **1.** [sudden] abrupt - **2.** [person] kurz angebunden; [manner] brüsk.

abscess ['æbsɪs] *n* Abszess *der*.

abscond [əb'skɒnd] *vi* [from detention centre] entfliehen; [from boarding school] wegllaufen.

abseil ['æbseɪl] *vi* sich abseilen.

absence ['æbsəns] *n* - **1.** [of person] Abwesenheit *die* - **2.** [lack] Mangel *der*.

absent ['æbsənt] *adj* [not present]: **~ (from)** abwesend (von).

absentee [,æbsən'tiː] *n* Abwesende *der, die*.

absent-minded [-'maɪndɪd] *adj* zerstreut.

absolute ['æbsəluːt] *adj* - **1.** [complete, utter] absolut, vollkommen; **it's an ~ disgrace** es ist eine ausgesprochene Schande - **2.** [ruler, power] absolut.

absolutely [æbsə'luːtlɪ] <> *adv* [completely, utterly] vollkommen, ausgesprochen; **I'm**

~ starving ich bin ausgesprochen hungrig <> *excl* [expressing agreement] auf jeden Fall!

absolve [əb'zɒlv] *vt*: **to ~ sb (from sthg)** [from crime] jn (von etw) freilsprechen; [from sin] jn (von etw) loslsprechen; [from responsibility] jn (von etw) entbinden.

absorb [əb'zɔːb] *vt* - **1.** [liquid] auflsaugen; [gas, heat] absorbieren - **2.** *fig* [learn] auflnehmen - **3.** [interest] fesseln; **to be ~ed in sthg** in etw (A) vertieft OR versunken sein - **4.** [take over] übernehmen.

absorbent [əb'zɔːbənt] *adj* absorbierend.

abstain [əb'steɪn] *vi* - **1.**: **to ~ from sthg** [drinking, smoking] sich einer Sache (G) enthalten; [sex, food] auf etw (A) verzichten - **2.** [in vote] sich der Stimme enthalten.

abstention [əb'stenʃn] *n* [in vote] Enthaltung *die*.

abstract ['æbstrækt] <> *adj* abstrakt <> *n* [summary] Abstract *der*.

absurd [əb'sɜːd] *adj* absurd.

abundant [ə'bʌndənt] *adj* reichlich.

abundantly [ə'bʌndəntlɪ] *adv* [extremely]: **it's ~ clear** es ist mehr als klar.

abuse [*n* ə'bjuːs, *vb* ə'bjuːz] <> *n* - **1.** (U) [offensive remarks] Beschimpfungen *pl*, Schimpfworte *pl* - **2.** [maltreatment] Missbrauch *der* - **3.** [of alcohol, drugs, power] Missbrauch *der* <> *vt* - **1.** [insult] beschimpfen - **2.** [maltreat, misuse] missbrauchen.

abusive [ə'bjuːsɪv] *adj* ausfallend.

abysmal [ə'bɪzml] *adj* [behaviour, performance, weather] miserabel; [failure] erbärmlich.

abyss [ə'bɪs] *n* Abgrund *der*; *fig* [between people, groups] Kluft *die*, Abgründe *pl*.

a/c (*abbr of* account (current)) Kto.

AC *n abbr of* alternating current.

academic [,ækə'demɪk] <> *adj* - **1.** [of college, university] wissenschaftlich - **2.** [studious] intellektuell - **3.** [hypothetical] theoretisch <> *n* Akademiker *der*, -in *die*.

academy [ə'kædəmɪ] *n* Akademie *die*.

accede [æk'siːd] *vi* - **1.** *fml* [agree]: **to ~ to sthg** in etw (A) einlwilligen - **2.** [monarch]: **to ~ to the throne** den Thron besteigen.

accelerate [ək'seləreɪt] <> *vt* [pace, rhythm, decline, event] beschleunigen <> *vi* - **1.** [car, driver] beschleunigen - **2.** [inflation, growth] sich beschleunigen, zulnehmen.

acceleration [ək,selə'reɪʃn] *n* Beschleunigung *die*.

accelerator [ək'seləreɪtə'] *n* Gaspedal *das*.

accent ['æksent] *n* [gen] Akzent *der*.

accept [ək'sept] *vt* - **1.** [gift, advice, apology, invitation, offer] anlnehmen - **2.** [change, situation] akzeptieren, hinlnehmen - **3.** [defeat, blame] einlgestehen; [responsibility] übernehmen - **4.** [person - as part of group] akzeptieren; [- for job] nehmen; [- as member of club] auflnehmen - **5.** [admit]: **to ~ that...** zugeben, dass ...; **it is generally ~ed that ...** es ist allgemein anerkannt, dass ... - **6.** [subj: shop, bank] akzeptieren; [subj: machine] nehmen.

acceptable [ək'septəbl] *adj* akzeptabel.

acceptance [ək'septəns] *n* - **1.** [of gift, piece of work] Annahme *die* - **2.** [of change, situation] Hinnahme *die* - **3.** [of defeat, blame] Eingeständnis *das*; [of responsibility] Übernehmen *das* - **4.** [of person - as part of group] Akzeptierung *die*; [- for job] Anstellung *die*; [- as member of club] Aufnahme *die*.

access ['ækses] *n (U)* - **1.** [entry, way in] Zutritt *der*, Zugang *der* - **2.** [opportunity to use, see]: **to have ~ to sthg** zu etw Zugang haben.

accessible [ək'sesəbl] *adj* - **1.** [place] zugänglich - **2.** [available] verfügbar.

accessory [ək'sesərɪ] *n* - **1.** [extra part, device] Extra *das*; **accessories** Zubehör *das* - **2.** LAW Helfershelfer *der*, -in *die*.

accident ['æksɪdənt] *n* - **1.** [unpleasant event] Unfall *der*; [more serious] Unglück *das*; [mishap] Missgeschick *das*; **to have an ~** [in car] einen Autounfall haben - **2.** [unintentional act] Versehen *das* - **3.** *(U)* [chance]: **we met by ~** wir haben uns zufällig getroffen.

accidental [,æksɪ'dentl] *adj* [meeting, discovery] zufällig.

accidentally [,æksɪ'dentəlɪ] *adv* [meet, find, discover] zufällig.

accident-prone *adj*: **he is ~** er ist vom Pech verfolgt.

acclaim [ə'kleɪm] <> *n* Anerkennung *die*, Beifall *der* <> *vt* feiern.

acclimatize, -ise [ə'klaɪmətaɪz], **acclimate** *Am* ['æklɪmeɪt] *vi*: **to ~ (to sthg)** sich (in etw *(D)*) akklimatisieren.

accommodate [ə'kɒmədeɪt] *vt* - **1.** [subj: building, car] Platz bieten für; [subj: person] unterbringen - **2.** [oblige] entgegenkommen *(+ D)*, berücksichtigen.

accommodating [ə'kɒmədeɪtɪŋ] *adj* entgegenkommend.

accommodation *Br* [ə,kɒmə'deɪʃn] *n*, **accommodations** *Am* [ə,kɒmə'deɪʃnz] *npl* [lodging] Unterkunft *die*.

accompany [ə'kʌmpənɪ] *vt* - **1.** [gen] begleiten - **2.** MUS: **to ~ sb (on sthg)** jn (auf etw *(D)*) begleiten.

accomplice [ə'kʌmplɪs] *n* Komplize *der*, -zin *die*.

accomplish [ə'kʌmplɪʃ] *vt* [achieve] erreichen, leisten; [complete] vollbringen.

accomplishment [ə'kʌmplɪʃmənt] *n* - **1.** [feat, deed] Leistung *die* - **2.** [action] Vollendung *die*. ➤ **accomplishments** *npl* Fähigkeiten *pl*.

accord [ə'kɔːd] *n* - **1.** [settlement] Einigung *die* - **2.** [agreement, harmony]: **to be in ~ (with sthg)** (mit etw) im Einklang sein; **to do sthg of one's own ~** etw aus eigenem Antrieb tun, etw aus freien Stücken tun.

accordance [ə'kɔːdəns] *n*: **in ~ with** entsprechend *(+ D)*, gemäß *(+ D)*; **in ~ with your wishes** Ihren Wünschen entsprechend.

according to [ə'kɔːdɪŋ-] *prep* - **1.** [as stated or shown by] zufolge *(+ D)*, laut *(+ D)*; **to go ~ plan** nach Plan gehen - **2.** [with regard to, depending on] entsprechend *(+ D)*.

accordingly [ə'kɔːdɪŋlɪ] *adv* - **1.** [appropriately] (dem)entsprechend - **2.** [consequently] folglich, demgemäß.

accordion [ə'kɔːdjən] *n* Akkordeon *das*.

accost [ə'kɒst] *vt* belästigen.

account [ə'kaʊnt] *n* - **1.** [with bank, building society] Konto *das* - **2.** [with shop, company] Kundenkonto *das* - **3.** [report] Bericht *der* - **4.** *phr*: **to take ~ of sthg**, **to take sthg into ~** etw berücksichtigen; **to be of no ~** ohne Bedeutung sein; **on no ~** auf keinen Fall. ➤ **accounts** *npl* [of business] Buchführung *die*. ➤ **by all accounts** *adv* nach allem, was man hört. ➤ **on account of** *prep* aufgrund *(+ G)*. ➤ **account for** *vt fus* - **1.** [explain] erklären; **all the missing people have been ~ed for** der Verbleib aller vermissten Personen ist geklärt worden - **2.** [represent] ausmachen.

accountable [ə'kaʊntəbl] *adj*: **~ (for sb/ sthg)** verantwortlich (für etw/jn).

accountancy [ə'kaʊntənsɪ] *n* Buchhaltung *die*, Buchführung *die*.

accountant [ə'kaʊntənt] *n* Buchhalter *der*, -in *die*.

accounts department *n* Buchhaltungsabteilung *die*, Buchführungsabteilung *die*.

accrue [ə'kruː] *vi* FIN sich ansammeln.

accumulate [ə'kjuːmjuleɪt] <> *vt* [money, belongings] anhäufen; [evidence] sammeln <> *vi* [money, belongings] sich anhäufen.

accuracy ['ækjurəsɪ] *n* - **1.** [truth, correctness] Korrektheit *die*, Richtigkeit *die* - **2.** [precision - of weapon, marksman] Präzision *die*; [- of typing, typist] Fehlerlosigkeit *die*; [- of figures, estimate] Genauigkeit *die*.

accurate ['ækjurət] *adj* - **1.** [true] korrekt, richtig - **2.** [precise - weapon, marksman] präzis(e); [- typing, typist] fehlerlos; [- figures, estimate] genau.

accurately ['ækjurətlɪ] *adv* - **1.** [truthfully] korrekt, richtig - **2.** [precisely - aim, estimate] genau; [- type] fehlerlos.

accusation [,ækju'zeɪʃn] *n* - **1.** [charge, criticism] Vorwurf *der*, Beschuldigung *die* - **2.** LAW [formal charge] Anklage *die*.

accuse [ə'kjuːz] *vt* - **1.** [charge, criticize]: **to ~ sb of sthg** jn einer Sache *(G)* beschuldigen; **to ~ sb of doing sthg** jn beschuldigen, etw getan zu haben - **2.** LAW: **to be ~d of murder/ fraud** des Mordes/Betrugs angeklagt sein OR werden; **to be ~d of doing sthg** beschuldigt werden, etwas getan zu haben.

accused [əˈkjuːzd] *n* LAW: **the ~** der/die Angeklagte.

accustomed [əˈkʌstəmd] *adj:* **to be ~ to sthg** etw gewöhnt sein, an etw *(A)* gewöhnt sein; **to be ~ to doing sthg** gewohnt sein, etw zu tun.

ace [eɪs] *n* [gen] Ass *das*.

ache [eɪk] ⇔ *n* [dull pain] (dumpfer) Schmerz ⇔ *vi* - **1.** [be painful] weh tun, schmerzen; **my head ~s** mein Kopf tut mir weh - **2.** *fig* [want]: **to be aching for sthg** sich nach etw sehnen; **to be aching to do sthg** sich danach sehnen, etw zu tun.

achieve [əˈtʃiːv] *vt* [success] erzielen; [goal] erreichen; [ambition] verwirklichen; [victory] erringen; [fame] erlangen.

achievement [əˈtʃiːvmənt] *n* [feat, deed] Leistung *die*.

acid [ˈæsɪd] *n* - **1.** CHEM Säure *die* - **2.** *inf* [LSD] Acid *das*.

acid rain *n* saurer Regen.

acknowledge [əkˈnɒlɪdʒ] *vt* - **1.** [accept, admit] eingestehen, zugeben - **2.** [recognize]: **to ~ sb as sthg** jn als etw anerkennen - **3.** [letter]: **to ~ (receipt of) sthg** den Eingang OR Empfang von etw bestätigen - **4.** [greet] grüßen.

acknowledg(e)ment [əkˈnɒlɪdʒmənt] *n* - **1.** [thanks] Anerkennung *die* - **2.** [acceptance] Eingeständnis *das* - **3.** [letter] Empfangsbestätigung *die*. ◆ **acknowledg(e)ments** *npl* [in book] Danksagungen *pl*.

acne [ˈæknɪ] *n* Akne *die*.

acorn [ˈeɪkɔːn] *n* Eichel *die*.

acoustic [əˈkuːstɪk] *adj* akustisch. ◆ **acoustics** *npl* [of room] Akustik *die*.

acquaint [əˈkweɪnt] *vt:* **to ~ sb with sthg** [information] jn über etw *(A)* informieren; [method, technique] jn mit etw vertraut machen; **to be ~ed with sb** mit jm bekannt sein.

acquaintance [əˈkweɪntəns] *n* [personal associate] Bekannte, der, die.

acquire [əˈkwaɪər] *vt* - **1.** [house, company, book] erwerben; [information, document] erhalten - **2.** [habit] annehmen; [skill, knowledge] erwerben; **to ~ a taste for sthg** Gefallen an etw *(D)* finden.

acquisitive [əˈkwɪzɪtɪv] *adj* habgierig.

acquit [əˈkwɪt] *vt* - **1.** LAW: **to ~ sb (of sthg)** jn (von etw) freisprechen - **2.** [conduct]: **to ~ o.s. well/badly** seine Sache gut/schlecht machen.

acquittal [əˈkwɪtl] *n* LAW Freispruch *der*.

acre [ˈeɪkər] *n* ≃ Morgen *der*, = 4047,9 *m²*.

acrid [ˈækrɪd] *adj* [smoke, smell] beißend; [taste] bitter.

acrimonious [ˌækrɪˈməʊnjəs] *adj* erbittert.

acrobat [ˈækrəbæt] *n* Akrobat *der*, -in *die*.

across [əˈkrɒs] ⇔ *adv* - **1.** [to the other side] hinüber; [from the other side] herüber - **2.** [in measurements] breit; [of circle] im Durchmesser - **3.** [in crossword] waag(e)recht ⇔ *prep* - **1.** [from one side to the other] über (+ *A*) - **2.** [on the other side of] auf der anderen Seite (+ *G*). ◆ **across from** *prep* gegenüber von.

acrylic [əˈkrɪlɪk] ⇔ *adj* Acryl-, aus Acryl ⇔ *n* Acryl *das*.

act [ækt] ⇔ *n* - **1.** [action, deed] Tat *die*, Akt *der*; **an ~ of mercy** ein Gnadenakt - **2.** LAW Gesetz *das* - **3.** [of play, opera] Akt *der*; [in cabaret *etc*] Nummer *die* - **4.** *fig* [pretence] Komödie *die*, Schau *die*; **to put on an ~** Komödie spielen - **5.** *phr:* **get your ~ together!** reiß dich mal am Riemen! ⇔ *vi* - **1.** [take action] handeln - **2.** [behave] sich benehmen - **3.** [in play, film] spielen - **4.** *fig* [pretend] Komödie spielen; **to ~ innocent** unschuldig tun - **5.** [take effect] wirken - **6.** [fulfil function]: **to ~ as sthg** als etw fungieren ⇔ *vt* [role] spielen.

acting [ˈæktɪŋ] ⇔ *adj* [interim] stellvertretend ⇔ *n* (*U*) [performance] Spiel *das*; [profession] Schauspielerei *die*.

action [ˈækʃn] *n* - **1.** (*U*) [fact of doing sthg] Handeln *das*; **to take ~** etwas unternehmen; **to put sthg into ~** etw in die Tat umsetzen; **in ~** [person] in Aktion; [machine] in Betrieb; **out of ~** [person] nicht in Aktion; [machine] außer Betrieb - **2.** [deed] Tat *die* - **3.** (*U*) [in battle, war] Gefecht *das* - **4.** LAW [trial] Prozess *der*; [charge] Klage *die* - **5.** [in play, book, film] Handlung *die* - **6.** [effect] Wirkung *die*.

action replay *n* Wiederholung *die*.

activate [ˈæktɪveɪt] *vt* [device, machine] in Gang setzen; [alarm] auslösen.

active [ˈæktɪv] *adj* aktiv; [mind, interest] rege.

actively [ˈæktɪvlɪ] *adv* aktiv.

activity [ækˈtɪvətɪ] *n* - **1.** (*U*) [movement, action] Geschäftigkeit *die* - **2.** [pastime, hobby] Betätigung *die*. ◆ **activities** *npl* Aktivitäten *pl*.

actor [ˈæktər] *n* Schauspieler *der*.

actress [ˈæktrɪs] *n* Schauspielerin *die*.

actual [ˈæktʃʊəl] *adj* eigentlich; [cost, amount, cause] tatsächlich, wirklich.

📖 **actual**

Das englische Wort actual beziehungsweise die adverbiale Form actually bedeutet nicht „aktuell", sondern entspricht dem deutschen „wirklich" oder „eigentlich". Die Frage What did he actually say? bedeutet also „Was hat er eigentlich gesagt?"
Das deutsche „aktuell" dagegen wird im Englischen meist mit current ausgedrückt. „Ein Thema von aktuellem Interesse" kann man mit a topic of current interest übersetzen.

actually ['æktʃʊəlɪ] *adv* - **1.** [really, in truth] wirklich - **2.** [by the way] übrigens.

acumen ['ækjʊmen] *n*: **business** ~ Geschäftssinn *der.*

acupuncture ['ækjʊpʌŋktʃəʳ] *n* Akupunktur *die.*

acute [ə'kjuːt] *adj* - **1.** [pain, shortage] akut; [embarrassment, anxiety] groß - **2.** [observer, mind] scharf; [analysis, judgement, person] scharfsinnig - **3.** [sight] scharf; [hearing, sense of smell] fein - **4.** MATH spitz.

ad [æd] (*abbr of* **advertisement**) *n inf* [in newspaper] Inserat *das*, Annonce *die*; [on TV] Werbung *die*; [in shop window] Angebot *das.*

AD (*abbr of* **Anno Domini**) A. D.

adamant ['ædəmənt] *adj*: **to be** ~ **(about sthg)** (in Bezug auf etw *(A)*) unnachgiebig sein; **to be** ~ **that ...** darauf bestehen, dass ...

Adam's apple ['ædəmz-] *n* Adamsapfel *der.*

adapt [ə'dæpt] <> *vt* - **1.** [adjust, modify] anlpassen; [machine, system] umlstellen; [text, materials] umlarbeiten - **2.** [book, play] adaptieren <> *vi*: **to** ~ **to sthg** sich etw *(D)* anlpassen; [idea] sich mit etw anlfreunden.

adaptable [ə'dæptəbl] *adj* anpassungsfähig.

adapter, adaptor [ə'dæptəʳ] *n* [for foreign plug] Adapter *der*; [for several plugs] Mehrfachstecker *der.*

add [æd] *vt* - **1.** [gen]: **to** ~ **sthg (to)** etw hinzulfügen (zu) - **2.** [total] addieren. ◆ **add on** *vt sep* - **1.** [build on, attach]: **to** ~ **sthg on (to sthg)** etw (an etw *(A)*) anlbauen - **2.** [include]: **to** ~ **sthg on (to sthg)** etw (zu etw) hinzulfügen; [number, amount] etw (zu etw) dazulrechnen. ◆ **add to** *vt fus* [increase] vergrößern, vermehren. ◆ **add up** *vt sep* [total up] zusammenlrechnen. ◆ **add up to** *vt fus* [represent] ergeben.

adder ['ædəʳ] *n* [snake] Viper *die.*

addict ['ædɪkt] *n* - **1.** [taking drugs] Süchtige *der, die*, Abhängige *der, die* - **2.** *fig* [fan]: **to be a chocolate** ~ süchtig nach Schokolade sein; **to be an exercise** ~ ein Sportfanatiker sein.

addicted [ə'dɪktɪd] *adj lit & fig*: ~ **(to)** süchtig (nach).

addiction [ə'dɪkʃn] *n lit & fig*: ~ **(to)** Sucht *die* (nach).

addictive [ə'dɪktɪv] *adj*: **to be** ~ [drug] süchtig machen; *fig* [exercise, food, TV] zu einer Sucht werden können.

addition [ə'dɪʃn] *n* - **1.** MATH Addition *die* - **2.** [extra thing] Zusatz *der*, Ergänzung *die* - **3.** [act of adding] Hinzufügen *das*; **in** ~ außerdem; **in** ~ **to** zusätzlich zu.

additional [ə'dɪʃənl] *adj* zusätzlich.

additive ['ædɪtɪv] *n* Zusatz *der.*

address [ə'dres] <> *n* - **1.** [location] Adresse *die* - **2.** [speech] Ansprache *die* <> *vt* - **1.** [letter, parcel] adressieren - **2.** [meeting, confer-

ence] eine Ansprache halten bei - **3.** [person] ansprechen; **to** ~ **sb as sthg** jn etw nennen.

address book *n* Adressbuch *das.*

adenoids ['ædɪnɔɪdz] *npl* Polypen *pl.*

adept ['ædept] *adj*: **to be** ~ **(at sthg)** (in etw *(D)*) geschickt sein.

adequate ['ædɪkwət] *adj* - **1.** [sufficient] ausreichend - **2.** [good enough] adäquat.

adhere [əd'hɪəʳ] *vi* - **1.** [stick]: **to** ~ **(to)** kleben (an (+ *D*)) - **2.** [observe]: **to** ~ **to sthg** sich an etw *(A)* halten, etw befolgen - **3.** [uphold]: **to** ~ **to sthg** an etw *(D)* festlhalten.

adhesive [əd'hiːsɪv] <> *adj* klebend; ~ **label** Haftetikett *das* <> *n* Klebstoff *der.*

adhesive tape *n* Klebestreifen *der.*

adjacent [ə'dʒeɪsənt] *adj* angrenzend, Neben-; **to be** ~ **to sthg** an etw *(A)* anlgrenzen.

adjective ['ædʒɪktɪv] *n* Adjektiv *das.*

adjoining [ə'dʒɔɪnɪŋ] *adj* angrenzend.

adjourn [ə'dʒɜːn] <> *vt*: **to** ~ **sthg (until)** etw vertagen (auf (+ *A*)) <> *vi* sich vertagen.

adjudicate [ə'dʒuːdɪkeɪt] *vi* als Preisrichter fungieren; **to** ~ **on** OR **upon sthg** entscheiden OR urteilen über etw.

adjust [ə'dʒʌst] <> *vt* regulieren; [settings] einlstellen; [clothing] zurechtlrücken <> *vi*: **to** ~ **(to sthg)** sich (auf etw *(A)*) einlstellen.

adjustable [ə'dʒʌstəbl] *adj* [machine] regulierbar; [chair] verstellbar.

adjustment [ə'dʒʌstmənt] *n* - **1.** [gen] Regulierung *die*; [of settings] Einstellung *die* - **2.** [to situation]: ~ **(to)** Anpassung *die* (an (+ *A*)).

ad lib [,æd'lɪb] <> *adv* [freely] aus dem Stegreif <> *n* [improvised joke] Stegreifwitz *der.* ◆ **ad-lib** *vi* improvisieren.

administer [əd'mɪnɪstəʳ] *vt* - **1.** [company] verwalten - **2.** [punishment] verhängen; **to** ~ **justice** Recht sprechen - **3.** [drug, medication] verabreichen.

administration [əd,mɪnɪ'streɪʃn] *n* - **1.** [gen] Verwaltung *die* - **2.** [of punishment] Verhängung *die*; **the** ~ **of justice** die Rechtsprechung.

administrative [əd'mɪnɪstrətɪv] *adj* Verwaltungs-, administrativ.

admirable ['ædmərəbl] *adj* [worthy of admiration] bewundernswert; [excellent] großartig.

admiral ['ædmərəl] *n* Admiral *der.*

admiration [,ædmə'reɪʃn] *n* Bewunderung *die.*

admire [əd'maɪəʳ] *vt* bewundern; **to** ~ **sb for sthg** jn wegen etw *(G)* bewundern.

admirer [əd'maɪərəʳ] *n* - **1.** [suitor] Verehrer *der*, -in *die* - **2.** [enthusiast, fan] Bewunderer *der*, -in *die.*

admission [əd'mɪʃn] *n* - **1.** [permission to enter] Zulassung *die*; [to museum *etc*] Eintritt *der* - **2.** [cost of entrance] Eintrittspreis *der*

- 3. [confession - of crime] Geständnis *das;* [- of guilt, mistake] Eingeständnis *das.*

admit [əd'mɪt] ◇ *vt* **- 1.** [crime] gestehen; [mistake] einlgestehen; **to ~ that ...** zulgeben, dass ...; **to ~ doing sthg** zulgeben, etw getan zu haben; **to ~ defeat** *fig* auflgeben **- 2.** [allow to enter] hereinllassen, hineinllassen; **to be ~ted to hospital** *Br* OR **to the hospital** *Am* ins Krankenhaus eingeliefert werden **- 3.** [allow to join]: **to ~ sb (to sthg)** jn (in etw *(A)*) auflnehmen ◇ *vi:* **to ~ to sthg** etw zulgeben.

admittance [əd'mɪtəns] *n:* '**no ~**' 'kein Zutritt'.

admittedly [əd'mɪtɪdlɪ] *adv* zugegebenermaßen.

admonish [əd'mɒnɪʃ] *vt fml* ermahnen.

ad nauseam [ˌæd'nɔ:zɪæm] *adv* bis zum Überdruss.

ado [ə'du:] *n:* **without further** OR **more ~** ohne weitere Umstände.

adolescence [ˌædə'lesns] *n* Jugend *die.*

adolescent [ˌædə'lesnt] ◇ *adj* **- 1.** [teenage] jugendlich **- 2.** *pej* [immature] unreif ◇ *n* [teenager] Jugendliche *der, die.*

adopt [ə'dɒpt] *vt* **- 1.** [child] adoptieren **- 2.** [plan, method] übernehmen; [attitude, mannerism, recommendation] anlnehmen.

adoption [ə'dɒpʃn] *n* **- 1.** [of child] Adoption *die* **- 2.** *(U)* [of plan, method] Übernahme *die;* [of recommendation] Annahme *die.*

adore [ə'dɔ:ʳ] *vt* über alles lieben; **I ~ these chocolate biscuits** ich esse diese Schokoladenkekse für mein Leben gern.

adorn [ə'dɔ:n] *vt* schmücken.

adrenalin [ə'drenəlɪn] *n* Adrenalin *das.*

Adriatic [ˌeɪdrɪ'ætɪk] *n:* **the ~ (Sea)** die Adria.

adrift [ə'drɪft] *adj* [boat, ship] treibend.

adult ['ædʌlt] ◇ *adj* erwachsen; [animal] ausgewachsen; [book, film] für Erwachsene ◇ *n* [person] Erwachsene *der, die.*

adultery [ə'dʌltərɪ] *n (U)* Ehebruch *der.*

advance [əd'vɑ:ns] ◇ *n* **- 1.** [of army] Vorrücken *das* **- 2.** [improvement, progress] Fortschritt *der* **- 3.** [money] Vorschuss *der* ◇ *comp:* **~ booking** Vorbestellung *die;* **~ payment** Vorauszahlung *die;* **~ warning** Vorwarnung *die* ◇ *vt* **- 1.** [improve - cause] voranlbringen, fördern; [- interest] fördern **- 2.** [bring forward in time] vorlverlegen **- 3.:** **to ~ sb sthg** [money] jm etw vorlschießen ◇ *vi* **- 1.** [go forward - army] vorlrücken **- 2.** [improve] Fortschritte machen. ◆ **advances** *npl:* **to make ~s to sb** [sexual] bei jm Annäherungsversuche machen. ◆ **in advance** *adv* im Voraus.

advanced [əd'vɑ:nst] *adj* **- 1.** [developed - plan] weit entwickelt; [- stage] vorgerückt **- 2.** [student, pupil] fortgeschritten.

advantage [əd'vɑ:ntɪdʒ] *n* Vorteil *der;* **to**

be to one's ~ für jn von Vorteil sein; **to have** OR **hold the ~ (over sb)** (jm gegenüber) im Vorteil sein; **to take ~ of** auslnutzen.

advent ['ædvənt] *n* [of invention] Aufkommen *das;* [of period] Beginn *der.* ◆ **Advent** *n* RELIG Advent *der.*

adventure [əd'ventʃəʳ] *n* Abenteuer *das.*

adventure playground *n* Abenteuerspielplatz *der.*

adventurous [əd'ventʃərəs] *adj* **- 1.** [person] abenteuerlustig **- 2.** [life, project] abenteuerlich.

adverb ['ædvɜ:b] *n* Adverb *das.*

adverse ['ædvɜ:s] *adj* [weather] schlecht; [conditions] ungünstig; [criticism] negativ, nachteilig; [effect] nachteilig.

advert ['ædvɜ:t] *n Br* = advertisement.

advertise ['ædvətaɪz] *vt* [job, product] Reklame OR Werbung machen für; **to ~ for sb/ sthg** jn/etw per Anzeige suchen.

advertisement [əd'vɜ:tɪsmənt] *n* **- 1.** [in newspaper] Inserat *das;* [on TV] Werbung *die;* [in shop window] Angebot *das* **- 2.** *fig* [recommendation] Aushängeschild *das.*

advertising ['ædvətaɪzɪŋ] *n (U)* **- 1.** [advertisements] Werbung *die,* Reklame *die* **- 2.** [industry] Werbebranche *die.*

advice [əd'vaɪs] *n (U)* Rat *der;* **to give sb ~** jm einen Rat geben; **to take sb's ~** js Rat befolgen; **a piece of ~** ein Ratschlag.

advisable [əd'vaɪzəbl] *adj* ratsam.

advise [əd'vaɪz] ◇ *vt* **- 1.** [give advice to]: **to ~ sb to do sthg** jm raten, etw zu tun; **to ~ sb against sthg** jm von etw ablraten; **to ~ sb against doing sthg** jm davon ablraten, etw zu tun **- 2.** [professionally]: **to ~ sb on sthg** jn in etw *(D)* beraten **- 3.** *fml* [inform]: **to ~ sb of sthg** jn über etw *(A)* unterrichten ◇ *vi:* **to ~ against sthg** von etw ablraten; **to ~ against doing sthg** davon ablraten, etw zu tun.

advisedly [əd'vaɪzɪdlɪ] *adv* mit Bedacht.

adviser *Br,* **advisor** *Am* [əd'vaɪzəʳ] *n* Berater *der,* -in *die.*

advisory [əd'vaɪzərɪ] *adj* [group, organization] beratend.

advocate [*n* 'ædvəkət, *vb* 'ædvəkeɪt] ◇ *n* **- 1.** *Scot* LAW (Rechts)anwalt *der,* -wältin *die* **- 2.** [supporter] Befürworter *der,* -in *die,* Verfechter *der,* -in *die* ◇ *vt* befürworten.

Aegean [i:'dʒi:ən] *n:* **the ~ (Sea)** die Ägäis.

aeon *Br,* **eon** *Am* ['i:ən] *n* Äon *der; fig* [very long time] Ewigkeit *die.*

aerial ['eərɪəl] ◇ *adj* Luft-; **~ photograph** Luftaufnahme *die* ◇ *n Br* [antenna] Antenne *die.*

aerobics [eə'rəʊbɪks] *n (U)* Aerobic *das.*

aerodynamic [ˌeərəʊdaɪ'næmɪk] *adj* aerodynamisch. ◆ **aerodynamics** ◇ *n (U)* [science] Aerodynamik *die* ◇ *npl* [aerodynamic qualities] Aerodynamik *die.*

aeroplane Br ['eərəpleɪn], **airplane** Am n Flugzeug das.

aerosol ['eərəsɒl] n Spraydose die.

aesthetic, esthetic Am [es'θetɪk] adj ästhetisch.

afar [ə'fɑ:ʳ] adv: **from ~** aus der Ferne.

affable ['æfəbl] adj umgänglich.

affair [ə'feəʳ] n - 1. [event, concern] Angelegenheit die, Sache die - 2. [extramarital relationship] Verhältnis das.

affect [ə'fekt] vt - 1. [influence] beeinflussen; [health] beeinträchtigen - 2. [move emotionally] berühren - 3. [feign] vortäuschen.

affection [ə'fekʃn] n Zuneigung die.

affectionate [ə'fekʃnət] adj liebevoll.

affirm [ə'fɜ:m] vt - 1. [declare] versichern - 2. [confirm] bestätigen.

affix [ə'fɪks] vt [stamp] kleben.

afflict [ə'flɪkt] vt plagen; **to be ~ed with sthg** von etw geplagt sein.

affluence ['æfluəns] n Wohlstand der.

affluent ['æfluənt] adj wohlhabend.

afford [ə'fɔ:d] vt - 1. [gen]: **to be able to ~ sthg** sich (D) etw leisten können; **to be able to ~ the time (to do sthg)** die Zeit haben (etw zu tun); **I can't ~ two weeks off work** ich kann mir zwei Wochen Urlaub nicht leisten; **we can't ~ to let this happen** wir können es uns nicht leisten, dies geschehen zu lassen - 2. fml [provide - protection, shelter] gewähren; [- assistance] leisten.

affront [ə'frʌnt] ◇ n Beleidigung die, Affront der ◇ vt beleidigen.

Afghanistan [æf'gænɪstæn] n Afghanistan nt.

afield [ə'fiːld] adv: **far ~** weit weg.

afloat [ə'fləʊt] adj - 1. [above water] schwimmend - 2. fig [out of debt]: **to stay ~** sich über Wasser halten.

afoot [ə'fʊt] adj: **there's something ~** da ist irgendetwas im Gange.

afraid [ə'freɪd] adj - 1. [frightened, reluctant]: **to be ~ (of sb/sthg)** (vor jm/etw) Angst haben; **to be ~ of doing** OR **to do sthg** Angst (davor) haben, etw zu tun - 2. [in apologies]: **I'm ~ we can't come** wir können leider nicht kommen; **I'm ~ so/not** leider ja/nicht.

afresh [ə'freʃ] adv: **to start ~** noch einmal von vorn anfangen; **to look at sthg ~** etw erneut betrachten.

Africa ['æfrɪkə] n Afrika nt.

African ['æfrɪkən] ◇ adj afrikanisch ◇ n Afrikaner der, -in die.

aft [ɑ:ft] adv achtern; **to go ~** nach achtern gehen.

after ['ɑ:ftəʳ] ◇ prep - 1. [in time] nach; **day ~ day** Tag für Tag; **time ~ time** immer wieder; **the day ~ tomorrow** übermorgen; **the week ~ next** übernächste Woche - 2. [in order] nach; **~ you!** nach Ihnen!; **shut the door ~ you** schließe die Tür hinter dir - 3. [in

search of]: **to be ~ sb/sthg** jn/etw suchen - 4. [with the name of] nach; **he is named ~ his father** er ist nach seinem Vater benannt - 5. [directed at sb moving away]: **to call (sthg) ~ sb** jm (etw) nachrufen - 6. [enquiring]: **to ask ~ sb/sthg** sich nach jm/etw erkundigen - 7. [telling the time] nach; **a quarter ~ ten** Am Viertel nach zehn ◇ adv danach ◇ conj nachdem; **I came ~ he had gone** ich kam, nachdem er gegangen war. ◆ **afters** npl Br inf Nachtisch der. ◆ **after all** adv - 1. [in spite of everything] doch - 2. [it should be remembered] schließlich.

aftereffects ['ɑ:ftərɪˌfekts] npl [of war, storm] Folgen pl.

afterlife ['ɑ:ftəlaɪf] (pl -lives [-laɪvz]) n Leben das nach dem Tode.

aftermath ['ɑ:ftəmæθ] n Nachwirkungen pl; **in the ~ of sthg** nach etw.

afternoon [ˌɑ:ftə'nu:n] n Nachmittag der; **in the ~** am Nachmittag; **good ~** guten Tag. ◆ **afternoons** adv esp Am nachmittags.

after-sales service n Kundendienst der.

aftershave ['ɑ:ftəʃeɪv] n Rasierwasser das.

aftersun (lotion) ['ɑ:ftəsʌn-] n Aftersunlotion die.

aftertaste ['ɑ:ftəteɪst] n lit & fig Nachgeschmack der.

afterthought ['ɑ:ftəθɔ:t] n nachträgliche Idee.

afterwards ['ɑ:ftəwədz], **afterward** esp Am ['ɑ:ftəwəd] adv danach; **three weeks ~** drei Wochen später.

again [ə'gen] adv - 1. [one more time] wieder; **~ and ~** immer wieder; **time and ~** immer wieder; **never ~** nie wieder; **all over ~** noch einmal von vorn - 2. [once more as before] wieder; **he was ill, but he's well ~ now** er ist krank gewesen, aber jetzt ist er wieder gesund - 3. [asking for repetition] wieder, noch einmal; **what is his name ~?** wie heißt er noch gleich? - 4. [besides] außerdem; **~, we must remember his age** außerdem müssen wir sein Alter berücksichtigen - 5. phr: **half as much ~** noch mal halb so viel; **(twice) as much ~** doppelt so viel; **come ~?** inf wie bitte?; **then** OR **there ~** andererseits.

against [ə'genst] ◇ prep - 1. [gen] gegen; **he was leaning ~ the wall** er stand an die Wand gelehnt; **~ the law** rechtswidrig - 2. [in contrast to]: **as ~** verglichen mit ◇ adv: **are you for or ~?** bist du dafür oder dagegen?

age [eɪdʒ] (cont ageing OR aging) ◇ n - 1. [gen] Alter das; **she's 20 years of ~** sie ist 20 Jahre alt; **he's about my ~** er ist ungefähr mein Alter; **he was still writing at the ~ of 80** mit 80 schrieb er immer noch; **what ~ are you?** wie alt sind Sie?; **to come of ~** volljährig werden; **to be under ~** minderjährig sein - 2. [of history] Zeitalter das ◇ vt altern lassen ◇ vi [person] altern; [wine] reifen.

ages *npl* [a long time]: **that was ~s ago** das ist schon ewig her; **I haven't seen her for ~s** ich habe sie eine Ewigkeit nicht gesehen.

aged [*adj sense 1* eɪdʒd, *adj sense 2 & npl* 'eɪdʒɪd] ◇ *adj* - **1.** [of the stated age]: **a girl ~ 5** ein fünfjähriges Mädchen - **2.** [very old] betagt ◇ *npl*: **the ~** die alten Menschen.

age group *n* Altersgruppe *die*.

agency ['eɪdʒənsɪ] *n* - **1.** [business] Agentur *die* - **2.** [organization] Organisation *die*.

agenda [ə'dʒendə] (*pl* -s) *n* Tagesordnung *die*; **what's on the ~ for today?** was steht heute auf dem Programm?

agent ['eɪdʒənt] *n* - **1.** COMM [representative] Agent *der*, -in *die* - **2.** [spy] Agent *der*, -in *die*.

aggravate ['ægrəveɪt] *vt* - **1.** [make worse] verschlimmern - **2.** [annoy] ärgern.

aggregate ['ægrɪgət] ◇ *adj* Gesamt-; **~ earnings** Gesamtverdienst *der* ◇ *n* [total] Gesamtsumme *die*; **on ~** insgesamt.

aggressive [ə'gresɪv] *adj* - **1.** [belligerent - person] aggressiv - **2.** [forceful - person] energisch; [- campaign] aggressiv.

aggrieved [ə'griːvd] *adj* gekränkt.

aghast [ə'gɑːst] *adj*: **~ (at)** entsetzt (über (+ A)).

agile [*Br* 'ædʒaɪl, *Am* 'ædʒəl] *adj* [person] beweglich, agil; [body] gelenkig.

agitate ['ædʒɪteɪt] ◇ *vt* - **1.** [disturb, worry] aufregen - **2.** [shake] schütteln ◇ *vi* [campaign actively]: **to ~ for/against sthg** für/gegen etw Propaganda machen.

AGM (*abbr of* annual general meeting) *n Br* JHV *die*.

agnostic [æg'nɒstɪk] ◇ *adj* agnostisch ◇ *n* Agnostiker *der*, -in *die*.

ago [ə'gəʊ] *adv* vor; **that was a long time ~** das ist schon lange her; **three days/years ~** vor drei Tagen/Jahren.

agog [ə'gɒg] *adj* gespannt.

agonizing ['ægənaɪzɪŋ] *adj* qualvoll.

agony ['ægənɪ] *n* Qual *die*; **to be in ~** Qualen erleiden.

agony aunt *n Br inf* Kummerkastentante *die*.

agree [ə'griː] ◇ *vi* - **1.** [concur - two or more people] einer Meinung sein; [- one person] der gleichen Meinung sein; **to ~ with sb/sthg** jm/etw zulstimmen; **to ~ on sthg** sich auf etw (A) einigen - **2.** [consent] einlwilligen; **to ~ to sthg** mit etw einverstanden erklären - **3.** [statements] übereinlstimmen - **4.** [food]: **curries don't ~ with me** Currygerichte bekommen mir nicht - **5.** GRAMM: **to ~ (with)** übereinlstimmen (mit) ◇ *vt* - **1.** [price, terms] vereinbaren - **2.** [concur]: **I ~ that ... ich** bin auch der Meinung, dass ...; **it was ~d that ...** man einigte sich darauf, dass ... - **3.** [consent]: **to ~ to do sthg** sich bereit OR einverstanden erklären,

etw zu tun - **4.** [concede]: **to ~ that ... zuge-**ben, dass ...

agreeable [ə'grɪəbl] *adj* - **1.** [weather, experience] angenehm; [person] nett - **2.** [willing]: **to be ~ to sthg** mit etw einverstanden sein.

agreed [ə'griːd] *adj*: **to be ~ on sthg** sich über etw (A) einig sein.

agreement [ə'griːmənt] *n* - **1.** [accord] Einigkeit *die*; **to be in ~ with sb/sthg** mit jm/etw übereinlstimmen - **2.** [settlement] Vereinbarung *die*; [contract] Vertrag *der* - **3.** [consent] Einwilligung *die* - **4.** GRAMM Übereinstimmung *die*.

agricultural [ˌægrɪ'kʌltʃərəl] *adj* landwirtschaftlich.

agriculture ['ægrɪkʌltʃə] *n* Landwirtschaft *die*.

aground [ə'graʊnd] *adv*: **to run ~** auf Grund laufen, stranden.

ahead [ə'hed] *adv* - **1.** [in front]: **the road ~** die Straße vor uns/ihnen/ *etc*; **straight ~** geradeaus - **2.** [in competition, game]: **to be ~** führen - **3.** [indicating success]: **to get ~** vorwärts kommen - **4.** [in time]: **to plan ~** vorauslplanen; **the weeks ~ are going to be difficult** die nächsten Wochen werden schwierig sein. ◆ **ahead of** *prep* - **1.** [in front of] vor (+ D); **the road ~ of them** die Straße vor ihnen - **2.** [in competition, game]: **they are 10 points ~ of the other teams** sie sind den anderen Mannschaften um 10 Punkte voraus - **3.** [in time] vor; **~ of schedule** früher als geplant.

aid [eɪd] *vt* - **1.** [help] unterstützen - **2.** LAW: **to ~ and abet** Beihilfe leisten (+ D).

AIDS, Aids [eɪdz] (*abbr of* acquired immune deficiency syndrome) ◇ *n* Aids *das* ◇ *comp*: **~ patient** Aidspatient *der*, -in *die*.

ailing ['eɪlɪŋ] *adj lit & fig* kränkelnd.

ailment ['eɪlmənt] *n* Leiden *das*.

aim [eɪm] ◇ *n* - **1.** [objective] Ziel *das* - **2.** [in firing gun, arrow] Zielen *das*; **to take ~ at sthg** auf etw (A) zielen ◇ *vt* - **1.**: **to ~ a gun at sb/sthg** mit einem Gewehr auf jn/etw zielen; **to ~ a camera at sb/sthg** eine Kamera auf jn/etw richten - **2.** [plan, programme]: **to be ~ed at doing sthg** darauf ausgerichtet sein, etw zu tun - **3.** [remark, criticism]: **to be ~ed at sb** gegen jn gerichtet sein ◇ *vi* - **1.** [point weapon]: **to ~ (at)** zielen (auf (+ A)) - **2.** [intend]: **to ~ at OR for sthg** etw anlstreben; **to ~ to do sthg** vorlhaben, etw zu tun.

aimless ['eɪmlɪs] *adj* [person, life] ziellos; [task, activity] planlos.

ain't [eɪnt] *inf* = am not, are not, is not, have not, has not.

air [eə] ◇ *n* - **1.** [gen] Luft *die*; **to throw sthg into the ~** etw in die Luft werfen; **by ~** [travel] mit dem Flugzeug; **to be (up) in the ~** *fig* ungewiss sein - **2.** [look] Aussehen *das*; [facial expression] Miene *die* - **3.** RADIO & TV: **to**

be on the ~ [programme] gesendet werden ◇ *comp* Luft- ◇ *vt* - **1.** [washing] nachtrocknen lassen - **2.** [room, bed] lüften - **3.** [feelings, opinions] äußern - **4.** [broadcast] senden ◇ *vi* [washing] nachtrocknen.

air bag *n* AUT Airbag *der.*

airbase ['eəbeɪs] *n* Luftstützpunkt *der.*

airbed ['eəbed] *n Br* Luftmatratze *die.*

airborne ['eəbɔːn] *adj* - **1.** [troops, regiment] Luftlande- - **2.** [plane] in der Luft.

air-conditioned [-kən'dɪʃnd] *adj* klimatisiert.

air-conditioning [-kən'dɪʃnɪŋ] *n* [device] Klimaanlage *die;* [process] Klimatisierung *die.*

aircraft ['eəkrɑːft] (*pl inv*) *n* Flugzeug *das.*

aircraft carrier *n* Flugzeugträger *der.*

airfield ['eəfiːld] *n* Flugplatz *der.*

airforce ['eəfɔːs] *n* Luftwaffe *die.*

air freshener [-ˌfreʃnə'] *n* Raumspray *das.*

airgun ['eəgʌn] *n* Luftgewehr *das.*

airhostess ['eəˌhəʊstɪs] *n* Stewardess *die.*

airlift ['eəlɪft] ◇ *n* Luftbrücke *die* ◇ *vt* über eine Luftbrücke befördern.

airline ['eəlaɪn] *n* Fluglinie *die.*

airliner ['eəlaɪnə'] *n* Verkehrsflugzeug *das.*

airmail ['eəmeɪl] *n* Luftpost *die;* **by ~** mit OR per Luftpost.

airplane ['eəpleɪn] *n Am* = aeroplane.

airport ['eəpɔːt] *n* Flughafen *der.*

air raid *n* Luftangriff *der.*

air rifle *n* Luftgewehr *das.*

airsick ['eəsɪk] *adj:* **I often get ~** im Flugzeug wird mir leicht übel.

airspace ['eəspeɪs] *n* Luftraum *der.*

air steward *n* Steward *der.*

airstrip ['eəstrɪp] *n* Start- und Landebahn *die.*

air terminal *n* Terminal *das* OR *der.*

airtight ['eətaɪt] *adj* luftdicht.

air-traffic controller *n* Fluglotse *der,* -sin *die.*

airy ['eərɪ] *adj* - **1.** [room] luftig - **2.** [notions] abstrus; [promises] vage - **3.** [nonchalant] lässig, nonchalant.

aisle [aɪl] *n* - **1.** [in church - central] Mittelgang *der;* [- at side] Seitenschiff *das* - **2.** [in plane, theatre, shop] Gang *der.*

ajar [ə'dʒɑː'] *adj* angelehnt.

aka (*abbr of* also known as) alias.

akin [ə'kɪn] *adj:* **~ to** vergleichbar mit.

alacrity [ə'lækrətɪ] *n fml* [eagerness] Eifer *der;* **she accepted our offer with ~** sie nahm unser Angebot ohne zu zögern an.

alarm [ə'lɑːm] ◇ *n* - **1.** [fear] Beunruhigung *die* - **2.** [device] Alarmanlage *die;* **to raise** OR **sound the ~** [by activating device] Alarm geben; [by shouting] Alarm schlagen ◇ *vt* [scare] beunruhigen, alarmieren.

alarm clock *n* Wecker *der.*

alarming [ə'lɑːmɪŋ] *adj* beunruhigend.

alas [ə'læs] *excl literary* leider.

Albania [æl'beɪnjə] *n* Albanien *nt.*

Albanian [æl'beɪnjən] ◇ *adj* albanisch ◇ *n* [person] Albaner *der,* -in *die.*

albeit [ɔːl'biːɪt] *conj fml* wenn auch.

albino [æl'biːnəʊ] (*pl* -s) *n* Albino *der.*

album ['ælbəm] *n* Album *das.*

alcohol ['ælkəhɒl] *n* Alkohol *der.*

alcoholic [ˌælkə'hɒlɪk] ◇ *adj* [drink] alkoholisch ◇ *n* Alkoholiker *der,* -in *die.*

alcove ['ælkəʊv] *n* [in room] Alkoven *der;* [in wall] Nische *die.*

ale [eɪl] *n* Ale *das.*

alert [ə'lɜːt] ◇ *adj* - **1.** [vigilant] wachsam - **2.** [perceptive] aufmerksam; [as character trait] aufgeweckt - **3.** [aware]: **to be ~ to sthg** sich (*D*) einer Sache (*G*) bewusst sein ◇ *n* Alarm *der;* **on the ~** [watchful] auf der Hut; MIL in Gefechtsbereitschaft ◇ *vt* - **1.** [police, fire brigade] alarmieren; [to imminent danger] warnen - **2.** [make aware]: **to ~ sb to sthg** jm etw bewusst machen.

A level (*abbr of* Advanced level) *n einzelne Prüfung des Schulabschlusses weiterführender Schulen in England, Wales und Nordirland.*

A level

Die A level-Prüfungen entsprechen in etwa dem deutschen Abitur bzw. der schweizerischen Matura und werden von Schülern im Alter von 18 Jahren abgelegt. Ihr Bestehen ist Voraussetzung für ein Hochschulstudium in Großbritannien. Im britischen Schulsystem wählen die Schüler bis zu vier Fächer, und in jedem Fach wird eine A level-Prüfung abgelegt. Die A level-Endnoten sind sehr wichtig, da sie mit entscheiden, ob ein Schüler an der Universität der eigenen Wahl angenommen wird.

alfresco [æl'freskəʊ] *adj & adv* im Freien.

algae ['ældʒiː] *npl* Algen *pl.*

algebra ['ældʒɪbrə] *n* Algebra *die.*

Algeria [æl'dʒɪərɪə] *n* Algerien *nt.*

alias ['eɪlɪəs] (*pl* -es) ◇ *adv* alias ◇ *n* Deckname *der.*

alibi ['ælɪbaɪ] *n* Alibi *das.*

alien ['eɪljən] ◇ *adj* - **1.** [foreign] ausländisch - **2.** [from outer space] außerirdisch - **3.** [unfamiliar] fremd ◇ *n* - **1.** [from outer space] Außerirdische *der, die* - **2.** LAW [foreigner] Ausländer *der,* -in *die.*

alienate ['eɪljəneɪt] *vt* [voters, supporters] verärgern, entfremden.

alight [ə'laɪt] (*pt & pp* -ed *or* alit) ◇ *adj:* **to be ~** brennen; **to set sthg ~** etw anzünden ◇ *vi fml* - **1.** [bird, insect] sich niederlassen - **2.** [from train, bus] aussteigen.

align [ə'laɪn] vt [line up] ausrichten.

alike [ə'laɪk] adj & adv [similar] ähnlich; [identical] gleich; **to look ~** [similar] ähnlich aussehen; [identical] gleich aussehen.

alimony ['ælɪmənɪ] n Unterhaltszahlung die.

alive [ə'laɪv] adj [living, lively] lebendig; **is he still ~?** lebt er noch?; **to keep a tradition ~** eine Tradition aufrechterhalten.

alkali ['ælkəlaɪ] (pl -s OR -es) n Alkali das.

all [ɔːl] <> adj - **1.** [the whole of – with sg noun] ganze; **~ the money** das ganze Geld; **~ the time** immer; **~ day/evening** den ganzen Tag/Abend; **~ his life** sein ganzes Leben lang - **2.** [every one of – with pl noun] alle, -r, -s; **~ the people** alle Menschen; **~ three died** alle drei starben; **at ~ hours** zu jeder Tages- und Nachtzeit <> pron - **1.** [everything]: **~ of the cake** der ganze Kuchen; **is that ~?** [in shop] ist das alles?; **she ate it ~, she ate ~ of it** sie aß alles auf; **it's ~ gone** es ist nichts mehr da - **2.** [everybody] alle; **~ of us went, we ~ went** wir sind alle gegangen - **3.** (with superl): **the best of ~** der/die/das Allerbeste; **the biggest of ~** der/die/das Allergrößte; **he is the cleverest of ~** er ist der klügste von allen; **and, best of ~, ...** und (was) das Beste ist, ... <> adv - **1.** [completely] ganz; **~ alone** ganz allein; **dressed ~ in red** ganz in rot gekleidet; **the water spilled ~ over the carpet** das Wasser ergoss sich über den Teppichboden; **I'd forgotten ~ about that** das hatte ich völlig vergessen; **~ told** [in total] insgesamt - **2.** [in scores] beide; **it's two ~** es steht zwei beide - **3.** (with compar): **you'll feel ~ the better for it** du wirst dich danach umso besser fühlen; **to run ~ the faster** noch schneller laufen - **4.** [in phrases]: **~ over** [finished] alles vorbei. ◆ **above all** adv ▷ above. ◆ **after all** adv ▷ after. ◆ **all but** adv fast; **~ but empty** fast leer. ◆ **all in all** adv alles in allem. ◆ **at all** adv ▷ at. ◆ **in all** adv [in total] zusammen; [in summary] alles in allem.

Allah ['ælə] n Allah.

all-around adj Am = all-round.

allay [ə'leɪ] vt fml [fears, doubts] weitgehend zerstreuen; [anger] vermindern.

all clear n - **1.** [signal] Entwarnung die - **2.** fig [go-ahead] Bewilligung die.

allegation [,ælɪ'geɪʃn] n Behauptung die.

allege [ə'ledʒ] vt behaupten; **he is ~d to have passed on the information** er soll die Informationen weitergegeben haben.

allegedly [ə'ledʒɪdlɪ] adv angeblich.

allergic [ə'lɜːdʒɪk] adj: **~ (to)** allergisch (gegen).

allergy ['ælədʒɪ] n Allergie die; **to have an ~ to sthg** eine Allergie gegen etw haben.

alleviate [ə'liːvɪeɪt] vt mildern.

alley(way) ['ælɪ(weɪ)] n [street] (enge) Gasse die; [in garden] Weg der.

alliance [ə'laɪəns] n Bündnis das.

allied ['ælaɪd] adj - **1.** MIL verbündet, alliiert - **2.** [related] verwandt.

alligator ['ælɪgeɪtə'] (pl inv OR -s) n Alligator der.

all-important adj [crucial] entscheidend.

all-in adj Br [price] Pauschal-. ◆ **all in** <> adj [tired] völlig OR total erledigt <> adv Br [inclusive] alles inklusive.

all-night adj [party, session] die ganze Nacht dauernd; [shop] nachts durchgehend geöffnet.

allocate ['æləkeɪt] vt: **to ~ sthg to sb** [money, resources] jm etw zur Verfügung stellen; [task, seats] jm etw zuweisen; [tickets] etw an jn verteilen.

allot [ə'lɒt] vt [task] zuweisen; [money, resources] zur Verfügung stellen; [time] vorlsehen.

allotment [ə'lɒtmənt] n - **1.** Br [garden] Schrebergarten der - **2.** [sharing out - of task] Zuweisung die; [- of money, resources] Verteilung die; [- of time] Vorsehen das - **3.** [share - of money, resources] Anteil der; [- of time] Zeitrahmen der.

all-out adj [effort] äußerst; [war] total; [attack] massiv.

allow [ə'laʊ] vt - **1.** [permit] erlauben; **to ~ sb to do sthg** jm erlauben, etw zu tun; **to be ~ed to do sthg** etw tun dürfen - **2.** [allocate - money] einlrechnen; [- time] einlplanen - **3.** [admit]: **to ~ that ...** einlräumen, dass ... ◆ **allow for** vt fus einlkalkulieren.

allowance [ə'laʊəns] n - **1.** [grant] finanzielle Unterstützung; **travel ~** Reisekostenzuschuss der; **clothing ~** Kleidungsgeld das - **2.** Am [pocket money] Taschengeld das - **3.** [excuse]: **to make ~s for sb** mit jm Nachsicht haben; **to make ~s for sthg** etw berücksichtigen.

alloy ['ælɔɪ] n Legierung die.

all right <> adv - **1.** [healthy, unharmed]: **to feel ~** sich ganz gut fühlen; **did you get home ~?** bist du gut nach Hause gekommen? - **2.** inf [acceptably] ganz gut - **3.** inf [indicating agreement] **okay - 4.** inf [certainly]: **it's pneumonia ~** es ist sicher Lungenentzündung - **5.** [do you understand?]: **all right?** okay? - **6.** [now then]: **~, let's go** okay, auf gehts <> adj - **1.** [healthy, unharmed]: **are you ~?** bist du in Ordnung? - **2.** inf [acceptable]: **it was ~** es war ganz ordentlich; **that's ~** [never mind] das ist schon in Ordnung - **3.** [permitted]: **is it ~ if I make a phone call?** haben Sie etwas dagegen, wenn ich (kurz) telefoniere?

all-round Br, **all-around** Am adj [athlete] Allround-; [worker] vielseitig begabt.

all-time adj [record, best] absolut.

allude [ə'lu:d] *vi*: **to ~ to sthg** auf etw (A) an|spielen.

alluring [ə'ljʊərɪŋ] *adj* verführerisch.

allusion [ə'lu:ʒn] *n* Anspielung *die*.

ally ['ælaɪ] *n* Verbündete *der, die*.

almighty [ɔ:l'maɪtɪ] *adj inf* [noise, fuss] Riesen-.

almond ['ɑ:mənd] *n* Mandel *die*.

almost ['ɔ:lməʊst] *adv* fast, beinahe; **I ~ missed the bus** ich hätte beinahe den Bus verpasst.

alms [ɑ:mz] *npl dated* Almosen *pl*.

aloft [ə'lɒft] *adv* [in the air]: **to hold sthg ~** etw in die Höhe halten.

alone [ə'ləʊn] <> *adj* allein, -e <> *adv* - **1.** [without others] allein, -e - **2.** [only] nur, allein; **you ~ can help me** nur du OR du allein kannst mir helfen - **3.** [untouched, unchanged]: **to leave sthg ~** etw in Ruhe lassen; **leave me ~!** lass mich in Ruhe! ➠ **let alone** *conj* geschweige denn.

along [ə'lɒŋ] <> *adv* - **1.** [indicating movement]: **to stroll ~** dahin|schlendern; **they went ~ to the demonstration** sie gingen zu der Vorführung - **2.** [with others]: **to take sb/sthg ~** jn/etw mit|nehmen; **to come ~** mit|kommen <> *prep* entlang (+ A); **they walked ~ the river** sie liefen den Fluss entlang; **they walked ~ the forest path** sie folgten dem Waldweg; **the trees ~ the path** die Bäume neben dem Weg. ➠ **all along** *adv* die ganze Zeit. ➠ **along with** *prep* zusammen mit.

alongside [ə,lɒŋ'saɪd] <> *prep* neben (+ D); [with verbs of motion] neben (+ A) <> *adv* daneben.

aloof [ə'lu:f] <> *adj* unnahbar <> *adv*: **to remain ~ (from)** sich fern|halten (von).

aloud [ə'laʊd] *adv* laut.

alphabet ['ælfəbet] *n* Alphabet *das*.

alphabetical [,ælfə'betɪkl] *adj* alphabetisch.

Alps [ælps] *npl*: **the ~** die Alpen *pl*.

already [ɔ:l'redɪ] *adv* schon.

alright [,ɔ:l'raɪt] *adv & adj* = all right.

Alsatian [æl'seɪʃn] *n* [dog] (deutscher) Schäferhund.

also ['ɔ:lsəʊ] *adv* auch.

altar ['ɔ:ltə'] *n* Altar *der*.

alter ['ɔ:ltə'] <> *vt* ändern; [appearance] verändern; [text] ab|ändern <> *vi* sich ändern; [appearance] sich verändern.

alteration [,ɔ:ltə'reɪʃn] *n* Änderung *die*; [of appearance] Veränderung *die*; [of text] Abänderung *die*.

alternate [*adj Br* ɔ:l'tɜ:nət, *Am* 'ɔ:ltərnət, *vb* 'ɔ:ltərneɪt] <> *adj* - **1.** [by turns] abwechselnd - **2.** [every other]: **on ~ days** jeden zweiten Tag <> *vt* ab|wechseln <> *vi*: **to ~ (with)** sich ab|wechseln (mit); **to ~ between sthg**

and sthg zwischen etw (D) und etw (D) (abl) wechseln.

alternately [ɔ:l'tɜ:nətlɪ] *adv* abwechselnd.

alternating current ['ɔ:ltəneɪtɪŋ-] *n* ELEC Wechselstrom *der*.

alternative [ɔ:l'tɜ:nətɪv] <> *adj* - **1.** [different, other] andere, -r, -s - **2.** [nontraditional] alternativ <> *n* Alternative *die*; **an ~ to sb/ sthg** eine Alternative zu jm/etw; **to have no ~ (but to do sthg)** keine (andere) Wahl haben(, als etw zu tun).

alternatively [ɔ:l'tɜ:nətɪvlɪ] *adv* oder aber, aber auch.

alternative medicine *n* (U) alternative Heilmethoden *pl*.

alternator ['ɔ:ltəneɪtə'] *n* ELEC Wechselstromgenerator *der*; [in car] Lichtmaschine *die*.

although [ɔ:l'ðəʊ] *conj* obwohl.

altitude ['æltɪtju:d] *n* Höhe *die*.

altogether [,ɔ:ltə'geðə'] *adv* - **1.** [completely] vollkommen - **2.** [in general, in total] insgesamt.

aluminium *Br* [,æljʊ'mɪnɪəm], **aluminum** *Am* [ə'lu:mɪnəm] <> *n* Aluminium *das* <> *comp* Aluminium-.

always ['ɔ:lweɪz] *adv* immer; **you can ~ stay at my place** du kannst auch bei mir übernachten.

am [æm] *vb* ➠ be.

a.m. (*abbr of* ante meridiem) vormittags; **at 3 ~** um 3 Uhr morgens OR früh; **12 ~** 12 Uhr.

amalgamate [ə'mælgəmeɪt] <> *vt* mischen <> *vi* sich verbinden.

amass [ə'mæs] *vt* [fortune, power, information] anhäufen.

amateur ['æmətə'] <> *adj* - **1.** [nonprofessional] Amateur- - **2.** *pej* [unprofessional] dilettantisch <> *n* [nonprofessional] Amateur *der*, *-in die*.

amateurish ['æmətərɪʃ] *adj pej* [unprofessional] dilettantisch.

amaze [ə'meɪz] *vt* erstaunen, verblüffen.

amazed [ə'meɪzd] *adj* erstaunt, verblüfft.

amazement [ə'meɪzmənt] *n* Erstaunen *das*.

amazing [ə'meɪzɪŋ] *adj* erstaunlich.

Amazon ['æməzn] *n* - **1.** [river]: **the ~** der Amazonas - **2.** [region]: **the ~ (Basin)** das Amazonasbecken; **the ~ rainforest** der Regenwald am Amazonas.

ambassador [æm'bæsədə'] *n* Botschafter *der*, *-in die*.

amber ['æmbə'] *n* - **1.** [substance] Bernstein *der* - **2.** *Br* [colour of traffic light] Gelb *das*.

ambiguous [æm'bɪɡjʊəs] *adj* [two possible meanings] zweideutig; [many possible meanings] mehrdeutig.

ambition [æm'bɪʃn] *n* - **1.** Ehrgeiz *der* - **2.** [objective, goal] Ambition *die*.

ambitious [æm'bɪʃəs] *adj* ehrgeizig.

amble ['æmbl] *vi* schlendern.

ambulance ['æmbjʊləns] *n* Krankenwagen *der*, Ambulanz *die*.

ambush ['æmbʊʃ] <> *n* Hinterhalt *der* <> *vt* [attack] aus dem Hinterhalt überfallen.

amenable [ə'miːnəbl] *adj*: ~ **(to sthg)** (einer Sache *(D)*) zugänglich.

amend [ə'mend] *vt* [change] abändern.
◆ **amends** *npl*: **to make ~s (for sthg)** Entschädigungen (für etw) bieten.

amendment [ə'mendmənt] *n* Änderung *die*.

amenities [ə'miːnətɪz] *npl* Einrichtungen *pl*.

America [ə'merɪkə] *n* Amerika *nt*.

American [ə'merɪkn] <> *adj* amerikanisch <> *n* Amerikaner *der*, -in *die*.

American football *n* Br American Football *der*.

American Indian *n* Indianer *der*, -in *die*.

amiable ['eɪmjəbl] *adj* freundlich.

amicable ['æmɪkəbl] *adj* freundschaftlich; [agreement] gütlich.

amid(st) [ə'mɪd(st)] *prep fml* inmitten *(+ G)*.

amiss [ə'mɪs] <> *adj*: **is there anything ~?** stimmt etwas nicht? <> *adv*: **to take sthg ~** etw übel nehmen.

ammonia [ə'məʊnjə] *n* Ammoniak *der*.

ammunition [,æmjʊ'nɪʃn] *n* Munition *die*.

amnesia [æm'niːzjə] *n* Amnesie *die*.

amnesty ['æmnəstɪ] *n* Amnestie *die*.

amok [ə'mɒk] *adv*: **to run ~** Amok laufen.

among(st) [ə'mʌŋ(st)] *prep* unter *(+ D)*; ~ **other things** unter anderem; **I count him ~ my friends** ich zähle ihn zu meinen Freunden; **they were talking ~ themselves** sie unterhielten sich.

amoral [,eɪ'mɒrəl] *adj* amoralisch.

amorous ['æmərəs] *adj* amourös.

amount [ə'maʊnt] *n* - **1.** [quantity] Menge *die* - **2.** [sum of money] Betrag *der*.
◆ **amount to** *vt fus* - **1.** [total] sich belaufen auf *(+ A)* - **2.** [be equivalent to] hinauslaufen auf *(+ A)*.

amp [æmp] *n abbr of* ampere.

ampere ['æmpeə'] *n* Ampere *das*.

amphibious [æm'fɪbɪəs] *adj* amphibisch.

ample ['æmpl] *adj* - **1.** [enough] reichlich - **2.** [large] großzügig.

amplifier ['æmplɪfaɪə'] *n* Verstärker *der*.

amputate ['æmpjʊteɪt] *vt & vi* amputieren.

Amsterdam [,æmstə'dæm] *n* Amsterdam *nt*.

amuck [ə'mʌk] *adv* = amok.

amuse [ə'mjuːz] *vt* - **1.** [make laugh] amüsieren - **2.** [entertain] unterhalten; **to ~ o.s. (with sthg)** sich *(D)* (mit etw) die Zeit vertreiben.

amused [ə'mjuːzd] *adj* amüsiert; **to be ~ at** OR **by sthg** von etw erheitert sein; **to keep o.s. ~** sich die Zeit vertreiben.

amusement [ə'mjuːzmənt] *n* - **1.** [enjoyment] Vergnügen *das* - **2.** [diversion, game] Unterhaltungsmöglichkeit *die*.

amusement arcade *n* Spielhalle *die*.

amusement park *n* Vergnügungspark *der*.

amusing [ə'mjuːzɪŋ] *adj* [funny] amüsant.

an [*stressed* æn, *unstressed* ən] *indef art* ⊳ a².

anaemic Br, **anemic** Am [ə'niːmɪk] *adj* [suffering from anaemia] anämisch.

anaesthetic Br, **anesthetic** Am [,ænɪs'θetɪk] *n* Anästhetikum *das*, Narkosemittel *das*; **under ~** unter Narkose, in der Narkose.

analogue Br, **analog** Am ['ænəlɒg] *adj* analog.

analogy [ə'nælədʒɪ] *n* Analogie *die*; **by ~** analog dazu.

analyse Br, **-lyze** Am ['ænəlaɪz] *vt* analysieren.

analysis [ə'næləsɪs] (*pl* -ses [ə'næləsiːz]) *n* [gen] Analyse *die*.

analyst ['ænəlɪst] *n* - **1.** [political, computer, statistics] Analytiker *der*, -in *die* - **2.** [psychoanalyst] Psychoanalytiker *der*, -in *die*.

analytic(al) [,ænə'lɪtɪk(l)] *adj* analytisch.

analyze *vt Am* = analyse.

anarchist ['ænəkɪst] *n* Anarchist *der*, -in *die*.

anarchy ['ænəkɪ] *n* Anarchie *die*.

anathema [ə'næθəmə] *n* Anathema *das*.

anatomy [ə'nætəmɪ] *n* Anatomie *die*.

ancestor ['ænsestə'] *n* [person] Vorfahr *der*.

anchor ['æŋkə'] <> *n* - **1.** NAUT Anker *der*; **to drop/weigh ~** Anker werfen/lichten - **2.** TV Moderator *der*, -in *die* <> *vt* - **1.** [secure] sichern - **2.** TV moderieren <> *vi* NAUT ankern.

anchovy ['æntʃəvɪ] (*pl inv* OR -ies) *n* Sardelle *die*.

ancient ['eɪnʃənt] *adj* - **1.** [dating from distant past] alt - **2.** *hum* [very old] alt, uralt.

ancillary [æn'sɪlərɪ] *adj* [staff, device] Hilfs-.

and [*stressed* ænd, *unstressed* ənd, ən] *conj* - **1.** [gen] und; ~ **you?** und du/Sie?; **my wife ~ I** meine Frau und ich; **nice ~ warm** schön warm - **2.** [in numbers]: **a hundred ~ one** hunderteins; **an hour ~ a quarter** eineinviertel Stunden - **3.** [with repetition]: **more ~ more** immer mehr; **for days ~ days** tagelang - **4.** *(with infinitive)* [in order to]: **to try ~ do sthg** versuchen, etw zu tun; **wait ~ see!** warte es ab!, warten Sie es ab! ◆ **and all that** *adv* und dergleichen. ◆ **and so on, and so forth** *adv* und so weiter, und so fort.

Andes ['ændiːz] *n*: **the ~** die Anden *pl*.

anecdote ['ænɪkdəʊt] *n* Anekdote *die*.

anemic *adj Am* = anaemic.

anesthetic *etc Am* = anaesthetic *etc*.

anew [ə'njuː] *adv* von neuem.

angel ['eɪndʒl] *n lit & fig* Engel *der*.

anger ['æŋgə'] <> *n* Zorn *der* <> *vt* ärgern.

angina [æn'dʒaɪnə] *n* Angina pectoris *die*.

angle ['æŋgl] *n* - **1.** MATH [corner] Winkel *der*

- **2.** [point of view] Standpunkt *der* - **3.** [slope] Schräge *die*; **at an ~** im schrägen Winkel.

angler ['æŋglə'] *n* Angler *der*, -in *die*.

Anglican ['æŋglɪkən] <> *adj* anglikanisch <> *n* Anglikaner *der*, -in *die*.

angling ['æŋglɪŋ] *n* Angeln *das*.

angry ['æŋgrɪ] *adj* böse; **to be ~ (with sb)** (jm) böse sein; **to get ~ (with sb)** böse werden (auf jn).

anguish ['æŋgwɪʃ] *n* Qual *die*.

angular ['æŋgjʊlə'] *adj* [face, jaw, body] kantig; [furniture, car] eckig.

animal ['ænɪml] <> *adj* - **1.** [gen] Tier- - **2.** [physical] animalisch <> *n* - **1.** [living creature] Tier *das* - **2.** *inf pej* [brutal person] Bestie *die*.

animate ['ænɪmət] *adj* [alive] lebend.

animated ['ænɪmeɪtɪd] *adj* [lively] lebhaft.

aniseed ['ænɪsiːd] *n* Anis *der*.

ankle ['æŋkl] <> *n* Knöchel *der* <> *comp* Knöchel-; **~ socks** Söckchen *pl*.

annex ['æneks] *vt* annektieren.

annexe ['æneks] *n* [building] Anbau *der*.

annihilate [ə'naɪəleɪt] *vt* vernichten.

anniversary [ˌænɪ'vɜːsərɪ] *n* Jahrestag *der*.

announce [ə'naʊns] *vt* - **1.** [make public] anlkündigen - **2.** [state, declare] verkünden.

announcement [ə'naʊnsmənt] *n* [public statement] Bekanntmachung *die*; **government ~** Regierungserklärung *die*.

announcer [ə'naʊnsə'] *n* Ansager *der*, -in *die*; **television ~** Fernsehansager *der*, -in *die*; **radio ~** Radioansager *der*, -in *die*.

annoy [ə'nɔɪ] *vt* ärgern.

annoyance [ə'nɔɪəns] *n* Ärgernis *das*.

annoyed [ə'nɔɪd] *adj* verärgert; **to be ~ at sthg/with sb** über etw/jn verärgert sein; **to get ~** sich ärgern.

annoying [ə'nɔɪŋ] *adj* ärgerlich.

annual ['ænjʊəl] <> *adj* jährlich, Jahres- <> *n* - **1.** [plant] einjährige Pflanze - **2.** [book] Jahrbuch *das*.

annual general meeting *n* Jahreshauptversammlung *die*.

annul [ə'nʌl] *vt* annullieren.

annulment [ə'nʌlmənt] *n* Annullierung *die*.

annum ['ænəm] *n*: **per ~** pro Jahr.

anomaly [ə'nɒməlɪ] *n* Anomalie *die*.

anonymous [ə'nɒnɪməs] *adj* anonym.

anorak ['ænəræk] *n esp Br* Anorak *der*.

anorexia (nervosa) [ˌænə'reksɪə (nɜː'vəʊsə)] *n* Anorexie *die*, Magersucht *die*.

anorexic [ˌænə'reksɪk] <> *adj* magersüchtig <> *n* Magersüchtige *der*, *die*.

another [ə'nʌðə'] <> *adj* - **1.** [additional] noch eine, -r, -s; **in ~ few minutes** in einigen Minuten - **2.** [different] ein anderer, eine andere, ein anderes <> *pron* - **1.** [an additional one] noch eine, -r, -s; **one after ~** einer/eine/

eines nach dem/der anderen - **2.** [a different one] etwas anderes; **they love one ~** sie lieben einander, sie lieben sich; **they are always arguing with one ~** sie streiten immer miteinander, sie streiten (sich) immer.

answer ['ɑːnsə'] <> *n* - **1.** [reply] Antwort *die*; **in ~ to** als Antwort auf (+ *A*) - **2.** [solution] Lösung *die* <> *vt* - **1.** [reply to - question, letter, advertisement] beantworten - **2.** [respond to]: **to ~ the door** die Tür öffnen; **to ~ the phone** den Hörer ablnehmen <> *vi* [reply] antworten. **◆ answer back** *vt sep & vi* widersprechen (+ *D*). **◆ answer for** *vt fus* verantworten.

answerable ['ɑːnsərəbl] *adj* [accountable] verantwortlich; **~ to sb/for sthg** jm gegenüber/für etw verantwortlich.

answering machine ['ɑːnsərɪŋ-] *n* Anrufbeantworter *der*.

ant [ænt] *n* Ameise *die*.

antagonism [æn'tægənɪzm] *n* Feindlichkeit *die*, Feindseligkeit *die*.

antagonize, -ise [æn'tægənaɪz] *vt*: **to ~ sb** jn gegen sich auflbringen.

Antarctic [æn'tɑːktɪk] <> *n*: **the ~** die Antarktis <> *adj* antarktisch.

antelope ['æntɪləʊp] (*pl inv* OR **-s**) *n* Antilope *die*.

antenatal [ˌæntɪ'neɪtl] *adj* Schwangerschafts-.

antenatal clinic *n* Sprechstunde *die* für Schwangere.

antenna [æn'tenə] (*pl sense 1* **-nae** [-niː], *pl sense 2* **-s**) *n* - **1.** [of insect, lobster] Fühler *der* - **2.** *Am* [aerial] Antenne *die*.

anthem ['ænθəm] *n* Hymne *die*.

anthology [æn'θɒlədʒɪ] *n* Anthologie *die*.

anthrax ['ænθræks] *n* Milzbrand *der*.

antibiotic [ˌæntɪbaɪ'ɒtɪk] *n* Antibiotikum *das*.

antibody ['æntɪˌbɒdɪ] *n* Antikörper *der*.

anticipate [æn'tɪsɪpeɪt] *vt* - **1.** [expect] erwarten, vorauslsehen - **2.** [preempt]: **to ~ sb** jm zuvorlkommen.

anticipation [ænˌtɪsɪ'peɪʃn] *n* Erwartung *die*; **in ~ of** in Erwartung von.

anticlimax [ˌæntɪ'klaɪmæks] *n* Enttäuschung *die*.

anticlockwise *Br* [ˌæntɪ'klɒkwaɪz] <> *adj* [direction] Links- <> *adv* gegen den Uhrzeigersinn, nach links.

antics ['æntɪks] *npl* - **1.** [of children, animals] Possen *pl* - **2.** *pej* [of politician *etc*] Eskapaden *pl*.

anticyclone [ˌæntɪ'saɪkləʊn] *n* Hoch *das*.

antidepressant [ˌæntɪdɪ'presnt] *n* Antidepressivum *das*.

antidote ['æntɪdəʊt] *n lit & fig*: **~ (to)** Gegenmittel *das* (gegen).

antifreeze ['æntɪfriːz] *n* Frostschutzmittel *das*.

antihistamine [ˌæntɪˈhɪstəmɪn] n Antihistamin das.

antiperspirant [ˌæntɪˈpɜːspərənt] n Deodorant das.

antiquated [ˈæntɪkweɪtɪd] adj antiquiert.

antique [ænˈtiːk] ◇ adj antik ◇ n Antiquität die.

antique shop n Antiquitätenhandlung die.

anti-Semitism [ˌæntɪˈsemɪtɪzəm] n Antisemitismus der.

antiseptic [ˌæntɪˈseptɪk] ◇ adj steril, desinfiziert ◇ n Antiseptikum das.

antisocial [ˌæntɪˈsəʊʃl] adj - 1. [damaging to society] unsozial - 2. [unsociable] ungesellig; [working hours] unsozial.

antlers [ˈæntləz] npl Geweih das.

anus [ˈeɪnəs] n After der.

anvil [ˈænvɪl] n Amboss der.

anxiety [æŋˈzaɪətɪ] n - 1. [worry, cause of worry] Sorge die - 2. [keenness] Ungeduld die.

anxious [ˈæŋkʃəs] adj - 1. [worried] besorgt; **to be ~ about sb/sthg** sich um jn/etw sorgen - 2. [keen]: **to be ~ to do sthg** darauf brennen, etw zu tun.

any [ˈenɪ] ◇ adj - 1. (in questions): **have you got ~ money?** hast du Geld?; **have you got ~ postcards?** haben Sie Postkarten?; **can I be of ~ help?** kann ich Ihnen irgendwie behilflich sein? - 2. (with negatives): **I haven't got ~ money** ich habe kein Geld; **we don't have ~ rooms** wir haben keine Zimmer frei; **he never does ~ housework** er tut nie etwas im Haushalt - 3. [no matter which] irgendein, -e; **take ~ one you like** nimm, welches du willst; **~ beer will do** jedes Bier ist recht; **at ~ time** jederzeit; ⊳ case, day, moment, rate ◇ pron - 1. (in questions) welche; **I'm looking for a hotel – are there ~ nearby?** ich suche ein Hotel – gibts hier welche in der Nähe?; **can ~ of you change a tyre?** kann jemand von euch einen Reifen wechseln? - 2. (with if): **if ~** wenn überhaupt; **few foreign films, if ~, are successful here** nur wenige ausländische Filme haben hier Erfolg - 3. (with negatives): **I don't want ~ (of them)** ich möchte keinen/keines/keine (von denen) - 4. [no matter which one] jede, -r, -s; **take ~ you like** nimm, welches du willst; **you can sit at ~ of the tables** Sie können sich an jeden beliebigen Tisch setzen ◇ adv - 1. (in questions): **is there ~ more ice cream?** ist noch Eis da?; **is that ~ better?** ist das besser? - 2. (with negatives): **we can't wait ~ longer** wir können nicht mehr länger warten; **I can't see it ~ more** ich kann es nicht mehr sehen.

anybody [ˈenɪˌbɒdɪ] pron = anyone.

anyhow [ˈenɪhaʊ] adv - 1. [in spite of that] trotzdem - 2. [carelessly] durcheinander, wahllos - 3. [returning to topic] jedenfalls.

anyone [ˈenɪwʌn] pron - 1. [any person] jeder; **~ can tell you that** (ein) jeder kann dir das sagen; **~ else would have given up** jeder andere hätte es aufgegeben; **if ~ asks, you haven't seen me** wenn jemand fragt, du hast mich nicht gesehen - 2. (in questions) irgendjemand; **has ~ seen my book?** hat irgendjemand mein Buch gesehen?; **do you know ~ else?** kennst du sonst noch jemanden? - 3. (in negative statements): **there wasn't ~ in** niemand war zu Hause; **I didn't see ~ else** ich habe sonst niemanden gesehen; **there was hardly ~ there** es war kaum jemand dort.

anyplace [ˈenɪpleɪs] adv Am = anywhere.

anything [ˈenɪθɪŋ] pron - 1. [no matter what] alles; **he eats ~** er isst alles; **if ~ should happen to him** falls ihm irgendetwas zustoßen sollte - 2. (in questions) irgendetwas; **would you like ~ else?** darf es noch etwas sein? - 3. (in negative statements): **I don't want ~ at all** ich möchte überhaupt nichts (haben); **he didn't tell me ~** er hat mir nichts gesagt; **hardly ~** kaum etwas; **not for ~** um keinen Preis.

anyway [ˈenɪweɪ] adv - 1. [in any case] sowieso - 2. [in spite of that] trotzdem - 3. [in conversation] jedenfalls; **~, there we were, ...** nun ja, jedenfalls standen wir da ...

anywhere [ˈenɪweə'] adv - 1. [any place] überall; **sit ~ you like** setz dich einfach irgendwohin; **~ else** woanders, anderswo - 2. (in questions) irgendwo; **have you seen my jacket ~?** hast du meine Jacke irgendwo gesehen?; **did you go ~ else?** bist du/seid Ihr noch irgendwo anders hingegangen? - 3. (in negative statements): **I can't find it ~** ich kann es nirgends finden; **we didn't see ~ interesting** wir haben nichts Interessantes gesehen.

apart [əˈpɑːt] adv - 1. [separated in space] getrennt; **she stood ~ from the group** sie hielt sich abseits der Gruppe - 2. [in several pieces] auseinander; **to fall ~** auseinander fallen; **to take sthg ~** etw auseinander nehmen - 3. [aside, excepted] beiseite; **joking ~** Spaß beiseite. ◆ **apart from** ◇ prep [except for] mit Ausnahme von ◇ conj [in addition to] abgesehen von.

apartheid [əˈpɑːtheɪt] n Apartheid die.

apartment [əˈpɑːtmənt] n esp Am Wohnung die.

apartment building n Am Wohnblock der.

apathy [ˈæpəθɪ] n Teilnahmslosigkeit die.

ape [eɪp] ◇ n [animal] Menschenaffe der ◇ vt pej [imitate] nachläffen.

aperitif [əperəˈtiːf] n Aperitif der.

aperture [ˈæpəˌtjʊə'] n - 1. [hole, opening] Öffnung die - 2. PHOT Blende die.

apex [ˈeɪpeks] (pl -es OR apices) n [top] lit Spitze der; fig Gipfel der.

APEX [ˈeɪpeks] (abbr of advance purchase

excursion) *n Br* zeitlich reglementierter Vorverkauf verbilligter Flugtickets und Bahnfahrkarten.

apices ['eɪpɪsiːz] *pl* ⊏▷ apex.

apiece [ə'piːs] *adv* [object] pro Stück.

apocalypse [ə'pɒkəlɪps] *n* Apokalypse *die*.

apologetic [ə,pɒlə'dʒetɪk] *adj* entschuldigend; **to be ~ (about sthg)** sich (für etw OR wegen etw *(G)*) entschuldigen.

apologize, -ise [ə'pɒlədʒaɪz] *vi* sich entschuldigen; **to ~ to sb for sthg** sich bei jm für etw entschuldigen.

apology [ə'pɒlədʒɪ] *n* Entschuldigung *die*.

apostle [ə'pɒsl] *n* RELIG Apostel *der*.

apostrophe [ə'pɒstrəfɪ] *n* GRAMM Apostroph *der*.

appal *Br*, **appall** *Am* [ə'pɔːl] *vt* entsetzen.

appalling [ə'pɔːlɪŋ] *adj* entsetzlich.

apparatus [,æpə'reɪtəs] *(pl inv OR -es) n* Apparat *der*; [device] Gerät *das*; [in gym] Geräte *pl*.

apparel [ə'pærəl] *n Am* Kleidung *die*.

apparent [ə'pærənt] *adj* - 1. [evident] offensichtlich - 2. [seeming] scheinbar.

apparently [ə'pærəntlɪ] *adv* - 1. [according to rumour] anscheinend - 2. [seemingly] scheinbar.

appeal [ə'piːl] ⟨▷ *vi* - 1. [request] (dringend) bitten; **to ~ to sb for sthg** jn (dringend) um etw bitten; **to ~ to the public to do sthg** die Öffentlichkeit dazu aufrufen, etw zu tun - 2. [to sb's honour, common sense]: **to ~ to** appellieren an *(+ A)* - 3. LAW: **to ~ (against)** Berufung einlegen (gegen) - 4. [attract, interest]: **to ~ to sb** jm gefallen, jm zusagen ⟨▷ *n* - 1. [for help, money] Aufruf *der*, Appell *der*; [for mercy] Gesuch *das* - 2. LAW Berufung *die* - 3. [charm, interest] Reiz *der*.

appealing [ə'piːlɪŋ] *adj* [person] ansprechend; [baby] süß; [idea] reizvoll.

appear [ə'pɪə'] ⟨▷ *vi* - 1. [gen] erscheinen - 2. [in play] auftreten ⟨▷ *vt* [seem] scheinen; **it would ~ that ...** es hat den Anschein, OR es scheint, als ob ...

appearance [ə'pɪərəns] *n* - 1. [gen] Erscheinen *das*; [of symptoms] Auftreten *das* - 2. [outward aspect] äußere Erscheinung; [facial features] Aussehen *das* - 3. [in play, film, on TV] Auftritt *der*.

appease [ə'piːz] *vt* [person, anger] (durch Zugeständnisse) beschwichtigen.

append [ə'pend] *vt fml*: **to ~ sthg (to)** [add] etw hinzufügen (zu); [enclose] etw beifügen *(+ D)*.

appendices [ə'pendɪsiːz] *pl* ⊏▷ appendix.

appendicitis [ə,pendɪ'saɪtɪs] *n (U)* Blinddarmentzündung *die*.

appendix [ə'pendɪks] *(pl -dixes OR -dices) n* - 1. MED Blinddarm *der*; **to have one's ~ out** OR **removed** sich *(D)* den Blinddarm herausnehmen lassen - 2. [in book] Anhang *der*.

appetite ['æpɪtaɪt] *n*: **~ (for)** Appetit *der* (auf *(+ A)*).

appetizer, -iser ['æpɪtaɪzə'] *n* (appetitanregendes) Häppchen; [starter] Vorspeise *die*.

appetizing, -ising ['æpɪtaɪzɪŋ] *adj* appetitlich.

applaud [ə'plɔːd] ⟨▷ *vt* - 1. [person] applaudieren *(+ D)* - 2. *fig* [effort] loben; [decision] begrüßen ⟨▷ *vi* applaudieren.

applause [ə'plɔːz] *n* Applaus *der*.

apple ['æpl] *n* Apfel *der*.

apple tree *n* Apfelbaum *der*.

appliance [ə'plaɪəns] *n* Gerät *das*.

applicable [ə'plɪkəbl] *adj* zutreffend; **delete where not ~** Nichtzutreffendes streichen; **to be ~ to sb/sthg** auf jn/etw zutreffen.

applicant ['æplɪkənt] *n*: **~ (for)** [for job] Bewerber *der*, -in *die* (um OR für); [for state benefit] Antragsteller *der*, -in *die* (für).

application [,æplɪ'keɪʃn] *n* - 1. [for job, college]: **~ (for)** Bewerbung *die* (um OR für) - 2. [for club]: **~ (for)** Antrag *der* (auf *(+ A)*) - 3. [of knowledge, rule] Anwendung *die*; [of invention] Einsatz *der* - 4. [use] Verwendung *die* - 5. [diligence] Fleiß *der* - 6. COMPUT: **~ (program)** Anwendungsprogramm *das*.

application form *n* [for job] Bewerbungsformular *das*; [for state benefit, club] Antragsformular *das*.

applied [ə'plaɪd] *adj* [science] angewandt.

apply [ə'plaɪ] ⟨▷ *vt* - 1. [rule, skill] anlwenden - 2. [paint, ointment] aufltragen; **to ~ the brakes** bremsen ⟨▷ *vi* - 1. [for work, grant]: **to ~ (for)** sich bewerben (um OR für); **to ~ to sb for sthg** sich bei jm um OR für etw bewerben - 2. [be relevant]: **to ~ (to)** zutreffen (auf *(+ A)*).

appoint [ə'pɔɪnt] *vt* [to job, position] einlstellen; [to office] ernennen.

appointment [ə'pɔɪntmənt] *n* - 1. *(U)* [to job, position] Einstellung *die*; [to office] Ernennung *die* - 2. [job, position] Stelle *die* - 3. [with doctor, hairdresser, in business] Termin *der*; **to have an ~** einen Termin haben; **to make an ~** einen Termin vereinbaren.

apportion [ə'pɔːʃn] *vt* [money] aufteilen; [blame] zulweisen.

appraisal [ə'preɪzl] *n* Beurteilung *die*.

appreciable [ə'priːʃəbl] *adj* [difference] merklich; [amount] beträchtlich.

appreciate [ə'priːʃɪeɪt] ⟨▷ *vt* - 1. [value] schätzen; **her books were not ~d at the time** ihre Bücher wurden damals nicht gewürdigt - 2. [recognize, understand] sich *(D)* bewusst sein *(+ G)* - 3. [help, advice] dankbar sein für; **thanks, I really ~ it!** danke schön, sehr nett von dir/Ihnen! ⟨▷ *vi* FIN im Wert steigen.

appreciation [ə,priːʃɪ'eɪʃn] *n* - 1. [liking] Anerkennung *die* - 2. [understanding] Verständnis *das* - 3. [gratitude] Dankbarkeit *die*.

appreciative [ə'pri:ʃjətɪv] *adj* [person, audience] dankbar; **to be ~ of sthg** etw zu schätzen wissen.

apprehensive [ˌæprɪ'hensɪv] *adj:* **~ (about)** besorgt (wegen (+ G)).

apprentice [ə'prentɪs] *n* Lehrling *der;* **an ~ mechanic** ein Mechanikerlehrling.

apprenticeship [ə'prentɪsʃɪp] *n* Lehre *die.*

approach [ə'prəʊtʃ] <> *n* **- 1.** [arrival] (Heran)nahen *das.* **- 2.** [access] Zugang *der;* [road] Zufahrt *die.* **- 3.** [method] Ansatz *der.* **- 4.** [proposal]: **to make an ~ to sb** an jn heranltreten <> *vt* **- 1.** [come near to] sich nähern (+ D); **temperatures ~ing 35°C** Temperaturen von bis zu 35°C **- 2.** [speak to]: **to ~ sb about sthg** wegen etw an jn heranltreten (G) **- 3.** [problem, task] anlgehen <> *vi* sich nähern.

approachable [ə'prəʊtʃəbl] *adj* **- 1.** [person] umgänglich **- 2.** [place] erreichbar.

appropriate [*adj* ə'prəʊprɪət, *vb* ə'prəʊprɪeɪt] <> *adj* angemessen; [clothing, moment] passend <> *vt* **- 1.** LAW [steal] sich anleignen **- 2.** [allocate] bestimmen.

approval [ə'pru:vl] *n* **- 1.** [liking, admiration] Anerkennung *die* **- 2.** [official agreement] Genehmigung *die* **- 3.** COMM: **on ~** zur Probe.

approve [ə'pru:v] <> *vi:* **to ~ of sb** von jm etwas halten; **to ~ of sthg** mit etw einverstanden sein <> **I don't ~ of him** ich halte nichts von ihm <> *vt* genehmigen.

approx. [ə'prɒks] *abbr of* approximately.

approximate [ə'prɒksɪmət] *adj* ungefähr.

approximately [ə'prɒksɪmətlɪ] *adv* ungefähr, circa.

apricot ['eɪprɪkɒt] *n* [fruit] Aprikose *die.*

April ['eɪprəl] *n* April *der; see also* September.

April Fools' Day *n* der erste April.

apron ['eɪprən] *n* [clothing] Schürze *die.*

apt [æpt] *adj* **- 1.** [pertinent] treffend **- 2.** [likely]: **to be ~ to do sthg** dazu neigen, etw zu tun.

aptitude ['æptɪtjuːd] *n* Begabung *die;* **to have an ~ for sthg** eine Begabung für etw haben.

aptly ['æptlɪ] *adv* treffend.

aqualung ['ækwəlʌŋ] *n* Presslufttauchgerät *das.*

aquarium [ə'kweərɪəm] (*pl* -riums OR -ria [-rɪə]) *n* Aquarium *das.*

Aquarius [ə'kweərɪəs] *n* Wassermann *der.*

aquatic [ə'kwætɪk] *adj* Wasser-.

aqueduct ['ækwɪdʌkt] *n* Aquädukt *der* OR *das.*

Arab ['ærəb] <> *adj* arabisch <> *n* [person] Araber *der,* -in *die.*

Arabian [ə'reɪbjən] *adj* arabisch.

Arabic ['ærəbɪk] <> *adj* arabisch <> *n* [language] Arabisch(e) *das.*

Arabic numeral *n* arabische Ziffer.

arable ['ærəbl] *adj:* **~ land** Ackerland *das.*

arbitrary ['ɑːbɪtrərɪ] *adj* willkürlich.

arbitration [ˌɑːbɪ'treɪʃn] *n* Schlichtungsverfahren *das;* **to go to ~** vor eine Schlichtungskommission gehen.

arcade [ɑː'keɪd] *n* **- 1.** [for shopping] Passage *die.* **- 2.** ARCHIT [covered passage] Arkade *die.*

arch [ɑːtʃ] <> *adj* [knowing] schelmisch <> *n* **- 1.** ARCHIT Bogen *der;* [arched entrance] Torbogen *der.* **- 2.** [of foot] Wölbung *die* <> *vt* [back] krümmen <> *vi* sich wölben.

archaeologist [ˌɑːkɪ'ɒlədʒɪst] *n* Archäologe *der,* -in *die.*

archaeology [ˌɑːkɪ'ɒlədʒɪ] *n* Archäologie *die.*

archaic [ɑː'keɪɪk] *adj* [language] veraltet.

archbishop [ˌɑːtʃ'bɪʃəp] *n* Erzbischof *der.*

archenemy [ˌɑːtʃ'enɪmɪ] *n* Erzfeind *der,* -in *die.*

archeology *etc* [ˌɑːkɪ'ɒlədʒɪ] = archaeology *etc.*

archer ['ɑːtʃə^r] *n* Bogenschütze *der.*

archery ['ɑːtʃərɪ] *n* Bogenschießen *das.*

archetypal [ˌɑːkɪ'taɪpl] *adj* typisch.

architect ['ɑːkɪtekt] *n* **- 1.** [of buildings] Architekt *der,* -in *die* **- 2.** *fig* [of plan, event] Urheber *der,* -in *die.*

architecture ['ɑːkɪtektʃə^r] *n* **- 1.** [gen & COMPUT] Architektur *die* **- 2.** [style of building] Baustil *der.*

archives ['ɑːkaɪvz] *npl* [of documents] Archiv *das.*

archway ['ɑːtʃweɪ] *n* Torbogen *der.*

Arctic ['ɑːktɪk] <> *adj* **- 1.** GEOGR arktisch **- 2.** *inf* [cold] eiskalt <> *n:* **the ~ die** Arktis.

ardent ['ɑːdənt] *adj* leidenschaftlich; [desire] brennend.

arduous ['ɑːdjʊəs] *adj* [task] mühselig; [climb, journey] anstrengend.

are [weak form ə^r, strong form ɑː^r] *vb* ⊏> be.

area ['eərɪə] *n* **- 1.** [region] Gegend *die;* [in town] Viertel *das;* **in the Bristol ~** im Raum Bristol **- 2.** *fig* [approximate size, number]: **in the ~ of** im Bereich von **- 3.** [surface size] Fläche *die* **- 4.** [space] Bereich *der;* **a parking ~** ein Parkplatz **- 5.** [of knowledge, interest, subject] Gebiet *das.*

area code *n Am* Vorwahl *die.*

arena [ə'riːnə] *n lit* & *fig* Arena *die.*

aren't [ɑːnt] = are not.

Argentina [ˌɑːdʒən'tiːnə] *n* Argentinien *nt.*

Argentine ['ɑːdʒəntaɪn], **Argentinian** [ˌɑːdʒən'tɪnɪən] <> *adj* argentinisch <> *n* Argentinier *der,* -in *die.*

arguably [ə'gjʊəblɪ] *adv* möglicherweise.

argue ['ɑːgjuː] <> *vi* **- 1.** [quarrel]: **to ~ (with sb about sthg)** sich (mit jm über etw (A)) streiten **- 2.** [reason] argumentieren; **to ~ for/against sthg** für/gegen etw einltreten <> *vt:* **to ~ the case for sthg** für etw einltreten; **to ~ that ...** die Meinung vertreten, dass ...

argument ['ɑːgjʊmənt] *n* **- 1.** [quarrel]

Streit *der;* **to have an ~ (with sb)** sich (mit jm) streiten - **2.** [reason] Argument *das* - **3.** (U) [reasoning] Diskussion *die.*

argumentative [ˌɑːgjuˈmentətɪv] *adj* streitsüchtig.

arise [əˈraɪz] (*pt* arose; *pp* arisen [əˈrɪzn]) *vi* [problems, difficulties] aufltreten; [opportunities] sich ergeben; **to ~ from sthg** sich aus etw ergeben; **if the need ~s** falls sich die Notwendigkeit ergibt.

aristocrat [*Br* ˈærɪstəkræt, *Am* əˈrɪstəkræt] *n* Aristokrat *der,* -in *die,* Adlige *der, die.*

arithmetic [əˈrɪθmətɪk] *n* Arithmetik *die,* Rechnen *das;* [calculation] Rechnung *die.*

ark [ɑːk] *n* [ship] Arche *die.*

arm [ɑːm] ◇ *n* - **1.** [of person] Arm *der;* **~ in ~** Arm in Arm; **to keep sb at ~'s length** *fig* jn auf Distanz halten - **2.** [of garment] Ärmel *der* - **3.** [of chair] Armlehne *die* ◇ *vt* [with weapons] bewaffnen. **➙ arms** *npl* [weapons] Waffen *pl;* **to take up ~s** zu den Waffen greifen; **to be up in ~s (about sthg)** (wegen etw (*G*)) aufgebracht sein.

armaments [ˈɑːməmənts] *npl* Waffen *pl.*

armband [ˈɑːm bænd] *n* Armbinde *die;* [for swimming] Schwimmflügel *der.*

armchair [ˈɑːmtʃeəʳ] *n* Sessel *der.*

armed [ɑːmd] *adj* - **1.** [police, thieves] bewaffnet - **2.** *fig* [with information] : **~ with sthg** mit etw ausgestattet.

armed forces *npl* Streitkräfte *pl.*

armhole [ˈɑːmhəʊl] *n* Armloch *das.*

armour *Br,* **armor** *Am* [ˈɑːməʳ] *n* - **1.** [for person] Rüstung *die* - **2.** [for military vehicle] Panzerung *die.*

armoured car [ˈɑːməd-] *n* MIL Panzerwagen *der.*

armoury *Br,* **armory** *Am* [ˈɑːmərɪ] *n* Arsenal *das.*

armpit [ˈɑːmpɪt] *n* Achselhöhle *die.*

armrest [ˈɑːmrest] *n* Armlehne *die.*

arms control [ˈɑːmz-] *n* Rüstungskontrolle *die.*

army [ˈɑːmɪ] *n* - **1.** MIL Heer *das,* Armee *die;* **to be in the ~** beim Militär sein - **2.** *fig* [large group] Heer *das.*

A road *n Br ≃* Bundesstraße *die.*

aroma [əˈrəʊmə] *n* Duft *der.*

arose [əˈrəʊz] *pt* ▷ arise.

around [əˈraʊnd] ◇ *adv* - **1.** [here and there] herum; **to travel ~** herumlreisen; **to sit ~ doing nothing** untätig herumlsitzen - **2.** [on all sides] herum; **all ~** auf allen Seiten - **3.** [present, nearby]: **is she ~?** ist sie da?; **~ here** [in the area] hier in der Gegend; **cars have been ~ for over a century** Autos gibt es schon seit über hundert Jahren - **4.** [in a circle]: **to go ~** sich drehen; **to spin ~ (and ~)** sich im Kreis drehen - **5.** [to the other side]: **to go ~** herumlgehen; **to turn ~** sich umldrehen; **to look ~** sich umlsehen - **6.** *phr:* **to have been ~** *inf* [travelled a lot] (viel) herumgekommen

sein ◇ *prep* - **1.** [surrounding] um ... herum - **2.** [near]: **~ here/there** hier/dort in der Nähe; **is there a bank anywhere ~ here?** gibt es hier irgendwo eine Bank? - **3.** [all over]: **150 offices ~ the world** 150 Büros in der ganzen Welt; **all ~ the country** im ganzen Land; **we walked ~ the town** wir spazierten durch die Stadt - **4.** [in a circle]: **we walked ~ the lake** wir gingen um den See herum; **to go/drive ~ sthg** um etw herumlgehen/herumlfahren; **~ the clock** *fig* rund um die Uhr - **5.** [approximately] ungefähr - **6.** [in circumference]: **she measures 30 inches ~ the waist** um die Taille misst sie 75 cm - **7.** [so as to avoid]: **~ an obstacle** um ein Hindernis herumlgehen; **to find a way ~ a problem** einen Ausweg für ein Problem finden.

arouse [əˈraʊz] *vt* - **1.** [excite] erregen; [interest, suspicion] erwecken - **2.** [wake] wecken, auflwecken.

arrange [əˈreɪndʒ] *vt* - **1.** [flowers] arrangieren; [books, objects] (an)lordnen; [furniture] (um)lstellen - **2.** [event] planen; [meeting] vereinbaren; [party] arrangieren; **to ~ to do sthg** vereinbaren, etw zu tun - **3.** MUS bearbeiten, arrangieren.

arrangement [əˈreɪndʒmənt] *n* - **1.** [agreement] Vereinbarung *die;* **to come to an ~** eine Einigung erzielen - **2.** [of objects] Anordnung *die* - **3.** MUS Bearbeitung *die,* Arrangement *das.* **➙ arrangements** *npl* [preparations] Vorbereitungen *pl;* **please make your own ~s for accommodation** bitte arrangieren Sie Ihre Unterkunft selbst.

array [əˈreɪ] ◇ *n* [of objects, people, ornaments] Aufgebot *das* ◇ *vt* [ornaments] auflstellen.

arrears [əˈrɪəz] *npl* [money owed] Rückstände *pl;* **to be paid in ~** rückwirkend bezahlt werden; **to be in ~** im Rückstand sein.

arrest [əˈrest] ◇ *n* [by police] Verhaftung *die;* **to be under ~** verhaftet sein ◇ *vt* - **1.** [subj: police] verhaften - **2.** *fml* [sb's attention] erregen - **3.** *fml* [stop - development] hemmen; [- spread of disease] auflhalten.

arrival [əˈraɪvl] *n* - **1.** [at place] Ankunft *die;* **on ~** bei der Ankunft; **late ~** [of train, bus, mail] verspätete Ankunft - **2.** [of new system, technology] Aufkommen *das* - **3.** [person] Ankömmling *der;* **new ~** [person] Neuankömmling *der.*

arrive [əˈraɪv] *vi* - **1.** [gen] anlkommen; **to ~ at a conclusion/decision** zu einem Schluss/ einer Entscheidung kommen - **2.** [moment, event] kommen.

arrogant [ˈærəgənt] *adj* arrogant.

arrow [ˈærəʊ] *n* Pfeil *der.*

arse *Br* [ɑːs], **ass** *Am* [æs] *n vulg* [buttocks] Arsch *der.*

arsenic [ˈɑːsnɪk] *n* Arsen *das.*

arson [ˈɑːsn] *n* Brandstiftung *die.*

art [ɑːt] ◇ *n* Kunst *die* ◇ *comp* Kunst-.
◆ **arts** *npl* - **1.** SCH & UNIV [humanities]
Geisteswissenschaften *pl* - **2.** [fine arts]: **the
~s** die schönen Künste *pl*.

artefact ['ɑːtɪfækt] *n* = artifact.

artery ['ɑːtərɪ] *n* Arterie *die*.

art gallery *n* Kunstgalerie *die*.

arthritis [ɑː'θraɪtɪs] *n* Arthritis *die*.

artichoke ['ɑːtɪtʃəʊk] *n* Artischocke *die*.

article ['ɑːtɪkl] *n* - **1.** [item] Gegenstand *der*;
COMM Ware *die*, Artikel *der*; **~ of clothing**
Kleidungsstück *das* - **2.** [in newspaper, maga-
zine] Artikel *der* - **3.** [in agreement, contract]
Paragraph *der*; [in constitution] Artikel *der*
- **4.** GRAMM Artikel *der*.

articulate [*adj* ɑː'tɪkjʊlət, *vb* ɑː'tɪkjʊleɪt]
◇ *adj* [speech] leichtverständlich; **to be
~** [person] sich gut ausdrücken können
◇ *vt* [thought, wish] zum Ausdruck bringen, artikulieren.

articulated lorry [ɑː'tɪkjʊleɪtɪd-] *n Br* Sat-
telschlepper *der*.

artifact ['ɑːtɪfækt] *n* Artefakt *das*.

artificial [ˌɑːtɪ'fɪʃl] *adj* - **1.** [non-natural]
künstlich - **2.** [insincere] gekünstelt.

artillery [ɑː'tɪlərɪ] *n* Artillerie *die*.

artist ['ɑːtɪst] *n* Künstler *der*, -in *die*.

artistic [ɑː'tɪstɪk] *adj* - **1.** [gen] künstlerisch;
[person] künstlerisch begabt - **2.** [attractive]
kunstvoll.

artistry ['ɑːtɪstrɪ] *n* Kunstwertigkeit *die*.

as [unstressed əz, stressed æz] ◇ *conj* - **1.** [re-
ferring to time] als - **2.** [referring to manner]
wie; **~ expected** ... er erwartet ...; **do ~ I
say** tu, was ich dir sage; **it's hard enough ~ it
is** es ist ohnehin schon schwierig genug
- **3.** [introducing a statement] wie; **~ I told you
...** wie ich dir bereits gesagt habe ...; **~ you
know, ...** wie du weißt, ... - **4.** [because]
weil, da ◇ *adv (in comparisons)*: **~ ... ~ so ...**
wie; **he's ~ tall ~ I am** er ist so groß wie ich;
~ many ~ so viele wie; **~ much ~** so viel wie
◇ *prep* als; **she works ~ a nurse** sie arbeitet
als Krankenschwester; **to consider sb ~ a
friend** jn als Freund betrachten. ◆ **as for**
prep: **~ for me** was mich betrifft. ◆ **as
from, as of** *prep* ab; **~ from** OR **of Monday** ab
Montag. ◆ **as if, as though** *conj* als ob, als
wenn; **he looked at me ~ if I were mad** er sah
mich an, als ob ich verrückt wäre; **~ if by
chance** wie durch Zufall. ◆ **as to** *prep Br*:
she questioned him ~ to his motives sie fragte ihn nach seinen Beweggründen.

a.s.a.p. *(abbr of* as soon as possible) bald-
möglichst.

asbestos [æs'bestəs] *n* Asbest *der*.

ascend [ə'send] ◇ *vt* [hill] besteigen; [stair-
case] hinaufgehen; [ladder] hinaufsteigen
◇ *vi* [climb] aufsteigen; [subj: path, road *etc*]
an|steigen.

ascendant [ə'sendənt] *n*: **to be in the ~** im
Aufstieg begriffen sein.

ascent [ə'sent] *n* - **1.** [gen] Aufstieg *der*
- **2.** [upward slope] Steigung *die*.

ascertain [ˌæsə'teɪn] *vt* ermitteln.

ascribe [ə'skraɪb] *vt*: **to ~ sthg to sthg** einer
Sache *(D)* etw zulschreiben; **to ~ sthg to sb**
jm etw zulschreiben.

ash [æʃ] *n* - **1.** [from cigarette, fire] Asche *die*
- **2.** [tree] Esche *die*.

ashamed [ə'ʃeɪmd] *adj* beschämt; **to be ~ of
sb/sthg** sich js/einer Sache *(G)* schämen; **to
be ~ to do sthg** sich schämen, etw zu tun.

ashore [ə'ʃɔːr] *adv* [go, swim] an Land.

ashtray ['æʃtreɪ] *n* Aschenbecher *der*.

Ash Wednesday *n* Aschermittwoch *der*.

Asia [Br 'eɪʃə, Am 'eɪʒə] *n* Asien *nt*.

Asian [Br 'eɪʃn, Am 'eɪʒn] ◇ *adj* asiatisch
◇ *n* [from Far East] Asiat *der*, -in *die*.

aside [ə'saɪd] ◇ *adv* - **1.** [to one side] beiseite, zur Seite; **step ~!** treten Sie zur Seite!; **to
take sb ~** jn beiseite nehmen - **2.** [apart]: **joking ~, ...** Spaß beiseite, ...; **~ from** abgesehen von ◇ *n* - **1.** [in play] Apart *das* - **2.** [re-
mark] beiläufige Bemerkung.

ask [ɑːsk] ◇ *vt* - **1.** [gen] fragen; **to ~ a question** eine Frage stellen; **to ~ sb sthg** jn etw
fragen - **2.** [request - permission, forgiveness]
bitten um; **to ~ sb for sthg** jn um etw bitten;
to ~ sb for advice jn um Rat fragen; **to ~ sb to
do sthg** jn (darum) bitten, etw zu tun - **3.** [in-
vite] einladen; **to ~ sb (round) to dinner** jn
zum Abendessen einladen - **4.** [price] verlangen ◇ *vi* - **1.** [enquire] fragen - **2.** [request]
bitten. ◆ **ask after** *vt fus* sich erkundigen
nach. ◆ **ask for** *vt fus* - **1.** [ask to talk to]
verlangen; **he's ~ing for you** er will Sie sprechen - **2.** [request] bitten um.

askance [ə'skæns] *adv*: **to look ~ at sb** jn
missbilligend anlschauen; **to look ~ at sthg** einer Sache *(D)* ablehnend gegenüberlstehen.

askew [ə'skjuː] *adj* schief.

asking price ['ɑːskɪŋ-] *n* Verkaufspreis *der*.

asleep [ə'sliːp] *adj* schlafend; **to fall ~** einlschlafen.

asparagus [ə'spærəgəs] *n* Spargel *der*.

aspect ['æspekt] *n* - **1.** [facet] Aspekt *der*
- **2.** [appearance] Aussehen *das*.

aspersions [ə'spɜːʃnz] *npl*: **to cast ~ (on
sthg)** abfällige Bemerkungen (über etw *(A)*)
machen.

asphalt ['æsfælt] *n (U)* Asphalt *der*.

asphyxiate [əs'fɪksɪeɪt] *vt* ersticken.

aspiration [ˌæspə'reɪʃn] *n* [desire, ambi-
tion] Bestrebung *die*.

aspire [ə'spaɪər] *vi*: **to ~ to sthg** nach etw
streben; **to ~ to do sthg** danach streben, etw
zu tun.

aspirin ['æsprɪn] *n* Aspirin® *das*.

ass [æs] *n* - **1.** Esel *der* - **2.** *Am vulg* = arse.

assailant [ə'seɪlənt] *n* Angreifer *der*, -in *die*.

assassin [əˈsæsɪn] n Attentäter der, -in die (dessen Mordanschlag glückt).

assassinate [əˈsæsɪneɪt] vt ermorden; **to be ~d** einem Attentat zum Opfer fallen.

assassination [ə,sæsɪˈneɪʃn] n (geglücktes) Attentat, (politischer) Mord.

assault [əˈsɔːlt] ◇ n - 1. MIL: ~ **(on sthg)** Sturmangriff der (auf etw (A)) - 2. [physical attack]: ~ **(on sb)** (tätlicher) Angriff (auf jn) ◇ vt [attack - physically] (tätlich) anlgreifen; [- sexually] belästigen.

assemble [əˈsembl] ◇ vt - 1. [gather - people] zusammenlrufen; [- evidence, material] zusammenltragen; [- Parliament] einlberufen - 2. [fit together] zusammenlbauen ◇ vi [people] sich versammeln; [Parliament] zusammenltreten.

assembly [əˈsemblɪ] n - 1. [gen] Versammlung die; [at school] Morgenandacht die - 2. (U) [fitting together] Zusammenbau der; [of device, machine] Montage die.

assembly line n Fließband das.

assent [əˈsent] ◇ n Zustimmung die ◇ vi zulstimmen; **to ~ to sthg** einer Sache (D) zulstimmen.

assert [əˈsɜːt] vt - 1. [conviction, belief] behaupten; [innocence] beteuern - 2. [authority] geltend machen.

assertive [əˈsɜːtɪv] adj [person, tone] energisch; [attitude] selbstbewusst.

assess [əˈses] vt - 1. [judge] einlschätzen, beurteilen - 2. [estimate - value] schätzen; [- damages] festlsetzen.

assessment [əˈsesmənt] n - 1. [judgement] Einschätzung die - 2. [estimate - of value] Schätzung die; [- of damages] Festsetzung die.

asset [ˈæset] n - 1. [valuable quality] Vorteil der - 2. [valuable person] Stütze die. ◆ **assets** npl COMM Vermögen das.

assign [əˈsaɪn] vt - 1. [allot]: **to ~ sthg (to sb/ sthg)** (jm/etw) etw zulteilen OR zulweisen - 2. [appoint]: **to ~ sb (to sthg)** jn (einer Sache (D)) zulteilen OR zulweisen; **to ~ sb to do sthg** jn damit beauftragen, etw zu tun.

assignment [əˈsaɪnmənt] n - 1. [task] Aufgabe die; [at school] Projekt das; [job] Auftrag der - 2. [act of appointing] Zuteilung die; [to task] Betrauung die; [to post] Berufung die.

assimilate [əˈsɪmɪleɪt] vt - 1. [gen] auflnehmen - 2. [people]: **to ~ sb (into sthg)** jn (in etw (A)) integrieren.

assist [əˈsɪst] vt helfen (+ D); **to ~ sb with sthg** jm bei etw helfen; **to ~ sb in doing sthg** jm helfen, etw zu tun.

assistance [əˈsɪstəns] n (U) Hilfe die; **to be of ~ (to sb)** (jm) behilflich sein.

assistant [əˈsɪstənt] ◇ n - 1. [helper] Assistent der, -in die - 2. [in shop] Verkäufer der, -in die ◇ comp stellvertretend; ~ **editor** Redaktionsassistent der, -in die.

associate [adj & n əˈsəʊʃɪət, vb əˈsəʊʃɪeɪt] ◇ adj [member] außerordentlich ◇ n [business partner] Partner der, -in die ◇ vt [connect] in Verbindung bringen, assoziieren; **to ~ sb/sthg with sb/sthg** jn/etw mit jm/etw in Verbindung bringen; **to be ~d with sb/sthg** mit jm/etw in Verbindung gebracht werden ◇ vi: **to ~ with sb** mit jm verkehren.

association [ə,səʊsɪˈeɪʃn] n - 1. [organization] Verband der - 2. (U) [relationship] Verkehr der, Umgang der; **in ~ with sb/sthg** in Zusammenarbeit mit jm/etw.

assorted [əˈsɔːtɪd] adj [colours, sizes] verschieden; [sweets] gemischt.

assortment [əˈsɔːtmənt] n [mixture - of people] Mischung die; [- of goods] Auswahl die.

assume [əˈsjuːm] vt - 1. [suppose, adopt] anlnehmen - 2. [undertake] übernehmen.

assumed name [əˈsjuːmd-] n falscher Name.

assuming [əˈsjuːmɪŋ] conj: ~ **(that)** ... vorausgesetzt(, dass) ...

assumption [əˈsʌmpʃn] n [supposition] Annahme die.

assurance [əˈʃʊərəns] n - 1. [promise] Zusicherung die - 2. [confidence] Selbstsicherheit die - 3. (U) FIN [insurance] Versicherung die.

assure [əˈʃʊəʳ] vt [reassure] versichern (+ D); **to ~ sb of sthg** jn einer Sache (G) versichern; **to be ~d of sthg** [be certain] sich (D) einer Sache (G) sicher sein.

assured [əˈʃʊəd] adj selbstsicher.

asterisk [ˈæstərɪsk] n Sternchen das.

asthma [ˈæsmə] n Asthma das.

astonish [əˈstɒnɪʃ] vt erstaunen.

astonished [əˈstɒnɪʃd] adj erstaunt.

astonishment [əˈstɒnɪʃmənt] n Erstaunen das.

astound [əˈstaʊnd] vt verblüffen.

astray [əˈstreɪ] adv: **to go ~** [object] verloren gehen; [animal] sich verirren; **to lead sb ~** fig jn vom rechten Weg ablbringen.

astride [əˈstraɪd] ◇ adv rittlings ◇ prep rittlings auf (+ D).

astrology [əˈstrɒlədʒɪ] n Astrologie die.

astronaut [ˈæstrənɔːt] n Astronaut der, -in die.

astronomical [,æstrəˈnɒmɪkl] adj lit & fig astronomisch.

astronomy [əˈstrɒnəmɪ] n Astronomie die.

astute [əˈstjuːt] adj clever.

asylum [əˈsaɪləm] n - 1. dated [mental hospital] psychiatrische Anstalt - 2. (U) [protection] Asyl das.

at [unstressed ət, stressed æt] prep - 1. [indicating place, position]: **there was a knock ~ the door** es klopfte an der Tür; **he studies ~ Cambridge** er studiert in Cambridge; ~ **the bottom of the hill** am Fuß(e) des Hügels;

~ my father's bei meinem Vater; **~ home** zu Hause; **~ school** in der Schule; **~ work** bei der Arbeit **- 2.** [indicating direction]: **to aim ~ sb/ sthg** auf jn/etw zielen; **to smile ~ sb** jn anlächeln; **to look ~ sb/sthg** jn/etw ansehen **- 3.** [indicating a particular time]: **~ midnight/ noon/eleven o'clock** um Mitternacht/zwölf Uhr mittags/elf Uhr; **~ Christmas/Easter** zu OR an Weihnachten/Ostern; **~ night** bei Nacht, nachts **- 4.** [indicating age, speed, rate]: **~ your age** in deinem Alter; **~ 52 (years of age)** mit 52 (Jahren); **~ 100 miles per hour** mit 100 Meilen pro Stunde; **~ high speed** mit hoher Geschwindigkeit **- 5.** [indicating price]: **~ £50 (a pair)** für 50 Pfund (das Paar) **- 6.** [indicating particular state, condition]: **~ peace/war** im Frieden/Krieg; **~ lunch** beim Mittagessen **- 7.** (after adjectives): **amused/ appalled/puzzled ~ sthg** über etw (A) belustigt/entsetzt/verblüfft; **to be bad/ good ~ sthg** in etw (D) schlecht/gut sein. ➡ **at all** adv **- 1.** (with negative): **not ~ all** [when thanked] keine Ursache; [when answering a question] überhaupt nicht; **she's not ~ all happy** sie ist überhaupt nicht glücklich **- 2.** [in the slightest]: **have you done anything ~ all today?** hast du heute überhaupt irgendetwas gemacht?; **do you know her ~ all?** kennst du sie überhaupt?

ate [Br et, Am eɪt] pt ⊏▷ eat.

atheist ['eɪθɪɪst] n Atheist der, -in die.

Athens ['æθɪnz] n Athen nt.

athlete ['æθliːt] n Leichtathlet der, -in die.

athletic [æθ'letɪk] adj **- 1.** [relating to athletics] athletisch **- 2.** [sporty] sportlich. ➡ **athletics** npl Leichtathletik die.

Atlantic [ət'læntɪk] ◇ adj atlantisch ◇ n: **the ~ (Ocean)** der Atlantik.

atlas ['ætləs] n Atlas der.

atmosphere ['ætmə,sfɪə'] n **- 1.** [gen] Atmosphäre die **- 2.** [in room] Luft die.

atmospheric [,ætməs'ferɪk] adj **- 1.** [pressure, pollution] atmosphärisch **- 2.** [music, place, film] stimmungsvoll.

atom ['ætəm] n TECH Atom das.

atom bomb n Atombombe die.

atomic [ə'tɒmɪk] adj Atom-.

atone [ə'təʊn] vi: **to ~ for sthg** [crime, sin] (für) etw büßen; [mistake, behaviour] etw wieder gutmachen.

A to Z n Stadtplan der (im Buchformat).

atrocious [ə'trəʊʃəs] adj grauenhaft.

atrocity [ə'trɒsətɪ] n Greueltat die.

attach [ə'tætʃ] vt **- 1.** [fasten] befestigen; [document] beilheften; **to ~ sthg to sthg** an etw (D) befestigen; [document] einer Sache (D) etw beilheften **- 2.** [attribute]: **to ~ sthg to sthg** [importance] einer Sache (D) etw beilmessen; [blame] einer Sache (D) etw zulschreiben **- 3.** COMPUT anlheften, anlhängen.

attaché case [ə'tæʃeɪ-]n Aktenkoffer der.

attached [ə'tætʃt] adj [fond]: **to be ~ to sb/ sthg** an jm/etw hängen.

attachment [ə'tætʃmənt] n **- 1.** [device] Zusatzgerät das **- 2.** COMPUT Attachment das, Anhang der.

attack [ə'tæk] ◇ n **- 1.** [physical]: **~ (on sb)** [on person] Überfall der (auf jn); [on enemy] Angriff der (auf jn) **- 2.** [verbal]: **~ (on sthg)** Angriff der (auf etw (A)) **- 3.** [of illness] Anfall der ◇ vt **- 1.** [physically - person] überfallen; [- enemy] anlgreifen **- 2.** [verbally] anlgreifen **- 3.** [affect] befallen **- 4.** [deal with] in Angriff nehmen ◇ vi anlgreifen.

attacker [ə'tækə'] n Angreifer der, -in die.

attain [ə'teɪn] vt [rank, objectives] erreichen; [success, happiness] erlangen.

attainment [ə'teɪnmənt] n [skill] Fertigkeit die.

attempt [ə'tempt] ◇ n Versuch der; **an ~ at a smile** ein Versuch zu lächeln; **to make an ~ on sb's life** einen Mordanschlag auf jn verüben ◇ vt [try] versuchen; **to ~ to do sthg** versuchen, etw zu tun.

attend [ə'tend] ◇ vt **- 1.** [meeting] teilllnehmen an (+ D); [party] gehen zu **- 2.** [school, church] besuchen ◇ vi **- 1.** [be present] anwesend sein **- 2.** [pay attention]: **to ~ (to sthg)** auflpassen (bei etw). ➡ **attend to** vt fus **- 1.** [deal with] sich kümmern um **- 2.** [look after - customer] bedienen; [- patient] behandeln.

attendance [ə'tendəns] n **- 1.** [number present - at meeting] Teilnehmerzahl die; [- at concert, cinema] Besucherzahl die **- 2.** [presence] Anwesenheit die, Teilnahme die; **to have a poor ~ record** oft fehlen.

attendant [ə'tendənt] n [at museum] Aufseher der, -in die; [at petrol station] Tankwart der; **car park ~** Parkplatzwächter der, -in die.

attention [ə'tenʃn] ◇ n (U) **- 1.** [awareness, interest] Aufmerksamkeit die; **to attract sb's ~** jn auf sich (A) aufmerksam machen; **to bring sthg to sb's ~, to draw sb's ~ to sthg** jn auf etw (A) aufmerksam machen; **to pay ~ to sb/sthg** jm/etw Aufmerksamkeit schenken; **to pay ~** auflpassen **- 2.** [care] Fürsorge die **- 3.** COMM: **for the ~ of** zu Händen (von) ◇ excl MIL stillgestanden!

attentive [ə'tentɪv] adj aufmerksam.

attic ['ætɪk] n Dachboden der.

attitude ['ætɪtjuːd] n **- 1.** [way of thinking]: **~ (to OR towards sb/sthg)** Einstellung die (gegenüber jm/zu etw) **- 2.** [behaviour, posture] Haltung die.

attn (abbr of for the attention of) z. Hd.

attorney [ə'tɜːnɪ] n Am [lawyer] (Rechts)anwalt der, -wältin die.

attorney general (pl attorneys general) n ≃ Generalbundesanwalt der, -wältin die.

attract [ə'trækt] vt **- 1.** [draw, cause to come near] anlziehen, anllocken **- 2.** [be attractive to] anziehend wirken auf *(+ A)* - **3.** [support] gewinnen; [criticism] auf sich *(A)* ziehen - **4.** [magnetically] anziehen.

attraction [ə'trækʃn] *n* - **1.** [liking] Anziehungskraft *die;* **to feel an ~ to sb** sich zu jm hingezogen fühlen - **2.** *(U)* [appeal, charm] Reiz *der* - **3.** [attractive feature, event] Attraktion *die.*

attractive [ə'træktɪv] *adj* - **1.** [person] anziehend - **2.** [thing, idea] attraktiv.

attribute [*vb* ə'trɪbjuːt, *n* 'ætrɪbjuːt] ⬦ *vt* - **1.** [ascribe]: **to ~ sthg to sb/sthg** etw jm/etw zuschreiben - **2.** [work of art, remark]: **to ~ sthg to sb** jm etw zuschreiben ⬦ *n* [quality] Eigenschaft *die.*

aubergine ['əʊbəʒiːn] *n Br* Aubergine *die.*

auburn ['ɔːbən] *adj* [hair] rotbraun.

auction ['ɔːkʃn] ⬦ *n* Auktion *die,* Versteigerung *die;* **at** OR **by ~** bei einer Auktion OR Versteigerung; **to put sthg up for ~** etw zur Versteigerung anbieten ⬦ *vt* versteigern.
➤ **auction off** *vt sep* versteigern.

auctioneer [ˌɔːkʃəˈnɪəʳ] *n* Auktionator *der.*

audacious [ɔːˈdeɪʃəs] *adj* [daring] kühn; [impudent] dreist.

audible ['ɔːdəbl] *adj* hörbar.

audience ['ɔːdjəns] *n* [gen] Publikum *das;* [of TV programme] Zuschauer *pl;* [of radio programme] Zuhörer *pl.*

audio-visual [ˌɔːdɪəʊ-] *adj* audiovisuell.

audit ['ɔːdɪt] ⬦ *n* Buchprüfung *die* ⬦ *vt* prüfen.

audition [ɔːˈdɪʃn] *n* [of actor] Vorsprechen *das;* [of singer] Probesingen *das;* [of musician] Probespiel *das.*

auditor ['ɔːdɪtəʳ] *n* Buchprüfer *der,* -in *die.*

auditorium [ˌɔːdɪˈtɔːrɪəm] *(pl* -riums OR -ria [-rɪə]*) n* Zuschauerraum *der.*

augur ['ɔːgəʳ] *vi:* **to ~ well/badly** etwas Gutes/nichts Gutes verheißen.

August ['ɔːgəst] *n* August *der; see also* September.

aunt [ɑːnt] *n* Tante *die.*

auntie, aunty ['ɑːntɪ] *n inf* Tantchen *das.*

au pair [ˌəʊ'peəʳ] *n* Aupairmädchen *das.*

aura ['ɔːrə] *n* Aura *die.*

aural ['ɔːrəl] *adj* SCH: **~ comprehension** Hörverständnis *die.*

auspices ['ɔːspɪsɪz] *npl:* **under the ~ of** unter der Schirmherrschaft *(+ G).*

auspicious [ɔːˈspɪʃəs] *adj* [start] vielversprechend; [day, occasion] günstig.

Aussie ['ɒzɪ] *inf* ⬦ *adj* australisch ⬦ *n* Australier *der,* -in *die.*

austere [ɒ'stɪəʳ] *adj* - **1.** [person] streng; [life] asketisch - **2.** [room, building] karg.

austerity [ɒ'sterətɪ] *n* - **1.** [of person] Strenge *die;* [of life - for religious reasons] Entsagung *die;* [- for economic reasons] Entbehrung *die* - **2.** [of room, building] Kargheit *die.*

Australia [ɒ'streɪljə] *n* Australien *nt.*

Australian [ɒ'streɪljən] ⬦ *adj* australisch ⬦ *n* Australier *der,* -in *die.*

Austria ['ɒstrɪə] *n* Österreich *nt.*

Austrian ['ɒstrɪən] ⬦ *adj* österreichisch ⬦ *n* Österreicher *der,* -in *die.*

authentic [ɔːˈθentɪk] *adj* authentisch.

author ['ɔːθəʳ] *n* Autor *der,* -in *die;* [by profession] Schriftsteller *der,* -in *die.*

authoritarian [ɔːˌθɒrɪˈteərɪən] *adj* autoritär.

authoritative [ɔːˈθɒrɪtətɪv] *adj* - **1.** [person, voice] Respekt einflößend - **2.** [report] verlässlich.

authority [ɔːˈθɒrətɪ] *n* - **1.** [official organization] Behörde *die,* Amt *das* - **2.** *(U)* [power] Autorität *die;* **to have ~ over sb** Weisungsbefugnis gegenüber jm haben; **in ~** verantwortlich - **3.** [permission] Erlaubnis *die* - **4.** [expert] Autorität *die.* ➤ **authorities** *npl:* **the authorities** die Behörden.

authorize, -ise ['ɔːθəraɪz] *vt* genehmigen; [biography] autorisieren; [money] bewilligen; **to ~ sb to do sthg** jn ermächtigen, etw zu tun.

autistic [ɔːˈtɪstɪk] *adj* autistisch.

auto ['ɔːtəʊ] *(pl* -s*) n Am* Auto *das.*

autobiography [ˌɔːtəbaɪˈɒgrəfɪ] *n* Autobiografie *die.*

autocratic [ˌɔːtəˈkrætɪk] *adj* autokratisch.

autograph ['ɔːtəgrɑːf] ⬦ *n* Autogramm *das* ⬦ *vt* signieren.

automate ['ɔːtəmeɪt] *vt* automatisieren.

automatic [ˌɔːtəˈmætɪk] ⬦ *adj* automatisch ⬦ *n* - **1.** [car] Wagen *der* mit Automatikgetriebe - **2.** [gun] automatische Waffe - **3.** [washing machine] Waschautomat *der.*

automatically [ˌɔːtəˈmætɪklɪ] *adv* automatisch.

automobile ['ɔːtəməbiːl] *n Am* Auto(mobil) *das.*

autonomy [ɔːˈtɒnəmɪ] *n (U)* Autonomie *die.*

autopsy ['ɔːtɒpsɪ] *n* Autopsie *die.*

autumn ['ɔːtəm] *n* Herbst *der.*

auxiliary [ɔːgˈzɪljərɪ] ⬦ *adj* - **1.** [providing assistance] Hilfs-; **~ nurse** Schwesternhelferin *die* - **2.** GRAMM [verb] Hilfs- ⬦ *n* [in hospital] Hilfskraft *die.*

Av. *abbr of* avenue.

avail [ə'veɪl] ⬦ *n:* **to no ~** vergeblich, ohne Erfolg ⬦ *vt:* **to ~ o.s. of sthg** von etw Gebrauch machen.

available [ə'veɪləbl] *adj* verfügbar; [product] lieferbar; **to be ~** [person] zur Verfügung stehen.

avalanche ['ævəlɑːnʃ] *n lit & fig* Lawine *die.*

avarice ['ævərɪs] *n* Habgier *die.*

Ave. *abbr of* avenue.

avenge [ə'vendʒ] *vt* rächen.

avenue ['ævənjuː] *n* Allee *die (in der Stadt).*

average ['ævərɪdʒ] <> *adj* - **1.** [mean] durchschnittlich - **2.** [typical]: **the ~ Englishman** der Durchschnittsengländer - **3.** *pej* [mediocre] durchschnittlich, mittelmäßig <> *n* Durchschnitt *der;* **on ~** im Durchschnitt <> *vt:* **we ~d 80 miles per hour** wir sind durchschnittlich 80 Meilen pro Stunde gefahren. ◆ **average out** *vi:* **to ~ out at** durchschnittlich betragen.

aversion [ə'vɜːʃn] *n* [dislike]: **~ (to)** Abneigung *die* (gegen).

avert [ə'vɜːt] *vt* - **1.** [problem] vermeiden; [accident, disaster] verhindern - **2.** [eyes, glance] abwenden.

aviary ['eɪvjərɪ] *n* Vogelhaus *das.*

avid ['ævɪd] *adj* begeistert, passioniert; **~ for sthg** begierig auf etw *(A).*

avocado [,ævə'kɑːdəʊ] *(pl* -s OR -es) *n:* **~ (pear)** Avocado *die.*

avoid [ə'vɔɪd] *vt* - **1.** [problem, accident, mistake] vermeiden; **to ~ doing sthg** vermeiden, etw zu tun - **2.** [keep away from] meiden.

await [ə'weɪt] *vt* erwarten.

awake [ə'weɪk] *(pt* awoke OR awaked) *pp* awoken) <> *adj* [not sleeping] wach <> *vt* - **1.** [person] wecken - **2.** *fig* [memories, feelings] erwecken <> *vi* aufwachen.

awakening [ə'weɪknɪŋ] *n* Erwachen *das.*

award [ə'wɔːd] <> *n* [prize] Preis *der;* [for bravery] Auszeichnung *die* <> *vt:* **to ~ sb sthg, to ~ sthg to sb** [prize] jm etw verleihen; [free kick, penalty] jm etw geben; [damages, compensation] jm etw zulsprechen.

aware [ə'weəʳ] *adj* - **1.** [conscious]: **to be ~ of sthg** sich *(D)* einer Sache *(G)* bewusst sein; **to be ~ that ...** sich *(D)* bewusst sein, dass ... - **2.** [informed, sensitive] (gut) informiert; **to be ~ of sthg** über etw *(A)* informiert sein.

awareness [ə'weənɪs] *n* Bewusstsein *das.*

away [ə'weɪ] <> *adv* - **1.** [indicating movement] weg; **to walk ~ (from)** weglgehen (von); **to run ~ (from)** weglaufen (von); **to look ~ (from)** weglsehen (von); **to turn ~ (from)** sich ablwenden (von) - **2.** [at a distance]: **far ~** weit entfernt; **10 miles ~ (from here)** 10 Meilen (von hier) entfernt; **it's still two weeks ~** bis dahin sind es noch zwei Wochen - **3.** [absent] weg; [not at home or in the office] nicht da; **Mr Stone is ~ on a business trip** Herr Stone ist auf Geschäftsreise - **4.** [in a safe place]: **to put sthg ~** etw weglräumen - **5.** [indicating removal or disappearance]: **to fade ~** verblassen; **to take sthg ~ (from sb)** (jm) etw weglnehmen; **to give sthg ~** [as a present] etw verschenken - **6.** [continuously]: **to work ~** in einem fort arbeiten - **7.** *phr:* **straight ~** OR **right ~** sofort <> *adj* SPORT: **~ game** Auswärtsspiel *das.*

awe [ɔː] *n* Ehrfurcht *die;* **to be in ~ of sb** Ehrfurcht vor jm haben.

awesome ['ɔːsəm] *adj* [impressive] Ehrfurcht gebietend.

awful ['ɔːfʊl] *adj* - **1.** [terrible] furchtbar, schrecklich - **2.** *inf* [very great]: **an ~ lot** sehr viel; **an ~ lot of time/money/books** eine Menge Zeit/Geld/Bücher.

awfully ['ɔːflɪ] *adv inf* [very] furchtbar.

awkward ['ɔːkwəd] *adj* - **1.** [clumsy - movement] ungeschickt, unbeholfen; [- position] ungünstig; [- person] unbeholfen - **2.** [embarrassed - person] verlegen; [- silence] betreten; [- situation, questions] peinlich - **3.** [uncooperative] unkooperativ - **4.** [inconvenient] ungünstig - **5.** [difficult, delicate] schwierig.

awning ['ɔːnɪŋ] *n* - **1.** [of tent] Vordach *das* - **2.** [of shop] Markise *die.*

awoke [ə'wəʊk] *pt* awake.

awoken [ə'wəʊkn] *pp* awake.

awry [ə'raɪ] <> *adj* schief <> *adv:* **to go ~** schief gehen.

axe *Br,* **ax** *Am* [æks] <> *n* Axt *die* <> *vt* [project] auflgeben; [jobs] streichen, kürzen.

axes ['æksiːz] *pl* axis.

axis ['æksɪs] *(pl* axes) *n* Achse *die.*

axle ['æksl] *n* Achse *die.*

aye [aɪ] <> *adv* - **1.** *Scot* [yes] ja - **2.** NAUT [yes] zu Befehl, jawohl <> *n* [vote] Jastimme *die.*

Azores [ə'zɔːz] *npl:* **the ~** die Azoren *pl.*

B

b *(pl* b's OR bs), **B** *(pl* B's OR Bs) [biː] *n* [letter] b *das,* B *das.* ◆ **B** *n* - **1.** MUS H *das* - **2.** SCH [mark] ≃ zwei.

BA *n abbr of* Bachelor of Arts.

babble ['bæbl] <> *n* [noise] Gemurmel *das* <> *vi* plappern.

baboon [bə'buːn] *n* Pavian *der.*

baby ['beɪbɪ] *n* Baby *das;* **don't be such a ~!** benimm dich nicht wie ein Baby!

baby buggy *n* - **1.** *Br* [pushchair] Sportwagen *der* - **2.** *Am* = baby carriage.

baby carriage *n Am* Kinderwagen *der.*

baby food *n* Babynahrung *die.*

baby-sit *vi* babysitten.

baby-sitter [-,sɪtəʳ] *n* Babysitter *der,* -in *die.*

bachelor ['bætʃələʳ] *n* Junggeselle *der.*

Bachelor of Arts *n* [degree] erster akademischer Grad der Geisteswissenschaften an Universitäten in englischsprachigen Ländern.

Bachelor of Science *n* [degree] erster akademischer Grad der Naturwissenschaften an Universitäten in englischsprachigen Ländern.

back [bæk] <> *adv* - **1.** [backwards] zurück; **stand ~ (please)!** (bitte) zurück|treten!; **to tie ~** zurück|binden; **to push ~** [shove] zurück|schieben - **2.** [to former position or state] zurück; **when will you be ~?** wann bist du wieder da?; **~ and forth** hin und her; **to give sthg ~** etw zurück|geben; **we went ~ to sleep** wir sind wieder eingeschlafen; **~ home** bei uns zu Hause - **3.** [earlier]: **two weeks ~** vor zwei Wochen; **it dates ~ to 1960** es stammt aus dem Jahr(e) 1960; **I found out ~ in January** ich habe es schon im Januar erfahren; **to think ~ to sthg** an etw *(A)* zurück|denken - **4.** [in reply, in return]: **to write/phone/pay ~** zurück|schreiben/-rufen/-zahlen - **5.** [in fashion again]: **to be ~ (in fashion)** wieder modern sein <> *n* - **1.** [of person, animal, hand] Rücken *der;* [of chair] Lehne *die;* **to do sthg behind sb's ~** etw hinter js Rücken tun; **to put one's ~ into sthg** sich bei etw an|strengen; **get off my ~!** *inf* lass mich in Ruhe! - **2.** [opposite or reverse side - of banknote, page] Rückseite *die;* **~ of the head** Hinterkopf *der* - **3.** [not front - inside car] Rücksitz *der;* [- of room] hinterer Teil; **at the ~ of, in ~ of** *Am* hinter (+ *D);* **at the ~ of the cupboard** hinten im Schrank - **4.** SPORT [player] Verteidiger *der;* [in rugby] Spieler *der* der Hintermannschaft <> *adj (in compounds)* - **1.** [at the back - wheels, legs, door] Hinter- - **2.** [overdue - rent] überfällig <> *vt* - **1.** [reverse] zurück|setzen - **2.** [support] unterstützen - **3.** [bet on]: **to ~ a horse** (Geld) auf ein Pferd setzen <> *vi* [car, driver] rückwärts fahren. **back to back** *adv* [stand] Rücken an Rücken. **back to front** *adv* [the wrong way round] verkehrt herum. **back down** *vi* nach|geben. **back out** *vi* [of arrangement] aus|steigen. **back up** <> *vt sep* - **1.** [support] unterstützen - **2.** [confirm] bestätigen - **3.** [reverse] zurück|setzen - **4.** COMPUT ein Backup machen <> *vi* [car, driver] zurück|setzen.

backache ['bækeɪk] *n (U)* Rückenschmerzen *pl.*

backbencher [ˌbæk'bentʃəʳ] *n Br* POL parlamentarischer Hinterbänkler.

backbone ['bækbəʊn] *n lit & fig* Rückgrat *das.*

backcloth ['bækklɒθ] *n Br* = backdrop.

backdate [ˌbæk'deɪt] *vt* zurück|datieren.

back door *n* Hintertür *die.*

backdrop ['bækdrɒp] *n lit & fig* Hintergrund *der.*

backfire [ˌbæk'faɪəʳ] *vi* - **1.** [motor vehicle] Fehlzündungen haben - **2.** [plan] fehl|schlagen; **to ~ on sb** auf jn zurück|fallen.

backgammon ['bækˌgæmən] *n* Backgammon *das.*

background ['bækgraʊnd] *n* - **1.** [gen] Hintergrund *der;* **in the ~** *lit & fig* im Hintergrund - **2.** [upbringing] Herkunft *die.*

backhand ['bækhænd] *n* Rückhand *die.*

backhanded ['bækhændɪd] *adj fig* [compliment] zweifelhaft.

backhander ['bækhændəʳ] *n Br inf* [bribe] Schmiergeld *das.*

backing ['bækɪŋ] *n* - **1.** *(U)* [support] Unterstützung *die* - **2.** [lining] Verstärkung *die.*

backing group *n* MUS Begleitband *die.*

backlash ['bæklæʃ] *n* Gegenschlag *der.*

backlog ['bæklɒg] *n* Rückstände *pl;* **to have a ~ of work** mit der Arbeit im Rückstand sein.

back number *n* alte Ausgabe.

backpack ['bækpæk] *n* Rucksack *der.*

back pay *n* ausstehender Lohn.

back seat *n* [in car] Rücksitz *der;* **to take a ~** *fig* sich im Hintergrund halten.

backside [ˌbæk'saɪd] *n inf* Hintern *der.*

backstage [ˌbæk'steɪdʒ] *adv* hinter den Kulissen.

back street *n Br* kleine Seitenstraße.

backstroke ['bækstrəʊk] *n* Rückenschwimmen *das.*

backup ['bækʌp] *n* - **1.** *(U)* [support] Unterstützung *die* - **2.** COMPUT Sicherungskopie *die.*

backward ['bækwəd] <> *adj* - **1.** [gen] rückwärts gerichtet; **a ~ glance** ein Blick über die Schulter - **2.** *pej* [child, country] zurückgeblieben <> *adv Am* = backwards.

backwards ['bækwədz], **backward** *Am* ['bækwəd] *adv* [towards the rear] rückwärts; **to fall ~** nach hinten fallen; **~ and forwards** hin und her; **to look ~** zurück|blicken.

backwater ['bækˌwɔːtəʳ] *n* [place] Kaff *das.*

backyard [ˌbæk'jɑːd] *n* - **1.** *Br* [yard] Hinterhof *der* - **2.** *Am* [garden] Garten *der* hinter dem Haus.

bacon ['beɪkən] *n (U)* Schinkenspeck *der.*

bacteria [bæk'tɪərɪə] *npl* Bakterien *pl.*

bad [bæd] (*compar* worse; *superl* worst) <> *adj* - **1.** [unpleasant, unfavourable - gen] schlecht; [- smell] übel; **~ breath** Mundgeruch *der;* **he is in a ~ way** es geht ihm gar nicht gut; **smoking is ~ for you** Rauchen ist schädlich; **too ~!** Pech! - **2.** [serious] schwer; **to have a ~ cold** einen starken Schnupfen haben - **3.** [inadequate - eyesight, excuse] schwach; **to be ~ at sthg** etw schlecht können; **he's ~ at English** er ist schlecht in Englisch; **not ~** nicht schlecht - **4.** [injured, unhealthy] schlimm; **my ~ leg** mein schlimmes Bein; **he has a ~ heart** er hat ein schwaches Herz - **5.** [naughty] ungezogen; [wicked] böse, übel; **he's a ~ lot** er ist ein übler Bursche - **6.** [food - rotten, off] verdorben; **to go ~** verderben - **7.** [guilty]: **he really feels ~ about it** es tut ihm wirklich leid <> *adv Am* = badly.

baddy ['bædɪ] (*pl* -ies) *n inf* Böse *der.*

badge [bædʒ] *n* - **1.** [for fun] Button *der* - **2.** [for employee, visitor] Schild(chen) *das* - **3.** [sewn-on] Abzeichen *das* - **4.** [on car] Emblem *das*.

badger ['bædʒə'] ⬦ *n* Dachs *der* ⬦ *vt* [pester]: **to ~ sb** jm keine Ruhe lassen.

badly ['bædlɪ] (*compar* worse; *superl* worst) *adv* - **1.** [poorly] schlecht; **to treat sb ~** jn schlecht behandeln - **2.** [wounded, beaten, affected] schwer - **3.** [very much]: **to be ~ in need of sthg** dringend benötigen.

badly-off *adj* [poor] nicht gut gestellt.

badminton ['bædmɪntən] *n* (U) Federball *das;* SPORT Badminton *das*.

bad-tempered [-'tempəd] *adj* - **1.** [by nature] übellaunig - **2.** [in a bad mood] schlecht gelaunt.

baffled [bæfld] *adj* ratlos.

bag [bæg] ⬦ *n* - **1.** [container] Tasche *die;* [for shopping] Tüte *die;* [large, for coal, cement] Sack *der;* [of tea, rice] Beutel *der;* **to pack one's ~s** *fig* [leave] seine Sachen packen - **2.** [handbag] Handtasche *die;* [when travelling] Reisetasche *die* - **3.** [bagful]: **a ~ of crisps** *Br* eine Tüte Chips; **a ~ of potatoes** ein Sack Kartoffeln ⬦ *vt* - **1.** *Br inf* [get] sich (D) schnappen - **2.** *Br inf* [reserve] belegen, besetzen. ➡ **bags** *npl* - **1.** [under eyes] Tränensäcke *pl* - **2.** [lots]: **~s of time/room** *inf* eine Menge OR jede Menge Zeit/Platz.

bagel ['beɪgəl] *n* kleines ringförmiges Brötchen.

baggage ['bægɪdʒ] *n* Gepäck *das*.

baggage reclaim *n* Gepäckausgabe *die*.

baggy ['bægɪ] *adj* weit (geschnitten).

bagpipes ['bægpaɪps] *npl* Dudelsack *der*.

Bahamas [bə'hɑːməz] *npl*: **the ~** die Bahamas.

bail [beɪl] *n* (U) LAW Kaution *die;* **on ~** gegen Kaution. ➡ **bail out** ⬦ *vt sep* - **1.** LAW [pay bail for] (die) Kaution stellen für - **2.** [rescue] aus der Klemme helfen (+ D) - **3.** [boat] auslschöpfen ⬦ *vi* [from plane] ablspringen.

bailiff ['beɪlɪf] *n* [in charge of repossession] Gerichtsvollzieher *der;* [in court] Gerichtsdiener *der*.

bait [beɪt] ⬦ *n* (U) Köder *der* ⬦ *vt* - **1.** [hook, trap] mit einem Köder versehen - **2.** [torment - person] piesacken; [- bear, badger] quälen.

bake [beɪk] ⬦ *vt* - **1.** [bread, cake *etc*] backen - **2.** [ground] ausldörren; [clay, brick] brennen ⬦ *vi* backen.

baked beans [beɪkt-] *npl* weiße Bohnen *pl* in Tomatensoße.

baked potato *n* in der Schale gebackene Kartoffel.

baker ['beɪkə'] *n* Bäcker *der*, -in *die;* **~'s (shop)** Bäckerei *die*, Bäckerladen *der*.

bakery ['beɪkərɪ] *n* Bäckerei *die*.

baking ['beɪkɪŋ] *n* [cooking] Backen *das*.

balaclava [ˌbælə'klɑːvə] *n Br* eng anliegende Kopfbedeckung, die nur das Gesicht frei lässt.

balance ['bæləns] ⬦ *n* - **1.** [equilibrium] Gleichgewicht *das;* **to keep/lose one's ~** das Gleichgewicht halten/verlieren; **off ~** aus dem Gleichgewicht - **2.** *fig* [counterweight] Ausgleich *der* - **3.** *fig* [weight, force]: **~ of power** Gleichgewicht *das* der Kräfte - **4.** [scales] Waage *die* - **5.** [remainder] Rest *der* - **6.** [of bank account] Kontostand *der* ⬦ *vt* - **1.** [keep in balance] im Gleichgewicht halten - **2.** [compare]: **to ~ sthg against sthg** etw gegen etw ablwägen - **3.** [in accounting]: **to ~ the books/the budget** die Bilanz machen ⬦ *vi* - **1.** [maintain equilibrium] das Gleichgewicht halten - **2.** [in accounting] sich auslgleichen. ➡ **on balance** *adv* alles in allem.

balanced diet [ˌbælənst-] *n* ausgewogene Ernährung.

balance of payments *n* Zahlungsbilanz *die*.

balance of trade *n* Handelsbilanz *die*.

balance sheet *n* Bilanz *die*.

balcony ['bælkənɪ] *n* - **1.** [on building] Balkon *der* - **2.** [in theatre] oberster Rang.

bald [bɔːld] *adj* - **1.** [head, man] glatzköpfig, kahl(köpfig) - **2.** [tyre] völlig abgenutzt - **3.** *fig* [unadorned] nüchtern, unverblümt.

bale [beɪl] *n* Ballen *der*. ➡ **bale out** *Br* ⬦ *vt sep* [boat] auslschöpfen ⬦ *vi* [from plane] ablspringen.

Balearic Islands [ˌbælɪ'ærɪk-], **Balearics** [ˌbælɪ'ærɪks] *npl*: **the ~** die Balearen.

balk [bɔːk] *vi*: **to ~ (at)** zurücklschrecken (vor (+ D)).

Balkans ['bɔːlkənz], **Balkan States** ['bɔːlkən-]*npl*: **the ~** der Balkan.

ball [bɔːl] *n* - **1.** [in game] Ball *der;* [in snooker, bowling] Kugel *die;* **to be on the ~** auf Draht sein; **to play ~** *fig* mitlmachen - **2.** [of wool] Knäuel *das* - **3.** [of foot] Ballen *der* - **4.** [dance] Ball *der*. ➡ **balls** *vinf* ⬦ *n* (U) [nonsense] Schwachsinn *der* ⬦ *npl* [testicles] Eier *pl* ⬦ *excl* Scheiße!

ballad ['bæləd] *n* Ballade *die*.

ballast ['bæləst] *n* Ballast *der*.

ball bearing *n* Kugellager *das*.

ball boy *n* Balljunge *der*.

ballerina [ˌbælə'riːnə] *n* Ballerina *die*.

ballet ['bæleɪ] *n* Ballett *das*.

ballet dancer *n* Balletttänzer *der*, -in *die*.

ball game *n* - **1.** *Am* [baseball match] Baseballspiel *das* - **2.** *fig* [situation]: **it's a whole new ~** *inf* das ist eine ganz neue Lage.

balloon [bə'luːn] *n* - **1.** [toy] Luftballon *der* - **2.** [hot-air balloon] Heißluftballon *der*.

ballot ['bælət] ⬦ *n* [voting process] Abstimmung *die* ⬦ *vt* [members] abstimmen lassen.

ballot box *n* Wahlurne *die*.

ballot paper *n* Stimmzettel *der*.

ball park *n Am* Baseballstadion *das*.

ballpoint (pen) ['bɔːlpɔɪnt-] *n* Kugelschreiber *der*.

ballroom ['bɔːlrʊm] *n* Ballsaal *der*.

ballroom dancing *n (U)* Gesellschaftstanz *der*.

balmy ['bɑːmɪ] *adj* [evening] mild.

balsawood ['bɒlsəwʊd] *n* Balsaholz *das*.

Baltic ['bɔːltɪk] <> *adj* [port, coast] Ostsee-, baltisch <> *n*: **the ~ (Sea)** die Ostsee.

Baltic State *n*: **the ~s** die Baltischen Staaten.

bamboo [bæm'buː] *n* Bambus *der*.

bamboozle [bæm'buːzl] *vt inf* verwirren.

ban [bæn] <> *n* Verbot *das*; **~ on smoking** Rauchverbot *das* <> *vt* verbieten; **to ~ sb from doing sthg** jm etw verbieten.

banal [bə'nɑːl] *adj pej* banal.

banana [bə'nɑːnə] *n* Banane *die*.

band [bænd] *n* **- 1.** [musical - pop] Gruppe *die*; [- traditional, classical] Kapelle *die*; [- jazz] Band *die* **- 2.** [gang] Bande *die* **- 3.** [of colour, metal] Streifen *der* **- 4.** [range] Klasse *die*.
➤ **band together** *vi* sich zusammenschließen.

bandage ['bændɪdʒ] <> *n* Verband *der* <> *vt* verbinden.

Band-Aid® *n* Heftpflaster *das*.

bandit ['bændɪt] *n* Bandit *der*.

bandstand ['bændstænd] *n* Musikpavillon *der*.

bandwagon ['bændwægən] *n*: **to jump on the ~** auf den fahrenden Zug auflspringen.

bandy ['bændɪ] ➤ **bandy about, bandy around** *vt sep* [words] um sich werfen mit.

bang [bæŋ] <> *adv* [right]: **~ in the middle** genau in der Mitte; **his description was ~ on** seine Beschreibung passte aufs Haar; **~ on time** auf die Minute pünktlich <> *n* **- 1.** [blow] Schlag *der* **- 2.** [loud noise] Knall *der* <> *vt* **- 1.** [hit] anlschlagen **- 2.** [door] zulschlagen <> *vi* **- 1.** [knock]: **to ~ on the door/wall** [once] gegen die Tür/die Wand schlagen; [more than once] gegen die Tür/die Wand hämmern **- 2.** [make a loud noise] (heruml)poltern **- 3.** [crash]: **to ~ into sb/sthg** gegen jn/etw stoßen <> *excl* peng!
➤ **bangs** *npl Am* Pony *der*.

banger ['bæŋər] *n Br* **- 1.** *inf* [sausage] Würstchen *das* **- 2.** *inf* [old car] alte Kiste **- 3.** [firework] Knallkörper *der*.

bangle ['bæŋgl] *n* Armreif *der*.

banish ['bænɪʃ] *vt lit & fig* verbannen.

banister ['bænɪstər] *n*, **banisters** ['bænɪstəz] *npl* Geländer *das*.

bank [bæŋk] <> *n* **- 1.** FIN Bank *die* **- 2.** [of data, blood *etc*] Bank *die* **- 3.** [of river, lake] Ufer *das* **- 4.** [slope] Böschung *die* **- 5.** [of fog, cloud] Bank *die*; **a ~ of snow** eine Schneeverwehung <> *vt* FIN einlzahlen <> *vi* **- 1.** FIN: **who do you ~ with?** bei welcher Bank sind Sie?

- 2. [plane] sich in die Kurve legen. ➤ **bank on** *vt fus* sich verlassen auf (+ *A*).

bank account *n* Bankkonto *das*.

bank balance *n* Kontostand *der*.

bank card *n* = banker's card.

bank charges *npl* Bankgebühren *pl*.

bank draft *n* Banküberweisung *die*.

banker ['bæŋkər] *n* FIN Bankier *der*.

banker's card *n Br* Scheckkarte *die*.

bank holiday *n Br* Feiertag *der*.

banking ['bæŋkɪŋ] *n* Bankwesen *das*.

bank manager *n* Filialleiter *der*, -in *die*.

bank note *n* Banknote *die*, Geldschein *der*.

bank rate *n* Diskontsatz *der*.

bankrupt ['bæŋkrʌpt] *adj* bankrott; **to go ~** bankrott machen, in Konkurs gehen.

bankruptcy ['bæŋkrəptsɪ] *n* Bankrott *der*.

bank statement *n* Kontoauszug *der*.

banner ['bænər] *n* Transparent *das*.

bannister *n*, **bannisters** *npl* = banister.

banquet ['bæŋkwɪt] *n* Festessen *das*.

banter ['bæntər] *n (U)* Frotzeleien *pl*.

bap [bæp] *n Br* weiches Brötchen.

baptism ['bæptɪzm] *n* Taufe *die*.

Baptist ['bæptɪst] *n* Baptist *der*, -in *die*.

baptize, -ise [*Br* bæp'taɪz, *Am* 'bæptaɪz] *vt* taufen.

bar [bɑːr] <> *n* **- 1.** [of wood, metal] Stange *die*; [of gold] Barren *der*; [of soap] Stück *das*; [of chocolate - slab] Tafel *die*; [- long and thin] Riegel *der*; **to be behind ~s** hinter Gittern sitzen; **the ~** [in gymnastics] der Balken **- 2.** *fig* [obstacle] Hindernis *das* **- 3.** [in hotel] Bar *die*; [pub] Kneipe *die* **- 4.** [counter] Theke *die* **- 5.** MUS Takt *der* <> *vt* **- 1.** [door, window] verriegeln **- 2.** [block] (ver)sperren; **to ~ sb's way** jm den Weg versperren <> *prep* [except] ausgenommen, außer (+ *D*); **~ none** ohne Ausnahme. ➤ **Bar** *n*: **to be called to the Bar** *Br* als Anwalt zugelassen werden.

barbaric [bɑː'bærɪk] *adj* barbarisch.

barbecue ['bɑːbɪkjuː] *n* **- 1.** [grill] Grill *der* **- 2.** [party] Barbecue *das*, Grillparty *die*.

barbed wire [bɑːbd-] *n* Stacheldraht *der*.

barber ['bɑːbər] *n* (Herren)friseur *der*; **~'s (shop)** (Herren)friseurladen *der*.

barbiturate [bɑː'bɪtjʊrət] *n* Barbiturat *das*.

bar code *n* Strichkodierung *die*.

bare [beər] <> *adj* **- 1.** [feet, legs, body] nackt, bloß; [rock, branches, landscape] kahl **- 2.** [basic]: **the ~ facts** die reinen Tatsachen; **the ~ minimum** das strikte Minimum **- 3.** [room, cupboard] leer <> *vt* entblößen; **to ~ one's teeth** die Zähne fletschen.

barefaced ['beəfeɪst] *adj* schamlos, frech.

barefoot(ed) [ˌbeə'fʊt(ɪd)] <> *adj* barfüßig <> *adv* barfuß.

barely ['beəlɪ] *adv* [scarcely] kaum, knapp.

bargain ['bɑːgɪn] <> *n* **- 1.** [agreement] Geschäft *das*; **into the ~** obendrein **- 2.** [good buy] Schnäppchen *das* ◇ *vi* (ver)handeln; **to ~ with sb for sthg** mit jm um etw handeln OR feilschen. ➡ **bargain for, bargain on** *vt fus* erwarten, rechnen mit.

barge ['bɑːdʒ] ◇ *n* Schleppkahn *der*, Lastkahn *der* ◇ *vi inf*: **to ~ into a room** in ein Zimmer hereinlplatzen; **to ~ past sb/sthg** an jm/etw vorbeilstürmen. ➡ **barge in** *vi*: **to ~ in (on sb)** hereinlplatzen (bei jm).

baritone ['bærɪtəun] *n* Bariton *der*.

bark [bɑːk] ◇ *n* - 1. [of dog] Bellen *das* - 2. [on tree] Rinde *die*, Borke *die* ◇ *vi* [dog] bellen; **to ~ at sb/sthg** jn/etw anlbellen.

barley ['bɑːlɪ] *n* Gerste *die*.

barley sugar *n Br* Malzbonbon *der* OR *das*.

barmaid ['bɑːmeɪd] *n* Bardame *die*.

barman ['bɑːmən] (*pl* **-men** [-mən]) *n* Barkeeper *der*.

barn [bɑːn] *n* Scheune *die*.

barometer [bə'rɒmɪtər] *n lit & fig* Barometer *das*.

baron ['bærən] *n* Baron *der*; **oil ~** Ölmagnat *der*; **press ~** Pressezar *der*.

baroness ['bærənɪs] *n* Baronin *die*; [not married] Baronesse *die*.

barrack ['bærək] *vt Br* auslpfeifen, auslbuhen. ➡ **barracks** *npl* Kaserne *die*.

barrage ['bærɑːʒ] *n* - 1. [of firing] Sperrfeuer *das*; **a ~ of complaints/questions** eine Flut von Beschwerden/Fragen - 2. *Br* [dam] Staudamm *der*.

barrel ['bærəl] *n* - 1. [for beer, wine] Fass *das* - 2. [for oil] Tonne *die*; [as measure] Barrel *das* - 3. [of gun] Lauf *der*.

barren ['bærən] *adj* [woman, land, soil] unfruchtbar.

barricade [ˌbærɪ'keɪd] *n* Barrikade *die*.

barrier ['bærɪər] *n* Barriere *die*; [at car park, level crossing] Schranke *die*.

barring ['bɑːrɪŋ] *prep*: **~ accidents** falls nichts passiert.

barrister ['bærɪstər] *n Br* Rechtsanwalt *der*, -wältin *die*.

barrow ['bærəu] *n* [market stall] Karren *der*.

bartender ['bɑːtendər] *n Am* Barkeeper *der*.

barter ['bɑːtər] ◇ *n* Tauschhandel *der* ◇ *vt & vi* tauschen.

base [beɪs] ◇ *n* - 1. [of post, lamp, mountain] Fuß *der*; [of triangle] Basis *die*; [of box] Boden *der* - 2. [of food, paint] Basis *die* - 3. [centre of activities - gen] Standort *der*; [- military, in mountaineering] Stützpunkt *der* - 4. [in baseball] Mal *das* ◇ *vt* - 1. [locate - MIL] stationieren; **he's ~d in Paris** sein Büro ist in Paris - 2. [use as starting point]: **to ~ sthg (up)on sthg** etw auf etw (A) gründen OR basieren ◇ *adj pej* [dishonourable] niederträchtig.

baseball ['beɪsbɔːl] *n* (U) Baseball *der*.

baseball cap *n* Baseballkappe *die*.

basement ['beɪsmənt] *n* [of house] Keller *der*; [of department store] Untergeschoss *das*.

base rate *n* Leitzins *der*.

bases ['beɪsiːz] *pl* ⊳ **basis**.

bash [bæʃ] *inf* ◇ *n* - 1. [blow] (heftiger) Schlag - 2. [attempt]: **to have a ~ (at sthg)** (etw) mal probieren ◇ *vt* [hit] schlagen; **to ~ one's head** sich (D) den Kopf anlhauen.

bashful ['bæʃful] *adj* schüchtern.

basic ['beɪsɪk] *adj* grundlegend, wesentlich; [vocabulary, principle] Grund-; [meal, accommodation] einfach. ➡ **basics** *npl*: **the ~s** die Grundlagen *pl*.

BASIC ['beɪsɪk] (*abbr of* Beginner's All-purpose Symbolic Instruction Code) *n* BASIC *nt*.

basically ['beɪsɪklɪ] *adv* grundsätzlich.

basil ['bæzl] *n* Basilikum *das*.

basin ['beɪsn] *n* - 1. [sink] Waschbecken *das* - 2. *Br* [bowl] Schüssel *die*.

basis ['beɪsɪs] (*pl* **-ses**) *n* - 1. [reason] Grundlage *die*, Basis *die*; **on the ~ that ...** in der Annahme, dass ... - 2. [foundation, arrangement] Basis *die*; **on a weekly ~** wöchentlich; **on the ~ of** auf der Grundlage (+ G).

bask [bɑːsk] *vi* sich aalen.

basket ['bɑːskɪt] *n* Korb *der*.

basketball ['bɑːskɪtbɔːl] *n* Basketball *der*.

bass [beɪs] *adj* [part, singer] Bass-.

bass drum *n* große Trommel.

bass guitar *n* Bassgitarre *die*.

bassoon [bə'suːn] *n* Fagott *das*.

bastard ['bɑːstəd] *n* - 1. [illegitimate child] Bastard *der* - 2. *vinf pej* [unpleasant person] Scheißkerl *der*; **the poor ~** die arme Sau.

bastion ['bæstɪən] *n fig* Bastion *die*.

bat [bæt] *n* - 1. [animal] Fledermaus *die* - 2. [for cricket, baseball] Schlagholz *das*; [for table tennis] Schläger *der* - 3. *phr*: **to do sthg off one's own ~** etw auf eigene Faust tun.

batch [bætʃ] *n* - 1. [of papers, letters, work] Stapel *der* - 2. [of products] Ladung *die* - 3. [of people] Schwung *der*.

bated ['beɪtɪd] *adj*: **with ~ breath** mit angehaltenem Atem.

bath [bɑːθ] ◇ *n* Bad *das*; [bathtub] (Bade)wanne *die*; **to have** OR **take a ~** ein Bad nehmen, baden ◇ *vt* baden. ➡ **baths** *npl Br* Bad *das*.

bathe [beɪð] ◇ *vt* - 1. [wound] auslwaschen, baden - 2. [in light, sweat] baden ◇ *vi* baden.

bathing ['beɪðɪŋ] *n* Baden *das*.

bathing cap *n* Badekappe *die*.

bathing costume, bathing suit *n* Badeanzug *der*.

bathrobe ['bɑːθrəub] *n* Bademantel *der*.

bathroom ['bɑːθrum] *n* - 1. *Br* [room with bath] Badezimmer *das* - 2. *Am* [toilet] Toilette *die*.

bath towel *n* Badetuch *das*.

bathtub ['ba:θtʌb] n Badewanne die.

baton ['bætən] n - 1. [of conductor] Taktstock der - 2. [in relay race] Staffelstab der - 3. Br [of policeman] Schlagstock der.

batsman ['bætsmən] (pl -men [-mən]) n Schlagmann der.

battalion [bə'tæljən] n Bataillon das.

batter ['bætə'] <> n CULIN Teig der <> vt [person] schlagen, verprügeln <> vi [on door, wall] hämmern, trommeln.

battered ['bætəd] adj - 1. [person] verprügelt - 2. [car, hat, suitcase] verbeult - 3. CULIN im Teigmantel.

battery ['bætəri] n Batterie die.

battle ['bætl] <> n - 1. [in war] Schlacht die - 2. [struggle]: ~ (for/against) Kampf der (für/gegen); **that's half the ~** damit ist schon eine Menge gewonnen <> vi: **to ~ (for/against)** kämpfen (für/gegen).

battlefield ['bætlfi:ld], **battleground** [-graund] n lit & fig Schlachtfeld das.

battlements ['bætlmənts] npl Zinnen pl.

battleship ['bætlʃip] n Schlachtschiff das.

bauble ['bɔ:bl] n Christbaumkugel die.

baulk [bɔ:k] vi = balk.

bawdy ['bɔ:di] adj derb.

bawl [bɔ:l] <> vt [shout] brüllen <> vi - 1. [shout] brüllen - 2. [weep] heulen.

bay [bei] n - 1. GEOGR Bucht die - 2. [for loading] Ladeplatz der - 3. [for parking] Parkbucht die - 4. phr: **to keep sb at ~** jn auf Abstand halten.

bay leaf n Lorbeerblatt das.

bay window n Erkerfenster das.

bazaar [bə'zɑ:'] n - 1. [market] Basar der - 2. Br [charity sale] Wohltätigkeitsbasar der.

B & B n abbr of bed and breakfast.

BBC (abbr of British Broadcasting Corporation) n BBC die.

📖 **BBC**

Seit der Schaffung des weltweit ersten öffentlichen Fernsehsenders durch die BBC im Jahre 1936 ist die Zahl der terrestrisch zu empfangenden Sender in Großbritannien auf fünf gestiegen: BBC1, BBC2, ITV, Channel 4 und Channel 5. Die BBC ist eine öffentlich-rechtliche Anstalt (alle Besitzer von Fernsehgeräten müssen wie auch in Deutschland Rundfunkgebühren bezahlen) und ist von der Regierung unabhängig.

BC (abbr of before Christ) v. Chr.

be [bi:] (pt was OR were; pp been) <> vi - 1. [exist] sein; **there is/are** es ist/sind ... da, es gibt; **are there any shops near here?** gibt es hier in der Nähe irgendwelche Geschäfte?; **there is someone in the room** es ist jemand im Zimmer; **~ that as it may** wie dem auch sei - 2. [referring to location] sein; **the hotel is near the airport** das Hotel befindet sich in der Nähe des Flughafens; **he will ~ here tomorrow** er kommt morgen - 3. [referring to movement] sein; **have you ever been to California?** warst du schon mal in Kalifornien?; **I'll ~ there in ten minutes** ich komme in zehn Minuten; **where have you been?** wo bist du gewesen? - 4. [occur] sein; **my birthday is in June** mein Geburtstag ist im Juni - 5. [identifying, describing] sein; **he's a doctor** er ist Arzt; **I'm British** ich bin Brite/Britin; **I'm hot/cold** mir ist heiß/kalt; **you are right** du hast Recht; **~ quiet!** sei still!, seid still!; **one and one are two** eins und eins ist zwei - 6. [referring to health]: **how are you?** wie geht es Ihnen?; **I'm fine** mir geht es gut; **she is ill** sie ist krank - 7. [referring to age]: **how old are you?** wie alt bist du?; **I am 14 (years old)** ich bin 14 (Jahre alt) - 8. [referring to cost] kosten; **how much is it?** wie viel kostet es?; **it's £10** es kostet 10 Pfund - 9. [referring to time, dates] sein; **what time is it?** wie viel Uhr ist es?, wie spät ist es?; **it's ten o'clock** es ist zehn Uhr; **today is February 17th** heute haben wir den 17. Februar - 10. [referring to measurement] sein; **it's ten metres long/high** es ist zehn Meter lang/hoch; **I'm 8 stone** ich wiege 50 Kilo - 11. [referring to the weather] sein; **it's hot/cold** es ist heiß/kalt - 12. [for emphasis] sein; **is that you?** bist du das?; **yes, it's me** ja, ich bins <> aux vb - 1. (in combination with present participle to form continuous tense): **I'm learning German** ich lerne Deutsch; **what is he doing?** was macht er?; **it's snowing** es schneit; **we've been visiting the museum** wir waren im Museum; **I've been living in London for 10 years** ich wohne seit 10 Jahren in London; **he is going on holiday next week** nächste Woche fährt er in Urlaub - 2. (forming passive) werden; **they were defeated** sie wurden geschlagen; **the flight was delayed** das Flugzeug hatte Verspätung; **it is said ...** man sagt ... - 3. (with infinitive to express an order): **all rooms are to ~ vacated by 10.00 a.m.** alle Zimmer müssen bis 10 Uhr geräumt sein; **you are not to tell anyone** das darfst du niemandem erzählen - 4. (with infinitive to express future tense): **the race is to start at noon** das Rennen ist für 12 Uhr angesetzt - 5. (in tag questions): **it's cold, isn't it?** es ist kalt, nicht wahr?; **you're not going now, are you?** willst du schon gehen?

beach [bi:tʃ] n Strand der.

beacon ['bi:kən] n - 1. [fire, lighthouse] Leuchtfeuer das - 2. [radio beacon] Funkfeuer das.

bead [bi:d] n [of glass, wood, sweat] Perle die.

beak [bi:k] n [of bird] Schnabel der.

beaker ['bi:kə'] n Becher der.

beam [bi:m] ⬦ n - **1.** [of wood] Balken der; [of steel] Träger der - **2.** [of light] Strahl der - **3.** Am AUT: **high/low ~s** Fern-/Abblendlicht das ⬦ vt [signal, news] ausstrahlen ⬦ vi strahlen.

bean [bi:n] n Bohne die; **to be full of ~s** inf voller Tatendrang sein; **to spill the ~s** inf [confess] singen.

beanbag ['bi:nbæg] n [seat] Sitzsack der.

beanshoot ['bi:nʃu:t], **beansprout** ['bi:nspraʊt] n (Soja)bohnensprosse die.

bear [beəʳ] (pt bore; pp borne) ⬦ n [animal] Bär der ⬦ vt - **1.** [gen] tragen - **2.** [tolerate] ertragen, aushalten - **3.** [ill will, hatred] hegen ⬦ vi - **1.** [turn]: **to ~ left/right** sich links/rechts halten - **2.** [have effect]: **to bring pressure/influence to ~ on sb** auf jm Druck/Einfluss geltend machen. ➡ **bear down** vi: **to ~ down on sb/sthg** auf jn/etw zusteuern. ➡ **bear out** vt sep bestätigen. ➡ **bear up** vi: **to ~ up well** sich tapfer halten. ➡ **bear with** vt fus: **~ with me for a minute, will you?** einen Moment Geduld, bitte.

beard [bɪəd] n Bart der.

bearer ['beərəʳ] n - **1.** [of stretcher, coffin] Träger der - **2.** [of news, letter] Überbringer der, -in die - **3.** [of cheque, passport] Inhaber der, -in die - **4.** [of name, title] Träger der, -in die.

bearing ['beərɪŋ] n - **1.** [relevance] Bedeutung die; **to have a ~ on sthg** bei etw eine Rolle spielen - **2.** [deportment] (Körper)haltung die - **3.** TECH Lager das - **4.** [on compass]: **to take a ~** die Richtung bestimmen; **to get one's ~s** fig sich orientieren; **to lose one's ~s** fig die Orientierung verlieren.

beast [bi:st] n - **1.** [animal] Tier das - **2.** inf pej [person - unpleasant] Ekel das; [- evil] Bestie die.

beat [bi:t] (pt beat; pp beaten) ⬦ n - **1.** [of drum, heart, pulse] Schlag der - **2.** [MUS - rhythm] Rhythmus der; [- measure] Takt der - **3.** [of policeman] Runde die ⬦ vt - **1.** [gen] schlagen; **to ~ a record** einen Rekord brechen; **it ~s me** inf ich habe keine Ahnung - **2.** MUS: **to ~ time** (den) Takt schlagen OR anlgeben - **3.** phr: **~ it!** inf [go away] verschwinde!, hau ab! ⬦ vi - **1.** [rain - on roof] trommeln - **2.** [heart, pulse] schlagen. ➡ **beat off** vt sep [resist] abwehren. ➡ **beat up** vt sep inf [person] zusammenschlagen.

beating ['bi:tɪŋ] n - **1.** [punishment] Prügel pl; **to give sb a ~** jm eine Tracht Prügel verabreichen - **2.** [defeat] Niederlage die.

beautiful ['bju:tɪfʊl] adj - **1.** [person] schön - **2.** [picture, music, weather] wundervoll, herrlich - **3.** inf [goal, player] herrlich, toll.

beautifully ['bju:təflɪ] adv - **1.** [dressed, decorated] bezaubernd - **2.** inf [cook, sing, play] wunderbar.

beauty ['bju:tɪ] n Schönheit die.

beauty parlour n Schönheitssalon der.

beauty salon n = beauty parlour.

beauty spot n - **1.** [place] schönes Fleckchen - **2.** [on skin] Schönheitsfleck der.

beaver ['bi:vəʳ] n Biber der.

became [bɪ'keɪm] pt ▷ become.

because [bɪ'kɒz] conj weil. ➡ **because of** prep wegen (+ G, D).

beck [bek] n: **to be at sb's ~ and call** nach js Pfeife tanzen.

beckon ['bekən] ⬦ vt [make a signal to] zulwinken (+ D) ⬦ vi: **to ~ to sb** jm zulwinken.

become [bɪ'kʌm] (pt became; pp become) vt werden; **to ~ old/rich/famous** alt/reich/berühmt werden; **to ~ accustomed to sthg** sich an etw (A) gewöhnen.

to become

Das englische Verb to become, das „werden" bedeutet, wird leicht mit dem falschen Freund „bekommen" verwechselt. Die Aussage He's become a real pain lately sagt keineswegs aus, dass jemand Schmerzen hat, sondern lautet übersetzt etwa „Er ist in letzter Zeit zu einer richtigen Nervensäge geworden". Dem deutschen „bekommen" entspricht das englische Wort to get. „Was hast du denn zum Geburtstag geschenkt bekommen?" fragt man im Englischen mit What did you get for your birthday?

becoming [bɪ'kʌmɪŋ] adj - **1.** [attractive]: **it's very ~** es steht ihr/dir/etc gut - **2.** [appropriate] schicklich.

bed [bed] n - **1.** [to sleep on] Bett das; **to go to ~** zu OR ins Bett gehen; **to get out of ~** auflstehen; **to go to ~ with sb** euphemism mit jm ins Bett gehen - **2.** [flowerbed] Beet das - **3.** [of sea] Meeresgrund der; [of river] Flussbett das.

bed and breakfast n Zimmer das mit Frühstück.

bedclothes ['bedkləʊðz] npl Bettzeug das.

bedlam ['bedləm] n Chaos das.

bed linen n Bettwäsche die.

bedraggled [bɪ'drægld] adj schmutzig und nass.

bedridden ['bed,rɪdn] adj bettlägerig.

bedroom ['bedrom] n Schlafzimmer das.

bedside ['bedsaɪd] n: **at sb's ~** an js Bett.

bedside table n Nachttisch der.

bed-sit(ter) n Br Wohnschlafzimmer das.

bedsore ['bedsɔ:ʳ] n wundgelegene Stelle.

bedspread ['bedspred] n Tagesdecke die.

bedtime ['bedtaɪm] n Schlafenszeit die.

bee [bi:] n Biene die.

beech [bi:tʃ] n - **1.** [tree] Buche die - **2.** [wood] Buchenholz das.

beef [bi:f] n Rindfleisch das.

beefburger ['bi:f,bɜ:gə'] n Hamburger der.

beefsteak ['bi:f,steɪk] n Beefsteak das.

beehive ['bi:haɪv] n Bienenstock der.

beeline ['bi:laɪn] n: **to make a ~ for sb/sthg** inf geradewegs auf jn/etw zusteuern.

been [bi:n] pp ⊳ be.

beer [bɪə'] n Bier das.

beer garden n Biergarten der.

beermat ['bɪə,mæt] n Bierdeckel der.

beet [bi:t] n - 1. [sugar beet] Zuckerrübe die - 2. Am [beetroot] rote Rübe, rote Bete.

beetle ['bi:tl] n Käfer der.

beetroot ['bi:tru:t] n rote Rübe, rote Bete.

before [bɪ'fɔ:'] ⋄ prep - 1. [in time] vor (+ D); **they arrived ~ us** sie sind vor uns angekommen; **the week ~ last** vorletzte Woche; **the day ~ yesterday** vorgestern; **the day ~** der Tag zuvor; **~ long** bald - 2. [in front of, facing] vor (+ D); **~ my (very) eyes** vor meinen Augen; **we have a difficult task ~ us** wir haben eine schwierige Aufgabe vor uns ⋄ adv [previously] schon einmal; **never ~** noch nie ⋄ conj bevor.

beforehand [bɪ'fɔ:hænd] adv vorher.

befriend [bɪ'frend] vt sich anfreunden mit.

beg [beg] ⋄ vt - 1. [money, food] betteln um - 2. [favour, forgiveness] bitten um; **to ~ sb for sthg** jn um etw bitten; **to ~ sb to do sthg** jn bitten, etw zu tun ⋄ vi - 1. [for money, food]: **to ~ (for)** betteln (um) - 2. [for favour, forgiveness]: **to ~ (for)** bitten (um).

began [bɪ'gæn] pt ⊳ begin.

beggar ['begə'] n Bettler der, -in die.

begin [bɪ'gɪn] (pt began; pp begun; cont -ning) ⋄ vt beginnen, anfangen; **to ~ doing** OR **to do sthg** beginnen OR anfangen, etw zu tun ⋄ vi beginnen, anfangen; **to ~ with** zunächst, zu Anfang.

beginner [bɪ'gɪnə'] n Anfänger der, -in die.

beginning [bɪ'gɪnɪŋ] n Anfang der; **from the ~** von Anfang an.

begrudge [bɪ'grʌdʒ] vt - 1. [envy]: **to ~ sb sthg** jm etw missgönnen - 2. [do unwillingly]: **to ~ doing sthg** etw widerwillig tun.

begun [bɪ'gʌn] pp ⊳ begin.

behalf [bɪ'hɑ:f] n: **on** Br OR **in** Am **~ of** in Namen (+ G), im Auftrag (+ G).

behave [bɪ'heɪv] ⋄ vt: **to ~ o.s.** sich benehmen ⋄ vi sich verhalten; [with good manners] sich benehmen.

behaviour Br, **behavior** Am [bɪ'heɪvjə'] n Benehmen das.

behead [bɪ'hed] vt enthaupten, köpfen.

beheld [bɪ'held] pt & pp ⊳ behold.

behind [bɪ'haɪnd] ⋄ prep - 1. [at the back of] hinter (+ D); [with verbs of motion] hinter (+ A) - 2. [causing, responsible for] hinter (+ D); **what's ~ this campaign?** was hat es mit dieser Kampagne auf sich?; **what's ~ it?** was steckt dahinter? - 3. [supporting]: **to be ~ sb** fig jn unterstützen - 4. [indicating deficiency,

delay]: **~ schedule** im Rückstand ⋄ adv - 1. [at, in the back] hinten; **the others followed ~** die anderen kamen hinterher; **to leave sthg ~** etw zurücklassen; **to stay ~** (da)bleiben - 2. [late]: **to be ~ (with sthg)** (mit etw) im Verzug sein ⋄ n inf Hintern der.

behold [bɪ'həʊld] (pt & pp beheld) vt literary erblicken.

beige [beɪʒ] ⋄ adj beige ⋄ n Beige das.

being ['bi:ɪŋ] n - 1. [creature] Wesen das, Geschöpf das - 2. [existence]: **in ~** existierend, vorhanden; **to come into ~** entstehen.

belated [bɪ'leɪtɪd] adj verspätet.

belch [beltʃ] ⋄ n Rülpser der ⋄ vt [smoke, fire] (aus)speien ⋄ vi [person] rülpsen.

beleaguered [bɪ'li:gəd] adj lit & fig belagert.

Belgian ['beldʒən] ⋄ adj belgisch ⋄ n Belgier der, -in die.

Belgium ['beldʒəm] n Belgien nt.

Belgrade [,bel'greɪd] n Belgrad nt.

belief [bɪ'li:f] n - 1. [gen]: **~ (in)** Glaube der (an (+ A)) - 2. [opinion] Meinung die; **it's my ~ that ...** ich bin davon überzeugt, dass ...

believe [bɪ'li:v] ⋄ vt glauben; **to ~ sb** jm glauben; **I ~ so** ich glaube ja; **I don't ~ it!** das darf (ja wohl) nicht wahr sein!; **~ it or not** ob du/Sie es glaubst/glauben oder nicht ⋄ vi glauben; **to ~ in sb/sthg** an jn/etw glauben.

believer [bɪ'li:və'] n RELIG Gläubige der, die; **I'm a never ~ in corporal punishment** ich halte viel von der Prügelstrafe.

belittle [bɪ'lɪtl] vt schmälern.

bell [bel] n Glocke die; [of phone, door, bike] Klingel die.

belligerent [bɪ'lɪdʒərənt] adj - 1. [at war] kriegführend - 2. [aggressive] angriffslustig.

bellows ['beləʊz] npl Blasebalg der.

belly ['belɪ] n Bauch der.

bellyache ['belɪeɪk] n Bauchschmerzen pl.

belly button n inf Bauchnabel der.

belong [bɪ'lɒŋ] vi gehören; **to ~ to sb** jm gehören; **to ~ to a party/club** einer Partei/einem Verein angehören.

belongings [bɪ'lɒŋɪŋz] npl Sachen pl.

beloved [bɪ'lʌvd] adj geliebt.

below [bɪ'ləʊ] ⋄ adv - 1. [in a lower position] unten; **they live on the floor ~** sie wohnen ein Stockwerk tiefer; **see ~** [in text] siehe unten - 2. [with numbers, quantities]: **children of 5 and ~** Kinder bis zu 5 Jahre - 3. NAUT: **to go ~** unter Deck gehen ⋄ prep - 1. [lower than] unter (+ D); [with verbs of motion] unter (+ A) - 2. [in rank, status] unter (+ D); **a sergeant is ~ a captain** ein Feldwebel steht unter einem Hauptmann - 3. [less than] unter (+ D); **10 degrees ~ (zero)** 10 Grad unter Null; **~ average** unter dem Durchschnitt.

belt [belt] ⋄ n - 1. [for clothing] Gürtel der - 2. TECH Riemen der ⋄ vt inf [hit] verprügeln.

beltway ['belt,weɪ] *n Am* Umgehungs-
straße *die*.

bemused [bɪ'mjuːzd] *adj* verwirrt.

bench [bentʃ] *n* - 1. POL [seat] Bank *die* - 2. [in
workshop] Werkbank *die*; [in laboratory] La-
bortisch *der*.

benchmark ['bentʃmɑːk] *n* [standard] Standard *der*; COMPUT Benchmark *die*.

bend [bend] *(pt & pp bent)* ◇ *n* - 1. [in
river, pipe] Biegung *die*; [in road] Kurve *die*
- 2. *phr*: **round the ~ inf** verrückt ◇ *vt* [arm,
leg, knee] beugen; [back] krümmen; [head]
neigen; [wire, fork, tube] (ver)biegen ◇ *vi*
- 1. [arm, leg] beugen; [branch, tree] biegen
- 2. [person] sich bücken - 3. [road] eine Kurve machen; [river] eine Biegung machen.
◆ **bend down** *vi* sich bücken. ◆ **bend
over** *vi* sich bücken; **to ~ over backwards for
sb** alles für jn tun.

beneath [bɪ'niːθ] ◇ *adv* [below] unten
◇ *prep* - 1. [under] unter (+ D); [with verbs of
motion] unter (+ A); **she shoved it ~ the bed**
sie schob es unter das Bett - 2. [unworthy of]:
that is ~ him das ist unter seiner Würde.

benefactor ['benɪfæktə'] *n* Wohltäter *der*,
-in *die*.

beneficial [,benɪ'fɪʃl] *adj* nützlich; **to be
~ to sb/sthg** jm/etw zugute kommen.

beneficiary [,benɪ'fɪʃərɪ] *n* LAW [of will] Be-
günstigte *der, die*.

benefit ['benɪfɪt] ◇ *n* - 1. (U) [advantage]
Nutzen *der*; **to be to sb's ~**, **to be of ~ to sb** zu
js Nutzen sein; **for the ~ of** zum Nutzen
(+ G); **to give sb the ~ of the doubt** jm trotz
Zweifels Glauben schenken - 2. [good point]
Vorteil *der* - 3. [allowance of money] Unter-
stützung *die* ◇ *vt* nützen (+ D) ◇ *vi*: **to
~ from sthg** von etw profitieren.

Benelux ['benɪlʌks] *n*: **the ~ countries** die
Beneluxstaaten, die Beneluxländer.

benevolent [bɪ'nevələnt] *adj* wohlwollend.

benign [bɪ'naɪn] *adj* - 1. [influence] gut; [cli-
mate] mild - 2. MED gutartig.

bent [bent] ◇ *pt & pp* ▷ **bend** ◇ *adj*
- 1. [wire, bar] gebogen, verbogen - 2. [per-
son, body] gebeugt - 3. *Br inf* [dishonest] korrupt - 4. [determined]: **to be ~ on sthg** etw
unbedingt wollen/haben wollen; **to be ~ on
doing sthg** etw unbedingt tun wollen ◇ *n*
[natural aptitude]: **~ (for)** Neigung *die* (zu).

bequeath [bɪ'kwiːð] *vt lit & fig* hinterlassen.

bequest [bɪ'kwest] *n* Nachlass *der*.

berate [bɪ'reɪt] *vt* schelten.

bereaved [bɪ'riːvd] *(pl inv)* ◇ *adj*: **to be ~**
trauern ◇ *npl*: **the ~** die Hinterbliebenen *pl*.

beret ['bereɪ] *n* Baskenmütze *die*.

berk [bɜːk] *n Br inf* [dishonest] Dussel *der*.

Berlin [bɜː'lɪn] *n* Berlin *nt*.

berm [bɜːm] *n Am* Grünstreifen *der*.

Bermuda [bə'mjuːdə] *n* Bermudainseln *pl*.

Bern [bɜːn] *n* Bern *nt*.

berry ['berɪ] *n* Beere *die*.

berserk [bə'zɜːk] *adj*: **to go ~** wild werden.

berth [bɜːθ] ◇ *n* - 1. [in harbour] Liegeplatz
der - 2. [on ship] Koje *die*; [on train] Schlafwa-
genplatz *der* ◇ *vi* [ship] anlegen.

beseech [bɪ'siːtʃ] *(pt & pp* besought OR be-
seeched) *vt literary* [implore]: **to ~ sb (to do
sthg)** jn anflehen(, etw zu tun).

beset [bɪ'set] *(pt & pp* beset) ◇ *adj*: **~ with**
OR **by sthg** von etw heimgesucht ◇ *vt*
heimsuchen.

beside [bɪ'saɪd] *prep* - 1. [next to] neben (+
A, D) - 2. [compared with] verglichen mit
- 3. *phr*: **to be ~ o.s. with joy/anger** vor
Freude/Wut außer sich sein.

besides [bɪ'saɪdz] ◇ *adv* außerdem
◇ *prep* außer (+ D); **~ being expensive, it's
also ugly** es ist nicht nur teuer, sondern
auch hässlich.

besiege [bɪ'siːdʒ] *vt lit & fig* belagern.

besotted [bɪ'sɒtɪd] *adj*: **~ (with sb)** vernarrt
(in jn).

besought [bɪ'sɔːt] *pt & pp* ▷ **beseech**.

best [best] ◇ *adj* beste, -r, -s; **my ~ friend**
mein bester Freund/meine beste Freundin
◇ *adv* am besten; **which car do you like ~?**
welches Auto gefällt dir am besten?; **what
type of beer do you like ~?** welches Bier
magst du am liebsten? ◇ *n* - 1. Beste *der,
die, das*; **to do one's ~** sein Bestes tun - 2. *phr*:
to make the ~ of sthg das Beste aus etw machen; **for the ~** nur zum Guten; **all the ~!** alles Gute! ◆ **at best** *adv* bestenfalls.

best man *n* Trauzeuge *der*.

bestow [bɪ'stəʊ] *vt fml*: **to ~ sthg on sb** jm
etw gewähren.

best-seller *n* [book] Bestseller *der*.

bet [bet] *(pt & pp* bet OR -ted) ◇ *n* - 1. [wa-
ger] Wette *die*; **to have a ~ on sthg** auf etw
(A) wetten - 2. *fig* [prediction]: **it's a safe
~ that ...** man kann sicher sein, dass ... ◇ *vt*
wetten ◇ *vi* - 1. [gamble]: **to ~ (on sthg)** (auf
etw (A)) wetten - 2. *fig* [predict]: **to ~ on sthg**
sich auf etw (A) verlassen.

betray [bɪ'treɪ] *vt* verraten; [trust] missbrauchen.

betrayal [bɪ'treɪəl] *n* Verrat *der*.

better ['betə'] ◇ *adj (compar of good, well)*
besser; **to get ~** besser werden; **I hope you
get ~ soon** ich hoffe, es geht dir bald besser;
to get ~ and ~ immer besser werden ◇ *adv*
besser; [like] lieber ◇ *n* [better one] Bessere
der, die, das; **to get the ~ of sb** die Oberhand
über jn gewinnen; **my curiosity got the ~ of
me** meine Neugier war stärker ◇ *vt* [im-
prove] verbessern; **to ~ o.s.** sich verbessern.

better off *adj* besser dran.

betting ['betɪŋ] *n (U)* - 1. [bets] Wetten *das*
- 2. [odds] Wetten *pl*.

betting shop *n Br* Wettannahmestelle *die*.

between [bɪ'twiːn] <> *prep* zwischen (+ *D*); [with verbs of motion] zwischen (+ *A*); ~ **now and next month** bis nächsten Monat; **we had only twenty pounds** ~ **us** wir hatten (zusammen) nur zwanzig Pfund <> *adv*: **(in)** ~ zwischen.

beverage ['bevərɪdʒ] *n fml* Getränk *das*.

beware [bɪ'weə'] *vi* sich in Acht nehmen; **to** ~ **of sthg** sich vor etw in Acht nehmen; '~ **of the dog**' 'Vorsicht bissiger Hund'.

bewildered [bɪ'wɪldəd] *adj* verwirrt.

beyond [bɪ'jɒnd] <> *prep* - **1.** [in space] jenseits (+ *G*), über (+ *A*) ... hinaus; **it's just** ~ **the park** es ist direkt auf der anderen Seite des Parks - **2.** [in time]: ~ **the year 2010** über das Jahr 2010 hinaus; ~ **midnight** bis nach Mitternacht; ~ **the age of five** ab dem fünften Lebensjahr - **3.** [outside the range of] über (+ *A*, *D*); **the town has changed** ~ **all recognition** die Stadt hat sich bis zur Unkenntlichkeit verändert <> *adv* - **1.** [in space] jenseits (davon) - **2.** [in time] darüber hinaus, danach.

bias ['baɪəs] *n* - **1.** [prejudice] Voreingenommenheit *die* - **2.** [tendency] Tendenz *die*.

biased ['baɪəst] *adj* - **1.** [person]: **to be** ~ **(against)** voreingenommen sein (gegenüber) - **2.** [system]: **to be** ~ **against/towards sb** jn benachteiligen/bevorteilen.

bib [bɪb] *n* [for baby] Latz *der*, Lätzchen *das*.

Bible ['baɪbl] *n* Bibel *die*.

bicarbonate of soda [baɪ'kɑːbənət-] *n* Natron *das*.

biceps ['baɪseps] (*pl inv*) *n* Bizeps *der*.

bicker ['bɪkə'] *vi* sich zanken.

bicycle ['baɪsɪkl] *n* Fahrrad *das*.

bicycle path *n* Fahrradweg *der*.

bicycle pump *n* Luftpumpe *die*.

bid [bɪd] (*pt & pp* bid) <> *n* - **1.** [attempt] Versuch *der* - **2.** [at auction] Gebot *das* - **3.** COMM Angebot *das* <> *vt* [at auction] bieten - <> *vi* [at auction]: **to** ~ **(for)** bieten (für).

bidder ['bɪdə'] *n* Bietende *der, die*.

bidding ['bɪdɪŋ] *n* [at auction] Bieten *das*.

bide [baɪd] *vt*: **to** ~ **one's time** (eine Gelegenheit) ablwarten.

bifocals [ˌbaɪ'fəʊklz] *npl* Brille *die* mit Bifokalgläsern.

big [bɪg] *adj* - **1.** [gen] groß; **how** ~ **is it?** wie groß ist es?; **my** ~ **brother** mein großer Bruder; ~ **ideas** hochfliegende Ideen - **2.** [important] bedeutend; **the** ~ **day** der große Tag - **3.** [conceited]: **to have a** ~ **head** eingebildet sein - **4.** [phr] *inf*: **he's into motorbikes in a** ~ **way** er ist vernarrt in Motorräder.

bigamy ['bɪgəmɪ] *n* Bigamie *die*.

big deal *inf* <> *n*: **it's no** ~ das ist kein Problem; **what's the** ~? was ist schon dabei? <> *excl* und wenn schon!

Big Dipper [-'dɪpə'] *n* - **1.** *Br* [rollercoaster]

Achterbahn *die* - **2.** *Am* ASTRON: **the** ~ der Große Bär.

bigheaded [ˌbɪg'hedɪd] *adj inf* eingebildet.

bigot ['bɪgət] *n* bigotter Mensch.

bigoted ['bɪgətɪd] *adj* bigott.

bigotry ['bɪgətrɪ] *n* Bigotterie *die*.

big time *n inf*: **to make** OR **hit the** ~ ganz groß rauslkommen.

big toe *n* großer Zeh.

big top *n* Zirkuszelt *das*.

big wheel *n Br* [at fairground] Riesenrad *das*.

bike [baɪk] *n inf* - **1.** [cycle] Rad *das* - **2.** [motorcycle] Motorrad *das*.

bikeway ['baɪkweɪ] *n Am* Radweg *der*.

bikini [bɪ'kiːnɪ] *n* Bikini *der*.

bile [baɪl] *n* Galle *die*.

bilingual [baɪ'lɪŋgwəl] *adj* zweisprachig.

bill [bɪl] <> *n* - **1.** [statement of cost] Rechnung *die* - **2.** [in parliament] Gesetzentwurf *der* - **3.** [of show, concert] Programm *das* - **4.** *Am* [bank note] Geldschein *der*, Banknote *die* - **5.** [poster]: '**post** OR **stick no** ~**s**' 'Plakate ankleben verboten' - **6.** [of bird] Schnabel *der* <> *vt*: **to** ~ **sb (for sthg)** jm eine Rechnung (für etw) schicken.

billboard ['bɪlbɔːd] *n* Plakatwand *die*.

billet ['bɪlɪt] *n* Quartier *das*.

billfold ['bɪlfəʊld] *n Am* Brieftasche *die*.

billiards ['bɪljədz] *n (U)* Billard *das*.

billion ['bɪljən] *num* - **1.** [thousand million] Milliarde *die* - **2.** *Br dated* [million million] Billion *die*.

bimbo ['bɪmbəʊ] (*pl* -s OR -es) *n inf pej* Tussi *die*.

bin [bɪn] *n Br* [for rubbish] Abfalleimer *der*.

bind [baɪnd] (*pt & pp* bound) *vt* - **1.** [gen] binden - **2.** [bandage] verbinden - **3.** [constrain] verpflichten.

binder ['baɪndə'] *n* [cover] Ordner *der*.

binding ['baɪndɪŋ] <> *adj* verbindlich, bindend <> *n* [of book] Einband *der*.

binge [bɪndʒ] *inf* <> *n*: **to go on a** ~ [on drink] auf Sauftour gehen; [on food] eine Fresstour machen <> *vi*: **to** ~ **on sthg** [drink] etw saufen; [food] etw fressen.

bingo ['bɪŋgəʊ] *n* Bingo *das*.

binoculars [bɪ'nɒkjʊləz] *npl* Fernglas *das*.

biochemistry [ˌbaɪəʊ'kemɪstrɪ] *n* Biochemie *die*.

biodegradable [ˌbaɪəʊdɪ'greɪdəbl] *adj* biologisch abbaubar.

biography [baɪ'ɒgrəfɪ] *n* Biografie *die*.

biological [ˌbaɪə'lɒdʒɪkl] *adj* biologisch.

biology [baɪ'ɒlədʒɪ] *n* Biologie *die*.

birch [bɜːtʃ] *n* [tree] Birke *die*.

bird [bɜːd] *n* - **1.** [creature] Vogel *der* - **2.** *inf* [woman] Braut *die*.

birdie ['bɜːdɪ] *n* [in golf] Birdie *das*.

bird's-eye view *n* Vogelperspektive *die*.

bird-watcher [-ˌwɒtʃəʳ] *n* Vogelbeobachter *der*, -in *die*.

Biro® [ˈbaɪərəʊ] *n* Kugelschreiber *der*.

birth [bɜːθ] *n* - **1.** [of baby] Geburt *die*; **to give ~ (to)** gebären - **2.** *fig* [of idea, system, country] Geburtsstunde *die*.

birth certificate *n* Geburtsurkunde *die*.

birth control *n* (U) Geburtenregelung *die*; **to use ~** verhüten.

birthday [ˈbɜːθdeɪ] *n* Geburtstag *der*.

birthmark [ˈbɜːθmɑːk] *n* Muttermal *das*.

birthrate [ˈbɜːθreɪt] *n* Geburtenrate *die*.

biscuit [ˈbɪskɪt] *n* - **1.** *Br* [thin dry cake] Keks *der* - **2.** *Am* [bread-like cake] Hefebrötchen, *das üblicherweise mit Bratensaft gegessen wird*.

bisect [baɪˈsekt] *vt* - **1.** GEOM halbieren - **2.** [cut in two] durchschneiden.

bishop [ˈbɪʃəp] *n* - **1.** [in church] Bischof *der* - **2.** [in chess] Läufer *der*.

bison [ˈbaɪsn] (*pl inv* OR **-s**) *n* Bison *der*.

bit [bɪt] *pt* ⊳ **bite** ⬦ *n* - **1.** [small piece] Stück *das*; **~s and pieces** *Br* [objects] Krimskrams *der*; **to fall to ~s** kaputtgehen, auseinander fallen - **2.** [unspecified amount]: **a ~ of** ein bisschen; **quite a ~ of** eine ganze Menge - **3.** [short time]: **for a ~** für ein Weilchen - **4.** [of drill] Bohrer *der* - **5.** [of bridle] Trensengebiss *das* - **6.** COMPUT Bit *das*. ⬦ **a bit** *adv* [tired, late, confused] ein bisschen.
➤ **bit by bit** *adv* Stück für Stück.

bitch [bɪtʃ] *n* - **1.** [female dog] Hündin *die* - **2.** *vinf* [woman] Miststück *das*.

bitchy [ˈbɪtʃɪ] *adj inf* gehässig, gemein.

bite [baɪt] (*pt* bit; *pp* bitten) ⬦ *n* Biss *der*; **to have a ~ (to eat)** eine Happen essen ⬦ *vt* beißen ⬦ *vi* - **1.** [animal, person, insect] beißen; **to ~ into sthg** in etw (hinein)beißen - **2.** [tyres, clutch] greifen - **3.** *fig* [sanction, law] greifen.

biting [ˈbaɪtɪŋ] *adj* - **1.** [wind, cold] schneidend, beißend - **2.** [caustic - comment] bissig.

bitmap [ˈbɪtmæp] *n* COMPUT Bitmap *das*.

bitten [ˈbɪtn] *pp* ⊳ **bite**.

bitter [ˈbɪtəʳ] ⬦ *adj* - **1.** [gen] bitter; **it's ~ (weather) today** es ist heute bitterkalt - **2.** [argument, war] erbittert - **3.** [resentful] verbittert ⬦ *n* *Br* [beer] *dem Altbier ähnliches Bier*.

bitter lemon *n* Bitter Lemon *das*.

bitterness [ˈbɪtənɪs] *n* Bitterkeit *die*.

bizarre [bɪˈzɑːʳ] *adj* exzentrisch; [house, landscape] bizarr.

blab [blæb] *vi inf* quatschen.

black [blæk] ⬦ *adj* - **1.** [gen] schwarz - **2.** [future] finster, düster ⬦ *n* - **1.** [colour] Schwarz *das*; **in ~ and white** [in writing] schwarz auf weiß; **in the ~** [solvent] in den schwarzen Zahlen - **2.** [person] Schwarze *der*, *die* ⬦ *vt* *Br* [boycott] boykottieren.
➤ **black out** *vi* [faint] ohnmächtig werden.

blackberry [ˈblækbərɪ] *n* Brombeere *die*.

blackbird [ˈblækbɜːd] *n* Amsel *die*.

blackboard [ˈblækbɔːd] *n* Tafel *die*.

blackcurrant [ˌblækˈkʌrənt] *n* schwarze Johannisbeere.

blacken [ˈblækn] ⬦ *vt* [in colour] schwärzen ⬦ *vi* [sky] sich verdunkeln.

black eye *n* schwarzes Auge.

Black Forest *n* Schwarzwald *der*.

blackhead [ˈblækhed] *n* Mitesser *der*.

black ice *n* (U) Glatteis *das*.

blackleg [ˈblækleg] *n pej* Streikbrecher *der*, -in *die*.

blacklist [ˈblæklɪst] ⬦ *n* schwarze Liste ⬦ *vt* auf die schwarze Liste setzen.

blackmail [ˈblækmeɪl] ⬦ *n* Erpressung *die* ⬦ *vt* erpressen.

black market *n* Schwarzmarkt *der*.

blackout [ˈblækaʊt] *n* - **1.** [in wartime] Verdunkelung *die* - **2.** [power cut] Stromausfall *der* - **3.** [suppression of news] Nachrichtensperre *die* - **4.** [fainting] Ohnmachtsanfall *der*.

black pudding *n Br* Blutwurst *die*.

Black Sea *n*: **the ~** das Schwarze Meer.

black sheep *n* schwarzes Schaf.

blacksmith [ˈblæksmɪθ] *n* Schmied *der*, -in *die*.

black spot *n* [for road accidents] Gefahrenstelle *die*.

bladder [ˈblædəʳ] *n* ANAT Blase *die*.

blade [bleɪd] *n* - **1.** [of knife, razor] Klinge *die* - **2.** [of propeller, saw, oar] Blatt *das* - **3.** [of grass] Halm *der*.

blame [bleɪm] ⬦ *n* Schuld *die*; **to take the ~ for sthg** die Schuld für etw auf sich (A) nehmen ⬦ *vt* beschuldigen; **to ~ sthg on sb/sthg** jm/etw die Schuld an etw (D) geben; **they ~d her for the defeat** sie gaben ihr die Schuld an der Niederlage; **to be to ~ for sthg** an etw (D) schuld sein.

📖 **to blame**

Das englische Verb *to blame* bedeutet nicht „blamieren", sondern „verantwortlich machen" oder „die Schuld geben". *You can't* <u>blame</u> *him for that* hieße im Deutschen „Dafür kann man ihm nicht die Schuld geben".
Was „blamieren" betrifft, so muss zwischen der transitiven und der reflexiven Form des Verbs unterschieden werden. „Jemanden <u>blamieren</u>" heißt auf Englisch *to disgrace someone*, „sich <u>blamieren</u>" entspricht dem Ausdruck *to disgrace oneself*. „Er hat sich vor allen Leuten <u>blamiert</u>" würde man im Englischen mit *He* <u>disgraced</u> *himself in front of everybody* übersetzen.

bland [blænd] *adj* - **1.** [person] farblos - **2.** [food] fad - **3.** [music, style] nichtssagend.

blank [blæŋk] ◇ *adj* leer ◇ *n* - **1.** [empty space] Leere *die*, leere Stelle - **2.** MIL [cartridge] Platzpatrone *die*.

blank cheque *n* Blankoscheck *der*; **to give sb a ~ to do sthg** *fig* jm freie Hand lassen, etw zu tun.

blanket ['blæŋkıt] *n* - **1.** [bed cover] Decke *die* - **2.** [layer] Schicht *die*.

blare [bleə^r] *vi* plärren.

blasphemy ['blæsfəmı] *n* Blasphemie *die*.

blast [blɑːst] ◇ *n* - **1.** [of bomb] Explosion *die* - **2.** [of air] Windstoß *der* ◇ *vt* [hole, tunnel] sprengen ◇ *excl* Br *inf* verdammt!
➡ **(at) full blast** *adv* - **1.** [maximum volume] auf höchster Lautstärke - **2.** [maximum effort, speed] auf Hochtouren.

blasted ['blɑːstıd] *adj inf* verdammt.

blast-off *n* SPACE Start *der*.

blatant ['bleıtənt] *adj* [shameless] unverhohlen.

blaze [bleız] ◇ *n* - **1.** [fire] Brand *der* - **2.** *fig* [of colour, light] Pracht *die* ◇ *vi* - **1.** [fire] lodern - **2.** *fig* [with colour, emotion] brennen.

blazer ['bleızə^r] *n* Blazer *der*.

bleach [bliːtʃ] ◇ *n (U)* [for clothes] Bleichmittel *das*; [for cleaning] Reinigungsmittel *das* ◇ *vt* [hair, clothes] bleichen.

bleachers ['bliːtʃəz] *npl* Am SPORT *nicht überdachte Zuschauertribüne.*

bleak [bliːk] *adj* - **1.** [weather] trüb, trostlos; [place] trostlos - **2.** [future, face, person] trüb.

bleary-eyed [ˌblıərı'aıd] *adj* verschlafen.

bleat [bliːt] *vi* - **1.** [sheep] blöken; [goat] meckern - **2.** *fig* [person] meckern.

bleed [bliːd] (*pt & pp* bled [bled]) ◇ *vt* [drain] entlüften ◇ *vi* bluten.

bleeper ['bliːpə^r] *n* Piepser *der*.

blemish ['blemıʃ] *n lit & fig* Makel *der*.

blend [blend] ◇ *n lit & fig* Mischung *die* ◇ *vt* (ver)mischen; **to ~ sthg with sthg** etw mit etw mischen ◇ *vi* [colours, sounds] sich (ver)mischen.

blender ['blendə^r] *n* [food mixer] Mixer *der*.

bless [bles] (*pt & pp* -ed OR blest) *vt* - **1.** RELIG segnen - **2.** *phr*: **~ you!** [after sneezing] Gesundheit!; [thank you] du bist ein Engel!

blessing ['blesıŋ] *n lit & fig* Segen *der*.

blest [blest] *pt & pp* ⟶ bless.

blew [bluː] *pt* ⟶ blow.

blight [blaıt] *vt* beeinträchtigen.

blimey ['blaımı] *excl* Br *inf* herrje!

blind [blaınd] ◇ *adj* [gen] blind; **to be ~ to sthg** *fig* gegenüber einer Sache (D) OR für etw blind sein ◇ *n* [for window] Jalousie *die* ◇ *npl*: **the ~** die Blinden *pl* ◇ *vt* blenden; **to ~ sb to sthg** *fig* jn für etw blind machen.

blind alley *n lit & fig* Sackgasse *die*.

blind date *n* Rendezvous *mit einem oder einer Unbekannten.*

blinders ['blaındəz] *npl* Am Scheuklappen *pl.*

blindfold ['blaındfəʊld] ◇ *adv* mit verbundenen Augen ◇ *n* Augenbinde *die* ◇ *vt*: **to ~ sb** jm die Augen verbinden.

blindingly ['blaındıŋlı] *adv* [obvious] völlig.

blindly ['blaındlı] *adv lit & fig* blindlings.

blindness ['blaındnıs] *n* Blindheit *die*.

blind spot *n* - **1.** [when driving] toter Winkel - **2.** *fig* [inability to understand]: **to have a ~ about sthg** (überhaupt) keine Begabung für etw haben.

blink [blıŋk] ◇ *n phr*: **to be on the ~** *inf* [machine] eine Macke haben ◇ *vt* [eyes] anlblinzeln ◇ *vi* [light] auflscheinen.

blinkered ['blıŋkəd] *adj fig* [view, attitude] engstirnig.

blinkers ['blıŋkəz] *npl* Br [for horse] Scheuklappen *pl.*

bliss [blıs] *n* Glück *das*, (Glück)seligkeit *die*; **it was sheer ~** es war die reinste Wonne.

blissful ['blısfʊl] *adj* herrlich; **in ~ ignorance** in völliger Ahnungslosigkeit.

blister ['blıstə^r] ◇ *n* Blase *die* ◇ *vi* - **1.** [skin] Blasen bekommen - **2.** [paint] Blasen werfen.

blithely ['blaıðlı] *adv* unbekümmert.

blitz [blıts] *n* MIL Luftangriff *der*.

blizzard ['blızəd] *n* Schneesturm *der*.

bloated ['bləʊtıd] *adj* - **1.** [body, face] aufgedunsen - **2.** [with food] übersatt.

blob [blɒb] *n* - **1.** [of paint] Klecks *der*; [of cream] Klacks *der* - **2.** [indistinct form] Fleck *der*.

block [blɒk] ◇ *n* - **1.** [building]: **~ (of flats)** Wohnhaus *das*; **office ~** Bürohaus *das* - **2.** [of ice, wood, stone] Klotz *der* - **3.** Am [of buildings] Block *der* - **4.** [mental] geistige Sperre ◇ *vt* - **1.** [road, path, law] blockieren; [pipe] verstopfen - **2.** [view] versperren.

blockade [blɒ'keıd] ◇ *n* Blockade *die* ◇ *vt* blockieren, sperren.

blockage ['blɒkıdʒ] *n* Verstopfung *die*.

blockbuster ['blɒkbʌstə^r] *n inf* Kassenschlager *der*.

block capitals *npl* Blockschrift *die*.

block letters *npl* Blockschrift *die*.

bloke [bləʊk] *n* Br *inf* Typ *der*.

blond [blɒnd] *adj* blond.

blonde [blɒnd] ◇ *adj* blond ◇ *n* [woman] Blondine *die*.

blood [blʌd] *n* Blut *das*; **in cold ~** kaltblütig.

bloodbath ['blʌdbɑːθ] *n* Blutbad *das*.

blood cell *n* Blutzelle *die*.

blood donor *n* Blutspender *der*.

blood group *n* Blutgruppe *die*.

bloodhound ['blʌdhaʊnd] *n* Bluthund *der*.

blood poisoning *n* Blutvergiftung *die*.

blood pressure *n* Blutdruck *der*.

bloodshed ['blʌdʃed] *n* Blutvergießen *das.*

bloodshot ['blʌdʃɒt] *adj* [eyes] blutunterlaufen.

bloodstream ['blʌdstri:m] *n* Blutstrom *der.*

blood test *n* Blutprobe *die.*

bloodthirsty ['blʌd θɜːstɪ] *adj* blutrünstig.

blood transfusion *n* Transfusion *die.*

bloody ['blʌdɪ] <> *adj* - 1. [gen] blutig - 2. *Br vinf* [for emphasis] verdammt; **~ hell!** verdammt noch mal! <> *adv Br vinf* verdammt.

bloody-minded [-'maɪndɪd] *adj Br inf* stur.

bloom [blu:m] <> *n* Blüte <> *vi* blühen.

blooming ['blu:mɪŋ] <> *adj Br inf* [for emphasis] verflixt <> *adv Br inf* verflixt.

blossom ['blɒsəm] <> *n* Blüte *die;* **in ~** in Blüte <> *vi* - 1. [tree] blühen - 2. *fig* [person] aufblühen.

blot [blɒt] <> *n* - 1. [of ink *etc*] (Tinten)klecks *der* - 2. *fig* [blemish] Makel *der;* **a ~ on the landscape** ein Schandfleck in der Landschaft <> *vt* - 1. [dry] ablöschen - 2. [spot with ink] beklecksen. ◆ **blot out** *vt sep* [memory] auslöschen.

blotchy ['blɒtʃɪ] *adj* fleckig.

blotting paper ['blɒtɪŋ-] *n* (U) Löschpapier *das.*

blouse [blaʊz] *n* Bluse *die.*

blow [bləʊ] (*pt* blew; *pp* blown) <> *vi* - 1. [wind] wehen; [stronger] blasen - 2. [move in the wind] wehen; **the door blew open/shut** die Tür flog auf/zu - 3. [person] blasen - 4. [fuse] durchbrennen - 5. [whistle] ertönen <> *vt* - 1. [subj: wind] wehen; [stronger] blasen - 2. [clear]: **to ~ one's nose** sich (*D*) die Nase putzen - 3. [whistle, horn, trumpet] blasen <> *n* Schlag *der.* ◆ **blow away** *vi* wegfliegen. ◆ **blow out** <> *vt sep* ausblasen <> *vi* - 1. [candle] ausgehen - 2. [tyre] platzen. ◆ **blow over** *vi* - 1. [storm] sich legen - 2. [argument] in Vergessenheit geraten. ◆ **blow up** <> *vt sep* - 1. [inflate] aufblasen; [with pump] aufpumpen - 2. [with bomb] in die Luft jagen - 3. [photograph] vergrößern <> *vi* [explode] explodieren.

blow-dry <> *n* Fönen *das;* **a cut and ~** Schneiden und Fönen <> *vt* fönen.

blowlamp *Br* ['bləʊlæmp], **blowtorch** *esp Am* ['bləʊtɔːtʃ] *n* Lötlampe *die.*

blown [bləʊn] *pp* → blow.

blowout ['bləʊaʊt] *n* [of tyre]: **he had a ~** ihm platzte ein Reifen.

blowtorch *n esp Am* = blowlamp.

blubber ['blʌbər] <> *n* Walfischspeck *der* <> *vi pej* flennen, heulen.

bludgeon ['blʌdʒən] *vt* prügeln.

blue [blu:] <> *adj* - 1. [in colour] blau - 2. *inf* [sad] trübsinnig - 3. [film] Porno-; [joke] unanständig <> *n* Blau *das;* **out of the ~** aus heiterem Himmel. ◆ **blues** *npl* - 1. MUS:

the ~s der Blues - 2. *inf* [sad feeling]: **the ~s** ein Anfall von Melancholie.

bluebell ['blu:bel] *n* Glockenblume *die.*

blueberry ['blu:bərɪ] *n* Heidelbeere *die.*

blue cheese *n* Blauschimmelkäse *der.*

blue-collar *adj:* **~ worker** Arbeiter *der,* -in *die.*

blue jeans *npl Am* (Blue) Jeans *die.*

blueprint ['blu:prɪnt] *n* - 1. CONSTR Blaupause *die* - 2. *fig* [plan, programme] Entwurf *der.*

bluff [blʌf] <> *adj* [person, manner] raubeinig <> *n* - 1. [deception] Bluff *der;* **to call sb's ~** in dazu auffordern, seine Drohung wahr zu machen - 2. [cliff] Steilhang *der* <> *vi* bluffen.

blunder ['blʌndər] <> *n* Schnitzer *der* <> *vi* [make mistake] einen Schnitzer machen; [socially] sich blamieren.

blunt [blʌnt] <> *adj* - 1. [knife, pencil, instrument] stumpf - 2. [person] geradeheraus; [manner, question] unverblümt <> *vt fig* [enthusiasm] dämpfen; [impact] abschwächen.

blur [blɜːr] <> *n* verschwommener Fleck; **he couldn't remember anything about the accident, it was all a ~** er konnte sich an nichts bezüglich des Unfalls erinnern, alles war verschwommen <> *vt* - 1. [outline, photograph] unscharf machen - 2. [distinction] undeutlich machen.

blurb [blɜːb] *n inf* [on book] Klappentext *der.*

blurt [blɜːt] ◆ **blurt out** *vt sep* herausplatzen mit.

blush [blʌʃ] <> *n* Röte *die* <> *vi* rot werden.

blusher ['blʌʃər] *n* Rouge *das.*

blustery ['blʌstərɪ] *adj* stürmisch.

BMX (*abbr of* bicycle motorcross) *n:* **~ bike** BMX-Rad *das.*

BO *n abbr of* body odour.

boar [bɔːr] *n* - 1. [male pig] Eber *der* - 2. [wild pig] Keiler *der.*

board [bɔːd] <> *n* - 1. [plank] Brett *das* - 2. [for notices - large] schwarzes Brett; [- small] Pinnwand *die* - 3. [for games] Spielbrett *das* - 4. [blackboard] Tafel *die* - 5. ADMIN: **~ (of directors)** Vorstand *der;* **~ of examiners** Prüfungskommission *die;* **~ of enquiry** Untersuchungsausschuss *der* - 6. *Br* [at hotel, guesthouse] Verpflegung *die;* **~ and lodging** Unterkunft und Verpflegung; **full/half ~** Voll-/Halbpension *die* - 7. *phr:* **above ~** offen <> *vt* [train, bus] einsteigen in (+ *A*); **to ~ a ship/aircraft** an Bord eines Schiffes/Flugzeugs gehen. ◆ **across the board** <> *adj* [increase] generell <> *adv* [apply] überall. ◆ **on board** <> *prep* [ship, plane] an Bord (+ *G*); [bus, train] in (+ *D*) <> *adv:* **to be on ~** [on ship, plane] an Bord sein; [on train] im Zug sein; **to take sthg on ~** [knowledge] etw berücksichtigen; [advice] etw anlnehmen. ◆ **board up** *vt sep* mit Brettern vernageln.

boarder ['bɔːdə*r*] *n* - **1.** [lodger] Pensionsgast *der* - **2.** [at school] Internatsschüler *der*, -in *die*.

boarding card ['bɔːdɪŋ-] *n* Bordkarte *die*.

boardinghouse ['bɔːdɪŋhaʊs, *pl* -haʊzɪz] *n* Pension *die*.

boarding school ['bɔːdɪŋ-] *n* Internat *das*.

Board of Trade *n Br*: **the ~** das Handelsministerium.

boardroom ['bɔːdrʊm] *n* Sitzungssaal *der*.

boast [bəʊst] ⬦ *n* Prahlerei *die* ⬦ *vi* prahlen; **to ~ about sthg** mit etw prahlen.

boastful ['bəʊstfʊl] *adj* prahlerisch.

boat [bəʊt] *n* Boot *das*; [large] Schiff *das*; **by ~** mit dem Boot; [large] mit dem Schiff.

boater ['bəʊtə*r*] *n* [hat] steifer Strohhut.

boatswain ['bəʊsn] *n* NAUT Bootsmann *der*.

bob [bɒb] ⬦ *n* - **1.** [hairstyle] Bubikopf *der* - **2.** *Br inf dated* [shilling] Schilling *der* - **3.** [bobsleigh] Bob *der* ⬦ *vi* [boat, ship] auf und ab schaukeln.

bobbin ['bɒbɪn] *n* Spule *die*.

bobby ['bɒbɪ] *n Br inf* [policeman] Polizist *der*.

bobsleigh ['bɒbsleɪ] *n* Bob *der*.

bode [bəʊd] *vi literary*: **to ~ well/ill (for sb/sthg)** ein gutes/schlechtes Zeichen (für jn/etw) sein.

bodily ['bɒdɪlɪ] ⬦ *adj* körperlich; **~ functions** Körperfunktionen *pl* ⬦ *adv* [carry, lift] mit dem ganzen Körper.

body ['bɒdɪ] *n* - **1.** [of human, animal] Körper *der* - **2.** [corpse] Leiche *die* - **3.** [organization] Organisation *die* - **4.** [of car] Karosserie *die*; [of plane] Rumpf *der* - **5.** [group] Gruppe *die* - **6.** [of wine] Körper *der* - **7.** [of hair] Volumen *das* - **8.** [garment] Body *der*.

body building *n* Bodybuilding *das*.

bodyguard ['bɒdɪgɑːd] *n* [one person] Leibwächter *der*; [group of people] Leibwache *die*.

body odour *n* Körpergeruch *der*.

bodywork ['bɒdɪwɜːk] *n* Karosserie *die*.

bog [bɒg] *n* - **1.** [marsh] Sumpf *der* - **2.** *Br inf* [toilet] Klo *das*.

bogged down [‚bɒgd-] *adj*: **~ (in sthg)** *lit & fig* (in etw (*D*)) festgefahren.

boggle ['bɒgl] *vi*: **the mind ~s!** es übersteigt den Verstand!

bog-standard *adj inf* stinknormal.

bogus ['bəʊgəs] *adj* [identity] falsch; [emotion] geheuchelt.

boil [bɔɪl] ⬦ *n* - **1.** [on skin] Furunkel *der* - **2.** [boiling point]: **to bring sthg to the ~** etw zum Kochen bringen; **to come to the ~** zu kochen beginnen ⬦ *vt* kochen; **to ~ the kettle** Wasser aufsetzen ⬦ *vi* kochen; **the kettle is ~ing** das Wasser im Kessel kocht. ◆ **boil down to** *vt fus fig* hinauslaufen auf

(+ A). ◆ **boil over** *vi* - **1.** [liquid] überlkochen - **2.** *fig* [feelings] ihren Höhepunkt erreichen.

boiled ['bɔɪld] *adj* gekocht; **~ potatoes** Salzkartoffeln *pl*; **~ sweets** Bonbons *pl*; **~ egg** gekochtes Ei.

boiler ['bɔɪlə*r*] *n* Boiler *der*.

boiler suit *n Br* Overall *der*, Blaumann *der*.

boiling ['bɔɪlɪŋ] *adj* [hot liquid] kochend heiß; [weather] wahnsinnig heiß; **I'm ~ (hot)!** mir ist fürchterlich heiß!

boiling point *n* Siedepunkt *der*.

boisterous ['bɔɪstərəs] *adj* ungestüm.

bold [bəʊld] *adj* - **1.** [person, plan] kühn, mutig - **2.** ART [lines, colour] kräftig; [design] kühn - **3.** TYPO: **~ type** OR **print** Fettdruck *der*.

bollard ['bɒlɑːd] *n* Poller *der*.

bollocks ['bɒləks] *Br vinf* ⬦ *npl* Eier *pl* ⬦ *excl* Scheiße!

bolster ['bəʊlstə*r*] ⬦ *n* Nackenrolle *die* ⬦ *vt* [confidence] stärken.

bolt [bəʊlt] ⬦ *n* - **1.** [on door, window] Riegel *der* - **2.** [type of screw] Bolzen *der* ⬦ *adv*: **~ upright** kerzengerade ⬦ *vt* - **1.** [fasten together] verschrauben - **2.** [close] verriegeln - **3.** [food] hinunterlschlingen ⬦ *vi* [run - horse] durchlgehen; [- person] flüchten.

bomb [bɒm] ⬦ *n* Bombe *die* ⬦ *vt* [from the air] bombardieren; [on the ground] einen Bombenanschlag verüben auf (+ A).

bombard [bɒm'bɑːd] *vt* [from the air] bombardieren; [from gun] beschießen; **to ~ sb with sthg** *fig* jn mit etw bombardieren.

bomb disposal squad *n* Bombenräumkommando *das*.

bomber ['bɒmə*r*] *n* - **1.** [plane] Bomberflugzeug *das* - **2.** [person] Bombenleger *der*, -in *die*.

bombing ['bɒmɪŋ] *n* [from the air] Bombardierung *die*; [on the ground] Bombenanschlag *der*.

bombshell ['bɒmʃel] *n fig* schwerer Schlag.

bona fide [‚bəʊnə'faɪd] *adj* [genuine] echt.

bond [bɒnd] ⬦ *n* - **1.** [emotional link] enge Beziehung; **~s of friendship** freundschaftliche Bande *pl* - **2.** [binding promise]: **my word is my ~** was ich verspreche, halte ich auch - **3.** FIN Obligation *die* ⬦ *vt* - **1.** [glue]: **to ~ sthg to sthg** etw an etw (*D*) kleben - **2.** *fig* [people]: **the experience ~ed them together** die Erfahrung band sie aneinander.

bone [bəʊn] ⬦ *n* [in human] Knochen *der*; [of fish] Gräte *die*; **~s** [of skeleton] Gebeine *pl* ⬦ *vt* [meat] von den Knochen lösen; [fish] entgräten.

bone-dry *adj* knochentrocken.

bone-idle *adj inf* stinkfaul.

bonfire ['bɒn‚faɪə*r*] *n* großes Feuer (*im Freien*).

bonfire night n Br 5. November, Jahrestag der Pulververschwörung; ▷ **Guy Fawkes' Night.**

bonk vt & vi Br vinf bumsen.

Bonn [bɒn] n Bonn nt.

bonnet ['bɒnɪt] n - 1. Br [of car] Kühlerhaube die, Motorhaube die - 2. [hat - for woman] Haube die; [- for baby] Häubchen das.

bonny ['bɒnɪ] adj Scot [baby] prächtig; [girl] hübsch.

bonus ['bəʊnəs] (pl -es) n - 1. [extra money] Prämie die; **Christmas ~** Weihnachtsgratifikation die - 2. fig [added advantage] Pluspunkt der.

bony ['bəʊnɪ] adj [person, hand, face] knochig.

boo [buː] (pl -s) <> excl buh! <> n Buhruf der <> vt auslbuhen, auslpfeifen <> vi buhen.

boob [buːb] n inf [mistake] Schnitzer der. ◆ **boobs** npl Br vinf [breasts] Möpse pl.

booby trap ['buːbɪ-] n - 1. [bomb] getarnte Bombe - 2. [prank] Falle die (mit deren Hilfe ein Streich gespielt wird).

book [bʊk] <> n - 1. [for reading] Buch das - 2. [of stamps, matches, tickets] Heftchen das; [of cheques] Heft das <> vt - 1. [table, room] reservieren lassen; [ticket] bestellen; [performer] engagieren; [plane seat] buchen; **to be fully ~ed** [restaurant, hotel] ausgebucht sein; [performance] ausverkauft sein - 2. inf [subj: police] auflschreiben - 3. Br FTBL verwarnen <> vi [book table, room] reservieren lassen; [book ticket] vorlbestellen; [book plane seat] buchen. ◆ **books** npl COMM Bücher die. ◆ **book up** vt sep buchen; **to be ~ed up** [restaurant, hotel] ausgebucht sein; [performance] ausverkauft sein.

bookcase ['bʊkkeɪs] n Bücherregal das.

bookie ['bʊkɪ] n inf Buchmacher der.

booking ['bʊkɪŋ] n - 1. esp Br [of seat, room] Reservierung die; [of ticket] Bestellung die - 2. FTBL Verwarnung die.

booking office n esp Br [in station] Fahrkartenschalter der.

bookkeeping ['bʊkˌkiːpɪŋ] n COMM Buchhaltung die.

booklet ['bʊklɪt] n Broschüre die.

bookmaker ['bʊkˌmeɪkə'] n Buchmacher der.

bookmark ['bʊkmɑːk] n Lesezeichen das.

bookseller ['bʊkˌselə'] n Buchhändler der, -in die.

bookshelf ['bʊkʃelf] (pl -shelves [-ʃelvz]) n Bücherbord das.

bookshop Br ['bʊkʃɒp], **bookstore** Am ['bʊkstɔːʳ] n Buchhandlung die.

book token n esp Br Büchergutschein der.

boom [buːm] <> n - 1. [of cannons, guns] Donnern das; [of voice] Dröhnen das - 2. [in business, economy] Boom der, Aufschwung der - 3. NAUT Baum der - 4. [for TV camera, microphone] Galgen der <> vi - 1. [cannons, guns] donnern; [voice] dröhnen - 2. [business, economy] einen Aufschwung nehmen.

boon [buːn] n Segen der.

boost [buːst] <> n - 1. [in profits, production] Zunahme die - 2. [in popularity] Steigerung die; [in spirits, morale] Verbesserung die; **to give sb a ~** [encourage] jm Auftrieb geben <> vt - 1. [profits, production] anlkurbeln - 2. [popularity] steigern; [morale, spirits] heben.

booster ['buːstə'] n [vaccine] Auffrischimpfung die.

boot [buːt] <> n - 1. [footwear] Stiefel der; [for football, rugby] Schuh der - 2. Br [of car] Kofferraum der <> vt - 1. inf [kick] einen Tritt geben (+ D); [ball] kicken - 2. COMPUT booten, hochfahren. ◆ **to boot** adv noch dazu. ◆ **boot up** vi COMPUT booten.

booth [buːð] n - 1. [at fair] (Markt)bude die - 2. [for telephone] Telefonzelle die - 3. [for voting] Kabine die.

booty ['buːtɪ] n literary Beute die.

booze [buːz] inf <> n [alcohol] Alkohol der <> vi saufen.

bop [bɒp] inf <> n [dance]: **to have a ~** rocken <> vi [dance] rocken.

border ['bɔːdə'] <> n - 1. [between countries] Grenze die - 2. [of dress, handkerchief] Bordüre die; [of plate] Rand der - 3. [outer limit] Rand der - 4. [in garden] Rabatte die <> vt - 1. [country] grenzen an (+ A) - 2. [field, garden] umschließen; [path] säumen. ◆ **border on** vt fus [verge on] grenzen an (+ A).

borderline ['bɔːdəlaɪn] <> adj: **~ case** Grenzfall der <> n fig Grenze die.

bore [bɔːʳ] <> pt ▷ bear <> n - 1. [person] Langweiler der; [situation, event] Plage die - 2. [of gun] Kaliber das; **a 12-~ shotgun** eine Flinte vom Kaliber 12 <> vt - 1. [not interest] langweilen; **to ~ sb stiff** OR **to ~ sb to tears** OR **to ~ sb to death** jn zu Tode langweilen - 2. [drill] bohren.

bored [bɔːd] adj gelangweilt; **she is ~ with always staying in** es langweilt sie, immer zu Hause zu bleiben.

boredom ['bɔːdəm] n Langeweile die.

boring ['bɔːrɪŋ] adj langweilig.

born [bɔːn] adj: **to be ~** geboren werden; **I was ~ in London/1968** ich bin OR wurde in London/1968 geboren; **a ~ entertainer** ein geborener Entertainer.

borne [bɔːn] pp ▷ bear.

borough ['bʌrə] n Regierungsbezirk, der entweder eine Stadt oder einen Stadtteil umfasst.

borrow ['bɒrəʊ] vt sich (D) leihen; [book from library] auslleihen; **to ~ sthg from sb** sich (D) etw von jm leihen OR borgen.

Bosnia ['bɒznɪə] n Bosnien nt.

Bosnian ['bɒznɪən] <> adj bosnisch <> n Bosnier der, -in die.

bosom ['buzəm] n - **1.** [breasts] Busen der; [of dress] Brustteil der - **2.** fig [of family] Schoß der; ◆ **friend** Busenfreund der, -in die.

boss [bɒs] n - **1.** [gen] Chef der, -in die - **2.** fig [of gang] Boss der. ◆ **boss about, boss around** vt sep pej herumkommandieren.

bossy ['bɒsɪ] adj herrisch.

bosun ['bəʊsn] n = boatswain.

botany ['bɒtənɪ] n Botanik die.

botch [bɒtʃ] ◆ **botch up** vt sep inf mehr schlecht als recht machen.

both [bəʊθ] ◇ pron beide; ~ **of us** wir beide; ~ **of them speak German** sie sprechen beide Deutsch; **do you prefer music or painting? – I like them** – bevorzugst du Musik oder Malerei? – ich mag beides ◇ adj beide ◇ adv: ~ **my sister and I** sowohl meine Schwester als auch ich.

bother ['bɒðə'] ◇ vt - **1.** [worry, hurt] stören; **what you told me yesterday has been ~ing me** was du mir gestern gesagt hast, hat mich beschäftigt; **she can't be ~ed to do it** sie hat keine Lust, das zu tun - **2.** [annoy] ärgern; [pester] belästigen; **I'm sorry to ~ you** entschuldigen Sie die Störung ◇ vi sich bemühen; **no, don't ~!** nein, das ist nicht nötig!; **to ~ about sthg** sich um etw kümmern; **don't ~ to phone me** Sie brauchen mich nicht anzurufen; **I didn't ~ to lock up** ich habe mir nicht die Mühe gemacht, abzuschließen; **don't ~ getting up** bleiben Sie doch sitzen ◇ n Mühe die; **no ~ at all** überhaupt kein Problem; **if it isn't too much of a ~** wenn es Ihnen nichts ausmacht ◇ excl verflixt!

bothered ['bɒðəd] adj [annoyed] verärgert.

bottle ['bɒtl] ◇ n - **1.** [container, quantity] Flasche die - **2.** [for baby] Fläschchen das, Flasche die - **3.** (U) Br inf [courage] Mumm der ◇ vt - **1.** [wine] in Flaschen abfüllen - **2.** [fruit] einlmachen. ◆ **bottle up** vt sep [feelings] in sich (D) auflstauen.

bottle bank n Altglascontainer der.

bottleneck ['bɒtlnek] n Engpass der.

bottle-opener n Flaschenöffner der.

bottom ['bɒtəm] ◇ adj - **1.** [lowest] unterste, -r, -s - **2.** [least successful] schlechteste, -r, -s; **to be ~ in sthg** [subject] der Schlechteste in etw (D) sein ◇ n - **1.** [of glass, bottle, bag] Boden der; [of page, list, ladder] unteres Ende; [of sea, lake] Grund der; [of hill, mountain] Fuß der; **at the ~** unten - **2.** [of street, garden]: **at the ~ of** am Ende (+ G) - **3.** [of organization] unteres Ende; **he worked his way up from the ~** er hat sich hoch gearbeitet - **4.** [buttocks] Hintern der - **5.** [cause]: **to get to the ~ of sthg** einer Sache (D) auf den Grund gehen. ◆ **bottom out** vi den Tiefstand erreichen.

bottom line n fig [result]: **the ~** das Endergebnis.

bough [baʊ] n Ast der.

bought [bɔːt] pt & pp ⇨ buy.

boulder ['bəʊldə'] n (gerundeter) Felsbrocken.

bounce [baʊns] ◇ vi - **1.** [ball] springen; **the ball ~d onto the car** der Ball prallte auf das Auto - **2.** [person - with energy, enthusiasm] hüpfen; **to ~ on sthg** [jump up and down] auf etw (D) springen - **3.** inf [cheque] platzen ◇ vt [ball] aufprallen lassen ◇ n [rebound] Aufprall der.

bouncer ['baʊnsə'] n inf Rausschmeißer der.

bound [baʊnd] ◇ pt & pp ⇨ bind ◇ adj - **1.** [certain]: **to be ~ to do sthg** etw bestimmt tun; **it was ~ to happen** das musste so kommen; **he's ~ to win** er gewinnt hundertprozentig - **2.** [forced, morally obliged]: ~ **by sthg** durch etw gebunden; ~ **to do sthg** gezwungen, etw zu tun; **I'm ~ to say** OR **admit ... ich** muss sagen OR zugeben ... - **3.** [en route]: **to be ~ for** unterwegs sein nach ◇ n [leap] Sprung der ◇ vt [border]: **to be ~ed by** begrenzt sein von. ◆ **bounds** npl Grenzen pl; **out of ~s** verboten.

boundary ['baʊndrɪ] n Grenze die.

bourbon ['bɜːbən] n Bourbon der.

bout [baʊt] n - **1.** [attack, session] Anfall der - **2.** [boxing match] Kampf der.

bow¹ [baʊ] n - **1.** [act of bowing] Verbeugung der - **2.** [of ship] Bug der ◇ vt [lower] beugen ◇ vi - **1.** [make a bow] sich verbeugen - **2.** [defer]: **to ~ to sthg** sich einer Sache (D) beugen.

bow² [bəʊ] n - **1.** [weapon, for musical instrument] Bogen der - **2.** [knot] Schleife die.

bowels ['baʊəlz] npl lit & fig Eingeweide pl.

bowl [bəʊl] n [container] Schüssel die; [of pipe] Kopf der ◇ vi [in cricket] den Ball werfen. ◆ **bowls** n britische Variante des französischen Boulespiels, bei der die Spielkugeln gerollt werden. ◆ **bowl over** vt sep umlwerfen.

bow-legged [ˌbəʊ'legɪd] adj O-beinig.

bowler ['bəʊlə'] n - **1.** [in cricket] Werfer der, -in die - **2.** [headgear]: ~ **(hat)** Melone die.

bowling ['bəʊlɪŋ] n: **(tenpin) ~** Bowling das.

bowling alley n Bowlingbahn die.

bowling green n Rasen- oder Kunstrasenfläche, auf der „bowls" gespielt wird.

bow tie [bəʊ-] n Fliege die.

box [bɒks] ◇ n - **1.** [made of wood or metal] Kiste die; [smaller] Kasten der; [made of cardboard] Karton der; [smaller] Schachtel die; **a ~ of chocolates** eine Schachtel Pralinen - **2.** [in theatre] Loge die - **3.** [on form] Kästchen das - **4.** Br inf [television]: **the ~** die Glotze ◇ vi [fight] boxen.

boxer ['bɒksə'] n - **1.** [fighter] Boxer der - **2.** [dog] Boxer der, -hündin die.

boxer shorts npl Boxershorts pl.

boxing ['bɒksɪŋ] *n* Boxen *das*.

Boxing Day *n* Zweiter Weihnachtsfeiertag.

boxing glove *n* Boxhandschuh *der*.

box office *n* Kasse *die (von Kino, Theater, bei Konzert)*.

boy [bɔɪ] ⬦ *n* [young male, son] Junge *der* ⬦ *excl*: **(oh)** ~! *inf* oh, Mann!

boycott ['bɔɪkɒt] ⬦ *n* Boykott *der* ⬦ *vt* boykottieren.

boyfriend ['bɔɪfrend] *n* Freund *der*.

boyish ['bɔɪɪʃ] *adj* jungenhaft.

bra [brɑː] *n* Büstenhalter *der*, BH *der*.

brace [breɪs] ⬦ *n* - **1.** [on teeth] Klammer *die* - **2.** [on leg] Stützapparat *der* ⬦ *vt* - **1.** [steady, support]: **to ~ o.s.** sich festlhalten - **2.** *fig* [mentally prepare]: **to ~ o.s. (for sthg)** sich (auf etw (A)) gefasst machen. ⬦ **braces** *npl Br* [for trousers] Hosenträger *pl*.

bracelet ['breɪslɪt] *n* Armband *das*.

bracken ['brækn] *n* (U) Farnkraut *das*.

bracket ['brækɪt] ⬦ *n* - **1.** [support] Halterung *die;* **(angle)** ~ Winkelträger *der* - **2.** [parenthesis] Klammer *die;* **in ~s** in Klammern - **3.** [group] Klasse *die* ⬦ *vt* [enclose in brackets] einlklammern, in Klammern setzen.

brag [bræg] *vi* prahlen.

braid [breɪd] ⬦ *n* - **1.** (U) [on uniform] Tresse *die* - **2.** *esp Am* [hairstyle] Zopf *der* ⬦ *vt esp Am* flechten.

brain [breɪn] *n* - **1.** [organ] Gehirn *das* - **2.** [mind, person] Kopf *der*. ⬦ **brains** *npl* [intelligence] Grips *der*, Intelligenz *die*.

brainchild ['breɪntʃaɪld] *n* Geistesprodukt *das*.

brainwash ['breɪnwɒʃ] *vt*: **to ~ sb** jn einer Gehirnwäsche unterziehen.

brainwave ['breɪnweɪv] *n* Geistesblitz *der*.

brainy ['breɪnɪ] *adj inf* gescheit.

brake [breɪk] ⬦ *n* - **1.** [on vehicle] Bremse *die* - **2.** *fig* [restraint] Zurückhaltung *die* ⬦ *vi* bremsen.

brake light *n* Bremslicht *das*.

bramble ['bræmbl] *n* [bush] Brombeerbusch *der;* [fruit] Brombeere *die*.

bran [bræn] *n* (U) Kleie *die*.

branch [brɑːntʃ] ⬦ *n* - **1.** [of tree] Zweig *der*, Ast *der* - **2.** [of river] Arm *der;* [of railway] Nebenstrecke *die* - **3.** [of company, bank, organization] Zweigstelle *die* - **4.** [of subject] Zweig *der* ⬦ *vi* [road] sich teilen. ⬦ **branch out** *vi* sein Tätigkeitsfeld erweitern.

brand [brænd] ⬦ *n* - **1.** COMM [make] Marke *die* - **2.** *fig* [type, style] Sorte *die*, Art *die* ⬦ *vt* - **1.** [cattle] mit einem Brandzeichen versehen - **2.** *fig* [classify]: **to ~ sb (as) sthg** jn als etw brandmarken.

brandish ['brændɪʃ] *vt* schwingen.

brand name *n* Markenname *der*.

brand-new *adj* nagelneu, brandneu.

brandy ['brændɪ] *n* Brandy *der*.

brash [bræʃ] *adj pej* [person, manner] laut.

brass [brɑːs] *n* - **1.** [metal] Messing *das* - **2.** MUS: **the ~** die Blechbläser *pl*.

brass band *n* Blaskapelle *die*.

brat [bræt] *n inf pej* Balg *das*.

bravado [brə'vɑːdəʊ] *n* Wagemut *der*.

brave [breɪv] ⬦ *adj* mutig, tapfer ⬦ *n* [warrior] Krieger *der* ⬦ *vt* [weather] trotzen (+ D); [anger, displeasure, punishment] über sich (A) ergehen lassen.

📖 **brave**

Das englische Wort brave und das deutsche „brav" sind zwar sprachgeschichtlich eng verwandt, brave bedeutet aber „tapfer" oder auch „mutig". Brave soldiers sind also „tapfere Soldaten". „Brav" dagegen korrespondiert mit dem englischen good im Sinne von well-behaved. Das Versprechen „Wenn du brav bist, bekommst du ein Eis" lautet im Englischen If you're good, you'll get an ice-cream.

---

bravery ['breɪvərɪ] *n* Mut *der*.

brawl [brɔːl] *n* Handgemenge *das*.

brawn [brɔːn] *n* (U) - **1.** [muscle] Muskelkraft *die* - **2.** *Br* [meat] Schweinskopfsülze *die*.

bray [breɪ] *vi* [donkey] schreien.

brazen ['breɪzn] *adj* unverschämt, frech. ⬦ **brazen out** *vt sep*: **to ~ it out** sich (D) nichts anmerken lassen.

brazier ['breɪzjə'] *n* Kohlenbecken *das*.

Brazil [brə'zɪl] *n* Brasilien *nt*.

Brazilian [brə'zɪljən] ⬦ *adj* brasilianisch ⬦ *n* Brasilianer *der*, -in *die*.

brazil nut *n* Paranuss *die*.

breach [briːtʃ] ⬦ *n* - **1.** [of law, agreement] Bruch *der;* **to be in ~ of sthg** gegen etw verstoßen; **~ of contract** Vertragsbruch *der* - **2.** [opening, gap] Bresche *die* ⬦ *vt* - **1.** [disobey] verletzen - **2.** [make hole in] durchbrechen.

breach of the peace *n* öffentliche Ruhestörung.

bread [bred] *n* (U) [food] Brot *das;* **~ and butter** [food] Butterbrot *das; fig* [main income] Lebensunterhalt *der*.

bread bin *Br*, **bread box** *Am n* Brotkasten *der*.

breadcrumbs ['bredkrʌmz] *npl* Brotkrümel *pl;* [for coating food] Paniermehl *das*.

breadline ['bredlaɪn] *n*: **to be on the ~** am Existenzminimum leben.

breadth [bretθ] *n* - **1.** [in measurements] Breite *die* - **2.** *fig* [scope] Spektrum *das*.

breadwinner ['bred,wɪnə'] *n* Ernährer *der*, -in *die*.

break [breɪk] (*vt* broke; *pp* broken) ⬦ *n*

- 1. [gap, interruption] Unterbrechung *die;* **~ in sthg** Unterbrechung in etw *(D)* - **2.** [fracture, rupture, change] Bruch *der;* **~ with sthg** Bruch *der* mit etw - **3.** [pause, rest] Unterbrechung *die;* SCH Pause *die;* **weekend ~** Urlaubswochenende *das;* **to take** OR **have a ~** - eine (kurze) Pause machen; **to have a ~ from sthg** mit etw pausieren; **without a ~** ohne Unterbrechung - **4.** *inf* [luck, chance] Chance *die* ◇ *vt* - **1.** [gen] brechen; [smash] zerbrechen; [windows] einlschlagen - **2.** [cause to stop working] kaputtlmachen - **3.** [interrupt - journey, silence] unterbrechen; **to ~ sb's fall** js Fall bremsen - **4.** [tell]: **to ~ the news of sthg to sb** jm etw mitlteilen ◇ *vi* - **1.** [gen] brechen - **2.** [stop working] kaputtlgehen - **3.** [pause] eine Pause machen - **4.** [weather] umlschlagen - **5.** [escape]: **to ~ loose** OR **free** loslbrechen - **6.** [voice] brechen - **7.** [news] bekannt werden - **8.** *phr:* **to ~ even** seine Kosten decken. ◆ **break away** *vi* [escape] weglaufen. ◆ **break down** ◇ *vt sep* - **1.** [destroy] einlschlagen - **2.** [analyse] auflschlüsseln ◇ *vi* [gen] zusammenlbrechen; **the car has broken down** das Auto hat eine Panne. ◆ **break in** ◇ *vi* - **1.** [enter by force] einlbrechen - **2.** [interrupt]: **to ~ in (on sb/sthg)** (jn/etw) unterbrechen ◇ *vt sep* - **1.** [horse] zulreiten - **2.** [person] einlarbeiten. ◆ **break into** *vt fus* - **1.** [enter by force] einlbrechen in *(+ A)* - **2.** [begin suddenly] auslbrechen in *(+ A)*. ◆ **break off** *vt sep* & *vi* ablbrechen. ◆ **break out** *vi* - **1.** [begin suddenly] auslbrechen - **2.** [escape]: **to ~ out (of)** auslbrechen (aus). ◆ **break up** ◇ *vt sep* - **1.** [object] zerbrechen; [ice, soil] auflbrechen - **2.** [bring to an end]: **the police broke up the party** die Polizei sprengte die Party; **she broke up the fight** sie trennte die Kämpfenden ◇ *vi* - **1.** [object] auseinander brechen - **2.** [relationship] in die Brüche gehen; [fight, party] enden; **to ~ up with sb** sich von jm trennen - **3.** [crowd] auseinander treiben - **4.** [school] enden; [pupils, teachers] in die Ferien gehen.

breakage ['breɪkɪdʒ] *n* Bruchschaden *der.*

breakdown ['breɪkdaʊn] *n* - **1.** [of system] Zusammenbruch *der;* [of car] Panne *die;* [of machine] Störung *die;* [in talks] Scheitern *das* - **2.** [analysis] Aufschlüsselung *die.*

breakfast ['brekfəst] *n* Frühstück *das;* **to have ~** frühstücken.

break-in *n* Einbruch *der.*

breakneck ['breɪknek] *adj:* **at ~ speed** in halsbrecherischem Tempo.

breakthrough ['breɪkθruː] *n* Durchbruch *der.*

breakup ['breɪkʌp] *n* [of relationship] Scheitern *das.*

breast [brest] *n* Brust *die.*

breast-feed *vt* & *vi* stillen.

breaststroke ['breststrəʊk] *n* Brustschwimmen *das.*

breath [breθ] *n* Atem *der;* **bad ~** Mundruch *der;* **he took a deep ~** er holte tief Atem; **out of ~** außer Atem; **to get one's ~ back** Luft holen.

breathalyse *Br,* **-yze** *Am* ['breθəlaɪz] *vt* (ins Röhrchen) blasen lassen.

breathe [briːð] ◇ *vi* atmen ◇ *vt* [inhale] einlatmen. ◆ **breathe in** *vt sep* & *vi* einlatmen. ◆ **breathe out** *vi* auslatmen.

breather ['briːðəʳ] *n inf* Atempause *die.*

breathing ['briːðɪŋ] *n* Atmen *das.*

breathless ['breθlɪs] *adj* atemlos.

breathtaking ['breθˌteɪkɪŋ] *adj* atemberaubend.

breed [briːd] (*pt* & *pp* **bred** [bred]) ◇ *n* - **1.** [of animal] Rasse *die* - **2.** *fig* [sort, style] Art *die* ◇ *vt* - **1.** [animals, plants] züchten - **2.** *fig* [suspicion] säen ◇ *vi* züchten.

breeding ['briːdɪŋ] *n* (U) - **1.** [of animals] Aufzucht *die;* [of plants] Züchtung *die* - **2.** [manners] Erziehung *die.*

breeze [briːz] *n* Brise *die.*

breezy ['briːzɪ] *adj* - **1.** [windy] windig - **2.** [cheerful] leichtherzig, fröhlich.

brevity ['brevɪtɪ] *n* Kürze *die.*

brew [bruː] ◇ *vt* [beer] brauen; [tea, coffee] auflgießen ◇ *vi* - **1.** [tea, coffee] ziehen - **2.** *fig* [trouble, storm] sich zusammenlbrauen.

brewery ['bruːərɪ] *n* Brauerei *die.*

bribe [braɪb] ◇ *n* Bestechung *die* ◇ *vt:* **to ~ sb (to do sthg)** jn bestechen(, etw zu tun).

bribery ['braɪbərɪ] *n* (U) Bestechung *die.*

brick [brɪk] *n* Ziegelstein *der,* Backstein *der.*

bricklayer ['brɪkˌleɪəʳ] *n* Maurer *der.*

bridal ['braɪdl] *adj* Braut-.

bride [braɪd] *n* Braut *die.*

bridegroom ['braɪdgrʊm] *n* Bräutigam *der.*

bridesmaid ['braɪdzmeɪd] *n* Brautjungfer *die.*

bridge [brɪdʒ] ◇ *n* - **1.** [gen] Brücke *die* - **2.** [card game] Bridge *das* ◇ *vt fig* [gap] überbrücken.

bridle ['braɪdl] *n* Zaum *der.*

bridle path *n* Reitweg *der.*

brief [briːf] ◇ *adj* - **1.** [short] kurz - **2.** [skimpy, concise] knapp; **please be ~** fassen Sie sich kurz; **in ~** kurz (gesagt) ◇ *n* - **1.** LAW [statement] Unterlagen *pl* - **2.** *Br* [instructions] Auftrag *der* ◇ *vt:* **to ~ sb (on sthg)** jn (über etw *(A)*) unterrichten. ◆ **briefs** *npl* [underwear] Slip *der;* **a pair of ~s** ein Slip.

briefcase ['briːfkeɪs] *n* Aktentasche *die.*

briefing ['briːfɪŋ] *n* Einsatzbesprechung *die.*

briefly ['briːflɪ] *adv* kurz.

brigade [brɪˈgeɪd] *n* - **1.** MIL Brigade *die* - **2.** [organization] Truppe *die.*

brigadier [ˌbrɪɡəˈdɪəʳ] *n Br* Brigadegeneral *der*.

bright [braɪt] *adj* - 1. [room, light] hell - 2. [colour] leuchtend - 3. [lively, cheerful] strahlend - 4. [intelligent] klug, gescheit; **a ~ girl** ein aufgewecktes Mädchen - 5. [future, prospects] glänzend. ◆ **brights** *npl Am inf* AUT Fernlicht *das*.

brighten [ˈbraɪtn] *vi* sich auflhellen. ◆ **brighten up** *vt sep* - 1. [room, house] auflhellen - 2. [situation, prospects] auflheitern ◇ *vi* - 1. [become more cheerful] fröhlicher werden; [face] sich auflhellen - 2. [weather] sich auflhellen.

brilliance [ˈbrɪljəns] *n* - 1. [cleverness] Großartigkeit *die* - 2. [of colour, light] Strahlen *das*.

brilliant [ˈbrɪljənt] *adj* - 1. [gen] glänzend, brillant - 2. [colour, light] strahlend - 3. *inf* [wonderful, enjoyable] toll; *iron* oh ~! na toll!

brim [brɪm] ◇ *n* - 1. [edge] Rand *der* - 2. [of hat] Krempe *die* ◇ *vi* - 1. [with liquid]: **to ~ with sthg** randvoll mit etw sein - 2. [with feeling]: **to ~ with ideas** vor Ideen überlsprudeln; **to ~ with self-confidence** vor Selbstbewußtsein strotzen.

brine [braɪn] *n* (U) Sole *die*, Lake *die*.

bring [brɪŋ] (*pt & pp* brought) *vt* - 1. [take along] mitbringen; [move] bringen; **to ~ sb good luck** jm Glück bringen - 2. [cause] führen zu; **to ~ sthg to an end** etw zu Ende bringen; **to ~ sthg into being** etw ins Leben rufen. ◆ **bring about** *vt sep* verursachen. ◆ **bring around** *vt sep* [make conscious] zu Bewusstsein bringen. ◆ **bring back** *vt sep* - 1. [return] zurücklbringen - 2. [shopping, gift] mitlbringen - 3. [reinstate - custom] wieder einlführen; [- government] wieder an die Macht bringen - 4. [cause to remember]: **to ~ back memories** Erinnerungen wachlrufen. ◆ **bring down** *vt sep* - 1. [shoot down - plane] ablschießen - 2. [government, tyrant] stürzen - 3. [prices] senken - 4. THEATRE: **to ~ the house down** stürmischen Beifall ernten. ◆ **bring forward** *vt sep* - 1. [meeting, election] vorlverlegen - 2. [in bookkeeping] übertragen. ◆ **bring in** *vt sep* - 1. [introduce] einlführen - 2. [earn] einlbringen - 3. [involve] einlschalten. ◆ **bring off** *vt sep* [plan] in die Tat umlsetzen; [deal] zustande bringen; **you'll never ~ it off** das schaffst du nie. ◆ **bring out** *vt sep* - 1. [new product, book] herauslbringen - 2. [reveal - flavour] betonen; **to ~ sthg out in sb** [characteristic] etw in jm wachlrufen. ◆ **bring round, bring to** *vt sep* = **bring around**. ◆ **bring up** *vt sep* - 1. [child] erziehen; **I was brought up in Liverpool** ich bin in Liverpool aufgewachsen - 2. [subject] anlsprechen - 3. [food] erbrechen.

brink [brɪŋk] *n*: **on the ~ of** am Rand(e) (+ G).

brisk [brɪsk] *adj* - 1. [walk, swim] flott - 2. [manner, tone] forsch.

bristle [ˈbrɪsl] ◇ *n* Borste *die* ◇ *vi* - 1. [hair] sich sträuben - 2. [person]: **to ~ (at sthg)** zornig reagieren (auf etw (A)).

Britain [ˈbrɪtn] *n* Großbritannien *nt*.

British [ˈbrɪtɪʃ] ◇ *adj* britisch ◇ *npl*: **the ~** die Briten *pl*.

British Isles *npl*: **the ~** die Britischen Inseln.

Briton [ˈbrɪtn] *n* Brite *der*, -tin *die*.

brittle [ˈbrɪtl] *adj* [china] zerbrechlich; [material] spröde; [bones] schwach.

broach [brəʊtʃ] *vt* [subject] anlschneiden.

broad [brɔːd] ◇ *adj* - 1. [wide] breit - 2. [wide-ranging, extensive] weit - 3. [introduction, description] umfassend - 4. [hint] deutlich - 5. [accent] stark ◇ *n Am inf* [woman] Braut *die*. ◆ **in broad daylight** *adv* am helllichten Tag.

B road *n Br* ≃ Landstraße *die*.

broad bean *n* dicke Bohne, Saubohne *die*.

broadcast [ˈbrɔːdkɑːst] (*pt & pp* broadcast) RADIO & TV ◇ *n* Sendung *die*, Übertragung *die* ◇ *vt* senden, übertragen.

broaden [ˈbrɔːdn] ◇ *vt* - 1. [make wider] verbreitern, erweitern - 2. [make more wide-ranging] vergrößern; **to ~ one's mind** seinen Horizont erweitern ◇ *vi* [become wider] sich verbreitern.

broadly [ˈbrɔːdlɪ] *adv* [generally] allgemein.

broadminded [ˌbrɔːdˈmaɪndɪd] *adj* tolerant.

broccoli [ˈbrɒkəlɪ] *n* Broccoli *der*.

brochure [ˈbrəʊʃəʳ] *n* Prospekt *der*.

broil [brɔɪl] *vt Am* grillen.

broke [brəʊk] ◇ *pt* ⊏▷ break ◇ *adj inf* [penniless] pleite.

broken [ˈbrəʊkn] ◇ *pp* ⊏▷ break ◇ *adj* - 1. [damaged, in pieces] zerbrochen - 2. [fractured] gebrochen - 3. [not working] kaputt - 4. [interrupted] unterbrochen - 5. [marriage, home] kaputt, zerrüttet - 6. [hesitant, inaccurate] gebrochen.

broker [ˈbrəʊkəʳ] *n* [of shares, commodities] Broker *der*, -in *die*; (insurance) **~** Versicherungsmakler *der*, -in *die*.

brolly [ˈbrɒlɪ] *n Br inf* (Regen)schirm *der*.

bronchitis [brɒnˈkaɪtɪs] *n* (U) Bronchitis *die*.

bronze [brɒnz] *n* Bronze *die*.

brooch [brəʊtʃ] *n* Brosche *die*.

brood [bruːd] ◇ *n* Brut *die* ◇ *vi*: **to ~ (over** OR **about sthg)** (über etw (D)) brüten.

brook [brʊk] *n* Bach *der*.

broom [bruːm] *n* [brush] Besen *der*.

broomstick [ˈbruːmstɪk] *n* Besenstiel *der*.

Bros, bros (*abbr of* brothers) Gebr.

broth [brɒθ] *n* Brühe *die*.

brothel [ˈbrɒθl] *n* Bordell *das*.

brother-in-law (*pl* brothers-in-law) *n* Schwager *der*.
brought [brɔːt] *pt & pp* ⊳ bring.
brow [braʊ] *n* - 1. [forehead] Stirn *die* - 2. [eyebrow] Braue *die* - 3. [of hill] Bergkuppe *die*.
brown [braʊn] ⬦ *adj* - 1. [colour] braun; ~ **bread** Graubrot *das* - 2. [tanned] braun ⬦ *n* [colour] Braun *das* ⬦ *vt* [food] bräunen.
Brownie (Guide) ['braʊnɪ-] *n* Pfadfinderin *die*.
brown paper *n* (*U*) Packpapier *das*.
brown rice *n* brauner Reis.
brown sugar *n* brauner Zucker.
browse [braʊz] ⬦ *vt* COMPUT: **to ~ the Web** im Web surfen ⬦ *vi* - 1. [in shop] sich umlsehen - 2. [read]: **to ~ through sthg** in etw (*D*) blättern - 3. [graze] weiden.
browser ['braʊzəʳ] *n* COMPUT Browser *der*.
bruise [bruːz] ⬦ *n* Bluterguss *der*, blauer Fleck ⬦ *vt* - 1. [part of body] sich prellen; [fruit] beschädigen; **she ~d her arm** sie holte sich einen blauen Fleck am Arm - 2. *fig* [pride, feelings] verletzen.
brunch [brʌntʃ] *n* Brunch *der*.
brunette [bruːˈnet] *n* Brünette *die*.
brunt [brʌnt] *n*: **to bear** OR **take the ~ of sthg** die Hauptlast von etw tragen.
brush [brʌʃ] ⬦ *n* - 1. [with bristles] Bürste *die*; [for painting] Pinsel *der* - 2. [encounter]: **to have a ~ with the law** mit dem Gesetz in Konflikt kommen ⬦ *vt* - 1. [clean with brush - hair] bürsten; [- teeth] putzen - 2. [touch lightly] berühren. ◆ **brush aside** *vt sep* [disregard] vom Tisch wischen. ◆ **brush off** *vt sep* [dismiss] zurücklweisen; **to ~ sb off** jn ablblitzen lassen. ◆ **brush up** ⬦ *vt sep* *fig* [revise] auflfrischen ⬦ *vi*: **to ~ up (on sthg)** (etw) auflfrischen.
brush-off *n inf*: **to give sb the ~** jm ein Abfuhr erteilen.
brusque [bruːsk] *adj* brüsk.
Brussels ['brʌslz] *n* Brüssel *nt*.
brussels sprouts *npl* Rosenkohl *der*.
brutal ['bruːtl] *adj* brutal.
brute [bruːt] ⬦ *adj*: ~ **force** rohe Gewalt ⬦ *n* Tier *das*, Vieh *das*.
BSc *n abbr of* Bachelor of Science.
BSE (*abbr of* bovine spongiform encephalopathy) *die* BSE.
bubble ['bʌbl] ⬦ *n* (Luft)bläschen *das* ⬦ *vi* - 1. [produce bubbles] Bläschen bilden - 2. [make a bubbling sound] blubbern - 3. *fig* [person]: **to ~ with sthg** vor etw (*D*) sprühen.
bubble bath *n* (*U*) Schaumbad *das*.
bubble gum *n* (*U*) Kaugummi *das* OR *der*.
bubblejet printer ['bʌbldʒet-] *n* Tintenstrahldrucker *der*.
Bucharest [ˌbjuːkəˈrest] *n* Bukarest *nt*.
buck [bʌk] (*pl sense 1 inv* OR **-s**) ⬦ *n* - 1. [male animal - rabbit, hare] Rammler *der*; [- deer]

Bock *der* - 2. *esp Am inf* [dollar] Dollar *der* - 3. *inf* [responsibility]: **to pass the ~** die Verantwortung weiterlreichen ⬦ *vi* [horse] bocken. ◆ **buck up** *inf vi* - 1. [hurry up] sich beeilen - 2. [cheer up] auflleben.
bucket ['bʌkɪt] *n* Eimer *der*.
buckle ['bʌkl] ⬦ *n* Schnalle *die*, Spange *die* ⬦ *vt* - 1. [fasten] zulschnallen - 2. [bend] einldellen, verbeulen ⬦ *vi* [wheel] sich verbiegen; [knees, legs] nachlgeben.
bud [bʌd] ⬦ *n* Knospe *die* ⬦ *vi* Knospen treiben, auslschlagen.
Budapest [ˌbjuːdəˈpest] *n* Budapest *nt*.
Buddha ['bʊdə] *n* Buddha *der*.
Buddhism ['bʊdɪzm] *n* Buddhismus *der*.
budding ['bʌdɪŋ] *adj* [aspiring] angehend.
buddy ['bʌdɪ] *n esp Am inf* [friend] Kumpel *der*.
budge [bʌdʒ] ⬦ *vt* - 1. [move] bewegen - 2. [change mind of] beeinflussen ⬦ *vi* - 1. [move] sich rühren - 2. [change mind] nachlgeben.
budgerigar ['bʌdʒərɪgɑːʳ] *n* Wellensittich *der*.
budget ['bʌdʒɪt] ⬦ *adj* [cheap - travel, holiday] kostengünstig; [- prices] niedrig ⬦ *n* Budget *das*. ◆ **budget for** *vt fus* einlplanen.
budgie ['bʌdʒɪ] *n inf* Wellensittich *der*.
buff [bʌf] ⬦ *adj* [brown] braun ⬦ *n inf* [expert] Kenner *der*, -in *die*.
buffalo ['bʌfələʊ] (*pl inv* OR **-es** OR **-s**) *n* Büffel *der*, Buffalo *der*.
buffer ['bʌfəʳ] *n* - 1. [gen] Puffer *der* - 2. [for trains] Prellbock *der*.
buffet[1] ['bʊfeɪ] *n* - 1. [meal] Buffet *das* - 2. [cafeteria] Stehimbiss *das*.
buffet[2] ['bʌfɪt] *vt* [physically] rütteln.
buffet car ['bʊfeɪ-] *n* Speisewagen *der*.
bug [bʌg] ⬦ *n* - 1. *esp Am* [small insect] Insekt *das*; [beetle] Käfer *der* - 2. *inf* [germ] Bazillus *der* - 3. *inf* [listening device] Wanze *die* - 4. COMPUT Programmfehler *der* ⬦ *vt inf* - 1. [room, phone] verwanzen - 2. [annoy] nerven.
bugger ['bʌgəʳ] *Br vinf* ⬦ *n* [unpleasant person] Scheißkerl *der*; **he's a lazy ~!** er ist ein fauler Sack!; **the poor ~!** der arme Kerl! ⬦ *excl* Scheiße! ◆ **bugger off** *vi*: ~ **off!** hau ab!
buggy ['bʌgɪ] *n* Kinderwagen *der*.
bugle ['bjuːgl] *n* Signalhorn *das*.
build [bɪld] (*pt & pp* **built**) ⬦ *vt* - 1. [construct] bauen - 2. *fig* [form, create] auflbauen ⬦ *n* (*U*) Statur *die*. ◆ **build on** ⬦ *vt fus* [further] auflbauen ⬦ *vt sep* [base on]: **to ~ sthg on sthg** etw auf etw (*D*) auflbauen. ◆ **build up** ⬦ *vt sep* [strengthen] auflbauen ⬦ *vi* [increase] zulnehmen. ◆ **build upon** *vt fus & vt sep* = build on.
builder ['bɪldəʳ] *n* Bauarbeiter *der*, -in *die*.

building ['bɪldɪŋ] *n* - **1.** [structure] Gebäude *das* - **2.** (U) [profession] Bau *der*.

building and loan association *n Am* Bausparkasse *die*.

building site *n* Baustelle *die*.

building society *n Br* Bausparkasse *die*.

buildup ['bɪldʌp] *n* [increase] Steigerung *die*, Zunahme *die*.

built [bɪlt] *pt* & *pp* ⊏➤ build.

built-in *adj* - **1.** CONSTR eingebaut - **2.** [inherent] automatisch.

built-up *adj*: ~ **area** bebautes Gebiet.

bulb [bʌlb] *n* - **1.** [for lamp] (Glüh)birne *die* - **2.** [of plant] Zwiebel *die*.

Bulgaria [bʌl'geərɪə] *n* Bulgarien *nt*.

Bulgarian [bʌl'geərɪən] ◇ *adj* bulgarisch ◇ *n* - **1.** [person] Bulgare *der*, -rin *die* - **2.** [language] Bulgarisch(e) *das*.

bulge [bʌldʒ] ◇ *n* [lump] Beule *die* ◇ *vi*: **to ~ (with sthg)** (mit etw) voll gestopft sein.

bulk [bʌlk] ◇ *n* - **1.** [mass] Ausmaß *das* - **2.** [of person] Masse *die* - **3.** COMM: **in ~** en gros - **4.** [majority]: **the ~ of** der Großteil (+ G) ◇ *adj* en gros, Groß-.

bulky ['bʌlkɪ] *adj* sperrig, unhandlich; [garment] unhandlich.

bull [bʊl] *n* [male cow] Stier *der*, Bulle *der*.

bulldog ['bʊldɒg] *n* Bulldogge *die*.

bulldozer ['bʊldəʊzə*r*] *n* Bulldozer *der*.

bullet ['bʊlɪt] *n* [for gun] Kugel *die*.

bulletin ['bʊlətɪn] *n* - **1.** [brief report] Bericht *der* - **2.** [regular publication] Bulletin *das*.

bullet-proof *adj* kugelsicher.

bullfight ['bʊlfaɪt] *n* Stierkampf *der*.

bullfighter ['bʊl͵faɪtə*r*] *n* Torero *der*.

bullfighting ['bʊl͵faɪtɪŋ] *n* (U) Stierkampf *der*.

bullion ['bʊljən] *n* (U) Barren *der*.

bullock ['bʊlək] *n* Ochse *der*.

bullring ['bʊlrɪŋ] *n* Stierkampfarena *die*.

bull's-eye *n* Schwarze *das*, Zentrum *das*.

bully ['bʊlɪ] ◇ *n* Tyrann *der* ◇ *vt* drangsalieren, tyrannisieren; **to ~ sb into doing sthg** jn so drangsalieren, dass er/sie etw tut.

bum [bʌm] *n* - **1.** *esp Br inf* [bottom] Hintern *der* - **2.** *Am inf pej* [tramp] Gammler *der*, -in *die*.

bum bag *n inf* Gürteltasche *die*.

bumblebee ['bʌmblbi:] *n* Hummel *die*.

bump [bʌmp] ◇ *n* - **1.** [lump] Beule *die;* [in road] Unebenheit *die*, Hubbel *der* - **2.** [knock, blow] Delle *die* - **3.** [noise] Bums *der* ◇ *vt* [knock, damage] an schlagen. ◆ **bump into** *vt fus* [meet by chance] treffen.

bumper ['bʌmpə*r*] ◇ *adj* Riesen-; **~ harvest** Rekordernte *die* ◇ *n* - **1.** [on car] Stoßstange *die* - **2.** *Am* RAIL Rammbohle *die*.

bumpy ['bʌmpɪ] *adj* holp(e)rig.

bun [bʌn] *n* - **1.** [cake] Rosinenbrötchen *das* - **2.** [bread roll] Milchbrötchen *das* - **3.** [hairstyle] Knoten *der*.

bunch [bʌntʃ] ◇ *n* [group - of people] Traube *die*, Haufen *der;* [- of flowers] Strauß *der;* [- of grapes] Traube *die;* [- of parsley, asparagus, keys] Bund *der* ◇ *vi* sich bauschen. ◆ **bunches** *npl* [hairstyle] Zöpfe *pl*.

bundle ['bʌndl] ◇ *n* Bündel *das* ◇ *vt* stopfen.

bung [bʌŋ] ◇ *n* Stöpsel *der*, Zapfen *der* ◇ *vt Br inf* [put] schmeißen.

bungalow ['bʌŋgələʊ] *n* Bungalow *der*.

bungle ['bʌŋgl] *vt* verpfuschen.

bunion ['bʌnjən] *n* Ballen *der*.

bunk [bʌŋk] *n* - **1.** [bed] Koje *die;* [in dorm] Bett *das* - **2.** = bunk bed.

bunk bed *n* Etagenbett *das*.

bunker ['bʌŋkə*r*] *n* Bunker *der*.

bunny ['bʌnɪ] *n*: **~ (rabbit)** Häschen *das*.

bunting ['bʌntɪŋ] *n* (U) Wimpel *pl*.

buoy [*Br* bɔɪ, *Am* 'bu:ɪ] *n* Boje *die*. ◆ **buoy up** *vt sep* [encourage] beleben, stärken.

buoyant ['bɔɪənt] *adj* - **1.** [able to float] schwimmfähig - **2.** [optimistic] beschwingt.

burden ['bɜːdn] ◇ *n* Bürde *die*, Last *die;* **to be a ~ on sb** eine Last für jn sein ◇ *vt*: **to ~ sb with sthg** jn mit etw belasten.

bureau ['bjʊərəʊ] (*pl* -x) *n* - **1.** [office, branch] Büro *das* - **2.** *Br* [desk] Sekretär *der* - **3.** *Am* [chest of drawers] Kommode *die*.

bureaucracy [bjʊə'rɒkrəsɪ] *n* Bürokratie *die*.

bureau de change (*pl* bureaux de change) *n* Wechselstube *die*.

bureaux ['bjʊərəʊz] *pl* ⊏➤ bureau.

burger ['bɜːgə*r*] *n* Hamburger *der*.

burglar ['bɜːglə*r*] *n* Einbrecher *der*, -in *die*.

burglar alarm *n* Alarmanlage *die*.

burglarize *vt Am* = burgle.

burglary ['bɜːglərɪ] *n* Einbruch *der*.

burgle ['bɜːgl], **burglarize** *Am* ['bɜːgləraɪz] *vt* ein brechen in (+ *A*).

burial ['berɪəl] *n* Begräbnis *das*.

burly ['bɜːlɪ] *adj* stämmig, kräftig.

Burma ['bɜːmə] *n* Birma *nt*.

burn [bɜːn] (*pt* & *pp* burnt OR -ed) ◇ *vt* - **1.** [gen] verbrennen; [house] ab brennen - **2.** [overcook] anbrennen lassen - **3.** [use as fuel] verbrauchen - **4.** [with chemical] verätzen ◇ *vi* - **1.** [gen] brennen - **2.** [food] anbrennen - **3.** [face, cheeks] glühen - **4.** [get sunburned] einen Sonnenbrand bekommen ◇ *n* - **1.** [wound, injury] Brandwunde *die* - **2.** [mark - on carpet, sofa] Brandfleck *der*. ◆ **burn down** *vt sep* nieder brennen ◇ *vi* [building, town] ab brennen.

burner ['bɜːnə*r*] *n* [on cooker] Brenner *der*.

burnt [bɜːnt] *pt* & *pp* ⊏➤ burn.

burp [bɜːp] *inf* ◇ *n* Rülpser *der* ◇ *vi* auf stoßen.

burrow ['bʌrəʊ] ◇ *n* Bau *der* ◇ *vi* - **1.** [dig] graben - **2.** *fig* [search] wühlen.

bursar ['bɜːsəʳ] *n* Schatzmeister *der.*

bursary ['bɜːsərɪ] *n Br* Stipendium *das.*

burst [bɜːst] (*pt & pp* burst) ◇ *vi* - **1.** [break open] platzen - **2.** [explode] explodieren - **3.** [go suddenly]: **to ~ in** hineinⅼplatzen ◇ *vt* [tyre, balloon, bubble] platzen lassen; [dam, river bank] durchⅼbrechen ◇ *n* [bout] Explosion *die.* ◆ **burst into** *vt fus* auslⅼbrechen in (+ A); **the house ~ into flames** im Haus brach Feuer aus. ◆ **burst out** *vt fus* - **1.** [say suddenly] losⅼplatzen - **2.** [begin suddenly]: **to ~ out laughing/crying** in Gelächter/Tränen auslⅼbrechen.

bursting ['bɜːstɪŋ] *adj* [eager]: **to be ~ to do sthg** darauf brennen, etw zu tun.

bury ['berɪ] *vt* - **1.** [in ground - person] begraben; [- thing] vergraben - **2.** [hide] vergraben.

bus [bʌs] *n* Bus *der;* **by ~** mit dem Bus.

bush [buʃ] *n* - **1.** [gen] Busch *der* - **2.** *phr:* **to beat about the ~** um den heißen Brei herumⅼreden.

bushy ['buʃɪ] *adj* buschig.

business ['bɪznɪs] *n* - **1.** (U) [commerce] Geschäft *das;* **on ~** geschäftlich; **to mean ~** *inf* es ernst meinen; **to go out of ~** zulmachen, schließen - **2.** [company] Firma *die* - **3.** (U) [concern] Angelegenheit *die;* **mind your own ~!** *inf* kümmere dich um deine eigenen Sachen! - **4.** [affair, matter] Sache *die.*

businesslike ['bɪznɪslaɪk] *adj* sachlich.

businessman ['bɪznɪsmən] (*pl* -men [-men]) *n* Geschäftsmann *der.*

business trip *n* Geschäftsreise *die.*

businesswoman ['bɪznɪs‚wʊmən] (*pl* -women [-‚wɪmɪn]) *n* Geschäftsfrau *die.*

busker ['bʌskəʳ] *n Br* Straßenmusikant *der,* -in *die.*

bus shelter *n* Wartehäuschen *das.*

bus station *n* Busbahnhof *der.*

bus stop *n* Bushaltestelle *die.*

bust [bʌst] (*pt & pp* bust OR -ed) ◇ *adj inf* - **1.** [broken] kaputt - **2.** [bankrupt]: **to go ~** pleite gehen ◇ *n* - **1.** [bosom] Busen *der* - **2.** [statue] Büste *die* ◇ *vt inf* [break] kaputt machen ◇ *vi inf* kaputt gehen.

bustle ['bʌsl] ◇ *n* [activity] reges Treiben ◇ *vi:* **to ~ about** OR **around** hin und her eilen.

busy ['bɪzɪ] ◇ *adj* - **1.** [active] (viel) beschäftigt - **2.** [hectic - life] bewegt; [- week] hektisch; [- place] belebt; [- office] geschäftig; **to be ~ doing sthg** damit beschäftigt sein, etw zu tun - **3.** *esp Am* TELEC [engaged] besetzt ◇ *vt:* **to ~ o.s. doing sthg** sich damit beschäftigen, etw zu tun.

busybody ['bɪzɪ‚bɒdɪ] *n pej* Wichtigtuer *der,* -in *die.*

busy signal *n Am* TELEC Besetztzeichen *das.*

but [bʌt] ◇ *conj* aber; [with negatives] sondern; **we were poor ~ happy** wir waren arm, aber glücklich; **she owns not one ~ two**

houses sie hat nicht nur eins, sondern zwei Häuser ◇ *prep* [except] außer; **he has no one ~ himself to blame** das hat er sich (D) selbst zuzuschreiben; **the last ~ one** der/die/das Vorletzte; **anyone ~ him would have helped** jeder andere hätte geholfen ◇ *adv fml* [only] nur. ◆ **but for** *prep* ohne.

butcher ['bʊtʃəʳ] ◇ *n* - **1.** [shopkeeper] Fleischer *der,* Metzger *der;* **~'s (shop)** Fleischerei *die,* Metzgerei *die* - **2.** *fig* [killer] Schlächter *der* ◇ *vt* - **1.** [kill for meat] schlachten - **2.** *fig* [massacre] abⅼschlachten.

butler ['bʌtləʳ] *n* Butler *der.*

butt [bʌt] ◇ *n* - **1.** [of cigarette] Kippe *die;* [of cigar] Stummel *der* - **2.** [of rifle] Kolben *der* - **3.** [for water] Fass *das* - **4.** [target] Zielscheibe *die* - **5.** *esp Am inf* [bottom] Hintern *der* ◇ *vt* [hit with head] mit dem Kopf stoßen. ◆ **butt in** *vi* [interrupt] sich einⅼmischen, dazwischenⅼplatzen; **to ~ in on sb/sthg** sich bei jm/etw einⅼmischen.

butter ['bʌtəʳ] ◇ *n* Butter *die* ◇ *vt* buttern, mit Butter bestreichen.

buttercup ['bʌtəkʌp] *n* Butterblume *die.*

butter dish *n* Butterdose *die.*

butterfly ['bʌtəflaɪ] *n* - **1.** [insect] Schmetterling *der* - **2.** (U) [swimming style] Schmetterlingsstil *der.*

buttocks ['bʌtəks] *npl* Hintern *der.*

button ['bʌtn] *n* - **1.** [on clothes, machine] Knopf *der* - **2.** *Am* [badge] Anstecker *der* ◇ *vt* = button up. ◆ **button up** *vt sep* zulⅼknöpfen.

button mushroom *n* junger Champignon.

buttress ['bʌtrɪs] *n* Stützpfeiler *der.*

buxom ['bʌksəm] *adj* vollbusig.

buy [baɪ] (*pt & pp* bought) ◇ *vt* - **1.** [purchase] kaufen; [company] auflⅼkaufen; **to ~ sthg from sb** etw von jm kaufen - **2.** *fig* [bribe] kaufen, bestechen ◇ *n* Kauf *der.* ◆ **buy out** *vt sep* - **1.** [in business] auslⅼzahlen - **2.** [from army]: **to ~ o.s. out** sich freilⅼkaufen. ◆ **buy up** *vt sep* auflⅼkaufen.

buyer *n* - **1.** [purchaser] Käufer *der,* -in *die* - **2.** [profession] Einkäufer *der,* -in *die.*

buyout ['baɪaʊt] *n* Aufkauf *der.*

buzz [bʌz] ◇ *n* [noise - of insect, machinery] Summen *das;* [- of conversation] Gemurmel *das;* **to give sb a ~** *inf* [- TELEC] jn anⅼrufen ◇ *vi* - **1.** [insect, machinery] summen - **2.** *fig* [place]: **the office was ~ing with excitement** im Büro herrschte große Aufregung - **3.** *fig:* **my head was ~ing** mir schwirrte der Kopf ◇ *vt* [on intercom] rufen.

buzzer ['bʌzəʳ] *n* Summer *der.*

buzzword ['bʌzwɜːd] *n inf* Modewort *das.*

by [baɪ] ◇ *prep* - **1.** [expressing cause, agent] von; **he was hit ~ a car** er ist von einem Auto angefahren worden; **~ Mozart** von Mozart - **2.** [indicating method, means, manner] mit;

~ car/train mit dem Auto/Zug; **to pay - cred-it card** mit Kreditkarte bezahlen; **to take sb - the hand** jn an der Hand nehmen; **made - hand** handgemacht; **he got rich ~ buying land** er wurde durch Grundstückskäufe reich - **3.** [near to, beside] an (+ D); **~ the sea** am Meer; **~ my side** an meiner Seite, neben mir - **4.** [past] an (+ D) ... vorbei; **a car went ~ the house** ein Auto fuhr am Haus vorbei - **5.** [via] durch; **exit ~ the door on the left** Ausgang durch die Tür auf der linken Seite; **we came ~ way of Paris** wir kamen über Paris - **6.** [with time]: **it will be ready ~ tomor-row** bis morgen wird es fertig sein; **be there ~ nine** sei spätestens um neun da; **she should be there ~ now** sie müßte inzwischen da sein; **~ then it was too late** zu diesem Zeitpunkt war es bereits zu spät; **~ day** tagsüber; **~ night** nachts - **7.** [expressing quantity]: **sold ~ the dozen** im Dutzend verkauft; **prices fell ~ 20%** die Preise fielen um 20%; **~ the day/week/month/hour** pro Tag/Woche/Monat/Stunde - **8.** [expressing meaning]: **what do you mean ~ that?** was meinst du damit? - **9.** [in division] durch; [in multiplication] mit; **two metres ~ five** zwei mal fünf Meter - **10.** [according to] nach; **~ law** nach dem Gesetz; **it's fine ~ me** ich bin damit einverstanden; **~ nature** von Natur aus; **~ pro-fession** von Beruf - **11.** [expressing gradual process]: **day ~ day** Tag für Tag; **they came out one ~ one** sie kamen einer nach dem anderen heraus; **little ~ little** nach und nach - **12.** *phr:* **~ mistake** versehentlich; **~ chance** durch Zufall; **~ the way** übrigens ⬦ *adv* ▷ **go, pass** *etc.* ⬦ **by and large** adv im Großen und Ganzen. ⬤ **(all) by oneself** ⬦ *adv* allein; **did you do it all ~ yourself?** hast du das ganz allein gemacht? ⬦ *adj* allein; **I'm all ~ myself today** ich bin heute ganz allein.

bye(-bye) [baɪ(baɪ)] *excl* inf tschüs!

byelaw ['baɪlɔ:] *n* = bylaw.

by-election *n* Nachwahl *die*.

bygone ['baɪgɒn] *adj* vergangen. ⬤ **by-gones** *npl:* **to let ~s be ~s** die Vergangenheit ruhen lassen.

bylaw ['baɪlɔ:] *n* Verordnung *die*.

bypass ['baɪpɑːs] ⬦ *n* - **1.** [road] Umge-hungsstraße *die* - **2.** MED: **~ (operation)** By-passoperation *die* ⬦ *vt* - **1.** [place] umlfahren, umgehen - **2.** [issue, person] umge-hen.

by-product *n lit & fig* Nebenprodukt *das*.

bystanders ['baɪ,stændəz] *npl:* **the ~** die Umstehenden *pl*.

byte [baɪt] *n* COMPUT Byte *das*.

byword ['baɪwɜ:d] *n* [symbol]: **to be a ~ for sth** ein Synonym für etw sein.

C

c (*pl* c's OR cs), **C** (*pl* C's OR Cs) [si:] *n* [letter] c *das*, C *das*. ⬤ **C** *n* - **1.** MUS C *das;* **C major** C-Dur - **2.** SCH [mark] ≃ drei - **3.** (*abbr of* celsius, centrigrade) C.

c., ca. (*abbr of* circa) ca.

cab [kæb] *n* - **1.** [taxi] Taxi *das* - **2.** [of lorry] Führerhaus *das*.

cabaret ['kæbəreɪ] *n* Varieté *das*.

cabbage ['kæbɪdʒ] *n* [vegetable] Kohl *der*.

cabin ['kæbɪn] *n* - **1.** [on ship, in aircraft] Ka-bine *die* - **2.** [house] Hütte *die*.

cabin crew *n* Begleitpersonal *das*.

cabinet ['kæbɪnɪt] *n* - **1.** [cupboard] Vitrine *die* - **2.** POL Kabinett *das*.

cable ['keɪbl] ⬦ *n* - **1.** [rope] Seil *das* - **2.** [telegram] Telegramm *das* - **3.** ELEC Kabel *das* - **4.** TV = cable television ⬦ *vt* [telegraph] telegrafieren.

cable car *n* Drahtseilbahn *die*.

cable television, cable TV *n* Kabelfern-sehen *das*.

cache [kæʃ] *n* - **1.** [store] geheimes Lager, Versteck *das* - **2.** COMPUT Zwischenspeicher *der*.

cackle ['kækl] *vi* [person] kichern.

cactus ['kæktəs] (*pl* -tuses OR -ti [-taɪ]) *n* Kaktus *der*.

cadet [kə'det] *n* [in police] Kadett *der*, -in *die*.

cadge [kædʒ] *Br inf* ⬦ *vt:* **to ~ sthg (off OR from sb)** etw (von jm) schnorren ⬦ *vi:* **to ~ off** OR **from sb** von jm schnorren.

caesarean (section) [sə'zeərɪən-] *n Br* Kaiserschnitt *der*.

cafe, café ['kæfeɪ] *n* Café *das*.

cafeteria [,kæfɪ'tɪərɪə] *n* Cafeteria *die*.

caffeine ['kæfi:n] *n* Koffein *das*.

cage [keɪdʒ] *n* Käfig *der*.

cagey ['keɪdʒɪ] (*compar* -ier; *superl* -iest) *adj inf* zugeknöpft, verschlossen.

cagoule [kə'gu:l] *n Br* Regenjacke *die*.

cajole [kə'dʒəʊl] *vt* zu zureden; **to ~ sb into doing sthg** jn überreden, etw zu tun.

cake [keɪk] *n* - **1.** [sweet food] Kuchen *der;* **a piece of ~** *inf* fig ein Kinderspiel - **2.** [of soap] Stück *das*.

caked [keɪkt] *adj:* **~ with sthg** verkrustet mit etw.

calcium ['kælsɪəm] *n* Kalzium *das*.

calculate ['kælkjʊleɪt] *vt* - **1.** [work out] auslrechnen - **2.** [plan, intend]: **to be ~d to do sthg** darauf ausgelegt sein, etw zu tun.

calculating ['kælkjuleɪtɪŋ] *adj pej* berechnend.

calculation [ˌkælkjʊ'leɪʃn] *n* [sum] Berechnung *die*.

calculator ['kælkjuleɪtə'] *n* Taschenrechner *der*, Rechenmaschine *die*.

calendar ['kælɪndə'] *n* - **1.** [gen] Kalender *der* - **2.** [list of events] Veranstaltungskalender *der*.

calf [kɑːf] (*pl* calves) *n* - **1.** [young animal] Kalb *das* - **2.** [of leg] Wade *die*.

calibre, caliber *Am* ['kælɪbə'] *n* Kaliber *das*.

California [ˌkælɪ'fɔːnjə] *n* Kalifornien *nt*.

calipers *npl Am* = callipers.

call [kɔːl] ◇ *n* - **1.** [shout - of person, animal] Ruf *der;* **a - for help** Hilferuf *der* - **2.** [visit] Besuch *der;* **to pay sb a ~** bei jm vorbeigehen - **3.** [demand]: **she has a lot of ~s on her time** ihre Zeit ist stark beansprucht; **there are ~s for a referendum** verschiedentlich wird nach einem Referendum verlangt; **there's no ~ for that sort of behaviour!** das gehört sich nicht! - **4.** [telephone call] Anruf *der* - **5.** [for flight] Aufruf *der* ◇ *vt* - **1.** [name, describe] nennen; **to be ~ed** heißen; **what's he ~ed?** wie heißt er?; **to ~ sb names** jn beschimpfen; **let's ~ it £10** sagen wir 10 Pfund - **2.** [shout] rufen - **3.** [telephone - person; doctor] rufen - **4.** [meeting] einlberufen; [election] anlsetzen; [flight] auflrufen; [strike] auslrufen ◇ *vi* - **1.** [shout] rufen - **2.** [telephone] anlrufen; **who's ~ing?** wie war der Name? - **3.** [visit] vorbeilkommen; **this train ~s at ...** dieser Zug hält in ... ◆ **call** *adj:* **to be on ~** [doctor, nurse] Bereitschaftsdienst haben. ◆ **call back** ◇ *vt sep* zurücklrufen ◇ *vi* - **1.** [phone again] zurücklrufen - **2.** [visit again] wiederlkommen. ◆ **call for** *vt fus* - **1.** [come to fetch] abllholen - **2.** [demand] verlangen; [require] erfordern. ◆ **call in** ◇ *vt sep* - **1.** [send for - army, riot police] einllsetzen - **2.** FIN [loan] einllfordern ◇ *vi:* **to ~ in (on sb)** (bei jm) vorbeilschauen. ◆ **call off** *vt sep* - **1.** [cancel] abllsagen - **2.** [dog, attacker] zurücklrufen. ◆ **call on** *vt fus* - **1.** [visit] besuchen - **2.** [ask]: **to ~ on sb to do sthg** jn auflfordern, etw zu tun. ◆ **call out** ◇ *vt sep* - **1.** [shout out] auslrufen - **2.** [doctor, fire brigade] rufen ◇ *vi* [shout out] rufen. ◆ **call round** *vi* vorbeilkommen. ◆ **call up** *vt sep* - **1.** MIL einllberufen - **2.** [on telephone] anllrufen - **3.** COMPUT auflrufen.

call box *n Br* Telefonzelle *die*.

caller ['kɔːlə'] *n* - **1.** [visitor] Besucher *der*, -in *die* - **2.** [on telephone] Anrufer *der*, -in *die*.

calling ['kɔːlɪŋ] *n* - **1.** [profession, trade] Beruf *der* - **2.** [vocation] Berufung *die*.

calling card *n Am* Visitenkarte *die*.

callipers *Br*, **calipers** *Am* ['kælɪpəz] *npl*

- **1.** MATH Taster *der*, Zirkel *der* - **2.** MED Beinschienen *die*.

callous ['kæləs] *adj* gefühllos, herzlos.

callus ['kæləs] (*pl* -es) *n* Schwiele *die*.

calm [kɑːm] ◇ *adj* - **1.** [person, voice] ruhig - **2.** [weather, day] windstill - **3.** [water] still ◇ *n* Ruhe *die* ◇ *vt* beruhigen. ◆ **calm down** ◇ *vt sep* beruhigen ◇ *vi* sich beruhigen.

Calor gas® ['kælə'-] *n Br britische Handelsmarke für Butangas.*

calorie ['kælərɪ] *n* Kalorie *die*.

calves [kɑːvz] *pl* ▷ calf.

Cambodia [kæm'bəʊdjə] *n* Kambodscha *nt*.

camcorder ['kæmˌkɔːdə'] *n* Camcorder *der*.

came [keɪm] *pt* ▷ come.

camel ['kæml] *n* [animal] Kamel *das*.

cameo ['kæmɪəʊ] (*pl* -s) *n* - **1.** [piece of jewellery] Kamee *die* - **2.** [in film] *kleine Nebenrolle, in der ein berühmter Schauspieler zu sehen ist.*

camera ['kæmərə] *n* Kamera *die*. ◆ **in camera** *adv* LAW unter Ausschluss der Öffentlichkeit.

cameraman ['kæmərəmæn] (*pl* -men [-men]) *n* Kameramann *der*.

camouflage ['kæməflɑːʒ] ◇ *n* - **1.** MIL Tarnung *die* - **2.** [of bird] Tarngefieder *das;* [of animal] Tarnkleid *das* ◇ *vt* MIL tarnen.

camp [kæmp] ◇ *n* - **1.** [for tents] Lagerplatz *der* - **2.** MIL Feldlager *das* - **3.** [for refugees, faction] Lager *das* ◇ *vi* MIL lagern; [holiday] campen. ◆ **camp out** *vi* campen.

campaign [kæm'peɪn] ◇ *n* - **1.** [project, crusade] Kampagne *die* - **2.** [in war] Feldzug *der* ◇ *vi:* **to ~ for sthg** sich für etw einllsetzen; **to ~ against sthg** gegen etw anlgehen.

camp bed *n* Feldbett *das*.

camper ['kæmpə'] *n* - **1.** [person] Camper *der*, -in *die* - **2.** [vehicle]: **~ (van)** Wohnmobil *das*.

campground ['kæmpgraʊnd] *n Am* Campingplatz *der*, Zeltplatz *der*.

camping ['kæmpɪŋ] *n* Camping *das;* **to go ~** zelten gehen.

camping site, campsite ['kæmpsaɪt] *n* Campingplatz *der*, Zeltplatz *der*.

campus ['kæmpəs] (*pl* -es) *n* Universitätsgelände *das*, Campus *der*.

can¹ [*weak form* kən, *strong form* kæn] (*pt & pp* -ned; *cont* -ning) ◇ *n* [container] Dose *die* ◇ *vt* konservieren, einldosen.

can² [*weak form* kən, *strong form* kæn] (*pt & conditional* could; *negative* cannot OR can't) *aux vb* - **1.** [be able to] können; **~ you help me?** können Sie mir helfen?; **I - see you** ich kann dich sehen, ich sehe dich; **~ you see/ hear anything?** sehen/hören Sie etwas?, können Sie etwas sehen/hören? - **2.** [know how to] können; **~ you drive?** kannst du Auto fahren?; I ~ speak German/play the piano ich spreche Deutsch/spiele Klavier - 3. [be allowed to] können, dürfen; you ~'t smoke here Sie können OR dürfen hier nicht rauchen; you ~ use my car if you like du kannst mein Auto nehmen - 4. [in polite requests] können; ~ you tell me the time? können Sie mir sagen, wie viel Uhr es ist? - 5. [indicating disbelief, puzzlement] können; what ~ she have done with it? was hat sie bloß damit gemacht?; you ~'t be serious! das ist doch wohl nicht dein Ernst! - 6. [indicating possibility] können; they could be lost sie könnten sich verlaufen haben.

Canada ['kænədə] n Kanada nt.

Canadian [kə'neɪdjən] ◇ adj kanadisch ◇ n Kanadier der, -in die.

canal [kə'næl] n Kanal der.

Canaries [kə'neərɪz] npl: **the ~** die Kanaren pl.

canary [kə'neərɪ] n Kanarienvogel der.

cancel ◇ vt - 1. [call off - event, party] ausfallen lassen; [- appointment, meeting] absagen; [- order, booking] stornieren; **the concert has been ~led** das Konzert fällt aus; **the flight has been ~led** der Flug ist gestrichen worden - 2. [invalidate - stamp] entwerten; [- cheque] stornieren; [- debt] streichen; [- subscription] abbestellen ◇ vi: **we had to ~** wir mussten absagen. ◆ **cancel out** vt sep: **to ~ each other out** einander auslgleichen.

cancellation [,kænsə'leɪʃn] n Stornierung die; [of meeting, visit] Absage die; [of subscription] Abbestellung die.

cancer ['kænsə'] n Krebs der. ◆ **Cancer** n Krebs der.

candelabra [,kændɪ'lɑːbrə] n Leuchter der.

candid ['kændɪd] adj offen, ehrlich.

candidate ['kændɪdət] n - 1. [for job] Kandidat der, -in die - 2. [for exam] Prüfling der.

candle ['kændl] n Kerze die.

candlelight ['kændllaɪt] n Kerzenlicht das.

candlelit ['kændllɪt] adj im Kerzenschein.

candlestick ['kændlstɪk] n Kerzenständer der.

candour Br, **candor** Am ['kændə'] n Offenheit die.

candy ['kændɪ] n esp Am - 1. (U) [confectionery] Süßigkeiten pl - 2. [sweet] Bonbon das.

candy bar n Am Schokoriegel der.

candyfloss Br ['kændɪflɒs], **cotton candy** Am n (U) Zuckerwatte die.

cane [keɪn] n - 1. (U) [for making furniture] Rohr das - 2. [walking stick] Spazierstock der - 3. [for punishment]: **the ~** der Rohrstock - 4. [for supporting plant] Stock der ◇ vt mit dem Rohrstock züchtigen.

canine ['keɪnaɪn] ◇ adj Hunde- ◇ n: **~ (tooth)** Eckzahn der.

canister ['kænɪstə'] n Kanister der, Behälter der; [for tea, film] Dose die.

cannabis ['kænəbɪs] n Cannabis der.

canned [kænd] adj [food] Konserven-; [drink] Dosen-.

cannibal ['kænɪbl] n Kannibale der, -in die.

cannon ['kænən] (pl inv OR -s) n - 1. [on ground] Kanone die - 2. [on aircraft] Bordkanone die.

cannonball ['kænənbɔːl] n Kanonenkugel die.

cannot ['kænɒt] vb fml ▷ can².

canny ['kænɪ] adj umsichtig, sparsam.

canoe [kə'nuː] n Paddelboot das, Kanu das.

canoeing [kə'nuːɪŋ] n Kanufahren das.

canon ['kænən] n - 1. [clergyman] Domherr der - 2. [general principle] Grundregel die.

can opener n Dosenöffner der.

canopy ['kænəpɪ] n [over bed, seat] Baldachin der.

can't [kɑːnt] = cannot.

cantankerous [kæn'tæŋkərəs] adj streitsüchtig.

canteen [kæn'tiːn] n - 1. [restaurant - in workplace] Kantine die; [- in university] Mensa die - 2. [box of cutlery] Besteckkasten der.

canter ['kæntə'] ◇ n Kanter der ◇ vi im Handgalopp reiten.

canvas ['kænvəs] n - 1. (U) [cloth] Segeltuch das - 2. [art - for painting] Leinwand die; [- finished painting] Gemälde das.

canvass ['kænvəs] vt - 1. POL: **to ~ voters** um Wählerstimmen werben - 2. COMM: **to ~ opinion** eine Meinungsumfrage durchlführen.

canyon ['kænjən] n Cañon der.

cap [kæp] vt [outdo]: **to ~ it all** als Krönung des Ganzen.

capability [,keɪpə'bɪlətɪ] n - 1. [ability] Fähigkeit die - 2. MIL Potenzial das.

capable ['keɪpəbl] adj - 1. [able, having capacity]: **to be ~ of sthg** fähig sein; **to be ~ of doing sthg** fähig sein, etw zu tun - 2. [competent, skilful] kompetent.

capacity [kə'pæsɪtɪ] n - 1. (U) [limit] Fassungsvermögen die; [of room, hall] Sitzplätze pl; **the theatre has a ~ of 200** das Theater fasst 200 Personen - 2. [ability] Fähigkeit die; **~ for sthg** die Fähigkeit zu etw; **~ for doing** OR **to do sthg** die Fähigkeit, etw zu tun - 3. [position] Stellung die; **in a ... ~** in der Funktion (+ G) .

cape [keɪp] n - 1. GEOGR Kap das - 2. [cloak] Cape das, Umhang der.

caper ['keɪpə'] n - 1. [food] Kaper die - 2. inf [escapade] Eskapade die.

capita ▷ per capita.

capital ['kæpɪtl] ◇ adj - 1.: **~ letter** Großbuchstabe der - 2. [offence] Kapital- ◇ n - 1. [of country]: **~ (city)** Hauptstadt die - 2. [letter] Großbuchstabe der - 3. (U) [money] Kapital *das;* **to make ~ out of sthg** *fig* aus etw Kapital schlagen.

capital expenditure *n* Kapitalaufwand *der.*

capital gains tax *n* Kapitalertragssteuer *die.*

capitalism ['kæpɪtəlɪzm] *n* Kapitalismus *der.*

capitalist ['kæpɪtəlɪst] <> *adj* kapitalistisch <> *n* Kapitalist *der,* -in *die.*

capitalize, -ise ['kæpɪtəlaɪz] *vi:* **to ~ on sthg** aus etw Nutzen ziehen.

capital punishment *n (U)* Todesstrafe *die.*

capitulate [kə'pɪtjʊleɪt] *vi:* **to ~ (to sthg)** kapitulieren (vor etw *(D)*).

Capricorn ['kæprɪkɔːn] *n* Steinbock *der.*

capsize [kæp'saɪz] <> *vt* zum Kentern bringen <> *vi* kentern.

capsule ['kæpsjuːl] *n* **- 1.** [gen] Kapsel *die* **- 2.** [on spacecraft] Raumkapsel *die.*

captain ['kæptɪn] *n* Kapitän *der;* [in army] Hauptmann *der.*

caption ['kæpʃn] *n* Bildunterschrift *die.*

captivate ['kæptɪveɪt] *vt* bezaubern.

captive ['kæptɪv] <> *adj* **- 1.** [imprisoned] gefangen **- 2.** *fig* [unable to leave]: **~ audience** unfreiwilliges Publikum <> *n* Gefangene *der, die.*

captor ['kæptə^r] *n* Person, die jemanden gefangen nimmt.

capture ['kæptʃə^r] <> *vt* **- 1.** [take prisoner - person] gefangen nehmen; [- animal] einfangen **- 2.** [city, market, audience] erobern; [interest, imagination, votes] gewinnen **- 3.** COMPUT erfassen <> *n* Gefangennahme *die;* [of city] Eroberung *die.*

car [kɑː^r] <> *n* **- 1.** [motor car] Auto *das,* Wagen *der* **- 2.** [on train] Wagen *der* <> *comp* Automobil-, Auto-.

carafe [kə'ræf] *n* Karaffe *die.*

caramel ['kærəmel] *n* **- 1.** [burnt sugar] Karamell *der* **- 2.** [sweet] Karamellbonbon *das.*

carat ['kærət] *n Br* Karat *das.*

caravan ['kærəvæn] *n* **- 1.** *Br* [vehicle - towed by car] Wohnwagen *der,* Caravan *der;* [- towed by horse] Pferdewagen *der* **- 2.** [travelling group] Karawane *die.*

caravan site *n Br* Wohnwagenplatz *der.*

carbohydrate [ˌkɑːbəʊ'haɪdreɪt] *n (U)* Kohle(n)hydrat *das.* ◆ **carbohydrates** *npl* [food] Kohle(n)hydrate *pl.*

carbon ['kɑːbən] *n* [element] Kohlenstoff *der.*

carbonated ['kɑːbəneɪtɪd] *adj* mit Kohlensäure versetzt.

carbon copy *n* **- 1.** [document] Durchschlag *der* **- 2.** *fig* [exact copy]: **she's a ~ of her mother** sie ist ihrer Mutter wie aus dem Gesicht geschnitten.

carbon dioxide [-daɪ'ɒksaɪd] *n* Kohlendioxyd *das.*

carbon monoxide [-mɒn'ɒksaɪd] *n* Kohlenmonoxid *das.*

carbon paper *n (U)* Kohlepapier *das.*

car-boot sale *n Br* auf einem (Park)platz oder in einem Parkhaus stattfindender Trödelmarkt.

carburettor *Br,* **carburetor** *Am* [ˌkɑːbə'retə^r] *n* Vergaser *der.*

carcass ['kɑːkəs] *n* [of animal] Kadaver *der.*

card [kɑːd] *n* **- 1.** [playing card] Spielkarte *die* **- 2.** [for identification] Karte *die* **- 3.** [greetings card] Grußkarte *die* **- 4.** [postcard] Postkarte *die* **- 5.** *(U)* [cardboard] Pappe *die.* ◆ **cards** *npl* [game] Kartenspiel *das;* **to play ~s** Karten spielen. ◆ **on the cards** *Br,* **in the cards** *Am adv inf* durchaus möglich.

cardboard ['kɑːdbɔːd] <> *n (U)* Pappe *die* <> *comp* Papp-.

cardboard box *n* Pappkarton *der.*

cardiac ['kɑːdiæk] *adj* Herz-.

cardigan ['kɑːdɪgən] *n* Strickjacke *die.*

cardinal ['kɑːdɪnl] <> *adj* äußerste, -r, -s; **~ sin** Todsünde *die* <> *n* RELIG Kardinal *der.*

card index *n Br* Kartei *die.*

card table *n* Kartentisch *der.*

care [keə^r] *vi* **- 1.** [be concerned]: **you really don't ~, do you?** dir ist das wohl ganz egal, wie?; **to ~ about sb/sthg** an jn/etw denken **- 2.** [mind] sich kümmern; **I don't ~ if/that/ how ...** es ist mir egal, ob/dass/wie ...; **who ~s?** wen interessiert das schon?; **I don't honestly ~ what I look like** es kümmert OR interessiert mich ehrlich gesagt nicht, wie ich aussehe. ◆ **care of** *prep* bei. ◆ **care for** *vt fus* [like] Interesse haben für; **I don't much ~ for opera** ich mache mir nichts aus Oper; **does she still ~ for him?** bedeutet er ihr noch immer viel?; **would you ~ for a drink?** möchtest du etwas trinken?

career [kə'rɪə^r] <> *n* **- 1.** [job] Beruf *der;* **to make a ~ out of sthg** etw zum Beruf machen **- 2.** [working life] Laufbahn *die;* [in retrospect] Werdegang *der* **- 3.** [very successful] Karriere *die;* **to make a ~ for o.s.** Karriere machen <> *vi* rasen.

careers adviser *n* Berufsberater *der,* -in *die.*

carefree ['keəfriː] *adj* sorglos, sorgenfrei.

careful ['keəfʊl] *adj* **- 1.** [cautious] vorsichtig; **to be ~ with sthg** vorsichtig mit etw umlgehen; **to be ~ to do sthg** darauf achten, etw zu tun **- 2.** [thorough] gründlich.

carefully ['keəflɪ] *adv* **- 1.** [cautiously] vorsichtig **- 2.** [thoroughly] gründlich.

careless ['keəlɪs] *adj* **- 1.** [inattentive] unaufmerksam **- 2.** [unconcerned] nachlässig.

caress [kə'res] <> *n* Liebkosung *die* <> *vt* liebkosen.

caretaker ['keəˌteɪkə^r] *n Br* Hausmeister *der,* -in *die.*

car ferry *n* Autofähre *die.*

cargo ['kɑːgəʊ] (*pl* -es OR -s) *n* Ladung *die.*

car hire *n* (U) *Br* Autovermietung *die.*

Caribbean [*Br* kærɪ'biːən, *Am* kə'rɪbɪən] *n* - 1. [sea]: **the - (Sea)** das Karibische Meer, die Karibische See - 2. [region]: **the - die Karibik.**

caring ['keərɪŋ] *adj* mitfühlend.

carnage ['kɑːnɪdʒ] *n* (U) Gemetzel *das.*

carnal ['kɑːnl] *adj literary* fleischlich.

carnation [kɑː'neɪʃn] *n* Nelke *die.*

carnival ['kɑːnɪvl] *n* - 1. [festive occasion] Karneval *der* - 2. [fair] Volksfest *das.*

carnivorous [kɑː'nɪvərəs] *adj* Fleisch fressend.

carol ['kærəl] *n*: **(Christmas)** ~ Weihnachtslied *das.*

carousel [ˌkærə'sel] *n* - 1. *esp Am* [at fair] Karussell *das* - 2. [at airport] Gepäckband *das.*

carp [kɑːp] (*pl inv* OR -s) <> *n* Karpfen *der* <> *vi* nörgeln; **to ~ about sb** über jn meckern.

car park *n Br* Parkplatz *der.*

carpenter ['kɑːpəntəˀ] *n* [working on buildings] Zimmerer *der;* [making furniture] Tischler *der.*

carpentry ['kɑːpəntrɪ] *n* [working on buildings] Zimmerhandwerk *das;* [making furniture] Tischlerhandwerk *das.*

carpet ['kɑːpɪt] <> *n* [floor covering] Teppich(boden) *der* <> *vt* [floor] mit Teppich(boden) auslegen.

carpet sweeper [-ˌswiːpəˀ] *n* Teppichkehrmaschine *die.*

car phone *n* Autotelefon *das.*

car radio *n* Autoradio *das.*

car rental *n* (U) *Am* Autovermietung *die.*

carriage ['kærɪdʒ] *n* - 1. [horsedrawn vehicle] Kutsche *die* - 2. *Br* [railway coach] Wagen *der* - 3. [transport of goods] Transport *der;* **~ paid** OR **free** *Br* frachtfrei, frei Haus.

carriageway ['kærɪdʒweɪ] *n Br* Fahrbahn *die.*

carrier ['kærɪəˀ] *n* - 1. COMM Spediteur *der* - 2. [of disease] Überträger *der*, -in *die* - 3. = carrier bag.

carrier bag *n* Tragetasche *die.*

carrot ['kærət] *n* - 1. [vegetable] Möhre *die*, Karotte *die* - 2. *inf* [incentive] Köder *der.*

carry ['kærɪ] <> *vt* - 1. [transport] tragen - 2. [be equipped with] dabeilhaben, mit sich führen - 3. [disease] übertragen - 4. [involve] mit sich bringen - 5. [motion, proposal] anlnehmen - 6. [be pregnant with] tragen - 7. MATH: **5 ~ 15 Rest 1** <> *vi* [sound] tragen. <> **carry away** *vt fus*: **to get carried away** sich hinreißen lassen. <> **carry forward** *vt sep* übertragen. <> **carry off** *vt sep* - 1. [plan, performance] schaffen - 2. [prize] gewinnen. <> **carry on** <> *vt fus* [continue] fortlfahren; **to ~ on doing sthg** etw weiterhin tun <> *vi* - 1. [continue] weiterlmachen; **to ~ on with sthg** mit etw weiterlmachen

- 2. *inf* [make a fuss] sich auflführen. <> **carry out** *vt fus* [task, plan, order] auslführen; [experiment, investigation] durchlführen; [promise, threat] wahr machen. <> **carry through** *vt sep* [accomplish] durchlführen.

carryall ['kærɪɔːl] *n Am* Reisetasche *die.*

carrycot ['kærɪkɒt] *n esp Br* Babytragetasche *die.*

carry-out *n Am & Scot* Essen oder Getränke *zum Mitnehmen.*

carsick ['kɑːˌsɪk] *adj* reisekrank.

cart [kɑːt] <> *n* - 1. [vehicle] Wagen *der* - 2. *Am* [for shopping]: **(shopping** OR **grocery)** ~ Einkaufswagen *der* <> *vt inf* schleppen.

carton ['kɑːtn] *n* Karton *der;* [of cream, yoghurt] Becher *der;* [of milk] Tüte *die.*

cartoon [kɑː'tuːn] *n* - 1. [satirical drawing] Karikatur *die* - 2. [comic strip] Comic(strip) *der* - 3. [film] Zeichentrickfilm *der.*

cartridge ['kɑːtrɪdʒ] *n* - 1. [for gun, pen] Patrone *die* - 2. [for camera] Film *der.*

cartwheel ['kɑːtwiːl] *n* Rad *das;* **to do ~s** Rad schlagen.

carve [kɑːv] <> *vt* - 1. [wood] schnitzen; [stone] hauen - 2. [meat] auflschneiden - 3. [cut] ritzen <> *vi* den Braten/das Fleisch auflschneiden. <> **carve out** *vt sep*: **to ~ out a career** sich eine Karriere auflbauen. <> **carve up** *vt sep* [divide] auflteilen.

carving ['kɑːvɪŋ] *n* [object] Skulptur *die.*

carving knife *n* Tranchiermesser *das.*

car wash *n* [place] Autowaschanlage *die.*

case [keɪs] *n* - 1. [gen] Fall *der;* **in that ~** in dem Fall; **as** OR **whatever the ~ may be** je nachdem; **in ~ of emergency/doubt** im Notfall/Zweifelsfall - 2. [argument] Angelegenheit *die;* **the ~ for the defence** die Verteidigung - 3. [packing case] Kiste *die;* [small box] Kästchen *das;* [for glasses, cigarettes] Etui *das;* [for musical instrument] Kasten *der* - 4. *Br* [suitcase] Koffer *der.* <> **in any case** *adv* wie dem auch sei. <> **in case** <> *conj* falls <> *adv*: **(just) in ~** für alle Fälle.

cash [kæʃ] <> *n* (U) - 1. [notes and coins] Bargeld *das;* **to pay (in) ~** bar bezahlen - 2. *inf* [money] Geld *das;* **I'm a bit short of ~** ich bin etwas knapp bei Kasse - 3. [payment]: **~ in advance** Vorkasse *die;* **~ on delivery** zahlbar bei Empfang <> *vt* einllösen.

cash and carry *n* [for retailers] Großhandelsmarkt *der;* [for public] Verbrauchermarkt *der.*

cash box *n* Geldkassette *die.*

cash card *n* Kontokarte *die.*

cash desk *n Br* Kasse *die.*

cash dispenser [-dɪˌspensəˀ] *n* Geldautomat *der.*

cashew (nut) ['kæʃuː-] *n* Cashewnuss *die.*

cashier [kæ'ʃɪəˀ] *n* Kassierer *der*, -in *die.*

cash machine *n* = cash dispenser.

cashmere ['kæʃmɪəˀ] *n* Kaschmir *der.*

cashpoint (machine) ['kæʃpɔɪnt-] *n* Geldautomat *der.*

cash register *n* Registrierkasse *die.*

casing ['keɪsɪŋ] *n* Gehäuse *das;* [of cable] Hülle *die;* [of tyre] Mantel *der.*

casino [kə'siːnəʊ] (*pl* -s) *n* Kasino *das.*

cask [kɑːsk] *n* Fass *das.*

casket ['kɑːskɪt] *n* - 1. [for jewels] (Schmuck)kästchen *das* - 2. *Am* [coffin] Sarg *der.*

casserole ['kæsərəʊl] *n* - 1. [stew] Fleischeintopf *der* - 2. [pan] Schmortopf *der.*

cassette [kæ'set] *n* Kassette *die.*

cassette player *n* Kassettenspieler *der.*

cassette recorder *n* Kassettenrekorder *der.*

cast [kɑːst] (*pt & pp* cast) ◇ *n* - 1. [of play, film] Besetzung *die* - 2. MED Gipsverband *der* ◇ *vt* - 1. [gen] werfen; **to ~ one's eye over sthg** einen Blick auf etw (A) werfen; **to ~ doubt on sthg** etw in Zweifel ziehen - 2. [choose for play, film]: **she ~ him in the role of Hamlet** sie gab ihm die Rolle des Hamlet - 3. POL: **to ~ one's vote** seine Stimme abgeben - 4. [metal, statue] gießen. ◆ **cast aside** *vt sep* fallen lassen. ◆ **cast off** *vi* - 1. NAUT ablegen - 2. [in knitting] Maschen abnehmen. ◆ **cast on** *vi* [in knitting] Maschen anschlagen.

castaway ['kɑːstəweɪ] *n* Schiffbrüchige *der, die.*

caster ['kɑːstə'] *n* Rolle *die.*

caster sugar *n Br* Feinkristallzucker *der.*

casting vote ['kɑːstɪŋ-] *n* entscheidende Stimme.

cast iron *n* (U) Gusseisen *das.*

castle ['kɑːsl] *n* - 1. [fortress] Burg *die;* [mansion] Schloss *das* - 2. [in chess] Turm *der.*

castor ['kɑːstə'] *n* = caster.

castrate [kæ'streɪt] *vt* kastrieren.

casual ['kæʒʊəl] *adj* - 1. [relaxed] gleichgültig - 2. *pej* [offhand] nachlässig - 3. [chance] zufällig - 4. [clothes]: ~ **clothes** zwanglose Kleidung - 5. [work, worker] Gelegenheits-.

casually ['kæʒʊəlɪ] *adv* - 1. [in a relaxed manner] gleichgültig - 2. [dress] leger.

casualty ['kæʒjʊəltɪ] *n* - 1. [dead person] Todesopfer *das;* [injured person] Unfallopfer *das* - 2. = casualty department.

casualty department *n* Ambulanz *die.*

cat [kæt] *n* - 1. [domestic] Katze *die* - 2. [wild] Raubkatze *die.*

catalogue *Br,* **catalog** *Am* ['kætəlɒg] ◇ *n* [of items] Katalog *der* ◇ *vt* katalogisieren.

catalyst ['kætəlɪst] *n* - 1. CHEM Katalysator *der* - 2. *fig* [cause] Auslöser *der.*

catalytic converter [ˌkætə'kɪtɪk-] *n* Katalysator *der.*

catapult *Br* ['kætəpʌlt] ◇ *n* - 1. [hand-held] Katapult *das* - 2. HIST [machine] Katapult *das* ◇ *vt* schleudern; **she was ~ed to fame** *fig* sie wurde über Nacht berühmt.

cataract ['kætərækt] *n* MED grauer Star.

catarrh [kə'tɑː'] *n* Katarrh *der.*

catastrophe [kə'tæstrəfɪ] *n* Katastrophe *die.*

catch [kætʃ] (*pt & pp* caught) ◇ *vt* - 1. [ball, fish, animal] fangen - 2. [criminal] fassen - 3. [discover] überraschen; **to ~ sb doing sthg** jn bei etw ertappen - 4. [train, plane] erreichen - 5. [hear clearly] hören - 6. [interest] wecken; [imagination] anregen; **I tried to ~ his attention** ich versuchte, ihn auf mich aufmerksam zu machen - 7. [sight]: **to ~ sight of sb/sthg, to ~ a glimpse of sb/sthg** jn/etw flüchtig zu Gesicht bekommen - 8. [illness, disease]: **to ~ malaria/measles** an Malaria/Masern erkranken; **to ~ a cold** sich erkälten - 9. [trap]: **to ~ one's finger in the door** sich den Finger in der Tür einklemmen - 10. [strike] treffen ◇ *vi* - 1. [clothing] hängen bleiben; [foot, limb] stecken bleiben - 2. [fire] angehen ◇ *n* - 1. [of ball *etc*]: **good ~!** sehr gut gefangen! - 2. [of fish] Fang *der* - 3. [fastener] Verschluss *der* - 4. [snag] Haken *der.* ◆ **catch on** *vi* - 1. [become popular] Anklang finden - 2. *inf* [understand] begreifen; **to ~ on to sthg** hinter etw (A) kommen. ◆ **catch out** *vt sep* [trick] hereinlegen. ◆ **catch up** ◇ *vt sep* - 1. [come level with] einholen - 2. [involve]: **to get caught up in sthg** in etw (A) verwickelt werden ◇ *vi* aufholen; **to ~ up on sthg** etw nachholen. ◆ **catch up with** *vt fus* - 1. [in race, work] einholen - 2. [criminal] ausfindig machen.

catching ['kætʃɪŋ] *adj* ansteckend.

catchment area ['kætʃmənt-] *n* Einzugsgebiet *das.*

catchphrase ['kætʃfreɪz] *n* [of performer] Lieblingsspruch *der.*

catchy ['kætʃɪ] *adj:* **a ~ tune** ein Ohrwurm.

categorically [ˌkætɪ'gɒrɪklɪ] *adv* kategorisch.

category ['kætəgərɪ] *n* Kategorie *die.*

cater ['keɪtə'] *vi* [provide food]: **to ~ for sb** jn mit Lebensmitteln versorgen. ◆ **cater for** *vt fus Br* [tastes, needs] befriedigen.

caterer ['keɪtərə'] *n* Lebensmittellieferant *der,* -in *die.*

catering ['keɪtərɪŋ] *n* (U) [industry] Gaststättengewerbe *das;* [at wedding, party] Essen *das.*

caterpillar ['kætəpɪlə'] *n* Raupe *die.*

cathedral [kə'θiːdrəl] *n* Kathedrale *die.*

Catholic ['kæθlɪk] ◇ *adj* katholisch ◇ *n* Katholik *der,* -in *die.* ◆ **catholic** *adj:* **to have very ~ tastes** vielseitig interessiert sein.

cat litter *n* Katzenstreu *das.*

Catseyes® ['kætsaɪz] *npl Br* Katzenaugen *pl.*

cattle ['kætl] *npl* Vieh *das.*

catty ['kætɪ] *adj inf pej* [spiteful] gehässig.

catwalk ['kætwɔːk] n Laufsteg der.

caucus ['kɔːkəs] n - 1. Am POL Sitzung die, Versammlung die - 2. Br POL Gremium das.

caught [kɔːt] pt & pp ⊏ catch.

cauliflower ['kɒlɪˌflaʊəʳ] n Blumenkohl der.

cause [kɔːz] ⬦ n - 1. [reason why sthg happens] Ursache die - 2. [grounds]: ~ (for) Grund der (zu); to have no ~ to do sthg keinen Grund haben, etw zu tun; I have no ~ for complaint ich habe keinen Grund zur Klage - 3. [movement, aim] Sache die; for a good ~ für eine gute Sache ⬦ vt verursachen; to ~ sb to do sthg jn veranlassen, etw zu tun.

caustic ['kɔːstɪk] adj - 1. CHEM ätzend - 2. fig [comment] bissig.

caution ['kɔːʃn] ⬦ n - 1. [care] Vorsicht die; [prudence] Umsicht die; 'proceed with ~' 'vorsichtig vorgehen' - 2. [warning] Warnung die - 3. Br LAW Verwarnung die ⬦ vt - 1. [warn]: to ~ sb against doing sthg jn davor warnen, etw zu tun - 2. Br LAW verwarnen.

cautious ['kɔːʃəs] adj [careful] vorsichtig; [prudent] umsichtig.

cavalry ['kævlrɪ] n (U) - 1. [on horseback] Kavallerie die - 2. [in armoured vehicles] motorisierte Truppen pl.

cave [keɪv] n Höhle die. ◆ **cave in** vi [physically collapse] ein|stürzen.

caveman ['keɪvmæn] (pl -men [-men]) n Höhlenmensch der.

cavernous ['kævənəs] adj [room, building] höhlenartig.

caviar(e) ['kævɪɑːʳ] n Kaviar der.

cavity ['kævətɪ] n - 1. [in object, structure] Hohlraum der; [in body] Höhle die - 2. [in tooth] Loch das.

cavort [kə'vɔːt] vi herum|tollen.

CB n (abbr of Citizens' Band) CB.

CBI (abbr of Confederation of British Industry) n britischer Unternehmerverband.

cc ⬦ n (abbr of cubic centimetre) cm³ ⬦ abbr of carbon copy.

CD n (abbr of compact disc) CD die.

CD player n CD-Player der, CD-Spieler der.

CD-ROM [ˌsiːdiːˈrɒm] (abbr of compact disc read-only memory) n CD-ROM die.

cease [siːs] fml ⬦ vt beenden, ein|stellen; to ~ doing OR to do sthg aufhören, etw zu tun ⬦ vi auf|hören, enden.

cease-fire n Waffenruhe die.

ceaseless ['siːslɪs] adj fml unaufhörlich.

cedar (tree) ['siːdəʳ] n Zeder die.

cedilla [sɪ'dɪlə] n Cedille die.

ceiling ['siːlɪŋ] n - 1. [of room] Decke die - 2. [limit] oberste Grenze.

celebrate ['selɪbreɪt] ⬦ vt [victory, anniversary] feiern ⬦ vi feiern.

celebrated ['selɪbreɪtɪd] adj berühmt.

celebration [ˌselɪ'breɪʃn] n - 1. (U) [activity] Feiern das - 2. [event] Feier die.

celebrity [sɪ'lebrɪtɪ] n [star] Star der.

celery ['selərɪ] n Stangensellerie die OR die.

celibate ['selɪbət] adj RELIG zölibatär; fig enthaltsam.

cell [sel] n - 1. [gen] Zelle die - 2. COMPUT Feld das.

cellar ['seləʳ] n - 1. [basement] Keller der - 2. [stock of wine] Weinkeller der.

cello ['tʃeləʊ] (pl -s) n Cello das.

Cellophane® ['seləfeɪn] n Zellophan das.

Celsius ['selsɪəs] adj Celsius-, Celsius; 20 degrees ~ 20 Grad Celsius.

Celt [kelt] n Kelte der, -tin die.

Celtic ['keltɪk] adj keltisch.

cement [sɪ'ment] ⬦ n (U) [for concrete] Zement der ⬦ vt - 1. [cover with cement] betonieren - 2. fig [friendship] festigen.

cement mixer n Betonmischmaschine die.

cemetery ['semɪtrɪ] n Friedhof der.

censor ['sensəʳ] ⬦ n Zensor der ⬦ vt zensieren.

censorship ['sensəʃɪp] n Zensur die.

censure ['senʃəʳ] ⬦ n Tadel der ⬦ vt tadeln.

census ['sensəs] (pl censuses) n Volkszählung die.

cent [sent] n Cent der.

centenary Br ['sen'tiːnərɪ], **centennial** Am [sen'tenjəl] n Hundertjahrfeier die.

center n, adj & vt Am = centre.

centigrade ['sentɪgreɪd] adj Celsius-; 16 degrees ~ 16 Grad Celsius.

centilitre Br, **centiliter** Am ['sentɪˌliːtəʳ] n Zentiliter der.

centimetre Br, **centimeter** Am ['sentɪˌmiːtəʳ] n Zentimeter der.

centipede ['sentɪpiːd] n Tausendfüßler der.

central ['sentrəl] adj zentral.

Central America n Mittelamerika nt.

central heating n Zentralheizung die.

centralize, -ise ['sentrəlaɪz] vt zentralisieren.

central locking [-'lɒkɪŋ] n Zentralverriegelung die.

central reservation n Br Mittelstreifen der.

centre Br, **center** Am ['sentəʳ] ⬦ n - 1. [gen] Mitte die, Zentrum das; [of circle] Mittelpunkt der - 2. [building, place] Zentrum das - 3. [of event, activity] Zentrum das, Mittelpunkt der; she always wants to be the ~ of attention sie will immer im Mittelpunkt stehen; ~ of gravity Schwerpunkt der - 4. POL Mitte die - 5. [in basketball, netball] Center der ⬦ adj - 1. [middle] Mittel-, mittlere, -r, -s - 2. POL: ~ party Partei der Mitte ⬦ vt [text, image] zentrieren.

centre forward *n* Mittelstürmer *der*, -in *die*.

century ['sentʃʊrɪ] *n* Jahrhundert *das*.

ceramic [sɪ'ræmɪk] *adj* keramisch. ◆ **ceramics** *npl* [objects] Keramik *die*.

cereal ['sɪərɪəl] *n* - **1.** [crop] Getreide *das* - **2.** (U) [breakfast food] Frühstücksflocken *pl*.

ceremonial [ˌserɪ'məʊnjəl] *adj* feierlich.

ceremony ['serɪmənɪ] *n* - **1.** [event] Zeremonie *die* - **2.** [formality] Förmlichkeit *die*; **to stand on ~** sehr förmlich sein.

certain ['sɜːtn] *adj* - **1.** [gen] sicher; **he is ~ to be late** er kommt bestimmt zu spät; **to make ~** nachlprüfen; **I always make ~ of being on time** ich achte immer darauf, pünktlich zu sein; **for ~** sicher - **2.** [particular, individual] gewiss; **to a ~ extent** bis zu einem gewissen Grad.

certainly ['sɜːtnlɪ] *adv* sicher(lich); **can I bring a friend along? - ~!** kann ich einen Bekannten/eine Bekannte mitbringen? - na klar!; **do you dye your hair? - ~ not!** färbst du dir die Haare? - natürlich nicht!

certainty ['sɜːtntɪ] *n* Sicherheit *die*; **it's a ~ that he will win the race** es steht fest, dass er das Rennen gewinnen wird.

certificate [sə'tɪfɪkət] *n* Bescheinigung *die*; [from school, college] Zeugnis *das*; [of birth] Urkunde *die*.

certified ['sɜːtɪfaɪd] *adj* - **1.** [teacher, accountant] geprüft - **2.** [document] beglaubigt.

certified mail *n Am* Einschreiben *das*.

certified public accountant *n Am* Buchhalter *der*, -in *die*.

certify ['sɜːtɪfaɪ] *vt* - **1.** [declare true] bescheinigen; **this is to ~ that ...** hiermit wird bescheinigt, dass ... - **2.** [declare insane] für unzurechnungsfähig erklären.

cervical [sə'vaɪkl] *adj* Gebärmutter-.

cervical smear *n* Abstrich *der*.

cervix ['sɜːvɪks] (*pl* -ices [-ɪsiːz]) *n* Gebärmutterhals *der*.

cesarean (section) *n Am* = caesarean section.

cesspit ['sespɪt], **cesspool** ['sespuːl] *n* Senkgrube *die*.

cf. (*abbr of* confer) vgl.

CFC (*abbr of* chlorofluorocarbon) *n* FCKW *das*.

ch. (*abbr of* chapter) Kap.

chafe [tʃeɪf] *vt* [rub] scheuern.

chaffinch ['tʃæfɪntʃ] *n* Buchfink *der*.

chain [tʃeɪn] ◇ *n* Kette *die*; **a ~ of events** eine Kette von Ereignissen ◇ *vt* anlketten.

chain reaction *n* Kettenreaktion *die*.

chain saw *n* Kettensäge *die*.

chain smoker *n* Kettenraucher *der*, -in *die*.

chain store *n* Filiale *die* einer Ladenkette.

chair [tʃeəʳ] ◇ *n* - **1.** [gen] Stuhl *der* - **2.** [university post] Lehrstuhl *der* ◇ *vt* [meeting, discussion] den Vorsitz führen bei, leiten.

chair lift *n* Sessellift *der*.

chairman ['tʃeəmən] (*pl* -men [-mən]) *n* Vorsitzende *der*.

chairperson ['tʃeəˌpɜːsn] (*pl* -s) *n* Vorsitzende *der*, *die*.

chalet ['ʃæleɪ] *n* [in mountains] Chalet *das*.

chalk [tʃɔːk] *n* - **1.** [for drawing] Kreide *die* - **2.** (U) [type of rock] Kalkstein *der*.

chalkboard ['tʃɔːkbɔːd] *n Am* Tafel *die*.

challenge ['tʃælɪndʒ] ◇ *n* - **1.** [gen] Herausforderung *die* - **2.** [to authority] Infragestellung *die* ◇ *vt* - **1.** [to fight, competition]: **to ~ sb (to sthg)** jn (zu etw) herauslfordern - **2.** [question] in Frage stellen.

challenging ['tʃælɪndʒɪŋ] *adj* herausfordernd.

chamber ['tʃeɪmbəʳ] *n* Kammer *die*.

chambermaid ['tʃeɪmbəmeɪd] *n* Zimmermädchen *das*.

chamber music *n* Kammermusik *die*.

chamber of commerce *n* Handelskammer *die*.

chameleon [kə'miːljən] *n* Chamäleon *das*.

champagne [ˌʃæm'peɪn] *n* Champagner *der*.

champion ['tʃæmpjən] *n* - **1.** [of competition] Meister *der*, -in *die*, Champion *der* - **2.** [of cause] Verfechter *der*, -in *die*.

championship ['tʃæmpjənʃɪp] *n* Meisterschaft *die*.

chance [tʃɑːns] ◇ *n* - **1.** (U) [luck] Glück *das*; **by ~** zufällig; **by any ~** vielleicht - **2.** [likelihood] Chance *die*, Möglichkeit *die*; **she doesn't stand a ~ of winning the match** sie hat keine Chance, das Spiel zu gewinnen; **on the off ~** auf gut Glück - **3.** [opportunity] Gelegenheit *die*, Chance *die* - **4.** [risk]: **to take a ~** es riskieren ◇ *adj* [meeting] zufällig ◇ *vt* [risk] riskieren; **he's chancing his luck a bit** er fordert sein Glück heraus.

chancellor ['tʃɑːnsələʳ] *n* Kanzler *der*.

Chancellor of the Exchequer *n Br* Schatzkanzler *der*.

chandelier [ˌʃændə'lɪəʳ] *n* Kronleuchter *der*.

change [tʃeɪndʒ] ◇ *n* - **1.** [alteration] Änderung *die*; [difference] Veränderung *die*; **~ in sb/sthg** Veränderung in jm/etw; **a ~ for the better** eine Verbesserung; **a ~ for the worse** eine Verschlechterung - **2.** [contrast, for variety] Abwechslung *die*; **for a ~** zur Abwechslung - **3.** [switch, replacement] Wechsel *der*; **a ~ of clothes** Kleidung zum Wechseln - **4.** (U) [money returned after payment] Wechselgeld *das* - **5.** (U) [coins] Kleingeld *das*; **have you got ~ for a £5 note?** können Sie mir einen Fünfpfundschein wechseln? ◇ *vt* - **1.** [alter, make different] ändern; **to ~ sthg into sthg** etw in etw (A) umlwandeln; **to ~ one's mind** seine Meinung ändern - **2.** [replace] auslwechseln; [product purchased] umltauschen

- **3.** [switch] wechseln; **to ~ clothes, to get ~d** sich umlziehen; **to ~ trains/planes** umlsteigen - **4.** [money] wechseln - **5.** [bed] wechseln; [baby] trockenllegen <> *vi* - **1.** [alter, become different] sich ändern, sich verändern; **to ~ into sthg** sich in etw (A) verwandeln - **2.** [put on different clothes] sich umlziehen - **3.** [on train, bus] umlsteigen; **all ~!** alles auslsteigen! ◆ **change over** *vi*: **to ~ over to sthg** auf etw (A) umlstellen.

changeable ['tʃeɪndʒəbl] *adj* - **1.** [mood] wechselnd - **2.** [weather] wechselhaft.

change machine *n* Geldwechselautomat *der*.

changeover ['tʃeɪndʒ,əʊvə'] *n*: **~ (to sthg)** Umstellung *die* (auf etw (A)).

changing ['tʃeɪndʒɪŋ] *adj* sich (ver)ändernd, wechselnd.

changing room *n* [in sports] Umkleideraum *der*; [in shop] Umkleidekabine *die*.

channel ['tʃænl] <> *n* - **1.** [gen] Kanal *der* - **2.** [route] Fahrrinne *die* <> *vt* [water] leiten. ◆ **Channel** *n*: **the (English) Channel** der Ärmelkanal. ◆ **channels** *npl*: **to go through the proper ~s** sich an die richtigen Stellen wenden.

Channel Islands *npl*: **the ~** die Kanalinseln *pl*.

Channel Tunnel *n*: **the ~** der Kanaltunnel.

chant [tʃɑːnt] *n* - **1.** RELIG [song] Gesang *der* - **2.** [repeated words] Sprechchor *der*.

chaos ['keɪɒs] *n* Chaos *das*.

chaotic [keɪˈɒtɪk] *adj* chaotisch.

chap [tʃæp] *n Br inf* [man] Kerl *der*.

chapel ['tʃæpl] *n* [part of church, small church] Kapelle *die*.

chaplain ['tʃæplɪn] *n* Hausgeistliche *der*.

chapped [tʃæpt] *adj* aufgesprungen.

chapter ['tʃæptə'] *n* Kapitel *das*.

char [tʃɑː'] *vt* [burn] verkohlen.

character ['kærəktə'] *n* - **1.** [nature of place] Charakter *der*; [- of person] Wesen *das*; **in ~** typisch - **2.** [unusual quality, style] Originalität *die* - **3.** [in film, book, play] Gestalt *die* - **4.** *inf* [unusual person] Original *das* - **5.** [letter, symbol] Schriftzeichen *das*.

characteristic [,kærəktəˈrɪstɪk] <> *adj* charakteristisch <> *n* Kennzeichen *das*.

characterize, -ise ['kærəktəraɪz] *vt* - **1.** [typify] kennzeichnen - **2.** [portray]: **to ~ sthg as sthg** etw als etw beschreiben.

charade [ʃəˈrɑːd] *n* Farce *die*. ◆ **charades** *n* (U) Scharade *die*.

charcoal ['tʃɑːkəʊl] *n* (U) [for drawing] Kohle *die*; [for barbecue] Holzkohle *die*.

charge [tʃɑːdʒ] <> *n* - **1.** [cost] Gebühr *die*; **free of ~** gebührenfrei - **2.** LAW Anklage *die* - **3.** [command, control] Verantwortung *die*; **to take ~ (of sthg)** [of organization, group of people] die Leitung (einer Sache (G)) übernehmen; **in ~** zuständig; **in ~ of** verantwort-

lich für - **4.** ELEC Ladung *die* - **5.** MIL Sturmangriff *der* <> *vt* - **1.** [customer] berechnen (+ D); **to ~ £10 for sthg** für etw 10 Pfund verlangen; **to ~ sthg to sb** jm etw in Rechnung stellen - **2.** [suspect, criminal] anlklagen; **to ~ sb with sthg** jn wegen etw anlklagen - **3.** [attack] anlgreifen - **4.** ELEC auflladen <> *vi* - **1.** [rush] stürmen - **2.** [attack] anlgreifen.

charge card *n* Kundenkreditkarte *die*.

chargé d'affaires [,ʃɑːʒeɪdæˈfeə'] (*pl* **chargés d'affaires**) *n* Diplomat, der anstelle eines Botschafters ein Land vertritt.

charger ['tʃɑːdʒə'] *n* [for batteries] Ladegerät *das*.

chariot ['tʃærɪət] *n* Streitwagen *der*.

charisma [kəˈrɪzmə] *n* Charisma *das*.

charity ['tʃærətɪ] *n* - **1.** (U) [gifts, money] Spenden *pl* - **2.** [organization] Wohltätigkeitsorganisation *die*, karitative Einrichtung - **3.** [kindness] Nächstenliebe *die*.

charm [tʃɑːm] <> *n* - **1.** (U) [appeal, attractiveness] Charme *der* - **2.** [spell] Bann *der* - **3.** [on bracelet] Anhänger *der*; **lucky ~** Glücksbringer *der* <> *vt* bezaubern.

charming ['tʃɑːmɪŋ] *adj* bezaubernd; [person] charmant.

chart [tʃɑːt] <> *n* - **1.** [diagram] Diagramm *das*; [for weather forecast] Wetterkarte *die* - **2.** [map] Karte *die* <> *vt* - **1.** [map - seas, skies] kartieren; [- movements] auf einer Karte erfassen - **2.** *fig* [record] auflzeichnen. ◆ **charts** *npl*: **the ~s** die Hitparade.

charter ['tʃɑːtə'] <> *n* [document - of organization] Charta *die*; [- of town] Gründungsurkunde *die* <> *vt* [plane, boat] chartern.

chartered accountant [,tʃɑːtəd-] *n Br* Wirtschaftsprüfer *der*, -in *die*.

charter flight *n* Charterflug *der*.

charter plane *n* Charterflugzeug *das*.

chase [tʃeɪs] <> *n* Verfolgungsjagd *die*; [hunt] Jagd *die* <> *vt* - **1.** [pursue] jagen; [criminal] verfolgen - **2.** [drive away] fortljagen <> *vi*: **to ~ after sb/sthg** jm/etw nachljagen.

chasm ['kæzm] *n* - **1.** [deep crack] tiefe Felsspalte - **2.** *fig* [divide] Kluft *die*.

chassis ['ʃæsɪ] (*pl inv*) *n* [of vehicle] Fahrgestell *das*.

chat [tʃæt] <> *n* Plauderei *die*; **to have a ~** plaudern <> *vi* plaudern. ◆ **chat up** *vt sep Br inf* sich heranlmachen an (+ A).

chat room *n* COMPUT Diskussionsforum *das*, Chatroom *der*.

chat show *n Br* Talkshow *die*.

chatter ['tʃætə'] <> *n* [of person] Geplapper *das* <> *vi* - **1.** [person] plappern - **2.** [animal, bird] zwitschern - **3.** [teeth] klappern.

chatterbox ['tʃætəbɒks] *n inf* [child] Plappermäulchen *das*.

chatty ['tʃætɪ] *adj* - **1.** [person] gesprächig - **2.** [letter] im Plauderton geschrieben.

chauffeur [ˈʃəʊfəˈ] *n* Chauffeur *der.*

chauvinist [ˈʃəʊvɪnɪst] *n* Chauvinist *der.*

cheap [tʃiːp] ◇ *adj* - **1.** [inexpensive] billig - **2.** [reduced in price] preiswert - **3.** [poorquality] billig - **4.** [vulgar] billig; **to feel ~** sich schäbig fühlen ◇ *adv* billig.

cheapen [ˈtʃiːpn] *vt* [degrade - thing or place] herabsetzen; [- person] erniedrigen.

cheaply [ˈtʃiːplɪ] *adv* billig.

cheat [tʃiːt] ◇ *n* - **1.** [person] Betrüger *der,* -in *die;* [in exam, game] Mogler *der,* -in *die* - **2.** [act] Betrug *der* ◇ *vt* betrügen; **to ~ sb out of sthg** jn um etw betrügen ◇ *vi* [in exam, game] mogeln. ◆ **cheat on** *vt fus inf* [be unfaithful to] betrügen.

check [tʃek] ◇ *n* - **1.** [inspection, test]: **~ (on sthg)** Überprüfung *die* (von etw); **to keep a ~ on sthg** etw (regelmäßig) überprüfen - **2.** [restraint]: **to put a ~ on sthg** etw unter Kontrolle halten; **in ~** unter Kontrolle - **3.** *Am* [bill] Rechnung *die* - **4.** [pattern] Karomuster *das* - **5.** *Am* = **cheque** ◇ *vt* - **1.** [test, verify] kontrollieren - **2.** [restrain] unter Kontrolle halten; [advance] aufhalten; **to ~ o.s.** innehalten ◇ *vi* [have a look] nachsehen; [ask sb] nachfragen; **to ~ on sthg** etw überprüfen. ◆ **check in** ◇ *vt sep* [luggage] abfertigen lassen; [coat] abgeben ◇ *vi* - **1.** [at hotel] sich anlmelden - **2.** [at airport] einlchecken. ◆ **check out** ◇ *vt sep* [investigate] überprüfen ◇ *vi* [from hotel] sich ablmelden. ◆ **check up** *vi:* **to ~ up on sb** [supervise] jn kontrollieren; [investigate] über jn Nachforschungen anlstellen; **to ~ up on sthg** etw überprüfen.

checkbook *n Am* = **chequebook**.

checked [tʃekt] *adj* [patterned] kariert.

checkered *adj Am* = **chequered**.

checkers [ˈtʃekəz] *n (U) Am* Damespiel *das.*

check-in *n* Abfertigung *die;* [check-in desk] Abfertigungsschalter *der.*

checking account [ˈtʃekɪŋ-] *n Am* Girokonto *das.*

checkmate [ˈtʃekmeɪt] *n* Schachmatt *das.*

checkout [ˈtʃekaʊt] *n* [in supermarket] Kasse *die.*

checkpoint [ˈtʃekpɔɪnt] *n* Kontrollpunkt *der.*

checkup [ˈtʃekʌp] *n* Kontrolluntersuchung *die,* Vorsorgeuntersuchung *die.*

Cheddar (cheese) [ˈtʃedəˈ-] *n* Cheddar(käse) *der.*

cheek [tʃiːk] *n* - **1.** [of face] Backe *die,* Wange *die* - **2.** *inf* [impudence] Frechheit *die.*

cheekbone [ˈtʃiːkbəʊn] *n* Wangenknochen *der,* Backenknochen *der.*

cheeky [ˈtʃiːkɪ] *adj* frech.

cheer [tʃɪəˈ] ◇ *n* [shout] Hurraruf *der;* [cheering] Jubelgeschrei *das;* **three ~s for Linda!** ein dreifaches Hurra für Linda! ◇ *vt* - **1.** [shout approval, encouragement at] zul-

jubeln *(+ D)* - **2.** [gladden] auflmuntern ◇ *vi* jubeln. ◆ **cheers** *excl* - **1.** [said before drinking] prost! - **2.** *Br inf* [goodbye] tschüs! - **3.** *Br inf* [thank you] danke! ◆ **cheer up** ◇ *vt sep* auflmuntern ◇ *vi* vergnügter werden; **~ up!** Kopf hoch!

cheerful [ˈtʃɪəfʊl] *adj* heiter; [music, colour] fröhlich.

cheerio [ˌtʃɪərɪˈəʊ] *excl Br inf* tschüs!

cheese [tʃiːz] *n* Käse *der.*

cheeseboard [ˈtʃiːzbɔːd] *n* - **1.** [board] Käsebrett *das* - **2.** [on menu] Käseplatte *die.*

cheeseburger [ˈtʃiːzˌbɜːgəˈ] *n* Cheeseburger *der.*

cheesecake [ˈtʃiːzkeɪk] *n* Käsekuchen *der.*

cheetah [ˈtʃiːtə] *n* Gepard *der.*

chef [ʃef] *n* [cook] Koch *der,* Köchin *die;* [head cook] Chefkoch *der,* -köchin *die.*

chef

Das englische Wort chef ist ein falscher Freund, auf den man schnell hereinfällt. Eine so betitelte Person ist im Englischen kein Vorgesetzter in einer Firma, sondern ein Koch, und ein head chef ist ein Chefkoch oder Küchenchef. It's the chef's day off today bedeutet also, dass der Koch heute seinen freien Tag hat.
Was in Deutschland der „Chef" bzw. die „Chefin", ist im englischsprachigen Raum der boss oder head. „Da müssen Sie erst den Chef fragen" hieße auf Englisch in etwa You'll have to ask the boss about that first.

chemical [ˈkemɪkl] ◇ *adj* chemisch ◇ *n* Chemikalie *die.*

chemist [ˈkemɪst] *n* - **1.** *Br* [pharmacist] Apotheker *der,* -in *die;* **~'s (shop)** [dispensing] Apotheke *die;* [non-dispensing] Drogerie *die* - **2.** [scientist] Chemiker *der,* -in *die.*

chemistry [ˈkemɪstrɪ] *n* [science] Chemie *die.*

cheque *Br,* **check** *Am* [tʃek] *n* Scheck *der.*

chequebook *Br,* **checkbook** *Am* [ˈtʃekbʊk] *n* Scheckheft *das.*

cheque (guarantee) card *n Br* Scheckkarte *die.*

chequered *Br* [ˈtʃekəd], **checkered** *Am* [ˈtʃekerd] *adj* [varied] bewegt.

cherish [ˈtʃerɪʃ] *vt* [person] liebevoll sorgen für; [thing] hegen und pflegen; [hope] hegen.

cherry [ˈtʃerɪ] *n* - **1.** [fruit] Kirsche *die* - **2.: ~ (tree)** Kirschbaum *der.*

chess [tʃes] *n* Schach *das.*

chessboard [ˈtʃesbɔːd] *n* Schachbrett *das.*

chest [tʃest] *n* - **1.** ANAT Brust *die* - **2.** [trunk] Truhe *die.*

chestnut [ˈtʃesnʌt] ◇ *adj* [colour] kastani-

enbraun <> n - **1.** [nut] Kastanie die - **2.:** ~ **(tree)** Kastanienbaum der.

chest of drawers (pl chests of drawers) n Kommode die.

chew [tʃuː] <> n [sweet] Kaubonbon der OR das <> vt - **1.** [food] kauen - **2.** [nails, pencil] kauen an (+ D). **chew up** vt sep zerkauen, zerbeißen.

chewing gum ['tʃuːɪŋ-] n (U) Kaugummi der.

chic [ʃiːk] adj schick.

chick [tʃɪk] n - **1.** [baby bird] Junge das, Küken das - **2.** inf [girl] Braut die.

chicken ['tʃɪkɪn] n - **1.** [bird] Huhn das - **2.** (U) [food] Hähnchen das - **3.** inf [coward] Feigling der. **chicken out** vi inf: **to ~ out of sthg** vor etw (D) kneifen; **to ~ out of doing sthg** sich (aus Angst) davor drücken, etw zu tun.

chickenpox ['tʃɪkɪnpɒks] n Windpocken pl.

chickpea ['tʃɪkpiː] n Kichererbse die.

chicory ['tʃɪkərɪ] n [vegetable] Chicorée die.

chief [tʃiːf] <> adj - **1.** [most important] Haupt- - **2.** [head] leitend <> n - **1.** [of organization] Leiter der, -in die, Chef der, -in die; ~ **of police** Polizeipräsident der, -in die - **2.** [of tribe] Häuptling der.

chief executive n [of company] Direktor der, -in die.

chiefly ['tʃiːflɪ] adv hauptsächlich.

chiffon ['ʃɪfɒn] n Chiffon der.

chilblain ['tʃɪlbleɪn] n Frostbeule die.

child [tʃaɪld] (pl children) n Kind das.

child benefit n Br Kindergeld das.

childhood ['tʃaɪldhʊd] n Kindheit die.

childish ['tʃaɪldɪʃ] adj pej kindisch.

childlike ['tʃaɪldlaɪk] adj kindlich.

childminder ['tʃaɪldˌmaɪndə'] n Br Tagesmutter die.

childproof ['tʃaɪldpruːf] adj kindersicher.

children ['tʃɪldrən] pl [> child.

children's home n Kinderheim das.

Chile ['tʃɪlɪ] n Chile nt.

chili ['tʃɪlɪ] n = chilli.

chill [tʃɪl] <> adj kühl <> n - **1.** [illness] Erkältung die mit leichtem Fieber - **2.** [in temperature]: **there's a ~ in the air** es ist kühl draußen - **3.** [feeling of fear] Schauder der <> vt - **1.** [drink] kühlen; [food] kalt stellen - **2.** [person - with cold]: **I'm ~ed to the bone** ich bin bis auf die Knochen durchgefroren <> vi [drink, food] kühl werden.

chilli ['tʃɪlɪ] (pl -ies) n [vegetable] Chili der; ~ **con carne** Chili con carne.

chilling ['tʃɪlɪŋ] adj - **1.** [very cold] eisig - **2.** [frightening] schaudererregend.

chilly ['tʃɪlɪ] adj kühl.

chime [tʃaɪm] <> n [of bells] Geläut das; [of clock] Schlagen das; [of door bell] Läuten das <> vt [time] schlagen <> vi [bell] läuten;

[clock] schlagen. **chime in** vi sich einschalten.

chimney ['tʃɪmnɪ] n Schornstein der.

chimneypot ['tʃɪmnɪpɒt] n Schornsteinaufsatz der.

chimneysweep ['tʃɪmnɪswiːp] n Schornsteinfeger der.

chimp [tʃɪmp] n inf Schimpanse der.

chimpanzee [tʃɪmpən'ziː] n Schimpanse der.

chin [tʃɪn] n Kinn das.

china ['tʃaɪnə] n Porzellan das.

China ['tʃaɪnə] n China nt.

Chinese [tʃaɪ'niːz] <> adj chinesisch <> n [language] Chinesisch(e) das <> npl: **the ~** die Chinesen pl.

chink [tʃɪŋk] n [narrow opening] Ritze die; **a ~ of light** ein dünner Lichtstrahl.

chip [tʃɪp] <> n - **1.** Br [fried potato]: ~**s** Pommes frites pl - **2.** Am [potato crisp] Chip der - **3.** [fragment - of wood] Span der; [- of stone, metal] Splitter der - **4.** [flaw] angeschlagene Stelle - **5.** [microchip, token] Chip der <> vt [damage] anschlagen. **chip in** inf vi - **1.** [contribute] etwas beisteuern - **2.** [interrupt] sich einschalten. **chip off** vt sep abkratzen.

chipboard ['tʃɪpbɔːd] n (U) Spanplatte die.

chip shop n Br Imbissbude die.

chiropodist [kɪ'rɒpədɪst] n Fußpfleger der, -in die.

chirp [tʃɜːp] vi [bird] zwitschern.

chirpy ['tʃɜːpɪ] adj esp Br inf munter.

chisel ['tʃɪzl] <> n [for stone] Meißel der; [for wood] Beitel der <> vt [in stone] meißeln; [in wood] stemmen.

chit [tʃɪt] n Zettel der.

chitchat ['tʃɪttʃæt] n inf Geplauder das.

chivalry ['ʃɪvlrɪ] n - **1.** literary [of knights] Rittertum das - **2.** [courtesy] Ritterlichkeit die.

chives [tʃaɪvz] npl Schnittlauch der.

chlorine ['klɔːriːn] n Chlor das.

choc-ice ['tʃɒkaɪs] n Br Eis mit Schokoladenüberzug.

chock [tʃɒk] n Keil der.

chock-a-block, chock-full adj inf überfüllt.

chocolate ['tʃɒkələt] <> n - **1.** (U) [food] Schokolade die - **2.** [sweet] Praline die - **3.** [drink]: **(hot) ~** heiße Schokolade <> comp [made of chocolate] Schokoladen-.

choice [tʃɔɪs] <> n - **1.** [gen] Wahl die - **2.** [variety, selection] Auswahl die <> adj erlesen, ausgesucht.

choir ['kwaɪə'] n Chor der.

choirboy ['kwaɪəbɔɪ] n Chorknabe der.

choke [tʃəʊk] <> n AUT Choke der <> vt - **1.** [strangle] würgen; **to ~ sb to death** jn erwürgen; **the fumes ~d her** durch den Rauch bekam sie keine Luft mehr - **2.** [block] ver-

stopfen <> *vi* keine Luft mehr kriegen; [on fishbone] sich verschlucken; **to ~ to death** ersticken.

cholera ['kɒlərə] *n* Cholera *die*.

choose [tʃu:z] (*pt* chose; *pp* chosen) <> *vt* - **1.** [select - career] wählen; [- cake, dress] auslwählen - **2.** [opt]: **to ~ to do sthg** beschließen, etw zu tun <> *vi* [select]: **to ~ (from sthg)** eine Wahl treffen (zwischen etw *(D)*).

choos(e)y ['tʃu:zɪ] (*compar* -ier; *superl* -iest) *adj* wählerisch.

chop [tʃɒp] <> *n* [meat] Kotelett *das* <> *vt* - **1.** [wood] hacken; [food] schneiden - **2.** *inf* [funding, budget] kürzen - **3.** *phr*: **to ~ and change** es sich *(D)* dauernd anders überlegen. ◆ **chop down** *vt sep* fällen. ◆ **chop up** *vt sep* [wood] klein hacken; [food] klein schneiden.

chopper ['tʃɒpə'] *n* - **1.** [axe] Hackbeil *das* - **2.** *inf* [helicopter] Hubschrauber *der*.

choppy ['tʃɒpɪ] *adj* kabbelig.

chopsticks ['tʃɒpstɪks] *npl* Stäbchen *pl*.

chord [kɔ:d] *n* MUS Akkord *der*.

chore [tʃɔ:'] *n* lästige Pflicht; **household ~s** Hausarbeit *die*.

chorus ['kɔ:rəs] *n* - **1.** [part of song] Refrain *der* - **2.** [singers] Chor *der*.

chose [tʃəʊz] *pt* ▷ choose.

chosen ['tʃəʊzn] *pp* ▷ choose.

Christ [kraɪst] <> *n* Christus *der* <> *excl* oh Gott!

christen ['krɪsn] *vt* taufen.

christening ['krɪsnɪŋ] *n* Taufe *die*.

Christian ['krɪstʃən] <> *adj* christlich <> *n* Christ *der*, -in *die*.

Christianity [ˌkrɪstɪ'ænətɪ] *n* Christentum *das*.

Christian name *n* Vorname *der*.

Christmas ['krɪsməs] *n* Weihnachten *das*; **Happy OR Merry ~!** Frohe Weihnachten!

Christmas card *n* Weihnachtskarte *die*.

Christmas Day *n* erster Weihnachtstag.

Christmas Eve *n* Heiligabend *der*.

Christmas pudding *n Br* schwere Süßspeise mit Trockenfrüchten, die an Weihnachten gegessen wird.

Christmas tree *n* Weihnachtsbaum *der*.

chrome [krəʊm], **chromium** ['krəʊmɪəm] <> *n* Chrom *das* <> *comp* Chrom-.

chronic ['krɒnɪk] *adj* - **1.** [illness, unemployment] chronisch - **2.** [alcoholic] Gewohnheits-; [liar] chronisch.

chronicle ['krɒnɪkl] *n* Chronik *die*.

chronological [ˌkrɒnə'lɒdʒɪkl] *adj* chronologisch.

chrysanthemum [krɪ'sænθəməm] (*pl* -s) *n* Chrysantheme *die*.

chubby ['tʃʌbɪ] *adj* mollig.

chuck [tʃʌk] *vt inf* - **1.** [throw] schmeißen - **2.** [job] hinlschmeißen; [girlfriend, boy-

friend] Schluss machen mit. ◆ **chuck away, chuck out** *vt sep inf* weglschmeißen.

chuckle ['tʃʌkl] *vi* in sich *(A)* hineinllachen.

chug [tʃʌg] *vi* tuckern.

chum [tʃʌm] *n inf* [friend] Kumpel *der*.

chunk [tʃʌŋk] *n* - **1.** [of bread, cheese] Stück *das* - **2.** *inf* [large amount] großer Teil.

church [tʃɜ:tʃ] *n* Kirche *die*; **to go to ~** in die Kirche gehen.

Church of England *n*: **the ~** die Anglikanische Kirche.

churchyard ['tʃɜ:tʃjɑːd] *n* Friedhof *der*.

churlish ['tʃɜ:lɪʃ] *adj* [impolite] unhöflich; [loutish] ungehobelt.

churn [tʃɜ:n] <> *n* - **1.** [for making butter] Butterfass *das* - **2.** [for milk] Milchkanne *die* <> *vt* [stir up] auflwühlen. ◆ **churn out** *vt sep inf* am laufenden Band produzieren.

chute [ʃu:t] *n* Rutsche *die*; [for rubbish] Müllschlucker *der*.

chutney ['tʃʌtnɪ] *n* Chutney *das*.

CIA (*abbr of* Central Intelligence Agency) *n* CIA *der* OR *die*.

CID (*abbr of* Criminal Investigation Department) *n* = Kripo *die*.

cider ['saɪdə'] *n* Cidre *der*, Apfelwein *der*.

cigar [sɪ'gɑ:'] *n* Zigarre *die*.

cigarette [ˌsɪgə'ret] *n* Zigarette *die*.

cinder ['sɪndə'] *n* Asche *die*.

Cinderella [ˌsɪndə'relə] *n* Aschenputtel *das*.

cinecamera ['sɪnɪˌkæmərə] *n* Filmkamera *die*.

cinefilm ['sɪnɪˌfɪlm] *n* Film für eine Filmkamera.

cinema ['sɪnəmə] *n* Kino *das*.

cinnamon ['sɪnəmən] *n* Zimt *der*.

cipher ['saɪfə'] *n* [secret writing system] Chiffre *die*, Kode *der*.

circa ['sɜːkə] *prep* etwa, zirka.

circle ['sɜːkl] <> *n* - **1.** [gen] Kreis *der*; **to go round in ~s** sich im Kreis bewegen - **2.** [in theatre, cinema] Balkon *der* <> *vt* - **1.** [draw a circle round] einlkreisen - **2.** [move round] umkreisen <> *vi* kreisen.

circuit ['sɜːkɪt] *n* - **1.** ELEC Stromkreis *der* - **2.** [lap] Runde *die* - **3.** [motor racing track] Rennstrecke *die* - **4.** [series of venues] Tour *die*.

circuitous [sə'kjuːɪtəs] *adj* umständlich.

circular ['sɜːkjʊlə'] <> *adj* - **1.** [in shape] rund, kreisförmig - **2.** [route] Rund- <> *n* - **1.** [letter, memo] Rundschreiben *das* - **2.** [advertisement] Wurfsendung *die*.

circulate ['sɜːkjʊleɪt] <> *vi* - **1.** [gen] zirkulieren - **2.** [rumour, story] umlgehen, kursieren - **3.** [socialize] sich unter die Leute mischen <> *vt* - **1.** [document] zirkulieren lassen - **2.** [rumour, story] in Umlauf setzen.

circulation [ˌsɜːkjʊ'leɪʃn] *n* - **1.** [of blood] Zirkulation *die*, Kreislauf *der* - **2.** [of money, document] Umlauf *der;* **in** ~ im Umlauf - **3.** [of magazine, newspaper] Auflage *die* - **4.** [of heat, air] Zirkulation *die.*

circumcision [ˌsɜːkəmˈsɪʒn] *n* Beschneidung *die.*

circumference [səˈkʌmfərəns] *n* Umfang *der.*

circumflex [ˈsɜːkəmfleks] *n:* ~ **(accent)** Zirkumflex *der.*

circumspect [ˈsɜːkəmspekt] *adj* umsichtig.

circumstances [ˈsɜːkəmstənsɪz] *npl* Umstände *pl;* **under** OR **in no** ~ unter keinen Umständen, auf keinen Fall; **under** OR **in the** ~ unter diesen Umständen.

circumvent [ˌsɜːkəmˈvent] *vt fml* umgehen.

circus [ˈsɜːkəs] *n* Zirkus *der.*

cistern [ˈsɪstən] *n* - **1.** *Br* [in roof] Wassertank *der* - **2.** [in toilet] Spülkasten *der.*

cite [saɪt] *vt* - **1.** [mention, quote] zitieren - **2.** LAW vorladen.

citizen [ˈsɪtɪzn] *n* - **1.** [of country] Staatsbürger *der,* -in *die* - **2.** [of town] Bürger *der,* -in *die.*

Citizens' Advice Bureau *n* Bürgerberatungsstelle *die.*

Citizens' Band *n* CB-Funk *der.*

citizenship [ˈsɪtɪznʃɪp] *n* [nationality] Staatsangehörigkeit *die.*

citrus fruit [ˈsɪtrəs-] *n* Zitrusfrucht *die.*

city [ˈsɪtɪ] *n* Stadt *die;* [large] Großstadt *die.*
➤ **City** *n Br:* **the City** Londoner Finanzviertel.

city centre *n* Innenstadt *die.*

city hall *n Am* Rathaus *das.*

civic [ˈsɪvɪk] *adj* - **1.** [leader, event] Stadt- - **2.** [duty, pride] bürgerlich, Bürger-.

civil [ˈsɪvl] *adj* - **1.** [disorder, marriage] zivil - **2.** [polite] höflich.

civil engineering *n* Hoch- und Tiefbau *der.*

civilian [sɪˈvɪljən] ◇ *n* Zivilist *der,* -in *die* ◇ *comp* [government] Zivil-; [organization] zivil; **in** ~ **clothes** in Zivil.

civilization [ˌsɪvəlaɪˈzeɪʃn] *n* - **1.** [advanced world] Zivilisation *die* - **2.** [society, culture] Kultur *die.*

civilized [ˈsɪvəlaɪzd] *adj* - **1.** [advanced] zivilisiert - **2.** [polite] zivilisiert.

civil law *n* bürgerliches Recht *n*

civil liberties *npl* Freiheitsrechte *pl.*

civil rights *npl* Bürgerrechte *pl.*

civil servant *n* Beamte *der,* -in *die* (im Staatsdienst).

civil service *n* Staatsdienst *der.*

civil war *n* Bürgerkrieg *der.*

CJD *(abbr of Creutzfeldt-Jakob disease) n* CJK *die.*

cl *(abbr of centilitre) n* cl.

clad [klæd] *adj literary* [dressed]: ~ **in sthg** in etw *(D)* gekleidet.

claim [kleɪm] ◇ *n* - **1.** [for territory, expen-

ses, refund] Anspruch *der;* [demand] Forderung *die;* **to lay** ~ **to sthg** etw für sich beanspruchen - **2.** [assertion] Behauptung *die* ◇ *vt* - **1.** [money] beantragen; [lost property] beanspruchen; [expenses] einreichen; [credit] für sich in Anspruch nehmen; **the** ~ **responsibility for it** er bekannte, dafür verantwortlich zu sein - **2.** [assert] behaupten ◇ *vi:* **to** ~ **for sthg** Ansprüche auf etw *(A)* geltend machen.

claimant [ˈkleɪmənt] *n* Antragsteller *der,* -in *die;* LAW Kläger *der,* -in *die.*

clairvoyant [kleəˈvɔɪənt] *n* Hellseher *der,* -in *die.*

clam [klæm] *n* Klaffmuschel *die.*

clamber [ˈklæmbə] *vi* klettern.

clammy [ˈklæmɪ] *adj inf* [skin] feucht und klamm; [weather] schwül.

clamour *Br,* **clamor** *Am* [ˈklæmə] ◇ *n* ◇ *vi:* **to** ~ **for sthg** etw lautstark fordern.

clamp [klæmp] ◇ *n* - **1.** [fastener] Schraubzwinge *die* - **2.** MED & TECH Klemme *die* ◇ *vt* - **1.** [with fastener] festlklemmen - **2.** [parked car] Parkkralle anlegen (+ *D*).
➤ **clamp down** *vi:* **to** ~ **down (on)** durchlgreifen (gegen).

clan [klæn] *n* Clan *der.*

clandestine [klænˈdestɪn] *adj* geheim.

clang [klæŋ] *n* [of bell] lautes Tönen.

clap [klæp] ◇ *vt* Beifall klatschen (+ *D*); **to** ~ **one's hands** in die Hände klatschen; **to** ~ **eyes on sb/sthg** jn/etw zu Gesicht bekommen ◇ *vi* Beifall klatschen.

clapping [ˈklæpɪŋ] *n* Beifall *der.*

claret [ˈklærət] *n* [wine] roter Bordeaux.

clarify [ˈklærɪfaɪ] *vt* [näher] erläutern.

clarinet [ˌklærəˈnet] *n* Klarinette *die.*

clarity [ˈklærətɪ] *n* Klarheit *die.*

clash [klæʃ] ◇ *n* - **1.** [incompatibility]: **a** ~ **of interests** ein Interessenkonflikt; **a** ~ **of personalities** ein Zusammenprall verschiedener Persönlichkeiten - **2.** [fight] Zusammenstoß *der* - **3.** [disagreement] Meinungsverschiedenheit *die* ◇ *vi* - **1.** [ideas, beliefs] aufeinander prallen; [colours] sich beißen - **2.** [fight]: **to** ~ **(with sb)** (mit jm) zusammenlstoßen - **3.** [disagree]: **to** ~ **(with sb)** (mit jm) aneinander geraten - **4.** [coincide]: **to** ~ **(with sthg)** sich (mit etw) überschneiden.

clasp [klɑːsp] ◇ *n* [on necklace, bracelet] Verschluss *der;* [on belt] Schnalle *die* ◇ *vt* erlgreifen.

class [klɑːs] ◇ *n* - **1.** [gen] Klasse *die* - **2.** [lesson] Stunde *die;* **an evening** ~ ein Abendkurs - **3.** [social group] Schicht *die;* **upper** ~ Oberschicht *die;* **the working** ~ die Arbeiterklasse ◇ *vt* einlstufen; **to** ~ **sb as sthg** jn als etw einlstufen.

classic [ˈklæsɪk] ◇ *adj* [gen] klassisch ◇ *n* Klassiker *der.*

classical ['klæsɪkl] *adj* - **1.** klassisch - **2.** [sculpture, architecture] klassizistisch.

classified ['klæsɪfaɪd] *adj* [secret]: ~ **information** Verschlusssache *die*.

classified ad *n* Annonce *die*.

classify ['klæsɪfaɪ] *vt* klassifizieren.

classmate ['klɑːsmeɪt] *n* Klassenkamerad *der*, -in *die*.

classroom ['klɑːsrom] *n* Klassenzimmer *das*.

classy ['klɑːsɪ] *adj inf* [clothes, restaurant] nobel; [car] edel; [person] vornehm.

clatter ['klætə] *n* Geklapper *das*.

clause [klɔːz] *n* - **1.** [in legal document] Klausel *die* - **2.** GRAMM Satz *der*.

claw [klɔː] *n* [of animal, bird] Kralle *die* *vt* kratzen *vi*: **to ~ at sthg** sich an etw (A) krallen.

clay [kleɪ] *n* [soil] Lehm *der*; [for pottery] Ton *der*.

clean [kliːn] *adj* - **1.** [gen] sauber - **2.** [reputation, driving licence] tadellos - **3.** [joke] harmlos - **4.** [line, movement] klar - **5.** [break] glatt *vt* sauber machen; **to ~ one's teeth** *Br* sich (D) die Zähne putzen *vi* putzen.

clean out *vt sep* [room, cupboard] gründlich aufräumen. **clean up** *vt sep* [mess] aufräumen; [with cloth] sauber machen; **to ~ o.s. up** sich waschen.

cleaner ['kliːnə] *n* - **1.** [person] Putzfrau *die* - **2.** [substance] Reiniger *der*.

cleaning ['kliːnɪŋ] *n*: **to do the ~** sauber machen.

cleanliness ['klenlɪnɪs] *n* Reinlichkeit *die*.

cleanse [klenz] *vt* [skin, wound] säubern.

cleanser ['klenzə] *n* - **1.** [for skin] Reinigungsmilch *die* - **2.** [detergent] Reinigungsmittel *das*.

clean-shaven [-'ʃeɪvn] *adj* glatt rasiert.

clear [klɪə] *adj* - **1.** [gen] klar; **to make sthg ~ (to sb)** (jm) etw klar machen; **to make it ~ that ...** deutlich machen, dass ...; **to make o.s. ~** sich klar ausdrücken - **2.** [obvious] eindeutig - **3.** [sound] deutlich; [speaker] deutlich hörbar - **4.** [skin, complexion, conscience] rein - **5.** [road, view] frei; **try and keep Friday** ~ versuch dir Freitag freizuhalten *adv*: **stand ~!** zurücktreten!; **to be ~ of sthg** etw nicht berühren; **to stay ~ of sb, to steer ~ of sb** jm aus dem Wege gehen; **to stay ~ of sthg, to steer ~ of sthg** etw meiden *vt* - **1.** [path, road] räumen; [pipe] reinigen; **to ~ the table** den Tisch abräumen - **2.** [take out of the way] aus dem Weg räumen - **3.** [jump over] überspringen - **4.** [debt] begleichen - **5.** [authorize] genehmigen - **6.** [prove not guilty] freisprechen; **to ~ one's name** seinen Namen reinwaschen; **to be ~ed of sthg** von etw freigesprochen werden *vi* [fog, smoke] sich verziehen; [weather] sich auflklären. **clear away** *vt sep* wegl-

räumen. **clear off** *vi Br inf* ablhauen. **clear out** *vt sep* [room, cupboard] gründlich auflräumen *vi inf* [leave] verschwinden. **clear up** *vt sep* - **1.** [tidy] auflräumen; [toys, litter] weglräumen - **2.** [mystery] auflklären; [problem, confusion] klären *vi* - **1.** [weather] sich auflklären - **2.** [tidy up] auflräumen.

clearance ['klɪərəns] *n (U)* [permission] Genehmigung *die*; [for takeoff] Starterlaubnis *die*.

clear-cut *adj* klar umrissen.

clearing ['klɪərɪŋ] *n* [in forest] Lichtung *die*.

clearly ['klɪəlɪ] *adv* - **1.** [speak, write] deutlich - **2.** [think, explain] klar - **3.** [obviously] eindeutig.

cleavage ['kliːvɪdʒ] *n* [between breasts] Dekolletee *das*.

cleaver ['kliːvə] *n* Hackbeil *das*.

clef [klef] *n* Notenschlüssel *der*.

cleft [kleft] *n* [in rock] Spalt *der*.

clench [klentʃ] *vt* umklammern; [fist] ballen; [teeth] zusammenlbeißen.

clergy ['klɜːdʒɪ] *npl*: **the ~** die Geistlichkeit.

clergyman ['klɜːdʒɪmən] (*pl* -men [-mən]) *n* Geistliche *der*.

clerical ['klerɪkl] *adj* - **1.** [in office] Büro- - **2.** [in church] geistlich.

clerk [*Br* klɑːk, *Am* klɜːrk] *n* - **1.** [in office] Büroangestellte *der, die* - **2.** [in court] Gerichtsschreiber *der*, -in *die* - **3.** *Am* [shop assistant] Verkäufer *der*, -in *die*.

clever ['klevə] *adj* - **1.** [person] klug; **to be ~ with one's hands** geschickte Hände haben - **2.** [idea, device] raffiniert.

click [klɪk] *n* Klicken *das* *vt* [fingers] schnippen mit; [tongue] schnalzen mit *vi* [gen & COMPUT] klicken; **to ~ on sthg** COMPUT etw anlklicken; **suddenly it all ~ed** plötzlich wurde alles klar.

client ['klaɪənt] *n* Kunde *der*, -din *die*; [of lawyer] Klient *der*, -in *die*.

cliff [klɪf] *n* [by sea] Klippe *die*.

climate ['klaɪmɪt] *n lit & fig* Klima *das*.

climax ['klaɪmæks] *n* [culmination] Höhepunkt *der*.

climb [klaɪm] *n* [of mountain] Aufstieg *der* *vt* [tree, wall] hochlklettern; [rope] hochlklettern an (+ D); [ladder, stairs] hinauflsteigen; [hill] steigen auf (+ A); [mountain] besteigen *vi* - **1.** [person, plant] klettern - **2.** [road, prices, costs] anlsteigen; [plane] (auf)lsteigen.

climber ['klaɪmə] *n* [person] Kletterer *der*, -in *die*; [mountaineer] Bergsteiger *der*, -in *die*.

climbing ['klaɪmɪŋ] *n* Klettern *das*; [mountaineering] Bergsteigen *das*; **to go ~** bergsteigen gehen.

clinch [klɪntʃ] *vt* [deal] ablschließen.

cling [klɪŋ] (*pt* & *pp* clung) *vi* - **1.** [hold tightly]: **to ~ to** sich klammern an (+ A)

- 2. [clothes]: **to ~ (to sthg)** sich (an etw (A)) anschmiegen.

clingfilm ['klɪŋfɪlm] n (U) Br Frischhaltefolie die.

clinic ['klɪnɪk] n Klinik die.

clinical ['klɪnɪkl] adj **- 1.** MED klinisch **- 2.** [coldly rational] nüchtern.

clink [klɪŋk] vi klirren.

clip [klɪp] ⬦ n **- 1.** [fastener] Klammer die; [on earring] Klipp der **- 2.** [of film, video] Ausschnitt der, Clip der ⬦ vt **- 1.** [fasten]: **to ~ sthg onto sthg** [papers] etw an etw (A) heften **- 2.** [cut] schneiden.

clipboard ['klɪpbɔːd] n Klemmbrett das.

clippers ['klɪpəz] npl **- 1.** [for hair] Haarschneidemaschine die **- 2.** [for nails] Nagelknipser der, Nagelzange die.

clipping ['klɪpɪŋ] n [newspaper cutting] Zeitungsausschnitt der.

cloak [kləʊk] n [garment] Umhang der.

cloakroom ['kləʊkrʊm] n **- 1.** [for clothes] Garderobe die **- 2.** Br [toilets] Waschraum der.

clock [klɒk] n **- 1.** [gen] Uhr die; **round the ~** rund um die Uhr **- 2.** [mileometer] Tachometer der. ⬥ **clock in** vi Br [at work] (den Arbeitsbeginn) stechen. ⬥ **clock off** vi Br [at work] (das Arbeitsende) stechen.

clockwise ['klɒkwaɪz] adj & adv im Uhrzeigersinn.

clockwork ['klɒkwɜːk] ⬦ n: **like ~** wie am Schnürchen ⬦ comp [toy, train] zum Aufziehen.

clog [klɒg] vt verstopfen. ⬥ **clogs** npl Clogs pl. ⬥ **clog up** vt sep & vi verstopfen.

close[1] [kləʊs] ⬦ adj **- 1.** [near] nahe; **~ to** nahe an (+ D); [with verbs of motion] nahe an (+ A); **the house is ~ to the river** das Haus steht nahe am Fluss; **she sat down ~ to me** sie setzte sich in meine Nähe; **don't get too ~ to the edge** geh nicht zu nahe an den Abgrund; **that was a ~ shave** OR **thing** OR **call** das war knapp; **when seen from ~ up** OR **to** aus der Nähe betrachtet **- 2.** [friend, contact, link] eng; **to be ~ to sb** jm nahe stehen **- 3.** [resemblance] stark **- 4.** [examination, inspection] genau; **on ~r examination** bei näherer Betrachtung **- 5.** [weather] schwül **- 6.** [race, contest] knapp ⬦ adv nah; **~ by, ~ at hand** in der Nähe; **~ behind** dicht dahinter; **to stand ~ together** nahe beieinander stehen. ⬥ **close on, close to** prep [almost] beinahe.

close[2] [kləʊz] ⬦ vt **- 1.** [gen] schließen **- 2.** [road] sperren **- 3.** [meeting, event] beenden; [speech, novel] beschließen **- 4.** [bank account] auflösen **- 5.** [deal] abschließen ⬦ vi **- 1.** [door, eyes, wound] sich schließen **- 2.** [shop, office, book, share price] schließen **- 3.** [deadline, offer] enden ⬦ n [end] Schluss der; **to draw to a ~** zu Ende gehen. ⬥ **close down** ⬦ vt sep [shut] schließen ⬦ vi [shut down] stillgelegt werden.

closed [kləʊzd] adj geschlossen.

close-knit [ˌkləʊs-] adj eng verbunden.

closely ['kləʊslɪ] adv **- 1.** [gen] eng; [resemble] stark **- 2.** [watch, guard, listen] genau; [follow] dicht.

closet ['klɒzɪt] ⬦ adj inf heimlich; **he's a ~ socialist** er ist ein verkappter Sozialist ⬦ n Am Schrank der.

close-up ['kləʊs-] n Nahaufnahme die.

closing time ['kləʊzɪŋ-] n [for pubs] Sperrstunde die; [for shops] Ladenschlusszeit die.

closure ['kləʊʒə] n **- 1.** [of business, company] Schließung die **- 2.** [of road, railway line] Sperrung die.

clot [klɒt] ⬦ n **- 1.** [lump] Klumpen der; [of blood] Blutgerinnsel das **- 2.** Br inf [fool] Hornochse der ⬦ vi [blood] gerinnen.

cloth [klɒθ] n **- 1.** (U) [material] Stoff der **- 2.** [for cleaning] Lappen der **- 3.** [tablecloth] Tischtuch das.

clothe [kləʊð] vt fml [dress] kleiden.

clothes [kləʊðz] npl Kleider pl; **to put one's ~ on** sich anziehen; **to take one's ~ off** sich ausziehen.

clothes brush n Kleiderbürste die.

clothesline ['kləʊðzlaɪn] n Wäscheleine die.

clothes peg Br, **clothespin** Am ['kləʊðzpɪn] n Wäscheklammer die.

clothing ['kləʊðɪŋ] n Kleidung die; **a piece of ~** ein Kleidungsstück.

cloud [klaʊd] n Wolke die. ⬥ **cloud over** vi [sky] sich bewölken.

cloudy ['klaʊdɪ] adj **- 1.** [day, sky] bedeckt **- 2.** [beer, water] trüb.

clout [klaʊt] inf ⬦ n (U) [influence] Schlagkraft die ⬦ vt [hit] schlagen.

clove [kləʊv] n: **a ~ of garlic** eine Knoblauchzehe. ⬥ **cloves** npl [spice] Gewürznelken pl.

clover ['kləʊvə] n Klee der.

clown [klaʊn] ⬦ n **- 1.** [performer] Clown der **- 2.** [fool] Idiot der ⬦ vi herumalbern.

cloying ['klɔɪɪŋ] adj **- 1.** [scent] süßlich **- 2.** [sentimentality] kitschig.

club [klʌb] ⬦ n **- 1.** [association] Klub der **- 2.** [nightclub] Nachtklub der **- 3.** [weapon] Knüppel der, Prügel der **- 4.** SPORT [equipment]: **(golf) ~** (Golf)schläger der ⬦ vt [hit] prügeln. ⬥ **clubs** npl [playing cards] Kreuz das; **the six of ~s** die Kreuzsechs. ⬥ **club together** vi Br zusammenlegen.

clubhouse ['klʌbhaʊs, pl -haʊzɪz] n Klubhaus das.

cluck [klʌk] vi [hen] gackern.

clue [kluː] n [hint] Hinweis der; [in crime] Spur die; [in crossword] Frage die; **I haven't (got) a ~ (about)** ich habe keine Ahnung (von).

clued-up [kluːd-] adj Br inf gut informiert.

clump [klʌmp] *n* [of trees, flowers] Gruppe *die*.

clumsy ['klʌmzɪ] *adj* [person] tollpatschig; [movement, remark] ungeschickt.

clung [klʌŋ] *pt & pp* ⊏━ cling.

cluster ['klʌstə'] ⟨⟩ *n* Gruppe *die*; [of grapes] Traube *die* ⟨⟩ *vi* - 1. [people] sich scharen - 2. [things] sich drängen.

clutch [klʌtʃ] ⟨⟩ *n* AUT Kupplung *die* ⟨⟩ *vt* festhalten ⟨⟩ *vi*: **to - at sb/sthg** nach jm/etw greifen.

clutter ['klʌtə'] *n* Unordnung *die*.

cm (*abbr of* centimetre) *n* cm.

c/o (*abbr of* care of) ⊏━ care.

Co. - 1. *abbr of* Company - 2. *abbr of* County.

coach [kəʊtʃ] ⟨⟩ *n* - 1. [bus] (Reise)bus *der* - 2. RAIL Wagen *der* - 3. [horsedrawn] Kutsche *die* - 4. SPORT Trainer *der*, -in *die* - 5. [tutor] Nachhilfelehrer *der*, -in *die* ⟨⟩ *vt* - 1. SPORT trainieren - 2. [tutor]: **to - sb (in sthg)** jm Nachhilfestunden (in etw (*D*)) geben.

coach station *n* Busbahnhof *der*.

coal [kəʊl] *n* (*U*) [mineral] Kohle *die*.

coalfield ['kəʊlfiːld] *n* Kohlenrevier *das*.

coalition [ˌkəʊə'lɪʃn] *n* POL Koalition *die*; **- government** Koalitionsregierung *die*.

coalmine ['kəʊlmaɪn] *n* Kohlenbergwerk *das*.

coarse [kɔːs] *adj* - 1. [rough - hair] dick; [- skin] derb; [- sandpaper, fabric] grob - 2. [vulgar - remark, laugh] ordinär; [- joke] derb; [- person] ordinär.

coast [kəʊst] ⟨⟩ *n* Küste *die* ⟨⟩ *vi* [car] im Leerlauf fahren.

coastal ['kəʊstl] *adj* Küsten-.

coaster ['kəʊstə'] *n* Untersetzer *der*.

coastguard ['kəʊstgɑːd] *n* - 1. [person] Mitglied *das* der Küstenwache - 2. [organization]: **the -** die Küstenwache.

coastline ['kəʊstlaɪn] *n* Küste *die*.

coat [kəʊt] ⟨⟩ *n* - 1. [garment] Mantel *der* - 2. [of animal] Fell *das* - 3. [of paint, varnish] Schicht *die* ⟨⟩ *vt*: **to - sthg (with sthg)** etw (mit etw) überziehen.

coat hanger *n* Kleiderbügel *der*.

coating ['kəʊtɪŋ] *n* [of chocolate] Überzug *der*; [of dust] Schicht *die*.

coat of arms (*pl* coats of arms) *n* Wappen *das*.

coax [kəʊks] *vt*: **to - sb (to do** OR **into doing sthg)** jn überreden(, etw zu tun).

cob [kɒb] *n* ⊏━ corn on the cob.

cobbles ['kɒblz], **cobblestones** ['kɒblstəʊnz] *npl* Kopfsteinpflaster *das*.

cobweb ['kɒbweb] *n* Spinnennetz *das*.

cocaine [kəʊ'keɪn] *n* Kokain *das*.

cock [kɒk] ⟨⟩ *n* - 1. [male chicken] Hahn *der* - 2. [male bird] Männchen *das* - 3. *vulg* [penis] Schwanz *der* ⟨⟩ *vt* - 1.: **to - a gun** den Hahn einer Schusswaffe spannen - 2. [head]: **to**

- one's head (to one side) den Kopf auf die Seite legen. ◆ **cock up** *vt sep Br vinf* versauen.

cockerel ['kɒkrəl] *n* junger Hahn.

cockle ['kɒkl] *n* Herzmuschel *die*.

Cockney ['kɒknɪ] (*pl* -s) *n* - 1. [person] Cockney *der* - 2. [dialect, accent] Cockney *das*.

cockpit ['kɒkpɪt] *n* Cockpit *das*.

cockroach ['kɒkrəʊtʃ] *n* Küchenschabe *die*.

cocktail ['kɒkteɪl] *n* Cocktail *der*.

cocktail party *n* Cocktailparty *die*.

cock-up *n vinf*: **to make a -** Scheiße bauen; **to make a - of sthg** etw versauen.

cocky ['kɒkɪ] *adj inf* überheblich.

cocoa ['kəʊkəʊ] *n* Kakao *der*.

coconut ['kəʊkənʌt] *n* Kokosnuss *die*.

cod [kɒd] (*pl inv* OR -s) *n* Kabeljau *der*.

COD *abbr of* cash on delivery.

code [kəʊd] ⟨⟩ *n* - 1. [cipher] Kode *der* - 2. [set of rules] Kodex *der*; **- of behaviour** Verhaltenskodex *der* - 3. TELEC Vorwahl *die* ⟨⟩ *vt* - 1. [encode] verschlüsseln, chiffrieren - 2. [give identifier to] kennzeichnen.

cod-liver oil *n* Lebertran *der*.

coerce [kəʊ'ɜːs] *vt* zwingen; **to - sb into doing sthg** jn dazu nötigen, etw zu tun.

C of E *n abbr of* Church of England.

coffee ['kɒfɪ] *n* Kaffee *der*.

coffee bar *n Br* Café *das*.

coffee break *n* Kaffeepause *die*.

coffee morning *n Br morgendliches Kaffeetrinken, das zu Wohltätigkeitszwecken organisiert wird.*

coffeepot ['kɒfɪpɒt] *n* Kaffeekanne *die*.

coffee shop *n* - 1. *Br* [café] Café *das* - 2. *Am* [restaurant] Café *das* - 3. [shop selling coffee] Kaffeegeschäft *das*.

coffee table *n* Couchtisch *der*.

coffin ['kɒfɪn] *n* Sarg *der*.

cog [kɒg] *n* - 1. [tooth on wheel] Zahn *der*; [wheel] Zahnrad *das*.

coherent [kəʊ'hɪərənt] *adj* [answer] folgerichtig; [theory, ideas, story, speech] schlüssig; [account] zusammenhängend.

cohesive [kəʊ'hiːsɪv] *adj* [united - group] einheitlich; [- image] stimmig.

coil [kɔɪl] ⟨⟩ *n* - 1. [of rope, wire] Rolle *die*; [of hair] Locke *die*; [of smoke] Kringel *der* - 2. ELEC Spule *die* - 3. *Br* [contraceptive device] Spirale *die* ⟨⟩ *vt* aufrollen; **to - sthg around sb/sthg** etw um jn/etw wickeln ⟨⟩ *vi* sich ringeln. ◆ **coil up** *vt sep* aufrollen.

coin [kɔɪn] ⟨⟩ *n* Münze *die* ⟨⟩ *vt* [invent] prägen.

coincide [ˌkəʊɪn'saɪd] *vi* - 1. [occur simultaneously]: **to - (with sthg)** (mit etw) zusammenfallen - 2. [be in agreement] übereinstimmen.

coincidence [kəʊ'ɪnsɪdəns] *n* Zufall *der*.

coincidental [kəʊˌɪnsɪ'dentl] *adj* zufällig.

coke [kəʊk] n - **1.** [fuel] Koks der - **2.** drugs sl [cocaine] Koks der.

cola ['kəʊlə] n Cola die OR das.

colander ['kʌləndə] n Sieb das.

cold [kəʊld] <> adj - **1.** [gen] kalt; **I'm ~** mir ist kalt - **2.** [unfriendly - eyes, smile, voice] kalt; [- person] gefühlskalt <> n - **1.** [illness] Erkältung die; **to catch (a) ~** sich erkälten - **2.** [low temperature] Kälte die.

cold-blooded [-'blʌdɪd] adj - **1.** [unfeeling - person] gefühllos; [- attitude] herzlos - **2.** [ruthless] kaltblütig.

cold sore n Bläschenausschlag der.

cold war n: **the ~** der Kalte Krieg.

coleslaw ['kəʊlslɔː] n (U) Krautsalat der.

collaborate [kə'læbəreɪt] vi - **1.** [work together]: **to ~ (with sb)** (mit jm) zusammenarbeiten - **2.** pej [with enemy]: **to ~ (with sb)** (mit jm) kollaborieren.

collapse [kə'læps] <> n - **1.** [destruction] Einsturz der - **2.** [failure - of marriage, government] Scheitern das; [- of empire] Untergang der; [- of system, business, company] Zusammenbruch der - **3.** MED Kollaps der <> vi - **1.** [fall down, fall in - house, building, roof] einIstürzen; [- stage, bridge] zusammenIbrechen; [- lung] zusammenIfallen; **I ~d into bed** ich ließ mich aufs Bett fallen - **2.** [fail - marriage, government] scheitern; [- system, business, company] zusammenIbrechen - **3.** MED kollabieren - **4.** [folding table, chair] sich zusammenklappen lassen.

collapsible [kə'læpsəbl] adj zusammenklappbar.

collar ['kɒlə] <> n - **1.** [on clothes] Kragen der - **2.** [for dog] Halsband das - **3.** TECH Bund der <> vt inf [detain] fassen.

collarbone ['kɒləbəʊn] n Schlüsselbein das.

collate [kə'leɪt] vt - **1.** [information, evidence] sammeln - **2.** [pages, photocopies] sortieren.

collateral [kə'lætərəl] n Sicherheit die.

colleague ['kɒliːg] n Kollege der, -gin die.

collect [kə'lekt] <> vt - **1.** [gen] sammeln; [empty glasses, bottles] einIsammeln; [dust] anIziehen; [one's belongings] zusammenIsuchen; [taxes] einIziehen; **to ~ o.s.** sich sammeln - **2.** [go to get, fetch] abIholen <> vi - **1.** [dust, dirt] sich anIsammeln - **2.** [for charity, gift] sammeln <> adv Am TELEC: **to call (sb) ~** ein R-Gespräch (mit jm) führen.

collection [kə'lekʃn] n - **1.** [gen] Sammlung die - **2.** (U) [of taxes] Einziehen das; [of rubbish] Abfuhr die; [of mail] Leerung die.

collective [kə'lektɪv] <> adj kollektiv <> n Produktionsgenossenschaft die.

collector [kə'lektə] n [as a hobby] Sammler der, -in die.

college ['kɒlɪdʒ] n - **1.** [for further education] ≈ Fachhochschule die; **~ of technology**

technische Hochschule - **2.** [of university] College das.

college of education n pädagogische Hochschule.

collide [kə'laɪd] vi: **to ~ (with sb/sthg)** (mit jm/etw) zusammenIstoßen.

colliery ['kɒljərɪ] n Kohlengrube die.

collision [kə'lɪʒn] n [crash]: **~ (with sb/sthg)** Zusammenstoß der (mit jm/etw), Kollision die (mit jm/etw); **to be on a ~ course with sb/ sthg** fig mit jm/etw auf Kollisionskurs sein.

colloquial [kə'ləʊkwɪəl] adj umgangssprachlich.

collude [kə'luːd] vi: **to ~ with sb** mit jm gemeinsame Sache machen.

Colombia [kə'lɒmbɪə] n Kolumbien nt.

colon ['kəʊlən] n - **1.** ANAT Dickdarm der - **2.** [punctuation mark] Doppelpunkt der.

colonel ['kɜːnl] n Oberst der.

colonial [kə'ləʊnjəl] adj kolonial-.

colonize, -ise ['kɒlənaɪz] vt kolonisieren.

colony ['kɒlənɪ] n Kolonie die.

color etc Am = colour etc.

colossal [kə'lɒsl] adj gewaltig.

colour Br, **color** Am ['kʌlə] <> n Farbe die; **in ~** in Farbe <> adj [not black and white] Farb- <> vt - **1.** [give colour to] färben; [with pen, crayon] kolorieren - **2.** fig [affect] beeinflussen <> vi [blush] erröten.

colour bar n Rassenschranke die.

colour-blind adj farbenblind.

coloured Br, **colored** Am ['kʌləd] adj farbig.

colourful Br, **colorful** Am ['kʌləful] adj - **1.** [brightly coloured] farbenfroh - **2.** [story] ereignisreich; [description] farbig - **3.** [person] schillernd.

colouring Br, **coloring** Am ['kʌlərɪŋ] n - **1.** [dye] Farbstoff der - **2.** [complexion] Gesichtsfarbe die; [of hair] Farbe die - **3.** [colours] Farben pl.

colour scheme n Farbzusammenstellung die.

colt [kəʊlt] n Hengstfohlen das.

column ['kɒləm] n - **1.** [structure, of smoke] Säule die - **2.** [of people, vehicles, numbers] Kolonne die - **3.** [of text] Spalte die - **4.** [article] Kolumne die.

columnist ['kɒləmnɪst] n Kolumnist der, -in die.

coma ['kəʊmə] n Koma das.

comb [kəʊm] <> n Kamm der <> vt - **1.** [hair] kämmen - **2.** [search] durchkämmen.

combat ['kɒmbæt] <> n Kampf der <> vt bekämpfen.

combination [ˌkɒmbɪ'neɪʃn] n - **1.** (U) [act of combining] Verbindung die - **2.** [mixture, for safe] Kombination die.

combine [vb kəm'baɪn, n 'kɒmbaɪn] <> vt

vereinigen; **to ~ sthg with sthg** [two substances, activities] etw mit etw verbinden; [two qualities] etw mit etw vereinigen ◇ vi [businesses, political parties]: **to ~ (with sb/sthg)** sich (mit jm/etw) zusammen|schließen ◇ n [group] Firmengruppe die.

combined [kəm'baɪnd] adj: **~ with sb/sthg** zusammen mit jm/etw; **~ efforts** vereinte Anstrengungen pl; **~ attack** gemeinsamer Angriff.

come [kʌm] (pt came; pp come) vi - **1.** [move] kommen; **~ here!** komm her!; **coming!** ich komme schon! - **2.** [arrive] kommen; **to ~ home** nach Hause kommen; **the news came as a shock (to him)** die Nachricht war ein Schock (für ihn) - **3.** [in competition, in order]: **to ~ first/last** Erster/Letzter werden; **P ~s before Q** P kommt vor Q - **4.** [become] werden; **to ~ true** wahr werden; **to ~ undone** aufgehen - **5.** [be sold]: **they ~ in packs of six** es gibt sie im Sechserpack - **6.** [happen]: **~ what may** was auch geschehen - **7.** [begin gradually]: **we have ~ to think that ...** wir sind zu der Ansicht gekommen, dass ...; **he has ~ to like Baltimore** inzwischen gefällt ihm Baltimore recht gut - **8.** inf [have orgasm] kommen - **9.** phr: **~ to think of it ...** wenn ich es mir recht überlege ... ◆ **to come** adv: **for generations to ~** auf Generationen hin; **in years to ~ we will look back on today with pride** wir werden später mit Stolz auf diesen Tag zurückblicken. ◆ **come about** vi [happen] geschehen; **how did it ~ about?** wie ist es dazu gekommen? ◆ **come across** vt fus [find] stoßen auf (+ A). ◆ **come along** vi - **1.** [arrive] kommen - **2.** [progress] voran|kommen. ◆ **come apart** vi auseinander fallen. ◆ **come at** vt fus [attack] los|gehen auf (+ A). ◆ **come back** vi - **1.** [gen] zurück|kommen; **to ~ back to sthg** auf etw (A) zurück|kommen - **2.** [memory]: **it will ~ back to me in a minute** es wird mir gleich einfallen. ◆ **come by** vt fus [get, obtain]: **to ~ by sthg** an etw (A) kommen; **they are hard to ~ by** sie sind schwer zu finden. ◆ **come down** vi - **1.** [price, rain] fallen - **2.** [descend] herunter|kommen. ◆ **come down to** vt fus: **it ~s down to a choice between money and happiness** es läuft auf eine Entscheidung zwischen Geld und Glück hinaus; **it all ~s down to profitability** letztlich ist die Rentabilität entscheidend. ◆ **come down with** vt fus [illness] bekommen. ◆ **come forward** vi sich melden. ◆ **come from** vt fus - **1.** [person]: **I ~ from Ireland** ich komme aus Irland; **my family ~s from Belgium** meine Familie stammt aus Belgien - **2.** [originate from]: **caviar ~s from sturgeon** Kaviar stammt vom Stör; **where is that noise coming from?** woher kommt dieses Geräusch? ◆ **come in**

vi - **1.** [enter] herein|kommen; **~ in!** herein! - **2.** [finish race] an|kommen; **to ~ in first** Erste/Erster werden. ◆ **come in for** vt fus [criticism] einstecken müssen. ◆ **come into** vt fus - **1.** [inherit] erben - **2.** [begin to be]: **to ~ into being** entstehen. ◆ **come off** vi - **1.** [button, top] ab|gehen - **2.** [succeed] klappen - **3.** [dirt, mud] ab|gehen - **4.** phr: **~ off it!** inf hör doch auf! ◆ **come on** vi - **1.** [start] an|fangen; **the rain came on** es fing an zu regnen - **2.** [start working - light, machine] an|gehen - **3.** [progress] voran|kommen - **4.** phr: **~ on!** [as encouragement, hurry up] komm!; [in disbelief] hör doch auf! ◆ **come out** vi - **1.** [become known] heraus|kommen - **2.** [appear - book, record] erscheinen; [- stars] zu sehen sein - **3.** [go on strike] streiken - **4.** [declare publicly]: **to ~ out for/against sthg** sich für/gegen etw aus|sprechen - **5.** [stain] heraus|gehen. ◆ **come out with** vt fus [idea] an|kommen mit; [remark] machen. ◆ **come round** vi - **1.** [visit] vorbei|kommen - **2.** [regain consciousness] zu sich kommen. ◆ **come through** ◇ vt fus [war, illness, difficult situation] überstehen ◇ vi [survive] durch|kommen. ◆ **come to** ◇ vt fus - **1.** [reach]: **to ~ to an end** zu Ende gehen; **to ~ to a decision** zu einer Entscheidung kommen - **2.** [amount to]: **the bill ~s to £20** das macht 20 Pfund ◇ vi [regain consciousness] zu sich kommen. ◆ **come under** vt fus - **1.** [be governed by - jurisdiction, rules] fallen unter (+ A); **to ~ under sb's influence** unter js Einfluss geraten - **2.** [suffer]: **to ~ under attack (from)** angegriffen werden (von). ◆ **come up** vi - **1.** [go upstairs] herauf|kommen - **2.** [be mentioned] erwähnt werden; **to ~ up for discussion** zur Diskussion kommen - **3.** [happen] passieren - **4.** [job] frei werden - **5.** [sun, moon] auf|gehen - **6.** [be imminent] bevor|stehen; **my birthday is coming up** ich habe bald Geburtstag. ◆ **come up against** vt fus [difficulties, obstacles] stoßen auf (+ A); [opponent] treffen auf (+ A). ◆ **come up to** vt fus - **1.** [approach - person, object] kommen zu; **it's coming up to Christmas/six o'clock** es ist bald Weihnachten/gleich sechs Uhr - **2.** [reach]: **the water ~s up to my waist** das Wasser reicht mir bis zur Taille. ◆ **come up with** vt fus [answer, idea, solution] sich (D) aus|denken.

comeback ['kʌmbæk] n [of person] Comeback das; **to make a ~** [person] ein Comeback schaffen; [activity, style] wieder in Mode kommen.

comedian [kə'miːdjən] n Komiker der, -in die.

comedown ['kʌmdaʊn] n inf Abstieg der.

comedy ['kɒmədɪ] n - **1.** [play, film] Komödie die - **2.** [humour] Komik die.

comet ['kɒmɪt] n Komet der.

come-uppance [ˌkʌmˈʌpəns] n inf: **to get one's ~** die Quittung kriegen.

comfort ['kʌmfət] <> n - 1. [ease] Behaglichkeit die - 2. [luxury] Komfort der - 3. [solace] Trost der; **to take ~ from sthg** Trost in etw (D) finden <> vt trösten.

comfortable ['kʌmftəbl] adj - 1. [chair, shoes, sofa, life] bequem; [house, hotel, coach] komfortabel - 2. [at ease]: **to be ~** sich wohl fühlen; **make yourself ~** machen Sie es sich bequem - 3. [financially secure - income] ausreichend; **to be ~** keine finanziellen Sorgen haben - 4. [after operation, accident]: **his condition is ~** ihm geht es (den Umständen entsprechend) gut - 5. [lead] sicher; [victory] leicht.

comfortably ['kʌmftəblɪ] adv - 1. [sit] bequem; [sleep] gut - 2. [without financial difficulty] bequem - 3. [win] mühelos.

comfort station n Am euphemism Bedürfnisanstalt die.

comic ['kɒmɪk] <> adj komisch <> n - 1. [comedian] Komiker der, -in die - 2. [magazine] Comicheft das.

comical ['kɒmɪkl] adj ulkig, komisch.

comic strip n Comicstrip der.

coming ['kʌmɪŋ] <> adj [future] kommend <> n: **~s and goings** Kommen und Gehen das.

comma ['kɒmə] n Komma das.

command [kəˈmɑːnd] <> n - 1. [order] Befehl der; MIL Kommando das - 2. (U) [control] Kommando das - 3. [mastery] Beherrschung die; **to have sthg at one's ~** etw zur Verfügung haben - 4. COMPUT Befehl der <> vt - 1. [order]: **to ~ sb (to do sthg)** jm befehlen(, etw zu tun) - 2. MIL [control] befehligen - 3. [deserve - respect, attention, admiration] verdienen.

commandeer [ˌkɒmənˈdɪər] vt MIL beschlagnahmen.

commander [kəˈmɑːndər] n - 1. [in army] Kommandant der, Befehlshaber der - 2. [in navy] Fregattenkapitän der.

commando [kəˈmɑːndəʊ] (pl -s OR -es) n - 1. [unit] Kommandotrupp der - 2. [soldier] Angehörige der, die eines Kommandotrupps.

commemorate [kəˈmeməreɪt] vt - 1. [honour] gedenken (+ G) - 2. [subj: statue, plaque] erinnern an (+ A).

commemoration [kəˌmeməˈreɪʃn] n: **in ~ of** zum Gedenken an (+ A).

commence [kəˈmens] fml <> vt beginnen; **to ~ doing sthg** (damit) beginnen, etw zu tun <> vi beginnen.

commend [kəˈmend] vt - 1. [praise]: **to ~ sb (on OR for sthg)** jn (wegen etw) loben - 2. [recommend]: **to ~ sthg (to sb)** (jm) etw empfehlen.

commensurate [kəˈmensərət] adj fml: **to be ~ with sthg** etw (D) entsprechen.

comment ['kɒment] <> n Bemerkung die; **no ~** kein Kommentar <> vt: **to ~ that** ... bemerken OR äußern, dass ... <> vi: **to ~ (on sthg)** sich (über etw (A)) äußern.

commentary ['kɒməntrɪ] n - 1. RADIO & TV Livereportage die - 2. [written] Kommentar der.

commentator ['kɒmənteɪtər] n RADIO & TV Reporter der, -in die.

commerce ['kɒmɜːs] n Handel der.

commercial [kəˈmɜːʃl] <> adj - 1. [regarding business - law, organization] Handels-; [- premises] Geschäfts- - 2. [profit-making] kommerziell <> n [advert] Werbespot der.

commercial break n Werbepause die.

commiserate [kəˈmɪzəreɪt] vi: **to ~ (with sb)** (jm) sein Mitgefühl ausⅼsprechen.

commission [kəˈmɪʃn] <> n - 1. (U) [money] Provision die - 2. [piece of work] Auftrag der - 3. [investigative body] Kommission die <> vt [work] in Auftrag geben; **to ~ sb to do sthg** jn damit beauftragt(, etw zu tun).

commissionaire [kəˌmɪʃəˈneər] n Br Portier der.

commissioner [kəˈmɪʃnər] n [of police] Präsident der, -in die.

commit [kəˈmɪt] vt - 1. [crime, sin] begehen - 2. [money, resources]: **to ~ sthg to sthg** etw für etw bestimmen; **to ~ o.s. (to sthg)** sich (auf etw (A)) festlegen; **to ~ o.s. to doing sthg** sich verpflichten, etw zu tun - 3. [consign] einⅼweisen; **to ~ sthg to memory** sich (D) etw merken.

commitment [kəˈmɪtmənt] n - 1. [dedication] Engagement das - 2. [responsibility] Verpflichtung die.

committee [kəˈmɪtɪ] n Ausschuss der.

commodity [kəˈmɒdətɪ] n [product] Produkt das.

common ['kɒmən] <> adj - 1. [ordinary, widespread] häufig; [practice] weit verbreitet; **the ~ cold** die Erkältung; **the ~ man** der Normalbürger - 2. [shared] gemeinsam; **it's ~ to us all** es ist uns allen gemein - 3. Br pej [vulgar] gewöhnlich <> n [land] Gemeinde die. ◆ **in common** adv gemein; **we've got a lot in ~** wir haben viel gemein.

common-law adj: **she is his common-law wife** sie lebt mit ihm in eheähnlicher Gemeinschaft.

commonly ['kɒmənlɪ] adv [generally] allgemein.

Common Market n: **the ~** der Gemeinsame Markt.

commonplace ['kɒmənpleɪs] adj alltäglich.

common room n Aufenthaltsraum der.

Commons ['kɒmənz] npl Br: **the ~** das (britische) Unterhaus.

common sense *n* gesunder Menschenverstand.

Commonwealth ['kɒmənwelθ] *n:* **the ~** das Commonwealth.

commotion [kə'məʊʃn] *n* [activity] Aufregung *die;* [noise] Lärm *der;* **to cause a ~** für Aufregung sorgen.

communal ['kɒmjʊnl] *adj* [kitchen] Gemeinschafts-; [garden, ownership] gemeinsam.

commune ['kɒmjuːn] *n* Kommune *die.*

communicate [kə'mjuːnɪkeɪt] <> *vt* mitteilen <> *vi* sich verständigen; **to ~ with** kommunizieren mit.

communication [kə,mjuːnɪ'keɪʃn] *n* - **1.** (U) [contact] Kommunikation *die;* **to be in ~ with sb** Kontakt mit jm haben - **2.** [letter, phone call] Mitteilung *die.*

communication cord *n Br* Notbremse *die.*

Communion [kə'mjuːnjən] *n* [Protestant] Abendmahl *das;* [Catholic] Kommunion *die.*

Communism ['kɒmjʊnɪzm] *n* Kommunismus *der.*

Communist ['kɒmjʊnɪst] <> *adj* kommunistisch <> *n* Kommunist *der,* -in *die.*

community [kə'mjuːnətɪ] *n* - **1.** [group] Gemeinschaft *die;* [local] Gemeinde *die;* [ethnic] Bevölkerungsgruppe *die* - **2.** [people in general]: **the ~** die Gesellschaft.

community centre *n* Gemeindezentrum *das.*

commutation ticket [,kɒmjuː'teɪʃn] *n Am* Zeitnetzkarte *die.*

commute [kə'mjuːt] <> *vt* LAW umwandeln <> *vi* [to work] pendeln.

commuter [kə'mjuːtəʳ] *n* Pendler *der,* -in *die.*

compact [*adj* kəm'pækt, *n* 'kɒmpækt] <> *adj* kompakt; [style, text] gedrängt <> *n* - **1.** [for face powder] Puderdose *die* - **2.** *Am* AUT: **~ (car)** Kompaktauto *das.*

compact disc *n* Compactdisc *die.*

compact disc player *n* CD-Player *der.*

companion [kəm'pænjən] *n* [person] Gefährte *der,* -tin *die.*

companionship [kəm'pænjənʃɪp] *n (U)* Gesellschaft *die.*

company ['kʌmpənɪ] *n* - **1.** [business] Firma *die;* **insurance ~** Versicherung *die* - **2.** [of actors] Schauspieltruppe *die* - **3.** (U) [companionship] Gesellschaft *die;* **she's good ~** es ist schön, mit ihr zusammen zu sein; **to keep sb ~** jm Gesellschaft leisten - **4.** [guests] Besuch *der* - **5.** MIL Kompanie *die* - **6.** NAUT Besatzung *die.*

comparable ['kɒmprəbl] *adj:* **~ (to** OR **with)** vergleichbar (mit).

comparative [kəm'pærətɪv] *adj* - **1.** [relative] relativ - **2.** [study, literature] vergleichend - **3.** GRAMM: **~ form** Komparativ *der.*

comparatively [kəm'pærətɪvlɪ] *adv* [relatively] relativ, verhältnismäßig.

compare [kəm'peəʳ] <> *vt* vergleichen; **to ~ sb/sthg with** OR **to** jn/etw vergleichen mit; **~d with** OR **to** verglichen mit, im Vergleich zu <> *vi:* **to ~ (with sb/sthg)** sich (mit jm/etw) vergleichen lassen.

comparison [kəm'pærɪsn] *n* Vergleich *der;* **in ~ (with** OR **to)** im Vergleich (zu).

making comparisons

Er ist mindestens so alt wie sie. He's at least as old as she is.

Wir sind gleich alt. We're the same age.

Er arbeitet nur halb so viel wie sein Kollege. He only works half as much as his colleague.

Im Vergleich zu damals ist sie heute richtig dynamisch. Compared with what she was like then, she's full of energy these days.

Sie hat die gleiche Art wie ihre Mutter. She's just like her mother.

compartment [kəm'pɑːtmənt] *n* - **1.** [in fridge, desk, drawer] Fach *das* - **2.** RAIL Abteil *das.*

compass ['kʌmpəs] *n* [for finding direction] Kompass *der.* **◆ compasses** *npl:* **(a pair of) ~es** ein Zirkel.

compassion [kəm'pæʃn] *n* Mitgefühl *das.*

compassionate [kəm'pæʃənət] *adj* mitfühlend.

compatible [kəm'pætəbl] *adj* - **1.** [people]: **to be ~** zueinander passen - **2.** COMPUT kompatibel.

compel [kəm'pel] *vt* [force] zwingen; **to ~ sb to do sthg** jn (dazu) zwingen, etw zu tun.

compelling [kəm'pelɪŋ] *adj* zwingend.

compensate ['kɒmpenseɪt] <> *vt:* **to ~ sb for sthg** [financially] jn für etw entschädigen <> *vi:* **to ~ for sthg** etw gutmachen.

compensation [,kɒmpen'seɪʃn] *n:* **~ (for sthg)** Entschädigung *die* (für etw).

compete [kəm'piːt] *vi* - **1.** [vie]: **to ~ (for sthg)** (um etw) kämpfen - **2.** COMM: **to ~ (with sb/sthg)** (mit jm/etw) konkurrieren; **to ~ for sthg** [contract, business] um etw kämpfen - **3.** [take part] teilnehmen.

competence ['kɒmpɪtəns] *n* Fähigkeit *die.*

competent ['kɒmpɪtənt] *adj* fähig.

competition [,kɒmpɪ'tɪʃn] *n* - **1.** [rivalry & COMM] Konkurrenz *die* - **2.** [race, contest] Wettbewerb *der.*

competitive [kəm'petətɪv] *adj* - **1.** [person] vom Konkurrenzdenken geprägt - **2.** [exam] Auswahl-; [sport] Wettkampf- - **3.** COMM [goods, prices, company] konkurrenzfähig.

competitor [kəm'petɪtəʳ] *n* - **1.** COMM Konkurrent *der*, -in *die* - **2.** [in race, contest] Teilnehmer *der*, -in *die*.

compile [kəm'paɪl] *vt* [programme, album] zusammen|stellen; [book, report] ab|fassen.

complacency [kəm'pleɪsnsɪ] *n* Selbstzufriedenheit *die*.

complain [kəm'pleɪn] *vi* - **1.** [moan]: **to ~ (about)** sich beschweren (über (+ A)) - **2.** MED: **to ~ of sthg** über etw (A) klagen.

complaint [kəm'pleɪnt] *n* - **1.** [gen] Beschwerde *die*; **to have no ~s** [be satisfied] sich nicht beklagen können - **2.** MED Leiden *das*.

complement [*n* 'komplɪmənt, *vb* 'komplɪ,ment] *vt* gut ergänzen; [food] vervollkommnen <> *n* [accompaniment & GRAMM] Ergänzung *die*.

complementary [,komplɪ'mentərɪ] *adj* [colour] (einander) ergänzend.

complete [kəm'pliːt] <> *adj* - **1.** [entire] vollständig; **- with** komplett mit - **2.** [finished] abgeschlossen, fertig - **3.** [total - disaster, surprise] völlig; **she was a ~ stranger to me** sie war mir völlig fremd <> *vt* - **1.** [make whole] vervollständigen - **2.** [finish] beenden - **3.** [questionnaire, form] aus|füllen.

completely [kəm'pliːtlɪ] *adv* vollkommen.

completion [kəm'pliːʃn] *n* [finishing] Beendigung *die*.

complex ['kompleks] <> *adj* [complicated] kompliziert <> *n* - **1.** [of buildings] (Gebäude)komplex *der* - **2.** PSYCH Komplex *der*.

complexion [kəm'plekʃn] *n* - **1.** [of face] Teint *der* - **2.** [aspect] Aspekt *der*.

compliance [kəm'plaɪəns] *n* Einverständnis *das*; **~ with sthg** [with rules] Einhalten *das* einer Sache (G).

complicate ['komplɪkeɪt] *vt* komplizieren.

complicated ['komplɪkeɪtɪd] *adj* kompliziert.

complication [,komplɪ'keɪʃn] *n* - **1.** [complexity] Kompliziertheit *die* - **2.** MED Komplikation *die*.

compliment [*n* 'komplɪmənt, *vb* 'komplɪ,ment] <> *n* Kompliment *das* <> *vt*: **to ~ sb (on sthg)** jm ein Kompliment/Komplimente (wegen etw (G)) machen.

➡ **compliments** *npl fml*: **with ~s** mit den besten Empfehlungen; **my ~s to the chef!** mein Kompliment an den Küchenchef!

complimentary [,komplɪ'mentərɪ] *adj* - **1.** [admiring] schmeichelhaft; **to be ~** [person] sich bewundernd äußern - **2.** [drink] Frei-.

complimentary ticket *n* Freikarte *die*.

comply [kəm'plaɪ] *vi*: **to ~ with sthg** [contract] etw erfüllen; [request] etw (D) nach|kommen; [law, standards] etw ein|halten.

component [kəm'pəʊnənt] *n* Teil *das*.

compose [kəm'pəʊz] *vt* - **1.** [constitute] bilden; **to be ~d of sthg** sich aus etw zusammen|setzen - **2.** [poem] verfassen;

[music] komponieren; [letter] ab|fassen - **3.** [make calm]: **to ~ o.s.** sich fassen.

composed [kəm'pəʊzd] *adj* [calm] beherrscht, gelassen.

composer [kəm'pəʊzər] *n* Komponist *der*, -in *die*.

composition [,kompə'zɪʃn] *n* - **1.** [piece of music] Komposition *die* - **2.** [contents] Zusammensetzung *die* - **3.** [essay] Aufsatz *der*.

compost [*Br* 'kompost, *Am* 'kompəʊst] *n* Kompost *der*.

composure [kəm'pəʊʒər] *n* Beherrschung *die*, Fassung *die*.

compound ['kompaʊnd] *n* - **1.** CHEM Verbindung *die* - **2.** [mixture] Mischung *die* - **3.** [enclosed area] umzäuntes Gelände - **4.** GRAMM zusammengesetztes Wort.

comprehend [,komprɪ'hend] *vt* [understand] begreifen, verstehen.

comprehension [,komprɪ'henʃn] *n* Verständnis *das*; **it's beyond my ~** es ist mir unbegreiflich.

comprehensive [,komprɪ'hensɪv] *adj* - **1.** [wide-ranging] umfassend - **2.** [insurance] Vollkasko-.

comprehensive (school) *n Br* Gesamtschule *die*.

📖 **comprehensive school**

Die heute am meisten verbreitete weiterführende Schule in Großbritannien wird von ca. 87% aller Kinder über elf Jahren besucht. Anders als die Grammar Schools, deren Besuch an Aufnahmeprüfungen gebunden ist, stehen die Comprehensives Schülern jeder Leistungs- und Eignungsstufe offen. Dieser Schultyp entspricht etwa der deutschen Gesamtschule.

compress [*n* 'kompres, *vb* kəm'pres] <> *n* MED Kompresse *die* <> *vt* - **1.** [squeeze] zusammen|pressen; **~ed air** Pressluft *die* - **2.** [text] kürzen.

comprise [kəm'praɪz] *vt* - **1.** [consist of]: **to be ~d of** bestehen aus - **2.** [constitute] bilden.

compromise ['komprəmaɪz] <> *n* Kompromiss *der* <> *vt* kompromittieren <> *vi* einen Kompromiss schließen.

compulsion [kəm'pʌlʃn] *n* Zwang *der*.

compulsive [kəm'pʌlsɪv] *adj* [behaviour, gambler, liar] zwanghaft.

compulsory [kəm'pʌlsərɪ] *adj* [retirement] Zwangs-; **it is ~ to do sthg** es ist Pflicht, etw zu tun; **attendance is ~** die Teilnahme ist verpflichtend.

computer [kəm'pjuːtər] <> *n* Computer *der* <> *comp* Computer-.

computer game *n* Computerspiel *das*.

computerized [kəm'pjuːtəraɪzd] *adj* computerisiert.

computer science *n* Informatik *die*.

computing [kəm'pjuːtɪŋ] *n* elektronische Datenverarbeitung; [subject] Informatik *die*.

comrade ['kɒmreɪd] *n* - **1.** POL Genosse *der*, -sin *die* - **2.** [companion] Kamerad *der*, -in *die*.

con [kɒn] *inf* ⟨⟩ *n* [trick] Schwindel *der* ⟨⟩ *vt* [trick] reinlegen; **to ~ sb out of sthg** jn um etw bringen; **to ~ sb into doing sthg** jn durch einen Trick dazu bringen, etw zu tun.

concave [ˌkɒn'keɪv] *adj* konkav.

conceal [kən'siːl] *vt:* **to ~ sthg (from sb)** [object] etw (vor jm) verstecken; [feelings, information] etw (vor jm) verbergen.

concede [kən'siːd] *vt* [a point] zulgeben; [defeat] einlgestehen.

conceit [kən'siːt] *n* Arroganz *die*.

conceited [kən'siːtɪd] *adj* eingebildet.

conceive [kən'siːv] ⟨⟩ *vt* - **1.** [plan, idea] sich *(D)* ausldenken - **2.** MED [child] empfangen ⟨⟩ *vi* - **1.** MED empfangen - **2.** [imagine]: **to ~ of sthg** sich *(D)* etw vorlstellen.

concentrate ['kɒnsəntreɪt] ⟨⟩ *vt* konzentrieren ⟨⟩ *vi:* **to ~ (on)** sich konzentrieren (auf *(+ A)*).

concentration [ˌkɒnsən'treɪʃn] *n* Konzentration *die*.

concentration camp *n* Konzentrationslager *das*, KZ *das*.

concept ['kɒnsept] *n* [idea] Vorstellung *die;* [principle] Konzept *das*.

concern [kən'sɜːn] ⟨⟩ *n* - **1.** [worry] Besorgnis *die;* [cause of worry] Sorge *die;* **to show ~ for sb/sthg** sich um jn/etw Gedanken machen - **2.** COMM [company] Unternehmen *das* ⟨⟩ *vt* - **1.** [worry] beunruhigen; **to be ~ed (about)** besorgt sein (um) - **2.** [involve] anlgehen; **to be ~ed with sthg** [subj: person] mit etw zu tun haben; **to ~ o.s. with sthg** sich mit etw befassen; **as far as I'm ~ed** was mich betrifft - **3.** [subj: book, film] handeln von.

concerning [kən'sɜːnɪŋ] *prep* bezüglich *(+ G)*.

concert ['kɒnsət] *n* Konzert *das*.

concerted [kən'sɜːtɪd] *adj* [effort] vereint.

concert hall *n* Konzerthalle *die*.

concertina [ˌkɒnsə'tiːnə] *n* Konzertina *die*.

concerto [kən'tʃɜːtəʊ] *(pl* -s*) n* Konzert *das*.

concession [kən'seʃn] *n* - **1.** [allowance] Zugeständnis *das* - **2.** COMM [franchise] Konzession *die* - **3.** [special price] Preisermäßigung *die*.

concise [kən'saɪs] *adj* präzis(e), exakt.

conclude [kən'kluːd] ⟨⟩ *vt* - **1.** [end] beenden - **2.** [deduce]: **to ~ (that)** ... schließen(, dass) ..., folgern(, dass) ... - **3.** [agreement, deal] ablschließen ⟨⟩ *vi* [finish] enden, schließen.

conclusion [kən'kluːʒn] *n* - **1.** [opinion] Schlussfolgerung *die* - **2.** [ending] Abschluss *der* - **3.** [of agreement, deal] Abschluss *der*.

conclusive [kən'kluːsɪv] *adj* eindeutig.

concoct [kən'kɒkt] *vt* - **1.** [story, excuse, alibi] sich *(D)* auslkenken - **2.** [meal] kreieren; [drink] zusammenlbrauen.

concoction [kən'kɒkʃn] *n* [meal] selbst kreiertes Gericht; [drink] Gebräu *das*.

concourse ['kɒŋkɔːs] *n* [hall] Eingangshalle *die*.

concrete ['kɒŋkriːt] ⟨⟩ *adj lit & fig* konkret ⟨⟩ *n* Beton *der* ⟨⟩ *comp* [made of concrete] Beton-.

concur [kən'kɜːr] *vi* [agree]: **to ~ (with sthg)** (etw *(D)*) zulstimmen.

concurrently [kən'kʌrəntlɪ] *adv* gleichzeitig.

concussion [kən'kʌʃn] *n* Gehirnerschütterung *die*.

condemn [kən'dem] *vt* - **1.** [disapprove of]: **to ~ sb (for sthg)** jn (wegen etw *(G)*) verurteilen - **2.** [force] verdammen - **3.** LAW [sentence]: **to ~ sb to sthg** jn zu etw verurteilen - **4.** [building] für unbewohnbar erklären.

condensation [ˌkɒnden'seɪʃn] *n* [on windows *etc*] Kondenswasser *das*.

condense [kən'dens] *vt* [text] zusammenlfassen.

condensed milk [kən'denst-] *n* Kondensmilch *die*.

condescending [ˌkɒndɪ'sendɪŋ] *adj* herablassend.

condition [kən'dɪʃn] ⟨⟩ *n* - **1.** [of object, building] Zustand *der;* [of person, patient] Verfassung *die;* **out of ~** schlecht in Form - **2.** MED [illness] Leiden *das* - **3.** [requirement] Bedingung *die*, Voraussetzung *die;* **on ~ that** ... unter der Bedingung, dass ... ⟨⟩ *vt* - **1.** PSYCH konditionieren - **2.** [determine] bestimmen - **3.** [hair] pflegen.

conditional [kən'dɪʃənl] ⟨⟩ *adj* [provisional] vorbehaltlich ⟨⟩ *n* GRAMM Konditional *der*.

conditioner [kən'dɪʃnər] *n* - **1.** [for hair] Pflegespülung *die* - **2.** [for clothes] Weichspüler *der*.

condolences [kən'dəʊlənsɪz] *npl* Beileid *das*.

condom ['kɒndəm] *n* Kondom *das* OR *der*.

condominium [ˌkɒndə'mɪnɪəm] *n Am* - **1.** [apartment] Eigentumswohnung *die* - **2.** [building] Apartmenthaus *das*.

condone [kən'dəʊn] *vt* hinweglsehen über *(+ A)*.

conducive [kən'djuːsɪv] *adj:* **to be ~ to sthg** einer Sache *(D)* förderlich sein.

conduct [*n* 'kɒndʌkt *vb* kən'dʌkt] ⟨⟩ *n* - **1.** [behaviour] Verhalten *das* - **2.** [of business, talks] Durchführung *die* ⟨⟩ *vt* - **1.** [carry out] durchlführen - **2.** [behave]: **to ~ o.s. well/badly** sich gut/schlecht benehmen - **3.** MUS dirigieren - **4.** PHYS [heat, electricity] leiten.

conducted tour [kən'dʌktɪd-] *n* Führung *die*.

conductor [kən'dʌktər] *n* - **1.** MUS Dirigent

der, -in die - 2. [on bus] Schaffner der - 3. Am [on train] Zugführer der.

cone [kəʊn] n - 1. [shape] Kegel der - 2. [for ice cream] Eistüte die - 3. [from tree] Zapfen der - 4. [on roads] Pylon der, Pylone die.

confectionery [kən'fekʃnəri] n (U) Süßwaren pl.

confederation [kən,fedə'reiʃn] n Bund der.

confer [kən'fɜː'] <> vt fml: **to ~ sthg (on sb)** [title, degree] (jm) etw verleihen <> vi: **to ~ (with sb on OR about sthg)** sich (mit jm über etw (A)) beraten.

conference ['kɒnfərəns] n Konferenz die.

confess [kən'fes] <> vt - 1. RELIG beichten - 2. [admit] gestehen <> vi [admit]: **to ~ (to sthg)** (etw) gestehen.

confession [kən'feʃn] n - 1. [of guilt] Geständnis das - 2. (U) RELIG Beichte die.

confetti [kən'feti] n (U) Konfetti pl.

confide [kən'faid] vi: **to ~ in sb** sich jm anlvertrauen.

confidence ['kɒnfidəns] n - 1. (U) [self-assurance] Selbstvertrauen das - 2. (U) [trust] Vertrauen das; **to have ~ in sb** Vertrauen zu jm haben - 3. [secrecy]: **in ~** im Vertrauen - 4. [secret] vertrauliche Information.

confidence trick n Schwindel der.

confident ['kɒnfidənt] adj - 1. [self-assured] selbstbewusst - 2. [sure] überzeugt; **to be ~ of sthg** von etw überzeugt sein.

confidential [,kɒnfi'denʃl] adj vertraulich.

confine [kən'fain] vt beschränken; **to be ~d to** beschränkt sein auf (+ A); **to ~ o.s. to sthg** sich auf etw (A) beschränken; **to ~ o.s. to doing sthg** sich darauf beschränken, etw zu tun. ◆ **confines** npl Grenzen pl.

confined [kən'faind] adj [space, area] beschränkt.

confinement [kən'fainmənt] n [state of imprisonment] Haft die.

confirm [kən'fɜːm] vt - 1. [gen] bestätigen - 2. RELIG konfirmieren; [Roman Catholic] firmen.

confirmation [,kɒnfə'meiʃn] n (U) - 1. [ratification] Bestätigung die - 2. RELIG Konfirmation die; [of Roman Catholic] Firmung die.

confirmed [kən'fɜːmd] adj [bachelor, spinster] überzeugt.

confiscate ['kɒnfiskeit] vt beschlagnahmen, konfiszieren.

conflict [n 'kɒnflikt, vb kən'flikt] <> n Konflikt der <> vi [clash] sich (D) widersprechen; **to ~ with sb/sthg** im Widerspruch zu jm/etw stehen.

conflicting [kən'fliktiŋ] adj widersprüchlich.

conform [kən'fɔːm] vi - 1. [behave as expected] sich anlpassen - 2. [be in accordance]: **to ~ (to OR with sthg)** sich (nach etw (D)) richten.

confound [kən'faund] vt [confuse] verblüffen.

confront [kən'frʌnt] vt - 1. [opponent, enemy, problem] sich stellen (+ D); **to be ~ed with a problem** mit einem Problem konfrontiert werden; **the problem that ~s us** das Problem, das sich uns stellt - 2. [present]: **to ~ sb (with sthg)** jn (mit etw) konfrontieren.

confrontation [,kɒnfrʌn'teiʃn] n Konfrontation die, Auseinandersetzung die.

confuse [kən'fjuːz] vt - 1. [bewilder] verwirren - 2. [mix up]: **to ~ sb/sthg (with)** jn/etw verwechseln (mit) - 3. [complicate - situation] verworren machen.

confused [kən'fjuːzd] adj [person] verwirrt; [ideas, thoughts, situation] verworren; **to get ~** konfus werden.

confusing [kən'fjuːziŋ] adj verwirrend.

confusion [kən'fjuːʒn] n - 1. [perplexity] Verwirrung die - 2. [mixing up] Verwechslung die - 3. [bewilderment] Verlegenheit die - 4. [disorder] Durcheinander das.

congeal [kən'dʒiːl] vi [blood] gerinnen; [food] fest werden.

congenial [kən'dʒiːnjəl] adj angenehm.

congested [kən'dʒestid] adj [roads, nose] verstopft.

congestion [kən'dʒestʃn] n (U) - 1. [overcrowding] Stau der - 2. MED Blutandrang der.

conglomerate [kən'glɒmərət] n COMM Großkonzern der (aus mehreren Firmen bestehend).

congratulate [kən'grætʃuleit] vt: **to ~ sb (on sthg)** jm (zu etw) gratulieren.

congratulations [kən,grætʃu'leiʃənz] <> npl Glückwunsch der, Glückwünsche pl <> excl herzlichen Glückwunsch!

congregate ['kɒŋgrigeit] vi [people] sich versammeln; [animals] sich sammeln.

congregation [,kɒŋgri'geiʃn] n RELIG Gemeinde die.

congress ['kɒŋgres] n [meeting] Kongress der. ◆ **Congress** n Am POL der Kongress.

📖 Congress

Der Kongress, das Gesetzgebungsorgan der USA, besteht aus zwei Häusern: dem Senate (Senat) und dem House of Representatives (Repräsentantenhaus). Gesetzesvorlagen müssen separat von beiden Häusern verabschiedet werden, um Gesetzeskraft zu erlangen. Ein Amtsenthebungsverfahren (Impeachment) gegen einen US-Präsidenten kann nur durch den Kongress betrieben werden (die Anklage muss durch das Repräsentantenhaus erhoben werden, das eigentliche Verfahren obliegt dem Senat). Der Kongress hat auch die Befugnis, die amerikanische Verfassung zu ändern.

congressman ['kɒŋgresmən] (*pl* -men [-mən]) *n Am* POL Kongressabgeordnete *der.*

conifer ['kɒnɪfər] *n* Nadelbaum *der.*

conjugation [ˌkɒndʒʊ'geɪʃn] *n* GRAMM Konjugation *die.*

conjunction [kən'dʒʌŋkʃn] *n* - 1. GRAMM Konjunktion *die* - 2. [combination] Verbindung *die;* [of events] Zusammentreffen *das.*

conjunctivitis [kənˌdʒʌŋktɪ'vaɪtɪs] *n* (U) Bindehautentzündung *die.*

conjure ['kʌndʒər] ◆ **conjure up** *vt sep* [evoke] heraufbeschwören.

conjurer ['kʌndʒərər] *n* Zauberer *der,* -in *die.*

conjuror ['kʌndʒərər] *n* = conjurer.

conker ['kɒŋkər] *n Br* (Ross)kastanie *die.*

conman ['kɒnmæn] (*pl* -men [-men]) *n* Betrüger *der.*

connect [kə'nekt] ◇ *vt* - 1. [join]: **to ~ sthg (to sthg)** etw (mit etw) verbinden - 2. [on telephone] verbinden - 3. [associate] in Verbindung OR Zusammenhang bringen; **to ~ sb/sthg to, to ~ sb/sthg with** jn/etw in Verbindung bringen mit; **to be ~ed** [two things] miteinander zu tun haben - 4. ELEC [to power supply]: **to ~ sthg (to sthg)** etw (an etw (A)) anschließen ◇ *vi* [train, plane, bus]: **to ~ with** Anschluss haben an (+ A).

connected [kə'nektɪd] *adj* [related]: **to be ~ with sthg** mit etw in Zusammenhang stehen.

connection [kə'nekʃn] *n* - 1. [relationship]: **to have a ~ with** in Zusammenhang stehen mit; **~ between** Zusammenhang zwischen; **in ~ with** im Zusammenhang mit - 2. ELEC [between wires] Schaltung *die* - 3. [on telephone] Verbindung *die* - 4. [plane, train, bus] Anschluss *der* - 5. [professional acquaintance]: **-s** Beziehungen *pl.*

connive [kə'naɪv] *vi* - 1. [plot]: **to ~ (with sb)** sich (mit jm) verschwören - 2. [allow to happen]: **to ~ at sthg** etw dulden.

connoisseur [ˌkɒnə'sɜːr] *n* Kenner *der,* -in *die;* **a ~ of wine** ein Weinkenner.

conquer ['kɒŋkər] *vt* - 1. [take by force - land, city] erobern; [- people] besiegen - 2. *fig* [overcome] besiegen.

conqueror ['kɒŋkərə] *n* [of land, city] Eroberer *der,* -in *die;* [of people] Sieger *der,* -in *die.*

conquest ['kɒŋkwest] *n* - 1. [act - of land, city] Eroberung *die;* [- of people] Sieg *der* - 2. [thing conquered] Eroberung *die.*

cons [kɒnz] *npl* - 1. *Br inf* (*abbr of* conveniences): **all mod ~** mit allem modernen Komfort - 2. ▷ pro.

conscience ['kɒnʃəns] *n* Gewissen *das.*

conscientious [ˌkɒnʃɪ'enʃəs] *adj* gewissenhaft.

conscious ['kɒnʃəs] *adj* - 1. [awake] bei Bewusstsein - 2. [aware]: **to be ~ of sthg** sich einer Sache (G) bewusst sein; **fashion-~** modebewusst; **to be money-~** sehr auf Geld achten - 3. [intentional - effort, decision] bewusst; [- insult] absichtlich.

consciousness ['kɒnʃəsnɪs] *n* Bewusstsein *das.*

conscript ['kɒn'skrɪpt] MIL *n* Wehrpflichtige *der.*

conscription [kən'skrɪpʃn] *n* Wehrpflicht *die.*

consecutive [kən'sekjʊtɪv] *adj* aufeinanderfolgend; [numbers] fortlaufend; **for four ~ days** vier Tage hintereinander.

consent [kən'sent] ◇ *n* (U) - 1. [permission] Zustimmung *die* - 2. [agreement]: **he is, by common ~, a good minister** man hält ihn allgemein für einen guten Minister ◇ *vi:* **~ (to sthg)** (einer Sache (D)) zustimmen.

consequence ['kɒnsɪkwəns] *n* - 1. [result] Folge *die;* **to take the ~s** die Konsequenzen tragen; **in ~** folglich - 2. (U) [importance] Bedeutung *die;* **a person of ~** eine bedeutende Person.

consequently ['kɒnsɪkwəntlɪ] *adv* folglich.

conservation [ˌkɒnsə'veɪʃn] *n* [of buildings] Schutz *der,* Erhaltung *die;* **nature ~** Naturschutz *der;* **~ of energy/water** sorgsamer Umgang mit Energie/Wasser.

conservative [kən'sɜːvətɪv] ◇ *adj* - 1. [traditional] konservativ - 2. [cautious] vorsichtig ◇ *n* Konservative *der, die.* ◆ **Conservative** POL ◇ *adj* konservativ ◇ *n* Konservative *der, die.*

Conservative Party *n:* **the ~** die Konservative Partei.

conservatory [kən'sɜːvətrɪ] *n* Wintergarten *der.*

conserve [*n* 'kɒnsɜːv, *vb* kən'sɜːv] ◇ *n* Marmelade *die* ◇ *vt* [energy, supplies, electricity] sorgsam umgehen mit; [nature, wildlife] schützen.

consider [kən'sɪdər] *vt* - 1. [think about] er-

wägen - 2. [take into account] berücksichtigen; **all things ~ed** alles in allem **- 3.** [believe]: **I ~ him (to be) an expert** ich halte ihn für einen Experten.

considerable [kən'sɪdrəbl] *adj* beträchtlich.

considerably [kən'sɪdrəblɪ] *adv* beträchtlich.

considerate [kən'sɪdərət] *adj* rücksichtsvoll.

consideration [kən,sɪdə'reɪʃn] *n* **- 1.** [thought] Überlegung *die;* **to take sthg into ~** etw berücksichtigen **- 2.** [thoughtfulness] Rücksichtnahme *die* **- 3.** [factor] Gesichtspunkt *der* **- 4.** [discussion]: **the matter is under ~** die Angelegenheit wird zur Zeit geprüft.

considering [kən'sɪdərɪŋ] <> *prep* in Anbetracht (+ *G*) <> *conj* wenn man bedenkt, dass <> *adv* eigentlich; **the play was quite good, ~** das Stück war eigentlich ganz gut.

consign [kən'saɪn] *vt:* **to ~ sthg to the attic/shed**/*etc* etw auf den Dachboden/in den Schuppen/*etc* verbannen; **to ~ sthg to the scrapheap** *fig* etw rauswerfen.

consignment [kən'saɪnmənt] *n* Sendung *die;* [bigger] Ladung *die.*

consist [kən'sɪst] ◆ **consist in** *vt fus:* **to ~ in sthg** in etw (*D*) bestehen; **to ~ in doing sthg** darin bestehen, etw zu tun. ◆ **consist of** *vt fus* bestehen aus.

consistency [kən'sɪstənsɪ] *n* **- 1.** [coherence] Beständigkeit *die;* [of several things] Einheitlichkeit *die* **- 2.** [texture] Konsistenz *die.*

consistent [kən'sɪstənt] *adj* **- 1.** [constant] beständig **- 2.** [steady] stetig **- 3.** [coherent]: **to be ~ (with)** im Einklang stehen (mit).

consolation [kɒnsə'leɪʃn] *n* Trost *der.*

console [*n* 'kɒnsəʊl, *vt* kən'səʊl] <> *n* [control panel] Bedienungsfeld *das;* [of computer game] Spielkonsole *die* <> *vt* trösten.

consoling

Mach dir nichts daraus. Don't let it bother you.
Das wird schon wieder werden. It'll be alright.
Kopf hoch! Keep your chin up!
Lass den Kopf nicht hängen. Don't give up!
Nimms nicht so schwer! Don't take it so seriously!

consonant ['kɒnsənənt] *n* Konsonant *der.*

consortium [kən'sɔːtjəm] (*pl* -tiums OR -tia [-tjə]) *n* Konsortium *das.*

conspicuous [kən'spɪkjʊəs] *adj* auffällig.

conspiracy [kən'spɪrəsɪ] *n* Verschwörung *die.*

conspire [kən'spaɪəʳ] *vt:* **to ~ to do sthg** heimlich planen, etw zu tun.

constable ['kʌnstəbl] *n* Br Wachtmeister *der,* -in *die.*

constant ['kɒnstənt] *adj* **- 1.** [unvarying] konstant, beständig **- 2.** [recurring] ständig.

constantly ['kɒnstəntlɪ] *adv* [always] dauernd, ständig.

consternation [kɒnstə'neɪʃn] *n* Bestürzung *die.*

constipated ['kɒnstɪpeɪtɪd] *adj* verstopft.

constipation [kɒnstɪ'peɪʃn] *n* (U) Verstopfung *die.*

constituency [kən'stɪtjʊənsɪ] *n* Wahlkreis *der.*

constituent [kən'stɪtjʊənt] *n* **- 1.** [voter] Wähler *der,* -in *die* **- 2.** [element] Bestandteil *der.*

constitute ['kɒnstɪtjuːt] *vt* **- 1.** [represent] darstellen **- 2.** [form] bilden **- 3.** [set up] einrichten.

constitution [kɒnstɪ'tjuːʃn] *n* **- 1.** [health] Konstitution *die* **- 2.** [composition] Zusammensetzung *die.*

constraint [kən'streɪnt] *n* **- 1.** [restriction] Beschränkung *die* **- 2.** [coercion]: **under ~** unter Zwang.

construct [kən'strʌkt] *vt* [build] bauen.

construction [kən'strʌkʃn] *n* **- 1.** [act of building] Bau *der;* **under ~** im Bau **- 2.** [building industry] Bauindustrie *die* **- 3.** [structure] Konstruktion *die.*

constructive [kən'strʌktɪv] *adj* konstruktiv.

construe [kən'struː] *vt fml* [interpret]: **to ~ sthg as** etw auffassen als.

consul ['kɒnsəl] *n* Konsul *der.*

consulate ['kɒnsjʊlət] *n* Konsulat *das.*

consult [kən'sʌlt] <> *vt* **- 1.** [ask advice of - doctor, lawyer] konsultieren; [- friend] um Rat fragen **- 2.** [refer to - dictionary] nachschlagen in (+ *D*); [- map] nachsehen auf (+ *D*) <> *vi:* **to ~ with sb** sich mit jm beraten.

consultant [kən'sʌltənt] *n* **- 1.** [expert] Berater *der,* -in *die* **- 2.** Br [hospital doctor] Facharzt *der,* -ärztin *die.*

consultation [kɒnsəl'teɪʃn] *n* [meeting, discussion] Beratung *die.*

consulting room [kən'sʌltɪŋ-] *n* Sprechzimmer *das.*

consume [kən'sjuːm] *vt* **- 1.** [food, drink] zu sich nehmen **- 2.** [fuel, energy] verbrauchen.

consumer [kən'sjuːməʳ] *n* Verbraucher *der,* -in *die.*

consumer goods *npl* Konsumgüter *pl.*

consumer society *n* Konsumgesellschaft *die.*

consummate ['kɒnsəmeɪt] *vt* [marriage] vollziehen.

consumption [kən'sʌmpʃn] *n* (U) **- 1.** [of

food, drink] Konsum *der* - **2.** [of fuel, energy] Verbrauch *der.*

cont. *(abbr of* continued) Forts.

contact ['kɒntækt] <> *n* Kontakt *der;* **to be in ~ with sthg** [touching] etw berühren; **to lose ~ with sb** den Kontakt zu jm verlieren; **to make ~ with sb** mit jm Kontakt aufInehmen; **in ~ (with sb)** in Kontakt (mit jm) <> *vt* sich in Verbindung setzen mit.

contact lens *n* Kontaktlinse *die.*

contagious [kən'teɪdʒəs] *adj lit & fig* ansteckend.

contain [kən'teɪn] *vt* - **1.** [hold, include] entIhalten - **2.** *fml* [control - enthusiasm, anger, excitement] unter Kontrolle halten; [- epidemic, riot] unter Kontrolle bringen; [- enemy troops] in Schach halten; [- population growth] in Grenzen halten.

container [kən'teɪnə'] *n* - **1.** [box, bottle *etc*] Behälter *der* - **2.** COMM [for transporting goods] Container *der.*

contaminate [kən'tæmɪneɪt] *vt* [make impure] verunreinigen; [make poisonous] verseuchen.

cont'd *(abbr of* continued) Forts.

contemplate ['kɒntempleɪt] *vt* - **1.** [consider] erwägen - **2.** *literary* [look at] betrachten.

contemporary [kən'tempərərɪ] <> *adj* [life] zeitgenössisch <> *n* Zeitgenosse *der,* -sin *die.*

contempt [kən'tempt] *n (U)* - **1.** [scorn]: **~ (for)** Verachtung *die* (für) - **2.** LAW: **~ (of court)** Missachtung *die* des Gerichts.

contemptuous [kən'temptʃʊəs] *adj* verächtlich; **to be ~ of sthg** etw verachten.

contend [kən'tend] <> *vi* - **1.** [deal]: **to ~ with sthg** mit etw zu kämpfen haben - **2.** [compete]: **to ~ for sthg** um etw kämpfen <> *vt fml* [claim]: **to ~ that ...** behaupten, dass ...

contender [kən'tendə'] *n* - **1.** [in fight, race] Konkurrent *der,* -in *die* - **2.** [in election] Kandidat *der,* -in *die.*

content [*n* 'kɒntent, *adj & vb* kən'tent] <> *adj*: **~ (with)** zufrieden (mit); **to be ~ to do sthg** etw gerne tun <> *n* - **1.** [amount contained] Gehalt *der* - **2.** [subject matter] Inhalt *der* <> *vt*: **to ~ o.s. with sthg** sich mit etw zufrieden geben. <> **contents** *npl* - **1.** [of container, document] Inhalt *der* - **2.** [at front of book] Inhaltsverzeichnis *das.*

contented [kən'tentɪd] *adj* zufrieden.

contention [kən'tenʃn] *n* - **1.** [assertion] Behauptung *die* - **2.** *(U)* [disagreement]: **to be a source of ~** ein Streitpunkt sein.

contest [*n* 'kɒntest, *vb* kən'test] <> *n* - **1.** [competition] Wettkampf *der;* **a beauty ~** ein Schönheitswettbewerb - **2.** [for power, control] Kampf *der* <> *vt* - **1.** [compete for] kämpfen um - **2.** [dispute - statement] be-

streiten; [- decision] Einspruch erheben gegen; [- will] anIfechten.

contestant [kən'testənt] *n* [in sports] WettkampfteilInehmer *der,* -in *die;* [in quiz, election] Kandidat *der,* -in *die.*

context ['kɒntekst] *n* - **1.** [of word, phrase] Kontext *der* - **2.** [of event, idea] Zusammenhang *der.*

continent ['kɒntɪnənt] *n* Kontinent *der.*
  ➡ **Continent** *n Br:* **the Continent** Kontinentaleuropa *das.*

continental [,kɒntɪ'nentl] *adj* kontinental.

continental breakfast *n* Frühstück mit Kaffee oder Tee, Brötchen und Marmelade.

continental quilt *n Br* Steppdecke *die.*

contingency [kən'tɪndʒənsɪ] *n* Eventualität *die.*

contingency plan *n* Ausweichplan *der.*

continual [kən'tɪnjʊəl] *adj* - **1.** [without interruption - noise] pausenlos; [- growth] ununterbrochen - **2.** [- jealousy] dauernd - **2.** [frequently repeated] ständig, dauernd.

continually [kən'tɪnjʊəlɪ] *adv* - **1.** [without interruption] ununterbrochen - **2.** [frequently] ständig.

continuation [kən,tɪnjʊ'eɪʃn] *n* Fortsetzung *die.*

continue [kən'tɪnjuː] <> *vt* [carry on] fortIsetzen; **to ~ singing/working/** *etc* OR **to sing/ work/** *etc* weiterlsingen/arbeiten/ *etc;* **'And now ...,' he ~d** „Und nun ...," fuhr er fort <> *vi* - **1.** [carry on] anIdauern; **to ~ with sthg** etw fortIsetzen - **2.** [begin again - gen] weiterIgehen; [- people] weiterlmachen - **3.** [resume speaking] fortIfahren - **4.** [resume travelling] weiterlfahren; [on foot] weiterIgehen.

continuous [kən'tɪnjʊəs] *adj* ununterbrochen.

continuously [kən'tɪnjʊəslɪ] *adv* ununterbrochen.

contort [kən'tɔːt] *vt* [face, image] verzerren; [one's body] verrenken.

contortion [kən'tɔːʃn] *n* [position] Verrenkung *die.*

contour ['kɒn,tʊə'] *n* - **1.** [outline] Kontur *die* - **2.** [on map] Höhenlinie *die.*

contraband ['kɒntrəbænd] <> *adj* geschmuggelt <> *n (U)* Schmuggelware *die.*

contraception [,kɒntrə'sepʃn] *n* Empfängnisverhütung *die.*

contraceptive [,kɒntrə'septɪv] <> *adj* Verhütungs-; [advice] zur Empfängnisverhütung <> *n* Verhütungsmittel *das.*

contract [*n* 'kɒntrækt, *vb* kən'trækt] <> *n* Vertrag *der;* **a ~ of employment** ein Arbeitsvertrag <> *vt* - **1.** [through legal agreement]: **to ~ to do sthg** sich vertraglich verpflichten, etw zu tun - **2.** *fml* [disease] sich (D) zulIziehen <> *vi* [decrease in size, length] sich zusammenlziehen.

contraction [kən'trækʃn] *n* - **1.** [of muscle,

material] Zusammenziehen das. - **2.** LING Kontraktion die.

contractor [kən'træktər] n [person] Auftragnehmer der, -in die; [company] beauftragte Firma.

contradict [ˌkɒntrə'dɪkt] vt widersprechen (+ D).

contradiction [ˌkɒntrə'dɪkʃn] n Widerspruch der.

contraflow ['kɒntrəfləʊ] n Umleitung auf die Gegenfahrbahn (bei Baustellen auf der Fahrbahn).

contraption [kən'træpʃn] n Apparat der.

contrary ['kɒntrəri, adj sense 2 kən'treəri] ◇ adj - **1.** [opposing] gegensätzlich; **to be ~ to sthg** im Gegensatz zu etw stehen - **2.** [stubborn] widerspenstig ◇ n Gegenteil das; **on the ~** im Gegenteil. ◆ **contrary to** prep im Gegensatz zu.

contrast [n 'kɒntrɑːst, vb kən'trɑːst] ◇ n: **~ (with OR to)** Gegensatz der (zu); **the ~ between** der Unterschied zwischen; **by OR in ~** im Gegensatz dazu; **in ~ with OR to sthg** im Gegensatz zu etw ◇ vt: **to ~ sthg with sthg** etw einer Sache (D) gegenüberstellen ◇ vi: **to ~ (with sthg)** im Gegensatz (zu etw) stehen; [colours] sich (gegen etw) abheben.

contravene [ˌkɒntrə'viːn] vt verstoßen gegen.

contribute [kən'trɪbjuːt] ◇ vt [ideas] beitragen; [money] beisteuern; [help, advice] zur Verfügung stellen ◇ vi - **1.** [donate]: **to ~ (to sthg)** (für etw) spenden - **2.** [be part of cause]: **to ~ to sthg** zu etw beitragen - **3.** [write material]: **to ~ to sthg** für etw einen Beitrag/Beiträge schreiben.

contribution [ˌkɒntrɪ'bjuːʃn] n: **~ (to sthg)** Beitrag der (zu etw).

contributor [kən'trɪbjuːtər] n - **1.** [of money] Spender der, -in die - **2.** [to magazine, newspaper] freier Mitarbeiter, freie Mitarbeiterin; [regular] Mitarbeiter der, -in die.

contrive [kən'traɪv] vt fml - **1.** [engineer] entwickeln; [meeting] arrangieren - **2.** [manage]: **to ~ to do sthg** es zuwege bringen, etw zu tun.

contrived [kən'traɪvd] adj gewollt.

control [kən'trəʊl] ◇ n - **1.** (U) [power to manage - of situation, language] Beherrschung die; [- of traffic] Regelung die; [- of disease, crowd, fire] Kontrolle die; [- of budget] Aufsicht die; **to be in ~ of** [situation, place] unter Kontrolle haben; **under ~** unter Kontrolle; **to get a situation under ~** eine Situation in den Griff bekommen - **2.** [of emotions] Beherrschung die; **to lose ~** [become angry] die Beherrschung verlieren - **3.** [limit] Beschränkung die - **4.** COMPUT Control die ◇ vt - **1.** [have power to manage - company] leiten; [- government] unter sich (D) haben; [- country] beherrschen; [- traffic] regulieren; [- crowds, rioters] unter Kontrolle ha-

ben - **2.** [operate - car, plane] steuern; [- machine] bedienen - **3.** [curb] unter Kontrolle bringen - **4.** [emotions] beherrschen; **to ~ o.s.** sich beherrschen. ◆ **controls** npl [of machine, plane] Bedienungsfeld das.

control panel n [of car] Armaturenbrett das; [of plane, machine] Bedienungsfeld das.

control tower n Kontrollturm der.

controversial [ˌkɒntrə'vɜːʃl] adj umstritten.

controversy ['kɒntrəvɜːsɪ, Br kən'trɒvəsɪ] n Streit der.

convalesce [ˌkɒnvə'les] vi genesen.

convene [kən'viːn] ◇ vt [meeting, conference] einberufen ◇ vi sich versammeln; [court, parliament] zusammentreten.

convenience [kən'viːnjəns] n - **1.** [ease of use]: **I like the ~ of** it ich finde es so praktisch; **for ~** aus praktischen Gründen - **2.** [benefit]: **please reply at your earliest ~** ich bitte um baldmöglichste Antwort; **a telephone is provided for your ~** ein Telefon wird Ihnen zur Verfügung gestellt.

convenient [kən'viːnjənt] adj - **1.** [suitable] günstig; **to be ~ for sb** jm passen - **2.** [handy] praktisch; **to be ~ for the shops** günstig in der Nähe von Geschäften gelegen sein.

convent ['kɒnvənt] n Kloster das (für Frauen).

convention [kən'venʃn] n - **1.** [practice] Brauch der; [social rule] Konvention die - **2.** [agreement] Abkommen das - **3.** [assembly] Tagung die.

conventional [kən'venʃənl] adj - **1.** pej [dull] konventionell; [person] konventionsgebunden - **2.** [traditional] üblich - **3.** [weapon, war] konventionell.

converge [kən'vɜːdʒ] vi - **1.** [come together] zusammenlaufen; **to ~ on sb/sthg** von überall her zu jm/etw strömen - **2.** [become similar] sich einander annähern.

conversant [kən'vɜːsənt] adj fml: **~ with sthg** mit etw vertraut.

conversation [ˌkɒnvə'seɪʃn] n Gespräch das; **to have a ~** sich unterhalten.

🗣 starting a conversation

Hätten Sie mal einen Augenblick Zeit? Have you got a minute?

Darf ich Sie kurz unterbrechen? Can I just interrupt a second?

Entschuldigen Sie, ich hätte da eine Frage. Excuse me, can I ask a question?

Hör mal, … Listen, …

Also, die Sache ist folgendermaßen. Right then, here's the plan.

---

converse [kən'vɜːs] vi fml [talk]: **to ~ (with sb)** sich (mit jm) unterhalten.

conversely [kən'vɜːslɪ] adv fml umgekehrt.

conversion [kən'vɜːʃn] n - 1. [process] Umwandlung die - 2. [converted building, room] Umbau der - 3. RELIG [change in belief] Bekehrung die - 4. [in rugby] Verwandlung die.

convert [vb kən'vɜːt, n 'kɒnvɜːt] ◇ vt - 1. [change]: **to ~ sthg (in)to sthg** [miles, pounds] etw in etw (A) umrechnen; [energy] etw in etw (A) umwandeln - 2. RELIG & fig: **to ~ sb (to sthg)** jn (zu etw) bekehren - 3. [building, room, ship]: **to ~ sthg (in)to sthg** etw zu etw umbauen ◇ vi: **to ~ from sthg to sthg** [gas, electricity] sich von etw auf etw (A) umstellen; [religion] von etw zu etw konvertieren ◇ n Bekehrte der, die.

convertible [kən'vɜːtəbl] n [car] Kabrio das.

convex [kɒn'veks] adj konvex.

convey [kən'veɪ] vt - 1. fml [people, cargo] befördern - 2. [feelings, thoughts] vermitteln; **to ~ sthg to sb** jm etw vermitteln.

conveyor belt [kən'veɪə-] n [in factory] Fließband das; [at airport] Förderband das.

convict [n 'kɒnvɪkt, vb kən'vɪkt] ◇ n Strafgefangene der, die ◇ vt: **to ~ sb of sthg** jn wegen etw verurteilen.

conviction [kən'vɪkʃn] n - 1. [gen] Überzeugung die - 2. LAW [of criminal] Verurteilung die; **previous ~s** Vorstrafen pl.

convince [kən'vɪns] vt [persuade] überzeugen; **to ~ sb of sthg** jn von etw überzeugen; **to ~ sb to do sthg** jn überreden, etw zu tun.

convincing [kən'vɪnsɪŋ] adj - 1. [person, argument, speech] überzeugend - 2. [win, victory] klar.

convoluted ['kɒnvəluːtɪd] adj [plot, reasoning] verwickelt; [sentence] gewunden.

convoy ['kɒnvɔɪ] n Konvoi der.

convulse [kən'vʌls] vt: **to be ~d with laughter** sich vor Lachen schütteln; **to be ~d with pain** sich vor Schmerzen krümmen.

convulsion [kən'vʌlʃn] n MED Konvulsion die.

cook [kʊk] ◇ n Koch der, Köchin die ◇ vt - 1. [food, meal] machen; [boil] kochen; [roast, fry] braten; **to ~ sthg (in the oven)** etw im Ofen garen lassen - 2. inf [falsify] frisieren ◇ vi [boil] kochen; [roast, fry] braten.

cookbook ['kʊkˌbʊk] n = cookery book.

cooker ['kʊkə-] n esp Br [stove] Herd der.

cookery ['kʊkərɪ] n Kochen das.

cookery book n Kochbuch das.

cookie ['kʊkɪ] n Keks der, Plätzchen das.

cooking ['kʊkɪŋ] n (U) - 1. [activity] Kochen das - 2. [food] Küche die; **her ~'s awful** ihre Kochkünste sind grauenvoll.

cool [kuːl] ◇ adj - 1. [gen] kühl; [dress] leicht - 2. [person] ruhig; **to keep a ~ head** einen kühlen Kopf behalten - 3. inf [excellent, fashionable] cool ◇ vt kühlen ◇ vi abkühlen ◇ n inf [calm]: **to keep one's ~** die Ruhe bewahren; **to lose one's ~** die Nerven verlieren. ◆ **cool down** vi [become less warm] abkühlen; [person] kühler werden.

cool bag n Kühltasche die.

cool box Br, **cooler** Am ['kuːlə-] n Kühlbox die.

coop [kuːp] n Käfig der. ◆ **coop up** vt sep inf einpferchen.

co-op ['kəʊˌɒp] n abbr of cooperative.

cooperate [kəʊ'ɒpəreɪt] vi: **to ~ (with sb)** (mit jm) zusammenarbeiten.

cooperation [kəʊˌɒpə'reɪʃn] n (U) - 1. [collaboration] Zusammenarbeit die - 2. [assistance] Mitarbeit die, Kooperation die.

cooperative [kəʊ'ɒpərətɪv] ◇ adj - 1. [helpful] kooperativ - 2. [collective] auf Genossenschaftsbasis ◇ n [enterprise] Genossenschaft die, Kooperative die.

coordinate [n kəʊ'ɔːdɪnət, vt kəʊ'ɔːdɪneɪt] ◇ n [on map, graph] Koordinate die ◇ vt koordinieren. ◆ **coordinates** npl [clothes] Kleidung die zum Kombinieren.

coordination [kəʊˌɔːdɪ'neɪʃn] n Koordination die.

cop [kɒp] n inf Polizist der, -in die.

cope [kəʊp] vi zurechtkommen; **to ~ with sthg** etw schaffen.

Copenhagen [ˌkəʊpən'heɪgən] n Kopenhagen nt.

copier ['kɒpɪə-] n [photocopier] Kopierer der.

cop-out n inf Rückzieher der.

copper ['kɒpə-] n - 1. [metal] Kupfer das - 2. Br inf [policeman] Polizist der, -in die.

coppice ['kɒpɪs], **copse** [kɒps] n Wäldchen das.

copy ['kɒpɪ] ◇ n - 1. [gen] Kopie die - 2. [of book, magazine] Exemplar das ◇ vt - 1. [imitate] nachahmen - 2. [photocopy] kopieren.

copyright ['kɒpɪraɪt] n Copyright das.

coral ['kɒrəl] n (U) Koralle die.

cord [kɔːd] n - 1. [string] Schnur die - 2. [wire] Kabel das - 3. (U) [fabric] Kord der. ◆ **cords** npl inf Kordhose die.

cordial ['kɔːdjəl] ◇ adj freundlich ◇ n Fruchtsirup der.

cordon ['kɔːdn] n Kette die. ◆ **cordon off** vt sep absperren.

corduroy ['kɔːdərɔɪ] n (U) Kord der.

core [kɔːʳ] vt entkernen.

coriander [ˌkɒrɪ'ændəʳ] n Koriander der.

cork [kɔːk] n - 1. [material] Kork der - 2. [stopper] Korken der.

corkscrew ['kɔːkskruː] n Korkenzieher der.

corn [kɔːn] n - 1. (U) Br [cereal] Korn das, Getreide das - 2. (U) esp Am [maize] Mais der - 3. [callus] Hühnerauge das.

corned beef [kɔːnd-] n Corned beef das.

corner ['kɔːnəʳ] ◇ n Ecke die; **to cut ~s** oberflächlich arbeiten ◇ vt - 1. fig [person, animal] in die Enge treiben - 2. [market] monopolisieren.

corner shop *n* Laden *der* an der Ecke.

cornerstone ['kɔːnəstəʊn] *n fig* Grundstein *der*.

cornet ['kɔːnɪt] *n* - 1. [instrument] Kornett *das* - 2. *Br* [ice-cream cone] Hörnchen *das*.

cornflakes ['kɔːnfleɪks] *npl* Cornflakes *pl*.

cornflour *Br* ['kɔːnflaʊə'], **cornstarch** *Am* [-stɑːtʃ] *n (U)* Stärkemehl *das*.

corn on the cob *n* Maiskolben *der*.

corny ['kɔːnɪ] *adj inf* abgedroschen.

coronary ['kɒrənrɪ], **coronary thrombosis** [-θrɒm'bəʊsɪs] *(pl coronary thromboses [-siːz])* *n* Herzinfarkt *der*.

coronation [ˌkɒrə'neɪʃn] *n* Krönung *die*.

coroner ['kɒrənə'] *n für die Untersuchung ungeklärter Todesfälle zuständiger Beamter.*

corporal ['kɔːpərəl] *n* Hauptgefreite *der*.

corporal punishment *n (U)* körperliche Züchtigung, Prügelstrafe *die*.

corporate ['kɔːpərət] *adj* - 1. [business] körperschaftlich - 2. [collective] gemeinsam.

corporation [ˌkɔːpə'reɪʃn] *n* - 1. [council] Gemeindeverwaltung *die* - 2. [large company] Handelsgesellschaft *die*.

corps [kɔː'] *(pl inv)* *n* Korps *das*.

corpse [kɔːps] *n* Leiche *die*.

correct [kə'rekt] <> *adj* - 1. [right, accurate] korrekt, richtig; **you're quite ~** du hast ganz Recht - 2. [appropriate, suitable] angemessen <> *vt* korrigieren.

correction [kə'rekʃn] *n* - 1. *(U)* [act of correcting] Korrigieren *das* - 2. [change] Korrektur *die*, Berichtigung *die*.

correlation [ˌkɒrə'leɪʃn] *n (U)*: **~ (between)** Wechselbeziehung *die* (zwischen).

correspond [ˌkɒrɪ'spɒnd] *vi* - 1. [be equivalent]: **to ~ with** OR **to sthg** etw *(D)* entsprechen - 2. [tally]: **to ~ (with** OR **to sthg)** (mit etw) übereinstimmen - 3. [write letters]: **to ~ (with sb)** (mit jm) korrespondieren.

correspondence [ˌkɒrɪ'spɒndəns] *n* - 1. [letters] Briefe *pl* - 2. *(U)* [letter-writing]: **~ with/between** Briefwechsel *der* mit/zwischen *(D)*.

correspondence course *n* Fernkurs *der*.

correspondent [ˌkɒrɪ'spɒndənt] *n* Korrespondent *der*, -in *die*.

corridor ['kɒrɪdɔː'] *n* Gang *der*.

corroborate [kə'rɒbəreɪt] *vt* bestätigen.

corrode [kə'rəʊd] <> *vt* zerfressen <> *vi* korrodieren.

corrosion [kə'rəʊʒn] *n (U)* Korrosion *die*.

corrugated iron *n* Wellblech *das*.

corrupt [kə'rʌpt] <> *adj* - 1. [gen] korrupt - 2. [depraved] verdorben <> *vt* - 1. [deprave] verderben - 2. COMPUT [damage] beschädigen.

corruption [kə'rʌpʃn] *n (U)* - 1. [dishonesty] Korruption *die* - 2. [depravity] Verdorbenheit *die* - 3. [debasement] Verführung *die*.

corset ['kɔːsɪt] *n* Korsett *das*.

cosh [kɒʃ] *n* Knüppel *der*.

cosmetic [kɒz'metɪk] <> *adj fig* [superficial] kosmetisch <> *n* Kosmetikum *das*. **cosmetics** *npl* Kosmetik *die*.

cosmopolitan [ˌkɒzmə'pɒlɪtn] *adj* [place] kosmopolitisch; [person] welterfahren.

cosset ['kɒsɪt] *vt* verhätscheln.

cost [kɒst] *(pt & pp sense 1 cost; pt & pp sense 2 -ed)* <> *n* - 1. [price] Kosten *pl* - 2. *fig* [loss, damage] Preis *der;* **at the ~ of his health** auf Kosten seiner Gesundheit; **at all ~s** um jeden Preis <> *vt* - 1. [gen] kosten - 2. COMM [estimate price of] die Kosten kalkulieren (+ G). **costs** *npl* LAW Kosten *pl*.

co-star *n*: **to be the ~ in a film** eine der Hauptrollen in einem Film spielen.

Costa Rica [ˌkɒstə'riːkə] *n* Costa Rica *nt*.

cost-effective *adj* kosteneffektiv.

costing ['kɒstɪŋ] *n* Kalkulation *die*.

costly ['kɒstlɪ] *adj* kostspielig, teuer.

cost of living *n*: **the ~** die Lebenshaltungskosten *pl*.

cost price *n* Selbstkostenpreis *der*.

costume ['kɒstjuːm] *n* - 1. THEATRE Kostüm *das* - 2. *(U)* [dress] Tracht *die* - 3. [swimming costume] Badeanzug *der*.

costume jewellery *n* Modeschmuck *der*.

cosy *Br*, **cozy** *Am* ['kəʊzɪ] *adj* [warm and comfortable] gemütlich.

cot [kɒt] *n* - 1. *Br* [for child] Kinderbett *das* - 2. *Am* [folding bed] Feldbett *das*.

cottage ['kɒtɪdʒ] *n* Häuschen *das*.

cottage cheese *n (U)* Hüttenkäse *der*.

cottage pie *n Br* Hackfleisch mit einer Lage Kartoffelbrei, im Ofen überbacken.

cotton ['kɒtn] *n* - 1. [fabric] Baumwolle *die* - 2. [thread] Faden *der* <> *comp* [fabric] Baumwoll-. **cotton on** *vi inf*: **to ~ on (to sthg)** (etw) kapieren.

cotton candy *n Am* = candyfloss.

cotton wool *n* Watte *die*.

couch [kaʊtʃ] *n* - 1. [sofa] Sofa *das*, Couch *die* - 2. [in doctor's surgery] Liege *die*.

cough [kɒf] *n* Husten *der*.

cough mixture *n Br* Hustensaft *der*.

cough sweet *n Br* Hustenpastille *die*.

cough syrup *n* = cough mixture.

could [kʊd] *pt* ▷ can².

couldn't ['kʊdnt] = could not.

could've ['kʊdəv] = could have.

council ['kaʊnsl] *n* - 1. [local authority] Stadtverwaltung *die* - 2. [group, organization] Rat *der* - 3. [meeting] Beratung *die*.

council estate *n* Sozialsiedlung *die*.

council house *n Br* ≃ Sozialwohnung *die*, *mit öffentlichen Mitteln gebautes Einfamilienhaus für eine Familie mit niedrigem Einkommen.*

councillor ['kaʊnsələr] *n* Stadtrat *der*, -rätin *die*.

council tax *n Br* Gemeindesteuer *die*.

counsel ['kaʊnsəl] n - 1. (U) fml [advice] Rat der - 2. [lawyer] Rechtsanwalt der, -wältin die; ~ for the defence Verteidiger der, -in die; ~ for the prosecution Anklagevertreter der, -in die.

counsellor Br, **counselor** Am ['kaʊnsələ'] n - 1. [adviser] Berater der, -in die - 2. Am [lawyer] Rechtsanwalt der, -wältin die.

count [kaʊnt] <> n - 1. [total] Zählung die; to keep ~ of sthg etw mitzählen; to lose ~ of sthg den Überblick über etw (A) verlieren - 2. [aristocrat] Graf der <> vt - 1. [add up] zählen - 2. [consider, include]: to ~ sb/sthg as sthg jn/etw als etw ansehen; there are six, not ~ing the broken ones es sind sechs, die zerbrochenen nicht mitgezählt <> vi zählen; to ~ (up) to zählen bis; to ~ for nothing umsonst gewesen sein; to ~ as sthg als etw zählen. ◆ count against vt fus sprechen gegen. ◆ count on vt fus - 1. [rely on] zählen auf (+ A) - 2. [expect] rechnen mit. ◆ count up vt fus zusammenzählen. ◆ count upon vt fus = count on.

countdown ['kaʊntdaʊn] n Countdown der.

counter ['kaʊntə'] <> n - 1. [in shop] Ladentisch der - 2. [in board game] Spielmarke die - 3. Am [in kitchen] Theke die <> vt: to ~ sthg with sthg etw (D) mit etw begegnen <> vi: to ~ with sthg mit etw reagieren. ◆ counter to adv entgegen (+ D); to run ~ to sthg etw (D) zuwiderlaufen.

counteract [ˌkaʊntə'rækt] vt entgegenwirken (+ D).

counterattack ['kaʊntərəˌtæk] vi einen Gegenangriff führen.

counterclockwise [ˌkaʊntə'klɒkwaɪz] adj & adv Am gegen den Uhrzeigersinn.

counterfeit ['kaʊntəfɪt] adj gefälscht.

counterfoil ['kaʊntəfɔɪl] n Kontrollabschnitt der.

counterpart ['kaʊntəpɑːt] n Gegenstück das.

counterproductive [ˌkaʊntəprə'dʌktɪv] adj die entgegengesetzte Wirkung habend.

countess ['kaʊntɪs] n Gräfin die.

countless ['kaʊntlɪs] adj unzählig.

country ['kʌntrɪ] n - 1. [nation] Land das; the ~ [countryside] das Land; they live in the ~ sie leben auf dem Land - 2. [area of land, region] Gebiet das.

country house n Landhaus das.

countryman ['kʌntrɪmən] (pl -men [-mən]) n Landsmann der.

countryside ['kʌntrɪsaɪd] n (U) Landschaft die.

county ['kaʊntɪ] n Grafschaft die.

county council n Br Grafschaftsrat der.

coup [kuː] n - 1. [rebellion]: ~ (d'état) Staatsstreich der - 2. [masterstroke] Coup der.

couple ['kʌpl] <> n - 1. [in relationship] Paar

das - 2. [small number]: a ~ (of) [two] zwei; [a few] ein paar <> vt [join]: to ~ sthg (to sthg) etw (an etw (A)) koppeln.

coupon ['kuːpɒn] n Gutschein der.

courage ['kʌrɪdʒ] n Mut der; to take ~ (from sthg) sich (durch etw) ermutigt fühlen.

courgette [kɔː'ʒet] n Br Zucchini die.

courier ['kʊrɪə'] n - 1. [on holiday tour] Reiseleiter der, -in die - 2. [to deliver letters, packages] Kurier der.

course [kɔːs] n - 1. [of study - for student] Kurs(us) der; [- for employee] Lehrgang der; a ~ of lectures eine Vorlesungsreihe - 2. MED [of treatment] Reihe die - 3. [path, route] Kurs der; in the ~ of time im Laufe der Zeit; during the ~ of the negotiations im Verlauf der Verhandlungen; on~ lit & fig auf Kurs; off ~ vom Kurs abgewichen - 4. [plan]: ~ (of action) Vorgehensweise die - 5. [of time]: in due ~ zu gegebener Zeit; in the ~ of im Laufe (+ G) - 6. [in meal] Gang der - 7. SPORT [for horseracing] Bahn die, Strecke die; [for golf] Platz der. ◆ of course adv natürlich; of ~ not natürlich nicht.

coursebook ['kɔːsbʊk] n Lehrbuch das.

coursework ['kɔːswɜːk] n (U) Mitarbeit die im Unterricht.

court [kɔːt] n - 1. [for trial] Gericht das; to take sb to ~ jn verklagen - 2. SPORT Platz der - 3. [courtyard, of monarch] Hof der.

courteous ['kɜːtjəs] adj höflich.

courtesy ['kɜːtɪsɪ] n Höflichkeit die. ◆ courtesy of prep [thanks to] dank (+ G).

courthouse ['kɔːthaʊs, pl -haʊzɪz] n Am Gerichtsgebäude das.

court-martial [-'mɑːʃl] (pl -s or courts-martial) n [trial] Kriegsgerichtsverhandlung die.

courtroom ['kɔːtrʊm] n Gerichtssaal der.

courtyard ['kɔːtjɑːd] n Hof der.

cousin ['kʌzn] n Cousin der, Cousine die.

cove [kəʊv] n Bucht die.

covenant ['kʌvənənt] n [of money] Zahlungsverpflichtung die.

cover ['kʌvə'] <> n - 1. [of machine, typewriter] Abdeckung die; [of seat, cushion] Überzug der - 2. [lid] Deckel der - 3. [of book, magazine] Einband der - 4. [blanket] Decke die - 5. (U) [protection, shelter, insurance] Schutz der; to take ~ [from weather] sich unterlstellen; [from gunfire] in Deckung gehen; under ~ [from weather] geschützt - 6. [disguise] Tarnung die <> vt - 1. [gen] bedecken; to be ~ed in blood blutüberströmt sein - 2. [insure]: to ~ sb (against sthg) [subj: policy] jn (gegen etw) versichern - 3. [report on] berichten über (+ A) - 4. [deal with] behandeln - 5. [pay for - damage] decken. ◆ cover up vt sep fig [to conceal] vertuschen.

coverage ['kʌvərɪdʒ] n (U) [of news] Berichterstattung die.

cover charge n Gedeckgebühr die.

covering ['kʌvərɪŋ] n Belag der.

covering letter Br, **cover letter** Am n Begleitbrief der.

cover note n Br vorläufiger Versicherungsschein.

covert ['kʌvət] adj verdeckt, versteckt; [look, glance] verstohlen.

cover-up n Vertuschung die.

covet ['kʌvɪt] vt fml begehren.

cow [kaʊ] ⟨⟩ n Kuh die ⟨⟩ vt einlschüchtern.

coward ['kaʊəd] n Feigling der.

cowardly ['kaʊədlɪ] adj feige.

cowboy ['kaʊbɔɪ] n [cattlehand] Cowboy der.

cower ['kaʊəʳ] vi sich ducken; [squat] kauern.

cox [kɒks], **coxswain** ['kɒksən] n Steuermann der.

coy [kɔɪ] adj kokett, neckisch.

cozy adj & n Am = cosy.

crab [kræb] n Krabbe die, Krebs der.

crack [kræk] ⟨⟩ n - **1.** [fault] Riss der; [in cup, glass, mirror] Sprung der - **2.** [in curtains, door] Spalt der; [in wall] Ritze die - **3.** [sharp noise] Knall der - **4.** inf [attempt]: **to have a ~ at** sthg sich an etw (D) versuchen - **5.** [cocaine] Crack das ⟨⟩ adj toll, erstklassig ⟨⟩ vt - **1.** [damage] einen Riss machen in (+ D); [cup, glass, mirror] anlschlagen; [skin] rissig machen - **2.** [whip] knallen mit - **3.** [bang, hit] anlschlagen; **I ~ed my head on the doorpost** ich habe mir den Kopf am Türrahmen gestoßen - **4.** [solve] lösen; [code] knacken - **5.** inf [make]: **to ~ a joke** einen Witz reißen ⟨⟩ vi - **1.** [be damaged] einen Riss bekommen; [cup, glass, mirror] springen; [skin] auflspringen - **2.** [person] zusammenlbrechen.

⟐ **crack down** vi: **to ~ down (on sb/sthg)** (bei jm/etw) hart durchlgreifen. ⟐ **crack up** vi durchldrehen.

cracker ['krækəʳ] n - **1.** [biscuit] Keks der - **2.** Br [for Christmas] Knallbonbon der.

crackers ['krækəz] adj Br inf [mad] verrückt.

crackle ['krækl] vi knacken.

cradle ['kreɪdl] ⟨⟩ n [bed, birthplace] Wiege die ⟨⟩ vt an sich (A) drücken.

craft [krɑːft] (pl sense 2 inv) n - **1.** [trade, skill] Handwerk das - **2.** [boat] Boot das.

craftsman ['krɑːftsmən] (pl -men [-mən]) n Handwerker der.

craftsmanship ['krɑːftsmənʃɪp] n (U) Handwerkskunst die.

crafty ['krɑːftɪ] adj schlau.

crag [kræg] n Felszacken der.

cram [kræm] ⟨⟩ vt - **1.** [stuff]: **to ~ sthg into** sthg etw in etw (A) stopfen - **2.** [overfill]: **to**

be ~med (with sthg) (mit etw) vollgestopft sein ⟨⟩ vi [study] pauken, büffeln.

cramp [kræmp] ⟨⟩ n Krampf der; **I've got ~** ich habe einen Krampf; **stomach ~s** Magenkrämpfe ⟨⟩ vt [hinder] hemmen, behindern.

cranberry ['krænbərɪ] n Preiselbeere die.

crane [kreɪn] n [machine] Kran der.

crank [kræŋk] ⟨⟩ n - **1.** TECH Kurbel die - **2.** inf [eccentric] Spinner der, -in die ⟨⟩ vt [handle, mechanism] kurbeln.

crankshaft ['kræŋkʃɑːft] n Kurbelwelle die.

cranny ['krænɪ] n ▷ nook.

crap [kræp] n vinf Scheiße die.

crash [kræʃ] ⟨⟩ n - **1.** [of car] Unfall der; [of plane] Absturz der; [of train] Unglück das; [collision] Zusammenstoß der; **to have a ~** verunglücken; [collide] zusammenlstoßen - **2.** [loud noise] Krachen das ⟨⟩ vt [car] einen Unfall haben mit; **she ~ed her car into a tree** sie krachte mit dem Auto gegen einen Baum ⟨⟩ vi - **1.** [car driver] verunglücken; [plane] ablstürzen; [collide] zusammenlstoßen; **to ~ into** sthg [in car] mit dem Auto gegen etw krachen - **2.** FIN [business, company] bankrott gehen; [stock market] zusammenlbrechen.

crash course n Intensivkurs der.

crash helmet n Sturzhelm der.

crash-land vi eine Bruchlandung machen.

crass [kræs] adj dumm und geschmacklos.

crate [kreɪt] n Kiste die; [of milk bottles, beer] Kasten der.

crater ['kreɪtəʳ] n Krater der.

cravat [krə'væt] n Halstuch das.

crave [kreɪv] ⟨⟩ vt sich sehnen nach ⟨⟩ vi: **to ~ for** sthg sich nach etw sehnen.

crawl [krɔːl] ⟨⟩ vi - **1.** [gen] kriechen; [baby, insect] krabbeln; **to ~ along** [traffic] im Schneckentempo vorwärtslkommen - **2.** inf [be covered]: **to be ~ing with** wimmeln von ⟨⟩ n [swimming stroke]: **the ~** das Kraulen; **to do the ~** kraulen.

crayfish ['kreɪfɪʃ] (pl inv OR -es) n [saltwater] Languste die.

crayon ['kreɪɒn] n [pencil] Buntstift der; [of wax] Wachsmalstift der.

craze [kreɪz] n Mode die (die gerade „in" ist); **the latest ~** der letzte Schrei.

crazy ['kreɪzɪ] adj inf - **1.** [mad] verrückt - **2.** [enthusiastic]: **to be ~ about** sthg/sb auf etw (A) /nach jm verrückt sein.

creak [kriːk] vi [door, floorboard] knarren; [bed, hinge, handle] quietschen.

cream [kriːm] ⟨⟩ adj [in colour] creme(farben) ⟨⟩ n - **1.** [food] Sahne die; [filling for chocolates, biscuits] Creme die - **2.** (U) [cosmetic] Creme die.

cream cake n Br Sahnetorte die; [bun] Sahnetörtchen das.

cream cheese n Frischkäse der.

cream cracker n Br Kräcker der.

cream tea *n* *Br* Nachmittagstee mit Gebäck, Marmelade und Sahne.

crease [kri:s] ◇ *n* [in fabric - deliberate] Bügelfalte *die*; [- accidental] Falte *die* ◇ *vt* [deliberately] **falten**; [accidentally] **zerknittern** ◇ *vi* [fabric] **knittern**.

create [kri:'eɪt] *vt* - **1.** [gen] **schaffen**; [the world] **erschaffen** - **2.** [noise, fuss] **verursachen**; [impression] **machen**; [difficulties] **bereiten**.

creation [kri:'eɪʃn] *n* - **1.** [gen] **Schaffung** *die*; [of the world] **Erschaffung** *die* - **2.** [work of art] **Werk** *das*; [dress, hat, hairstyle] **Kreation** *die*.

creative [kri:'eɪtɪv] *adj* kreativ.

creature ['kri:tʃə'] *n* [animal] Lebewesen *das*, Geschöpf *das*.

crèche [kreʃ] *n* *Br* (Kinder)hort *der*.

credence ['kri:dns] *n:* **to give** OR **lend ~ to sthg** etw glaubwürdig machen.

credentials [krɪ'denʃlz] *npl* - **1.** [papers] (Ausweis)papiere *pl* - **2.** *fig* [qualifications] Qualifikationen *pl*.

credibility [ˌkredə'bɪlətɪ] *n* Glaubwürdigkeit *die*.

credit ['kredɪt] ◇ *n* - **1.** [financial aid] Kredit *der*; **to be in ~** im Plus sein; **on ~** auf Kredit - **2.** *(U)* [honour] Ehre *die*; [approval] Anerkennung *die*; **he was never given any ~ for** man hat ihm nie Anerkennung dafür gezollt - **3.** SCH & UNIV [mark] Auszeichnung *die*; [unit of money credit] Schein *die* - **4.** FIN [money credited] Guthaben *das* ◇ *vt* - **1.** FIN gutschreiben - **2.** *inf* [believe] glauben - **3.** [attribute]: **to ~ sb with sthg** jm etw zulschreiben. ◆ **credits** *npl* CINEMA Nachspann *der*.

credit card *n* Kreditkarte *die*.

credit note *n* COMM & FIN Gutschrift *die*.

creditor ['kredɪtə'] *n* Gläubiger *der*, -in *die*.

creed [kri:d] *n* - **1.** [political] Kredo *das* - **2.** RELIG Konfession *die*.

creek [kri:k] *n* - **1.** [of sea] Meeresarm *der* - **2.** *Am* [stream] Bach *der*.

creep [kri:p] *(pt & pp* crept) ◇ *vi* [gen] **kriechen**; [person] **schleichen** ◇ *n* *inf* [loathsome person] **widerlicher Typ**; [groveller] **Schleimer** *der*. ◆ **creeps** *npl:* **to give sb the ~s** *inf* jm nicht geheuer sein.

creeper ['kri:pə'] *n* [plant - growing along ground] Kriechpflanze *die*; [- growing upwards] Kletterpflanze *die*.

creeping ['kri:pɪŋ] *adj* [gradual] schleichend.

creepy ['kri:pɪ] *adj* *inf* unheimlich.

creepy-crawly [ˌkri:pɪ'krɔ:lɪ] *(pl* creepy-crawlies) *n* *inf* Krabbeltier *das*.

cremate [krɪ'meɪt] *vt* einläschern.

cremation [krɪ'meɪʃn] *n* Einäscherung *die*.

crematorium [ˌkremə'tɔ:rɪəm] *(pl* -riums OR -ria [-rɪə]), **crematory** *Am* ['kremətrɪ] *n* Krematorium *das*.

crepe [kreɪp] *n* - **1.** [cloth] Krepp *der* - **2.** [rubber] Kreppgummi *der* - **3.** [thin pancake] Crêpe *die*.

crepe bandage *n* *Br* elastische Binde.

crepe paper *n* Krepppapier *das*.

crept [krept] *pt & pp* ⊳ creep.

crescent ['kresnt] *n* - **1.** [shape] Halbmond *der* - **2.** [street] halbkreisförmig verlaufende Straße.

cress [kres] *n* Kresse *die*.

crest [krest] *n* - **1.** [of bird] Haube *die*; [of cock, hill, wave] Kamm *der* - **2.** [of school, noble family] Wappen *das*.

crestfallen ['krest,fɔ:ln] *adj* geknickt.

Crete [kri:t] *n* Kreta *nt*.

cretin ['kretɪn] *n* *inf pej* Idiot *der*, -in *die*.

crevice ['krevɪs] *n* Spalte *die*.

crew [kru:] *n* - **1.** [of ship, plane] Besatzung *die*, Crew *die* - **2.** CINEMA & TV Crew *die*.

crew cut *n* Bürstenschnitt *der*.

crew-neck *n* runder Halsausschnitt.

crib [krɪb] ◇ *n* - **1.** [cradle] Krippe *die* - **2.** *Am* [cot] Kinderbett *das* ◇ *vt* *inf* [copy]: **to ~ sthg off** OR **from sb** etw von jm ablschreiben.

crick [krɪk] *n:* **I've got a ~ in my neck** ich habe einen steifen Hals.

cricket ['krɪkɪt] *n* - **1.** [game] Kricket *das* - **2.** [insect] Grille *die*.

📖 cricket

Kricket mit seinen für Laien schwer durchschaubaren Regeln ist Englands nationaler Sommersport. Zwei Mannschaften von je elf Spielern in weißem Dress versuchen sich abwechselnd beim **bat** (Schlag) und **bowl** (Wurf) mit dem Ziel, den Ball in das von einem Spieler der Gegenmannschaft mit dem Schlagholz verteidigte Tor zu werfen und insgesamt mehr **runs** (Läufe) zu erzielen als die Gegenmannschaft. Im professionellen Kricket wird das Spiel als fünf Tage dauerndes **International Test Match** gespielt, bei Amateuren dauert es dagegen meist einen halben Tag.

---

crime [kraɪm] *n* - **1.** [gen] Verbrechen *das*; **~ is on the decrease** die Zahl der Verbrechen nimmt ab - **2.** *fig* [shameful act] Schande *die*.

criminal ['krɪmɪnl] ◇ *adj* kriminell; [act, offence] strafbar ◇ *n* Kriminelle *der, die*.

crimson ['krɪmzn] *adj* - **1.** [in colour] purpurrot - **2.** [with embarrassment] knallrot.

cringe [krɪndʒ] *vi* - **1.** [out of fear] zurücklweichen - **2.** *inf* [with embarrassment] schaudern; **to ~ at sthg** vor etw *(D)* zurückschrecken.

crinkle ['krɪŋkl] *vt* [paper, clothes] zerknittern.

cripple ['krɪpl] ◇ *n* offensive Krüppel *der* ◇ *vt* - **1.** MED [disable] zum Krüppel machen

- 2. [ship, plane] aktionsunfähig machen **- 3.** fig [country, industry] lähmen.

crisis ['kraɪsɪs] (pl **crises** ['kraɪsiːz]) n Krise die.

crisp [krɪsp] adj **- 1.** [pastry, bacon] knusprig; [apple, vegetables] frisch und knackig **- 2.** [weather] frisch. ➡ **crisps** npl Br Chips pl.

crisscross ['krɪskrɒs] ◇ adj [pattern] gitterartig ◇ vt [subj: roads] kreuz und quer führen durch.

criterion [kraɪ'tɪərɪən] (pl **-rions** OR **-ria** [-rɪə]) n Kriterium das.

critic ['krɪtɪk] n Kritiker der, -in die.

critical ['krɪtɪkl] adj kritisch; [illness] schwer; [crucial] entscheidend; **to be ~ of sb/ sthg** jn/etw kritisieren.

critically ['krɪtɪklɪ] adv kritisch; [ill] schwer; **to be ~ important** von entscheidender Bedeutung sein.

criticism ['krɪtɪsɪzm] n **- 1.** [gen] Kritik die **- 2.** [unfavourable comment] Kritikpunkt der.

criticize, -ise ['krɪtɪsaɪz] vt & vi kritisieren.

croak [krəʊk] vi [frog] quaken; [raven, person] krächzen.

Croat ['krəʊæt] ◇ adj kroatisch ◇ n [person] Kroate der, -tin die.

Croatia [krəʊ'eɪʃə] n Kroatien nt.

Croatian [krəʊ'eɪʃn] adj & n = Croat.

crochet ['krəʊʃeɪ] n Häkeln das.

crockery ['krɒkərɪ] n Geschirr das.

crocodile ['krɒkədaɪl] (pl inv OR -s) n Krokodil das.

crocus ['krəʊkəs] (pl -cuses) n Krokus der.

crony ['krəʊnɪ] n inf [friend] Kumpel der.

crook [krʊk] n [criminal] Gauner der.

crooked ['krʊkɪd] adj **- 1.** [picture, tie, teeth] schief; [path] gewunden **- 2.** inf [dishonest - person] unehrlich; [- deal] krumm.

crop [krɒp] n **- 1.** [kind of plant] Feldfrucht die **- 2.** [harvest] Ernte die **- 3.** [whip] Reitpeitsche die **- 4.** [haircut] Kurzhaarschnitt die. ➡ **crop up** vi [problem] auftauchen.

croquette [krɒ'ket] n Krokette die.

cross [krɒs] ◇ adj [angry] böse; **to be ~ with sb** böse auf jn sein ◇ n **- 1.** [gen] Kreuz das **- 2.** [hybrid] Kreuzung die ◇ vt **- 1.** [street, road, river] überqueren; [room, desert] durchqueren; **it ~ed my mind that ...** der Gedanke ging mir durch den Kopf, dass ... **- 2.** [place one across the other] (über)kreuzen; [arms] verschränken; [legs] übereinander schlagen **- 3.** Br [cheque] als Verrechnungsscheck kennzeichnen ◇ vi [intersect] sich kreuzen. ➡ **cross off** vt sep streichen. ➡ **cross out** vt sep auslstreichen.

crossbar ['krɒsbɑːr] n **- 1.** [of goal] Querlatte die **- 2.** [of bicycle] Stange die.

cross-Channel ferry n Fähre die über den Ärmelkanal.

cross-country ◇ adj [run] Querfeldein-; [skiing] Langlauf- ◇ n Querfeldeinlauf der.

cross-examine vt lit & fig ins Kreuzverhör nehmen.

cross-eyed [-aɪd] adj: **to be ~** schielen.

crossfire ['krɒsˌfaɪər] n Kreuzfeuer das.

crossing ['krɒsɪŋ] n -1. [place] Übergang der -2. [sea journey] Überfahrt die.

cross-legged [-legd] adv im Schneidersitz.

cross-purposes npl: **to talk at ~** aneinander vorbeireden.

cross-reference n Querverweis der.

crossroads ['krɒsrəʊdz] (pl inv) n Kreuzung die.

cross-section n Querschnitt der.

crosswalk ['krɒswɔːk] n Am Fußgängerüberweg der.

crossword (puzzle) ['krɒswɜːd-] n Kreuzworträtsel das.

crotch [krɒtʃ] n **- 1.** [of man] Hodengegend die; [of woman] Schamgegend die **- 2.** [of clothes] Schritt der.

crotchet ['krɒtʃɪt] n Viertel(note) die.

crotchety ['krɒtʃɪtɪ] adj Br inf griesgrämig.

crouch [kraʊtʃ] vi kauern.

crow [krəʊ] ◇ n Krähe die; **10 miles as the ~ flies** 10 Meilen Luftlinie ◇ vi **- 1.** [cock] krähen **- 2.** inf [gloat]: **to ~ over sthg** sich mit etw brüsten.

crowbar ['krəʊbɑːr] n Brecheisen das.

crowd [kraʊd] ◇ n [mass of people] Menschenmenge die; **-s of people** große Menschenmengen ◇ vi sich drängen ◇ vt [streets, town] bevölkern; **we were ~ed into a small room** wir wurden in ein kleines Zimmer gedrängt.

crowded ['kraʊdɪd] adj voll; [train, shop, bar] überfüllt; [timetable, flat] eng; **to be ~ with people** voller Menschen sein.

crown [kraʊn] ◇ n **- 1.** [of monarch, tooth] Krone die **- 2.** [top - of hat] oberes Ende; [- of head] Scheitel der; [- of hill] Kuppe die ◇ vt **- 1.** [king, queen] krönen **- 2.** [tooth] überkronen **- 3.** [top] bedecken. ➡ **Crown** n: **the Crown** [monarchy] die Krone.

crown jewels npl Kronjuwelen pl.

crow's feet npl Krähenfüße pl.

crucial ['kruːʃl] adj entscheidend.

crucifix ['kruːsɪfɪks] n Kruzifix das.

Crucifixion [ˌkruːsɪ'fɪkʃn] n: **the ~** die Kreuzigung.

crude [kruːd] adj **- 1.** [raw] Roh-, roh **- 2.** [vulgar] derb, ordinär **- 3.** [drawing] grob; [method, shelter] primitiv.

crude oil n Rohöl das.

cruel [krʊəl] adj grausam.

cruelty ['krʊəltɪ] n Grausamkeit die; **~ to children** Kindesmisshandlung die; **~ to animals** Tierquälerei die.

cruet ['kruːɪt] n Menage die.

cruise [kru:z] ◇ *n* Kreuzfahrt *die* ◇ *vi* [ship] kreuzen; [plane] fliegen.

cruiser ['kru:zə'] *n* - 1. [warship] Kreuzer *der* - 2. [cabin cruiser] Vergnügungsjacht *die*.

crumb [krʌm] *n* [of food] Krümel *der*.

crumble ['krʌmbl] ◇ *n* mit Streuseln bedeckte überbackene Obstnachspeise ◇ *vt* zerkrümeln; [into larger pieces] zerbröckeln ◇ *vi* - 1. [plaster] bröckeln; [bread] krümeln; [building, wall] zerbröckeln - 2. *fig* [society, empire] verfallen; [hopes] dahinschwinden.

crumbly ['krʌmblɪ] *adj* [plaster] bröckelig; [bread, cake] krümelig.

crumpet ['krʌmpɪt] *n* kleines rundes Hefeteigbrot zum Toasten.

crumple ['krʌmpl] *vt* [clothes] zerknittern; [paper] zerknüllen.

crunch [krʌntʃ] ◇ *n*: if OR when it comes to the ~ *inf* wenn es darauf ankommt ◇ *vt* [with teeth] (krachend) kauen.

crunchy ['krʌntʃɪ] *adj* [apple, vegetables] frisch und knackig; [chocolate bar] knusprig.

crusade [kru:'seɪd] *n lit & fig* Kreuzzug *der*.

crush [krʌʃ] ◇ *n* - 1. [crowd] Gedränge *das* - 2. *inf* [infatuation]: **to have a ~ on sb** für jn schwärmen ◇ *vt* - 1. [squeeze - limb] quetschen; [- clothes, garlic] zerdrücken - 2. [ice, tablet] zerstoßen - 3. [destroy] zerquetschen; **to be ~ed to death** zu Tode gequetscht werden - 4. *fig* [army, hopes] vernichten; [opposition] niederschlagen.

crust [krʌst] *n* Kruste *die*.

crutch [krʌtʃ] *n* [stick] Krücke *die*.

crux [krʌks] *n* Kern *der*; **the ~ of the matter** der springende Punkt.

cry [kraɪ] *n* - 1. [shout] Ruf *der*; [louder] Schrei *der*; **a ~ of pain** ein Schmerzensschrei; **a ~ for help** ein Hilferuf - 2. [of bird] Schrei *der*. ◆ **cry off** *vi* einen Rückzieher machen. ◆ **cry out** *vt sep* & *vi* schreien.

cryptic ['krɪptɪk] *adj* rätselhaft.

crystal ['krɪstl] *n* Kristall *der*.

cub [kʌb] *n* - 1. [young animal] Junge *das* - 2. [boy scout] Wölfling *der*.

Cuba ['kju:bə] *n* Kuba *nt*.

Cuban ['kju:bən] ◇ *adj* kubanisch ◇ *n* Kubaner *der*, -in *die*.

cubbyhole ['kʌbɪhəul] *n* [room] Kabäuschen *das*; [compartment] Fach *das*.

cube [kju:b] ◇ *n* - 1. [object, shape] Würfel *der* - 2. MATH dritte Potenz ◇ *vt* MATH in die dritte Potenz erheben; **3 ~d** 3 hoch 3.

cubic ['kju:bɪk] *adj* Kubik-.

cubicle ['kju:bɪkl] *n* Kabine *die*.

Cub Scout *n* Wölfling *der*.

cuckoo ['kuku:] *n* Kuckuck *der*.

cuckoo clock *n* Kuckucksuhr *die*.

cucumber ['kju:kʌmbə'] *n* Gurke *die*.

cuddle ['kʌdl] ◇ *n*: **to give sb a ~** jn in den Arm nehmen ◇ *vt* an sich (A) drücken; [doll, dog] knuddeln ◇ *vi* schmusen.

cuddly toy ['kʌdl-] *n* Knuddeltier *das*.

cue [kju:] *n* - 1. RADIO, THEATRE & TV Stichwort *das*; **on ~** wie gerufen - 2. [in snooker, pool] Queue *das*.

cuff [kʌf] *n* - 1. [of sleeve] Manschette *die* - 2. *Am* [of trouser] Aufschlag *der*.

cuff link *n* Manschettenknopf *der*.

cul-de-sac ['kʌldəsæk] *n* Sackgasse *die*.

cull [kʌl] ◇ *n* Kontrolle der Größe eines Viehbestands durch das Töten der schwächsten Tiere ◇ *vt* - 1. [kill]: **to ~ seals** Robbenschlag betreiben - 2. *fml* [gather] sammeln.

culminate ['kʌlmɪneɪt] *vi*: **to ~ in sthg** in etw (D) gipfeln.

culmination [ˌkʌlmɪ'neɪʃn] *n* Höhepunkt *der*.

culottes [kju:'lɒts] *npl* Hosenrock *der*.

culpable ['kʌlpəbl] *adj fml* [person] schuldig.

culprit ['kʌlprɪt] *n* Schuldige *der*, *die*; [guilty of a crime] Täter *der*, -in *die*.

cult [kʌlt] ◇ *n* - 1. RELIG Kult *der* - 2. [book, film] Kultsymbol *das* ◇ *comp* [book, film] Kult-.

cultivate ['kʌltɪveɪt] *vt* - 1. [farm - land] bebauen; [- crops] anbauen - 2. [develop - interest, taste] entwickeln; [- friendship] pflegen; [- image] kultivieren.

cultural ['kʌltʃərəl] *adj* kulturell.

culture ['kʌltʃə'] *n* Kultur *die*.

cultured ['kʌltʃəd] *adj* kultiviert.

cumbersome ['kʌmbəsəm] *adj* [object] unhandlich; [parcel] sperrig.

cunning ['kʌnɪŋ] ◇ *adj* [plan] schlau; [person] gerissen; [device] schlau ausgedacht ◇ *n* [of plan] Schlauheit *die*; [of person] Gerissenheit *die*.

cup [kʌp] *n* - 1. [gen] Tasse *die*; **a ~ of tea** eine Tasse Tee - 2. [trophy, competition] Pokal *der* - 3. [of bra] Körbchen *das*.

cupboard ['kʌbəd] *n* Schrank *der*.

Cup Final *n*: **the ~** das Pokalendspiel.

curate ['kjuərət] *n* Vikar *der*.

curator [ˌkjuə'reɪtə'] *n* [of museum] Kustos *der*.

curb [kɜ:b] ◇ *n* - 1. [control]: **to put a ~ on sthg** etw im Zaum halten - 2. *Am* [of road] Bordstein *der* ◇ *vt* zügeln.

curdle ['kɜ:dl] *vi* gerinnen.

cure [kjuə'] ◇ *n* - 1. MED: **~ (for)** Heilmittel *das* (für) - 2. [solution]: **~ (for sthg)** Mittel *das* (gegen etw) ◇ *vt* - 1. MED [illness, person] heilen - 2. [solve] beheben - 3. [rid]: **to ~ sb of sthg** *fig* jn von etw heilen - 4. [preserve - smoke] räuchern; [- salt] pökeln; [- dry] trocknen.

cure-all *n* Allheilmittel *das*.

curfew ['kɜ:fju:] *n* Ausgangssperre *die*.

curio ['kjuərɪəu] (*pl* -s) *n* Kuriosität *die*.

curiosity [ˌkjuərɪ'ɒsɪtɪ] *n* - 1. [inquisitiveness] Neugier *die* - 2. [rarity] Kuriosität *die*.

curious ['kjʊərɪəs] *adj* - **1.** [inquisitive]: ~ **(about)** neugierig (auf (+ A)) - **2.** [strange] merkwürdig, seltsam.

curl [kɜːl] <> *n* [of hair] Locke *die* <> *vt* - **1.** [hair] in Locken legen - **2.** [tail, ribbon] (ein)rollen <> *vi* - **1.** [hair] sich locken - **2.** [paper, leaf] sich zusammenrollen - **3.** [smoke, snake] sich schlängeln. ◆ **curl up** *vi* [person, animal] sich zusammenrollen; **to ~ up in bed** sich ins Bett kuscheln.

curler ['kɜːlər] *n* Lockenwickler *der*.

curling tongs ['kɜːlɪŋ] *npl* Lockenstab *der*.

curly ['kɜːlɪ] *adj* [hair] lockig.

currant ['kʌrənt] *n* Korinthe *die*.

currency ['kʌrənsɪ] *n* - **1.** [money] Währung *die* - **2.** *fml* [acceptability]: **to gain ~** sich verbreiten, Verbreitung finden.

current ['kʌrənt] <> *adj* gegenwärtig <> *n* [flow - of water] Strömung *die*; [- of air] Luftströmung *die*; [- of electricity] Strom *der*.

current account *n* *Br* Girokonto *das*.

current affairs *npl* aktuelle Fragen *pl*.

currently ['kʌrəntlɪ] *adv* gegenwärtig.

curriculum [kə'rɪkjələm] (*pl* -lums OR -la [-lə]) *n* Lehrplan *der*.

curriculum vitae [-'viːtaɪ] (*pl* curricula vitae) *n* Lebenslauf *der*.

curry ['kʌrɪ] *n* Currygericht *das*; **chicken ~** Huhn mit Curry(sauce).

curse [kɜːs] <> *n* - **1.** [evil spell, swearword] Fluch *der* - **2.** [source of problems] Plage *die* <> *vt* verfluchen <> *vi* [swear] fluchen.

cursor ['kɜːsər] *n* COMPUT Cursor *der*.

cursory ['kɜːsərɪ] *adj* flüchtig.

curt [kɜːt] *adj* barsch.

curtail [kɜː'teɪl] *vt* [visit] abkürzen.

curtain ['kɜːtn] *n* [gen] Vorhang *der*.

curts(e)y ['kɜːtsɪ] (*pt & pp* curtsied) <> *n* Knicks *der* <> *vi* knicksen.

curve [kɜːv] <> *n* Kurve *die* <> *vi* [road, river] einen Bogen machen; [surface] sich wölben.

cushion ['kʊʃn] <> *n* [for sitting on] Kissen *das* <> *vt* dämpfen, abfangen.

cushy ['kʊʃɪ] *adj inf* bequem, lässig.

custard ['kʌstəd] *n* ≃ Vanillesoße *die*.

custody ['kʌstədɪ] *n* - **1.** [of child] Sorgerecht *das* - **2.** [of suspect]: **in ~** in Untersuchungshaft.

custom ['kʌstəm] *n* - **1.** [tradition] Brauch *der*; [habit] Gepflogenheit *die* - **2.** COMM [trade] Einkauf *der*. ◆ **customs** *n* (*U*) [place] Zoll *der*.

customary ['kʌstəmrɪ] *adj* üblich.

customer ['kʌstəmər] *n* Kunde *der*, -din *die*.

customize, -ise ['kʌstəmaɪz] *vt* - **1.** [make] individuell herrichten - **2.** [modify] anlpassen, modifizieren.

Customs and Excise *n* (*U*) *Br* britische Finanzbehörde, die indirekte Steuern (Ex- und Importsteuer, Mehrwertsteuer und Verbrauchssteuer) einzieht und verwaltet.

customs duty *n* (*U*) Zoll *der*.

customs officer *n* Zollbeamte *der*, -tin *die*.

cut [kʌt] (*pt & pp* cut) <> *n* - **1.** [slit] Schnitt *der* - **2.** [wound] Schnittwunde *die* - **3.** [of meat] Fleischstück *das* - **4.** [in salary, film, article] Kürzung *die* - **5.** [style - of clothes, hair] Schnitt *der* <> *vt* - **1.** [gen] schneiden; **to ~ one's finger** sich (*D*) in den Finger schneiden - **2.** [salary, costs, expenditure] reduzieren - **3.** [grass] mähen - **4.** [cards] abheben - **5.** *inf* [lecture, class] schwänzen <> *vi* - **1.** [gen] schneiden - **2.** [intersect] sich kreuzen. ◆ **cut back** <> *vt sep* - **1.** [prune] zurückschneiden - **2.** [reduce] reduzieren <> *vi*: **to ~ back on sthg** etw einschränken. ◆ **cut down** <> *vt sep* - **1.** [chop down] fällen - **2.** [reduce] reduzieren <> *vi*: **to ~ down on sthg** etw einschränken. ◆ **cut in** *vi* - **1.** [interrupt]: **to ~ in (on sb)** (jn) unterbrechen - **2.** [in car]: **to ~ in on** OR **in front of sb** jn schneiden. ◆ **cut off** *vt sep* - **1.** [sever] ablschneiden - **2.** [disconnect - electricity, gas, telephone] ablstellen; **I got ~ off** [on telephone] das Gespräch wurde unterbrochen - **3.** [isolate]: **to be ~ off (from sb/sthg)** (jm/etw) abgeschnitten sein - **4.** [discontinue] stoppen. ◆ **cut out** *vt sep* - **1.** [article, photo] auslschneiden; [tumour] herauslschneiden - **2.** [sewing] zulschneiden - **3.** [stop] auflhören mit; **~ it out!** lass das sein! - **4.** [exclude] auslschließen. ◆ **cut up** *vt sep* [vegetables] schneiden; [wood] hacken; [meat] auflschneiden.

cutback ['kʌtbæk] *n*: ~ **(in)** Kürzung *die* (von).

cute [kjuːt] *adj* süß.

cuticle ['kjuːtɪkl] *n* Nagelhaut *die*.

cutlery ['kʌtlərɪ] *n* (*U*) Besteck *das*.

cutlet ['kʌtlɪt] *n* Kotelett *das*.

cutout ['kʌtaʊt] *n* - **1.** [on machine] Stopschalter *der* - **2.** [shape] Ausschneidemodell *das*.

cut-price, cut-rate *Am adj* Billig-.

cut-throat *adj* [ruthless] gnadenlos.

cutting ['kʌtɪŋ] <> *adj* [wit] scharf; [remark] spitz, verletzend; [person] sarkastisch <> *n* - **1.** [of plant] Ableger *der* - **2.** [from newspaper] Ausschnitt *der* - **3.** *Br* [for road, railway] Durchstich *der*.

CV *n abbr of* curriculum vitae.

cwt. *abbr of* hundredweight.

cyanide ['saɪənaɪd] *n* Cyanid *das*.

cycle ['saɪkl] <> *n* - **1.** [series of events] Kreislauf *der*, Zyklus *der* - **2.** [of machine] Durchlauf *der*, Durchgang *der* - **3.** [bicycle] Fahrrad *das* - **4.** [of poems, songs] Zyklus *der* <> *comp* Fahrrad- <> *vi* Fahrrad fahren.

cycling ['saɪklɪŋ] *n* Fahrradfahren *das*.

cyclist ['saɪklɪst] *n* Fahrradfahrer *der*, -in *die*.

cylinder ['sɪlɪndə'] n - 1. [gen] Zylinder der
- 2. [for gas, oxygen] Flasche die.

cymbals ['sɪmblz] npl Becken das.

cynic ['sɪnɪk] n Zyniker der, -in die.

cynical ['sɪnɪkl] adj zynisch.

cynicism ['sɪnɪsɪzm] n Zynismus der.

Cypriot ['sɪprɪət] n Zypriot der, -in die.

Cyprus ['saɪprəs] n Zypern nt.

cyst [sɪst] n Zyste die.

czar [zɑː'] n Zar der.

Czech [tʃek] <> adj tschechisch <> n
- 1. [person] Tscheche der, -hin die - 2. [language] Tschechisch(e) das.

Czechoslovakia [ˌtʃekəslə'vækɪə] n
Tschechoslowakei die.

Czech Republic n: the ~ die Tschechische
Republik.

D

d (pl d's OR ds), **D** (pl D's OR Ds) [diː] n [letter] d
das, D das. ◆ **D** n - 1. MUS D das; **D flat** Des
das - 2. SCH [mark] ≃ vier.

DA n abbr of district attorney.

dab [dæb] <> n [small amount] Klecks der
<> vt - 1. [skin, wound] abtupfen - 2. [cream,
ointment]: **to ~ sthg on(to) sthg** etw auf etw
(A) tupfen.

dabble ['dæbl] vi: **to ~ (in sthg)** (in etw (D))
planschen OR plantschen.

dachshund ['dækshʊnd] n Dackel der.

dad [dæd], **daddy** ['dædɪ] n inf Vati der.

daddy longlegs [-'lɒŋlegz] (pl inv) n
Schnake die.

daffodil ['dæfədɪl] n Osterglocke die.

daft [dɑːft] adj Br inf doof, blöd.

dagger ['dægə'] n Dolch der.

daily ['deɪlɪ] <> adj & adv täglich <> n
[newspaper] Tageszeitung die.

dainty ['deɪntɪ] adj zierlich.

dairy ['deərɪ] n - 1. [on farm] Molkerei die
- 2. [shop] Milchgeschäft die.

dairy products npl Molkereiprodukte pl.

dais ['deɪɪs] n Podium das.

daisy ['deɪzɪ] n Gänseblümchen das.

daisy-wheel printer n Typenraddrucker
der.

dam [dæm] <> n (Stau)damm der <> vt
(auf)stauen.

damage ['dæmɪdʒ] <> n: ~ **(to sthg)** Schaden der (an etw (D)) <> vt - 1. [physically] beschädigen - 2. fig [chances, reputation] scha-

den (+ D). ◆ **damages** npl LAW
Schaden(s)ersatz der.

damn [dæm] <> adj & adv inf verdammt
<> n inf: **not to give a ~ or care a ~ (about sthg)**
sich einen Dreck scheren (um etw) <> vt RE-
LIG [condemn] verdammen <> excl inf verdammt!, Mist!

damned [dæmd] inf <> adj verdammt; **well
I'll be OR I'm ~!** Donnerwetter! <> adv verdammt.

damning ['dæmɪŋ] adj vernichtend.

damp [dæmp] <> adj feucht <> n Feuchtigkeit die <> vt anfeuchten.

dampen ['dæmpən] vt - 1. [make wet] anl-
feuchten - 2. fig [emotion] dämpfen.

damson ['dæmzn] n Damaszenerpflaume
die.

dance [dɑːns] <> n - 1. [gen] Tanz der
- 2. [social event] Tanzabend der - 3. [art form]
Tanzen das <> vi tanzen.

dancer ['dɑːnsə'] n Tänzer der, -in die.

dancing ['dɑːnsɪŋ] n Tanzen das.

dandelion ['dændɪlaɪən] n Löwenzahn der.

dandruff ['dændrʌf] n Schuppen pl.

Dane [deɪn] n Däne der, -nin die.

danger ['deɪndʒə'] n Gefahr die; **in ~** in Gefahr; **out of ~** außer Gefahr; **~ to sb/sthg** Gefahr für jn/etw; **to be in ~ of doing sthg** Gefahr laufen, etw zu tun.

dangerous ['deɪndʒərəs] adj gefährlich.

dangle ['dæŋgl] <> vt baumeln lassen; **to
~ sthg in front of sb** fig jn mit etw locken
<> vi baumeln.

Danish ['deɪnɪʃ] <> adj dänisch <> n [lan-
guage] Dänisch(e) das.

Danish (pastry) n Hefeteilchen das.

dank [dæŋk] adj naßkalt.

dapper ['dæpə'] adj adrett.

dappled ['dæpld] adj scheckig.

dare [deə'] <> vt - 1. [be brave enough]: **to
~ to do sthg** sich trauen, etw zu tun - 2. [chal-
lenge]: **to ~ sb to do sthg** jn herausfordern,
etw zu tun - 3. phr: **I ~ say** ich glaube schon
<> vi es wagen, sich trauen; **how ~ you!** was
fällt dir ein! <> n Mutprobe die.

daredevil ['deə,devl] n Draufgänger der,
-in die.

daring ['deərɪŋ] <> adj [person, action]
kühn, verwegen; [comment, clothes] gewagt
<> n Wagemut der, Kühnheit die.

dark [dɑːk] <> adj [gen] dunkel <> n
- 1. [darkness]: **the ~** die Dunkelheit; **to be in
the ~ about sthg** fig keine Ahnung von etw
haben - 2. [night]: **before/after ~** vor/nach
Einbruch der Dunkelheit.

darken ['dɑːkn] <> vt verdunkeln <> vi
[gen] sich verdunkeln.

dark glasses npl Sonnenbrille die.

darkness ['dɑːknɪs] n Dunkelheit die.

darkroom ['dɑːkrʊm] n Dunkelkammer
die.

darling ['dɑːlɪŋ] ◇ *adj* [dear] lieb ◇ *n* - 1. [loved person, term of address] Schatz *der* - 2. [favourite] Liebling *der*.

darn [dɑːn] ◇ *adj* & *adv inf* verdammt, verflixt ◇ *vt* [repair] stopfen.

dart [dɑːt] ◇ *n* [arrow] (Wurf)pfeil *der* ◇ *vi* [move quickly] flitzen. ✦ **darts** *n (U)* [game] Darts *pl*.

dartboard ['dɑːtbɔːd] *n* Dartscheibe *die*.

dash [dæʃ] ◇ *n* - 1. [of liquid] Schuß *der* - 2. [in punctuation] Gedankenstrich *der* - 3. [rush]: **to make a ~ for sthg** sich auf etw *(A)* stürzen ◇ *vt* - 1. *literary* [throw] schleudern - 2. [hopes] zerstören ◇ *vi* stürzen.

dashboard ['dæʃbɔːd] *n* Armaturenbrett *das*.

dashing ['dæʃɪŋ] *adj* [man] schneidig, flott.

data ['deɪtə] *n* Daten *pl*.

database ['deɪtəbeɪs] *n* Datenbank *die*.

data processing *n* Datenverarbeitung *die*.

date [deɪt] ◇ *n* - 1. [in time] Datum *das;* **to bring sb up to ~** jn über den Stand der Dinge informieren; **to bring sthg up to ~** etw auf den neuesten Stand bringen; **out of ~** [fashion, dictionary] veraltet; [passport] abgelaufen; **to keep sb/sthg up to ~** jn/etw auf dem Laufenden halten; **to ~** bis heute - 2. [appointment, person] Verabredung *die* - 3. [fruit] Dattel *die* ◇ *vt* - 1. [gen] datieren - 2. [go out with] ausgehen mit ◇ *vi* [go out of fashion] altmodisch werden.

dated ['deɪtɪd] *adj* altmodisch.

date of birth *n* Geburtsdatum *das*.

daub [dɔːb] *vt*: **to ~ sthg with sthg** etw mit etw beschmieren; **to ~ sthg on sthg** etw auf etw *(A)* schmieren.

daughter ['dɔːtə[r]] *n* Tochter *die*.

daughter-in-law *(pl* daughters-in-law) *n* Schwiegertochter *die*.

daunting ['dɔːntɪŋ] *adj* überwältigend.

dawdle ['dɔːdl] *vi* trödeln.

dawn [dɔːn] ◇ *n* - 1. [of day] Morgengrauen *das*, Tagesanbruch *der* - 2. *fig* [of era, peri-

od] Beginn *der* ◇ *vi lit* & *fig* anbrechen; **the day is ~ing** es dämmert. ✦ **dawn (up)on** *vt fus*: **it finally ~ed on me that ...** mir dämmerte schließlich, dass ...

day [deɪ] *n* - 1. [gen] Tag *der;* **the ~ before/after** am Tag zuvor/danach; **the ~ before yesterday** vorgestern; **the ~ after tomorrow** übermorgen; **any ~ now** jeden Tag *(in Kürze);* **one ~, some ~, one of these ~s** irgendwann, eines Tages; **to make sb's ~** jn sehr erfreuen - 2. [period]: **in those ~s** damals; **in my ~** zu meiner Zeit. ✦ **days** *adv* [work] tagsüber.

daybreak ['deɪbreɪk] *n* Tagesanbruch *der;* **at ~** bei Tagesanbruch.

daycentre ['deɪsentə[r]] *n Br* [for old people] Altentagesstätte *die;* [for children] Kindertagesstätte *die*.

daydream ['deɪdriːm] *vi* [not concentrate] vor sich hin träumen; [be idealistic] Luftschlösser bauen.

daylight ['deɪlaɪt] *n* - 1. [light] Tageslicht *das* - 2. [dawn] Tagesanbruch *der*.

day off *(pl* days off) *n* arbeitsfreier Tag.

day return *n Br* Tagesrückfahrkarte *die*.

daytime ['deɪtaɪm] ◇ *n* Tag *der* ◇ *comp:* **~ job** Arbeit am Tage OR über Tag; **~ television** *tagsüber ausgestrahlte Fernsehprogramme.*

day-to-day *adj* [routine, life] (all)täglich; **on a ~ basis** tageweise.

day trip *n* Tagesausflug *der*.

daze [deɪz] ◇ *n*: **in a ~** benommen, betäubt ◇ *vt* benommen machen.

dazzle ['dæzl] *vt* blenden.

DC *n abbr of* direct current.

deacon ['diːkn] *n* Diakon *der*.

deactivate [ˌdiːˈæktɪveɪt] *vt* entschärfen.

dead [ded] ◇ *adj* - 1. [person, animal, flower] tot; **the ~ man/woman** der/die Tote; **to shoot sb ~** jn erschießen - 2. [battery] leer; [telephone line, radio] tot - 3. [numb - arm, fingers] wie abgestorben, taub - 4. [lifeless - town] wie ausgestorben; [- party] öde ◇ *adv* - 1. [precisely] genau; **it's ~ ahead** es ist genau geradeaus; **~ on time** auf die Minute pünktlich - 2. *inf* [very] total; **'~ slow'** 'Schrittgeschwindigkeit'; **~ tired** todmüde - 3. [suddenly]: **to stop ~** [in car] plötzlich stehen bleiben ◇ *npl:* **the ~** die Toten *pl*.

deaden ['dedn] *vt* - 1. [noise] dämpfen - 2. [feeling] betäuben.

dead end *n lit* & *fig* Sackgasse *die*.

dead heat *n* totes Rennen.

deadline ['dedlaɪn] *n* letztmöglicher Termin.

deadlock ['dedlɒk] *n* Stillstand *der*.

dead loss *n inf* Reinfall *der;* **~ at sthg** Niete *die* in etw *(D)*.

deadly ['dedlɪ] ◇ *adj* tödlich; [enemy, sin] Tod- ◇ *adv* tödlich.

deadpan ['dedpæn] *adj* [delivery, manner] ausdruckslos; [humour] trocken.

deaf [def] ⬦ *adj* taub; **to be ~ to sthg** *fig* sich in Bezug auf etw *(A)* taub stellen ⬦ *npl:* **the ~** die Gehörlosen *pl.*

deaf-aid *n Br* Hörgerät *das.*

deaf-and-dumb *adj* taubstumm.

deafen ['defn] *vt* taub machen.

deafness ['defnɪs] *n* Taubheit *die.*

deal [di:l] *(pt & pp* dealt) ⬦ *n* **- 1.** [quantity]: **a good** OR **great ~** (sehr) viel; **a good** OR **great ~ of** eine Menge **- 2.** [business agreement] Geschäft *das;* **to do** OR **strike a ~ with sb** ein Geschäft mit jm abschließen **- 3.** *inf* [treatment]: **to give sb a fair/rough ~** jn fair/unfair behandeln ⬦ *vt* **- 1.** [strike]: **to ~ sb/sthg a blow,** **to ~ a blow to sb/sthg** jm/etw einen Schlag versetzen **- 2.** [cards] austeilen ⬦ *vi* **- 1.** [in cards] geben **- 2.** [in drugs, arms] handeln. **◆ deal in** *vt fus* COMM handeln mit. **◆ deal out** *vt sep* **- 1.** [cards] austeilen **- 2.** [share out] verteilen. **◆ deal with** *vt fus* **- 1.** [handle, cope with] sich kümmern um **- 2.** [be concerned with] handeln von **- 3.** [be faced with] es zu tun haben mit.

dealer ['di:lə*r*] *n* **- 1.** [trader] Händler *der,* -in *die.* **- 2.** [in cards] Kartengeber *der,* -in *die.*

dealing ['di:lɪŋ] *n* [trading] Handel *der.* **◆ dealings** *npl* [relations] Umgang *der;* **to have ~s with sb** mit jm (geschäftlich) zu tun haben.

dealt [delt] *pt & pp* ➪ deal.

dean [di:n] *n* UNIV & RELIG Dekan *der.*

dear [dɪə*r*] ⬦ *adj* **- 1.** [loved] lieb; **to be ~ to sb** jm lieb und teuer sein **- 2.** *esp Br* [expensive] teuer **- 3.** [in letter]: **Dear Tony** Lieber Tony; **Dear Mr Blair** Sehr geehrter Herr Blair; **Dear Sir** OR **Madam** Sehr geehrte Damen und Herren ⬦ *n:* **my ~** mein Lieber, meine Liebe ⬦ *excl:* **oh ~!** ach je!; **~ me!** du meine Güte!

dearly ['dɪəlɪ] *adv* [love] von ganzem Herzen; [hope, wish] sehr.

death [deθ] *n* Tod *der;* **to frighten/worry sb to ~** jn zu Tode erschrecken; **to be sick to ~ of sthg** etw gründlich satt haben.

death certificate *n* Totenschein *der.*

death duty *Br,* **death tax** *Am n* Erbschaftssteuer *die.*

deathly ['deθlɪ] *adj* [silence] tödlich.

death penalty *n* Todesstrafe *die.*

death rate *n* Sterblichkeitsrate *die.*

death tax *n Am* ➪ death duty.

death trap *n inf* Todesfalle *die.*

debar [di:'ba:*r*] *vt* ausschließen.

debase [dɪ'beɪs] *vt* [quality, value, concept] entwerten; **to ~ o.s.** sich erniedrigen.

debate [dɪ'beɪt] ⬦ *n* Debatte *die;* **to be open to ~** zur Debatte stehen ⬦ *vt* debattieren, diskutieren; **to ~ whether to do sthg**

darüber diskutieren, ob etw getan werden soll ⬦ *vi* debattieren, diskutieren.

debauchery [dɪ'bɔːtʃərɪ] *n* Ausschweifung *die.*

debit ['debɪt] ⬦ *n* Soll *das,* Debet *das* ⬦ *vt* debitieren, belasten.

debris ['deɪbriː] *n (U)* Trümmer *pl.*

debt [det] *n* Schuld *die;* **to be in ~** Schulden haben; **to be in sb's ~** in js Schuld stehen.

debt collector *n* Schuldeneintreiber *der.*

debtor ['detə*r*] *n* Schuldner *der,* -in *die.*

debug [ˌdiː'bʌg] *vt* COMPUT [program] Fehler beseitigen in.

debunk [ˌdiː'bʌŋk] *vt* entlarven.

debut ['deɪbjuː] *n* Debüt *das.*

decade ['dekeɪd] *n* Jahrzehnt *das.*

decadence ['dekədəns] *n* Dekadenz *die.*

decadent ['dekədənt] *adj* dekadent.

decaffeinated [dɪ'kæfɪneɪtɪd] *adj* entkoffeiniert.

decanter [dɪ'kæntə*r*] *n* Karaffe *die.*

decathlon [dɪ'kæθlɒn] *n* Zehnkampf *der.*

decay [dɪ'keɪ] ⬦ *n* **- 1.** [of body] Verwesung *die;* [of plant, wood] Verrotten *das;* **(tooth) ~** Karies *die* **- 2.** *fig* [of building] Zerfall *der;* [of society] Untergang *der* ⬦ *vi* **- 1.** [tooth] faulen; [body] verwesen; [plant, wood] verrotten **- 2.** *fig* [building] zerfallen; [society] untergehen.

deceased [dɪ'siːst] *(pl inv) fml* ⬦ *adj* verstorben ⬦ *n:* **the ~** der/die Verstorbene.

deceit [dɪ'siːt] *n* Betrug *der.*

deceitful [dɪ'siːtfʊl] *adj* betrügerisch.

deceive [dɪ'siːv] *vt* [trick] betrügen; [subj: memory, eyes] täuschen; **to deceive o.s.** sich *(D)* selbst etwas vormachen.

December [dɪ'sembə*r*] *n* Dezember *der;* siehe *also* September.

decency ['diːsnsɪ] *n* [respectability] Anstand *der;* **he didn't have the ~ to thank me** er hat es nicht für nötig gehalten, sich bei mir zu bedanken.

decent ['diːsnt] *adj* anständig; **are you ~?** [dressed] hast du was an?

deception [dɪ'sepʃn] *n* Täuschung *die.*

deceptive [dɪ'septɪv] *adj* irreführend.

decide [dɪ'saɪd] ⬦ *vt* **- 1.** [resolve] entscheiden, beschließen; **to ~ to do sthg** (sich) entscheiden, etw zu tun; **to ~ that ...** entscheiden, dass ..., beschließen, dass ... **- 2.** [issue, case, match] entscheiden; **what finally ~d you?** was hat dich schließlich dazu gebracht? ⬦ *vi* [make up one's mind] (sich) entscheiden, (sich) entschließen. **◆ decide (up)on** *vt fus* sich entscheiden für.

decided [dɪ'saɪdɪd] *adj* **- 1.** [distinct] entschieden **- 2.** [resolute] bestimmt.

decidedly [dɪ'saɪdɪdlɪ] *adv* **- 1.** [distinctly] entschieden **- 2.** [resolutely] bestimmt.

deciduous [dɪ'sɪdjʊəs] *adj* Laub-.

decimal ['desɪml] <> *adj* dezimal <> *n* Dezimalzahl *die*.

decimal point *n* Dezimalpunkt *der*.

decimate ['desɪmeɪt] *vt* dezimieren.

decipher [dɪ'saɪfə^r] *vt* entziffern.

decision [dɪ'sɪʒn] *n* [choice, judgement] Entscheidung *die*.

decisive [dɪ'saɪsɪv] *adj* - 1. [person] entschlossen - 2. [factor, event] entscheidend.

deck [dek] *n* - 1. [of ship, bus, plane] Deck *das* - 2. [of cards] Spiel *das* - 3. *Am* [of house] Terrasse *die*.

deckchair ['dektʃeə^r] *n* Liegestuhl *der*.

declaration [ˌdeklə'reɪʃn] *n* - 1. [statement, proclamation] Erklärung *die* - 2. [to customs] Zollerklärung *die*.

Declaration of Independence *n*: the ~ die (amerikanische) Unabhängigkeitserklärung.

Declaration of Independence

Die amerikanische Unabhängigkeitserklärung ist das von Thomas Jefferson, dem späteren Präsidenten der Vereinigten Staaten, verfasste Dokument, das 1776 vom konstitutionellen Kongress aufgenommen wurde und worin die Abspaltung der 13 Kolonien von Großbritannien erklärt wird. Die Gründung der ersten 13 Staaten verkörpert zusammen mit den ersten Staatsverfassungen den Ursprung der heutigen USA.

declare [dɪ'kleə^r] *vt* - 1. [state, proclaim] erklären - 2. [goods at customs, taxes] deklarieren.

decline [dɪ'klaɪn] <> *n* Niedergang *der;* to be in ~ sich verschlechtern; to be on the ~ (abl)sinken <> *vt* [offer, request] ablehnen; to ~ to do sthg es ablehnen, etw zu tun <> *vi* - 1. [deteriorate] sich verschlechtern - 2. [refuse] ablehnen.

decode [ˌdiː'kəʊd] *vt* entschlüsseln.

decompose [ˌdiːkəm'pəʊz] *vi* [vegetable matter] verfaulen; [flesh] verwesen.

decongestant [ˌdiːkən'dʒestənt] *n* schleimlösendes Mittel.

decorate ['dekəreɪt] *vt* - 1. [make pretty - cake, dessert] verzieren; [- with balloons, streamers, flags] dekorieren, schmücken - 2. [with paint] streichen; [with wallpaper] tapezieren - 3. [with medal] auszeichnen.

decoration [ˌdekə'reɪʃn] *n* - 1. [ornament] Dekoration *die;* [on cake] Verzierung *die;* **Christmas tree ~s** Christbaumschmuck *der* - 2. [appearance of room, building] Dekor *das* - 3. [medal] Auszeichnung *die*.

decorator ['dekəreɪtə^r] *n* Maler *der*, -in *die*.

decoy [*n* 'diːkɔɪ, *vt* dɪ'kɔɪ] <> *n* - 1. [for hunt-ing] Köder *der* - 2. [person] Lockvogel *der* <> *vt* anlocken.

decrease [*n* 'diːkriːs, *vb* dɪ'kriːs] <> *n*: ~ **(in sthg)** [crime, unemployment] Rückgang *der* (an etw (D)); [size, spending] Abnahme *die* (einer Sache (G)) <> *vt* verringern; [price] herabsetzen <> *vi* [in size] abnehmen; [of numbers] zurücklgehen, sinken.

decree [dɪ'kriː] <> *n* - 1. [order, decision] Erlass *der* - 2. *Am* [judgment] Urteil *das* <> *vt* verordnen.

decree nisi [-'naɪsaɪ] (*pl* decrees nisi) *n Br* LAW vorläufiges Scheidungsurteil.

decrepit [dɪ'krepɪt] *adj* [person] altersschwach; [house, car] heruntergekommen.

dedicate ['dedɪkeɪt] *vt* - 1. [book, song, poem]: **to ~ sthg to sb** jm etw widmen - 2. [devote]: **to ~ one's life to sthg** sein Leben einer Sache (D) widmen.

dedication [ˌdedɪ'keɪʃn] *n* - 1. [commitment] Hingabe *die* - 2. [in book] Widmung *die*.

deduce [dɪ'djuːs] *vt* schließen; **to ~ sthg from sthg** etw aus etw schließen.

deduct [dɪ'dʌkt] *vt*: **to ~ sthg (from)** etw ablziehen (von).

deduction [dɪ'dʌkʃn] *n* - 1. [conclusion] Folgerung *die* - 2. [of money, number] Abzug *der*.

deed [diːd] *n* - 1. [action] Tat *die* - 2. LAW Urkunde *die;* ~ of sale Kaufvertrag *der*.

deem [diːm] *vt fml* erachten; **to ~ it wise to do sthg** es für sinnvoll erachten, etw zu tun.

deep [diːp] <> *adj* - 1. [gen] tief - 2. [colour] dunkel - 3. [thoughts, feeling] stark - 4. [sigh, breath] schwer <> *adv* tief; ~ **down** *fig* innerlich.

deepen ['diːpn] *vi* - 1. [river, sea] tiefer werden - 2. [crisis, recession, feeling] sich verstärken.

deep freeze *n* Tiefkühltruhe *die*.

deep-fry *vt* frittieren.

deeply ['diːplɪ] *adv* - 1. [gen] tief - 2. [grateful, sorry, regret, moving] zutiefst.

deep-sea *adj* Tiefsee-.

deer [dɪə^r] (*pl inv*) *n* [male] Hirsch *der;* [female] Reh *das*.

deface [dɪ'feɪs] *vt* [poster] verunstalten.

defamatory [dɪ'fæmətrɪ] *adj fml* verleumderisch.

default [dɪ'fɔːlt] <> *n* - 1. [failure]: **to win by ~** durch Nichtantreten des Gegners gewinnen - 2. COMPUT Voreinstellung *die* <> *vi* [in sports] nicht anltreten.

defeat [dɪ'fiːt] <> *n* Niederlage *die;* [of motion] Ablehnung *die;* **to admit ~** sich geschlagen geben <> *vt* - 1. [team, opponent] schlagen - 2. [motion, proposal] ablehnen.

defeatist [dɪ'fiːtɪst] <> *adj* defätistisch <> *n* Defätist *der*.

defect [n 'diːfekt, vi diˈfekt] ⬦ n Mangel der, Fehler der ⬦ vi POL überlaufen.

defective [dɪˈfektɪv] adj defekt.

defence Br, **defense** Am [dɪˈfens] n - 1. [gen] Verteidigung die; **in my ~** zu meiner Verteidigung - 2. [protective device, system] Abwehr die.

defenceless Br, **defenseless** Am [dɪˈfenslɪs] adj schutzlos.

defend [dɪˈfend] vt verteidigen; **to ~ sb against sb/sthg** jn gegen jn/etw verteidigen.

defendant [dɪˈfendənt] n Angeklagte der, die, Beklagte der, die.

defender [dɪˈfendəʳ] n Verteidiger der, -in die.

defense n Am = defence.

defenseless adj Am = defenceless.

defensive [dɪˈfensɪv] ⬦ adj - 1. [weapons, tactics] Verteidigungs- - 2. [person] defensiv ⬦ n: **on the ~** in der Defensive.

defer [dɪˈfɜːʳ] ⬦ vt verschieben ⬦ vi: **to ~ to sb** sich jm beugen, sich jm fügen.

deferential [ˌdefəˈrenʃl] adj respektvoll.

defiance [dɪˈfaɪəns] n Trotz der; **in ~ of sb/sthg** jm/etw zum Trotz.

defiant [dɪˈfaɪənt] adj trotzig.

deficiency [dɪˈfɪʃnsɪ] n - 1. [lack] Mangel der - 2. [inadequacy] Mangelhaftigkeit die.

deficient [dɪˈfɪʃnt] adj - 1. [lacking]: **he is ~ in sthg** es mangelt ihm an etw (D) - 2. [inadequate] ungenügend.

deficit [ˈdefɪsɪt] n Defizit das.

defile [dɪˈfaɪl] vt besudeln.

define [dɪˈfaɪn] vt - 1. [give meaning of] definieren - 2. [describe] bestimmen, festlegen.

definite [ˈdefɪnɪt] adj - 1. [plan, date] bestimmt, definitiv - 2. [answer] eindeutig; [improvement, difference] deutlich - 3. [confident - person] bestimmt.

definitely [ˈdefɪnɪtlɪ] adv definitiv.

definition [defɪˈnɪʃn] n - 1. [of word, expression, concept] Definition die - 2. [of image] Bildschärfe die.

deflate [dɪˈfleɪt] ⬦ vt [balloon, tyre] die Luft ablassen aus ⬦ vi [balloon, tyre] Luft verlieren.

deflation [dɪˈfleɪʃn] n ECON Deflation die.

deflect [dɪˈflekt] vt ablenken.

defogger [ˌdiːˈfɒgəʳ] n Am AUT Scheibenbelüftung die.

deformed [dɪˈfɔːmd] adj deformiert.

defraud [dɪˈfrɔːd] vt betrügen.

defrost [ˌdiːˈfrɒst] ⬦ vt - 1. [fridge] abltauen; [frozen food] aufltauen - 2. Am AUT [de-ice] enteisen; [demist] belüften ⬦ vi - 1. [fridge] abltauen - 2. [frozen food] aufltauen.

deft [deft] adj geschickt.

defunct [dɪˈfʌŋkt] adj [organization] nicht mehr bestehend.

defuse [ˌdiːˈfjuːz] vt Br lit & fig entschärfen.

defy [dɪˈfaɪ] vt - 1. [disobey] trotzen (+ D) - 2. [challenge]: **to ~ sb to do sthg** jn herauslfordern, etw zu tun - 3. fig: **that defies description** das spottet jeder Beschreibung.

degenerate [adj dɪˈdʒenərət, vb dɪˈdʒenəreɪt] ⬦ adj degeneriert, entartet ⬦ vi: **to ~ (into)** auslarten (zu).

degrading [dɪˈgreɪdɪŋ] adj entwürdigend.

degree [dɪˈgriː] n - 1. [unit of measurement] Grad der - 2. [qualification] akademischer Grad; **to have/take a ~ (in sthg)** einen akademischen Abschluss (in etw (D)) haben/machen - 3. [amount - of risk, truth] Maß das; **to a (certain) ~** bis zu einem gewissen Grad; **by ~s** allmählich, nach und nach.

dehydrated [ˌdiːhaɪˈdreɪtɪd] adj [person] ausgetrocknet.

de-ice [diːˈaɪs] vt enteisen.

deign [deɪn] vi: **to ~ to do sthg** sich herabllassen, etw zu tun.

deity [ˈdiːɪtɪ] n Gottheit die.

dejected [dɪˈdʒektɪd] adj niedergeschlagen.

delay [dɪˈleɪ] ⬦ n Verspätung die ⬦ vt - 1. [plane, train, traveller] auflhalten; [start, operation, recovery] verzögern - 2. [postpone - meeting, journey, decision] verschieben; **to ~ doing sthg** es auflschieben, etw zu tun ⬦ vi zögern.

delayed [dɪˈleɪd] adj verspätet.

delectable [dɪˈlektəbl] adj - 1. [food] köstlich - 2. [person] reizend.

delegate [n ˈdelɪgət, vb ˈdelɪgeɪt] ⬦ n Delegierte der, die ⬦ vt delegieren; **to ~ sb to do sthg** jn beauftragen, etw zu tun; **to ~ sthg to sb** jn mit etw beauftragen.

delegation [delɪˈgeɪʃn] n - 1. [group of people] Delegation die - 2. (U) [act of delegating] Delegieren das.

delete [dɪˈliːt] vt [word, line, name] streichen; COMPUT löschen, entfernen.

deli [ˈdelɪ] n abbr of delicatessen.

deliberate [adj dɪˈlɪbərət, vb dɪˈlɪbəreɪt] ⬦ adj - 1. [intentional] absichtlich - 2. [slow] bedächtig ⬦ vi fml beraten.

deliberately [dɪˈlɪbərətlɪ] adv [on purpose] absichtlich.

delicacy [ˈdelɪkəsɪ] n - 1. [of lace, china] Feinheit die; [of health, instrument] Empfindlichkeit die - 2. (U) [tact] Feingefühl das - 3. [food] Delikatesse die.

delicate [ˈdelɪkət] adj - 1. [lace, china, flavour] fein; [fingers, colour] zart - 2. [child, person, health, instrument] empfindlich - 3. [situation, subject] heikel.

delicatessen [ˌdelɪkəˈtesn] n Delikatessengeschäft das.

delicious [dɪˈlɪʃəs] adj [tasty] köstlich.

delight [dɪ'laɪt] ◇ n Freude die; **to take ~ in doing sthg** Freude daran haben, etw zu tun ◇ vt erfreuen ◇ vi: **to ~ in doing sthg** sich damit vergnügen, etw zu tun.

---

delight

Ich bin froh, dass wir uns gesehen haben. I'm glad we met.

Ich freue mich schon auf den Urlaub. I'm looking forward to the holidays.

Es freut mich, dass es dir besser geht. I'm glad you're feeling better.

Wie schön, dich zu sehen. It's lovely to see you.

Was für eine angenehme Überraschung. What a nice surprise!

---

delighted [dɪ'laɪtɪd] adj sehr erfreut; **~ by** OR **with sthg** hocherfreut über etw (A); **to be ~ to do sthg** etw mit Vergnügen tun.

delightful [dɪ'laɪtfʊl] adj reizend; [meal] köstlich.

delinquent [dɪ'lɪŋkwənt] ◇ adj straffällig ◇ n Straftäter der, -in die.

delirious [dɪ'lɪrɪəs] adj - 1. MED im Delirium - 2. [ecstatic] ekstatisch.

deliver [dɪ'lɪvər] vt - 1. [distribute]: **to ~ sthg (to sb)** [mail, newspaper] (jm) etw zustellen; COMM (jm) etw liefern - 2. [give - speech, lecture] halten; [- message, warning] überbringen - 3. [a blow, kick] versetzen - 4.: **to ~ a woman's baby** eine Frau von ihrem Baby entbinden - 5. fml [liberate]: **to ~ sb (from sthg)** jn (von etw) erlösen - 6. Am POL [votes] stellen.

delivery [dɪ'lɪvərɪ] n - 1. [of goods] Lieferung die; [of letters] Zustellung die - 2. (U) [way of speaking] Vortragsweise die - 3. [birth] Entbindung die.

delude [dɪ'luːd] vt täuschen; **to ~ o.s.** sich etwas vormachen.

delusion [dɪ'luːʒn] n Täuschung die.

delve [delv] vi - 1. [into mystery]: **to ~ into sthg** sich in etw (A) vertiefen - 2. [in bag, cupboard] greifen.

demand [dɪ'mɑːnd] ◇ n - 1. [claim, firm request] Forderung die; **it makes great ~s on my time** es nimmt viel von meiner Zeit in Anspruch; **on ~** bei Bedarf - 2. (U) COMM: **~ (for)** Nachfrage die (nach); **in ~** [product, person] gefragt ◇ vt - 1. [request forcefully] fordern, verlangen; **to ~ to do sthg** verlangen, etw zu tun - 2. [enquire forcefully] zu wissen verlangen - 3. [require] erfordern.

demanding [dɪ'mɑːndɪŋ] adj - 1. [job] anstrengend - 2. [person, people] anspruchsvoll.

demean [dɪ'miːn] vt erniedrigen.

demeaning [dɪ'miːnɪŋ] adj erniedrigend.

demeanour Br, **demeanor** Am [dɪ'miːnər] n (U) fml Verhalten das.

demented [dɪ'mentɪd] adj wahnsinnig.

demise [dɪ'maɪz] n (U) fml - 1. [death] Ableben das - 2. fig [of company, custom] Ende das.

demister [,diː'mɪstər] n Br AUT Scheibenbelüftung die.

demo ['deməʊ] (pl -s) n inf abbr of demonstration.

democracy [dɪ'mɒkrəsɪ] n Demokratie die.

democrat ['deməkræt] n Demokrat der, -in die. ◆ **Democrat** n Am Wähler bzw. Angehöriger der Demokratischen Partei der USA.

democratic [,demə'krætɪk] adj demokratisch. ◆ **Democratic** adj Am die Demokratische Partei der USA betreffend.

Democratic Party n Am: **the ~** die Demokraten.

demolish [dɪ'mɒlɪʃ] vt - 1. [building] abreißen - 2. [idea, argument] zunichte machen.

demonstrate ['demənstreɪt] ◇ vt - 1. [prove] beweisen - 2. [appliance, machine] vorführen - 3. [ability, talent] zeigen ◇ vi: **to ~ (for/against)** demonstrieren (für/gegen).

demonstration [,demən'streɪʃn] n - 1. [public meeting] Demonstration die - 2. [of new appliance, machine] Vorführung die - 3. fml [of feelings] Ausdruck der.

demonstrator ['demənstreɪtər] n [protester] Demonstrant der, -in die.

demoralized [dɪ'mɒrəlaɪzd] adj demoralisiert, entmutigt.

demote [,diː'məʊt] vt degradieren.

demure [dɪ'mjʊər] adj sittsam.

den [den] n [of animal] Höhle die.

denial [dɪ'naɪəl] n - 1. [refutation] Leugnung die - 2. (U) [refusal] Verweigerung die.

denier ['denɪər] n Denier das.

denigrate ['denɪgreɪt] vt fml verunglimpfen.

denim ['denɪm] n (U) Jeansstoff der. ◆ **denims** npl Jeans pl.

denim jacket n Jeansjacke die.

Denmark ['denmɑːk] n Dänemark nt.

denomination [dɪ,nɒmɪ'neɪʃn] n - 1. RELIG Konfession die - 2. FIN Nennwert der.

denounce [dɪ'naʊns] vt [person] anlgreifen; [actions] anlprangern.

dense [dens] adj - 1. [thick] dicht - 2. inf [stupid] schwer von Begriff.

dent [dent] ◇ n Beule die ◇ vt einlbeulen.

dental ['dentl] adj Zahn-; **~ appointment** Termin der beim Zahnarzt.

dental floss n Zahnseide die.

dental surgeon n Zahnarzt der, -ärztin die.

dentist ['dentɪst] n Zahnarzt der, -ärztin die; **to go to the dentist('s)** zum Zahnarzt gehen.

dentures ['dentʃəz] npl Gebiss das.

deny [dɪ'naɪ] vt - 1. [refute] bestreiten; [publicly] dementieren - 2. *fml* [refuse] verweigern; **to ~ sb sthg** jm etw verweigern.

deodorant [diː'əʊdərənt] *n* Deodorant *das*.

depart [dɪ'pɑːt] *vi fml* - 1. [leave] weglgehen; [by car, bus *etc*] weglfahren; [on journey] ablreisen; **to ~ from** [train] ablfahren von; [plane] ablfliegen von - 2. [differ]: **to ~ from sthg** von etw ablweichen.

department [dɪ'pɑːtmənt] *n* - 1. [in organization, shop] Abteilung *die* - 2. SCH & UNIV Fachbereich *der* - 3. [in government] Ministerium *das*.

department store *n* Kaufhaus *das*.

departure [dɪ'pɑːtʃə'] *n* - 1. [leaving - on journey] Abreise *die*; [- of train] Abfahrt *die*; [- of plane] Abflug *der*; **'departures'** [in airport] 'Abflug' - 2. [variation]: **~ (from sthg)** Abweichung *die* (von etw.).

departure lounge *n* Abflughalle *die*.

depend [dɪ'pend] *vi* - 1.: **to ~ on sb/sthg** [financially] von jm/etw ablhängen; [to rely on] auf jn/etw angewiesen sein; **I can ~ on you** ich kann mich auf dich verlassen - 2. [be determined]: **to ~ on sb/sthg** von jm/etw ablhängen; **it ~s on what happens/who is there** das hängt davon ab, was passiert/wer da ist; **~ing on the weather** je nachdem, wie das Wetter wird.

dependable [dɪ'pendəbl] *adj* verlässlich.

dependant [dɪ'pendənt] *n* versorgungsabhängige Angehörige *der*, *die*.

dependent [dɪ'pendənt] *adj* - 1. [reliant]: **to be ~ (on sb/sthg)** [financially] abhängig sein (von jm/etw); [rely on] angewiesen sein (auf jn/etw) - 2. [addicted] abhängig - 3. [determined by]: **to be ~ on sb/sthg** (von jm/etw) abhängig sein.

depict [dɪ'pɪkt] *vt* - 1. [show in picture] darstellen - 2. [describe]: **to ~ sb/sthg as sthg** jn/ etw als etw beschreiben.

deplete [dɪ'pliːt] *vt* vermindern.

deplorable [dɪ'plɔːrəbl] *adj* beklagenswert.

deplore [dɪ'plɔː'] *vt* verurteilen.

deploy [dɪ'plɔɪ] *vt* auslsetzen.

deport [dɪ'pɔːt] *vt* auslweisen.

depose [dɪ'pəʊz] *vt* [king, ruler] ablsetzen.

deposit [dɪ'pɒzɪt] <> *n* - 1. GEOL [of gold, oil] Ablagerung *die* - 2. [in wine] Bodensatz *der* - 3. [payment into bank] Einzahlung *die* - 4. [down payment] Anzahlung *die* - 5. [returnable payment - on bottle] Pfand *das*; [- on hired goods] Kaution *die* <> *vt* - 1. [in bank] deponieren - 2. [bag, case, shopping] abllegen.

deposit account *n Br* Sparkonto *das*.

depot ['depəʊ] *n* - 1. [storage area - for buses] Depot *das*; [- for goods] Lagerhaus *das* - 2. *Am* [terminus - for trains] Bahnhof *der*; [- for buses] Busbahnhof *der*.

depreciate [dɪ'priːʃɪeɪt] *vi* an Wert verlieren.

depress [dɪ'pres] *vt* - 1. [sadden] deprimieren - 2. ECON [economy, market] sich hemmend auswirken auf (+ A); [prices, share values] verringern.

depressed [dɪ'prest] *adj* - 1. [person] deprimiert, niedergeschlagen - 2. [area] unterentwickelt *(in wirtschaftlicher Hinsicht)*.

depressing [dɪ'presɪŋ] *adj* deprimierend.

depression [dɪ'preʃn] *n* - 1. [sadness] Niedergeschlagenheit *die*; MED Depression *die* - 2. ECON Depression *die* - 3. *fml* [hollow] Vertiefung *die*.

deprivation [ˌdeprɪ'veɪʃn] *n* Entbehrung *die*; **sleep ~** Schlafentzug *der*.

deprive [dɪ'praɪv] *vt*: **to ~ sb of sthg** [to take sthg away] jn einer Sache (G) berauben; [to prevent sb from having sthg] jm etw vorlenthalten.

depth [depθ] *n* Tiefe *die*; **to be out of one's ~** [in water] nicht mehr stehen können; *fig* [unable to cope] überfordert sein; **in ~** eingehend. **depths** *npl*: **the ~s of the sea** die Tiefen des Meeres; **in the ~s of winter** im tiefsten Winter; **to be in the ~s of despair** in tiefster Verzweiflung sein.

deputize, -ise ['depjʊtaɪz] *vi*: **to ~ for sb** jn vertreten *(eine Person höheren Rangs)*.

deputy ['depjʊtɪ] <> *adj* stellvertretend <> *n* - 1. [second-in-command] Stellvertreter *der*, -in *die* - 2. *Am* [deputy sheriff] Hilfssheriff *der*.

derail [dɪ'reɪl] *vt* [train] entgleisen lassen.

deranged [dɪ'reɪndʒd] *adj* geistesgestört.

derby [*Br* 'dɑːbɪ, *Am* 'dɜːbɪ] *n* - 1. [sports event] Derby *das* - 2. *Am* [hat] Melone *die*.

derelict ['derəlɪkt] *adj* verfallen.

deride [dɪ'raɪd] *vt* verhöhnen.

derisory [də'raɪzərɪ] *adj* - 1. [ridiculous] lächerlich - 2. [scornful] höhnisch.

derivative [dɪ'rɪvətɪv] <> *adj pej* nachgeahmt <> *n* Derivat *das*.

derive [dɪ'raɪv] <> *vt* - 1.: **to ~ pleasure from sthg** Freude an etw (D) haben; **to ~ satisfaction from sthg** Befriedigung aus etw ziehen - 2.: **to be ~d from sthg** [from language] aus etw stammen; [from word] von etw abgeleitet sein <> *vi*: **to ~ from sthg** [from language] aus etw stammen; [from word] von etw abgeleitet sein.

derogatory [dɪ'rɒgətrɪ] *adj* abfällig.

derv [dɜːv] *n Br* Diesel *der*.

descend [dɪ'send] <> *vi* - 1. *fml* [go down - person] herunterlgehen/hinunterlgehen; [- in vehicle] herunterlfahren/hinunterlfahren; [- from carriage, ladder *etc*] herunterlsteigen/hinunterlsteigen; [- plane] die Flughöhe verringern - 2. [fall]: **to ~ on sb/ sthg** [silence] sich über jn/etw legen; [gloom] jn/etw befallen <> *vt fml* [go down] hinunterlgehen.

descendant [dɪ'sendənt] *n* Nachkomme *der*.

descended [dɪ'sendɪd] *adj*: **to be ~ from sb** von jm ablstammen.

descent [dɪ'sent] *n* - **1.** [downwards movement]: **a steep ~** ein steiler Abstieg - **2.** *(U)* [origin] Abstammung *die*.

describe [dɪ'skraɪb] *vt* beschreiben.

description [dɪ'skrɪpʃn] *n* - **1.** [account] Beschreibung *die* - **2.** [type] Art *die*.

desecrate ['desɪkreɪt] *vt* entweihen.

desert [*n* 'dezət, *vb & npl* dɪ'zɜ:t] ⟨⟩ *n* GEOGR Wüste *die* ⟨⟩ *vt* [abandon - place] verlassen; [- person] im Stich lassen ⟨⟩ *vi* MIL desertieren. ➡ **deserts** *npl*: **to get one's just ~s** bekommen, was man verdient hat.

deserted [dɪ'zɜ:tɪd] *adj* verlassen, öde.

deserter [dɪ'zɜ:tə'] *n* Deserteur *der*.

desert island ['dezət-] *n* einsame Insel.

deserve [dɪ'zɜ:v] *vt* verdienen; **to ~ to do sthg** verdienen, etw zu tun.

deserving [dɪ'zɜ:vɪŋ] *adj* verdienstvoll.

design [dɪ'zaɪn] ⟨⟩ *n* - **1.** [plan, drawing] Entwurf *der* - **2.** [art] Design *das* - **3.** [pattern] Muster *das* - **4.** [shape] Konstruktion *die*; [of dress] Schnitt *der* - **5.** [intention] Absicht *die*; **by ~** absichtlich; **to have ~s on sb/sthg** es auf jn/etw abgesehen haben ⟨⟩ *vt* entwerfen; **to be ~ed to do sthg** dafür vorgesehen sein, etw zu tun.

designate ['dezɪgneɪt] *vt* [appoint - area] bestimmen; [- person] ernennen; **to ~ sb to do sthg** bestimmen, dass jd etw tut.

designer [dɪ'zaɪnə'] ⟨⟩ *adj* [jeans, glasses, stubble] Designer- ⟨⟩ *n* [in industry] Konstrukteur *der*; [in theatre] Bühnenbildner *der*, -in *die*; [of clothes] Modedesigner *der*, -in *die*.

desirable [dɪ'zaɪərəbl] *adj* - **1.** *fml* [appropriate] wünschenswert - **2.** [attractive] reizvoll - **3.** [sexually attractive] begehrenswert.

desire [dɪ'zaɪə'] ⟨⟩ *n* - **1.** [wish]: **~ (for sthg/ to do sthg)** der Wunsch (nach etw/etw zu tun) - **2.** *(U)* [sexual longing] Begierde *die* ⟨⟩ *vt* - **1.** [want] wünschen - **2.** [feel sexual longing for] begehren.

> **desiring**
>
> Ich würde gerne ins Kino gehen. I would love to go to the cinema.
> Wenn es nach mir ginge, wären wir schon längst dort. If I had my way, we would've been there ages ago.
> Am liebsten wäre mir ein heißes Bad. I'm dying for a hot bath.
> Ich fände es am schönsten, wenn wir alle zusammen blieben. I think it would be best if we all stayed together.
> Ich habe große Lust, mir einen Hamburger zu kaufen. I could murder a hamburger.

desist [dɪ'zɪst] *vi fml*: **to ~ (from doing sthg)** davon ablsehen(, etw zu tun).

desk [desk] *n* - **1.** [piece of furniture] Schreibtisch *der*; [in school] Pult *das* - **2.** [service point] Schalter *der*; [in hotel] Empfang *der*.

desk diary *n* Tischkalender *der*.

desktop publishing ['desktɒp-] *n* Desktop-Publishing *das*.

desolate ['desələt] *adj* - **1.** [place] trostlos - **2.** [person] tieftraurig.

despair [dɪ'speə'] ⟨⟩ *n* Verzweiflung *die* ⟨⟩ *vi* verzweifeln; **to ~ of sb/sthg** an jm/etw verzweifeln; **to ~ of doing sthg** die Hoffnung auflgeben, etw zu tun.

despairing [dɪ'speərɪŋ] *adj* verzweifelt.

despatch [dɪ'spætʃ] *n & vt* = dispatch.

desperate ['despərət] *adj* - **1.** [reckless - criminal, person] zum Äußersten entschlossen; [- attempt, measures] verzweifelt - **2.** [serious, hopeless] hoffnungslos - **3.** [despairing] verzweifelt - **4.** [in great need]: **to be ~ for sthg** etw dringend benötigen.

desperately ['despərətlɪ] *adv* - **1.** [seriously, hopelessly] hoffnungslos - **2.** [very - busy, sorry] äußerst; **she ~ wants to travel** sie wünscht sich nichts mehr als zu reisen.

desperation [,despə'reɪʃn] *n* Verzweiflung *die*; **in ~** aus Verzweiflung.

despicable [dɪ'spɪkəbl] *adj* [person] verachtenswert; [behaviour, act] verabscheuungswürdig.

despise [dɪ'spaɪz] *vt* [person] verachten; [racism] verabscheuen.

despite [dɪ'spaɪt] *prep* trotz *(+ G)*.

despondent [dɪ'spɒndənt] *adj* verzagt.

dessert [dɪ'zɜ:t] *n* Dessert *das*.

dessertspoon [dɪ'zɜ:tspu:n] *n* Dessertlöffel *der*.

destination [,destɪ'neɪʃn] *n* [of means of transport] Bestimmungsort *der*; [of traveller] Reiseziel *das*.

destined ['destɪnd] *adj* [intended]: **to be ~ for sthg** zu etw bestimmt sein; **to be ~ to do sthg** dazu bestimmt sein, etw zu tun.

destiny ['destɪnɪ] *n* Schicksal *das*.

destitute ['destɪtju:t] *adj* notleidend; **to be ~** Not leiden.

destroy [dɪ'strɔɪ] *vt* [ruin] zerstören.

destruction [dɪ'strʌkʃn] *n* *(U)* Zerstörung *die*, Vernichtung *die*.

detach [dɪ'tætʃ] *vt* [remove] ablnehmen; [tear off] abltrennen; **to ~ sthg from sthg** etw von etw ablnehmen/abltrennen.

detached [dɪ'tætʃt] *adj* [unemotional] distanziert, unbeteiligt.

detached house *n* Einfamilienhaus *das*.

detachment [dɪ'tætʃmənt] *n* [aloofness] Distanziertheit *die*.

detail ['di:teɪl] ⟨⟩ *n* - **1.** [small point] Detail *das*; [specific] Einzelheit *die* - **2.** *(U)* [collection of facts, points] Details *pl*; **to go into ~** ins Detail gehen; **in ~** im Detail ⟨⟩ *vt* [list] auflisten. ➡ **details** *npl* [information] Informationen *pl*; [personal information] Personalien *pl*.

detailed ['di:teɪld] *adj* detailliert.

detain [dɪ'teɪn] *vt* - **1.** [in police station] in polizeilichem Gewahrsam behalten; [in hospital] zur stationären Behandlung behalten - **2.** [delay] aufhalten.

detect [dɪ'tekt] *vt* - **1.** [subj: person] bemerken - **2.** [subj: machine] ausfindig machen.

detection [dɪ'tekʃn] *n* - **1.** (U) [discovery] Entdeckung *die* - **2.** [investigation] Ermittlungsarbeit *die*.

detective [dɪ'tektɪv] *n* [private] Detektiv *der*, -in *die*; [police officer] Kriminalbeamte *der*, -tin *die*.

detective novel *n* Kriminalroman *der*.

detention [dɪ'tenʃn] *n* - **1.** [of suspect] Untersuchungshaft *die* - **2.** [at school] Nachsitzen *das*.

___

📖 **detention** ___

Detention oder das Nachsitzen ist eine der Disziplinarmaßnahmen für Schüler, die in der Schule gegen die Regeln verstoßen, beispielsweise keine Hausaufgaben machen, zu spät kommen oder die Uniformpflicht missachten.
Normalerweise dauert das Nachsitzen zwischen 30 Minuten und einer Stunde und findet während der Mittagspause oder nach der Schule statt. Lehrer sind gesetzlich verpflichtet, die Eltern mindestens 24 Stunden im Voraus über diese Maßregelung zu informieren.

___

deter [dɪ'tɜːʳ] *vt* abhalten; **to ~ sb from doing sthg** jn davon abhalten, etw zu tun.

detergent [dɪ'tɜːdʒənt] *n* [for clothes] Waschmittel *das*; [for dishes] Spülmittel *das*.

deteriorate [dɪ'tɪərɪəreɪt] *vi* sich verschlechtern.

determination [dɪˌtɜːmɪ'neɪʃn] *n* [resolve] Entschlossenheit *die*.

determine [dɪ'tɜːmɪn] *vt* - **1.** [establish, find out] bestimmen, ermitteln - **2.** [control] entscheiden - **3.** *fml* [resolve]: **to ~ to do sthg** sich dazu entschließen, etw zu tun - **4.** [fix, establish] festlegen.

determined [dɪ'tɜːmɪnd] *adj* - **1.** [person] resolut; **to be ~ to do sthg** fest entschlossen sein, etw zu tun - **2.** [effort] angestrengt.

deterrent [dɪ'terənt] *n* Abschreckungsmittel *das*.

detest [dɪ'test] *vt* verabscheuen.

detonate ['detəneɪt] ⟨⟩ *vt* zur Detonation bringen ⟨⟩ *vi* detonieren.

detour ['diːˌtʊəʳ] *n* Umweg *der*.

detract [dɪ'trækt] *vi*: **to ~ from** [quality] beeinträchtigen; [enjoyment, achievement] schmälern.

detriment ['detrɪmənt] *n*: **to the ~ of sb/ sthg** zum Schaden von jm/etw.

detrimental [ˌdetrɪ'mentl] *adj* [effect] schädlich; [consequences] nachteilig.

deuce [djuːs] *n* TENNIS Einstand *der*.

devaluation [ˌdiːvæljʊ'eɪʃn] *n* FIN Abwertung *die*.

devastated ['devəsteɪtɪd] *adj* - **1.** [area, city] verwüstet - **2.** *fig* [person] am Boden zerstört.

devastating ['devəsteɪtɪŋ] *adj* - **1.** [disastrous - hurricane, storm] verheerend; [- news, experience] niederschmetternd - **2.** [very effective - charm, wit] umwerfend; [- remark, argument] vernichtend; [- player, speaker] überragend.

develop [dɪ'veləp] ⟨⟩ *vt* - **1.** [land, area, resources] erschließen - **2.** [illness] bekommen; [habit] annehmen; **the machine ~ed a fault** an der Maschine ist ein Fehler aufgetreten - **3.** [industry, sector] fördern - **4.** [machine, weapon, product] weiterentwickeln - **5.** [business, company] ausbauen; [idea, argument, plot] entfalten - **6.** PHOT entwickeln ⟨⟩ *vi* - **1.** [gen] sich entwickeln; [plot] sich entfalten - **2.** [fault, problem] auftauchen; [illness] sich entwickeln.

developing country [dɪ'veləpɪŋ-] *n* Entwicklungsland *das*.

development [dɪ'veləpmənt] *n* - **1.** [gen] Entwicklung *die*; [of business, company] Ausbau *der*; [of idea, argument, plot] Entfaltung *die* - **2.** (U) [of land, area, resources] Erschließung *die* - **3.** [developed land] Neubausiedlung *die*.

deviate ['diːvɪeɪt] *vi*: **to ~ (from sthg)** (von etw) abweichen.

device [dɪ'vaɪs] *n* - **1.** [apparatus] Gerät *das* - **2.** [plan, method] Mittel *das* - **3.** [bomb] Sprengkörper *der*.

devil ['devl] *n* - **1.** [evil spirit] Teufel *der* - **2.** *inf* [person] Teufel *der*; **poor ~!** armer Teufel!; **you silly ~!** du Trottel!; **you lucky ~!** Glückspilz! - **3.** [for emphasis]: **who/where/ why the ~ ...?** wer/wo/warum zum Teufel ...? ➤ **Devil** *n* [Satan]: **the Devil** der Teufel.

devious ['diːvjəs] *adj* [plan, means] fragwürdig; [person] verschlagen.

devise [dɪ'vaɪz] *vt* entwerfen.

devoid [dɪ'vɔɪd] *adj fml*: **~ of** bar (+ *G*).

devolution [ˌdiːvə'luːʃn] *n* POL Dezentralisierung *die*.

devote [dɪ'vəʊt] *vt*: **to ~ sthg to sthg** etw für etw verwenden.

devoted [dɪ'vəʊtɪd] *adj* [mother] hingebungsvoll; [husband, wife] liebevoll und treu; **to be ~ to sb/sthg** jn/etw innig lieben.

devotion [dɪ'vəʊʃn] *n*: **~ (to sb/sthg)** Hingabe *die* (an jn/etw).

devour [dɪ'vaʊəʳ] *vt lit & fig* verschlingen.

devout [dɪ'vaʊt] *adj* RELIG fromm.

dew [djuː] *n* Tau *die*.

diabetes [ˌdaɪə'biːtiːz] *n* Diabetes *der*.

diabetic [ˌdaɪə'betɪk] ◇ adj [person] zuckerkrank ◇ n Diabetiker der, -in die.

diabolic(al) [ˌdaɪə'bɒlɪk(l)] adj - 1. [evil] teuflisch - 2. inf [very bad] sauschlecht.

diagnose ['daɪəgnəʊz] vt [illness] diagnostizieren.

diagnosis [ˌdaɪəg'nəʊsɪs] (pl -oses [-əʊsiːz]) n [of illness] Diagnose die.

diagonal [daɪ'ægənl] ◇ adj diagonal ◇ n Diagonale die.

diagram ['daɪəgræm] n Schaubild das.

dial ['daɪəl] ◇ n - 1. [of watch, clock] Zifferblatt das; [of meter] Skala die - 2. [of radio] Skala die - 3. [of telephone] Wählscheibe die ◇ vt [number] wählen.

dialect ['daɪəlekt] n Dialekt der.

dialling code ['daɪəlɪŋ-] n Br Vorwahl die.

dialling tone Br ['daɪəlɪŋ-], **dial tone** Am n Amtszeichen das.

dialogue Br, **dialog** Am ['daɪəlɒg] n Dialog der.

dial tone n Am = dialling tone.

dialysis [daɪ'ælɪsɪs] n Dialyse die.

diameter [daɪ'æmɪtə'] n Durchmesser der.

diamond ['daɪəmənd] n - 1. [gem] Diamant der - 2. [shape] Raute die. ➤ **diamonds** npl Karo das; **the six of ~s** die Karosechs.

diaper ['daɪəpə'] n Am Windel die.

diaphragm ['daɪəfræm] n [contraceptive] Diaphragma das.

diarrh(o)ea [ˌdaɪə'rɪə] n Durchfall der.

diary ['daɪərɪ] n - 1. [appointment book] (Termin)kalender der - 2. [personal record] Tagebuch das.

dice [daɪs] (pl inv) ◇ n [for games] Würfel der ◇ vt würfeln.

dictate [dɪk'teɪt] vt - 1. [read out] diktieren - 2. [impose] vorlschreiben.

dictation [dɪk'teɪʃn] n Diktat das; **to take** OR **do ~** ein Diktat auflnehmen.

dictator [dɪk'teɪtə'] n POL Diktator der, -in die.

dictatorship [dɪk'teɪtəʃɪp] n Diktatur die.

dictionary ['dɪkʃənrɪ] n Wörterbuch das; [for a particular subject] Lexikon das.

did [dɪd] pt ▷ do.

diddle ['dɪdl] vt inf übers Ohr hauen.

didn't ['dɪdnt] = did not.

die [daɪ] (pt & pp died; cont dying; npl sense 2 only dice) ◇ vi - 1. [person] sterben; [animal, plant] einlgehen; **to be dying** im Sterben liegen; **to be dying for sthg** inf sich nach etw sehnen; **to be dying to do sthg** inf darauf brennen, etw zu tun - 2. fig [love, anger] vergehen; [memory] schwinden ◇ n esp Am [dice] Würfel der. ➤ **die away** vi [sound] leiser werden. ➤ **die down** vi [wind] sich legen; [sound] leiser werden; [fire] herunterlbrennen. ➤ **die out** vi auslsterben.

diehard ['daɪhɑːd] n Ewiggestrige der, die.

diesel ['diːzl] n - 1. [vehicle] Diesel der - 2. [fuel] Dieselöl das.

diesel engine n - 1. [of car] Dieselmotor der - 2. LOCOMOTIVE Dieselokomotive die.

diesel fuel, diesel oil n Dieselkraftstoff der, Dieselöl das.

diet ['daɪət] ◇ n - 1. [eating pattern] Ernährung die - 2. [to lose weight, for medical reasons] Diät die; **to be/go on a ~** eine Diät machen ◇ comp [low-calorie] Diät- ◇ vi [to lose weight] eine Diät machen.

differ ['dɪfə'] vi - 1. [be different] verschieden sein; **to ~ from sb/sthg** sich von jm/etw unterscheiden - 2. [disagree]: **to ~ with sb (about sthg)** mit jm (über etw (D)) verschiedener Meinung sein.

difference ['dɪfrəns] n Unterschied der; **it doesn't make any ~** es ist egal; **~ of opinion** Meinungsverschiedenheit die.

different ['dɪfrənt] adj - 1. [not like before] anders; [not identical] verschieden, unterschiedlich; [various] verschieden; **to be ~ from** Br or Am anders als; anders sein als jd/etw - 2. [unusual] außergewöhnlich.

differentiate [ˌdɪfə'renʃɪeɪt] ◇ vt: **to ~ sthg from sthg** etw von etw unterscheiden ◇ vi: **to ~ (between)** unterscheiden (zwischen (+ D)).

difficult ['dɪfɪkəlt] adj - 1. [hard] schwierig; **to make life ~ for sb** jm das Leben schwer machen - 2. [awkward] schwierig.

difficulty ['dɪfɪkəltɪ] n Schwierigkeit die; **to have ~ (in) doing sthg** Schwierigkeiten haben, etw zu tun.

diffident ['dɪfɪdənt] adj schüchtern.

diffuse [dɪ'fjuːz] vt - 1. [light] auslstrahlen - 2. [information] verbreiten.

dig [dɪg] (pt & pp dug) ◇ n - 1. fig [unkind remark] Seitenhieb der - 2. ARCHAEOL Ausgrabung die ◇ vt [hole] graben; [garden] umlgraben ◇ vi [in ground] graben. ➤ **dig up** vt sep lit & fig auslgraben.

digest [dɪ'dʒest] vt lit & fig verdauen.

digestion [dɪ'dʒestʃn] n Verdauung die.

digestive biscuit [daɪ'dʒestɪv-] n Br mürber Keks aus Vollkornmehl.

digestive system [daɪ'dʒestɪv-] n Verdauungsapparat der.

digger ['dɪgə'] n [machine] Bagger der.

digit ['dɪdʒɪt] n - 1. [figure] Ziffer die - 2. [finger] Finger der; [toe] Zehe die.

digital ['dɪdʒɪtl] adj digital.

digital camera n digitale Kamera.

digital television n digitales Fernsehen.

digital watch n Digitaluhr die.

dignified ['dɪgnɪfaɪd] adj würdevoll.

dignity ['dɪgnətɪ] n Würde die.

digress [daɪ'gres] vi: **to ~ (from sthg)** (von etw) ablschweifen.

digs [dɪgz] npl Br inf Bude die.

dike [daɪk] *n* - **1.** [wall, bank] Damm *der* - **2.** *inf pej* [lesbian] Lesbe *die*.

dilapidated [dɪˈlæpɪdeɪtɪd] *adj* baufällig.

dilemma [dɪˈlemə] *n* Dilemma *das*.

diligent [ˈdɪlɪdʒənt] *adj* sorgfältig.

dilute [daɪˈluːt] <> *adj* verdünnt <> *vt*: **to ~ sthg (with sthg)** etw (mit etw) verdünnen.

dim [dɪm] <> *adj* - **1.** [room] halbdunkel; [light] trüb - **2.** [indistinct - shape, sight] undeutlich; [- sound, memory] schwach - **3.** [eyes] schwach - **4.** *inf* [stupid] beschränkt <> *vt* dämpfen <> *vi* [light, hope] schwinden.

dime [daɪm] *n Am* Zehncentstück *das*.

dimension [dɪˈmenʃn] *n* Dimension *die*. ➤ **dimensions** *pl* [of room, object] Abmessungen *pl*; **in three ~s** dreidimensional.

diminish [dɪˈmɪnɪʃ] <> *vt* [subj: person] herabsetzen; [subj: thing] verringern <> *vi* [importance, popularity] abnehmen.

diminutive [dɪˈmɪnjʊtɪv] <> *adj fml* winzig <> *n* GRAMM Verkleinerungsform *die*.

dimmer [ˈdɪmə*ʳ*] *n* Dimmer *der*. ➤ **dimmers** *npl Am* - **1.** [dipped headlights] Abblendlicht *das* - **2.** [parking lights] Begrenzungsleuchten *pl*.

dimmer switch *n* = dimmer.

dimple [ˈdɪmpl] *n* Grübchen *das*.

din [dɪn] *n inf* Getöse *das*.

dine [daɪn] *vi fml* speisen. ➤ **dine out** *vi* auswärts speisen.

diner [ˈdaɪnə*ʳ*] *n* - **1.** [person] Gast *der (in einem Restaurant)* - **2.** *Am* [restaurant] Lokal *das*.

dinghy [ˈdɪŋgɪ] *n* [for sailing] kleines Segelboot; **(rubber)** ~ Schlauchboot *das*.

dingy [ˈdɪndʒɪ] *adj* schmuddelig.

dining car [ˈdaɪnɪŋ-] *n* Speisewagen *der*.

dining room [ˈdaɪnɪŋ-] *n* - **1.** [in house] Esszimmer *das* - **2.** [in hotel] Speisesaal *der*.

dinner [ˈdɪnə*ʳ*] *n* - **1.** [meal - in the evening] (warmes) Abendessen; [- at noon] Mittagessen *das* - **2.** [formal event] (Abend)essen *das*.

dinner jacket *n* [jacket] Smokingjacke *die*; [suit] Smoking *der*.

dinner party *n* Abendgesellschaft *die* (mit Essen).

dinnertime [ˈdɪnətaɪm] *n* Essenszeit *die*.

dinosaur [ˈdaɪnəsɔː*ʳ*] *n* Dinosaurier *der*.

dint [dɪnt] *n fml*: **by ~ of** mittels *(+ G)*.

dip [dɪp] <> *n* - **1.** [in road, ground] Senke *die* - **2.** [sauce] Dip *der* - **3.** [swim]: **to go for a ~** (kurz) schwimmen gehen <> *vt* - **1.** [into liquid]: **to ~ sthg in(to) sthg** etw in etw *(A)* eintauchen - **2.** *Br* [headlights] abblenden <> *vi* [wing, road, ground] sich senken.

diploma [dɪˈpləʊmə] (*pl* -s) *n* Diplom *das*.

diplomacy [dɪˈpləʊməsɪ] *n* Diplomatie *die*.

diplomat [ˈdɪpləmæt] *n* [official] Diplomat *der*, -in *die*.

diplomatic [ˌdɪpləˈmætɪk] *adj* diplomatisch.

dipstick [ˈdɪpstɪk] *n* AUT Ölmessstab *der*.

dire [ˈdaɪə*ʳ*] *adj* [serious - warning] dringend; [- consequences] schwerwiegend; **to be in ~ need of sthg** etw dringend brauchen.

direct [dɪˈrekt] <> *adj* - **1.** [gen] direkt - **2.** [exact] genau <> *vt* - **1.** [aim]: **to ~ sthg at sb** [question, remark] etw an jn richten; **the campaign is ~ed at teenagers** die Kampagne zielt auf Teenager ab - **2.** [person to place] den Weg erklären *(+ D)* - **3.** [manage, be in charge of] leiten - **4.** [TV programme] leiten; [film, play] Regie führen bei - **5.** [order]: **to ~ sb to do sthg** jn anweisen, etw zu tun <> *adv* direkt.

direct current *n* Gleichstrom *der*.

direct debit *n Br* Dauerauftrag *der*.

direction [dɪˈrekʃn] *n* - **1.** [orientation] Richtung *die* - **2.** [of play, film] Regie *die*; [of TV programme] Leitung *die*. ➤ **directions** *npl* - **1.** [to place] Wegbeschreibung *die*; **to ask (sb) for ~** (jn) nach dem Weg fragen - **2.** [for use] Gebrauchsanweisung *die*.

directly [dɪˈrektlɪ] *adv* - **1.** [gen] direkt - **2.** [exactly] genau - **3.** [very soon] sofort.

director [dɪˈrektə*ʳ*] *n* - **1.** [of company] Direktor *der*, -in *die* - **2.** [of film, play] Regisseur *der*, -in *die*; [of TV programme] Leiter *der*, -in *die*.

directory [dɪˈrektərɪ] *n* - **1.** [book, list] Verzeichnis *das*; **(telephone)** ~ Telefonbuch *das* - **2.** COMPUT Directory *das*.

directory enquiries *n Br* Fernsprechauskunft *die*.

dire straits *npl*: **in ~** in großen Nöten.

dirt [dɜːt] *n* - **1.** [mud, dust] Schmutz *der* - **2.** [earth] Erde *die*.

dirt cheap *inf adj* spottbillig.

dirty [ˈdɜːtɪ] <> *adj* - **1.** [not clean] schmutzig - **2.** [unfair] gemein; **to play a ~ trick on sb** jm übel mitspielen - **3.** [smutty] schmutzig, unanständig <> *vt* beschmutzen.

disability [ˌdɪsəˈbɪlətɪ] *n* Behinderung *die*.

disabled [dɪsˈeɪbld] <> *adj* behindert <> *npl*: **the ~** die Behinderten *pl*.

disadvantage [ˌdɪsədˈvɑːntɪdʒ] *n* Nachteil *der*; **to be at a ~** im Nachteil sein.

disagree [ˌdɪsəˈgriː] *vi* - **1.** [with another person] nicht übereinstimmen; [two people] sich nicht einig sein; **to ~ with sb** mit jm nicht übereinstimmen; **to ~ with sthg** etw nicht einverstanden sein - **2.** [statements, accounts] nicht übereinstimmen - **3.** [subj: food, drink]: **to ~ with sb** jm nicht bekommen.

disagreeable [ˌdɪsəˈgriːəbl] *adj* - **1.** [smell, job] unangenehm - **2.** [person] unfreundlich.

disagreement [ˌdɪsəˈgriːmənt] *n* - **1.** [of opinions] Uneinigkeit *die*; [of records] Diskrepanz *die* - **2.** [argument] Meinungsverschiedenheit *die*; **to be in ~ about sthg** [people] verschiedener Ansicht in Bezug auf etw *(A)* sein.

disallow [ˌdɪsəˈlaʊ] *vt* - **1.** *fml* [appeal, claim] zurücklweisen - **2.** [goal] nicht anlerkennen.

disappear [ˌdɪsəˈpɪəʳ] *vi* verschwinden.

disappearance [ˌdɪsəˈpɪərəns] *n* Verschwinden *das*.

disappoint [ˌdɪsəˈpɔɪnt] *vt* enttäuschen.

disappointed [ˌdɪsəˈpɔɪntɪd] *adj*: ~ **(in** OR **with sthg)** (von etw) enttäuscht.

disappointing [ˌdɪsəˈpɔɪntɪŋ] *adj* enttäuschend.

disappointment [ˌdɪsəˈpɔɪntmənt] *n* Enttäuschung *die*.

🔲 disappointment

Das finde ich aber schade. That's a shame.
Schade, dass das Konzert ausfällt. It's a pity the concert has been cancelled.
So ein Pech! That's bad luck!
Das habe ich nicht erwartet. I wasn't expecting that.
Und jetzt war alle Mühe umsonst. All that work for nothing!
Das hätte ich nie von ihm gedacht. I would never have expected that of him.

---

disapproval [ˌdɪsəˈpruːvl] *n* Missfallen *das*.

disapprove [ˌdɪsəˈpruːv] *vi*: **to ~ of sthg** etw missbilligen; **to ~ of sb** etwas gegen jn haben.

disarm [dɪsˈɑːm] *vi* ablrüsten.

disarmament [dɪsˈɑːməmənt] *n* Abrüstung *die*.

disarray [ˌdɪsəˈreɪ] *n*: **to be in ~** *fml* [clothes, hair, room] in Unordnung sein; [group] schlecht organisiert sein.

disaster [dɪˈzɑːstəʳ] *n* Katastrophe *die*.

disastrous [dɪˈzɑːstrəs] *adj* katastrophal.

disband [dɪsˈbænd] <> *vt* aufllösen <> *vi* sich aufllösen.

disbelief [ˌdɪsbɪˈliːf] *n*: **in** OR **with ~** ungläubig.

disc *Br*, **disk** *Am* [dɪsk] *n* - **1.** [shape] Scheibe *die* - **2.** MED Bandscheibe *die* - **3.** [record] Platte *die*.

discard [dɪˈskɑːd] *vt* weglwerfen.

discern [dɪˈsɜːn] *vt* - **1.** [see] wahrlnehmen - **2.** [detect] erkennen.

discerning [dɪˈsɜːnɪŋ] *adj* kritisch.

discharge [*n* ˈdɪstʃɑːdʒ, *vt* dɪsˈtʃɑːdʒ] <> *n* - **1.** [of patient, prisoner, soldier] Entlassung *die* - **2.** [toxic emission] Ausstoß *der* - **3.** MED [from wound] Ausfluss *der* <> *vt* - **1.** [patient, prisoner, soldier] entlassen - **2.** *fml* [fulfil] erlfüllen - **3.** [emit] auslstoßen.

disciple [dɪˈsaɪpl] *n* - **1.** RELIG Jünger *der* - **2.** *fig* [follower] Anhänger *der*, -in *die*.

discipline [ˈdɪsɪplɪn] <> *n* Disziplin *die* <> *vt* - **1.** [train] disziplinieren - **2.** [punish] bestrafen.

disc jockey *n* Discjockey *der*.

disclose [dɪsˈkləʊz] *vt* enthüllen.

disclosure [dɪsˈkləʊʒəʳ] *n* Enthüllung *die*.

disco [ˈdɪskəʊ] (*pl* -s) *n* abbr of discotheque.

discomfort [dɪsˈkʌmfət] *n* - **1.** (*U*) [physical pain] Beschwerden *pl*; **to be in ~** Beschwerden haben - **2.** [anxiety, embarrassment] Unbehagen *das*.

disconcert [ˌdɪskənˈsɜːt] *vt* verunsichern.

disconnect [ˌdɪskəˈnekt] *vt* - **1.** [detach] trennen - **2.** [remove plug of] den Stecker herauslziehen von; [from water/gas supply] von der Wasserzufuhr/Gaszufuhr trennen; **to ~ sb's telephone** jm das Telefon ablstellen; **we've been ~ed** man hat uns das Telefon/das Gas/den Wasser/den Strom abgestellt - **3.** [when talking]: **we've been ~ed** die Verbindung wurde unterbrochen.

disconsolate [dɪsˈkɒnsələt] *adj* untröstlich.

discontent [ˌdɪskənˈtent] *n*: ~ **(with sthg)** Unzufriedenheit *die* (mit etw).

discontented [ˌdɪskənˈtentɪd] *adj*: **to be ~ (with sthg)** (mit etw) unzufrieden sein.

discontinue [ˌdɪskənˈtɪnjuː] *vt* [service, supply] einlstellen; [visits] beenden; [production] auslaufen lassen.

discord [ˈdɪskɔːd] *n* - **1.** *fml* [conflict] Uneinigkeit *die* - **2.** MUS Disharmonie *die*.

discotheque [ˈdɪskəʊtek] *n* Diskothek *die*.

discount [*n* ˈdɪskaʊnt, *vb*, *Br* dɪsˈkaʊnt, *Am* ˈdɪskaʊnt] <> *n* Rabatt *der* <> *vt* - **1.** [disregard] verwerfen - **2.** COMM [product] zu einem geringeren Preis anlbieten.

discourage [dɪsˈkʌrɪdʒ] *vt* - **1.** [dishearten] entmutigen - **2.** [dissuade]: **to ~ sb from doing sthg** jn davon ablbringen, etw zu tun.

discover [dɪˈskʌvəʳ] *vt* - **1.** [find] entdecken; [cause of sthg] herauslfinden - **2.** [realize] festlstellen.

discovery [dɪˈskʌvərɪ] *n* Entdeckung *die*.

discredit [dɪsˈkredɪt] *vt* diskreditieren.

discreet [dɪˈskriːt] *adj* diskret.

discrepancy [dɪˈskrepənsɪ] *n*: ~ **(in/between)** Diskrepanz *die* (zwischen (+ *D*)).

discretion [dɪˈskreʃn] *n* - **1.** [tact] Diskretion *die* - **2.** [judgment]: **use your own ~** handeln Sie nach eigenem Ermessen; **at the ~ of** nach Ermessen (+ *G*).

discriminate [dɪˈskrɪmɪneɪt] *vi* - **1.** [distinguish]: **to ~ (between)** unterscheiden (zwischen (+ *D*)) - **2.** [treat unfairly]: **to ~ against sb** jn diskriminieren.

discriminating [dɪˈskrɪmɪneɪtɪŋ] *adj* [person, eye, audience] kritisch; [taste] fein.

discrimination [dɪˌskrɪmɪˈneɪʃn] *n* - **1.** [prejudice] Diskriminierung *die* - **2.** [good judgment] Urteilsvermögen *das*.

discus [ˈdɪskəs] (*pl* -es) *n* Diskus *der*.

discuss [dɪˈskʌs] *vt* besprechen; [in political,

academic context] diskutieren; **to ~ sthg with sb** etw mit jm besprechen.

discussion [dr'skʌʃn] *n* **- 1.** *(U)* [act of discussing] Besprechen *das;* [in political, academic context] Diskussion *die;* **to be under ~** zur Diskussion stehen **- 2.** [talk] Gespräch *das;* [in political, academic context] Diskussion *die.*

disdain [dɪs'deɪn] *fml n:* **~ (for sb/sthg)** Verachtung *die* (für jn/etw).

disease [dɪ'ziːz] *n lit & fig* Krankheit *die.*

disembark [ˌdɪsɪm'bɑːk] *vi* von Bord gehen.

disenchanted [ˌdɪsɪn'tʃɑːntɪd] *adj:* **~ (with sthg)** (von etw) ernüchtert.

disengage [ˌdɪsɪn'geɪdʒ] *vt* **- 1.** [release]: **to ~ o.s./sthg (from sthg)** sich/etw (von etw) losmachen **- 2.** TECH [gears, mechanism] auslrücken.

disfigure [dɪs'fɪgə^r] *vt* verunstalten.

disgrace [dɪs'greɪs] ⟨⟩ *n* Schande *die;* **to be in ~** in Ungnade gefallen sein ⟨⟩ *vt:* **to ~ sb** jm Schande machen; **to ~ o.s.** sich blamieren.

disgraceful [dɪs'greɪsfʊl] *adj* skandalös.

disgruntled [dɪs'grʌntld] *adj* verstimmt.

disguise [dɪs'gaɪz] ⟨⟩ *n* Verkleidung *die;* **in ~** verkleidet ⟨⟩ *vt* **- 1.** [dress up] verkleiden **- 2.** [voice, handwriting] verstellen **- 3.** [disappointment, surprise] verbergen; [fact] verschleiern; [taste of sthg] überdecken.

disgust [dɪs'gʌst] ⟨⟩ *n:* **~ (at sthg)** Abscheu *der* (vor etw *(D)*) ⟨⟩ *vt* anlekeln.

disgusting [dɪs'gʌstɪŋ] *adj* ekelhaft.

dish [dɪʃ] *n* **- 1.** [bowl] Schüssel *die;* [shallow] Schale *die* **- 2.** *Am* [plate] Teller *der* **- 3.** [food] Gericht *das.* ⟨⟩ **dishes** *npl* Geschirr *das;* **to do** OR **wash the ~es** Geschirr spülen OR ablwaschen. ⟨⟩ **dish out** *vt sep inf* austeilen. ⟨⟩ **dish up** *vt sep inf* [food] aufltun.

dish aerial *Br,* **dish antenna** *Am* *n* Parabolantenne *die,* Satellitenschüssel *die.*

dishcloth ['dɪʃklɒθ] *n* Spültuch *das.*

disheartened [dɪs'hɑːtnd] *adj* entmutigt.

dishevelled *Br,* **disheveled** *Am* [dɪ'ʃevəld] *adj* [hair] zerzaust; [person] unordentlich.

dishonest [dɪs'ɒnɪst] *adj* **- 1.** [person] unehrlich; [trader] unredlich **- 2.** [action] unredlich, unlauter.

dishonor *n* & *vt Am* = dishonour.

dishonorable *adj Am* = dishonourable.

dishonour *Br,* **dishonor** *Am* [dɪs'ɒnə^r] ⟨⟩ *n* Unehre *die* ⟨⟩ *vt* entehren.

dishonourable *Br,* **dishonorable** *Am* [dɪs'ɒnərəbl] *adj* unehrenhaft.

dish towel *n Am* Geschirrtuch *das.*

dishwasher ['dɪʃˌwɒʃə^r] *n* [machine] Geschirrspülmaschine *die.*

disillusioned [ˌdɪsɪ'luːʒnd] *adj* desillusioniert; **~ with sb/sthg** von jm/etw enttäuscht.

disincentive [ˌdɪsɪn'sentɪv] *n* Abschreckungsmittel *das.*

disinclined [ˌdɪsɪn'klaɪnd] *adj:* **to be ~ to do sthg** abgeneigt sein, etw zu tun.

disinfect [ˌdɪsɪn'fekt] *vt* desinfizieren.

disinfectant [ˌdɪsɪn'fektənt] *n* Desinfektionsmittel *das.*

disintegrate [dɪs'ɪntɪgreɪt] *vi* [object] zerfallen.

disinterested [ˌdɪs'ɪntrəstɪd] *adj* **- 1.** [objective] unparteiisch **- 2.** *inf* [uninterested]: **~ (in sb/sthg)** nicht interessiert (an jm/etw).

disjointed [dɪs'dʒɔɪntɪd] *adj* zusammenhanglos.

disk [dɪsk] *n* **- 1.** COMPUT: **(floppy) ~** Diskette *die;* **(hard) ~** Festplatte *die* **- 2.** *Am* = disc.

disk drive *Br,* **diskette drive** *Am* *n* COMPUT [for floppy disk] Diskettenlaufwerk *das.*

diskette [dɪs'ket] *n* COMPUT Diskette *die.*

diskette drive *n Am* = disk drive.

dislike [dɪs'laɪk] ⟨⟩ *n:* **~ (of)** Abneigung *die* (gegen); **to take a ~ to sb/sthg** eine Abneigung gegen jn/etw empfinden ⟨⟩ *vt* nicht mögen.

dislocate ['dɪsləkeɪt] *vt* MED auslrenken.

dislodge [dɪs'lɒdʒ] *vt:* **to ~ sb/sthg (from)** jn/etw entfernen (von OR aus).

disloyal [ˌdɪs'lɔɪəl] *adj:* **~ (to sb)** illoyal (gegenüber jm).

dismal ['dɪzml] *adj* **- 1.** [gloomy, depressing] trist **- 2.** [attempt, failure] kläglich.

dismantle [dɪs'mæntl] *vt* auseinander nehmen.

dismay [dɪs'meɪ] ⟨⟩ *n* Bestürzung *die* ⟨⟩ *vt* bestürzen.

dismiss [dɪs'mɪs] *vt* **- 1.** [employee, class, troops]: **to ~ sb (from sthg)** jn (aus etw) entlassen **- 2.** [refuse to take seriously] abltun **- 3.** LAW [case] ablweisen.

dismissal [dɪs'mɪsl] *n* [from job] Entlassung *die.*

dismount [ˌdɪs'maʊnt] *vi:* **to ~ (from sthg)** ablsteigen (von etw).

disobedience [ˌdɪsə'biːdjəns] *n* Ungehorsam *der.*

disobedient [ˌdɪsə'biːdjənt] *adj* ungehorsam.

disobey [ˌdɪsə'beɪ] *vt* [rule] übertreten; [person] nicht gehorchen (+ *D*).

disorder [dɪs'ɔːdə^r] *n* **- 1.** [disarray]: **in ~** in Unordnung **- 2.** [rioting] Unruhen *pl* **- 3.** MED Funktionsstörung *die.*

disorderly [dɪs'ɔːdəlɪ] *adj* **- 1.** [untidy] unordentlich **- 2.** [unruly - behaviour] ungehörig.

disorganized, -ised [dɪs'ɔːgənaɪzd] *adj* [person] unorganisiert; [system] unstrukturiert.

disorientated *Br* [dɪs'ɔːrɪənteɪtɪd], **disoriented** *Am* [dɪs'ɔːrɪəntɪd] *adj* desorientiert.

disown [dɪs'əʊn] *vt* [son, daughter] verstoßen; [friend] verleugnen.

disparaging [dɪ'spærɪdʒɪŋ] *adj* geringschätzig.

dispassionate [dɪ'spæʃnət] *adj* objektiv.

dispatch [dɪ'spætʃ] ⬦ *n* Bericht *der* ⬦ *vt* [person, troops, submarine] entsenden; [message, letter, parcel] senden.

dispel [dɪ'spel] *vt* [doubts, fears] zerstreuen; [illusions] nehmen.

dispense [dɪ'spens] *vt* - **1.** [advice] erteilen; **to** ~ **justice** Recht sprechen - **2.** [drugs, medicine] abgeben. ⬦ **dispense with** *vt fus* - **1.** [do without] verzichten auf (+ A) - **2.** [make unnecessary] unnötig machen.

dispensing chemist *Br*, **dispensing pharmacist** *Am* [dɪ'spensɪŋ-] *n* Apotheker *der*, -in *die*.

disperse [dɪ'spɜːs] ⬦ *vt* [crowd] zerstreuen ⬦ *vi* [crowd] sich zerstreuen.

dispirited [dɪ'spɪrɪtɪd] *adj* entmutigt.

displace [dɪs'pleɪs] *vt* [supplant] ablösen.

display [dɪ'spleɪ] ⬦ *n* - **1.** [of goods, merchandise] Auslage *die*; [in museum] Ausstellung *die* - **2.**: **it was a fine ~ of courage/skill from him** er zeigte viel Mut/Geschick - **3.** [performance] Vorführung *die* - **4.** COMPUT Display *das* ⬦ *vt* - **1.** [goods, merchandise] ausstellen - **2.** [courage, skill, self-control] zeigen.

displease [dɪs'pliːz] *vt* verärgern; **to be ~d with sthg** mit etw unzufrieden sein.

displeasure [dɪs'pleʒəʳ] *n* Missfallen *das*.

disposable [dɪ'spəʊzəbl] *adj* - **1.** [to be thrown away after use] Wegwerf-; [~ **nappy** *Br*, ~ **diaper** *Am* Wegwerfwindel *die* - **2.** [available] verfügbar.

disposal [dɪ'spəʊzl] *n* (U) - **1.** [removal] Beseitigung *die* - **2.** [availability]: **to be at sb's ~** jm zur Verfügung stehen; **to put sthg at sb's ~** jm etw zur Verfügung stellen.

dispose [dɪ'spəʊz] ⬦ **dispose of** *vt fus* [rubbish, problem] beseitigen.

disposed [dɪ'spəʊzd] *adj* - **1.** [willing]: **to be ~ to do sthg** geneigt sein, etw zu tun - **2.** [friendly]: **to be well ~ to** OR **towards sb** jm wohlwollend gegenüber stehen.

disposition [ˌdɪspə'zɪʃn] *n* [temperament] Naturell *das*; **he has a cheerful ~** er ist ein fröhlicher Mensch.

disprove [ˌdɪs'pruːv] *vt* widerlegen.

dispute [dɪ'spjuːt] ⬦ *n* - **1.** [quarrel] Streit *der* - **2.** (U) [disagreement] Meinungsverschiedenheit *die*; **they are in ~** zwischen ihnen herrschen Unstimmigkeiten - **3.** IND Auseinandersetzung *die* ⬦ *vt* - **1.** [question, challenge] bestreiten - **2.** [fight for - championship] jm streitig machen; [- territory] beanspruchen.

disqualify [ˌdɪs'kwɒlɪfaɪ] *vt* - **1.** [subj: illness, criminal record]: **to ~ sb from doing sthg** jn dafür ungeeignet machen, etw zu tun - **2.** SPORT disqualifizieren - **3.** *Br*: **to ~ sb from driving** jm den Führerschein entziehen.

disquiet [dɪs'kwaɪət] *n* Unruhe *die*.

disregard [ˌdɪsrɪ'gɑːd] ⬦ *n*: ~ **(for sthg)** Geringschätzung *die* (für etw) ⬦ *vt* ignorieren.

disrepair [ˌdɪsrɪ'peəʳ] *n* Baufälligkeit *die*; **to fall into** ~ verfallen.

disreputable [dɪs'repjʊtəbl] *adj* in einem schlechten Ruf stehend.

disrepute [ˌdɪsrɪ'pjuːt] *n*: **to bring sthg into** ~ etw in Verruf bringen.

disrupt [dɪs'rʌpt] *vt* [meeting, lesson] stören; [transport system] behindern.

dissatisfaction [ˈdɪsˌsætɪs'fækʃn] *n* Unzufriedenheit *die*.

dissatisfied [ˌdɪs'sætɪsfaɪd] *adj*: ~ **(with sthg)** unzufrieden (mit etw).

dissect [dɪ'sekt] *vt* MED [animal] sezieren; [plant] präparieren.

dissent [dɪ'sent] ⬦ *n* (U) Nichtübereinstimmung *die* ⬦ *vi*: **to ~ from sthg** in Bezug auf etw anderer Meinung sein.

dissertation [ˌdɪsə'teɪʃn] *n* [for degree] schriftliche Abschlussarbeit; [for PhD] Dissertation *die*.

disservice [ˌdɪs'sɜːvɪs] *n*: **to do sb a ~** jm einen schlechten Dienst erweisen.

dissimilar [ˌdɪ'sɪmɪləʳ] *adj*: ~ **(to)** verschieden (von); **to be not ~ to sthg** etw *(D)* nicht unähnlich sein.

dissipate ['dɪsɪpeɪt] *vt* [efforts, money] verschwenden, vergeuden.

dissociate [dɪ'səʊʃɪeɪt] *vt*: **to ~ o.s. from sthg** sich von etw distanzieren.

dissolute ['dɪsəluːt] *adj* [way of life] ausschweifend; [person, behaviour] zügellos.

dissolve [dɪ'zɒlv] ⬦ *vt* auflösen ⬦ *vi* [substance] sich auflösen.

dissuade [dɪ'sweɪd] *vt*: **to ~ sb from doing sthg** jn davon abbringen, etw zu tun.

distance ['dɪstəns] *n* - **1.** [between two places] Entfernung *die*; [distance covered] Strecke *die* - **2.** [distant point]: **at a ~ of five metres** in 5 Metern Entfernung; **to follow sb at a ~** jm in einiger Entfernung folgen; **from a ~** aus der Entfernung; **in the ~** in der Ferne.

distant ['dɪstənt] *adj* - **1.** [place]: ~ **(from)** weit entfernt (von) - **2.** [future] fern; **it's all in the ~ past** das ist alles schon lange her - **3.** [relative] entfernt - **4.** [manner] kühl.

distaste [dɪs'teɪst] *n* (U): ~ **(for sthg)** Widerwille *der* (gegen etw).

distasteful [dɪs'teɪstfʊl] *adj* sehr unangenehm.

distended [dɪs'tendɪd] *adj* aufgebläht.

distil *Br*, **distill** *Am* [dɪ'stɪl] *vt* - **1.** [water] destillieren; [whisky] brennen - **2.** *fig* [information] herausdestillieren.

distillery [dɪ'stɪlərɪ] *n* Brennerei *die*.

distinct [dɪ'stɪŋkt] *adj* - **1.** [different]: ~ **(from)** verschieden (von); **as ~ from** im Unterschied zu - **2.** [clear] deutlich, klar.

distinction [dɪ'stɪŋkʃn] *n* - **1.** [difference] Unterschied *der;* **to draw** OR **make a ~ between** einen Unterschied machen zwischen (+ D) - **2.** (U) [excellence] Rang *der* - **3.** [in exam result] Auszeichnung *die.*

distinctive [dɪ'stɪŋktɪv] *adj* unverkennbar.

distinguish [dɪ'stɪŋwɪʃ] ⟨⟩ *vt* - **1.** [tell apart]: **to ~ sthg from sthg** etw von etw unterscheiden - **2.** [discern, perceive] erkennen - **3.** [make different] unterscheiden ⟨⟩ *vi:* **to ~ between** unterscheiden zwischen (+ D).

distinguished [dɪ'stɪŋwɪʃt] *adj* [visitor, politician] bedeutend; [career] glänzend.

distinguishing [dɪ'stɪŋwɪʃɪŋ] *adj* charakteristisch.

distort [dɪ'stɔːt] *vt* - **1.** [shape, face, sound] verzerren - **2.** [truth, facts] verzerrt darstellen.

distract [dɪ'strækt] *vt:* **to ~ sb (from sthg)** jn (von etw) ablenken.

distracted [dɪ'stræktɪd] *adj* geistesabwesend.

distraction [dɪ'strækʃn] *n* [interruption, diversion] Ablenkung *die.*

distraught [dɪ'strɔːt] *adj* verzweifelt.

distress [dɪ'stres] ⟨⟩ *n* (U) [suffering - mental] Kummer *der;* [- physical] Leiden *das* ⟨⟩ *vt* [upset] Kummer machen (+ D).

distressing [dɪ'stresɪŋ] *adj* bestürzend.

distribute [dɪ'strɪbjuːt] *vt* - **1.** [gen] verteilen; [prizes] verleihen - **2.** COMM [goods] vertreiben.

distribution [ˌdɪstrɪ'bjuːʃn] *n* - **1.** [gen] Verteilung *die;* [of prizes] Verleihung *die* - **2.** COMM [of goods] Vertrieb *der.*

distributor [dɪ'strɪbjʊtəʳ] *n* COMM & AUT Verteiler *der.*

district ['dɪstrɪkt] *n* - **1.** [of country] Gebiet *das;* [of city] Stadtteil *der* - **2.** [administrative area] Bezirk *der.*

district attorney *n Am* LAW Bezirksstaatsanwalt *der,* -anwältin *die.*

district nurse *n Br* Gemeindeschwester *die.*

distrust [dɪs'trʌst] ⟨⟩ *n* Misstrauen *das* ⟨⟩ *vt* misstrauen (+ D).

disturb [dɪ'stɜːb] *vt* - **1.** [interrupt] stören - **2.** [upset, worry] beunruhigen - **3.** [alter - surface of water] bewegen; [- papers] durcheinander bringen.

disturbance [dɪ'stɜːbəns] *n* - **1.** [fight] Krawall *der* - **2.** (U) [interruption, disruption] Störung *die.*

disturbed [dɪ'stɜːbd] *adj* - **1.** [upset, ill] gestört - **2.** [worried] beunruhigt.

disturbing [dɪ'stɜːbɪŋ] *adj* beunruhigend.

disuse [ˌdɪs'juːs] *n:* **to fall into ~** [regulation]

außer Gebrauch kommen; [building, mine] nicht mehr genutzt werden.

disused [ˌdɪs'juːzd] *adj* stillgelegt.

ditch [dɪtʃ] ⟨⟩ *n* Graben *der* ⟨⟩ *vt inf* - **1.** [boyfriend, girlfriend] abservieren - **2.** [plan] fallen lassen - **3.** [old car] (einfach) zurücklassen.

dither ['dɪðəʳ] *vi* zaudern.

ditto ['dɪtəʊ] *adv* dito.

dive [daɪv] (*Br pt & pp* -d, *Am pt & pp* -d OR **dove**) ⟨⟩ *vi* - **1.** [goalkeeper] hechten; [bird, aircraft] einen Sturzflug machen; [submarine] abtauchen - **2.** [as sport - from board] einen Kopfsprung machen; [- underwater] tauchen; **he ~d into the water** er sprang kopfüber ins Wasser - **3.** [rush] stürzen ⟨⟩ *n* - **1.** [of swimmer] Kopfsprung *der;* **to go into a ~** [bird, aircraft] einen Sturzflug machen; [submarine] abtauchen - **2.** *inf pej* [bar, restaurant] Kaschemme *die.*

diver ['daɪvəʳ] *n* [from board] Springer *der,* -in *die;* [underwater] Taucher *der,* -in *die.*

diverge [daɪ'vɜːdʒ] *vi* - **1.** [opinions, interests] voneinander abweichen; **to ~ from sthg** von etw abweichen - **2.** [roads, paths] sich trennen.

diversify [daɪ'vɜːsɪfaɪ] *vt & vi* diversifizieren.

diversion [daɪ'vɜːʃn] *n* - **1.** [distraction] Ablenkung *die* - **2.** [of traffic, river] Umleitung *die* - **3.** [of funds] Umverteilung *die.*

diversity [daɪ'vɜːsətɪ] *n* Mannigfaltigkeit *die.*

divert [daɪ'vɜːt] *vt* - **1.** [traffic, river] umleiten - **2.** [funds] umverteilen - **3.** [person, attention] ablenken.

divide [dɪ'vaɪd] ⟨⟩ *vt* - **1.** [form barrier between] trennen - **2.** [barrier] aufteilen - **3.** [split up]: **to ~ sthg into** etw aufteilen in (+ A) - **4.** MATH: **to ~ 9 by 3, to ~ 3 into 9** 9 durch 3 teilen - **5.** [disunite] spalten ⟨⟩ *vi* [split into two] sich teilen.

dividend ['dɪvɪdend] *n* Dividende *die.*

divine [dɪ'vaɪn] *adj lit & fig* göttlich.

diving ['daɪvɪŋ] *n* [from board] Springen *das;* [underwater] Tauchen *das.*

divingboard ['daɪvɪŋbɔːd] *n* Sprungbrett *das.*

divinity [dɪ'vɪnətɪ] *n* - **1.** [godliness] Göttlichkeit *die* - **2.** [study] Theologie *die.*

division [dɪ'vɪʒn] *n* - **1.** [barrier] Trennung *die;* [of country, group] Teilung *die;* ~ **between** Trennung zwischen (+ D) - **2.** [sharing out, distribution] Teilung *die* - **3.** MATH Division *die* - **4.** [disagreement] Uneinigkeit *die* - **5.** [department] Abteilung *die* - **6.** *Br* [in sports league] Liga *die.*

divorce [dɪ'vɔːs] ⟨⟩ *n* LAW Scheidung *die* ⟨⟩ *vt* LAW [husband, wife] sich scheiden lassen von.

divorced [dɪ'vɔːst] *adj* - **1.** LAW geschieden; **to get ~** sich scheiden lassen - **2.** *fig* [separated]: **to be ~ from sthg** keine Beziehung haben zu etw.

divorcee [dɪvɔːˈsiː] *n* geschiedener Mann, geschiedene Frau.

divulge [daɪˈvʌldʒ] *vt* preislgeben.

DIY *n Br abbr of* do-it-yourself.

dizzy [ˈdɪzɪ] *adj* [person] schwind(e)lig.

DJ *n abbr of* disc jockey.

DNA (*abbr of* deoxyribonucleic acid) *n* DNS die.

do [duː] (*pt* did; *pp* done; *pl* dos OR do's) ⟨⟩ *aux vb* - **1.** (*in negatives*): **don't ~ that!** tu das nicht!; **she didn't listen** sie hat nicht zugehört; **don't park your car there** stell den Auto nicht dort ab - **2.** (*in questions*): **did he like it?** hat es ihm gefallen?; **how ~ you ~ it?** wie machst du das?; **what did he want?** was wollte er? - **3.** (*referring back to previous verb*): **I eat more than you ~** ich esse mehr als du; **no I didn't!** nein, habe ich nicht!; **so ~ I** ich auch - **4.** (*in question tags*): **so, you like Denver, ~ you?** Sie mögen Denver also, nicht wahr?; **you come from Ireland, don't you?** Sie kommen aus Irland, oder?; **I like coffee – ~ you?** ich mag Kaffee – du auch? - **5.** (*for emphasis*): **I ~ like this bedroom** das Schlafzimmer gefällt mir wirklich; **~ come in!** kommen Sie doch herein! ⟨⟩ *vt* - **1.** [perform] machen, tun; **I've a lot to ~** ich habe viel zu tun; **to ~ one's homework** seine Hausaufgaben machen; **what is she ~ing?** was macht sie?; **what can I ~ for you?** was kann ich für Sie tun?; **to ~ aerobics/gymnastics** Aerobic/ Gymnastik machen; **to ~ the cooking** kochen; **well done!** bravo! - **2.** [clean, brush, cook *etc*]: **to ~ one's make-up** sich schminken; **to ~ one's teeth** sich *(D)* die Zähne putzen; **how would you like the steak done?** wie möchten Sie Ihr Steak (haben)? - **3.** [take action] tun, machen; **he couldn't ~ anything about it** er konnte nichts dagegen tun OR machen; **I'll ~ my best to help** ich helfe, so gut ich kann - **4.** [cause]: **the storm did a lot of damage** der Sturm hat viel Schaden angerichtet - **5.** [have as job]: **what ~ you ~?** was machen Sie beruflich?; **what ~ you want to ~ when you leave school?** was willst du machen, wenn du mit der Schule fertig bist? - **6.** [provide, offer]: **~ you ~ vegetarian food?** haben Sie vegetarisches Essen?; **we ~ pizzas for under £4** wir bieten Pizzas für weniger als 4 Pfund an - **7.** [study] studieren, machen; **I did physics at school** ich habe Physik in der Schule gehabt OR gemacht - **8.** [subj: vehicle] fahren; **the car can ~ 110 mph** das Auto schafft 175 km/h - **9.** *inf* [visit]: **we did Switzerland in a week** wir haben uns in einer Woche die Schweiz angesehen - **10.** [be good enough for] genügen (+ *D*); **that'll ~ me nicely** das genügt mir - **11.** *inf* [cheat]: **to ~ sb** jn übers Ohr hauen ⟨⟩ *vi* - **1.** [behave, act] tun; **~ as I say** tu, was ich sage; **you would**

~ **well to reconsider** Sie sollten es sich lieber noch einmal überlegen - **2.** [progress, get on]: **to ~ well/badly** gut/schlecht vorankommen; [in exam] gut/schlecht abschneiden; **he will ~ well** er wird Erfolg haben - **3.** [be sufficient] reichen, genügen; **will £5 ~?** genügen 5 Pfund OR sind 5 Pfund genug?; **that will ~ (nicely)** das genügt OR reicht; **that will ~!** [showing annoyance] das reicht! - **4.** *phr*: **how ~ you ~?** Guten Tag!; **how are you ~ing?** wie gehts? ⟨⟩ *n* [party] Party *die*. ⟨⟩ **dos** *npl*: **~s and don'ts** was man tun und lassen sollte.

⟨⟩ **do away with** *vt fus* [law, practice] ablschaffen. ⟨⟩ **do out of** *vt sep*: **to ~ sb out of £10** jn um 10 Pfund betrügen. ⟨⟩ **do up** *vt sep* - **1.** [fasten] zumachen; **~ your shoes up** binde dir die Schuhe - **2.** [decorate] renovieren - **3.** [wrap up] einpacken. ⟨⟩ **do with** *vt fus* - **1.** [need]: **I could ~ with a drink** ich könnte einen Drink gebrauchen; **the floor could ~ with a wash** der Boden könnte mal (wieder) geputzt werden - **2.** [have connection with]: **what has that got to ~ with it?** was hat das damit zu tun?; **that has nothing to ~ with you** das geht dich gar nichts an. ⟨⟩ **do without** ⟨⟩ *vt fus*: **to ~ without sthg** ohne etw auskommen; **I can ~ without your sarcasm** [expressing annoyance] Sie können sich Ihren Sarkasmus sparen ⟨⟩ *vi*: **we'll just have to ~ without then** dann müssen wir eben so auskommen.

docile [*Br* ˈdəʊsaɪl, *Am* ˈdɒsəl] *adj* fügsam.

dock [dɒk] ⟨⟩ *n* - **1.** [in harbour] Dock *das* - **2.** [in court] Anklagebank *die* ⟨⟩ *vi* [ship] anlegen.

docker [ˈdɒkəʳ] *n* Hafenarbeiter *der*, -in *die*.

dockyard [ˈdɒkjɑːd] *n* Werft *die*.

doctor [ˈdɒktəʳ] ⟨⟩ *n* - **1.** [of medicine] Arzt *der*, Ärztin *die*; **to go to the ~'s** zum Arzt gehen - **2.** [holder of PhD] Doktor *der* ⟨⟩ *vt* [tamper with - results] fälschen; [- text] verfälschen.

doctorate [ˈdɒktərət], **doctor's degree** *n* Doktorwürde *die*.

doctrine [ˈdɒktrɪn] *n* Doktrin *die*, Lehre *die*.

document [ˈdɒkjʊmənt] *n* Dokument *das*.

documentary [ˌdɒkjʊˈmentərɪ] ⟨⟩ *adj* dokumentarisch ⟨⟩ *n* Dokumentarfilm *der*.

dodge [dɒdʒ] ⟨⟩ *n inf* Trick *der* ⟨⟩ *vt* [avoid] auslweichen ⟨⟩ *vi*: **to ~ out of the way/to one side** zur Seite springen.

dodgy [ˈdɒdʒɪ] *adj Br inf* [business, deal] windig; [plan] dubios.

doe [dəʊ] *n* [female deer - roe deer] Ricke *die*; [- red deer] Hirschkuh *die*.

does [*weak form* dəz, *strong form* dʌz] *vb* ▷ do.

doesn't [ˈdʌznt] = does not.

dog [dɒg] ⟨⟩ *n* [animal] Hund *der* ⟨⟩ *vt* [subj: problems, bad luck]: **~ged by problems** von Problemen geplagt; **~ged by bad luck** von Pech verfolgt.

dog collar n - **1.** [of dog] Halsband das - **2.** [of clergyman] steifer weißer Kragen.

dog-eared [-ɪəd] adj mit Eselsohren.

dog food n Hundefutter das.

dogged ['dɒgɪd] adj beharrlich.

dogsbody ['dɒgˌbɒdɪ] n Br inf Mädchen das für alles.

doing ['duːɪŋ] n: **is this your ~?** ist das dein Werk? ◆ **doings** npl [activities] Taten pl.

do-it-yourself n Heimwerken das.

doldrums ['dɒldrəmz] npl: **to be in the ~** fig [industry] in einer Flaute stecken; [person] Trübsal blasen.

dole [dəʊl] n Br [unemployment benefit] Arbeitslosenunterstützung die; **to be on the ~** Arbeitslosenunterstützung beziehen. ◆ **dole out** vt sep austeilen.

doll [dɒl] n Puppe die.

dollar ['dɒləʳ] n Dollar der.

dollop ['dɒləp] n inf Klacks der.

dolphin ['dɒlfɪn] n Delfin der.

domain [də'meɪn] n [sphere of interest] Gebiet das.

dome [dəʊm] n ARCHIT Kuppel die.

domestic [də'mestɪk] ◇ adj - **1.** [internal - flight] Inland-; [- policy] Innen- **2.** [household, home-loving] häuslich - **3.** [not wild] Haus- ◇ n Hausangestellte der, die.

domestic science n Hauswirtschaftslehre die.

dominant ['dɒmɪnənt] adj [personality] dominant; [nation, group, colour] dominierend.

dominate ['dɒmɪneɪt] vt dominieren.

domineering [ˌdɒmɪ'nɪərɪŋ] adj herrisch.

domino ['dɒmɪnəʊ] (pl -es) n Dominostein der. ◆ **dominoes** npl [game] Domino das.

don [dɒn] n Br UNIV Universitätsdozent der, -in die.

donate [də'neɪt] vt spenden.

done [dʌn] ◇ pp ➩ **do** ◇ adj - **1.** [finished] erledigt; **I'm nearly ~** ich bin fast fertig - **2.** [cooked] gar ◇ excl [to conclude deal] abgemacht!

donkey ['dɒŋkɪ] (pl -s) n Esel der.

donor ['dəʊnəʳ] n Spender der, -in die.

donor card n Organspenderausweis der.

don't [dəʊnt] = do not.

doodle ['duːdl] ◇ n Kritzelei die ◇ vi vor sich hin kritzeln.

doom [duːm] n (U) Verhängnis das.

doomed [duːmd] adj zum Scheitern verurteilt; **to be ~ to sthg** zu etw verurteilt sein.

door [dɔːʳ] n Tür die.

doorbell ['dɔːbel] n Türklingel die.

doorknob ['dɔːnɒb] n Türknauf der.

doorman ['dɔːmən] (pl -men [-mən]) n Portier der.

doormat ['dɔːmæt] n lit & fig Fußabtreter der.

doorstep ['dɔːstep] n Eingangsstufe die;

the supermarket's right on her ~ sie hat den Supermarkt direkt vor der Tür.

doorway ['dɔːweɪ] n Eingang der.

dope [dəʊp] ◇ n - **1.** drugs sl [cannabis] Hasch das - **2.** [for athlete, horse] Aufputschmittel das - **3.** inf [fool] Trottel der ◇ vt dopen.

dopey ['dəʊpɪ] (compar -ier; superl -iest) adj inf - **1.** [groggy] benommen - **2.** [stupid] blöd.

dormant ['dɔːmənt] adj - **1.** [volcano] untätig - **2.**: **to lie ~** [talents] schlummern.

dormitory ['dɔːmɪtrɪ] n - **1.** [room] Schlafsaal der - **2.** Am [in university] Wohnheim das.

DOS [dɒs] (abbr of disk operating system) n DOS das.

dose [dəʊs] n - **1.** [of medicine, drug] Dosis die - **2.** [of illness] Anfall der.

dot [dɒt] ◇ n Punkt der ◇ vt verstreuen. ◆ **on the dot** adv: **at four on the ~** Punkt vier Uhr; **to arrive on the ~** auf die Minute pünktlich (an)kommen.

dote [dəʊt] ◆ **dote upon** vt fus vernarrt sein in (+ A).

dot-matrix printer n Matrixdrucker der.

dotted line ['dɒtɪd-] n punktierte Linie.

double ['dʌbl] ◇ adj doppelt; [row, door] Doppel-; **to have a ~ meaning** doppeldeutig sein; **two ~ one** zwei eins eins; **Susanne with a ~ 'n'** Susanne mit zwei „n" ◇ adv - **1.** [twice]: **~ the amount/number** doppelt so viel/viele - **2.** [two of the same] doppelt; **to see ~** doppelt sehen - **3.** [in two - fold] einmal; **to bend ~** sich zusammen|krümmen ◇ n - **1.** [twice the amount] Doppelte das - **2.** [of alcohol] Doppelter der - **3.** [look-alike] Ebenbild das - **4.** CINEMA Double das ◇ vt [increase twofold] verdoppeln ◇ vi [increase twofold] verdoppeln. ◆ **doubles** npl TENNIS Doppel das.

double-barrelled Br, **double-barreled** Am [-'bærəld] adj - **1.** [shotgun] doppelläufig - **2.** [name] Doppel-.

double bass n Kontrabass der.

double bed n Doppelbett das.

double-breasted [-'brestɪd] adj zweireihig.

double-check vt noch einmal überprüfen.

double chin n Doppelkinn das.

double cream n Br Schlagsahne die.

double-cross vt doppeltes Spiel treiben mit.

double-decker [-'dekəʳ] n Doppeldecker der.

double-dutch n Br hum Kauderwelsch das.

double fault n TENNIS Doppelfehler der.

double-glazing [-'gleɪzɪŋ] n Doppelverglasung die.

double-park vi AUT in der zweiten Reihe parken.

double room n Doppelzimmer das.

double vision n doppeltes Sehen.

doubly ['dʌblɪ] adv: ~ difficult/important/ etc umso schwieriger/wichtiger/ etc.

doubt [daʊt] ◇ n Zweifel der; there is no ~ that ... es besteht kein Zweifel, dass ...; to cast ~ on sthg etw in Zweifel ziehen; no ~ ohne Zweifel; without (a) ~, beyond (all) ~ ohne Zweifel; to be in ~ ungewiss sein ◇ vt - 1. [distrust] zweifeln an (+ D) - 2. [consider unlikely] bezweifeln.

doubtful ['daʊtfʊl] adj - 1. [unlikely, dubious] zweifelhaft - 2. [uncertain] ungewiss.

doubtless ['daʊtlɪs] adv ohne Zweifel.

dough [dəʊ] n (U) - 1. [for baking] Teig der - 2. vinf [money] Knete die.

doughnut ['dəʊnʌt] n ≃ Berliner der.

douse [daʊs] vt - 1. [fire, light] löschen - 2. [person] übergießen.

dove[1] [dʌv] n [bird] Taube die.

dove[2] [dəʊv] pt Am ▷ dive.

dowdy ['daʊdɪ] adj ohne jeden Schick.

down [daʊn] ◇ adv - 1. [towards the bottom] nach unten, hinunter/herunter; to fall ~ [person] hinfallen; [thing] herunterfallen; to bend ~ sich bücken; head ~ mit gesenktem Kopf - 2. [along]: I'm going ~ to the shops ich gehe einkaufen - 3. [downstairs] herunter; I'll come ~ later ich komme später herunter - 4. [southwards] hinunter/ herunter; we're going ~ to London wir fahren hinunter nach London - 5. [reduced]: prices are coming ~ die Preise fallen - 6. [as far as]: ~ to the last detail bis ins letzte Detail; ~ to the present bis in die heutige Zeit ◇ prep - 1. [towards the bottom of]: they ran ~ the hill sie liefen den Hügel hinunter; to fall ~ the stairs die Treppe hinunterlfallen - 2. [along] entlang; I was walking ~ the street when ... ich lief gerade die Straße entlang, als ... ◇ adj - 1. inf [depressed] down - 2. [not in operation]: the computers are ~ again die Computer tun es wieder (mal) nicht ◇ n (U) [feathers] Daunen pl ◇ vt - 1. [knock over] niederlschlagen - 2. [swallow] hastig trinken - 3. phr: to ~ tools die Arbeit niederllegen. ◆ **downs** npl Br Hügelland das. ◆ **down with** excl: ~ with the King! nieder mit dem König!

down-and-out ◇ adj heruntergekommen ◇ n Landstreicher der, -in die.

down-at-heel adj esp Br heruntergekommen.

downbeat ['daʊnbi:t] adj inf [ending] undramatisch.

downcast ['daʊnkɑ:st] adj fml niedergeschlagen.

downfall ['daʊnfɔ:l] n - 1. (U) [ruin - of dictator] Sturz der; [- of business] Ruin der - 2. [cause of ruin] Ruin der.

downhearted [ˌdaʊn'hɑ:tɪd] adj niedergeschlagen.

downhill [ˌdaʊn'hɪl] ◇ adj [path] bergab führend ◇ adv - 1. [downwards] bergab, ab-

wärts - 2. fig: her career went ~ after that mit ihrer Karriere ging es danach bergab ◇ n SKIING Abfahrtslauf der.

Downing Street ['daʊnɪŋ-] n Straße, in der sich der offizielle Wohnsitz des britischen Premierministers und des Schatzkanzlers befindet.

down payment n Anzahlung die.

downpour ['daʊnpɔːr] n Platzregen der.

downright ['daʊnraɪt] ◇ adj [fool, cheat, cheek] ausgesprochen; [lie] glatt; [insult] grob ◇ adv ausgesprochen.

downstairs [ˌdaʊn'steəz] ◇ adj: a ~ flat eine Parterre- OR Erdgeschosswohnung ◇ adv [be, live] unten; to go ~ (die Treppe) hinunterlgehen; to come ~ (die Treppe) herunterlkommen.

downstream [ˌdaʊn'stri:m] adv flussabwärts, stromabwärts.

down-to-earth adj sachlich, nüchtern.

downtown [ˌdaʊn'taʊn] esp Am ◇ adj: ~ New York im Stadtzentrum von New York ◇ adv [go] ins Stadtzentrum; [live] im Stadtzentrum.

downturn ['daʊntɜ:n] n: ~ (in sthg) Abnahme die (von etw).

down under adv Br [live] in Australien/ Neuseeland; [go] nach Australien/ Neuseeland.

downward ['daʊnwəd] ◇ adj - 1. [towards ground] abwärts gerichtet; ~ glance Blick nach unten; ~ movement Abwärtsbewegung die - 2. [decreasing] abnehmend, fallend ◇ adv Am = downwards.

downwards ['daʊnwədz] adv [look, move] nach unten.

dowry ['daʊərɪ] n Mitgift die.

doz. abbr of dozen.

doze [dəʊz] ◇ n Nickerchen das ◇ vi dösen. ◆ **doze off** vi einlnicken.

dozen ['dʌzn] ◇ num n Dutzend das; a ~ eggs ein Dutzend Eier. ◇ dozens npl inf: ~s of Dutzende (von). ~s of times x-mal.

dozy ['dəʊzɪ] adj - 1. [sleepy] schläfrig - 2. Br inf [stupid] blöd.

Dr. - 1. abbr of Drive - 2. abbr of Doctor.

drab [dræb] adj - 1. [colour, buildings] trist; [clothes] langweilig; [place] trostlos - 2. [life] eintönig, farblos.

draft [drɑːft] ◇ n - 1. [early version] Entwurf der; [picture, plan] Skizze die - 2. [money order] Zahlungsanweisung die - 3. Am MIL: the ~ die Einberufung - 4. Am = draught ◇ vt - 1. [write] entwerfen - 2. Am MIL einlberufen, einlziehen - 3. [recruit] rekrutieren.

draftsman n Am = draughtsman.

drafty adj Am = draughty.

drag [dræg] ◇ vt - 1. [pull] ziehen - 2. [lake, river] (mit dem Schleppnetz) absuchen ◇ vi - 1. [trail]: to ~ on the ground auf dem Boden schleifen - 2. [pass slowly] sich in die Länge ziehen ◇ n - 1. inf [bore] langweilige

Sache/Person; **what a ~!** wie öde! - **2.** *inf* [on cigarette] Zug *der* - **3.** [cross-dressing]: **in ~** in Frauenkleidern. **◆ drag on** *vi* sich in die Länge ziehen.

dragon ['drægən] *n lit & fig* Drache *der*.

dragonfly ['drægnflaɪ] *n* Libelle *die*.

drain [dreɪn] ◇ *n* - **1.** [pipe] Abflussrohr *das*; [grating in street] Gully *der*; **that's £50 down the ~** *fig* die 50 Pfund sind zum Fenster rausgeworfen - **2.** [depletion]: **~ on sthg** [resources, funds] Belastung *die* für etw; [energy, time] Verlust *der* von etw ◇ *vt* - **1.** [remove water from - vegetables] abgießen; [- marsh, field] entwässern - **2.** [deplete - funds, resources] erschöpfen; [- strength, energy] entziehen; **to feel ~ed** sich ausgelaugt fühlen - **3.** [drink, glass] ausltrinken ◇ *vi* [dry] abltropfen.

drainage ['dreɪnɪdʒ] *n* [ditches, channels] Entwässerungssystem *das*; [in city] Kanalisation *die*.

draining board *Br* ['dreɪnɪŋ-], **drainboard** *Am* ['dreɪnbɔːrd] *n* Abtropfbrett *das*.

drainpipe ['dreɪnpaɪp] *n* Abflussrohr *das*.

drama ['drɑːmə] *n* - **1.** [play, genre, event] Drama *das* - **2.** [dramatic quality] Dramatik *die*.

dramatic [drə'mætɪk] *adj* dramatisch.

dramatist ['dræmətɪst] *n* Dramatiker *der*, -in *die*.

dramatize, -ise ['dræmətaɪz] *vt* dramatisieren.

drank [dræŋk] *pt* ▷ drink.

drape [dreɪp] *vt* drapieren; **to be ~d with** OR **in sthg** mit etw drapiert sein. **◆ drapes** *npl Am* Vorhänge *pl*.

drastic ['dræstɪk] *adj* drastisch.

draught *Br*, **draft** *Am* [drɑːft] *n* - **1.** [air current] Luftzug *der*; **there's a ~ in here** hier zieht es - **2.** [from barrel]: **on ~** [beer] vom Fass. **◆ draughts** *n Br* Damespiel *das*; **to play ~s** Dame spielen.

draught beer *n Br* Fassbier *das*.

draughtsman *Br*, **draftsman** *Am* ['drɑːftsmən] (*pl* -men [-mən]) *n* technischer Zeichner.

draughty *Br*, **drafty** *Am* ['drɑːftɪ] *adj* zugig.

draw [drɔː] (*pt* drew; *pp* drawn) ◇ *vt* - **1.** [sketch] zeichnen - **2.** [pull, pull out] ziehen - **3.** [conclusion, comparison, distinction] ziehen - **4.** [criticism, support] hervorlrufen; **to ~ sb's attention to sthg** js Aufmerksamkeit auf etw (*A*) lenken ◇ *vi* - **1.** [sketch] zeichnen - **2.** [move]: **to ~ away** weglziehen; **to ~ near** heranlziehen - **3.** SPORT unentschieden spielen; **to ~ with sb** gegen jn unentschieden spielen ◇ *n* - **1.** SPORT [result] Unentschieden *das* - **2.** [lottery] Ziehung *die* - **3.** [attraction] Anziehungspunkt *der*. **◆ draw out** *vt sep* - **1.** [encourage] aus der Reserve locken - **2.** [prolong] in die Länge

ziehen - **3.** [withdraw] ablheben. **◆ draw up** ◇ *vt sep* [draft] auflsetzen; [list] auflstellen ◇ *vi* [stop] anlhalten.

drawback ['drɔːbæk] *n* Nachteil *der*.

drawbridge ['drɔːbrɪdʒ] *n* Zugbrücke *die*.

drawer [drɔːʳ] *n* Schublade *die*.

drawing ['drɔːɪŋ] *n* - **1.** [picture] Zeichnung *die* - **2.** [skill, act] Zeichnen *das*.

drawing pin *n Br* Reißzwecke *die*.

drawing room *n* Salon *der*.

drawl [drɔːl] *n* gedehntes Sprechen.

drawn [drɔːn] *pp* ▷ draw.

dread [dred] ◇ *n* Furcht *die* ◇ *vt* fürchten; **to ~ doing sthg** es schrecklich finden, etw tun zu müssen.

dreadful ['dredfʊl] *adj* schrecklich, furchtbar; **I feel ~** [guilty] es ist mir sehr peinlich.

dreadfully ['dredfʊlɪ] *adv* - **1.** [badly] furchtbar - **2.** [extremely] schrecklich.

dream [driːm] (*pt & pp* -ed OR dreamt) ◇ *n* Traum *der* ◇ *adj* Traum- ◇ *vt* [during sleep] träumen ◇ *vi*: **to ~ (of** OR **about sthg)** (von etw) träumen; **I wouldn't ~ of it** *fig* das würde mir nicht im Traum einlfallen; **to ~ of doing sthg** davon träumen, etw zu tun. **◆ dream up** *vt sep* sich (*D*) einfallen lassen OR auslldenken.

dreamt [dremt] *pt & pp* ▷ dream.

dreamy ['driːmɪ] *adj* - **1.** [distracted] verträumt - **2.** [languorous] traumhaft.

dreary ['drɪərɪ] *adj* - **1.** [gloomy, depressing] trostlos - **2.** [dull, boring] langweilig, öde.

dredge [dredʒ] *vt* auslbaggern. **◆ dredge up** *vt sep* - **1.** [from lake, river] herauflholen, herauslholen - **2.** *fig* [from past] auslgraben.

dregs [dregz] *npl* - **1.** [of liquid] (Boden)satz *der* - **2.** *fig* [of society] Abschaum *der*.

drench [drentʃ] *vt* durchlnässen; **to be ~ed in** OR **with sweat** in Schweiß gebadet sein.

dress [dres] ◇ *n* - **1.** [frock] Kleid *das* - **2.** [type of clothing] Kleidung *die* ◇ *vt* - **1.** [clothe] anlziehen; **to be ~ed** angezogen sein; **to be ~ed in** gekleidet sein in (+ *A*); **to get ~ed** sich anlziehen - **2.** [wound] verbinden - **3.** [salad] anlmachen ◇ *vi* sich anlziehen, sich kleiden. **◆ dress up** *vi* - **1.** [in costume] sich verkleiden - **2.** [in best clothes] sich festlich anlziehen.

dress circle *n* THEATRE erster Rang.

dresser ['dresəʳ] *n* - **1.** [for dishes] Küchenbüffet *das* (mit Tellerbord) - **2.** *Am* [chest of drawers] Frisiertisch *der*, Frisierkommode *die*.

dressing ['dresɪŋ] *n* - **1.** [bandage] Verband *der* - **2.** [for salad] Dressing *das*, Salatsoße *die* - **3.** *Am* [for turkey etc] Füllung *die*.

dressing gown *n* Bademantel *der*.

dressing room *n* - **1.** SPORT Umkleidekabine *die* - **2.** THEATRE Garderobe *die*.

dressing table *n* Frisiertisch *der*.

dressmaker ['dres,meɪkə'] n Schneider der, -in die.

dress rehearsal n Generalprobe die.

dressy ['dresɪ] adj elegant.

drew [druː] pt ⊳ draw.

dribble ['drɪbl] ⊳ n [trickle] Rinnsal das ⊳ vt SPORT [footballer] dribbeln ⊳ vi - 1. [drool] sabbern - 2. [spill] tropfen - 3. SPORT [ball] dribbeln.

dried [draɪd] ⊳ pt & pp ⊳ dry ⊳ adj getrocknet; ~ **milk** Trockenmilch die.

drier ['draɪə'] n = dryer.

drift [drɪft] ⊳ n - 1. [mass - of snow, leaves, sand] Verwehung die - 2. [meaning]: **I get her general** ~ ich verstehe, worauf sie hinaus-will ⊳ vi [boat, snow, sand, leaves] treiben.

drill [drɪl] ⊳ n - 1. [tool] Bohrer der - 2. [exercise, training] Übung die (für den Ernstfall) ⊳ vt - 1. [metal, wood, hole] bohren - 2. [instruct] drillen ⊳ vi: **to ~ (into sthg)** bohren (in etw (A)).

drink [drɪŋk] (pt drank; pp drunk) ⊳ n - 1. [gen] Getränk das; **a ~ of water** ein Glas Wasser - 2. [alcoholic beverage] Drink der; **to have a ~** etwas trinken - 3. [alcohol] Alkohol der ⊳ vt trinken ⊳ vi trinken.

drink-driving Br, **drunk-driving** Am n Trunkenheit die am Steuer.

drinker ['drɪŋkə'] n Trinker der, -in die.

drinking water ['drɪŋkɪŋ-] n Trinkwasser das.

drip [drɪp] ⊳ n - 1. [drop] Tropfen der - 2. MED Tropf der, Infusion die; **to be on a ~** am Tropf hängen ⊳ vi tropfen.

drip-dry adj bügelfrei.

drive [draɪv] (pt drove; pp driven) ⊳ n - 1. [journey] Fahrt die; **an hour's ~** eine Stunde Fahrt; **to go for a ~** spazieren fahren - 2. [urge] Trieb der - 3. [campaign] Aktion die - 4. (U) [energy] Energie die - 5. [in front of house] Einfahrt die - 6. [stroke - in golf] Treibschlag der; [- in tennis] Drive der - 7. AUT: **left-/right-hand ~** Links-/Rechtslenkung die - 8. COMPUT Laufwerk das ⊳ vt - 1. [vehicle, passenger] fahren; **to ~ sb home** jn nach Hause fahren - 2. TECH [operate] an|treiben; **~n by electricity** mit elektrischem Antrieb - 3. [chase - cattle, clouds, people] treiben; **they were ~n from their homeland** sie wurden aus ihrer Heimat vertrieben - 4. [motivate]: **~n by greed/ambition** von Gier/Ehrgeiz getrieben - 5. [force]: **to ~ sb to do sthg** jn dazu treiben, etw zu tun; **to ~ sb hard** jn schinden; **to ~ sb mad** OR **crazy** jn verrückt machen - 6. [hammer] schlagen ⊳ vi fahren; **can you ~?** kannst du Auto fahren?

drivel ['drɪvl] n inf Quatsch der.

driven ['drɪvn] pp ⊳ drive.

driver ['draɪvə'] n [of vehicle] Fahrer der, -in die.

driver's license n Am = driving licence.

driveway ['draɪvweɪ] n Auffahrt die.

driving ['draɪvɪŋ] ⊳ adj [rain] strömend; [wind] stürmisch ⊳ n Fahren das.

driving instructor n Fahrlehrer der, -in die.

driving lesson n Fahrstunde die.

driving licence Br, **driver's license** Am n Führerschein der.

driving school n Fahrschule die.

driving test n Fahrprüfung die.

drizzle ['drɪzl] ⊳ n Sprühregen der ⊳ v impers: **it's drizzling** es nieselt.

drone [drəʊn] n - 1. [sound - of machine, engine, loudspeaker] Dröhnen das; [- of insect] Summen das - 2. [male bee] Drohne die.

drool [druːl] vi - 1. [dribble] sabbern - 2. fig [admire]: **he stood there ~ing over the sports car** er konnte sich an dem Sportwagen nicht satt sehen.

droop [druːp] vi [hang down] herunter|hängen; [flower] den Kopf hängen lassen.

drop [drɒp] ⊳ n - 1. [of liquid] Tropfen der - 2. [sweet] Drops der OR das - 3. [decrease]: **~ (in sthg)** Rückgang der (von etw); [in salary] Minderung die (von etw) - 4. [vertical distance] Höhenunterschied der; **there's a 50 m ~ here** hier geht es 50 m (senkrecht) hinunter ⊳ vt - 1. [gen] fallen lassen; **to ~ (sb) a hint** (jm gegenüber) eine Anspielung machen - 2. [decrease, lower] senken - 3. [leave out] weg|lassen - 4. [let out of car] ab|setzen - 5. [write]: **to ~ sb a line** OR **note** jm ein paar Zeilen schreiben ⊳ vi - 1. [fall] fallen; [with exhaustion] um|fallen - 2. [decrease] sinken - 3. [voice] leiser werden. ◆ **drops** npl MED Tropfen pl. ◆ **drop in** vi inf: **to ~ in (on sb)** vorbei|kommen (bei jm). ◆ **drop off** ⊳ vt sep [person] ab|setzen; [letter, package] ab|schicken ⊳ vi - 1. [fall asleep] ein|nicken - 2. [grow less] zurück|gehen. ◆ **drop out** vi: **to ~ out (of** OR **from sthg)** aus|steigen (aus etw).

dropout ['drɒpaʊt] n - 1. [from society] Aussteiger der, -in die - 2. [from university] Studienabbrecher der, -in die.

droppings ['drɒpɪŋz] npl Kot der; [of horses] Äpfel pl.

drought [draʊt] n Dürre die.

drove [drəʊv] pt ⊳ drive.

drown [draʊn] ⊳ vt [person, animal] ertränken ⊳ vi ertrinken.

drowsy ['draʊzɪ] adj schläfrig.

drudgery ['drʌdʒərɪ] n Schinderei die.

drug [drʌg] ⊳ n - 1. [medication] Arzneimittel das - 2. [illegal substance] Droge die; **to be on ~s** drogen- OR rauschgiftabhängig sein ⊳ vt [person, animal] Drogen verabreichen (+ D); [food, drink] mit Drogen versetzen.

drug abuse n Drogenmissbrauch der.

drug addict n Drogensüchtige der, die.

druggist ['drʌgɪst] n Am Apotheker der, -in die.

drugstore ['drʌgstɔːʳ] n Am Drugstore der.

drum [drʌm] n - 1. [instrument, cylinder] Trommel die - 2. [container] Tonne die ⟨⟩ vt & vi trommeln. ❖ **drums** npl Schlagzeug das. ❖ **drum up** vt sep [business] ankurbeln.

drummer ['drʌməʳ] n Schlagzeuger der, -in die.

drumstick ['drʌmstɪk] n - 1. [for drum] Trommelschlägel der - 2. [of chicken] Keule die.

drunk [drʌŋk] ⟨⟩ pp ▷ drink ⟨⟩ adj [on alcohol] betrunken ⟨⟩ n [on one occasion] Betrunkene der, die; [habitual] Trinker der, -in die.

drunkard ['drʌŋkəd] n Trinker der, -in die.

drunk-driving n Am = drink-driving.

drunken ['drʌŋkn] adj [person] betrunken; a ~ evening ein feuchtfröhlicher Abend; in a ~ stupor sinnlos betrunken.

dry [draɪ] ⟨⟩ adj - 1. [gen] trocken - 2. [river, lake] ausgetrocknet - 3. [thirsty] durstig; to feel OR be ~ durstig sein, Durst haben ⟨⟩ vt & vi trocknen. ❖ **dry up** ⟨⟩ vt sep [dishes] abtrocknen ⟨⟩ vi - 1. [river, lake, well] austrocknen - 2. [supplies, inspiration] zur Neige gehen - 3. [actor, speaker] stecken bleiben - 4. [dry dishes] abtrocknen.

dry cleaner n: ~'s chemische Reinigung.

dryer ['draɪəʳ] n [for clothes] Trockner der.

dry land n Festland das.

dry rot n Trockenfäule die.

dry ski slope n Sommerskihang der.

DSS (abbr of Department of Social Security) n britisches Sozialamt.

DTI (abbr of Department of Trade and Industry) n Handels- und Industrieministerium das.

DTP (abbr of desktop publishing) n DTP das.

dual ['djuːəl] adj doppelt, Doppel-.

dual carriageway n Br vierspurige Straße.

dubbed [dʌbd] adj - 1. CINEMA synchronisiert - 2. [nicknamed] genannt.

dubious ['djuːbjəs] adj - 1. [suspect, questionable] dubios, zweifelhaft - 2. [uncertain, undecided]: to be ~ about doing sthg nicht wissen, ob man etw tun soll.

Dublin ['dʌblɪn] n Dublin nt.

duchess ['dʌtʃɪs] n Herzogin die.

duck [dʌk] ⟨⟩ n Ente die ⟨⟩ vt - 1. [head] ducken, einziehen - 2. [responsibility, duty] ausweichen (+ D) ⟨⟩ vi sich ducken.

duckling ['dʌklɪŋ] n - 1. [animal] Entenküken das - 2. (U) [food] junge Ente.

duct [dʌkt] n - 1. [pipe] Leitung die, Rohr das - 2. ANAT Kanal der.

dud [dʌd] ⟨⟩ adj - 1. [false] falsch - 2. [useless] wertlos - 3.: a ~ bomb/shell ein Blindgänger ⟨⟩ n [bomb, shell] Blindgänger der.

dude [djuːd] n Am inf Typ der.

due [djuː] ⟨⟩ adj - 1. [expected] fällig; the book's ~ (out) in May das Buch soll im Mai erscheinen - 2. [proper] ordnungsgemäß, nötig; in ~ course zu gegebener Zeit - 3. [owed, owing] fällig ⟨⟩ adv: ~ west genau nach Westen. ❖ **dues** npl Abgaben pl, Gebühren pl. ❖ **due to** prep wegen (+ G, D).

duel ['djuːəl] n Duell das.

duet [djuːˈet] n Duett das.

duffel bag ['dʌfl-] n Seesack der.

duffel coat ['dʌfl-] n Dufflecoat der.

dug [dʌg] pt & pp ▷ dig.

duke [djuːk] n Herzog der.

dull [dʌl] ⟨⟩ adj - 1. [boring] langweilig - 2. [colour, light] matt - 3. [day, weather] trüb - 4. [noise, pain] dumpf ⟨⟩ vt - 1. [senses] abstumpfen; [pain] dämpfen - 2. [make less bright - metal] stumpf werden lassen.

duly ['djuːlɪ] adv - 1. [properly] ordnungsgemäß - 2. [as expected] erwartungsgemäß.

dumb [dʌm] adj - 1. [unable to speak] stumm; to be struck ~ sprachlos sein - 2. esp Am inf [stupid] dumm.

dumbfound [dʌmˈfaʊnd] vt verblüffen; to be ~ed verblüfft sein, sprachlos sein.

dummy ['dʌmɪ] ⟨⟩ adj unecht; a ~ gun eine Spielzeugpistole ⟨⟩ n - 1. [model of human figure - for tailoring] Schneiderpuppe die; [- for crash testing] Dummy der; [- in shop] Schaufensterpuppe die - 2. [copy, fake object] Attrappe die - 3. Br [for baby] Schnuller der.

dump [dʌmp] ⟨⟩ n - 1. [for rubbish] Müllhalde die - 2. [for ammunition] Munitionslager das ⟨⟩ vt - 1. inf [put down] abladen - 2. [dispose of - waste, rubbish] wegwerfen; [- car] zurücklassen - 3. inf [jilt] in die Wüste schicken.

dumper (truck) ['dʌmpəʳ-] Br, **dump truck** Am n Kipper der, Kipplaster der.

dumping ['dʌmpɪŋ] n [of waste] Abladen das; 'no ~' 'Schutt abladen verboten'.

dumpling ['dʌmplɪŋ] n CULIN Kloß der.

dump truck n Am = dumper truck.

dumpy ['dʌmpɪ] adj inf dicklich, untersetzt.

dunce [dʌns] n Ignorant der.

dune [djuːn] n Düne die.

dung [dʌŋ] n Dung der, Mist der.

dungarees [ˌdʌŋgəˈriːz] npl Br [for work] Arbeitshose die; [fashion garment] Segeltuch das.

dungeon ['dʌndʒən] n Verlies das.

duo ['djuːəʊ] n - 1. [of singers, musicians] Duett das; [on stage] Duo das - 2. [couple] Duo das.

duplex ['djuːpleks] n Am - 1. [apartment] Doppelapartment das - 2. [house] Zweifamilienhaus das.

duplicate [adj & n 'djuːplɪkət, vb 'djuːplɪkeɪt] ⟨⟩ adj [document] kopiert; a ~ key ein Nachschlüssel ⟨⟩ n Kopie die; in ~ in dop-

pelter Ausfertigung ◇ *vt* [copy - document] kopieren; [- key] nachlmachen.

durable ['djʊərəbl] *adj* strapazierfähig.

duration [djʊ'reɪʃn] *n* Dauer *die*; **for the ~ of** für die Dauer von.

duress [djʊ'res] *n*: **under ~** unter Zwang.

during ['djʊərɪŋ] *prep* während (+ G).

dusk [dʌsk] *n* Abenddämmerung *die*.

dust [dʌst] ◇ *n* Staub *der* ◇ *vt* - **1.** [clean] ablstauben - **2.** [cover]: **to ~ sthg with sthg** etw mit etw bestäuben.

dustbin ['dʌstbɪn] *n Br* Mülltonne *die*.

dustcart ['dʌstkɑːt] *n Br* Müllwagen *der*.

duster ['dʌstə'] *n* [cloth] Staubtuch *das*.

dust jacket *n* [on book] Schutzumschlag *der*.

dustman ['dʌstmən] (*pl* -men [-mən]) *n Br* Müllmann *der*.

dustpan ['dʌstpæn] *n* Kehrschaufel *die*.

dusty ['dʌstɪ] *adj* staubig, verstaubt.

Dutch [dʌtʃ] ◇ *adj* niederländisch, holländisch ◇ *n* [language] Niederländisch(e) *das* ◇ *adv*: **to go ~** getrennt bezahlen.

dutiful ['djuːtɪfʊl] *adj* pflichtbewusst.

duty ['djuːtɪ] *n* - **1.** (*U*) [responsibility] Pflicht *die*; **to do one's ~** seine Pflicht tun - **2.** (*U*) [work] Dienst *der*; **to be on ~** Dienst haben; **to be off ~** dienstfrei haben - **3.** [tax] Zoll *der*. ◆ **duties** *npl* [tasks] Aufgaben *pl*.

duty-free *adj* (*U*) zollfrei.

duvet ['duːveɪ] *n Br* Daunendecke *die*.

duvet cover *n Br* Bettbezug *der* (*für eine Daunendecke*).

DVD (*abbr of* Digital Versatile Disk) *n* DVD *die*.

dwarf [dwɔːf] (*pl* -s OR dwarves [dwɔːvz]) ◇ *n* Zwerg *der*, -in *die* ◇ *vt* [tower over] winzig erscheinen lassen.

dwell [dwel] (*pt* & *pp* dwelt OR -ed) *vi literary* [live] wohnen. ◆ **dwell on** *vt fus* [talk about] sich lange befassen mit; [think about] lange nachldenken über (+ A).

dwelling ['dwelɪŋ] *n literary* Wohnung *die*.

dwelt [dwelt] *pt* & *pp* ➣ **dwell.**

dwindle ['dwɪndl] *vi* dahinlschwinden.

dye [daɪ] ◇ *n* Farbstoff *der* ◇ *vt* färben.

dying ['daɪɪŋ] ◇ *cont* ➣ **die** ◇ *adj* - **1.** [person, animal] sterbend - **2.** *fig* [tradition, language] aussterbend.

dyke [daɪk] *n* = dike.

dynamic [daɪ'næmɪk] *adj* dynamisch.

dynamite ['daɪnəmaɪt] *n* (*U*) - **1.** [explosive] Dynamit *das* - **2.** *inf fig* [story, news]: **to be ~** viel Zündstoff enthalten - **3.** *inf fig* [excellent]: **to be ~** eine Wucht sein.

dynamo ['daɪnəməʊ] (*pl* -s) *n* TECH Dynamo *der*; AUT Lichtmaschine *die*.

dynasty [*Br* 'dɪnəstɪ, *Am* 'daɪnəstɪ] *n* Dynastie *die*.

dyslexia [dɪs'leksɪə] *n* (*U*) Legasthenie *die*.

dyslexic [dɪs'leksɪk] *adj* legasthenisch; **to be ~** Legastheniker/Legasthenikerin sein.

E

e (*pl* e's OR es), **E** (*pl* E's OR Es) [iː] *n* [letter] e *das*, E *das*. ◆ **E** *n* - **1.** MUS E *das* - **2.** *abbr of* east - **3.** *inf* (*abbr of* ecstasy) E *das*.

each [iːtʃ] ◇ *adj* jede, -r, -s ◇ *pron*: **~ (one)** jede, -r, -s; **one another, ~ other** einander; **separated from ~ other** voneinander getrennt; **they know ~ other** sie kennen sich; **they kissed ~ other on the cheek** sie küssten sich auf die Wange; **there's one ~** es ist für jeden eins da; **I'd like one of ~** ich möchte von jedem/jeder eins; **they cost £10 ~** sie kosten je 10 Pfund.

eager ['iːgə'] *adj* [person] eifrig; **to be ~ for sthg** auf etw (*A*) erpicht sein; **to be ~ to do sthg** etw unbedingt tun wollen.

eagle ['iːgl] *n* Adler *der*.

ear [ɪə'] *n* - **1.** [of person, animal] Ohr *das*; **I'll play it by ~** ich werde es auf mich zukommen lassen - **2.** [of corn] Ähre *die*.

earache ['ɪəreɪk] *n* Ohrenschmerzen *pl*.

eardrum ['ɪədrʌm] *n* Trommelfell *das*.

earl [ɜːl] *n* Graf *der*.

earlier ['ɜːlɪə'] *adj* & *adv* früher; **~ on** früher.

earliest ['ɜːlɪəst] ◇ *adj* - **1.** [first] frühstmöglich; **at the ~ opportunity** so bald wie möglich - **2.** [most early] frühest ◇ *adv*: **she'll not be back till four o'clock at the ~** sie wird frühestens um vier Uhr wieder hier sein.

earlobe ['ɪələʊb] *n* Ohrläppchen *das*.

early ['ɜːlɪ] ◇ *adj* früh; **~ death** vorzeitiger Tod; **at an ~ hour** zu früher Stunde; **at an ~ age** [early in life] schon früh; [as a child] im Kindesalter; **in the ~ afternoon** am frühen Nachmittag; **to have an ~ breakfast/night** früh frühstücken/zu Bett gehen ◇ *adv* früh; **to leave ~** [person] früher gehen; [bus, train] zu früh ablfahren; **as ~ as next week** schon nächste Woche; **~ on** früh.

early closing *n*: **today is ~** heute schließen die Geschäfte früher.

early retirement *n*: **to take ~** in den vorzeitigen Ruhestand gehen.

earmark ['ɪəmɑːk] *vt*: **to be ~ed for sthg** für etw vorgesehen sein.

earn [ɜːn] *vt* - **1.** [gen] verdienen - **2.** COMM erwirtschaften.

earnest ['ɜːnɪst] *adj* ernsthaft. ◆ **in earnest** ◇ *adj*: **I'm in ~** ich meine es ernst *adv* ernsthaft; **to begin in** ~ richtig anlfangen.

earnings ['ɜːnɪŋz] *npl* [of person] Einkommen *das;* [of business] Ertrag *der.*

earphones ['ɪəfəʊnz] *npl* Kopfhörer *der.*

earpiece *n* [of telephone] Hörmuschel *die;* [of radio, mobile phone] ≈ Kopfhörer *der.*

earplugs ['ɪəplʌgz] *npl* Ohropax® *pl.*

earring ['ɪərɪŋ] *n* Ohrring *der.*

earshot ['ɪəʃɒt] *n:* **within/out of** ~ in/außer Hörweite.

earth [ɜːθ] *n* Erde *die;* **how/what/where/why on** ~ ...? wie/was/wo/warum um Himmels willen ...?; **to cost the** ~ **Br** ein Vermögen kosten *vt* **Br: to be** ~**ed** geerdet sein.

earthenware ['ɜːθnweə'] *n (U)* Töpferwaren *pl.*

earthquake ['ɜːθkweɪk] *n* Erdbeben *das.*

earthy ['ɜːθɪ] *adj* [humour, person] derb.

ease [iːz] *n* **- 1.** [in doing sthg] Leichtigkeit *die;* **to do sthg with** ~ etw mit Leichtigkeit tun **- 2.** [comfort]: **a life of** ~ ein komfortables Leben; **to put sb at** ~ jm die Befangenheit nehmen; **I feel at** ~ **(with him)** ich fühle mich (in seiner Gegenwart) wohl; **ill at** ~ unbehaglich *vt* **- 1.** [make less severe - pain] lindern; [- restriction, problem] verringern **- 2.** [move carefully]: **she** ~**d herself out of the armchair** sie erhob sich behutsam aus dem Sessel; **she** ~**d the window open** sie öffnete behutsam das Fenster *vi* [pain, rain] nachllassen; [grip] sich lockern.

◆ **ease off** *vi* [pain, rain] nachllassen.

◆ **ease up** *vi* **- 1.** [rain] nachllassen **- 2.** [relax] sich *(D)* mehr Ruhe gönnen.

easel ['iːzl] *n* Staffelei *die.*

easily ['iːzɪlɪ] *adv* **- 1.** [without difficulty] leicht **- 2.** [undoubtedly] zweifellos **- 3.** [in a relaxed manner] entspannt.

east [iːst] *adj* Ost-, östlich; ~ **wind** Ostwind *der vt* [travel, face] ostwärts, nach Osten; ~ **of** östlich von *n* **- 1.** [direction] Osten *der* **- 2.** [region]: **the** ~ der Osten.

◆ **East** *n:* **the East** [Asia & POL] der Osten.

East End *n:* **the** ~ *der Londoner Osten nördlich der Themse.*

Easter ['iːstə'] *n* Ostern *pl.*

Easter egg *n* Osterei *das.*

easterly ['iːstəlɪ] *adj* östlich; ~ **wind** Ostwind *der;* **in an** ~ **direction** in östlicher Richtung.

eastern ['iːstən] *adj* Ost-. ◆ **Eastern** *adj* **- 1.** [from Asia] östlich **- 2.** POL Ost-.

East German *adj* ostdeutsch *n* Ostdeutsche *der, die.*

East Germany *n:* **(the former)** ~ Ostdeutschland *nt.*

eastward ['iːstwəd] *adj* (in) Richtung Osten *adv* = eastwards.

eastwards ['iːstwədz] *adv* ostwärts.

easy ['iːzɪ] *adj* **- 1.** [not difficult] leicht;

[route] einfach **- 2.** [comfortable] leicht; **an** ~ **life** ein bequemes Leben **- 3.** [relaxed] ungezwungen *adv:* **to take it** OR **things** ~ *inf* [ease up] sich *(D)* mehr Ruhe gönnen; [have a rest] eine ruhige Kugel schieben.

easy chair *n* [armchair] Sessel *der.*

easygoing [,iːzɪ'gəʊɪŋ] *adj* [person] unbekümmert; [manner] lässig.

eat [iːt] *(pt* ate; *pp* eaten) *vt* [subj: person] essen; [subj: animal] fressen. ◆ **eat away** *vt sep,* **eat into** *vt fus* **- 1.** [subj: rust, acid] zerfressen **- 2.** [savings] aufzehren.

eaten ['iːtn] *pp* ⊳ eat.

eaves ['iːvz] *npl* [of house] Dachvorsprung *der.*

eavesdrop ['iːvzdrɒp] *vi* lauschen; **to** ~ **on sb** jn belauschen.

ebb [eb] *n* Ebbe *die vi* [tide, sea] zurücklgehen.

ebony ['ebənɪ] *n* Ebenholz *das.*

EC *(abbr of* European Community) *n* EG *die.*

e-cash *n* COMPUT elektronisches Geld.

ECB *(abbr of* European Central Bank) *n* EZB *die.*

eccentric [ɪk'sentrɪk] *adj* exzentrisch *n* Exzentriker *der, -in die.*

echo ['ekəʊ] *(pl* -es; *pt* & *pp* -ed) *n* **- 1.** [sound] Echo *das* **- 2.** [reminder] Reminiszenz *die vi* [repeat - opinion] wiederlgeben *vi* widerlhallen.

eclipse [ɪ'klɪps] *n* **- 1.** [of sun, moon] Eklipse *die,* Finsternis *die* **- 2.** *fig* [decline] Niedergang *der vt fig* [overshadow] in den Schatten stellen.

eco-friendly [,iːkəʊ-] *adj* umweltfreundlich.

ecological [,iːkə'lɒdʒɪkl] *adj* ökologisch; **an** ~ **group** eine Gruppe von Umweltschützern.

ecology [ɪ'kɒlədʒɪ] *n* Ökologie *die.*

economic [,iːkə'nɒmɪk] *adj* **- 1.** [growth, system, policy] Wirtschafts- **- 2.** [business] wirtschaftlich.

economical [,iːkə'nɒmɪkl] *adj* wirtschaftlich; [person] sparsam.

economics [,iːkə'nɒmɪks] *n (U)* [study] Wirtschaftswissenschaften *pl npl* [of plan, business, trade] Wirtschaftlichkeit *die.*

economize, -ise [ɪ'kɒnəmaɪz] *vi* sparen; **to** ~ **on sthg** an etw *(D)* sparen.

economy [ɪ'kɒnəmɪ] *n* **- 1.** [system] Wirtschaft *die* **- 2.** [saving]: **it is a failure** ~ es hilft nicht zu sparen; **to make economies** Sparmaßnahmen treffen; ~ **measure** Sparmaßnahme *die.*

economy class *n* Touristenklasse *die.*

ecstasy ['ekstəsɪ] *n* **- 1.** [great happiness] Ekstase *die;* **to go into ecstasies about sthg** über etw *(A)* in Verzückung geraten **- 2.** *(U)* [drug] Ecstasy *das.*

ecstatic [ek'stætɪk] *adj* ekstatisch.

eczema ['eksɪmə] *n (U)* Ekzem *das.*

edge [edʒ] <> n - 1. [of cliff, path, forest] Rand *der;* [of table, coin, book] Kante *die* - 2. [of blade] Schneide *die* - 3. [advantage]: **to have an ~ over sb, to have the ~ on sb** jm gegenüber einen Vorteil haben; **to have an ~ over sthg, to have the ~ on sthg** etw (D) überlegen sein <> vi [move slowly]: **to ~ forwards** sich Stück für Stück vorwärtsbewegen; **to ~ away** sich langsam zurückziehen. ◆ **on edge** *adj:* **to be on ~** [person] nervös sein; [nerves] gereizt sein.

edgeways ['edʒweɪz], **edgewise** ['edʒwaɪz] *adv* seitwärts.

edgy ['edʒɪ] *adj* nervös.

edible ['edɪbl] *adj* essbar.

Edinburgh ['edɪnbrə] *n* Edinburgh *nt.*

edit ['edɪt] *vt* - 1. [correct, select material for] redigieren - 2. CINEMA, RADIO & TV schneiden - 3. [newspaper, magazine] herausIgeben - 4. COMPUT editieren.

edition [ɪ'dɪʃn] *n* - 1. [of book, newspaper] Ausgabe *die* - 2. [broadcast] Sendung *die.*

editor ['edɪtə'] *n* - 1. [of newspaper, magazine, book] Herausgeber *der,* -in *die* - 2. [of section of newspaper, programme] Redakteur *der,* -in *die* - 3. [copy editor] Lektor *der,* -in *die* - 4. CINEMA, RADIO & TV Cutter *der,* -in *die* - 5. COMPUT Editor *der.*

editorial [,edɪ'tɔ:rɪəl] <> *adj* redaktionell; **~ department/staff** Redaktion *die* <> *n* Leitartikel *der.*

educate ['edʒʊkeɪt] *vt* - 1. SCH & UNIV auslbilden; [subj: parents] erziehen - 2. [inform] informieren.

education [,edʒʊ'keɪʃn] *n* - 1. [gen] Ausbildung *die;* [by parents] Erziehung *die.*

educational [,edʒʊ'keɪʃənl] *adj* - 1. [establishment, policy] Bildungs-; **~ background** Ausbildung *die* - 2. [toy] didaktisch; [experience] lehrreich.

EEC (*abbr of* European Economic Community) *n* EWG *die.*

eel [i:l] *n* Aal *der.*

eerie ['ɪərɪ] *adj* unheimlich.

efface [ɪ'feɪs] *vt* [mark, inscription] entfernen; [memory] auslöschen.

effect [ɪ'fekt] <> *n* - 1. [result] Wirkung *die;* **to have an ~ on sb/sthg** eine Wirkung auf jn/ etw haben; **to take ~** [law, rule] in Kraft treten; [drug] wirken; **to put sthg into ~** etw in Kraft setzen - 2. [impression] Wirkung *die,* Effekt *der;* **for ~** aus Effekthascherei <> *vt* bewirken. ◆ **effects** *npl* - 1.: **(special) ~s** (Spezial)effekte *pl* - 2. [property] Habe *die.* ◆ **in effect** *adv* in Wirklichkeit.

effective [ɪ'fektɪv] *adj* - 1. [successful] effektiv - 2. [actual] eigentlich - 3. [in operation] wirksam.

effectively [ɪ'fektɪvlɪ] *adv* - 1. [successfully] effektiv - 2. [in fact] in Wirklichkeit.

effectiveness [ɪ'fektɪvnɪs] *n* [success] Effektivität *die.*

effeminate [ɪ'femɪnət] *adj pej* weibisch.

effervescent [,efə'vesnt] *adj* sprudelnd.

efficiency [ɪ'fɪʃnsɪ] *n* [of person] Tüchtigkeit *die;* [of machine] Leistungsfähigkeit *die;* [of system] Effizienz *die.*

efficient [ɪ'fɪʃnt] *adj* [person] tüchtig; [machine] leistungsfähig; [method] effizient.

effluent ['efluənt] *n* Abwasser *das.*

effort ['efət] *n* - 1. [exertion] Anstrengung *die;* **it's not worth the ~** es ist nicht der Mühe wert; **to make the ~ to do sthg** sich bemühen, etw zu tun; **with ~** mit Mühe - 2. [attempt] Versuch *der;* **to make an/no ~ to do sthg** sich anstrengen/sich nicht anstrengen, etw zu tun.

effortless ['efətlɪs] *adj* mühelos.

effusive [ɪ'fju:sɪv] *adj* überschwenglich.

e.g. (*abbr of* exempli gratia) *adv* z. B.

egg [eg] *n* Ei *das.* ◆ **egg on** *vt sep* anlstacheln.

eggcup ['egkʌp] *n* Eierbecher *der.*

eggplant ['egplɑ:nt] *n Am* Aubergine *die.*

eggshell ['egʃel] *n* Eierschale *die.*

egg white *n* Eiweiß *das.*

egg yolk *n* Eigelb *das.*

ego ['i:gəʊ] (*pl* -s) *n* [opinion of self] Selbstbewusstsein *das;* PSYCH Ego *das.*

egoism ['i:gəʊɪzm] *n* Egoismus *der.*

egoistic [,i:gəʊ'ɪstɪk] *adj* egoistisch.

egotistic(al) [,i:gə'tɪstɪk(l)] *adj* egoistisch.

Egypt ['i:dʒɪpt] *n* Ägypten *nt.*

Egyptian [ɪ'dʒɪpʃn] <> *adj* ägyptisch <> *n* Ägypter *der,* -in *die.*

eiderdown ['aɪdədaʊn] *n esp Br* [bed cover] Daunendecke *die.*

eight [eɪt] *num* acht; *see also* six.

eighteen [,eɪ'ti:n] *num* achtzehn; *see also* six.

eighth [eɪtθ] *num* achte, -r, -s; *see also* sixth.

eighty ['eɪtɪ] *num* achtzig; *see also* sixty.

Eire ['eərə] *n* Irland *nt.*

either ['aɪðə', 'i:ðə'] <> *adj* - 1. [one or the other]: **~ will do** es ist egal, welches (von beiden); **~ way I will lose** wie ich es auch mache, ich werde dabei verlieren - 2. [each] beide; **on ~ side** auf beiden Seiten <> *pron:* **I'll take ~ (of them)** ich nehme einen/eine/eins (von beiden); **I don't like ~ (of them)** ich mag keinen/keine/keins (von beiden) <> *adv (in negatives):* **I can't ~** ich auch nicht <> *conj:* **~ ... or ...** entweder ... oder; **I don't like ~ him or her** ich mag weder ihn noch sie; **without ~ writing or phoning** ohne zu schreiben oder anzurufen.

eject [ɪ'dʒekt] *vt* - 1. [object] auslstoßen - 2. [person]: **to ~ sb (from)** jn hinauslwerfen (aus).

eke ◆ **eke out** *vt sep* strecken.

elaborate [*adj* ɪ'læbrət, *vb* ɪ'læbəreɪt] <> *adj* [explanation] ausführlich; [plan] ausgefeilt; [carving] kunstvoll; [ceremony] kom-

pliziert ⟨⟩ *vi:* **to ~ (on sthg)** (etw) näher erläutern.

elapse [ɪ'læps] *vi* [time] verstreichen.

elastic [ɪ'læstɪk] ⟨⟩ *adj -* **1.** [stretchy] elastisch *-* **2.** *fig* [flexible] flexibel ⟨⟩ *n (U)* [material] Gummiband *das.*

elasticated [ɪ'læstɪkeɪtɪd] *adj* [waistband] mit Gummizug.

elastic band *n Br* Gummiband *das.*

elated [ɪ'leɪtɪd] *adj* in Hochstimmung.

elbow ['elbəʊ] *n* Ellbogen *der.*

elder ['eldəʳ] ⟨⟩ *adj* ältere, -r, -s ⟨⟩ *n -* **1.** [older person]: **show respect to your ~s** zeige Respekt gegenüber älteren Menschen *-* **2.** [of church] Presbyter *der.*

elderly ['eldəlɪ] *adj* ältere, -r, -s ⟨⟩ *npl:* **the ~** ältere Menschen *pl.*

eldest ['eldɪst] *adj* älteste, -r, -s.

elect [ɪ'lekt] ⟨⟩ *adj:* **president ~** designierter Präsident ⟨⟩ *vt* [by voting] wählen; **he was ~ed (as) party leader** er wurde zum Parteivorsitzenden gewählt.

election [ɪ'lekʃn] *n* Wahl *die;* **to have** OR **hold an ~** eine Wahl abhalten.

elector [ɪ'lektəʳ] *n* [voter] Wähler *der,* -in *die.*

electorate [ɪ'lektərət] *n:* **the ~** die Wählerschaft.

electric [ɪ'lektrɪk] *adj -* **1.** [gen] elektrisch *-* **2.** *fig* [atmosphere] elektrisiert. ◆ **electrics** *npl Br inf* [in car, machine] Elektrik *die.*

electrical [ɪ'lektrɪkl] *adj* elektrisch; **~ goods** Elektrowaren *pl.*

electrical shock *n Am* = electric shock.

electric blanket *n* Heizdecke *die.*

electric cooker *n* Elektroherd *der.*

electric fire *n* Heizstrahler *der.*

electrician [ˌɪlek'trɪʃn] *n* Elektriker *der,* -in *die.*

electricity [ˌɪlek'trɪsətɪ] *n* [current] Strom *der;* [in physics] Elektrizität *die.*

electric shock *Br,* **electrical shock** *Am n* Stromschlag *der.*

electrify [ɪ'lektrɪfaɪ] *vt -* **1.** [railway line] elektrifizieren *-* **2.** *fig* [excite] elektrisieren.

electrocute [ɪ'lektrəkjuːt] *vt:* **to ~ o.s., to be ~d** sich durch Stromschlag töten; **to be ~d** [executed] auf dem elektrischen Stuhl hingerichtet werden.

electrolysis [ˌɪlek'trɒləsɪs] *n* Elektrolyse *die.*

electron [ɪ'lektrɒn] *n* Elektron *das.*

electronic [ˌɪlek'trɒnɪk] *adj* elektronisch. ◆ **electronics** ⟨⟩ *n (U)* [technology] Elektronik *die* ⟨⟩ *npl* [of car, machine] Elektronik *die.*

electronic data processing *n* elektronische Datenverarbeitung.

elegant ['elɪgənt] *adj* elegant.

element ['elɪmənt] *n -* **1.** [gen] Element *das;* [component] Bestandteil *der;* **an ~ of truth**

ein Körnchen Wahrheit *-* **2.** [of heater, kettle] Heizelement *das.* ◆ **elements** *npl -* **1.** [basics] Grundlagen *pl -* **2.** [weather]: **the ~s** die Elemente *pl.*

elementary [ˌelɪ'mentərɪ] *adj* [precautions, mistake, question] simpel; [education, maths] Elementar-.

elementary school *n Am* Grundschule *die.*

elephant ['elɪfənt] *n (pl inv* OR *-s) n* Elefant *der.*

elevate ['elɪveɪt] *vt -* **1.** [raise] heben *-* **2.** [give importance to] erheben; [promote] befördern.

elevator ['elɪveɪtəʳ] *n Am* Fahrstuhl *der.*

eleven [ɪ'levn] *num* elf; *see also* six.

elevenses [ɪ'levnzɪz] *n Br* zweites Frühstück.

eleventh [ɪ'levnθ] *num* elfte, -r, -s; *see also* sixth.

elicit [ɪ'lɪsɪt] *vt fml:* **to ~ sthg (from sb)** (jm) etw entlocken.

eligible ['elɪdʒəbl] *adj* [suitable, qualified] geeignet; **to be ~ for sthg** für etw in Frage kommen.

eliminate [ɪ'lɪmɪneɪt] *vt -* **1.** [remove] ausschließen; [disease, poverty] eliminieren *-* **2.** [from competition]: **to be ~d from sthg** aus etw ausscheiden.

elite [ɪ'liːt] ⟨⟩ *adj* Elite- ⟨⟩ *n* Elite *die.*

elitist [ɪ'liːtɪst] *adj* elitär.

elk [elk] *n (pl inv* OR *-s) n* Elch *der;* [Canadian] Elk *der.*

elm [elm] *n:* **~ (tree)** Ulme *die.*

elongated ['iːlɒŋgeɪtɪd] *adj* [face, shape] lang gezogen.

elope [ɪ'ləʊp] *vi* durch|brennen.

eloquent ['eləkwənt] *adj -* **1.** [speaker] wortgewandt *-* **2.** [speech, words] wohlgesetzt.

else [els] *adv:* **I don't want anything ~** ich will nichts mehr; **anything ~?** sonst noch etwas?; **everyone ~** alle anderen; **nobody ~** niemand anders; **nothing ~** sonst nichts; **somebody ~** [additional person] noch jemand anders; [different person] jemand anders; **anybody ~ (but you) would have given up** jeder andere (außer dir) hätte aufgegeben; **something ~** [additional thing] noch etwas; [different thing] etwas anderes; **somewhere ~** woanders; **to go somewhere ~** woandershin gehen; **what ~?** [in addition] was (sonst) noch?; [instead] was sonst?; **who ~?** [in addition] wer (sonst) noch?; [instead] wer sonst? ◆ **or else** *conj* [or if not] sonst, oder; **come in or ~ go out** komm entweder herein oder geh hinaus.

elsewhere [els'weəʳ] *adv* woanders.

elude [ɪ'luːd] *vt -* **1.** [police, pursuers] entwischen *-* **2.** [subj: fact, name] entfallen sein *(+ D).*

elusive [ɪ'luːsɪv] *adj* [quality] schwer fassbar; [success] schwer erreichbar; **he is very ~** er ist selten anzutreffen.

e-mail ⋄ *n* E-Mail *die;* **by ~** per E-Mail ⋄ *vt:* **to ~ sb** jm eine E-mail schicken.

e-mail address *n* COMPUT E-Mail-Adresse *die.*

emanate ['eməneɪt] *fml vi:* **to ~ from** [idea] stammen von; [smell] kommen von/aus.

emancipate [ɪ'mænsɪpeɪt] *vt* befreien; [women] emanzipieren.

embankment [ɪm'bæŋkmənt] *n* **- 1.** [along road, path] Böschung *die* **- 2.** [along river] Damm *der;* [along railway] Bahndamm *der.*

embark [ɪm'bɑːk] *vi* **- 1.** [board ship] sich einlschiffen **- 2.** [start]: **to ~ (up)on sthg** mit etw beginnen.

embarrass [ɪm'bærəs] *vt* in Verlegenheit bringen.

embarrassed [ɪm'bærəst] *adj* verlegen.

embarrassing [ɪm'bærəsɪŋ] *adj* peinlich.

embarrassment [ɪm'bærəsmənt] *n* Verlegenheit *die;* **to be an ~ to sb** jn in Verlegenheit bringen.

embassy ['embəsɪ] *n* Botschaft *die.*

embedded [ɪm'bedɪd] *adj* **- 1.** [in rock, wood, mud]: **to be ~ in sthg** in etw *(D)* festlstecken **- 2.** *fig* [feeling] fest verwurzelt.

embellish [ɪm'belɪʃ] *vt* **- 1.** [decorate]: **to ~ sthg with sthg** etw mit etw schmücken **- 2.** *fig* [story] auslschmücken.

embers ['embəz] *npl* Glut *die.*

embezzle [ɪm'bezl] *vt* unterschlagen.

embittered [ɪm'bɪtəd] *adj* verbittert.

emblem ['embləm] *n* Emblem *das.*

embody [ɪm'bɒdɪ] *vt* **- 1.** [epitomize] verkörpern **- 2.** [include] enthalten.

embossed [ɪm'bɒst] *adj* geprägt.

embrace [ɪm'breɪs] ⋄ *n* Umarmung *die* ⋄ *vt* [hug] umarmen ⋄ *vi* sich umarmen.

embroider [ɪm'brɔɪdə'] *vt* **- 1.** [design] sticken; [tablecloth, blouse] besticken **- 2.** [story] auslschmücken.

embroidery [ɪm'brɔɪdərɪ] *n* **- 1.** [skill] Sticken *das* **- 2.** [designs] Stickerei *die.*

embroil [ɪm'brɔɪl] *vt:* **to get ~ed (in sthg)** (in etw *(A)*) verwickelt werden.

embryo ['embrɪəʊ] *(pl* **-s)** *n* Embryo *der.*

emerald ['emərəld] *n* Smaragd *der.*

emerge [ɪ'mɜːdʒ] ⋄ *vi* **- 1.** [come out] auf-tauchen; **to ~ from sthg** aus etw herauslkommen **- 2.** [facts, truth] herauslkommen ⋄ *vt:* **it ~d that ...** es stellte sich heraus, dass ...

emergency [ɪ'mɜːdʒənsɪ] ⋄ *adj* Not- ⋄ *n* Notfall *der;* **in an ~** im Notfall.

emergency brake *n Am* Notbremse *die.*

emergency exit *n* Notausgang *der.*

emergency landing *n* Notlandung *die.*

emergency room *n Am* Unfallstation *die.*

emergency services *npl* Hilfsdienste *pl.*

emigrant ['emɪɡrənt] *n* Auswanderer *der.*

emigrate ['emɪɡreɪt] *vi* auslwandern.

eminent ['emɪnənt] *adj* berühmt und anerkannt.

emit [ɪ'mɪt] *vt fml* [light] auslstrahlen; [radiation, smoke] emittieren; [sound, heat] ablgeben.

emotion [ɪ'məʊʃn] *n* **- 1.** [particular feeling] Gefühl *das,* Emotion *die* **- 2.** *(U)* [strength of feeling] Gemütsbewegung *die;* **she showed no ~** sie blieb vollkommen unbewegt; **to speak with ~** ergriffen sprechen.

emotional [ɪ'məʊʃənl] *adj* **- 1.** [person - by nature] gefühlsbetont; [- temporarily] emotional; **to get ~** emotional werden **- 2.** [scene, farewell] emotionsgeladen; [music] gefühlvoll; [appeal, speech] gefühlsbetont **- 3.** [problems, needs, reasons] emotional.

emperor ['empərə'] *n* Kaiser *der.*

emphasis ['emfəsɪs] *(pl* **-ases** [-əsiːz]*) n* Betonung *die;* **to lay** OR **place ~ on sthg** großen Wert auf etw *(A)* legen.

emphasize, -ise ['emfəsaɪz] *vt* betonen; [point, feature] hervorlheben.

emphatic [ɪm'fætɪk] *adj* [forceful] entschieden.

emphatically [ɪm'fætɪklɪ] *adv* **- 1.** [with emphasis] mit Nachdruck **- 2.** [deny] entschieden.

empire ['empaɪə'] *n* POL Reich *das.*

employ [ɪm'plɔɪ] *vt* **- 1.** [give work to] beschäftigen; [recruit] anlstellen; **to be ~ed as a secretary** als Sekretär(in) arbeiten **- 2.** *fml* [use] anlwenden.

employee [ɪm'plɔɪiː] *n* Angestellte *der, die.*

employer [ɪm'plɔɪə'] *n* Arbeitgeber *der,* -in *die.*

employment [ɪm'plɔɪmənt] *n (U)* Arbeit *die;* [recruitment] Anstellung *die;* **to be in ~** eine Stelle haben.

employment agency *n* Stellenvermittlung *die.*

empower [ɪm'paʊə'] *vt fml:* **to be ~ed to do sthg** ermächtigt sein, etw zu tun.

empress ['empris] *n* Kaiserin *die.*

empty ['emptɪ] ⋄ *adj* leer; **on an ~ stomach** MED auf nüchternen Magen ⋄ *vt* leeren; [bin] auslleeren; [room] auslräumen; **to ~ sthg into/out of sthg** [pour] etw in etw *(A)* /aus etw schütten ⋄ *vi* [room, theatre] sich leeren ⋄ *n inf* [bottle] leere Flasche; [glass] leeres Glas.

empty-handed [-'hændɪd] *adv* unverrichteter Dinge.

EMU *(abbr of* **European Monetary Union)** *n* WWU *die.*

emulate ['emjʊleɪt] *vt* [person, example] nachleifern *(+ D)*; [system] nachlahmen.

emulsion [ɪ'mʌlʃn] n: ~ **(paint)** Dispersionsfarbe die.

enable [ɪ'neɪbl] vt: **to ~ sb to do sthg** es jm möglich machen, etw zu tun.

enact [ɪ'nækt] vt - 1. LAW erlassen - 2. [scene, play] aufführen.

enamel [ɪ'næml] n - 1. [on metal, glass] Email das - 2. [on tooth] Zahnschmelz der - 3. [paint] Emaillack der.

encapsulate [ɪn'kæpsjʊleɪt] vt fig zusammenfassen.

enchanting [ɪn'tʃɑːntɪŋ] adj bezaubernd.

encircle [ɪn'sɜːkl] vt umgeben; [subj: troops] umringen.

enclose [ɪn'kləʊz] vt - 1. [surround] umgeben; ~d space abgeschlossener Raum; **to be ~d by** OR **with sthg** von etw umgeben sein - 2. [put in envelope] beilegen; **please find ~d ... als Anlage senden wir Ihnen ...**

enclosure [ɪn'kləʊʒə^r] n - 1. [place] eingezäuntes Grundstück; [for animals] Gehege das - 2. [in letter] Anlage die.

encompass [ɪn'kʌmpəs] vt fml umfassen.

encore ['ɒŋkɔː^r] <> n Zugabe die <> excl Zugabe!

encounter [ɪn'kaʊntə^r] <> n Begegnung die; [battle] Kampf der <> vt fml - 1. [meet] begegnen (+ D) - 2. [experience] stoßen auf (+ A).

encourage [ɪn'kʌrɪdʒ] vt - 1. [person] ermutigen; **to ~ sb to do sthg** jn ermutigen OR ermuntern, etw zu tun - 2. [foster] fördern.

encouragement [ɪn'kʌrɪdʒmənt] n Ermutigung die; [support] Förderung die.

encroach [ɪn'krəʊtʃ] vi: **to ~ (up)on sthg** [on territory] in etw (A) vordringen; [on rights, privacy] in etw (A) eingreifen.

encyclop(a)edic [ɪn‚saɪkləʊ'piːdɪk] adj enzyklopädisch.

end [end] <> n - 1. [finish] Ende das; **from beginning to ~** von vorn bis hinten; **at the ~ of May** Ende Mai; **at an ~** zu Ende; **to come to an ~** enden; **to put an ~ to sthg** etw (D) ein Ende setzen; **at the ~ of the day** fig schließlich und endlich; **in the ~** [finally] schließlich - 2. [extremity] Ende das; [of box] Seite die; [of finger, stick] Spitze die; **to make ~s meet** [financially] zurechtkommen - 3. [leftover part] Rest der; [of candle] Stummel der - 4. fml [purpose] Ziel das - 5. literary [death] Ende das <> vt beenden <> vi enden; **to ~ in failure** in einem Misserfolg enden.

◆ **on end** adv - 1. [upright] hoch kant - 2. [continuously]: **for days on ~** tagelang.

◆ **end up** vi: **to ~ up in prison** im Gefängnis landen; **to ~ up doing sthg** schließlich etw tun.

endanger [ɪn'deɪndʒə^r] vt gefährden.

endearing [ɪn'dɪərɪŋ] adj liebenswert.

endeavour Br, **endeavor** Am [ɪn'devə^r] fml <> n Bemühung die <> vt: **to ~ to do sthg** sich bemühen, etw zu tun.

ending ['endɪŋ] n - 1. [of story, film] Ende das, Schluss der - 2. GRAMM Endung die.

endive ['endaɪv] n - 1. [salad vegetable] Endivie die - 2. [chicory] Chicorée die OR der.

endless ['endlɪs] adj endlos; [possibilities, desert] unendlich.

endorse [ɪn'dɔːs] vt - 1. [approve] billigen - 2. [cheque] auf der Rückseite unterschreiben, indossieren.

endorsement [ɪn'dɔːsmənt] n - 1. [approval] Billigung die - 2. Br [on driving licence] Strafvermerk der (auf dem Führerschein).

endow [ɪn'daʊ] vt [equip]: **to be ~ed with sthg** mit etw ausgestattet sein; **to be ~ed with charm/talent** Charme/Talent haben.

endurance [ɪn'djʊərəns] n Durchhaltevermögen das; **it was beyond ~** es war nicht auszuhalten.

endure [ɪn'djʊə^r] <> vt ertragen <> vi fml Bestand haben.

endways Br ['endweɪz], **endwise** Am ['endwaɪz] adv - 1. [lengthways] mit dem Ende nach vorn - 2. [end to end] mit dem Enden aneinander.

enemy ['enɪmɪ] <> n Feind der <> comp feindlich.

energetic [‚enə'dʒetɪk] adj - 1. [lively] energiegeladen; **to feel/be ~** viel Energie haben - 2. [game, activity] viel Energie erfordernd - 3. [supporter, campaigner] tatkräftig.

energy ['enədʒɪ] n [gen] Energie die.

enforce [ɪn'fɔːs] vt [high standards, discipline] sorgen für; **to ~ a law** für die Einhaltung eines Gesetzes sorgen.

enforced [ɪn'fɔːst] adj aufgezwungen.

engage [ɪn'geɪdʒ] <> vt - 1. [attract - attention] in Anspruch nehmen; [- interest] fesseln - 2. TECH [gear] einlegen; **to ~ the clutch** kuppeln - 3. fml [employ] anstellen; **to be ~d in** OR **on sthg** mit etw beschäftigt sein <> vi: **to ~ in sthg** sich mit etw befassen.

engaged [ɪn'geɪdʒd] adj - 1. [couple]: ~ **(to sb)** (mit jm) verlobt; **to get ~** sich verloben - 2. [busy] beschäftigt - 3. [toilet, telephone, number] besetzt.

engaged tone n Br Besetztzeichen das.

engagement [ɪn'geɪdʒmənt] n - 1. [of couple] Verlobung die - 2. [appointment - gen] Verpflichtung die; [- business] Termin der.

engagement ring n Verlobungsring der.

engaging [ɪn'geɪdʒɪŋ] adj [manner, personality] einnehmend; [smile] gewinnend.

engender [ɪn'dʒendə^r] vt fml erzeugen.

engine ['endʒɪn] n - 1. [of car, plane] Motor der; [of ship] Maschine die - 2. RAIL Lokomotive die.

engine driver n Br Lokomotivführer der.

engineer [‚endʒɪ'nɪə^r] n - 1. [of roads, machines, bridges] Techniker der, -in die; [with degree] Ingenieur der, -in die - 2. Am [engine driver] Lokomotivführer der.

engineering [ˌendʒɪˈnɪərɪŋ] *n (U)* Technik *die*; [mechanical] Maschinenbau *der*.

England [ˈɪŋglənd] *n* England *nt*.

English [ˈɪŋglɪʃ] <> *adj* englisch <> *n* Englisch(e) *das* <> *npl*: **the ~** die Engländer *pl*.

English breakfast *n* englisches Frühstück.

English Channel *n*: **the ~** der Ärmelkanal.

Englishman [ˈɪŋglɪʃmən] (*pl* -men [-mən]) *n* Engländer *der*.

Englishwoman [ˈɪŋglɪʃˌwʊmən] (*pl* -women [-wɪmɪn]) *n* Engländerin *die*.

engrave [ɪnˈgreɪv] *vt* [metal, glass] gravieren; [design] eingravieren.

engraving [ɪnˈgreɪvɪŋ] *n* [design] Gravierung *die*; [print] Stich *der*.

engrossed [ɪnˈgrəʊst] *adj*: **to be ~ (in sthg)** (in etw *(A)*) vertieft sein.

engulf [ɪnˈgʌlf] *vt* [subj: fire, water] verschlingen; [subj: panic, fear] überwältigen.

enhance [ɪnˈhɑːns] *vt* [value, chances] steigern, erhöhen; [beauty] betonen.

enjoy [ɪnˈdʒɔɪ] *vt* - **1.** [like] genießen; **she ~ed the film/book** der Film/das Buch hat ihr gefallen; **did you ~ it?** hast du es genossen?, hat es dir gefallen?; **to ~ doing sthg** etw gern(e) tun; **to ~ o.s.** sich amüsieren; **~ yourself!** viel Spaß! - **2.** *fml* [possess] genießen; **to ~ good health** sich guter Gesundheit erfreuen.

enjoyable [ɪnˈdʒɔɪəbl] *adj* [job, work, experience] angenehm; [holiday, day] schön; [film, book] unterhaltsam.

enjoyment [ɪnˈdʒɔɪmənt] *n* [gen] Vergnügen *das*.

enlarge [ɪnˈlɑːdʒ] *vt* vergrößern; [scope, interest, circle of friends] erweitern. ◆ **enlarge (up)on** *vt fus* sich genauer äußern über (+ *A*).

enlargement [ɪnˈlɑːdʒmənt] *n* Vergrößerung *die*.

enlighten [ɪnˈlaɪtn] *vt fml* aufklären.

enlightened [ɪnˈlaɪtnd] *adj* [person] aufgeklärt; [approach] fortschrittlich.

enlist [ɪnˈlɪst] <> *vt* - **1.** MIL [recruit] einziehen - **2.** [support, help] in Anspruch nehmen <> *vi* MIL: **to ~ (in)** sich melden (zu).

enmity [ˈenmətɪ] *n* Feindschaft *die*.

enormity [ɪˈnɔːmətɪ] *n* ungeheueres Ausmaß.

enormous [ɪˈnɔːməs] *adj* ungeheuer groß.

enough [ɪˈnʌf] <> *adj* genug; **~ time** Zeit genug; **have you got ~ money?** hast du genügend Geld? <> *pron* genug; **is that ~?** reicht das?; **to have had ~ (of sthg)** genug (von etw) haben; **I've had ~!** [expressing annoyance] jetzt reichts mir aber!; **more than ~** mehr als genug; **it's ~ to drive you crazy!** es ist zum Verrücktwerden! <> *adv* - **1.** [sufficiently] genug; **good ~** gut genug; **would you**

be good ~ to open the door for me? *fml* wärst du so gut und öffnest mir die Tür? - **2.** [rather]: **he seems a nice ~ chap** er ist ganz nett zu sein; **strangely ~** merkwürdigerweise; **sure ~** tatsächlich.

enquire [ɪnˈkwaɪəʳ] *vt & vi* = inquire.

enquiry [ɪnˈkwaɪərɪ] *n* = inquiry.

enraged [ɪnˈreɪdʒd] *adj* wütend.

enrol, enroll *Am* [ɪnˈrəʊl] <> *vt* einschreiben; SCH anmelden <> *vi*: **to ~ (on** OR **in)** sich einschreiben (für).

ensue [ɪnˈsjuː] *vi fml* folgen.

ensure [ɪnˈʃʊəʳ] *vt* sicherstellen; [safety, privacy] gewährleisten; **to ~ (that)** ... dafür sorgen, dass ...

ENT (*abbr of* Ear, Nose & Throat) HNO.

entail [ɪnˈteɪl] *vt* mit sich bringen.

enter [ˈentəʳ] <> *vt* - **1.** [house, room] eintreten in (+ *A*), betreten; [car, bus, train] einsteigen in (+ *A*); [subj: vehicle] fahren in (+ *A*); [subj: ship] einlaufen in (+ *A*); [country] einreisen in (+ *A*) - **2.** [army] eintreten in (+ *A*); [competition, race] teilnehmen an (+ *D*) - **3.** [horse, competitor] anmelden; [poem, story] einreichen - **4.** [write down] eintragen - **5.** COMPUT eingeben <> *vi* - **1.** [come or go in] eintreten; [enter bus, train] einsteigen; [enter country] einreisen - **2.** [register]: **to ~ (for sthg)** sich (für etw) anmelden. ◆ **enter into** *vt fus* [negotiations] treten in (+ *A*); **to ~ into an agreement with sb** mit jm ein Abkommen schließen.

enter key *n* COMPUT Eingabetaste *die*.

enterprise [ˈentəpraɪz] *n* - **1.** [company, project] Unternehmen *das*; **private ~** Privatwirtschaft *die* - **2.** *(U)* [initiative] Initiative *die*.

enterprising [ˈentəpraɪzɪŋ] *adj* [person] einfallsreich; [plan, idea] innovativ.

entertain [ˌentəˈteɪn] *vt* - **1.** [amuse] unterhalten - **2.** [dinner guest] bewirten - **3.** *fml* [idea, proposal] erwägen; [hopes] nähren; [suspicion, ambition] hegen.

entertainer [ˌentəˈteɪnəʳ] *n* Unterhalter *der*, -in *die*, Entertainer *der*, -in *die*.

entertaining [ˌentəˈteɪnɪŋ] *adj* unterhaltsam.

entertainment [ˌentəˈteɪnmənt] *n* - **1.** [amusement] Unterhaltung *die* - **2.** [show] Darbietung *die*.

enthral, enthrall *Am* [ɪnˈθrɔːl] *vt* fesseln.

enthusiasm [ɪnˈθjuːzɪæzm] *n* - **1.** [eagerness] Begeisterung *die*, Enthusiasmus *der* - **2.** [hobby] Leidenschaft *die*.

enthusiast [ɪnˈθjuːzɪæst] *n* Enthusiast *der*, -in *die*.

enthusiastic [ɪnˌθjuːzɪˈæstɪk] *adj* begeistert, enthusiastisch.

entice [ɪnˈtaɪs] *vt* locken; **to ~ sb away from sthg** jn von etw weglocken.

entire [ɪnˈtaɪəʳ] *adj* ganz; [amount, population] gesamt; [confidence, attention] voll.

entirely [ɪn'taɪəlɪ] *adv* ganz; **I agree ~** ich stimme voll und ganz zu.

entirety [ɪn'taɪrətɪ] *n fml*: **in its ~** in seiner Gesamtheit.

entitle [ɪn'taɪtl] *vt* [allow]: **to ~ sb to sthg** jn zu etw berechtigen; **to ~ sb to do sthg** jn dazu berechtigen, etw zu tun.

entitled [ɪn'taɪtld] *adj* - **1.** [allowed] berechtigt; **to be ~ to sthg** das Recht auf etw (A) haben - **2.** [called]: **to be ~** den Titel haben.

entitlement [ɪn'taɪtlmənt] *n* Berechtigung *die;* [to compensation, holiday] Anspruch *der.*

entrance [*n* 'entrəns, *vt* ɪn'trɑ:ns] <> *n* - **1.** [way in]: **~ (to)** Eingang *der* (zu) - **2.** [arrival] Eintritt *der;* [of actor] Auftritt *der* - **3.** [admission] Eintritt *der;* **to gain ~ to sthg** *fml* [building] Zutritt zu etw erhalten; [society, university] die Zulassung zu etw erhalten; **'no ~'** 'Zutritt verboten' <> *vt* [delight] bezaubern.

entrance examination *n* Aufnahmeprüfung *die.*

entrance fee *n* Eintrittsgeld *das;* [for club] Aufnahmegebühr *die.*

entrant ['entrənt] *n* [in competition, exam, race] Teilnehmer *der,* -in *die.*

entreat [ɪn'tri:t] *vt*: **to ~ sb to do sthg** jn inständig bitten, etw zu tun.

entrenched [ɪn'trentʃt] *adj* (fest) verwurzelt.

entrepreneur [ˌɒntrəprə'nɜ:ʳ] *n* Unternehmer *der,* -in *die.*

entrust [ɪn'trʌst] *vt*: **to ~ sthg to sb** jm etw anvertrauen; **to ~ sb with sthg** jn mit etw betrauen.

entry ['entrɪ] *n* - **1.** [entrance, arrival]: **~ (into)** Eingang *der* (in (+ A)) - **2.** (U) [admission]: **~ (to)** [to country] Einreise *die* (in (+ A)); [to building] Zutritt *der* (zu); [to event] Einlass *der* (in (+ A)); **to gain ~ to** [house] gelangen in (+ A); [organization] beitreten (+ D); **'no ~'** 'Zutritt verboten'; AUT 'Durchfahrt verboten' - **3.** [for race] Nennung *die;* [for competition] Einsendung *die* - **4.** [in diary, dictionary, ledger] Eintragung *die.*

entry form *n* Anmeldeformular *das.*

entry phone *n* Türsprechanlage *die.*

envelop [ɪn'veləp] *vt*: **to ~ sb/sthg in sthg** jn/etw in etw (A) (ein)hüllen.

envelope ['envələʊp] *n* Briefumschlag *der.*

envious ['envɪəs] *adj*: **~ (of sb/sthg)** neidisch (auf jn/etw).

environment [ɪn'vaɪərənmənt] *n* - **1.** [surroundings] Umgebung *die* - **2.** [natural world]: **the ~** die Umwelt.

environmental [ɪnˌvaɪərən'mentl] *adj* Umwelt-.

environmentally [ɪnˌvaɪərən'mentəlɪ] *adv* umwelt-; **~ friendly** umweltfreundlich.

envisage [ɪn'vɪzɪdʒ], **envision** *Am* [ɪn'vɪʒn] *vt* sich vorlstellen.

envoy ['envɔɪ] *n* Gesandte *der, die.*

envy ['envɪ] <> *n* Neid *der* <> *vt* beneiden; **to ~ sb sthg** jn um etw beneiden.

eon *n Am* = aeon.

epic ['epɪk] <> *adj* [poetry] episch; [journey] lang und abenteuerlich; [story] monumental <> *n* [book, film] Epos *das.*

epidemic [ˌepɪ'demɪk] *n* Epidemie *die.*

epileptic [ˌepɪ'leptɪk] <> *adj* epileptisch <> *n* Epileptiker *der,* -in *die.*

episode ['epɪsəʊd] *n* - **1.** [event] Episode *die* - **2.** [broadcast] Folge *die.*

epitaph ['epɪtɑ:f] *n* Epitaph *das.*

epitome [ɪ'pɪtəmɪ] *n*: **the ~ of** der Inbegriff (+ G).

epitomize, -ise [ɪ'pɪtəmaɪz] *vt* beispielhaft zeigen.

epoch ['i:pɒk] *n* Epoche *die.*

equal ['i:kwəl] <> *adj* - **1.** [of the same quantity, size, shape, degree] gleich; **they're of ~ size** sie sind gleich groß; **to be ~ to sthg** [sum] etw (D) entsprechen - **2.** [in status] gleich(berechtigt); **~ rights** Gleichberechtigung *die* - **3.** [capable]: **to be ~ to sthg** (D) gewachsen sein <> *n* [person] Gleichgestellte *der, die* <> *vt* - **1.** MATH gleichen - **2.** [in standard] gleichlkommen (+ D).

equality [i:'kwɒlətɪ] *n* Gleichheit *die.*

equalize, -ise ['i:kwəlaɪz] *vt & vi* SPORT auslgleichen.

equalizer, -iser ['i:kwəlaɪzəʳ] *n* SPORT Ausgleich *der.*

equally ['i:kwəlɪ] *adv* - **1.** [to the same extent] ebenso - **2.** [divide, share] in gleiche Teile - **3.** [by the same token] gleichzeitig.

equal opportunities *npl* Chancengleichheit *die.*

equate [ɪ'kweɪt] *vt*: **to ~ sthg with sthg** etw mit etw gleichlsetzen.

equation [ɪ'kweɪʒn] *n* MATH Gleichung *die.*

equator [ɪ'kweɪtəʳ] *n*: **the ~** der Äquator.

equilibrium [ˌi:kwɪ'lɪbrɪəm] *n* Gleichgewicht *das.*

equip [ɪ'kwɪp] *vt* - **1.** [provide with equipment] auslstatten; **to ~ sb/sthg with sthg** jn/etw mit etw auslrüsten - **2.** [prepare mentally]: **to ~ sb for sthg** jn für etw vorlbereiten.

equipment [ɪ'kwɪpmənt] *n (U)* Ausrüstung *die;* **electrical ~** Elektrogeräte *pl.*

equity *n (U)* FIN [market value] Eigenkapital *das.* ◆ **equities** *npl* ST EX Stammaktien *pl.*

equivalent [ɪ'kwɪvələnt] <> *adj* entsprechend, äquivalent; **to be ~ to sthg** etw (D) entsprechen <> *n* Gegenstück *das.*

equivocal [ɪ'kwɪvəkl] *adj* [statement, remark] zweideutig.

er [ɜ:ʳ] *excl* äh.

era ['ɪərə] (*pl* -s) *n* Ära *die.*

eradicate [ɪ'rædɪkeɪt] *vt* auslrotten.

erase [ɪ'reɪz] *vt* - **1.** [rub out] auslradieren;

[tape, recording] **löschen - 2.** *fig* [memory] (aus dem Gedächtnis) **tilgen.**

eraser [ɪ'reɪzə'] *n esp Am* Radiergummi *der.*

erect [ɪ'rekt] ⟨⟩ *adj* **- 1.** [person, posture] **aufrecht - 2.** [penis] **erigiert** ⟨⟩ *vt* **- 1.** [building, statue] **errichten, bauen - 2.** [tent] **aufbauen;** [roadblock, sign] **aufstellen.**

erection [ɪ'rekʃn] *n* **- 1.** *(U)* [of building, statue] **Errichtung** *die,* **Bau** *der* **- 2.** [erect penis] **Erektion** *die.*

ERM *(abbr of Exchange Rate Mechanism) n* **WUM** *der.*

erode [ɪ'rəʊd] *vt* **- 1.** GEOL **erodieren - 2.** *fig* [destroy] **unterlgraben.**

erosion [ɪ'rəʊʒn] *n* GEOL **Erosion** *die.*

erotic [ɪ'rɒtɪk] *adj* **erotisch.**

err [ɜː'] *vi* **sich irren.**

errand [ˈerənd] *n* **Besorgung** *die;* **to go on** OR **run an ~ (for sb)** (für jn) **eine Besorgung** OR **einen Botengang machen.**

erratic [ɪ'rætɪk] *adj* **wechselhaft;** [movement, bus service] **unregelmäßig;** [performance] **variabel;** [player] **unberechenbar.**

error [ˈerə'] *n* **- 1.** [mistake] **Fehler** *der* **- 2.** *(U)* [making mistakes]: **in ~ aus Versehen.**

erupt [ɪ'rʌpt] *vi* **auslbrechen.**

eruption [ɪ'rʌpʃn] *n* **Ausbruch** *der.*

escalate [ˈeskəleɪt] *vi* **eskalieren.**

escalator [ˈeskəleɪtə'] *n* **Rolltreppe** *die.*

escapade [ˌeskə'peɪd] *n* **Eskapade** *die.*

escape [ɪ'skeɪp] ⟨⟩ *n* **- 1.** [from person, place, situation]: **~ (from sb/sthg)** **Flucht** *die* **(vor jn/vor** OR **aus etw); there was no ~ es gab kein Entkommen; to make an** OR **one's ~ (from) flüchten (aus) - 2.** [from danger]: **to have a narrow ~ mit knapper Not entkommen - 3.** [leakage] **Ausströmen** *das* **- 4.** COMPUT **Escape** *das* ⟨⟩ *vt* **- 1.** [avoid] **entkommen (+ D) - 2.** [subj: fact, name] **entfallen; her name ~s me just now ihr Name fällt mir momentan nicht ein** ⟨⟩ *vi* **- 1.** [from person, place, situation]: **to ~ (from sb/sthg) fliehen** OR **flüchten (vor jm/vor** OR **aus etw); to ~ from prison aus dem Gefängnis fliehen - 2.** [from danger] **davonlkommen - 3.** [leak] **auslströmen.**

escapism [ɪ'skeɪpɪzm] *n* **Realitätsflucht** *die.*

escort [*n* ˈeskɔːt, *vb* ɪ'skɔːt] ⟨⟩ *n* **- 1.** [guard] **Geleitschutz** *der,* **Eskorte** *die;* **under ~ unter Bewachung - 2.** [companion] **Begleiter** *der,* **-in** *die* ⟨⟩ *vt* [accompany] **begleiten;** [for protection] **eskortieren.**

Eskimo [ˈeskɪməʊ] *(pl -s) n* [person] **Eskimo** *der,* **-frau** *die.*

especially [ɪ'speʃəlɪ] *adv* **- 1.** [in particular, more than usually] **besonders - 2.** [specifically] **speziell.**

espionage [ˈespɪəˌnɑːʒ] *n* **Spionage** *die.*

Esquire [ɪ'skwaɪə'] *n* ≈ **Herr/Herrn,** *britische Höflichkeitsanrede in der Postanschrift.*

essay [ˈeseɪ] *n* **- 1.** SCH **Aufsatz** *der* **- 2.** LITERATURE & UNIV **Essay** *der.*

essence [ˈesns] *n* **- 1.** [nature] **Wesentliche** *das,* **Kern** *der;* **in ~ im Wesentlichen - 2.** *(U)* CULIN **Essenz** *die.*

essential [ɪ'senʃl] *adj* **- 1.** [necessary]: **~ (to** OR **for sthg)** (unbedingt) **notwendig (für etw) - 2.** [basic] **wesentlich.** ◆ **essentials** *npl* **- 1.** [basic commodities] **Notwendigste** *das* **- 2.** [most important elements] **Grundlagen** *pl.*

essentially [ɪ'senʃəlɪ] *adv* **im Grunde.**

establish [ɪ'stæblɪʃ] *vt* **- 1.** [create - company, organization] **gründen;** [- system, law, post] **schaffen - 2.** [initiate]: **to ~ contact with sb Kontakt mit jm auflnehmen - 3.** [ascertain] **festlstellen, ermitteln - 4.** [cause to be accepted] **bestätigen.**

establishment [ɪ'stæblɪʃmənt] *n* **- 1.** *(U)* [creation, foundation] **Gründung** *die,* **Errichtung** *die* **- 2.** [shop, business] **Unternehmen** *das.* ◆ **Establishment** *n:* **the Establishment das Establishment.**

estate [ɪ'steɪt] *n* **- 1.** [land, property] **Gut** *das* **- 2.** [for housing] **Wohnsiedlung** *die;* [for industry] **Industriegebiet** *das* **- 3.** LAW [inheritance] **Besitz** *der,* **Besitztümer** *pl.*

estate agent *n Br* **Grundstücksmakler** *der,* **-in** *die;* **~'s Immobilienbüro** *das.*

estate car *n Br* **Kombiwagen** *der.*

esteem [ɪ'stiːm] ⟨⟩ *n* **Achtung** *die,* **Wertschätzung** *die* ⟨⟩ *vt* **schätzen, achten.**

esthetic *etc adj Am* = **aesthetic** *etc.*

estimate [*n* ˈestɪmət, *vb* ˈestɪmeɪt] ⟨⟩ *n* **- 1.** [calculation, reckoning] **Schätzung** *die* **- 2.** COMM **Kostenvoranschlag** *der* ⟨⟩ *vt* **schätzen, einlschätzen.**

estimation [ˌestɪ'meɪʃn] *n* *(U)* **- 1.** [opinion] **Urteil** *das,* **Einschätzung** *die;* **to go up/down in one's ~ in js Achtung steigen/sinken - 2.** [calculation] **Schätzung** *die.*

Estonia [e'stəʊnɪə] *n* **Estland** *nt.*

estranged[ɪ'streɪndʒd]*adj*getrennt**lebend.**

estuary [ˈestjʊərɪ] *n* **Flußmündung** *die.*

etc. *(abbr of et cetera)* **usw.**

etching [ˈetʃɪŋ] *n* **Radierung** *die.*

eternal [ɪ'tɜːnl] *adj* **ewig.**

eternity [ɪ'tɜːnətɪ] *n* **Ewigkeit** *die.*

ethic [ˈeθɪk] *n* **Ethik** *die.* ◆ **ethics** ⟨⟩ *n* [study] **Ethik** *die* ⟨⟩ *npl* [morals] **Moral** *die.*

ethical [ˈeθɪkl] *adj* **ethisch.**

Ethiopia [ˌiːθɪ'əʊpɪə] *n* **Äthiopien** *nt.*

ethnic cleansing [ˌeθnɪk'klenzɪŋ] *n* **ethnische Säuberung.**

etiquette [ˈetɪket] *n* **Etikette** *die.*

EU *(abbr of European Union) n* **EU** *die.*

euphemism [ˈjuːfəmɪzm] *n* **Euphemismus** *der.*

euphoria [juː'fɔːrɪə] *n* **Euphorie** *die.*

Euro, euro [ˈjʊərəʊ] *n* **Euro** *der.*

euro cent *n* **Eurocent** *der.*

Eurocheque [ˈjʊərəʊˌtʃek] *n* **Euroscheck** *der.*

Euroland *n* Euroland *das.*
Euro MP *n* Europaabgeordnete *der, die.*
Europe ['juərəp] *n* Europa *nt.*
European [,juərə'pi:ən] ◇ *adj* europäisch
◇ *n* Europäer *der,* -in *die.*
European Community *n:* **the** ~ die Europäische Gemeinschaft.
European Monetary System *n:* **the** ~ das Europäische Währungssystem.
European Parliament *n:* **the** ~ das Europäische Parlament.
European Union *n:* **the** ~ die Europäische Union.
euro zone *n* Eurozone *die.*
euthanasia [,ju:θə'neɪzjə] *n* Euthanasie *die.*
evacuate [ɪ'vækjʊeɪt] *vt* evakuieren.
evade [ɪ'veɪd] *vt* - **1.** [pursuers, capture] sich entziehen (+ *D*) - **2.** [issue, question] ausweichen (+ *D*) - **3.** [subj: love, success]: **love/success has always ~d him** ihm ist die Liebe/ der Erfolg immer versagt geblieben.
evaluate [ɪ'væljʊeɪt] *vt* bewerten.
evaporate [ɪ'væpəreɪt] *vi* - **1.** [liquid] verdunsten - **2.** *fig* [feeling] schwinden.
evaporated milk [ɪ'væpəreɪtɪd-] *n* Kondensmilch *die.*
evasion [ɪ'veɪʒn] *n* - **1.** [of responsibility, payment *etc*] Ausweichen *das,* Umgehen *das* - **2.** [lie] Ausflucht *die.*
evasive [ɪ'veɪsɪv] *adj* - **1.** [to avoid question, subject] ausweichend - **2.** [to avoid being hit]: **to take ~ action** ein Ausweichmanöver machen.
eve [i:v] *n* [day before] Vortag *der.*
even ['i:vn] ◇ *adj* - **1.** [rate, speed] gleichmäßig - **2.** [calm] ausgeglichen - **3.** [level, flat] eben - **4.** [teams] gleich stark; **the scores were ~** es herrschte Gleichstand; **to get ~ with sb** es jm heimlzahlen - **5.** [number] gerade ◇ *adv* - **1.** [for emphasis] sogar; **not ~** nicht einmal; **without ~ thinking** ohne auch nur einen Moment nachzudenken; ~ **now** sogar jetzt; ~ **then** selbst dann - **2.** [in comparisons] noch; ~ **better** noch besser. ◆ **even if** *conj* selbst OR auch wenn. ◆ **even out** ◇ *vt sep* - **1.** [gen] auslgleichen; **to ~ things out** das Kräfteverhältnis auslgleichen - **2.** [surface] ebnen ◇ *vi* sich auslgleichen. ◆ **even so** *adv* trotzdem. ◆ **even though** *conj* obwohl.
evening ['i:vnɪŋ] *n* Abend *der;* **in the ~s** am Abend. ◆ **evenings** *adv* Am am Abend.
evening class *n* Abendkurs *der.*
evening dress *n* - **1.** [formal clothes] Abendkleidung *die* - **2.** [woman's garment] Abendkleid *das.*
event [ɪ'vent] *n* - **1.** [happening] Ereignis *das* - **2.** SPORT Wettkampf *der* - **3.** [case] Fall *der;* **in the ~ of** im Falle (+ *G*); **in the ~ of rain** bei Regen; **in the ~ that** falls. ◆ **in any event** *adv*

[all the same] wie dem auch sei, wie auch immer. ◆ **in the event** *adv* Br letztlich.
eventful [ɪ'ventfʊl] *adj* ereignisreich; [life] bewegt.
eventual [ɪ'ventʃʊəl] *adj:* **the ~ winner was ...** der Sieger war schließlich ...

📖 **eventual**

Das englische Adjektiv- und Adverbgespann eventual und eventually scheint auf den ersten Blick „eventuell" zu bedeuten, die zutreffenden Übersetzungen lauten jedoch „schließlich" oder „letztendlich". You'll get used to it eventually meint also „Du wirst dich letztendlich daran gewöhnen".
„Eventuell" kann je nach Kontext verschiedene Übersetzungen haben, darunter possible, perhaps und maybe. Die Aussage Ich werde eventuell auch mitspielen, wenn es nicht regnet könnte im Englischen mit „I might play as well if it doesn't rain" ausgedrückt werden.

eventuality [ɪ,ventʃʊ'ælətɪ] *n* (möglicher) Fall, Eventualität *die.*
eventually [ɪ'ventʃʊəlɪ] *adv* schließlich.
ever ['evə] *adv* - **1.** [at any time] je, jemals; **the worst film I've ~ seen** der schlechteste Film, den ich je gesehen habe; **have you ~ been to Chicago?** sind Sie jemals in Chicago gewesen?; **don't ~ speak to me like that again!** so redest du nicht noch einmal mit mir!; **hardly ~** fast nie - **2.** [all the time] immer; **for ~** [eternally] für immer; [for a long time] seit Ewigkeiten; **as ~** wie immer; ~ **larger** immer größer - **3.** [for emphasis]: **why/how ~ did you do it?** warum/wie hast du das bloß gemacht?; **what ~ is the matter with you?** was ist denn mit dir los?; ~ **such a mess** ein fürchterliches Durcheinander. ◆ **ever since** ◇ *adv* seitdem ◇ *prep & conj* seit.
evergreen ['evəgri:n] *n* [plant] immergrüne Pflanze; [tree] immergrüner Baum.
everlasting [,evə'lɑ:stɪŋ] *adj* ewig; [peace] immer während.
every ['evrɪ] *adj* [each] jede, -r, -s; ~ **day** jeden Tag; ~ **few days** alle paar Tage; **one in ~ ten** eine, -r, -s von zehn. ◆ **every now and then, every so often** *adv* dann und wann, ab und zu. ◆ **every other** *adj:* ~ **other day/car** jeden zweiten Tag/Wagen. ◆ **every which way** *adv* Am überallhin.
everybody ['evrɪ,bɒdɪ] *pron* = everyone.
everyday ['evrɪdeɪ] *adj* (all)täglich.
everyone ['evrɪwʌn] *pron* alle; [each person] jeder; **as ~ knows** wie jeder weiß.
everyplace ['evrɪpleɪs] *adv* Am = everywhere.

everything ['evrɪθɪŋ] *pron* alles; **money isn't ~** Geld ist nicht alles.

everywhere, ['evrɪweə'] **everyplace** *Am adv* überall; [go] überallhin.

evict [ɪ'vɪkt] *vt*: **to ~ sb (from a house)** jn zur Räumung zwingen (eines Hauses).

evidence ['evɪdəns] *n* (U) **- 1.** [proof] Beweis *der* **- 2.** LAW Beweismaterial *das*; **piece of ~** Beweisstück *das*; **to give ~** (als Zeuge/Zeugin) auslsagen.

evident ['evɪdənt] *adj* offensichtlich.

evidently ['evɪdəntlɪ] *adv* offensichtlich.

evil ['i:vl] <> *adj* [morally bad] böse, schlecht; [practice] übel <> *n* **- 1.** [wickedness] Böse *das* **- 2.** [wicked thing] Übel *das*.

evoke [ɪ'vəʊk] *vt* hervorlrufen.

evolution [,i:və'lu:ʃn] *n* **- 1.** BIOL Evolution *die* **- 2.** [development] Entwicklung *die*.

evolve [ɪ'vɒlv] <> *vt* entwickeln <> *vi* **- 1.** BIOL: **to ~ (into/from)** sich entwickeln (in (+ D) /aus) **- 2.** [develop] sich entwickeln.

ewe [ju:] *n* Mutterschaf *das*.

ex- [eks] *prefix* Ex-, ehemalige, -r, -s.

exacerbate [ɪg'zæsəbeɪt] *vt* verschlimmern.

exact [ɪg'zækt] <> *adj* genau; **to be ~** um genau zu sein <> *vt*: **to ~ sthg (from sb)** etw (von jm) erzwingen OR erpressen.

exacting [ɪg'zæktɪŋ] *adj* **- 1.** [demanding, tiring] anspruchsvoll **- 2.** [rigorous] streng.

exactly [ɪg'zæktlɪ] <> *adv* genau, exakt; **not ~** [not really] nicht gerade; [as reply] nicht wirklich <> *excl* genau!

exaggerate [ɪg'zædʒəreɪt] *vt & vi* übertreiben.

exaggeration [ɪg,zædʒə'reɪʃn] *n* Übertreibung *die*.

exalted [ɪg'zɔ:ltɪd] *adj* [important - person] hoch gestellt; [- position] hoch.

exam [ɪg'zæm] (*abbr of* examination) *n* Prüfung *die*; **to take** OR **sit an ~** eine Prüfung machen OR ablegen.

examination [ɪg,zæmɪ'neɪʃn] *n* **- 1.** [test, inspection, consideration] Prüfung *die* **- 2.** MED Untersuchung *die* **- 3.** LAW [of witness, suspect] Vernehmung *die*, Verhör *das*.

examine [ɪg'zæmɪn] *vt* **- 1.** [look at, inspect] überprüfen **- 2.** MED untersuchen **- 3.** [consider, test knowledge of] prüfen **- 4.** LAW vernehmen.

examiner [ɪg'zæmɪnə'] *n* Prüfer *der*, -in *die*.

example [ɪg'zɑ:mpl] *n* **- 1.** [instance] Beispiel *das*; **for ~** zum Beispiel **- 2.** [model] Vorbild *das*.

exasperate [ɪg'zæspəreɪt] *vt* zum Verzweifeln bringen.

exasperation [ɪg,zæspə'reɪʃn] *n* Verzweiflung *die*.

excavate ['ekskəveɪt] *vt* **- 1.** ARCHAEOL auslgraben **- 2.** CONSTR auslheben.

exceed [ɪk'si:d] *vt* **- 1.** [be bigger than] übersteigen **- 2.** [go beyond, go over] übersteigen;

[limit] überschreiten; [expectations] übertreffen.

exceedingly [ɪk'si:dɪŋlɪ] *adv* äußerst.

excel [ɪk'sel] <> *vi*: **to ~ (in** OR **at sthg)** sich hervorltun (in etw (D)) <> *vt*: **to ~ o.s.** *Br* sich selbst übertreffen.

excellence ['eksələns] *n* [high quality] hervorragende Qualität; [high performance] hervorragende Leistung.

excellent ['eksələnt] *adj* ausgezeichnet.

except [ɪk'sept] <> *prep* außer; **everyone ~ her** alle außer ihr <> *conj*: **he does nothing ~ sleep** er tut nichts anderes als schlafen; **I'll do anything ~ typing** ich mache alles, nur nicht Maschine schreiben <> *vt*: **present company ~ed** Anwesende ausgenommen.

➠ **except for** *prep & conj* abgesehen von.

excepting [ɪk'septɪŋ] *prep & conj* = except.

exception [ɪk'sepʃn] *n* **- 1.** [exclusion] Ausnahme *die*; **an ~ to the rule** die Ausnahme von der Regel; **with the ~ of** mit Ausnahme von **- 2.** [offence]: **to take ~ to sthg** an etw (D) Anstoß nehmen.

exceptional [ɪk'sepʃənl] *adj* außergewöhnlich.

excerpt ['eksɜ:pt] *n*: **~ (from)** [from text] Auszug *der* (aus); [from film, play, piece of music] Ausschnitt *der* (aus).

excess [ɪk'ses, *before nouns* 'ekses] <> *adj* [fat in diet] überschüssig; [weight] über- <> *n* Übermaß *das*.

excess baggage *n* Übergewicht *das*.

excess fare *n Br* Nachlösegebühr *die*.

excessive [ɪk'sesɪv] *adj* übermäßig; [price] überhöht.

exchange [ɪks'tʃeɪndʒ] <> *n* **- 1.** [of information, students] Austausch *der*; **to be on an ~** [student] Austauschstudent, -in sein **- 2.** [swap] Tausch *der*; **in ~** dafür; **in ~ for** im Tausch gegen **- 3.** TELEC: **(telephone) ~** Fernmeldeamt *das* <> *vt* [houses, seats, jobs] tauschen; [addresses] auslltauschen; [in shop] umltauschen; **to ~ sthg for sthg** etw gegen etw einltauschen; [foreign currency] etw in etw (A) umltauschen; [in shop] etw gegen etw umltauschen; **to ~ sthg with sb** etw mit jm (aus)ltauschen.

exchange rate *n* FIN Wechselkurs *der*.

Exchequer [ɪks'tʃekə'] *n Br*: **the ~** das Schatzamt.

excise ['eksaɪz] *n* (U) Verbrauchssteuer *die*.

excite [ɪk'saɪt] *vt* **- 1.** [person] begeistern **- 2.** [interest, curiosity, feeling] erregen.

excited [ɪk'saɪtɪd] *adj* aufgeregt.

excitement [ɪk'saɪtmənt] *n* Aufregung *die*.

exciting [ɪk'saɪtɪŋ] *adj* aufregend; [story, race, film] spannend.

exclaim [ɪk'skleɪm] <> *vt* auslrufen <> *vi*: **to ~ in delight/horror** vor Freude/Entsetzen auflschreien.

exclamation mark *Br*, **exclamation point** *Am* [eksklə'meɪʃn-] *n* Ausrufezeichen *das*.

exclude [ɪk'sklu:d] *vt* - 1. [not include]: to ~ sb/sthg (from sthg) jn/etw (von etw) ausnehmen - 2. [prevent from entering]: to ~ sb (from) jm den Zutritt verweigern (zu) - 3. [reject, rule out] ausschließen.

excluding [ɪk'sklu:dɪŋ] *prep* außer (+ D).

exclusive [ɪk'sklu:sɪv] <> *adj* - 1. [high-class] exklusiv - 2. [sole] ausschließlich - 3. PRESS Exklusiv- <> *n* [interview] Exklusivinterview *das*; [report] Exklusivbericht *der*. ◆ **exclusive of** *prep* exklusive (+ G).

excrement ['ekskrɪmənt] *n* (U) *fml* Exkremente *pl*.

excruciating [ɪk'skru:ʃɪeɪtɪŋ] *adj* - 1. [pain, headache] schrecklich - 2. [embarrassment, experience] unerträglich.

excursion [ɪk'skɜ:ʃn] *n* Ausflug *der*.

excuse [*n* ɪk'skju:s, *vb* ɪk'skju:z] <> *n*: ~ (for) Entschuldigung *die* (für); that's just an ~ das ist nur eine Ausrede <> *vt* - 1. [justify] entschuldigen - 2. [forgive] verzeihen; to ~ sb for sthg jm etw verzeihen - 3. [let off]: to ~ sb (from sthg) jn (von etw) befreien - 4. *phr*: ~ me! [to attract attention] entschuldigen Sie bitte!; [forgive me] Entschuldigung!; *Am* [sorry] Verzeihung!

ex-directory *adj Br*: to be ~ nicht im Telefonbuch stehen.

execute ['eksɪkju:t] *vt* - 1. [kill] hin|richten - 2. *fml* [order, plan, movement] aus|führen.

execution [,eksɪ'kju:ʃn] *n* [killing] Hinrichtung *die*.

executive [ɪg'zekjʊtɪv] <> *adj*: ~ position leitende Position <> *n* COMM leitende Angestellte *der, die*.

executor [ɪg'zekjʊtə'] *n* Testamentsvollstrecker *der*.

exemplify [ɪg'zemplɪfaɪ] *vt* [typify] ein typisches Beispiel sein für.

exempt [ɪg'zempt] <> *adj*: ~ (from) befreit (von) <> *vt*: to ~ sb/sthg from jn/etw befreien von.

exercise ['eksəsaɪz] <> *n* - 1. (U) [physical movement] Bewegung *die* - 2. [series of movements] gymnastische Übung - 3. [activity]: it's a pointless ~ das ist eine sinnlose Übung <> *vt* - 1. [horse] bewegen; [dog] aus|führen - 2. *fml* [power] aus|üben; [right] wahr-nehmen; [caution] walten lassen <> *vi* sich bewegen.

exercise book *n* Heft *das*.

exert [ɪg'zɜ:t] *vt* aus|üben; to ~ o.s. sich anstrengen.

exertion [ɪg'zɜ:ʃn] *n* - 1. [of influence, power] Ausübung *die* - 2. [effort] Anstrengung *die*.

exhale [eks'heɪl] *vt & vi* aus|atmen.

exhaust [ɪg'zɔ:st] <> *n* - 1. (U) [fumes] Abgase *pl* - 2. [on car]: ~ (pipe) Auspuff *der* <> *vt* - 1. [tire] erschöpfen - 2. [use up] auf|brauchen; [subject] erschöpfen; my patience is ~ed meine Geduld ist zu Ende.

exhausted [ɪg'zɔ:stɪd] *adj* erschöpft.

exhausting [ɪg'zɔ:stɪŋ] *adj* anstrengend.

exhaustion [ɪg'zɔ:stʃn] *n* Erschöpfung *die*.

exhaustive [ɪg'zɔ:stɪv] *adj* [search, study] eingehend; [list] erschöpfend.

exhibit [ɪg'zɪbɪt] <> *n* - 1. ART Ausstellungsstück *das* - 2. LAW Beweisstück *das* <> *vt* - 1. *fml* [demonstrate] zeigen - 2. ART aus|stellen.

exhibition [,eksɪ'bɪʃn] *n* - 1. ART Ausstellung *die* - 2. [demonstration]: it was a fine ~ of skill er/sie zeigte viel Geschick - 3. *phr*: to make an ~ of o.s. *Br* sich lächerlich machen.

exhilarating [ɪg'zɪləreɪtɪŋ] *adj* aufregend.

exile ['eksaɪl] <> *n* - 1. [condition] Exil *das*; in ~ im Exil - 2. [person] Person *die*, die im Exil lebt <> *vt*: to ~ sb (to) jn aus|weisen OR verbannen (nach).

exist [ɪg'zɪst] *vi* existieren.

existence [ɪg'zɪstəns] *n* - 1. [state of being] Existenz *die*; to be in ~ existieren; to come into ~ entstehen - 2. [life] Dasein *das*.

existing [ɪg'zɪstɪŋ] *adj* bestehend; [government] gegenwärtig.

exit ['eksɪt] <> *n* - 1. [way out] Ausgang *der*; [from motorway] Ausfahrt *die* - 2. [departure]: to make an ~ hinaus|gehen <> *vi* [from building] hinaus|gehen; [from stage] ab|gehen; [from motorway] ab|fahren.

exodus ['eksədəs] *n* Auszug *der*.

exonerate [ɪg'zɒnəreɪt] *vt*: to ~ sb (from) jn entlasten (von).

exorbitant [ɪg'zɔ:bɪtənt] *adj* [cost, price] übertrieben hoch; [demands] übertrieben.

exotic [ɪg'zɒtɪk] *adj* exotisch.

expand [ɪk'spænd] <> *vt* [department, influence, area] vergrößern; [business, production, knowledge] erweitern <> *vi* sich vergrößern; [business] erweitern; [metal] sich aus|dehnen. ◆ **expand (up)on** *vt fus* weiter aus|führen.

expanse [ɪk'spæns] *n*: an ~ of water/sand eine Wasserfläche/Sandfläche.

expansion [ɪk'spænʃn] *n* [of business, production, knowledge] Erweiterung *die*; [of department, influence, area] Vergrößerung *die*.

expect [ɪk'spekt] <> *vt* - 1. [anticipate] erwarten; [count on] rechnen mit; to ~ sthg from sb etw von jm erwarten; to ~ to do sthg damit rechnen, etw zu tun; what do you expect? was willst du denn? - 2. [suppose]: to ~ (that) ... glauben, dass ...; I ~ so denke schon - 3. [be pregnant with]: to be ~ing a baby ein Kind erwarten <> *vi* [be pregnant]: to be ~ing in anderen Umständen sein.

expectancy *n* ⊏ life expectancy.

expectant [ɪk'spektənt] *adj* [crowd, person] erwartungsvoll.

expectant mother *n* werdende Mutter.

expectation [,ekspek'teɪʃn] *n*: they have no ~ of winning sie erwarten nicht, dass sie gewinnen; **against** OR **contrary to all ~(s)** wider Erwarten.

expedient [ɪkˈspiːdjənt] *adj fml* angebracht.

expedition [ˌekspɪˈdɪʃn] *n* - **1.** [organized journey] Expedition *die* - **2.** [short trip] Tour *die*.

expel [ɪkˈspel] *vt:* - **1.** [person]: **to ~ sb (from)** [country] jn auslweisen (aus); [school] jn verweisen (von) - **2.** [liquid, gas] auslstoßen.

expend [ɪkˈspend] *vt:* **to ~ sthg (on)** etw auflwenden (auf (+ A)).

expendable [ɪkˈspendəbl] *adj* [person] entbehrlich.

expenditure [ɪkˈspendɪtʃəʳ] *n (U)* [of money] Ausgaben *pl*.

expense [ɪkˈspens] *n* - **1.** [amount spent] Ausgabe *die* - **2.** *(U)* [cost] Kosten *pl*; **at the ~ of** auf Kosten (+ G); **at his ~** auf seine Kosten. ➡ **expenses** *npl* COMM Spesen *pl*.

expense account *n* Spesenkonto *das*.

expensive [ɪkˈspensɪv] *adj* - **1.** [financially] teuer - **2.** *fig* [mistake] schwerwiegend.

experience [ɪkˈspɪərɪəns] <> *n* - **1.** *(U)* [knowledge, practice] Erfahrung *die* - **2.** [event] Erlebnis *das* <> *vt* erfahren; [change] erleben.

experienced [ɪkˈspɪərɪənst] *adj:* **~ (at** OR **in)** erfahren (in (+ D)).

experiment [ɪkˈsperɪmənt] <> *n* - **1.** [science] Experiment *das* - **2.** [exploratory attempt] Versuch *der* <> *vi lit & fig:* **to ~ (with)** experimentieren (mit).

expert [ˈekspɜːt] <> *adj* [player] ausgezeichnet; [advice] fachmännisch <> *n* Fachmann *der*, -frau *die*.

expertise [ˌekspɜːˈtiːz] *n* Sachkenntnis *die*.

expire [ɪkˈspaɪəʳ] *vi* [licence, passport] abllaufen.

expiry [ɪkˈspaɪərɪ] *n* Ablauf *der*.

explain [ɪkˈspleɪn] <> *vt* erklären; **'my car broke down',** she ~ed „mein Auto ist kaputtgegangen", sagte sie; **to ~ to o.s.** [justify o.s.] sich rechtfertigen; [clarify one's meaning] sich klar auslldrücken; **to ~ sthg to sb** jm etw erklären <> *vi* erklären.

explanation [ˌekspləˈneɪʃn] *n:* **~ (for)** Erklärung *die* (für).

explicit [ɪkˈsplɪsɪt] *adj* - **1.** [clearly expressed] explizit - **2.** [graphic] eindeutig.

explode [ɪkˈspləʊd] <> *vt* [bomb] explodieren <> *vi* - **1.** [bomb] explodieren - **2.** *fig* [with feeling]: **to ~ in anger** (vor Wut) explodieren.

exploit [*n* ˈeksplɔɪt, *vb* ɪkˈsplɔɪt] <> *n* Heldentat *die* <> *vt* - **1.** [workers] auslbeuten; [friend] auslnutzen - **2.** [resources] auslschöpfen; [opportunity] nutzen.

exploitation [ˌeksplɔɪˈteɪʃn] *n* - **1.** [of workers] Ausbeutung *die;* [of friend] Ausnutzung *die* - **2.** [of resources] Ausschöpfung *die*.

exploration [ˌekspləˈreɪʃn] *n* - **1.** [of place]

Erforschung *die* - **2.** [of idea, theory] Untersuchung *die*.

explore [ɪkˈsplɔːʳ] <> *vt* - **1.** [place] erforschen - **2.** [idea, theory] untersuchen <> *vi* auf Erkundungstour gehen.

explorer [ɪkˈsplɔːrəʳ] *n* Erforscher *der*, -in *die*.

explosion [ɪkˈspləʊʒn] *n lit & fig* Explosion *die*.

explosive [ɪkˈspləʊsɪv] <> *adj* [material, situation] explosiv; [question] heikel; [temper] explosiv <> *n* Sprengstoff *der*.

export [*n & comp* ˈekspɔːt, *vb* ɪkˈspɔːt] <> *n* Export *der*, Ausfuhr *die* <> *comp* Export- <> *vt lit & fig* exportieren.

exporter [ekˈspɔːtəʳ] *n* Exporteur *der;* [country] Exportland *das*.

expose [ɪksˈpəʊz] *vt* - **1.** [uncover - skin] entblößen; [- underlying layer] freillegen; **to be ~d to sthg** einer Sache (D) ausgesetzt sein - **2.** [crime] aufldecken; [criminal] entlarven - **3.** PHOT belichten.

exposed [ɪkˈspəʊzd] *adj* [place] ungeschützt.

exposure [ɪkˈspəʊʒəʳ] *n* - **1.** [to light, sun, radiation]: **~ (to)** Ausgesetztsein *das* (+ D) - **2.**: **to die from ~** [hypothermia] erfrieren - **3.** [PHOT - time] Belichtung *die;* [- photograph] Aufnahme *die* - **4.** [publicity] Publicity *die*.

exposure meter *n* Belichtungsmesser *der*.

expound [ɪkˈspaʊnd] *vt fml* darllegen.

express [ɪkˈspres] <> *adj* - **1.** *Br* [letter, delivery] Eil- - **2.** *fml* [request] ausdrücklich; [purpose] bestimmt <> *adv* [send] per Express <> *n:* **~ (train)** D-Zug *der* <> *vt* [feeling, opinion] ausldrücken.

expression [ɪkˈspreʃn] *n* - **1.** [gen] Ausdruck *der* - **2.** [of feeling, opinion] Äußerung *die* - **3.** [look on face] Gesichtsausdruck *der*.

expressive [ɪkˈspresɪv] *adj* ausdrucksvoll.

expressly [ɪkˈspreslɪ] *adv* ausdrücklich.

expressway [ɪkˈspresweɪ] *n Am* Schnellstraße *die*.

exquisite [ɪkˈskwɪzɪt] *adj* [object, jewellery] exquisit; [food] köstlich; [painting, manners] ausgezeichnet; [taste] erlesen.

ext., extn. (*abbr of* extension) App.

extend [ɪkˈstend] <> *vt* - **1.** [road, building] auslbauen - **2.** [visit, visa, deadline] verlängern - **3.** [authority, law] ausldehnen - **4.** *fml* [head, arm] auslstrecken - **5.** [offer - credit, help] gewähren; **to ~ a welcome to sb** jn willkommen heißen <> *vi* - **1.** [stretch - in space] sich erstrecken; [- in time] anldauern - **2.** [rule, law]: **to ~ to sb/sthg** sich auf jn/etw erstrecken.

extension [ɪkˈstenʃn] *n* - **1.** [new room, building] Anbau *der* - **2.** [of visit, visa, deadline] Verlängerung *die* - **3.** TELEC Nebenanschluss *der* - **4.** ELEC Verlängerungskabel *das*.

extension lead *n* Verlängerungsschnur *die.*

extensive [ɪk'stensɪv] *àdj* - **1.** [damage] beträchtlich - **2.** [land, area] ausgedehnt - **3.** [discussions, tests] ausgedehnt; [use] häufig.

extensively [ɪk'stensɪvlɪ] *adv* - **1.** [modify, damage] beträchtlich - **2.** [discuss] ausführlich; [read] viel.

extent [ɪk'stent] *n* - **1.** [of land, area] Ausdehnung *die* - **2.** [of knowledge, damage] Umfang *der;* [of problem] Größe *die* - **3.** [degree]: **to what ~ ...?** inwieweit ...?; **to the ~ that** [in that, in so far as] insofern dass; [to the point where] derart ..., dass; **to a certain ~** in gewissem Maße; **to a large** OR **great ~** in hohem Maße; **to some ~** bis zu einem gewissen Grade.

extenuating circumstances [ɪk'stenjʊeɪtɪŋ-] *npl* mildernde Umstände *pl.*

exterior [ɪk'stɪərɪəᵊ] ◇ *adj* [wall, lights] Außen- ◇ *n* [of house, car, person] Äußere *das.*

exterminate [ɪk'stɜːmɪneɪt] *vt* ausrotten.

external [ɪk'stɜːnl] *adj* - **1.** [outside] äußere, -r, -s; **for ~ use only** nur äußerlich anzuwenden - **2.** [foreign - debt] Auslands-; [- affairs] auswärtig.

extinct [ɪk'stɪŋkt] *adj* - **1.** [species] ausgestorben - **2.** [volcano] erloschen.

extinguish [ɪk'stɪŋgwɪʃ] *vt fml* [fire] löschen; [cigarette] ausdrücken.

extinguisher [ɪk'stɪŋgwɪʃəᵊ] *n:* **(fire) ~** Feuerlöscher *der.*

extol, extoll *Am* [ɪk'stəʊl] *vt* rühmen.

extort [ɪk'stɔːt] *vt:* **to ~ sthg from sb** etw von jm erpressen.

extortionate [ɪk'stɔːʃnət] *adj* [price] Wucher-; [demand] ungeheuer.

extra ['ekstrə] ◇ *adj* [additional] zusätzlich; **~ charge** Zuschlag *der* ◇ *n* - **1.** [addition] Extra *das* - **2.** CINEMA & THEATRE Statist *der,* -in *die* ◇ *adv* [to pay, charge] extra. ➡ **extras** *npl* [in price] zusätzliche Kosten *pl.*

extra- ['ekstrə] *prefix* besonders; **an ~special present** ein ganz besonderes Geschenk.

extract [*n* 'ekstrækt, *vb* ɪk'strækt] ◇ *n* - **1.** [from book] Auszug *der;* [from film, piece of music] Ausschnitt *der* - **2.** [substance] Extrakt *der* ◇ *vt* - **1.** [pull out]: **to ~ sthg (from)** etw ziehen (aus) - **2.** [information, confession]: **to ~ sthg (from sb)** etw (aus jm) herausholen - **3.** [coal, oil]: **to ~ sthg (from)** etw gewinnen (aus).

extradite ['ekstrədaɪt] *vt:* **to ~ sb (from/to)** jn ausliefern (von/an).

extramural [ˌekstrə'mjʊərəl] *adj* UNIV: **~ studies** Studium *für* Teilzeitstudenten.

extraordinary [ɪk'strɔːdnrɪ] *adj* - **1.** [very special] außergewöhnlich - **2.** [strange] merkwürdig.

extraordinary general meeting *n* außerordentliche Hauptversammlung.

extravagance [ɪk'strævəgəns] *n* - **1.** [excessive spending] Verschwendung *die* - **2.** [luxury] Extravaganz *die.*

extravagant [ɪk'strævəgənt] *adj* - **1.** [wasteful - person, use] verschwenderisch; [- tastes] kostspielig - **2.** [gift, party, behaviour] extravagant - **3.** [claim] übertrieben.

extreme [ɪk'striːm] ◇ *adj* - **1.** [gen] äußerste, -r, -s; **~ heat** extreme Hitze - **2.** [conditions, views, politician] extrem ◇ *n* [furthest limit] Extrem *das.*

extremely [ɪk'striːmlɪ] *adv* [very] äußerst.

extremist [ɪk'striːmɪst] ◇ *adj* extremistisch ◇ *n* Extremist *der,* -in *die.*

extricate ['ekstrɪkeɪt] *vt:* **to ~ sthg (from)** etw befreien (aus); **to ~ o.s. (from)** sich herauswinden (aus); *fig* sich befreien (aus).

extrovert ['ekstrəvɜːt] ◇ *adj* extrovertiert ◇ *n* extrovertierter Mensch.

exuberance [ɪg'zjuːbərəns] *n* Ausgelassenheit *die.*

exultant [ɪg'zʌltənt] *adj* [person, crowd] jubelnd; [smile] triumphierend.

eye [aɪ] *n* (*cont* eyeing OR eying) ◇ *n* - **1.** [gen] Auge *das;* **to cast** OR **run one's ~ over sthg** etw überfliegen; **to catch the waiter's ~** die Aufmerksamkeit des Kellners erregen; **to have one's ~ on sb/sthg** ein Auge auf jn/etw haben; **to keep one's ~s open for, to keep an ~ out for** Ausschau halten nach (+ D); **to keep an ~ on** aufpassen auf (+ A) - **2.** [of needle] Öhr *das* ◇ *vt* [suspiciously] beäugen; [with desire] sehnsüchtig anschauen.

eyeball ['aɪbɔːl] *n* Augapfel *der.*

eyebath ['aɪbɑːθ] *n* Augenbad *das.*

eyebrow ['aɪbraʊ] *n* Augenbraue *die.*

eyebrow pencil *n* Augenbrauenstift *der.*

eyedrops ['aɪdrɒps] *npl* Augentropfen *pl.*

eyeglasses ['aɪˌglɑːsɪz] *npl Am* Brille *die.*

eyelash ['aɪlæʃ] *n* Augenwimper *die.*

eyelid ['aɪlɪd] *n* Augenlid *das.*

eyeliner ['aɪˌlaɪnəᵊ] *n* Eyeliner *der.*

eye-opener *n inf:* **it was an ~ for me** das hat mir die Augen geöffnet.

eye shadow *n* Lidschatten *der.*

eyesight ['aɪsaɪt] *n* (*U*) Sehkraft *die;* **to have good/bad ~** gute/schlechte Augen haben.

eyesore ['aɪsɔːᵊ] *n* Schandfleck *der.*

eyestrain ['aɪstreɪn] *n* Überanstrengung *die* der Augen.

eyewitness [ˌaɪ'wɪtnɪs] *n* Augenzeuge *der,* -gin *die.*

F

f (*pl* **f's** OR **fs**), **F** (*pl* **F's** OR **Fs**) [ef] *n* [letter] **f** *das*, **F** *das*. **F** *n* - **1.** MUS **F** *das* - **2.** (*abbr of* Fahrenheit) **F.**

fable ['feɪbl] *n* Fabel *die*.

fabric ['fæbrɪk] *n* - **1.** [cloth] Stoff *der* - **2.** [of building] Bausubstanz *die* - **3.** [of society] Gefüge *das*.

fabrication [ˌfæbrɪ'keɪʃn] *n* [lie] Lüge *die*.

fabulous ['fæbjʊləs] *adj inf* [excellent] toll.

facade [fə'sɑːd] *n lit & fig* Fassade *die*.

face [feɪs] ◇ *n* - **1.** [of person] Gesicht *das*; **~ to ~** [with person] von Angesicht zu Angesicht; **to come ~ to ~ with sthg** mit etw konfrontiert werden; **to say sthg to sb's ~** jm etw offen ins Gesicht sagen - **2.** [expression] Gesicht *das*; **to make** OR **pull a ~** ein Gesicht ziehen - **3.** [of cliff] Wand *die*; [of coin] Vorderseite *die*; [of building] Fassade *die*; **on the ~ of it** auf den ersten Blick - **4.** [of clock, watch] Zifferblatt *das* - **5.** [respect]: **to lose ~** das Gesicht verlieren; **to save ~** das Gesicht wahren ◇ *vi* - **1.** [look towards] gegenüberstehen (+ D); **my house ~s south** mein Haus liegt nach Süden; **the hotel ~s the harbour** das Hotel liegt gegenüber vom Hafen - **2.** [confront] sich stellen (+ D); **to be ~d with sthg** [problem, decision] mit etw konfrontiert werden - **3.** [facts, truth] ins Auge sehen (+ D); **let's ~ it!** machen wir uns nichts vor! - **4.** *inf* [cope with]: **I can't ~ another omelette** ich kann kein Omelett mehr sehen!; **I can't ~ it!** ich bringe es einfach nicht über mich. **► face down** *adv* [person] mit dem Gesicht nach unten; [playing card] mit der Bildseite nach unten. **► face up** *adv* [person] mit dem Gesicht nach oben; [playing card] mit der Bildseite nach oben. **► in the face of** *prep* [in spite of] trotz (+ G). **► face up to** *vt fus* [responsibility] auf sich (*A*) nehmen; [problem] sich stellen (+ D).

facecloth ['feɪsklɒθ] *n Br* Waschlappen *der*.

face cream *n* Gesichtscreme *die*.

face-lift *n* - **1.** [on face] Gesichtsstraffung *die* - **2.** *fig* [on building]: **to give sthg a ~** etw verschönern.

face-saving [-ˌseɪvɪŋ] *adj*: **a ~ agreement/ measure** eine Vereinbarung/Maßnahme, um das Gesicht zu wahren.

facet ['fæsɪt] *n* - **1.** [aspect] Seite *die* - **2.** [of jewel] Facette *die*.

facetious [fə'siːʃəs] *adj* leicht spöttisch.

face value *n* [of coin, stamp] Nennwert *der*;

to take sthg at ~ *fig* etw für bare Münze nehmen.

facility [fə'sɪlətɪ] *n* [feature] Einrichtung *die*. **► facilities** *npl* [amenities] Ausstattung *die*; **cooking facilities** Kochgelegenheiten *pl*.

facing ['feɪsɪŋ] *adj* [opposite] gegenüber befindlich.

facsimile [fæk'sɪmɪlɪ] *n* - **1.** [message] Fax *das* - **2.** [exact copy] Faksimile *das*.

fact [fækt] *n* Tatsache *die*; **it is a ~ that ...** es steht fest, dass ...; **to know sthg for a ~** etw genau wissen. **► in fact** *adv* [in reality] tatsächlich; [moreover] sogar.

fact of life *n* Tatsache *die* (mit der man sich abfinden muss). **► facts of life** *npl* euphemism: **to tell sb the ~s of life** jn aufklären.

factor ['fæktə*] *n* Faktor *der*.

factory ['fæktərɪ] *n* Fabrik *die*.

fact sheet *n Br* Informationsblatt *das*.

factual ['fæktʃʊəl] *adj* [account] auf Tatsachen beruhend.

faculty ['fækltɪ] *n* - **1.** [ability] Fähigkeit *die* - **2.** UNIV [section] Fakultät *die*; [staff] Lehrkörper *der*.

fad [fæd] *n* Tick *der*.

fade [feɪd] ◇ *vi* - **1.** [material, colour] verbleichen; [flower] verwelken - **2.** [light] nachlassen - **3.** [sound] verklingen - **4.** [feeling, interest, smile] schwinden; [memory] verblassen ◇ *vt* [material, colour] ausbleichen.

faeces *Br*, **feces** *Am* ['fiːsiːz] *npl* Fäkalien *pl*.

fag [fæg] *n* - **1.** *Br inf* [cigarette] Glimmstengel *der* - **2.** *Am pej* [homosexual] Schwuler *der*.

Fahrenheit ['færənhaɪt] *adj* Fahrenheit.

fail [feɪl] ◇ *vt* - **1.** [not succeed in]: **to ~ to do sthg** etw nicht tun können; **you can't ~ to notice it** du kannst es nicht übersehen; **he ~ed to persuade her** es gelang ihm nicht, sie zu überreden - **2.** [exam, test] durchfallen; [candidate] durchfallen lassen ◇ *vi* - **1.** [not succeed] scheitern - **2.** [in exam, test] durchfallen - **3.** [brakes, engine, heart] versagen; [lights] ausfallen - **4.** [eyesight] nachlassen; [health] sich verschlechtern.

failing ['feɪlɪŋ] ◇ *n* [weakness] Schwäche *die* ◇ *prep* wenn ... nicht; **~ any renewed fighting** wenn es keine neuen Kampfhandlungen gibt; **~ that** andernfalls.

failure ['feɪljə*] *n* - **1.** [gen] Misserfolg *der* - **2.** [person] Versager *der* - **3.** [of engine, brakes, heart] Versagen *das*; [of lights] Ausfall *der*.

faint [feɪnt] ◇ *adj* - **1.** [slight] schwach; [image] kaum sichtbar; [chance] gering; **I haven't the ~est idea** ich habe keinen blassen Schimmer - **2.** [dizzy] schwindelig ◇ *vi* ohnmächtig werden.

fair [feə*] ◇ *adj* - **1.** [just - judge, person] gerecht; [- result, decision, trial] fair; **it's not ~!**

das ist ungerecht! - **2.** [quite large] ziemlich groß - **3.** [quite good] ziemlich gut - **4.** [hair, person] blond - **5.** [skin, complexion] hell - **6.** [weather] schön ⬦ n - **1.** Br [funfair] Jahrmarkt der - **2.** [trade fair] Messe die ⬦ adv [play, fight] fair. ➤ **fair enough** excl Br inf na gut!

fair-haired [-'heəd] adj blond.

fairly ['feəlɪ] adv - **1.** [rather] ziemlich - **2.** [treat, distribute] gerecht; [describe, fight, play] fair.

fairy ['feərɪ] n Fee die.

fairy tale n Märchen das.

faith [feɪθ] n - **1.** [trust]: ~ (in) Vertrauen das (zu); **in bad** ~ mit böser Absicht; **I told you that in good** ~ ich habe dir das im Vertrauen gesagt - **2.** [particular religion] Religion die - **3.** (U) [religious belief] Glaube der.

faithful ['feɪθfʊl] adj - **1.** [friend, dog, lover] treu - **2.** [account, translation] getreu, genau.

faithfully ['feɪθfʊlɪ] adv: **Yours** ~ Br [in letter] hochachtungsvoll.

fake [feɪk] ⬦ adj [painting, passport] gefälscht; [gun, jewellery] unecht ⬦ n - **1.** [of painting, passport] Fälschung die; [of gun, jewellery] Imitation die - **2.** [person] Schwindler der, -in die ⬦ vt - **1.** [signature, results] fälschen - **2.** [simulate] vortäuschen; [illness] simulieren ⬦ vi: **he's faking** er tut nur so.

falcon ['fɔːlkən] n Falke der.

fall [fɔːl] (pt fell; pp fallen) ⬦ vi - **1.** [gen] fallen; [person] hinfallen; [from great height, heavily, in sport] stürzen; [thing to ground] herunter-/hinunterfallen; **the city fell to the enemy troops** die Stadt fiel in die Hände der feindlichen Truppen; **to** ~ **flat** [joke] daneben gehen - **2.** [decrease - temperature] fallen; [- number] abnehmen; [- demand, wind] nachlassen - **3.** [become - ill, silent, vacant] werden; **to** ~ **asleep** einschlafen; **to** ~ **in love** sich verlieben; **to** ~ **open** sich öffnen; **to** ~ **to bits** OR **pieces** auseinander fallen - **4.** [occur]: **to** ~ **(on)** fallen (auf (+ D)); **they** ~ **into two groups** sie lassen sich zwei Gruppen zuordnen ⬦ n - **1.** [accident, from power] Sturz der; **to have a** ~ stürzen - **2.** [- of snow] Schneefall der - **3.** [of city, country] Eroberung die - **4.** [decrease]: ~ **(in)** Abnahme die (+ G) - **5.** Am [autumn] Herbst der. ➤ **falls** npl [waterfall] Wasserfall der. ➤ **fall apart** vi - **1.** [book, chair] auseinander fallen - **2.** fig [country, person] zusammenbrechen. ➤ **fall back** vi - **1.** [retreat] zurückweichen - **2.** [lag behind] zurückfallen. ➤ **fall back on** vt fus [resort to] zurückgreifen auf (+ A). ➤ **fall behind** vi - **1.** [in race] zurückfallen - **2.** [with rent, work] in Rückstand geraten. ➤ **fall for** vt fus - **1.** inf [fall in love with] sich verlieben in (+ A) - **2.** [trick] hereinfallen auf (+ A). ➤ **fall in** vi [roof, ceiling] einstürzen.

➤ **fall off** vi - **1.** [drop off] herunter-/hinunterfallen - **2.** [diminish] zurückgehen. ➤ **fall out** vi - **1.** [hair, tooth] ausfallen - **2.** [quarrel]: **to** ~ **out (with sb)** sich (mit jm) zerstreiten. ➤ **fall over** vt fus [step, obstacle] fallen über (+ A) ⬦ vi [lose balance - person] hinfallen; [- chair, jug] umkippen. ➤ **fall through** vi [plan, deal] fehlschlagen.

fallacy ['fæləsɪ] n Irrtum der.

fallen ['fɔːln] pp ▷ fall.

fallible ['fæləbl] adj [person] fehlbar; [method, plan] nicht unfehlbar.

fallout ['fɔːlaʊt] n [radiation] radioaktiver Niederschlag.

fallow ['fæləʊ] adj [land] brach; **to lie** ~ brachliegen.

false [fɔːls] adj - **1.** [gen] falsch - **2.** [fake - nose, eyelashes] künstlich; [- passport] gefälscht; ~ **ceiling** Einschubdecke die.

false alarm n falscher Alarm.

falsely ['fɔːlslɪ] adv - **1.** [accused, imprisoned] zu Unrecht - **2.** [laugh] gekünstelt.

false teeth npl künstliches Gebiss.

falsify ['fɔːlsɪfaɪ] vt [facts, accounts] verfälschen.

falter ['fɔːltə*] vi - **1.** [move unsteadily] wankend - **2.** [voice] stocken - **3.** [hesitate] zögern.

fame [feɪm] n Ruhm der.

familiar [fə'mɪljə*] adj - **1.** [known] vertraut - **2.** [conversant]: **to be** ~ **with sthg** sich mit etw auskennen - **3.** pej [overly informal] vertraulich.

familiarity [fə,mɪlɪ'ærətɪ] n [gen] Vertrautheit die.

familiarize, -ise [fə'mɪljəraɪz] vt: **to** ~ **o.s. with sthg** sich mit etw vertraut machen; **to** ~ **sb with sthg** jn mit etw vertraut machen.

family ['fæmlɪ] n Familie die.

family credit n (U) Br staatlicher Zuschuss an einkommensschwache Familien.

family planning n Familienplanung die.

famine ['fæmɪn] n Hungersnot die.

famished ['fæmɪʃt] adj inf [very hungry]: **I'm** ~ ich sterbe vor Hunger.

famous ['feɪməs] adj: ~ **(for)** berühmt (für).

---

 famous

Das Wort famous entspricht nicht dem deutschen „famos", sondern bedeutet „berühmt". Aus the <u>famous</u> pyramids at Giza wird also „Die <u>berühmten</u> Pyramiden von Gizeh".
Das leicht veraltete deutsche „famos" drückt man im Englischen am besten mit marvellous aus. „Eine <u>famose</u> Erfindung" wäre im Englischen a <u>marvellous</u> invention.

fan [fæn] ⬦ n - **1.** [held in hand] Fächer der - **2.** [electric] Ventilator der - **3.** [enthusiast] Fan der ⬦ vt - **1.** [cool]: **to ~ one's face** sich (D) das Gesicht fächeln - **2.** [stimulate - fire, flames] anfachen; [- feelings] entfachen; [- fears] schüren. ● **fan out** vi [army, search party] ausІ́schwärmen.

fanatic [fə'nætık] n Fanatiker der, -in die.

fan belt n Keilriemen der.

fanciful ['fænsıful] adj - **1.** [odd] abstrus - **2.** [elaborate] fantastisch.

fancy ['fænsı] ⬦ adj - **1.** [elaborate - clothes, design, restaurant, hotel] ausgefallen; [- food, cakes] fein - **2.** [expensive] exklusiv ⬦ n - **1.** [liking] Lust die; **to take a ~ to** angetan sein von; **to take sb's ~** jm gefallen, jn ansprechen - **2.** [whim] Laune die ⬦ vt - **1.** inf [want] Lust haben auf (+ A); **to ~ doing sthg** Lust dazu haben, etw zu tun - **2.** [person] scharf sein auf (+ A).

fancy dress n (Masken)kostüm das.

fancy-dress party n Kostümfest das.

fanfare ['fænfeəʳ] n MUS Fanfare die.

fang [fæŋ] n - **1.** [of snake] Giftzahn der - **2.** [of wolf] Reißzahn der.

fan heater n Heizlüfter der.

fanny ['fænı] n Am inf [buttocks] Po der.

fantasize, -ise ['fæntəsaız] vi fantasieren; **to ~ about doing sthg** sich vorstellen, etw zu tun.

fantastic [fæn'tæstık] adj inf [gen] fantastisch.

fantasy ['fæntəsı] n Fantasie die.

📖 **fantasy**

Fantasy ist nicht unbedingt ein falscher Freund, wird aber doch häufig falsch verwendet. Es entspricht dem deutschen „Fantasie" nicht im Sinne von „Vorstellungskraft", sondern im Sinne von „Hirngespinst" oder „Traum". Der Satz For years my <u>fantasy</u> was to buy an island in the Caribbean würde übersetzt ungefähr so lauten: „Ich hatte schon seit Jahren den <u>Traum</u>, eine Karibikinsel zu kaufen." „Fantasie" im Sinne von Vorstellungskraft drückt man dagegen mit <u>imagination</u> aus. „Dieses Kind hat eine lebhafte <u>Fantasie</u>" ist mit this child has a vivid <u>imagination</u> zutreffend übersetzt.

---

fao (abbr of for the attention of) z. H. (von).

far [fɑːʳ] (compar farther OR further; superl farthest OR furthest) ⬦ adv - **1.** [in distance, time] weit; **have you come ~?** sind Sie von weit her gekommen?; **how ~ is it (to London)?** wie weit ist es (bis London)?; **as ~ as** [town, country] bis nach; [station, school] bis zu; **so ~** [until now] bisher; **~ and wide** über-

all; **he will go ~** fig er wird es weit bringen - **2.** [in degree]: **~ better/quicker** weitaus besser/schneller; **as ~ as I'm concerned** was mich betrifft; **as ~ as I know** so weit ich weiß; **~ and away, by ~** bei weitem; **~ from it** keineswegs ⬦ adj: **at the ~ end** am anderen Ende; **the ~ right/left** [in politics] die extreme Rechte/Linke.

faraway ['fɑːrəweı] adj - **1.** [place, country] weit entfernt - **2.** [look] abwesend.

farce [fɑːs] n THEATRE & fig Farce die.

farcical ['fɑːsıkl] adj lächerlich.

fare [feəʳ] n - **1.** [payment] Fahrpreis der; [for flight] Flugpreis der - **2.** fml [food] Kost die.

Far East n: **the ~** der Ferne Osten.

farewell [feə'wel] n Lebewohl das; **they said their ~s** sie verabschiedeten sich.

farm [fɑːm] ⬦ n Bauernhof der ⬦ vt bewirtschaften.

farmer ['fɑːməʳ] n Bauer der, Bäuerin die.

farmhouse ['fɑːmhaus, pl -hauzız] n Bauernhaus das.

farming ['fɑːmıŋ] n Landwirtschaft die.

farmland ['fɑːmlænd] n (U) Ackerland das.

farmstead ['fɑːmsted] n Am Gehöft das.

farmyard ['fɑːmjɑːd] n Hof der.

far-reaching [-'riːtʃıŋ] adj weitreichend.

farsighted [fɑː'saıtıd] adj - **1.** [person] weitblickend; [plan] auf weite Sicht konzipiert - **2.** Am [longsighted] weitsichtig.

fart [fɑːt] inf ⬦ n [wind] Furz der ⬦ vi furzen.

farther ['fɑːðəʳ] compar ⬅ far.

farthest ['fɑːðəst] superl ⬅ far.

fascinate ['fæsıneıt] vt faszinieren.

fascinating ['fæsıneıtıŋ] adj faszinierend.

fascination [fæsı'neıʃn] n Faszination die.

fascism ['fæʃızm] n Faschismus der.

fashion ['fæʃn] ⬦ n - **1.** [current style] Mode die; **to be in/out of ~** modern/unmodern sein - **2.** [manner] Art die; **after a ~** so einiger maßen ⬦ vt fml [shape] formen.

fashionable ['fæʃnəbl] adj [clothes, hairstyle] modisch.

fashion show n Modeschau die.

fast [fɑːst] ⬦ adj - **1.** [rapid] schnell; [journey] kurz - **2.** [clock, watch]: **to be ~** vorgehen - **3.** [dye] farbecht ⬦ adv - **1.** [rapidly] schnell - **2.** [firmly] fest; **to hold ~ to sthg** [grip firmly] an etw (D) festІhalten; **to be ~ asleep** fest schlafen ⬦ n [act] Fasten das; [period] Fastenzeit die ⬦ vi fasten.

fasten ['fɑːsn] ⬦ vt - **1.** [coat, door, bag, window] zumachen; **to ~ one's seat belt** sich anİschnallen - **2.** [attach]: **to ~ sthg to sthg** etw an etw (D) befestigen ⬦ vi: **to ~ on to sthg** etw an etw (D) befestigt werden.

📖 to fasten

Das englische Verb to fasten kann fälschlicherweise mit „fasten" oder „fassen" in Verbindung gebracht werden, aber es bedeutet „befestigen" oder „festmachen". Der Satz I <u>fastened</u> the bookshelves to the wall lautet im Deutschen richtig „Ich habe das Bücherregal an der Wand <u>befestigt</u>".

Das deutsche Wort „fasten" findet seine Entsprechung im ähnlichen englischen Verb to fast. „Sie muss drei Tage <u>fasten</u>" hieße auf Englisch She has to <u>fast</u> for three days. Die Fastenzeit nennt man im Englischen fasting period.

---

fastener ['fɑːsnə'] n Verschluss der.

fastening ['fɑːsnɪŋ] n Verschluss der.

fast food n Fastfood das.

fastidious [fə'stɪdɪəs] adj sehr genau.

fat [fæt] <> adj [gen] dick <> n Fett das.

fatal ['feɪtl] adj - **1.** [mistake, decision] fatal - **2.** [accident, illness] tödlich.

fatality [fə'tælətɪ] n [accident victim] Todesopfer das.

fate [feɪt] n Schicksal das.

fateful ['feɪtful] adj verhängnisvoll.

father ['fɑːðə'] n Vater der.

Father Christmas n Br Weihnachtsmann der.

father-in-law (pl father-in-laws OR fathers-in-law) n Schwiegervater der.

fathom ['fæðəm] <> n Faden der <> vt: to ~ sb/sthg (out) jn/etw ergründen.

fatigue [fə'tiːg] n - **1.** [exhaustion] Erschöpfung die - **2.** [in metal] Ermüdung die.

fatten ['fætn] vt mästen.

fattening ['fætnɪŋ] adj dick machend; **to be ~** dick machen.

fatty ['fætɪ] adj - **1.** [food, meat] fett - **2.** BIOL [tissue, acid] Fett-.

fatuous ['fætjʊəs] adj albern.

faucet ['fɔːsɪt] n Am Wasserhahn der.

fault ['fɔːlt] <> n - **1.** [responsibility] Schuld die; **it's my ~** es ist meine Schuld; **whose ~ is it?** wer ist schuld daran? - **2.** [error, defect, in tennis] Fehler der; **to find ~ with sb/sthg** etwas an jm/etw auszusetzen haben; **at ~** im Unrecht - **3.** GEOL Verwerfung die <> vt: to ~ sb (on sthg) jm widerlegen (in Bezug auf etw (A)).

faultless ['fɔːltlɪs] adj fehlerfrei.

faulty ['fɔːltɪ] adj fehlerhaft.

fauna ['fɔːnə] n Fauna die.

favour Br, **favor** Am ['feɪvə'] <> n - **1.** (U) [approval] Gunst die; **in sb's ~** zu js Gunsten; **to be in/out of ~ (with sb)** (bei jm) beliebt/unbeliebt sein; **to curry ~ with sb** sich bei jm einschmeicheln - **2.** [kind act] Gefallen der,

Gefälligkeit die; **to do sb a ~** jm einen Gefallen tun <> vt - **1.** [prefer] bevorzugen - **2.** [benefit] begünstigen. ⇒ **in favour** adv [in agreement]: **to be in ~** dafür sein. ⇒ **in favour of** prep - **1.** [in preference to] zugunsten (+ G) - **2.** [in agreement with]: **to be in ~ of sthg** für etw sein; **to be in ~ of doing sthg** dafür sein, etw zu tun.

favourable Br, **favorable** Am ['feɪvrəbl] adj - **1.** [conditions, weather] günstig - **2.** [review, impression] positiv.

favourite Br, **favorite** Am ['feɪvrɪt] <> adj Lieblings- <> n - **1.** [person] Liebling der; **this jacket is my ~** das ist meine Lieblingsjacke - **2.** [in race, contest] Favorit der, -in die.

favouritism Br, **favoritism** Am ['feɪvrɪtɪzm] n Günstlingswirtschaft die.

fawn [fɔːn] <> adj rehbraun <> vi: **to ~ on sb** sich bei jm einschmeicheln.

fax [fæks] <> n - **1.** [device] Faxgerät das - **2.** [message] Fax das <> vt [document] faxen; **to ~ sb sthg** jm etw faxen.

fax machine n Faxgerät das.

FBI (abbr of Federal Bureau of Investigation) n FBI das.

fear [fɪə'] <> n - **1.** [gen] Angst die, Furcht die - **2.** [risk] Gefahr die; **for ~ of waking him** aus Angst, dass er aufwachen könnte; **no ~!** inf auf keinen Fall! <> vt Angst haben vor (+ D); **to ~ the worst** das Schlimmste befürchten.

fearful ['fɪəful] adj - **1.** fml: **to be ~ of sthg** vor etw (D) Angst haben - **2.** [noise, temper] furchterregend.

fearless ['fɪələs] adj furchtlos.

feasible ['fiːzəbl] adj [plan] durchführbar.

feast [fiːst] n Festessen das.

feat [fiːt] n Meisterleistung die.

feather ['feðə'] n Feder die.

feature ['fiːtʃə'] <> n - **1.** [characteristic - gen] Merkmal das; [- of personality] Charakterzug der - **2.** [facial] Gesichtszug der - **3.** [article] Reportage die - **4.** RADIO & TV [programme] Feature das - **5.** CINEMA Kinofilm der <> vt: **the film ~s Brad Pitt** Brad Pitt spielt in dem Film mit; **the exhibition ~s the work of two young artists** die Ausstellung zeigt das Werk zweier junger Künstler <> vi: **to ~ (in)** vorkommen (in (+ D)).

feature film n Spielfilm der.

February ['februərɪ] n Februar der; see also September.

feces npl Am = faeces.

fed [fed] pt & pp ▷ feed.

federal ['fedrəl] adj Bundes-.

federation [,fedə'reɪʃn] n - **1.** [country] Föderation die - **2.** [association] Zusammenschluss der.

fed up adj: **to be ~ with sb/sthg** etw/jn satt haben; **I'm (feeling) ~** ich habe keine Lust mehr.

fee [fi:] *n* (for service) Gebühr *die;* (for membership) Beitrag *der;* (for doctor) Honorar *das;* **school -s** Schulgeld *das.*

feeble ['fi:bəl] *adj* - **1.** [weak] schwach - **2.** [excuse, joke] lahm.

feed [fi:d] (*pt & pp* fed) *vt* - **1.** [baby, animal] füttern - **2.** [insert]: **to ~ sthg into sthg** etw in etw (A) einlführen; [coins] etw in etw (A) einlwerfen *vi* [baby] essen; [animal] fressen *n* - **1.** [for baby] Mahlzeit *die* - **2.** [for animal] Futter *das.*

feedback ['fi:dbæk] *n* (U) - **1.** [reaction] Feedback *das* - **2.** ELEC Rückkoppelung *die.*

feeding bottle ['fi:dɪŋ-] *n Br* Saugflasche *die.*

feel [fi:l] (*pt & pp* felt) *vt* - **1.** [touch] fühlen; [examine] befühlen - **2.** [be aware of - tension, presence] spüren - **3.** [think]: **to ~ that** glauben, dass; **he felt it (to be) his duty** er hielt es für seine Pflicht - **4.** [experience - sensation] spüren, fühlen; [- emotion] empfinden; **I ~ the cold a lot** ich leide sehr unter der Kälte; **I felt myself blushing** ich fühlte, wie ich rot wurde - **5.** *phr:* **I'm not ~ing myself today** ich bin heute nicht ich selbst *vi* - **1.** [happy, angry, sleepy] sein; [lonely, fit, uncomfortable] sich fühlen; **I ~ cold** mir ist kalt; **I ~ stupid** ich komme mir blöd vor; **I ~ ill** ich fühle mich nicht gut; **to ~ like sthg** Lust haben auf etw (A); **I don't ~ like it** ich habe keine Lust dazu - **2.** [seem - light, heavy, soft *etc*] sich anlfühlen - **3.** [by touch]: **to ~ for sthg** nach etw (D) tasten *n* - **1.** [of material]: **it has a soft ~** es fühlt sich weich an - **2.** [atmosphere] Atmosphäre *die.*

feeler ['fi:lə'] *n* [of insect, snail] Fühler *der.*

feeling ['fi:lɪŋ] *n* - **1.** [gen] Gefühl *das* - **2.** [impression] Eindruck *der;* [opinion] Meinung *die.* **feelings** *npl* Gefühle *pl;* **to hurt sb's ~s** jn verletzen.

feet [fi:t] *pl* ▷ **foot.**

feign [feɪn] *vt fml* vorltäuschen.

fell [fel] *pt* ▷ **fall** *vt* - **1.** [tree] fällen - **2.** [person] niederlstrecken.

fellow ['feləʊ] *adj* Mit-; **~ passenger** Mitreisende *der, die;* **~ sufferer** Leidensgenosse *der,* -sin *die;* **~ student** Kommilitone *der,* -nin *die* *n* - **1.** *dated* [man] Kerl *der* - **2.** [comrade] Kamerad *der* - **3.** [of society] Mitglied *das;* [of college] Fellow *der.*

fellowship ['feləʊʃɪp] *n* - **1.** [organization] Vereinigung *die* - **2.** [UNIV - scholarship] Stipendium *das;* [- post] Stellung *die* eines Fellows.

felt [felt] *pt & pp* ▷ **feel** *n* Filz *der.*

felt-tip pen *n* Filzstift *der.*

female ['fi:meɪl] *adj* weiblich; **~ worker** Arbeiterin *die;* **~ student** Studentin *die* *n* - **1.** [animal] Weibchen *das* - **2.** *pej inf* [woman] Weib *das.*

feminine ['femɪnɪn] *adj* feminin *n* GRAMM Femininum *das.*

feminist ['femɪnɪst] *n* Feminist *der,* -in *die.*

fence [fens] *n* Zaun *der;* **to sit on the ~** *fig* nicht Partei ergreifen *vt* einlzäunen.

fencing ['fensɪŋ] *n* - **1.** SPORT Fechten *das* - **2.** [fences] Zäune *pl.*

fend [fend] *vi:* **to ~ for o.s.** für sich selbst sorgen. **fend off** *vt sep* ablwehren.

fender ['fendə'] *n* - **1.** [round fireplace] Kamingitter *das* - **2.** [on boat] Fender *der* - **3.** *Am* [over car wheel] Kotflügel *der.*

ferment [*n* 'fɜ:ment, *vb* fə'ment] *n* [unrest] Aufruhr *der* *vi* [beer, wine] gären.

fern [fɜ:n] *n* Farn *der.*

ferocious [fə'rəʊʃəs] *adj* [animal] wild; [attack, criticism] heftig.

ferret ['ferɪt] *n* Frettchen *das.* **ferret about, ferret around** *vi inf* herum stöbern.

ferry ['ferɪ] *n* Fähre *die* *vt* transportieren.

fertile ['fɜ:taɪl] *adj* - **1.** [gen] fruchtbar - **2.** [imagination] reich.

fertilizer ['fɜ:tɪlaɪzə'] *n* Dünger *der.*

fervent ['fɜ:vənt] *adj* leidenschaftlich.

fester ['festə'] *vi* [wound, sore] eitern.

festival ['festəvl] *n* - **1.** [series of organized events] Festival *das* - **2.** [holiday] Feiertag *der.*

festive ['festɪv] *adj* festlich.

festive season *n:* **the ~** die Weihnachtszeit.

festivities [fes'tɪvətɪz] *npl* Feierlichkeiten *pl.*

festoon [fe'stu:n] *vt* schmücken.

fetch [fetʃ] *vt* - **1.** [go and get] holen; [person from station, school *etc*] ablholen - **2.** [sell for] einlbringen; **to ~ a high price** einen hohen Preis erzielen.

fetching ['fetʃɪŋ] *adj* attraktiv.

fete, fête [feɪt] *n* Wohltätigkeitsbasar *der* *vt* durch Feiern ehren.

fetish ['fetɪʃ] *n* - **1.** [sexual obsession] Fetisch *der* - **2.** [mania] Manie *die.*

fetus ['fi:təs] *n* = **foetus.**

feud [fju:d] *n* Fehde *die* *vi* in Fehde liegen.

feudal ['fju:dl] *adj* feudal; [system, lord] Feudal-.

fever ['fi:və'] *n lit & fig* Fieber *das.*

feverish ['fi:vərɪʃ] *adj* - **1.** MED fiebrig - **2.** [frenzied] fieberhaft.

few [fju:] *adj* wenige; **the first ~ times** die ersten paar Male; **in a ~ minutes** in einigen Minuten *pron:* **a ~** ein paar; **a ~ more** noch ein paar; **quite a ~, a good ~** eine ganze Menge; **~ and far between** dünn gesät.

fewer ['fju:ə'] *adj* weniger *pron* weniger; **there are far ~ (of them) now** heute gibt es weit weniger.

fewest ['fju:əst] *adj:* **(the) ~** die wenigsten.

fiancé [fɪˈɒnseɪ] *n* Verlobte *der*.

fiancée [fɪˈɒnseɪ] *n* Verlobte *die*.

fiasco [fɪˈæskəʊ] (*Br pl* -s, *Am pl* -s OR -es) *n* Fiasko *das*.

fib [fɪb] *inf* ◇ *n* Schwindelei *die*; **to tell ~s** schwindeln ◇ *vi* schwindeln.

fibre *Br*, **fiber** *Am* [ˈfaɪbəʳ] *n* - **1.** [gen] Faser *die* - **2.** (*U*) [roughage] Ballaststoffe *pl* - **3.** [strength]: **moral ~** Charakterstärke *die*.

fibreglass *Br*, **fiberglass** *Am* [ˈfaɪbəglɑːs] *n* Fiberglas *das*.

fickle [ˈfɪkl] *adj* wankelmütig.

fiction [ˈfɪkʃn] *n* - **1.** (*U*) [literature] Belletristik *die* - **2.** [lie] Fiktion *die*.

fictional [ˈfɪkʃənl] *adj* [work] erzählend; [character] fiktiv; [event] erfunden.

fictitious [fɪkˈtɪʃəs] *adj* frei erfunden.

fiddle [ˈfɪdl] ◇ *n* - **1.** [violin] Geige *die* - **2.** *Br inf* [fraud] Schiebung *die*; **tax ~** Steuermanipulation *die* ◇ *vt Br inf* frisieren ◇ *vi* - **1.** [fidget]: **to ~ (about** OR **around)** (herum)zappeln; **to ~ (about** OR **around) with sthg** an etw (*D*) OR mit etw (herum)spielen - **2.** [waste time]: **to ~ about** OR **around** herumtrödeln.

fiddly [ˈfɪdlɪ] *adj Br inf* knifflig.

fidget [ˈfɪdʒɪt] *vi* zappeln.

field [fiːld] ◇ *n* - **1.** [gen] Feld *das*; **in the ~** in der Praxis - **2.** [for sports] Spielfeld *das* - **3.** [of knowledge] Gebiet *das* - **4.** COMPUT Datenfeld *das* ◇ *vt* [question] parieren.

field day *n*: **to have a ~** *fig* seinen großen Tag haben.

field marshal *n* Feldmarschall *der*.

field trip *n* Exkursion *die*.

fieldwork [ˈfiːldwɜːk] *n* Arbeit *die* im Gelände.

fiend [fiːnd] *n* - **1.** [cruel person] Teufel *der* - **2.** *inf* [fanatic] Fanatiker *der*, -in *die*.

fiendish [ˈfiːndɪʃ] *adj* - **1.** [evil] teuflisch - **2.** *inf* [very difficult, complex] verteufelt schwer.

fierce [fɪəs] *adj* [dog] bissig; [lion, warrior] aggressiv; [storm, temper] heftig; [competition] hart; [criticism] scharf; [heat] glühend.

fiery [ˈfaɪərɪ] *adj* - **1.** [burning] brennend - **2.** [speech] feurig; [temper] hitzig.

fifteen [fɪfˈtiːn] *num* fünfzehn; *see also* six.

fifth [fɪfθ] *num* fünfte, -r, -s; *see also* sixth.

Fifth Amendment *n Am*: **to take the ~** *die Aussage verweigern.*

fifty [ˈfɪftɪ] (*pl* -ies) *num* fünfzig; *see also* sixty.

fifty-fifty *adj* & *adv* fifty-fifty.

fig [fɪg] *n* Feige *die*.

fight [faɪt] (*pt* & *pp* fought) ◇ *n* - **1.** [brawl] Schlägerei *die*; [between boxers] Kampf *der*; **to have a ~ with sb** sich mit jm schlagen; **to put up a ~** sich heftig zur Wehr setzen - **2.** *fig* [struggle] Kampf *der* - **3.** [argu-

ment] Streit *der*; **to have a ~ (with sb)** Streit (mit jm) haben - **4.** [fighting spirit]: **there was no ~ left in him** er war kampfmüde ◇ *vt* - **1.** [physically] sich schlagen mit; [in battle, war] kämpfen mit OR gegen - **2.** [battle] austragen; [war] führen - **3.** [prejudice, racism] bekämpfen ◇ *vi* - **1.** [physically] sich schlagen; [in war] kämpfen - **2.** *fig* [struggle]: **to ~ for/against sthg** für/gegen etw kämpfen - **3.** [argue] sich streiten; **to ~ about** OR **over sthg** sich um OR über etw (*A*) streiten.

◆ **fight back** ◇ *vt fus* [tears, anger] zurückhalten ◇ *vi* sich zur Wehr setzen.

fighter [ˈfaɪtəʳ] *n* - **1.** [plane] Jagdflugzeug *das* - **2.** [soldier] Kämpfer *der* - **3.** [combative person] Kämpfernatur *die*.

fighting [ˈfaɪtɪŋ] *n* (*U*) [in war] Kämpfe *pl*; [brawling] Schlägereien *pl*.

figment [ˈfɪgmənt] *n*: **a ~ of your/his imagination** ein Hirngespinst von dir/ihm.

figurative [ˈfɪgərətɪv] *adj* - **1.** [language] bildlich - **2.** ART gegenständlich.

figure [*Br* ˈfɪgəʳ, *Am* ˈfɪgjər] ◇ *n* - **1.** [number] Zahl *die*; [digit] Ziffer *die*; **in single/ double ~s** in ein-/zweistelligen Zahlen - **2.** [outline of person] Gestalt *die* - **3.** [personality] Persönlichkeit *die*; **a father ~** eine Vaterfigur - **4.** [shape of body] Figur *die* - **5.** [diagram] Abbildung *die* ◇ *vt esp Am* [suppose] schätzen ◇ *vi* [feature] auftauchen; **to ~ prominently** eine wichtige Rolle spielen.

◆ **figure out** *vt sep* [answer] herausbekommen; [puzzle, problem] lösen.

figurehead [ˈfɪgəhed] *n lit* & *fig* Galionsfigur *die*.

figure of speech *n* Redensart *die*.

file [faɪl] ◇ *n* - **1.** [folder] Aktenordner *der* - **2.** [report] Akte *die*; **on ~**, **on the ~s** in der Akte, in den Akten - **3.** COMPUT Datei *die* - **4.** [tool] Feile *die* - **5.** [line]: **in single ~** hintereinander ◇ *vt* - **1.** [put in folder] ablheften - **2.** [complaint, petition, lawsuit] einlreichen - **3.** [wood, metal] feilen; **to ~ one's fingernails** sich (*D*) die Fingernägel feilen ◇ *vi* - **1.** [walk in single file]: **to ~ in/out** nacheinander hinein-/hinauslgehen - **2.** LAW: **to ~ for divorce** die Scheidung einlreichen.

filet *n Am* = fillet.

filing cabinet [ˈfaɪlɪŋ-] *n* Aktenschrank *der*.

fill [fɪl] ◇ *vt* - **1.** [gen] füllen - **2.** [repair - crack] zulspachteln; [- hole in ground] zulschütten - **3.** [fulfil - role] spielen; [- vacancy] besetzen; [- need] befriedigen ◇ *vi* sich füllen ◇ *n*: **to eat one's ~** sich satt essen. ◆ **fill in** ◇ *vt sep* - **1.** [form, questionnaire] auslfüllen; [name, address] einlsetzen - **2.** [inform]: **to ~ sb in (on sthg)** jn (über etw (*A*)) ins Bild setzen ◇ *vi*: **to ~ in for sb** für jn einlspringen. ◆ **fill out** ◇ *vt sep* [form, questionnaire] auslfüllen ◇ *vi* [get fatter] fülliger werden. ◆ **fill up** ◇ *vt sep* voll füllen ◇ *vi* sich füllen.

fillet, **filet** *Am* ['fɪlɪt] *n* Filet *das.*

fillet steak *n* Filetsteak *das.*

filling ['fɪlɪŋ] ◇ *adj* [food] sättigend ◇ *n* Füllung *die.*

filling station *n* Tankstelle *die.*

film [fɪlm] ◇ *n* **- 1.** [movie, for camera] Film *der* **- 2.** [layer] Schicht *die* ◇ *vt* filmen; [book, play] verfilmen ◇ *vi* drehen.

film star *n* Filmstar *der.*

Filofax® ['faɪləufæks] *n* Filofax® *das.*

filter ['fɪltər] ◇ *n* Filter *der* ◇ *vt* filtern.

filter coffee *n* Filterkaffee *der.*

filter lane *n Br* Abbiegespur *die.*

filter-tipped [-'tɪpt] *adj* mit Filter.

filth [fɪlθ] *n* (U) **- 1.** [dirt] Dreck *der* **- 2.** [obscenity] Obszönitäten *pl.*

filthy ['fɪlθɪ] *adj* **- 1.** [very dirty] dreckig **- 2.** [obscene] obszön.

fin [fɪn] *n* **- 1.** [on fish] Flosse *die* **- 2.** *Am* [for swimmer] Schwimmflosse *die.*

final ['faɪnl] ◇ *adj* **- 1.** [last] letzte, -r, -s **- 2.** [at end]: **the ~ score** der Schlussstand **- 3.** [decision, version, defeat] endgültig; **I said no, and that's ~!** ich sagte nein, und damit basta! ◇ *n* [of ball games] Endspiel *das;* [of races] Endrunde *die.* ◆ **finals** *npl* UNIV Examen *das.*

finale [fɪ'nɑːlɪ] *n* Finale *das.*

finalize, **-ise** ['faɪnəlaɪz] *vt* [arrangements, details, dates] endgültig festlegen; [deal] zum Abschluss bringen.

finally ['faɪnəlɪ] *adv* **- 1.** [at last] schließlich; [with relief] endlich **- 2.** [lastly] zum Schluss.

finance [*n* 'faɪnæns, *vb* faɪ'næns] ◇ *n* (U) **- 1.** [money] Geldmittel *pl* **- 2.** [money management] Finanzwesen *das* ◇ *vt* finanzieren. ◆ **finances** *npl* Finanzen *pl.*

financial [fɪ'nænʃl] *adj* finanziell.

find [faɪnd] (*pt & pp* found) ◇ *vt* **- 1.** [gen] finden **- 2.** [discover]: **to ~ that** festlstellen, dass; **I found myself back where I started** ich stellte fest, dass ich wieder da angekommen war, wo ich angefangen hatte **- 3.** LAW: **to be found guilty/not guilty** für schuldig/nicht schuldig befunden werden ◇ *n* Fund *der.* ◆ **find out** ◇ *vi* herauslfinden ◇ *vt fus* [information, truth] herauslfinden ◇ *vt sep* [person] auf die Schliche kommen (+ *D*).

findings ['faɪndɪŋz] *npl* Ergebnis *das.*

fine [faɪn] ◇ *adj* **- 1.** [good - food, work] ausgezeichnet; [- building] prächtig; [- weather, day] schön; **how are you? - ~,** **thanks** wie gehts? - gut, danke **- 2.** [satisfactory] in Ordnung, gut; **everything OK? - yes,** **~! is** alles OK? - ja, alles in Ordnung!; **more** **tea? - no, I'm ~, thanks** noch mehr Tee? - danke, ich habe genug; **it's ~ by me** ich habe nichts dagegen **- 3.** [hair] fein; [thread, wire]

dünn **- 4.** [sand, powder, sandpaper] fein **- 5.** [small, exact - detail] klein **- 6.** [grand - clothes, people] vornehm ◇ *adv* **- 1.** [quite well] gut; **that suits me** – das passt mir gut **- 2.** [thinly] fein ◇ *n* Geldstrafe *die* ◇ *vt* zu einer Geldstrafe verurteilen.

fine arts *npl* schöne Künste *pl.*

fine-tune *vt lit & fig* fein ablstimmen.

finger ['fɪŋgər] ◇ *n* Finger *der* ◇ *vt* [feel] anlfassen.

fingernail ['fɪŋgəneɪl] *n* Fingernagel *der.*

fingerprint ['fɪŋgəprɪnt] *n* Fingerabdruck *der.*

fingertip ['fɪŋgətɪp] *n* Fingerspitze *die;* **to have sthg at one's ~s** etw parat haben.

finicky ['fɪnɪkɪ] *adj pej* [eater] wählerisch; [person] pingelig; [task] knifflig.

finish ['fɪnɪʃ] ◇ *n* **- 1.** [end] Ende *das;* [of race] Finish *das* **- 2.** [on furniture, pottery] Oberfläche *die* ◇ *vt* **- 1.** [complete] beenden; **to ~ doing the ironing/eating breakfast/***etc* mit dem Bügeln/dem Frühstück/*etc* fertig sein; **to ~ writing a letter** einen Brief zu Ende schreiben **- 2.** [food] auslessen; [drink] austrinken; [supplies] auflbrauchen; [cigarette] zu Ende rauchen; [book] auslesen **- 3.** [work, school]: **I ~ work at half past five** ich mache um halb sechs Feierabend; **I ~ school at half** **past three** ich habe um halb vier Schule aus ◇ *vi* **- 1.** [end] zu Ende sein; **when do you ~?** [stop work] wann machst du Feierabend? **- 2.** [complete task] fertig werden; **I haven't** **~ed yet** ich bin noch nicht fertig **- 3.** [in race, competition]: **to ~ top of the league** Tabellenführer werden; **to ~ fifth** Fünfter werden. ◆ **finish off** *vt sep* **- 1.** [complete] beenden **- 2.** [food] auslessen; [drink] austrinken. ◆ **finish up** *vi:* **we ~ed up in a pub** wir sind schließlich in einer Kneipe gelandet; **she ~ed up running her own company** zum Schluss leitete sie ihre eigene Firma.

finishing line ['fɪnɪʃɪŋ-] *n* Ziellinie *die.*

finite ['faɪnaɪt] *adj* **- 1.** [limited] begrenzt **- 2.** GRAMM finit.

Finland ['fɪnlənd] *n* Finnland *nt.*

Finn [fɪn] *n* Finne *der,* -nin *die.*

Finnish ['fɪnɪʃ] ◇ *adj* finnisch ◇ *n* [language] Finnisch(e) *das.*

fir [fɜːr] *n* Tanne *die.*

fire ['faɪər] ◇ *n* **- 1.** [gen] Feuer *das;* **to be on** **~** brennen; **to catch ~** Feuer fangen; [forest, building] in Brand geraten; **to set ~ to sthg** etw anlzünden; [deliberately] etw in Brand setzen **- 2.** [in forest, of building] Brand *der* **- 3.** *Br* [heater] Ofen *der* **- 4.** (U) [shooting]: **under ~** unter Beschuss; **to open ~ (on sb)** das Feuer eröffnen (auf jn) ◇ *vt* **- 1.** [shoot - bullet, missile] ablfeuern; [- gun] ablschießen **- 2.** [from job] feuern **- 3.** [imagination] beflügeln **- 4.** [pottery] brennen ◇ *vi:* **to ~ (on** OR **at sb/sthg)** (auf jn/etw) schießen OR feuern.

fire alarm *n* Feueralarm *der.*

firearm ['faɪərɑːm] *n* Schusswaffe *die.*

firebomb ['faɪəbɒm] *n* Brandbombe *die.*

fire brigade *Br*, **fire department** *Am n* Feuerwehr *die.*

fire engine *n* Feuerwehrauto *das.*

fire escape *n* [stairs] Feuertreppe *die;* [ladder] Feuerleiter *die.*

fire extinguisher *n* Feuerlöscher *der.*

fireguard ['faɪəgɑːd] *n* Kamingitter *das.*

firelighter ['faɪəlaɪtəʳ] *n* Feueranzünder *der.*

fireman ['faɪəmən] *(pl* -men [-mən]) *n* Feuerwehrmann *der.*

fireplace ['faɪəpleɪs] *n* Kamin *der.*

fireproof ['faɪəpruːf] *adj* feuerfest.

fireside ['faɪəsaɪd] *n:* **by the ~** am Kamin.

fire station *n* Feuerwache *die.*

firewood ['faɪəwʊd] *n* Brennholz *das.*

firework ['faɪəwɜːk] *n* Feuerwerkskörper *der;* **~s** Feuerwerk *das.*

firing squad ['faɪrɪŋ-] *n* Exekutionskommando *das.*

firm [fɜːm] *<> adj* - **1.** [in texture] fest - **2.** [structure, shelf] stabil - **3.** [forceful, strong - pressure, hold, control] fest; [- leader, voice] energisch; **you must be ~ with him** sie müssen ihm gegenüber bestimmt auftreten; **to stand ~** standhaft bleiben - **4.** [belief] unerschütterlich; [answer] entschieden; [evidence] sicher *<> n* Firma *die.*

first [fɜːst] *<> adj* erste, -r, -s; **for the ~ time** zum ersten Mal; **I'll do it ~ thing (in the morning)** das ist das Erste, was ich morgen tun werde; **at ~ sight** auf den ersten Blick; **in the ~ place, ...** zunächst einmal ... *<> adv* - **1.** [firstly] zuerst; [arrive, speak etc] als erste, -r, -s; **~ of all** zuallererst; **what should I do ~?** was soll ich zuerst tun? - **2.** [for the first time] zum ersten Mal *<> pron* erste *der, die, das;* **the ~ of January** der erste Januar *<> n* - **1.** [event]: **the balloon race was a world ~** der Ballonweltflug war der erste seiner Art auf der Welt - **2.** *Br* UNIV Abschluss mit „Sehr gut" - **3.** AUT: **~ (gear)** erster Gang. ◆ **at first** *adv* zuerst. ◆ **at first hand** *adv* aus erster Hand.

first aid *n* Erste Hilfe.

first-aid kit *n* Verbandskasten *der.*

first-class *adj* - **1.** [excellent] erstklassig - **2.** [ticket] erster Klasse; [stamp] für Briefe, die innerhalb Großbritanniens schneller befördert werden sollen; **~ compartment** Erste-Klasse-Abteil *das.*

first course *n* erster Gang.

first floor *n* - **1.** *Br* [above ground level] erster Stock - **2.** *Am* [at ground level] Erdgeschoss *das.*

firsthand [fɜːstˈhænd] *adj & adv* aus erster Hand.

first lady *n* POL First Lady *die,* Frau des US-Präsidenten.

firstly ['fɜːstlɪ] *adv* zuerst; [followed by "secondly"] erstens.

first name *n* Vorname *der.*

first-rate *adj* erstklassig.

fish [fɪʃ] *(pl* - OR -es) *<> n* Fisch *der <> vi:* **to ~ (for)** fischen; [with rod] angeln; **to ~ for compliments** *fig* auf Komplimente aus sein.

fish and chips *npl Br* frittierter Fisch mit Pommes frites.

fish and chips

Ein traditionelles englisches Gericht, das aus frittiertem Fisch und Pommes frites besteht und das man in den fish and chip shops (einer Art Imbissstube) zum Mitnehmen in braunes Packpapier oder Zeitungspapier eingepackt bekommt. Fish and chip shops sind landauf, landab zu finden und bieten neben Fisch und Pommes frites auch eine Auswahl an anderen frittierten Schnellgerichten wie Würstchen, Hähnchen, Blutwurst und meat pies (Fleischpasteten) an.

fish and chip shop *n Br* Imbissstube, *die hauptsächlich frittierten Fisch mit Pommes frites verkauft.*

fishcake ['fɪʃkeɪk] *n* Fischfrikadelle *die.*

fisherman ['fɪʃəmən] *(pl* -men [-mən]) *n* Fischer *der;* [angler] Angler *der,* -in *die.*

fish fingers *Br*, **fish sticks** *Am npl* Fischstäbchen *das.*

fishing ['fɪʃɪŋ] *n* Fischen *das;* [with rod] Angeln *das;* [industry] Fischerei *das;* **to go ~** auf Fischfang gehen; [with rod] angeln gehen.

fishing boat *n* Fischerboot *das.*

fishing rod *n* Angelrute *die.*

fishmonger ['fɪʃˌmʌŋgəʳ] *n esp Br* Fischhändler *der,* -in *die;* **~'s (shop)** Fischgeschäft *das.*

fish shop *n* Fischgeschäft *das.*

fish sticks *npl Am* = fish fingers.

fish tank *n* [in house] Aquarium *das.*

fishy ['fɪʃɪ] *adj* - **1.** [smell, taste] Fisch- - **2.** *fig* [suspicious]: **there's something ~ about it** daran ist etwas faul.

fist [fɪst] *n* Faust *die.*

fit [fɪt] *<> adj* - **1.** [suitable]: **~ (for)** geeignet (für); **to be ~ to do sthg** die richtige Person sein, um etw zu tun; **he's not ~ to drive** [drunk] er ist nicht mehr in der Lage, Auto zu fahren; **~ to eat** essbar - **2.** [healthy] fit; **to keep/get ~** fit bleiben/werden *<> n* - **1.** [of clothes, shoes *etc*]: **to be a good ~** gut passen - **2.** [epileptic, of anger, coughing] Anfall *der;* **to have a ~** MED einen Anfall haben OR erleiden; *fig* [be angry] einen Wutanfall kriegen, ruckweise; **to work in ~s and starts** die Arbeit mehrmals unterbrechen <> *vt* - 1. [subj: clothes, shoes] **passen** (+ *D*); [subj: key] **passen in** (+ *A*) - 2. [insert]: **to ~ sthg into sthg** etw in etw (*A*) stecken - 3. [install] einlbauen; **to ~ sthg with sthg** etw mit etw auslstatten - 4. [correspond to] entsprechen (+ *D*); **he ~s the description** die Beschreibung passt auf ihn <> *vi* passen. ◆ **fit in** <> *vt sep* [find time for - person] dazwischenlschieben; [- task] zusätzlich erledigen <> *vi* [belong]: **he's never ~ted in here** er hat hier nie hingepasst.

fitness ['fitnis] *n* - 1. [health] Fitness *die*, Kondition *die* - 2. [suitability - for job]: **~ (for)** Eignung *die* (für).

fitted carpet [,fitid-] *n* Teppichboden *der*.

fitted kitchen [,fitid-] *n Br* Einbauküche *die*.

fitter ['fitər] *n* [mechanic] Monteur *der*, -in *die*, Installateur *der*, -in *die*.

fitting ['fitiŋ] <> *adj fml* angemessen <> *n* - 1. [part] Zubehörteil *das* - 2. [for clothing] Anprobe *die*. ◆ **fittings** *npl* Ausstattung *die*; [electrical, pipes] Installation *die*.

fitting room *n* Umkleidekabine *die*.

five [faiv] *num* fünf; *see also* six.

fiver ['faivər] *n inf* - 1. *Br* [amount] fünf britische Pfund *pl*; [note] Fünfpfundschein *der* - 2. *Am* [amount] fünf Dollar *pl*; [note] Fünfdollarschein *der*.

fix [fiks] <> *vt* - 1. [attach] befestigen; **to ~ sthg to sthg** etw an etw (*D*) befestigen; **to ~ one's eyes on sthg** seine Augen auf etw (*A*) heften - 2. [decide - date, amount, price] festlsetzen; **I've ~ed it with him** ich habe es mit ihm abgemacht; **how are you ~ed for money?** wie sieht es bei dir mit dem Geld aus? - 3. [repair] reparieren - 4. *inf* [rig - race, fight] manipulieren - 5. *esp Am* [food, drink] machen <> *n* - 1. *inf* [difficult situation]: **to be in a ~** in der Patsche sitzen - 2. *drugs sl* Fix *der*. ◆ **fix up** *vt sep* - 1. [provide]: **to ~ sb up with sthg** jm etw besorgen - 2. [arrange] arrangieren.

fixation [fik'seiʃn] *n* Fixierung *die*.

fixed [fikst] *adj* - 1. [attached] fest - 2. [charge, rate] festgesetzt - 3. [smile, stare, belief] starr.

fixture ['fikstʃər] *n* - 1. [in building] festes Inventar; **~s and fittings** *zu einer Wohnung gehörende Ausstattung und Installationen* - 2. [sports event] Spiel *das*.

fizz [fiz] *vi* [drink] sprudeln.

fizzle ['fizl] ◆ **fizzle out** *vi* [fire, enthusiasm] verpuffen.

fizzy ['fizi] *adj* kohlensäurehaltig.

flabbergasted ['flæbəga:stid] *adj* platt.

flabby ['flæbi] *adj* wabbelig.

flag [flæg] <> *n* Fahne *die*, Fahne *die* <> *vi* [person] ermüden; [enthusiasm, energy] nachllassen. ◆ **flag down** *vt sep* anlhalten.

flagpole ['flægpəʊl] *n* Fahnenstange *die*.

flagrant ['fleigrənt] *adj* himmelschreiend.

flagstone ['flægstəʊn] *n* Steinplatte *die*; [on floors] Fliese *die*.

flair [fleər] *n* - 1. [talent]: **~ (for)** Talent *das* (für) - 2. [stylishness - of person] Ausstrahlung *die*.

flak [flæk] *n inf* [criticism]: **to get a lot of ~** unter schweren Beschuss geraten.

flake [fleik] <> *n* [of snow] Flocke *die*; [of skin] Schuppe *die* <> *vi* [paint] ablblättern; [skin] sich schuppen.

flamboyant [flæm'bɔiənt] *adj* extravagant; [design, decoration] üppig.

flame [fleim] *n* Flamme *die*; **to be in ~s** in Flammen stehen; **to burst into ~s** in Brand geraten.

flamingo [flə'miŋgəʊ] (*pl* -s OR -es) *n* Flamingo *der*.

flammable ['flæməbl] *adj* leicht entflammbar.

flan [flæn] *n* [sweet] Torte *die*; [savoury] Quiche *die*.

flank [flæŋk] <> *n* Flanke *die* <> *vt*: **to be ~ed by sb/sthg** von jm/etw flankiert sein.

flannel ['flænl] *n* - 1. [fabric] Flannel *der* - 2. *Br* [facecloth] Waschlappen *der*.

flap [flæp] <> *n* - 1. [of pocket] Klappe *die*; [of envelope] Lasche *die*; [of table] hochklappbarer Teil - 2. *inf* [panic]: **in a ~** in Panik <> *vt* [wings] schlagen mit; [arms] wedeln mit <> *vi* [sail, flag, clothes] flattern.

flapjack ['flæpdʒæk] *n* - 1. *Br* [biscuit] Haferflockenkeks *der* - 2. *Am* [pancake] Pfannkuchen *der*.

flare [fleər] <> *n* [distress signal] Leuchtsignal *das* <> *vi* - 1. [fire]: **to ~ (up)** (aufl)lodern - 2.: **to ~ (up)** [war, violence, disease] auslbrechen - 3. [trousers, skirt] ausgestellt sein - 4. [nostrils] sich blähen. ◆ **flares** *npl Br* [trousers] Hose *die* mit Schlag.

flash [flæʃ] <> *n* - 1. [of light - bright] Aufblitzen *das*; **a ~ of lightning** ein Blitz; **a ~ of inspiration** *fig* ein Geistesblitz; **in a ~** blitzartig - 2. PHOT Blitz *der* <> *vt* - 1. [torch]: **to ~ a torch on sthg** etw mit etw anleuchten; **to ~ one's headlights** die Lichthupe benutzen; **to ~ sb a look/smile** jn plötzlich (kurz) anlschauen/anllächeln - 2. [show briefly - passport, pass] kurz zeigen <> *vi* [light] auflblinken; **to ~ by** OR **past** vorbeilsausen.

flashback ['flæʃbæk] *n* [in film] Rückblende *die*.

flashbulb ['flæʃbʌlb] *n* Blitzlicht *das*.

flashgun ['flæʃgʌn] *n* Blitzgerät *das*.

flashlight ['flæʃlait] *n* [torch] Taschenlampe *die*.

flashy ['flæʃi] *adj inf* protzig.

flask [flɑ:sk] *n* - 1. [Thermos] Thermosflasche *die* - 2. [hip flask] Flachmann *der*.

flat [flæt] <> *adj* - **1.** [gen] flach; [feet, tyre] platt; ~ **roof** Flachdach *das* - **2.** [refusal, denial] glatt - **3.** [voice] monoton - **4.** [MUS - singer, instrument] zu tief; **C** ~ Ces *das*; **D** ~ Des *das*; **A** ~ As *das*; **B** ~ B *das* - **5.** COMM [fare, fee] Pauschal- - **6.** [drink] abgestanden - **7.** [battery] leer <> *adv* - **1.** [level] flach - **2.** [exactly]: **in five minutes** ~ in ganzen fünf Minuten <> *n* - **1.** *Br* [apartment] Wohnung *die* - **2.** [MUS - note] erniedrigter Ton; [- symbol] Erniedrigungszeichen *das*. ◆ **flat out** *adv* [work] auf Hochtouren.

flatly ['flætlɪ] *adv* [refuse, deny] rundweg.

flatmate ['flætmeɪt] *n Br* Mitbewohner *der*, -in *die*.

flat rate *n* Pauschalpreis *der*.

flatten ['flætn] *vt* - **1.** [surface] glätten; [paper] glatt streichen - **2.** [destroy] dem Erdboden gleich machen. ◆ **flatten out** <> *vi* eben(er) werden <> *vt sep* [surface] glätten; [paper] glatt streichen.

flatter ['flætər] *vt* schmeicheln (+ *D*).

flattering ['flætərɪŋ] *adj* schmeichelhaft.

flattery ['flætərɪ] *n (U)* Schmeicheleien *pl*.

flaunt [flɔːnt] *vt* zur Schau stellen.

flavour *Br*, **flavor** *Am* ['fleɪvər] <> *n* - **1.** [taste] Geschmack *der* - **2.** *fig* [atmosphere] Touch *der* <> *vt* [food, drink] Geschmack verleihen (+ *D*).

flavouring *Br*, **flavoring** *Am* ['fleɪvərɪŋ] *n* Aroma *das*.

flaw [flɔː] *n* Fehler *der*.

flawless ['flɔːlɪs] *adj* fehlerlos.

flax [flæks] *n* [plant] Flachs *der*.

flea [fliː] *n* Floh *der*.

flea market *n* Flohmarkt *der*.

fleck [flek] <> *n* Tupfen *der* <> *vt*: **-ed (with)** besprenkelt (mit).

fled [fled] *pt* & *pp* ⊳ **flee.**

flee [fliː] (*pt* & *pp* **fled**) <> *vt* [country] fliehen aus; [enemy] fliehen vor (+ *D*) <> *vi* fliehen.

fleece [fliːs] <> *n* - **1.** [of sheep] Schaffell *das* - **2.** [material] Fleece *das*; [jacket] Fleecejacke *die* <> *vt inf* [cheat] abzocken.

fleet [fliːt] *n* - **1.** [of ships] Flotte *die* - **2.** [of cars, buses] Fuhrpark *der*.

fleeting ['fliːtɪŋ] *adj* flüchtig.

Flemish ['flemɪʃ] <> *adj* flämisch <> *n* [language] Flämisch(e) *das*.

flesh [fleʃ] *n* Fleisch *das*; [of fruit] Fruchtfleisch *das*; [of vegetable] Mark *das*; ~ **and blood** [family] Fleisch und Blut.

flesh wound *n* Fleischwunde *die*.

flew [fluː] *pt* ⊳ **fly.**

flex [fleks] <> *n* ELEC Kabel *das* <> *vt* [arm, knee] beugen.

flexible ['fleksəbl] *adj* - **1.** [material, bar] biegsam - **2.** [person, system] flexibel.

flexitime ['fleksɪtaɪm] *n* Gleitzeit *die*.

flick [flɪk] <> *n* [with finger] Schnippen *das* <> *vt* [switch - turn on] anknipsen; [- turn off] ausknipsen. ◆ **flick through** *vt fus* durchblättern.

flicker ['flɪkər] *vi* [light, candle] flackern; [TV, screen] flimmern; [shadow, eyelids] zucken.

flick knife *n Br* Klappmesser *das*.

flight [flaɪt] *n* - **1.** [of plane, bird] Flug *der* - **2.**: **a** ~ **of steps/stairs** eine Treppe - **3.** [escape] Flucht *die*.

flight attendant *n* Flugbegleiter *der*, -in *die*.

flight deck *n* - **1.** [of aircraft carrier] Flugdeck *das* - **2.** [of aircraft] Cockpit *das*.

flight recorder *n* Flugschreiber *der*.

flimsy ['flɪmzɪ] *adj* - **1.** [material, clothes, shoes] dünn; [paper] hauchdünn; [structure] nicht sehr stabil - **2.** [excuse] schwach; [argument] fadenscheinig.

flinch [flɪntʃ] *vi* zurückzucken.

fling [flɪŋ] (*pt* & *pp* **flung**) <> *n* [affair] Affäre *die* <> *vt* [throw] schleudern.

flint [flɪnt] *n* Feuerstein *der*.

flip [flɪp] <> *vt* - **1.** [omelette, steak *etc*] wenden; **to** ~ **a coin** eine Münze werfen; **to** ~ **open** aufklappen; **to** ~ **over** umdrehen; **to** ~ **through** [magazine] durchblättern - **2.** [switch - turn on] anknipsen; [- turn off] ausknipsen <> *vi inf* [become angry] ausflippen <> *n* [of coin]: **it was decided on the** ~ **of a coin** wir haben eine Münze geworfen, um zu entscheiden.

flip-flops *npl Br* [shoes] Badelatschen *pl*.

flippant ['flɪpənt] *adj* leichtfertig.

flipper ['flɪpər] *n* - **1.** [of animal] Flosse *die* - **2.** [for swimmer, diver] Schwimmflosse *die*.

flirt [flɜːt] <> *n*: **he's a terrible** ~ er flirtet mit allen <> *vi* [with person]: **to** ~ **(with)** flirten (mit).

flirtatious [flɜːˈteɪʃəs] *adj* kokett.

flit [flɪt] *vi* [bird] flattern.

float [fləʊt] <> *n* - **1.** [for fishing] Schwimmer *der*; [for swimming] Schwimmbrett *das* - **2.** [in procession] Festwagen *der* - **3.** [money] Wechselgeld *das* <> *vi* - **1.** [on water - not sink] schwimmen; [- move] treiben - **2.** [through air] schweben.

flock [flɒk] *n* [of birds] Schwarm *der*; [of sheep] Herde *die*; [of people] Schar *die*.

flog [flɒg] *vt* - **1.** [whip] auspeitschen - **2.** *Br inf* [sell] verklopppen.

flood [flʌd] <> *n* Flut *die* <> *vt* - **1.** [gen] überschwemmen; [kitchen] unter Wasser setzen - **2.** [with light] durchfluten.

flooding ['flʌdɪŋ] *n* Überschwemmung *die*.

floodlight ['flʌdlaɪt] *n* Scheinwerfer *der*.

floor <> *n* - **1.** [of room] Fußboden *der* - **2.** [storey] Stock *der* - **3.** [at meeting, debate]

Publikum *das* - **4.** [for dancing] Tanzfläche *die* ◇ *vt* - **1.** [knock down] zu Boden schlagen - **2.** [subj: comment, question]: **to ~ sb** jm die Sprache verschlagen.

floorboard ['flɔːbɔːd] *n* Diele *die*.

flop [flɒp] *n inf* [failure] Flop *der*.

floppy ['flɒpɪ] *adj* schlaff herunterhängend.

floppy (disk) *n* Diskette *die*.

flora ['flɔːrə] *n* Flora *die*.

florid ['flɒrɪd] *adj* - **1.** [face, complexion] gerötet - **2.** [style] blumig.

florist ['flɒrɪst] *n* Florist *der*, -in *die*; **~'s (shop)** *n* Blumengeschäft *das*.

flotsam ['flɒtsəm] *n*: **~ and jetsam** Treibgut und Strandgut.

flounder ['flaʊndə'] *vi* - **1.** [in water] sich abstrampeln - **2.** [in conversation, speech] ins Schwimmen kommen.

flour ['flaʊə'] *n* Mehl *das*.

flourish ['flʌrɪʃ] ◇ *vi* - **1.** [plant, flower] prächtig gedeihen - **2.** [company, business] florieren ◇ *vt* schwenken.

flout [flaʊt] *vt* missachten.

flow [fləʊ] ◇ *n* - **1.** [river, of liquid] Fluss *der*; [of words] Redefluss *der*; **~ of information/traffic** Informations-/Verkehrsfluss - **2.** [of tide] Flut *die* ◇ *vi* - **1.** [gen] fließen; [air, people] strömen - **2.** [hair, dress] wallen.

flowchart ['fləʊtʃɑːt], **flow diagram** *n* Flussdiagramm *das*.

flower ['flaʊə'] ◇ *n* [plant] Blume *die*; [blossom] Blüte *die*; **in ~** in Blüte ◇ *vi* blühen.

flowerbed ['flaʊəbed] *n* Blumenbeet *das*.

flowerpot ['flaʊəpɒt] *n* Blumentopf *der*.

flowery ['flaʊərɪ] *adj* - **1.** [dress, material] geblümt - **2.** *pej* [language] blumig.

flown [fləʊn] *pp* ⊏⊐ fly.

flu [fluː] *n (U)* Grippe *die*.

fluctuate ['flʌktʃʊeɪt] *vi* schwanken.

fluency ['fluːənsɪ] *n* - **1.** [in a foreign language] Gewandtheit *die* - **2.** [in speaking, writing] Flüssigkeit *die*.

fluent ['fluːənt] *adj* - **1.** [in a foreign language] fließend - **2.** [writing] flüssig; [speaker] gewandt.

fluffy ['flʌfɪ] *adj* [animal] flaumweich; [jumper] flauschig.

fluid ['fluːɪd] ◇ *n* Flüssigkeit *die* ◇ *adj* - **1.** [movement] fließend; [style] flüssig - **2.** [situation] Veränderungen unterworfen.

fluid ounce *n* = 28,41 *cm³*.

fluke [fluːk] *n inf* [chance]: **it was a ~** das war reiner Dusel.

flummox ['flʌməks] *vt esp Br inf* durcheinander bringen.

flung [flʌŋ] *pt & pp* ⊏⊐ fling.

flunk [flʌŋk] *Am inf vt* [SCH & UNIV - exam, test] fallen durch; [- student] durchfallen lassen.

fluorescent [flʊə'resənt] *adj* fluoreszierend.

fluoride ['flʊəraɪd] *n* Fluorid *das*.

flurry ['flʌrɪ] *n* [of snow] Gestöber *das*; **there was a ~ of activity** es herrschte eine rege Betriebsamkeit.

flush [flʌʃ] ◇ *adj* [level]: **to be ~ with sthg** bündig mit etw abschließen ◇ *n* - **1.** [in toilet] Spülung *die* - **2.** [blush] Röte *die* ◇ *vt* [with water]: **to ~ the toilet** spülen ◇ *vi* - **1.** [toilet] spülen - **2.** [blush] erröten.

flushed [flʌʃt] *adj* - **1.** [face] gerötet - **2.** [excited]: **to be ~ with sthg** über etw *(A)* aufgeregt und glücklich sein.

flustered ['flʌstəd] *adj* konfus.

flute [fluːt] *n MUS* Querflöte *die*.

flutter ['flʌtə'] ◇ *n* ◇ *vi* flattern.

flux [flʌks] *n*: **to be in a state of ~** im Fluss sein.

fly [flaɪ] ◇ *n* - **1.** [insect] Fliege *die* - **2.** [of trousers] Hosenschlitz *der* ◇ *vt* - **1.** [plane] fliegen; [kite] steigen lassen; [model aircraft] fliegen lassen; [passengers, goods] fliegen; [airline] fliegen mit - **2.** [flag] gehisst haben ◇ *vi* - **1.** [gen] fliegen; **the days flew by** OR **past** die Tage sind schnell verflogen - **2.** [flag] wehen. ◆ **fly away** *vi* wegfliegen.

fly-fishing *n* Fliegenfischen *das*.

flying ['flaɪɪŋ] ◇ *adj* [animal] Flug-; **~ leap** großer Sprung ◇ *n* Fliegen *das*.

flying colours *npl*: **to pass (sthg) with ~** (etw) glänzend bestehen.

flying saucer *n* fliegende Untertasse.

flying start *n*: **to get off to a ~** einen glänzenden Start haben.

flying visit *n* Stippvisite *die*.

flyover ['flaɪˌəʊvə'] *n Br* Überführung *die*.

flysheet ['flaɪʃiːt] *n* Überzelt *das*.

FM (*abbr of* frequency modulation) UKW.

foal [fəʊl] *n* Fohlen *das*.

foam [fəʊm] ◇ *n* - **1.** [bubbles] Schaum *der* - **2.** [material]: **~ (rubber)** Schaumgummi *der* ◇ *vi* schäumen.

fob [fɒb] ◆ **fob off** *vt sep*: **to ~ sthg off on sb** jm etw andrehen; **to ~ sb off with sthg** jn mit etw abspeisen.

focal point ['fəʊkl-] *n fig* Mittelpunkt *der*.

focus ['fəʊkəs] (*pl* -cuses OR -ci [-kaɪ]) ◇ *n* PHOT Fokus *der*; [of rays] Brennpunkt *der*; [of discussion] Mittelpunkt *der*; **in ~** [image] scharf; **out of ~** [image] unscharf ◇ *vt* - **1.** [lens, camera]: **to ~ sthg (on)** etw einstellen (auf *(+ A)*) - **2.** [mentally]: **to ~ one's attention on sb/sthg** seine Aufmerksamkeit auf jn/etw richten ◇ *vi*: **to ~ on** [with eyes] den Blick richten auf *(+ A)*; [with camera] mit der Kamera scharf stellen auf *(+ A); fig* [mentally] konzentrieren auf *(+ A)*.

focused, focussed ['fəʊkəst] *adj* [mentally] konzentriert.

fodder ['fɒdə^r] *n* Futter *das*.

foe [fəʊ] *n literary* Feind *der*.

foetus ['fi:təs] *n* Fötus *der*.

fog [fɒg] *n* Nebel *der*.

foggy ['fɒgɪ] *adj* neblig.

foghorn ['fɒghɔ:n] *n* Nebelhorn *das*.

fog lamp *n* Nebelscheinwerfer *der*.

foible ['fɔɪbl] *n* Eigenheit *die*.

foil [fɔɪl] ◇ *n (U)* [material] Folie *die* ◇ *vt* [criminal] einen Strich durch die Rechnung machen *(+ D)*; [plot, plan] vereiteln.

fold [fəʊld] ◇ *vt* - **1.** [sheet, blanket, paper] falten; **to ~ one's arms** die Arme verschränken - **2.** [wrap] einwickeln ◇ *vi* - **1.** [bed, chair, bicycle] sich zusammenklappen lassen - **2.** *inf* [business] eingehen ◇ *n* [in material, paper] Falte *die*. ◆ **fold up** ◇ *vt sep* - **1.** [sheet, blanket, paper] zusammen|falten - **2.** [chair, bed, bicycle] zusammen|klappen ◇ *vi* [chair, bed, bicycle] sich zusammen|klappen lassen.

folder ['fəʊldə^r] *n* [for papers] Mappe *die*.

folding ['fəʊldɪŋ] *adj* [chair, table] Klapp-.

foliage ['fəʊlɪɪdʒ] *n (U)* Blätter *pl*.

folk [fəʊk] ◇ *adj* Volks- ◇ *npl* [people] Leute *pl*. ◆ **folks** *npl inf* [relatives]: **my ~s** meine Leute.

folklore ['fəʊklɔ:^r] *n* Folklore *die*.

folk music *n* [popular] Folk *der*; [traditional] Volksmusik *die*.

folk song *n* [popular] Folksong *der*; [traditional] Volkslied *das*.

folksy ['fəʊksɪ] *adj Am inf* gemütlich.

follow ['fɒləʊ] ◇ *vt* - **1.** [gen] folgen *(+ D)*; **a presentation, ~ed by a discussion** ein Vortrag, gefolgt von einer Diskussion - **2.** [pursue] verfolgen - **3.** [advice, instructions] befolgen - **4.** [news, sb's career] verfolgen; [fashion] sich interessieren für ◇ *vi* folgen; **it ~s that …** daraus folgt, dass …; **I don't quite ~** [understand] da komm ich nicht ganz mit. ◆ **follow up** *vt sep* - **1.** [complaint] nachlgehen *(+ D)*; [suggestion] auflgreifen - **2.** [supplement]: **to ~ sthg up with sthg** etw auf etw *(A)* folgen lassen.

follower ['fɒləʊə^r] *n* [disciple, believer] Anhänger *der*, -in *die*.

following ['fɒləʊɪŋ] ◇ *adj* folgend; **the ~ day** am nächsten Tag ◇ *n* [supporters] Anhängerschaft *die* ◇ *prep* [after] nach.

folly ['fɒlɪ] *n* [foolishness] Torheit *die*.

fond [fɒnd] *adj* [affectionate] liebevoll; **to be ~ of sb** jn gerne haben; **to be ~ of sthg/of doing sthg** etw gerne haben/tun.

fondle ['fɒndl] *vt* streicheln.

font [fɒnt] *n* - **1.** [in church] Taufstein *der* - **2.** COMPUT & TYPO Schrift *die*.

food [fu:d] *n* Essen *das*; [for animals] Futter *das*; **health ~s** Reformkost *die*.

food poisoning [-ˌpɔɪznɪŋ] *n* Lebensmittelvergiftung *die*.

food processor [-ˌprəʊsesə^r] *n* Küchenmaschine *die*.

foodstuffs ['fu:dstʌfs] *npl* Nahrungsmittel *pl*.

fool [fu:l] ◇ *n* [idiot] Narr *der* ◇ *vt* täuschen; **to ~ sb into doing sthg** jn durch Tricks dazu bringen, etw zu tun. ◆ **fool about, fool around** *vi* - **1.** [behave foolishly]: **to ~ about (with sthg)** (mit etw) herumlalbern - **2.** [be unfaithful]: **to ~ about (with sb)** (mit jm) eine Affäre haben - **3.** *Am* [tamper]: **to ~ around with sthg** mit etw Blödsinn machen.

foolhardy ['fu:lˌhɑ:dɪ] *adj* tollkühn.

foolish ['fu:lɪʃ] *adj* - **1.** [unwise, silly] töricht - **2.** [laughable, undignified] dumm; **to look ~** albern aussehen; **to feel ~** sich *(D)* albern vorlkommen.

foolproof ['fu:lpru:f] *adj* absolut sicher.

foot [fʊt] *(pl sense 1* feet; *pl sense 2 inv* OR feet) ◇ *n* - **1.** [gen] Fuß *der*; [of sheep, cow] Huf *der*; [of bed] Fußende *das*; [of page] Ende *das*; **to be on one's feet** auf den Beinen sein; **to get to one's feet** auflstehen; **on** OR **by ~** zu Fuß; **to find one's feet** Fuß fassen; **to have/get cold feet** kalte Füße bekommen; **to put one's ~ in it** ins Fettnäpfchen treten; **to put one's feet up** die Beine hochlegen - **2.** [measurement] Fuß *der*, = 30,48 cm ◇ *vt inf*: **to ~ the bill (for sthg)** die Rechnung (für etw) bezahlen.

▱ **feet and inches**

Obwohl seit den 60er Jahren mehrere Anläufe unternommen wurden, metrische Maßeinheiten in der britischen und amerikanischen Industrie zu etablieren, halten die meisten Briten und Amerikaner im täglichen Leben weiter an den gewohnten britischen Maßeinheiten fest. Autofahrer messen den Verbrauch ihrer Fahrzeuge in miles per gallon, Immobilienmakler veräußern Büroräume nach cubic feet, und das eigene Gewicht und die Größe misst man immer noch in stones bzw. feet und inches. Die Umrechnung von britischem zu metrischem Maß ist dabei gar nicht so einfach: 1 Inch entspricht 2,54 cm, 12 Inch ergeben 1 Fuß, 3 Fuß ergeben 1 Yard, und 1760 Yards sind 1 Meile, was 1,61 km entspricht.

foot-and-mouth (disease) *n* Maul- und Klauenseuche *die*.

football ['fʊtbɔ:l] *n* - **1.** *Br* [soccer] Fußball *der* - **2.** *Am* [American football] Football *der*

- 3. [ball - in soccer] Fußball *der;* [- in American football] Ball *der.*

footballer ['fʊtbɔːlə'] *n* Br Fußballspieler *der,* -in *die.*

football player *n* Fußballspieler *der,* -in *die.*

footbridge ['fʊtbrɪdʒ] *n* Fußgängerbrücke *die.*

foothills ['fʊthɪlz] *npl* Gebirgsausläufer *pl.*

foothold ['fʊthəʊld] *n* Halt *der.*

footing ['fʊtɪŋ] *n* **- 1.** [foothold] Halt *der;* **to lose one's ~** den Halt verlieren **- 2.** [basis] Basis *die;* **to be on a war ~** auf einen Krieg vorbereitet sein.

footlights ['fʊtlaɪts] *npl* Rampenlicht *das.*

footnote ['fʊtnəʊt] *n* Fußnote *die.*

footpath ['fʊtpɑːθ, *pl* -pɑːðz] *n* Fußweg *der.*

footprint ['fʊtprɪnt] *n* Fußabdruck *der.*

footstep ['fʊtstep] *n* [sound] Schritt *der.*

footwear ['fʊtweə'] *n* Schuhwerk *das.*

for [fɔː'] <> *prep* **- 1.** [expressing purpose, reason, destination] für; **this is ~ you** dieses Buch ist für dich; **a ticket ~ Manchester** eine Fahrkarte nach Manchester; **~ this reason** aus diesem Grund; **a cure ~ sore throats** ein Mittel gegen Halsschmerzen; **what did you do that ~?** wozu OR warum hast du das getan?; **to jump ~ joy** vor Freude an die Decke springen; **what's it ~?** wofür ist das?; **to go ~ a walk** spazieren gehen; **it's time ~ bed** es ist Zeit schlafen OR ins Bett zu gehen; **'~ sale'** 'zu verkaufen' **- 2.** [during] seit; **I've lived here ~ ten years** ich lebe seit zehn Jahren hier; **we talked ~ hours** wir redeten stundenlang **- 3.** [by, before] für; **be there ~ 8 p.m.** sei um acht Uhr abends da; **I'll do it ~ tomorrow** ich mache es bis morgen; **be there at 7.30 ~ 8 o'clock** versucht um 19.30 Uhr da zu sein, damit wir um 20.00 Uhr anfangen können **- 4.** [on the occasion of]: **I got socks ~ Christmas** ich habe Socken zu Weihnachten bekommen; **what's ~ dinner?** was gibt's zum Abendessen? **- 5.** [on behalf of] für; **to do sthg ~ for sb** etw für jn tun **- 6.** [with time and space] für; **there's no room ~ it** dafür ist kein Platz; **to have time ~ for sthg** für etw Zeit haben **- 7.** [expressing distance]: **we drove ~ miles** wir fuhren meilenweit; **road works ~ 20 miles** Straßenarbeiten auf 20 Meilen **- 8.** [expressing price] für; **I bought it ~ five pounds** ich habe es für fünf Pfund gekauft; **~ free** gratis **- 9.** [expressing meaning]: **what's the German ~ 'boy'?** wie heißt „boy" auf Deutsch?; **P ~ Peter** P wie Peter **- 10.** [with regard to] für; **it's warm ~ November** es ist warm für November; **it's too far ~ him to walk** zum Gehen ist es für ihn zu weit; **to feel sorry ~ sb** jn bemitleiden; **to be glad ~ sb** sich für jn freuen **- 11.** [in favour of] für; **is she ~ or against it?** ist sie dafür oder dagegen?; **to vote ~ sthg** für etw stimmen; **I'm all ~ doing it** ich bin sehr dafür, dass wir das tun **- 12.** [in ratios] für; **~ every person who passes the test there are five who fail** auf jede Person, die die Prüfung besteht, kommen fünf, die durchfallen **- 13.** *phr:* **you'll be ~ it when ...** du kannst dich auf etwas gefasst machen, wenn ... <> *conj literary* denn. **◆ for all** <> *prep* **- 1.** [in spite of] trotz; **~ all that** trotzdem **- 2.** [considering how little]: **~ all the good it's done me** so wenig, wie es mir genützt hat <> *conj:* **~ all I care** meinetwegen; **~ all I know** so viel ich weiß.

forage ['fɒrɪdʒ] *vi* [search] herumlstöbern; **to ~ for sthg** nach etw stöbern.

foray ['fɒreɪ] *n* (Raub)überfall *der.*

forbad [fə'bæd], **forbade** [fə'beɪd] *pt* ⊳ forbid.

forbid [fə'bɪd] (*pt* -bade OR -bad; *pp* forbid OR -bidden) *vt* verbieten; **to ~ sb to do sthg** jm verbieten, etw zu tun.

forbidden [fə'bɪdn] <> *pp* ⊳ forbid <> *adj* [activity] verboten; **~ subject** Tabuthema *das.*

forbidding [fə'bɪdɪŋ] *adj* [person] abweisend; [landscape] unwirtlich.

force [fɔːs] <> *n* **- 1.** [strength, magnitude] Stärke *die;* [of explosion, blow] Wucht *die;* **a ~ ten gale** ein Sturm mit Windstärke zehn **- 2.** [violence] Gewalt *die;* **by ~** mit Gewalt **- 3.** PHYSICS Kraft *die* **- 4.** [powerful person, influence] Macht *die* **- 5.** [effect]: **to be in/come into ~** in Kraft sein/treten <> *vt* **- 1.** [compel] zwingen; **to ~ sb to do sthg** jn zwingen, etw zu tun; **to ~ sthg on sb** jm etw aufzwingen **- 2.** [lock, door] aufbrechen **- 3.** [push] pressen. **◆ forces** *npl:* **the ~s** die Streitkräfte *pl;* **to join ~s (with sb)** (mit jm) sich zusammenltun.

force-feed *vt* zwangsernähren.

forceful ['fɔːsfʊl] *adj* [person] energisch; [words] eindringlich; [speech] überzeugend.

forceps ['fɔːseps] *npl* Zange *die.*

forcibly ['fɔːsəblɪ] *adv* [seize, enter, remove] gewaltsam.

ford [fɔːd] *n* Furt *die.*

fore [fɔː'] <> *adj* NAUT vordere, -r, -s; **~ deck** Vordeck *das* <> *n:* **to come to the ~** *fig* [become well-known] bekannt werden; [become important] bedeutend werden.

forearm ['fɔːrɑːm] *n* Unterarm *der.*

foreboding [fɔː'bəʊdɪŋ] *n* Vorahnung *die.*

forecast ['fɔːkɑːst] (*pt & pp* forecast OR -ed) <> *n* Prognose *die;* **(weather) forecast** (Wetter)vorhersage *die* <> *vt* vorhersagen.

foreclose [fɔː'kləʊz] *vt & vi:* **to ~ (on) a mortgage** eine (durch eine Hypothek gesicherte) Schuldforderung geltend machen.

forecourt ['fɔːkɔːt] *n* Vorhof *der.*

forefront ['fɔːfrʌnt] *n:* **to be in OR at the**

~ of sthg [campaign, movement] an der Spitze einer Sache *(G)* stehen.

forego [fɔːˈgəʊ] *vt* = forgo.

foregone conclusion [ˈfɔːgɒn-] *n*: **it's a ~** es stand von vornherein fest.

foreground [ˈfɔːgraʊnd] *n* Vordergrund *der.*

forehand [ˈfɔːhænd] *n* Vorhand *die.*

forehead [ˈfɔːhed] *n* Stirn *die.*

foreign [ˈfɒrən] *adj* [gen] ausländisch; [correspondent, debt] Auslands-; [policy] Außen-; **~ person** Ausländer *der*, -in *die*; **~ holiday** Urlaub *der* im Ausland; **~ country** fremdes Land; **~ countries** das Ausland.

foreign affairs *npl* Außenpolitik *die.*

foreign currency *n* (U) Devisen *pl.*

foreigner [ˈfɒrənəʳ] *n* Ausländer *der*, -in *die.*

foreign language *n* Fremdsprache *die.*

foreign minister *n* Außenminister *der*, -in *die.*

Foreign Office *n* Br: **the ~** das Außenministerium.

Foreign Secretary *n* Br Außenminister *der*, -in *die.*

foreman [ˈfɔːmən] *(pl* -men [-mən]) *n* - **1.** [of workers] Vorarbeiter *der* - **2.** [of jury] Obmann *der*, -männin *die.*

foremost [ˈfɔːməʊst] <> *adj* führend <> *adv:* **first and ~** vor allem.

forensic [fəˈrensɪk] *adj* [examination] gerichtsmedizinisch.

forerunner [ˈfɔːˌrʌnəʳ] *n* [precursor] Vorläufer *der*, -in *die.*

foresee [fɔːˈsiː] *(pt* -saw [-ˈsɔː], *pp* -seen) *vt* vorhersehen, voraussehen.

foreseeable [fɔːˈsiːəbl] *adj* vorhersehbar; **for the ~ future** in absehbarer Zeit.

foreseen [fɔːˈsiːn] *pp* ▷ foresee.

foreshadow [fɔːˈʃædəʊ] *vt* ahnen lassen.

foresight [ˈfɔːsaɪt] *n* (U) Weitsicht *die.*

forest [ˈfɒrɪst] *n* Wald *der.*

forestall [fɔːˈstɔːl] *vt* zuvorkommen (+ D).

forestry [ˈfɒrɪstrɪ] *n* Forstwirtschaft *die*; [science] Forstwissenschaft *die.*

foretaste [ˈfɔːteɪst] *n* Vorgeschmack *der.*

foretell [fɔːˈtel] *(pt & pp* -told) *vt* vorhersagen.

foretold [fɔːˈtəʊld] *pt & pp* ▷ foretell.

forever [fəˈrevəʳ] *adv* [eternally] ewig; [disappear, exile] für immer.

forewarn [fɔːˈwɔːn] *vt* vorwarnen.

foreword [ˈfɔːwɜːd] *n* Vorwort *das.*

forfeit [ˈfɔːfɪt] <> *n* Strafe *die* <> *vt* [deposit, chance] einbüßen; [right] verwirken.

forgave [fəˈgeɪv] *pt* ▷ forgive.

forge [fɔːdʒ] <> *n* [place] Schmiede *die* <> *vt* - **1.** [metal] schmieden - **2.** [friendship, alliance] schließen; [relationship] knüpfen

- **3.** [signature, passport, banknotes] fälschen.
◆ **forge ahead** *vi* voran|kommen.

forger [ˈfɔːdʒəʳ] *n* Fälscher *der*, -in *die.*

forgery [ˈfɔːdʒərɪ] *n* Fälschung *die.*

forget [fəˈget] *(pt* -got; *pp* -gotten) <> *vt* vergessen; **to ~ to do sthg** vergessen, etw zu tun; **to ~ how to dance** das Tanzen verlernen; **~ it!** vergiss es! <> *vi* es vergessen; **to ~ about sthg** etw vergessen.

forgetful [fəˈgetfʊl] *adj* vergesslich.

forgive [fəˈgɪv] *(pt* -gave, *pp* -given [-ˈgɪvən]) *vt* [person] verzeihen (+ D); [sins] vergeben; **to ~ sb for sthg** jm etw verzeihen.

forgiveness [fəˈgɪvnɪs] *n* Verzeihung *die.*

forgo [fɔːˈgəʊ] *(pt* -went, *pp* -gone [-ˈgɒn]) *vt* verzichten auf (+ A).

forgot [fəˈgɒt] *pt* ▷ forget.

forgotten [fəˈgɒtn] *pp* ▷ forget.

fork [fɔːk] <> *n* - **1.** [for food, gardening] Gabel *die* - **2.** [in road, path, river] Gabelung *die* <> *vi* [road, river] sich gabeln; **to ~ left/right** [driver] links/rechts abbiegen.
◆ **fork out** *inf* <> *vt fus* blechen <> *vi:* **to ~ out (for sthg)** (für etw) blechen.

forklift truck [ˈfɔːklɪft-] *n* Gabelstapler *der.*

forlorn [fəˈlɔːn] *adj* - **1.** [expression] betrübt; [cry] verzweifelt - **2.** [desolate - person] einsam und unglücklich; [- place] trostlos - **3.** [hope] schwach; [attempt] verzweifelt.

form [fɔːm] <> *n* - **1.** [shape, type] Form *die*; [shape of person] Gestalt *die*; **in the ~ of** in Form von - **2.** [health & SPORT] Form *die*; **on ~** *Br*, **in ~** *Am* in Form; **off ~** nicht in Form; **according to ~, true to ~** wie erwartet - **3.** [piece of paper] Formular *das*; [application form] Bewerbungsbogen *der* - **4.** Br SCH [class] Klasse *die* - **5.** [etiquette]: **it is bad ~ to arrive late** es ist schlechtes Benehmen, zu spät zu kommen; **for ~'s sake** der Form halber <> *vt* - **1.** [plan] entwerfen; [friendship] schließen; [character] formen; **to ~ an idea of sthg** sich (D) eine Vorstellung von etw machen - **2.** [circle, sentence, plural, government] bilden - **3.** [constitute] sein; **to ~ part of sthg** ein Teil von etw sein <> *vi* sich bilden.

formal [ˈfɔːml] *adj* - **1.** [language] formell; [person] förmlich - **2.** [event] feierlich; **~ clothes** Gesellschaftskleidung *die* - **3.** [offer, decision] offiziell; **~ education** Ausbildung *die* in einer Institution.

formality [fɔːˈmælətɪ] *n* - **1.** (U) [correctness] Förmlichkeit *die* - **2.** [convention] Formalität *die.*

format [ˈfɔːmæt] <> *n* - **1.** [size & COMPUT] Format *das* <> **2.** [structure, arrangement] Struktur *die* <> *vt* COMPUT formatieren.

formation [fɔːˈmeɪʃn] *n* - **1.** (U) [of company] Gründung *die*; [of government] Bildung *die* - **2.** [arrangement] Formation *die.*

formative ['fɔːmətɪv] *adj* prägend; **~ years** entscheidende Jahre.

former ['fɔːməʳ] ⬦ *adj* - 1. [previous] früher, ehemalig; **in ~ times** früher - 2. [first] erstere, -r, -s ⬦ *n*: **the ~** der/die/das Erstere.

formerly ['fɔːməlɪ] *adv* früher.

formidable ['fɔːmɪdəbl] *adj* Respekt einflößend; [task] gewaltig.

formula ['fɔːmjʊlə] *(pl* -as OR -ae [-iː]) *n* [gen] Formel *die.*

formulate ['fɔːmjʊleɪt] *vt* - 1. [express] formulieren - 2. [plan] ausarbeiten.

forsake [fə'seɪk] *(pt* -sook; *pp* -saken) *vt literary* [person] verlassen; [habit] aufgeben.

forsook [fə'sʊk] *pt* ➣ forsake.

fort [fɔːt] *n* Fort *das.*

forth [fɔːθ] *adv literary* [outwards, onwards]: **to go/send ~** fortlgehen/-schicken; **to bring ~** hervorlbringen.

forthcoming [ˌfɔːθ'kʌmɪŋ] *adj* - 1. [future - election, events] bevorstehend; [- book] in Kürze erscheinend - 2. [willing to talk] mitteilsam.

forthright ['fɔːθraɪt] *adj* [person, manner] direkt; [opinions] unbümt.

forthwith [ˌfɔːθ'wɪθ] *adv fml* unverzüglich.

fortified wine ['fɔːtɪfaɪd-] *n* mit zusätzlichem Alkohol angereicherter Wein.

fortify ['fɔːtɪfaɪ] *vt* - 1. [place] befestigen - 2. *fig* [person, resolve] bestärken.

fortnight ['fɔːtnaɪt] *n* vierzehn Tage *pl.*

fortnightly ['fɔːtˌnaɪtlɪ] ⬦ *adj* [visit, meeting] alle zwei Wochen stattfindend; [magazine] alle zwei Wochen erscheinend ⬦ *adv* alle vierzehn Tage, alle zwei Wochen.

fortress ['fɔːtrɪs] *n* Festung *die.*

fortunate ['fɔːtjʊnət] *adj* glücklich; **to be ~** Glück haben; **it's ~ that ...** es ist ein Glück, dass ...

fortunately ['fɔːtʃnətlɪ] *adv* zum Glück.

fortune ['fɔːtʃuːn] *n* - 1. [money] Vermögen *das;* **it costs a ~** *inf* es kostet ein Vermögen - 2. [luck] Glück *das* - 3. [fate] Schicksal *das* - 4. [future]: **to tell sb's ~** jm die Zukunft voraussagen.

fortune-teller [-ˌteləʳ] *n* Wahrsager *der,* -in *die.*

forty ['fɔːtɪ] *num* vierzig; *see also* sixty.

forward ['fɔːwəd] ⬦ *adj* - 1. [movement] vorwärts- - 2. [planning] Voraus-; **we're no further ~ now than we were last year** wir sind jetzt nicht weiter als letztes Jahr - 3. [impudent] dreist ⬦ *adv* - 1. [in space - go, move] vorwärts; [- look, lean] nach vorn; [- fall] vornüber - 2. [in time]: **to bring a meeting ~** ein Treffen vorlverlegen; **from this time ~** [now] von jetzt an; [then] seitdem; **to put a clock ~** eine Uhr vorlstellen ⬦ *n* SPORT Stürmer *der,* -in *die* ⬦ *vt* [letter,

parcel] nachlsenden; **'please ~'** 'bitte nachsenden'.

forwarding address ['fɔːwədɪŋ-] *n* Nachsendeadresse *die.*

forwards ['fɔːwədz] *adv* = forward.

forwent [fɔː'went] *pt* ➣ forgo.

fossil ['fɒsl] *n* Fossil *das.*

foster ['fɒstəʳ] ⬦ *adj* [family, mother] Pflege- ⬦ *vt* - 1. [child] in Pflege nehmen - 2. [idea, hope] hegen; [relations] fördern.

foster child *n* Pflegekind *das.*

foster parents *npl* Pflegeeltern *pl.*

fought [fɔːt] *pt* & *pp* ➣ fight.

foul [faʊl] ⬦ *adj* - 1. [water] faulig; [air] verpestet; [food] verdorben; [smell, taste] übel - 2. [very unpleasant] schrecklich; **she's in a ~ mood today** sie ist heute in sehr schlechter Stimmung - 3. [language] unflätig ⬦ *n* SPORT Foul *das* ⬦ *vt* - 1. [make dirty] verunreinigen - 2. SPORT foulen.

found [faʊnd] ⬦ *pt* & *pp* ➣ find ⬦ *vt* - 1. [organization, town] gründen; [hospital, school] errichten - 2. [base]: **to be ~ed on sthg** auf etw *(D)* basieren.

foundation [faʊn'deɪʃn] *n* - 1. [basis] Grundlage *die;* **without ~** unbegründet - 2. [organization] Stiftung *die* - 3. [cosmetic]: **~ (cream)** Grundierungscreme *die.* ➣ **foundations** *npl* CONSTR Fundament *das.*

founder ['faʊndəʳ] ⬦ *n* [person] Gründer *der,* -in *die* ⬦ *vi* [sink] sinken.

foundry ['faʊndrɪ] *n* Gießerei *die.*

fountain ['faʊntɪn] *n* [man-made] Springbrunnen *der.*

fountain pen *n* Füllfederhalter *der.*

four [fɔːʳ] *num* vier; **on all ~s** auf allen vieren; *see also* six.

four-letter word *n* Vulgärausdruck *der.*

four-poster (bed) *n* Himmelbett *das.*

foursome ['fɔːsəm] *n* Quartett *das.*

fourteen [ˌfɔː'tiːn] *num* vierzehn; *see also* six.

fourth [fɔːθ] *num* vierte, -r, -s; *see also* sixth.

Fourth of July *n*: **the ~** der vierte Juli, Nationalfeiertag *(Unabhängigkeitstag)* in den USA.

four-wheel drive *n* - 1. [vehicle] Fahrzeug *das* mit Allradantrieb - 2. [system] Allradantrieb *der.*

fowl [faʊl] *(pl inv* OR -s) *n* [chicken] Huhn *das;* [turkey] Truthahn *der.*

fox [fɒks] ⬦ *n* Fuchs *der* ⬦ *vt* - 1. [outwit] täuschen - 2. [baffle] vor ein Rätsel stellen.

foxcub ['fɒkskʌb] *n* Fuchswelpe *der.*

foyer ['fɔɪeɪ] *n* - 1. [of hotel, theatre] Foyer *das* - 2. *Am* [of house] Diele *die.*

fracas ['frækɑː, *Am* 'freɪkəs] *(Br pl inv, Am pl* fracases) *n* Tumult *das.*

fraction ['frækʃn] n **- 1.** MATH Bruch der **- 2.** [small part] Bruchteil der.

fraction

Das englische Wort fraction bietet sich nicht als Übersetzung für „Fraktion" an, denn es bedeutet seinem lateinischen Ursprung getreu „Bruchteil". It was all over in a fraction of a second heißt also „Im Bruchteil einer Sekunde war alles vorbei".
Der deutsche Begriff Fraktion kann am ehesten mit „parliamentary party" übersetzt werden. Der Fraktionsvorsitzende der Grünen wäre dann im Englischen „the leader of the parliamentary Green Party".

fractionally ['frækʃnəlɪ] adv geringfügig.
fracture ['fræktʃər] ◇ n Bruch der ◇ vt brechen; **to ~ one's arm** sich (D) den Arm brechen.
fragile ['frædʒaɪl] adj zerbrechlich; [health] anfällig.
fragment ['frægmənt] n **- 1.** [of china, glass] Scherbe die **- 2.** [of text] Fragment das; [of conversation] Fetzen der.
fragrance ['freɪɡrəns] n Duft der.
fragrant ['freɪɡrənt] adj duftend.
frail [freɪl] adj **- 1.** [person, health] zart **- 2.** [structure] brüchig.
frame [freɪm] ◇ n **- 1.** [gen] Rahmen der; [of glasses, bed] Gestell das; [of house, boat] Gerippe das **- 2.** [physique] Körper der **- 3.** phr: **~ of mind** Gemütsverfassung die ◇ vt **- 1.** [painting, photograph] rahmen **- 2.** fig [surround] umrahmen **- 3.** [thoughts, answer] formulieren **- 4.** inf [falsely incriminate]: **to ~ sb** jm eine Sache anhängen.
framework ['freɪmwɜːk] n **- 1.** [of boat, house] Gerippe das **- 2.** [of society, democracy] (Grund)struktur die; [of essay] Gliederung die; **within the ~ of** im Rahmen (+ G).
France [frɑːns] n Frankreich nt.
franchise ['fræntʃaɪz] n **- 1.** POL Wahlrecht das **- 2.** COMM Lizenz die.
frank [fræŋk] ◇ adj offen; **to be ~, ...** offen gestanden, ... ◇ vt [letter] (freil)stempeln.
frankly ['fræŋklɪ] adv **- 1.** [talk] offen **- 2.** [to be honest] offen gestanden.
frantic ['fræntɪk] adj **- 1.** [person] außer sich **- 2.** [activity, day, pace] hektisch.
fraternity [frə'tɜːnətɪ] n **- 1.** [community]: **the medical/banking ~** die Mediziner/ Bankfachleute **- 2.** Am [of students] Studentenverbindung die.
fraternize, -ise ['frætənaɪz] vi: **to ~ (with sb)** sich (mit jm) verbrüdern; **to ~ with the enemy** mit dem Feind fraternisieren.
fraud [frɔːd] n **- 1.** (U) [crime] Betrug der **- 2.** [deceitful act] Schwindel der **- 3.** pej [impostor] Betrüger der, -in die.
fraught [frɔːt] adj **- 1.** [full]: **~ with danger** gefährlich; **~ with problems** voller Probleme **- 2.** Br [frantic - person] gestresst.
fray [freɪ] ◇ vi [clothing, fabric] ausfransen; [rope] sich durchscheuern ◇ n literary: **to join in the ~** sich in den Kampf/ Streit einlmischen.
frayed [freɪd] adj **- 1.** [clothing, fabric] ausgefranst; [rope] durchgescheuert **- 2.** fig [nerves] strapaziert; **tempers were ~** Gemüter waren erhitzt.
freak [friːk] ◇ adj außergewöhnlich ◇ n **- 1.** [strange creature - in appearance] Missgeburt die; [- in behaviour] Irre der, die **- 2.** [unusual event] außergewöhnliche Begebenheit **- 3.** inf [fanatic]: **a fitness ~** ein Fitnessfanatiker; **a computer ~** ein Computerfreak. ◆ **freak out** inf vi **- 1.** [get angry] ausl-flippen **- 2.** [panic] durchldrehen.
freckle ['frekl] n Sommersprosse die.
free [friː] (compar freer; superl freest; pt & pp freed) ◇ adj **- 1.** [gen] frei; **~ period** SCH Freistunde die; **she is ~ to leave** es steht ihr frei, zu gehen; **feel ~ to disagree** sie sind nicht gezwungen, zuzustimmen; **feel ~!** nur zu!; **to set sb/an animal ~** jn/ein Tier freillassen; **if you have a ~ moment** wenn Sie einen Moment Zeit haben **- 2.** [costing nothing] kostenlos; **'admission ~'** 'Eintritt frei'; **~ of charge** umsonst ◇ adv **- 1.** [without payment] kostenlos; **for ~** umsonst **- 2.** [without restraint]: **to cut ~** los/schneiden; [from wrecked vehicle] befreien; **to work ~** sich lockern ◇ vt **- 1.** [prisoner, animal] freillassen; [country, city] befreien **- 2.** [make available] zur Verfügung stellen **- 3.** [extricate - person] befreien; [- object] herauslkriegen.
freedom ['friːdəm] n Freiheit die; **~ of speech** Redefreiheit die.
freefone ['friːfəʊn] adj Br: **a ~ number** eine gebührenfreie Telefonnummer.
free-for-all n **- 1.** [brawl] allgemeine Schlägerei **- 2.** [argument] allgemeine lautstarke Auseinandersetzung.
free gift n Gratisgabe die.
freehand ['friːhænd] ◇ adj [drawing] Freihand- ◇ adv aus der Hand.
free house n Wirtshaus, das keiner bestimmten Brauerei gehört und daher Bier verschiedener Marken ausschenken darf.
free kick n Freistoß der.
freelance ['friːlɑːns] ◇ adj [work] freiberuflich; [translator, journalist] freiberuflich tätig ◇ n Freiberufler der, -in die.
freely ['friːlɪ] adv **- 1.** [available, move] frei; [admit, talk] offen; [travel] ungehindert **- 2.** [generously] großzügig.
Freemason ['friː,meɪsn] n Freimaurer der.
freepost ['friːpəʊst] adv [send] portofrei.

free-range adj Br [eggs] von frei laufenden Hühnern; [hens] frei laufend.

freestyle ['fri:staɪl] n [in swimming] Freistil der.

free time n Freizeit die.

free trade n Freihandel der.

freeware ['fri:weəʳ] n COMPUT Freeware die.

freeway ['fri:weɪ] n Am Autobahn die.

freewheel [ˌfri:'wi:l] vi [cyclist] (mit dem Fahrrad) rollen; [motorist] im Leerlauf fahren.

free will n freier Wille; **to do sthg of one's own ~** etw aus freien Stücken tun.

freeze [fri:z] (pt froze; pp frozen) <> vt einlfrieren; [pond, river] zufrieren lassen; [lock, pipes] einfrieren lassen <> vi - 1. [pond, river] zulfrieren; [pipes] einlfrieren - 2. METEOR frieren - 3. [stop moving] in der Bewegung erlstarren; **freeze!** keine Bewegung! <> n - 1. [cold weather] Frost der - 2.: **wage/price ~** Lohn-/Preisstopp der.

freezer ['fri:zəʳ] n [upright] Tiefkühlschrank der; [chest] Tiefkühltruhe die; [part of fridge] Gefrierfach das.

freezing ['fri:zɪŋ] <> adj eiskalt; **I'm ~** mir ist eiskalt <> n inf: **above/below ~** über/unter dem Gefrierpunkt.

freezing point n Gefrierpunkt der.

freight [freɪt] n [goods] Fracht die.

freight train n Güterzug der.

French [frentʃ] <> adj französisch <> n [language] Französisch(e) das <> npl: **the ~** die Franzosen pl.

French bean n grüne Bohne.

French doors npl = French windows.

French dressing n - 1. [in UK] Vinaigrette die - 2. [in US] Salatsoße mit Majonäse und Ketschup.

French fries npl esp Am Pommes frites pl.

Frenchman ['frentʃmən] (pl -men [-mən]) n Franzose der.

French stick n Br Baguette das.

French windows npl große zweiflügelige Glastür.

Frenchwoman ['frentʃˌwʊmən] (pl -women [-ˌwɪmɪn]) n Französin die.

frenetic [frə'netɪk] adj [activity] hektisch; [pace] rasend.

frenzy ['frenzɪ] n: **in a ~** hektisch.

frequency ['fri:kwənsɪ] n - 1. [rate] Häufigkeit die - 2. [radio wave] Frequenz die.

frequent [adj 'fri:kwənt, vb frɪ'kwent] <> adj häufig; **she is a ~ visitor** sie kommt häufig zu Besuch <> vt häufig besuchen.

frequently [frɪ'kwentlɪ] adv häufig.

fresh [freʃ] adj - 1. [gen] frisch; [information] neu; **~ water** Süßwasser das - 2. [new] neu; **to make a ~ pot of tea** noch einmal eine Kanne Tee machen; **to give sthg a ~ coat of**

paint etw neu streichen - 3. [refreshing] erfrischend; **to get some ~ air** an die frische Luft gehen - 4. [original] originell.

freshen ['freʃn] vi [wind] auflfrischen.
◆ **freshen up** vi [person] sich frisch machen.

fresher ['freʃəʳ] n Br inf Erstsemester das.

freshly ['freʃlɪ] adv frisch.

freshman ['freʃmən] (pl -men [-mən]) n Erstsemester das.

freshness ['freʃnɪs] n - 1. [of food, air, taste] Frische die - 2. [originality] Originalität die.

freshwater ['freʃˌwɔ:təʳ] adj Süßwasser-.

fret [fret] vi [worry] sich (D) Sorgen machen.

friction ['frɪkʃn] n (U) - 1. [force] Reibung die - 2. [rubbing] Reiben das - 3. [conflict] Reibereien pl.

Friday ['fraɪdɪ] n Freitag der; see also Saturday.

fridge [frɪdʒ] n esp Br Kühlschrank der.

fridge-freezer n Br Kühlgefrierkombination die.

fried [fraɪd] <> pt & pp > fry <> adj gebraten; **~ egg** Spiegelei das.

friend [frend] n [gen] Freund der, -in die; **to be ~s (with sb)** (mit jm) befreundet sein; **to make ~s (with sb)** sich (mit jm) anlfreunden.

friendly ['frendlɪ] adj freundlich; [country] befreundet; **to be ~ with sb** mit jm befreundet sein.

friendship ['frendʃɪp] n Freundschaft die.

fries [fraɪz] npl = French fries.

frieze [fri:z] n ARCHIT Fries der; [on wallpaper] Bordüre die.

fright [fraɪt] n - 1. (U) [fear] Angst die; **to take ~** es mit der Angst zu tun bekommen - 2. [shock] Schreck der; **to give sb a ~** jn erlschrecken, jm einen Schreck einljagen.

frighten ['fraɪtn] vt Angst machen (+ D).

frightened ['fraɪtnd] adj [person] verängstigt; [voice, expression] angsterfüllt; **to be ~ (of)** Angst haben (vor (+ D)).

frightening ['fraɪtnɪŋ] adj beängstigend.

frightful ['fraɪtfʊl] adj schrecklich.

frigid ['frɪdʒɪd] adj [sexually] frigide.

frill [frɪl] n - 1. [on clothes] Rüsche die - 2. inf [extra]: **with no ~s** ohne Extras.

fringe [frɪndʒ] n - 1. [on clothes, curtain] Fransen pl - 2. Br [of hair] Pony der - 3. [edge] Rand der.

frisk [frɪsk] vt [search] durchsuchen.

frisky ['frɪskɪ] adj inf quicklebendig.

fritter ['frɪtəʳ] n CULIN in Pfannkuchenteig getauchtes und gebratenes Obst-, Gemüse- oder Fleischstück. ◆ **fritter away** vt sep vergeuden.

frivolous ['frɪvələs] adj frivol.

frizzy ['frɪzɪ] adj kraus.

fro [frəʊ] > to.

frock [frɒk] *n dated* Kleid *das*.

frog [frɒg] *n* [animal] Frosch *der;* **to have a ~ in one's throat** einen Frosch im Hals haben.

frolic ['frɒlɪk] (*pt & pp* -ked; *cont* -king) *vi* herumltollen.

from [*weak form* frəm, *strong form* frɒm] *prep* - 1. [expressing origin, source] von; **where did you get that ~?** woher hast du das?; **I'm ~ England** ich bin aus England; **I bought it ~ a supermarket** ich habe es in einem Supermarkt gekauft; **the train ~ Manchester** der Zug aus Manchester; **we moved ~ Boston to Denver** wir sind von Boston nach Denver umgezogen - 2. [expressing removal, deduction] von; **away ~ home** weg von zu Hause; **to take sthg away ~ sb** jm etw weglnehmen; **take 5 (away) ~ 9** ziehe 5 von 9 ab; **he took a notebook ~ his pocket** er nahm ein Notizbuch aus der Tasche; **to drink ~ a cup** aus einer Tasse trinken - 3. [expressing distance] von; **five miles ~ London** fünf Meilen von London entfernt; **it's not far ~ here** es ist nicht weit von hier - 4. [expressing position] von; **~ here you can see the valley** von hier aus kann man das Tal sehen - 5. [expressing starting time] von ... an; **open ~ nine to five** von neun bis fünf geöffnet; **~ next year** ab nächstem Jahr; **~ now on** von nun an - 6. [expressing change] von; **the price has gone up ~ one to two pounds** der Preis ist von einem Pfund auf zwei Pfund gestiegen - 7. [expressing range]: **tickets cost ~ $10** Karten gibt es ab 10 Dollar; **it could take ~ two to six months** es könnte zwischen zwei und sechs Monaten dauern - 8. [as a result of] von; **I'm tired ~ walking** ich bin vom Gehen müde; **to suffer ~ asthma** an Asthma leiden - 9. [expressing protection] vor (+ *D*); **sheltered ~ the wind** windgeschützt - 10. [in comparisons]: **different ~** anders als; **to distinguish good ~ bad** gut und böse auseinander halten - 11. [indicating material]: **made ~ wood/plastic** aus Holz/Kunststoff (gemacht) - 12. [on the evidence of]: **to speak ~ experience** aus Erfahrung sprechen; **what I can see** so wie ich es verstehe; **to judge ~ appearances** nach dem Äußeren urteilen.

front [frʌnt] ◇ *n* - 1. [most forward part] Vorderseite *die;* [of house] Vorderfront *die;* **at the ~** vorne; **at the ~ of the train** vorne im Zug; **on the ~ of her dress** vorn auf ihrem Kleid; **to lie on one's ~** auf dem Bauch liegen - 2. MIL & METEOR Front *die* - 3. [by the sea] (Strand)promenade *die* - 4. [outward appearance]: **it's all a ~** es ist alles nur Fassade ◇ *adj* Vorder-, vordere, -r, -s; [row, page] erste, -r, -s; **~ garden** Vorgarten *der.* ◆ **in front** *adv* vorne; **the people in ~** die vorne sitzenden/stehenden Leute. ◆ **in front of** *prep* vor (+ *D*).

frontbench [ˌfrʌnt'bentʃ] *n* POL führende Mitglieder der Regierung oder der Opposition.

front door *n* [of house] Haustür *die.*

frontier ['frʌn.tɪəʳ, *Am* frʌn'tɪər] *n lit & fig* Grenze *die.*

front room *n* Wohnzimmer *das.*

front-runner *n* SPORT Läufer *der,* -in *die* an der Spitze; *fig* Spitzenkandidat *der,* -in *die.*

frost [frɒst] *n* - 1. (*U*) [layer of ice] Frost *der,* Reif *der* - 2. [weather] Frost *der.*

frostbite ['frɒstbaɪt] *n* (*U*) Erfrierungen *pl.*

frosted ['frɒstɪd] *adj* - 1. [opaque]: **~ glass** Milchglas *das* - 2. *Am* CULIN mit Zuckerguss überzogen.

frosting ['frɒstɪŋ] *n Am* CULIN Zuckerguss *der.*

frosty ['frɒstɪ] *adj* - 1. *lit & fig* [cold] frostig - 2. [field] bereift; [ground] gefroren.

froth [frɒθ] *n* Schaum *der.*

frown [fraʊn] *vi* die Stirn runzeln. ◆ **frown (up)on** *vt fus* missbilligen.

froze [frəʊz] *pt* ▷ freeze.

frozen [frəʊzn] ◇ *pp* ▷ freeze ◇ *adj* - 1. [ground] gefroren; [pipes] eingefroren; [lake] zugefroren - 2. [food] tiefgefroren - 3. [very cold] eiskalt; **I'm ~** mir ist eiskalt.

frugal ['fruːgl] *adj* - 1. [meal] einfach - 2. [person] sparsam.

fruit [fruːt] (*pl inv* OR -s) *n* - 1. [food] Obst *das;* [variety of fruit] Frucht *die* - 2. *fig* [result] Frucht *die.*

fruitcake ['fruːtkeɪk] *n* Kuchen mit Trockenfrüchten.

fruiterer ['fruːtərəʳ] *n Br* Obsthändler *der,* -in *die.*

fruitful ['fruːtfʊl] *adj* fruchtbar.

fruition [fruː'ɪʃn] *n:* **to come to ~** [plans] Wirklichkeit werden.

fruit juice *n* Fruchtsaft *der.*

fruitless ['fruːtlɪs] *adj* fruchtlos.

fruit machine *n Br* Spielautomat *der.*

fruit salad *n* Obstsalat *der.*

frumpy ['frʌmpɪ] *adj inf* [clothes] unmodisch; [person] unmodisch gekleidet.

frustrate [frʌ'streɪt] *vt* - 1. [person] frustrieren - 2. [plan, attempt] vereiteln.

frustrated [frʌ'streɪtɪd] *adj* - 1. [person] frustriert - 2. [poet, artist] gescheitert.

frustration [frʌ'streɪʃn] *n* Frustration *die.*

fry [fraɪ] ◇ *vt* [food] braten; **~ to an egg** ein Spiegelei machen ◇ *vi* [food] braten.

frying pan ['fraɪŋ-] *n* Bratpfanne *die.*

ft. (*abbr of* foot) ft.

fuck [fʌk] *vt & vi vulg* ficken. ◆ **fuck off** *excl vulg* verpiss dich!

fudge [fʌdʒ] *n* (*U*) [sweet] weiches Bonbon aus Milch, Zucker und Butter.

fuel [fjʊəl] ◇ *n* [for fire] Brennmaterial *das;* [for aircraft, ship] Treibstoff *der;* [for vehicle]

Benzin *das* ◇ *vt* [argument, violence] anlheizen.

fuel tank *n* Benzintank *der*.

fugitive ['fjuːdʒətɪv] *n*: **to be a ~ from justice** vor der Justiz auf der Flucht sein.

fulfil, fulfill *Am* [fʊl'fɪl] *vt* - **1.** [carry out - duty] erfüllen; [- promise] halten; [- role] ausfüllen - **2.** [satisfy - need] befriedigen; [- requirement] entsprechen *(+ D)*; [- hope, ambition] erfüllen.

fulfilment, fulfillment *Am* [fʊl'fɪlmənt] *n (U)* - **1.** [satisfaction] Befriedigung *die* - **2.** [carrying through - of ambition, dream] Erfüllung *die*; [- of need] Befriedigung *die*.

full [fʊl] ◇ *adj* - **1.** [filled] voll; **I'm ~ (up)** [after meal] ich bin satt; **the bus is ~** der Bus ist voll besetzt; **the room was ~ of furniture** das Zimmer war voll mit Möbeln; **his pockets were ~ of sweets** er hatte die Taschen voller Süßigkeiten - **2.** [complete - day, amount] ganz; [- details] genau; [- report] ausführlich - **3.** [plump - face] voll; [- figure] mollig - **4.** [skirt, sleeve] weit - **5.** [flavour] voll ◇ *adv* [very]: **he knows ~ well that ...** er weiß ganz genau, dass ... ◇ *n*: **in ~** vollständig.

full-blown [-'bləʊn] *adj* [heart attack] groß; [war] richtig; **~ Aids** Vollbild-Aids *das*.

full board *n (U)* Vollpension *die*.

full-fledged *adj Am* = fully-fledged.

full moon *n* Vollmond *der*.

full-scale *adj* - **1.** [life-size] in Originalgröße - **2.** [thorough - inquiry] umfassend; [- war] total.

full stop *n* Punkt *der*.

full time *n Br* SPORT Spielende *das*. ◆ **full-time** ◇ *adj* [job, employment] Ganztags-; [worker] Vollzeit- ◇ *adv* ganztags.

full up *adj* - **1.** [after meal] satt - **2.** [bus, train] voll.

fully ['fʊlɪ] *adv* - **1.** [completely] vollkommen; **~ trained/automatic** vollausgebildet/automatisch - **2.** [in detail - answer] ausführlich; [- describe] detailliert.

fully-fledged *Br*, **full-fledged** *Am* [-'fledʒd] *adj fig* [doctor, lawyer] vollausgebildet.

fumble ['fʌmbl] *vi* [in bag, pocket] wühlen; **to ~ for sthg** [for light switch] nach etw tasten; [for words] nach etw suchen.

fume [fjuːm] *vi* [with anger] kochen. ◆ **fumes** *npl* Dämpfe *pl*; [from car] Abgase *pl*; [from fire] Rauch *der*.

fumigate ['fjuːmɪgeɪt] *vt* [room, building] ausräuchern.

fun [fʌn] *n* - **1.** [gen] Spaß *der*; **it's good ~** es macht viel Spaß; **to have ~** sich amüsieren; **for ~, for the ~ of it** aus OR zum Spaß - **2.** [ridicule]: **to make ~ of sb, to poke ~ at sb** sich über jn lustig machen.

function ['fʌŋkʃn] ◇ *n* - **1.** [gen] Funktion

die - **2.** [social event] Veranstaltung *die* ◇ *vi* - **1.** [work] funktionieren - **2.** [serve]: **to ~ as** dienen als.

functional ['fʌŋkʃnəl] *adj* - **1.** [practical] funktionell - **2.** [operational] funktionsfähig.

fund [fʌnd] ◇ *n* - **1.** [amount of money] Fonds *der* - **2.** *fig* [of knowledge, experience] Fundus *der* ◇ *vt* finanzieren. ◆ **funds** *npl* Gelder *pl*; **public ~s** öffentliche Mittel *pl*.

fundamental [,fʌndə'mentl] *adj* - **1.** [basic - idea] grundlegend; [- principle, change, error] fundamental - **2.** [vital]: **to be ~ (to)** von fundamentaler Bedeutung sein (für).

funding ['fʌndɪŋ] *n* Gelder *pl*.

funeral ['fjuːnərəl] *n* Beerdigung *die*.

funeral parlour *n* Beerdigungsinstitut *das*.

funfair ['fʌnfeə'] *n* Kirmes *die*.

fungus ['fʌŋgəs] *(pl* -gi [-gaɪ] OR -guses) *n* BOT Pilz *der*.

funnel ['fʌnl] *n* - **1.** [tube] Trichter *der* - **2.** [on ship] Schornstein *der*.

funny ['fʌnɪ] *adj* - **1.** [amusing] lustig - **2.** [odd] komisch - **3.** [ill]: **I feel ~** mir ist komisch. ◆ **funnies** *npl Am* Cartoons *pl*.

fur [fɜː'] *n* - **1.** [on animal] Fell *das* - **2.** [garment] Pelz *der*.

fur coat *n* Pelzmantel *der*.

furious ['fjʊərɪəs] *adj* - **1.** [very angry] wütend - **2.** [violent] heftig; **at a ~ pace/speed** mit rasender Geschwindigkeit.

furlong ['fɜːlɒŋ] *n* Achtelmeile *die*.

furnace ['fɜːnɪs] *n* [for melting metal] Schmelzofen *der*.

furnish ['fɜːnɪʃ] *vt* - **1.** [room, house] einrichten - **2.** *fml* [provide - proof, explanation] liefern; **to ~ sb with sthg** jm etw liefern.

furnished ['fɜːnɪʃt] *adj* möbliert.

furnishings ['fɜːnɪʃɪŋz] *npl* Einrichtungsgegenstände *pl*.

furniture ['fɜːnɪtʃə'] *n (U)* Möbel *pl*; **a piece of ~** ein Möbelstück.

furrow ['fʌrəʊ] *n* - **1.** [in field] Furche *die* - **2.** [on forehead] Runzel *die*.

furry ['fɜːrɪ] *adj* - **1.** [animal] mit dichtem Fell - **2.** [material] flauschig; **~ toy** Plüschtier *das*.

further ['fɜːðə'] ◇ *compar* ⤐ far ◇ *adv* - **1.** [gen] weiter; **~ back** weiter hinten; [in time] weiter zurück; **~ on** weiter; **the police decided not to take the matter any ~** die Polizei entschied, die Angelegenheit nicht weiterzuverfolgen - **2.** [in addition] darüber hinaus ◇ *adj* [additional] weitere, -r, -s; **until ~ notice** bis auf weiteres ◇ *vt* [career] voranbringen; [aim] unterstützen.

further education *n Br* Erwachsenenbildung *die*.

furthermore [,fɜːðə'mɔː'] *adv* außerdem.

furthest ['fɜːðɪst] ◇ *superl* ⤐ far ◇ *adj*

am weitesten entfernt ⬦ *adv* am weitesten.

furtive ['fɜ:tɪv] *adj* [glance] verstohlen; [behaviour] heimlichtuerisch.

fury ['fjʊərɪ] *n* Wut *die*.

fuse *Br*, **fuze** *Am* [fju:z] ⬦ *n* - **1.** [of plug] Sicherung *die* - **2.** [of bomb, firework] Zünder *der* ⬦ *vt* [ideas, styles] verbinden ⬦ *vi* ELEC: **the lights have ~d** die Sicherung (für das Licht) ist durchgebrannt.

fusebox ['fju:zbɒks] *n* Sicherungskasten *der*.

fused [fju:zd] *adj* [plug] gesichert.

fuselage ['fju:zəlɑ:ʒ] *n* (Flugzeug)rumpf *der*.

fuss [fʌs] ⬦ *n* Theater *das*; **to make a ~** Aufhebens machen ⬦ *vi* sich aufregen.

fussy ['fʌsɪ] *adj* - **1.** [person] pingelig - **2.** [design, dress] verspielt.

futile ['fju:taɪl] *adj* zwecklos.

futon ['fu:tɒn] *n* Futon *der*.

future ['fju:tʃəʳ] ⬦ *n* - **1.** [time ahead] Zukunft *die*; **in ~** in Zukunft; **in the ~** in der Zukunft - **2.** GRAMM: **~ (tense)** Futur *das* ⬦ *adj* künftig; **at a ~ date** zu einem späteren Zeitpunkt.

fuze *n, vt & vi Am* = fuse.

fuzzy ['fʌzɪ] *adj* - **1.** [hair] kraus - **2.** [image, photo] unscharf - **3.** [ideas] wirr.

G

g[1] (*pl* **g's** OR **gs**), **G** (*pl* **G's** OR **Gs**) [dʒi:] *n* [letter] g *das*, G *das*. ⬥ **G** ⬦ *n* MUS G *das* ⬦ *abbr* of good.

g[2] [dʒi:] (*abbr of* gram) g.

gab [gæb] *n* ⬥ gift.

gabble ['gæbl] ⬦ *vt* herunterrasseln ⬦ *vi* brabbeln ⬦ *n* Gebrabbel *das*.

gable ['geɪbl] *n* Giebel *der*.

gadget ['gædʒɪt] *n* Gerät *das*.

Gaelic ['geɪlɪk] ⬦ *adj* gälisch ⬦ *n* Gälisch(e) *das*.

gag [gæg] ⬦ *n* - **1.** [for mouth] Knebel *der* - **2.** *inf* [joke] Gag *der* ⬦ *vt* knebeln.

gage *n & vt Am* = gauge.

gaiety ['geɪətɪ] *n* Fröhlichkeit *die*.

gaily ['geɪlɪ] *adv* [cheerfully] fröhlich; [dressed] in leuchtenden Farben; **~ coloured** farbenfroh.

gain [geɪn] ⬦ *n* - **1.** [profit] Gewinn *der*; [advantage] Vorteil *der* - **2.** [increase] Zunahme *die* ⬦ *vt* - **1.** [support] gewinnen; [advantage]

sich verschaffen; [reputation] erwerben; [victory] erringen - **2.** [increase]: **to ~ weight** zunehmen; **to ~ speed** schneller werden; **to ~ strength/popularity** an Stärke/Beliebtheit gewinnen ⬦ *vi* - **1.** [increase]: **to ~ in sthg** etw (D) gewinnen - **2.** [profit]: **to ~ (from/by sthg)** (von/durch etw) profitieren - **3.** [watch, clock] vorgehen. ⬥ **gain on** *vt fus*: **to ~ on sb** jm (immer) näher kommen.

gait [geɪt] *n* Gang *der*.

gala ['gɑ:lə] *n* [celebration] Festveranstaltung *die*.

galaxy ['gæləksɪ] *n* Galaxis *die*.

gale [geɪl] *n* Sturm *der*.

gall [gɔ:l] *n*: **to have the ~ to do sthg** die Frechheit haben, etwas zu tun.

gallant [*sense 1* 'gælənt, *sense 2* gə'lænt, 'gælənt] *adj* - **1.** [courageous] mutig - **2.** [polite to women] galant.

gall bladder *n* Gallenblase *die*.

gallery ['gælərɪ] *n* - **1.** [gen] Galerie *die* - **2.** THEATRE dritter Rang.

galley ['gælɪ] (*pl* -s) *n* [kitchen - of ship] Kombüse *die*; [- of aircraft] Bordküche *die*.

Gallic ['gælɪk] *adj* gallisch.

galling ['gɔ:lɪŋ] *adj* ärgerlich.

gallivant [,gælɪ'vænt] *vi inf* sich herumtreiben.

gallon ['gælən] *n* Gallone *die*.

gallop ['gæləp] ⬦ *n* - **1.** [pace of horse] Galopp *der* - **2.** [horse ride] Galoppritt *der* ⬦ *vi* [horse] galoppieren.

gallows ['gæləʊz] (*pl inv*) *n* Galgen *der*.

gallstone ['gɔ:lstəʊn] *n* Gallenstein *der*.

galore [gə'lɔ:ʳ] *adv* in Hülle und Fülle.

galvanize, -ise ['gælvənaɪz] *vt* - **1.** TECH galvanisieren - **2.** [impel]: **to ~ sb into action** jn dazu veranlassen, aktiv zu werden.

gamble ['gæmbl] ⬦ *n* [risk] Risiko *das* ⬦ *vi* - **1.** [bet] (um Geld) spielen - **2.** [take risk]: **to ~ on sthg** sich auf etw (A) verlassen.

gambler ['gæmbləʳ] *n* Spieler *der*, -in *die*.

gambling ['gæmblɪŋ] *n* Spielen *das* (um Geld).

game [geɪm] ⬦ *n* - **1.** [gen] Spiel *das*; **fancy a ~ of chess/cards?** hast du Lust auf eine Partie Schach/Karten? - **2.** [hunted animals, meat] Wild *das* - **3.** *phr*: **the ~'s up** das Spiel ist aus; **to give the ~ away** alles verderben; **to play ~s with sb** sein Spiel mit jm treiben ⬦ *adj* - **1.** [brave] mutig - **2.** [willing]: **to be ~ for sthg** für etw bereit sein; **to be ~ to do sthg** bereit sein, etw zu tun. ⬥ **games** ⬦ *n* SCH Sport *der* ⬦ *npl* [sporting event] Spiele *pl*.

gamekeeper ['geɪm,ki:pəʳ] *n* Wildhüter *der*.

game reserve *n* Wildreservat *das*.

gammon ['gæmən] *n* geräucherter und gekochter Vorderschinken.

gamut ['gæmət] n Skala die.

gang [gæŋ] n [of criminals] Bande die, Gang die; [of young people] Clique die. ➠ **gang up** vi inf sich zusammen|tun; **to ~ up on sb** sich gegen jn verbünden.

gangrene ['gæŋgri:n] n Wundbrand der.

gangster ['gæŋstə'] n Gangster der.

gangway ['gæŋweɪ] n - 1. Br [aisle] Gang der - 2. [gangplank] Gangway die.

gaol [dʒeɪl] n & vt Br = jail.

gap [gæp] n - 1. [empty space, omission] Lücke die - 2. [in time] Abstand der - 3. fig [disparity] Kluft die.

gape [geɪp] vi - 1. [person] gaffen; **to ~ at sb/ sthg** jn/etw begaffen - 2. [hole, shirt, wound] klaffen.

gaping ['geɪpɪŋ] adj - 1. [person] gaffend - 2. [hole, shirt, wound] klaffend.

gap year n einjährige Pause zwischen Schule und Studium.

📖 **gap year**

Britische Schulabgänger sind bei Erreichen der A-levels (Abitur) selten älter als 18 Jahre, da "sitzen bleiben" im britischen Schulsystem die absolute Ausnahme darstellt. Viele Schulabgänger entscheiden sich daher dafür, zwischen Schule und Universität ein Jahr Pause einzulegen, wissend, dass der angestrebte Kurs an Universität oder College nur drei oder vier Jahre dauern wird. Das gap year bietet den jungen Leuten die Chance, ausgiebig zu reisen oder wertvolle Arbeitserfahrung zu sammeln.

---

garage [Br 'gɑːrɑːʒ, 'gærɪdʒ, Am gə'rɑːʒ] n - 1. [for keeping car] Garage die - 2. Br [for fuel] Tankstelle die - 3. [for car repair] Werkstatt die - 4. [for selling cars] Autohändler der.

garbage ['gɑːbɪdʒ] n esp Am - 1. [refuse] Müll der - 2. inf [nonsense] Unsinn der.

garbage can n Am Mülltonne die.

garbage truck n Am Müllauto das.

garbled ['gɑːbld] adj entstellt.

garden ['gɑːdn] ⬦ n - 1. [private] Garten der - 2. [public] Grünanlage die ⬦ vi gärtnern.

garden centre n Gartencenter das.

gardener ['gɑːdnə'] n - 1. [professional] Gärtner der, -in die - 2. [amateur] Hobbygärtner der, -in die.

gardening ['gɑːdnɪŋ] n Gartenarbeit die.

gargle ['gɑːgl] vi gurgeln.

gargoyle ['gɑːgɔɪl] n Wasserspeier der.

garish ['geərɪʃ] adj grell.

garland ['gɑːlənd] n Girlande die.

garlic ['gɑːlɪk] n Knoblauch der.

garlic bread n (U) Knoblauchbrot das.

garment ['gɑːmənt] n Kleidungsstück das.

garnish ['gɑːnɪʃ] CULIN ⬦ n Garnierung die ⬦ vt garnieren.

garrison ['gærɪsn] n Garnison die.

garter ['gɑːtə'] n - 1. [around leg] Strumpfband das - 2. Am [suspender] Strumpfhalter der.

gas [gæs] (pl gases OR gasses) ⬦ n - 1. [gen] Gas das - 2. Am [fuel for vehicle] Benzin das; **to step on the ~** inf aufs Gas treten OR steigen ⬦ vt [poison] vergasen.

gas cooker n Br Gasherd der.

gas fire n Br Gasofen der.

gas gauge n Am Benzinuhr die.

gash [gæʃ] ⬦ n tiefe Schnittwunde ⬦ vt: **to ~ one's hand/arm** sich in die Hand/den Arm schneiden.

gasket ['gæskɪt] n Dichtung die.

gas mask n Gasmaske die.

gas meter n Gaszähler der, Gasuhr die.

gasoline ['gæsəliːn] n Am Benzin das.

gasp [gɑːsp] ⬦ n Keuchen das ⬦ vi - 1. [breathe quickly] keuchen - 2. [in shock, surprise] nach Luft schnappen.

gas pedal n Am Gaspedal das.

gas station n Am Tankstelle die.

gas stove n = gas cooker.

gas tank n Am Benzintank der.

gastroenteritis ['gæstrəʊ,entə'raɪtɪs] n Magen-Darm-Katarrh der.

gastronomy [gæs'trɒnəmɪ] n Gastronomie die.

gasworks ['gæswɜːks] (pl inv) n Gaswerk das.

gate [geɪt] n - 1. [in wall, fence] Tor das - 2. [at airport] Flugsteig der.

gatecrash ['geɪtkræʃ] vt inf herein|platzen.

gateway ['geɪtweɪ] n Tor das.

gather ['gæðə'] ⬦ vt - 1. [collect] sammeln; **to ~ together** sich versammeln - 2. [speed]: **to ~ speed** schneller werden - 3. [understand]: **to ~ that ...** annehmen, dass ...; **as far as I can ~** soweit ich weiß - 4. [into folds] raffen, kräuseln ⬦ vi [come together - people] sich versammeln; [- crowd] sich an|sammeln; [- clouds] sich zusammen|ziehen.

gathering ['gæðərɪŋ] n Versammlung die.

gaudy ['gɔːdɪ] adj grell.

gauge, gage Am ['geɪdʒ] ⬦ n - 1. [measuring instrument] Messinstrument das - 2. [calibre] Kaliber das - 3. RAIL Spurweite die ⬦ vt - 1. [measure, calculate] messen - 2. [judge, predict] beurteilen.

gaunt [gɔːnt] adj hager.

gauntlet ['gɔːntlɪt] n: **to run the ~** Spießbruten laufen; **to throw down the ~ (to sb)** (jm) den Fehdehandschuh hin|werfen.

gauze [gɔːz] n Gaze die.

gave [geɪv] pt ⬑ give.

gawky ['gɔːkɪ] adj unbeholfen.

gawp [gɔːp] *vi* gaffen; **to ~ at** sb/sthg jn/ etw anlgaffen.

gay [geɪ] <> *adj* - **1.** [homosexual] schwul - **2.** [cheerful, lively] fröhlich - **3.** [brightly coloured] **bunt** <> *n* [homosexual] Schwule *der*.

gay rights *npl* Rechte *pl* von Homosexuellen.

gaze [geɪz] <> *n* Blick *der* <> *vi*: **to ~ (at** sb/ sthg) (jn/etw) anlstarren.

GB (*abbr of* Great Britain) *n* GB.

GCSE (*abbr of* General Certificate of Secondary Education) *n* Abschlussprüfung an weiterführenden Schulen in England, Wales und Nordirland.

GCSE

Das GCSE wurde 1988 in England, Wales und Nordirland eingeführt und ersetzt die bis dahin üblichen O level-Prüfungen. Es handelt sich um Schulabschlussprüfungen in verschiedenen Fächern, die im Alter von 15 oder 16 Jahren abgelegt werden müssen. Will der Schüler oder die Schülerin eine weiterführende Schule besuchen und die A level-Prüfungen machen, muss das GCSE in mindestens fünf Schächern absolviert werden. Im Gegensatz zu den O levels fließen beim GCSE neben dem Prüfungsergebnis auch die im Laufe des Schuljahres erzielten Ergebnisse in die Endnote mit ein.

GDP (*abbr of* gross domestic product) *n* BIP *das*.

gear [gɪəʳ] <> *n* - **1.** TECH [mechanism] Zahnrad *das* - **2.** [on car, bicycle] Gang *der*; **out of ~** im Leerlauf; **in ~** mit eingelegtem Gang - **3.** (U) [equipment, clothes] Ausrüstung *die* <> *vt*: **to ~ sthg to** sb/sthg etw auf jn/etw auslrichten. ◆ **gear up** *vi*: **to ~ up for sthg** sich für etw rüsten; **to ~ up to do sthg** sich dafür rüsten, etw zu tun.

gearbox ['gɪəbɒks] *n* Getriebegehäuse *das*; **six-speed ~** Sechsganggetriebe *das*.

gear lever, gear stick *Br*, **gear shift** *Am* *n* Schaltknüppel *der*.

geese [giːs] *pl* ➞ goose.

gel [dʒel] <> *n* Gel *das* <> *vi fig* [idea, plan] Gestalt anlnehmen.

gelatin ['dʒelətɪn], **gelatine** [ˌdʒelə'tiːn] *n* Gelatine *die*.

gelignite ['dʒelɪgnaɪt] *n* Plastiksprengstoff *der*.

gem [dʒem] *n* - **1.** [jewel] (geschliffener) Edelstein - **2.** *fig* [person] Juwel *das*.

Gemini ['dʒemɪnaɪ] *n* [sign] Zwillinge *pl*.

gender ['dʒendəʳ] *n* Geschlecht *das*.

gene [dʒiːn] *n* Gen *das*.

general ['dʒenərəl] <> *adj* [gen] allgemein <> *n* MIL General *der*. ◆ **in general** *adv*

- **1.** [as a whole] im Allgemeinen - **2.** [usually] gewöhnlich.

general anaesthetic *n* Vollnarkose *die*.

general delivery *adv* *Am* postlagernd.

general election *n* Parlamentswahlen *pl*.

general election

Die general election (das Äquivalent zur deutschen Bundestagswahl) findet, wenn nicht außergewöhnliche Umstände vorliegen, mindestens alle fünf Jahre statt. Bei dieser Wahl werden die Parlamentsabgeordneten für jeden der 650 Wahlkreise in Großbritannien und Nordirland gewählt. Der genaue Zeitpunkt der general election, die traditionell an einem Donnerstag stattfindet, wird vom Premierminister bestimmt, der durch die Wahl des Termins unter Umständen das Wahlergebnis beeinflussen kann. In Großbritannien und Nordirland gilt das first past the post-System (relatives Mehrheitswahlrecht), bei dem der Kandidat mit einer einfachen Mehrheit ins Parlament einzieht.

generalization [ˌdʒenərəlaɪ'zeɪʃn] *n* Verallgemeinerung *die*.

general knowledge *n* Allgemeinbildung *die*.

generally ['dʒenərəlɪ] *adv* - **1.** [usually] im Allgemeinen - **2.** [in a general way] allgemein.

general practitioner [-præk'tɪʃənəʳ] *n* Arzt *der*, Ärztin *die* für Allgemeinmedizin.

general public *n*: **the ~** die breite Öffentlichkeit.

general store *n* Gemischtwarenhandlung *die*.

general strike *n* Generalstreik *der*.

generate ['dʒenəreɪt] *vt* - **1.** [energy, power, heat] erzeugen - **2.** [interest, excitement] hervorlrufen; [jobs, employment] schaffen.

generation [ˌdʒenə'reɪʃn] *n* - **1.** [gen] Generation *die* - **2.** [of energy, power, heat] Erzeugung *die*.

generator ['dʒenəreɪtəʳ] *n* Generator *der*.

generosity [ˌdʒenə'rɒsətɪ] *n* Freigebigkeit *die*, Großzügigkeit *die*.

generous ['dʒenərəs] *adj* großzügig.

genetic [dʒɪ'netɪk] *adj* genetisch. ◆ **genetics** *n* Genetik *die*, Vererbungslehre *die*.

genetically modified [dʒɪ'netɪklɪ-] *adj* genmanipuliert, gentechnisch verändert.

Geneva [dʒɪ'niːvə] *n* Genf *nt*.

genial ['dʒiːnjəl] *adj* jovial.

genitals ['dʒenɪtlz] *npl* Genitalien *pl*.

genius ['dʒiːnjəs] (*pl* -es) *n* Genie *das*.

gent [dʒent] *n* *Br inf* Gentleman *der*. ◆ **gents** *n* *Br* [toilets] Herrentoilette *die*.

genteel [dʒen'ti:l] *adj* - **1.** [refined] vornehm - **2.** [affected] geziert.

gentle ['dʒentl] *adj* - **1.** [person] sanftmütig - **2.** [rain, breeze, movement] sanft, leicht - **3.** [slope, curve] sanft - **4.** [hint] zart.

gentleman ['dʒentlmən] (*pl* -men [-mən]) *n* - **1.** [well-bred man] Gentleman *der* - **2.** [man] Herr *der*.

gently ['dʒentlɪ] *adv* - **1.** [speak] sanft - **2.** [blow] leicht; [move, heat] behutsam - **3.** [slope, curve] allmählich.

genuine ['dʒenjʊɪn] *adj* - **1.** [real] echt - **2.** [sincere] aufrichtig.

geography [dʒɪ'ɒɡrəfɪ] *n* [science] Geografie *die*; [in school] Erdkunde *die*.

geology [dʒɪ'ɒlədʒɪ] *n* Geologie *die*.

geometric(al) [ˌdʒɪə'metrɪk(l)] *adj* geometrisch.

geometry [dʒɪ'ɒmɪtrɪ] *n* Geometrie *die*.

geranium [dʒɪ'reɪnjəm] (*pl* -s) *n* Geranie *die*.

geriatric [ˌdʒerɪ'ætrɪk] *adj* - **1.** [of old people] geriatrisch - **2.** *pej* [very old, inefficient] veraltet, altersschwach.

germ [dʒɜːm] *n lit & fig* Keim *der*.

German ['dʒɜːmən] ◇ *adj* deutsch ◇ *n* - **1.** [person] Deutsche *der, die* - **2.** [language] Deutsch(e) *das*.

German measles *n* Röteln *die*.

Germany ['dʒɜːmənɪ] *n* Deutschland *nt*.

germinate ['dʒɜːmɪneɪt] *vi lit & fig* keimen.

gesticulate [dʒes'tɪkjʊleɪt] *vi* gestikulieren.

gesture ['dʒestʃəʳ] ◇ *n* Geste *die* ◇ *vi*: **to ~ to** OR **towards sb** auf jn deuten.

get [get] (*pt* & *pp* got, *Am pp* gotten) ◇ *vt* - **1.** [obtain] bekommen; [buy] kaufen; **she got a job** sie hat eine Stelle gefunden; **he got us two tickets** er hat uns zwei Karten besorgt - **2.** [receive] bekommen; **I got a book for Christmas** ich habe zu Weihnachten ein Buch bekommen; **when did you ~ the news?** wann haben Sie die Nachricht bekommen? - **3.** [train, plane, bus] nehmen; **let's ~ a taxi** lass uns ein Taxi nehmen - **4.** [fetch] holen; **could you ~ me the manager?** [on phone] könnten Sie mir den Geschäftsführer geben?; **can I ~ you something to eat/drink?** möchtest du etwas essen/trinken? - **5.** [illness] bekommen; **I got this cold while I was on holiday** ich habe mir diese Erkältung im Urlaub zugezogen - **6.** [catch] fangen; **the police have got the killer** die Polizei hat den Mörder gefasst - **7.** [cause to be done]: **to ~ sthg done** etw machen lassen; **can I ~ my car repaired here?** kann ich mein Auto hier reparieren lassen? - **8.** [cause to become]: **she got the children ready for school** sie machte die Kinder für die Schule fertig; **I can't ~ the car started** ich

kriege das Auto nicht an; **to ~ lunch** das Mittagessen zubereiten - **9.** [ask, tell]: **to ~ sb to do sthg** jn bitten, etw zu tun - **10.** [move]: **I can't ~ it through the door** ich bekomme es nicht durch die Tür - **11.** [understand] verstehen; **I don't ~ it** *inf* das verstehe ich nicht - **12.** [time, chance] haben; **we didn't ~ the chance to see everything** wir hatten nicht die Gelegenheit, uns alles anzuschauen; **I haven't got (the) time** ich habe keine Zeit - **13.** [idea, feeling] haben; **I ~ a lot of enjoyment from it** ich habe viel Spaß daran - **14.** [answer - phone]: **could you ~ the phone?** könntest du ans Telefon gehen? - **15.** *phr*: **we ~ a lot of German tourists here** zu uns kommen viele deutsche Touristen; **we ~ a lot of rain here in winter** hier regnet es viel im Winter; ▷ have ◇ *vi* - **1.** [become] werden; **it's getting late** es wird spät; **to ~ lost** sich verirren; **~ lost!** *inf* hau ab!; **to ~ ready** sich fertig machen - **2.** [into particular state, position]: **to ~ into trouble** in Schwierigkeiten geraten; **how do you ~ to the river from here?** wie kommt man von hier zum Fluss?; **to ~ dressed** sich anziehen; **to ~ married** heiraten - **3.** [arrive] ankommen; **when does the train ~ here?** wann kommt der Zug hier an? - **4.** [eventually succeed]: **I finally got to meet him last week** letzte Woche habe ich ihn endlich getroffen; **she got to like the class** allmählich gefiel ihr der Kurs; **to ~ to know sb** jn kennen lernen - **5.** [progress]: **how far have you got?** wie weit bist du gekommen?; **we're ~ting nowhere** so kommen wir nicht weiter ◇ *aux vb* werden; **to ~ delayed** aufgehalten werden; **to ~ killed** getötet werden; **to ~ excited** aufgeregt werden; **let's ~ going** OR **moving!** also los!

◆ **get about** *vi* - **1.** [move from place to place] herumkommen; **he ~s about a lot** er kommt viel herum - **2.** [news, rumour] sich verbreiten. ◆ **get along** *vi* - **1.** [manage]: **to ~ along (without sb/sthg)** (ohne jn/etw) zurechtkommen - **2.** [progress]: **how are you ~ting along?** wie kommst du voran? - **3.** [in relationship]: **to ~ along (with sb)** (mit jm) auskommen - **4.** [leave] gehen; **I must be ~ting along** ich muss jetzt gehen. ◆ **get around, get round** ◇ *vt fus* [problem] umgehen ◇ *vi* - **1.** [move from place to place] herumkommen - **2.** [circulate - news] sich verbreiten - **3.** [eventually do]: **to ~ around to sthg/to doing sthg** dazu kommen, etw zu tun. ◆ **get at** *vt fus* - **1.** [reach] heranlkommen an (+ A); [truth] herauslbekommen - **2.** [imply]: **what are you ~ting at?** worauf willst du hinaus? - **3.** *inf* [nag]: **stop ~ting at me!** nörgel nicht dauernd an mir rum! ◆ **get away** ◇ *vt sep*: **~ him away from here** bring ihn von hier weg ◇ *vi* - **1.** [leave] weglkommen; **I need to ~ away by five** ich muss um fünf Uhr gehen OR weg - **2.** [escape]

entkommen. **get away with** vt fus durchkommen mit. **get back** <> vt sep - 1. [recover, regain] zurück|bekommen - 2. [take revenge on]: **to ~ sb back for sthg** jm etw heim|zahlen <> vi - 1. [return] zurück|kommen - 2. [move away] zurück|treten. **get back to** vt fus - 1. [return to previous state, activity]: **to ~ back to sleep** wieder ein|schlafen; **to ~ back to work** zur Arbeit zurück|kehren - 2. [phone back]: **I'll ~ back to you later** ich rufe Sie später zurück. **get by** vi [manage, survive] zurecht|kommen; **to ~ by on sthg** mit etw aus|kommen. **get down** vt sep - 1. [depress] deprimieren; **don't let it ~ you down** lass dich davon nicht unter|kriegen - 2. [fetch from higher level] herunter|holen - 3. [write] auf|schreiben. **get down to** vt fus: **to ~ down to doing sthg** sich daran machen, etw zu tun; **to ~ down to sthg** sich an etw (A) machen. **get in** vi - 1. [arrive] an|kommen - 2. [into car, bus] ein|steigen. **get into** vt fus - 1. [car] ein|steigen in (+ A) - 2. [become involved in] geraten in (+ A); **to ~ into an argument with sb** mit jm in Streit geraten - 3. [enter into a particular situation, state] geraten in (+ A); **to ~ into a panic** in Panik geraten; **to ~ into trouble** in Schwierigkeiten geraten. **get off** <> vt sep [remove - clothes, shoes] aus|ziehen; [- stain] heraus|bekommen; [- lid] ab|bekommen; **to ~ sb/sthg off one's hands** jn/etw los|werden <> vt fus [bus, train] aus|steigen aus; [bicycle] ab|steigen von <> vi - 1. [from train, bus] aus|steigen; [from bicycle] ab|steigen - 2. [leave] los|gehen; [in car] los|fahren - 3. [escape punishment] davon|kommen. **get on** <> vt fus [bus, train] ein|steigen in (+ A); [bicycle] steigen auf (+ A) <> vi - 1. [on train, bus] ein|steigen; [on bicycle] auf|steigen - 2. [in relationship] sich verstehen; **how do you ~ on with his family?** wie kommst du mit seiner Familie aus? - 3. [progress]: **how are you ~ting on?** wie kommst du voran? - 4. [proceed]: **to ~ on (with sthg)** (mit etw) weiter|machen - 5. [have success] Erfolg haben. **get out** <> vt sep - 1. [take out] heraus|nehmen - 2. [remove]: **how do you ~ wine stains out?** wie bekommt man Weinflecken heraus? <> vi - 1. [from car, bus] aus|steigen - 2. [become known - news] heraus|kommen. **get out of** vt fus - 1. [car, bus, train] aus|steigen aus - 2. [escape from] heraus|kommen aus; **to ~ out of a difficult situation** sich aus einer schwierigen Lage befreien - 3. [avoid]: **to ~ out of sthg** um etw herum|kommen; **to ~ out of doing sthg** darum herum|kommen, etw zu tun. **get over** <> vt fus - 1. [recover from] hinweg|kommen über (+ A) - 2. [overcome] überwinden <> vt sep [communicate] verständlich machen. **get round** vt fus &

vi = get around. **get through** <> vt fus - 1. [work, task] erledigen - 2. [exam] bestehen - 3. [food, drink] verbrauchen - 4. [survive] überstehen <> vi - 1. [on phone] durch|kommen; **I couldn't ~ through to her** ich konnte sie nicht erreichen - 2. [make oneself understood]: **I can't ~ through to her** ich konnte es ihr nicht verständlich machen. **get to** vt fus inf [annoy] auf die Nerven gehen; **don't let him ~ to you** lass dich von ihm nicht ärgern. **get together** <> vt sep - 1. [organize - team, report] zusammen|stellen; [- demonstration] organisieren - 2. [gather - people] zusammen|bringen; [- belongings] zusammen|packen <> vi zusammen|kommen. **get up** <> vi auf|stehen <> vt fus - 1. [organize - petition etc] organisieren - 2. [gather]: **to ~ up speed in** Fahrt kommen. **get up to** vt fus inf an|stellen; **I wonder what they're ~ting up to** ich frage mich, was die da treiben.

get-together n inf Zusammenkunft die.

ghastly ['gɑːstlɪ] adj - 1. inf [very bad, unpleasant] scheußlich, grässlich - 2. [horrifying, macabre] schrecklich, schauerlich.

gherkin ['gɜːkɪn] n Gewürzgurke die.

ghetto ['getəʊ] n (pl -s OR -es) Ghetto das.

ghetto blaster [-,blɑːstəʳ] n inf Ghettoblaster der.

ghost [gəʊst] n Geist der, Gespenst das.

giant ['dʒaɪənt] <> adj riesig <> n [very tall man] Riese der.

gibberish ['dʒɪbərɪʃ] n [meaningless] Unsinn der, Quatsch der; [hard to understand] Kauderwelsch das.

gibe [dʒaɪb] n Seitenhieb der.

Gibraltar [dʒɪ'brɔːltəʳ] n Gibraltar nt.

giddy ['gɪdɪ] adj [dizzy] schwindelig.

gift [gɪft] n - 1. [present] Geschenk das - 2. [talent] Talent das, Begabung die; **to have a ~ for sthg** ein Talent OR eine Begabung für etw haben; **to have a ~ for doing sthg** ein Talent OR eine Begabung haben, etw zu tun; **the ~ of the gab** die Überzeugungsgabe.

---

gift

Wenn man im englischsprachigen Ausland ein gift bekommt, ist das kein Grund zur Panik – es handelt sich um ein Geschenk. They bought me a really nice gift for my birthday heißt also: „Sie haben mir ein wirklich schönes <u>Geschenk</u> zum Geburtstag gekauft."
Todbringendes „Gift" bezeichnet man im Englischen dagegen mit dem ursprünglich französischen Wort poison. „Wegen der Ratten haben wir <u>Gift</u> ausgelegt" lautet übersetzt We've put <u>poison</u> down for the rats.

---

gift certificate n Am = gift token.

gifted ['gɪftɪd] *adj* talentiert, begabt.

gift token, gift voucher *Br*, **gift certificate** *Am n* Geschenkgutschein *der*.

gift wrap *n* Geschenkpapier *das*.

gig [gɪg] *n inf* Gig *der*, Konzert *das*.

gigantic [dʒaɪ'gæntɪk] *adj* gigantisch.

giggle ['gɪgl] *vi* [laugh] kichern.

gilded ['gɪldɪd] *adj* = gilt.

gills [gɪlz] *npl* Kiemen *pl*.

gilt [gɪlt] <> *adj* vergoldet <> *n* [gold layer] Vergoldung *die*.

gimmick ['gɪmɪk] *n pej* Spielerei *die*.

gin [dʒɪn] *n* Gin *der*; **~ and tonic** Gin Tonic *der*.

ginger ['dʒɪndʒəʳ] <> *adj Br* [colour - hair] rotblond; [- cat] rötlichbraun <> *n* Ingwer *der*.

ginger ale *n* Ginger Ale *das*.

ginger beer *n* Ingwerbier *das*.

gingerbread ['dʒɪndʒəbred] *n* (U) [biscuit] Pfefferkuchen mit Ingwergeschmack.

gingerly ['dʒɪndʒəlɪ] *adv* vorsichtig.

gipsy ['dʒɪpsɪ] <> *adj* Zigeuner- <> *n* Zigeuner *der*, -in *die*.

giraffe [dʒɪ'rɑːf] (*pl inv* OR -s) *n* Giraffe *die*.

girder ['gɜːdəʳ] *n* Träger *der*.

girdle ['gɜːdl] *n* [corset] Mieder *das*.

girl [gɜːl] *n* Mädchen *das*; [daughter] Tochter *die*, Mädchen *das*.

girlfriend ['gɜːlfrend] *n* Freundin *die*.

girl guide *Br*, **girl scout** *Am n* Pfadfinderin *die*.

giro ['dʒaɪrəʊ] (*pl* -s) *n Br* [system] Giro *das*; **~ (cheque)** Giroscheck für Sozialhilfeempfänger.

gist [dʒɪst] *n* Wesentliche *das*; **to get the ~ (of sthg)** das Wesentliche (einer Sache (G)) mitbekommen.

give [gɪv] (*pt* gave; *pp* given) <> *vt* - 1. [gen] geben; **to ~ sb sthg** jm etw geben; **to ~ sb a push/kiss** jm einen Schubs/Kuss geben; **to ~ sb a look/smile** jn anlsehen/anllächeln; **to ~ a cry** aufIschreien - 2. [as present]: **to ~ sb sthg** jm etw schenken; [as donation] jm etw spenden - 3. [speech] halten - 4. [attention, time]: **he ~s the issue a lot of attention** er widmet der Sache viel Aufmerksamkeit - 5. [communicate] geben; **when will you ~ me your decision?** wann werden Sie mir Ihre Entscheidung mitteilen?; **~ her my regards** grüß sie schön von mir - 6. [produce] machen; **to ~ sb a surprise** jm eine Überraschung bereiten; **to ~ sb pleasure/trouble** jm Freude/Probleme bereiten OR machen; **to ~ sb a fright** jn erschrecken; **what gave you that idea?** wie bist du auf diese Idee gekommen? <> *vi* [yield] nachlgeben <> *n* [elasticity] Nachgiebigkeit *die*. ◆ **give or take** *prep*: **5,000 people, ~ or take a few hundred** schätzungsweise 5000 Leute. ◆ **give away** *vt sep* - 1. [hand over] weglgeben - 2. [reveal] verraten; **to ~ the game away** al-

les verraten. ◆ **give back** *vt sep* zurücklgeben. ◆ **give in** *vi* - 1. [agree unwillingly] nachlgeben; **to ~ in to sb/sthg** jm/etw nachlgeben - 2. [admit defeat] sich geschlagen geben. ◆ **give off** *vt fus* ablgeben. ◆ **give out** <> *vt sep* [distribute] auslteilen <> *vi* [fail - legs, machine] versagen; [- strength, supply] zu Ende gehen. ◆ **give up** <> *vt sep* - 1. [stop, abandon] auflgeben; **to ~ up doing sthg** aufIhören, etw zu tun - 2. [surrender]: **to ~ o.s. up (to sb)** sich (jm) ergeben <> *vi* [admit defeat] auflgeben.

given ['gɪvn] <> *adj* - 1. [fixed] bestimmt - 2. [prone]: **to be ~ to sthg** zu etw neigen; **to be ~ to doing sthg** die Angewohnheit haben, etw zu tun <> *prep* [taking into account] angesichts (+ G); **~ that ...** angesichts der Tatsache, dass ...

given name *n Am* Vorname *der*.

glacier ['glæsjəʳ] *n* Gletscher *der*.

glad [glæd] *adj* - 1. [happy] froh; **to be ~ about sthg** sich über etw (A) freuen - 2. [grateful]: **to be ~ of sthg** dankbar für etw sein.

gladly ['glædlɪ] *adv* [willingly, eagerly] gern(e).

glamor *n Am* = glamour.

glamorous ['glæmərəs] *adj* [film star, lifestyle] glamourös; [job] Traum-.

glamour *Br*, **glamor** *Am* ['glæməʳ] *n* [of film star, lifestyle] Glamour *der*; [of job] Reiz *der*.

glance [glɑːns] <> *n* Blick *der*; **at a ~** auf einen Blick; **at first ~** auf den ersten Blick <> *vi*: **to ~ at sb** jn kurz anlsehen; **to ~ at sthg** einen Blick auf etw (A) werfen. ◆ **glance off** *vt fus* [subj: ball, bullet] abIprallen an (+ D); [subj: light] reflektiert werden von.

gland [glænd] *n* Drüse *die*.

glandular fever [ˌglændjʊlə-] *n* Drüsenfieber *das*.

glare [gleəʳ] <> *n* - 1. [scowl] langer wütender Blick - 2. (U) [of light, sun] greller Schein; **the ~ of publicity** das Rampenlicht der Öffentlichkeit <> *vi* - 1. [scowl] böse blicken; **to ~ at sb/sthg** jn/etw böse anlstarren - 2. [light, sun] grell scheinen.

glaring ['gleərɪŋ] *adj* - 1. [error, example] eklatant - 2. [light, sun] grell.

glass [glɑːs] <> *n* - 1. [gen] Glas *das*; **a ~ of wine** ein Glas Wein - 2. (U) [glassware] Glaswaren *pl* <> *comp* Glas-. ◆ **glasses** *npl* [spectacles] Brille *die*; [binoculars] Fernglas *das*; **a pair of ~es** eine Brille.

glaze [gleɪz] <> *n* Glasur *die* <> *vt* [pottery & CULIN] glasieren.

glazier ['gleɪzjəʳ] *n* Glaser *der*, -in *die*.

gleam [gliːm] <> *n* [of surface] Schimmer *der*; [of light, sunset] Schein *der* <> *vi* [surface, object] schimmern; [gold, brass] glänzen; [light] scheinen; [eyes] funkeln.

gleaming ['gliːmɪŋ] *adj* [surface, object] schimmernd; [gold, brass] glänzend; [light] scheinend; [eyes] funkelnd.

glean [gliːn] *vt* [gather] zusammen|tragen.

glee [gliː] *n* [joy] Freude *die;* [gloating] Schadenfreude *die.*

glen [glen] *n Irish & Scot* enges Tal.

glib [glɪb] *adj pej* - **1.** [answer, excuse] leichthin gesagt - **2.** [person] aalglatt.

glide [glaɪd] *vi* - **1.** [move smoothly - boat] gleiten; [- dancer] schweben - **2.** [fly] schweben.

glider ['glaɪdə'] *n* Segelflugzeug *das.*

gliding ['glaɪdɪŋ] *n* Segelfliegen *das.*

glimmer ['glɪmə'] *n* - **1.** [faint light] schwacher Schein - **2.** *fig:* **she didn't show a ~ of interest/understanding** sie zeigte nicht die leiseste Spur von Interesse/Verständnis.

glimpse [glɪmps] <> *n* [look] flüchtiger Blick <> *vt* - **1.** [catch sight of] flüchtig OR kurz sehen - **2.** [perceive]: **to ~ sb's true feelings** einen Eindruck von js wahren Gefühlen bekommen.

glint [glɪnt] <> *n* - **1.** [of metal, sunlight] Glitzern *das* - **2.** [in eyes]: **there was a ~ of anger in his eyes** seine Augen funkelten böse <> *vi* - **1.** [metal, sunlight] glitzern - **2.** [eyes] funkeln.

glisten ['glɪsn] *vi* [gold, lips] glänzen; [lake, raindrops] glitzern.

glitter ['glɪtə'] <> *n* - **1.** [of object, light] Glitzern *das;* [of diamonds, stars] Funkeln *das* - **2.** [decoration, make-up] Glitzerstaub *der* <> *vi* glitzern; [diamonds, stars] funkeln.

gloat [gləʊt] *vi:* **to ~ (over sthg)** [over sb's misfortune] sich hämisch (über etw *(A)*) freuen; [over one's own success] sich selbstzufrieden (über etw *(A)*) freuen.

global ['gləʊbl] *adj* global; [economy, peace] Welt-.

global warming [-'wɔːmɪŋ] *n* Erwärmung *die* der Erdatmosphäre.

globe [gləʊb] *n* - **1.** [Earth]: **the ~** die Erde - **2.** [sphere representing world] Globus *der.*

gloom [gluːm] *n* - **1.** [darkness] Düsterkeit *die* - **2.** [unhappiness] Trübsinn *der.*

gloomy ['gluːmɪ] *adj* - **1.** [place, landscape, weather] düster - **2.** [person, atmosphere] trübsinnig - **3.** [outlook] düster; [news] bedrückend.

glorious ['glɔːrɪəs] *adj* - **1.** [illustrious] glorreich - **2.** [wonderful] herrlich.

glory ['glɔːrɪ] *n* - **1.** [fame, honour] Ruhm *der* - **2.** [splendour] Herrlichkeit *die.*

gloss [glɒs] *n* - **1.** [shine] Glanz *der* - **2.:** **~ (paint)** Lackfarbe *die.* <> **gloss over** *vt fus* [treat briefly] nur ganz kurz erwähnen; [hide] unter den Teppich kehren.

glossary ['glɒsərɪ] *n* Glossar *das.*

glossy ['glɒsɪ] *adj* glänzend; [photo, paper] Glanz-.

glove [glʌv] *n* Handschuh *der;* **to fit like a ~** [garment] wie angegossen passen.

glove compartment *n* Handschuhfach *das.*

glow [gləʊ] <> *n* [of fire, light, sunset] Schein *der* <> *vi* [light] scheinen; [fire, sky] glühen.

glower ['glaʊə'] *vi* wütend drein|blicken; **to ~ at sb/sthg** jn/etw wütend an|blicken.

glucose ['gluːkəʊs] *n* Glukose *die.*

glue [gluː] (*cont* glueing OR gluing) <> *n* Klebstoff *der* <> *vt* kleben; **to ~ sthg to sthg** etw an etw *(A)* kleben.

glum [glʌm] *adj* trübsinnig.

glut [glʌt] *n:* **~ (of sthg)** Überangebot *das* (an etw *(D)*).

glutton ['glʌtn] *n* Vielfraß *der;* **to be a ~ for punishment** ein Masochist sein.

GM *adj abbr of* genetically modified.

GMO (*abbr of* genetically modified organism) *n* GVO *der.*

gnarled [nɑːld] *adj* knorrig.

gnat [næt] *n* Mücke *die.*

gnaw [nɔː] *vt* nagen an (+ *D*); [fingernails] kauen an (+ *D*); **to ~ a hole in sthg** ein Loch in etw *(A)* nagen.

gnome [nəʊm] *n* Gnom *der;* [in garden] Gartenzwerg *der.*

GNP (*abbr of* gross national product) *n* BSP *das.*

go [gəʊ] (*pt* went; *pp* gone; *pl* goes) <> *vi* - **1.** [move] gehen; [by vehicle, travel] fahren; [by plane] fliegen; **to ~ shopping/for a walk** einkaufen/spazieren gehen; **I'll ~ and collect the cases** ich gehe die Koffer abholen; **to ~ home/to school** nach Hause/in die Schule gehen; **to ~ to Austria** nach Österreich fahren; **to ~ by bus** mit dem Bus fahren; **to ~ by plane** fliegen; **to ~ to work** zur Arbeit gehen - **2.** [leave] gehen; [in vehicle] fahren; **it's time we went** es wird Zeit, dass wir gehen; **let's ~!** gehen wir!; **when does the bus ~?** wann fährt der Bus ab?; **~ away!** geh weg! - **3.** [lead]: **where does this path ~?** wohin führt dieser Weg? - **4.** [time] vergehen - **5.** [progress - negotiations, preparations, business] laufen; **how are your studies ~ing?** wie läuft es mit deinem Studium?; **how did the party ~?** wie war die Party?; **to ~ well** gut gehen; **how's it ~ing?** wie gehts? - **6.** [become] werden; **she went pale** sie wurde bleich; **to ~ bankrupt** Bankrott machen - **7.** [be]: **our cries went unheard** unsere Rufe blieben ungehört; **to ~ hungry** hungern - **8.** [expressing future tense]: **to be ~ing to do sthg** etw tun werden; **it's ~ing to rain tomorrow** morgen wird es regnen; **we're ~ing to go to Switzerland** wir fahren in die Schweiz; **she's ~ing to have a baby** sie be-

goad

kommt ein Baby - **9.** [function - gen] laufen; [- watch, clock] gehen - **10.** [become damaged] kaputt|gehen; **the fuse has gone die Sicherung ist herausgesprungen - 11.** [bell, alarm] los|gehen; **the bell went** es klingelte - **12.** [match] zusammen|passen; **to ~ with** passen zu; **red wine doesn't ~ with fish** Rotwein passt nicht zu Fisch - **13.** [fit] passen, gehen; **it won't ~ into my case** es geht OR passt nicht in meinen Koffer - **14.** [belong] kommen; **the plates ~ in the cupboard** die Teller kommen in den Schrank - **15.** [in division] gehen; **three into two won't ~** zwei durch drei geht nicht - **16.** *inf* [with negative - giving advice]: **now, don't ~ catching cold** erkälte dich bloß nicht - **17.** *inf* [expressing irritation]: **he's gone and broken my computer!** er hat doch tatsächlich meinen Computer kaputtgemacht!; **now what's he gone and done?** was hat er jetzt wieder gemacht?; **you've gone and done it now!** jetzt hast du es geschafft! <> *n* - **1.** [turn]: **it's your ~ du bist dran - 2.** *inf* [attempt] Versuch *der*; **to have a ~ at sthg** etw versuchen; **to have a ~ on sthg** etw aus|probieren; **'50p a ~'** 'jede Runde 50 Pence' - **3.** *phr*: **to have a ~ at sb** [criticize] jn zur Schnecke machen. **to go** *adv* [remaining]: **how long is there to ~ until Christmas?** wie lange ist es noch bis Weihnachten? <> **go about** <> *vt fus* [perform]: **to ~ about one's business** seinen Geschäften nach|gehen <> *vi* = go around. <> **go ahead** *vi* - **1.**: **to ~ ahead (with sthg)** (mit etw) an|fangen OR beginnen; **~ ahead!** bitte! - **2.** [take place] statt|finden. <> **go along** *vi*: **he was making it up as he went along** er sagte einfach, was ihm gerade im Sinn kam. <> **go along with** *vt fus* [idea, plan] zu|stimmen *(+ D).* <> **go around** *vi* - **1.** [associate]: **to ~ around with sb** mit jm herum|ziehen - **2.** [joke, illness, story] herum|gehen; [rumour] um|gehen. <> **go away** *vi* weg|gehen; [by vehicle] weg|fahren; **~ away!** geh weg! <> **go back** *vi* - **1.** [return] zurück|gehen; [by vehicle] zurück|fahren - **2.** [to activity]: **to ~ back to work** [after interruption] die Arbeit wieder auf|nehmen; [after holiday] wieder arbeiten gehen; **to ~ back to sleep** wieder ein|schlafen - **3.** [date from]: **their friendship goes back to 1955** sie sind schon seit 1955 befreundet. <> **go back on** *vt fus*: **to ~ back on one's word** sein Wort nicht halten. <> **go by** <> *vi* [time] vergehen <> *vt fus* - **1.** [be guided by - instincts] folgen *(+ D);* [- instructions] befolgen - **2.** [judge by - appearances] gehen nach; **~ing by her accent, I'd say she was French** ihrem Akzent nach ist sie Französin. <> **go down** <> *vi* - **1.** [decrease - prices, value, temperature] sinken - **2.** [sun] unter|gehen - **3.** [tyre] platt werden - **4.** [be accepted]: **to ~ down well/badly** gut/schlecht an|kommen <> *vt fus* [stairs,

road] hinunter|gehen. <> **go for** *vt fus* - **1.** [choose] wählen; [buy] nehmen - **2.** [be attracted to]: **to ~ for sb/sthg** jn/etw bevorzugen - **3.** [attack]: **to ~ for sb** auf jn los|gehen - **4.** [try to obtain] aus sein auf *(+ A);* **just ~ for it and ask her out!** frag sie einfach, ob sie mit dir ausgehen will! <> **go in** *vi* hinein|gehen. <> **go in for** *vt fus* - **1.** [enter - competition] mit|machen bei; [- exam] machen - **2.** *inf* [activity]: **he goes in for sports in a big way** er ist ein großer Sportfan. <> **go into** *vt fus* - **1.** [investigate] sich befassen mit - **2.** [take up as a profession]: **to ~ into teaching** Lehrer werden. <> **go off** <> *vi* - **1.** [alarm] los|gehen; [bomb] explodieren - **2.** [food] schlecht werden - **3.** [light, heating] aus|gehen <> *vt fus inf* [lose interest in] nicht mehr mögen. <> **go on** <> *vi* - **1.** [happen] los sein; **what's ~ing on next door?** was ist nebenan los? - **2.** [light, heating] an|gehen - **3.** [continue]: **to ~ on doing sthg** etw weiter tun - **4.** [pass - time] vergehen - **5.** [talk for too long]: **to ~ on (and on) about sthg** auf etw *(D)* herum|reiten; **don't ~ on about it!** hör doch mal (damit) auf! <> *vt fus* [be guided by]: **I've got nothing to ~ on** ich habe keine Anhaltspunkte. <> **go on at** *vt fus* [nag]: **to ~ on at sb** an jm herum|nörgeln. <> **go out** *vi* - **1.** [light, heating] aus|gehen - **2.** [move outside] hinaus|gehen; **to ~ out for a meal** essen gehen; **to ~ out for a walk** einen Spaziergang machen - **3.** [have relationship]: **to ~ out with sb** mit jm zusammen sein; **we've been ~ing out for six years** wir sind seit sechs Jahren zusammen - **4.** [tide]: **the tide is ~ing out** die Ebbe hat eingesetzt. <> **go over** *vt fus* - **1.** [check] überprüfen - **2.** [repeat]: **to ~ over sthg again** etw wiederholen. <> **go round** *vi* [revolve] sich drehen. <> **go through** *vt fus* - **1.** [experience] durch|machen - **2.** [search] durchsuchen. <> **go through with** *vt fus*: **the government is ~ing through with the plan** die Regierung setzt den Plan in die Tat um; **she couldn't ~ through with it** sie brachte es nicht fertig. <> **go towards** *vt fus* [contribute to] bestimmt sein für. <> **go under** *vi lit & fig* unter|gehen. <> **go up** <> *vi* - **1.** [increase] steigen - **2.** [move upwards - balloon] auf|steigen; [- person] auf|steigen <> *vt fus* [stairs, hill] hinauf|steigen. <> **go without** *vt fus*: **to ~ without sthg** ohne etw aus|kommen.

goad [gəʊd] *vt* [provoke] provozieren.

go-ahead <> *adj* fortschrittlich <> *n* Erlaubnis *die*.

goal [gəʊl] *n* - **1.** SPORT Tor *das*; **to score a ~** ein Tor erzielen - **2.** [aim] Ziel *das*.

goalkeeper ['gəʊlˌkiːpəʳ] *n* Torwart *der*.

goalpost ['gəʊlpəʊst] *n* Torpfosten *der*.

goat [gəʊt] *n* Ziege *die*.

goat's cheese *n* Ziegenkäse *der*.

gob [gɒb] *n Br inf* [mouth] Maul *das*.

gobble ['gɒbl] *vt* hinunterschlingen.

go-between *n* Vermittler *der*, -in *die*.

gobsmacked ['gɒbsmækt] *adj Br inf* platt.

go-cart *n* = go-kart.

god [gɒd] *n* Gott *der*. ◆ **God** ◇ *n* Gott *der;* **God knows** keine Ahnung; **for God's sake!** um Gottes willen!; **thank God!** Gott sei Dank! ◇ *excl:* **(my) God!** (mein) Gott!

godchild ['gɒdtʃaild] (*pl* -children [-ˌtʃildrən]) *n* Patenkind *das*.

goddaughter ['gɒdˌdɔːtə^r] *n* Patentochter *die*.

goddess ['gɒdɪs] *n* Göttin *die*.

godfather ['gɒdˌfɑːðə^r] *n* Pate *der*.

godforsaken ['gɒdfəˌseikn] *adj* gottverlassen.

godmother ['gɒdˌmʌðə^r] *n* Patin *die*.

godsend ['gɒdsend] *n* Geschenk *das* des Himmels.

godson ['gɒdsʌn] *n* Patensohn *der*.

goes [gəʊz] *vb* ⊳ go.

goggles ['gɒglz] *npl* [in industry] Schutzbrille *die;* [for diving] Taucherbrille *die;* [for skiing] Skibrille *die*.

going ['gəʊiŋ] ◇ *adj* - **1.** [rate, salary] üblich - **2.** *Br* [available]: **any jobs ~?** gibt es freie Stellen? ◇ *n* - **1.** [progress]: **have you finished already? - that's good** ~ bist du schon fertig? - du bist gut OR schnell vorangekommen; **it was slow** ~ es ging nur langsam voran - **2.** [in horse racing] Geläuf *das;* **the ~ is good** die Bahn ist gut; **this novel is heavy** ~ dieser Roman liest sich schwer.

go-kart [-kɑːt] *n Br* Go-Kart *der*.

gold [gəʊld] ◇ *adj* [gold-coloured] golden ◇ *n* [gen] Gold *das* ◇ *comp* [made of gold] Gold-.

golden ['gəʊldən] *adj* - **1.** [made of gold] Gold- - **2.** [gold-coloured] golden.

goldfish ['gəʊldfɪʃ] (*pl inv*) *n* Goldfisch *der*.

gold leaf *n* Blattgold *das*.

gold medal *n* Goldmedaille *die*.

goldmine ['gəʊldmaɪn] *n* - **1.** [mine] Goldmine *die* - **2.** [profitable business] Goldgrube *die*.

gold-plated [-'pleitɪd] *adj* vergoldet.

goldsmith ['gəʊldsmɪθ] *n* Goldschmied *der*, -in *die*.

golf [gɒlf] *n* Golf *das*.

golf ball *n* [for golf] Golfball *der*.

golf club *n* - **1.** [place, society] Golfklub *der* - **2.** [equipment] Golfschläger *der*.

golf course *n* Golfplatz *der*.

golfer ['gɒlfə^r] *n* Golfspieler *der*, -in *die*.

gone [gɒn] ◇ *pp* ⊳ go ◇ *adj* [no longer here] weg ◇ *prep* [past] nach; **it's ~ twelve (o'clock)** es ist zwölf Uhr vorbei.

gong [gɒŋ] *n* Gong *der*.

good [gʊd] (*compar* **better;** *superl* **best**) ◇ *adj* - **1.** [gen] gut; **it's ~ to see you again** schön, Sie wieder zu sehen; **to have a ~ time** sich gut amüsieren; **to feel ~** sich wohl fühlen; **it tastes/smells** ~ es schmeckt/riecht gut; **is this meat still ~?** kann man das Fleisch noch essen?; **it's ~ for you** [beneficial] das wird dir gut tun; [food] das ist gesund; **a ~ opportunity** eine günstige Gelegenheit; **to be ~ at sthg** etw gut können; **~ at French** gut in Französisch; **she's ~ with her hands** sie ist geschickt mit den Händen - **2.** [suitable] geeignet; **he would make a ~ president** er eignet sich zum Präsidenten - **3.** [kind] lieb; **that's very ~ of you** das ist sehr nett von Ihnen; **to be ~ to sb** gut zu jm sein; **would you be ~ enough to open the door?** wären Sie so liebenswürdig, mir die Tür zu öffnen? - **4.** [well-behaved] artig, brav; **be ~!** sei brav! - **5.** [thorough] gründlich - **6.** [considerable]: **a ~ while/deal** ziemlich lange/viel; **a ~ ten minutes** gute zehn Minuten - **7.** [moral correctness] Gute *das;* **to be up to no ~** nichts Gutes im Schilde führen - **2.** [use]: **it's no ~** [there's no point] es hat keinen Zweck - **3.** [benefit]: **it will do him ~** es wird ihm gut tun. ◆ **goods** *npl* Waren *pl*. ◆ **as good as** *adv* so gut wie; **as ~ as new** so gut wie neu. ◆ **for good** *adv* für immer. ◆ **good afternoon** *excl* guten Tag! ◆ **good evening** *excl* guten Abend! ◆ **good morning** *excl* guten Morgen! ◆ **good night** *excl* gute Nacht!

goodbye [ˌgʊd'bai] ◇ *excl* auf Wiedersehen!; [on phone] auf Wiederhören! ◇ *n:* **to say** ~ auf Wiedersehen sagen; **to wave** ~ zum Abschied winken.

saying goodbye

Ich muss jetzt leider gehen. I'm afraid I must be going.

Ich bin in Eile. I'm in a hurry.

Ja, dann bis zum nächsten Mal. OK then, see you again soon.

Es war schön, Sie getroffen zu haben. It was nice meeting you/to have met you.

Es hat mich sehr gefreut, Sie kennengelernt zu haben. I very much enjoyed meeting you.

good deed *n* gute Tat.

good fortune *n* Glück *das*.

Good Friday *n* Karfreitag *der*.

good-humoured [-'hjuːməd] *adj* [person - temporarily] gut gelaunt; [- by nature] gutmütig; [rivalry] freundschaftlich.

good-looking [-'lʊkiŋ] *adj* gut aussehend.

good-natured [-'neitʃəd] *adj* [person] gutmütig; [rivalry] freundschaftlich; [argument] friedlich.

goodness ['gʊdnɪs] ◇ *n* - **1.** [kindness] Güte *die* - **2.** [of food] Nährgehalt *der* ◇ *excl:*

(my) ~! meine Güte!; **for ~' sake!** um Himmels willen!; **thank ~!** Gott sei Dank!

goods train *n* Br Güterzug *der*.

goodwill [ˌgʊdˈwɪl] *n* (U) guter Wille; [between countries & COMM] Goodwill *der*.

goody ['gʊdɪ] ◇ *n inf* [in story] Gute *der, die* ◇ *excl* toll!, prima! ➜ **goodies** *npl inf* - **1.** [delicious food] Leckerbissen *pl* - **2.** [desirable objects] schöne Dinge *pl*.

goose [guːs] (*pl* geese) *n* Gans *die*.

gooseberry ['gʊzbərɪ] *n* Stachelbeere *die*.

gooseflesh ['guːsfleʃ] *n*, **goose pimples** Br *npl*, **goosebumps** Am ['guːsbʌmps] *npl* Gänsehaut *die*.

gore [gɔːʳ] ◇ *n* (U) *literary* [blood] Blut *das* ◇ *vt* [subj: bull] mit den Hörnern verletzen.

gorge [gɔːdʒ] ◇ *n* Schlucht *die* ◇ *vt*: **to ~ o.s. on** OR **with sthg** sich mit etw vollstopfen.

gorgeous ['gɔːdʒəs] *adj* - **1.** [place, present, weather] herrlich, wunderschön - **2.** *inf* [person] toll aussehend; **to be ~** toll auslsehen.

gorilla [gəˈrɪlə] *n* Gorilla *der*.

gormless ['gɔːmlɪs] *adj* Br *inf* dämlich.

gory ['gɔːrɪ] *adj* [story, film] blutrünstig.

gosh [gɒʃ] *excl inf* mein Gott!, Mensch!

go-slow *n* Br Bummelstreik *der*.

gospel ['gɒspl] *n* [doctrine] Lehre *die*. ➜ **Gospel** *n* [in Bible] Evangelium *das*.

gossip ['gɒsɪp] ◇ *n* - **1.** [conversation] Klatsch *der*; **to have a ~** klatschen - **2.** [person] Klatschbase *die* ◇ *vi* klatschen.

gossip column *n* Klatschspalte *die*.

got [gɒt] *pt & pp* ➜ get.

gotten ['gɒtn] *pp* Am ➜ get.

goulash ['guːlæʃ] *n* Gulasch *das*.

gourmet ['gʊəmeɪ] *n* Feinschmecker *der*, -in *die*.

gout [gaʊt] *n* Gicht *die*.

govern ['gʌvən] ◇ *vt* - **1.** POL regieren - **2.** [determine] bestimmen ◇ *vi* POL regieren.

governess ['gʌvənɪs] *n* Gouvernante *die*.

government ['gʌvnmənt] *n* Regierung *die*.

governor ['gʌvənəʳ] *n* - **1.** POL Gouverneur *der*, -in *die* - **2.** [of school] Mitglied *das* des Schulbeirats; [of bank] Mitglied *das* des Direktoriums - **3.** [of prison] Direktor *der*, -in *die*.

gown [gaʊn] *n* - **1.** [dress] Kleid *das*; [evening gown] Abendkleid *das* - **2.** UNIV & LAW Talar *der* - **3.** MED Kittel *der*.

GP *n abbr of* general practitioner.

grab [græb] ◇ *vt* - **1.** [with hands]: **to ~ (hold of)** [person] packen; [object] schnappen; **to ~ (hold of) sb's arm** jn am Arm packen - **2.** *fig* [opportunity] (beim Schopf) ergreifen; [sandwich, lunch] schnell essen - **3.** *inf* [appeal to]: **how does that ~ you?** wie findest du das? ◇ *vi*: **to ~ at sthg** [with hands] nach etw greifen.

grace [greɪs] ◇ *n* - **1.** (U) [elegance] Grazie *die*, Anmut *die* - **2.** [extra time]: **ten days' ~** zehn Tage Aufschub - **3.** [prayer] Tischgebet *das* ◇ *vt* [adorn] schmücken.

graceful ['greɪsfʊl] *adj* [beautiful] graziös, anmutig; [line, curve] gefällig.

gracious ['greɪʃəs] ◇ *adj* [polite] höflich ◇ *excl*: **(good) ~!** ach du meine Güte!

grade [greɪd] ◇ *n* - **1.** [quality] Güteklasse *die*; **high-~** hochwertig - **2.** [in company, organization]: **(salary) ~** Gehaltsstufe *die* - **3.** Am [class] Klasse *die* - **4.** [in exam, test] Note *die* - **5.** Am [gradient] Gefälle *das* ◇ *vt* - **1.** [classify] klassifizieren - **2.** [test, exam] benoten.

grade crossing *n* Am Bahnübergang *der*.

grade school *n* Am Grundschule *die*.

gradient ['greɪdɪənt] *n* [of road - upward] Steigung *die*; [- downward] Gefälle *das*.

gradual ['grædʒʊəl] *adj* allmählich.

gradually [n 'grædʒʊəlɪ] *adv* allmählich.

graduate [n 'grædʒʊət, vb 'grædʒʊeɪt] ◇ *n* - **1.** [person with a degree] Graduierte *der, die* - **2.** Am [of high school] ≃ Abiturient *der*, -in *die (mit bestandenem Abitur)* ◇ *vi* - **1.** [with a degree]: **to ~ (from)** seinen Hochschulabschluss machen (an (+ D)) - **2.** Am [from high school]: **to ~ (from)** ≃ das Abitur machen (an (+ D)).

graduation [ˌgrædʒʊˈeɪʃn] *n* [university or school ceremony] Abschlussfeier *die*.

graffiti [grəˈfiːtɪ] *n* (U) Graffiti *pl*.

graft [grɑːft] ◇ *n* - **1.** [from plant] Pfropfreis *das* - **2.** MED Transplantat *das* - **3.** Br *inf* [hard work] Plackerei *die* - **4.** Am *inf* [corruption] Schiebung *die* ◇ *vt* - **1.** [plant]: **to ~ sthg (onto)** etw pfropfen (auf (+ A)) - **2.** MED: **to ~ sthg (onto)** etw transplantieren (in (+ A)).

grain [greɪn] *n* - **1.** [of corn, rice, salt, sand] Korn *das* - **2.** (U) [crops] Getreide *das*, Korn *das* - **3.** [in wood] Maserung *die*.

gram [græm] *n* Gramm *das*.

grammar ['græməʳ] *n* Grammatik *die*.

grammar school *n* - **1.** [in UK] ≃ Gymnasium *das* - **2.** [in US] ≃ Grundschule *die*.

grammatical [grəˈmætɪkl] *adj* grammatisch; **it's not ~** es ist nicht grammatikalisch richtig.

gramme [græm] *n* Br = gram.

gramophone ['græməfəʊn] *n* dated Grammofon *das*.

gran [græn] *n* Br *inf* Oma *die*, Omi *die*.

grand [grænd] (*pl inv*) ◇ *adj* [house, style] prachtvoll; [design, plan] ehrgeizig; [person, job] bedeutend ◇ *n inf* [thousand pounds] tausend Pfund *pl*; [thousand dollars] tausend Dollar *pl*.

grandad ['grændæd] *n inf* Opa *der*, Opi *die*.

grandchild ['græntʃaɪld] (*pl* -children [-ˌtʃɪldrən]) *n* Enkelkind *das*.

granddad ['grændæd] *n inf* = grandad.

granddaughter ['grænˌdɔːtər] *n* Enkelin *die.*

grandeur ['grændʒər] *n* [of building] Pracht *die;* [of scenery] Herrlichkeit *die.*

grandfather ['grændˌfɑːðər] *n* Großvater *der.*

grandma ['grænmɑː] *n inf* Oma *die*, Omi *die.*

grandmother ['grænˌmʌðər] *n* Großmutter *die.*

grandpa ['grænpɑː] *n inf* Opa *der*, Opi *der.*

grandparents ['grænˌpeərənts] *npl* Großeltern *pl.*

grand piano *n* Flügel *der.*

grand slam *n* SPORT Grand Slam *der.*

grandson ['grænsʌn] *n* Enkel *der.*

grandstand ['grændstænd] *n* (überdachte) Tribüne.

grand total *n* Endsumme *die.*

granite ['grænɪt] *n* Granit *der.*

granny ['grænɪ] *n inf* Oma *die*, Omi *die.*

grant [grɑːnt] <> *n* [money] Zuschuss *der;* [for study] Stipendium *das* <> *vt fml* - 1. [request, right] gewähren; [appeal] nachkommen (+ D); [wish] erfüllen - 2. [admit] zulgeben - 3. *phr:* **to take sthg for ~ed** etw als selbstverständlich betrachten.

granule ['grænjuːl] *n* Körnchen *das.*

grape [greɪp] *n* (Wein)traube *die.*

grapefruit ['greɪpfruːt] (*pl inv* OR **-s**) *n* Grapefruit *die*, Pampelmuse *die.*

grapevine ['greɪpvaɪn] *n* Weinstock *der;* **we heard on the ~ that ...** *fig* wir haben gehört, dass ...

graph [grɑːf] *n* Diagramm *das.*

graphic ['græfɪk] *adj* - 1. [vivid] anschaulich - 2. ART grafisch. **graphics** *npl* [pictures] grafische Darstellungen *pl.*

graphic artist *n* Grafiker *der*, -in *die.*

graphite ['græfaɪt] *n* Graphit *das.*

graph paper *n* Millimeterpapier *das.*

grapple ['græpl] **grapple with** *vt fus lit & fig* ringen mit.

grasp [grɑːsp] <> *n* - 1. [grip] Griff *der* - 2. [understanding]: **to have a good ~ of sthg** [language] etw gut beherrschen; [situation] etw verstehen <> *vt* - 1. [with hands] ergreifen - 2. [understand] begreifen.

grasping ['grɑːspɪŋ] *adj pej* [greedy] habgierig.

grass [grɑːs] *n* - 1. [on ground] Gras *das;* [lawn] Rasen *der* - 2. *drugs sl* [marijuana] Gras *das.*

grasshopper ['grɑːsˌhɒpər] *n* Heuschrecke *die.*

grass roots <> *npl* [ordinary people] Basis *die* <> *comp:* ~ **opinion/support** Meinung/Unterstützung der Basis; **at ~ level** an der Basis.

grass snake *n* Ringelnatter *die.*

grate [greɪt] <> *n* [in fireplace] (Kamin)rost *der* <> *vt* [cheese, carrots] reiben <> *vi* [irritate] auf die Nerven gehen.

grateful ['greɪtfʊl] *adj:* **to be ~ to sb (for sthg)** jm (für etw) dankbar sein.

grater ['greɪtər] *n* Reibe *die.*

gratify ['grætɪfaɪ] *vt* [please]: **to be gratified to hear/discover that ...** mit Genugtuung hören/entdecken, dass ...

grating ['greɪtɪŋ] <> *adj* nervend <> *n* [grille] Gitter *das.*

gratitude ['grætɪtjuːd] *n:* ~ **(to sb)** Dankbarkeit *die* (gegenüber jm).

gratuitous [grəˈtjuːɪtəs] *adj fml* unnötig.

grave [greɪv] <> *adj* - 1. [solemn] ernst - 2. [serious - situation, threat, illness] ernst; [- news] schlimm <> *n* Grab *das.*

gravel ['grævl] *n* Kies *der.*

gravestone ['greɪvstəʊn] *n* Grabstein *der.*

graveyard ['greɪvjɑːd] *n* Friedhof *der.*

gravity ['grævətɪ] *n* (*U*) - 1. [force] Schwerkraft *die* - 2. *fml* [seriousness] Ernst *der.*

gravy ['greɪvɪ] *n* (*U*) [meat juice] Bratensaft *der;* [sauce] Soße *die.*

gray *adj & n Am* = grey.

graze [greɪz] <> *vt* - 1. [cattle] grasen OR weiden lassen - 2. [knee, elbow] auflschürfen - 3. [touch lightly] streifen <> *vi* [animals] grasen, weiden <> *n* [wound] Schürfwunde *die.*

grease [griːs] <> *n* (*U*) - 1. [animal fat] Fett *das* - 2. [lubricant] Schmiere *die* <> *vt* [engine, machine] schmieren; [baking tray] einlfetten.

greaseproof paper [ˌgriːspruːf-] *n Br* Pergamentpapier *das.*

greasy ['griːsɪ] *adj* - 1. [food, hair, hands] fettig - 2. [clothes] schmierig.

great [greɪt] <> *adj* - 1. [large] groß; **to a ~ extent** in hohem Maße; **the ~ majority** die überwiegende Mehrheit; **a ~ deal of money** eine Menge OR sehr viel Geld - 2. [very good] großartig; **we had a ~ time** wir haben uns toll amüsiert <> *excl:* **(that's) ~!** (das ist) toll!

Great Britain *n* Großbritannien *nt.*

greatcoat ['greɪtkəʊt] *n langer schwerer Mantel.*

great-grandchild *n* Urenkel *der*, -in *die.*

great-grandfather *n* Urgroßvater *der.*

great-grandmother *n* Urgroßmutter *die.*

greatly ['greɪtlɪ] *adv* sehr.

greatness ['greɪtnɪs] *n* [importance] Bedeutung *die;* [size] Größe *die.*

Greece [griːs] *n* Griechenland *nt.*

greed [griːd] *n* - 1. [for food] Gefräßigkeit *die* - 2. *fig* [for money, power] Gier *die.*

greedy ['griːdɪ] *adj* - 1. [for food] gefräßig - 2. *fig* [for money, power]: ~ **for money/power** geld-/machtgierig.

Greek [griːk] <> *adj* griechisch <> *n* - 1. [person] Grieche *der*, -chin *die* - 2. [language] Griechisch(e) *das.*

green [griːn] <> *adj* grün; ~ **(with envy)**

blass OR grün (vor Neid) ◇ n - 1. [colour] Grün das - 2. [in village]: **(village)** ~ (Dorf)wiese die - 3. GOLF Grün das. ➤ **Green** n POL Grüne der, die; **the Greens** die Grünen. ➤ **greens** npl [vegetables] Grüngemüse das.

greenback ['gri:nbæk] n Am inf [banknote] Dollarschein der.

green belt n Br Grüngürtel der.

green card n - 1. Br [for insuring vehicle] grüne Versicherungskarte - 2. Am [resident's permit] Aufenthaltserlaubnis die.

greenfly ['gri:nflaɪ] (pl inv OR -ies) n (grüne) Blattlaus.

greengrocer ['gri:n,grəʊsə'] n Obst- und Gemüsehändler der, -in die; ~'s **(shop)** Obst- und Gemüsegeschäft das.

greenhouse ['gri:nhaʊs, pl -haʊzɪz] n Gewächshaus das, Treibhaus das.

greenhouse effect n: **the** ~ der Treibhauseffekt.

Greenland ['gri:nlənd] n Grönland nt.

green salad n grüner Salat.

greet [gri:t] vt lit & fig begrüßen; [say hello to in passing] grüßen.

greeting ['gri:tɪŋ] n Gruß der; **to exchange** ~**s** sich grüßen. ➤ **greetings** npl [on card]: **Christmas** ~**s** Weihnachtsgrüße; **birthday** ~**s** Glückwünsche zum Geburtstag.

greetings card Br, **greeting card** Am n Glückwunschkarte die.

grenade [grə'neɪd] n: **(hand)** ~ (Hand)granate die.

grew [gru:] pt ▷ grow.

grey Br, **gray** Am [greɪ] ◇ adj grau; [life] trostlos; **to go** ~ grau werden ◇ n Grau das.

grey-haired [-'heəd] adj grauhaarig.

greyhound ['greɪhaʊnd] n Windhund der.

grid [grɪd] n - 1. [grating] Gitter das - 2. [for maps] Gitternetz das; ELEC Überlandleitungsnetz das.

griddle ['grɪdl] n gusseiserne Platte zum Backen von Pfannkuchen.

gridlock ['grɪdlɒk] n [in traffic] Zusammenbruch der des Verkehrs.

grief [gri:f] n - 1. [sorrow] Trauer die - 2. inf [trouble] Ärger der - 3. phr: **to come to** ~ [in an accident] verunglücken; [plan] scheitern; **good** ~! ach du lieber Himmel!

grievance ['gri:vns] n [complaint] Beschwerde die.

grieve [gri:v] vi: **to** ~ **(for sb/sthg)** (um jn/ etw) trauern.

grievous ['gri:vəs] adj fml [wound] schlimm; [mistake] schwer wiegend.

grill [grɪl] ◇ n [of cooker] Grill der; [over fire] Bratrost der ◇ vt - 1. [cook] grillen - 2. inf [interrogate - interviewee] ausquetschen; [- prisoner, suspect] ins Verhör nehmen.

grille [grɪl] n Gitter das; **radiator** ~ AUT Kühlergrill der.

grim [grɪm] adj - 1. [face, smile] grimmig; [determination] eisern - 2. [place, situation] trostlos; [prospect] düster; [news] grauenvoll.

grimace ['grɪməs] ◇ n Grimasse die ◇ vi Grimassen schneiden; **to** ~ **with pain** vor Schmerz das Gesicht verziehen.

grime [graɪm] n Schmutz der; [soot] Ruß der.

grimy ['graɪmɪ] adj schmutzig; [sooty] verrußt.

grin [grɪn] ◇ n Grinsen das ◇ vi grinsen; **to** ~ **at sb/sthg** jn/etw angrinsen.

grind [graɪnd] (pt & pp ground) ◇ vt [coffee, pepper, flour] mahlen ◇ vi [car, gears] knirschen ◇ n [hard, boring work] Schinderei die; **the daily** ~ der tägliche Trott. ➤ **grind down** vt sep [oppress] unterdrücken. ➤ **grind up** vt sep zermahlen.

grinder ['graɪndə'] n [for coffee, pepper] Mühle die.

grip [grɪp] ◇ n - 1. [physical hold]: **to release one's** ~ **on sb/sthg** jn/etw loslassen - 2. [control]: **to have a (good)** ~ **on a situation** eine Situation im Griff haben; **to get to** ~**s with sthg** etw in den Griff bekommen; **to get a** ~ **on o.s.** sich zusammenreißen - 3. [of tyres] Haftung die; [of shoes] Halt der - 4. [handle] Griff der ◇ vt - 1. [grasp] festhalten - 2. [subj: tyres] haften auf (+ D) - 3. [imagination, attention, audience] fesseln.

gripe [graɪp] inf ◇ n [complaint] Gemecker das ◇ vi: **to** ~ **(about sthg)** (über etw (A)) meckern.

gripping ['grɪpɪŋ] adj [story, film] fesselnd.

grisly ['grɪzlɪ] adj grausig.

gristle ['grɪsl] n Knorpel der.

grit [grɪt] ◇ n (U) - 1. [for roads, in winter] Streusand der - 2. inf [courage] Schneid der ◇ vt [road, steps] streuen.

groan [grəʊn] ◇ n Stöhnen das ◇ vi - 1. [moan] stöhnen - 2. [door, table] ächzen - 3. [complain] sich beklagen.

grocer ['grəʊsə'] n Lebensmittelhändler der, -in die; ~'s **(shop)** Lebensmittelgeschäft das.

groceries ['grəʊsərɪz] npl Lebensmittel pl.

groggy ['grɒgɪ] adj geschwächt.

groin [grɔɪn] n Leiste die.

groom [gru:m] ◇ n - 1. [of horses] Stallbursche der, Stallgehilfin die - 2. [bridegroom] Bräutigam der ◇ vt - 1. [horse] striegeln; [dog] bürsten - 2. [candidate]: **to** ~ **sb (for)** jn vorbereiten (auf (+ A)).

groomed [gru:md] adj: **well** ~ gepflegt.

groove [gru:v] n Rille die.

grope [grəʊp] vi: **to** ~ **(about) for sthg** [object] nach etw tasten.

gross [grəʊs] (pl inv OR -es) ◇ adj

- 1. [weight, income] Brutto- **- 2.** *fml* [error, misconduct] grob; [exaggeration] krass **- 3.** *inf* [coarse, vulgar - person, behaviour] ordinär **- 4.** *inf* [obese] fett ◇ *n* Gros *das*.

grossly ['grəʊslɪ] *adv* [for emphasis] äußerst.

grotesque [grəʊ'tesk] *adj* grotesk.

grotto ['grɒtəʊ] (*pl* -es OR -s) *n* Grotte *die*.

grotty ['grɒtɪ] *adj Br inf* mies.

ground [graʊnd] ◇ *pt & pp* ▷ grind ◇ *n* **- 1.** [gen] Boden *der;* **above ~** über der Erde; **below ~** unter der Erde; **on the ~** auf dem Boden; *fig* vor Ort; **to gain/lose ~** an Boden gewinnen/verlieren; **to cut the ~ from under sb's feet** jm den Boden unter den Füßen wegziehen; **to stand one's ~** nicht von der Stelle weichen; *fig* auf seinem Standpunkt beharren **- 2.** SPORT Sportplatz *der;* [stadium] Stadion *das;* **football ~** Fußballplatz *der;* [stadium] Fußballstadion *das* ◇ *vt* **- 1.** [base]: **to be ~ed on** OR **in sthg** auf etw (D) basieren **- 2.** [aircraft, pilot] *inf* nicht fliegen lassen **- 3.** *esp Am* [child]: **to be ~ed** Hausarrest haben **- 4.** *Am* ELEC: **to be ~ed** geerdet sein. ◆ **grounds** *npl* **- 1.** [reason] Grund *der;* **to have ~s for doing sthg** einen Grund dafür haben, etw zu tun; **on health ~s** aus gesundheitlichen Gründen **- 2.** [of building] Gelände *das* **- 3.**: **coffee ~s** Kaffeesatz *der*.

ground crew *n* Bodenpersonal *das*.

ground floor *n* Erdgeschoss *das*.

grounding ['graʊndɪŋ] *n*: **to have a ~ in sthg** Grundkenntnisse in etw (D) haben.

groundless ['graʊndlɪs] *adj* grundlos.

groundsheet ['graʊndʃi:t] *n* Bodenplane *die*.

ground staff *n Br* [at airport] Bodenpersonal *das*.

groundwork ['graʊndwɜ:k] *n* (U) Vorarbeit *pl*.

group [gru:p] ◇ *n* [gen] Gruppe *die* ◇ *vt* gruppieren; [classify] klassifizieren ◇ *vi*: **to ~ (together)** sich zusammen tun.

groupie ['gru:pɪ] *n inf* Groupie *das*.

grouse [graʊs] (*pl inv* OR -s) ◇ *n* [bird] Schottisches Moorschneehuhn ◇ *vi inf* meckern.

grove [grəʊv] *n* Hain *der*.

grovel ['grɒvl] *vi* kriechen; **to ~ to sb** vor jm kriechen.

grow [grəʊ] (*pt* grew; *pp* grown) ◇ *vi* **- 1.** [gen] wachsen; [problem] sich vergrößern; [love] stärker werden; [idea] Formen an nehmen; **to ~ in popularity** an Beliebtheit gewinnen **- 2.** [become] werden; **to ~ old** alt werden; **to ~ to do sthg** allmählich etw tun ◇ *vt* [crops, vegetables] anbauen; [flowers] züchten; **to ~ one's hair/a beard** sich (D) die Haare/einen Bart wachsen lassen. ◆ **grow on** *vt fus inf* [subj: music,

idea]: **it'll ~ on you** es wird dir mit der Zeit immer besser gefallen. ◆ **grow out of** *vt fus* **- 1.** [clothes, shoes] herauswachsen aus **- 2.** [habit] ablegen. ◆ **grow up** *vi* [person] aufwachsen; [become adult] erwachsen werden; **~ up!** werd endlich erwachsen!

grower ['grəʊəʳ] *n* [of flowers] Züchter *der,* -in *die;* [of crops, vegetables] Anbauer *der,* -in *die*.

growl [graʊl] *vi* knurren; [bear, engine] brummen.

grown [grəʊn] ◇ *pp* ▷ grow ◇ *adj* erwachsen.

grown-up ◇ *adj* [fully grown] ausgewachsen; [mature] erwachsen ◇ *n* Erwachsene *der, die*.

growth [grəʊθ] *n* **- 1.** [increase - of economy, company, population] Wachstum *das;* [- of research, opposition, nationalism] Zunahme *die* **- 2.** [development - of person] Entwicklung *die* **- 3.** MED Geschwulst *die*.

grub [grʌb] *n* **- 1.** [insect] Larve *die* **- 2.** *inf* [food] Futter *das*.

grubby ['grʌbɪ] *adj* [clothes] schmuddelig; [hands, child] schmutzig.

grudge [grʌdʒ] ◇ *n* Groll *der;* **to bear sb a ~, to have a ~ against sb** einen Groll gegen jn hegen ◇ *vt*: **to ~ sb sthg** jm etw missgönnen.

gruelling *Br*, **grueling** *Am* ['grʊəlɪŋ] *adj* strapaziös.

gruesome ['gru:səm] *adj* grausig.

gruff [grʌf] *adj* **- 1.** [voice] rau **- 2.** [person, manner] barsch.

grumble ['grʌmbl] *vi* [complain]: **to ~ (about)** murren (über (+ A)).

grumpy ['grʌmpɪ] *adj inf* mürrisch.

grunt [grʌnt] ◇ *n* Grunzen *das* ◇ *vi* grunzen.

G-string *n* **- 1.** MUS G-Saite *die* **- 2.** [clothing] Tangaslip *der*.

guarantee [ˌgærən'ti:] ◇ *n* Garantie *die;* [document] Garantieschein *der;* **to give sb a ~ that ...** jm garantieren, dass ... ◇ *vt* **- 1.** COMM Garantie geben auf (+ A) **- 2.** [promise] garantieren.

guard [gɑ:d] ◇ *n* **- 1.** [person] Wachposten *der;* [for prisoner] Gefängniswärter *der,* -in *die;* [group of guards] Wache *die* **- 2.** [supervision] Überwachung *die;* **to be on ~** Wache haben; **to catch sb off ~** jn überrumpeln **- 3.** *Br* RAIL Schaffner *der,* -in *die* **- 4.** [protective device] Schutz *der;* [for machine] Schutzvorrichtung *die;* [for fire] Schutzgitter *das* **- 5.** [in boxing] Deckung *die* ◇ *vt* bewachen.

guard dog *n* Wachhund *der*.

guarded ['gɑ:dɪd] *adj* [reply, statement] vorsichtig.

guardian ['gɑ:djən] *n* **- 1.** LAW [of child] Vormund *der* **- 2.** [protector] Wächter *der,* -in *die*.

guardrail ['gɑːdreɪl] n Geländer das.

guard's van n Br Schaffnerabteil das.

guerilla [gə'rɪlə] n = guerrilla.

Guernsey ['gɜːnzɪ] n [place] Guernsey nt.

guerrilla [gə'rɪlə] n Guerillakämpfer der, -in die.

guerrilla warfare n (U) Guerillakrieg der.

guess [ges] ◇ n - 1. [at facts, figures] Schätzung die; **at a ~** schätzungsweise - 2. [hypothesis] Vermutung die ◇ vt [answer, name] raten; [correctly] erraten, richtig schätzen; [figure, weight] schätzen; **~ what!** stell dir vor! ◇ vi - 1. [gen] raten; **to ~ at sthg** etw zu erraten versuchen - 2. [suppose] glauben, denken; **I ~ (so)** ich glaube (schon).

guesswork ['geswɜːk] n (U) (reine) Vermutung.

guest [gest] n Gast der; **be my ~!** nur zu!

guesthouse ['gesthaʊs, pl -haʊzɪz] n Pension die.

guestroom ['gestrʊm] n Gästezimmer das.

guffaw [gʌ'fɔː] vi schallend lachen.

guidance ['gaɪdəns] n (U) - 1. [help from teacher, parents] Anleitung die; [counselling] Beratung die - 2. [leadership] Führung die.

guide [gaɪd] ◇ n - 1. [for tourists] Fremdenführer der, -in die; **tour ~** Reiseleiter der, -in die - 2. [guide book] Führer der; [manual] Handbuch das - 3. [indication] Orientierungshilfe die; **to use sthg as a ~** etw als Vorbild nehmen - 4. = girl guide ◇ vt - 1. [lead] führen; **to be ~d by sb/sthg** [influenced] sich von jm/etw leiten lassen - 2. [plane, missile] lenken.

guide book n Führer der.

guide dog n Blindenhund der.

guided tour ['gaɪdɪd-] n Führung die.

guideline ['gaɪdlaɪn] n Richtlinie die.

guild [gɪld] n [association] Vereinigung die.

guile [gaɪl] n literary List die.

guillotine ['gɪləˌtiːn] n - 1. [for executions] Guillotine die - 2. [for paper] Papierschneidemaschine die ◇ vt [execute] guillotinieren.

guilt [gɪlt] n Schuld die.

guilty ['gɪltɪ] adj - 1. [gen] schuldig; [smile, look] schuldbewusst - 2.: **to be found ~/not ~** LAW für schuldig/nicht schuldig befunden werden.

guinea pig ['gɪnɪ-] n - 1. [animal] Meerschweinchen das - 2. [subject of experiment] Versuchskaninchen das.

guise [gaɪz] n fml: **to present sthg in a new ~** etw anders darstellen; **under the ~ of friendship** unter dem Deckmantel der Freundschaft.

guitar [gɪ'tɑːʳ] n Gitarre die.

guitarist [gɪ'tɑːrɪst] n Gitarrist der, -in die.

gulf [gʌlf] n - 1. [sea] Golf der - 2. lit & fig [gap] Kluft die. ◆ **Gulf** n: **the Gulf** der Golf.

gull [gʌl] n Möwe die.

gullet ['gʌlɪt] n Speiseröhre die.

gullible ['gʌləbl] adj leichtgläubig.

gully ['gʌlɪ] n - 1. [valley] Schlucht die - 2. [ditch] Graben der.

gulp [gʌlp] ◇ n Schluck der ◇ vt hinunterlschlucken ◇ vi schlucken. ◆ **gulp down** vt sep hinunterlschlucken.

gum [gʌm] ◇ n - 1. [chewing gum] Kaugummi der - 2. [adhesive] Klebstoff der - 3. ANAT Zahnfleisch das ◇ vt [stick] kleben.

gummed [gʌmd] adj gummiert.

gun [gʌn] n - 1. [weapon - revolver] Pistole die, Revolver der; [- rifle, shotgun] Gewehr das; [- cannon] Kanone die - 2. SPORT [starting pistol] Startpistole die - 3. [for paint, spraying] Pistole die. ◆ **gun down** vt sep [person, animal] niederlschießen.

gunfire ['gʌnfaɪəʳ] n (U) MIL Geschützfeuer das; [of small arms] Schießerei die.

gunman ['gʌnmən] (pl -men [-mən]) n (mit einer Schußwaffe) bewaffneter Mann.

gunpoint ['gʌnpɔɪnt] n: **to hold sb at ~** jn mit einer Pistole/einem Gewehr bedrohen.

gunpowder ['gʌnˌpaʊdəʳ] n Schießpulver das.

gunshot ['gʌnʃɒt] n Schuss der.

gurgle ['gɜːgl] vi - 1. [water] gluckern - 2. [baby] glucksen.

guru ['gʊruː] n Guru der.

gush [gʌʃ] ◇ n Strahl der ◇ vi - 1. [flow out] herauslschießen - 2. pej [enthuse] schwärmen.

gust [gʌst] n Windstoß der, Böe die.

gusto ['gʌstəʊ] n: **with ~** mit Genuss.

gut [gʌt] ◇ n - 1. MED Darm der - 2. inf [stomach] Bauch der ◇ vt - 1. [animal, fish] auslnehmen - 2. [building]: **the fire ~ted the house** das Haus brannte völlig aus. ◆ **guts** npl inf - 1. [intestines] Eingeweide pl; **to hate sb's ~s** jn absolut nicht ausstehen können - 2. [courage] Mumm der.

gutter ['gʌtəʳ] n - 1. [beside road] Rinnstein der - 2. [on roof] Dachrinne die.

guy [gaɪ] n - 1. inf [man] Typ der - 2. esp Am [person]: **are you ready, ~s?** seid ihr fertig? - 3. Br [dummy] Puppe, die Guy Fawkes darstellt und in der „Guy Fawkes' Night" verbrannt wird.

Guy Fawkes' Night n Nacht des 5. November, Jahrestag der Pulververschwörung gegen König James I und das Parlament 1605.

guzzle ['gʌzl] ◇ vt [food] hinunterlschlingen; [drink] hinunterlkippen ◇ vi [eat] sich volllfressen.

gym [dʒɪm] n inf - 1. [gymnasium - in school] Turnhalle die; [- in hotel] Fitnessraum der; [- health club] Fitnessstudio das - 2. [exercises] Turnen das.

gymnasium [dʒɪm'neɪzjəm] (*pl* -iums OR -ia [-jə]) *n* [in school] Turnhalle *die*; [in hotel] Fitnessraum *der*; [health club] Fitnessstudio *das*.

📖 gymnasium

Ein gymnasium ist im Englischen eine „Turnhalle" und keine weiterführende Schule. Die Kurzform gym ist außerdem die geläufige Bezeichnung für ein „Fitnessstudio".
Das deutsche „Gymnasium" hat im britischen und amerikanischen Schulsystem keine exakte Entsprechung. Am ehesten kann diese Schulform jedoch mit der britischen grammar school beziehungsweise der amerikanischen senior high school verglichen werden.

---

gymnast ['dʒɪmnæst] *n* Turner *der*, -in *die*.
gymnastics [dʒɪm'næstɪks] *n* (U) [exercises] Gymnastik *die*; [discipline] Turnen *das*.
gym shoes *npl* Turnschuhe *pl*.
gynaecologist *Br*, **gynecologist** *Am* [,gaɪnə'kɒlədʒɪst] *n* Gynäkologe *der*, -gin *die*.
gynaecology, **gynecology** *Am* [,gaɪnə'kɒlədʒɪ] *n* Gynäkologie *die*.
gypsy ['dʒɪpsɪ] *adj* & *n* = gipsy.
gyrate [dʒaɪ'reɪt] *vi* sich schnell drehen; [disco dancer] ausgelassen tanzen.

H

h (*pl* h's OR hs), **H** (*pl* H's OR Hs) [eɪtʃ] *n* [letter] h *das*, H *das*.
haberdashery ['hæbədæʃərɪ] *n* (U) [goods] Kurzwaren *pl*.
habit ['hæbɪt] *n* - 1. [usual practice] Gewohnheit *die*; **to get into the ~ of doing sthg** sich (D) daran gewöhnen, etw zu tun - 2. [drug addiction] Abhängigkeit *die* - 3. [garment] Habit *das*.
habitat ['hæbɪtæt] *n* Lebensraum *der*.
habitual [hə'bɪtʃʊəl] *adj* - 1. [customary] gewohnt - 2. [offender, smoker, drinker] Gewohnheits-.
hack [hæk] ◇ *n pej* [writer] Schreiberling *der* ◇ *vt* [cut] hacken; **to ~ sthg to pieces** etw zerhacken. ◆ **hack into** *vt fus* COMPUT eindringen in (+ A).
hacker ['hækər] *n* COMPUT Hacker *der*.
hackneyed ['hæknɪd] *adj pej* abgedroschen.
hacksaw ['hæksɔː] *n* Metallsäge *die*.

had [*weak form* həd, *strong form* hæd] *pt* & *pp* ⊳ have.
haddock ['hædək] (*pl inv*) *n* Schellfisch *der*.
hadn't ['hædnt] = had not.
haemorrhage ['hemərɪdʒ] *n* & *vi* = hemorrhage.
haemorrhoids ['hemərɔɪdz] *npl* = hemorrhoids.
haggard ['hægəd] *adj* verhärmt.
haggis ['hægɪs] *n* schottische Spezialität aus Schafsinnereien, im Schafsmagen gekocht.
haggle ['hægl] *vi*: **to ~ (over** OR **about)** feilschen (um).
Hague [heɪg] *n*: **The ~** Den Haag *nt*.
hail [heɪl] ◇ *n lit* & *fig* Hagel *der*; **a ~ of bullets** ein Kugelhagel ◇ *vt* - 1. [call] rufen; [taxi] heranwinken, anhalten - 2. [acclaim]: **to ~ sb/sthg as sthg** jn/etw als etw feiern ◇ *v impers* METEOR hageln.
hailstone ['heɪlstəʊn] *n* Hagelkorn *das*.
hailstorm ['heɪlstɔːm] *n* Hagelsturm *der*.
hair [heər] ◇ *n* - 1. (U) [on human head] Haare *pl*, Haar *das*; [single hair] Haar *das*; **to have one's ~ cut** sich (D) die Haare schneiden lassen; **to do one's ~** sich (D) die Haare machen - 2. [on animal, insect, plant] Haar *das* - 3. [on human skin] Haar *das* ◇ *comp* Haar-.
hairbrush ['heəbrʌʃ] *n* Haarbürste *die*.
haircut ['heəkʌt] *n* Haarschnitt *der*; **to get a ~ sich** (D) die Haare schneiden lassen.
hairdo ['heəduː] (*pl* -s) *n inf* Frisur *die*.
hairdresser ['heə,dresər] *n* Friseur *der*, -euse *die*; **~'s (salon)** Friseur *der*.
hairdryer ['heə,draɪər] *n* [handheld] Föhn *der*; [with hood] Trockenhaube *die*.
hair gel *n* Haargel *das*.
hairgrip ['heəgrɪp] *n Br* Haarklammer *die*.
hairpin ['heəpɪn] *n* Haarnadel *die*.
hairpin bend *n* Haarnadelkurve *die*.
hair-raising [-,reɪzɪŋ] *adj* haarsträubend.
hair remover [-rɪ,muːvər] *n* Enthaarungscreme *die*.
hairspray ['heəspreɪ] *n* Haarspray *das*.
hairstyle ['heəstaɪl] *n* Frisur *die*.
hairy ['heərɪ] *adj* - 1. [animal, person, body] behaart - 2. *inf* [dangerous] haarig.
half [*Br* hɑːf, *Am* hæf] (*pl senses 1, 2 and 3* halves; *pl senses 4 and 5* halves OR halfs) ◇ *adj* halb, -e, -er, -es; **~ my life** mein halbes Leben (lang); **a dozen** ein halbes Dutzend; **~ an hour** eine halbe Stunde ◇ *adv* halb; **as big** halb so groß; **as much again** noch einmal halb soviel; **past ten** *Br*, **after ten** *Am* halb elf; **it's ~ past** es ist halb; **isn't ~ cold** *Br inf* es ist unheimlich kalt; **--and~** halb und halb ◇ *n* - 1. [50%] Hälfte *die*; **of it** die Hälfte davon; **in ~** [cut, tear] in zwei Hälften; **to go halves (with sb)** (mit jm) halbe-halbe machen - 2. [fraction] Halbe(s) *das*; **four and a ~** viereinhalb - 3. SPORT [of sports match] Spielhälfte *die* - 4. [of beer] kleines Bier - 5. [child's ticket] Fahrkarte *die* zum

halben Preis; **one and a ~** ein Erwachsener und ein Kind.

half board *n* (*U*) *esp Br* Halbpension *die*.

half-caste [-kɑːst] <> *adj* Halbblut- <> *n* Mischling *der*.

half-fare *n* halber Fahrpreis.

half-hearted [-ˈhɑːtɪd] *adj* halbherzig.

half hour *n* halbe Stunde.

half-mast *n* Br: **at ~** [flag] auf halbmast.

half moon *n* Halbmond *der*.

half note *n* Am MUS halbe Note.

halfpenny [ˈheɪpnɪ] (*pl* **-pennies** OR **-pence**) *n* halber Penny.

half-price *adj & adv* zum halben Preis.

half term *n Br* kurze Schulferien in der Mitte des Trimesters.

half time *n* Halbzeit *die*.

halfway [hɑːfˈweɪ] <> *adj*: **at the ~ stage** OR **point of sthg** in der Mitte von etw <> *adv*: **to go ~** die Hälfte des Weges zurücklegen; **~ through the holidays** mitten im Urlaub.

hall [hɔːl] *n* - 1. [in house] Diele *die*, Flur *der* - 2. [meeting room] Saal *der* - 3. [public building] Halle *die* - 4. Br UNIV [hall of residence] Studentenwohnheim *das* - 5. [country house] Herrensitz *der*.

hallmark [ˈhɔːlmɑːk] *n* - 1. [typical feature] Kennzeichen *das* - 2. [on metal] Feingehaltsstempel *der*.

hallo [həˈləʊ] *excl* = hello.

hall of residence (*pl* **halls of residence**) *n Br* UNIV Studentenwohnheim *das*.

Hallowe'en, Halloween [ˌhæləʊˈiːn] *n* Abend vor Allerheiligen, an dem sich Kinder oft als Gespenster verkleiden.

hallucinate [həˈluːsɪneɪt] *vi* halluzinieren.

hallway [ˈhɔːlweɪ] *n* Diele *die*, Flur *der*.

halo [ˈheɪləʊ] (*pl* **-es** OR **-s**) *n* [of saint, angel] Heiligenschein *der*.

halt [hɔːlt] <> *n*: **to come to a ~** *lit & fig* zum Stillstand kommen; **to call a ~ to sthg** etw (*D*) Einhalt gebieten <> *vt* [person] anhalten; [development, activity] zum Stillstand bringen <> *vi* [vehicle] anhalten, halten; [person] stehen bleiben; [development, activity] stillstehen.

halve [Br hɑːv, Am hæv] *vt* - 1. [reduce by half] halbieren - 2. [divide] teilen.

halves [Br hɑːvz, Am hævz] *pl* ➪ half.

ham [hæm] <> *n* [meat] Schinken *der* <> *comp* [salad, sandwich] Schinken-.

hamburger [ˈhæmbɜːgə] *n* - 1. [burger] Hamburger *der* - 2. (*U*) Am [mince] Hackfleisch *das*.

hamlet [ˈhæmlɪt] *n* kleines Dorf.

hammer [ˈhæmə] <> *n* Hammer *der* <> *vt* - 1. [with tool - nail] einschlagen; [- panel] hämmern - 2. *inf fig* [fact, order]: **to ~ sthg into sb** jm etw einbläuen - 3. *inf fig* [team, player] abservieren <> *vi*: **to ~ (on)** hämmern (an (+ A)). ➪ **hammer out** *vt fus* [agree-

ment, solution] ausarbeiten <> *vt sep* [metal] aushämmern; [dent] ausbeulen.

hammock [ˈhæmək] *n* Hängematte *die*.

hamper [ˈhæmpə] <> *n* - 1. [for picnic] Picknickkorb *der* - 2. Am [for laundry] Wäschekorb *der* <> *vt* [impede] behindern.

hamster [ˈhæmstə] *n* Hamster *der*.

hand [hænd] <> *n* - 1. [part of body] Hand *die*; **to hold ~s** Händchen halten; **by ~** von Hand; **to get** OR **lay one's ~s on sb/sthg** an jm/etw herankommen; **to have one's ~s full** alle Hände voll zu tun haben; **to try one's ~ at sthg** sich in etw (*D*) versuchen - 2. [help] Hilfe *die*; **do you need a ~?** kann ich dir helfen?; **to give** OR **lend sb a ~** jm helfen - 3. [worker] Arbeiter *der*, -in *die*; [on ship] Besatzungsmitglied *das* - 4. [of clock, watch] Zeiger *der* - 5. [handwriting] Handschrift *die* - 6. [of cards] Blatt *das* <> *vt*: **to ~ sthg to sb, to ~ sb sthg** jm etw geben OR reichen. ➪ **(close) at hand** *adv* nah in Reichweite. ➪ **in hand** *adv* - 1. [time, money]: **I have ten pounds in ~** ich habe zehn Pfund übrig; **we have an hour in ~** es bleibt uns noch eine Stunde - 2. [problem, situation]: **to have sthg in ~** etw in Bearbeitung haben. ➪ **on hand** *adv* zur Stelle. ➪ **on the one hand** *adv* einerseits. ➪ **on the other hand** *adv* andererseits. ➪ **out of hand** <> *adj* [situation]: **to get out of ~** außer Kontrolle geraten <> *adv* [completely] rundweg. ➪ **to hand** *adv* zur Hand. ➪ **hand down** *vt sep* [heirloom] hinterlassen; [knowledge] weitergeben. ➪ **hand in** *vt sep* [lost property] abgeben; [essay, application] einreichen. ➪ **hand out** *vt sep* austeilen. ➪ **hand over** <> *vt sep* - 1. [gen] übergeben - 2. TELEC: **I'll ~ you over to the manager** ich gebe Ihnen (mal) den Manager <> *vi*: **to ~ over (to sb)** (an jn) übergeben.

handbag [ˈhændbæg] *n* Handtasche *die*.

handball [ˈhændbɔːl] *n* [game] Handball *der*.

handbook [ˈhændbʊk] *n* Handbuch *das*.

handbrake [ˈhændbreɪk] *n* Handbremse *die*.

handcuffs [ˈhændkʌfs] *npl* Handschellen *pl*.

handful [ˈhændfʊl] *n* [gen] Hand *die* voll; [of grass, hair] Büschel *das*.

handgun [ˈhændgʌn] *n* Handfeuerwaffe *die*.

handicap [ˈhændɪkæp] <> *n* - 1. [disability] Behinderung *die* - 2. *fig* [disadvantage] Nachteil *der* - 3. SPORT Handicap *das* <> *vt* [hinder] behindern.

handicapped [ˈhændɪkæpt] *adj* [disabled] behindert.

handicraft [ˈhændɪkrɑːft] *n* [skill] Handwerk *das*.

handiwork [ˈhændɪwɜːk] *n* (*U*) Handarbeit *die*.

handkerchief ['hæŋkətʃɪf] (*pl* -chiefs OR -chieves [-tʃiːvz]) *n* Taschentuch *das*.

handle ['hændl] ⬦ *n* Griff *der;* [of door] Klinke *die;* [of broom, spade, frying pan] Stiel *der;* [of jug, cup] Henkel *der* ⬦ *vt* - 1. [with hands] anfassen - 2. [control - tool, machine, words] handhaben; [- car, ship] steuern - 3. [process - orders, complaints] bearbeiten; [- stolen goods] verschieben - 4. [cope with - situation, crisis, death] umgehen mit.

handlebars ['hændlbɑːz] *npl* Lenker *der*.

handler ['hændlə'] *n*: **(baggage)** ~ Gepäck-abfertiger *der*, -in *die*.

hand luggage *n* (U) *Br* Handgepäck *das*.

handmade [‚hænd'meɪd] *adj* in Handarbeit hergestellt.

handout ['hændaʊt] *n* - 1. [of money, food] Almosen *das* - 2. [leaflet] Flugblatt *das* - 3. [for lecture, discussion] Handout *das*.

handrail ['hændreɪl] *n* Geländer *das*.

handset ['hændset] *n* TELEC Hörer *der*.

handshake ['hændʃeɪk] *n* Händedruck *der*.

handsome ['hænsəm] *adj* - 1. [man] gut aussehend ⬦ *vt* [reward] großzügig; [profit] groß.

handstand ['hændstænd] *n* Handstand *der*.

hand towel *n* Händehandtuch *das*.

handwriting ['hænd‚raɪtɪŋ] *n* Handschrift *die*.

handy ['hændɪ] *adj inf* - 1. [useful] praktisch; **to come in** ~ nützlich sein - 2. [person] geschickt - 3. [near]: **the newsagent's is very** ~ der Zeitungshändler ist gleich um die Ecke.

---

handy

Das englische Adjektiv handy ist erst seit dem Siegeszug des Mobiltelefons ein falscher Freund. Es bedeutet „praktisch". Die deutsche Aussage „Ein Handy ist heute sehr praktisch" kann man mit a mobile (phone) comes in very handy these days übersetzen.
Wie das Beispiel bereits zeigt, wird ein Handy im Englischen als mobile phone oder kurz mobile bezeichnet.

---

handyman ['hændɪmæn] (*pl* -men [-men]) *n* Heimwerker *der*.

hang [hæŋ] (*pt & pp sense 1* hung; *pt & pp sense 2* hung OR hanged) ⬦ *vt* - 1. [suspend] aufhängen; **to** ~ **sthg on sthg** etw an etw (A) hängen - 2. [execute] hängen ⬦ *vi* hängen ⬦ *n*: **to get the** ~ **of sthg** *inf* kapieren, wie etw funktioniert. ⬦ **hang about, hang around** *vi* - 1. [loiter] herumlungen - 2. [wait] warten. ⬦ **hang down** *vi* herunterhängen. ⬦ **hang on** *vi* - 1. [keep hold]: **to** ~ **on (to)** sich festhalten (an (+ D)) - 2. *inf* [continue waiting] warten; ~ **on!** Moment mal!; [on telephone] bleiben Sie am Apparat! - 3. [persevere] aushalten.

⬦ **hang out** *vi inf* [spend time] herumhängen. ⬦ **hang round** *vi* = hang about. ⬦ **hang up** ⬦ *vt sep* [suspend] aufhängen ⬦ *vi* [on telephone] auflegen. ⬦ **hang up on** *vt fus* TELEC: **he hung up on me** er hat einfach aufgelegt.

hangar ['hæŋə'] *n* Hangar *der*.

hanger ['hæŋə'] *n* [coat hanger] Kleiderbügel *der*.

hangers-on *npl* Gefolgsleute *pl*.

hang gliding *n* Drachenfliegen *das*.

hangover ['hæŋ‚əʊvə'] *n* [from drinking] Kater *der*.

hang-up *n inf* PSYCH Komplex *der*.

hanker ['hæŋkə'] ⬦ **hanker after, hanker for** *vt fus* sich sehnen nach.

hankie, hanky ['hæŋkɪ] *n inf abbr of* handkerchief.

haphazard [‚hæp'hæzəd] *adj* willkürlich.

happen ['hæpən] *vi* - 1. [occur] geschehen, passieren; **to** ~ **to sb** jm passieren - 2. [chance]: **to** ~ **to do sthg** zufällig etw (A) tun; **as it** ~**s** zufälligerweise.

happening ['hæpənɪŋ] *n* Ereignis *das*.

happily ['hæpɪlɪ] *adv* - 1. [contentedly]: **the children were playing** ~ die Kinder spielten vergnügt - 2. [fortunately] glücklicherweise - 3. [willingly] gern.

happiness ['hæpɪnɪs] *n* Glück *das*.

happy ['hæpɪ] *adj* - 1. [contented] glücklich - 2. [causing contentment - life, day] glücklich; [- story] erfreulich; **Happy Christmas!** frohe OR fröhliche Weihnachten!; **Happy New Year!** frohes neues Jahr!; **Happy Birthday!** herzlichen Glückwunsch zum Geburtstag! - 3. [satisfied] zufrieden; **to be** ~ **with** OR **about sthg** glücklich OR zufrieden mit etw sein - 4. [willing]: **to be** ~ **to do sthg** etw gerne tun .

happy-go-lucky *adj inf* unbeschwert.

harangue [hə'ræŋ] ⬦ *n* Standpauke *die* ⬦ *vt*: **to** ~ **sb** jm eine Standpauke halten.

harass ['hærəs] *vt* belästigen.

harbour *Br*, **harbor** *Am* ['hɑːbə'] ⬦ *n* Hafen *der* ⬦ *vt* - 1. [feeling] hegen - 2. [person] versteckt halten.

hard [hɑːd] ⬦ *adj* - 1. [gen] hart; **to be** ~ **on sb** streng mit jm sein - 2. [difficult, strenuous] schwer; **it is** ~ **to believe that ...** es ist kaum zu glauben, dass ...; ~ **of hearing** schwerhörig - 3. [kick, push] heftig - 4. [fact] nackt - 5. *Br* POL: **the** ~ **left/right** der linke/rechte Flügel der Partei ⬦ *adv* - 1. [work, hit] hart; **to try** ~ sich (D) viel Mühe geben; **to listen** ~ genau hinhören - 2. [rain] heftig - 3. *phr*: **to be** ~ **pushed** OR **put** OR **pressed to do sthg** Schwierigkeiten haben, etw zu tun; **to feel** ~ **done by** sich benachteiligt fühlen.

hardback ['hɑːdbæk] ⬦ *adj* gebunden ⬦ *n* [book] gebundene Ausgabe.

hardboard ['hɑːdbɔːd] *n* Pressspanplatte *die*.

hard-boiled adj [egg] hart gekocht.

hard cash n Bargeld das.

hard copy n COMPUT Papierausdruck der.

hard disk n Festplatte die.

harden ['ha:dn] ◇ vt - 1. fig [person] abl-härten - 2.: **to ~ sb's opinion/attitude** jn in seiner Meinung/Einstellung bestärken ◇ vi - 1. [glue, concrete] härten - 2. [attitude, ideas, opinion] sich verhärten.

hardheaded [,ha:d'hedɪd] adj nüchtern.

hard-hearted [-'ha:tɪd] adj hartherzig.

hard labour n Zwangsarbeit die.

hard-liner n Hardliner der, -in die.

hardly ['ha:dlɪ] adv - 1. [scarcely, not really] kaum; **~ ever** fast nie; **~ anything** fast nichts - 2. [only just] gerade erst.

hardship ['ha:dʃɪp] n Entbehrung die.

hard shoulder n Br AUT Standspur die.

hard up adj inf knapp bei Kasse.

hardware ['ha:dweə⁹] n (U) - 1. [tools, equipment] Eisenwaren pl - 2. COMPUT Hardware die.

hardware shop n Eisenwarenhandlung die.

hardwearing [,ha:d'weərɪŋ] adj Br strapazierfähig.

hardworking [,ha:d'wɜ:kɪŋ] adj fleißig.

hardy ['ha:dɪ] adj - 1. [person, animal] abgehärtet - 2. [plant] mehrjährig.

hare [heə⁹] n Hase die, Feldhase der.

haricot (bean) ['hærɪkəʊ-] n weiße Bohne.

harm [ha:m] ◇ n [physical] Verletzung die; [psychological] Schaden der; **to do ~ to sb/ sthg, to do sb/sthg ~** jm/etw Schaden zufügen, jm/etw schaden; **to be out of ~'s way** [person] in Sicherheit sein; [thing] aus dem Weg sein ◇ vt [physically] verletzen; [psychologically] schädigen.

harmful ['ha:mfʊl] adj schädlich.

harmless ['ha:mlɪs] adj harmlos; [substance] unschädlich.

harmonica [ha:'mɒnɪkə] n Mundharmonika die.

harmonize, -ise ['ha:mənaɪz] ◇ vt [views, policies] in Einklang bringen ◇ vi - 1. [sounds, colours] **to ~ (with sthg)** harmonieren (mit etw) - 2. MUS harmonisieren.

harmony ['ha:mənɪ] n Harmonie die.

harness ['ha:nɪs] ◇ n - 1. [for horse] Geschirr das - 2. [for person, child] Gurt der ◇ vt - 1. [horse] anlschirren - 2. [energy, solar power] nutzbar machen.

harp [ha:p] n MUS Harfe die. ◆ **harp on** vi: **to ~ on (about sthg)** immer wieder anlfangen (von etw).

harpoon [ha:'pu:n] ◇ n Harpune die ◇ vt harpunieren.

harpsichord ['ha:psɪkɔ:d] n Cembalo das.

harrowing ['hærəʊɪŋ] adj grauenvoll.

harsh [ha:ʃ] adj - 1. [person, criticism, treatment, words] hart, streng - 2. [conditions, weather] rau - 3. [voice] barsch; [cry] schrill

- 4. [colour, contrast, light] grell - 5. [landscape] trostlos - 6. [taste] streng.

harvest ['ha:vɪst] ◇ n Ernte die ◇ vt ernten.

has [weak form həz, strong form hæz] vb ➤ have.

has-been n inf pej vergessene Größe.

hash [hæʃ] n - 1. [meat] Haschee das - 2. inf [mess]: **to make a ~ of sthg** etw vermasseln.

hashish ['hæʃi:ʃ] n Haschisch das.

hasn't ['hæznt] = has not.

hassle ['hæsl] inf ◇ n Ärger der ◇ vt ärgern.

haste [heɪst] n - 1. [rush] Eile die; **to do sthg in ~** etw in Eile tun - 2. [speed] Eile die.

hasten ['heɪsn] ◇ vt beschleunigen ◇ vi: **to ~ (to do sthg)** sich beeilen (, etw zu tun).

hastily ['heɪstɪlɪ] adv - 1. [rashly] übereilt - 2. [quickly] hastig.

hasty ['heɪstɪ] adj - 1. [rash] übereilt - 2. [quick] hastig.

hat [hæt] n Hut der.

hatch [hætʃ] ◇ vt - 1. [egg] auslbrüten - 2. fig [scheme, plot] auslhecken ◇ vi [chick] auslschlüpfen ◇ n [for serving food] Durchreiche die.

hatchback ['hætʃ,bæk] n Schräghecklimousine die.

hatchet ['hætʃɪt] n Beil das.

hate [heɪt] ◇ n [emotion] Hass der ◇ vt hassen, verabscheuen; **to ~ doing sthg** es hassen, etw zu tun.

hateful ['heɪtfʊl] adj abscheulich.

hatred ['heɪtrɪd] n Hass der.

hat trick n SPORT Hattrick der.

haughty ['hɔ:tɪ] adj hochmütig.

haul [hɔ:l] ◇ n - 1. [of drugs, stolen goods] Beute die - 2. [distance]: **a long ~** ein langer Weg ◇ vt [pull] ziehen.

haulage ['hɔ:lɪdʒ] n (U) [business] Transportunternehmen das.

haulier Br ['hɔ:lɪə⁹], **hauler** Am ['hɔ:lər] n [business] Spedition die.

haunch [hɔ:ntʃ] n - 1. [of person] Gesäß das - 2. [of animal] Keule die.

haunt [hɔ:nt] ◇ n [place] Lieblingsort der; [pub] Stammlokal das ◇ vt - 1. [subj: ghost] spuken in (+ D), umlgehen in (+ D) - 2. [subj: memory, fear, problem] verfolgen.

have [hæv] (pt & pp had) ◇ aux vb (to form perfect tenses) haben/sein; **I ~ burnt it** ich habe es verbrannt; **he has come** er ist gekommen; **I ~ finished** ich bin fertig; **I ~ lived here for three years** ich wohne hier seit drei Jahren; **~ you seen the film?** hast du den Film gesehen?; **~ you been there?** - no, **I haven't/yes, I ~** warst du schon mal dort? - nein, noch nie/ja; **she hasn't gone yet, has she?** sie ist noch nicht gegangen, oder?; **we had already left** wir waren schon gegangen; **I would never ~ gone if I'd known** ich wäre nie gegangen, wenn ich das gewusst hätte ◇ mo-

dal vb [be obliged]: **to ~ (got) to do sthg** etw tun müssen; **do you ~ to go, ~ you got to go?** musst du wirklich gehen?; **I've got to go to work** ich muss arbeiten gehen; **do you ~ to pay?** muss man bezahlen? ◇ vt - **1.** [possess]: **to ~ (got) haben; I ~ no money, I haven't got any money** ich habe kein Geld; **she has (got) brown hair** sie hat braunes Haar - **2.** [illness] haben; **to ~ a cold** eine Erkältung haben - **3.** [need to deal with]: **to ~ (got) haben; I've got things to do** ich habe einiges zu erledigen - **4.** [receive - news, letter] bekommen; **we don't ~ many visitors** wir haben OR bekommen wenig Besuch - **5.** [instead of another verb] haben; **to ~ a read of sthg** etw lesen; **to ~ a bath** ein Bad nehmen; **to ~ breakfast** frühstücken; **to ~ a cigarette** eine Zigarette rauchen; **to ~ a game of chess** eine Partie Schach spielen; **to ~ lunch/dinner** zu Mittag/zu Abend essen; **to ~ a shower** duschen; **to ~ a swim** schwimmen; **I've had a bad day** heute ist alles schief gegangen - **6.** [give birth to]: **to ~ a baby** ein Kind bekommen - **7.** [cause to be done]: **to ~ sb do sthg** jn etw tun lassen; **to ~ sthg done** etw machen lassen; **I'm having the house decorated** ich lasse das Haus tapezieren; **to ~ one's hair cut** sich (D) die Haare schneiden lassen - **8.** [experience, suffer - accident] haben; **to ~ a good time** sich großartig amüsieren - **9.** [organize - party] machen; [- meeting] abhalten - **10.** *inf* [cheat]: **you've been had!** du bist reingelegt worden! - **11.** *phr*: **to ~ it in for sb** es auf jn abgesehen haben; **to ~ had it** [car, machine, clothes] hinüber sein; **I've had it** [be tired] ich kann nicht mehr; [be in trouble] ich bin geliefert.

◆ have on vt sep - **1.** [be wearing] anhaben - **2.** [tease] anführen; **you're having me on!** du willst wohl auf den Arm nehmen!

◆ have out vt sep - **1.** [appendix, tonsils] herausgenommen bekommen; **to ~ a tooth out** einen Zahn gezogen bekommen - **2.** [discuss frankly]: **to ~ it out with sb** sich mit jm ausisprechen.

haven ['heɪvn] n Zufluchtsort *der.*

haven't ['hævnt] = have not.

havoc ['hævək] n Chaos *das,* Verwüstung *die;* **to play ~ with sthg** [health] etw ruinieren; [plans] etw über den Haufen werfen.

Hawaii [hə'waiɪ] n Hawaii *nt.*

hawk [hɔːk] n lit & fig Falke *der.*

hawker ['hɔːkə'] n - **1.** [street vendor] Straßenhändler *der,* -in *die* - **2.** [door-to-door] Hausierer *der,* -in *die.*

hay [heɪ] n Heu *das.*

hay fever n Heuschnupfen *der.*

haystack ['heɪˌstæk] n Heuschober *der.*

haywire ['heɪˌwaɪə'] adj inf: **to go ~** [person] durchldrehen; [machine] verrückt spielen.

hazard ['hæzəd] ◇ n [danger] Gefahr *die;* [risk] Risiko *das* ◇ vt - **1.** [life, reputation] riskieren - **2.** [guess, suggestion] wagen.

hazardous ['hæzədəs] adj [risky] riskant; [dangerous] gefährlich.

hazard warning lights npl Br Warnblinkanlage *die.*

haze [heɪz] n - **1.** [mist] Dunst *der* - **2.** [state of confusion] Verwirrtheit *die.*

hazelnut ['heɪzl,nʌt] n Haselnuss *die.*

hazy ['heɪzɪ] adj - **1.** [misty] dunstig - **2.** [vague, confused] verwirrt.

he [hiː] pers pron er; **~'s tall** er ist groß; **~ doesn't care** ihm ist es egal; **there ~ is** dort ist er; HE **can't do it** DER kann das nicht tun.

head [hed] ◇ n - **1.** [part of body] Kopf *der;* **a** OR **per ~** pro Kopf; **to laugh one's ~ off** sich totllachen; **to sing/shout one's ~ off** aus vollem Halse singen/schreien - **2.** [mind, brain] Verstand *der;* **to have a ~ for figures** eine Begabung für Zahlen haben; **to be off one's ~** *Br,* **to be out of one's ~** *Am* [mad] verrückt OR durchgedreht sein; *inf* [drunk] besoffen sein; **to go to sb's ~** [alcohol, success, praise] jm zu Kopf steigen; **to keep one's ~** den Kopf nicht verlieren; **to lose one's ~** den Kopf verlieren - **3.** [top, extremity - of stairs] oberer Absatz; [- of queue] Anfang *der;* [- of table, bed] Kopfende *das;* [- of procession, arrow] Spitze *die* - **4.** [of flower, cabbage] Kopf *der* - **5.** [leader - gen] Leiter *der,* -in *die;* [- of family] Oberhaupt *das* - **6.** [head teacher] Schulleiter *der,* -in *die* ◇ vt - **1.** [procession, queue, list] anlführen - **2.** [organization, delegation] leiten - **3.** FTBL köpfen ◇ vi [gen] gehen; [by car, bus, train] fahren; **where are you ~ing?** wohin gehst/fährst du?

◆ heads npl [on coin] Kopf *der;* **~s or tails?** Kopf oder Zahl? **◆ head for** vt fus - **1.** [place]: **to ~ for Glasgow** Richtung Glasgow fahren - **2.** *fig* [trouble, disaster] zulsteuern auf (+ A).

head of year

Die meisten Schulen der Sekundarstufe in England und Wales, ob staatlich oder privat, sind nach Jahrgangsstufen organisiert, beginnend mit der 7. und abschließend mit der 13. Klasse, dem zweiten Jahr der sixth form (Oberstufe). Für jede Jahrgangsstufe wird eine Lehrkraft ernannt, die die Rolle des Tutors ausübt und eine Vielzahl von Angelegenheiten bis hin zu Disziplinfragen und verlorenem Eigentum regelt. Der head of year fungiert auch als Vertrauenslehrer bei persönlichen Problemen und nimmt Kontakt mit den Eltern auf, wenn im Verlauf des Jahres schulische Probleme auftreten.

headache ['hedeɪk] n Kopfschmerzen *pl;* **to have a ~** Kopfschmerzen haben.

headband ['hedbænd] *n* Stirnband *das*.

headdress ['hed,dres] *n* Kopfschmuck *der*.

header ['hedə'] *n* - 1. FTBL Kopfball *der* - 2. [at top of page] Kopfzeile *die*.

headfirst [,hed'fɜːst] *adv* kopfüber.

heading ['hedɪŋ] *n* Überschrift *die*.

headlamp ['hedlæmp] *n* Br Scheinwerfer *der*.

headland ['hedlənd] *n* Landspitze *die*.

headlight ['hedlaɪt] *n* Scheinwerfer *der*.

headline ['hedlaɪn] *n* - 1. [in newspaper] Schlagzeile *die* - 2. [of news broadcast]: **the news ~s** die Kurznachrichten *pl*.

headlong ['hedlɒŋ] *adv* - 1. [at great speed] halsbrecherisch - 2. [impetuously] blindlings - 3. [dive, fall] kopfüber.

headmaster [,hed'mɑːstə'] *n* Schulleiter *der*.

headmistress [,hed'mɪstrɪs] *n* Schulleiterin *die*.

head office *n* Hauptsitz *der*.

head-on <> *adj* [collision] frontal; [confrontation] direkt <> *adv* frontal; [meet] direkt.

headphones ['hedfəʊnz] *npl* Kopfhörer *der*.

headquarters [,hed'kwɔːtəz] *npl* [of business, organization] Hauptniederlassung *die*; [of armed forces] Hauptquartier *das*.

headrest ['hedrest] *n* Kopfstütze *die*.

headroom ['hedrʊm] *n* [in car] Kopfraum *der*; [below bridge] lichte Höhe.

headscarf ['hedskɑːf] (*pl* -s OR -scarves [-skɑːvz]) *n* Kopftuch *das*.

headset ['hedset] *n* Kopfhörer *der*.

head start *n*: ~ **(on** OR **over sb)** Vorsprung *der* (vor OR gegenüber jm).

headstrong ['hedstrɒŋ] *adj* eigenwillig.

head waiter *n* Oberkellner *der*.

headway ['hedweɪ] *n*: **to make ~** vorankommen.

headword ['hedwɜːd] *n* Stichwort *das*.

heady ['hedɪ] *adj* [exciting] aufregend.

heal [hiːl] <> *vt* - 1. [person, wound] heilen - 2. *fig* [breach, division] schlichten, beilegen <> *vi* heilen.

healing ['hiːlɪŋ] <> *adj* heilend <> *n* (*U*) Heilung *die*.

health [helθ] *n* Gesundheit *die*.

health centre *n* Ärztezentrum *das*.

health food *n* Reformkost *die*.

health food shop *n* Reformhaus *das*.

health service *n* Gesundheitsdienst *der*.

healthy ['helθɪ] *adj* - 1. [gen] gesund - 2. [profit, sum] ordentlich - 3. [attitude] vernünftig; [respect] angebracht.

heap [hiːp] <> *n* Haufen *der* <> *vt* [pile up] aufhäufen; **to ~ sthg on(to) sthg** etw auf etw (*A*) häufen. **heaps** *npl inf*: **~s of money/people/books** ein Haufen Geld/Leute/Bücher; **~s of time** eine Menge Zeit.

hear [hɪə'] (*pt* & *pp* heard [hɜːd]) <> *vt* - 1. [perceive] hören - 2. [learn of] hören; **to ~ (that)** ... hören, dass ... - 3. LAW [listen to] anhören <> *vi* - 1. [gen] hören; **to ~ from sb** von jm hören - 2. [know]: **to ~ about sthg** etw erfahren - 3. *phr*: **to have heard of sb/sthg** von jm/etw gehört haben; **I won't ~ of it!** ich möchte nichts davon hören!

hearing ['hɪərɪŋ] *n* - 1. [sense] Gehör *das* - 2. LAW [trial] Verhandlung *die*.

hearing aid *n* Hörgerät *das*.

hearsay ['hɪəseɪ] *n* Hörensagen *das*.

hearse [hɜːs] *n* Leichenwagen *der*.

heart [hɑːt] *n* - 1. [gen] Herz *das*; **from the ~** von Herzen; **to break sb's ~** jm das OR js Herz brechen - 2. (*U*) [courage] Mut *der*; **to lose ~** den Mut verlieren - 3. [core - of city] Herz *das*; [- of problem] Kern *der*. **hearts** *npl* [playing cards] Herz *das*; **the six of ~s** die Herzsechs. **at heart** *adv* im Grunde. **by heart** *adv* auswendig.

heartache ['hɑːteɪk] *n* Kummer *der*.

heart attack *n* Herzanfall *der*.

heartbeat ['hɑːtbiːt] *n* Herzschlag *der*.

heartbroken ['hɑːt,brəʊkn] *adj* untröstlich.

heartburn ['hɑːtbɜːn] *n* Sodbrennen *das*.

heart failure *n* Herzversagen *das*.

heartfelt ['hɑːtfelt] *adj* tief empfunden.

hearth [hɑːθ] *n* Kamin *der*.

heartless ['hɑːtlɪs] *adj* herzlos.

heartwarming ['hɑːt,wɔːmɪŋ] *adj* herzerfreuend.

hearty ['hɑːtɪ] *adj* - 1. [laughter, praise, welcome] herzlich - 2. [meal, appetite] herzhaft.

heat [hiːt] <> *n* - 1. [warmth] Wärme *die* - 2. (*U*) [specific temperature] Temperatur *die* - 3. (*U*) [fire, source of heat] Feuer *das* - 4. (*U*) [hot weather] Hitze *die* - 5. *fig* [pressure]: **in the ~ of the moment** in der Hitze des Gefechts - 6. [eliminating round - in race] Vorlauf *der*; [- in competition] Vorrunde *die* - 7. ZOOL: **on ~** *Br*, **in ~** *Am* brünstig; [dog, cat] läufig; [horse] rossig <> *vt* heiß machen, erhitzen; [house, pool] heizen. **heat up** <> *vt sep* heiß machen <> *vi* sich erwärmen.

heated ['hiːtɪd] *adj* - 1. [room, swimming pool] beheizt - 2. [argument, discussion, person] hitzig.

heater ['hiːtə'] *n* [in car] Heizung *die*; [in room, water tank] Heizgerät *das*.

heath [hiːθ] *n* Heide *die*.

heathen ['hiːðn] <> *adj* heidnisch <> *n* Heide *der*, -din *die*.

heather ['heðə'] *n* Heidekraut *das*.

heating ['hiːtɪŋ] *n* Heizung *die*.

heatstroke ['hiːtstrəʊk] *n* Hitzschlag *der*.

heat wave *n* Hitzewelle *die*.

heave [hiːv] <> *vt* - 1. [pull] hieven; [push] schieben - 2. *inf* [throw] schmeißen - 3. [give out]: **to ~ a sigh** einen Seufzer ausstoßen

◇ *vi* - 1. [pull] ziehen - 2. [rise and fall] sich heben und senken - 3. [retch] brechen.

heaven ['hevn] *n* [Paradise] Himmel *der.*
  ◆ **heavens** ◇ *npl*: **the ~s** *literary* der Himmel ◇ *excl*: **(good) ~s!** du lieber Himmel!

heavenly ['hevnlɪ] *adj inf* [delightful] himmlisch, herrlich.

heavily ['hevɪlɪ] *adv* - 1. [smoke, drink] stark; [rain] heftig - 2. [built] solide - 3. [breathe, sigh] schwer, laut - 4. [fall, land] schwerfällig - 5. [sleep] tief.

heavy ['hevɪ] *adj* - 1. [in weight] schwer - 2. [fighting, losses] schwer; [rain] heftig; [traffic, smoker, drinker] stark; **to be a ~ sleeper** immer tief und fest schlafen - 3. [person - fat] dick; [- solidly built] untersetzt - 4. [coat, sweater] dick - 5. [food, responsibility] schwer - 6. [breathing, step, fall] schwerfällig - 7. [schedule, week] arbeitsreich - 8. [work, job] anstrengend.

heavy cream *n Am* Schlagsahne *die.*

heavy goods vehicle *n Br* Schwertransporter *der.*

heavyweight ['hevɪweɪt] ◇ *adj* SPORT Schwergewichts- ◇ *n* - 1. [boxer] Schwergewichtler *der* - 2. [intellectual] Größe *die.*

Hebrew ['hiːbruː] ◇ *adj* hebräisch ◇ *n* [language] Hebräisch(e) *das.*

heck [hek] *excl*: **what/where/why the ~ ...?** was/wo/warum zum Teufel ...?; **a ~ of a nice guy** ein wahnsinnig netter Kerl; **a ~ of a lot of people** wahnsinnig viele Leute.

heckle ['hekl] ◇ *vt* (durch Zwischenrufe) unterbrechen ◇ *vi* zwischenrufen.

hectic ['hektɪk] *adj* hektisch.

he'd [hiːd] = he had, he would.

hedge [hedʒ] ◇ *n* [shrub] Hecke *die* ◇ *vi* [prevaricate] Ausflüchte machen.

hedgehog ['hedʒhɒg] *n* Igel *der.*

heed [hiːd] ◇ *n*: **to take ~ of sthg** etw *(D)* Beachtung schenken ◇ *vt fml* beachten.

heedless ['hiːdlɪs] *adj*: **to be ~ of sthg** etw nicht beachten.

heel [hiːl] *n* - 1. [of foot] Ferse *die* - 2. [of shoe] Absatz *der.*

hefty ['heftɪ] *adj inf* - 1. [person] kräftig - 2. [fee, fine] saftig; [salary] dick.

heifer ['hefə'] *n* Färse *die.*

height [haɪt] *n* - 1. [gen] Höhe *die;* [of person] Größe *die;* **5 metres in ~** 5 Meter hoch; **what ~ are you?** wie groß sind Sie? - 2. [zenith] Höhepunkt *der.*

heighten ['haɪtn] ◇ *vt* [feeling, awareness] verstärken ◇ *vi* [anxiety] steigern ◇ *vi* sich verstärken.

heir [eə'] *n* Erbe *die,* -bin *die.*

heiress ['eərɪs] *n* Erbin *die.*

heirloom ['eəluːm] *n* Erbstück *das.*

heist [haɪst] *n inf* Raubüberfall *der.*

held [held] *pt & pp* ▷ hold.

helicopter ['helɪkɒptə'] *n* Hubschrauber *der.*

hell [hel] ◇ *n* - 1. [gen] Hölle *die* - 2. *inf* [for emphasis]: **what/where/why the ~ ...?** was/wo/warum zum Teufel ...?; **one** OR **a ~ of a mess** ein wahnsinniges Durcheinander; **one** OR **a ~ of a nice guy** ein wahnsinnig netter Kerl - 3. *phr*: **to ~ with the expense!** (es ist mir) egal, was es kostet!; **to do sthg for the ~ of it** *inf* etw aus Jux machen; **to give sb ~** *inf* jm die Hölle heiß machen; **go to ~!** *vinf* hau ab! ◇ *excl inf* verdammt!

he'll [hiːl] = he will.

hellish ['helɪʃ] *adj inf* höllisch, schrecklich.

hello [hə'ləʊ] *excl* hallo.

helm [helm] *n lit & fig* Ruder *das.*

helmet ['helmɪt] *n* Helm *der.*

help [help] ◇ *n* Hilfe *die;* **to be of ~** behilflich sein; **to be a ~** eine Hilfe sein; **with sb's ~** mit js Hilfe; **with the ~ of sthg** mit Hilfe einer Sache *(G)* ◇ *vt* - 1. [assist] helfen *(+ D);* **to ~ sb (to) do sthg** jm helfen, etw zu tun; **to ~ sb with sthg** jm bei etw helfen - 2. [make easier for] erleichtern; **to ~ sb (to) do sthg** es jm erleichtern, etw zu tun - 3. [contribute to]: **to ~ (to) do sthg** helfen, etw zu tun - 4. [avoid]: **I can't ~ it** ich kann nichts dafür; **I couldn't ~ laughing** ich mußte einfach lachen - 5. *phr*: **to ~ o.s.** sich bedienen; **to ~ o.s. to sthg** sich *(D)* etw nehmen ◇ *vi* helfen; **to ~ with sthg** bei etw helfen ◇ *excl* Hilfe!
  ◆ **help out** ◇ *vt sep* aushelfen *(+ D)* ◇ *vi* aushelfen.

helper ['helpə'] *n* - 1. [on any task] Helfer *der,* -in *die* - 2. *Am* [to do housework] Hausgehilfe *der,* -fin *die.*

helpful ['helpfʊl] *adj* - 1. [willing to help] hilfsbereit - 2. [useful] nützlich, hilfreich.

helping ['helpɪŋ] *n* Portion *die.*

helpless ['helplɪs] *adj* hilflos.

helpline ['helplaɪn] *n* Servicenummer *die;* COMPUT Hotline *die.*

Helsinki [hel'sɪŋkɪ] *n* Helsinki *nt.*

hem [hem] ◇ *n* Saum *der* ◇ *vt* säumen.
  ◆ **hem in** *vt sep* einlengen.

hemisphere ['hemɪˌsfɪə'] *n* Hemisphäre *die.*

hemline ['hemlaɪn] *n* Saum *der.*

hemorrhage ['hemərɪdʒ] *n* Blutung *die.*

hemorrhoids ['hemərɔɪdz] *npl* Hämorrhoiden *pl.*

hen [hen] *n* [female chicken] Huhn *das.*

hence [hens] *adv fml* - 1. [therefore] folglich - 2. [from now]: **ten years ~** in zehn Jahren.

henceforth [ˌhens'fɔːθ] *adv fml* fortan.

henchman ['hentʃmən] *(pl* -men [-mən]) *n pej* Helfershelfer *der.*

henna ['henə] *n* Henna *die* OR *das.*

henpecked ['henpekt] *adj pej*: **to be ~** unter dem Pantoffel stehen; **a ~ husband** ein Pantoffelheld.

her [hɜːʳ] <> *pers pron (accusative)* sie; *(dative)* ihr; **I know ~** ich kenne sie; **it's ~** sie ist es; **send it to ~** schick es ihr; **tell ~ ...** sag ihr ...; **he's worse than ~** er ist schlimmer als sie; **she took her luggage with ~** sie nahm ihr Gepäck mit <> *poss adj* ihr; **~ friend** ihr Freund/ihre Freundin; **~ children** ihre Kinder; **she washed ~ hair** sie hat sich die Haare gewaschen.

herald ['herəld] *vt fml* anlkünd(ig)en.

herb [hɜːb] *n* Kraut *das*.

herd [hɜːd] <> *n lit & fig* Herde *die* <> *vt* treiben.

here [hɪəʳ] *adv* hier; **come ~!** komm her!; **~ you are!** [when giving sthg] bitte!; [greeting sb] da bist du ja!; **~ we are** da sind wir; **~ and there** hier und da; **~ and now** sofort; **~'s to you!** [in toast] auf Ihr Wohl!

hereabouts *Br* [ˌhɪərə'bauts], **hereabout** *Am* [ˌhɪərə'baut] *adv* in dieser Gegend.

hereafter [ˌhɪər'ɑːftəʳ] <> *adv fml* im Folgenden <> *n*: **the ~** das Jenseits.

hereby [ˌhɪə'baɪ] *adv fml* hiermit.

hereditary [hɪ'redɪtrɪ] *adj* erblich, Erb-.

heresy ['herəsɪ] *n* Ketzerei *die*, Häresie *die*.

herewith [ˌhɪə'wɪð] *adv fml* anbei.

heritage ['herɪtɪdʒ] *n* Erbe *das*.

hermit ['hɜːmɪt] *n* Einsiedler *der*, -in *die*.

hernia ['hɜːnɪə] *n* Bruch *der*, Hernie *die*.

hero ['hɪərəu] *(pl* -es) *n* [gen] Held *der*.

heroic [hɪ'rəuɪk] *adj* [person, deed] heldenhaft. **heroics** *npl pej* Heldenstücke *pl*.

heroin ['herəuɪn] *n* Heroin *das*.

heroine ['herəuɪn] *n* Heldin *die*.

heron ['herən] *(pl inv OR* -s) *n* Reiher *der*.

herring ['herɪŋ] *(pl inv OR* -s) *n* Hering *der*.

hers [hɜːz] *poss pron* ihre, -r, -s; **a friend of ~** ein Freund von ihr; **these shoes are ~** diese Schuhe gehören ihr; **she ate my portion and ~** sie aß meine und ihre Portion.

herself [hɜː'self] *pron* - **1.** *(reflexive)* sich; **she hurt ~** sie hat sich verletzt - **2.** *(after prep)* sich selbst; **she did it ~** [stressed] sie hat es selbst getan; **by ~** allein.

he's [hiːz] = he is, he has.

hesitant ['hezɪtənt] *adj* [person] unentschlossen, zögerlich.

hesitate ['hezɪteɪt] *vi* zögern; **to ~ to do sthg** Bedenken haben, etw zu tun.

hesitation [ˌhezɪ'teɪʃn] *n* Zögern *das*.

heterosexual [ˌhetərəu'sekʃuəl] <> *adj* heterosexuell <> *n* Heterosexuelle *der*, *die*.

het up [ˌhet-] *adj inf* aufgeregt.

hexagon ['heksəgən] *n* Sechseck *das*.

hey [heɪ] *excl* he!

heyday ['heɪdeɪ] *n* Glanzzeit *die*.

HGV *(abbr of heavy goods vehicle) n* LKW *der*.

hi [haɪ] *excl inf* hallo!

hiatus [haɪ'eɪtəs] *(pl* -es) *n fml* Unterbrechung *die*.

hibernate ['haɪbəneɪt] *vi* Winterschlaf halten.

hiccough, hiccup ['hɪkʌp] <> *n* - **1.** [sound] Schluckauf *der*; **to have ~s** (den) Schluckauf haben - **2.** *fig* [difficulty] kleines Problem <> *vi* schlucksen.

hid [hɪd] *pt* └> hide.

hidden ['hɪdn] <> *pp* └> hide <> *adj* versteckt; **~ costs** verdeckte Unkosten.

hide [haɪd] *(pt* hid; *pp* hidden) <> *vt* - **1.** [conceal - person, item] verstecken; [- emotions, facts] verbergen; **to ~ sthg (from sb)** etw (vor jm) verstecken/verbergen - **2.** [cover] verdecken <> *vi* sich verstecken <> *n* [animal skin] Haut *die*.

hide-and-seek *n* Versteckspiel *das*.

hideaway ['haɪdəweɪ] *n inf* Versteck *das*.

hideous ['hɪdɪəs] *adj* grässlich.

hiding ['haɪdɪŋ] *n* - **1.** [concealment]: **to be in ~** sich verstecken - **2.** *inf* [beating]: **to give sb a (good) ~** jm eine (ordentliche) Abreibung verpassen.

hiding place *n* Versteck *das*.

hierarchy ['haɪərɑːkɪ] *n* Hierarchie *die*.

hi-fi ['haɪfaɪ] *n* Hi-Fi *das*.

high [haɪ] <> *adj* - **1.** [gen] hoch; *(before noun)* hohe, -r, -s; **how ~ is it?** wie hoch ist es?; **it's 10 metres ~** es ist 10 Meter hoch; **~ winds** starker Wind - **2.** *inf* [from drugs] high <> *n* - **1.** [weather front] Hoch *das* - **2.** [highest point] Höchststand *der* <> *adv* hoch; **to aim ~** hoch hinauslwollen.

highbrow ['haɪbrau] *adj* intellektuell; [literature, tastes] anspruchsvoll.

high chair *n* (Kinder)hochstuhl *der*.

high-class *adj* [superior - hotel, restaurant] vornehm; [- performance] hochwertig.

High Court *n Br* LAW oberster Gerichtshof.

higher ['haɪəʳ] *adj* [exam, qualification] höher. **Higher** *n* SCH: **Higher (Grade)** schottischer Abiturabschluss in einem Fach.

higher education *n* Hochschulbildung *die*.

high jump *n* SPORT Hochsprung *der*.

Highlands ['haɪləndz] *npl*: **the ~** [of Scotland] das schottische Hochland.

highlight ['haɪlaɪt] <> *n* [of event, occasion] Höhepunkt *der* <> *vt* hervorlheben. **highlights** *npl* [in hair] Strähnchen *pl*.

highlighter (pen) ['haɪlaɪtəʳ-] *n* Textmarker *der*.

highly ['haɪlɪ] *adv* - **1.** [very, extremely] höchst - **2.** [very well] sehr gut - **3.** [at an important level]: **~ placed** hoch plaziert - **4.** [favourably] sehr gut; **I ~ recommend it** ich kann es sehr empfehlen.

highly-strung [-'strʌŋ] *adj* nervös.

Highness ['haɪnɪs] *n*: **His/Her/Your (Royal) ~** Seine/Ihre/Eure (Königliche) Hoheit.

high-pitched [-'pɪtʃt] *adj* [voice] hoch; [shout, scream] schrill.

high point *n* Höhepunkt *der.*

high-powered [-'pauəd] *adj* [dynamic - activity, place] anspruchsvoll, leistungsorientiert; [- person] dynamisch.

high-ranking [-'ræŋkɪŋ] *adj* ranghoch.

high-rise *adj*: ~ **building** Hochhaus *das.*

high school *n* höhere Schule.

high season *n* Hochsaison *die.*

high spot *n* Höhepunkt *der.*

high street *n Br* Hauptstraße *die.*

high-tech [-'tek] *adj* Hightech-.

high tide *n* Flut *die.*

highway ['haɪweɪ] *n* **- 1.** *Am* [main road between cities] Schnellstraße *die* **- 2.** *Br* [any main road] Landstraße *die.*

Highway Code *n Br*: **the** ~ die Straßenverkehrsordnung.

hijack ['haɪdʒæk] ◇ *n* Entführung *die* ◇ *vt* entführen.

hijacker ['haɪdʒækə'] *n* [of aircraft] Flugzeugentführer *der*, -in *die*; [of vehicle] Entführer *der*, -in *die.*

hike [haɪk] ◇ *n* Wanderung *die* ◇ *vi* wandern.

hiker ['haɪkə'] *n* Wanderer *der*, -in *die.*

hiking ['haɪkɪŋ] *n* Wandern *das*; **to go** ~ wandern gehen.

hilarious [hɪ'leərɪəs] *adj* urkomisch.

hill [hɪl] *n* **- 1.** [mound] Hügel *der* **- 2.** [slope] Hang *der.*

hillside ['hɪlsaɪd] *n* Hang *der.*

hilly ['hɪlɪ] *adj* hügelig.

hilt [hɪlt] *n* Heft *das*; **to support/defend sb to the** ~ jn voll und ganz unterstützen/verteidigen.

him [hɪm] *pers pron (accusative)* ihn; *(dative)* ihm; **I know** ~ ich kenne ihn; **it's** ~ er ist es; **send it to** ~ schick es ihm; **tell** ~ **say** ihm; **she's worse than** ~ sie ist schlimmer als er; **he took his luggage with** ~ er nahm sein Gepäck mit.

Himalayas [ˌhɪmə'leɪəz] *npl*: **the** ~ der Himalaja.

himself [hɪm'self] *pron* **- 1.** *(reflexive)* sich; **he hurt** ~ er hat sich verletzt **- 2.** *(after prep)* sich selbst; **he did it** ~ [stressed] er hat es selbst getan; **by** ~ allein.

hind [haɪnd] *(pl inv OR -s)* ◇ *adj*: ~ **legs** Hinterbeine *pl* ◇ *n* Hirschkuh *die.*

hinder ['hɪndə'] *vt* behindern.

hindrance ['hɪndrəns] *n* **- 1.** [obstacle] Hindernis *das* **- 2.** (U) [delay] Behinderung *die.*

hindsight ['haɪndsaɪt] *n* (U): **with the benefit of** ~ im Nachhinein.

Hindu ['hɪndu:] *(pl -s)* ◇ *adj* Hindu-, hinduistisch ◇ *n* Hindu *der.*

hinge [hɪndʒ] *n* [on door, window] Angel *die*; [on lid] Scharnier *das.* ◆ **hinge (up)on** *vt fus* [depend on] abhängen von.

hint [hɪnt] ◇ *n* **- 1.** [indirect suggestion] Andeutung *die*; **to drop a** ~ eine Andeutung ma-

chen **- 2.** [useful suggestion, tip] Tipp *der* **- 3.** [small amount, trace] Spur *die* ◇ *vi*: **to** ~ **at sthg** etw andeuten ◇ *vt*: **to** ~ **that ...** andeuten, dass ...

hip [hɪp] *n* [part of body] Hüfte *die.*

hippie ['hɪpɪ] *n* Hippie *der.*

hippo ['hɪpəʊ] *(pl -s)* *n* Nilpferd *das.*

hippopotamus [ˌhɪpə'pɒtəməs] *(pl -muses OR -mi [-maɪ])* *n* Nilpferd *das.*

hippy ['hɪpɪ] *n* = **hippie.**

hire ['haɪə'] ◇ *n* (U) [of car, television, venue] Mieten *das*; [of suit] Leihen *das*; **'for** ~' 'zu vermieten'; [taxi sign] 'frei' ◇ *vt* **- 1.** [rent - car, television, venue] mieten; [- suit] leihen **- 2.** [employ] anstellen. ◆ **hire out** *vt sep* [car, television, venue] vermieten; [suit] verleihen.

hire car *n Br* Mietwagen *der.*

hire purchase *n* Ratenkauf *der.*

his [hɪz] ◇ *poss adj* sein; ~ **friend** sein Freund/seine Freundin; ~ **children** seine Kinder; **he has washed** ~ **hair** er hat sich die Haare gewaschen ◇ *poss pron* seine, -r, -s; **a friend of** ~ ein Freund von ihm; **these shoes are** ~ diese Schuhe gehören ihm; **he ate my portion and** ~ er aß meine und seine Portion.

hiss [hɪs] *vi* zischen; [cat] fauchen.

historic [hɪ'stɒrɪk] *adj* historisch.

historical [hɪ'stɒrɪkəl] *adj* historisch.

history ['hɪstərɪ] *n* **- 1.** [gen] Geschichte *die* **- 2.** [past record] Vorgeschichte *die.*

hit [hɪt] *(pt & pp hit)* ◇ *n* **- 1.** [blow] Schlag *der* **- 2.** [successful strike] Treffer *der* **- 3.** [success] Erfolg *der*; [record] Hit *der* **- 4.** COMPUT [of website] Treffer *der* ◇ *comp* Erfolgs-; [record] Hit- ◇ *vt* **- 1.** [strike] schlagen **- 2.** [subj: stones, bullet] treffen; [subj: vehicle - tree, wall] fahren gegen; [- person] erwischen **- 3.** [reach] erreichen **- 4.** *phr*: **to** ~ **it off (with sb)** sich gut (mit jm) verstehen.

hit-and-miss *adj* = hit-or-miss.

hit-and-run ◇ *n*: ~ **(accident)** Unfall *der* mit Fahrerflucht ◇ *adj* [driver] unfallflüchtig.

hitch [hɪtʃ] ◇ *n* [problem, snag] Problem *das* ◇ *vt* **- 1.** [solicit]: **to** ~ **a lift** trampen **- 2.** [fasten]: **to** ~ **sthg on(to) sthg** etw an etw (D) befestigen ◇ *vi* [hitchhike] trampen. ◆ **hitch up** *vt sep* [skirt, trousers] hochziehen.

hitchhike ['hɪtʃhaɪk] *vi* trampen.

hitchhiker ['hɪtʃhaɪkə'] *n* Anhalter *der*, -in *die*, Tramper *der*, -in *die.*

hi-tech [ˌhaɪ'tek] *adj* = high-tech.

hitherto [ˌhɪðə'tu:] *adv fml* bisher.

hit-or-miss *adj* willkürlich.

HIV *(abbr of human immunodeficiency virus)* *n* HIV; **to be --positive** HIV-positiv sein.

hive [haɪv] *n* [for bees] Bienenstock *der*; **to be a** ~ **of activity** *fig* der reinste Bienenstock

sein. ◆ **hive off** vt sep [separate] ablspalten, ausgliedern.

HNC (abbr of Higher National Certificate) n
britische Qualifikation in technischen Fächern.

HND (abbr of Higher National Diploma) n britische Hochschulqualifikation in technischen Fächern.

hoard [hɔːd] ◇ n Vorrat der ◇ vt horten.

hoarding ['hɔːdɪŋ] n Br Plakatwand die.

hoarse [hɔːs] adj heiser.

hoax [həʊks] n [joke] Streich der; [threat,
alarm] blinder Alarm.

hob [hɒb] n Br [on cooker] Kochfläche die.

hobble ['hɒbl] vi humpeln.

hobby ['hɒbɪ] n Hobby das.

hobbyhorse ['hɒbɪhɔːs] n [favourite topic]
Lieblingsthema das.

hobo ['həʊbəʊ] (pl -es OR -s) n Am Landstreicher der, Penner der.

hockey ['hɒkɪ] n - 1. [on grass] Hockey das
- 2. Am [ice hockey] Eishockey das.

hockey stick n Hockeyschläger der.

hoe [həʊ] ◇ n Hacke die ◇ vt hacken.

hog [hɒg] ◇ n - 1. Am [pig] Schwein das
- 2. inf [greedy person] Vielfraß der - 3. phr: **to
go the whole ~** aufs Ganze gehen ◇ vt inf
[monopolize - road] in Beschlag nehmen;
[- attention] mit Beschlag belegen.

Hogmanay ['hɒgmaneɪ] n Scot Silvester der
OR das.

Hogmanay

Hogmanay ist in Schottland die Bezeichnung für Silvester und die traditionellen
Feste an diesem Tag. Das Wort stammt
vermutlich aus dem Altfranzösischen und
bedeutet „Neujahrsgeschenk". Diese Bedeutung passt jedenfalls zum Brauch des
firstfooting, nach dessen Regeln der Erste, der nach Mitternacht die Schwelle eines Hauses überschreitet, „etwas fürs
Feuer, etwas für den Tisch und etwas in
einer Flasche" mitzubringen hat. Dieser
erste Besucher beeinflusst dem Glauben
nach das Glück des Haushalts für das
kommende Jahr. Zu Hogmanay fassen
sich traditionell um Mitternacht alle An-
wesenden an den Händen und singen
Auld Lang Syne.

---

hoist [hɔɪst] ◇ n [device for lifting] Lasten-
aufzug der ◇ vt - 1. [load, person] heben,
hieven - 2. [sail, flag] hissen.

hold [həʊld] (pt & pp held) ◇ vt - 1. [gen]
halten; **to ~ sb prisoner/hostage** jn gefangen
halten/als Geisel festhalten - 2. [position, responsibility, title, driving licence] haben; [be-
lief, principle] vertreten - 3. [meeting, talks]
abhalten; [conversation] führen - 4. fml [con-
sider]: **to ~ sthg to be necessary/important**

etw für notwendig/wichtig erachten OR halten; **to ~ (that)** der Meinung sein, dass; **to
~ sb responsible for sthg** jn für etw verantwortlich machen - 5. [on telephone]: **please
~ the line** bitte bleiben Sie am Apparat
- 6. [attention, interest] fesseln - 7. [support]
tragen - 8. [contain] enthalten; **what does
the future ~ for him?** was birgt die Zukunft
für ihn? - 9. [have space for] Platz haben für
- 10. phr: **~ it!**, **~ everything!** halt!; **to ~ one's
own** sich behaupten können ◇ vi
- 1. [promise, objection] gelten; [weather] sich
halten; **his luck held** das Glück blieb ihm
treu; **to ~ still** OR **steady** still halten - 2. [on
phone] am Apparat sein ◇ n - 1. [grip]
Griff der; **to keep ~ of sthg** [with hand] etw
festhalten; [save] etw behalten; **to take** OR
lay ~ of sthg etw fassen OR packen; **to get
~ of sthg** [obtain] etw bekommen; **to get ~ of
sb** [find] jn erreichen - 2. [of ship, aircraft] La-
deraum der, Frachtraum der - 3. [control, in-
fluence]: **to have a ~ over sb** [person] jn in der
Hand haben; [feeling, idea] von jm Besitz ergreifen. ◆ **hold back** vt sep [gen] zurücklhalten. ◆ **hold down** vt sep: **to ~ down a
job** sich in einer Stelle halten. ◆ **hold off**
vt sep [fend off] abwehren. ◆ **hold on** vi
- 1. [wait, on phone] warten; **~ on!** [on phone]
einen Moment, bitte! - 2. [grip]: **to ~ on (to
sthg)** sich (an etw (D)) festhalten. ◆ **hold
out** ◇ vt sep [hand] ausstrecken; [arms]
ausbreiten ◇ vi - 1. [supply] reichen - 2. [resist]:
to ~ out (against sb/sthg) sich (gegen jn/
etw) behaupten. ◆ **hold up** vt sep
- 1. [raise] hochheben - 2. [delay - traffic, pro-
duction] aufhalten; [- plans] verzögern.

holdall ['həʊldɔːl] n Br Reisetasche die.

holder ['həʊldə] n - 1. [container] Halter der;
[for cigarette] Spitze die - 2. [owner] Inhaber
der, -in die.

holding ['həʊldɪŋ] n - 1. [investment] Akti-
enbesitz der - 2. [farm] Gut das.

holdup ['həʊldʌp] n - 1. [robbery] bewaffneter Raubüberfall - 2. [delay] Verzögerung
die; [of traffic] stockender Verkehr.

hole [həʊl] n - 1. [gen] Loch das; **~ in one** [in
golf] As das - 2. inf [horrible place] Loch das;
[town] Kaff das - 3. inf [predicament]: **to get
o.s. into a ~** in die Bredouille kommen; **to be
in a ~** in der Bredouille sein.

holiday ['hɒlɪdeɪ] n - 1. [vacation] Urlaub
der; **~s** Urlaub der; SCH Ferien pl; **to be on ~** im
Urlaub sein; **to go on ~** in Urlaub fahren
- 2. [public holiday] Feiertag der.

holiday camp n Br ≃ Feriendorf das.

holidaymaker ['hɒlɪdɪˌmeɪkə] n Br Urlauber der, -in die.

holiday pay n Br Urlaubsgeld das.

holiday resort n Br Ferienort der.

holistic [həʊ'lɪstɪk] adj holistisch.

Holland ['hɒlənd] n Holland nt.

holler ['hɒlə'] *vt & vi inf* brüllen.

hollow ['hɒləʊ] ⬦ *adj* hohl; [cheeks] eingefallen; [victory, success] wertlos; [promise] leer ⬦ *n* - 1. [in tree] Höhlung *die* - 2. [in ground, pillow] Mulde *die*; **the ~ of one's hand/back** die hohle Hand/das Kreuz. ◆ **hollow out** *vt sep* aushöhlen.

holly ['hɒlɪ] *n* Stechpalme *die*.

holocaust ['hɒləkɔːst] *n*: **a nuclear ~** ein atomarer Holocaust. ◆ **Holocaust** *n*: **the Holocaust** der Holocaust.

holster ['həʊlstə'] *n* Pistolenhalfter *das*.

holy ['həʊlɪ] *adj* heilig; [ground] geweiht.

Holy Ghost *n*: **the ~** der Heilige Geist.

Holy Land *n*: **the ~** das Heilige Land.

Holy Spirit *n*: **the ~** der Heilige Geist.

home [həʊm] ⬦ *n* - 1. [place of residence, institution] Heim *das* - 2. [place of origin] Heimat *die* - 3. [family unit] Zuhause *das*; **to leave ~** von zu Hause weglgehen ⬦ *adj* - 1. [market, product] inländisch - 2. SPORT Heim- ⬦ *adv*: **to go ~** nach Hause gehen; [from abroad] zurücklfahren/zurücklfliegen; **to be ~** zu Hause sein. ◆ **at home** *adv* - 1. [in one's house, flat] daheim, zu Hause - 2. [comfortable]: **to feel at ~ somewhere** sich irgendwo wohl fühlen; **to make o.s. at ~** es sich (D) bequem machen - 3. [in one's own country]: **at ~ the shops close at five** bei uns machen die Geschäfte um fünf zu.

home address *n* Privatadresse *die*.

home brew *n* (U) selbstgebrautes Bier.

home computer *n* Heimcomputer *der*.

home cooking *n* bürgerliche Küche.

Home Counties *npl Br*: **the ~** *die London umgebenden Grafschaften*.

home economics *n* (U) Hauswirtschaft(slehre) *die*.

home help *n Br* Haushaltshilfe *die*.

homeland ['həʊmlænd] *n* [country of birth] Heimatland *das*.

homeless ['həʊmlɪs] ⬦ *adj* obdachlos ⬦ *npl*: **the ~** die Obdachlosen.

homely ['həʊmlɪ] *adj* - 1. [simple, unpretentious - place] schlicht; **~ fare** Hausmannskost *die* - 2. [ugly] unattraktiv.

homemade [ˌhəʊm'meɪd] *adj* selbstgemacht; [bread] selbstgebacken; [food] hausgemacht.

Home Office *n Br*: **the ~** das Innenministerium.

homeopathy [ˌhəʊmɪ'ɒpəθɪ] *n* Homöopathie *die*.

home page *n* COMPUT Homepage *die*.

Home Secretary *n Br* Innenminister *der*, -in *die*.

homesick ['həʊmsɪk] *adj* heimwehkrank; **to be/feel ~** Heimweh haben.

hometown ['həʊmtaʊn] *n* Heimatstadt *die*.

homework ['həʊmwɜːk] *n* (U) - 1. SCH

Hausaufgaben *pl* - 2. *inf* [preparation]: **he's really done his ~** er hat sich gut vorbereitet.

homey, homy ['həʊmɪ] *adj Am* [place, atmosphere] heimelig.

homicide ['hɒmɪsaɪd] *n* Mord *der*.

homogeneous [ˌhɒmə'dʒiːnɪəs] *adj* homogen.

homophobic [ˌhɒmə'fəʊbɪk] *adj* homosexuellenfeindlich, homophob.

homosexual [ˌhɒmə'sekʃʊəl] ⬦ *adj* homosexuell ⬦ *n* Homosexuelle *der*, *die*.

homy *adj Am* = homey.

hone [həʊn] *vt* - 1. [knife, sword] schleifen, wetzen - 2. [intellect, wit] schärfen.

honest ['ɒnɪst] ⬦ *adj* - 1. [trustworthy, legal] redlich - 2. [truthful] ehrlich; **to be ~, ...** ehrlich gesagt, ... ⬦ *adv* ehrlich.

honestly ['ɒnɪstlɪ] ⬦ *adv* - 1. [in a trustworthy manner] redlich - 2. [truthfully] ehrlich ⬦ *excl* also wirklich!

honesty ['ɒnɪstɪ] *n* - 1. [trustworthiness] Redlichkeit *die* - 2. [truthfulness] Ehrlichkeit *die*.

honey ['hʌnɪ] *n* - 1. [food] Honig *der* - 2. *esp Am* [dear] Liebling *der*.

honeycomb ['hʌnɪkəʊm] *n* - 1. [in wax] Bienenwabe *die* - 2. [pattern] Wabenmuster *das*.

honeymoon ['hʌnɪmuːn] ⬦ *n* - 1. [after wedding] Flitterwochen *pl*; [trip] Hochzeitsreise *die* - 2. *fig* [initial trouble-free period] Schonzeit *die* ⬦ *vi* Hochzeitsreise machen.

Hong Kong [ˌhɒŋ'kɒŋ] *n* Hongkong *nt*.

honk [hɒŋk] ⬦ *vi* [motorist] hupen ⬦ *vt*: **to ~ one's horn** auf die Hupe drücken.

honor *etc Am* = honour *etc*.

honorary [*Br* 'ɒnərərɪ, *Am* ɒnə'reərɪ] *adj* - 1. [given as an honour] Ehren-; **~ degree** ehrenhalber verliehener akademischer Grad - 2. [unpaid] ehrenamtlich.

honour *Br*, **honor** *Am* ['ɒnə'] ⬦ *n* Ehre *die*; **a man of ~** ein Ehrenmann; **in her ~** zu ihren Ehren ⬦ *vt* - 1. [fulfil - debt] begleichen; [- promise, agreement] erfüllen; [- cheque] akzeptieren - 2. *fml* [bring honour to] ehren. ◆ **honours** *npl* - 1. [tokens of respect] Ehren *pl* - 2. UNIV *der erste erreichbare akademische Grad, der in ein oder zwei Fächern erlangt wird*.

honourable *Br*, **honorable** *Am* ['ɒnrəbl] *adj* ehrenhaft.

hood [hʊd] *n* - 1. [on cloak, jacket] Kapuze *die*; [of robber] Maske *die* - 2. [of cooker] Abzugshaube *die*; [of pram, convertible car] Verdeck *das* - 3. *Am* [car bonnet] Motorhaube *die*.

hoodlum ['huːdləm] *n Am inf* [youth] Rowdy *der*; [gangster] Gangster *der*.

hoof [huːf, hʊf] (*pl* -s OR hooves) *n* Huf *der*.

hook [hʊk] ⬦ *n* Haken *der* ⬦ *vt* - 1. [fasten with hook]: **to ~ sthg on to sthg** etw an etw (D) festlhaken - 2. [fish] an die Angel bekommen. ◆ **off the hook** *adv* - 1. TELEC: **the telephone is off the ~** der Hörer ist abgenommen; **to leave the phone off the ~** den Hörer nicht auflegen - **2.** [out of trouble]: **to be off the ~** aus dem Schneider sein. ◆ **hook up** *vt sep*: **to ~ sthg up to sthg** COMPUT & TELEC etw an etw *(A)* anschließen.

hooked [hukt] *adj* - **1.** [shaped like a hook] gebogen; **~ nose** Hakennase *die* - **2.** *inf* [addicted]: **to be ~ on sthg** [on drugs] von etw abhängig sein; [on music, money, art] auf etw *(A)* ganz versessen sein.

hook(e)y ['huki] *n Am inf*: **to play ~** (die Schule) schwänzen.

hooligan ['hu:ligən] *n* Rowdy *der*.

hoop [hu:p] *n* Reifen *der*.

hooray [hu'rei] *excl* = hurray.

hoot [hu:t] <> *n* - **1.** [of owl] Schrei *der* - **2.** [of horn] Hupen *das* - **3.** *Br inf* [amusing thing, person]: **to be a ~** zum Schießen sein <> *vi* - **1.** [owl] schreien - **2.** [horn] hupen <> *vt* [horn]: **to ~ one's horn** hupen.

hooter ['hu:tə'] *n* [horn - of car] Hupe *die*; [- of factory] Sirene *die*.

Hoover® ['hu:və'] *n Br* Staubsauger *der*. ◆ **hoover** *vt & vi* (staub)saugen.

hooves [hu:vz] *pl* ⟹ hoof.

hop [hɒp] *n* [of person, animal, bird] Hüpfer *der* <> *vi* - **1.** [jump] hüpfen - **2.** *inf* [move nimbly] springen; **to ~ on a bus/train/ plane** kurz entschlossen den Bus/den Zug/ das Flugzeug nehmen <> *vt inf phr*: **~ it!** verschwinde! ◆ **hops** *npl* [for making beer] Hopfen *der*.

hope [həup] <> *vi* hoffen; **to ~ for sthg** auf etw *(A)* hoffen; **I ~ so** hoffentlich; **I ~ not** hoffentlich nicht <> *vt*: **to ~ (that) ...** hoffen, dass ...; **to ~ to do sthg** hoffen, etw zu tun <> *n* - **1.** *(U)* [belief, optimism] Hoffnung *die*; **to be beyond ~** [situation] aussichtslos OR hoffnungslos sein - **2.** [expectation, chance] Hoffnung *die*; **in the ~ of doing sthg** in der Hoffnung, etw zu tun.

hopeful ['həupful] *adj* - **1.** [person] hoffnungsvoll; **to be ~ that ...** zuversichtlich sein, dass ...; **to be ~ of doing sthg** zuversichtlich sein, etw zu tun - **2.** [sign, future] vielversprechend.

hopefully ['həupfəli] *adv* - **1.** [in a hopeful way] hoffnungsvoll - **2.** [with luck] hoffentlich.

hopeless ['həuplıs] *adj* - **1.** [despairing, impossible] hoffnungslos - **2.** *inf* [useless] miserabel.

hopelessly ['həuplıslı] *adv* hoffnungslos.

horizon [hə'raızn] *n* [of sky] Horizont *der*; **on the ~** *lit & fig* am Horizont.

horizontal [ˌhɒrı'zɒntl] <> *adj* horizontal <> *n*: **the ~** die Horizontale.

hormone ['hɔ:məun] *n* Hormon *das*.

horn [hɔ:n] *n* - **1.** [gen] Horn *das* - **2.** [on car] Hupe *die*; [on ship] Signalhorn *das*.

hornet ['hɔ:nıt] *n* Hornisse *die*.

horny ['hɔ:nı] *adj* - **1.** [scale, body] hornig; [hand] schwielig - **2.** *vinf* [sexually excited] geil.

horoscope ['hɒrəskəup] *n* Horoskop *das*.

horrendous [hɒ'rendəs] *adj* - **1.** [horrific] entsetzlich - **2.** *inf* [unpleasant - bill, amount] horrend; [- weather] scheußlich.

horrible ['hɒrəbl] *adj* schrecklich.

horrid ['hɒrıd] *adj esp Br* fürchterlich; **don't be so ~** sei nicht so gemein.

horrific [hɒ'rıfık] *adj* entsetzlich.

horrify ['hɒrıfaı] *vt* entsetzen.

horror ['hɒrə'] *n* - **1.** [alarm, fear] Entsetzen *das* - **2.** [horrifying thing] Schrecken *der*; **the ~s of war** die Gräuel des Krieges.

horror film *n* Horrorfilm *der*.

horse [hɔ:s] *n* Pferd *das*.

horseback ['hɔ:sbæk] <> *adj*: **~ riding** *Am* Reiten *das* <> *n*: **on ~** zu Pferd.

horse chestnut *n* [tree, nut] Rosskastanie *die*.

horseman ['hɔ:smən] (*pl* -men [-mən]) *n* Reiter *der*.

horsepower ['hɔ:sˌpaʊə'] *n (U)* Pferdestärke *die*.

horse racing *n* Pferderennen *das*.

horseradish ['hɔ:sˌrædıʃ] *n (U)* [plant] Meerrettich *der*.

horse riding *n* Reiten *das*.

horseshoe ['hɔ:sˌʃu:] *n* Hufeisen *das*.

horsewoman ['hɔ:sˌwʊmən] (*pl* -women [-ˌwımın]) *n* Reiterin *die*.

horticulture ['hɔ:tıˌkʌltʃə'] *n* Gartenbau *der*.

hose [həuz] <> *n* [hosepipe] Schlauch *der* <> *vt* [garden] sprengen.

hosepipe ['həuzpaıp] *n* Schlauch *der*.

hosiery ['həuzıərı] *n (U)* Strumpfwaren *pl*.

hospitable [hɒ'spıtəbl] *adj* gastfreundlich.

hospital ['hɒspıtl] *n* Krankenhaus *das*.

hospitality [ˌhɒspı'tælətı] *n* Gastfreundschaft *die*.

host [həust] <> *n* - **1.** [gen] Gastgeber *der*; **~ country** Gastland *das* - **2.** [compere] Moderator *der* - **3.** *literary* [large number]: **a ~ of sthg** eine Schar von etw <> *vt* moderieren.

hostage ['hɒstıdʒ] *n* Geisel *die*.

hostel ['hɒstl] *n* Wohnheim *das*; **(youth) ~** Jugendherberge *die*.

hostess ['həustes] *n* [at party] Gastgeberin *die*.

hostile [*Br* 'hɒstaıl, *Am* 'hɒstl] *adj* - **1.** [antagonistic, unfriendly]: **~ (to sb/sthg)** feindselig (gegenüber jm/etw) - **2.** [weather conditions] widrig; [climate] unwirtlich - **3.** MIL [territory, forces] feindlich.

hostility [hɒ'stılətı] *n (U)* Feindseligkeit *die*. ◆ **hostilities** *npl* Feindseligkeiten *pl*.

hot [hɒt] *adj* - **1.** [gen] heiß; **I'm ~** mir ist heiß - **2.** [cooked] warm - **3.** [spicy] scharf - **4.** *inf* [expert] stark; **to be ~ on** OR **at sthg** super in etw *(D)* sein **- 5.** [recent]: **a ~ piece of news** das Neueste vom Neuesten **- 6.** [temper] hitzig.

hot-air balloon *n* Heißluftballon *der.*

hotbed ['hɒtbed] *n* Brutstätte *die.*

hot-cross bun *n* Rosinenbrötchen *mit kleinem Teigkreuz, das um Ostern gegessen wird.*

hot dog *n* Hot Dog *der* OR *das.*

hotel [həʊ'tel] *n* Hotel *das.*

hot flush *Br,* **hot flash** *Am n* Hitzewallung *die;* **~es** fliegende Hitze.

hotheaded [ˌhɒt'hedɪd] *adj* hitzköpfig.

hothouse ['hɒthaʊs, *pl* -haʊzɪz] *n* [greenhouse] Treibhaus *das.*

hot line *n* **- 1.** [between government heads] heißer Draht **- 2.** [for crisis, disaster] Hotline *die.*

hotly ['hɒtlɪ] *adv* **- 1.** [argue, debate, deny] heftig **- 2.** [pursue]: **they were ~ pursued by a policeman** ein Polizist war ihnen dicht auf den Fersen.

hotplate ['hɒtpleɪt] *n* Kochplatte *die.*

hot-tempered [-'tempəd] *adj* jähzornig.

hot-water bottle *n* Wärmflasche *die.*

hound [haʊnd] <> *n* Jagdhund *der* <> *vt* verfolgen.

hour ['aʊə'] *n* Stunde *die;* **half an ~** eine halbe Stunde; **per** OR **an ~** pro OR die Stunde; **on the ~** zur vollen Stunde; **every ~, on the ~** jede volle Stunde. ◆ **hours** *npl* [of business] Geschäftszeiten *pl;* [of pub, museum etc] Öffnungszeiten *pl;* [of doctor] Sprechstunde *die.*

hourly ['aʊəlɪ] <> *adj* **- 1.** [happening every hour] stündlich **- 2.** [per hour] Stunden- <> *adv* **- 1.** [every hour] stündlich **- 2.** [per hour] pro Stunde.

house [*n & adj* haʊs, *pl* 'haʊzɪz, *vb* haʊz] <> *n* **- 1.** [gen] Haus *das;* **to move ~** umziehen; **on the ~** auf Kosten des Hauses; **to bring the ~ down** das Publikum zum Toben bringen **- 2.** SCH *eine der traditionellen Schülergemeinschaften innerhalb einer Schule, die untereinander Wettbewerbe veranstalten* <> *vt* [subj: person] unterbringen; **the building ~s three families/offices** im Gebäude sind drei Familien/Büros untergebracht <> *adj* Haus-; **~ style** hauseigener Stil; **~ red/white** [wine] Hausmarke *die (Rot-/Weißwein).*

houseboat ['haʊsbəʊt] *n* Hausboot *das.*

household ['haʊshəʊld] <> *adj* **- 1.** [domestic] Haushalts- **- 2.** [familiar]: **to be a ~ name** ein Begriff sein <> *n* Haushalt *der.*

housekeeper ['haʊsˌkiːpə'] *n* Haushälterin *die.*

housekeeping ['haʊsˌkiːpɪŋ] *n* **- 1.** [work] Haushaltsführung *die* **- 2.** [budget]: **~ (money)** Haushaltsgeld *das.*

house music *n* Hausmusik *die.*

House of Commons *n Br:* **the ~** das britische Unterhaus.

House of Lords *n Br:* **the ~** das britische Oberhaus.

House of Representatives *n Am:* **the ~** das Repräsentantenhaus.

houseplant ['haʊsplɑːnt] *n* Zimmerpflanze *die.*

Houses of Parliament *npl Br:* **the ~** Sitz des britischen Parlaments.

housewarming (party) ['haʊsˌwɔːmɪŋ-] *n* Einzugsparty *die.*

housewife ['haʊswaɪf] *(pl* -wives [-waɪvz]) *n* Hausfrau *die.*

housework ['haʊswɜːk] *n* Hausarbeit *die.*

housing ['haʊzɪŋ] *n (U)* [accommodation] Wohnungen *pl;* [act] Unterbringung *die.*

housing association *n Br* Wohnungsbaugesellschaft *die.*

housing benefit *n (U) Br* Wohngeld *das.*

housing estate *Br,* **housing project** *Am n* Wohnsiedlung *die.*

hovel ['hɒvl] *n* armselige Hütte.

hover ['hɒvə'] *vi* [fly] schweben.

hovercraft ['hɒvəkrɑːft] *(pl inv* OR -s) *n* Luftkissenfahrzeug *das.*

how [haʊ] *adv* **- 1.** [referring to way, manner] wie; **~ do you get there?** wie kommt man dahin?; **tell me ~ to do it** sag mir, wie man das macht **- 2.** [referring to health, general state] wie; **~ are you?** wie gehts dir?; **~ are you doing?, ~ are things?** wie gehts dir?; **~ is your room?** wie ist dein Zimmer?; **~ do you do?** guten Tag! **- 3.** [referring to degree, amount] wie; **~ far?** wie weit?; **~ long?** wie lang?; **~ many?** wie viele?; **~ much?** wie viel?; **~ much is it?** wie viel kostet es?; **~ old are you?** wie alt bist du? **- 4.** [in exclamations] wie; **~ nice/awful!** wie schön/schrecklich!; **~ I wish I could!** wenn ich doch nur könnte! ◆ **how about** *adv:* **~ about a drink?** wie wäre es mit einem Drink?; **I could do with a night off, ~ about you?** ich könnte einen freien Abend gebrauchen, du auch?

however [haʊ'evə'] <> *conj* [in whatever way] wie (immer) <> *adv* **- 1.** [nevertheless] jedoch; **~, it was not to be** es sollte jedoch nicht sein **- 2.** [no matter how] wie ... auch; **~ difficult/good it is** wie schwierig/gut es auch ist **- 3.** [how] wie ... bloß; **~ did you know?** woher hast du das bloß gewusst?

howl [haʊl] *vi* **- 1.** [animal, wind] heulen **- 2.** [person] schreien; **to ~ with laughter** brüllen vor Lachen.

hp *(abbr of* horsepower) *n* PS.

HP *n* **- 1.** *(abbr of* hire purchase): **to buy sthg on ~** etw auf Raten kaufen **- 2.** = hp.

HQ *(abbr of* headquarters) *n* HQ *das.*

hr *(abbr of* hour) Std.

hrs *(abbr of* hours) Std.

hub [hʌb] n - **1.** [of wheel] (Rad)nabe die - **2.** [of activity] Zentrum das.

hubbub ['hʌbʌb] n Lärm der.

hubcap ['hʌbkæp] n Radkappe die.

huddle ['hʌdl] vi - **1.** [crouch, curl up] kauern - **2.** [crowd together]: **to ~ (together)** sich (zusammen)drängen.

hue [hju:] n [colour] Farbton der.

huff [hʌf] n: **in a ~** beleidigt.

hug [hʌg] <> n Umarmung die; **to give sb a ~** jn umarmen <> vt - **1.** [embrace] umarmen - **2.** [hold - one's knees] umfassen - **3.** [stay close to]: **to ~ the coast/kerb** dicht an der Küste/am Straßenrand entlangfahren.

huge [hju:dʒ] adj riesig; [subject] vielfältig.

hulk [hʌlk] n - **1.** [of ship] (Schiffs)rumpf der - **2.** [person] Koloss der.

hull [hʌl] n [of ship] Schiffskörper der.

hullo [hə'ləʊ] excl = hello.

hum [hʌm] <> vi - **1.** [bee] summen; [car, machine] brummen - **2.** [sing] summen - **3.** [be busy - place] voller Leben sein; [- office] voller Aktivität sein <> vt [tune] summen.

human ['hju:mən] <> adj menschlich <> n: **~ (being)** Mensch der.

humane [hju:'meɪn] adj [compassionate] human.

humanitarian [hju:ˌmænɪ'teərɪən] adj humanitär.

humanity [hju:'mænətɪ] n - **1.** [kindness, sympathy] Humanität die - **2.** [mankind] Menschheit die. ◆ **humanities** npl: **the humanities** die Geisteswissenschaften.

human race n: **the ~** die menschliche Rasse.

human resources npl Humankapital das.

human rights npl Menschenrechte pl.

humble ['hʌmbl] <> adj [position, job, origins] niedrig; [clerk] einfach; [home, room, opinion] bescheiden; [person] demütig <> vt demütigen.

humbug ['hʌmbʌg] n Br [sweet] Pfefferminzbonbon der OR das.

humdrum ['hʌmdrʌm] adj [life] eintönig.

humid ['hju:mɪd] adj feucht.

humidity [hju:'mɪdətɪ] n (Luft)feuchtigkeit die.

humiliate [hju:'mɪlɪeɪt] vt demütigen.

humiliation [hju:ˌmɪlɪ'eɪʃn] n Demütigung die.

humility [hju:'mɪlətɪ] n Demut die.

humor n & vt Am = humour.

humorous ['hju:mərəs] adj [remark, story] lustig; [person] humorvoll.

humour Br, **humor** Am ['hju:mə'] <> n [comedy] Humor der; [of situation, remark] Komik die <> vt: **to ~ sb** jm seinen Willen lassen.

hump [hʌmp] n - **1.** [hill] Hügel der - **2.** [of camel] Höcker der; [of person] Buckel der.

hunch [hʌntʃ] n inf Gefühl das, Ahnung die.

hunchback ['hʌntʃbæk] n Bucklige der, die.

hundred ['hʌndrəd] num hundert; **a** OR **one ~** (ein)hundert; see also **six.** ◆ **hundreds** npl Hunderte pl.

hundredth ['hʌndrəθ] num hundertste, -r, -s; see also **sixth.**

hundredweight ['hʌndrədweɪt] n - **1.** [in UK] ≃ Zentner der, = 50,8 kg - **2.** [in US] ≃ Zentner der, = 45,36 kg.

hung [hʌŋ] pt & pp ▷ hang.

Hungarian [hʌŋ'geərɪən] <> adj ungarisch <> n - **1.** [person] Ungar der, -in die - **2.** [language] Ungarisch(e) das.

Hungary ['hʌŋgərɪ] n Ungarn nt.

hunger ['hʌŋgə'] n lit & fig Hunger der.

hunger strike n Hungerstreik der.

hung over adj inf verkatert.

hungry ['hʌŋgrɪ] adj hungrig; **to be ~** Hunger haben; **to be ~ for sthg** fig sich nach etw sehnen.

hung up adj inf: **to be ~ (on** OR **about)** sich verrückt machen (wegen (+ G)).

hunk [hʌŋk] n - **1.** [of bread, cheese] Stück das - **2.** inf [attractive man]: **he's a real ~** er ist ein richtiger Mann.

hunt [hʌnt] <> n - **1.** SPORT Jagd die; Br [for foxes] Fuchsjagd die; [hunters] Jagdgesellschaft die - **2.** [search] Suche die <> vi - **1.** [for food, sport] jagen - **2.** Br [for foxes] auf die Fuchsjagd gehen - **3.** [search]: **to ~ (for)** suchen (nach) <> vt - **1.** [animals, birds] jagen - **2.** [criminal] fahnden nach.

hunter ['hʌntə'] n [of animals, birds] Jäger der.

hunting ['hʌntɪŋ] n (U) - **1.** SPORT Jagd die - **2.** Br [foxhunting] Fuchsjagd die.

hurdle ['hɜ:dl] n lit & fig Hürde die. ◆ **hurdles** npl SPORT Hürdenlauf der.

hurl [hɜ:l] vt schleudern; **to ~ abuse at sb** jm Beschimpfungen an den Kopf werfen.

hurray [hʊ'reɪ] excl hurra!

hurricane ['hʌrɪkən] n Orkan der; [tropical] Hurrikan der.

hurried ['hʌrɪd] adj [meal] hastig; [departure] überstürzt; [glance] flüchtig; [note] eilig geschrieben.

hurriedly ['hʌrɪdlɪ] adv [eat] hastig; [leave, write] eilig.

hurry ['hʌrɪ] <> vt [person] (zur Eile) antreiben; [process] beschleunigen; **don't ~ me** hetz mich nicht; **to ~ to do sthg** sich beeilen, etw zu tun <> vi sich beeilen <> n Eile die; **to be in a ~** in Eile sein; **to do sthg in a ~** etw in Eile tun. ◆ **hurry up** vi sich beeilen.

hurt [hɜ:t] (pt & pp hurt) <> vt - **1.** [cause physical pain to] wehtun (+ D); **to ~ one's leg/arm** sich am Bein/Arm wehtun; **to ~ o.s.** sich (D) wehtun - **2.** [injure, upset] verletzen; **to ~ sb's feelings** js Gefühle verletzen - **3.** [harm] schaden (+ D) <> vi - **1.** [gen]

wehltun - 2. [harm] schaden <> adj [leg, arm, feelings] verletzt; [look, voice] gekränkt.

hurtful ['hɜːtful] adj verletzend.

hurtle ['hɜːtl] vi sausen.

husband ['hʌzbənd] n Ehemann der; **my ~** mein Mann.

hush [hʌʃ] <> n Schweigen das <> excl still!
➡ **hush up** vt sep [affair] vertuschen.

husk [hʌsk] n [of seed] Hülse die; [of grain] Spelze die.

husky ['hʌskɪ] <> adj [voice] rau <> n [dog] Husky der, Eskimohund der.

hustle ['hʌsl] <> vt [hurry]: **he ~d her out of the room** er drängte sie schnell aus dem Raum <> n: ~ **and bustle** geschäftiges Treiben.

hut [hʌt] n Hütte die; [temporary building] Baracke die.

hutch [hʌtʃ] n Stall der.

hyacinth ['haɪəsɪnθ] n Hyazinthe die.

hydrant ['haɪdrənt] n Hydrant der.

hydraulic [haɪ'drɔːlɪk] adj hydraulisch.

hydroelectric [ˌhaɪdrəʊɪ'lektrɪk] adj hydroelektrisch; **~ power** durch Wasserkraft erzeugte Energie.

hydrofoil ['haɪdrəfɔɪl] n Tragflächenboot das.

hydrogen ['haɪdrədʒən] n Wasserstoff der.

hyena [haɪ'iːnə] n Hyäne die.

hygiene ['haɪdʒiːn] n Hygiene die; **personal ~** Körperpflege die.

hygienic [haɪ'dʒiːnɪk] adj hygienisch.

hymn [hɪm] n Kirchenlied das.

hype [haɪp] inf <> n Publicity die <> vt Publicity machen für.

hyperactive [ˌhaɪpər'æktɪv] adj überaktiv.

hypermarket ['haɪpəˌmɑːkɪt] n Großmarkt der.

hyphen ['haɪfn] n Bindestrich der; [at end of line] Trennungsstrich der.

hypnosis [hɪp'nəʊsɪs] n Hypnose die.

hypnotic [hɪp'nɒtɪk] adj hypnotisch.

hypnotize, -ise ['hɪpnətaɪz] vt hypnotisieren.

hypocrisy [hɪ'pɒkrəsɪ] n Heuchelei die.

hypocrite ['hɪpəkrɪt] n Heuchler der, -in die.

hypocritical [ˌhɪpə'krɪtɪkl] adj heuchlerisch.

hypothesis [haɪ'pɒθɪsɪs] (pl -theses [-θɪsiːz]) n Hypothese die.

hypothetical [ˌhaɪpə'θetɪkl] adj hypothetisch.

hysteria [hɪs'tɪərɪə] n Hysterie die.

hysterical [hɪs'terɪkl] adj - 1. [gen] hysterisch - 2. inf [very funny] urkomisch.

hysterics [hɪs'terɪks] npl [panic] hysterischer Anfall; **to be in ~** inf [with laughter] sich auslschütten vor Lachen.

i (pl i's OR is), **I** (pl I's OR Is) [aɪ] n [letter] i das, I das.

I [aɪ] pers pron ich; **I'm tall** ich bin groß; **she and I were at college together** ich war mit ihr zusammen im College.

ice [aɪs] <> n - 1. (U) [gen] Eis das; [on pond] Eisschicht die; [on road] Glatteis das - 2. Br [ice cream] (Speise)eis das, Eiskrem <> vt Br [cake] glasieren. ➡ **ice over, ice up** vi [windscreen] vereisen; [lake] zulfrieren.

iceberg ['aɪsbɜːg] n Eisberg der.

iceberg lettuce n Eisbergsalat der.

icebox ['aɪsbɒks] n - 1. Br [in refrigerator] Eisfach das - 2. Am [refrigerator] Eisschrank der.

ice cream n Eis das, Eiskrem die.

ice cube n Eiswürfel der.

ice hockey n Eishockey das.

Iceland ['aɪslənd] n Island nt.

Icelandic [aɪs'lændɪk] <> adj isländisch <> n [language] Isländisch(e) das.

ice lolly n Br Eis das am Stiel.

ice pick n Eispickel der.

ice rink n Schlittschuhbahn die.

ice skate n Schlittschuh der. ➡ **ice-skate** vi Schlittschuh laufen, Eis laufen.

ice-skating n Schlittschuhlaufen das, Eislaufen das; [sport] Eiskunstlauf der; **to go ~** Schlittschuh laufen gehen.

icicle ['aɪsɪkl] n Eiszapfen der.

icing ['aɪsɪŋ] n [of cake] Zuckerguss der.

icing sugar n Br Puderzucker der.

icon ['aɪkɒn] n - 1. RELIG Ikone die - 2. COMPUT Icon das.

icy ['aɪsɪ] adj - 1. [wind, cold, weather] eisig; **it's ~ cold** es ist eiskalt - 2. [road, pavement] vereist - 3. fig [welcome, atmosphere] eisig.

I'd [aɪd] = I would, I had.

ID n (abbr of identification) Ausweis der.

idea [aɪ'dɪə] n - 1. [plan, suggestion] Idee die - 2. [notion] Vorstellung die; **you have no ~ how difficult it is** du kannst dir nicht vorstellen, wie schwer es ist; **can you give me an ~ of the price?** können Sie mir einen ungefähren Preis nennen?; **to have an ~ that ...** glauben, dass ...; **to have no ~** keine Ahnung haben - 3. [intention] Absicht die; **what's the big ~?** inf was soll das (heißen)?

ideal [aɪ'dɪəl] <> adj ideal <> n Ideal das.

ideally [aɪ'dɪəlɪ] adv - 1. [located] ideal; **he was ~ suited to the job** er war perfekt geeignet für die Stelle - **2.** [preferably] idealerweise, im Idealfall.

identical [aɪ'dentɪkl] *adj* identisch.

identification [aɪˌdentɪfɪ'keɪʃn] *n* - **1.** [gen] Identifizierung *die* - **2.** *(U)* [documentation] Ausweispapiere *pl*; **do you have any ~?** können Sie sich ausweisen?

identify [aɪ'dentɪfaɪ] <> *vt* - **1.** [gen] identifizieren; [cause, need] erkennen; **to ~ o.s.** sich ausweisen - **2.** [connect]: **to ~ sb with sthg** jn mit etw in Verbindung bringen <> *vi* [empathize]: **to ~ with sb/sthg** sich mit jm/etw identifizieren.

identity [aɪ'dentətɪ] *n* Identität *die.*

identity card *n* Personalausweis *der.*

ideology [ˌaɪdɪ'ɒlədʒɪ] *n* Weltanschauung *die; pej* Ideologie *die.*

idiom ['ɪdɪəm] *n* - **1.** [phrase] Redewendung *die* - **2.** *fml* [style] Idiom *das.*

idiomatic [ˌɪdɪə'mætɪk] *adj* idiomatisch.

idiosyncrasy [ˌɪdɪə'sɪŋkrəsɪ] *n* [of person] Eigenheit *die;* [of thing] Besonderheit *die.*

idiot ['ɪdɪət] *n* Idiot *der.*

idiotic [ˌɪdɪ'ɒtɪk] *adj* idiotisch.

idle ['aɪdl] <> *adj* - **1.** [person - inactive] untätig, müßig; [- lazy] faul - **2.** [machine, factory] stillstehend; [workers] unbeschäftigt - **3.** [threat] leer - **4.** [glance] flüchtig - **5.** [futile] sinnlos <> *vi* [engine] im Leerlauf sein.
<> **idle away** *vt sep* [time] vertrödeln.

idol ['aɪdl] *n* - **1.** [hero] Idol *das* - **2.** RELIG Götze *der.*

idolize, -ise ['aɪdəlaɪz] *vt* vergöttern.

idyllic [ɪ'dɪlɪk] *adj* idyllisch.

i.e. *(abbr of* id est) d. h.

if [ɪf] *conj* wenn, falls; *(in indirect questions after "know", "wonder")* ob; **~ I were you** wenn ich du wäre; **pleasant weather, ~ rather cold** schönes Wetter, wenn auch ziemlich kalt; **as ~** als ob. <> **if not** *conj* wenn nicht, falls nicht. <> **if only** <> *conj* - **1.** [expressing regret] wenn ... nur; **~ only I had known** wenn ich das nur OR bloß gewusst hätte - **2.** [providing a reason] (und) sei es nur; **go and see him, ~ only to please me** geh ihn besuchen, und sei es nur mir zuliebe <> *excl:* **~ only!** das wäre schön!

igloo ['ɪgluː] *(pl* -s) *n* Iglu *der* OR *das.*

ignite [ɪg'naɪt] <> *vt* entzünden; AUT zünden <> *vi* sich entzünden; AUT zünden.

ignition [ɪg'nɪʃn] *n* [in car] Zündung *die.*

ignition key *n* Zündschlüssel *der.*

ignorance ['ɪgnərəns] *n* Unwissenheit *die;* [of particular subject, information *etc*] Unkenntnis *die.*

ignorant ['ɪgnərənt] *adj* - **1.** [uneducated] ungebildet; [lacking information] unwissend - **2.** *fml* [unaware]: **to be ~ of sthg** von etw nichts wissen - **3.** *inf* [rude] ungehobelt.

ignore [ɪg'nɔː] *vt* ignorieren.

ilk [ɪlk] *n*: **people of that ~** solche Leute; **and others of that ~** und seines-/ihresgleichen.

ill [ɪl] <> *adj* - **1.** [sick] krank; **to feel ~** sich unwohl OR krank fühlen; **to be taken ~, to fall ~** krank werden - **2.** [bad - omen, treatment] schlecht; [- effects] nachteilig; **~ at ease** unbehaglich <> *adv* schlecht; **to speak/think ~ of sb** schlecht über jn reden/denken.

I'll [aɪl] = I will, I shall.

ill-advised [-əd'vaɪzd] *adj* unklug.

illegal [ɪ'liːgl] *adj* [action] gesetzwidrig; [organization] illegal.

illegible [ɪ'ledʒəbl] *adj* unleserlich.

illegitimate [ˌɪlɪ'dʒɪtɪmət] *adj* - **1.** [child] unehelich - **2.** [activity] unzulässig.

ill-equipped [-ɪ'kwɪpt] *adj:* **to be ~ to do sthg** [unsuited] nicht dafür geeignet sein, etw zu tun.

ill-fated [-'feɪtɪd] *adj* unglückselig.

ill feeling *n* Feindseligkeit *die.*

ill health *n* schwache Gesundheit.

illicit [ɪ'lɪsɪt] *adj* illegal.

illiteracy [ɪ'lɪtərəsɪ] *n* Analphabetentum *das.*

illiterate [ɪ'lɪtərət] <> *adj* - **1.** [unable to read] des Lesens und Schreibens unkundig; **to be ~** Analphabet, -in sein - **2.** [uneducated] ungebildet <> *n* Analphabet *der,* -in *die.*

illness ['ɪlnɪs] *n* Krankheit *die.*

illogical [ɪ'lɒdʒɪkl] *adj* unlogisch.

ill-suited *adj* nicht zusammenpassend; **to be ~ to sthg** für etw ungeeignet sein.

ill-treat *vt* misshandeln; [worker] schlecht behandeln.

illuminate [ɪ'luːmɪneɪt] *vt* - **1.** [light up] beleuchten - **2.** [problem, subject] erhellen.

illumination [ɪˌluːmɪ'neɪʃn] *n* [lighting] Beleuchtung *die.* <> **illuminations** *npl Br* festliche Beleuchtung.

illusion [ɪ'luːʒn] *n* Illusion *die;* **to be under the ~ that ...** sich einbilden, dass ...; **optical ~** optische Täuschung.

illustrate ['ɪləstreɪt] *vt* illustrieren.

illustration [ˌɪlə'streɪʃn] *n* - **1.** [picture] Illustration *die* - **2.** [example] Beispiel *das.*

illustrious [ɪ'lʌstrɪəs] *adj fml* berühmt; [career] glanzvoll.

ill will *n* böses Blut; **he didn't bear anyone any ~** er war niemandem feindlich gesinnt.

I'm [aɪm] = I am.

image ['ɪmɪdʒ] *n* - **1.** [gen] Bild *das;* [in mirror] Spiegelbild *das* - **2.** [in mind] Vorstellung *die* - **3.** [of company, public figure] Image *das.*

imagery ['ɪmɪdʒrɪ] *n* [in writing] Metaphorik *die;* [in visual arts] Bildersymbolik *die.*

imaginary [ɪ'mædʒɪnrɪ] *adj* imaginär.

imagination [ɪˌmædʒɪ'neɪʃn] *n* - **1.** [ability, fantasy] Fantasie *die* - **2.** [mind] Einbildung *die;* **it's all in her ~** das bildet sie sich nur ein.

imaginative [ɪˈmædʒɪnətɪv] *adj* fantasievoll; [concerning new ideas] einfallsreich.

imagine [ɪˈmædʒɪn] *vt* - **1.** [visualize] sich *(D)* vorstellen, sich *(D)* denken; **to ~ doing sthg** sich *(D)* vorstellen, etw zu tun; **~ (that)!** stell dir das mal vor! - **2.** [dream] sich *(D)* einbilden; **you ~d it** du hast es dir (nur) eingebildet - **3.** [suppose] anlnehmen, vermuten.

imbalance [ˌɪmˈbæləns] *n* Ungleichgewicht *das*.

imbecile [ˈɪmbɪsiːl] *n* Idiot *der*.

IMF *(abbr of* International Monetary Fund*) n* IWF *der*.

imitate [ˈɪmɪteɪt] *vt* nachlahmen.

imitation [ˌɪmɪˈteɪʃn] <> *n* - **1.** [gen] Nachahmung *die* - **2.** [copy] Kopie *die* <> *adj* unecht, imitiert; **~ leather** Kunstleder *das*.

immaculate [ɪˈmækjʊlət] *adj* - **1.** [clean and tidy] makellos - **2.** [behaviour] tadellos.

immaterial [ˌɪməˈtɪərɪəl] *adj* [irrelevant] unwichtig.

immature [ˌɪməˈtjʊəˡ] *adj* - **1.** [person, behaviour] unreif - **2.** BOT & ZOOL noch nicht voll entwickelt.

immediate [ɪˈmiːdjət] *adj* - **1.** [response, attention] unverzüglich; [need, problem] dringend; **to take ~ action** sofort OR unverzüglich handeln - **2.** [future, neighbourhood] unmittelbar; **the ~ area** das Gebiet in unmittelbarer Nähe; **the ~ family** die engste Familie.

immediately [ɪˈmiːdjətlɪ] <> *adv* - **1.** [at once] sofort - **2.** [directly] unmittelbar, direkt <> *conj* [as soon as] sobald.

immense [ɪˈmens] *adj* enorm.

immerse [ɪˈmɜːs] *vt* - **1.** [in liquid]: **to ~ sthg in sthg** etw in etw *(A)* einltauchen - **2.** *fig* [involve]: **to ~ o.s. in sthg** sich in etw *(A)* stürzen.

immersion heater [ɪˈmɜːʃn-] *n* Heißwasserbereiter *der*.

immigrant [ˈɪmɪgrənt] *n* Einwanderer *der*, -derin *die*.

immigration [ˌɪmɪˈgreɪʃn] *n* Einwanderung *die*.

imminent [ˈɪmɪnənt] *adj* [danger] drohend; [death, disaster] unmittelbar bevorstehend.

immobilize, -ise [ɪˈməʊbɪlaɪz] *vt* [machine, lift] lahm legen; [vehicle] gegen Wegfahren sichern.

immoral [ɪˈmɒrəl] *adj* unmoralisch.

immortal [ɪˈmɔːtl] *adj* unsterblich.

immortalize, -ise [ɪˈmɔːtəlaɪz] *vt* unsterblich machen.

immovable [ɪˈmuːvəbl] *adj* - **1.** [fixed] unbeweglich - **2.** [obstinate] unnachgiebig.

immune [ɪˈmjuːn] *adj* - **1.** MED: **~ (to)** immun (gegen) - **2.** *fig:* **to be ~ to criticism** gegen Kritik unempfindlich sein.

immunity [ɪˈmjuːnətɪ] *n* MED: **~ (to)** Immunität *die* (gegen).

immunize, -ise [ˈɪmjuːnaɪz] *vt:* **to ~ sb (against)** MED jn immunisieren (gegen).

impact [ˈɪmpækt] *n* - **1.** [force of contact] Aufprall *der;* [of two moving objects] Zusammenprall *der* - **2.** [effect] Auswirkung *die;* **to make an ~ on sb** Eindruck auf jn machen; **to make an ~ on sthg** einen Einfluss auf etw *(A)* haben.

impair [ɪmˈpeəˡ] *vt* beeinträchtigen.

impart [ɪmˈpɑːt] *vt fml* - **1.** [knowledge, skills]: **to ~ sthg to sb** jm etw vermitteln - **2.** [feeling, quality]: **to ~ sthg to sthg** etw *(D)* etw verleihen.

impartial [ɪmˈpɑːʃl] *adj* [person] unparteiisch; [news report] objektiv.

impassable [ɪmˈpɑːsəbl] *adj* unpassierbar.

impassive [ɪmˈpæsɪv] *adj* unbewegt.

impatience [ɪmˈpeɪʃns] *n* Ungeduld *die*.

impatient [ɪmˈpeɪʃnt] *adj* ungeduldig; **to be ~ to do sthg** es nicht erwarten können, etw zu tun.

impeccable [ɪmˈpekəbl] *adj* untadelig.

impede [ɪmˈpiːd] *vt* [person] hindern; [progress, activity] behindern.

impediment [ɪmˈpedɪmənt] *n* - **1.** [obstacle] Hindernis *das* - **2.** [disability] Behinderung *die*.

impel [ɪmˈpel] *vt:* **to ~ sb to do sthg** jn (dazu) nötigen, etw zu tun.

impending [ɪmˈpendɪŋ] *adj* [doom, disaster] drohend; [interview, test] bevorstehend.

imperative [ɪmˈperətɪv] <> *adj* dringend notwendig <> *n* - **1.** [necessity] dringende Notwendigkeit - **2.** GRAMM Imperativ *der*.

imperfect [ɪmˈpɜːfɪkt] <> *adj* [work, copy] fehlerhaft; [knowledge] mangelhaft <> *n* GRAMM: **~ (tense)** Imperfekt *das*.

imperial [ɪmˈpɪərɪəl] *adj* - **1.** [of an empire] imperial; [of an emperor] kaiserlich - **2.** [measurement] britisch.

imperil [ɪmˈperɪl] *vt fml* gefährden.

impersonal [ɪmˈpɜːsnl] *adj* - **1.** [unemotional] unpersönlich - **2.** GRAMM: **~ verb** unpersönlich gebrauchtes Verb.

impersonate [ɪmˈpɜːsəneɪt] *vt* - **1.** [mimic] imitieren, nachlahmen - **2.** [pretend to be] sich auslgeben als.

impersonation [ɪmˌpɜːsəˈneɪʃn] *n* [by mimic] Imitation *die*, Nachahmung *die*.

impertinent [ɪmˈpɜːtɪnənt] *adj* unverschämt.

impervious [ɪmˈpɜːvɪəs] *adj:* **to be ~ to charm** für Charme unempfänglich sein; **to be ~ to criticism** von Kritik unberührt sein.

impetuous [ɪmˈpetjʊəs] *adj* impulsiv.

impetus [ˈɪmpɪtəs] *n* - **1.** *(U)* [momentum] Schwung *der* - **2.** [stimulus] Impuls *der*.

impinge [ɪmˈpɪndʒ] *vi:* **to ~ on sb/sthg** sich auf jn/etw auslwirken.

implant [*n* ˈɪmplɑːnt, *vb* ɪmˈplɑːnt] <> *n*

Implantat *das* <> *vt* - **1.** [instil]: **to ~ sthg in sb** jm etw einimpfen - **2.** MED: **to ~ sthg in(to) sb** jm etw implantieren.

implausible [ɪmˈplɔːzəbl] *adj* [story] unglaubwürdig.

implement [*n* ˈɪmplɪmənt, *vb* ˈɪmplɪment] <> *n* [tool] Werkzeug *das*; [piece of equipment] Gerät *das* <> *vt* [plan] ausführen; [law] vollziehen; [policy] in die Praxis umlsetzen.

implication [ˌɪmplɪˈkeɪʃn] *n* - **1.** *(U)* [involvement] Verwicklung *die* - **2.** [inference] Auswirkung *die*; **by ~** implizit.

implicit [ɪmˈplɪsɪt] *adj* - **1.** [inferred] implizit; [acknowledgement] stillschweigend; [criticism] unausgesprochen - **2.** [faith, belief] blind.

implore [ɪmˈplɔː] *vt*: **to ~ sb (to do sthg)** jn inständig bitten(, etw zu tun).

imply [ɪmˈplaɪ] *vt* - **1.** [suggest]: **I'm not ~ing that ...** ich will damit nicht sagen, dass ... - **2.** [responsibility] mit einlschließen.

impolite [ˌɪmpəˈlaɪt] *adj* unhöflich.

import [*n* ˈɪmpɔːt, *vb* ɪmˈpɔːt] <> *n* - **1.** [product] Importware *die* - **2.** *(U)* [act of importing] Import *der* <> *vt* - **1.** [goods] importieren - **2.** COMPUT importieren.

importance [ɪmˈpɔːtns] *n (U)* Wichtigkeit *die*; [significance] Bedeutung *die*.

important [ɪmˈpɔːtnt] *adj* wichtig; [significant] bedeutend; [person] einflussreich; **to be ~ to sb** für jn wichtig sein.

importer [ɪmˈpɔːtə] *n* [person, firm] Importeur *der*; [country] Importland *das*.

impose [ɪmˈpəʊz] <> *vt*: **to ~ sthg (on sb/ sthg)** (jm/etw) etw auflerlegen; **to ~ a tax on sb** jn besteuern <> *vi*: **to ~ (on sb)** (jm) zur Last fallen.

imposing [ɪmˈpəʊzɪŋ] *adj* beeindruckend.

imposition [ˌɪmpəˈzɪʃn] *n* - **1.** [enforcement - gen] Auferlegung *die*; [- of tax] Erhebung *die* - **2.** [burden] Zumutung *die*.

impossible [ɪmˈpɒsəbl] *adj* unmöglich.

impostor, imposter *Am* [ɪmˈpɒstə] *n* Hochstapler *der*, -in *die*.

impotent [ˈɪmpətənt] *adj* - **1.** [sexually] impotent - **2.** [powerless] machtlos.

impound [ɪmˈpaʊnd] *vt* beschlagnahmen.

impoverished [ɪmˈpɒvərɪʃt] *adj lit* & *fig* verarmt.

impractical [ɪmˈpræktɪkl] *adj* praxisfern.

impregnable [ɪmˈpregnəbl] *adj* [fortress, defences] uneinnehmbar; *fig* [person] unangreifbar; [position, argument] unanfechtbar.

impregnate [ˈɪmpregneɪt] *vt* - **1.** [saturate]: **to ~ sthg with sthg** etw mit etw tränken; [to protect material] etw mit etw imprägnieren - **2.** *fml* [fertilize] befruchten.

impress [ɪmˈpres] *vt* - **1.** [make impression on] beeindrucken; [deliberately] imponieren (+ *D*); **to be favourably/unfavourably ~ed**

einen guten/schlechten Eindruck haben - **2.** [make clear]: **to ~ sthg on sb** jm etw einlschärfen.

impression [ɪmˈpreʃn] *n* - **1.** [gen] Eindruck *der*; **to make an ~** Eindruck machen; **to be under the ~ (that) ...** den Eindruck haben, dass ... - **2.** [impersonation] Nachahmung *die*, Imitation *die*; **to do an ~ of sb** jn imitieren OR nachlahmen - **3.** [of book] Nachdruck *der*.

impressive [ɪmˈpresɪv] *adj* beeindruckend.

imprint [ˈɪmprɪnt] *n* [mark] Abdruck *der*.

imprison [ɪmˈprɪzn] *vt* inhaftieren.

improbable [ɪmˈprɒbəbl] *adj* [unlikely] unwahrscheinlich.

impromptu [ɪmˈprɒmptjuː] *adj* improvisiert.

improper [ɪmˈprɒpə] *adj* - **1.** [unsuitable - treatment] unangebracht; [- behaviour] unpassend - **2.** [dishonest - actions] unehrenhaft; [- dealings] unlauter - **3.** [rude] unanständig.

improve [ɪmˈpruːv] <> *vi* [weather, work, student] besser werden; [delinquent, health] sich bessern; [productivity] sich steigern; **to ~ (up)on** übertreffen; [offer] überbieten <> *vt* - **1.** [make better] verbessern - **2.** [increase - vocabulary, knowledge] erweitern; [- productivity] erhöhen, steigern - **3.** [cultivate]: **to ~ one's mind** sich (weiter)bilden; **to ~ o.s.** an sich *(D)* arbeiten.

improvement [ɪmˈpruːvmənt] *n* Verbesserung *die*; [in health, sb's behaviour, weather] Besserung *die*; [in productivity, sports] Steigerung *die*.

improvise [ˈɪmprəvaɪz] <> *vt* improvisieren; [shelter] notdürftig erstellen <> *vi* improvisieren.

impudence [ˈɪmpjʊdəns] *n* Unverschämtheit *die*.

impudent [ˈɪmpjʊdənt] *adj* unverschämt.

impulse [ˈɪmpʌls] *n* Impuls *der*; **to do sthg on ~** etw aus einem Impuls heraus tun.

impulsive [ɪmˈpʌlsɪv] *adj* impulsiv.

impunity [ɪmˈpjuːnətɪ] *n*: **with ~** ungestraft.

impurity [ɪmˈpjʊərətɪ] *n* Unreinheit *die*.

in [ɪn] <> *prep* - **1.** [indicating place, position] in (+ *D*); (with verbs of motion) in (+ *A*); **it's ~ the box/garden** es ist in der Schachtel/im Garten; **put it ~ the box/garden** leg es in die Schachtel/in den Garten; **~ the street/world** auf der Straße/Welt; **~ the country** auf dem Lande; **~ the sky** am Himmel; **~ Paris/ Belgium** in Paris/Belgien; **to be ~ hospital/ prison** im Krankenhaus/Gefängnis sein; **~ here/there** hier/dort drinnen - **2.** [wearing] in (+ *D*); **she was still ~ her nightclothes** war noch im Nachthemd; **(dressed) ~ red** rot gekleidet - **3.** [at a particular time, during] in (+ *D*); **~ April** im April; **she was born ~ 1999** sie wurde 1999 geboren; ~ (the) spring/winter im Frühling/Winter; ~ the afternoon/morning am Nachmittag/Morgen; ten o'clock ~ the morning zehn Uhr morgens - 4. [within, after] in (+ D); he learned to type ~ two weeks er lernte in zwei Wochen Maschine schreiben; it'll be ready ~ an hour es ist in einer Stunde fertig - 5. [expressing time passed] seit; it's my first decent meal ~ weeks das ist meine erste anständige Mahlzeit seit Wochen - 6. [indicating situation, circumstances]: ~ the sun/rain in der Sonne/im Regen; to be ~ pain Schmerzen haben; ~ danger/difficulty in Gefahr/Schwierigkeiten; ~ these circumstances unter diesen Umständen - 7. [indicating manner]: to write ~ ink mit Tinte schreiben; ~ a soft voice mit sanfter Stimme; they were talking ~ English sie sprachen Englisch; ~ writing schriftlich - 8. [indicating emotional state]: ~ anger/delight/amazement/despair wütend/entzückt/erstaunt/verzweifelt; ~ my excitement in meiner Aufregung - 9. [specifying area of activity]: advances ~ medicine Fortschritte in der Medizin; he's ~ computers er ist in der Computerbranche - 10. [referring to quantity]: to buy sthg ~ large/small quantities etw in großen/kleinen Mengen kaufen; ~ (their) thousands zu Tausenden - 11. [referring to age]: she's ~ her twenties sie ist in den Zwanzigern - 12. [describing arrangement] in (+ D); ~ a circle/line im Kreis/in einer Reihe; to stand ~ twos zu zweit dastehen - 13. [indicating colour] in (+ D); it comes ~ green or blue es gibt es in grün oder blau - 14. [as regards]: a rise ~ prices ein Preisanstieg; to be 3 metres ~ length 3 Meter lang sein; a change ~ direction ein Richtungswechsel - 15. [in ratios]: one ~ ten jeder Zehnte; an increase of five pence ~ the pound eine Preiserhöhung von fünf Prozent - 16. (after superl) in (+ D); the best ~ the world der/die/das Beste in der Welt - 17. (+ present participle): she made a mistake ~ accepting the offer sie machte einen Fehler, indem sie das Angebot annahm ◇ adv - 1. [inside] herein/hinein; you can go ~ now du kannst jetzt hineingehen - 2. [at home, work] da; is Judith ~? ist Judith da?; to stay ~ zu Hause bleiben - 3. [of train, boat, plane]: to get ~ ankommen; the train isn't ~ yet der Zug ist noch nicht angekommen - 4. [in shop]: is my new TV ~ yet? ist mein neuer Fernseher schon da? - 5. [of tide]: the tide is ~ es ist Flut - 6. phr: you're ~ for a surprise du wirst eine Überraschung erleben; he's ~ for it inf der kann sich auf etwas gefasst machen; my luck is ~ das Glück ist auf meiner Seite ◇ adj inf in; short skirts are ~ this year kurze Röcke sind dieses Jahr in. ◆ ins npl: she knows the ~s and outs of

the matter sie ist mit allen Feinheiten der Sache vertraut.

in. abbr of inch.

inability [ˌɪnəˈbɪlətɪ] n Unfähigkeit die.

inaccessible [ˌɪnəkˈsesəbl] adj - 1. [place] unzugänglich - 2. [book, film, music] schwer verständlich.

inaccurate [ɪnˈækjʊrət] adj [imprecise] ungenau; [incorrect] inkorrekt.

inadequate [ɪnˈædɪkwət] adj unzureichend.

inadvertently [ˌɪnədˈvɜːtəntlɪ] adv [forget, break] aus Versehen; [discover] zufällig.

inadvisable [ˌɪnədˈvaɪzəbl] adj nicht ratsam.

inane [ɪˈneɪn] adj dumm.

inanimate [ɪnˈænɪmət] adj leblos.

inappropriate [ˌɪnəˈprəʊprɪət] adj unpassend.

inarticulate [ˌɪnɑːˈtɪkjʊlət] adj [person]: to be ~ sich nicht gut ausdrücken können.

inasmuch [ˌɪnəzˈmʌtʃ] ◆ inasmuch as conj fml [because] da; [to the extent that] insofern als.

inaudible [ɪˈnɔːdɪbl] adj unhörbar.

inaugural [ɪˈnɔːgjʊrəl] adj [meeting] Eröffnungs-; [speech] Antritts-.

inauguration [ɪˌnɔːgjʊˈreɪʃn] n - 1. [of leader, president] Amtseinführung die - 2. [of building] Einweihung die.

inborn [ˌɪnˈbɔːn] adj angeboren.

inbound [ˈɪnbaʊnd] adj ankommend.

inbred [ˌɪnˈbred] adj [characteristic, quality] angeboren.

inbuilt [ˌɪnˈbɪlt] adj [quality, defect] angeboren.

inc. (abbr of inclusive) inkl.

Inc. [ɪŋk] abbr of incorporated.

incapable [ɪnˈkeɪpəbl] adj - 1. [unable]: to be ~ of sthg zu etw nicht fähig sein; to be ~ of doing sthg nicht fähig sein, etw zu tun - 2. [incompetent] unfähig.

incapacitated [ˌɪnkəˈpæsɪteɪtɪd] adj [for work] arbeitsunfähig.

incarcerate [ɪnˈkɑːsəreɪt] vt fml einkerkern.

incendiary device [ɪnˈsendjərɪ-] n Brandsatz der.

incense [n ˈɪnsens, vb ɪnˈsens] ◇ n Weihrauch der ◇ vt [anger] erbosen, erzürnen.

incentive [ɪnˈsentɪv] n Anreiz der.

incentive scheme n Anreizsystem das.

inception [ɪnˈsepʃn] n fml Beginn der; [of institution] Gründung die.

incessant [ɪnˈsesnt] adj unaufhörlich.

incessantly [ɪnˈsesntlɪ] adv unaufhörlich.

incest [ˈɪnsest] n Inzest der.

inch [ɪntʃ] ◇ n Zoll der, = 2,54 cm ◇ vi: to ~ forward/through sich zentimeterweise vorwärts bewegen/hindurchbewegen.

incidence ['ɪnsɪdəns] n Häufigkeit die.

incident ['ɪnsɪdənt] n - 1. [event] Vorfall der; **the meeting went off without ~** das Treffen verlief ohne Zwischenfälle - 2. POL Zwischenfall der.

incidental [ˌɪnsɪ'dentl] adj [minor] nebensächlich; **~ expenses** Nebenausgaben pl.

incidentally [ˌɪnsɪ'dentlɪ] adv [by the way] übrigens.

incinerate [ɪn'sɪnəreɪt] vt verbrennen.

incipient [ɪn'sɪpɪənt] adj fml beginnend.

incisive [ɪn'saɪsɪv] adj [person] scharfsinnig; [comment, writing] pointiert.

incite [ɪn'saɪt] vt aufhetzen; **to ~ sb to do sthg** jn dazu aufstacheln, etw zu tun.

incl. (abbr of inclusive) inkl.

inclination [ˌɪnklɪ'neɪʃn] n - 1. [desire, slope] Neigung die - 2. [tendency]: **to have an ~ to do sthg** die Neigung (dazu) haben, etw zu tun.

incline [n 'ɪnklaɪn, vb ɪn'klaɪn] <> n [slope] Hang der; [angle] Neigung die <> vt [head, body] neigen.

inclined [ɪn'klaɪnd] adj - 1. [tending] geneigt; **to be ~ to do sthg** dazu neigen, etw zu tun - 2. [wanting]: **to be ~ to do sthg** Lust haben, etw zu tun - 3. [sloping] geneigt.

include [ɪn'kluːd] vt - 1. [gen] (mit) einschließen; [contain] enthalten - 2. [add, count] mitrechnen.

included [ɪn'kluːdɪd] adj eingeschlossen; **service is not ~** die Bedienung ist nicht inbegriffen.

including [ɪn'kluːdɪŋ] prep einschließlich (+ G); **up to and ~ last month** bis einschließlich des letzten Monats.

inclusive [ɪn'kluːsɪv] adj einschließlich, inklusive; **~ price** Pauschalpreis der; **from the 8th to the 16th ~** vom 8. bis einschließlich 16.; **~ of** einschließlich (+ G).

incoherent [ˌɪnkəʊ'hɪərənt] adj [speech] zusammenhanglos; **he was ~** er drückte sich unklar aus.

income ['ɪŋkʌm] n Einkommen das.

income support n Br Sozialhilfe die.

income tax n Einkommensteuer die.

incompatible [ˌɪnkəm'pætɪbl] adj [ideas, jobs, characters] unvereinbar; [computers] inkompatibel; **to be ~ with sb** nicht zu jm passen.

incompetent [ɪn'kɒmpɪtənt] adj unfähig, inkompetent; [work] unzulänglich.

incomplete [ˌɪnkəm'pliːt] adj unvollständig; [story] nicht abgeschlossen.

incomprehensible [ɪnˌkɒmprɪ'hensəbl] adj unverständlich.

inconceivable [ˌɪnkən'siːvəbl] adj undenkbar, unvorstellbar.

inconclusive [ˌɪnkən'kluːsɪv] adj [meeting, debate] ergebnislos; [evidence, argument] nicht schlüssig.

incongruous [ɪn'kɒŋgrʊəs] adj [clothes, behaviour] unpassend.

inconsequential [ˌɪnkɒnsɪ'kwenʃl] adj [insignificant] unbedeutend.

inconsiderate [ˌɪnkən'sɪdərət] adj rücksichtslos.

inconsistency [ˌɪnkən'sɪstənsɪ] n Widersprüchlichkeit die.

inconsistent [ˌɪnkən'sɪstənt] adj widersprüchlich; [performance] schwankend; [work] unbeständig; [behaviour] inkonsequent; **to be ~ with sthg** mit etw nicht übereinstimmen.

inconspicuous [ˌɪnkən'spɪkjʊəs] adj unauffällig.

inconvenience [ˌɪnkən'viːnjəns] <> n Unannehmlichkeit die <> vt Unannehmlichkeiten OR Umstände bereiten.

inconvenient [ˌɪnkən'viːnjənt] adj ungünstig; **to be ~ for sb** jm ungelegen kommen.

incorporate [ɪn'kɔːpəreɪt] vt einschließen; **to ~ sb/sthg in(to) sthg** jn/etw in etw (A) aufnehmen.

incorporated company n COMM (im Handelsregister) eingetragene Gesellschaft.

incorrect [ˌɪnkə'rekt] adj falsch; [behaviour] inkorrekt.

incorrigible [ɪn'kɒrɪdʒəbl] adj unverbesserlich.

increase [n 'ɪnkriːs, vb ɪn'kriːs] <> n: **~ (in)** [number, unemployment] Zunahme die (+ G); [price, demand, speed] Erhöhung die (+ G); [output] Steigerung die (+ G); **to be on the ~** (ständig) zunehmen <> vt [price, wages, speed] erhöhen; [output] steigern; [fear, efforts] verstärken <> vi steigen; [unemployment, pain] zunehmen; [anxiety] wachsen.

increasing [ɪn'kriːsɪŋ] adj [number, use, frequency] zunehmend; [anxiety, demand] wachsend.

increasingly [ɪn'kriːsɪŋlɪ] adv zunehmend.

incredible [ɪn'kredəbl] adj - 1. [wonderful] sagenhaft - 2. [very large, unbelievable] unglaublich.

incredulous [ɪn'kredjʊləs] adj ungläubig.

increment ['ɪnkrɪmənt] n Zuwachs der; [of salary] Gehaltserhöhung die.

incriminating [ɪn'krɪmɪneɪtɪŋ] adj belastend.

incubator ['ɪnkjʊbeɪtə'] n [for baby] Brutkasten der.

incur [ɪn'kɜː'] vt [loss] erleiden; [expenses] haben; [debts] machen.

indebted [ɪn'detɪd] adj [grateful]: **to be ~ to sb** jm zu Dank verpflichtet sein.

indecent [ɪn'diːsnt] adj unanständig.

indecisive [ˌɪndɪ'saɪsɪv] adj - 1. [person] unentschlossen - 2. [result] unklar.

indeed [ɪn'diːd] adv wirklich, tatsächlich;

[certainly] natürlich; **very big** ~ wirklich sehr groß; **thank you very much** ~ vielen herzlichen Dank; ~? [in surprise] wirklich?, so?

indefinite [ɪnˈdefɪnɪt] *adj* - **1.** [period, number] unbestimmt - **2.** [answer] unklar.

indefinitely [ɪnˈdefɪnətlɪ] *adv* [wait] unbegrenzt lange; [closed] bis auf weiteres; [postpone] auf unbestimmte Zeit.

indent [ɪnˈdent] *vt* [text] einrücken.

independence [ˌɪndɪˈpendəns] *n* - **1.** [gen] Unabhängigkeit *die* - **2.** [in character] Selbstständigkeit *die*.

Independence Day *n* (amerikanischer) Unabhängigkeitstag *(4. Juli)*.

independent [ˌɪndɪˈpendənt] *adj* - **1.** [gen]: ~ **(of)** unabhängig (von) - **2.** [person - in character] selbstständig.

independent school *n Br* nichtstaatliche Schule.

in-depth *adj* eingehend.

indescribable [ˌɪndɪˈskraɪbəbl] *adj* unbeschreiblich.

indestructible [ˌɪndɪˈstrʌktəbl] *adj* unzerstörbar.

index [ˈɪndeks] *(pl senses 1 and 2 -es; pl sense 3 -es OR indices) n* - **1.** [of book] Register *das* - **2.** [in library] Kartei *die* - **3.** ECON Index *der*.

index card *n* Karteikarte *die*.

index finger *n* Zeigefinger *der*.

index-linked [-ˌlɪŋkt] *adj* der Inflationsrate angepasst.

India [ˈɪndɪə] *n* Indien *nt*.

Indian [ˈɪndɪən] <> *adj* - **1.** [from India] indisch - **2.** [from the Americas] indianisch, Indianer- <> *n* - **1.** [from India] Inder *der*, -in *die* - **2.** [from the Americas] Indianer *der*, -in *die*.

Indian Ocean *n*: **the** ~ der Indische Ozean.

indicate [ˈɪndɪkeɪt] <> *vt* - **1.** [with finger, pointer] zeigen auf (+ A); [subj: dial, arrow, gauge] anzeigen - **2.** [intention, fact] andeuten - **3.** [mention - desire, preference] zum Ausdruck bringen - **4.** [suggest] hindeuten auf (+ A) <> *vi* [when driving] blinken.

indication [ˌɪndɪˈkeɪʃn] *n* - **1.** [suggestion]: **can you give me an** ~ **of when you will arrive?** können Sie mir ungefähr sagen, wann Sie ankommen? - **2.** [sign] (An)zeichen *das*; [hint] Hinweis *der*.

indicative [ɪnˈdɪkətɪv] <> *adj*: **to be** ~ **of sthg** auf etw (A) hindeuten, auf etw (A) schließen lassen <> *n* GRAMM Indikativ *der*.

indicator [ˈɪndɪkeɪtə*] *n* - **1.** [sign] Indikator *der* - **2.** [on car] Blinker *der*.

indices [ˈɪndɪsiːz] *pl* ▷ **index.**

indict [ɪnˈdaɪt] *vt*: **to** ~ **sb (for)** jn anklagen (wegen (+ G)).

indictment [ɪnˈdaɪtmənt] *n* - **1.** LAW Anklageerhebung *die* - **2.** [criticism]: **an** ~ **of** ein Armutszeugnis für.

indifference [ɪnˈdɪfrəns] *n* Gleichgültigkeit *die*.

---

indifference

Das ist mir vollkommen egal. I couldn't care less.

Das geht doch mich nichts an. That doesn't concern me.

So ein Pech. What bad luck!

Meinetwegen. Yes, for all I care.

Das ist Ihre Sache. That's your business.

Wenn du meinst. If you like.

---

indifferent [ɪnˈdɪfrənt] *adj* - **1.** [uninterested] gleichgültig; **to be** ~ **to sthg** sich für etw nicht interessieren - **2.** [mediocre] mittelmäßig.

indigenous [ɪnˈdɪdʒɪnəs] *adj* [culture, traditions] einheimisch, landeseigen.

indigestion [ˌɪndɪˈdʒestʃn] *n (U)* Magenverstimmung *die*.

indignant [ɪnˈdɪgnənt] *adj*: **to be** ~ **(at)** empört sein (über (+ A)).

indignity [ɪnˈdɪgnətɪ] *n* Demütigung *die*.

indigo [ˈɪndɪgəʊ] *adj* indigoblau.

indirect [ˌɪndɪˈrekt] *adj* indirekt; **an** ~ **route** ein Umweg.

indiscreet [ˌɪndɪˈskriːt] *adj* indiskret; [tactless] taktlos.

indiscriminate [ˌɪndɪˈskrɪmɪnət] *adj* wahllos; [treatment] willkürlich; [person] unkritisch.

indispensable [ˌɪndɪˈspensəbl] *adj* unentbehrlich.

indisputable [ˌɪndɪˈspjuːtəbl] *adj* unbestreitbar; [evidence] unanfechtbar.

indistinguishable [ˌɪndɪˈstɪŋgwɪʃəbl] *adj*: **to be** ~ **(from sb/sthg)** (von jm/etw) nicht zu unterscheiden sein.

individual [ˌɪndɪˈvɪdʒʊəl] <> *adj* - **1.** [single] einzeln; [tuition] Einzel-; ~ **case** Einzelfall *der* - **2.** [distinctive] individuell <> *n* Einzelne *der, die*, Individuum *das*.

individually [ˌɪndɪˈvɪdʒʊəlɪ] *adv* einzeln.

Indonesia [ˌɪndəˈniːzɪə] *n* Indonesien *nt*.

indoor [ˈɪndɔː*] *adj* [swimming pool, sports] Hallen-; [plant] Zimmer-.

indoors [ˌɪnˈdɔːz] *adv* [stay] drinnen; [go] nach drinnen.

induce [ɪnˈdjuːs] *vt* [persuade]: **to** ~ **sb to do sthg** jn dazu bringen, etw zu tun.

inducement [ɪnˈdjuːsmənt] *n* [incentive] Anreiz *der*.

induction course [ɪnˈdʌkʃn-] *n* Einführungskurs *der*.

indulge [ɪnˈdʌldʒ] <> *vt* - **1.** [whim] nachgeben (+ D); [passion] frönen (+ D) - **2.** [child, person] verwöhnen <> *vi*: **to** ~ **in sthg** etw (D) frönen.

indulgence [ɪnˈdʌldʒəns] *n* - **1.** *(U)* [tolerance, kindness] Nachsicht *die* - **2.** [special treat] Luxus *der*.

indulgent [ɪnˈdʌldʒənt] *adj* nachsichtig; [giving way] nachgiebig.

industrial [ɪnˈdʌstrɪəl] *adj* industriell; [city, area, society] Industrie-.

industrial action *n*: **to take ~** in den Ausstand treten.

industrial estate *Br,* **industrial park** *Am n* Industriegebiet *das*.

industrialist [ɪnˈdʌstrɪəlɪst] *n* Industrielle *der, die*.

industrial park *n Am* = industrial estate.

industrial relations *npl* Beziehungen *pl* zwischen Arbeitgebern und Gewerkschaften.

industrial revolution *n* Industrielle Revolution.

industrious [ɪnˈdʌstrɪəs] *adj* fleißig.

industry [ˈɪndəstrɪ] *n* - 1. [gen] Industrie *die;* **the tourist ~** die Tourismusbranche - 2. [hard work] Fleiß *der*.

inebriated [ɪˈniːbrɪeɪtɪd] *adj fml* betrunken.

inedible [ɪnˈedɪbl] *adj* - 1. [unpleasant to eat] ungenießbar - 2. [poisonous] nicht essbar.

ineffective [ˌɪnɪˈfektɪv] *adj* unwirksam.

ineffectual [ˌɪnɪˈfektʃʊəl] *adj* [person] unfähig; [plan] ineffizient.

inefficiency [ˌɪnɪˈfɪʃnsɪ] *n* [of person] Unfähigkeit *die;* [of process] Unproduktivität *die;* [of machine] Unwirtschaftlichkeit *die*.

inefficient [ˌɪnɪˈfɪʃnt] *adj* [person] unfähig, ineffizient; [process] unproduktiv; [machine] unwirtschaftlich.

ineligible [ɪnˈelɪdʒəbl] *adj*: **to be ~ for sthg** [promotion] für etw nicht in Frage kommen; [benefits] auf etw *(A)* keinen Anspruch haben.

inept [ɪˈnept] *adj* [person] unfähig; [comment] unpassend; [performance, attempt] ungeschickt.

inequality [ˌɪnɪˈkwɒlətɪ] *n* - 1. [gen] Ungleichheit *die* - 2. [difference] Unterschied *der*.

inert [ɪˈnɜːt] *adj* [person] reglos.

inertia [ɪˈnɜːʃə] *n* [gen] Trägheit *die*.

inescapable [ˌɪnɪˈskeɪpəbl] *adj* unausweichlich.

inevitable [ɪnˈevɪtəbl] <> *adj* unvermeidlich <> *n*: **the ~** das Unvermeidliche.

inevitably [ɪnˈevɪtəblɪ] *adv* zwangsläufig.

inexcusable [ˌɪnɪkˈskjuːzəbl] *adj* unverzeihlich, unentschuldbar.

inexhaustible [ˌɪnɪgˈzɔːstəbl] *adj* unerschöpflich.

inexpensive [ˌɪnɪkˈspensɪv] *adj* preiswert.

inexperienced [ˌɪnɪkˈspɪərɪənst] *adj* unerfahren; **to be ~ in sthg** mit etw wenig vertraut sein.

inexplicable [ˌɪnɪkˈsplɪkəbl] *adj* unerklärlich.

infallible [ɪnˈfæləbl] *adj* unfehlbar.

infamous [ˈɪnfəməs] *adj* berüchtigt.

infancy [ˈɪnfənsɪ] *n* frühe Kindheit; **to be in its ~** *fig* (noch) in den Kinderschuhen stecken.

infant [ˈɪnfənt] *n* - 1. [baby] Säugling *der* - 2. [young child] Kleinkind *das*.

infantry [ˈɪnfəntrɪ] *n* Infanterie *die*.

infant school *n Br* Vorschule *die (für 5- bis 7-jährige)*.

infatuated [ɪnˈfætjʊeɪtɪd] *adj*: **to be ~ (with sb/ sthg)** (in jn/etw) vernarrt sein.

infatuation [ɪnˌfætjʊˈeɪʃn] *n*: **~ (with sb/ sthg)** Vernarrtheit *die* (in jn/etw).

infect [ɪnˈfekt] *vt* MED infizieren.

infection [ɪnˈfekʃn] *n* MED Infektion *die;* **ear ~** Ohrenentzündung *die*.

infectious [ɪnˈfekʃəs] *adj lit & fig* ansteckend.

infer [ɪnˈfɜː] *vt* - 1. [deduce]: **to ~ that ...** folgern, dass ...; **to ~ sthg (from sthg)** etw (aus etw) folgern - 2. *inf* [imply] andeuten.

inferior [ɪnˈfɪərɪə] <> *adj* - 1. [lower in status] untergeordnet; **to be ~ (to sb/sthg)** (jm/ etw) untergeordnet sein - 2. [lower in quality] minderwertig; **to feel ~** sich unterlegen fühlen; **to be ~ to sthg** von geringerer Qualität als etw sein <> *n* [in status] Untergebene *der, die*.

inferiority [ɪnˌfɪərɪˈɒrətɪ] *n* - 1. [in status] untergeordnete Stellung - 2. [in quality] Minderwertigkeit *die*.

inferiority complex *n* Minderwertigkeitskomplex *der*.

inferno [ɪnˈfɜːnəʊ] *(pl -s) n* Flammenmeer *das*.

infertile [ɪnˈfɜːtaɪl] *adj* unfruchtbar.

infested [ɪnˈfestɪd] *adj*: **~ with sthg** [vermin, insects] von etw befallen; [weeds] von etw überwuchert.

infighting [ˈɪnˌfaɪtɪŋ] *n (U)* [rivalry] interne Machtkämpfe *pl;* [quarrelling] interne Querelen *pl*.

infiltrate [ˈɪnfɪltreɪt] *vt* [territory] infiltrieren; [party, organization] unterwandern.

infinite [ˈɪnfɪnət] *adj* unendlich.

infinitive [ɪnˈfɪnɪtɪv] *n* Infinitiv *der*.

infinity [ɪnˈfɪnətɪ] *n* - 1. [unreachable point] Unendlichkeit *die* - 2. MATH Unendliche *das*.

infirm [ɪnˈfɜːm] *adj* gebrechlich.

infirmary [ɪnˈfɜːmərɪ] *n* - 1. [hospital] Krankenhaus *das* - 2. [room] Krankenzimmer *das*.

infirmity [ɪnˈfɜːmətɪ] *n* - 1. [individual weakness or illness] Gebrechen *das* - 2. [state of being weak or ill] Gebrechlichkeit *die*.

inflamed [ɪnˈfleɪmd] *adj* MED entzündet.

inflammable [ɪnˈflæməbl] *adj* leicht entzündlich.

inflammation [ˌɪnfləˈmeɪʃn] *n* MED Entzündung *die*.

inflatable [ɪn'fleɪtəbl] *adj* aufblasbar.

inflate [ɪn'fleɪt] *vt* - **1.** [fill with air - tyre] aufpumpen; [- life-jacket, balloon] aufblasen - **2.** ECON [increase] in die Höhe treiben.

inflation [ɪn'fleɪʃn] *n* ECON Inflation *die*.

inflationary [ɪn'fleɪʃnrɪ] *adj* ECON [policy, spiral] Inflations-; [trend, wage rise] inflationär.

inflation rate *n* ECON Inflationsrate *die*.

inflict [ɪn'flɪkt] *vt:* **to ~ sthg on sb** [pain] jm etw zufügen; [problem] jn mit etw belasten; [punishment] jn mit etw belegen.

influence ['ɪnfluəns] ⬦ *n:* **~ (on sb/sthg), ~ (over sb/sthg)** Einfluss *der* (auf jn/etw); **under the ~ of** unter dem Einfluss von ⬦ *vt* beeinflussen.

influential [ˌɪnflu'enʃl] *adj* einflussreich.

influenza [ˌɪnflu'enzə] *n fml* Grippe *die*.

influx ['ɪnflʌks] *n* Zustrom *der*.

inform [ɪn'fɔːm] *vt* benachrichtigen; [police] verständigen; **to ~ sb of/about sthg** jm etw mitteilen. ➡ **inform on** *vt fus* anlzeigen.

informal [ɪn'fɔːml] *adj* - **1.** [casual, relaxed - party, clothes] zwanglos; [- language] informell - **2.** [non-official] inoffiziell.

informant [ɪn'fɔːmənt] *n* Informant *der*, -in *die*.

information [ˌɪnfə'meɪʃn] *n (U):* **~ (on** OR **about sthg)** Informationen *pl* (über etw (A)); **to get ~** sich informieren; **a piece of ~** eine Auskunft, eine Information; **'Information' 'Information', 'Auskunft'; for your ~** COMM zu Ihrer Kenntnisnahme OR Information.

information desk *n* Auskunftsschalter *der*.

information technology *n* Informationstechnologie *die*.

informative [ɪn'fɔːmətɪv] *adj* [person] auskunftsfreudig; [book, film] informativ.

informer [ɪn'fɔːmə'] *n* [denouncer] Informant *der*, -in *die*.

infrared [ˌɪnfrə'red] *adj* Infrarot-.

infrastructure ['ɪnfrəˌstrʌktʃə'] *n* Infrastruktur *die*.

infringe [ɪn'frɪndʒ] ⬦ *vt* - **1.** [right] verletzen - **2.** [law, agreement] verstoßen gegen ⬦ *vi:* **to ~ on sb's rights** js Rechte verletzen.

infringement [ɪn'frɪndʒmənt] *n* - **1.** [of right] Verletzung *die* - **2.** [of law, agreement] Verstoß *der*.

infuriating [ɪn'fjʊərɪeɪtɪŋ] *adj:* **he/his behaviour is ~!** er/sein Benehmen macht mich rasend!

ingenious [ɪn'dʒiːnɪəs] *adj* genial; [device, method] raffiniert; [person] einfallsreich.

ingenuity [ˌɪndʒɪ'njuːətɪ] *n* [of person] Genialität *die*, Einfallsreichtum *der;* [of device, method] Raffiniertheit *die*.

ingot ['ɪŋgət] *n* [of gold, silver] Barren *der*.

ingrained [ˌɪn'greɪnd] *adj* - **1.** [dirt] tief sitzend - **2.** [belief] unerschütterlich; [hatred] tief.

ingratiating [ɪn'greɪʃɪeɪtɪŋ] *adj* [smile] zuckersüß; [person, manner] schmeichlerisch.

ingredient [ɪn'griːdɪənt] *n* - **1.** [in cooking] Zutat *die* - **2.** [element] Element *das*.

inhabit [ɪn'hæbɪt] *vt* bewohnen.

inhabitant [ɪn'hæbɪtənt] *n* [of country, city] Einwohner *der*, -in *die;* [of house] Bewohner *der*, -in *die*.

inhale [ɪn'heɪl] ⬦ *vt* einlatmen ⬦ *vi* [breathe in] einlatmen; [smoker] Lungenzüge machen.

inhaler [ɪn'heɪlə'] *n* MED Inhalationsapparat *der*.

inherent [ɪn'hɪərənt, ɪn'herənt] *adj:* **her ~ laziness** die ihr eigene Faulheit; **the dangers ~ in this sport** die mit diesem Sport verbundenen Gefahren.

inherently [ɪn'hɪərəntlɪ, ɪn'herəntlɪ] *adv* von Natur aus.

inherit [ɪn'herɪt] ⬦ *vt:* **to ~ sthg (from sb)** etw (von jm) erben ⬦ *vi* erben.

inheritance [ɪn'herɪtəns] *n* Erbe *das*.

inhibit [ɪn'hɪbɪt] *vt* hemmen.

inhibition [ˌɪnhɪ'bɪʃn] *n* Hemmung *die*.

inhospitable [ˌɪnhɒ'spɪtəbl] *adj* - **1.** [person] ungastlich - **2.** [climate, area] unwirtlich.

in-house ⬦ *adj* hausintern; **~ staff** festangestellte Mitarbeiter ⬦ *adv* im Hause.

inhuman [ɪn'hjuːmən] *adj* [cruel] unmenschlich.

initial [ɪ'nɪʃl] ⬦ *adj* - **1.** [early] anfänglich - **2.:** **~ letter** Initiale *die* ⬦ *vt* mit seinen Initialen unterschreiben; [as authorization] ablzeichnen. ➡ **initials** *npl* Initialen *pl*.

initially [ɪ'nɪʃəlɪ] *adv* anfangs.

initiate [ɪ'nɪʃɪeɪt] *vt* - **1.** [start] initiieren; [talks, scheme] in die Wege leiten - **2.** [teach]: **to ~ sb (into sthg)** [into mystery, secret] jn (in etw (A)) einlweihen; [into group] jn (in etw (A)) feierlich auflnehmen.

initiative [ɪ'nɪʃətɪv] *n* Initiative *die*.

inject [ɪn'dʒekt] *vt* - **1.** MED: **to ~ sb with sthg, to ~ sthg into sb** jm etw spritzen OR injizieren - **2.** *fig* [add]: **to ~ sthg into sthg** [fun, excitement] etw in etw (A) bringen; [money, funds] etw in etw (A) pumpen.

injection [ɪn'dʒekʃn] *n* - **1.** MED Spritze *die*, Injektion *die* - **2.** [of funds] Zuschuss *der*.

injure ['ɪndʒə'] *vt* [hurt physically, offend] verletzen.

injured [ɪn'dʒəd] ⬦ *adj* [physically hurt, offended] verletzt ⬦ *npl:* **the ~ die** Verletzten.

injury ['ɪndʒərɪ] *n (U)* - **1.** [physical harm] Verletzungen *pl* - **2.** [wound, to one's feelings] Verletzung *die;* **to do o.s. an ~** sich verletzen.

injury time *n (U)* Nachspielzeit *die*.

injustice [ɪn'dʒʌstɪs] *n* Ungerechtigkeit *die;* **to do sb an ~** jm unrecht tun.

ink [ɪŋk] *n* (U) [for writing] Tinte *die;* [for drawing] Tusche *die;* [for printing] Druckfarbe *die.*

ink-jet printer *n* Tintenstrahldrucker *der.*

inkling ['ɪŋklɪŋ] *n:* **to have an ~ of sthg** etw ahnen.

inlaid [ˌɪn'leɪd] *adj:* **~ (with sthg)** (mit etw) eingelegt.

inland [*adj* 'ɪnlənd, *adv* ɪn'lænd] <> *adj* Binnen- <> *adv* landeinwärts.

Inland Revenue *n Br:* **the ~** ≃ das Finanzamt.

in-laws *npl inf* angeheiratete Verwandte *pl;* [parents-in-law] Schwiegereltern *pl.*

inlet ['ɪnlet] *n* - **1.** [stretch of water - from lake] (schmale) Bucht; [- from sea] Meeresarm *der* - **2.** [way in] Zuleitung *die.*

inmate ['ɪnmeɪt] *n* Insasse *der,* -sin *die.*

inn [ɪn] *n* Wirtshaus *das.*

innate [ɪ'neɪt] *adj* angeboren.

inner ['ɪnə'] *adj* - **1.** [most central] innere, -r, -s; [room] innen liegend; [courtyard] Innen-; **~ ear** Innenohr *das;* **Inner London** Innenstadt *die* Londons - **2.** [unexpressed, secret] innere.

inner city *n:* **the ~** die Innenstadt, *die Innenberzirke einer Stadt, in denen es oft soziale Probleme gibt.*

inner tube *n* Schlauch *der.*

innings ['ɪnɪŋz] (*pl inv*) *n Br* [in cricket] Durchgang *der.*

innocence ['ɪnəsəns] *n* (U) Unschuld *die.*

innocent ['ɪnəsənt] *adj* unschuldig; **to be ~ of sthg** an etw (D) unschuldig sein.

innocuous [ɪ'nɒkjʊəs] *adj* harmlos.

innovation [ˌɪnə'veɪʃn] *n* Innovation *die.*

innovative ['ɪnəvətɪv] *adj* innovativ.

innuendo [ˌɪnjuː'endəʊ] (*pl* -es OR -s) *n* - **1.** [individual remark] versteckte Andeutung, Anspielung *die* - **2.** (U) [style of speaking] Anspielungen *pl.*

innumerable [ɪ'njuːmərəbl] *adj* unzählig.

inoculate [ɪ'nɒkjʊleɪt] *vt* impfen.

inordinately [ɪ'nɔːdɪnətlɪ] *adv fml* außerordentlich.

in-patient *n* stationärer Patient, stationäre Patientin.

input ['ɪnpʊt] (*pt & pp* input OR -ted) <> *n* (U) - **1.** [contribution - money, resources] Investition *die;* [- labour, effort] Beitrag *der* - **2.** COMPUT Eingabe *die* - **3.** ELEC Energiezufuhr *die* <> *vt* COMPUT einlgeben.

inquest ['ɪnkwest] *n* LAW gerichtliche Untersuchung der Todesursache.

inquire [ɪn'kwaɪə'] <> *vt:* **to ~ when/ whether** OR **if/how ...** sich erkundigen wann/ob/wie ... <> *vi* [ask for information] sich erkundigen; **to ~ about sthg** sich nach

etw erkundigen, nach etw fragen. ◆ **inquire after** *vt fus* sich erkundigen nach. ◆ **inquire into** *vt fus* untersuchen.

inquiry [ɪn'kwaɪərɪ] *n* - **1.** [question] Anfrage *die;* **to make inquiries** Erkundigungen einlziehen; [police] Nachforschungen anlstellen - **2.** [investigation] Untersuchung *die.*

inquisitive [ɪn'kwɪzətɪv] *adj* [curious] neugierig; [for knowledge] wissbegierig.

inroads ['ɪnrəʊdz] *npl:* **to make ~ into sthg** [savings, supplies] etw anlgreifen; [field of knowledge] in etw (A) vorldringen.

insane [ɪn'seɪn] *adj* - **1.** MED [mad] geisteskrank - **2.** *fig* [person, idea, jealousy] verrückt.

insanity [ɪn'sænətɪ] *n* (U) MED [madness] Geisteskrankheit *die.*

insatiable [ɪn'seɪʃəbl] *adj* unersättlich.

inscription [ɪn'skrɪpʃn] *n* - **1.** [on wall, headstone, plaque - written] Aufschrift *die;* [- cut] Inschrift *die* - **2.** [in book] Widmung *die.*

inscrutable [ɪn'skruːtəbl] *adj* unergründlich; [look] undurchdringlich.

insect ['ɪnsekt] *n* Insekt *das.*

insecticide [ɪn'sektɪsaɪd] *n* (U) Insektizid *das.*

insect repellent *n* (U) Insektenschutzmittel *das.*

insecure [ˌɪnsɪ'kjʊə'] *adj* unsicher.

insensitive [ɪn'sensətɪv] *adj* - **1.** [unkind, thoughtless] unsensibel - **2.** [unresponsive]: **~ to sthg** unempfänglich für etw - **3.** [to pain, cold]: **~ to sthg** unempfindlich gegen etw.

inseparable [ɪn'seprəbl] *adj* - **1.** [subjects, facts]: **to be ~ (from sthg)** (mit etw) untrennbar verbunden sein - **2.** [people] unzertrennlich.

insert [*vb* ɪn'sɜːt, *n* 'ɪnsɜːt] <> *vt* - **1.** [put inside]: **to ~ sthg (in** OR **into sthg)** etw (in etw (A)) einlführen - **2.** [include, add]: **to ~ sthg (in** OR **into sthg)** etw (in etw (A)) einlfügen <> *n* Einlage *die.*

insertion [ɪn'sɜːʃn] *n* - **1.** [act of inserting] Einführen *das* - **2.** [thing inserted - in text] Einfügung *die.*

in-service training *n Br* (berufsbegleitende) Fortbildung.

inshore [*adj* 'ɪnʃɔː', *adv* ɪn'ʃɔː'] <> *adj* Küsten- <> *adv* [be situated] in Küstennähe.

inside [ɪn'saɪd] <> *prep* - **1.** [indicating place, position] in (+ D); (with verbs of motion) in (+ A); **it's ~ the box** es ist in der Schachtel; **put it ~ the box** leg es in die Schachtel; **come ~ the house!** komm ins Haus! - **2.** [indicating time, limit]: **~ three weeks** in weniger als drei Wochen; **he was just ~ the record** er lag knapp unter der Rekordzeit <> *adv* - **1.** [referring to place, object, building] innen; **to be ~ drinnen** sein; **to come ~** hereinlkommen; **to go ~** hineinlgehen; **there was something**

~ es war etwas drin - **2.** [referring to body, mind] innerlich - **3.** *prison sl inf* im Kittchen OR Knast; **to be** ~ sitzen <> *adj* Innen-; **an** ~ **toilet** eine Toilette im Haus; ~ **information** vertrauliche Information <> *n* [interior, inner part]: **the** ~ das Innere; **lock the door from the** ~ schließ die Tür von innen ab; **on the** ~ innen; ~ **out** [clothes] links (herum); **to turn sthg** ~ **out** etw auf links drehen; **to know sthg** ~ **out** *fig* etw in- und auswendig kennen. ◆ **insides** *npl inf* [intestines] Eingeweide *pl.* ◆ **inside of** *prep Am* [building, object] in.

inside lane *n* AUT [in UK] linke Fahrspur; [in Europe, US *etc*] rechte Fahrspur.

insight ['ɪnsaɪt] *n* - **1.** *(U)* [wisdom]: ~ **(into sthg)** Verständnis *das* (für etw) - **2.** [glimpse]: ~ **(into sthg)** Einblick *das* (in etw (A)).

insignificant [ˌɪnsɪg'nɪfɪkənt] *adj* unbedeutend.

insincere [ˌɪnsɪn'sɪəʳ] *adj* [person, remark] unaufrichtig; [smile] falsch.

insinuate [ɪn'sɪnjueɪt] *vt pej* [imply]: **to** ~ **(that)** an|deuten(, dass).

insipid [ɪn'sɪpɪd] *adj pej* - **1.** [taste, colour, music] fade; [person, character] geistlos - **2.** [food, drink] fade, geschmacklos.

insist [ɪn'sɪst] <> *vt* - **1.** [state firmly]: **to** ~ **that** darauf beharren, dass - **2.** [demand]: **to** ~ **that** bestehen, dass <> *vi*: **to** ~ **on sthg** auf etw (D) bestehen; **to** ~ **on doing sthg** darauf bestehen, etw zu tun.

insistent [ɪn'sɪstənt] *adj* - **1.** [determined] beharrlich; **to be** ~ **on sthg** auf etw (D) beharren OR bestehen - **2.** [continual] anhaltend.

insofar [ˌɪnsəʊ'fɑːʳ] ◆ **insofar as** *conj* insofern als.

insole ['ɪnsəʊl] *n* Einlegesohle *die.*

insolent ['ɪnsələnt] *adj* frech.

insolvent [ɪn'sɒlvənt] *adj* zahlungsunfähig, insolvent.

insomnia [ɪn'sɒmnɪə] *n* Schlaflosigkeit *die.*

inspect [ɪn'spekt] *vt* - **1.** [letter, person] genau betrachten - **2.** [factory, troops, premises] inspizieren; [machine] prüfen.

inspection [ɪn'spekʃn] *n* - **1.** [examination] Prüfung *die* - **2.** [of factory, troops, premises] Inspektion *die;* [of machine] Prüfung *die.*

inspector [ɪn'spektəʳ] *n* - **1.** [official] Inspektor *der,* -in *die;* [on bus, train] Kontrolleur *der,* -in *die* - **2.** [of police] ≃ Kommissar *der,* -in *die.*

inspiration [ˌɪnspə'reɪʃn] *n* - **1.** *(U)* [source of ideas] Inspiration *die* - **2.** [brilliant idea] Eingebung *die.*

inspire [ɪn'spaɪəʳ] *vt* inspirieren; **to** ~ **sb with sthg, to** ~ **sthg in sb** [confidence, passion, enthusiasm] in jm etw wecken; [respect] jm etw ein|flößen.

install *Br,* **instal** *Am* [ɪn'stɔːl] *vt* [machinery, equipment] installieren.

installation [ˌɪnstə'leɪʃn] *n* - **1.** [base, site] Anlage *die* - **2.** *(U)* [act of fitting] Installation *die.*

instalment *Br,* **installment** *Am* [ɪn'stɔːlmənt] *n* - **1.** [payment] Rate *die;* **to pay in** ~**s** in Raten zahlen - **2.** [episode - of story] Fortsetzung *die;* [- of TV, radio programme] Folge *die.*

instance ['ɪnstəns] *n* Fall *der;* **for** ~ zum Beispiel.

instant ['ɪnstənt] <> *adj* - **1.** [immediate] sofort, unmittelbar - **2.** [food]: ~ **coffee** Instant- OR Pulverkaffee *der;* ~ **mashed potato** fertiges Kartoffelpüree <> *n* [moment] Augenblick *der,* Moment *der;* **the** ~ **(that)** ... in dem Augenblick, in dem ...; **this** ~ sofort.

instantly ['ɪnstəntlɪ] *adv* sofort.

instead [ɪn'sted] *adv* stattdessen; ~ **of** statt (+ G); ~ **of him** an seiner Stelle.

instep ['ɪnstep] *n* Spann *der,* Fußrücken *der.*

instigate ['ɪnstɪgeɪt] *vt* [discussions] den Anstoß geben zu; [meeting] in die Wege leiten; [investigation] ein|leiten; [strike, revolt] an|stiften zu.

instil *Br,* **instill** *Am* [ɪn'stɪl] *vt*: **to** ~ **sthg in(to) sb** jm etw beibringen.

instinct ['ɪnstɪŋkt] *n* - **1.** *(U)* [natural ability] Instinkt *der;* **by** ~ instinktiv - **2.** [impulse] Impuls *der.*

instinctive [ɪn'stɪŋktɪv] *adj* instinktiv.

institute ['ɪnstɪtjuːt] <> *n* Institut *das* <> *vt* - **1.** [establish] ein|führen - **2.** [proceedings] an|strengen.

institution [ˌɪnstɪ'tjuːʃn] *n* - **1.** [tradition, system, organization] Institution *die* - **2.** [home] Heim *das,* Anstalt *die.*

instruct [ɪn'strʌkt] *vt* - **1.** [tell, order]: **to** ~ **sb to do sthg** jn an|weisen, etw zu tun - **2.** [teach] unterrichten; **to** ~ **sb in sthg** jn in etw (D) unterrichten.

instruction [ɪn'strʌkʃn] *n* - **1.** [order] Anweisung *die* - **2.** *(U)* [teaching] Unterricht *der.* ◆ **instructions** *npl* [for use] Gebrauchsanleitung *die.*

instructor [ɪn'strʌktəʳ] *n* Lehrer *der,* -in *die.*

instrument ['ɪnstrʊmənt] *n* - **1.** [gen] Instrument *das* - **2.** *literary* [means] Mittel *das.*

instrumental [ˌɪnstrʊ'mentl] *adj* [important, helpful]: **to be** ~ **in sthg** eine entscheidende Rolle bei etw spielen.

instrument panel *n* Armaturenbrett *das.*

insubordinate [ˌɪnsə'bɔːdɪnət] *adj fml* aufsässig; MIL ungehorsam.

insubstantial [ˌɪnsəb'stænʃl] *adj* - **1.** [fragile] zerbrechlich - **2.** [unsatisfying - meal] dürftig; [- book] ohne Substanz.

insufficient [ˌɪnsə'fɪʃnt] *adj fml*: ~ **(for sthg)** unzureichend (für etw); **to be** ~ **to do sthg** nicht dafür aus|reichen, um etw zu tun.

insular ['ɪnsjʊləʳ] *adj* [narrow-minded] engstirnig.

insulate ['ɪnsjʊleɪt] *vt* - 1. [house, tank &
ELEC] isolieren - 2. [protect] schützen; **to ~ sb
against** OR **from sthg** jn gegen etw ab-
schirmen.

insulating tape ['ɪnsjʊleɪtɪŋ-] *n (U) Br* Isolierband *das*.

insulation [,ɪnsjʊ'leɪʃn] *n (U)* [material]
Isolierung *die*.

insulin ['ɪnsjʊlɪn] *n* Insulin *das*.

insult [*vb* ɪn'sʌlt, *n* 'ɪnsʌlt] <> *vt* beleidigen
<> *n* Beleidigung *die*.

insuperable [ɪn'suːprəbl] *adj fml* unüber-
windlich.

insurance [ɪn'ʃʊərəns] *n lit & fig:* ~ **(against
sthg)** Versicherung (gegen etw).

insurance policy *n* Versicherungspolice
die.

insure [ɪn'ʃʊəʳ] <> *vt* - 1. [against fire, accident, theft] **to ~ sb/sthg against sthg** jn/etw
gegen etw versichern - 2. *Am* [make certain]
sicher stellen <> *vi* [protect] **to ~ against
sthg** sich gegen etw absichern.

insurer [ɪn'ʃʊərəʳ] *n* Versicherungsgeber
der, -in *die*.

insurmountable [,ɪnsə'maʊntəbl] *adj* un-
überwindlich.

intact [ɪn'tækt] *adj* unversehrt, intakt.

intake ['ɪnteɪk] *n* - 1. [amount consumed]
Aufnahme *die* - 2. [people recruited]: **this
year's ~ includes several overseas students**
dieses Jahr wurden einige ausländische Studenten aufgenommen - 3. [inlet] Einlass *der*.

integral ['ɪntɪgrəl] *adj* [part, feature] wesentlich; **to be ~ to sthg** für etw wesentlich
sein.

integrate ['ɪntɪgreɪt] *vt* - 1. [include in a
larger unit, combine] integrieren - 2. [minorit-
ies, marginalized people] integrieren, einl-
gliedern.

integrity [ɪn'tegrətɪ] *n* - 1. [honour] Integri-
tät *die* - 2. *fml* [wholeness] Einheit *die*.

intellect ['ɪntəlekt] *n* - 1. [ability to reason]
Verstand *der* - 2. [mind, intelligence] Intellekt
der.

intellectual [,ɪntə'lektjʊəl] <> *adj* intellektuell <> *n* Intellektuelle *der*, *die*.

intelligence [ɪn'telɪdʒəns] *n (U)* - 1. [ability
to reason] Intelligenz *die* - 2. [information
service] Nachrichtendienst *der* - 3. [informa-
tion] Information *die*.

intelligent [ɪn'telɪdʒənt] *adj* intelligent.

intend [ɪn'tend] *vt* beabsichtigen; **to be ~ed
as sthg** als etw gemeint sein; **it was ~ed to
be a surprise** es sollte eine Überraschung
sein; **to ~ doing** OR **to do sthg** beabsichtigen,
etw zu tun.

intended [ɪn'tendɪd] *adj* [result] beabsichtigt.

intense [ɪn'tens] *adj* - 1. [competition, pain,

emotion] heftig; [concentration] äußerst;
[colour, light] intensiv; [heat] stark - 2. [per-
son - serious] ernsthaft; [- emotional] heftig.

intensely [ɪn'tenslɪ] *adv* äußerst.

intensify [ɪn'tensɪfaɪ] <> *vt* intensivieren
<> *vi* [cold, heat] zunehmen; [pressure,
problem] sich verschärfen.

intensity [ɪn'tensətɪ] *n* - 1. [of competition,
pain, emotion] Heftigkeit *die*; [of colour, light,
concentration] Intensität *die*; [of heat] Stärke
die - 2. [of person - seriousness] Ernsthaftig-
keit *die*; [- of emotional nature] Heftigkeit *die*.

intensive [ɪn'tensɪv] *adj* intensiv.

intensive care *n:* **to be in ~** auf der Inten-
sivstation sein.

intent [ɪn'tent] <> *adj* - 1. [expression] gespannt - 2. [determined]: **to be ~ (up)on
doing sthg** fest entschlossen sein, etw zu
tun <> *n fml* Absicht *die*; **to all ~s and purposes** im Grunde, so gut wie.

intention [ɪn'tenʃn] *n* Absicht *die*.

intentional [ɪn'tenʃənl] *adj* absichtlich.

intently [ɪn'tentlɪ] *adv* konzentriert.

interact [,ɪntər'ækt] *vi* - 1. [people]: **to
~ (with sb)** (mit jm) Kontakt haben
- 2. [forces, ideas]: **to ~ (with sthg)** (mit etw)
in Wechselwirkung stehen.

intercede [,ɪntə'siːd] *vi fml:* **to ~ (with sb)**
sich (bei jm) einlsetzen .

intercept [,ɪntə'sept] *vt* abfangen.

interchange [*n* 'ɪntətʃeɪndʒ] *n* [road junc-
tion] Kreuzung *die*.

interchangeable [,ɪntə'tʃeɪndʒəbl] *adj:*
~ **(with sb/ sthg)** austauschbar (mit jm/etw).

intercom ['ɪntəkɒm] *n* Gegensprechanlage
die.

intercourse ['ɪntəkɔːs] *n:* **(sexual) ~** (Geschlechts)verkehr *der*.

interest ['ɪntrəst] <> *n* - 1. [enthusiasm, appeal, advantage] Interesse *das*; ~ **in sb/sthg**
Interesse an jm/etw - 2. [hobby] Hobby *das*
- 3. *(U)* [financial charge] Zinsen *pl* - 4. [share
in company] Anteil *der* <> *vt* interessieren;
can I ~ you in buying my car? wären Sie interessiert, mein Auto zu kaufen?

interested ['ɪntrəstɪd] *adj* - 1. [enthusiastic,
curious] interessiert; **to be ~ in sthg** [in job]
Interesse an etw (+ D) haben; [in butterflies,
films] sich für etw (A) interessieren; **to be
~ in doing sthg** interessiert sein, etw zu tun
- 2. [concerned] beteiligt.

interesting ['ɪntrəstɪŋ] *adj* interessant.

interest rate *n* Zinssatz *der*.

interface ['ɪntəfeɪs] *n* COMPUT Schnittstelle
die.

interfere [,ɪntə'fɪəʳ] *vi* - 1. [meddle]: **to ~ (in
sthg)** sich (in etw *(A)*) einlmischen - 2. [cause
disruption]: **to ~ with sthg** etw stören.

interference [,ɪntə'fɪərəns] *n (U)* - 1. [med-
dling]: ~ **(with** OR **in sthg)** Einmischung *die* (in
etw *(A)*) - 2. RADIO & TV Störung *die*.

interim ['ɪntərɪm] <> *adj* [measure] Übergangs-; [report] Zwischen- <> *n*: **in the ~** in der Zwischenzeit.

interior [ɪn'tɪərɪə'] <> *adj* Innen- <> *n* [inside] Innere *das*.

interlock [ˌɪntə'lɒk] *vi* TECH ineinander greifen; **to ~ with sthg** in etw (A) greifen.

interlude ['ɪntəlu:d] *n* [period of time] Zwischenzeit *die*.

intermediary [ˌɪntə'mi:djərɪ] *n* Mittelsmann *der*, -person *die*.

intermediate [ˌɪntə'mi:djət] *adj* - **1.** [transitional] Zwischen- - **2.** [post-beginner] fortgeschritten.

interminable [ɪn'tɜ:mɪnəbl] *adj* endlos.

intermission [ˌɪntə'mɪʃn] *n* Pause *die*.

intermittent [ˌɪntə'mɪtənt] *adj* in Abständen auftretend.

intern [*vb* ɪn'tɜ:n, *n* 'ɪntɜ:n] <> *vt* internieren <> *n esp Am* [trainee - teacher] Assistent *der*, -in *die*; [- doctor] Assistenzarzt *der*, -ärztin *die*.

internal [ɪn'tɜ:nl] *adj* - **1.** [within the body] innere, -r, -s - **2.** [within a country - flight] Inlands-; [- trade] Binnen- - **3.** [within an organization] intern.

internally [ɪn'tɜ:nəlɪ] *adv* - **1.** [within the body] innerlich - **2.** [within a country] landesintern - **3.** [within an organization] intern.

Internal Revenue *n Am*: **the ~** das Finanzamt.

international [ˌɪntə'næʃənl] <> *adj* international <> *n Br* SPORT - **1.** [match] Länderspiel *das* - **2.** [player] Nationalspieler *der*, -in *die*.

Internet ['ɪntənet] *n*: **the ~** das Internet.

Internet service provider *n* COMPUT Internetprovider *der*.

interpret [ɪn'tɜ:prɪt] <> *vt* [understand] auslegen, interpretieren; **to ~ sthg as** etw interpretieren als <> *vi* dolmetschen.

interpreter [ɪn'tɜ:prɪtə'] *n* [person] Dolmetscher *der*, -in *die*.

interpreting [ɪn'tɜ:prɪtɪŋ] *n* [occupation] Dolmetschen *das*.

interrelate [ˌɪntərɪ'leɪt] *vi*: **to ~ (with sthg)** (mit etw) in Beziehung stehen.

interrogate [ɪn'terəgeɪt] *vt* [question] verhören.

interrogation [ɪnˌterə'geɪʃn] *n* Verhör *das*.

interrogation mark *n Am* Fragezeichen *das*.

interrogative [ˌɪntə'rɒgətɪv] GRAMM <> *adj* Frage- <> *n* - **1.** [form]: **the ~** die Frageform - **2.** [word] Fragefürwort *das*.

interrupt [ˌɪntə'rʌpt] *vt & vi* unterbrechen.

interruption [ˌɪntə'rʌpʃn] *n* Unterbrechung *die*.

intersect [ˌɪntə'sekt] <> *vi* sich kreuzen <> *vt* kreuzen.

intersection [ˌɪntə'sekʃn] *n* [junction] Kreuzung *die*.

intersperse [ˌɪntə'spɜ:s] *vt*: **to be ~d with sthg** von etw unterbrochen OR durchsetzt sein.

interstate (highway) ['ɪntəsteɪt-] *n Am* Interstate Highway *der*, Autobahn *zwischen den US-Bundesstaaten*.

interval ['ɪntəvl] *n* - **1.** [period of time]: **~ (between)** Abstand *der* (zwischen (+ D)); **at ~s of** in Abständen von - **2.** *Br* [at play, concert] Pause *die*.

intervene [ˌɪntə'vi:n] *vi* - **1.** [person, government] einlgreifen; **to ~ in sthg** in etw (A) einlgreifen - **2.** [event] dazwischenlkommen.

intervention [ˌɪntə'venʃn] *n* Eingreifen *das*.

interview ['ɪntəvju:] <> *n* - **1.** [for job] Vorstellungsgespräch *das* - **2.** PRESS Interview *das* <> *vt* - **1.** [for job] ein Vorstellungsgespräch führen mit - **2.** PRESS interviewen.

interviewer ['ɪntəvju:ə'] *n* - **1.** [for job] Leiter *der*, -in *die* des Vorstellungsgesprächs - **2.** PRESS Interviewer *der*, -in *die*.

intestine [ɪn'testɪn] *n* Darm *der*.

intimacy ['ɪntɪməsɪ] *n* [closeness]: **~ (between/with)** Vertrautheit *die* (zwischen (+D) /mit). ◆ **intimacies** *npl* Vertraulichkeiten *pl*.

intimate ['ɪntɪmət] *adj* - **1.** [friend, relationship] vertraut; **to be on ~ terms with sb** mit jm auf vertrautem Fuße stehen - **2.** [place, atmosphere, dinner] intim - **3.** [thoughts, details] persönlich - **4.** [thorough - knowledge] gründlich.

intimately ['ɪntɪmətlɪ] *adv* - **1.** [directly] direkt - **2.** [as close friends] vertraulich; **to know sb ~** jn gut kennen - **3.** [thoroughly] gründlich.

intimidate [ɪn'tɪmɪdeɪt] *vt* einlschüchtern.

into ['ɪntʊ] *prep* - **1.** [inside] in (+ A); **to put sthg ~ sthg** [lying down] etw in etw (A) legen; [upright] etw in etw (A) stellen; **to put sthg ~ one's pocket** etw in die Tasche stecken; **to go ~ the house** ins Haus hineinlgehen - **2.** [against]: **to bump/crash into sthg** gegen etw stoßen/knallen - **3.** [indicating transformation, change] in (+ A); **to change ~ sthg** [become] zu etw werden; [clothes] sich (D) etw anlziehen; **to translate ~ German** ins Deutsche übersetzen - **4.** [concerning, about] über (+ A) - **5.** MATH: **4 ~ 20 goes 5 (times)** 20 (geteilt) durch 4 ist 5 - **6.** [indicating elapsed time]: **I was a week ~ my holiday when ...** in meiner zweiten Urlaubswoche ...; **late ~ the night** bis tief in die Nacht hinein - **7.** *inf* [interested in]: **to be ~ sthg** etw mögen; **she's ~ jazz** sie ist ein Jazzfan.

intolerable [ɪn'tɒlrəbl] *adj* unerträglich.

intolerance [ɪn'tɒlərəns] *n* Intoleranz *die*.

intolerant [ɪn'tɒlərənt] *adj* intolerant.

intoxicated [ɪn'tɒksɪkeɪtɪd] *adj* - 1. [drunk]: **to be ~** berauscht sein - 2. *fig* [excited]: **to be ~ by** OR **with sthg** von etw berauscht sein.

intractable [ɪn'træktəbl] *adj fml* [insoluble] hartnäckig.

intramural [ˌɪntrə'mjʊərəl] *adj* innerhalb der Universität.

intransitive [ɪn'trænzɪtɪv] *adj* intransitiv.

intravenous [ˌɪntrə'viːnəs] *adj* intravenös.

in-tray *n* Eingangsablage *die*.

intricate ['ɪntrɪkət] *adj* knifflig.

intrigue [*n* 'ɪntriːg *vb* ɪn'triːg] ⬥ *n* Intrige *die* ⬥ *vt* faszinieren.

intriguing [ɪn'triːgɪŋ] *adj* faszinierend.

intrinsic [ɪn'trɪnsɪk] *adj* immanent.

introduce [ˌɪntrə'djuːs] *vt* - 1. [one person to another] vor|stellen; **to ~ sb to sb** jm in vor|stellen - 2. RADIO & TV [programme] vor|stellen - 3. [animal, plant, method]: **to ~ sthg (to** OR **into)** etw ein|führen (in (+ *D*)) - 4. [to new experience]: **to ~ sb to sthg** jn in etw (*A*) ein|führen - 5. [signal start of] ein|leiten.

introduction [ˌɪntrə'dʌkʃn] *n* - 1. [of method, technology] Einführung *die* - 2. [preface]: **~ to sthg** Einleitung zu etw.

introductory [ˌɪntrə'dʌktrɪ] *adj* einleitend; **an ~ offer** ein Eröffnungsangebot.

introvert ['ɪntrəvɜːt] *n* introvertierter Mensch.

introverted ['ɪntrəvɜːtɪd] *adj* introvertiert.

intrude [ɪn'truːd] *vi* stören; **to ~ (up)on sb/ sthg** jn/etw stören.

intruder [ɪn'truːdə'] *n* Eindringling *der*.

intrusive [ɪn'truːsɪv] *adj* aufdringlich.

intuition [ˌɪntjuː'ɪʃn] *n* - 1. (*U*) [sense] Intuition *die* - 2. [hunch] Vorahnung *die*.

inundate ['ɪnʌndeɪt] *vt* - 1. *fml* [flood] überschwemmen - 2. [overwhelm]: **to be ~d with sthg** von etw überschwemmt werden.

invade [ɪn'veɪd] *vt* - 1. MIL ein|marschieren in (+ *A*) - 2. [subj: shoppers, fans] ein|fallen - 3. [privacy, calm] stören.

invalid [*adj* ɪn'vælɪd, *n* 'ɪnvəlɪd] ⬥ *adj* - 1. [ticket, contract, vote] ungültig - 2. [argument, theory] nicht schlüssig ⬥ *n* Invalide *der*, -din *die*.

invaluable [ɪn'væljʊəbl] *adj*: **~ (to sb/sthg)** unschätzbar (für jn/etw).

invariably [ɪn'veərɪəblɪ] *adv* stets.

invasion [ɪn'veɪʒn] *n* - 1. MIL Invasion *die* - 2. *fig* [intrusion] Eingriff *der*.

invent [ɪn'vent] *vt* erfinden.

invention [ɪn'venʃn] *n* - 1. [creation, untruth] Erfindung *die* - 2. (*U*) [inventiveness] Vorstellungsgabe *die*.

inventive [ɪn'ventɪv] *adj* einfallsreich.

inventor [ɪn'ventə'] *n* Erfinder *der*, -in *die*.

inventory ['ɪnvəntrɪ] *n* - 1. [list] Inventar *das* - 2. *Am* [goods] Bestand *der*.

invert [ɪn'vɜːt] *vt fml* um|drehen.

inverted commas [ɪnˌvɜːtɪd-] *npl Br* Anführungszeichen *die*.

invest [ɪn'vest] ⬥ *vt* - 1. [money]: **to ~ sthg (in sthg)** etw (in etw (*A*)) investieren - 2. [time, energy]: **to ~ sthg in sthg** etw in etw (*A*) investieren ⬥ *vi* - 1. [financially]: **to ~ (in sthg)** (in etw (*A*)) investieren - 2. *fig* [in sthg useful]: **to ~ in sthg** in etw (*A*) investieren.

investigate [ɪn'vestɪgeɪt] *vt* untersuchen.

investigation [ɪnˌvestɪ'geɪʃn] *n* Untersuchung *die*; **an ~ into sthg** eine Untersuchung von etw.

investment [ɪn'vestmənt] *n* - 1. [gen] Investition *die* - 2. [financial product, purchase] Anlage *die*.

investor [ɪn'vestə'] *n* Anleger *der*, -in *die*.

inveterate [ɪn'vetərət] *adj* [liar, gambler] unverbesserlich.

invidious [ɪn'vɪdɪəs] *adj* - 1. [unfair] ungerecht - 2. [unpleasant] unangenehm.

invigilate [ɪn'vɪdʒɪleɪt] *Br* ⬥ *vt* Aufsicht führen bei ⬥ *vi* Aufsicht führen.

invigorating [ɪn'vɪgəreɪtɪŋ] *adj* erfrischend, belebend.

invincible [ɪn'vɪnsɪbl] *adj* unschlagbar.

invisible [ɪn'vɪzɪbl] *adj* unsichtbar.

invitation [ˌɪnvɪ'teɪʃn] *n* [request to attend] Einladung *die*.

invite [ɪn'vaɪt] *vt* - 1. [request to attend] ein|laden; **to ~ sb to sthg** jn zu etw ein|laden - 2. [ask politely]: **to ~ sb to do sthg** jn ersuchen, etw zu tun - 3. [trouble, criticism] heraus|fordern.

inviting [ɪn'vaɪtɪŋ] *adj* einladend.

invoice ['ɪnvɔɪs] ⬥ *n* Rechnung *die* ⬥ *vt* - 1. [customer] eine Rechnung schicken an (+ *A*) - 2. [goods] in Rechnung stellen.

invoke [ɪn'vəʊk] *vt* [feeling] hervor|rufen.

involuntary [ɪn'vɒləntrɪ] *adj* [movement] unwillkürlich.

involve [ɪn'vɒlv] *vt* - 1. [entail, require - work, travelling] mit sich bringen; [- special equipment, knowledge] erfordern - 2. [concern, affect] betreffen - 3. [make part of sthg]: **to ~ sb in sthg** jn in etw (*A*) hinein|ziehen.

involved [ɪn'vɒlvd] *adj* - 1. [complex] kompliziert - 2. [participating]: **to be ~ in sthg** an etw (*D*) beteiligt sein - 3. [in a relationship]: **to be/get ~ with sb** mit jm eine enge Beziehung haben/ein|gehen - 4. [entailed]: **what is ~ (in it)?** worum geht es (dabei)?

involvement [ɪn'vɒlvmənt] *n* - 1. [participation]: **~ (in sthg)** Beteiligung (an etw (*D*)) - 2. [commitment]: **~ (in sthg)** Engagement (für etw).

inward ['ɪnwəd] <> adj - **1.** [feelings, satisfaction] innerlich - **2.** [flow, movement] nach innen gehend <> adv Am = **inwards**.

inwards ['ɪnwədz], **inward** Am adv nach innen.

iodine [Br 'aɪədiːn, Am 'aɪədaɪn] n (U) Jod das.

iota [aɪ'əʊtə] n Jota das.

IOU (abbr of I owe you) n Schuldschein der.

IQ (abbr of intelligence quotient) n IQ der.

IRA (abbr of Irish Republican Army) n IRA die.

Iran [ɪ'rɑːn] n Iran der.

Iranian [ɪ'reɪnɪən] <> adj iranisch <> n [person] Iraner der, -in die.

Iraq [ɪ'rɑːk] n Irak der.

Iraqi [ɪ'rɑːkɪ] <> adj irakisch <> n [person] Iraker der, -in die.

irate [aɪ'reɪt] adj zornig.

Ireland ['aɪələnd] n Irland nt.

iris ['aɪərɪs] (pl -es) n - **1.** [flower] Schwertlilie, die, Iris die - **2.** [of eye] Iris die.

Irish ['aɪrɪʃ] <> adj irisch <> n [language] Irisch(e) das <> npl: **the** ~ die Iren.

Irishman ['aɪrɪʃmən] (pl -men [-mən]) n Ire der.

Irish Sea n: **the** ~ die Irische See.

Irishwoman ['aɪrɪʃˌwʊmən] (pl -women [-ˌwɪmɪn]) n Irin die.

iron ['aɪən] <> adj - **1.** [made of iron] eisern; ~ **bar** Eisenstange die - **2.** fig [very strict] eisern <> n - **1.** [metal, golf club] Eisen das - **2.** [for clothes] Bügeleisen das <> vt bügeln.

⇒ **iron out** vt sep fig [problems] ausbügeln.

ironic(al) [aɪ'rɒnɪk(l)] adj - **1.** [using irony] ironisch - **2.** [paradoxical] paradox.

ironing ['aɪənɪŋ] n - **1.** [work] Bügeln das - **2.** [clothes] Bügelwäsche die.

ironing board n Bügelbrett das.

ironmonger ['aɪənˌmʌŋgə] n Br Eisenwarenhändler der, -in die; ~'**s (shop)** Eisenwarenhandlung die.

irony ['aɪrənɪ] n Ironie die.

irrational [ɪ'ræʃənl] adj irrational.

irreconcilable [ɪˌrekən'saɪləbl] adj [views, differences] unvereinbar.

irregular [ɪ'regjʊlə] adj [gen & GRAMM] unregelmäßig; [surface] uneben.

irrelevant [ɪ'reləvənt] adj unwichtig.

irreparable [ɪ'repərəbl] adj irreparabel.

irreplaceable [ˌɪrɪ'pleɪsəbl] adj unersetzlich.

irrepressible [ˌɪrɪ'presəbl] adj unerschütterlich; **he's** ~ er ist nicht unterzukriegen.

irresistible [ˌɪrɪ'zɪstəbl] adj unwiderstehlich.

irrespective [ˌɪrɪ'spektɪv] ⇒ **irrespective of** prep ungeachtet (+ G).

irresponsible [ˌɪrɪ'spɒnsəbl] adj unverantwortlich.

irrigation [ˌɪrɪ'geɪʃn] <> n [of land] Bewässerung die <> comp Bewässerungs-.

irritable ['ɪrɪtəbl] adj [person, mood] reizbar; [voice, reply] gereizt.

irritate ['ɪrɪteɪt] vt - **1.** [make angry] ärgern - **2.** [make sore] reizen.

irritated ['ɪrɪteɪtɪd] adj [angry, sore] gereizt.

irritating ['ɪrɪteɪtɪŋ] adj - **1.** [person, noise] ärgerlich - **2.** [substance, material] reizend.

irritation [ˌɪrɪ'teɪʃn] n - **1.** [anger] Ärger der - **2.** [cause of anger] Ärgernis das - **3.** [soreness] Reizung die.

IRS (abbr of Internal Revenue Service) n Am: **the** ~ das Finanzamt.

is [ɪz] vb ⊳ **be**.

Islam ['ɪzlɑːm] n [religion] Islam der.

island ['aɪlənd] n lit & fig Insel die.

islander ['aɪləndə] n Inselbewohner der, -in die.

isle [aɪl] n Insel die.

Isle of Man n: **the** ~ die Insel Man.

Isle of Wight [-waɪt] n: **the** ~ Wight.

isn't ['ɪznt] = **is not**.

isobar ['aɪsəbɑː] n METEOR Isobare die.

isolate ['aɪsəleɪt] vt isolieren.

isolated ['aɪsəleɪtɪd] adj - **1.** [place] abgelegen - **2.** [person] isoliert - **3.** [example, incident] einzeln.

Israel ['ɪzreɪl] n Israel nt.

Israeli [ɪz'reɪlɪ] <> adj israelisch <> n Israeli der, die.

issue ['ɪʃuː] <> n - **1.** [important subject] Frage die; **to make an** ~ **of sthg** ein Problem aus etw machen - **2.** [edition] Ausgabe die - **3.** [of stamps, bank notes, shares] Ausgabe die <> vt - **1.** [statement] abgeben; [decree] erlassen; [warning] aussprechen - **2.** [stamps, bank notes, shares] ausstellen; [passport, documents] ausstellen; [uniforms] ausgeben.

it [ɪt] pron - **1.** [referring to specific person or thing] (subj) er/sie/es; (direct object) ihn/sie/es; (indirect object) ihm/ihr; ~'**s big** er/sie/es ist groß; **she hit** ~ sie hat ihn/sie/es getroffen; **get the cat/dog and give** ~ **a drink** hole die Katze/den Hund und gib ihr/ihm etwas zu trinken - **2.** (with prepositions): **tell me about** ~ erzähl mir davon; **you're good at** ~ du kannst das gut; **a table with a chair beside** ~ ein Tisch mit einem Stuhl daneben; **what did you learn from** ~? was hast du daraus gelernt?; **put your hand in** ~ steck deine Hand hinein; **stand on top of** ~ stell dich darauf; **put the books on** ~ leg die Bücher darauf; **it had a sheet over** ~ darüber lag ein Tuch; **shall we go to** ~? sollen wir hingehen?; **put the box under** ~ stell die Schachtel darunter; **a free book came with** ~ es war ein kostenloses Buch dabei - **3.** (impersonal use) es; ~'**s hot** es ist heiß; ~'**s raining** es regnet; ~'**s Sunday** es ist Sonntag; ~'**s six o'clock** es ist sechs

Uhr; **~'s the children that worry me most** am meisten mache ich mir um die Kinder Sorgen; **~'s said that ...** man sagt, dass ... - **4.** *(nonspecific)* es; **~'s easy** es ist einfach; **~'s a difficult question** das ist eine schwierige Frage; **who is ~? – ~'s Mary/me** wer ist da? – Mary/ich bins.

IT *n abbr of* information technology.

Italian [ɪ'tæljən] <> *adj* italienisch <> *n* - **1.** [person] Italiener *der,* -in *die* - **2.** [language] Italienisch(e) *das.*

italic [ɪ'tælɪk] *adj* kursiv. **italics** *npl* Kursivschrift *die.*

Italy ['ɪtəlɪ] *n* Italien *nt.*

itch [ɪtʃ] <> *n* Juckreiz *der* <> *vi* [part of body] jucken; **I'm ~ing** es juckt mich; **I'm ~ing to do it** es juckt mich, das zu tun.

itchy ['ɪtʃɪ] *adj* juckend; **to be ~** [part of body] jucken; **I feel ~** es juckt mich.

it'd ['ɪtəd] = it would, it had.

item ['aɪtəm] *n* - **1.** [object] Gegenstand *der;* [in shop] Artikel *der;* [on agenda] Punkt *der;* COMM Posten *der;* **~ of clothing** Kleidungsstück *das* - **2.** [of news] Meldung *die.*

itemize, -ise ['aɪtəmaɪz] *vt* auf einer Liste einzeln aufführen.

itinerary [aɪ'tɪnərərɪ] *n* Reiseroute *die.*

it'll [ɪtl] = it will.

its [ɪts] *poss adj* [masculine, neuter subject] sein; [feminine subject] ihr; **the dog wagged ~ tail** der Hund wedelte mit dem Schwanz.

it's [ɪts] = it is, it has.

itself [ɪt'self] *pron* - **1.** *(reflexive)* sich - **2.** *(after prep)* sich selbst; **by ~** allein; **in ~** an sich - **3.** *(stressed)* selbst; **the house ~ is fine** das Haus selbst ist in Ordnung.

I've [aɪv] = I have.

ivory ['aɪvərɪ] *n* Elfenbein *das.*

ivy ['aɪvɪ] *n* Efeu *der.*

Ivy League *n Am* Gruppe von alten, angesehenen Universitäten im Osten der USA.

J

j (*pl* j's OR js), **J** (*pl* J's OR Js) [dʒeɪ] *n* [letter] j *das,* J *das.*

jab [dʒæb] <> *n* - **1.** [push] Stoß *der;* [with needle, knife] Stich *der* - **2.** *Br inf* [injection] Spritze *die* <> *vt* [with sthg] stechen; **to ~ sthg into sb/sthg** etw in jn/etw (hinein)-stoßen.

jabber ['dʒæbər] *vi* plappern.

jack [dʒæk] *n* - **1.** [for car] Wagenheber *der* - **2.** [playing card] Bube *der.* **jack up** *vt sep* [car] aufbocken.

jackal ['dʒækəl] *n* Schakal *der.*

jackdaw ['dʒækdɔː] *n* Dohle *die.*

jacket ['dʒækɪt] *n* - **1.** [garment] Jacke *die;* [of suit] Jackett *das* - **2.** [of book] Schutzumschlag *der* - **3.** *Am* [of record] Plattenhülle *die.*

jacket potato *n in der Schale gebackene Kartoffel.*

jack knife *n* Klappmesser *das.* **jackknife** *vi* [lorry] sich querstellen.

jack plug *n* Bananenstecker *der.*

jackpot ['dʒækpɒt] *n* Jackpot *der.*

jaded ['dʒeɪdɪd] *adj* abgestumpft.

jagged ['dʒægɪd] *adj* [metal] scharfig; [edge] ausgezackt; [rocks] zerklüftet.

jail [dʒeɪl] <> *n* Gefängnis *das;* **in ~** im Gefängnis; **to go to ~** ins Gefängnis kommen <> *vt* einlsperren.

jailer ['dʒeɪlər] *n* Gefängniswärter *der,* -in *die.*

jam [dʒæm] <> *n* - **1.** [preserve] Marmelade *die* - **2.** [of traffic] Stau *der* - **3.** *inf* [difficult situation] Klemme *die* <> *vt* - **1.** [mechanism, brakes] blockieren; **to get one's finger ~med** sich *(D)* den Finger einlquetschen - **2.** [cram]: **to ~ sthg into sthg** etw in etw *(A)* stopfen - **3.** [streets, town] verstopfen - **4.** TELEC: **thousands of callers ~med the switchboard** Tausende von Anrufern blockierten die Leitungen der (Telefon)zentrale - **5.** RADIO stören <> *vi* [stick - window, door] klemmen; [- brakes, lever] sich verklemmen. **jam on** *vt sep:* **to ~ the brakes on** eine Vollbremsung machen.

Jamaica [dʒə'meɪkə] *n* Jamaika *nt;* **in ~** auf Jamaika.

jam-packed [-'pækt] *adj inf* proppenvoll.

jangle ['dʒæŋgl] *vt* [keys] klimpern mit.

janitor ['dʒænɪtər] *n Am & Scot* [caretaker] Hausmeister *der.*

January ['dʒænjʊərɪ] *n* Januar *der; see also* September.

177

Japan [dʒə'pæn] *n* Japan *nt*.

Japanese [ˌdʒæpə'niːz] *(pl inv)* ⬦ *adj* japanisch ⬦ *n* [language] Japanisch(e) *das* ⬦ *npl* [people]: **the** - die Japaner *pl*.

jar [dʒɑːʳ] ⬦ *n* Glas *das* ⬦ *vt* [shake] durch|schütteln ⬦ *vi* - **1.** [noise, voice]: **to ~ (on sb)** unangenehm (für jn) sein - **2.** [colours] sich beißen.

jargon ['dʒɑːgən] *n* Fachsprache *die*.

jaundice ['dʒɔːndɪs] *n* Gelbsucht *die*.

jaundiced ['dʒɔːndɪst] *adj fig* [attitude, view] verbittert.

jaunt [dʒɔːnt] *n* Ausflug *der*.

jaunty ['dʒɔːntɪ] *adj* [hat, wave] flott; [person] munter.

javelin ['dʒævlɪn] *n* Speer *der*.

jaw [dʒɔː] *n* [of person, animal] Kiefer *der*.

jawbone ['dʒɔːbəʊn] *n* Kieferknochen *der*.

jay [dʒeɪ] *n* Eichelhäher *der*.

jaywalker ['dʒeɪwɔːkəʳ] *n* im Straßenverkehr unachtsamer Fußgänger.

jazz [dʒæz] *n* MUS Jazz *der*. ➡ **jazz up** *vt sep inf* auf|peppen.

jazzy ['dʒæzɪ] *adj* [colour, clothes] poppig.

jealous ['dʒeləs] *adj* [envious]: **to be ~ (of)** neidisch (auf (+ A)) sein.

jealousy ['dʒeləsɪ] *n* - **1.** [envy] Neid *der* - **2.** [possessiveness] Eifersucht *die*.

jeans [dʒiːnz] *npl* Jeans *pl*.

Jeep® [dʒiːp] *n* Jeep® *der*.

jeer [dʒɪəʳ] ⬦ *vt* verhöhnen ⬦ *vi* [crowd, fans] höhnisch johlen; **to ~ at sb** jn verhöhnen.

Jello® ['dʒeləʊ] *n Am* Wackelpudding *der*.

jelly ['dʒelɪ] *n* - **1.** [dessert] Wackelpudding *der* - **2.** [jam] Gelee *das*.

jellyfish ['dʒelɪfɪʃ] *(pl inv OR -es)* *n* Qualle *die*.

jeopardize, -ise ['dʒepədaɪz] *vt* gefährden.

jerk [dʒɜːk] ⬦ *n* - **1.** [movement] Ruck *der* - **2.** *inf pej* [fool] Trottel *der* ⬦ *vi* einen Satz machen.

jersey ['dʒɜːzɪ] *(pl -s)* *n* - **1.** [sweater] Pullover *der* - **2.** *(U)* [cloth] Jersey *der*.

Jersey ['dʒɜːzɪ] *n* Jersey *nt;* **in ~** auf Jersey.

jest [dʒest] *n* Scherz *der;* **in ~** im Spaß.

Jesus (Christ) ['dʒiːzəs-] ⬦ *n* Jesus (Christus) ⬦ *interj inf* Menschenskind!

jet [dʒet] *n* - **1.** [aircraft] Jet *der*, Düsenflugzeug *das* - **2.** [of liquid, gas, steam] Strahl *der*.

jet-black *adj* pechschwarz.

jet engine *n* Düsentriebwerk *das*.

jetfoil ['dʒetfɔɪl] *n* Tragflügelboot *das*.

jet lag *n* Jetlag *der*.

jetsam ['dʒetsəm] *n* ⟼ **flotsam**.

jettison ['dʒetɪsən] *vt* - **1.** [cargo, bombs - from plane] ab|werfen; [- from ship] über Bord werfen - **2.** *fig* [discard - ideas,

hope] über Bord werfen; [- unwanted possession] weg|werfen.

jetty ['dʒetɪ] *n* Landungssteg *der*.

Jew [dʒuː] *n* Jude *der*, Jüdin *die*.

jewel ['dʒuːəl] *n* Edelstein *der;* [in watch] Stein *der*, **~s** [jewellery] Schmuck *der*.

jeweller *Br*, **jeweler** *Am* ['dʒuːələʳ] *n* Juwelier *der;* **~'s (shop)** Juweliergeschäft *das*.

jewellery *Br*, **jewelry** *Am* ['dʒuːəlrɪ] *n* Schmuck *der;* **piece of ~** Schmuckstück *das*.

Jewish ['dʒuːɪʃ] *adj* jüdisch.

jibe [dʒaɪb] *n* spöttische Bemerkung.

jiffy ['dʒɪfɪ] *n inf*: **in a ~** sofort.

Jiffy bag® *n* Versandtasche *die*.

jig [dʒɪg] *n* [dance] lebhafter Schreittanz, vor allem auf dem Land früher beliebt.

jigsaw (puzzle) ['dʒɪgsɔː-] *n* Puzzle(spiel) *das*.

jilt [dʒɪlt] *vt* sitzen lassen.

jingle ['dʒɪŋgl] ⬦ *n* [in advertising] Jingle *der* ⬦ *vi* [bells] bimmeln; [keys] klimpern.

jinx [dʒɪŋks] *n*: **there's a ~ on it** es ist verhext.

jitters ['dʒɪtəz] *npl inf*: **the ~** das große Zittern.

job [dʒɒb] *n* - **1.** [paid work] Stelle *die;* **to lose one's ~** entlassen werden - **2.** [task] Arbeit *die;* **on the ~** bei der Arbeit - **3.** [difficult time]: **to have a ~ doing sthg** (große) Mühe haben, etw zu tun - **4.** *phr*: **that's just the ~** *Br inf* das ist genau das Richtige.

job centre *n Br* Arbeitsamt *das*.

jobless ['dʒɒblɪs] *adj* arbeitslos.

jobsharing ['dʒɒbʃeərɪŋ] *n* Jobsharing *das*.

jockey ['dʒɒkɪ] *(pl -s)* ⬦ *n* Jockey *der* ⬦ *vi*: **to ~ for position** um eine gute Position kämpfen.

jocular ['dʒɒkjʊləʳ] *adj* witzig, lustig.

jodhpurs ['dʒɒdpəz] *npl* Reithose *die*.

jog [dʒɒg] ⬦ *n* [run]: **to go for a ~** joggen gehen ⬦ *vt* [nudge - person] an|stoßen; [- table, sb's arm, elbow] stoßen gegen; **to ~ sb's memory** js Gedächtnis nach|helfen ⬦ *vi* [run] joggen.

jogging ['dʒɒgɪŋ] *n* Joggen *das;* **to go ~** joggen gehen.

john [dʒɒn] *n Am inf* [toilet] Klo *das*.

join [dʒɔɪn] ⬦ *n* Naht(stelle) *die* ⬦ *vt* - **1.** [connect] verbinden; **to ~ sthg to sthg** etw mit etw verbinden - **2.** [other people] sich an|schließen (+ D); **I'll ~ you in a moment** [follow you] ich komme gleich nach - **3.** [club, organization] bei|treten (+ D); [company] an|fangen bei; [army] gehen zu - **4.** [take part in] teil|nehmen an (+ D); **to ~ the queue** *Br*, **to ~ the line** *Am* sich in die Schlange ein|reihen ⬦ *vi* - **1.** [connect - rivers] ineinander fließen; [- edges, pieces] miteinander verbunden sein - **2.** [become a

member] Mitglied werden. ◆ **join in** ◇ vt
fus mitlmachen bei ◇ vi mitlmachen.
◆ **join up** vi MIL zum Militär gehen.

joiner ['dʒɔɪnə'] n Tischler der, -in die.

joint [dʒɔɪnt] ◇ adj [effort] vereint; [re-
sponsibility] gemeinsam; [owner] Mit- ◇ n
- **1.** ANAT Gelenk das - **2.** [in structure] Verbin-
dungsstelle die; [in carpentry] Fuge die - **3.** Br
[of meat] Braten der - **4.** inf pej [place] Laden
der - **5.** drugs sl [cannabis cigarette] Joint der.

joint account n gemeinsames Konto.

jointly ['dʒɔɪntlɪ] adv gemeinsam.

joke [dʒəʊk] ◇ n Witz der; **to play a ~ on sb**
jm einen Streich spielen; **it's no ~** [not easy]
das ist keine Kleinigkeit; **to be a ~** [person]
eine Witzfigur sein ◇ vi Witze machen; **to
~ about sthg** über etw (A) Witze machen;
you must be joking! das meinst du doch
nicht im Ernst!

joker ['dʒəʊkə'] n - **1.** [person] Spaßvogel der
- **2.** [playing card] Joker der.

jolly ['dʒɒlɪ] ◇ adj lustig, fröhlich ◇ adv
Br [very] super.

jolt [dʒəʊlt] ◇ n - **1.** [jerk] Ruck der
- **2.** [shock] **to give sb a ~** jm einen Schock
versetzen ◇ vt - **1.** [jerk] durchlschütteln
- **2.** [shock] **to ~ sb into doing sthg** jn so auf-
rütteln, dass er etw tut.

jostle ['dʒɒsl] ◇ vt anlrempeln ◇ vi drängeln.

jot [dʒɒt] n: **there isn't a ~ of truth in it** es ist
kein Funken Wahrheit darin. ◆ **jot down**
vt sep sich (D) notieren.

journal ['dʒɜːnl] n - **1.** [magazine] Zeitschrift die - **2.** [diary] Tagebuch das.

journalism ['dʒɜːnəlɪzm] n Journalismus
der.

journalist ['dʒɜːnəlɪst] n Journalist der, -in
die.

journey ['dʒɜːnɪ] (pl -s) n Reise die; **to go on
a ~** verreisen; **an hour's ~** eine Stunde Fahrt.

jovial ['dʒəʊvɪəl] adj fröhlich.

joy [dʒɔɪ] n Freude die.

joyful ['dʒɔɪfʊl] adj [person] froh; [shout]
freudig; [scene, news] erfreulich.

joystick ['dʒɔɪstɪk] n - **1.** [in aircraft] Steuer-
knüppel der - **2.** [for computers] Joystick der.

Jr. (abbr of Junior) jun.

jubilant ['dʒuːbɪlənt] adj [person, fans]
überglücklich; [shout] Jubel-.

jubilee ['dʒuːbɪliː] n Jubiläum das.

judge [dʒʌdʒ] ◇ n - **1.** LAW Richter der, -in
die - **2.** SPORT Schiedsrichter der, -in die; [of
competition] Preisrichter der, -in die ◇ vt
- **1.** LAW [case] verhandeln - **2.** [competition]
beurteilen - **3.** [estimate] (ein)schätzen ◇ vi
[decide] (be)urteilen; **to ~ from** OR **by sthg**,
judging from OR **by sthg** nach etw zu urteilen.

judg(e)ment ['dʒʌdʒmənt] n - **1.** LAW Urteil
das - **2.** [opinion] Urteil das - **3.** [ability to form
opinion] Urteilsvermögen das.

judicial [dʒuː'dɪʃl] adj Gerichts-.

judiciary [dʒuː'dɪʃərɪ] n: **the ~** das Ge-
richtswesen.

judicious [dʒuː'dɪʃəs] adj klug.

judo ['dʒuːdəʊ] n Judo das.

jug [dʒʌg] n Krug der.

juggernaut ['dʒʌgənɔːt] n [truck] Laster
der.

juggle ['dʒʌgl] vt & vi - **1.** [throw] jonglieren - **2.**: **to ~ (with) figures** die Zahlen so
hinldrehen, wie man sie haben will.

juggler ['dʒʌglə'] n Jongleur der, -in die.

juice [dʒuːs] n Saft der.

juicy ['dʒuːsɪ] adj [fruit] saftig.

jukebox ['dʒuːkbɒks] n Musikbox die.

July [dʒuː'laɪ] n Juli der; see also September.

jumble ['dʒʌmbl] ◇ n [mixture] Durcheinander das ◇ vt: **to ~ (up)** [objects] durcheinander werfen; [words] durcheinander bringen.

jumble sale n Br in Pfarrsälen oder Gemeinde-
und Stadthallen abgehaltener Trödelmarkt, dessen Erlös wohltätigen Vereinen zugute kommt.

jumbo jet ['dʒʌmbə-] n Jumbo-Jet der.

jumbo-sized [-saɪzd] adj Riesen-.

jump [dʒʌmp] ◇ n - **1.** [leap] Sprung der
- **2.** [rapid increase] Sprung der ◇ vt
- **1.** [fence, stream] überlspringen - **2.**: **to ~ the
queue** sich vorldrängen - **2.** inf [attack] überfallen ◇ vi - **1.** [gen] springen; **to ~ over sthg**
über etw (A) springen - **2.** [with fright, sur-
prise] einen Satz machen; **you made me ~!**
du hast mich erschreckt! - **3.** [increase]
sprunghaft anlsteigen. ◆ **jump at** vt fus fig
[opportunity] ergreifen. ◆ **jump in** vi
hereinlspringen; **~ in!** [get in car] spring rein!
◆ **jump out** vi herauslspringen; **to ~ out
(of) the window** aus dem Fenster springen.
◆ **jump up** vi [get up quickly] auf-
springen.

jumper ['dʒʌmpə'] n - **1.** Br [pullover] Pullover der - **2.** Am [dress] Trägerkleid das.

jump leads npl Starthilfekabel pl.

jump-start vt mit Starthilfe zünden.

jumpsuit ['dʒʌmpsuːt] n Overall der.

jumpy ['dʒʌmpɪ] adj nervös.

junction ['dʒʌŋkʃn] n [of roads] Kreuzung
die; [of railway lines, pipes] Knotenpunkt der;
[on motorway] Anschlussstelle die.

June [dʒuːn] n Juni der; see also September.

jungle ['dʒʌŋgl] n lit & fig Dschungel der.

junior ['dʒuːnɪə'] ◇ adj - **1.** [younger] jünger - **2.** [lower in rank] untergeordnet; **~ partner** Juniorpartner der - **3.** Am [after name] junior ◇ n - **1.** [person of lower rank] Person

niedrigeren Ranges - **2.** [younger person] Jüngere *der, die;* **he is two years my** ~ er ist zwei Jahre jünger als ich - **3.** *Am* SCH & UNIV *Schüler/Student im vorletzten Jahr.*

junior high school *n Am Schule zwischen Grund- und Oberschule.*

junior school *n Br* Grundschule *die (für 7- bis 11-jährige).*

junk [dʒʌŋk] *n* - **1.** *inf* [unwanted things] Ramsch *der* - **2.** [boat] Dschunke *die.*

junk food *n pej* ungesundes Essen wie Fast Food, Chips, Süßigkeiten.

junkie ['dʒʌŋkɪ] *n drugs sl* Junkie *der,* Fixer *der, -in die.*

junk mail *n (U) pej* Reklamemüll *der (der mit der Post kommt).*

junk shop *n* Trödelladen *der.*

Jupiter ['dʒuːpɪtə'] *n* [planet] Jupiter *der.*

jurisdiction [,dʒuərɪs'dɪkʃn] *n* [of court] Zuständigkeitsbereich *der.*

juror ['dʒuərə'] *n* Geschworene *der, die.*

jury ['dʒuərɪ] *n* - **1.** [in court of law] **the** ~ die Geschworenen *pl* - **2.** [in contest] Jury *die.*

just [dʒʌst] <> *adv* - **1.** [recently] gerade; **to have** ~ **done sthg** gerade etw getan haben - **2.** [at this or that moment] gerade; **I was** ~ **about to pick up the phone, when ...** ich wollte gerade den Hörer abnehmen, als ...; **we were** ~ **leaving, when ...** wir wollten gerade gehen, als ...; **I'm** ~ **coming** ich komme schon - **3.** [exactly] genau; ~ **what I need** genau das, was ich brauche; **it's** ~ **as good** es ist genauso gut - **4.** [only] nur; ~ **a bit** nur ein bisschen; ~ **over an hour** etwas über eine Stunde; ~ **a minute!** einen Moment! - **5.** [simply] einfach; **'~ add water'** 'nur Wasser zugeben' - **6.** [almost not]: **(only)** ~ gerade (noch) - **7.** [for emphasis]: **look what you've done!** sieh nur, was du gemacht hast! - **8.** [in requests]: **could you** ~ **open your mouth?** können Sie mal den Mund aufmachen? <> *adj* [fair] gerecht; **it's only** ~ es ist nur recht und billig. ◆ **just about** *adv* [almost] fast. ◆ **just now** *adv* - **1.** [a short time ago] gerade; **I was speaking to her** ~ **now** ich habe gerade mit ihr gesprochen - **2.** [at this moment] im Moment.

justice ['dʒʌstɪs] *n (U)* - **1.** [fairness] Gerechtigkeit *die* - **2.** LAW [power of law] Justiz *die* - **3.** [of cause, claim] Rechtmäßigkeit *die.*

justify ['dʒʌstɪfaɪ] *vt* - **1.** [gen] rechtfertigen - **2.** TYPO justieren; COMPUT ausrichten.

justly ['dʒʌstlɪ] *adv* zu Recht, mit Recht.

jut [dʒʌt] *vi:* **to** ~ **(out)** (her)vorragen.

juvenile ['dʒuːvənaɪl] <> *adj* - **1.** LAW jugendlich; ~ **crime** die Jugendkriminalität - **2.** *pej* [childish] infantil <> *n* LAW Jugendliche *der, die.*

juxtapose [,dʒʌkstə'pəʊz] *vt:* **to** ~ **sthg with sthg** etw neben etw (*A*) stellen.

k (*pl* **k's** OR **ks**), **K** (*pl* **K's** OR **Ks**) [keɪ] *n* [letter] k *das,* K *das.* ◆ **K** *n* - **1.** (*abbr of* kilobyte) Kb *das* - **2.** (*abbr of* thousand) Tsd.

kaleidoscope [kə'laɪdəskəʊp] *n* Kaleidoskop *das.*

kangaroo [,kæŋgə'ruː] *n* Känguruh *das.*

kaput [kə'pʊt] *adj inf* kaputt.

karaoke [,kærɪ'əʊkiː] *n* Karaoke *das.*

karat ['kærət] *n Am* Karat *das.*

karate [kə'rɑːtɪ] *n* Karate *das.*

kayak ['kaɪæk] *n* Kajak *der* OR *das.*

KB (*abbr of* kilobyte(s)) *n* COMPUT Kb *das.*

kcal (*abbr of* kilocalorie) kcal.

kebab [kɪ'bæb] *n:* **(shish)** ~ Kebab *der;* **(doner)** ~ Gyros *der.*

keel [kiːl] *n* Kiel *der;* **to get sthg back on an even** ~ etw wieder auf die Beine bringen. ◆ **keel over** *vi* [ship] kentern; [person] umkippen.

keen [kiːn] *adj* - **1.** [enthusiastic] begeistert; **to be** ~ **on sthg** etw sehr mögen; **to be** ~ **to do** OR **on doing sthg** etw unbedingt tun wollen; **she wasn't** ~ **on the idea** sie war von der Sache nicht angetan - **2.** [interest, desire, competition] stark - **3.** [edge] [eyesight, hearing] gut - **4.** [wind] scharf.

keep [kiːp] (*pt & pp* kept) <> *vt* - **1.** [retain] behalten; **please** ~ **the change** bitte behalten Sie das Wechselgeld; **to** ~ **a seat for sb** einen Platz für jn freihalten - **2.** [store] aufbewahren - **3.** [maintain] halten; **to** ~ **sb waiting** jn warten lassen; **to** ~ **sb awake** jn wach halten - **4.** [promise, appointment] einhalten - **5.** [secret] für sich behalten; **to** ~ **sthg from sb** etw vor jm geheim halten - **6.** [delay]: **what kept you?** wo bist du denn so lang gewesen? - **7.** [record, diary] führen; **to** ~ **a note of sthg** etw aufschreiben - **8.** [prevent]: **to** ~ **sb from doing sthg** jn davon abhalten, etw zu tun; **the noise kept me from sleeping** der Lärm ließ mich nicht schlafen - **9.** [own - farm animals] halten - **10.** *phr:* **they** ~ **themselves to themselves** sie bleiben für sich <> *vi* - **1.** [remain] bleiben; **to** ~ **fit** fit bleiben; **to** ~ **silent** schweigen; **to** ~ **warm** sich warm halten; **to** ~ **clear of sthg** sich von etw fern halten - **2.** [continue]: **to** ~ **doing sthg** [continuously] etw weiter tun; [repeatedly] etw dauernd tun; **to** ~ **going** [walking] weiterlgehen; [driving] weiterlfahren; [working] weiterlmachen; **'~ left'** 'links fahren';

~ straight on [walking] gehen Sie immer geradeaus; [driving] fahren Sie immer geradeaus - **3.** [food] sich halten - **4.** *Br* [in health]: **how are you ~ing?** wie geht es dir? ◇ *n* [food, lodging] Unterhalt *der;* **to earn one's ~** sein eigenes Brot verdienen. ◆ **for keeps** *adv* für immer. ◆ **keep back** ◇ *vt sep* - **1.** [information] verschweigen - **2.** [money] zurück|behalten ◇ *vi* [stand back] zurückbleiben. ◆ **keep off** *vt fus* [subject, food, drink] vermeiden; **'~ off the grass'** 'Rasen betreten verboten'. ◆ **keep on** *vi* - **1.** [continue]: **to ~ on doing sthg** [continuously] etw weiter tun; [repeatedly] etw dauernd tun - **2.** [talk incessantly]: **to ~ on (about sthg)** dauernd (über etw (A)) reden. ◆ **keep out** ◇ *vt sep* nicht herein|lassen ◇ *vi:* **'~ out!'** 'Betreten verboten!'. ◆ **keep to** *vt fus* - **1.** [rule, promise, plan]: **to ~ to sthg** sich an etw (A) halten - **2.** [not deviate from]: **to ~ to the point** bei der Sache bleiben; **~ to the path!** auf dem Weg bleiben! ◆ **keep up** ◇ *vt sep* - **1.** [prevent from falling] halten - **2.** [maintain - standards, friendship] aufrecht|erhalten; [- house, garden] instand halten; **~ it up!** weiter so! - **3.** [prevent from going to bed]: **to ~ sb up** jm vom Schlafen ab|halten ◇ *vi* [maintain pace, level] mit|halten; **to ~ up with sb/sthg** mit jm/etw mit|halten können; **to ~ up with the news** sich auf dem Laufenden halten.

keeper ['ki:pə^r] *n* - **1.** [in zoo] Wärter *der,* -in *die* - **2.** [of museum] Kustos *der.*

keep-fit *Br n* Fitness *die.*

keeping ['ki:pɪŋ] *n* - **1.** [care]: **in safe ~** sicher verwahrt; **for safe ~** zur Verwahrung - **2.** [conformity]: **to be in ~ with sthg** [regulations, decision] etw (D) entsprechen; [clothes, furniture, style] zu etw passen.

keepsake ['ki:pseɪk] *n* Andenken *das.*

kennel ['kenl] *n* - **1.** [for dog] Hundehütte *die;* [for many dogs] Zwinger *der* - **2.** *Am* = **kennels**. ◆ **kennels** *npl Br* [for boarding pets] Tierpension *die.*

Kenya ['kenjə] *n* Kenia *nt.*

kept [kept] *pt & pp* ⊳ **keep.**

kerb [kɜ:b] *n Br* Bordsteinkante *die.*

kernel ['kɜ:nl] *n* [of nut] Kern *der.*

kerosene ['kerəsi:n] *n* Petroleum *das.*

ketchup ['ketʃəp] *n* Ketschup *das* OR *der.*

kettle ['ketl] *n* Kessel *der;* **to put the ~ on** Wasser auf|setzen.

key [ki:] ◇ *n* - **1.** [gen] Schlüssel *der* - **2.** [of typewriter, computer, piano] Taste *die* - **3.** MUS Tonart *die* ◇ *adj* [main] Schlüssel-.

keyboard ['ki:bɔ:d] *n* - **1.** [of typewriter, computer] Tastatur *die,* Keyboard *das* - **2.** [of piano] Klaviatur *die;* [of organ] Manual *das.*

keyed up [ˌki:d-] *adj* aufgeregt, nervös.

keyhole ['ki:həʊl] *n* Schlüsselloch *das.*

keynote ['ki:nəʊt] *n* [main point] Hauptgedanke *der.*

keypad ['ki:pæd] *n* COMPUT Tastenfeld *das.*

key ring *n* Schlüsselring *der.*

kg (*abbr of* kilogram) kg.

khaki ['kɑ:kɪ] ◇ *adj* kakifarben ◇ *n* [colour] Kaki *das.*

kHz (*abbr of* kilohertz) *n* kHz.

kick [kɪk] ◇ *n* - **1.** [with foot] (Fuß)tritt *der* - **2.** *inf* [excitement]: **to do sthg for ~s** etw aus Spaß tun; **to get a ~ from sthg** an etw (D) Spaß haben ◇ *vt* - **1.** [with foot - gen] treten; [- ball] kicken; **I could have ~ed myself!** ich hätte mich ohrfeigen können! - **2.** *inf* [habit] auf|geben ◇ *vi* [person] treten; [baby] strampeln; [animal] aus|schlagen, treten. ◆ **kick off** *vi* - **1.** FTBL an|stoßen - **2.** *inf fig* [start] an|fangen. ◆ **kick out** *vt sep inf* raus|schmeißen.

kid [kɪd] ◇ *n* - **1.** *inf* [child] Kind *das* - **2.** [young goat] Zicklein *das* ◇ *comp inf* [brother, sister] kleine, -r ◇ *vt inf* - **1.** [tease] veralbern - **2.** [delude]: **to ~ o.s.** sich (D) etwas vor|machen ◇ *vi inf:* **to be ~ding** Spaß machen; **you're ~ding!** das ist nicht dein Ernst!

kidnap ['kɪdnæp] (*Am pt & pp* -ed; *cont* -ing) *vt* entführen, kidnappen.

kidnapper *Br,* **kidnaper** *Am* ['kɪdnæpə^r] *n* Kidnapper *der,* -in *die,* Entführer *der,* -in *die.*

kidnapping *Br,* **kidnaping** *Am* ['kɪdnæpɪŋ] *n* Kidnapping *das.*

kidney ['kɪdnɪ] (*pl* kidneys) *n* Niere *die.*

kidney bean *n* Kidneybohne *die.*

kill [kɪl] ◇ *vt* - **1.** [person, animal] töten; [murder] um|bringen; [plant] ein|gehen lassen; **to ~ o.s.** sich um|bringen - **2.** *fig* [hope] zerstören; [conversation, desire] zum Erliegen bringen; [pain] ab|töten ◇ *vi* töten.

killer ['kɪlə^r] *n* [person] Mörder *der,* -in *die.*

killing ['kɪlɪŋ] *n* - **1.** [murder] Tötung *die* - **2.** *inf* [profit]: **to make a ~** ein Riesengeschäft machen.

killjoy ['kɪldʒɔɪ] *n* Spielverderber *der.*

kiln [kɪln] *n* [for bricks, pottery] Brennofen *der;* [for hops] Darrofen *der.*

kilo ['ki:ləʊ] (*pl* -s) (*abbr of* kilogram) *n* Kilo *das.*

kilobyte ['kɪləbaɪt] *n* Kilobyte *das.*

kilogram(me) ['kɪləgræm] *n* Kilogramm *das.*

kilohertz ['kɪləhɜ:ts] (*pl inv*) *n* Kilohertz *das.*

kilometre *Br* ['kɪləˌmi:tə^r], **kilometer** *Am* [kɪ'lɒmɪtər] *n* Kilometer *der.*

kilowatt ['kɪləwɒt] *n* Kilowatt *das.*

kilt [kɪlt] *n* Kilt *der,* Schottenrock *der.*

kin [kɪn] *n* ⊳ **kith.**

kind [kaɪnd] ◇ *adj* nett; **that's very ~ of you** das ist sehr nett von dir ◇ *n* Art *die;* [of cheese, wine *etc*] Sorte *die;* **what ~ of music**

do you like? welche Musik magst du?; **what ~ of car do you drive?** was für ein Auto hast du?; **- of** *inf* irgendwie; **they're two of a ~** sie sind vom gleichen Schlag; **all ~s of animals** allerlei Tiere; **in ~** [payment] in Naturalien.

kindergarten ['kındə,gɑːtn] *n* Kindergarten *der*.

kind-hearted [-'hɑːtɪd] *adj* gutherzig.

kindle ['kındl] *vt fig* [idea, feeling] entfachen.

kindly ['kaɪndlɪ] ◇ *adj* gütig, wohltätig ◇ *adv* - **1.** [speak, smile] freundlich - **2.** [please] freundlicherweise.

kindness ['kaɪndnɪs] *n* - **1.** [gentleness] Freundlichkeit *die* - **2.** [helpful act] Gefälligkeit *die*.

kindred ['kındrıd] *adj* ähnlich; **~ spirit** verwandte Seele.

king [kıŋ] *n* König *der*.

kingdom ['kıŋdəm] *n* - **1.** [country] Königreich *das* - **2.** [of animals, plants] Reich *das*.

kingfisher ['kıŋ,fıʃəʳ] *n* Eisvogel *der*.

king-size(d) [-saɪz(d)] *adj* Kingsize-.

kinky ['kıŋkı] *adj inf* abartig.

kiosk ['kiːɒsk] *n* - **1.** [small shop] Kiosk *der* - **2.** *Br* [telephone box] Telefonzelle *die*.

kip [kıp] *Br inf* ◇ *n*: **to have a ~** eine Runde schlafen ◇ *vi* eine Runde schlafen.

kipper ['kıpəʳ] *n* Räucherhering *der*.

kiss [kıs] ◇ *n* Kuss *der*; **to give sb a ~** jm einen Kuss geben ◇ *vt* küssen ◇ *vi* sich küssen.

kiss of life *n*: **the ~** die Mund-zu-Mund-Beatmung.

kit [kıt] *n* - **1.** [set] Ausrüstung *die*, Satz *der*; **repair ~** Flickzeug *das* - **2.** *(U)* [sports clothes] Sportsachen *pl* - **3.** [to be assembled] Bausatz *der*.

kitchen ['kıtʃın] *n* Küche *die*.

kitchen roll *n* Küchenrolle *die*.

kitchen sink *n* Spülbecken *das*.

kitchen unit *n* Küchenelement *das*.

kite [kaɪt] *n* [toy] Drachen *der*.

kith [kıθ] *n*: **~ and kin** Kind und Kegel.

kitten ['kıtn] *n* Kätzchen *das*.

kitty ['kıtı] *n* [for bills, drinks] Gemeinschaftskasse *die*; [in card games] Bank *die*.

kiwi ['kiːwiː] *n* [bird] Kiwi *der*.

kiwi fruit *n* Kiwi *die*.

km *(abbr of* kilometre*)* km.

km/h *(abbr of* kilometres per hour*)* km/h.

knack [næk] *n* Trick *der*; **to have a ~ the ~ of doing sthg** [ability] den Dreh rauslhaben, etw zu tun; **he has a** OR **the ~ of turning up late** er hat das Talent, (immer) zu spät zu kommen.

knackered ['nækəd] *adj Br inf* kaputt.

knapsack ['næpsæk] *n* Rucksack *der*.

knead [niːd] *vt* [dough, clay] kneten.

knee [niː] *n* Knie *das*.

kneecap ['niːkæp] *n* Kniescheibe *die*.

kneel [niːl] *(Br pt & pp* knelt, *Am pt & pp* knelt OR -ed*) vi* knien. ◆ **kneel down** *vi* niederlknien.

knelt [nelt] *pt & pp* ▷ kneel.

knew [njuː] *pt* ▷ know.

knickers ['nıkəz] *npl* - **1.** *Br* [underwear] Schlüpfer *der* - **2.** *Am* [knickerbockers] Knickerbockers *pl*.

knick-knacks ['nıknæks] *npl* Nippes *pl*.

knife [naɪf] *(pl* knives*)* ◇ *n* Messer *das* ◇ *vt* einlstechen auf (+ A).

knight [naɪt] ◇ *n* - **1.** [gen] Ritter *der* - **2.** [in chess] Springer *der* ◇ *vt* in den Adelsstand erheben.

knighthood ['naɪthʊd] *n*: **to get** OR **be given a ~** in den Adelsstand erhoben werden.

knit [nıt] *(pt & pp* knit OR -ted*)* ◇ *adj*: **closely** OR **tightly ~** *fig* eng verbunden ◇ *vt* stricken ◇ *vi* - **1.** [with wool] stricken - **2.** [join] zusammenlwachsen.

knitting ['nıtıŋ] *n (U)* - **1.** [activity] Stricken *das* - **2.** [thing being knitted] Strickzeug *das*.

knitting needle *n* Stricknadel *die*.

knitwear ['nıtweəʳ] *n (U)* Strickwaren *pl*.

knives [naɪvz] *pl* ▷ knife.

knob [nɒb] *n* - **1.** [handle] Griff *der*, Knauf *der* - **2.** [on TV, radio] Knopf *der*.

knock [nɒk] ◇ *n* - **1.** [hit - on body] Schlag *der*; [- on door] Klopfen *das* - **2.** *inf* [piece of bad luck] Schlag *der* ◇ *vt* - **1.** [hit] (an)lschlagen, (an)lstoßen - **2.** *inf* [criticize] stark kritisieren ◇ *vi* - **1.** [on door]: **to ~ (at** OR **on)** klopfen (auf *or* an (+ A)) - **2.** [car engine] klopfen. ◆ **knock down** *vt sep* - **1.** [pedestrian] anlfahren - **2.** [building] niederlreißen. ◆ **knock off** *vi inf* [stop working] Feierabend machen. ◆ **knock out** *vt sep* - **1.** [make unconscious - subj: person, punch] k.o. schlagen; [- subj: drug] bewusstlos werden lassen - **2.** [from competition] auslscheiden. ◆ **knock over** *vt sep* - **1.** [push over] umlstoßen; [person] umlwerfen - **2.** [pedestrian] überfahren.

knocker ['nɒkəʳ] *n* [on door] Türklopfer *der*.

knock-on effect *n Br* Auswirkung *die*.

knockout ['nɒkaʊt] *n* - **1.** [in boxing] Knockout *der*, K.O. *der* - **2.** *inf* [sensation]: **she's a ~** sie ist toll.

knot [nɒt] ◇ *n* - **1.** [in rope, string] Knoten *der*; **to tie/untie a ~** einen Knoten machen/lösen - **2.** [in wood] Ast *der* - **3.** [ship's speed] Knoten *der* ◇ *vt* [rope, string] knoten.

know [nəʊ] *(pt* knew, *pp* known*)* ◇ *vt* - **1.** [fact, information] wissen; **as far as I ~** so viel ich weiß; **to let sb ~ sthg** jn etw wissen lassen - **2.** [person, place] kennen; **to get to ~ sb** jn kennen lernen - **3.** [language, skill] können; **to ~ how to do sthg** etw tun können - **4.** [recognize] erkennen - **5.** [call]: **to be ~n as** bekannt sein als - **6.** [distinguish] unterscheiden können; **to ~ right from wrong** Gut und Böse unterscheiden können <> vi: I ~ das weiß ich; **to ~ about sthg** [understand] sich mit etw auslkennen; [have heard about] etw wissen; **to ~ of** kennen, wissen von; **you ~** [for emphasis] weißt du <> n: **to be in the ~** im Bilde sein.

know-all n Br Besserwisser der, -in die.

know-how n Know-how das.

knowing ['nəʊɪŋ] adj [look, smile] wissend.

knowingly ['nəʊɪŋlɪ] adv - **1.** [look, smile] wissend - **2.** [act] wissentlich.

know-it-all n = know-all.

knowledge ['nɒlɪdʒ] n (U) - **1.** [learning] Kenntnisse pl - **2.** [awareness] Wissen das; **I had no ~ of it** ich wusste nichts davon; **to the best of my ~** soweit OR soviel ich weiß.

knowledgeable ['nɒlɪdʒəbl] adj sachkundig.

known [nəʊn] pp >> know.

knuckle ['nʌkl] n ANAT (Finger)knöchel der.

koala (bear) [kəʊ'ɑːlə-] n Koala(bär) der.

Koran [kɒ'rɑːn] n: **the ~** der Koran.

Korea [kə'rɪə] n Korea nt.

Korean [kə'rɪən] <> adj koreanisch <> n - **1.** [person] Koreaner der, -in die - **2.** [language] Koreanisch(e) das.

kosher ['kəʊʃər] adj koscher.

kung fu [ˌkʌŋ'fuː] n Kung-Fu das.

Kurd [kɜːd] n Kurde der, -din die.

Kuwait [kʊ'weɪt] n - **1.** [country] Kuwait nt - **2.** [city] Kuwait-City nt.

L

l¹ (pl l's OR ls), **L** (pl L's OR Ls) [el] n [letter] l das, L das.

l² (abbr of litre) [el] l.

lab [læb] n inf Labor das.

label ['leɪbl] <> n - **1.** [on bottle, clothing] Etikett das; [tied on] Anhänger der; [stuck on] Aufkleber der - **2.** [of record] Label das <> vt - **1.** [fix label to - bottle, clothing] etikettieren; [- with tied-on label] mit Anhänger versehen; [- with stuck-on label] mit Aufkleber versehen - **2.** [describe] **to ~ sb (as) sthg** jn als etw einlstufen.

labor etc n Am = labour etc.

laboratory [Br lə'bɒrətrɪ, Am 'læbrəˌtɔːrɪ] n Labor(atorium) das.

laborious [lə'bɔːrɪəs] adj mühsam.

labor union n Am (Arbeiter)gewerkschaft die.

labour Br, **labor** Am ['leɪbər] <> n - **1.** [work] Arbeit die - **2.** (U) [workers] Arbeiterschaft die, Arbeiter pl - **3.** MED (Geburts)wehen pl <> vi - **1.** [work] arbeiten - **2.** [struggle]: **to ~ at** OR **over sthg** sich mit etw plagen. ◆ **Labour** Br POL <> adj Labour- <> n Labour Party die.

laboured Br, **labored** Am ['leɪbəd] adj [breathing] schwer; [style] schwerfällig.

labourer Br, **laborer** Am ['leɪbərər] n Arbeiter der, -in die.

Labour Party n Br: **the ~** die Labour Party die.

Labrador ['læbrədɔːr] n [dog] Labrador der.

labyrinth ['læbərɪnθ] n Labyrinth das.

lace [leɪs] <> n - **1.** (U) [material] Spitze die - **2.** [for shoe] Schnürsenkel der <> vt - **1.** [shoe, boot] (zu)schnüren - **2.** [drink] mit einem Schuss Alkohol versetzen. ◆ **lace up** vt sep zulschnüren.

lack [læk] <> n: **~ (of)** Mangel der (an (+ D)); **for ~ of money** aus Geldmangel; **there is no ~ of ...** es mangelt nicht an (+ D) ... <> vt: **he ~s confidence/intelligence** es mangelt ihm an Selbstvertrauen/Intelligenz <> vi: **to be ~ing** fehlen; **he is ~ing in confidence/ intelligence** es mangelt ihm an Selbstvertrauen/Intelligenz.

lackadaisical [ˌlækə'deɪzɪkl] adj pej lustlos.

lacklustre Br, **lackluster** Am ['lækˌlʌstər] adj [performance] glanzlos; [person, party] langweilig.

laconic [lə'kɒnɪk] adj lakonisch.

lacquer ['lækər] n - **1.** [for wood, metal] Lack der - **2.** [for hair] Haarspray das.

lacrosse [lə'krɒs] n Lacrosse das.

lad [læd] n inf - **1.** [young boy] Junge der - **2.** [male friend] Kumpel der.

ladder ['lædər] <> n - **1.** [for climbing] Leiter die - **2.** Br [in tights] Laufmasche die <> vt Br: **I've ~ed my tights** ich habe eine Laufmasche.

laden ['leɪdn] adj: **~ (with)** beladen (mit).

ladies Br ['leɪdɪz], **ladies room** Am n Damentoilette die.

ladle ['leɪdl] n (Schöpf)kelle die.

lady ['leɪdɪ] <> n - **1.** [woman] Dame die - **2.** [by birth or upbringing] Lady die <> comp: **~ doctor** Ärztin; **~ dentist** Zahnärztin. ◆ **Lady** n [member of nobility] Lady die.

ladybird Br ['leɪdɪbɜːd], **ladybug** Am ['leɪdɪbʌg] n Marienkäfer der.

ladylike ['leɪdɪlaɪk] adj damenhaft.

lag [læg] <> vi: **to ~ (behind)** zurücklbleiben <> vt isolieren <> n [time lag] zeitliche Verzögerung.

lager ['lɑːgər] n helles Bier.

lagoon [lə'guːn] n Lagune die.

laid [leɪd] pt & pp >> lay.

laid-back adj inf gelassen.

lain [leɪn] pp >> lie.

lair [leəʳ] *n* Lager *das*.

lake [leɪk] *n* See *der*.

Lake District *n*: **the ~** der Lake District, *Seenlandschaft in Nordwestengland*.

lamb [læm] *n* Lamm *das*.

lambswool ['læmzwʊl] *n* Lambswool *die*.

lame [leɪm] *adj lit & fig* lahm.

lament [lə'ment] ⟨⟩ *n* Klage *die*; [song] Klagelied *das* ⟨⟩ *vt* beklagen.

lamentable ['læməntəbl] *adj* beklagenswert.

laminated ['læmɪneɪtɪd] *adj* geschichtet.

lamp [læmp] *n* Lampe *die*; [on street] Laterne *die*.

lampoon [læm'puːn] *vt* verspotten.

lamppost ['læmppəʊst] *n* Laternenpfahl *der*.

lampshade ['læmpʃeɪd] *n* Lampenschirm *der*.

lance [lɑːns] ⟨⟩ *n* [spear] Lanze *die* ⟨⟩ *vt* MED aufschneiden.

land [lænd] ⟨⟩ *n* **- 1.** [gen] Land *das* **- 2.** [property] Land *das* ⟨⟩ *vt* **- 1.** [landen] **- 2.** [cargo] löschen **- 3.** [fish] an Land ziehen **- 4.** *inf* [job, contract] kriegen **- 5.** *inf* [put]: **to ~ sb in trouble/jail** jn in Schwierigkeiten/ins Gefängnis bringen **- 6.** *inf* [encumber]: **to ~ sb with sb/sthg** jm jn/etw aufhalsen ⟨⟩ *vi* **- 1.** [plane, passenger] landen; [from ship] an Land gehen **- 2.** [fall] fallen. ◆ **land up** *vi inf* [in place] landen; [in situation] enden.

landing ['lændɪŋ] *n* **- 1.** [between stairs] Treppenabsatz *der* **- 2.** [of aeroplane] Landung *die*.

landing card *n* Einreisekarte *die*.

landlady ['lænd,leɪdɪ] *n* **- 1.** [of pub] Wirtin *die* **- 2.** [of lodgings] Vermieterin *die*.

landlord ['lændlɔːd] *n* **- 1.** [of pub] Wirt *der* **- 2.** [of lodgings] Vermieter *der*.

landmark ['lændmɑːk] *n* **- 1.** [prominent feature] Wahrzeichen *das* **- 2.** *fig* [in history] Meilenstein *der*.

landowner ['lænd,əʊnəʳ] *n* Grundbesitzer *der*, -in *die*.

landscape ['lændskeɪp] *n* [scenery] Landschaft *die*.

landslide ['lændslaɪd] *n lit & fig* Erdrutsch *der*.

lane [leɪn] *n* **- 1.** [country road] (enge) Landstraße **- 2.** [division of road] Fahrspur *die*, Fahrstreifen *der*; **'get in ~'** 'Bitte einordnen'; **'keep in ~'** 'Auf der Fahrspur bleiben' **- 3.** [in swimming pool, on racetrack] Bahn *die* **- 4.** [for shipping] Schifffahrtsweg *der*; [for aircraft] Flugroute *die*.

language ['læŋgwɪdʒ] *n* Sprache *die*; **bad ~** Kraftausdrücke *pl*.

language laboratory *n* Sprachlabor *das*.

languid ['læŋgwɪd] *adj* [gesture] lässig; [person] träge.

languish ['læŋgwɪʃ] *vi* **- 1.** [suffer] schmach-

ten **- 2.** [become weak - person, plant] verkümmern.

lank [læŋk] *adj* [hair] strähnig.

lanky ['læŋkɪ] *adj* schlaksig.

lantern ['læntən] *n* Laterne *die*.

lap [læp] ⟨⟩ *n* **- 1.** [knees] Schoß *der* **- 2.** SPORT Runde *die* ⟨⟩ *vt* **- 1.** [subj: animal] (auf)schlecken **- 2.** SPORT [runner, car] überrunden ⟨⟩ *vi* [water, waves] plätschern.

lapel [lə'pel] *n* Revers *das*.

lapse [læps] ⟨⟩ *n* **- 1.** [failing]: **~ of concentration** Konzentrationsschwäche *die*; **memory ~** Gedächtnislücke *die* **- 2.** [in behaviour] Lapsus *der* **- 3.** [of time]: **after a ~ of three years** nach drei Jahren ⟨⟩ *vi* **- 1.** [licence, passport] ablaufen; [law] nicht mehr gelten; [custom] aussterben **- 2.** [standards] verfallen; [quality] sich verschlechtern **- 3.** [subj: person]: **to ~ into sthg** in etw *(A)* verfallen; [coma] in etw *(A)* fallen.

lap-top (computer) *n* Laptop *der*.

lard [lɑːd] *n* Schweineschmalz *das*.

larder ['lɑːdəʳ] *n* [room] Vorratsraum *der*; [cupboard] Vorratsschrank *der*.

large [lɑːdʒ] *adj* groß; [person] korpulent. ◆ **at large** ⟨⟩ *adj*: **to be at ~** [prisoner] auf freiem Fuß sein; [animal] frei herumlaufen ⟨⟩ *adv* [as a whole]: **society/the world at ~** die ganze Gesellschaft/Welt.

largely ['lɑːdʒlɪ] *adv* zum größten Teil.

lark [lɑːk] *n* **- 1.** [bird] Lerche *die* **- 2.** *inf* [joke] Jux *der*. ◆ **lark about** *vi* herumalbern.

laryngitis [,lærɪn'dʒaɪtɪs] *n (U)* Kehlkopfentzündung *die*.

lasagna, lasagne [lə'zænjə] *n (U)* Lasagne *pl*.

laser ['leɪzəʳ] *n* Laser *der*.

laser printer *n* Laserdrucker *der*.

lash [læʃ] ⟨⟩ *n* **- 1.** [eyelash] Wimper *die* **- 2.** [blow with whip] Peitschenhieb *der* ⟨⟩ *vt* **- 1.** [whip as punishment] auspeitschen **- 2.** [subj: wind, rain, waves] peitschen gegen **- 3.** [tie]: **to ~ sthg to sthg** etw an etw *(D)* festlbinden. ◆ **lash out** *vi* **- 1.** [physically] um sich schlagen; **to ~ out at** OR **against sb** (auf jn) einlschlagen OR loslschlagen **- 2.** [verbally]: **to ~ out at** OR **against sb** Schimpftiraden auf jn losllassen, jn beschimpfen.

lass [læs] *n* Mädel *das*.

lasso [læ'suː] (*pl* -s) ⟨⟩ *n* Lasso *das* ⟨⟩ *vt* mit dem Lasso einlfangen.

last [lɑːst] ⟨⟩ *adj* letzte, -r, -s; **~ Tuesday** letzten Dienstag; **~ but one** vorletzte, -r, -s; **that's the ~ thing I want** das ist das Letzte, was ich will ⟨⟩ *adv* zuletzt ⟨⟩ *pron*: **to be the ~ to arrive/sit down**/*etc* als Letzte(r) anlkommen/sich hinlsetzen/*etc*; **I'm always the ~ to be told** ich bin immer der Letzte, der etwas erfährt; **to leave sthg till ~** etw bis zuletzt auflschieben; **the Saturday before ~** vorletzten Samstag; **the ~ but one** der/die/

das Vorletzte <> n [final thing]: **the ~ I saw/ heard of him** das Letzte, was ich von ihm sah/hörte <> vi - **1.** [continue to exist or function] dauern; [shoes] halten; [luck, feeling] an|halten - **2.** [keep fresh] sich halten - **3.** [be enough for]: **this will ~ a week** das wird für eine Woche reichen. ◆ **at (long) last** adv endlich.

last-ditch adj allerletzte, -r, -s.

lasting ['lɑːstɪŋ] adj [peace] dauerhaft; [effect, mistrust] anhaltend.

lastly ['lɑːstlɪ] adv zum Schluss.

last-minute adj in letzter Minute; [flight, ticket] Last-Minute-.

last name n Familienname der.

latch [lætʃ] n Riegel der. ◆ **latch onto** vt fus inf [idea] ab|fahren auf; [person] sich hängen an.

late [leɪt] <> adj - **1.** [not on time]: **to be ~** [person] zu spät dran sein; [train, bus] Verspätung haben; **to be ~ for sthg** zu etw zu spät kommen - **2.** [near end of]: **in the ~ evening/afternoon/morning** am späten Abend/Nachmittag/Vormittag; **he arrived in ~ December** er kam Ende Dezember - **3.** [later than normal] spät - **4.** [deceased] verstorben - **5.** [former] vorige <> adv - **1.** [not on time]: **to arrive (20 minutes) ~** [bus, train] (20 Minuten) Verspätung haben; [person] (20 Minuten) zu spät kommen - **2.** [later than normal, near end of period] spät; **~ in the afternoon** am späten Nachmittag; **~ in August** Ende August; **I worked ~** ich habe lange gearbeitet. ◆ **of late** adv in letzter Zeit.

latecomer ['leɪtˌkʌmə'] n Zuspätkommende,der, die.

lately ['leɪtlɪ] adv in letzter Zeit.

latent ['leɪtənt] adj latent vorhanden.

later ['leɪtə'] <> adj später <> adv: **~ (on)** später.

lateral ['lætərəl] adj seitlich.

latest ['leɪtɪst] <> adj [most recent] neueste, -r, -s <> n: **at the ~** spätestens.

lather ['lɑːðə'] <> n [Seifen]schaum der <> vt ein|seifen.

Latin ['lætɪn] <> adj [studies, student] Latein- <> n [language] Latein(ische) das.

Latin America n Lateinamerika nt.

Latin American adj lateinamerikanisch.

latitude ['lætɪtjuːd] n GEOGR Breite die.

latter ['lætə'] <> adj - **1.** [later - years] spätere; **in the ~ part of the century** in der zweiten Hälfte des Jahrhunderts - **2.** [second] zweite, -r, -s; [opposed to former] letzte, -r, -s <> n: **the ~** der/die/das Letztere.

lattice ['lætɪs] n Gitter das.

Latvia ['lætvɪə] n Lettland nt.

laudable ['lɔːdəbl] adj lobenswert.

laugh [lɑːf] <> n - **1.** [sound] Lachen das - **2.** inf [fun, joke] Spaß der; **to do sthg for ~s** OR **a ~** etw aus OR zum Spaß machen <> vi lachen. ◆ **laugh at** vt fus [mock] sich lustig machen über (+ A). ◆ **laugh off** vt sep [dismiss] mit einem Lachen ab|tun.

laughable ['lɑːfəbl] adj pej lächerlich.

laughingstock ['lɑːfɪŋstɒk] n Zielscheibe die des Spotts.

laughter ['lɑːftə'] n Gelächter das.

launch [lɔːntʃ] <> n - **1.** [of new ship] Stapellauf der - **2.** [into air - of missile] Abschuss der - **3.** [start] Beginn der - **4.** COMM [of new book, product] Lancieren das - **5.** [boat] Barkasse die <> vt - **1.** [into water - boat] zu Wasser lassen; [- new ship] vom Stapel lassen - **2.** [into air - space rocket, satellite] in den Weltraum schießen; [- missile] abschießen - **3.** [start - campaign] beginnen; **to ~ an attack** einen Angriff durch|führen - **4.** COMM [new book, product] lancieren.

launch(ing) pad ['lɔːntʃ(ɪŋ)-] n [for rocket, missile, satellite] Abschussrampe die.

launder ['lɔːndə'] vt - **1.** [clothes] waschen und bügeln - **2.** inf [money] waschen.

laund(e)rette ['lɔːndəræt], **Laundromat®** Am n Waschsalon der.

laundry ['lɔːndrɪ] n - **1.** (U) [clothes] Wäsche die - **2.** [business] Wäscherei die.

laurel ['lɒrəl] n Lorbeer der.

lava ['lɑːvə] n Lava die.

lavatory ['lævətrɪ] n Toilette die.

lavender ['lævəndə'] n [plant] Lavendel der.

lavish ['lævɪʃ] <> adj - **1.** [generous] großzügig; **to be ~ with sthg** [with money, time] mit etw großzügig sein - **2.** [sumptuous - decoration] aufwendig; [- banquet] üppig <> vt: **to ~ sthg on sb** [praise, attention, money] jn mit etw förmlich überhäufen.

law [lɔː] n - **1.** [legislation, rule, natural or scientific principle] Gesetz das; **to become ~** rechtskräftig werden; **to break the ~** das Gesetz brechen; **against the ~** gesetzeswidrig; **~ and order** Recht und Ordnung - **2.** (U) [legal system]: **(the) ~** das Recht - **3.** [subject studied] Jura.

law-abiding [-əˌbaɪdɪŋ] adj gesetzestreu.

law court n Gericht das.

lawful ['lɔːfʊl] adj fml rechtmäßig.

lawn [lɔːn] n Rasen der.

lawnmower ['lɔːnˌməʊə'] n Rasenmäher der.

lawn tennis n Rasentennis das.

law school n juristische Fakultät.

lawsuit ['lɔːsuːt] n Klage die.

lawyer ['lɔːjə'] n (Rechts)anwalt der, -anwältin die.

lax [læks] adj lax; [discipline] lasch; [behaviour] locker.

laxative ['læksətɪv] n Abführmittel das.

lay [leɪ] (pt & pp laid) <> pt ⊳ lie <> vt - **1.** [in specified position] legen - **2.** [prepare - trap, snare] auf|stellen; **to ~ the table** den Tisch decken - **3.** [carpet, cable, pipes] verlegen; [bricks, foundations] legen - **4.** [egg] legen - **5.: to ~ the blame (for sthg) on sb** jm die Schuld (für etw) geben; **to ~ emphasis on sthg** Wert auf etw (A) legen ◇ adj - **1.** RELIG Laien- - **2.** [untrained, unqualified] laienhaft; **~ person** Laie der. ◆ **lay aside** vt sep - **1.** [save - food, money] zur Seite legen - **2.** [knitting, book] weglegen. ◆ **lay down** vt sep - **1.** [regulations] auflstellen - **2.** [arms, tools] niederllegen. ◆ **lay off** ◇ vt sep [workers] entlassen ◇ vt fus inf - **1.** [leave alone] in Ruhe lassen - **2.** [stop, give up]: **to ~ off alcohol/cigarettes** mit dem Trinken/Rauchen aufhören. ◆ **lay on** vt sep Br [provide, supply] sorgen für. ◆ **lay out** vt sep - **1.** [clothes, tools, ingredients] bereitlegen - **2.** [garden, house, town] planen.

layabout ['leɪəbaʊt] n Br inf Faulenzer der.

lay-by (pl -s) n Br [small] Parkbucht die; [large] Rastplatz der.

layer ['leɪəʳ] n - **1.** [of substance, material] Schicht die - **2.** fig [level] Ebene die.

layman ['leɪmən] (pl -men [-mən]) n RELIG & fig Laie der.

layout ['leɪaʊt] n [of house] Raumaufteilung die; [of garden] Anlage die; [of text] Layout das.

laze [leɪz] vi: **to ~ (about** OR **around)** faulenzen.

lazy ['leɪzɪ] adj - **1.** [person] faul - **2.** [action] träge.

lazybones ['leɪzɪbəʊnz] (pl inv) n Faulpelz der.

lb abbr of pound.

LCD (abbr of liquid crystal display) n LCD; **~ display** LCD-Anzeige die.

lead¹ [liːd] (pt & pp led) ◇ n - **1.** (U) [winning position] Führung die; **to be in** OR **have the ~** in Führung liegen - **2.** [amount ahead] Vorsprung der - **3.** (U) [initiative, example]: **to take the ~** [do sthg first] mit gutem Beispiel voranlgehen; **I followed his ~** ich folgte seinem Beispiel - **4.** (U) [stage or film role]: **the ~** die Hauptrolle - **5.** [clue] Anhaltspunkt der - **6.** [for dog] Leine die - **7.** [wire, cable] Kabel das ◇ adj [most important]: **~ singer** Leadsänger der, -in die; **~ actor** Hauptdarsteller der; **~ story** Leitartikel der ◇ vt - **1.** [procession, parade] anlführen - **2.** [person, existence] führen - **3.** [team, investigation] leiten - **4.** [political party] führen - **4.** [strike, campaign] organisieren - **5.** [cause, influence]: **to ~ sb to do sthg** jn veranlassen, etw zu tun ◇ vi - **1.** [go] führen - **2.** [give access to]: **to ~ to/ into sthg** zu etw/in etw (A) führen - **3.** [be winning] führen - **4.** [result in]: **to ~ to sthg** zu etw führen. ◆ **lead up to** vt fus - **1.** [precede]: **the events that led up to the disaster** die Ereignisse, die der Katastrophe vorausgingen - **2.** [in conversation - topic] zulsteuern

auf (+ A); **what are you ~ing up to?** worauf willst du hinaus?

lead² [led] ◇ n - **1.** [metal] Blei das - **2.** [in pencil] Mine die ◇ comp Blei-.

leaded ['ledɪd] adj [petrol] verbleit.

leader ['liːdəʳ] n - **1.** [head - of organization] Leiter der, -in die; [- of political party] Vorsitzende der, die; [- of gang] Anführer der, -in die - **2.** [in race, competition] Führende der, die; **to be the ~** in Führung liegen - **3.** Br [in newspaper] Leitartikel der.

leadership ['liːdəʃɪp] n [position, people in charge] Führung die; [quality] Führungsqualitäten pl.

lead-free [led-] adj bleifrei.

leading ['liːdɪŋ] adj [prominent] führend.

leading light n herausragende Persönlichkeit.

leaf [liːf] (pl leaves) n - **1.** [of tree, plant, book] Blatt das - **2.** [of table] Platte die (zur Vergrößerung eines Tisches). ◆ **leaf through** vt fus durchlblättern.

leaflet ['liːflɪt] n Broschüre die; [commercial] Prospekt der; [political] Flugblatt das.

league [liːg] n - **1.** [group - of people, countries] Bündnis das; **to be in ~ with sb** mit jm verbündet sein - **2.** SPORT Liga die.

leak [liːk] ◇ n - **1.** [in pipe, tank, roof] undichte Stelle; [in boat] Leck das - **2.** [disclosure]: **there has been a ~** es ist etwas durchgesickert ◇ vt [make known] durchsickern lassen ◇ vi [pipe, tank, roof, shoe] undicht sein; [boat] lecken; [gas] auslströmen; [liquid] auslaufen; **to ~ (out) from sthg** aus etw auslströmen/auslaufen. ◆ **leak out** vi [news, secret] auslsickern.

lean [liːn] (pt & pp leant OR -ed) ◇ adj - **1.** [person - thin] dünn; [- slim] schlank - **2.** [meat, harvest, year] mager ◇ vt: **to ~ sthg against sthg** etw gegen OR an etw (A) lehnen ◇ vi - **1.** [bend, slope - person] sich beugen; [- wall] sich neigen; **to ~ forward** sich vorlbeugen - **2.** [rest]: **to ~ on/against sthg** sich an etw (A)/gegen etw lehnen. ◆ **lean back** vi sich zurückllehnen.

leaning ['liːnɪŋ] n: **~ (towards sthg)** Neigung die (zu etw).

leant [lent] pt & pp ▷ lean.

lean-to (pl -s) n angebauter Schuppen.

leap [liːp] (pt & pp leapt OR -ed) ◇ n - **1.** [jump] Sprung der - **2.** [increase] sprunghafter Anstieg ◇ vi [jump] springen.

leapfrog ['liːpfrɒg] ◇ n (U) Bockspringen das ◇ vt fig überlspringen.

leapt [lept] pt & pp ▷ leap.

leap year n Schaltjahr das.

learn [lɜːn] (pt & pp -ed OR learnt) ◇ vt - **1.** [acquire knowledge, skill of] (er)lernen; **to ~ (how) to cook/read/etc** kochen/lesen/etc lernen - **2.** [memorize] (auswendig) lernen - **3.** [hear] erfahren; **to ~ that ...** erfahren, dass ... ⬦ vi - 1. [acquire knowledge, skill] lernen - 2. [hear]: to ~ of OR about sthg von etw erfahren.

learned ['lɜːnɪd] adj - 1. [person] gelehrt - 2. [journal, paper, book] wissenschaftlich.

learner ['lɜːnəʳ] n: she's a quick ~ sie lernt schnell; ~s of English Englischlerner pl.

learner (driver) n Fahrschüler der, -in die.

learning ['lɜːnɪŋ] n (U) [process] Lernen das; [knowledge] Wissen das; [result] Gelehrsamkeit die.

learnt [lɜːnt] pt & pp ⬦ learn.

lease [liːs] ⬦ n LAW [of premises] Pacht die; [contract] Pachtvertrag der; [of car] Leasing das; [contract] Leasingvertrag der ⬦ vt [premises - to sb] verpachten; [- car] leasen; [- from sb] pachten; [- car] leasen.

leasehold ['liːshəʊld] adj [property] Pacht-.

leash [liːʃ] n (Hunde)leine die.

least [liːst] (superl of **little**) ⬦ adj wenigste, -r, -s; he earns the ~ money er verdient am wenigsten ⬦ pron: (the) ~ das Wenigste; it's the ~ I can do das ist das Mindeste, was ich tun kann; not in the ~ nicht im Geringsten; to say the ~ gelinde gesagt ⬦ adv am wenigsten. ◆ at least adv wenigstens. ◆ least of all adv am allerwenigsten.

leather ['leðəʳ] ⬦ n Leder das ⬦ comp Leder-.

leave [liːv] (pt & pp **left**) ⬦ vt - 1. [gen] verlassen; ~ the door open lass die Tür offen; let's ~ it at that lassen wir es dabei - 2. [not take away] lassen - 3. [not use, not eat] übrig lassen - 4. [a mark, scar, message, in will] hinterlassen; to ~ one's money to sb jm sein Geld hinterlassen - 5. [space, gap] lassen - 6. [entrust] überlassen; he left it to her to decide er hat ihr die Entscheidung überlassen; ⬦ left vi [go] gehen; [train, bus] abfahren ⬦ n (U) - 1. [time off work] Urlaub der; on ~ auf Urlaub - 2. fml [permission] Erlaubnis die. ◆ leave behind vt sep zurücklassen. ◆ leave out vt sep auslassen.

leave of absence n Urlaub der.

leaves [liːvz] pl ⬦ leaf.

Lebanon ['lebənən] n Libanon der.

lecherous ['letʃərəs] adj lüstern.

lecture ['lektʃəʳ] ⬦ n - 1. [talk - at university] Vorlesung die; [- at conference] Vortrag der - 2. [criticism, reprimand] Strafpredigt die ⬦ vt [scold]: to ~ sb jm eine Strafpredigt halten ⬦ vi [give talk]: to ~ (on/in sthg) eine Vorlesung/einen Vortrag (über etw (A)) halten.

lecturer ['lektʃərəʳ] n - 1. [teacher] Dozent der, -in die - 2. [speaker] Redner der, -in die.

led [led] pt & pp ⬦ lead¹.

ledge [ledʒ] n [of window - outside] Fenstersims der; [- inside] Fensterbrett das.

ledger ['ledʒəʳ] n Hauptbuch das.

leek [liːk] n: a ~ eine Stange Lauch.

leer [lɪəʳ] ⬦ n lüsterner Blick ⬦ vi: to ~ at sb jm einen lüsternen Blick zuwerfen.

leeway ['liːweɪ] n [room to manoeuvre] Spielraum der.

left [left] ⬦ pt & pp ⬦ leave ⬦ adj - 1. [remaining] übrig; to be ~ übrig geblieben sein - 2. [side, hand, foot] linke, -r, -s ⬦ adv links ⬦ n [direction]: on the ~ auf der linken Seite; to the ~ [position] auf der linken Seite; [movement] auf die linke Seite; keep to the ~! sich links halten! ◆ Left n POL: the Left die Linke.

left-hand adj linke, -r, -s; the ~ side die linke Seite.

left-hand drive adj mit Linkssteuer.

left-handed [-'hændɪd] adj [person] linkshändig.

left luggage (office) n Br Gepäckaufbewahrung die.

leftover ['leftəʊvəʳ] adj übrig geblieben. ◆ leftovers npl Reste pl.

left wing n POL linker Flügel. ◆ left-wing adj POL linke, -r, -s.

leg [leg] n - 1. [gen] Bein das; to pull sb's ~ jn auf den Arm nehmen - 2. CULIN [of chicken] Schenkel der; [of lamb, pork] Keule die - 3. [of journey] Etappe die; [of tournament] Runde die.

legacy ['legəsɪ] n - 1. [gift of money] Erbschaft die - 2. fig [consequence] Erbe das.

legal ['liːgl] adj - 1. [concerning the law - system] Rechts-; [- advice] juristisch; the ~ profession die Juristenschaft - 2. [lawful] legal.

legalize, -ise ['liːgəlaɪz] vt legalisieren.

legal tender n (U) legales Zahlungsmittel.

legend ['ledʒənd] n - 1. [myth] Sage die - 2. fig [person] Legende die.

leggings ['legɪŋz] npl Leggings pl.

legible ['ledʒəbl] adj lesbar.

legislation [ˌledʒɪs'leɪʃn] n (U) [laws] Gesetze pl.

legislature ['ledʒɪsleɪtʃəʳ] n Legislative die.

legitimate [lɪ'dʒɪtɪmət] adj - 1. [government] rechtmäßig; [business, action] legal - 2. [argument] stichhaltig; [complaint, question] berechtigt - 3. [child] ehelich.

legroom ['legrʊm] n Beinfreiheit die.

leg-warmers [-ˌwɔːməz] npl Legwärmer pl.

leisure [Br 'leʒəʳ, Am 'liːʒəʳ] n Freizeit die; do it at (your) ~ machen Sie es, wenn Sie Zeit haben.

leisure centre n Freizeitzentrum das.

leisurely [Br 'leʒəlɪ, Am 'liːʒəʳlɪ] adj & adv gemächlich.

leisure time n Freizeit die.

lemon ['lemən] n [fruit] Zitrone die.

lemonade [ˌlemə'neɪd] n - 1. Br [fizzy] Limonade die - 2. [made with fresh lemons] Zitronensaftgetränk (aus Zitronen, Zucker und Wasser bestehend).

lemon juice *n (U)* Zitronensaft *der*.

lemon sole *n* Seezunge *die*.

lemon squash *n (U) Br* Zitronengetränk *das*.

lemon squeezer [-ˌskwiːzəʳ] *n* Zitronenpresse *die*.

lemon tea *n* Zitronentee *der*.

lend [lend] *(pt & pp* lent) *vt* - **1.** [money, book]: **to ~ sb sthg, to ~ sthg to sb** jm etw leihen; **I don't like ~ing money** ich verleihe nicht gerne Geld - **2.** [support, assistance]: **to ~ one's support to sb** jn unterstützen; **to ~ one's assistance to sb** jm helfen - **3.** [credibility, quality]: **to ~ sthg to sb/sthg** jm/einer Sache etw verleihen.

lending rate ['lendɪŋ-] *n* Darlehenszinssatz *der*.

length [leŋθ] *n* - **1.** [gen] Länge *die*; **in ~** in der Länge, lang - **2.** [whole distance]: **we walked the ~ of the street** wir gingen die ganze Straße entlang - **3.** [of swimming pool] Länge *die* - **4.** [of string, wood, cloth] Stück *das* - **5.** *phr*: **he went to great ~s to achieve his goal** er tat alles Mögliche, um sein Ziel zu erreichen. ◆ **at length** *adv* - **1.** [eventually] endlich - **2.** [in detail] ausführlich.

lengthen ['leŋθən] ◇ *vt* verlängern ◇ *vi* länger werden.

lengthways ['leŋθweɪz] *adv* der Länge nach, längs.

lengthy ['leŋθɪ] *adj* lang, langwierig; [stay, visit] ausgedehnt; [discussions] langwierig.

lenient ['liːnɪənt] *adj* [person] nachsichtig; [verdict, sentence] mild.

lens [lenz] *n* - **1.** PHOT & ANAT Linse *die*; [of glasses] Glas *das* - **2.** [contact lens] Kontaktlinse *die*.

lent [lent] *pt & pp* ▷ lend.

Lent [lent] *n* Fastenzeit *die*.

lentil ['lentɪl] *n* Linse *die*.

Leo ['liːəʊ] *n* Löwe *der*.

leopard ['lepəd] *n* Leopard *der*.

leotard ['liːətɑːd] *n einteiliger Anzug für Artisten und Showtänzer*.

leper ['lepəʳ] *n* Leprakranke *der, die*.

leprosy ['leprəsɪ] *n* Lepra *die*.

lesbian ['lezbɪən] *n* Lesbe *die*, Lesbierin *die*.

less [les] *(compar of* little) ◇ *adj* weniger; **~ ... than** weniger ... als; **of ~ value** von geringerem Wert ◇ *pron* weniger; **~ than 20** weniger als 20 ◇ *adv* weniger; **~ and ~** immer weniger ◇ *prep* [minus] weniger; **purchase price - 10%** Kaufpreis abzüglich 10%.

lessen ['lesn] ◇ *vt* [risk, chances, effect] verringern; [pain] lindern ◇ *vi* nachlassen.

lesser ['lesəʳ] *adj* geringer; **to a ~ extent** OR **degree** in geringerem Umfang.

lesson ['lesn] *n* - **1.** [class] (Unterrichts)stunde *die* - **2.** [example]: **to teach sb a ~** jm eine Lektion erteilen.

let [let] *(pt & pp* let) *vt* - **1.** [allow] lassen; **to ~ sb do sthg** jn etw tun lassen; **she ~ her hair grow** sie ließ sich *(D)* die Haare wachsen; **to ~ go of sthg** etw loslassen; **to ~ sthg go** [release] jn loslassen; **to ~ o.s. go** [neglect] sich gehen lassen; **to ~ sb have sthg** [permanently] jm etw überlassen; **he wouldn't ~ me have the book** er wollte mir das Buch nicht geben; **to ~ sb know sthg** jn etw wissen lassen; **~ me know as soon as possible** sagen Sie mir so bald wie möglich Bescheid - **2.** [in verb forms]: **~'s go!** gehen wir!; **~ me see** lass mich überlegen - **3.** [rent out] vermieten; **'to ~'** 'zu vermieten'. ◆ **let alone** *conj* geschweige denn. ◆ **let down** *vt sep* - **1.** [person - disappoint] enttäuschen; [- not help] im Stich lassen - **2.** [let air out of]: **to ~ sb's tyres down** jm die Luft aus den Reifen lassen. ◆ **let in** *vt sep* hereinlassen; **to ~ o.s. in for sthg** sich auf etw *(A)* einlassen; **to ~ sb in on sthg** [secret, plan] jn in etw *(A)* einweihen. ◆ **let off** *vt sep* - **1.** [excuse] davonkommen lassen - **2.** [from vehicle] aussteigen lassen - **3.** [cannon, missile] abfeuern; [firework] loslassen. ◆ **let on** *vi*: **to ~ on about sthg** etw verraten. ◆ **let out** *vt sep* heraus-/hinauslassen; **~ me out!** lass mich heraus!; **to ~ out a scream** einen Schrei ausstoßen. ◆ **let up** *vi* nachlassen.

letdown ['letdaʊn] *n inf* Enttäuschung *die*.

lethal ['liːθl] *adj* tödlich.

lethargic [lə'θɑːdʒɪk] *adj* träge, lethargisch.

let's [lets] = let us.

letter ['letəʳ] *n* - **1.** [written message] Brief *der* - **2.** [of alphabet] Buchstabe *der*.

letter bomb *n* Briefbombe *die*.

letterbox ['letəbɒks] *n Br* Briefkasten *der*.

lettuce ['letɪs] *n* Kopfsalat *der*.

letup ['letʌp] *n* Nachlassen *das*.

leuk(a)emia [luː'kiːmɪə] *n* Leukämie *die*.

level ['levl] ◇ *adj* - **1.** [equal in height]: **to be ~ (with sthg)** (mit etw) auf gleicher Höhe sein - **2.** [equal in standard] ebenbürtig - **3.** [flat] waagerecht; [teaspoon] gestrichen ◇ *n* - **1.** [amount - gen] Niveau *das*; [- of noise] Pegel *der*; [- of temperature] Höhe *die* - **2.** [of liquid] Stand *der* - **3.** [standard] Niveau *das* - **4.** *Am* [spirit level] Wasserwaage *die* - **5.** [storey] Geschoss *das*; [of multistorey car park] Ebene *die* - **6.** *phr*: **to be on the ~** *inf* ehrlich sein ◇ *vt* - **1.** [make flat] ebnen - **2.** [demolish] dem Erdboden gleichmachen. ◆ **level off, level out** *vi* - **1.** [unemployment, inflation] aufhören zu steigen - **2.** AERON [aircraft] abfangen. ◆ **level with** *vt fus inf* ehrlich sein mit.

level crossing *n Br* ebener Bahnübergang.

level-headed [-'hedɪd] *adj* vernünftig.

lever [*Br* 'liːvəʳ, *Am* 'levər] *n* [handle, bar] Hebel *der*.

leverage [*Br* 'liːvərɪdʒ, *Am* 'levərɪdʒ] *n (U)*

- 1. fig [influence] Einfluss der **- 2.** [principle] Hebelwirkung die; [force] Hebelkraft die.

levy ['levɪ] (pl **levies**) ⟨⟩ n: **~ (on sthg)** Steuer die (auf etw (A)) ⟨⟩ vt erheben.

lewd [lju:d] adj [joke, song] unanständig; [remark] anzüglich.

liability [ˌlaɪə'bɪlətɪ] n **- 1.** [hindrance] Belastung die **- 2.** LAW [legal responsibility]: **~ (for sthg)** Haftung die (für etw). ⟜ **liabilities** npl FIN Verbindlichkeiten pl, Schulden pl.

liable ['laɪəbl] adj **- 1.** [likely]: **to be ~ to do sthg** die Neigung haben, etw zu tun **- 2.** [prone]: **to be ~ to sthg** für etw anfällig OR empfänglich sein **- 3.** LAW: **to be ~ (for sthg)** [debt, accident, damage] (für etw) verantwortlich sein; **to be ~ to sthg** [fine, arrest, imprisonment] für etw haftbar sein.

liaise [lɪ'eɪz] vi: **to ~ with** Kontakt aufnehmen mit; **to ~ between** als Verbindungsperson agieren zwischen (+ D).

liar ['laɪə] n Lügner der, -in die.

libel ['laɪbl] ⟨⟩ n (schriftliche) Verleumdung ⟨⟩ vt (schriftlich) verleumden.

liberal ['lɪbərəl] adj **- 1.** [tolerant] liberal **- 2.** [generous] großzügig. ⟜ **Liberal** POL ⟨⟩ adj liberal ⟨⟩ n Liberale der, die.

Liberal Democrat ⟨⟩ adj liberaldemokratisch ⟨⟩ n Liberaldemokrat der, -in die.

liberate ['lɪbəreɪt] vt befreien.

liberation [ˌlɪbə'reɪʃn] n Befreiung die.

liberty ['lɪbətɪ] n Freiheit die; **at ~** auf freiem Fuß; **you are at ~ to leave** es steht dir frei zu gehen; **to take liberties (with sb)** sich (D) (jm gegenüber) Freiheiten herausInehmen.

Libra ['li:brə] n Waage die.

librarian [laɪ'breərɪən] n Bibliothekar der, -in die.

library ['laɪbrərɪ] n Bibliothek die.

library book n Leihbuch das.

libretto [lɪ'bretəʊ] (pl **-s**) n Libretto das.

Libya ['lɪbɪə] n Libyen nt.

lice [laɪs] pl ⟹ **louse**.

licence ['laɪsns] ⟨⟩ n **- 1.** [permit - for dog] Genehmigung die; [- for TV] Anmeldung die; [- for driver] Führerschein der; [- for marriage] Erlaubnis die, Lizenz die; [- for bar, pub] Konzession die; [- for pilot] Pilotenschein der **- 2.** COMM Lizenz die ⟨⟩ vt Am = license.

license ['laɪsns] ⟨⟩ vt COMM: **to ~ sb to do sthg** jm eine Lizenz erteilen, etw zu tun; **to ~ sthg** eine Lizenz OR Konzession für etw erteilen ⟨⟩ n Am = licence.

licensed ['laɪsnst] adj **- 1.** [person]: **to be ~ to do sthg** die Genehmigung haben, etw zu tun **- 2.** [object] zugelassen **- 3.** Br [premises] mit Schankerlaubnis OR Schankkonzession.

license plate n Am Nummernschild das.

lick [lɪk] vt [with tongue] lecken.

licorice ['lɪkərɪs] n = liquorice.

lid [lɪd] n **- 1.** [cover] Deckel der **- 2.** [eyelid] Augenlid das.

lie [laɪ] (pt sense 1 **lied**; pt senses 2-5 **lay**; pp sense 1 **lied**; pp senses 2-5 **lain**; cont all senses **lying**) ⟨⟩ n Lüge die; **to tell ~s** lügen ⟨⟩ vi **- 1.** [tell lie] lügen; **to ~ to sb** jn anlügen; **to ~ about sthg** über etw (A) nicht die Wahrheit sagen **- 2.** [be horizontal, be situated] liegen; **to ~ in wait for sb** jm aufIauern; **to ~ idle** [machine] stillstehen **- 3.** [lie down] sich legen **- 4.** [difficulty, answer, responsibility etc] liegen **- 5.** phr: **to ~ low** sich versteckt halten. ⟜ **lie about, lie around** vi herumIliegen. ⟜ **lie down** vi sich hinIlegen. ⟜ **lie in** vi Br im Bett bleiben.

lie-down n Br Nickerchen das; **to have a ~** sich (kurz) hinIlegen.

lie-in n Br: **to have a ~** richtig ausIschlafen.

lieutenant [Br lef'tenənt, Am lu:'tenənt] n [in army] Oberleutnant der; [in navy] Kapitänleutnant der.

life [laɪf] (pl **lives**) n **- 1.** [gen] Leben das; **to come to ~** zum Leben erwachen; **that's ~!** so ist das Leben!; **he was sent to prison for ~** er wurde zu einer lebenslänglichen Haftstrafe verurteilt; **to scare the ~ out of sb** jn zu Tode erschrecken **- 2.** inf [life imprisonment] lebenslängliche Freiheitsstrafe; **to get ~** inf lebenslänglich kriegen.

life assurance n = life insurance.

life belt n Rettungsring der.

lifeboat ['laɪfbəʊt] n Rettungsboot das.

life buoy n Rettungsboje die.

life cycle n Lebenszyklus der.

life expectancy [-ɪk'spektənsɪ] n Lebenserwartung die.

lifeguard ['laɪfgɑ:d] n Rettungsschwimmer der, -in die.

life insurance n Lebensversicherung die.

life jacket n Schwimmweste die.

lifeless ['laɪflɪs] adj leblos.

lifelike ['laɪflaɪk] adj lebensecht.

lifeline ['laɪflaɪn] n **- 1.** [rope] Rettungsleine die **- 2.** fig [with outside] Verbindung die mit der Außenwelt.

life preserver [-prɪˌzɜ:vər] n Am **- 1.** [belt] Rettungsring der **- 2.** [jacket] Schwimmweste die, Rettungsweste die.

life raft n Rettungsfloß das.

lifesaver ['laɪfˌseɪvər] n Lebensretter der.

life sentence n lebenslange Freiheitsstrafe.

life-size(d) [-saɪz(d)] adj lebensgroß.

lifespan ['laɪfspæn] n **- 1.** [of person, animal] Lebenserwartung die **- 2.** [of product, machine] Lebensdauer die.

lifestyle ['laɪfstaɪl] n Lebensstil der.

lifetime ['laɪftaɪm] n Lebenszeit die.

lift [lɪft] ⟨⟩ n **- 1.** [ride]: **to give sb a ~** jn (im Auto) mitlnehmen **- 2.** Br [elevator] Fahrstuhl der ⟨⟩ vt **- 1.** [hand, arm, leg] heben **- 2.** [object] hochlheben - **3**. [ban, embargo] auflheben - **4**. [plagiarize - idea] stehlen; [- writing] ablschreiben - **5**. *inf* [steal] klauen ⬦ *vi* - **1**. [lid, top] sich heben - **2**. [mist, fog, clouds] sich lichten.

lift-off *n* Abheben *das*.

light [laɪt] (*pt & pp* lit OR -ed) ⬦ *adj* - **1**. [gen] leicht - **2**. [pale, bright] hell; **~ blue** hellblau ⬦ *n* - **1**. (*U*) [brightness] Licht *das* - **2**. [device - lamp] Lampe *die*; [- on car] Scheinwerfer *der*; [- in street] Laterne *die*; **to put** OR **turn the ~ on** das Licht einlschalten - **3**. [for cigarette, pipe] Feuer *das*; **to set ~ to sthg** etw anlzünden - **4**. [perspective]: **in the ~ of** *Br*, **in ~ of** *Am* angesichts (+ *G*) - **5**. *phr*: **to come to ~** ans Licht kommen ⬦ *vt* - **1**. [ignite] anlzünden - **2**. [illuminate] erleuchten ⬦ *adv*: **to travel ~** mit wenig Gepäck reisen.
◆ **light up** ⬦ *vt sep* - **1**. [sky, room, stage] erleuchten - **2**. [cigarette, cigar, pipe] anlzünden ⬦ *vi* - **1**. [face, eyes] aufleuchten - **2**. *inf* [start smoking] sich (*D*) eine anlzünden.

light bulb *n* Glühbirne *die*.

lighten [laɪtn] ⬦ *vt* - **1**. [make brighter - gen] heller machen; [- hair] aufhellen - **2**. [make less heavy - load] leichter machen; [- workload] erleichtern ⬦ *vi* [mood, atmosphere] lockerer OR entspannter werden.

lighter [laɪtə^r] *n* Feuerzeug *das*.

light-headed [-hedɪd] *adj* schwindlig.

light-hearted [-hɑːtɪd] *adj* - **1**. [cheerful] heiter, unbeschwert - **2**. [amusing] fröhlich.

lighthouse [laɪthaʊs, *pl* -haʊzɪz] *n* Leuchtturm *der*.

lighting [laɪtɪŋ] *n* Beleuchtung *die*.

light meter *n* PHOT Belichtungsmesser *der*.

lightning [laɪtnɪŋ] *n* (*U*) Blitz *der*.

lightweight [laɪtweɪt] ⬦ *adj* [object] leicht ⬦ *n* Leichtgewicht *das*; **political ~s** Schmalspurpolitiker *pl*.

likable [laɪkəbl] *adj* sympathisch.

like [laɪk] ⬦ *prep* wie; **~ this/that** so; **what's it ~?** wie ist es?; **to look ~ sb/sthg** jm/etw ähnlich sehen; **it looks ~ rain** es sieht nach Regen aus ⬦ *vt* mögen; **to ~ doing sthg** etw gern tun; **do you ~ it?** gefällt es dir?; **as you ~** wie Sie wollen/wie du willst; **I don't ~ to bother her** ich will sie nicht stören; **I'd ~ to sit down** ich würde mich gern hinsetzen; **I'd ~ a drink** ich würde gern etwas trinken; **we'd ~ you to come for dinner** wir möchten Sie zum Essen einladen ⬦ *n*: **and the ~** und dergleichen.

likeable [laɪkəbl] *adj* = likable.

likelihood [laɪklɪhʊd] *n* Wahrscheinlichkeit *die*.

likely [laɪklɪ] *adj* - **1**. [probable] wahrscheinlich; **they're ~ to win** sie werden wahrscheinlich gewinnen; **a ~ story!** *iron* na klar! - **2**. [suitable] geeignet.

liken [laɪkn] *vt*: **to ~ sb/sthg to** jn/etw vergleichen mit.

likeness [laɪknɪs] *n* - **1**. [resemblance]: **~ (to sb/sthg)** Ähnlichkeit *die* (mit jm/etw) - **2**. [portrait] Bildnis *die*, Porträt *das*.

likewise [laɪkwaɪz] *adv* gleichfalls, ebenfalls; **to do ~** das Gleiche tun.

liking [laɪkɪŋ] *n*: **~ for sb/sthg** Vorliebe *die* für jn/etw; **to have a ~ for sb/sthg** für jn/etw eine Vorliebe haben; **that's not to my ~** das ist nicht nach meinem Geschmack.

lilac [laɪlək] ⬦ *adj* [colour] lila ⬦ *n* - **1**. [tree] Flieder *der* - **2**. [colour] Lila *das*.

Lilo® [laɪləʊ] (*pl* -s) *n Br* Luftmatratze *die*.

lily [lɪlɪ] *n* Lilie *die*.

limb [lɪm] *n* - **1**. [of body] Glied *das*; **~s** Glieder *pl*, Gliedmaßen *pl* - **2**. [of tree] Ast *der*.

limber [lɪmbə^r] ◆ **limber up** *vi* sich auflockern, Lockerungsübungen machen.

limbo [lɪmbəʊ] (*pl* -s) *n* [uncertain state]: **to be in ~** in der Schwebe sein.

lime [laɪm] *n* - **1**. [fruit] Limone *die*; **~ juice** Limonensaft *der* - **2**. [linden tree] Linde *die*.

limelight [laɪmlaɪt] *n*: **the ~** das Rampenlicht.

limerick [lɪmərɪk] *n* Limerick *der*.

limestone [laɪmstəʊn] *n* Kalkstein *der*.

limit [lɪmɪt] ⬦ *n* - **1**. [restriction] Begrenzung *die* - **2**. [boundary, greatest extent] Grenze *die*; **'off ~s'** *esp Am* 'Zutritt verboten'; **that subject is off ~s** das Thema ist tabu; **within ~s** [to a certain extent] innerhalb bestimmter Grenzen ⬦ *vt* begrenzen.

limitation [ˌlɪmɪteɪʃn] *n* - **1**. [restriction, control] Begrenzung *die* - **2**. [shortcoming]: **~s** Grenzen *pl*.

limited [lɪmɪtɪd] *adj* begrenzt.

limited company, limited liability company *n* Gesellschaft *die* mit beschränkter Haftung.

limousine [lɪməziːn] *n* luxuriöse Limousine.

limp [lɪmp] ⬦ *adj* schlaff; [lettuce, flowers] welk ⬦ *n* Hinken *das*; **to walk with a ~** hinken ⬦ *vi* hinken.

line [laɪn] ⬦ *n* - **1**. [mark] Linie *die*; **to draw the ~ at sthg** *fig* bei etw den Schlussstrich ziehen - **2**. [row] Reihe *die* - **3**. [queue] Schlange *die*; **to stand** OR **wait in ~** Schlange stehen OR anstehen - **4**. [direction of movement] Gerade *die*; **he can't walk in a straight ~** er kann nicht (mehr) geradeaus gehen - **5**. [alignment]: **in ~ (with)** in einer Linie (mit); **to step out of ~** [misbehave] aus der Reihe tanzen - **6**. [RAIL - railway track] Gleise *pl*; [- route] Bahnlinie *die*; **the ~ was blocked** die Strecke war blockiert - **7**. [of poem, song, text] Zeile *die* - **8**. [wrinkle] Falte *die* - **9**. [rope] Leine *die*; [wire] Kabel *das*; [string] Schnur *die* - **10**. TELEC [telephone connection] Leitung *die*; **hold the ~** bleiben Sie am Apparat - **11**. *inf* [short letter] kurze Nachricht; **to drop sb a ~** jm ein paar Zeilen schreiben **- 12.** *inf* [field of activity] Branche *die* **- 13.** MIL: **enemy ~s** feindliche Linien **- 14.** [limit, borderline] Grenze *die* **- 15.** COMM [type of product] Modell *das*; [group of products] Kollektion *die* ⬦ *vt* [cover inside surface of - drawer] ausschlagen; [- garment, curtains] füttern. ➡ **out of line** *adj* fehl am Platz. ➡ **line up** ⬦ *vt sep* **- 1.** [in rows] aufstellen **- 2.** *inf* [organize] arrangieren ⬦ *vi* **- 1.** [in a row] sich aufstellen **- 2.** [in a queue] sich anstellen.

lined [laɪnd] *adj* **- 1.** [paper] liniert **- 2.** [face] faltig.

linen ['lɪnɪn] *(U) n (U)* **- 1.** [cloth] Leinen *das* **- 2.** [tablecloths] Wäsche *die*.

liner ['laɪnə'] *n* [ship] Linienschiff *das*.

linesman ['laɪnzmən] *(pl* -men [-mən]) *n* SPORT Linienrichter *der*.

linger ['lɪŋgə'] *vi* **- 1.** [dawdle]: **we ~ed over our meal** wir gaben in aller Gemütlichkeit; **she ~ed behind after school** sie blieb nach Schulschluss noch da **- 2.** [persist] zurückbleiben.

lingo ['lɪŋgəʊ] *(pl* -es) *n inf* **- 1.** [language] Sprache *die* **- 2.** [specialist jargon] (Fach)jargon *der*.

linguist ['lɪŋgwɪst] *n* **- 1.** [person good at languages] Sprachkundige *der, die* **- 2.** [student or teacher of linguistics] Linguist *der,* -in *die*.

lining ['laɪnɪŋ] *n* **- 1.** [of garment, curtains, box] Futter *das* **- 2.** [of stomach, nose] Schleimhaut *die* **- 3.** *(U)* AUT [of brakes] Belag *der*.

link [lɪŋk] ⬦ *n* **- 1.** [of chain] Glied *das* **- 2.** [connection]: **~ (between/with)** Verbindung *die* (zwischen (+ *D*)/mit OR zu) ⬦ *vt* verbinden; **to ~ arms with sb** sich bei jm unterhaken. ➡ **link up** *vt sep* verbinden; **to ~ sthg up with sthg** etw mit etw verbinden.

lino ['laɪnəʊ], **linoleum** [lɪ'nəʊlɪəm] *n* Linoleum *das*.

lion ['laɪən] *n* Löwe *der*.

lip [lɪp] *n* **- 1.** [of mouth] Lippe *die* **- 2.** [of container] Rand *der*.

lip-read *vi* von den Lippen lesen.

lip salve [-sælv] *n Br* Lippenbalsam *der*.

lip service *n*: **to pay ~ to sthg** ein Lippenbekenntnis zu etw ablegen.

lipstick ['lɪpstɪk] *n* Lippenstift *der*.

liqueur [lɪ'kjʊə'] *n* Likör *der*.

liquid ['lɪkwɪd] ⬦ *adj* flüssig ⬦ *n* Flüssigkeit *die*.

liquidation [ˌlɪkwɪ'deɪʃn] *n* Liquidation *die*.

liquidize, -ise ['lɪkwɪdaɪz] *vt Br* CULIN mit dem Mixer pürieren.

liquidizer, -iser ['lɪkwɪdaɪzə'] *n Br* (elektrischer) Mixer.

liquor ['lɪkə'] *n esp Am* [alcoholic drink] Alkohol *der*; [spirits] Spirituosen *pl*.

liquorice ['lɪkərɪʃ, 'lɪkərɪs] *n* Lakritze *die*.

liquor store *n Am* Wein- und Spirituosenhandlung *die*.

Lisbon ['lɪzbən] *n* Lissabon *nt*.

lisp [lɪsp] ⬦ *n* Lispeln *das* ⬦ *vi* lispeln.

list [lɪst] ⬦ *n* Liste *die* ⬦ *vt* **- 1.** [in writing] auflisten **- 2.** [in speech] aufführen.

listed building [ˌlɪstɪd-] *n Br* unter Denkmalschutz stehendes Gebäude.

listen ['lɪsn] *vi* **- 1.** [give attention] zuhören; **to ~ to sb/sthg** jm/etw zuhören; **to ~ for sthg** auf etw *(A)* horchen **- 2.** [heed advice] hören; **to ~ to sb/sthg** auf jn/etw hören.

listener ['lɪsnə'] *n* Zuhörer *der,* -in *die*; [of radio] Hörer *der,* -in *die*.

listless ['lɪstlɪs] *adj* apathisch.

lit [lɪt] *pt & pp* ▷ **light**.

liter *n Am* = litre.

literacy ['lɪtərəsɪ] *n (U)* Lese- und Schreibfähigkeit *die*.

literal ['lɪtərəl] *adj* wörtlich.

literally ['lɪtərəlɪ] *adv* **- 1.** [for emphasis] im wahrsten Sinne des Wortes, buchstäblich **- 2.** [not figuratively] wörtlich.

literary ['lɪtərərɪ] *adj* literarisch; **a ~ critic** ein Literaturkritiker.

literate ['lɪtərət] *adj* **- 1.** [able to read and write] des Lesens und Schreibens kundig **- 2.** [well-read] gebildet.

literature ['lɪtrətʃə'] *n* **- 1.** [novels, plays, poetry] Literatur *die* **- 2.** [printed information] Informationsmaterial *das*.

lithe [laɪð] *adj* geschmeidig.

Lithuania [ˌlɪθjʊ'eɪnɪə] *n* Litauen *nt*.

litigation [ˌlɪtɪ'geɪʃn] *n (U) fml* Prozess *der*.

litre *Br*, **liter** *Am* ['liːtə'] *n* Liter *der*.

litter ['lɪtə'] ⬦ *n* **- 1.** [waste material] Abfall *der* **- 2.** [newborn animals] Wurf *der* **- 3.** [for litter tray]: **(cat) ~** (Katzen)streu *die* ⬦ *vt*: **to be ~ed with sthg** mit etw übersät sein.

litterbin ['lɪtəˌbɪn] *n Br* Mülleimer *der*.

little ['lɪtl] *(compar sense 3* less; *superl sense 3* least) ⬦ *adj* **- 1.** [small, younger] klein; **the ~ ones** die Kleinen *pl* **- 2.** [in distance, time] kurz **- 3.** [not much] wenig; **he speaks ~ English** er spricht wenig Englisch; **he speaks a ~ English** er spricht ein bisschen Englisch ⬦ *pron* wenig; **a ~** ein bisschen ⬦ *adv* wenig; **~ by ~** nach und nach; **as ~ as possible** so wenig wie möglich.

little finger *n* kleiner Finger.

live¹ [lɪv] ⬦ *vi* **- 1.** [have home] wohnen **- 2.** [be alive] leben; **to ~ to a great age** ein hohes Alter erreichen **- 3.** [survive] überleben ⬦ *vt* führen; **to ~ a happy life** ein glückliches Leben führen; **to ~ it up** *inf* in Saus und Braus leben. ➡ **live down** *vt sep*: **she'll never ~ this down** das wird ihr auf ewig anhängen. ➡ **live off** *vt fus* [savings, land] leben von. ➭ **live on** ⬦ *vt fus* [savings] leben von; [food] sich ernähren von; **I have enough to ~ on** ich habe genug zum Leben ⬦ *vi* [continue] weiterlleben. ➭ **live together** *vi* zusammenlwohnen. ➭ **live up to** *vt fus* [reputation] gerecht werden (+ *D*); [expectations] entsprechen (+ *D*). ➭ **live with** *vt fus* - **1.** [in same house] zusammenlwohnen mit - **2.** *inf* [problem, situation] sich abllfinden mit.

live² [laɪv] *adj* - **1.** [alive] lebendig - **2.** [programme, performance] Live-; ELEC [wire] gelalden - **3.** [ammunition] scharf.

livelihood ['laɪvlɪhʊd] *n* Lebensunterhalt *der.*

lively ['laɪvlɪ] *adj* lebhaft.

liven ['laɪvn] ➭ **liven up** ⬦ *vt sep* beleben ⬦ *vi* [person] auflleben.

liver ['lɪvə'] *n* Leber *die.*

lives [laɪvz] *pl* ⟾ life.

livestock ['laɪvstɒk] *n* Nutzvieh *das.*

livid ['lɪvɪd] *adj inf* [angry] wütend.

living ['lɪvɪŋ] ⬦ *adj* - **1.** [person] lebend - **2.** [language] lebendig ⬦ *n* - **1.** [means of earning money] Lebensunterhalt *der;* **what do you do for a ~?** was machen Sie beruflich? - **2.** [lifestyle] Leben *das.*

living conditions *npl* Lebensbedingungen *pl.*

living room *n* Wohnzimmer *das.*

living standards *npl* Lebensstandard *der.*

living wage *n* zum Leben ausreichender Lohn.

lizard ['lɪzəd] *n* Eidechse *die.*

llama ['lɑːmə] (*pl inv* OR -s) *n* Lama *das.*

load [ləʊd] ⬦ *n* - **1.** [something carried] Ladung *die* - **2.** [large amount]: **~s of, a ~ of** *inf* eine Menge; **what a ~ of rubbish!** *inf* was für ein Blödsinn! ⬦ *vt* - **1.** [container, vehicle] beladen; **to ~ sthg with sthg** etw mit etw beladen - **2.** [gun, cannon]: **to ~ sthg (with sthg)** etw (mit etw) laden - **3.** [camera]: **to ~ a camera with a film** einen Film in eine Kamera einllegen - **4.** COMPUT [program] laden. ➭ **load up** ⬦ *vt sep* beladen ⬦ *vi* auflladen.

loaded ['ləʊdɪd] *adj* - **1.** [question, statement] gewichtig - **2.** [gun] geladen; [camera] mit eingelegtem Film - **3.** *inf* [rich] stinkreich.

loaf [ləʊf] (*pl* loaves) *n* Laib *der.*

loan [ləʊn] ⬦ *n* - **1.** [money lent] Darlehen *das,* Kredit *der* - **2.** [act of lending] Ausleihen *das;* **on ~** ausgeliehen ⬦ *vt:* **to ~ sthg (to sb),** **to ~ (sb) sthg** etw (jm) verleihen.

loath [ləʊθ] *adj:* **to be ~ to do sthg** etw nur ungern tun.

loathe [ləʊð] *vt* verabscheuen; **to ~ doing sthg** es verabscheuen, etw zu tun.

loaves [ləʊvz] *pl* ⟾ loaf.

lob [lɒb] ⬦ *n* TENNIS Lob *der* ⬦ *vt* - **1.** [throw] (in hohem Bogen) werfen - **2.** TENNIS lobben.

lobby ['lɒbɪ] ⬦ *n* - **1.** [anteroom] Vorraum *der;* [in hotel] Empfangshalle *die;* [in theatre] Foyer *das* - **2.** [pressure group] Lobby *die* ⬦ *vt* Einfluss nehmen auf (+ *A*).

lobe [ləʊb] *n* [of ear] Ohrläppchen *das.*

lobster ['lɒbstə'] *n* Hummer *der.*

local ['ləʊkl] ⬦ *adj* - **1.** [of the immediate area - tradition, hospital, shop, inhabitants] örtlich; [- phone call] Orts- - **2.** ADMIN & POL [services, council] Kommunal- ⬦ *n inf* - **1.** [person]: **the ~s** die Einheimischen *pl* - **2.** *Br* [pub] Stammkneipe *die.*

📖 **local**

Das Wort local als Substantiv kann im Englischen zwar eine Gaststätte bezeichnen, entspricht dann aber nicht dem deutschen Wort „Lokal", sondern bedeutet „Stammkneipe". Our local is just around the corner heißt auf Deutsch „Unsere Stammkneipe ist gleich um die Ecke".
Personen, die als locals bezeichnet werden, sind „Einheimische". Only locals go to that bar hieße auf Deutsch in etwa: „In diese Kneipe gehen nur Einheimische".
Wenn mit dem deutschen „Lokal" eine Kneipe gemeint ist, lautet die zutreffende Übersetzung pub oder bar; handelt es sich um eine Speisegaststätte, spricht man von einem restaurant.

---

local authority *n Br* Kommunalverwaltung *die.*

local call *n* Ortsgespräch *das.*

local government *n* Kommunalverwaltung *die.*

locality [ləʊˈkælətɪ] *n* Gegend *die.*

localized, -ised ['ləʊkəlaɪzd] *adj* örtlich begrenzt.

locally ['ləʊkəlɪ] *adv* [in region] am Ort; [in neighbourhood] in der Nachbarschaft.

locate [*Br* ləʊˈkeɪt, *Am* 'ləʊkeɪt] *vt* - **1.** [find] ausfindig machen, lokalisieren - **2.** [situate]: **to be ~d** sich befinden.

location [ləʊˈkeɪʃn] *n* - **1.** [place] Ort *der* - **2.** CINEMA: **the film was shot on ~ in China** die Außenaufnahmen zu diesem Film wurden in China gemacht.

loch [lɒk, lɒx] *n Scot* See *der.*

lock [lɒk] ⬦ *n* - **1.** [of door, window, box] Schloss *das* - **2.** [on canal] Schleuse *die* - **3.** AUT [steering lock] Einschlag *der* - **4.** [of hair] Locke *die* ⬦ *vt* - **1.** [fasten securely] abllschließen; [bicycle] anllschließen - **2.** [keep safely]: **to ~ sthg in sthg** etw in etw (*A*) einllschließen - **3.** [immobilize] sperren ⬦ *vi* - **1.** [fasten securely] verschließen - **2.** [become immobilized] blockieren. ➭ **lock away** *vt sep* weglschließen. ➭ **lock in** *vt* *sep* einlschließen. ◆ **lock out** *vt sep* auslsperren. ◆ **lock up** *vt sep* - **1.** [person] einlsperren - **2.** [house] ablschließen - **3.** [valuables] weglschließen.

locker ['lɒkə'] *n* [at gym, work] Spind *der*; [at station] Schließfach *das*.

locker room *n Am* Umkleideraum *der*.

locket ['lɒkɪt] *n* Medaillon *das*.

locomotive [ˌləʊkə'məʊtɪv] *n* Lokomotive *die*.

locust ['ləʊkəst] *n* Heuschrecke *die*.

lodge [lɒdʒ] ◇ *n* - **1.** [caretaker's room, of Freemasons] Loge *die* - **2.** [of manor house] Pförtnerhaus *das* - **3.** [for hunting] Jagdhütte *die* ◇ *vi* - **1.** [stay, live]: **to ~ with sb** bei jm (zur Untermiete) wohnen - **2.** [become stuck] steckenlbleiben - **3.** *fig* [in mind] sich festlsetzen ◇ *vt fml* [register] einlreichen.

lodger ['lɒdʒə'] *n* Untermieter *der*, -in *die*.

lodging ['lɒdʒɪŋ] *n* ➭ **board**. ◆ **lodgings** *npl* möblierte Zimmer *pl*.

loft [lɒft] *n* Dachboden *der*.

lofty ['lɒftɪ] *adj* - **1.** [noble] hoch; [feelings] erhaben; [aims] hoch gesteckt - **2.** *pej* [haughty] hochmütig - **3.** *literary* [high] hoch.

log [lɒg] ◇ *n* - **1.** [of wood] Holzscheit *das* - **2.** [written record of ship] Logbuch *das*; [- of plane] Bordbuch *das* ◇ *vt* - **1.** [information - on paper] einltragen; [- in computer] einlgeben - **2.** [speed, distance, time] zurückllegen. ◆ **log in** *vi* COMPUT (sich) einlloggen. ◆ **log out** *vi* COMPUT (sich) auslloggen.

logbook ['lɒgbʊk] *n* [of car] Fahrtenbuch *das*.

loggerheads ['lɒgəhedz] *n*: **to be at ~** sich (D) in den Haaren liegen.

logic ['lɒdʒɪk] *n* Logik *die*.

logical ['lɒdʒɪkl] *adj* logisch.

logistics [lə'dʒɪstɪks] *n* (U) Logistik *die*.

logo ['ləʊgəʊ] (*pl* -s) *n* Logo *das*.

loin [lɔɪn] *n* Lende *die*.

loiter ['lɔɪtə'] *vi* - **1.** [hang about] herumllungern - **2.** [dawdle] trödeln, bummeln.

loll [lɒl] *vi* [sit, lie about] (sich) lümmeln, herumllümmeln.

lollipop ['lɒlɪpɒp] *n* Lutscher *der*, Lolli *der*.

lollipop lady *n Br meist* ältere Dame in der Funktion eines Schülerlotsen.

lollipop man *n Br meist* älterer Herr in der Funktion eines Schülerlotsen.

lolly ['lɒlɪ] *n* [lollipop] Lutscher *der*, Lolli *der*.

London ['lʌndən] *n* London *nt*.

Londoner ['lʌndənə'] *n* Londoner *der*, -in *die*.

lone [ləʊn] *adj* [lonely] einsam; [only] einzig.

loneliness ['ləʊnlɪnɪs] *n* Einsamkeit *die*.

lonely ['ləʊnlɪ] *adj* einsam.

loner ['ləʊnə'] *n* Einzelgänger *der*, -in *die*.

lonesome ['ləʊnsəm] *adj Am inf* einsam.

long [lɒŋ] ◇ *adj* lang; **it's 2 metres ~** es ist 2 Meter lang; **it's two hours ~** es dauert zwei Stunden; **the book is 500 pages ~** das Buch hat 500 Seiten; **how ~ is it?** [in distance] wie lang ist es?; [in time] wie lange dauert es?; **a ~ time ago** *adv* lange; **I won't be ~** ich komme gleich wieder; **how ~ will it take?** wie lange dauert es?; **all day ~** den ganzen Tag; **before ~** bald; **no ~er** nicht mehr; **so ~!** *inf* tschüs! ◇ *vt*: **to ~ to do sthg** sich danach sehnen, etw zu tun. ◆ **as long as, so long as** *conj* [if] solange. ◆ **long for** *vt fus* sich sehnen nach.

long-distance *adj*: **a ~ race** ein Langstreckenrennen; **he's a ~ lorry driver** er ist Fernfahrer.

long-distance call *n* Ferngespräch *das*.

longhand ['lɒŋhænd] *n* Langschrift *die*.

long-haul *adj*: **~ flight** Langstreckenflug *der*.

longing ['lɒŋɪŋ] ◇ *adj* sehnsüchtig ◇ *n*: **~ (for sthg)** Sehnsucht *die* (nach etw).

longitude ['lɒndʒɪtju:d] *n* GEOGR (geografische) Länge.

long jump *n* Weitsprung *der*.

long-life *adj* [battery] mit langer Lebensdauer; **~ milk** H-Milch *die*.

long-range *adj* - **1.** [missile, bomber] Langstrecken- - **2.** [plan, forecast] langfristig.

long shot *n fig*: **it's a ~, but it might work** es ist ein gewagtes Unternehmen, aber es könnte klappen.

longsighted [ˌlɒŋ'saɪtɪd] *adj* weitsichtig.

long-standing *adj* (schon) lange bestehend.

longsuffering [ˌlɒŋ'sʌfərɪŋ] *adj* geduldig.

long term *n*: **in the ~** auf lange Sicht.

long wave *n* Langwelle *die*.

longwinded [ˌlɒŋ'wɪndɪd] *adj* langatmig.

loo [lu:] (*pl* -s) *n Br inf* Klo *das*.

look [lʊk] ◇ *n* - **1.** [with eyes] Blick *der*; **to give sb a ~** jm einen Blick zulwerfen; **to have a ~ at sthg** sich (D) etw anlsehen; **let me have a ~!** lass mich mal sehen! - **2.** [search]: **to have a ~ (for sthg)** (etw) suchen - **3.** [appearance] Aussehen *das*; **by the ~ OR ~s of it** allem Anschein nach ◇ *vi* - **1.** [with eyes] sehen; **to ~ at sb/sthg** jn/etw anlsehen; **I'm just ~ing** [in shop] ich wollte mich nur umsehen - **2.** [search] suchen - **3.** [building, room]: **to ~ onto** gehen auf (+ A) - **4.** [seem] auslsehen; **he ~s as if he hasn't slept** er sieht aus, als hätte er nicht geschlafen; **it ~s like rain** es sieht nach Regen aus; **she ~s like her mother** sie sieht ihrer Mutter ähnlich. ◆ **looks** *npl*: **(good) ~s** gutes Aussehen. ◆ **look after** *vt fus* [take care of] sich kümmern um. ◆ **look at** *vt fus* anlsehen; **he ~ed at his watch** er sah OR schaute auf seine Uhr. ◆ **look down on** *vt fus* [condescend to] herablsehen auf (+ A). ◆ **look for** *vt fus* suchen. **look forward to** *vt fus* sich freuen auf (+ A). **look into** *vt fus* [examine] untersuchen. **look on** *vi* [watch] zulsehen. **look out** *vi* auflpassen; ~ **out!** Vorsicht! **look out for** *vt fus* [person, place] Ausschau halten nach; [opportunity] suchen nach. **look round** <> *vt fus* [city, museum] besichtigen; **to ~ round the shops** einen Einkaufsbummel machen <> *vi* - **1.** [look at surroundings] sich umlsehen - **2.** [turn] sich umldrehen. **look to** *vt fus* - **1.** [depend on] sich verlassen auf (+ A); **they ~ed to her for help** sie verließen sich darauf, dass sie ihnen helfen würde - **2.** [think about] planen. **look up** <> *vt* - **1.** [in dictionary] nachlschlagen; [in phone book] herauslsuchen - **2.** [visit]: **to ~ sb up** jn auflsuchen <> *vi* sich bessern. **look up to** *vt fus* [admire]: **to ~ up to sb** zu jm auflsehen.

lookout ['lukaut] *n* - **1.** [place] Ausguck *der* - **2.** [person] Wachposten *der* - **3.** [search]: **to be on the ~ for sthg** nach etw Ausschau halten.

loom [lu:m] *vi* - **1.** [rise up] (plötzlich) aufltauchen - **2.** *fig* [be imminent - date] bevorlstehen; [- threat, difficulties] sich ablzeichnen.

loony ['lu:nɪ] *inf* <> *adj* bekloppt, verrückt <> *n* Bekloppte *der, die*, Verrückte *der, die*.

loop [lu:p] *n* - **1.** [shape] Schleife *die*, Schlinge *die* - **2.** [contraceptive] Spirale *die*.

loophole ['lu:phəul] *n fig* Schlupfloch *das*.

loose [lu:s] *adj* - **1.** [not firmly fixed - joint, tooth, handle] lose, locker - **2.** [unpackaged - sweets, nails, paper] lose - **3.** [not tightfitting - clothes, fit] locker sitzend, leger - **4.** [animal - free, not restrained] frei laufend; [- which has escaped] entlaufen; [hair] offen - **5.** [translation, definition] frei.

loose change *n* Kleingeld *das*.

loose end *n*: **to be at a ~** *Br*, **to be at ~s** *Am* nichts zu tun haben.

loosely ['lu:slɪ] *adv* - **1.** [hold, connect, tie] locker - **2.** [translate, define] frei.

loosen ['lu:sn] *vt* lockern. **loosen up** *vi* - **1.** [before game, race] sich auflwärmen - **2.** *inf* [relax] sich entspannen.

loot [lu:t] <> *n* Beute *die* <> *vt* auslplündern, auslrauben.

looting ['lu:tɪŋ] *n* Plündern *das*.

lop [lɒp] **lop off** *vt sep* ablschneiden.

lop-sided [-'saɪdɪd] *adj* [uneven] schief.

lord [lɔ:d] *n Br* Lord *der*. **Lord** *n* - **1.** RELIG: **the Lord** [God] der Herr; **good Lord!** *Br* Grundgütiger!, oh mein Gott! - **2.** [in titles] Lord *der*. **Lords** *npl Br* POL: **the (House of) Lords** das Oberhaus.

lorry ['lɒrɪ] *n Br* Lastkraftwagen *der*.

lorry driver *n Br* Lastkraftwagenfahrer *der*.

lose [lu:z] (*pt & pp* lost) <> *vt* - **1.** [gen] verlieren; **to ~ sight of sb/sthg** jn/etw aus den

Augen verlieren; **to ~ one's way** sich verirren - **2.** [waste - time] verschwenden; [- opportunity] versäumen - **3.** [subj: clock, watch] nachlgehen - **4.** [pursuers] ablschütteln <> *vi* verlieren. **lose out** *vi*: **to ~ out (on sthg)** (bei etw) den Kürzeren ziehen.

loser ['lu:zə'] *n* - **1.** [of competition] Verlierer *der*, -in *die* - **2.** *pej* [unsuccessful person] Loser *der*.

loss [lɒs] *n* - **1.** [gen] Verlust *der*; **to make a ~** Verlust machen - **2.** [of match, competition] Niederlage *die* - **3.** *phr*: **I'm at a ~ to explain it** ich weiß nicht, wie ich es erklären soll; **he was at a ~ for words** ihm fehlten die Worte.

lost [lɒst] <> *pt & pp* >> lose <> *adj* - **1.** [unable to find way] verirrt; **to get ~** sich verirren, sich verlieren; **get ~!** *inf* verschwinde!, hau ab! - **2.** [keys, wallet] verloren.

lost-and-found office *n Am* Fundbüro *das*.

lost property office *n Br* Fundbüro *das*.

lot [lɒt] *n* - **1.** [large amount]: **a ~ of**, **~s of** eine Menge - **2.** *inf* [group of things]: **put this ~ in my office** bring das hier in mein Büro - **3.** [destiny] Los *das* - **4.** [at auction] Posten *der* - **5.** [entire amount]: **the ~** alles, das Ganze - **6.** *Am* [of land] Parzelle *die*; [car park] Stellfläche *die*, Parkplatz *der* - **7.** *phr*: **to draw ~s** losen. **a lot** *adv* (sehr) viel.

lotion ['ləuʃn] *n* Lotion *die*.

lottery ['lɒtərɪ] *n* - **1.** [raffle] Lotterie *die* - **2.** [risky venture] Glücksspiel *das*.

loud [laud] <> *adj* - **1.** [not quiet, noisy] laut - **2.** [garish] grell <> *adv* laut; **out ~** laut.

loudhailer [,laud'heɪlə'] *n Br* Megafon *das*.

loudly ['laudlɪ] *adv* [noisily] laut.

loudspeaker [,laud'spi:kə'] *n* Lautsprecher *der*.

lounge [laundʒ] <> *n* - **1.** [in house] Wohnzimmer *das* - **2.** [in airport, hotel] Lounge *die* - **3.** *Br* = lounge bar <> *vi* sich lümmeln.

lounge bar *n Br* abgetrennter, meist gemütlicherer Teil eines Pubs, in dem die Getränke teurer sind.

louse [laus] (*pl sense 1* lice; *pl sense 2* -s) *n* - **1.** [insect] Laus *die* - **2.** *fig* [person] Laus *die*.

lousy ['lauzɪ] *adj inf* [poor-quality] lausig.

lout [laut] *n* Flegel *der*, Lümmel *der*.

lovable ['lʌvəbl] *adj* liebenswert.

love [lʌv] <> *n* - **1.** [gen] Liebe *die*; **a ~ of OR for sthg** eine Liebe zu OR für etw; **give her my ~** grüße sie herzlich von mir; **~ from** [at end of letter] alles Liebe von; **to be in ~ (with sb)** verliebt sein; **to fall in ~ (with sb)** sich (in jn) verlieben; **to make ~** miteinander schlafen - **2.** *inf* [term of address] Schatz *der* - **3.** TENNIS Null <> *vt* - **1.** [gen] lieben; **to do sthg OR doing sthg** etw sehr OR wahnsinnig gern tun.

love affair *n* Affäre *die*.

love life *n* Liebesleben *das*.

lovely ['lʌvlɪ] *adj* - **1.** [in looks - child] reizend; [- person] sehr hübsch; [in character] reizend - **2.** [good, nice] wunderschön; **it was ~ to meet you** es war sehr nett, Sie kennen zu lernen.

lover ['lʌvə] n - **1.** [sexual partner] Geliebte der, die - **2.** [enthusiast]: **a ~ of** ein Liebhaber, eine Liebhaberin (+ G).

loving ['lʌvɪŋ] adj liebevoll.

low [ləʊ] <> adj - **1.** [gen] niedrig; **to keep a ~ profile** sich unauffällig benehmen - **2.** [standard, quality, opinion] schlecht - **3.** [level, sound, note, neckline] tief - **4.** [light, heat] schwach - **5.** [supplies] knapp - **6.** [voice] leise - **7.** [depressed] niedergeschlagen <> adv [fly, bend, sink] tief <> n - **1.** [low point] Tiefstand der - **2.** [area of low pressure] Tief das.

low-calorie adj kalorienarm.

low-cut adj tief ausgeschnitten.

lower ['ləʊə] <> adj untere, -r, -s; [lip] Unter-; - **leg** Unterschenkel der <> vt - **1.** [move downwards - drawbridge, car window] herunterlassen; [- flag] einholen; [- head, eyes] senken - **2.** [reduce] senken; [resistance] schwächen - **3.** [voice]: **to ~ one's voice** leiser sprechen.

low-fat adj fettarm.

low-key adj [negotiations] informell; [approach] zurückhaltend.

low-lying adj tief gelegen.

loyal ['lɔɪəl] adj: **to be ~ to sb** [friend, supporter] jm treu sein; [king, boss] gegenüber jm loyal sein.

loyalty ['lɔɪəltɪ] n [of friend, supporter] Treue die; [to government] Loyalität die.

lozenge ['lɒzɪndʒ] n [tablet] Pastille die.

LP (abbr of long-playing record) n LP die.

L-plate n Br Schild mit einem L, welches anzeigt, dass der Fahrer des Wagens Fahrschüler ist.

Ltd, ltd (abbr of limited) GmbH.

lubricant ['lu:brɪkənt] n Schmiermittel das.

lubricate ['lu:brɪkeɪt] vt schmieren.

luck [lʌk] n: **(good)** ~ Glück das; **good ~!** viel Glück!; **bad** ~ Pech das; **bad ~!, hard ~!** so ein Pech!; **to be in** ~ Glück haben; **with (any)** ~ mit (ein bisschen) Glück.

wishing good luck

Hals- und Beinbruch! Best of luck!
Halt die Ohren steif! Keep smiling!
Viel Glück. Good luck.
Toi, toi, toi. All the very best.
Ich drücke dir die Daumen. I'll keep my fingers crossed for you.

luckily ['lʌkɪlɪ] adv glücklicherweise.

lucky ['lʌkɪ] adj - **1.** [fortunate] glücklich; **to be ~** Glück haben; **it was a ~ guess** das war gut geraten - **2.** [bringing good luck] Glück bringend; [number] Glücks-.

lucrative ['lu:krətɪv] adj lukrativ.

ludicrous ['lu:dɪkrəs] adj lächerlich.

lug [lʌg] vt inf schleppen.

luggage ['lʌgɪdʒ] n Br Gepäck das.

luggage rack n Br (in train) Gepäckablage die; [on car] Dachgepäckträger der.

lukewarm ['lu:kwɔ:m] adj - **1.** [tepid] lauwarm - **2.** [unenthusiastic] lau.

lull [lʌl] <> n Pause die; **a ~ in the fighting** eine Kampfpause <> vt - **1.** [make sleepy]: **to ~ sb to sleep** jn in den Schlaf lullen - **2.** [reassure]: **to ~ sb into a false sense of security** jn in Sicherheit wiegen.

lullaby ['lʌləbaɪ] n Schlaflied das.

lumber ['lʌmbə] n (U) - **1.** Am [timber] Bauholz das - **2.** Br [bric-a-brac] Gerümpel das.
◆ **lumber with** vt sep Br inf: **to ~ sb with sthg** jm etw aufhalsen.

lumberjack ['lʌmbədʒæk] n Holzfäller der.

luminous ['lu:mɪnəs] adj [armband] leuchtend; [dial, paint] Leucht-.

lump [lʌmp] <> n - **1.** [piece - of earth, in sauce] Klumpen der; [- of coal, cheese] Stück das - **2.** [MED - bump] Beule die; [- tumour] Knoten der - **3.** [of sugar] Stück das <> vt: **to ~ together** nicht differenziert behandeln; in einen Topf werfen; **you'll just have to ~ it** inf du musst dich damit abfinden.

lump sum n Pauschalbetrag der.

lunacy ['lu:nəsɪ] n Wahnsinn der.

lunar ['lu:nə] adj Mond-.

lunatic ['lu:nətɪk] pej <> adj wahnwitzig <> n Wahnsinnige der, die, Irre der, die.

lunch [lʌntʃ] <> n Mittagessen das; **to have ~** zu Mittag essen <> vi zu Mittag essen.

luncheon meat n Frühstücksfleisch das.

luncheon voucher n Br Essensbon der.

lunch hour n Mittagspause die.

lunchtime ['lʌntʃtaɪm] n Mittagszeit die.

lung [lʌŋ] n Lunge die.

lunge [lʌndʒ] vi: **to ~ forward** nach vorn springen; **to ~ at sb** sich auf jn stürzen.

lurch [lɜ:tʃ] <> n: **to leave sb in the ~** jn im Stich lassen <> vi [person] taumeln; [drunkard] torkeln; [ship] schlingern; [car] sich ruckartig bewegen.

lure [ljʊə] <> n [attraction] Reiz der <> vt [tempt] locken.

lurid ['ljʊərɪd] adj - **1.** [brightly coloured] grell; [clothes] in grellen Farben - **2.** [sensational] reißerisch.

lurk [lɜ:k] vi [person, danger] lauern.

luscious ['lʌʃəs] adj [fruit] saftig.

lush [lʌʃ] adj - **1.** [grass] saftig; [vegetation] üppig - **2.** inf [decorations] üppig.

lust [lʌst] n (U) [sexual desire] (sexuelle) Begierde - **2.** [greed]: ~ **for sthg** Gier die nach etw. ◆ **lust after, lust for** vt fus - **1.** [money, power] gieren nach - **2.** [person] begehren.

Luxembourg ['lʌksəmbɜ:g] n Luxemburg nt.

luxurious [lʌg'ʒʊərɪəs] adj - **1.** [expensive] luxuriös - **2.** [voluptuous] üppig.

luxury ['lʌkʃərɪ] ◇ n Luxus der; [expensive item] Luxusartikel der ◇ comp Luxus-.

LW (abbr of long wave) LW.

Lycra® ['laɪkrə] ◇ n (U) Lycra® das ◇ comp aus Lycra®.

lying ['laɪɪŋ] ◇ adj lügnerisch, verlogen ◇ n [dishonesty] Lügen das.

lynch [lɪntʃ] vt lynchen.

lyric ['lɪrɪk] adj: ~ poetry Lyrik die. ◆ **lyrics** npl [of song] Text der.

lyrical ['lɪrɪkl] adj - 1. [poetic] lyrisch - 2. [enthusiastic]: **to wax ~ about sthg** von etw schwärmen.

M

m¹ (pl m's OR ms), **M** (pl M's OR Ms) [em] n [letter] m das, M das. ◆ **M** Br abbr of motorway.

m² - 1. abbr of metre - 2. abbr of million - 3. abbr of mile.

MA n abbr of Master of Arts.

mac [mæk] n Br inf abbr of mackintosh.

macaroni [,mækə'rəʊnɪ] n (U) Makkaroni pl.

machine [mə'ʃiːn] n - 1. [device] Maschine die - 2. [organization] Apparat der.

machinegun [mə'ʃiːngʌn] n Maschinengewehr das.

machinery [mə'ʃiːnərɪ] n (U) - 1. [machines] Maschinen pl - 2. fig [system] Maschinerie die.

macho ['mætʃəʊ] adj inf machohaft.

mackerel ['mækrəl] (pl inv OR -s) n Makrele die.

mackintosh ['mækɪntɒʃ] n Br Regenmantel der.

mad [mæd] adj - 1. [insane, foolish] verrückt; **to go ~** verrückt werden - 2. [furious] wütend; **to go ~ at sb** auf jn sehr wütend werden - 3. [very enthusiastic]: **to be ~ about sb/sthg** ganz verrückt nach jm/auf etw (A) sein.

madam ['mædəm] n fml [form of address] gnädige Frau.

mad cow disease n Rinderwahnsinn der.

madden ['mædn] vt wahnsinnig machen.

made [meɪd] pt & pp ▷ make.

made-to-measure adj maßgeschneidert.

made-up adj - 1. [face, eyes] geschminkt - 2. [story, excuse] erfunden.

madly ['mædlɪ] adv [frantically] wie verrückt; **to be ~ in love (with sb)** bis über beide Ohren (in jn) verliebt sein.

madman ['mædmən] (pl -men [-mən]) n Verrückte der, Irre der.

madness ['mædnɪs] n Wahnsinn der.

Mafia ['mæfɪə] n: **the ~** die Mafia.

magazine [,mægə'ziːn] n - 1. [periodical] Zeitschrift die, Magazin das - 2. [news programme, of gun] Magazin das.

maggot ['mægət] n Made die.

magic ['mædʒɪk] ◇ adj - 1. [potion, spell, trick] Zauber- - 2. inf [moment, feeling] wundervoll ◇ n - 1. [sorcery] Magie die - 2. [conjuring] Zauberei die - 3. [special quality] Zauber der.

magical ['mædʒɪkl] adj magisch.

magician [mə'dʒɪʃn] n Zauberer der.

magistrate ['mædʒɪstreɪt] n Friedensrichter der, -in die.

magnanimous [mæg'nænɪməs] adj großmütig.

magnate ['mægneɪt] n Magnat der.

magnesium [mæg'niːzɪəm] n Magnesium das.

magnet ['mægnɪt] n lit & fig Magnet der.

magnetic [mæg'netɪk] adj - 1. [force, object] magnetisch - 2. fig: **to have a ~ personality** ein sehr anziehendes Wesen haben.

magnificent [mæg'nɪfɪsənt] adj [building, gown] prächtig; [idea, book] großartig.

magnify ['mægnɪfaɪ] vt [TECH - image] vergrößern; [- sound] verstärken.

magnifying glass ['mægnɪfaɪɪŋ-] n Lupe die.

magnitude ['mægnɪtjuːd] n (U) - 1. [size] Größe die - 2. [importance] Bedeutung die; **a problem of this ~** ein Problem dieser Größenordnung.

magpie ['mægpaɪ] n Elster die.

mahogany [mə'hɒgənɪ] n [wood] Mahagoni das.

maid [meɪd] n [servant] Dienstmädchen das; [in hotel] Zimmermädchen das.

maiden ['meɪdn] ◇ adj [voyage, flight] Jungfern- ◇ n literary [young girl] Maid die.

maiden name n Mädchenname der.

mail [meɪl] ◇ n (U) Post die; **by ~** mit der Post ◇ vt esp Am (mit der Post) (ver)schicken OR senden.

mailbox ['meɪlbɒks] n Am - 1. [for letters] Briefkasten der - 2. COMPUT Mailbox die.

mailing list ['meɪlɪŋ-] n Adressenliste die.

mailman ['meɪlmən] (pl -men [-mən]) n Am Postbote der, Briefträger der.

mail order n Versandhandel der.

mailshot ['meɪlʃɒt] n - 1. [material] Postwurfsendung die - 2. [activity]: **to do a ~** Postwurfsendungen verschicken.

maim [meɪm] vt verstümmeln.

main [meɪn] ◇ adj Haupt- ◇ n Hauptleitung die; **a gas ~** eine Hauptgasleitung. ◆ **mains** npl: **to turn the water/gas off at the ~s** den Haupthahn für das Wasser/Gas abldrehen. ◆ in the main *adv* im Allgemeinen.

main course *n* Hauptgericht *das.*

mainframe (computer) ['meɪnfreɪm] *n* Großrechner *der.*

mainland ['meɪnlənd] ◇ *adj:* ~ Britain das britische Festland ◇ *n:* the ~ das Festland.

mainly ['meɪnlɪ] *adv* hauptsächlich.

main road *n* Hauptstraße *die.*

mainstay ['meɪnsteɪ] *n* [person] wichtigste Stütze; **tourism is the ~ of the economy** der Tourismus ist der Hauptpfeiler der Wirtschaft.

mainstream ['meɪnstriːm] *adj* vorherrschend; [music] Mainstream-.

maintain [meɪn'teɪn] *vt* - 1. [friendship, order, image] aufrecht erhalten - 2. [speed, temperature] beibehalten - 3. [family, children] unterhalten - 4. [vehicle, building] instand halten - 5. [assert - one's innocence] beteuern; **to ~ (that)** ... behaupten, dass ...

maintenance ['meɪntənəns] *n* (U) - 1. [of vehicle, building] Instandhaltung *die* - 2. [paid to ex-wife] Unterhalt *der* - 3. [of law and order] Aufrechterhaltung *die.*

maize [meɪz] *n* Mais *der.*

majestic [mə'dʒestɪk] *adj* majestätisch.

majesty ['mædʒəstɪ] *n* Erhabenheit *die.* ◆ **Majesty** *n:* **His/Her/Your Majesty** Seine/Ihre/Eure Majestät.

major ['meɪdʒər] ◇ *adj* - 1. [important] bedeutend; [problem] : **a ~ operation** eine größere Operation - 2. [main] Haupt- - 3. MUS [key, scale] Dur-; **C - C-Dur** ◇ *n* Major *der.*

majority [mə'dʒɒrətɪ] *n* Mehrheit *die;* **in a** OR **the ~** in der Mehrzahl.

make [meɪk] (*pt & pp* made) ◇ *vt* - 1. [produce] machen; [manufacture] herstellen; **it's made of wood** es ist aus Holz - 2. [prepare] machen; **to ~ lunch** das Mittagessen machen - 3. [perform, do] machen; **to ~ a decision** eine Entscheidung treffen; **to ~ an effort** sich anstrengen; **to ~ a phone call** telefonieren; **to ~ a speech** eine Rede halten - 4. [cause to be] machen; **to ~ sb happy/sad** jn glücklich/ traurig machen; **to ~ sthg into sthg** etw zu etw machen - 5. [cause to do]: **to ~ sb/sthg do sthg** jn/etw dazubringen OR veranlassen, etw zu tun - 6. [force] zwingen; **to ~ sb do sthg** jn zwingen, etw zu tun - 7. [add up to] machen; **that ~s £5** das macht 5 Pfund - 8. [calculate]: **I ~ it 50** ich komme auf 50; **what time do you ~ it?** wie spät hast du? - 9. [earn] verdienen; **to ~ a profit/loss** einen Gewinn/Verlust machen - 10. [reach, be able to attend]: **we didn't ~ the train** wir haben den Zug nicht geschafft - 11. [gain - friend, enemy] machen; **to ~ friends with sb** mit jm Freundschaft schließen - 12. *phr:* **to ~ it** es schaffen; **I won't be able to ~ it tonight** ich schaffe es heute Abend nicht; **to ~ do with**

sthg mit etw auslkommen ◇ *n* [brand] Marke *die.* ◆ **make for** *vt fus* - 1. [move towards] zulhalten auf (+ A) - 2. [contribute to, enable] fördern. ◆ **make of** *vt sep* halten von. ◆ **make off** *vi* sich davonlmachen. ◆ **make out** *vt sep* - 1. *inf* [see] auslmachen; [hear, understand] verstehen - 2. [cheque, receipt] auslstellen; [application form] auslfüllen; [list] auflstellen ◇ *vt fus* [pretend, claim]: **to ~ out (that)** ... vorlgeben, dass ... ◆ **make up** *vt sep* - 1. [compose, constitute] bilden; **to be made up of sthg** aus etw bestehen - 2. [invent] erfinden, sich *(D)* ausldenken; **she made it up** sie hat es erfunden - 3. [face] schminken - 4. [become friends again]: **to ~ up with sb** sich mit jm versöhnen.

make-up *n* (U) - 1. [cosmetics] Make-up *das* - 2. [composition] Beschaffenheit *die;* [of team] Zusammensetzung *die.*

making ['meɪkɪŋ] *n* [of product] Herstellung *die;* [of cake] Backen *das.*

malaria [mə'leərɪə] *n* Malaria *die.*

Malaysia [mə'leɪzɪə] *n* Malaysia *nt.*

male [meɪl] ◇ *adj* - 1. [staff, members] männlich; **~ cat** Kater *der* - 2. [concerning men - problems] Männer-; [- hormone] männlich ◇ *n* - 1. [animal] Männchen *das* - 2. [human] Mann *der.*

malevolent [mə'levələnt] *adj* boshaft; [intention, action] böswillig.

malfunction [mæl'fʌŋkʃn] ◇ *n* Fehlfunktion *die* ◇ *vi* nicht richtig funktionieren.

malice ['mælɪs] *n* Boshaftigkeit *die.*

malicious [mə'lɪʃəs] *adj* boshaft; [act, intention] böswillig.

malign [mə'laɪn] ◇ *adj* [influence] schädlich; [behaviour] Unheil bringend ◇ *vt* verleumden.

malignant [mə'lɪgnənt] *adj* MED bösartig.

mall [mɔːl] *n esp Am:* **(shopping) ~** Einkaufszentrum *das.*

mallet ['mælɪt] *n* [tool] Holzhammer *der.*

malnutrition [ˌmælnjuːˈtrɪʃn] *n* Unterernährung *die.*

malpractice [ˌmælˈpræktɪs] *n* LAW Amtsmissbrauch *der.*

malt [mɔːlt] *n* [grain] Malz *das.*

mammal ['mæml] *n* Säugetier *das.*

mammoth ['mæməθ] ◇ *adj* ungeheuer groß ◇ *n* Mammut *das.*

man [mæn] (*pl* men [men]) ◇ *n* - 1. [gen] Mann *der* - 2. [type]: **he's not a betting ~** er macht sich nicht viel aus Wetten - 3. (U) [human beings] Mensch *der* ◇ *vt* [ship, spaceship] bemannen.

manage ['mænɪdʒ] ◇ *vi* zurechtkommen; **thanks, I can ~!** danke, ich komme schon zurecht! ◇ *vt* - 1. [succeed]: **to ~ to do sthg** es schaffen, etw zu tun - 2. [control - company, organization] leiten; [- popstar, boxer, football team] **managen - 3.** [be available for]: **I could ~ a few hours on Friday** Freitag hätte ich ein paar Stunden Zeit; **I can't ~ four o'clock** vier Uhr schaffe ich nicht.

management ['mænɪdʒmənt] *n* **- 1.** *(U)* [control - of company, organization] Leitung *die* **- 2.** [people in control - of business] Geschäftsführung *die;* [- of operation] Leitung *die.*

manager ['mænɪdʒə'] *n* [of company, shop] Geschäftsführer *der,* -in *die;* [of organization] Leiter *der,* -in *die;* [of popstar, boxer, football team] Manager *der,* -in *die.*

managerial [ˌmænɪˈdʒɪəriəl] *adj* [post] leitend.

mandate ['mændeɪt] *n* **- 1.** [elected right or authority] Mandat *das* **- 2.** [task] Auftrag *der.*

mane [meɪn] *n* Mähne *die.*

mangle ['mæŋgl] *vt* [body, car] (übel) zurichten.

mango ['mæŋgəʊ] (*pl* -es OR -s) *n* Mango *die.*

manhandle ['mænˌhændl] *vt* [person] grob behandeln.

manhole ['mænhəʊl] *n* Kanalschacht *der.*

mania ['meɪnɪə] *n* [excessive liking]: **~ (for)** Leidenschaft *die* (für).

maniac ['meɪnɪæk] *n* **- 1.** [madman] Wahnsinnige *der, die* **- 2.** [fanatic]: **a TV/sex ~** ein Fernseh-/Sexbesessener, eine Fernseh-/Sexbesessene.

manic ['mænɪk] *adj* [overexcited - person] aufgedreht.

manicure ['mænɪˌkjʊə'] *n* Maniküre *die.*

manifest ['mænɪfest] *fml vt* bekunden, zum Ausdruck bringen; **to ~ itself** sich zeigen.

manifesto [ˌmænɪ'festəʊ] (*pl* -s OR -es) *n* Manifest *das.*

manipulate [mə'nɪpjʊleɪt] *vt* **- 1.** [people] manipulieren **- 2.** [machine, controls] bedienen.

manipulative [mə'nɪpjʊlətɪv] *adj* manipulativ.

mankind [mæn'kaɪnd] *n* Menschheit *die.*

manly ['mænlɪ] *adj* [voice, bearing] männlich; [behaviour] mannhaft.

man-made *adj* [fibre] Kunst-; [environment] von Menschen geschaffen.

manner ['mænə'] *n* **- 1.** [method] Art *die,* Weise *die;* **in this ~** auf diese Art und Weise **- 2.** [attitude] Auftreten *das;* **I don't like your ~!** mir gefällt nicht, wie Sie mit mir reden! ◆ **manners** *npl* Manieren *pl.*

manoeuvre *Br,* **maneuver** *Am* [mə'nuːvə'] ◇ *n* [movement] Manöver *das* ◇ *vt* [car, ship] manövrieren.

manor ['mænə'] *n* Herrenhaus *das.*

manpower ['mænˌpaʊə'] *n (U)* Arbeitskräfte *pl.*

mansion ['mænʃn] *n* Villa *die.*

manslaughter ['mænˌslɔːtə'] *n (U)* Totschlag *der.*

manual ['mænjʊəl] ◇ *adj* [work, system] manuell ◇ *n* [handbook] Handbuch *das.*

manufacture [ˌmænjʊ'fæktʃə'] *vt* [make] herstellen.

manufacturer [ˌmænjʊ'fæktʃərə'] *n* Hersteller *der.*

manure [mə'njʊə'] *n* Dung *der.*

manuscript ['mænjʊskrɪpt] *n* [untyped copy] Manuskript *das.*

many ['menɪ] (*compar* more; *superl* most) ◇ *adj* viele; **~ people** viele Leute ◇ *pron* viele; **how ~?** wie viele?

map [mæp] *n* (Land)karte *die;* [of town] Stadtplan *der.*

maple ['meɪpl] *n* Ahorn *der.*

marathon ['mærəθn] *n* Marathon(lauf) *der.*

marble ['mɑːbl] *n* [stone] Marmor *der.*

march [mɑːtʃ] ◇ *n* MIL Marsch *der* ◇ *vi* **- 1.** [soldiers, protesters] **marschieren - 2.** [walk briskly]: **to ~ up to sb** schnurstracks auf jn zulmarschieren.

March [mɑːtʃ] *n* März *der; see also* September.

marcher ['mɑːtʃə'] *n* [protester] Demonstrant *der,* -in *die.*

mare [meə'] *n* Stute *die.*

margarine [ˌmɑːdʒə'riːn, ˌmɑːgə'riːn] *n* Margarine *die.*

margin ['mɑːdʒɪn] *n* **- 1.** [in contest] Spielraum *der* **- 2.** COMM: **profit ~** Gewinnspanne *die* **- 3.** [edge - of page, wood] Rand *der.*

marginal ['mɑːdʒɪnl] *adj* [unimportant] von geringer Bedeutung; [effect, adjustment] geringfügig.

marigold ['mærɪgəʊld] *n* Ringelblume *die.*

marihuana, marijuana [ˌmærɪ'wɑːnə] *n* Marihuana *das.*

marine [mə'riːn] ◇ *adj* [plant] im Meer lebend ◇ *n* Marineinfanterist *der.*

marital ['mærɪtl] *adj* [happiness, crisis] Ehe-; [sex, rights] ehelich.

marital status *n* Familienstand *der.*

maritime ['mærɪtaɪm] *adj* See-.

mark [mɑːk] ◇ *n* **- 1.** [stain] Fleck *der;* [on person's skin] Mal *das* **- 2.** [sign] Zeichen *das* **- 3.** SCH & UNIV Note *die* **- 4.** [stage, level]: **we've reached the halfway ~** wir haben die Hälfte hinter uns **- 5.** [currency] Mark *die* ◇ *vt* **- 1.** [stain] fleckig machen; [scratch] zerkratzen **- 2.** [label] kennzeichnen **- 3.** SCH & UNIV korrigieren **- 4.** [identify] markieren **- 5.** [commemorate] begehen.

marked [mɑːkt] *adj* [noticeable] merklich.

market ['mɑːkɪt] ◇ *n* Markt *der* ◇ *vt* vermarkten.

marketing ['mɑːkɪtɪŋ] *n* COMM Marketing *das.*

marketplace ['mɑːkɪtpleɪs] *n* [in a town] Marktplatz *der.*

marmalade ['mɑ:məleɪd] *n (U):* **(orange) ~** Orangenmarmelade *die.*

---

marmalade

Das britische Wort marmalade ist ein falscher Freund, weil es nur die Bezeichnung für Orangen- oder Zitronenmarmelade ist. Alle anderen Fruchtsorten heißen jam. Möchte man zum Frühstück Erdbeermarmelade haben, fragt man also nach strawberry jam. Zu beachten ist auch die unterschiedliche Schreibweise im Deutschen und Englischen.

---

marriage ['mærɪdʒ] *n* - **1.** [wedding] Hochzeit *die,* Heirat *die;* [ceremony] Trauung *die* - **2.** [state] Ehe *die.*

marrow ['mærəʊ] *n* - **1.** *Br* [vegetable] Speisekürbis *der* - **2.** *(U)* [in bones] (Knochen)mark *das.*

marry ['mærɪ] ⋄ *vt* - **1.** [become spouse of] heiraten; **to get married** heiraten - **2.** [subj: priest, minister, registrar] trauen ⋄ *vi* heiraten.

Mars [mɑ:z] *n* [planet] Mars *der.*

marsh [mɑ:ʃ] *n* Sumpf *der.*

marshal ['mɑ:ʃl] ⋄ *n* MIL Marschall *der* ⋄ *vt* [support] sichern.

martial arts [,mɑ:ʃl-] *npl* Kampfsportarten *pl.*

martial law [,mɑ:ʃl-] *n* Kriegsrecht *das.*

martyr ['mɑ:tə'] *n* Märtyrer *der,* -in *die.*

marvel ['mɑ:vl] ⋄ *n* Wunder *das;* **you're a ~!** du bist ja unglaublich! ⋄ *vi:* **to ~ (at sthg)** staunen (über etw *(A)*).

marvellous *Br,* **marvelous** *Am* ['mɑ:vələs] *adj* wunderbar.

Marxism ['mɑ:ksɪzm] *n* Marxismus *der.*

Marxist ['mɑ:ksɪst] ⋄ *adj* marxistisch ⋄ *n* Marxist *der,* -in *die.*

masculine ['mæskjʊlɪn] *adj* - **1.** [typically male] männlich - **2.** GRAMM & [woman] maskulin.

mash [mæʃ] *vt* (zu Brei) zerdrücken.

mashed potatoes [mæʃt-] *npl* Kartoffelbrei *der.*

mask [mɑ:sk] ⋄ *n* Maske *die* ⋄ *vt* - **1.** [truth, feelings] verbergen - **2.** [smell, flavour] überdecken.

masochist ['mæsəkɪst] *n* Masochist *der,* -in *die.*

mason ['meɪsn] *n* - **1.** [stonemason] Steinmetz *der* - **2.** [Freemason] Freimaurer *der.*

mass [mæs] ⋄ *n* - **1.** [gen & PHYS] Masse *die* - **2.** [large quantity] Unmenge *die;* **a ~ of people** eine große Menschenmenge ⋄ *adj* [unemployment, protest *etc*] Massen-. ◆ **Mass** *n* RELIG Messe *die.*

massacre ['mæsəkə'] *n* Massaker *das.*

massage [*Br* 'mæsɑ:ʒ, *Am* mə'sɑ:ʒ] ⋄ *n* Massage *die* ⋄ *vt* massieren.

massive ['mæsɪv] *adj* riesig; [dose] sehr groß.

mass media *n or npl:* **the ~** die Massenmedien *pl.*

mast [mɑ:st] *n* - **1.** [on boat] Mast *der* - **2.** RADIO & TV Sendemast *der.*

master ['mɑ:stə'] ⋄ *n* - **1.** [gen] Herr *der* - **2.** *Br* [teacher] Lehrer *der* ⋄ *vt* [job, skill, language] beherrschen.

Master of Arts (*pl* **Masters of Arts**) *n* - **1.** [degree] ≃ Magister Artium *der* - **2.** [person] Inhaber des „Master of Arts".

Master of Science (*pl* **Masters of Science**) *n* - **1.** [degree] ≃ Magister rerum naturalium *der* - **2.** [person] Inhaber des „Master of Science".

masterpiece ['mɑ:stəpi:s] *n* lit & fig Meisterwerk *das.*

master's degree *n* Magister(titel) *der.*

mat [mæt] *n* [on table] Untersetzer *der;* [on floor] (Fuß)matte *die;* [in sport] Matte *die.*

match [mætʃ] ⋄ *n* - **1.** [game] Spiel *das;* [in boxing, wrestling] Kampf *der* - **2.** [for lighting] Streichholz *das* - **3.** [equal]: **to be no ~ for sb** jm nicht gewachsen sein; **to meet one's ~** seinen Meister finden ⋄ *vt* - **1.** [views, feelings, ideas] übereinstimmen mit - **2.** [in colour, design] passen zu (+ *D*) - **3.** [be as good as] gleichkommen (+ *D*) ⋄ *vi* - **1.** [views, ideas] übereinstimmen - **2.** [in colour, design] zusammenpassen.

matchbox ['mætʃbɒks] *n* Streichholzschachtel *die.*

matching ['mætʃɪŋ] *adj* (dazu) passend.

mate [meɪt] ⋄ *n* - **1.** *inf* [friend] Kumpel *der* - **2.** *Br inf* [term of address] Kumpel *der* - **3.** [of animal - male] Männchen *das;* [- female] Weibchen *das* - **4.** NAUT: **(first) ~** Maat *der* ⋄ *vi* [animals]: **to ~ (with)** sich paaren (mit).

material [mə'tɪərɪəl] ⋄ *adj* - **1.** [physical] materiell - **2.** [important] wesentlich ⋄ *n* - **1.** [substance] Material *das* - **2.** [fabric] Stoff *der* - **3.** *(U)* [ideas, information] Stoff *der,* Material *das.* ◆ **materials** *npl:* **building ~s** Baumaterialien *pl;* **writing ~s** Schreibzeug *das;* **cleaning ~s** Putzzeug *das.*

materialistic [mə,tɪərɪə'lɪstɪk] *adj* materialistisch.

materialize, -ise [mə'tɪərɪəlaɪz] *vi* - **1.** [happen - crisis] eintreten; [- threat] in die Tat umgesetzt werden - **2.** [appear] auftauchen.

maternal [mə'tɜ:nl] *adj* - **1.** [instinct] Mutter-; [person] mütterlich - **2.** [on mother's side]: **~ grandparents** Großeltern mütterlicherseits.

maternity [mə'tɜ:nətɪ] *n* Mutterschaft *die.*

maternity dress *n* Umstandskleid *das.*

maternity leave *n (U)* Mutterschaftsurlaub *der.*

maternity ward *n* Entbindungsstation *die*.

math *n Am* = maths.

mathematical [ˌmæθə'mætɪkl] *adj* mathematisch.

mathematics [ˌmæθə'mætɪks] *n (U)* Mathematik *die*.

maths *Br* [mæθs], **math** *Am* [mæθ] *(abbr of mathematics) inf n (U)* Mathe *die*.

matinée ['mætɪneɪ] *n* Nachmittagsvorstellung *die*.

matriculation [məˌtrɪkjʊ'leɪʃn] *n* UNIV Immatrikulation *die*.

matrimonial [ˌmætrɪ'məʊnɪəl] *adj* [problems, dispute] Ehe-; [harmony] ehelich.

matrimony ['mætrɪmənɪ] *n* Ehestand *der*.

matron ['meɪtrən] *n Br* [in hospital] Oberschwester *die*.

matt *Br*, **matte** *Am* [mæt] *adj* matt.

matted ['mætɪd] *adj* verfilzt.

matter ['mætər] <> *n* - **1.** [question, situation] Angelegenheit *die*; **that's quite another** OR **a different ~** das ist etwas ganz anderes; **that's a ~ of opinion** das ist Ansichtssache; **to make ~s worse** die Sache noch schlimmer machen; **and to make ~s worse, ...** zu allem Unglück ..., und obendrein ...; **as a ~ of course** selbstverständlich - **2.** [trouble]: **there's something the ~ with my radio** etwas stimmt nicht mit dem Radio; **what's the ~?** was ist (denn) los?; **what's the ~ with it/her?** was ist (los) damit/mit ihr? - **3.** [substance] Materie *die* - **4.** *(U)* [material] Stoff *der*; **reading ~** Lesestoff *der* <> *vi* von Bedeutung sein; **it doesn't ~** das macht nichts; **it doesn't ~ what I do, ...** ganz gleich was ich tue, ... **◆ as a matter of fact** *adv* sogar. **◆ for that matter** *adv* eigentlich. **◆ no matter** *adv*: **no ~ how ...** ganz gleich wie ...; **no ~ what** ganz egal was.

matter-of-fact *adj* sachlich, nüchtern.

mattress ['mætrɪs] *n* Matratze *die*.

mature [mə'tjʊər] <> *adj* - **1.** [person] reif - **2.** [cheese] reif; [wine] ausgereift <> *vi* - **1.** [child] erwachsen werden; [animal] zur vollen Größe heranlwachsen; [plant] die volle Größe erreichen - **2.** *fig* [grow up] reifer werden - **3.** [cheese] reifen; [wine] auslreifen - **4.** [insurance policy] fällig werden.

mature student *n Br* UNIV *Person, die erst einige Jahre nach dem Schulabschluss ein Studium aufnimmt*.

maul [mɔːl] *vt* übel zulrichten.

mauve [məʊv] *adj* mauve.

max. [mæks] *abbr of* maximum.

maxim ['mæksɪm] *(pl -s) n* Maxime *die*.

maxima ['mæksɪmə] *pl* ⊳ maximum.

maximum ['mæksɪməm] *(pl* maxima OR -s) <> *adj* maximal; [speed, weight, temperature] Höchst- <> *n* Maximum *das*.

may [meɪ] *aux vb* - **1.** [expressing possibility]

können; **it ~ be done as follows** man kann wie folgt vorgehen; **it ~ rain** es könnte regnen; **they ~ have got lost** sie haben sich vielleicht verirrt; **be that as it ~** wie dem auch sei; **come what ~** komme, was wolle - **2.** [expressing permission] können; **~ I smoke?** darf ich rauchen?; **you ~ sit, if you wish** Sie dürfen sich setzen, wenn Sie wollen - **3.** [when conceding a point]: **it ~ be a long walk, but it's worth it** es ist vielleicht ein langer Weg, aber es lohnt sich - **4.** *fml* [expressing wish, hope]: **~ you be very happy!** ich wünsche dir, dass du glücklich wirst!; ⊳ might.

May [meɪ] *n* Mai *der; see also* September.

maybe ['meɪbiː] *adv* vielleicht.

May Day *n der* 1. Mai.

mayhem ['meɪhem] *n* Chaos *das*.

mayonnaise [ˌmeɪə'neɪz] *n* Majonäse *die*.

mayor [meər] *n* Bürgermeister *der*.

mayoress ['meərɪs] *n* [female mayor] Bürgermeisterin *die*; [mayor's wife] Frau *die* des Bürgermeisters.

maze [meɪz] *n* - **1.** [system of paths] Irrgarten *der* - **2.** *fig* [of ideas] Wirrwarr *der*; [of streets] Labyrinth *das*.

MB *(abbr of* megabyte) Mb *das*.

MD *n (abbr of* Doctor of Medicine) Dr. med.

me [miː] *pers pron* (accusative) mich; (dative) mir; **she knows ~** sie kennt mich; **it's ~** ich bins; **send it to ~** schick es mir; **tell ~** sagen Sie mal, sag mal; **he's worse than ~** er ist schlechter als ich.

meadow ['medəʊ] *n* Wiese *die*.

meagre *Br*, **meager** *Am* ['miːgər] *adj* dürftig.

meal [miːl] *n* - **1.** [occasion] Mahlzeit *die*; **to go out for a ~** essen gehen - **2.** [food] Essen *das*, Gericht *das*.

mealtime ['miːltaɪm] *n* Essenszeit *die*.

mean [miːn] *(pt & pp* meant) <> *vt* - **1.** [signify] bedeuten; **the name ~s nothing to me** der Name sagt mir nichts - **2.** [intend] beabsichtigen; **to ~ to do sthg** vorhaben, etw zu tun; **the bus was meant to leave at eight** der Bus hätte eigentlich um acht Uhr abfahren sollen; **it's meant to be good** das soll gut sein; **he ~s well** er meint es gut - **3.** [with remark] meinen; **what do you ~ by that?** was meinst du damit? - **4.** [be serious about] ernst meinen; **I didn't ~ it!** ich habe es nicht so gemeint!; **I ~ it!** es ist mein Ernst!, ich meine es ernst! - **5.** *phr:* **Paul, I ~ Peter** [when correcting o.s.] Paul, ich meine (natürlich) Peter <> *adj* - **1.** [miserly] geizig - **2.** [unkind] gemein; **to be ~ to sb** gemein zu jm sein - **3.** [average] durchschnittlich <> *n* [average] Durchschnitt *der;* ⊳ means.

meander [mɪ'ændər] *vi* - **1.** [river, road] sich schlängeln - **2.** [person] schlendern.

meaning ['miːnɪŋ] *n* Bedeutung *die;* [of

film, work of art, life] Sinn *der;* **what's the ~ of this?** was soll denn das?

meaningful ['miːnɪŋfʊl] *adj* - **1.** [look, comment] vielsagend - **2.** [discussion, relationship] ernsthaft.

meaningless ['miːnɪŋlɪs] *adj* - **1.** [word, lyrics] ohne Sinn - **2.** [futile] sinnlos.

means [miːnz] *(pl inv)* <> *n* [method] Mittel *das;* **a ~ of transport** Verkehrsmittel *das;* **by ~ of** mittels *(+ G),* durch <> *npl* [money] Mittel *pl;* **it is beyond my ~** das kann ich mir nicht leisten; **can I have one? – by all ~!** darf ich eins haben? – (aber) selbstverständlich!
  ◆ **by no means** *adv* keineswegs.

meant [ment] *pt & pp* ⇨ mean.

meantime ['miːnˌtaɪm] *n:* **in the ~** in der Zwischenzeit.

meanwhile ['miːnˌwaɪl] *adv* inzwischen.

measles ['miːzlz] *n:* **(the) ~** Masern *pl.*

measly ['miːzlɪ] *adj inf* mick(e)rig.

measure ['meʒə'] <> *n* - **1.** [step, action] Maßnahme *die* - **2.** [of alcohol] ausgeschenkte Menge - **3.** [indication]: **to be a ~ of sthg** ein Zeichen für etw sein <> *vt* messen; [room] ausˈmessen; [damage, harm] abˈschätzen.

measurement ['meʒəmənt] *n* - **1.** [figure] Maß *das* - **2.** *(U)* [act of measuring] Messung *die.* ◆ **measurements** *npl* [of sb's body] Maße *pl;* **to take sb's ~s** bei jm Maß nehmen.

meat [miːt] *n* Fleisch *das.*

meatball ['miːtbɔːl] *n* Fleischklößchen *das.*

meat pie *n Br* Fleischpastete *die.*

meaty ['miːtɪ] *adj fig* [full of ideas] aussagehaltig.

Mecca ['mekə] *n* GEOGR Mekka *nt.*

mechanic [mɪ'kænɪk] *n* Mechaniker *der,* -in *die.* ◆ **mechanics** <> *n (U)* [study] Mechanik *die* <> *npl* [way sthg works] Funktionsweise *die.*

mechanical [mɪ'kænɪkl] *adj* [device, action, smile] mechanisch.

mechanism ['mekənɪzm] *n* - **1.** [of machine, behaviour] Mechanismus *der* - **2.** [procedure] Verfahren *das.*

medal ['medl] *n* Medaille *die.*

medallion [mɪ'dæljən] *n* Medaillon *das.*

meddle ['medl] *vi:* **to ~ (in/with sthg)** sich (in etw *(A)*) einˈmischen; **to ~ with sb** sich mit jm einˈlassen.

media ['miːdɪə] <> *pl* ⇨ medium <> *n or npl:* **the ~** die Medien *pl.*

mediaeval [ˌmedɪ'iːvl] *adj* = medieval.

median ['miːdɪən] *n Am* [of road] Mittelstreifen *der.*

mediate ['miːdɪeɪt] *vi:* **to ~ (for/between)** vermitteln (für/zwischen *(+ D)).*

mediator ['miːdɪeɪtə'] *n* Vermittler *der,* -in *die.*

Medicaid ['medɪkeɪd] *n Am staatliche Ge-*

sundheitsfürsorge für einkommensschwache US-Bürger.

medical ['medɪkl] <> *adj* medizinisch <> *n* ärztliche Untersuchung.

Medicare ['medɪkeə'] *n Am staatliche Gesundheitsfürsorge für ältere US-Bürger.*

medicated ['medɪkeɪtɪd] *adj* medizinisch.

medicine ['medsɪn] *n* - **1.** [treatment of illness] Medizin *die* - **2.** [substance] Medikament *das.*

medieval [ˌmedɪ'iːvl] *adj* mittelalterlich.

mediocre [ˌmiːdɪ'əʊkə'] *adj* mittelmäßig.

meditate ['medɪteɪt] *vi* - **1.** [reflect, ponder]: **to ~ (on OR upon)** nachˈdenken (über *(+ A)*) - **2.** [practise meditation] meditieren.

Mediterranean [ˌmedɪtə'reɪnɪən] <> *n* - **1.** [sea]: **the ~ (Sea)** das Mittelmeer - **2.** [area around sea]: **the ~** der Mittelmeerraum <> *adj* Mittelmeer-, mediterran.

medium ['miːdɪəm] <> *adj* mittlere, -r, -s <> *n* Medium *das.*

medium-size(d) [-saɪz(d)] *adj* mittelgroß.

medium wave *n* Mittelwelle *die.*

medley ['medlɪ] *(pl medleys)* *n* - **1.** [mixture] Gemisch *das* - **2.** [selection of music] Medley *das,* Potpourri *das.*

meek [miːk] *adj* sanftmütig; [voice] sanft.

meet [miːt] *(pt & pp met)* <> *vt* - **1.** [by arrangement] sich treffen mit; [by chance] treffen; [get to know] kennen lernen; **to arrange to ~ sb** sich mit jm verabreden; **pleased to ~ you!** sehr erfreut! - **2.** [go to collect] abˈholen - **3.** [need, requirement] erfüllen - **4.** [cost, expense] begleichen - **5.** [join - subj: road, river] treffen auf *(+ A)* <> *vi* - **1.** [by arrangement, by chance] sich treffen; [committee *etc*] zusammenˈkommen - **2.** [get to know each other] sich kennen lernen - **3.** [intersect] aufeinander treffen - **4.** [join] zusammenˈkommen <> *n Am* [sports meeting] Sportfest *das.* ◆ **meet up** *vi:* **to ~ up (with sb)** sich (mit jm) treffen. ◆ **meet with** *vt fus* - **1.** [problems, resistance] stoßen auf *(+ A)* - **2.** [by arrangement] sich treffen mit.

meeting ['miːtɪŋ] *n* - **1.** [for discussions, business] Meeting *das,* Sitzung *die* - **2.** [coming together - by chance] Begegnung *die;* [- by arrangement] Treffen *das.*

megabyte ['megəbaɪt] *n* COMPUT Megabyte *das.*

megaphone ['megəfəʊn] *n* Megafon *das.*

melancholy ['melənkəlɪ] *adj* melancholisch; [facts, news] traurig.

mellow ['meləʊ] <> *adj* - **1.** [light] warm - **2.** [smooth, pleasant] angenehm; [sound, tones] lieblich, sanft; [wine] ausgereift; [whisky] mild - **3.** [gentle, relaxed] milde, sanft <> *vi* [person] abˈgeklärt werden.

melody ['melədɪ] *n* Melodie *die.*

melon ['melən] *n* Melone *die.*

melt [melt] <> *vt* [make liquid - chocolate,

snow] schmelzen; [butter] zerlassen ⟷ vi - 1. [become liquid] schmelzen - 2. fig [soften - person] dahinlschmelzen; [- heart] überlgehen - 3. fig [disappear]: **to ~ away** [savings, anger] dahinlschmelzen, weglschmelzen.
➤ **melt down** vt sep einlschmelzen.

meltdown ['meltdaun] n Kernschmelze die.

melting pot ['meltiŋ-] n fig Schmelztiegel der.

member ['membər] n Mitglied das; **a ~ of staff** ein Firmenangehöriger, eine Firmenangehörige.

Member of Congress (pl Members of Congress) n Am Kongressmitglied das.

Member of Parliament (pl Members of Parliament) n Parlamentsabgeordnete der, die.

membership ['membəʃip] n (U) - 1. [fact of belonging] Mitgliedschaft die - 2. [number of members] Mitgliederzahl die - 3. [people]: **the ~** die Mitglieder.

membership card n Mitgliedskarte die.

memento [mɪ'mentəu] (pl -s) n Andenken das.

memo ['meməu] (pl -s) n Mitteilung die.

memoirs ['memwɑːz] npl Memoiren pl.

memorandum [ˌmemə'rændəm] (pl -da [-də] OR -dums) n fml Memorandum das.

memorial [mɪ'mɔːrɪəl] ⟷ adj Gedenk- ⟷ n Denkmal das.

memorize, -ise ['meməraɪz] vt auswendig lernen.

memory ['memərɪ] n - 1. [ability to remember] Gedächtnis das - 2. (U) [things remembered] Erinnerung die; **I have no ~ of it** ich kann mich nicht daran erinnern; **from ~** auswendig - 3. [event, experience remembered] Erinnerung die - 4. (U) [of dead person] Andenken das - 5. COMPUT Speicher der.

men [men] pl ⟻ **man**.

menace ['menəs] ⟷ n - 1. [threat] Drohung die; [danger] drohende Gefahr - 2. (U) [threatening quality] Bedrohung die - 3. inf [nuisance, pest] Plage die ⟷ vt bedrohen.

menacing ['menəsɪŋ] adj bedrohlich.

mend [mend] ⟷ n inf: **to be on the ~** auf dem Weg der Besserung sein ⟷ vt [repair] reparieren; [clothes] flicken.

menial ['miːnɪəl] adj niedrig.

meningitis [ˌmenɪn'dʒaɪtɪs] n MED Hirnhautentzündung die, Meningitis die.

menopause ['menəpɔːz] n (U): **the ~** die Wechseljahre, die Menopause.

men's room n Am: **the ~** die Herrentoilette.

menstruation [ˌmenstru'eɪʃn] n (U) Menstruation die, Periode die.

menswear ['menzweər] n (U) Herrenbekleidung die.

mental ['mentl] adj - 1. [intellectual] geistig

- 2. [psychiatric] psychiatrisch; **~ illness** Geisteskrankheit die; **her ~ health** ihr Geisteszustand - 3. [performed in the mind] im Kopf; **~ arithmetic** Kopfrechnen das.

mental hospital n Nervenklinik die.

mentality [men'tælətɪ] n (U) Mentalität die.

mentally handicapped npl: **the ~** die geistig Behinderten pl.

mention ['menʃn] ⟷ vt erwähnen; **to ~ sthg to sb** etw jm gegenüber erwähnen; **not to ~ ...** ganz zu schweigen von ...; **don't ~ it!** gern geschehen! ⟷ n Erwähnung die; **to get a ~** erwähnt werden.

menu ['menjuː] n - 1. [in restaurant - card] Speisekarte die; [- dishes] Menü das - 2. COMPUT Menü das.

meow n & vi Am = miaow.

MEP (abbr of Member of the European Parliament) n MdEP das.

mercenary ['mɜːsɪnrɪ] ⟷ adj - 1. [only interested in money] gewinnsüchtig - 2. MIL Söldner- ⟷ n [soldier] Söldner der.

merchandise ['mɜːtʃəndaɪz] n (U) Ware die.

merchant ['mɜːtʃənt] n Händler der, -in die.

merchant bank n Br Handelsbank die.

merchant navy Br, **merchant marine** Am n Handelsmarine die.

merciful ['mɜːsɪful] adj [person] barmherzig.

merciless ['mɜːsɪlɪs] adj gnadenlos.

mercury ['mɜːkjurɪ] n Quecksilber das.

Mercury ['mɜːkjurɪ] n [planet] Merkur der.

mercy ['mɜːsɪ] n - 1. [kindness, pity] Gnade die; **to be at the ~ of sb/sthg** fig jm/etw ausgeliefert sein - 2. [blessing] Segen der.

mere [mɪər] adj: **a ~ £10 is all it costs** es kostet bloß OR nur 10 Pfund; **it took him a ~ two hours** er brauchte bloß OR nur zwei Stunden; **she's a ~ child!** sie ist ja noch ein Kind!

merely ['mɪəlɪ] adv bloß, nur.

merge [mɜːdʒ] ⟷ vt - 1. COMM fusionieren - 2. COMPUT mischen ⟷ vi - 1. COMM: **to ~ (with)** fusionieren (mit) - 2. [roads, lines] zusammenllaufen - 3. [blend] ineinander überlgehen; **to ~ into the landscape/ background** mit der Landschaft/dem Hintergrund verschmelzen.

merger ['mɜːdʒər] n COMM Fusion die.

meringue [mə'ræŋ] n Baiser das.

merit ['merɪt] ⟷ n (U) [value] Wert der; **she was chosen for the post on ~** sie bekam die Stelle aufgrund ihrer guten Leistungen ⟷ vt verdienen. ➤ **merits** npl Vorteile pl.

mermaid ['mɜːmeɪd] n Meerjungfrau die.

merry ['merɪ] adj - 1. [party] fröhlich; **Merry Christmas!** frohe OR fröhliche Weihnachten! - 2. inf [tipsy] angeheitert.

merry-go-round n Karussell das.

mesh [meʃ] *n (U)* [netting]: **(wire)** ~ Maschendraht *der*.

mesmerize, -ise ['mezməraɪz] *vt*: **to be ~d by sb/sthg** fasziniert OR gebannt sein von jm/etw.

mess [mes] *n* - **1.** [untidy state] Durcheinander *das* - **2.** [sthg spilt, knocked over] Schweinerei *die* - **3.** [muddle] Durcheinander *das*; [problematic situation] Schlamassel *der* - **4.** MIL Messe *die*. ◆ **mess about, mess around** *inf* ⬦ *vt sep* [person] an der Nase herumlführen ⬦ *vi* - **1.** [fool around, waste time] herumlgammeln - **2.** [interfere]: **to ~ about with** [machine] herumlbasteln an (+ D); [sb's papers] durcheinander bringen. ◆ **mess up** *vt sep inf* - **1.** [make dirty] verdrecken; [make untidy] in Unordnung bringen - **2.** [plan, evening] verderben.

message ['mesɪdʒ] *n* - **1.** [piece of information] Nachricht *die* - **2.** [idea, moral] Botschaft *die*.

messenger ['mesɪndʒər] *n* Bote *der*.

Messrs, Messrs. ['mesəz] *(abbr of messieurs)*: **~ Wilson and Williams** die Herren Wilson und Williams.

messy ['mesɪ] *adj* - **1.** [untidy] unordentlich; [dirty] dreckig - **2.** *inf* [complicated, confused] kompliziert.

met [met] *pt & pp* ⬡ meet.

metal ['metl] ⬦ *n* Metall *das* ⬦ *adj* Metall-, metallen.

metallic [mɪ'tælɪk] *adj* - **1.** [sound] metallisch - **2.** [shiny]: **~ paint** Metalliclackierung *die*; **~ blue** metallicblau.

metalwork ['metəlwɜːk] *n (U)* [craft] Metallarbeit *die*.

metaphor ['metəfər] *n* [symbol, image] Metapher *die*.

mete [miːt] ◆ **mete out** *vt sep*: **to ~ sthg out to sb** jm etw zulmessen.

meteor ['miːtɪər] *n* Meteor *der*.

meteorology [miːtɪə'rɒlədʒɪ] *n* Meteorologie *die*.

meter ['miːtər] ⬦ *n* - **1.** [device - for gas, electricity] Zähler *der*; [- in taxi] Uhr *die*; [- for parking] Parkuhr *die* - **2.** *Am* = metre ⬦ *vt* messen.

method ['meθəd] *n* Methode *die*.

methodical [mɪ'θɒdɪkl] *adj* methodisch.

Methodist ['meθədɪst] ⬦ *adj* Methodisten- ⬦ *n* Methodist *der*, -in *die*.

meths [meθs] *n (U) Br inf* Brennspiritus *der*.

methylated spirits [ˌmeθɪleɪtɪd-] *n (U)* Brennspiritus *der*.

meticulous [mɪ'tɪkjʊləs] *adj* genau.

metre *Br*, **meter** *Am* ['miːtər] *n* [unit of measurement] Meter *der*.

metric ['metrɪk] *adj* metrisch.

metronome ['metrənəʊm] *n* Metronom *das*.

metropolitan [ˌmetrə'pɒlɪtn] *adj* Stadt-.

mettle ['metl] *n (U)*: **to be on one's ~** sein Bestes geben; **to show one's ~** zeigen, was man kann.

mew [mjuː] *n & vi* = miaow.

mews [mjuːz] *(pl inv) n Br* [stables] Stallungen *pl*; [street] *Gasse mit ehemaligen Stallungen*.

Mexican ['meksɪkn] ⬦ *adj* mexikanisch ⬦ *n* Mexikaner *der*, -in *die*.

Mexico ['meksɪkəʊ] *n* Mexiko *nt*.

MI5 *(abbr of Military Intelligence 5) n* MI5 *der*, *britische Spionageabwehr*.

miaow *Br* [miːˈaʊ], **meow** *Am* [mɪˈaʊ] ⬦ *n* Miau *das* ⬦ *vi* miauen.

mice [maɪs] *pl* ⬡ mouse.

mickey ['mɪkɪ] *n*: **to take the ~ out of sb** *Br inf* jn auf den Arm nehmen.

microchip ['maɪkrəʊtʃɪp] *n* Mikrochip *der*.

microcomputer [ˌmaɪkrəʊkəmˈpjuːtər] *n* Mikrocomputer *der*.

microfilm ['maɪkrəʊfɪlm] *n* Mikrofilm *der*.

microphone ['maɪkrəfəʊn] *n* Mikrofon *das*.

microscope ['maɪkrəskəʊp] *n* Mikroskop *das*.

microscopic [ˌmaɪkrəˈskɒpɪk] *adj* [very small] mikroskopisch.

microwave (oven) [ˌmaɪkrəweɪv-] *n* Mikrowellenherd *der*.

mid- [mɪd] *prefix*: **in ~June** Mitte Juni; **a ~morning snack** ein zweites Frühstück; **he is in his ~fifties** er ist Mitte fünfzig; **in the ~20th century** Mitte des 20. Jahrhunderts.

midair [ˌmɪdˈeər] ⬦ *adj*: **~ collision** Zusammenstoß in der Luft ⬦ *n*: **in ~** in der Luft.

midday [mɪdˈdeɪ] *n* Mittag *der*; **at ~** mittags.

middle ['mɪdl] ⬦ *adj* [central] Mittel-, mittlere, -r, -s ⬦ *n* - **1.** [gen] Mitte *die*; **in the ~ (of sthg)** in der Mitte (von etw); **in the ~ of the night** mitten in der Nacht; **to be in the ~ of doing sthg** gerade dabei sein, etw zu tun - **2.** [waist] Taille *die*.

middle-aged [-'eɪdʒd] *adj* im mittleren Alter, mittleren Alters.

Middle Ages *npl*: **the ~** das Mittelalter.

middle-class *adj* Mittelklasse-.

middle classes *npl*: **the ~** die Mittelklasse.

Middle East *n*: **the ~** der Nahe Osten.

middleman ['mɪdlmæn] *(pl -men [-men])* *n* - **1.** COMM Zwischenhändler *der* - **2.** [in negotiations] Vermittler *der*.

middle name *n* zweiter Vorname.

midfield [ˌmɪdˈfiːld] *n* FTBL Mittelfeld *das*.

midge [mɪdʒ] *n* Mücke *die*.

midget ['mɪdʒɪt] *n* Zwerg *der*.

Midlands ['mɪdləndz] *npl*: **the ~** Region im Zentrum von England.

midnight ['mɪdnaɪt] *n* Mitternacht *die*; **at ~** um Mitternacht.

midriff ['mɪdrɪf] *n* Bauch *der*.

midst [mɪdst] *n*: **in the ~ of** mitten in (+ D);

to be in the ~ of doing sthg gerade dabei sein, etw zu tun.

midsummer ['mɪd ˌsʌməʳ] *n (U)* Hochsommer *der*.

midway [ˌmɪd'weɪ] *adv* - **1.** [in space]: **~ (between)** auf halbem Wege (zwischen) - **2.** [in time] in der Mitte; **~ through** mitten in *(+ D)*.

midweek [*adj* 'mɪdwiːk, *adv* ˌmɪd'wiːk] <> *adj*: **a ~ meeting/match** ein Mitte der Woche stattfindendes Treffen/Spiel <> *adv* Mitte der Woche.

midwife ['mɪdwaɪf] *(pl* -wives [-waɪvz]) *n* Hebamme *die*.

might [maɪt] <> *modal vb* - **1.** [expressing possibility] können; **they ~ still come** sie könnten noch kommen; **they ~ have been killed** sie sind vielleicht umgekommen - **2.** [expressing suggestion]: **you ~ have told me!** das hättest du mir doch sagen können!; **it ~ be better to wait** sie sollten vielleicht lieber warten - **3.** *fml* [asking permission]: **~ I have a few words?** könnte ich Sie mal sprechen?; **he asked if he ~ leave the room** er fragte, ob er das Zimmer verlassen dürfte - **4.** [when conceding a point]: **it ~ be expensive, but it's good quality** es ist zwar teuer, aber es ist eine gute Qualität - **5.** [would]: **I'd hoped you ~ come too** ich hatte gehofft, du würdest auch mitkommen - **6.** *phr*: **I ~ have known/guessed** das hätte ich eigentlich wissen/mir eigentlich denken können <> *n (U)* Macht *die*; **with all one's ~** mit aller Macht OR Kraft.

mighty ['maɪtɪ] <> *adj* [powerful] mächtig <> *adv Am inf* mächtig.

migraine ['miːgreɪn, 'maɪgreɪn] *n* Migräne *die*.

migrant ['maɪgrənt] *n* - **1.** [bird] Zugvogel *der* - **2.** [worker] Wanderarbeiter *der*, -in *die*.

migrate [*Br* maɪ'greɪt, *Am* 'maɪgreɪt] *vi* - **1.** [bird] in den Süden ziehen - **2.** [person] abwandern.

mike [maɪk] *(abbr of* microphone) *n inf* Mikro *das*.

mild [maɪld] *adj* - **1.** [gen] mild; [sedative, illness] leicht - **2.** [person, manner] sanft.

mildew ['mɪldjuː] *n* [on books, walls] Schimmel *der*.

mildly ['maɪldlɪ] *adv* milde; **to put it ~** gelinde gesagt.

mile [maɪl] *n* Meile *die*; **to be ~s away** [distracted] (mit seinen Gedanken) ganz woanders sein. ◆ **miles** *adv (in comparisons)* weit; **~s better** weit besser.

mileage ['maɪlɪdʒ] *n* - **1.** [recorded] Meilenzahl *die* - **2.** *(U) inf* [advantage] Vorteil *der*.

mileometer [maɪ'lɒmɪtəʳ] *n* ≃ Kilometerzähler *der*.

milestone ['maɪlstəʊn] *n lit & fig* Meilenstein *der*.

militant ['mɪlɪtənt] <> *adj* militant <> *n* militanter Student/Arbeiter/ *etc.*

military ['mɪlɪtrɪ] <> *adj* Militär-, militärisch <> *n*: **the ~** das Militär.

militia [mɪ'lɪʃə] *n* Miliz *die*.

milk [mɪlk] <> *n* Milch *die* <> *vt* - **1.** [cow, goat] melken - **2.** [company] schröpfen; *fig* [situation, scandal] auslnutzen.

milk chocolate *n* Milchschokolade *die*.

milkman ['mɪlkmən] *(pl* -men [-mən]) *n* Milchmann *der*.

milk shake *n* Milchshake *der*.

milky ['mɪlkɪ] *adj* - **1.** *Br* [coffee] Milch-; [tea] mit Milch - **2.** [complexion] milchig.

Milky Way *n*: **the ~** die Milchstraße.

mill [mɪl] *n* - **1.** [flour mill, grinder] Mühle *die* - **2.** [cloth factory] Weberei *die*. ◆ **mill about, mill around** *vi* umherlaufen.

millennium [mɪ'lenɪəm] *(pl* -nnia [-nɪə]) *n* Millennium *das;* **the ~ bug** das Jahr-2000-Computerproblem.

millet ['mɪlɪt] *n (U)* Hirse *die*.

milligram(me) ['mɪlɪgræm] *n* Milligramm *das*.

millimetre *Br,* **millimeter** *Am* ['mɪlɪˌmiːtəʳ] *n* Millimeter *der*.

million ['mɪljən] *n* - **1.** [1,000,000] Million *die* - **2.** [enormous number]: **a ~, ~s of** zig.

millionaire [ˌmɪljə'neəʳ] *n* Millionär *der*, -in *die*.

milometer [maɪ'lɒmɪtəʳ] *n* = mileometer.

mime [maɪm] <> *n* - **1.** [acting, act] Pantomime *die* - **2.** [actor]: **~ (artist)** Pantomime *der*, -min *die* <> *vt* mimen.

mimic ['mɪmɪk] *(pt & pp* -ked; *cont* -king) <> *n* Imitator *der*, -in *die* <> *vt* nachlahmen.

min. - **1.** *abbr of* minute - **2.** *abbr of* minimum.

mince [mɪns] <> *n (U) Br* Hackfleisch *das* <> *vt* - **1.** [meat] durchldrehen - **2.**: **not to ~ one's words** kein Blatt vor den Mund nehmen <> *vi* [walk] trippeln.

mincemeat ['mɪnsmiːt] *n (U)* - **1.** [fruit] *Mischung aus Äpfeln, Rosinen, Fett und Gewürzen, die im Teigmantel gebacken wird* - **2.** *Am* [minced meat] Hackfleisch *das*.

mince pie *n mit Mincemeat gefüllte Pastete*.

mincer ['mɪnsəʳ] *n* Fleischwolf *der*.

mind [maɪnd] <> *n* - **1.** [reason] Verstand *der;* **to be out of one's ~** nicht bei Sinnen OR verrückt sein; **no one in their right ~ would do that** kein vernünftiger Mensch würde das tun; **state of ~** Geisteszustand *der* - **2.** [thoughts] Gedanken *pl;* **I can't get her out of my ~** sie geht mir nicht aus dem Kopf; **to come into/cross sb's ~** jm in den Sinn kommen; **to have sthg on one's ~** etw auf dem Herzen haben - **3.** [intellect] Geist *der* - **4.** [attention]: **to keep one's ~ on sthg** sich auf etw *(A)* konzentrieren; **if you put your ~ to it** wenn du dich anstrengst - **5.** [opinion]: **to my ~** meiner Ansicht OR Meinung nach; **to**

change one's ~ seine Meinung ändern; **to keep an open** ~ sich nicht festlegen; **to make one's ~ up** sich entschließen; **to speak one's** ~ seine Meinung frei äußern; **to be in two ~s about sthg** hinsichtlich einer Sache *(G)* unentschlossen sein - **6.** [memory] Gedächtnis *das;* **to bear sthg in** ~ etw nicht vergessen - **7.** [intention]: **to have sthg in** ~ an etw *(A)* denken; **to have a ~ to do sthg** die Absicht haben, etw zu tun - **8.** [intelligent person, thinker] Geist *der;* **he is one of the greatest ~s of the 19th century** er ist einer der größten Köpfe des 19. Jahrhunderts ◇ *vi* - **1.** [object]: **I don't** ~ ich habe nichts dagegen; **do you ~ if …?** macht es Ihnen etwas aus, wenn …?, stört es Sie, wenn …? - **2.** [care, worry]: **I don't ~ if …** es macht mir nichts aus, wenn …; **never** ~ [don't worry] mach dir nichts draus; [it's not important] es macht nichts ◇ *vt* - **1.** [object to]: **I don't ~ it/him** ich habe nichts dagegen/gegen ihn; **do you ~ waiting?** macht es dir etwas aus, zu warten? - **2.** [bother about]: **I don't ~ what he says** es ist mir gleichgültig, was er sagt - **3.** [pay attention to] achten auf *(+ A)* - **4.** [take care of] sich kümmern um. ◆ **mind you** *adv* allerdings.

minder ['maɪndəʳ] *n Br* [bodyguard] Leibwächter *der,* -in *die.*

mindful ['maɪndfʊl] *adj:* **to be ~ of sthg** sich *(D)* einer Sache *(G)* bewusst sein.

mindless ['maɪndlɪs] *adj* - **1.** [stupid] sinnlos - **2.** [not requiring thought] geistlos.

mine¹ [maɪn] ◇ *n* - **1.** [for excavating minerals] Bergwerk *das;* [for gold, diamond] Mine *die* - **2.** [bomb] Mine *die* ◇ *vt* - **1.** [coal, gold] fördern - **2.** [lay mines in] verminen.

mine² [maɪn] *poss pron* meine, -r, -s; **it's ~** es gehört mir; **a friend of ~** ein Freund von mir.

minefield ['maɪnfiːld] *n lit & fig* Minenfeld *das.*

miner ['maɪnəʳ] *n* Bergarbeiter *der,* -in *die.*

mineral ['mɪnərəl] GEOL ◇ *adj* mineralisch ◇ *n* Mineral *das.*

mineral water *n (U)* Mineralwasser *das.*

mingle ['mɪŋgl] *vi* - **1.** [combine]: **to ~ (with)** sich mischen (mit) - **2.** [at party]: **to ~ (with the guests)** sich unter die Gäste mischen.

miniature ['mɪnətʃəʳ] ◇ *adj* Miniatur- ◇ *n* - **1.** [painting] Miniatur *die* - **2.** [of alcohol] Miniflasche *die* - **3.** [small scale]: **in ~** im Kleinen, Miniatur-.

minibus ['mɪnɪbʌs] *(pl* -es) *n* Kleinbus *der.*

minicab ['mɪnɪkæb] *n Br* Kleintaxi *das.*

minima ['mɪnɪmə] *pl* ▷ **minimum.**

minimal ['mɪnɪml] *adj* minimal.

minimum ['mɪnɪməm] *(pl* -mums OR -ma) ◇ *adj* Mindest- ◇ *n* Minimum *das.*

mining ['maɪnɪŋ] ◇ *n* Bergbau *der* ◇ *adj* Bergbau-; [accident] Gruben-.

miniskirt ['mɪnɪskɜːt] *n* Minirock *der.*

minister ['mɪnɪstəʳ] *n* - **1.** POL: ~ **(of** OR **for sthg)** Minister *der,* -in *die* (für etw) - **2.** RELIG Pastor *der,* -in *die.* ◆ **minister to** *vt fus* sich kümmern um; **to ~ to sb's needs** js Bedürfnisse befriedigen.

ministerial [ˌmɪnɪ'stɪərɪəl] *adj* POL Ministerial-, ministeriell.

minister of state *n:* ~ **(for sthg)** Staatsminister *der,* -in *die* (für etw).

ministry ['mɪnɪstrɪ] *n* - **1.** POL Ministerium *das* - **2.** RELIG: **the** ~ das geistliche Amt.

mink [mɪŋk] *(pl inv) n* [fur, animal] Nerz *der.*

minor ['maɪnəʳ] ◇ *adj* - **1.** [unimportant] unbedeutend - **2.** MUS [key] Moll-; **in B** ~ in H-Moll ◇ *n* [in age] Minderjährige *der, die.*

minority [maɪ'nɒrətɪ] *n* Minderheit *die.*

mint [mɪnt] ◇ *n* - **1.** *(U)* [herb] Minze *die* - **2.** [sweet] Pfefferminzbonbon *das* - **3.** [for coins]: **the Mint** die Münze; **in ~ condition** in neuwertigem OR tadellosem Zustand ◇ *vt* [coins] prägen.

minus ['maɪnəs] *(pl* -es) ◇ *prep* - **1.** MATH minus, weniger - **2.** [in temperatures] minus ◇ *adj* - **1.** MATH negativ - **2.** SCH [in grades] minus ◇ *n* - **1.** MATH Minus *das* - **2.** [disadvantage] Nachteil *der.*

minus sign *n* Minuszeichen *das.*

minute¹ ['mɪnɪt] *n* - **1.** [period of 60 seconds] Minute *die* - **2.** [moment] Moment *der;* **at any** ~ jederzeit; **this** ~ sofort, auf der Stelle. ◆ **minutes** *npl* [of meeting] Protokoll *das.*

minute² [maɪ'njuːt] *adj* [tiny] winzig.

miracle ['mɪrəkl] *n* Wunder *das.*

miraculous [mɪ'rækjʊləs] *adj* - **1.** RELIG wundersam - **2.** *fig* [recovery, escape] wunderbar.

mirage [mɪ'rɑːʒ] *n* [in desert] Fata Morgana *die.*

mire [maɪəʳ] *n* Morast *der,* Schlamm *der.*

mirror ['mɪrəʳ] ◇ *n* Spiegel *der* ◇ *vt* [copy] widerspiegeln.

misadventure [ˌmɪsəd'ventʃəʳ] *n* [unfortunate accident] Missgeschick *das.*

misapprehension [ˌmɪsæprɪ'henʃn] *n* Missverständnis *das.*

misbehave [ˌmɪsbɪ'heɪv] *vi* sich schlecht benehmen.

miscalculate [ˌmɪs'kælkjʊleɪt] ◇ *vt* - **1.** [amount, time, distance] falsch berechnen - **2.** *fig* [misjudge] falsch einschätzen ◇ *vi* - **1.** MATH sich verrechnen - **2.** *fig* [misjudge] sich verschätzen.

miscarriage [ˌmɪs'kærɪdʒ] *n* Fehlgeburt *die.*

miscarriage of justice *n* Justizirrtum *der.*

miscellaneous [ˌmɪsə'leɪnɪəs] *adj* verschieden.

mischief ['mɪstʃɪf] *n (U)* - **1.** [naughty behaviour] Unfug *der* - **2.** [harm] Schaden *der.*

mischievous ['mɪstʃɪvəs] *adj* - **1.** [playful] schelmisch - **2.** [naughty] unartig.

misconception [ˌmɪskən'sepʃn] *n* falsche Vorstellung, falsche Auffassung.

misconduct [ˌmɪs'kɒndʌkt] *n* [bad behaviour] schlechtes Benehmen.

miscount [ˌmɪs'kaʊnt] ⬦ *vt* falsch zählen ⬦ *vi* sich verzählen.

misdemeanour *Br*, **misdemeanor** *Am* [ˌmɪsdɪ'miːnəʳ] *n* LAW Vergehen *das*.

miser ['maɪzəʳ] *n* Geizhals *der*.

miserable ['mɪzrəbl] *adj* - 1. [person, life] elend; **don't look so ~** guck nicht so jämmerlich - 2. [conditions, pay, weather] miserabel; [evening, holiday] schrecklich - 3. [failure] kläglich.

miserly ['maɪzəlɪ] *adj* geizig.

misery ['mɪzərɪ] *n* - 1. [unhappiness] Kummer *der* - 2. [poverty] Elend *das*, Armut *die*.

misfire [ˌmɪs'faɪəʳ] *vi* - 1. [gun, car engine] fehlzünden - 2. [plan] fehlschlagen.

misfit ['mɪsfɪt] *n* Außenseiter *der*, -in *die*.

misfortune [mɪs'fɔːtʃuːn] *n* - 1. [bad luck] Pech *das* - 2. [piece of bad luck] Unglück *das*.

misgivings [mɪs'gɪvɪŋz] *npl* Bedenken *pl*.

misguided [ˌmɪs'gaɪdɪd] *adj* [opinion] töricht.

mishandle [ˌmɪs'hændl] *vt* - 1. [person, animal] schlecht behandeln - 2. [negotiations, business] falsch handhaben.

mishap ['mɪshæp] *n* [unfortunate event] Missgeschick *das*.

misinterpret [ˌmɪsɪn'tɜːprɪt] *vt* falsch auslegen OR deuten.

misjudge [ˌmɪs'dʒʌdʒ] *vt* - 1. [calculate wrongly] falsch einschätzen - 2. [appraise wrongly] falsch beurteilen.

mislay [ˌmɪs'leɪ] (*pt & pp* -laid [-'leɪd]) *vt* verlegen.

mislead [ˌmɪs'liːd] (*pt & pp* -led) *vt* irreführen.

misleading [ˌmɪs'liːdɪŋ] *adj* irreführend.

misled [ˌmɪs'led] *pt & pp* ⊳ mislead.

misplace [ˌmɪs'pleɪs] *vt* verlegen.

misprint ['mɪsprɪnt] *n* Druckfehler *der*.

miss [mɪs] ⬦ *vt* - 1. [person in crowd, film, turning, opportunity, train, flight] verpassen - 2. [subj: bullet, ball, footballer] verfehlen - 3. [wife, family, home] vermissen; **I ~ reading English newspapers** ich vermisse es, englische Zeitungen zu lesen - 4. [meeting, appointment, school] versäumen - 5. [disaster] entkommen (+ D); **I just ~ed being run over** ich wäre beinahe überfahren worden ⬦ *vi* [fail to hit] nicht treffen ⬦ *n*: **to give sthg a ~** *inf* sich (D) etw verkneifen. ⬧ **miss out** ⬦ *vt sep* [omit - by accident] übersehen; [- deliberately] auslassen ⬦ *vi*: **to ~ out on sthg** etw verpassen.

Miss [mɪs] *n* Fräulein *nt*.

misshapen [mɪs'ʃeɪpn] *adj* [hands, fingers, toes] missgebildet; [biscuits, cake] missraten.

missile [*Br* 'mɪsaɪl, *Am* 'mɪsl] *n* - 1. [weap-

on] Rakete *die*, Flugkörper *der* - 2. [thrown object] Wurfgeschoss *das*.

missing ['mɪsɪŋ] *adj* - 1. [lost] verschwunden; **~ in action** vermisst; **sixty people are still ~** sechzig Personen werden immer noch vermisst - 2. [not present] fehlend; **who's ~?** wer fehlt?

mission ['mɪʃn] *n* - 1. [task, duty] Auftrag *der* - 2. [delegation] Delegation *die*, Gesandtschaft *die* - 3. ASTRON & MIL Mission *die* - 4. [RELIG - building, teaching] Mission *die*.

missionary ['mɪʃənrɪ] *n* Missionar *der*, -in *die*.

misspend [ˌmɪs'spend] (*pt & pp* -spent [-'spent]) *vt* [money, talent, youth] vergeuden.

mist [mɪst] *n* Nebel *der*. ⬧ **mist over**, **mist up** *vi* beschlagen.

mistake [mɪ'steɪk] (*pt* -took; *pp* -taken) ⬦ *n* Fehler *der*; **to make a ~** [in writing, work] einen Fehler machen; [be mistaken] sich irren; **by ~** irrtümlich ⬦ *vt* - 1. [misunderstand] falsch verstehen, missverstehen - 2. [fail to distinguish]: **to ~ sb/sthg for** jn/etw verwechseln mit.

mistaken [mɪ'steɪkn] ⬦ *pp* ⊳ mistake ⬦ *adj* - 1. [person]: **to be ~** sich irren; **to be ~ about sb/sthg** sich in jm/etw irren - 2. [belief, idea] irrig, falsch.

mistletoe ['mɪsltəʊ] *n (U)* Mistel *die*.

mistook [mɪ'stʊk] *pt* ⊳ mistake.

mistreat [ˌmɪs'triːt] *vt* schlecht behandeln.

mistress ['mɪstrɪs] *n* - 1. [of house, situation] Herrin *die* - 2. [female lover] Geliebte *die*.

mistrust [ˌmɪs'trʌst] ⬦ *n* Misstrauen *das* ⬦ *vt* misstrauen (+ D).

misty ['mɪstɪ] *adj* neblig.

misunderstand [ˌmɪsʌndə'stænd] (*pt & pp* -stood) ⬦ *vt* missverstehen ⬦ *vi* falsch verstehen.

misunderstanding [ˌmɪsʌndə'stændɪŋ] *n* - 1. [lack of understanding, wrong interpretation] Missverständnis *das* - 2. [disagreement] Meinungsverschiedenheit *die*.

misunderstood [ˌmɪsʌndə'stʊd] *pt & pp* ⊳ misunderstand.

misuse [*n* ˌmɪs'juːs, *vb* ˌmɪs'juːz] ⬦ *n* Missbrauch *der*; [of funds] Zweckentfremdung *die* ⬦ *vt* [abuse] missbrauchen; [funds] zweckentfremden.

mitigate ['mɪtɪgeɪt] *vt fml* lindern.

mitten ['mɪtn] *n* Fausthandschuh *der*.

mix [mɪks] ⬦ *vt* - 1. [substances] mischen; [activities] miteinander verbinden; **to ~ sthg with sthg** etw mit etw vermischen - 2. [drink, song] mixen; [cement] mischen ⬦ *vi* - 1. [substances] sich vermischen - 2. [socially]: **to ~ with sb** mit jm verkehren, Umgang pflegen mit jm ⬦ *n* - 1. [combination] Mischung *die* - 2. MUS Mix *der*. ⬧ **mix**

up *vt sep* - **1.** [confuse] verwechseln - **2.** [disorder] durcheinander bringen.

mixed [mɪkst] *adj* gemischt.

mixed grill *n* gemischter Grillteller.

mixed up *adj* - **1.** [confused] verwirrt - **2.** [involved]: **to be ~ in sthg** in etw (A) verwickelt sein.

mixer ['mɪksə'] *n* - **1.** [device] Mixer *der*; [cement] Mischer *der* - **2.** [soft drink] *alkoholfreies Getränk, wie z. B. Fruchtsaft, das zum Mischen mit Spirituosen verwendet wird.*

mixture ['mɪkstʃə'] *n* Mischung *die*.

mix-up *n inf* Verwechslung *die*.

ml (*abbr of* millilitre) ml.

mm (*abbr of* millimetre) mm.

moan [məʊn] ◇ *n* [of pain] Stöhnen *das*; [of sadness] Seufzer *der* ◇ *vi* - **1.** [in pain] stöhnen; [in sadness] seufzen - **2.** *inf* [complain] jammern; **to ~ about sb/sthg** jammern OR sich beklagen über jn/etw.

moat [məʊt] *n* [around castle] Burggraben *der*; [in zoo] Wassergraben *der*.

mob [mɒb] ◇ *n* Mob *der* ◇ *vt* belagern.

mobile ['məʊbaɪl] ◇ *adj* - **1.** [able to move] beweglich - **2.** *inf* [having transport] motorisiert ◇ *n* [phone] Handy *das*.

mobile home *n* Wohnmobil *das*.

mobile phone *n* Handy *das*.

mobilize, -ise ['məʊbɪlaɪz] ◇ *vt* - **1.** [support, workforce] mobilisieren - **2.** MIL mobil machen ◇ *vi* MIL mobil machen.

mock [mɒk] ◇ *adj* [surprise] gespielt; [Georgian house] Pseudo-; [exam] Übungs- ◇ *vt* [deride] verspotten.

mockery ['mɒkərɪ] *n* - **1.** [scorn] Spott *der* - **2.** [travesty] Farce *die*.

mode [məʊd] *n* [manner] Art (und Weise) *die*; **~ of transport** Transportmittel *das*.

model ['mɒdl] ◇ *n* - **1.** [gen] Modell *das* - **2.** [basis for imitation] Vorlage *die*; [person, society] Vorbild *das* - **3.** [best example] Musterbeispiel *das* ◇ *adj* - **1.** [miniature] Modell- - **2.** [exemplary] Muster-, musterhaft ◇ *vt* - **1.** [shape] modellieren - **2.** [in fashion show] vorführen - **3.** [copy]: **to ~ o.s. on sb** sich (D) jn zum Vorbild nehmen ◇ *vi* [in fashion show] als Modell arbeiten, modeln.

modem ['məʊdem] *n* COMPUT Modem *das*.

moderate [*adj & n* 'mɒdərət, *vb* 'mɒdəreɪt] ◇ *adj* - **1.** [views, habits] gemäßigt; [demands] bescheiden - **2.** [heat] mäßig; [quantity] angemessen; **of ~ height/size** mittelgroß - **3.** [success, ability] mittelmäßig ◇ *n* POL Gemäßigte *der*, *die* ◇ *vt* mäßigen.

moderation [ˌmɒdə'reɪʃn] *n* Mäßigung *die*; **in ~** in Maßen.

modern ['mɒdən] *adj* modern.

modernize, -ise ['mɒdənaɪz] *vt & vi* modernisieren.

modern languages *npl* neue Sprachen *pl*.

modest ['mɒdɪst] *adj* bescheiden.

modesty ['mɒdɪstɪ] *n* Bescheidenheit *die*.

modicum ['mɒdɪkəm] *n fml*: **a ~ of** ein bisschen; **a ~ of truth** ein Körnchen Wahrheit.

modify ['mɒdɪfaɪ] *vt* - **1.** [alter] ändern, abländern - **2.** [tone down] mäßigen.

module ['mɒdjuːl] *n* - **1.** [unit] Modul *das*; SCH & UNIV *zu einem Kurs gehörende Unterrichtseinheit* - **2.** [of spacecraft] Raumkapsel *die*.

mogul ['məʊgl] *n* [magnate] Mogul *der*.

mohair ['məʊheə'] *n* (*U*) Mohair *der*.

moist [mɔɪst] *adj* feucht.

moisten ['mɔɪsn] *vt* befeuchten.

moisture ['mɔɪstʃə'] *n* Feuchtigkeit *die*.

moisturizer, -iser ['mɔɪstʃəraɪzə'] *n* Feuchtigkeitscreme *die*.

molar ['məʊlə'] *n* Backenzahn *der*.

molasses [mə'læsɪz] *n* (*U*) Melasse *die*.

mold *etc n & vt Am* = **mould**.

mole [məʊl] *n* - **1.** [animal] Maulwurf *der* - **2.** [on skin] Muttermal *das*, Leberfleck *der* - **3.** [spy] Spion *der*.

molecule ['mɒlɪkjuːl] *n* Molekül *das*.

molest [mə'lest] *vt* - **1.** [attack sexually] sexuell belästigen - **2.** [bother] belästigen.

mollusc, mollusk *Am* ['mɒləsk] *n* Weichtier *das*.

mollycoddle ['mɒlɪˌkɒdl] *vt inf* verhätscheln, verzärteln.

molt *vt & vi Am* = **moult**.

molten ['məʊltn] *adj* geschmolzen.

mom [mɒm] *n Am inf* Mutter *die*; [within speaker's family] Mutti *die*.

moment ['məʊmənt] *n* - **1.** [very short period of time] Moment *der*, Augenblick *der* - **2.** [particular point in time] Zeitpunkt *der*; **at any ~** jeden Moment; **at the ~** im Moment; **for the ~** vorerst.

momentarily ['məʊməntərɪlɪ] *adv* - **1.** [for a short time] momentan - **2.** *Am* [immediately] jeden Moment OR Augenblick.

momentary ['məʊməntrɪ] *adj* kurz.

momentous [mə'mentəs] *adj* bedeutsam.

momentum [mə'mentəm] *n* [speed] Schwung *der*; **to gain** OR **gather ~** [object, campaign] in Fahrt kommen.

momma ['mɒmə], **mommy** ['mɒmɪ] *n Am* Mama *die*, Mami *die*.

Monaco ['mɒnəkəʊ] *n* Monaco *nt*.

monarch ['mɒnək] *n* Monarch *der*, -in *die*.

monarchy ['mɒnəkɪ] *n* Monarchie *die*.

monastery ['mɒnəstrɪ] *n* Kloster *das*.

Monday ['mʌndɪ] *n* Montag *der*; *see also* Saturday.

monetary ['mʌnɪtrɪ] *adj* Währungs-.

money ['mʌnɪ] *n* (*U*) Geld *das*; **to make ~** Geld machen; **to get one's ~'s worth** etw für sein Geld bekommen.

moneybox ['mʌnɪbɒks] *n* Sparbüchse *die*.

money order *n* Zahlungsanweisung *die*.

mongrel ['mʌŋgrəl] n [dog] Mischling der.

monitor ['mɒnɪtə'] ⋄ n Monitor der ⋄ vt - 1. [check] überwachen, kontrollieren - 2. [listen to] ablhören, mitlhören.

monk [mʌŋk] n Mönch der.

monkey ['mʌŋkɪ] (pl monkeys) n [animal] Affe der.

mono ['mɒnəʊ] ⋄ adj [with noun] Mono-; [with adj] mono- ⋄ n inf [sound] Mono das.

monochrome ['mɒnəkrəʊm] adj monochrom, schwarzweiß.

monocle ['mɒnəkl] n Monokel das.

monologue, monolog Am ['mɒnəlɒg] n Monolog der.

monopolize, -ise [mə'nɒpəlaɪz] vt monopolisieren; [conversation] beherrschen; [person] in Beschlag nehmen.

monopoly [mə'nɒpəlɪ] n: ~ (on OR of) Monopol das (auf (+ A)).

monotonous [mə'nɒtənəs] adj monoton.

monotony [mə'nɒtənɪ] n Monotonie die.

monsoon [mɒn'suːn] n Monsun der.

monster ['mɒnstə'] n Monster das.

monstrosity [mɒn'strɒsətɪ] n Monstrosität die, Ungeheuerlichkeit die.

monstrous ['mɒnstrəs] adj - 1. [appalling] abscheulich - 2. [hideous] scheußlich - 3. [very large] riesig.

month [mʌnθ] n Monat der.

monthly ['mʌnθlɪ] ⋄ adj monatlich; [magazine] Monats- ⋄ adv monatlich ⋄ n [magazine] Monatsmagazin das.

monument ['mɒnjʊmənt] n - 1. [memorial] Monument das - 2. [historic building] Denkmal das.

monumental [ˌmɒnjʊ'mentl] adj - 1. [very large] monumental - 2. [important] bedeutend - 3. [extremely bad] ungeheuerlich.

moo [muː] (pl -s) vi muhen.

mood [muːd] n Stimmung die; [of person] Laune die; to be in a (bad) ~ schlechte Laune haben; to be in a good ~ gute Laune haben.

moody ['muːdɪ] adj pej - 1. [changeable] launisch - 2. [bad-tempered] schlecht gelaunt.

moon [muːn] n Mond der.

moonlight ['muːnlaɪt] (pt & pp -ed) n Mondlicht das.

moonlighting ['muːnlaɪtɪŋ] n [illegal work] Schwarzarbeit die.

moonlit ['muːnlɪt] adj [place] mondbeschienen; [night] mondhell.

moor [mɔː'] ⋄ vt vertäuen ⋄ vi anllegen.

moorland ['mɔːlənd] n esp Br Heideland das.

moose [muːs] (pl inv) n Elch der.

mop [mɒp] ⋄ n - 1. [for cleaning] Mopp der - 2. inf [of hair]: ~ of hair (Haar)mähne die ⋄ vt wischen. ◆ **mop up** vt sep [liquid, dirt] auflwischen.

mope [məʊp] vi pej Trübsal blasen.

moped ['məʊped] n Moped das.

moral ['mɒrəl] ⋄ adj - 1. [relating to morals] moralisch - 2. [behaving correctly] moralisch einwandfrei ⋄ n [lesson] Moral die. ◆ **morals** npl [principles] Moral die.

morale [mə'rɑːl] n Moral die.

morality [mə'rælətɪ] n Moralität die.

morbid ['mɔːbɪd] adj morbid.

more [mɔː'] ⋄ adv - 1. (in comparatives): ~ difficult (than) schwieriger (als); speak ~ clearly, please sprich bitte deutlicher; much ~ quickly viel schneller - 2. [to a greater degree] mehr; we ought to go to the cinema ~ wir sollten öfters ins Kino gehen; I couldn't agree ~ ich stimme dem völlig zu; she's ~ like a mother to me than a sister sie ist mehr wie eine Mutter als wie eine Schwester; we were ~ hurt than angry wir waren eher verletzt als zornig; we'd be ~ than happy to help wir würden sehr gerne helfen; ~ than ever mehr denn je - 3. [referring to time]: once/twice ~ noch einmal/zweimal; I don't go there any ~ ich gehe da nicht mehr hin ⋄ adj - 1. [larger number, amount of] mehr; there are ~ tourists than usual es sind mehr Touristen als gewöhnlich da; ~ than ten men mehr als zehn Männer - 2. [additional] mehr; we need ~ money/time wir brauchen mehr Geld/Zeit; two ~ bottles noch zwei Flaschen; is there any ~ cake? ist noch mehr Kuchen da?; there's no ~ wine es ist kein Wein mehr da; have some ~ tea nehmen Sie noch etwas Tee ⋄ pron - 1. [larger number, amount] mehr; I've got ~ than you ich habe mehr als du; ~ than 20 mehr als 20 - 2. [additional amount] mehr; we need ~ wir brauchen mehr; I'd like two ~ ich möchte noch zwei; to see ~ of sb jn öfter sehen; is there any ~? ist noch mehr da?; there's no ~ es ist nichts mehr da; I have no ~ (of them) ich habe keine mehr; have some ~ nimm dir noch; (and) what's ~ außerdem; the ~ he has, the ~ he wants je mehr er hat, desto mehr will er haben. ◆ **more and more** ⋄ adv - 1. [increasingly] immer mehr; ~ and - depressed/difficult immer deprimierter/schwieriger - 2. [increasingly often] immer mehr OR öfter ⋄ adj immer mehr; there are ~ and ~ cars on the roads es gibt immer mehr Autos auf den Straßen ⋄ pron immer mehr; we are spending ~ and ~ on petrol wir geben immer mehr für Benzin aus. ◆ **more or less** adv [almost] mehr oder weniger; she ~ or less suggested I had stolen it sie hat mehr oder weniger behauptet, dass ich es gestohlen hätte; it cost $500, ~ or less es kostete um die $500.

moreover [mɔː'rəʊvə'] adv fml außerdem.

morgue [mɔːg] n Leichenhalle die.

morning ['mɔːnɪŋ] n - 1. [first part of day] Morgen der, Vormittag der; in the ~ [before lunch] morgens; [tomorrow morning] mor-

gen - 2. [between midnight and noon] Morgen *der.* ◆ **mornings** *adv Am* morgens.

Morocco [mə'rɒkəʊ] *n* Marokko *nt.*

moron ['mɔːrɒn] *n inf* Bekloppte *der, die.*

morose [mə'rəʊs] *adj* griesgrämig.

morphine ['mɔːfiːn] *n* Morphium *das.*

Morse (code) [mɔːs-] *n* (U) Morsezeichen *pl.*

morsel ['mɔːsl] *n* Bissen *der,* Happen *der.*

mortal ['mɔːtl] ◇ *adj* **- 1.** [not eternal] sterblich **- 2.** [causing death] tödlich **- 3.** [danger, fear] Todes-; ~ **enemy** Todfeind *der;* ~ **combat** Kampf *der* um Leben und Tod ◇ *n* Sterbliche *der, die.*

mortality [mɔː'tælətɪ] *n* Sterblichkeit *die.*

mortar ['mɔːtəʳ] *n* **- 1.** [cement mixture] Mörtel *der* **- 2.** [gun, bowl] Mörser *der.*

mortgage ['mɔːgɪdʒ] ◇ *n* Hypothek *die* ◇ *vt* mit einer Hypothek belasten.

mortified ['mɔːtɪfaɪd] *adj* beschämt.

mortuary ['mɔːtʃʊərɪ] *n* Leichenhalle *die.*

mosaic [mə'zeɪɪk] *n* Mosaik *das.*

Moscow ['mɒskəʊ] *n* Moskau *nt.*

Moslem ['mɒzləm] *adj* & *n* = Muslim.

mosque [mɒsk] *n* Moschee *die.*

mosquito [mə'skiːtəʊ] (*pl* -es OR -s) *n* Moskito *der.*

moss [mɒs] *n* (U) Moos *das.*

most [məʊst] (*superl* of **many** & **much**) ◇ *adj* **- 1.** [the majority of] die meisten; ~ **people agree** die meisten Leute sind dieser Meinung **- 2.** [the largest amount of] der/die/das meiste; **I drank (the) ~ beer** ich habe das meiste Bier getrunken ◇ *adv* **- 1.** [in superlatives]: **she spoke (the) ~ clearly** sie sprach am deutlichsten; **the ~ expensive hotel in town** das teuerste Hotel in der Stadt **- 2.** [to the greatest degree] am meisten; **I like this one ~** mir gefällt dieses am besten **- 3.** *fml* [very] äußerst, höchst; **it was a ~ pleasant evening** es war ein äußerst angenehmer Abend ◇ *pron* **- 1.** [the majority] die meisten *pl;* ~ **of the villages** die meisten Dörfer; ~ **of the time** die meiste Zeit; ~ **of the work** der größte Teil der Arbeit **- 2.** [the largest amount] das meiste; **she earns (the) ~** sie verdient am meisten **- 3.** *phr:* **at ~** höchstens; **to make the ~ of sthg** das Beste aus etw machen; **to make the ~ of an opportunity** eine Gelegenheit voll ausnutzen.

mostly ['məʊstlɪ] *adv* hauptsächlich.

MOT *n* (*abbr of* Ministry of Transport (test)) ≈ TÜV *der.*

motel [məʊ'tel] *n* Motel *das.*

moth [mɒθ] *n* Nachtfalter *der;* [eating clothes] Motte *die.*

mothball ['mɒθbɔːl] *n* Mottenkugel *die.*

mother ['mʌðəʳ] ◇ *n* Mutter *die* ◇ *vt pej* [spoil] bemuttern.

motherhood ['mʌðəhʊd] *n* Mutterschaft *die.*

mother-in-law (*pl* mothers-in-law OR mother-in-laws) *n* Schwiegermutter *die.*

motherly ['mʌðəlɪ] *adj* mütterlich.

mother-of-pearl *n* Perlmutt *das.*

mother-to-be (*pl* mothers-to-be) *n* werdende Mutter.

mother tongue *n* Muttersprache *die.*

motif [məʊ'tiːf] *n* [pattern] Muster *das.*

motion ['məʊʃn] ◇ *n* **- 1.** [movement] Bewegung *die;* **to set sthg in ~** etw in Bewegung setzen **- 2.** [proposal] Antrag *der* ◇ *vt* & *vi:* **to ~ (to) sb to do sthg** jm durch Zeichen zu verstehen geben, etw zu tun.

motionless ['məʊʃənlɪs] *adj* bewegungslos.

motion picture *n Am* Film *der.*

motivated ['məʊtɪveɪtɪd] *adj* motiviert.

motivation [‚məʊtɪ'veɪʃn] *n* Motivation *die.*

motive ['məʊtɪv] *n* Motiv *das.*

motor ['məʊtəʳ] ◇ *adj Br* [relating to cars] Auto- ◇ *n* [engine] Motor *der.*

motorbike ['məʊtəbaɪk] *n inf* Motorrad *das.*

motorboat ['məʊtəbəʊt] *n* Motorboot *das.*

motorcar ['məʊtəkɑːʳ] *n Br fml* Automobil *das.*

motorcycle ['məʊtə‚saɪkl] *n* Motorrad *das.*

motorcyclist ['məʊtə‚saɪklɪst] *n* Motorradfahrer *der,* -in *die.*

motoring ['məʊtərɪŋ] *adj Br* [offence] Verkehrs-; [magazine] Auto-.

motorist ['məʊtərɪst] *n* Autofahrer *der,* -in *die.*

motor racing *n* Autorennen *das.*

motor scooter *n* Motorroller *der.*

motor vehicle *n* Kraftfahrzeug *das.*

motorway ['məʊtəweɪ] *n Br* Autobahn *die.*

mottled ['mɒtld] *adj* [leaf] gesprenkelt; [skin, face] fleckig.

motto ['mɒtəʊ] (*pl* -s OR -es) *n* [maxim] Motto *das.*

mould, mold *Am* [məʊld] ◇ *n* **- 1.** [growth] Schimmel *der* **- 2.** [shape] Form *die* ◇ *vt* formen.

mouldy, moldy *Am* ['məʊldɪ] *adj* schimmelig.

moult, molt *Am* [məʊlt] *vi* [bird] sich mausern; [animal] im Fellwechsel OR Haarwechsel sein.

mound [maʊnd] *n* **- 1.** [small hill] Hügel *der* **- 2.** [untidy pile] Haufen *der;* [of papers, blankets] Stapel *der.*

mount [maʊnt] ◇ *n* **- 1.** [support, frame - for photograph] Rahmen *der;* [- for jewel] Fassung *die;* [- for machine] Sockel *der* **- 2.** [horse, pony] Reittier *das* **- 3.** [mountain]: **Mount Everest** Mount Everest; **Mount Etna** Etna ◇ *vt* **- 1.** [climb onto] besteigen **- 2.** *fml* [climb up - stairs] hochsteigen **- 3.** [organize] organisieren **- 4.** [fix in place - jewel] einlfassen; [- photographic slide] rahmen; **to ~ sthg on the wall** etw an die Wand hängen ◇ vi [increase] sich erhöhen.

mountain ['maʊntɪn] n lit & fig Berg der.

mountain bike n Mountainbike das.

mountaineer [ˌmaʊntɪ'nɪəʳ] n Bergsteiger der, -in die.

mountaineering [ˌmaʊntɪ'nɪərɪŋ] n Bergsteigen das.

mountainous ['maʊntɪnəs] adj [full of mountains] bergig.

mourn [mɔːn] ◇ vt trauern um ◇ vi trauern; **to ~ for sb** um jn trauern.

mourner ['mɔːnəʳ] n Trauernde der, die.

mournful ['mɔːnfʊl] adj traurig.

mourning ['mɔːnɪŋ] n: **to be in ~** [mourn] trauern.

mouse [maʊs] (pl mice) n [animal & COMPUT] Maus die.

mouse mat, mouse pad n COMPUT Mousepad das.

mousetrap ['maʊstræp] n Mausefalle die.

mousse [muːs] n - **1.** [food] Mousse die - **2.** [for hair] Schaumfestiger der.

moustache Br [mə'stɑːʃ], **mustache** Am ['mʌstæʃ] n Schnurrbart der.

mouth [maʊθ] n - **1.** [of person] Mund der - **2.** [entrance - of cave, tunnel] Eingang der; [- of river] Mündung die.

mouthful ['maʊθfʊl] n [amount - of food] Bissen der; [- of drink] Schluck der.

mouthorgan ['maʊθˌɔːgən] n Mundharmonika die.

mouthpiece ['maʊθpiːs] n - **1.** [of telephone] Sprechmuschel die - **2.** [of musical instrument] Mundstück das - **3.** [spokesperson] Sprachrohr das.

mouthwash ['maʊθwɒʃ] n (U) Mundwasser das.

mouth-watering [-ˌwɔːtərɪŋ] adj appetitlich, appetitanregend.

movable ['muːvəbl] adj beweglich.

move [muːv] ◇ n - **1.** [movement] Bewegung die; **to get a ~ on** inf sich beeilen - **2.** [to new house] Umzug der; [to higher position in company] Aufstieg der - **3.** [in board game] Zug der; **it's your ~** du bist am Zug - **4.** [course of action]: **it would be a good ~** es wäre klug ◇ vt - **1.** [arm, head] bewegen; [piece of furniture] rücken; [car] weglfahren; [piece in board game] einen Zug machen mit - **2.** [change]: **to ~ house** umlziehen; **to ~ sb to another job** jn versetzen - **3.** [affect emotionally] bewegen, rühren - **4.** [in debate]: **to ~ that ...** beantragen, dass ... - **5.** fml [cause]: **to ~ sb to do sthg** jn dazu bewegen, etw zu tun ◇ vi - **1.** [shift] sich bewegen - **2.** [act] handeln - **3.** [to new house] umlziehen. ➤ **move about** vi - **1.** [fidget] sich unruhig (hin und her) bewegen - **2.** [travel] unterwegs sein. ➤ **move along** ◇ vt sep [per-

son, crowds] zum Weitergehen veranlassen ◇ vi weiterlgehen; [in car] weiterlfahren. ➤ **move around** vi = move about. ➤ **move away** vi [go in opposite direction] weglgehen; [car] weglfahren. ➤ **move in** vi - **1.** [to new house] umlziehen - **2.** [troops] einlrücken; [competitors] auf den Plan treten. ➤ **move on** vi - **1.** [after stopping] weiterlgehen; [in car] weiterlfahren - **2.** [in discussion] fortlfahren. ➤ **move out** vi [from house] auslziehen. ➤ **move over** vi zur Seite rutschen OR rücken. ➤ **move up** vi [on seat] auflrutschen, auflrücken.

moveable ['muːvəbl] adj = movable.

movement ['muːvmənt] n - **1.** [motion, gesture, group] Bewegung die - **2.** [transportation] Beförderung die - **3.** [trend] Trend der - **4.** MUS Satz der.

movie ['muːvɪ] n esp Am Film der; **to go to the ~s** zum Kino gehen.

movie camera n Filmkamera die.

moving ['muːvɪŋ] adj - **1.** [touching] bewegend - **2.** [not fixed] beweglich.

mow [məʊ] (pt -ed; pp -ed OR mown) vt mähen. ➤ **mow down** vt sep niederlmähen.

mower ['məʊəʳ] n [lawnmower] Rasenmäher der.

mown [məʊn] pp ➤ mow.

MP n Br abbr of Member of Parliament.

mpg (abbr of miles per gallon) n: **31 ~ 9,1 l auf 100 km.**

mph (abbr of miles per hour) n: **he was doing 50 ~** er fuhr 80 km/h (schnell).

Mr ['mɪstəʳ] n Herr.

Mrs ['mɪsɪz] n Frau, Fr.

Ms [mɪz] n Frau, Fr.

MSc n abbr of Master of Science.

much [mʌtʃ] (compar more; superl most) ◇ adj viel; **I haven't got ~ money** ich habe nicht viel Geld; **as ~ food as you can eat** so viel du essen kannst; **how ~ is left?** wie viel ist übrig?; **we have too ~ work** wir haben zu viel Arbeit ◇ adv - **1.** [to a great extent] viel; **it's ~ better** es ist viel besser; **I like it very ~** es gefällt mir sehr gut; **it's not ~ good** inf es ist nicht besonders; **nothing ~** nichts Besonderes; **thank you very ~** vielen Dank; **~ as I like him** so gern ich ihn auch mag; **~ to my surprise** sehr zu meiner Überraschung; **~ the same** ziemlich das Gleiche; **he's not so ~ stupid as lazy** er ist weniger dumm als faul; **he left without so ~ as a goodbye** er hat sich nicht einmal verabschiedet - **2.** [often] oft; **we don't go there ~** wir gehen da nicht oft hin ◇ pron viel; **I haven't got ~** ich habe nicht viel; **as ~ as you like** so viel Sie wollen; **how ~ is it?** wie viel kostet es?; **you've got too ~** du hast zu viel; **I don't think ~ of him** ich halte nicht viel von ihm; **I thought as ~** das habe ich mir gedacht; **I'm not ~ of a cook**

ich bin kein großer Koch; **so ~ for his friendship!** und das nennt sich Freundschaft!

muck [mʌk] n (U) inf - **1.** [dirt] Dreck der - **2.** [manure] Mist der. ◆ **muck about, muck around** Br inf ◇ vt sep [person] an der Nase herumlführen ◇ vi herumlalbern. ◆ **muck up** vt sep Br inf vermasseln.

mucky ['mʌkɪ] adj inf dreckig.

mucus ['mjuːkəs] n (U) Schleim der.

mud [mʌd] n Schlamm der.

muddle ['mʌdl] ◇ n [disorder] Durcheinander das ◇ vt - **1.** [put into disorder] durcheinander bringen - **2.** [confuse - person] verwirren. ◆ **muddle along** vi vor sich (A) hin wursteln. ◆ **muddle through** vi sich durchlwursteln OR durchschlagen. ◆ **muddle up** vt sep durcheinander bringen.

muddy ['mʌdɪ] ◇ adj [floor, boots] schmutzig; [river] schlammig ◇ vt fig [issue, situation] verworren machen.

mudguard ['mʌdɡɑːd] n [on car] Kotflügel der; [on motorcycle] Schutzblech das.

muesli ['mjuːzlɪ] n Br Müsli das.

muff [mʌf] ◇ n [for hands] Muff der; [for ears] Ohrenwärmer der ◇ vt inf verpatzen.

muffin ['mʌfɪn] n - **1.** Br [bread roll] kleines flaches Milchbrötchen, das warm und mit Butter gegessen wird - **2.** Am [cake] kleiner Kuchen.

muffle ['mʌfl] vt [quieten] dämpfen.

muffler ['mʌflər] n Am [for car] Auspuff der.

mug [mʌɡ] ◇ n - **1.** [cup, mugful] Tasse die - **2.** inf [fool] Trottel der ◇ vt [attack and rob] überfallen und berauben.

mugging ['mʌɡɪŋ] n Straßenraub der.

muggy ['mʌɡɪ] adj schwül.

mule [mjuːl] n - **1.** [animal] Maultier das - **2.** [slipper] Schlappen der.

mull [mʌl] ◆ **mull over** vt sep gründlich durch denken.

mulled [mʌld] adj: **~ wine** Glühwein der.

multicoloured Br, **multicolored** Am ['mʌltɪˌkʌləd] adj bunt, mehrfarbig.

multilateral [ˌmʌltɪˈlætərəl] adj multilateral.

multilingual [ˌmʌltɪˈlɪŋɡwəl] adj mehrsprachig.

multinational [ˌmʌltɪˈnæʃənl] n multinationales Unternehmen.

multiple ['mʌltɪpl] ◇ adj vielfach ◇ n MATH Vielfache das.

multiple sclerosis [-sklɪˈrəʊsɪs] n (U) multiple Sklerose.

multiplex (cinema) ['mʌltɪpleks-] n großes Kino mit mehreren Vorführsälen.

multiplication [ˌmʌltɪplɪˈkeɪʃn] n (U) - **1.** MATH Multiplikation die - **2.** [increase] Vervielfachung die, Vermehrung die.

multiply ['mʌltɪplaɪ] ◇ vt - **1.** MATH multiplizieren - **2.** [increase] vermehren ◇ vi

- **1.** MATH multiplizieren - **2.** [increase] sich vervielfältigen - **3.** [breed] sich vermehren.

multistorey Br, **multistory** Am [ˌmʌltɪˈstɔːrɪ] adj mehrstöckig; **~ car park** Parkhaus das.

multitude ['mʌltɪtjuːd] n [large number] Vielzahl die.

mum [mʌm] Br inf ◇ n Mutter die; [within speaker's family] Mutti die ◇ adj: **to keep ~** den Mund halten.

mumble ['mʌmbl] ◇ vt [response] murmeln; [words] nuscheln ◇ vi vor sich (A) hin murmeln; **stop mumbling** hör auf zu nuscheln.

mummy ['mʌmɪ] n - **1.** Br inf [mother] Mami die - **2.** [preserved body] Mumie die.

mumps [mʌmps] n (U) Mumps der.

munch [mʌntʃ] vt & vi mampfen.

mundane [mʌnˈdeɪn] adj [ordinary] alltäglich.

municipal [mjuːˈnɪsɪpl] adj städtisch; [park, administration] Stadt-.

municipality [mjuːˌnɪsɪˈpælətɪ] n Stadt die.

mural ['mjuːərəl] n Wandgemälde das.

murder ['mɜːdər] ◇ n Mord der ◇ vt ermorden.

murderer ['mɜːdərər] n Mörder der, -in die.

murderous ['mɜːdərəs] adj [thugs] mordgierig; [attack] mörderisch.

murky ['mɜːkɪ] adj - **1.** [dark - place] düster; [- water] trüb - **2.** [shameful] dunkel, finster.

murmur ['mɜːmər] ◇ n - **1.** [low sound - of voices] Gemurmel das; [- of disapproving voices] Murmeln das - **2.** MED [of heart] Herzgeräusch das ◇ vt & vi murmeln.

muscle ['mʌsl] n - **1.** [organ] Muskel der - **2.** (U) MED [tissue] Muskelgewebe das - **3.** (U) fig [power] Macht die. ◆ **muscle in** vi mitlmischen.

muscular ['mʌskjʊlər] adj - **1.** [of muscles] Muskel- - **2.** [strong] muskulös.

muse [mjuːz] ◇ n Muse die ◇ vi sinnieren.

museum [mjuːˈzɪəm] n Museum das.

mushroom ['mʌʃrʊm] ◇ n [cultivated] Pilz der, Champignon der ◇ vi [grow quickly - organization, movement] sehr schnell wachsen; [- houses] wie Pilze aus dem Boden schießen.

music ['mjuːzɪk] n - **1.** [gen] Musik die; **a piece of ~** ein Musikstück - **2.** [subject studied] Musik die - **3.** [written] Noten pl.

musical ['mjuːzɪkl] ◇ adj - **1.** [education, director] Musik- - **2.** [talented in music] musikalisch - **3.** [voice, sound] melodiös ◇ n Musical das.

musical instrument n Musikinstrument das.

music centre n Kompaktanlage die.

music hall n Br Varieté das.

musician [mjuːˈzɪʃn] n Musiker der, -in die.

Muslim ['mʊzlɪm] <> *adj* moslemisch <> *n* Moslem *der,* Moslime *die.*

mussel ['mʌsl] *n* Miesmuschel *die.*

must [mʌst] <> *aux vb* müssen; [with negative] dürfen; **I ~ go** ich muss gehen; **you ~n't be late** du darfst nicht zu spät kommen; **do it, if you ~** tu es, wenn es sein muss; **the room ~ be vacated by ten** das Zimmer ist bis zehn Uhr zu räumen; **you ~ have seen it** du musst es doch gesehen haben; **you ~ see that film** du musst dir diesen Film ansehen; **you ~ be joking!** das kann doch nicht dein Ernst sein! <> *n:* **it's a ~** *inf* das ist ein Muss.

mustache *n Am* = **moustache.**

mustard ['mʌstəd] *n* Senf *der.*

muster ['mʌstə'] <> *vt* **- 1.** [summon - strength, courage] zusammen|nehmen; [- support] zusammen|bekommen **- 2.** [assemble - volunteers, helpers] versammeln; [- troops] zusammen|ziehen <> *vi* [troops] sich sammeln.

mustn't [mʌsnt] = must not.

must've ['mʌstəv] = must have.

musty ['mʌstɪ] *adj* [smell, room, air] muffig; [books] moderig.

mute [mjuːt] *adj* [person] stumm.

muted ['mjuːtɪd] *adj* **- 1.** [sound, colour] gedämpft **- 2.** [protest] schwach.

mutilate ['mjuːtɪleɪt] *vt* **- 1.** [maim] verstümmeln **- 2.** [damage, spoil] ruinieren.

mutiny ['mjuːtɪnɪ] <> *n* Meuterei *die* <> *vi* meutern.

mutter ['mʌtə'] <> *vt* murmeln <> *vi* murmeln; [grumble] murren.

mutton ['mʌtn] *n* Hammelfleisch *das.*

mutual ['mjuːtʃʊəl] *adj* **- 1.** [aid] gegenseitig; **by ~ consent** in gegenseitigem Einverständnis **- 2.** [friend, interest] gemeinsam.

mutually ['mjuːtʃʊəlɪ] *adv* [reciprocally - beneficial, convenient] für beide Seiten; [- agreed] von beiden Seiten.

muzzle ['mʌzl] <> *n* **- 1.** [dog's nose and jaws] Schnauze *die* **- 2.** [for dog] Maulkorb *der* **- 3.** [of gun] Mündung *die* <> *vt* **- 1.** [dog] einen Maulkorb anlegen (+ D) **- 2.** *fig* [press, opposition] knebeln.

MW *(abbr of medium wave)* MW.

my [maɪ] <> *poss adj* mein; **~ friend** mein Freund, meine Freundin; **~ children** meine Kinder; **I washed ~ hair** ich habe mir die Haare gewaschen <> *excl:* **(oh) ~!** meine Güte!

myself [maɪ'self] *pron* **- 1.** (reflexive: accusative) mich; (reflexive: dative) mir; **I have hurt ~** ich habe mich verletzt; **I bought ~ some new clothes** ich habe mir neue Kleider gekauft **- 2.** (after prep: accusative) mich selbst; (after prep: dative) mir selbst; **I did it ~** ich habe es selbst gemacht; **by ~** allein.

mysterious [mɪ'stɪərɪəs] *adj* **- 1.** [puzzling - illness, sound] rätselhaft; [- disappearance] mysteriös **- 2.** [secretive] geheimnisvoll.

mystery ['mɪstərɪ] *n* **- 1.** [puzzle] Rätsel *das* **- 2.** [secret] Geheimnis *das.*

mystical ['mɪstɪkl] *adj* mystisch.

mystified ['mɪstɪfaɪd] *adj* verwirrt.

mystifying ['mɪstɪfaɪɪŋ] *adj* [action] rätselhaft; [decision] unerklärlich.

mystique [mɪ'stiːk] *n (U)* geheimnisvoller Nimbus.

myth [mɪθ] *n* **- 1.** [legend] Mythos *der* **- 2.** [false belief] Irrglauben *der.*

mythical ['mɪθɪkl] *adj* **- 1.** [legendary] mythisch **- 2.** [imaginary - place, time] fiktiv.

mythology [mɪ'θɒlədʒɪ] *n* Mythologie *die.*

N

n *(pl* n's OR ns), **N** *(pl* N's OR Ns) [en] *n* [letter] *n das,* N *das.* ◆ **N** *(abbr of* north) N.

n/a, N/A **- 1.** *(abbr of* not applicable) entf. **- 2.** *(abbr of* not available) n. bez.

nab [næb] *vt inf* **- 1.** [arrest] schnappen **- 2.** [claim quickly] sich (D) schnappen.

nag [næg] <> *vt* [pester] keine Ruhe lassen (+ D); [find fault with] herum|nörgeln an (+ D); **to ~ sb to do sthg** jm zusetzen, damit er/ sie etw tut <> *n Br inf* [horse] Klepper *der.*

nagging ['nægɪŋ] *adj* [thought, doubt, pain] quälend.

nail [neɪl] <> *n* [gen] Nagel *der* <> *vt:* **to ~ sthg to sthg** etw an etw (A) nageln. ◆ **nail down** *vt sep lit & fig* festl|nageln.

nailbrush ['neɪlbrʌʃ] *n* Nagelbürste *die.*

nail clippers [-ˌklɪpəz] *npl* Nagelknipser *der.*

nail file *n* Nagelfeile *die.*

nail polish *n* Nagellack *der.*

nail scissors *npl* Nagelschere *die.*

nail varnish *n* Nagellack *der.*

nail varnish remover [-rɪ'muːvə'] *n* Nagellackentferner *der.*

naive, naïve [naɪ'iːv] *adj* naiv.

naked ['neɪkɪd] *adj* **- 1.** [nude] nackt **- 2.** [flame] offen; [light bulb] nackt; **with the ~ eye** mit bloßem Auge **- 3.** [truth, aggression] nackt.

name [neɪm] <> *n* **- 1.** [gen] Name *der;* **what's your ~?** wie heißen Sie?; **my ~ is ...** ich heiße ...; **to know sb by ~** jn mit Namen kennen; **to know sb only by ~** jn nur dem Namen nach kennen; **in the ~ of** im Namen (+ G); **the account is in her ~** das Konto läuft auf ihren Namen; **to call sb ~s** jn beschimpfen - **2.** [reputation] Name *der*, Ruf *der*; **to clear one's ~** seine Unschuld beweisen ⟨⟩ *vt* - **1.** [baby, place, ship] einen Namen geben (+ D); **they ~d their daughter Kate** sie nannten ihre Tochter Kate; **I ~ this ship 'Bounty'** ich taufe das Schiff auf den Namen „Bounty"; **to ~ sb after sb** *Br,* **to ~ sb for sb** *Am* jn nach jm nennen; **to ~ sthg after sthg** *Br,* **to ~ sthg for sthg** *Am* etw nach etw benennen - **2.** [reveal identity of]: **to ~ sb** js Namen nennen - **3.** [choose - price, date] nennen; [- successor] ernennen.

namely ['neɪmlɪ] *adv* nämlich.

namesake ['neɪmseɪk] *n* Namensvetter *der*, -in *die*.

nanny ['nænɪ] *n* [childminder] Kindermädchen *das*.

nap [næp] ⟨⟩ *n* [sleep] Nickerchen *das*; **to take** OR **have a ~** ein Nickerchen machen ⟨⟩ *vi* [sleep] ein Nickerchen machen; **to be caught ~ping** *inf* überrumpelt werden.

nape [neɪp] *n*: ~ **(of the neck)** Nacken *der*.

napkin ['næpkɪn] *n* [serviette] Serviette *die*.

nappy ['næpɪ] *n Br* Windel *die*.

narcotic [nɑː'kɒtɪk] *n* Betäubungsmittel *das*. ➤ **narcotics** *npl* Rauschgift *das*.

narrative ['nærətɪv] ⟨⟩ *adj* [ability; skill] erzählerisch; [poem] narrativ ⟨⟩ *n* [account] Schilderung *die*.

narrator [*Br* nə'reɪtə', *Am* 'næreɪtər] *n* [in book] Erzähler *der*, -in *die*; [of documentary] Kommentator *der*, -in *die*.

narrow ['nærəʊ] ⟨⟩ *adj* - **1.** [not wide] schmal; [valley, lane] eng - **2.** [attitude, beliefs] engstirnig - **3.** [victory, defeat, majority] knapp ⟨⟩ *vt* - **1.**: **to ~ one's eyes** die Augen zu Schlitzen verengen - **2.** [difference, gap] verringern ⟨⟩ *vi* - **1.** [become less wide] sich verengen - **2.** [eyes] zu Schlitzen werden - **3.** [difference, gap] sich verringern. ➤ **narrow down** *vt sep* [restrict - choice] einschränken; [- possibilities] beschränken.

narrowly ['nærəʊlɪ] *adv* [just] knapp; [escape] mit knapper Not.

narrow-minded [-'maɪndɪd] *adj* engstirnig.

nasal ['neɪzl] *adj* - **1.** [sound] näselnd - **2.** ANAT Nasen-.

nasty ['nɑːstɪ] *adj* - **1.** [unkind - person, behaviour] gemein; [- remark] gehässig - **2.** [smell, taste, weather] scheußlich - **3.** [problem, question] schwierig - **4.** [injury, accident, fall] schlimm.

nation ['neɪʃn] *n* Nation *die*; [people] Volk *das*.

national ['næʃənl] ⟨⟩ *adj* - **1.** [nationwide - strike] national, landesweit; [- newspaper] überregional; [- library, debt] Staats- - **2.** [typical of nation] landestypisch; [custom] Volks- ⟨⟩ *n* Staatsbürger *der*, -in *die*.

national anthem *n* Nationalhymne *die*.

national curriculum *n* Programm, das die Fächer und zu erreichenden Standards in den staatlichen Schulen in England und Wales festlegt.

national curriculum

Bis zur Verabschiedung des Gesetzes zur Bildungsreform 1988 hatten staatliche Schulen in England und Wales kein vorgeschriebenes Curriculum. Heute werden die Inhalte des Lehrstoffs von einer Regierungsbehörde bestimmt, die auch die unterschiedlichen Lernziele (SATs) definiert. Verpflichtend ist der Unterricht in drei Hauptfächern (Englisch, Mathematik und Naturwissenschaft) und sieben Basisoder Nebenfächern. Das National Curriculum legt vier Zeitpunkte fest, zu denen der allgemeine Leistungsstand der Schüler geprüft wird: im Alter von 7, 11, 14 und 16 Jahren.

national dress *n* Landestracht *die*.

National Health Service *n* staatlicher britischer Gesundheitsdienst.

National Insurance *n* (U) *Br* - **1.** [system] Sozialversicherung *die* - **2.** [payments] Sozialversicherungsbeiträge *pl*.

nationalism ['næʃnəlɪzm] *n* Nationalismus *der*.

nationalist ['næʃnəlɪst] ⟨⟩ *adj* nationalistisch ⟨⟩ *n* Nationalist *der*, -in *die*.

nationality [,næʃə'nælətɪ] *n* Nationalität *die*.

nationalize, -ise ['næʃnəlaɪz] *vt* verstaatlichen.

national service *n* Wehrdienst *der*.

National Trust *n* britische Organisation, die im Besitz historischer Bauwerke ist und diese unterhält.

nationwide ['neɪʃənwaɪd] *adj & adv* landesweit.

native ['neɪtɪv] ⟨⟩ *adj* [customs, population, plant] einheimisch; ~ **country** Heimatland *das*; **a ~ Italian** ein gebürtiger Italiener; ~ **speaker** Muttersprachler *der*; ~ **language** Muttersprache *die*; ~ **to** [plant, animal] beheimatet in (+ D) ⟨⟩ *n* [person] Einheimische *der*, *die*; *offensive* [of colony] Eingeborene *der*, *die*.

Native American *n* Indianer *der*, -in *die*.

Nativity [nə'tɪvətɪ] *n*: **the ~ die** Geburt Christi.

NATO ['neɪtəʊ] (*abbr of* North Atlantic Treaty Organization) *n* NATO *die*.

natural ['nætʃrəl] *adj* - **1.** [gen] natürlich - **2.** [inborn - instinct, skill] angeboren; [- footballer, musician *etc*] geboren - **3.** [disaster, phenomenon] Natur-.

natural gas *n* Erdgas *das*.

naturalize, -ise ['nætʃrəlaız] *vt* [make citizen] einbürgern.

naturally ['nætʃrəlı] *adv* - **1.** [of course] natürlich - **2.** [behave, speak] natürlich - **3.** [cheerful, talented] von Natur aus.

natural yoghurt *n* Naturjoghurt *der OR das.*

nature ['neıtʃə'] *n* - **1.** [gen] Natur *die* - **2.** [temperament] Wesen *das;* **by ~** von Natur aus - **3.** [type] Art *die.*

nature reserve *n* Naturschutzgebiet *das.*

naughty ['nɔːtı] *adj* - **1.** [child] ungezogen - **2.** [word, story] unanständig.

nausea ['nɔːzıə] *n* Übelkeit *die.*

nauseating ['nɔːzıeıtıŋ] *adj fig* [disgusting] abscheulich.

nautical ['nɔːtıkl] *adj* nautisch; [map] See-; [term] seemännisch.

naval ['neıvl] *adj* Marine-; [battle, forces] See-.

nave [neıv] *n* Kirchenschiff *das.*

navel ['neıvl] *n* Nabel *der.*

navigate ['nævıgeıt] ⟨⟩ *vt* [steer - plane, ship] navigieren ⟨⟩ *vi* [in plane, ship] navigieren; **I'll drive, and you ~** ich fahre, und du dirigierst mich.

navigation [,nævı'geıʃn] *n* Navigation *die.*

navigator ['nævıgeıtə'] *n* Navigator *der.*

navvy ['nævı] *n Br inf* Bauarbeiter *der.*

navy ['neıvı] *n* [armed force] (Kriegs)marine *die.*

navy (blue) ⟨⟩ *adj* marineblau ⟨⟩ *n* Marineblau *das.*

Nazi ['nɑːtsı] *(pl* -s) *n* Nazi *der.*

NB *(abbr of* nota bene) NB.

near [nıə'] ⟨⟩ *adj* nahe; **in the ~ future** demnächst; **the ~est hospital** das nächste Krankenhaus; **a ~ disaster** beinahe ein Unglück; **it was a ~ thing (for us)** wir sind gerade noch davongekommen ⟨⟩ *adv* nahe; **~ at hand** (ganz) in der Nähe; **to come** OR **draw ~ to sb/sthg** sich jm/etw nähern; **a ~ impossible task** eine nahezu unmögliche Aufgabe ⟨⟩ *prep:* **~ (to)** nahe an *(+ D);* **the door** bei der Tür; **~ to death/despair** dem Tode/der Verzweiflung nahe ⟨⟩ *vt* sich nähern *(+ D);* **the road is ~ing completion** die Straße ist fast fertig ⟨⟩ *vi* sich nähern.

nearby [nıə'baı] ⟨⟩ *adj* nahe gelegen ⟨⟩ *adv* in der Nähe.

nearly ['nıəlı] *adv* [almost] fast, beinahe; **I ~ fell** ich bin fast OR beinahe gefallen; **not ~** bei weitem nicht.

near miss *n* [between aircraft] Beinahezusammenstoß *der.*

nearside ['nıəsaıd] *n* Beifahrerseite *die.*

nearsighted [,nıə'saıtıd] *adj Am* kurzsichtig.

neat [niːt] *adj* - **1.** [tidy] ordentlich; [sb's appearance] adrett - **2.** [skilful - solution] elegant; [- manoeuvre] geschickt - **3.** [whisky, vodka *etc*] pur - **4.** *Am inf* [very good] super.

neatly ['niːtlı] *adv* - **1.** [tidily] ordentlich; [dress] adrett - **2.** [skilfully] geschickt.

necessarily [,nesə'serılı, *Br* 'nesəsrəlı] *adv* notwendigerweise; **not ~** nicht unbedingt.

necessary ['nesəsrı] *adj* - **1.** [required] notwendig, nötig; **to make it ~ for sb to do sthg** es erforderlich machen, dass jd etw tut - **2.** [inevitable] unausweichlich.

necessity [nı'sesətı] *n* - **1.** [need] Notwendigkeit *die;* **of ~** notwendigerweise - **2.** [necessary thing] Notwendigkeit *die.*

neck [nek] *n* - **1.** [gen] Hals *der* - **2.** [of shirt] Kragen *der;* [of dress] Ausschnitt *der.*

➤ **neck and neck** *adj* gleichauf; **the two horses are ~ and ~** zwischen den beiden Pferden gibt es ein Kopf-an-Kopf-Rennen.

necklace ['neklıs] *n* (Hals)kette *die.*

neckline ['neklaın] *n* Ausschnitt *der.*

necktie ['nektaı] *n Am* Krawatte *die.*

nectarine ['nektərın] *n* Nektarine *die.*

need [niːd] ⟨⟩ *n* - **1.** [requirement, necessity] Bedürfnis *das;* **to be in** OR **have ~ of sthg** etw brauchen; **in ~ of repair** reparaturbedürftig; **there is no ~ (for you) to cry** du brauchst nicht zu weinen; **if ~ be** notfalls - **2.** [distress, poverty] Not *die* ⟨⟩ *vt* brauchen; **to ~ to do sthg** etw tun müssen; **you don't ~ to wait for me** du brauchst nicht auf mich zu warten; **that's all I ~!** *fig* das hat mir gerade noch gefehlt! ⟨⟩ *aux vb:* **~ we go?** müssen wir gehen?; **it ~ not happen** es muss nicht dazu kommen.

needle ['niːdl] *n* Nadel *die.*

needless ['niːdlıs] *adj* unnötig; **~ to say ...** selbstverständlich ...

needlework ['niːdlwɜːk] *n* (U) Handarbeit *die.*

needn't ['niːdnt] = need not.

needy ['niːdı] *adj* bedürftig.

negative ['negətıv] ⟨⟩ *adj* - **1.** [not affirmative] negativ - **2.** [pessimistic] pessimistisch ⟨⟩ *n* - **1.** PHOT Negativ *das* - **2.** LING Verneinung *die;* [word] Verneinungswort *das;* **to answer in the ~** mit „Nein" antworten.

neglect [nı'glekt] ⟨⟩ *n* Vernachlässigung *die* ⟨⟩ *vt* - **1.** [not take care of] vernachlässigen - **2.** [not do - duty] versäumen; [- task, work] unerledigt lassen; **to ~ to do sthg** es versäumen, etw zu tun.

negligee ['neglıʒeı] *n* Negligee *das.*

negligence ['neglıdʒəns] *n* Nachlässigkeit *die;* [causing danger & LAW] Fahrlässigkeit *die.*

negligible ['neglıdʒəbl] *adj* unerheblich.

negotiate [nı'gəʊʃıeıt] ⟨⟩ *vt* - **1.** [agreement, deal] auslhandeln - **2.** [obstacle] überwinden; [bend] nehmen; [hill, rapids] passieren ⟨⟩ *vi* verhandeln; **to ~ with sb for sthg** mit jm über etw *(A)* verhandeln.

negotiation [nı,gəʊʃı'eıʃn] *n* Verhandlung *die.*

neigh [neɪ] *vi* wiehern.

neighbor *etc n Am* = neighbour *etc*.

neighbour *Br*, **neighbor** *Am* ['neɪbə'] *n* Nachbar *der*, -in *die*; [at table] Tischnachbar *der*, -in *die*; [country] Nachbarland *das*.

neighbourhood *Br*, **neighborhood** *Am* ['neɪbəhʊd] *n* [small area of town] Gegend *die*; [people] Nachbarschaft *die*; **it costs in the ~ of £3,000** [approximately] es kostet so um die 3000 Pfund.

neighbouring *Br*, **neighboring** *Am* ['neɪbərɪŋ] *adj* angrenzend.

neighbourly *Br*, **neighborly** *Am* ['neɪbəlɪ] *adj* [relations, deed] gutnachbarlich.

neither ['naɪðə', 'niːðə'] <> *adj*: **~ bag is big enough** keine der beiden Taschen ist groß genug <> *pron*: **~ of us** keiner von uns beiden <> *conj*: **~ do I** ich auch nicht; **~ ... nor ...** weder ... noch ...; **that's ~ here nor there** *fig* das hat nichts mit der Sache zu tun.

neon light [ˌniːɒn-] *n* Neonlicht *das*.

nephew ['nefjuː] *n* Neffe *der*.

Neptune ['neptjuːn] *n* [planet] Neptun *der*.

nerd [nɜːd] *n inf*: **computer ~** Computerfreak *der*.

nerve [nɜːv] *n* - **1.** ANAT Nerv *der* - **2.** [courage] Mut *der*; **to lose/keep one's ~** seine Nerven verlieren/behalten - **3.** [cheek] Frechheit *die*. ◆ **nerves** *npl* Nerven *pl*; **to get on sb's ~s** jm auf die Nerven gehen.

nerve-racking [-ˌrækɪŋ] *adj* nervenaufreibend.

nervous ['nɜːvəs] *adj* [condition, twitch] nervös; [tissue, illness] Nerven-; **to be ~ of** Angst haben von (+ *D*); **to be ~ about sthg** nervös wegen etw sein.

nervous breakdown *n* Nervenzusammenbruch *der*.

nest [nest] <> *n* - **1.** [gen] Nest *das* - **2.** [of tables] Satz *der* <> *vi* [bird] nisten.

nest egg *n* [money] Notgroschen *der*.

nestle ['nesl] *vi* [make o.s. comfortable] es sich bequem machen.

net [net] <> *adj* - **1.** [profit, weight] Netto-, netto - **2.** [final] End- <> *n* [gen] Netz *das* <> *vt* - **1.** [catch] mit dem Netz fangen - **2.** *fig* [husband] sich (*D*) angeln; [criminal] fangen; [fortune] verdienen - **3.** [profit, sum - subj: deal] netto einlbringen; [- subj: person] netto einlnehmen. ◆ **Net** *n* COMPUT: **the Net** das Internet.

netball ['netbɔːl] *n* Korbball *der*.

net curtains *npl* Tüllgardinen *pl*.

Netherlands ['neðələndz] *npl*: **the ~** die Niederlande *pl*.

nett [net] *adj* = net.

netting ['netɪŋ] *n* (*U*) - **1.** [gen] Netz *das*; [metal] Maschendraht *der* - **2.** [fabric] Tüll *der*.

nettle ['netl] *n* Nessel *die*.

network ['netwɜːk] *n* - **1.** [gen] Netz *das*

- **2.** RADIO & TV [station] Sendenetz *das*
- **3.** COMPUT Netzwerk *das*.

neurosis [ˌnjʊə'rəʊsɪs] (*pl* -ses [siːz]) *n* Neurose *die*.

neurotic [ˌnjʊə'rɒtɪk] <> *adj* neurotisch <> *n* Neurotiker *der*, -in *die*.

neuter ['njuːtə'] <> *adj* GRAMM sächlich <> *vt* [animal] kastrieren.

neutral ['njuːtrəl] <> *adj* - **1.** POL & ELEC neutral - **2.** [inexpressive] ausdruckslos - **3.** [pale grey-brown] naturfarben - **4.** [colourless] farblos <> *n* (*U*) AUT Leerlauf *der*; **in ~** im Leerlauf.

neutrality [njuː'trælətɪ] *n* POL Neutralität *die*.

neutralize, -ise ['njuːtrəlaɪz] *vt* [effects] neutralisieren.

never ['nevə'] *adv* nie; *(simple negative)* nicht; **she's ~ late** sie kommt nie zu spät; **he ~ said a word about it** er hat gar nichts davon gesagt; **~ mind!** macht nichts!; **you've ~ asked him to dinner!** [in disbelief] hast du ihn wirklich zum Essen eingeladen!; **well I ~!** na so was!

never-ending *adj* endlos.

nevertheless [ˌnevəðə'les] *adv* trotzdem.

new [*adj* njuː, *n* njuːz] *adj* neu; **as good as ~** so gut wie neu. ◆ **news** *n* (*U*) - **1.** [information] Nachricht *die*; **that's ~ to me** das ist mir neu - **2.** RADIO & TV Nachrichten *pl*.

newborn ['njuːbɔːn] *adj* neugeboren.

newcomer ['njuːˌkʌmə'] *n*: **~ (to sthg)** Neuling *der* (in etw (*D*)).

newfangled [ˌnjuː'fæŋgld] *adj inf pej* neumodisch.

new-found *adj* [confidence, strength] neu gefunden.

newly ['njuːlɪ] *adv* neu; **~ painted** frisch gestrichen.

newlyweds ['njuːlɪwedz] *npl* Frischvermählte *pl*.

new moon *n* Neumond *der*.

news agency *n* Nachrichtenagentur *die*.

newsagent *Br* ['njuːzeɪdʒənt], **newsdealer** *Am* ['njuːzdiːlər] *n* Zeitungshändler *der*, -in *die*; **~'s (shop)** Zeitungshändler *der*.

newsflash ['njuːzflæʃ] *n* Kurzmeldung *die*.

newsletter ['njuːzˌletə'] *n* Rundschreiben *das*, Mitteilungsblatt *das*.

newspaper ['njuːzˌpeɪpə'] *n* - **1.** [publication, company] Zeitung *die* - **2.** [paper] Zeitungspapier *das*.

newsreader ['njuːzˌriːdə'] *n* Nachrichtensprecher *der*, -in *die*.

newsstand ['njuːzstænd] *n* Zeitungskiosk *der*.

newt [njuːt] *n* Wassermolch *der*.

New Year *n* Neujahr *das*; **Happy ~!** frohes neues Jahr!

New Year's Day *n* Neujahrstag *der*.

New Year's Eve *n* Silvester *der* OR *das*.

New York [-'jɔːk] *n* New York *nt*.

New Zealand [-'ziːlənd] *n* Neuseeland *nt*.

New Zealander [-'ziːləndə'] *n* Neuseeländer *der*, -in *die*.

next [nekst] <> *adj* nächste, -r, -s; **when does the ~ bus leave?** wann fährt der nächste Bus ab? <> *adv* - **1.** [afterwards] als nächstes, danach - **2.** [on next occasion] das nächste Mal; **the ~ week after ~** übernächste Woche - **3.** *(with superlatives):* **the ~ most expensive** der/die/das nächstteuerste; **the ~ best thing to do would be to ...** das nächstbeste wäre, zu ... <> *pron:* **~ please!** der Nächste bitte! **→ next to** *prep* - **1.** [near] neben - **2.** [in comparisons]: **~ to music** I like the theatre best nach Musik mag ich Theater am liebsten - **3.** [almost] fast; **~ to nothing** fast nichts; **I got it for ~ to nothing** ich habe es fast umsonst bekommen.

next door *adv* nebenan. **→ next-door** *adj:* **next-door neighbour** direkter Nachbar, direkte Nachbarin.

next of kin *n* nächste Angehörige *der*, *die*.

NHS *n abbr of* National Health Service.

NI *n abbr of* National Insurance.

nib [nɪb] *n* Feder *die*.

nibble ['nɪbl] *vt* knabbern.

nice [naɪs] *adj* - **1.** [car, picture, weather] schön; [dress] hübsch; [food] gut; **to have a ~ time** Spaß haben; **it's ~ and warm** es ist schön warm - **2.** [kind, pleasant] nett, sympathisch; **to be ~ to sb** nett zu jm sein.

nice-looking [-'lʊkɪŋ] *adj* [person] gut aussehend; [car, house] schön.

nicely ['naɪslɪ] *adv* - **1.** [well, attractively - dressed, decorated] hübsch; [- made] schön - **2.** [politely - ask] höflich; [- behave] gut - **3.** [satisfactorily] gut; **that will do ~** das ist genau richtig.

niche [niːʃ] *n* [in wall] Nische *die*.

nick [nɪk] <> *n* - **1.** [cut] Kerbe *die*, Einkerbung *die* - **2.** *Br inf* [condition]: **to be in good/bad ~** [object] gut/schlecht erhalten sein; [person] in guter/schlechter Verfassung sein - **3.** *phr:* **in the ~ of time** in letzter Minute <> *vt* - **1.** [cut - wood] einkerben - **2.** *Br inf* [steal] klauen - **3.** *Br inf* [arrest] schnappen.

nickel ['nɪkl] *n* - **1.** [metal] Nickel *das* - **2.** *Am* [coin] Fünfcentstück *das*.

nickname ['nɪkneɪm] *n* Spitzname *der*.

nicotine ['nɪkətiːn] *n* Nikotin *das*.

niece [niːs] *n* Nichte *die*.

niggle ['nɪgl] *vt* [worry] zu schaffen machen *(+ D)*.

night [naɪt] *n* - **1.** [not day] Nacht *die;* **at ~** nachts - **2.** [evening] Abend *der;* **at ~** abends - **3.** *phr:* **to have an early/a late ~** früh/spät ins Bett gehen. **→ nights** *adv* - **1.** *Am* [at night] nachts - **2.** *Br* [night shift]: **to work ~s** Nachtschicht arbeiten.

nightcap ['naɪtkæp] *n* [drink] Schlummertrunk *der*.

nightclub ['naɪtklʌb] *n* Nightclub *der*.

nightdress ['naɪtdres] *n* Nachthemd *das*.

nightfall ['naɪtfɔːl] *n:* **at ~** bei Einbruch der Dunkelheit.

nightgown ['naɪtgaʊn] *n* Nachthemd *das*.

nightie ['naɪtɪ] *n inf* Nachthemd *das*.

nightingale ['naɪtɪŋgeɪl] *n* Nachtigall *die*.

nightlife ['naɪtlaɪf] *n* Nachtleben *das*.

nightly ['naɪtlɪ] <> *adj* nächtlich <> *adv* [every evening] jeden Abend; [every night] jede Nacht.

nightmare ['naɪtmeə'] *n lit & fig* Albtraum *der*.

night porter *n* Nachtportier *der*.

night school *n (U)* Abendschule *die*.

night shift *n* Nachtschicht *die*.

nightshirt ['naɪtʃɜːt] *n* Nachthemd *das (für Herren)*.

nighttime ['naɪttaɪm] *n (U)* Nacht *die*.

nil [nɪl] *n* - **1.** [nothing] null - **2.** *Br* SPORT: **two ~** zwei zu null.

Nile [naɪl] *n:* **the ~** der Nil.

nimble ['nɪmbl] *adj* - **1.** [person] wendig; [fingers] geschickt - **2.** [mind] beweglich.

nine [naɪn] *num* neun; *see also* six.

nineteen [ˌnaɪn'tiːn] *num* neunzehn; *see also* six.

ninety ['naɪntɪ] *num* neunzig; *see also* sixty.

ninth [naɪnθ] *num* neunte, -r, -s; *see also* sixth.

nip [nɪp] <> *n* - **1.** [bite] leichter Biss; [pinch] Kniff *der* - **2.** [of drink] Schluck *der* <> *vt* [bite] beißen; [pinch] kneifen.

nipple ['nɪpl] *n* - **1.** [of breast] Brustwarze *die* - **2.** [of baby's bottle] Schnuller *der*.

nit [nɪt] *n* - **1.** [in hair] Nisse *die* - **2.** *Br inf* [idiot] Blödmann *der*.

nitpicking ['nɪtpɪkɪŋ] *n inf (U)* Spitzfindigkeit *die*.

nitrogen ['naɪtrədʒən] *n* Stickstoff *der*.

nitty-gritty [ˌnɪtɪ'grɪtɪ] *n inf:* **to get down to the ~** zur Sache kommen.

no [nəʊ] *(pl* -es*)* <> *adv* nein; **to answer ~** mit einem Nein antworten; **I am ~ richer than he is** ich bin nicht reicher als er <> *adj* kein; **I have ~ money left** ich habe kein Geld übrig; **it's ~ easy job** es ist keine leichte Aufgabe; **it's ~ good** OR **use** es nützt nichts; **in ~ time** im Nu; **'~ smoking'** 'Rauchen verboten'; **~ way!** *inf* auf keinen Fall! <> *n* Nein *das;* **she won't take ~ for an answer** sie lässt sich nicht davon abbringen.

No., no. *(abbr of* number*)* Nr.

nobility [nə'bɪlətɪ] *n* - **1.** [aristocracy]: **the ~** der Adel - **2.** [nobleness] Vornehmheit *die*.

noble ['nəʊbl] *adj* - **1.** [aristocratic] adlig - **2.** [fine, distinguished] edel, nobel.

nobody ['nəʊbədɪ] <> *pron* niemand;

~ else can do it das kann sonst keiner ◇ *n pej* Niemand *der*.

no-claim(s) bonus *n* Schadenfreiheitsrabatt *der*.

nocturnal [nɒk'tɜ:nl] *adj* **- 1.** [at night] nächtlich **- 2.** [animal] Nacht-.

nod [nɒd] ◇ *vt*: **to ~ one's head** mit dem Kopf nicken ◇ *vi* nicken; **to ~ to sb** jm zulnicken. ➡ **nod off** *vi* einlnicken.

noise [nɔiz] *n* **- 1.** [sound] Geräusch *das* **- 2.** (U) [unpleasant sound] Krach *der*.

noisy ['nɔizi] *adj* laut.

nominal ['nɒmɪnl] *adj* **- 1.** [in name only] nominell **- 2.** [very small] gering.

nominate ['nɒmɪneɪt] *vt* **- 1.** [propose]: **to ~ sb (for/as sthg)** jn (für/als etw) nominieren **- 2.** [appoint]: **to ~ sb to sthg** jn zu etw ernennen.

nominee [ˌnɒmɪ'ni:] *n* Kandidat *der*, -in *die*.

non- [nɒn] *prefix* [with noun] Nicht-; [with adj] nicht-.

nonalcoholic [ˌnɒnælkə'hɒlɪk] *adj* nichtalkoholisch, ohne Alkohol.

nonaligned [ˌnɒnə'laɪnd] *adj* blockfrei.

nonchalant [*Br* 'nɒnʃələnt, *Am* ˌnɒnʃə'lɑ:nt] *adj* nonchalant, lässig.

noncommittal [ˌnɒnkə'mɪtl] *adj* [reply, attitude] unverbindlich; **he was ~** er legte sich nicht fest.

nonconformist [ˌnɒnkən'fɔ:mɪst] ◇ *adj* nonkonformistisch ◇ *n* Nonkonformist *der*, -in *die*.

nondescript [*Br* 'nɒndɪskrɪpt, *Am* ˌnɒndɪ'skrɪpt] *adj* unscheinbar.

none [nʌn] ◇ *pron* [not any] keine, -r, -s; **~ of us** keiner von uns; **~ of the money** nichts von dem Geld; **I'll have ~ of your nonsense** ich will nichts von dem Unsinn hören; **it is ~ of his business** es geht ihn gar nichts an ◇ *adv*: **I'm ~ the wiser** ich bin um nichts schlauer geworden; **I like him ~ the worse for it** ich mag ihn deshalb nicht weniger. ➡ **none too** *adv*: **~ too soon** keine Minute zu früh.

nonentity [nɒ'nentətɪ] *n* Null *die*.

nonetheless [ˌnʌnðə'les] *adv* nichtsdestoweniger.

non-event *n* Reinfall *der*.

nonexistent [ˌnɒnɪg'zɪstənt] *adj* nicht existierend; **to be ~** nicht existieren.

nonfiction [ˌnɒn'fɪkʃn] *n* (U) Sachliteratur *die*.

no-nonsense *adj* sachlich.

nonpayment [ˌnɒn'peɪmənt] *n* (U) Nichtzahlung *die*.

nonplussed, nonplused *Am* [ˌnɒn'plʌst] *adj* verblüfft.

nonreturnable [ˌnɒnrɪ'tɜ:nəbl] *adj* [bottle] Einweg-.

nonsense ['nɒnsəns] ◇ *n* (U) **- 1.** [meaningless words, foolish idea] Unsinn *der*

- 2. [foolish behaviour] Dummheiten *pl* ◇ *excl* Unsinn!

nonsensical [nɒn'sensɪkl] *adj* unsinnig.

nonsmoker [ˌnɒn'sməukə*r*] *n* Nichtraucher *der*, -in *die*.

nonstick [ˌnɒn'stɪk] *adj* antihaftbeschichtet.

nonstop [ˌnɒn'stɒp] ◇ *adj* [flight, race] Nonstop-; [activity, rain] ohne Unterbrechung ◇ *adv* ununterbrochen.

noodles ['nu:dlz] *npl* Nudeln *pl*.

nook [nuk] *n* [of room] Winkel *der*; **in every ~ and cranny** in allen Ecken OR Winkeln.

noon [nu:n] *n* Mittag *der*.

no one *pron* = nobody.

noose [nu:s] *n* Schlinge *die*.

no-place *adv Am* = nowhere.

nor [nɔ:*r*] *conj* auch nicht; **~ do I** ich auch nicht; **I don't know, ~ do I care** das weiß ich nicht, und es ist mir auch egal.

norm [nɔ:m] *n* Norm *die*.

normal ['nɔ:ml] *adj* normal.

normality [nɔ:'mælɪtɪ] *n* Normalität *die*.

normally ['nɔ:məlɪ] *adv* **- 1.** [usually] normalerweise **- 2.** [in a normal way] normal.

north [nɔ:θ] ◇ *adj* Nord- ◇ *adv* nach Norden; **~ of** nördlich von OR Norden *der*.

North Africa *n* Nordafrika *nt*.

North America *n* Nordamerika *nt*.

North American ◇ *adj* nordamerikanisch ◇ *n* Nordamerikaner *der*, -in *die*.

northeast [ˌnɔ:θ'i:st] ◇ *n* Nordosten *der* ◇ *adj* nordöstlich, Nordost- ◇ *adv* nordostwärts; **~ of** nordöstlich von.

northerly ['nɔ:ðəlɪ] *adj* [direction] nördlich; [area] im Norden; [wind] Nord-.

northern ['nɔ:ðən] *adj* [region, dialect] nördlich; [Europe] Nord-.

Northern Ireland *n* Nordirland *nt*.

northernmost ['nɔ:ðənməust] *adj* nördlichste, -r, -s.

North Pole *n*: **the ~** der Nordpol.

North Sea *n*: **the ~** die Nordsee.

northward ['nɔ:θwəd] ◇ *adj* [migration] nördlich ◇ *adv* = northwards.

northwards ['nɔ:θwədz] *adv* nach Norden.

northwest [ˌnɔ:θ'west] ◇ *n* Nordwesten *der* ◇ *adj* nordwestlich, Nordwest- ◇ *adv* nordwestwärts; **~ of** nordwestlich von.

Norway ['nɔ:weɪ] *n* Norwegen *nt*.

Norwegian [nɔ:'wi:dʒən] ◇ *adj* norwegisch ◇ *n* **- 1.** [person] Norweger *der*, -in *die* **- 2.** [language] Norwegisch(e) *das*.

nose [nəuz] *n* [of person] Nase *die*; **it's under your ~** es ist vor deiner Nase; **to keep one's ~ out of sthg** sich aus etw herauslhalten; **to look down one's ~ at sb/sthg** *fig* von oben auf jn/etw herablschauen; **to poke OR stick one's ~ into sthg** *inf* seine Nase in etw (A) stecken; **to turn up one's ~ at sthg** seine Nase über etw *(A)* rümpfen. ◆ **nose about, nose around** *vi* herumschnüffeln.

nosebleed ['nəʊzbliːd] *n* Nasenbluten *das.*

nosey ['nəʊzi] *adj* = nosy.

nostalgia [nɒ'stældʒə] *n (U)* Nostalgie *die;* ~ **for sthg** Sehnsucht *die* nach etw.

nostril ['nɒstrəl] *n* Nasenloch *das.*

nosy ['nəʊzi] *adj* neugierig.

not [nɒt] *adv* nicht; **she's** ~ **there** sie ist nicht da; ~ **any** kein; ~ **yet** noch nicht; ~ **at all** [pleased, interested] überhaupt nicht; [in reply to thanks] gern geschehen; ~ **that I'm afraid of him** nicht etwa, dass ich Angst vor ihm habe; ~ **to worry!** keine Sorge!

notable ['nəʊtəbl] *adj* [person] bedeutend; [success] bemerkenswert; [improvement] beachtlich, beträchtlich; **to be** ~ **for sthg** durch etw auffallen; **with the** ~ **exception of** mit Ausnahme von.

notably ['nəʊtəbli] *adv* **- 1.** [in particular] vor allem **- 2.** [noticeably] deutlich.

notary ['nəʊtəri] *n:* ~ **(public)** Notar *der,* -in *die.*

notch [nɒtʃ] *n* [cut] Kerbe *die.*

note [nəʊt] ◇ *n* **- 1.** [short letter] Zettel *der* **- 2.** [written reminder, record] Notiz *die;* **to take** ~ **of sthg** etw bemerken **- 3.** [paper money] Geldschein *der;* **a £5** ~ eine Fünfpfundnote **- 4.** [MUS - symbol] Note *die;* [- sound] Klang *der* **- 5.** [tone] Ton *der* ◇ *vt* **- 1.** [observe] bemerken **- 2.** [mention] erwähnen. ◆ **notes** *npl* [in book] Anmerkungen *pl.* ◆ **note down** *vt sep* aufschreiben.

notebook ['nəʊtbʊk] *n* **- 1.** [for writing in] Notizbuch *das* **- 2.** COMPUT Notebook *das.*

noted ['nəʊtɪd] *adj:* ~ **(for sthg)** bekannt (für etw).

notepad ['nəʊtpæd] *n* Notizblock *der.*

notepaper ['nəʊtpeɪpə^r] *n* Briefpapier *das.*

noteworthy ['nəʊtˌwɜːði] *adj* bemerkenswert.

nothing ['nʌθɪŋ] ◇ *pron* nichts; ~ **new/ interesting** nichts Neues/Interessantes; **for** ~ [for free] umsonst; [in vain] vergeblich; **she is** ~ **if not discreet** diskret ist sie auf jeden Fall; ~ **but** nichts als; **he does** ~ **but complain** er beschwert sich dauernd; **he thinks** ~ **of walking ten miles** es macht ihm nichts aus, zehn Meilen zu gehen ◇ *adv:* ~ **like** [very unlike] ganz anders als; ~ **like enough** lange nicht genug; ~ **like as good** längst nicht so gut.

notice ['nəʊtɪs] ◇ *n* **- 1.** [piece of paper - announcing sthg] Ankündigung *die;* [- informing of sthg] Mitteilung *die* **- 2.** [attention]: **it escaped her** ~ es entging ihrer Aufmerksamkeit; **to take** ~**/no** ~ **of sb/sthg** jn/etw beachten/nicht beachten **- 3.** *(U)* [warning] Bescheid *der;* **at short** ~ kurzfristig; **until further** ~ bis auf weiteres **- 4.** [at work]: **to be given one's** ~ gekündigt werden; **to hand in**

one's ~ seine Kündigung einJreichen ◇ *vt* bemerken.

noticeable ['nəʊtɪsəbl] *adj* deutlich.

notice board *n* Anschlagbrett *das.*

notify ['nəʊtɪfaɪ] *vt:* **to** ~ **sb (of sthg)** jn benachrichtigen (über etw *(A)*).

notion ['nəʊʃn] *n* [concept, idea] Idee *die,* Vorstellung *die.* ◆ **notions** *npl Am* [haberdashery] Kurzwaren *pl.*

notorious [nəʊ'tɔːrɪəs] *adj* [person] berühmt; [criminal, event] berühmt-berüchtigt; [place] verrufen.

notwithstanding [ˌnɒtwɪð'stændɪŋ] *fml* ◇ *prep* trotz (+ *G*) ◇ *adv* trotzdem.

nought [nɔːt] *num* Null *die;* ~**s and crosses** Kreuzchen- und Kringelspiel *das.*

noun [naʊn] *n* Substantiv *das.*

nourish ['nʌrɪʃ] *vt* [feed] ernähren.

nourishing ['nʌrɪʃɪŋ] *adj* nahrhaft.

nourishment ['nʌrɪʃmənt] *n* Nahrung *die.*

novel ['nɒvl] ◇ *adj* neuartig ◇ *n* Roman *der.*

novelist ['nɒvəlɪst] *n* Romanschriftsteller *der,* -in *die.*

novelty ['nɒvltɪ] *n* **- 1.** [quality] Neuartigkeit *die* **- 2.** [unusual object, event] Neuheit *die* **- 3.** [cheap object] Krimskrams *der.*

November [nə'vembə^r] *n* November *der; see also* September.

novice ['nɒvɪs] *n* **- 1.** [inexperienced person] Neuling *der* **- 2.** RELIG Novize *der,* -zin *die.*

now [naʊ] ◇ *adv* **- 1.** [gen] jetzt; **just** ~ gerade eben; **right** ~ [at the moment] im Moment; [immediately] sofort; **by** ~ inszwischen; **from** ~ **on** von jetzt an; **three days from** ~ heute in drei Tagen; **any day/time** ~ jeden Tag/ Moment; **(every)** ~ **and then OR** ~ **again** hin und wieder; **for** ~ erst einmal **- 2.** [introducing statement]: ~ **(then), ...** also ... ◇ *conj:* ~ **(that) ...** jetzt, wo ...

nowadays ['naʊədeɪz] *adv* heutzutage.

nowhere *Br* ['nəʊweə^r], **no-place** *Am adv* nirgendwo, nirgends; ~ **near** nicht annähernd; **dinner is** ~ **near ready** das Abendessen ist noch lange nicht fertig; **to be getting** ~ [achieve nothing] nichts erreichen; [make no progress] nicht vorankommen.

nozzle ['nɒzl] *n* Düse *die.*

nuance ['njuːɒns] *n* Nuance *die.*

nuclear ['njuːklɪə^r] *adj* nuklear, Nuklear-.

nuclear bomb *n* Atombombe *die.*

nuclear disarmament *n* nukleare Abrüstung.

nuclear energy *n* Atomenergie *die.*

nuclear power *n* Atomkraft *die,* Kernkraft *die;* ~ **station** Atomkraftwerk *das.*

nuclear reactor *n* Atomreaktor *der.*

nuclear war *n* Atomkrieg *der.*

nucleus ['njuːklɪəs] *(pl* -lei [-lɪaɪ]) *n* Kern *der;* **atomic** ~ Atomkern *der.*

nude [nju:d] ⬦ *adj* nackt ⬦ *n* [figure, painting] Akt *der;* **in the ~** nackt.

nudge [nʌdʒ] *vt* [with elbow] anlstupsen.

nudist ['nju:dɪst] ⬦ *adj* Nudisten-; **~ beach** Nacktbadestrand *der* ⬦ *n* Nudist *der,* -in *die.*

nugget ['nʌgɪt] *n* - 1. [of gold] Nugget *das,* Goldklümpchen *das* - 2. *fig:* **a ~ of information** ein wertvolles Stück Information.

nuisance ['nju:sns] *n* - 1. [annoying thing, situation] Ärgernis *das;* **what a ~!** wie ärgerlich! - 2. [annoying person] Nervensäge *die;* **to make a ~ of o.s.** lästig werden.

null [nʌl] *adj:* **~ and void** null und nichtig.

numb [nʌm] *adj* [shoulder, hand] taub, gefühllos; [person] benommen; **to be ~ with sthg** [with cold, fear, shock] starr vor etw *(D)* sein; [with grief] benommen vor etw *(D)* sein.

number ['nʌmbə'] ⬦ *n* - 1. [numeral] Zahl *die,* Ziffer *die* - 2. [of telephone, house, car] Nummer *die* - 3. [quantity] Anzahl *die,* Zahl *die;* **a ~ of** mehrere; **any ~ of** unzählig - 4. [song] Nummer *die* ⬦ *vt* - 1. [amount to] zählen - 2. [give a number to] nummerieren - 3. [include]: **he is ~ed among the greatest politicians of this century** er zählt zu den größten Politikern dieses Jahrhunderts.

number one ⬦ *adj* [main] vorrangig ⬦ *n inf* [oneself] Nummer eins.

numberplate ['nʌmbəpleɪt] *n Br* Nummernschild *das.*

Number Ten *n:* **~ (Downing Street)** Sitz des *britischen Premierministers.*

numeral ['nju:mərəl] *n* Ziffer *die.*

numerate ['nju:mərət] *adj Br* rechenkundig.

numerical [nju:'merɪkl] *adj* numerisch.

numerous ['nju:mərəs] *adj* zahlreich.

nun [nʌn] *n* Nonne *die.*

nurse [nɜ:s] ⬦ *n* Krankenschwester *die;* [male] Krankenpfleger *der* ⬦ *vt* - 1. MED [person] pflegen - 2. [desire, dream, hope] hegen, nähren - 3. [breast-feed] stillen.

nursery ['nɜ:səri] *n* - 1. [for children] Kinderzimmer *das* - 2. [for plants] Gärtnerei *die.*

nursery rhyme *n* Kinderreim *der.*

nursery school *n* Kindergarten *der.*

nursing ['nɜ:sɪŋ] *n* (U) - 1. [profession] Krankenpflege *die* - 2. [care] Pflege *die.*

nursing home *n* [for old people] Pflegeheim *das.*

nurture ['nɜ:tʃə'] *vt* - 1. [children] nähren; [plants] hegen - 2. [hope, desire, plan] hegen.

nut [nʌt] *n* - 1. [to eat] Nuss *die* - 2. TECH Schraubenmutter *die* - 3. *inf* [mad person] Spinner *der,* -in *die.* ◆ **nuts** *inf* ⬦ *adj:* **to be ~s** verrückt sein ⬦ *excl Am* verdammt!

nutcrackers ['nʌt,krækəz] *npl* Nussknacker *der.*

nutmeg ['nʌtmeg] *n* Muskatnuss *die.*

nutritious [nju:'trɪʃəs] *adj* nahrhaft.

nutshell ['nʌt,ʃel] *n:* **in a ~** kurz gefasst.

nuzzle ['nʌzl] *vi:* **to ~ (up) against sb/sthg** sich an jn/etw anlschmiegen OR drücken.

nylon ['naɪlɒn] ⬦ *n* [fabric] Nylon *das* ⬦ *comp* Nylon-.

O

o (*pl* o's OR os), **O** (*pl* O's OR Os) [əʊ] *n* - 1. [letter] o *das,* O *das* - 2. [zero] Null *die.*

oak [əʊk] ⬦ *n* - 1. [tree] Eiche *die* - 2. (U) [wood] Eichenholz *das* ⬦ *comp* Eichenholz-.

OAP *n abbr of* old age pensioner.

oar [ɔ:'] *n* Ruder *das.*

oasis [əʊ'eɪsɪs] (*pl* oases [əʊ'eɪsi:z]) *n lit & fig* Oase *die.*

oath [əʊθ] *n* - 1. [promise] Eid *der;* **on** OR **under ~** unter Eid - 2. [swearword] Fluch *der.*

oatmeal ['əʊtmi:l] *n* [food] Hafermehl *das.*

oats [əʊts] *npl* Hafer *der.*

obedience [ə'bi:dɪəns] *n:* **~ (to sb)** Gehorsam *der* (gegenüber jm).

obedient [ə'bi:dɪənt] *adj* gehorsam.

obese [əʊ'bi:s] *adj* fettleibig.

obey [ə'beɪ] ⬦ *vt* [person] gehorchen (+ *D*); [orders, command, law] befolgen ⬦ *vi* gehorchen.

obituary [ə'bɪtʃʊəri] *n* Nachruf *der.*

object [*n* 'ɒbdʒɪkt, *vb* əb'dʒekt] ⬦ *n* - 1. [thing] Gegenstand *der* - 2. [aim] Ziel *das;* **the ~ of the exercise** der Zweck der Übung - 3. GRAMM Objekt *das* ⬦ *vt:* **to ~ that ...** einlwenden, dass ... ⬦ *vi* dagegen sein; **to ~ to sthg** gegen etw sein; **to ~ to doing sthg** etwas dagegen haben, etw zu tun.

objection [əb'dʒekʃn] *n* Einwand *der;* **to have no ~ to sthg** keinen Einwand gegen etw haben; **to have no ~ to doing sthg** nichts dagegen haben, etw zu tun.

objectionable [əb'dʒekʃənəbl] *adj* [behaviour, language] anstößig; [person] unausstehlich, widerwärtig.

objective [əb'dʒektɪv] ⬦ *adj* objektiv ⬦ *n* Ziel *das.*

obligation [,ɒblɪ'geɪʃn] *n* - 1. [compulsion] Zwang *der* - 2. [duty] Verpflichtung *die.*

obligatory [ə'blɪgətrɪ] *adj* obligatorisch; **to be ~** Pflicht sein.

oblige [ə'blaɪdʒ] *vt* - 1. [force]: **to ~ sb to do sthg** jn zwingen, etw zu tun - 2. *fml* [do a favour for]: **to ~ sb** jm einen Gefallen tun.

obliging [ə'blaɪdʒɪŋ] *adj* zuvorkommend.

oblique [ə'bliːk] <> *adj* - 1. [look, compliment] indirekt; [hint] versteckt - 2. [line] Schräg-, schräg <> *n* TYPO Schrägstrich *der*.

obliterate [ə'blɪtəreɪt] *vt* ausllöschen.

oblivion [ə'blɪvɪən] *n* - 1. [unconsciousness] Bewusstlosigkeit *die* - 2. [state of being forgotten] Vergessenheit *die*, Vergessen *das*.

oblivious [ə'blɪvɪəs] *adj*: **to be ~ to sthg** sich (D) einer Sache (G) nicht bewusst sein.

oblong ['ɒblɒŋ] <> *adj* rechteckig <> *n* Rechteck *das*.

obnoxious [əb'nɒkʃəs] *adj* [smell] widerlich; [remark] gemein; [person] unausstehlich.

oboe ['əʊbəʊ] *n* Oboe *die*.

obscene [əb'siːn] *adj* obszön.

obscure [əb'skjʊə³] <> *adj* - 1. [not well-known] unbekannt - 2. [difficult to understand, see] unklar <> *vt* - 1. [make difficult to understand] unklar machen - 2. [hide] verdecken.

observance [əb'zɜːvəns] *n (U)* Einhaltung *die*.

observant [əb'zɜːvnt] *adj* aufmerksam.

observation [,ɒbzə'veɪʃn] *n* - 1. (U) [action of watching] Beobachtung *die* - 2. [remark] Bemerkung *die*, Äußerung *die*.

observatory [əb'zɜːvətrɪ] *n* Observatorium *das*, Sternwarte *die*.

observe [əb'zɜːv] *vt* - 1. *fml* [notice] bemerken - 2. [watch carefully] beobachten - 3. [obey] einhalten - 4. [remark] bemerken.

observer [əb'zɜːvə³] *n* - 1. [watcher] Zuschauer *der*, -in *die* - 2. [commentator] Beobachter *der*, -in *die*.

obsess [əb'ses] *vt*: **to be ~ed by** OR **with sb/sthg** von jm/etw besessen sein.

obsessive [əb'sesɪv] *adj* obsessiv, zwanghaft.

obsolete ['ɒbsəliːt] *adj* veraltet, überholt.

obstacle ['ɒbstəkl] *n* Hindernis *das*.

obstetrics [ɒb'stetrɪks] *n* Geburtshilfe *die*.

obstinate ['ɒbstənət] *adj* - 1. [person] verbohrt - 2. [cough, resistance] hartnäckig.

obstruct [əb'strʌkt] *vt* - 1. [road, path] blockieren, versperren - 2. [progress, justice, traffic] behindern.

obstruction [əb'strʌkʃn] *n* - 1. [in road, pipe] Blockierung *die* - 2. [of justice] Behinderung *die* - 3. SPORT Behinderung *die*.

obtain [əb'teɪn] *vt* erhalten.

obtainable [əb'teɪnəbl] *adj* erhältlich.

obtrusive [əb'truːsɪv] *adj* [person, behaviour] aufdringlich; [colour] auffällig; [smell] penetrant.

obtuse [əb'tjuːs] *adj* - 1. *fml* [person] begriffsstutzig - 2. GEOM [angle] stumpf.

obvious ['ɒbvɪəs] *adj* offensichtlich.

obviously ['ɒbvɪəslɪ] *adv* - 1. [of course] selbstverständlich - 2. [clearly] eindeutig.

occasion [ə'keɪʒn] *n* - 1. [circumstance, time] Gelegenheit *die*; **on one ~** einmal - 2. [important event] Anlass *der*; **to rise to the ~** sich der Lage gewachsen zeigen - 3. *fml* [reason, motive] Grund *der*.

occasional [ə'keɪʒənl] *adj* gelegentlich.

occasionally [ə'keɪʒnəlɪ] *adv* gelegentlich.

occult [ɒ'kʌlt] *adj* okkult.

occupant ['ɒkjʊpənt] *n* - 1. [of building, room] Bewohner *der*, -in *die* - 2. [of chair] Inhaber *der*, -in *die*; [of vehicle] Insasse *der*, -in *die*.

occupation [,ɒkjʊ'peɪʃn] *n* - 1. [job] Beruf *der* - 2. [pastime] Beschäftigung *die* - 3. MIL Besetzung *die*, Okkupation *die*.

occupational hazard [ɒkjʊ,peɪʃnl-] *n* Berufsrisiko *das*.

occupier ['ɒkjʊpaɪə³] *n* Bewohner *der*, -in *die*.

occupy ['ɒkjʊpaɪ] *vt* - 1. [house, room] bewohnen; [seat] belegen - 2. MIL besetzen, okkupieren - 3. [keep busy]: **to ~ o.s.** sich beschäftigen - 4. [time, space] in Anspruch nehmen; **how do you ~ your evenings?** wie füllst du deine Abende aus?

occur [ə'kɜː³] *vi* - 1. [happen] sich ereignen; [change] stattfinden; [difficulty] auftreten - 2. [exist, be found] vorkommen - 3. [come to mind]: **to ~ to sb** jm in den Sinn kommen.

occurrence [ə'kʌrəns] *n* [event] Vorkommnis *das*, Ereignis *das*.

ocean ['əʊʃn] *n* - 1. [in names] Ozean *der* - 2. *Am* [sea] Meer *das*.

ochre *Br*, **ocher** *Am* ['əʊkə³] *adj* ockerfarben.

o'clock [ə'klɒk] *adv* Uhr; **five ~** fünf Uhr.

octave ['ɒktɪv] *n* MUS Oktave *die*.

October [ɒk'təʊbə³] *n* Oktober *der; see also* September.

octopus ['ɒktəpəs] (*pl* -puses OR -pi [-paɪ]) *n* Tintenfisch *der*.

OD *abbr of* overdose.

odd [ɒd] *adj* - 1. [strange] seltsam - 2. [not part of pair] einzeln - 3. [number] ungerade - 4. [leftover] überzählig - 5. [occasional] gelegentlich - 6. *inf* [approximately] ungefähr; **twenty ~ years** mehr als zwanzig Jahre.
◆ **odds** *npl* - 1. [probability] Wahrscheinlichkeit *die*; **the ~s are that ...** aller Wahrscheinlichkeit nach ...; **against all** OR **the ~s** wider Erwarten - 2. [bits]: **~s and ends** Krimskrams *der* - 3. *phr*: **to be at ~s with sb/sthg** sich mit jm/etw uneinig sein.

oddity ['ɒdɪtɪ] *n* - 1. [strange person] Sonderling *der*; [strange thing] Kuriosität *die* - 2. [strangeness] Eigenartigkeit *die*.

odd jobs *npl* Gelegenheitsarbeiten *pl*.

oddly ['ɒdlɪ] *adv* seltsam.

oddments ['ɒdmənts] *npl* Einzelstücke *pl*.

odds-on ['ɒdz-] *adj inf*: **the ~ favourite** der

klare Favorit; **it's ~ that ...** es ist sehr wahrscheinlich, dass ...

odometer [əʊ'dɒmɪtəʳ] n Kilometerzähler der.

odour Br, **odor** Am ['əʊdəʳ] n Geruch der.

of [unstressed əv, stressed ɒv] prep - 1. [gen] von (the genitive case is often used instead of „von"); **the cover ~ the book** der Umschlag des Buches; **the handle ~ the door** der Türgriff; **a friend ~ mine** ein Freund von mir; **the works ~ Shakespeare** die Werke Shakespeares OR von Shakespeare; **the Queen ~ England** die Königin von England; **the University ~ Leeds** die Universität Leeds; **south ~ Boston/the river** südlich von Boston/des Flusses - 2. [expressing quantity, contents, age]: **a pound ~ sweets** ein Pfund Bonbons; **a piece ~ cake** ein Stück Kuchen; **a cup ~ coffee** eine Tasse Kaffee; **a rise ~ 20%** ein Anstieg um 20%; **a town ~ 50,000 people** eine Stadt mit 50 000 Einwohnern; **thousands ~ people** Tausende von Leuten; **a girl ~ six** ein sechsjähriges Mädchen; **both/one ~ us** beide/einer von uns; **a man ~ courage** ein mutiger Mann - 3. [made from] aus; **a house ~ stone** ein Haus aus Stein; **it's made ~ wood** es ist aus Holz - 4. [with emotions]: **a love ~ France** eine Liebe zu Frankreich; **a fear ~ flying** Angst vor dem Fliegen - 5. [on the part of] von; **that was very kind ~ you** das war sehr nett von Ihnen - 6. [referring to place names]: **the city ~ Birmingham** die Stadt Birmingham - 7. [indicating resemblance] von; **it was the size ~ a pea** es war so groß wie eine Erbse, es hatte die Größe einer Erbse - 8. [with dates, periods of time]: **the 26th ~ April** der 26. April; **the summer ~ 1969** der Sommer 1969; **in September ~ last year** im September letzten Jahres - 9. [indicating cause of death]: **to die ~ sthg** an etw (D) sterben - 10. Am [in telling the time] vor; **it's ten ~ four** es ist zehn vor vier.

off [ɒf] ⇔ adv - 1. [away] weg; **to get ~** [from bus, train, plane] auslsteigen; **we're ~ to Austria next week** wir fahren nächste Woche nach Österreich; **to go** OR **drop ~ to sleep** einlschlafen - 2. [expressing removal] ab; **to take sthg ~** [clothes, shoes] etw auslziehen; [lid, wrapper] etw ablnehmen; **with his shoes ~** ohne Schuhe - 3. [not working]: **to turn sthg ~** [TV, radio, engine] etw auslschalten; [tap] etw zuldrehen - 4. [expressing distance or time away]: **it's 10 miles ~** es sind noch 10 Meilen bis dahin; **it's a long way ~** [in distance] es ist noch ein weiter Weg bis dahin; [in time] bis dahin ist es noch lange hin - 5. [not at work]: **I'm taking a week ~** ich nehme mir eine Woche frei ⇔ prep - 1. [away from] von; **to get ~ sthg** [bed, chair] von etw auflstehen; [bus, train, plane] aus etw auslsteigen; [ship] etw verlassen; **~ the coast** vor der Küste; **it's just ~ the main road**

es ist gleich in der Nähe der Hauptstraße - 2. [absent from]: **to be ~ work** frei haben - 3. inf [from] von; **I bought it ~ her** ich habe es von ihr gekauft - 4. inf [no longer liking or needing]: **I'm ~ my food at the moment** ich habe zur Zeit keinen Appetit; **she's ~ drugs now** sie nimmt keine Drogen mehr ⇔ adj - 1. [meat, cheese, milk, beer] schlecht - 2. [not working] aus; [tap] zu - 3. [cancelled] abgesagt; **the deal is ~** die Sache ist abgeblasen - 4. [not available]: **the soup's ~** es ist keine Suppe mehr da.

offal ['ɒfl] n Innereien pl.

off-chance n: **on the ~** auf gut Glück.

off colour adj kränklich.

off duty adv außer Dienst, dienstfrei. ◆ **off-duty** adj außer Dienst.

offence Br, **offense** Am [ə'fens] n - 1. [crime] Verbrechen das - 2. [displeasure, hurt] Beleidigung die; **to take ~** beleidigt sein.

offend [ə'fend] vt beleidigen.

offender [ə'fendəʳ] n - 1. [criminal] Straftäter der, -in die - 2. [culprit] Schuldige der, die.

offense [sense 2 'ɒfens] n Am = offence.

offensive [ə'fensɪv] ⇔ adj - 1. [causing offence] beleidigend; [behaviour] anstößig - 2. [aggressive] Angriffs-, aggressiv ⇔ n - 1. MIL Offensive die, Angriff der - 2. fig [attack]: **to go on** OR **take the ~** in die Offensive gehen.

offer ['ɒfəʳ] ⇔ n Angebot das; **on ~** [available] verkäuflich; [at a special price] im Angebot ⇔ vt anlbieten; **to ~ sthg to sb, to ~ sb sthg** jm etw anlbieten; **to ~ to do sthg** anlbieten, etw zu tun ⇔ vi sich anlbieten.

offering ['ɒfərɪŋ] n - 1. [something offered] Gabe die - 2. RELIG [sacrifice] Opfer das.

off guard adv unvorbereitet.

offhand [ˌɒf'hænd] ⇔ adj lässig ⇔ adv auf Anhieb.

office ['ɒfɪs] n - 1. [gen] Büro das - 2. [government department] Behörde die - 3. [position of authority] Amt das; **in ~** im Amt.

office block n Bürogebäude das.

office hours npl Bürostunden pl.

officer ['ɒfɪsəʳ] n - 1. MIL Offizier der - 2. [in organization] Vertreter der, -in die - 3. [in police force] Polizeibeamte der, -tin die.

office worker n Büroangestellte der, die.

official [ə'fɪʃl] ⇔ adj offiziell ⇔ n Beamte der, -tin die; SPORT Funktionär der, -in die.

offing ['ɒfɪŋ] n: **in the ~** in Sicht.

off-licence n Br Wein- und Spirituosenhandlung die.

off-line adj COMPUT offline.

off-peak adj: **~ electricity** Nachtstrom der; **~ fares** verbilligter Tarif; **during ~ hours** außerhalb der Stoßzeiten.

off-putting [-ˌpʊtɪŋ] adj abstoßend.

off season n: **the ~** die Nebensaison.

offset [ˌɒf'set] (pt & pp offset) vt ausl-gleichen.

offshore [ˌɒf'ʃɔːr] ⬦ adj - **1.** [in or on the sea] Offshore- - **2.** [near coast] in Küstennä-he; ~ **waters** Küstengewässer pl ⬦ adv - **1.** [out at sea] offshore, im offenen Meer - **2.** [near coast] in Küstennähe.

offside [adv ˌɒf'saɪd, n 'ɒfsaɪd] ⬦ adv SPORT im Abseits ⬦ n [of vehicle] Fahrersei-te die.

offspring ['ɒfsprɪŋ] (pl inv) n - **1.** fml or hum [of people] Nachwuchs der - **2.** [of animals] Junge(s) das.

offstage [ˌɒf'steɪdʒ] adj & adv hinter der Bühne, hinter den Kulissen.

off-the-cuff adj & adv unüberlegt.

off-the-peg adj Br: ~ **suit** Anzug der von der Stange.

off-the-record adj & adv inoffiziell.

off-white adj gebrochen weiß.

often ['ɒfn, 'ɒftn] adv oft; **how ~ do the buses run?** wie oft fährt der Bus?; **every so ~** gelegentlich; **as ~ as not, more ~ than not** meistens.

ogle ['əʊgl] vt pej begaffen.

oh [əʊ] excl - **1.** [to introduce comment] ach! - **2.** [expressing hesitation, joy, surprise, fear] oh!; ~ **no!** oh nein!

oil [ɔɪl] ⬦ n Öl das ⬦ vt ölen, schmieren.

oilcan ['ɔɪlkæn] n Ölkanne die.

oilfield ['ɔɪlfiːld] n Ölfeld das.

oil filter n Ölfilter der.

oil-fired [-ˌfaɪəd] adj ölbefeuert; ~ **central heating** Ölheizung die.

oil painting n - **1.** [picture] Ölgemälde das - **2.** [art] Ölmalerei die.

oilrig ['ɔɪlrɪg] n Ölbohrinsel die.

oil slick n Ölteppich der.

oil tanker n - **1.** [ship] Öltanker der - **2.** [lorry] Tankwagen der.

oil well n Ölquelle die.

oily ['ɔɪlɪ] adj [rag, clothes] ölig; [food] fettig.

ointment ['ɔɪntmənt] n Salbe die.

OK (pt & pp OKed; cont OKing), **okay** [ˌəʊ'keɪ] inf ⬦ adj in Ordnung; **are you ~?** ist alles in Ordnung?; **is that ~ with you?** ist dir das recht? ⬦ adv [well] gut ⬦ excl - **1.** [expressing agreement] okay! - **2.** [to intro-duce new topic]: ~, **let's get started** Okay, fangen wir an ⬦ vt sein Okay geben zu.

old [əʊld] ⬦ adj - **1.** [gen] alt; **how ~ are you?** wie alt bist du?; **I'm 36 years ~** ich bin 36 (Jahre alt); **to get ~** alt werden; **in the ~ days** früher - **2.** [for emphasis]: **any ~ thing** das erste beste; **good ~ George!** der gute alte Georg! ⬦ npl: **the ~** ältere Leute.

old age n (U) Alter das.

old age pensioner n Br Rentner der, -in die.

old-fashioned [-'fæʃnd] adj [person, clothes] altmodisch; [ideas] überholt.

old people's home n Altersheim das.

O level (abbr of ordinary level) n Br ≃ mitt-lere Reife, früherer Schulabschluss in England und Wales, 1988 durch das GCSE ersetzt.

olive ['ɒlɪv] n Olive die.

olive green adj olivgrün.

olive oil n Olivenöl das.

Olympic [ə'lɪmpɪk] adj olympisch.
➡ **Olympics** npl: **the ~s** die Olympischen Spiele.

Olympic Games npl: **the ~** die Olympi-schen Spiele.

omelet(te) ['ɒmlɪt] n Omelett das.

omen ['əʊmən] n Omen das.

ominous ['ɒmɪnəs] adj ominös.

omission [ə'mɪʃn] n Auslassung die.

omit [ə'mɪt] vt auslassen; **to ~ to do sthg** es unterlassen, etw zu tun; [unintentionally] es versäumen, etw zu tun.

on [ɒn] ⬦ prep - **1.** [indicating position, loca-tion] auf (+ D); (with verbs of motion) auf (+ A); **it's ~ the table** es ist auf dem Tisch; **put it ~ the table** leg es auf den Tisch; ~ **the wall/ceiling** an der Wand/der Decke; ~ **page four** auf Seite vier; ~ **my left/right** zu meiner Linken/Rechten; ~ **the left/right** auf der linken/rechten Seite; **we stayed ~ a farm** wir übernachteten auf einem Bauernhof; ~ **the Rhine** am Rhein; ~ **the main road** an der Hauptstraße; **he had a scar ~ his face** er hat-te eine Narbe im Gesicht; **do you have any money ~ you?** hast du Geld bei dir? - **2.** [indi-cating means] auf (+ D); **recorded ~ tape** auf Band; ~ **TV/the radio** im Radio/Fernsehen; **it runs ~ unleaded petrol** es fährt mit blei-freiem Benzin; **he lives ~ fruit and yoghurt** er lebt von Obst und Joghurt; **to cut o.s. ~ sthg** sich an etw (D) schneiden - **3.** [indica-ting mode of transport]: **to be ~ the train/plane** im Zug/Flugzeug sein; **to travel ~ the bus/train** mit dem Bus/Zug fahren; **to get ~ a bus** in einen Bus einsteigen; ~ **foot** zu Fuß - **4.** [using, supported by]: **to stand ~ one leg** auf einem Bein stehen; **he was lying ~ his back** er lag auf dem Rücken; **to be ~ medica-tion** Medikamente nehmen; **to be ~ drugs** [addicted] drogensüchtig sein; **to be ~ social security** Sozialhilfe bekommen - **5.** [about] über (+ A); **a book ~ Germany** ein Buch über Deutschland - **6.** [indicating time] an (+ D); ~ **Tuesday** am Dienstag; ~ **Tuesdays** diens-tags; ~ **25 August** am 25. August; ~ **arrival** bei Ankunft; ~ **my return**, ~ **returning** bei meiner Rückkehr - **7.** [indicating activity]: **to work** ~ **sthg** an etw (D) arbeiten; **he's here** ~ **business** er ist geschäftlich hier; ~ **holiday** im Urlaub; **she's** ~ **the telephone** [talking] sie telefoniert gerade; **to be** ~ **fire** brennen - **8.** [according to]: ~ **good authority** aus guter Quelle; ~ **this evidence ...** aufgrund dieser Beweise ... - **9.** [indicating influence, effect] auf (+ A); **the effect ~ Britain** die Auswirkungen auf Großbritannien; **a tax ~ imports** eine Steuer auf Importe - 10. [earning]: **she's ~ £25,000 a year** sie verdient £25.000 pro Jahr; **to be ~ a low income** ein niedriges Einkommen haben - 11. [referring to musical instrument] auf (+ D); **the violin/flute** auf der Geige/Flöte - 12.: ~ **the cheap** billig; ~ **the sly** hintenherum - 13. inf [paid by]: **the drinks are ~ me** die Drinks gehen auf mich ⟨◇⟩ adv - 1. [in place, covering]: **to have sthg ~** [clothes, hat] etw anhaben; **put the lid ~** mach den Deckel drauf; **to put one's clothes ~** sich (D) (seine Kleider) anziehen - 2. [film, play, programme]: **the news is ~** die Nachrichten laufen; **what's ~ at the cinema?** was läuft im Kino?; **there's nothing ~ tonight** heute abend kommt nichts - 3. [working on; you left the heater ~** du hast das Heizgerät angelassen; **to turn sthg ~** [TV, radio, engine] etw einschalten; [tap] etw aufdrehen - 4. [indicating continuing action] weiter; **to work ~** weiterarbeiten; **we talked ~ into the night** wir redeten noch bis in die Nacht hinein; **he kept ~ walking** er ging immer weiter - 5. [forward]: **send my mail ~ (to me)** senden Sie mir die Post nach - 6. [with transport]: **to get ~** einsteigen; **is everyone ~?** sind alle eingestiegen? - 7. phr: **earlier ~** früher; **later ~** später; **it's just not ~!** inf das geht einfach nicht!; **to be** OR **go ~ at sb (to do sthg)** [pester] jm zusetzen(, etw zu tun). ◆ **from ... on** adv: **from that moment ~** von dem Moment an; **from now ~** von jetzt an, ab jetzt; **from then ~** von da an. ◆ **on and off** adv ab und zu. ◆ **on to, onto** prep (only written as onto for senses 4 and 5) - 1. [to a position on top of] auf (+ A); **she jumped ~ to the chair** sie sprang auf den Stuhl - 2. [into a vehicle] in (+ A); **she got ~ to the bus** sie stieg in den Bus ein - 3. [wall, door] an (+ A); **stick the photo ~ to the page** kleb das Foto auf die Seite - 4. [aware of]: **to be ~to sb** [subj: police] jm auf der Spur sein; **she's ~to something** sie hat etwas entdeckt - 5. [into contact with]: **to get ~to sb** sich an jn wenden.

once [wʌns] ⟨◇⟩ adv einmal; **not ~** kein einziges Mal; **for ~** ausnahmsweise; ~ **more** [one more time] noch einmal; [again] wieder; ~ **and for all** ein für allemal; ~ **(upon a time) there was ...** es war einmal ... ⟨◇⟩ conj wenn. ◆ **at once** adv - 1. [immediately] sofort - 2. [at the same time] gleichzeitig; **all at ~** auf einmal.

oncoming [ˈɒnˌkʌmɪŋ] adj: ~ **traffic** Gegenverkehr der.

one [wʌn] ⟨◇⟩ num - 1. [the number 1] eins; **thirty-~** einunddreißig; **at ~/~ thirty** [time] um eins/halb zwei; **in ~s and twos** vereinzelt - 2. (with masculine and neuter nouns) ein; (with feminine nouns) eine; ~ **brother and ~ sister** ein Bruder und eine Schwester;

~ **hundred/thousand** (ein)hundert/ (ein)tausend; **page ~** Seite eins; **~-fifth** ein Fünftel; ~ **or two** einige ⟨◇⟩ adj - 1. [only] einzige, -r, -s; **it's her ~ ambition** das ist ihr einziger Ehrgeiz - 2. [indefinite]: ~ **day** [in past, future] eines Tages; ~ **of these days** irgendwann einmal; ~ **afternoon/night** an einem Nachmittag/Abend - 3. fml [a certain] ein gewisser, eine gewisse; ~ **James Smith** ein gewisser James Smith ⟨◇⟩ pron - 1. [referring to a particular thing or person]: **the red/blue ~** der/die/das Rote/Blaue; **the best ~s** die besten; **the ~ on the table** der/die/das auf dem Tisch; **the ~ I told you about** der/die/das, von dem/der/dem ich dir erzählt habe; **the ~s you want** die OR diejenigen, die du willst; **I like that ~** ich mag den/die/das (da); **which ~?** welche, -r, -s?; **a red dot and a blue ~** ein roter Punkt und ein blauer - 2. [indefinite] eine/einer/eins; **there's only ~ left** es ist nur eine/einer/eins übrig; **have you got ~?** hast du eine/einen/eins?; ~ **of my friends** einer meiner Freunde; **not ~ (of them)** keiner (von ihnen); ~ **by ~** einer nach dem anderen - 3. [referring to money]: ~ **fifty, please** eins fünfzig, bitte - 4. fml [you, anyone] man; ~ **never knows** man weiß nie; **to give ~'s opinion** seine Meinung sagen; **to cut ~'s finger** sich (D) in den Finger schneiden. ◆ **for one** adv: **I for ~ will come** ich jedenfalls werde kommen.

one-armed bandit [-ɑːmd-] n einarmiger Bandit.

one-man adj Einmann-.

one-off inf ⟨◇⟩ adj [event, offer, concert] einmalig; ~ **object/product** Einzelstück das ⟨◇⟩ n - 1. [unique event] einmalige Sache - 2. [unique object, product] Einzelstück das.

one-on-one adj Am = one-to-one.

one-parent family n Einelternfamilie die.

oneself [wʌnˈself] pron fml - 1. (reflexive) sich; **to make ~ comfortable** es sich (D) bequem machen - 2. (after prep) sich selbst; **to look at ~ in the mirror** sich (selbst) im Spiegel betrachten - 3. (stressed) selbst; **to do sthg ~** etw selbst tun.

one-sided [-ˈsaɪdɪd] adj einseitig.

one-to-one Br, **one-on-one** Am adj: ~ **discussion** Diskussion die unter vier Augen; ~ **tuition** Einzelunterricht der.

one-way adj: ~ **street** Einbahnstraße die; ~ **traffic** Einbahnverkehr der; ~ **ticket** einfache Fahrkarte.

ongoing [ˈɒnˌgəʊɪŋ] adj [situation] andauernd; [project] laufend; [discussions] im Gang befindlich.

onion [ˈʌnjən] n Zwiebel die.

online [adj ˈɒnlaɪn adv ˌɒnˈlaɪn] COMPUT ⟨◇⟩ adj Online- ⟨◇⟩ adv online.

onlooker [ˈɒnˌlʊkəʳ] n Zuschauer der, -in die; [at accident scene] Schaulustige der, die.

only ['əʊnlɪ] <> *adj* einzige, -r, -s; **an ~ child** ein Einzelkind <> *adv* nur; **I ~ want one** ich möchte nur einen/eine/eines; **I ~ wish I could** ich würde es wirklich gern tun; **~ yesterday** erst gestern; **we've ~ just arrived** wir sind gerade erst angekommen; **there's ~ just enough** es ist gerade noch genug da; **not ~** nicht nur <> *conj* aber; **I would go, ~ I'm too tired** ich würde gehen, aber ich bin zu müde.

onset ['ɒnset] *n* Beginn *der*; [of war, illness] Ausbruch *der*.

onshore [ˌɒn'ʃɔːʳ] *adv* an Land.

onslaught ['ɒnslɔːt] *n* - **1.** [physical] (heftiger) Angriff - **2.** [verbal] (verbale) Attacke.

onto ['ɒntuː] *prep* <> on.

onus ['əʊnəs] *n*: **the ~ is on him to convince us** es liegt an ihm, uns zu überzeugen.

onward ['ɒnwəd] <> *adj*: **~ journey** Weiterreise *die* <> *adv* = onwards.

onwards ['ɒnwədz] *adv* [forwards] vorwärts; **to travel ~** weiterreisen; **from now ~** von jetzt an; **from October ~** ab Oktober.

ooze [uːz] <> *vt fig* [charm] aus|strahlen; [confidence] strotzen vor (+ D) <> *vi* [liquid, blood] triefen; [mud] (heraus)quellen.

opaque [əʊ'peɪk] *adj* - **1.** [not transparent] undurchsichtig - **2.** *fig* [text, meaning] unverständlich.

open ['əʊpn] <> *adj* - **1.** [gen] offen; **wide ~** weit offen - **2.** [receptive - mind, person]: **to be ~ to sthg** [ready to accept] für etw offen sein; **~ to question** fraglich; **two options are ~ to us** zwei Möglichkeiten stehen uns offen - **3.** [shop, office, library] geöffnet; **~ to the public** der Öffentlichkeit zugänglich - **4.** [inaugurated] eröffnet - **5.** [unobstructed - road, passage] frei; [- view] weit - **6.** [not enclosed]: **~ country** freies Land; **in the ~ air** im Freien <> *n*: **in the ~** [in the fresh air] im Freien; **to bring sthg out into the ~** etw ans Licht bringen <> *vt* - **1.** [gen] öffnen; **to ~ fire** das Feuer eröffnen - **2.** [bank account, meeting, event, new building] eröffnen <> *vi* - **1.** [door, window, eyes, flower] sich öffnen - **2.** [begin business] öffnen - **3.** [commence] beginnen. ◆ **open on to** *vt fus* [subj: door] führen auf (+ A). ◆ **open up** <> *vt sep* - **1.** [gen] öffnen - **2.** [for development - country, market] erschließen <> *vi* - **1.** [unlock door] aufschließen - **2.** [for business] öffnen - **3.** [become available - possibilities, chances] sich eröffnen - **4.** [become less reserved] offener werden.

opener ['əʊpnəʳ] *n* Öffner *der*.

opening ['əʊpnɪŋ] <> *adj* [speech, scene] Eröffnungs- <> *n* - **1.** [beginning] Anfang *der* - **2.** [gap] Öffnung *die* - **3.** [opportunity, business possibility] Möglichkeit *die* - **4.** [job vacancy] freie Stelle.

opening hours *npl* Öffnungszeiten *pl*.

openly ['əʊpənlɪ] *adv* [frankly] offen; [publicly] öffentlich.

open-minded [-'maɪndɪd] *adj* aufgeschlossen.

open-plan *adj* [office] Großraum-.

Open University *n Br*: **the ~** britische Fernuniversität.

opera ['ɒpərə] *n* Oper *die*.

opera house *n* Opernhaus *das*.

operate ['ɒpəreɪt] <> *vt* - **1.** [machine] bedienen - **2.** COMM [business] leiten, führen <> *vi* - **1.** [law] sich aus|wirken; [system] funktionieren; [machine - function] funktionieren; [- be in operation] in Betrieb sein - **2.** COMM [business] arbeiten - **3.** MED: **to ~ (on sb/sthg)** (jn/etw) operieren.

operating theatre *Br*, **operating room** *Am* ['ɒpəreɪtɪŋ-] *n* Operationssaal *der*.

operation [ˌɒpə'reɪʃn] *n* - **1.** [planned activity - MIL] Operation *die*; [- of police force] Einsatz *der*; **rescue ~** Rettungsaktion *die*; **relief ~** Hilfsaktion *die* - **2.** (U) [COMM - management] Leitung *die*; [- company, business] Unternehmen *das* - **3.** (U) [of machine - running] Betrieb *der*; [- control] Bedienung *die*; **to be in ~** [machine] in Betrieb sein; [law] in Kraft sein; [system] angewendet werden - **4.** MED Operation *die*; **to have an ~** operiert werden.

operational [ˌɒpə'reɪʃənl] *adj* [machine]: **to be ~** [ready for use] betriebsbereit sein; [in use] in Betrieb sein.

operator ['ɒpəreɪtəʳ] *n* - **1.** [TELEC - at telephone exchange] Vermittlung *die*; [- at switchboard] Telefonist *der*, **-in** *die* - **2.** [of machine] Maschinenarbeiter *der*, **-in** *die*; [of computer] Operator *der*, **-in** *die* - **3.** COMM [person in charge] Unternehmer *der*, **-in** *die*.

opinion [ə'pɪnjən] *n* Meinung *die*, Ansicht *die*; MED Gutachten *das*; **what's your ~ of him?** was halten Sie von ihm?; **to be of the ~ that ...** der Meinung OR Ansicht sein, dass ...; **to have a high/low ~ of sb** eine hohe/schlechte Meinung von jm haben; **in my ~** meiner Meinung OR Ansicht nach.

giving opinions

Meiner Meinung/Ansicht nach muss man etwas unternehmen. In my opinion, we have to do something.

Wenn ihr mich fragt, ist das ein abgekartetes Spiel. If you ask me, the whole thing has been rigged.

Ich glaube, Sie irren sich. I think you've made a mistake.

Ich finde, man sollte die Gelegenheit nutzen. I think we should make the most of the opportunity.

Was mich angeht, könnt ihr auf mich zählen. You can count on me.

opinionated [ə'pɪnjəneɪtɪd] *adj pej* rechthaberisch.

opinion poll *n* Meinungsumfrage *die.*

opponent [ə'pəʊnənt] *n* Gegner *der,* -in *die.*

opportune ['ɒpətjuːn] *adj* [moment] günstig.

opportunist [ˌɒpə'tjuːnɪst] *n* Opportunist *der,* -in *die.*

opportunity [ˌɒpə'tjuːnətɪ] *n* Gelegenheit *die;* **to take the ~ to do** OR **of doing sthg** die Gelegenheit ergreifen, um etw zu tun.

oppose [ə'pəʊz] *vt* [resist] sich widersetzen (+ *D*); [ideas, views] abllehnen.

opposed [ə'pəʊzd] *adj:* **to be ~ to sthg** gegen etw sein; **as ~ to** im Gegensatz zu.

opposing [ə'pəʊzɪŋ] *adj* [points of view] entgegengesetzt; [teams] gegnerisch.

opposite ['ɒpəzɪt] ◇ *adj* - 1. [facing] gegenüberliegend; **the houses ~** die Häuser gegenüber - 2. [very different] entgegengesetzt ◇ *adv* gegenüber ◇ *prep* [facing] gegenüber (+ *D*) ◇ *n* Gegenteil *das.*

opposite number *n* Pendant *das.*

opposition [ˌɒpə'zɪʃn] *n* - 1. [disapproval] Widerstand *der,* Opposition *die* - 2. [opposing team] Gegner *pl.* ◆ **Opposition** *n Br* POL: **the Opposition** die Opposition.

oppress [ə'pres] *vt* - 1. [persecute] unterdrücken - 2. [subj: anxiety, atmosphere] bedrücken.

oppressive [ə'presɪv] *adj* - 1. [regime, government, society] repressiv - 2. [heat, weather] drückend - 3. [situation, silence] bedrückend.

opt [ɒpt] ◇ *vt:* **to ~ to do sthg** sich dafür entscheiden, etw zu tun ◇ *vi:* **to ~ for sthg** sich für etw entscheiden. ◆ **opt in** *vi:* **to ~ in to sthg** etw (*D*) beiltreten. ◆ **opt out** *vi:* **to ~ out (of)** [scheme, system] ausltreten (aus).

optical ['ɒptɪkl] *adj* optisch.

optician [ɒp'tɪʃn] *n* Optiker *der,* -in *die;* **to go to the ~'s** zum Optiker gehen.

optimist ['ɒptɪmɪst] *n* Optimist *der,* -in *die.*

optimistic [ˌɒptɪ'mɪstɪk] *adj:* **she's ~ about passing her driving test** sie ist optimistisch, dass sie die Fahrprüfung bestehen wird.

optimum ['ɒptɪməm] *adj* optimal.

option ['ɒpʃn] *n* [choice] Wahl *die;* [alternative to be chosen] (Wahl)möglichkeit *die;* **to have the ~ to do** OR **of doing sthg** die Möglichkeit haben, etw zu tun.

optional ['ɒpʃənl] *adj* [subject] Wahl-; [course] fakultativ; **~ extra** Extra *das.*

or [ɔːʳ] *conj* - 1. [linking alternatives] oder; **either one ~ the other** entweder das eine oder das andere; **~ (else)** [otherwise] sonst; **ten kilometres ~ so** [approximately] ungefähr zehn Kilometer - 2. *(after negatives)* noch; **he can-**

not read ~ write er kann weder lesen noch schreiben.

oral ['ɔːrəl] ◇ *adj* - 1. [exam] mündlich - 2. MED [medicine] zum Einnehmen; [hygiene] Mund-; **~ vaccine** Schluckimpfung *die* ◇ *n* mündliche Prüfung.

orally ['ɔːrəlɪ] *adv* MED oral; **to take sthg ~** etw einlnehmen.

orange ['ɒrɪndʒ] ◇ *adj* [colour] orange ◇ *n* - 1. [fruit] Orange *die,* Apfelsine *die* - 2. (*U*) [colour] Orange *das.*

orator ['ɒrətəʳ] *n* Redner *der,* -in *die.*

orbit ['ɔːbɪt] ◇ *n* [in space] Umlaufbahn *die* ◇ *vt* umkreisen.

orchard ['ɔːtʃəd] *n* Obstgarten *der.*

orchestra ['ɔːkɪstrə] *n* Orchester *das.*

orchid ['ɔːkɪd] *n* Orchidee *die.*

ordain [ɔː'deɪn] *vt* RELIG: **to be ~ed** (zum Priester) geweiht werden.

ordeal [ɔː'diːl] *n* Tortur *die.*

order ['ɔːdəʳ] ◇ *n* - 1. [instruction] Anweisung *die,* MIL Befehl *der;* **until further ~s** bis auf weiteren Befehl; **to be under ~s** to do sthg MIL den Befehl haben, etw zu tun - 2. COMM [request, in restaurant] Bestellung *die;* **to place an ~ with sb for sthg** bei jm eine Bestellung für etw auflgeben; [contract to manufacture or supply goods] Auftrag *der;* **to place an ~ with sb for sthg** jm für etw einen Auftrag erteilen; **to ~ auf Bestellung - 3.** (*U*) [sequence] Reihenfolge *die;* **arranged in ~ of importance** nach Wichtigkeit geordnet; **in alphabetical ~** in alphabetischer Reihenfolge - 4. (*U*) [neatness, discipline, system] Ordnung *die* - 5. [fitness for use]: **in ~** [valid] in Ordnung; **in working ~** funktionstüchtig; **out of ~** [machine, lift] außer Betrieb; **you're out of ~!** *inf* pass auf, was du sagst/machst! - 6. RELIG Orden *der* - 7. Am [portion] Portion *die* ◇ *vt* - 1. [command] anlordnen; MIL befehlen (+ *D*); [subj: court] verfügen; **to ~ sb to do sthg** jn anweisen, etw zu tun; MIL jm befehlen, etw zu tun; **to ~ that ...** anlordnen, dass ...; MIL befehlen, dass ... - 2. COMM [request] bestellen; [to be manufactured: suit, aircraft, ship] in Auftrag geben. ◆ **in the order of** *Br,* **on the order of** *Am adv* etwa. ◆ **in order that** *conj* damit. ◆ **in order to** *conj* um ... zu; **in ~ to get a better view** um eine bessere Sicht zu bekommen. ◆ **order about, order around** *vt sep* herumlkommandieren.

order form *n* Bestellschein *der.*

orderly ['ɔːdəlɪ] ◇ *adj* ordentlich ◇ *n* [in hospital] Pfleger *der,* -in *die.*

ordinarily ['ɔːdənrəlɪ] *adv* [normally] gewöhnlich, normalerweise.

ordinary ['ɔːdɪnrɪ] ◇ *adj* - 1. [normal] gewöhnlich, normal; **~ people** einfache Leute

- 2. *pej* [unexceptional] gewöhnlich ⬦ *n:* **out of the ~** außergewöhnlich.

📖 **ordinary**

Das englische ordinary bedeutet übersetzt so viel wie „gewöhnlich" oder „normal". Obwohl auch das deutsche „ordinär" in dieser Bedeutung gebraucht werden kann, ist es fast nie die richtige Übersetzung. This is no ordinary computer heißt im Deutschen daher „Dies ist kein gewöhnlicher Computer."

Möchte man auf Englisch sagen, dass etwas „ordinär" ist, lauten die geeigneten Begriffe vulgar or crude. Der Feststellung „Er ist ein ordinärer Mensch" entspricht das englische he is a vulgar man.

---

ore [ɔːʳ] *n* Erz *das.*

oregano [ˌɒrɪˈɡɑːnəʊ] *n* Oregano *der.*

organ [ˈɔːɡən] *n* **- 1.** ANAT Organ *das* **- 2.** MUS Orgel *die.*

organic [ɔːˈɡænɪk] *adj* **- 1.** [of animals, plants] organisch **- 2.** [food] biodynamisch.

organization [ˌɔːɡənaɪˈzeɪʃn] *n* **- 1.** [gen] Organisation *die* **- 2.** *(U)* [arrangement] Ordnung *die.*

organize, -ise [ˈɔːɡənaɪz] *vt* organisieren; [affairs, thoughts] ordnen.

organizer, -iser [ˈɔːɡənaɪzəʳ] *n* [person] Organisator *der*, **-in** *die.*

orgasm [ˈɔːɡæzm] *n* Orgasmus *der.*

orgy [ˈɔːdʒɪ] *n* Orgie *die.*

oriental [ˌɔːrɪˈentl] *adj* orientalisch.

origami [ˌɒrɪˈɡɑːmɪ] *n* Origami *das.*

origin [ˈɒrɪdʒɪn] *n* **- 1.** [starting point] Ursprung *der* **- 2.** *(U)* [birth] Herkunft *die;* **country of ~** Herkunftsland *das.* ◆ **origins** *npl* Herkunft *die.*

original [əˈrɪdʒənl] ⬦ *adj* **- 1.** [first] ursprünglich **- 2.** [document] Original-; **~ painting** Original *das* **- 3.** [new, unusual] originell ⬦ *n* Original *das.*

originally [əˈrɪdʒənəlɪ] *adv* [initially] ursprünglich.

originate [əˈrɪdʒəneɪt] ⬦ *vt* [scheme, policy] ins Leben rufen; [new style] begründen ⬦ *vi:* **to ~ in/from** seinen Ursprung haben in *(+ D).*

ornament [ˈɔːnəmənt] *n* **- 1.** [object] Ziergegenstand *der* **- 2.** *(U)* [decoration] Verzierungen *pl.*

ornamental [ˌɔːnəˈmentl] *adj* dekorativ; **~ garden** Ziergarten *der.*

ornate [ɔːˈneɪt] *adj* reich verziert; [language] blumig.

ornithology [ˌɔːnɪˈθɒlədʒɪ] *n* Ornithologie *die.*

orphan [ˈɔːfn] ⬦ *n* Waise *die*, Waisenkind *das* ⬦ *vt:* **to be ~ed** (zur) Waise werden.

orphanage [ˈɔːfənɪdʒ] *n* Waisenhaus *das.*

orthodox [ˈɔːθədɒks] *adj* **- 1.** [conventional] konventionell **- 2.** RELIG orthodox.

orthopaedic [ˌɔːθəˈpiːdɪk] *adj* orthopädisch.

Oslo [ˈɒzləʊ] *n* Oslo *nt.*

ostensible [ɒˈstensəbl] *adj* angeblich.

ostentatious [ˌɒstənˈteɪʃəs] *adj* [person] protzenhaft; [behaviour] betont auffällig.

osteopath [ˈɒstɪəpæθ] *n* Osteopath *der*, **-in** *die.*

ostracize, -ise [ˈɒstrəsaɪz] *vt* ächten.

ostrich [ˈɒstrɪtʃ] *n* Strauß *der.*

other [ˈʌðəʳ] ⬦ *adj* andere, -r, -s; **the ~ one** der/die/das andere; **the ~ day** neulich; **every ~ day** jeden zweiten Tag; **any ~ questions?** sonst noch Fragen? ⬦ *pron* andere, -r, -s; **one or ~ (of us)** der eine oder andere (von uns); **one after the ~** hintereinander ⬦ *adv:* **~ than** außer; **it was none ~ than the king** es war kein anderer als der König.

otherwise [ˈʌðəwaɪz] ⬦ *adv* **- 1.** [apart from that] ansonsten, sonst **- 2.** [differently] anders; **to be ~ engaged** anderweitig beschäftigt sein; **~ known as** auch bekannt als ⬦ *conj* [or else] sonst, andernfalls.

otter [ˈɒtəʳ] *n* Otter *der.*

ouch [aʊtʃ] *excl* au!, aua!

ought [ɔːt] *aux vb:* **I ~ to go now** ich sollte jetzt gehen; **you ~ not to have said that** du hättest das nicht sagen sollen; **you ~ to see a doctor** du solltest zum Arzt gehen; **the car ~ to be ready by Friday** das Auto sollte Freitag fertig sein; **it ~ to be enough for three** das dürfte für drei Personen genügen.

ounce [aʊns] *n* **- 1.** [unit of measurement] Unze *die (= 28,35 g)* **- 2.** *fig* [of truth, intelligence] Funken *der.*

our [ˈaʊəʳ] *poss adj* unser; **~ children** unsere Kinder; **we washed ~ hair** wir haben uns die Haare gewaschen; **a home of ~ own** ein eigenes Haus.

ours [ˈaʊəz] *poss pron* unsere, -r, -s; **this suitcase is ~** dieser Koffer gehört uns; **a friend of ~** ein Freund von uns.

ourselves [aʊəˈselvz] *pron* *(reflexive, after prep)* uns; **we did it ~** wir haben es selbst gemacht; **(all) by ~** (ganz) allein.

oust [aʊst] *vt fml:* **to ~ sb from sthg** [position, job] jn aus etw verdrängen.

out [aʊt] ⬦ *adj* [light, cigarette] aus ⬦ *adv* **- 1.** [outside] draußen; **to come ~ (of)** herauskommen (aus); **to get ~ (of)** aussteigen (aus); **it's cold ~ today** es ist heute kalt draußen; **~ you go!** raus mit dir!; **~ here/there** hier/dort draußen **- 2.** [not at home, work]: **she's ~** sie ist nicht da; **to go ~** ausgehen; **to go ~ for a walk** einen Spaziergang machen **- 3.** [so as to be extinguished] aus; **put your cigarette ~!** mach deine Zigarette aus! **- 4.** [of tides]: **the tide is ~** es ist Ebbe **- 5.** [expressing removal]: **to take sthg ~ (of)** etw herauslnehmen (aus); [money] etw ablheben (von); **he poured the water ~** er schüttete das Wasser aus - **6.** [expressing distribution]: **to hand sthg ~** etw auslteilen - **7.** [wrong]: **the bill's £10 ~** die Rechnung stimmt um 10 Pfund nicht - **8.** [published, known]: **the book is just ~** das Buch ist soeben erschienen; **the secret is ~** das Geheimnis ist gelüftet - **9.** [in flower] aufgeblüht; **the roses are ~** die Rosen blühen - **10.** [visible]: **the moon is ~** der Mond scheint - **11.** [out of fashion] aus der Mode - **12.** *inf* [on strike]: **they've been ~ for months now** sie streiken schon seit Monaten - **13.** [determined]: **to be ~ for revenge** auf Rache aus sein; **I'm not ~ to make money** ich bin nicht darauf aus, Geld zu verdienen. ◆ **out of** *prep* - **1.** [away from, outside]: **stay ~ of the sun** bleib aus der Sonne; **I was ~ of the country** ich war im Ausland - **2.** [indicating cause, origin] aus *(+ D)*; **~ of respect/curiosity** aus Respekt/Neugierde; **made ~ of wood** aus Holz (gemacht) - **3.** [without]: **I'm ~ of** OR **I've run ~ of cigarettes** ich habe keine Zigaretten mehr - **4.** [to indicate proportion]: **five ~ of ten** fünf von zehn - **5.** *phr:* **~ of danger/control** außer Gefahr/Kontrolle. ◆ **out of doors** *adv* im Freien.

out-and-out *adj* [liar, fool, crook] ausgemacht.

outback ['aʊtbæk] *n:* **the ~** weit abseits der Städte gelegener Teil Australiens.

outboard (motor) ['aʊtbɔ:d-] *n* Außenbordmotor *der.*

outbreak ['aʊtbreɪk] *n* [of war, disease] Ausbruch *der.*

outburst ['aʊtbɜ:st] *n* [of emotion, violence] Ausbruch *der.*

outcast ['aʊtkɑ:st] *n* [socially] Außenseiter *der,* -in *die;* [from family, group] Verstoßene *der, die.*

outcome ['aʊtkʌm] *n* Ergebnis *das.*

outcry ['aʊtkraɪ] *n* Aufschrei *der* der Empörung.

outdated [,aʊt'deɪtɪd] *adj* [belief, concept, method] überholt; [language] antiquiert.

outdid [,aʊt'dɪd] *pt* ⊳ outdo.

outdo [,aʊt'du:] *(pt* -did; *pp* -done [-'dʌn]) *vt* übertreffen.

outdoor ['aʊtdɔ:'] *adj* [life, activity] im Freien; **~ swimming pool** Freibad *das;* **~ clothes** Straßenkleidung *die.*

outdoors [aʊt'dɔ:z] *adv* draußen, im Freien; [go] nach draußen.

outer ['aʊtə'] *adj* [wall] Außen-; [layer] äußere, -r, -s.

outer space *n* Weltraum *der.*

outfit ['aʊtfɪt] *n* - **1.** [clothes] Kleider *pl;* [fancy dress] Kostüm *das* - **2.** *inf* [organization] Laden *der,* Verein *der.*

outgoing ['aʊt,gəʊɪŋ] *adj* - **1.** [from job] (aus dem Amt) scheidend - **2.** [friendly, sociable] kontaktfreudig. ◆ **outgoings** *npl Br* Ausgaben *pl.*

outgrow [,aʊt'grəʊ] *(pt* -grew [-'gru:]; *pp* -grown [-'grəʊn]) *vt* - **1.** [grow too big for] herauslwachsen aus - **2.** [habit] ablegen.

outhouse ['aʊthaʊs, *pl* -haʊzɪz] *n* Nebengebäude *das.*

outing ['aʊtɪŋ] *n* [trip] Ausflug *der.*

outlandish [aʊt'lændɪʃ] *adj* sonderbar.

outlaw ['aʊtlɔ:] ⬦ *n* Geächtete *der, die;* [in the Wild West] Bandit *der* ⬦ *vt* [make illegal] verbieten.

outlay ['aʊtleɪ] *n* Kostenaufwand *der.*

outlet ['aʊtlet] *n* - **1.** [for feelings] Ventil *das* - **2.** [hole, pipe] Auslass *der* - **3.** [shop] Verkaufsstelle *die* - **4.** *Am* ELEC Steckdose *die.*

outline ['aʊtlaɪn] ⬦ *n* - **1.** [brief description] Abriss *der;* **in ~** in Grundzügen - **2.** [silhouette] Umriss *der* ⬦ *vt* [describe briefly] umreißen, skizzieren.

outlive [,aʊt'lɪv] *vt* [subj: person] überleben.

outlook ['aʊtlʊk] *n* - **1.** [attitude, disposition] Einstellung *die* - **2.** [prospect] Aussichten *pl.*

outlying ['aʊt,laɪɪŋ] *adj* [villages] abgelegen; **~ district** Außenbezirk *der.*

outmoded [,aʊt'məʊdɪd] *adj* überholt.

outnumber [,aʊt'nʌmbə'] *vt* zahlenmäßig überlegen sein *(+ D).*

out-of-date *adj* [passport, season ticket] abgelaufen; [clothes] altmodisch; [belief] überholt.

out of doors *adv* draußen, im Freien; [go] nach draußen.

out-of-the-way *adj* [isolated] abgelegen.

outpatient ['aʊt,peɪʃnt] *n* ambulanter Patient, ambulante Patientin; **~s (department)** Ambulanz *die.*

output ['aʊtpʊt] *n (U)* - **1.** [production - of factory, writer] Produktion *die;* [- in agriculture] Ertrag *der* - **2.** [COMPUT - printing out] Ausdrucken *das;* [- printout] Ausdruck *der.*

outrage ['aʊtreɪdʒ] ⬦ *n* - **1.** *(U)* [anger, shock] Empörung *die* - **2.** [atrocity] Verbrechen *das* ⬦ *vt* empören; [sense of morality] zuwiderllaufen *(+ D).*

outrageous [aʊt'reɪdʒəs] *adj* - **1.** [offensive, shocking - crime] verabscheuungswürdig; [- language] unflätig; [- behaviour] unerhört - **2.** [extravagant, wild - outfit, idea] exzentrisch.

outright [*adj* 'aʊtraɪt, *adv* ,aʊt'raɪt] ⬦ *adj* [refusal, denial] kategorisch; [disaster] total; [winner, victory] klar; [lie] glatt ⬦ *adv* [ask] ohne Umschweife; [deny] kategorisch; [win, fail] klar.

outset ['aʊtset] *n*: **at the ~** zu OR am Anfang; **from the ~** von Anfang an.

outside [*adv* ˌaʊt'saɪd, *adj, prep & n* 'aʊt-saɪd] ◇ *adv* draußen; **to go ~** nach draußen gehen ◇ *prep* - 1. [gen] außerhalb (+ *G*); **we live just ~ London** wir wohnen gleich außerhalb Londons; **~ (office) hours** außerhalb der Dienststunden - 2. [in front of] vor (+ *A, D*); **~ the door** vor der Tür ◇ *adj* - 1. [exterior] Außen- - 2. [help, advice] von außen; **~ influence** äußere Einflüsse - 3. [unlikely]: **there's an ~ chance** es besteht eine geringe Chance ◇ *n* [of building, car, container] Außenseite *die*; **to open the door from the ~** die Tür von außen öffnen. ◆ **outside of** *prep* - 1. *Am* [on the outside of] außerhalb (+ *G*) - 2. [apart from] außer.

outside lane *n* Überholspur *die*.

outside line *n* Amtsleitung *die*.

outsider [ˌaʊt'saɪdəʳ] *n* Außenseiter *der*, -in *die*.

outsize ['aʊtsaɪz] *adj* - 1. [book, portion] überdimensional - 2.: **~ clothes** Kleidung *die* in Übergröße.

outskirts ['aʊtskɜːts] *npl*: **the ~** die Außenbezirke *pl*; **on the ~** am Stadtrand.

outspoken [ˌaʊt'spəʊkn] *adj* freimütig.

outstanding [ˌaʊt'stændɪŋ] *adj* - 1. [excellent - person] außergewöhnlich; [- performance, achievement] hervorragend - 2. [very obvious, important] bemerkenswert - 3. [not paid - money] ausstehend; [- bill] unbezahlt - 4. [still to be done - work] unerledigt; [- problem] ungeklärt.

outstay [ˌaʊt'steɪ] *vt*: **to ~ one's welcome** länger bleiben als erwünscht.

outstretched [ˌaʊt'stretʃt] *adj* ausgestreckt.

outstrip [ˌaʊt'strɪp] *vt* - 1. [do better than] übertreffen - 2. [run faster than] überholen.

out-tray *n* Ablage *die* für Ausgänge.

outward ['aʊtwəd] ◇ *adj* - 1. [going away]: **~ journey** Hinreise *die* - 2. [external, visible]: **she maintained her ~ composure** sie blieb äußerlich ruhig; **he shows no ~ sign of his grief** nach außen hin zeigt er nichts von seinem Kummer ◇ *adv Am* = outwards.

outwardly ['aʊtwədlɪ] *adv* nach außen hin.

outwards *Br* ['aʊtwədz], **outward** *Am adv* nach außen.

outweigh [ˌaʊt'weɪ] *vt* überwiegen.

outwit [ˌaʊt'wɪt] *vt* überlisten.

oval ['əʊvl] ◇ *adj* oval ◇ *n* Oval *das*.

Oval Office *n*: **the ~** Büro des US-Präsidenten im Weißen Haus.

ovary ['əʊvərɪ] *n* ANAT Eierstock *der*.

ovation [əʊ'veɪʃn] *n* Ovation *die*, begeisterter Beifall; **to give a standing ~** jm stehende Ovationen darlbringen.

oven ['ʌvn] *n* [for cooking] Backofen *der*.

ovenproof ['ʌvnpruːf] *adj* feuerfest.

over ['əʊvəʳ] ◇ *prep* - 1. [directly above] über (+ *D*); **a bridge ~ the road** eine Brücke über der Straße - 2. [indicating place, position] über (+ *D*); [indicating direction] über (+ *A*); **she wore a veil ~ her face** sie trug einen Schleier vor dem Gesicht; **put your coat ~ the chair** leg deinen Mantel über den Stuhl - 3. [across] über (+ *A*); **to walk ~ sth** über etw laufen; **he threw it ~ the wall** er warf es über die Mauer; **it's just ~ the road** es ist gleich gegenüber; **it's ~ the river** es ist auf der anderen Seite des Flusses; **with a view ~ the gardens** mit Blick auf die Gärten - 4. [more than] über (+ *A*); **it cost ~ $1,000** es hat über 1000 Dollar gekostet; **~ and above this amount** über den Betrag hinaus - 5. [about] über (+ *A*); **an argument ~ the price** ein Streit über den Preis - 6. [during]: **~ the weekend** übers Wochenende; **~ the past two years** in den letzten zwei Jahren; **to discuss sth ~ lunch/a cup of coffee** etw beim Essen/bei einer Tasse Kaffee besprechen - 7. [to do]: **he took a long time ~ it** er hat lange dazu gebraucht - 8. [recovered from] über (+ *A*); **to be ~ sth** über etw (*A*) hinweg sein - 9. [by means of] über (+ *A*); **~ the phone** am Telefon; **~ the radio** im Radio ◇ *adv* - 1. [referring to distance away]: **~ by the gate** drüben beim Tor; **here/there** hier/da drüben - 2. [across] herüber/hinüber; **to drive ~** herüberlfahren/hinüberlfahren - 3. [round to other side]: **to turn sth ~** etw umldrehen; **to roll ~** sich umldrehen - 4. [more]: **children aged 12 and ~** Kinder ab 12; **sums of £100 and ~** Summen von 100 Pfund und mehr - 5. [remaining] übrig; **to be (left) ~** übrig bleiben - 6. [at/to sb's house]: **to invite sb ~ for dinner** jn zu sich zum Essen einladen; **I was ~ at my mum's yesterday** ich war gestern bei meiner Mutter - 7. RADIO over; **~ and out!** over and out! - 8. [involving repetitions]: **(all) ~ again** wieder von vorne; **~ and ~ (again)** immer wieder ◇ *adj* [finished]: **to be ~** zu Ende sein.

overall [*adj & n* ˌəʊvər'ɔːl, *adv* ˌəʊvər'ɔːl] ◇ *adj* - 1. [total] Gesamt- - 2. [general] allgemein ◇ *adv* - 1. [in total] insgesamt - 2. [in general] im Großen und Ganzen ◇ *n* - 1. [coat] Kittel *der* - 2. *Am* [with trousers] Overall *der*. ◆ **overalls** *npl* - 1. [with long sleeves] Overall *der* - 2. *Am* [with bib] Latzhose *die*.

overawe [ˌəʊvər'ɔː] *vt* [subj: person - make feel fear] einlschüchtern; [- make feel respect] Ehrfurcht einlflößen (+ *D*); [subj: surroundings] überwältigen.

overbalance [ˌəʊvə'bæləns] *vi* das Gleichgewicht verlieren.

overbearing [ˌəʊvə'beərɪŋ] *adj pej* herrisch.

overboard ['əʊvəbɔːd] adv NAUT: **to fall ~** über Bord gehen.

overcame [ˌəʊvə'keɪm] pt ⟶ overcome.

overcast [ˌəʊvə'kɑːst] adj bedeckt.

overcharge [ˌəʊvə'tʃɑːdʒ] vt: **to ~ sb (for sthg)** jm zu viel berechnen (für etw).

overcoat ['əʊvəkəʊt] n Mantel der.

overcome [ˌəʊvə'kʌm] (pt -came; pp -come) vt - 1. [control, deal with] überwinden - 2. [overwhelm]: **to be ~ with emotion** gerührt sein; **to be ~ by fear** von Furcht ergriffen werden; **he was ~ by the fumes** die Dämpfe machten ihn bewusstlos.

overcrowded [ˌəʊvə'kraʊdɪd] adj [room, pub, prison] überfüllt; [town] übervölkert.

overcrowding [ˌəʊvə'kraʊdɪŋ] n [of room, pub, prison] Überfüllung die; [of town] Übervölkerung die.

overdo [ˌəʊvə'duː] (pt -did [-'dɪd]; pp -done [-'dʌn]) vt - 1. [exaggerate, do too much] es übertreiben mit; **to ~ it** es übertreiben; [work too hard] sich übernehmen - 2. [overcook - vegetables] verkochen; [- steak] verbraten.

overdose ['əʊvədəʊs] n Überdosis die.

overdraft ['əʊvədrɑːft] n Kontoüberziehung die.

overdrawn [ˌəʊvə'drɔːn] adj [account] überzogen; **I'm (£200) ~** mein Konto ist (um 200 Pfund) überzogen.

overdue [ˌəʊvə'djuː] adj - 1. [late - library book] überfällig; **the train is 20 minutes ~** der Zug hat 20 Minuten Verspätung - 2. [reform, rent, bill] überfällig.

overestimate [ˌəʊvər'estɪmeɪt] vt - 1. [guess too high a value for] zu hoch (ein)schätzen - 2. [overrate] überschätzen.

overflow [vb ˌəʊvə'fləʊ, n 'əʊvəfləʊ] vi - 1. [bath] überlaufen; [river] über die Ufer treten - 2. [place, container]: **to be ~ing (with sthg)** [room] überfüllt sein (mit etw); [drawer, box] überquellen (vor etw) n [pipe, hole] Überlauf der.

overgrown [ˌəʊvə'grəʊn] adj [garden, path] überwuchert.

overhaul [n 'əʊvəhɔːl, vb ˌəʊvə'hɔːl] n - 1. [service] Überholung die - 2. [revision] Überarbeitung die vt - 1. [service] überholen - 2. [revise] überarbeiten.

overhead [adv ˌəʊvə'hed, adj & n 'əʊvəhed] adj: **~ cable** ELEC Hochspannungsleitung die; **~ lighting** Deckenbeleuchtung die adv über uns/ihm/etc; **the clouds ~** die Wolken am Himmel n (U) Am Gemeinkosten pl. ⟶ **overheads** npl Br Gemeinkosten pl.

overhead projector n Overheadprojektor der.

overhear [ˌəʊvə'hɪə] (pt & pp -heard [-'hɜːd]) vt [remark] zufällig hören; [conversation] zufällig mithören.

Das Verb to overhear scheint auf den ersten Blick dem deutschen „überhören" zu entsprechen, bedeutet aber „zufällig hören". I overheard them plotting together hat im Deutschen die Bedeutung „ich hörte zufällig, wie sie gemeinsam etwas ausheckten".
Das deutsche „überhören" kann im Englischen mit to ignore ausgedrückt werden, wenn etwas absichtlich überhört wird, oder mit not to hear, wenn jemand etwas nicht mitbekommen hat. Der Satz „Sie hat das wohl überhört" lautet im Englischen I don't think she heard.

overheat [ˌəʊvə'hiːt] vt [room] überheizen vi [engine, car] heißlaufen; [photocopier, toaster] zu heiß werden.

overjoyed [ˌəʊvə'dʒɔɪd] adj: **to be ~ (at sthg)** (über etw (A)) überglücklich sein.

overkill ['əʊvəkɪl] n [excess]: **to be ~** zu viel des Guten sein.

overladen [ˌəʊvə'leɪdn] pp ⟶ overload adj zu schwer beladen.

overland ['əʊvəlænd] adj & adv auf dem Landweg.

overlap [ˌəʊvə'læp] vi - 1. [cover each other] einander teilweise überdecken - 2. [be similar]: **to ~ (with sthg)** [ideas, systems] sich teilweise decken (mit etw); [timetable, holiday] sich überschneiden (mit etw).

overleaf [ˌəʊvə'liːf] adv auf der Rückseite.

overload [ˌəʊvə'ləʊd] (pp -loaded OR -laden) vt - 1. [put too much in] überladen - 2. ELEC überlasten - 3. [with work, problems]: **to be ~ed (with sthg)** überlastet sein (mit etw).

overlook [ˌəʊvə'lʊk] vt - 1. [look over] eine Aussicht haben auf (+ A); **a room ~ing the square** ein Zimmer mit Blick auf den Platz - 2. [disregard, miss] übersehen - 3. [excuse] hinwegsehen über (+ A).

overnight [adj 'əʊvənaɪt, adv ˌəʊvə'naɪt] adj: **~ stay** Übernachtung die; **~ bag** kleine Reisetasche; **to be an ~ success** [person] über Nacht großen Erfolg haben; [play] über Nacht ein großer Erfolg sein adv über Nacht.

overpass ['əʊvəpɑːs] n Am Überführung die.

overpower [ˌəʊvə'paʊə] vt überwältigen.

overpowering [ˌəʊvə'paʊərɪŋ] adj [feeling] überwältigend; [heat] unerträglich; [smell] penetrant; [person] einschüchternd.

overran [ˌəʊvə'ræn] pt ⟶ overrun.

overrated [ˌəʊvə'reɪtɪd] adj: **to be ~** überschätzt werden.

override [ˌəʊvə'raɪd] (pt -rode; pp -ridden

[-'rɪdɪŋ]) *vt* - **1.** [be more important than] Vorrang haben vor (+ D) - **2.** [overrule - decision] auflheben.

overriding [ˌəʊvə'raɪdɪŋ] *adj* vorrangig.

overrode [ˌəʊvə'rəʊd] *pt* ⊏⇒ override.

overrule [ˌəʊvə'ruːl] *vt* [person] überstimmen; [decision] auflheben; [objection] ablweisen.

overrun [ˌəʊvə'rʌn] (*pt* -ran; *pp* -run) ◇ *vt* - **1.** MIL [occupy] einlfallen in (+ A) - **2.** fig: **to be ~ with** [insects, rats] wimmeln von; [weeds] überwuchert sein von; [tourists] überlaufen sein von ◇ *vi* [last too long] länger als vorgesehen dauern.

oversaw [ˌəʊvə'sɔː] *pt* ⊏⇒ oversee.

overseas [*adj* 'əʊvəsiːz, *adv* ˌəʊvə'siːz] ◇ *adj* - **1.** [in or to foreign countries] Auslands-; **~ aid** Entwicklungshilfe *die* - **2.** [from abroad] aus dem Ausland ◇ *adv* [travel] nach Übersee; [study, live] in Übersee.

oversee [ˌəʊvə'siː] (*pt* -saw; *pp* -seen [-'siːn]) *vt* beaufsichtigen.

overshadow [ˌəʊvə'ʃædəʊ] *vt* - **1.** fig [outweigh, eclipse]: **to be ~ed by sb/sthg** von jm/etw in den Schatten gestellt werden - **2.** fig [mar, cloud]: **to be ~ed by sthg** [subj: party, victory] von etw überschattet werden; [subj: happiness, peace of mind] durch etw stark beeinträchtigt werden.

overshoot [ˌəʊvə'ʃuːt] (*pt* & *pp* -shot [-ʃɒt]) *vt* [go past - turning] vorbeilfahren an (+ D); [- runway] hinauslrollen über (+ A).

oversight ['əʊvəsaɪt] *n* Versehen *das*.

oversleep [ˌəʊvə'sliːp] (*pt* & *pp* -slept [-'slept]) *vi* verschlafen.

overstep [ˌəʊvə'step] *vt* überschreiten; **to ~ the mark** zu weit gehen.

overt ['əʊvɜːt] *adj* unverhohlen.

overtake [ˌəʊvə'teɪk] (*pt* -took; *pp* -taken [-'teɪk]) ◇ *vt* - **1.** AUT überholen - **2.** [subj: disaster, misfortune] ereilen ◇ *vi* überholen.

overthrow [*n* 'əʊvəθrəʊ, *vb* ˌəʊvə'θrəʊ] (*pt* -threw [-'θruː]; *pp* -thrown [-'θrəʊn]) ◇ *n* [of government] Sturz *der* ◇ *vt* [government, president] stürzen.

overtime ['əʊvətaɪm] ◇ *n* (U) - **1.** [extra time worked] Überstunden *pl* - **2.** Am SPORT Verlängerung *die* ◇ *adv*: **to work ~** Überstunden machen.

overtones ['əʊvətəʊnz] *npl* Untertöne *pl*.

overtook [ˌəʊvə'tʊk] *pt* ⊏⇒ overtake.

overture ['əʊvəˌtjʊəʳ] *n* MUS Ouvertüre *die*.

overturn [ˌəʊvə'tɜːn] ◇ *vt* - **1.** [turn over] umlwerfen - **2.** [overrule] auflheben - **3.** [overthrow] stürzen ◇ *vi* [boat] kentern; [lorry] umlstürzen.

overweight [ˌəʊvə'weɪt] *adj* [person] übergewichtig.

overwhelm [ˌəʊvə'welm] *vt* überwältigen.

overwhelming [ˌəʊvə'welmɪŋ] *adj* - **1.** [feeling, quality] überwältigend - **2.** [vic-

tory, majority] überwältigend; [defeat] vernichtend.

overwork [ˌəʊvə'wɜːk] ◇ *n* (U) Überlastung *die* ◇ *vt* [give too much work to] mit Arbeit überlasten.

owe [əʊ] *vt*: **to ~ sthg to sb, to ~ sb sthg** [money, respect, gratitude] jm etw schulden; [good looks, success] jm etw verdanken.

owing ['əʊɪŋ] *adj*: **the amount ~** der ausstehende Betrag; **to be ~** auslstehen. ◆ **owing to** *prep* wegen (+ G).

owl [aʊl] *n* Eule *die*.

own [əʊn] ◇ *adj* eigen; **I have my ~ bedroom** ich habe ein eigenes Zimmer; **she makes her ~ clothes** sie näht ihre Kleider selbst ◇ *pron*: **it has a taste all of its ~** es hat einen ganz eigenen Geschmack; **on my ~** allein; **to get one's ~ back** *inf* sich revanchieren; **he can hold his ~** er kann sich behaupten ◇ *vt* [possess] besitzen; **who ~s this car?** wem gehört dieses Auto? ◆ **own up** *vi*: **to ~ up (to sthg)** (etw) zulgeben.

owner ['əʊnəʳ] *n* Besitzer *der*, -in *die*; [of firm, shop] Inhaber *der*, -in *die*.

ownership ['əʊnəʃɪp] *n* Besitz *der*.

ox [ɒks] (*pl* oxen) *n* Ochse *der*.

Oxbridge ['ɒksbrɪdʒ] *n* die Universitäten Oxford und Cambridge.

oxen ['ɒksn] *pl* ⊏⇒ ox.

oxtail soup [ˌɒksteɪl-] *n* Ochsenschwanzsuppe *die*.

oxygen ['ɒksɪdʒən] *n* Sauerstoff *der*.

oxygen mask *n* Sauerstoffmaske *die*.

oyster ['ɔɪstəʳ] *n* Auster *die*.

oz. *abbr of* ounce.

ozone ['əʊzəʊn] *n* Ozon *das*.

ozone-friendly *adj* FCKW-frei.

ozone layer *n* Ozonschicht *die*.

P

p¹ (*pl* p's OR ps), **P** (*pl* P's OR Ps) [piː] *n* [letter] p *das*, P *das*.

p² [piː] - **1.** *abbr of* page - **2.** *abbr of* penny, pence.

P45 [ˌpiːfɔːtɪ'faɪv] *n Br* ≃ Lohnsteuerkarte *die, Steuerbescheinigung, die bei einem Arbeitsplatzwechsel dem neuen Arbeitgeber vorgelegt werden muss.*

pa [pɑː] *n esp Am inf* Papa *der*, Vati *der*.

p.a. (*abbr of* per annum) p. a.

PA *n* - **1.** *Br abbr of* personal assistant - **2.** (*abbr of* public address system) Lautsprecheranlage *die*.

pace [peɪs] ⬦ *n* - **1.** [speed, rate] Tempo *das;* **to keep ~ (with sb/sthg)** (mit jm/etw) Schritt halten - **2.** [step] Schritt *der* ⬦ *vi* [walk up and down] auf und ab gehen.

pacemaker ['peɪsˌmeɪkə'] *n* MED Herzschrittmacher *der.*

Pacific [pə'sɪfɪk] ⬦ *adj* pazifisch; [coast] Pazifik- ⬦ *n*: **the ~ (Ocean)** der Pazifik.

pacifier ['pæsɪfaɪər] *n Am* [for child] Schnuller *der.*

pacifist ['pæsɪfɪst] *n* Pazifist *der,* -in *die.*

pacify ['pæsɪfaɪ] *vt* - **1.** [person] beruhigen - **2.** [country, region] befriedigen.

pack [pæk] ⬦ *n* - **1.** [bag - on back] Rucksack *der;* [- carried by animal] Last *die* - **2.** [packet - of cigarettes, tissues] Packung *die;* [- of washing powder] Paket *das* - **3.** [of cards] (Karten)spiel *das* - **4.** [group - of wolves] Rudel *das;* [- of hounds] Meute *die;* [- of thieves] Bande *die* ⬦ *vt* - **1.** [for journey, holiday - bag, suitcase] packen; [- clothes, toothbrush] einlpacken - **2.** [put in container, parcel] einlpacken; [product] verpacken - **3.** [crowd into] füllen; **to be ~ed into sthg** in etw (A) gezwängt sein ⬦ *vi* [for journey, holiday] packen. ⬟ **pack in** ⬦ *vt sep Br inf* [job] hinlschmeißen; [boyfriend] sausen lassen; [smoking] auflhören mit; **~ it in!** [stop annoying me, shut up] hör (doch) auf damit! ⬦ *vi inf* [break down] den Geist auflgeben. ⬟ **pack off** *vt sep inf* fortlschicken.

package ['pækɪdʒ] ⬦ *n* - **1.** [gen & COMPUT] Paket *das* - **2.** *esp Am* [packet - of cigarettes, tissues] Packung *die;* [- of washing powder] Paket *das* ⬦ *vt* [wrap up, pack up] verpacken.

package deal *n* Paket *das.*

package tour *n* Pauschalreise *die.*

packaging ['pækɪdʒɪŋ] *n (U)* [wrapping] Verpackung *die.*

packed [pækt] *adj* - **1.** [place]: **~ (with)** (über)voll (mit) - **2.** [magazine, information pack]: **~ with** voll mit.

packed lunch *n Br* Lunchpaket *das.*

packet ['pækɪt] *n* - **1.** [box, bag, contents - of biscuits, cigarettes] Packung *die;* [- of washing powder] Paket *das* - **2.** [parcel] Päckchen *das.*

packing ['pækɪŋ] *n (U)* - **1.** [protective material] Verpackungsmaterial *das* - **2.** [for journey, holiday] Packen *das.*

packing case *n* Kiste *die.*

pact [pækt] *n* Pakt *der.*

pad [pæd] ⬦ *n* - **1.** [for garment] Polster *das* - **2.** [for protection] Schützer *der* - **3.** [notepad] Block *der* - **4.** [for absorbing liquid]: **~ of cotton wool** Wattebausch *der;* **sanitary ~** Damenbinde *die* - **5.** SPACE: **(launch) ~** Abschussrampe *die* - **6.** *inf dated* [home] Bude *die* ⬦ *vt* [furniture] polstern; [clothing] wattieren.

padding ['pædɪŋ] *n (U)* - **1.** [protective material] Polsterung *die* - **2.** [in speech, essay, letter] Füllwerk *das.*

paddle ['pædl] ⬦ *n* - **1.** [for canoe, dinghy] Paddel *das* - **2.** [wade]: **to have a ~** durchs Wasser waten ⬦ *vi* - **1.** [in canoe, dinghy] paddeln - **2.** [wade] waten.

paddle boat, paddle steamer *n* Raddampfer *der.*

paddling pool ['pædlɪŋ-] *n* - **1.** [in park] Plantschbad *das* - **2.** [inflatable] Plantschbecken *das.*

paddock ['pædək] *n* - **1.** [small field] Koppel *die* - **2.** [at racecourse] Sattelplatz *der.*

paddy field ['pædɪ-] *n* Reisfeld *das.*

padlock ['pædlɒk] ⬦ *n* Vorhängeschloss *das* ⬦ *vt* (mit einem Vorhängeschloss) verschließen.

paediatrics [ˌpiːdɪ'ætrɪks] *n* = pediatrics.

pagan ['peɪgən] ⬦ *adj* heidnisch ⬦ *n* Heide *der,* -din *die.*

page [peɪdʒ] ⬦ *n* - **1.** [side of paper] Seite *die* - **2.** [leaf, sheet of paper] Blatt *das* ⬦ *vt* [call out name of] ausrufen lassen; **paging Miss Smith!** Miss Smith, bitte!

pageant ['pædʒənt] *n* [show] historisches Schauspiel; [parade] Festumzug *der.*

pageantry ['pædʒəntrɪ] *n* Prunk *der.*

page break *n* COMPUT Seitenumbruch *der.*

paid [peɪd] ⬦ *pt & pp* ⮕ **pay** ⬦ *adj* bezahlt.

pail [peɪl] *n* Eimer *der.*

pain [peɪn] *n* - **1.** [ache] Schmerz *der* - **2.** *(U)* [physical suffering] Schmerzen *pl;* **to be in ~** Schmerzen haben - **3.** *(U)* [mental suffering] Qualen *pl.* ⬟ **pains** *npl* [effort] Mühe *die;* **to be at ~s to do sthg** sich *(D)* große Mühe geben, etw zu tun; **to take ~s to do sthg** sich *(D)* Mühe geben, etw zu tun.

pained [peɪnd] *adj* [expression] gequält.

painful ['peɪnfʊl] *adj* - **1.** [physically] schmerzhaft; **to be ~** wehtun, schmerzen - **2.** [distressing] schmerzlich.

painfully ['peɪnfʊlɪ] *adv* - **1.** [physically] unter Schmerzen - **2.** [distressingly] schmerzlich.

painkiller ['peɪnˌkɪlə'] *n* schmerzstillendes Mittel.

painless ['peɪnlɪs] *adj* - **1.** [physically] schmerzlos - **2.** [unproblematic] unproblematisch; [exam, decision] leicht.

painstaking ['peɪnzˌteɪkɪŋ] *adj* sorgfältig.

paint [peɪnt] ⬦ *n* Farbe *die;* [on car, furniture] Lack *der* ⬦ *vt* - **1.** [picture, portrait] malen - **2.** [wall, room] streichen; [car, fingernails] lackieren; [lips, face] schminken ⬦ *vi* ART malen.

paintbrush ['peɪntbrʌʃ] *n* Pinsel *der.*

painter ['peɪntə'] *n* Maler *der,* -in *die.*

painting ['peɪntɪŋ] *n* - **1.** [picture] Gemälde *das* - **2.** [artistic] Malen *das;* [activity] Malerei *die* - **3.** [by decorator] Anstreichen *das.*

paintwork ['peɪntwɜːk] *n (U)* [on wall] Anstrich *der;* [on car] Lack *der.*

pair [peə⁽ʳ⁾] *n* Paar *das;* **in ~s** paarweise; **a ~ of pliers** eine Zange; **a ~ of scissors** eine Schere; **a ~ of shorts** Shorts *pl;* **a ~ of spectacles** eine Brille; **a ~ of tights** eine Strumpfhose; **a ~ of trousers** eine Hose.

pajamas [pə'dʒɑːməz] *npl Am* = pyjamas.

Pakistan [*Br* ˌpɑːkɪ'stɑːn, *Am* ˌpækɪ'stæn] *n* Pakistan *nt*.

Pakistani [*Br* ˌpɑːkɪ'stɑːnɪ, *Am* 'pækɪstænɪ] ◇ *adj* pakistanisch ◇ *n* Pakistaner *der,* -in *die.*

pal [pæl] *n inf* Kumpel *der;* **be a ~!** sei so nett!

palace ['pælɪs] *n* Palast *der;* [of bishop, aristocracy] Palais *das;* [grand house] Schloss *das.*

palatable ['pælətəbl] *adj* **- 1.** [food] wohlschmeckend **- 2.** [suggestion, idea] annehmbar.

palate ['pælət] *n* Gaumen *der.*

palaver [pə'lɑːvə⁽ʳ⁾] *n inf* [fuss] Theater *das.*

pale [peɪl] *adj* [colour, face] blass; [clothes] hell; [light] fahl.

Palestine ['pæləˌstaɪn] *n* Palästina *nt.*

Palestinian [ˌpælə'stɪnɪən] ◇ *adj* palästinensisch ◇ *n* [person] Palästinenser *der,* -in *die.*

palette ['pælət] *n* ART Palette *die.*

pall [pɔːl] ◇ *n* **- 1.:** **a ~ of smoke** eine Rauchglocke **- 2.** *Am* [over coffin] Sargtuch *das* ◇ *vi* an Reiz verlieren.

pallet ['pælɪt] *n* Palette *die.*

palm [pɑːm] *n* **- 1.** [tree] Palme *die* **- 2.** [of hand] Handfläche *die;* **to read sb's ~** jm aus der Hand lesen. ➡ **palm off** *vt sep inf:* **to ~ sthg off on sb** jm etw abdrehen; **to ~ sb off with sthg** jn mit etw abspeisen.

Palm Sunday *n* Palmsonntag *der.*

palmtop ['pɑːmtɒp] *n* COMPUT Palmtopcomputer *der.*

palm tree *n* Palme *die.*

palpable ['pælpəbl] *adj* [obvious] offensichtlich.

paltry ['pɔːltrɪ] *adj* armselig.

pamper ['pæmpə⁽ʳ⁾] *vt* verhätscheln.

pamphlet ['pæmflɪt] *n* [for information] Broschüre *die;* [for publicity] (Werbe)prospekt *der;* [political] Pamphlet *das.*

pan [pæn] ◇ *n* **- 1.** [for frying] Pfanne *die;* [saucepan] Topf *der* **- 2.** *Am* [for baking] Backform *die* ◇ *vt inf* [criticize] verreißen ◇ *vi* CINEMA schwenken.

panacea [ˌpænə'sɪə] *n* Allheilmittel *das.*

panama [ˌpænə'mɑː] *n:* **~ (hat)** Panamahut *der.*

Panama Canal *n:* **the ~** der Panamakanal.

pancake ['pænkeɪk] *n* Pfannkuchen *der.*

Pancake Day *n Br* Fastnachtsdienstag *der.*

panda ['pændə] (*pl inv* OR *-s*) *n* Panda *der.*

pandemonium [ˌpændɪ'məʊnɪəm] *n* Chaos *das.*

pander ['pændə⁽ʳ⁾] *vi:* **to ~ to sb/sthg** jm/etw nachgeben.

pane [peɪn] *n* Scheibe *die.*

panel ['pænl] *n* **- 1.** [of experts, interviewers] Gremium *das;* [on TV and radio programmes] Diskussionsrunde *die* **- 2.** [of wood] Platte *die* **- 3.** [of machine] Schalttafel *die.*

panelling *Br,* **paneling** *Am* ['pænəlɪŋ] *n* Täfelung *die.*

pang [pæŋ] *n* [of guilt, fear, regret] Anfall *der;* **~s of conscience** Gewissensbisse *pl.*

panic ['pænɪk] (*pt & pp* **-ked**; *cont* **-king**) ◇ *n* Panik *die* ◇ *vi* in Panik geraten; **don't ~!** keine Panik!

panicky ['pænɪkɪ] *adj* [feeling] panisch; **to feel ~** Angst bekommen.

panic-stricken *adj* von Panik erfasst OR ergriffen.

panorama [ˌpænə'rɑːmə] *n* Panorama *das.*

pansy ['pænzɪ] *n* **- 1.** [flower] Stiefmütterchen *das* **- 2.** *inf pej* [man] Tunte *die.*

pant [pænt] *vi* keuchen; [dog] hecheln. ➡ **pants** *npl* **- 1.** *Br* [underpants - for men] Unterhose *die;* [- for women] Schlüpfer *der* **- 2.** *Am* [trousers] Hose *die.*

panther ['pænθə⁽ʳ⁾] (*pl inv* OR *-s*) *n* Panther *der.*

panties ['pæntɪz] *npl inf* Schlüpfer *der.*

pantihose ['pæntɪhəʊz] *npl Am* = panty hose.

pantomime ['pæntəmaɪm] *n Br* meist um die Weihnachtszeit aufgeführtes Märchenspiel.

pantry ['pæntrɪ] *n* Speisekammer *die.*

panty hose ['pæntɪhəʊz] *npl Am* Strumpfhose *die.*

papa [*Br* pə'pɑː, *Am* 'pæpə] *n dated* [father] Papa *der.*

paper ['peɪpə⁽ʳ⁾] ◇ *n* **- 1.** [for writing on] Papier *das;* **a piece of ~** [scrap] ein Stück Papier; [sheet] ein Blatt Papier; **on ~** [written down] schriftlich; [in theory] auf dem Papier **- 2.** [newspaper] Zeitung *die* **- 3.** [exam] Klausur *die* **- 4.** [essay] Arbeit *die* **- 5.** [at conference] Referat *das* ◇ *adj* **- 1.** [cup, napkin, hat] Papier-, aus Papier **- 2.** [qualifications] auf dem Papier; [profits] nominell ◇ *vt* [with wallpaper] tapezieren. ➡ **papers** *npl* **- 1.** [identity papers] Papiere *pl* **- 2.** [documents] Dokumente *pl*, Unterlagen *pl.*

paperback ['peɪpəbæk] *n:* **~ (book)** Taschenbuch *das.*

paper bag *n* Papiertüte *die.*

paper clip *n* Büroklammer *die.*

paper handkerchief *n* Papiertaschentuch *das.*

paper shop *n Br* Zeitungsgeschäft *das.*

paperweight ['peɪpəweɪt] *n* Briefbeschwerer *der.*

paperwork ['peɪpəwɜːk] *n (U)* Schreibarbeit *die.*

paprika ['pæprɪkə] *n* Paprika *der.*

par [pɑː⁽ʳ⁾] *n* **- 1.: to be on a ~ with sb/sthg** [person] sich mit jm/etw messen können; [company, country] mit jm/etw vergleichbar sein - 2. [in golf] Par *das*; **above/below** ~ *fig* über/unter den Durchschnitt - 3. [good health]: **to feel below** OR **under** ~ nicht ganz auf dem Posten OR Damm sein.

parable ['pærəbl] *n* REL Gleichnis *das*; [moral story] Parabel *die*.

parachute ['pærəʃuːt] <> *n* Fallschirm *der* <> *vi* mit dem Fallschirm abspringen.

parade [pə'reɪd] <> *n* - 1. [procession] Umzug *der* - 2. MIL Parade *die* <> *vt* - 1. [people - soldiers] marschieren lassen; [- captives] zur Schau stellen - 2. [object] vor sich *(D)* herltragen - 3. *fig* [flaunt] zur Schau stellen <> *vi* paradieren; [soldiers] marschieren.

paradise ['pærədaɪs] *n* Paradies *das*.

paradox ['pærədɒks] *n* Paradox(on) *das*.

paradoxically [,pærə'dɒksɪklɪ] *adv* paradoxerweise.

paraffin ['pærəfɪn] *n* Paraffin *das*.

paragon ['pærəgən] *n* Muster *das*.

paragraph ['pærəgrɑːf] *n* Absatz *der*.

parallel ['pærəlel] <> *adj* lit & fig: ~ **(to** OR **with)** parallel (zu) <> *n* - 1. [gen] Parallele *die* - 2. GEOGR Breitenkreis *der*; **the 38th** ~ der 38. Breitengrad.

paralyse *Br*, **paralyze** *Am* ['pærəlaɪz] *vt* - 1. MED lähmen - 2. *fig* [immobilize] lahm legen.

paralysis [pə'rælɪsɪs] *(pl* -lyses [-lɪsiːz]) *n* MED Lähmung *die*.

paralyze *vt Am* = paralyse.

paramedic [,pærə'medɪk] *n* Sanitäter *der*, -in *die*.

parameter [pə'ræmɪtə'] *n* Parameter *der*.

paramount ['pærəmaunt] *adj*: **to be** ~ Vorrang OR Priorität haben; **of - importance** von äußerster Wichtigkeit.

paranoid ['pærənɔɪd] *adj* - 1. MED paranoid - 2. [worried, suspicious]: **she's** ~ **about being on time** sie hat ständig Angst, zu spät zu kommen; **you're getting** ~! dein Misstrauen ist ja krankhaft!

paraphernalia [,pærəfə'neɪlɪə] *n* Drum und Dran *das*.

parasite ['pærəsaɪt] *n lit & fig* Schmarotzer *der*, Parasit *der*.

parasol ['pærəsɒl] *n* Sonnenschirm *der*.

paratrooper ['pærətruːpə'] *n* Fallschirmjäger *der*.

parcel ['pɑːsl] *n* Paket *das*. ➡ **parcel up** *vt sep* als Paket verpacken.

parched [pɑːtʃt] *adj* - 1. [very dry - grass, plain] ausgetrocknet, verdorrt; [- throat, lips] trocken - 2. *inf* [very thirsty]: **I'm** ~ ich habe riesigen Durst.

parchment ['pɑːtʃmənt] *n* Pergament *das*.

pardon ['pɑːdn] <> *n* - 1. LAW Begnadigung *die* - 2. [forgiveness]: **I beg your** ~? [showing surprise or offence] erlauben Sie mal!; [what did you say?] (wie) bitte?; **I beg your** ~! [apologizing] Entschuldigung! <> *vt* - 1. LAW be-

gnadigen - 2. [forgive] verzeihen, vergeben; **to** ~ **sb for sthg** jm etw verzeihen; ~? [what did you say?] wie bitte?; ~ **me!** Entschuldigung!, Verzeihung!

parent ['peərənt] *n* [father] Vater *der*; [mother] Mutter *die*; ~**s** Eltern *pl*.

parental [pə'rentl] *adj* elterlich.

parenthesis [pə'renθɪsɪs] *(pl* -theses [-θɪsiːz]) *n*: **in parentheses** in Klammern.

Paris ['pærɪs] *n* Paris *nt*.

parish ['pærɪʃ] *n* Gemeinde *die*.

parity ['pærətɪ] *n* [state] Gleichheit *die*.

park [pɑːk] <> *n* Park *der* <> *vt* parken; [bicycle] ablstellen <> *vi* parken.

parking ['pɑːkɪŋ] *n (U)* - 1. [act] Parken *das*; **'no** ~' 'Parken verboten' - 2. [space] Parkplätze *pl*.

parking lot *n Am* Parkplatz *der*.

parking meter *n* Parkuhr *die*.

parking ticket *n* Strafzettel *der*.

parlance ['pɑːləns] *n*: **in common/legal** ~ im allgemeinen/juristischen Sprachgebrauch.

parliament ['pɑːləmənt] *n* Parlament *das*.

parliamentary [,pɑːlə'mentərɪ] *adj* parlamentarisch.

parlour *Br*, **parlor** *Am* ['pɑːlə'] *n* [cafe]: **ice cream** ~ Eisdiele *die*.

parochial [pə'rəukɪəl] *adj pej* [person] engstirnig; [view, approach] eng, beschränkt.

parody ['pærədɪ] <> *n* Parodie *die*; **a** ~ **of** eine Parodie auf *(+ A)* <> *vt* parodieren.

parole [pə'rəul] *n (U)* Bewährung *die*; **on** ~ auf Bewährung.

parrot ['pærət] *n* Papagei *der*.

parry ['pærɪ] *vt lit & fig* abwehren.

parsley ['pɑːslɪ] *n* Petersilie *die*.

parsnip ['pɑːsnɪp] *n* Pastinak *der*.

parson ['pɑːsn] *n* Pfarrer *der*, -in *die*.

part [pɑːt] <> *n* - 1. [gen] Teil *der*; **in this** ~ **of Germany** in dieser Gegend Deutschlands; **for the better** ~ **of two hours** fast zwei Stunden; **for the most** ~ zum größten Teil - 2. [of TV serial] Fortsetzung *die* - 3. [component] Teil *das*; **to form** ~ **of sthg** Teil von etw sein - 4. [acting role] Rolle *die*; *fig* [involvement] Anteil *der*; **his** ~ **in the crime** seine Rolle bei dem Verbrechen; **to play an important** ~ **in sthg** eine wichtige Rolle bei etw spielen; **to take** ~ **in sthg** an etw *(D)* teillnehmen; **for my/his/**etc ~ was mich/ihn/etc anbetrifft; **on the** ~ **of** vonseiten *(+ G)* - 5. *Am* [hair parting] Scheitel *der* <> *adv* teils <> *vt* - 1. [separate] trennen - 2. [curtains] öffnen; [branches] zur Seite schieben; [legs] auflmachen; [hair] scheiteln <> *vi* - 1. [people] sich trennen - 2. [curtains, lips, legs] sich öffnen; [crowd, branches] sich teilen. ➡ **parts** *npl*: **in these** ~**s** in dieser Gegend; **in foreign** ~**s** in fremden Ländern. ➡ **part with** *vt fus* sich trennen von.

part exchange n: **in ~ (for)** in Zahlung (für).

partial ['pɑːʃl] adj - **1.** [incomplete] Teil-, teilweise - **2.** [biased] parteiisch - **3.** [fond]: **to be ~ to sthg** eine Schwäche für etw haben.

participant [pɑː'tɪsɪpənt] n Teilnehmer der, -in die.

participate [pɑː'tɪsɪpeɪt] vi: **to ~ (in)** teillnehmen (an (+ D)).

participation [pɑː,tɪsɪ'peɪʃən] n Teilnahme die.

participle ['pɑːtɪsɪpl] n Partizip das.

particle ['pɑːtɪkl] n - **1.** [tiny piece] Teilchen das - **2.** GRAMM Partikel die.

particular [pə'tɪkjʊləʳ] adj - **1.** [specific] bestimmt - **2.** [special] besondere, -r, -s - **3.** [fussy] eigen. ➡ **particulars** npl Einzelheiten pl. ➡ **in particular** adv besonders; **nothing in ~** nichts Besonderes.

particularly [pə'tɪkjʊləlɪ] adv [very] besonders.

parting ['pɑːtɪŋ] n - **1.** [farewell] Abschied der - **2.** Br [in hair] Scheitel der.

partisan [,pɑːtɪ'zæn] ◇ adj parteiisch ◇ n [freedom fighter] Partisan der, -in die.

partition [pɑː'tɪʃn] ◇ n [wall, screen] Trennwand die ◇ vt teilen.

partly ['pɑːtlɪ] adv zum Teil, teilweise.

partner ['pɑːtnəʳ] ◇ n - **1.** [gen] Partner der, -in die - **2.** [in a business] Geschäftspartner der, -in die - **3.** [in crime] Komplize der, -zin die ◇ vt: **to ~ sb** js Partner sein.

partnership ['pɑːtnəʃɪp] n - **1.** [relationship] Partnerschaft die - **2.** [business] (Personen)gesellschaft die.

partridge ['pɑːtrɪdʒ] (pl inv OR -s) n Rebhuhn das.

part-time ◇ adj Teilzeit- ◇ adv: **to work ~** Teilzeit arbeiten.

party ['pɑːtɪ] ◇ n - **1.** POL & LAW Partei die - **2.** [social gathering] Party die; **to have a ~** eine Party geben - **3.** [group of people] Gruppe die ◇ vi inf feiern.

party line n - **1.** POL Parteilinie die - **2.** TELEC Gemeinschaftsanschluss der.

pass [pɑːs] ◇ vt - **1.** [walk past] vorbeilgehen an (+ D); [drive past] vorbeilfahren an (+ D) - **2.** AUT [overtake] überholen - **3.** [hand over] reichen; **to ~ sthg to sb, to ~ sb sthg** etw reichen - **4.** [in football, hockey etc]: **to ~ sb the ball, to ~ the ball to sb** jm den Ball zulspielen or passen - **5.** [exam, test] bestehen - **6.** [candidate] bestehen lassen - **7.** [approve - law] verabschieden; [- motion] anlnehmen; **this product has been ~ed as fit for sale** dieses Produkt ist für den Verkauf freigegeben worden - **8.** [life, time] verbringen - **9.** [exceed] überschreiten - **10.** [judgement] fällen; [sentence] verhängen ◇ vi - **1.** [walk past] vorbeilgehen; [drive past] vorbeilfahren; **to let sb ~** jn vorbeillassen; **if you're ~ing this way** falls Sie hier vorbeikommen - **2.** AUT [overtake] überholen - **3.** [road, river, path] führen; [pipe, cable] verlaufen - **4.** [time, holiday, lesson] vergehen - **5.** [in test, exam] bestehen - **6.** [in football, hockey etc] einen Pass spielen ◇ n - **1.** [document] Ausweis der - **2.** Br [in exam] Bestehen das; **to get a ~** bestehen - **3.** [between mountains] Pass der - **4.** [in football, hockey etc] Pass der; [in tennis] Passierschlag der - **5.** phr: **to make a ~ at sb** inf bei jm Annäherungsversuche machen. ➡ **pass as** vt fus durchlgehen für. ➡ **pass away** vi entschlafen. ➡ **pass by** ◇ vt fus [walk past] vorbeilgehen an (+ D); [drive past] vorbeilfahren an (+ D) ◇ vt sep fig [subj: news, events] vorbeilgehen an (+ D) ◇ vi [walk past] vorbeilgehen; [drive past] vorbeilfahren. ➡ **pass for** vt fus = pass as. ➡ **pass on** ◇ vt sep lit & fig: **to ~ sthg on (to sb)** etw (an jn) weiterlgeben ◇ vi - **1.** [move on] weiterlmachen; **let's ~ on to the next question** gehen wir zur nächsten Frage über - **2.** = pass away. ➡ **pass out** vi - **1.** [faint] ohnmächtig werden - **2.** Br MIL ernannt werden. ➡ **pass over** vt fus [subject, problem] übergehen; **to be ~ed over for promotion** bei der Beförderung übergangen werden. ➡ **pass through** vi durchlkommen; **we're just ~ing through** wir sind nur auf der Durchreise. ➡ **pass up** vt sep [opportunity] vorübergehen lassen; [invitation, offer] abllehnen.

passable ['pɑːsəbl] adj - **1.** [satisfactory] passabel - **2.** [road, path] passierbar.

passage ['pæsɪdʒ] n - **1.** [corridor] Gang der; [between houses] Durchgang der - **2.** [through crowd] Weg der - **3.** ANAT Gang der - **4.** (U) fml [transition] Übergang der; **the ~ of time** der Strom der Zeit - **5.** [sea journey] Überfahrt die.

passageway ['pæsɪdʒweɪ] n Gang der; [between houses] Durchgang der.

passbook ['pɑːsbʊk] n Sparbuch das.

passenger ['pæsɪndʒəʳ] n [gen] Passagier der; [in taxi] Fahrgast der; [in car] Insasse der, -sin die.

passerby [,pɑːsə'baɪ] (pl passersby [,pɑːsəz'baɪ]) n Passant der, -in die.

passing ['pɑːsɪŋ] adj [remark] beiläufig; [fashion, mood] vorübergehend. ➡ **in passing** adv [mention] beiläufig.

passion ['pæʃn] n Leidenschaft die.

passionate ['pæʃənət] adj leidenschaftlich.

passive ['pæsɪv] adj - **1.** [person] passiv - **2.** GRAMM passivisch, Passiv-.

Passover ['pɑːs,əʊvəʳ] n Passah das.

passport ['pɑːspɔːt] n (Reise)pass der.

passport control n Passkontrolle die.

password ['pɑːswɜːd] n Passwort das.

past [pɑːst] ◇ adj - **1.** [former] ehemalig - **2.** [earlier] vergangene, -r, -s; **in ~ times** in früheren Zeiten - **3.** [most recent, last] letzte,

-r, -s; the ~ month der letzte Monat **- 4.** [finished] **vorbei** <> n **- 1.** [time]: **the ~ die** Vergangenheit; **in the ~** früher **- 2.** [personal history] Vergangenheit die **- 3.** GRAMM Vergangenheit die <> adv **- 1.** [telling the time] nach; **it's ten/a quarter ~** es ist zehn/viertel nach **- 2.** [by] vorbei; **to run ~** vorbeilaufen <> prep **- 1.** [telling the time] nach; **twenty ~ four** zwanzig nach vier; **at half/a quarter ~ eight** um halb/viertel neun **- 2.** [by] an (+ D) ... vorbei; **he drove ~ the house** er fuhr am Haus vorbei **- 3.** [beyond] hinter (+ D).

pasta ['pæstə] n (U) Nudeln pl.

paste [peɪst] <> n **- 1.** [smooth mixture] Brei der **- 2.** [U] CULIN Brotaufstrich der **- 3.** [glue] Kleister der <> vt kleben; COMPUT einfügen.

pastel ['pæstl] adj pastellfarben.

pasteurize, -ise ['pɑːstʃəraɪz] vt pasteurisieren.

pastille ['pæstɪl] n Pastille die.

pastime ['pɑːstaɪm] n Hobby das.

pastor ['pɑːstəʳ] n Pfarrer der, -in die.

past participle n Partizip Perfekt das.

pastry ['peɪstrɪ] n **- 1.** [mixture] Teig der **- 2.** [cake] Teilchen das.

past tense n Vergangenheit die.

pasture ['pɑːstʃəʳ] n [field] Weide die.

pasty ['peɪstɪ] n (Br) CULIN Pastete die.

pat [pæt] <> adv: **to have sthg off ~** etw parat haben <> n **- 1.** [light stroke] Klaps der **- 2.** [of butter] Portion die <> vt [dog, hand] tätscheln; [back, shoulder] (leicht) klopfen auf (+ A).

patch [pætʃ] <> n **- 1.** [piece of material] Flicken der **- 2.** [over eye] Augenklappe die **- 3.** [small area] Fleck der; **there were still ~es of snow** es lag vereinzelt OR stellenweise noch Schnee; **a bald ~** eine kahle Stelle **- 4.** [of land] Stück (Land) das; **vegetable ~** Gemüsebeet das **- 5.** [period of time]: **to be going through a difficult ~** eine schwierige Zeit durchmachen <> vt flicken. ◆ **patch up** vt sep **- 1.** [mend] zusammenflicken **- 2.** fig [quarrel] beilegen; [marriage] kitten.

patchy ['pætʃɪ] adj **- 1.** [fog, sunshine] vereinzelt; [colour] fleckig **- 2.** [knowledge] lückenhaft **- 3.** [performance, game] unterschiedlich (in der Qualität).

pâté ['pæteɪ] n (U) Pastete die.

patent [Br 'peɪtənt, Am 'pætənt] <> adj [obvious] offensichtlich <> n Patent das <> vt patentieren lassen.

patent leather n Lackleder das.

paternal [pəˈtɜːnl] adj **- 1.** [love, attitude] väterlich **- 2.** [on father's side]: **~ grandmother/grandfather** Großmutter die/Großvater der väterlicherseits.

path [pɑːθ, pl pɑːðz] n **- 1.** [track] Weg der; [narrower] Pfad der **- 2.** [way ahead, course of action] Weg der **- 3.** [trajectory] Bahn die.

pathetic [pəˈθetɪk] adj **- 1.** [causing pity]

Mitleid erregend; **to be a ~ sight** ein Bild des Jammers bieten **- 2.** [useless - attempt, effort] erbärmlich; **she's ~** sie ist ein hoffnungsloser Fall.

pathological [ˌpæθəˈlɒdʒɪkl] adj **- 1.** MED. pathologisch **- 2.** [uncontrollable] krankhaft.

pathology [pəˈθɒlədʒɪ] n Pathologie die.

pathos ['peɪθɒs] n Pathos das.

pathway ['pɑːθweɪ] n Weg der; [narrower] Pfad der.

patience ['peɪʃns] n **- 1.** [quality] Geduld die **- 2.** [card game] Patience die.

patient ['peɪʃnt] <> adj geduldig <> n Patient der, -in die.

patio ['pætɪəʊ] (pl -s) n Terrasse die.

patriotic [Br ˌpætrɪˈɒtɪk, Am ˌpeɪtrɪˈɒtɪk] adj patriotisch.

patrol [pəˈtrəʊl] <> n [of police] Streife die; [of soldiers] Patrouille die <> vt [subj: police - in vehicle] Streife fahren in (+ D); [- on foot] seine Runden machen in (+ D); [subj: soldiers] patrouillieren.

patrol car n Streifenwagen der.

patrolman [pəˈtrəʊlmən] (pl -men [-mən]) n Am (Streifen)polizist der.

patron ['peɪtrən] n **- 1.** [sponsor] Förderer der, -derin die **- 2.** Br [of charity, campaign] Schirmherr der, -in die.

patronize, -ise ['pætrənaɪz] vt pej [talk down to] von oben herab behandeln.

patronizing, -ising ['pætrənaɪzɪŋ] adj pej gönnerhaft.

patter ['pætəʳ] <> n **- 1.** [of feet] Getrappel das; [of raindrops] Platschen das **- 2.** [talk] Sprüche pl <> vi [dog, feet] trappeln; [rain] platschen.

pattern ['pætən] n **- 1.** [design] Muster das **- 2.** [of life, work] Ablauf der **- 3.** [of distribution] Schema das **- 4.** [for sewing] Schnittmuster das; [for knitting] Strickanleitung die **- 5.** [model] Vorbild das.

paunch [pɔːntʃ] n Bauch der.

pauper ['pɔːpəʳ] n Arme der, die.

pause [pɔːz] <> n Pause die; **without a ~** ohne Unterbrechung <> vi **- 1.** [stop speaking] innehalten **- 2.** [stop doing sthg] eine Pause machen OR einlegen.

pave [peɪv] vt pflastern; **to ~ the way for sb/ sthg** jm/etw den Weg ebnen.

pavement ['peɪvmənt] n **- 1.** Br [at side of road] Bürgersteig der **- 2.** Am [road surface] Fahrbahnbelag der.

pavilion [pəˈvɪljən] n **- 1.** [at sports field] Klubhaus das **- 2.** [at exhibition] Pavillon der.

paving stone ['peɪvɪŋ-] n Pflasterstein der.

paw [pɔː] n Pfote die; [of lion, bear] Tatze die.

pawn [pɔːn] <> n **- 1.** [chesspiece] Bauer der **- 2.** [unimportant person] Schachfigur die <> vt verpfänden.

pawnbroker ['pɔːnˌbrəʊkəʳ] n Pfandleiher der, -in die.

pawnshop ['pɔːnʃɒp] *n* Pfandhaus *das*.

pay [peɪ] (*pt & pp* paid) ◇ *vt* - **1.** [bill, debt, person] bezahlen; [fine, taxes, fare, sum of money] zahlen; **to ~ sb for sthg** jm das Geld für etw geben; **how much did you ~ for it?** wie viel hast du dafür gezahlt? - **2.** [be profitable, advantageous to]: **it won't ~ you to sell the house just now** es wird sich für dich nicht lohnen, das Haus jetzt zu verkaufen; **it will ~ you to keep quiet** es wird für dich von Vorteil sein, wenn du schweigst - **3.**: **to ~ sb a compliment** jm ein Kompliment machen; **to ~ a visit to sb/a place** jn/einen Ort besuchen ◇ *vi* - **1.** [for services, work, goods] (be)zahlen; **to ~ for sthg** etw bezahlen - **2.** [be profitable - crime] sich lohnen; [- work] sich rentieren - **3.** *fig* [suffer] bezahlen; **to ~ dearly for sthg** teuer für etw bezahlen ◇ *n* [wages] Lohn *der*; [salary] Gehalt *das*. ◆ **pay back** *vt sep* - **1.** [return money to]: **I'll ~ you back (the money) tomorrow** ich zahle dir morgen das Geld zurück - **2.** [revenge o.s. on]: **I'll ~ you back for that!** das werde ich dir heimzahlen! ◆ **pay off** ◇ *vt sep* - **1.** [debt] abbezahlen; [loan] tilgen - **2.** [employee] auszahlen - **3.** [informer, blackmailer] Schweigegeld zahlen (+ *D*) ◇ *vi* [be successful] sich auszahlen. ◆ **pay up** *vi* zahlen.

payable ['peɪəbl] *adj* - **1.** [debt, loan]: **to be ~** fällig sein - **2.** [cheque]: **to be ~ to sb** an jn zu zahlen sein; **to make a cheque ~ to sb** einen Scheck auf jn auslstellen.

paycheck ['peɪtʃek] *n Am* [cheque] Lohnscheck *der*; [money] Lohn *der*.

payday ['peɪdeɪ] *n* Zahltag *der*.

payee [peɪ'iː] *n* Zahlungsempfänger *der*, -in *die*.

pay envelope *n Am* Lohntüte *die*.

payment ['peɪmənt] *n* - **1.** [act of paying] Bezahlung *die* - **2.** [amount of money] Zahlung *die*.

pay packet *n Br* - **1.** [envelope] Lohntüte *die* - **2.** [wages] Lohn *der*.

pay-per-view *adj* Pay-per-View-.

pay phone, pay station *Am n* Münzfernsprecher *der*.

payroll ['peɪrəʊl] *n*: **to be on the ~** angestellt sein.

payslip *Br* ['peɪslɪp], **paystub** *Am* ['peɪstʌb] *n* [for wages] Lohnstreifen *der*; [for salary] Gehaltsstreifen *der*.

pay station *n Am* = pay phone.

paystub *n Am* = payslip.

PC *n* - **1.** (*abbr of* personal computer) PC *der* - **2.** *abbr of* police constable.

PE *n abbr of* physical education.

pea [piː] *n* Erbse *die*.

peace [piːs] *n* - **1.** [tranquillity] Ruhe *die*; **~ of mind** Seelenfrieden *der*; **to be at ~ with o.s.** mit sich selbst im Reinen sein - **2.** [no war] Frieden *der*; **to make (one's) ~ with sb/sthg**

mit jm/etw Frieden schließen - **3.** [law and order] Ruhe *die* und Ordnung.

peaceful ['piːsfʊl] *adj* friedlich.

peacetime ['piːstaɪm] *n (U)* Friedenszeiten *pl*.

peach [piːtʃ] ◇ *adj* [in colour] pfirsichfarben ◇ *n* [fruit] Pfirsich *der*.

peacock ['piːkɒk] *n* Pfau *der*.

peak [piːk] ◇ *n* - **1.** [mountain top] Gipfel *der* - **2.** [highest point] Höhepunkt *der*; **to be at one's ~** auf dem Höhepunkt seiner Leistungen sein - **3.** [of cap] Schirm *der* ◇ *adj*: **in ~ condition** in Höchstform ◇ *vi* den Höchststand erreichen.

peaked [piːkt] *adj*: **~ cap** Schirmmütze *die*.

peak hour *n* TELEC & ELEC Hauptbelastungszeit *die*; [for traffic] Hauptverkehrszeit *die*.

peak period *n* Hochsaison *die*.

peak rate *n* Höchsttarif *der*.

peal [piːl] ◇ *n* - **1.** [of bells] Glockenläuten *das* - **2.**: **~s of laughter** schallendes Gelächter; **~ of thunder** Donnerschlag *der* ◇ *vi* [bells] läuten.

peanut ['piːnʌt] *n* Erdnuss *die*.

peanut butter *n* Erdnussbutter *die*.

pear [peəʳ] *n* Birne *die*.

pearl [pɜːl] *n* Perle *die*.

peasant ['peznt] *n* [in countryside] (armer) Bauer, (arme) Bäuerin.

peat [piːt] *n* Torf *der*.

pebble ['pebl] *n* Kiesel(stein) *der*.

peck [pek] ◇ *n* [kiss] Küsschen *das* ◇ *vt* - **1.** [with beak - hand] picken nach - **2.** [kiss] ein Küsschen geben (+ *D*).

peckish ['pekɪʃ] *adj Br inf* (etwas) hungrig.

peculiar [pɪ'kjuːlɪəʳ] *adj* - **1.** [odd] seltsam, eigenartig - **2.** [slightly ill]: **to feel ~** sich komisch fühlen - **3.** [characteristic]: **to be ~ to sb/sthg** jm/etw eigentümlich sein.

peculiarity [pɪ,kjuːlɪ'ærətɪ] *n* - **1.** [strange habit] Eigenheit *die* - **2.** [individual characteristic] Charakteristikum *das* - **3.** [oddness] Eigenartigkeit *die*.

pedal ['pedl] *n* Pedal *das*.

pedal bin *n* Treteimer *der*.

pedantic [pɪ'dæntɪk] *adj pej* pedantisch.

peddle ['pedl] *vt* - **1.** [drugs] handeln mit - **2.** [rumour, gossip] verbreiten.

pedestal ['pedɪstl] *n* Sockel *der*.

pedestrian [pɪ'destrɪən] ◇ *adj pej* langweilig ◇ *n* Fußgänger *der*, -in *die*.

pedestrian crossing *n Br* Fußgängerüberweg *der*.

pedestrian precinct *Br*, **pedestrian zone** *Am n* Fußgängerzone *die*.

pediatrics [,piːdɪ'ætrɪks] *n* Kinderheilkunde *die*, Pädiatrie *die*.

pedigree ['pedɪgriː] ◇ *adj* mit einem Stammbaum ◇ *n* Stammbaum *der*.

pedlar Br, **peddler** Am ['pedlə'] n: **(drug)** ~ Drogenhändler der, -in die.

pee [pi:] inf ⬥ ~ **1.** [act of urinating]: **to have a ~** pinkeln; **to go for a ~** pinkeln gehen - **2.** [urine] Urin der ⬥ vi pinkeln.

peek [pi:k] inf ⬥ n: **to have** OR **take a ~ at sthg** einen kurzen Blick auf etw (A) werfen ⬥ vi gucken.

peel [pi:l] ⬥ n (U) Schale die ⬥ vt schälen ⬥ vi [walls, paint] abblättern; [wallpaper] sich lösen; [skin, nose, back] sich schälen.

peelings ['pi:lɪŋz] npl Schalen pl.

peep [pi:p] ⬥ n - **1.** [look]: **to have** OR **take a ~ at sthg** einen kurzen Blick auf etw (A) werfen - **2.** inf [sound] Piep(s) der; **I haven't heard a ~ from them** ich habe keinen Pieps von ihnen gehört ⬥ vi [look] gucken.

peephole ['pi:phəʊl] n [in door] Spion der.

peer [pɪə'] ⬥ n - **1.** [noble] Angehöriger des hohen Adels in Großbritannien - **2.** [equal]: **he is respected by his ~s** er ist sehr anerkannt bei seinesgleichen ⬥ vi angestrengt schauen.

peer group n Peergroup die.

peeved [pi:vd] adj inf eingeschnappt.

peevish ['pi:vɪʃ] adj [remark, mood] gereizt; [person - as characteristic] reizbar; [- temporarily] gereizt.

peg [peg] ⬥ n - **1.** [hook] Haken der - **2.** [for washing line] (Wäsche)klammer die - **3.** [for tent] Hering der ⬥ vt [price] festsetzen.

pejorative [pɪ'dʒɒrətɪv] adj abwertend.

pekinese [,pi:kə'ni:z] (pl inv OR -s) n Pekinese der.

Peking [pi:'kɪŋ] n Peking nt.

pelican ['pelɪkən] (pl inv OR -s) n Pelikan der.

pelican crossing n Br Ampelübergang der.

pellet ['pelɪt] n [for gun] Schrotkugel die.

pelt [pelt] ⬥ vt: **to ~ sb (with sthg)** jn (mit etw) bewerfen ⬥ vi - **1.** [rain]: **it's ~ing (with rain)** es schüttet - **2.** [run very fast] rasen.

pelvis ['pelvɪs] (pl -vises) n Becken das.

pen [pen] n - **1.** [for writing]: **(ballpoint)** ~ Kugelschreiber der; **(fountain)** ~ Füllfederhalter der; **(felt-tipped)** ~ Filzstift der - **2.** [enclosure] Pferch der.

penal ['pi:nl] adj LAW: **~ system** Strafrecht das; **~ reform** Strafrechtsreform die.

penalize, -ise ['pi:nəlaɪz] vt - **1.** [punish & SPORT] bestrafen - **2.** [put at a disadvantage] benachteiligen.

penalty ['penltɪ] n - **1.** [punishment] Strafe die; **to pay the ~ (for sthg)** fig (für etw) büßen müssen - **2.** [fine] Geldstrafe die - **3.** SPORT: **~ (kick)** FTBL Strafstoß der; RUGBY Straftritt der.

penance ['penəns] n (U) - **1.** RELIG Buße die - **2.** fig [punishment] Strafe die.

pence [pens] Br pl ⬥ penny.

penchant [pā pā̃, Am 'pentʃənt] n: **to have a ~ for sthg** eine Schwäche OR Vorliebe für etw haben.

pencil ['pensl] n Bleistift der; **in ~** mit Blei-

stift. ⬥ **pencil in** vt sep [person] vormerken; [date] vorläufig festhalten.

pencil case n Federmäppchen das.

pencil sharpener [-'ʃɑ:pnə'] n (Blei-stift)spitzer der.

pendant ['pendənt] n [jewel on chain] Anhänger der.

pending ['pendɪŋ] fml ⬥ adj: **to be ~** [about to happen] bevorstehen; LAW [waiting to be dealt with] noch anhängig sein ⬥ prep bis zu; **~ further inquiries** bis weitere Untersuchungen durchgeführt worden sind.

pendulum ['pendjʊləm] (pl -s) n Pendel das.

penetrate ['penɪtreɪt] vt - **1.** [get into - subj: person] vordringen in (+ A); [- subj: wind, rain, light] durchdringen; [- subj: sharp object, bullet] eindringen in (+ A) - **2.** [infiltrate] sich einschleusen in (+ A).

pen friend n Brieffreund der, -in die.

penguin ['peŋgwɪn] n Pinguin der.

penicillin [,penɪ'sɪlɪn] n Penizillin das.

peninsula [pə'nɪnsjʊlə] (pl -s) n Halbinsel die.

penis ['pi:nɪs] (pl penises ['pi:nɪsɪz]) n Penis der.

penitentiary [,penɪ'tenʃərɪ] n Am Gefängnis das.

penknife ['pennaɪf] (pl -knives [-naɪvz]) n Taschenmesser das.

pen name n Pseudonym das.

pennant ['penənt] n Wimpel der.

penniless ['penɪlɪs] adj mittellos.

penny ['penɪ] (pl senses 1 & 2 -ies; pl sense 3 pence) n - **1.** Br [coin] Penny der - **2.** Am [coin] Centstück das - **3.** Br [value]: **30 pence** 30 Pence.

pen pal n inf Brieffreund der, -in die.

pension ['penʃn] n - **1.** Rente die - **2.** [disability pension] Erwerbsunfähigkeitsrente die.

pensioner ['penʃənə'] n Br: **(old-age)** ~ Rentner der, -in die.

pensive ['pensɪv] adj nachdenklich.

pentagon ['pentəgən] n Fünfeck das. ⬥ **Pentagon** n Am: **the Pentagon** das Pentagon.

Pentecost ['pentɪkɒst] n - **1.** [Christian] Pfingsten das - **2.** [Jewish] Ernte(dank)fest das.

penthouse ['penthaʊs, pl -haʊzɪz] n Penthouse das.

pent up ['pent-] adj [emotions] unterdrückt; [energy] angestaut.

penultimate [pe'nʌltɪmət] adj vorletzte, -r, -s.

people ['pi:pl] ⬥ n [nation, race] Volk das ⬥ npl - **1.** [persons] Menschen pl, Leute pl; **a lot of ~** viele Menschen OR Leute; **five ~** fünf Personen OR Leute - **2.** [in indefinite uses] Leute die; **~ say that ...** man sagt OR es heißt, dass ... - **3.** [inhabitants - of country] Bevölkerung *die;* [- of town, city] Einwohner *pl* - **4.** POL: **the ~ das Volk** ◇ *vt:* **to be ~d by** OR **with** bevölkert sein von.

pep [pep] *n inf* Schwung *der.* ◆ **pep up** *vt sep inf* - **1.** [person] munter machen - **2.** [party, event] in Schwung bringen.

pepper ['pepə'] *n* - **1.** [spice] Pfeffer *der* - **2.** [vegetable] Paprika *der.*

pepperbox *n Am* = pepper pot.

peppermint ['pepəmınt] *n* - **1.** [sweet] Pfefferminz(bonbon) *das* - **2.** [herb] Pfefferminze *die.*

pepper pot *Br,* **pepperbox** *Am* ['pepəbɒks] *n* Pfefferstreuer *der.*

pep talk *n inf:* **to give sb a ~** jm ein paar aufmunternde Worte sagen.

per [pɜːʳ] *prep* [expressing rate, ratio] pro; **as ~ instructions** gemäß Anweisung.

per annum [pər'ænəm] *adv* pro Jahr.

per capita [pə'kæpɪtə] *adv* pro Kopf.

perceive [pə'siːv] *vt* - **1.** [see] wahrnehmen - **2.** [notice, realize] erkennen - **3.** [conceive, consider]: **to ~ sb/sthg as** jn/etw betrachten als.

percent [pə'sent] *n* Prozent *das.*

percentage [pə'sentɪdʒ] *n* Prozentsatz *der.*

perception [pə'sepʃn] *n* - **1.** [of colour, sound, time] Wahrnehmung *die* - **2.** [insight] Auffassungsvermögen *das.*

perceptive [pə'septɪv] *adj* scharfsinnig.

perch [pɜːtʃ] ◇ *n* [for bird] (Sitz)stange *die* ◇ *vi* - **1.** [bird]: **to ~ (on sthg)** sich (auf etw (D)) niederlassen - **2.** [person]: **to ~ on (the edge of) a desk** sich auf die Kante eines Schreibtisches setzen.

percolator ['pɜːkəleɪtəʳ] *n* Kaffeemaschine *die.*

percussion [pə'kʌʃn] *n* MUS: **~ instrument** Schlaginstrument *das.*

perennial [pə'renɪəl] ◇ *adj* - **1.** [continual] immer wieder auftretend - **2.** BOT perennierend ◇ *n* BOT perennierende Pflanze.

perfect [*adj & n* 'pɜːfɪkt, *vb* pə'fekt] ◇ *adj* - **1.** [ideal, faultless] perfekt, vollkommen - **2.** [for emphasis - nuisance] ausgesprochen; **~ strangers** wildfremde Leute ◇ *n* GRAMM: **~ (tense)** Perfekt *das* ◇ *vt* vervollkommnen.

perfection [pə'fekʃn] *n* [faultlessness] Perfektion *die;* **to do sthg to ~** etw perfekt machen.

perfectionist [pə'fekʃənɪst] *n* Perfektionist *der,* -in *die.*

perfectly ['pɜːfɪktlɪ] *adv* - **1.** [for emphasis - honest, frank, ridiculous] absolut; **you know ~ well ...** du weißt ganz genau ... - **2.** [to perfection] exakt, genau.

perforate ['pɜːfəreɪt] *vt* [paper - with one hole] lochen; [- with row of holes] perforieren; [lung, eardrum] durchstechen.

perform [pə'fɔːm] ◇ *vt* - **1.** [carry out - op-

eration] durch|führen; [- miracle] vollbringen; [- service, function] erfüllen - **2.** [play, concert] auf|führen; [part] spielen; [dance] vor|tanzen ◇ *vi* - **1.** [car, machine] laufen; [in exam] ab|schneiden; **he is ~ing well** [employee] er leistet gute Arbeit; [sportsman] er ist in Hochform - **2.** [actor, singer] auf|treten.

performance [pə'fɔːməns] *n* - **1.** [of task, duty] Erfüllung *die;* [of operation] Durchführung *die* - **2.** [at cinema] Vorstellung *die;* [of play, concert] Aufführung *die* - **3.** [by actor, singer, of car, engine] Leistung *die.*

performer [pə'fɔːməʳ] *n* Künstler *der,* -in *die.*

perfume ['pɜːfjuːm] *n* - **1.** [for woman] Parfüm *das* - **2.** [pleasant smell] Duft *der.*

perfunctory [pə'fʌŋktərɪ] *adj* [search, read] oberflächlich; [kiss, glance] flüchtig; [explanation, apology] der Form halber.

perhaps [pə'hæps] *adv* vielleicht; **~ so** (das) mag sein; **~ not** vielleicht nicht.

peril ['perɪl] *n* (U) literary Gefahr *die.*

perimeter [pə'rɪmɪtəʳ] *n* Begrenzung *die;* **~ fence** Umzäunung *die.*

period ['pɪərɪəd] ◇ *n* - **1.** [of time] Zeit *die;* **over a ~ of several years** über einen Zeitraum von mehreren Jahren - **2.** HIST Zeitalter *das,* Epoche *die;* **the Elizabethan ~** die elisabethanische Zeit - **3.** SCH (Schul)stunde *die;* **free ~** Freistunde *die* - **4.** [menstruation] Periode *die* - **5.** *Am* [full stop] Punkt *der* ◇ *comp* [dress, furniture] zeitgenössisch.

periodic [,pɪərɪ'ɒdɪk] *adj* [events] regelmäßig wiederkehrend; [visits] regelmäßig.

periodical [,pɪərɪ'ɒdɪkl] ◇ *adj* = periodic ◇ *n* [magazine] Zeitschrift *die.*

peripheral [pə'rɪfərəl] ◇ *adj* - **1.** [of little importance] nebensächlich - **2.** [vision] peripher; [region, group] Rand- ◇ *n* COMPUT peripheriegerät *das.*

perish ['perɪʃ] *vi* - **1.** [die] um|kommen - **2.** [food] verderben; [rubber] verschleißen.

perishable ['perɪʃəbl] *adj* verderblich. ◆ **perishables** *npl* verderbliche Waren *pl.*

perjury ['pɜːdʒərɪ] *n* (U) LAW Meineid *der.*

perk [pɜːk] *n inf* Vergünstigung *die.* ◆ **perk up** *vi* [become more energetic] munter werden; [become more cheerful] auf|leben.

perky ['pɜːkɪ] *adj inf* munter.

perm [pɜːm] *n* Dauerwelle *die.*

permanent ['pɜːmənənt] ◇ *adj* - **1.** [not temporary] dauerhaft; [job] fest - **2.** [continuous] ständig; [constant] konstant ◇ *n Am* [perm] Dauerwelle *die.*

permeate ['pɜːmɪeɪt] *vt lit & fig* durch|dringen.

permissible [pə'mɪsəbl] *adj* erlaubt.

permission [pə'mɪʃn] *n* (U) Erlaubnis *die;* [official] Genehmigung *die.*

asking permission

Darf ich das Fenster aufmachen? May I open the window?

Kann ich mal kurz telefonieren? Could I make a quick telephone call?

Würde es Ihnen etwas ausmachen, wenn ich die Tür schließe? Would you mind if I closed the door?

Könnte ich bitte mal vorbei? Excuse me, could I get through please?

Wenn Sie nichts dagegen haben, würde ich jetzt gerne gehen. If you don't mind, I really ought to be going now.

permit [*vb* pə'mɪt, *n* 'pɜːmɪt] ⬦ *vt* - **1.** [allow] erlauben; **to ~ sb to do sthg** jm erlauben, etw zu tun; **to ~ sb sthg** jm etw gestatten - **2.** [enable] zullassen ⬦ *n* Genehmigung *die*.

perpendicular [ˌpɜːpən'dɪkjʊləʳ] ⬦ *adj:* **~ (to)** senkrecht (zu) ⬦ *n* MATH Senkrechte *die*.

perpetrate ['pɜːpɪtreɪt] *vt fml* [crime, murder] begehen.

perpetual [pə'petʃʊəl] *adj* - **1.** *pej* [continuous] ständig - **2.** [everlasting] ewig.

perplexing [pə'pleksɪŋ] *adj* verblüffend.

persecute ['pɜːsɪkjuːt] *vt* verfolgen.

persevere [ˌpɜːsɪ'vɪəʳ] *vi* - **1.** [with difficulty] durchhalten; **to ~ with sthg** [studies, job] mit etw weitermachen; [search] etw nicht aufgeben - **2.** [with determination]: **to ~ in doing sthg** darauf beharren, etw zu tun.

Persian ['pɜːʃn] *adj* persisch.

persist [pə'sɪst] *vi* - **1.** [problem, situation, rain] anhalten, fortdauern - **2.** [person]: **to ~ in doing sthg** etw unaufhörlich tun.

persistence [pə'sɪstəns] *n* - **1.** [continuation] Fortdauer *die*, Anhalten *das* - **2.** [determination] Beharrlichkeit *die*.

persistent [pə'sɪstənt] *adj* - **1.** [constant] fortdauernd - **2.** [determined] hartnäckig.

person ['pɜːsn] (*pl* people OR persons *fml*) *n* - **1.** [man or woman] Mensch *der*; **in ~** persönlich - **2.** GRAMM Person *die*.

personable ['pɜːsnəbl] *adj* von angenehmem Äußeren.

personal ['pɜːsənl] *adj* - **1.** [gen] persönlich - **2.** [letter, message] privat.

personal assistant *n* persönlicher Assistent, persönliche Assistentin.

personal column *n* Privatanzeigen *pl*.

personal computer *n* Personalcomputer *der*.

personality [ˌpɜːsə'nælətɪ] *n* Persönlichkeit *die*.

personally ['pɜːsnəlɪ] *adv* persönlich.

personal organizer, -iser *n* Terminplaner *der*.

personal property *n* (*U*) LAW Privateigentum *das*.

personal stereo *n* Walkman® *der*.

personify [pə'sɒnɪfaɪ] *vt* [represent] verkörpern; **she's evil personified** sie ist das Böse in Person.

personnel [ˌpɜːsə'nel] ⬦ *n* (*U*) [department] Personalabteilung *die* ⬦ *npl* [staff] Personal *das*.

perspective [pə'spektɪv] *n* Perspektive *die*.

Perspex® ['pɜːspeks] *n Br* Plexiglas® *das*.

perspiration [ˌpɜːspə'reɪʃn] *n* - **1.** [sweat] Schweiß *der* - **2.** [sweating] Schwitzen *das*.

persuade [pə'sweɪd] *vt* [convince] überzeugen; **to ~ sb to do sthg** jn überreden, etw zu tun; **to ~ sb that ...** jn davon überzeugen, dass ...; **to ~ sb of sthg** jn von etw überzeugen.

persuasion [pə'sweɪʒn] *n* - **1.** (*U*) [act of persuading] Überredung *die* - **2.** [belief] Überzeugung *die*.

persuasive [pə'sweɪsɪv] *adj* überzeugend.

pertain [pə'teɪn] *vi fml:* **to ~ to** gehören zu.

pertinent ['pɜːtɪnənt] *adj* relevant.

perturb [pə'tɜːb] *vt fml* beunruhigen.

peruse [pə'ruːz] *vt* [read - thoroughly] sorgfältig durchlesen; [- quickly] überfliegen.

pervade [pə'veɪd] *vt* durchdringen.

perverse [pə'vɜːs] *adj* pervers.

perversion [*Br* pə'vɜːʃn, *Am* pərˈvɜːrʒn] *n* [sexual deviation] Perversion *die*.

pervert [*n* 'pɜːvɜːt, *vb* pə'vɜːt] ⬦ *n* Perverse *der*, *die* ⬦ *vt* - **1.** [distort - truth] verzerren; [- course of justice] behindern - **2.** [corrupt morally - person, mind] verderben.

pessimist ['pesɪmɪst] *n* Pessimist *der*, -in *die*.

pessimistic [ˌpesɪ'mɪstɪk] *adj* pessimistisch.

pest [pest] *n* - **1.** [in garden, on farm] Schädling *der* - **2.** *inf* [annoying person, thing] Pest *die*, Plage *die*.

pester ['pestəʳ] *vt* belästigen.

pet [pet] ⬦ *adj* [favourite] Lieblings- ⬦ *n* - **1.** [animal] Haustier *das* - **2.** [favourite person] Liebling *der* ⬦ *vt* [stroke] streicheln ⬦ *vi* [sexually] Petting machen.

petal ['petl] *n* Blütenblatt *das*.

peter ['piːtəʳ] ➤ **peter out** *vi* [supply] versiegen; [path] auslaufen.

petite [pə'tiːt] *adj* zierlich.

petition [pɪ'tɪʃn] ⬦ *n* - **1.** [supporting campaign] Petition *die* - **2.** LAW: **~ for divorce** Scheidungsantrag *der* ⬦ *vt* [lobby]: **to ~ sb** eine Petition bei jm einreichen.

petrified ['petrɪfaɪd] *adj* [terrified] verängstigt, gelähmt vor Angst.

petrol ['petrəl] *n Br* Benzin *das*.

petrol bomb *n Br* Benzinbombe *die*.

petrol can *n Br* Benzinkanister *der*.

petrol pump *n Br* Zapfsäule *die*.

petrol station *n* Br Tankstelle *die*.

petrol tank *n* Br Benzintank *der*.

petticoat ['petɪkəʊt] *n* Unterrock *der*.

petty ['petɪ] *adj* - **1.** [small-minded] kleinlich - **2.** [trivial] geringfügig.

petty cash *n* Portokasse *die*.

petulant ['petjʊlənt] *adj* mürrisch; [child] bockig.

pew [pjuː] *n* Kirchenbank *die*.

pewter ['pjuːtə'] *n* Zinn *das*.

phantom ['fæntəm] ◇ *adj* [imaginary] Phantom- ◇ *n* [ghost] Phantom *das*.

pharmaceutical [ˌfɑːmə'sjuːtɪkl] *adj* pharmazeutisch.

pharmacist ['fɑːməsɪst] *n* [in shop] Apotheker *der*, -in *die*.

pharmacy ['fɑːməsɪ] *n* [shop] Apotheke *die*.

phase [feɪz] *n* Phase *die*. ◆ **phase in** *vt sep* schrittweise OR allmählich einlführen. ◆ **phase out** *vt sep* ausllaufen lassen.

PhD (*abbr of* Doctor of Philosophy) *n* Dr. Phil.

pheasant ['feznt] (*pl inv* OR **-s**) *n* Fasan *der*.

phenomena [fɪ'nɒmɪnə] *pl* ▷ phenomenon.

phenomenal [fɪ'nɒmɪnl] *adj* [remarkable] phänomenal.

phenomenon [fɪ'nɒmɪnən] (*pl* **-mena**) *n* Phänomen *das*.

philanthropist [fɪ'lænθrəpɪst] *n* Philanthrop *der*, Menschenfreund *der*.

philosopher [fɪ'lɒsəfə'] *n* Philosoph *der*, -in *die*.

philosophical [ˌfɪlə'sɒfɪkl] *adj* - **1.** [gen] philosophisch - **2.** [stoical] gelassen.

philosophy [fɪ'lɒsəfɪ] *n* Philosophie *die*.

phlegm [flem] *n* (U) [mucus] Schleim *der*.

phobia ['fəʊbɪə] *n* Phobie *die*.

phone [fəʊn] ◇ *n* Telefon *das*; **to be on the ~** [speaking] telefonieren, am Telefon sein; Br [connected to network] Telefon haben ◇ *comp* Telefon- ◇ *vt & vi* anlrufen. ◆ **phone back** *vt sep & vi* zurücklrufen. ◆ **phone up** *vt sep & vi* anlrufen.

phone book *n* Telefonbuch *das*.

phone booth *n* Br Telefonkabine *die*.

phone box *n* Br Telefonzelle *die*.

phone call *n* Telefonanruf *der*, Telefongespräch *das*; **to make a ~** telefonieren.

phonecard ['fəʊnkɑːd] *n* Telefonkarte *die*.

phone-in *n* Radio- oder TV-Programm, bei dem Zuhörer bzw. Zuschauer anrufen können, um ihre Meinung zu äußern.

phone number *n* Telefonnummer *die*.

phonetics [fə'netɪks] *n* (U) Fonetik *die*.

phoney Br, **phony** Am ['fəʊnɪ] *inf* ◇ *adj* - **1.** [false] falsch - **2.** [insincere] unaufrichtig ◇ *n* [person] Hochstapler *der*, -in *die*.

photo ['fəʊtəʊ] *n* Foto *das*; **to take a ~ (of)** ein Foto machen (von).

photocopier ['fəʊtəʊˌkɒpɪə'] *n* Fotokopierer *der*.

photocopy ['fəʊtəʊˌkɒpɪ] ◇ *n* Fotokopie *die* ◇ *vt* fotokopieren.

photograph ['fəʊtəgrɑːf] ◇ *n* Fotografie *die*, Aufnahme *die*; **to take a ~ (of sb/sthg)** jn/etw fotografieren ◇ *vt* fotografieren.

photograph

Photograph ist ein falscher Freund, weil dieses Wort sich auf das Bild und nicht auf die fotografierende Person bezieht. What a great photograph bedeutet also „was für eine großartige Aufnahme". In diesem Zusammenhang ist der Unterschied zum Begriff photography zu beachten: photography bedeutet nicht Aufnahme, sondern „Fotografie" im Sinne von „das Fotografieren".
Die englische Berufsbezeichnung für einen Fotografen oder eine Fotografin lautet photographer.

photographer [fə'tɒgrəfə'] *n* Fotograf *der*, -in *die*.

photography [fə'tɒgrəfɪ] *n* (U) Fotografie *die*.

phrasal verb [ˌfreɪzl-] *n* Verb *das* mit Präposition.

phrase [freɪz] ◇ *n* - **1.** [part of sentence] Satzglied *das* - **2.** [expression] Wendung *die* ◇ *vt* [express] ausldrücken.

phrasebook ['freɪzbʊk] *n* Sprachführer *der*.

physical ['fɪzɪkl] ◇ *adj* - **1.** [relating to body] körperlich - **2.** [world, object] fassbar, materiell - **3.** [relating to physics] physikalisch ◇ *n* ärztliche Untersuchung.

physical education *n* Sportunterricht *der*.

physically ['fɪzɪklɪ] *adv* - **1.** [bodily] körperlich - **2.** [materially] materiell, physisch.

physically handicapped ◇ *adj* körperbehindert ◇ *npl*: **the ~** die Körperbehinderten *pl*.

physician [fɪ'zɪʃn] *n* Arzt *der*, Ärztin *die*.

physicist ['fɪzɪsɪst] *n* Physiker *der*, -in *die*.

physics ['fɪzɪks] *n* (U) Physik *die*.

physiotherapy [ˌfɪzɪəʊ'θerəpɪ] *n* Physiotherapie *die*.

physique [fɪ'ziːk] *n* Körperbau *der*.

pianist ['pɪənɪst] *n* Pianist *der*, -in *die*.

piano [pɪ'ænəʊ] (*pl* **-s**) *n* Klavier *das*.

pick [pɪk] ◇ *n* - **1.** [tool] Spitzhacke *die* - **2.** [selection]: **take your ~** such dir einen/eine/eins aus - **3.** [best]: **the ~ of** das Beste von ◇ *vt* - **1.** [choose] auslsuchen; [winner] auslwählen - **2.** [fruit, flowers] pflücken - **3.** [remove] entfernen - **4.** [nose, teeth]: **to ~ one's nose** in der Nase bohren; **to ~ one's teeth** in seinen Zähnen stochern - **5.** [provoke]: **to ~ a fight (with sb)** (mit jm) einen

Streit an|fangen - **6.** [lock] knacken. ◆ **pick on** *vt fus* auf dem Kieker haben. ◆ **pick out** *vt sep* - **1.** [recognize] erkennen - **2.** [select] aus|suchen; [winner] aus|wählen. ◆ **pick up** ◇ *vt sep* - **1.** [lift up] hoch|heben; [after dropping] auf|heben - **2.** [collect - gen] ab|holen; [- hitchhiker] mit|nehmen - **3.** [acquire - habit] an|nehmen; [- tips] bekommen; [- skill, language] lernen; **to ~ up speed** schneller werden - **4.** *inf* [man, woman] an|machen - **5.** RADIO & TELEC [signal] empfangen - **6.** [conversation, work] wieder auf|nehmen ◇ *vi* - **1.** [improve] sich verbessern - **2.** [resume] weiter|machen.

pickaxe *Br*, **pickax** *Am* ['pɪkæks] *n* Spitzhacke *die*.

picket ['pɪkɪt] ◇ *n* [at place of work] Streikposten *der* ◇ *vt* [place of work] Streikposten auf|stellen vor (+ D).

picket line *n* Streikpostenkette *die*.

pickle ['pɪkl] ◇ *n* - **1.** (U) [food] Pickles *pl* - **2.** *inf* [difficult situation]: **to be in a ~** in der Tinte sitzen ◇ *vt* ein|legen.

pickpocket ['pɪk,pɒkɪt] *n* Taschendieb *der*, -in *die*.

pick-up *n* - **1.** [of record player] Tonabnehmer *der* - **2.** [truck] Pick-up *der*.

picnic ['pɪknɪk] (*pt & pp* -ked; *cont* -king) ◇ *n* Picknick *das* ◇ *vi* picknicken.

pictorial [pɪk'tɔːrɪəl] *adj* [illustrated] bebildert.

picture ['pɪktʃə'] ◇ *n* - **1.** [gen] Bild *das*; [painting] Gemälde *das*; **as pretty as a ~** bildhübsch - **2.** [movie] Film *der* - **3.** [in one's mind] Vorstellung *die* - **4.** [prospect] Aussicht *die* - **5.** *phr*: **to get the ~** *inf* kapieren; **to put sb in the ~** jn ins Bild setzen ◇ *vt* - **1.** [in mind] sich (D) vor|stellen - **2.** [in photo] fotografieren; [in painting, drawing] dar|stellen. ◆ **pictures** *npl Br*: **the ~s** [cinema] das Kino.

picture book *n* Bilderbuch *das*.

picturesque [,pɪktʃə'resk] *adj* malerisch.

pie [paɪ] *n* - **1.** [sweet] Obstkuchen *der* - **2.** [savoury] Pastete *die*.

piece [piːs] *n* - **1.** [gen] Stück *das*; [component] Teil *das*; **a ~ of news** eine Neuigkeit; **a ~ of advice** ein Rat; **a ~ of furniture** ein Möbelstück; **a fifty pence ~** ein Fünfzigpencestück; **to fall to ~s** auseinander|fallen; **to take sthg to ~s** auseinander nehmen; **in one ~** [intact, unharmed] heil - **2.** [in chess] Figur *die*; [in backgammon, draughts] Stein *der* - **3.** [of journalism] Artikel *der*. ◆ **piece together** *vt sep* [facts] zusammen|fügen.

piecemeal ['piːsmiːl] *adj & adv* stückweise.

piecework ['piːswɜːk] *n* (U) Akkordarbeit *die*.

pier [pɪə'] *n* [at seaside] Pier *der*.

pierce [pɪəs] *vt* [subj: bullet, noise, light] durch|dringen; [subj: needle] durch|stechen;

to have one's ears ~d sich (D) Ohrlöcher stechen lassen.

piercing ['pɪəsɪŋ] ◇ *adj* [sound, voice] durchdringend; [wind] schneidend; [look, eyes] stechend ◇ *n* Piercing *das*.

pig [pɪg] *n* - **1.** [animal] Schwein *das* - **2.** *inf pej* [greedy eater] Vielfraß *der* - **3.** *inf pej* [unkind person] Schwein *das*.

pigeon ['pɪdʒɪn] (*pl inv* OR -s) *n* Taube *die*.

pigeonhole ['pɪdʒɪnhəʊl] ◇ *n* [compartment] Fach *das* ◇ *vt fig* [classify] in eine Kategorie ein|ordnen.

piggybank ['pɪgɪbæŋk] *n* Sparschwein *das*.

pigheaded [,pɪg'hedɪd] *adj* stur.

pigment ['pɪgmənt] *n* Pigment *das*.

pigpen *n Am* = pigsty.

pigskin ['pɪgskɪn] *n* Schweinsleder *das*.

pigsty ['pɪgstaɪ], **pigpen** *Am* ['pɪgpen] *n lit & fig* Schweinestall *der*.

pigtail ['pɪgteɪl] *n* Zopf *der*.

pilchard ['pɪltʃəd] *n* Sardine *die*.

pile [paɪl] ◇ *n* - **1.** [heap] Haufen *der*; **a ~** OR **~s of money/work** *inf* ein Haufen Geld/ Arbeit - **2.** [neat stack] Stapel *der*, Stoß *der* - **3.** [of carpet, fabric] Flor *der* ◇ *vt* stapeln; **to be ~d high with sthg** mit etw voll gestapelt sein. ◆ **piles** *npl* MED Hämorrhoiden *pl*. ◆ **pile into** *vt fus inf* [car] sich zwängen in (+ A); [room] drängen in (+ A). ◆ **pile up** ◇ *vt sep* [books, boxes] auf|stapeln ◇ *vi* [accumulate] sich an|häufen.

pileup ['paɪlʌp] *n* Massenkarambolage *die*.

pilfer ['pɪlfə'] *vt & vi* stehlen.

pilgrim ['pɪlgrɪm] *n* Pilger *der*, -in *die*.

pilgrimage ['pɪlgrɪmɪdʒ] *n* Pilgerfahrt *die*.

pill [pɪl] *n* Pille *die*; [contraceptive]: **the ~** die Pille; **to be on the ~** die Pille nehmen.

pillage ['pɪlɪdʒ] *vt* plündern.

pillar ['pɪlə'] *n* Pfeiler *der*.

pillar box *n Br* Briefkasten *der*.

pillion ['pɪljən] *n* Soziussitz *der*; **to ride ~** auf dem Soziussitz mit|fahren.

pillow ['pɪləʊ] *n* - **1.** [for bed] Kopfkissen *das* - **2.** *Am* [on sofa, chair] Kissen *das*.

pillowcase ['pɪləʊkeɪs], **pillowslip** ['pɪləʊslɪp] *n* Kopfkissenbezug *der*.

pilot ['paɪlət] ◇ *n* - **1.** [of plane] Pilot *der*, -in *die* - **2.** NAUT Lotse *der* - **3.** TV Pilotfilm *der* ◇ *comp* [trial] Pilot- ◇ *vt* - **1.** [plane] führen, fliegen - **2.** NAUT lotsen - **3.** [scheme] testen.

pilot light *n* Zündflamme *die*.

pimp [pɪmp] *n inf* Zuhälter *der*.

pimple ['pɪmpl] *n* Pickel *der*.

pin [pɪn] ◇ *n* - **1.** [for sewing] Nadel *die*; **I've got ~s and needles in my feet** *fig* meine Füße sind eingeschlafen - **2.** [drawing pin] Reißzwecke *die*; [safety pin] Sicherheitsnadel *die* - **3.** [of plug] Kontaktstift *der* - **4.** TECH Bolzen *der*, Stift *der* - **5.** *Am* [brooch] Brosche *die*; [badge] Anstecknadel *die* ◇ *vt*: **to ~ sthg to** OR **on etw heften an (+ A); **to ~ sb to the**

wall/ground jn gegen die Wand/auf den Boden drücken; **to ~ the blame for sthg on sb** jm die Schuld an etw zulschieben. ➡ **pin down** vt sep **- 1.** [identify] bestimmen **- 2.** [force to make a decision] festlegen.

pinafore ['pɪnəfɔːr] n **- 1.** [apron] Schürze die **- 2.** Br [dress] Trägerkleid das.

pinball ['pɪnbɔːl] n (U) Flipper der.

pincers ['pɪnsəz] npl **- 1.** [tool] Kneifzange die **- 2.** [of crab, lobster] Schere die.

pinch [pɪntʃ] <> n **- 1.** [nip] Kneifen das **- 2.** [of salt, herbs etc] Prise die <> vt **- 1.** [nip] kneifen **- 2.** inf [steal] klauen. ➡ **at a pinch** Br, **in a pinch** Am adv zur Not.

pincushion ['pɪn‚kʊʃn] n Nadelkissen das.

pine [paɪn] <> n **- 1.** [tree] Kiefer die **- 2.** [wood] Kiefernholz das <> vi: **to ~ for** sich sehnen nach.

pineapple ['paɪnæpl] n Ananas die.

ping [pɪŋ] n [sound] Ping das.

pink [pɪŋk] <> adj rosa; **to go ~** erröten <> n [colour] Rosa das.

pinnacle ['pɪnəkl] n fig [of career, success] Höhepunkt der.

pinpoint ['pɪnpɔɪnt] vt bestimmen.

pin-striped [-‚straɪpt] adj Nadelstreifen-.

pint [paɪnt] n **- 1.** Br [unit of measurement] Pint das, = 0,568 l. **- 2.** Am [unit of measurement] Pint das, = 0,473 l. **- 3.** Br [beer]: **let's go for a ~** lass uns ein Bier trinken gehen; **a ~ of Guinness** ein großes (Glas) Guinness.

pioneer [‚paɪə'nɪər] n Pionier der.

pious ['paɪəs] adj **- 1.** [religious] fromm **- 2.** pej [sanctimonious] scheinheilig.

pip [pɪp] n **- 1.** [seed] Kern der **- 2.** Br: **the ~s** [on radio] das Zeitzeichen; [on public telephone] Warnton, der ertönt, wenn Geld nachgeworfen werden muss.

pipe [paɪp] <> n **- 1.** [for gas, water] Rohr das, Leitung die **- 2.** [for smoking] Pfeife die <> vt [liquid, gas] leiten. ➡ **pipes** npl MUS [bagpipes] Dudelsack der. ➡ **pipe down** vi inf still sein. ➡ **pipe up** vi inf sich (spontan) zu Wort melden.

pipe cleaner n Pfeifenreiniger der.

pipeline ['paɪplaɪn] n Pipeline die.

piper ['paɪpər] n MUS [on bagpipes] Dudelsackspieler der, -in die.

piping hot [‚paɪpɪŋ-] adj siedend heiß.

pirate ['paɪrət] <> adj [video, copy etc] Piraten-, Raub- <> n [sailor] Pirat der <> vt [copy illegally] Raubkopien machen von.

pirouette [‚pɪru'et] <> n Pirouette die <> vi Pirouetten drehen.

Pisces ['paɪsiːz] n Fische pl; **I'm (a) ~** ich bin Fisch.

piss [pɪs] vinf <> n [urine] Pisse die; **to have a ~** pissen gehen <> vi pissen.

pissed [pɪst] adj vinf **- 1.** Br [drunk] voll, besoffen **- 2.** Am [annoyed] stocksauer.

pissed off adj vinf stocksauer.

pistol ['pɪstl] n Pistole die.

piston ['pɪstən] n Kolben der.

pit [pɪt] <> n **- 1.** [large hole, coalmine] Grube die **- 2.** [for orchestra] Orchestergraben der **- 3.** Am [of fruit] Kern der <> vt: **to be ~ted against sb** [in game] gegen jn spielen (müssen); [in fight] gegen jn kämpfen (müssen). ➡ **pits** npl [in motor racing]: **the ~s** die Boxen pl.

pitch [pɪtʃ] <> n **- 1.** SPORT Feld das, Platz der **- 2.** MUS Tonhöhe die; [of voice] Stimmlage die; [of instrument] Tonlage die **- 3.** [level, degree] Ausmaß das **- 4.** [in market, on street] Standplatz der **- 5.** inf [sales talk] Verkaufsvortrag der **- 6.** [of roof] Neigung die <> vt **- 1.** [throw] werfen **- 2.** [set level of] ansetzen **- 3.** [camp, tent] aufschlagen <> vi **- 1.** [fall] fallen; **to ~ forward** nach vorne fallen **- 2.** [ship] stampfen; [plane] absacken.

pitch-black adj stockfinster.

pitcher ['pɪtʃər] n Am **- 1.** [jug] Krug der **- 2.** [in baseball] Pitcher der.

pitchfork ['pɪtʃfɔːk] n Mistgabel die.

pitfall ['pɪtfɔːl] n [hazard] Falle die.

pith [pɪθ] n [of fruit] weiße Haut.

pithy ['pɪθɪ] adj prägnant.

pitiful ['pɪtɪfʊl] adj **- 1.** [arousing pity] Mitleid erregend **- 2.** [arousing contempt] jämmerlich.

pitiless ['pɪtɪlɪs] adj erbarmungslos.

pit stop n Boxenstopp der.

pittance ['pɪtəns] n Hungerlohn der.

pity ['pɪtɪ] <> n **- 1.** [compassion] Mitleid das; **to take** OR **have ~ on sb** Mitleid mit jm haben **- 2.** [shame]: **it's a ~ (that)** ... (es ist) schade(, dass) ...; **what a ~!** wie schade! <> vt bemitleiden.

pivot ['pɪvət] n **- 1.** TECH [joint] Drehgelenk das **- 2.** fig [crux] Dreh- und Angelpunkt der.

pizza ['piːtsə] n Pizza die.

placard ['plækɑːd] n Plakat das.

placate [plə'keɪt] vt beschwichtigen.

place [pleɪs] <> n **- 1.** [location] Ort der; [spot, place in text & MATH] Stelle die; **~ of birth** Geburtsort; **to two decimal ~s** bis auf zwei Stellen nach dem Komma **- 2.** [home] Zuhause das; **let's go to my ~** gehen wir zu mir **- 3.** [post, vacancy] Stelle die **- 4.** [role, function] Rolle die **- 5.** [table setting] Gedeck das **- 6.** [instance]: **in the first ~** am Anfang; **why didn't you say so in the first ~?** warum hast du das nicht gleich OR direkt gesagt?; **in the first ~ ..., and in the second ~ ...** erstens ..., zweitens ... **- 7.** phr: **to take ~** stattfinden; **to take sb's ~** js Platz einlnehmen <> vt **- 1.** [put] stellen; [put flat] legen; **to ~ the blame on sb** jm die Schuld zulschieben; **to ~ an ad in the paper** eine Anzeige in die Zeitung setzen **- 2.** [identify] einlordnen **- 3.** [make]: **to ~ an order** COMM eine Bestellung aufgeben; **to ~ a bet on sthg** auf etw (D) wetten **- 4.** [be situated]: **the house is**

well ~d for the tube das Haus liegt ganz in der Nähe der U-Bahn; **how are we ~d for money/time?** wie viel Geld/Zeit haben wir? **- 5.** [in race]: **to be ~d** sich platzieren. ◆ **all over the place** *adv* überall. ◆ **in place** *adv* **- 1.** [in proper position] an seinem Platz **- 2.** [established, set up] eingerichtet. ◆ **in place of** *prep* anstatt (+ G). ◆ **out of place** *adv* **- 1.** [in wrong position] nicht an seinem Platz **- 2.** [unsuitable] unpassend.

place mat *n* Platzset *das*.

placement ['pleɪsmənt] *n* [work experience] Praktikum *das*.

placid ['plæsɪd] *adj* **- 1.** [person, child, animal] ausgeglichen **- 2.** [place] ruhig.

plagiarize, -ise ['pleɪdʒəraɪz] *vt* plagiieren.

plague [pleɪg] ◇ *n* **- 1.** MED Seuche *die;* (U) [specific disease] Pest *die* **- 2.** [nuisance] Plage *die* ◇ *vt* plagen; **to be ~d by bad luck** vom Pech verfolgt sein.

plaice [pleɪs] (*pl inv*) *n* Scholle *die*.

plain [pleɪn] ◇ *adj* **- 1.** [simple] einfach, schlicht; [paper] unliniert; [in colour] einfarbig; [unpatterned] uni; [yoghurt] Natur-; **in ~ clothes** in Zivil **- 2.** [clear] klar **- 3.** [blunt - statement, answer] unverblümt; **the ~ truth** die reine Wahrheit **- 4.** [absolute - madness, stupidity] absolut, schier **- 5.** [not pretty] unattraktiv ◇ *adv inf* [completely] einfach ◇ *n* GEOGR Ebene *die*.

plain chocolate *n Br* Bitterschokolade *die*.

plain-clothes *adj* in Zivil.

plainly ['pleɪnlɪ] *adv* **- 1.** [upset, angry] sichtlich; [remember, hear] deutlich **- 2.** [frankly] offen **- 3.** [simply] einfach, schlicht.

plaintiff ['pleɪntɪf] *n* Kläger *der,* -in *die*.

plait [plæt] ◇ *n* Zopf *der* ◇ *vt* flechten.

plan [plæn] ◇ *n* **- 1.** [gen] Plan *der;* **to make ~s** Pläne machen; **have you got any ~s for tonight?** hast du heute Abend etwas vor?; **to go according to ~** nach Plan verlaufen **- 2.** [of story, project] Konzept *das,* Entwurf *der* ◇ *vt* **- 1.** [organize] planen **- 2.** [intend]: **to ~ to do sthg** vorhaben, etw zu tun **- 3.** [design] entwerfen ◇ *vi* planen; **to ~ for sthg** Pläne für etw machen. ◆ **plan on** *vt fus:* **to ~ on doing sthg** vorhaben, etw zu tun.

plane [pleɪn] *n* **- 1.** [aircraft] Flugzeug *das* **- 2.** GEOM Ebene *die* **- 3.** *fig* [level] Niveau *das* **- 4.** [tool] Hobel *der* **- 5.** [tree] Platane *die*.

planet ['plænɪt] *n* Planet *der*.

plank [plæŋk] *n* [piece of wood] (langes) Brett.

planning ['plænɪŋ] *n* Planung *die*.

planning permission *n* (U) Baugenehmigung *die*.

plant [plɑːnt] ◇ *n* **- 1.** BOT Pflanze *die* **- 2.** [factory] Werk *das,* Fabrik *die* **- 3.** (U) [heavy machinery] Maschinen *pl* ◇ *vt* **- 1.** [tree, vegetable] pflanzen; [seed] säen; [field, garden] bepflanzen **- 2.** [place firmly] aufstellen; **he ~ed a kiss on her cheek** er gab

ihr einen Kuss auf die Wange **- 3.** [bomb, microphone, spy] platzieren, anbringen; [thought, idea] pflanzen, setzen.

plantation [plæn'teɪʃn] *n* **- 1.** [piece of land] Plantage *die* **- 2.** [of trees] Anpflanzung *die*.

plaque [plɑːk] *n* **- 1.** [plate] Gedenktafel *die* **- 2.** (U) [on teeth] Zahnbelag *der*.

plaster ['plɑːstə^r] ◇ *n* **- 1.** [for wall, ceiling] Putz *der* **- 2.** [for broken bones] Gips *der* **- 3.** *Br* [for cut]: **(sticking) ~** Pflaster *das* ◇ *vt* **- 1.** [wall, ceiling] verputzen **- 2.** [cover] pflastern.

plaster cast *n* **- 1.** [for broken bones] Gipsverband *der* **- 2.** [model, statue] Gipsform *die*.

plastered ['plɑːstəd] *adj inf* [drunk] besoffen.

plasterer ['plɑːstərə^r] *n* Putzer *der,* -in *die*.

plaster of paris *n* Gips *der*.

plastic ['plæstɪk] ◇ *adj* Plastik- ◇ *n* [material] Plastik *das*.

Plasticine® *Br* ['plæstɪsiːn], **play dough** *Am n* Plastilin *das*.

plastic surgery *n* plastische Chirurgie *die*.

plate [pleɪt] ◇ *n* **- 1.** ... to be ~d **with silver/gold** versilbert/vergoldet sein.

plateau ['plætəʊ] (*pl* -s OR -x [-z]) *n* **- 1.** GEOGR Plateau *das* **- 2.** *fig* [steady level]: **prices have reached a ~** die Preise haben sich stabilisiert.

plate-glass *adj* Spiegelglas-.

platform ['plætfɔːm] *n* **- 1.** [gen & COMPUT] Plattform *die;* [for speaker, performer] Podium *das* **- 2.** [at railway station] Bahnsteig *der;* **~ 12** Gleis 12.

platinum ['plætɪnəm] *n* Platin *das*.

platoon [plə'tuːn] *n* Zug *der*.

platter ['plætə^r] *n* [dish] Platte *die*.

plausible ['plɔːzəbl] *adj* [reason, excuse] plausibel; [person] überzeugend.

play [pleɪ] ◇ *n* **- 1.** [gen] Spiel *das;* **in ~** SPORT im Spiel; **out of ~** SPORT im Aus; **to come into ~** *fig* eine Rolle spielen; **~ on words** Wortspiel *das* **- 2.** [in theatre] Schauspiel *das,* Stück *das;* [on radio] Hörspiel *das;* [on television] Fernsehspiel *das* ◇ *vt* spielen; **to ~ sb/sthg** [opposing player or team] spielen gegen; **to ~ the piano** Klavier spielen; **to ~ a trick on sb** jm einen Streich spielen; **to ~ a part OR role in sthg** *fig* eine Rolle in etw (D) spielen; **to ~ it cool** so tun, als sei nichts gewesen ◇ *vi* spielen; **to ~ for time** versuchen, Zeit zu gewinnen; **to ~ safe** auf Nummer Sicher gehen. ◆ **play along** *vi:* **to ~ along (with sb)** sich (jm) vorübergehend fügen. ◆ **play down** *vt sep* herunterspielen. ◆ **play up** ◇ *vt sep* [emphasize] betonen ◇ *vi* [machine, part of body] Schwierigkeiten machen; [children] sich wie wild gebärden.

play-act *vi* schauspielern.

playboy ['pleɪbɔɪ] *n* Playboy *der*.

play dough *n Am* = Plasticine®.

player ['pleɪəʳ] *n* [gen] Spieler *der*, -in *die*.

playful ['pleɪfʊl] *adj* [comment] neckisch; [person, animal] verspielt.

playground ['pleɪgraʊnd] *n* [at school] Schulhof *der*; [in park] Spielplatz *der*.

playgroup ['pleɪgru:p] *n* Krabbelgruppe *die*.

playing card ['pleɪɪŋ-] *n* Spielkarte *die*.

playing field ['pleɪɪŋ-] *n* Sportplatz *der*.

playmate ['pleɪmeɪt] *n* Spielkamerad *der*, -in *die*.

play-off *n* Entscheidungsspiel *das*.

playpen ['pleɪpen] *n* Laufstall *der*.

playschool ['pleɪsku:l] *n* Krabbelgruppe *die*.

plaything ['pleɪθɪŋ] *n lit & fig* Spielzeug *das*.

playtime ['pleɪtaɪm] *n* (U) [at school]: **at ~ in** der großen Pause.

playwright ['pleɪraɪt] *n* Dramatiker *der*, -in *die*.

plc (*abbr of* public limited company) AG *die*.

plea [pli:] *n* - 1. [appeal] Appell *der* - 2. LAW Plädoyer *das*; **what's your ~?** wie plädieren Sie?

plead [pli:d] (*pt & pp* -ed OR pled) <> *vt* - 1. LAW plädieren; **to ~ guilty/not guilty** sich schuldig/nicht schuldig bekennen - 2. [ignorance] sich berufen auf (+ A) <> *vi* - 1. [beg] flehen; **to ~ with sb to do sthg** jn anflehen, etw zu tun; **to ~ for sthg** um etw flehen - 2. LAW: **to ~ sb's case** jn in einer Sache vertreten.

pleasant ['pleznt] *adj* angenehm; [smile] freundlich; [day] schön.

pleasantry ['plezntrɪ] *n*: **to exchange pleasantries** Nettigkeiten austauschen.

please [pli:z] <> *vt* gefallen (+ D); **there's no pleasing him** man kann ihm nichts recht machen; **he's hard to ~** er ist nicht leicht zufrieden zu stellen; **~ yourself!** wie du willst! <> *vi* gefallen; **may I? ~ ~ do!** darf ich? ~ bitte sehr!; **he does as he ~s** er macht, was ihm gefällt <> *adv* bitte; **yes, ~!** ja, bitte!

pleased [pli:zd] *adj* [happy] erfreut; [satisfied] zufrieden; **to be ~ about sthg** sich über etw (A) freuen; **to be ~ with sb/sthg** mit jm/etw zufrieden sein; **~ to meet you!** angenehm!

pleasing ['pli:zɪŋ] *adj* erfreulich.

pleasure ['pleʒəʳ] *n* - 1. [gen] Freude *die*; **with ~** gern(e); **it's a ~!, my ~!** gern geschehen! - 2. (U) [enjoyment] Vergnügen *das*.

pleat [pli:t] <> *n* Falte *die* <> *vt* fälteln.

pled [pled] *pt & pp* ▷ plead.

pledge [pledʒ] <> *n* - 1. [promise] Versprechen *das* - 2. [token] Pfand *das* <> *vt* - 1. [promise] versprechen - 2. [commit]: **to be ~d to sthg** zu etw verpflichtet werden; **to ~ o.s. to sthg** sich zu etw verpflichten - 3. [pawn] verpfänden.

plentiful ['plentɪfʊl] *adj* reichlich.

plenty ['plentɪ] <> *n* (U) Überfluss *der* <> *pron*: **we've got ~** wir haben mehr als genug; **five will be ~** fünf sind mehr als genug; **~ of** viel, eine Menge <> *adv* Am [very] sehr.

pliable ['plaɪəbl], **pliant** ['plaɪənt] *adj* - 1. [metal] biegsam; [material] geschmeidig - 2. [person] anpassungsfähig.

pliers ['plaɪəz] *npl* Zange *die*.

plight [plaɪt] *n* Elend *das*.

plimsoll ['plɪmsəl] *n Br* Turnschuh *der*.

plinth [plɪnθ] *n* Plinthe *die*.

plod [plɒd] *vi* - 1. [walk slowly] schwerfällig gehen - 2. [work slowly] sich abmühen.

plonk [plɒŋk] *n* (U) Br inf [wine] billiger Wein. ◆ **plonk down** *vt sep inf* hinknallen.

plot [plɒt] <> *n* - 1. [conspiracy] Komplott *das* - 2. [of story, film, play] Handlung *die* - 3. [of land] Stück *das* Land; [allotment] Parzelle *die* <> *vt* - 1. [conspire] planen; **to ~ to do sthg** gemeinsam planen, etw zu tun - 2. [chart] einzeichnen; MATH aufzeichnen <> *vi*: **to ~ (against)** sich verschwören (gegen).

plough Br, **plow** Am [plaʊ] <> *n* Pflug *der* <> *vt* pflügen; **to ~ money into sthg** Geld in etw (A) stecken <> *vi* [crash]: **to ~ into sthg** in etw (A) rasen.

ploughman's ['plaʊmənz] (*pl inv*) *n* Br: **~ (lunch)** Pubmahlzeit aus Käse, Brot und Pickles.

plow *etc n & vb Am* = plough *etc*.

ploy [plɔɪ] *n* Trick *der*.

pluck [plʌk] <> *vt* - 1. [flower, fruit] pflücken - 2. [pull] ziehen - 3. [chicken] rupfen - 4. [eyebrows, guitar, harp] zupfen <> *n* (U) *dated* Mut *der*. ◆ **pluck up** *vt sep*: **to ~ up the courage to do sthg** den Mut aufbringen, etw zu tun.

plug [plʌg] <> *n* - 1. ELEC Stecker *der*; [socket] Steckdose *die* - 2. [for bath, sink] Stöpsel *der* <> *vt* - 1. [hole, ears] verstopfen - 2. *inf* [advertise] Schleichwerbung machen für. ◆ **plug in** *vt sep* ELEC einstecken.

plughole ['plʌghəʊl] *n* Abfluss *der*.

plum [plʌm] *n* [fruit] Pflaume *die*.

plumb [plʌm] <> *adv* - 1. Br [exactly] genau; **~ in the middle** genau in der/die Mitte - 2. Am [completely] völlig, komplett <> *vt*: **to ~ the depths of sthg** den Tiefpunkt von etw erreichen.

plumber ['plʌməʳ] *n* Klempner *der*.

plumbing ['plʌmɪŋ] *n* (U) - 1. [fittings] Leitungen *pl* - 2. [work] Installieren *das* von Sanitäranlagen.

plume [plu:m] *n* - 1. [on bird, hat] Feder *die*; [on helmet] Federbusch *der* - 2. [column]: **a ~ of smoke** eine Rauchfahne.

plummet ['plʌmɪt] *vi* - 1. [plane, bird] (senkrecht) hinunterstürzen - 2. [prices, value, shares] rapide fallen.

plump [plʌmp] ⇔ adj rundlich, mollig ⇔ vi: **to - for sthg** sich für etw entscheiden. ➣ **plump up** vt sep aufschütteln.

plunder ['plʌndə] vt plündern.

plunge [plʌndʒ] ⇔ n - 1. [rapid decrease] Sturz der - 2. [dive] Sprung der; [head-on] Kopfsprung der; **to take the -** den Schritt wagen ⇔ vt - 1. [immerse]: **to - sthg into sthg** etw in etw (A) werfen - 2. [thrust]: **to - sthg into sthg** etw in etw (A) treiben; **-d into darkness** in Dunkelheit getaucht ⇔ vi - 1. [dive] springen; [out of control] stürzen - 2. [prices, value] fallen.

plunger ['plʌndʒə] n [for sinks, drains] Saugglocke die.

pluperfect [ˌpluːˈpɜːfɪkt] n: **- (tense)** Plusquamperfekt das.

plural ['plʊərəl] ⇔ adj GRAMM im Plural ⇔ n Plural der; **in the -** im Plural.

plus [plʌs] (pl -es OR -ses) ⇔ adj - 1. [over, more than]: **30 -** mehr als 30, über 30 - 2. [in school marks] plus ⇔ n - 1. MATH [sign] Pluszeichen das - 2. inf [bonus] Plus das ⇔ prep - 1. MATH plus, und - 2. [as well as] und ⇔ conj [moreover] und (außerdem).

plush [plʌʃ] adj luxuriös.

plus sign n Pluszeichen das.

Pluto ['pluːtəʊ] n [planet] Pluto der.

plutonium [pluːˈtəʊnɪəm] n Plutonium das.

ply [plaɪ] vt - 1. [work at]: **to - a trade** ein Gewerbe betreiben - 2.: **to - sb with drink** jm Alkohol aufdrängen; **to - sb with questions** jn mit Fragen bedrängen.

-ply [plaɪ] suffix: **four-** [wood] vierschichtig; [wool] vierfädig.

plywood ['plaɪwʊd] n Sperrholz das.

p.m., pm (abbr of post meridiem) nachmittags; **at 9 -** um 21 Uhr OR 9 Uhr abends.

PM n abbr of prime minister.

PMT n abbr of premenstrual tension.

pneumatic [njuːˈmætɪk] adj pneumatisch.

pneumatic drill n Pressluftbohrer der.

pneumonia [njuːˈməʊnɪə] n (U) Lungenentzündung die.

poach [pəʊtʃ] ⇔ vt - 1. [hunt illegally] wildern - 2. [idea] kopieren - 3. [egg] pochieren ⇔ vi wildern.

poacher ['pəʊtʃə] n [person] Wilderer der.

poaching ['pəʊtʃɪŋ] n Wildern das.

PO Box n abbr of Post Office Box.

pocket ['pɒkɪt] ⇔ n - 1. [in clothes] Tasche die; **to be out of -** draufzahlen; **to pick sb's -** jm etwas (aus der Tasche) stehlen - 2. [of warm air, mineral] Einschluss der; **- of resistance** Widerstandsnest das - 3. [of snooker, pool table] Loch das ⇔ adj Taschen- ⇔ vt einlstecken.

pocketbook ['pɒkɪtbʊk] n - 1. [notebook] Notizbuch das - 2. Am [handbag] Handtasche die.

pocketknife ['pɒkɪtnaɪf] (pl -knives [-naɪvz]) n Taschenmesser das.

pocket money n Taschengeld das.

pod [pɒd] n [of plants] Hülse die.

podgy ['pɒdʒɪ] adj inf pummelig.

podia ['pəʊdɪə] npl ⇨ podium.

podiatrist [pəˈdaɪətrɪst] n Am Fußpfleger der, -in die.

podium ['pəʊdɪəm] (pl -diums OR -dia) n Podium das.

poem ['pəʊɪm] n Gedicht das.

poet ['pəʊɪt] n Dichter der, -in die.

poetic [pəʊˈetɪk] adj poetisch.

poetry ['pəʊɪtrɪ] n (U) [poems] Dichtung die.

poignant ['pɔɪnjənt] adj [moving] ergreifend.

point [pɔɪnt] ⇔ n - 1. [tip] Spitze die - 2. [in discussion, debate] Punkt der; **to make a -** eine Anmerkung machen; **to make one's -** seinen Standpunkt deutlich machen - 3. [meaning] Sinn der; **you've missed the - of what he is trying to say** du hast nicht verstanden, worauf er hinauswill; **to get OR come to the -** zur Sache kommen; **that's beside the -** das tut hier nichts zur Sache - 4. [feature]: **good OR strong -** Stärke die; **bad OR weak -** Schwäche die - 5. [purpose] Zweck der; **there's no -** es hat keinen Sinn - 6. MATH Komma das; **five - seven** fünf Komma sieben - 7. [in scores] Punkt der - 8. Br ELEC Steckdose die - 9. Am [full stop] Punkt der - 10. phr: **to make a - of doing sthg** Wert darauf legen, etw zu tun ⇔ vt: **to - sthg (at)** etw richten (auf (+ A)) ⇔ vi - 1. [person]: **to - at OR to** zeigen auf (+ A) - 2. fig [evidence, facts]: **to - to sb/sthg** auf jn/etw hinlweisen. ➣ **points** npl Br RAIL Weiche die. ➣ **on the point of** prep: **to be on the - of doing sthg** im Begriff sein, etw zu tun; **I was on the - of going** ich wollte gerade gehen. ➣ **up to a point** adv bis zu einem gewissen Punkt. ➣ **point out** vt sep - 1. [indicate] zeigen - 2. [call attention to] hinlweisen auf (+ A).

point-blank adv - 1. [directly] direkt; [ask] geradeheraus; [refuse] rundweg - 2. [shoot] aus nächster Nähe.

pointed ['pɔɪntɪd] adj - 1. [sharp] spitz - 2. [meaningful] betont; [remark] spitz.

pointer ['pɔɪntə] n - 1. [tip] Hinweis der - 2. [needle on dial] Zeiger der - 3. [stick] Zeigestock der - 4. COMPUT Mauszeiger der.

pointless ['pɔɪntlɪs] adj zwecklos, sinnlos.

point of view (pl points of view) n [attitude] Standpunkt der.

poise [pɔɪz] n (U) [composure] Selbstsicherheit die.

poised [pɔɪzd] adj - 1. [ready] bereit; **to be - to do sthg** bereit sein, etw zu tun; **to be - for sthg** bereit sein für etw OR zu etw - 2. [composed] gefasst.

poison ['pɔɪzn] ⇔ n Gift das ⇔ vt - 1. [gen]

vergiften - 2. *fig* [corrupt] verschmutzen - 3. [atmosphere, water] verderben.

poisoning ['pɔɪznɪŋ] *n* Vergiftung *die*.

poisonous ['pɔɪznəs] *adj* [gen] giftig.

poke [pəʊk] <> *vt* - 1. [with finger, stick] stoßen; **to ~ sb in the ribs** jm einen Stoß in die Rippen geben - 2. [thrust] stecken; **he ~d his head round the door** er steckte den Kopf zur Tür herein - 3. [fire] schüren <> *vi:* **to ~ out of** hervorlschauen aus. **◆ poke about, poke around** *vi inf* herumlstochern.

poker ['pəʊkə'] *n* - 1. [game] Poker *das* - 2. [for fire] Schürhaken *der*.

poker-faced [-ˌfeɪst] *adj* mit einem Pokerface.

poky ['pəʊkɪ] *adj pej* eng.

Poland ['pəʊlənd] *n* Polen *nt*.

polar ['pəʊlə'] *adj* GEOGR polar.

Polaroid® ['pəʊlərɔɪd] *n* - 1. [camera] Polaroidkamera® *die* - 2. [photograph] Polaroidfoto *das*.

pole [pəʊl] *n* - 1. [for electricity] Pfahl *der*; [for flag] Mast *der*; [for skiing] Stock *der* - 2. GEOGR & ELEC Pol *der*.

Pole [pəʊl] *n* Pole *der*, -lin *die*.

pole vault *n* **the ~** der Stabhochsprung.

police [pə'liːs] <> *npl* - 1. [police force] **the ~** die Polizei - 2. [policemen] Polizisten *pl* <> *vt* [area] kontrollieren.

police car *n* Streifenwagen *der*.

police constable *n Br* Wachtmeister *der*, -in *die*.

police force *n* Polizei *die*.

policeman [pə'liːsmən] (*pl* -men [-mən]) *n* Polizist *der*.

police officer *n* Polizeibeamte *der*, -tin *die*.

police station *n Br* Polizeiwache *die*.

policewoman [pə'liːsˌwʊmən] (*pl* -women [-ˌwɪmɪn]) *n* Polizistin *die*.

policy ['pɒləsɪ] *n* - 1. [plan] Politik *die* - 2. [for insurance] Police *die*.

polio ['pəʊlɪəʊ] *n* (U) Kinderlähmung *die*.

polish ['pɒlɪʃ] <> *n* - 1. [cleaning material] Politur *die;* **window ~** Glasreiniger *der* - 2. [shine] Glanz *der;* [of furniture] Politur *die* - 3. *fig* [of performance] Brillanz *die;* [of style, manners] Schliff *der* <> *vt* - 1. [shine] polieren - 2. *fig* [perfect]: **to ~ sthg (up)** etw verfeinern. **◆ polish off** *vt sep inf* - 1. [meal] verputzen - 2. [job] schnell erledigen; [book] verschlingen.

Polish ['pəʊlɪʃ] <> *adj* polnisch <> *n* [language] Polnisch(e) *das*.

polished ['pɒlɪʃt] *adj* - 1. [surface] poliert - 2. [person, manners] geschliffen - 3. [performance] brilliant.

polite [pə'laɪt] *adj* höflich.

political [pə'lɪtɪkl] *adj* politisch.

politically correct [pə'lɪtɪklɪ-] *adj* politisch korrekt.

politician [ˌpɒlɪ'tɪʃn] *n* Politiker *der*, -in *die*.

politics ['pɒlətɪks] <> *n* (U) Politik *die*

<> *npl* - 1. [personal beliefs] politische Ansichten - 2. [of a group, area] Politik *die*.

poll [pəʊl] <> *n* - 1. [election] Wahl *die* - 2. [survey] Umfrage *die* <> *vt* - 1. [people] befragen - 2. [votes] erhalten. **◆ polls** *npl:* **to go to the ~s** wählen gehen.

pollen ['pɒlən] *n* Blütenstaub *der*.

polling booth ['pəʊlɪŋ-] *n* Wahlkabine *die*.

polling day ['pəʊlɪŋ-] *n Br* Wahltag *der*.

polling station ['pəʊlɪŋ-] *n* Wahllokal *das*.

pollute [pə'luːt] *vt* verschmutzen.

pollution [pə'luːʃn] *n* Verschmutzung *die*.

polo ['pəʊləʊ] *n* Polo *das*.

polo neck *n Br* - 1. [collar] Rollkragen *der* - 2. [jumper] Rollkragenpullover *der*.

polo shirt *n* Polohemd *das*.

polyethylene *n Am* = polythene.

polystyrene [ˌpɒlɪ'staɪriːn] *n* Styropor® *das*.

polytechnic [ˌpɒlɪ'teknɪk] *n Br* Polytechnikum *das*, ≈ technische Hochschule.

polythene *Br* ['pɒlɪθiːn], **polyethylene** *Am* [ˌpɒlɪ'eθɪliːn] *n* Polyethylen *das*.

polythene bag *n Br* Plastiktüte *die*.

pomegranate ['pɒmɪˌgrænɪt] *n* Granatapfel *der*.

pomp [pɒmp] *n* Pomp *der*.

pompom ['pɒmpɒm] *n* Pompon *der*.

pompous ['pɒmpəs] *adj* [pretentious] aufgeblasen; [speech] geschwollen.

pond [pɒnd] *n* Teich *der*.

ponder ['pɒndə'] *vt & vi* nachldenken; **to ~ on** OR **over sthg** über etw (A) nachldenken.

ponderous ['pɒndərəs] *adj* schwerfällig.

pong [pɒŋ] *Br inf n* Gestank *der*, Mief *der*.

pontoon [pɒn'tuːn] *n* - 1. [bridge] Ponton *der* - 2. *Br* [game] Siebzehnundvier *der*.

pony ['pəʊnɪ] *n* Pony *das*.

ponytail ['pəʊnɪteɪl] *n* Pferdeschwanz *der*.

poodle ['puːdl] *n* Pudel *der*.

pool [puːl] <> *n* - 1. [of water, blood] Lache *die;* [of light] Lichtkegel *der;* [of rain] Pfütze *die* - 2. [swimming pool] Swimmingpool *der;* [small pond] Teich *der* - 3. [game] Poolbillard *das* <> *vt* zusammenllegen. **◆ pools** *npl Br:* **the ~s** das Fußballtoto.

poor [pɔː'] <> *adj* - 1. [impoverished, unfortunate] arm - 2. [not very good] schlecht <> *npl:* **the ~** die Armen *pl*.

poorly ['pɔːlɪ] <> *adj Br inf* krank <> *adv* [badly] schlecht.

pop [pɒp] <> *n* - 1. [music] Pop *der* - 2. *inf* [fizzy drink] Brause *die* - 3. *esp Am inf* [father] Papa *der* - 4. [noise] Knall *der* <> *vt* - 1. [balloon, bubble] platzen, zerplatzen - 2. [put] stecken <> *vi* [balloon] platzen; [cork] knallen; **my ears are ~ping** ich habe Druck auf den Ohren. **◆ pop in** *vi* [visit] vorbeilschauen. **◆ pop up** *vi* aufltauchen.

pop concert *n* Popkonzert *das*.

popcorn ['pɒpkɔːn] *n* Popcorn *das*.

pope [pəʊp] *n* Papst *der*.

pop group *n* Popgruppe *die*.

poplar ['pɒplə'] *n* Pappel *die*.

poppy ['pɒpɪ] *n* Mohn *der*.

Popsicle® ['pɒpsɪkl] *n Am* Eis *das* am Stiel.

popular ['pɒpjʊlə'] *adj* **- 1.** [well-liked] populär, beliebt **- 2.** [common] weit verbreitet **- 3.** [newspaper, politics] volksnah; [entertainment] volkstümlich; [debate] öffentlich.

popularize, -ise ['pɒpjʊləraɪz] *vt* **- 1.** [make popular] popularisieren **- 2.** [simplify] vereinfachen.

population [ˌpɒpjʊ'leɪʃn] *n* [gen] Bevölkerung *die*.

porcelain ['pɔːsəlɪn] *n* Porzellan *das*.

porch [pɔːtʃ] *n* **- 1.** [entrance] Windfang *der* **- 2.** *Am* [veranda] Veranda *die*.

porcupine ['pɔːkjʊpaɪn] *n* Stachelschwein *das*.

pore [pɔː'] *n* Pore *die*. ➡ **pore over** *vt fus* (eingehend) studieren.

pork [pɔːk] *n* Schweinefleisch *das*.

pork pie *n* Schweinefleischpastete *die*.

pornography [pɔː'nɒgrəfɪ] *n* Pornografie *die*.

porous ['pɔːrəs] *adj* porös.

porridge ['pɒrɪdʒ] *n* Haferbrei *der*.

port [pɔːt] *n* **- 1.** [coastal town] Hafenstadt *die*; [harbour] Hafen *der* **- 2.** NAUT Backbord *das* **- 3.** [drink] Portwein *der* **- 4.** COMPUT Anschluss *der*.

portable ['pɔːtəbl] *adj* tragbar.

porter ['pɔːtə'] *n* **- 1.** *Br* [at hotel, museum] Pförtner *der*, Portier *der* **- 2.** [at station, airport] Gepäckträger *der* **- 3.** *Am* [on train] Schlafwagenschaffner *der*.

portfolio [ˌpɔːt'fəʊlɪəʊ] *(pl* -s) *n* **- 1.** [case] Aktentasche *die* **- 2.** [sample of work] Mappe *die* **- 3.** FIN Portefeuille *das*.

porthole ['pɔːthəʊl] *n* Bullauge *das*.

portion ['pɔːʃn] *n* **- 1.** [part, share] Teil *der* **- 2.** [of food] Portion *die*.

portrait ['pɔːtreɪt] *n lit & fig* Porträt *das*.

portray [pɔː'treɪ] *vt* **- 1.** [gen] darstellen **- 2.** [subj: artist] porträtieren.

Portugal ['pɔːtʃʊgl] *n* Portugal *nt*.

Portuguese [ˌpɔːtʃʊ'giːz] *(pl inv)* ◇ *adj* portugiesisch ◇ *n* **- 1.** [person] Portugiese *der*, -sin *die* **- 2.** [language] Portugiesisch(e) *das* ◇ *npl*: **the ~** die Portugiesen *pl*.

pose [pəʊz] ◇ *n* **- 1.** [position] Haltung *die* **- 2.** *pej* [pretence] Pose *die* ◇ *vt* **- 1.** [problem, danger, threat] darstellen **- 2.** [a question] stellen ◇ *vi* **- 1.** [for photo] posieren; [for painting] Modell stehen **- 2.** *pej* [behave affectedly] posieren **- 3.** [pretend to be]: **to ~ as a tourist** sich als Tourist ausgeben.

posh [pɒʃ] *adj inf* nobel.

position [pə'zɪʃn] ◇ *n* **- 1.** [place, situation] Lage *die* **- 2.** [of plane, ship] Position *die* **- 3.** [of body] Haltung *die* **- 4.** [setting, rank] Stellung *die* **- 5.** [in race, combat] Platz *der* **- 6.** [job] Stelle *die* **- 7.** [stance, opinion]: **~ on sthg** Haltung *die* gegenüber etw *(D)* ◇ *vt* positionieren.

positive ['pɒzətɪv] *adj* **- 1.** [gen] positiv **- 2.** [sure, certain] sicher; **to be ~ about sthg** sich einer Sache *(G)* sicher sein **- 3.** [evidence, fact] definitiv **- 4.** [for emphasis] total.

possess [pə'zes] *vt* besitzen; **what ~ed you to do that?** was ist in Sie gefahren, dass Sie das gemacht haben?

possession [pə'zeʃn] *n* Besitz *der*. ➡ **possessions** *npl* Habe *die*; **his personal ~s** all seine Sachen.

possessive [pə'zesɪv] ◇ *adj* **- 1.** *pej* [person] besitzergreifend **- 2.** GRAMM Possessiv- ◇ *n* GRAMM Possessivfunktion *die*.

possibility [ˌpɒsə'bɪlətɪ] *n* Möglichkeit *die*.

possible ['pɒsəbl] *adj* möglich; **would it be ~ for me to ...?** könnte ich vielleicht ...?; **as soon as ~** so bald wie möglich; **as much as ~** so viel wie möglich; **if ~** wenn möglich.

possibly ['pɒsəblɪ] *adv* **- 1.** [perhaps] möglicherweise **- 2.** [conceivably] möglich; **I'll do all I ~ can** ich werde mein Möglichstes tun; **I can't ~ do that** das kann ich unmöglich tun.

post [pəʊst] ◇ *n* **- 1.** [service, letters, delivery] Post *die*; **by ~** per Post **- 2.** [pole] Pfosten *der*; **to pip sb at the ~** in race] jn knapp schlagen; *fig* jm etw vor der Nase weg|schnappen **- 3.** [job & MIL] Posten *der* ◇ *vt* **- 1.** [by mail] per OR mit der Post schicken **- 2.** [employee] versetzen.

postage ['pəʊstɪdʒ] *n* Porto *das*; **~ and packing** Porto und Verpackung.

postal ['pəʊstl] *adj* Post-, postalisch.

postal order *n* Postanweisung *die*.

postbox ['pəʊstbɒks] *n Br* Briefkasten *der*.

postcard ['pəʊstkɑːd] *n* Postkarte *die*.

postcode ['pəʊstkəʊd] *n Br* Postleitzahl *die*.

postdate [ˌpəʊst'deɪt] *vt* vor|datieren.

poster ['pəʊstə'] *n* Poster *das*, Plakat *das*.

poste restante [ˌpəʊst'restɑːnt] *n (U) esp Br*: **to send sthg ~** etw postlagernd schicken.

posterior [pɒ'stɪərɪə'] ◇ *adj* [rear] hintere, -r, -s ◇ *n hum* Hinterteil *das*.

postgraduate [ˌpəʊst'grædʒʊət] ◇ *adj* [studies, course] Aufbau- ◇ *n*: **~ (student)** Student, der ein Aufbaustudium absolviert.

posthumous ['pɒstjʊməs] *adj* postum.

postman ['pəʊstmən] *(pl* -men [-mən]) *n* Briefträger *der*, Postbote *der*.

postmark ['pəʊstmɑːk] ◇ *n* Poststempel *der* ◇ *vt* stempeln.

postmortem [ˌpəʊst'mɔːtəm] *n* **- 1.** [autopsy]: **~ (examination)** Obduktion *die* **- 2.** *fig* [analysis] Analyse *die*.

post office *n* Post *die*.

post office box *n* Postfach *das*.

postpone [ˌpəʊst'pəʊn] *vt* verschieben; [decision] auf|schieben.

postscript ['pəʊstskrɪpt] *n* [to letter] Postskriptum *das*.

posture ['pɒstʃə'] *n lit & fig* Haltung *die.*

postwar [ˌpəʊst'wɔː'] *adj* Nachkriegs-.

posy ['pəʊzɪ] *n* Blumensträußchen *das.*

pot [pɒt] <> *n* **- 1.** [for cooking, flowers] Topf *der* **- 2.** [for tea, coffee] Kanne *die* **- 3.** [for paint] Büchse *die;* [for jam] Glas *das* **- 4.** (U) *drugs sl* [cannabis] Hasch *das* <> *vt* [plant] einltopfen.

potassium [pə'tæsɪəm] *n* Kalium *das.*

potato [pə'teɪtəʊ] (*pl* -es) *n* Kartoffel *die.*

potato peeler [-ˌpiːlə'] *n* Kartoffelschäler *der.*

potent ['pəʊtənt] *adj* **- 1.** [argument] stichhaltig **- 2.** [drink, drug] stark.

potential [pə'tenʃl] <> *adj* potenziell <> *n* (U) [of person] Potenzial *das;* **to have ~** [person] das Potenzial haben; [scheme, plan, company, business] entwicklungsfähig sein.

potentially [pə'tenʃəlɪ] *adv* potenziell.

pothole ['pɒthəʊl] *n* **- 1.** [in road] Schlagloch *das* **- 2.** [underground] Höhle *die.*

potholing ['pɒtˌhəʊlɪŋ] *n Br* Höhlenforschung *die;* **to go ~** eine Höhle erforschen (gehen).

potion ['pəʊʃn] *n* Trank *der.*

potluck [ˌpɒt'lʌk] *n:* **to take ~** aufs Geratewohl auslwählen; [at meal] mit dem vorlieb nehmen, was gerade da ist.

potshot ['pɒtˌʃɒt] *n:* **to take a ~ at sthg** aufs Geratewohl auf etw (A) schießen.

potted ['pɒtɪd] *adj* **- 1.** [grown in pot] Topf- **- 2.** [meat] eingemacht.

potter ['pɒtə'] <> **potter about, potter around** *vi Br* [do minor work] herumlwerkeln; [work slowly] herumltrödeln.

pottery ['pɒtərɪ] *n* **- 1.** (U) [clay objects] Töpferwaren *pl* **- 2.** [craft] Töpfern *das.*

potty ['pɒtɪ] *Br inf* <> *adj* verrückt; **to be ~ about sb/sthg** nach jm/etw verrückt sein <> *n* Töpfchen *das.*

pouch [paʊtʃ] *n* Beutel *der.*

poultry ['pəʊltrɪ] <> *n* [meat] Geflügel *das* <> *npl* [birds] Geflügel *das.*

pounce [paʊns] *vi:* **to ~ on** OR **upon** sich stürzen auf (+ A).

pound [paʊnd] <> *n* **- 1.** *Br* [unit of money, currency system] Pfund *das* **- 2.** [unit of weight] ≈ Pfund *das* (= 454g) **- 3.** [for cars] Abstellplatz *der* (für abgeschleppte Fahrzeuge); [for dogs] Asyl *das* <> *vt* [pulverize] pulverisieren <> *vi* **- 1.** [strike loudly]: **to ~ on sthg** [wall, door] an OR gegen etw (A) hämmern; [table] auf etw (A) hämmern **- 2.** [beat, throb - heart] pochen; [- head] brummen.

pound coin *n* Einpfundmünze *die.*

pound sterling <> *n* Pfund *das* Sterling.

pour [pɔː'] <> *vt:* **to ~ sthg (into sthg)** [liquid] etw (in etw (A)) gießen; [grain, sugar] etw (in etw (A)) schütten; **to ~ sb a drink, to ~ a drink for sb** jm einen Drink einlgießen <> *vi lit & fig* strömen; **sweat was ~ing off him** ihm lief der Schweiß herunter <> *v impers* [rain hard] gießen; **it was ~ing (with rain)** es goss (wie aus Eimern) <> **pour in** *vi* (in großen Mengen) einltreffen. <> **pour out** *vt sep* **- 1.** [from container] auslschütten **- 2.** [drink] einlschenken.

pouring ['pɔːrɪŋ] *adj* [rain] strömend.

pout [paʊt] *vi* schmollen.

poverty ['pɒvətɪ] *n* (U) [hardship] Armut *die.*

poverty-stricken [-ˌstrɪkən] *adj* verarmt.

powder ['paʊdə'] <> *n* [for baking, washing] Pulver *das;* [for face, body] Puder *der* <> *vt* [face, body] pudern.

powder compact *n* Puderdose *die.*

powdered ['paʊdəd] *adj* **- 1.** [in powder form]: **~ milk** Trockenmilch *die;* **~ eggs** Trockenei *das* **- 2.** [covered in powder] gepudert.

powder puff *n* Puderquaste *die.*

powder room *n* Damentoilette *die.*

power ['paʊə'] <> *n* **- 1.** (U) [control, influence] Macht *die;* **to be in ~** an der Macht sein; **to come to ~** an die Macht kommen; **to take ~** die Macht übernehmen **- 2.** [ability, capacity] Vermögen *das,* Fähigkeit *die;* **to be (with)in one's ~** to do sthg in js Macht liegen, etw zu tun **- 3.** [legal authority] Macht *die;* **to have the ~ to do sthg** das Recht haben, etw zu tun **- 4.** (U) [strength] Stärke *die* **- 5.** (U) TECH [energy] Energie *die* **- 6.** (U) [electricity] Strom *der* **- 7.** [powerful person, group] Macht *die* <> *vt* [machine] anltreiben.

powerboat ['paʊəbəʊt] *n* Rennboot *das.*

power cut *n* Stromsperre *die.*

power failure *n* Stromausfall *der.*

powerful ['paʊəfʊl] *adj* **- 1.** [influential] mächtig **- 2.** [strong] kräftig; [drug, smell] stark; [blow, kick] kraftvoll; [machine] leistungsstark **- 3.** [very convincing, very moving - piece of writing, speech] überzeugend; [- work of art] überwältigend.

powerless ['paʊəlɪs] *adj* machtlos; **he was ~ to help** es stand nicht in seiner Macht zu helfen.

power point *n Br* Steckdose *die.*

power station *n* Kraftwerk *das.*

power steering *n* Servolenkung *die.*

pp (*abbr of* per procurationem) pp.

p & p (*abbr of* postage and packing) *n* Post- und Verpackung *die.*

PR *n* **- 1.** *abbr of* proportional representation **- 2.** *abbr of* public relations.

practicable ['præktɪkəbl] *adj* durchführbar.

practical ['præktɪkl] <> *adj* **- 1.** [gen] praktisch **- 2.** [practicable] durchführbar, umsetzbar <> *n* Praktikum *das.*

practicality [ˌpræktɪ'kælətɪ] *n* Praxisbezogenheit *die.*

practical joke *n* Streich *der.*

practically ['præktıklı] *adv* - **1.** [sensibly] praktisch - **2.** [almost] fast.

practice, practise *Am* ['præktıs] *n* - **1.** *(U)* [training] Übung *die*; [for sport] Training *das*; [for music] Üben *das*; **to be out of ~** aus der Übung sein - **2.** [training session - of choir] Probe *die*; [- of sport] Training *das* - **3.** [implementation]: **to put sthg into ~** etw in die Praxis umsetzen; **in ~** [in fact] in Wirklichkeit, tatsächlich - **4.** [habit, regular activity - of group] Brauch *der*; [- of person] Gewohnheit *die* - **5.** [business] Praxis *die*.

practicing *adj Am* = practising.

practise, practice *Am* ['præktıs] <> *vt* - **1.** [musical instrument, movement in sport] üben; [foreign language] sprechen - **2.** [customs, beliefs] ausüben - **3.** [do as profession] praktizieren <> *vi* - **1.** [train] üben - **2.** [doctor, lawyer] praktizieren.

practising, practicing *Am* ['præktısıŋ] *adj* praktizierend.

Prague [prɑːg] *n* Prag *nt*.

prairie ['preərı] *n* Prärie *die*.

praise [preız] <> *n* Lob *das*; **to sing sb's ~s** ein Loblied auf jn singen <> *vt* loben.

praiseworthy ['preız‚wɜːðı] *adj* lobenswert.

pram [præm] *n Br* Kinderwagen *der*.

prance [prɑːns] *vi* - **1.** [vain person] (heruml)stolzieren; [child] herumlhüpfen - **2.** [horse] tänzeln.

prank [præŋk] *n* Streich *der*.

prawn [prɔːn] *n* Garnele *die*.

pray [preı] *vi* RELIG beten; **to ~ to God** zu Gott beten.

prayer [preə^r] *n* - **1.** *(U)* [act of praying] Beten *das*, Gebet *das* - **2.** [set of words] Gebet *das* - **3.** *fig* [strong hope] starke Hoffnung.

prayer book *n* Gebetsbuch *das*.

preach [priːtʃ] <> *vt lit & fig* predigen <> *vi* - **1.** RELIG predigen - **2.** *pej* [pontificate]: **to ~ (at sb)** (jm) eine Predigt halten.

preacher ['priːtʃə^r] *n* Prediger *der*, -in *die*.

precarious [prı'keərıəs] *adj* wackelig; [situation] prekär.

precaution [prı'kɔːʃn] *n* Vorsichtsmaßnahme *die*.

precede [prı'siːd] *vt* vorauslgehen (+ *D*).

precedence ['presıdəns] *n*: **to take ~ over sb/sthg** den Vorrang vor jm/gegenüber etw haben.

precedent ['presıdənt] *n* Präzedenzfall *der*.

precinct ['priːsıŋkt] *n* - **1.** *Br* [for pedestrians] Fußgängerzone *die*; [for shopping] verkehrsfreies Einkaufsviertel - **2.** *Am* [district] Bezirk *der*; **police ~** Polizeirevier *das*.
➤ **precincts** *npl* [around building] Umgebung *die*, Bereich *der*.

precious ['preʃəs] *adj* - **1.** [gen] kostbar - **2.** *inf iron* [damned] verflixt, verdammt - **3.** [affected] affektiert.

precipice ['presıpıs] *n* Steilwand *die*.

precise [prı'saıs] *adj* genau.

precisely [prı'saıslı] *adv* genau.

precision [prı'sıʒn] *n (U)* Genauigkeit *die*.

preclude [prı'kluːd] *vt fml* [possibility, misunderstanding] ausschließen; [event, action] unmöglich machen; **to ~ sb from doing sthg** es jm unmöglich machen, etw zu tun.

precocious [prı'kəʊʃəs] *adj* frühreif.

preconceived [‚priːkən'siːvd] *adj* vorgefasst.

precondition [‚priːkən'dıʃn] *n fml* (Vor)bedingung *die*.

predator ['predətə^r] *n* [animal] Raubtier *das*; [bird] Raubvogel *der*.

predecessor ['priːdısesə^r] *n* - **1.** [person] Vorgänger *der*, -in *die* - **2.** [thing] Vorläufer *der*.

predicament [prı'dıkəmənt] *n* missliche Lage.

predict [prı'dıkt] *vt* vorherlsagen.

predictable [prı'dıktəbl] *adj* [result, reaction] vorhersehbar; [person, behaviour] berechenbar.

prediction [prı'dıkʃn] *n* [something foretold] Voraussage *die*.

predispose [‚priːdıs'pəʊz] *vt*: **to be ~d to do sthg** dazu neigen, etw zu tun; **to be ~d to sthg** zu etw neigen.

predominant [prı'dɒmınənt] *adj* vorherrschend.

predominantly [prı'dɒmınəntlı] *adv* überwiegend.

preempt [‚priː'empt] *vt* zuvorlkommen (+ *D*).

preen [priːn] *vt* - **1.** [subj: bird] putzen - **2.** *fig* [subj: person]: **to ~ o.s.** sich zurechtlmachen.

prefab ['priːfæb] *n inf* Fertighaus *das*.

preface ['prefıs] *n* [in book] Vorwort *das*; **~ to sthg** [to text] Vorwort einer Sache (*G*); [to speech] Einleitung *die* einer Sache (*G*).

prefect ['priːfekt] *n Br* [pupil] Aufsichtsschüler *der*, -in *die*.

prefer [prı'fɜː^r] *vt* vorziehen, bevorzugen; **to ~ sthg to sthg** etw einer Sache (*D*) vorlziehen; **to ~ to do sthg** es vorlziehen, etw zu tun.

preferable ['prefrəbl] *adj*: **to be ~ (to sthg)** (etw (*D*)) vorzuziehen sein.

preferably ['prefrəblı] *adv* vorzugsweise.

preference ['prefərəns] *n* - **1.** [liking]: **~ (for sthg)** Vorliebe *die* (für etw) - **2.** [precedence]: **to give sb/sthg ~, to give ~ to sb/sthg** jm/etw den Vorzug geben.

preferential [‚prefə'renʃl] *adj* [treatment] bevorzugt.

prefix ['priːfıks] *n* GRAMM Präfix *das*.

pregnancy ['pregnənsı] *n* Schwangerschaft *die*.

pregnant ['pregnənt] *adj* [woman] schwanger; [animal] trächtig.

prehistoric [ˌpriːhɪ'stɒrɪk] *adj* prähistorisch, vorgeschichtlich.

prejudice ['predʒʊdɪs] <> *n* [bias]: ~ **(against)** Vorurteil *das* (gegen) <> *vt* [jeopardize] schaden *(+ D).*

prejudiced ['predʒʊdɪst] *adj* voreingenommen.

prejudicial [ˌpredʒʊ'dɪʃl] *adj*: **to be ~ to sb** für jn schädlich sein; **to be ~ to sthg** einer Sache *(D)* abträglich sein.

preliminary [prɪ'lɪmɪnərɪ] *adj* [activity] vorbereitend; [talks, investigation] Vor-; [report, results] vorläufig.

prelude ['preljuːd] *n* [event]: ~ **to sthg** Auftakt *der* zu etw.

premarital [ˌpriː'mærɪtl] *adj* vor der Ehe.

premature [ˌpremə'tjʊəʳ] *adj* **- 1.** [death, baldness] vorzeitig **- 2.**: ~ **birth/child** Frühgeburt *die* **- 3.** *pej* [decision, action] übereilt.

premeditated [ˌpriː'medɪteɪtɪd] *adj* vorsätzlich.

premenstrual syndrome, premenstrual tension [priːˌmenstrʊəl-] *n* prämenstruelles Syndrom.

premier ['premjəʳ] <> *adj* führend <> *n* Premierminister *der*, -in *die*.

premiere ['premɪeəʳ] *n* Premiere *die*.

premise ['premɪs] *n* Voraussetzung *die*.
◆ **premises** *npl* Räumlichkeiten *pl*; **on the ~s** im Hause.

premium ['priːmɪəm] *n* **- 1.**: **to sell sthg at a ~** [above usual value] etw über Wert verkaufen; **to be at a ~** [in great demand] sehr gefragt sein **- 2.** [insurance payment] Prämie *die*.

premium bond *n Br* Prämienanleihe *die*, *britische Staatsanleihe, die eine monatliche Verlosungsteilnahme beinhaltet.*

premonition [ˌpremə'nɪʃn] *n* Vorahnung *die*.

preoccupied [priː'ɒkjʊpaɪd] *adj* in Gedanken vertieft OR versunken; **to be ~ with sthg** mit etw beschäftigt sein.

prepaid ['priːpeɪd] *adj* [envelope] portofrei; [items] im Voraus bezahlt.

preparation [ˌprepə'reɪʃn] *n* **- 1.** *(U)* [act of preparing] Vorbereitung *die* **- 2.** [prepared mixture - food] Fertigmischung *die*; [- medicine, cosmetics] Präparat *das*. ◆ **preparations** *npl* [plans] Vorbereitungen *pl*.

preparatory [prɪ'pærətrɪ] *adj* vorbereitend.

preparatory school *n* **- 1.** [in UK] *private Grundschule, die auf die Aufnahme in eine Public School vorbereitet* **- 2.** [in US] *private höhere Schule, die auf die Aufnahme in eine Hochschule vorbereitet.*

prepare [prɪ'peəʳ] <> *vt* **- 1.** [make ready] vorlbereiten; **to ~ to do sthg** sich anlschicken, etw zu tun **- 2.** [make, assemble] zulbereiten <> *vi*: **to ~ for sthg** sich auf etw *(A)* vorlbereiten.

prepared [prɪ'peəd] *adj* **- 1.** [organized, done beforehand] vorbereitet **- 2.** [willing]: **to be ~ to do sthg** bereit sein, etw zu tun **- 3.** [ready]: **to be ~ for sthg** auf etw *(A)* vorbereitet sein.

preposition [ˌprepə'zɪʃn] *n* Präposition *die*.

preposterous [prɪ'pɒstərəs] *adj* absurd.

prep school [prep-] *n abbr of* preparatory school.

prerequisite [ˌpriː'rekwɪzɪt] *n*: ~ **(of** OR **for)** Voraussetzung *die* (für).

prerogative [prɪ'rɒgətɪv] *n* Vorrecht *das*.

preschool [ˌpriː'skuːl] *adj* Vorschul-.

prescribe [prɪ'skraɪb] *vt* **- 1.** MED verschreiben **- 2.** [order] vorlschreiben.

prescription [prɪ'skrɪpʃn] *n* MED Rezept *das*.

presence ['prezns] *n* **- 1.** [being present] Anwesenheit *die*, Gegenwart *die*; **in his ~** in seiner Gegenwart **- 2.** *(U)* [personality, charisma] Ausstrahlung *die*.

presence of mind *n* Geistesgegenwart *die*.

present [*adj & n* 'preznt, *vb* prɪ'zent] <> *adj* **- 1.** [current] gegenwärtig, derzeitig **- 2.** [in attendance] anwesend; **to be ~ at sthg** bei etw anwesend sein <> *n* **- 1.** [current time]: **the ~** die Gegenwart; **at ~** zur Zeit **- 2.** [gift] Geschenk *das* **- 3.** GRAMM: ~ **(tense)** Präsens *das*, Gegenwart *die* <> *vt* **- 1.** [gift, award] überreichen; **to ~ sb with sthg, to ~ sthg to sb** jm etw überreichen **- 2.** [opportunity] bieten; [problem] auflwerfen **- 3.** [introduce - person] vorlstellen; **to ~ sb to sb** jm jn vorlstellen **- 4.** [TV, radio programme] moderieren **- 5.** [facts, figures, report] vorllegen **- 6.** [portray] darlstellen **- 7.** [arrive, go]: **to ~ o.s.** [at reception] sich melden; [for interview] erscheinen **- 8.** [perform] darlbieten.

presentable [prɪ'zentəbl] *adj* präsentabel.

presentation [ˌprezn'teɪʃn] *n* **- 1.** *(U)* [publication, broadcasting] Präsentation *die* **- 2.** *(U)* [of product] Aufmachung *die*; [of policy, text] Präsentation *die* **- 3.** [ceremony] Verleihung *die* **- 4.** [talk] Präsentation *die* **- 5.** [performance] Darbietung *die*.

present day *n*: **the ~** der heutige Tag, jetzt. ◆ **present-day** *adj* heutig.

presenter [prɪ'zentəʳ] *n Br* Moderator *der*, -in *die*.

presently ['prezntlɪ] *adv* **- 1.** [soon] bald **- 2.** [now] gegenwärtig, jetzt.

preservation [ˌprezə'veɪʃn] *n* *(U)* **- 1.** [of democracy, law and order] Aufrechterhaltung *die*; [of building, wildlife, countryside] Erhaltung *die* **- 2.** [of food] Konservierung *die*.

preservative [prɪ'zɜːvətɪv] *n* [in food] Konservierungsmittel *das*; [for wood] Schutzmittel *das*.

preserve [prɪ'zɜːv] <> *vt* **- 1.** [democracy, peace, situation] aufrechtlerhalten; [building, wildlife, way of life] erhalten **- 2.** [food] konservieren; [fruit] ein|wecken <> *n* [jam] Konfitüre *die*.

preset [ˌpriːˈset] (*pt* & *pp* **preset**) *vt* [oven] vorheizen; [VCR] programmieren.

president [ˈprezɪdənt] *n* Präsident *der*, -in *die*.

presidential [ˌprezɪˈdenʃl] *adj* [decision] des Präsidenten; [campaign, election] Präsidentschafts-; [staff, limousine] Präsidenten-.

press [pres] <> *n* **- 1.** [push]: **to give sthg a ~** etw drücken; **at the ~ of a button** auf Knopfdruck **- 2.** [journalism]: **the ~** die Presse **- 3.** [printing machine, pressing machine] Presse *die* <> *vt* **- 1.** [push firmly] drücken; **to ~ sthg against sthg** etw gegen etw pressen **- 2.** [squeeze] drücken; [grapes] keltern; [flowers] pressen **- 3.** [iron] bügeln **- 4.** [urge, force] drängen; **to ~ sb to do sthg** OR **into doing sthg** jn drängen OR zwingen, etw zu tun **- 5.** [pursue - claim, point] beharren auf (+ D) <> *vi* **- 1.** [push hard]: **to ~ (on)** drücken (auf (+ A)) **- 2.** [surge] drängen. ◆ **press on** *vi* [continue]: **to ~ on with** weiter|machen (mit).

press agency *n* Presseagentur *die*.

press conference *n* Pressekonferenz *die*.

pressed [prest] *adj*: **to be ~ for time/money** unter Zeitdruck/finanziellem Druck stehen.

pressing [ˈpresɪŋ] *adj* [urgent] dringend.

press officer *n* Pressesprecher *der*, -in *die*.

press release *n* Pressemitteilung *die*.

press-stud *n Br* Druckknopf *der*.

press-up *n Br* Liegestütz *der*.

pressure [ˈpreʃər] *n* (*U*) *lit* & *fig* Druck *der*; **to put ~ on sb (to do sthg)** auf jn Druck aus|üben(, etw zu tun).

pressure cooker *n* Schnellkochtopf *der*.

pressure gauge *n* Druckmesser *der*.

pressure group *n* Interessengruppe *die*.

pressurize, -ise [ˈpreʃəraɪz] *vt* **- 1.** TECH unter Druck setzen **- 2.** *Br* [force]: **to ~ sb to do** OR **into doing sthg** jn (dazu) drängen, etw zu tun.

prestige [preˈstiːʒ] *n* Prestige *das*.

presumably [prɪˈzjuːməblɪ] *adv* vermutlich.

presume [prɪˈzjuːm] *vt* [assume] an|nehmen; **to ~ (that)** ... an|nehmen, dass ...; **he is ~d dead** es wird davon ausgegangen, dass er tot ist.

presumption [prɪˈzʌmpʃn] *n* **- 1.** [assumption] Annahme *die* **- 2.** (*U*) [audacity] Vermessenheit *die*.

presumptuous [prɪˈzʌmptʃuəs] *adj* anmaßend.

pretence, pretense *Am* [prɪˈtens] *n*: **he made no ~ of being interested** er gab nicht vor, interessiert zu sein; **under false ~s** unter Vortäuschung falscher Tatsachen.

pretend [prɪˈtend] <> *vt* **- 1.** [make believe]: **to ~ to do sthg** vorgeben, etw zu tun; **to ~ (that)** ... so tun, als ob ... **- 2.** [claim]: **to ~ to**

do sthg behaupten, dass man etw tut <> *vi* [feign] nur so tun.

pretense *n Am* = pretence.

pretension [prɪˈtenʃn] *n* [claim] Anspruch *der*.

pretentious [prɪˈtenʃəs] *adj* [person] wichtigtuerisch; [film, book] prätentiös.

pretext [ˈpriːtekst] *n* Vorwand *der*; **on** OR **under the ~ that** ... unter dem Vorwand, dass ...; **on** OR **under the ~ of doing sthg** unter dem Vorwand, etw zu tun wollen.

pretty [ˈprɪtɪ] <> *adj* hübsch <> *adv* [quite, rather] ziemlich; **~ much** OR **well** so ziemlich.

prevail [prɪˈveɪl] *vi* **- 1.** [be widespread] vorlherrschen; [custom] weit verbreitet sein **- 2.** [triumph] sich durch|setzen; **to ~ over sb/ sthg** sich gegen jn/etw durch|setzen **- 3.** [persuade]: **to ~ (up)on sb to do sthg** jn dazu bringen, etw zu tun.

prevailing [prɪˈveɪlɪŋ] *adj* **- 1.** [belief, opinion] vorherrschend; [fashion] aktuell **- 2.** [wind] vorherrschend.

prevalent [ˈprevələnt] *adj* vorherrschend; [illness] weit verbreitet.

prevent [prɪˈvent] *vt* verhindern; [illness] vor|beugen (+ D); **to ~ sb (from) doing sthg** jn daran hindern, etw zu tun.

preventive [prɪˈventɪv] *adj* vorbeugend; [measures, medicine] Präventiv-.

preview [ˈpriːvjuː] *n* **- 1.** [early showing of film, play] Voraufführung *die*; [- of exhibition] Vorbesichtigung *die* **- 2.** [trailer for films] Vorschau *die*.

previous [ˈpriːvɪəs] *adj* **- 1.** [earlier, prior] früher; **~ conviction** Vorstrafe *die* **- 2.** [with days and dates] vorhergehend; **in ~ years** in früheren Jahren **- 3.** [former] vorherig.

previously [ˈpriːvɪəslɪ] *adv* **- 1.** [formerly] vorher **- 2.** [with days and dates] zuvor.

prewar [ˌpriːˈwɔːr] *adj* Vorkriegs-.

prey [preɪ] *n* (*U*) Beute *die*. ◆ **prey on** *vt fus* **- 1.** [subj: animal, bird] Beute machen auf (+ A) **- 2.** [trouble]: **to ~ on sb's mind** jn bedrücken.

price [praɪs] <> *n* **- 1.** [cost] Preis *der* **- 2.** [value] Wert *der*; **to be without ~** (mit Geld) nicht zu bezahlen sein <> *vt* [set cost of] den Preis fest|setzen von; **it was ~d at £100** es sollte 100 Pfund kosten.

priceless [ˈpraɪslɪs] *adj* **- 1.** [very valuable] von unschätzbarem Wert **- 2.** *inf* [funny] wahnsinnig komisch.

price list *n* Preisliste *die*.

price tag *n* [label] Preisschild *das*.

pricey [ˈpraɪsɪ] (*compar* -ier; *superl* -iest) *adj inf* teuer.

prick [prɪk] <> *n* **- 1.** [scratch, wound] Stich *der* **- 2.** *vulg* [penis] Schwanz *der* **- 3.** *vulg* [stupid person] Arschloch *das* <> *vt* [jab, pierce] stechen in (+ A); **to ~ one's finger** sich (D) in den Finger stechen. ◆ **prick up** *vt sep*: **to ~ up one's ears** *lit* & *fig* seine Ohren spitzen.

prickle ['prɪkl] ◇ n - 1. [thorn] Stachel der - 2. [sensation] Prickeln das ◇ vi prickeln.

prickly ['prɪklɪ] adj - 1. [thorny] stachelig - 2. fig [touchy] reizbar.

pride [praɪd] ◇ n Stolz der; **to take ~ in sthg** auf etw (A) stolz sein ◇ vt: **to ~ o.s. on sthg** auf etw (A) stolz sein.

priest [priːst] n Priester der.

priestess ['priːstɪs] n Priesterin die.

priesthood ['priːsthʊd] n (U) - 1. [position, office]: **the ~** das Priesteramt - 2. [priests collectively]: **the ~** die Priesterschaft.

prig [prɪg] n Tugendbold der.

prim [prɪm] adj [person, behaviour] sittsam.

primarily ['praɪmərɪlɪ] adv in erster Linie.

primary ['praɪmərɪ] ◇ adj [main - concern, aim, reason] Haupt- ◇ n POL Vorwahl die (zur Bestimmung der Präsidentschaftskandidaten einer Partei).

primary school n Grundschule die.

primary teacher n [in UK] Grundschullehrer der, -in die.

primate ['praɪmeɪt] n - 1. ZOOL Primat der - 2. RELIG Primas der.

prime [praɪm] ◇ adj - 1. [main - concern, aim, reason] Haupt- - 2. [excellent] erstklassig ◇ n [peak]: **to be in one's ~** in den besten Jahren sein ◇ vt [paint] grundieren.

prime minister n Premierminister der, -in die.

primer ['praɪmə'] n - 1. [paint] Grundierung die - 2. [textbook] Fibel die.

primitive ['prɪmɪtɪv] adj primitiv.

primrose ['prɪmrəʊz] n Himmelschlüssel der.

Primus stove® ['praɪməs-] n Campingkocher der.

prince [prɪns] n - 1. [son of king, queen] Prinz der - 2. [ruler] Fürst der.

princess [prɪn'ses] n Prinzessin die.

principal ['prɪnsəpl] ◇ adj Haupt- ◇ n [of school, college] Direktor der, -in die.

principle ['prɪnsəpl] n - 1. [gen] Prinzip das - 2. [integrity] Prinzipien pl; **to do sthg on ~** OR **as a matter of ~** etw aus Prinzip tun. ◆ **in principle** adv im Prinzip.

print [prɪnt] ◇ n - 1. (U) [printed characters] Schrift die; [printed matter] Gedruckte das; **in large/small ~** groß/klein gedruckt; **in ~** [available] erhältlich; [in newspaper] gedruckt; **to be out of ~** vergriffen sein - 2. ART Druck der - 3. [photograph] Abzug der - 4. [fabric] bedruckter Stoff - 5. [footprint, fingerprint] Abdruck der ◇ vt - 1. [gen] drucken - 2. [write clearly] in Druckschrift schreiben ◇ vi [printer] drucken. ◆ **print out** vt sep COMPUT ausdrucken.

printed matter ['prɪntɪd-] n (U) Drucksache die.

printer ['prɪntə'] n [person & COMPUT] Drucker der; [firm] Druckerei die.

printing ['prɪntɪŋ] n (U) - 1. [act] Drucken das - 2. [trade] Druckereigewerbe das.

printout ['prɪntaʊt] n Ausdruck der.

prior ['praɪə'] ◇ adj - 1. [previous - agreement] vorherig; [- warning] Vor-; **a ~ engagement** eine anderweitige Verpflichtung - 2. [more important] vorrangig ◇ n [monk] Prior der. ◆ **prior to** prep vor (+ D); **~ to leaving** bevor ich/er/etc ging.

priority [praɪ'ɒrətɪ] n - 1. [matter] vordringliche Sache - 2. [urgency] Vorrang der; **to have** OR **take ~ (over sthg)** Vorrang (vor etw (D)) haben.

prise [praɪz] vt: **to ~ sthg open** etw aufbrechen.

prison ['prɪzn] n Gefängnis das.

prisoner ['prɪznə'] n Gefangene der, die.

prisoner of war (pl prisoners of war) n Kriegsgefangene der, die.

privacy [Br 'prɪvəsɪ, Am 'praɪvəsɪ] n (U) Privatsphäre die.

private ['praɪvɪt] ◇ adj - 1. [gen] privat; [hospital, house, industry, life] Privat- - 2. [confidential] vertraulich - 3. [personal - belongings, plans] persönlich - 4. [secluded] abgelegen - 5. [reserved] in sich zurückgezogen ◇ n - 1. [soldier] einfacher Soldat; **Private Smith** Soldat Smith - 2. [secrecy]: **in ~** [of conversation between two people] unter vier Augen; [of meeting] hinter geschlossenen Türen.

private enterprise n (U) freies Unternehmertum.

private eye n Privatdetektiv der, -in die.

privately ['praɪvɪtlɪ] adv - 1. [not by the state] privat; **~ owned** in Privatbesitz - 2. [confidentially - discuss between two people] unter vier Augen; [- discuss in meeting] hinter verschlossenen Türen; [- meet, agree] insgeheim - 3. [personally] persönlich.

private property n (U) Privatgrundstück das.

private school n Privatschule die.

📖 private school

Die britischen Privatschulen sind nicht Bestandteil des staatlichen Bildungssystems. Die Eltern der meisten Schüler zahlen Schulgeld, viele Privatschulen bieten guten Schülern aber auch Stipendien. Verwirrenderweise werden manche kostenpflichtigen Schulen auch public schools oder independent schools genannt.
In den USA sind die Bezeichnungen private school und public school dagegen strikt voneinander getrennt: nur der Besuch der public school ist kostenlos.

privatize, -ise ['praɪvɪtaɪz] vt privatisieren.

privet ['prɪvɪt] n (U) Liguster der.

privilege ['prɪvɪlɪdʒ] n - 1. [special advantage] Privileg das - 2. [honour] Ehre die.

privy ['prɪvɪ] adj: **to be ~ to sthg** fml in etw (A) eingeweiht sein.

prize [praɪz] ◇ adj - 1. [prizewinning] preisgekrönt - 2. [perfect]: **~ idiot** Vollidiot ◇ n Preis der ◇ vt [value] (hoch)schätzen.

prize-giving [-,ɡɪvɪŋ] n Br Preisverleihung die.

prizewinner ['praɪz,wɪnə'] n Preisträger der, -in die.

pro [prəʊ] n - 1. inf [professional] Profi der - 2. [advantage]: **the ~s and cons** das Für und Wider.

probability [,prɒbə'bɪlətɪ] n [gen] Wahrscheinlichkeit die.

probable ['prɒbəbl] adj wahrscheinlich.

probably ['prɒbəblɪ] adv wahrscheinlich.

probation [prə'beɪʃn] n (U) - 1. [of prisoner] Bewährung die; **to put sb on ~** jm Bewährung geben - 2. [trial period] Probezeit die; **I'm on ~** ich bin in der Probezeit.

probe [prəʊb] ◇ n - 1. [investigation]: **~ (into)** Untersuchung die (+ G) - 2. MED & TECH Sonde die ◇ vt - 1. [investigate] sondieren; [mystery] erforschen - 2. [prod - with stick] suchend herumlstochern in (+ D).

problem ['prɒbləm] ◇ n Problem das; **no ~!** inf kein Problem! ◇ comp Problem-.

procedure [prə'siːdʒə'] n Verfahren das.

proceed [vb prə'siːd, npl 'prəʊsiːdz] ◇ vt: **to ~ to do sthg** dazu übergehen, etw zu tun ◇ vi - 1. [continue] fortlfahren; [party] fortgesetzt werden; [event] weiterlgehen; **to ~ with sthg** mit etw fortfahren - 2. fml [go, advance - on foot] gehen; [- in vehicle] fahren; **to ~ somewhere** sich irgendwohin begeben. ► **proceeds** npl Erlös der.

proceedings [prə'siːdɪŋz] npl - 1. [series of actions] Vorgänge pl; [event] Veranstaltung die - 2. [legal action] Verfahren das.

process ['prəʊses] ◇ n - 1. [series of actions] Prozess die; [electoral - **~** Wahlverfahren das; **in the ~** dabei; **to be in the ~ of doing sthg** dabei sein, etw zu tun - 2. [method] Verfahren das ◇ vt - 1. [treat - materials] verarbeiten; [- food] behandeln - 2. [examine, deal with - application] bearbeiten; [- information, data] verarbeiten.

processing ['prəʊsesɪŋ] n (U) - 1. [treating - of materials] Verarbeitung die; [- of food] Behandeln das - 2. [examining - of applications] Bearbeitung die; [- of information, data] Verarbeitung die.

procession [prə'seʃn] n Zug der; **in ~** in einem langen Zug.

proclaim [prə'kleɪm] vt [independence] proklamieren; [innocence, loyalty] beteuern; **to ~ sb king** jn zum König ernennen.

procure [prə'kjʊə'] vt [tickets, supplies] beschaffen; [somebody's release] bewirken.

prod [prɒd] vt [push, poke - person] anlstupsen; [- ground, food] herumlstochern in (+ D).

prodigy ['prɒdɪdʒɪ] n Wunderkind das.

produce [n 'prɒdjuːs, vb prə'djuːs] ◇ n (U) - 1. [goods] Erzeugnisse pl - 2. [fruit and vegetables] Obst und Gemüse das ◇ vt - 1. [manufacture, make] produzieren; [work of art] schaffen - 2. [yield - raw materials] liefern; [- heat, crop, gas] erzeugen; [- interest, profit] einlbringen - 3. [cause - results, agreements] erzielen; [- disaster] hervorlrufen - 4. [give birth to - subj: woman] gebären; [- subj: animal] werfen - 5. [leaves, flowers] hervorlbringen - 6. [present, show - evidence, argument] vorllegen; [- passport, letter] vorlzeigen - 7. [gen] produzieren.

producer [prə'djuːsə'] n - 1. [gen] Produzent der, -in die - 2. [manufacturer] Hersteller der, -in die.

product ['prɒdʌkt] n [thing manufactured or grown] Produkt das.

production [prə'dʌkʃn] n - 1. (U) [process - of goods] Produktion die; [- of electricity, heat] Erzeugung die; [- of blood cells] Bildung die - 2. (U) [output] Produktion die - 3. CINEMA, THEATRE & TV Produktion die.

production line n Fertigungsstraße die.

productive [prə'dʌktɪv] adj - 1. [worker] produktiv; [land] ertragreich; [business] leistungsfähig - 2. [meeting, relationship, experience] Gewinn bringend.

productivity [,prɒdʌk'tɪvətɪ] n Produktivität die.

profane [prə'feɪn] adj [vulgar] gotteslästerlich.

profession [prə'feʃn] n - 1. [career] Beruf der; **by ~** von Beruf - 2. [body of people] Berufsstand der; **the medical/teaching ~** die Ärzteschaft/Lehrerschaft.

professional [prə'feʃənl] ◇ adj - 1. [relating to a profession - qualifications] beruflich; [- advice, help, opinion] fachmännisch; **~ people** hochqualifizierte Personen - 2. [full-time, of high standard] professionell; [army, actor] Berufs-; [footballer] Profi- ◇ n - 1. [full-time sportsperson] Profi der; [full-time actor] Berufsschauspieler der - 2. [skilled person]: **he's a real ~** er ist ein echter Profi.

professor [prə'fesə'] n - 1. Br [head of department] Professor der, -in die - 2. Am & Can [teacher, lecturer] Dozent der, -in die.

proficiency [prə'fɪʃənsɪ] n (U): **~ (in)** Kompetenz die (in (+ D)).

profile ['prəʊfaɪl] n - 1. [outline of face] Profil das; **to keep a low ~** fig sich unauffällig verhalten - 2. [biography] Porträt das.

profit ['prɒfɪt] ⬦ *n* - **1.** [financial gain] Gewinn *der*, Profit *der* - **2.** [advantage]: **you may learn something to your** ~ du könntest etwas lernen, was nützlich für dich ist ⬦ *vi*: **to** ~ **(from** OR **by sthg)** (von etw) profitieren.

profitability [ˌprɒfɪtə'bɪlətɪ] *n* Rentabilität *die*.

profitable ['prɒfɪtəbl] *adj* Gewinn bringend.

profound [prə'faʊnd] *adj* - **1.** [intense - feeling, silence] tief; [- change] tief greifend; [- effect] nachhaltig - **2.** [penetrating, wise - idea, book] tiefgründig.

profusely [prə'fjuːslɪ] *adv* - **1.** [bleed, sweat] sehr stark - **2.** [thank] überschwenglich; **to apologize** ~ sich vielmals entschuldigen.

profusion [prə'fjuːʒn] *n*: ~ **(of)** (Über)fülle *die* (von).

prognosis [prɒg'nəʊsɪs] *(pl* -noses [-'nəʊsiːz]) *n* Prognose *die*.

program ['prəʊgræm] *(pt & pp* -med OR -ed; *cont* -ming) ⬦ *n* - **1.** COMPUT Programm *das* - **2.** *Am* = programme ⬦ *vt* - **1.** COMPUT programmieren - **2.** *Am* = programme.

programer *n Am* = programmer.

programme *Br*, **program** *Am* ['prəʊgræm] ⬦ *n* - **1.** [gen] Programm *das* - **2.** RADIO & TV Sendung *die* ⬦ *vt* programmieren.

programmer *Br*, **programer** *Am* ['prəʊgræmə'] *n* COMPUT Programmierer *der*, -in *die*.

programming ['prəʊgræmɪŋ] *n* COMPUT Programmieren *das*.

progress [*n* 'prəʊgres, *vb* prə'gres] ⬦ *n* - **1.** [physical movement] Vorwärtskommen *das* - **2.** [headway] Voranschreiten *das*; **to make** ~ **(in sthg)** (bei etw) Fortschritte machen; **in** ~ im Gange - **3.** [evolution] Fortschritt *der* ⬦ *vi* - **1.** [improve - science, technology, work] voran|kommen; [- patient, student] Fortschritte machen - **2.** [continue]: **as the journey/meeting** ~**ed** im Laufe der Reise/des Treffens.

progressive [prə'gresɪv] *adj* - **1.** [forward-looking] fortschrittlich - **2.** [gradual] fortschreitend.

prohibit [prə'hɪbɪt] *vt* verbieten; **to** ~ **sb from doing sthg** jm verbieten, etw zu tun.

project [*n* 'prɒdʒekt, *vb* prə'dʒekt] ⬦ *n* - **1.** [plan, idea] Vorhaben *das*, Projekt *das* - **2.** SCH [study] Projekt *das* ⬦ *vt* - **1.** [plan] planen - **2.** [estimate] voraus|sagen; [costs] überschlagen - **3.** [film, light] projizieren - **4.** [present] dar|stellen; [image] vermitteln ⬦ *vi* [jut out] hervor|ragen.

projectile [prə'dʒektaɪl] *n* Geschoss *das*.

projection [prə'dʒekʃn] *n* - **1.** [estimate] Voraussage *die*; [of costs] Überschlagen *das* - **2.** *(U)* [of film, light] Projektion *die*.

projector [prə'dʒektə'] *n* Projektor *der*.

proletariat [ˌprəʊlɪ'teərɪət] *n* Proletariat *das*.

prolific [prə'lɪfɪk] *adj* sehr produktiv.

prologue, prolog *Am* ['prəʊlɒg] *n* - **1.** [introduction] Prolog *der* - **2.** *fig* [preceding event]: **to be the** ~ **to sthg** die Vorstufe für etw sein.

prolong [prə'lɒŋ] *vt* verlängern.

prom [prɒm] *n* - **1.** *(abbr of promenade)* *Br inf* [at seaside] Strandpromenade *die* - **2.** *Am* [ball - at high school] Schulball *der;* [- at college] Studentenball *der*.

promenade [ˌprɒmə'nɑːd] *n Br* [at seaside] Strandpromenade *die*.

prominent ['prɒmɪnənt] *adj* - **1.** [important - person] prominent; [- ideas, issues] wichtig - **2.** [noticeable - building, landmark] exponiert; [- features] markant.

promiscuous [prɒ'mɪskjʊəs] *adj* promiskuitiv.

promise ['prɒmɪs] ⬦ *n* - **1.** [vow] Versprechen *das* - **2.** *(U)* [hope, prospect]: ~ **(of)** Aussicht *die* (auf (+ A)) ⬦ *vt* versprechen; **to** ~ **sb sthg** jm etw versprechen; **to** ~ **(sb) to do sthg** (jm) versprechen, etw zu tun ⬦ *vi* versprechen.

---

 promising

> Du kannst dich auf mich verlassen. You can rely on me.
>
> Das verspreche ich dir hoch und heilig. I give you my word.
>
> Ich werde mich darum kümmern. I'll take care of that.
>
> Das geht in Ordnung. No problem, that's fine.
>
> Versprochen! I promise!

---

promising ['prɒmɪsɪŋ] *adj* vielversprechend.

promontory ['prɒməntrɪ] *n* Kap *das*.

promote [prə'məʊt] *vt* - **1.** [foster] fördern - **2.** [push, advertise] Werbung machen für - **3.** [in job] befördern - **4.** SPORT: **to be** ~**d** auf|steigen.

promoter [prə'məʊtə'] *n* - **1.** [of event, concert] Veranstalter *der*, -in *die* - **2.** [of cause, idea] Förderer *der*.

promotion [prə'məʊʃn] *n* - **1.** [in job] Beförderung *die* - **2.** [advertising] Werbung *die* - **3.** [campaign] Werbekampagne *die*.

prompt [prɒmpt] ⬦ *adj* - **1.** [quick] prompt; [action] sofortig - **2.** [punctual] pünktlich ⬦ *adv*: **at nine o'clock** ~ Punkt 9 Uhr ⬦ *vt* - **1.** [provoke, persuade]: **to** ~ **sb to do sthg** jn dazu veranlassen, etw zu tun - **2.** THEATRE soufflieren (+ D).

promptly ['prɒmptlɪ] *adv* - **1.** [quickly] prompt - **2.** [punctually] pünktlich.

prone [prəʊn] *adj* [susceptible]: **to be ~ to sthg** zu etw neigen; **to be ~ to do sthg** dazu neigen, etw zu tun.

prong [prɒŋ] *n* Zinke *die*.

pronoun ['prəʊnaʊn] *n* Pronomen *das*.

pronounce [prə'naʊns] *vt* - 1. [say aloud] auslsprechen - 2. [declare, state - verdict, opinion] verkünden; **to ~ sb fit for work/dead** jn für arbeitsfähig/tot erklären.

pronounced [prə'naʊnst] *adj* [accent] stark; [improvement, deterioration] deutlich.

pronouncement [prə'naʊnsmənt] *n* Erklärung *die*.

pronunciation [prə,nʌnsɪ'eɪʃn] *n* Aussprache *die*.

proof [pruːf] *n* - 1. [evidence] Beweis *der* - 2. PRESS [first copy] Korrekturfahne *die* - 3. [of alcohol] Alkoholgehalt *der*.

prop [prɒp] ⇔ *n lit & fig* Stütze *die* ⇔ *vt*: **to ~ sthg against sthg** etw gegen etw lehnen. ◆ **props** *npl* [in film, play] Requisiten *pl*. ◆ **prop up** *vt sep* - 1. [support physically - wall] ablstützen; [- ladder] anllehnen - 2. *fig* [sustain - regime] stützen; [- organization] unterstützen; [- company] vor dem Konkurs bewahren.

propel [prə'pel] *vt* anltreiben.

propeller [prə'pelə*] *n* [of plane] Propeller *der*; [of ship] Schraube *die*.

propelling pencil [prə'pelɪŋ-] *n Br* Drehbleistift *der*.

propensity [prə'pensətɪ] *n fml*: **~ for** OR **to sthg** Hang *der* zu etw; **to have a ~ to do sthg** dazu neigen, etw zu tun.

proper ['prɒpə*] *adj* - 1. [real] richtig - 2. [correct] korrekt - 3. [decent] anständig.

properly ['prɒpəlɪ] *adv* - 1. [satisfactorily, correctly] richtig - 2. [decently] anständig.

proper noun *n* Eigenname *der*.

property ['prɒpətɪ] *n* - 1. [possession] Eigentum *das* - 2. [specific building] Haus *das*; [piece of land] Grundstück *das* - 3. (U) [buildings, land] Immobilien *pl* - 4. [quality] Eigenschaft *die*.

property owner *n* [of house] Hausbesitzer *der*, -in *die*; [of land] Grundbesitzer *der*, -in *die*.

prophecy ['prɒfɪsɪ] *n* Prophezeiung *die*.

prophesy ['prɒfɪsaɪ] *vt* prophezeien.

prophet ['prɒfɪt] *n* RELIG Prophet *der*.

proportion [prə'pɔːʃn] *n* - 1. [part] Teil *der*, Anteil *der* - 2. [ratio, comparison] Verhältnis *das* - 3. (U) ART: **in ~** in den richtigen Proportionen; **out of ~** mit verschobenen Proportionen; **a sense of ~** *fig* ein vernünftiger Maßstab.

proportional [prə'pɔːʃənl] *adj* im Verhältnis stehend; MATH proportional; **to be ~ to sthg** zu etw im Verhältnis stehen; MATH zu etw proportional sein.

proportional representation *n* (U) Verhältniswahlsystem *das*.

proportionate [prə'pɔːʃnət] *adj*: **~ (to sthg)** im Verhältnis (zu etw).

proposal [prə'pəʊzl] *n* - 1. [plan, suggestion] Vorschlag *der* - 2. [offer of marriage] Heiratsantrag *der*.

propose [prə'pəʊz] ⇔ *vt* - 1. [plan, solution, person] vorlschlagen; [toast] auslbringen - 2. [motion] einlbringen, stellen - 3. [intend]: **to ~ doing** OR **to do sthg** vorlhaben OR beabsichtigen, etw zu tun ⇔ *vi*: **to ~ (to sb)** (jm) einen Heiratsantrag machen.

proposition [,prɒpə'zɪʃn] *n* - 1. [statement of theory] These *die* - 2. [suggestion] Vorschlag *der*.

proprietor [prə'praɪətə*] *n* Besitzer *der*, -in *die*.

propriety [prə'praɪətɪ] *n fml* [moral correctness] Anstand *der*.

pro rata [-'rɑːtə] *adj & adv* anteilig.

prose [prəʊz] *n* Prosa *die*.

prosecute ['prɒsɪkjuːt] *vt* LAW strafrechtlich verfolgen.

prosecution [,prɒsɪ'kjuːʃn] *n* - 1. [criminal charge] strafrechtliche Verfolgung - 2. [lawyers]: **the ~** die Anklage(vertretung).

prosecutor ['prɒsɪkjuːtə*] *n esp Am* Ankläger *der*, -in *die*.

prospect [*n* 'prɒspekt, *vb* prə'spekt] ⇔ *n* Aussicht *die* ⇔ *vi*: **to ~ (for sthg)** [gold] schürfen (nach etw); [oil] bohren (nach etw). ◆ **prospects** *npl*: **~s (for sthg)** Aussichten *pl* (auf etw (A)); **he has good ~s** er hat gute Erfolgschancen.

📖 **prospect**

Vorsicht ist bei der Verwendung des Wortes prospect angebracht, denn es bedeutet „Aussicht" im Sinne von „Erwartung" oder „Möglichkeit" und nicht etwa „Prospekt". A job with good **prospects** ist ein Job mit guten beruflichen Aussichten. Ein „Prospekt" heißt dagegen im Englischen brochure. „Ich habe <u>Prospekte</u> aus der Touristeninformation mitgebracht" liest sich auf Englisch ungefähr so: I picked up some <u>brochures</u> from the tourist office.

prospective [prə'spektɪv] *adj* voraussichtlich.

prospectus [prə'spektəs] (*pl* -es) *n* (Werbe)prospekt *der*.

prosper ['prɒspə*] *vi* [business, country] blühen; [person] Erfolg haben.

prosperity [prɒ'sperətɪ] *n* Wohlstand *der*.

prosperous ['prɒspərəs] *adj* [person] wohlhabend; [business, place] blühend.

prostitute ['prɒstɪtjuːt] *n* Prostituierte *die;* **(male)** ~ Stricher *der,* Strichjunge *der.*

prostrate ['prɒstreɪt] *adj* [lying flat] (auf dem Bauch) ausgestreckt.

protagonist [prə'tægənɪst] *n* Hauptfigur *die,* Protagonist *der,* -in *die.*

protect [prə'tekt] *vt* schützen; **to ~ sb/sthg from/against** jn/etw schützen vor *(+ D)*/gegen.

protection [prə'tekʃn] *n:* ~ **(from/against)** Schutz *der* (vor *(+ D)*/gegen).

protective [prə'tektɪv] *adj* - **1.** [layer, clothing] Schutz-, schützend - **2.** [feelings, instinct] Beschützer-.

protein ['prəʊtiːn] *n* Protein *das.*

protest [*n* 'prəʊtest, *vb* prə'test] ◇ *n* - **1.** [complaint] Protest *der* - **2.** [demonstration] Protestkundgebung *die* ◇ *vt* - **1.** [one's innocence] beteuern - **2.** *Am* [protest against] protestieren gegen ◇ *vi* [complain]: **to ~ (about/against sthg)** protestieren (gegen etw).

Protestant ['prɒtɪstənt] ◇ *adj* protestantisch ◇ *n* Protestant *der,* -in *die.*

protester [prə'testə'] *n* [demonstrator] Protestierende *der, die.*

protest march *n* Protestmarsch *der.*

protocol ['prəʊtəkɒl] *n (U)* Protokoll *das.*

prototype ['prəʊtətaɪp] *n* Prototyp *der.*

protracted [prə'træktɪd] *adj* langwierig.

protrude [prə'truːd] *vi:* **to ~ (from sthg)** (aus etw) hervorlstehen.

protuberance [prə'tjuːbərəns] *n* Auswuchs *der.*

proud [praʊd] *adj* stolz; **to be ~ of sb/sthg** auf jn/etw stolz sein.

prove [pruːv] (*pp* -d OR proven) *vt* - **1.** [show to be true] beweisen - **2.** [show o.s. to be]: **to ~ (to be) sthg** sich als etw erweisen; **to ~ o.s. to be sthg** sich als etw erweisen.

proven ['pruːvn, 'prəʊvn] ◇ *pp* ▷ prove ◇ *adj* [fact] erwiesen, bewiesen; [liar] ausgewiesen.

proverb ['prɒvɜːb] *n* Sprichwort *das.*

provide [prə'vaɪd] *vt* [food, money, information] zur Verfügung stellen; [opportunity] bieten; **to ~ sb with sthg, to ~ sthg for sb** jm etw zur Verfügung stellen. ◆ **provide for** *vt fus* - **1.** [support] sorgen für - **2.** *fml* [make arrangements for] vorlsorgen für.

provided [prə'vaɪdɪd] ◆ **provided (that)** *conj* vorausgesetzt, dass.

providing [prə'vaɪdɪŋ] ◆ **providing (that)** *conj* vorausgesetzt, dass.

province ['prɒvɪns] *n* - **1.** [part of country] Provinz *die* - **2.** [specialist subject] Fachgebiet *das;* [area of responsibility] Aufgabenbereich *der.*

provincial [prə'vɪnʃl] *adj* - **1.** [of a province] Provinz- - **2.** *pej* [narrow-minded] provinziell.

provision [prə'vɪʒn] *n* - **1.** [act of supplying] Bereitstellung *die* - **2.** *(U)* [arrangement] Vorkehrung *die* - **3.** [in agreement, law] Bestimmung *die.* ◆ **provisions** *npl* [supplies] Vorräte *pl.*

provisional [prə'vɪʒənl] *adj* provisorisch.

proviso [prə'vaɪzəʊ] (*pl* -s) *n* Vorbehalt *der;* **with the ~ that …** unter dem Vorbehalt, dass …

provocative [prə'vɒkətɪv] *adj* - **1.** [controversial] provokativ - **2.** [sexy] aufreizend.

provoke [prə'vəʊk] *vt* - **1.** [annoy] provozieren - **2.** [cause - criticism, reaction] hervorlrufen, erregen; [- argument] provozieren.

prow [praʊ] *n* Bug *der.*

prowess ['praʊɪs] *n (U) fml* Erfahrenheit *die.*

prowl [praʊl] ◇ *n:* **to be on the ~** (auf Beutezug) herumlstreifen ◇ *vt* durchstreifen ◇ *vi* herumlstreifen, umherlstreifen.

prowler ['praʊlə'] *n* Herumtreiber *der,* -in *die.*

proxy ['prɒksɪ] *n:* **by ~** in Vertretung.

prudent ['pruːdnt] *adj* [person] umsichtig; [action] überlegt.

prudish ['pruːdɪʃ] *adj* prüde.

prune [pruːn] ◇ *n* [fruit] Backpflaume *die* ◇ *vt* [hedge, tree] beschneiden.

pry [praɪ] *vi* neugierig sein; **to ~ into sthg** seine Nase in etw stecken.

PS *n abbr of* postscript.

psalm [sɑːm] *n* Psalm *der.*

pseudonym ['sjuːdənɪm] *n* Pseudonym *das.*

psyche ['saɪkɪ] *n* Psyche *die.*

psychiatric [ˌsaɪkɪ'ætrɪk] *adj* [hospital, department] psychiatrisch; [illness, problem] psychisch.

psychiatrist [saɪ'kaɪətrɪst] *n* Psychiater *der,* -in *die.*

psychiatry [saɪ'kaɪətrɪ] *n (U)* Psychiatrie *die.*

psychic ['saɪkɪk] ◇ *adj* - **1.** [clairvoyant - powers] übersinnlich; **she is ~** sie hat übersinnliche Kräfte - **2.** [mental] psychisch ◇ *n* Person *die* mit übersinnlichen Kräften.

psychoanalysis [ˌsaɪkəʊə'næləsɪs] *n* Psychoanalyse *die.*

psychoanalyst [ˌsaɪkəʊ'ænəlɪst] *n* Psychoanalytiker *der,* -in *die.*

psychological [ˌsaɪkə'lɒdʒɪkl] *adj* psychologisch.

psychologist [saɪ'kɒlədʒɪst] *n* Psychologe *der,* -gin *die.*

psychology [saɪ'kɒlədʒɪ] *n* Psychologie *die.*

psychopath ['saɪkəpæθ] *n* Psychopath *der,* -in *die.*

psychotic [saɪ'kɒtɪk] ◇ *adj* psychotisch ◇ *n* Psychotiker *der,* -in *die.*

pt - **1.** *abbr of* pint - **2.** (*abbr of* point) Pkt.

PTO (*abbr of* please turn over) b.w.

pub [pʌb] *n* Pub *der*, Bierlokal *das*.

pub

Pubs, kurz für public houses, haben ihren eigenständigen Charakter im viktorianischen Großbritannien erworben, existieren aber schon länger (der älteste Pub das Landes ist angeblich der Trip to Jerusalem in Nottingham, wo bereits 1189 die zum Kreuzzug aufbrechenden Ritter ihren Durst gelöscht haben sollen). Der britische Pub ist ein wichtiger sozialer Treffpunkt besonders in dörflichen Gemeinschaften. Bis vor kurzem waren die Gastwirte (publicans oder landlords) an streng überwachte Schankzeiten zwischen 11 Uhr und 23 Uhr gebunden, aber jetzt werden diese Beschränkungen allmählich gelockert. Die anstehende Polizeistunde wird meist durch Läuten einer Glocke und den Ruf Last orders, please oder Time, ladies and gentlemen angezeigt.

puberty ['pjuːbətɪ] *n* Pubertät *die*.

pubic ['pjuːbɪk] *adj* Scham-.

public ['pʌblɪk] ◇ *adj* - 1. [of people in general, open to all] öffentlich - 2. [of, by the state] staatlich, Staats- - 3. [known to everyone]: ~ figure bekannte Persönlichkeit; it's ~ knowledge that ... es ist allgemein bekannt, dass ... ◇ *n*: the ~ die Öffentlichkeit; in ~ in der Öffentlichkeit.

public-address system *n* Lautsprecheranlage *die*.

publican ['pʌblɪkən] *n Br* Wirt *der*, -in *die*.

publication [ˌpʌblɪ'keɪʃn] *n* - 1. (U) [act of publishing] Veröffentlichung *die* - 2. [book, article] Publikation *die*.

public bar *n Br* schlicht eingerichteter Teil eines Pubs, in dem die Getränke billiger als in der „Lounge Bar" sind.

public company *n* Aktiengesellschaft *die*.

public convenience *n Br* öffentliche Toilette.

public holiday *n* gesetzlicher Feiertag.

public house *n Br fml* Gaststätte *die*.

publicity [pʌb'lɪsɪtɪ] *n (U)* - 1. [media attention] Publicity *die* - 2. [information] Werbung *die*, Reklame *die*.

publicize, -ise ['pʌblɪsaɪz] *vt* bekannt machen.

public limited company *n* ≈ Aktiengesellschaft *die*.

public opinion *n (U)* öffentliche Meinung.

public relations ◇ *n (U)* [work] Öffentlichkeitsarbeit *die*, Public Relations *pl* ◇ *npl*: it would be good for ~ es wäre gut für unser öffentliches Ansehen.

public school *n* - 1. *Br* [private school] hö-

here Privatschule - 2. *Am & Scot* [state school] staatliche Schule.

public transport *n (U)* öffentliche Verkehrsmittel *pl.*

publish ['pʌblɪʃ] *vt* veröffentlichen.

publisher ['pʌblɪʃəʳ] *n* - 1. [company] Verlag *der* - 2. [person] Verleger *der*, -in *die*.

publishing ['pʌblɪʃɪŋ] *n* Verlagswesen *das*.

pub lunch *n* Mittagessen *das* im Pub.

pucker ['pʌkəʳ] *vt* [lips for kissing] spitzen.

pudding ['pʊdɪŋ] *n* - 1. [sweet food] Nachspeise *die* - 2. (U) *Br* [part of meal] Nachtisch *der*, Dessert *das*.

puddle ['pʌdl] *n* Pfütze *die*.

puff [pʌf] ◇ *n* - 1. [of cigarette, pipe] Zug *der* - 2. of wind Windhauch *der*; ~ of smoke Rauchwölkchen *das* ◇ *vt* paffen ◇ *vi* - 1. [smoke]: to ~ at OR on sthg an etw (D) paffen - 2. [pant] keuchen, schnaufen. ◆ **puff out** *vt sep* [cheeks] aufblasen; [chest] anschwellen lassen; [feathers] aufplustern.

puffed [pʌft] *adj* [swollen]: ~ up angeschwollen.

puff pastry, puff paste *Am n (U)* Blätterteig *der*.

puffy ['pʌfɪ] *adj* aufgedunsen.

pull [pʊl] ◇ *vt* - 1. [rope, hair] ziehen an (+ D); [cart] ziehen; to ~ sthg to pieces in Stücke reißen; *fig* etw scharf kritisieren - 2. [curtains - open] aufziehen; [- close] zuziehen - 3. [trigger] drücken; [lever] ziehen - 4. [take out - cork] herausziehen; [- gun, tooth] ziehen - 5. [muscle, hamstring] sich (D) zerren - 6. [crowd, voters] anziehen ◇ *vi* [tug with hand] ziehen ◇ *n* - 1. [tug with hand] Ziehen *das*, Zug *der*; to give the rope a ~ am Seil ziehen - 2. (U) [influence] Einfluss *der*. ◆ **pull apart** *vt sep* [separate] auseinander ziehen. ◆ **pull at** *vt fus* ziehen an (+ D). ◆ **pull away** *vi* - 1. [from roadside]: to ~ away (from) wegziehen (von) - 2. [in race]: to ~ away (from) sich absetzen (von). ◆ **pull down** *vt sep* [demolish] abreißen. ◆ **pull in** *vi* [car, bus] anhalten; [train] einfahren. ◆ **pull off** *vt sep* - 1. [take off] ausziehen - 2. [succeed in - coup, robbery] landen; [- deal] an Land ziehen. ◆ **pull out** ◇ *vt sep* [withdraw] zurückziehen ◇ *vi* - 1. [train] abfahren - 2. [vehicle - from kerb] abfahren; [- from lane] ausscheren - 3. [withdraw] sich zurückziehen. ◆ **pull over** *vi* [vehicle, driver] an den Straßenrand fahren. ◆ **pull through** *vi* [patient] durchkommen. ◆ **pull together** *vt sep*: to ~ o.s. together sich zusammenreißen. ◆ **pull up** ◇ *vt sep* - 1. [raise] hochziehen - 2. [move closer] heranziehen ◇ *vi* anhalten.

pulley ['pʊlɪ] *(pl* -s) *n* [wheel] Rolle *die*; [whole system] Flaschenzug *der*.

pullover ['pʊlˌəʊvəʳ] *n* Pullover *der*.

pulp [pʌlp] ◇ *adj*: ~ novel Schundroman

der; ~ **fiction** Schundliteratur *die* ⟨⟩ *n* [soft mass] Brei *der*.

pulpit ['pʊlpɪt] *n* Kanzel *die*.

pulsate [pʌl'seɪt] *vi* pulsieren; [air, sound] vibrieren.

pulse [pʌls] ⟨⟩ *n* - **1.** [in body] Puls *der* - **2.** TECH Impuls *der* ⟨⟩ *vi* [blood, music] pulsieren. ⟜ **pulses** *npl* [food] Hülsenfrüchte *pl*.

puma ['pjuːmə] (*pl inv* OR **-s**) *n* Puma *der*.

pummel ['pʌml] *vt* mit den Fäusten bearbeiten, einschlagen auf (+ *A*).

pump [pʌmp] ⟨⟩ *n* - **1.** [machine] Pumpe *die* - **2.** [for petrol] Zapfsäule *die*, Tanksäule *die* ⟨⟩ *vt* [convey by pumping] pumpen ⟨⟩ *vi* [machine, person, heart] pumpen. ⟜ **pumps** *npl* [shoes] Pumps *pl*.

pumpkin ['pʌmpkɪn] *n* Kürbis *der*.

pun [pʌn] *n* Wortspiel *das*.

punch [pʌntʃ] ⟨⟩ *n* - **1.** [blow] (Faust)schlag *der* - **2.** [for making holes in paper] Locher *der* - **3.** (*U*) [drink - cold] Bowle *die*; [- hot] Punsch *der* ⟨⟩ *vt* - **1.** [hit] (mit der Faust) schlagen - **2.** [perforate - ticket] lochen; **to ~ a hole in sthg** ein Loch in etw machen.

Punch-and-Judy show [ˌpʌntʃənˈdʒuːdɪ-] *n* Kasperletheater *das*.

punch ball *n* Punchingball *der*.

punch line *n* Pointe *die*.

punch-up *n Br inf* Schlägerei *die*.

punchy ['pʌntʃɪ] *adj inf* [style] prägnant; [slogan] durchschlagend.

punctual ['pʌŋktʃʊəl] *adj* pünktlich.

punctuation [ˌpʌŋktʃʊ'eɪʃn] *n* Zeichensetzung *die*, Interpunktion *die*.

punctuation mark *n* Satzzeichen *das*.

puncture ['pʌŋktʃər] ⟨⟩ *n* [in tyre, ball] (kleines) Loch; **I had a ~** ich hatte einen Platten ⟨⟩ *vt* - **1.** [tyre, ball] ein Loch machen in (+ *A*) - **2.** [lung, skin] punktieren.

pundit ['pʌndɪt] *n* Experte *der*, -tin *die*.

pungent ['pʌndʒənt] *adj* - **1.** [smell] stechend, beißend; [taste] scharf - **2.** *fig* [criticism, remark] scharf.

punish ['pʌnɪʃ] *vt* bestrafen; **to ~ sb for sthg** jn für etw bestrafen.

punishing ['pʌnɪʃɪŋ] *adj* [work, schedule] strapaziös.

punishment ['pʌnɪʃmənt] *n* - **1.** (*U*) [act of punishing] Bestrafung *die* - **2.** [means of punishment] Strafe *die*.

punk [pʌŋk] ⟨⟩ *adj* Punker- ⟨⟩ *n* - **1.** [music]: **~ (rock)** Punk(rock) *der* - **2.** [person]: **~ (rocker)** Punker *der*, -in *die* - **3.** *Am inf* [lout] Rowdy *der*, Randalierer *der*.

punt [pʌnt] *n* - **1.** [boat] Stechkahn *der* - **2.** [Irish currency] Punt *das*.

punter ['pʌntər] *n Br inf* [customer] Kunde *der*, -din *die*.

puny ['pjuːnɪ] *adj* [person] kümmerlich; [limbs] schwächlich; [effort] erbärmlich.

pup [pʌp] *n* - **1.** [young dog] Hundejunge *das* - **2.**: **seal ~** Robbenjunge *das*.

pupil ['pjuːpl] *n* - **1.** [student, follower] Schüler *der*, -in *die* - **2.** [of eye] Pupille *die*.

puppet ['pʌpɪt] *n* - **1.** [string puppet] & *fig* Marionette *die* - **2.** [glove puppet] Handpuppe *die*.

puppy ['pʌpɪ] *n* Hundejunge *das*.

purchase ['pɜːtʃəs] *fml* ⟨⟩ *n* - **1.** (*U*) [act of buying] Kauf *der* - **2.** [thing bought]: **~s** Einkäufe *pl*; **this was a good ~** das war ein guter Kauf - **3.** (*U*) [grip] Halt *der* ⟨⟩ *vt* kaufen.

purchaser ['pɜːtʃəsər] *n* Käufer *der*, -in *die*.

pure [pjʊər] *adj* - **1.** [unadulterated, untainted] rein - **2.** [voice, sound] klar - **3.** *literary* [chaste] rein - **4.** [science, maths] theoretisch - **5.** [for emphasis] pur.

puree ['pjʊəreɪ] *n* Püree *das*.

purely ['pjʊəlɪ] *adv* rein.

purge [pɜːdʒ] ⟨⟩ *n* POL Säuberungsaktion *die* ⟨⟩ *vt* - **1.** POL säubern - **2.** [rid]: **to ~ sthg/ o.s. of sthg** etw/sich von etw befreien.

purify ['pjʊərɪfaɪ] *vt* [air, water] reinigen.

purist ['pjʊərɪst] *n* Purist *der*, -in *die*.

purity ['pjʊərətɪ] *n* (*U*) - **1.** [of air, water] Reinheit *die* - **2.** [of sound, voice] Klarheit *die*.

purple ['pɜːpl] ⟨⟩ *adj* violett, lila ⟨⟩ *n* Violett *das*, Lila *das*.

purport [pə'pɔːt] *vi fml*: **to ~ to do/be sthg** vorgeben, etw zu tun/sein.

purpose ['pɜːpəs] *n* - **1.** [objective, reason] Zweck *der* - **2.** [use]: **to no ~** umsonst - **3.** [determination] Entschlossenheit *die*. ⟜ **on purpose** *adv* absichtlich, mit Absicht.

purposeful ['pɜːpəsfʊl] *adj* zielbewusst.

purr [pɜːr] *vi* - **1.** [cat, person] schnurren - **2.** [engine, machine] summen.

purse [pɜːs] ⟨⟩ *n* - **1.** [for money] Portmonee *das* - **2.** *Am* [handbag] Handtasche *die* ⟨⟩ *vt* [lips] aufwerfen, schürzen.

purser ['pɜːsər] *n* Zahlmeister *der*, -in *die*.

pursue [pə'sjuː] *vt* - **1.** [criminal, car] verfolgen - **2.** [hobby, interest] nachgehen (+ *D*); [aim] verfolgen - **3.** [matter] weiterlverfolgen.

pursuer [pə'sjuːər] *n* Verfolger *der*, -in *die*.

pursuit [pə'sjuːt] *n fml* [attempt to obtain, achieve]: **the ~ of sthg** das Streben nach etw - **2.** [chase] Verfolgung *die* - **3.** [occupation, activity] Beschäftigung *die*.

pus [pʌs] *n* Eiter *der*.

push [pʊʃ] ⟨⟩ *vt* - **1.** [press, move - button] drücken; [- bicycle, person] schieben; **to ~ the door open/to** die Tür auf/zumachen - **2.** [encourage] (nachdrücklich) ermutigen; **to ~ sb to do sthg** jn (nachdrücklich) ermutigen, etw zu tun - **3.** [force] drängen; **to ~ sb into doing sthg** jn drängen, etw zu tun - **4.** *inf* [promote] Werbung machen für ⟨⟩ *vi* - **1.** [shove] schieben; [in crowd] drängen - **2.** [on button, bell] drücken - **3.** [campaign]:

to ~ for sthg auf etw (A) drängen ◇ n
- **1.** [shove] Stoß der, Schubs der - **2.** [on button, bell]: **to give sthg a ~** etw drücken
- **3.** [campaign] (großangelegte) Aktion.
◆ **push around** vt sep inf fig [bully] herumlschubsen. ◆ **push in** vi [in queue] (sich) vorldrängen. ◆ **push off** vi inf [go away] verschwinden. ◆ **push on** vi [continue] weiterlmachen. ◆ **push through** vt sep [new law, reform] durchlbringen.

pushchair ['pʊʃtʃeəʳ] n Br Sportwagen der.

pushed [pʊʃt] adj inf: **to be ~ for time** unter Zeitdruck stehen; **to be ~ for money** in Geldnöten sein; **to be hard ~ to do sthg** es schwer finden, etw zu tun.

pusher ['pʊʃəʳ] n drugs sl Dealer der, -in die.

pushover ['pʊʃ‚əʊvəʳ] n inf [sucker]: **he's a ~** er lässt sich leicht reinlegen.

push-up n esp Am Liegestütz der.

pushy ['pʊʃɪ] adj pej aufdringlich, aggressiv.

puss [pʊs], **pussy (cat)** ['pʊsɪ-] n inf Mieze(katze) die.

put [pʊt] (pt & pp **put**) vt - **1.** [place] tun; [place upright] stellen; [lay flat] legen; **to ~ sthg into sthg** etw in etw (A) hineinltun/hineinlstellen/hineinllegen; **he ~ his arm round her shoulder** er legte ihr den Arm um die Schulter; **I ~ the children first** bei mir kommen die Kinder zuerst; **he ~ his hand in his pocket** er steckte die Hand in die Tasche; **that ~s me in a difficult position** das bringt mich in eine schwierige Lage - **2.** [send]: **to ~ sb in prison/hospital** jn ins Gefängnis stecken/ins Krankenhaus schicken; **to ~ a child to bed** ein Kind ins Bett bringen - **3.** [express] sagen - **4.** [ask]: **to ~ a question (to sb)** (jm) eine Frage stellen - **5.** [make]: **to ~ a proposal to sb** jm einen Vorschlag machen - **6.** [write] schreiben - **7.** [cause]: **to ~ sb to a lot of trouble** jm viel Mühe machen - **8.** [estimate]: **to ~ sthg at** etw schätzen auf (+ A) - **9.** [invest - money, time, energy]: **to ~ sthg into sthg** etw in etw (A) investieren - **10.** [apply]: **to ~ the blame on sb** jm die Schuld geben. ◆ **put across** vt sep [ideas] verständlich machen. ◆ **put away** vt sep - **1.** [tidy away] weglräumen - **2.** inf [lock up] einlsperren - **3.** inf [eat] verdrücken; [drink] schlucken. ◆ **put back** vt sep - **1.** [replace] zurückllegen; [upright] zurücklstellen; **~ it back in the bag** stecke es wieder in die Tasche - **2.** [postpone] verschieben - **3.** [clock, watch] zurücklstellen. ◆ **put by** vt sep [money] zurückllegen. ◆ **put down** vt sep - **1.** [place] setzen; [place upright] (hinl)stellen; [lay flat] (hinl)legen - **2.** [passenger] ablsetzen - **3.** [deposit] anlzahlen - **4.** [riot, rebellion] niederlschlagen - **5.** [write down] auflschreiben; **to ~ sthg down in writing** etw schriftlich niederllegen - **6.** Br [animal] einlschläfern. ◆ **put down to** vt sep: **to**

~ sthg down to sthg etw einer Sache (D) zulschreiben. ◆ **put forward** vt sep - **1.** [plan, theory, name] vorlschlagen; [proposal] machen - **2.** [meeting, date] vorlverlegen - **3.** [clock, watch] vorlstellen. ◆ **put in** vt sep - **1.** [spend - time] verwenden - **2.** [submit] einlreichen - **3.** [install] einlbauen. ◆ **put in for** vt fus [request] sich bewerben um. ◆ **put off** vt sep - **1.** [postpone] verschieben; **to ~ off doing sthg** es verschieben, etw zu tun - **2.** [switch off] auslschalten, auslmachen - **3.** [cause to wait] hinlhalten - **4.** [discourage]: **to ~ sb off doing sthg** jn davon ablbringen, etw zu tun - **5.** [distract] ablenken - **6.** [cause to dislike]: **to ~ sb off doing sthg** es jm verleiden, etw zu tun - **7.** [passenger] ablsetzen. ◆ **put on** vt sep - **1.** [clothes] anlziehen; [hat, glasses] auflsetzen; [make-up] aufllegen; **~ your clothes on!** zieh dich an! - **2.** [play, show] auflführen; [exhibition] veranstalten - **3.** [gain in weight]: **to ~ on weight** zulnehmen; **I've ~ on two kilos** ich habe zwei Kilo zugenommen - **4.** [TV, radio, light] anlschalten; [handbrake] anlziehen - **5.** [CD, record] aufllegen; [tape] einllegen; [music] anlstellen - **6.** [start cooking] auflstellen; **to ~ the kettle on** Wasser auflsetzen - **7.** [feign] vorltäuschen - **8.** [add] auflschlagen - **9.** [provide - bus, train] einlsetzen. ◆ **put out** vt sep - **1.** [place outside - milk bottles] hinauslstellen; [- rubbish] hinauslbringen; [- cat] hinauslsetzen - **2.** [issue - book, record] veröffentlichen; [- statement] ablgeben - **3.** [cigarette, fire, light] auslmachen - **4.** [hand, arm, leg] auslstrecken - **5.** [annoy]: **to be ~ out** verärgert sein - **6.** [inconvenience]: **to ~ sb out** jm Umstände machen. ◆ **put through** vt sep [phonecall] durchlstellen; **to ~ sb through to sb** jn mit jm verbinden. ◆ **put up** ◇ vt sep - **1.** [tent, statue, building] auflstellen - **2.** [umbrella] auflspannen; [flag] hochlziehen - **3.** [notice] anlschlagen; [sign] anlbringen; [curtains] auflhängen - **4.** [provide - money] stellen - **5.** [propose - candidate] auflstellen - **6.** [increase - price, cost] hochltreiben - **7.** [provide accommodation for] unterlbringen ◇ vt fus [resistance] leisten; **to ~ up a fight** sich wehren ◇ vi Br [in hotel] unterlkommen. ◆ **put up with** vt fus dulden.

putrid ['pju:trɪd] adj fml [decayed] faulig.

putt [pʌt] ◇ n Schlag der ◇ vt & vi putten, einllochen.

putty ['pʌtɪ] n Kitt der.

puzzle ['pʌzl] ◇ n - **1.** [game] Rätsel das; [toy] Geduldsspiel das; **(jigsaw) ~** Puzzle das - **2.** [mystery] Rätsel das ◇ vt verblüffen ◇ vi: **to ~ over sthg** sich (D) über etw (A) den Kopf zerbrechen. ◆ **puzzle out** vt sep herauslfinden.

puzzling ['pʌzlɪŋ] adj verblüffend.

pyjamas [pə'dʒɑːməz] npl Schlafanzug der.

pylon ['paɪlən] n ELEC Mast der.
pyramid ['pɪrəmɪd] n Pyramide die.
Pyrex® ['paɪreks] n (U) ≃ Jenaer Glas® das.
python ['paɪθn] n (pl inv OR -s) n Python-schlange die.

Q

q (pl q's OR qs), **Q** (pl Q's OR Qs) [kjuː] n q das, Q das.
quack [kwæk] n - 1. [noise] Quaken das - 2. inf pej [doctor] Quacksalber der.
quad [kwɒd] n abbr of quadrangle.
quadrangle ['kwɒdræŋgl] n - 1. [figure] Viereck das - 2. [courtyard] (viereckiger) Hof.
quadruple [kwɒ'druːpl] ⬦ adj vierfach ⬦ vt vervierfachen ⬦ vi sich vervierfachen.
quadruplets ['kwɒdruplɪts] npl Vierlinge pl.
quail [kweɪl] (pl inv OR -s) n Wachtel die.
quaint [kweɪnt] adj [cottage] urig; [tradition] kurios.
quake [kweɪk] ⬦ n inf (abbr of earthquake) Beben das ⬦ vi beben, zittern.
qualification [ˌkwɒlɪfɪ'keɪʃn] n - 1. [examination, certificate, skill] Qualifikation die - 2. [qualifying statement] Einschränkung die.
qualified ['kwɒlɪfaɪd] adj - 1. [trained] ausgebildet - 2. [able]: **to be ~ to do sthg** qualifiziert sein, etw zu tun - 3. [limited] eingeschränkt.
qualify ['kwɒlɪfaɪ] ⬦ vt - 1. [statement] einschränken - 2. [entitle]: **to ~ sb to do sthg** jn berechtigen, etw zu tun ⬦ vi - 1. [pass exams & SPORT] sich qualifizieren - 2. [be entitled]: **to ~ for sthg** zu etw berechtigt sein.
quality ['kwɒlətɪ] ⬦ n - 1. [gen] Qualität die - 2. [characteristic] Eigenschaft die ⬦ comp Qualitäts-.
qualms [kwɑːmz] npl Skrupel pl.
quandary ['kwɒndərɪ] n: **to be in a ~ about** OR **over sthg** in einer Zwickmühle stecken wegen etw OR in Bezug auf etw (A).
quantify ['kwɒntɪfaɪ] vt in Zahlen ausldrücken.
quantity ['kwɒntətɪ] n Menge die; **to be an unknown ~** eine unbekannte Größe sein.
quarantine ['kwɒrəntiːn] ⬦ n Quarantäne die ⬦ vt unter Quarantäne stellen.
quarrel ['kwɒrəl] ⬦ n Streit der ⬦ vi sich streiten; **to ~ with sb** sich mit jm streiten; **to ~ with sthg** an etw (D) etwas auszusetzen haben.

quarrelsome ['kwɒrəlsəm] adj streitsüchtig.
quarry ['kwɒrɪ] n - 1. [place] Steinbruch der - 2. [prey] Beute die.
quart [kwɔːt] n [unit of measurement] Br Quart das (= 1,14 l); Am Quart das (= 0,95 l).
quarter ['kwɔːtər] n - 1. [fraction, area in town] Viertel das - 2. [in telling time]: **a ~ past (two)** Br, **a ~ after (two)** Am Viertel nach (zwei); **a ~ to (two)** Br, **a ~ of (two)** Am Viertel vor (zwei) - 3. [of year] Vierteljahr das, Quartal das - 4. Am [coin] Vierteldollar der - 5. [four ounces] ≃ Viertelpfund das - 6. [direction] Richtung die; **from an unexpected ~** von unerwarteter Seite. ⬦ **quarters** npl [rooms] Quartier das. ⬦ **at close quarters** adv aus der Nähe.
quarterfinal [ˌkwɔːtə'faɪnl] n Viertelfinalspiel das.
quarterly ['kwɔːtəlɪ] ⬦ adj & adv vierteljährlich ⬦ n Vierteljahresschrift die.
quartet [kwɔː'tet] n Quartett das.
quartz [kwɔːts] n (U) Quarz der.
quartz watch n Quarzuhr die.
quash [kwɒʃ] vt - 1. [decision, sentence] aufheben - 2. [rebellion] unterdrücken.
quasi- ['kweɪzaɪ] prefix quasi-.
quaver ['kweɪvər] n MUS Achtelnote die.
quay [kiː] n Kai der.
quayside ['kiːsaɪd] n Kai der.
queasy ['kwiːzɪ] adj unwohl.
queen [kwiːn] n - 1. [royalty, bee] Königin die - 2. [in chess, playing card] Dame die.
queen mother n: **the ~** die Königinmutter.
queer [kwɪər] ⬦ adj [odd] seltsam, eigenartig; **I'm feeling a bit ~** mir ist nicht ganz wohl ⬦ n inf pej [homosexual] Schwule der.
quell [kwel] vt unterdrücken.
quench [kwentʃ] vt stillen.
query ['kwɪərɪ] ⬦ n Frage die ⬦ vt [decision] in Frage stellen; [invoice] beanstanden.
quest [kwest] n literary: **~ (for sthg)** Suche die (nach etw).
question ['kwestʃn] ⬦ n Frage die; **to ask (sb) a ~** (jm) eine Frage stellen; **to bring** OR **call sthg into ~** etw in Frage stellen; **to be beyond ~** außer Zweifel OR Frage stehen; **without ~** ohne Zweifel; **there's no ~ of doing it** es kommt nicht in Frage, es zu tun ⬦ vt - 1. [interrogate] befragen - 2. [express doubt about] bezweifeln. ⬦ **in question** adv: **the ... in ~** der/die/das betreffende ... ⬦ **out of the question** adj ausgeschlossen.
questionable ['kwestʃənəbl] adj - 1. [uncertain] fraglich - 2. [not right, not honest] fragwürdig.
question mark n Fragezeichen das.
questionnaire [ˌkwestʃə'neər] n Fragebogen der.
queue [kjuː] Br ⬦ n Schlange die ⬦ vi

Schlange stehen; **to ~ (up) for sthg** für etw anlstehen.

quibble ['kwɪbl] *pej* <> *n* Spitzfindigkeit *die* <> *vi* spitzfindig sein; **to ~ over** OR **about sthg** über etw *(A)* streiten.

quiche [kiːʃ] *n* Quiche *die.*

quick [kwɪk] *adj & adv* schnell.

quicken ['kwɪkn] <> *vt* [make faster] beschleunigen <> *vi* [get faster] schneller werden.

quickly ['kwɪklɪ] *adv* schnell.

quicksand ['kwɪksænd] *n* Treibsand *der.*

quick-witted [-'wɪtɪd] *adj* [person] geistesgegenwärtig; [response] schlagkräftig.

quid [kwɪd] (*pl inv*) *n* Br *inf* Pfund *das.*

quiet ['kwaɪət] <> *adj* - **1.** [not noisy, calm] ruhig - **2.** [not talkative, silent] still; **to keep ~ about sthg** über etw *(A)* nichts sagen; **be ~!** sei/seid still! - **3.** [discreet - clothes, colours] dezent; **to have a ~ word with sb** mit jm unter vier Augen reden - **4.** [wedding] im kleinen Kreis <> *n* Ruhe *die;* **on the ~** *inf* heimlich <> *vt Am* zum Schweigen bringen. ◆ **quiet down** *Am* <> *vt sep* beruhigen <> *vi* sich beruhigen.

quieten ['kwaɪətn] *vt* beruhigen. ◆ **quieten down** <> *vt sep* beruhigen <> *vi* sich beruhigen.

quietly ['kwaɪətlɪ] *adv* - **1.** [without noise] leise - **2.** [without excitement] ruhig - **3.** [without fuss] in aller Stille.

quilt [kwɪlt] *n* Steppdecke *die.*

quintet [kwɪn'tet] *n* Quintett *das.*

quintuplets [kwɪn'tjuːplɪts] *npl* Fünflinge *pl.*

quip [kwɪp] <> *n* geistreiche Bemerkung <> *vt* witzeln.

quirk [kwɜːk] *n* - **1.** [habit] Marotte *die* - **2.** [strange event]: **a ~ of fate** eine Laune des Schicksals.

quit [kwɪt] (*Br pt & pp* quit OR -ted, *Am pt & pp* quit) <> *vt* - **1.** [resign from - job] auflgeben, kündigen; [- army] verlassen - **2.** [stop] auflhören mit <> *vi* - **1.** [resign] kündigen - **2.** [stop] auflhören.

quite [kwaɪt] *adv* - **1.** [fairly] ziemlich; **~ a lot** ziemlich viel; **~ a few** ziemlich viele - **2.** [completely] ganz; **I ~ agree** das finde ich auch - **3.** [after negative]: **not ~ big enough** nicht groß genug; **I don't ~ understand** ich verstehe nicht ganz - **4.** [for emphasis]: **it was ~ a surprise** es war eine ziemliche Überraschung; **she's ~ a singer** sie singt ganz gut - **5.** [to express agreement]: **~ (so)!** richtig!

quits [kwɪts] *adj inf*: **to be ~ (with sb)** (mit jm) quitt sein; **we'll call it ~** [forget the debt] es ist schon in Ordnung; [stop doing sthg] lassen Sie uns jetzt auflhören.

quiver ['kwɪvə'] *vi* zittern.

quiz [kwɪz] (*pl* -zes; *pt & pp* -zed) <> *n* - **1.** [competition, game] Quiz *das* - **2.** *Am* SCH Prüfung *die* <> *vt*: **to ~ sb (about sthg)** jn (über etw *(A)*) auslfragen.

quizzical ['kwɪzɪkl] *adj* fragend.

quota ['kwəʊtə] *n* Quote *die.*

quotation [kwəʊ'teɪʃn] *n* - **1.** [citation] Zitat *das* - **2.** COMM Kostenvoranschlag *der.*

quotation marks *npl* Anführungszeichen *pl;* **in ~** in Anführungszeichen.

quote [kwəʊt] <> *n* - **1.** [citation] Zitat *das* - **2.** COMM Kostenvoranschlag *der* <> *vt* [cite] zitieren <> *vi* [cite] zitieren; **to ~ from sthg** aus etw zitieren.

quotient ['kwəʊʃnt] *n* Quotient *der.*

R

r (*pl* r's OR rs), **R** (*pl* R's OR Rs) [ɑːʳ] *n* r *das,* R *das.*

rabbi ['ræbaɪ] *n* Rabbiner *der.*

rabbit ['ræbɪt] *n* Kaninchen *das.*

rabbit hutch *n* Kaninchenstall *der.*

rabble ['ræbl] *n* - **1.** [disorderly crowd] auflwieglerische Menge - **2.** [riffraff]: **the ~** der Pöbel.

rabies ['reɪbiːz] *n* Tollwut *die.*

RAC (*abbr of* Royal Automobile Club) *n* ≃ ADAC *der.*

race [reɪs] <> *n* - **1.** [competition] Rennen *das* - **2.** *fig* [for power, control] Wettlauf *der;* **arms ~** Wettrüsten *das* - **3.** [people, ethnic background] Rasse *die* <> *vt* - **1.** [compete against]: **to ~ sb** mit jm um die Wette laufen/fahren/etc - **2.** [animal, vehicle] antreten lassen <> *vi* - **1.** [compete]: **to ~ against sb** gegen jn anltreten - **2.** [rush] rennen - **3.** [heart, pulse] rasen - **4.** [engine] durchldrehen.

race car *n Am* = racing car.

racecourse ['reɪskɔːs] *n* Rennbahn *die.*

race driver *n Am* = racing driver.

racehorse ['reɪshɔːs] *n* Rennpferd *das.*

racetrack ['reɪstræk] *n* Rennbahn *die.*

racial ['reɪʃl] *adj* Rassen-.

racial discrimination *n* Rassendiskriminierung *die.*

racing ['reɪsɪŋ] *n* [motor racing] Rennsport *der;* [horse racing] Pferderennsport *der.*

racing car *Br,* **race car** *Am n* Rennwagen *der.*

racing driver *Br,* **race driver** *Am n* Rennfahrer *der,* -in *die.*

racism ['reɪsɪzm] *n* Rassismus *der.*

racist ['reɪsɪst] <> *adj* rassistisch <> *n* Rassist *der,* -in *die.*

rack [ræk] *n* - **1.** [frame] Ständer *der* - **2.** [for luggage] Ablage *die*.

racket ['rækɪt] *n* - **1.** [noise] Krach *der* - **2.** [illegal activity] Gaunerei *die* - **3.** SPORT Schläger *der*.

racquet ['rækɪt] *n* Schläger *der*.

racy ['reɪsɪ] *adj* feurig.

radar ['reɪdɑː] *n* Radar *der*.

radiant ['reɪdɪənt] *adj* strahlend.

radiate ['reɪdɪeɪt] *vt* auslstrahlen.

radiation [ˌreɪdɪ'eɪʃn] *n (U)* [radioactive] radioaktive Strahlung.

radiator ['reɪdɪeɪtə] *n* - **1.** [in house] Heizkörper *der* - **2.** AUT Kühler *der*.

radical ['rædɪkl] <> *adj* - **1.** POL radikal - **2.** [fundamental] fundamental <> *n* POL Radikale *der, die*.

radically ['rædɪklɪ] *adv* radikal.

radii ['reɪdɪaɪ] *pl* [> radius.

radio ['reɪdɪəʊ] *(pl -s)* <> *n* - **1.** [system of communication] Rundfunk *der* - **2.** [broadcasting, equipment] Radio *das* <> *comp* Radio- <> *vt* [message] funken; [person] anlfunken.

radioactive [ˌreɪdɪəʊ'æktɪv] *adj* radioaktiv.

radio alarm *n* Radiowecker *der*.

radio-controlled [-kən'trəʊld] *adj* ferngesteuert.

radiology [ˌreɪdɪ'ɒlədʒɪ] *n* Radiologie *die*.

radish ['rædɪʃ] *n* Radieschen *das*.

radius ['reɪdɪəs] *(pl radii)* *n* - **1.** MATH Radius *der* - **2.** ANAT Speiche *die*.

RAF [ɑː'reɪ'ef, ræf] *n abbr of* Royal Air Force.

raffle ['ræfl] <> *n* Tombola *die* <> *vt* verlosen.

raffle ticket *n* Los *das*.

raft [rɑːft] *n* Floß *das*.

rafter ['rɑːftə] *n* Dachsparren *der*.

rag [ræg] *n* - **1.** [piece of cloth] Lumpen *der* - **2.** *pej* [newspaper] Käseblatt *das*. ◆ **rags** *npl* [clothes] Lumpen *pl*.

rag-and-bone man *n* Lumpensammler *der*.

rag doll *n* Flickenpuppe *die*.

rage [reɪdʒ] <> *n* - **1.** [fury] Wut *die*; **to fly into a ~** in Rage geraten - **2.** *inf* [fashion]: **to be all the ~** der letzte Schrei sein <> *vi* toben; [disease] wüten.

ragged ['rægɪd] *adj* - **1.** [person, clothes] zerlumpt - **2.** [coastline] zerklüftet - **3.** [performance] stümperhaft.

raid [reɪd] <> *n* - **1.** MIL [attack] Angriff *der* - **2.** [forced entry - by thieves] Überfall *der*; [- by police] Razzia *die* <> *vt* - **1.** MIL [attack] anlgreifen - **2.** [enter by force - subj: thieves] einlbrechen in *(+ A)*; [- subj: police] eine Razzia machen in *(+ D)*.

raider ['reɪdə] *n* - **1.** [attacker] Angreifer *der*, -in *die* - **2.** [thief] Einbrecher *der*, -in *die*.

rail [reɪl] <> *n* - **1.** [fence] Geländer *das;* [on ship] Reling *die* - **2.** [bar, of railway] Schiene *die* - **3.** *(U)* [form of transport] (Eisen)bahn *die* <> *comp* Eisenbahn-, Bahn-.

railcard ['reɪlkɑːd] *n Br* ≃ Bahncard *die*.

railing ['reɪlɪŋ] *n* Geländer *das;* [on ship] Reling *die*.

railway *Br* ['reɪlweɪ], **railroad** *Am* ['reɪlrəʊd] *n* - **1.** [track] Gleis *das* - **2.** [company, system] (Eisen)bahn *die*.

railway line *n* - **1.** [route] (Eisen)bahnlinie *die* - **2.** [track] Gleis *das*.

railwayman ['reɪlweɪmən] *(pl -men [-mən]) n Br* Eisenbahner *der*.

railway station *n* Bahnhof *der*.

railway track *n* Gleis *das*.

rain [reɪn] <> *n* Regen *der* <> *v impers & vi* regnen; **it's ~ing** es regnet.

rainbow ['reɪnbəʊ] *n* Regenbogen *der*.

rain check *n Am:* **to take a ~ on sthg** etw auf ein andermal verschieben.

raincoat ['reɪnkəʊt] *n* Regenmantel *der*.

raindrop ['reɪndrɒp] *n* Regentropfen *der*.

rainfall ['reɪnfɔːl] *n (U)* Niederschlag *der*.

rain forest *n* Regenwald *der*.

rainy ['reɪnɪ] *adj* regnerisch.

raise [reɪz] <> *vt* - **1.** [lift up] heben; [window] hochlziehen; **to ~ o.s.** sich auflrichten - **2.** [increase, improve] anlheben; **to ~ one's voice** [make louder] seine Stimme heben; [in protest] seine Stimme erheben - **3.** [obtain - from donations] auflbringen; [- by selling, borrowing] auftreiben - **4.** [evoke] (herauf)beschwören - **5.** [child, animal] auflziehen - **6.** [crop] anlbauen - **7.** [mention] auflwerfen <> *n Am* Erhöhung *die*.

raisin ['reɪzn] *n* Rosine *die*.

rake [reɪk] <> *n* [implement] Harke *die*, Rechen *der* <> *vt* - **1.** [smooth] harken, rechen - **2.** [gather] zusammenlrechen.

rally ['rælɪ] <> *n* - **1.** [meeting] Versammlung *die* - **2.** [car race] Rallye *die* - **3.** SPORT [exchange of shots] Ballwechsel *der* <> *vt* sammeln <> *vi* - **1.** [come together] sich sammeln - **2.** [recover] sich erholen. ◆ **rally round** <> *vt fus* sich scharen um <> *vi* sich seiner/ihrer/etc anlnehmen.

ram [ræm] <> *n* [animal] Widder *der* <> *vt* rammen.

RAM [ræm] *(abbr of* random access memory) *n* RAM.

ramble ['ræmbl] <> *n* Wanderung *die* <> *vi* - **1.** [walk] wandern - **2.** [talk] schwafeln.

rambler ['ræmblə] *n* [walker] Spaziergänger *der*, -in *die*.

rambling ['ræmblɪŋ] *adj* - **1.** [building] weitläufig - **2.** [conversation, book] weitschweifig.

ramp [ræmp] *n* Rampe *die*.

rampage [ræm'peɪdʒ] n: **to go on the ~** randalieren.

rampant ['ræmpənt] adj - 1. [unrestrained] wuchernd; **to be ~** wüten - 2. [widespread] weit verbreitet.

ramparts ['ræmpɑːts] npl Schutzwall der.

ramshackle ['ræm,ʃækl] adj heruntergekommen.

ran [ræn] pt ⊳ run.

ranch [rɑːntʃ] n Ranch die.

rancher ['rɑːntʃə'] n Viehzüchter der, -in die.

rancid ['rænsɪd] adj ranzig.

rancour Br, **rancor** Am ['ræŋkə'] n Bitterkeit die.

random ['rændəm] ⋄ adj willkürlich; **~ sample** Stichprobe die ⋄ n: **at ~** [choose, sample] willkürlich; [fire, hit out] ziellos.

random access memory n (U) COMPUT Arbeitsspeicher der.

randy ['rændɪ] adj inf scharf.

rang [ræŋ] pt ⊳ ring.

range [reɪndʒ] ⋄ n - 1. [distance covered] Reichweite die; **at close ~** auf kurze Entfernung - 2. [variety] Auswahl die; **there was a wide ~ of people there** es waren ganz unterschiedliche Leute da - 3. [bracket] Klasse die - 4. [of mountains, hills] Kette die - 5. [shooting area] Platz der - 6. MUS [of voice] Stimmumfang der ⋄ vt [place in row] aufstellen ⋄ vi - 1. [vary]: **to ~ from ... to ...** reichen von ... bis ...; **to ~ between ... and ...** liegen zwischen ... und ... - 2. [deal with, include]: **to ~ over sthg** sich erstrecken auf etw (A).

ranger ['reɪndʒə'] n [of park] Aufseher der, -in die; [of forest] Förster der, -in die.

rank [ræŋk] ⋄ adj - 1. [utter, absolute] ausgesprochen - 2. [offensive] übel ⋄ n - 1. [in army, police] Rang der; **the ~ and file** MIL die Mannschaft; [of political party, organization] die Basis - 2. [social class] Stand der - 3. [row, line] Reihe die; **taxi ~** Taxistand der ⋄ vt [classify]: **to ~ sb among the great writers** jn zu den großen Schriftstellern zählen; **he is ~ed fourth in the world** er steht an vierter Stelle in der Weltrangliste ⋄ vi: **to ~ as** gelten als; **to ~ among** zählen zu. ◆ **ranks** npl - 1. MIL: **the ~s** die einfachen Soldaten - 2. fig [members] Reihen pl.

rankle ['ræŋkl] vi: **it still ~s with me** es wurmt mich noch immer.

ransack ['rænsæk] vt - 1. [plunder] plündern - 2. [search] durchwühlen.

ransom ['rænsəm] n Lösegeld das; **to hold sb to ~** [keep prisoner] jn als Geisel halten; fig [put in impossible position] jn erpressen.

rant [rænt] vi schwadronieren.

rap [ræp] ⋄ n - 1. [knock] Klopfen das - 2. MUS Rap der ⋄ vt [on table] klopfen auf (+ A); **to ~ sb on the knuckles** jm auf die Finger klopfen.

rape [reɪp] ⋄ n - 1. [crime, attack] Vergewaltigung die - 2. fig [destruction]: **the ~ of the countryside** der Raubbau an der Landschaft - 3. [plant] Raps der ⋄ vt vergewaltigen.

rapid ['ræpɪd] adj rapide, schnell. ◆ **rapids** npl Stromschnelle die.

rapidly ['ræpɪdlɪ] adv schnell.

rapist ['reɪpɪst] n Vergewaltiger der.

rapport [ræ'pɔː'] n: **a (good) ~ with/ between** ein gutes Verhältnis mit/zwischen (+ D).

rapture ['ræptʃə'] n: **to go into ~s over** OR **about sb/sthg** über jn/etw in Verzückung geraten.

rapturous ['ræptʃərəs] adj begeistert.

rare [reə'] adj - 1. [scarce, infrequent] selten - 2. [exceptional] rar - 3. CULIN [underdone] blutig.

rarely ['reəlɪ] adv selten.

raring ['reərɪŋ] adj: **to be ~ to go** in den Startlöchern sein.

rarity ['reərətɪ] n - 1. [unusual object, person] Rarität die - 2. (U) [scarcity] Seltenheit die.

rascal ['rɑːskl] n [mischievous child] Frechdachs der.

rash [ræʃ] ⋄ adj [person] unbesonnen; [action, decision, promise] voreilig ⋄ n - 1. MED Ausschlag der - 2. [spate] Serie die.

rasher ['ræʃə'] n Streifen der.

raspberry ['rɑːzbərɪ] n [fruit] Himbeere die.

rat [ræt] n - 1. [animal] Ratte die - 2. pej [person] Schwein das.

rate [reɪt] ⋄ n - 1. [speed] Tempo das; **at this ~** bei diesem Tempo - 2. [ratio, proportion] Rate die - 3. [of taxation, interest] Satz der ⋄ vt - 1. [consider]: **to ~ sb/sthg (as)** jn/etw einschätzen (als); **to ~ sb/sthg among** jn/ etw zählen zu - 2. [deserve] verdienen. ◆ **at any rate** adv auf jeden Fall.

ratepayer ['reɪt,peɪə'] n Br Steuerzahler der, -in die.

rather ['rɑːðə'] adv - 1. [slightly, a bit] ziemlich; **he's had ~ too much to drink** er hat ziemlich viel getrunken - 2. [for emphasis] recht; **I ~ thought so** das habe ich mir fast gedacht; **I ~ like him** ich mag ihn recht gern - 3. [expressing a preference] lieber; **would you ~ ...?** möchtest du lieber ...?; **I'd ~ not** lieber nicht - 4. [more exactly]: **or ~ ...** vielmehr ... - 5. [on the contrary]: **(but) ~ ...** vielmehr ... ◆ **rather than** conj statt.

ratify ['rætɪfaɪ] vt ratifizieren.

rating ['reɪtɪŋ] n [standing]: **popularity ~** Beliebtheitsgrad der; **what is her ~ in the polls?** wie hoch ist ihr Beliebtheitsgrad?

ratio ['reɪʃɪəʊ] (pl -s) n Verhältnis das.

ration ['ræʃn] ⋄ n Ration die ⋄ vt [goods] rationieren. ◆ **rations** npl Rationen pl.

rational ['ræ∫ənl] *adj* - 1. [reasonable] ratio-nal - 2. [capable of reason] vernünftig.

rationale [ˌræ∫ə'nɑːl] *n* Gründe *pl*.

rationalize, -ise ['ræ∫ənəlaɪz] *vt* rationali-sieren.

rat race *n* ständiger Konkurrenzkampf.

rattle ['rætl] ⟨⟩ *n* [toy] Klapper *die* ⟨⟩ *vt* - 1. [make rattling noise with - keys] klimpern mit; [subj: wind - windows] rütteln an (+ D) - 2. [unsettle] durcheinander bringen ⟨⟩ *vi* [make rattling noise] klappern; [bottles] klirren.

rattlesnake ['rætlsneɪk], **rattler** *Am* ['rætləʳ] *n* Klapperschlange *die*.

raucous ['rɔːkəs] *adj* [voice, laughter] rau; [behaviour] wüst.

ravage ['rævɪdʒ] *vt* verheeren, verwüsten.
 ➡ **ravages** *npl* Verheerung *die*.

rave [reɪv] ⟨⟩ *adj* glänzend ⟨⟩ *n* Br inf [event] Rave *der* OR *das* ⟨⟩ *vi* - 1. [talk angrily]: **to ~ about/against sthg** gegen etw (A)/gegen etw wettern - 2. [talk enthusiastically]: **to ~ about sthg** von etw schwärmen.

raven ['reɪvn] *n* Rabe *der*.

ravenous ['rævənəs] *adj* ausgehungert; **I'm ~!** ich habe einen Bärenhunger!

ravine [rə'viːn] *n* Schlucht *die*.

raving ['reɪvɪŋ] *adj*: **he's a ~ lunatic** er ist total verrückt.

ravioli [ˌrævɪ'əʊlɪ] *n* (U) Ravioli *pl*.

ravishing ['rævɪ∫ɪŋ] *adj* hinreißend.

raw [rɔː] *adj* - 1. [uncooked] roh - 2. [untreated] roh, Roh- - 3. [painful - wound] offen; [- skin] wund - 4. [inexperienced] unerfahren.

raw deal *n*: **to get a ~** schlecht wegkommen.

raw material *n* - 1. [natural substance] Rohstoff *der* - 2. (U) *fig* [basis] Grundlage *die*.

ray [reɪ] *n* - 1. [beam] Strahl *der* - 2. *fig* [glimmer] Schimmer *der*.

rayon ['reɪɒn] *n* Reyon *das*.

raze [reɪz] *vt*: **the house was ~d to the ground** das Haus wurde dem Erdboden gleichgemacht.

razor ['reɪzəʳ] *n* Rasierapparat *der*.

razor blade *n* Rasierklinge *die*.

RC (*abbr of* Roman Catholic) *adj* röm.-kath.

Rd (*abbr of* Road) Str.

R & D (*abbr of* research and development) *n* F & E.

re [riː] *prep* betreffs (+ G).

RE *n* (*abbr of* religious education) Religionsunterricht *der*.

reach [riːt∫] ⟨⟩ *vt* - 1. [arrive at] anlkommen in (+ D) - 2. [be able to touch] heranlkommen an (+ A) - 3. [contact, extend as far as, attain, achieve] erreichen ⟨⟩ *vi* - 1. [person, arm, hand] greifen; **to ~ (out) for sthg** nach etw greifen - 2. [land] reichen ⟨⟩ *n* [of boxer] Reichweite *die*; **within sb's ~** [easily touched]

innerhalb js Reichweite; **within easy ~ of the station** vom Bahnhof leicht zu erreichen; **out of** OR **beyond sb's ~** [not easily touched] außerhalb js Reichweite.

react [rɪ'ækt] *vi* - 1. [rebel]: **to ~ against sthg** sich gegen etw auflehnen - 2. CHEM: **to ~ with sthg** auf etw (A) reagieren.

reaction [rɪ'æk∫n] *n* - 1. [response & MED]: **~ (to sthg)** Reaktion *die* (auf etw (A)) - 2. [re-bellion]: **~ (against sthg)** Gegenreaktion *die* (auf etw (A)) - 3. [reflex] Reaktionsfähigkeit *die*; **she's got very quick ~s** sie hat sehr gute Reflexe.

reactionary [rɪ'æk∫ənrɪ] ⟨⟩ *adj* reaktionär ⟨⟩ *n* Reaktionär *der*, -in *die*.

reactor [rɪ'æktəʳ] *n* [nuclear reactor] Reaktor *der*.

read [riːd] (*pt & pp* read [red]) ⟨⟩ *vt* - 1. [book, magazine, music] lesen; **to ~ music** Noten lesen - 2. [say aloud]: **to ~ sb sthg** jm etw vorlesen - 3. [subj: sign, notice] besagen; [subj: gauge, meter, barometer] anlzeigen - 4. [take reading from - meter, gauge] abllesen - 5. [interpret] verstehen; [sb's thoughts] lesen - 6. *Br* UNIV studieren ⟨⟩ *vi* - 1. [in book, magazine] lesen; **to ~ about sthg** von etw lesen - 2. [out loud]: **to ~ to sb (from)** jm vorlesen (aus). ➡ **read out** *vt sep* vorlesen. ➡ **read over, read through** *vt sep* durchllesen. ➡ **read up on** *vt fus* nachllesen über (+ A).

readable ['riːdəbl] *adj* [book] lesenswert.

reader ['riːdəʳ] *n* [person who reads] Leser *der*, -in *die*.

readership ['riːdə∫ɪp] *n* [total number of readers] Leser *pl*.

readily ['redɪlɪ] *adv* - 1. [willingly] bereitwillig - 2. [easily] leicht.

reading ['riːdɪŋ] *n* - 1. [act of reading] Lesen *das* - 2. [reading material] Lektüre *die* - 3. [recital] Lesung *die* - 4. [taken from meter] Zählerstand *der*; [taken from thermometer] Thermometerstand *der* - 5. [POL - of bill] Lesung *die*.

readjust [ˌriːə'dʒʌst] ⟨⟩ *vt* [mechanism, instrument] nachlstellen; [mirror] einlstellen; [policy] neu anlpassen ⟨⟩ *vi*: **to ~ to sthg** sich wieder an etw (A) gewöhnen.

readout ['riːdaʊt] *n* COMPUT Anzeige *die*.

ready ['redɪ] ⟨⟩ *adj* - 1. [prepared] fertig; **to be ~ to do sthg** bereit sein, etw zu tun; **to be ~ for sthg** für etw bereit sein; **to get ~** sich fertig machen; **to get sthg ~** etw fertig machen - 2. [willing]: **to be ~ to do sthg** bereit sein, etw zu tun - 3. [in need of]: **to be ~ for sthg** etw gebrauchen können; **I'm ~ for bed** ich bin bettreif - 4. [likely]: **to be ~ to collapse** zum Umfallen müde sein; **she was ~ to cry** sie war den Tränen nahe ⟨⟩ *vt* vorlbereiten.

ready cash *n* Bargeld *das*.

ready-made adj - **1.** [product] Fertig- - **2.** fig [reply, excuse] vorgefertigt.

ready money n Bargeld das.

ready-to-wear adj: ~ clothes Konfektionskleidung die, Kleidung die von der Stange.

real ['rıəl] <> adj - **1.** [authentic, for emphasis] echt; **this is the ~ thing!** [marvellous] das ist unglaublich toll!; **this time it's for ~** diesmal ist es echt - **2.** [actually existing] real - **3.** [cost, value] tatsächlich; **in ~ terms** real <> adv Am wirklich.

real estate n (U) Immobilien pl.

realign [ˌriːə'laın] vt [brakes] nachlstellen.

realism ['rıəlızm] n Realismus der.

realistic [ˌrıə'lıstık] adj realistisch.

reality [rı'ælətı] n Realität die.

realization [ˌrıəlaı'zeıʃn] n (U) - **1.** [awareness, recognition] Realisation die - **2.** [achievement] Realisierung die.

realize, -ise ['rıəlaız] vt - **1.** [become aware of, understand] begreifen - **2.** [achieve] verwirklichen - **3.** COMM erzielen.

really ['rıəlı] <> adv - **1.** [for emphasis] wirklich; ~ good/bad wirklich gut/schlecht; **you ~ ought to see this film** du solltest dir den Film unbedingt ansehen - **2.** [actually] eigentlich; **not ~** eigentlich nicht - **3.** [honestly] wirklich - **4.** [to sound less negative] eigentlich <> excl - **1.** [expressing doubt, surprise]: **really?** wirklich? - **2.** [expressing disapproval]: **really!** also wirklich!

realm [relm] n - **1.** [field] Bereich der - **2.** [kingdom] Reich das.

realtor ['rıəltər] n Am Grundstücksmakler der, -in die.

reap [riːp] vt lit & fig ernten.

reappear [ˌriːə'pıər] vi wieder erscheinen.

rear [rıər] <> adj [wheel] Hinter-; ~ **window** [of car] Heckscheibe die <> n - **1.** [back] Rückseite die; **to bring up the ~** die Nachhut bilden - **2.** inf [buttocks] Hintern der <> vt [children, animals, plants] auflziehen <> vi: **to ~ (up)** sich auflbäumen.

rearm [riː'ɑːm] <> vt wieder bewaffnen <> vi wieder auflrüsten.

rearrange [ˌriːə'reındʒ] vt - **1.** [arrange differently] umlstellen - **2.** [reschedule] verlegen.

rearview mirror ['rıəvjuː-] n Rückspiegel der.

reason ['riːzn] <> n - **1.** [cause]: ~ **(for sthg)** Grund der (für etw) ; **for some ~** aus irgendeinem Grund - **2.** [justification]: **to have ~ to do sthg** Grund haben, etw zu tun - **3.** [common sense] Vernunft die; **to listen to ~** auf die Stimme der Vernunft hören; **it stands to ~** es ist logisch <> vt [conclude]: **to ~ that ...** folgern, dass ... <> vi vernünftig denken. **reason with** vt fus vernünftig reden mit.

reasonable ['riːznəbl] adj - **1.** [sensible]

vernünftig - **2.** [acceptable - decision, explanation] angemessen; [- work] ganz gut; [- offer] akzeptabel; [- price] vernünftig - **3.** [fairly large]: **a ~ amount/number** ziemlich viel/ viele.

reasonably ['riːznəblı] adv - **1.** [quite] ziemlich - **2.** [sensibly] vernünftig.

reasoned ['riːznd] adj durchdacht.

reasoning ['riːznıŋ] n (U) Argumentation die.

reassess [ˌriːə'ses] vt [position, opinion] neu einlschätzen.

reassurance [ˌriːə'ʃʊərəns] n - **1.** [comfort] Beruhigung die - **2.** [promise] Versicherung die.

reassure [ˌriːə'ʃʊər] vt beruhigen.

 reassuring

Du wirst sehen, das klappt schon. Everything will be alright, you'll see.

Keine Sorge, sie kommt bestimmt wieder. Don't worry, she'll be back.

Das ist nicht schlimm. That's not a problem.

Es wird schon nichts passiert sein. Everything's OK.

Immer mit der Ruhe, bis jetzt ist alles gut gegangen. Relax, everything has gone fine until now.

reassuring [ˌriːə'ʃʊərıŋ] adj beruhigend.

rebate ['riːbeıt] n Nachlass der.

rebel [n 'rebl, vb rı'bel] <> n Rebell der, -in die <> vi: **to ~ (against)** rebellieren (gegen).

rebellion [rı'beljən] n Rebellion die.

rebellious [rı'beljəs] adj rebellisch.

rebound [rı'baʊnd] vi [ball] ablprallen.

rebuff [rı'bʌf] n Abfuhr die.

rebuild [ˌriː'bıld] (pt & pp -built [ˌriː'bılt]) vt wieder auflbauen.

rebuke [rı'bjuːk] <> n Tadel der <> vt: **to ~ sb (for sthg)** jn (für etw) tadeln.

recall [rı'kɔːl] <> n (U) [memory] Erinnerung die <> vt - **1.** [remember] sich erinnern an (+ A) - **2.** [summon back] zurücklrufen.

recap ['riːkæp] inf vt & vi [summarize] zusammenlfassen.

recapitulate [ˌriːkə'pıtjʊleıt] vt & vi zusammenlfassen.

recd, rec'd abbr of received.

recede [rı'siːd] vi - **1.** [move away] zurücklweichen; **his hair is receding** er bekommt eine leichte Stirnglatze - **2.** fig [disappear, fade] schwinden.

receding [rı'siːdıŋ] adj [chin] fliehend; [hairline] zurückweichend.

receipt [rı'siːt] n - **1.** [piece of paper] Quittung die - **2.** (U) [act of receiving] Empfang der.

receipts *npl* [money taken] Einnahmen *pl.*

📖 receipt

Dieses Wort ähnelt sehr dem deutschen „Rezept", meint aber „Quittung". Should I write you out a receipt? fragt also, ob man eine Quittung ausgestellt haben möchte.
„Rezept" im Sinne von Kochrezept heißt im Englischen recipe, und das „Rezept" vom Arzt nennt man prescription. Die Wendung „Nur auf Rezept erhältlich" lautet im Englischen Only available on prescription.

---

receive [rɪ'siːv] *vt* - 1. [gift, letter] erhalten - 2. [news] erfahren - 3. [setback] erfahren; **to ~ an injury** verletzt werden - 4. [visitor, guest] empfangen - 5. [greet]: **to be well/badly ~d** gut/schlecht aufgenommen werden.

receiver [rɪ'siːvə^r] *n* - 1. [of telephone] Hörer *der* - 2. [radio, TV set] Empfänger *der* - 3. FIN [official] Konkursverwalter *der*, -in *die*.

recent ['riːsnt] *adj* neueste, -r, -s.

recently ['riːsntlɪ] *adv* kürzlich.

receptacle [rɪ'septəkl] *n* Behälter *der*.

reception [rɪ'sepʃn] *n* Empfang *der*.

reception desk *n* Empfang *der*.

receptionist [rɪ'sepʃənɪst] *n* Empfangschef *der*, Empfangsdame *die*.

recess ['riːses, *Br* rɪ'ses] *n* - 1. [vacation] Ferien *pl*; **to be in/go into** ~ eine Sitzungspause haben/beginnen - 2. [alcove] Nische *die* - 3. [of mind, memory] Winkel *der* - 4. *Am* SCH Pause *die*.

recession [rɪ'seʃn] *n* Rezession *die*.

recharge [ˌriːˈtʃɑːdʒ] *vt* (auf)laden.

recipe ['resɪpɪ] *n lit & fig* Rezept *das*.

recipient [rɪ'sɪpɪənt] *n* Empfänger *der*, -in *die*.

reciprocal [rɪ'sɪprəkl] *adj* wechselseitig.

recital [rɪ'saɪtl] *n* [of poetry] Vortrag *der*; [of music] Konzert *das*.

recite [rɪ'saɪt] *vt* - 1. [perform aloud] vortragen - 2. [list] aufzählen.

reckless ['reklɪs] *adj* leichtsinnig.

reckon ['rekn] *vt* - 1. *inf* [think]: **to ~ (that)** ... schätzen, dass ... - 2. [consider, judge]: **to be ~ed to be sthg** als etw eingeschätzt werden - 3. [calculate] schätzen. ◆ **reckon on** *vt fus* zählen auf (+ *A*). ◆ **reckon with** *vt fus* [expect] rechnen mit.

reckoning ['rekənɪŋ] *n (U)* [calculation] Schätzung *die*.

reclaim [rɪ'kleɪm] *vt* - 1. [claim back - lost item, luggage] abholen; [- tax, expenses] zurückerlangen - 2. [make fit for use] gewinnen.

recline [rɪ'klaɪn] *vi* [lie back] sich zurücklehnen.

reclining [rɪ'klaɪnɪŋ] *adj* verstellbar.

recluse [rɪ'kluːs] *n* Einsiedler *der*, -in *die*.

recognition [ˌrekəg'nɪʃn] *n (U)* - 1. [identification] Erkennen *das*; **to have changed beyond** OR **out of all** ~ nicht wiederzuerkennen sein - 2. [acknowledgement] Anerkennung *die*; **in ~ of** in Anerkennung (+ *G*).

recognizable ['rekəgnaɪzəbl] *adj* erkennbar.

recognize, -ise ['rekəgnaɪz] *vt* - 1. [gen] erkennen - 2. [officially accept, approve] anerkennen.

recoil [*vb* rɪ'kɔɪl, *n* 'riːkɔɪl] ◇ *vi* - 1. [draw back] zurückweichen - 2. *fig* [shrink from]: **to ~ from/at sthg** vor etw (*D*) zurückschrecken ◇ *n* [of gun] Rückstoß *der*.

recollect [ˌrekə'lekt] *vt* sich erinnern an (+ *A*).

recollection [ˌrekə'lekʃn] *n* Erinnerung *die*.

recommend [ˌrekə'mend] *vt* - 1. [commend, speak in favour of]: **to ~ sb/sthg (to sb)** (jm) jn/etw empfehlen - 2. [advise] raten zu.

recompense ['rekəmpens] ◇ *n*: ~ **(for sthg)** Entschädigung *die* (für etw) ◇ *vt*: **to ~ sb (for sthg)** jn (für etw) entschädigen.

reconcile ['rekənsaɪl] *vt* - 1. [beliefs, ideas] (miteinander) vereinbaren; **to ~ sthg with sthg** etw mit etw vereinbaren - 2. [people] versöhnen - 3. [resign]: **to ~ o.s. to sthg** sich mit etw aussöhnen.

reconditioned [ˌriːkən'dɪʃnd] *adj* überholt.

reconnaissance [rɪ'kɒnɪsəns] *n (U)* Erkundung *die*.

reconsider [ˌriːkən'sɪdə^r] ◇ *vt* neu überdenken ◇ *vi*: **it's not too late to** ~ Sie können es sich noch einmal überlegen.

reconstruct [ˌriːkən'strʌkt] *vt* - 1. [building, bridge, country] wieder aufbauen - 2. [event, crime] rekonstruieren.

record [*n & adj* 'rekɔːd, *vb* rɪ'kɔːd] ◇ *n* - 1. [written account] Aufzeichnung *die*; **off the** ~ inoffiziell - 2. [vinyl disc] (Schall)platte *die* - 3. [best achievement] Rekord *der* - 4. [history]: **to have a good** ~ gute Leistungen aufweisen können; **to have a criminal** ~ vorbestraft sein ◇ *adj* Rekord- ◇ *vt* - 1. [write down] aufzeichnen - 2. [put on tape *etc*] aufnehmen.

recorded delivery [rɪ'kɔːdɪd-] *n*: **to send sthg by** ~ etw per Einschreiben schicken.

recorder [rɪ'kɔːdə^r] *n* - 1. [machine]: **(tape)** ~ Tonbandgerät *das*; **(cassette)** ~ Kassettenrekorder *der*; **(video)** ~ Videorekorder *der* - 2. [musical instrument] Blockflöte *die*.

record holder *n* Rekordinhaber *der*, -in *die*.

recording [rɪ'kɔːdɪŋ] *n* - 1. [individual recording] Aufnahme *die* - 2. *(U)* [process of recording] Aufzeichnung *die*.

record player n Plattenspieler der.

recount [n 'riːkaʊnt, vt sense 1 rɪ'kaʊnt, sense 2 ˌriː'kaʊnt] ◇ n Nachzählung die ◇ vt - **1.** [narrate] erzählen - **2.** [count again] nachlzählen.

recoup [rɪ'kuːp] vt [recover] wieder einlbringen.

recourse [rɪ'kɔːs] n fml: **to have ~ to sthg** Zuflucht zu etw nehmen.

recover [rɪ'kʌvə'] ◇ vt - **1.** [stolen goods, money] zurücklbekommen; **to ~ sthg from sb/somewhere** etw von jm/irgendwo zurücklbekommen - **2.** [one's strength, balance, senses] wiederlgewinnen ◇ vi [from illness]: **to ~ (from)** genesen (von).

recovery [rɪ'kʌvərɪ] n - **1.** [from illness]: **~ (from)** Genesung die (von) - **2.** fig [of currency, economy] Erholung die - **3.** [of stolen goods, money] Wiedererlangung die.

recreation [ˌrekrɪ'eɪʃn] n [leisure] Erholung die.

recrimination [rɪˌkrɪmɪ'neɪʃn] n (U) Gegenbeschuldigung die. ◆ **recriminations** npl gegenseitige Beschuldigungen pl.

recruit [rɪ'kruːt] ◇ n [in armed forces] Rekrut der, -in die; [in company, organization] neues Mitglied ◇ vt - **1.** [find, employ - in armed forces] rekrutieren; [- in company, organization] einlstellen - **2.** [persuade to join] werben; **they ~ed her to help out** sie haben sie zur Hilfe herangezogen ◇ vi [look for new staff] einlstellen.

recruitment [rɪ'kruːtmənt] n (U) [of staff] Einstellung die; [of soldiers] Rekrutierung die.

rectangle ['rekˌtæŋgl] n Rechteck das.

rectangular [rek'tæŋgjʊlə'] adj rechteckig.

rectify ['rektɪfaɪ] vt fml berichtigen.

rector ['rektə'] n - **1.** [priest] Pfarrer der - **2.** Scot [head - of school] Direktor der, -in die; [- of college, university] Rektor der, -in die.

rectory ['rektərɪ] n Pfarrhaus das.

recuperate [rɪ'kuːpəreɪt] vi fml: **to ~ (from)** genesen (von).

recur [rɪ'kɜː'] vi wiederlkehren; [problem, error] wieder auflltreten.

recurrence [rɪ'kʌrəns] n fml Wiederkehr die; [of problem, error] Wiederauftreten das.

recurrent [rɪ'kʌrənt] adj immer wiederkehrend; [problem, error] immer wieder auftretend.

recycle [ˌriː'saɪkl] vt recyceln.

red [red] ◇ adj rot ◇ n [colour] Rot das; **to be in the ~** inf in den roten Zahlen sein.

red card n FTBL: **to be shown the ~, to get a ~** die rote Karte gezeigt bekommen.

red carpet n: **to roll out the ~ for sb** für jn den roten Teppich auslrollen.

Red Cross n: **the ~** das Rote Kreuz.

redcurrant ['red,kʌrənt] n (rote) Johannisbeere.

redden ['redn] vi [person, face] erröten.

redecorate [ˌriː'dekəreɪt] vt & vi renovieren.

redeem [rɪ'diːm] vt - **1.** [save, rescue] retten - **2.** [from pawnbroker] einllösen.

redeeming [rɪ'diːmɪŋ] adj: **her one ~ feature is …** ihre einzige positive Eigenschaft ist …

redeploy [ˌriːdɪ'plɔɪ] vt [troops] umverlegen; [workers, staff] an anderer Stelle einlsetzen.

red-faced [-'feɪst] adj [with embarrassment] mit rotem Kopf.

red-haired [-'heəd] adj rothaarig.

red-handed [-'hændɪd] adj: **to catch sb ~** jn auf frischer Tat ertappen.

redhead ['redhed] n Rotkopf der.

red herring n fig falsche Spur.

red-hot adj - **1.** [extremely hot] rot glühend - **2.** [very good] inf klasse, super.

redid [ˌriː'dɪd] pt ▷ redo.

redirect [ˌriːdɪ'rekt] vt - **1.** [mail] nachllsenden - **2.** [aircraft, aid] umlleiten; [one's energies] anders einlsetzen.

rediscover [ˌriːdɪ'skʌvə'] vt - **1.** [reexperience] wieder entdecken - **2.** [make popular, famous again]: **to be ~ed** wieder entdeckt werden.

red light n [traffic signal] rote Ampel.

red-light district n Rotlichtviertel das.

redo [ˌriː'duː] (pt -did; pp -done) vt [do again] noch einmal machen; [letter, essay] noch einmal schreiben.

redolent ['redələnt] adj: **to be ~ of sthg** literary [reminiscent] an etw (A) erinnern.

redone [ˌriː'dʌn] pp ▷ redo.

redouble [ˌriː'dʌbl] vt: **to ~ one's efforts (to do sthg)** seine Anstrengungen verdoppeln (etw zu tun).

redraft [ˌriː'drɑːft] vt neu abfassen.

red tape n fig Bürokratie die.

reduce [rɪ'djuːs] ◇ vt - **1.** [make smaller, less] reduzieren - **2.** [force, bring]: **to be ~d to doing sthg** dazu gezwungen sein, etw zu tun; **to be ~d to tears** zum Weinen gebracht werden ◇ vi Am [lose weight] ablnehmen.

reduction [rɪ'dʌkʃn] n - **1.** [decrease]: **~ (in sthg)** Reduzierung die (einer Sache (G)) - **2.** [amount of decrease]: **~ (of)** Ermäßigung die (um).

redundancy [rɪ'dʌndənsɪ] n Br - **1.** [job loss]: **redundancies** Entlassungen pl - **2.** [jobless state] Arbeitslosigkeit die.

redundant [rɪ'dʌndənt] adj - **1.** Br [jobless]: **to be made ~** den Arbeitsplatz verlieren - **2.** [superfluous] überflüssig.

reed [riːd] n - **1.** [plant] Schilfrohr das - **2.** [of musical instrument] Rohrblatt das.

reef [riːf] n [in sea] Riff das.

reek [riːk] ◇ n Gestank der ◇ vi: **to ~ (of sthg)** (nach etw) stinken.

reel [riːl] ◇ *n* - **1.** [roll] Spule *die* - **2.** [on fishing rod] Rolle *die* ◇ *vi* [stagger] torkeln. ➤ **reel in** *vt sep* [fishing line] einlrollen; [fish] einlholen. ➤ **reel off** *vt sep* [list] ablspulen.

reenact [ˌriːɪˈnækt] *vt* nachlspielen.

ref *n* - **1.** *inf* (*abbr of* referee) SPORT Schiri *der* - **2.** ADMIN *abbr of* reference.

refectory [rɪˈfektərɪ] *n* [in school, college] Speisesaal *der*.

refer [rɪˈfɜːʳ] *vt* - **1.** [person]: **to ~ sb to sb** jn an jn verweisen; **to ~ sb to sthg** [document, article] jn auf etw (*A*) verweisen - **2.** [report, case, decision]: **to ~ sthg to sb/sthg** etw an jn/etw weiterlleiten. ➤ **refer to** *vt fus* - **1.** [mention] erwähnen; [as support for argument] sich beziehen auf (+ *A*) - **2.** [apply to, concern] betreffen - **3.** [consult] zu Rate ziehen.

referee [ˌrefəˈriː] ◇ *n* - **1.** SPORT Schiedsrichter *der*, -in *die* - **2.** *Br* [for job application] Referenz *die* ◇ *vt* SPORT leiten ◇ *vi* SPORT Schiedsrichter sein.

reference [ˈrefrəns] *n* - **1.** [act of mentioning]: **to make ~ to sb/sthg** jn/etw erwähnen; **with ~ to** *fml* mit Bezug auf (+ *A*) - **2.** [mention]: **~ (to)** Anspielung die (auf (+ *A*)) - **3.** [in catalogue, on map] Verweis *der* - **4.** COMM [in letter, for job application] Referenz *die*.

reference book *n* Nachschlagewerk *das*.

reference number *n* [for customer] Kundennummer *die*; [for member] Mitgliedsnummer *die*; [on file] Aktenzeichen *das*.

referendum [ˌrefəˈrendəm] (*pl* -s OR -da [-də]) *n* POL Referendum *das*.

refill [*n* ˈriːfɪl, *vb* ˌriːˈfɪl] ◇ *n* - **1.** [for pen, lighter] Nachfüllpatrone *die* - **2.** *inf* [drink]: **would you like a ~?** möchten Sie nachgeschenkt haben? ◇ *vt* nachlfüllen.

refine [rɪˈfaɪn] *vt* - **1.** [oil, food] raffinieren - **2.** [details, speech] verfeinern.

refined [rɪˈfaɪnd] *adj* - **1.** [genteel] fein - **2.** [highly developed, purified] raffiniert.

refinement [rɪˈfaɪnmənt] *n* - **1.** [improvement]: **~ (on sthg)** Verfeinerung *die* (von etw) - **2.** (*U*) [gentility] Feinheit *die*.

reflect [rɪˈflekt] ◇ *vt* - **1.** [show, be a sign of] widerlspiegeln - **2.** [throw back - light, heat] reflektieren; [- image] spiegeln - **3.** [think, consider]: **to ~ that ...** daran denken, dass ... ◇ *vi* [think, consider]: **to ~ (on** OR **upon sthg)** reflektieren (über etw (*A*)).

reflection [rɪˈflekʃn] *n* - **1.** [sign, consequence] Widerspiegelung *die* - **2.** [criticism]: **this is no ~ on your judgement** das ist keine Kritik an Ihrem Urteil - **3.** [image] Spiegelung *die* - **4.** (*U*) *literary* [thinking] Reflexion *die*; **on ~** bei näherer Überlegung.

reflector [rɪˈflektəʳ] *n* Rückstrahler *der*.

reflex [ˈriːfleks] *n*: **~ (action)** Reflex *der*.

reflexive [rɪˈfleksɪv] *adj* GRAMM reflexiv.

reform [rɪˈfɔːm] ◇ *n* Reform *die* ◇ *vt* - **1.** [change] reformieren - **2.** [improve behaviour of] bessern ◇ *vi* [behave better] sich bessern.

Reformation [ˌrefəˈmeɪʃn] *n*: **the ~ die** Reformation.

reformatory [rɪˈfɔːmətrɪ] *n Am* Besserungsanstalt *die*.

reformer [rɪˈfɔːməʳ] *n* Reformer *der*, -in *die*.

refrain [rɪˈfreɪn] ◇ *n* Refrain *der* ◇ *vi fml*: **to ~ from doing sthg** es unterlassen, etw zu tun.

refresh [rɪˈfreʃ] *vt* erfrischen.

refresher course [rɪˈfreʃəʳ-] *n* Auffrischungskurs *der*. (

refreshing [rɪˈfreʃɪŋ] *adj* erfrischend.

refreshments [rɪˈfreʃmənts] *npl* Erfrischungen *pl*.

refrigerator [rɪˈfrɪdʒəreɪtəʳ] *n* Kühlschrank *der*.

refuel [ˌriːˈfjuəl] *vt & vi* aufltanken.

refuge [ˈrefjuːdʒ] *n* - **1.** [place of safety] Zuflucht *die* - **2.** [safety]: **to seek** OR **take ~** [hide] Zuflucht suchen; **to seek** OR **take ~ in sthg** *fig* in etw (*D*) Zuflucht suchen.

refugee [ˌrefjuˈdʒiː] *n* Flüchtling *der*.

refund [*n* ˈriːfʌnd, *vb* rɪˈfʌnd] ◇ *n* Rückzahlung *die* ◇ *vt*: **to ~ sthg to sb, to ~ sb sthg** etw an jn zurücklzahlen.

refurbish [ˌriːˈfɜːbɪʃ] *vt* renovieren.

refusal [rɪˈfjuːzl] *n*: **~ (to do sthg)** Weigerung *die* (etw zu tun).

refuse¹ [rɪˈfjuːz] ◇ *vt* - **1.** [withhold, deny]: **to ~ sb sthg, to ~ sthg to sb** jm etw verweigern - **2.** [decline] abllehnen; **to ~ to do sthg** sich weigern, etw zu tun ◇ *vi* sich weigern.

refuse² [ˈrefjuːs] *n* Müll *der*.

refuse collection [ˈrefjuːs-] *n* Müllabfuhr *die*.

refute [rɪˈfjuːt] *vt fml* widerlegen.

regain [rɪˈgeɪn] *vt* [recover] wiederlgewinnen; **to ~ consciousness** wieder zu Bewusstsein kommen.

regal [ˈriːgl] *adj* majestätisch.

regard [rɪˈgɑːd] ◇ *n* - **1.** (*U*) *fml* [respect, esteem]: **~ (for sb/sthg)** Achtung *die* (vor jm/etw); **to hold sb/sthg in high/low ~** jn/etw hoch/gering achten - **2.** [aspect]: **in this/that ~** in dieser/jener Hinsicht ◇ *vt*: **to ~ o.s./sb/sthg as** sich/jn/etw halten für; **to be highly ~ed** hoch geachtet sein. ➤ **regards** *npl* [in greetings] Grüße *pl*; **send her my ~s** grüße sie von mir. ➤ **as regards** *prep* in Bezug auf (+ *A*). ➤ **in regard to, with regard to** *prep* bezüglich (+ *G*).

regarding [rɪˈgɑːdɪŋ] *prep* in Bezug auf (+ *A*).

regardless [rɪˈgɑːdlɪs] *adv* trotzdem. ➤ **regardless of** *prep* ohne Rücksicht auf (+ *A*).

regime [reɪˈʒiːm] *n pej* Regime *das*.

regiment ['redʒɪmənt] *n* MIL Regiment *das.*
region ['riːdʒən] *n* - **1.** [of country] Gebiet *das,* Region *die* - **2.** [of body] Bereich *der* - **3.** [range]: **in the ~ of** ungefähr.
regional ['riːdʒənl] *adj* regional.
register ['redʒɪstəʳ] ◇ *n* [of school class] Klassenbuch *das* ◇ *vt* - **1.** [record officially, show, measure] registrieren - **2.** [express] zeigen ◇ *vi* - **1.** [enrol]: **to ~ as/for sthg** sich als/ für etw (an)melden - **2.** [book in] sich einltragen - **3.** *inf* [be properly understood]: **it didn't ~ (with her)** sie registrierte es gar nicht.
registered ['redʒɪstəd] *adj* - **1.** [officially listed - company, charity] eingetragen - **2.** [letter, parcel] eingeschrieben.
registered trademark *n* eingetragenes Warenzeichen.
registrar [ˌredʒɪ'strɑːʳ] *n* [keeper of records] Standesbeamte *der,* -tin *die.*
registration [ˌredʒɪ'streɪʃn] *n* - **1.** [in records] Eintragung *die* - **2.** [on course] Anmeldung *die* - **3.** AUT = registration number.
registration number *n* AUT Kennzeichen *das.*
registry ['redʒɪstrɪ] *n* Registratur *die.*
registry office *n* Standesamt *das.*
regret [rɪ'gret] ◇ *n* Bedauern *das;* **I have no ~s about it** ich bedauere es nicht ◇ *vt* bedauern; **to ~ doing sthg** bedauern, etw getan zu haben.

🖉 **regretting**

Ich bedaure, dass sie gegangen ist. I'm sorry she's gone.
Das tut mir Leid. I'm terribly sorry about that.
Leider habe ich ihn nicht erreicht. Unfortunately I couldn't get hold of him.
Unglücklicherweise habe ich ausgerechnet an diesem Tag eine Verabredung. Unfortunately, I'm afraid I already have an appointment on that day.
Wirklich schade, dass wir uns nicht mehr sehen können. It's a real shame we shan't be able to see each other again.

regretfully [rɪ'gretfʊlɪ] *adv* mit Bedauern.
regrettable [rɪ'gretəbl] *adj* bedauerlich.
regroup [ˌriː'gruːp] *vi* sich neu gruppieren; [soldiers] sich neu formieren.
regular ['regjʊləʳ] ◇ *adj* - **1.** [gen & GRAMM] regelmäßig - **2.** [usual] üblich - **3.** *Am* [in size] klein - **4.** *Am* [pleasant]: **he's a ~ guy** er ist O.K. - **5.** *Am* [normal] normal ◇ *n* [customer, client] Stammkunde *der,* -din *die.*
regularly ['regjʊləlɪ] *adv* regelmäßig.
regulate ['regjʊleɪt] *vt* - **1.** [control] regulieren - **2.** [adjust] regeln.
regulation [ˌregjʊ'leɪʃn] ◇ *adj* [standard]

vorgeschrieben ◇ *n* - **1.** [rule] Vorschrift *die* - **2.** *(U)* [control] Regulierung *die.*
rehabilitate [ˌriːə'bɪlɪteɪt] *vt* rehabilitieren.
rehearsal [rɪ'hɜːsl] *n* Probe *die.*
rehearse [rɪ'hɜːs] *vt* & *vi* proben.
reheat [ˌriː'hiːt] *vt* aufwärmen.
reign [reɪn] ◇ *n lit* & *fig* Herrschaft *die* ◇ *vi* - **1.** [rule]: **to ~ (over)** herrschen (über (+ A)) - **2.** [prevail]: **to ~ over** sich auslbreiten über (+ D).
reimburse [ˌriːɪm'bɜːs] *vt* [person] entschädigen; [expenses] zurücklerstatten; **to ~ sb for sthg** jm etw zurücklerstatten.
rein [reɪn] *n fig:* **to give sb (a) free ~** jm freie Hand lassen. ◆ **reins** *npl* [for horse] Zügel *pl.*
reindeer ['reɪnˌdɪəʳ] *(pl inv)* *n* Rentier *das.*
reinforce [ˌriːɪn'fɔːs] *vt* - **1.** [ceiling, frame, cover]: **to ~ sthg (with sthg)** etw (mit etw) verstärken - **2.** [dislike, prejudice] bestärken - **3.** [argument, claim] stützen.
reinforced concrete [ˌriːɪn'fɔːst-] *n* Stahlbeton *der.*
reinforcement [ˌriːɪn'fɔːsmənt] *n* [in construction] Verstärkung *die.* ◆ **reinforcements** *npl* MIL Verstärkung *die.*
reinstate [ˌriːɪn'steɪt] *vt* - **1.** [employee] wieder einlstellen - **2.** [payment, policy] wieder auflnehmen.
reissue [ˌriː'ɪʃuː] ◇ *n* Neuausgabe *die;* [of book] Neuauflage *die* ◇ *vt* neu herauslgeben; [book] neu aufllegen.
reiterate [riː'ɪtəreɪt] *vt fml* wiederholen.
reject [*n* 'riːdʒekt, *vb* rɪ'dʒekt] ◇ *n:* **~s** [from factory] Ausschuss *der* ◇ *vt* abllehnen.
rejection [rɪ'dʒekʃn] *n* - **1.** [of offer, values, religion] Ablehnung *die* - **2.** [for job] Absage *die.*
rejoice [rɪ'dʒɔɪs] *vi:* **to ~ (at** OR **in sthg)** sich freuen (über etw (A)).
rejuvenate [rɪ'dʒuːvəneɪt] *vt* verjüngen.
rekindle [ˌriː'kɪndl] *vt fig* wieder entflammen.
relapse [rɪ'læps] *n* Rückfall *der.*
relate [rɪ'leɪt] ◇ *vt* - **1.** [connect]: **to ~ sthg to sthg** etw zu etw in Beziehung bringen OR setzen - **2.** [tell] erzählen ◇ *vi* - **1.** [connect]: **to ~ to sthg** mit etw zusammenhängen - **2.** [concern]: **to ~ to sb/sthg** jm/etw betreffen - **3.** [empathize]: **to ~ to sb/sthg** einen Bezug zu jm/etw haben. ◆ **relating to** *prep* im Zusammenhang mit.
related [rɪ'leɪtɪd] *adj* - **1.** [in same family] verwandt; **to be ~ to sb** mit jm verwandt sein - **2.** [connected] zusammenhängend; **to be ~ to sthg** mit etw zusammenhängen.
relation [rɪ'leɪʃn] *n* - **1.** *(U)* [connection]: **~ to/between** Beziehung *die* zu/zwischen (+ D) - **2.** [family member] Verwandte *der, die.*

➤ **relations** *npl* [relationship]: **~s (between/with)** Beziehungen *pl* (zwischen (+ *D*)/mit).

relationship [rɪ'leɪʃnʃɪp] *n* Beziehung *die*.

relative ['relətɪv] ⬦ *adj* - **1.** [gen] relativ - **2.** [respective] jeweilig ⬦ *n* Verwandte *der, die*. ➤ **relative to** *prep fml* - **1.** [compared to] im Vergleich zu - **2.** [connected with] sich beziehend auf (+ *A*).

relatively ['relətɪvlɪ] *adv* relativ.

relax [rɪ'læks] ⬦ *vt* - **1.** [mind, muscle, person] entspannen - **2.** [grip, discipline, regulation] lockern ⬦ *vi* - **1.** [person, body, muscle] sich entspannen - **2.** [grip] sich lockern.

relaxation [ˌriːlæk'seɪʃn] *n* (*U*) [rest] Entspannung *die*.

relaxed [rɪ'lækst] *adj* entspannt.

relaxing [rɪ'læksɪŋ] *adj* entspannend.

relay ['riːleɪ] ⬦ *n* - **1.** SPORT: **~ (race)** Staffellauf *der*; **to work in ~s** *fig* sich (bei der Arbeit) abllösen - **2.** RADIO & TV Relais *das* ⬦ *vt* - **1.** RADIO & TV [broadcast] übertragen - **2.** [message, news]: **to ~ sthg (to sb)** (jm) etw auslrichten.

release [rɪ'liːs] ⬦ *n* - **1.** (*U*) [from captivity] Freilassung *die* - **2.** (*U*) [from pain, suffering] Erlösung *die* - **3.** [statement] Verlautbarung *die* - **4.** [of gas, fumes] Freisetzen *das* - **5.** [of film, video, CD] Freigabe *die*; **the movie is on ~ from Friday** der Film ist von Freitag an im Kino (zu sehen) - **6.** [video, CD]: **new ~** Neuerscheinung *die*; [film] neuer Film ⬦ *vt* - **1.** [set free] freillassen; **to ~ sb from prison/captivity** jm aus dem Gefängnis/der Gefangenschaft entlassen; **to ~ sb from sthg** [promise, contract] jn von etw befreien - **2.** [make available] freisetzen - **3.** [from control, grasp] losllassen - **4.** [brake, lever, handle] lösen - **5.** [let out, emit]: **to be ~d (from/into sthg)** freigesetzt werden (aus etw/in etw (*A*)) - **6.** [film, video, CD] herauslbringen; [statement, news story] veröffentlichen.

relegate ['relɪgeɪt] *vt* - **1.** [lower status of]: **to ~ sb/sthg (to)** jn/etw verbannen (in (+ *A*)) - **2.** *Br* SPORT: **to be ~d** ablsteigen.

relent [rɪ'lent] *vi* [person] nachlgeben.

relentless [rɪ'lentlɪs] *adj* erbarmungslos.

relevant ['reləvənt] *adj* - **1.** [connected]: **~ (to)** relevant (für) - **2.** [important]: **~ (to)** wichtig (für) - **3.** [appropriate] entsprechend.

reliable [rɪ'laɪəbl] *adj* zuverlässig.

reliably [rɪ'laɪəblɪ] *adv* zuverlässig.

reliant [rɪ'laɪənt] *adj*: **~ on** abhängig von (+ *D*).

relic ['relɪk] *n* - **1.** [old object, custom - still in use] Überbleibsel *das*; [- no longer in use] Relikt *das* - **2.** RELIG Reliquie *die*.

relief [rɪ'liːf] *n* - **1.** [comfort] Erleichterung *die* - **2.** (*U*) [for poor, refugees] Hilfe *die* - **3.** *Am* [social security] Fürsorge *die*.

🔲 **relief**

Zum Glück kommen wir noch rechtzeitig.
Fortunately we'll still get there in time.
Gott sei Dank ist die Vase nicht kaputt!
Thank God the vase didn't get broken!
Da kommt sie endlich! Here she is at last!
Jetzt bin ich aber erleichtert. What a relief!
Mir fällt ein Stein vom Herzen. That's a
weight off my mind.

relieve [rɪ'liːv] *vt* - **1.** [ease, lessen] lindern; **to ~ sb of sthg** jn von etw befreien - **2.** [take over from]: **to ~ sb of sthg** jn einer Sache (*G*) entheben - **3.** [give help to] helfen (+ *D*).

religion [rɪ'lɪdʒn] *n* - **1.** [belief in a god] Glaube *der* - **2.** [system of belief] Religion *die*.

religious [rɪ'lɪdʒəs] *adj* religiös.

relinquish [rɪ'lɪŋkwɪʃ] *vt* auflgeben.

relish ['relɪʃ] ⬦ *n* - **1.** [enjoyment]: **with (great) ~** genüsslich - **2.** [pickle] Soße *die* ⬦ *vt* [enjoy] genießen; **to ~ the idea** OR **thought of doing sthg** sich darauf freuen, etw zu tun.

relocate [ˌriːləʊ'keɪt] ⬦ *vt* verlegen ⬦ *vi* den Standort wechseln.

reluctance [rɪ'lʌktəns] *n* Widerwille *der*.

reluctant [rɪ'lʌktənt] *adj* widerwillig; **to be ~ to do sthg** abgeneigt sein, etw zu tun.

reluctantly [rɪ'lʌktəntlɪ] *adv* widerwillig.

rely [rɪ'laɪ] ➤ **rely on** *vt fus* - **1.** [count on] sich verlassen auf (+ *A*) - **2.** [be dependent on]: **to ~ on sb/sthg for sthg** wegen etw auf jn/etw angewiesen sein.

remain [rɪ'meɪn] ⬦ *vt*: **that ~s to be done** das bleibt (noch) zu tun ⬦ *vi* bleiben. ➤ **remains** *npl* - **1.** [of meal, ancient civilization, building] Überreste *pl* - **2.** [corpse] menschliche Überreste *pl*.

remainder [rɪ'meɪndə'] *n* Rest *der*.

remaining [rɪ'meɪnɪŋ] *adj* verbleibend.

remand [rɪ'mɑːnd] LAW ⬦ *n*: **on ~** in Untersuchungshaft ⬦ *vt*: **to be ~ed in custody** in Untersuchungshaft bleiben.

remark [rɪ'mɑːk] ⬦ *n* Bemerkung *die* ⬦ *vt*: **to ~ that ...** bemerken, dass ...

remarkable [rɪ'mɑːkəbl] *adj* bemerkenswert.

remarry [ˌriː'mærɪ] *vi* wieder heiraten.

remedial [rɪ'miːdjəl] *adj* - **1.** SCH Förder- - **2.** [corrective - action] abhelfend.

remedy ['remədɪ] ⬦ *n*: **~ (for sthg)** [for ill health] Heilmittel *das* (für OR gegen etw); [solution] Lösung *die* (für etw) ⬦ *vt* ablhelfen (+ *D*).

remember [rɪ'membə'] ⬦ *vt* - **1.** [recollect] sich erinnern an (+ *A*); **to ~ doing sthg** sich daran erinnern, etw getan zu haben - **2.** [not forget] denken an (+ *A*); **to ~ to do sthg** daran denken, etw zu tun ⬦ *vi* sich erinnern.

remembrance [rɪ'membrəns] *n fml:* **in ~ of** zur Erinnerung an (+ A).

Remembrance Day *n* nationaler britischer Trauertag zum Gedenken an die in den beiden Weltkriegen gefallenen Soldaten. Er wird am dem 11. November nächstliegenden Sonntag begangen.

remind [rɪ'maɪnd] *vt* - **1.** [tell]: **to ~ sb about sthg** jn an etw (A) erinnern; **to ~ sb to do sthg** jn daran erinnern, etw zu tun - **2.** [be reminiscent of]: **to ~ sb of sb/sthg** jn an jn/ etw erinnern.

reminder [rɪ'maɪndəʳ] *n* - **1.** [to jog memory]: **to give sb a ~ to do sthg** jn daran erinnern, etw zu tun - **2.** [for bill, membership, licence] Mahnung *die.*

reminisce [‚remɪ'nɪs] *vi:* **to ~ (about sthg)** in Erinnerungen (an etw (A)) schwelgen.

reminiscent [‚remɪ'nɪsnt] *adj:* **to be ~ of sb/sthg** an jn/etw erinnern.

remiss [rɪ'mɪs] *adj* nachlässig.

remit [*n* 'ri:mɪt, *vb* rɪ'mɪt] ⬦ *n Br* Aufgabenbereich *der* ⬦ *vt* [send] überweisen.

remittance [rɪ'mɪtns] *n* Überweisung *die.*

remnant ['remnənt] *n* Rest *der.*

remold *n Am* = remould.

remorse [rɪ'mɔ:s] *n* Reue *die.*

remorseful [rɪ'mɔ:sful] *adj* reuig.

remorseless [rɪ'mɔ:slɪs] *adj* - **1.** [pitiless] unbarmherzig - **2.** [unstoppable] unaufhaltsam.

remote [rɪ'məʊt] *adj* - **1.** [distant - place] abgelegen; [- time] entfernt - **2.** [aloof] unnahbar - **3.** [unconnected, irrelevant]: **~ from** entfernt von - **4.** [slight - resemblance] entfernt; [- chance, possibility] gering.

remote control *n* - **1.** (U) [system] Fernsteuerung *die* - **2.** [machine, device] Fernbedienung *die.*

remotely [rɪ'məʊtlɪ] *adv* - **1.** [slightly]: **not ~** nicht im Entferntesten, nicht im Geringsten - **2.** [distantly] entfernt.

remoulds *Br*, **remolds** *Am* ['ri:məʊldz] *npl* runderneuerte Reifen *pl.*

removable [rɪ'mu:vəbl] *adj* [detachable] abnehmbar.

removal [rɪ'mu:vl] *n* - **1.** *Br* [change of house] Umzug *der* - **2.** [act of removing] Entfernen *das.*

removal van *n Br* Möbelwagen *der.*

remove [rɪ'mu:v] *vt* - **1.** [take away, clean]: **to ~ sthg (from)** etw entfernen (aus/von) - **2.** [clothes, hat] ablegen - **3.** [from a job]: **to ~ sb (from)** jn entfernen (von) - **4.** [problem] beseitigen; [suspicion] zerstreuen.

remuneration [rɪ‚mju:nə'reɪʃn] *n fml* - **1.** [pay] Bezahlung *die* - **2.** [amount of money] Vergütung *die.*

render ['rendəʳ] *vt* - **1.** [make] machen - **2.** [give - help, service] leisten.

rendezvous ['rɒndɪvu:] (*pl inv*) *n* - **1.** [meet-

ing] Rendezvous *das* - **2.** [place] Treffpunkt *der.*

renegade ['renɪgeɪd] *n* Abtrünnige *der, die.*

renew [rɪ'nju:] *vt* - **1.** [repeat, restart] wieder aufnehmen - **2.** [extend validity of] verlängern - **3.** [increase]: **with ~ed enthusiasm/ interest** mit neuem Enthusiasmus/ Interesse.

renewable [rɪ'nju:əbl] *adj* - **1.** [resources] erneuerbar - **2.** [contract, licence, membership] verlängerbar.

renewal [rɪ'nju:əl] *n* (U) [of contract, licence, membership] Verlängerung *die.*

renounce [rɪ'naʊns] *vt* - **1.** [reject] abschwören (+ D) - **2.** *fml* [relinquish] verzichten auf (+ A).

renovate ['renəveɪt] *vt* renovieren.

renown [rɪ'naʊn] *n* Ruf *der.*

renowned [rɪ'naʊnd] *adj:* **~ (for sthg)** berühmt (für etw).

rent [rent] ⬦ *n* Miete *die* ⬦ *vt* - **1.** [subj: tenant, hirer] mieten - **2.** [subj: owner] vermieten.

📖 **rent**

Das Substantiv **rent** hat nichts mit Altersversorgung zu tun, sondern bedeutet „Miete". Three months' **rent** in advance heißt „drei Monatsmieten im Voraus". Die im Alter ausgezahlte „Rente" heißt im Englischen **pension**. „Meine Mutter ist letztes Jahr in Rente gegangen" kann mit my mother began drawing her **pension** last year übersetzt werden.

---

rental ['rentl] ⬦ *adj* Miet- ⬦ *n* [money] Leihgebühr *die;* [for house] Miete *die.*

rental car *n* Mietwagen *der.*

renunciation [rɪ‚nʌnsɪ'eɪʃn] *n* (U) - **1.** [relinquishing]: **~ of sthg** Verzicht *der* auf etw (A) - **2.** [rejection]: **~ of sthg** Abschwörung *die* von etw.

reorganize, -ise [‚ri:'ɔ:gənaɪz] *vt* neu organisieren.

rep [rep] *n* - **1.** *abbr of* representative - **2.** *abbr of* repertory company.

repaid [‚ri:'peɪd] *pt & pp* ⬦ repay.

repair [rɪ'peəʳ] ⬦ *n* Reparatur *die;* **in good/ bad ~** in gutem/schlechtem Zustand ⬦ *vt* - **1.** [fix, mend] reparieren; [puncture, crack] ausbessern - **2.** [make amends for] wieder gutmachen.

repair kit *n* Flickzeug *das.*

repartee [‚repɑ:'ti:] *n* (U) Schlagabtausch *der.*

repatriate [‚ri:'pætrɪeɪt] *vt* repatriieren.

repay [‚ri:'peɪ] (*pt & pp* repaid) *vt* - **1.** [money] zurückzahlen; **to ~ sb sthg, to ~ sthg to sb** jm etw zurückzahlen - **2.** [kindness] vergelten.

repayment [rɪ'peɪmənt] *n* Rückzahlung *die*.

repeal [rɪ'piːl] *vt* auflheben.

repeat [rɪ'piːt] ◇ *vt* wiederholen ◇ *n* [broadcast] Wiederholung *die*.

repeatedly [rɪ'piːtɪdlɪ] *adv* wiederholt.

repel [rɪ'pel] *vt* - 1. [disgust] ablstoßen - 2. [drive away] ablwehren.

repellent [rɪ'pelənt] ◇ *adj* abstoßend ◇ *n*: (insect) ~ Insektenabwehrmittel *das*.

repent [rɪ'pent] ◇ *vt* bereuen ◇ *vi*: **to ~ of sthg** über etw (A) Reue empfinden.

repentance [rɪ'pentəns] *n* Reue *die*.

repercussions [ˌriːpə'kʌʃnz] *npl* Auswirkungen *pl*.

repertoire ['repətwɑːʳ] *n* Repertoire *das*.

repertory ['repətrɪ] *n* [repertoire] Repertoire *das*.

repetition [ˌrepɪ'tɪʃn] *n* Wiederholung *die*.

repetitious [ˌrepɪ'tɪʃəs], **repetitive** [rɪ'petɪtɪv] *adj* monoton.

replace [rɪ'pleɪs] *vt* - 1. [gen] ersetzen; **to ~ sb/sthg with sb/sthg** jn/etw durch jn/etw ersetzen - 2. [put back - upright] zurückllstellen; [- lying flat] zurückllegen.

replacement [rɪ'pleɪsmənt] *n* - 1. [act of replacing] Ersetzen *das* - 2. [new person, object]: ~ **(for sthg)** Ersatz *der* (für etw); ~ **(for sb)** [in job - temporary] Vertretung *die* (von jm); [- permanent] Nachfolger *der*, -in *die* (von jm).

replay [*n* 'riːpleɪ, *vb* ˌriː'pleɪ] ◇ *n* - 1. [recording]: **(action) ~** Wiederholung *die* - 2. [game] Wiederholungsspiel *das* ◇ *vt* - 1. [match, game] wiederholen - 2. [film, tape] nochmals ablspielen.

replenish [rɪ'plenɪʃ] *vt fml*: **to ~ sthg (with sthg)** etw (mit etw) wieder aufllfüllen.

replica ['replɪkə] *n* Kopie *die*.

reply [rɪ'plaɪ] ◇ *n*: ~ **(to sthg)** Antwort *die* (auf etw (A)) ◇ *vt* antworten ◇ *vi* antworten; **to ~ to sb/sthg** jm/auf etw (A) antworten.

reply coupon *n* Antwortschein *der*.

report [rɪ'pɔːt] ◇ *n* - 1. [description, account] Bericht *der* - 2. PRESS Reportage *die* - 3. *Br* SCH Zeugnis *das* ◇ *vt* - 1. [news, crime] melden - 2. [make known]: **to ~ that ...** berichten, dass ...; **to ~ sthg (to sb)** (jm) etw berichten - 3. [complain about]: **to ~ sb (to sb)** jn (bei jm) anlzeigen; **to ~ sb for sthg** jn wegen etw anlzeigen ◇ *vi* - 1. [give account]: **to ~ (on sthg)** (über etw (A)) berichten - 2. PRESS: **this is John Smith, ~ing from Moscow** John Smith (mit einem Bericht) aus Moskau; **to ~ on sthg** über etw (A) berichten - 3. [present o.s.]: **to ~ to** sich melden bei; **to ~ for duty** sich zum Dienst melden.

report card *n Am* SCH Zeugnis *das*.

reportedly [rɪ'pɔːtɪdlɪ] *adv* angeblich.

reporter [rɪ'pɔːtəʳ] *n* [in TV, radio, press] Reporter *der*, -in *die*, Berichterstatter *der*, -in *die*.

repossess [ˌriːpə'zes] *vt* wieder in Besitz nehmen.

reprehensible [ˌreprɪ'hensəbl] *adj fml* verwerflich.

represent [ˌreprɪ'zent] *vt* - 1. [act for] vertreten - 2. [constitute, symbolize] darlstellen.

representation [ˌreprɪzen'teɪʃn] *n* [depiction] Darstellung *die*. ◆ **representations** *npl fml*: **to make ~s to sb** sich mit einem Anliegen an jn wenden.

representative [ˌreprɪ'zentətɪv] ◇ *adj* - 1. [acting for main group] stellvertretend - 2. [typical]: ~ **(of)** repräsentativ (für) ◇ *n* - 1. [of company, organization, group] Vertreter *der*, -in *die* - 2. *Am* POL Abgeordnete *der*, *die*.

repress [rɪ'pres] *vt* unterdrücken.

repression [rɪ'preʃn] *n (U)* Unterdrückung *die*.

reprieve [rɪ'priːv] ◇ *n* - 1. [of death sentence] Begnadigung *die* - 2. [respite] Gnadenfrist *die* ◇ *vt* begnadigen.

reprimand ['reprɪmɑːnd] ◇ *n* Tadel *der* ◇ *vt* tadeln.

reprisal [rɪ'praɪzl] *n* - 1. [counterblow] Vergeltungsmaßnahme *die* - 2. [revenge]: **in ~ (for)** als Vergeltung (für).

reproach [rɪ'prəʊtʃ] ◇ *n* Vorwurf *der*; **to be beyond ~** über jeden Vorwurf erhaben sein ◇ *vt*: **to ~ sb (for OR with sthg)** jm (wegen etw) Vorwürfe machen.

reproduce [ˌriːprə'djuːs] ◇ *vt* [copy] reproduzieren ◇ *vi* BIOL sich fortlpflanzen.

reproduction [ˌriːprə'dʌkʃn] *n* - 1. [replica] Reproduktion *die*; ~ **furniture** Stilmöbel *pl* - 2. *(U)* [copying, simulation] Reproduktion *die*; **sound ~** Tonwiedergabe *die* - 3. BIOL Fortpflanzung *die*.

reprove [rɪ'pruːv] *vt*: **to ~ sb (for sthg)** jn (wegen etw) tadeln.

reptile ['reptaɪl] *n* Reptil *das*.

republic [rɪ'pʌblɪk] *n* Republik *die*.

republican [rɪ'pʌblɪkən] ◇ *adj* republikanisch ◇ *n* Republikaner *der*, -in *die*. ◆ **Republican** ◇ *adj* - 1. [in USA] republikanisch; **the Republican Party** die Republikanische Partei - 2. [in Northern Ireland] bezeichnet einen Befürworter einer vereinten unabhängigen Republik Irland bzw. dessen Ideen ◇ *n* - 1. [in USA] Republikaner *der*, -in *die* - 2. [in Northern Ireland] Befürworter einer vereinten unabhängigen Republik Irland.

repulse [rɪ'pʌls] *vt* - 1. [refuse] zurücklweisen; [person] verstoßen - 2. MIL [drive back] ablwehren.

repulsive [rɪ'pʌlsɪv] *adj* abstoßend.

reputable ['repjʊtəbl] *adj* seriös.

reputation [ˌrepjʊ'teɪʃn] *n* Ruf *der*.

repute [rɪ'pjuːt] n fml [reputation]: **of good/ill ~** von gutem/schlechtem Ruf.

reputed [rɪ'pjuːtɪd] adj: **he is a ~ expert/millionaire** er soll ein Fachmann/Millionär sein; **to be ~ to be sthg** als etw gelten.

reputedly [rɪ'pjuːtɪdlɪ] adv: **he is ~ the best surgeon** er gilt als der beste Chirurg.

request [rɪ'kwest] <> n: **~ (for sthg)** Bitte die (um etw); **on ~** auf Wunsch <> vt bitten um; **to ~ sb to do sthg** jn bitten, etw zu tun.

require [rɪ'kwaɪəʳ] vt erfordern; **to be ~d to do sthg** aufgefordert werden, etw zu tun.

requirement [rɪ'kwaɪəmənt] n - 1. [condition] Erfordernis das - 2. [need] Bedarf der.

reran [ˌriː'ræn] pt [> rerun.

rerun [n 'riːrʌn, vb ˌriː'rʌn] (pt reran; pp rerun) <> n Wiederholung die <> vt [gen] wiederholen.

resat [ˌriː'sæt] pt & pp [> resit.

rescind [rɪ'sɪnd] vt LAW annullieren.

rescue ['reskjuː] <> n Rettung die <> vt retten; **to ~ sb/sthg from sb/sthg** jn/etw vor jm/aus etw retten.

rescuer ['reskjuəʳ] n Retter der, -in die.

research [ˌrɪ'sɜːtʃ] <> n (U): **~ (on OR into sthg)** Forschung die (über etw (A)); **~ and development** Forschung und Entwicklung <> vt erforschen; [article, book] recherchieren.

researcher [rɪ'sɜːtʃəʳ] n Forscher der, -in die.

resemblance [rɪ'zembləns] n: **~ (to/between)** Ähnlichkeit die (mit/zwischen (+ D)).

resemble [rɪ'zembl] vt ähneln.

resent [rɪ'zent] vt sich ärgern über (+ A); **I ~ that!** das ärgert mich!

resentful [rɪ'zentfʊl] adj verärgert.

resentment [rɪ'zentmənt] n Groll der.

reservation [ˌrezə'veɪʃn] n - 1. [booking] Reservierung die - 2. [doubt]: **without ~** ohne Vorbehalt - 3. Am [for Native Americans] Reservat das. ◆ **reservations** npl [doubts] Vorbehalte pl.

reserve [rɪ'zɜːv] <> n - 1. [supply] Reserve die; **in ~** in Reserve - 2. SPORT [substitute] Reservespieler der, -in die - 3. [sanctuary] Reservat das - 4. (U) [restraint, shyness] Reserve die <> vt - 1. [keep for particular purpose]: **to ~ sthg for sb/sthg** etw für jn/etw reservieren - 2. [book] reservieren - 3. [retain]: **to ~ the right to do sthg** sich das Recht vorbehalten, etw zu tun.

reserved [rɪ'zɜːvd] adj reserviert.

reservoir ['rezəvwɑːʳ] n [lake] Reservoir das.

reset [ˌriː'set] (pt & pp reset) vt - 1. [clock] neu stellen; [meter] zurückstellen - 2. COMPUT rücksetzen.

reshape [ˌriː'ʃeɪp] vt [policy, thinking] umlformen.

reshuffle [ˌriː'ʃʌfl] POL <> n Umbildung die <> vt umlbilden.

reside [rɪ'zaɪd] vi fml - 1. [live] seinen Wohnsitz haben - 2. [be located, found]: **to ~ in sthg** in etw (D) liegen.

residence ['rezɪdəns] n [house] Wohnsitz der.

residence permit n Aufenthaltserlaubnis die.

resident ['rezɪdənt] <> adj - 1. [settled, living] wohnhaft - 2. [on-site, live-in] Haus- <> n [of town, street] Bewohner der, -in die; [in hotel] Gast der.

residential [ˌrezɪ'denʃl] adj: **~ course** Kurs, bei dem die Teilnehmer auf dem Schulgelände untergebracht werden; **~ care** Pflege die im Haus.

residential area n Wohngebiet das.

residue ['rezɪdjuː] n CHEM Rückstand der.

resign [rɪ'zaɪn] <> vt - 1. [give up - job] kündigen; [- post] zurückltreten von - 2. [accept calmly]: **to ~ o.s. to sthg** sich mit etw ablfinden <> vi [from job] kündigen; [from post] zurückltreten.

resignation [ˌrezɪg'neɪʃn] n - 1. [from job] Kündigung die; [from post] Rücktritt der - 2. [calm acceptance] Resignation die.

resigned [rɪ'zaɪnd] adj: **to be ~ to sthg** sich mit etw abgefunden haben.

resilient [rɪ'zɪlɪənt] adj - 1. [material] elastisch - 2. [person] widerstandsfähig.

resist [rɪ'zɪst] vt Widerstand leisten gegen; [temptation, offer] widerstehen (+ D).

resistance [rɪ'zɪstəns] n (U): **~ (to sthg)** Widerstand der (gegen etw).

resit [n 'riːsɪt, vb ˌriː'sɪt] (pt & pp resat) Br <> n Wiederholungsprüfung die <> vt wiederholen.

resolute ['rezəluːt] adj energisch.

resolution [ˌrezə'luːʃn] n - 1. [motion, decision] Resolution die - 2. [vow, promise] Vorsatz der - 3. [determination] Entschlossenheit die - 4. (U) [solution - of problem] Lösung die; [- of dispute, argument] Beilegung die.

resolve [rɪ'zɒlv] <> n [determination] Entschlossenheit die <> vt - 1. [vow, promise]: **to ~ that ...** beschließen, dass ...; **to ~ to do sthg** sich entschließen, etw zu tun - 2. [solve - problem] lösen; [- dispute, argument] beilegen.

resort [rɪ'zɔːt] n - 1. [for holidays] Urlaubsort der - 2. [solution]: **as a last ~** als letzte Möglichkeit; **in the last ~** im schlimmsten Fall. ◆ **resort to** vt fus [lying, begging] sich verlegen auf (+ A); [violence] anlwenden.

resound [rɪ'zaʊnd] vi - 1. [noise] schallen - 2. [place]: **to ~ with** widerhallen von.

resounding [rɪ'zaʊndɪŋ] adj - 1. [noise, voice] schallend - 2. [success, victory] gewaltig.

resource [rɪ'zɔːs] n [asset] Resourcen pl; **natural ~s** Naturschätze pl.

resourceful [rɪ'zɔːsfʊl] *adj* einfallsreich.

respect [rɪ'spekt] ⬦ *n* - **1.** (U) [admiration]: **~ (for)** Respekt *der* (vor (+ D)); **with ~,** … bei allem Respekt, … - **2.** (U) [observance]: **~ for sthg** Achtung *die* vor etw (+ D) - **3.** [aspect] Hinsicht *die*; **in this/that ~** in dieser/jener Hinsicht ⬦ *vt* - **1.** [admire] anerkennen; **to ~ sb for sthg** jn für etw respektieren - **2.** [observe] achten. ⬦ **respects** *npl* Grüße *pl*; **give my ~s to your wife** grüßen Sie Ihre Frau von mir. ⬦ **with respect to** *prep* in Bezug auf (+ A).

respectable [rɪ'spektəbl] *adj* - **1.** [morally correct] ehrbar - **2.** [adequate, quite good] ansehnlich.

respectful [rɪ'spektfʊl] *adj* respektvoll.

respective [rɪ'spektɪv] *adj* jeweilig.

respectively [rɪ'spektɪvlɪ] *adv* beziehungsweise; **Jill and John are four and six years old** – Jill und John sind vier und sechs beziehungsweise sechs Jahre alt.

respite ['respaɪt] *n* - **1.** [pause] Atempause *die*; **without ~** ohne Unterbrechung - **2.** [delay] Aufschub *der*.

resplendent [rɪ'splendənt] *adj literary* prachtvoll.

respond [rɪ'spɒnd] *vi*: **to ~ (to sthg)** antworten (auf etw (A)).

response [rɪ'spɒns] *n* Antwort *die*.

responsibility [rɪ,spɒnsə'bɪlətɪ] *n* - **1.** [charge, blame]: **~ (for sthg)** Verantwortung *die* (für etw) - **2.** [duty - of job, position] Aufgabe *die*; **~ (to sb)** Verantwortung *die* (jm gegenüber).

responsible [rɪ'spɒnsəbl] *adj* - **1.** [in charge, to blame]: **~ (for sthg)** verantwortlich (für etw) - **2.** [answerable]: **~ to sb** jm (gegenüber) verantwortlich - **3.** [sensible] vernünftig - **4.** [position, task] verantwortungsvoll.

responsibly [rɪ'spɒnsəblɪ] *adv* verantwortungsbewusst.

responsive [rɪ'spɒnsɪv] *adj*: **to be ~** (audience) mitgehen; (class) mitlmachen.

rest [rest] ⬦ *n* - **1.** [remainder]: **the ~** der Rest; **the ~ of the cake/customers** der Rest des Kuchens/der Kunden - **2.** [relaxation] Ruhe *die* - **3.** [break] Pause *die* - **4.** [support] Stütze *die* ⬦ *vt* - **1.** [relax] auslruhen - **2.** [support, lean]: **to ~ sthg on/against sthg** etw auf (+ A) /gegen etw lehnen - **3.** *phr*: **~ assured (that)** … seien Sie versichert, dass … ⬦ *vi* - **1.** [relax, be still] sich auslruhen - **2.** [depend]: **to ~ (up)on sb/sthg** von jm/etw abhängen - **3.** [be supported]: **to ~ on sthg** auf etw (D) ruhen; **to ~ against sthg** an etw (D) lehnen.

restaurant ['restərɒnt] *n* Restaurant *das*.

restful ['restfʊl] *adj* ruhig.

rest home *n* Pflegeheim *das*.

restive ['restɪv] *adj* unruhig.

restless ['restlɪs] *adj* - **1.** [bored, fidgety] rastlos - **2.** [sleepless] schlaflos.

restoration [,restə'reɪʃn] *n* (U) - **1.** [reestab-

lishment] Wiederherstellung *die* - **2.** [renovation] Restaurierung *die*.

restore [rɪ'stɔːʳ] *vt* - **1.** [reestablish] wiederherlstellen; **the palace has been ~d to its former glory** dem Palast ist seine alte Pracht wiedergegeben worden - **2.** [renovate] restaurieren - **3.** [give back] zurücklgeben.

restrain [rɪ'streɪn] *vt* - **1.** [hold back] zurücklhalten; **to ~ o.s. from doing sthg** sich zurücklhalten (davon), etw zu tun - **2.** [dog, attacker] bändigen - **3.** [repress] unterdrücken.

restrained [rɪ'streɪnd] *adj* - **1.** [person] beherrscht - **2.** [tone] verhalten.

restraint [rɪ'streɪnt] *n* - **1.** [rule, check] Beschränkung *die* - **2.** [self-control] Selbstbeherrschung *die*.

restrict [rɪ'strɪkt] *vt* [limit] einlschränken; **to ~ sb/sthg to sb/sthg** jn/etw auf jn/etw beschränken.

restriction [rɪ'strɪkʃn] *n* [limitation, regulation] Einschränkung *die*.

restrictive [rɪ'strɪktɪv] *adj* einschränkend.

rest room *n Am* Toilette *die*.

result [rɪ'zʌlt] ⬦ *n* - **1.** [gen] Ergebnis *das* - **2.** [consequence] Folge *die*; **as a ~** folglich; **as a ~ of sthg** als Folge von etw ⬦ *vi*: **to ~ in sthg** zu etw führen; **to ~ from sthg** aus etw folgen.

resume [rɪ'zjuːm] ⬦ *vt* [activity] wieder auflnehmen ⬦ *vi* wieder beginnen.

résumé ['rezjuːmeɪ] *n* - **1.** [summary] Resümee *das*, Zusammenfassung *die* - **2.** *Am* [of career, qualifications] Lebenslauf *der*.

resumption [rɪ'zʌmpʃn] *n* Wiederaufnahme *die*.

resurgence [rɪ'sɜːdʒəns] *n* Wiederaufleben *das*.

resurrection [,rezə'rekʃn] *n* [of policy, festival, legal case] Wiederbelebung *die*.

resuscitation [rɪ,sʌsɪ'teɪʃn] *n* Wiederbelebung *die*.

retail ['riːteɪl] ⬦ *n* Einzelhandel *der* ⬦ *adv* im Einzelhandel ⬦ *vi*: **it ~s at £10** es kostet im Einzelhandel 10 Pfund.

retailer ['riːteɪləʳ] *n* Einzelhändler *der*, -in *die*.

retail price *n* Einzelhandelspreis *der*.

retain [rɪ'teɪn] *vt* - **1.** [pride, power, independence] behalten - **2.** [heat] speichern.

retainer [rɪ'teɪnəʳ] *n* [fee] Vorschuss *der*.

retaliate [rɪ'tælɪeɪt] *vi* zurücklschlagen.

retaliation [rɪ,tælɪ'eɪʃn] *n* Vergeltung *die*.

retarded [rɪ'tɑːdɪd] *adj offensive* [child] zurückgeblieben.

retch [retʃ] *vi* würgen.

reticent ['retɪsənt] *adj* zurückhaltend.

retina ['retɪnə] (*pl* -nas OR -nae [-niː]) *n* Netzhaut *die*, Retina *die*.

retinue ['retɪnjuː] *n* Gefolge *das*.

retire [rɪ'taɪəʳ] *vi* - **1.** [from work] in den Ruhestand treten - 2. *fml* [to another place, to bed] sich zurücklziehen.

retired [rɪ'taɪəd] *adj* pensioniert; **to be ~** im Ruhestand sein.

retirement [rɪ'taɪəmənt] *n (U)* - 1. [act of retiring] Pensionierung *die* - 2. [life after work] Ruhestand *der*.

retiring [rɪ'taɪərɪŋ] *adj* [shy] zurückhaltend.

retort [rɪ'tɔːt] ◇ *n* [sharp reply] (scharfe) Erwiderung ◇ *vt:* **to ~ that ...** erwidern, dass ...

retrace [rɪ'treɪs] *vt:* **to ~ one's steps** denselben Weg zurücklgehen.

retract [rɪ'trækt] ◇ *vt* - 1. [take back] zurücklnehmen - 2. [draw in] einlziehen ◇ *vi* [be drawn in] eingezogen werden.

retrain [ˌriː'treɪn] *vt* umlschulen.

retreat [rɪ'triːt] ◇ *n* - 1. MIL [withdrawal]: **~ (from)** Rückzug *der* (aus) - 2. [refuge] Zuflucht *die* ◇ *vi* - 1. [withdraw]: **to ~ (to)** sich zurücklziehen (in (+ A)); **she ~ed hastily** sie wich hastig zurück - 2. MIL: **to ~ (from)** den Rückzug anltreten (aus) - 3. [from principle, policy, lifestyle]: **to ~ from sthg** etw auflgeben.

retribution [ˌretrɪ'bjuːʃn] *n* Vergeltung *die*.

retrieval [rɪ'triːvl] *n* COMPUT Wiederauffinden *das*.

retrieve [rɪ'triːv] *vt* - 1. [get back] zurücklbekommen - 2. COMPUT wiederauffinden - 3. [situation] retten.

retriever [rɪ'triːvəʳ] *n* [dog] Apportierhund *der;* [of specific breed] Retriever *der*.

retrospect ['retrəspekt] *n:* **in ~** im Nachhinein.

retrospective [ˌretrə'spektɪv] *adj* - 1. [mood] (zu)rückblickend - 2. [law, pay rise] rückwirkend.

return [rɪ'tɜːn] ◇ *n* - 1. [arrival back]: **~ (to)** Rückkehr *die* (nach); **~ to sthg** *fig* Rückkehr *die* zu etw - 2. [giving back] Rückgabe *die* - 3. TENNIS Return *der* - 4. *Br* [ticket] Rückfahrkarte *die;* [for plane] Rückflugticket *das* - 5. [profit] Ertrag *der* - 6. COMPUT [on keyboard] Eingabetaste *die* ◇ *vt* - 1. [give back] zurücklgeben; [loan] zurücklzahlen - 2. [visit, compliment, love] erwidern - 3. [replace] zurücklstellen - 4. LAW [verdict] fällen - 5. POL [candidate] wählen ◇ *vi* [come back] zurücklkommen; [go back] zurücklgehen; [pain] wiederlkehren; **to ~ from Germany** aus Deutschland zurücklkehren OR zurücklkommen; **to ~ to London** nach London zurücklkehren OR zurücklkommen; **to ~ to work** wieder arbeiten; **to ~ to a subject** auf ein Thema zurücklkommen. ◆ **returns** *npl* - 1. COMM Gewinn *der* - 2. [on birthday]: **many happy ~s (of the day)!** herzlichen

Glückwunsch (zum Geburtstag)! ◆ **in return** *adv* dafür. ◆ **in return for** *prep* für.

return ticket *n Br* Rückfahrkarte *die*.

reunification [ˌriːjuːnɪfɪ'keɪʃn] *n* Wiedervereinigung *die*.

reunion [ˌriː'juːnjən] *n* - 1. [party] Treffen *das* - 2. *(U)* [meeting again] Wiedersehen *das*.

reunite [ˌriːjuː'naɪt] *vt* wieder vereinigen; **to be ~d with sb/sthg** mit jm/etw wieder vereint sein.

rev [rev] *inf* ◇ *n* (*abbr of* revolution) Umdrehung *die* ◇ *vt:* **to ~ the engine (up)** den Motor hoch drehen lassen.

revamp [ˌriː'væmp] *vt inf* - 1. [reorganize] auf Vordermann bringen - 2. [redecorate] auflmöbeln.

reveal [rɪ'viːl] *vt* enthüllen.

revealing [rɪ'viːlɪŋ] *adj* - 1. [dress, blouse] offenherzig - 2. [comment] aufschlussreich.

revel ['revl] *vi:* **to ~ in sthg** [freedom, success] etw in vollen Zügen genießen; [gossip] in etw *(D)* schwelgen.

revelation [ˌrevə'leɪʃn] *n* - 1. [surprising fact] Enthüllung *die* - 2. [surprising experience] Offenbarung *die;* **to be a ~ to sb** jm die Augen öffnen.

revenge [rɪ'vendʒ] ◇ *n* Rache *die;* [in game] Revanche *die;* **to take ~ (on sb)** sich (an jm) rächen ◇ *vt:* **to ~ o.s. on sb/ sthg** sich an jm/etw rächen.

revenue ['revənjuː] *n* [income] Einnahmen *pl;* [of State] Staatseinnahmen *pl*.

reverberate [rɪ'vɜːbəreɪt] *vi* - 1. [re-echo] widerhallen; [shock wave] sich fortsetzen - 2. [have repercussions] Auswirkungen haben.

reverberations [rɪˌvɜːbə'reɪʃnz] *npl* - 1. [echoes] Widerhall *der* - 2. [repercussions] Auswirkungen *pl*.

revere [rɪ'vɪəʳ] *vt fml* verehren.

Reverend ['revərənd] *n:* **(the) ~ Peter James** Pfarrer Peter James.

reversal [rɪ'vɜːsl] *n* - 1. [of order, position, trend] Umkehrung *die;* [of decision] Umstoßung *die;* [of roles] Vertauschung *die* - 2. [piece of ill luck] Rückschlag *der*.

reverse [rɪ'vɜːs] ◇ *adj* umgekehrt; [side] Rück- ◇ *n* - 1. AUT: **~ (gear)** Rückwärtsgang *der* - 2. [opposite]: **the ~** das Gegenteil - 3. [back]: **the ~** die Rückseite; [of coin] die Kehrseite ◇ *vt* - 1. AUT rückwärts fahren mit - 2. [order, position, trend] umlkehren; [decision] umlstoßen; [roles] tauschen - 3. [turn over] umldrehen - 4. *Br* TELEC: **to ~ the charges** ein R-Gespräch führen ◇ *vi* AUT rückwärts fahren.

reverse-charge call *n Br* R-Gespräch *das*.

reversing light [rɪ'vɜːsɪŋ-] *n Br* Rückfahrscheinwerfer *der*.

revert [rɪ'vɜːt] *vi:* **to ~ to sthg** zu etw

zurück|kehren; **to ~ to type** *fig* wieder in die alten Gewohnheiten verfallen.
review [rɪ'vjuː] ◇ *n* - **1.** [examination] Überprüfung *die* - **2.** [critique] Besprechung *die*, Rezension *die* ◇ *vt* - **1.** [reassess] überprüfen - **2.** [write critique of] besprechen - **3.** [troops] inspizieren, mustern - **4.** *Am* [study] wiederholen.
reviewer [rɪ'vjuːəʳ] *n* Rezensent *der*, -in *die*.
revile [rɪ'vaɪl] *vt literary* schmähen.
revise [rɪ'vaɪz] ◇ *vt* - **1.** [alter] revidieren - **2.** [rewrite] überarbeiten - **3.** *Br* [study] wiederholen ◇ *vi* **Br: to ~ (for sthg)** (für etw) den Stoff wiederholen.
revision [rɪ'vɪʒn] *n* - **1.** [alteration] Revision *die* - **2.** *Br* [study]: **to do some ~** den Stoff wiederholen.
revitalize, -ise [ˌriː'vaɪtəlaɪz] *vt* wieder beleben.
revival [rɪ'vaɪvl] *n* [economy, interest] Wiederbelebung *die*.
revive [rɪ'vaɪv] ◇ *vt* wieder beleben; [tradition, memories] wieder aufleben lassen; [play] wieder auff|führen ◇ *vi* - **1.** [regain consciousness] wieder zu sich kommen - **2.** [plant, economy, interest] wieder aufleben, wieder erblühen.
revolt [rɪ'vəʊlt] ◇ *n* Aufstand *der*, Revolte *die* ◇ *vt* an|widern ◇ *vi*: **to ~ (against)** revoltieren (gegen).
revolting [rɪ'vəʊltɪŋ] *adj* widerlich.
revolution [ˌrevə'luːʃn] *n* - **1.** POL & *fig* Revolution *die* - **2.** TECH [circular movement] Umdrehung *die*.
revolutionary [ˌrevə'luːʃnərɪ] ◇ *adj lit* & *fig* revolutionär ◇ *n* POL Revolutionär *der*, -in *die*.
revolve [rɪ'vɒlv] *vi* sich drehen; **to ~ (a)round** *lit* & *fig* sich drehen um.
revolver [rɪ'vɒlvəʳ] *n* Revolver *der*.
revolving [rɪ'vɒlvɪŋ] *adj* Dreh-.
revolving door *n* Drehtür *die*.
revue [rɪ'vjuː] *n* Revue *die*.
revulsion [rɪ'vʌlʃn] *n* Ekel *der*.
reward [rɪ'wɔːd] ◇ *n* Belohnung *die* ◇ *vt* belohnen; **to ~ sb for/with sthg** jn für/mit etw belohnen.
rewarding [rɪ'wɔːdɪŋ] *adj* lohnend; **it is a ~ book** es lohnt sich, das Buch zu lesen.
rewind [ˌriː'waɪnd] (*pt* & *pp* rewound) *vt* [tape] zurück|spulen.
rewire [ˌriː'waɪəʳ] *vt* [house] neu verkabeln; [plug] neu an|schließen.
reword [ˌriː'wɜːd] *vt* neu formulieren.
rewound [ˌriː'waʊnd] *pt* & *pp* ▷ rewind.
rewrite [ˌriː'raɪt] (*pt* rewrote [ˌriː'rəʊt]; *pp* rewritten [ˌriː'rɪtn]) *vt* neu schreiben.
Reykjavik ['rekjəvɪk] *n* Reykjavik *nt*.
rhapsody ['ræpsədɪ] *n* - **1.** MUS Rhapsodie *die* - **2.** [strong approval]: **to go into rhapso-**

dies over sthg von etw zu schwärmen beginnen.
rhetoric ['retərɪk] *n (U)* Rhetorik *die*.
rhetorical question [rɪ'tɒrɪkl-] *n* rhetorische Frage.
rheumatism ['ruːmətɪzm] *n* Rheuma *das*.
Rhine [raɪn] *n*: **the ~** der Rhein.
rhino ['raɪnəʊ] (*pl inv* OR -s) *n inf* Nashorn *das*, Rhinozeros *das*.
rhinoceros, rhinoceros [raɪ'nɒsərəs] (*pl inv* OR -es) *n* Nashorn *das*, Rhinozeros *das*.
rhododendron [ˌrəʊdə'dendrən] *n* Rhododendron *der* OR *das*.
rhubarb ['ruːbɑːb] *n* Rhabarber *der*.
rhyme [raɪm] ◇ *n* Reim *der* ◇ *vi*: **to ~ (with sthg)** sich (mit etw) reimen.
rhythm ['rɪðm] *n* Rhythmus *der*.
rib [rɪb] *n* [of body, framework] Rippe *die*.
ribbon ['rɪbən] *n* - **1.** [for decoration] Band *das* - **2.** [for typewriter] Farbband *das*.
rice [raɪs] *n* Reis *der*.
rice pudding *n* Milchreis *der*.
rich [rɪtʃ] ◇ *adj* - **1.** [gen] reich; **to be ~ in sthg** reich an etw *(D)* sein - **2.** [soil] fruchtbar - **3.** [food, cake] schwer ◇ *npl*: **the ~** die Reichen *pl*. ◆ **riches** *npl* Reichtümer *pl*.
richly ['rɪtʃlɪ] *adv* - **1.** [well - rewarded] reich - **2.** [abundantly] reichlich - **3.** [sumptuously, expensively] reich.
richness ['rɪtʃnɪs] *n (U)* - **1.** [of deposit] Reichtum *der* - **2.** [of soil] Fruchtbarkeit *die* - **3.** [of food] Schwere *die*.
rickety ['rɪkətɪ] *adj* wackelig.
ricochet ['rɪkəʃeɪ] (*pt* & *pp* -ed OR -ted; *cont* -ing) ◇ *n* Abprall *der* ◇ *vi*: **to ~ (off sthg)** (von etw) ab|prallen.
rid [rɪd] (*pt* & *pp* -ded; *pp* rid) *vt*: **to ~ sb/sthg of sthg** jn/etw von etw befreien; **to ~ o.s. of sthg** sich von etw befreien.
ridden ['rɪdn] *pp* ▷ ride.
riddle ['rɪdl] *n* Rätsel *das*.
riddled ['rɪdld] *adj*: **to be ~ with holes** ganz durchlöchert sein; **to be ~ with errors** voller Fehler sein.
ride [raɪd] (*pt* rode; *pp* ridden) ◇ *n* - **1.** [on horseback] Ritt *der*; **to go for a ~** reiten gehen - **2.** [on bicycle, motorbike, in car] Fahrt *die*; **to go for a ~** eine Fahrt/Tour machen - **3.** *phr*: **to take sb for a ~** *inf* [trick] jn rein|legen ◇ *vt* - **1.** [horse] reiten - **2.** [bicycle, motorbike] fahren; **to ~ a bicycle/motorbike** Rad/Motorrad fahren - **3.** [distance - on horse] reiten; [- on bicycle, motorbike] fahren - **4.** *Am* [train, bus, elevator] fahren mit ◇ *vi* - **1.** [on horseback] reiten - **2.** [on bicycle, motorbike] fahren - **3.** [in car, bus]: **to ~ in sthg** mit etw fahren.
rider ['raɪdəʳ] *n* - **1.** [on horseback] Reiter *der*, -in *die* - **2.** [on bicycle, motorbike] Fahrer *der*, -in *die*.
ridge [rɪdʒ] *n* - **1.** [on mountain] Kamm *der*, Rücken *der* - **2.** [on flat surface] Riffel *die*.

ridicule ['rɪdɪkjuːl] ◇ n Spott der ◇ vt lächerlich machen, verspotten.

ridiculous [rɪ'dɪkjʊləs] adj lächerlich.

riding ['raɪdɪŋ] n Reiten das.

riding school n Reitschule die.

rife [raɪf] adj: to be ~ grassieren.

riffraff ['rɪfræf] n Gesindel das.

rifle ['raɪfl] n Gewehr das.

rifle range n Schießstand der.

rift [rɪft] n - 1. GEOL Spalt der - 2. [quarrel]: a ~ between eine Kluft zwischen (+ D).

rig [rɪɡ] ◇ n: (oil) ~ Bohrinsel die ◇ vt [fix outcome of] manipulieren. ◆ **rig up** vt sep aufstellen, montieren.

rigging ['rɪɡɪŋ] n (U) [on ship] Takelung die.

right [raɪt] ◇ adj - 1. [gen] richtig; **have you got the ~ time?** haben Sie die genaue Zeit?; **to be ~ (about sthg)** (bezüglich etw) Recht haben; **to get the answer ~** die richtige Antwort geben - 2. [going well]: **things aren't ~ between them** sie kommen nicht gut miteinander aus - 3. [not left] rechte, -r, -s - 4. Br inf [idiot, mess] richtig, total ◇ n - 1. [moral correctness, entitlement] Recht das; **to be in the ~** im Recht sein; **human ~s** Menschenrechte pl; **.by ~s** rechtmäßig, von Rechts wegen - 2. [right-hand side] rechte Seite; **on your ~** zu Ihrer Rechten; **on the ~** rechts ◇ adv - 1. [correctly] richtig - 2. [not left] rechts - 3. [emphatic use] ganz; **stay ~ here** bleib hier; **to turn ~ round** sich ganz herumdrehen - 4. [immediately] gleich; **~ now** [immediately] (jetzt) gleich; [at this very moment] (jetzt) gerade; **~ away** sofort ◇ vt - 1. [correct] wieder gutmachen - 2. [make upright] aufrichten ◇ excl gut!, O. K.! ◆ **Right** n POL: **the Right** die Rechte.

right angle n rechter Winkel; **at ~s to sthg** im rechten Winkel zu etw.

righteous ['raɪtʃəs] adj [person] rechtschaffen; [anger] selbstgerecht.

rightful ['raɪtfʊl] adj rechtmäßig.

right-hand adj [on the right] rechte, -r, -s.

right-hand drive adj rechts gesteuert.

right-handed [-'hændɪd] adj rechtshändig.

right-hand man n rechte Hand.

rightly ['raɪtlɪ] adv - 1. [correctly, without error] ganz richtig - 2. [appropriately, aptly] korrekt - 3. [justifiably] mit Recht.

right of way n - 1. AUT Vorfahrt die - 2. [access] Durchgangsrecht das.

right wing n: **the ~** der rechte Flügel. ◆ **right-wing** adj rechtsgerichtet.

rigid ['rɪdʒɪd] adj - 1. [hard, stiff, inflexible] starr - 2. [strict] strikt.

rigor n Am = rigour.

rigorous ['rɪɡərəs] adj streng.

rigour Br, **rigor** Am ['rɪɡə'] n Strenge die. ◆ **rigours** npl Unbilden pl.

rile [raɪl] vt ärgern.

rim [rɪm] n Rand der; [of spectacles] Fassung die; [of wheel] Felge die.

rind [raɪnd] n [of fruit] Schale die; [of cheese] Rinde die; [of bacon] Schwarte die.

ring [rɪŋ] (pt rang; pp vt senses 1 & 2 & vi rung; pt & pp vt senses 3 & 4 only -ed) ◇ n - 1. [telephone call]: **to give sb a ~** jn anlrufen - 2. [sound of bell] Klingeln das - 3. [quality, tone]: **her excuse had a familiar ~ (about it)** ihre Ausrede kam mir bekannt vor; **there's a ~ of truth about it** es klingt sehr wahrscheinlich - 4. [object, jewellery, for boxing] Ring der - 5. [of people, trees] Kreis der - 6. [people working together] Ring der; **crime ~** Verbrecherring der ◇ vt - 1. Br [phone] anlrufen - 2. [bell] läuten; **to ~ the doorbell** (an der Tür) klingeln OR läuten - 3. [draw a circle round] einlkreisen - 4. [surround] umringen; **to be ~ed with sthg** von etw umringt sein ◇ vi - 1. Br [phone] klingeln - 2. [doorbell, person at door] klingeln, läuten - 3. [to attract attention]: **to ~ (for sb)** (nach jm) läuten. ◆ **ring back** vt sep & vi Br zurücklrufen. ◆ **ring off** vi Br auflhängen. ◆ **ring up** vt sep Br Umgebungsstraße die.

ring binder n Ringbuch das.

ringing ['rɪŋɪŋ] n [of bell] Läuten das; [of telephone] Klingeln das; [in ears] Klingen das.

ringing tone n Br TELEC Freizeichen das.

ringleader ['rɪŋˌliːdə'] n Anführer der, -in die.

ringlet ['rɪŋlɪt] n Ringellocke die.

ring road n Br Umgebungsstraße die.

rink [rɪŋk] n [for ice-skating] Eisbahn die; [for roller-skating] Rollschuhbahn die.

rinse [rɪns] vt [clothes; vegetables] waschen; [hands; mouth] spülen; **to ~ one's hands** die Hände ablspülen; **to ~ one's mouth out** sich (D) den Mund auslspülen.

riot ['raɪət] ◇ n Aufruhr der; **to run ~** [hooligans] randalieren; [children] außer Rand und Band sein; [plants] wuchern ◇ vi einen Aufruhr machen.

rioter ['raɪətə'] n Aufrührer der, -in die.

riotous ['raɪətəs] adj [mob] randalierend; [party, behaviour] ausgelassen, wild.

riot police npl Bereitschaftspolizei die.

rip [rɪp] ◇ n Riss der ◇ vt - 1. [tear, shred] zerreißen - 2. [remove]: **to ~ sthg from** OR **off sthg** etw von etw ablreißen ◇ vi reißen.

RIP (abbr of rest in peace) R. I. P.

ripe [raɪp] adj [ready to eat] reif; **to be ~ for sthg** fig für etw reif sein.

ripen ['raɪpn] ◇ vt reifen lassen ◇ vi reifen.

rip-off n inf [excessive charge] Wucher der.

ripple ['rɪpl] ◇ n - 1. [in water] kleine Welle - 2. [sound]: **a ~ of laughter** sanftes Gelächter; **a ~ of applause** kurzer Applaus ◇ vt kräuseln.

rise [raɪz] (pt rose; pp risen ['rɪzn]) ◇ n

- **1.** *Br* [increase in amount]: ~ **(in sth)** Anstieg *der* (einer Sache *(G)*) - **2.** *Br* [increase in salary] Gehaltserhöhung *die* - **3.** [to power, fame] Aufstieg *der* - **4.** [slope] Steigung *die* - **5.** *phr:* **to give ~ to sth** zu etw führen ◇ *vi* - **1.** [go upwards, become higher, increase] steigen - **2.** [sun, bread] aufgehen - **3.** [stand up, get out of bed] aufstehen - **4.** [slope upwards] (an)steigen - **5.** [become louder - voice] lauter werden - **6.** [become higher in pitch] höher werden - **7.** [prove o.s.]: **to ~ to the occasion** der Lage gewachsen sein; **to ~ to the challenge** die Herausforderung anlnehmen - **8.** [rebel] sich erheben - **9.** [in status] aufsteigen; **to ~ to power** an die Macht kommen.

rising ['raɪzɪŋ] ◇ *adj* - **1.** [sloping upwards] (an)steigend - **2.** [increasing, tide] steigend - **3.** [increasingly successful] aufsteigend ◇ *n* [rebellion] Aufstand *der*, Erhebung *die*.

risk [rɪsk] ◇ *n* Risiko *das;* **to run the ~ of doing sth** Gefahr laufen, etw zu tun; **to take a ~** ein Risiko einlgehen; **at one's own ~** auf eigenes Risiko; **at ~** in Gefahr; **to put at ~** gefährden ◇ *vt* - **1.** [put in danger] riskieren - **2.** [take the chance of]: **to ~ doing sth** riskieren, etw zu tun.

risky ['rɪskɪ] *adj* riskant.

risqué [rɪ'skeɪ] *adj* gewagt, schlüpfrig.

rite [raɪt] *n* Ritus *der*.

ritual ['rɪtʃʊəl] ◇ *adj* rituell ◇ *n* Ritual *das*.

rival ['raɪvl] ◇ *adj* Konkurrenz-, konkurrierend ◇ *n* Rivale *der*, -lin *die*; COMM Konkurrent *der*, -in *die* ◇ *vt* sich messen mit, konkurrieren mit.

rivalry ['raɪvlrɪ] *n* Rivalität *die*.

river ['rɪvə*r*] *n* Fluss *der;* **the River Thames** *Br,* **the Thames River** *Am* die Themse.

river bank *n* Flussufer *das*.

riverbed ['rɪvəbed] *n* Flussbett *das*.

riverside ['rɪvəsaɪd] *n:* **the ~** das Flussufer.

rivet ['rɪvɪt] ◇ *n* Niete *die* ◇ *vt* - **1.** [fasten with rivets] nieten - **2.** *fig* [fascinate]: **to be ~ed by sth** von etw gefesselt sein.

road [rəʊd] *n* Straße *die;* **by ~** [send] per Spedition; [travel] mit dem Auto/Bus/*etc;* **on the ~ to victory/success/recovery** auf dem Weg zum Sieg/zum Erfolg/der Besserung.

roadblock ['rəʊdblɒk] *n* Straßensperre *die*.

road map *n* Straßenkarte *die*.

road safety *n* Verkehrssicherheit *die*.

roadside ['rəʊdsaɪd] *n:* **by the ~** am Straßenrand.

road sign *n* Verkehrszeichen *das*.

road tax *n* Kraftfahrzeugsteuer *die*.

roadway ['rəʊdweɪ] *n* Fahrbahn *die*.

road works *npl* (Straßen)bauarbeiten *pl*.

roam [rəʊm] ◇ *vt* [countryside] durchstreifen; [streets] herumlziehen in (+ *D*) ◇ *vi* [in

countryside] wandern; [in streets] herumlziehen.

roar [rɔː*r*] ◇ *vi* - **1.** [lion, person] brüllen; **to ~ with laughter** vor Lachen brüllen - **2.** [wind, engine] heulen ◇ *vt* brüllen ◇ *n* - **1.** [of lion, person] Brüllen *das* - **2.** [of wind, engine] Heulen *das;* [of traffic] Lärm *der*.

roaring ['rɔːrɪŋ] ◇ *adj* - **1.** [traffic] lärmend; [wind, engine] heulend - **2.** [fire] prasselnd - **3.** [for emphasis]: **a ~ success** ein Riesenerfolg; **to do a ~ trade** ein Riesengeschäft machen ◇ *adv:* **~ drunk** sternhagelvoll.

roast [rəʊst] ◇ *adj:* **~ beef** Rinderbraten *der*, Roastbeef *das;* **~ chicken** Brathähnchen *das;* **~ pork** Schweinebraten *der* ◇ *n* Braten *der* ◇ *vt* - **1.** [meat] braten; [potatoes] *im Ofen* in Fett backen - **2.** [coffee beans, nuts] rösten.

rob [rɒb] *vt* [person] bestehlen; [bank, house] auslrauben; **to ~ sb of sth** [of money, goods] jm etw stehlen; *fig* [of opportunity, glory] jn einer Sache *(G)* berauben.

robber ['rɒbə*r*] *n* Räuber *der*, -in *die*.

robbery ['rɒbərɪ] *n* Raub *der*.

robe [rəʊb] *n* - **1.** [of priest, judge, monarch] Robe *die* - **2.** *Am* [dressing gown] Morgenrock *der*.

robin ['rɒbɪn] *n* Rotkehlchen *das*.

robot ['rəʊbɒt] *n* Roboter *der*.

robust [rəʊ'bʌst] *adj* [person, health] robust; [economy] stabil; [criticism, defence] stark.

rock [rɒk] ◇ *n* - **1.** (*U*) [substance] Stein *der* - **2.** [boulder] Fels(en) *der* - **3.** *Am* [pebble] Stein *der* - **4.** [music] Rock *der* - **5.** *Br* [sweet]: **stick of ~** Zuckerstange *die* ◇ *comp* [band, concert, singer] Rock- ◇ *vt* - **1.** [cause to move] schaukeln; [baby] wiegen - **2.** [shock] erschüttern ◇ *vi* [boat, cradle, in chair] schaukeln. ◆ **on the rocks** *adv* - **1.** [drink] mit Eis - **2.** [marriage, relationship] kaputt.

rock bottom *n:* **to be at ~** auf dem Tiefpunkt sein; **to hit ~** den Tiefpunkt erreichen. ◆ **rock-bottom** *adj* [prices] Schleuder-.

rockery ['rɒkərɪ] *n* Steingarten *der*.

rocket ['rɒkɪt] ◇ *n* Rakete *die* ◇ *vi* hoch schießen.

rocket launcher [-ˌlɔːntʃə*r*] *n* Raketenwerfer *der*.

rocking chair ['rɒkɪŋ-] *n* Schaukelstuhl *der*.

rocking horse ['rɒkɪŋ-] *n* Schaukelpferd *das*.

rocky ['rɒkɪ] *adj* - **1.** [full of rocks] steinig - **2.** [unsteady] wackelig.

Rocky Mountains *npl:* **the ~** die Rocky Mountains.

rod [rɒd] *n* Stange *die;* [for fishing] Angel *die*.

rode [rəʊd] *pt* ▷ ride.

rodent ['rəʊdənt] *n* Nagetier *das*.

roe [rəʊ] *n* [of fish] Rogen *der*.

rogue [rəʊg] *n* - **1.** [likable rascal] Frech-

dachs der - **2.** dated [dishonest person] Schurke der.

role [rəʊl] n Rolle die.

roll [rəʊl] ◇ n - **1.** [of material, paper, film] Rolle die - **2.** [of bread] Brötchen das; **a cheese ~** ein Käsebrötchen - **3.** [list] Liste die; **electoral ~** Wählerverzeichnis das - **4.** [sound - of thunder] Rollen das; [- of drums] Wirbel der ◇ vt - **1.** [turn over] rollen - **2.** [make into cylinder] auflrollen; [umbrella] zusammenlrollen; **~ed into one** fig in einem ◇ vi - **1.** [gen] rollen - **2.** [make loud noise - thunder] rollen; [- drums] wirbeln. ● **roll about, roll around** vi herumlrollen; [person] sich wälzen. ● **roll over** vi [person] sich umlldrehen. ● **roll up** ◇ vt sep - **1.** [make into cylinder] auflrollen, zusammenlrollen - **2.** [sleeves] hochlkrempeln ◇ vi - **1.** [vehicle] vorlfahren - **2.** inf [person] auflkreuzen.

roll call n Namensaufruf der; MIL Appell der.

roller ['rəʊlə'] n - **1.** [cylinder] Walze die - **2.** [curler] (Locken)wickler der.

roller blades npl Rollerblades pl.

roller coaster n Achterbahn die.

roller skate n Rollschuh der.

rolling ['rəʊlɪŋ] adj - **1.** [hills] wellig - **2.** phr: **to be ~ in it** inf im Geld schwimmen.

rolling pin n Nudelholz das.

roll-on adj & n: **~ (deodorant)** Deoroller der.

ROM [rɒm] (abbr of read only memory) n ROM.

Roman ['rəʊmən] ◇ adj römisch ◇ n Römer der, -in die.

Roman Catholic ◇ adj römischkatholisch ◇ n Katholik der, -in die.

romance [rəʊ'mæns] n - **1.** [romantic quality] Romantik die - **2.** [love affair] Romanze die - **3.** [novel] Liebesroman der.

Romania [ru:'meɪnjə] n Rumänien nt.

Romanian [ru:'meɪnjən] ◇ adj rumänisch ◇ n - **1.** [person] Rumäne der, -nin die - **2.** [language] Rumänisch(e) das.

romantic [rəʊ'mæntɪk] adj - **1.** [gen] romantisch - **2.** [novel, film, play] Liebes-.

Rome [rəʊm] n Rom nt.

romp [rɒmp] ◇ n: **to have a ~** herumltoben, herumltollen ◇ vi [play noisily] herumltoben, herumltollen.

rompers ['rɒmpəz] npl, **romper suit** ['rɒmpə'-] n Strampelhose die.

roof [ru:f] n - **1.** [of building, vehicle] Dach das; **to go through** OR **hit the ~** an die Decke gehen - **2.** [upper part - of cave] Gewölbe das; **~ of the mouth** Gaumen der.

roofing ['ru:fɪŋ] n (U) [material] Deckung die.

roof rack n Dachträger der.

rooftop ['ru:ftɒp] n Dach das.

rook [rʊk] n - **1.** [bird] Krähe die - **2.** [chess piece] Turm der.

rookie ['rʊkɪ] n Am inf Grünschnabel der.

room [ru:m, rʊm] n - **1.** [in house, hotel] Zimmer das; [in office, public building etc] Raum der - **2.** (U) [space] Platz der; **to make ~ for sb/sthg** für jn/etw Platz machen - **3.** (U) [opportunity, possibility]: **there is still ~ for improvement** es könnte besser sein; **there is no ~ for sentimentality in politics** Sentimentalität hat in der Politik nichts zu suchen.

roommate ['ru:mmeɪt] n Zimmergenosse der, -sin die.

room service n (U) Zimmerservice der.

roomy ['ru:mɪ] adj [house, car] geräumig; [garment] weit.

roost [ru:st] ◇ n Hühnerstange die ◇ vi [hens] auf der Stange sitzen.

rooster ['ru:stə'] n Hahn der.

root [ru:t] ◇ n lit & fig Wurzel die; **to take ~** [plant] Wurzel fassen; [idea] Fuß fassen; **the ~ of the problem** die Ursache des Problems ◇ vi [search] wühlen. ● **roots** npl [origins] Wurzeln pl. ● **root for** vt fus esp Am inf anlfeuern. ● **root out** vt sep [eradicate] auslrotten.

rope [rəʊp] ◇ n Seil das; **to know the ~s** sich auslkennen ◇ vt: **to ~ together** zusammenlbinden; [climbers] anlseilen. ● **rope in** vt sep inf [involve] ranlkriegen.

rosary ['rəʊzərɪ] n Rosenkranz der.

rose [rəʊz] ◇ pt ⊳ rise ◇ adj [pink] rosa ◇ n [flower] Rose die.

rosé ['rəʊzeɪ] n Rosé der.

rose bush n Rosenstrauch der.

rosemary ['rəʊzmərɪ] n Rosmarin der.

rosette [rəʊ'zet] n Rosette die.

roster ['rɒstə'] n Dienstplan der.

rostrum ['rɒstrəm] (pl -trums OR -tra [-trə]) n [for speaker, conductor] Pult das.

rosy ['rəʊzɪ] adj lit & fig rosig.

rot [rɒt] ◇ n - **1.** (U) [decay - of wood, food] Fäulnis die; [- in society, organization] Verfall der; **dry ~** Trockenfäule die; **to stop the ~** den Verfall auflhalten; **the ~ set in** es ging abwärts - **2.** Br dated [nonsense] Quatsch der ◇ vt faulen lassen ◇ vi faulen.

rota ['rəʊtə] n Dienstplan der.

rotary ['rəʊtərɪ] ◇ adj rotierend, Rotations- ◇ n Am [roundabout] Kreisverkehr der.

rotate [rəʊ'teɪt] ◇ vt [turn] drehen ◇ vi [turn] sich drehen, rotieren.

rotation [rəʊ'teɪʃn] n [turning movement] Drehung die, Rotation die.

rote [rəʊt] n: **by ~** auswendig.

rotten ['rɒtn] adj - **1.** [decayed] verfault - **2.** inf [poor-quality, unskilled] lausig - **3.** inf [mean] gemein - **4.** inf [unpleasant, unenjoyable] mies - **5.** inf [unwell]: **to feel ~** sich mies fühlen.

rouge [ru:ʒ] n Rouge das.

rough [rʌf] ◇ *adj* - **1.** [not smooth - surface] rau; [- road] uneben, holprig - **2.** [violent] grob, rau - **3.** [crude, basic - shelter, conditions] primitiv; [- people, manners] rau - **4.** [not detailed, not exact] grob; **~ draft** Rohentwurf *der*; **at a ~ guess** grob geschätzt; **can you give me a ~ idea of the cost?** können Sie mir sagen, wie viel es ungefähr kostet? - **5.** [unpleasant, tough - life, time] hart; [- journey] anstrengend; [- area] rau; **to be ~ on sb** hart für jn sein - **6.** [stormy] stürmisch - **7.** [harsh - voice] rau; [- wine] sauer ◇ *adv:* **to sleep ~** im Freien übernachten ◇ *n* - **1.** GOLF: **the ~** das Rough - **2.** [draft]: **to write sthg in ~** ein Konzept für etw machen ◇ *vt phr:* **to ~ it** primitiv leben.

rough and ready *adj* primitiv; [person] rau(beinig).

roughen ['rʌfn] *vt* [surface] aufrauen.

roughly ['rʌflɪ] *adv* - **1.** [gen] grob - **2.** [approximately] etwa.

roulette [ruːˈlet] *n* Roulette *das*.

round [raʊnd] ◇ *adj* rund ◇ *prep* - **1.** [surrounding] um … herum; **there were soldiers all ~ the building** rund um das Gebäude waren Soldaten - **2.** [near]: **~ here/there** hier/dort in der Nähe; **is there a bank anywhere ~ here?** gibt es hier irgendwo eine Bank? - **3.** [all over]: **150 offices ~ the world** 150 Büros in der ganzen Welt; **all ~ the country** in ganzen Land; **to go ~ a museum** ein Museum besuchen; **to show sb ~ sthg** jn in etw (D) herumlführen - **4.** [in a circle]: **we walked ~ the lake** wir gingen um den See herum; **to go/drive ~ sthg** um etw herumlgehen/herumlfahren; **~ the clock** *fig* rund um die Uhr - **5.** [in circumference]: **she measures 30 inches ~ the waist** um die Taille misst sie 75 cm - **6.** [on or to the other side of]: **to go ~ the corner** um die Ecke sein/gehen - **7.** [so as to avoid] um … herum; **to get ~ an obstacle** um ein Hindernis herumlgehen; **to find a way ~ a problem** einen Ausweg für ein Problem finden ◇ *adv* - **1.** [on all sides] herum; **all ~** auf allen Seiten, rundherum - **2.** [near]: **~ about** [in distance] in der Nähe; [approximately] rund; **~ about ten o'clock** gegen zehn Uhr - **3.** [here and there] herum; **to travel ~** herumlreisen - **4.** [in a circle]: **to go ~** sich drehen; **to spin ~ (and ~)** sich im Kreis drehen - **5.** [to the other side]: **to go ~** herumlgehen; **to turn ~** sich umldrehen; **to look ~** sich umlsehen; **it's a long way ~** das ist ein Umweg - **6.** [on a visit]: **why don't you come ~?** warum kommst du nicht vorbei?; **I spent the day ~ at her house** ich war den ganzen Tag bei ihr (zu Hause) - **7.** [when sharing]: **to hand sthg ~** etw herumlreichen - **8.** [continuously]: **all year ~** das ganze Jahr über ◇ *n* - **1.** [gen & SPORT] Runde *die*; **a ~ of applause** eine Runde Applaus - **2.** [of ammunition] Schuss *der* - **3.** [of drinks] Runde *die*; **it's my ~**

es ist meine Runde - **4.**: **a ~ of sandwiches** ein Sandwich - **5.** [of toast] Scheibe *die* ◇ *vt* [turn]: **to ~ a bend** um eine Kurve fahren. ➤ **round off** *vt sep* ablrunden. ➤ **round up** *vt sep* - **1.** [animals] zusammenltreiben - **2.** [number] auflrunden.

roundabout ['raʊndəbaʊt] ◇ *adj* umständlich ◇ *n Br* - **1.** [on road] Kreisverkehr *der* - **2.** [at fairground, playground] Karussell *das*.

rounders ['raʊndəz] *n* (U) *Br* Schlagball *der*.

roundly ['raʊndlɪ] *adv* [criticize] scharf; [defeated] vernichtend.

round trip *n* Rundreise *die*.

roundup ['raʊndʌp] *n* [summary] Zusammenfassung *die*.

rouse [raʊz] *vt* - **1.** [wake up] wecken - **2.** [impel]: **to ~ o.s. to do sthg** sich dazu auflraffen, etw zu tun; **to ~ sb to action** jn zum Handeln bewegen - **3.** [subj: orator] in Erregung versetzen - **4.** [give rise to] hervorlrufen; [emotions, interest] wecken, wachlrufen.

rousing ['raʊzɪŋ] *adj* [speech] mitreißend; [cheer] stürmisch.

rout [raʊt] ◇ *n* Niederlage *die* ◇ *vt* in die Flucht schlagen.

route [ruːt] ◇ *n* - **1.** [line of travel] Strecke *die*, Route *die* - **2.** [fixed itinerary]: **air/bus/shipping ~** Flug-/Bus-/Schifffahrtslinie *die* - **3.** *fig* [to achievement] Weg *der* ◇ *vt* [flight, traffic] legen; [goods] schicken.

route map *n* [for public transport] Streckenkarte *die*; [for holiday route] Tourenplan *der*.

routine [ruːˈtiːn] ◇ *adj* routinemäßig, Routine- ◇ *n* Routine *die*.

row[1] [rəʊ] ◇ *n* Reihe *die*; **in a ~** nacheinander ◇ *vt* & *vi* rudern.

row[2] [raʊ] ◇ *n* - **1.** [quarrel] Streit *der*, Krach *der* - **2.** *inf* [noise] Krach *der*, Krawall *der* ◇ *vi* [quarrel] sich streiten.

rowboat ['rəʊbəʊt] *n Am* Ruderboot *das*.

rowdy ['raʊdɪ] *adj* [person] wild, randalierend; [party, atmosphere] laut.

row house [rəʊ-] *n Am* Reihenhaus *das*.

rowing ['rəʊɪŋ] *n* Rudern *das*.

rowing boat *n Br* Ruderboot *das*.

royal ['rɔɪəl] ◇ *adj* [regal] königlich ◇ *n inf* Angehörige *der*, *die* der königlichen Familie.

Royal Air Force *n:* **the ~** die Königliche Luftwaffe.

royal family *n* königliche Familie.

Royal Mail *n Br:* **the ~** die Königliche Post.

Royal Navy *n:* **the ~** die Königliche Marine.

royalty ['rɔɪəltɪ] *n* (U) [persons] Königshaus *das*. ➤ **royalties** *npl* Tantiemen *pl*.

rpm (*abbr of* revolutions per minute) *npl* U/min.

RSPCA (*abbr of* Royal Society for the Preven-

tion of Cruelty to Animals) n britischer Tierschutzverein.

RSVP (abbr of répondez s'il vous plaît) u.A.w.g.

rub [rʌb] <> vt reiben; **to ~ one's hands together** sich (D) die Hände reiben; **he ~bed sun cream into her back** er rieb ihren Rücken mit Sonnencreme ein; **to ~ sb up the wrong way** Br, **to ~ sb the wrong way** Am fig jn verstimmen <> vi: **to ~ against** OR **on sthg** an etw (D) reiben; [person, animal] sich an etw (D) reiben; **to ~ together** sich reiben. ➤ **rub off on** vt fus [subj: quality] abfärben auf (+ A). ➤ **rub out** vt sep [erase] ausradieren.

rubber ['rʌbə'] <> adj [made of rubber] Gummi- <> n - 1. [substance] Gummi der - 2. Br [eraser] Radiergummi der - 3. [in cards] Robber der - 4. Am inf [condom] Gummi der.

rubber band n Gummiband das.

rubber plant n Gummibaum der.

rubber stamp n Stempel der. ➤ **rubber-stamp** vt stempeln.

rubbish ['rʌbɪʃ] <> n (U) - 1. [refuse] Abfall der, Müll der - 2. inf fig [worthless thing] Mist der - 3. inf [nonsense] Quatsch der, Blödsinn der <> vt inf [person, opinion] lächerlich machen; [play, book] verreißen <> excl inf Quatsch!

rubbish bag n Br Müllsack der.

rubbish bin n Br Mülleimer der.

rubbish dump, rubbish tip n Br Mülladeplatz der.

rubble ['rʌbl] n Schutt der.

ruby ['ru:bɪ] n [gem] Rubin der.

rucksack ['rʌksæk] n Rucksack der.

rudder ['rʌdə'] n Ruder das.

ruddy ['rʌdɪ] adj - 1. [reddish] rot; [complexion] gesund - 2. Br dated [for emphasis] verdammt.

rude [ru:d] adj - 1. [impolite] unhöflich - 2. [dirty, naughty] unanständig - 3. [unexpected]: **~ awakening** böses Erwachen.

rudimentary [ˌru:dɪ'mentərɪ] adj [basic] elementar.

rueful ['ru:fʊl] adj reumütig; [smile] wehmütig.

ruffian ['rʌfjən] n Grobian der.

ruffle ['rʌfl] vt - 1. [hair, fur] zersausen; [water] kräuseln - 2. [pride] verletzen; **to ~ sb's composure** jn aus der Ruhe bringen.

rug [rʌg] n - 1. [carpet] kleiner Teppich; [by bed] Bettvorleger der - 2. [blanket] Decke die.

rugby ['rʌgbɪ] n Rugby das.

rugged ['rʌgɪd] adj - 1. [rocky, uneven - landscape] wild; [- cliffs] zerklüftet - 2. [sturdy] stabil.

rugger ['rʌgə'] n Br inf Rugby das.

ruin ['ru:ɪn] <> n - 1. [financial downfall] Ruin der - 2. [ruined building] Ruine die <> vt ruinieren; [chances, atmosphere] verderben.

➤ **in ruins** adv: **to be in ~s** [town, country] in Ruinen liegen; [building] eine Ruine sein; [marriage, career, plans] ruiniert sein.

rule [ru:l] <> n - 1. [regulation, guideline] Regel die - 2. [norm]: **the ~** die Regel; **as a ~** in der Regel - 3. (U) [control] Herrschaft die <> vt - 1. [control, guide] beherrschen - 2. [govern] regieren - 3. [decide]: **to ~ that ...** entscheiden, dass ... <> vi - 1. [give decision] entscheiden - 2. fml [be paramount] herrschen - 3. [govern] regieren. ➤ **rule out** vt sep ausschließen.

ruled [ru:ld] adj [lined] liniert.

ruler ['ru:lə'] n - 1. [for measurement] Lineal das - 2. [leader] Herrscher der, -in die.

ruling ['ru:lɪŋ] <> adj [in control] herrschend <> n [decision] Entscheidung die.

rum [rʌm] n Rum der.

Rumania [ru:'meɪnjə] n = Romania.

Rumanian [ru:'meɪnjən] adj & n = Romanian.

rumble ['rʌmbl] <> n [of thunder] Grollen das; [of lorry, train] Rumpeln das; [of stomach] Knurren das <> vi [thunder] grollen; [train] rumpeln; [stomach] knurren.

rummage ['rʌmɪdʒ] vi wühlen, stöbern.

rumour Br, **rumor** Am ['ru:mə'] n Gerücht das.

rumoured Br, **rumored** Am ['ru:məd] adj: **he is ~ to be married already** er soll angeblich schon verheiratet sein.

rump [rʌmp] n - 1. [of animal] Hinterteil das - 2. inf [of person] Hinterteil das.

rump steak n Rumpsteak das.

rumpus ['rʌmpəs] n inf Spektakel das, Krach der.

run [rʌn] (pt ran; pp run) <> n - 1. [on foot] Lauf der; **to go for a ~** laufen gehen; **at a ~** im Lauf; **on the ~** auf der Flucht - 2. [in car] Fahrt die; **to go for a ~** eine Fahrt machen - 3. [series] Reihe die; **a ~ of bad luck** eine Pechsträhne - 4. THEATRE: **it had an eight-week ~ on Broadway** es wurde für acht Wochen am Broadway gespielt - 5. [great demand]: **a ~ on sthg** ein Ansturm auf etw (A) - 6. [in tights] Laufmasche die - 7. [in cricket, baseball] Lauf der - 8. [for skiing] Abfahrt die; [for bobsleigh] Bahn die - 9. [term, period]: **in the long/short ~** auf lange/kurze Sicht (gesehen) <> vt - 1. [on foot] rennen, laufen; **to ~ a race** ein Rennen laufen - 2. [business, hotel] führen; [course, event] leiten - 3. [operate - machine, film, computer program] laufen lassen; [- experiment] durchführen - 4. [have and use - car] halten - 5. [water, tap] laufen lassen; **to ~ a bath** ein Bad einlassen - 6. [article, headline] veröffentlichen - 7. inf [drive] fahren; **I'll ~ you home** ich fahre dich nach Hause - 8. [move, pass]: **to ~ one's hand along sthg/over sthg** mit der Hand an etw (D) entlang/über etw (A) fahren <> vi - 1. [on foot, in race] laufen; [fast] rennen; **we had to ~ for the bus** wir mussten rennen, um den Bus zu erwischen - **2.** [road, track] führen, verlaufen; [river] fließen; [pipe, cable] verlaufen; **the path ~s along the coast** der Weg verläuft entlang der Küste - **3.** [in election]: **to ~ (for)** kandidieren (für) - **4.** [progress, develop] laufen; **to ~ smoothly** gut laufen - **5.** [operate - machine, engine] laufen; [- factory] arbeiten; **to ~ on unleaded petrol** mit bleifreiem Benzin fahren; **to ~ off mains electricity** mit Netzstrom laufen - **6.** [bus, train] fahren; **the bus ~s every hour** der Bus fährt jede Stunde - **7.** [liquid, tears, tap] laufen - **8.** [eyes] tränen; **my nose is ~ning** mir läuft die Nase - **9.** [colour] auslaufen; [clothes] abfärben - **10.** [continue - contract] gültig sein, laufen; [- play] laufen. ◆ **run about** vi herumlaufen. ◆ **run across** vt fus [meet] zufällig treffen. ◆ **run around** vi = run about. ◆ **run away** vi [flee]: **to ~ away (from)** weglaufen (von); [fast] weglrennen (von). ◆ **run down** ◇ vt sep - **1.** [in vehicle] überfahren - **2.** [criticize] herunterlmachen - **3.** [allow to decline] abllbauen ◇ vi [battery] leer werden; [clock] abllaufen. ◆ **run into** vt fus - **1.** [meet - person] zufällig treffen - **2.** [encounter - problem] stoßen auf (+ A); **to ~ into debt** in Schulden geraten - **3.** [in vehicle] laufen OR fahren gegen. ◆ **run off** ◇ vt sep [copy] drucken ◇ vi: **to ~ off (with sthg)** durchlbrennen; **to ~ off with sb** mit jm durchlbrennen. ◆ **run out** vi - **1.** [supply, fuel] ausllgehen; **time is ~ning out** die Zeit wird knapp - **2.** [licence, contract] abllaufen. ◆ **run out of** vt fus: **we've ~ out of petrol/money** wir haben kein Benzin/Geld mehr. ◆ **run over** vt sep [knock down] überfahren. ◆ **run through** vt fus - **1.** [practise] durchlgehen - **2.** [read through] schnell durchllesen. ◆ **run to** vt fus [amount to] sich belaufen auf (+ A). ◆ **run up** vt sep [debt] machen; [bill] zusammenkommen lassen. ◆ **run up against** vt fus stoßen auf (+ A).

runaway ['rʌnəweɪ] ◇ adj [child] ausgerissen; [horse] durchgegangen; [inflation] galoppierend; [victory] sehr überzeugend ◇ n [escapee] Ausreißer der, -in die.

rundown ['rʌndaʊn] n - **1.** [report] Bericht der - **2.** [decline] Abbau der. ◆ **run-down** adj - **1.** [dilapidated] heruntergekommen - **2.** [tired] erschöpft.

rung [rʌŋ] ◇ pp ➞ ring ◇ n lit & fig Sprosse die.

runner ['rʌnər] n - **1.** [athlete] Läufer der, -in die - **2.** [of sledge, skate] Kufe die; [of drawer] Schiene die.

runner bean n Br Stangenbohne die.

runner-up (pl runners-up) n Zweite der, die.

running ['rʌnɪŋ] ◇ adj - **1.** [continuous]

ständig - **2.** [consecutive] hintereinander; **three weeks ~** drei Wochen hintereinander - **3.** [water] fließend ◇ n - **1.** SPORT Laufen das - **2.** [management, control] Leitung die - **3.** [of machine] Betrieb der - **4.** phr: **to be in the ~ (for sthg)** im Rennen (für etw) liegen; **to be out of the ~ (for sthg)** aus dem Rennen (für etw) sein.

runny ['rʌnɪ] adj - **1.** [food] flüssig - **2.** [nose] laufend; [eyes] wässerig; **he had a ~ nose** ihm lief die Nase.

run-of-the-mill adj durchschnittlich, nullachtfünfzehn.

runt [rʌnt] n - **1.** [animal] kleinstes Tier eines Wurfs - **2.** pej [person] mickriger Kerl.

run-up n - **1.** [preceding time]: **in the ~ to** in der Zeit vor (+ D) - **2.** SPORT Anlauf der.

runway ['rʌnweɪ] n Start- und Landebahn die; [for takeoff] Startbahn die; [for landing] Landebahn die.

rupture ['rʌptʃər] n - **1.** MED Bruch der - **2.** [of relationship] (Ab)bruch der.

rural ['rʊərəl] adj ländlich.

ruse [ru:z] n List die.

rush [rʌʃ] ◇ n - **1.** [hurry] Eile die; **to be in a ~** es sehr eilig haben; **to make a ~ for sthg** auf etw (A) zulstürzen OR zulleilen - **2.** [demand]: **~ (for** OR **on sthg)** Ansturm der (auf etw (A)) - **3.** [busiest period] Stoßzeit die - **4.** [surge - of blood] Andrang der; [- of water] Schwall der ◇ vt - **1.** [hurry - work] hastig erledigen; [- meal] hastig essen; [- person] drängen - **2.** [send quickly - people] schnell bringen; [- supplies, troops] schnell schicken; **to ~ sb to hospital** jn schnell ins Krankenhaus bringen - **3.** [attack suddenly] zulstürmen auf (+ A); [enemy, position] stürmen ◇ vi - **1.** [hurry] sich beeilen - **2.** [crowd] stürzen; [air, blood, water] schießen. ◆ **rushes** npl BOT Binsen pl.

rush hour n Hauptverkehrszeit die, Stoßzeit die.

rusk [rʌsk] n Zwieback der.

Russia ['rʌʃə] n Russland nt.

Russian ['rʌʃn] ◇ adj russisch ◇ n - **1.** [person] Russe der, -sin die - **2.** [language] Russisch(e) das.

rust [rʌst] ◇ n [on metal] Rost der ◇ vi rosten.

rustle ['rʌsl] ◇ vt - **1.** [paper] rascheln mit; [subj: wind - leaves] rascheln lassen - **2.** Am [cattle] stehlen ◇ vi [paper, leaves] rascheln.

rusty ['rʌstɪ] adj - **1.** [metal] rostig - **2.** fig [skill] eingerostet; **I'm ~** ich bin aus der Übung.

rut [rʌt] n [furrow] Furche die; **to get into a ~** in einen Trott kommen.

ruthless ['ru:θlɪs] adj [person] rücksichtslos; [investigation, destruction] schonungslos; [murder] brutal.

RV n Am (abbr of recreational vehicle) Wohnmobil das.

rye [raɪ] n [grain] Roggen der.

rye bread n (U) Roggenbrot das.

S

s (pl **ss** OR **s's**), **S** (pl **Ss** OR **S's**) [es] n [letter] s das, S das. ◆ **S** (abbr of south) S.

Sabbath ['sæbəθ] n: **the ~** der Sabbat.

sabotage ['sæbətɑːʒ] ◇ n Sabotage die ◇ vt sabotieren.

sachet ['sæʃeɪ] n [of shampoo, cream] Einzelpackung die; [of sugar, coffee] Portionspackung die.

sack [sæk] ◇ n - **1.** [bag] Sack der - **2.** Br inf [dismissal]: **to get** OR **be given the ~** rausgeschmissen werden ◇ vt Br inf [dismiss] rausschmeißen.

sacred ['seɪkrɪd] adj lit & fig heilig.

sacrifice ['sækrɪfaɪs] ◇ n lit & fig Opfer das ◇ vt lit & fig opfern.

sacrilege ['sækrɪlɪdʒ] n lit & fig Sakrileg das.

sad [sæd] adj traurig.

sadden ['sædn] vt traurig machen; **I was ~ed to hear of her death** die Nachricht von ihrem Tod machte mich sehr traurig.

saddle ['sædl] ◇ n Sattel der ◇ vt - **1.** [put saddle on] satteln - **2.** fig [burden]: **to ~ sb with sthg** jm etw aufhalsen; **to be ~d with sthg** etw am Hals haben.

saddlebag ['sædlbæg] n Satteltasche die.

sadistic [sə'dɪstɪk] adj sadistisch.

sadly ['sædlɪ] adv - **1.** [sorrowfully] traurig - **2.** [regrettably] leider.

sadness ['sædnɪs] n - **1.** [sorrow] Trauer die - **2.** [distressing nature] Traurigkeit die.

s.a.e., **sae** n abbr of stamped addressed envelope.

safari [sə'fɑːrɪ] n Safari die.

safe [seɪf] ◇ adj sicher; [product] ungefährlich; **it's not ~ for young children** es ist gefährlich für kleine Kinder; **have a ~ journey!** gute Reise!; **~ and sound** wohlbehalten; **it's ~ to say that ...** man kann mit Sicherheit sagen, dass ...; **to be on the ~ side** um sicher zu gehen ◇ n Safe der.

safe-conduct n - **1.** [document giving protection] Geleitbrief der - **2.** [protection] sicheres Geleit.

safe-deposit box n Banksafe der.

safeguard ['seɪfgɑːd] ◇ n: **~ (against sthg)** Schutz der (gegen etw) ◇ vt: **to ~ sb/**

sthg (against sthg) jn/etw (vor etw (D)) schützen.

safekeeping [ˌseɪf'kiːpɪŋ] n (sichere) Aufbewahrung.

safely ['seɪflɪ] adv sicher; [arrive] wohlbehalten; **I can ~ say (that) ...** ich kann mit Sicherheit sagen, dass ...

safe sex n Safersex der.

safety ['seɪftɪ] n Sicherheit die.

safety belt n Sicherheitsgurt der.

safety pin n Sicherheitsnadel die.

sag [sæg] vi [sink downwards] durchhängen.

sage [seɪdʒ] ◇ adj [wise] weise ◇ n - **1.** [herb] Salbei der - **2.** [wise man] Weise der.

Sagittarius [ˌsædʒɪ'teərɪəs] n Schütze der.

Sahara [sə'hɑːrə] n: **the ~ (Desert)** die (Wüste) Sahara.

said [sed] pt & pp ⊳ say.

sail [seɪl] ◇ n - **1.** [of boat] Segel das; **to set ~** losfahren - **2.** [journey by boat]: **to go for a ~** segeln gehen ◇ vt - **1.** [ship] steuern; [sailing boat] segeln mit - **2.** [sea] befahren ◇ vi - **1.** [person - travel] mit dem Schiff fahren; [- leave] abfahren; [- SPORT] segeln - **2.** [ship - move] fahren; [- leave] abfahren - **3.** [sailing boat] segeln - **4.** fig [through air] segeln. ◆ **sail through** vt fus [exam] spielend bestehen.

sailboat n Am = sailing boat.

sailing ['seɪlɪŋ] n - **1.** SPORT Segeln das; **plain ~** ganz einfach - **2.** [trip by ship]: **there are ten ~s a day** das Schiff fährt zehnmal am Tag.

sailing boat Br, **sailboat** Am ['seɪlbəʊt] n Segelboot das.

sailing ship n Segelschiff das.

sailor ['seɪlə'] n Seemann der; [in navy] Matrose der; SPORT Segler der, -in die.

saint [seɪnt] n RELIG Heilige der, die.

saintly ['seɪntlɪ] adj [person] gütig.

sake [seɪk] n - **1.** [benefit, advantage]: **for the ~ of sb** jm zuliebe; **for my/your ~** mir/dir zuliebe - **2.** [purpose]: **for the ~ of peace/ your health** um des Friedens/deiner Gesundheit willen; **let us say, for the ~ of argument, that ...** sagen wir spaßeshalber, dass ... - **3.** phr: **for God's** OR **Heaven's ~!** um Gottes willen!

salad ['sæləd] n Salat der.

salad bowl n Salatschüssel die.

salad cream n Br majonäseartige Salatsoße.

salad dressing n Salatsoße die, Dressing das.

salami [sə'lɑːmɪ] n Salami die.

salary ['sælərɪ] n Gehalt das.

sale [seɪl] n - **1.** [instance of selling] Verkauf der; **to make a ~** etwas verkaufen - **2.** (U) [selling] Verkauf der; **to be on ~** verkauft werden; **to be for ~** zu verkaufen sein - **3.** [at reduced prices] Ausverkauf der - **4.** [auction] Auktion die. ◆ **sales** npl - **1.** [quantity sold] Absatz *der* - **2.** [at reduced prices]: **the ~s** der Schlussverkauf.

saleroom *Br* ['seɪlrʊm], **salesroom** *Am* ['seɪlzrʊm] *n* [for auction] Auktionsraum *der*.

sales assistant ['seɪlz-], **salesclerk** ['seɪlzklɜːrk] *Am n* Verkäufer *der*, -in *die*.

salesman ['seɪlzmən] (*pl* -men [-mən]) *n* Verkäufer *der*; [representative] Vertreter *der*.

sales rep *n inf* Vertreter *der*, -in *die*.

salesroom *n Am* = saleroom.

saleswoman ['seɪlz,wʊmən] (*pl* -women [-,wɪmɪn]) *n* Verkäuferin *die*; [representative] Vertreterin *die*.

saliva [sə'laɪvə] *n* Speichel *der*.

salmon ['sæmən] (*pl inv* OR -s) *n* Lachs *der*.

salmonella [,sælmə'nelə] *n* (*U*): ~ **(poisoning)** Salmonellenvergiftung *die*.

salon ['sælɒn] *n* Salon *der*.

saloon [sə'luːn] *n* - **1.** *Br* [car] Limousine *die* - **2.** *Am* [bar] Wirtschaft *die*; [in the Wild West] Saloon *der* - **3.** [on ship] Salon *der*.

salt [sɔːlt, sɒlt] *n* Salz *das*; **to take sthg with a pinch of ~** etw nicht wörtlich nehmen *vt* - **1.** [food] salzen - **2.** [roads] streuen. **salt away** *vt sep inf* [money] auf die hohe Kante legen.

SALT [sɔːlt] (*abbr of* Strategic Arms Limitation Talks/Treaty) *n* SALT.

saltcellar *Br* ['sɔːlt,selə'], **salt shaker** *Am* [-,ʃeɪkə'] *n* Salzstreuer *der*.

saltwater ['sɔːlt,wɔːtə'] *n* Salzwasser *das* *adj* Meeres-.

salty ['sɔːltɪ] *adj* [tasting of salt] salzig.

salute [sə'luːt] *n* - **1.** MIL [with hand] Gruß *der*; **to give a ~** salutieren - **2.** MIL [firing of guns] Salut *der* - **3.** [formal acknowledgement]: **~ (to sthg)** Würdigung *die* (von etw) *vt* - **1.** MIL salutieren vor (+ *D*) - **2.** [acknowledge formally, honour] würdigen; [person] ehren *vi* MIL salutieren.

salvage ['sælvɪdʒ] *n* (*U*) - **1.** [rescue of ship] Bergung *die* - **2.** [property rescued] Bergungsgut *das* *vt* - **1.** [rescue]: **to ~ sthg (from)** etw bergen (aus) - **2.** *fig*: **to ~ one's reputation** seinen Ruf retten.

salvation [sæl'veɪʃn] *n* (*U*) - **1.** [saviour] Rettung *die* - **2.** RELIG Erlösung *die*.

Salvation Army *n*: **the ~** die Heilsarmee.

same [seɪm] *adj* - **1.** [identical]: **the ~** derselbe/dieselbe/dasselbe, dieselben *pl*; **you've got the ~ book as me** du hast das gleiche Buch wie ich; **the ~ thing** dasselbe; **the ~ ones** dieselben; **at the ~ time** [simultaneously] zur gleichen Zeit; [nevertheless] andererseits; **one and the ~** ein und derselbe/dieselbe/dasselbe - **2.** [unchanged]: **the ~** der/die/das Gleiche, die Gleichen *pl*; **the ~ ones** die Gleichen *pron* - **1.** [identical]: **the ~** derselbe/dieselbe/dasselbe, dieselben *pl*; **I'll have the ~ as her** ich möchte das Gleiche wie sie; **all** OR **just the ~** [nevertheless] trotzdem; **it's all the ~ to me** es ist mir

gleich; **they are all the ~** sie sind alle gleich; **the ~ to you** gleichfalls; **(the) ~ again, please** noch einen/eine/eins, bitte; **it's not the ~** es ist nicht dasselbe - **2.** [unchanged]: **the ~** der/die/das Gleiche, die Gleichen *pl*; **her views are still the ~** sie hat immer noch die gleichen Ansichten *adv* [identically]: **to dress/feel the ~** sich gleich anziehen/fühlen; **they look the ~** sie sehen gleich aus.

sample ['sɑːmpl] *n* - **1.** [of product] Probe *die*; [of fabric] Muster *das* - **2.** [for analysis] Probe *die* - **3.** [representative portion - of work] Musterbeispiel *das*; [- of people in survey] Auswahl *die* *vt* - **1.** [taste] kosten - **2.** [try out, test] ausprobieren.

sanatorium, sanitorium *Am* [,sænə-'tɔːrɪəm] (*pl* -riums OR -ria [-rɪə]) *n* Sanatorium *das*.

sanctimonious [,sæŋktɪ'məʊnjəs] *adj pej* frömmlerisch.

sanction ['sæŋkʃn] *n* - **1.** [formal approval] Billigung *die* - **2.** [punishment] Strafe *die* *vt* [authorize] billigen.

sanctuary ['sæŋktʃʊərɪ] *n* - **1.** [for birds, wildlife] Schutzgebiet *das* - **2.** [safety, place of safety] Zufluchtsort *der*.

sand [sænd] *n* Sand *der* *vt* [make smooth] schmirgeln.

sandal ['sændl] *n* Sandale *die*.

sandalwood ['sændlwʊd] *n* Sandelholz *das*.

sandbox *n Am* = sandpit.

sandcastle ['sænd,kɑːsl] *n* Sandburg *die*.

sand dune *n* Sanddüne *die*.

sandpaper ['sænd,peɪpə'] *n* Sandpapier *das* *vt* mit Sandpapier abl-schmirgeln.

sandpit *Br* ['sændpɪt], **sandbox** *Am* ['sændbɒks] *n* Sandkasten *der*.

sandwich ['sænwɪdʒ] *n* Sandwich *das*; **ham/cheese** ~ Schinken-/Käsebrot *das* *vt* *fig*: **to be ~ed between** eingeklemmt sein zwischen (+ *D*).

sandwich board *n* zweiteilige Reklametafel zum Umhängen.

sandwich course *n Br* Kurs, bei dem sich Studium und Praktikum abwechseln.

sandy ['sændɪ] *adj* - **1.** [beach] sandig - **2.** [sand-coloured] sandfarben.

sane [seɪn] *adj* - **1.** [not mad] normal, bei Verstand - **2.** [sensible] vernünftig.

sang [sæŋ] *pt* sing.

sanitary ['sænɪtrɪ] *adj* - **1.** [connected with health - officer, system] Gesundheits-; [- procedures] sanitär - **2.** [clean, hygienic] hygienisch.

sanitary towel, sanitary napkin *Am n* Damenbinde *die*.

sanitation [,sænɪ'teɪʃn] *n* (*U*) sanitäre Einrichtungen *pl*.

sanitorium *n Am* = sanatorium.

sanity ['sænəti] *n (U)* - **1.** [saneness] Verstand *der* - **2.** [good sense] Vernunft *die*.

sank [sæŋk] *pt* ▷ sink.

Santa (Claus) ['sæntə (ˌklɔːz)] *n* der Weihnachtsmann.

sap [sæp] ◇ *n (U)* [of plant] Saft *der* ◇ *vt* [weaken] schwächen.

sapling ['sæplɪŋ] *n* junger Baum.

sapphire ['sæfaɪə'] *n* Saphir *der*.

sarcastic [sɑːˈkæstɪk] *adj* sarkastisch.

sardine [sɑːˈdiːn] *n* Sardine *die*.

Sardinia [sɑːˈdɪnjə] *n* Sardinien *nt*.

sardonic [sɑːˈdɒnɪk] *adj* [smile, look] hämisch.

SAS *(abbr of Special Air Service) n* Spezialeinheit der britischen Armee.

SASE *n Am abbr of self-addressed stamped envelope*.

sash [sæʃ] *n* [strip of cloth] Schärpe *die*.

sat [sæt] *pt & pp* ▷ sit.

SAT [sæt] *n* - **1.** *(abbr of Standard Assessment Task) Eignungstest für Schulkinder in England und Wales* - **2.** *(abbr of Scholastic Aptitude Test) Zulassungsprüfung an US-Universitäten.*

📖 **SATs**

Der SAT (Scholastic Aptitude Test) ist eine in den USA übliche, aus zwei Teilen bestehende Aufnahmeprüfung für die Universität, die die sprachlichen (Lesen und Schreiben) und mathematischen Fertigkeiten der Schüler im letzten Jahr der High School testet. Anders als die englischen A-level examinations ist sie nicht auf bestimmte Leistungskurse o. Ä. bezogen.

Satan ['seɪtn] *n* Satan *der*.

satchel ['sætʃəl] *n* Schultasche *die*.

satellite ['sætəlaɪt] ◇ *n lit & fig* Satellit *der* ◇ *comp* Satelliten-.

satellite TV *n* Satellitenfernsehen *das*.

satin ['sætɪn] ◇ *n* Satin *der* ◇ *comp* - **1.** [made of satin] Satin- - **2.** [wallpaper, paint, finish] seidenmatt.

satire ['sætaɪə'] *n* Satire *die*.

satisfaction [ˌsætɪsˈfækʃn] *n* - **1.** [pleasure] Befriedigung *die* - **2.** [something that pleases]: **the job has few ~s** die Arbeit ist nicht sehr befriedigend - **3.** [fulfilment - of need, demand] Befriedigung *die;* [- of criteria] Erfüllung *die*.

satisfactory [ˌsætɪsˈfæktərɪ] *adj* befriedigend.

satisfied ['sætɪsfaɪd] *adj* [happy] zufrieden; **to be ~ with sthg** mit etw zufrieden sein.

satisfy ['sætɪsfaɪ] *vt* - **1.** [make happy] zufrieden stellen - **2.** [convince] überzeugen; **to ~ sb/o.s. that ...** jn/sich davon überzeugen,

dass ... - **3.** [fulfil - need, demand] befriedigen; [- requirements] genügen *(+ D)*.

satisfying ['sætɪsfaɪɪŋ] *adj* befriedigend.

satsuma [ˌsætˈsuːmə] *n* Satsuma *die*.

saturate ['sætʃəreɪt] *vt* - **1.** [drench] tränken; [subj: rain] durchnässen - **2.** [fill completely, swamp - area, town] überschwemmen; [- market] sättigen.

saturated *adj* - **1.** [drenched] getränkt; [with rain] durchnässt - **2.** [fat] gesättigt.

Saturday ['sætədɪ] ◇ *n* Samstag *der;* **what day is it? – it's ~** was ist heute? – es ist Samstag; **on ~** am Samstag; **on ~s** samstags; **last/this/next ~** letzten/diesen/nächsten Samstag; **every ~** jeden Samstag; **every other ~** jeden zweiten Samstag; **the ~ before** den Samstag davor, am vorhergehenden Samstag; **the ~ before last** vorletzten Samstag; **the ~ after next, ~ week, a week on ~** übernächsten Samstag, Samstag in einer Woche ◇ *comp* Samstags-; **~ morning/afternoon/evening/night** Samstagmorgen *der/*-nachmittag *der/*-abend *der/*-nacht *die*.

sauce [sɔːs] *n* CULIN Soße *die*, Sauce *die*.

saucepan ['sɔːspən] *n* Kochtopf *der*.

saucer ['sɔːsə'] *n* Untertasse *die*.

saucy ['sɔːsɪ] *adj inf* frech.

Saudi Arabia ['saʊdɪ-] *n* Saudi-Arabien *nt*.

sauna ['sɔːnə] *n* Sauna *die;* **to have a ~** in die Sauna gehen.

saunter ['sɔːntə'] *vi* schlendern.

sausage ['sɒsɪdʒ] *n* Wurst *die*.

sausage roll *n Br* Würstchen in Blätterteig.

sauté [Br 'səʊteɪ, Am səʊˈteɪ] (*pt & pp* sautéed OR sautéd) ◇ *adj* [potatoes] Röst-, Brat- ◇ *vt* [potatoes] rösten, braten; [meat] sautieren.

savage ['sævɪdʒ] ◇ *adj* [attack, criticism, person] brutal; [dog] bissig ◇ *n* Wilde *der, die* ◇ *vt* [attack physically] anfallen.

save [seɪv] ◇ *vt* - **1.** [rescue] retten; **to ~ sb from sthg** jn vor etw *(D)* retten; **to ~ sb's life** jm das Leben retten - **2.** [money, time, space] sparen - **3.** [reserve] aufheben; **to ~ a seat for sb** jm einen Platz freihalten; **to ~ one's strength/voice** seine Kräfte/Stimme schonen - **4.** [make unnecessary - trouble, work] ersparen; [- expense] vermeiden; **to ~ sb from doing sthg** es jm ersparen, etw zu tun - **5.** SPORT abwehren - **6.** COMPUT speichern ◇ *vi* [save money] sparen ◇ *n* SPORT Parade *die* ◇ *prep fml:* **~ (for)** außer *(+ D)*. ◆ **save on** *vt fus* sparen. ◆ **save up** *vi:* **to ~ up (for sthg)** (auf etw *(A)*) sparen.

savings ['seɪvɪŋz] *npl* Ersparnisse *pl*.

savings account *n Am* Sparkonto *das*.

savings and loan association *n Am* Bausparkasse *die*.

savings bank *n* Sparkasse *die*.

saviour *Br*, **savior** *Am* ['seɪvjə'] *n* Retter *der*, -in *die*.

savour *Br*, **savor** *Am* ['seɪvəʳ] *vt* genießen.
savoury *Br*, **savory** *Am* ['seɪvərɪ] <> *adj*
- **1.** [not sweet] pikant - **2.** [respectable, pleasant] angenehm <> *n* (pikantes) Häppchen.
saw [sɔː] (*Br pt* -ed; *pp* sawn, *Am pt* & *pp* -ed) <> *pt* □► see <> *n* Säge *die* <> *vt* sägen.
sawdust ['sɔːdʌst] *n* Sägemehl *das*.
sawed-off shotgun *n Am* = sawn-off shotgun.
sawmill ['sɔːmɪl] *n* Sägewerk *das*.
sawn [sɔːn] *pp Br* □► saw.
sawn-off shotgun *Br*, **sawed-off shotgun** ['sɔːd-] *Am n Gewehr mit abgesägtem Lauf*.
saxophone ['sæksəfəʊn] *n* Saxofon *das*.
say [seɪ] (*pt* & *pp* said) <> *vt* - **1.** [gen] sagen; **to ~ sthg again** etw nochmal sagen, etw wiederholen; **who should I ~ it is?** wen darf ich melden?; **he's said to be good** er soll gut sein - **2.** [subj: clock, meter] an|zeigen; [subj: sign] besagen; **the letter ~s ...** in dem Brief steht ...; **it ~s here that ...** hier heißt es, dass ... - **3.** [assume]: **I'd ~ he's lying** meiner Meinung nach lügt er; **(let's) ~ you were to lose** nehmen wir an, du verlierst; **shall we ~ nine (o'clock)?** sagen wir um neun? - **4.** *phr*: **that goes without ~ing** das versteht sich von selbst; **that's not ~ing much** das will nicht viel heißen; **it has a lot to be said for it** es spricht vieles dafür <> *n*: **to have a/no ~ (in sthg)** etw/nichts (bei etw) zu sagen haben; **to have one's ~** seine Meinung äußern.
  ◆ **that is to say** *adv* das heißt.
saying ['seɪɪŋ] *n* Redensart *die*.
scab [skæb] *n* - **1.** [of wound] Schorf *der* - **2.** *pej* [non-striker] Streikbrecher *der*, -in *die*.
scaffold ['skæfəʊld] *n* - **1.** [frame] Gerüst *das* - **2.** [for executions] Schafott *das*.
scaffolding ['skæfəldɪŋ] *n* (U) Gerüst *das*.
scald [skɔːld] <> *n* Verbrühung *die* <> *vt* [burn] verbrühen.
scale [skeɪl] <> *n* - **1.** [set of numbers] Skala *die*; [of pay] Tarif *der* - **2.** [of ruler, thermometer] Einteilung *die* - **3.** [size] Größe *die*; [extent] Ausmaß *das*; **on a small/large ~** im Kleinen/Großen; **the project is on a large ~** das Projekt ist groß angelegt - **4.** [size ratio] Maßstab *der*; **to ~** maßstab(s)getreu - **5.** MUS Tonleiter *die* - **6.** [of fish, snake] Schuppe *die* - **7.** *Am* = scales <> *vt* - **1.** [climb] erklimmen - **2.** [remove scales from] schuppen.
  ◆ **scales** *npl* Waage *die*. ◆ **scale down** *vt sep* [industry] ab|bauen; [investment] reduzieren; [production] drosseln.
scallop ['skɒləp] <> *n* [shellfish] Kammmuschel *die*; CULIN Jakobsmuschel *die* <> *vt* [decorate] mit einem Bogenrand verzieren.
scalp [skælp] <> *n* - **1.** ANAT Kopfhaut *die* - **2.** [removed from head] Skalp *der* <> *vt* skalpieren.
scalpel ['skælpəl] *n* Skalpell *das*.
scamper ['skæmpəʳ] *vi* [children, dog] flit-

zen; [mouse] huschen; **to ~ around** [children] herum|tollen.
scampi ['skæmpɪ] *n* (U) Scampi *pl*.
scan [skæn] <> *n* MED & TECH Scan *der*; [on pregnant woman] Ultraschalluntersuchung *die* <> *vt* - **1.** [examine carefully - map] studieren; [- area] ab|suchen; [- crowd] mit den Augen ab|suchen - **2.** [glance at] überfliegen - **3.** MED computertomografisch untersuchen - **4.** COMPUT & TECH scannen.
scandal ['skændl] *n* - **1.** [scandalous event, outrage] Skandal *der* - **2.** (U) [rumours] Skandalgeschichten *pl*.
scandalize, -ise ['skændəlaɪz] *vt* schockieren.
Scandinavia [ˌskændɪ'neɪvjə] *n* Skandinavien *nt*.
Scandinavian [ˌskændɪ'neɪvjən] <> *adj* skandinavisch <> *n* [person] Skandinavier *der*, -in *die*.
scant [skænt] *adj* wenig.
scanty ['skæntɪ] *adj* [amount, resources] dürftig, spärlich; [dress] knapp.
scapegoat ['skeɪpgəʊt] *n* Sündenbock *der*.
scar [skɑːʳ] *n lit* & *fig* Narbe *die*.
scarce ['skeəs] *adj* knapp.
scarcely ['skeəslɪ] *adv* kaum.
scare [skeəʳ] <> *n* - **1.** [sudden fright] Schreck(en) *der*; **to give sb a ~** jn erschrecken - **2.** [public panic] Panik *die*; **a bomb ~** ein Bombenalarm <> *vt* [frighten] erschrecken.
  ◆ **scare away**, **scare off** *vt sep* verscheuchen.
scarecrow ['skeəkrəʊ] *n* Vogelscheuche *die*.
scared ['skeəd] *adj* - **1.** [very frightened] verängstigt; **to be ~** Angst haben; **to be ~ stiff** OR **to death** fürchterliche Angst haben - **2.** [nervous, worried]: **to be ~ that ...** befürchten, dass ...
scarf [skɑːf] (*pl* -s OR scarves) *n* Schal *der*; [headscarf] Kopftuch *das*.
scarlet ['skɑːlət] *adj* scharlachrot.
scarves [skɑːvz] *pl* □► scarf.
scathing ['skeɪðɪŋ] *adj* [remark, criticism] scharf.
scatter ['skætəʳ] <> *vt* [spread out] verstreuen; [seed] streuen <> *vi* [crowd] sich zerstreuen; [birds] auf|fliegen.
scatterbrained ['skætəbreɪnd] *adj inf* zerstreut.
scenario [sɪ'nɑːrɪəʊ] (*pl* -s) *n* Szenario *das*.
scene [siːn] *n* Szene *die*; [location] Ort *der*; **behind the ~s** hinter den Kulissen; **it's not my ~** das ist nicht mein Fall; **to set the ~** [give background information] Hintergrundinformationen geben; **to set the ~ for sthg** den Nährboden für etw bilden.
scenery ['siːnərɪ] *n* (U) - **1.** [of countryside] Landschaft *die* - **2.** [in theatre] Kulissen *pl*.
scenic ['siːnɪk] *adj* [view] schön.

scent [sent] n - **1.** [smell - of flowers] Duft der; [- of animal] Witterung die - **2.** [perfume] Parfüm das.

scepter n Am = sceptre.

sceptic Br, **skeptic** Am ['skeptɪk] n Skeptiker der, -in die.

sceptical Br, **skeptical** Am ['skeptɪkl] adj skeptisch; **to be ~ about sthg** bezüglich etw (G) skeptisch sein.

sceptre Br, **scepter** Am ['septə^r] n Zepter das.

schedule [Br 'ʃedjuːl, Am 'skedʒʊl] <> n - **1.** [plan] Plan der, Programm das; **ahead of/behind ~** früher/später als geplant; **on ~** pünktlich, planmäßig - **2.** [written list] Verzeichnis das <> vt: **to ~ sthg (for)** etw planen OR anlsetzen (für).

scheduled flight [Br 'ʃedjuːld-, Am 'skedjʊld-] n Linienflug der.

scheme [skiːm] <> n - **1.** [plan] Programm das; **pension ~** Altersversorgung die - **2.** pej [dishonest plan] raffinierter Plan - **3.** [arrangement, decoration - of room] Einrichtung die; **colour ~** Farbzusammenstellung die <> vi pej Pläne schmieden.

scheming ['skiːmɪŋ] adj raffiniert; [politician] intrigant.

schizophrenic [ˌskɪtsə'frenɪk] <> adj schizophren <> n Schizophrene der, die.

scholar ['skɒlə^r] n - **1.** [expert] Gelehrte der, die - **2.** dated [school student] Schüler der, -in die - **3.** [holder of scholarship] Stipendiat der, -in die.

scholarship ['skɒləʃɪp] n - **1.** [grant] Stipendium das - **2.** [learning] Gelehrsamkeit die.

school [skuːl] n - **1.** [gen] Schule die; **to go to ~** in die Schule gehen; **at ~** in der Schule - **2.** UNIV [department] Fachbereich der; **~ of medicine/law** medizinische/juristische Fakultät - **3.** Am [university] Universität die - **4.** [group of fish, dolphins] Schwarm der.

schoolbook ['skuːlbʊk] n Schulbuch das.

schoolboy ['skuːlbɔɪ] n Schuljunge der, Schüler der.

schoolchild ['skuːltʃaɪld] (pl -children [-tʃɪldrən]) n Schulkind das.

schooldays ['skuːldeɪz] npl Schulzeit die.

schoolgirl ['skuːlgɜːl] n Schulmädchen das, Schülerin die.

schooling ['skuːlɪŋ] n [education] Ausbildung die.

school-leaver [-ˌliːvə^r] n Br Schulabgänger der, -in die.

schoolmaster ['skuːlˌmɑːstə^r] n dated Schulmeister der.

schoolmistress ['skuːlˌmɪstrɪs] n dated Schulmeisterin die.

schoolteacher ['skuːlˌtiːtʃə^r] n Lehrer der, -in die.

school year n Schuljahr das.

sciatica [saɪ'ætɪkə] n Ischias der.

science ['saɪəns] n - **1.** (U) [system of knowledge] Wissenschaft die - **2.** [branch of knowledge] Naturwissenschaft die.

science fiction n Sciencefiction die.

scientific [ˌsaɪən'tɪfɪk] adj wissenschaftlich.

scientist ['saɪəntɪst] n Wissenschaftler der, -in die; [of physical or natural sciences] Naturwissenschaftler der, -in die.

scintillating ['sɪntɪleɪtɪŋ] adj [conversation, speaker] vor Geist sprühend.

scissors ['sɪzəz] npl Schere die; **a pair of ~** eine Schere.

sclerosis [sklɪ'rəʊsɪs] n ⊳ multiple sclerosis.

scoff [skɒf] <> vt Br inf verputzen <> vi [mock] spotten; **to ~ at sb/sthg** über jn/etw spotten.

scold [skəʊld] vt auslschimpfen.

scone [skɒn, skəʊn] n kleiner brötchenartiger Kuchen, der mit Butter oder Marmelade und Schlagsahne bestrichen gegessen wird.

scoop [skuːp] <> n - **1.** [kitchen implement] Schaufel die; [for potato, ice-cream] Portionierer der - **2.** [scoopful] Kugel die - **3.** [news report] Exklusivbericht der <> vt [with hands, spoon] schaufeln; [liquid] schöpfen. ◆ **scoop out** vt sep [remove] herauslöffeln.

scooter ['skuːtə^r] n - **1.** [toy] (Tret)roller der - **2.** [motorcycle] (Motor)roller der.

scope [skəʊp] n (U) - **1.** [opportunity] Möglichkeit die - **2.** [range] Umfang der.

scorch [skɔːtʃ] vt - **1.** [clothes] versengen; [food] anlbrennen; [skin] verbrennen - **2.** [grass, fields] versengen.

scorching ['skɔːtʃɪŋ] adj inf: **~ (hot)** [day, weather] knallheiß; [sun] sengend.

score [skɔː^r] <> n - **1.** SPORT Spielstand der; [at end of game] Ergebnis das; **the ~ is 4–3** es steht 4 zu 3 - **2.** [in test, competition] Punkte pl - **3.** dated [twenty] zwanzig - **4.** MUS Noten pl - **5.** [subject]: **on that ~** in dieser Hinsicht <> vt - **1.** SPORT erzielen; [goal] schießen - **2.** [achieve - success] erzielen; [- victory] erringen; [- hit] landen - **3.** [win in an argument]: **to ~ a point over sb** jn auslstechen - **4.** [cut - surface] einlkerben; [- line] einlritzen <> vi SPORT Punkte erzielen; **to ~ a goal** [in football] ein Tor schießen; [in handball] ein Tor werfen. ◆ **score out** vt sep Br durchlstreichen.

scoreboard ['skɔːbɔːd] n Anzeigetafel die.

scorer ['skɔːrə^r] n - **1.** [official] Anschreiber der, -in die - **2.** [player]: **(goal) ~** Torschütze der, -zin die.

scorn [skɔːn] <> n (U) Verachtung die <> vt - **1.** [despise] verachten - **2.** fml [refuse to accept] verschmähen.

scornful ['skɔːnfʊl] adj [laugh, remark] verächtlich; **to be ~ of sthg** etw verachten.

Scorpio ['skɔːpɪəʊ] (pl -s) n Skorpion der.

scorpion ['skɔːpjən] n Skorpion der.

Scot [skɒt] n Schotte der, -tin die.

scotch [skɒtʃ] vt [idea, rumour] ein Ende setzen (+ D).

Scotch [skɒtʃ] ◇ adj schottisch ◇ n [whisky] Scotch der.

Scotch (tape)® n Am Tesafilm® der.

scot-free adj inf: **to get off ~** ungeschoren davonlkommen.

Scotland ['skɒtlənd] n Schottland nt.

Scots [skɒts] ◇ adj schottisch ◇ n [dialect] Schottisch das.

Scotsman ['skɒtsmən] (pl -men [-mən]) n Schotte der.

Scotswoman ['skɒtswʊmən] (pl -women [-ˌwɪmɪn]) n Schottin die.

Scottish ['skɒtɪʃ] adj schottisch.

scoundrel ['skaʊndrəl] n dated Schurke der.

scour [skaʊəʳ] vt - 1. [clean] scheuern - 2. [search] durchkämmen.

scourge [skɜːdʒ] n Geißel die.

scout [skaʊt] n MIL Kundschafter der, -in die.
◆ **Scout** n [boy scout] Pfadfinder der.
◆ **scout around** vi: **to ~ around (for sthg)** (nach etw) herumlsuchen.

scowl [skaʊl] ◇ n finsterer OR böser Blick ◇ vi ein finsteres OR böses Gesicht machen; **to ~ at sb** jn finster OR böse anlsehen.

scrabble ['skræbl] vi - 1. [scramble] klettern - 2. [feel around] herumlwühlen; **to ~ around for sthg** nach etw wühlen.

scramble ['skræmbl] ◇ n [rush] Gedrängel das ◇ vi - 1. [climb] klettern - 2. [struggle]: **to ~ for sthg** um etw kämpfen.

scrambled eggs ['skræmbld-] npl Rührei das.

scrap [skræp] ◇ n - 1. [small piece] Stückchen das; [of paper, material, conversation] Fetzen der; **not a ~ of evidence** kein einziger Beweis - 2. [metal] Schrott der - 3. inf [fight] Rauferei die; [quarrel] Streit der ◇ vt [plan, system] auflgeben; [car, ship] verschrotten.
◆ **scraps** npl [food] (Essens)reste pl.

scrapbook ['skræpbʊk] n Erinnerungsalbum das.

scrape [skreɪp] ◇ n - 1. [scraping noise] Kratzen das - 2. dated [difficult situation]: **to get into a ~** in die Klemme geraten ◇ vt - 1. [remove]: **to ~ sthg off sthg** etw von etw ablschaben - 2. [peel] schaben - 3. [rub against - car, bumper] schrammen; [- glass] verkratzen; [- knee, skin] auflschürfen ◇ vi [rub]: **to ~ against sthg** etw streifen.
◆ **scrape through** vt fus [exam, test] mit knapper Not bestehen.

scraper ['skreɪpəʳ] n [for paint] Spachtel der.

scrap merchant n Br Schrotthändler der, -in die.

scrap paper Br, **scratch paper** Am n Schmierpapier das.

scrapyard ['skræpjɑːd] n Schrottplatz der.

scratch [skrætʃ] ◇ n - 1. [on skin, surface]

Kratzer der - 2. phr: **to start sthg from ~** etw ganz von vorne anlfangen; **to be up to ~** den Erwartungen entsprechen ◇ vt - 1. [skin] kratzen; **to ~ o.s.** sich kratzen - 2. [surface] verkratzen ◇ vi - 1. [branch, knife, thorn]: **to ~ at/against sthg** an etw (D)/gegen etw kratzen - 2. [person, animal] sich kratzen.

scratch card n Rubbellos das.

scratch paper n Am = scrap paper.

scrawl [skrɔːl] ◇ n [scribble] Kritzelei die ◇ vt [scribble] hinlkritzeln.

scrawny ['skrɔːnɪ] adj [person, legs, arms] dürr; [animal] mager.

scream [skriːm] ◇ n [of person] Schrei der ◇ vt schreien ◇ vi [person] schreien.

scree [skriː] n Geröll das.

screech [skriːtʃ] ◇ n - 1. [of person, bird] Kreischen das - 2. [of tyres, brakes] Quietschen das ◇ vt kreischen ◇ vi - 1. [person, bird] kreischen - 2. [tyres] quietschen.

screen [skriːn] n - 1. [viewing surface] Bildschirm der; [in cinema] Leinwand die - 2. [films]: **the (big) ~** der Film - 3. [protective panel] Wandschirm der ◇ vt - 1. [in cinema] zeigen - 2. [on TV] auslstrahlen - 3. [hide] ablschirmen - 4. [shield]: **to ~ sthg (from sb/sthg)** etw (gegen jn/etw) ablschirmen - 5. [candidate, luggage] überprüfen.

screening ['skriːnɪŋ] n - 1. [in cinema] Vorführung die - 2. [on TV] Ausstrahlung die - 3. (U) [for security] Überprüfung die - 4. (U) MED [examination] Untersuchung die.

screenplay ['skriːnpleɪ] n Drehbuch das.

screw [skruː] ◇ n [nail] Schraube die ◇ vt - 1. [fix with screws]: **to ~ sthg to sthg** etw an etw (A) schrauben - 2. [lid]: **to ~ sthg on/off** etw zu-/auflschrauben - 3. vulg [have sex with] bumsen, vögeln ◇ vi [lid]: **to ~ on/off** sich zu-/auflschrauben lassen; **to ~ together** sich zusammenlschrauben lassen.
◆ **screw up** vt sep - 1. [crumple up] zusammenlknüllen - 2. [contort, twist - eyes] zusammenlkneifen; [- face] verziehen - 3. vinf [ruin] vermasseln.

screwdriver ['skruːˌdraɪvəʳ] n [tool] Schraubenzieher der.

scribble ['skrɪbl] ◇ n Gekritzel das ◇ vt hinlkritzeln ◇ vi [write] (vor sich hin)-schreiben; [messily] kritzeln.

script [skrɪpt] n - 1. [of film] Skript das - 2. [system of writing] Schrift die - 3. [handwriting] Handschrift die.

scriptwriter ['skrɪptˌraɪtəʳ] n Textautor der, -in die; [of film] Filmautor der, -in die.

scroll [skrəʊl] n [roll of paper] Schriftrolle die.

scrounge [skraʊndʒ] inf vt: **to ~ sthg (off sb)** etw (bei jm) ablstauben OR schnorren.

scrounger ['skraʊndʒəʳ] n inf Schnorrer der, -in die.

scrub [skrʌb] n - 1. [rub]: **to give sthg a**

(good) ~ etw (gründlich) schrubben - **2.** [undergrowth] Gestrüpp *das* ⬦ *vt* schrubben.

scruff [skrʌf] *n:* **by the ~ of the neck** am Genick.

scruffy ['skrʌfɪ] *adj* [person, clothes] ungepflegt; [part of town] heruntergekommen.

scrum(mage) ['skrʌm(ɪdʒ)] *n* RUGBY Gedränge *das*.

scrunchy ['skrʌntʃɪ] *n* Zopfband *das*.

scruples ['skruːplz] *npl* Skrupel *pl*.

scrutinize, -ise ['skruːtɪnaɪz] *vt* (genau) untersuchen; [face] prüfend anlsehen.

scrutiny ['skruːtɪnɪ] *n* (U) (genaue) Untersuchung OR Prüfung.

scuff [skʌf] *vt* - **1.** [drag]: **to ~ one's feet** schlurfen - **2.** [damage - shoes, floor] ablwetzen; [- furniture] ablnutzen.

scuffle ['skʌfl] *n* Rauferei *die*.

scullery ['skʌlərɪ] *n* Spülküche *die*.

sculptor ['skʌlptə*r*] *n* Bildhauer *der*, -in *die*.

sculpture ['skʌlptʃə*r*] ⬦ *n* - **1.** [work of art] Skulptur *die*, Plastik *die* - **2.** (U) [art] Bildhauerei *die*, Skulptur *die* ⬦ *vt* formen; [in stone, wood] hauen.

scum [skʌm] *n* - **1.** [froth] Schaum *der* - **2.** *vinf pej* [worthless people] Abschaum *der*.

scupper ['skʌpə*r*] *vt* - **1.** NAUT [sink] versenken - **2.** *Br fig* [plan] zerschlagen; [chance] ruinieren.

scurrilous ['skʌrələs] *adj fml* verleumderisch.

scurry ['skʌrɪ] *vi* hasten; [mouse] huschen.

scuttle ['skʌtl] ⬦ *n:* **(coal)** ~ Kohleneimer *der* ⬦ *vi* [rush] hasten; [mouse] huschen.

scythe [saɪð] *n* Sense *die*.

SDLP (*abbr of* Social Democratic and Labour Party) *n gemäßigte pro-irische Partei Nordirlands.*

sea [siː] ⬦ *n* [ocean] Meer *das*, See *die;* **to be at ~** [ship, sailor] auf See sein; **to be all at ~** *fig* [person] verwirrt sein; **by ~** [send] auf dem Seeweg; [travel] mit dem Schiff fahren; **by the ~** am Meer; **out to ~** aufs Meer hinaus ⬦ *comp* See-.

seabed ['siːbed] *n:* **the ~** der Meeresgrund.

seafood ['siːfuːd] *n* (U) Meeresfrüchte *pl*.

seafront ['siːfrʌnt] *n* Strandpromenade *die*.

seagull ['siːgʌl] *n* Möwe *die*.

seal [siːl] (*pl sense 1 only inv* OR **-s**) ⬦ *n* - **1.** [animal] Robbe *die* - **2.** [official mark] Siegel *das* - **3.** [official fastening] Versiegelung *die;* [on letter] Siegel *das;* [of metal] Plombe *die* ⬦ *vt* - **1.** [stick down] zulkleben - **2.** [block up] abldichten. ◆ **seal off** *vt sep* ablriegeln.

sea level *n* Meeresspiegel *der*.

sea lion (*pl inv* OR **-s**) *n* Seelöwe *der*.

seam [siːm] *n* - **1.** SEWING Naht *die* - **2.** [of coal] Flöz *das*.

seaman ['siːmən] (*pl* **-men** [-mən]) *n* Seemann *der*.

seamy ['siːmɪ] *adj* anrüchig.

séance ['seɪɒns] *n* spiritistische Sitzung.

seaplane ['siːpleɪn] *n* Wasserflugzeug *das*.

seaport ['siːpɔːt] *n* Seehafen *der*.

search [sɜːtʃ] ⬦ *n* - **1.** [for lost person, object]: ~ **(for)** Suche *die* (nach); **in ~ of** auf der Suche nach - **2.** [of person, luggage, house] Durchsuchung *die* ⬦ *vt* durchsuchen; [city] ablsuchen; [one's mind, memory] durchlforschen ⬦ *vi:* **to ~ (for)** suchen (nach).

search engine *n* COMPUT Suchmaschine *die.*

searching ['sɜːtʃɪŋ] *adj* [look] prüfend, forschend; [question] tiefschürfend; [examination] gründlich.

searchlight ['sɜːtʃlaɪt] *n* Suchscheinwerfer *der.*

search party *n* Suchmannschaft *die.*

search warrant *n* Durchsuchungsbefehl *der.*

seashell ['siːʃel] *n* Muschel *die.*

seashore ['siːʃɔː*r*] *n:* **the ~** der Strand.

seasick ['siːsɪk] *adj* seekrank.

seaside ['siːsaɪd] *n:* **the ~** das Meer.

season ['siːzn] ⬦ *n* - **1.** [time of year] Jahreszeit *die* - **2.** [for particular activity] Zeit *die* - **3.** [of holiday] Saison *die;* **out of ~** außerhalb der Saison - **4.** [of food]: **strawberries are out of ~** zu dieser Jahreszeit gibt es keine Erdbeeren - **5.** [series - of films] Saison *die;* [- of lectures] Reihe *die* ⬦ *vt* [food] würzen.

seasonal ['siːzənl] *adj* [change] saisonal; [work] Saison-.

seasoned ['siːznd] *adj* [experienced] erfahren.

seasoning ['siːznɪŋ] *n* [for food] Gewürz *das.*

season ticket *n* Dauerkarte *die;* [for train] Zeitkarte *die;* [for theatre] Abonnement *das.*

seat [siːt] ⬦ *n* - **1.** [chair, part of chair, in parliament] Sitz *der* - **2.** [place to sit] (Sitz)platz *der;* **take** OR **have a ~** nehmen Sie Platz - **3.** [of skirt] Sitz *der;* [of trousers] Hosenboden *der* ⬦ *vt* [person, guests] setzen.

seat belt *n* Sicherheitsgurt *der.*

seawater ['siː‚wɔːtə*r*] *n* Meerwasser *das*, Seewasser *das.*

seaweed ['siːwiːd] *n* Seetang *das.*

seaworthy ['siː‚wɜːðɪ] *adj* seetüchtig.

sec. (*abbr of* second) *n* sek.

secede [sɪ'siːd] *vi fml:* **to ~ (from sthg)** sich (von etw) ablspalten.

secluded [sɪ'kluːdɪd] *adj* abgelegen.

seclusion [sɪ'kluːʒn] *n* Abgeschiedenheit *die.*

second ['sekənd] ⬦ *n* - **1.** [of time, of angle] Sekunde *die* - **2.** *Br* UNIV [Note an britischen Universitäten, die dem deutschen „gut" entspricht] - **3.** [moment] Moment *der;* **wait a ~!** einen

Moment! - **4.** AUT: **~ (gear)** zweiter Gang <> *num* zweite, -r, -s; **the ~** der/die/das Zweite; **on the ~ (of March)** am zweiten (März); **she's ~ only to him** nur er ist besser als sie; **to come ~** den zweiten Platz belegen; *see also* sixth. **→ seconds** *npl* - **1.** COMM Waren *pl* zweiter Wahl - **2.** [of food] zweite Portion.

secondary ['sekəndrɪ] *adj* - **1.** SCH: **~ education** höhere Schulbildung - **2.** [less important - road, cause] Neben-; [- issue] nebensächlich; **to be ~ to sthg** weniger wichtig als etw sein.

secondary school *n* höhere Schule.

second-class *adj* - **1.** *pej* [less important] zweitklassig; [citizen] zweiter Klasse - **2.** [ticket, seat] Zweite-Klasse- - **3.** [postage]: **~ stamp** billigere Briefmarke für Post, die weniger schnell befördert wird - **4.** Br UNIV Note an britischen Universitäten, die dem deutschen „gut" entspricht.

second-hand <> *adj* - **1.** [goods] gebraucht; [clothes] Secondhand- - **2.** [shop] Gebrauchtwaren-; [selling clothes] Secondhand- - **3.** *fig* [indirect] aus zweiter Hand <> *adv* [not new] gebraucht.

second hand *n* [of clock] Sekundenzeiger *der*.

secondly ['sekəndlɪ] *adv* zweitens.

secondment [sɪ'kɒndmənt] *n* Br einstweilige Versetzung.

second-rate *adj pej* zweitklassig, zweitrangig.

second thought *n*: **to have ~s about sthg** sich (D) etw anders überlegen; **on ~s** Br, **on ~** Am nach nochmaligem Überlegen.

secrecy ['si:krəsɪ] *n* (U) - **1.** [being kept secret] Geheimhaltung *die* - **2.** [secretiveness] Heimlichtuerei *die*.

secret ['si:krɪt] <> *adj* geheim; [admirer] heimlich <> *n* Geheimnis *das*; **in ~** im Geheimen.

secretarial [ˌsekrə'teərɪəl] *adj*: **~ staff** Büroangestellte *pl*.

secretary [Br 'sekrətrɪ, Am 'sekrəˌterɪ] *n* - **1.** [clerical worker] Sekretär *der*, -in *die* - **2.** [head of organization] Geschäftsführer *der*, -in *die* - **3.** POL [minister] Minister *der*, -in *die*.

Secretary of State *n* - **1.** Br [minister]: **~ (for sthg)** Minister *der*, -in *die* (für etw) - **2.** Am [in charge of foreign affairs] Außenminister *der*, -in *die*.

secretive ['si:krətɪv] *adj* [person] heimlichtuerisch.

secretly ['si:krɪtlɪ] *adv* [privately] heimlich.

sect [sekt] *n* Sekte *die*.

sectarian [sek'teərɪən] *adj* konfessionsbedingt; [war, quarrel] Konfessions-.

section ['sekʃn] *n* - **1.** [portion] Teil *der*; [of book, road] Abschnitt *der*; [of law] Absatz

der; [of community] Gruppe *die*; [of fruit] Stück *das*; **the sports ~ of the newspaper** der Sportteil der Zeitung - **2.** GEOM Schnitt *der*.

sector ['sektə'] *n* Sektor *der*.

secular ['sekjʊlə'] *adj* säkular, weltlich; [music] profan.

secure [sɪ'kjʊə'] <> *adj* - **1.** [gen] sicher - **2.** [building] einbruchsicher, sicher OR fest verschlossen <> *vt* - **1.** [obtain] sich (D) sichern; [agreement] erzielen - **2.** [make safe] sichern - **3.** [fasten] festmachen; [door, window, lid] sicher verschließen.

security [sɪ'kjʊərətɪ] *n* Sicherheit *die*. **→ securities** *npl* FIN Wertpapiere *pl*.

security guard *n* Wache *die*.

sedan [sɪ'dæn] *n* Am Limousine *die*.

sedate [sɪ'deɪt] <> *adj* ruhig <> *vt* Beruhigungsmittel geben (+ D).

sedation [sɪ'deɪʃn] *n*: **they've got him under ~** er hat Beruhigungsmittel bekommen.

sedative ['sedətɪv] *n* Beruhigungsmittel *das*.

sediment ['sedɪmənt] *n* [Boden]satz *der*; CHEM & GEOL Sediment *das*.

seduce [sɪ'dju:s] *vt* verführen; **to ~ sb into doing sthg** jn dazu verleiten, etw zu tun.

seductive [sɪ'dʌktɪv] *adj* verführerisch.

see [si:] (*pt* saw, *pp* seen) <> *vt* - **1.** [gen] sehen; **as I ~ it** wie ich es sehe; **what do you ~ in him?** was findest du bloß an ihm?; **~ p. 10** siehe S. 10; **do you ~ what I mean?** verstehst du, was ich meine? - **2.** [visit] besuchen; [doctor, solicitor] gehen zu; **to ~ sb about sthg** jn wegen etw sprechen; **~ you!** tschüs!; **~ you soon/later!** bis bald!; **~ you tomorrow/on Thursday!** bis morgen/Donnerstag! - **3.** [accompany] begleiten - **4.** [make sure]: **to ~ that ...** dafür sorgen, dass ... <> *vi* - **1.** [with eyes] sehen; **let me ~** [have a look] lass mich mal sehen - **2.** [understand] verstehen; **I ~** ich verstehe; **you ~, it's not that far at all** du siehst ja, es ist gar nicht weit - **3.** [find out]: **I'll go and ~** ich sehe mal nach; **let's ~, let me ~** [when thinking] warten Sie mal, also - **4.** [decide]: **I'll (have to) ~** ich muss es mir überlegen. **→ seeing as, seeing that** *conj inf* da. **→ see about** *vt fus* - **1.** [organize] sich kümmern um - **2.** [expressing doubt]: **we'll ~ about that** das werden wir sehen. **→ see off** *vt sep* - **1.** [say goodbye to] verabschieden - **2.** Br [chase away] verjagen. **→ see through** <> *vt fus* [person, scheme] durchschauen <> *vt sep* - **1.** [not abandon - deal, project] zu Ende bringen - **2.** [help to survive] durch|bringen. **→ see to** *vt fus* [deal with] sich kümmern um; [repair] reparieren; **I'll ~ to it that he gets it** ich sorge dafür, dass er es bekommt.

seed [si:d] *n* - **1.** [of plant] Samen *der*; [pip] Kern *der* - **2.** SPORT: **to be the top/fourth ~** als Nummer eins/vier gesetzt sein. **→ seeds** *npl fig* [beginnings] Keim *der*.

seedling ['si:dlɪŋ] *n* Sämling *der*.

seedy ['si:dɪ] *adj* [shabby] schäbig; [disreputable] zwielichtig.

seek [si:k] (*pt & pp* sought) *vt fml* suchen; **to ~ sb's advice/help** jn um Rat fragen/Hilfe bitten; **to ~ to do sthg** danach streben, etw zu tun.

seem [si:m] ⟨⟩ *vi* scheinen; **he ~s better** es scheint ihm besser zu gehen; **they ~ to believe that ...** sie glauben anscheinend, dass ...; **I ~ to remember his name was John** ich glaube, er hieß John ⟨⟩ *v impers* scheinen; **it ~s to me (that) you're right** mir scheint, du hast Recht; **so it would ~** so scheint es wenigstens.

seemingly ['si:mɪŋlɪ] *adv* scheinbar.

seen [si:n] *pp* ⟹ see.

seep [si:p] *vi* sickern.

seesaw ['si:sɔ:] *n* Wippe *die*.

seethe [si:ð] *vi* - **1.** [person] vor Wut schäumen - **2.** [place]: **to be seething with sthg** von etw wimmeln.

see-through *adj* durchsichtig.

segment ['segmənt] *n* - **1.** [of report, audience] Teil *der*; [of market] Segment *das* - **2.** [of fruit] Stück *das*.

segregate ['segrɪgeɪt] *vt* trennen.

seize [si:z] *vt* - **1.** [grab] packen, greifen - **2.** [win - control, power] übernehmen; [- town] einlnehmen - **3.** [arrest] festlnehmen - **4.** [chance, opportunity] ergreifen. ◆ **seize (up)on** *vt fus* [suggestion, idea] sich stützen auf (+ A). ◆ **seize up** *vi* - **1.** [body] versagen - **2.** [engine] sich festlfressen.

seizure ['si:ʒə'] *n* - **1.** MED Anfall *der* - **2.** *(U)* [taking - of town] Einnahme *die*; [- of control, power] Übernahme *die*; [- of goods by customs] Beschlagnahme *die*.

seldom ['seldəm] *adv* selten.

select [sɪ'lekt] ⟨⟩ *adj* - **1.** [carefully chosen] auserlesen - **2.** [exclusive] exklusiv ⟨⟩ *vt* auslwählen.

selection [sɪ'lekʃn] *n* [choice, assortment, range] Auswahl *die*.

selective [sɪ'lektɪv] *adj* - **1.** [not general, limited] selektiv - **2.** [choosy] wählerisch.

self [self] (*pl* selves) *n* Selbst *das*; **she's her old ~ again** sie ist wieder ganz die Alte.

self-addressed stamped envelope [-ə'drest-] *n Am* adressierter und frankierter Rückumschlag.

self-assured *adj* selbstbewusst.

self-catering *adj* mit Selbstversorgung.

self-centred [-'sentəd] *adj* egozentrisch.

self-confessed [-kən'fest] *adj* erklärt.

self-confidence *n* Selbstbewusstsein *das*.

self-confident *adj* selbstbewusst.

self-conscious *adj* verlegen, befangen.

self-contained [-kən'teɪnd] *adj* - **1.** [person - independent] unabhängig; [- reserved] reserviert - **2.** [flat] abgeschlossen.

self-control *n* Selbstbeherrschung *die*.

self-defence *n* Selbstverteidigung *die*.

self-discipline *n* Selbstdisziplin *die*.

self-employed [-ɪm'plɔɪd] *adj* selbstständig.

self-esteem *n* Selbstachtung *die*.

self-explanatory [-ek'splænətrɪ] *adj* aus sich heraus verständlich.

self-important *adj pej* überheblich.

self-indulgent *adj pej* [person] genusssüchtig.

self-interest *n pej* Eigennutz *der*.

selfish ['selfɪʃ] *adj* selbstsüchtig, egoistisch.

selfishness ['selfɪʃnɪs] *n* Selbstsucht *die*, Egoismus *der*.

selfless ['selflɪs] *adj* selbstlos.

self-made *adj* [man] Selfmade-.

self-opinionated *adj pej* rechthaberisch.

self-pity *n pej* Selbstmitleid *das*.

self-portrait *n* Selbstporträt *das*.

self-possessed [-pə'zesd] *adj* beherrscht.

self-preservation *n* Selbsterhaltung *die*; **instinct for ~** Selbsterhaltungstrieb *der*.

self-raising flour *Br* [-ˌreɪzɪŋ-], **self-rising flour** *Am n (U)* Mehl *das* mit Backpulverzusatz.

self-reliant *adj* selbstständig.

self-respect *n* Selbstachtung *die*.

self-respecting [-rɪs'pektɪŋ] *adj*: **no ~ parent would dress their child so badly** Eltern, die etwas auf sich halten, würden ihr Kind nicht so furchtbar anziehen.

self-restraint *n* Selbstbeherrschung *die*.

self-righteous *adj pej* selbstgerecht.

self-rising flour *n Am* = self-raising flour.

self-satisfied *adj pej* selbstzufrieden.

self-service *n* Selbstbedienung *die*.

self-sufficient *adj* [person, community]: **to be ~ (in sthg)** sich selbst (mit etw) versorgen.

self-taught *adj* autodidaktisch.

sell [sel] (*pt & pp* sold) *vt* - **1.** [goods] verkaufen; **to ~ sthg to sb, to ~ sb sthg** etw an jn verkaufen, jm etw verkaufen; **I sold it for fifty pounds** ich habe es für fünfzig Pfund verkauft - **2.** [promote sale of]: **such a cover will ~ the magazine** mit so einem Titelbild verkauft sich die Zeitschrift garantiert gut - **3.** *fig* [make enthusiastic about]: **to ~ sthg to sb, to ~ sb sthg** jm etw schmackhaft machen; **I'm not sold on the idea** ich bin von der Idee nicht begeistert ⟨⟩ *vi* - **1.** [person] verkaufen - **2.** [product] sich verkaufen; **to ~ for** OR **at** verkauft werden OR zu. ◆ **sell off** *vt sep* verkaufen. ◆ **sell out** ⟨⟩ *vt sep* [performance]: **to be sold out** auslverkauft sein ⟨⟩ *vi* - **1.** [shop, ticket office]: **we've sold out** wir sind ausverkauft; **we've**

sold out of bread wir haben kein Brot mehr - **2.** [betray one's principles] sich verkaufen.

sell-by date n Br Verfallsdatum das.

seller ['selə^r] n [vendor] Verkäufer der, -in die.

selling price ['selɪŋ-] n Verkaufspreis der.

Sellotape® ['seləteɪp] n Br Tesafilm® der, Klebeband das.

sell-out n [performance, match]: **to be a ~** ausverkauft sein.

selves [selvz] pl ⊳ self.

semaphore ['seməfɔː^r] n (U) Flaggenzeichen pl.

semblance ['sembləns] n fml Anschein der.

semen ['siːmen] n (U) Samen der.

semester [sɪ'mestə^r] n Semester das.

semicircle ['semɪˌsɜːkl] n Halbkreis der.

semicolon [ˌsemɪ'kəʊlən] n Semikolon das.

semidetached [ˌsemɪdɪ'tætʃt] adj & n Br: **~ (house)** Doppelhaushälfte die.

semifinal [ˌsemɪ'faɪnl] n Halbfinale das.

seminar ['semɪnɑː^r] n Seminar das.

seminary ['semɪnəri] n RELIG Priesterseminar das.

semiskilled [ˌsemɪ'skɪld] adj angelernt.

semolina [ˌsemə'liːnə] n Grieß der.

Senate ['senɪt] n POL: **the ~** der Senat.

senator ['senətə^r] n Senator der, -in die.

send [send] (pt & pp sent) vt - **1.** [letter, message, money] schicken; [signal] senden; **to ~ sb sthg, to ~ sthg to sb** jm etw schicken, etw an jn schicken - **2.** [tell to go]: **to ~ sb (to)** jn schicken (zu); **to ~ sb for sthg** jn nach etw schicken - **3.** [into a specific state]: **to ~ sb to sleep** jn zum Einschlafen bringen; **to ~ sb into a rage** jn wütend machen. ◆ **send back** vt sep zurückschicken. ◆ **send for** vt fus - **1.** [person] holen lassen - **2.** [by post] anlfordern. ◆ **send in** vt sep - **1.** [visitor] hereinlschicken - **2.** [troops, police] entsenden, schicken - **3.** [submit] einlreichen. ◆ **send off** vt sep - **1.** [by post] ablschicken - **2.** SPORT [player] vom Platz verweisen. ◆ **send off for** vt fus [by post] schriftlich anlfordern. ◆ **send up** vt sep inf Br [imitate] parodieren.

sender ['sendə^r] n Absender der, -in die.

sender

Ein sender ist im Englischen der Absender eines Briefes oder eines Pakets und hat nichts mit Radio oder Fernsehen zu tun. „Sender" wie ARD und ZDF in Deutschland oder BBC und ITV in Großbritannien bezeichnet man im Englischen als TV oder radio station. Der „Sender" als elektrisches Gerät zum Aussenden von Signalen heißt dagegen auf Englisch transmitter.

send-off n Verabschiedung die.

senile ['siːnaɪl] adj senil.

senior ['siːnjə^r] ⟨⟩ adj - **1.** [high-ranking - position, manager] leitend; [- official] höher; [- nurse, doctor] Ober-; [- police officer] ranghoch - **2.** [higher-ranking]: **to be ~ to sb** höher als jd gestellt sein - **3.** SCH [classes] höher; [pupils] älter ⟨⟩ n - **1.** [older person]: **I'm five years his ~, I'm his ~ by five years** ich bin fünf Jahre älter als er - **2.** SCH Schüler/Student im letzten Schul-/Studienjahr.

senior citizen n Senior der, -in die.

sensation [sen'seɪʃn] n - **1.** [feeling] Gefühl das - **2.** [cause of excitement] Sensation die.

sensational [sen'seɪʃənl] adj [news, victory, show] sensationell; [person, appearance] toll.

sense [sens] ⟨⟩ n - **1.** [faculty] Sinn der - **2.** [feeling, sensation] Gefühl das; **~ of guilt** Schuldgefühl das; **~ of justice** Gerechtigkeitssinn der - **3.** [natural ability] Gefühl das; **business ~** Geschäftssinn der; **a ~ of humour** Humor der - **4.** [wisdom, reason] Vernunft der - **5.** [meaning] Bedeutung die; **to make ~** [have clear meaning] Sinn haben; [be logical] sinnvoll sein; **to make no ~** keinen Sinn machen - **6.** phr: **to come to one's ~s** [be sensible again] (wieder) zur Vernunft kommen; [regain consciousness] (wieder) zu Bewusstsein kommen ⟨⟩ vt [feel] spüren; **to ~ (that) ...** spüren, dass ... ◆ **in a sense** adv in gewissem Sinne.

senseless ['senslɪs] adj - **1.** [stupid] sinnlos - **2.** [unconscious] bewusstlos.

sensibilities [ˌsensɪ'bɪlətɪz] npl [delicate feelings] Empfindlichkeit die.

sensible ['sensəbl] adj vernünftig.

sensible

Dieses Wort wird sehr leicht in der Annahme verwendet, es bedeute „sensibel". Die richtige Übersetzung lautet jedoch „vernünftig". A very sensible person beschreibt also „einen sehr <u>vernünftigen</u> Menschen".
„Sensibel" heißt auf Englisch sensitive. „Sie ist immer ein <u>sensibles</u> Kind gewesen" kann man daher mit She has always been a <u>sensitive</u> child übersetzen.

sensitive ['sensɪtɪv] adj - **1.** [eyes, skin] empfindlich; **~ to heat/light** hitze-/lichtempfindlich - **2.** [understanding, aware]: **to be ~ (to sthg)** (gegenüber etw) aufmerksam sein - **3.** [easily hurt, touchy]: **to be ~ to sthg** gegenüber etw empfindlich sein; **to be ~ about sthg** wegen etw empfindlich sein - **4.** [controversial] heikel - **5.** [instrument] empfindlich.

sensual ['sensjʊəl] *adj* sinnlich.

sensuous ['sensjʊəs] *adj* sinnlich.

sent [sent] *pt* & *pp* ⊳ send.

sentence ['sentəns] ◇ *n* - **1.** [group of words] Satz *der* - **2.** LAW [decision] Urteil *das*; **a ~ of five years** eine fünfjährige Haftstrafe ◇ *vt*: **to ~ sb (to sthg)** jn (zu etw) verurteilen.

sentiment ['sentɪmənt] *n* [feeling] Gefühl *das*; [opinion] Meinung *die*.

sentimental [ˌsentɪ'mentl] *adj* sentimental.

sentry ['sentrɪ] *n* Wache *die*.

separate [*adj* 'seprət, *vb* 'sepəreɪt] ◇ *adj* - **1.** [not joined, apart]: **~ (from sthg)** getrennt (von etw) - **2.** [individual, distinct] verschieden; **write on a ~ piece of paper** schreiben Sie auf ein neues Blatt ◇ *vt* - **1.** [keep or set apart]: **to ~ (from)** trennen (von); **to ~ sb/sthg into** jn/etw einteilen in (+ A) - **2.** [distinguish] unterscheiden; **to ~ sb/sthg from** jn/etw unterscheiden von ◇ *vi* - **1.** [go different ways]: **to ~ (from)** sich trennen (von) - **2.** [come apart, divide] auseinander gehen - **3.** [couple] sich trennen.

separately ['seprətlɪ] *adv* getrennt.

separation [ˌsepə'reɪʃn] *n* Trennung *die*; [division] Einteilung *die*.

September [sep'tembə] *n* September *der*; **in ~** im September; **last/this/next ~** letzten/diesen/nächsten September; **by ~** bis September; **every ~** jeden September, jedes Jahr im September; **during ~** im September; **at the beginning/end of ~** Anfang/Ende September; **in the middle of ~** Mitte September.

septic ['septɪk] *adj* eitrig; MED septisch.

septic tank *n* Klärgrube *die*.

sequel ['siːkwəl] *n* - **1.** [book, film]: **~ (to sthg)** Fortsetzung *die* (von etw) - **2.** [consequence]: **~ to sthg** Folge *die* von etw.

sequence ['siːkwəns] *n* - **1.** [series] Reihe *die* - **2.** (U) [order] Reihenfolge *die* - **3.** [of film] Sequenz *die*.

Serbia ['sɜːbjə] *n* Serbien *nt*.

serene [sɪ'riːn] *adj* [person] gelassen.

sergeant ['sɑːdʒənt] *n* - **1.** [in the army] Feldwebel *der* - **2.** [in the police] Wachtmeister *der*, -in *die*.

sergeant major *n* Hauptfeldwebel *der*.

serial ['sɪərɪəl] *n* [on TV] Serie *die*; [on radio] Sendereihe *die*; [in newspaper] Fortsetzungsroman *der*.

series ['sɪəriːz] (*pl inv*) *n* - **1.** [sequence] Reihe *die* - **2.** RADIO & TV Serie *die*.

serious ['sɪərɪəs] *adj* - **1.** [gen] ernst; [situation, problem, illness, loss] schwer; [shortage] groß - **2.** [newspaper] seriös; **are you ~?** ist das dein Ernst?

serious

Das Wort **serious** sollte man nicht mit „seriös" verwechseln. Wenn es sich auf Personen bezieht, lautet die Übersetzung „ernst" oder „ernsthaft". Is he **serious** about her? kann mit „Meint er es **ernst** mit ihr?" wiedergegeben werden. In Bezug auf einen Unfall lautet die passende Übersetzung „schwer": He was in a **serious** accident recently – „Er hat vor kurzem einen **schweren** Autounfall gehabt". Will man im Englischen ausdrücken, dass jemand „seriös" ist, verwendet man am besten **respectable** oder **reliable**: Aus „Dieser Händler macht einen **seriösen** Eindruck" würde also This dealer seems **respectable**.

seriously ['sɪərɪəslɪ] *adv* - **1.** [earnestly] ernsthaft; **to take sb/sthg ~** jn/etw ernst nehmen - **2.** [very badly - ill] schwer; [- lacking] sehr.

seriousness ['sɪərɪəsnɪs] *n* - **1.** [of person, expression, situation] Ernst *der* - **2.** [of illness, loss] Schwere *die*.

sermon ['sɜːmən] *n* - **1.** [in church] Predigt *die* - **2.** *fig* & *pej* [lecture] Moralpredigt *die*.

serrated [sɪ'reɪtɪd] *adj* gezackt.

servant ['sɜːvənt] *n* [in household] Diener *der*, -in *die*.

serve [sɜːv] ◇ *vt* - **1.** [work for] dienen (+ D) - **2.** [have effect]: **this only ~d to make him more angry** das führte nur dazu, dass er noch ärgerlicher wurde; **to ~ a purpose** einem Zweck dienen - **3.** [provide - with gas, electricity, water] versorgen; **which motorways ~ Birmingham?** welche Autobahnen führen nach Birmingham? - **4.** [food or drink]: **to ~ sthg to sb, to ~ sb sthg** jm etw servieren - **5.** [customer] bedienen - **6.** LAW: **to ~ sb with a writ** jn vor Gericht laden - **7.** [complete, carry out - prison sentence] verbüßen; [- apprenticeship] absolvieren; **to ~ a term of office** im Amt sein - **8.** SPORT aufschlagen - **9.** *phr*: **it ~s you right** das geschieht dir recht ◇ *vi* - **1.** [be employed - as soldier] dienen; [- in profession] arbeiten; **to ~ on** [committee] angehören (+ D) - **2.** [function]: **to ~ as sthg** als etw dienen - **3.** [with food, drink] servieren - **4.** [in shop, bar etc] bedienen - **5.** SPORT aufschlagen ◇ *n* SPORT Aufschlag *der*. ◆ **serve out, serve up** *vt sep* [food] servieren.

service ['sɜːvɪs] ◇ *n* - **1.** [organization, system] Dienst *der*; **bus/train ~** Bus-/Zugverbindung *die* - **2.** [amenity] Dienstleistung *die*, Service *der* - **3.** [employment - length of time] Dienstzeit *die* - **4.** (U) [in shop, bar etc] Bedienung *die*, Service *der*; **'~ not included'** 'Trinkgeld nicht inbegriffen' - **5.** MIL Militär-

dienst *der* - **6.** [mechanical check - of car] Durchsicht *die;* [- of machine] Wartung *die* - **7.** RELIG Gottesdienst *der* - **8.** [set of tableware] Service *das* - **9.** [operation] Betrieb *der;* **in/out of ~** in/außer Betrieb - **10.** SPORT Aufschlag *der* - **11.** [help]: **to be of ~ to sb** [person] jm behilflich sein; [thing] jm von Nutzen sein <> *vt* [car, machine] warten. ◆ **services** *npl* - **1.** [on motorway] Raststätte *die (mit Tankstelle).* - **2.** [armed forces]: **the ~s** das Militär - **3.** [help] Hilfe *die,* Dienste *pl.*

serviceable ['sɜːvɪsəbl] *adj* praktisch.

service area *n* Raststätte *die (mit Tankstelle).*

service charge *n* Bedienungszuschlag *der,* Service *der.*

serviceman ['sɜːvɪsmən] (*pl* -men [-mən]) *n* MIL Militärangehörige *der.*

service provider *n* COMPUT Internetprovider *der.*

service station *n* Raststätte *die (mit Tankstelle).*

serviette [ˌsɜːvɪ'et] *n* Serviette *die.*

session ['seʃn] *n* - **1.** [of court, parliament] Sitzung *die* - **2.** [meeting] Treffen *das;* **recording ~** Aufnahme *die* - **3.** Am [school term] Semester *das.*

set [set] (*pt & pp* set) <> *adj* - **1.** [specified, prescribed] festgelegt, festgesetzt; [book, text] vorgeschrieben - **2.** [fixed - phrase, expression] fest; [- ideas, routine] starr - **3.** [ready]: **to be (all) ~ (to do sthg)** startbereit sein(, etw zu tun) - **4.** [determined]: **to be ~ on doing sthg** entschlossen sein, etw zu tun; **to be dead ~ against sthg** völlig gegen etw sein <> *n* - **1.** [collection, group] Satz *der;* **~ of teeth** Gebiss *das;* chess **~** Schachspiel *das* - **2.** [television, radio] Apparat *der* - **3.** [of film] Filmkulisse *die;* [of play] Kulisse *die* - **4.** TENNIS Satz *der* <> *vt* - **1.** [put in specified position, place] stellen; [lying down] legen - **2.** [fix, insert]: **to ~ sthg in(to) sthg** etw in etw *(A)* einlassen - **3.** [indicating change of state or activity]: **to ~ sb free** jn befreien; **to ~ sb's mind at rest** jn beruhigen; **to ~ sthg on fire** etw anlzünden; **her remark ~ me thinking** ihre Bemerkung brachte mich zum Nachdenken - **4.** [prepare in advance - trap] auflstellen; [- table] decken - **5.** [clock, meter] stellen - **6.** [time, deadline, minimum wage] festlsetzen, festllegen - **7.** [create - trend] setzen; [- example] geben; [- precedent] schaffen; [- record] auflstellen - **8.** [assign - target] setzen; [- essay, homework] auflgeben; [- exam] auslarbeiten - **9.** MED [bone, broken leg] richten - **10.** [story, film] spielen - **11.** [hair] legen <> *vi* - **1.** [sun] unterlgehen - **2.** [jelly, cement] fest werden. ◆ **set about** *vt fus* [start]: **to ~ about sthg** etw in Angriff nehmen; **to ~ about doing sthg** sich daranmachen, etw zu tun. ◆ **set aside** *vt sep* - **1.** [keep, save - food] auflheben; [- money] beiseite legen; [- time] einlplanen - **2.** [not

consider] außer Acht lassen. ◆ **set back** *vt sep* [delay] zurücklwerfen. ◆ **set off** <> *vt sep* - **1.** [initiate, cause] ausllösen - **2.** [trigger - bomb] zünden; [- alarm] ausllösen <> *vi* [on journey] auflbrechen. ◆ **set out** <> *vt sep* - **1.** [arrange, spread out] zurechtllegen; [chairs] auflstellen; [food] anlrichten - **2.** [clarify, explain] darllegen <> *vt fus* [intend]: **to ~ out to do sthg** sich *(D)* vorlnehmen, etw zu tun <> *vi* [on journey] auflbrechen. ◆ **set up** *vt sep* - **1.** [establish, arrange - fund, organization] gründen; [- interview, meeting] anlsetzen - **2.** [erect - roadblock] errichten; **to ~ up camp** Zelte auflschlagen - **3.** [install] auflstellen - **4.** *inf* [incriminate] als Schuldigen hinlstellen.

setback ['setbæk] *n* Rückschlag *der.*

settee [se'tiː] *n* Sofa *das,* Couch *die.*

setting ['setɪŋ] *n* - **1.** [surroundings] Umgebung *die* - **2.** [of dial, control] Einstellung *die.*

settle ['setl] <> *vt* - **1.** [argument, differences] beillegen - **2.** [pay - bill, debt] begleichen; [- account] auslgleichen - **3.** [nerves, stomach] beruhigen <> *vi* - **1.** [go to live] sich niederllassen - **2.** [make o.s. comfortable] es sich *(D)* bequem machen - **3.** [come to rest - dust] sich legen; [- sediment] sich setzen. ◆ **settle down** *vi* - **1.** [give one's attention]: **to ~ down to work** sich an die Arbeit machen; **to ~ down to doing sthg** sich daranlmachen, etw zu tun - **2.** [assume stable lifestyle] sesshaft werden - **3.** [make o.s. comfortable] es sich *(D)* bequem machen - **4.** [become calm] sich beruhigen. ◆ **settle for** *vt fus* sich zufriedenlgeben mit. ◆ **settle in** *vi* [in house] sich einlleben; [in job] sich einlgewöhnen. ◆ **settle on** *vt fus* [choose] sich entscheiden für. ◆ **settle up** *vi* [financially]: **to ~ up (with sb)** ablrechnen (mit jm).

settlement ['setlmənt] *n* - **1.** [agreement] Übereinkunft *die,* Einigung *die* - **2.** [village] (An)siedlung *die* - **3.** [payment] Begleichung *die,* Bezahlung *die.*

settler ['setlə'] *n* Siedler *der,* -in *die.*

set-up *n inf* - **1.** [system] System *das;* [organization] Organisation *die* - **2.** [deception to incriminate] Falle *die.*

seven ['sevn] *num* sieben; *see also* six.

seventeen [ˌsevn'tiːn] *num* siebzehn; *see also* six.

seventeenth [ˌsevn'tiːnθ] *num* siebzehnte, -r, -s; *see also* sixth.

seventh ['sevnθ] *num* siebte, -r, -s; *see also* sixth.

seventy ['sevntɪ] *num* siebzig; *see also* sixty.

sever ['sevə'] *vt* - **1.** [limb] abltrennen; [rope] durchlschneiden; [ligament] reißen - **2.** [relationship, ties] ablbrechen.

several ['sevrəl] <> *adj* [some] mehrere, einige <> *pron* mehrere, einige.

severe [sɪ'vɪə'] *adj* - **1.** [shock, pain, gale]

stark; [illness, injury] schwer; [problem] ernst - 2. [stern - person] streng; [- criticism] heftig.

severity [sɪ'verətɪ] n (U) - 1. [of storm] Stärke die; [of illness] Schwere die; [of problem] Ernst der - 2. [sternness - of person] Strenge die; [- of criticism] Heftigkeit die.

sew [səʊ] (Br pp sewn, Am pp sewed OR sewn) vt & vi nähen. ◆ **sew up** vt sep [join] zusammennähen.

sewage ['su:ɪdʒ] n (U) Abwasser das.

sewer ['sʊə'] n Abwasserkanal der.

sewing ['səʊɪŋ] n (U) - 1. [activity] Nähen das - 2. [items] Näharbeit die.

sewing machine n Nähmaschine die.

sewn [səʊn] pp ⊳ sew.

sex [seks] n - 1. [gender] Geschlecht das - 2. [sexual intercourse] Sex der; **to have ~ (with sb)** (mit jm) Sex haben.

sexist ['seksɪst] ◇ adj sexistisch ◇ n Sexist der, -in die.

sexual ['sekʃʊəl] adj - 1. [of sexuality, sexual intercourse] sexuell; [disease, organ] Geschlechts- - 2. [of gender]: **~ equality/rivalry** Gleichheit/Rivalität zwischen den Geschlechtern.

sexual discrimination n Diskriminierung die aufgrund des Geschlechts.

sexual harassment n (U) sexuelle Belästigung.

sexual intercourse n (U) Geschlechtsverkehr der.

sexually transmitted disease ['seksʃʊəlɪ-] n sexuell übertragbare Krankheit.

sexy ['seksɪ] adj inf sexy.

shabby ['ʃæbɪ] adj schäbig; [street] heruntergekommen.

shack [ʃæk] n Hütte die.

shackle ['ʃækl] vt - 1. [chain] fesseln - 2. literary [restrict] (be)hindern.

shade [ʃeɪd] ◇ n - 1. (U) [shadow] Schatten der - 2. [lampshade] Lampenschirm der - 3. [colour] Farbton der - 4. [nuance] Schattierung die ◇ vt - 1. [from light] beschatten - 2. [drawing] schattieren. ◆ **shades** npl inf [sunglasses] Sonnenbrille die.

shadow ['ʃædəʊ] n Schatten der; **there's not a OR the ~ of a doubt** es gibt nicht den geringsten Zweifel.

shadow cabinet n Schattenkabinett das.

shadowy ['ʃædəʊɪ] adj - 1. [dark] dunkel - 2. [unknown, sinister] mysteriös.

shady ['ʃeɪdɪ] adj - 1. [place] schattig - 2. [tree] Schatten spendend - 3. inf [dishonest, sinister] zweifelhaft.

shaft [ʃɑ:ft] n - 1. [vertical passage] Schacht der - 2. [rod - of tool] Stiel der; [- of column] Schaft der; [- of propeller] Welle die - 3. [of light] Strahl der.

shaggy ['ʃægɪ] adj [hair, beard, dog] struppig; [carpet] verfilzt.

shake [ʃeɪk] (pt shook; pp shaken) ◇ vt

- 1. [move vigorously] schütteln; **to ~ hands** sich (D) die Hände schütteln; **to ~ sb's hand, to ~ hands with sb** jm die Hand schütteln, js Hand schütteln; **to ~ one's head** den Kopf schütteln - 2. [upset, undermine] erschüttern ◇ vi zittern. ◆ **to give sthg a ~** etw schütteln. ◆ **shake off** vt sep [police, pursuer] abschütteln; [illness] loslwerden. ◆ **shake up** vt sep [upset] stark mitlnehmen.

shaken ['ʃeɪkn] pp ⊳ shake.

shaky ['ʃeɪkɪ] adj - 1. [unsteady - chair, table] wackelig; [- hand, writing, voice] zitternd; [- person] zitterig - 2. [weak, uncertain] schwach; [finances] unsicher.

shall [weak form ʃəl, strong form ʃæl] aux vb - 1. (1st person sg & 1st person pl) [to express future tense] werden; **I ~ be late tomorrow** morgen werde ich später kommen; **I ~ be ready soon** ich bin bald fertig; **will you be there? - we ~** werdet ihr dort sein? - ja - 2. (esp 1st person sg & 1st person pl) [in questions] sollen; ~ **I buy some wine?** soll ich Wein kaufen?; **where ~ we go?** wo gehen wir hin?; **I'll tell her too, ~ I?** ich sag es ihr auch, OK? - 3. [in orders] sollen; **you ~ tell me what happened!** du wirst mir erzählen, was passiert ist!; **payment ~ be made within a week** die Zahlung muss innerhalb einer Woche erfolgen.

shallow ['ʃæləʊ] adj - 1. [in size] flach - 2. pej [superficial] seicht.

sham [ʃæm] ◇ adj [feeling] vorgetäuscht ◇ n [piece of deceit] Schein der.

shambles ['ʃæmblz] n - 1. [disorder] Chaos das - 2. [fiasco] Disaster das.

shame [ʃeɪm] ◇ n - 1. [remorse] Scham die - 2. [dishonour]: **to bring ~ (up)on sb** Schande über jn bringen - 3. [pity]: **it's a ~ (that) ...** schade, dass ...; **what a ~!** (wie) schade! ◇ vt beschämen; **to ~ sb into doing sthg** jn moralisch zwingen, etw zu tun.

shameful ['ʃeɪmfʊl] adj schändlich.

shameless ['ʃeɪmlɪs] adj schamlos.

shampoo [ʃæm'pu:] (pl -s; pt & pp -ed; cont -ing) ◇ n - 1. [liquid] Shampoo das - 2. [act of shampooing]: **to give one's hair a ~** sich (D) das Haar schampunieren ◇ vt [hair] schampunieren; [carpet] reinigen.

shamrock ['ʃæmrɒk] n Klee der.

shandy ['ʃændɪ] n [in Northern Germany] Alsterwasser das; [in Southern Germany] Radler das.

shan't [ʃɑ:nt] = shall not.

shantytown ['ʃæntɪtaʊn] n Slum der.

shape [ʃeɪp] ◇ n - 1. [outer form] Form die - 2. [figure, abstract structure] Gestalt die; **to take ~** Gestalt anlnehmen - 3. [form, health]: **to be in good/bad ~** [person] in guter/schlechter Form sein; **his business is in bad ~** seine Geschäfte laufen schlecht ◇ vt

- 1. [mould physically]: **to ~ sthg (into)** etw formen (in (+ A)) **- 2.** [influence - person, character] formen; [- ideas, life, future] beeinflussen. ➡ **shape up** vi [develop] sich entwickeln.

-shaped ['ʃeɪpt] suffix -förmig; **egg~** eiförmig.

shapeless ['ʃeɪplɪs] adj formlos.

shapely ['ʃeɪplɪ] adj [legs] wohlproportioniert; [woman] wohlgeformt.

share [ʃeəʳ] ◇ n: to do one's ~ of sthg seinen Beitrag zu etw leisten ◇ vt teilen ◇ vi [share book] zusammen hineinschauen; **there's only one room left – we'll have to ~** es gibt nur noch ein Zimmer – wir müssen es teilen; **to ~ in sthg** sich an etw (D) beteiligen. ➡ **shares** npl FIN Aktien pl. ➡ **share out** vt sep verteilen.

shareholder ['ʃeəˌhəʊldəʳ] n Aktionär der, -in die.

shark [ʃɑːk] (pl inv OR -s) n [fish] Hai der.

sharp [ʃɑːp] ◇ adj **- 1.** [not blunt] scharf; [needle, pencil] spitz **- 2.** [well-defined] scharf **- 3.** [intelligent, keen - person, mind] scharfsinnig; [- eyesight, hearing] scharf **- 4.** [sudden - increase, fall] abrupt; [- turn] scharf; [- slope] steil **- 5.** [angry, severe] scharf; **she was rather ~ with me** sie war recht schroff zu mir **- 6.** [piercing, loud] schrill **- 7.** [painful] schneidend **- 8.** [bitter] herb **- 9.** [MUS - raised a semitone] um einen Halbton erhöht; **C ~** Cis das; **D ~** Dis das; **A ~** Ais das ◇ adv **-◣.** [punctually] pünktlich; **at eight o'clock ~** Punkt acht Uhr **- 2.** [quickly, suddenly]: **to turn ~ right/left** scharf nach rechts/links abbiegen ◇ n [MUS - note] erhöhter Ton; [- symbol] Kreuz das.

sharpen ['ʃɑːpn] vt [make sharp] schärfen; [pencil] (an)spitzen.

sharpener ['ʃɑːpnəʳ] n [for pencil] Spitzer der; [for knife] Messerschärfer der.

sharply ['ʃɑːplɪ] adv **- 1.** [distinctly] scharf **- 2.** [suddenly - increase, fall] abrupt; [- turn] scharf; [- slope] steil **- 3.** [harshly] scharf.

shatter ['ʃætəʳ] ◇ vt **- 1.** [glass, window] zerschmettern **- 2.** fig [beliefs, hopes, dreams] zerschlagen ◇ vi [glass, window] zerspringen.

shattered ['ʃætəd] adj **- 1.** [shocked, upset] niedergeschmettert **- 2.** Br inf [very tired] völlig fertig.

shave [ʃeɪv] ◇ n [with razor] Rasur die; **to have a ~** sich rasieren ◇ vt **- 1.** [with razor] rasieren **- 2.** [wood] abhobeln ◇ vi sich rasieren.

shaver ['ʃeɪvəʳ] n Rasierapparat der.

shaving brush ['ʃeɪvɪŋ-] n Rasierpinsel der.

shaving cream ['ʃeɪvɪŋ-] n Rasiercreme die.

shaving foam ['ʃeɪvɪŋ-] n Rasierschaum der.

shawl [ʃɔːl] n Schultertuch das.

she [ʃiː] ◇ pers pron **- 1.** [referring to woman, girl, animal] sie; **~'s tall** sie ist groß; **there ~ is** da ist sie; **SHE can't do it** SIE kann es nicht tun; **if I were** OR **was** ~ fml wenn ich sie wäre **- 2.** [referring to boat, car, country] es; **~ sails tomorrow** es fährt morgen ab ◇ comp: **~-bear** Bärin die.

sheaf [ʃiːf] (pl sheaves) n **- 1.** [of papers, letters] Bündel das **- 2.** [of corn, grain] Garbe die.

shear [ʃɪəʳ] (pt -ed; pp -ed OR shorn) vt scheren. ➡ **shears** npl **- 1.** [for garden] Heckenschere die **- 2.** [for dressmaking] große Schere.

sheath [ʃiːθ] (pl -s [ʃiːðz]) n **- 1.** [for knife] Scheide die **- 2.** [for cable] Umhüllung die, Ummantelung die **- 3.** Br [condom] Kondom das.

sheaves [ʃiːvz] pl ▷ sheaf.

shed [ʃed] (pt & pp shed) ◇ n Schuppen der ◇ vt **- 1.** [gen] verlieren **- 2.** [employees] entlassen; [inhibitions] überwinden **- 3.** [tears, blood] vergießen.

she'd [weak form ʃɪd, strong form ʃiːd] = she had, she would.

sheen [ʃiːn] n Glanz der.

sheep [ʃiːp] (pl inv) n Schaf das.

sheepdog ['ʃiːpdɒg] n Hütehund der.

sheepish ['ʃiːpɪʃ] adj verlegen.

sheepskin ['ʃiːpskɪn] n Schaffell das.

sheer [ʃɪəʳ] adj **- 1.** [absolute] rein **- 2.** [very steep] senkrecht **- 3.** [delicate] hauchdünn.

sheet [ʃiːt] n **- 1.** [for bed] Bettuch das, Laken das **- 2.** [of paper] Blatt das **- 3.** [of glass] Scheibe die; [of metal] Blech das; [of wood] Platte die.

shelf [ʃelf] (pl shelves) n Regal das.

shell [ʃel] ◇ n **- 1.** [of egg, nut] Schale die **- 2.** [of tortoise] Panzer der; [of snail] Haus das **- 3.** [on beach] Muschel die **- 4.** [of building] Rohbau der; [of car] Karosserie die; [of boat] Rumpf der **- 5.** MIL [Granate die ◇ vt **- 1.** [remove covering from] schälen; [peas] enthülsen **- 2.** MIL beschießen.

she'll [ʃiːl] = she will, she shall.

shellfish ['ʃelfɪʃ] (pl inv) n **- 1.** [creature] Schalentier das **- 2.** (U) [food] Meeresfrüchte pl.

shell suit n Br Jogginganzug der (aus Nylon).

shelter ['ʃeltəʳ] ◇ n **- 1.** [building, structure] Unterstand der; [against air raids] (Luftschutz)bunker der; [in mountains] Berghütte die **- 2.** [cover, protection] Schutz der **- 3.** [accommodation] Obdach das ◇ vt **- 1.** [from rain, sun, bombs]: **to be ~ed by/from sthg** von/vor etw (D) geschützt sein **- 2.** [give asylum to - refugee] Obdach geben (+ D); [- fugitive, criminal] Unterschlupf gewähren (+ D)

◇ *vi:* **to ~ from/in sthg** vor/in etw (D) Schutz suchen.

sheltered ['ʃeltəd] *adj* - **1.** [place] geschützt - **2.** [life, childhood] behütet - **3.** [accommodation, housing] betreut.

shelve [ʃelv] *vt* [plan] aufschieben.

shelves [ʃelvz] *pl* ⊳ shelf.

shepherd ['ʃepəd] ◇ *n* Schäfer *der* ◇ *vt fig* führen.

shepherd's pie ['ʃepədz-] *n* mit Kartoffelbrei überbackenes Hackfleisch.

sheriff ['ʃerif] *n* Am [law officer] Sheriff *der*.

sherry ['ʃeri] *n* Sherry *der*.

she's [ʃiːz] = she is, she has.

shield [ʃiːld] ◇ *n* - **1.** [armour] Schild *der* - **2.** Br [sports trophy] Trophäe *die* - **3.** [protection]: **~ against sthg** Schutz *der* gegen etw ◇ *vt:* **to ~ sb/o.s. (from sthg)** jn/sich (vor etw (D)) schützen.

shift [ʃift] ◇ *n* - **1.** [slight change] Veränderung *die* - **2.** [period of work, workers] Schicht *die* ◇ *vt* - **1.** [move, put elsewhere] verschieben - **2.** [change slightly] ändern - **3.** Am AUT: **to ~ gear** schalten ◇ *vi* - **1.** [move] sich bewegen; [move up - person] rutschen; [- thing] verrutschen - **2.** [change slightly - attitude, opinion] sich ändern; [- wind] umlschlagen - **3.** Am AUT schalten.

shifty ['ʃifti] *adj inf* verschlagen.

shilling ['ʃiliŋ] *n* Br Shilling *der*.

shimmer ['ʃimər] ◇ *n* Schimmer *der;* [in heat] Flimmern *das* ◇ *vi* schimmern; [in heat] flimmern.

shin [ʃin] *n* Schienbein *das*.

shinbone ['ʃinbəʊn] *n* Schienbein *das*.

shine [ʃain] (*pt* & *pp* shone) ◇ *n* Glanz *der* ◇ *vt* - **1.** [torch, lamp]: **to ~ sthg on sthg** mit etw auf etw (A) leuchten - **2.** [polish] polieren ◇ *vi* [moon, sun] scheinen; [stars, light] leuchten; [eyes, metal, shoes] glänzen.

shingle ['ʃiŋgl] *n* [on beach] Strandkies *der*. ◆ **shingles** (U) *n* MED Gürtelrose *die*.

shiny ['ʃaini] *adj* glänzend.

ship [ʃip] ◇ *n* Schiff *das* ◇ *vt* [send] versenden; [send by ship - people] befördern; [- goods] verschiffen.

shipbuilding ['ʃip,bildiŋ] *n* Schiffbau *der*.

shipment ['ʃipmənt] *n* - **1.** [cargo] Sendung *die;* [in ship] Ladung *die* - **2.** [act of shipping] Versand *der;* [by ship] Verschiffung *die*.

shipping ['ʃipiŋ] *n* (U) - **1.** [transport] Versand *der;* [by ship] Verschiffung *die* - **2.** [ships] Schiffe *pl*.

shipshape ['ʃipʃeip] *adj* tipptopp in Ordnung.

shipwreck ['ʃiprek] ◇ *n* - **1.** [destruction of ship] Schiffbruch *der* - **2.** [wrecked ship] Schiffswrack *das* ◇ *vt:* **to be ~ed** Schiffbruch erleiden.

shipyard ['ʃipjɑːd] *n* (Schiffs)werft *die*.

shirk [ʃɜːk] *vt* sich drücken vor (+ D).

shirt [ʃɜːt] *n* Hemd *das*.

shirtsleeves ['ʃɜːtsliːvz] *npl:* **to be in (one's) ~** in Hemdsärmeln sein.

shit [ʃit] (*pt* & *pp* shit OR -ted OR shat) *vulg* ◇ *n* [excrement, nonsense] Scheiße *die* ◇ *vi* scheißen ◇ *excl* Scheiße!

shiver ['ʃivər] ◇ *n* Schauder *der* ◇ *vi:* **to ~ (with sthg)** (vor etw (D)) zittern.

shoal [ʃəʊl] *n* [of fish] Schwarm *der*.

shock [ʃɒk] ◇ *n* - **1.** [surprise, reaction] Schock *der* - **2.** MED: **to be suffering from ~, to be in (a state of) ~** unter Schock stehen - **3.** [impact] Wucht *die* - **4.** ELEC Schlag *der* ◇ *vt* & *vi* [upset] schockieren.

shock absorber [-əb,zɔːbər] *n* Stoßdämpfer *der*.

shocking ['ʃɒkiŋ] *adj* - **1.** [very bad] miserabel - **2.** [scandalous, horrifying] schockierend.

shod [ʃɒd] ◇ *pt* & *pp* ⊳ shoe ◇ *adj:* **well/poorly ~** gut/schlecht beschuht.

shoddy ['ʃɒdi] *adj* schäbig.

shoe [ʃuː] (*pt* & *pp* -d OR shod) ◇ *n* [for person] Schuh *der* ◇ *vt* [horse] beschlagen.

shoebrush ['ʃuːbrʌʃ] *n* Schuhbürste *die*.

shoehorn ['ʃuːhɔːn] *n* Schuhanzieher *der*.

shoelace ['ʃuːleis] *n* Schnürsenkel *der*.

shoe polish *n* (U) Schuh(putz)creme *die*.

shoe shop *n* Schuhgeschäft *das*.

shoestring ['ʃuːstriŋ] *n fig:* **on a ~** mit minimalen (finanziellen) Mitteln.

shone [ʃɒn] *pt* & *pp* ⊳ shine.

shoo [ʃuː] ◇ *vt* verscheuchen ◇ *excl* husch!

shook [ʃʊk] *pt* ⊳ shake.

shoot [ʃuːt] (*pt* & *pp* shot) ◇ *vt* - **1.** [fire gun at - killing] erschießen; [- wounding] anlschießen; **to ~ o.s.** [kill o.s.] sich erschießen - **2.** Br [hunt] jagen - **3.** [arrow] ablschießen - **4.** CINEMA drehen ◇ *vi* - **1.** [fire gun]: **to ~ (at sb/sthg)** (auf jn/etw) schießen - **2.** Br [hunt] jagen - **3.** [move quickly]: **to ~ in/out/past** herein-/heraus-/vorbeischießen - **4.** CINEMA drehen - **5.** SPORT schießen ◇ *n* - **1.** Br [hunting expedition] Jagd *die* - **2.** [of plant] Trieb *der*. ◆ **shoot down** *vt sep* [plane, helicopter] ablschießen; [person] niederlschießen. ◆ **shoot up** *vi* - **1.** [grow quickly] schnell wachsen - **2.** [increase quickly] in die Höhe schießen.

shooting ['ʃuːtiŋ] *n* - **1.** [killing] Schießerei *die* - **2.** [hunting] Jagd *die*.

shooting star *n* Sternschnuppe *die*.

shop [ʃɒp] ◇ *n* - **1.** [store] Geschäft *das*, Laden *der* - **2.** [workshop] Werkstatt *die* ◇ *vi* einkaufen; **to go ~ping** einkaufen gehen.

shop assistant *n* Br Verkäufer *der*, -in *die*.

shop floor *n:* **the ~** [workers] die Arbeiter *pl;* **on the ~** bei den Arbeitern.

shopkeeper ['ʃɒp,kiːpər] *n* Ladenbesitzer *der*, -in *die*.

shoplifting ['ʃɒp.lɪftɪŋ] *n (U)* Ladendiebstahl der.

shopper ['ʃɒpər] *n* Käufer der, -in die.

shopping ['ʃɒpɪŋ] *n (U)* - 1. [purchases] Einkäufe *pl* - 2. [act of shopping] Einkaufen das; **to do the ~** einkaufen (gehen).

shopping bag *n* Einkaufstasche die.

shopping centre *Br*, **shopping mall** *Am*, **shopping plaza** *Am* [-.plɑːzə] *n* Einkaufszentrum das.

shop steward *n* gewerkschaftliche Vertrauensperson.

shopwindow [.ʃɒp'wɪndəʊ] *n* Schaufenster das.

shore [ʃɔːʳ] *n* Ufer das; **on ~** [not at sea] an Land. ◆ **shore up** *vt sep* - 1. [prop up] abstützen - 2. *fig* [sustain] stützen.

shorn [ʃɔːn] *pp* ⇨ **shear** ⇨ *adj* [head, sheep] geschoren; [hair] kurz geschoren.

short [ʃɔːt] ⇨ *adj* - 1. [gen] kurz - 2. [in height] klein - 3. [curt]: **to be ~ (with sb)** (zu jm) schroff OR barsch sein - 4. [lacking] knapp; **we're £10 ~** uns fehlen 10 Pfund; **he is ~ on intelligence/money** es mangelt ihm an Intelligenz/Geld - 5. [abbreviated]: **to be ~ for sthg** die Kurzform von etw sein ⇨ *adv* - 1. [lacking]: **we're running ~ of food** unsere Lebensmittelvorräte gehen langsam zur Neige - 2. [suddenly, abruptly]: **to cut sthg ~** etw vorzeitig abbrechen; **to stop ~** plötzlich stehenbleiben ⇨ *n* - 1. *Br* [alcoholic drink] Schnaps der - 2. CINEMA Kurzfilm der. ◆ **shorts** *npl* - 1. [short trousers] Shorts *pl* - 2. *Am* [underwear] Boxershorts *pl*. ◆ **for short** *adv*: **he's called Bob for ~** er wird kurz Bob genannt. ◆ **in short** *adv* kurz gesagt. ◆ **nothing short of** *prep* nichts anderes als. ◆ **short of** *prep* [apart from]: **~ of ringing up, I don't see how I can find out** ich kann es nur herausfinden, wenn ich anrufe.

shortage ['ʃɔːtɪdʒ] *n* Mangel der, Knappheit die.

shortbread ['ʃɔːtbred] *n (U)* Buttergebäck das.

short-change *vt* - 1. [in shop, restaurant] zu wenig herausgeben (+ D) - 2. *fig* [reward unfairly] übers Ohr gehauen werden.

short circuit *n* Kurzschluss der.

shortcomings ['ʃɔːt.kʌmɪŋz] *npl* Unzulänglichkeiten *pl*.

short cut *n* - 1. [quick route] Abkürzung die - 2. [quick method] schneller Weg.

shorten ['ʃɔːtn] ⇨ *vt* - 1. [in time] verkürzen - 2. [in length] kürzen ⇨ *vi* [days, nights] kürzer werden.

shortfall ['ʃɔːtfɔːl] *n*: **~ (in/of sthg)** Defizit das (bei/von etw).

shorthand ['ʃɔːthænd] *n (U)* [writing system] Stenografie die, Kurzschrift die.

shorthand typist *n Br* Stenotypist der, -in die.

short list *n Br* engere Wahl.

shortly ['ʃɔːtlɪ] *adv* [soon] bald; **~ before/after our arrival** kurz vor/nach unserer Ankunft.

shortsighted [.ʃɔːt'saɪtɪd] *adj lit & fig* kurzsichtig.

short-staffed [-'stɑːft] *adj*: **to be ~** an Personalmangel leiden.

short story *n* Kurzgeschichte die.

short-tempered [-'tempəd] *adj* reizbar.

short-term *adj* kurzfristig.

short wave *n* Kurzwelle die.

shot [ʃɒt] ⇨ *pt & pp* ⇨ **shoot** ⇨ *n* - 1. [gunshot, injection, drink] Schuss der; **like a ~** [quickly] wie der Blitz - 2. [marksman] Schütze der, -zin die - 3. [SPORT - in football] Schuss der; [- in golf, tennis] Schlag der - 4. [photograph] Aufnahme die - 5. CINEMA Einstellung die - 6. *inf* [try, go] Versuch der.

shotgun ['ʃɒtgʌn] *n* Schrotflinte die.

should [ʃʊd] *aux vb* - 1. [expressing desirability]: **we ~ leave now** wir sollten jetzt gehen; **you ~ have seen her!** du hättest sie sehen sollen! - 2. [asking for advice, permission]: **~ I go too?** soll ich auch gehen?; **~ I do it now?** soll ich es jetzt tun? - 3. [as suggestion]: **I ~ deny everything** ich würde alles abstreiten; **I ~n't take too much notice** kümmern Sie sich nicht zu sehr darum - 4. [expressing probability]: **she ~ be home soon** sie müsste bald zu Hause sein - 5. [ought to]: **they ~ have won the match** sie hätten das Spiel gewinnen müssen; **that ~ do** das dürfte genügen - 6. *fml* [expressing wish]: **I ~ like to come with you** ich würde gerne mit dir kommen - 7. *(as conditional)*: **you ~ need anything, call reception** *fml* sollten Sie irgendetwas brauchen, rufen Sie die Rezeption an; **how ~ I know?** wie soll ich das wissen? - 8. *(in subordinate clauses)*: **we decided that you ~ meet him** wir beschlossen, dass du ihn kennenlernen solltest - 9. [expressing uncertain opinion]: **I ~ imagine he's about 50** meiner Meinung nach ist er etwa 50.

shoulder ['ʃəʊldər] ⇨ *n* Schulter die ⇨ *vt* - 1. [load] auf die Schulter(n) nehmen - 2. [responsibility] übernehmen.

shoulder blade *n* Schulterblatt das.

shoulder strap *n* - 1. [on dress] Träger der - 2. [on bag] Schulterriemen der.

shouldn't ['ʃʊdnt] = should not.

should've ['ʃʊdəv] = should have.

shout [ʃaʊt] ⇨ *n* Schrei der ⇨ *vt* schreien ⇨ *vi* schreien; **to ~ at sb** jn anschreien. ◆ **shout down** *vt sep* niederschreien.

shouting ['ʃaʊtɪŋ] *n* Geschrei das.

shove [ʃʌv] *inf* ⇨ *n*: **to give sb a ~** jm einen Schubs geben; **to give sthg a ~** etw rücken; [car] etw anschieben ⇨ *vt* [push - person] schubsen; [- thing] schieben; [stuff] stopfen.

shove off *vi* - 1. [in boat] (vom Ufer) ablstoßen - 2. *inf* [go away] verschwinden.

shovel ['ʃʌvl] <> *n* Schaufel *die* <> *vt* [with a shovel] schaufeln.

show [ʃəʊ] (*pt* -ed; *pp* shown OR -ed) <> *n* - 1. [entertainment] Show *die* - 2. CINEMA Vorstellung *die* - 3. [exhibition] Ausstellung *die* - 4. [display - of strength] Zurschaustellen *das;* [- of temper] Anfall *der,* Ausbruch *der* <> *vt* zeigen; [subj: thermometer, dial] anlzeigen; [profit, loss] auflweisen; [work of art] auslstellen; **to ~ sb sthg, to ~ sthg to sb** jm etw zeigen; **to ~ sb to the door/his table** jn zur Tür bringen/zu seinem Tisch führen <> *vi* - 1. [indicate, make clear] zeigen - 2. [be visible] zu sehen sein - 3. CINEMA: **what's ~ing tonight?** welcher Film läuft heute Abend? **show off** <> *vt sep* vorlführen <> *vi* anlgeben. **show up** <> *vt sep* [embarrass] blamieren <> *vi* - 1. [stand out] hervorlstehen, hervorltreten - 2. [arrive] aufltauchen.

show business *n* Showbusiness *das,* Showgeschäft *das.*

showdown ['ʃəʊdaʊn] *n:* **to have a ~ with sb** mit jm eine klärende Auseinandersetzung haben.

shower ['ʃaʊəʳ] <> *n* - 1. [device] Dusche *die* - 2. [wash]: **to have** OR **take a ~** duschen - 3. [of rain] Schauer *der* - 4. [of confetti, sparks] Regen *der;* [of insults, abuse] Flut *der* <> *vt:* **to ~ sb with sthg** jn mit etw überschütten <> *vi* [wash] duschen.

shower cap *n* Duschhaube *die.*

showing ['ʃəʊɪŋ] *n* CINEMA Vorstellung *die.*

show jumping [-ˌdʒʌmpɪŋ] *n* Springreiten *das.*

shown [ʃəʊn] *pp* ▷ show.

show-off *n inf* Angeber *der,* -in *die.*

showpiece ['ʃəʊpiːs] *n* [main attraction] Paradestück *das.*

showroom ['ʃəʊrʊm] *n* Ausstellungsraum *der.*

shrank [ʃræŋk] *pt* ▷ shrink.

shrapnel ['ʃræpnl] *n (U)* Granatsplitter *pl.*

shred [ʃred] <> *n* - 1. [of paper] Schnitzel *der;* [of fabric] Fetzen *der* - 2. *fig* [of truth] Funken *der;* [of evidence] Hauch *der* <> *vt* - 1. CULIN [cabbage, lettuce] in Streifen schneiden - 2. [paper in shredder] in den Reißwolf stecken.

shredder ['ʃredəʳ] *n* - 1. CULIN [in food processor] Zerkleinerer *der* - 2. [for documents] Aktenvernichter *der.*

shrewd [ʃruːd] *adj* scharfsinnig; [person] klug; [action, judgement, move] klug.

shriek [ʃriːk] <> *n* Schrei *der* <> *vi:* **to ~ (with/in)** auflschreien (vor (+ D)).

shrill [ʃrɪl] *adj* [high-pitched] schrill.

shrimp [ʃrɪmp] *n* Garnele *die.*

shrine [ʃraɪn] *n* Schrein *der.*

shrink [ʃrɪŋk] (*pt* shrank; *pp* shrunk) <> *vt* eingehen lassen <> *vi* - 1. [become smaller] schrumpfen; [person] kleiner werden; [clothing] einlgehen - 2. *fig* [contract, diminish] zusammenlschrumpfen; [of trade] zurücklgehen - 3. [recoil]: **to ~ away from sb/ sthg** vor jm/etw zurücklweichen <> *n inf* [psychoanalyst] Nervenklempner *der.*

shrink-wrap *vt* einlschweißen.

shrivel ['ʃrɪvl] <> *vt:* **to ~ (up)** [plant] welken lassen; [skin] runzelig werden lassen <> *vi:* **to ~ (up)** [plant] welken; [skin] runzelig werden.

shroud [ʃraʊd] <> *n* [cloth] Leichentuch *das* <> *vt:* **to be ~ed in sthg** in etw (A) eingehüllt sein.

Shrove Tuesday ['ʃrəʊv-] *n* Faschingsdienstag *der,* Fastnachtsdienstag *der.*

shrub [ʃrʌb] *n* Strauch *der,* Busch *der.*

shrubbery ['ʃrʌbərɪ] *n* Gebüsch *das.*

shrug [ʃrʌg] <> *vt:* **to ~ one's shoulders** mit den Achseln zucken <> *vi* mit den Achseln zucken. **shrug off** *vt sep* beiseite schieben.

shrunk [ʃrʌŋk] *pp* ▷ shrink.

shudder ['ʃʌdəʳ] *vi* - 1. [person]: **to ~ (with sthg)** (vor etw (D)) schauern OR schaudern - 2. [machine, vehicle] beben.

shuffle ['ʃʌfl] *vt* - 1. **to ~ one's feet** mit den Füßen scharren; [when walking] schlurfen - 2. [cards] mischen - 3. [papers] durchlsortieren.

shun [ʃʌn] *vt* meiden (+ D).

shunt [ʃʌnt] *vt* RAIL rangieren.

shut [ʃʌt] (*pt & pp* shut) <> *adj* geschlossen <> *vt* schließen, zulmachen <> *vi* schließen; [eyes] zulfallen. **shut away** *vt sep* - 1. [criminal] einlsperren - 2. [valuables] einlschließen. **shut down** *vt sep & vi* [factory, business] schließen. **shut out** *vt sep* - 1. [person, cat] auslsperren; [light, noise] am Eindringen hindern. **shut up** <> *vt sep* - 1. [lock up] ablschließen - 2. [silence] zum Schweigen bringen <> *vi* - 1. *inf* [be quiet] den Mund halten; **~ up!** halt den Mund! - 2. [close] schließen.

shutter ['ʃʌtəʳ] *n* - 1. [on window] Fensterladen *der* - 2. [in camera] Blende *die.*

shuttle ['ʃʌtl] <> *adj:* **~ service** Shuttle-Service *der,* Pendelverkehr *der* <> *n* [plane] Pendelflugzeug *das;* [train] Pendelzug *der;* [bus] Pendelbus *der.*

shuttlecock ['ʃʌtlkɒk] *n* Federball *der.*

shy [ʃaɪ] <> *adj* [timid] schüchtern <> *vi* scheuen.

Siberia [saɪˈbɪərɪə] *n* Sibirien *nt.*

siblings ['sɪblɪŋz] *npl* Geschwister *pl.*

Sicily [ˈsɪsɪlɪ] *n* Sizilien *nt.*

sick [sɪk] *adj* - 1. [unwell] krank; **she's off ~ this week** sie fehlt diese Woche wegen Krankheit - 2. [nauseous]: **she felt ~** ihr war schlecht OR übel - 3. [vomiting]: **to be ~** *Br* sich übergeben (müssen) - 4. [fed up]: **to be ~ of sthg** etw satt haben; **to be ~ of doing sthg** es satt haben, etw zu tun - 5. [offensive - joke] makaber; [- humour] schwarz.

sicken ['sɪkn] ◇ *vt* [disgust] krank machen ◇ *vi Br:* **to be ~ing for sthg** etw auslbrüten.

sickening ['sɪkɪŋ] *adj* - 1. [disgusting] widerlich - 2. *hum* [infuriating] unerträglich.

sickle ['sɪkl] *n* Sichel *die*.

sick leave *n:* **to be on ~** krankgeschrieben sein.

sickly ['sɪklɪ] *adj* - 1. [unhealthy] kränklich - 2. [nauseating] widerlich.

sickness ['sɪknɪs] *n* - 1. [illness] Krankheit *die* - 2. *Br* [nausea] Übelkeit *die;* [vomiting] Erbrechen *das.*

sick pay *n (U)* Lohnfortzahlung *die* im Krankheitsfall.

side [saɪd] ◇ *n* - 1. [gen] Seite *die;* **on every ~, on all ~s** auf allen Seiten; **from ~ to ~** von einer Seite auf die andere, hin und her; **at** OR **by sb's ~** an js Seite; **~ by ~** Seite an Seite; on one's mother's ~ mütterlicherseits; on one's father's ~ väterlicherseits - 2. [inner surface - of cave, crate, bathtub] Wand *die* - 3. [of river, lake] Ufer *das;* [of road] Rand *der* - 4. [team] Mannschaft *die* - 5. [of argument] Standpunkt *der;* **to take sb's ~** für jn Partei ergreifen - 6. [aspect - of character, personality] Seite *die;* [- of situation] Aspekt *der;* **to be on the safe ~** um sicherzugehen ◇ *adj* [situated on side] Seiten-. ◆ **side with** *vt fus* Partei ergreifen für.

sideboard ['saɪdbɔːd] *n* Anrichte *die*, Büfett *das.*

sideboards *Br* ['saɪdbɔːdz], **sideburns** *Am* ['saɪdbɜːnz] *npl* Koteletten *pl.*

side effect *n* - 1. MED [secondary effect] Nebenwirkung *die* - 2. [unplanned result] Nebeneffekt *der.*

sidelight ['saɪdlaɪt] *n* Seitenlicht *das.*

sideline ['saɪdlaɪn] *n* - 1. [extra business] Nebenbeschäftigung *die* - 2. SPORT [painted line] Seitenlinie *die.*

sidelong ['saɪdlɒŋ] ◇ *adj* Seiten- ◇ *adv:* **to look ~ at sb/sthg** jn/etw aus dem Augenwinkel anlschauen.

sidesaddle ['saɪd͵sædl] *adv:* **to ride ~** im Damensitz reiten.

sideshow ['saɪdʃəʊ] *n* Nebenattraktion *die.*

sidestep ['saɪdstep] *vt lit & fig* auslweichen (+ *D*).

side street *n* Nebenstraße *die*, Seitenstraße *die.*

sidetrack ['saɪdtræk] *vt:* **to be ~ed** abgelenkt werden.

sidewalk ['saɪdwɔːk] *n Am* Bürgersteig *der.*

sideways ['saɪdweɪz] ◇ *adj* [movement] zur Seite; [look] Seiten- ◇ *adv* seitwärts.

siding ['saɪdɪŋ] *n* Abstellgleis *das.*

siege [siːdʒ] *n* - 1. [by army] Belagerung *die* - 2. [by police] Umstellen *das.*

sieve [sɪv] ◇ *n* Sieb *das* ◇ *vt* sieben.

sift [sɪft] ◇ *vt* - 1. [sieve] sieben - 2. *fig* [examine carefully] sichten, durchlsehen ◇ *vi:* **to ~ through sthg** etw durchlsehen OR durchlgehen.

sigh [saɪ] ◇ *n* Seufzer *der* ◇ *vi* seufzen.

sight [saɪt] ◇ *n* - 1. [vision] Sehvermögen *das;* **he has good/poor ~** er sieht gut/ schlecht - 2. [act of seeing]: **it was their first ~ of their grandchild** sie haben ihr Enkelkind zum ersten Mal gesehen; **in ~** in Sicht; **out of ~** außer Sicht; **at first ~** auf den ersten Blick - 3. [spectacle] Anblick *der* - 4. [on gun] Visier *das* ◇ *vt* [see] erspähen; [land] sichten. ◆ **sights** *npl* [on tour] Sehenswürdigkeiten *pl.*

sightseeing ['saɪt͵siːɪŋ] *n* Sightseeing *das;* **to do some** OR **go ~** Sehenswürdigkeiten besichtigen.

sightseer ['saɪt͵siːəʳ] *n* Tourist *der*, -in *die.*

sign [saɪn] ◇ *n* - 1. [written symbol, gesture] Zeichen *das* - 2. [notice] Schild *das* - 3. [indication] Anzeichen *das;* **there's no ~ of him yet** von ihm ist noch nichts zu sehen ◇ *vt* [letter] unterschreiben; [document] unterzeichnen; [painting] signieren; **to ~ one's name** unterschreiben. ◆ **sign on** *vi* - 1. [enrol - for course] sich einlschreiben; [- MIL] sich verpflichten - 2. [register as unemployed] sich beim Arbeitsamt melden. ◆ **sign up** ◇ *vt sep* [employee] einlstellen; [recruit] verpflichten ◇ *vi* [enrol - for course] sich einlschreiben; [- MIL] sich verpflichten.

signal ['sɪgnl] ◇ *n* Signal *das* ◇ *vt:* **to ~ sb to do sthg** jm ein Zeichen geben, etw zu tun ◇ *vi* - 1. AUT blinken - 2. [indicate]: **to ~ to sb to do sthg** jm ein Zeichen geben, etw zu tun.

signature ['sɪgnətʃəʳ] *n* [name] Unterschrift *die.*

significance [sɪg'nɪfɪkəns] *n (U)* Bedeutung *die.*

significant [sɪg'nɪfɪkənt] *adj* - 1. [large, important] bedeutend - 2. [full of hidden meaning] bedeutsam.

signify ['sɪgnɪfaɪ] *vt* bedeuten.

signpost ['saɪnpəʊst] *n* Wegweiser *der.*

Sikh [siːk] ◇ *adj* Sikh- ◇ *n* Sikh *der*, *die.*

silence ['saɪləns] ◇ *n* - 1. [of person, on topic] Schweigen *das* - 2. [of place] Stille *die*, Ruhe *die* ◇ *vt* zum Schweigen bringen.

silencer ['saɪlənsəʳ] *n* Schalldämpfer *der.*

silent ['saɪlənt] *adj* - 1. [speechless] still - 2. [taciturn] schweigsam - 3. [noiseless] ruhig, leise - 4. CINEMA Stumm- - 5. LING stumm.

silhouette [͵sɪluː'et] *n* Silhouette *die.*

silicon chip ['sɪlɪkn-] *n* Siliziumchip *der.*

silk [sɪlk] <> *n* Seide *die* <> *comp* Seiden-.

silky ['sɪlkɪ] *adj* seidig; [voice] samtig.

sill [sɪl] *n* [of window] (Fenster)sims *der*.

silly ['sɪlɪ] *adj* - 1. [foolish] dumm - 2. [comical] komisch - 3. [childish, ridiculous]: **don't be so ~!** sei nicht so albern!

silo ['saɪləʊ] (*pl* -s) *n* Silo *das*.

silt [sɪlt] *n* Schlick *der*, Schlamm *der*.

silver ['sɪlvə'] <> *adj* [greyish-white] silbern <> *n* (U) - 1. [metal, silverware] Silber *das* - 2. [coins] Silbermünzen *pl* <> *comp* [made of silver] Silber-.

silver foil, silver paper *n* (U) Alufolie *die*.

silver-plated [-'pleɪtɪd] *adj* versilbert.

silverware ['sɪlvəweə'] *n* - 1. [objects made of silver] Silber *das* - 2. *Am* [cutlery] Besteck *das*.

similar ['sɪmɪlə'] *adj* ähnlich; **to be ~ to sthg** so ähnlich wie etw sein.

similarly ['sɪmɪləlɪ] *adv* ebenso.

simmer ['sɪmə'] *vt & vi* auf kleiner Flamme kochen.

simple ['sɪmpl] *adj* - 1. [easy] einfach - 2. [plain - clothing, furniture, style] schlicht; [- fact, truth] rein; [- way of life] einfach - 3. [mentally retarded] einfältig.

simple-minded [-'maɪndɪd] *adj* [person] einfältig; [view] vereinfacht.

simplicity [sɪm'plɪsətɪ] *n* [ease] Einfachheit *die*; [plainness - of clothing, furniture, style] Schlichtheit *die*.

simplify ['sɪmplɪfaɪ] *vt* vereinfachen.

simply ['sɪmplɪ] *adv* - 1. [merely] einfach - 2. [for emphasis]: **you ~ must go** du musst unbedingt gehen; **the weather is ~ dreadful** das Wetter ist einfach scheußlich - 3. [in an uncomplicated way - live] einfach; [- dress] schlicht.

simulate ['sɪmjʊleɪt] *vt* - 1. [feign - gen] vortäuschen; [- illness] simulieren - 2. [produce effect, appearance of] simulieren.

simultaneous [*Br* ˌsɪmʊl'teɪnjəs, *Am* ˌsaɪməl'teɪnjəs] *adj* gleichzeitig; [broadcast] direkt; [interpreting] Simultan-.

sin [sɪn] <> *n* Sünde *die* <> *vi*: **to ~ (against)** sündigen (gegen).

since [sɪns] <> *adv* seitdem; **I haven't seen them ~** ich habe sie seitdem nicht mehr gesehen; **she has ~ moved to London** inzwischen ist sie nach London umgezogen; **~ then** seitdem <> *prep* seit; **I've been here ~ six o'clock** ich bin hier seit sechs Uhr <> *conj* - 1. [in time] seit; **it's ages ~ I saw her** ich habe sie schon seit langem nicht mehr gesehen - 2. [because] da.

sincere [sɪn'sɪə'] *adj* aufrichtig.

sincerely [sɪn'sɪəlɪ] *adv* aufrichtig; **Yours ~** [at end of letter] mit freundlichen Grüßen.

sincerity [sɪn'serətɪ] *n* Aufrichtigkeit *die*.

sinew ['sɪnjuː] *n* Sehne *die*.

sinful ['sɪnfʊl] *adj* sündig.

sing [sɪŋ] (*pt* sang; *pp* sung) <> *vt* singen <> *vi* singen.

Singapore [ˌsɪŋə'pɔː'] *n* Singapur *nt*.

singe [sɪndʒ] *vt* versengen.

singer ['sɪŋə'] *n* Sänger *der*, -in *die*.

singing ['sɪŋɪŋ] *n* (U) Gesang *der*.

single ['sɪŋgl] <> *adj* - 1. [sole] einzig; **every ~** jede/jeder/jedes einzelne - 2. [unmarried] ledig - 3. *Br* [one-way] einfach <> *n* - 1. *Br* [one-way ticket] einfache Fahrkarte - 2. MUS Single *die*. ◆ **singles** *npl* TENNIS Einzel *das*. ◆ **single out** *vt sep*: **to ~ sb out (for sthg)** jn (für etw) auslsuchen OR auslwählen.

single bed *n* Einzelbett *das*.

single-breasted [-'brestɪd] *adj* einreihig.

single cream *n* (U) *Br* Sahne mit niedrigem Fettgehalt.

single file *n*: **in ~** im Gänsermarsch.

single-handed [-'hændɪd] *adv* eigenhändig.

single-minded [-'maɪndɪd] *adj* zielstrebig.

single parent *n* [mother] alleinerziehende Mutter; [father] alleinerziehender Vater.

single-parent family *n* Familie *die* mit nur einem Elternteil.

single room *n* Einzelzimmer *das*.

singlet ['sɪŋglɪt] *n* - 1. *Br* [underwear] Unterhemd *das* - 2. SPORT ärmelloses Trikot.

singular ['sɪŋgjʊlə'] <> *adj* - 1. GRAMM im Singular, in der Einzahl - 2. [unusual] eigentümlich; [unique] einzigartig <> *n* Singular *der*, Einzahl *die*.

sinister ['sɪnɪstə'] *adj* finster, unheimlich.

sink [sɪŋk] (*pt* sank; *pp* sunk) <> *n* - 1. [in kitchen] Spülbecken *das* - 2. [in bathroom] Waschbecken *das* <> *vt* - 1. [in water] versenken - 2. [teeth, claws]: **to ~ sthg into sthg** etw in etw (A) graben <> *vi* - 1. [gen] sinken; [person - in water] unterlgehen; **to ~ to one's knees** auf die Knie sinken - 2. *fig* [heart, spirits]: **my heart sank when I read the news** meine Stimmung sank, als ich die Nachricht hörte - 3. [building, ground] sich senken. ◆ **sink in** *vi*: **it hasn't sunk in yet** ich habe/er hat/*etc* es noch nicht realisiert.

sink unit *n* Spüle *die*.

sinner ['sɪnə'] *n* Sünder *der*, -in *die*.

sinus ['saɪnəs] (*pl* -es) *n* Stirnhöhle *die*.

sip [sɪp] <> *n* kleiner Schluck <> *vt* nippen an (+ D), in kleinen Schlucken trinken.

siphon ['saɪfn] <> *n*: (soda) **~** Siphon *der* <> *vt* - 1.: **to ~ (off)** ablsaugen - 2. *fig* [transfer] verlagern.

sir [sɜː'] *n* - 1. [form of address] mein Herr - 2. [in titles] Sir *der*.

siren ['saɪərən] *n* Sirene *die*.

sirloin (steak) [ˈsɜːlɔɪn-] *n* Lendensteak *das*.

sissy ['sɪsɪ] *n inf* Waschlappen *der*.

sister ['sɪstə'] *n* - 1. [gen] Schwester *die* - 2. *Br* [senior nurse] Oberschwester *die*.

sister-in-law (*pl* sisters-in-law OR sister-in-laws) *n* Schwägerin *die*.

sit [sɪt] (*pt & pp* sat) <> *vt* - **1.** [place] setzen - **2.** *Br* [examination] ablegen <> *vi* - **1.** [be in seated position] sitzen - **2.** [sit down] sich hinsetzen - **3.** [be member]: **to ~ on sthg** in etw (*D*) sitzen - **4.** [be in session] tagen. ◆ **sit about, sit around** *vi* herumsitzen. ◆ **sit down** *vi* sich setzen. ◆ **sit in on** *vt fus* beiwohnen (+ *D*). ◆ **sit through** *vt fus* bis zum Ende durchhalten. ◆ **sit up** *vi* - **1.** [be sitting upright] aufrecht sitzen; [move into upright position] sich aufsetzen - **2.** [stay up] aufbleiben.

sitcom ['sɪtkɒm] *n inf* Situationskomödie *die*.

site [saɪt] <> *n* - **1.**: archaeological ~ Ausgrabungsstätte *die*; building ~ Baustelle *die* - **2.** [location, place] Ort *der*, Stelle *die* <> *vt*: **to be ~d** gelegen sein.

sit-in *n* Sit-in *das*.

sitting ['sɪtɪŋ] *n* - **1.**: dinner is served in two ~s das Abendessen wird in zwei Schichten serviert - **2.** [session] Sitzung *die*.

sitting room *n* Wohnzimmer *das*.

situated ['sɪtjʊeɪtɪd] *adj* [located]: **to be ~** sich befinden.

situation [ˌsɪtjʊ'eɪʃn] *n* - **1.** [circumstances] Lage *die*, Situation *die* - **2.** [location] Lage *die* - **3.** [job] Stelle *die*; **'Situations Vacant'** *Br* 'Stellenangebote'.

six [sɪks] <> *num adj* - **1.** [numbering six] sechs - **2.** [referring to age]: **she's ~ (years old)** sie ist sechs (Jahre alt) <> *num pron* sechs; **I want ~** ich möchte sechs (Stück); **there were ~ of us** wir waren zu sechst; **groups of ~** [people] Sechsergruppen; [objects] Gruppen von jeweils sechs <> *num n* - **1.** [the number six] Sechs *die*; **two hundred and ~** zweihundertsechs - **2.** [six o'clock]: **at ~** um sechs (Uhr) - **3.** [in addresses]: **~ Peyton Place** Peyton Place sechs - **4.** [group of six]: **the batteries come in ~es** die Batterien werden im Sechserpack verkauft; **we need one more person to make a ~** wir brauchen noch eine Person, um eine Sechsergruppe zu bilden - **5.** [in scores]: **~~zero** sechs zu null - **6.** [in cards] Sechs *die*; **the ~ of hearts** die Herzsechs.

sixteen [sɪks'ti:n] *num* sechzehn; *see also* six.

sixteenth [sɪks'ti:nθ] *num* sechzehnte, -r, -s; *see also* sixth.

sixth [sɪksθ] <> *num adj* sechste, -r, -s <> *num adv* [on list] an sechster Stelle; **he came ~** er wurde Sechster <> *num pron* [in series] Sechste, -r, -s <> *n* - **1.** [fraction] Sechstel *das* - **2.** [in dates] Sechste *der*; **the ~ of March** der sechste März.

sixth form *n Br* SCH ≃ Oberstufe *die*.

sixth form college *n Br* zu den A-Levels führende Schule für Schüler ab 16 Jahren.

sixty ['sɪkstɪ] *num* sechzig; *see also* six. ◆ **sixties** *npl* - **1.** [decade]: **the sixties** die Sechzigerjahre - **2.** [in ages]: **to be in one's sixties** in den Sechzigern sein.

size [saɪz] *n* Größe *die*; **to cut sb down to ~** jn zurechtstutzen. ◆ **size up** *vt sep* [situation] einschätzen; [person] abschätzen.

sizeable ['saɪzəbl] *adj* ziemlich groß.

sizzle ['sɪzl] *vi* brutzeln.

skate [skeɪt] (*pl sense 3 only inv* OR **-s**) <> *n* - **1.** [ice skate] Schlittschuh *der* - **2.** [roller skate] Rollschuh *der* - **3.** [fish] Rochen *der* <> *vi* - **1.** [on ice skates] Schlittschuh laufen - **2.** [on roller skates] Rollschuh laufen.

skateboard ['skeɪtbɔ:d] *n* Skateboard *das*.

skater ['skeɪtə'] *n* - **1.** [on ice] Schlittschuhläufer *der*, -in *die* - **2.** [on roller skates] Rollschuhläufer *der*, -in *die*.

skating ['skeɪtɪŋ] *n* - **1.** [on ice] Schlittschuhlaufen *das* - **2.** [on roller skates] Rollschuhlaufen *das*.

skeleton ['skelɪtn] *n* Skelett *das*.

skeleton key *n* Dietrich *der*.

skeptic *etc n Am* = sceptic *etc*.

sketch [sketʃ] <> *n* - **1.** [drawing] Skizze *die* - **2.** [brief description] kurze Darstellung - **3.** [on TV, radio, stage] Sketch *der* <> *vt* - **1.** [draw] skizzieren - **2.** [describe] kurz darlegen.

sketchbook ['sketʃbʊk] *n* Skizzenbuch *das*.

sketchpad ['sketʃpæd] *n* Skizzenblock *der*.

sketchy ['sketʃɪ] *adj* oberflächlich.

skewer ['skjʊə'] <> *n* Spieß *der* <> *vt* aufspießen.

ski [ski:] (*pt & pp* skied; *cont* skiing) <> *n* Ski *der* <> *vi* Ski fahren.

ski boots *npl* Skistiefel *pl*.

skid [skɪd] <> *n* Schleudern *das*; **to go into a ~** ins Schleudern geraten <> *vi* schleudern.

skier ['ski:ə'] *n* Skiläufer *der*, -in *die*.

skiing ['ski:ɪŋ] *n* Skifahren *das*.

ski jump *n* - **1.** [slope] Sprungschanze *die* - **2.** [sporting event] Skispringen *das*.

skilful, skillful *Am* ['skɪlfʊl] *adj* geschickt.

ski lift *n* Skilift *der*.

skill [skɪl] *n* - **1.** [expertise] Geschicklichkeit *die* - **2.** [craft, technique] Fertigkeit *die*.

skilled [skɪld] *adj* - **1.** [skilful] geschickt; **~ in** OR **at doing sthg** geschickt darin sein, etw zu tun - **2.** [trained - worker] ausgebildet; [- work, labour] fachmännisch.

skillful *etc Am* = skilful *etc*.

skim [skɪm] <> *vt* [remove] abschöpfen <> *vi* - **1.** [bird]: **to ~ over sthg** hinweggleiten über (+ *A*) - **2.** [read]: **to ~ through sthg** etw überfliegen.

skim(med) milk [skɪm(d)-] *n* Magermilch *die*.

skimp [skɪmp] <> *vt* sparen an (+ *D*) <> *vi*: **to ~ on sthg** an etw (*D*) sparen.

skimpy ['skɪmpɪ] adj dürftig; [clothes] knapp.
skin [skɪn] ⬦ n - 1. [of person, on liquid] Haut die - 2. [of animal] Fell das - 3. [of fruit, vegetable] Schale die ⬦ vt - 1. [animal] häuten - 2. [graze] aufschürfen.
skin-deep adj oberflächlich.
skinny ['skɪnɪ] adj inf dürr.
skin-tight adj hauteng.
skip [skɪp] ⬦ n - 1. [little jump] Hüpfer der - 2. Br [large container] Sperrmüllcontainer der ⬦ vt [miss - page] überspringen; [- meal] auslllassen; **to ~ school** die Schule schwänzen ⬦ vi - 1. [move in little jumps] hüpfen - 2. Br [jump over rope] seillspringen.
ski pants npl Skihosen pl.
ski pole n Skistock der.
skipper ['skɪpə'] n Kapitän der.
skipping rope n Br Springseil das.
skirmish ['skɜːmɪʃ] n - 1. MIL Gefecht das - 2. fig [disagreement] Auseinandersetzung die.
skirt [skɜːt] ⬦ n [garment] Rock der ⬦ vt lit & fig umlgehen.
ski tow n Skilift der.
skittle ['skɪtl] n Br Kegel der; **to have a game of ~s** kegeln (gehen).
skive [skaɪv] vi Br inf: **to ~ (off)** [from school] schwänzen; [from work] blau machen.
skulk [skʌlk] vi - 1. [hide] sich verstecken - 2. [prowl] herumlschleichen.
skull [skʌl] n Schädel der.
skunk [skʌŋk] n Stinktier das.
sky [skaɪ] n Himmel der.
skylight ['skaɪlaɪt] n Dachfenster das.
skyscraper ['skaɪ,skreɪpə'] n Wolkenkratzer der.
slab [slæb] n - 1. [of concrete, stone] Platte die; [of wood] Tafel die - 2. [of meat, chocolate, cake] großes Stück.
slack [slæk] ⬦ adj - 1. [not taut] locker - 2. [not busy] flau - 3. [careless] nachlässig ⬦ n: **there is too much ~ in the rope** das Seil ist nicht straff genug.
slacken ['slækn] ⬦ vt - 1. [make slower] verlangsamen - 2. [make looser] lockern ⬦ vi [become slower] langsamer werden.
slagheap ['slæghiːp] n Halde die.
slam [slæm] ⬦ vt - 1. [shut] zulknallen - 2. [place roughly]: **to ~ sthg on(to) sthg** etw auf etw (A) knallen ⬦ vi [shut] zulknallen.
slander ['slɑːndə'] ⬦ n (U) Verleumdung die ⬦ vt verleumden.
slang [slæŋ] n Slang der.
slant [slɑːnt] ⬦ n - 1. [diagonal angle] Schräge die - 2. [point of view] Blickwinkel der ⬦ vt [bias] zurechtlbiegen ⬦ vi schräg sein.
slanting ['slɑːntɪŋ] adj schräg.
slap [slæp] ⬦ n Schlag der; [in face] Ohrfeige die; [on back] Klaps der ⬦ vt - 1. [person]

schlagen; **to ~ sb's face** jm eine Ohrfeige geben; **to ~ sb on the back** jm auf den Rücken klopfen - 2. [put]: **to ~ sthg on(to) sthg** etw auf etw (A) knallen ⬦ adv inf [directly] direkt.
slapdash ['slæpdæʃ], **slaphappy** ['slæp,hæpɪ] adj inf schlampig.
slapstick ['slæpstɪk] n Slapstick der.
slap-up adj Br inf Super-.
slash [slæʃ] ⬦ n - 1. [long cut] Schnitt der - 2. esp Am [oblique stroke] Schrägstrich der ⬦ vt - 1. [cut - material] (zer)schneiden; [- tyres] zerschlitzen, auflschlitzen; **to ~ one's wrists** sich die Pulsadern auflschneiden - 2. inf [reduce drastically] stark reduzieren.
slat [slæt] n [in blind] Lamelle die; [in bench] Latte die.
slate [sleɪt] ⬦ n - 1. (U) [rock] Schiefer der - 2. [on roof] Schieferplatte die ⬦ vt [criticize] verreißen.
slaughter ['slɔːtə'] ⬦ n - 1. [of animals] Schlachten das - 2. [of people] Abschlachten das ⬦ vt - 1. [animals] schlachten - 2. [people] ablschlachten.
slaughterhouse ['slɔːtəhaʊs, pl -haʊzɪz] n Schlachthof der.
slave [sleɪv] ⬦ n [servant] Sklave der, -vin die ⬦ vi: **to ~ (over sthg)** sich (mit etw) ablplagen.
slavery ['sleɪvərɪ] n Sklaverei die.
sleaze ['sliːz] n Korruption die.
sleazy ['sliːzɪ] adj [area, bar] schäbig; [behaviour] korrupt.
sledge [sledʒ], **sled** Am [sled] n Schlitten der.
sledgehammer ['sledʒ,hæmə'] n Vorschlaghammer der.
sleek [sliːk] adj - 1. [hair, fur] seidig glänzend - 2. [car, plane] schnittig.
sleep [sliːp] (pt & pp slept) ⬦ n Schlaf der; **to go to ~** [doze off, go numb] einlschlafen ⬦ vi schlafen. ➠ **sleep in** vi [oversleep] verschlafen. ➠ **sleep with** vt fus euphemism schlafen mit.
sleeper ['sliːpə'] n - 1. [person]: **to be a heavy/light ~** einen tiefen/leichten Schlaf haben - 2. [sleeping compartment] Schlafwagenabteil das - 3. [train] Schlafwagenzug der - 4. Br [on railway track] Schwelle die.
sleeping bag ['sliːpɪŋ-] n Schlafsack der.
sleeping car ['sliːpɪŋ-] n Schlafwagen der.
sleeping pill ['sliːpɪŋ-] n Schlaftablette die.
sleepless ['sliːplɪs] adj schlaflos.
sleepwalk ['sliːpwɔːk] vi schlaflwandeln.
sleepy ['sliːpɪ] adj [person] schläfrig.
sleet [sliːt] ⬦ n Schneeregen der ⬦ v impers: **it's ~ing** es fällt Schneeregen.
sleeve [sliːv] n - 1. [of garment] Ärmel der - 2. [for record] Hülle die.
sleigh [sleɪ] n Schlitten der.

slender ['slendə'] *adj* - **1.** [thin] schlank - **2.** [scarce - resources] knapp; [- hope, chance] gering.

slept [slept] *pt & pp* ▭► sleep.

slice [slaɪs] ◇ *n* - **1.** [thin piece] Scheibe *die*; [of pizza] Stück *das* - **2.** [proportion] Teil *der* - **3.** SPORT Slice *der* ◇ *vt* - **1.** [cut into slices] in Scheiben schneiden - **2.** SPORT slicen.
◆ **slice off** *vt sep* [sever] abtrennen.

slick [slɪk] ◇ *adj* - **1.** [smoothly efficient] geschickt gemacht - **2.** *pej* [person] aalglatt; [answer, argument] glatt ◇ *n:* (oil) - Ölteppich *der.*

slide [slaɪd] (*pt & pp* slid [slɪd]) ◇ *n* - **1.** PHOT Dia(positiv) *das* - **2.** [in playground] Rutsche *die* - **3.** *Br* [for hair] Haarspange *die* - **4.** [decline - of person] Abrutschen *das*; [- in prices, standards] Absinken *das* ◇ *vt* gleiten lassen ◇ *vi* - **1.** [on ice, slippery surface] schlittern - **2.** [move quietly] gleiten - **3.** [decline - person] abrutschen; [- prices, standards] absinken.

sliding door [.slaɪdɪŋ-] *n* Schiebetür *die.*

slight [slaɪt] ◇ *adj* - **1.** [minor] leicht; **not the ~est interest** nicht die geringste Interesse; **not in the ~est** nicht im Geringsten - **2.** [slender] schmal ◇ *n* [insult] Kränkung *die* ◇ *vt* [offend] kränken.

slightly ['slaɪtlɪ] *adv* [to small extent] etwas.

slim [slɪm] ◇ *adj* - **1.** [person] schlank - **2.** [object] schmal - **3.** [chance, possibility] gering ◇ *vi* [lose weight] abnehmen; [diet] eine Diät machen.

slime [slaɪm] *n* Schleim *der.*

slimming ['slɪmɪŋ] *n* Abnehmen *das.*

sling [slɪŋ] (*pt & pp* slung) ◇ *n* - **1.** [for injured arm] Armschlinge *die* - **2.** [for carrying things] Trageriemen *der* ◇ *vt* - **1.** [hang roughly]: **she slung the bag over her shoulder** sie hängte sich die Tasche über die Schulter - **2.** *inf* [throw] schleudern - **3.** [hang by both ends] spannen.

slip [slɪp] ◇ *n* - **1.** [mistake] Versehen *das*; **a ~ of the tongue** ein Versprecher - **2.** [form] Abschnitt *der* - **3.** [of paper]: ~ **(of paper)** Zettel *der* - **4.** [underwear] Unterrock *der* - **5.** *phr*: **to give sb the ~** *inf* jm entkommen ◇ *vt* - **1.** [put, slide] stecken - **2.** [clothes]: **to ~ sthg on/off** etw überziehen/ausziehen - **3.** [escape]: **it ~ped my mind** ich habe es vergessen ◇ *vi* - **1.** [lose balance] ausrutschen - **2.** [move unexpectedly - hand, foot] rutschen; **it ~ped out of my hand** es rutschte mir aus der Hand; **I let it ~** [revealed it] es ist mir herausgerutscht - **3.** [decline] sinken - **4.** [move discreetly] schlüpfen; **to ~ into/out of sthg** [clothes] in etw *(A)* /aus etw schlüpfen. ◆ **slip away** *vi* [leave] sich davonschleichen. ◆ **slip on** *vt sep* [clothes] überziehen; [shoes] anziehen. ◆ **slip up** *vi* sich vertun.

slipped disc [.slɪpt-] *n* Bandscheibenvorfall *der.*

slipper ['slɪpə'] *n* Hausschuh *der.*

slippery ['slɪpərɪ] *adj* - **1.** [surface, soap] rutschig - **2.** [person] windig.

slip road *n Br* [onto motorway] Auffahrt *die*; [leaving motorway] Ausfahrt *die.*

slip-up *n inf* Versehen *das.*

slit [slɪt] (*pt & pp* slit) ◇ *n* Schlitz *der* ◇ *vt* aufschlitzen.

slither ['slɪðə'] *vi* - **1.** [car, person] rutschen - **2.** [snake] gleiten.

sliver ['slɪvə'] *n* - **1.** [splinter] Splitter *der* - **2.** [slice] hauchdünne Scheibe.

slob [slɒb] *n inf* Dreckschwein *das.*

slog [slɒg] *inf* ◇ *n* [tiring work] Schinderei *die* ◇ *vi* [work]: **to ~ (away) at sthg** sich mit etw abplagen.

slogan ['sləʊgən] *n* Slogan *der.*

slop [slɒp] ◇ *vt* verschütten ◇ *vi* überschwappen.

slope [sləʊp] ◇ *n* - **1.** [of roof, ground] Neigung *die* - **2.** [hill] Hang *der* ◇ *vi* [shelf, table] schräg sein.

sloping ['sləʊpɪŋ] *adj* schräg; [land] abfallend.

sloppy ['slɒpɪ] *adj* [careless] schlampig.

slot [slɒt] *n* - **1.** [opening] Schlitz *der* - **2.** [groove] Nut *die* - **3.** [place in broadcasting schedule] Sendezeit *die.*

slot machine *n* - **1.** [vending machine] Münzautomat *der* - **2.** [arcade machine] Spielautomat *der.*

slouch [slaʊtʃ] *vi* [when sitting] sich hinlümmeln; [when standing] schlaff dastehen.

Slovakia [slə'vækɪə] *n* Slowakei *die.*

slovenly ['slʌvnlɪ] *adj* schlampig.

slow [sləʊ] ◇ *adj* - **1.** [not fast] langsam - **2.** [clock, watch]: **to be ~** nachgehen - **3.** [not intelligent] langsam ◇ *adv*: **to go ~** [driver] langsam fahren; [workers] Bummelstreik machen ◇ *vt* verlangsamen ◇ *vi* [person] langsam werden; [car] langsamer fahren; [increase, progress] sich verlangsamen. ◆ **slow down, slow up** ◇ *vt sep* verlangsamen ◇ *vi* langsamer werden; [car] langsamer fahren; [walker] langsamer gehen.

slowdown ['sləʊdaʊn] *n* Verlangsamung *die.*

slowly ['sləʊlɪ] *adv* langsam.

slow motion *n* Zeitlupe *die.*

sludge [slʌdʒ] *n* Schlamm *der.*

slug [slʌg] *n* - **1.** ZOOL Nacktschnecke *die* - **2.** *inf* [of alcohol] Schluck *der* - **3.** *Am inf* [bullet] Kugel *die.*

sluggish ['slʌgɪʃ] *adj* träge; [business] flau.

sluice [slu:s] *n* Schleuse *die.*

slum [slʌm] *n* [area] Slum *der.*

slumber ['slʌmbə'] *literary* ◇ *n* Schlummer *der* ◇ *vi* schlummern.

slump [slʌmp] ◇ *n* - **1.** [decline]: ~ **(in sthg)**

Abfall *der* (einer Sache *(G)*) - **2.** [period of economic depression] Konjunkturabschwung *der* ⬦ *vi* - **1.** [business, market] plötzlich zurückgehen; [prices] stürzen - **2.** [person] sich fallen lassen.

slung [slʌŋ] *pt* & *pp* ⊳ sling.

slur [slɜːʳ] ⬦ *n* [insult]: - **(on sb/sthg)** Schande *die* (für jn/etw) ⬦ *vt* [speech]: **to ~ one's words** mit schwerer Zunge sprechen.

slush [slʌʃ] *n* Schneematsch *der*.

slut [slʌt] *n inf* Schlampe *die*.

sly [slaɪ] (*compar* slyer OR slier; *superl* slyest OR sliest) *adj* - **1.** [look, smile, grin] wissend - **2.** [cunning] listig.

smack [smæk] ⬦ *n* [slap] Klaps *der*; [on face] Ohrfeige *die* ⬦ *vt* - **1.** [slap] einen Klaps geben (+ *D*); [in the face] ohrfeigen - **2.** [put] knallen.

small [smɔːl] ⬦ *adj* klein; **a ~ number** eine geringe Anzahl; **a ~ matter** eine Kleinigkeit; **a ~ business** ein Kleinbetrieb; **to feel ~** sich schämen ⬦ *adv*: **to chop stng up ~** etw kleinschneiden.

small ads [-ædz] *npl Br* Kleinanzeigen *pl*.

small change *n* Kleingeld *das*.

smallholder ['smɔːlˌhəʊldəʳ] *n Br* Kleinbauer *der*, -bäuerin *die*.

small hours *npl* frühe Morgenstunden *pl*.

smallpox ['smɔːlpɒks] *n (U)* Pocken *pl*.

small print *n*: **the ~ das** Kleingedruckte.

small talk *n* Smalltalk *der*.

smarmy ['smɑːmɪ] *adj* schleimig.

smart [smɑːt] ⬦ *adj* - **1.** [elegant] elegant - **2.** *esp Am* [clever] klug - **3.** [fashionable, exclusive] exklusiv - **4.** [rapid] flott ⬦ *vi* - **1.** [sting] brennen - **2.** [feel anger and humiliation] verletzt sein.

smarten ['smɑːtn] ◆ **smarten up** *vt sep* [room] aufräumen; **to ~ up one's appearance** sich herrichten.

smash [smæʃ] ⬦ *n* - **1.** [sound] Krach *der* - **2.** *inf* [car crash] Unfall *der* - **3.** TENNIS Schmetterball *der* ⬦ *vt* - **1.** [break into pieces] zerschlagen - **2.** *fig* [defeat] zerschlagen ⬦ *vi* - **1.** [break into pieces] zerbrechen - **2.** [crash, collide]: **to ~ through stng** durch etw rasen; **the car ~ed into the tree** das Auto krachte gegen den Baum.

smashing ['smæʃɪŋ] *adj inf* klasse, toll.

smattering ['smætərɪŋ] *n*: **to have a ~ of stng** Grundkenntnisse in etw *(D)* haben; **I have a ~ of German** ich kann ein bisschen Deutsch.

smear [smɪəʳ] ⬦ *n* - **1.** [dirty mark] Fleck *der* - **2.** MED Abstrich *der* - **3.** [slander] Verleumdung *die* ⬦ *vt* - **1.** [smudge - page, painting] verschmieren; [- paint, ink] verwischen - **2.** [spread]: **to ~ stng onto stng** etw auf etw *(A)* schmieren - **3.** [slander] verleumden.

smell [smel] (*pt* & *pp* -ed OR smelt) ⬦ *n* - **1.** [odour] Geruch *der*; [unpleasant] Gestank

der - **2.** *(U)* [sense of smell] Geruchssinn *der* - **3.** [sniff]: **to have a ~ of stng** an etw *(D)* riechen ⬦ *vt* - **1.** [notice an odour of, sense] riechen - **2.** [sniff at] riechen an (+ *D*); [subj: dog] schnuppern an (+ *D*) ⬦ *vi* - **1.** [have sense of smell] riechen - **2.** [have particular smell]: **to ~ of stng** nach etw riechen; **to ~ like stng** wie etw riechen; **to ~ good/bad** gut/schlecht riechen - **3.** [smell unpleasantly] übel riechen.

smelly ['smelɪ] *adj* übel riechend.

smelt [smelt] *pt* & *pp* ⊳ smell.

smile [smaɪl] ⬦ *n* Lächeln *das* ⬦ *vi* lächeln.

smiley ['smaɪlɪ] *n* COMPUT Smiley *der*.

smirk [smɜːk] *n* Grinsen *das*.

smock [smɒk] *n* Kittel *der*.

smog [smɒg] *n* Smog *der*.

smoke [sməʊk] ⬦ *n* [from fire] Rauch *der* ⬦ *vt* - **1.** [cigarette, cigar] rauchen - **2.** [fish, meat, cheese] räuchern ⬦ *vi* rauchen.

smoked [sməʊkt] *adj* [food] geräuchert.

smoker ['sməʊkəʳ] *n* - **1.** [person who smokes] Raucher *der* - **2.** RAIL [compartment] Raucherabteil *das*.

smoke shop *n Am* Tabakladen *der*.

smoking ['sməʊkɪŋ] *n* Rauchen *das*; **'no ~'** 'Rauchen verboten'.

smoky ['sməʊkɪ] *adj* rauchig.

smolder *vi Am* = smoulder.

smooth [smuːð] ⬦ *adj* - **1.** [surface] glatt - **2.** [sauce, paste] sämig - **3.** [flow, pace, supply] gleichmäßig - **4.** [taste] weich - **5.** [flight, ride] ruhig; [takeoff, landing] weich; [engine] ruhig laufend - **6.** *pej* [person, manner] aalglatt - **7.** [trouble-free] glatt verlaufend; [transition] reibungslos ⬦ *vt* - **1.** [hair, skirt, tablecloth] glatt streichen - **2.** [rub]: **~ the oil into your skin** reiben Sie Ihre Haut mit dem Öl ein. ◆ **smooth out** *vt sep* - **1.** [skirt, sheet, crease] glatt streichen - **2.** [difficulties] aus dem Weg räumen.

smother ['smʌðəʳ] *vt* - **1.** [cover thickly]: **to ~ stng in OR with stng** etw mit etw bedecken - **2.** [suffocate, extinguish] ersticken - **3.** *fig* [repress] unterdrücken - **4.** [suffocate with love] (mit Liebe) erdrücken.

smoulder *Br*, **smolder** *Am* ['sməʊldəʳ] *vi lit* & *fig* schwelen.

SMS (*abbr of* Short Message System) *n* SMS *die*.

smudge [smʌdʒ] ⬦ *n* [dirty mark] Fleck *der*; [of ink] verwischte Stelle ⬦ *vt* [spoil - by blurring] verschmieren; [- outline, ink] verwischen; [- by dirtying] beschmutzen.

smug [smʌg] *adj pej* selbstzufrieden.

smuggle ['smʌgl] *vt* schmuggeln.

smuggler ['smʌglə'] *n* Schmuggler *der*, -in *die*.

smuggling ['smʌglɪŋ] *n* Schmuggel *der*.

smutty ['smʌtɪ] *adj inf pej* [lewd] schmutzig.

snack [snæk] *n* Snack *der*, Imbiss *der*.

snack bar *n* Snackbar *die*, Imbissstube *die*.

snag [snæg] ◇ *n* [problem] Haken *der* ◇ *vi*: **to ~ on sthg** an etw *(D)* hängenbleiben.

snail [sneɪl] *n* Schnecke *die*.

snake [sneɪk] *n* Schlange *die*.

snap [snæp] ◇ *adj* spontan; [election] Spontan- ◇ *n* - **1.** [of twig, branch] Knacken *das*; [of whip] Knallen *das* - **2.** *inf* [photograph] Schnappschuss *der* - **3.** [card game] Schnippschnappschnurr *das* ◇ *vt* - **1.** [break - rope] zerreißen; **to ~ one's fingers** mit den Fingern schnippen - **2.** [say sharply] hervorstoßen ◇ *vi* - **1.** [break] (zer)brechen; [rope] (zer)reißen - **2.** [attempt to bite]: **to ~ (at sb/sthg)** (nach jm/etw) schnappen - **3.** [speak sharply]: **to ~ at sb** jn anfahren. **◆ snap up** *vt sep* zuschlagen bei (+ *D*).

snappy ['snæpɪ] *adj inf* [stylish, quick] flott; **make it ~!** mach hin!

snapshot ['snæpʃɒt] *n* Schnappschuss *der*.

snare [sneəʳ] ◇ *n* Falle *die* ◇ *vt* in einer Falle fangen.

snarl [snɑːl] ◇ *n* Knurren *das* ◇ *vi* knurren.

snatch [snætʃ] ◇ *n* [of song, conversation] Bruchstück *das* ◇ *vt* [grab] schnappen.

sneak [sniːk] (*Am pt* snuck) ◇ *n Br inf* Petze *die* ◇ *vt* [bring secretly] schmuggeln; **to ~ a look at sb/sthg** jn/etw heimlich anlsehen ◇ *vi* [move quietly] schleichen; **to ~ up on sb** sich an jn heranlschleichen.

sneakers ['sniːkəz] *npl Am* Sportschuhe *pl*.

sneaky ['sniːkɪ] *adj inf* hinterhältig.

sneer [snɪəʳ] ◇ *n* spöttisches Lächeln ◇ *vi* [smile unpleasantly] spöttisch lächeln.

sneeze [sniːz] ◇ *n* Niesen *das* ◇ *vi* niesen.

snide [snaɪd] *adj* abfällig.

sniff [snɪf] ◇ *vt* - **1.** [smell] riechen an (+ *D*) - **2.** [drug] schnüffeln ◇ *vi* schniefen.

snigger ['snɪgəʳ] ◇ *n* hämisches Kichern ◇ *vi* hämisch kichern.

snip [snɪp] ◇ *n inf* [bargain] Schnäppchen *das* ◇ *vt* [cut] schnippeln.

sniper ['snaɪpəʳ] *n* Heckenschütze *der*.

snippet ['snɪpɪt] *n* Bruchstück *das*.

snob [snɒb] *n* Snob *der*.

snobbish ['snɒbɪʃ], **snobby** ['snɒbɪ] *adj* snobistisch.

snooker ['snuːkəʳ] *n* Snooker *das*.

snoop [snuːp] *vi inf* (heruml)schnüffeln.

snooty ['snuːtɪ] *adj* hochnäsig.

snooze [snuːz] ◇ *n* Nickerchen *das*; **to have a ~** ein Nickerchen machen ◇ *vi* ein Nickerchen machen.

snore [snɔːʳ] ◇ *n* Schnarchen *das* ◇ *vi* schnarchen.

snoring ['snɔːrɪŋ] *n* Schnarchen *das*.

snorkel ['snɔːkl] *n* Schnorchel *der*.

snort [snɔːt] ◇ *n* Schnauben *das* ◇ *vi* schnauben.

snout [snaʊt] *n* Schnauze *die*.

snow [snəʊ] ◇ *n* Schnee *der* ◇ *v impers*: **it's ~ing** es schneit.

snowball ['snəʊbɔːl] ◇ *n* Schneeball *der* ◇ *vi fig* lawinenartig anlwachsen.

snowdrift ['snəʊdrɪft] *n* Schneewehe *die*.

snowdrop ['snəʊdrɒp] *n* Schneeglöckchen *das*.

snowfall ['snəʊfɔːl] *n* Schneefall *der*.

snowflake ['snəʊfleɪk] *n* Schneeflocke *die*.

snowman ['snəʊmæn] (*pl* -men [-men]) *n* Schneemann *der*.

snowplough *Br*, **snowplow** *Am* ['snəʊplaʊ] *n* [vehicle] Schneepflug *der*.

snowstorm ['snəʊstɔːm] *n* Schneesturm *der*.

SNP (*abbr of* Scottish National Party) *n* nationalistische Partei in Schottland.

Snr, snr (*abbr of* senior) sen.

snub [snʌb] ◇ *n* Abfuhr *die* ◇ *vt*: **to ~ sb** jm eine Abfuhr erteilen.

snuck [snʌk] *pt Am* ⊏▷ sneak.

snug [snʌg] *adj* - **1.** [person, feeling, place] gemütlich - **2.** [close-fitting] gut sitzend.

snuggle ['snʌgl] *vi*: **to ~ up to sb** sich an jn kuscheln; **to ~ down in bed** sich ins Bett kuscheln.

so [səʊ] ◇ *adv* - **1.** [to such a degree] so; **it's ~ difficult that ...** es ist so schwierig, dass ...; **don't be ~ stupid!** sei nicht so dumm!; **I (do) ~ hope you can come** ich hoffe so sehr, dass du kommen kannst; **~ much money/many cars** so viel Geld/viele Autos; **I liked it ~ much that ...** es gefiel mir so sehr OR gut, dass ...; **~ much ~ that ...** dermaßen, dass ... - **2.** [referring back]: **what's the point then?** was soll das also?; **you knew already?** du hast es also schon gewusst?; **I think ~** ich glaube (schon); **I don't think ~** ich glaube nicht; **I'm afraid ~** leider ja; **I told you ~** das habe ich dir gleich gesagt; **if ~** falls ja; **is that ~?** tatsächlich? - **3.** [also] auch; **can I ~** ich auch; **do I** ich auch; **he is clever and ~ is she** er ist intelligent und sie auch - **4.** [in this way] so - **5.** [in expressing agreement]: **~ there is** ja, stimmt; **that's her car** - **it is!** das ist ihr Auto - tatsächlich!; **~ I see** das sehe ich - **6.** [referring to unspecified amount, limit]: **they pay us ~ much a week** sie zahlen uns so viel die Woche; **or ~** oder so ◇ *conj* - **1.** [consequently] also; **he said yes and ~ we got married** er sagte ja, also heirateten wir; **I'm away next week ~ I won't be there** ich bin nächste Woche weg, also werde ich nicht kommen - **2.** [to introduce a statement]: **what have you been up to?** na, was treibst du so?; **~ that's who she is!** das ist sie also!; **~ what?** *inf* na und?; **~ there!** *inf* das wars! **◆ and so on, and so forth** *adv* und so weiter.

so as *conj* um; **we didn't knock ~ as not to disturb them** wir klopften nicht an, um sie nicht zu stören. **so that** *conj* damit.

soak [səʊk] ⟨⟩ *vt* - **1.** [leave immersed] einlweichen - **2.** [wet thoroughly] durchnässen; **to be ~ed with sthg** mit etw durchtränkt sein ⟨⟩ *vi* - **1.** [become thoroughly wet]: **to leave sthg to ~, to let sthg ~** etw einlweichen - **2.** [spread]: **to ~ into sthg** in etw *(A)* einsickern; **to ~ through sthg** durch etw (hindurch)sickern. **soak up** *vt sep* [liquid] auflsaugen.

soaking ['səʊkɪŋ] *adj*: **to be ~ (wet)** völlig durchnässt sein.

so-and-so *n inf* - **1.** [to replace a name]: **Mr So-and-so** Herr Soundso - **2.** [annoying person]: **you little ~!** du Biest!

soap [səʊp] *n* - **1.** *(U)* [for washing] Seife *die* - **2.** TV Seifenoper *die*.

soap dish *n* Seifenschale *die*.

soap opera *n* Seifenoper *die*.

soap powder *n* Seifenpulver *das*.

soapy ['səʊpɪ] *adj* seifig.

soar [sɔːʳ] *vi* - **1.** [bird, kite, rocket] auflsteigen - **2.** [increase rapidly] rapide anlsteigen.

sob [sɒb] *n* Schluchzer *der*.

sober ['səʊbəʳ] *adj* - **1.** [not drunk] nüchtern - **2.** [serious] ernsthaft - **3.** [plain] einfach. **sober up** *vi* nüchtern werden.

sobering ['səʊbərɪŋ] *adj* ernüchternd.

so-called [-kɔːld] *adj* so genannt.

soccer ['sɒkəʳ] *n (U)* Fußball *der*.

sociable ['səʊʃəbl] *adj* gesellig.

social ['səʊʃl] *adj* - **1.** [behaviour, background, conditions] sozial, gesellschaftlich - **2.** [gathering, drinking] gesellig.

socialism ['səʊʃəlɪzm] *n* Sozialismus *der*.

socialist ['səʊʃəlɪst] ⟨⟩ *adj* sozialistisch ⟨⟩ *n* Sozialist *der*, -in *die*.

socialize, -ise ['səʊʃəlaɪz] *vi*: **to ~ with sb** mit jm gesellschaftlich verkehren; **she ~s a lot** sie geht viel aus.

social security *n (U)* Sozialversicherung *die*.

social services *npl* Sozialeinrichtungen *pl*.

social worker *n* Sozialarbeiter *der*, -in *die*.

society [sə'saɪətɪ] *n* - **1.** [mankind, community] Gesellschaft *die* - **2.** [club, organization] Verein *der*, Klub *der*.

sociology [,səʊsɪ'ɒlədʒɪ] *n* Soziologie *die*.

sock [sɒk] *n* Socke *die*, Socken *der*.

socket ['sɒkɪt] *n* - **1.** ELEC Steckdose *die* - **2.** ANAT [of joint] Gelenkpfanne *die*; [of eye] Augenhöhle *die*.

sod [sɒd] *n* - **1.** [of turf] Sode *die* - **2.** *vinf* [man] Scheißkerl *der*; [woman] Miststück *das*.

soda ['səʊdə] *n* - **1.** CHEM Soda *das*, Natron *das* - **2.** [soda water] Soda *das* - **3.** *Am* [fizzy drink] Limonade *die*.

soda water *n* Sodawasser *das*.

sodden ['sɒdn] *adj* durchnässt.

sodium ['səʊdɪəm] *n* Natrium *das*.

sofa ['səʊfə] *n* Sofa *das*.

Sofia ['səʊfjə] *n* Sofia *nt*.

soft [sɒft] *adj* - **1.** [gen] weich - **2.** [breeze, sound, knock, nature] sanft - **3.** [light, colour, music] gedämpft - **4.** [not strict] mild.

softball ['sɒftbɔːl] *n* Softball *der*.

soft drink *n* alkoholfreies Getränk.

soften ['sɒfn] ⟨⟩ *vt* - **1.** [substance] weich machen; [water] enthärten - **2.** [punch, impact, effect, light] dämpfen; [blow, attitude] mildern ⟨⟩ *vi* - **1.** [substance] weich werden - **2.** [eyes, voice, expression] sanft werden.

softhearted [,sɒft'hɑːtɪd] *adj* weichherzig.

softly ['sɒftlɪ] *adv* - **1.** [move, touch] sanft - **2.** [speak, sing, shine] leise - **3.** [smile, look] sanft.

soft return *n* COMPUT weicher Zeilenumbruch.

software ['sɒftweəʳ] *n* COMPUT Software *die*.

soggy ['sɒgɪ] *adj* durchnässt; [ground] matschig.

soil [sɔɪl] ⟨⟩ *n* - **1.** [earth] Erde *die*; [ground & GEOGR] Boden *der* - **2.** *fig* [territory] Boden *der* ⟨⟩ *vt* [dirty] beschmutzen.

soiled [sɔɪld] *adj* schmutzig.

solar ['səʊləʳ] *adj* Sonnen-.

solar energy *n* Solarenergie *die*.

sold [səʊld] *pt & pp* ⟩ sell.

solder ['səʊldəʳ] ⟨⟩ *n (U)* TECH Lot *das* ⟨⟩ *vt* löten.

soldier ['səʊldʒəʳ] *n* Soldat *der*.

sold out *adj* ausverkauft.

sole [səʊl] *(pl sense 2 only inv OR -s)* ⟨⟩ *adj* - **1.** [only] einzig - **2.** [exclusive] alleinig ⟨⟩ *n* - **1.** [of foot] Sohle *die* - **2.** [fish] Seezunge *die*.

solemn ['sɒləm] *adj* - **1.** [person, face, voice] ernst - **2.** [agreement, promise, occasion, music] feierlich.

solicit [sə'lɪsɪt] ⟨⟩ *vt fml* [request] werben um ⟨⟩ *vi* [prostitute] sich anlbieten.

solicitor [sə'lɪsɪtəʳ] *n Br* Rechtsanwalt *der*, -anwältin *die*.

solid ['sɒlɪd] ⟨⟩ *adj* - **1.** [not liquid or gas] fest - **2.** [gold, silver, wood] massiv - **3.** [building, base, relationship, person] solide - **4.** [support] einmütig; [evidence] handfest; [majority] solide - **5.** [line] ununterbrochen, durchgängig; **two hours ~, two ~ hours** zwei volle Stunden ⟨⟩ *adv*: **to be packed ~** brechend voll sein ⟨⟩ *n* [not liquid or gas] fester Stoff. **solids** *npl* [food] feste Nahrung.

solidarity [,sɒlɪ'dærətɪ] *n* Solidarität *die*.

solitaire [,sɒlɪ'teəʳ] *n* - **1.** [jewel] Solitär *der* - **2.** [board game] Solitaire *das* - **3.** *Am* [card game] Patience *die*.

solitary ['sɒlɪtrɪ] *adj* - **1.** [involving one person, single] einzeln **- 2.** [enjoying solitude] einsam.

solitary confinement *n* Einzelhaft *die*.

solitude ['sɒlɪtjuːd] *n* Einsamkeit *die*.

solo ['səʊləʊ] *(pl* -s*)* ◇ *adj* **- 1.** MUS Solo- **- 2.** [attempt, flight] Allein- ◇ *n* MUS Solo *das* ◇ *adv* **- 1.** MUS solo **- 2.** [fly, climb] allein.

soloist ['səʊləʊɪst] *n* Solist *der*, -in *die*.

soluble ['sɒljʊbl] *adj* **- 1.** [substance] löslich **- 2.** [problem] lösbar.

solution [sə'luːʃn] *n* Lösung *die*; **a ~ to sthg** eine Lösung für etw.

solve [sɒlv] *vt* lösen.

solvent ['sɒlvənt] ◇ *adj* FIN solvent ◇ *n* [substance] Lösungsmittel *das*.

Somalia [sə'mɑːlɪə] *n* Somalia *nt*.

sombre *Br*, **somber** *Am* ['sɒmbəʳ] *adj* düster.

some [sʌm] ◇ *adj* **- 1.** [a certain amount of] etwas; **~ money** etwas Geld; **~ meat** ein bisschen Fleisch; **would you like ~ (more) tea?** möchtest du (noch) Tee? **- 2.** [a certain number of] einige; **~ people** einige Leute; **I bought ~ sweets** ich habe Bonbons gekauft; **can I have ~ sweets?** kann ich Bonbons haben?; **I've known her for ~ years** ich kenne sie schon seit einigen Jahren **- 3.** *(contrastive use)* [certain] manche; **~ jobs are better paid than others** manche Jobs sind besser bezahlt als andere **- 4.** [in imprecise statements] irgendein, -e; **she married ~ Italian (or other)** sie hat irgend so einen Italiener geheiratet; **there must be ~ mistake** das muss ein Irrtum sein **- 5.** *inf iron* [not very good]: **~ welcome that was!** das war vielleicht ein enttäuschender Empfang!; **~ friend you are!** du bist mir vielleicht ein Freund! ◇ *pron* **- 1.** [a certain amount] etwas; **I've read ~ of the article** ich habe einen Teil des Artikels gelesen; **~ of it is mine** ein Teil davon gehört mir; **take ~ bread – I've already got ~** nimm dir Brot – ich habe schon **- 2.** [a certain number] einige; **can I have ~?** [books, pens, potatoes *etc*] kann ich welche haben?; **have ~ strawberries – I've already got ~** nimm dir Erdbeeren - ich habe schon welche; **~ (of them) left early** einige (von ihnen) gingen vorher **- 3.** [some people] manche; **~ say he lied** manche sagen, dass er gelogen hat ◇ *adv* ungefähr; **there were ~ 7,000 people there** es waren ungefähr OR um die 7000 Leute da.

somebody ['sʌmbədɪ] *pron* jemand; **ask ~ else** frag jemand anders; **~ or other** irgend jemand; **he really thinks he's ~** [important person] er glaubt wirklich, er ist wer.

someday ['sʌmdeɪ] *adv* eines Tages.

somehow ['sʌmhaʊ], **someway** *Am* ['sʌmweɪ] *adv* irgendwie.

someone ['sʌmwʌn] *pron* = somebody.

someplace *adv Am* = somewhere.

somersault ['sʌməsɔːlt] ◇ *n* Purzelbaum

der; SPORT Salto *der* ◇ *vi* einen Purzelbaum schlagen; SPORT einen Salto machen.

something ['sʌmθɪŋ] ◇ *pron* etwas; **I saw ~ moving** ich sah, wie sich etwas bewegte; **~ nice** etwas Schönes; **there's ~ about him I don't like** er hat etwas an sich, das mir nicht gefällt; **~ else** sonst etwas; **~ or other** irgend etwas; **or ~** *inf* oder so etwas; **well, at least that's ~** nun, das ist immerhin etwas; **there's ~ in what you say** es ist schon etwas Wahres an dem, was du sagst; **it's really ~!** es ist ganz toll!; **it came as ~ of a surprise to me** es war schon irgendwie eine Überraschung für mich ◇ *adv* [in approximations]: **~ like/in the region of** ungefähr; **it looks ~ like a rose** es sieht so ähnlich wie eine Rose aus.

sometime ['sʌmtaɪm] ◇ *adj* ehemalig ◇ *adv* irgendwann.

sometimes ['sʌmtaɪmz] *adv* manchmal.

someway *adv Am* = somehow.

somewhat ['sʌmwɒt] *adv* ziemlich.

somewhere *Br* ['sʌmweəʳ], **someplace** *Am* ['sʌmpleɪs] *adv* **- 1.** [gen - with verbs of position] irgendwo; [- with verbs of motion] irgendwohin; **~ else** irgendwo anders/ irgendwo andershin; **~ or other** irgendwo/irgendwohin **- 2.** [in approximations] ungefähr; **~ around** OR **in the region of 50** ungefähr 50.

son [sʌn] *n* Sohn *der*.

song [sɒŋ] *n* Lied *das;* [of bird] Gesang *der*.

sonic ['sɒnɪk] *adj* Schall-.

son-in-law *(pl* sons-in-law OR son-in-laws*) n* Schwiegersohn *der*.

soon [suːn] *adv* **- 1.** [in a short time] bald; **~ after** OR **afterwards** kurz danach **- 2.** [early]: **how ~ can you be ready?** wie schnell kannst du fertig sein?; **too ~** zu früh; **not a minute too ~** keine Minute zu früh; **as ~ as** sobald; **as ~ as possible** so bald wie möglich.

sooner ['suːnəʳ] *adv* **- 1.** [earlier] früher; **no ~ ... than ...** kaum ... als (auch schon) ...; **~ or later** früher oder später; **the ~ the better** je früher, desto besser **- 2.** [expressing preference] lieber.

soot [sʊt] *n* Ruß *der*.

soothe [suːð] *vt* **- 1.** [pain] lindern **- 2.** [person, fear] beruhigen.

sophisticated [sə'fɪstɪkeɪtɪd] *adj* **- 1.** [stylish] hochelegant **- 2.** [intelligent] kultiviert **- 3.** [complicated] hoch entwickelt.

sophomore ['sɒfəmɔːʳ] *n Am* Student *der*, -in *die* im zweiten Studienjahr.

soporific [ˌsɒpə'rɪfɪk] *adj* einschläfernd.

sopping ['sɒpɪŋ] *adj*: **~ (wet)** klatschnass.

soppy ['sɒpɪ] *adj inf pej* rührselig.

soprano [sə'prɑːnəʊ] *(pl* -s*) n* **- 1.** [person] Sopranistin *die* **- 2.** [voice] Sopran *der*.

sorbet ['sɔːbeɪ] *n* Sorbet *das*.

sordid ['sɔːdɪd] *adj* [desires, thoughts, past] schmutzig.

sore [sɔːʳ] ⬦ adj - 1. [painful] wund, entzündet; **to have a ~ throat/head** Halsschmerzen/Kopfschmerzen haben - 2. Am inf [angry] sauer ⬦ n MED wunde OR entzündete Stelle.

sorrow ['sɒrəʊ] n - 1. [feeling of sadness] Kummer der - 2. [cause of sadness] Leid das.

sorry ['sɒrɪ] ⬦ adj - 1. [expressing apology]: **I'm ~** es tut mir leid; **I'm ~ about the mess** entschuldige bitte die Unordnung; **I'm ~ for what I did** was ich getan habe, tut mir leid; **I'm ~ to bother you, but could you …** Verzeihung, könnten Sie … - 2. [expressing disappointment]: **I'm ~ you couldn't come** schade, dass du nicht kommen konntest; **we were ~ about his resignation** wir finden es schade, dass er seinen Rücktritt; **we're ~ to see you go** wir finden es schade, dass du gehst - 3. [expressing regret]: **I'm ~ I ever came here** ich bereue, jemals hierhergekommen zu sein; **I'm ~ to have to announce …** ich muss Ihnen leider mitteilen … - 4. [expressing sympathy]: **to be** OR **feel ~ for sb** jn bedauern OR bemitleiden - 5. [expressing polite disagreement]: **I'm ~, but …** Entschuldigung OR Verzeihung, aber … - 6. [poor, pitiable] bedauernswert ⬦ excl - 1. [expressing apology] Entschuldigung!, Verzeihung! - 2. [asking for repetition] wie bitte? - 3. [to correct o.s.] ich meine (natürlich).

sort [sɔːt] ⬦ n [kind, type] Sorte die; **what ~ of car have you got?** was für ein Auto hast du?; **a ~ of** eine Art (von) ⬦ vt [classify, separate] sortieren. ➤ **sort of** adv [rather] irgendwie. ➤ **sort out** vt sep - 1. [into groups] sortieren - 2. [tidy up - papers, clothes] weglräumen; [- room] auflräumen; [- affairs, finances] regeln - 3. [work out, arrange] sich (D) überlegen.

SOS (abbr of save our souls) n SOS das.

so-so adj & adv inf so la la.

sought [sɔːt] pt & pp ▷ seek.

soul [səʊl] n - 1. [gen] Seele die - 2. [perfect example] Inbegriff der; **I'm the ~ of discretion** ich bin die Verschwiegenheit in Person - 3. [music] Soul der.

soul-destroying [-dɪˌstrɔɪŋ] adj [boring] geisttötend; [discouraging] sehr entmutigend.

sound [saʊnd] ⬦ adj - 1. [mind, body] gesund - 2. [building, structure] intakt - 3. [advice, investment] vernünftig - 4. [thorough] ordentlich ⬦ adv: **to be ~ asleep** tief OR fest schlafen ⬦ n - 1. [noise] Geräusch das; [of music, voice, instrument] Klang der; [of person, animal] Laut der - 2. (U) PHYS Schall der - 3. [volume] Lautstärke die - 4. [impression, idea] Gedanke der; **I don't like the ~ of this new plan** der neue Plan behagt mir nicht; **by the ~ of it** allem Anschein nach ⬦ vt ertönen lassen; [alarm] ausllösen; [bell] läuten; [horn] hupen ⬦ vi - 1. [make a noise] ertö-

nen; **to ~ like sthg** wie etw klingen - 2. [seem] klingen, zu sein scheinen; **she ~s nice** sie scheint nett zu sein; **it ~s like a good investment** das hört sich nach einer guten Investition an. ➤ **sound out** vt sep: **to ~ sb out** bei jm vorlfühlen; [furtively] jn auslhorchen.

sound barrier n Schallmauer die.

sound effects npl Klangeffekte pl.

soundly ['saʊndlɪ] adv - 1. [beat, defeat] vernichtend - 2. [sleep] tief, fest.

soundproof ['saʊndpruːf] adj schalldicht.

soundtrack ['saʊndtræk] n Soundtrack der.

soup [suːp] n Suppe die.

soup plate n Suppenteller der.

soup spoon n Suppenlöffel der.

sour ['saʊəʳ] ⬦ adj sauer; [relationship] erkalten ⬦ vt [person] verbittern; [relationship] erkalten lassen.

source [sɔːs] n Quelle die.

south [saʊθ] ⬦ adj Süd-, südlich ⬦ adv nach Süden, südwärts; **~ of** südlich von; **in the ~ of England** im Süden Englands ⬦ n - 1. [direction] Süden der - 2. [region]: **the ~ der** Süden.

South Africa n Südafrika nt.

South America n Südamerika nt.

southeast [ˌsaʊθˈiːst] ⬦ adj südöstlich, Südost- ⬦ adv südostwärts, nach Südosten; **~ of** südöstlich von ⬦ n [direction] Südosten der.

southerly ['sʌðəlɪ] adj - 1. [direction] südlich; [area] im Süden - 2. [wind] Süd-.

southern ['sʌðən] adj [region, dialect] südlich; [Europe] Süd-.

South Korea n Südkorea nt.

South Pole n: **the ~** der Südpol.

southward ['saʊθwəd] ⬦ adj südlich, nach Süden ⬦ adv = southwards.

southwards ['saʊθwədz] adv nach Süden.

southwest [ˌsaʊθˈwest] ⬦ adj südwestlich, Südwest- ⬦ adv südwestwärts, nach Südwesten; **~ of** südwestlich von ⬦ n Südwesten der.

souvenir [ˌsuːvəˈnɪəʳ] n Souvenir das, Andenken das.

sovereign ['sɒvrɪn] n - 1. [ruler] Herrscher der, -in die - 2. [coin] Sovereign der.

soviet ['səʊvɪət] n Sowjet der. ➤ **Soviet** ⬦ adj sowjetisch ⬦ n [person] Sowjetbürger der, -in die.

Soviet Union n: **the (former) ~** die (ehemalige) Sowjetunion.

sow¹ [səʊ] (pt -ed; pp sown OR -ed) vt - 1. [seeds] säen, auslsäen - 2. fig [doubt] säen.

sow² [saʊ] n [pig] Sau die.

sown [səʊn] pp ▷ sow¹.

soya ['sɔɪə] n Soja das.

soy(a) bean ['sɔɪ(ə)-] n Sojabohne die.

spa [spɑː] n [spring] Mineralquelle die; [place] Bad das.

space [speɪs] ⬦ *n* - **1.** (U) [room] Raum *der*; **there isn't enough ~ in here** hier ist nicht genug Platz - **2.** [outer space] Weltraum *der* - **3.** [gap] Zwischenraum *der* - **4.** [area] Fläche *die*, Raum *der* - **5.** TYPO Leerzeichen *das* - **6.** [period of time] Zeitraum *der*; **within the ~ of ten minutes** innerhalb von zehn Minuten; **in a short ~ of time** [in future] in Kürze; [in past] nach kurzer Zeit - **7.** [seat, place] Platz *der* ⬦ *comp* Weltraum- ⬦ *vt* in regelmäßigen Abständen anlordnen. ◆ **space out** *vt sep* [arrange] in regelmäßigen Abständen anlordnen.

spacecraft ['speɪskrɑːft] (*pl inv*) *n* Raumschiff *das*.

spaceman ['speɪsmæn] (*pl* -men [-men]) *n* [astronaut] Raumfahrer *der*.

spaceship ['speɪsʃɪp] *n* Raumschiff *das*.

space shuttle *n* Spaceshuttle *das*.

spacesuit ['speɪssuːt] *n* Raumanzug *der*.

spacious ['speɪʃəs] *adj* geräumig.

spade [speɪd] *n* - **1.** [tool] Spaten *der* - **2.** [playing card] Pik *das*. ◆ **spades** *npl* Pik *das*; **the six of ~s** die Pik Sechs.

spaghetti [spə'getɪ] *n* (U) Spaghetti *pl*.

Spain [speɪn] *n* Spanien *nt*.

span [spæn] ⬦ *pt* ⬐ spin ⬦ *n* - **1.** [in time] Zeitraum *der*, Zeitspanne *die* - **2.** [range] Reihe *die* - **3.** [of hands, wings, bridge] Spannweite *die* ⬦ *vt* - **1.** [encompass] umfassen - **2.** [cross] überspannen.

Spaniard ['spænjəd] *n* Spanier *der*, -in *die*.

spaniel ['spænjəl] *n* Spaniel *der*.

Spanish ['spænɪʃ] ⬦ *adj* spanisch ⬦ *n* [language] Spanisch(e) *das*.

spank [spæŋk] *vt*: **to ~ sb** [once] jm einen Klaps auf den Hintern geben; [several times] jm den Hintern versohlen.

spanner ['spænə'] *n* Schraubenschlüssel *der*.

spar [spɑː'] *vi* BOXING sparren.

spare [speə'] ⬦ *adj* - **1.** [surplus] zusätzlich, Ersatz-; **have you got a ~ pencil?** hast du einen Bleistift übrig? - **2.** [free] frei ⬦ *n inf* [part] Ersatzteil *das* ⬦ *vt* - **1.** [make available] entbehren können, übrig haben; **can you ~ five minutes?** hast du (mal) fünf Minuten Zeit?; **to ~** [extra] übrig, zur Verfügung; **we had an hour to ~** wir hatten (noch) eine Stunde Zeit - **2.** [not harm] verschonen - **3.** [effort, trouble] scheuen; **to ~ no expense** keine Kosten scheuen - **4.** [save, protect from]: **to ~ sb sthg** jm etw ersparen.

spare part *n* AUT Ersatzteil *das*.

spare time *n* Freizeit *die*.

spare wheel *n* Ersatzrad *das*.

sparing ['speərɪŋ] *adj*: **to be ~ with sthg** mit etw sparsam sein.

sparingly ['speərɪŋlɪ] *adv* sparsam.

spark [spɑːk] *n* - **1.** [from fire, electricity] Funke *der* - **2.** *fig* [of understanding, interest, humour] Funken *der*.

sparkle ['spɑːkl] ⬦ *n* [of jewel, frost, stars, sea] Glitzern *das*; [of eyes] Funkeln *das* ⬦ *vi* [jewel, frost, stars, sea] glitzern; [eyes] funkeln.

sparkling ['spɑːklɪŋ] *adj* - **1.** [mineral water] sprudelnd - **2.** [wit] sprühend.

sparkling wine *n* Schaumwein *der*, Sekt *der*.

spark plug *n* Zündkerze *die*.

sparrow ['spærəʊ] *n* Spatz *der*, Sperling *der*.

sparse ['spɑːs] *adj* spärlich; [hair] schütter, dünn.

spasm ['spæzm] *n* - **1.** MED [muscular contraction] Krampf *der* - **2.** [fit] Anfall *der*.

spastic ['spæstɪk] MED *n* Spastiker *der*, -in *die*.

spat [spæt] *pt & pp* ⬐ spit.

spate [speɪt] *n* Flut *die*.

spatter ['spætə'] *vt* bespritzen.

spawn [spɔːn] ⬦ *n* Laich *der* ⬦ *vt fig* [produce] erzeugen ⬦ *vi* ZOOL laichen.

speak [spiːk] (*pt* spoke; *pp* spoken) ⬦ *vt* sprechen ⬦ *vi* - **1.** [say words] sprechen; **to ~ to** OR **with sb** mit jm sprechen OR reden; **to ~ to sb about sthg** mit jm über etw (A) sprechen OR reden; **to ~ about sb/sthg** über jn/ etw sprechen OR reden - **2.** [make a speech] sprechen, reden; **to ~ on sthg** über etw (A) sprechen - **3.** [in giving an opinion]: **generally ~ing** im Allgemeinen, im Großen und Ganzen; **personally ~ing** meiner Ansicht nach. ◆ **so to speak** *adv* sozusagen. ◆ **speak for** *vt fus* [represent] sprechen für. ◆ **speak up** *vi* - **1.** [say something] sprechen; **to ~ up for sb/sthg** für jn/etw einltreten - **2.** [speak louder] lauter sprechen.

speaker ['spiːkə'] *n* - **1.** [person talking] Sprecher *der*, -in *die* - **2.** [in lecture] Redner *der*, -in *die* - **3.** [of a language]: **a German ~** ein Sprecher/eine Sprecherin des Deutschen - **4.** [loudspeaker, in hi-fi] Lautsprecher *der*. ◆ **Speaker** *n Br* [in House of Commons] Präsident *der*, -in *die* des Unterhauses.

spear [spɪə'] *n* Speer *der*.

spearhead ['spɪəhed] *vt* anlführen.

spec [spek] *n Br inf*: **on ~** aufs Geratewohl.

special ['speʃl] *adj* - **1.** [specific, out of the ordinary] besondere, -r, -s, spezielle, -r, -s - **2.** [valued]: **to be ~ to sb** jm viel bedeuten.

special delivery *n* Eilzustellung *die*.

specialist ['speʃəlɪst] ⬦ *adj* Fach- ⬦ *n* [expert] Spezialist *der*, -in *die*; [doctor] Facharzt *der*, -ärztin *die*.

speciality [ˌspeʃɪ'ælətɪ], **specialty** *Am* ['speʃltɪ] *n* - **1.** [field of knowledge] Spezialgebiet *das* - **2.** [service, product] Spezialität *die*.

specialize, -ise ['speʃəlaɪz] *vi*: **to ~ (in sthg)** sich (auf etw (A)) spezialisieren; [have special qualifications] (auf etw (A)) spezialisiert sein.

specially ['speʃəlɪ] adv - **1.** [on purpose, specifically] speziell - **2.** [really] besonders.

specialty n Am = speciality.

species ['spiːʃiːz] (pl inv) n Spezies die, Art die.

specific [spə'sɪfɪk] adj bestimmt, spezifisch; **to be ~ to sb/sthg** jm/etw eigen sein.

specifically [spə'sɪfɪklɪ] adv - **1.** [explicitly] ausdrücklich - **2.** [particularly, precisely] im Besonderen.

specify ['spesɪfaɪ] vt spezifizieren, herauslstellen; **to ~ that ...** deutlich machen, dass ..., herauslstellen, dass ...

specimen ['spesɪmən] n - **1.** [example] Exemplar das - **2.** [sample] Probe die.

speck [spek] n - **1.** [small stain] Fleck der; [of paint, mud] Spritzer der - **2.** [small particle - of dust] Körnchen das; [- of soot] Flocke die.

speckled ['spekld] adj: **~ (with sthg)** gesprenkelt (mit etw).

specs [speks] npl inf Brille die.

spectacle ['spektəkl] n - **1.** [sight] Anblick der; **to make a ~ of o.s.** sich unmöglich benehmen - **2.** [event] Spektakel das. ◆ **spectacles** npl Br [glasses] Brille die.

spectacular [spek'tækjʊləʳ] adj spektakulär.

spectator [spek'teɪtəʳ] n Zuschauer der, -in die.

spectre Br, **specter** Am ['spektəʳ] n - **1.** fml [ghost] Gespenst das - **2.** fig [frightening prospect] Schreckgespenst das.

speculation [,spekjʊ'leɪʃn] n Spekulation die.

sped [sped] pt & pp ▷ speed.

speech [spiːtʃ] n - **1.** (U) [ability to speak, dialect] Sprache die - **2.** [formal talk] Rede die - **3.** THEATRE Text der - **4.** [manner of speaking] Sprechweise die; **his ~ is clear and precise** er spricht klar und deutlich - **5.** GRAMM: **direct/indirect ~** direkte/indirekte Rede.

speechless ['spiːtʃlɪs] adj: **to be ~ (with sthg)** (vor etw (D)) sprachlos sein.

speed [spiːd] (pt & pp -ed OR sped) ◇ n - **1.** [pace, rapid rate] Geschwindigkeit die, Tempo das; **~ of light/sound** Licht-/Schallgeschwindigkeit die; **at high/low ~** mit hoher/niedriger Geschwindigkeit; **at top** OR **full ~** mit Höchstgeschwindigkeit - **2.** [gear] Gang der - **3.** PHOT [of film] Lichtempfindlichkeit die ◇ vi - **1.** [move fast]: **to ~ along/away/by** entlang-/davon-/vorbeiljagen - **2.** AUT [go too fast] zu schnell fahren. ◆ **speed up** ◇ vt sep beschleunigen; [person] auf Trab bringen ◇ vi [worker] sich beeilen; [driver, vehicle] beschleunigen; [production] sich erhöhen.

speedboat ['spiːdbəʊt] n Rennboot das.

speeding ['spiːdɪŋ] n zu schnelles Fahren; LAW Geschwindigkeitsüberschreitung die.

speed limit n Geschwindigkeitsbeschränkung die.

speedometer [spɪ'dɒmɪtəʳ] n Tachometer der OR das.

speedway ['spiːdweɪ] n - **1.** SPORT Speedwayrennen das - **2.** Am [road] Schnellstraße die.

speedy ['spiːdɪ] adj schnell.

spell [spel] (Br pt & pp spelt OR -ed, Am pt & pp -ed) ◇ n - **1.** [period of time] Weile die; **with some sunny ~s** mit sonnigen Abschnitten; **for a ~** eine Weile - **2.** [enchantment] Zauber der; **to cast** OR **put a ~ on sb** jn verzaubern - **3.** [magic word] Zauberspruch der ◇ vt - **1.** [word, name] schreiben; [aloud] buchstabieren - **2.** fig [signify] bedeuten; [aloud] buchstabieren; **it ~s disaster** das bedeutet Unglück ◇ vi: **to be able to ~** fehlerfrei schreiben können. ◆ **spell out** vt sep - **1.** [read aloud] buchstabieren - **2.** [explain]: **to ~ sthg out (for** OR **to sb)** (jm) etw klarlmachen.

spellbound ['spelbaʊnd] adj gebannt.

spelling ['spelɪŋ] n - **1.** [of a particular word] Schreibweise die - **2.** [ability to spell] Rechtschreibung die.

spelt [spelt] pt & pp Br ▷ spell.

spend [spend] (pt & pp spent) vt - **1.** [pay out] auslgeben; **she ~s a lot of money on clothes** sie gibt viel Geld für Kleidung aus - **2.** [time, life] verbringen; **he spent two hours shopping** er ist zwei Stunden lang einkaufen gewesen.

📖 **to spend**

Dieses englische Verb ist ein falscher Freund, der nichts mit „spenden" zu tun hat. Es kann in folgenden Zusammenhängen verwendet werden: To spend money bedeutet „Geld ausgeben", und to spend the weekend heißt „das Wochenende verbringen".
Möchte man sagen, dass man Geld gespendet hat, sagt man I've donated money. Handelt es sich dagegen um Blut, verwendet man oft to give: „Bitte spenden Sie Blut" – please give blood.

---

spent [spent] ◇ pt & pp ▷ spend ◇ adj [fuel, matches] verbraucht; [ammunition] verschossen; [patience, energy] erschöpft.

sperm [spɜːm] (pl inv OR -s) n - **1.** [cell] Spermium das - **2.** (U) [fluid] Sperma das.

spew [spjuː] ◇ vt [flames, lava] speien ◇ vi: **to ~ (out) from sthg** aus etw hervorlschießen.

sphere [sfɪəʳ] n - **1.** [globe] Kugel die - **2.** [of interest, activity] Bereich der; **~ of influence** Einflussbereich der.

spice [spaɪs] n - **1.** CULIN Gewürz das - **2.** (U) fig [excitement] Würze die.

spick-and-span [ˌspɪkən'spæn] adj blitzblank.

spicy ['spaɪsɪ] adj pikant.

spider ['spaɪdə'] n Spinne die.

spike [spaɪk] n - **1.** [on railings] Spitze die; [on shoe] Spike der - **2.** [on plant] Stachel der ⬥ vt [drink] einen Schuss (Alkohol) zulgeben.

spill [spɪl] (Br pt & pp spilt OR -ed, Am pt & pp -ed) ⬥ vt - **1.** [liquid, salt] verschütten - **2.** [blood] vergießen ⬥ vi [liquid, salt] sich ergießen.

spilt [spɪlt] pt & pp Br ▷ spill.

spin [spɪn] (pt span OR spun; pp spun) ⬥ n - **1.** [turn] Drehung die - **2.** AERON Trudeln das; **the plane went into a ~ das** Flugzeug begann zu trudeln - **3.** inf [in car] Spritztour die; **to go for a ~** eine Spritztour machen - **4.** SPORT [on ball] Effet der ⬥ vt - **1.** [gen] schnell drehen - **2.** [in spin-dryer] schleudern; [coin in the air] hochlwerfen - **3.** [thread, cloth, wool] spinnen - **4.** SPORT [ball] einen Effet geben (+ D) ⬥ vi - **1.** [gen] sich schnell drehen; [plane] trudeln - **2.** [spinner of thread] spinnen - **3.** [in spin-dryer] schleudern. ⬥ **spin out** vt sep [story, explanation] in die Länge ziehen; [money, food] strecken.

spinach ['spɪnɪdʒ] n Spinat der.

spinal column ['spaɪnl-] n Wirbelsäule die.

spinal cord ['spaɪnl-] n Rückenmark das.

spindly ['spɪndlɪ] adj [arms, legs] spindeldürr; [plant] zierlich.

spin-dryer n Br Wäscheschleuder die.

spine [spaɪn] n - **1.** ANAT Wirbelsäule die - **2.** [of book] Rücken der - **3.** [of hedgehog, plant] Stachel der.

spin-off n [by-product] Nebenprodukt das.

spinster ['spɪnstə'] n Unverheiratete die.

spiral ['spaɪərəl] ⬥ adj spiralförmig ⬥ n lit & fig Spirale die ⬥ vi [move in spiral curve - staircase, path] sich (hoch) winden; [- smoke] spiralförmig auflsteigen.

spiral staircase n Wendeltreppe die.

spire [spaɪə'] n Turmspitze die.

spirit ['spɪrɪt] n - **1.** [soul, ghost] Geist der; **to be with sb in ~** in Gedanken bei jm sein - **2.** (U) [courage] Mut der - **3.** (U) [attitude] Geist der; [mood] Stimmung die; **fighting ~** Kampfgeist der - **4.** [essence] Geist der, Sinn der. ⬥ **spirits** npl - **1.** [mood] Stimmung die, Laune die; **to be in high/low ~s** guter/ schlechter Laune sein - **2.** [alcohol] Spirituosen pl.

spirited ['spɪrɪtɪd] adj [action, defence] beherzt; [performance] lebendig; [debate] lebhaft.

spirit level n Wasserwaage die.

spiritual ['spɪrɪtʃʊəl] adj - **1.** [of the spirit] geistig, spirituell - **2.** [religious] geistlich.

spit [spɪt] (Br pt & pp spat, Am pt & pp spit) ⬥ n - **1.** [saliva] Spucke die - **2.** [skewer] Spieß der ⬥ vi [from mouth] spucken ⬥ v impers Br [rain lightly] tröpfeln.

spite [spaɪt] ⬥ n (U) Bosheit die ⬥ vt ärgern. ⬥ **in spite of** prep trotz (+ G).

spiteful ['spaɪtfʊl] adj boshaft.

spittle ['spɪtl] n Spucke die.

splash [splæʃ] ⬥ n - **1.** [sound] Platschen das - **2.** [patch - of colour] Tupfen der; [- of light] Fleck der ⬥ vt - **1.** [subj: person] bespritzen - **2.** [subj: water] spritzen auf (+ A) - **3.** [apply haphazardly] klatschen ⬥ vi - **1.** [person]: **to ~ about** OR **around** herumlspritzen - **2.** [water, liquid]: **to ~ on/against sthg** an etw (A)/gegen etw klatschen.

spleen [spli:n] n - **1.** ANAT Milz die - **2.** (U) fig [anger]: **to vent one's ~ on sb** seine Wut OR schlechte Laune an jm ausllassen.

splendid ['splendɪd] adj - **1.** [very good] großartig - **2.** [magnificent, beautiful] prachtvoll.

splint [splɪnt] n Schiene die.

splinter ['splɪntə'] ⬥ n Splitter der ⬥ vi [glass, bone, wood] splittern.

split [splɪt] (pt & pp split; cont -ting) ⬥ n - **1.** [crack] Spalt der - **2.** [tear] Riss der - **3.** [division, schism] Spaltung die, Riss der ⬥ vt - **1.** [crack, divide] spalten; **the collision ~ the ship in two** bei dem Zusammenstoß zerbrach das Schiff in zwei Teile - **2.** [tear] zerreißen - **3.** [share] teilen; **we'll ~ the costs** wir werden uns die Kosten teilen; **to ~ the difference** sich in der Mitte treffen ⬥ vi - **1.** [crack - wood, stone] sich spalten; [- ship] auseinanderlbrechen - **2.** [tear - fabric] reißen; [- seam, trousers] platzen; **the bag ~ open** die Tasche platzte auf - **3.** [divide] sich teilen. ⬥ **split up** vi sich trennen; **to ~ up with sb** sich von jm trennen.

split second n Bruchteil der einer Sekunde.

splutter ['splʌtə'] vi - **1.** [person speaking, engine] stottern - **2.** [fire, flames] zischen.

spoil [spɔɪl] (pt & pp -ed OR spoilt) vt - **1.** [ruin] verderben; **to ~ sb's fun** jm den Spaß verderben - **2.** [pamper] verwöhnen; **to be ~t for choice** die Qual der Wahl haben. ⬥ **spoils** npl Beute die.

spoiled [spɔɪld] adj = spoilt.

spoilsport ['spɔɪlspɔ:t] n Spielverderber der, -in die.

spoilt [spɔɪlt] ⬥ pt & pp ▷ spoil ⬥ adj - **1.** [child] verzogen - **2.** [food, dinner] verdorben.

spoke [spəʊk] ⬥ pt ▷ speak ⬥ n Speiche die.

spoken ['spəʊkn] pp ▷ speak.

spokesman ['spəʊksmən] (pl -men [-mən]) n Sprecher der.

spokeswoman [ˈspəʊksˌwʊmən]   (*pl* -women [-ˌwɪmɪn]) *n* Sprecherin *die*.

sponge [spʌndʒ] (*Br cont* spongeing, *Am cont* sponging) ◇ *n* - **1**. [for cleaning, washing] Schwamm *der* - **2**. [cake] Biskuitkuchen *der* ◇ *vt* [face] ablwischen; [wall, car] mit einem Schwamm ablwaschen ◇ *vi inf:* **to ~ off sb** jm auf der Tasche liegen.

sponge bag *n Br* Kulturbeutel *der*.

sponge cake *n* Biskuitkuchen *der*.

sponsor [ˈspɒnsər] ◇ *n* - **1**. [of team, film, TV programme] Sponsor *der* - **2**. [of student, museum, for charity] Förderer *der*, -in *die* ◇ *vt* - **1**. [team, film, TV programme] sponsern - **2**. [student, museum, for charity] finanziell unterstützen - **3**. [bill, appeal, proposal] unterstützen.

sponsored walk [ˌspɒnsəd-] *n* Wohltätigkeitsmarsch *der*.

sponsorship [ˈspɒnsəʃɪp] *n (U)* finanzielle Unterstützung.

spontaneous [spɒnˈteɪnjəs] *adj* spontan.

spooky [ˈspuːkɪ] *adj inf* unheimlich.

spool [spuːl] *n* Spule *die*.

spoon [spuːn] *n* Löffel *der*.

spoon-feed *vt* - **1**. [feed with spoon] füttern - **2**. *fig* [students, pupils] gängeln.

spoonful [ˈspuːnfʊl] (*pl* -s OR spoonsful) *n* Löffel *der*; **a ~ of salt** ein Löffel Salz.

sporadic [spəˈrædɪk] *adj* sporadisch; [showers, shooting] vereinzelt.

sport [spɔːt] *n* - **1**. [games] Sport *der*; [type of sport] Sportart *die*; **she's good at ~** sie ist sportlich - **2**. *dated* [cheerful person]: **he's a (good) ~** er ist in Ordnung.

sporting [ˈspɔːtɪŋ] *adj* - **1**. [relating to sport] sportlich; **~ event** Wettkampf *der* - **2**. [generous, fair] anständig, fair.

sports car [ˈspɔːts-] *n* Sportwagen *der*.

sportsman [ˈspɔːtsmən] (*pl* -men [-mən]) *n* Sportler *der*.

sportsmanship [ˈspɔːtsmənʃɪp] *n* sportliche Fairness.

sportswear [ˈspɔːtsweər] *n (U)* [in sport] Sportbekleidung *die*; [for leisure] Freizeitkleidung *die*.

sportswoman [ˈspɔːtsˌwʊmən] (*pl* -women [-ˌwɪmɪn]) *n* Sportlerin *die*.

sporty [ˈspɔːtɪ] *adj inf* sportlich.

spot [spɒt] ◇ *n* - **1**. [of blood, ink, paint] Fleck *der* - **2**. [pimple] Pickel *der* - **3**. *inf* [small amount]: **a few ~s of rain** ein paar Regentropfen; **a ~ of** ein bisschen, etwas; **to have a ~ of lunch** eine Kleinigkeit zu Mittag essen; **to do a ~ of work** ein bisschen arbeiten - **4**. [place] Stelle *die*; **what a lovely ~!** was für ein schönes Plätzchen!; **to do sthg on the ~** etw auf der Stelle tun ◇ *vt* [notice] sehen; [mistake] finden.

spot check *n* Stichprobe *die*.

spotless [ˈspɒtlɪs] *adj* [clean] blitzsauber.

spotlight [ˈspɒtlaɪt] *n* [in theatre, TV] Scheinwerfer *der*; [at home] Spot *der*; **to be in the ~** *fig* im Rampenlicht stehen.

spotted [ˈspɒtɪd] *adj* [material, garment] gepunktet.

spotty [ˈspɒtɪ] *adj Br* [skin] pick(e)lig.

spouse [spaʊs] *n* Gatte *der*, -tin *die*.

spout [spaʊt] ◇ *n* - **1**. [of kettle, watering can] Schnabel *der* - **2**. [of water - from fountain, geyser] Strahl *der* ◇ *vi:* **to ~ from** OR **out of sthg** [liquid] aus etw hervorlspritzen; [flames] aus etw hervorlschießen.

sprain [spreɪn] ◇ *n* Verstauchung *die* ◇ *vt:* **to ~ one's ankle/wrist** sich *(D)* den Knöchel/das Handgelenk verstauchen.

sprang [spræŋ] *pt* ⊳ spring.

sprawl [sprɔːl] *vi* - **1**. [person] sich auslstrecken - **2**. [city, suburbs] sich unkontrolliert auslbreiten.

spray [spreɪ] ◇ *n* - **1**. [droplets] Sprühnebel *der*; [of sea] Gischt *die* - **2**. [pressurized liquid] Spray *das* - **3**. [can, container] Sprühdose *die* ◇ *vt* - **1**. [plant, field] besprühen; [crops] spritzen; **to ~ one's hair** sich das Haar mit Haarspray stylen - **2**. [paint, perfume] sprühen.

spread [spred] (*pt & pp* spread) ◇ *n* - **1**. CULIN [paste] Brotaufstrich *der*; **cheese ~** Streichkäse *der* - **2**. [diffusion, growth] Ausbreitung *die* - **3**. [range] Umfang *der* - **4**. *Am* [bedspread] Decke *die* ◇ *vt* - **1**. [open out - map, tablecloth, arms] auslbreiten; [- fingers, legs] spreizen - **2**. [apply]: **to ~ sthg with butter** etw mit Butter bestreichen; **to ~ butter/jam on one's bread** Butter/Marmelade aufs Brot streichen - **3**. [diffuse, disseminate] verbreiten - **4**. [over a surface, share evenly] verteilen ◇ *vi* - **1**. [disease, fire, rumour, news] sich auslbreiten - **2**. [water, cloud] sich ausldehnen. ◆ **spread out** *vi* [disperse] sich verteilen.

spread-eagled [-ˌiːgld] *adj:* **to be** OR **lie ~** ausgestreckt dalliegen.

spreadsheet [ˈspredʃiːt] *n* COMPUT Tabelle *die*.

spree [spriː] *n:* **to go on a spending/shopping ~** groß einkaufen gehen.

sprightly [ˈspraɪtlɪ] *adj* [old person] rüstig.

spring [sprɪŋ] (*pt* sprang; *pp* sprung) ◇ *n* - **1**. [season] Frühling *der*, Frühjahr *das*; **in (the) ~** im Frühling, im Frühjahr - **2**. [coil] Feder *die* - **3**. [water source] Quelle *die* ◇ *vi* - **1**. [leap] springen; **to ~ to one's feet** auflspringen - **2**. [be released]: **the branch sprang back** der Zweig schnellte zurück; **to ~ shut** zulfallen; **to ~ open** auflspringen - **3**. [originate]: **to ~ from sthg** aus etw entstehen. ◆ **spring up** *vi* - **1**. [get up] auflspringen - **2**. [grow in size, height] wachsen - **3**. [appear - building] aus dem Boden schießen; [- wind] auflkommen; [- problem] aufltauchen.

springboard ['sprɪŋbɔːd] *n lit & fig* Sprungbrett *das*.

spring-clean *vt*: **to ~ the house** Frühjahrsputz machen.

spring onion *n Br* Frühlingszwiebel *die*.

springtime ['sprɪŋtaɪm] *n*: **in (the) ~** im Frühling.

springy ['sprɪŋɪ] *adj* [carpet, mattress, step] federnd; [ground, rubber] elastisch.

sprinkle ['sprɪŋkl] *vt* [liquid] sprenkeln, sprengen; [powder, salt] streuen; **to ~ sthg with sthg** [liquid] etw mit etw (be)sprengen; [powder, salt] etw mit etw bestreuen.

sprinkler ['sprɪŋklə'] *n* **- 1.** [for gardens] Rasensprenger *der* **- 2.** [for extinguishing fires]: **a ~ system** Sprinkleranlage *die*.

sprint [sprɪnt] ◇ *n* [race] Lauf *der*, Sprint *der*; **to break into** OR **put on a ~** losspurten ◇ *vi* rennen; SPORT sprinten.

sprout [spraʊt] ◇ *n* **- 1.** CULIN: **(brussels) ~** Rosenkohl *der* **- 2.** [shoot] Trieb *der* ◇ *vt* **- 1.** [germinate] keimen lassen **- 2.** [grow - leaves, shoots] (aus)treiben; [- beard, moustache] sich *(D)* wachsen lassen ◇ *vi* **- 1.** [germinate] keimen **- 2.** [grow] wachsen, sprießen.

spruce [spruːs] ◇ *adj* gepflegt ◇ *n* [tree] Fichte *die*. ◆ **spruce up** *vt sep* [room, house] auf Vordermann bringen.

sprung [sprʌŋ] *pp* ▷ spring.

spry [spraɪ] *adj* rüstig.

spun [spʌn] *pt & pp* ▷ spin.

spur [spɜː'] ◇ *n* **- 1.** [incentive]: **~ (to sthg)** Ansporn *der* OR Antrieb *der* (für etw) **- 2.** [on rider's boot] Sporn *der* ◇ *vt* **- 1.** [horse] die Sporen geben *(+ D)* **- 2.** [encourage]: **to ~ sb to do sthg** jn anlspornen, etw zu tun. ◆ **on the spur of the moment** *adv* ganz spontan. ◆ **spur on** *vt sep* [encourage] anlspornen.

spurn [spɜːn] *vt* verschmähen.

spurt [spɜːt] ◇ *n* **- 1.** [of water, steam] Strahl *der* **- 2.** [of energy] Anfall *der* **- 3.** [burst of speed] Spurt *der* ◇ *vi*: **to ~ (out of** OR **from sthg)** [water, steam, flames] herauslschießen (aus etw).

spy [spaɪ] ◇ *n* Spion *der*, -in *die* ◇ *vt* sichten ◇ *vi* **- 1.** [work as spy] spionieren **- 2.** [watch secretly]: **to ~ on sb** jm nachlspionieren.

spying ['spaɪɪŋ] *n* Spionage *die*.

Sq., sq. *abbr of* square.

squabble ['skwɒbl] ◇ *n* Zank *der* ◇ *vi*: **to ~ (about** OR **over sthg)** sich (wegen etw) zanken.

squad [skwɒd] *n* **- 1.** [police department] Dezernat *das* **- 2.** MIL Trupp *der* **- 3.** SPORT Mannschaft *die*.

squadron ['skwɒdrən] *n* [of fighter planes] Staffel *die*; [of warships] Geschwader *das*.

squalid ['skwɒlɪd] *adj* **- 1.** [filthy - place] dre-

ckig und verkommen; [- conditions] erbärmlich **- 2.** [base, dishonest] schmutzig.

squall [skwɔːl] *n* [storm] Bö(e) *die*.

squalor ['skwɒlə'] *n* Schmutz *der*.

squander ['skwɒndə'] *vt* [money] verschwenden; [opportunity] vertun.

square [skweə'] ◇ *adj* **- 1.** [in shape] quadratisch; [face, brackets] eckig **- 2.** *Br* [MATH - referring to area] Quadrat-; [- when each side is of same length] im Quadrat **- 3.** [not owing money]: **to be ~** quitt sein ◇ *n* **- 1.** [shape] Quadrat *das* **- 2.** [in town, city] Platz *der* **- 3.** *inf* [unfashionable person] Spießer *der*, -in *die* ◇ *vt* **- 1.** MATH [multiply by itself] quadrieren; **4 ~d is 16** 4 hoch 2 ist 16, 4 (zum) Quadrat ist 16 **- 2.** [balance, reconcile]: **to ~ sthg with sthg** etw mit etw in Einklang bringen. ◆ **square up** *vi* [settle up]: **to ~ up with sb** mit jm ablrechnen.

squarely ['skweəlɪ] *adv* **- 1.** [directly] genau **- 2.** [honestly] offen und ehrlich.

squash [skwɒʃ] ◇ *n* **- 1.** SPORT Squash *das* **- 2.** *Br* [drink]: **lemon/orange ~** Fruchtsaftgetränk mit Zitronen-/Orangengeschmack **- 3.** *Am* [vegetable] Kürbis *der* ◇ *vt* [hat] zerdrücken; [box] zusammenldrücken; [fruit] zerquetschen.

squat [skwɒt] ◇ *adj* gedrungen ◇ *vi* [crouch]: **to ~ (down)** sich (hinl)hocken; **he was ~ting** er hockte.

squatter ['skwɒtə'] *n Br* [in empty building] Hausbesetzer *der*, -in *die*.

squawk [skwɔːk] *n* [of bird] Kreischen *das*.

squeak [skwiːk] *n* **- 1.** [of animal] Quieken *das* **- 2.** [of door, hinge] Quietschen *das*.

squeal [skwiːl] *vi* [person] kreischen; [animal] quieken.

squeamish ['skwiːmɪʃ] *adj* zart besaitet.

squeeze [skwiːz] ◇ *n* [pressure]: **to give sthg a ~** etw drücken ◇ *vt* **- 1.** [press firmly] drücken; [orange, lemon] auslpressen **- 2.** [extract, press out - juice] herauslpressen; **to ~ sthg out of sthg** etw aus etw drücken **- 3.** [cram]: **to ~ sthg into sthg** etw in etw *(A)* hineinlpressen OR zwängen.

squelch [skweltʃ] *vi* [through mud] patschen.

squid [skwɪd] *(pl inv* OR **-s)** *n* Tintenfisch *der*.

squiggle ['skwɪgl] *n* Schnörkel *der*.

squint [skwɪnt] ◇ *n* MED: **to have a ~** schielen ◇ *vi* **- 1.** MED schielen **- 2.** [halfclose one's eyes]: **to ~ at sthg** etw blinzelnd anlsehen.

squirm [skwɜːm] *vi lit & fig* sich winden.

squirrel [*Br* 'skwɪrəl, *Am* 'skwɜːrəl] *n* Eichhörnchen *das*.

squirt [skwɜːt] ◇ *vt* [force out] spritzen ◇ *vi*: **to ~ (out of sthg)** (herausl)spritzen (aus etw).

Sr *abbr of* senior.

Sri Lanka [ˌsriːˈlæŋkə] *n* Sri Lanka *nt*.

St - 1. *abbr of* saint - 2. *abbr of* street.

stab [stæb] ⟨⟩ *n* - 1. [with knife] Stich der - 2. *inf* [attempt]: **to have a ~ at sthg** etw probieren - 3. [twinge]: **a ~ of pain** ein stechender Schmerz ⟨⟩ *vt* - 1. [with knife] einlstechen (auf (+ A)); **to ~ sb to death** jn erstechen; **to ~ sb in the back** *fig* jm in den Rücken fallen - 2. [with fork] auflspießen.

stable ['steɪbl] ⟨⟩ *adj* - 1. [steady, unchanging] stabil; [job] sicher - 2. [solid, anchored - ladder, shelf] stabil; [- ship, aircraft] sicher - 3. [person, personality]: **(mentally) ~** innerlich gefestigt ⟨⟩ *n* [building] Reitstall der; [horses] Rennstall der.

stack [stæk] ⟨⟩ *n* [pile] Stoß der, Stapel der ⟨⟩ *vt* [pile up] stapeln.

stadium ['steɪdjəm] (*pl* -diums OR -dia [-djə]) *n* Stadion das.

staff [stɑːf] ⟨⟩ *n* [employees] Personal das ⟨⟩ *vt* mit Personal auslstatten.

stag [stæg] (*pl inv* OR -s) *n* [deer] Hirsch der.

stage [steɪdʒ] ⟨⟩ *n* - 1. [period, phase] Stadium das, Phase die; **at this ~** zu diesem Zeitpunkt - 2. [platform] Bühne die ⟨⟩ *vt* - 1. THEATRE auflführen, inszenieren - 2. [organize] veranstalten.

stagecoach ['steɪdʒkəʊtʃ] *n* Postkutsche die.

stage fright *n* Lampenfieber das.

stagger ['stægər] ⟨⟩ *vt* - 1. [astound] die Sprache verschlagen (+ D) - 2. [arrange at different times] staffeln ⟨⟩ *vi* [totter] schwanken.

stagnant ['stægnənt] *adj* - 1. [water] stehend; [air] verbraucht - 2. [business, career, economy] stagnierend.

stagnate [stæg'neɪt] *vi* - 1. [water] stehen; [air] verbraucht werden - 2. [business, career, economy] stagnieren.

stag night, stag party *n feucht-fröhlicher Männerabend, mit dem ein Bräutigam am Abend vor der Hochzeit sein Junggesellendasein beschließt.*

staid [steɪd] *adj* [person] seriös, gesetzt; [appearance, attitude] bieder.

stain [steɪn] ⟨⟩ *n* [mark] Fleck der ⟨⟩ *vt* [discolour] Flecken hinterlassen auf (+ D).

stained glass *n* farbiges Glas.

stainless steel ['steɪnlɪs-] *n* Edelstahl der.

stain remover [-ˌrɪmuːvər] *n* Fleckenentferner der.

stair [steər] ⟨⟩ *n* [step] Stufe die. **stairs** *npl* Treppe die.

staircase ['steəkeɪs] *n* Treppe die.

stairway ['steəweɪ] *n* Treppenaufgang der, Treppe die.

stairwell ['steəwel] *n* Treppenhaus das.

stake [steɪk] ⟨⟩ *n* - 1. [share]: **to have a ~ in sthg** einen Anteil an etw (D) haben - 2. [wooden post] Pfahl der - 3. [in gambling] Einsatz der ⟨⟩ *vt* - 1. [risk]: **to ~ sthg on sthg** etw auf etw (A) setzen - 2. [in gambling] setzen. **to be at stake** *adv* auf dem Spiel stehen.

stale [steɪl] *adj* [bread] altbacken; [cake] trocken; [water, beer, air] abgestanden.

stalemate ['steɪlmeɪt] *n* - 1. [deadlock] Sackgasse die - 2. CHESS Patt das.

stalk [stɔːk] ⟨⟩ *n* Stiel der; [of cabbage] Strunk der ⟨⟩ *vt* [animal] sich heranlpirschen an (+ A); [person] nachlstellen (+ D).

stall [stɔːl] ⟨⟩ *n* - 1. [table] Stand der - 2. [in stable] Box die ⟨⟩ *vt* AUT ablwürgen ⟨⟩ *vi* - 1. AUT ablsterben - 2. [delay]: **to ~ for time** versuchen, Zeit zu schinden. **stalls** *npl* Br [in theatre, cinema] Parkett das.

stallion ['stæljən] *n* Hengst der.

stamina ['stæmɪnə] *n* Ausdauer die.

stammer ['stæmər] ⟨⟩ *n* Stottern das; **to have a ~** stottern ⟨⟩ *vi* stottern.

stamp [stæmp] ⟨⟩ *n* - 1. [postage stamp] Briefmarke die - 2. [rubber stamp] Stempel der ⟨⟩ *vt* - 1. [produce by stamping] auflstempeln - 2. [stomp]: **to ~ one's foot** auflstampfen (mit dem Fuß) ⟨⟩ *vi* - 1. [walk] stampfen, trampeln - 2. [with one foot]: **to ~ on sthg** auf etw (A) treten.

stamp album *n* Briefmarkenalbum das.

stamp-collecting [-kəˌlektɪŋ] *n* Briefmarkensammeln das.

stamped addressed envelope ['stæmptəˌdrest-] *n* Br frankierter Rückumschlag.

stampede [stæm'piːd] *n* - 1. [of animals] panische Flucht - 2. [of people] Massenandrang der.

stance [stæns] *n* - 1. [posture] Haltung die - 2. [attitude]: **~ (on)** Einstellung die (zu).

stand [stænd] (*pt & pp* stood) ⟨⟩ *n* - 1. [stall] Stand der - 2. [for umbrellas, coats, bicycle] Ständer der - 3. [at sports stadium] Tribüne die MIL & *fig*: **to make a ~** Widerstand leisten - 5. [position] Standpunkt der - 6. Am LAW Zeugenstand der ⟨⟩ *vt* - 1. [place] stellen - 2. [withstand - pressure, heat] ertragen; **I can't ~ him** ich kann ihn nicht ausstehen - 3. [put up with] auslhalten ⟨⟩ *vi* - 1. [gen] stehen; **to be ~ing** stehen - 2. [rise to one's feet] auflstehen - 3. Br LAW [be a candidate] kandidieren. **stand back** *vi* zurücklltreten. **stand by** ⟨⟩ *vt fus* - 1. [person] halten zu - 2. [promise] halten; [decision, offer] bleiben bei ⟨⟩ *vi* - 1. [in readiness] sich bereitlhalten - 2. [not intervene] daneben stehen. **stand down** *vi* [resign] zurücklltreten. **stand for** *vt fus* - 1. [signify] stehen für - 2. [tolerate] hinlnehmen. **stand in** *vi*: **to ~ in for sb** für jn einlspringen. **stand out** *vi* - 1. [be clearly visible] herauslstechen - 2. [be superior] sich ablheben. **stand up** ⟨⟩ *vt sep inf* [boyfriend, girlfriend etc] versetzen ⟨⟩ *vi* - 1. [be on one's feet] stehen - 2. [rise to one's feet] auflstehen - 3. [be upright] aufrecht stehen.

◆ **stand up for** vt fus ein|treten für.
◆ **stand up to** vt fus - **1.** [bad treatment] sich wehren gegen; [weather, heat] trotzen (+ D) - **2.** [person, boss] sich behaupten gegenüber.

standard ['stændəd] ◇ adj Standard-; [spelling, pronunciation] korrekt ◇ n - **1.** [level] Niveau das; **up to ~** der Norm entsprechend - **2.** [point of reference] Maßstab der - **3.** [flag] Fahne die. ◆ **standards** npl [principles] Wertvorstellungen pl.

standard lamp n Br Stehlampe die.
standard of living (pl standards of living) n Lebensstandard der.

standby ['stændbaɪ] (pl standbys) ◇ n [substitute] Ersatz der; **on ~** in Bereitschaft ◇ comp [ticket] Standby-.

stand-in n - **1.** [replacement] Vertretung die - **2.** [stunt person] Double das.

standing ['stændɪŋ] ◇ adj [permanent] ständig; [army] stehend ◇ n - **1.** [reputation] Ruf der - **2.** [duration] Dauer die.

standing order n Dauerauftrag der.
standing room n (U) Stehplätze pl.
standoffish [ˌstænd'ɒfɪʃ] adj kühl.
standpoint ['stændpɔɪnt] n Standpunkt der.

standstill ['stændstɪl] n: **to come to a ~** [stop moving] stehen bleiben; fig zum Erliegen kommen.

stand-up adj: **~ comedian** Komiker der, -in die; **~ comedy** Comedyshow die.

stank [stæŋk] pt ⊳ **stink**.

staple ['steɪpl] ◇ adj [principal] Haupt- ◇ n - **1.** [for paper] (Heft)klammer die - **2.** [principal commodity] Grundnahrungsmittel das ◇ vt zusammen|heften.

stapler ['steɪplər] n Hefter der.

star [stɑːr] ◇ n - **1.** [gen] Stern - **2.** [celebrity] Star der ◇ comp [performer] Star-; ◆ **attraction** Spitzenattraktion die ◇ vi [actor]: **to ~ (in)** die Hauptrolle spielen (in (+ D)). ◆ **stars** npl [horoscope] Sterne pl.

starboard ['stɑːbəd] ◇ adj Steuerbord- ◇ n: **to ~** nach Steuerbord.

starch [stɑːtʃ] n Stärke die.

stardom ['stɑːdəm] n Ruhm der.

stare [steər] ◇ n starrer Blick ◇ vi starren; **to ~ at sb/sthg** jn/etw an|starren.

stark [stɑːk] ◇ adj - **1.** [landscape, room] kahl - **2.** [fact, truth] nackt; [contrast] scharf ◇ adv: **~ naked** splitternackt.

starling ['stɑːlɪŋ] n Star der.

starry ['stɑːrɪ] adj sternenklar.

Stars and Stripes n: **the ~** das Sternenbanner.

start [stɑːt] ◇ n - **1.** [beginning] Anfang der, Beginn der - **2.** [jump] Schreck(en) der - **3.** SPORT Start der - **4.** [lead, advantage] Vorsprung der ◇ vt - **1.** [begin] an|fangen, beginnen; **to ~ work** anfangen zu arbeiten; **to**

~ a race ein Rennen starten; **to ~ doing** OR **to do sthg** an|fangen, etw zu tun; **it ~ed me thinking** es gab mir zu denken - **2.** [engine, car] starten; [cassette player] ein|schalten; **to ~ a fire** [arson] Feuer legen; [for warmth] Feuer machen - **3.** [business] gründen; [shop] auf|machen; [society] ins Leben rufen ◇ vi - **1.** [begin] beginnen, an|fangen; **to ~ with sb/sthg** mit jm/etw beginnen; **~ing from next week** ab nächster Woche; **to ~ with** [at first] zuerst; [in the first place] erstens; [when ordering meal] als Vorspeise - **2.** [car, engine] starten; [tape] laufen - **3.** [on journey] auf|brechen - **4.** [jump] zusammen|schrecken.

◆ **start off** ◇ vt sep [meeting, discussion] beginnen; [rumour] in Umlauf bringen; **this should be enough to ~ you off** das sollte für den Anfang reichen ◇ vi - **1.** [begin] beginnen, an|fangen - **2.** [on journey] auf|brechen.

◆ **start out** vi - **1.** [in life, career] an|fangen; **to ~ out as sthg** ursprünglich etw sein - **2.** [on journey] auf|brechen. ◆ **start up** ◇ vt sep - **1.** [business] gründen; [shop] auf|machen; [society] ins Leben rufen - **2.** [car, engine] starten ◇ vi - **1.** [guns, music, noise] los|gehen - **2.** [car, engine] starten - **3.** [set up business] an|fangen.

starter ['stɑːtər] n - **1.** Br [of meal] Vorspeise die - **2.** AUT Anlasser der - **3.** SPORT [official] Starter, -in die; [competitor] Teilnehmer der, -in die.

starting point ['stɑːtɪŋ-] n Ausgangspunkt der.

startle ['stɑːtl] vt erschrecken.

startling ['stɑːtlɪŋ] adj überraschend.

starvation [stɑːˈveɪʃn] n Hunger der; **to die of ~** verhungern.

starve [stɑːv] ◇ vt [deprive of food] aus|hungern ◇ vi [have no food] hungern; [die of hunger] verhungern; **I'm starving!** ich habe einen Mordshunger.

state [steɪt] ◇ n - **1.** [condition] Zustand der - **2.**: **to get into a ~** sich auf|regen - **3.** [country, region] Staat der ◇ comp Staats- ◇ vt [declare] erklären; [specify] an|geben. ◆ **State** n [government]: **the State** der Staat. ◆ **States** npl [USA]: **the States** die Vereinigten Staaten pl.

State Department n Am Außenministerium das.

stately ['steɪtlɪ] adj [building] stattlich; [person] würdevoll.

statement ['steɪtmənt] n - **1.** [declaration & LAW] Aussage die - **2.** [from bank] Kontoauszug der.

state of mind (pl states of mind) n [mood] Verfassung die.

statesman ['steɪtsmən] (pl -men [-mən]) n Staatsmann der.

static ['stætɪk] ◇ adj [unchanging] konstant ◇ n [on TV, radio] Empfangsstörung die.

static electricity n Reibungselektrizität die.

station ['steɪʃn] <> n - 1. [for trains] Bahnhof der; [for buses] Busbahnhof der - 2. RADIO Sender der - 3. [police or fire station] Wache die - 4. [position] Platz der <> vt - 1. [position] auflstellen - 2. MIL stationieren.

stationary ['steɪʃnəri] adj stehend.

stationer ['steɪʃnəʳ] n: ~'s (shop) Schreibwarenhandlung die.

stationery ['steɪʃnəri] n (U) Schreibwaren pl.

stationmaster ['steɪʃn,mɑːstəʳ] n Bahnhofsvorsteher der, -in die.

station wagon n Am Kombiwagen der.

statistic [stə'tɪstɪk] n [number] statistisches Ergebnis; ~s Statistik die. ◆ **statistics** n (U) [science] Statistik die.

statistical [stə'tɪstɪkl] adj statistisch.

statue ['stætʃuː] n Statue die.

stature ['stætʃəʳ] n - 1. [height, size] Statur die - 2. [importance] Format das.

status ['steɪtəs] n - 1. [legal or social position] Status der - 2. [prestige] Prestige das.

status symbol n Statussymbol das.

statute ['stætjuːt] n - 1. [law] Gesetz das - 2. [of organization] Statut das.

statutory ['stætjutri] adj gesetzlich.

staunch [stɔːntʃ] <> adj treu <> vt [blood] stillen; [flow] stauen.

stave [steɪv] (pt & pp -d or stove) n MUS Notenlinien pl. ◆ **stave off** vt sep [danger, disaster] ablwenden; [hunger] lindern.

stay [steɪ] <> vi bleiben; [as guest] übernachten; **I'm ~ing at the hotel/with friends** ich wohne im Hotel/bei Freunden; **to ~ for dinner** zum Abendessen bleiben; **to ~ the night** übernachten <> n [visit] Aufenthalt der. ◆ **stay in** vi [stay at home] zu Hause bleiben. ◆ **stay on** vi bleiben. ◆ **stay out** vi - 1. [not come home]: **he ~ed out last night** er ist letzte Nacht nicht nach Hause gekommen - 2. [not get involved]: **to ~ out of sthg** sich aus etw rauslhalten. ◆ **stay up** vi - 1. [not go to bed] auflbleiben - 2. [shelf, picture] hängen bleiben; [socks] oben bleiben.

stead [sted] n: **to stand sb in good ~** jm zustatten kommen.

steadfast ['stedfɑːst] adj - 1. [supporter] treu - 2. [resolve] unerschütterlich - 3. [gaze] unverwandt.

steadily ['stedɪli] adv - 1. [improve, increase] stetig - 2. [breathe, move] gleichmäßig - 3. [look, say] ruhig.

steady ['stedi] <> adj - 1. [gradual] stetig - 2. [regular, constant] konstant - 3. [not shaking, calm] ruhig - 4. [boyfriend, job] fest - 5. [worker] zuverlässig <> vt - 1. [boat, camera] ins Gleichgewicht bringen - 2. [voice, nerves] beruhigen.

steak [steɪk] n - 1. [meat] Steak das - 2. [fish] Fischsteak das.

steal [stiːl] (pt stole; pp stolen) <> vt lit & fig stehlen; **to ~ sthg from sb** jm etw stehlen <> vi [move stealthily] schleichen.

stealthy ['stelθɪ] adj verstohlen.

steam [stiːm] <> n Dampf der <> vt CULIN dämpfen <> vi dämpfen. ◆ **steam up** <> vt sep [window] beschlagen lassen <> vi [window, glasses] beschlagen.

steamboat ['stiːmbəʊt] n Dampfer der.

steam engine n Dampflok die.

steamroller ['stiːm,rəʊləʳ] n Dampfwalze die.

steamy ['stiːmi] adj - 1. [room] voll Dampf - 2. inf [erotic] heiß.

steel [stiːl] <> n Stahl der <> comp Stahl-.

steelworks ['stiːlwɜːks] (pl inv) n Stahlwerk das.

steep [stiːp] <> adj - 1. [gen] steil - 2. inf [expensive] gesalzen <> vt [soak] einlweichen.

steeple ['stiːpl] n Kirchturm der.

steer ['stɪəʳ] <> n [bullock] junger Ochse <> vt - 1. [boat] steuern; [car] lenken - 2. [person] lotsen <> vi steuern; **to ~ clear of sb/sthg** fig einen großen Bogen um jn/etw machen.

steering ['stɪərɪŋ] n Lenkung die.

steering wheel n Lenkrad das.

stem [stem] <> n - 1. [of plant, glass] Stiel der - 2. [of pipe] Hals der - 3. GRAMM Stamm der <> vt [stop] einldämmen. ◆ **stem from** vt fus herlrühren von.

stench [stentʃ] n Gestank der.

stencil ['stensl] <> n Schablone die <> vt [design, pattern] mit einer Schablone zeichnen; [words] mit einer Schablone schreiben.

step [step] <> n - 1. [pace, stage] Schritt der; **to be in ~/out of ~ with public opinion** fig im Einklang/nicht im Einklang mit der öffentlichen Meinung sein; **to keep in ~ with sthg** mit etw Schritt halten; **~ by ~** Schritt für Schritt - 2. [measure] Maßnahme die; **it's a ~ in the right direction** das ist immerhin ein Anfang - 3. [of staircase, ladder] Stufe die <> vi treten; **~ this way** folgen Sie mir bitte; **she ~ped off the bus** sie stieg aus dem Bus; **to ~ on/in sthg** auf/in etw (A) treten; **to ~ on it** inf [drive fast] aufs Gas drücken; [hurry up] hinlmachen. ◆ **steps** npl - 1. [stairs] Stufen pl - 2. Br [stepladder] Trittleiter die. ◆ **step down** vi [resign] zurückltreten. ◆ **step in** vi [intervene] einlschreiten. ◆ **step up** vt sep [increase] steigern.

stepbrother ['step,brʌðəʳ] n Stiefbruder der.

stepdaughter ['step,dɔːtəʳ] n Stieftochter die.

stepfather ['step,fɑːðəʳ] n Stiefvater der.

stepladder ['step,lædəʳ] n Trittleiter die.

stepmother ['step,mʌðə'] *n* Stiefmutter *die.*

stepping-stone ['stepɪŋ-] *n* - **1.** [in river] Trittstein *der* - **2.** *fig* [way to success] Sprungbrett *das.*

stepsister ['step,sɪstə'] *n* Stiefschwester *die.*

stepson ['stepsʌn] *n* Stiefsohn *der.*

stereo ['sterɪəʊ] (*pl* -s) ◇ *adj* Stereo- ◇ *n* - **1.** [stereo system] Stereoanlage *die* - **2.** [stereo sound] Stereo *das.*

stereotype ['sterɪətaɪp] *n* Klischee *das.*

sterile ['steraɪl] *adj* - **1.** [germ-free] steril - **2.** [man, woman, animal] unfruchtbar.

sterilize, -ise ['sterəlaɪz] *vt* sterilisieren.

sterling ['stɜːlɪŋ] ◇ *adj* - **1.** [pound]: £100 ~ 100 Pfund Sterling - **2.** [excellent] gediegen ◇ *n* (*U*) Pfund *das* Sterling.

sterling silver *n* Sterlingsilber *das.*

stern [stɜːn] ◇ *adj* streng ◇ *n* Heck *das.*

steroid ['stɪərɔɪd] *n* Steroid *das.*

stethoscope ['steθəskəʊp] *n* Stethoskop *das.*

stew [stjuː] ◇ *n* Eintopf *der* ◇ *vt* schmoren.

steward ['stjʊəd] *n* - **1.** *Br* [on plane, ship] Steward *der* - **2.** *Br* [at public event] Ordner *der*, -in *die.*

stewardess ['stjʊədɪs] *n* Stewardess *die.*

stick [stɪk] (*pt & pp* stuck) ◇ *n* - **1.** [piece of wood] Stock *der* - **2.** [of dynamite, celery, cinnamon, rhubarb] Stange *die;* [of chewing gum, chalk] Stück *das* - **3.** SPORT Schläger *der* ◇ *vt* - **1.** [with adhesive] kleben; **to ~ sthg on** OR **to sthg** etw an etw (*A*) kleben - **2.** [push, insert] stecken; **to ~ sthg in(to) sthg** etw in etw (*A*) stechen - **3.** *inf* [put] tun - **4.** *Br inf* [tolerate] ertragen ◇ *vi* - **1.** [arrow, dart, spear] stecken - **2.** [adhere]: **to ~ (to)** kleben (an OR auf (+ *D*)) - **3.** [become jammed] klemmen.

◆ **stick out** ◇ *vt sep* - **1.** [extend - tongue, head] herausstrecken; [- hand] ausstrecken - **2.** *inf* [endure]: **to ~ it out** es durchhalten ◇ *vi* - **1.** [protrude] vorstehen; [ears] abstehen - **2.** *inf* [be noticeable] auffallen.

◆ **stick to** *vt fus* [person, decision] bleiben bei; [path] bleiben auf (+ *D*); [promise] halten. ◆ **stick up** *vi* vorstehen; [hair] hochstehen. ◆ **stick up for** *vt fus* eintreten für.

sticker ['stɪkə'] *n* Aufkleber *der.*

sticking plaster ['stɪkɪŋ-] *n* Heftpflaster *das.*

stick shift *n Am* - **1.** [gear lever] Schalthebel *der* - **2.** [car] Auto *das* mit Handschaltung.

sticky ['stɪkɪ] *adj* - **1.** [hands] klebrig; **~ tape** Klebeband *das;* **~ label** Aufkleber *der* - **2.** *inf* [awkward] heikel.

stiff [stɪf] ◇ *adj* - **1.** [gen] steif; [rod, brush] hart; [shoes] fest; [drawer, door] widerspenstig - **2.** [resistance, drink] stark; [penalty] hart - **3.** [difficult] schwer ◇ *adv inf:* **to be bored**

~ sich zu Tode langweilen; **to be scared** ~ starr vor Angst sein.

stiffen ['stɪfn] ◇ *vt* - **1.** [material] steif machen - **2.** [resistance, resolve] verstärken ◇ *vi* - **1.** [gen] steif werden; [with horror] erstarren - **2.** [resistance, resolve] sich verstärken.

stifle ['staɪfl] ◇ *vt* - **1.** [suffocate] ersticken - **2.** [suppress] unterdrücken ◇ *vi* [suffocate] ersticken.

stifling ['staɪflɪŋ] *adj* drückend.

stigma ['stɪgmə] *n* - **1.** [social disgrace] Schande *die* - **2.** BOT Stigma *das.*

stile [staɪl] *n* Zaunübertritt *der.*

stiletto [stɪ'letəʊ] *n Br* [shoe] Stöckelschuh *der.*

still [stɪl] ◇ *adv* - **1.** [gen] noch; **we've ~ got ten minutes** wir haben noch zehn Minuten; **I ~ haven't seen it** ich habe es noch nicht gesehen; **~ bigger/more important** noch größer/wichtiger; **~ more money** noch mehr Geld - **2.** [even now] immer noch; **she could ~ change her mind** sie könnte es sich immer noch anders überlegen - **3.** [nevertheless] trotzdem; **you ~ have to pay** Sie müssen trotzdem zahlen - **4.** [motionless]: **to stand ~** stillstehen; **sit ~!** sitz still! ◇ *adj* - **1.** [motionless] bewegungslos; **please be ~!** sitz/steh bitte still! - **2.** [calm, quiet] ruhig - **3.** [not windy] windstill - **4.** [not fizzy] ohne Kohlensäure ◇ *n* - **1.** PHOT Standfoto *das* - **2.** [for making alcohol] Destillierapparat *der.*

stillborn ['stɪlbɔːn] *adj* tot geboren.

still life (*pl* -s) *n* Stillleben *das.*

stilted ['stɪltɪd] *adj* gespreizt.

stilts ['stɪlts] *npl* - **1.** [for person] Stelzen *pl* - **2.** [for building] Pfähle *pl.*

stimulate ['stɪmjʊleɪt] *vt* - **1.** [interest] anlregen; [growth, economy] anlkurbeln - **2.** [person - physically] erregen; [- mentally] stimulieren.

stimulating ['stɪmjʊleɪtɪŋ] *adj* - **1.** [physically] belebend - **2.** [mentally] stimulierend.

stimulus ['stɪmjʊləs] (*pl* -li [-laɪ]) *n* - **1.** [gen] Anreiz *der* - **2.** BIOL Reiz *der.*

sting [stɪŋ] (*pt & pp* stung) ◇ *n* - **1.** [wound, pain, mark] Stich *der* - **2.** [part of bee, wasp, scorpion] Stachel *der* ◇ *vt* - **1.** [subj: bee, wasp, scorpion] stechen; **I was stung by the nettles** ich habe mich an den Brennnesseln verbrannt - **2.** *fig* [subj: remark, criticism] schmerzen ◇ *vi* [bee, wasp, scorpion] stechen; [nettle, smoke, eyes, skin] brennen.

stingy ['stɪndʒɪ] *adj inf* geizig.

stink [stɪŋk] (*pt* stank OR stunk; *pp* stunk) ◇ *n* Gestank *der* ◇ *vi* [smell] stinken.

stint [stɪnt] ◇ *n* [period of time] Zeit *die;* **he did a two-year ~ as editor** er arbeitete zwei Jahre lang als Redakteur ◇ *vi:* **to ~ on sthg** mit etw sparen.

stipulate ['stɪpjʊleɪt] *vt* festlegen.

stir [stɜːʳ] ⋄ *n* [excitement] Aufsehen *das* ⋄ *vt* - 1. [mix] umrühren - 2. [subj: wind] spielen mit - 3. [excite] bewegen ⋄ *vi* - 1. [move] sich bewegen - 2. [emotion] wach werden. ◆ **stir up** *vt sep* - 1. [dust, mud] aufwühlen - 2. [trouble, feelings, memories] wachrufen.

stirrup ['stɪrəp] *n* Steigbügel *der*.

stitch [stɪtʃ] ⋄ *n* - 1. [in sewing, for wound] Stich *der*; [in knitting] Masche *die* - 2. [pain]: **to have a ~** Seitenstechen haben ⋄ *vt* nähen.

stoat [stəʊt] *n* Hermelin *das*.

stock [stɒk] ⋄ *n* - 1. [supply] Vorrat *der* - 2. (U) COMM [of shop] Lagerbestand *der*; **in ~** vorrätig; **out of ~** nicht vorrätig - 3. FIN: **~s and shares** Wertpapiere und Aktien - 4. (U) [ancestry] Herkunft *die* - 5. CULIN Brühe *die* - 6. [livestock] Nutzvieh *das* - 7. *phr*: **to take ~ (of)** Bilanz ziehen (über (+ A)) ⋄ *adj* [typical] stereotyp ⋄ *vt* - 1. [have in stock] auf Lager haben - 2. [shelves] auffüllen; [lake with fish] bestücken. ◆ **stock up** *vi*: **to ~ up (on** OR **with)** sich eindecken (mit).

stockbroker ['stɒk,brəʊkəʳ] *n* Börsenmakler *der*, -in *die*.

stock cube *n* Br Brühwürfel *der*.

stock exchange *n* Börse *die*.

stockholder ['stɒk,həʊldəʳ] *n* Am Aktionär *der*, -in *die*.

Stockholm ['stɒkhəʊm] *n* Stockholm *nt*.

stocking ['stɒkɪŋ] *n* Strumpf *der*.

stock market *n* Börse *die*.

stockpile ['stɒkpaɪl] ⋄ *n* Lager *das* ⋄ *vt* horten.

stocktaking ['stɒk,teɪkɪŋ] *n* (U) Inventur *die*.

stocky ['stɒkɪ] *adj* stämmig.

stodgy ['stɒdʒɪ] *adj* [food] schwer.

stoical ['stəʊɪkl] *adj* stoisch.

stoke [stəʊk] *vt* [fire] schüren.

stole [stəʊl] *pt* ⟃ steal.

stolen ['stəʊln] *pp* ⟃ steal.

stolid ['stɒlɪd] *adj* stur.

stomach ['stʌmək] ⋄ *n* - 1. [organ] Magen *der* - 2. [belly] Bauch *der* ⋄ *vt* [tolerate] ertragen.

stomachache ['stʌməkeɪk] *n* Magenschmerzen *pl*.

stomach upset *n* Magenverstimmung *die*.

stone [stəʊn] (*pl sense 3 only inv* OR *-s*) ⋄ *n* - 1. [gen] Stein *der* - 2. [unit of measurement] = 6,35 kg ⋄ *comp* aus Stein; [bridge, wall] Stein- ⋄ *vt* mit Steinen bewerfen.

stone-cold *adj* eiskalt.

stonework ['stəʊnwɜːk] *n* Mauerwerk *das*.

stood [stʊd] *pt* & *pp* ⟃ stand.

stool [stuːl] *n* [seat] Hocker *der*.

stoop [stuːp] ⋄ *n* [bent back]: **to walk with**

a ~ gebeugt gehen ⋄ *vi* - 1. [bend forwards] sich bücken - 2. [have a stoop] gebeugt gehen.

stop [stɒp] ⋄ *n* - 1. [of bus] Haltestelle *die*; [of train] Station *die* - 2. [in journey] Halt *der*; [longer] Aufenthalt *der* - 3. [standstill]: **to put a ~ to sthg** einer Sache (D) ein Ende machen - 4. [in punctuation] Punkt *der* ⋄ *vt* - 1. [halt - person, car] anlhalten; [- machine, engine] ablstellen; [- ball] stoppen; **to ~ doing sthg** auflhören, etw zu tun; **to ~ smoking** mit dem Rauchen auflhören - 2. [prevent] verhindern; **to ~ sb from doing sthg** jn daran hindern, etw zu tun; **to ~ sthg from happening** verhindern, dass etw geschieht - 3. [hole, gap] stopfen ⋄ *vi* - 1. [come to an end] auflhören - 2. [halt] anlhalten; [walker, machine, watch] stehen bleiben; [on journey] Halt machen - 3. [stay] bleiben. ◆ **stop off** *vi* Halt machen. ◆ **stop up** *vt sep* [block] zulstopfen.

stopgap ['stɒpgæp] *n* Notlösung *die*.

stopover ['stɒp,əʊvəʳ] *n* Zwischenstation *die*.

stoppage ['stɒpɪdʒ] *n* - 1. [strike] Streik *der* - 2. Br [deduction] Abzug *der*.

stopper ['stɒpəʳ] *n* Pfropfen *der*.

stopwatch ['stɒpwɒtʃ] *n* Stoppuhr *die*.

storage ['stɔːrɪdʒ] *n* - 1. [act of storing] Lagerung *die* - 2. COMPUT Speichern *das*.

store [stɔːʳ] ⋄ *n* - 1. *esp Am* [shop] Laden *der*, Geschäft *das*; [department store] Kaufhaus *das* - 2. [supply]: **~ of sthg** Vorrat an etw (D) - 3. [storage place] Lager *das* ⋄ *vt* - 1. [keep, save - address, details] auflbewahren; [- goods, provisions] lagern; [- furniture] einlstellen - 2. COMPUT speichern. ◆ **store up** *vt sep* [information] anlsammeln; **to ~ food** Lebensmittelvorräte anlegen.

storekeeper ['stɔː,kiːpəʳ] *n* Am Ladenbesitzer *der*, -in *die*.

storeroom ['stɔːrʊm] *n* Lagerraum *der*.

storey Br (*pl* -s), **story** Am (*pl* -ies) ['stɔːrɪ] *n* Stockwerk *das*.

stork [stɔːk] *n* Storch *der*.

storm [stɔːm] ⋄ *n* - 1. [bad weather] Sturm *der* - 2. [violent reaction - of abuse, tears] Flut *die*; [- of protest] Sturm *der* ⋄ *vt* - 1. MIL stürmen - 2. [say angrily] toben ⋄ *vi* [go angrily] stürmen.

stormy ['stɔːmɪ] *adj lit & fig* stürmisch.

story ['stɔːrɪ] *n* - 1. [tale, history] Geschichte *die* - 2. [article - in newspaper] Artikel *der*; [- on TV/radio news] Bericht *der* - 3. *euphemism* [lie] Märchen *das* - 4. *Am* = storey.

stout [staʊt] ⋄ *adj* - 1. [corpulent] korpulent - 2. [strong] kräftig; [boots] fest - 3. [brave] tapfer ⋄ *n* Starkbier *das*.

stove [stəʊv] ⋄ *pt* & *pp* ⟃ stave ⋄ *n*

- 1. [for cooking] Herd der **- 2.** [for heating] Ofen der.

stow [stəʊ] vt: **to ~ sthg (away)** etw verstauen.

stowaway ['stəʊəweɪ] n blinder Passagier.

straddle ['strædl] vt **- 1.** [subj: person - chair] rittlings sitzen auf (+ D); [- gap] breitbeinig stehen über (+ D) **- 2.** [subj: bridge] überspannen; **the town ~s the border** der Ort erstreckt sich zu beiden Seiten der Grenze.

straggle ['strægl] vi **- 1.** [buildings] verstreut liegen; [plant] wuchern **- 2.** [person, group] zurücklbleiben.

straggler ['stræglə'] n Nachzügler der, -in die.

straight [streɪt] <> adj **- 1.** [not curved, level, upright] gerade **- 2.** [not curly] glatt **- 3.** [honest, frank] ehrlich, offen **- 4.** [tidy] ordentlich; **to put a room ~** ein Zimmer auflräumen **- 5.** [simple - exchange] einfach; [- choice] klar **- 6.** [undiluted] pur **- 7.** phr: **to get sthg ~** etw klarlstellen <> adv **- 1.** [in a straight line, upright] gerade **- 2.** [directly, immediately] direkt **- 3.** [honestly, frankly] offen **- 4.** [undiluted] pur. **straight off** adv sofort. **straight out** adv rundheraus.

straightaway [ˌstreɪtə'weɪ] adv sofort.

straighten ['streɪtn] vt **- 1.** [tidy - dress] gerade ziehen; [- room, desk] auflräumen **- 2.** [make straight] begradigen **- 3.** [make level] auslrichten. **straighten out** vt sep [sort out] klären.

straightforward [ˌstreɪt'fɔːwəd] adj **- 1.** [easy] einfach **- 2.** [honest, frank] offen, ehrlich.

strain [streɪn] <> n **- 1.** [gen] Belastung die **- 2.** MED [of muscle] Zerrung die; [of back] Überanstrengung die <> vt **- 1.** [work hard - eyes] überanstrengen **- 2.** MED [injure]: **to ~ a muscle/one's back** sich einen Muskel zerren/seinen Rücken überanstrengen **- 3.** [overtax - resources] überbeanspruchen; [- patience] auf die Probe stellen **- 4.** [drain] durch ein Sieb gießen **- 5.** TECH [rope, girder, ceiling] belasten <> vi: **to ~ to do sthg** sich anlstrengen, etw zu tun. **strains** npl literary [of music] Klänge pl.

strained [streɪnd] adj **- 1.** [forced] angestrengt **- 2.** [tense] angespannt **- 3.** MED [sprained] gezerrt.

strainer ['streɪnə'] n Sieb das.

strait [streɪt] n GEOGR Meerenge die. **straits** npl: **in dire** OR **desperate ~s** in einer Notlage.

straitjacket ['streɪtˌdʒækɪt] n Zwangsjacke die.

straitlaced [ˌstreɪt'leɪst] adj pej spießig.

strand [strænd] n Faden der; [of hair] Strähne die.

stranded ['strændɪd] adj [person, car] festsitzend.

strange [streɪndʒ] adj **- 1.** [unusual, unexpected] seltsam **- 2.** [unfamiliar] fremd.

stranger ['streɪndʒə'] n [unknown person] Unbekannte der, die; **she's a complete ~ to me** ich kenne sie überhaupt nicht **- 2.** [person from elsewhere] Fremde der, die.

strangle ['stræŋgl] vt **- 1.** [kill] erwürgen **- 2.** fig [stifle] ersticken.

strap [stræp] <> n **- 1.** [for carrying] Riemen der **- 2.** [for fastening - of dress, bra] Träger der; [- of watch] Armband das <> vt [fasten]: **to ~ sthg (on)to sthg** etw auf etw (A) schnallen.

strapping ['stræpɪŋ] adj stramm.

strategic [strə'tiːdʒɪk] adj strategisch.

strategy ['strætɪdʒɪ] n Strategie die.

straw [strɔː] n **- 1.** [dried corn] Stroh das **- 2.** [for drinking] Strohhalm der.

strawberry ['strɔːbərɪ] <> n Erdbeere die <> comp Erdbeer-.

stray [streɪ] <> adj **- 1.** [cat, dog] streunend **- 2.** [bullet] verirrt <> vi **- 1.** [person, animal] herumlstreunen; **to ~ from the path** vom Weg ablweichen **- 2.** [thoughts, mind] ablschweifen.

streak [striːk] <> n **- 1.** [mark, line] Streifen der; **a ~ of lightning** ein Blitz(strahl) **- 2.** [in character] Zug der <> vi [move quickly] sausen.

stream [striːm] <> n **- 1.** [gen] Strom der **- 2.** [brook] Bach der **- 3.** [of abuse, complaints] Flut die **- 4.** Br SCH Leistungsgruppe die <> vt Br SCH in Leistungsgruppen einlteilen <> vi strömen.

streamer ['striːmə'] n [for party] Luftschlange die.

streamlined ['striːmlaɪnd] adj **- 1.** [aerodynamic] stromlinienförmig **- 2.** [efficient] rationalisiert.

street [striːt] n Straße die.

streetcar ['striːtkɑː'] n Am Straßenbahn die.

street lamp, street light n Straßenlaterne die.

street plan n Stadtplan der.

strength [streŋθ] n **- 1.** [gen] Stärke die **- 2.** (U) [confidence, courage] Kraft die **- 3.** [solidity] Stabilität die.

strengthen ['streŋθn] vt **- 1.** [gen] stärken **- 2.** [team, structure, resolve] verstärken **- 3.** [friendship, ties, bond] festigen **- 4.** [make braver, more confident] bestärken.

strenuous ['strenjʊəs] adj [exercise] anstrengend; [effort] gewaltig.

stress [stres] <> n **- 1.** [emphasis]: **to lay** OR **put ~ on sthg** etw besonders betonen **- 2.** [tension, anxiety] Stress der **- 3.** TECH [physical pressure]: **~ (on sthg)** Druck der (auf etw (A)) **- 4.** LING [on word, syllable] Betonung die <> vt [emphasize & LING] betonen.

stressful ['stresfʊl] adj stressig.

stretch [stretʃ] <> n **- 1.** [area] Stück das

- 2. [period of time] Zeitspanne *die*; **for a five-year ~** für fünf Jahre ◇ *vt* **- 1.** [pull longer or wider] dehnen **- 2.** [pull taut] spannen **- 3.** [extend to full length] auslstrecken **- 4.** [rules, meaning, truth]: **to ~ the rules** eine Ausnahme machen; **to ~ the truth** übertreiben **- 5.** [budget, resources] strecken **- 6.** [provide challenge for] fordern ◇ *vi* **- 1.** [area]: **to ~ over** sich ausldehnen über *(+ A)*; **to ~ from ... to** reichen von ... bis **- 2.** [person, animal] sich strecken **- 3.** [material, elastic] sich dehnen. ◆ **stretch out** ◇ *vt sep* [hold out] auslstrecken ◇ *vi* [lie down] sich auslstrecken.

stretcher ['stretʃəʳ] *n* Trage *die*.

strew [struː] *(pt* -ed; *pp* strewn [struːn] OR -ed) *vt* [scatter untidily]: **to be ~n with sthg** [freckles, confetti] mit etw übersät sein; **the streets were ~n with litter** die Straßen waren voller Müll.

stricken ['strikn] *adj*: **to be ~ by** OR **with sthg** [doubt, horror, panic] von etw erfüllt sein; [illness] an etw *(D)* leiden.

strict [strikt] *adj* **- 1.** [severe] streng **- 2.** [exact, precise] genau; **in the ~est sense of a word** im engsten Sinne des Wortes.

strictly ['striktli] *adv* **- 1.** [severely, rigidly, absolutely] streng **- 2.** [precisely, exactly] genau; **~ speaking** genau genommen **- 3.** [exclusively] ausschließlich.

stride [straid] *(pt* strode; *pp* stridden ['stridn]) ◇ *n* [step] Schritt *der*; **to take sthg in one's ~** *fig* mit etw leicht fertig werden ◇ *vi* schreiten.

strident ['straidnt] *adj* **- 1.** [voice, sound] durchdringend **- 2.** [demand] lautstark.

strike [straik] *(pt & pp* struck) ◇ *n* **- 1.** [refusal to work, do sthg] Streik *der*; **to be (out) on ~** streiken; **to go on ~** in Streik treten **- 2.** MIL [attack] Angriff *der* **- 3.** [find] Fund *der* ◇ *vt* **- 1.** [hit deliberately] schlagen; [hit accidentally - car] fahren gegen; [- boat] auflaufen auf *(+ A)* **- 2.** [subj: hurricane, disaster, lightning] treffen **- 3.** [subj: thought]: **it ~s me that ...** mir fällt auf, dass ...; **he ~s me as very capable** er scheint mir sehr fähig zu sein **- 4.** [bargain] auslhandeln **- 5.** [match] anlzünden **- 6.** [chime] schlagen ◇ *vi* **- 1.** [stop working] streiken **- 2.** [happen suddenly - disaster, hurricane] loslbrechen; [- lightning] einlschlagen **- 3.** [attack] anlgreifen **- 4.** [chime] schlagen. ◆ **strike down** *vt sep* niederlschlagen. ◆ **strike out** ◇ *vt sep* durchlstreichen ◇ *vi* **- 1.** [head out] loslziehen **- 2.** [do sthg different]: **to ~ out on one's own** eigene Wege gehen. ◆ **strike up** *vt fus* **- 1.** [friendship, conversation] anlfangen **- 2.** [music] anlfangen zu spielen.

striker ['straikəʳ] *n* **- 1.** [person on strike] Streikende *der*, *die* **- 2.** FTBL Stürmer *der*, *-in die*.

striking ['straikiŋ] *adj* **- 1.** [noticeable, unusual] auffallend **- 2.** [attractive] umwerfend.

string [striŋ] *(pt & pp* strung) *n* **- 1.** [gen] Schnur *die*; **to pull ~s** Beziehungen spielen lassen **- 2.** [of onions] Zopf *der*; **~ of pearls** [necklace] Perlenkette *die* **- 3.** [series] Reihe *die*; [for musical instrument, tennis racket] Saite *die*; [for bow] Sehne *die*. ◆ **strings** *npl* MUS: **the ~s** die Streicher *pl*. ◆ **string out** *vt sep* [disperse]: **to be strung out** verteilt sein. ◆ **string together** *vt sep fig* [words, sentences] aneinander fügen.

string bean *n* Stangenbohne *die*.

stringent ['strindʒənt] *adj* streng.

strip [strip] ◇ *n* **- 1.** [of fabric, paper, land, water] Streifen *der* **- 2.** *Br* SPORT [clothes] Trikot *das* ◇ *vt* **- 1.** [undress] auslziehen **- 2.** [remove - paint] ablkratzen; [- wallpaper] ablziehen ◇ *vi* [undress] sich auslziehen. ◆ **strip off** *vi* sich auslziehen.

strip cartoon *n Br* Comic *der*.

stripe [straip] *n* **- 1.** [band of colour] Streifen *der* **- 2.** [sign of rank] Ärmelstreifen *der*.

striped [straipt] *adj* gestreift.

stripper ['stripəʳ] *n* **- 1.** [performer of striptease] Stripper *der*, *-in die* **- 2.** [liquid] Entferner *der*; [tool] Spachtel *der*.

striptease ['stripti:z] *n* Striptease *der*.

strive [straiv] *(pt* strove; *pp* striven ['strivn]) *vi fml*: **to ~ for sthg** nach etw streben; **to ~ to do sthg** bemüht sein, etw zu tun.

strode [strəud] *pt* ▷ stride.

stroke [strəuk] ◇ *n* **- 1.** MED Schlaganfall *der* **- 2.** [of pen, brush] Strich *der* **- 3.** [in swimming - movement] Zug *der*; [- style] Stil *der* **- 4.** [in rowing, in ball game, of clock] Schlag *der* **- 5.** *Br* TYPO [oblique] Schrägstrich *der* **- 6.** [piece]: **a ~ of genius** ein Geniestreich; **a ~ of luck** ein Glücksfall; **at a ~** mit einem Streich ◇ *vt* streicheln.

stroll [strəul] ◇ *n* Spaziergang *der* ◇ *vi* spazieren gehen.

stroller ['strəuləʳ] *n Am* [for baby] Sportwagen *der*.

strong [stroŋ] *adj* **- 1.** [gen] stark; **~ point** Stärke *die* **- 2.** [physically powerful, healthy] kräftig **- 3.** [solid, sturdy] stabil; [measures] energisch **- 4.** [argument, case, evidence] überzeugend.

stronghold ['stroŋhəuld] *n fig* Hochburg *die*.

strongly ['stroŋli] *adv* **- 1.** [sturdily, solidly] solide **- 2.** [in degree or intensity] stark **- 3.** [support] energisch; **do you feel ~ about it?** ist es Ihnen wichtig?

strong room *n* Tresorraum *der*.

strove [strəuv] *pt* ▷ strive.

struck [strʌk] *pt & pp* ▷ strike.

structure ['strʌktʃəʳ] *n* **- 1.** [organization, arrangement] **Struktur** *die* - **2.** [building, construction] **Konstruktion** *die*.

struggle ['strʌgl] ⬦ *n* Kampf *der;* **a ~ for sth** ein Kampf um etw; **it will be a ~ to finish on time** wir werden uns sehr anstrengen müssen, um rechtzeitig fertig zu werden ⬦ *vi* - **1.** [try hard, strive] kämpfen; **to ~ for sth** um etw kämpfen; **she ~d to reach the switch** sie hatte Mühe, an den Schalter zu kommen - **2.** [fight]: **to ~ (with sb)** (mit jm) kämpfen.

strum [strʌm] *vt* klimpern; [guitar] klimpern auf (+ *D*).

strung [strʌŋ] *pt & pp* ▭ string.

strut [strʌt] ⬦ *n* CONSTR Strebe *die* ⬦ *vi* stolzieren.

stub [stʌb] ⬦ *n* - **1.** [of cigarette, pencil] Stummel *der* - **2.** [of ticket, cheque] Abschnitt *der* ⬦ *vt*: **to ~ one's toe** sich den Zeh stoßen. ➡ **stub out** *vt sep* ausdrücken.

stubble ['stʌbl] *n* (*U*) Stoppeln *pl*.

stubborn ['stʌbən] *adj* - **1.** [person - resolute] hartnäckig; [- unreasonable] dickköpfig, stur - **2.** [stain] hartnäckig.

stuck [stʌk] ⬦ *pt & pp* ▭ stick ⬦ *adj* - **1.** [fixed tightly, jammed - window, lid] verklemmt; [- finger, toe, garment] eingeklemmt - **2.** [stumped]: **I'm ~** ich komme nicht weiter - **3.** [stranded]: **he got ~ in Birmingham** er saß in Birmingham fest - **4.** [in an unpleasant situation, trapped]: **to be ~** festsitzen.

stuck-up *adj inf pej* hochnäsig.

stud [stʌd] *n* - **1.** [metal decoration] Niete *die* - **2.** [earring] Ohrstecker *der* - **3.** Br [on boot, shoe] Stollen - **4.** [place for breeding horses] Gestüt *das*.

studded ['stʌdɪd] *adj*: **~ with sth** mit etw besetzt.

student ['stjuːdnt] ⬦ *n* - **1.** [at college, university] Student *der*, -in *die* - **2.** [scholar]: **to be a ~ of history/human nature** sich für Geschichte/die menschliche Natur interessieren ⬦ *comp* Studenten-.

student loan *n* Br Studentendarlehen *das*.

studio ['stjuːdɪəʊ] (*pl* -s) *n* - **1.** [artist's workroom] Atelier *das* - **2.** CINEMA, RADIO & TV Studio *das*.

studio flat *Br*, **studio apartment** *Am n* Atelierwohnung *die*.

studious ['stjuːdɪəs] *adj* fleißig.

study ['stʌdɪ] ⬦ *n* - **1.** (*U*) [learning] Studium *das* - **2.** [piece of research] Untersuchung *die* - **3.** [room] Arbeitszimmer *das* ⬦ *vt & vi* studieren.

stuff [stʌf] ⬦ *n* (*U*) *inf* - **1.** [matter, things, substance] Zeug *das* - **2.** [belongings] Sachen *pl* ⬦ *vt* - **1.** [push, put] stopfen - **2.** [fill, cram]: **to ~ sth (with sth)** etw (mit etw) voll stopfen - **3.** CULIN füllen.

stuffed [stʌft] *adj* - **1.** [filled, crammed]:

~ with sth mit etw voll gestopft - **2.** *inf* [with food] voll - **3.** CULIN gefüllt - **4.** [animal] ausgestopft.

stuffing ['stʌfɪŋ] *n* (*U*) - **1.** [for furniture] Polsterung *die* - **2.** [for toys & CULIN] Füllung *die*.

stuffy ['stʌfɪ] *adj* - **1.** [room] stickig - **2.** [formal, old-fashioned] spießig.

stumble ['stʌmbl] *vi* - **1.** [trip] stolpern - **2.** [hesitate, make mistake] stocken. ➡ **stumble across, stumble on** *vt fus* stoßen auf (+ *A*); [person] stolpern über (+ *A*).

stumbling block ['stʌmblɪŋ-] *n* Hindernis *das*.

stump [stʌmp] ⬦ *n* [remaining part] Stumpf *der* ⬦ *vt* [subj: question, problem]: **to be ~ed by a problem/question** keine Lösung/Antwort wissen.

stun [stʌn] *vt* - **1.** [knock unconscious] bewusstlos schlagen - **2.** [shock, surprise] verblüffen.

stung [stʌŋ] *pt & pp* ▭ sting.

stunk [stʌŋk] *pt & pp* ▭ stink.

stunning ['stʌnɪŋ] *adj* - **1.** [beautiful] atemberaubend - **2.** [shocking] schrecklich; [surprising] sensationell.

stunt [stʌnt] ⬦ *n* - **1.** [for publicity] Werbetrick *der* - **2.** CINEMA Stunt *der* ⬦ *vt* hemmen.

stunt man *n* Stuntman *der*.

stupefy ['stjuːpɪfaɪ] *vt* - **1.** [tire, bore] abstumpfen lassen - **2.** [surprise] verblüffen.

stupendous [stjuːˈpendəs] *adj inf* - **1.** [wonderful] toll - **2.** [very large] enorm.

stupid ['stjuːpɪd] *adj* - **1.** [foolish] dumm - **2.** *inf* [wretched, damned] blöd.

stupidity [stjuːˈpɪdətɪ] *n* Dummheit *die*.

sturdy ['stɜːdɪ] *adj* kräftig; [furniture, bridge] stabil.

stutter ['stʌtər] *vi* [in speaking] stottern.

sty [staɪ] *n* Schweinestall *der*.

stye [staɪ] *n* Gerstenkorn *das*.

style [staɪl] ⬦ *n* - **1.** [gen] Stil *der;* **in ~** im großen Stil; **that's not my ~** das ist nicht meine Art - **2.** [fashion, design] Mode *die* ⬦ *vt* [hair] stylen.

stylish ['staɪlɪʃ] *adj* elegant.

stylist ['staɪlɪst] *n* [hairdresser] Stylist *der*, -in *die*.

stylus ['staɪləs] (*pl* -es) *n* [on record player] Nadel *die*.

suave [swɑːv] *adj* gewandt; *pej* glatt.

sub [sʌb] *n inf* - **1.** SPORT (*abbr of* substitute) Ersatz *der* - **2.** *abbr of* submarine - **3.** Br *abbr of* subscription.

subconscious [ˌsʌbˈkɒnʃəs] ⬦ *adj* unterbewusst ⬦ *n*: **the ~** das Unterbewusstsein.

subcontract [ˌsʌbkənˈtrækt] *vt* an (ein) Subunternehmen vergeben.

subdue [səbˈdjuː] *vt* - **1.** [enemy, rioters, crowds] unterwerfen - **2.** [feelings, passions] unter|drücken.

subdued [səb'dju:d] *adj* - **1.** [person] ruhig - **2.** [sound, feelings, lighting, colour] gedämpft.

subject [*adj, n & prep* 'sʌbdʒekt, *vt* səb'dʒekt] <> *adj* - **1.** [subordinate]: ~ **to sthg** etw *(D)* unterworfen - **2.** [liable]: ~ **to sthg** [disease] anfällig für etw; ~ **to tax** steuerpflichtig; **prices ~ to change** COMM Preisänderungen vorbehalten <> *n* - **1.** [topic under consideration] Thema *das;* **he is the ~ of an inquiry** es wird eine Untersuchung über ihn durchgeführt - **2.** GRAMM Subjekt *das* - **3.** SCH & UNIV Fach *das* - **4.** [citizen] Staatsbürger *der,* -in *die* <> *vt* - **1.** [subjugate] unterwerfen - **2.** [force to experience]: **to ~ sb to sthg** [punishment, inquiry] einer Sache *(D)* unterziehen. ▸ **subject to** *prep* [depending on] abhängig von.

subjective [səb'dʒektɪv] *adj* subjektiv.

subject matter *n* Stoff *der.*

subjunctive [səb'dʒʌŋktɪv] *n* GRAMM: ~ **(mood)** Konjunktiv *der.*

sublet [ˌsʌb'let] *(pt & pp* sublet) *vt* untervermieten.

sublime [sə'blaɪm] *adj* [wonderful] erhaben.

submachine gun [ˌsʌbmə'ʃiːn-] *n* Maschinenpistole *die.*

submarine [ˌsʌbmə'riːn] *n* U-Boot *das.*

submerge [səb'mɜːdʒ] <> *vt* - **1.** [flood] überschwemmen - **2.** [plunge into liquid] eintauchen <> *vi* tauchen.

submission [səb'mɪʃn] *n* - **1.** [obedience, capitulation] Unterwerfung *die* - **2.** [presentation] Einreichen *das.*

submissive [səb'mɪsɪv] *adj* unterwürfig.

submit [səb'mɪt] <> *vt* [present] einlreichen <> *vi* [admit defeat] sich ergeben; **to ~ to sb/sthg** sich jm/etw unterwerfen.

subordinate [sə'bɔːdɪnət] <> *adj fml* [less important]: ~ **(to sthg)** (einer Sache *(D)*) untergeordnet <> *n* Untergebene *der, die.*

subpoena [sə'piːnə] *(pt & pp* -ed) LAW <> *n* Vorladung *die* <> *vt* vorlladen.

subscribe [səb'skraɪb] *vi* - **1.** [to magazine, newspaper]: **to ~ to sthg** etw abonnieren - **2.** [to view, belief]: **to ~ to sthg** sich einer Sache *(D)* anlschließen.

subscriber [səb'skraɪbəʳ] *n* - **1.** [to magazine, newspaper] Abonnent *der,* -in *die* - **2.** [to service] Teilnehmer *der,* -in *die.*

subscription [səb'skrɪpʃn] *n* [to newspaper, magazine] Abonnement *das;* [to club, organization] Mitgliedsbeitrag *der.*

subsequent ['sʌbsɪkwənt] *adj* nachfolgend.

subsequently ['sʌbsɪkwəntlɪ] *adv* anschließend.

subservient [səb'sɜːvjənt] *adj* [servile]: ~ **(to sb)** (jm gegenüber) unterwürfig.

subside [səb'saɪd] *vi* - **1.** [grow less intense]

nachllassen - **2.** [grow quieter] leiser werden - **3.** [sink - building, ground] sich senken; [- river] sinken.

subsidence [səb'saɪdns, 'sʌbsɪdns] *n (U)* CONSTR Bodensenkung *die.*

subsidiary [səb'sɪdjərɪ] <> *adj* untergeordnet <> *n*: ~ **(company)** Tochter(gesellschaft) *die.*

subsidize, -ise ['sʌbsɪdaɪz] *vt* subventionieren.

subsidy ['sʌbsɪdɪ] *n* Subvention *die.*

substance ['sʌbstəns] *n* - **1.** [material, tangibility] Substanz *die* - **2.** [essence, gist] Kern *der* - **3.** *(U)* [importance] Gewicht *das.*

substantial [səb'stænʃl] *adj* - **1.** [large, considerable] beträchtlich - **2.** [solid, well-built] solide.

substantially [səb'stænʃəlɪ] *adv* - **1.** [quite a lot] beträchtlich - **2.** [mainly] im Wesentlichen.

substitute ['sʌbstɪtjuːt] <> *n* - **1.** [replacement]: ~ **(für)** Ersatz *der* (für) - **2.** SPORT Ersatzspieler *der,* -in *die* <> *vt*: **to ~ sb/sthg for sb/ sthg** jn/etw durch jn/etw ersetzen.

subtitle ['sʌbˌtaɪtl] *n* [of book] Untertitel *der.* ▸ **subtitles** *npl* CINEMA Untertitel *pl.*

subtle ['sʌtl] *adj* - **1.** [nuance, difference] fein; [colour, music] zart - **2.** [comment, method] subtil.

subtlety ['sʌtltɪ] *n* - **1.** [of difference] Feinheit *die;* [of colour, music] Zartheit *die* - **2.** [of comment, method] Subtilität *die.*

subtotal ['sʌbˌtəʊtl] *n* Zwischensumme *die.*

subtract [səb'trækt] *vt*: **to ~ sthg (from sthg)** etw (von etw) subtrahieren OR abziehen.

subtraction [səb'trækʃn] *n* Subtraktion *die.*

suburb ['sʌbɜːb] *n* Vorort *der.* ▸ **suburbs** *npl* Vororte *pl.*

suburban [sə'bɜːbn] *adj* - **1.** [of suburbs] Vorort- - **2.** *pej* [boring] spießig.

suburbia [sə'bɜːbɪə] *n (U)* die Vororte *pl.*

subversive [səb'vɜːsɪv] *adj* subversiv.

subway ['sʌbweɪ] *n* - **1.** *Br* [underground walkway] Unterführung *die* - **2.** *Am* [underground railway] U-Bahn *die.*

succeed [sək'siːd] <> *vt* nachlfolgen (+ *D*); [thing, event] folgen (+ *D*) <> *vi* [be successful] erfolgreich sein; **he ~ed in persuading her** es gelang ihm, sie zu überreden.

succeeding [sək'siːdɪŋ] *adj fml* nachfolgend.

success [sək'ses] *n* Erfolg *der.*

successful [sək'sesfʊl] *adj* erfolgreich.

succession [sək'seʃn] *n* [series] Folge *die.*

successive [sək'sesɪv] *adj* aufeinander folgend.

succinct [sək'sɪŋkt] *adj* prägnant.

succumb [sə'kʌm] *vi* [to a bad influence]: **to ~ to sthg** einer Sache *(D)* erliegen.

such [sʌtʃ] ◇ *adj* - **1.** [gen] solche, -r, -s; **~ people** solche Leute; **I've never heard ~ nonsense** ich habe noch nie so einen Unsinn gehört!; **shoplifting and ~ crimes** Ladendiebstahl und derartige Delikte; **there's no ~ thing** so etwas gibt es nicht; **countries ~ as Spain and France** Länder wie Spanien und Frankreich - **2.** [whatever]: **I've spent ~ money as I had** ich habe mein weniges Geld ausgegeben - **3.** [so great]: **there are ~ differences that ...** die Unterschiede sind so groß, dass ...; **~ was their skill that ...** sie waren so geschickt, dass ... ◇ *adv*: **~ big houses** so große Häuser, solche großen Häuser; **~ a man** ein solcher Mann, so ein Mann; **it's ~ a lovely day** es ist so ein schöner Tag; **~ a thing should never have happened** so etwas hätte nie passieren dürfen; **~ a lot** so viel; **~ a long time** so lange; **in ~ a way that ...** auf solche Weise, dass ... ◇ *pron*: **and ~ (like)** und dergleichen. ◆ **as such** *adv* als solche, -r, -s. ◆ **such and such** *adj* das und das; **on ~ and ~ a day** an dem und dem Tag.

suck [sʌk] *vt* - **1.** [by mouth] saugen; [lollipop, thumb] lutschen - **2.** [draw in] einlsaugen.

sucker ['sʌkə'] *n* - **1.** [suction pad] Saugnapf *der* - **2.** *inf* [gullible person] Depp *der*.

suction ['sʌkʃn] *n* - **1.** [drawing in] Sogwirkung *die* - **2.** [adhesion] Saugwirkung *die*.

Sudan [suː'dɑːn] *n* Sudan *der*.

sudden ['sʌdn] *adj* plötzlich; **all of a ~** plötzlich.

suddenly ['sʌdnli] *adv* plötzlich.

sue [suː] *vt* verklagen; **to ~ sb for sthg** [libel *etc*] jn wegen etw verklagen; [sum of money] jn auf etw *(A)* verklagen.

suede [sweid] *n* Wildleder *das*.

suet ['soit] *n* Nierenfett *das*.

suffer ['sʌfə'] ◇ *vt* erleiden ◇ *vi* leiden; **to ~ from sthg** MED an etw *(D)* leiden.

sufferer ['sʌfrə'] *n*: **rheumatism ~** Rheumakranke *der, die*; **hay fever ~** an Heuschnupfen Leidende *der, die*.

suffering ['sʌfrɪŋ] *n* Leiden *das*.

suffice [sə'fais] *vi* *fml* genügen.

sufficient [sə'fiʃnt] *adj* genügend.

sufficiently [sə'fiʃntli] *adv* genug.

suffocate ['sʌfəkeit] *vt & vi* ersticken.

suffuse [sə'fjuːz] *vt*: **~d with sthg** von etw durchdrungen.

sugar ['ʃʊgə'] ◇ *n* Zucker *der* ◇ *vt* zuckern.

sugar beet *n (U)* Zuckerrübe *die*.

sugarcane ['ʃʊgəkein] *n* Zuckerrohr *das*.

sugary ['ʃʊgəri] *adj* [high in sugar] süß.

suggest [sə'dʒest] *vt* - **1.** [propose] vorlschlagen - **2.** [imply] anldeuten.

suggesting

Kann ich Ihnen helfen? Can I help you?

Was kann ich für Sie tun? How can I be of help?

Wenn Sie möchten, übernehme ich das für Sie. I'll do that for you if you like.

Ich schlage vor, wir gehen alle zusammen ins Kino. Why don't we all go to the movies?

Ich hätte da eine Idee. I've got an idea.

suggestion [sə'dʒestʃn] *n* - **1.** [proposal, idea] Vorschlag *der* - **2.** *(U)* [implication]: **there was no ~ of corruption** nichts deutete auf Korruption hin.

suggestive [sə'dʒestɪv] *adj* - **1.** [implying sexual connotation] anzüglich - **2.** [implying a certain conclusion]: **to be ~ of sthg** auf etw *(A)* hinldeuten - **3.** [reminiscent]: **to be ~ of sthg** an etw *(A)* denken lassen.

suicide ['soisaid] *n* *lit & fig* Selbstmord *der*; **to commit ~** Selbstmord begehen.

suit [suːt] ◇ *n* - **1.** [matching clothes] Anzug *der*; [for woman] Kostüm *das* - **2.** [in cards] Farbe *die* - **3.** LAW Prozess *der* ◇ *vt* - **1.** [look attractive on] stehen *(+ D)* - **2.** [be convenient or appropriate on] passen *(+ D)*; **~ yourself!** mach, was du willst! ◇ *vi*: **does that ~?** passt dir das?

suitable ['suːtəbl] *adj*: **~ (for)** geeignet (für).

suitably ['suːtəbli] *adv* [dressed] passend; [impressed] gehörig.

suitcase ['suːtkeis] *n* Koffer *der*.

suite [swiːt] *n* - **1.** [of rooms] Suite *die* - **2.** [of furniture] Garnitur *die*.

suited ['suːtid] *adj* - **1.** [suitable]: **to be ~ to/ for sthg** für etw geeignet sein - **2.** [compatible]: **to be well/ideally ~** gut/ideal zusammenpassen.

sulfur *n Am* = sulphur.

sulk [sʌlk] *vi* schmollen.

sulky ['sʌlki] *adj* [remark] beleidigt; [child] schmollend; **to be in a ~ mood** schmollen.

sullen ['sʌlən] *adj* missmutig.

sulphur *Br*, **sulfur** *Am* ['sʌlfə'] *n* Schwefel *der*.

sultana [səl'tɑːnə] *n Br* [dried grape] Sultanine *die*.

sultry ['sʌltri] *adj* - **1.** [weather, day] schwül - **2.** [woman] sinnlich.

sum [sʌm] *n* Summe *die*. ◆ **sum up** *vt sep & vi* [summarize] zusammenlfassen.

summarize, -ise ['sʌməraiz] *vt & vi* zusammenlfassen.

summary ['sʌməri] *n* Zusammenfassung *die*.

summer ['sʌmə'] ◇ *n* Sommer *der*; **in (the) ~** im Sommer ◇ *comp* Sommer-.

summerhouse ['sʌməhaʊs, *pl* -haʊzɪz] *n* Gartenhaus *das*.

summer school *n* Ferienkurs *der*.

summertime ['sʌmətaɪm] *n*: **in (the) ~** im Sommer.

summit ['sʌmɪt] *n* [mountain top, meeting] Gipfel *der*.

summon ['sʌmən] *vt* [to sb's office] herbeizitieren; [doctor, fire brigade] rufen. ◆ **summon up** *vt sep* [courage, energy] aufbringen.

summons ['sʌmənz] (*pl* summonses) LAW ◇ *n* Vorladung *die* ◇ *vt* vorladen.

sumptuous ['sʌmptʃʊəs] *adj* [decor, fittings] prächtig; [meal] üppig; [hotel] luxuriös.

sun [sʌn] *n* Sonne *die*.

sunbathe ['sʌnbeɪð] *vi* sich sonnen.

sunbed ['sʌnbed] *n* Sonnenbank *die*.

sunburn ['sʌnbɜːn] *n (U)* Sonnenbrand *der*.

sunburned ['sʌnbɜːnd], **sunburnt** ['sʌnbɜːnt] *adj* sonnengebräunt; [excessively] sonnenverbrannt.

Sunday ['sʌndɪ] *n* Sonntag *der*; **~ lunch** Sonntagsessen *das*; *see also* Saturday.

Sunday school *n* Sonntagsschule *die*.

sundial ['sʌndaɪəl] *n* Sonnenuhr *die*.

sundown ['sʌndaʊn] *n* Sonnenuntergang *der*.

sundry ['sʌndrɪ] *adj fml* verschiedene; **all and ~** = jedermann. ◆ **sundries** *npl fml* Verschiedenes *nt*.

sunflower ['sʌn,flaʊə^r] *n* Sonnenblume *die*.

sung [sʌŋ] *pp* ⊳ sing.

sunglasses ['sʌn,glɑːsɪz] *npl* Sonnenbrille *die*.

sunk [sʌŋk] *pp* ⊳ sink.

sunlight ['sʌnlaɪt] *n* Sonnenlicht *das*.

sunny ['sʌnɪ] *adj lit & fig* sonnig; **~ side up** *Am* [fried egg] einseitig gebraten.

sunrise ['sʌnraɪz] *n* Sonnenaufgang *der*.

sunroof ['sʌnruːf] *n* [of car] Schiebedach *das*.

sunset ['sʌnset] *n* Sonnenuntergang *der*.

sunshade ['sʌnʃeɪd] *n* Sonnenschirm *der*.

sunshine ['sʌnʃaɪn] *n* Sonnenschein *der*.

sunstroke ['sʌnstrəʊk] *n* Sonnenstich *der*.

suntan ['sʌntæn] *n* Sonnenbräune *die*.

super ['suːpə^r] *adj inf* toll.

superb [suːˈpɜːb] *adj* erstklassig.

supercilious [,suːpəˈsɪlɪəs] *adj* hochnäsig.

superficial [,suːpəˈfɪʃl] *adj* oberflächlich.

superfluous [suːˈpɜːfluəs] *adj* überflüssig.

superhuman [,suːpəˈhjuːmən] *adj* übermenschlich.

superimpose [,suːpərɪmˈpəʊz] *vt*: **to ~ sthg on sthg** etw mit etw überlagern.

superintendent [,suːpərɪnˈtendənt] *n* - 1. *Br* [of police] Polizeikommissar *der*, -in *die* - 2. *fml* [of department] Direktor *der*, -in *die*.

superior [suːˈpɪərɪə^r] ◇ *adj* - 1. [better]:

~ (to) besser (als) - 2. [of high quality - goods] besonders hochwertig; **a person of ~ intelligence** ein Mensch von überragender Intelligenz - 3. [of higher rank]: **~ (to sb)** höher (als jd) - 4. *pej* [arrogant] überheblich ◇ *n* [senior] Vorgesetzte *der, die*.

superlative [suːˈpɜːlətɪv] ◇ *adj* [of the highest quality - performance] unübertrefflich; [- player] überragend ◇ *n* GRAMM Superlativ *der*.

supermarket ['suːpə,mɑːkɪt] *n* Supermarkt *der*.

supernatural [,suːpəˈnætʃrəl] *adj* übernatürlich.

superpower ['suːpə,paʊə^r] *n* Supermacht *die*.

supersede [,suːpəˈsiːd] *vt* ablösen.

supersonic [,suːpəˈsɒnɪk] *adj* Überschall-.

superstitious [,suːpəˈstɪʃəs] *adj* abergläubisch.

superstore ['suːpəstɔː^r] *n* Verbrauchermarkt *der*; **DIY ~** Heimwerkermarkt *der*.

supervise ['suːpəvaɪz] *vt* beaufsichtigen.

supervisor ['suːpəvaɪzə^r] *n* Aufsicht *die*; [of university students] Tutor *der*, -in *die*.

supper ['sʌpə^r] *n* - 1. [main evening meal] Abendessen *das* - 2. [light evening meal] Abendbrot *das*.

supple ['sʌpl] *adj* - 1. [person] beweglich - 2. [material] geschmeidig.

supplement [*n* 'sʌplɪmənt, *vb* 'sʌplɪment] ◇ *n* - 1. [addition - to charge] Zuschlag *der*; [- to diet] Ergänzung *die* - 2. [of newspaper] Beilage *die*; [in book] Nachtrag *der* ◇ *vt* ergänzen.

supplementary [,sʌplɪˈmentərɪ] *adj* [additional] zusätzlich.

supplier [səˈplaɪə^r] *n* Lieferant *der*, -in *die*.

supply [səˈplaɪ] ◇ *n* - 1. [store, reserve] Vorrat *der* - 2. [network]: **the water/electricity ~** die Wasser-/Stromversorgung - 3. *(U)* ECON Angebot *das* ◇ *vt*: **to ~ sthg (to sb)** [deliver] etw liefern (an jn); **to ~ sb (with sthg)** [deliver] jn (mit etw) beliefern; **he supplied the police with the necessary information** er lieferte der Polizei die nötigen Informationen; **to ~ sthg with sthg** etw mit etw versorgen. ◆ **supplies** *npl* Vorräte *pl*; [for office] Bürobedarf *der*; [for army] Nachschub *der*.

support [səˈpɔːt] ◇ *n* - 1. [gen] Unterstützung *die* - 2. [object, person] Stütze *die* ◇ *vt* - 1. [gen] unterstützen - 2. [physically] stützen - 3. [theory] untermauern.

supporter [səˈpɔːtə^r] *n* - 1. [of person, plan] Anhänger *der*, -in *die* - 2. SPORT Fan *der*.

suppose [səˈpəʊz] ◇ *vt* [assume] annehmen ◇ *vi* [assume]: **I ~ (so)** das nehme ich an; **I ~ not** wahrscheinlich nicht - 2. [agree]: **I ~ so** ja, gut; **I ~ not** wahrscheinlich nicht.

supposed [sə'pəʊzd] *adj* - **1.** [doubtful] angeblich - **2.** [intended]: **to be ~ to do sthg** etw tun sollen - **3.** [reputed]: **it is ~ to be good** es soll gut sein.

supposedly [sə'pəʊzɪdlɪ] *adv* angeblich.

supposing [sə'pəʊzɪŋ] *conj*: **~ you are right** ... angenommen, dass Sie Recht haben ...; **~ he came back?** wenn er nun zurückkäme?

suppress [sə'pres] *vt* unterdrücken.

supreme [su'pri:m] *adj* - **1.** [highest in rank] Ober- - **2.** [great] größte, -r, -s.

surcharge ['sɜːtʃɑːdʒ] *n*: **~ (on sthg)** Zuschlag *der* (auf etw (*A*)).

sure [ʃʊə'] <> *adj* sicher; **to be ~ of sthg** sich einer Sache (*G*) sicher sein; **with such qualifications she can be ~ of getting a job** mit so einer Qualifikation findet sie mit Sicherheit eine Stelle; **be ~ to lock the door** denke daran, die Tür abzuschließen; **to make ~ (that)** ... sicherstellen, dass ...; **I'm ~ (that)** ... ich bin (mir) sicher, dass ...; **to be ~ of o.s.** selbstsicher sein; [about specific matter] sich (*D*) seiner Sache sicher sein <> *adv* - **1.** *esp Am inf* [yes] sicher - **2.** *Am* [really] wirklich. ▶ **for sure** *adv*: **I don't know for ~** da bin ich nicht ganz sicher; **she'll come for ~** sie kommt bestimmt. ▶ **sure enough** *adv* tatsächlich.

surely ['ʃʊəlɪ] *adv* [expressing surprise] sicherlich; **you can't be serious?** das ist doch nicht dein Ernst?

surf [sɜːf] <> *n* Brandung *die* <> *vt*: **to ~ the Internet** im Internet surfen.

surface ['sɜːfɪs] <> *n lit & fig* Oberfläche *die;* **on the ~** [of person] äußerlich; **to scratch the ~ of sthg** *fig* etw oberflächlich behandeln <> *vi lit & fig* auftauchen.

surface mail *n* Post, die auf dem Land-/Seeweg befördert wird.

surfboard ['sɜːfbɔːd] *n* Surfbrett *das.*

surfeit ['sɜːfɪt] *n fml*: **~ of sthg** Übermaß *das* an etw (*D*).

surfing ['sɜːfɪŋ] *n* Surfen *das.*

surge [sɜːdʒ] <> *n* [of water] Schwall *der;* [of electricity] Stoß *der;* [of interest, support] Woge *die* <> *vi* strömen; [interest, support] anlschwellen; [sales, applications] in die Höhe schießen.

surgeon ['sɜːdʒən] *n* Chirurg *der,* -in *die.*

surgery ['sɜːdʒərɪ] *n* - **1.** MED [performing operations] Chirurgie *die;* **to have ~** operiert werden - **2.** *Br* MED [place] Praxis *die.*

surgical ['sɜːdʒɪkl] *adj* - **1.** [connected with surgery] chirurgisch - **2.** [worn as treatment] orthopädisch.

surgical spirit *n Br* Wunddesinfektionsmittel *das.*

surly ['sɜːlɪ] *adj* mürrisch.

surmount [sɜː'maʊnt] *vt* [overcome] überwinden.

surname ['sɜːneɪm] *n* Nachname *der.*

surpass [sə'pɑːs] *vt fml* [exceed] übertreffen.

surplus ['sɜːpləs] <> *adj* überschüssig <> *n*: **~ (of sthg)** Überschuss *der* (an etw (*D*)).

surprise [sə'praɪz] <> *n* Überraschung *die* <> *vt* überraschen.

---

surprise

So eine Überraschung! What a surprise!
Wer hätte das gedacht? Who would have thought it?
Was für ein Zufall! What a coincidence!
Das wundert mich. I'm amazed.
Wie merkwürdig! How strange!
Das hätte ich nicht für möglich gehalten. I would never have thought it possible.

---

surprised [sə'praɪzd] *adj* überrascht.

surprising [sə'praɪzɪŋ] *adj* überraschend.

surprisingly [sə'praɪzɪŋlɪ] *adv* überraschenderweise.

surrender [sə'rendə'] <> *n* Kapitulation *die* <> *vi* - **1.** [stop fighting]: **to ~ (to sb)** sich (jm) ergeben - **2.** *fig* [give in]: **to ~ (to sthg)** (etw (*D*)) nachlgeben.

surreptitious [ˌsʌrəp'tɪʃəs] *adj* heimlich.

surrogate ['sʌrəgeɪt] <> *adj* Ersatz- <> *n* Ersatz *der.*

surrogate mother *n* Leihmutter *die.*

surround [sə'raʊnd] *vt* - **1.** [gen] umlgeben - **2.** [trap] umzingeln.

surrounding [sə'raʊndɪŋ] *adj* [area, countryside] umliegend. ▶ **surroundings** *npl* Umgebung *die.*

surveillance [sɜː'veɪləns] *n* (*U*) Überwachung *die;* **to keep sb under ~** jn überwachen.

survey [*n* 'sɜːveɪ, *vb* sə'veɪ] <> *n* - **1.** [statistical investigation] Untersuchung *die;* [of public opinion] Umfrage *die* - **2.** [physical examination - of land] Vermessung *die;* [- of building] Begutachtung *die* <> *vt* - **1.** [contemplate] betrachten - **2.** [investigate statistically] untersuchen - **3.** [examine, assess - land] vermessen; [- building] begutachten.

surveyor [sə'veɪə'] *n* [of land] Landvermesser *der,* -in *die;* [of building] Baugutachter *der,* -in *die.*

survival [sə'vaɪvl] *n* [continuing to live] Überleben *das.*

survive [sə'vaɪv] <> *vt* überleben <> *vi* - **1.** [continue to exist] überleben - **2.** *inf* [cope successfully] es auslhalten.

survivor [sə'vaɪvə'] *n* - **1.** [person who escapes death] Überlebende *der, die* - **2.** *fig* [fighter] Kämpfernatur *die.*

susceptible [sə'septəbl] *adj* - **1.** [likely to be influenced]: **~ to sthg** empfänglich für etw - **2.** MED: **to sthg** anfällig für etw.

suspect [*adj & n* 'sʌspekt, *vb* sə'spekt] ◇ *adj* verdächtig ◇ *n* Verdächtige *der, die* ◇ *vt* - **1.** [distrust] zweifeln an (+ *D*) - **2.** [think likely] vermuten - **3.** [consider guilty]: **to ~ sb (of sthg)** jn (einer Sache (*G*)) verdächtigen.

suspend [sə'spend] *vt* - **1.** [hang] aufhängen - **2.** [temporarily discontinue] zeitweilig einstellen - **3.** [temporarily remove - from job] suspendieren; [- from school] zeitweilig von der Schule verweisen.

suspender belt [sə'spendə'-] *n Br* Strumpfhaltergürtel *der*.

suspenders [sə'spendəz] *npl* - **1.** *Br* [for stockings] Strumpfhalter *pl*, Strapse *pl* - **2.** *Am* [for trousers] Hosenträger *pl*.

suspense [sə'spens] *n (U)* Spannung *die*.

suspension [sə'spenʃn] *n* - **1.** [temporary discontinuation] Einstellung *die* - **2.** [removal - from job] Suspendierung *die*; [- from school] zeitweiliger Schulverweis - **3.** AUT Federung *die*.

suspension bridge *n* Hängebrücke *die*.

suspicion [sə'spɪʃn] *n* - **1.** *(U)* [distrust] Misstrauen *das* - **2.** [idea, theory] Verdacht *der*.

suspicious [sə'spɪʃəs] *adj* - **1.** [having suspicions] misstrauisch - **2.** [causing suspicion] verdächtig.

sustain [sə'steɪn] *vt* - **1.** [maintain - interest, opposition, activity] aufrechterhalten; [- hope] bewahren; [- rate, speed] beibehalten - **2.** [nourish – physically] ernähren - **3.** [injury, damage] davon|tragen - **4.** [withstand - weight] aus|halten.

sustenance ['sʌstɪnəns] *n (U) fml* Nahrung *die*.

SW (*abbr of* short wave) KW.

swab [swɒb] *n* [cotton wool] Tupfer *der*.

swagger ['swægə'] *vi* stolzieren.

swallow ['swɒləʊ] ◇ *n* [bird] Schwalbe *die* ◇ *vt* - **1.** [food, drink] schlucken - **2.** *fig* [accept] schlucken - **3.** *fig* [anger, tears] hinunter|schlucken ◇ *vi* schlucken.

swam [swæm] *pt* ⊳ swim.

swamp [swɒmp] ◇ *n* Sumpf *der* ◇ *vt* - **1.** [flood] unter Wasser setzen - **2.** [overwhelm]: **to ~ sb/sthg (with sthg)** jn/etw (mit etw) überfluten.

swan [swɒn] *n* [bird] Schwan *der*.

swap [swɒp] *vt* - **1.** [exchange]: **to ~ sthg (with sb)** etw (mit jm) tauschen; **to ~ sthg (over** OR **round)** etw (aus)|tauschen - **2.** [replace]: **to ~ sthg for sthg** etw gegen etw ein|tauschen.

swarm [swɔːm] *n* Schwarm *der*.

swarthy ['swɔːðɪ] *adj* dunkel.

swastika ['swɒstɪkə] *n* Hakenkreuz *das*.

swat [swɒt] *vt* tot|schlagen.

sway [sweɪ] ◇ *vt* [influence] beeinflussen ◇ *vi* sich wiegen; [drunk person] schwanken.

swear [sweə'] (*pt* swore; *pp* sworn) ◇ *vt* schwören; **to ~ to do sthg** schwören, etw zu tun ◇ *vi* - **1.** [state emphatically] schwören - **2.** [use swearwords] fluchen.

swearword ['sweəwɜːd] *n* Kraftausdruck *der*.

sweat [swet] ◇ *n* [perspiration] Schweiß *der* ◇ *vi lit & fig* schwitzen.

sweater ['swetə'] *n* Pullover *der*.

sweatshirt ['swetʃɜːt] *n* Sweatshirt *das*.

sweaty ['swetɪ] *adj* [clothes] verschwitzt; [skin] schweißnass.

swede [swiːd] *n Br* Steckrübe *die*.

Swede [swiːd] *n* Schwede *der*, -din *die*.

Sweden ['swiːdn] *n* Schweden *nt*.

Swedish ['swiːdɪʃ] ◇ *adj* schwedisch ◇ *n* [language] Schwedisch(e) *das*.

sweep [swiːp] (*pt & pp* swept) ◇ *n* - **1.** [of arm, hand] Schwung *der* - **2.** [with brush]: **to give sthg a ~** etw kehren OR fegen - **3.** [chimneysweep] Schornsteinfeger *der*, -in *die* ◇ *vt* - **1.** [with brush] fegen, kehren - **2.** [scan] ab|suchen - **3.** [spread through] überrollen.

➡ **sweep up** *vt sep & vi* [with brush] zusammen|kehren OR |-fegen.

sweeping ['swiːpɪŋ] *adj* - **1.** [effect, change] tief greifend - **2.** [statement] pauschal.

sweet [swiːt] ◇ *adj* - **1.** [gen] süß - **2.** [gentle, kind] lieb ◇ *n Br* - **1.** [candy] Bonbon *das* - **2.** [dessert] Nachtisch *der*, Dessert *das*.

sweet corn *n* Mais *der*.

sweeten ['swiːtn] *vt* [add sugar to] süßen.

sweetheart ['swiːthɑːt] *n* - **1.** [term of endearment] Liebling *der* - **2.** [boyfriend or girlfriend] Freund *der*, -in *die*.

sweetness ['swiːtnɪs] *n* - **1.** [gen] Süße *die* - **2.** [of character, voice] Liebenswürdigkeit *die*.

sweet pea *n* Wicke *die*.

swell [swel] (*pt* -ed; *pp* swollen OR -ed) ◇ *vi* - **1.** [become larger]: **to ~ (up)** an|schwellen - **2.** [fill with air - lungs, balloons] sich füllen; [- sails] sich blähen - **3.** [increase in number] an|wachsen - **4.** [become louder] an|schwellen ◇ *vt* [increase] steigern ◇ *n* [of sea]: **there is a heavy ~** es herrscht starker Seegang ◇ *adj Am inf* klasse, prima.

swelling ['swelɪŋ] *n* [on body] Schwellung *die*.

sweltering ['sweltərɪŋ] *adj* [heat] drückend; [weather, day] drückend heiß.

swept [swept] *pt & pp* ⊳ sweep.

swerve [swɜːv] *vi* [vehicle, driver] aus|schwenken.

swift [swɪft] ◇ *adj* - **1.** [fast] schnell - **2.** [prompt] prompt ◇ *n* [bird] Mauersegler *der*.

swig [swɪg] *n inf* Schluck *der*.

swill [swil] <> n (U) [pig food] Schweine-futter das <> vt Br [wash] waschen; [glass, cup] auslspülen.

swim [swim] (pt swam; pp swum) <> n: **to have a ~** schwimmen; **to go for a ~** schwimmen gehen <> vi - **1.** [move through water] schwimmen - **2.** [feel dizzy]: **my head was ~ming** mir war ganz schwindlig.

swimmer ['swimə'] n Schwimmer der, -in die.

swimming ['swimɪŋ] n Schwimmen das; **to go ~** schwimmen gehen.

swimming cap n Badekappe die.

swimming costume n Br Badeanzug der.

swimming pool n Schwimmbad das.

swimming trunks npl Badehose die.

swimsuit ['swimsuːt] n Badeanzug der.

swindle ['swindl] <> n Betrug der <> vt betrügen; **to ~ sb out of sthg** jn um etw betrügen.

swine [swain] n inf pej [person] Schwein das.

swing [swiŋ] (pt & pp swung) <> n - **1.** [child's toy] Schaukel die - **2.** [change - in opinion, mood] Umschwung der - **3.** [swaying movement] Schwingen das - **4.** inf [blow]: **to take a ~ at sb** nach jm schlagen - **5.** phr: **to be in full ~** in vollem Gange sein <> vt - **1.** [move back and forth] hin und her schwingen; [arms] schwingen mit - **2.** [turn] schwenken <> vi - **1.** [move back and forth] hin und her schwingen; [dangle - legs] baumeln - **2.** [turn]: **the door swung open** die Tür schwang auf; **he swung round** er drehte sich um - **3.** [change] umlschwenken; **the party has swung to the left** die Partei hat einen Linksschwenk gemacht.

swing bridge n Drehbrücke die.

swing door n Pendeltür die.

swingeing ['swindʒiŋ] adj esp Br [cuts] drastisch; [criticism] scharf.

swipe [swaip] <> vt - **1.** inf [steal] klauen - **2.** [plastic card] durchlziehen <> vi: **to ~ at sb** nach jm schlagen.

swirl [swɜːl] <> n Wirbel der <> vi wirbeln.

swish [swiʃ] <> adj inf [posh] schick <> vt [tail] schlagen mit.

Swiss [swis] <> adj Schweizer, schweizerisch <> n Schweizer der, -in die <> npl: **the ~** die Schweizer pl.

switch [switʃ] <> n - **1.** [control device] Schalter der - **2.** [change - of policy] Änderung die; **the ~ to a different system** die Umstellung auf ein anderes System <> vt - **1.** [transfer] wechseln; **to ~ sthg to sthg** [conversation, attention] etw auf etw (A) lenken; [allegiance] etw auf etw (A) übertragen - **2.** [swap, exchange] vertauschen; **to ~ jobs** den Arbeitsplatz wechseln. ◆ **switch off** vt sep [device] auslschalten. ◆ **switch on** vt sep [device] anlschalten.

switchboard ['switʃbɔːd] n Zentrale die.

Switzerland ['switsələnd] n Schweiz die.

swivel ['swivl] <> vt drehen <> vi sich drehen.

swivel chair n Drehstuhl der.

swollen ['swəuln] <> pp ⊳ swell <> adj [part of body] geschwollen; [river] angeschwollen; **~ with pride** stolzgeschwellt.

swoop [swuːp] <> n [raid] Razzia die <> vi [plane] einen Sturzflug machen; [bird] herablstoßen.

swop [swɒp] n, vt & vi = swap.

sword [sɔːd] n Schwert das.

swordfish ['sɔːdfɪʃ] (pl inv OR -es) n Schwertfisch der.

swore [swɔːʳ] pt ⊳ swear.

sworn [swɔːn] pp ⊳ swear.

swot [swɒt] Br inf <> n pej Streber der, -in die <> vi: **to ~ (for sthg)** büffeln (für etw).

swum [swʌm] pp ⊳ swim.

swung [swʌŋ] pt & pp ⊳ swing.

sycamore ['sikəmɔːʳ] n Bergahorn der.

syllable ['siləbl] n Silbe die.

syllabus ['siləbəs] (pl -buses OR -bi [-bai]) n Lehrplan der.

symbol ['simbl] n Symbol das.

symbolize, -ise ['simbəlaiz] vt symbolisieren.

symmetry ['simətri] n (U) Symmetrie die.

sympathetic [ˌsimpə'θetik] adj - **1.** [understanding] verständnisvoll - **2.** [willing to support] wohlgesinnt; **to be ~ to sthg** einer Sache (D) wohlwollend gegenüberstehen; [new ideas] für etw zugänglich sein.

📖 **sympathetic**

Dieser falsche Freund bedeutet „verständnisvoll" und nur in wenigen Fällen „sympathisch". Our teacher is always <u>sympathetic</u> if we've got something on our minds bedeutet „unser Lehrer ist immer <u>verständnisvoll</u>, wenn wir etwas auf dem Herzen haben."
„Sympathisch" kann im Englischen mit likable ausgedrückt werden, in der Praxis sagt man jedoch meist einfach nice: „Ein wirklich <u>sympathischer</u> Mensch" – a really <u>nice</u> person.

sympathize, -ise ['simpəθaiz] vi - **1.** [feel sorry] mitfühlen, Mitleid haben; **to ~ with sb** mit jm mitfühlen - **2.** [understand]: **to ~ with sthg** für etw Verständnis haben - **3.** [support]: **to ~ with sthg** mit etw sympathisieren.

sympathizer, -iser ['simpəθaizəʳ] n [supporter] Sympathisant der, -in die.

sympathy ['simpəθi] n [compassion] Mitgefühl das, Mitleid das; **to have ~ for sb** Mitleid mit jm haben.

symphony ['simfəni] n Sinfonie die.

symposium [sɪm'pəʊzjəm] (*pl* -siums OR -sia [-zjə]) *n fml* Symposium *das*.
symptom ['sɪmptəm] *n lit & fig* Symptom *das*.
synagogue ['sɪnəgɒg] *n* Synagoge *die*.
syndicate ['sɪndɪkət] *n* Syndikat *das*.
syndrome ['sɪndrəum] *n* MED [set of symptoms] Syndrom *das*.
synonym ['sɪnənɪm] *n*: ~ (for OR of sthg) Synonym *das* (für OR von etw).
synopsis [sɪ'nɒpsɪs] (*pl* -ses [-si:z]) *n* Zusammenfassung *die*.
syntax ['sɪntæks] *n* LING Syntax *die*.
synthetic [sɪn'θetɪk] *adj* - 1. [man-made] synthetisch; ~ fibre Kunstfaser *die* - 2. *pej* [insincere] künstlich.
syphilis ['sɪfɪlɪs] *n* Syphilis *die*.
syphon ['saɪfn] *n* & *vt* = siphon.
Syria ['sɪrɪə] *n* Syrien *nt*.
syringe [sɪ'rɪndʒ] *n* Spritze *die*.
syrup ['sɪrəp] *n* (*U*) - 1. [sugar and water] Sirup *der* - 2. *Br*: (golden) ~ Sirup *der* (*Brotaufstrich*) - 3. [medicine]: cough ~ Hustensaft *der*.
system ['sɪstəm] *n* System *das*; road/railway/transport ~ Straßen-/Bahn-/Transportnetz *das*; stereo ~ Stereoanlage *die*; to get sthg out of one's ~ *inf* etw loswerden.
systematic [ˌsɪstə'mætɪk] *adj* systematisch.
systems analyst ['sɪstəmz-] *n* COMPUT Systemanalytiker *der*, -in *die*.

T

t (*pl* t's OR ts), **T** (*pl* T's OR Ts) [ti:] *n* t *das*, T *das*.
ta [tɑː] *excl Br inf* danke.
tab [tæb] *n* - 1. [of maker] Etikett *das*; [bearing owner's name] Namensschild *das* - 2. [for opening can] Verschluss *der* - 3. *Am* [bill] Rechnung *die*; to pick up the ~ die Rechnung übernehmen - 4. *phr*: to keep ~s on sb jn genau beobachten.
tabby ['tæbɪ] *n*: ~ (cat) getigerte Katze.
table ['teɪbl] <> *n* - 1. [piece of furniture] Tisch *der* - 2. [diagram] Tabelle *die* <> *vt Br* [propose] einbringen.
tablecloth ['teɪblklɒθ] *n* Tischdecke *die*, Tischtuch *das*.
table football *n* Tischfußball *der*.
table lamp *n* Tischlampe *die*.
tablemat ['teɪblmæt] *n* Set *das*.
tablespoon ['teɪblspu:n] *n* Servierlöffel *der*.

tablet ['tæblɪt] *n* - 1. [pill] Tablette *die* - 2. [piece of stone] Tafel *die* - 3. [of soap] Stück *das*.

📖 **tablet**

Dieses Wort sollte man nicht mit dem deutschen „Tablett" in Verbindung bringen, denn es bedeutet „Tablette". A tablet of soap bezeichnet allerdings „ein Stück Seife".
Das „Tablett" zum Transportieren von Tassen und Tellern ist im Englischen ein tray. „Sie servierte den Kaffee auf einem Tablett" heißt auf Englisch She brought in the coffee on a tray.

table tennis *n* Tischtennis *das*.
tabloid ['tæblɔɪd] *n*: ~ (newspaper) Boulevardzeitung *die*; the ~ press die Boulevardpresse.

📖 **tabloids**

Tabloids sind Tageszeitungen von handlichem Format. Der Begriff tabloid ist generell die Bezeichnung für Boulevardzeitungen wie die aggressiv auftretende „Sun", den „Mirror" und den „Express". Diese bieten ihren Lesern viel trivialen und sensationsheischenden Lesestoff, haben aber, ähnlich den deutschen „Bildzeitung", aufgrund ihrer großen Leserschaft enormen Einfluss auf die ernsten Themen. Mit einer täglichen Auflage von fast vier Millionen ist die „Sun" mit Abstand Großbritanniens größte Zeitung.

tacit ['tæsɪt] *adj* stillschweigend.
taciturn ['tæsɪtɜ:n] *adj* schweigsam.
tack [tæk] <> *n* - 1. [nail] kleiner Nagel - 2. NAUT Kurs *der* - 3. *fig* [course of action] Weg *der* <> *vt* - 1. [fasten with nail]: to ~ sthg to sthg etw an etw (*A*) nageln - 2. [in sewing] heften <> *vi* NAUT kreuzen.
tackle ['tækl] <> *n* - 1. FTBL Tackling *das* - 2. RUGBY Fassen *das* - 3. [equipment, gear] Ausrüstung *die* - 4. [for lifting] Flaschenzug *der* <> *vt* - 1. [deal with] angehen - 2. [attack & FTBL] angreifen - 3. RUGBY fassen.
tacky ['tækɪ] *adj* - 1. *inf* [cheap] billig; [tasteless] geschmacklos - 2. [sticky] klebrig.
tact [tækt] *n* Takt *der*; he has no ~ er hat kein Taktgefühl.
tactful ['tæktful] *adj* taktvoll.
tactic ['tæktɪk] *n* Taktik *die*. ◆ tactics *n* (*U*) MIL Taktik *die*.
tactical ['tæktɪkl] *adj* taktisch.
tactile *adj*: a ~ person eine Person, die Körperkontakt mag.
tactless ['tæktlɪs] *adj* taktlos.
tadpole ['tædpəʊl] *n* Kaulquappe *die*.

tag [tæg] *n* - **1.** [on clothing - of maker] Etikett *das;* [- bearing owner's name] Namensschild *das* - **2.** [of paper] Schild *das;* [price - Preisschild *das;* luggage ~ Gepäckanhänger *der.* ◆ **tag along** *vi inf* mitlkommen.

tail [teɪl] ◇ *n* - **1.** [of animal, bird, fish] Schwanz *der* - **2.** [of coat] Schoß *der;* [of shirt] Zipfel *der* ◇ *vt inf* [follow - person] beschatten; [- car] folgen (+ D). ◆ **tails** ◇ *adv* [side of coin] Zahl *die;* heads or ~s? Kopf oder Zahl? ◇ *npl* [formal dress] Frack *der.* ◆ **tail off** *vi* [decrease in volume] leiser werden.

tailback ['teɪlbæk] *n Br* Rückstau *der.*

tailcoat ['teɪlkəʊt] *n* Frack *der.*

tail end *n* Ende *das.*

tailgate ['teɪlgeɪt] *n* [of hatchback car] Heckklappe *die.*

tailor ['teɪlə[r]] ◇ *n* Schneider *der,* -in *die* ◇ *vt* [adjust]: to ~ sthg to sthg [plans, policy] etw auf etw (A) zulschneiden; [product] etw auf etw (A) ablstimmen.

tailor-made *adj fig:* to be ~ for sb [role, job] genau auf jn zugeschnitten sein.

tailwind ['teɪlwɪnd] *n* Rückenwind *der.*

tainted ['teɪntɪd] *adj* - **1.** [reputation] beschmutzt; [money] schmutzig - **2.** *Am* [food] verdorben.

Taiwan [ˌtaɪ'wɑːn] *n* Taiwan *nt.*

take [teɪk] (*pt* took; *pp* taken) ◇ *vt* - **1.** [gen] nehmen; she took my arm sie nahm mich beim Arm; to ~ the train/bus den Zug/Bus nehmen; to ~ a bath ein Bad nehmen; to ~ an exam/a photo/a walk eine Prüfung/ein Foto/einen Spaziergang machen; to ~ risks Risiken einlgehen; to ~ a decision eine Entscheidung treffen; to ~ an interest in sthg sich für etw interessieren; to ~ pity on sb Mitleid mit jm haben; I ~ the view that ... ich bin der Meinung, dass ...; to ~ a seat Platz nehmen; to be ~n ill krank werden - **2.** [bring, accompany] bringen; [take along] mitlnehmen; to ~ sthg to sb jm etw bringen; to ~ sb to the station jn zum Bahnhof bringen; he took her to the theatre er ging mit ihr ins Theater - **3.** [remove, steal] mitlnehmen; to ~ sthg from sb jm etw ablnehmen; [steal] jm etw weglnehmen - **4.** [capture - city] einlnehmen, erobern; [- prisoner] machen - **5.** [control, power] übernehmen; to ~ charge die Leitung übernehmen - **6.** [accept] anlnehmen; [subj: machine] nehmen; [opportunity] wahrlnehmen; [responsibility] übernehmen; do you ~ travellers' cheques? nehmen Sie Travellerschecks?; to ~ sb's advice js Rat (D) folgen - **7.** [receive - prize, praise] bekommen; to ~ criticism kritisiert werden - **8.** [contain] fassen; the car can ~ six people in dem Auto haben sechs Leute Platz - **9.** [size in clothes, shoes] haben; what size do you ~? welche Größe haben Sie?; I ~ a (size) 34 ich habe

Größe 34 - **10.** [bear] ertragen; I can't ~ any more mir reichts - **11.** [require] erfordern; how long will it ~? wie lange wird es dauern?, wie lange braucht es? - **12.** [react to] auflnehmen; to ~ sthg seriously etw ernst nehmen; to ~ sthg badly etw schlecht auflnehmen; is it to ~ away? zum Mitnehmen? - **2.** [deduct] ablziehen - **13.** [temperature, pulse] messen - **14.** [rent] mieten - **15.** [make - sum of money] einlnehmen - **16.** GRAMM: this verb ~s the dative dieses Verb wird mit dem Dativ konstruiert - **17.** [assume]: I ~ it (that) ... ich gehe davon aus, dass ... ◇ *vi* CINEMA Einstellung *die.* ◆ **take after** *vt fus* nachlschlagen (+ D); he ~s after his mother/father er schlägt nach seiner Mutter/seinem Vater.

◆ **take apart** *vt sep* [dismantle] auseinander nehmen. ◆ **take away** *vt sep* - **1.** [remove]: to ~ sthg away (from sb) (jm) etw weglnehmen; is it to ~ away? zum Mitnehmen? - **2.** [deduct] ablziehen. ◆ **take back** *vt sep* - **1.** [return] zurücklbringen - **2.** [faulty goods, statement] zurücklnehmen. ◆ **take down** *vt sep* - **1.** [pictures, curtains] abl nehmen; [scaffolding, tent] ablbauen - **2.** [from shelf] herunterlnehmen - **3.** [write down] auflschreiben - **4.** [lower] herunterllassen. ◆ **take in** *vt sep* - **1.** [bring inside - washing] hereinlbringen - **2.** [deceive] hereinllegen; to be ~n in (by sb/sthg) (auf jn/ etw) hereinlfallen - **3.** [understand] auflnehmen - **4.** [include] einlschließen - **5.** [provide accommodation for] auflnehmen - **6.** [clothes] enger machen. ◆ **take off** ◇ *vt sep* - **1.** [remove] ablnehmen; [clothing] auslziehen; to ~ one's clothes off sich auslziehen - **2.** [have as holiday]: to ~ time off sich (D) freilnehmen; to ~ a week off sich (D) eine Woche freilnehmen - **3.** *Br inf* [imitate] nachläffen ◇ *vi* - **1.** [plane] ablheben - **2.** [go away suddenly] verschwinden. ◆ **take on** *vt sep* - **1.** [job, responsibility] anlnehmen - **2.** [employ] anlstellen, einlstellen - **3.** [confront] sich anllegen mit; [competitor, sports team] anltreten gegen. ◆ **take out** *vt sep* - **1.** [remove - from container] herauslnehmen; [- tooth] ziehen; [- money from bank] ablheben - **2.** [library book] auslleihen - **3.** [loan] auflnehmen; [insurance policy] ablschließen; [patent] anlmelden - **4.** [go out with] auslgehen mit. ◆ **take over** ◇ *vt sep* [company, job] übernehmen ◇ *vi* - **1.** [take control] die Kontrolle übernehmen - **2.** [in job]: to ~ over from sb jn ablösen. ◆ **take to** *vt fus* - **1.** [come to like] mögen - **2.** [begin]: to ~ to doing sthg anlfangen, etw zu tun; she's ~n to getting up earlier sie steht nun früher auf; to ~ to drink zu trinken anlfangen. ◆ **take up** *vt sep* - **1.** [begin - post] anltreten; [- job] auflnehmen; to ~ up the clarinet anfangen, Klarinette zu spielen - **2.** [time, effort, space] in Anspruch nehmen - **3.** [trousers, dress] kürzen. **take up on** vt sep [accept]: **to ~ sb up on an offer** js Angebot anlnehmen.

takeaway Br ['teɪkə,weɪ], **takeout** Am ['teɪkaʊt] <> n [food] Essen das zum Mitnehmen <> comp [food] zum Mitnehmen.

taken ['teɪkn] pp ▷ take.

takeoff ['teɪkɒf] n [of plane] Start der.

takeout n Am = takeaway.

takeover ['teɪk,əʊvə'] n Übernahme die.

takings ['teɪkɪŋz] npl Einnahmen pl.

talc [tælk], **talcum (powder)** ['tælkəm-] n Talk der.

tale [teɪl] n Geschichte die.

talent ['tælənt] n Talent das.

talented ['tæləntɪd] adj talentiert.

talk [tɔːk] <> n - **1.** [conversation] Gespräch das, Unterhaltung die; **to have a ~** sich unterhalten; [more formal] ein Gespräch führen - **2.** [gossip] Gerede das - **3.** [lecture] Vortrag der <> vi - **1.** [speak] sprechen, reden; **to ~ to sb** mit jm reden OR sprechen; **to ~ to o.s.** Selbstgespräche führen; **to ~ about sb/sthg** über jn/etw sprechen OR reden; **~ing of him/ that, ...** da wir gerade von ihm/davon sprechen ...; **he's ~ing of buying a car** er redet davon, sich ein neues Auto kaufen will - **2.** [gossip] klatschen - **3.** [make a speech] eine Rede halten; **to ~ on** OR **about sthg** über etw (A) sprechen <> vt - **1.** [politics, sport, business] reden über (+ A) or etw - **2.** [nonsense] reden. **talks** npl Gespräche pl. **talk into** vt sep: **to ~ sb into doing sthg** jn dazu überreden, etw zu tun. **talk out of** vt sep: **to ~ sb out of doing sthg** jm auslreden, etw zu tun. **talk over** vt sep [discuss] bereden, besprechen.

talkative ['tɔːkətɪv] adj gesprächig.

talk show n Am Talkshow die.

tall [tɔːl] adj - **1.** [person] groß; **I'm 5 feet ~** ich bin 1,50 m groß; **how ~ are you?** wie groß bist du? - **2.** [building, tree] hoch.

tally ['tælɪ] <> n [record]: **to keep a ~ of sthg** über etw (A) Buch führen <> vi übereinlstimmen.

talon ['tælən] n Kralle die.

tambourine [,tæmbə'riːn] n Tamburin das.

tame [teɪm] <> adj - **1.** [animal, bird] zahm - **2.** pej [dull] lahm <> vt - **1.** [animal, bird] zähmen; [lion] bändigen - **2.** [person] bändigen.

tamper ['tæmpə'] **tamper with** vt fus sich (D) zu schaffen machen an (+ D).

tampon ['tæmpɒn] n Tampon der.

tan [tæn] <> adj [light brown] hellbraun <> n [from sun] Bräune die; **to get a ~** braun werden <> vi braun werden.

tangent ['tændʒənt] n GEOM Tangente die; **to go off at a ~** fig plötzlich vom Thema ablschweifen.

tangerine [,tændʒə'riːn] n Mandarine die.

tangible ['tændʒəbl] adj [difference, benefit] merklich; [results] greifbar.

tangle ['tæŋgl] n - **1.** [mass] Gewirr das - **2.** fig [mess] Durcheinander das; **to get (o.s.) into a ~** sich verstricken.

tank [tæŋk] n - **1.** [container] Tank der; **(fish) ~ Aquarium** das - **2.** MIL Panzer der.

tanker ['tæŋkə'] n - **1.** [ship] Tanker der - **2.** [truck] Tankwagen der.

tanned [tænd] adj [suntanned] braun (gebrannt).

Tannoy® ['tænɔɪ] n Lautsprecheranlage die.

tantalizing ['tæntəlaɪzɪŋ] adj verlockend.

tantamount ['tæntəmaʊnt] adj: **to be ~ to sthg** einer Sache (D) gleichlkommen.

tantrum ['tæntrəm] (pl -s) n Wutanfall der.

Tanzania [,tænzə'nɪə] n Tansania nt.

tap [tæp] <> n - **1.** [device] Hahn der; **the hot(-water)/cold(-water) ~** der Warmwasser-/Kaltwasserhahn - **2.** [light blow] Klaps der; **she gave him a ~ on the shoulder** sie klopfte ihm auf die Schulter; [on door] Klopfen <> vt - **1.** [knock] klopfen - **2.** [make use of] erschließen - **3.** [listen secretly to] ablhören.

tap dance n Stepptanz der.

tape [teɪp] <> n - **1.** [magnetic tape] Magnetband das - **2.** [cassette] Kassette die - **3.** [adhesive material] Klebeband das <> vt - **1.** [record] auflnehmen - **2.** [fasten with adhesive tape] (mit Klebeband) verklleben OR zulkleben; **to ~ together** zusammenlkleben.

tape measure n Maßband das.

taper ['teɪpə'] vi [corridor] sich verengen; [trousers] nach unten enger werden.

tape recorder n Tonbandgerät das; [cassette recorder] Kassettenrekorder der.

tapestry ['tæpɪstrɪ] n [piece of work] Wandteppich der.

tar [tɑː'] n Teer der.

target ['tɑːgɪt] <> n - **1.** [of missile, bomb] Ziel das - **2.** [for archery, shooting] Zielscheibe die - **3.** fig [butt of criticism] Zielscheibe die - **4.** fig [goal] Ziel das <> vt - **1.** [aim weapon at] zielen auf (+ A) - **2.** [channel resources towards] sich (D) zum Ziel setzen; **to ~ the young** die Jugendlichen als Zielgruppe haben.

tariff ['tærɪf] n - **1.** [tax] Zoll der - **2.** Br [price list] Preisliste die.

Tarmac® ['tɑːmæk] n [material] Makadam der. **tarmac** n AERON: **the tarmac** die Rollbahn.

tarnish ['tɑːnɪʃ] vt - **1.** [make dull] stumpf werden lassen - **2.** fig [reputation] beflecken.

tarpaulin [tɑː'pɔːlɪn] n [sheet] Plane die.

tart [tɑːt] <> adj - **1.** [bitter-tasting] herb; [fruit] sauer - **2.** [sarcastic] scharf <> n - **1.** [sweet pastry] Kuchen der; [small] Törtchen das; **fruit ~** Obstkuchen-/törtchen - **2.** Br vinf [prostitute] Nutte die. **tart up**

vt sep Br inf pej [building, room] auflmotzen; **to - o.s. up** sich aufltakeln.

tartan ['tɑːtn] ⬦ *n* - **1.** *(U)* [cloth] Schottenstoff *der* - **2.** [pattern] Schottenkaro *das* ⬦ *comp* im Schottenkaro.

task [tɑːsk] *n* Aufgabe *die.*

task force *n* - **1.** MIL Spezialeinheit *die* - **2.** [group of helpers] Kommando *das.*

tassel ['tæsl] *n* Quaste *die.*

taste [teɪst] ⬦ *n* - **1.** [sense of taste] Geschmackssinn *der* - **2.** [flavour] Geschmack *der;* **to have a funny ~** komisch schmecken - **3.** [try] Kostprobe *die;* **to have a ~** probieren - **4.** *fig* [liking, preference]: **~ (for sthg)** Vorliebe *die* (für etw) - **5.** *fig* [experience]: **his first ~ of success** sein erstes Erfolgserlebnis; **I've had a ~ of power** ich habe erfahren, wie es ist, Macht zu haben - **6.** *(U)* [discernment] Geschmack *der;* **she has (good) ~** sie hat (guten) Geschmack; **in bad ~** geschmacklos; **in good ~** geschmackvoll ⬦ *vt* - **1.** [food - experience flavour of] schmecken; [- test, try] probieren, kosten - **2.** *fig:* **to ~ success** ein Erfolgserlebnis haben ⬦ *vi* schmecken; **to ~ of/like sthg** nach/wie etw schmecken.

taste

Die sinngemäße Übersetzung dieses falschen Freundes lautet keinesfalls „Taste", sondern „Geschmack", wobei der Geschmack einer Speise, das Stilempfinden einer Person oder der Geschmackssinn gemeint sein kann. In der Frage *Could I have a taste of that wine?* bedeutet *taste* jedoch „Kostprobe" und kann mit „Könnte ich bitte einmal diesen Wein *probieren?"* übersetzt werden.

Die „Taste" zum Drücken heißt im Englischen *key,* wenn sie zu einem Musikinstrument oder einer Computertastatur gehört, und *button* an elektrischen Geräten, deren Fernbedienungen und der (Computer-)Maus.

tasteful ['teɪstfʊl] *adj* geschmackvoll.

tasteless ['teɪstlɪs] *adj lit & fig* geschmacklos.

tasty ['teɪstɪ] *adj* schmackhaft.

tatters ['tætəz] *npl:* **to be in ~** [clothes] in Fetzen sein; *fig* [confidence, reputation] sehr angeschlagen sein.

tattoo [tə'tuː] *(pl -s)* ⬦ *n* [design] Tätowierung *die* ⬦ *vt* tätowieren.

tatty ['tætɪ] *adj Br inf pej* schäbig.

taught [tɔːt] *pt & pp* ⊳ teach.

taunt [tɔːnt] ⬦ *vt* verspotten ⬦ *n* spöttische Bemerkung.

Taurus ['tɔːrəs] *n* Stier *der;* **I'm a ~** ich bin Stier.

taut [tɔːt] *adj* straff.

tawdry ['tɔːdrɪ] *adj pej* geschmacklos.

---

tax [tæks] ⬦ *n* [money paid to government] Steuer *die* ⬦ *vt* - **1.** [gen] besteuern - **2.** [patience, ingenuity] strapazieren.

taxable ['tæksəbl] *adj* steuerpflichtig.

tax allowance *n* Steuerfreibetrag *der.*

taxation [tæk'seɪʃn] *n* - **1.** [system] Besteuerung *die* - **2.** [amount] Steuer *die.*

tax collector *n* Finanzbeamte *der,* -tin *die.*

tax disc *n Br* Steuermarke *die.*

tax-free *Br,* **tax-exempt** *Am adj* steuerfrei.

taxi ['tæksɪ] ⬦ *n* Taxi *das* ⬦ *vi* [plane] rollen.

taxi driver *n* Taxifahrer *der,* -in *die.*

tax inspector *n* Steuerprüfer *der,* -in *die.*

taxi rank *Br,* **taxi stand** *n* Taxistand *der.*

taxpayer ['tæks,peɪə'] *n* Steuerzahler *der,* -in *die.*

tax return *n* Steuererklärung *die.*

TB *(abbr of tuberculosis) n* TB *die.*

tea [tiː] *n* - **1.** [drink] Tee *der* - **2.** *Br* [afternoon meal] Nachmittagstee *der* - **3.** *Br* [evening meal] Abendessen *das.*

tea

Das britische Nationalgetränk ist nicht nur eine beliebte Erfrischung, sondern gilt auch als probates Mittel gegen Müdigkeit, Schock und alles mögliche andere. Angestellte haben *tea breaks,* Damen pflegen ihren *afternoon tea* (inklusive *Sandwiches, Scones* und Gebäck), und Schulkinder haben ihren *tea* (leichte Abendmahlzeit nach der Schule). Für die Briten ist *tea* mit Essen und Behaglichkeit verbunden.

teabag ['tiːbæg] *n* Teebeutel *der.*

tea break *n Br* Teepause *die.*

teach [tiːtʃ] *(pt & pp taught)* ⬦ *vt* - **1.** [gen] unterrichten; **to ~ sb sthg** jm Unterricht geben in etw *(D),* jn in etw *(D)* unterrichten; **to ~ sb to swim** jm das Schwimmen beilbringen; **to ~ sb(s) that ...** (jn) (be)lehren, dass ... - **2.** [advocate] lehren; **to ~ sb sthg, to ~ sthg to sb** jn etw lehren; **to ~ sb to do sthg** jn lehren, etw zu tun ⬦ *vi* unterrichten.

teacher ['tiːtʃə'] *n* Lehrer *der,* -in *die.*

teaching ['tiːtʃɪŋ] *n* - **1.** [profession, work] Unterrichten *das* - **2.** [thing taught] Lehre *die.*

tea cloth *n* - **1.** [tablecloth] (kleine) Tischdecke *die* - **2.** [tea towel] Geschirrtuch *das.*

tea cosy *Br,* **tea cozy** *Am n* Teewärmer *der.*

teacup ['tiːkʌp] *n* Teetasse *die.*

teak [tiːk] *n* Teakholz *das.*

team [tiːm] *n* - **1.** SPORT Team *das,* Mannschaft *die* - **2.** [group] Team *das.*

teammate ['tiːmmeɪt] *n* Mannschaftsmitglied *das.*

teamwork ['ti:mwɜ:k] n (U) Teamarbeit die.

teapot ['ti:pɒt] n Teekanne die.

tear[1] [tɪə[r]] n [when crying] Träne die.

tear[2] [teə[r]] (pt tore; pp torn) ⬦ vt - 1. [rip] zerreißen - 2. [remove roughly] reißen ⬦ vi - 1. [rip] (zer)reißen - 2. inf [move quickly] rasen ⬦ n [rip] Riss der. ◆ **tear apart** vt sep - 1. [rip up] zerreißen - 2. [upset greatly] fertig machen. ◆ **tear down** vt sep [building, poster] abreißen. ◆ **tear up** vt sep zerreißen.

teardrop ['tɪədrɒp] n Träne die.

tearful ['tɪəfʊl] adj [person] tränenüberströmt.

tear gas [tɪə[r]-] n Tränengas das.

tearoom ['ti:rʊm] n Teestube die.

tease [ti:z] ⬦ n inf - 1. [joker] Witzbold der - 2. [sexually] Schäker der, -in die ⬦ vt: to ~ sb (about sthg) jn (wegen etw) aufziehen.

tea service, tea set n Teeservice das.

teaspoon ['ti:spu:n] n Teelöffel der.

teat [ti:t] n - 1. [of animal] Zitze die - 2. [of bottle] Sauger der.

teatime ['ti:taɪm] n (U) Br [in evening] Abendessenszeit die; [in afternoon] Teezeit die.

tea towel n Geschirrtuch das.

technical ['teknɪkl] adj technisch; ~ **term** Fachbegriff der.

technical college n Br ≃ Fachhochschule die.

technicality [ˌteknɪ'kælətɪ] n - 1. [intricacy] technische Einzelheit - 2. [petty rule] Formsache die.

technically ['teknɪklɪ] adv - 1. [theoretically] theoretisch - 2. [scientifically] technisch.

technician [tek'nɪʃn] n [worker] Techniker der, -in die.

technique [tek'ni:k] n Technik die.

technological [ˌteknə'lɒdʒɪkl] adj technologisch.

technology [tek'nɒlədʒɪ] n Technologie die.

teddy ['tedɪ] n: ~ (**bear**) Teddy(bär) der.

tedious ['ti:dʒəs] adj langweilig.

tee [ti:] n GOLF Tee das, Abschlag der.

teem [ti:m] vi - 1. [rain] gießen - 2. [be busy]: to be ~ing with wimmeln von.

teenage ['ti:neɪdʒ] adj Teenager-; [children] halbwüchsig.

teenager ['ti:nˌeɪdʒə[r]] n Teenager der.

teens [ti:nz] npl: to be in one's ~ im Teenageralter sein.

tee shirt n T-Shirt das.

teeter ['ti:tə[r]] vi - 1. [wobble] schwanken - 2. fig [be in danger]: to be ~ing on the brink of disaster am Rande einer Katastrophe stehen.

teeth [ti:θ] pl ⊏ tooth.

teethe [ti:ð] vi [baby] zahnen.

teething troubles npl fig Anfangsschwierigkeiten pl.

teetotaller Br, **teetotaler** Am [ti:'təʊtlə[r]] n Abstinenzler der, -in die.

tel. (abbr of telephone) Tel.

telecommunications ['telɪkəˌmju:nɪ-'keɪʃnz] npl Telekommunikationswesen das.

telegram ['telɪgræm] n Telegramm das.

telegraph ['telɪgrɑ:f] ⬦ n Telegraf der ⬦ vt telegrafieren.

telegraph pole, telegraph post Br n Telegrafenmast der.

telepathy [tɪ'lepəθɪ] n Telepathie die.

telephone ['telɪfəʊn] ⬦ n Telefon das; to be on the ~ Br [connected] Telefon haben; [speaking] am Telefon sein ⬦ vt anlrufen ⬦ vi telefonieren.

telephone book n Telefonbuch das.

telephone booth n Br Telefonkabine die.

telephone box n Br Telefonzelle die.

telephone call n Telefonanruf der, Telefongespräch das; to make a ~ telefonieren.

telephone directory n Telefonbuch das.

telephone number n Telefonnummer die.

telephonist [tɪ'lefənɪst] n Br Telefonist der, -in die.

telescope ['telɪskəʊp] n Teleskop das.

teletext ['telɪtekst] n Videotext der.

televise ['telɪvaɪz] vt im Fernsehen übertragen.

television ['telɪˌvɪʒn] n - 1. [medium, industry] Fernsehen das; on ~ im Fernsehen - 2. [apparatus] Fernseher der.

television set n Fernseher der.

telex ['teleks] ⬦ n Telex das ⬦ vt (ein) Telex schicken (+ D); [message] telexen.

tell [tel] (pt & pp told) ⬦ vt - 1. [fact] sagen; [story, joke, lie] erzählen; to ~ sb (that) ... jm sagen, dass ...; to ~ sb sthg, to ~ sthg to sb jm etw erzählen; to ~ the truth die Wahrheit sagen; to ~ sb the time jm sagen, wie spät es ist - 2. [instruct, reveal] sagen; to ~ sb to do sthg jm sagen, dass er/sie etw tun soll; to ~ sb (that ...) jm sagen, dass ... - 3. [judge, recognize] wissen; to ~ the time die Uhr lesen können ⬦ vi - 1. [reveal secret]: he won't ~ er wird nichts sagen - 2. [judge] beurteilen - 3. [have effect] sich zeigen. ◆ **tell apart** vt sep unterscheiden. ◆ **tell off** vt sep auslschimpfen.

telling ['telɪŋ] adj - 1. [effective] wirkungsvoll - 2. [revealing] aufschlussreich.

telly ['telɪ] n Br inf - 1. [medium] Fernsehen das; on ~ im Fernsehen - 2. [apparatus] Flimmerkiste die.

temp [temp] Br inf ⬦ n (abbr of temporary (employee)) Zeitarbeitskraft die ⬦ vi als Zeitarbeitskraft arbeiten.

temper ['tempə[r]] ⬦ n - 1. [state of mind,

mood] Laune *die;* **to lose one's ~** die Beherrschung verlieren - **2.** [angry state]: **to be in a ~** wütend sein - **3.** [temperament] Temperament *das* <> *vt fml* [moderate] mäßigen.

temperament ['tempramant] *n* Temperament *das.*

temperamental [,tempra'mentl] *adj* launisch, launenhaft.

📖 **temperamental**

Dieses Wort sollte man mit Bedacht verwenden, denn in Verbindung mit einer Person oder einer Maschine bedeutet es nicht „temperamentvoll", sondern „launisch" oder „launenhaft". Der Satz The children are always a bit temperamental first thing in the morning könnte auf Deutsch so heißen: „Die Kinder sind immer etwas launisch am frühen Morgen". Das Adjektiv „temperamentvoll" dagegen hat die englische Entsprechung lively. „Ein temperamentvolles Pferd" ist daher a lively horse.

---

temperature ['tempratʃaʳ] *n* Temperatur *die;* **to have a ~** Fieber haben.

tempestuous [tem'pestjʊəs] *adj lit & fig* stürmisch.

template ['templɪt] *n* [of shape, pattern] Schablone *die.*

temple ['templ] *n* - **1.** RELIG Tempel *der* - **2.** ANAT Schläfe *die.*

temporarily [,tempə'rerəlɪ] *adv* vorübergehend.

temporary ['tempərərɪ] *adj* vorübergehend; [job] befristet.

tempt [tempt] *vt* [entice]: **to ~ sb to do sthg** jn dazu verlocken, etw zu tun.

temptation [temp'teɪʃn] *n* - **1.** [state] Versuchung *die* - **2.** [tempting thing] Verlockung *die.*

tempting ['temptɪŋ] *adj* verlockend.

ten [ten] *num* zehn; *see also* six.

tenable ['tenəbl] *adj* [reasonable, credible] haltbar.

tenacious [tɪ'neɪʃəs] *adj* hartnäckig.

tenancy ['tenənsɪ] *n* - **1.** [period - of building] Mietdauer *die;* [- of land] Pachtzeit *die* - **2.** [possession of building] Mieten *das;* [- of land] Pachten *das.*

tenant ['tenənt] *n* Mieter *der,* -in *die.*

tend [tend] *vt* - **1.** [have tendency]: **to ~ to do sthg** [person] dazu neigen, etw zu tun - **2.** [look after] sich kümmern um.

tendency ['tendənsɪ] *n* - **1.** [trend]: **~ towards sthg** Tendenz *die* zu etw - **2.** [leaning, habit] Neigung *die;* **to have the ~ to do sthg** die Neigung haben, etw zu tun.

tender ['tendəʳ] <> *adj* - **1.** [caring, gentle] zärtlich - **2.** [meat] zart - **3.** [sore] empfindlich <> *n* COMM Angebot *das* <> *vt fml* [of-

fer - money] anlbieten; [- resignation] einlreichen.

tendon ['tendən] *n* Sehne *die.*

tenement ['tenəmənt] *n* Mietshaus *das.*

tennis ['tenɪs] *n* Tennis *das.*

tennis ball *n* Tennisball *der.*

tennis court *n* Tennisplatz *der.*

tennis racket *n* Tennisschläger *der.*

tenor ['tenəʳ] *n* Tenor *der.*

tense [tens] <> *adj* angespannt <> *n* GRAMM Zeit(form) *die* <> *vt* [muscles] anlspannen.

tension ['tenʃn] *n* (U) - **1.** [anxiety] Anspannung *die;* [between people] Spannung *die* - **2.** TECH [tightness] Spannung *die.*

tent [tent] *n* Zelt *das.*

tentacle ['tentəkl] *n* Fangarm *der,* Tentakel *der* OR *das.*

tentative ['tentətɪv] *adj* - **1.** [person, step, smile] zögernd - **2.** [agreement, plan] vorläufig.

tenterhooks ['tentəhʊks] *npl:* **to be on ~** auf glühenden Kohlen sitzen.

tenth [tenθ] *num* zehnte, -r, -s; *see also* sixth.

tent peg *n* Hering *der,* Zeltpflock *der.*

tent pole *n* Zeltstange *die.*

tenuous ['tenjʊəs] *adj* schwach.

tepid ['tepɪd] *adj lit & fig* lauwarm.

term [tɜːm] <> *n* - **1.** [word, expression] Begriff *der,* Ausdruck *der* - **2.** SCH & UNIV Trimester *das* - **3.** [period of time]: **a prison ~** eine Haftstrafe; **in the long/short ~** auf lange/kurze Sicht <> *vt* bezeichnen; **to ~ sb/ sthg sthg** jn/etw als etw bezeichnen. ◆ **terms** *npl* - **1.** [of contract, agreement] Konditionen *pl* - **2.** [conditions]: **in international ~s** im internationalen Vergleich; **in real ~s** effektiv - **3.** [of relationship]: **to be on good ~s (with sb)** (mit jm) gut auslkommen - **4.** *phr:* **to come to ~s with sthg** sich mit etw ablfinden. ◆ **in terms of** *prep* in Bezug auf (+ A).

terminal ['tɜːmɪnl] <> *adj* MED unheilbar <> *n* - **1.** RAIL Endbahnhof *der;* AERON Terminal *der* - **2.** COMPUT Terminal *das* - **3.** ELEC Pol *der.*

terminate ['tɜːmɪneɪt] <> *vt fml* beenden; [contract] auflösen; [pregnancy] ablbrechen <> *vi* [bus, train] enden.

terminus ['tɜːmɪnəs] (*pl* -ni OR -nuses) *n* Endstation *die.*

terrace ['terəs] *n* - **1.** *Br* [of houses] Häuserreihe *die* - **2.** [patio] Terrasse *die.* ◆ **terraces** *npl* FTBL: **the ~s** die Ränge *pl.*

terraced house *n Br* Reihenhaus *das.*

terrain [te'reɪn] *n* Gelände *das.*

terrible ['terəbl] *adj* furchtbar, schrecklich.

terribly ['terəblɪ] *adv* [extremely] furchtbar, schrecklich.

terrier ['terɪəʳ] *n* Terrier *der.*

terrific [tə'rɪfɪk] *adj* - **1.** [wonderful] großartig - **2.** [enormous] enorm.

terrified ['terɪfaɪd] *adj:* **to be ~ (of sb/sthg)** wahnsinnige Angst haben (vor jm/etw).

terrifying ['terɪfaɪɪŋ] *adj* fürchterlich.

territory ['terətrɪ] *n* - **1.** [political area] Territorium *das* - **2.** [terrain] Gelände *das*.

terror ['terə'] *n* - **1.** [fear] panische Angst - **2.** *inf* [rascal] Teufel *der*.

terrorism ['terərɪzm] *n* Terrorismus *der*.

terrorist ['terərɪst] *n* Terrorist *der*, -in *die*.

terrorize, -ise ['terəraɪz] *vt* terrorisieren.

terse [tɜːs] *adj* - **1.** [reply, remark] knapp - **2.** [person] kurz angebunden.

Terylene® ['terəliːn] *n* Trevira® *das*.

test [test] ◇ *n* - **1.** [trial] Test *der;* [of friendship, courage] Probe *die* - **2.** [examination of knowledge, skill - SCH] Klassenarbeit *die;* [- UNIV] Klausur *die;* **driving ~** Fahrprüfung *die* - **3.** MED [medical check] Test *der* ◇ *vt* - **1.** [car, method] testen; [friendship, courage] auf die Probe stellen; **to have one's eyes ~ed** seine Augen testen lassen - **2.** [pupil] prüfen; **to ~ sb on sthg** jn in etw (D) prüfen.

test-drive *vt* Probe fahren.

testicles ['testɪklz] *npl* Hoden *pl.*

testify ['testɪfaɪ] ◇ *vt* **to ~ that ...** bezeugen, dass ... ◇ *vi* - **1.** LAW auslsagen - **2.** [be proof]: **to ~ to sthg** von etw zeugen.

testimony [*Br* 'testɪmənɪ, *Am* 'testəməʊnɪ] *n* (U) LAW Aussage *die*.

testing ['testɪŋ] *adj* [difficult] schwer.

test match *n Br* internationales Cricket- oder Rugbyspiel.

test tube *n* Reagenzglas *das*.

test-tube baby *n* Retortenbaby *das*.

tetanus ['tetənəs] *n* Tetanus *der*, Wundstarrkrampf *der*.

tether ['teðə'] ◇ *vt* anlbinden ◇ *n:* **to be at the end of one's ~** am Ende sein.

text [tekst] *n* - **1.** [gen] Text *der* - **2.** [of speech, interview] Wortlaut *die*.

textbook ['tekstbʊk] *n* Lehrbuch *das*.

textile ['tekstaɪl] *n* Textilie *die*.

texture ['tekstʃə'] *n* Beschaffenheit *die*.

Thai [taɪ] ◇ *adj* thailändisch ◇ *n* - **1.** [person] Thailänder *der*, -in *die* - **2.** [language] Thai *das*.

Thailand ['taɪlænd] *n* Thailand *nt*.

Thames [temz] *n:* **the ~** die Themse.

than [weak form ðən, strong form ðæn] ◇ *prep* als; **you're better ~ me** du bist besser als ich; **more ~ ten** mehr als zehn ◇ *conj* als; **I'd rather stay in ~ go out** ich bleibe lieber zu Hause als auszugehen; **no sooner had we arrived ~ the music began** kaum waren wir angekommen, da begann die Musik zu spielen.

thank [θæŋk] *vt:* **to ~ sb (for sthg)** jm (für etw) danken; **~ God** OR **goodness** OR **heavens!** Gott sei Dank! ◆ **thanks** ◇ *npl*

Dank *der* ◇ *excl* danke. ◆ **thanks to** *prep* dank (+ D).

thankful ['θæŋkfʊl] *adj* - **1.** [grateful]: **~ (for sthg)** dankbar (für etw) - **2.** [relieved] erleichtert.

thankless ['θæŋklɪs] *adj* undankbar.

thanksgiving ['θæŋks‚gɪvɪŋ] *n* Danksagung *die*. ◆ **Thanksgiving (Day)** *n* amerikanisches Erntedankfest.

📖 Thanksgiving

In den USA ist Thanksgiving (Erntedankfest) ein Feiertag, der an jedem vierten Donnerstag im November zum Dank für die Ernte, aber auch für alle anderen Segnungen des vergangenen Jahres gefeiert wird. Das Fest geht zurück auf das Jahr 1621, als die ersten Siedler aus Großbritannien, die Pilgrims, ihre erste Ernte einbrachten. Das traditionelle Thanksgiving-Essen besteht aus Truthahnbraten und pumpkin pie, einem Kürbisgericht.

thank you *excl* danke schön!; **~ for ...** danke für ...

that [ðæt, *weak form of pron senses 3–5 & conj* ðət] (*pl* those) ◇ *pron* - **1.** (*demonstrative use*) das, die *pl;* **who's/what's ~?** wer/was ist das?; **~'s interesting** das ist interessant; **is ~ Lucy?** [on phone] bist du das, Lucy?; [pointing] ist das Lucy?; **how much are those?** wieviel kosten die (da)?; **all those I saw** all die, die ich sah; **after ~** danach; **what do you mean by ~?** was willst du damit sagen? - **2.** (*referring to thing or person further away*) jene-, -r, -s, jene *pl;* **this is new, ~ is old** dies ist neu, jenes ist alt; **I want those there** ich möchte die da - **3.** (*introducing relative clause: subject*) der/die/das, die *pl;* **a shop ~ sells antiques** ein Geschäft, das Antiquitäten verkauft - **4.** (*introducing relative clause: object*) den/die/das, die *pl;* **the film ~ I saw** der Film, den ich gesehen habe; **everything ~ I have done** alles, was ich gemacht habe; **the best ~ he could do** das Beste, was er machen konnte - **5.** (*introducing relative clause: after prep + D*) dem/der/dem, denen *pl;* (*introducing relative clause: after prep + A*) den/die/das, die *pl;* **the place ~ I'm looking for** der Ort, nach dem ich suche; **the envelope ~ I put it in** der Umschlag, in den ich es steckte; **the night ~ we went to the theatre** der Abend, an dem wir ins Theater gingen ◇ *adj* - **1.** (*demonstrative use*) der/die/das, die *pl;* **~ film was good** der Film war gut; **who's ~ man?** wer ist der Mann?; **what's ~ noise?** was ist das für ein Lärm?; **those chocolates are delicious** die Pralinen da schmecken köstlich - **2.** (*referring to thing or person further away*) jene-, -r, -s, jene *pl;* **I prefer ~ book** ich bevorzuge das Buch da; **I'll have ~ one** ich nehme das da ◇ *adv* so; **it wasn't ~ bad/good** es war nicht so schlecht/gut ⟨⟩ *conj* dass; **he recommended ~ I phone you** er empfahl mir, dich anzurufen. **➠ that is (to say)** *adv* das heißt.

thatched [θætʃt] *adj*: **~ roof** Reetdach *das*.

that's [ðæts] = that is.

thaw [θɔː] ⟨⟩ *vt* auftauen ⟨⟩ *vi* - **1.** [ice, frozen food] tauen - **2.** *fig* [atmosphere] sich entspannen ⟨⟩ *n* Tauwetter *das*.

the [weak form ðə, before vowel ðɪ, strong form ðiː] *def art* - **1.** [gen] der/die/das, die *pl*; **~ man** der Mann; **~ woman** die Frau; **~ book** das Buch; **~ girls** die Mädchen; **~ Wilsons** die Wilsons; **to play ~ piano** Klavier spielen; **ten pence in ~ pound** zehn Pence pro Pfund; **you're not** THE **Jack Straw, are you?** Sie sind nicht DER Jack Straw, oder? **it's the place to go to in Paris** da geht man in Paris hin - **2.** *(with an adj to form a noun)*: **~ British/poor** die Briten/Armen; **~ impossible** das Unmögliche - **3.** [in dates] der; **~ twelfth (of May)** der Zwölfte (Mai); **~ forties** die Vierziger - **4.** [in comparisons]: **~ more I see of her, ~ less I like her** je mehr ich sie sehe, desto weniger mag ich sie; **~ sooner ~ better** je eher, desto besser - **5.** [in titles]: **Elizabeth ~ Second** Elisabeth die Zweite.

theatre *Br*, **theater** *Am* ['θɪətə'] *n* - **1.** [building] Theater *das* - **2.** [art, industry]: **the ~** das Theater - **3.** [in hospital] Operationssaal *der* - **4.** *Am* [cinema] Kino *das*.

theatregoer *Br*, **theatergoer** *Am* ['θɪətə,gəʊə'] *n* Theaterbesucher *der*, -in *die*.

theatrical [θɪ'ætrɪkl] *adj* - **1.** [of the theatre] Theater- - **2.** *fig* [for effect] theatralisch.

theft [θeft] *n* Diebstahl *der*.

their [ðeə'] *poss adj* ihr; **~ house** ihr Haus; **~ children** ihre Kinder; **they brushed ~ teeth** sie putzten sich (D) die Zähne; **it wasn't** THEIR **fault** das war nicht IHRE Schuld.

theirs [ðeəz] *poss pron* ihre, -r, -s; **that is ~** das ist ihres; **this house is ~** dieses Haus gehört ihnen; **a friend of ~** ein Freund von ihnen; **it wasn't our fault, it was** THEIRS das war nicht unsere Schuld, es war IHRE.

them [weak form ðəm, strong form ðem] *pers pron pl (accusative)* sie; *(dative)* ihnen; **I know ~** ich kenne sie; **I like ~** sie gefallen mir; **it's ~** sie sind es; **send it to ~** schicke es ihnen; **tell ~ ...** sage ihnen ...; **he's worse than ~** er ist schlimmer als sie; **if I were** OR **was ~** wenn ich sie wäre; **you can't expect** THEM **to do it** du kannst nicht erwarten, dass SIE das tun; **all of ~** sie alle; **none of ~** keiner von ihnen; **some/a few of ~** einige von ihnen; **most of ~** die meisten; **both of ~** alle beide; **there are three of ~** es gibt drei davon; [people] sie sind zu dritt; **neither of ~** keiner/keine/keines von beiden.

theme [θiːm] *n* [gen] Thema *das*.

theme tune *n* [of film] Titelmelodie *die*; [of

TV, radio programme] Erkennungsmelodie *die*.

themselves [ðem'selvz] *pron* sich; **they washed ~** sie wuschen sich; **by ~** [alone] allein; **they did it (by) ~** sie machten es selbst; **they have the garden (all) to ~** sie haben den Garten (ganz) für sich allein.

then [ðen] ⟨⟩ *adv* - **1.** [not now, next, afterwards] dann; [in the past] damals; **the film starts at eight – I'll see you ~** der Film fängt um acht an – bis dann; **I had breakfast, ~ I went to work** ich frühstückte und ging dann zur Arbeit; **we were much younger ~** wir waren damals viel jünger; **before ~** vorher; **by/until ~** bis dahin; **from ~ on** von da an; **since ~** seitdem - **2.** [in that case] also; **go on, ~ also machs!; you knew all along, ~?** du hast es also die ganze Zeit gewusst? - **3.** [therefore] also; **these, ~, were the reasons for our failure** das waren also die Gründe für unser Versagen - **4.** [with "if" clauses] dann; **if you help me now, ~ I'll help you later** wenn Sie mir jetzt helfen, dann helfe ich Ihnen später - **5.** [furthermore, also] außerdem; **(and) ~ there are the children to consider ...** und dann müssen wir an die Kinder denken ⟨⟩ *adj* damalig; **the ~ president** der damalige Präsident.

theoretical [θɪə'retɪkl] *adj* theoretisch.

theorize, -ise ['θɪəraɪz] *vi*: **to ~ (about sthg)** theoretisieren (über etw (A)).

theory ['θɪərɪ] *n* Theorie *die*; **in ~** theoretisch, in der Theorie.

therapist ['θerəpɪst] *n* Therapeut *der*, -in *die*.

therapy ['θerəpɪ] *n* Therapie *die*.

there [ðeə'] ⟨⟩ *pron* [indicating existence]: **~ is/are** es gibt; **are ~ any left?** sind noch welche übrig?; **~ are three of us** wir sind zu dritt; **~'s a page missing** es fehlt eine Seite; **~ must be some mistake** das muss ein Irrtum sein ⟨⟩ *adv* - **1.** [in existence, present] da; **is anyone ~?** ist da jemand?; **is John ~, please?** [on phone] ist John da? - **2.** [at/in that place] dort; [to that place] dorthin; **that man ~ der** Mann dort; **I'm going ~ next week** nächste Woche hin; **we're ~ at last!** endlich sind wir da!; **it's 6 kilometres ~ and back** es sind 6 Kilometer hin und zurück; **~ it/he is** da ist es/er; **in/over ~** da drinnen/drüben; **up ~** dort oben ⟨⟩ *excl*: **~, I told you so!** ich habe es dir doch gleich gesagt!; **~, ~ (don't cry)** na, na (weine nicht). **➠ there and then, then and there** *adv* auf der Stelle.

thereabouts [ðeərə'baʊts], **thereabout** *Am* [ðeərə'baʊt] *adv*: **at eight o'clock or ~** so um acht Uhr herum; **fifty or ~** so ungefähr fünfzig; **somewhere ~** da irgendwo.

thereafter [,ðeər'ɑːftə'] *adv fml* danach.

thereby [,ðeər'baɪ] *adv fml* damit.

therefore ['ðeəfɔː'] *adv* deshalb, deswegen.

there's [ðeəz] = there is.

thermal ['θɜ:ml] *adj* [clothes] Thermo-.

thermometer [θə'mɒmɪtə'] *n* Thermometer *das*.

Thermos (flask)® ['θɜ:məs-] *n* Thermosflasche® *die*.

thermostat ['θɜ:məstæt] *n* Thermostat *der*.

thesaurus [θɪ'sɔ:rəs] (*pl* -es) *n* Thesaurus *der*.

these [ði:z] *pl* ⇨ this.

thesis ['θi:sɪs] (*pl* theses ['θi:si:z]) *n* - 1. [argument] These *die* - 2. [doctoral dissertation] Dissertation *die*, Doktorarbeit *die*.

they [ðeɪ] *pers pron* *pl* - 1. [gen] sie; ~'re happy sie sind glücklich; ~'re pretty earrings das sind hübsche Ohrringe; it is ~ who are responsible sie sind es, die verantwortlich sind; THEY can't do it DIE können es nicht tun - 2. [unspecified people] man; ~ still haven't repaired the road sie haben immer noch nicht die Straße repariert; ~ say that ... man sagt, dass ...

they'd [ðeɪd] = they had, they would.

they'll [ðeɪl] = they shall, they will.

they're [ðeə'] = they are.

they've [ðeɪv] = they have.

thick [θɪk] ⇨ *adj* - 1. [gen] dick; it is one metre ~ es ist einen Meter dick - 2. [dense] dicht; ~ with smoke voller Rauch - 3. *inf* [stupid] dumm - 4. [accent] stark ⇨ *n*: to be in the ~ of it mittendrin sein.

thicken ['θɪkn] ⇨ *vt* [soup, sauce] eindicken ⇨ *vi* [forest, crowd, fog] dichter werden; [soup, sauce] dicker werden.

thickness ['θɪknɪs] *n* - 1. [width, depth] Dicke *die* - 2. [density] Dichte *die* - 3. [viscosity] Dickflüssigkeit *die*.

thickset [θɪk'set] *adj* gedrungen.

thick-skinned [-'skɪnd] *adj* dickfellig.

thief [θi:f] (*pl* thieves) *n* Dieb *der*, -in *die*.

thieve [θi:v] *vt* & *vi* stehlen.

thieves [θi:vz] *pl* ⇨ thief.

thigh [θaɪ] *n* Oberschenkel *der*.

thimble ['θɪmbl] *n* Fingerhut *der*.

thin [θɪn] *adj* - 1. [gen] dünn - 2. [sparse] gering; [mist] leicht; [hair] dünn, schütter - 3. [poor - excuse] fadenscheinig. ◆ **thin down** *vt sep* verdünnen.

thing [θɪŋ] *n* - 1. [affair, item, subject] Sache *die*, Ding *das*; the (best) ~ to do would be ... das Beste wäre (es) ...; the ~ is ... die Sache ist die, dass ... - 2. [anything]: not a ~ gar nichts - 3. [object, creature] Ding *das*; the lucky ~! der/die Glückliche!; you poor ~! du Armer/Arme! ◆ **things** *npl* - 1. [clothes, possessions] Sachen *pl* - 2. *inf* [life] Dinge *pl*.

think [θɪŋk] (*pt* & *pp* thought) ⇨ *vt* - 1. [believe]: to ~ (that) ... denken(, dass) ..., glauben(, dass) ...; I ~ so ich glaube schon; I don't ~ so ich glaube nicht - 2. [have in mind]:

to ~ (that) ... denken(, dass) ...; what are you ~ing? woran denkst du? - 3. [imagine] sich (*D*) denken, sich (*D*) vorstellen - 4. [in polite requests]: do you ~ you could help me? könnten Sie mir vielleicht helfen? ⇨ *vi* - 1. [use mind] denken; I thought for a long time ich dachte lange nach - 2. [have stated opinion]: what do you ~ of OR about his new film? was hältst du von seinem neuen Film?; I don't ~ much of them/it ich halte nicht viel von ihnen/davon; to ~ a lot of sb/sthg viel von jm/etw halten - 3. *phr*: to ~ twice before doing sthg es sich (*D*) genau überlegen, bevor man etw tut. ◆ **think about** *vt fus* [consider] nachdenken über (+ *A*); to ~ about doing sthg daran denken, etw zu tun. ◆ **think of** *vt fus* - 1. [consider, remember, show consideration for] denken an (+ *A*); to ~ of doing sthg daran denken, etw zu tun; I can't ~ of her name ich kann mich nicht an ihren Namen erinnern, ich komme nicht auf ihren Namen - 2. [conceive] sich (*D*) ausdenken; to ~ of doing sthg die Idee haben, etw zu tun; we'll ~ of sthg wir werden uns (*D*) etw einfallen lassen. ◆ **think over** *vt sep* überdenken. ◆ **think up** *vt sep* sich (*D*) ausdenken.

think tank *n* Expertenkommission *die*.

third [θɜ:d] ⇨ *num* dritte, -r, -s ⇨ *n* - 1. [fraction] Drittel *das* - 2. *Br* UNIV Abschluss mit „befriedigend"; *see also* sixth.

thirdly ['θɜ:dlɪ] *adv* drittens.

third-rate *adj pej* drittklassig.

Third World *n*: the ~ die Dritte Welt.

thirst [θɜ:st] *n* Durst *der*; a ~ for sthg *fig* ein Durst nach etw; ~ for adventure Abenteuerlust *die*.

thirsty ['θɜ:stɪ] *adj*: to be OR feel ~ Durst haben, durstig sein; this is ~ work diese Arbeit macht durstig.

thirteen [,θɜ:'ti:n] *num* dreizehn; *see also* six.

thirty ['θɜ:tɪ] *num* dreißig; *see also* sixty.

this [ðɪs] (*pl* these) ⇨ *pron* - 1. [referring to thing, person mentioned] das; ~ is for you das ist für dich; who's/what's ~? wer/was ist das?; what are these? was ist das?; ~ is Daphne Logan [introducing someone] das ist Daphne Logan; [introducing o.s. on phone] hier ist Daphne Logan; before ~ früher - 2. [referring to thing, person nearer speaker] diese, -r, -s, diese *pl*; which shoes do you want, these or those? welche Schuhe wollen Sie, die hier oder die da?; I want these here ich möchte die hier ⇨ *adj* - 1. [referring to thing, person] diese, -r, -s, diese *pl*; I prefer ~ book ich bevorzuge dieses Buch; these chocolates are delicious diese Pralinen schmecken köstlich; I'll have ~ one/these ones ich nehme dieses/diese; ~ morning/evening diesen Morgen/Abend; ~ week diese Woche; ~ Sunday/summer diesen Sonntag/Sommer

- 2. *inf* [a certain]: **there was ~ man ...** da war dieser Mann ...; **~ woman came over to my table** diese Frau kam an meinen Tisch ◇ *adv* so; **it was ~ big** es war so groß; **~ far** bis hier.

thistle ['θɪsl] *n* Distel *die*.

thorn [θɔːn] *n* [prickle] Dorn *der*.

thorny ['θɔːnɪ] *adj* **- 1.** [prickly] dornig **- 2.** *fig* [tricky, complicated] heikel.

thorough ['θʌrə] *adj* **- 1.** [exhaustive, meticulous] gründlich; [worker] sorgfältig, gewissenhaft **- 2.** [complete, utter] völlig; **that's a ~ nuisance** das ist wirklich lästig.

thoroughbred ['θʌrəbred] *n* [horse] Vollblut *das*.

thoroughfare ['θʌrəfeəʳ] *n fml* Durchgangsstraße *die*.

thoroughly ['θʌrəlɪ] *adv* **- 1.** [fully, in detail] gründlich **- 2.** [completely, utterly] durch und durch.

those [ðəʊz] *pl* ▷ that.

though [ðəʊ] ◇ *conj* **- 1.** [in spite of the fact that] obwohl, obgleich **- 2.** [even if] wenn auch ◇ *adv* [nevertheless] aber; **he's quite intelligent, ~** er ist aber ziemlich intelligent.

thought [θɔːt] ◇ *pt & pp* ▷ think ◇ *n* **- 1.** [notion] Gedanke *der* **- 2.** (U) [act of thinking] Nachdenken *das;* **to give some ~ to sthg** über etw (A) nachdenken; **after much ~** nach langem Überlegen **- 3.** [philosophy] Denken *das* **- 4.** [gesture]: **it's the ~ that counts** der gute Wille zählt. ◆ **thoughts** *npl* Gedanken *pl*.

thoughtful ['θɔːtfʊl] *adj* **- 1.** [pensive - person, mood] nachdenklich **- 2.** [considerate - person] rücksichtsvoll; [- action, remark] wohl überlegt.

thoughtless ['θɔːtlɪs] *adj* [person, behaviour] rücksichtslos; [remark] unüberlegt.

thousand ['θaʊznd] *num* **- 1.** [number] tausend; **a/one ~** (ein)tausend; **five ~ and forty-two** fünftausend(und)zweiundvierzig; **~s of** Tausende von **- 2.** *fig* [umpteen]: **a ~** tausend; **I have a ~ things to do** ich habe tausend Dinge zu tun; *see also* six.

thousandth ['θaʊzntθ] ◇ *num* tausendste, -r, -s; *see also* sixth ◇ *n* [fraction] Tausendstel *das*.

thrash [θræʃ] *vt* **- 1.** [beat, hit] prügeln **- 2.** *inf* [trounce] fertig machen. ◆ **thrash about, thrash around** *vi* sich hin und her werfen. ◆ **thrash out** *vt sep* durchdiskutieren.

thread [θred] ◇ *n* **- 1.** [of cotton, wool] Faden *der* **- 2.** [of screw] Gewinde *das* **- 3.** *fig* [theme]: **to follow the ~ of sb's argument** js Gedankengang (D) folgen; **she lost the ~ (of what she was saying)** sie hat den Faden verloren ◇ *vt* [needle] ein|fädeln; [beads] auf|ziehen.

threadbare ['θredbeəʳ] *adj* [garment] abgetragen; [carpet] abgewetzt.

threat [θret] *n* **- 1.** [warning] Drohung *die* **- 2.** [menace]: **~ (to sb/sthg)** Bedrohung *die* OR Gefahr *die* (für jn/etw) **- 3.** [risk]: **the ~ of war/inflation** die Gefahr eines Krieges/einer Inflation; **there is a ~ of storms** es kann Stürme geben.

threaten ['θretn] ◇ *vt* **- 1.** [issue threat]: **to ~ sb (with sthg)** jm (mit etw) drohen; **to ~ to do sthg** drohen, etw zu tun **- 2.** [be likely]: **to ~ to do sthg** drohen, etw zu tun **- 3.** [endanger] bedrohen, gefährden ◇ *vi* drohen.

three [θriː] *num* drei; *see also* six.

three-dimensional [-dɪˈmenʃənl] *adj* dreidimensional.

threefold ['θriːfəʊld] *adj & adv* dreifach.

three-piece *adj* dreiteilig.

three-ply *adj* [wool] dreifädig; [wood] dreischichtig.

thresh [θreʃ] *vt* dreschen.

threshold ['θreʃhəʊld] *n* **- 1.** [doorway] Türschwelle *die* **- 2.** [level] Schwelle *die*.

threw [θruː] *pt* ▷ throw.

thrift shop *n Am* Secondhandladen, dessen Erlöse einem wohltätigen Zweck zugute kommen.

thrifty ['θrɪftɪ] *adj* [person] sparsam.

thrill [θrɪl] ◇ *n* **- 1.** [sudden feeling] Erregung *die;* **a ~ of horror** im Schauder des Entsetzens; **I felt a ~ of joy** ich war freudig erregt **- 2.** [exciting experience] (aufregendes) Erlebnis ◇ *vt* begeistern, mitreißen.

thrilled [θrɪld] *adj*: **to be ~ (with sthg)** (von etw) begeistert sein; **I was ~ to meet her** ich fand es sehr aufregend, sie zu treffen.

thriller ['θrɪləʳ] *n* Thriller *der*.

thrilling ['θrɪlɪŋ] *adj* [match, book, film] spannend; [news] umwerfend.

thrive [θraɪv] (*pt* -d OR **throve**; *pp* -d) *vi* [person - be successful] erfolgreich sein; [plant] prächtig gedeihen; [business] blühen.

thriving ['θraɪvɪŋ] *adj* [person - successful] erfolgreich; [plant] prächtig gedeihend; [business] blühend.

throat [θrəʊt] *n* **- 1.** [inside mouth] Hals *der* **- 2.** [front of neck] Kehle *die*.

throb [θrɒb] *vi* **- 1.** [beat - pulse, heart] pochen; [- blood] pulsieren; [- engine, machine, music] dröhnen **- 2.** [be painful]: **my head is ~bing** ich habe pochende Kopfschmerzen.

throes [θrəʊz] *npl*: **to be in the ~ of sthg** mitten in etw (D) stecken.

throne [θrəʊn] *n* Thron *der*.

throng [θrɒŋ] ◇ *n* [crowd] Menschenmenge *die;* **a ~ of** Scharen *pl* von ◇ *vt* [place] belagern; [streets] sich drängen in (+ D).

throttle ['θrɒtl] ◇ *n* **- 1.** [valve] Drosselklappe *die* **- 2.** [lever] Gashebel *der;* [Pedal] Gaspedal *das;* **at full ~** mit Vollgas ◇ *vt* [strangle] erwürgen.

through [θruː] ◇ *adj* **- 1.** [finished]: **to be ~ (with sthg)** (mit etw) fertig sein **- 2.** [referring to transport]: **~ traffic** Durchgangsver-

kehr *der;* **a ~ train** ein durchgehender Zug
$\Leftrightarrow$ *adv* - **1.** [from one end to another] durch;
to let sb ~ in jn durchllassen; **wet ~ völlig**
durchnässt - **2.** [until]: **I slept ~ till ten** ich
schlief bis zehn durch; **we stayed ~ till Fri-
day** wir blieben bis Freitag $\Leftrightarrow$ *prep* - **1.** [from
one side to another] durch; **he went ~ the
park** er ging durch den Park; **to drill ~ sthg**
etw durchlbohren; **I'm halfway ~ this book**
ich habe das Buch schon halb gelesen
- **2.** [during, throughout] während *(+ G);* **all
~ his life** sein ganzes Leben hindurch - **3.** [be-
cause of] wegen *(+ G);* **absent ~ illness** wegen Krankheit abwesend; **~ fear** aus Furcht
- **4.** [by means of] durch; **I got the job ~ a
friend** ich bekam die Stelle durch einen
Freund - **5.** *Am* [up until and including]: **Monday ~ Thursday** Montag bis Donnerstag.
$\blacktriangleright$ **through and through** *adv* - **1.** [com-
pletely] durch und durch - **2.** [thorough-
ly - know] gründlich.

throughout [θruː'aʊt] $\Leftrightarrow$ *prep* - **1.** [during]:
~ the day/morning den ganzen Tag/Morgen
(über); **~ the year** das ganze Jahr (hindurch);
~ her life ihr ganzes Leben lang - **2.** [every-
where in] überall in *(+ D);* **~ the country** im
ganzen Land $\Leftrightarrow$ *adv* - **1.** [all the time] die
ganze Zeit (über) - **2.** [everywhere] überall;
[completely] ganz.

throve [θrəʊv] *pt* $\Longrightarrow$ thrive.

throw [θrəʊ] *(pt* threw; *pp* thrown) $\Leftrightarrow$ *vt*
- **1.** [propel, put] werfen - **2.** [move suddenly]:
he threw himself to the floor/onto the bed
er warf sich auf den Boden/das Bett - **3.**
[rider] ablwerfen - **4.** *fig* [force]: **to ~ sb into
confusion** jn durcheinander bringen - **5.** *fig*
[confuse] aus dem Konzept bringen $\Leftrightarrow$ *n*
[toss, pitch] Wurf *der.* $\blacktriangleright$ **throw away** *vt sep*
- **1.** [discard] weglwerfen - **2.** *fig* [money, time]
vergeuden; [opportunity] nicht nutzen.
$\blacktriangleright$ **throw out** *vt sep* - **1.** [discard] weglwerfen - **2.** *fig* [reject] abllehnen - **3.** [force to
leave] hinauslwerfen. $\blacktriangleright$ **throw up** *vi inf*
[vomit] sich übergeben.

throwaway ['θrəʊə,weɪ] *adj* - **1.** [product,
bottle] Wegwerf- - **2.** [remark] beiläufig.

throw-in *n Br* FTBL Einwurf *der.*

thrown [θrəʊn] *pp* $\Longrightarrow$ throw.

thru [θruː] *adj, adv & prep Am inf =* through.

thrush [θrʌʃ] *n* [bird] Drossel *die.*

thrust [θrʌst] *(pt & pp* thrust) $\Leftrightarrow$ *n* - **1.** [for-
ward movement - of knife, sword] Stoß *der;*
[- MIL] Vorstoß *der* - **2.** [main aspect] Tenor
der $\Leftrightarrow$ *vt* [jab, shove]: **to ~ sthg into sthg**
[knife, stick] etw in etw *(A)* stoßen; **she ~ the
money into her pocket** sie stopfte das Geld
in ihre Tasche.

thud [θʌd] $\Leftrightarrow$ *n* dumpfer Aufschlag $\Leftrightarrow$ *vi*
dumpf auflschlagen; [feet] stampfen.

thug [θʌg] *n* Schläger *der.*

thumb [θʌm] $\Leftrightarrow$ *n* [of hand] Daumen *der*
$\Leftrightarrow$ *vt inf* [hitch]: **to ~ a lift** per Anhalter fah-

ren. $\blacktriangleright$ **thumb through** *vt fus* durchlblättern.

thumbs down [,θʌmz-] *n:* **to get** OR **be giv-
en the ~ abgelehnt werden.**

thumbs up *n* [go-ahead]: **to get** OR **be given
the ~ grünes Licht bekommen.**

thumbtack ['θʌmtæk] *n Am* Reißzwecke
die.

thump [θʌmp] $\Leftrightarrow$ *n* - **1.** [blow] Schlag *der*
- **2.** [thud] Bums *der* $\Leftrightarrow$ *vt* [punch] schlagen
$\Leftrightarrow$ *vi* [heart] heftig pochen.

thunder ['θʌndə'] $\Leftrightarrow$ *n (U)* - **1.** METEOR
Donner *der* - **2.** *fig* [loud sound] Donnern *das*
$\Leftrightarrow$ *v impers* METEOR: **it is ~ing** es donnert.

thunderbolt ['θʌndəbəʊlt] *n* - **1.** METEOR
Blitz *der* - **2.** *fig* [shock]: **the news was a ~ die**
Nachricht schlug wie ein Blitz ein.

thunderclap ['θʌndəklæp] *n* Donnerschlag *der.*

thunderstorm ['θʌndəstɔːm] *n* Gewitter
das.

Thursday ['θɜːzdɪ] *n* Donnerstag *der; see also* Saturday.

thus [ðʌs] *adv fml* - **1.** [as a consequence] daher - **2.** [in this way] auf diese Weise - **3.** [as
follows] folgendermaßen.

thwart [θwɔːt] *vt* vereiteln; [person] einen
Strich durch die Rechnung machen *(+ D).*

thyme [taɪm] *n* Thymian *der.*

tiara [tɪ'ɑːrə] *n* [piece of jewellery] Diadem
das.

Tibet [tɪ'bet] *n* Tibet *nt.*

tic [tɪk] *n* Zucken *das.*

tick [tɪk] $\Leftrightarrow$ *n* - **1.** [written mark] Häkchen
das - **2.** [sound] Ticken *das* - **3.** [insect] Zecke
die $\Leftrightarrow$ *vt* [name] ablhaken; [answer, box on
form] anlkreuzen $\Leftrightarrow$ *vi* [make ticking sound]
ticken. $\blacktriangleright$ **tick off** *vt sep* - **1.** [mark off] ablhaken - **2.** [tell off] *inf:* **to ~ sb off (for sthg)** jn
(wegen etw) rüffeln. $\blacktriangleright$ **tick over** *vi*
- **1.** [engine] im Leerlauf sein - **2.** [business, or-
ganization] ganz gut laufen.

ticket ['tɪkɪt] *n* - **1.** [for match, concert] Ein-
trittskarte *die;* [for bus, train, tram] Fahrkarte
die, Fahrschein *der;* [for plane] Ticket *das;* [for
lottery, raffle] Los *das;* [for library] Ausweis
der; [for car park] Parkschein *der* - **2.** [on prod-
uct]: **(price)** ~ Preisschild *das* - **3.** [notice of
traffic offence] Strafzettel *der.*

ticket collector *n Br* [on train] Schaffner
der, -in *die;* [in station] Fahrkartenkontrolleur
der, -in *die.*

ticket inspector *n Br* [on bus, tram] Fahrkartenkontrolleur *der,* -in *die;* [on train]
Schaffner *der,* -in *die.*

ticket machine *n* [for public transport]
Fahrscheinautomat *der;* [in car park] Park-
scheinautomat *der.*

ticket office *n* [at railway station] Fahrkartenschalter *der;* [at theatre] Theaterkasse *die.*

tickle ['tɪkl] $\Leftrightarrow$ *vt* [touch lightly] kitzeln;

[subj: beard, wool] **kratzen** ⬦ *vi* [foot, back] **jucken**; [beard, wool] **kratzen**.

ticklish ['tɪklɪʃ] *adj* [sensitive to touch] **kitzlig**.

tidal ['taɪdl] *adj* **Gezeiten-**.

tidal wave *n* **Flutwelle** *die*.

tidbit ['tɪdbɪt] *n Am* = titbit.

tiddlywinks ['tɪdlɪwɪŋks], **tiddledywinks** *Am* ['tɪdldɪwɪŋks] *n (U)* [game] **Flohhüpfspiel** *das*.

tide [taɪd] *n* - 1. [of sea] **Gezeiten** *pl*; **high ~ Flut** *die*; **low ~ Ebbe** *die*; **the ~ is in/out** es ist **Flut/Ebbe** - 2. *fig* [trend]: **the ~ of (public) opinion** der **Trend** der **öffentlichen Meinung**; **to swim with/against the ~** mit dem/gegen den **Strom schwimmen** - 3. *fig* [large quantity]: **a ~ of protest** eine **Flut** von **Protesten**.

tidy ['taɪdɪ] ⬦ *adj* [gen] **ordentlich**; [appearance] **gepflegt** ⬦ *vt* **aufräumen**. ➤ **tidy up** *vt sep* & *vi* **aufräumen**.

tie [taɪ] (*pt* & *pp* **tied**; *cont* **tying**) ⬦ *n* - 1. [necktie] **Krawatte** *die* - 2. [in game, competition] **Unentschieden** *das* ⬦ *vt* - 1. [attach]: **to ~ sthg (on)to sthg** etw an etw *(A)* **binden**; **to ~ sthg round sthg** etw um etw **binden**; **my hands are ~d** *fig* mir sind die **Hände gebunden**; **to ~ sthg with sthg** etw mit etw **zusammenlbinden** - 2. [do up, fasten] **binden**; [knot] **machen** - 3. *fig* [link]: **to be ~d to sb/sthg** an jn/etw **gebunden sein** ⬦ *vi* [in sport] **unentschieden spielen**. ➤ **tie down** *vt sep fig* [restrict]: **to be ~d down by sthg** durch etw **eingeschränkt sein**. ➤ **tie in with** *vt fus* **passen zu**. ➤ **tie up** *vt sep* - 1. [parcel, papers] **verschnüren**; [person] **fesseln**; [animal] **anlbinden** - 2. [shoelaces] **binden** - 3. *fig* [savings] **fest anllegen** - 4. *fig* [link]: **to be ~d up with sthg** mit etw **zusammenlhängen**.

tiebreak(er) ['taɪbreɪk(əʳ)] *n* - 1. **TENNIS Tiebreak** *das* - 2. [extra question] **Entscheidungsfrage** *die*.

tiepin ['taɪpɪn] *n* **Krawattennadel** *die*.

tier [tɪəʳ] *n* [of seats] **Rang** *der*; [of cake] **Etage** *die*.

tiff [tɪf] *n* **Krach** *der*.

tiger ['taɪgəʳ] *n* **Tiger** *der*.

tight [taɪt] ⬦ *adj* - 1. [close-fitting] **eng**; **the dress was a very ~ fit** das **Kleid** war sehr **eng** - 2. [secure - lid] **fest sitzend**; [- screw] **fest angezogen**; [- knot] **fest** - 3. [taut] **straff** - 4. [close together - bundle] **fest zusammengebunden**; **they stood in a ~ group** sie standen **eng zusammen** - 5. [schedule] **knapp**; [money, match, finish] **knapp** - 6. [rule, control] **streng** - 7. [bend] **scharf**, **eng** - 8. *inf* [drunk] **voll** - 9. *inf* [miserly] **knauserig** ⬦ *adv* - 1. [firmly, securely] **fest**; **to hold ~** **festlhalten**; **to shut** OR **close sthg ~** [eyes] etw **fest schließen**; [lid] etw **fest verschließen**

- 2. [tautly] **straff**. ➤ **tights** *npl* **Strumpfhose** *die*.

tighten ['taɪtn] ⬦ *vt* - 1. [knot, belt, screw] **anlziehen** - 2. [make tauter] **straffen**, **spannen** - 3. [strengthen]: **to ~ one's hold** OR **grip on sthg** etw **fester halten**; *fig* [on party, country] seine **Macht in etw** *(D)* **auslbauen** - 4. [grip, control, security] **verschärfen** ⬦ *vi* [grip, hold] **fester werden**; [rope, chain] sich **spannen**.

tightfisted [ˌtaɪt'fɪstɪd] *adj inf pej* **knauserig**.

tightly ['taɪtlɪ] *adv* [firmly, securely] **fest**.

tightrope ['taɪtrəʊp] *n* **Drahtseil** *das*.

tile [taɪl] *n* - 1. [on roof] **Dachziegel** *der* - 2. [on floor, wall] **Fliese** *die*, **Kachel** *die*.

tiled [taɪld] *adj* [floor, wall, bath] **gefliest**.

till [tɪl] ⬦ *prep* & *conj* **bis** ⬦ *n* **Kasse** *die*.

tilt [tɪlt] ⬦ *vt* [object, chair] **kippen**; [head] **neigen** ⬦ *vi* [person, chair] **kippen**; [head] sich **neigen**.

timber ['tɪmbəʳ] *n* - 1. *(U)* [wood] **Holz** *das* - 2. [beam] **Balken** *der*.

time [taɪm] ⬦ *n* - 1. [gen] **Zeit** *die*; **at that ~** zu der **Zeit**, **damals**; **now is the ~ to do it** jetzt ist der richtige **Zeitpunkt** OR die richtige **Zeit**, es zu tun; **it will take ~** es wird einige **Zeit dauern**; **to have no ~ for sb/sthg** keine **Zeit für jn/etw haben**; **to pass the ~** sich *(D)* die **Zeit vertreiben**; **to play for ~** **versuchen**, **Zeit zu gewinnen** - 2. [as measured by clock]: **what ~ is it?**, **what's the ~?** wie **spät ist es?**, wie viel **Uhr ist es?**; **at this ~ of the day** zu dieser **Tageszeit**; **in a week's/year's ~** in einer **Woche/einem Jahr**; **could you tell me the ~?** **können Sie mir sagen**, wie **spät es ist?**; **can she tell the ~?** kann sie schon die **Uhr lesen?** - 3. [while, spell]: **it was a long ~ before ...** es dauerte lange, **bevor ...**; **in a short ~** **bald**; **for a ~** **einige Zeit(lang)** - 4. [era] **Zeit** *die*; **in ancient ~s** zur **Zeit der Antike**; **in modern ~s** **heutzutage** - 5. [occasion] **Mal** *das*; **this ~** **diesmal**, **dieses Mal**; **(the) last ~** **letztes Mal**, **das letzte Mal**; **three ~s a week** **dreimal pro** OR **in der Woche**; **from ~ to ~** von **Zeit zu Zeit**; **~ after ~, ~ and again** **immer wieder** - 6. [experience]: **we had a good ~** es war **schön**; **to have a hard ~** **viel durchlmachen**; **to have a hard ~ doing sthg** **Schwierigkeiten haben**, etw zu tun - 7. [degree of lateness]: **to be in good ~** OR **ahead of ~** **früh dran sein**; **on ~** **pünktlich**; **did you get there on ~?** **warst du rechtzeitig dort?** - 8. MUS **Takt** *der*; **to beat ~** den **Takt anlgeben**; **in 4/4 ~** im **Viervierteltakt** ⬦ *vt* - 1. [schedule]: **the meeting was ~d to start at nine o'clock** der **Beginn** der **Sitzung** war auf neun **Uhr angesetzt** - 2. [measure - race, runner] die **Zeit stoppen** von; **I ~d how long it took him** ich habe gestoppt, wie lange er **gebraucht hat** - 3. [choose appropriate moment for] **zeitlich ablstimmen**. ➤ **times** ⬦ *npl*

four ~s as much/many viermal so viel/viele; **three ~s as big** dreimal so groß <> *prep* MATH mal; **10 ~s 4 is 40** 10 mal 4 ist 40. <> **about time** *adv*: **it's about ~ (that)** ... es wird (langsam) Zeit, dass ... <> **at a time** *adv*: **three/four at a ~** drei/vier auf einmal; **one at a ~** eine, -r, -s nach den anderen; **for months at a ~** monatelang. <> **at times** *adv* manchmal. <> **at the same time** *adv* - 1. [simultaneously] gleichzeitig, zur gleichen Zeit - 2. [equally] trotzdem, dennoch. <> **for the time being** *adv* vorläufig. <> **in time** *adv* - 1. [not late] rechtzeitig; **to be in ~ for sthg** rechtzeitig für etw kommen - 2. [eventually] schließlich; [over a long period] mit der Zeit.

time bomb *n lit & fig* Zeitbombe *die.*

time lag *n* Zeitabstand *der.*

timeless ['taɪmlɪs] *adj* zeitlos.

time limit *n* Frist *die.*

timely ['taɪmlɪ] *adj* rechtzeitig.

time off *n* (U) freie Zeit.

time-out (*pl* time-outs) *n* SPORT Auszeit *die.*

timer ['taɪmə^r] *n* [time switch] Schaltuhr *die.*

time scale *n* [for project] Zeitspanne *die.*

time-share *n Br* Ferienwohnung, an der man einen Besitzanteil hat.

time switch *n* Schaltuhr *die.*

timetable ['taɪmˌteɪbl] *n* - 1. SCH Stundenplan *der* - 2. [of buses, trains] Fahrplan *der* - 3. [schedule] Programm *das.*

time zone *n* Zeitzone *die.*

timid ['tɪmɪd] *adj* schüchtern.

timing ['taɪmɪŋ] *n* (U) - 1. [of actor, musician, tennis player] Timing *das* - 2. [chosen moment]: **the ~ of the remark/election was unfortunate** der Zeitpunkt der Bemerkung/Wahlen war unglücklich gewählt - 3. SPORT [measuring] Stoppen *das.*

tin [tɪn] *n* - 1. (U) [metal] Blech *das* - 2. *Br* [can] Dose *die* - 3. [for storing] Dose *die.*

tin can *n* Blechdose *die.*

tinfoil ['tɪnfɔɪl] *n* (U) Alufolie *die.*

tinge [tɪndʒ] *n* Spur *die.*

tinged [tɪndʒd] *adj*: **~ with sthg** mit einer Spur von etw.

tingle ['tɪŋgl] *vi* kribbeln.

tinker ['tɪŋkə^r] <> *vi*: **to ~ (with sthg)** (an etw (D)) herumbasteln.

tinned [tɪnd] *adj Br* Dosen-.

tin opener *n Br* Dosenöffner *der.*

tinsel ['tɪnsl] *n* <> Lametta *das.*

tint [tɪnt] *n* Ton *der.*

tinted ['tɪntɪd] *adj* getönt.

tiny ['taɪnɪ] *adj* winzig.

tip [tɪp] <> *n* - 1. [end] Spitze *die* - 2. *Br* [dump] Müllkippe *die* - 3. [gratuity] Trinkgeld *das* - 4. [piece of advice] Tipp *der* <> *vt* - 1. [tilt] kippen - 2. [spill] schütten - 3. [give a gratuity to] Trinkgeld geben (+ D) <> *vi* - 1. [tilt] kippen - 2. [spill] herauslfallen; [li-

quid] sich ergießen. <> **tip over** *vt sep & vi* umlkippen.

tip-off *n* Tipp *der.*

tipped [tɪpt] *adj* [cigarette] mit Filter.

tipsy ['tɪpsɪ] *adj inf* beschwipst.

tiptoe ['tɪptəʊ] <> *n*: **on ~** auf Zehenspitzen <> *vi* auf Zehenspitzen gehen.

tire ['taɪə^r] <> *n Am* = tyre <> *vt* ermüden <> *vi* - 1. [get tired] müde werden - 2. [get fed up]: **to ~ of sb/sthg** von jm/etw genug haben.

tired ['taɪəd] *adj* - 1. [sleepy] müde - 2. [fed up]: **to be ~ of sthg** etw leid sein; **to be ~ of doing sthg** es leid sein, etw zu tun.

tireless ['taɪəlɪs] *adj* unermüdlich.

tiresome ['taɪəsəm] *adj* lästig.

tiring ['taɪərɪŋ] *adj* ermüdend.

tissue ['tɪʃuː] *n* - 1. [paper handkerchief] Tempo® *das*, Papiertaschentuch *das* - 2. (U) BIOL Gewebe *das.*

tissue paper *n* (U) Seidenpapier *das.*

tit [tɪt] *n* - 1. [bird] Meise *die* - 2. *vulg* [breast] Titte *die.*

titbit *Br* ['tɪtbɪt], **tidbit** *Am* ['tɪdbɪt] *n lit & fig* Leckerbissen *der.*

tit for tat [-'tæt] *n* wie du mir, so ich dir.

titillate ['tɪtɪleɪt] *vt* [person] anlregen.

title ['taɪtl] *n* Titel *der.*

titter ['tɪtə^r] *vi* kichern.

TM *abbr of* trademark.

to [unstressed before consonant tə, unstressed before vowel tʊ, stressed tuː] <> *prep* - 1. [indicating direction] nach; **to go ~ Liverpool/Spain** nach Liverpool/Spanien fahren; **to go ~ the USA** in die USA fahren; **to go ~ school/the cinema** in die Schule/ins Kino gehen; **to go ~ university** auf die Universität gehen; **to go ~ work/the doctor's** zur Arbeit/zum Arzt gehen; **the road ~ Bakersfield** die Straße nach Bakersfield - 2. [indicating position]: **I nailed it ~ the wall** ich habe es an die Wand genagelt; **~ the left** links; **~ the right** rechts; **~ the east/west (of the river)** östlich/westlich (des Flusses) - 3. (to express indirect object): **to give sthg ~ sb** jm etw geben; **to talk ~ sb** mit jm sprechen; **to listen ~ the radio** Radio hören; **we added milk ~ the mixture** wir fügten Milch zu der Mischung hinzu - 4. [as far as] bis; **from here ~ London** von hier bis London; **to count ~ ten** bis zehn zählen; **we work from nine ~ five** wir arbeiten von 9 bis 5; **a year ~ the day** ein Jahr auf den Tag genau - 5. *Br* [in telling the time] vor; **it's ten ~ three** es ist zehn vor drei - 6. [per] pro; **10 kilometres ~ the litre** 10 Kilometer pro Liter - 7. [in ratios]: **six votes ~ four** sechs Stimmen gegen vier; **he's ten ~ one to win** es steht zehn zu eins, dass er gewinnt - 8. [of, for]: **the key ~ the car** der Schlüssel für das Auto; **a letter ~ my daughter** ein Brief an meine Tochter - 9. [indicating reaction, effect]

tonsil

zu; **~ my surprise** zu meiner Überraschung; **it would be ~ your advantage** es wäre zu Ihrem Vorteil - **10.** [in stating opinion]: **~ me, he's lying** meiner Meinung nach lügt er; **it seemed quite unnecessary ~ me/him**/*etc* mir/ihm/*etc* erschien dies recht unnötig - **11.** [indicating process, change of state]: **to turn ~ ice** zu Eis werden; **it could lead ~ trouble** das könnte Ärger geben ◇ *with infinitive* - **1.** (forming simple infinitive): **~ walk** gehen; **~ laugh** lachen - **2.** (following another vb): **begin/try ~ do sthg** anfangen/versuchen, etw zu tun; **to want ~ do sthg** etw tun wollen - **3.** (following an adj) zu; **difficult ~ do** schwer zu tun; **ready ~ go** bereit zu gehen - **4.** (indicating purpose) um zu; **we came here ~ look at the castle** wir sind hierher gekommen, um das Schloss anzuschauen - **5.** (replacing a relative clause): **he is the first ~ complain** er ist der erste, der sich beschwert; **to have a lot ~ do** viel zu tun haben; **he told me ~ leave** er sagte, ich solle gehen - **6.** (to avoid repetition of infinitive): **I meant to call him, but I forgot ~** ich wollte ihn eigentlich anrufen, vergaß es aber; **you ought ~** du solltest es tun - **7.** [in comments]: **~ be honest ...** um ehrlich zu sein ...; **~ sum up ...** um zusammenzufassen ... ◇ *adv* [shut]: **push the door ~** drück die Tür zu. ◆ **to and fro** *adv* hin und her; **to go ~ and fro** kommen und gehen.

toad [təʊd] *n* Kröte *die.*

toadstool ['təʊdstu:l] *n* Giftpilz *der.*

toast [təʊst] ◇ *n* (U) [bread, drink] Toast *der* ◇ *vt* - **1.** [bread] toasten - **2.** [person] trinken auf (+ A).

toasted sandwich [ˌtəʊstɪd-] *n* getoastetes Sandwich.

toaster ['təʊstə'] *n* Toaster *der.*

tobacco [tə'bækəʊ] *n* Tabak *der.*

tobacconist [tə'bækənɪst] *n*: **~'s (shop)** Tabakwarenhandlung *die.*

toboggan [tə'bɒgən] *n* Schlitten *der.*

today [tə'deɪ] *n & adv* (U) heute.

toddler ['tɒdlə'] *n* Kleinkind *das.*

to-do (*pl* -s) *n inf dated* Getue *das.*

toe [təʊ] ◇ *n* - **1.** [of foot] Zeh *der,* Zehe *die* - **2.** [of sock, shoe] Spitze *die* ◇ *vt*: **to ~ the line** sich an die Regeln halten; [in political party] sich an die Parteilinie halten.

toenail ['təʊneɪl] *n* Zehennagel *der.*

toffee ['tɒfɪ] *n* - **1.** [sweet] Karamellbonbon *das* - **2.** [substance] Karamell *das.*

together [tə'geðə'] *adv* - **1.** [gen] zusammen; **to go ~** [belong together] zusammengehören - **2.** [at the same time] zur gleichen Zeit. ◆ **together with** *prep* zusammen mit.

toil [tɔɪl] *fml* ◇ *n* Mühe *die* ◇ *vi* sich abmühen.

toilet ['tɔɪlɪt] *n* Toilette *die;* **to go to the ~** zur Toilette gehen.

toilet bag *n* Kulturbeutel *der.*

toilet paper *n* Toilettenpapier *das.*

toiletries ['tɔɪlɪtrɪz] *npl* Toilettenartikel *pl.*

toilet roll *n* Rolle *die* Toilettenpapier.

token ['təʊkn] ◇ *adj* symbolisch ◇ *n* - **1.** [voucher, disc] Gutschein *der* - **2.** [symbol] Zeichen *das.* ◆ **by the same token** *adv* ebenso.

told [təʊld] *pt & pp* ⊳ tell.

tolerable ['tɒlərəbl] *adj* [reasonable] annehmbar.

tolerance ['tɒlərəns] *n* Toleranz *die.*

tolerant ['tɒlərənt] *adj* - **1.** [not bigoted]: **~ of sb/sthg** tolerant gegenüber jm/etw - **2.** [resistant]: **~ to sthg** unempfindlich gegen etw.

tolerate ['tɒləreɪt] *vt* - **1.** [put up with - noise, heat, behaviour] ertragen - **2.** [permit] dulden, tolerieren.

toll [təʊl] *n* - **1.** [number] Zahl *die;* **the death ~ die** Zahl der Toten - **2.** [fee] Gebühr *die* - **3.** *phr*: **to take its ~** seinen Tribut fordern.

tomato [*Br* tə'mɑːtəʊ, *Am* tə'meɪtəʊ] (*pl* -es) *n* Tomate *die.*

tomb [tu:m] *n* Grab *das.*

tomboy ['tɒmbɔɪ] *n*: **she was a bit of a ~** sie war wie ein Junge.

tombstone ['tu:mstəʊn] *n* Grabstein *der.*

tomcat ['tɒmkæt] *n* Kater *der.*

tomorrow [tə'mɒrəʊ] *n & adv* morgen.

ton [tʌn] (*pl inv* OR -s) *n* - **1.** *Br* [imperial unit of measurement] ≃ Tonne *die* (= 1016 kg) - **2.** *Am* [unit of measurement] ≃ Tonne *die* (= 907 kg) - **3.** [metric unit of measurement] Tonne *die* (= 1000 kg). ◆ **tons** *npl Br inf*: **-s of** ein Haufen (+ G).

tone [təʊn] *n* [gen] Ton *der;* **to lower the ~** das Niveau senken. ◆ **tone down** *vt sep* mäßigen. ◆ **tone up** *vt sep* in Form bringen.

tone-deaf *adj*: **to be ~** kein musikalisches Gehör haben.

tongs [tɒŋz] *npl* - **1.** [for sugar] Zange *die* - **2.** [for hair] Lockenstab *der.*

tongue [tʌŋ] *n* - **1.** [gen] Zunge *die;* **to hold one's ~** *fig* den Mund halten; **to have a sharp ~** eine scharfe Zunge haben - **2.** *fml* [language] Sprache *die.*

tongue-in-cheek *adj* ironisch.

tongue-tied *adj*: **to be ~** kein Wort herausbringen.

tonic ['tɒnɪk] *n* - **1.** [tonic water] Tonic *das* - **2.** [medicine] Tonikum *das.*

tonic water *n* Tonic *das.*

tonight [tə'naɪt] *n & adv* heute Abend; [during night] heute Nacht.

tonne [tʌn] (*pl inv* OR -s) *n* Tonne *die.*

tonsil ['tɒnsl] *n* Mandel *die.*

tonsil(l)itis [ˌtɒnsɪˈlaɪtɪs] n (U) Mandelentzündung die.

too [tuː] adv - 1. [also] auch - 2. [excessively] zu; ~ **many** zu viel; **it's ~ late to go out** es ist zu spät zum Ausgehen; **I know her all** OR **only ~ well** ich kenne sie nur zu gut; **it was none ~ comfortable** es war nicht gerade bequem; **not ~ good** nicht besonders gut; **how do you feel? – not ~ bad** wie fühlst du dich? – ganz gut; **I'd be only ~ happy to help** ich würde wirklich OR nur zu gerne helfen.

took [tʊk] pt ⊳ take.

tool [tuːl] n - 1. [implement] Werkzeug das - 2. fig [means] Hilfsmittel das.

tool box n Werkzeugkasten der.

tool kit n Werkzeugsatz der.

toot [tuːt] ⬦ n: **to give a ~** hupen ⬦ vi hupen.

tooth [tuːθ] (pl teeth) n Zahn der.

toothache ['tuːθeɪk] n (U) Zahnschmerzen pl.

toothbrush ['tuːθbrʌʃ] n Zahnbürste die.

toothpaste ['tuːθpeɪst] n Zahnpasta die.

toothpick ['tuːθpɪk] n Zahnstocher der.

top [tɒp] ⬦ adj - 1. [highest] oberste, -r, -s - 2. [most important, successful] Spitzen-; **she was ~ in the exam** sie war die Beste in der Prüfung - 3. [maximum] Höchst- ⬦ n - 1. [highest point - of road] Ende das; [- of stairs] oberste Stufe; [- of hill] Gipfel der; [- of tree] Krone die; **at the ~ of the page** oben auf der Seite; **on ~** oben; **at the ~ of one's voice** aus vollem Halse - 2. [lid, cap - of bottle, jar] Deckel der; [- of pen, tube] Kappe die - 3. [upper side - of table] Platte die; [- of box] Oberseite - 4. [clothing] Oberteil das - 5. [toy] Kreisel der - 6. [in organization, league, table] Spitze die; **to be ~ of the class** Klassenbeste, -r sein ⬦ vt - 1. [be first in - table, chart] anführen; [- poll, league] an erster Stelle liegen in (+ D) - 2. [better] übertreffen; [offer] überbieten - 3. [exceed] übersteigen - 4. [cover]: **to ~ with cream** Sahne geben auf (+ A); **~ped with** mit. ⬦ **on top of** prep - 1. [indicating position] auf (+ D); [indicating direction] auf (+ A) - 2. [in addition to] zusätzlich zu. ⬦ **top up** Br, **top off** Am vt sep nachfüllen.

top floor n oberstes Stockwerk.

top hat n Zylinder der.

top-heavy adj kopflastig.

topic ['tɒpɪk] n Thema das.

topical ['tɒpɪkl] adj aktuell.

topless ['tɒplɪs] adj [barebreasted] oben ohne.

topmost ['tɒpməʊst] adj oberste, -r, -s.

topping ['tɒpɪŋ] n Garnierung die.

topple ['tɒpl] ⬦ vt [government, leader] stürzen ⬦ vi fallen.

top-secret adj streng geheim.

topspin ['tɒpspɪn] n (U) Topspin der.

topsy-turvy [ˌtɒpsɪˈtɜːvɪ] adj - 1. [messy] durcheinander - 2. [haywire] verkehrt.

torch [tɔːtʃ] n - 1. Br [electric] Taschenlampe die - 2. [flaming stick] Fackel die.

tore [tɔːr] pt ⊳ tear².

torment [n 'tɔːment, vb tɔːˈment] ⬦ n Qual die ⬦ vt [worry, annoy] quälen.

torn [tɔːn] pp ⊳ tear².

tornado [tɔːˈneɪdəʊ] (pl -es OR -s) n Tornado der.

torpedo [tɔːˈpiːdəʊ] (pl -es) n Torpedo der.

torrent ['tɒrənt] n - 1. [rushing water] reißender Strom - 2. [of words] Schwall der.

torrid ['tɒrɪd] adj lit & fig heiß.

tortoise ['tɔːtəs] n Schildkröte die.

tortoiseshell ['tɔːtəʃel] ⬦ adj [cat] Schildpatt- ⬦ n [material] Schildpatt das.

torture ['tɔːtʃər] ⬦ n - 1. (U) [punishment] Folter die - 2. fig [cruel treatment] Qual die ⬦ vt foltern.

Tory ['tɔːrɪ] ⬦ adj Tory-, konservativ ⬦ n Tory der, die, Konservative der, die.

toss [tɒs] ⬦ vt - 1. [throw carelessly] werfen; **she ~ed back her head** sie warf ihren Kopf zurück - 2. [food] schwenken; [salad] mischen; [pancake] wenden - 3. [coin] werfen; **I'll ~ you for it** lass uns eine Münze werfen - 4. [boat, passengers] hin und her werfen ⬦ vi [move about]: **to ~ and turn** sich hin und her werfen. ⬦ **toss up** vi eine Münze werfen.

tot [tɒt] n - 1. inf [small child] kleines Kind - 2. [of drink] Schluck der.

total ['təʊtl] ⬦ adj - 1. [complete - dedication, despair, darkness] völlig; [- eclipse, failure] total; **~ fool** Vollidiot der - 2. [amount, number] Gesamt- ⬦ n Gesamtsumme die; **a ~ of 50 people** insgesamt 50 Leute ⬦ vt - 1. [add up] zusammenlzählen - 2. [amount to] sich belaufen auf (+ A).

totally ['təʊtəlɪ] adv völlig.

totter ['tɒtər] vi - 1. [walk unsteadily] taumeln - 2. fig [government] schwanken.

touch [tʌtʃ] ⬦ n - 1. (U) [act of touching] Berührung die; **to be soft to the ~** sich weich anlfühlen - 2. [detail] Detail das - 3. (U) [style] Note die - 4. [contact]: **to get in ~ with sb** sich mit jm in Verbindung setzen; **to keep in ~ (with sb)** (mit jm) in Kontakt bleiben; **to lose ~ with sb** jn aus den Augen verlieren; **to be out of ~ with sthg** in Bezug auf etw (A) nicht auf dem Laufenden sein - 5. [small amount]: **a ~ (of sthg)** eine Spur (von etw) - 6. SPORT: **in ~** im Aus ⬦ vt - 1. [make contact with] anlfassen - 2. [move emotionally] rühren - 3. [eat, drink] anlrühren ⬦ vi - 1. [make contact - people, things] sich berühren; **don't ~!** nicht anlfassen! - 2. [be in contact] aneinander stoßen. ⬦ **touch down** vi [plane] auflsetzen. ⬦ **touch on** vt fus rühren an (+ A).

touch-and-go *adj* ungewiss.

touchdown ['tʌtʃdaʊn] *n* - **1.** [of plane] Aufsetzen *das* - **2.** [in American football] Touchdown *der*.

touched [tʌtʃt] *adj* - **1.** [moved] bewegt - **2.** *inf* [slightly mad] nicht ganz richtig im Kopf.

touching ['tʌtʃɪŋ] *adj* rührend.

touchline ['tʌtʃlaɪn] *n* Auslinie *die*.

touchy ['tʌtʃɪ] *adj* - **1.** [person] empfindlich - **2.** [subject, question] heikel.

tough [tʌf] *adj* - **1.** [gen] hart - **2.** [meat] zäh - **3.** [decision, life] schwer - **4.** [criminal, neighbourhood] rau.

toughen ['tʌfn] *vt* - **1.** [character] hart machen - **2.** [material] härten.

toupee ['tuːpeɪ] *n* Toupet *das*.

tour [tʊəʳ] ◇ *n* - **1.** [trip] Tour *die* - **2.** [of building, town, museum] Rundgang *der* - **3.** [of pop group etc] Tournee *die*; **to be on ~** auf Tournee sein ◇ *vt* - **1.** [visit - city, museum] besichtigen; [- country] reisen durch - **2.** SPORT & THEATRE eine Tournee machen durch.

touring ['tʊərɪŋ] *n* Herumreisen *das*.

tourism ['tʊərɪzm] *n* Tourismus *der*, Fremdenverkehr *der*.

tourist ['tʊərɪst] *n* Tourist *der*, -in *die*.

tourist (information) office *n* Touristeninformation *die*, Fremdenverkehrsbüro *das*.

tournament ['tɔːnəmənt] *n* Turnier *das*.

tour operator *n* Reiseveranstalter *der*.

tout [taʊt] ◇ *n* Schwarzhändler *der*, -in *die* ◇ *vt* [tickets, goods] anbieten ◇ *vi*: **to ~ for custom** auf Kundenfang sein.

tow [təʊ] ◇ *n*: **to give sb a ~** jn abschleppen; **to be on ~** *Br* abgeschleppt werden ◇ *vt* abschleppen.

towards *Br* [tə'wɔːdz], **toward** *Am* [tə'wɔːd] *prep* - **1.** [in the direction of] zu; **to run ~ sb** auf jn zullaufen; **efforts ~ his release** Bemühungen um seine Freilassung - **2.** [facing] nach - **3.** [with regard to] gegenüber; **his feelings ~ me** seine Gefühle mir gegenüber OR für mich - **4.** [in time] gegen; **~ nine o'clock** gegen neun Uhr - **5.** [in space]: **to sit ~ the back/front** hinten/vorne sitzen - **6.** [as contribution] für; **he gave £20 ~ animal research** er spendete £20 für die Tierforschung.

towel ['taʊəl] *n* Handtuch *das*.

towelling *Br*, **toweling** *Am* ['taʊəlɪŋ] *n* (U) Frotteestoff *der*.

towel rail *n* Handtuchhalter *der*.

tower ['taʊəʳ] ◇ *n* Turm *der* ◇ *vi* hochragen; **to ~ over sb/sthg** jn/etw überragen.

tower block *n* *Br* Hochhaus *das*.

town [taʊn] *n* Stadt *die*; **to go out on the ~** einen draufmachen; **to go to ~** *fig* [spend a lot] es sich (D) was kosten lassen; [take trouble] sich ins Zeug legen.

town centre *n* Stadtmitte *die*.

town council *n* Stadtrat *der*.

town hall *n* - **1.** [building] Rathaus *das* - **2.** (U) *fig* [council] Stadtrat *der*.

town plan *n* Stadtplan *der*.

town planning *n* (U) Stadtplanung *die*.

towpath ['təʊpɑːθ, *pl* -pɑːðz] *n* Leinpfad *der*.

towrope ['təʊrəʊp] *n* Abschleppseil *das*.

tow truck *n* *Am* Abschleppwagen *der*.

toxic ['tɒksɪk] *adj* giftig.

toy [tɔɪ] *n* Spielzeug *das*. ◆ **toy with** *vt fus* spielen mit.

toy shop *n* Spielwarenladen *der*.

trace [treɪs] ◇ *n* Spur *die* ◇ *vt* - **1.** [find] aufspüren - **2.** [follow progress of] verfolgen - **3.** [mark outline of] nachzeichnen; [with tracing paper] durchpausen.

tracing paper *n* (U) Transparentpapier *das*.

track [træk] ◇ *n* - **1.** [path] Pfad *der* - **2.** SPORT Bahn *die* - **3.** RAIL Gleis *das* - **4.** [mark, trace] Spur *die* - **5.** [on record, tape, CD] Stück *das* - **6.** *phr*: **to lose ~ of sb/sthg** jn/etw aus den Augen verlieren; **to be on the right/wrong ~** auf der richtigen/falschen Spur sein ◇ *vt* [follow] nachspüren (+ D). ◆ **track down** *vt sep* [person, animal] aufspüren; [book, address] aufstöbern.

track record *n*: **to have a good ~** gute Erfolge aufzuweisen haben.

tracksuit ['træksuːt] *n* Trainingsanzug *der*.

traction ['trækʃn] *n* (U) PHYSICS Zugkraft *die*; **in ~** im Streckverband.

tractor ['træktəʳ] *n* Traktor *der*.

trade [treɪd] ◇ *n* - **1.** [commerce] Handel *der* - **2.** [job] Handwerk *das*; **by ~** von Beruf ◇ *vt* [exchange] tauschen; **to ~ sthg for sthg** etw gegen etw eintauschen ◇ *vi* COMM [do business]: **to ~ (with sb)** (mit jm) Handel treiben. ◆ **trade in** *vt sep* [exchange] in Zahlung geben.

trade fair *n* Messe *die*.

trade-in *n*: **they gave her a ~ on her old cooker** sie nahmen ihren alten Herd in Zahlung.

trademark ['treɪdmɑːk] *n* - **1.** COMM Warenzeichen *das* - **2.** *fig* [characteristic]: **honesty is his ~** er ist für seine Ehrlichkeit bekannt.

trade name *n* COMM Handelsname *der*.

trader ['treɪdəʳ] *n* Händler *der*, -in *die*.

tradesman ['treɪdzmən] (*pl* -men [-mən]) *n* [shopkeeper, trader] Händler *der*.

trades union *n* *Br* = trade union.

Trades Union Congress *n* *Br*: **the ~** der Gewerkschaftsbund.

trade union *n* Gewerkschaft *die*.

trading ['treɪdɪŋ] *n* Handel *der*.

trading estate *n* *Br* Industriegebiet *das*.

tradition [trə'dɪʃn] *n* - **1.** (U) [system of customs] Tradition *die* - **2.** [established practice] Brauch *der*.

traditional [trə'dɪʃənl] *adj* traditionell.

traffic ['træfɪk] (*pt & pp* -ked; *cont* -king) ◇ *n* - **1.** [vehicles] Verkehr *der* - **2.** [illegal trade] Handel *der*; **the ~ in drugs/arms** der Drogen-/Waffenhandel ◇ *vi*: **to ~ in sthg** mit etw handeln.

traffic circle *n Am* Kreisverkehr *der*.

traffic jam *n* Stau *der*.

trafficker ['træfɪkə'] *n* Händler *der*, -in *die*.

traffic lights *npl* Ampel *die*.

traffic warden *n Br* Hilfspolizist *der*, Politesse *die*.

tragedy ['trædʒədɪ] *n* Tragödie *die*.

tragic ['trædʒɪk] *adj* tragisch.

trail [treɪl] ◇ *n* - **1.** [path] Weg *der* - **2.** [traces] Spur *die* ◇ *vt* - **1.** [drag behind, tow] hinter sich (*D*) her schleifen - **2.** [lag behind] zurückliegen hinter (+ *D*) ◇ *vi* - **1.** [drag behind] schleifen - **2.** [move slowly] trotten - **3.** SPORT [lose] zurückliegen. **➤ trail away, trail off** *vi*: **his voice ~ed away** seine Stimme wurde leiser und verstummte schließlich.

trailer ['treɪlə'] *n* - **1.** [vehicle for luggage] Anhänger *der* - **2.** *esp Am* [for living in] Wohnwagen *der* - **3.** CINEMA Trailer *der*.

train [treɪn] ◇ *n* - **1.** RAIL Zug *der*; **by ~** mit dem Zug - **2.** [of dress] Schleppe *die* - **3.** [connected sequence]: **~ of thought** Gedankengang *der* ◇ *vt* - **1.** [teach - animal] dressieren; **to ~ sb to do sthg** jm beibringen, etw zu tun - **2.** [for job] ausbilden; **to ~ sb as sthg** jn zu etw ausbilden - **3.** SPORT trainieren - **4.** [gun, camera]: **to ~ sthg on sb/sthg** etw auf jn/etw richten ◇ *vi* - **1.** [for job]: **to ~ (as)** eine Ausbildung machen (als) - **2.** SPORT: **to ~ (for sthg)** (für etw) trainieren.

train driver *n* Zugführer *der*, -in *die*.

trained [treɪnd] *adj* ausgebildet.

trainee [treɪ'niː] *n* Auszubildende *der, die*; [academic, technical] Praktikant *der*, -in *die*.

trainer ['treɪnə'] *n* - **1.** [of dogs] Dresseur *der*, -euse *die*; [of horses] Trainer *der*, -in *die* - **2.** SPORT Trainer *der*, -in *die*. **➤ trainers** *npl Br* [shoes] Turnschuhe *pl*.

training ['treɪnɪŋ] *n* - **1.** [for job] Ausbildung *die* - **2.** SPORT Training *das*.

training shoes *npl Br* Turnschuhe *pl*.

traipse [treɪps] *vi* latschen.

trait [treɪt] *n* Charakterzug *der*.

traitor ['treɪtə'] *n*: **~ (to sthg)** Verräter *der*, -in *die* (an etw (*D*)).

trajectory [trə'dʒektərɪ] *n* TECH Flugbahn *die*.

tram [træm] *n Br* Straßenbahn *die*.

tramp [træmp] ◇ *n* [homeless person] Landstreicher *der*, -in *die* ◇ *vi* [trudge] trotten.

trample ['træmpl] *vt* niedertrampeln.

trampoline ['træmpəliːn] *n* Trampolin *das*.

trance [trɑːns] *n* [hypnotic state] Trance *die*.

tranquil ['træŋkwɪl] *adj literary* friedlich.

tranquillizer *Br*, **tranquilizer** *Am* ['træŋkwɪlaɪzə'] *n* Beruhigungsmittel *das*.

transaction [træn'zækʃn] *n* [piece of business] Transaktion *die*.

transcend [træn'send] *vt fml* [go beyond] hinausgehen über (+ *A*).

transcript ['trænskrɪpt] *n* [of speech, conversation] Mitschrift *die*.

transfer [*n* 'trænsfɜːr', *vb* træns'fɜːr'] ◇ *n* - **1.** (*U*) [from one place to another - of money] Überweisung *die*; [- of prisoner] Überführung *die*; [- of patient] Verlegung *die* - **2.** (*U*) [from one person to another] Übertragung *die* - **3.** [for job] Versetzung *die* - **4.** SPORT Wechsel *der*, Transfer *der* - **5.** [design] Abziehbild *das* ◇ *vt* - **1.** (*U*) [from one place to another - money] überweisen; [- prisoner] überführen; [- patient] verlegen - **2.** [from one person to another]: **to ~ sthg to sb** jm etw übertragen - **3.** [for job] versetzen - **4.** SPORT transferieren ◇ *vi* [to different job *etc* & SPORT] wechseln.

transfix [træns'fɪks] *vt* [immobilize] erstarren lassen.

transform [træns'fɔːm] *vt*: **to ~ sb/sthg (into)** jn/etw verwandeln (in (+ *A*)).

transfusion [træns'fjuːʒn] *n* Transfusion *die*.

transistor [træn'zɪstə'] *n* ELECTRON Transistor *der*.

transit ['trænsɪt] *n*: **in ~** [goods] auf dem Transport.

transition [træn'zɪʃn] *n*: **~ from sthg to sthg** Übergang *der* von etw zu etw.

transitive ['trænzɪtɪv] *adj* GRAMM transitiv.

transitory ['trænzɪtrɪ] *adj* vergänglich.

translate [træns'leɪt] *vt* - **1.** [languages] übersetzen - **2.** *fig* [transform]: **to ~ a plan into action** einen Plan in die Tat umsetzen.

translation [træns'leɪʃn] *n* Übersetzung *die*.

translator [træns'leɪtə'] *n* Übersetzer *der*, -in *die*.

transmission [trænz'mɪʃn] *n* - **1.** [passing on & ELECTRON] Übertragung *die* - **2.** RADIO & TV [programme] Sendung *die*.

transmit [trænz'mɪt] *vt* übertragen.

transmitter [trænz'mɪtə'] *n* ELECTRON Sender *der*.

transparency [trans'pærənsɪ] *n* - **1.** PHOT Dia(positiv) *das* - **2.** [for overhead projector] Folie *die*.

transparent [træns'pærənt] *adj* - **1.** [see-through] durchsichtig - **2.** [obvious] offensichtlich.

transpire [træn'spaɪə'] *fml* ◇ *vt*: **it ~s that ...** es stellt sich heraus, dass ... ◇ *vi* [happen] passieren.

transplant [*n* 'trænsplɑːnt, *vb* træns'plɑːnt] ⬦ *n* [MED - operation] Transplantation *die;* [- organ, tissue] Transplantat *das* ⬦ *vt* - 1. MED transplantieren - 2. BOT [seedlings] umlpflanzen.

transport [*n* 'trænspɔːt, *vb* træn'spɔːt] ⬦ *n* - 1. [system] Verkehrsmittel *pl* - 2. [of goods, people] Beförderung *die,* Transport *der* ⬦ *vt* [goods, people] befördern, transportieren.

transportation [ˌtrænspɔː'teɪʃn] *n (U) esp Am* = transport.

transpose [træns'pəʊz] *vt* [change round] umlstellen.

trap [træp] ⬦ *n* Falle *die* ⬦ *vt* - 1. [animal, bird] fangen - 2. *fig* [trick] eine Falle stellen (+ *D*) - 3. [immobilize, catch]: **to be ~ped in a relationship** in einer Beziehung gefangen sein - 4. [energy] speichern.

trapdoor ['træp'dɔːʳ] *n* Falltür *die.*

trapeze [trə'piːz] *n* Trapez *das.*

trappings ['træpɪŋz] *npl* äußere Zeichen *pl.*

trash [træʃ] *n* - 1. *Am* [refuse] Abfall *der* - 2. *inf pej* [sthg of poor quality] Ramsch *der;* [book, film] Schund *der.*

trashcan ['træʃkæn] *n Am* Abfalleimer *der.*

traumatic [trɔː'mætɪk] *adj* traumatisch.

travel ['trævl] ⬦ *n (U)* Reisen *das* ⬦ *vt* [distance] fahren; **to ~ the world/country** durch die Welt/das Land reisen ⬦ *vi* - 1. [journey] reisen - 2. [go, move - train] fahren; [- light] sich fortlbewegen; [- current] fließen; [- news] sich verbreiten.

travel agency *n* Reisebüro *das.*

travel agent *n* Reiseveranstalter *der,* -in *die;* **~'s** Reisebüro *das.*

travelcard ['trævlkɑːd] *n* Zeitkarte *die.*

traveller *Br,* **traveler** *Am* ['trævləʳ] *n* - 1. [person on journey] Reisende *der, die* - 2. [itinerant] Herumreisende *der, die.*

traveller's cheque *n* Travellerscheck *der.*

travelling *Br,* **traveling** *Am* ['trævlɪŋ] *adj* - 1. [itinerant] Wander- - 2. [for taking on journeys, of travel] Reise-.

travelsick ['trævlsɪk] *adj* reisekrank.

travesty ['trævəstɪ] *n:* **it was a ~ of justice** es war eine Verhöhnung der Gerechtigkeit.

trawler ['trɔːləʳ] *n* Trawler *der.*

tray [treɪ] *n* - 1. [for carrying] Tablett *das* - 2. [for papers, mail] Korb *der.*

treacherous ['tretʃərəs] *adj* - 1. [person, behaviour] verräterisch - 2. [rock, tides] tückisch.

treachery ['tretʃərɪ] *n* Verrat *der.*

treacle ['triːkl] *n Br* Sirup *der.*

tread [tred] (*pt* trod; *pp* trodden) ⬦ *n* - 1. [on tyre, shoe] Profil *das* - 2. [sound or way of walking] Schritt *der,* Tritt *der* ⬦ *vi* [place foot]: **to ~ on sthg** auf etw *(A)* treten.

treason ['triːzn] *n* Verrat *der.*

treasure ['treʒəʳ] ⬦ *n* Schatz *der* ⬦ *vt* [memory] bewahren; [object] sorgfältig auflbewahren.

treasurer ['treʒərəʳ] *n* Schatzmeister *der,* -in *die.*

treasury ['treʒərɪ] *n* [room] Schatzkammer *die.* ⬥ **Treasury** *n:* **the Treasury** das Finanzministerium.

treat [triːt] ⬦ *vt* - 1. [gen] behandeln; **to ~ sthg as a joke** etw als Witz anlsehen - 2. [give sthg special]: **to ~ sb (to sthg)** jn (zu etw) einlladen ⬦ *n* [sthg special]: **what a ~!** was für ein Genuss!; **to give sb a ~** jm eine Freude bereiten; **this is my ~** ich lade dich ein.

treatment ['triːtmənt] *n* [gen] Behandlung *die;* [specific method of medical care] Behandlungsmethode *die.*

treaty ['triːtɪ] *n* Vertrag *der.*

treble ['trebl] ⬦ *adj* [with numbers]: **~ 4** dreimal 4 ⬦ *n* MUS - 1. *(U)* [musical range] Oberstimme *die* - 2. [boy singer] Knabensopran *der* ⬦ *vt* verdreifachen ⬦ *vi* sich verdreifachen.

treble clef *n* Violinschlüssel *der.*

tree [triː] *n* [plant & COMPUT] Baum *der.*

treetop ['triːtɒp] *n* Baumkrone *die.*

tree-trunk *n* Baumstamm *der.*

trek [trek] *n* anstrengender Marsch.

tremble ['trembl] *vi* zittern.

tremendous [trɪ'mendəs] *adj* - 1. [impressive, large] enorm - 2. *inf* [really good] sagenhaft.

tremor ['treməʳ] *n* - 1. [of body, voice] Zittern *das* - 2. [small earthquake] Beben *das.*

trench [trentʃ] *n* - 1. [channel] Graben *der* - 2. MIL Schützengraben *der.*

trend [trend] *n* [tendency] Trend *der,* Tendenz *die.*

trendy [trendɪ] *adj inf* in, angesagt.

trepidation [ˌtrepɪ'deɪʃn] *n (U) fml:* **in** OR **with ~** mit einem beklommenen Gefühl.

trespass ['trespəs] *vi:* **to ~ (on sb's land)** ein Grundstück unbefugt betreten; **'no ~ing'** 'Betreten verboten'.

trespasser ['trespəsəʳ] *n* Unbefugte *der, die.*

trial ['traɪəl] *n* - 1. LAW Prozess *der;* **to be on ~ (for sthg)** (wegen etw) vor Gericht stehen - 2. [test, experiment] Versuch *der;* **on ~** zur Probe; **by ~ and error** durch Ausprobieren - 3. [unpleasant experience] Qual *die.*

triangle ['traɪæŋgl] *n* - 1. [shape] Dreieck *das* - 2. MUS Triangel *der.*

tribe [traɪb] *n* [social group] Stamm *der.*

tribunal [traɪ'bjuːnl] *n* Tribunal *das.*

tributary ['trɪbjʊtrɪ] *n* GEOGR Nebenfluss *der.*

tribute ['trɪbjuːt] *n* - 1. [respect] Tribut *der;* **to pay ~ to sb/sthg** jm/etw Tribut zollen - 2. [evidence]: **it's a ~ to his strength of char-**

acter that ... es ist ein Beweis für seine Charakterstärke, dass ...

trice [traɪs] *n*: in a ~ im Nu.

trick [trɪk] <> *n* - 1. [to deceive] Streich *der*; **to play a ~ on sb** jm einen Streich spielen - 2. [to entertain] Trick *der* - 3. [ability, knack] Trick *der*; **that will do the ~** damit ist das Problem gelöst <> *vt* austricksen; **to ~ sb into doing sthg** jn durch List dazu bringen, etw zu tun.

trickery [ˈtrɪkərɪ] *n* Betrug *der*.

trickle [ˈtrɪkl] <> *n* [of liquid] Rinnsal *das*; [drip] Tröpfeln *das* <> *vi* - 1. [liquid] rinnen - 2. [people]: **to ~ in/out** nach und nach herein-/herauslkommen.

tricky [ˈtrɪkɪ] *adj* [difficult] verzwickt.

tricycle [ˈtraɪsɪkl] *n* Dreirad *das*.

tried [traɪd] *adj*: **~ and tested** erprobt, bewährt.

trifle [ˈtraɪfl] *n* - 1. CULIN Dessert aus Biskuit, Früchten, Vanillecreme und Sahne in Schichten - 2. [unimportant thing] Kleinigkeit *die*. ◆ **a trifle** *adv fml* eine Spur.

trifling [ˈtraɪflɪŋ] *adj pej* unbedeutend.

trigger [ˈtrɪgə] *n* [on gun] Abzug *der*. ◆ **trigger off** *vt sep* = trigger.

trill [trɪl] *n* - 1. MUS Triller *der* - 2. [of birds] Trällern *das*.

trim [trɪm] <> *adj* - 1. [neat and tidy] gepflegt - 2. [slim] schlank <> *n* [cut]: **to give sb OR sb's hair a ~** jm die Haare nachlschneiden <> *vt* - 1. [cut - hedge] zurücklschneiden; [- hair] nachlschneiden; [- lawn] mähen; [- nails] schneiden - 2. [decorate]: **to ~ sthg (with sthg)** etw (mit etw) verzieren.

trinket [ˈtrɪŋkɪt] *n* Schmuckstück *das*.

trio [ˈtriːəʊ] (*pl* -s) *n* Trio *das*.

trip [trɪp] <> *n* - 1. [journey] Ausflug *der* - 2. *drugs sl* [experience] Trip *der* <> *vt* [make stumble] ein Bein stellen (+ *D*) <> *vi* [stumble]: **to ~ (over sthg)** (über etw (*A*)) stolpern. ◆ **trip up** *vt sep* [make stumble] ein Bein stellen (+ *D*).

tripe [traɪp] *n* (*U*) - 1. CULIN Kaldaunen *pl* - 2. *inf* [nonsense] Quatsch *der*.

triple [ˈtrɪpl] <> *adj* dreifach <> *vt* verdreifachen <> *vi* sich verdreifachen.

triple jump *n*: **the ~** der Dreisprung.

triplets [ˈtrɪplɪts] *npl* Drillinge *pl*.

tripod [ˈtraɪpɒd] *n* Stativ *das*.

trite [traɪt] *adj pej* banal.

triumph [ˈtraɪəmf] <> *n* Triumph *der* <> *vi*: **to ~ (over)** triumphieren (über (+ *A*)).

trivia [ˈtrɪvɪə] *n* (*U*) Belanglosigkeiten *pl*.

trivial [ˈtrɪvɪəl] *adj pej* trivial.

trod [trɒd] *pt* ⟳ tread.

trolley [ˈtrɒlɪ] (*pl* trolleys) *n* - 1. *Br* [for shopping] Einkaufswagen *der*; [for luggage] Gepäckwagen *der* - 2. *Br* [for food, drinks] Servierwagen *der* - 3. *Am* [vehicle] Straßenbahn *die*.

trombone [trɒmˈbəʊn] *n* Posaune *die*.

troop [truːp] <> *n* [large group] Schar *die* <> *vi* strömen. ◆ **troops** *npl* MIL Truppen *pl*.

trophy [ˈtrəʊfɪ] *n* SPORT Trophäe *die*.

tropical [ˈtrɒpɪkl] *adj* tropisch.

tropics [ˈtrɒpɪks] *npl*: **the ~** die Tropen.

trot [trɒt] <> *n* Trab *der* <> *vi* traben. ◆ **on the trot** *adv inf* hintereinander.

trouble [ˈtrʌbl] <> *n* - 1. (*U*) [difficulty] Problem *das*; **to be in ~** [having problems] in Schwierigkeiten stecken - 2. [bother]: **it's no ~** es macht mir keine Mühe; **to take the ~ to do sthg** sich (*D*) die Mühe machen, etw zu tun - 3. (*U*) [pain, illness] Beschwerden *pl*; **to have heart/kidney ~** es mit dem Herzen/den Nieren haben - 4. [fighting & POL] Unruhen *pl* <> *vt* - 1. [worry, upset] beunruhigen - 2. [interrupt, disturb] stören - 3. [cause pain to] zu schaffen machen (+ *D*). ◆ **troubles** *npl* - 1. [worries] Sorgen *pl* - 2. POL [unrest] Unruhen *pl*.

troubled [ˈtrʌbld] *adj* - 1. [worried, upset] besorgt - 2. [disturbed - sleep] unruhig; [- place] von Unruhen geschüttelt; **~ times** turbulente Zeiten.

troublemaker [ˈtrʌblˌmeɪkə] *n* Unruhestifter *der*, -in *die*.

troublesome [ˈtrʌblsəm] *adj* lästig.

trough [trɒf] *n* - 1. [for animals] Trog *der* - 2. [low point] Tal *das*.

troupe [truːp] *n* Truppe *die*.

trousers [ˈtraʊzəz] *npl* Hose *die*; **a pair of ~** eine Hose.

trout [traʊt] (*pl inv* OR -s) *n* Forelle *die*.

trowel [ˈtraʊəl] *n* - 1. [for the garden] Pflanzkelle *die* - 2. [for cement, plaster] Kelle *die*.

truant [ˈtruːənt] *n* [child] Schwänzer *der*, -in *die*; **to play ~** (die Schule) schwänzen.

truck [trʌk] *n* - 1. *esp Am* [lorry] Lastwagen *der* - 2. RAIL Güterwaggon *der*.

truck driver *n esp Am* Lastwagenfahrer *der*, -in *die*.

trucker [ˈtrʌkə] *n Am* Lastwagenfahrer *der*, -in *die*.

truck farm *n Am* Gemüsegärtnerei *die*.

trudge [trʌdʒ] *vi* sich schleppen; [through snow, mud] stapfen.

true [truː] *adj* - 1. [factual] wahr; **to come ~** wahr werden - 2. [genuine] echt, wahr - 3. [faithful] getreu - 4. [precise, exact] gerade.

truffle [ˈtrʌfl] *n* Trüffel *die*.

truly [ˈtruːlɪ] *adv* - 1. wirklich - 2. *phr*: **yours ~** [at end of letter] mit freundlichen Grüßen.

trump [trʌmp] *n* [card] Trumpf *der*.

trumped-up [ˈtrʌmpt-] *adj pej* konstruiert.

trumpet [ˈtrʌmpɪt] *n* MUS Trompete *die*.

truncheon [ˈtrʌntʃən] *n* Knüppel *der*.

trundle [ˈtrʌndl] *vi* entlanglzockeln; [downhill] hinunterlzockeln.

trunk [trʌŋk] *n* - **1.** [of tree] Stamm *der* - **2.** ANAT Rumpf *der* - **3.** [of elephant] Rüssel *der* - **4.** [luggage] Schrankkoffer *der* - **5.** *Am* [of car] Kofferraum *der*. **trunks** *npl* [for swimming] Badehose *die*.

trunk road *n Br* Fernstraße *die*.

truss [trʌs] *n* MED Bruchband *das*.

trust [trʌst] <> *vt* - **1.** [have confidence in] trauen (+ *D*), vertrauen (+ *D*); **to ~ sb to do sthg** jm zutrauen, etw zu tun - **2.** [entrust]: **to ~ sb with sthg** jm mit etw vertrauen - **3.** *fml* [hope]: **I ~ (that)** ... ich hoffe(, dass) ... <> *n*. **1.** (U) [faith] Vertrauen *das*; **~ in sb/sthg** Vertrauen zu jm/etw - **2.** (U) [responsibility] Verantwortung *die* - **3.** FIN Treuhandschaft *die* - **4.** COMM Trust *der*.

trusted ['trʌstɪd] *adj* bewährt.

trustee [trʌs'tiː] *n* - **1.** FIN & LAW Treuhänder *der*, -in *die* - **2.** [manager of institution] Verwalter *der*, -in *die*.

trust fund *n* Treuhandvermögen *das*.

trusting ['trʌstɪŋ] *adj* vertrauensvoll.

trustworthy ['trʌst,wɜːðɪ] *adj* vertrauenswürdig.

truth [truːθ] *n* Wahrheit *die*; **to tell the ~,** ... um die Wahrheit zu sagen, ...; **in (all) ~** in aller Wahrhaftigkeit.

truthful ['truːθfʊl] *n* ehrlich.

try [traɪ] <> *vt* - **1.** [attempt] versuchen; **to ~ to do sthg** versuchen, etw zu tun - **2.** [sample] probieren; [test] ausprobieren - **3.** LAW [case] gerichtlich verhandeln; [criminal] vor Gericht stellen - **4.** [tax, strain] auf die Probe stellen <> *vi* versuchen; **to ~ for sthg** sich um etw bemühen <> *n* [attempt & SPORT] Versuch *der*; **to give sthg a ~** etw mal versuchen. **try on** *vt sep* [clothes] anprobieren. **try out** *vt sep* ausprobieren.

trying ['traɪɪŋ] *adj* schwierig.

T-shirt *n* T-Shirt *das*.

tub [tʌb] *n* - **1.** [of margarine, ice cream] Becher *der* - **2.** *inf* [bath] Wanne *die*.

tubby ['tʌbɪ] *adj inf* rundlich.

tube [tjuːb] *n* - **1.** [hollow cylinder - inflexible] Röhrchen *das*, Rohr *das*; [- flexible] Schlauch *der* - **2.** [of toothpaste, glue] Tube *die* - **3.** *Br* [underground train] U-Bahn *die*; **by ~** mit der U-Bahn.

tuberculosis [tjuː,bɜːkjʊ'ləʊsɪs] *n* Tuberkulose *die*.

tubular ['tjuːbjʊlə'] *adj* Röhren-.

TUC *n abbr of* Trades Union Congress.

tuck [tʌk] *vt* [place neatly] stecken. **tuck away** *vt sep* [store] verstecken. **tuck in** <> *vt sep* - **1.** [child, patient] zudecken - **2.** [clothes] hineinstecken <> *vi inf* zullangen. **tuck up** *vt sep* zudecken.

tuck shop *n Br* Schulkiosk *der*.

Tuesday ['tjuːzdɪ] *n* Dienstag *der*; *see also* Saturday.

tuft [tʌft] *n* Büschel *das*.

tug [tʌg] <> *n* - **1.** [pull] Ruck *der* - **2.** [boat] Schleppkahn *der* <> *vt* (ruckartig) ziehen; **she ~ged his sleeve** sie zupfte ihn am Ärmel <> *vi*: **to ~ at sthg** (ruckartig) an etw (*D*) ziehen.

tug-of-war *n* Tauziehen *das*.

tuition [tjuː'ɪʃn] *n* (U) Unterricht *der*.

tulip ['tjuːlɪp] *n* Tulpe *die*.

tumble ['tʌmbl] <> *vi* - **1.** [person, prices] fallen - **2.** [water] stürzen <> *n* Sturz *der*.

tumbledown ['tʌmbldaʊn] *adj* baufällig.

tumble-dryer [-,draɪə'] *n* Wäschetrockner *der*.

tumbler ['tʌmblə'] *n* [glass - short] Whiskyglas *das*; [- tall] Becherglas *das*.

tummy ['tʌmɪ] *n inf* - **1.** [outside of stomach] Bauch *der* - **2.** [inside of stomach] Magen *der*.

tumour *Br*, **tumor** *Am* ['tjuːmə'] *n* Tumor *der*.

tuna [*Br* 'tjuːnə, *Am* 'tuːnə] (*pl inv* OR -s), **tuna fish** (*pl* tuna fish) *n* Thunfisch *der*.

tune [tjuːn] <> *n* [song, melody] Melodie *die* <> *vt* - **1.** MUS stimmen - **2.** [engine, RADIO & TV] einstellen. **tune in** *vi* RADIO & TV einschalten; **to ~ in to sthg** etw einschalten. **tune up** *vi* MUS stimmen. **in tune** <> *adj* MUS (richtig) gestimmt <> *adv* - **1.** MUS richtig - **2.** [in agreement]: **to be in ~ with sb/sthg** mit jm/etw im Einklang stehen. **out of tune** <> *adj* MUS verstimmt <> *adv* - **1.** MUS falsch - **2.** [not in agreement]: **out of ~ with sb/sthg** mit jm/etw nicht im Einklang stehen.

tuneful ['tjuːnfʊl] *adj* melodisch.

tuner ['tjuːnə'] *n* - **1.** RADIO & TV Tuner *der* - **2.** MUS Stimmer *der*, -in *die*.

tunic ['tjuːnɪk] *n* [clothing] Hemdbluse *die*; [of uniform] Uniformjacke *die*.

tuning fork ['tjuːnɪŋ-] *n* Stimmgabel *die*.

Tunisia [tjuː'nɪzɪə] *n* Tunesien *das*.

tunnel ['tʌnl] <> *n* Tunnel *der* <> *vi* graben.

turban ['tɜːbən] *n* [man's headdress] Turban *der*.

turbine ['tɜːbaɪn] *n* Turbine *die*.

turbocharged ['tɜːbəʊtʃɑːdʒd] *adj* mit Turboaufladung.

turbulence ['tɜːbjʊləns] *n* (U) *lit & fig* Turbulenz *die*.

turbulent ['tɜːbjʊlənt] *adj* - **1.** [period of time & PHYS] turbulent - **2.** [winds, weather] stürmisch - **3.** [crowd] ungestüm.

tureen [tə'riːn] *n* Suppenterrine *die*.

turf [tɜːf] (*pl* -s OR turves) <> *n* - **1.** (U) [grass surface] Rasen *der* - **2.** [clod] Grassode *die* <> *vt* [with grass] mit Rollrasen bedecken. **turf out** *vt sep Br inf* [evict] rausschmeißen.

Turk [tɜːk] *n* Türke *der*, -kin *die*.

turkey ['tɜːkɪ] (*pl* turkeys) *n* Truthahn *der*.

Turkey ['tɜːkɪ] *n* Türkei *die;* **in ~** in der Türkei.

Turkish ['tɜːkɪʃ] ◇ *adj* türkisch ◇ *n* [language] Türkisch(e) *das.*

Turkish delight *n* (U) türkischer Honig.

turmoil ['tɜːmɔɪl] *n* (U) Aufruhr *der.*

turn ['tɜːn] ◇ *n* - **1.** [in road, river] Kurve *die* - **2.** [of knob, key, switch] Drehung *die* - **3.** [change] Wendung *die* - **4.** [in game, order]: **it's my ~** ich bin an der Reihe, ich bin dran; **in ~** der Reihe nach - **5.** [performance] Nummer *die* - **6.** MED Anfall *der* - **7.** *phr:* **to do sb a good ~** jm etwas Gutes tun ◇ *vt* - **1.** [key, head, wheel, chair] drehen - **2.** [corner] biegen um - **3.** [page, omelette] wenden - **4.** [direct]: **to ~ one's attention to sb/sthg** jm/etw seine Aufmerksamkeit zuwenden - **5.** [transform]: **to ~ sthg into sthg** etw in etw (A) verwandeln - **6.** [make]: **to ~ sthg red** etw rot werden lassen; **to ~ sthg inside out** das Innere von etw nach außen drehen ◇ *vi* - **1.** [change direction] wenden; **his thoughts ~ed to his family** er dachte an seine Familie - **2.** [wheel, knob, head, person] sich drehen - **3.** [in book]: **to ~ to sthg** etw aufschlagen - **4.** [for consolation, advice]: **to ~ to sb/sthg** sich an jn/etw wenden - **5.** [become] werden; **to ~ into sthg** sich in etw (A) verwandeln. ◆ **turn around** *vt sep* & *vi* = **turn round.** ◆ **turn away** ◇ *vt sep* [refuse entry to] abweisen ◇ *vi* sich ablwenden. ◆ **turn back** ◇ *vt sep* - **1.** [force to return] zurücklschicken - **2.** [fold back] auflschlagen ◇ *vi* [return] umlkehren. ◆ **turn down** *vt sep* - **1.** [reject] abweisen, abllehnen - **2.** [heating, lighting, sound] herunterldrehen. ◆ **turn in** *vi inf* [go to bed] sich aufs Ohr legen. ◆ **turn off** ◇ *vt fus* [leave - road, path] abllbiegen von ◇ *vt sep* [switch off] ablschalten ◇ *vi* [leave path, road] abllbiegen. ◆ **turn on** ◇ *vt sep* - **1.** [make work] einlschalten - **2.** *inf* [excite sexually] anlmachen ◇ *vt fus* [attack] losllgehen auf (+ A). ◆ **turn out** ◇ *vt sep* - **1.** [switch off] auslschalten - **2.** [empty] leeren ◇ *vt fus:* **to ~ out to be sthg** sich als etw erweisen; **it ~s out that ...** es stellt sich heraus, dass ... ◇ *vi* - **1.** [end up]: **it will ~ out all right** es wird (schon) alles in Ordnung kommen - **2.** [attend]: **to ~ out (for sthg)** (zu etw) erscheinen. ◆ **turn over** ◇ *vt sep* - **1.** [playing card, stone, page] umldrehen - **2.** [consider] überdenken - **3.** [hand over]: **to ~ sb/sthg over to sb** jm jn/etw überlgeben ◇ *vi* - **1.** [roll over] sich umldrehen - **2.** *Br* TV umlschalten. ◆ **turn round** *vt sep* - **1.** [rotate] umldrehen - **2.** [words, sentence] umldrehen - **3.** [quantity of work] bearbeiten ◇ *vi* [person] sich umldrehen. ◆ **turn up** ◇ *vt sep* [heat, lighting, radio, TV] aufldrehen ◇ *vi inf* - **1.** [appear, arrive, be found] aufltauchen - **2.** [happen] sich ergeben.

turning ['tɜːnɪŋ] *n* [side road] Abzweigung *die.*

turning point *n* Wendepunkt *der.*

turnip ['tɜːnɪp] *n* Rübe *die.*

turnout ['tɜːnaʊt] *n* [attendance] Teilnahme *die.*

turnover ['tɜːn‚əʊvə'] *n* (U) - **1.** [of personnel] Fluktuation *die* - **2.** FIN Umsatz *der.*

turnpike ['tɜːnpaɪk] *n Am* gebührenpflichtige Autobahn.

turnstile ['tɜːnstaɪl] *n* Drehkreuz *das.*

turntable ['tɜːn‚teɪbl] *n* [on record player] Plattenteller *der.*

turn-up *n Br* - **1.** [on trousers] Aufschlag *der* - **2.** *inf* [surprise]: **a ~ for the books** eine echte Überraschung.

turpentine ['tɜːpəntaɪn] *n* (U) Terpentin *das.*

turquoise ['tɜːkwɔɪz] ◇ *adj* türkis ◇ *n* - **1.** [mineral, gem] Türkis *der* - **2.** [colour] Türkis *das.*

turret ['tʌrɪt] *n* [on castle] Eckturm *der.*

turtle ['tɜːtl] (*pl inv* OR **-s**) *n* Schildkröte *die.*

turtleneck ['tɜːtlnek] *n* - **1.** [garment] Rollkragenpullover *der* - **2.** [neck] Rollkragen *der.*

turves [tɜːvz] *pl* ⟩ **turf.**

tusk [tʌsk] *n* Stoßzahn *der.*

tussle ['tʌsl] ◇ *n* Gerangel *das* ◇ *vi:* **to ~ over sthg** *lit* (sich) um etw (A) raufen; *fig* eine Auseinandersetzung wegen etw haben.

tutor ['tjuːtə'] *n* - **1.** [private] Privatlehrer *der,* -in *die* - **2.** UNIV Tutor *der,* -in *die.*

tutorial [tjuː'tɔːrɪəl] *n* Tutorium *das.*

tuxedo [tʌk'siːdəʊ] (*pl* **-s**) *n Am* Smoking *der.*

TV (*abbr of* television) *n* - **1.** (U) [medium, industry] Fernsehen *das* - **2.** [apparatus] Fernseher *der.*

twang [twæŋ] *n* - **1.** [of spring, guitar string] vibrierender Ton; [of rubber band] schnappender Ton - **2.** [accent] Tonfall *der.*

tweed [twiːd] *n* Tweed *der.*

tweezers ['twiːzəz] *npl* Pinzette *die.*

twelfth [twelfθ] *num* zwölfte, -r, -s; *see also* sixth.

twelve [twelv] *num* zwölf; *see also* six.

twentieth ['twentɪəθ] *num* zwanzigste, -r, -s; *see also* sixth.

twenty ['twentɪ] *num* zwanzig; *see also* sixty.

twice [twaɪs] *adv* zweimal.

twiddle ['twɪdl] *vt* [knob, button] herumldrehen an (+ D).

twig [twɪg] *n* Zweig *der.*

twilight ['twaɪlaɪt] *n* [in evening] Dämmerung *die.*

twin [twɪn] ◇ *adj* - **1.** [child, sibling] Zwillings-; **~ girls** Zwillingsschwestern - **2.** [towns] Partner-; **~ beds** zwei Einzelbetten ◇ *n* [sibling] Zwilling *der.*

twine [twaɪn] ◇ *n* (U) Schnur *die* ◇ *vt:* **to ~ sthg round sthg** etw um etw wickeln.

twinge [twɪndʒ] *n* Stich *der.*

twinkle ['twɪŋkl] *vi* funkeln.

twin room *n* Zweibettzimmer *das.*

twin town *n* Partnerstadt *die.*

twirl [twɜ:l] ◇ *vt* - **1.** [spin] herumlwirbeln - **2.** [twist, moustache] zwirbeln ◇ *vi* wirbeln.

twist [twɪst] ◇ *n* - **1.** [in road, staircase, river] Biegung *die* - **2.** *fig* [in plot] Wendung *die* ◇ *vt* - **1.** [gen] verdrehen - **2.** [lid, knob, dial] drehen - **3.** MED [sprain]: **to ~ one's ankle** sich (D) den Fuß verrenken ◇ *vi* - **1.** [road, river] sich schlängeln - **2.** [body] sich winden; [face] sich verziehen.

twit [twɪt] *n Br inf* Trottel *der.*

twitch [twɪtʃ] ◇ *n* Zucken *das* ◇ *vi* zucken.

two [tu:] *num* zwei; **in ~** in zwei Teile; *see also* **six.**

twofaced [ˌtu:'feɪst] *adj pej* falsch.

twofold ['tu:fəʊld] *adj & adv* zweifach.

two-piece *adj* [suit, swimsuit] zweiteilig.

twosome ['tu:səm] *n inf* Paar *das.*

two-way *adj* [in both directions] in beiden Richtungen.

tycoon [taɪ'ku:n] *n* Magnat *der.*

type [taɪp] ◇ *n* - **1.** [sort, kind] Art *die*; **what ~ of car are you looking for?** was für ein Auto suchen Sie denn? - **2.** [in classification] Gruppe *die* - **3.** (U) TYPO Schrift *die* ◇ *vt & vi* tippen.

typecast ['taɪpkɑ:st] (*pt & pp* typecast) *vt* festllegen (auf eine bestimmte Rolle).

typeface ['taɪpfeɪs] *n* TYPO Schrift *die.*

typescript ['taɪpskrɪpt] *n* Manuskript *das.*

typewriter ['taɪpˌraɪtə'] *n* Schreibmaschine *die.*

typhoid (fever) ['taɪfɔɪd-] *n* (U) Typhus *der.*

typhoon [taɪ'fu:n] *n* Taifun *der.*

typical ['tɪpɪkl] *adj* typisch; **~ of sb/sthg** typisch für jn/etw.

typing ['taɪpɪŋ] *n* Tippen *das*, Maschineschreiben *das.*

typist ['taɪpɪst] *n* Schreibkraft *die.*

typography [taɪ'pɒgrəfɪ] *n* Typografie *die.*

tyranny ['tɪrənɪ] *n* (U) [of person, government] Tyrannei *die.*

tyrant ['taɪrənt] *n* Tyrann *der*, -in *die.*

tyre *Br*, **tire** *Am* ['taɪə'] *n* Reifen *der.*

tyre pressure *n* (U) Reifendruck *der.*

u (*pl* u's OR us), **U** (*pl* U's OR Us) [ju:] *n* [letter] u *das*, U *das.*

U-bend *n* U-Bogen *der.*

udder ['ʌdə'] *n* Euter *der.*

UFO (*abbr of* unidentified flying object) *n* UFO *das.*

Uganda [ju:'gændə] *n* Uganda *nt.*

ugly ['ʌglɪ] *adj* - **1.** [unattractive] hässlich - **2.** *fig* [unpleasant] unerfreulich.

UHF (*abbr of* ultra-high frequency) *n* UHF.

UK *n abbr of* United Kingdom.

Ukraine [ju:'kreɪn] *n:* **the ~** die Ukraine.

ulcer ['ʌlsə'] *n* - **1.** [in stomach] Geschwür *das* - **2.** [in mouth, stomach] Aphthe *die.*

Ulster ['ʌlstə'] *n* Ulster *nt.*

ulterior [ʌl'tɪərɪə'] *adj:* **an ~ motive** Hintergedanke *der.*

ultimata [ˌʌltɪ'meɪtə] *pl* ⊏▷ ultimatum.

ultimate ['ʌltɪmət] ◇ *adj* - **1.** [final, longterm] letzte, -r, -s - **2.** [most powerful] absolut ◇ *n:* **the ~ in sthg** das Höchste an etw (D).

ultimately ['ʌltɪmətlɪ] *adv* [finally, in the long term] letztlich.

ultimatum [ˌʌltɪ'meɪtəm] (*pl* -tums OR -ta [-tə]) *n* Ultimatum *das.*

ultrasound ['ʌltrəsaʊnd] *n* Ultraschall *der.*

ultraviolet [ˌʌltrə'vaɪələt] *adj* ultraviolett.

umbilical cord [ʌm'bɪlɪkl-] *n* Nabelschnur *die.*

umbrella [ʌm'brelə] ◇ *n* - **1.** [portable] Regenschirm *der* - **2.** [fixed] Sonnenschirm *der* ◇ *adj* Schirm-.

umpire ['ʌmpaɪə'] ◇ *n* Schiedsrichter *der*, -in *die* ◇ *vt* Schiedsrichter sein bei.

umpteen [ˌʌmp'ti:n] *num adj inf* zigmal.

umpteenth [ˌʌmp'ti:nθ] *num adj inf:* **for the ~ time** zum x-ten Mal.

UN (*abbr of* United Nations) *n* UNO *die*, UN *die.*

unabated [ˌʌnə'beɪtɪd] *adj* unvermindert.

unable [ʌn'eɪbl] *adj:* **to be ~ to do sthg** außer Stande sein, etw zu tun.

unacceptable [ˌʌnək'septəbl] *adj* unannehmbar.

unaccompanied [ˌʌnə'kʌmpənɪd] *adj* [luggage] aufgegeben; [child, song] ohne Begleitung.

unaccountably [ˌʌnə'kaʊntəblɪ] *adv* [inexplicably] unerklärlicherweise.

unaccounted [ˌʌnə'kaʊntɪd] *adj:* **~ for** unauffindbar.

unaccustomed [ˌʌnə'kʌstəmd] *adj* [unused]: **to be ~ to sthg** an etw *(A)* nicht gewöhnt sein; **to be ~ to doing sthg** nicht daran gewöhnt sein, etw zu tun.

unadulterated [ˌʌnə'dʌltəreɪtɪd] *adj* rein.

unanimous [juː'nænɪməs] *adj* einstimmig.

unanimously [juː'nænɪməslɪ] *adv* einstimmig.

unanswered [ˌʌn'ɑːnsəd] *adj* unbeantwortet.

unappetizing, -ising [ˌʌn'æpɪtaɪzɪŋ] *adj* unappetitlich.

unarmed [ˌʌn'ɑːmd] *adj* unbewaffnet.

unashamed [ˌʌnə'ʃeɪmd] *adj* schamlos.

unassuming [ˌʌnə'sjuːmɪŋ] *adj* bescheiden.

unattached [ˌʌnə'tætʃt] *adj* - **1.** [not fastened, linked]: **~ to sthg** unabhängig von etw - **2.** [without partner] ungebunden.

unattended [ˌʌnə'tendɪd] *adj* unbeaufsichtigt.

unattractive [ˌʌnə'træktɪv] *adj* unattraktiv.

unauthorized, -ised [ˌʌn'ɔːθəraɪzd] *adj* unrechtmäßig; [biography] nicht autorisiert.

unavailable [ˌʌnə'veɪləbl] *adj* nicht verfügbar; [person] nicht zu erreichen.

unavoidable [ˌʌnə'vɔɪdəbl] *adj* unvermeidlich.

unaware [ˌʌnə'weəʳ] *adj*: **to be ~ of sthg** sich *(D)* einer Sache *(G)* nicht bewusst sein; **she was ~ of my presence** sie bemerkte mich nicht.

unawares [ˌʌnə'weəz] *adv*: **to catch** OR **take sb ~** jn überraschen.

unbalanced [ˌʌn'bælənst] *adj* - **1.** [biased] unausgewogen - **2.** [deranged] psychisch labil.

unbearable [ʌn'beərəbl] *adj* unerträglich.

unbeatable [ˌʌn'biːtəbl] *adj* unschlagbar.

unbeknown(st) [ˌʌnbɪ'nəʊn(st)] *adv*: **~ to him** ohne sein Wissen.

unbelievable [ˌʌnbɪ'liːvəbl] *adj* unglaublich.

unbia(s)sed [ˌʌn'baɪəst] *adj* unvoreingenommen.

unborn [ˌʌn'bɔːn] *adj* [child] ungeboren.

unbreakable [ˌʌn'breɪkəbl] *adj* unzerbrechlich.

unbridled [ˌʌn'braɪdld] *adj* ungezügelt.

unbutton [ˌʌn'bʌtn] *vt* aufknöpfen.

uncalled-for [ˌʌn'kɔːld-] *adj* unnötig.

uncanny [ʌn'kænɪ] *adj* unheimlich.

unceasing [ʌn'siːsɪŋ] *adj fml* beständig.

unceremonious [ˈʌnˌserɪ'məʊnjəs] *adj* [abrupt] brüsk.

uncertain [ʌn'sɜːtn] *adj* - **1.** [person, plans] unsicher; **in no ~ terms** unmissverständlich - **2.** [weather] unvorhersehbar; [future] ungewiss - **3.** [cause, motive] unklar.

---

uncertainty

Meinst du wirklich? Do you really think so?
Ich bin mir nicht so sicher. I'm not so sure.
Es könnte doch sein, dass er seine Meinung
geändert hat. It could just be that he
changed his mind.
Ich weiß nicht so recht. I'm not so sure.
Ich frage mich, ob ich richtig gehandelt habe. I wonder if I did the right thing.

---

unchanged [ˌʌn'tʃeɪndʒd] *adj* unverändert.

unchecked [ˌʌn'tʃekt] *adj & adv* [unrestrained] uneingeschränkt.

uncivilized, -ised [ˌʌn'sɪvɪlaɪzd] *adj* [barbaric] unzivilisiert.

uncle ['ʌŋkl] *n* Onkel *der*.

unclear [ˌʌn'klɪəʳ] *adj* - **1.** [meaning, instructions] unklar - **2.** [future, person] unsicher - **3.** [motives, details] undurchsichtig.

uncomfortable [ˌʌn'kʌmftəbl] *adj* - **1.** [shoes, chair, clothes] unbequem - **2.** *fig* [fact, truth] unbequem - **3.** [person]: **to feel ~** [in physical discomfort] sich nicht wohl fühlen; [ill at ease] sich unbehaglich fühlen.

uncommon [ʌn'kɒmən] *adj* - **1.** [rare] selten - **2.** *fml* [extreme] außergewöhnlich.

uncompromising [ˌʌn'kɒmprəmaɪzɪŋ] *adj* unnachgiebig.

unconcerned [ˌʌnkən'sɜːnd] *adj* [not anxious] unbesorgt.

unconditional [ˌʌnkən'dɪʃənl] *adj* bedingungslos.

unconscious [ʌn'kɒnʃəs] ⬦ *adj* - **1.** [having lost consciousness] bewusstlos - **2.** *fig* [unaware]: **to be ~ of sthg** sich *(D)* einer Sache *(G)* nicht bewusst sein - **3.** PSYCH unbewusst ⬦ *n* PSYCH: **the ~** das Unbewusste.

unconsciously [ʌn'kɒnʃəslɪ] *adv* unbewusst.

uncontrollable [ˌʌnkən'trəʊləbl] *adj* - **1.** [irrepressible] unbezwingbar - **2.** [inflation, growth, epidemic] unkontrollierbar - **3.** [child, animal] nicht zu bändigen.

unconventional [ˌʌnkən'venʃənl] *adj* unkonventionell.

unconvinced [ˌʌnkən'vɪnst] *adj* nicht überzeugt.

uncouth [ʌn'kuːθ] *adj* ungehobelt.

uncover [ʌn'kʌvəʳ] *vt lit & fig* aufdecken.

undecided [ˌʌndɪ'saɪdɪd] *adj* - **1.** [person] unentschlossen - **2.** [issue] unentschieden.

undeniable [ˌʌndɪ'naɪəbl] *adj* unbestreitbar.

under ['ʌndəʳ] ⬦ *prep* - **1.** [beneath, below] unter (+ *D*); (with verbs of motion) unter (+ *A*); **it's ~ the table** es ist unter dem Tisch; **put it ~ the table** leg es unter den Tisch - **2.** [less than] unter (+ *D*); **children ~ ten** Kinder unter zehn; **in ~ two hours** in weniger als zwei Stunden - **3.** [indicating conditions or circumstances]: **~ the circumstances** unter diesen Umständen; **to be ~ pressure** unter Druck sein - **4.** [undergoing]: **to be ~ review/discussion** revidiert/diskutiert werden; **~ construction** im Bau - **5.** [directed, governed by] unter (+ D); **Britain ~ Blair** Großbritannien unter Blair - **6.** [according to] nach; **~ the terms of the will** nach dem Testament - **7.** [in classification, name, title] unter (+ D) <> adv - **1.** [beneath] unten; **how long can you stay ~?** [underwater] wie lange kannst du unter Wasser bleiben?; **she lifted the blanket and crawled ~** sie hob die Decke hoch und kroch darunter - **2.** [less]: **children of 12 and ~** Kinder bis zu 12 Jahren.

underage [ˌʌndərˈeɪdʒ] adj minderjährig.

undercarriage [ˈʌndəˌkærɪdʒ] n Fahrgestell das.

undercharge [ˌʌndəˈtʃɑːdʒ] vt zu wenig berechnen (+ D).

underclothes [ˈʌndəkləʊðz] npl Unterwäsche die.

undercoat [ˈʌndəkəʊt] n [of paint] Grundierung die.

undercover [ˈʌndəˌkʌvəʳ] adj [agent] Geheim-.

undercurrent [ˈʌndəˌkʌrənt] n fig [tendency] Unterton der.

undercut [ˌʌndəˈkʌt] (pt & pp undercut) vt [in price] unterbieten.

underdeveloped [ˌʌndədɪˈveləpt] adj unterentwickelt.

underdog [ˈʌndədɒg] n: **the ~** der/die Schwächere.

underdone [ˌʌndəˈdʌn] adj nicht gar.

underestimate [ˌʌndərˈestɪmeɪt] vt - **1.** [time, money, amount] zu niedrig schätzen - **2.** [strength, abilities] unterschätzen.

underfoot [ˌʌndəˈfʊt] adv unter den Füßen.

undergo [ˌʌndəˈgəʊ] (pt -went; pp -gone [-ˈgɒn]) vt [operation, examination] sich unterziehen (+ D); [training] teilnehmen an (+ D); [difficulties] durchmachen.

undergraduate [ˌʌndəˈgrædjʊət] n Student der, -in die.

underground [adj & n ˈʌndəgraʊnd, adv ˌʌndəˈgraʊnd] <> adj - **1.** [below ground] unterirdisch - **2.** fig [secret, illegal] Untergrund- <> adv: **to go/be forced ~** in den Untergrund gehen/gedrängt werden <> n - **1.** Br [transport system] U-Bahn die - **2.** [activist movement] Untergrund der.

undergrowth [ˈʌndəgrəʊθ] n (U) Unterholz das.

underhand [ˌʌndəˈhænd] adj hinterhältig.

underline [ˌʌndəˈlaɪn] vt lit & fig unterstreichen.

underlying [ˌʌndəˈlaɪɪŋ] adj zugrunde liegend.

undermine [ˌʌndəˈmaɪn] vt fig [weaken] untergraben.

underneath [ˌʌndəˈniːθ] <> prep [indicating location] unter (+ D); [indicating direction] unter (+ A); **from ~ sthg** unter etw (D) hervor <> adv darunter <> n [underside]: **the ~** die Unterseite.

underpaid [ˈʌndəpeɪd] adj unterbezahlt.

underpants [ˈʌndəpænts] npl Unterhose die.

underpass [ˈʌndəpɑːs] n Unterführung die.

underprivileged [ˌʌndəˈprɪvɪlɪdʒd] adj unterprivilegiert.

underrated [ˌʌndəˈreɪtɪd] adj unterschätzt.

undershirt [ˈʌndəʃɜːt] n Am Unterhemd das.

underside [ˈʌndəsaɪd] n: **the ~** die Unterseite.

understand [ˌʌndəˈstænd] (pt & pp -stood) <> vt - **1.** [gen] verstehen - **2.** fml [have meant]: **to ~ that ...** glauben, dass ... <> vi verstehen.

understandable [ˌʌndəˈstændəbl] adj verständlich.

understanding [ˌʌndəˈstændɪŋ] <> n - **1.** [knowledge, insight] Kenntnis die - **2.** (U) [sympathy] Verständnis das - **3.** [interpretation, conception] Auffassung die; **it was my ~ that ...** ich dachte, dass ... - **4.** [informal agreement] Übereinkunft die <> adj [sympathetic] verständnisvoll.

understated [ˌʌndəˈsteɪtɪd] adj untertrieben.

understatement [ˌʌndəˈsteɪtmənt] n - **1.** [inadequate statement] Untertreibung die - **2.** (U) [quality of understating] Understatement das.

understood [ˌʌndəˈstʊd] pt & pp ▷ understand.

understudy [ˈʌndəˌstʌdɪ] n zweite Besetzung.

undertake [ˌʌndəˈteɪk] (pt -took; pp -taken [-ˈteɪkn]) vt - **1.** [take on] auf sich (A) nehmen - **2.** [promise]: **to ~ to do sthg** sich verpflichten, etw zu tun.

undertaker [ˈʌndəˌteɪkəʳ] n Leichenbestatter der, -in die.

undertaking [ˌʌndəˈteɪkɪŋ] n - **1.** [task] Aufgabe die - **2.** [promise] Versprechen das.

undertone [ˈʌndətəʊn] n - **1.** [quiet voice] leise Stimme - **2.** [underlying feeling] Unterton der.

undertook [ˌʌndəˈtʊk] pt ▷ undertake.

underwater [ˌʌndəˈwɔːtəʳ] <> adj Unterwasser- <> adv unter Wasser.

underwear [ˈʌndəweəʳ] n Unterwäsche die.

underwent [ˌʌndəˈwent] pt ▷ undergo.

underwriter ['ʌndəˌraɪtə'] n Versicherer der.

undid [ʌn'dɪd] pt ⤳ undo.

undies ['ʌndɪz] npl inf Unterwäsche die.

undisputed [ˌʌndɪ'spjuːtɪd] adj unbestritten.

undistinguished [ˌʌndɪ'stɪŋgwɪʃt] adj mittelmäßig.

undo [ʌn'duː] (pt -did; pp -done) vt - 1. [unfasten] aufmachen - 2. [nullify] zunichte machen.

undoing [ʌn'duːɪŋ] n (U) fml Verderben das.

undone [ʌn'dʌn] ⟨⟩ pp ⤳ undo ⟨⟩ adj - 1. [unfastened] offen - 2. fml [not done] ungetan.

undoubted [ʌn'daʊtɪd] adj unbestritten.

undoubtedly [ʌn'daʊtɪdlɪ] adv fml zweifellos.

undress [ˌʌn'dres] ⟨⟩ vt ausziehen ⟨⟩ vi sich ausziehen.

undue [ˌʌn'djuː] adj fml unangemessen.

undulate ['ʌndjʊleɪt] vi fml - 1. [in movement - snake, road] sich schlängeln - 2. [in shape - landscape] sich wellenförmig erstrecken.

unduly [ˌʌn'djuːlɪ] adv fml unnötig.

unearth [ʌn'ɜːθ] vt - 1. [dig up] ausgraben - 2. fig [discover] aufstöbern.

unease [ʌn'iːz] n (U) Unbehagen das.

uneasy [ʌn'iːzɪ] adj - 1. [person, feeling] unbehaglich - 2. [silence] verlegen - 3. [peace] unsicher.

uneconomic ['ʌnˌiːkə'nɒmɪk] adj unökonomisch.

uneducated [ˌʌn'edjʊkeɪtɪd] adj - 1. [person] ungebildet - 2. [behaviour, manners, speech] unkultiviert.

unemployed [ˌʌnɪm'plɔɪd] ⟨⟩ adj [out-of-work] arbeitslos ⟨⟩ npl: **the -** die Arbeitslosen pl.

unemployment [ˌʌnɪm'plɔɪmənt] n Arbeitslosigkeit die.

unemployment benefit Br n (U) Arbeitslosenunterstützung die.

unerring [ˌʌn'ɜːrɪŋ] adj untrüglich.

uneven [ˌʌn'iːvn] adj - 1. [not flat] uneben - 2. [inconsistent] ungleichmäßig - 3. [unfair] ungleich.

unexpected [ˌʌnɪk'spektɪd] adj unerwartet.

unexpectedly [ˌʌnɪk'spektɪdlɪ] adv unerwartet.

unfailing [ʌn'feɪlɪŋ] adj [loyalty, support, good humour] unerschöpflich.

unfair [ˌʌn'feə'] adj ungerecht.

unfaithful [ˌʌn'feɪθfʊl] adj [sexually] untreu.

unfamiliar [ˌʌnfə'mɪljə'] adj - 1. [not well-known] unbekannt - 2. [not acquainted]: **to be ~ with sb/sthg** jn/etw nicht kennen.

unfashionable [ˌʌn'fæʃnəbl] adj unmodisch.

unfasten [ˌʌn'fɑːsn] vt aufmachen; [rope] aufknoten.

unfavourable Br, **unfavorable** Am [ˌʌn'feɪvrəbl] adj - 1. [not conducive] ungünstig - 2. [negative] unvorteilhaft.

unfeeling [ʌn'fiːlɪŋ] adj herzlos.

unfinished [ʌn'fɪnɪʃt] adj unerledigt.

unfit [ˌʌn'fɪt] adj - 1. [not in good shape] nicht fit - 2. [not suitable]: **~ (for sthg)** ungeeignet (für etw).

unfold [ʌn'fəʊld] ⟨⟩ vt [open out] auseinanderfalten ⟨⟩ vi [story, truth] an den Tag kommen.

unforeseen [ˌʌnfɔː'siːn] adj unvorhergesehen.

unforgettable [ˌʌnfə'getəbl] adj unvergesslich.

unforgivable [ˌʌnfə'gɪvəbl] adj unverzeihlich.

unfortunate [ʌn'fɔːtʃnət] adj - 1. [unlucky] unglücklich - 2. [regrettable] bedauernswert.

unfortunately [ʌn'fɔːtʃnətlɪ] adv leider.

unfounded [ˌʌn'faʊndɪd] adj unbegründet.

unfriendly [ʌn'frendlɪ] adj unfreundlich.

unfurnished [ˌʌn'fɜːnɪʃt] adj unmöbliert.

ungainly [ʌn'geɪnlɪ] adj unbeholfen.

ungrateful [ʌn'greɪtfʊl] adj undankbar.

unhappy [ʌn'hæpɪ] adj - 1. [sad] unglücklich - 2. [not pleased]: **to be ~ (about OR with sthg)** nicht glücklich (über etw (A) OR mit etw) sein - 3. fml [unfortunate] unglückselig.

unharmed [ʌn'hɑːmd] adj unverletzt.

unhealthy [ʌn'helθɪ] adj ungesund.

unheard-of [ʌn'hɜːdɒv] adj - 1. [unknown] unbekannt - 2. [unprecedented] unerhört.

unhook [ˌʌn'hʊk] vt - 1. [unfasten hooks of] aufhaken - 2. [remove from hook] abhaken, vom Haken nehmen.

unhurt [ˌʌn'hɜːt] adj unverletzt.

unhygienic [ˌʌnhaɪ'dʒiːnɪk] adj unhygienisch.

unidentified flying object n unbekanntes Flugobjekt.

unification [ˌjuːnɪfɪ'keɪʃn] n (U) Vereinigung die.

uniform ['juːnɪfɔːm] ⟨⟩ adj gleichförmig ⟨⟩ n Uniform die.

unify ['juːnɪfaɪ] vt vereinen.

unilateral [ˌjuːnɪ'lætərəl] adj einseitig.

unimportant [ˌʌnɪm'pɔːtənt] adj unwichtig.

uninhabited [ˌʌnɪn'hæbɪtɪd] adj unbewohnt.

uninjured [ˌʌn'ɪndʒəd] adj unverletzt.

unintelligent [ˌʌnɪn'telɪdʒənt] adj nicht intelligent.

unintentional [ˌʌnɪn'tenʃənl] adj unabsichtlich.

union ['ju:njən] <> *n* - **1.** [trade union] Gewerkschaft *die* - **2.** [alliance] Union *die* <> *comp* Gewerkschafts-.

Union Jack *n:* **the ~** der Union Jack, *britische Nationalflagge.*

unique [ju:'ni:k] *adj* - **1.** [unparalleled] einzigartig - **2.** *fml* [peculiar, exclusive]: **this custom is ~ to our country** diesen Brauch gibt es nur in unserem Land.

unison ['ju:nɪzn] *n* (U) [agreement] Einklang *der;* **in ~** [simultaneously] unisono.

unit ['ju:nɪt] *n* - **1.** [gen] Einheit *die* - **2.** [part of machine or system, piece of furniture] Element *das* - **3.** [department] Abteilung *die.*

unite [ju:'naɪt] <> *vt* vereinigen <> *vi* sich vereinigen.

united [ju:'naɪtɪd] *adj* - **1.** [in harmony] vereint - **2.** [unified] vereinigt.

United Kingdom *n:* **the ~** das Vereinigte Königreich.

United Nations *n:* **the ~** die Vereinten Nationen *pl.*

United States *n:* **the ~ (of America)** die Vereinigten Staaten (von Amerika); **in the ~** in den Vereinigten Staaten.

unity ['ju:nətɪ] *n* - **1.** [union] Einheit *die* - **2.** [harmony] Einigkeit *die.*

universal [ˌju:nɪ'vɜ:sl] *adj* universal.

universe ['ju:nɪvɜ:s] *n* ASTRON Universum *das.*

university [ˌju:nɪ'vɜ:sətɪ] <> *n* Universität *die* <> *comp* Universitäts-; **~ student** Student *der,* -in *die.*

unjust [ˌʌn'dʒʌst] *adj* ungerecht.

unkempt [ˌʌn'kempt] *adj* [hair, beard, appearance] ungepflegt.

unkind [ʌn'kaɪnd] *adj* [uncharitable] gemein.

unknown [ˌʌn'nəʊn] *adj* unbekannt.

unlawful [ˌʌn'lɔ:fʊl] *adj* ungesetzlich.

unleaded [ˌʌn'ledɪd] *adj* bleifrei.

unleash [ˌʌn'li:ʃ] *vt literary* entfesseln.

unless [ən'les] *conj* es sei denn, wenn … nicht; **~ you know more** es sei denn, Sie wissen mehr; **you'll be late ~ you set off at once** wenn du dich nicht gleich auf den Weg machst, wirst du zu spät kommen; **~ I'm mistaken** wenn ich mich nicht irre; **~ there's a miracle** falls nicht ein Wunder geschieht.

unlike [ˌʌn'laɪk] *prep* - **1.** [different from] nicht ähnlich (+ D) - **2.** [in contrast to] im Gegensatz zu - **3.** [not typical of]: **it's very ~ you to complain** es sieht dir gar nicht ähnlich, dich zu beschweren.

unlikely [ʌn'laɪklɪ] *adj* - **1.** [not probable] unwahrscheinlich - **2.** [bizarre] merkwürdig.

unlisted [ʌn'lɪstɪd] *adj Am* [phone number]: **to be ~** nicht im Telefonbuch stehen.

unload [ˌʌn'ləʊd] *vt* - **1.** [remove] ausladen - **2.** [remove load from] entladen.

unlock [ˌʌn'lɒk] *vt* aufschließen.

unlucky [ʌn'lʌkɪ] *adj* - **1.** [unfortunate] unglücklich; [person] unglücksselig - **2.** [bringing bad luck] Unglücks-.

unmarried [ˌʌn'mærɪd] *adj* unverheiratet.

unmistakable [ˌʌnmɪ'steɪkəbl] *adj* unverwechselbar.

unmitigated [ʌn'mɪtɪgeɪtɪd] *adj* vollkommen.

unnatural [ʌn'nætʃrəl] *adj* - **1.** [unusual, strange] unnatürlich - **2.** [affected] aufgesetzt.

unnecessary [ʌn'nesəsərɪ] *adj* unnötig.

unnerving [ˌʌn'nɜ:vɪŋ] *adj* [experience] verunsichernd; [silence] beunruhigend.

unnoticed [ˌʌn'nəʊtɪst] *adj:* **to go** OR **pass ~** nicht bemerkt werden.

unobtainable [ˌʌnəb'teɪnəbl] *adj* nicht erhältlich.

unofficial [ˌʌnə'fɪʃl] *adj* inoffiziell.

unorthodox [ʌn'ɔ:θədɒks] *adj* unorthodox.

unpack [ˌʌn'pæk] *vt* & *vi* auslpacken.

unparalleled [ʌn'pærəleld] *adj* einmalig.

unpleasant [ʌn'pleznt] *adj* unangenehm.

unplug [ʌn'plʌg] *vt* ELEC: **to ~ sthg** den Stecker von etw herauslziehen.

unpopular [ˌʌn'pɒpjʊləʳ] *adj* unpopulär.

unprecedented [ʌn'presɪdəntɪd] *adj* beispiellos.

unpredictable [ˌʌnprɪ'dɪktəbl] *adj* unvorhersehbar; [person] unberechenbar.

unprofessional [ˌʌnprə'feʃənl] *adj* unprofessionell.

unqualified [ˌʌn'kwɒlɪfaɪd] *adj* - **1.** [not qualified] unqualifiziert; [teacher, nurse] nicht ausgebildet - **2.** [total, complete - success, support] uneingeschränkt; [- denial] vollständig.

unquestionable [ʌn'kwestʃənəbl] *adj* unbestreitbar.

unquestioning [ʌn'kwestʃənɪŋ] *adj* bedingungslos.

unravel [ʌn'rævl] *vt* - **1.** [undo - knitting] aufltrennen; [- threads] entwirren - **2.** *fig* [solve] lösen.

unreal [ˌʌn'rɪəl] *adj* [strange] unwirklich.

unrealistic [ˌʌnrɪə'lɪstɪk] *adj* unrealistisch.

unreasonable [ʌn'ri:znəbl] *adj* - **1.** [person]: **he's so ~** mit ihm kann man überhaupt nicht vernünftig reden - **2.** [demand, decision] unangemessen.

unrelated [ʌn'reɪtɪd] *adj:* **to be ~ (to sthg)** in keinem Zusammenhang (mit etw) stehen.

unrelenting [ˌʌnrɪ'lentɪŋ] *adj* [struggle, questions] unerbittlich; [pressure] unablässig.

unreliable [ˌʌnrɪ'laɪəbl] *adj* unzuverlässig.

unremitting [ˌʌnrɪ'mɪtɪŋ] *adj* [effort, activity] unablässig, unaufhörlich.

unrequited [ˌʌnrɪ'kwaɪtɪd] *adj* unerwidert.

unreserved [ˌʌnrɪ'zɜːvd] *adj* [admiration, support, approval] uneingeschränkt.

unresolved [ˌʌnrɪ'zɒlvd] *adj* ungelöst.

unrest [ʌn'rest] *n* (U) Unruhen *pl*.

unrivalled *Br*, **unrivaled** *Am* [ʌn'raɪvld] *adj* unübertroffen.

unroll [ʌn'rəʊl] *vt* aufrollen.

unruly [ʌn'ruːlɪ] *adj* - 1. [person, group] undiszipliniert; [child] unartig; [behaviour] ungezügelt - 2. [hair] widerspenstig.

unsafe [ʌn'seɪf] *adj* - 1. [dangerous] gefährlich - 2. [in danger] nicht sicher.

unsaid [ʌn'sed] *adj*: **to leave sthg ~** etw unausgesprochen lassen.

unsatisfactory ['ʌnˌsætɪs'fæktərɪ] *adj* unbefriedigend.

unsavoury, **unsavory** *Am* [ʌn'seɪvərɪ] *adj* - 1. [person] zwielichtig; [appearance] abstoßend; [reputation, behaviour, area] zweifelhaft - 2. [smell] widerwärtig.

unscathed [ʌn'skeɪðd] *adj* unversehrt.

unscrew [ʌn'skruː] *vt* - 1. [lid, bottle top] losdrehen - 2. [sign, mirror] abschrauben.

unscrupulous [ʌn'skruːpjʊləs] *adj* skrupellos.

unseemly [ʌn'siːmlɪ] *adj* unpassend, unschicklich.

unselfish [ʌn'selfɪʃ] *adj* selbstlos.

unsettled [ʌn'setld] *adj* - 1. [disturbed - person] beunruhigt; [- weather] unbeständig - 2. [unfinished, unresolved - argument] nicht beigelegt; [- issue] ungeklärt - 3. [account, bill] ausstehend.

unshak(e)able [ʌn'ʃeɪkəbl] *adj* [faith, belief] unerschütterlich; [decision] unumstößlich.

unshaven [ʌn'ʃeɪvn] *adj* unrasiert.

unsightly [ʌn'saɪtlɪ] *adj* unansehnlich.

unskilled [ʌn'skɪld] *adj* [worker] ungelernt; [work] einfach.

unsociable [ʌn'səʊʃəbl] *adj* ungesellig.

unsocial [ʌn'səʊʃl] *adj*: **to work ~ hours** früh/morgens/nachts/am Wochenende arbeiten.

unsound [ʌn'saʊnd] *adj* - 1. [conclusion, theory, decision] zweifelhaft - 2. [building, structure] instabil.

unspeakable [ʌn'spiːkəbl] *adj* fürchterlich.

unstable [ʌn'steɪbl] *adj* - 1. [structure, government] instabil; [weather] wechselhaft - 2. [mentally, emotionally] labil.

unsteady [ʌn'stedɪ] *adj* wackelig.

unstoppable [ʌn'stɒpəbl] *adj* unaufhaltsam.

unstuck [ʌn'stʌk] *adj*: **to come ~** [notice, stamp, label] sich ablösen; *fig* [plan, system] schief gehen; [person] auf die Nase fallen.

unsuccessful [ˌʌnsək'sesfʊl] *adj* erfolglos; [attempt] vergeblich.

unsuccessfully [ˌʌnsək'sesfʊlɪ] *adv* erfolglos, vergeblich.

unsuitable [ʌn'suːtəbl] *adj* unpassend; **to be ~ for sthg** für etw ungeeignet sein.

unsure [ʌn'ʃɔː'] *adj* - 1. [not confident]: **to be ~ of o.s.** unsicher sein - 2. [not certain]: **to be ~ (about/of sthg)** sich (D) (einer Sache (G)) nicht sicher sein.

unsuspecting [ˌʌnsə'spektɪŋ] *adj* nichts ahnend.

unsympathetic ['ʌnˌsɪmpə'θetɪk] *adj* [unfeeling] nicht mitfühlend.

untangle [ʌn'tæŋgl] *vt* entwirren.

untapped [ʌn'tæpt] *adj* ungenutzt; [mineral resources] unerschlossen.

untenable [ʌn'tenəbl] *adj* unhaltbar.

unthinkable [ʌn'θɪŋkəbl] *adj* undenkbar, unvorstellbar.

untidy [ʌn'taɪdɪ] *adj* unordentlich.

untie [ʌn'taɪ] *(cont* untying) *vt* [string, knot, bonds] lösen; [package] aufbinden; [prisoner] losbinden.

until [ən'tɪl] *<> prep* bis; **~ the evening/end** bis zum Abend/Ende; **not ~ ... erst ...;** **she won't come ~ two o'clock** sie kommt erst um zwei Uhr *<> conj* bis; **wait ~ he comes** warte, bis er kommt; **she won't come ~ she is invited** sie kommt erst, wenn sie eingeladen wird.

untimely [ʌn'taɪmlɪ] *adj* - 1. [premature] vorzeitig - 2. [inopportune] ungelegen, unpassend.

untold [ʌn'təʊld] *adj* [amount] ungezählt; [wealth] unermesslich; [suffering, joy] unsäglich.

untoward [ˌʌntə'wɔːd] *adj* [event] unglücklich; [behaviour] ungebührlich.

untrue [ʌn'truː] *adj* [inaccurate] unwahr, falsch.

unused [*sense 1* ʌn'juːzd, *sense 2* ʌn'juːst] *adj* - 1. [new] unbenutzt - 2. [unaccustomed]: **to be ~ to sthg** an etw (A) nicht gewöhnt sein; **to be ~ to doing sthg** nicht daran gewöhnt sein, etw zu tun.

unusual [ʌn'juːʒl] *adj* ungewöhnlich.

unusually [ʌn'juːʒəlɪ] *adv* außergewöhnlich.

unveil [ʌn'veɪl] *vt lit & fig* enthüllen.

unwanted [ʌn'wɒntɪd] *adj* [clothes, furniture] ausrangiert; [child, pregnancy] ungewollt; **to feel ~** das Gefühl haben, unerwünscht zu sein.

unwelcome [ʌn'welkəm] *adj* - 1. [news, experience] unerfreulich - 2. [visitor] unwillkommen.

unwell [ʌn'wel] *adj*: **to be/feel ~** sich unwohl fühlen.

unwieldy [ʌn'wiːldɪ] *adj* - 1. [tool] unhandlich; [piece of furniture] sperrig - 2. *fig* [system, method] umständlich; [organization] schwerfällig.

unwilling [ˌʌn'wɪlɪŋ] *adj* unwillig.

unwind [ˌʌn'waɪnd] (*pt & pp* -wound) ⋄ *vt* ablwickeln ⋄ *vi fig* [person] sich entspannen.

unwise [ˌʌn'waɪz] *adj* unklug.

unworkable [ˌʌn'wɜːkəbl] *adj* undurchführbar.

unworthy [ʌn'wɜːðɪ] *adj*: **to be ~ of sthg** einer Sache (G) unwürdig sein.

unwound [ʌn'waʊnd] *pt & pp* ⊳ unwind.

unwrap [ˌʌn'ræp] *vt* auslpacken.

up [ʌp] ⋄ *adv* - **1.** [towards higher position, level] hoch; **we walked ~ to the top** wir sind zum Gipfel gelaufen; **to throw sthg ~** etw in die Höhe werfen; **prices are going ~** die Preise steigen; **~ and ~** immer höher - **2.** [in higher position] oben; **she's ~ in her room** sie ist oben in ihrem Zimmer; **~ here/there** hier/da OR dort oben - **3.** [into an upright position]: **to stand ~** aufstehen; **to sit ~** [from lying position] sich auflsetzen; [sit straight] sich gerade hinlsetzen; **help me ~** hilf mir auf - **4.** [northwards]: **to live ~ north** oben im Norden wohnen; **I'm going ~ to York** ich fahre hoch nach York - **5.** [facing upwards] nach oben gerichtet; **he was lying face ~** er lag mit dem Gesicht nach oben - **6.** [along river] oben; **their house is a little further ~** ihr Haus liegt ein bisschen weiter in dieser Richtung - **7.** [ahead]: **to be two goals ~** mit zwei Toren führen ⋄ *prep* - **1.** [towards higher position]: **to walk ~ a hill** einen Hügel hinauflgehen; **I went ~ the stairs** ich ging die Treppe hinauf - **2.** [in higher position]: **to be ~ a hill** oben auf einem Hügel sein - **3.** [towards far end of]: **they live ~ the road from us** sie wohnen weiter oben in unserer Straße ⋄ *adj* - **1.** [out of bed] auf; **I was ~ at six today** ich war heute um sechs auf; **to be ~ all night** die ganze Nacht auflbleiben - **2.** [at an end] um, zu Ende; **time's ~** die Zeit ist um - **3.** *inf* [wrong]: **there's something ~** es liegt etwas in der Luft; **what's ~ (with you)?** was ist (mit dir) los? ⋄ *n*: **~s and downs** Höhen und Tiefen *pl*. ⟐ **up and down** ⋄ *adv*: **to walk/jump ~ and down** auf und ab gehen/springen ⋄ *prep* [backwards and forwards]: **we walked ~ and down the avenue** wir gingen die Allee auf und ab. ⟐ **up to** *prep* - **1.** [indicating position, level] bis zu; **the water came ~ to my knees** das Wasser reichte mir bis an die Knie; **~ to this point** bis zu diesem Punkt; **~ to six weeks/ten people** bis zu sechs Wochen/zehn Personen - **2.** [in time] bis; **I felt fine ~ to last month** bis letzten Monat ging es mir gut - **3.** [well or able enough for]: **my French isn't ~ to much** *inf* mein Französisch ist nicht besonders gut; **to be ~ to a task** einer Aufgabe gewachsen sein; **I'm not**

~ to going out tonight ich schaffe es heute abend nicht auszugehen - **3.** *phr*: **what are you ~ to?** *inf* [doing] was machst du da?; [planning] sie haben etwas vor; **they're ~ to something** sie haben etwas vor; **it's ~ to you** das liegt bei dir. ⟐ **up until** *prep* bis; **~ until ten o'clock** bis um zehn Uhr.

up-and-coming *adj* [athlete, actor] kommend; [business] aufstrebend.

upbringing ['ʌpˌbrɪŋɪŋ] *n* Erziehung *die*.

update [ˌʌp'deɪt] *vt* aktualisieren.

upheaval [ʌp'hiːvl] *n* Aufruhr *der*.

upheld [ʌp'held] *pt & pp* ⊳ uphold.

uphill [ʌp'hɪl] ⋄ *adj* - **1.** [rising] ansteigend - **2.** *fig* [difficult] mühsam ⋄ *adv* bergauf.

uphold [ʌp'həʊld] (*pt & pp* -held) *vt* - **1.** [law] beilbehalten - **2.** [decision, system] unterstützen.

upholstery [ʌp'həʊlstərɪ] *n (U)* Polsterung *die*.

upkeep ['ʌpkiːp] *n* Instandhaltung *die*; [of garden] Pflege *die*.

uplifting [ʌp'lɪftɪŋ] *adj* [cheering] erhebend.

up-market *adj* [hotel, restaurant, area] vornehm; [goods] edel.

upon [ə'pɒn] *prep fml* - **1.** [on, on top of - indicating place, position] auf (+ D); [- indicating direction] auf (+ A); **summer/the weekend is ~ us** es ist beinahe Sommer/Wochenende - **2.** [when] als; **~ hearing the news, I rushed to the telephone** als ich die Neuigkeiten hörte, rannte ich sofort zum Telefon.

upper ['ʌpə'] ⋄ *adj* - **1.** [physically higher & GEOGR] obere, -r, -s; **~ lip** Oberlippe *die* - **2.** [higher in order, rank] höher ⋄ *n* [of shoe] Obermaterial *das*.

upper class *n*: **the ~** die Oberschicht. ⟐ **upper-class** *adj* vornehm.

upper-crust *adj* vornehm.

upper hand *n*: **to have the ~** die Oberhand haben; **to gain** OR **get the ~** die Oberhand gewinnen.

Upper House *n* POL Oberhaus *das*.

uppermost ['ʌpəməʊst] *adj* - **1.** [highest] oberste, -r, -s - **2.** [most important]: **my father's illness is ~ in my mind at the moment** die Krankheit meines Vaters beschäftigt mich momentan am meisten.

upright ['ʌpraɪt] ⋄ *adj lit & fig* aufrecht ⋄ *adv* aufrecht ⋄ *n* [of goal] Pfosten *der*; [of bookshelf] Seitenteil *das*; [of door] Türpfosten *der*.

uprising ['ʌpˌraɪzɪŋ] *n* Aufstand *der*.

uproar ['ʌprɔː'] *n* Aufruhr *der*.

uproot [ʌp'ruːt] *vt* entwurzeln.

upset [ʌp'set] (*pt & pp* upset) ⋄ *adj* - **1.** [distressed] aufgeregt; [shocked] bestürzt; [offended] beleidigt - **2.** MED: **to have an**

~ stomach eine Magenverstimmung haben <> n - 1. MED: **to have a stomach ~** eine Magenverstimmung haben - 2. [surprise result] Überraschungsergebnis das <> vt - 1. [distress] aufregen; **the news ~ him** der Nachricht bestürzte ihn - 2. [mess up] durcheinander bringen - 3. [overturn, knock over] umlkippen, umlstoßen; [boat] zum Kentern bringen.

upshot ['ʌpʃɒt] n Ergebnis das.

upside down [ˌʌpsaɪd-] <> adj [inverted] verkehrt herum <> adv verkehrt herum; **to turn sthg ~** fig [disorder] etw auf den Kopf stellen.

upstairs [ˌʌp'steəz] <> adj oben, im oberen Stockwerk <> adv - 1. [not downstairs] oben; [with motion] nach oben - 2. [on the floor above] oben, im oberen Stockwerk <> n oberes Stockwerk.

upstart ['ʌpstɑːt] n Emporkömmling der.

upstream [ˌʌp'striːm] <> adj: **~ (from sthg)** stromaufwärts (von etw) <> adv stromaufwärts.

upsurge ['ʌpsɜːdʒ] n: **~ of/in sthg** Zunahme die an etw (D).

uptake ['ʌpteɪk] n: **to be quick on the ~** schnell verstehen; **to be slow on the ~** schwer von Begriff sein.

uptight [ʌp'taɪt] adj inf verkrampft.

up-to-date adj - 1. [machinery, methods] modern - 2. [news, information] neueste, -r, -s, aktuell; **to keep ~ with sthg** über etw (A) auf dem Laufenden bleiben.

upturn ['ʌptɜːn] n: **~ (in sthg)** Aufschwung der (in etw (D)).

upward ['ʌpwəd] <> adj [movement, trend] Aufwärts- <> adv Am = upwards.

upwards ['ʌpwədz] adv - 1. [to a higher place] nach oben - 2. [to a higher number, degree, rate]: **to climb** OR **move ~** anlsteigen. ➡ **upwards of** prep über (+ A), mehr als.

uranium [jʊ'reɪnjəm] n Uran das.

urban ['ɜːbən] adj städtisch; **~ development** Stadtentwicklung die.

urbane [ɜː'beɪn] adj gewandt.

Urdu ['ʊədu:] n Urdu das.

urge [ɜːdʒ] <> n Drang der; **to have an ~ to do sthg** den Drang verspüren, etw zu tun <> vt - 1. [try to persuade]: **to ~ sb to do sthg** jn drängen, etw zu tun - 2. [advocate] eindringlich raten zu.

urgency ['ɜːdʒənsɪ] n Dringlichkeit die.

urgent ['ɜːdʒənt] adj - 1. [pressing] dringend - 2. [desperate] verzweifelt.

urinal [ˌjʊə'raɪnl] n [receptacle] Urinal das; [room] Pissoir das.

urinate ['jʊərɪneɪt] vi urinieren.

urine ['jʊərɪn] n Urin der.

urn [ɜːn] n - 1. [for ashes] Urne die - 2. [for tea, coffee] Heißwasserbehälter mit Zapfhahn.

Uruguay ['jʊərəgwaɪ] n Uruguay nt.

us [ʌs] pers pron uns; **they know ~** sie kennen uns; **they like ~** wir gefallen ihnen; **it's ~** wir sinds; **send it to ~** schicke es uns; **tell ~** sag uns; **they're worse than ~** sie sind schlimmer als wir; **you can't expect us to do it** du kannst nicht erwarten, dass WIR das tun; **all of ~** wir alle; **none of ~** keiner von uns; **some/a few of ~** einige von uns; **most of ~** die meisten von uns; **both of ~** wir beide; **there are three of ~** wir sind zu dritt; **neither of ~** keiner von uns.

US (abbr of United States) n: **the ~** die USA pl.

USA n (abbr of United States of America): **the ~** die USA pl.

usage ['juːzɪdʒ] n - 1. (U) [use of language] Gebrauch der - 2. [meaning] Bedeutung die - 3. (U) [treatment] Behandlung die; [handling] Gebrauch der.

use [n u & aux vb juːs, vt juːz] <> n - 1. [act of using] Gebrauch der, Benutzung die; [for specific purpose] Verwendung die; [of method] Anwendung die; **to be in/out of ~** im/außer Gebrauch sein; **to make ~ of sthg** von etw Gebrauch machen - 2. [purpose, usefulness] Nutzen der; **can you find a ~ for this?** kannst du damit etwas anfangen?; **to be of ~** nützlich sein; **it's no ~!** es hat keinen Zweck!; **what's the ~ (of doing that)?** was hat es für einen Zweck(, das zu tun)? <> aux vb: **I ~d to go for a run every day** ich bin früher jeden Tag laufen gegangen; **he didn't ~ to be so fat** er war früher nicht so dick <> vt - 1. [utilize] gebrauchen, benutzen; [for specific purpose] verwenden; [method] anlwenden - 2. pej [exploit] benutzen. ➡ **use up** vt sep aufbrauchen.

used [senses 1 and 2 juːzd, sense 3 juːst] adj - 1. [dirty] benutzt, schmutzig - 2. [secondhand] gebraucht, Gebraucht- - 3. [accustomed]: **to be ~ to sthg** an etw (A) gewöhnt sein; **to be ~ to doing sthg** daran gewöhnt sein OR es gewohnt sein, etw zu tun; **to get ~ to sthg** sich an etw (A) gewöhnen.

useful ['juːsfʊl] adj [handy] nützlich.

useless ['juːslɪs] adj - 1. [unusable] nutzlos - 2. [pointless] zwecklos, unnütz - 3. inf [hopeless] **to be ~** zu nichts zu gebrauchen sein.

user ['juːzə'] n Benutzer der, -in die; **drug ~** Drogenkonsument der, -in die.

user-friendly adj benutzerfreundlich.

usher ['ʌʃə'] <> n Platzanweiser der, -in die <> vt führen.

usherette [ˌʌʃə'ret] n Platzanweiserin die.

USSR (abbr of Union of Soviet Socialist Republics) n UdSSR die.

usual ['juːʒəl] adj üblich; **as ~** wie üblich.

usually ['juːʒəlɪ] adv normalerweise.

utensil [juː'tensl] n Utensil das.

uterus ['juːtərəs] (pl -ri [-raɪ] OR -ruses) n Uterus der, Gebärmutter die.

utility [juːˈtɪlətɪ] n - 1. [usefulness] Nützlichkeit die - 2. [company]: **(public) ~** (öffentlicher) Versorgungsbetrieb - 3. COMPUT Dienstprogramm das.

utility room n ≃ Waschküche die.

utilize, -ise [ˈjuːtəlaɪz] vt nutzen.

utmost [ˈʌtməʊst] ⟨⟩ adj äußerste, -r, -s ⟨⟩ n - 1. [best effort]: **to do one's ~ (to achieve sthg)** sein Möglichstes tun(, um etw zu erreichen) - 2. [maximum] Äußerste das; **to the ~** bis zum Äußersten.

utter [ˈʌtə⁰] ⟨⟩ adj völlig, komplett ⟨⟩ vt [sound, cry] ausstoßen; [word] sagen.

utterly [ˈʌtəlɪ] adv völlig.

U-turn n - 1. [turning movement] Wende die - 2. fig [complete change] Kehrtwendung die.

v¹ (pl v's OR vs), **V** (pl V's OR Vs) [viː] n [letter] v das, V das.

v² - 1. abbr of verse - 2. abbr of versus - 3. abbr of volt.

vacancy [ˈveɪkənsɪ] n - 1. [job, position] offene Stelle, freie Position - 2. [room available] freies Zimmer; **'vacancies'** 'frei'; **'no vacancies'** 'belegt'.

vacant [ˈveɪkənt] adj - 1. [house] leer stehend; [chair] unbesetzt; [toilet] nicht besetzt; [room] frei - 2. [post, job] offen, frei - 3. [look] leer.

vacant lot n Baugrundstück das.

vacate [vəˈkeɪt] vt - 1. [post, job] aufgeben - 2. [seat] frei machen - 3. [hotel, room] ausziehen aus.

vacation [vəˈkeɪʃn] n - 1. UNIV [period when closed] Ferien pl - 2. Am [holiday] Ferien pl, Urlaub der.

vacationer [vəˈkeɪʃənə⁰] n Am Urlauber der, -in die.

vaccinate [ˈvæksɪneɪt] vt: **to ~ sb (against sthg)** jn (gegen etw) impfen.

vaccine [Br ˈvæksiːn, Am vækˈsiːn] n Impfstoff der.

vacuum [ˈvækjʊəm] ⟨⟩ n - 1. TECH Vakuum das - 2. [cleaning machine] Staubsauger der ⟨⟩ vt & vi Staub saugen.

vacuum cleaner n Staubsauger der.

vacuum-packed adj vakuumverpackt.

vagina [vəˈdʒaɪnə] n Scheide die, Vagina die.

vagrant [ˈveɪɡrənt] n Landstreicher der, -in die.

vague [veɪɡ] adj - 1. [imprecise, evasive] va-

ge - 2. [feeling] leicht - 3. [absent-minded] zerstreut - 4. [shape, outline] schemenhaft.

vaguely [ˈveɪɡlɪ] adv - 1. [imprecisely] vage - 2. [slightly, not very] leicht - 3. [absent-mindedly] zerstreut - 4. [indistinctly] undeutlich.

vain [veɪn] adj - 1. pej [conceited] eitel - 2. [attempt, hope] vergeblich. ◆ **in vain** adv vergeblich, vergebens.

valentine card [ˈvæləntaɪn-] n Grußkarte die zum Valentinstag.

Valentine's Day [ˈvæləntaɪnz-] n: **(St) ~** Valentinstag der.

valet [ˈvælɪt, ˈvælɪt] n Kammerdiener der.

valid [ˈvælɪd] adj - 1. [argument] stichhaltig; [explanation] einleuchtend; [decision] begründet; [claim] berechtigt - 2. [ticket, passport, driving licence] gültig; [contract] rechtsgültig.

valley [ˈvælɪ] (pl valleys) n Tal das.

valour Br, **valor** Am [ˈvælə⁰] n fml & literary Heldenmut der.

valuable [ˈvæljʊəbl] adj wertvoll. ◆ **valuables** npl Wertsachen pl.

valuation [ˌvæljuˈeɪʃn] n - 1. (U) [pricing] Schätzung die - 2. [estimated price] Schätzwert der.

value [ˈvæljuː] ⟨⟩ n (U) Wert der; **to be good** ~ preisgünstig sein; **to be ~ for money** ein gutes Preis-Leistungs-Verhältnis haben ⟨⟩ vt schätzen. ◆ **values** npl [morals] Werte pl, Wertvorstellungen pl.

value-added tax [-ædɪd-] n Mehrwertsteuer die.

valued [ˈvæljuːd] adj geschätzt.

valve [vælv] n - 1. [in pipe, tube] Absperrhahn der - 2. [on tyre] Ventil das.

van [væn] n - 1. AUT Transporter der, Lieferwagen der - 2. Br RAIL Wagon der, Wagen der.

vandal [ˈvændl] n Vandale der, -lin die.

vandalism [ˈvændəlɪzm] n Vandalismus der.

vandalize, -ise [ˈvændəlaɪz] vt mutwillig beschädigen.

vanguard [ˈvænɡɑːd] n: **in the ~ of sthg** an der Spitze einer Sache (G).

vanilla [vəˈnɪlə] n Vanille die.

vanish [ˈvænɪʃ] vi - 1. [no longer be visible] verschwinden - 2. [no longer exist - race, species] aussterben; [- hopes, chances] schwinden.

vanity [ˈvænətɪ] n (U) pej [of person] Eitelkeit die.

vapour Br, **vapor** Am [ˈveɪpə⁰] n (U) Dampf der.

variable [ˈveərɪəbl] adj - 1. [changeable] unbeständig - 2. [uneven - quality] unterschiedlich; [- performance] unbeständig.

variance [ˈveərɪəns] n fml: **to be at ~ with sthg** mit etw nicht übereinstimmen.

variation [ˌveərɪˈeɪʃn] n - 1. (U) [fact of difference] Unterschied der - **2.** [change in level or quantity] Schwankung die - **3.** [different version & MUS] Variation die.

varicose veins ['værɪkəʊs-] npl Krampfadern pl.

varied ['veərɪd] adj [life] bewegt; [group] gemischt; [work, diet] abwechslungsreich.

variety [və'raɪətɪ] n - **1.** (U) [difference in type] Abwechslung die - **2.** [selection] Auswahl die - **3.** [type] Art die, Sorte die - **4.** (U) THEATRE Varietee das.

various ['veərɪəs] adj verschieden.

varnish ['vɑːnɪʃ] <> n [for wood, fingernails] Lack der; [for pottery] Glasur die <> vt [wood, fingernails] lackieren; [pottery] glasieren.

vary ['veərɪ] <> vt verändern, variieren <> vi [differ] sich unterscheiden; [fluctuate] sich ändern; [prices] schwanken.

vase [Br vɑːz, Am veɪz] n Vase die.

vast [vɑːst] adj riesig; [expense, difference] enorm.

vat [væt] n [open] Bottich der; [closed] Fass das.

VAT [væt, viːeɪˈtiː] (abbr of value added tax) n Mehrwertsteuer die, MwSt.

Vatican ['vætɪkən] n: **the ~ der** Vatikan.

vault [vɔːlt] <> n - **1.** [in bank] Tresorraum der - **2.** [under church] Gruft die - **3.** [roof] Gewölbe das <> vt springen über (+ A) <> vi: to ~ **over sthg** über etw (A) springen.

VCR (abbr of video cassette recorder) n Videorekorder der.

VD n abbr of venereal disease.

VDU (abbr of visual display unit) n Bildschirm der.

veal [viːl] n Kalbfleisch das.

veer [vɪə'] vi - **1.** [vehicle] ausscheren; [road] eine Kurve machen; [wind] (sich) drehen - **2.** fig [conversation, mood] schwanken.

vegan ['viːgən] <> adj veganisch <> n Veganer der, -in die.

vegetable ['vedʒtəbl] <> n Gemüse das <> adj Gemüse-.

vegetarian [ˌvedʒɪ'teərɪən] <> adj vegetarisch <> n Vegetarier der, -in die.

vegetation [ˌvedʒɪ'teɪʃn] n Vegetation die.

vehement ['viːəmənt] adj heftig; [denial, protest, defence] vehement; [debate] hitzig.

vehicle ['viːəkl] n [for transport] Fahrzeug das.

veil [veɪl] n Schleier der; **to draw a ~ over sthg** fig etw verschweigen.

vein [veɪn] n [gen] Ader die.

velocity [vɪ'lɒsətɪ] n PHYSICS Geschwindigkeit die.

velvet ['velvɪt] n Samt der.

vendetta [ven'detə] n Blutrache die; [in the press] Hetzkampagne die.

vending machine ['vendɪŋ-] n Automat der.

vendor ['vendə'] n Verkäufer der, -in die; **street ~** Straßenhändler der, -in die.

veneer [və'nɪə'] n - **1.** [of wood] Furnier das - **2.** fig [appearance]: **to give sthg a ~ of respectability** einer Sache (D) einen seriösen Anstrich geben.

venereal disease [vɪ'nɪərɪəl-] n (U) Geschlechtskrankheit die.

venetian blind [vɪˌniːʃn-] n Jalousie die.

Venezuela [ˌvenɪz'weɪlə] n Venezuela nt.

vengeance ['vendʒəns] n (U) Vergeltung die, Rache die; **with a ~** gewaltig; **to work with a ~** hart arbeiten.

venison ['venɪzn] n (U) Wild das (Damwild).

venom ['venəm] n - **1.** [poison] Gift das - **2.** fig [spite, bitterness] Gehässigkeit die.

vent [vent] <> n [in car] Öffnung die; [in chimney, for ventilation] Abzug der; **to give ~ to sthg** [feelings] etw (D) freien Lauf lassen; [anger] etw (D) Luft machen <> vt [express - feelings] freien Lauf lassen (+ D); [- anger] Luft machen (+ D); **to ~ one's anger on sb** seinen Ärger an jm ausllassen.

ventilate ['ventɪleɪt] vt (be)lüften.

ventilator ['ventɪleɪtə'] n - **1.** [in room, building] Ventilator der - **2.** MED Beatmungsgerät das.

ventriloquist [ven'trɪləkwɪst] n Bauchredner der, -in die.

venture ['ventʃə'] <> n Unternehmen das <> vt [proffer - opinion, advice] zu äußern wagen; [- guess] wagen; [- suggestion, remark] sich (D) erlauben; **to ~ to do sthg** (D) erlauben, etw zu tun <> vi - **1.** [go somewhere dangerous] sich wagen - **2.** [embark]: **to ~ into politics** den Schritt in die Politik wagen.

venue ['venjuː] n [for concert, conference] Veranstaltungsort der; [for match] Austragungsort der.

veranda(h) [və'rændə] n Veranda die.

verb [vɜːb] n Verb das.

verbal ['vɜːbl] adj - **1.** [spoken - agreement] mündlich; [- skills] sprachlich; **~ abuse** Beschimpfung die - **2.** GRAMM Verb-, verbal.

verbatim [vɜː'beɪtɪm] adj & adv (wort)wörtlich.

verbose [vɜː'bəʊs] adj fml langatmig.

verdict ['vɜːdɪkt] n Urteil das; **what's your ~ on his new film?** was hältst du von seinem neuen Film?

verge [vɜːdʒ] n - **1.** [edge, side] Rand der; [of road] Bankett das - **2.** [brink]: **to be on the ~ of sthg** [ruin, mental breakdown] am Rand einer Sache (G) stehen; [success] kurz vor etw (D) stehen; **to be on the ~ of doing sthg** kurz davor stehen, etw zu tun. ◆ **verge (up)on** vt fus grenzen an (+ A).

verify ['verɪfaɪ] vt - **1.** [check] prüfen, überprüfen - **2.** [confirm] bestätigen.

veritable ['verɪtəbl] adj fml or hum wahr.

vermin ['vɜːmɪn] *npl* - **1.** ZOOL [insects] Ungeziefer *das;* [rodents] Schädlinge *pl* - **2.** *pej* [people] Abschaum *der.*

vermouth [vɜː'muːθ] *n* Wermut *der.*

versa ▷ vice versa.

versatile ['vɜːsətaɪl] *adj* - **1.** [person] vielseitig - **2.** [machine, tool] vielseitig verwendbar.

verse [vɜːs] *n* - **1.** (U) [poetry] Lyrik *die* - **2.** [stanza] Strophe *die* - **3.** [in Bible] Vers *der.*

version ['vɜːʃn] *n* [form, account of events] Version *die.*

versus ['vɜːsəs] *prep* - **1.** SPORT gegen - **2.** [as opposed to] im Gegensatz zu.

vertebra ['vɜːtɪbrə] (*pl* -brae [-briː]) *n* Rückenwirbel *der.*

vertical ['vɜːtɪkl] *adj* senkrecht, vertikal.

vertigo ['vɜːtɪɡəʊ] *n* (U) Gleichgewichtsstörungen *pl.*

verve [vɜːv] *n* Schwung *der.*

very ['verɪ] ◇ *adv* sehr; **much** sehr; **not** nicht sehr ◇ *adj* genau; **the opposite** genau das Gegenteil; **the person I was looking for!** nach Ihnen habe ich gerade gesucht!; **that afternoon** am selben Nachmittag; **the next day** gleich am nächsten Tag; **my own room** mein eigenes Zimmer; **the best** das Allerbeste; **for the first/last time** zum allerersten/allerletzten Mal; **at the beginning** ganz am Anfang; **the thought makes me shudder** mich schaudert beim bloßen Gedanken. ◆ **very well** *adv* - **1.** [all right] schön, also gut - **2.** *phr:* **I/you**/*etc* **can't well say no** ich kann/du kannst/*etc* wohl kaum nein sagen.

vessel ['vesl] *n fml* - **1.** [boat] Schiff *das* - **2.** [container] Gefäß *das.*

vest [vest] *n* - **1.** *Br* [undershirt] Unterhemd *das* - **2.** *Am* [waistcoat] Weste *die.*

vestibule ['vestɪbjuːl] *n fml* [entrance hall] Eingangshalle *die.*

vestige ['vestɪdʒ] *n fml* Spur *die.*

vestry ['vestrɪ] *n* Sakristei *die.*

vet [vet] ◇ *n Br abbr of* veterinary surgeon ◇ *vt Br* [check] überprüfen.

veteran ['vetrən] ◇ *adj* [experienced] mit langjähriger Erfahrung ◇ *n* Veteran *der,* -in *die.*

veterinarian [,vetərɪ'neərɪən] *n Am* Tierarzt *der,* -ärztin *die.*

veterinary surgeon ['vetərɪnrɪ-] *n Br fml* Tierarzt *der,* -ärztin *die.*

veto ['viːtəʊ] (*pl* -es; *pt & pp* -ed; *cont* -ing) ◇ *n* Veto *das* ◇ *vt* sein Veto einlegen gegen.

vex [veks] *vt fml* [annoy] (ver)ärgern.

VHF (*abbr of* very high frequency) *n* UKW.

VHS (*abbr of* video home system) *n* VHS.

via ['vaɪə] *prep* - **1.** [travelling through] über (+ A), via (+ A) - **2.** [by means of]: **a friend**

durch einen Freund; **satellite** via OR per Satellit.

viable ['vaɪəbl] *adj* - **1.** [plan, programme, scheme] durchführbar - **2.** ECON lebensfähig.

Viagra® [vaɪ'æɡrə] *n* Viagra® *das.*

vibrate [vaɪ'breɪt] *vi* vibrieren; PHYS schwingen.

vicar ['vɪkə'] *n* Pfarrer *der,* -in *die.*

vicarage ['vɪkərɪdʒ] *n* Pfarrhaus *das.*

vicarious [vɪ'keərɪəs] *adj* [enjoyment, pleasure] indirekt.

vice [vaɪs] *n* - **1.** [immorality, fault] Laster *das* - **2.** [tool] Schraubstock *der.*

vice-chairman *n* stellvertretender Vorsitzender.

vice-chancellor *n* UNIV Leiter der Universitätsverwaltung und Vorsitzender des Senats.

vice-president *n* Vizepräsident *der,* -in *die.*

vice versa [,vaɪsɪ'vɜːsə] *adv* umgekehrt.

vicinity [vɪ'sɪnətɪ] *n* - **1.** [neighbourhood] Umgebung *die;* **in the (of)** in der Nähe (von OR (+ G)) - **2.** [approximate figures]: **in the of £80,000 a year** um die £80 000 pro Jahr.

vicious ['vɪʃəs] *adj* - **1.** [attack, blow, killer] brutal - **2.** [person, gossip] boshaft, gehässig - **3.** [dog] bösartig.

vicious circle *n* Teufelskreis *der.*

victim ['vɪktɪm] *n* Opfer *das;* **to fall to sb/ sthg** jm/etw zum Opfer fallen.

victimize, -ise ['vɪktɪmaɪz] *vt* schikanieren.

victor ['vɪktə'] *n* Sieger *der,* -in *die.*

victorious [vɪk'tɔːrɪəs] *adj* [winning] siegreich.

victory ['vɪktərɪ] *n* Sieg *der;* **to win a over sb/sthg** jn/etw besiegen.

video ['vɪdɪəʊ] (*pl* -s; *pt & pp* -ed; *cont* -ing) ◇ *n* - **1.** [gen] Video *das;* **I've got it on** ich habe es auf Video - **2.** [machine] Videorekorder *der* ◇ *comp* Video- ◇ *vt* - **1.** [using videorecorder] (auf Video) auflnehmen - **2.** [using camera] filmen.

video camera *n* Videokamera *die.*

video cassette *n* Videokassette *die.*

video game *n* Videospiel *das.*

videorecorder ['vɪdɪəʊrɪ,kɔːdə'] *n* Videorekorder *der.*

video shop *n* Videothek *die.*

videotape ['vɪdɪəʊteɪp] *n* Videoband *das.*

vie [vaɪ] (*pt & pp* vied; *cont* vying) *vi*: **to (with sb) for sthg** (mit jm) um etw wetteifern; **to with sb to do sthg** mit jm darum wetteifern, etw zu tun.

Vienna [vɪ'enə] *n* Wien *nt.*

Vietnam [*Br* ,vjet'næm, *Am* ,vjet'nɑːm] *n* Vietnam *nt.*

Vietnamese [,vjetnə'miːz] ◇ *adj* vietnamesisch ◇ *n* [language] Vietnamesisch(e) *das* ◇ *npl*: **the** die Vietnamesen.

view [vjuː] ◇ *n* - **1.** [opinion] Ansicht *die,* Meinung *die;* **in my** meiner Ansicht OR Mei-

nung nach - **2.** [vista] Aussicht *die*, Blick *der*
- **3.** [ability to see] Sicht *die;* **to come into ~** in
Sicht kommen ◇ *vt* - **1.** [consider] sehen; **he
~ed her with suspicion** er betrachtete sie mit
Argwohn - **2.** *fml* [house] besichtigen. ◆ **in
view of** *prep* angesichts *(+ G).* ◆ **with a
view to** *conj:* **with a ~ to doing sthg** mit der
Absicht, etw zu tun.

viewer ['vju:ə'] *n* - **1.** [person] Zuschauer
der, -in *die* - **2.** [for slides] Diabetrachter *der*.

viewfinder ['vju:ˌfaɪndə'] *n* Sucher *der*.

viewpoint ['vju:pɔɪnt] *n* - **1.** [opinion]
Standpunkt *der* - **2.** [place] Aussichtspunkt
der.

vigilante [ˌvɪdʒɪ'læntɪ] *n* (militante) Bür-
gerwehr.

vigorous ['vɪgərəs] *adj* - **1.** [walk] flott;
[shake, scrub] kräftig - **2.** [protest, denial, at-
tempt] energisch.

vile [vaɪl] *adj* [act, person] abscheulich;
[food] scheußlich.

villa ['vɪlə] *n* Villa *die*.

village ['vɪlɪdʒ] *n* Dorf *das*.

villager ['vɪlɪdʒə'] *n* Dorfbewohner *der*, -in
die.

villain ['vɪlən] *n* - **1.** [of film, book, play] Bösewicht *der* - **2.** *dated* [criminal] Schurke *der*.

vindicate ['vɪndɪkeɪt] *vt* [confirm] bestätigen; [justify] rechtfertigen; **to ~ o.s.** seine
Unschuld beweisen.

vindictive [vɪn'dɪktɪv] *adj* rachsüchtig.

vine [vaɪn] *n* [grapevine] Weinrebe *die*.

vinegar ['vɪnɪgə'] *n* Essig *der*.

vineyard ['vɪnjəd] *n* Weinberg *der*.

vintage ['vɪntɪdʒ] ◇ *adj* [wine] erlesen
◇ *n* [wine] Jahrgang *der*.

vinyl ['vaɪnɪl] *n* Vinyl *das*.

viola [vɪ'əʊlə] *n* - **1.** MUS Bratsche *die* - **2.** BOT
Veilchen *das*.

violate ['vaɪəleɪt] *vt* - **1.** [human rights, law,
treaty] verstoßen gegen - **2.** [peace, privacy]
stören - **3.** [grave] schänden.

violence ['vaɪələns] *n* (U) - **1.** [physical
force] Gewalt *die;* [of people] Gewalttätigkeit
die; [of actions] Brutalität *die* - **2.** [of words, re-
action] Heftigkeit *die*.

violent ['vaɪələnt] *adj* - **1.** [person] gewalttätig; [attack] heftig; [crime] Gewalt-; [death]
gewaltsam - **2.** [intense] heftig.

violet ['vaɪələt] ◇ *adj* violett ◇ *n*
- **1.** [flower] Veilchen *das* - **2.** [colour] Violett
das.

violin [ˌvaɪə'lɪn] *n* Violine *die*, Geige *die*.

violinist [ˌvaɪə'lɪnɪst] *n* Violinist *der*, -in *die*,
Geiger *der*, -in *die*.

VIP (*abbr of* very important person) *n* Promi-
nente *der, die*, VIP *der*.

viper ['vaɪpə'] *n* Viper *die*.

virgin ['vɜːdʒɪn] ◇ *adj* - **1.** [gen] jungfräu-
lich - **2.** [forest, soil] unberührt ◇ *n* Jungfrau
die.

Virgo ['vɜːgəʊ] (*pl* -s) *n* Jungfrau *die*.

virile ['vɪraɪl] *adj* männlich.

virtually ['vɜːtʃʊəlɪ] *adv* [almost] so gut
wie, praktisch.

virtual reality *n* virtuelle Realität.

virtue ['vɜːtjuː] *n* - **1.** [goodness] Tugend-
haftigkeit *die* - **2.** [merit, quality] Tugend *die*
- **3.** [benefit] Vorteil *der*. ◆ **by virtue of**
prep fml aufgrund *(+ G).*

virtuous ['vɜːtʃʊəs] *adj* tugendhaft.

virus ['vaɪrəs] *n* MED & COMPUT Virus *das*.

visa ['viːzə] *n* Visum *das;* **entry/exit ~**
Einreise-/Ausreisevisum *das*.

vis-à-vis *prep fml* [in comparison to] gegenüber *(+ D);* [regarding] bezüglich *(+ G).*

viscose ['vɪskəʊs] *n* Viskose *die*.

visibility [ˌvɪzɪ'bɪlətɪ] *n* - **1.** [being visible]
Sichtbarkeit *die* - **2.** [range of vision] Sichtweite *die;* **good/poor ~** gute/schlechte Sicht.

visible ['vɪzəbl] *adj* - **1.** [which can be physically seen] sichtbar - **2.** [evident] sichtlich.

vision ['vɪʒn] *n* - **1.** [ability to see] Sehvermögen *das* - **2.** *fig* [foresight] Weitblick *der;* **a
man of ~** ein Mann mit Weitblick - **3.** [im-
pression, dream] Vision *die*.

visit ['vɪzɪt] ◇ *n* Besuch *der;* [stay] Aufenthalt *der* ◇ *vt* besuchen.

visiting hours ['vɪzɪtɪŋ-] *npl* Besuchszei-
ten *pl*.

visitor ['vɪzɪtə'] *n* Besucher *der*, -in *die;* **she
has ~s** sie hat Besuch.

visitors' book *n* Gästebuch *das*.

visor ['vaɪzə'] *n* [on helmet] Visier *das*.

vista ['vɪstə] *n* [view] Ausblick *der*.

visual ['vɪʒʊəl] *adj* Seh-; [joke, memory,
image] visuell.

visual display unit *n* Bildschirm *der*.

visualize, -ise ['vɪʒʊəlaɪz] *vt* sich (D) vorstellen.

vital ['vaɪtl] *adj* - **1.** [essential] unerlässlich,
unbedingt notwendig; [essential to life] lebenswichtig - **2.** [full of life - person] vital.

vitally ['vaɪtəlɪ] *adv:* **~ important** von entscheidender Bedeutung.

vitamin [*Br* 'vɪtəmɪn, *Am* 'vaɪtəmɪn] *n* Vitamin *das*.

vivacious [vɪ'veɪʃəs] *adj* lebhaft, lebendig.

vivid ['vɪvɪd] *adj* - **1.** [colour] kräftig
- **2.** [memory] lebhaft; [description] lebendig.

vividly ['vɪvɪdlɪ] *adv* - **1.** [painted] in kräftigen Farben - **2.** [remember] lebhaft; [describe]
lebendig.

vixen ['vɪksn] *n* Füchsin *die*.

VLF (*abbr of* very low frequency) *n* VLF.

V-neck *n* - **1.** [sweater, dress] Pullover *der*/
Kleid *das* mit V-Ausschnitt - **2.** [neck] V-
Ausschnitt *der*.

vocabulary [və'kæbjʊlərɪ] *n* - **1.** [gen]
Wortschatz *der*, Vokabular *das* - **2.** [list of
words] Wörterverzeichnis *das*.

vocal ['vəʊkl] adj - 1. [outspoken] lautstark - 2. [of the voice] stimmlich.

vocal cords npl Stimmbänder pl.

vocation [vəʊ'keɪʃn] n [calling] Berufung die.

vocational [vəʊ'keɪʃənl] adj berufsbezogen.

vociferous [və'sɪfərəs] adj fml lautstark.

vodka ['vɒdkə] n Wodka der.

vogue [vəʊg] n Mode die; **to be in ~** in Mode sein.

voice [vɔɪs] <> n [gen] Stimme die <> vt [opinion, emotion] zum Ausdruck bringen.

void [vɔɪd] <> adj - 1. [contract, result] ungültig, nichtig ▷ null - 2. fml [empty]: **~ of interest** ohne jegliches Interesse <> n - 1. literary [feeling of emptiness]: **the ~ left by his death** die Lücke, die sein Tod hinterlassen hat - 2. [chasm] Nichts das.

volatile [Br 'vɒlətaɪl, Am 'vɒlətl] adj [situation] brisant; [person] aufbrausend; [market] unbeständig.

volcano [vɒl'keɪnəʊ] (pl -es OR -s) n Vulkan der.

volition [və'lɪʃn] n fml: **of one's own ~** aus freiem Willen.

volley ['vɒlɪ] (pl volleys) <> n - 1. [of gunfire] Salve die - 2. [of insults] Flut die - 3. [in tennis] Volley der; [in football] Volleyschuss der <> vt [in tennis] volley spielen; [in football] volley nehmen.

volleyball ['vɒlɪbɔːl] n SPORT Volleyball der.

volt [vəʊlt] n Volt das.

voltage ['vəʊltɪdʒ] n Spannung die.

voluble ['vɒljʊbl] adj fml redselig.

volume ['vɒljuːm] n - 1. [of sound] Lautstärke die - 2. [of container, object] Volumen das, Rauminhalt der - 3. [of work] Umfang der; **~ of traffic** Verkehrsaufkommen das - 4. [book] Band der.

voluntarily [Br 'vɒləntrɪlɪ, Am ˌvɒlən'terəlɪ] adv freiwillig; [work] ehrenamtlich.

voluntary ['vɒləntrɪ] adj - 1. [not obligatory] freiwillig - 2. [unpaid] ehrenamtlich.

voluntary work n freiwillige OR ehrenamtliche Tätigkeit.

volunteer [ˌvɒlən'tɪər] <> n - 1. [gen & MIL] Freiwillige der, die - 2. [unpaid worker] freiwillige Helfer der, -in die <> vt - 1. [of one's free will]: **to ~ to do sthg** sich bereit erklären, etw zu tun - 2. [information] geben; **to ~ advice** Ratschläge erteilen <> vi sich freiwillig melden.

vomit ['vɒmɪt] <> n Erbrochene das <> vi sich übergeben.

vote [vəʊt] <> n - 1. [individual decision] Stimme die; **a ~ for/against sb/sthg** eine Stimme für/gegen jn/etw - 2. [session, ballot] Abstimmung die - 3. [result of ballot]: **the ~**

das Abstimmungsergebnis - 4. [suffrage] Stimmrecht das <> vt - 1. [gen] wählen; **to ~ to do sthg** (per Abstimmung) beschließen, etw zu tun - 2. [suggest] vorschlagen <> vi wählen; **to ~ for/against sb/sthg** für/gegen jn/etw stimmen; **to ~ on an issue** über eine Frage abstimmen.

voter ['vəʊtər] n Wähler die, -in die.

voting ['vəʊtɪŋ] n Wahl die, Abstimmung die.

vouch [vaʊtʃ] ◆ **vouch for** vt fus - 1. [person] bürgen für - 2. [character, accuracy] sich verbürgen für.

voucher ['vaʊtʃər] n Gutschein der.

vow [vaʊ] <> n Gelöbnis das; RELIG Gelübde das <> vt: **to ~ to do sthg** geloben, etw zu tun; **to ~ (that) ...** schwören(, dass) ...

vowel ['vaʊəl] n Vokal der.

voyage ['vɔɪɪdʒ] n Reise die; [by sea] Seereise die; [through space] Flug der.

vs abbr of versus.

VSO (abbr of Voluntary Service Overseas) n britische Hilfsorganisation, die Freiwillige mit Berufsausbildung in Entwicklungsländern einsetzt.

vulgar ['vʌlgər] adj - 1. [tasteless - décor] geschmacklos; [- person] ordinär - 2. [rude] vulgär.

vulnerable ['vʌlnərəbl] adj - 1. [easily hurt - emotionally] verletzlich; [- physically] verwundbar - 2. [easily influenced]: **~ (to sthg)** anfällig (für etw).

vulture ['vʌltʃər] n lit & fig Geier der.

w (pl w's OR ws), **W** (pl W's OR Ws) ['dʌbljuː] n w das, W das. ◆ **W** (abbr of west, watt) W.

wad [wɒd] n - 1. [of cotton wool] Bausch der - 2. [of bank notes, documents] Bündel das.

waddle ['wɒdl] vi watscheln.

wade [weɪd] vi waten. ◆ **wade through** vt fus fig durchackern.

wading pool ['weɪdɪŋ-] n Am Plantschbecken das.

wafer ['weɪfər] n [thin biscuit] Waffel die.

waffle ['wɒfl] <> n - 1. CULIN Waffel die - 2. Br inf [vague talk] Geschwafel das <> vi schwafeln.

wag [wæg] <> vt [tail] wedeln mit <> vi [tail] wedeln.

wage [weɪdʒ] <> n Lohn der <> vt: **to ~ war against sb/sthg** einen Kampf gegen jn/etw führen. ◆ **wages** npl Lohn der.

wage packet n - 1. [envelope] Lohntüte die - 2. [pay] Lohn der.

wager ['weɪdʒə'] n Wette die.

waggle ['wægl] inf vt [tail] wedeln mit; [ears] wackeln mit.

wagon, waggon Br ['wægən] n - 1. [horse-drawn vehicle] Fuhrwerk das - 2. Br RAIL Waggon der.

wail [weɪl] <> n - 1. [of baby] Geschrei das; [of mourner] Klagen das - 2. [of wind, siren] Heulen das <> vi [baby] schreien; [mourner] klagen.

waist [weɪst] n Taille die.

waistcoat ['weɪskəʊt] n Br Weste die.

waistline ['weɪstlaɪn] n Taille die.

wait [weɪt] <> n Wartezeit die <> vi warten; **to ~ and see** abwarten(, was passiert) <> vt - 1. [person]: **I/he/she can't ~ to do it** ich/er/sie kann es kaum erwarten, es zu tun - 2.: **to ~ tables** kellnern. ◆ **wait for** vt fus warten auf (+ A); **to ~ for sb to do sthg** darauf warten, dass jd etw tut. ◆ **wait on** vt fus [serve food to] bedienen. ◆ **wait up** vi aufbleiben.

waiter ['weɪtə'] n Kellner der.

waiting list ['weɪtɪŋ-] n Warteliste die.

waiting room ['weɪtɪŋ-] n Warteraum der; [at doctor's] Wartezimmer das; [at railway station] Wartesaal der.

waitress ['weɪtrɪs] n Kellnerin die, Serviererin die.

waive [weɪv] vt fml [entrance fee] verzichten auf (+ A); [rule] nicht anwenden.

wake [weɪk] (pt woke OR -d; pp woken OR -d) <> n [of ship, boat] Kielwasser das <> vt wecken <> vi aufwachen. ◆ **wake up** <> vt sep aufwecken <> vi [wake] aufwachen.

waken ['weɪkən] fml <> vt wecken <> vi erwachen.

Wales [weɪlz] n Wales nt.

walk [wɔːk] <> n - 1. [stroll] Spaziergang der; **to go for a ~** einen Spaziergang machen; **to take the dog for a ~** mit dem Hund spazieren gehen; **it's quite a long ~ to the station** zu Fuß ist es ganz schön weit bis zum Bahnhof - 2. [gait] Gang der <> vt - 1. [escort]: **I'll ~ you back to the car park** ich gehe mit dir zurück bis zum Parkplatz - 2. [dog] spazieren führen - 3. [cover on foot] laufen, (zu Fuß) gehen <> vi gehen, laufen; [hike] wandern; **he ~s to work** er geht zu Fuß zur Arbeit. ◆ **walk out** vi - 1. [leave suddenly] hinausgehen - 2. [go on strike] in Streik treten. ◆ **walk out on** vt fus sitzen lassen.

walker ['wɔːkə'] n [for pleasure] Spaziergänger der, -in die; [for hiking] Wanderer der, -derin die; SPORT Geher der, -in die.

walkie-talkie [ˌwɔːkɪ'tɔːkɪ] n Walkie-Talkie das.

walking ['wɔːkɪŋ] n [for pleasure] Spazierengehen das; [hiking] Wandern das; SPORT Gehen das.

walking shoes npl Wanderschuhe pl.

walking stick n Spazierstock der.

Walkman® ['wɔːkmən] n Walkman® der.

walkout ['wɔːkaʊt] n [of workers] Arbeitsniederlegung die.

walkover ['wɔːkˌəʊvə'] n Br inf [victory] spielender Sieg.

walkway ['wɔːkweɪ] n Fußweg der.

wall [wɔːl] n - 1. [inside building, of stomach, cell] Wand die - 2. [outside] Mauer die.

wallchart ['wɔːltʃɑːt] n Schautafel die.

walled [wɔːld] adj von Mauern umgeben.

wallet ['wɒlɪt] n [for money] Brieftasche die; [for documents] Etui das.

wallop ['wɒləp] inf vt [person] versohlen, verdreschen; [ball] dreschen.

wallow ['wɒləʊ] vi [in mud] sich wälzen, sich suhlen.

wallpaper ['wɔːlˌpeɪpə'] <> n (U) Tapete die <> vt tapezieren.

Wall Street n Wall Street die.

wally ['wɒlɪ] n Br inf Dussel der.

walnut ['wɔːlnʌt] n - 1. [nut] Walnuss die - 2. [tree] Walnussbaum der, Nussbaum der - 3. [wood] Nussbaumholz das.

walrus ['wɔːlrəs] (pl inv OR -es) n Walross das.

waltz [wɔːls] <> n Walzer der <> vi [dance] Walzer tanzen.

wan [wɒn] adj [person, complexion] bleich; [smile] matt.

wand [wɒnd] n Zauberstab der.

wander ['wɒndə'] vi - 1. [person] herumlaufen, umherwandern - 2. [thoughts] schweifen, wandern.

wane [weɪn] vi - 1. [popularity, enthusiasm] schwinden - 2. [moon] abnehmen.

wangle ['wæŋgl] vt inf organisieren; **to ~ sthg out of sb** jm etw aus dem Kreuz leiern.

want [wɒnt] <> vt - 1. [desire] wollen; **to ~ to do sthg** etw tun wollen; **to ~ sb to do sthg** wollen, dass jd etw tut; **what do you ~ to eat?** was möchtest du (zu) essen?; **you're ~ed on the phone** Sie werden am Telefon verlangt - 2. [need] brauchen; **you ~ to be more careful** du solltest vorsichtiger sein - 3. [seek] suchen; **he is ~ed by the police** er wird von der Polizei gesucht <> n - 1. [need] Bedürfnis das - 2. [lack] Mangel der; **his ~ of understanding** seine mangelnde Einsicht; **for ~ of** aus Mangel an (+ D) - 3. [poverty] Not die; **to be in ~** Not leiden.

wanted ['wɒntɪd] adj: **to be ~ (by the police)** (polizeilich) gesucht werden.

wanton ['wɒntən] adj fml [destruction] mutwillig; [neglect] sträflich.

war [wɔː'] n Krieg der; **to be at ~** sich im Kriegszustand befinden.

ward [wɔːd] *n* **- 1.** [part of hospital] Station *die;* [room in hospital] Krankensaal *der;* **maternity ~** Entbindungsstation *die* **- 2.** Br POL Wahlbezirk *der* **- 3.** LAW Mündel *das.*
◆ **ward off** *vt fus* [blow, evil spirits] ablwehren; [disease] schützen vor (+ D).

warden ['wɔːdn] *n* **- 1.** [of park] Aufseher *der,* -in *die;* [of game reserve] Wildhüter *der,* -in *die* **- 2.** Br [of youth hostel] Herbergsvater *der,* -mutter *die;* [of hall of residence] Heimleiter *der,* -in *die* **- 3.** Am [prison governor] Gefängnisdirektor *der,* -in *die.*

warder ['wɔːdə] *n* [in prison] Wärter *der,* -in *die.*

wardrobe ['wɔːdrəʊb] *n* **- 1.** [piece of furniture] Kleiderschrank *der,* Schrank *der* **- 2.** [collection of clothes] Garderobe *die.*

warehouse ['weəhaʊs, *pl* -haʊzɪz] *n* Lagerhaus *das.*

📖 **warehouse**

Ein warehouse ist im Englischen kein Warenhaus, sondern ein Lagerhaus oder Lager. The goods are stored in a warehouse at the harbour hieße also übersetzt „die Ware ist in einem Lagerhaus im Hafen untergebracht". Ein „Warenhaus" ist im Englischen ein department store. Der Satz „Herrenbekleidung finden Sie im ersten Stock dieses Warenhauses" würde im Englischen The men's clothing department is on the first floor of this store lauten.

---

warfare ['wɔːfeə] *n* (U) [war] Krieg *der;* [technique] Kriegsführung *die.*

warhead ['wɔːhed] *n* Sprengkopf *der.*

warily ['weərɪlɪ] *adv* [carefully] vorsichtig; [suspiciously] misstrauisch.

warm [wɔːm] ◇ *adj* **- 1.** [gen] warm; **are you ~ enough?** ist dir warm genug? **- 2.** [friendly - person, feelings, welcome] herzlich; [- atmosphere] freundlich ◇ *vt* [food, milk] warm machen. ◆ **warm to** *vt fus* [idea, place] Gefallen finden an (+ D).
◆ **warm up** ◇ *vt sep* **- 1.** [heat - food] warm machen; [- room] heizen **- 2.** [reheat] aufwärmen ◇ *vi* **- 1.** [get warmer] wärmer werden **- 2.** [machine, engine] warm laufen; [audience] in Stimmung kommen **- 3.** [athlete, footballer] sich aufwärmen; [orchestra, musician] sich einspielen.

warm-hearted [-'hɑːtɪd] *adj* [person] warmherzig; [action, gesture] herzlich.

warmly ['wɔːmlɪ] *adv* **- 1.** [in warm clothes]: **to dress ~** sich warm anziehen **- 2.** [in a friendly way] herzlich.

warmth [wɔːmθ] *n* **- 1.** [of temperature, clothes] Wärme *die* **- 2.** [of welcome, smile, support] Herzlichkeit *die.*

warn [wɔːn] *vt* **- 1.** [advise] warnen; **to ~ sb of** OR **about sthg** jn vor etw (D) warnen

- 2. [inform] Bescheid geben (+ D); **to ~ sb that ...** jn darauf hinleisen, dass ...

warning ['wɔːnɪŋ] *n* **- 1.** [cautionary advice] Warnung *die;* [from police, judge] Verwarnung *der* **- 2.** [notice]: **to give sb ~** jm rechtzeitig Bescheid sagen.

warning light *n* Warnleuchte *die.*

warp [wɔːp] ◇ *vt* **- 1.** [wood]: **the sun will ~ the wood** in der Sonne wird sich das Holz verziehen **- 2.** [mind] psychisch schwer schädigen ◇ *vi* [wood] sich verziehen.

warrant ['wɒrənt] ◇ *n* LAW [written order] Befehl *der;* [for arrest] Haftbefehl *der;* [for search] Durchsuchungsbefehl *der* ◇ *vt fml* [justify] rechtfertigen.

warranty ['wɒrəntɪ] *n* [guarantee] Garantie *die.*

warren ['wɒrən] *n* Kaninchenbau *der.*

warrior ['wɒrɪə] *n literary* Krieger *der.*

Warsaw ['wɔːsɔː] *n* Warschau *nt.*

warship ['wɔːʃɪp] *n* Kriegsschiff *das.*

wart [wɔːt] *n* Warze *die.*

wartime ['wɔːtaɪm] *n* Kriegszeit *die;* **in ~** in Kriegszeiten.

wary ['weərɪ] *adj* [careful] vorsichtig; [suspicious] misstrauisch; **to be ~ of sthg** sich vor etw (D) in Acht nehmen.

was [*weak form* wəz, *strong form* wɒz] *pt* ▷ be.

wash [wɒʃ] ◇ *n* **- 1.** [act of washing]: **she/it needs a ~** sie/es muss gewaschen werden; **to have a ~** sich waschen; **to give sthg a ~** etw waschen **- 2.** [clothes to be washed] Wäsche *die* **- 3.** [from boat] Kielwasser *das* ◇ *vt* [clean] waschen; [dishes] spülen ◇ *vi* [clean o.s.] sich waschen.
◆ **wash away** *vt sep* wegspülen.
◆ **wash up** ◇ *vt sep Br* [dishes] ablwaschen, spülen ◇ *vi* **- 1.** Br [wash the dishes] abwaschen, spülen **- 2.** Am [wash o.s.] sich waschen.

washable ['wɒʃəbl] *adj* waschbar.

washbasin Br ['wɒʃˌbeɪsn], **washbowl** Am ['wɒʃbəʊl] *n* Waschbecken *das.*

washcloth ['wɒʃˌklɒθ] *n Am* Waschlappen *der.*

washer ['wɒʃə] *n* **- 1.** TECH Dichtungsring *der* **- 2.** [washing machine] Waschmaschine *die.*

washing ['wɒʃɪŋ] *n* **- 1.** [act] Waschen *das* **- 2.** [clothes] Wäsche *die.*

washing line *n* Wäscheleine *die.*

washing machine *n* Waschmaschine *die.*

washing powder *n Br* Waschpulver *das.*

Washington ['wɒʃɪŋtən] *n* [city]: **~ D.C.** Washington *nt, Hauptstadt der USA.*

washing-up *n* **- 1.** Br [crockery, pans etc] Abwasch *der* **- 2.** [act]: **to do the ~** spülen, den Abwasch machen.

washing-up liquid *n Br* Spülmittel *das.*

washout ['wɒʃaʊt] *n inf* Reinfall *der.*

washroom ['wɒʃrum] *n Am* Toilette *die*.

wasn't [wɒznt] = was not.

wasp [wɒsp] *n* Wespe *die*.

wastage ['weɪstɪdʒ] *n (U)* [process] Verschwendung *die*; [amount] Verlust *der*.

waste [weɪst] <> *adj* [fuel] ungenutzt <> *n* - **1.** [misuse] Verschwendung *die*; **a ~ of time** eine Zeitverschwendung - **2.** [refuse] Abfall *der* <> *vt* verschwenden; [opportunity] vertun.

wastebasket ['weɪst,bɑːskɪt] *n Am* Papierkorb *der*.

waste disposal unit *n* Müllschlucker *der*.

wasteful ['weɪstful] *adj* verschwenderisch.

waste ground *n* Ödland *das*.

wastepaper basket, wastepaper bin [,weɪst'peɪpə'-], **wastebasket** *Am* ['weɪst,bɑːskɪt] *n* Papierkorb *der*.

watch [wɒtʃ] <> *n* - **1.** [timepiece] Uhr *die*, Armbanduhr *die* - **2.** [act of guarding]: **to keep ~ Wache halten; to keep (a) ~ on sb/sthg** auf jn/etw aufpassen - **3.** [guard - person] Wachmann *der*; [- group] Wache *die* <> *vt* - **1.** [look at] beobachten; [game, event] zusehen OR zuschauen bei; [film, play] sich (D) anlesen - **2.** [spy on] beobachten - **3.** [be careful about] aufpassen auf (+ A) <> *vi* [observe] zulsehen, zuschauen. ◆ **watch for** *vt fus* [person, thing] Ausschau halten nach; [opportunity] warten auf (+ A). ◆ **watch out** *vi* - **1.** [be careful]: **to ~ out (for sthg)** auflpassen (auf etw (A)), Acht geben (auf etw (A)); ~ **out!** Achtung!, Vorsicht! - **2.** [keep a lookout]: **to ~ out for sthg** nach etw Ausschau halten.

watchdog ['wɒtʃdɒg] *n* - **1.** [dog] Wachhund *der* - **2.** [organization] Aufsichtsbehörde *die*.

watchful ['wɒtʃful] *adj* [vigilant] wachsam.

watchmaker ['wɒtʃ,meɪkə'] *n* Uhrmacher *der*, -in *die*.

watchman ['wɒtʃmən] (*pl* -men [-mən]) *n* Wächter *der*.

water ['wɔːtə'] <> *n* Wasser *das* <> *vt* [plants] gießen; [garden, lawn] sprengen; [land, field] bewässern <> *vi* - **1.** [eyes] tränen - **2.** [mouth]: **my mouth was ~ing** mir lief das Wasser im Munde zusammen. ◆ **waters** *npl* [territory at sea] Gewässer *pl*. ◆ **water down** *vt sep* - **1.** [drink] verdünnen - **2.** *usu pej* [plan, criticism, novel] verwässern.

water bottle *n* Wasserflasche *die*.

watercolour ['wɔːtə,kʌlə'] *n* - **1.** [picture] Aquarell *das* - **2.** [paint] Aquarellfarbe *die*.

watercress ['wɔːtəkres] *n* Brunnenkresse *die*.

waterfall ['wɔːtəfɔːl] *n* Wasserfall *der*.

water heater *n* Heißwassergerät *das*, Boiler *der*.

waterhole ['wɔːtəhəul] *n* Wasserstelle *die*.

watering can ['wɔːtərɪŋ-] *n* Gießkanne *die*.

water lily *n* Seerose *die*.

waterline ['wɔːtəlaɪn] *n* NAUT Wasserlinie *die*.

waterlogged ['wɔːtəlɒgd] *adj* - **1.** [land, sports] (völlig) aufgeweicht - **2.** [vessel] voll Wasser.

water main *n* Hauptwasserleitung *die*.

watermark ['wɔːtəmɑːk] *n* - **1.** [in paper] Wasserzeichen *das* - **2.** [showing water level] Wasserstandsmarke *die*.

watermelon ['wɔːtə,melən] *n* Wassermelone *die*.

water polo *n* Wasserball *der*.

waterproof ['wɔːtəpruːf] <> *adj* [watch] wasserdicht; [anorak, shoes] wasserundurchlässig <> *n*: ~**s** Regenkleidung *die*.

watershed ['wɔːtəʃed] *n* [turning point] Wendepunkt *die*.

water skiing *n* Wasserskilaufen *das*.

water tank *n* Wassertank *der*.

watertight ['wɔːtətaɪt] *adj* - **1.** [waterproof] wasserdicht - **2.** [faultless] hieb- und stichfest.

waterworks ['wɔːtəwɜːks] (*pl inv*) *n* [building] Wasserwerk *das*.

watery ['wɔːtərɪ] *adj* - **1.** [food, juice] wässrig; [coffee, tea] dünn - **2.** [light, sun] blass.

watt [wɒt] *n* Watt *das*.

wave [weɪv] <> *n* - **1.** [gen] Welle *die* - **2.** [gesture]: **to give sb a ~** jm zulwinken <> *vt* - **1.** [flag, handkerchief] schwenken; [baton] schwingen; [gun, stick] fuchteln; **to ~ one's hand at sb** jm winken - **2.** [gesture to]: **to ~ sb on/over** jn weiter!-/herüberlwinken <> *vi* - **1.** [with hand] winken; **to ~ at** OR **to** jm zulwinken - **2.** [flag] wehen; [branches] sich hin und her bewegen, sich wiegen.

wavelength ['weɪvleŋθ] *n* Wellenlänge *die*; **to be on the same ~ (as sb)** *fig* auf der gleichen Wellenlänge (wie jd) funken.

waver ['weɪvə'] *vi* - **1.** [person, resolve, confidence] wanken - **2.** [voice] zittern - **3.** [flame, light] flackern.

wavy ['weɪvɪ] *adj* - **1.** [hair] wellig - **2.** [line] Schlangen-.

wax [wæks] <> *n* - **1.** [in candles, polish, for skis] Wachs *das* - **2.** [in ears] Ohrenschmalz *das* <> *vt* - **1.** [floor, table, skis] wachsen - **2.** [legs] mit Wachs enthaaren <> *vi* [moon] zulnehmen.

wax paper *n Am* Wachspapier *das*.

waxworks ['wækswɜːks] (*pl inv*) *n* [museum] Wachsfigurenkabinett *das*.

way [weɪ] <> *n* - **1.** [means, method] Art und Weise *die*; **this/that ~ so; this is the best ~ to do it** man macht es am besten so - **2.** [manner, style] Art *die*; **I feel the same ~ as you** mir geht es wie Ihnen; **she's behaving in a very**

odd ~ sie benimmt sich sehr seltsam; **if that's the** ~ **you feel ...** wenn du so denkst ...; **in the same** ~ auf die gleiche Weise - **3.** [thoroughfare, path] Weg der; **'give** ~' Br AUT 'Vorfahrt beachten' - **4.** [route] Weg der; **which** ~ **is the station?** wie kommt man zum Bahnhof?; **what's the best** ~ **to the station?** wie kommt man am besten zum Bahnhof?; **to be in the** ~ im Weg sein; **to be in sb's** ~ jm im Wege stehen; **on the** ~ **(to the station)** auf dem Weg (zum Bahnhof); **on the** ~ **home/to school** auf dem Heimweg/Schulweg; **on the** ~ **back/there** auf dem Rückweg/Hinweg; **out of the** ~ [place] abgelegen; **get out of the** OR **my** ~! geh mir aus dem Weg!; **to go out of one's** ~ **to do sthg** sich (D) besondere Mühe geben, etw zu tun; **to keep out of sb's** ~ jm aus dem Wege gehen; **to be under** ~ [ship] in Fahrt sein; [project, meeting] im Gange sein; **to get under** ~ [ship] in Fahrt kommen; [project, meeting] in Gang kommen; **to lose one's** ~ sich verlaufen; [in car] sich verfahren; **make your** ~ **to the exit** begeben Sie sich zum Ausgang; **to make** ~ **for sb/sthg** jm/einer Sache Platz machen; **to stand in sb's** ~ fig jm im Wege stehen - **5.** [direction] Richtung die; **which** ~ **are you going?** in welche Richtung gehst du?; **this/that** ~ hier/dort entlang; **look this** ~, **please** sehen Sie bitte hierher; ~ **in** Eingang der; ~ **out** Ausgang der - **6.** [side]: **the right** ~ **round** richtig herum; **the wrong** ~ **round** verkehrt herum; **the right/wrong** ~ **up** richtig/verkehrt herum; **the other** ~ **round** anders herum - **7.** [distance] Weg der; **all the** ~ den ganzen Weg; **we're with you all the** ~ fig wir stehen voll und ganz hinter dir; **it's a long** ~ **(away) from here** es liegt weit weg OR entfernt; **I have a long** ~ **to go** ich habe einen weiten Weg vor mir; **he's not as clever as her by a long** ~ er ist bei weitem nicht so klug wie sie - **8.** phr: **to give** ~ [under weight, pressure] nachlgeben; **in many** ~**s** in vieler Hinsicht; **no** ~! auf keinen Fall! ⟨⟩ adv inf [far] viel; ~ **ahead** weit voraus; ~ **off** weit entfernt; ~ **back in 1930** damals, 1930. ◆ **ways** npl [customs, habits] Art die. ◆ **by the way** adv übrigens.

waylay [ˌweɪ'leɪ] (pt & pp -laid [-'leɪd]) vt ablfangen.

wayward ['weɪwəd] adj eigenwillig.

WC (abbr of water closet) n WC das.

we [wiː] pers pron pl wir; ~ **British** wir Briten.

weak [wiːk] adj - **1.** [gen] schwach - **2.** [lacking knowledge, skill]: **to be** ~ **on sthg** in etw (D) schwach sein.

weaken ['wiːkn] ⟨⟩ vt schwächen; [argument] entkräften ⟨⟩ vi - **1.** [person] schwach werden - **2.** [influence, power & FIN] schwächer werden.

weakling ['wiːklɪŋ] n pej Schwächling der.

weakness ['wiːknɪs] n - **1.** [gen] Schwäche die; **to have a** ~ **for sthg** eine Schwäche für etw haben - **2.** [in plan, argument] Schwachpunkt der.

wealth [welθ] n - **1.** (U) [riches] Reichtum der - **2.** [abundance]: **a** ~ **of sthg** ein Reichtum an etw (D).

wealthy ['welθɪ] adj reich.

weapon ['wepən] n Waffe die.

weaponry ['wepənrɪ] n (U) Waffen pl.

wear [weə^r] (pt wore; pp worn) ⟨⟩ n - **1.** [type of clothes] Kleidung die - **2.** [damage]: ~ **(and tear)** Abnutzung die ⟨⟩ vt - **1.** [clothes, shoes, jewellery, spectacles] tragen - **2.** [damage] ablnutzen ⟨⟩ vi - **1.** [deteriorate] sich ablnutzen - **2.** [last]: **to** ~ **well/badly** gut/nicht gut halten. ◆ **wear away** ⟨⟩ vt sep [steps] ausltreten; [inscription] verwittern; [grass] ablnutzen ⟨⟩ vi [inscription] verwittern; [steps] ausgetreten werden; [inscription] verwittern; [grass] abgenutzt werden. ◆ **wear down** vt sep - **1.** [reduce size of] ablnutzen; [heel] abllaufen - **2.** [weaken] auslzehren; [resistance] zermürben. ◆ **wear off** vi nachllassen. ◆ **wear out** ⟨⟩ vt sep - **1.** [clothing, machinery] ablnutzen - **2.** [person, patience, strength] erschöpfen ⟨⟩ vi [clothing, shoes] sich ablnutzen.

weary ['wɪərɪ] adj - **1.** [exhausted] müde - **2.** [fed up]: **to be** ~ **of sthg** etw satt haben; **to be** ~ **of doing sthg** es satt haben, etw zu tun.

weasel ['wiːzl] n Wiesel das.

weather ['weðə^r] ⟨⟩ n Wetter das; **to be under the** ~ nicht ganz auf der Höhe sein ⟨⟩ vt [survive] überstehen.

weather-beaten [-ˌbiːtn] adj [face, skin] wettergegerbt.

weather forecast n Wettervorhersage die.

weatherman ['weðəmæn] (pl -men [-men]) n Meterologe der.

weather vane [-veɪn] n Wetterfahne die.

weave [wiːv] (pt wove; pp woven) ⟨⟩ vt [using loom] weben ⟨⟩ vi [move] sich durchlschlängeln.

weaver ['wiːvə^r] n Weber der, -in die.

web [web] n - **1.** [cobweb] Spinnennetz das - **2.** fig [of lies, intrigue] Netz das. ◆ **Web** n: **the Web** COMPUT das Netz, das Web.

website ['webˌsaɪt] n COMPUT Website die.

wed [wed] (pt & pp wed OR -ded) literary ⟨⟩ vt - **1.** [marry] heiraten - **2.** [subj: priest] trauen ⟨⟩ vi heiraten.

we'd [wiːd] = we had, we would.

wedding ['wedɪŋ] n Hochzeit die.

wedding anniversary n Hochzeitstag der.

wedding cake n Hochzeitskuchen der.

wedding dress n Hochzeitskleid das.

wedding ring n Ehering der.

wedge [wedʒ] ⬦ n - 1. [gen] Keil der - 2. [of cheese, cake, pie] Stück das ⬦ vt - 1. [secure] festlklemmen - 2. [squeeze, push] zwängen.

Wednesday ['wenzdɪ] n Mittwoch der; see also Saturday.

wee [wi:] ⬦ adj Scot klein ⬦ n inf: **to do/ have a ~** Pipi machen ⬦ vi inf Pipi machen.

weed [wi:d] ⬦ n - 1. [wild plant] Unkraut das - 2. Br inf [feeble person] Schwächling der ⬦ vt: **to ~ the garden** im Garten Unkraut jäten.

weedkiller ['wi:dˌkɪlə'] n Unkrautvertilgungsmittel das.

weedy ['wi:dɪ] adj Br inf [feeble] schwächlich.

week [wi:k] n Woche die; **in three ~s' time** in drei Wochen; **a ~ last Saturday** Samstag vor einer Woche.

weekday ['wi:kdeɪ] n Wochentag der.

weekend [ˌwi:k'end] n Wochenende das; **at the ~** am Wochenende.

weekly ['wi:klɪ] ⬦ adj wöchentlich; [newspaper] Wochen- ⬦ adv wöchentlich ⬦ n Wochenzeitung die.

weep [wi:p] (pt & pp wept) vt & vi weinen.

weeping willow [ˌwi:pɪŋ-] n Trauerweide die.

weigh [weɪ] ⬦ vt - 1. [find weight of] wiegen - 2. [consider carefully] ablwägen - 3. [raise]: **to ~ anchor** den Anker lichten ⬦ vi [have specific weight] wiegen. ➤ **weigh down** vt sep - 1. [physically]: **to be ~ed down with sthg** mit etw beladen sein - 2. [mentally]: **to be ~ed down by** OR **with sthg** mit etw belastet sein. ➤ **weigh up** vt sep [situation, pros and cons] ablwägen; [person, opposition] einlschätzen.

weight [weɪt] n - 1. [of person, package, goods & SPORT] Gewicht das; **to put on** OR **gain** ~ zulnehmen; **to lose** ~ ablnehmen - 2. fig [power, influence]: **the ~ of public opinion** die Übermacht der öffentlichen Meinung; **to throw one's ~ about** sich auflspielen - 3. lit & fig [burden] Last die; **it took a ~ off my mind** damit ist mir ein Stein vom Herzen gefallen - 4. phr: **to pull one's ~** seinen Beitrag leisten.

weighted ['weɪtɪd] adj: **to be ~ in favour of/against sb/sthg** jn/etw bevorteilen/benachteiligen.

weighting ['weɪtɪŋ] n (U) Zulage die.

weight lifting n Gewichtheben das.

weighty ['weɪtɪ] adj [serious, important] schwerwiegend.

weir [wɪə'] n Wehr das.

weird [wɪəd] adj seltsam.

welcome ['welkəm] ⬦ adj - 1. [guest] willkommen - 2. [free]: **to be ~ to do sthg** etw gerne tun können - 3. [pleasant, desirable] angenehm - 4. [in reply to thanks]: **you're ~** bitte, gern geschehen ⬦ n Willkommen

das; **to get/receive a warm ~** herzlich aufgenommen werden ⬦ vt - 1. [receive] empfangen - 2. [approve, support] willkommen heißen ⬦ excl willkommen!

weld [weld] ⬦ n ⬦ vt schweißen.

welfare ['welfeə'] ⬦ adj sozial; [work, worker] Sozial- ⬦ n - 1. [state of wellbeing] Wohl das - 2. Am [income support] Sozialhilfe die.

well [wel] (compar better; superl best) ⬦ adj - 1. [in health] gesund; **how are you? – (I'm) very ~, thanks** wie geht es Ihnen? – sehr gut, danke; **to feel ~** sich wohl fühlen; **to get ~** gesund werden; **get ~ soon!** gute Besserung! - 2. [good]: **all's ~** alles ist in Ordnung; **it's just as ~ you stayed** nur gut, dass du geblieben bist ⬦ adv - 1. [gen] gut; **the patient is doing ~** der Patient macht gute Fortschritte; **to ~ out of sthg** von etw profitieren; **you did ~ to come immediately** gut, dass du sofort gekommen bist; **~ done!** gut gemacht!; **to speak ~ of sb** jn lobend erwähnen; **~ beaten** restlos geschlagen; **to go ~** gut gehen - 2. [definitely, certainly]: **~ within one's rights** voll im Recht; **you know perfectly ~ that ...** du weißt ganz genau, dass ...; **it's ~ worth it** es lohnt sich unbedingt; **~ after six o'clock** viel später als sechs Uhr; **~ over 50** weit über 50 - 3. [easily, possibly]: **it may ~ happen** es kann durchaus passieren; **you may ~ laugh** lachen Sie nur!; **that may ~ be true** das mag wahr sein ⬦ n - 1. [for water] Brunnen der - 2. [oil well] Ölquelle die ⬦ excl - 1. [expressing hesitation]: **~, I don't really know** tja, das weiß ich nicht so recht - 2. [expressing resignation]: **oh ~!** na ja! - 3. [expressing surprise]: **~, I didn't expect to see you here!** na so was, ich habe nicht erwartet, Sie hier zu sehen!; **~ I never!** na, so was! - 4. [after interruption]: **~, as I was saying** ... also, wie gesagt ... ➤ **as well** adv [in addition] auch; **I might as ~ go home** ich könnte genauso gut nach Hause gehen. ➤ **as well as** conj sowohl ... als auch; **children as ~ as adults** sowohl Kinder als auch Erwachsene. ➤ **well up** vi hochlquellen.

we'll [wi:l] = we shall, we will.

well-advised [-əd'vaɪzd] adj klug; **he/you would be ~ to do sthg** er täte/du tätest gut daran, etw zu tun.

well-behaved [-bɪ'heɪvd] adj artig.

wellbeing [ˌwel'bi:ɪŋ] n Wohl das.

well-built adj [person] gut gebaut.

well-done adj [thoroughly cooked] durchgebraten.

well-dressed [-'drest] adj gut gekleidet.

well-earned [-'ɜ:nd] adj wohlverdient.

wellington (boot) ['welɪŋtən-] n Gummistiefel der.

well-kept adj - 1. [garden, village] gepflegt - 2. [secret] wohl gehütet.

well-known adj bekannt.

well-mannered [-ˈmænəd] *adj*: **to be ~** gute Manieren haben.

well-meaning *adj* [action, suggestion] gut gemeint; **she's very ~** sie meint es gut.

well-nigh [-naɪ] *adv* nahezu.

well-off *adj* **- 1.** [financially] wohlhabend **- 2.** [in a good position]: **to be ~ for sthg** mit etw gut versorgt sein.

well-read [-ˈred] *adj* belesen.

well-rounded [-ˈraʊndɪd] *adj* [varied] vielseitig.

well-timed [-ˈtaɪmd] *adj* gut abgepasst.

well-to-do *adj* wohlhabend.

well-wisher [-ˌwɪʃəʳ] *n* Symphatisant *der*, -in *die*.

Welsh [welʃ] <> *adj* walisisch <> *n* [language] Walisisch(e) *das*.

Welshman [ˈwelʃmən] (*pl* -men [-mən]) *n* Waliser *der*.

Welshwoman [ˈwelʃˌwʊmən] (*pl* -women [-ˌwɪmɪn]) *n* Waliserin *die*.

went [went] *pt* ⊏⊐ go.

wept [wept] *pt & pp* ⊏⊐ weep.

were [wɜːʳ] *vb* ⊏⊐ be.

we're [wɪəʳ] = we are.

weren't [wɜːnt] = were not.

west [west] <> *n* Westen *der*; **the ~** der Westen <> *adj* **- 1.** [area] West-, westlich **- 2.** [wind] West- <> *adv* nach Westen, westwärts; **~ of** westlich von. ◆ **West** *n* POL: **the West** der Westen.

West Bank *n*: **the ~** das Westjordanland.

West Country *n*: **the ~** der Südwesten Englands.

westerly [ˈwestəlɪ] *adj* **- 1.** [direction] westlich **- 2.** [area] im Westen **- 3.** [wind] West-.

western [ˈwestən] <> *adj* **- 1.** [part of country, continent] West- **- 2.** POL [relating to the West] westlich <> *n* [film] Western *der*.

West German *adj* westdeutsch <> *n* [person] Westdeutsche *der*, *die*.

West Germany *n*: **(former) ~** (ehemaliges) Westdeutschland *nt*.

West Indies [-ˈɪndiːz] *npl*: **the ~** die Westindischen Inseln.

Westminster [ˈwestmɪnstəʳ] *n* **- 1.** [area] Westminster *nt* **- 2.** *fig* [British parliament] *britisches Parlament*.

westward [ˈwestwəd] <> *adj* nach Westen <> *adv* = westwards.

westwards [ˈwestwədz] *adv* nach Westen, westwärts.

wet [wet] (*pt & pp* wet OR -ted) <> *adj* **- 1.** [damp, soaked] nass **- 2.** [rainy] regnerisch; [climate] feucht **- 3.** [ink, concrete] feucht **- 4.** *Br inf pej* [weak, feeble] lasch; **he's a ~** er ist ein Weichei <> *n inf Br* POL Gemäßigte *der*, *die* <> *vt* nass machen; **to ~ the bed** ins Bett machen.

wet blanket *n inf pej* Spielverderber *der*.

wet suit *n* Taucheranzug *der*.

we've [wiːv] = we have.

whack [wæk] *inf* <> *n* **- 1.** [share] Teil *der* **- 2.** [hit] Schlag *der* <> *vt* einen Schlag geben (+ *D*).

whale [weɪl] *n* [animal] Wal *der*.

wharf [wɔːf] (*pl* -s OR wharves [wɔːvz]) *n* Kai *der*.

what [wɒt] <> *adj* **- 1.** (*in questions*) welche, -r, -s; **~ colour is it?** welche Farbe hat es?; **he asked me ~ colour it was** er fragte mich, welche Farbe es hatte; **~ time is it?** wie viel Uhr OR wie spät ist es?; **~ sort of (an) animal is that?** was ist das für ein Tier? **- 2.** (*in exclamations*) was für; **~ a surprise!** was für eine Überraschung!; **~ a beautiful day!** was für ein schöner Tag! <> *pron* **- 1.** (*in questions*) was; **~ is going on?** was ist los?; **~ are they doing?** was tun sie da?; **~'s your name?** wie heißt du?; **she asked me ~ happened** sie fragte mich, was passiert war; **~ is it for?** wofür ist das?; **~ are they talking about?** worüber reden sie?; **~ if it rains?** was geschieht, wenn es regnet?; **~ did you say?** wie bitte? **- 2.** (*introducing relative clause*) was; **I didn't see ~ happened** ich habe nicht gesehen, was passiert ist; **you can't have ~ you want** du kannst nicht haben, was du willst **- 3.** *phr*: **~ for?** wozu?; **~ about going for a meal?** wie wäre es mit Essen gehen?; **so ~?** *inf* na und? <> *excl* was!

whatever [wɒtˈevəʳ] <> *adj*: **at ~ time you want** wann immer du willst; **they have no chance ~** sie haben überhaupt keine Chance <> *pron* **- 1.** [no matter what]: **take ~ you want** nimm, was du willst; **~ I do, I'll lose** was ich auch tue, ich verliere; **don't let go ~ happens** du darfst auf keinen Fall loslassen **- 2.** [indicating vagueness]: **~ that may be** was auch immer das sein mag **- 3.** [indicating surprise]: **~ did he say?** was hat er denn bloß gesagt? <> *excl Am inf* was aus!

what's-his-name *n inf* Dingsda *der*, *die*.

whatsit [ˈwɒtsɪt] *n inf* Dingsbums *das*.

whatsoever [ˌwɒtsəʊˈevəʳ] *adj*: **I had no interest ~** ich hatte keinerlei Interesse; **nothing ~** überhaupt nichts.

wheat [wiːt] *n* Weizen *der*.

wheedle [ˈwiːdl] *vt*: **to ~ sb into doing sthg** jn dazu kriegen, etw zu tun; **to ~ sthg out of sb** jm etw abschwatzen.

wheel [wiːl] <> *n* **- 1.** [of bicycle, car, train] Rad *das* **- 2.** AUT [steering wheel] Lenkrad *das* <> *vt* schieben <> *vi* [turn round]: **to ~ round** sich jäh umdrehen.

wheelbarrow [ˈwiːlˌbærəʊ] *n* Schubkarre *die*.

wheelchair [ˈwiːlˌtʃeəʳ] *n* Rollstuhl *der*.

wheel clamp *n* Parkkralle *die*. ◆ **wheel-clamp** *vt*: **my car was ~ed** an meinem Auto war eine Parkkralle.

wheeze [wiːz] *vi* pfeifend atmen.

whelk [welk] *n* Wellhornschnecke *die*.

when [wen] ◇ *adv (in questions)* wann; **~ does the plane arrive?** wann kommt das Flugzeug an?; **he asked me - I would be in London** er fragte mich, wann ich in London sei ◇ *conj* - **1.** [specifying time] wenn; [in the past] als; **on the day - it happened** an dem Tag, als es geschah - **2.** [although, seeing as] wo … doch; **you said it was black - in fact it was white** du hast gesagt, es wäre schwarz, wo es doch weiß war.

whenever [wen'evə^r] ◇ *conj* [every time] (immer) wenn; **~ you like** [no matter when] wann immer du willst ◇ *adv:* **~ did you find time to do it?** wann hast du bloß die Zeit dafür gefunden?; **next week or ~** nächste Woche oder wann auch immer.

where [weə^r] ◇ *adv (in questions)* wo; **~ do you come from?** woher kommst du?; **~ are you going?** wohin gehst du? ◇ *conj* - **1.** [referring to place, situation] wo; **at the place - it happened** dort, wo es passiert ist; **that's (just) ~ you're wrong** (genau) da irren Sie sich - **2.** [whereas] während.

whereabouts [*adv* weərə'bauts, *n* 'weərəbauts] ◇ *adv* wo ◇ *npl* Aufenthaltsort *der.*

whereas [weər'æz] *conj* während.

whereby [weə'bai] *conj fml* wodurch.

whereupon [ˌweərə'pɒn] *conj fml* woraufhin.

wherever [weər'evə^r] ◇ *conj* wo immer; [from any place] woher auch immer; [to any place] wohin auch immer; [everywhere] überall wo; **~ that may be** wo immer das sein mag ◇ *adv:* **~ did you hear that?** wo hast du das bloß gehört?

whet [wet] *vt:* **to ~ sb's appetite (for doing sthg)** jn auf den Geschmack bringen(, etw zu tun).

whether ['weðə^r] *conj* ob; **he didn't know ~ to go or not** er wusste nicht, ob er gehen sollte oder nicht; **~ I want to or not** ob ich nun will oder nicht.

which [wɪtʃ] ◇ *adj (in questions)* welche, -r, -s; **~ room do you want?** welches Zimmer willst du?; **~ one?** welches?; **she asked me ~ room I wanted** sie fragte mich, welches Zimmer ich wollte ◇ *pron* - **1.** *(in questions – subject)* welche, -r, -s; **~ is the cheapest?** welches ist das billigste?; **he asked me ~ was the best** er fragte mich, welcher der Beste sei - **2.** *(in questions – object)* welche, -n, -s; **~ do you prefer?** welches gefällt dir besser?; **he asked me ~ I preferred** er fragte mich, welches ich bevorzugen würde - **3.** *(in questions – after prep + A)* welche, -n, -s; **~ should I put the vase on?** auf welchen soll ich die Vase stellen? - **4.** *(in questions – after prep + D)* welcher/welchem/welchem; **he asked me ~ I was talking about** er fragte mich, von welchem ich spreche - **5.** *(introducing relative clause – after subject)* der/die/das, die *(pl)*; **the**

house ~ is on corner das Haus, das an der Ecke steht - **6.** *(introducing relative clause – object, after prep + A)* den/die/das, die *(pl)*; **the television ~ I bought** der Fernseher, den ich gekauft habe; **the book through ~ he became famous** das Buch, durch das er berühmt wurde - **7.** *(introducing relative clause – object, after prep + D)* dem/der/dem, denen *(pl)*; **the settee on ~ I'm sitting** das Sofa, auf dem ich sitze; **ten apples, of ~ six are bad** zehn Äpfel, von denen OR wovon sechs faul sind - **8.** *(introducing relative clause – object, after prep + G)* dessen/deren/dessen, deren *(pl)* - **9.** *(referring back)* was; **he's late, ~ annoys me** er ist spät dran, was mich ärgert; **he's always late, ~ I don't like** er verspätet sich immer, was ich nicht leiden kann.

whichever [wɪtʃ'evə^r] ◇ *adj* - **1.** [any] welche, -r, -s; **take ~ book you like** nehmen Sie welches Buch Sie (auch immer) wollen - **2.** [no matter which] egal welche; **~ way you look** wo man auch hinsieht ◇ *pron* [the one which] welche, -r, -s; **take ~ you like** nimm, welches du (auch) willst.

whiff [wɪf] *n* [smell] Hauch *der.*

while [waɪl] ◇ *n:* **a ~** eine Weile; **for a ~** eine Weile, eine Zeit lang; **in a ~** bald; **a short ~ ago** vor kurzem; **once in a ~** hin und wieder ◇ *conj* - **1.** [gen] während; **he fell asleep ~ (he was) reading** er schlief beim Lesen ein - **2.** [although] obgleich, während.
➜ **while away** *vt sep:* **to ~ away the time** sich (D) die Zeit vertreiben.

whilst [waɪlst] *conj* = while.

whim [wɪm] *n* Laune *die.*

whimper ['wɪmpə^r] *vi* [child] wimmern; [animal] winseln.

whimsical ['wɪmzɪkl] *adj* wunderlich.

whine [waɪn] *vi* [make sound] heulen; [dog] jaulen.

whinge [wɪndʒ] *vi Br:* **to ~ (about sb/sthg)** (über jn/etw) jammern.

whip [wɪp] ◇ *n* - **1.** [for hitting] Peitsche *die* - **2.** *Br* POL Einpeitscher *der* ◇ *vt* - **1.** [beat with whip] auspeitschen - **2.** [take quickly]: **to ~ stg out** etw zücken; **to ~ sthg off** etw herunterreißen - **3.** CULIN [whisk] schlagen.

whipped cream [wɪpt-] *n* Schlagsahne *die.*

whip-round *n Br inf:* **to have a ~** eine Sammlung machen.

whirl [wɜːl] ◇ *n* - **1.** [rotating movement] Wirbel *der* - **2.** *fig* [of activity] Trubel *der* ◇ *vt:* **to ~ sb/sthg round** jn etw herumlwirbeln ◇ *vi* [move around] wirbeln.

whirlpool ['wɜːlpuːl] *n* Strudel *der.*

whirlwind ['wɜːlwɪnd] *n* Wirbelsturm *der.*

whirr [wɜː^r] *vi* [of wings] schwirren; [machinery, camera] surren.

whisk [wɪsk] ◇ *n* CULIN Schneebesen *der* ◇ *vt* - **1.** [put or take quickly]: **she was ~ed into hospital** sie wurde schnellstens ins

Krankenhaus gebracht - **2.** CULIN (mit dem Schneebesen) schlagen.

whisker ['wɪskəʳ] *n* [of animal] Schnurrhaar *das.* ◆ **whiskers** *npl* [of man] Backenbart *der.*

whisky *Br,* **whiskey** *Am & Irish (pl* whiskeys) ['wɪskɪ] *n* Whisky *der.*

whisper ['wɪspəʳ] ◇ *vt* flüstern; **to ~ sthg to sb** jm etw zulflüstern ◇ *vi* flüstern.

whistle ['wɪsl] ◇ *n* - **1.** [through lips, from whistle] Pfiff *der* - **2.** [of kettle, train] Pfeifen *das* - **3.** [object] Pfeife *die* ◇ *vt* pfeifen ◇ *vi:* **to ~ at sb** jm nachlpfeifen.

white [waɪt] ◇ *adj* - **1.** [gen] weiß - **2.** [coffee, tea] mit Milch - **3.** [wine] Weiß- ◇ *n* - **1.** [colour] Weiß *das* - **2.** [person] Weiße *der, die* - **3.** [of egg] Eiweiß *das* - **4.** [of eye] Weiße *das.*

white-collar *adj:* **~ worker** Büroangestellte *der, die;* **~ job** Schreibtischarbeit *die.*

white-hot *adj* weißglühend.

White House *n* [residence of president, US government]: **the ~** das Weiße Haus.

white lie *n* Notlüge *die.*

whiteness ['waɪtnɪs] *n* Weiße *die.*

white paper *n* POL Weißbuch *das.*

white sauce *n* Béchamelsoße *die.*

white spirit *n (U) Br* Terpentinersatz *der.*

whitewash ['waɪtwɒʃ] ◇ *n* - **1.** *(U)* [paint] Tünche *die* - **2.** *pej* [cover-up] Verschleierung *die* ◇ *vt* [paint] tünchen.

Whitsun ['wɪtsn] *n* [day] Pfingstsonntag *der.*

whittle ['wɪtl] *vt* [reduce]: **to ~ sthg away** OR **down** etw allmählich reduzieren.

whiz, whizz [wɪz] *vi* sausen.

whiz(z) kid *n inf* Senkrechtstarter *der,* -in *die.*

who [huː] *pron* - **1.** *(in questions)* wer; *(accusative)* wen; *(dative)* wem; **~ are you?** wer bist du/sind Sie?; **~ does he think he is?** was bildet er sich eigentlich ein? - **2.** *(in relative clauses)* der/die/das, die *pl;* **the friend ~ came yesterday** der Freund, der gestern kam.

who'd [huːd] = who had, who would.

whodu(n)nit [ˌhuːˈdʌnɪt] *n inf* Krimi *der.*

whoever [huːˈevəʳ] *pron* [whichever person] wer immer; **~ it is** es auch ist; **~ could that be?** wer könnte das bloß sein?

whole [həʊl] ◇ *adj* - **1.** [entire, complete] ganz - **2.** *esp Am* [for emphasis]: **a ~ lot of questions** eine ganze Reihe von Fragen; **a ~ lot bigger** viel größer ◇ *adv esp Am* [for emphasis] völlig ◇ *n* - **1.** [all, entirety]: **the ~ of the school** die ganze Schule; **the ~ of the summer** den ganzen Sommer - **2.** [unit, complete thing] Ganze *das.* ◆ **as a whole** *adv* als Ganzes. ◆ **on the whole** *adv* im Großen und Ganzen.

whole-hearted [-ˈhɑːtɪd] *adj* [support, agreement] voll.

wholemeal *Br* ['həʊlmiːl], **whole wheat** *Am adj* Vollkorn-.

wholesale ['həʊlseɪl] ◇ *adj* - **1.** [bulk] Großhandels- - **2.** *pej* [excessive] Massen- ◇ *adv* - **1.** [in bulk] im Großhandel - **2.** *pej* [excessively] massenhaft.

wholesaler ['həʊlˌseɪləʳ] *n* Großhändler *der,* -in *die.*

wholesome ['həʊlsəm] *adj* gesund.

whole wheat *adj Am* = wholemeal.

who'll [huːl] = who will.

wholly ['həʊlɪ] *adv* völlig.

whom [huːm] *pron fml* - **1.** *(in direct, indirect questions)* wen; *(dative)* wem; **~ did you phone?** wen hast du angerufen?; **for/of/to ~?** nach/von/mit wem? - **2.** *(in relative clauses)* den/die/das, die *pl; (dative)* dem/der/dem, denen *(pl);* **the girl ~ he married** das Mädchen, das er geheiratet hat; **the man to ~ you were speaking** der Mann, mit dem du gesprochen hast; **several people came, none of ~ I knew** es kamen verschiedene Leute, von denen ich keinen kannte.

whooping cough ['huːpɪŋ-] *n (U)* Keuchhusten *der.*

whopping ['wɒpɪŋ] *adj inf* Mords-; [lie] faustdick.

whore [hɔːʳ] *n pej* Hure *die.*

who're ['huːəʳ] = who are.

whose [huːz] ◇ *pron (in direct, indirect questions)* wessen; **~ is this?** wem gehört das?; **tell me ~ this is** sag mir, wem das gehört ◇ *adj* - **1.** *(in questions)* wessen; **~ car is that?** wessen Auto ist das? - **2.** *(in relative clauses)* dessen/deren/dessen, deren *(pl);* **that's the boy ~ father's an MP** das ist der Junge, dessen Vater Abgeordneter ist.

who've [huːv] = who have.

why [waɪ] ◇ *adv* warum; **~ not?** warum nicht?; **I didn't ask** ~ ich habe nicht gefragt, weshalb ◇ *conj* warum; **there are several reasons ~ he left** es gibt mehrere Gründe dafür, dass er wegging ◇ *excl:* **~, it's David!** sieh da, (da kommt) David! ◆ **why ever** *adv:* **~ ever did you do that?** warum hast du das bloß getan?

wick [wɪk] *n* [of candle] Docht *der.*

wicked ['wɪkɪd] *adj* - **1.** [evil] böse, schlecht - **2.** [mischievous] schelmisch.

wicker ['wɪkəʳ] *adj:* **~ chair** Korbstuhl *der.*

wicket ['wɪkɪt] *n* CRICKET - **1.** [stumps] Mal *das,* Wicket *das* - **2.** [pitch] Spielbahn *die* - **3.** [dismissal] Wicket *das.*

wide [waɪd] ◇ *adj* - **1.** [broad] breit - **2.** [variety, selection, gap, difference] groß - **3.** [coverage, knowledge] umfassend - **4.** [far-reaching] weit reichend ◇ *adv* - **1.** [as far as possible] weit - **2.** [off-target] daneben.

wide-awake *adj* hellwach.

widely ['waɪdlɪ] *adv* - **1.** [broadly] breit - **2.** [extensively] weit; **~ read** belesen; **to be**

~ experienced viel Erfahrung haben; **~ known** allgemein bekannt - **3.** [considerably] beträchtlich.

widen ['waɪdn] *vt* - **1.** [road, hole] verbreitern - **2.** [search, activity, range] auslweiten; [choice] erweitern - **3.** [gap, difference] vergrößern.

wide open *adj* - **1.** [window, door] weit offen - **2.** [eyes] weit aufgerissen.

wide-ranging ['waɪd'reɪndʒɪŋ] *adj* umfassend.

widespread ['waɪdspred] *adj* weit verbreitet.

widow ['wɪdəʊ] *n* Witwe *die*.

widowed ['wɪdəʊd] *adj* verwitwet.

widower ['wɪdəʊəʳ] *n* Witwer *der*.

width [wɪdθ] *n* Breite *die*; **3 metres in ~** 3 Meter breit.

wield [wiːld] *vt* - **1.** [weapon] schwingen - **2.** [power] auslüben.

wife [waɪf] (*pl* **wives**) *n* Ehefrau *die*.

wig [wɪg] *n* Perücke *die*.

wiggle ['wɪgl] *inf vt*: **to ~ one's ears/toes** mit seinen Ohren/Zehen wackeln.

wild [waɪld] *adj* - **1.** [gen] wild - **2.** [violent, dangerous] gewalttätig - **3.** [weather, sea] stürmisch - **4.** [hair, look] wirr. ◆ **wilds** *npl*: **the ~s** die Wildnis.

wilderness ['wɪldənɪs] *n* Wildnis *die*.

wild-goose chase *n inf* hoffnungslose Suche.

wildlife ['waɪldlaɪf] *n* Tierwelt *die*.

wildly ['waɪldlɪ] *adv* - **1.** [gen] wild - **2.** [talk, throw] aufs Geratewohl - **3.** [very] äußerst.

wilful *Br*, **willful** *Am* ['wɪlfʊl] *adj* - **1.** [determined] stur - **2.** [deliberate] beabsichtigt.

will[1] [wɪl] ◇ *n* - **1.** [gen] Wille *der*; **against his ~** gegen seinen Willen; **~ to live** Lebenswille *der* - **2.** [document] Testament *das* ◇ *vt*: **to ~ sb to do sthg** (sich *(D)*) mit aller Kraft wünschen, dass jd etw tut.

will[2] [wɪl] *aux vb* - **1.** (*expressing future tense*) werden; **~ you be here next Friday?** bist du nächsten Freitag hier?; **~ you do that for me?** – no **I won't**/**yes I ~** wirst du das für mich tun? – nein(, werde ich nicht)/ja(, werde ich); **when ~ you have finished it?** wann seid ihr damit fertig?; **I think he WILL come** ich glaube schon, dass er kommt - **2.** [expressing willingness] wollen, werden; **I won't do it** ich werde das nicht tun; **no one ~ do it** keiner wird das machen - **3.** [expressing polite question]: **~ you have some more tea?** möchten Sie noch mehr Tee? - **4.** [in commands, requests]: **~ you please be quiet!** sei bitte ruhig!; **close that window, ~ you?** mach doch bitte das Fenster zu - **5.** [expressing possibility]: **the hall ~ hold up to 1,000 people** die Halle fasst bis zu 1000 Leute; **pensions ~ be paid monthly** Pensionen werden monatlich ausgezahlt - **6.** [expressing an assumption]: **that'll be your father** das wird

dein Vater sein; **as you ~ have gathered, ...** wie Sie sich wohl gedacht haben, ... - **7.** [indicating irritation]: **well, if you WILL leave your toys everywhere** na ja, wenn ihr auch dauernd eure Spielsachen überall herumliegen lasst; **she WILL keep phoning me** sie ruft mich aber auch dauernd an.

willful *adj Am* = **wilful**.

willing ['wɪlɪŋ] *adj* - **1.** [prepared]: **to be ~ (to do sthg)** bereit sein(, etw zu tun) - **2.** [eager] bereitwillig.

willingly ['wɪlɪŋlɪ] *adv* bereitwillig, gerne.

willow (tree) ['wɪləʊ-] *n* Weide *die*.

willpower ['wɪl,paʊəʳ] *n* Willenskraft *die*.

willy-nilly [,wɪlɪ'nɪlɪ] *adv* - **1.** [at random] aufs Geratewohl - **2.** [wanting to or not] wohl oder übel.

wilt [wɪlt] *vi* - **1.** [plant] verwelken - **2.** *fig* [person] schlapp werden.

wily ['waɪlɪ] *adj* listig.

wimp [wɪmp] *n inf pej* Waschlappen *der*.

win [wɪn] (*pt* & *pp* **won**) ◇ *n* Sieg *der* ◇ *vt* gewinnen ◇ *vi* gewinnen; [in battle] siegen. ◆ **win over, win round** *vt sep* für sich gewinnen.

wince [wɪns] *vi*: **to ~ at/with sthg** bei/vor etw *(D)* zusammenlzucken.

winch [wɪntʃ] *n* Winde *die*.

wind[1] [wɪnd] ◇ *n* - **1.** METEOR Wind *der* - **2.** (*U*) [breath] Atem *der* - **3.** (*U*) [in stomach] Blähungen *pl* ◇ *vt* [knock breath out of]: **I was ~ed by the fall** durch den Sturz blieb mir die Luft weg.

wind[2] [waɪnd] (*pt* & *pp* **wound**) ◇ *vt* - **1.** [string, thread] wickeln - **2.** [clock] auflziehen ◇ *vi* [river, road] sich schlängeln. ◆ **wind down** ◇ *vt sep* - **1.** [car window] herunterlkurbeln - **2.** [production] allmählich einlstellen ◇ *vi* [relax] entspannen. ◆ **wind up** *vt sep* - **1.** [finish - meeting] ablschließen; [- business] aufllösen - **2.** [clock] auflziehen - **3.** [car window] hochlkurbeln - **4.** *Br inf* [deliberately annoy] auflziehen.

windfall ['wɪndfɔːl] *n* [unexpected gift] unerhoffter Gewinn.

winding ['waɪndɪŋ] *adj* kurvenreich; [river] gewunden.

wind instrument [wɪnd-] *n* Blasinstrument *das*.

windmill ['wɪndmɪl] *n* Windmühle *die*.

window ['wɪndəʊ] *n* - **1.** [gen & COMPUT] Fenster *das* - **2.** [of shop] Schaufenster *das* - **3.** [free time] freie Zeit.

window box *n* Blumenkasten *der*.

window cleaner *n* Fensterputzer *der*, -in *die*.

window ledge *n* [outside] Fenstersims *das*; [inside] Fensterbrett *das*.

windowpane ['wɪndəʊ,peɪn] *n* Fensterscheibe *die*.

windowsill ['wɪndəʊsɪl] *n* [outside] Fenstersims *der* OR *das*; [inside] Fensterbrett *das*.

windpipe ['wɪndpaɪp] *n* Luftröhre *die*.

windscreen *Br* ['wɪndskriːn], **windshield** *Am* ['wɪndʃiːld] *n* Windschutzscheibe *die*.

windscreen washer *n* Scheibenwaschanlage *die*.

windscreen wiper *n* Scheibenwischer *der*.

windshield *n* *Am* = windscreen.

windsurfing ['wɪndˌsɜːfɪŋ] *n* Windsurfen *das*.

windswept ['wɪndswept] *adj* [landscape] windgepeitscht.

windy ['wɪndɪ] *adj* windig.

wine [waɪn] *n* Wein *der*.

wine bar *n* *Br* Weinbar *die*.

wineglass ['waɪnglɑːs] *n* Weinglas *das*.

wine list *n* Weinkarte *die*.

wine tasting [-ˌteɪstɪŋ] *n* - **1.** [practice] Weinverkosten *das* - **2.** [event] Weinprobe *die*.

wine waiter *n* Weinkellner *der*.

wing [wɪŋ] *n* - **1.** [gen] Flügel *der* - **2.** [of plane] Tragfläche *die* - **3.** [of car] Kotflügel *der*. ◆ **wings** *npl* THEATRE: **the ~s** die Kulissen.

winger ['wɪŋər] *n* SPORT Außenstürmer *der*, -in *die*.

wink [wɪŋk] ◇ *n* [of eye] Zwinkern *das* ◇ *vi* [eye] zwinkern; **to ~ at sb** jm zulzwinkern.

winkle ['wɪŋkl] *n* Strandschnecke *die*. ◆ **winkle out** *vt sep* herauslbekommen; **to ~ sthg out of sb** *fig* etw aus jm herauslbekommen.

winner ['wɪnər] *n* [person] Gewinner *der*, -in *die*; [in sport] Sieger *der*, -in *die*.

winning ['wɪnɪŋ] *adj* [victorious] siegreich; [successful] erfolgreich. ◆ **winnings** *npl* Gewinn *der*.

winning post *n* Zielpfosten *der*.

winter ['wɪntər] ◇ *n* Winter *der*; **in ~** im Winter ◇ *comp* Winter-.

winter sports *npl* Wintersport *der*.

wintertime ['wɪntətaɪm] *n* Winterzeit *die*.

wint(e)ry ['wɪntrɪ] *adj* winterlich.

wipe [waɪp] ◇ *n* [clean]: **he gave his face/the table a ~** er wischte sein Gesicht/den Tisch ab ◇ *vt* - **1.** [rub to clean - floor] wischen; [- face, table] ablwischen - **2.** [rub to dry] abltrocknen. ◆ **wipe out** *vt sep* - **1.** [erase] weglwischen - **2.** [eradicate - gen] vernichten; [- race] auslrotten. ◆ **wipe up** ◇ *vt sep* auflwischen ◇ *vi* [dry dishes] abltrocknen.

wire ['waɪər] ◇ *n* - **1.** [gen] Draht *der*; [electrical] Leitung *die* - **2.** *esp Am* [telegram] Telegramm *das* ◇ *vt* - **1.** ELEC [plug] anlschließen - **2.** *esp Am* [send telegram to] ein Telegramm schicken.

wireless ['waɪəlɪs] *n dated* Radio *das*.

wiring ['waɪərɪŋ] *n* (*U*) elektrische Leitungen *pl*.

wiry ['waɪərɪ] *adj* - **1.** [hair] borstig - **2.** [body, man] drahtig.

wisdom ['wɪzdəm] *n* Weisheit *die*.

wisdom tooth *n* Weisheitszahn *der*.

wise [waɪz] *adj* [prudent] weise.

wish [wɪʃ] ◇ *n* Wunsch *der*; **~ to do sthg** der Wunsch, etw zu tun; **~ for sthg** der Wunsch nach etw (*D*) ◇ *vt* - **1.** [want]: **to ~ to do sthg** *fml* etw zu tun wünschen; **I ~ed (that) he'd come** wenn er nur käme - **2.** [desire, request by magic]: **I ~ (that) I had a million pounds** ich wünschte, ich hätte eine Million Pfund - **3.** [in greeting]: **to ~ sb sthg** jm etw wünschen ◇ *vi* [by magic]: **to ~ for sthg** sich etw herbeilwünschen. ◆ **wishes** *npl*: **best ~es** alles Gute; **(with) best ~es** [at end of letter] herzliche Grüße.

wishy-washy ['wɪʃɪˌwɒʃɪ] *adj inf pej* [person] kraftlos; [ideas] vage.

wisp [wɪsp] *n* - **1.** [tuft] Büschel *das* - **2.** [small cloud]: **~ of smoke** Rauchfahne *die*.

wistful ['wɪstfʊl] *adj* wehmütig.

wit [wɪt] *n* - **1.** [humour] Witz *der* - **2.** [intelligence]: **to have the ~ to do sthg** klug genug sein, etw zu tun. ◆ **wits** *npl* [intelligence, mind]: **to have** OR **keep one's ~s about one** geistesgegenwärtig sein.

witch [wɪtʃ] *n* Hexe *die*.

with [wɪð] *prep* - **1.** [gen] mit; **come ~ me** komm mit mir; **a man ~ a beard** ein Mann mit Bart; **a room ~ a bathroom** ein Zimmer mit Bad; **be careful ~ that!** sei vorsichtig damit!; **bring it ~ you** bringen Sie es mit; **to argue ~ sb** (sich) mit jm streiten; **the war ~ Germany** der Krieg gegen Deutschland; **I can't do it ~ you watching me** ich kann es nicht tun, wenn du mir zuschaust - **2.** [at house of, in the hands of] bei; **we stayed ~ friends** wir haben bei Freunden übernachtet; **the decision rests ~ you** die Entscheidung liegt bei dir - **3.** [indicating emotion] vor (+ *D*); **to tremble ~ fear** vor Angst zittern - **4.** [because of] bei; **~ the weather as it is, we decided to stay at home** angesichts des Wetters beschlossen wir zu Hause zu bleiben; **~ my luck, I'll probably lose** bei meinem Glück werde ich wahrscheinlich verlieren - **5.** *phr*: **I'll be ~ you in a moment** ich komme gleich; **I'm not quite ~ you** [I don't understand] ich komme nicht ganz mit; **I'm ~ you there** [I'm on your side] da bin ich ganz deiner Ansicht.

withdraw [wɪðˈdrɔː] (*pt* -drew; *pp* -drawn) ◇ *vt* - **1.** *fml* [remove] weglnehmen; **to ~ sthg from sthg** etw von etw weglnehmen - **2.** FIN ablheben - **3.** MIL [troops] zurücklziehen - **4.** [retract] zurücklnehmen ◇ *vi* - **1.**: **to ~ (from)** sich zurücklziehen (aus) - **2.** [quit, give up) auflgeben; **to ~ from sthg** aus etw auslscheiden.

withdrawal [wɪð'drɔːəl] *n* **- 1.** [removal] Zurückziehen *das* **- 2.** MIL Rückzug *der* **- 3.** [retraction] Zurücknahme *die* **- 4.** [leaving, quitting]: **~ (from sthg)** Ausscheiden *das* (aus etw) **- 5.** FIN Abheben *das*.

withdrawal symptoms *npl* Entzugserscheinungen *pl*.

withdrawn [wɪð'drɔːn] <> *pp* ▷ withdraw <> *adj* [shy, quiet] verschlossen.

withdrew [wɪð'druː] *pt* ▷ withdraw.

wither ['wɪðə'] *vi* **- 1.** [dry up] verwelken **- 2.** [become weak] schwinden.

withhold [wɪð'həʊld] (*pt & pp* **-held** [-'held]) *vt* zurücklhalten.

within [wɪ'ðɪn] <> *prep* innerhalb (+ G); **~ sight** in Sichtweite; **~ the next week** innerhalb der nächsten Woche; **~ 10 miles** im Umkreis von 10 Meilen <> *adv* innen.

without [wɪð'aʊt] *prep* ohne; **~ doing sthg** ohne etw zu tun; **I left ~ him seeing me** ich ging (weg), ohne dass er mich sah.

withstand [wɪð'stænd] (*pt & pp* **-stood** [-'stʊd]) *vt* standlhalten (+ D).

witness ['wɪtnɪs] <> *n* **- 1.** [gen] Zeuge *der*, -gin *die* **- 2.**: **to bear ~ to sthg** [be proof of] von etw zeugen <> *vt* **- 1.**: **to ~ sthg** [murder, accident] Zeuge einer Sache (G) sein; [changes] etw erleben **- 2.** [countersign] als Zeuge unterschreiben.

witness box *Br*, **witness stand** *Am n* Zeugenstand *der*.

witticism ['wɪtɪsɪzm] *n* geistreiche Bemerkung.

witty ['wɪtɪ] *adj* geistreich und witzig.

wives [waɪvz] *pl* ▷ wife.

wizard ['wɪzəd] *n* **- 1.** [man with magic powers] Zauberer *der* **- 2.** [skilled person] Genie *das*.

wobble ['wɒbl] *vi* wackeln.

woe [wəʊ] *n literary* Leid *das*.

woke [wəʊk] *pt* ▷ wake.

woken ['wəʊkn] *pp* ▷ wake.

wolf [wʊlf] (*pl* wolves) *n* [animal] Wolf *der*.

woman ['wʊmən] (*pl* women) ['wɪmɪn] <> *n* Frau *die* <> *comp*: **~ doctor** Ärztin *die*; **~ teacher** Lehrerin *die*.

womanly ['wʊmənlɪ] *adj* fraulich.

womb [wuːm] *n* Gebärmutter *die*.

women ['wɪmɪn] *pl* ▷ woman.

women's liberation *n* **- 1.** [aim] Gleichstellung der Frau **- 2.** [movement] Frauenrechtsbewegung *die*.

won [wʌn] *pt & pp* ▷ win.

wonder ['wʌndə'] <> *n* **- 1.** [amazement] Staunen *das* **- 2.** [cause for surprise]: **it's a ~ that ...** es ist ein Wunder, dass ...; **no OR little OR small ~** kein Wunder; **no ~ she left!** kein Wunder, dass sie gegangen ist! **- 3.** [amazing thing] Wunder *das* <> *vt*

- 1. [speculate] sich fragen; **to ~ if** OR **whether** sich fragen, ob **- 2.** [in polite requests]: **I ~ whether you would mind shutting the window?** könnten Sie wohl bitte das Fenster schließen? <> *vi* [speculate] sich fragen; **to ~ about sthg** sich über etw (A) Fragen stellen.

wonderful ['wʌndəful] *adj* wundervoll, wunderbar.

wonderfully ['wʌndəfulɪ] *adv* **- 1.** [very well] wunderbar **- 2.** [for emphasis] sehr.

won't [wəʊnt] = will not.

woo [wuː] *vt* **- 1.** *literary* [court - woman] den Hof machen (+ D) **- 2.** *fig* [try to win over] umlwerben.

wood [wʊd] <> *n* **- 1.** (U) [timber] Holz *das* **- 2.** [group of trees] Wald *der* <> *comp* Holz-. ➤ **woods** *npl* [forest] Wald *der*.

wooded ['wʊdɪd] *adj* [forested] bewaldet.

wooden ['wʊdn] *adj* **- 1.** [of wood] Holz- **- 2.** *pej* [actor] hölzern.

woodpecker ['wʊd,pekə'] *n* Specht *der*.

woodwind ['wʊdwɪnd] *n*: **the ~** die Holzbläser *pl*.

woodwork ['wʊdwɜːk] *n* **- 1.** [wooden objects] Holzarbeiten *pl*; [part of house or room] Holzteile *pl* **- 2.** [craft] Tischlerei *die*.

wool [wʊl] *n* **- 1.** [gen] Wolle *die* **- 2.** *phr*: **to pull the ~ over sb's eyes** *inf* jn hinters Licht führen.

woollen *Br*, **woolen** *Am* ['wʊlən] *adj* [garment] Woll-. ➤ **woollens** *npl* Wollwaren *pl*.

woolly ['wʊlɪ] *adj* [woollen] Woll-.

word [wɜːd] <> *n* **- 1.** LING Wort *das*; **~ for ~** Wort für Wort; **in other ~s** mit anderen Worten; **in a ~** kurz gesagt; **can I have a ~ (with you)?** kann ich Sie mal sprechen?; **I/you/etc couldn't get a ~ in edgeways** ich bin/du bist/etc nicht zu Wort gekommen **- 2.** (U) [news] Nachricht *die*; **have you had ~ of John recently?** hast du in letzter Zeit etwas von John gehört? **- 3.** [promise] Wort *das*; **to give sb one's ~** jm sein Wort geben <> *vt* formulieren.

wording ['wɜːdɪŋ] *n* Wortlaut *der*.

word processing *n* Textverarbeitung *die*.

word processor [-,prəʊsesə'] *n* Textverarbeitungssystem *das*.

wore [wɔː'] *pt* ▷ wear.

work [wɜːk] <> *n* **- 1.** (U) [gen] Arbeit *die*; **to be in ~** Arbeit haben; **to be out of ~** arbeitslos sein **- 2.** ART & LITERATURE [created product] Werk *das* <> *vt* **- 1.** [person, staff]: **he ~s his staff too hard** er verlangt zu viel von seinen Angestellten **- 2.** [machine] bedienen **- 3.** [wood, clay, land] bearbeiten <> *vi* **- 1.** [do a job] arbeiten **- 2.** [function, be successful] funktionieren **- 3.** [gradually become]: **to ~ loose** sich lockern. ➤ **works** <> *n* [factory] Werk *das* <> *npl* **- 1.** [mechanism] Innere *das* **- 2.** [digging, building] Bauarbeiten *pl.* ◆ **work on** *vt fus* - **1.** [concentrate on] arbeiten an (+ *D*) - **2.** [principle, assumption, belief] ausgehen von - **3.** [try to persuade] bearbeiten. ◆ **work out** ◇ *vt sep* - **1.** [formulate] auslarbeiten - **2.** [calculate] auslrechnen ◇ *vi* - **1.** [figure, total]: **that ~s out at £10 each** das macht 10 Pfund pro Person - **2.** [turn out]: **to ~ out in sb's favour** für jn vorteilhaft sein - **3.** [be successful] gut auslgehen - **4.** [train, exercise] trainieren. ◆ **work up** *vt sep* - **1.** [excite]: **to ~ o.s. up into** sich hineinlsteigern in (+ *A*) - **2.** [generate - enthusiasm, courage] auflbringen; [- appetite] entwickeln.

workable ['wɜːkəbl] *adj* [practicable] durchführbar.

workaholic [ˌwɜːkəˈhɒlɪk] *n* Workaholic *der.*

worked up [ˌwɜːkt-] *adj* aufgeregt.

worker ['wɜːkəʳ] *n* [employee] Arbeiter *der*, -in *die.*

workforce ['wɜːkfɔːs] *n* Belegschaft *die.*

working ['wɜːkɪŋ] *adj* - **1.** [in operation] in Betrieb - **2.** [having employment] erwerbstätig - **3.** [relating to work] Arbeits-. ◆ **workings** *npl* [of system, machine] Funktionsweise *die.*

working class *n*: **the ~** die Arbeiterklasse. ◆ **working-class** *adj* Arbeiter-.

working order *n*: **in ~** funktionstüchtig.

workload ['wɜːkləʊd] *n* Arbeitsvolumen *das.*

workman ['wɜːkmən] (*pl* -men [-mən]) *n* [craftsman] Handwerker *der*; [worker] Arbeiter *der.*

workmanship ['wɜːkmənʃɪp] *n* (*U*) handwerkliches Können.

workmate ['wɜːkmeɪt] *n* Kollege *der*, -gin *die.*

work permit *n* Arbeitserlaubnis *die.*

workplace ['wɜːkpleɪs] *n* Arbeitsplatz *der.*

workshop ['wɜːkʃɒp] *n* - **1.** [room, building] Werkstatt *die* - **2.** [discussion] Workshop *der.*

workstation ['wɜːkˌsteɪʃn] *n* COMPUT Workstation *die.*

worktop ['wɜːktɒp] *n Br* Arbeitsfläche *die.*

world [wɜːld] ◇ *n* - **1.** [gen]: **the ~** die Welt; **to have the best of both ~s** die Vorteile beider Seiten genießen; **the next ~** das Jenseits - **2.** [great deal]: **to think the ~ of sb** große Stücke auf jn halten; **a ~ of difference** ein himmelweiter Unterschied ◇ *comp* Welt-.

world-class *adj* Weltklasse-.

world-famous *adj* weltberühmt.

worldly ['wɜːldlɪ] *adj* [not spiritual] weltlich.

World War I *n* Erster Weltkrieg.

World War II *n* Zweiter Weltkrieg.

worldwide ['wɜːldwaɪd] *adj & adv* weltweit.

World Wide Web *n*: **the ~** COMPUT das World Wide Web.

worm [wɜːm] *n* [animal] Wurm *der.*

worn [wɔːn] ◇ *pp* ▷ **wear** ◇ *adj* - **1.** [threadbare - carpet] abgenutzt; [- clothes] abgetragen; [- tyre] abgefahren - **2.** [tired] erschöpft.

worn-out *adj* - **1.** [old, threadbare] ganz abgenutzt; [clothes, shoes] ganz abgetragen - **2.** [tired] ausgelaugt.

worried ['wʌrɪd] *adj* besorgt; **I was ~ he'd be angry** ich hatte Angst, er würde böse sein.

worry ['wʌrɪ] ◇ *n* Sorge *die* ◇ *vt* [cause to be troubled] Sorgen machen (+ *D*) ◇ *vi*: **to ~ about sb/sthg** sich um jn/etw sorgen OR Sorgen machen; **not to ~!** keine Sorge!

worrying ['wʌrɪɪŋ] *adj* beunruhigend.

worse [wɜːs] ◇ *adj* - **1.** [not as good] schlechter; [situation] schlimmer; **to get ~** sich verschlechtern; [situation] sich verschlimmern - **2.** [sicker]: **he's ~** es geht ihm schlechter; **she seemed to get ~** ihr Zustand schien sich zu verschlechtern ◇ *adv* [more badly] schlechter; **~ off** [having less money] schlechter dran; [in a more unpleasant situation] schlimmer dran ◇ *n* Schlimmeres *das*; **a change for the ~** eine Verschlimmerung; [of health, weather] eine Verschlechterung.

worsen ['wɜːsn] ◇ *vt* [situation, crisis] verschlimmern ◇ *vi* [situation, crisis] sich verschlimmern; [weather, work] sich verschlechtern.

worship ['wɜːʃɪp] ◇ *vt* - **1.** RELIG anlbeten - **2.** [admire, adore] vergöttern ◇ *n* - **1.** (*U*) RELIG Verehrung *die*; [service] Gottesdienst *der* - **2.** (*U*) [adoration] Vergötterung *die.* ◆ **Worship** *n*: **Your Worship** Euer Ehren; **Her/His Worship (the Mayoress/Mayor)** die sehr verehrte Frau Bürgermeister/der sehr verehrte Herr Bürgermeister.

worst [wɜːst] ◇ *adj* schlimmste, -r, -s, schlechteste, -r, -s ◇ *adv* am schlimmsten, am schlechtesten ◇ *n*: **the ~** das Schlimmste; **if the ~ comes to the ~** wenn alle Stricke reißen. ◆ **at (the) worst** *adv* schlimmstenfalls.

worth [wɜːθ] ◇ *prep*: **how much is it ~?** wie viel ist das wert?; **it's ~ £50** es ist 50 Pfund wert; **it's ~ seeing** es ist sehenswert; **it's not ~ it** es lohnt sich nicht; **he's ~ millions** er besitzt Millionen; **to run for all one is ~** *fig* rennen, was man nur rennen kann ◇ *n* - **1.** [amount]: **£50 ~ of traveller's cheques** Reiseschecks im Wert von 50 Pfund; **a week's ~ of groceries** Lebensmittel *pl* für eine Woche - **2.** [value] Wert *der*; **he proved his ~** er hat sich bewährt.

worthless ['wɜːθlɪs] *adj* - **1.** [object] wertlos - **2.** [person] nichtsnutzig.

worthwhile [ˌwɜːθˈwaɪl] *adj* lohnend; **to be ~** sich lohnen.

worthy ['wɜːðɪ] *adj* - **1.** [deserving of respect] würdig; **for a ~ cause** für einen guten Zweck - **2.** [deserving]: **to be ~ of sthg** etw verdienen - **3.** *pej* [good but unexciting] ehrbar.

would [wʊd] *modal vb* - **1.** [in reported speech]: **she said she ~ come** sie sagte, sie würde kommen - **2.** [indicating condition]: **what ~ you do?** was würdest du tun?; **what ~ you have done?** was hättest du getan?; **I ~ be most grateful** ich wäre äußerst dankbar - **3.** [indicating willingness]: **she ~n't go sie wollte einfach nicht gehen; he ~ do anything for her** er würde alles für sie tun - **4.** [in polite questions]: **~ you like a drink?** möchtest du etwas trinken?; **~ you mind closing the window?** könntest du das Fenster zumachen? - **5.** [indicating inevitability]: **he ~ say that** er musste das sagen; **I quite forgot! – you ~!** das habe ich ganz vergessen! – das sieht dir ähnlich! - **6.** [giving advice]: **I ~ report it if I were you** an deiner Stelle würde ich es melden - **7.** [expressing opinions]: **I ~ prefer coffee** ich hätte lieber Kaffee; **I ~ prefer to go by bus** ich würde lieber mit dem Bus fahren; **I ~ have thought (that) ...** ich hätte gedacht, dass ... - **8.** [describing habitual past actions]: **she ~ often come home tired out** oft kam sie total erschöpft nach Hause.

would-be *adj* angehend.

wouldn't ['wʊdnt] = would not.

would've ['wʊdəv] = would have.

wound[1] [wuːnd] ◇ *n* Wunde *die* ◇ *vt* - **1.** [physically] verwunden - **2.** [emotionally] verletzen.

wound[2] [waʊnd] *pt & pp* ▷ wind[2].

wove [wəʊv] *pt* ▷ weave.

woven ['wəʊvn] *pp* ▷ weave.

WP *n* - **1.** *abbr of* word processing - **2.** *abbr of* word processor.

wrangle ['ræŋgl] ◇ *n* Streitigkeiten *pl* ◇ *vi* sich streiten; **to ~ with sb (over sthg)** mit jm (über etw (*A*)) streiten.

wrap [ræp] *vt* [cover in paper or cloth] einlwickeln; **to ~ sthg in sthg** etw in etw (*A*) einlwickeln; **to ~ sthg (a)round sthg** etw um etw wickeln. ◆ **wrap up** ◇ *vt sep* [cover in paper or cloth] einlwickeln ◇ *vi* [put warm clothes on]: **~ up well** OR **warmly!** zieh dich warm an!

wrapper ['ræpə'] *n* Hülle *die;* [of sweets] Papier *das.*

wrapping ['ræpɪŋ] *n* Verpackung *die.*

wrapping paper *n* (*U*) Geschenkpapier *das.*

wreak [riːk] *vt* [destruction, havoc] anlrichten; [revenge] üben.

wreath [riːθ] *n* [circle of flowers] Kranz *der.*

wreck [rek] ◇ *n* Wrack *das;* **a nervous ~** ein Nervenbündel; **a car ~** *Am* ein Autounfall ◇ *vt* - **1.** [break, destroy] demolieren; [car] zu Schrott fahren - **2.** NAUT [cause to run aground] versenken; **to be ~ed** [person] Schiffbruch erleiden - **3.** [spoil, ruin] ruinieren.

wreckage ['rekɪdʒ] *n* [of plane, building] Trümmer *pl;* [of car] Wrack *das.*

wren [ren] *n* Zaunkönig *der.*

wrench [rentʃ] ◇ *n* [tool] Schraubenschlüssel *der* ◇ *vt* - **1.** [pull violently] reißen - **2.** [twist and injure]: **to ~ one's arm/leg** sich den Arm/das Bein verrenken.

wrestle ['resl] *vi* - **1.** [fight]: **to ~ with sb** jm ringen - **2.** *fig* [struggle]: **to ~ with sthg** mit etw kämpfen.

wrestler ['reslə'] *n* Ringer *der,* -in *die;* [as entertainer] Wrestler *der,* -in *die.*

wrestling ['reslɪŋ] *n* Ringen *das;* [as entertainment] Wrestling *das.*

wretch [retʃ] *n* [unhappy person]: **poor ~!** armer Tropf!

wretched ['retʃɪd] *adj* - **1.** [miserable] elend; [conditions] erbärmlich - **2.** *inf* [damned] verflixt.

wriggle ['rɪgl] *vi* - **1.** [move about - person] zappeln; [- worm] sich winden - **2.** [twist]: **he ~d under the fence** er wand sich unter dem Zaun hindurch; **to ~ free** sich loslwinden.

wring [rɪŋ] (*pt & pp* wrung) *vt* [squeeze out water from] auslwringen.

wringing ['rɪŋɪŋ] *adj:* **~ (wet)** tropfnass.

wrinkle ['rɪŋkl] ◇ *n* - **1.** [on skin] Falte *die* - **2.** [in cloth] Knitterfalte *die* ◇ *vt* [screw up - nose] rümpfen; [- forehead] runzeln ◇ *vi* [crease] knittern.

wrist [rɪst] *n* Handgelenk *das.*

wristwatch ['rɪstwɒtʃ] *n* Armbanduhr *die.*

writ [rɪt] *n* Verfügung *die.*

write [raɪt] (*pt* wrote; *pp* written) ◇ *vt* - **1.** [gen] schreiben - **2.** [cheque, prescription] auslstellen - **3.** COMPUT speichern ◇ *vi* - **1.** [gen] schreiben - **2.** COMPUT ablspeichern. ◆ **write down** *vt sep* auflschreiben. ◆ **write off** *vt sep* - **1.** [project] auflgeben - **2.** [debt, investment, person] ablschreiben - **3.** *Br inf* [vehicle] zu Schrott fahren. ◆ **write up** *vt sep* [notes] auslarbeiten.

write-off *n* [car] Totalschaden *der.*

writer ['raɪtə'] *n* - **1.** [as profession] Schriftsteller *der,* -in *die* - **2.** [of letter, article, story] Verfasser *der,* -in *die.*

writhe [raɪð] *vi* sich winden; [with pain] sich krümmen.

writing ['raɪtɪŋ] *n* - **1.** [gen] Schrift *die;* **in ~** schriftlich - **2.** [activity] Schreiben *das.*

writing paper *n* (*U*) Briefpapier *das.*

written ['rɪtn] *pp* ▷ write ◇ *adj* schriftlich.

wrong [rɒŋ] ◇ *adj* - **1.** [amiss]: **there's nothing ~ with me** mir fehlt nichts; **is something ~?** stimmt etwas nicht?; **what's ~?** was ist los?; **there's something ~ with the car** mit dem Auto stimmt etwas nicht **- 2.** [not suitable] falsch **- 3.** [not correct - answer, decision, turning] falsch, verkehrt; **to be ~** [person] Unrecht haben; **I was ~ to ask** ich hätte nicht fragen sollen **- 4.** [morally bad] unrecht ⬦ *adv* [incorrectly] falsch, verkehrt; **to get sthg ~** sich nicht etw vertun; **to go ~** [make a mistake] einen Fehler machen; **the printer keeps going ~** der Drucker spielt ständig verrückt ⬦ *n* Unrecht *das;* **to be in the ~** Unrecht haben ⬦ *vt literary* Unrecht tun (+ *D).*

wrongful ['rɒŋfʊl] *adj* [unjust] ungerecht.

wrongly ['rɒŋlɪ] *adv* **- 1.** [unsuitably] falsch **- 2.** [mistakenly] zu Unrecht.

wrong number *n* falsche Nummer; **you've got the ~** Sie haben sich verwählt.

wrote [rəʊt] *pt* ▷ write.

wrung [rʌŋ] *pt & pp* ▷ wring.

wry [raɪ] *adj* [amused] ironisch; [humour, remark] trocken.

x (*pl* x's OR xs), **X** (*pl* X's OR Xs) [eks] *n* **- 1.** [letter] x *das,* X *das* **- 2.** [unknown name] X **- 3.** [quantity, in algebra] x **- 4.** [to mark place]: **X marks the spot** ein Kreuzchen markiert die Stelle **- 5.** [at end of letter] *ein Kreuzchen am Ende eines Briefes, das einen Kuss bedeutet.*

xenophobic [ˌzenə'fəʊbɪk] *adj* fremdenfeindlich, xenophob.

Xmas ['eksməs] *n* Weihnachten *das.*

X-ray ⬦ *n* **- 1.** [ray] Röntgenstrahl *der* **- 2.** [picture] Röntgenbild *das* ⬦ *vt* röntgen.

xylophone ['zaɪləfəʊn] *n* Xylofon *das.*

y (*pl* y's OR ys), **Y** (*pl* Y's OR Ys) [waɪ] *n* [letter] y *das,* Y *das.*

yacht [jɒt] *n* Jacht *die.*

yachting ['jɒtɪŋ] *n* Segeln *das.*

yachtsman ['jɒtsmən] (*pl* -men [-mən]) *n* Segler *der.*

Yank [jæŋk] *n Br inf pej* Ami *der.*

Yankee ['jæŋkɪ] *n Br inf pej* [American] Ami *der.*

yap [jæp] *vi* [dog] kläffen.

yard [jɑːd] *n* **- 1.** [unit of measurement] Yard *das,* = 91,44 *cm* **- 2.** [enclosed area] Hof *der* **- 3.** [place of work]: **ship ~** Schiffswerft *die;* **builder's ~** Bauhof *der* **- 4.** *Am* [attached to house] Garten *der.*

yardstick ['jɑːdstɪk] *n* Maßstab *der.*

yarn [jɑːn] *n* (U) [thread] Garn *das.*

yawn [jɔːn] ⬦ *n* [when tired] Gähnen *das* ⬦ *vi* gähnen.

yd *abbr of* yard.

yeah [jeə] *adv inf* ja.

year [jɪə] *n* Jahr *das;* **all (the) ~ round** das ganze Jahr über; **for seven ~s** sieben Jahre (lang). ▶ **years** *npl* [ages] Jahre *pl;* **for ~s** jahrelang.

yearly ['jɪəlɪ] ⬦ *adj* **- 1.** [event, inspection, report] jährlich **- 2.** [income, wage] Jahres- ⬦ *adv* jährlich.

yearn [jɜːn] *vi:* **to ~ for sthg** sich nach etw sehnen; **to ~ to do sthg** sich danach sehnen, etw zu tun.

yearning ['jɜːnɪŋ] *n:* **~ (for sb/sthg)** Sehnsucht *die* (nach jm/etw).

yeast [jiːst] *n* (U) Hefe *die.*

yell [jel] ⬦ *n* Schrei *der* ⬦ *vt & vi* schreien.

yellow ['jeləʊ] ⬦ *adj* [in colour] gelb ⬦ *n* Gelb *das.*

yellow card *n* FTBL gelbe Karte.

yelp [jelp] *vi* aufjaulen; [of person] aufschreien.

yes [jes] ⬦ *adv* **- 1.** [gen] ja; **~, please** ja, bitte; **to say ~ to sthg** einer Sache (D) zulstimmen **- 2.** [to encourage further speech] so **- 3.** [expressing disagreement] doch ⬦ *n* [vote in favour] Ja *das.*

yesterday ['jestədɪ] ⬦ *n* Gestern *das* ⬦ *adv* gestern.

yet [jet] ⬦ *adv* noch; *(in questions)* schon; **have you read the book ~?** hast du das Buch schon gelesen?; **not ~** noch nicht; **aren't you ready ~?** bist du bald fertig?; **as ~** bisher, bis jetzt; **I've ~ to do it** ich muss es noch tun; **~ another delay** noch eine Verspätung; **~ again** schon wieder; **he'll win ~** er wird schon noch gewinnen ⬦ *conj* doch; **simple ~ effective** einfach, aber wirksam; **and ~ I like him** und doch OR dennoch mag ich ihn.

yew [juː] *n* Eibe *die.*

yield [jiːld] ⬦ *n* Ertrag *der* ⬦ *vt* **- 1.** [produce] hervorlbringen; [fruit] tragen; [profits] ablwerfen; [result, answer, clue] ergeben **- 2.** [give up] ablgeben ⬦ *vi* **- 1.** [open, give way, break] nachlgeben **- 2.** *fml* [give up, surrender] sich ergeben **- 3.** *Am* AUT [give way]: **'~'** 'Vorfahrt beachten'.

YMCA (*abbr of* Young Men's Christian Association) *n* CVJM *der.*

yoga ['jəʊgə] *n* Yoga *der* OR *das.*

yoghourt, yoghurt, yogurt [*Br* 'jɒgət, *Am* 'jəʊgərt] *n* Joghurt *der* OR *das.*

yoke [jəʊk] *n* Joch *das.*

yolk [jəʊk] *n* Dotter *der* OR *das*, Eigelb *das.*

you [ju:] *pers pron* - **1.** *(subject – singular)* du; *(– plural)* ihr; *(– polite form)* Sie; ~ **Germans** ihr Deutschen; **I'm shorter than** ~ ich bin kleiner als du/Sie/ihr - **2.** *(direct object, after prep + A – singular)* dich; *(– plural)* euch; *(– polite form)* Sie; **I hate ~!** ich hasse dich/Sie/euch!; **I did it for** ~ ich habe es für dich/Sie/euch getan - **3.** *(direct object, after prep + D – singular)* dir; *(– plural)* euch; *(– polite form)* Ihnen; **I told ~!** ich habe es dir/Ihnen/euch gesagt; **after ~!** nach Ihnen! - **4.** *(indefinite use – subject)* man; *(– object)* einen; *(– indirect object)* einem; ~ **never know** man kann nie wissen; **it does ~ good** es tut einem gut.

you'd [ju:d] = you had, you would.

you'll [ju:l] = you will.

young [jʌŋ] <> *adj* [not old] jung <> *npl* - **1.** [young people]: **the ~ die** Jugend - **2.** [baby animals] Junge *pl.*

younger ['jʌŋgəʳ] *adj* jünger.

youngster ['jʌŋstəʳ] *n* - **1.** [child] Kind *das* - **2.** [young person] Jugendliche *der, die.*

your [jɔːʳ] *poss adj* - **1.** *(singular subject)* dein, -e, eine *pl; (plural subject)* euer/eure, eure *pl; (polite form)* Ihr, -e, Ihre *pl;* ~ **dog** dein/euer/Ihr Hund; ~ **house** dein/euer/Ihr Haus; ~ **children** deine/euer/Ihre Kinder - **2.** *(indefinite subject):* **it's good for ~ teeth** es ist gut für die Zähne; ~ **average Englishman** der durchschnittliche Engländer.

you're [jɔːʳ] = you are.

yours [jɔːz] *poss pron (singular subject)* deiner/deine/deins, deine *pl; (plural subject)* eurer/eure/eures, eure *pl; (polite form)* Ihrer/Ihre/Ihres, Ihre *pl;* **a friend of** ~ ein Freund von dir/euch/Ihnen; **that money is** ~ dieses Geld gehört dir/euch/Ihnen. ➤ **Yours** *adv* [in letter - gen] Dein/Deine; [- polite form] Ihr/Ihre; ⊏⊐ **faithfully, sincerely** *etc.*

yourself [jɔːˈself] *(pl* -selves [-ˈselvz]*) pron* - **1.** *(reflexive, after prep + A – singular)* dich; *(– plural)* euch; *(– polite form)* sich - **2.** *(reflexive, after prep + D – singular)* dir; *(– plural)* euch; *(– polite form)* sich; **did you do it ~?** hast du/haben Sie das selbst gemacht?; **did you do it yourselves?** habt ihr/haben Sie das selbst gemacht?; **by ~/yourselves** allein.

youth [ju:θ] *n* - **1.** [period of life, young people] Jugend *die* - **2.** [quality] Jugendlichkeit *die* - **3.** [boy] Junge *der;* [young man] junger Mann.

youth club *n* Jugendklub *der.*

youthful ['ju:θfʊl] *adj* jugendlich.

youth hostel *n* Jugendherberge *die.*

you've [ju:v] = you have.

Yugoslavia [ˌju:gəˈslɑːvɪə] *n* Jugoslawien *das.*

Yugoslavian [ˌju:gəˈslɑːvɪən] <> *adj* jugoslawisch <> *n* Jugoslawe *der*, -win *die.*

yuppie, yuppy ['jʌpɪ] *n* Yuppie *der.*

YWCA (*abbr of* Young Women's Christian Association) *n* CVJF *der.*

Z

z *(pl* z's OR zs), **Z** *(pl* Z's OR Zs) [*Br* zed, *Am* zi:] *n* [letter] z *das*, Z *das.*

zany ['zeɪnɪ] *adj inf* verrückt.

zeal [zi:l] *n fml* Eifer *der.*

zebra [*Br* 'zebrə, *Am* 'zi:brə] *(pl inv* OR -s) *n* Zebra *das.*

zebra crossing *n Br* Zebrastreifen *der.*

zenith [*Br* 'zenɪθ, *Am* 'zi:nəθ] *n lit & fig* Zenit *der.*

zero [*Br* 'zɪərəʊ, *Am* 'zi:rəʊ] *(pl* -s OR -es; *pt & pp* -ed; *cont* -ing) <> *adj* keinerlei; ~ **growth** Nullwachstum *das* <> *n* Null *die.*

zest [zest] *n* - **1.** [excitement] Schwung *der* - **2.** *(U)* [eagerness] Begeisterung *die* - **3.** *(U)* [of orange, lemon] Schale *der.*

zigzag ['zɪgzæg] *vi* [person, vehicle] im Zickzack laufen/fahren; [path] im Zickzack verlaufen.

Zimbabwe [zɪmˈbɑːbwɪ] *n* Simbabwe *nt.*

zinc [zɪŋk] *n* Zink *das.*

zip [zɪp] *n Br* [fastener] Reißverschluss *der.* ➤ **zip up** *vt sep* den Reißverschluss zulmachen an *(+ D).*

zip code *n Am* Postleitzahl *die.*

zip fastener *n Br* = zip.

zipper ['zɪpəʳ] *n Am* = zip.

zodiac ['zəʊdɪæk] *n:* **the ~** Tierkreis *der.*

zone [zəʊn] *n* [district] Zone *die.*

zoo [zu:] *n* Zoo *der.*

zoom [zu:m] *vi inf* [move quickly] sausen. ➤ **zoom off** *vi inf* ablrauschen.

zoom lens *n* Zoomobjektiv *das.*

zucchini [zu:ˈki:nɪ] *(pl inv* OR -s) *n Am* Zucchini *die.*